Koren Talmud Bavli

THE NOÉ EDITION

EIRUVIN · PART TWO

KOREN TALMUD BAVLI

THE NOÉ EDITION

עירובין ב

EIRUVIN · PART TWO

COMMENTARY BY

Rabbi Adin Even-Israel (Steinsaltz)

EDITOR-IN-CHIEF

Rabbi Dr Tzvi Hersh Weinreb

EXECUTIVE EDITOR

Rabbi Joshua Schreier

•

SHEFA FOUNDATION

KOREN PUBLISHERS JERUSALEM

Supported by the Matanel Foundation

Koren Talmud Bavli
Volume 5: Tractate Eiruvin, Part Two
The Noé Edition

ISBN 978 965 301 567 8

First Hebrew/English Edition, 2013

Koren Publishers Jerusalem Ltd.
PO Box 4044, Jerusalem 91040, ISRAEL
PO Box 8531, New Milford, CT 06776, USA
www.korenpub.com

Shefa Foundation

Shefa Foundation is the parent organization of institutions established by Rabbi Adin Even-Israel (Steinsaltz)

PO Box 45187, Jerusalem 91450 ISRAEL
Telephone: +972 2 646 0900, Fax +972 2 624 9454
www.hashefa.co.il

Hardcover design by Ben Gasner

הִנֵּה יָמִים בָּאִים, נְאֻם אֲדֹנָי יֱהֹוִה, וְהִשְׁלַחְתִּי רָעָב בָּאָרֶץ,
לֹא־רָעָב לַלֶּחֶם וְלֹא־צָמָא לַמַּיִם, כִּי אִם־לִשְׁמֹעַ אֵת דִּבְרֵי יהוה.

Behold, days are coming – says the Lord God –
I will send a hunger to the land, not a hunger for bread
nor a thirst for water, but to hear the words of the Lord.

(AMOS 8:11)

The Noé edition of the Koren Talmud Bavli
with the commentary of Rabbi Adin Steinsaltz (Even-Israel)
is dedicated to all those who open its cover
to quench their thirst for Jewish knowledge,
in our generation of Torah renaissance.

This beautiful edition is for the young, the aged,
the novice and the savant alike,
as it unites the depth of Torah knowledge
with the best of academic scholarship.

Within its exquisite and vibrant pages,
words become worlds.

It will claim its place in the library of classics,
in the bookcases of the Beit Midrash,
the classrooms of our schools,
and in the offices of professionals and business people
who carve out precious time to grapple with its timeless wisdom.

For the Student and the Scholar

DEDICATED BY LEO AND SUE NOÉ

Managing Editor
Rabbi Jason Rappoport

Senior Content Editor
Rabbi Dr. Shalom Z. Berger

Editors
Rabbi Joshua Amaru, *Coordinating Editor*
Rabbi David Jay Derovan
Rabbi Dov Karoll
Rabbi Adin Krohn
Sally Mayer
Rabbi Avishai Magence, *Content Curator*
Rabbi Jonathan Mishkin
Gavriel Reiss
Shira Shmidman
Rabbi Michael Siev
Avi Steinhart
Rabbi David Strauss
Rabbi Abe Y. Weschler

Copy Editors
Aliza Israel, *Coordinator*
Bracha Hermon
Ita Olesker
Shira Finson
Debbie Ismailoff
Ilana Sobel
Deena Nataf

Language Consultants
Dr. Stephanie E. Binder, *Greek & Latin*
Yaakov Hoffman, *Arabic*
Dr. Shai Secunda, *Persian*

Design & Typesetting
Raphaël Freeman, *Design & Typography*
Dena Landowne Bailey, *Typesetting*
Tani Bayer, *Jacket Design*

Images
Rabbi Eliahu Misgav, *Illustration*
Yehudit Cohen, *Image Acquisition*

Digital Edition
Raphaël Freeman, *Team Leader*
Eliyahu Skoczylas, *Senior Architect*
Tani Bayer, *User Interface Design*
Dena Landowne Bailey, *Concept*
Rabbi Hanan Benayahu, *Concept*
Laura Messinger, *Commercial Liaison*

We dedicate this volume
of Massekhet Eiruvin
to our cherished friends and mentors

Lotte and Ludwig Bravmann

whose lives express the spirit of inclusiveness
and responsibility symbolized by the "eiruv"
and who exemplify the principle of

כָּל יִשְׂרָאֵל עֲרֵבִים זֶה בָּזֶה

All Israel are responsible for one another

Giti and Jack Bendheim

Contents

For the vocalized Vilna Shas layout, please open as a Hebrew book.

Haskama

Rabbi Moshe Feinstein

RABBI MOSES FEINSTEIN
455 F. D. R. DRIVE
New York, N. Y. 10002
OREgon 7-1222

משה פיינשטיין
ר״מ תפארת ירושלים
בנוא יארק

בע״ה

בזה ראיתי הפירוש החשוב של הרב הגאון מוהר״ר עדין שטיינזלץ שליט״א מעיה״ק ירושלים, על מסכתות ביצה ור״ה. באמת כבר ידוע לי פירושו של הרה״ג הנ״ל על מסכתות התלמוד בבלי, וכבר כתבתי מכתב הסכמה עליהם. ובאתי בזה רק להדגיש מחדש איך שהפירושים של הרה״ג הנ״ל, שכולל פירוש חדש על הגמרא עצמו וגם פירוש שיש בו סיכום להלכה מהנידונים שבגמרא, נוסף לעוד כמה חלקים, הם באמת עבודה גדולה, שיכולים להיות לתועלת לא רק לאלו שכבר מורגלים בלמוד הגמרא, ורוצים להעמק יותר, אלא גם לאלו שמתחילים ללמוד, להדריכם בדרכי התורה איך להבין ולהעמיק בים התלמוד.

והריני מברך להרה״ג הנ״ל שיצליחהו השי״ת בספריו אלו ושיזכה לחבר עוד ספרים, להגדיל תורה ולהאדירה, לתפארת השם ותורתו.

ועל זה באתי על החתום לכבוד התורה ביום ז׳ לחודש אייר תשמ״ג.

משה פיינשטיין

משה פיינשטיין

…These new commentaries – which include a new interpretation of the Talmud, a halakhic summary of the debated issues, and various other sections – are a truly outstanding work; they can be of great benefit not only to those familiar with talmudic study who seek to deepen their understanding, but also to those who are just beginning to learn, guiding them through the pathways of the Torah and teaching them how to delve into the sea of the Talmud.

I would like to offer my blessing to this learned scholar. May the Holy One grant him success with these volumes and may he merit to write many more, to enhance the greatness of Torah, and bring glory to God and His word…

Rabbi Moshe Feinstein
New York, 7 Adar 5743

ר׳ משה פיינשטיין שליט״א

הנה ראיתי את מסכת אחת מהש״ס שנקד אותה וגם צייר צורות הצמחים וכדומה מדברים שלא ידוע לכמה אנשים הרה״ג ר׳ עדין שטיינזלץ מירושלים שליט״א וגם הוסיף שם בגליון פירושים וחידושים וניכר שהוא ת״ח וראויין לעיין בהם ת״ח ובני הישיבה וטוב גם לקנותם בבתי כנסיות ובבתי מדרשות שיש שיהיו להם לתועלת. — ועל זה באתי עה״ח ג׳ אדר ב׳ תש״ל.

נאם משה פיינשטיין

ר״מ תפארת ירושלים, ניו־יורק, ארה״ב

I have seen one tractate from the Talmud to which the great scholar Rabbi Adin Steinsaltz שליט״א has added *nikkud* (vowels) and illustrations to explain that which is unknown to many people; he has also added interpretations and innovations, and is evidently a *talmid hakham*. *Talmidei hakhamim* and yeshiva students ought to study these volumes, and synagogues and *batei midrash* would do well to purchase them, as they may find them useful.

Rabbi Moshe Feinstein
New York, Adar 5730

Haskama

Rabbi Menachem Mendel Schneerson

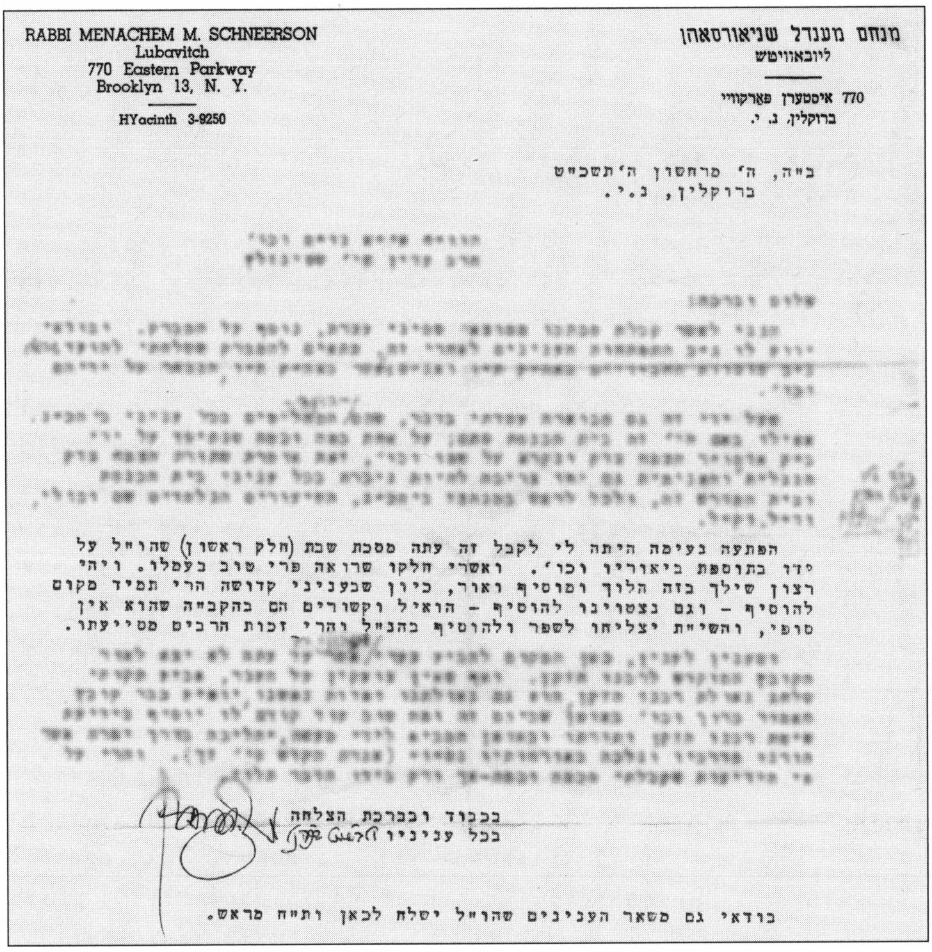

RABBI MENACHEM M. SCHNEERSON
Lubavitch
770 Eastern Parkway
Brooklyn 13, N. Y.

HYacinth 3-9250

מנחם מענדל שניאורסאהן
ליובאוויטש

770 איסטערן פארקוויי
ברוקלין, נ. י.

ב"ה, ה' מרחשון ה'תשכ"ט
ברוקלין, נ.י.

הפתעה נעימה היתה לי לקבל זה עתה מסכת שבת (חלק ראשון) שהו"ל על
ידו בתוספת ביאוריו וכו'. ואשרי חלקו שרואה פרי טוב בעמלו. ויהי
רצון שילך בזה הלוך ומוסיף ואור, כיון שבעניני קדושה הרי תמיד מקום
להוסיף – וגם נצטוינו להוסיף – הואיל וקשורים הם בהקב"ה שהוא אין
סופי, והשי"ת יצליחו לשפר ולהוסיף בהנ"ל והרי זכות הרבים מסייעתו.

בכבוד ובברכת הצלחה
בכל עניניו

בודאי גם משאר הענינים שהו"ל ישלח לכאן ותי"ח מראש.

…I have just had the pleasant surprise of receiving tractate *Shabbat* (part one), which has been published by [Rabbi Steinsaltz] along with his explanations, etc. Happy is the man who sees good fruits from his labors. May he continue in this path and increase light, for in the matters of holiness there is always room to add – and we have been commanded to add – for they are linked to the Holy One, Blessed be He, Who is infinite. And may the Holy One grant him success to improve and enhance this work, since the greater good strengthens his hand…

Rabbi Menachem Mendel Schneerson
The Lubavitcher Rebbe
Brooklyn, 5 Marḥeshvan, 5729

Haskama

Rabbi Moshe Zvi Neria

מכתבו של הרב משה צבי נריה

ב"ה

"ושמעו ביום ההוא החרשים דברי ספר"

(ישעי' כט' יח')

תרגום ספרי קדמונים לשפת דורות אחרונים – היא משימתם של חכמי דור ודור. ובישראל שמצוות "ושננתם לבניך" מקיפה את כל חלקי האומה, ודאי שהיתה זאת המשימה בכל עידן ועידן.

בכל דור כך, ובדורנו אשר רבים בו הקרובים שנתרחקו וחוזרים ומתקרבים – לא כל שכן. כי רבים היום האומרים "מי ישקנו מים מבאר" התלמוד, ומועטים הם הדולים ומשקים.

ראוי אפוא להערכה מיוחדת נסיונו המבורך של הצעיר המופלא, הרב עדין שטינזלץ, לפרש פרקי-תלמוד בהסברה מורחבת-תמציתית, אשר נוסף על הפרוש המלולי והעניני הוא מעלה גם את ההגיון של הדברים ומתרגמת אותם לשפת-המושגים של בן-דורנו.

דומה שכל הנגשים אל חומר למודי מתוך רצון להבינו – התלמיד החרוץ והמבוגר המשכיל – לא יתקלו בשום קושי בבואם ללמוד סוגיא תלמודית לפי פרוש זה. ולא עוד אלא שיש לקוות כי ההסברה הגיונית תעמידם מיד על טוב-הטעם של דף-הגמרא, והם ימשכו יותר ויותר אל הלמוד העיוני הזה אשר טובי המוחות בישראל לנו בעומקו, ואשר ממנו פינה, ממנו יתד לבנין חיינו.

נועם ד' על המפרש הנמרץ להמשיך במפעלו, וברוכים כל העוזרים להוצאתו לאור-עולם.

ביקר אורייתא

(חתימה)

The translation of the books of our past into the language of the present – this was the task of the sages of every generation. And in Israel, where the command to "teach them repeatedly to your children" applies to all parts of the nation, it was certainly the task of every era. This is true for every generation, and in our time – when many of those who have strayed far are once again drawing near – all the more so. For many today say, "Who will let us drink from the well" of Talmud, and few are those who offer up the waters to drink.

We must, therefore, particularly commend the blessed endeavor of Rabbi Adin Steinsaltz to explain the chapters of the Talmud in this extensive yet succinct commentary, which, in addition to its literal interpretation of the text, also explicates the latter's underlying logic and translates it into the language of our generation.

It appears that all those who seek to study Talmud – the diligent student and the learned adult – will have no difficulty understanding when using this commentary. Moreover, we may hope that the logical explanation will reveal to them the beauty of the talmudic page, and they will be drawn deeper and deeper into the intellectual pursuit which has engaged the best Jewish minds, and which serves as the cornerstone of our very lives…

Rabbi Moshe Zvi Neria

 THIS HASKAMA REFERS TO THE ORIGINAL HEBREW EDITION OF THE STEINSALTZ TALMUD, UPON WHICH THIS VOLUME IS BASED

Haskama

Rabbi Mordechai Eliyahu

ב"ה

MORDECHAI ELIAHU
FORMER CHIEF RABBI OF ISRAEL & RICHON LEZION

מרדכי אליהו
ראשון לציון והרב הראשי לישראל לשעבר

ז' בתשרי תשנ"ד
5-137.נד

מכתב ברכה

הגמרא בעירובין כ"א: אומרת: דרש רבא מאי דכתיב ויותר שהיה קהלת חכם, עוד לימד דעת את העם - ואזן וחקר תקן משלים הרבה". לימד דעת את העם - קבע כיצד לקרוא פסוק וסימנים בין תיבות המקרא וממשיכה הגמרא ואומרת: אמר עולא אמר ר' אליעזר בתחילה היתה תורה דומה לכפיפה שאין לה אזנים עד שבא שלמה ועשה לה אזנים". וכדברי רש"י שם: "וע"י כך אוחזין ישראל במצוות שנתרחקו מן העבירה כדרך שנוח לאחוז בכלי שיש לו בית יד וכו' (ערובין כ"א, י').

דברים מעין אלו אפשר לאמר על האי גברא יקירא, על איש מורם מעם, משכמו ומעלה בתורה ובמידות. ויותר ממה שעשה בתורה שבע"פ עושה בתורה שבכתב - מלמד דעת את העם. ולא זו בלבד אלא גם עושה אזנים לתורה, היא תורת התלמוד שהוא חתום וסתום בפני רבים. ורק מעט מזער מבני עליה שהם מועטים ומי שלומד בישיבה יכל כיום ללמוד בש"ס ולהבין מה שלפניו, ואף שיש לנו פירוש רש"י, עדין לא הכל ממששין בו. עד שקם הרב הגדול מעוז ומגדול הרה"ג ר' **עדין שטיינזלץ** שליט"א ועשה אזנים לתורה, שאפשר לאחוז גמרא ביד וללמוד, ואפי' לפשוטי העם ועשה פרושים ושם אותם בצד הארון, פרושים נאים בשפה ברורה ונעימה דבר דבור על אופניו. ועם הסברים וציורים להבין ולהשכיל, כדי שמי שרוצה לקרבה אל מלאכת ה' ללמוד יכל לעשות זאת.

ועיני ראו ולא זר שבשיעורי תורה בגמרא הרבה באים עם גמרות בידם ואלה שבאים עם "פירוש הרב שטיינזלץ לתלמוד הבבלי" הם מוכנים ומבינים טוב יותר. כי כבר יש להם הקדמה מפרושיו ומבאוריו.
ואמינא לפועלו יישר ומן שמיא זכו ליה ללמד דעת את העם .

ויהי רצון שחפץ בידו יצלח, וכל אשר יפנה ישכיל ויצליח, ויזכה להגדיל תורה ולהאדירה, ויוסיף לנו עוד גמרות מבוארות כהנה וכהנה עד לסיומו , "וישראל עושה חיל".

ובזכות לימוד תורה ואני זאת בריתי וכו', ובא לציון גואל, בב"א.

מרדכי אליהו
ראשון לציון הרב הראשי לישראל לשעבר

The Talmud in *Eruvin* 21b states: "Rava continued to interpret verses homiletically. What is the meaning of the verse: 'And besides being wise, Kohelet also taught the people knowledge; and he weighed, and sought out, and set in order many proverbs'? (Ecclesiastes 12:9). He explains: He taught the people knowledge; he taught it with the accentuation marks in the Torah, and explained each matter by means of another matter similar to it. And he weighed [*izen*], and sought out, and set in order many proverbs; Ulla said that Rabbi Eliezer said: At first the Torah was like a basket without handles [*oznayim*] until Solomon came and made handles for it." And as Rashi there explains: "And thus were Israel able to grasp the mitzvot and distance themselves from transgressions – just as a vessel with handles is easily held, etc."

Such things may be said of this beloved and eminent man, a great sage of Torah and of virtue. And far more than he has done with the Oral Torah, he does with the Written Torah – teaching the people knowledge. And beyond that, he also affixes handles to the Torah, i.e., to the Talmud, which is obscure and difficult for many. Only the intellectual elite, which are a precious few, and those who study in yeshiva, can today learn the Talmud and understand what it says – and even though we have Rashi, still not everyone uses him. But now the great scholar Rabbi Adin Steinsaltz שליט"א has come and affixed handles to the Torah, allowing the Talmud to be held and studied, even by simple men. And he has composed a commentary alongside the text, a fine commentary in clear, comprehensible language, "a word fitly spoken" with explanations and illustrations, so that all those who seek to study the work of God can do so.

Rabbi Mordechai Eliyahu
Former Chief Rabbi of Israel, 7 Tishrei, 5754

Message from Rabbi Adin Even-Israel (Steinsaltz)

The Talmud is the cornerstone of Jewish culture. True, our culture originated in the Bible and has branched out in directions besides the Talmud, yet the latter's influence on Jewish culture is fundamental. Perhaps because it was composed not by a single individual, but rather by hundreds and thousands of Sages in *batei midrash* in an ongoing, millennium-long process, the Talmud expresses not only the deepest themes and values of the Jewish people, but also of the Jewish spirit. As the basic study text for young and old, laymen and learned, the Talmud may be said to embody the historical trajectory of the Jewish soul. It is, therefore, best studied interactively, its subject matter coming together with the student's questions, perplexities, and innovations to form a single intricate weave. In the entire scope of Jewish culture, there is not one area that does not draw from or converse with the Talmud. The study of Talmud is thus the gate through which a Jew enters his life's path.

The *Koren Talmud Bavli* seeks to render the Talmud accessible to the millions of Jews whose mother tongue is English, allowing them to study it, approach it, and perhaps even become one with it.

This project has been carried out and assisted by several people, all of whom have worked tirelessly to turn this vision into an actual set of books to be studied. It is a joyful duty to thank the many partners in this enterprise for their various contributions. Thanks to Koren Publishers Jerusalem, both for the publication of this set and for the design of its very complex graphic layout. Thanks of a different sort are owed to the Shefa Foundation and its director, Rabbi Menachem Even-Israel, for their determination and persistence in setting this goal and reaching it. Many thanks to the translators, editors, and proofreaders for their hard and meticulous work. Thanks to the individuals and organizations that supported this project, chief among them the Matanel Foundation and the Noé family of London. And thanks in advance to all those who will invest their time, hearts, and minds in studying these volumes – to learn, to teach, and to practice.

Rabbi Adin Even-Israel (Steinsaltz)
Jerusalem 5772

Acknowledgments

We are indeed privileged to dedicate this edition of the *Koren Talmud Bavli* in honor of the generous support of Leo and Sue Noé of London.

The name Noé is synonymous with philanthropy. The family's charitable endeavors span a vast range of educational projects, welfare institutions, and outreach organizations across the globe, with a particular emphasis on the "nurturing of each individual." Among so many other charitable activities, the Noés have been deeply involved with *Kisharon*, which provides the British Jewish community with vital support for hundreds of people with learning difficulties and their families; they provide steadfast support of SEED, which stands at the forefront of adult Jewish education in the UK, and *Kemach*, an organization in Israel that "helps Haredi students sustain themselves in dignity," providing both professional and vocational training for the Haredi community in Israel.

The Noés are not simply donors to institutions. They are partners. Donors think of a sum. Partners think of a cause, becoming rigorously and keenly involved, and giving of their time and energy. We are honored that they have chosen to partner with our two organizations, *Shefa* and *Koren Publishers Jerusalem*, enabling us to further and deepen learning among all Jews.

Leo and Sue are the proud parents and grandparents of five children and their families. The next generation has been taught by example that with life's gifts come the responsibilities to be active within and contribute to society – both Jewish and non-Jewish – as is consistent with the noblest of Jewish values.

Rabbi Adin Even-Israel (Steinsaltz)
Matthew Miller, Publisher
Jerusalem 5773

Introduction by the Editor-in-Chief

The vastly expanded audience of Talmud study in our generation is a phenomenon of historical proportions. The reasons for this phenomenon are many, and include the availability of a wide array of translations, commentaries, and study aids.

One outstanding example of such a work is the translation of the Talmud into modern Hebrew by Rabbi Adin Even-Israel (Steinsaltz). The product of a lifetime of intense intellectual labor, this translation stands out in its uniqueness.

But what can the interested student do if he or she does not comprehend the Hebrew, even in its modern form? Where is the English speaker who wishes to access this instructive material to turn?

The *Koren Talmud Bavli* that you hold in your hand is designed to be the answer to those questions.

This work is the joint effort of Rabbi Steinsaltz himself, his closest advisory staff, and Koren Publishers Jerusalem. It is my privilege to have been designated Editor-in-Chief of this important project, and to have worked in close collaboration with a team of translators and proofreaders, artists and graphic designers, scholars and editors.

Together we are presenting to the English-speaking world a translation that has all the merits of the original Hebrew work by Rabbi Steinsaltz, and provides assistance for the beginner of any age who seeks to obtain the necessary skills to become an adept talmudist.

This is the fifth volume of the project, tractate *Eiruvin*, part II. It includes the entire original text, in the traditional configuration and pagination of the famed Vilna edition of the Talmud. This enables the student to follow the core text with the commentaries of Rashi, *Tosafot*, and the customary marginalia. It also provides a clear English translation in contemporary idiom, faithfully based upon the modern Hebrew edition.

At least equal to the linguistic virtues of this edition are the qualities of its graphic design. Rather than intimidate students by confronting them with a page-size block of text, we have divided the page into smaller thematic units. Thus, readers can focus their attention and absorb each discrete discussion before proceeding to the next unit. The design of each page allows for sufficient white space to ease the visual task of reading. The illustrations, one of the most innovative features of the Hebrew edition, have been substantially enhanced and reproduced in color.

The end result is a literary and artistic masterpiece. This has been achieved through the dedicated work of a large team of translators, headed by Rabbi Joshua Schreier, and through the unparalleled creative efforts of Raphaël Freeman and his gifted staff.

The group of individuals who surround Rabbi Steinsaltz and support his work deserve our thanks as well. I have come to appreciate their energy, initiative, and persistence. And I thank the indefatigable Rabbi Menachem Even-Israel, whom I cannot praise highly enough. The quality of his guidance and good counsel is surpassed only by his commitment to the dissemination and perpetuation of his father's precious teachings.

Finally, in humility, awe, and great respect, I acknowledge Rabbi Adin Even-Israel (Steinsaltz). I thank him for the inspirational opportunity he has granted me to work with one of the outstanding sages of our time.

Rabbi Tzvi Hersh Weinreb
Jerusalem 5772

Preface by the Executive Editor

Tractate *Eiruvin* is regarded as one of the most difficult tractates to comprehend both conceptually and technically. The discussions of the joining of courtyards and Shabbat limits, as well as the merging of alleyways, provide myriad challenges to beginners and accomplished scholars alike.

In the middle of the first chapter (13b), a roadmap to successful Torah study is provided in this famous talmudic passage: "Rabbi Abba said that Shmuel said: For three years Beit Shammai and Beit Hillel disagreed. These said: The *halakha* is in accordance with our opinion, and these said: The *halakha* is in accordance with our opinion. Ultimately, a Divine Voice emerged and proclaimed: Both these and those are the words of the living God. However, the *halakha* is in accordance with the opinion of Beit Hillel."

The message is clear. There is room for more than one legitimate opinion in the study of God's Torah.

The Gemara continues and asks: Since both these and those are the words of the living God, why were Beit Hillel privileged to have the *halakha* established in accordance with their opinion? If both are legitimate, why is the opinion of Beit Hillel preferred?

Surprisingly, the answer has little to do with scholarship. The reason is that they were agreeable and forbearing, showing restraint when affronted, and when they taught the *halakha* they would teach both their own statements and the statements of Beit Shammai. Moreover, when they formulated their teachings, in deference to Beit Shammai, when citing a dispute they prioritized the statements of Beit Shammai over their own statements.

Beit Hillel serve as paradigmatic role models for all those studying Torah. One who seeks preeminence must combine excellence in scholarship together with exemplary personal conduct. It is only the fulfillment of mitzvot between man and his Maker in tandem with mitzvot between man and his fellow man that is the hallmark of a true Torah scholar.

The *Koren Talmud Bavli* seeks to follow in the footsteps of Beit Hillel.

Its user-friendly layout, together with its accessible translation, takes the Steinsaltz commentary on the Talmud one step further. It opens the doors to even more students who might have previously felt excluded from the exciting give and take of the study hall, enabling them to take their place as full-fledged participants in the world of Talmud study.

My involvement in the production of the *Koren Talmud Bavli* has been both a privilege and a pleasure. The Shefa Foundation, headed by Rabbi Menachem Even-Israel and devoted to the dissemination of the wide-ranging, monumental works of Rabbi Adin Even-Israel (Steinsaltz), constitutes the Steinsaltz side of this partnership; Koren Publishers Jerusalem, headed by Matthew Miller, with the day-to-day management in the able hands of Raphaël Freeman, constitutes the publishing side of this partnership. In addition, I would like to note the invaluable contribution of Dena Landowne Bailey, who is responsible for laying out the *Koren Talmud Bavli*. The combination of the inspiration, which is the hallmark of Shefa, with the creativity and professionalism for which Koren is renowned and which I experience on a daily basis, has lent the *Koren Talmud Bavli* its outstanding quality in terms of both content and form.

I would like to express my appreciation for Rabbi Dr. Tzvi Hersh Weinreb, the Editor-in-Chief, whose insight and guidance have been invaluable. The contribution of my friend and colleague, Rabbi Dr. Shalom Z. Berger, the Senior Content Editor, cannot be overstated; his title does not begin to convey the excellent direction he has provided in all aspects of this project. The erudite and articulate men and women who serve as translators, editors and copy editors have ensured that this project adheres to the highest standards.

There are several others whose contributions to this project cannot be overlooked. On the Steinsaltz side: Meir HaNegbi, Yacov Elbert, and Tsipora Ifrah. On the Koren side, my colleagues at Koren: Rabbi David Fuchs, Rabbi Hanan Benayahu, Efrat Gross, Rachel Hanstater Meghnagi, Rabbi Eliyahu Misgav, and Rabbi Yinon Chen. Their assistance in all matters, large and small, is appreciated.

At the risk of being repetitious, I would like to thank Rabbi Dr. Berger for introducing me to the world of Steinsaltz. Finally, I would like to thank Rabbi Menachem Even-Israel, with whom it continues to be a pleasure to move forward in this great enterprise.

Rabbi Joshua Schreier
Jerusalem 5772

Introduction by the Publisher

The Talmud has sustained and inspired Jews for thousands of years. Throughout Jewish history, an elite cadre of scholars has absorbed its learning and passed it on to succeeding generations. The Talmud has been the fundamental text of our people.

Beginning in the 1960s, Rabbi Adin Even-Israel (Steinsaltz) שליט״א created a revolution in the history of Talmud study. His translation of the Talmud, first into modern Hebrew and then into other languages, as well the practical learning aids he added to the text, have enabled millions of people around the world to access and master the complexity and context of the world of Talmud.

It is thus a privilege to present the *Koren Talmud Bavli*, an English translation of the talmudic text with the brilliant elucidation of Rabbi Steinsaltz. The depth and breadth of his knowledge are unique in our time. His rootedness in the tradition and his reach into the world beyond it are inspirational.

Working with Rabbi Steinsaltz on this remarkable project has been not only an honor, but a great pleasure. Never shy to express an opinion, with wisdom and humor, Rabbi Steinsaltz sparkles in conversation, demonstrating his knowledge (both sacred and worldly), sharing his wide-ranging interests, and, above all, radiating his passion. I am grateful for the unique opportunity to work closely with him, and I wish him many more years of writing and teaching.

Our intentions in publishing this new edition of the Talmud are threefold. First, we seek to fully clarify the talmudic page to the reader – textually, intellectually, and graphically. Second, we seek to utilize today's most sophisticated technologies, both in print and electronic formats, to provide the reader with a comprehensive set of study tools. And third, we seek to help readers advance in their process of Talmud study.

To achieve these goals, the *Koren Talmud Bavli* is unique in a number of ways:

- The classic *tzurat hadaf* of Vilna, used by scholars since the 1800s, has been reset for great clarity, and opens from the Hebrew "front" of the book. Full *nikkud* has been added to both the talmudic text and Rashi's commentary, allowing for a more fluent reading with the correct pronunciation; the commentaries of *Tosafot* have been punctuated. Upon the advice of many English-speaking teachers of Talmud, we have separated these core pages from the translation, thereby enabling the advanced student to approach the text without the distraction of the translation. This also reduces the number of volumes in the set. At bottom of each *daf*, there is a reference to the corresponding English pages. In addition, the Vilna edition was read against other manuscripts and older print editions, so that texts which had been removed by non-Jewish censors have been restored to their rightful place.

- The English translation, which starts on the English "front" of the book, reproduces the *menukad* Talmud text alongside the English translation (in bold) and commentary and explanation (in a lighter font). The Hebrew and Aramaic text is presented in logical paragraphs. This allows for a fluent reading of the text for the non-Hebrew or non-Aramaic reader. It also allows for the Hebrew reader to refer easily to the text alongside. Where the original text features dialogue or poetry, the English text is laid out in a manner appropriate to the genre. Each page refers to the relevant *daf*.

- Critical contextual tools surround the text and translation: personality notes, providing short biographies of the Sages; language notes, explaining foreign terms borrowed from Greek, Latin, Persian, or Arabic; and background notes, giving information essential to the understanding of the text, including history, geography, botany, archeology, zoology, astronomy, and aspects of daily life in the talmudic era.
- Halakhic summaries provide references to the authoritative legal decisions made over the centuries by the rabbis. They explain the reasons behind each halakhic decision as well as the ruling's close connection to the Talmud and its various interpreters.
- Photographs, drawings, and other illustrations have been added throughout the text – in full color in the Noé and Electronic editions, and in black and white in the Daf Yomi edition – to visually elucidate the text.

This is not an exhaustive list of features of this edition, it merely presents an overview for the English-speaking reader who may not be familiar with the "total approach" to Talmud pioneered by Rabbi Steinsaltz.

Several professionals have helped bring this vast collaborative project to fruition. My many colleagues are noted on the Acknowledgements page, and the leadership of this project has been exceptional.

RABBI MENACHEM EVEN-ISRAEL, DIRECTOR OF THE SHEFA FOUNDATION, was the driving force behind this enterprise. With enthusiasm and energy, he formed the happy alliance with Koren and established close relationships among all involved in the work.

RABBI DR. TZVI HERSH WEINREB שליט״א, EDITOR-IN-CHIEF, brought to this project his profound knowledge of Torah, intellectual literacy of Talmud, and erudition of Western literature. It is to him that the text owes its very high standard, both in form and content, and the logical manner in which the beauty of the Talmud is presented.

RABBI JOSHUA SCHREIER, EXECUTIVE EDITOR, assembled an outstanding group of scholars, translators, editors, and proofreaders, whose standards and discipline enabled this project to proceed in a timely and highly professional manner.

RABBI MEIR HANEGBI, EDITOR OF THE HEBREW EDITION OF THE STEINSALTZ TALMUD, lent his invaluable assistance throughout the work process, supervising the reproduction of the Vilna pages.

RAPHAËL FREEMAN, EXECUTIVE EDITOR OF KOREN, created this Talmud's unique typographic design which, true to the Koren approach, is both elegant and user-friendly.

It has been an enriching experience for all of us at Koren Publishers Jerusalem to work with the Shefa Foundation and the Steinsaltz Center to develop and produce the *Koren Talmud Bavli*. We pray that this publication will be a source of great learning and, ultimately, greater *Avodat Hashem* for all Jews.

Matthew Miller, Publisher
Koren Publishers Jerusalem
Jerusalem 5772

Introduction to **Eiruvin**

See that God has given you the Shabbat, therefore He has given you on the sixth day the bread of two days; remain every man in his place, let no man go out of his place on the seventh day.

(Exodus 16:29)

If you turn away your foot because of the Shabbat, from pursuing your business on My holy day; and call the Shabbat a delight, and the holy of God honorable; and shall honor it by not doing your usual ways, nor pursuing your business, nor speaking of it; then you shall delight yourself in God, and I will make you ride upon the high places of the earth, and I will feed you with the heritage of Jacob your father; for the mouth of God has spoken it.

(Isaiah 58:13–14)

Neither carry forth a burden out of your houses on the Shabbat day, nor do any work; but make the Shabbat day holy, as I commanded your fathers.

(Jeremiah 17:22)

Tractate *Eiruvin*, in its entirety, is an elaboration and conclusion of the subject matter discussed in tractate *Shabbat*, as it focuses on one aspect of the *halakhot* of Shabbat that was not comprehensively elucidated. Tractate *Shabbat* opened with a discussion of the prohibited labor of carrying out on Shabbat. Tractate *Eiruvin* analyzes the details of the rabbinic laws that apply to this act. This prohibited labor is unique in that it is not an inherently creative act; rather, it is merely the act of transferring an object from one domain to another.

In essence, the labor of carrying out highlights the significance of Shabbat as a day of rest, not only a day during which specific activities are prohibited, but also a day on which a premium is placed on quiet, rest, and a sense of relaxation. Shabbat demands that one take a break from the everyday hustle and bustle of moving and carrying from the public to the private domain and vice versa. Similarly, the public thoroughfare calms down from its weekday business and trade. This is accomplished by the creation of domains that are unique to Shabbat. That is, they do not correspond to the domains in force with regard to the rules of commerce, nor those of ritual purity. Transference between different domains is forbidden, as is carrying in the public domain.

The laws of Shabbat recognize four basic domains:

- A private domain
- A public domain
- A *karmelit*, which is an intermediate domain, neither public nor private
- An exempt domain, which is not really a domain at all

In effect, there are only three domains on Shabbat: the private and the public, both of which are domains by Torah law, and the *karmelit*, which is a domain by rabbinic law. All other areas fall into the category of exempt domain.

The private domain is an area of four handbreadths by four handbreadths; a handbreadth is the distance from the tip of the thumb to the tip of the little finger, or slightly more. A private domain is separated from the area around it by walls that are at least ten handbreadths high. In terms of the *halakhot* of Shabbat, an area is a private domain even if it is open to the public and available for use.

The public domain is a thoroughfare at least sixteen cubits wide; a cubit is the distance from the elbow to the end of the index finger. According to some opinions, for an area to be defined as a public domain it must also be frequented by more than 600,000 people daily. The *halakhot* of the public domain apply only up to a height of ten handbreadths.

According to Torah law, these are the two primary domains. The Sages added a third, the *karmelit,* whose legal status by rabbinic law is that of a public domain. The *karmelit* is at least four handbreadths by four handbreadths and not surrounded by walls. Examples of this domain are fields, lakes, etc.

An exempt domain is an area of less than four handbreadths by four handbreadths. In addition, the airspace above ten handbreadths in a public domain or a *karmelit* is an exempt domain, where the *halakhot* of carrying do not apply.

For many years, these domains constituted the only restrictions with regard to carrying out and movement on Shabbat. After the Jewish people settled and began to develop their land, the rabbinic leadership grew concerned that in the course of mundane living in towns and villages, Shabbat was not accorded its due. In particular, the distinctions between the domains of Shabbat were obfuscated; their theoretical parameters did not correspond to the actual utilization of those areas, and the domains and their *halakhot* were interchanged. After all, a private domain full of people and activity could appear, at least superficially, indistinguishable from a public domain. Moreover, people were able to engage in most of their typical weekday activities without actually violating any of the Torah prohibitions. Consequently, the idea of Shabbat as a day of rest was not realized.

Already in the First Temple era, the rabbinic Sages began to issue decrees intended to raise the general level of consciousness concerning Shabbat observance. These decrees fall into the category of *shevut*, prohibitions by rabbinic law designed to enhance the character of Shabbat as a day of rest. Such decrees severely limited the permitted uses of the private domains and placed renewed emphasis on the plain meaning of the passage in Exodus that is the source for all of the Shabbat domains: "Let no man go out of his place on the seventh day." The Sages' decrees limited the designation of private domains to those places that actually belong to an individual and his family. Private domains utilized by more than one individual, e.g., a courtyard shared by several households, as well as the alleyways and paths into which courtyards open, were rendered public domains by rabbinic law.

The decrees issued by the Sages are the starting point for tractate *Eiruvin*. The tractate attempts to arrive at practical solutions for the problems created by these restrictions. The objective is not to abrogate the decrees, but rather to discover alternative methods to underscore the differences between the public and private domains. Similarly, the tractate attempts to discover how one could go beyond the Shabbat limits while maintaining the framework that requires limiting travel on Shabbat. The myriad ordinances that constitute the bulk of tractate *Eiruvin* work within the framework of the established principles of the *halakhot* of Shabbat. Within the halakhic framework, there is extensive use of a series of abstract concepts, e.g., domain, limit, partition, and space. Although these principles are often the basis for stringencies and restrictions, they can also serve as the basis for far-reaching leniencies. The two primary concepts analyzed in the framework of tractate *Eiruvin* are the essence of a partition and the essence of a residence.

The partition is a fundamental component of domains, alleyways, courtyards, houses, and more. Clearly a solid wall with no openings is a partition; however, in most cases the demarcation is less clear-cut. At times, the wall is not sturdy enough to serve as a partition. At times, there are windows, doorways, and other spaces in the wall. At times, the wall does not cover the entire opening. It was therefore necessary to create broader criteria that apply to all forms of partitions, despite their quantitative and qualitative differences: Concepts like *lavud*, which determines that objects less than three handbreadths apart are considered joined; *gode*, through which an incomplete partition can be extended upward or downward; *ḥavot*, through which a cross beam is lowered; and others that broaden the parameters of the concept of partition to include incomplete partitions, e.g., cross beam, side post, form of a doorway, and upright boards.

In a similar vein, it must be established what is considered one's fixed residence. Here too, there are clear-cut examples with regard to which there is no uncertainty. One who eats and sleeps and remains in a house that is his alone, certainly has a residence that is exclusively his. However, since reality is a bit more complex, as in practice most people do not live alone and do not spend all their lives in one place. Therefore, it was necessary to create a broader abstract definition of the concept of fixed residence and establish when it is that several people have the legal status of one person, where family relations and dependence unify them, and to what degree one must be tied to or be present at a certain place in order to be considered a resident. Once these definitions are determined, the simplistic distinction between resident and guest is no longer necessarily significant. The concept of one's residence can, on the one hand, be restricted to the individual alone, while on the other hand it can be expanded to include others. Based on the expansive interpretation of the concept of residence, the possibility of establishing the joining of courtyards, the merging of alleyways, and the joining of Shabbat boundaries becomes feasible.

While some of these solutions might appear to be a disingenuous attempt to circumvent the fundamental *halakha*, in fact, life in accordance with halakhic principles requires their formulation and definition in an abstract and expansive manner. Especially in the case of *eiruv*, where the original prohibitions are rabbinic in nature, there is room for far-reaching leniency in implementing these halakhic principles.

Tractate *Eiruvin* is divided into ten chapters, with the final six chapters included in the present volume:

Chapter Five deals with the methods used to measure the Shabbat limits for the city's residents, what are the borders of the city for that purpose, and how the two thousand cubits of the joining of Shabbat boundaries are measured.

Chapter Six, in which the Gemara returns to the original discussion with regard to the *halakhot* of the joining of courtyards, asks: How and when can residents of a courtyard become as one, enabling them to move objects in their courtyard, and in what cases are they unable to do so?

Chapter Seven continues the discussion of the joining of courtyards from a different perspective: Under what circumstances can two adjacent courtyards be considered as one, and when do the partitions between them render them two separate courtyards? Another topic addressed in this chapter is: How does one conduct oneself in practice when merging alleyways?

Chapter Eight continues addressing this topic. In addition, it discusses the subject of an *eiruv* established for inhabitants of two residences located on different floors of a single structure. In what manner can these be transformed into a single courtyard in every sense? In addition, the *halakhot* of the joining of courtyards when there is a pool of water in the courtyard and the special provisions instituted in that case are discussed.

Chapter Nine deals with clarification of the relationship between the various domains instituted by rabbinic ordinance with regard to Shabbat. It addresses houses, roofs, courtyards, and enclosures, and adjacent courtyards surrounded by fences and those not surrounded by fences. How and when is it permitted to move objects between them and beyond their borders?

Chapter Ten begins with a discussion of the *halakhot* of *eiruv* and the special cases where the Sages were lenient. The bulk of the chapter, however, deals with several *halakhot* whose sole connection to tractate *Eiruvin* lies in the fact that they fall into the category of *shevut*, decrees and preventive measures issued by the Sages to enhance the character of Shabbat as a day of rest. The discussion centers on what is permitted and what is prohibited on Shabbat in those areas where the Sages issued decrees and instituted ordinances. In addition, the degree to which those rabbinic laws are in effect inside and outside the Holy Temple is discussed.

The *halakhot* in this tractate are not merely theoretical. Hundreds of *eiruvin* have been established in cities and towns throughout the United States and around the world based on real-world application of the principles found in this tractate.

Introduction to **Perek V**

The primary focus of this chapter is the *halakhot* of the joining of Shabbat boundaries, concentrating on the joining of city boundaries. To this point, the discussions in the tractate have focused on the individual and how and when he measures his Shabbat limit. In this chapter the Gemara turns its attention to the Shabbat limit of a collective, an entire town.

The *halakhot* of the Shabbat boundaries of an individual are unlike those of a town, as the Shabbat limit of an individual is calculated from a single point from which one measures in all directions. In contrast, a town is a place with indeterminate contours and dimensions, which include sections, several houses, or even one isolated house that cannot be arranged into any uniform shape.

Since the objective of the ordinances of the Sages with regard to the *halakhot* of *eiruv* is leniency, not stricture, the first step must be delineation of the boundaries of the city itself, as anything inside the city is considered a single, four-cubit unit with regard to the Shabbat limit.

This determination of the boundaries of the city is no simple matter, as even a city surrounded by a wall is not typically constructed in a precise manner, and its borders are not straight lines. This is especially true when the fences, houses, and courtyards that are adjacent to the city on all sides, and are in many respects annexed to the city, are taken into consideration. Consequently, a method of determining when and how those areas are incorporated into the city proper must be adopted, so that its Shabbat limit can be measured from a defined border. In practice, the boundaries of the city must be delineated as straight lines, in order to simplify calculation of the measurement. Only then can the actual measurement of the Shabbat limit of the city begin.

The measurement of the Shabbat limits is also a complicated process, as only rarely is the area surrounding a city level and easily measured. When the city is surrounded by hills, numerous diverse difficulties confront one seeking to measure the Shabbat limits through mountains, valleys, and plains. Furthermore, cities are sometimes close enough to share the same Shabbat limit. When are they deemed a single unit, and when is each city or section of a city deemed an independent entity? These issues and related questions constitute the subject matter of this chapter.

מתני׳ כֵּיצַד מְעַבְּרִין אֶת הֶעָרִים? בַּיִת נִכְנָס בַּיִת יוֹצֵא, פָּגוּם נִכְנָס פָּגוּם יוֹצֵא. הָיוּ שָׁם גְּדוּדִיּוֹת גְּבוֹהוֹת עֲשָׂרָה טְפָחִים,

MISHNA **How does one extend** the boundaries of **cities** in order to ensure that all its protrusions are included within the borders of the city?[H] He extends a straight line across the edge of the city, and if **a house is recessed and** another **house protrudes,** or **a turret** [*pagum*][L] **is recessed and** another **turret protrudes** from that line, and similarly, if **there were remnants** of walls **ten handbreadths high,**

HALAKHA

Extending cities – עִיבּוּר הֶעָרִים: A city's Shabbat limits are not measured from each house separately. Rather, they are measured from the city's borders, which are established as a straight line that incorporates all structures that are part of the city (*Shulḥan Arukh, Oraḥ Ḥayyim* 398:6).

LANGUAGE

Turret [*pagum*] – פָּגוּם: From the Greek πῆγμα, *pègma*, meaning an addition to a construction, a stage, or a wooden structure meant to hold something.

וּגְשָׁרִים וּנְפָשׁוֹת שֶׁיֵּשׁ בָּהֶן בֵּית דִּירָה – מוֹצִיאִין אֶת הַמִּדָּה כְּנֶגְדָּן, וְעוֹשִׂין אוֹתָהּ כְּמִין טַבְלָא מְרוּבַּעַת, כְּדֵי שֶׁיְּהֵא נִשְׂכָּר אֶת הַזָּוִיּוֹת.

and bridges and monuments over graves **in which there is a residence, one extends the measure** of that side of the city as though there were other structures **opposite them** in the adjacent corner of the city. **And** prior to measuring the Shabbat limit, **one renders** the city **like a square tablet so that it gains the corners,** although there are actually no houses in those corners.

גמ׳ רַב וּשְׁמוּאֵל: חַד תָּנֵי ״מְעַבְּרִין״, וְחַד תָּנֵי ״מְאַבְּרִין״.

GEMARA The Gemara cites a dispute with regard to the mishna's terminology. **Rav and Shmuel** disagreed: **One taught** that the term in the mishna is ***me'abberin,*** with the letter *ayin,* **and one taught** that the term in the mishna is ***me'abberin,*** with the letter *alef.*

מַאן דְּתָנֵי ״מְאַבְּרִין״ – אֵבֶר אֵבֶר. וּמַאן דְּתָנֵי ״מְעַבְּרִין״ – כְּאִשָּׁה עוּבָּרָה.

The Gemara explains: **The one who taught *me'abberin*** with an *alef* explained the term in the sense of **limb** [*ever*] by **limb.** Determination of the city's borders involves the addition of limbs to the core section of the city. **And the one who taught *me'abberin*** with an *ayin* explained the term in the sense of **a pregnant woman** [*ubbera*] whose belly protrudes. In similar fashion, all the city's protrusions are incorporated in its Shabbat limit.[N]

מְעָרַת הַמַּכְפֵּלָה, רַב וּשְׁמוּאֵל; חַד אָמַר: שְׁנֵי בָתִּים זֶה לִפְנִים מִזֶּה, וְחַד אָמַר: בַּיִת וַעֲלִיָּיה עַל גַּבָּיו.

Apropos this dispute, the Gemara cites similar disputes between Rav and Shmuel. With regard to **the Machpelah Cave,** in which the Patriarchs and Matriarchs are buried, **Rav and Shmuel** disagreed. **One said:** The cave consists of **two rooms, one** farther **in** than **the other. And one said:** It consists of **a room and** a second **story above it.**

בִּשְׁלָמָא לְמַאן דְּאָמַר זֶה עַל גַּב זֶה – הַיְינוּ מַכְפֵּלָה. אֶלָּא לְמַאן דְּאָמַר שְׁנֵי בָתִּים זֶה לִפְנִים מִזֶּה, מַאי מַכְפֵּלָה?

The Gemara asks: **Granted,** this is understandable **according to the one who said** the cave consists of **one** room **above the other,** as **that is** the meaning of **Machpelah, double. However, according to the one who said** it consists of **two rooms, one** farther **in** than **the other,** in **what** sense is it **Machpelah?** Even ordinary houses contain two rooms.

שֶׁכְּפוּלָה בְּזוּגוֹת. ״מַמְרֵא קִרְיַת אַרְבַּע״, אָמַר רַבִּי יִצְחָק: קִרְיַת הָאַרְבַּע זוּגוֹת: אָדָם וְחַוָּה, אַבְרָהָם וְשָׂרָה, יִצְחָק וְרִבְקָה, יַעֲקֹב וְלֵאָה.

Rather, it is called Machpelah in the sense **that it is doubled with** the Patriarchs and Matriarchs, who are buried there **in pairs.** This is similar to the homiletic interpretation of the alternative name for Hebron mentioned in the Torah: **"Mamre** of **Kiryat Ha'Arba,** which is Hebron" (Genesis 35:27). **Rabbi Yitzḥak said:** The city is called Kiryat Ha'Arba, the city of four, because it is **the city of the four couples** buried there: **Adam and Eve, Abraham and Sarah, Isaac and Rebecca,** and **Jacob and Leah.**

NOTES

Me'abberin with an *ayin* and *me'abberin* with an *alef* – מְעַבְּרִין וּמְאַבְּרִין: The *Arukh* explains the word *me'abberin* with the letter *alef* as follows. Just as a person's limbs [*eivarim*] protrude from his body, so too, extra, protruding sections are added to a city. The *Me'iri* explains the word *me'abberin* with the letter *ayin* to mean that just as a pregnant woman [*me'ubberet*] contains an addition to her body in the form of a child, so too, the additions to a city's structures are added to the city's borders.

״וַיְהִי בִּימֵי אַמְרָפֶל״, רַב וּשְׁמוּאֵל; חַד אָמַר: נִמְרוֹד שְׁמוֹ, וְלָמָּה נִקְרָא שְׁמוֹ אַמְרָפֶל – שֶׁאָמַר וְהִפִּיל לְאַבְרָהָם אָבִינוּ בְּתוֹךְ כִּבְשַׁן הָאֵשׁ. וְחַד אָמַר: אַמְרָפֶל שְׁמוֹ, וְלָמָּה נִקְרָא שְׁמוֹ נִמְרוֹד – שֶׁהִמְרִיד אֶת כָּל הָעוֹלָם כּוּלּוֹ עָלָיו בְּמַלְכוּתוֹ.

They disagreed about this verse as well: **"And it came to pass in the days of Amraphel"** (Genesis 14:1). **Rav and Shmuel** both identified Amraphel with Nimrod. However, **one said: Nimrod was his name. And why was his name called Amraphel?** It is a contraction of two Hebrew words: **As he said [*amar*]** the command **and cast [*hippil*] our father Abraham into the fiery furnace,** when Abraham rebelled against and challenged his proclaimed divinity. **And one said: Amraphel was his name. And why was his name called Nimrod? Because he caused the entire world to rebel [*himrid*]**[N] against **God during his reign.**

״וַיָּקָם מֶלֶךְ חָדָשׁ עַל מִצְרָיִם״ רַב וּשְׁמוּאֵל; חַד אָמַר: חָדָשׁ מַמָּשׁ, וְחַד אָמַר: שֶׁנִּתְחַדְּשׁוּ גְּזֵירוֹתָיו.

They also disagreed about this verse: **"There arose a new king over Egypt,** who knew not Joseph" (Exodus 1:8). **Rav and Shmuel** disagreed. **One said:** He was **actually a new** king, **and one said:** He was in fact the old king, but **his decrees were new.**

מַאן דְּאָמַר חָדָשׁ מַמָּשׁ – דִּכְתִיב ״חָדָשׁ״, וּמַאן דְּאָמַר שֶׁנִּתְחַדְּשׁוּ גְּזֵירוֹתָיו – מִדְּלָא כְּתִיב ״וַיָּמָת וַיִּמְלוֹךְ״.

The Gemara explains. **The one who said** he was **actually** a **new** king based his opinion on the fact **that it is written** in the verse that he was **new. And the one who said that his decrees were new** derived his opinion **from** the fact **that it is not written: And** the king **died, and** his successor **reigned,** as it is written, for example, with regard to the kings of Edom (Genesis 36).

וּלְמַאן דְּאָמַר שֶׁנִּתְחַדְּשׁוּ גְּזֵירוֹתָיו, הָא כְּתִיב: ״אֲשֶׁר לֹא יָדַע אֶת יוֹסֵף״! מַאי ״אֲשֶׁר לֹא יָדַע אֶת יוֹסֵף״ – דַּהֲוָה דָּמֵי כְּמַאן דְּלָא יָדַע לֵיהּ לְיוֹסֵף כְּלָל.

The Gemara asks: **And according to the one who said that his decrees were new, isn't it written: "Who knew not Joseph"?** If it were the same king, how could he not know Joseph? The Gemara explains: **What is** the meaning of the phrase: **"Who knew not Joseph"?** It means **that he** conducted himself **like one who did not know Joseph at all.**

(סִימָן שְׁמוֹנֶה עֶשְׂרֵה וּשְׁנֵים עָשָׂר לָמַדְנוּ בְּדָוִד וְיָבֵן).

The Gemara cites a **mnemonic** of key words from a series of traditions cited below: **Eighteen and twelve**[N] **we studied, with regard to David, and he will understand.**

אָמַר רַבִּי יוֹחָנָן: שְׁמוֹנָה עָשָׂר יָמִים גִּידַּלְתִּי אֵצֶל רַבִּי אוֹשַׁעְיָא בְּרִיבִּי, וְלֹא לָמַדְתִּי מִמֶּנּוּ אֶלָּא דָּבָר אֶחָד בְּמִשְׁנָתֵינוּ: כֵּיצַד מְאַבְּרִין אֶת הֶעָרִים – בְּאָלֶף.

Rabbi Yoḥanan said: I spent eighteen days with Rabbi Oshaya[P] **the Distinguished [*Beribbi*],**[L] **and I learned from him only one matter in our Mishna.** In the phrase: **How does one extend cities,** the word *me'abberin* is spelled **with an *alef*.**

אִינִי?! וְהָאָמַר רַבִּי יוֹחָנָן: שְׁנֵים עָשָׂר תַּלְמִידִים הָיוּ לוֹ לְרַבִּי אוֹשַׁעְיָא בְּרִיבִּי, וּשְׁמוֹנָה עָשָׂר יָמִים גִּידַּלְתִּי בֵּינֵיהֶן, וְלָמַדְתִּי לֵב כָּל אֶחָד וְאֶחָד וְחָכְמַת כָּל אֶחָד וְאֶחָד!

The Gemara asks: **Is this so? Didn't Rabbi Yoḥanan say: Rabbi Oshaya the Distinguished had twelve students, and I spent eighteen days among them, and I learned the heart of each and every one,** i.e., the nature and character of each student, **and the** extent of the **wisdom of each and every one?** How could Rabbi Yoḥanan say that he learned only one matter?

לֵב כָּל אֶחָד וְאֶחָד וְחָכְמַת כָּל אֶחָד וְאֶחָד – גָּמַר, גְּמָרָא – לָא גָּמַר. אִיבָּעֵית אֵימָא: מִנַּיְיהוּ דִּידְהוּ – גָּמַר, מִינֵּיהּ דִּידֵיהּ – לָא גָּמַר. וְאִיבָּעֵית אֵימָא: דָּבָר אֶחָד בְּמִשְׁנָתֵינוּ קָאָמַר.

The Gemara answers: It is possible that **he learned the heart of each and every one and the wisdom of each and every one,** but **he did not learn** substantive **tradition.** And **if you wish, say** instead: **From** the students **themselves he learned** many things; **from** Rabbi Oshaya **himself he did not learn** anything beyond that one matter. **And if you wish, say** instead: Rabbi Yoḥanan meant to **say** that he learned only one matter **in our Mishna** from Rabbi Oshaya, but he learned other matters from him based on *baraitot* and other sources.

NOTES

Because he caused the entire world to rebel – שֶׁהִמְרִיד אֶת כָּל הָעוֹלָם כּוּלּוֹ: Rashi explains that Nimrod was the king of Babylonia who advised the generation of the Dispersion to build the Tower of Babel and rebel against God, consequently causing the entire world to rebel against Him.

Eighteen and twelve, etc. – שְׁמוֹנָה עֶשְׂרֵה וּשְׁנֵים עָשָׂר וכו׳: Some texts cite the mnemonic as: Eighteen and twelve, we studied, in his generation, the hearts. According to this version, it refers to the eighteen days Rabbi Yoḥanan spent with Rabbi Oshaya and his twelve students, Rabbi Yoḥanan's statement about studying with Rabbi Oshaya in crowded conditions, Rabbi Oshaya's greatness in his generation, and the hearts of the early and later Sages.

LANGUAGE

The Distinguished [*Beribbi*] – בְּרִיבִּי: This honorific title for a great person was added to the names of several Sages. The word is probably a contraction of the two words bar and Rabbi, which together means the son of a Sage. It was first used as a label for Sages who were sons of Sages. Its meaning was later broadened to refer also to great scholars who did not have distinguished fathers.

PERSONALITIES

Rabbi Oshaya – רַבִּי אוֹשַׁעְיָא: Referred to as Rabbi Oshaya the Great in the Jerusalem Talmud, Rabbi Oshaya was one of the greatest scholars of the transitional generation between the *tanna'im* and the *amora'im*. He was a third-generation scholar, the son of Rabbi Ḥama and the grandson of Rabbi Bisa. He studied Torah with his father and with bar Kappara, and with Rabbi Ḥiyya as a disciple-colleague. His greatest work was arranging collections of precisely worded *baraitot*, to such an extent that it was said that any *baraita* not taught in the schools of Rabbi Ḥiyya and Rabbi Oshaya is unreliable. For this reason, he was called the father of the Mishna.

He was a close associate of the house of the *Nasi*, and was on especially close terms with Rabbi Yehuda Nesia, grandson of Rabbi Yehuda HaNasi.

Rabbi Oshaya had many students, the greatest of whom was Rabbi Yoḥanan, who studied Torah with him for many years. The eighteen days mentioned in this context is probably referring to the beginning of his studies.

It seems that Rabbi Oshaya had a son who was also a Torah scholar, Rabbi Marinos, who continued the good relationship between his family and the house of the *Nasi*.

וְאָמַר רַבִּי יוֹחָנָן: כְּשֶׁהָיִינוּ לוֹמְדִין תּוֹרָה אֵצֶל רַבִּי אוֹשַׁעְיָא, הָיִינוּ יוֹשְׁבִין אַרְבָּעָה אַרְבָּעָה בָּאַמָּה. אָמַר רַבִּי: כְּשֶׁהָיִינוּ לוֹמְדִין תּוֹרָה אֵצֶל רַבִּי אֶלְעָזָר בֶּן שַׁמּוּעַ, הָיִינוּ יוֹשְׁבִין שִׁשָּׁה שִׁשָּׁה בָּאַמָּה.

And Rabbi Yoḥanan said about that period: **When we were studying Torah with Rabbi Oshaya,** it was so crowded with students that **we would sit four in each square cubit.** Similarly, **Rabbi** Yehuda HaNasi **said: When we were studying Torah with Rabbi Elazar ben Shamua, we would sit six in each** square **cubit.**

אָמַר רַבִּי יוֹחָנָן: רַבִּי אוֹשַׁעְיָא בְּרִיבִּי בְּדוֹרוֹ – כְּרַבִּי מֵאִיר בְּדוֹרוֹ, מָה רַבִּי מֵאִיר בְּדוֹרוֹ לֹא יָכְלוּ חֲבֵרָיו לַעֲמוֹד עַל סוֹף דַּעְתּוֹ – אַף רַבִּי אוֹשַׁעְיָא לֹא יָכְלוּ חֲבֵרָיו לַעֲמוֹד עַל סוֹף דַּעְתּוֹ.

Rabbi Yoḥanan said about his teacher: **Rabbi Oshaya the Distinguished** was as great **in his generation as Rabbi Meir** was **in his generation: Just as** with regard to **Rabbi Meir, in his generation his colleagues were unable to fully grasp** the profundity **of his thinking** due to the subtlety of his great mind, **so** it was with **Rabbi Oshaya; his colleagues were unable to fully grasp** the profundity of **his thinking.**

אָמַר רַבִּי יוֹחָנָן: לִבָּן שֶׁל רִאשׁוֹנִים כְּפִתְחוֹ שֶׁל אוּלָם, וְשֶׁל אַחֲרוֹנִים כְּפִתְחוֹ שֶׁל הֵיכָל, וְאָנוּ כִּמְלֹא נֶקֶב מַחַט סִידְקִית.

Similarly, **Rabbi Yoḥanan said: The hearts,** i.e., the wisdom, **of** the **early** Sages were **like the doorway to the Entrance Hall** of the Temple, which was twenty by forty cubits, **and** the hearts **of the later** Sages **were like the doorway to the Sanctuary,** which was ten by twenty cubits. **And we,** i.e., our hearts, **are like** the **eye of a fine needle.**

רִאשׁוֹנִים – רַבִּי עֲקִיבָא, אַחֲרוֹנִים – רַבִּי אֶלְעָזָר בֶּן שַׁמּוּעַ. אִיכָּא דְּאָמְרִי: רִאשׁוֹנִים – רַבִּי אֶלְעָזָר בֶּן שַׁמּוּעַ, אַחֲרוֹנִים – רַבִּי אוֹשַׁעְיָא בְּרִיבִּי, וְאָנוּ כִּמְלֹא נֶקֶב מַחַט סִידְקִית.

He explains: The term **early** Sages is referring to **Rabbi Akiva,** and the term **later** Sages is referring to his student, **Rabbi Elazar ben Shamua. Some say** that the term **early** Sages refers to **Rabbi Elazar ben Shamua** and that the term the **later** Sages refers to **Rabbi Oshaya the Distinguished. And we are like** the **eye of a fine needle.**

אָמַר אַבַּיֵי: וַאֲנַן כִּי סִיכְתָּא בְּגוּדָא לִגְמָרָא. אָמַר רָבָא: וַאֲנַן כִּי אֶצְבַּעְתָּא בְּקִירָא לִסְבָרָא. אָמַר רַב אַשִׁי: אֲנַן כִּי אֶצְבַּעְתָּא בְּבִירָא לִשְׁכְחָה.

On the topic of the steady decline of the generations, **Abaye said: And we,** as far as our capabilities are concerned, **are like a peg in the wall**[N] **with regard to** Torah **study.** Just as a peg enters a wall with difficulty, our studies penetrate our minds only with difficulty. **Rava said: And we are like a finger in wax [*kira*]**[LN] **with regard to logical reasoning.** A finger is not easily pushed into wax, and it extracts nothing from the wax. **Rav Ashi said: We are like a finger in a pit with regard to forgetfulness.** Just as a finger easily enters a large pit, similarly, we quickly forget our studies.

אָמַר רַב יְהוּדָה, אָמַר רַב: בְּנֵי יְהוּדָה שֶׁהִקְפִּידוּ עַל לְשׁוֹנָם – נִתְקַיְּימָה תּוֹרָתָם בְּיָדָם, בְּנֵי גָלִיל שֶׁלֹּא הִקְפִּידוּ עַל לְשׁוֹנָם – לֹא נִתְקַיְּימָה תּוֹרָתָם בְּיָדָם.

The Gemara continues the discussion relating to study and comprehension, and cites that which **Rav Yehuda said that Rav said:** With regard to **the people of Judea, who were particular in their speech** and always made certain that it was both precise and refined, **their Torah** knowledge **endured for them;** with regard to **the people of the Galilee, who were not particular in their speech, their Torah** knowledge **did not endure for them.**

מִידֵּי בְּקְפֵידָא תַּלְיָא מִילְּתָא? אֶלָּא בְּנֵי יְהוּדָה דְּדַיְיקִי לִישָּׁנָא, וּמִתְנַחֵי לְהוּ סִימָנָא – נִתְקַיְּימָה תּוֹרָתָן בְּיָדָן, בְּנֵי גָלִיל דְּלָא דַּיְיקִי לִישָּׁנָא וְלָא מִתְנַחֵי לְהוּ סִימָנָא – לֹא נִתְקַיְּימָה תּוֹרָתָן בְּיָדָם.

The Gemara asks: **Is this matter at all dependent on** being **particular** with one's language? **Rather,** with regard to **the people of Judea, who were precise in their language and** who **would formulate mnemonics**[N] for their studies, **their Torah** knowledge **endured for them;** with regard to **the people of the Galilee, who were not precise in their language and** who **would not formulate mnemonics, their Torah** knowledge **did not endure for them.**

LANGUAGE

Wax [*kira*] – קִירָא: From the Greek κῆρος, *kèros*, meaning wax.

NOTES

Like a peg in the wall – **כִּי סִיכְתָּא בְּגוּדָא**: Rabbeinu Ḥananel explains further that just as a peg in a wall does nothing to strengthen the wall, our studying is also ineffective.

Like a finger in wax – **כִּי אֶצְבַּעְתָּא בְּקִירָא**: Rabbeinu Ḥananel explains that this is referring to a finger inserted into very soft wax. As soon as one removes his finger, the depression he created disappears.

Who were precise in their language and who would formulate mnemonics – **דְּדַיְיקִי לִישָּׁנָא וּמִתְנַחֵי לְהוּ סִימָנָא**: One who is imprecise in his language is unable to use mnemonics to link the different sections of his studies, as the mnemonic will be ineffective. However, one who is exact in his phraseology can use mnemonics to remember the connections between various matters.

NOTES

Saul and David – **שָׁאוּל וְדָוִד**: Elsewhere, the Gemara describes Saul and David as the greatest Torah scholars of their generation, who would deliver public discourses. However, Saul's opinions were not in accordance with the accepted *halakha*, as indicated by the verse subsequently quoted in the Gemara, "And wherever he turned himself he did them mischief," whereas King David's teachings were in accordance with the accepted *halakha*.

בְּנֵי יְהוּדָה גָּמְרוּ מֵחַד רַבָּה – נִתְקַיְּימָה תּוֹרָתָן בְּיָדָם, בְּנֵי גָלִיל דְּלָא גָּמְרִי מֵחַד רַבָּה – לֹא נִתְקַיְּימָה תּוֹרָתָן בְּיָדָם.

Furthermore, with regard to **the people of Judea, who studied from one teacher, their Torah** knowledge **endured for them,** as their teacher provided them with a consistent approach; however, with regard to **the people of the Galilee, who did not study from one teacher,** but rather from several teachers, **their Torah** knowledge **did not endure for them,** as it was a combination of the approaches and opinions of a variety of Sages.

רָבִינָא אָמַר: בְּנֵי יְהוּדָה דְּגַלּוֹ מַסֶּכְתָּא – נִתְקַיְּימָה תּוֹרָתָן בְּיָדָם, בְּנֵי גָלִיל דְּלָא גַּלּוֹ מַסֶּכְתָּא – לֹא נִתְקַיְּימָה תּוֹרָתָן בְּיָדָם.

Ravina said: With regard to **the people of Judea, who would** publicly **disclose the tractate** to be studied in the coming term so that everyone could prepare and study it in advance (*ge'onim*), **their Torah** knowledge **endured for them;** with regard to **the people of the Galilee, who would not disclose the tractate** to be studied in the coming term, **their Torah** knowledge **did not endure for them.**

דָּוִד גַּלֵּי מַסֶּכְתָּא, שָׁאוּל לָא גַּלֵּי מַסֶּכְתָּא. דָּוִד דְּגַלֵּי מַסֶּכְתָּא כְּתִיב בֵּיהּ: ״יְרֵאֶיךָ יִרְאוּנִי וְיִשְׂמָחוּ״, שָׁאוּל דְּלָא גַּלֵּי מַסֶּכְתָּא כְּתִיב בֵּיהּ: (״אֶל כָּל) אֲשֶׁר יִפְנֶה

The Gemara relates that King **David would disclose the tractate** to be studied in advance, whereas **Saul would not disclose the tractate** to be studied.[N] **With regard to David, who would disclose the tractate, it is written: "Those who fear You will see me and be glad"** (Psalms 119:74), since all were prepared and could enjoy his Torah. **With regard to Saul, who would not disclose the tractate** to be studied, **it is written: "And wherever he turned himself**

Perek **V**
Daf **53** Amud **b**

NOTES

He did them mischief – **יַרְשִׁיעַ**: In other words, since the students did not know their topic of study in advance, they were comparable to wicked and ignorant people (*Me'iri*).

BACKGROUND

Like beets on the ground – **כִּתְרָדִין עֲלֵי אֲדָמָה**: The image below is of beet greens soon after they have sprouted.

Beet sprouts

יַרְשִׁיעַ״.

he did them mischief"[N] (I Samuel 14:47).

וְאָמַר רַבִּי יוֹחָנָן: מִנַּיִן שֶׁמָּחַל לוֹ הַקָּדוֹשׁ בָּרוּךְ הוּא עַל אוֹתוֹ עָוֹן – שֶׁנֶּאֱמַר: ״מָחָר אַתָּה וּבָנֶיךָ עִמִּי״ – עִמִּי בִּמְחִיצָתִי.

The Gemara concludes the mention of Saul on a positive note. **And Rabbi Yoḥanan said: From where** is it derived **that the Holy One, Blessed be He, forgave him for that sin,** the massacre of Nov, the city of priests? **As it is stated** that the spirit of Samuel said to him: "And the Lord will also deliver Israel with you into the hand of the Philistines, **and tomorrow shall you and your sons be with me"** (I Samuel 28:19); the phrase **"with me"** means **within my partition** together with me in heaven, i.e., on the same level as the righteous prophet Samuel.

אָמַר רַבִּי אַבָּא: אִי אִיכָּא דְּמַשְׁאִיל לְהוּ לִבְנֵי יְהוּדָה דְּדַיְיקִי לִשָּׁנֵי: ״מְאַבְּרִין״ תְּנַן, אוֹ ״מְעַבְּרִין״ תְּנַן? ״אַכּוּזוֹ״ תְּנַן, אוֹ ״עַכּוּזוֹ״ תְּנַן? יָדְעִי.

The Gemara returns to the earlier question with regard to the correct reading of the word *me'abberin*. **Rabbi Abba said: If there is anyone who can ask the people of Judea, who are precise in their language,** whether the term in the mishna that **we learned** is ***me'abberin*** with an *alef* **or *me'abberin*** with an *ayin*, he should ask them. Similarly, with regard to the blemishes of a firstborn animal, **was** the term meaning its hindquarters that **we learned** in the mishna ***akkuzo*** with an *alef*, **or did we learn *akkuzo*** with an *ayin*? **They would know.**

שְׁאֵילִינְהוּ, וְאָמְרִי לֵיהּ: אִיכָּא דְּתָנֵי ״מְאַבְּרִין״, וְאִיכָּא דְּתָנֵי ״מְעַבְּרִין״. אִיכָּא דְּתָנֵי ״אַכּוּזוֹ״, וְאִיכָּא דְּתָנֵי ״עַכּוּזוֹ״.

The Gemara answers: **One asked** the people of Judea, **and they said to him: Some teach *me'abberin*** with an *alef*, **and some teach *me'abberin*** with an *ayin*. **Some teach *akkuzo*** with an *alef*, **and some teach *akkuzo*** with an *ayin*. Both versions are well founded and neither one is erroneous.

בְּנֵי יְהוּדָה דַּיְיקִי לִישָּׁנָא מַאי הִיא? דְּהַהוּא בַּר יְהוּדָה דַּאֲמַר לְהוּ: טַלִּית יֵשׁ לִי לִמְכּוֹר. אָמְרוּ לֵיהּ: מַאי גַּוְון טַלִּיתָךְ? אֲמַר לְהוּ: כִּתְרָדִין עֲלֵי אֲדָמָה.

Having mentioned that **the people of Judea are precise in their speech,** the Gemara asks: **What is** the meaning of this? The Gemara answers with an example: **As** in the case of **a certain person from Judea who said to those** within earshot: **I have a cloak to sell. They said to him: What color is your cloak? He said to them: Like beets on the ground,**[B] providing an exceedingly precise description of the exact shade of the cloak, the green tint of beet greens when they first sprout.

בְּנֵי גָלִיל דְּלָא דַּיְיקִי לִישָּׁנָא מַאי הִיא? (דְּתַנְיָא:) דְּההוּא בַּר גָּלִילָא [דַּהֲוָה קָאָזֵיל] וַאֲמַר לְהוּ: אַמַּר לְמַאן, אַמַּר לְמַאן? אָמְרוּ לֵיהּ: גְּלִילָאָה שׁוֹטֶה, חֲמַר לְמִירְכַּב, אוֹ חֲמַר לְמִישְׁתִּי, עֲמַר לְמִילְבַּשׁ, אוֹ אִימַּר לְאִיתְכְּסָאָה?

The Gemara returns to **the people of the Galilee, who are not precise in their speech. What is** the meaning of this? The Gemara cites examples: **As it was taught** in a *baraita* **that** there was **a certain person from the Galilee who would walk and say** to people: **Who has *amar*? Who has *amar*? They said to him: Foolish Galilean,** what do you mean? Galileans did not pronounce the guttural letters properly, so it was unclear whether he sought **a donkey [*ḥamor*] to ride, or wine [*ḥamar*] to drink, wool [*amar*] to wear, or a lamb [*imar*] to slaughter.** This is an example of the lack of precision in the Galileans' speech.

הַהִיא אִיתְּתָא דְּבָעְיָא לְמֵימַר לַחֲבֶרְתָּהּ "תָּאִי דְּאוֹכְלִיךְ חֶלְבָּא", אָמְרָה לָהּ: שְׁלוֹכְתִּי, תּוֹכְלִיךְ לָבְיָא.

The Gemara cites another example of the lack of linguistic precision of the Galileans: There was **a certain woman who wanted to say to her friend:** My neighbor, **come and I will feed you milk [*ta'i de'okhlikh ḥelba*];** however, due to the imprecise articulation of her words, **she said to her: My neighbor,** may a **lioness eat you [*tokhlikh lavya*].**

הַהִיא אִתְּתָא דְּאָתְיָא לְקַמֵּיהּ דְּדַיָּינָא, אָמְרָה לֵיהּ: מָרִי כִּירִי, תַּפְלָא הָוֵית לִי וּגְנָבוּךְ מִין. וּכְדוּ הֲוָות דְּכַד שְׁדַרוּ לָךְ עִילָּוֵיהּ – לָא מָטֵי כַּרְעִיךְ אַאַרְעָא.

The Gemara cites another example of the ignorance and incivility of the Galileans: There was **a certain woman who came before a judge** intending to say: Master, sir [*Mari kiri*, spelled with a *kuf*], I had a board, and they stole it from me [*tavla havet li ugenavuha mimeni*]. But instead **she said to him: Master, servant [*Mari kiri*,[L] spelled with a *kaf*], I had a beam and they stole you from me [*tafla havet li ugenavukh min*]. And it was so** large, **that when they would hang you upon it, your feet would not reach the ground.**

אַמְהֲתָא דְּבֵי רַבִּי, כִּי הֲוָה מִשְׁתַּעְיָא בִּלְשׁוֹן חָכְמָה, אָמְרָה הָכִי: עָלֶת נָקְפַתְּ בַּכַּד, יִדְאוּן נִישְׁרַיָּא לְקִינֵּיהוֹן.

In contrast to the speech of the Galileans, which indicates ignorance and loutishness, the Gemara cites examples of the clever phraseology of the inhabitants of Judea and the Sages: **The maidservant in the house of Rabbi** Yehuda HaNasi,[N] **when she would speak enigmatically,** employing euphemistic terminology or in riddles, **she would say as follows: The ladle** used for drawing wine from the jug **is** already **knocking against** the bottom of **the jug,** i.e., the wine jug is almost empty. **Let the eagles fly to their nests,** i.e., let the students return home, as there is nothing left for them to drink.

וְכַד הֲוָה בָּעֵי דְּלֵיתְבוּן, הֲוָה אַמְרָה לְהוּ: יַעֲדֵי בָּתַר חֲבֶרְתָּהּ מִינָּהּ, וְתִתְקְפֵי עָלֶת בַּכַּד כְּאִילְפָא דְּאָזְלָא בְּיַמָּא.

And when Rabbi Yehuda HaNasi **wanted them to sit, she would say to them: Let us remove** the stopper **from another** jug, **and let the ladle** float **in the jug like a ship sailing in the sea.**

רַבִּי יוֹסֵי בַּר אַסְיָין, כִּי הֲוָה מִשְׁתָּעֵי בִּלְשׁוֹן חָכְמָה, אֲמַר: עֲשׂוּ לִי שׁוֹר בְּמִשְׁפָּט בְּטוּר מִסְכֵּן.

The Gemara also relates that **when Rabbi Yosei bar Asyan would speak enigmatically, he would say: Prepare for me an ox in judgment on a poor mountain.** His method was to construct words by combining words from Aramaic translations of Hebrew words or Hebrew translations of Aramaic words. Ox is *tor* in Aramaic; judgment is *din*. Combined they form *teradin*, beets. Mountain in Hebrew is *har*, which they pronounced *ḥar*; poor is *dal*. Together it spells *ḥardal*, mustard. Thus, Rabbi Yosei bar Asyan was requesting beets in mustard.

וְכַד הֲוָה שָׁאֵיל בְּאוּשְׁפִּיזָא, אֲמַר הָכִי: גְּבַר פּוּם דֵּין חַי, מַה זּוֹ טוֹבָה יֵשׁ?

And when he would inquire about an inn, he would say as follows: This man here is raw; what is this good that there is? The phrase "this man here is raw" is used in a similar syllable-by-syllable translation: Man in Hebrew is *ish*; here is *po*; this is *zeh*; and raw is *na*. All together, they sound like *ushpazikhna*, i.e., an innkeeper (Rabbeinu Ḥananel). In other words, Rabbi Yosei bar Asyan was asking after the innkeeper.

רַבִּי אַבָּהוּ, כִּי הֲוָה מִשְׁתָּעֵי בִּלְשׁוֹן חָכְמָה, הֲוָה אֲמַר הָכִי: אַתְרִיגוּ לְפֶחָמִין, אַרְקִיעוּ לְזְהָבִין, וַעֲשׂוּ לִי שְׁנֵי מַגִּידֵי בַּעֲלָטָה. אִיכָּא דְּאָמְרִי: וְיַעֲשׂוּ לִי בָּהֶן שְׁנֵי מַגִּידֵי בַּעֲלָטָה.

When Rabbi Abbahu would speak enigmatically,[N] **he would say as follows: Make the coals the color of an *etrog*; beat the golden ones,**[N] i.e., spread out the coals, which redden like gold when they glow; **and make me two speakers-in-the-dark,** i.e., roosters, which announce the dawn when it is still dark. **Some say** a slightly different version: **And they shall make me in them,** on the coals, i.e., roast for me on top of the coals, **two speakers-in-the-dark.**

LANGUAGE

Servant [*kiri*] – כִּירִי: From the Greek χείριος, *keyrios*, meaning enslaved or a servant. The woman apparently used the word *kiri*, spelled with the letter *kaf*, rather than the honorific term *kiri*, spelled with the letter *kuf*. The word *kiri* with the letter *kuf* is from the Greek κύριε, *kurie*, meaning sir.

NOTES

The maidservant in the house of Rabbi Yehuda HaNasi – אַמְהֲתָא דְּבֵי רַבִּי: Rabbeinu Ḥananel had a slightly different version of this text, which led him to offer a different interpretation. He explains that these statements were made by the maidservant to Rabbi Yehuda HaNasi himself when the wine in the barrel was finished. She wished to ask in cryptic fashion whether the students should be told to conclude their visit, or whether a new barrel should be opened and they should stay.

Speak enigmatically – מִשְׁתָּעֵי בִּלְשׁוֹן חָכְמָה: Rabbi Abbahu used these clever turns of phrase so that not everyone would understand what was being said. Apparently, the hints with regard to beets in mustard and to the preparation of roosters were so that the speaker would not appear gluttonous.

With regard to the innkeeper mentioned earlier in the Gemara, the Maharsha explains that Rabbi Yosei was inquiring after the health of the innkeeper's wife, and since this was unusual for him, he did so discreetly.

Make the coals the color of an *etrog*; beat the golden ones – אַתְרִיגוּ לְפֶחָמִין, אַרְקִיעוּ לְזְהָבִין: The *Arukh* explains that these verbs should be read as *hatrigo*, which means to hit, break, beat; and *harkiu*, move it outside under the sky [*rakia*].

NOTES

And some say it refers to a tractate – ואמרי לה מסכתא: The *Arukh* explains that the reference is to a section of the halakhic midrash, *Torat Kohanim*. According to this interpretation, the term *eiranit* is understood to mean a villager, as *Torat Kohanim* is not included in the Mishna.

He has taken counsel with the one who crowns – נתייעץ במכתיר: There is a tradition which states that Rabbi Abbahu took counsel with Rabbi Yoḥanan, the head of the academy, and went to join Rabbi Yehoshua, son of Rabban Gamliel, son of Rabbi Yehuda HaNasi, who lived in the South (*Sefer Yoḥasin HaShalem*). The *Ge'on Ya'akov* explains that Rabbi Abbahu took counsel with the authorities in Caesarea and dried out [*hingiv*], i.e., disturbed, Mephibosheth, those who would shame [*mevaishei*] the Sages, i.e., the heretics who would engage them in disputes.

A remainder in the pot – פאה באלפס: Etiquette does not require one to leave anything in the pot, as not everyone sees what is left in it, whereas all can see what a person leaves on his own plate.

HALAKHA

A remainder in the pot – פאה באלפס: It is not necessary to leave something in the pot to give to the attendant serving the meal. However, it is indeed proper to leave something for him from the plate itself, in accordance with Rashi's explanation of this gemara (*Shulḥan Arukh, Oraḥ Ḥayyim* 170:3).

LANGUAGE

Pot [*ilpas*] – אלפס: From the Greek λοπάς, *lopas*, meaning a cooking utensil that has a lid.

אמרו ליה רבנן לרבי אבהו: הצפינו היכן רבי אלעאי צפון: אמר להן: עלץ בנערה אהרונית אחרונית עירנית והנעירתו.

In a similarly clever manner, **the Sages said to Rabbi Abbahu: Show us [*hatzpinenu*] where Rabbi Elai is hiding [*tzafun*],** as we do not know his whereabouts. **He said to them: He rejoiced with the latter [*aḥaronit*] Aharonic [*Aharonit*] girl; she is lively [*eiranit*] and kept him awake [*vehiniratu*].**

אמרי לה: אשה,

There are two ways to understand this cryptic statement: **Some say** it refers to **a woman,** i.e., he married a young girl from a priestly family [Aharonic], who is his second [latter] wife, from a village [*eiranit*], and he is sleeping now because she kept him awake during the night.

ואמרי לה: מסכתא.

And some say it refers to **a tractate.**[N] The term girl refers to the tractate; Aharonic indicates that it is a tractate from the order of *Kodashim*, which deals with the priestly service. The phrase the latter means that it is his latest course of study, and lively alludes to the challenging nature of the subject matter. Since he was awake all night studying, he is presently sleeping.

אמרי ליה לרבי אלעאי: הצפינו היכן רבי אבהו [צפון]! אמר להן: נתייעץ במכתיר, והנגיב למפיבשת.

The Gemara continues: **They said to Rabbi Elai: Show us where Rabbi Abbahu is hiding,** as we do not know where he is. **He said to them: He has taken counsel with the one who crowns,**[N] i.e., the *Nasi*, who appoints the Sages, **and has gone south [*hingiv*] to Mephibosheth,** i.e., he has headed to the Sages of the south, referred to here as Mephibosheth, who was King Saul's grandson and a great Sage of his time.

אמר רבי יהושע בן חנניה: מימי לא נצחני אדם חוץ מאשה תינוק ותינוקת. אשה מאי היא? פעם אחת נתארחתי אצל אכסניא אחת, עשתה לי פולין. ביום ראשון אכלתים ולא שיירתי מהן כלום. שנייה ולא שיירתי מהן כלום. ביום שלישי הקדיחתן במלח. כיון שטעמתי – משכתי ידי מהן.

Having discussed the clever speech of various Sages, the Gemara relates that **Rabbi Yehoshua ben Ḥananya said** as follows: **In all my days, no person defeated me** in a verbal encounter **except for a woman, a young boy, and a young girl. What is** the encounter in which **a woman** got the better of me? **One time I was staying at a certain inn** and the hostess **prepared me beans. On the first day I ate them and left nothing over,** although proper etiquette dictates that one should leave over something on his plate. On the **second** day I again ate **and left nothing over.** On the third day **she over-salted them** so that they were inedible. **As soon as I tasted** them, **I withdrew my hands from them.**

אמרה לי: רבי, מפני מה אינך סועד? אמרתי לה: כבר סעדתי מבעוד יום. אמרה לי: היה לך למשוך ידיך מן הפת.

She said to me: My Rabbi, why aren't you eating beans as on the previous days? Not wishing to offend her, **I said to her: I have already eaten during the daytime. She said to me: You should have withdrawn your hand from bread** and left room for some beans.

אמרה לי: רבי, שמא לא הנחת פאה בראשונים? ולא כך אמרו חכמים: אין משיירין פאה באלפס, אבל משיירין פאה בקערה.

She then **said to me: My Rabbi, perhaps you did not leave a remainder** of food on your plate **on the first** days, which is why you are leaving over food today. **Isn't this what the Sages said: One need not leave a remainder in the pot**[NH] **[*ilpas*],**[L] **but one must leave a remainder on the plate** as an expression of etiquette (*Tosafot*). This is the incident in which a woman got the better of Rabbi Yehoshua ben Ḥananya.

תינוקת מאי היא? פעם אחת הייתי מהלך בדרך, והיתה דרך עוברת בשדה והייתי מהלך בה. אמרה לי תינוקת אחת: רבי, לא שדה היא זו? אמרתי לה: לא, דרך כבושה היא. אמרה לי: ליסטים כמותך כבשוה.

What is the incident with **a young girl? One time I was walking along the path, and the path passed through a field, and I was walking on it. A certain young girl said to me: My Rabbi, isn't this a field?** One should not walk through a field, so as not to damage the crops growing there. **I said to her: Isn't it a well-trodden path** in the field, across which one is permitted to walk? **She said to me: Robbers like you have trodden it.** In other words, it previously had been prohibited to walk through this field, and it is only due to people such as you, who paid no attention to the prohibition, that a path has been cut across it. Thus, the young girl defeated Rabbi Yehoshua ben Ḥananya in a debate.

תינוק מאי היא? פעם אחת הייתי מהלך בדרך, וראיתי תינוק יושב על פרשת דרכים. ואמרתי לו: באיזה דרך נלך לעיר? אמר לי: זו קצרה וארוכה, וזו ארוכה וקצרה. והלכתי בקצרה וארוכה, כיון שהגעתי לעיר מצאתי שמקיפין אותה גנות ופרדיסין.

What is the incident with **a young boy? One time I was walking along the path, and I saw a young boy sitting at the crossroads. And I said to him: On which path shall we walk** in order to get **to the city? He said to me: This** path **is short and long, and that** path **is long and short. I walked on the** path that was **short and long. When I approached the city I found that gardens and orchards surrounded it,** and I did not know the trails leading through them to the city.

חָזַרְתִּי לַאֲחוֹרַי. אָמַרְתִּי לוֹ: בְּנִי, הֲלֹא אָמַרְתָּ לִי קְצָרָה! אָמַר לִי: וְלֹא אָמַרְתִּי לְךָ אֲרוּכָּה?! נְשַׁקְתִּיו עַל רֹאשׁוֹ, וְאָמַרְתִּי לוֹ: אַשְׁרֵיכֶם יִשְׂרָאֵל שֶׁכּוּלְּכֶם חֲכָמִים גְּדוֹלִים אַתֶּם, מִגְּדוֹלְכֶם וְעַד קְטַנְּכֶם.

I went back and met the young boy again and **said to him: My son, didn't you tell me** that this way is **short? He said to me: And didn't I tell you** that it is also **long?**[N] **I kissed him on his head and said to him: Happy are you, O Israel, for you are all exceedingly wise, from your old to your young.**

רַבִּי יוֹסֵי הַגְּלִילִי הֲוָה קָא אָזֵיל בְּאוֹרְחָא, אַשְׁכַּחָהּ לִבְרוּרְיָה, אֲמַר לָהּ: בְּאֵיזוֹ דֶּרֶךְ נֵלֵךְ לְלוֹד? אָמְרָה לֵיהּ: גְּלִילִי שׁוֹטֶה, לֹא כָּךְ אָמְרוּ חֲכָמִים אַל תַּרְבֶּה שִׂיחָה עִם הָאִשָּׁה; הָיָה לְךָ לוֹמַר: בְּאֵיזֶה לְלוֹד.

Having discussed wise speech and the wisdom of Jewish women, the Gemara cites the following story: **Rabbi Yosei HaGelili was walking along the way,** and **met Berurya. He said to her: On which path shall we walk** in order to get **to Lod? She said to him: Foolish Galilean, didn't the Sages say: Do not talk much with women? You should have said** your question more succinctly: **Which way to Lod?**

בְּרוּרְיָה אַשְׁכַּחְתֵּיהּ לְהַהוּא תַּלְמִידָא דַּהֲוָה קָא גָּרֵיס בִּלְחִישָׁה,

The Gemara relates more of Berurya's wisdom: **Berurya came across a certain student who was whispering his studies** rather than raising his voice.

NOTES

Short and long – קְצָרָה וַאֲרוּכָּה: Rabbi Yehoshua thought the young boy meant that while one path is shorter than the other, it is still a very long road, whereas the other road is actually longer than the first, but is also called short, as it is not that much longer than the first (Maharshal).

בָּטְשָׁה בֵּיהּ, אָמְרָה לֵיהּ: לֹא כָּךְ כָּתוּב: "עֲרוּכָה בַכֹּל וּשְׁמוּרָה", אִם עֲרוּכָה בִּרְמ"ח אֵבָרִים שֶׁלְּךָ – מִשְׁתַּמֶּרֶת, וְאִם לָאו – אֵינָהּ מִשְׁתַּמֶּרֶת. תָּנָא: תַּלְמִיד אֶחָד הָיָה לְרַבִּי אֱלִיעֶזֶר שֶׁהָיָה שׁוֹנֶה בְּלַחַשׁ, לְאַחַר שָׁלֹשׁ שָׁנִים שָׁכַח תַּלְמוּדוֹ.

She kicked him and said to him: Isn't it written as follows: "Ordered in all things and secure" (II Samuel 23:5), which indicates that **if** the Torah **is ordered in your 248 limbs,** i.e., if you exert your entire body in studying it, **it will be secure, and if not, it will not be secure.** The Gemara relates that **it was** similarly **taught** in a *baraita*: **Rabbi Eliezer had a student who would study quietly,** and **after three years he forgot his studies.**

תָּנָא: תַּלְמִיד אֶחָד הָיָה לוֹ לְרַבִּי אֱלִיעֶזֶר שֶׁנִּתְחַיֵּיב בִּשְׂרֵיפָה לַמָּקוֹם. אָמְרוּ: הַנִּיחוּ לוֹ, אָדָם גָּדוֹל שִׁמֵּשׁ.

Incidental to the story cited above involving a student of Rabbi Eliezer, the Gemara cites the following episode: **It was taught** in a *baraita*: **Rabbi Eliezer had a student who was liable for** the punishment of death by **burning,** for his sins **against God,** but the Rabbis **said: Let him** alone and do not punish him as he deserves, because **he served a great person.**

אֲמַר לֵיהּ שְׁמוּאֵל לְרַב יְהוּדָה: שִׁינָּנָא, פְּתַח פּוּמֵיךְ קְרֵי, פְּתַח פּוּמֵיךְ תְּנֵי, כִּי הֵיכִי דְּתִתְקַיֵּים בִּיךְ וְתוֹרִיךְ חַיֵּי. שֶׁנֶּאֱמַר: "כִּי חַיִּים הֵם לְמֹצְאֵיהֶם וּלְכָל בְּשָׂרוֹ מַרְפֵּא", אַל תִּקְרֵי "לְמֹצְאֵיהֶם" אֶלָּא "לְמוֹצִיאֵיהֶם בַּפֶּה".

The Gemara cites instructions issued by Shmuel that are similar to those of Berurya. **Shmuel said to Rav Yehuda: Keen scholar** [*shinnana*],[L] **open your mouth and read** from the Torah, **open your mouth and study** the Talmud, **in order that** your studies **should endure in you and** that **you should live a long life, as it is stated: "For they are life to those who find them, and health to all their flesh"** (Proverbs 4:22). **Do not read: "To those who find them** [*lemotzeihem*]," **but** rather **"to those who express them** [*lemotzi'eihem*]," **with** their **mouth.**

אֲמַר לֵיהּ שְׁמוּאֵל לְרַב יְהוּדָה: שִׁינָּנָא, חֲטוֹף וֶאֱכוֹל, חֲטוֹף וְאִישְׁתֵּי, דְּעָלְמָא דְּאָזְלִינַן מִינֵּיהּ כְּהִלּוּלָא דָּמֵי.

The Gemara cites additional instructions issued by Shmuel: **Shmuel said to Rav Yehuda,** his beloved student: **Keen scholar, grab and eat,**[N] **grab and drink, as the world from which we are departing is like a wedding feast,** whose joy is only temporary, and one who does not take pleasure in it now will not be able to do so in the future.

אֲמַר לֵיהּ רַב לְרַב הַמְנוּנָא: בְּנִי, אִם יֵשׁ לְךָ – הֵיטֵב לָךְ, שֶׁאֵין בִּשְׁאוֹל תַּעֲנוּג וְאֵין לַמָּוֶת הִתְמַהְמֵהַּ. וְאִם תֹּאמַר אַנִּיחַ לְבָנַי – חוֹק בִּשְׁאוֹל מִי יַגִּיד לָךְ. בְּנֵי הָאָדָם דּוֹמִים לְעִשְׂבֵי הַשָּׂדֶה, הַלָּלוּ נוֹצְצִין וְהַלָּלוּ נוֹבְלִין.

Similarly, **Rav said to Rav Hamnuna: My son, if you have** money, **do well for yourself.** There is no point waiting, **as there is no pleasure in the netherworld, and death does not tarry. And if you say: I will** save up in order to **leave for my children, who told you the law**[N] **of the netherworld,** i.e., how do you know which of you will die first (*Arukh*)? **People are similar to grass of the field,** in that **these blossom,** i.e., grow, and their actions are blessed, **and these wither**[N] and die.

LANGUAGE

Keen scholar [*shinnana*] **– שִׁינָּנָא:** According to many commentaries, Rashi among them, *shinnana* means sharp, and it is an honorific that Shmuel conferred upon his most prominent student. However, the *ge'onim* explain, based on old Aramaic vernacular, that *shinnana* means the one with the large teeth, and that was Rav Yehuda's nickname.

NOTES

Grab and eat – חֲטוֹף וֶאֱכוֹל: The *Me'iri* explains: Eat and drink quickly so that you can return to Torah study, as the pleasures of this world are transient and pass quickly.

I will leave for my children, who told you the law – אַנִּיחַ לְבָנַי חוֹק...מִי יַגִּיד לָךְ: It appears that Rashi and the *Arukh* explain the word law [*ḥok*] to mean sustenance. Therefore, the statement can be understood as follows: If you say, I will leave sustenance for my children, who will tell you in the netherworld how your food is being used?

Blossom and wither – נוֹצְצִין וְנוֹבְלִין: Some explain this statement as emphasizing that every person has his own source of livelihood and does not need to rely on his father, just as grass in a field flourishes without being sown (*Ge'on Ya'akov*).

HALAKHA

Studying aloud – לימוד בקול רם: It is proper to study Torah out loud, as in this way one's studies will endure and will not be quickly forgotten (*Shulḥan Arukh, Yoreh De'a* 246:22).

אמר רבי יהושע בן לוי: המהלך בדרך ואין עמו לוייה – יעסוק בתורה, שנאמר: "כי לוית חן הם".

Having expounded the verse "For they are life to those who find them" as referring to the Torah, the Gemara cites another teaching related to this verse that praises the Torah. **Rabbi Yehoshua ben Levi said: One who is walking along the way without a companion** and is afraid **should engage in Torah** study, **as it is stated** with regard to the words of Torah: **"For they shall be a graceful wreath [*livyat ḥen*]** for your head, and chains about your neck" (Proverbs 1:9). The word *livyat* is understood here as a reference to *levaya*, accompaniment, so that the verse is interpreted to mean that Torah is a graceful accompaniment to one who is traveling.

חש בראשו – יעסוק בתורה, שנאמר: "כי לוית חן הם לראשך". חש בגרונו – יעסוק בתורה, שנאמר: "וענקים לגרגרותיך". חש במעיו – יעסוק בתורה, שנאמר: "רפאות תהי לשרך". חש בעצמותיו – יעסוק בתורה, שנאמר: "ושקוי לעצמותיך". חש בכל גופו – יעסוק בתורה, שנאמר: "ולכל בשרו מרפא".

One who feels pain **in his head should engage in Torah** study, as it is stated: **"For they shall be a graceful wreath for your head." One who feels** pain **in his throat should engage in Torah** study, as it is stated: **"And chains about your neck." One who feels** pain **in his intestines should engage in Torah** study, **as it is stated: "It shall be health to your navel"** (Proverbs 3:8). **One who feels** pain **in his bones should engage in Torah** study, **as it is stated: "And marrow to your bones"** (Proverbs 3:8). **One who feels** pain **in his entire body should engage in Torah** study, **as it is stated: "And health to all their flesh"** (Proverbs 4:22).

אמר רב יהודה ברבי חייא: בא וראה שלא כמדת הקדוש ברוך הוא מדת בשר ודם. מדת בשר ודם, אדם נותן סם לחבירו – לזה יפה ולזה קשה. אבל הקדוש ברוך הוא אינו כן, נתן תורה לישראל – סם חיים לכל גופו, שנאמר: "ולכל בשרו מרפא".

Rav Yehuda, son of Rabbi Ḥiyya, said: Come and see that the attribute of flesh and blood is unlike the attribute of the Holy One, Blessed be He. The attribute of flesh and blood is that when **a person gives a drug to his fellow, it is good for this** part of his body **and it is harmful to that** other part of his body. **But** the attribute of **the Holy One, Blessed be He, is not so; He gave the Torah to the Jewish people,** and **it is a drug of life for one's entire body, as it is stated: "And health to all their flesh."**

אמר רב אמי: מאי דכתיב: "כי נעים כי תשמרם בבטנך יכונו יחדיו על שפתיך", אימתי דברי תורה נעימים – בזמן שתשמרם בבטנך, ואימתי תשמרם בבטנך – בזמן שיכונו יחדו על שפתיך.

The Gemara continues with praise for Torah study and knowledge. **Rav Ami said: What is** the meaning of **that which is written: "For it is a pleasant thing if you keep them within you; let them be firmly attached together to your lips"** (Proverbs 22:18)? **When are words of Torah pleasant? When you keep them within you** and know them. **And when will you keep them within you? When they will be attached together to your lips,** i.e., when you articulate them audibly and expound them.[H]

רבי זירא אמר, מהכא: "שמחה לאיש במענה פיו ודבר בעתו מה טוב", אימתי "שמחה לאיש" – בזמן שמענה בפיו. לשון אחר: אימתי שמחה לאיש במענה פיו – בזמן שדבר בעתו מה טוב.

Rabbi Zeira said that this idea is derived **from here: "A man has joy in the answer of his mouth; and a word in due season, how good it is"** (Proverbs 15:23). **When does a man have joy? When an answer** related to Torah study **is in his mouth. Another version: When does a man have joy in the answer of his mouth? When** he experiences the fulfillment of: **A word in due season, how good it is,** i.e., when he knows when and how to address each issue.

רבי יצחק אמר, מהכא: "כי קרוב אליך הדבר מאד בפיך ובלבבך לעשותו", אימתי קרוב אליך – בזמן שבפיך ובלבבך לעשותו.

Rabbi Yitzḥak said that this idea is derived **from here: "But the matter is very near to you, in your mouth and in your heart, that you may do it"** (Deuteronomy 30:14). **When** is it **very near to you? When it is in your mouth and in your heart, that you may do it,** i.e., when you articulate your Torah study.

רבא אמר, מהכא: "תאות לבו נתתה לו וארשת שפתיו בל מנעת סלה", אימתי תאות לבו נתתה לו – בזמן שארשת שפתיו בל מנעת סלה.

Rava said that this idea is actually derived **from here: "You have given him his heart's desire, and have not withheld the request of his lips, Selah"** (Psalms 21:3). **When have You given him his heart's desire? When You have not withheld the request of his lips, Selah,** i.e., when he converses in words of Torah.

רבא רמי: כתיב: "תאות לבו נתתה לו", וכתיב: "וארשת שפתיו בל מנעת סלה"! זכה – תאות לבו נתתה לו, לא זכה – וארשת שפתיו בל מנעת סלה.

Rava raised an internal **contradiction** in that very verse: In the beginning of the verse **it is written: "You have given him his heart's desire,"** implying that it is enough for one to request in his heart, whereas in the end of the verse **it is written: "And You have not withheld the request of his lips, Selah,"** indicating that one must express his prayers verbally. Rava himself resolved the contradiction: If one **is fortunate, "You have given him his heart's desire,"** even if he does not give verbal expression to his wants. But if he **is not fortunate,** at least **"You have not withheld the request of his lips, Selah."**

תָּנָא דְּבֵי רַבִּי אֱלִיעֶזֶר בֶּן יַעֲקֹב: כׇּל מָקוֹם שֶׁנֶּאֱמַר ״נֶצַח״ ״סֶלָה״ ״וָעֶד״ – אֵין לוֹ הֶפְסֵק עוֹלָמִית. ״נֶצַח״ – דִּכְתִיב: ״כִּי לֹא לְעוֹלָם אָרִיב וְלֹא לָנֶצַח אֶקְצוֹף״.

With regard to the end of this verse, a Sage **of the school of Rabbi Eliezer ben Ya'akov taught** the following *baraita*: **Wherever it states** ***netzah***, **Selah,** or ***va'ed***, the matter **will never cease.** ***Netzah***, **as it is written: "For I will not contend forever; neither will I be eternally** [***lanetzah***] **angry"** (Isaiah 57:16), which demonstrates that *netzah* bears a similar meaning to forever.

״סֶלָה״ – דִּכְתִיב: ״כַּאֲשֶׁר שָׁמַעְנוּ כֵּן רָאִינוּ בְּעִיר ה׳ צְבָאוֹת בְּעִיר אֱלֹהֵינוּ אֱלֹהִים יְכוֹנְנֶהָ עַד עוֹלָם סֶלָה״. ״וָעֶד״ – דִּכְתִיב: ״ה׳ יִמְלוֹךְ לְעוֹלָם וָעֶד״.

Selah, as it is written: "As we have heard, so have we seen in the city of the Lord of Hosts, in the city of our God; may God establish it forever, Selah" (Psalms 48:9), which demonstrates that Selah means forever. ***Va'ed***, **as it is written: "The Lord shall reign forever and ever** [***va'ed***]**"** (Exodus 15:18).

(סִימָן עֲנָקִים לְחָיָיו לוּחוֹת חָרוּת). אָמַר רַבִּי (אֱלִיעֶזֶר), מַאי דִּכְתִיב: ״וַעֲנָקִים לְגַרְגְּרוֹתֶיךָ״ – אִם מֵשִׂים אָדָם עַצְמוֹ כַּעֲנָק זֶה שֶׁרָף עַל הַצַּוָּאר, וְנִרְאֶה וְאֵינוֹ נִרְאֶה – תַּלְמוּדוֹ מִתְקַיֵּים בְּיָדוֹ, וְאִם לָאו – אֵין תַּלְמוּדוֹ מִתְקַיֵּים בְּיָדוֹ.

In light of the previous discussion, the Gemara cites several expositions of verses proposed by Rabbi Eliezer, while first providing them with a **mnemonic: Chains, cheeks, tablets, engraved. Rabbi Eliezer said: What is** the meaning of **that which is written: "And chains about your neck"** (Proverbs 1:9)? **If a person makes himself like a chain that hangs loosely on the neck,** i.e., if a scholar is not pushy and disruptive to others, **and** he is also **seen but not seen,** i.e., just as a chain is covered by clothes and hair, so too, the scholar does not let himself be seen, **his** Torah **study will endure. But if not,** if he acts in a rude and arrogant manner, **his** Torah **study will not endure.**

וְאָמַר רַבִּי אֱלִיעֶזֶר, מַאי דִּכְתִיב: ״לְחָיָו כַּעֲרוּגַת הַבּוֹשֶׂם״ – אִם מֵשִׂים אָדָם עַצְמוֹ כַּעֲרוּגָה זוֹ שֶׁהַכֹּל דָּשִׁין בָּהּ, וּכְבוֹשֶׂם זֶה שֶׁהַכֹּל מִתְבַּשְּׂמִין בָּהּ – תַּלְמוּדוֹ מִתְקַיֵּים, וְאִם לָאו – אֵין תַּלְמוּדוֹ מִתְקַיֵּים.

And Rabbi Eliezer also **said: What is** the meaning of **that which is written: "His cheeks are like a bed of spices"** (Song of Songs 5:13)? **If a person makes himself** humble **like this** garden **bed upon which everyone treads, and like this spice with which everyone perfumes himself,** i.e., which benefits not only the one who wears it, **his** Torah **study will endure. But if not, his** Torah **study will not endure.**

וְאָמַר רַבִּי (אֱלִיעֶזֶר) , מַאי דִּכְתִיב: ״לוּחוֹת אֶבֶן״ – אִם אָדָם מֵשִׂים עַצְמוֹ אֶת לְחָיָיו כְּאֶבֶן זוֹ שֶׁאֵינָהּ נִמְחֵית – תַּלְמוּדוֹ מִתְקַיֵּים בְּיָדוֹ, וְאִם לָאו – אֵין תַּלְמוּדוֹ מִתְקַיֵּים בְּיָדוֹ.

And Rabbi Eliezer further **said: What is** the meaning **of that which is written: "Tablets** [***luhot***] **of stone"** (Exodus 31:18)? **If a person makes his cheeks** [***lehayav***] **like this stone that does not wear away,** **his** Torah **study will endure. But if not,** i.e., if he is not diligent in his studies, **his** Torah **study will not endure.**

וְאָמַר רַבִּי (אֱלִיעֶזֶר), מַאי דִּכְתִיב: ״חָרוּת עַל הַלּוּחוֹת״ – אִלְמָלֵי לֹא נִשְׁתַּבְּרוּ לוּחוֹת הָרִאשׁוֹנוֹת לֹא נִשְׁתַּכְּחָה תּוֹרָה מִיִּשְׂרָאֵל.

And, lastly, **Rabbi Eliezer said: What is** the meaning of **that which is written:** "And the tablets were the work of God, and the writing was the writing of God, **engraved upon the tablets"** (Exodus 32:16)? This teaches that **had the first tablets,** the subject of this verse, **not been broken, the Torah would never have been forgotten from the Jewish people,** as the Torah would have been engraved upon their hearts.

רַב אַחָא בַּר יַעֲקֹב אָמַר: אֵין כׇּל אוּמָּה וְלָשׁוֹן שׁוֹלֶטֶת בָּהֶן, שֶׁנֶּאֱמַר: ״חָרוּת״, אַל תִּיקְרֵי ״חָרוּת״ אֶלָּא ״חֵירוּת״.

Rav Aha bar Ya'akov said: Had the tablets not been broken, **no nation or tongue** would ever **have ruled over them, as it is stated: "Engraved"; do not read** it engraved [***harut***] **but** rather **freedom** [***heirut***].

אָמַר רַב מַתָּנָה, מַאי דִּכְתִיב: ״וּמִמִּדְבָּר מַתָּנָה״ – אִם מֵשִׂים אָדָם עַצְמוֹ כְּמִדְבָּר זֶה שֶׁהַכֹּל דָּשִׁין בּוֹ – תַּלְמוּדוֹ מִתְקַיֵּים בְּיָדוֹ, וְאִם לָאו – אֵין תַּלְמוּדוֹ מִתְקַיֵּים בְּיָדוֹ.

Similarly, **Rav Mattana said: What is** the meaning of **that which is written:** "The well that the princes dug out, that the nobles of the people delved, with the scepter, with their staves. **And from the wilderness they went to Mattanah"** (Numbers 21:18)? **If a person makes himself** humble **like this wilderness,**[H] which is open to all and **upon which everyone treads, his** Torah **study will endure** and be given to him as a gift [*mattana*]. **And if not, his** Torah **study will not endure.**

רָבָא בְּרֵיהּ דְּרַב יוֹסֵף בַּר חָמָא הֲוָה לֵיהּ מִלְּתָא לְרַב יוֹסֵף בַּהֲדֵיהּ, כִּי מְטָא מַעֲלֵי יוֹמָא דְּכִיפּוּרֵי אֲמַר: אֵיזִיל וַאֲפַיְּיסֵיהּ. אֲזַל, אַשְׁכְּחֵיהּ לְשַׁמָּעֵיהּ דְּקָא מָזֵיג לֵיהּ כָּסָא. אֲמַר: הַב לִי וְאִימְזְגֵיהּ אֲנָא. יְהַב לֵיהּ, מַזְגֵיהּ. כִּדְטַעְמֵיהּ אֲמַר: דָּמֵי הַאי מְזִיגָא לִמְזִיגָא דְּרָבָא בְּרֵיהּ דְּרַב יוֹסֵף בַּר חָמָא. אָמַר לֵיהּ: אֲנָא הוּא.

The Gemara relates that **Rav Yosef had a grievance**[N] **against Rava, son of Rav Yosef bar Hama,** who is usually referred to in the Gemara simply as Rava, and as a result of the grievance the two would never meet. **When the eve of Yom Kippur arrived,** Rava **said: I will go and appease him. He went and found** Rav Yosef's **attendant mixing him a cup** of wine. **He said to** the attendant: **Give it to me, and I will mix** it. **He gave it to** Rava, and Rava **mixed it.** Rav Yosef was blind and could not see his visitor, but **when he tasted** the wine **he said: This mixture is similar to the mixture** of **Rava,**[N] **son of Rav Yosef bar Hama,** who would add extra water to the wine. Rava **said to him: It is I.**

HALAKHA

Makes himself like this wilderness – מְשִׂים אָדָם עַצְמוֹ כְּמִדְבָּר זֶה: The arrogant do not truly possess Torah. Only one who humbles himself and sits at the feet of the Sages retains his Torah study (Rambam *Sefer HaMadda, Hilkhot Talmud Torah* 3:9).

NOTES

Rav Yosef had a grievance – הֲוָה לֵיהּ מִלְּתָא לְרַב יוֹסֵף: The basis of the dispute between Rava and Rav Yosef is found in tractate *Nedarim*. Rava sent Rav Yosef a query with regard to a certain halakhic issue. Upon receiving Rav Yosef's response, Rava stated that the response failed to address his difficulty. Rav Yosef, insulted by Rava's comments, retorted: If he does not need me, he should not send questions to me. Consequently, Rava had to go and appease him. In his conciliatory remarks and his exposition of the verses in Numbers, Rava alluded to a person who is arrogant due to his learning, and who regrets his haughtiness.

The mixture of Rava – מְזִיגָא דְּרָבָא: Rava's wine mixture was one part wine and three parts water, whereas the usual ratio was one to two. Therefore, Rava's wine mixture was unique.

HALAKHA

Makes himself like an animal – מֵשִׂים עַצְמוֹ כְּחַיָּה: Torah does not endure among those who study while providing themselves with comforts, including excessive eating or drinking (*Shulḥan Arukh, Yoreh De'a* 246:21).

NOTES

That tramples and eats…that soils and eats – שֶׁדּוֹרֶסֶת וְאוֹכֶלֶת...שֶׁמַּסְרַחַת וְאוֹכֶלֶת: One explanation is that a student is not particular with regard to his mealtimes when he is studying Torah. Sometimes he eats very quickly, and at other times he significantly delays his meal to enable him to attend various Torah classes.

אָמַר לֵיהּ: לָא תֵּתִיב אַכַּרְעָיךְ עַד דִּמְפָרְשַׁתְּ לִי הָנֵי קְרָאֵי, מַאי דִּכְתִיב: ״וּמִמִּדְבָּר מַתָּנָה וּמִמַּתָּנָה נַחֲלִיאֵל וּמִנַּחֲלִיאֵל בָּמוֹת וּמִבָּמוֹת הַגַּיְא״.

Rav Yosef **said to him: Do not sit on your knees until you have explained these verses to me: What is** the meaning of **that which is written: "And from the wilderness to Mattanah; and from Mattanah to Nahaliel; and from Nahaliel to Bamoth; and from Bamoth to the valley** in the field of Moab, to the top of Pisgah, which looks out toward the desert" (Numbers 21:19–20)?

אָמַר לֵיהּ: אִם אָדָם מֵשִׂים עַצְמוֹ כְּמִדְבָּר זֶה שֶׁהַכֹּל דָּשִׁין בּוֹ – תּוֹרָה נִיתְּנָה לוֹ בְּמַתָּנָה. וְכֵיוָן שֶׁנִּיתְּנָה לוֹ בְּמַתָּנָה – נְחָלוֹ אֵל, שֶׁנֶּאֱמַר: ״וּמִמַּתָּנָה נַחֲלִיאֵל״. וְכֵיוָן שֶׁנְּחָלוֹ אֵל – עוֹלֶה לִגְדוּלָּה, שֶׁנֶּאֱמַר: ״וּמִנַּחֲלִיאֵל בָּמוֹת״.

Rava **said to him: If a person makes himself** humble **like this wilderness,** which is open to all and **upon which everyone treads, the Torah will be given to him as a gift** [*mattana*]. **And once it is given to him as a gift, he inherits it** [*neḥalo*] and God [*El*] makes it His inheritance, **as it is stated: "And from Mattanah to Nahaliel." And once God has made it His inheritance, he rises to greatness, as it is stated: "And from Nahaliel to Bamoth,"** which means heights.

וְאִם מֵגִיס לִבּוֹ – הַקָּדוֹשׁ בָּרוּךְ הוּא מַשְׁפִּילוֹ, שֶׁנֶּאֱמַר: ״וּמִבָּמוֹת הַגַּיְא״. וְאִם חוֹזֵר בּוֹ – הַקָּדוֹשׁ בָּרוּךְ הוּא מַגְבִּיהוֹ, שֶׁנֶּאֱמַר: ״כׇּל גֶּיא יִנָּשֵׂא״.

And if he becomes haughty, the Holy One, Blessed be He, lowers him, as it is stated: "And from Bamoth to the valley." And if he repents, the Holy One, Blessed be He, raises him back **up, as it is stated: "Every valley shall be exalted"** (Isaiah 40:4).

אָמַר רַב הוּנָא, מַאי דִּכְתִיב: ״חַיָּתְךָ יָשְׁבוּ בָהּ תָּכִין בְּטוֹבָתְךָ לֶעָנִי אֱלֹהִים״ – אִם אָדָם מֵשִׂים עַצְמוֹ כְּחַיָּה זוֹ שֶׁדּוֹרֶסֶת וְאוֹכֶלֶת, וְאִיכָּא דְּאָמְרִי: שֶׁמַּסְרַחַת וְאוֹכֶלֶת – תַּלְמוּדוֹ מִתְקַיֵּים בְּיָדוֹ, וְאִם לָאו – אֵין תַּלְמוּדוֹ מִתְקַיֵּים בְּיָדוֹ. וְאִם עוֹשֶׂה כֵּן – הַקָּדוֹשׁ בָּרוּךְ הוּא עוֹשֶׂה לוֹ סְעוּדָה בְּעַצְמוֹ, שֶׁנֶּאֱמַר: ״תָּכִין בְּטוֹבָתְךָ לֶעָנִי אֱלֹהִים״.

Rav Huna said: What is the meaning of **that which is written: "Your flock found a dwelling in it; You, O God, prepare of Your goodness for the poor"** (Psalms 68:11)? **If a person makes himself like an animal**[H] **that tramples** its prey **and eats** it immediately, without being particular about its food, i.e., if a scholar immediately reviews what he has heard from his teacher; **and some say,** like an animal **that soils and eats,**[N] i.e., if a scholar is not particular about maintaining his honor during his Torah study, just as an animal is not particular about the quality of its food, **his** Torah **study will endure. And if not, his** Torah **study will not endure. And if he does so, the Holy One, Blessed be He, will Himself prepare him a feast, as it is stated: "You, O God, prepare of Your goodness for the poor,"** indicating that God in His goodness will Himself prepare a feast for that pauper.

אָמַר רַבִּי חִיָּיא בַּר אַבָּא, אָמַר רַבִּי יוֹחָנָן: מַאי דִּכְתִיב: ״נוֹצֵר תְּאֵנָה יֹאכַל פִּרְיָהּ״, לָמָּה נִמְשְׁלוּ דִּבְרֵי תוֹרָה כִּתְאֵנָה – מָה תְּאֵנָה זוֹ

Rabbi Ḥiyya bar Abba said that Rabbi Yoḥanan said: What is the meaning of **that which is written: "He who guards the fig tree shall eat its fruit"** (Proverbs 27:18)? **Why were matters of Torah compared to a fig tree? Just as this fig tree,**

Perek **V**
Daf **54** Amud **b**

כׇּל זְמַן שֶׁאָדָם מְמַשְׁמֵשׁ בָּהּ מוֹצֵא בָּהּ תְּאֵנִים – אַף דִּבְרֵי תוֹרָה כׇּל זְמַן שֶׁאָדָם הוֹגֶה בָּהֶן – מוֹצֵא בָּהֶן טַעַם.

whenever a person searches it for figs to eat, **he finds figs in it,** as the figs on a tree do not ripen all at once, so that one can always find a recently ripened fig, so too, with **matters of Torah. Whenever a person meditates upon them, he finds in them** new **meaning.**

אָמַר רַבִּי שְׁמוּאֵל בַּר נַחְמָנִי: מַאי דִּכְתִיב: ״אַיֶּלֶת אֲהָבִים וְיַעֲלַת חֵן וגו׳״ לָמָּה נִמְשְׁלוּ דִּבְרֵי תוֹרָה לְאַיֶּלֶת? לוֹמַר לָךְ: מָה אַיָּלָה רַחְמָהּ צַר וַחֲבִיבָה עַל בּוֹעֲלָהּ כׇּל שָׁעָה וְשָׁעָה כְּשָׁעָה רִאשׁוֹנָה – אַף דִּבְרֵי תוֹרָה חֲבִיבִין עַל לוֹמְדֵיהֶן כׇּל שָׁעָה וְשָׁעָה כְּשָׁעָה רִאשׁוֹנָה.

Rabbi Shmuel bar Naḥmani said: What is the meaning of **that which is written: "A loving hind and a graceful roe,** let her breasts satisfy you at all times, and be you ravished always with her love" (Proverbs 5:19)? **Why were matters of Torah compared to a hind? To tell you that just as with a hind, its womb is narrow and it is cherished by its mate each and every hour like the first hour, so too, matters of Torah are cherished by those who study them each and every hour like the first hour.**

״וְיַעֲלַת חֵן״ – שֶׁמַּעֲלַת חֵן עַל לוֹמְדֶיהָ. ״דַּדֶּיהָ יְרַוֻּךָ בְכׇל עֵת״, לָמָּה נִמְשְׁלוּ דִּבְרֵי תוֹרָה כַּדַּד? מָה דַּד זֶה כׇּל זְמַן שֶׁהַתִּינוֹק מְמַשְׁמֵשׁ בּוֹ מוֹצֵא בּוֹ חָלָב – אַף דִּבְרֵי תוֹרָה, כׇּל זְמַן שֶׁאָדָם הוֹגֶה בָּהֶן – מוֹצֵא בָּהֶן טַעַם.

"And a graceful roe" is expounded as follows: **That** the Torah **bestows grace upon those who study it. "Let her breasts satisfy you at all times"; why were matters of Torah compared to a breast? Just as with a breast, whenever a baby searches it** for milk to suckle, **he finds milk in it, so too, with matters of Torah. Whenever a person meditates upon them, he finds** new **meaning in them.**

״בְּאַהֲבָתָהּ תִּשְׁגֶּה תָמִיד״ – כְּגוֹן רַבִּי (אֱלִיעֶזֶר) בֶּן פְּדָת. אָמְרוּ עָלָיו עַל רַבִּי (אֱלִיעֶזֶר) שֶׁהָיָה יוֹשֵׁב וְעוֹסֵק בַּתּוֹרָה בַּשּׁוּק הַתַּחְתּוֹן שֶׁל צִיפּוֹרִי, וּסְדִינוֹ מוּטָּל בַּשּׁוּק הָעֶלְיוֹן שֶׁל צִיפּוֹרִי. (תַּנְיָא,) אָמַר רַבִּי יִצְחָק בֶּן אֶלְעָזָר: פַּעַם אַחַת בָּא אָדָם לִיטְּלוֹ וּמָצָא בּוֹ שָׂרָף.

"And be you ravished always with her love"; your love for Torah should always distract you from worldly matters, **as was** the case with **Rabbi Elazar ben Pedat. They said of him, of Rabbi Elazar, that he would sit and engage in Torah** study **in the lower marketplace of Tzippori, and his cloak was lying in the upper marketplace of Tzippori.** His mind was so focused on Torah study that he would act in this unusual manner. In this regard, the Gemara relates that **it was taught** in a *baraita* that **Rabbi Yitzḥak ben Elazar said: One time a person came to take** this cloak for himself **and found a serpent on it** guarding it.

תָּנָא דְּבֵי רַב עָנָן, מַאי דִּכְתִיב: ״רוֹכְבֵי אֲתוֹנוֹת צְחוֹרוֹת יוֹשְׁבֵי עַל מִדִּין [וְהוֹלְכֵי עַל דֶּרֶךְ שִׂיחוּ]״, ״רוֹכְבֵי אֲתוֹנוֹת״ – אֵלּוּ תַּלְמִידֵי חֲכָמִים שֶׁמְּהַלְּכִין מֵעִיר לְעִיר וּמִמְּדִינָה לִמְדִינָה לִלְמוֹד (בּוֹ) תּוֹרָה. ״צְחוֹרוֹת״ – שֶׁעוֹשִׂין אוֹתָהּ כְּצָהֳרַיִם. ״יֹשְׁבֵי עַל מִדִּין״ – שֶׁדָּנִין דִּין אֱמֶת לַאֲמִיתּוֹ. ״וְהוֹלְכֵי״ – אֵלּוּ בַּעֲלֵי מִקְרָא. ״עַל דֶּרֶךְ״ – אֵלּוּ בַּעֲלֵי מִשְׁנָה. ״שִׂיחוּ״ – אֵלּוּ בַּעֲלֵי תַלְמוּד, שֶׁכָּל שִׂיחָתָן דִּבְרֵי תוֹרָה.

In further praise of the Torah and those who study it, a Sage **of the school of Rav Anan taught: What is** the meaning of **that which is written: "You that ride on white donkeys, you that sit on rich cloths, and you that walk by the way, tell of it"**[N] (Judges 5:10)? **"You that ride on white donkeys"; these are Torah scholars, who travel from city to city and from province to province to study Torah. "White [*tzeḥorot*]"** are those **who make it** clear **as noon [*tzahorayim*]**, i.e., who make the Torah comprehensible. **"You that sit on couches [*midin*]"** refers to those **who judge [*danin*] an absolutely true judgment. "And you that walk"; these are the masters of Bible,** who are the least important of the scholars. **"By the way"; these are the** more important **masters of Mishna. "Tell of it"; these are the masters of Talmud,** the most important of all, **as all their conversation is** about **matters of Torah.**

אָמַר רַב שֵׁיזְבִי מִשּׁוּם רַבִּי אֶלְעָזָר בֶּן עֲזַרְיָה, מַאי דִּכְתִיב: ״לֹא יַחֲרוֹךְ רְמִיָּה צֵידוֹ״ – לֹא יִחְיֶה וְלֹא יַאֲרִיךְ יָמִים צַיָּיד הָרַמַּאי.

The Gemara continues with this topic: **Rav Sheizvi said in the name of Rabbi Elazar ben Azarya: What is** the meaning of **that which is written: "The slothful man [*remiyya*] will not roast [*yaḥarokh*] his catch"** (Proverbs 12:27)?[N] **The deceitful [*rammai*] hunter**[N] **will not live [*yiḥyeh*] a long life [*ya'arikh*].** A deceitful hunter continues to hunt more and more animals without holding on to the animals he has already caught. Similarly, someone who continues to study new material without reviewing what he has already learned will not be successful.

רַב שֵׁשֶׁת אָמַר: צַיָּיד הָרַמַּאי יַחֲרוֹךְ?

Rav Sheshet said: Will **a deceitful hunter** have something to **roast?**[N] One who acts in this way is a fool, but it is hard to describe him as deceitful.

כִּי אֲתָא רַב דִּימִי, אֲמַר: מָשָׁל לְצַיָּיד שֶׁצָּד צִפֳּרִים, אִם רִאשׁוֹן רִאשׁוֹן מְשַׁבֵּר כְּנָפָיו – מִשְׁתַּמֵּר, וְאִם לָאו – אֵין מִשְׁתַּמֵּר.

When Rav Dimi came from Eretz Yisrael to Babylonia, **he said: This is comparable to a hunter who is hunting birds; if he breaks** the **wings** of the birds **one by one** as he captures them so that they will be unable to fly off again, his prey **will be secured, and if not,** they **will not be secured.** According to this explanation, the word *rammai* is interpreted as cunning rather than deceitful. A cunning hunter secures his prey; similarly, a cunning student reviews each lesson and thereby retains that which he learns.

NOTES

You that walk by the way, tell of it – וְהוֹלְכֵי עַל דֶּרֶךְ שִׂיחוּ: Some explain this in the following manner: The expression "that walk" refers to masters of Bible, who are not on the highest level and are therefore described as walking rather than riding. Those who have mastered Mishna are referred to as traveling "by the way," as they are closer to the highest level of study, but are not equal to Talmud scholars. "Tell it" alludes to Talmud scholars, who constantly focus on the most important course of study (Maharsha; Rav Ya'akov Emden).

The slothful man will not roast his catch – לֹא יַחֲרוֹךְ רְמִיָּה צֵידוֹ: The *Arukh* explains the aphorism as referring to someone who prepares his catch in a slothful manner, without making the effort to break its wings properly; consequently, his prey will fly away. This is a metaphor for one who does not review his studies properly, and whose continued study will therefore be ineffective.

The deceitful hunter – צַיָּיד הָרַמַּאי: This refers to one who deceives others by showing off the breadth of his knowledge. However, since he does not review his studies, he will forget them and thereby shorten his life, as the Torah states: "For it is your life and length of days" (Rashi).

Will a deceitful hunter have something to roast – צַיָּיד הָרַמַּאי יַחֲרוֹךְ: Rashi reads this statement as a question. The *Arukh*, however, explains that it refers to a student who tells his teacher that he cannot grasp any more, and then uses the remaining time to review what he has just learned. Such a student will retain his knowledge.

HALAKHA

Until he learns it – עד שילמדנו: One who teaches Torah should not get angry with his students. Rather, he should review the lesson several times until the students understand (*Shulḥan Arukh, Yoreh De'a* 246:10).

אמר (רבה), אמר רב סחורה, אמר רב הונא, מאי דכתיב: "הון מהבל ימעט וקובץ על יד ירבה", אם עושה אדם תורתו חבילות חבילות – מתמעט, ואם לאו – קובץ על יד ירבה.

Similarly, **Rabba said that Rav Seḥora said that Rav Huna said: What is** the meaning of **that which is written: "Wealth gotten through vanity [*hevel*] shall be diminished; but he that gathers little by little shall increase"** (Proverbs 13:11)? **If a person turns his Torah into bundles [*ḥavilot*,** derived from the word *hevel* by replacing the *heh* with a *ḥet*], studying large amounts at the same time, his Torah **will diminish. And if not,** i.e., if he learns little by little and reviews what he has learned, **he that gathers little by little shall increase.**

אמר רבה: ידעי רבנן להא מלתא ועברי עלה. אמר רב נחמן בר יצחק: אנא עבדתה, ואיקיים בידאי.

Rabba said: The Sages know this, but nevertheless **transgress it,** i.e., they fail to heed this advice. **Rav Naḥman bar Yitzḥak said: I did this,** learning little by little and regularly reviewing what I had learned, **and** my learning **has** indeed **endured.**

תנו רבנן: כיצד סדר משנה? משה למד מפי הגבורה, נכנס אהרן ושנה לו משה פירקו. נסתלק אהרן וישב לשמאל משה. נכנסו בניו ושנה להן משה פירקן, נסתלקו בניו, אלעזר ישב לימין משה ואיתמר לשמאל אהרן. רבי יהודה אומר: לעולם אהרן לימין משה חוזר. נכנסו זקנים ושנה להן משה פירקן, נסתלקו זקנים, נכנסו כל העם ושנה להן משה פירקן. נמצאו ביד אהרן ארבעה, ביד בניו שלשה, וביד הזקנים שנים, וביד כל העם אחד.

The Gemara continues to discuss methods of Torah study. **The Sages taught** the following *baraita*: **What was the order of teaching** the Oral Law? How was the Oral Law first taught? **Moses learned** directly **from the mouth of the Almighty. Aaron entered** and sat before him, **and Moses taught him his lesson** as he had learned it from God. **Aaron moved** aside **and sat to the left of Moses.** Aaron's **sons entered, and Moses taught them their lesson** while Aaron listened. Aaron's **sons moved** aside; **Elazar sat to the right of Moses and Itamar** sat **to the left of Aaron. Rabbi Yehuda** disagreed with the first *tanna* with regard to the seating arrangements and **said: Actually, Aaron would return to** sit to **the right of Moses. The elders entered and Moses taught them their lesson. The elders moved** aside, and **the entire nation entered and Moses taught them their lesson. Therefore, Aaron had** heard the lesson **four times, his sons** heard it **three** times, **the elders** heard it **twice, and the entire nation** heard it **once.**

נסתלק משה, ושנה להן אהרן פירקו. נסתלק אהרן, שנו להן בניו פירקן. נסתלקו בניו, שנו להן זקנים פירקן. נמצא ביד הכל ארבעה.

Moses then **departed** to his tent, **and Aaron taught** the others **his lesson** as he had learned it from Moses. **Aaron** then **departed** and **his sons taught** the others **their lesson. His sons** then **departed** and **the elders taught** the rest of the people **their lesson. Hence everyone,** Aaron, his sons, the elders and all the people, heard the lesson taught by God **four times.**

מכאן אמר רבי אליעזר: חייב אדם לשנות לתלמידו ארבעה פעמים. וקל וחומר, ומה אהרן שלמד מפי משה, ומשה מפי הגבורה – כך, הדיוט מפי הדיוט – על אחת כמה וכמה.

From here Rabbi Eliezer said: A person is obligated to teach his student his lesson **four times. And** it follows by way of **an *a fortiori* inference: If Aaron, who learned from Moses** himself, **and Moses** had received the Torah directly **from the mouth of the Almighty,** needed **this** regimen; **an ordinary** student learning **from the mouth of an ordinary** teacher, **how much more so** must he review his studies four times.

רבי עקיבא אומר: מנין שחייב אדם לשנות לתלמידו עד שילמדנו – שנאמר: "ולמדה את בני ישראל". ומנין עד שתהא סדורה בפיהם – שנאמר: "שימה בפיהם".

Rabbi Akiva says: From where do we derive **that a person is obligated to teach his student until he learns** the material and understands it?[H] **As it is stated:** "Now therefore write this song for you, **and teach it to the children of Israel;** put it in their mouths, that this song may be a witness for me against the children of Israel" (Deuteronomy 31:19). This verse indicates that one must teach Torah to others. **And from where** do we derive that one must teach his students **until** the material **is organized in their mouths? As it is stated: "Put it in their mouths,"** so that they should be capable of teaching it to others.

ומניין שחייב להראות לו פנים – שנאמר: "ואלה המשפטים אשר תשים לפניהם".

And from where do we derive **that** a teacher **must show** his students **the reasons** for the teachings? **As it is stated: "Now these are the judgments which you shall set before them"** (Exodus 21:1), which indicates that the lesson must be set out in logical fashion for the students.

וליגמרו כולהו ממשה! כדי לחלוק כבוד לאהרן ובניו, וכבוד לזקנים.

With regard to the manner in which the Oral Law was taught, the Gemara asks: **They should all have studied from Moses** himself four times. The Gemara answers: The teaching was divided in this manner **in order to give honor to Aaron and his sons, and** also to give **honor to the elders.**

וְנֵיעוּל אַהֲרֹן וְנִיגְמַר מִמֹּשֶׁה, וְלֵיעַיְילוּ בָּנָיו וְלִיגְמְרוּ מֵאַהֲרֹן, וְלֵיעַיְילוּ זְקֵנִים וְלֵילְפוּ מִבָּנָיו, וְלֵיזְלוּ וְלִיגַמְרִינְהוּ לְכוּלְּהוּ יִשְׂרָאֵל! כֵּיוָן דְּמֹשֶׁה מִפִּי הַגְּבוּרָה גָּמַר – מִסְתַּיְּיעָא מִלְּתֵיהּ.

The Gemara asks why a different method was not adopted, one which would have involved less trouble for Moses: **Aaron should have entered and studied from Moses; his sons should** then **have entered and studied from Aaron; the elders should** then **have entered and studied from** Aaron's **sons; and** then **they should have gone out and taught all of the Jewish people.** The Gemara answers: **Since Moses had studied** directly **from the mouth of the Almighty, it would be** more **effective** for everyone to hear the Torah at least once from Moses himself.

אָמַר מָר, רַבִּי יְהוּדָה אוֹמֵר: לְעוֹלָם אַהֲרֹן לִימִין מֹשֶׁה חוֹזֵר. כְּמַאן אָזְלָא הָא דְּתַנְיָא: שְׁלֹשָׁה שֶׁהָיוּ מְהַלְּכִין בַּדֶּרֶךְ – הָרַב בָּאֶמְצַע, וְגָדוֹל בִּימִינוֹ, וְקָטָן בִּשְׂמֹאלוֹ. לֵימָא רַבִּי יְהוּדָה הִיא וְלָא רַבָּנַן!

The Master said in the *baraita* that **Rabbi Yehuda says: Actually, Aaron would return to** sit to **the right of Moses,** i.e., no matter how many people were present Aaron always sat to Moses' right. The Gemara asks: **In accordance with whose** opinion **was it taught** in a *baraita* dealing with the rules of etiquette: If **three** people **were walking along the way,**[H] **the teacher** should walk **in the middle and the greater** of the two students should be **to his right and the lesser** one should be **to his left?**[N] **Shall we say** that **it is** the opinion of **Rabbi Yehuda and not** that of **the Sages?** According to the Sages, the greater of the two students should be positioned to the left of the teacher so that the student's right side faces his teacher.

אֲפִילּוּ תֵּימָא רַבָּנַן, מִשּׁוּם טִירְחָא דְּאַהֲרֹן.

The Gemara answers: You can **even say** that this *baraita* was taught in accordance with the opinion of **the Sages,** and the reason they said that Aaron remained to Moses' left even after the others entered is **due to the trouble to Aaron** if he would have to stand up and sit down again.

רַבִּי פְּרִידָא הֲוָה לֵיהּ הַהוּא תַּלְמִידָא דַּהֲוָה תָּנֵי לֵיהּ אַרְבַּע מְאָה זִימְנֵי וְגָמַר. יוֹמָא חַד בָּעְיוּהּ לְמִלְּתָא דְּמִצְוָה, תְּנָא לֵיהּ וְלָא גְּמַר.

Having discussed the importance of reviewing one's Torah study, the Gemara relates that **Rabbi Perida had a certain student whom he would** have to **teach four hundred times, and** only then would he **learn** the material, as he was incapable of understanding it otherwise. **One day they requested** Rabbi Perida's presence **for a mitzva matter**[N] after the lesson. Rabbi Perida **taught** his student four hundred times as usual, **but** this time the student **did not** successfully **learn** the material.

אֲמַר לֵיהּ: הָאִידָּנָא מַאי שְׁנָא? אֲמַר לֵיהּ: מִדְּהַהִיא שַׁעְתָּא דַּאֲמַר לֵיהּ לְמָר אִיכָּא מִילְּתָא דְּמִצְוָה – אַסְּחַאי לְדַעְתַּאי, וְכׇל שַׁעְתָּא אָמֵינָא, הַשְׁתָּא קָאֵי מָר, הַשְׁתָּא קָאֵי מָר. אֲמַר לֵיהּ: הַב דַּעְתֵּיךְ וְאַתְנֵי לָיךְ. הֲדַר תְּנָא לֵיהּ אַרְבַּע מְאָה זִימְנֵי [אַחְרִינֵי].

Rabbi Perida **said to him: What is different now** that you are unable to grasp the lesson? **He said to him: From the time that they said to the Master** that **there is a mitzva matter** for which he is needed, **my mind was distracted** from the lesson **and every moment I said: Now the Master will get up, now the Master will get up** to go and perform the mitzva and he will not complete the lesson. Rabbi Perida **said to him: Pay attention** this time **and I will teach you,** and know that I will not leave until you have fully mastered the lesson. **He taught him again an additional four hundred times.**

נְפַקָא בַּת קָלָא וְאָמְרָה לֵיהּ: נִיחָא לָיךְ דְּלִיסְפּוּ לָךְ אַרְבַּע מְאָה שְׁנֵי, אוֹ דְּתִיזְכּוּ אַתְּ וְדָרָךְ לְעָלְמָא דְּאָתֵי? אֲמַר: דְּנִיזְכּוּ אֲנָא וְדָרַיי לְעָלְמָא דְּאָתֵי. אָמַר לָהֶן הַקָּדוֹשׁ בָּרוּךְ הוּא: תְּנוּ לוֹ זוֹ וָזוֹ.

Due to the merit of Rabbi Perida's great devotion to his students, **a Divine Voice emerged and said to him:** Is it **preferable to you that four hundred years be added** to your life, **or that you and** the rest of **your generation** will **merit the World-to-Come? He said:** I prefer **that I and my generation merit the World-to-Come. The Holy One, Blessed be He, said** to the angels: **Give him both;** he shall live a very long life and he and the rest of his generation will merit the World-to-Come.

אָמַר רַב חִסְדָּא: אֵין תּוֹרָה נִקְנֵית אֶלָּא בְּסִימָנִין, שֶׁנֶּאֱמַר: "שִׂימָהּ בְּפִיהֶם", אַל תִּקְרֵי "שִׂימָהּ" אֶלָּא "סִימָנָהּ".

The Gemara continues its discussion with regard to methods of Torah study: Rav **Ḥisda said: The Torah can be acquired only with** mnemonic **signs** that aid the memory, **as it is stated: "Put it in their mouths." Do not read** the phrase as: **Put it** [*simah*], **but** rather as: **Its sign** [*simanah*], thus indicating that mnemonic signs aid in memorizing the material.

שַׁמְעַהּ רַב תַּחְלִיפָא מִמַּעַרְבָא, אֲזַל אַמְרַהּ קַמֵּיהּ דְּרַבִּי אַבָּהוּ, אֲמַר: אַתּוּן מֵהָתָם מַתְנִיתוּ לַהּ, אֲנַן מֵהָכָא מַתְנִינַן לַהּ: "הַצִּיבִי לָךְ צִיּוּנִים שִׂימִי לָךְ וגו׳" עֲשׂוּ צִיּוּנִים לַתּוֹרָה. וּמַאי מַשְׁמַע דְּהַאי צִיּוּן לִישָּׁנָא דְּסִימָנָא הוּא – דִּכְתִיב: "וְרָאָה עֶצֶם אָדָם וּבָנָה אֶצְלוֹ צִיּוּן".

Rav Taḥalifa of the West, i.e., from Eretz Yisrael, **heard this** statement and **went** and **said it before Rabbi Abbahu,** who **said: You learn this** idea **from there; we learn it from here,** as the verse states: **"Set up signposts** [*tziyyunim*] **for yourself; establish you** markers" (Jeremiah 31:20), which is understood to mean: **Establish** mnemonic **signs for the Torah. And from where** may it be inferred **that this** term ***tziyyun*** **denotes a sign? As it is written** in a different verse: "And when they that pass through shall pass through the land, **and any sees a human bone, he shall set up a sign** [***tziyyun***] **by it"** (Ezekiel 39:15), i.e., a sign that there is a source of ritual impurity at that spot.

HALAKHA

If three people were walking along the way – **שְׁלֹשָׁה שֶׁהָיוּ מְהַלְּכִין בַּדֶּרֶךְ**: If three people are walking together along the road, the teacher should walk in the middle, with his leading disciple to his right and the other student to his left. The students should walk slightly behind the teacher and a little to the side (*Shakh*), as explained elsewhere (*Shulḥan Arukh, Yoreh De'a* 242:17).

NOTES

The rules of etiquette – **הִלְכוֹת דֶּרֶךְ אֶרֶץ**: If two people are walking or sitting together, the more important person should be on the right. If there are three people, the more important person should be in the middle, while the next in importance is to his right, and the least important of the three to his left. Some authorities, however, maintain that it is proper for the second person to be positioned on the left, so that his right side should face the leading member of the group.

A mitzva matter – **מִלְּתָא דְּמִצְוָה**: Whenever the Talmud refers to a mitzva without further detail, it can be assumed that the reference is to the collection of funds for charity.

רַבִּי אֱלִיעֶזֶר אָמַר, מֵהָכָא: ״אֱמוֹר לַחׇכְמָה אֲחוֹתִי אָתְּ וּמוֹדָע לַבִּינָה תִקְרָא״ – עֲשֵׂה מוֹדָעִים לַתּוֹרָה. רָבָא אָמַר: עֲשֵׂה מוֹעֲדִים לַתּוֹרָה.

Rabbi Eliezer said that we learn this same idea **from here: "Say to wisdom, you are my sister, and call understanding, your kinswoman [*moda*]"** (Proverbs 7:4), which means: **Establish signs [*moda'im*]** that convey knowledge of **the Torah. Rava said** with regard to this verse: **Set appointed times [*mo'adim*]** for Torah study.[H]

HALAKHA

Set appointed times for Torah study – עֲשֵׂה מוֹעֲדִים לַתּוֹרָה: It is proper to go to a house of study and study Torah for a fixed amount of time every day after prayers (*Shulḥan Arukh, Oraḥ Ḥayyim* 155:1).

Perek **V**
Daf **55** Amud **a**

וְהַיְינוּ דְּאָמַר אַבְדִּימִי בַּר חָמָא בַּר דּוֹסָא, מַאי דִּכְתִיב: ״לֹא בַשָּׁמַיִם הִיא וְלֹא מֵעֵבֶר לַיָּם הִיא״, ״לֹא בַשָּׁמַיִם הִיא״ – שֶׁאִם בַּשָּׁמַיִם הִיא אַתָּה צָרִיךְ לַעֲלוֹת אַחֲרֶיהָ, וְאִם מֵעֵבֶר לַיָּם הִיא – אַתָּה צָרִיךְ לַעֲבוֹר אַחֲרֶיהָ.

And this idea, that one must exert great effort to retain one's Torah knowledge, **is** in accordance with **what Avdimi bar Ḥama bar Dosa said: What is** the meaning of **that which is written: "It is not in heaven…nor is it beyond the sea"** (Deuteronomy 30:12–13)? **"It is not in heaven"** indicates **that if it were in heaven, you would have to ascend after it, and if it were beyond the sea, you would have to cross after it,** as one must expend whatever effort is necessary in order to study Torah.

רָבָא אָמַר: ״לֹא בַשָּׁמַיִם הִיא״ – לֹא תִּמָּצֵא בְּמִי שֶׁמַּגְבִּיהַּ דַּעְתּוֹ עָלֶיהָ כַּשָּׁמַיִם, וְלֹא תִּמָּצֵא בְּמִי שֶׁמַּרְחִיב דַּעְתּוֹ עָלֶיהָ כַּיָּם.

Expounding the verse differently, **Rava said: "It is not in heaven"** means that Torah **is not to be found in someone who raises his mind over it, like the heavens,** i.e., he thinks his mind is above the Torah and he does not need a teacher; **nor is it to be found in someone who expands his mind over it, like the sea,** i.e., he thinks he knows everything there is to know about the topic he has learned.[N]

רַבִּי יוֹחָנָן אָמַר: ״לֹא בַשָּׁמַיִם הִיא״ – לֹא תִּמָּצֵא בְּגַסֵּי רוּחַ, ״וְלֹא מֵעֵבֶר לַיָּם הִיא״ – לֹא תִּמָּצֵא לֹא בְּסַחְרָנִים וְלֹא בְּתַגָּרִים.

Rabbi Yoḥanan said: "It is not in heaven" means that Torah **is not to be found in the haughty,** those who raise their self-image as though they were in heaven. **"Nor is it beyond the sea"** means that **it is not to be found among merchants or traders** who are constantly traveling and do not have the time to study Torah properly.[H]

תָּנוּ רַבָּנַן: כֵּיצַד מְעַבְּרִין אֶת הֶעָרִים? אֲרוּכָּה – כְּמוֹת שֶׁהִיא, עֲגוּלָּה – עוֹשִׂין לָהּ זָוִיּוֹת. מְרוּבַּעַת – אֵין עוֹשִׂין לָהּ זָוִיּוֹת. הָיְתָה רְחָבָה מִצַּד אֶחָד וּקְצָרָה מִצַּד אַחֵר – רוֹאִין אוֹתָהּ כְּאִילּוּ הִיא שָׁוָה.

After the lengthy aggadic digression, the Gemara returns to the topic of the mishna, extending the outskirts of a city. **The Sages taught** in the *Tosefta*: **How does one extend** the boundaries of **cities?** If the city is **long,** in the shape of a rectangle, the Shabbat limit is measured from the boundary **as it is.** If the city is **round, one creates** simulated **corners for it,**[H] rendering it square, and the Shabbat limit is measured from there.[B] If it is **square, one does not create** additional **corners for it.** If the city **was wide on one side**[H] **and narrow on the other side, one regards it as though** the two sides **were** of **equal** length, adding to the narrow side to form a square.[B]

NOTES

Someone who raises his mind and someone who expands his mind – מַגְבִּיהַּ דַּעְתּוֹ, מַרְחִיב דַּעְתּוֹ: One who raises his mind is one who believes that his mind is so lofty that he no longer needs a teacher. One who expands his mind is one who has studied a topic and now thinks he knows everything there is to know about it (Maharsha).

HALAKHA

It is not in heaven or beyond the sea – לֹא בַשָּׁמַיִם וּמֵעֵבֶר לַיָּם: Torah is not found in one who spends too much of his time on business activities. It is appropriate for one to limit the time he spends on business so that he can study Torah (Rambam *Sefer HaMadda, Hilkhot Talmud Torah* 3:8).

One creates simulated corners for it – עוֹשִׂין לָהּ זָוִיּוֹת: In the case of a round city, one first squares its perimeter and then measures its Shabbat limit. The same rule applies if the city is triangular in shape or if it has an irregular perimeter (Rambam). The Gemara's statement: One does not create additional corners for it, applies only to a city that is already rectangular (Vilna Gaon; *Shulḥan Arukh, Oraḥ Ḥayyim* 398:2).

Wide on one side – רְחָבָה מִצַּד אֶחָד: If a city is wide on one side and narrow on the other, it is viewed as though both sides are the length of the longer side, and the Shabbat boundaries are measured from there (*Shulḥan Arukh, Oraḥ Ḥayyim* 398:4).

BACKGROUND

The boundaries of a round city – תְּחוּמֵי עִיר עֲגוּלָּה:

City
2000

Measurement of Shabbat limit for a round city

A city that is narrow on one side – עִיר צָרָה בְּצַד אֶחָד:

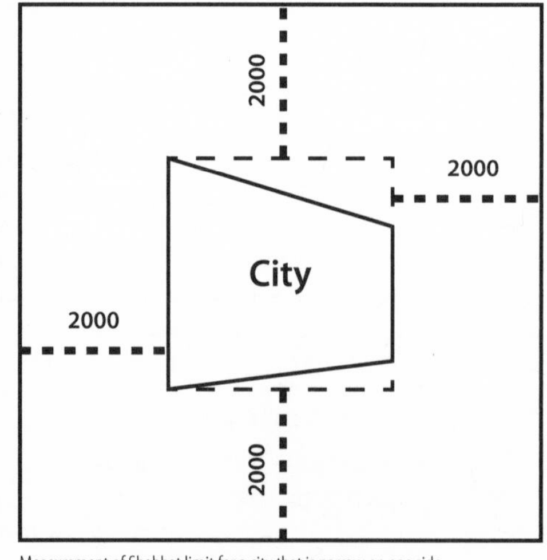

Measurement of Shabbat limit for a city that is narrow on one side

הָיָה בַּיִת אֶחָד יוֹצֵא כְּמִין פָּגוּם, אוֹ שְׁנֵי בָתִּים יוֹצְאִין כְּמִין שְׁנֵי פְגוּמִין – רוֹאִין אוֹתָן כְּאִילּוּ חוּט מָתוּחַ עֲלֵיהֶן, וּמוֹדֵד מִמֶּנּוּ וּלְהַלָּן אַלְפַּיִם אַמָּה. הָיְתָה עֲשׂוּיָה כְּמִין קֶשֶׁת אוֹ כְּמִין גַּאם – רוֹאִין אוֹתָהּ כְּאִילּוּ הִיא מְלֵאָה בָּתִּים וַחֲצֵירוֹת, וּמוֹדֵד מִמֶּנּוּ וּלְהַלָּן אַלְפַּיִם אַמָּה.

If **one house** in a row of dwellings **was protruding like a turret, or if two houses** were **protruding like two turrets, one regards them as though a cord is stretched over their** outer edge along the length of the city, **and one measures two thousand cubits** beginning **from there.** If the city **was shaped like a bow**[N] **or like** the Greek letter ***gamma*,**[N] **one regards it as though** the interior space were **full of houses and courtyards, and one measures two thousand cubits** beginning **from there.**

אָמַר מָר: אֲרוּכָּה – כְּמוֹת שֶׁהִיא, פְּשִׁיטָא! לָא צְרִיכָא, דַּאֲרִיכָא וְקַטִּינָא, מַהוּ דְּתֵימָא: לִיתֵּן לָהּ פּוּתְיָא אַאוֹרְכָּהּ, קָא מַשְׁמַע לַן.

The Gemara proceeds to analyze the *Tosefta*. **The Master said:** If the city is **long,** the Shabbat limit is measured from the boundary **as it is.** The Gemara expresses surprise: That is **obvious.** The Gemara explains: **It was necessary** to teach this *halakha* **only** with regard to a case **where** the city is **long and narrow.**[H] **Lest you say: Let us give its breadth** the dimension **of its length** and regard the city as if it were square, **it teaches us** that we do not do so.

"מְרוּבַּעַת – אֵין עוֹשִׂין לָהּ זָוִיּוֹת", פְּשִׁיטָא! לָא צְרִיכָא, דִּמְרַבְּעָא וְלָא מְרַבְּעָא בְּרִיבּוּעַ עוֹלָם. מַהוּ דְּתֵימָא: לִירַבְּעָא בְּרִיבּוּעַ עוֹלָם, קָא מַשְׁמַע לַן.

The *Tosefta* stated: If the city is **square, one does not create** additional **corners for it.** Once again the Gemara asks: That is **obvious.** The Gemara answers: **It was necessary** to teach this *halakha* **only** with regard to a case **where** the shape of the city **is square but** that **square is not** aligned with the **four** directions **of the world,**[H] i.e., north, south, east, and west. **Lest you say: Let us** align the **square with the four** directions of the **world, it teaches us** that this is not done.

"הָיָה בַּיִת אֶחָד יוֹצֵא כְּמִין פָּגוּם, אוֹ שְׁנֵי בָתִּים יוֹצְאִין כְּמִין שְׁנֵי פְגוּמִין", הַשְׁתָּא בַּיִת אֶחָד אָמְרַתְּ, שְׁנֵי בָתִּים מִיבַּעְיָא?!

The *Tosefta* also stated: If **one house** in a row of dwellings **was protruding like a turret, or** if **two houses** were **protruding like two turrets,** one regards them as though a cord is stretched over their outer edge along the length of the city, and one measures two thousand cubits beginning from there. The Gemara asks: **Now,** if with regard to **one house, you said** to extend the city's boundaries, with regard to **two houses, is it necessary** to say so?

לָא צְרִיכָא, מִשְּׁתֵּי רוּחוֹת. מַהוּ דְּתֵימָא: מֵרוּחַ אַחַת – אָמְרִינַן, מִשְּׁתֵּי רוּחוֹת – לָא אָמְרִינַן, קָא מַשְׁמַע לַן.

The Gemara answers: **It was necessary** to teach this *halakha* **only** with regard to a case where the two houses were protruding **on two** different **sides** of the city.[B] **Lest you say:** When a house protrudes **from one side, we say** that the city is extended even due to a single house, but if houses protrude **from two sides we do not say** so; therefore, **it teaches us** to regard the city as though it is extended on both sides.

HALAKHA

Long and narrow – אֲרִיכָא וְקַטִּינָא: A city which is long and narrow is measured as it is (*Shulḥan Arukh, Oraḥ Ḥayyim* 398:1).

That square is not aligned with the four directions of the world – לָא מְרַבְּעָא בְּרִיבּוּעַ עוֹלָם: The Shabbat limit of a square city is measured as it is, without adjusting it so that the sides align with the directions of the compass (*Shulḥan Arukh, Oraḥ Ḥayyim* 398:1).

BACKGROUND

A city with turrets – עִיר עִם פְּגוּמִים:

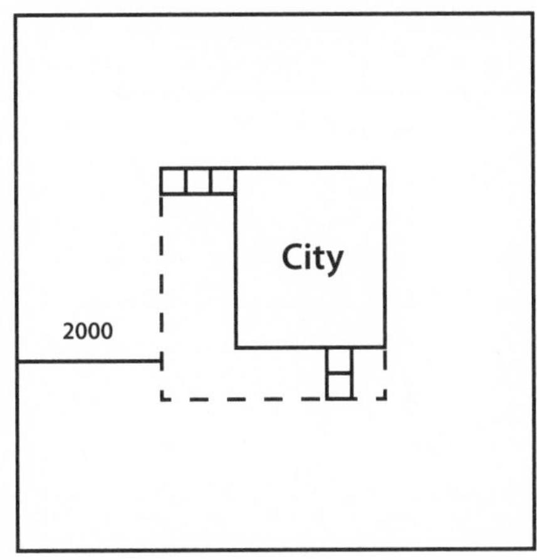

Measurement of Shabbat limit for a city that has turrets protruding from two different sides of the city

NOTES

If the city was shaped…like the letter *gamma* – ...עֲשׂוּיָה כְּמִין גַּאם: The early commentaries disagree about how to establish the boundaries of a *gamma*-shaped city. Although most commentaries understand that it is made into an actual rectangle, some of them maintain that it is squared as illustrated (see *Me'iri*; Ritva).

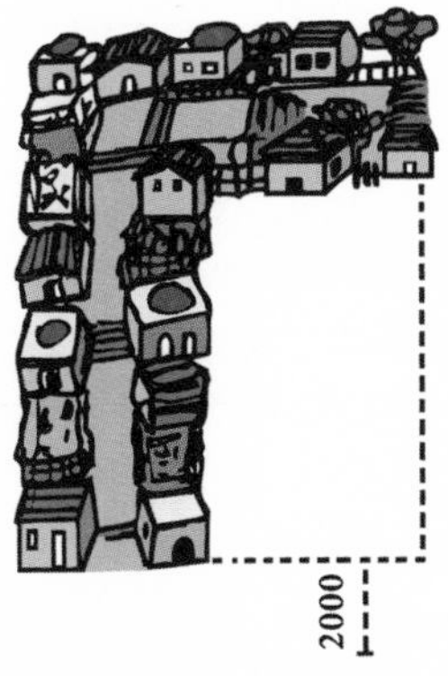

Measurement of Shabbat limit for a *gamma*-shaped city

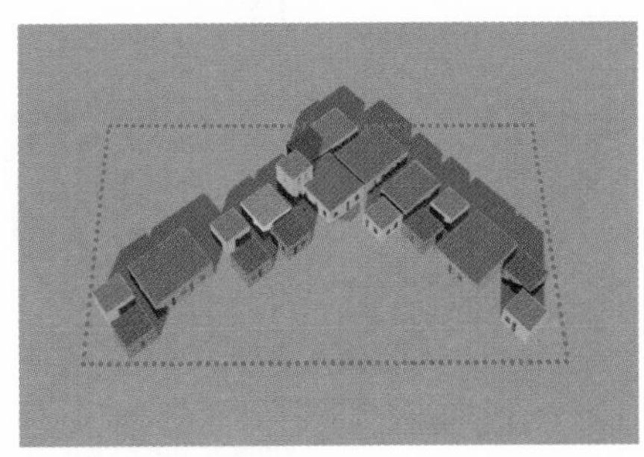

Alternative interpretation of the measurement of the Shabbat limit for a *gamma*-shaped city

NOTES

If the city was shaped like a bow – הָיְתָה עֲשׂוּיָה כְּמִין קֶשֶׁת: The early commentaries offer many opinions with regard to the relationship between Rav Huna's statement about a bow-shaped city and the rulings of the *Tosefta*. Several questions are raised in this regard. For example, does the principle with regard to a bow-shaped city apply also to one that is *gamma*-shaped? Moreover, doesn't the principle concerning the measurement of a town's boundaries according to the turrets, which is not limited to a width of four thousand cubits, contradict Rav Huna's statement? What is the difference between a city that is shaped like a bow and one that has protrusions separated by a significant distance?

The commentaries have suggested various answers. The Ra'avad states that the principle with regard to turrets applies only where the distance between them is less than four thousand cubits. The Rashba and other commentaries explain that there is a difference between the city's basic contours and a structure such as a turret or even the small watchtowers of a city. If the city is inhabited along an entire side and there are structures that protrude from that side, it is reasonable to assume that other structures will eventually be built there as well. However, if the entire city is shaped like a bow, it is clear that the space between the two ends of the bow is not meant to be inhabited, and if the residents add to the city, they will simply add to the ends of the bow.

HALAKHA

A city that is shaped like a bow – עִיר הָעֲשׂוּיָה כַּקֶּשֶׁת: If there are less than four thousand cubits between two ends of a city that is shaped like a bow or a *gamma*, the Shabbat boundary is measured from the imaginary bowstring between the two ends of the bow. If there are more than four thousand cubits between the two ends, the measurement is made from the actual perimeter of the city. Some hold that the measurement begins from the place where the two sides of the bow are separated by less than four thousand cubits (*Shulḥan Arukh, Oraḥ Ḥayyim* 398:4, and in the comment of the Rema).

The wall of a city that was breached – חוֹמַת הָעִיר שֶׁנִּפְרְצָה: In a case where the wall of a city was breached on opposite sides and the houses between the breaches were destroyed, if the gap between the two sections of the city is greater than 141⅓ cubits, the two sections are considered distinct entities with regard to the *halakhot* of *eiruv*. If the gap is smaller than that distance, the two sections have the status of a single city, as stated by Rav Huna (*Shulḥan Arukh, Oraḥ Ḥayyim* 398:7, and in the comment of the Rema).

"הָיְתָה עֲשׂוּיָה כְּמִין קֶשֶׁת אוֹ כְּמִין גַּאם – רוֹאִין אוֹתָהּ כְּאִילּוּ הִיא מְלֵאָה בָּתִּים וַחֲצֵירוֹת, וּמוֹדֵד מִמֶּנָּה וּלְהַלָּן אַלְפַּיִם אַמָּה". אָמַר רַב הוּנָא: עִיר הָעֲשׂוּיָה כַּקֶּשֶׁת, אִם יֵשׁ בֵּין שְׁנֵי רָאשֶׁיהָ פָּחוֹת מֵאַרְבַּעַת אֲלָפִים אַמָּה – מוֹדְדִין לָהּ מִן הַיֶּתֶר, וְאִם לָאו – מוֹדְדִין לָהּ מִן הַקֶּשֶׁת.

The *Tosefta* stated: If the city **was shaped like a bow or like** the Greek letter ***gamma*****, one regards it as if** the interior space were **full of houses and courtyards, and one measures two thousand cubits** beginning **from there. Rav Huna said:** With regard to **a city that is shaped like a bow,**[HB] the following distinction applies: **If there are less than four thousand cubits between** the **two ends** of the bow, so that the Shabbat limits measured from the two ends of the city overlap, the interior space of the bow is regarded as if it were filled with houses, and **one measures** the Shabbat limit of the city **from the** imaginary **bowstring** stretched between the two ends of the bow. **But if** that is **not** the case, and the distance between the two ends of the bow is four thousand cubits or more, **one measures** the Shabbat limit **from the bow** itself.

וּמִי אָמַר רַב הוּנָא הָכִי? וְהָאָמַר רַב הוּנָא: חוֹמַת הָעִיר שֶׁנִּפְרְצָה בְּמֵאָה וְאַרְבָּעִים וְאַחַת וּשְׁלִישׁ!

The Gemara asks: **Did Rav Huna** actually **say** that the distance between two sections of a single city that renders them separate entities is four thousand cubits? **Didn't Rav Huna say:** With regard to **the wall of a city that was breached,**[H] even if there is a gap between two sections of the city, the city is still considered a single entity if the breach is no more than **141⅓** cubits? However, if the breach is wider, the two sections are considered separate entities. Apparently, a distance of 141⅓ cubits suffices to separate between two sections of a city and to render them separate entities.

אָמַר רַבָּה בַּר עוּלָּא: לָא קַשְׁיָא; כָּאן – בְּרוּחַ אַחַת, כָּאן – מִשְּׁתֵּי רוּחוֹת.

Rabba bar Ulla said: That is **not difficult. Here,** where Rav Huna speaks of four thousand cubits, he is referring to a case where the gap is **on** only **one side,** as the other side, the bow, is inhabited; but **there,** where he speaks of 141⅓ cubits, he is referring to a case where the breach is **from two sides,** which truly renders the city two separate entities.[B]

וּמַאי קָא מַשְׁמַע לָן – דְּנוֹתְנִין קַרְפֵּף לָזוֹ וְקַרְפֵּף לָזוֹ? הָא אֲמָרָהּ רַב הוּנָא חֲדָא זִימְנָא! דִּתְנַן:

The Gemara asks: If so, **what is** Rav Huna **teaching us** in the case of the breached city wall, that **one allocates a *karpef*,** an area measuring slightly more than seventy cubits, **to this** section of the city **and** a ***karpef*** **to that** section of the city? **Didn't Rav Huna** already **say** this **on one occasion? As we learned** in a mishna:

BACKGROUND

A city that is shaped like a bow – עִיר הָעֲשׂוּיָה כַּקֶּשֶׁת: If there are less than four thousand cubits between the two ends of the bow, one measures the Shabbat limit of the city from the imaginary bowstring stretched between the two ends.

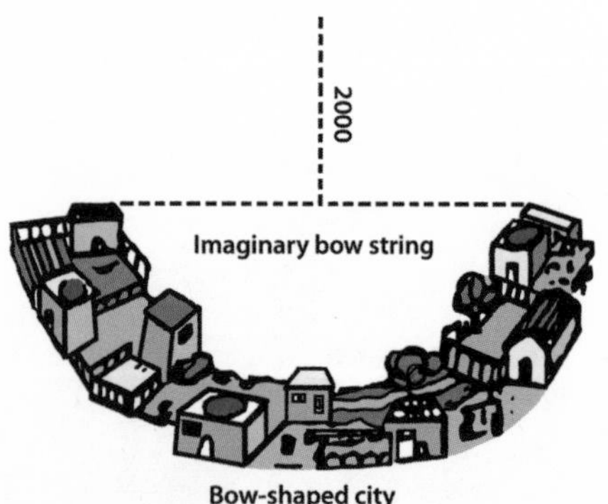

Measurement of Shabbat limit for a city that is shaped like a bow, where the two ends of the arc are separated by less than four thousand cubits

If the two ends of the bow are separated by more than four thousand cubits, one measures the city's boundary from all the sides of the perimeter of the city.

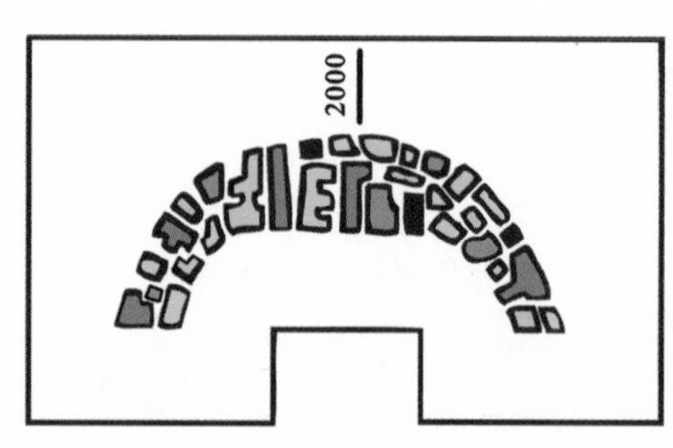

Measurement of Shabbat limit for a city that is shaped like a bow, where the two ends are separated by more than four thousand cubits

A city that was breached – עִיר שֶׁנִּפְרְצָה:

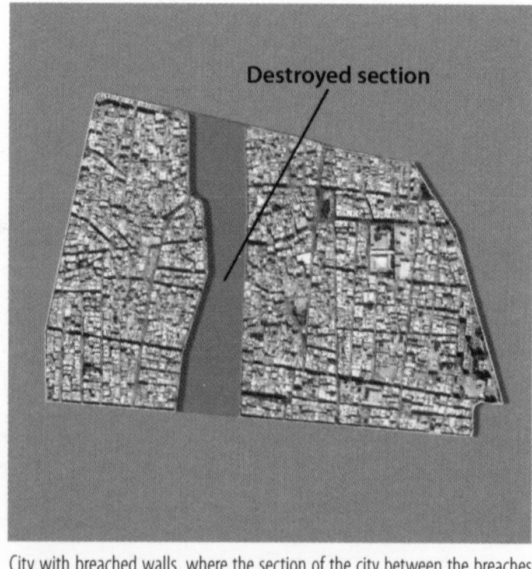

City with breached walls, where the section of the city between the breaches was destroyed

נוֹתְנִין קַרְפֵּף לָעִיר, דִּבְרֵי רַבִּי מֵאִיר. וַחֲכָמִים אוֹמְרִים: לֹא אָמְרוּ קַרְפֵּף אֶלָּא בֵּין שְׁתֵּי עֲיָירוֹת.

One allocates a ***karpef*** **to** every **city,** i.e., an area of slightly more than seventy cubits is added to the boundary of a city and the Shabbat limit is measured from there; this is **the statement of Rabbi Meir. And the Sages say: They spoke of** the measure of **a** ***karpef*** **only** with regard to the space **between two** adjacent **cities,** i.e., if adjacent cities are separated by a shorter distance than that, they are considered one city.

וְאִיתְּמַר, רַב הוּנָא אָמַר: קַרְפֵּף לָזוֹ וְקַרְפֵּף לָזוֹ. וְחִיָּיא בַּר רַב אָמַר: אֵין נוֹתְנִין אֶלָּא קַרְפֵּף אֶחָד לִשְׁנֵיהֶם.

And it was stated that the *amora'im* disputed this issue. **Rav Huna said: A** ***karpef*** is added **to this** city **and** another ***karpef*** is added **to that** city, so that as long as the cities are not separated by a distance of slightly more than 141 cubits, they are considered one entity. **And Ḥiyya bar Rav said: One allocates only one** ***karpef*** **to the two of them.** Accordingly, Rav Huna has already stated that the measure of a *karpef* is added to both cities in determining whether they are close enough to be considered a single entity.

צְרִיכָא, דְּאִי אַשְׁמְעִינַן הָכָא – מִשּׁוּם דַּהֲוָה לֵיהּ צַד הֶיתֵּר מֵעִיקָּרָא, אֲבָל הָתָם – אֵימָא לָא.

The Gemara answers: **It is necessary** for Rav Huna to state this *halakha* in both instances, **as, had he taught it to us** only **here,** in the case of the breached wall, one might have said that a *karpef* is allocated to each city only in that case **because it had an aspect of permissibility from the outset,** namely, the two sections originally formed one city. **But there,** with regard to the two cities, **say** that this is **not the case** and the two cities are only considered as one if they are separated by less than the measure of a single *karpef*.

וְאִי אַשְׁמְעִינַן הָתָם – מִשּׁוּם דִּדְחִיקָא תַּשְׁמִישְׁתַּיְיהוּ, אֲבָל הָכָא דְּלָא דְּחִיקָא תַּשְׁמִישְׁתַּיְיהוּ – אֵימָא לָא, צְרִיכָא.

And had he taught it to **us** only **there,** with regard to the two cities, one might have said that only in that case is a *karpef* allocated to each city **because** one *karpef* would be too **cramped for the use** of both cities. **But here,** in the case of the breached wall, **where** one *karpef* **would not be** too **cramped for the use of** both sections, as the vacant space is inside the city, in an area that had not been used in this fashion before the wall was breached, **say** that this is **not** the case and a single *karpef* is sufficient. Therefore, **it was necessary** to state this *halakha* in both cases.

וְכַמָּה הָוֵי בֵּין יֶתֶר לְקֶשֶׁת? רַבָּה בַּר רַב הוּנָא אָמַר: אַלְפַּיִם אַמָּה. רָבָא בְּרֵיהּ דְּרַבָּה בַּר רַב הוּנָא אָמַר: אֲפִילּוּ יָתֵר מֵאַלְפַּיִם אַמָּה.

The Gemara asks: **And how much** distance may there be **between** the imaginary **bowstring and** the center of the **bow**[N] in a city that is shaped like a bow?[H] **Rabba bar Rav Huna said: Two thousand cubits. Rava, son of Rabba bar Rav Huna, said: Even more than two thousand cubits.**

אָמַר אַבָּיֵי: כְּוָותֵיהּ דְּרָבָא בְּרֵיהּ דְּרַבָּה בַּר רַב הוּנָא מִסְתַּבְּרָא, דְּאִי בָּעֵי – הָדַר אָתֵי דֶּרֶךְ בָּתִּים.

Abaye said: It stands to reason in accordance with the opinion of **Rava, son of Rabba bar Rav Huna, as if one wants, he can return and go** anywhere within the bow **by way of the houses.** Since one can always walk to the end of the city, and from there he is permitted to walk down the line of the imaginary bowstring, he should also be permitted to walk from the middle of the bow to the bowstring, even if the distance is more than two thousand cubits.

"הָיוּ שָׁם גְּדוּדִיּוֹת גְּבוֹהוֹת עֲשָׂרָה טְפָחִים כו'". מַאי גְּדוּדִיּוֹת? אָמַר רַב יְהוּדָה: שָׁלֹשׁ מְחִיצוֹת שֶׁאֵין עֲלֵיהֶן תִּקְרָה.

We learned in the mishna: If **there were remnants** of walls **ten handbreadths high** on the outskirts of a city, they are considered part of the city, and the Shabbat limit is measured from them. The Gemara asks: **What are** these **remnants? Rav Yehuda said: Three partitions that do not have a roof over them,**[H] which are considered part of the city despite the fact that they do not comprise a proper house.

NOTES

Between the bowstring and the bow – בֵּין יֶתֶר לְקֶשֶׁת: Some commentaries explain that this issue stands alone and is unrelated to the previous statements on this topic. Other commentaries state that the dispute between Rabba bar Rav Huna and his son is about how to explain the opinion of their father and grandfather, Rav Huna (see Ritva).

HALAKHA

The distance between the bowstring and the bow – מֶרְחָק בֵּין יֶתֶר לְקֶשֶׁת: In a city shaped like a bow, if the distance between the imaginary bowstring and the bow is less than two thousand cubits, the Shabbat limit is measured from the bowstring, even if the two ends of the arc are more than four thousand cubits apart. The *halakha* is in accordance with the opinion of Rava, son of Rabba bar Rav Huna, whose opinion was supported by Abaye (*Kesef Mishne*; see Vilna Gaon; *Shulḥan Arukh, Oraḥ Ḥayyim* 398:4, and in the comment of the Rema).

Three partitions that do not have a roof over them – שָׁלֹשׁ מְחִיצוֹת שֶׁאֵין עֲלֵיהֶן תִּקְרָה: A structure that contains three walls even without a roof, encloses an area of four by four cubits, and is used as a residence (*Shulḥan Arukh HaRav*) constitutes a house that is considered part of the city from which the Shabbat limit is measured (*Shulḥan Arukh, Oraḥ Ḥayyim* 398:6).

אִיבַּעְיָא לְהוּ: שְׁתֵּי מְחִיצּוֹת וְיֵשׁ עֲלֵיהֶן תִּקְרָה מַהוּ? תָּא שְׁמַע: אֵלּוּ שֶׁמִּתְעַבְּרִין עִמָּהּ: נֶפֶשׁ שֶׁיֵּשׁ בָּהּ אַרְבַּע אַמּוֹת עַל אַרְבַּע אַמּוֹת, וְהַגֶּשֶׁר וְהַקֶּבֶר שֶׁיֵּשׁ בָּהֶן בֵּית דִּירָה, וּבֵית הַכְּנֶסֶת שֶׁיֵּשׁ בָּהּ בֵּית דִּירָה לַחַזָּן, וּבֵית עֲבוֹדָה זָרָה שֶׁיֵּשׁ בָּהּ בֵּית דִּירָה לַכּוֹמָרִים, וְהָאוּרָווֹת וְהָאוֹצָרוֹת שֶׁבַּשָּׂדוֹת וְיֵשׁ בָּהֶן בֵּית דִּירָה, וְהַבּוּרְגָּנִין שֶׁבְּתוֹכָהּ, וְהַבַּיִת שֶׁבַּיָּם – הֲרֵי אֵלּוּ מִתְעַבְּרִין עִמָּהּ.

The dilemma was raised before the Sages: In the case of **two partitions** that **have a roof over them,**[H] **what is the** *halakha*? Is this structure also treated like a house? **Come and hear** a proof from the *Tosefta*: **These** are the structures **that are included in** the city's **extension: A monument** [*nefesh*] over a grave[B] **that is four cubits by four cubits; and a bridge or a grave in which there is a residence;**[B] **and a synagogue in which there is a residence for the sexton** or synagogue attendant, and which is used not only for prayer services at specific times; **and an idolatrous temple in which there is a residence for the priests; and** similarly, horse **stables and storehouses in the fields in which there is a residence; and** small **watchtowers in** the fields; **and** similarly, **a house on** an island in **the sea** or lake, which is located within seventy cubits of the city; all of **these** structures **are included in the** city's boundaries.

וְאֵלּוּ שֶׁאֵין מִתְעַבְּרִין עִמָּהּ: נֶפֶשׁ שֶׁנִּפְרְצָה מִשְּׁתֵּי רוּחוֹתֶיהָ אֵילָךְ וְאֵילָךְ, וְהַגֶּשֶׁר וְהַקֶּבֶר שֶׁאֵין לָהֶן בֵּית דִּירָה, וּבֵית הַכְּנֶסֶת שֶׁאֵין לָהּ בֵּית דִּירָה לַחַזָּן, וּבֵית עֲבוֹדָה זָרָה שֶׁאֵין לָהּ בֵּית דִּירָה לַכּוֹמָרִים, וְהָאוּרָווֹת וְהָאוֹצָרוֹת שֶׁבַּשָּׂדוֹת שֶׁאֵין לָהֶן בֵּית דִּירָה, וּבוֹר וְשִׁיחַ וּמְעָרָה וְגָדֵר וְשׁוֹבָךְ שֶׁבְּתוֹכָהּ, וְהַבַּיִת שֶׁבַּסְּפִינָה – אֵין אֵלּוּ מִתְעַבְּרִין עִמָּהּ.

And these structures **are not included in** the boundaries of a city: **A tomb that was breached on both sides,** from **here** to **there,** i.e., from one side all the way to the other; **and** similarly, **a bridge and a grave that do not have a residence; and a synagogue that does not have a residence for the sexton; and an idolatrous temple that does not have a residence for the priests; and** similarly, **stables and storehouses in fields that do not have a residence,** and therefore are not used for human habitation; **and a cistern, and an** elongated water **ditch, and a cave,** i.e., a covered cistern, **and a wall, and a dovecote in** the field; **and** similarly, **a house on a boat** that is not permanently located within seventy cubits of the city; all of **these** structures **are not included in the** city's boundaries.[H]

קָתָנֵי מִיהַת: נֶפֶשׁ שֶׁנִּפְרְצָה מִשְּׁתֵּי רוּחוֹתֶיהָ אֵילָךְ וְאֵילָךְ. מַאי לָאו – דְּאִיכָּא תִּקְרָה? לָא, דְּלֵיכָּא תִּקְרָה.

In any case, it was taught that **a tomb that was breached on both sides,** from **here** to **there,** is not included in the city's boundaries. **What,** is this **not** referring to a case where **there is a roof** on the tomb, and the two remaining walls are not included in the city's boundaries even though they have a roof? The Gemara answers: **No,** the *Tosefta* is referring to a case **where there is no roof** on the tomb.

בֵּית שֶׁבַּיָּם לְמַאי חֲזֵי? אָמַר רַב פַּפָּא: בַּיִת שֶׁעָשׂוּי לְפַנּוֹת בּוֹ כֵּלִים שֶׁבַּסְּפִינָה.

The Gemara asks: **A house on** an island in **the sea, what is** it **suitable for** if it is not actually part of the inhabited area? **Rav Pappa said:** It is referring to **a house used to move a ship's utensils** into it for storage.

וּמְעָרָה אֵין מִתְעַבֶּרֶת עִמָּהּ? וְהָתָנֵי רַבִּי חִיָּיא: מְעָרָה מִתְעַבֶּרֶת עִמָּהּ! אָמַר אַבָּיֵי: כְּשֶׁיֵּשׁ בִּנְיָן עַל פִּיהָ.

The Gemara raises another question with regard to the *Tosefta*: **And is a cave** on the outskirts of a city really **not included in its extension? Didn't Rabbi Ḥiyya teach** in a *baraita*: **A cave is included in its extension? Abaye said:** That statement applies **when there is a structure** built **at its entrance,** which is treated like a house on the outskirts of the city.[H]

וְתֵיפּוֹק לֵיהּ מִשּׁוּם בִּנְיָן גּוּפֵיהּ! לָא צְרִיכָא, לְהַשְׁלִים.

The Gemara asks: If there is a structure at the entrance to the cave, why is the cave mentioned? **Let him derive** the *halakha* that it is treated like a house **because of the structure itself.** The Gemara answers: **No, it is necessary** only in a case where the cave serves **to complete** the structure,[N] i.e., where the area of the structure and cave combined are only four by four cubits, which is the minimum size of a house.

אָמַר רַב הוּנָא: יוֹשְׁבֵי צְרִיפִין אֵין מוֹדְדִין לָהֶן אֶלָּא מִפֶּתַח בָּתֵּיהֶן.

The discussion with regard to measuring Shabbat limits has been referring to a properly built city. **Rav Huna said: Those who dwell in huts,** i.e., in thatched hovels of straw and willow branches, are not considered inhabitants of a city. Therefore, **one measures** the Shabbat limit **for them only from the entrance to their homes;** the huts are not combined together and considered a city.

מְתִיב רַב חִסְדָּא: "וַיַּחֲנוּ עַל הַיַּרְדֵּן מִבֵּית הַיְשִׁימוֹת", וְאָמַר רַבָּה בַּר בַּר חָנָה, (אָמַר רַבִּי יוֹחָנָן): לְדִידִי חֲזִי לִי הַהוּא אַתְרָא, וְהָוֵי תְּלָתָא פַּרְסֵי עַל תְּלָתָא פַּרְסֵי.

Rav Ḥisda raised an objection: The Torah states with regard to the Jewish people in the desert: **"And they pitched by the Jordan, from Beit-HaYeshimot** to Avel-Shittim in the plains of Moab" (Numbers 33:49), **and Rabba bar bar Ḥana said that Rabbi Yoḥanan said: I myself saw that place, and it is three parasangs** [*parsa*], the equivalent of twelve *mil*, **by three parasangs.**

HALAKHA

Two partitions and a roof – שְׁתֵּי מְחִיצּוֹת וְתִקְרָה: Two walls that are covered by a roof and used as a residence (*Shulḥan Arukh HaRav*) are considered part of the city for the purpose of determining the Shabbat boundaries. This matter was left unresolved by the Gemara, and the general policy is to be lenient in cases of doubt concerning the *halakhot* of *eiruv* (*Be'er HaGola*; *Shulḥan Arukh*, *Oraḥ Ḥayyim* 398:6).

What is included in the city – מָה מִצְטָרֵף לָעִיר: Bridges, graves, warehouses, stables, idolatrous temples, houses, and any other structure used as a residence are all considered part of a city. If any of these structures does not serve as a residence, it is not considered part of the city (*Shulḥan Arukh*, *Oraḥ Ḥayyim* 398:6).

A cave as part of the city – מְעָרָה וְצֵירוּפָהּ לָעִיר: In this context, the word cave is referring to a covered cistern that has a structure at its entrance. The structure and cistern may combine to complete the required size of a house, in which case they are considered part of a city (*Shulḥan Arukh*, *Oraḥ Ḥayyim* 398:6).

BACKGROUND

A tomb – נֶפֶשׁ: A tomb in this context is a structure built over a grave, or more typically alongside it, to serve as a recognizable marking of the grave. Occasionally, it would also contain a residence for the guardian of the grave.

Since a tomb is merely a memorial of a grave, the Sages stated that it is not constructed for righteous people, because the words of righteous people are their memorial. They do not need any other monument.

Structure known as the Tomb of Zechariah

A bridge in which there is a residence – גֶּשֶׁר שֶׁיֵּשׁ בּוֹ דִּירָה:

Pont Valentre bridge in France with residential towers on it

NOTES

A cave that serves to complete – מְעָרָה שֶׁמַּשְׁלִימָה: The Ritva explains that if the house was more than seventy-plus cubits from the city and the cave was within that distance from the city, the cave is considered joined to the house, so that the house is within the boundary of the city.

וְתַנְיָא: כְּשֶׁהֵן נִפְנִין – אֵין נִפְנִין לֹא לִפְנֵיהֶם וְלֹא לְצִדֵּיהֶן, אֶלָּא לְאַחֲרֵיהֶן.

And it was taught in a *baraita*: **When they would defecate** in the wilderness, **they would not defecate in front of themselves,** i.e., in front of the camp, **and not to their sides,** due to respect for the Divine Presence; **rather,** they would do so **behind** the camp. This indicates that even on Shabbat, when people needed to defecate, they would walk the entire length of the camp, which was considerably longer than two thousand cubits, which equals one *mil*. It is apparent that the encampment of the Jewish people was considered to be a city despite the fact that it was composed of tents alone. How, then, did Rav Huna say that those who live in huts are not considered city dwellers?[NH]

אֲמַר לֵיהּ רָבָא: דִּגְלֵי מִדְבָּר קָאָמְרַתְּ? כֵּיוָן דִּכְתִיב בְּהוּ: ״עַל פִּי ה׳ יַחֲנוּ וְעַל פִּי ה׳ יִסָּעוּ״ – כְּמַאן דִּקְבִיעַ לְהוּ דָּמֵי.

Rava said to him: The banners of the desert, you say? Are you citing a proof from the practice of the Jewish people as they traveled through the desert according to their tribal banners? **Since it is written with regard to them: "According to the commandment of the Lord they remained encamped, and according to the commandment of the Lord they journeyed"** (Numbers 9:20), **it was considered as though it were a permanent** residence **for them.** A camp that is established in accordance with the word of God is regarded as a permanent settlement.

אָמַר רַב חִינָּנָא בַּר רַב כָּהֲנָא, אָמַר רַב אַשִׁי: אִם יֵשׁ שָׁם שָׁלֹשׁ חֲצֵירוֹת שֶׁל שְׁנֵי בָתִּים – הוּקְבְּעוּ.

Rav Ḥinnana bar Rav Kahana said that Rav Ashi said: If there are three courtyards of two properly built **houses** among a settlement of huts, **they have been established** as a permanent settlement, and the Shabbat limit is measured from the edge of the settlement.

אָמַר רַב יְהוּדָה, אָמַר רַב: יוֹשְׁבֵי צְרִיפִין וְהוֹלְכֵי מִדְבָּרוֹת – חַיֵּיהֶן אֵינָן חַיִּים, וּנְשֵׁיהֶן וּבְנֵיהֶן אֵינָן שֶׁלָּהֶן.

On the topic of people who dwell in huts, **Rav Yehuda said that Rav said: Those who dwell in huts,** such as shepherds who pass from one place to another and stay in a single location for only a brief period, **and desert travelers, their lives are not lives,** i.e., they lead extremely difficult lives, **and their wives and children are not** always **their** own, as will be explained below.

תַּנְיָא נַמִי הָכִי, אֱלִיעֶזֶר אִישׁ בִּירְיָא אוֹמֵר: יוֹשְׁבֵי צְרִיפִין כְּיוֹשְׁבֵי קְבָרִים, וְעַל בְּנוֹתֵיהֶם הוּא אוֹמֵר: ״אָרוּר שׁוֹכֵב עִם כָּל בְּהֵמָה״.

That was also taught in the following *baraita*: **Eliezer of Biriyya says: Those who dwell in huts are like those who dwell in graves. And with regard to** one who marries **their daughters,**[N] the verse **says: "Cursed be he who sleeps with any manner of beast"** (Deuteronomy 27:21).

מַאי טַעְמָא? עוּלָּא אָמַר: שֶׁאֵין לָהֶן מֶרְחֲצָאוֹת. וְרַבִּי יוֹחָנָן אָמַר: מִפְּנֵי שֶׁמַּרְגִּישִׁין זֶה לָזֶה בִּטְבִילָה.

The Gemara asks: **What is the reason** for this harsh statement with regard to the daughters of those who dwell in huts or travel in deserts? **Ulla said: They do not have bathhouses,** and therefore the men have to walk a significant distance in order to bathe. There is concern that while they are away their wives commit adultery, and that consequently their children are not really their own. **And Rabbi Yoḥanan said: Because they sense when one another immerses.** Similarly to the men, the women must walk a significant distance in order to immerse in a ritual bath. Since the settlement is very small and everyone knows when the women go to immerse, it is possible for an unscrupulous man to use this information to engage in adulterous relations with them by following them and taking advantage of the fact that they are alone.

מַאי בֵּינַיְיהוּ? אִיכָּא בֵּינַיְיהוּ נַהֲרָא דִּסְמִיךְ לְבֵיתָא.

The Gemara asks: **What is the** practical difference **between** the explanations of Ulla and Rabbi Yoḥanan? The Gemara explains: **There is** a practical difference **between them** in a case where there is **a river that is adjacent to the house,** and it is suitable for immersion but not for bathing. Consequently, the women would not have to go far to immerse themselves, but the men would still have to walk a significant distance in order to bathe.

אָמַר רַב הוּנָא: כָּל עִיר שֶׁאֵין בָּהּ יָרָק – אֵין תַּלְמִיד חָכָם רַשַּׁאי לָדוּר בָּהּ. לְמֵימְרָא דְּיָרָק מְעַלְּיָא? וְהָתַנְיָא: שְׁלֹשָׁה מַרְבִּין אֶת הַזֶּבֶל, וְכוֹפְפִין אֶת הַקּוֹמָה, וְנוֹטְלִין אֶחָד מֵחֲמֵשׁ מֵאוֹת מִמְּאוֹר עֵינָיו שֶׁל אָדָם, וְאֵלּוּ הֵן:

Having mentioned various places of residence, the Gemara cites what **Rav Huna said: Any city that does not have vegetables, a Torah scholar is not permitted to dwell there** for health reasons. The Gemara asks: **Is that to say that vegetables are beneficial** to a person's health? **Wasn't it taught** in a *baraita*: **Three** things **increase one's waste, bend** his **stature, and remove one five-hundredth of the light of a person's eyes; and they are**

NOTES

The Jewish people in the wilderness – יִשְׂרָאֵל בַּמִּדְבָּר: This difficulty is also raised in the Jerusalem Talmud and several solutions are suggested, including the possibility that Moses built several permanent houses for the encampment so that the entire camp would be considered a single city.

And with regard to one who marries their daughters – וְעַל בְּנוֹתֵיהֶם: In other words, the lives of traveling people are so difficult that they are unable to maintain appropriate standards of modesty and instead live like animals, leading to the fact that their daughters will be prohibited. For this reason, Eliezer of Biriyya cited this particular verse rather than a verse dealing with children born from illegitimate relationships (Ritva; Rashba).

HALAKHA

A settlement of huts – יִשּׁוּב צְרִיפִין: A settlement composed of huts and tents does not have the status of a permanent city. Therefore, the Shabbat limit of each resident is measured from the entrance to his hut. However, if the residents are permanently settled in a location, it is considered a city (*Magen Avraham*, based on the Gemara's discussion of the banners in the wilderness). The presence of three courtyards, each containing two permanent houses, transforms the entire settlement into a city (*Shulḥan Arukh*, *Oraḥ Ḥayyim* 398:10).

HALAKHA

He squares it with the four directions of the world – מְרַבְּעָה בְּרִיבּוּעַ הָעוֹלָם: A circular city, which must be squared for the calculation of its Shabbat limit, is squared in alignment with the directions of the compass (*Shulḥan Arukh, Oraḥ Ḥayyim* 398:3).

BACKGROUND

The constellation Scorpio – מַזָּל עַקְרָב:

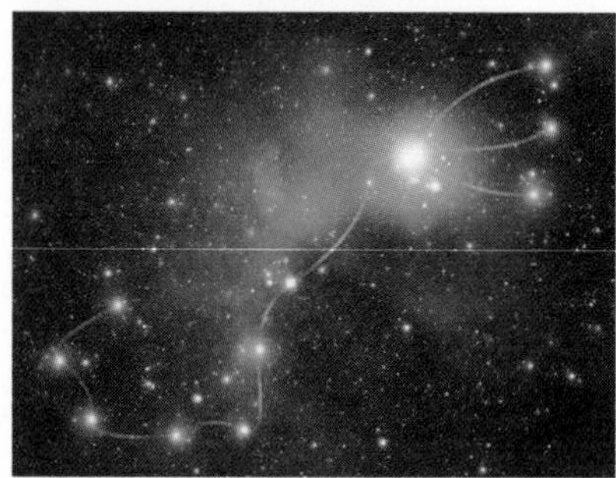

Stars of Scorpio against the background of the Milky Way, which the Sages called the River of Fire

Scorpio and Ursa Major – עַקְרָב וַעֲגָלָה: The map below presents the view of the night sky in July from the latitude of Jerusalem. Only the stars used by the Sages are displayed, because these are the ones utilized to determine the directions of the compass. The Ursa constellations, also known as the Great and Minor Bears, are always to the north. The North Star, at the edge of Ursa Major, marks the direction of due north, with only a very slight deviation. The situation is less straightforward with regard to the constellation Scorpio, since there are months it is not visible, and it does not always face exactly the same direction. In general, this constellation can be seen only in the summer months. Whenever it is visible it appears in the direction of south, but not due south. It is likely that these changes in the position of the Scorpio are among the factors that make it difficult to determine the directions of the compass according to the position of the stars. It should be noted that in the talmudic period the North Star was not due north; rather, due north was closer to the stars of Ursa Major.

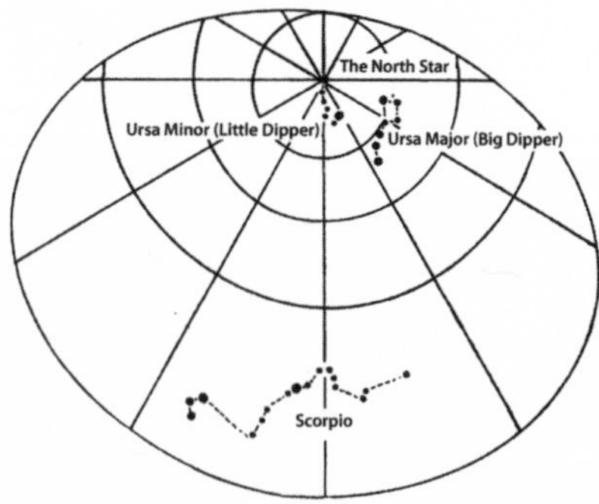

Map of the night sky marking Ursa Major, Ursa Minor, the North Star, and Scorpio

פַּת קִיבָר, וְשֵׁכָר חָדָשׁ, וְיָרָק! לָא קַשְׁיָא; הָא – בְּתוּמֵי וְכַרְתֵּי, הָא – בִּשְׁאָר יַרְקֵי. כִּדְתַנְיָא: שׁוּם – יָרָק, כְּרֵישִׁין – חֲצִי יָרָק, נִרְאֶה צְנוֹן – נִרְאֶה סַם חַיִּים.

coarse bread, made from coarse flour that has not been thoroughly sifted, **new beer, and vegetables.** This indicates that vegetables are harmful to one's well-being. The Gemara answers: This is **not difficult. This** statement of Rav Huna is referring **to garlic and leeks,** which are beneficial; **that** *baraita* is referring **to other vegetables,** which are harmful. **As it was taught** in a *baraita*: **Garlic is** a healthy **vegetable; leeks** are **a half-vegetable,** meaning they are half as healthful. If **radish has been seen, an elixir of life has been seen,** as it is very beneficial to the body.

וְהָא תַּנְיָא: נִרְאֶה צְנוֹן – נִרְאֶה סַם הַמָּוֶת! לָא קַשְׁיָא; כָּאן – בְּעָלִין, כָּאן – בְּאִמְּהוֹת; כָּאן – בִּימוֹת הַחַמָּה, כָּאן – בִּימוֹת הַגְּשָׁמִים.

The Gemara asks: **Wasn't it taught** in a different *baraita*: If **radish has been seen, a lethal drug has been seen?** The Gemara answers: This is **not difficult. Here,** in the *baraita* that deprecates radish, it is referring **to** its **leaves; there,** in the *baraita* that praises radish, it is referring **to the roots.** Alternatively, **here** it is referring **to the summer,** when radish is beneficial; **there,** it is referring **to the winter,** when it is harmful.

אָמַר רַב יְהוּדָה, אָמַר רַב: כׇּל עִיר שֶׁיֵּשׁ בָּהּ מַעֲלוֹת וּמוֹרָדוֹת – אָדָם וּבְהֵמָה שֶׁבָּהּ מֵתִים בַּחֲצִי יְמֵיהֶן. מֵתִים סָלְקָא דַּעְתָּךְ? אֶלָּא אֵימָא: מַזְקִינִים בַּחֲצִי יְמֵיהֶן. אָמַר רַב הוּנָא בְּרֵיהּ דְּרַב יְהוֹשֻׁעַ: הָנֵי מוּלְיָיתָא דְּבֵי בִּירִי וּדְבֵי נֶרֶשׁ אַזְקְנוּן.

On the topic of the attributes of different locations, **Rav Yehuda** also **said that Rav said:** In **any city that has** many **ascents and descents,** which can be taxing to the body, **people and animals die at half their days,** meaning half of their life expectancy. The Gemara expresses surprise: **Can it enter your mind** that Rav really meant to say that they **die** prematurely? Even in such cities they are known to have a regular life expectancy. **Rather, say: They grow old at half their days,** i.e., they age prematurely due to the strain of climbing up and down the inclines. Similarly, **Rav Huna, son of Rav Yehoshua, said: The ascents** and descents **between Beit Biri and Beit Neresh,** my place of residence, **made me grow old** prematurely.

תָּנוּ רַבָּנַן: בָּא לְרַבְּעָהּ – מְרַבְּעָהּ בְּרִיבּוּעַ עוֹלָם, נוֹתֵן צְפוֹנָהּ לִצְפוֹן עוֹלָם וּדְרוֹמָהּ לִדְרוֹם עוֹלָם. וְסִימָנֵיךְ: עֲגָלָה בַּצָּפוֹן וְעַקְרָב בַּדָּרוֹם.

With regard to the measurements of a city's boundaries, **the Sages taught** the following *baraita*: If, in order to measure the Shabbat limit, **one comes to square** a city, i.e., to extend the city's boundaries to include all of its protrusions within an imaginary square, **he squares it** so that the sides of the square align **with the four** directions **of the world.**[H] **He sets the northern** side of the square **to** align with **the north of the world, and its southern** side **to** align with **the south of the world. And your sign** by which you can recognize the directions of the world is as follows: The constellation of **Ursa Major is in the north and Scorpio**[B] **is in the south.** The directions of the city are determined by these constellations.[B]

רַבִּי יוֹסֵי אוֹמֵר: אִם אֵינוֹ יוֹדֵעַ לְרַבְּעָהּ בְּרִיבּוּעַ שֶׁל עוֹלָם – מְרַבְּעָהּ כְּמִין הַתְּקוּפָה. כֵּיצַד? חַמָּה יוֹצְאָה בְּיוֹם אָרוֹךְ וְשׁוֹקַעַת בְּיוֹם אָרוֹךְ – זֶה הוּא פְּנֵי צָפוֹן, חַמָּה יוֹצְאָה בְּיוֹם קָצָר וְשׁוֹקַעַת בְּיוֹם קָצָר – זֶה הוּא פְּנֵי דָרוֹם. תְּקוּפַת נִיסָן וּתְקוּפַת תִּשְׁרֵי – חַמָּה יוֹצְאָה בַּחֲצִי מִזְרָח וְשׁוֹקַעַת בַּחֲצִי מַעֲרָב,

Rabbi Yosei says: If one does not know how to square the city[N] in alignment **with the four** directions **of the world** based upon the constellations, **he should square it based upon the seasons,** although this is less precise. **How so?** Where **the sun rises and sets on the longest day** of the year, the summer solstice, **this** route of the sun **is the face of the north.** The sun rises in the northeast and sets in the northwest, and thus travels from east to west across the north side of the world. Conversely, where **the sun rises and sets on the shortest day** of the year, the winter solstice, **this** route of the sun **is the face of the south.** Whereas at **the vernal equinox and the autumnal equinox,** when day and night are equal in length, **the sun rises in the middle of the east and sets in the middle of the west.**[N]

NOTES

If one does not know how to square the city – אִם אֵינוֹ יוֹדֵעַ לְרַבְּעָהּ: When squaring a city in alignment with the directions of the world, the best method is to follow the stars, which provide an exact determination of the directions. Calculations based on the circuit of the sun are inexact (Ritva).

The sun and the directions – הַחַמָּה וְהַכִּיוּוּנִים: A slightly different and far simpler method to determine directions is offered in the Jerusalem Talmud. One notes the location of the sun at sunrise on the shortest day of the year, the winter solstice, and on the longest day of the year, the summer solstice. The midpoint between these locations is due east. The midpoint between the locations of the sun during sunset on these days is due west.

שֶׁנֶּאֱמַר: ״הוֹלֵךְ אֶל דָּרוֹם וְסוֹבֵב אֶל צָפוֹן״. ״הוֹלֵךְ אֶל דָּרוֹם״ – בַּיּוֹם, ״וְסוֹבֵב אֶל צָפוֹן״ – בַּלַּיְלָה. ״סוֹבֵב סוֹבֵב הוֹלֵךְ הָרוּחַ״ – אֵלּוּ פְּנֵי מִזְרָח וּפְנֵי מַעֲרָב, פְּעָמִים מְהַלַּכְתָּן וּפְעָמִים מְסַבַּבְתָּן.

As it is stated: "One generation passes away and another generation comes; but the earth abides forever. The sun also rises and the sun goes down, and hastens to its place, where it rises again. **It goes toward the south, and turns about to the north;** round and round goes the wind, and on its circuits the wind returns" (Ecclesiastes 1:4–6). The verse is understood as describing the sun's movements, as follows: **"It goes toward the south"**[N] **during the day; "and turns about to the north,"** on the other side of the earth, **at night. "Round and round goes the wind** [*ruaḥ*];" the word *ruaḥ* can also mean direction or side. Rabbi Yosei explains that **these are the face of the east and the face of the west; sometimes** the sun **traverses them** visibly, **and sometimes it turns about them** without being seen.

אָמַר רַב מְשַׁרְשְׁיָא: לֵיתְנְהוּ לְהָנֵי כְּלָלֵי. דְּתַנְיָא: לֹא יָצְאָה חַמָּה מֵעוֹלָם מִקֶּרֶן מִזְרָחִית צְפוֹנִית וְשָׁקְעָה בְּקֶרֶן מַעֲרָבִית צְפוֹנִית, וְלֹא יָצְאָה חַמָּה מִקֶּרֶן מִזְרָחִית דְּרוֹמִית וְשָׁקְעָה בְּקֶרֶן מַעֲרָבִית דְּרוֹמִית.

Rav Mesharshiya said: There is no validity to these **rules** established by Rabbi Yosei,[N] **as it was taught** in a *baraita*: **The sun has never risen**, even during the summer, **at the northeastern corner** of the sky **and set in the northwestern corner, nor has the sun** ever **risen**, even during the winter, **at the southeastern corner and set in the southwestern corner.** Therefore, one can establish the directions of the world according to the sun's path only during the autumn and spring.[B]

אָמַר שְׁמוּאֵל: אֵין תְּקוּפַת נִיסָן נוֹפֶלֶת אֶלָּא בְּאַרְבָּעָה רִבְעֵי הַיּוֹם, אוֹ בִּתְחִלַּת הַיּוֹם, אוֹ בִּתְחִלַּת הַלַּיְלָה, אוֹ בַּחֲצִי הַיּוֹם, אוֹ בַּחֲצִי הַלַּיְלָה.

On the topic of the previous discussion with regard to calculating the directions of the world based upon the seasons, **Shmuel said: The vernal equinox occurs only at** the beginning of one of **the four quarters of a day: Either** precisely **at the beginning of the day, or** precisely **at the beginning of the night, or at midday, or at midnight.**

וְאֵין תְּקוּפַת תַּמּוּז נוֹפֶלֶת אֶלָּא אוֹ בְּאַחַת וּמֶחֱצָה, אוֹ בְּשֶׁבַע וּמֶחֱצָה, בֵּין בַּיּוֹם וּבֵין בַּלַּיְלָה. וְאֵין תְּקוּפַת תִּשְׁרֵי נוֹפֶלֶת אֶלָּא אוֹ בְּשָׁלֹשׁ שָׁעוֹת, אוֹ בְּתֵשַׁע שָׁעוֹת, בֵּין בַּיּוֹם וּבֵין בַּלַּיְלָה. וְאֵין תְּקוּפַת טֵבֵת נוֹפֶלֶת אֶלָּא אוֹ בְּאַרְבַּע וּמֶחֱצָה, אוֹ בְּעֶשֶׂר וּמֶחֱצָה, בֵּין בַּיּוֹם וּבֵין בַּלַּיְלָה.

Similarly, **the summer solstice occurs only** at certain times of the day: **Either at** the conclusion of **one and a half** hours **or seven and a half** hours **of the day or night. And the autumnal equinox occurs only** at certain times: **Either at** the conclusion of **three hours or nine hours of the day or night. And the winter solstice occurs only** at certain times: **Either at** the conclusion of **four and a half** hours **or ten and a half** hours **of the day or night.**

וְאֵין בֵּין תְּקוּפָה לִתְקוּפָה אֶלָּא תִּשְׁעִים וְאֶחָד יוֹם וְשֶׁבַע שָׁעוֹת וּמֶחֱצָה. וְאֵין תְּקוּפָה מוֹשֶׁכֶת מֵחֲבֶרְתָּהּ אֶלָּא חֲצִי שָׁעָה.

And all this is based on the principle that **there are only ninety-one days and seven and a half hours between** the beginning of **one season and the next,** as he assumed that a year is exactly 365¼ days.[N] **And** similarly, each **season** begins precisely **one-half** planetary **hour past the** beginning of the **previous season.** There are seven heavenly bodies that are each ascendant for an hour at a time in a constant rotation: Mercury, Moon, Saturn, Jupiter, Mars, the Sun, and Venus. Each season begins half an hour later in this rotation than **the previous** season.

NOTES

It goes toward the south – הוֹלֵךְ אֶל דָּרוֹם: In countries north of the equator, the sun is always to the south rather than to the north. Consequently, during the day the sun goes to the south, so to speak, meaning that it moves slightly toward the south throughout the daylight hours. At night, however, the sun does the opposite; it is positioned on the opposite side of the earth and travels toward the north.

There is no validity to these rules – לֵיתְנְהוּ לְהָנֵי כְּלָלֵי: The sun never rises from the exact northeastern corner or sets precisely in the northwestern corner of the sky, but rather does so near the exact corner. Therefore, according to this explanation, one should not rely upon these signs (*Me'iri*).

The calculation of the seasons – חֶשְׁבּוֹן הַתְּקוּפוֹת: The calculation of the seasons cited here is in accordance with Shmuel's opinion that the solar year consists of exactly 365 days and six hours. The intercalation of the year, however, follows the opinion of Rav Adda, who calculated the solar year as a few moments shorter than that. According to Rav Adda, the calculations of the seasons offered here are incorrect.

BACKGROUND

The circuit of the sun – מַהֲלַךְ הַשֶּׁמֶשׁ: The center of the sun is not on the same plane as the equator; rather, the earth's axis is tilted in relation to it (this is known by astronomers as the obliquity of the ecliptic). Therefore, the seasons differ from one another both in the lengths of their respective days and nights and in the location of the rising sun. The earth's tilt changes every day. On the days mentioned by the Gemara, its tilt is as shown in the chart below. This chart shows that the sun indeed rises and sets toward the south and toward the north on the longest and shortest days. With regard to the extent of its tilt, the *baraita* cited by Rav Mesharshiya is also correct in that it never rises nor sets in the southeastern or southwestern corners (i.e., 45° from the easternmost or westernmost points).

Day	Sunrise	Sunset
Autumnal equinox (September 23)	Easternmost point	Westernmost point
Shortest day (winter solstice; December 22)	27° 55′ south of east	27° 55′ south of west
Vernal equinox (March 21)	Easternmost point	Westernmost point
Longest day (summer solstice; June 22)	27° 55′ north of east	27° 55′ north of west

BACKGROUND

Constellations and hours – מַזָּלוֹת וְשָׁעוֹת: Throughout the generations, the hours of day and night were associated with the seven moving heavenly bodies, in the following order: The Sun, Venus, Mercury, Moon, Saturn, Jupiter, and Mars. The table below lists the heavenly bodies for certain hours of the day and night for the different days of the week. One can use it to calculate the attribution of each hour of day or night for any day of the week.

וְאָמַר שְׁמוּאֵל: אֵין לְךָ תְּקוּפַת נִיסָן שֶׁנּוֹפֶלֶת בְּצֶדֶק שֶׁאֵינָהּ מְשַׁבֶּרֶת אֶת הָאִילָנוֹת, וְאֵין לְךָ תְּקוּפַת טֵבֵת שֶׁנּוֹפֶלֶת בְּצֶדֶק שֶׁאֵינָהּ מְיַיבֶּשֶׁת אֶת הַזְּרָעִים, וְהוּא דְּאִיתְלִיד לְבָנָה אוֹ בִּלְבָנָה אוֹ בְּצֶדֶק.

And Shmuel said: There is no instance when the **vernal equinox occurs in** the planetary hour of **Jupiter** and **it does not break the trees** with its strong winds; **and there is no** instance when **the winter solstice occurs in** the planetary hour of **Jupiter** and **it does not dry up the seeds. And this** applies only **where the new moon appeared either at** the hour of the **Moon or at** the hour of **Jupiter.**[B]

	Sunday	Monday	Tuesday	Wednesday	Thursday	Friday	Shabbat
First; sunrise	Mercury	Jupiter	Venus	Saturn	Sun	Moon	Mars
Three hours into the day	Saturn	Sun	Moon	Mars	Mercury	Jupiter	Venus
Three hours into the night	Venus	Saturn	Sun	Moon	Mars	Mercury	Jupiter
Eleven hours into the night	Moon	Mars	Mercury	Jupiter	Venus	Saturn	Sun

Perek **V**
Daf **56** Amud **b**

NOTES

Because he would lose the corners – מִפְּנֵי שֶׁהוּא מַפְסִיד אֶת הַזָּוִיּוֹת: Rashi explains that if one were to measure the two thousand cubits from the corners of the city, the Shabbat boundary would be significantly less than if he were to measure it from the side of the square. When one measures two thousand cubits from the side, the distance from the corner is approximately 2,800 cubits, whereas if one measures 2,000 from the corner the distance from the side is approximately 1,428 cubits. There are several difficulties with this approach based upon the language of the Gemara. Some early commentaries explain that the Gemara is assuming that the extended boundaries of a city are not square-shaped; rather, two thousand cubits are measured from the sides only, and the corners are subsequently filled, as in the diagram below. Slight variations of this shape are possible, but the basic principle remains the same (*Me'iri*).

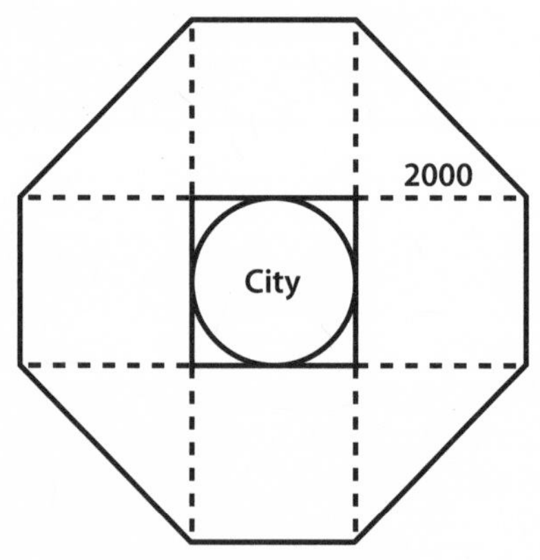

City measured from the corners only

תָּנוּ רַבָּנַן: הַמְרַבֵּעַ אֶת הָעִיר – עוֹשֶׂה אוֹתָהּ כְּמִין טַבְלָא מְרוּבַּעַת, וְחוֹזֵר וּמְרַבֵּעַ אֶת הַתְּחוּמִין, וְעוֹשֶׂה אוֹתָן כְּמִין טַבְלָא מְרוּבַּעַת.

The Sages taught: One who squares a city in order to determine its Shabbat limit **renders it like a square tablet, and then** he also **squares the** Shabbat **boundaries and renders them like a square tablet.** Consequently, after squaring the city, he adds additional squares of two thousand cubits to each of its sides.

וּכְשֶׁהוּא מוֹדֵד – לֹא יִמְדּוֹד מֵאֶמְצַע הַקֶּרֶן אַלְפַּיִם אַמָּה, מִפְּנֵי שֶׁהוּא מַפְסִיד אֶת הַזָּוִיּוֹת. אֶלָּא מֵבִיא טַבְלָא מְרוּבַּעַת שֶׁהִיא אַלְפַּיִם אַמָּה עַל אַלְפַּיִם אַמָּה, וּמַנִּיחָהּ בַּקֶּרֶן בַּאֲלַכְסוֹנָהּ.

And when he measures the Shabbat limit, **he should not measure** the **two thousand cubits** diagonally **from the middle of** each **corner** of the city, **because** if he were to do so, **he would lose the corners,**[N] i.e., the limit would extend only two thousand cubits on the diagonal from each of the corners. **Rather,** he measures the boundary as though **he brought a square tablet that is two thousand cubits by two thousand cubits, and places it at** each **corner at its diagonal.**

נִמְצֵאת הָעִיר מִשְׂתַּכֶּרֶת אַרְבַּע מֵאוֹת אַמּוֹת לְכָאן וְאַרְבַּע מֵאוֹת אַמּוֹת לְכָאן, נִמְצְאוּ תְּחוּמִין מִשְׂתַּכְּרִין שְׁמוֹנֶה מֵאוֹת אַמּוֹת לְכָאן וּשְׁמוֹנֶה מֵאוֹת לְכָאן, נִמְצְאוּ הָעִיר וּתְחוּמִין מִשְׂתַּכְּרִין אֶלֶף וּמָאתַיִם לְכָאן וְאֶלֶף וּמָאתַיִם לְכָאן.

As a result, **it will be found** that **the city gains four hundred cubits in this** corner **and** another **four hundred cubits in the** opposite corner. Assuming that the city itself is round and has a diameter of two thousand cubits, as will be explained below, when the borders of the city are squared, approximately four hundred cubits are added to the city at each corner. When one then squares the Shabbat boundaries, **it is found** that the Shabbat **boundaries gain eight hundred cubits in this** corner **and eight hundred cubits in the** opposite corner.[H] Consequently, by squaring both the city itself and its Shabbat boundaries, **it is found** that **the city and the** Shabbat **boundaries** together **gain 1,200** cubits **in this** corner **and 1,200** cubits **in the** opposite corner.[B]

BACKGROUND

Squaring a city – רִיבּוּעַ הָעִיר: The diagram illustrates how to square a city and add space to the corners of its extended boundaries. The diagram represents both the four hundred additional cubits between the circumference of the city and the surrounding square, and the eight hundred cubits added along the diagonal of the squared limit.

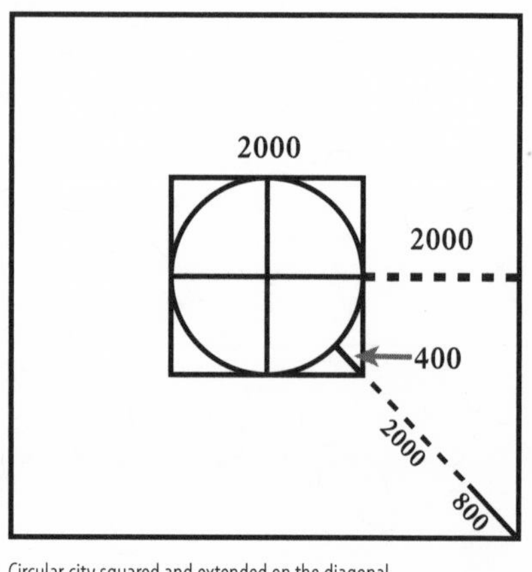

Circular city squared and extended on the diagonal

HALAKHA

How one squares the boundaries – כֵּיצַד מְרַבְּעִים אֶת הַתְּחוּמִים: The outer limits of a city are delineated as a square; one then adds an extended boundary of two thousand cubits in each direction, which is also delineated as a square (*Shulḥan Arukh, Oraḥ Ḥayyim* 399:10).

אָמַר אַבַּיֵי: וּמַשְׁכַּחַתְּ לָהּ בְּמָתָא דְּהָוְיָא תְּרֵי אַלְפֵי אַתְּרֵי אַלְפֵי.

Abaye said: And you find this projection of the additions to the city's borders and Shabbat boundaries to be correct **in** the case of a round **city that is two thousand** cubits **by two thousand** cubits.

תַּנְיָא, אָמַר רַבִּי אֱלִיעֶזֶר בְּרַבִּי יוֹסֵי: תְּחוּם עָרֵי לְוִיִּם אַלְפַּיִם אַמָּה, צֵא מֵהֶן אֶלֶף אַמָּה מִגְרָשׁ – נִמְצָא מִגְרָשׁ רְבִיעַ, וְהַשְּׁאָר שָׂדוֹת וּכְרָמִים.

The Gemara cites a similar discussion with regard to the Levite cities, the forty-eight cities given to the Levites in Eretz Yisrael instead of a tribal inheritance. **It was taught** in a *baraita* that **Rabbi Eliezer, son of Rabbi Yosei, said: The boundary of the cities of the Levites** extends **two thousand cubits** in each direction beyond the inhabited section of the city. **Remove from them a thousand cubits of open space** just beyond the inhabited area, which must be left vacant. **Consequently, the open space is one quarter** of the extended area, **and the rest is fields and vineyards.**[H]

מְנָא הָנֵי מִילֵּי? אָמַר רָבָא, דְּאָמַר קְרָא: "מִקִּיר הָעִיר וָחוּצָה אֶלֶף אַמָּה סָבִיב", אָמְרָה תּוֹרָה: סַבֵּב אֶת הָעִיר בְּאֶלֶף, נִמְצָא מִגְרָשׁ רְבִיעַ.

The Gemara asks: **From where are these matters?** From where is it derived that the open space surrounding the cities of the Levites measured a thousand cubits? **Rava said: As the verse states:** "And the open spaces of the cities, that you shall give to the Levites, **shall be from the wall of the city and outward a thousand cubits round about**" (Numbers 35:4). **The Torah states: Surround the city with a thousand** cubits on all sides to serve as an open space. **Consequently, the open space is one quarter** of the area.

רְבִיעַ?! פַּלְגָּא הָוֵי! אָמַר רָבָא: בַּר אַדָּא מְשׁוֹחָאָה אַסְבְּרָהּ לִי, מַשְׁכַּחַתְּ לָהּ בְּמָתָא דְּהָוְיָא תְּרֵי אַלְפֵי אַתְּרֵי אַלְפֵי. תְּחוּם כַּמָּה הָוְיָא – שִׁיתְסַר, קְרָנוֹת כַּמָּה הָוְיָין – שִׁיתְסַר. דַּל תְּמַנְיָא דִּתְחוּמִין, וְאַרְבָּעָה דִּקְרָנוֹת, כַּמָּה הָוֵי – תְּרֵיסַר.

The Gemara asks: Is it **one quarter?**[N] **It is one half.**[N] One thousand cubits is exactly half of the two thousand cubits incorporated into the boundary of the cities of the Levites. **Rava said: Bar Adda the surveyor explained** the calculation **to me: You will find** this **in a city that is two thousand** cubits **by two thousand** cubits. **How many** cubits is the extended **boundary** of the city itself, without the corners? **Sixteen** million square cubits. Squares measuring two thousand by two thousand cubits are appended to each of the four sides of the city. The area of each of these squares is four million square cubits, and the total area of all the additional squares is sixteen million square cubits. **How many** cubits **are the corners? Sixteen** million square cubits, as additional squares of two thousand by two thousand cubits are appended to the corners of the outer boundaries of the cities. **Subtract eight** million square cubits **from the** area of the extended **boundary** for the open space around the city; the first thousand cubits beyond the inhabited part of the city must be left as open space, which amounts to areas measuring one thousand by two thousand cubits on each of the four sides of the city, for a total of eight million square cubits. **And** subtract another **four** million square cubits **from the corners,** as sections of the corners are parallel to the open spaces. **How much is** the sum total of the area of the open spaces? **Twelve** million square cubits.[B]

נִמְצָא מִגְרָשׁ רְבִיעַ? טְפֵי מִתִּילְתָּא נִינְהוּ!

The Gemara asks: According to this calculation, how is **the open space found** to be **one quarter** of the area? **It is more than one-third.** The entire area of the extended boundary is thirty-two million square cubits and the open space occupies twelve million square cubits, which is more than one-third of the total area of the extended boundary.

אַיְיתֵי אַרְבָּעָה דְּמָתָא שְׁדֵי עֲלַיְיהוּ. אַכַּתִּי תִּילְתָּא הָוֵי!

The Gemara explains: **Bring the four** million square cubits **of the city** itself and **add them** to the area of the limit, and you will arrive at the correct ratio. The Gemara asks: The opens space **is still one-third,** as the total area of the city and its extended boundary is thirty-six million square cubits, and the area of the open space is twelve million square cubits.

מִי סָבְרַתְּ בְּרִיבּוּעָא קָאָמַר? בְּעִיגּוּלָא קָאָמַר.

The Gemara answers: **Do you think** that this *halakha* **was stated** with regard **to a square** city? **It was** in fact **stated** with regard **to a round** city. The open space beyond the city is also round; however, the total extended boundary is squared, so that the total area of a round city with a diameter of two thousand cubits and its extended boundary is thirty-six million square cubits.

כַּמָּה מְרוּבָּע יָתֵר עַל הָעִגּוּל – רְבִיעַ, דַּל רְבִיעַ מִינַּיְיהוּ – פְּשׁוּ לְהוּ תִּשְׁעָה, וְתִשְׁעָה מִתְּלָתִין וְשִׁיתָּא רִיבְעָא, הָוֵי.

The Gemara explains the calculation: **How much larger is** the area of **a square than** the area of **the circle? One quarter. Subtract one quarter from** the twelve million square cubits of open space, and **nine** million square cubits **are left; and nine is** precisely **one quarter of thirty-six.**

HALAKHA

The boundary of the Levite cities – תְּחוּם עִיר הַלְוִיִּם: One thousand cubits are measured outward in each direction from the city wall for the open space, to which two thousand cubits are added in each direction for the boundary. This follows the straightforward meaning of the mishna in tractate *Sota*, although it does not accord with the Gemara here (*Kesef Mishne*; Rambam *Sefer Zera'im, Hilkhot Shemitta VeYovel* 13:2).

NOTES

Quarter – רְבִיעַ: The Rambam maintains that the open space around the Levite cities was a thousand cubits, and that an additional two thousand cubits were added to the boundary beyond the open space. According to that opinion, the *baraita* can be read in a straightforward manner, since the area of the open space is one quarter of the total area of the extended boundary.

It is one half – פַּלְגָּא הָוֵי: *Tosafot* questioned this statement because the area of the open space does not appear to be half of the total area of the extended boundary according to any calculation. The Ritva explains that at this stage, the Gemara does not know whether or not the open space around a Levite city and its extended boundary have corners, similar to Ravina's statement on 57a, p. 30. If the extended boundary is calculated without the corners, the open space is indeed half the total area of the extended boundary.

BACKGROUND

Levite city – עִיר הַלְוִיִּם: This sketch features the open space and its corners, and also the extended boundary and its corners. It also indicates the measurements of the areas in units of one thousand by one thousand cubits.

Corners				Corners
	1	2	1	
	2	City	2	
	1	2	1	
Corners				Corners

Levite city and the areas around it

Round Levite city – **עִיר הַלְוִיִּם בְּעִיגּוּל**: The measurements in the diagram below follow Abaye's opinion that the city is one thousand by one thousand cubits in size.

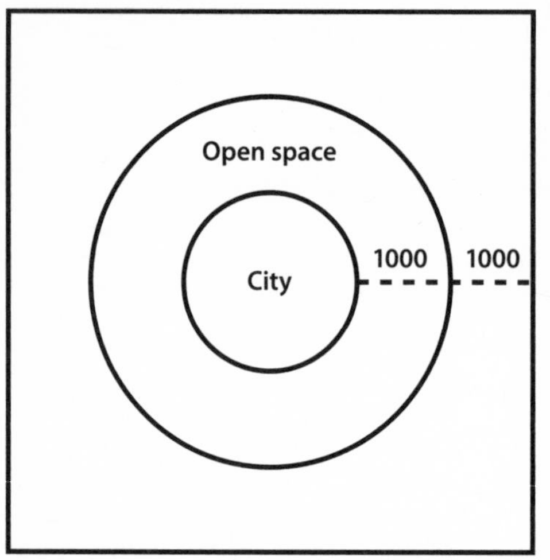

Levite city, its circular open space, and the square boundary surrounding it

אַבַּיֵי אָמַר: מַשְׁכַּחַתְּ לַהּ נַמִי בְּמָתָא דַּהֲוְיָא אַלְפָּא בְּאַלְפָּא. תְּחוּמִין כַּמָּה הָווּ – תְּמַנְיָא, קְרָנוֹת כַּמָּה הָוֵי – שִׁיתְסַר.

Abaye said: You will also find that the open space is one quarter of the total area **in a city that is a thousand** cubits **by a thousand** cubits.[B] **How many** cubits **is the** extended **boundary** of the city without the corners? It is **eight** million square cubits. Additional areas are appended along each side of the city and extending two thousand cubits beyond the city itself. Each of these areas is two thousand cubits by one thousand cubits, for a total area of two million square cubits. Since there are four of these zones, their total area is eight million square cubits. **How many** cubits **are the corners?** They are **sixteen** million square cubits, as squares of two thousand cubits by two thousand cubits are added to each of the four corners.

Perek **V**
Daf **57** Amud **a**

BACKGROUND

Ravina's opinion – **שִׁיטַת רָבִינָא**: According to Ravina, the city has open space only at the sides but not at the corners. Therefore, the open space is one quarter of the entire boundary.

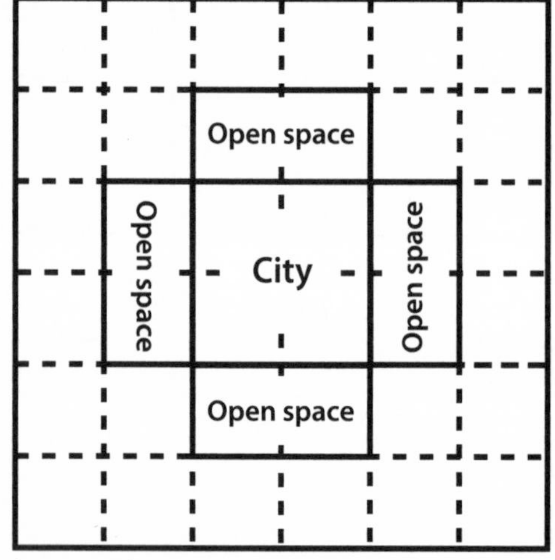

Open space according to Ravina

דַּל אַרְבַּע דִּתְחוּמִין וְאַרְבַּע דִּקְרָנוֹת, כַּמָּה הָוֵי – תְּמַנְיָא.

Subtract four million square cubits **of the** extended **boundary** for the area of the open space, which is a thousand cubits by a thousand cubits on each side, **and** an additional **four** million square cubits **from the corners,** a thousand cubits by a thousand cubits in each corner, which are connected to the open space. **How much is** the sum total? It is **eight** million square cubits.

תִּילְתָּא הָווּ! מִי סָבְרַתְּ בְּרִבּוּעָא קָאָמַר? בְּעִיגּוּלָא קָאָמַר. כַּמָּה מְרוּבָּע יָתֵר עַל הָעִגּוּל – רָבִיעַ, דַּל רָבִיעַ – פְּשׁוּ לָהּ שִׁיתָּא, וְשִׁיתָּא מֵעֶשְׂרִים וְאַרְבָּעָה רִיבְעָא הָוֵי.

The Gemara asks: According to this calculation, the eight million square cubits of open space **are one-third** of the total area of the extended boundary, which is twenty-four million square cubits. The Gemara answers as it answered above: **Do you think** that this *halakha* **was stated with regard to a square** city? **It was stated with regard to a round** city. **How much larger is** the area of **a square than** the area of **a circle?** It is **one quarter** of the area of the circle. **Subtract one quarter from** the eight million square cubits of open space, and **six** million square cubits **are left; and six is** precisely **one quarter of twenty-four.**

רָבִינָא אָמַר: מַאי רָבִיעַ – רָבִיעַ דִּתְחוּמִין.

Ravina said: What is the meaning of the statement that the open space is **one quarter?** It is **one quarter** of **the boundary.** This *halakha* was indeed stated with regard to a square city. However, there is open space only along the sides of the city but not at its corners. Accordingly, a city that is two thousand cubits by two thousand cubits has a total extended boundary of thirty-two million square cubits, of which eight million square cubits, two thousand cubits by one thousand cubits on each side, is open space. The open space is thus one quarter of the total.[BN]

NOTES

Ravina's opinion – **שִׁיטַת רָבִינָא**: Rabbeinu Ḥananel explains that the purpose of Ravina's statement is to explain that Abaye does not include the area of the city itself, but only the surrounding areas. Rabbi Zeraḥya HaLevi explains it completely differently: Ravina maintains that there are only five hundred cubits of open space on each side, which combine to form an area of a thousand by a thousand cubits, and beyond that there is an additional space of a thousand cubits on each side for the extended boundary, which combine to form two thousand by two thousand cubits. The extended boundary does not include corners. Consequently, the open space is one quarter of the area of the extended boundary.

רַב אַשִׁי אָמַר: מַאי רָבִיעַ – רָבִיעַ דִּקְרָנוֹת.

Rav Ashi said the opposite: **What is** the meaning of the statement that the open space is **one quarter** of the total extended boundary? **One quarter of the corners.** Open space is granted only in the corners, and not along the sides. Accordingly, the open space is one thousand cubits by a thousand cubits in each corner, for a total of four million square cubits. The total extended boundary in each corner is two thousand cubits by two thousand cubits, or four million square cubits per corner, which equals a grand total of sixteen million square cubits. Consequently, the open space is one quarter of the total extended boundary.[NB]

אֲמַר לֵיהּ רָבִינָא לְרַב אַשִׁי: וְהָא ״סָבִיב״ כְּתִיב!

Ravina said to Rav Ashi: Isn't it written in the verse: "And the open spaces of the cities, that you shall give to the Levites, shall be from the wall of the city and outward one thousand cubits **around**" (Numbers 35:4)? The verse indicates that the city is provided with open space on all sides and not merely at its corners

מַאי ״סָבִיב״ – סָבִיב דִּקְרָנוֹת. דְּאִי לָא תֵּימָא הָכִי, גַּבֵּי עוֹלָה דִּכְתִיב: ״וְזָרְקוּ (בְּנֵי אַהֲרֹן) אֶת הַדָּם עַל הַמִּזְבֵּחַ סָבִיב״ הָכִי נַמִי סָבִיב מַמָּשׁ? אֶלָּא מַאי סָבִיב – סָבִיב דִּקְרָנוֹת, הָכִי נַמִי: מַאי סָבִיב – סָבִיב דִּקְרָנוֹת.

Rav Ashi responded: **What is** the meaning of **around? Around at the corners,** i.e., an open space of this size is provided at each corner. **As, if you do not say so,** that the area of the corners is also called around, **with regard to** the **burnt-offering, as it is written: "And they shall sprinkle the blood around upon the altar"** (Leviticus 1:5), **here, too,** will you say that the blood must be sprinkled **literally "around"** the altar on all sides? The blood is sprinkled only upon the corners of the altar. **Rather, what is** the meaning of **around? Around the corners,** i.e., the mitzva is to sprinkle the blood at the corners, and this is considered sprinkling blood "around upon the altar." **Here too,** with regard to the open space of the cities of the Levites, **what is** the meaning of **around? Around the corners.**

אֲמַר לֵיהּ רַב חֲבִיבִי מְחוֹזְנָאָה לְרַב אַשִׁי: וְהָא אִיכָּא מוֹרְשָׁא דְּקַרְנָתָא!

The Gemara returns to its previous statement that the open space around a city of the Levites is one quarter of the total extended boundary when the city is round. It questions this statement based upon the mishna's ruling that the boundaries of a city are always delineated as a square. **Rav Ḥavivi from Meḥoza said to Rav Ashi: But aren't there the protrusions of the corners?**[N] How can there be a thousand cubits of open space on each side; when the city is squared, the corners of the square protrude into the open space, thus reducing its area?

בְּמָתָא עִיגּוּלְתָּא. וְהָא רִיבְּעוּהָ! אֵימוֹר דְּאָמְרִינַן: חָזֵינַן כְּמַאן דִּמְרַבְּעָא, רִבּוּעֵי וַדַּאי מִי מְרַבְּעִנַן?

Rav Ashi replied: We are dealing **with a circular city.** Rav Ḥavivi responded: **But haven't they squared** the city? Rav Ashi responded: **Say that we say** the following: **We view** the city **as if it were squared. Do we actually** add houses and **square it?** Although for the purpose of calculating the extended boundary we view the city as a square, in actuality the uninhabited sections are part of the open space.

אֲמַר לֵיהּ רַב חֲנִילָאִי מְחוֹזְנָאָה לְרַב אַשִׁי: מִכְּדִי, כַּמָּה מְרוּבָּע יָתֵר עַל הָעִגּוּל – רָבִיעַ, הָנֵי תְּמָנֵי מְאָה שִׁית מְאָה וְשִׁיתִּין וּשְׁבַע נְכֵי תִּילְתָּא הָוֵי!

Rav Ḥanilai from Meḥoza said to Rav Ashi: Now, how much larger is the area of **a square than** the area of **a circle? One quarter.** Therefore, if we calculate how much area a circular city with a diameter of two thousand cubits gains when it is squared, does it add up to **these eight hundred** cubits mentioned above? The extra area added **is** only **667 minus one-third** cubits.

אֲמַר לֵיהּ: הָנֵי מִילֵּי בְּעִיגּוּלָא מִגּוֹ רִבּוּעַ, אֲבָל בַּאֲלַכְסוֹנָא – בָּעֵינָא טְפֵי. דְּאָמַר מָר: כָּל אַמְּתָא בְּרִיבּוּעַ – אַמְּתָא וּתְרֵי חוּמְשֵׁי בַּאֲלַכְסוֹנָא.

Rav Ashi **said to him: This** statement **applies only to a circle** enclosed **within a square,** as the area of a circle is three-quarters the area of the square around it. **However, with regard to** the additional **diagonal** [*alakhsona*][L] space added in the corners of the square, **more is required. As the Master said: Every cubit** in the side **of a square is one and two-fifths cubits in its diagonal.** Based on this rule, the calculation is exact.

NOTES

Rav Ashi's opinion – שִׁיטַת רַב אַשִׁי: Although Rav Ashi's opinion does not appear to be consistent with the straightforward meaning of the verses, it has the great advantage of applying equally to all cities, large and small (Ritva).

The protrusions of the corners – מוֹרְשָׁא דְּקַרְנָתָא: The author of the *Me'iri* cites an explanation that claims that Rav Ḥavivi thought that the city itself is square while the surrounding open space is circular. In that case, the city does not gain the additional corners as calculated above.

BACKGROUND

Rav Ashi's opinion – שִׁיטַת רַב אַשִׁי: According to Rav Ashi, both the extended boundary and the open space are added only at the corners of the city. The area at the top right corner clearly shows that the open space takes up one quarter of the boundary.

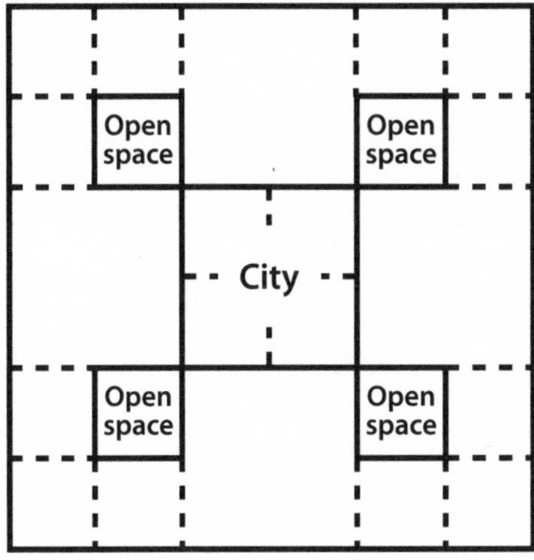

Open space according to Rav Ashi

LANGUAGE

Diagonal [*alakhsona*] – אֲלַכְסוֹנָא: From the Greek λοξός, *loxos*, meaning a diagonal. The corresponding indigenous Aramaic word is *karanzol*.

מתני׳ נוֹתְנִין קַרְפֵּף לָעִיר, דִּבְרֵי רַבִּי מֵאִיר. וַחֲכָמִים אוֹמְרִים: לֹא אָמְרוּ קַרְפֵּף אֶלָּא בֵּין שְׁתֵּי עֲיָירוֹת, אִם יֵשׁ לָזוֹ שִׁבְעִים אַמָּה וְשִׁירַיִים וְלָזוֹ שִׁבְעִים אַמָּה וְשִׁירַיִים – עוֹשֶׂה קַרְפֵּף אֶת שְׁתֵּיהֶן לִהְיוֹת אֶחָד.

MISHNA **One allocates a *karpef* to every city,**[H] i.e., the measure of a *karpef*, which is slightly more than seventy cubits, is added to every city, and the two thousand cubits of the Shabbat limit are measured from there; **this is the statement of Rabbi Meir. And the Rabbis say: They spoke of** the addition of **a *karpef* only** with regard to the space **between two** adjacent **cities.** How so? **If this** city **has seventy cubits and a remainder** vacant on one side, **and that** city **has seventy cubits and a remainder** vacant on the adjacent side, and the two areas of seventy-plus cubits overlap, **the *karpef* combines the two** cities **into one.**

וְכֵן שְׁלֹשָׁה כְּפָרִים הַמְשׁוּלָּשִׁין, אִם יֵשׁ בֵּין שְׁנַיִם חִיצוֹנִים מֵאָה וְאַרְבָּעִים וְאַחַת וּשְׁלִישׁ – עָשָׂה אֶמְצָעִי אֶת שְׁלָשְׁתָּן לִהְיוֹת אֶחָד.

And likewise, in the case of **three villages that are** arranged as **a triangle, if there are** only **141⅓** cubits separating **between the two outer** villages, the **middle** village **combines the three** villages **into one.**

גמ׳ מְנָא הָנֵי מִילֵּי? אָמַר רָבָא, דְּאָמַר קְרָא: ״מִקִּיר הָעִיר וָחוּצָה״, אָמְרָה תּוֹרָה: תֵּן חוּצָה וְאַחַר כָּךְ מְדוֹד.

GEMARA The Gemara asks: **From where are these matters,** that a *karpef* is added to a city, derived? **Rava said: As the verse states:** "And the open spaces of the cities, that you shall give to the Levites, shall be **from the wall of the city and outward** a thousand cubits around. And you shall measure from outside the city on the east side two thousand cubits" (Numbers 35:4–5). **The Torah says: Provide** a certain vacant space **outside**[N] the city, **and** only **afterward measure** the two thousand cubits.[N]

״וַחֲכָמִים אוֹמְרִים לֹא אָמְרוּ וכו׳״. אִיתְּמַר, רַב הוּנָא אָמַר: נוֹתְנִין קַרְפֵּף לָזוֹ וְקַרְפֵּף לָזוֹ. חִיָּיא בַּר רַב אָמַר: קַרְפֵּף [אֶחָד] לִשְׁתֵּיהֶן.

We learned in the mishna: **And the Rabbis say: They spoke** of the addition of a *karpef* **only** with regard to the space between two adjacent cities. **It was stated** that the *amora'im* disagreed with regard to this issue. **Rav Huna said: One allocates a *karpef* to this** city **and a *karpef* to that** city,[H] so that the two cities together are granted a total of slightly more than 141 cubits. **Ḥiyya bar Rav said:** One allocates only **one** common ***karpef* to the two of them.**

תְּנַן, וַחֲכָמִים אוֹמְרִים: לֹא אָמְרוּ קַרְפֵּף אֶלָּא בֵּין שְׁתֵּי עֲיָירוֹת. תְּיוּבְתָּא דְּרַב הוּנָא!

The Gemara raises possible proofs for each opinion. **We learned** in the mishna: **And the Rabbis say: They spoke** of the addition of **a *karpef* only with regard to** the space **between two** adjacent **cities.** This appears to be **a conclusive refutation of** the opinion of **Rav Huna,** as it states that one *karpef* is allocated rather than two.

אָמַר לָךְ רַב הוּנָא: מַאי קַרְפֵּף – תּוֹרַת קַרְפֵּף. וּלְעוֹלָם קַרְפֵּף לָזוֹ וְקַרְפֵּף לָזוֹ.

The Gemara answers that **Rav Huna** could have **said to you** in response to this difficulty: **What is** meant here by **a *karpef*?** It means **the principle of a *karpef*. In actuality,** one allocates **a *karpef* to this** city **and a *karpef* to that** city.

הָכִי נַמִי מִסְתַּבְּרָא, מִדְּקָתָנֵי סֵיפָא: אִם יֵשׁ לָזוֹ שִׁבְעִים אַמָּה וְשִׁירַיִים וְלָזוֹ שִׁבְעִים אַמָּה וְשִׁירַיִים – עוֹשֶׂה קַרְפֵּף לִשְׁתֵּיהֶן לִהְיוֹת אֶחָד. שְׁמַע מִינָּהּ.

The Gemara comments: **So, too, it is reasonable** to explain the mishna in the following manner: **From** the fact **that it teaches** in **the latter clause: If this** city **has seventy cubits and a remainder** vacant on one side, **and that** city **has seventy cubits and a remainder** vacant on the adjacent side, and the two areas of seventy-plus cubits overlap, **the *karpef* combines the two** cities **into one.** This indicates that an area of seventy cubits and a remainder is added to each city. The Gemara concludes: Indeed, **learn from this** that this is the correct understanding of the mishna.

לֵימָא תֶּיהֱוֵי תְּיוּבְתֵּיהּ דְּחִיָּיא בַּר רַב! אָמַר לָךְ חִיָּיא בַּר רַב:

The Gemara asks: **Let us say** that **this** mishna **is a conclusive refutation of** the opinion of **Ḥiyya bar Rav,** that two adjacent cities are granted only one *karpef*. The Gemara answers that **Ḥiyya bar Rav** could have **said to you:**

NOTES

Outside – חוּצָה: The size of the vacant area outside the city is not provided. However, it is apparently equal to a known measure, that of a standard courtyard, which is the same as the area of the courtyard of the Tabernacle (Ra'avad).

A city and its outside – עִיר וְחוּצָה לָהּ: The Ritva explains that the Rabbis do not accept Rabbi Meir's exposition of the verse. Rather, they assert that a *karpef* is added to the two cities only due to their proximity. In the Jerusalem Talmud it is indicated that the Rabbis also expound this verse in the following manner: If there is only one city, the measure begins at its wall. If there are two cities, the measurement begins from a point outside of each city.

HALAKHA

A *karpef* to every city – קַרְפֵּף לָעִיר: The Shabbat limit of two thousand cubits is calculated from the last residential house of the city, in accordance with the opinion of the Rabbis. However, some hold that an additional seventy cubits are added (Rema), in accordance with the lenient opinion of Rabbi Meir, as the *halakha* generally follows the lenient opinion with regard to the *halakhot* of *eiruv* (*Shulḥan Arukh, Oraḥ Ḥayyim* 398:5).

A *karpef* to this city and a *karpef* to that city – קַרְפֵּף לָזֶה וְלָזֶה: If two cities are situated near each other, a *karpef* is allocated to each, for a total of 141⅓ cubits. The *halakha* follows the opinion of Rav Huna over that of Ḥiyya bar Rav, since Rav Huna was older and was a greater Torah scholar. In addition, the *halakha* follows the lenient opinion with regard to the laws of *eiruv* (*Shulḥan Arukh, Oraḥ Ḥayyim* 398:7).

הָא מַנִּי – רַבִּי מֵאִיר הִיא.

In accordance with **whose** opinion is **this** clause of the mishna? **It is** the opinion of **Rabbi Meir,** who maintains that one allocates a *karpef* to each city.

אִי רַבִּי מֵאִיר הִיא, הָא תָּנֵי לֵיהּ רֵישָׁא: נוֹתְנִין קַרְפֵּף לָעִיר דִּבְרֵי רַבִּי מֵאִיר!

The Gemara continues to ask: **If it is** in accordance with the opinion **of Rabbi Meir, didn't we** already **learn in the first clause: One allocates a** ***karpef*** **to** each **city;** this is **the statement of Rabbi Meir?** What need is there to mention Rabbi Meir's opinion again?

צְרִיכָא, דְּאִי מֵהַהִיא הֲוָה אָמֵינָא: חַד לְחַדָא, וְחַד לְתַרְתֵּי, קָא מַשְׁמַע לַן דִּלְתַרְתֵּי תְּרֵי יָהֲבִינַן לְהוּ.

The Gemara answers: **It was necessary** to mention his opinion again, **as,** if we had learned his opinion only **from that** first clause, **I might have said** that one allocates **one** ***karpef*** **for one** city **and** also **one** *karpef* **for two** cities. Therefore, the mishna **teaches us that for two** cities, **one allocates two** ***karpef*** areas.

וְאִי אַשְׁמְעִינַן הָכָא – מִשּׁוּם דִּדְחִיקָא תַּשְׁמִישְׁתַּיְיהוּ, אֲבָל הָתָם דְּלָא דְּחִיקָא תַּשְׁמִישְׁתַּיְיהוּ – אֵימָא לָא, צְרִיכָא.

And conversely, **if** the mishna had **taught us** this law only **here,** with regard to two cities, one might have said that only in that case is each city granted a separate *karpef,* **because** a smaller space between the two adjacent cities would be too **crowded for the use** of both cities. **But there,** with regard to one city, **where** the area of the city itself **is not** too **crowded for the use of** its residents, one might **say** that it is **not** given any *karpef* whatsoever. Therefore, it was **necessary** for the mishna to teach both clauses.

תְּנַן: וְכֵן שְׁלֹשָׁה כְּפָרִים הַמְשׁוּלָּשִׁין, אִם יֵשׁ בֵּין שְׁנַיִם הַחִיצוֹנִים מֵאָה וְאַרְבָּעִים וְאַחַת אַמָּה וּשְׁלִישׁ – עוֹשֶׂה אֶמְצָעִי אֶת שְׁלָשְׁתָּן לִהְיוֹת אֶחָד. טַעְמָא דְּאִיכָּא אֶמְצָעִי, הָא לֵיכָּא אֶמְצָעִי – לָא. תְּיוּבְתָּא דְּרַב הוּנָא!

The Gemara tries again to adduce proof from the mishna, in which **we learned: And likewise,** in the case of **three villages that are aligned** in a row, **if there is** only **141⅓** cubits separating **between the two outer ones,** the **middle** village **combines the three** villages **into one.** At this point the Gemara understands that the mishna here is dealing with three villages arranged in a straight line. Therefore, it makes the following inference: **The reason** that the three villages are considered as one **is** only because **there is a middle** village, **but were there no middle** village, they would **not** be considered as one. This appears to be **a conclusive refutation of** the opinion of **Rav Huna.** According to Rav Huna, the two villages should be considered as one even without the middle village, due to the double *karpef.*

אָמַר לָךְ רַב הוּנָא: הָא אִתְּמַר עֲלַהּ, אָמַר רַבָּה אָמַר רַב אִידִי, אָמַר רַבִּי חֲנִינָא: לֹא מְשׁוּלָּשִׁין מַמָּשׁ, אֶלָּא רוֹאִין: כֹּל שֶׁאִילּוּ מַטִּיל אֶמְצָעִי בֵּינֵיהֶן וְיִהְיוּ מְשׁוּלָּשִׁין, וְאֵין בֵּין זֶה לָזֶה אֶלָּא מֵאָה וְאַרְבָּעִים אַמָּה וְאַחַת וּשְׁלִישׁ – עָשָׂה אֶמְצָעִי אֶת שְׁלָשְׁתָּן לִהְיוֹת אֶחָד.

The Gemara rejects this argument: **Rav Huna** could have **said to you: Wasn't it stated with regard to** that mishna that **Rabba said** that **Rav Idi said** that **Rabbi Ḥanina said:** It does **not** mean that the villages are **actually aligned** in a row of **three** villages[NHB] in a straight line. **Rather,** even if the middle village is off to one side and the outer villages are more than two *karpef* lengths apart, **we see** their spacing and make the following assessment: **Any** case **where, if the middle** village **were placed between** the other two **so that they were three** villages **aligned** in a row, **there would be only** a distance **of 141⅓ cubits between one and the other,** then the **middle** village **turns the three** villages **into one.** According to this explanation, the mishna can be understood even as a support for the opinion of Rav Huna.

אֲמַר לֵיהּ רָבָא לְאַבָּיֵי: כַּמָּה יְהֵא בֵּין חִיצוֹן לְאֶמְצָעִי? אֲמַר לֵיהּ: אַלְפַּיִם אַמָּה.

With regard to this case, **Rava said to Abaye: How much** distance can **there be between an outer** village **and the middle one,**[N] if the latter is still to combine the three villages into one? Abaye **said to him: Two thousand cubits.**

וְהָא אַתְּ הוּא דַּאֲמַרְתְּ: כְּוָותֵיהּ דְּרָבָא בְּרֵיהּ דְּרַבָּה בַּר רַב הוּנָא מִסְתַּבְּרָא, דְּאָמַר: יוֹתֵר מֵאַלְפַּיִם אַמָּה!

Rava replied: **Wasn't it you** yourself **who said: It is reasonable** to rule **in accordance with** the opinion of **Rava, son of Rabba bar Rav Huna, who said:** The Shabbat limit of a bow-shaped city is measured from the imaginary bowstring stretched between the two ends of the city, even if the distance between the center of the string and the center of the bow is **more than two thousand cubits.** Why shouldn't the three villages in this case be considered a single village also, even if they are separated by more than two thousand cubits?

NOTES

Three villages – שְׁלֹשָׁה כְּפָרִים: Among other points of contention, Ḥiyya bar Rav and Rav Huna disagree about the same point disputed by Shmuel and bar Kappara in the Jerusalem Talmud: Whether the villages referred to here are lined up in a row or arranged in a triangle.

Outer and middle ones – חִיצוֹנִים וְאֶמְצָעִים: In the Jerusalem Talmud, there is confusion with regard to the terms outer and middle. Since Rav Huna holds that the villages are in the form of a triangle rather than in a row, each of them could be the middle one. Indeed, some of the early commentators, including Rashi, maintain that there is in fact no difference between the villages, as any two of them can be seen as outer ones in relation to the third. Other commentaries state that the two outer villages must be closer to one another than the third village. Therefore, the two closest villages are considered the outer ones, while the middle one is farthest from them (see Ra'avad; Rashba). In the Jerusalem Talmud a different answer is apparently suggested: There are more than three villages. Another village is positioned next to each of the outer ones, so that the identity of the middle one is clear.

HALAKHA

Three villages – שְׁלֹשָׁה כְּפָרִים: If there are three villages positioned in a triangle with no more than two thousand cubits between the outer ones and the middle one, and it is possible to insert the middle one in between the two outer villages so there is less than 141⅓ cubits between them, they all assume the legal status of a single city. Consequently, the Shabbat limit for each is measured from the outskirts common to all the villages. The Rema maintains that this leniency applies only to the two outer ones, allowing their inhabitants to walk from one to the other; however, the middle village continues to measure its own boundary. However, other later commentaries rule leniently and maintain that the residents of the middle village are not confined to the Shabbat limit as measured from their own village (*Shulḥan Arukh HaRav; Mishna Berura*; see Ra'avad; *Shulḥan Arukh, Oraḥ Ḥayyim* 398:8).

BACKGROUND

Three villages – שְׁלֹשָׁה כְּפָרִים: This diagram displays the three villages according to the Gemara's conclusion. The dotted lines show the imaginary placement of the middle village, so that it is positioned in between the other two villages.

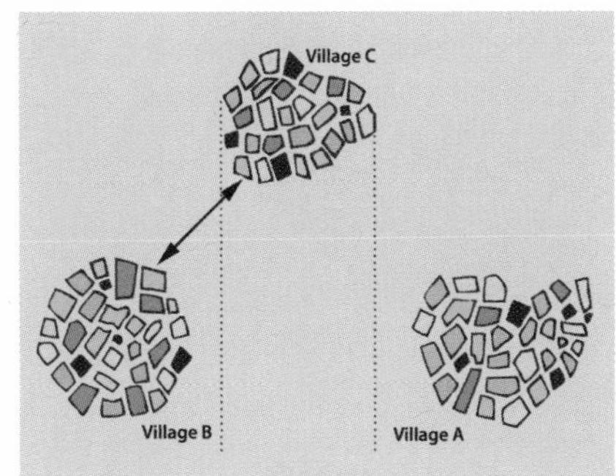

Three villages

הָכִי הָשְׁתָּא! הָתָם – אִיכָּא בָּתִּים, הָכָא – לֵיכָּא בָּתִּים.

Abaye rejected the comparison: **How can you compare? There,** in the case of the bow-shaped city, **there are houses** that combine the city into a single unit, whereas **here, there are no houses** linking the outer villages. Therefore, if two villages are separated by more than two thousand cubits, the measure of the Shabbat limit, they cannot be considered a single entity.

וַאֲמַר לֵיהּ רָבָא לְאַבַּיֵי: כַּמָּה יְהֵא בֵּין חִיצוֹן לְחִיצוֹן? כַּמָּה יְהֵא?! מַאי נָפְקָא לָךְ מִינָּהּ? כֹּל שֶׁאִילּוּ מַכְנִיס אֶמְצָעִי בֵּינֵיהֶן וְאֵין בֵּין זֶה לָזֶה אֶלָּא מֵאָה וְאַרְבָּעִים וְאַחַת וּשְׁלִישׁ.

And Rava said to Abaye: How much distance can **there be between** one **outer** village **and** the other **outer** village? Abaye expressed surprise at this question: **How much** distance can **there be** between them? **What is the** practical **difference to you? Any** case **where, if the middle** village **were placed between them, there would be only** a distance of **141⅓** cubits **between one and the other,** the middle village turns the three villages into one. Therefore, the critical detail is not the distance between the outer villages but the size of the middle village.

וַאֲפִילּוּ אַרְבַּעַת אֲלָפִים אַמָּה?! אֲמַר לֵיהּ: אִין. וְהָאָמַר רַב הוּנָא: עִיר הָעֲשׂוּיָה כַּקֶּשֶׁת, אִם יֵשׁ בֵּין שְׁנֵי רָאשֶׁיהָ פָּחוֹת מֵאַרְבַּעַת אֲלָפִים אַמָּה – מוֹדְדִין לָהּ מִן הַיֶּתֶר, וְאִם לָאו – מוֹדְדִין לָהּ מִן הַקֶּשֶׁת!

Rava continued his line of questioning: Is this true **even** if the distance between the two outer villages is **four thousand cubits?** Abaye **said to him: Yes.** Rava asked: **Didn't Rav Huna say** the following with regard to **a city shaped like a bow: If** the distance **between its two ends is less than four thousand cubits, one measures** the Shabbat limit **from the** imaginary **bowstring** stretched between the two ends of the bow; **and if not, one measures** the Shabbat limit **from the bow** itself? This indicates that even if there is an uninterrupted string of houses linking the two ends of the city, if the two ends are separated by more than four thousand cubits, the distance is too great for it to be considered a single city.

אֲמַר לֵיהּ: הָתָם – לֵיכָּא לְמֵימַר ״מַלֵּי״, הָכָא – אִיכָּא לְמֵימַר ״מַלֵּי״.

Abaye **said to him: There,** in the case of the bow-shaped city, **there is no** room **to say: Fill** it in,[N] as there is nothing with which to fill in the empty space between the two ends of the city. However, **here,** in the case of the villages, **there is** room **to say: Fill** it in, as the middle village is seen as though it were projected between the two outer villages, and therefore all three combine into a single village.

אֲמַר לֵיהּ רַב סָפְרָא לְרָבָא: הֲרֵי בְּנֵי אַקִּיסְטְפוֹן דְּמָשְׁחִינַן לְהוּ תְּחוּמָא מֵהַאי גִּיסָּא דְּאַרְדְּשִׁיר, וּבְנֵי תְחוּמָא דְּאַרְדְּשִׁיר מָשְׁחִינַן לְהוּ תְּחוּמָא מֵהַאי גִּיסָּא דְּאַקִּיסְטְפוֹן, הָא אִיכָּא דִּגְלַת דְּמַפְסַקָא יָתֵר מִמֵּאָה וְאַרְבָּעִים וְאַחַת וּשְׁלִישׁ!

Rav Safra said to Rava: With regard to **the people of** the city of **Akistefon, for whom we measure the** Shabbat **limit from the** far **end of** the city of **Ardeshir, and the people of Ardeshir, for whom we measure the** Shabbat **limit from the far end of Akistefon,**[B] as though the two settlements were a single city; **isn't there the Tigris** River, **which separates them by more than 141⅓** cubits? How can two cities that are separated by more than two *karpef*-lengths be considered a single entity?

נְפַק אַחֲוֵי לֵיהּ הָנָךְ אַטְמָהָתָא דְּשׁוּרָא, דְּמִבְלְעִי בְּדִגְלַת בְּשִׁבְעִים אַמָּה וְשִׁירַיִים.

Rava **went out** and **showed** Rav Safra **the foundations of a wall** of one of the cities, **which were submerged in the Tigris** River **at** a distance of **seventy cubits and a remainder** from the other city. In other words, the two cities were in fact linked through the remnants of a wall submerged in the river.

מתני׳ אֵין מוֹדְדִין אֶלָּא בְּחֶבֶל שֶׁל חֲמִשִּׁים אַמָּה, לֹא פָּחוֹת וְלֹא יוֹתֵר. וְלֹא יִמְדּוֹד אֶלָּא כְּנֶגֶד לִבּוֹ.

MISHNA **One may measure** a Shabbat limit **only with a rope fifty cubits** long, **no less and no more,** as will be explained in the Gemara. **And one may measure** the limit **only at the level of one's heart,** i.e., whoever comes to measure the limit must hold the rope next to his chest.[H]

הָיָה מוֹדֵד וְהִגִּיעַ לַגַּיְא אוֹ לַגָּדֵר – מַבְלִיעוֹ וְחוֹזֵר לְמִדָּתוֹ. הִגִּיעַ לָהָר – מַבְלִיעוֹ וְחוֹזֵר לְמִדָּתוֹ,

If **one was measuring** the limit **and he reached a canyon or a fence,** the height of the fence and the depth of the canyon are not counted toward the two thousand cubits; rather, **he spans it and** then **resumes his measurement.**[B] Two people hold the two ends of the rope straight across the canyon or the fence, and the distance is measured as though the area were completely flat. If **one reached a hill,** he does not measure its height; rather, **he spans** the hill as if it were not there **and** then **resumes his measurement,**

NOTES

There is no room to say fill it in – לֵיכָּא לְמֵימַר מַלֵּי: Various explanations have been offered for this statement. Based on *Tosafot*, the Rosh states that since it is impossible to insert the sides of the bow into the area created by the bowstring, the uninhabited area cannot be viewed as though it were filled in. The same applies if the middle village is larger than the gap between the two outer ones. The author of the *Me'iri* explains that in the case of a bow-shaped city, there is no presumption that the space will be filled in the future, since the city will likely expand in the direction of the ends of its semicircular arc. However, the vacant space between the three villages might very well be filled with houses over the course of time.

BACKGROUND

Ardeshir and Akistefon – אַרְדְּשִׁיר וְאַקִּיסְטְפוֹן: These names refer to ancient cities. According to the Talmud, Akistefon, or Katisifon, in Greek Κτεσιφων, *Ktesifon*, is the biblical Kalneh. Ardeshir is Seleucia on the Tigris, and was renamed Veh-Ardashir, after the Persian king Ardishir, founder of the Sassanid dynasty.

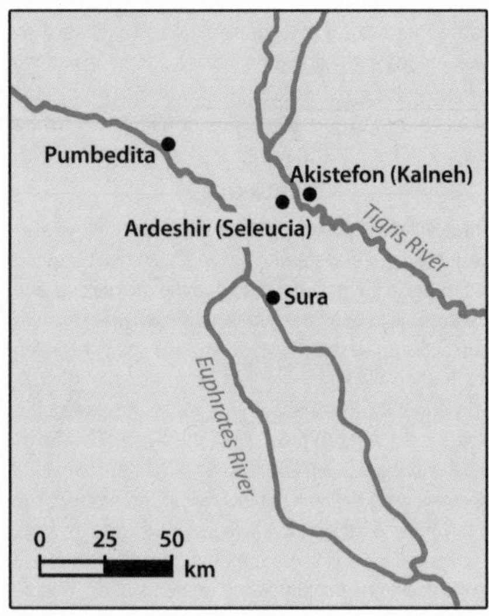

Ardeshir and Akistefon

Spanning a canyon – הַבְלָעַת גַּיְא: This illustration shows how a valley is spanned when measuring the limits of a city. There is no need to descend and measure the entire depth of the valley along the dotted line. Rather, it is sufficient to measure the area above the valley, spanned by means of a rope fifty cubits long.

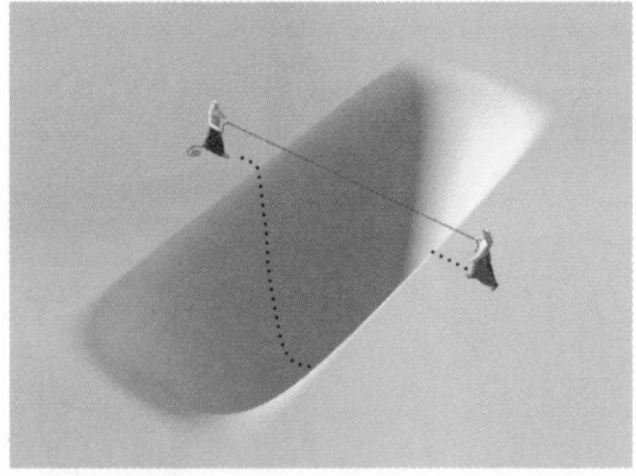

Measuring a canyon with rope

HALAKHA

Measuring at the level of one's heart – מְדִידָה כְּנֶגֶד לִבּוֹ: Whoever measures the Shabbat limit must hold the rope as taut as possible at the level of his heart (*Shulḥan Arukh, Oraḥ Ḥayyim* 399:3).

וּבִלְבַד שֶׁלֹּא יֵצֵא חוּץ לַתְּחוּם.

provided he does not thereby **go out beyond the** city's Shabbat **limit,** as those watching the surveyor might mistakenly think the limit extends to that point.

אִם אֵינוֹ יָכוֹל לְהַבְלִיעוֹ – בָּזוֹ אָמַר רַבִּי דּוֹסְתַּאי בַּר יַנַּאי מִשּׁוּם רַבִּי מֵאִיר: שָׁמַעְתִּי שֶׁמְּקַדְּרִין בֶּהָרִים.

If, due to the width of the canyon or hill, **he cannot span it, with regard to this** situation **Rabbi Dostai bar Yannai said in the name of Rabbi Meir: I heard that one may pierce**[N] **hills.** In other words, one measures the distance as if there were a hole from one side of the hill to the other, so that in effect, he measures only the horizontal distance and ignores the differences in elevation.

גמ׳ מְנָא הָנֵי מִילֵּי? אָמַר רַב יְהוּדָה, אָמַר רַב: דְּאָמַר קְרָא: ״אֹרֶךְ הֶחָצֵר מֵאָה בָּאַמָּה וְרוֹחַב חֲמִשִּׁים בַּחֲמִשִּׁים״, אָמְרָה תּוֹרָה: בְּחֶבֶל שֶׁל חֲמִשִּׁים אַמָּה מְדוֹד.

GEMARA The Gemara asks: **From where are these matters,** that the Shabbat limit must be measured with a rope fifty cubits long, derived? **Rav Yehuda said** that **Rav said:** They are derived from **that** which **the verse states: "The length of the courtyard shall be one hundred cubits, and the breadth fifty by fifty"** (Exodus 27:18). **The Torah states: Measure with a rope of fifty cubits,** i.e., the length and breadth of the courtyard must be measured "by fifty," with a rope fifty cubits long.

הַאי מִיבָּעֵי לֵיהּ לִיטּוֹל חֲמִשִּׁים וּלְסַבֵּב חֲמִשִּׁים!

The Gemara asks: **This** repetitive usage of the word fifty **is necessary** to teach us something else, namely, that the area of a courtyard is equivalent to a square the size of the Tabernacle's courtyard. To this end, the Torah states: **Take** a square of **fifty** cubits by fifty cubits, **and surround** it with the remaining **fifty** cubits in order to form a square, each side of which is just over seventy cubits long.

אִם כֵּן לֵימָא קְרָא: ״חֲמִשִּׁים חֲמִשִּׁים״, מַאי ״חֲמִשִּׁים בַּחֲמִשִּׁים״ – שְׁמַעַתְּ מִינַּהּ תַּרְתֵּי.

The Gemara answers: **If so, let the verse state: Fifty, fifty,** which would have sufficed to teach us the size and shape of a courtyard. **What is** the significance of the phrase: **Fifty by fifty? Conclude from this** that the verse comes to teach **two** things, both the matter of the square courtyard and that the length of the rope used to measure the Shabbat limit should be fifty cubits long.

״לֹא פָּחוֹת וְלֹא יוֹתֵר״. תָּנָא: לֹא פָּחוֹת – מִפְּנֵי שֶׁמַּרְבֶּה, וְלֹא יוֹתֵר – מִפְּנֵי שֶׁמְּמַעֵט.

We learned in the mishna: One may measure a Shabbat limit only with a rope fifty cubits long, **not less and not more. It was taught** in the *Tosefta*: **No less, because** a shorter rope improperly **increases** the Shabbat limit, as the rope is likely to be stretched. **And no more, because** a longer rope **reduces** the limit, as the rope is likely to sag due to its weight.

אָמַר רַבִּי אַסִי: אֵין מוֹדְדִין אֶלָּא בְּחֶבֶל שֶׁל אַפְסַקִימָא. מַאי אַפְסַקִימָא? אָמַר רַבִּי אַבָּא: נַרְגִּילָא. מַאי נַרְגִּילָא? אָמַר רַבִּי יַעֲקֹב: דִּיקְלָא דְּחַד נְבָרָא. אִיכָּא דְּאָמְרִי: מַאי אַפְסַקִימָא? רַבִּי אַבָּא אָמַר: נַרְגִּילָא, רַבִּי יַעֲקֹב אָמַר: דִּיקְלָא דְּחַד נְבָרָא.

Rabbi Asi said: One may measure only with a rope of *afsakima*.[LB] The Gemara asks: **What is *afsakima*? Rabbi Abba said:** It is the ***nargila***[L] plant. This name was also not widely known, and therefore the Gemara asks: **What is *nargila*?**[B] **Rabbi Ya'akov said: A palm tree** that has only **one fibrous vine** wrapped around it. **Some say** a different version of the previous discussion, according to which the Gemara asked: **What is *afsakima*? Rabbi Abba said:** It is the ***nargila*** plant. **Rabbi Ya'akov** disagreed and **said:** It is **a palm tree** with **one fibrous vine.**

תַּנְיָא, אָמַר רַבִּי יְהוֹשֻׁעַ בֶּן חֲנַנְיָא: אֵין לְךָ שֶׁיָּפֶה לִמְדִידָה יוֹתֵר מִשַּׁלְשְׁלָאוֹת שֶׁל בַּרְזֶל, אֲבָל מַה נַּעֲשֶׂה שֶׁהֲרֵי אָמְרָה תּוֹרָה ״וּבְיָדוֹ חֶבֶל מִדָּה״.

It was taught in a *baraita* that **Rabbi Yehoshua ben Ḥananya said: You have nothing better for measuring than iron chains,**[N] as they do not stretch. **But what shall we do, as the Torah states:** "I lifted up my eyes again and looked, and behold a man **with a measuring rope in his hand"** (Zechariah 2:5), from which it is derived that measurements must be made with a rope.

וְהָכְתִיב: ״וּבְיַד הָאִישׁ קְנֵה הַמִּדָּה״! הַהוּא לְתַרְעֵי.

The Gemara asks: **Isn't it** also **written: "And in the man's hand a measuring reed** of six cubits long, of one cubit and a handbreadth each" (Ezekiel 40:5), which indicates that reeds may also be used for measuring? The Gemara answers: **That is** used **for** measuring **gates,** which are too narrow to be measured with lengthy ropes.

תָּנֵי רַב יוֹסֵף: שְׁלֹשָׁה חֲבָלִים הֵם: שֶׁל מָגָג, שֶׁל נֶצֶר, וְשֶׁל פִּשְׁתָּן.

Rav Yosef taught that **there are three** kinds of **rope,** each required by *halakha* for a different purpose: A rope **of *magag*,**[N] a kind of bulrush reed; a rope **of *netzer*,** made from fibrous palm vines; **and** a rope **of flax.**

NOTES

Pierce [*mekadderin*] – מְקַדְּרִין: The term *kiddur* can be explained in several ways. Some commentaries explain that it denotes drilling a hole, while other commentaries suggest that it is related to the word *kiddud*, meaning cutting, because the calculation in this context is performed as though the slope were cut into pieces (*Arukh*). The author of the *Me'iri* explains that *kiddur* means to estimate or to approximate.

Iron chains – שַׁלְשְׁלָאוֹת שֶׁל בַּרְזֶל: The author of the *Me'iri* explains that Rabbi Yehoshua ruled that it is proper to measure with chains. However, a flax rope is also valid, since it is mentioned as a measuring implement in the Prophets.

Rope of *magag* – חֶבֶל שֶׁל מָגָג: A rope fashioned out of bulrush reeds [*magag*] was used for binding the red heifer. The entire ritual of the heifer had to be performed in a state of ritual purity, and a rope of this kind does not contract impurity (Rabbeinu Yehonatan). An alternative explanation is that it was used for this purpose due to its soft texture; it would not physically blemish the animal (*Me'iri*).

LANGUAGE

Afsakima – אַפְסַקִימָא: Probably derived with a reversal of letters from the Greek word σφήκωμα, *sfèkoma*, meaning a rope or a cord.

Nargila – נַרְגִּילָא: From the Middle Iranian word nārgīl, meaning coconut, and derived from Sanskrit.

BACKGROUND

Rope of *afsakima* – חֶבֶל שֶׁל אַפְסַקִימָא: Various types of rope are made from the coconut tree. The finest quality ones are manufactured from the fibrous layer of the coconut shell. These ropes are considered superior to all others due to their resistance to water and weather. They do not shrink or expand at all.

Nargila – נַרְגִּילָא: The coconut palm, *Cocos nucifera*, can grow to a height of 30 m. Its fruit, coconuts, have a diameter of up to 20 cm. The tree has been cultivated since ancient times. In its native areas, the tropical regions of Asia and the Pacific islands, the coconut palm is utilized in a variety of ways, including eating, drinking, weaving, building, and for firewood.

Coconut palm

שֶׁל מָגָג – לַפָּרָה, דִּתְנַן: כְּפָתוּהָ בְּחֶבֶל הַמָּגָג וּנְתָנוּהָ עַל גַּב מַעֲרַכְתָּהּ. שֶׁל נְצָרִים – לַסּוֹטָה, דִּתְנַן: וְאַחַר כָּךְ מֵבִיא חֶבֶל הַמִּצְרִי וְקוֹשְׁרוֹ לְמַעְלָה מִדַּדֶּיהָ. שֶׁל פִּשְׁתָּן – לְמְדִידָה.

They are used for the following purposes: A rope **of *magag*** is utilized **for** the burning of **the red heifer, as we learned** in a mishna: **They would bind** the heifer **with a rope of *magag*[H] and place it on its woodpile,** where it would be burned after it was slaughtered. A rope **of *netzer*** was required **for a *sota*,** a woman suspected of adultery, **as we learned** in a mishna: Before the *sota* is compelled to drink the bitter waters, her clothes are torn. **And after that** a priest **brings a *mitzri* rope,[N]** i.e., a rope made of reeds [*netzarim*],[H] **and binds it above her breasts,** so that her garments will not fall. A rope **of flax[H]** is used **for measuring.**

״הָיָה מוֹדֵד וְהִגִּיעַ״. מִדְּתָנֵי ״חוֹזֵר לְמִידָּתוֹ״ – מִכְּלָל דְּאִם אֵינוֹ יָכוֹל לְהַבְלִיעוֹ, הוֹלֵךְ לְמָקוֹם שֶׁיָּכוֹל לְהַבְלִיעוֹ, וּמַבְלִיעוֹ, וְצוֹפֶה כְּנֶגֶד מִידָּתוֹ וְחוֹזֵר.

It was stated in the mishna: If **he was measuring** the limit **and he reached** a canyon or a fence, he spans the area as if it were completely flat and then resumes his measurement. The Gemara comments: **From** the fact that **it taught** that **he resumes his measurement,** it may be derived **by inference that if he cannot span it** because it is too wide, **he goes to a place where** it is narrower so that **he can span it. And he spans it, and he** then **looks** for the spot at the same distance that is **aligned with his** original **measurement,[B] and he resumes** his measurement from there.[N]

תַּנְיָא לְהָא, דְּתָנוּ רַבָּנַן: הָיָה מוֹדֵד וְהִגִּיעַ הַמִּידָּה לַגַּיְא, אִם יָכוֹל לְהַבְלִיעוֹ בְּחֶבֶל שֶׁל חֲמִשִּׁים אַמָּה – מַבְלִיעוֹ, וְאִם לָאו – הוֹלֵךְ לְמָקוֹם שֶׁיָּכוֹל לְהַבְלִיעוֹ, וּמַבְלִיעוֹ, וְצוֹפֶה וְחוֹזֵר לְמִידָּתוֹ.

The Gemara comments that **we have** indeed **learned this, as the Sages taught** the following *baraita*: In the case of **one who was measuring** the Shabbat limit **and the measurement reached a canyon, if he can span** the canyon **with a rope of fifty cubits,** i.e., if the canyon is less than fifty cubits wide, **he spans it. And if not,** i.e., if the valley is more than fifty cubits wide, **he goes to a place where** it is narrower so that **he can span it, and he spans it, and he** then **looks** for the spot at the same distance that aligns with his original measurement, **and he resumes his measurement** from there.

אִם הָיָה גַּיְא מְעוּקָּם – מַקְדִּיר וְעוֹלֶה, מַקְדִּיר וְיוֹרֵד. הִגִּיעַ לַכּוֹתֶל – אֵין אוֹמְרִים יִקּוֹב הַכּוֹתֶל, אֶלָּא אוֹמְדוֹ וְהוֹלֵךְ לוֹ.

The *baraita* continues: **If the canyon was curved[B]** so that it surrounds the city on more than one side, and it cannot be spanned on the side where he wishes to measure the limit, **he pierces and ascends, pierces and descends,** thereby measuring the canyon's width bit by bit. If **he reached a wall, we do not say that he should pierce the wall** so that it can be precisely measured; **rather, he estimates** its width **and** then **leaves** and continues on.

וְהָא אֲנַן תְּנַן: מַבְלִיעוֹ וְחוֹזֵר לְמִידָּתוֹ! הָתָם נִיחָא תַּשְׁמִישְׁתָּא, הָכָא לָא נִיחָא תַּשְׁמִישְׁתָּא.

The Gemara asks: **Didn't we learn** in the mishna: If he reached a canyon or fence, **he spans it and** then **resumes his measurement?[N]** Why is a precise measurement required there, whereas in the case of a wall, an estimate is sufficient? The Gemara explains: **There,** in the mishna, we are dealing with a place whose **use is convenient,** i.e., where the slope is relatively gentle so that the area can be crossed. Therefore, the area must actually be measured. However, **here,** in the *baraita*, the wall's **use is not convenient.** Since one cannot walk through the wall, an estimate of its width is sufficient.

אָמַר רַב יְהוּדָה, אָמַר שְׁמוּאֵל: לֹא שָׁנוּ אֶלָּא שֶׁאֵין חוּט הַמִּשְׁקוֹלֶת יוֹרֵד כְּנֶגְדּוֹ,

Rav Yehuda said that **Shmuel said: They taught[N]** the method of piercing **only where a plumb line does not drop straight down,** i.e., where the canyon has a slope.[H]

HALAKHA

Rope of *magag* – חֶבֶל שֶׁל מָגָג: The red heifer is bound with a rope fashioned out of bulrush reeds [*magag*] (Rambam *Sefer Tahara, Hilkhot Para Aduma* 3:2).

Rope of reeds – חֶבֶל שֶׁל נְצָרִים: After the clothes of a *sota* are torn, her garments are bound with a rope so that they will not fall off entirely. The preferred rope for this purpose is one fashioned of reeds, a *mitzri* rope (Rambam *Sefer Nashim, Hilkhot Sota* 3:11).

Rope of flax – חֶבֶל שֶׁל פִּשְׁתָּן: The measurements for an *eiruv* are made with a rope of flax (*Shulḥan Arukh, Oraḥ Ḥayyim* 399:1).

Measurement and spanning – מְדִידָה וְהַבְלָעָה: In the case of one who is measuring the distance to determine the Shabbat limit and reaches a canyon up to two thousand cubits deep whose walls slope over a distance of more than four cubits, if the canyon is less than fifty cubits wide, he spans it; if not, he pierces it. If the canyon is more than two thousand cubits deep, one measures the area of the entire slope itself, in accordance with the opinion of the Rosh. If the area over which walls of the canyon slope is less than four cubits and the valley is narrower than fifty cubits, he spans it; if that is not possible, he measures only the width of the floor of the canyon. This ruling is in accordance with the view of the Rosh, who rules in accordance with the Gemara's second version of the mishna (*Shulḥan Arukh, Oraḥ Ḥayyim* 399:5).

BACKGROUND

Looks for the spot aligned with his measurement – צוֹפֶה כְּנֶגֶד מִידָּתוֹ: When measuring the distance from a city, if the surveyor arrives at an obstacle that cannot be circumvented, such as a mountain, he begins his measurements from a different place, along the dotted line in the diagram, until he passes the obstacle, at which point he resumes his measurement along the original line.

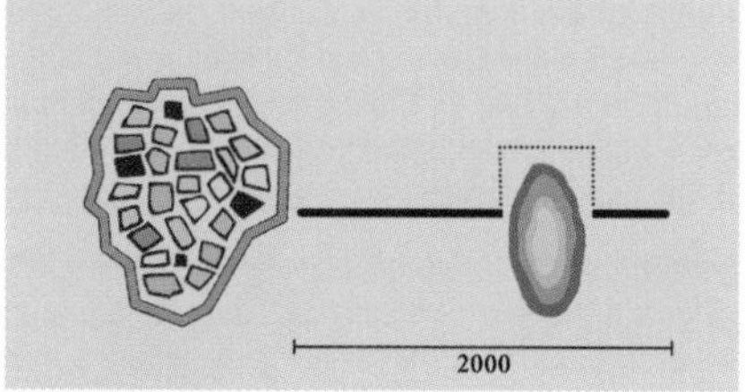

Measuring distance with an obstacle in the way

The canyon was curved – גַּיְא מְעוּקָּם: Generally, if one encounters a canyon while measuring the distance of the Shabbat limit, he may bypass it and measure the distance at a parallel location. When the canyon is curved, as depicted in the image, it cannot be bypassed efficiently. Therefore, other methods must be implemented in order to measure the limit correctly.

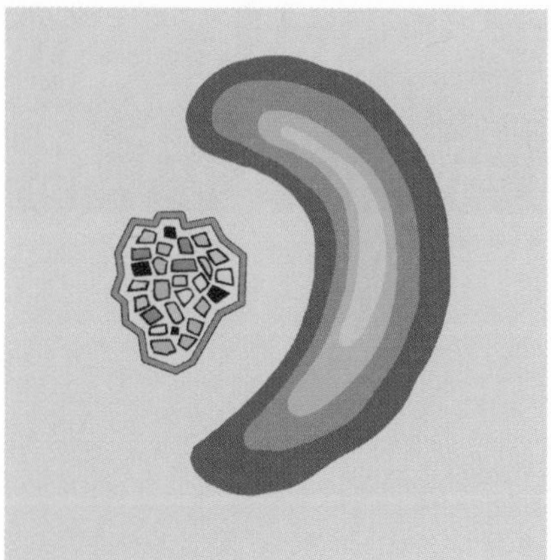

Curved canyon within the Shabbat limit of a city

NOTES

***Mitzri* rope – חֶבֶל הַמִּצְרִי:** In the Jerusalem Talmud it is stated that a *mitzri* rope, made of reeds, was used for the *sota* in order to hint that this woman acted in the manner of an Egyptian [*Mitzri*], as the Egyptians were known for their licentious behavior.

He looks for the spot that is aligned with his measurement and he resumes – צוֹפֶה כְּנֶגֶד מִידָּתוֹ וְחוֹזֵר: The early commentaries ask: Why does one return to his original measurement? Let him measure from the place where he circumvented the valley or mountain. The Ra'avad explains that were one to do this, the measurement would be inadequate, as it is necessary to perform at least two measurements on each side of the city, one at each end, to ensure that the limit will be measured accurately.

He spans it and resumes his measurement – מַבְלִיעוֹ וְחוֹזֵר לְמִידָּתוֹ: There are several variant readings and explanations of this passage. The Rif's version contains the following question: Wasn't it taught in a *baraita* that one must perform a proper measurement? According to this version, a wall that can be used is measured in the common manner, while a steep wall cannot be measured (see Rashba).

They taught only – לֹא שָׁנוּ: Some commentaries explain that this caveat is referring back to the mishna's statement with regard to spanning, namely, that a canyon can be spanned only if a plumb line does not drop straight below it (see Rashba and Ritva).

אֲבָל חוּט הַמִּשְׁקוֹלֶת יוֹרֵד כְּנֶגְדּוֹ – מוֹדְדוֹ מְדִידָה יָפָה.

However, if **a plumb line drops straight down**,[B] i.e., if the canyon wall is very steep, **he measures** the width of the canyon **properly** at the bottom of the canyon, without taking its walls into account.

וְכַמָּה עוֹמְקוֹ שֶׁל גַּיְא? אָמַר רַב יוֹסֵף: אַלְפַּיִם.

The Gemara asks: **And what is the depth of a canyon** that may be spanned if it is not more than fifty cubits wide? **Rav Yosef said:** Up to **two thousand** cubits; but if it is deeper than that, the slope must be measured as well.

אֵיתִיבֵיהּ אַבָּיֵי: עָמוֹק מֵאָה וְרוֹחַב חֲמִשִּׁים מַבְלִיעוֹ, וְאִם לָאו – אֵין מַבְלִיעוֹ. הוּא דְּאָמַר כַּאֲחֵרִים; דְּתַנְיָא, אֲחֵרִים אוֹמְרִים: אֲפִילּוּ עָמוֹק אַלְפַּיִם וְרוֹחַב חֲמִשִּׁים מַבְלִיעוֹ.

Abaye raised an objection from the following *baraita*: If a canyon is up to **one hundred** cubits **deep and** up to **fifty** cubits **wide, one may span it; and if not, one may not span it.** How could Rav Yosef say that the canyon may be spanned if its depth is less than two thousand cubits? The Gemara answers: **He stated** his opinion **in accordance with** the opinion of ***Aḥerim*; as it was taught** in a *baraita*: ***Aḥerim* say: Even** if the canyon is **two thousand** cubits **deep and fifty** cubits **wide, one may span it.**

אִיכָּא דְּאָמְרִי, אָמַר רַב יוֹסֵף: אֲפִילּוּ יָתֵר מֵאַלְפַּיִם. כְּמַאן? דְּלָא כְּתַנָּא קַמָּא וְלָא כַּאֲחֵרִים!

The Gemara cites an alternate version of the previous discussion. **Some say** that **Rav Yosef said: Even** if the canyon is **more than two thousand** cubits deep, it may be spanned. The Gemara asks: **In accordance with whose** opinion did Rav Yosef say this? It is **not in accordance with** the opinion of **the first *tanna*, and** it is **not in accordance with** the opinion of **the *Aḥerim*.**

הָתָם – שֶׁאֵין חוּט הַמִּשְׁקוֹלֶת יוֹרֵד כְּנֶגְדּוֹ, הָכָא – בְּחוּט הַמִּשְׁקוֹלֶת יוֹרֵד כְּנֶגְדּוֹ.

The Gemara answers: **There,** where the *tanna'im* disagree about the depth of a canyon that may be spanned, they refer to a case where **a plumb line does not drop straight down** and therefore there is reason to measure the slope. **Here,** however, where Rav Yosef says that the canyon may be spanned even if it is more than two thousand cubits deep, he is referring to a case where **a plumb line drops straight down.**[N]

וְכִי אֵין חוּט הַמִּשְׁקוֹלֶת יוֹרֵד כְּנֶגְדּוֹ עַד כַּמָּה? אָמַר אֲבִימִי: אַרְבַּע. וְכֵן תָּנֵי רָמִי בַּר יְחֶזְקֵאל: אַרְבַּע.

The Gemara asks: **And where a plumb line does not drop straight down, how much** must it extend from the top of the canyon in order for the wall of the canyon to be considered a slope rather than a vertical wall? **Avimi said: Four** cubits.[N] If the bed of the canyon lies four cubits beyond the top edge of the canyon, the wall is sloped and must be included in the measurement. **And similarly, Rami bar Ezekiel taught,** based upon a *baraita*, that the maximum run is **four** cubits.

״הִגִּיעַ לָהָר, מַבְלִיעוֹ, וְחוֹזֵר לְמִידָּתוֹ״. אָמַר רָבָא: לֹא שָׁנוּ אֶלָּא בְּהַר הַמִּתְלַקֵּט עֲשָׂרָה מִתּוֹךְ אַרְבַּע, אֲבָל בְּהַר הַמִּתְלַקֵּט עֲשָׂרָה מִתּוֹךְ חָמֵשׁ – מוֹדְדוֹ מְדִידָה יָפָה.

We learned in the mishna: If **he reached a hill,** he does not measure its height, but rather **he spans** the hill as if it were not there **and** then **resumes his measurement. Rava said: They taught** this *halakha* **only with regard to a hill that has an incline of ten** handbreadths **within** a run of **four** cubits. **However, with regard to** a gentler **hill,** e.g., one **that has an incline of ten** handbreadths **within five** cubits,[N] **one must measure** the hill **properly,** i.e., he must include the slope itself in his measurement.

רַב הוּנָא בְּרֵיהּ דְּרַב נָתָן מַתְנֵי לְקוּלָּא; אָמַר רָבָא: לֹא שָׁנוּ אֶלָּא בְּהַר הַמִּתְלַקֵּט עֲשָׂרָה מִתּוֹךְ חָמֵשׁ, אֲבָל בְּהַר הַמִּתְלַקֵּט עֲשָׂרָה מִתּוֹךְ אַרְבַּע – אוֹמְדוֹ וְהוֹלֵךְ לוֹ.

The Gemara notes that **Rav Huna, son of Rav Natan, teaches a lenient** formulation of this *halakha*: **Rava said** that **they only taught** this *halakha* **with regard to a hill that has an incline of ten** handbreadths **within** a run of **five** cubits. **However, with regard to** a steeper **hill that has an incline of ten** handbreadths **within four** cubits, one need not take any precise measurements; instead, **he estimates** the length of the hill, **and** then **leaves** and continues measuring from the other side.

״וּבִלְבַד שֶׁלֹּא יֵצֵא חוּץ לַתְּחוּם״. מַאי טַעְמָא? אָמַר רַב כָּהֲנָא: גְּזֵירָה שֶׁמָּא יֹאמְרוּ ״מִדַּת תְּחוּמִין בָּאָה לְכָאן״.

We learned in the mishna that one may measure a canyon or hill located within the Shabbat limit, **provided that one does not go out beyond the limit.** The Gemara asks: **What is the reason** for this restriction? **Rav Kahana said:** It is **a decree, lest** people **say: The measurement of the** Shabbat **limit comes to here.** Since people know that he set out to measure the Shabbat limit, if they see him measuring in a certain spot they will assume that the area is included in the Shabbat limit.

BACKGROUND

A plumb line drops straight down – חוּט הַמִּשְׁקוֹלֶת יוֹרֵד כְּנֶגְדּוֹ: This illustration depicts a canyon whose left side is so steep that a plumb line drops straight down. On the right side, a plumb line does not drop straight down. The distance between the plumb line that reaches the bottom of the valley and the bottom of the valley on the other side is greater than four cubits.

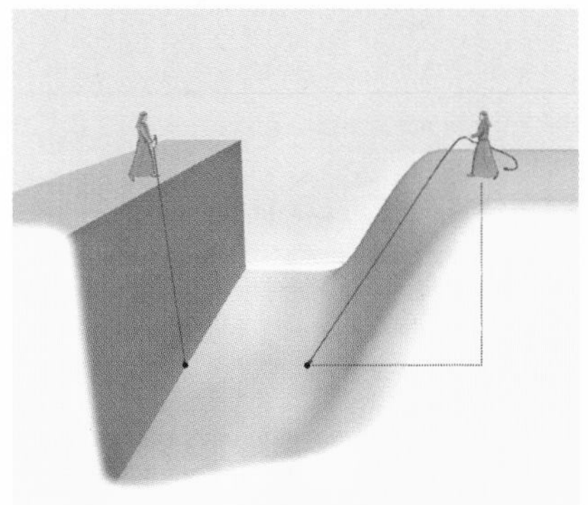

Dropping a plumb line into a valley

NOTES

The depth of a valley – עוֹמְקוֹ שֶׁל גַּיְא: According to the opinion that the depth of a valley can be only two thousand cubits, this measure corresponds to the Shabbat limit. The Rambam explains that according to the opinion that it can be more than two thousand cubits, the limit is four thousand cubits, corresponding to the view of Rav Huna with regard to a semicircular shaped city (Rashba; *Maggid Mishne*). According to the opinion that the depth of a valley can be only one hundred cubits, the measure corresponds to the courtyard of the Tabernacle (Rashba).

A plumb line up to four cubits – חוּט הַמִּשְׁקוֹלֶת עַד אַרְבַּע: Some explain this as follows: If the slope of the canyon is so steep at the top that a plumb line drops straight down for a length of four cubits, it is no longer considered a place that can be traversed by foot because this steep section makes it hard to reach the gentler slopes below it (Rashba; see *Tosafot*).

A hill that has an incline of ten handbreadths within five cubits – הַר הַמִּתְלַקֵּט עֲשָׂרָה מִתּוֹךְ חָמֵשׁ: An incline with this ratio, on which one walks without exertion, is based upon the incline of the ramp of the altar, which was thirty cubits long and nine cubits high (Rabbeinu Ḥananel; *Me'iri*).

BACKGROUND

Piercing – מְקַדְּרִין: Piercing is performed by means of a series of short measurements of four cubits each, which together equal the width or length of a particular area.

Measuring with piercing method

HALAKHA

Piercing mountains – קִידּוּר בֶּהָרִים: If a hill is so steep that a plumb line drops straight down without extending four cubits beyond the edge of the cliff, we do not measure its slope at all. If the elevation rises ten handbreadths within five cubits, and the canyon is less than fifty cubits wide, one spans it with a rope. If this method cannot be used, one figuratively pierces it using a rope of four cubits. If the elevation rises ten handbreadths within four cubits and the canyon is less than fifty cubits wide, it is sufficient to estimate the width of the canyon. However, if the canyon is wider than fifty cubits, one must pierce it (Rosh; *Shulḥan Arukh, Oraḥ Ḥayyim* 399:4).

One may not pierce for the rite of the beheaded heifer – אֵין מְקַדְּרִין...בְּעֶגְלָה עֲרוּפָה: When measuring the distance from the murder victim to the nearest city in order to perform the rite of the beheaded heifer, one does not pierce hills; rather, the slope is included in the measurement (Rambam *Sefer Nezikim, Hilkhot Rotze'aḥ UShemirat HaNefesh* 9:4).

Measurement by an expert – מְדִידָה עַל יְדֵי מוּמְחֶה: Only an expert surveyor may measure and establish Shabbat limits (*Shulḥan Arukh, Oraḥ Ḥayyim* 399:7).

Who is believed with regard to the Shabbat limit – מִי נֶאֱמָן עַל הַתְּחוּם: All adults are believed with regard to a Shabbat limit, including slaves and maidservants. Minors are not believed. However, an adult is believed when he says: I remember that we used to walk up until this point when I was young. This ruling is in accordance with the mishna here and the mishna in tractate *Ketubot* (*Shulḥan Arukh, Oraḥ Ḥayyim* 399:11).

"אִם אֵינוֹ יָכוֹל לְהַבְלִיעוֹ". תָּנוּ רַבָּנַן: כֵּיצַד מְקַדְּרִין? תַּחְתּוֹן כְּנֶגֶד לִבּוֹ, עֶלְיוֹן כְּנֶגֶד מַרְגְּלוֹתָיו. אָמַר אַבַּיֵי, נְקִיטִינַן: אֵין מְקַדְּרִין אֶלָּא בְּחֶבֶל שֶׁל אַרְבַּע אַמּוֹת.

We learned in the mishna: **If,** due to the width of the canyon or hill, **one cannot span it,** he may pierce it. **The Sages taught** a *baraita* which explains this procedure: **How does one** figuratively **pierce** a hill? Two people hold the two ends of a measuring rope. The one who is **lower** down on the hill holds the rope **at the level of his heart** while the one who is **higher** holds it **at the level of his feet,** and they proceed to measure in this fashion.[B] **Abaye said:** Based on tradition, **we hold** that **one may pierce only with a rope of four cubits.**[HN]

אָמַר רַב נַחְמָן, אָמַר רַבָּה בַּר אֲבוּהּ, (נְקִיטִינַן): אֵין מְקַדְּרִין לֹא בְּעֶגְלָה עֲרוּפָה וְלֹא בְּעָרֵי מִקְלָט, מִפְּנֵי שֶׁהֵן שֶׁל תּוֹרָה.

Rav Naḥman said that Rabba bar Avuh said: Based on tradition, **we hold** that **one may not pierce** when measuring distances for the rite of the **beheaded heifer.**[H] This rite is practiced when a murder victim is found, and it is not known who killed him. Judges measure the distance from the location of the corpse to the nearest town, in order to determine which town must perform the rite (Deuteronomy 21). Similarly, **one may not** pierce when measuring distances with regard to **cities of refuge,** in order to determine the boundaries within which an accidental murderer is protected from the blood redeemer (Numbers 32). **Because** these measurements **are from the Torah,** indirect methods of measurement are insufficient. The area must be measured as though it were flat.

מתני׳ אֵין מוֹדְדִין אֶלָּא מִן הַמּוּמְחֶה. רִיבָּה לְמָקוֹם אֶחָד וּמִיעֵט לְמָקוֹם אַחֵר – שׁוֹמְעִין לְמָקוֹם שֶׁרִיבָּה. רִיבָּה לְאֶחָד וּמִיעֵט לְאֶחָד – שׁוֹמְעִין לַמְרוּבֶּה.

MISHNA One **may measure** the Shabbat limit **only with an expert**[N] surveyor.[H] If it is discovered that the surveyor **extended** the limit **in one place and reduced it in another place,**[N] so that the line marking the Shabbat limit is not straight, **one accepts** the measurement of **the place where he extended** the limit and straightens the limit accordingly. Similarly, if the surveyor **extended** the limit **for one and reduced** it **for another, one accepts the extended** measurement.

וַאֲפִילּוּ עֶבֶד אֲפִילּוּ שִׁפְחָה נֶאֱמָנִין לוֹמַר "עַד כָּאן תְּחוּם שַׁבָּת". שֶׁלֹּא אָמְרוּ חֲכָמִים אֶת הַדָּבָר לְהַחְמִיר, אֶלָּא לְהָקֵל.

And furthermore, **even** a gentile **slave** and **even** a gentile **maidservant,** whose testimonies are generally considered unreliable, **are trustworthy to say: The Shabbat limit** extended **until here;**[H] **as the Sages did not state the matter,** the laws of Shabbat limits, **to be stringent, but** rather **to be lenient.** The prohibition to walk more than two thousand cubits is rabbinic in origin and is therefore interpreted leniently.

NOTES

The methods of measuring – שִׁיטוֹת הַמְּדִידָה: The Rambam distinguishes between the laws that are applicable to a canyon, a mountain, and a wall. Two principles apply to a canyon: If a plumb line does not drop straight down, and the canyon is up to two thousand cubits deep, one spans it; or, if the spanning will not work, he pierces it. If a plumb line does drop straight down, and the canyon is up to four thousand cubits deep, one spans or pierces it. If it is deeper than this, one must include the wall of the canyon in the measurement.

With regard to a mountain, if the slope rises ten handbreadths within five cubits, he spans or pierces it. If the slope rises ten handbreadths within four cubits, he estimates the distance. With regard to a wall, if its use is convenient, he measures it. If not, he estimates it. If a plumb line drops straight down, he measures only the level section.

The Rashba maintains that the *halakha* is the same with regard to a canyon, a fence, a wall, and a mountain, and the following four principles apply: If the slope rises ten handbreadths within more than five cubits, one must measure all of it. If it rises ten handbreadths within five cubits, he spans or pierces it. If it rises ten handbreadths within four cubits, he estimates it. If the plumb line drops straight down, he measures only the level section and disregards the inclined and upright parts.

According to the Rosh, one law applies to a mountain and a wall, whereas a canyon is treated differently. Three principles apply in the case of a mountain and a wall: If it rises ten handbreadths within five cubits, he spans or pierces it; if it rises ten handbreadths within four cubits, he estimates; and if the plumb line drops straight down, he only measures only the level part.

With regard to a canyon, four principles apply: If he can span it, he does so. If the plumb line drops straight down, he spans it even if it is more than two thousand cubits deep; if the plumb line does not drop straight down, he spans the canyon only if it is less than two thousand cubits deep. If he cannot span it and a plumb line drops straight down, he measures only the level section. If it does not drop straight down and it is less than two thousand cubits deep, he measures with the piercing method; if it is more than two thousand cubits deep, he must include the canyon wall in his measurement (*Ge'on Ya'akov*).

Expert [*mumḥe*] – מוּמְחֶה: The *ge'onim*, cited by Rabbeinu Ḥananel and the Rif, explain the term *mumḥe* as related to the verse: "And the border shall go down and shall strike [*umaḥa*] upon the slope of the Sea of Galilee" (Numbers 34:11). Therefore, they explain the mishna as follows: A level area near the city must selected for its measurement, so that it will not be necessary to adjust the measurements (see *Tosafot*).

Extended the limit in one place and reduced it in another place – רִיבָּה לְמָקוֹם אֶחָד וּמִיעֵט לְמָקוֹם אַחֵר: The Rambam explains the term extended to mean that one went beyond the previously accepted boundary in one place. Similarly, reduced means that one placed the boundary closer to the city than the previously accepted boundary (Rambam's Commentary on the Mishna).

גמ׳ לְמָקוֹם שֶׁרִיבָּה – אִין, לְמָקוֹם שֶׁמִּיעֵט – לָא?! אֵימָא: אַף לְמָקוֹם שֶׁרִיבָּה.

GEMARA The Gemara asks: Does this mean that in a **place where he extended** the limit, **yes,** the surveyor's measurements are accepted, but in **a place where he reduced** the limit,[N] **no,** his measurements are not accepted? If his extended measurement is accepted, his shortened measurement should certainly be accepted as well. The Gemara answers: **Say** that the mishna means that the surveyor's measurements are accepted **even in a place where he extended** the limit,[H] without concern that he might have erred (*Tosafot*), and that the surveyor's measurements are certainly accepted in places where he reduced the Shabbat limit.

״רִיבָּה לְאֶחָד וּמִיעֵט לְאֶחָד כו׳״. הָא תּוּ לָמָּה לִי? הַיְינוּ הָךְ! הָכִי קָאָמַר: רִיבָּה אֶחָד וּמִיעֵט אֶחָד – שׁוֹמְעִין לָזֶה שֶׁרִיבָּה.

We learned in the mishna: If the surveyor **extended** the limit **for one and reduced** it **for another,** one accepts the extended measurement. The Gemara asks: **Why do I need this as well? This** clause **is the same as that** previous clause in the mishna. The Gemara answers that **this is what** the mishna **said:** If two surveyors measured the Shabbat limit and **one extended** the Shabbat limit **and one reduced** it, **one accepts** the measurements of **the** surveyor **who extended** it.[H]

אָמַר אַבַּיֵי: וּבִלְבַד שֶׁלֹּא יְרַבֶּה יוֹתֵר מִמִּדַּת הָעִיר בַּאֲלַכְסוֹנָא.

Abaye said: The measurements of the surveyor who extended the limit are accepted only **as long as he does not extend** the limit **more than** the difference between **the measure** of the Shabbat limit **of the city** calculated **as a diagonal** line from the corner of the city[N] and as calculated as a straight line from the side of the city. If, however, the difference in measurements exceeds that amount, the Shabbat limit must be measured again.

״שֶׁלֹּא אָמְרוּ חֲכָמִים אֶת הַדָּבָר לְהַחְמִיר, אֶלָּא לְהָקֵל״. וְהָתַנְיָא: לֹא אָמְרוּ חֲכָמִים אֶת הַדָּבָר לְהָקֵל, אֶלָּא לְהַחְמִיר!

We learned in the mishna: **As the Sages did not state the matter,** the laws of Shabbat limits, **to be stringent, but** rather **to be lenient.** The Gemara asks: **Wasn't** the opposite **taught** in a *baraita*: **The Sages did not state the matter,** the laws of Shabbat limits, **to be lenient but** rather **to be stringent?**

אָמַר רָבִינָא: לֹא לְהָקֵל עַל דִּבְרֵי תוֹרָה, אֶלָּא לְהַחְמִיר עַל דִּבְרֵי תוֹרָה, וּתְחוּמִין דְּרַבָּנַן.

Ravina said that there is no contradiction between these two statements: The very institution of Shabbat limits was enacted **not to be** more **lenient** than **Torah law,** but **rather to be stringent** beyond **Torah law.** Nonetheless, since **Shabbat limits are rabbinic law,** the Sages permitted certain leniencies with regard to how the Shabbat limits are measured.

מתני׳ עִיר שֶׁל יָחִיד וְנַעֲשֵׂית שֶׁל רַבִּים – מְעָרְבִין אֶת כּוּלָּהּ.

MISHNA Although this chapter as a whole deals with *halakhot* governing the joining of Shabbat boundaries, this mishna returns to the *halakhot* governing a joining of courtyards. If **a private city,**[N] which does not have many residents, grows and **becomes** a heavily populated **public** city,[HN] **one may establish a joining of the courtyards for all of it,** as long as it does not include a public domain as defined by Torah law.

HALAKHA

Even in a place where he extended the limit – אַף לְמָקוֹם שֶׁרִיבָּה: If an expert surveyor adjusts the measurements of the Shabbat limit, his opinion is accepted whether he extends or reduces the limit. This *halakha* in accordance with the explanation of the Rambam. The Rema writes that if the two measurements taken on one side of the city do not match each other, one connects the two measurements by means of a straight line. This ruling is in accordance with the explanation of the Rosh and the *Tur*. Some authorities state that the shorter measurement is extended to be consistent with the longer measurement, in accordance with Rashi's explanation. The Vilna Gaon rules in accordance with the second opinion cited by the Rema (*Mishna Berura; Shulḥan Arukh, Oraḥ Ḥayyim* 399:8).

One accepts the measurements of the surveyor who extended it – שׁוֹמְעִין לָזֶה שֶׁרִיבָּה: If two surveyors measured the Shabbat limits separately, the conclusions of the one who extended the measure are accepted. This is the *halakha* as long as the difference between the two sets of measurements does not exceed 585 cubits, the approximate difference between the Shabbat limit as measured directly from the side of the city and the Shabbat limit as determined on the basis of diagonal lines of two thousand cubits from the four corners of the city (*Shulḥan Arukh, Oraḥ Ḥayyim* 399:9).

A private city becomes a public city – עִיר שֶׁל יָחִיד וְנַעֲשֵׂית שֶׁל רַבִּים: If a city was the private property of a single individual and subsequently becomes a public city, its residents may establish a single joining of the courtyards for the entire city, in accordance with the opinion of the Rambam and most early authorities. According to Rashi, a city is defined as a public city only if 600,000 people pass through it on a regular basis (*Shulḥan Arukh, Oraḥ Ḥayyim* 392:1).

NOTES

A place where he extended the limit…a place where he reduced the limit – מָקוֹם שֶׁרִיבָּה...מָקוֹם שֶׁמִּיעֵט: The early commentaries explain that the measurements for the Shabbat limit were taken from two locations on each side of the city. For example, on the eastern side, the city would be measured at both the northeastern corner and the southeastern corner. The case under discussion is where one of the measurements extended farther than the other measurement on the same side of the city. The commentaries disagree about whether the shorter measurement should be extended to match the longer measurement, or whether both measurements are accepted under the assumption that the difference in the terrain caused the perceived difference in the Shabbat limit.

Calculated as a diagonal line from the corner of the city – בַּאֲלַכְסוֹנָא: The Shabbat limit is calculated by measuring two thousand cubits in a perpendicular line from each side of the city. Each measurement is then extended perpendicularly until it intersects with the lines from the adjacent sides of the city. This creates a corner of the Shabbat limit that is 2,800 cubits from the corner of the city. However, if one were to measure two thousand cubits diagonally from the four corners of the city and then connect the four points via straight lines, the limit as measured from the sides of the city would be approximately 1,415 cubits. Consequently, if the difference between the measurements of two surveyors is less than 585 cubits, the extended measurement is accepted and the other measurement is presumed to have been taken by improperly measuring a diagonal line from the corner of the city. However, if the discrepancy between the two measurements is greater than this amount, it cannot be explained in this way, and the Shabbat limit must be measured again.

A private city, etc. – עִיר שֶׁל יָחִיד וכו׳: It is unclear why this mishna, which deals with the joining of courtyards, was included in this chapter, whose primary topic is the *halakhot* of the joining of Shabbat boundaries. Seemingly, one of the previous chapters would be a more natural context for this mishna. It is possible that this mishna is related to the previous mishna in the following way. The previous mishna mentions people's memories of the Shabbat limit. This mishna presents the case of city whose status has changed from public to private or vice versa, and it is assumed that people still recall the previous state of affairs (*Tosefot Ḥadashim*).

A private city becomes a public city – עִיר שֶׁל יָחִיד וְנַעֲשֵׂית שֶׁל רַבִּים: There are different interpretations of the term private city. Rashi explains that it does not refer to a privately owned city, but rather to a city that is not a public domain. Other commentaries maintain that it refers to a city that belonged to a single individual who subsequently rented or sold residential space to non-relatives. Since the city was originally owned by one person, it has a special status (Rashba; Ritva).

וְשֶׁל רַבִּים וְנַעֲשֵׂית שֶׁל יָחִיד – אֵין מְעָרְבִין אֶת כּוּלָּהּ, אֶלָּא אִם כֵּן עָשָׂה חוּצָה לָהּ כְּעִיר חֲדָשָׁה שֶׁבִּיהוּדָה, שֶׁיֵּשׁ בָּהּ חֲמִשִּׁים דִּיוּרִין, דִּבְרֵי רַבִּי יְהוּדָה. רַבִּי שִׁמְעוֹן אוֹמֵר: שָׁלֹשׁ חֲצֵירוֹת שֶׁל שְׁנֵי בָתִּים.

And if **a public** city loses residents over time and **becomes a private** city, **one may not establish an** ***eiruv*** **for all of it unless one maintains** an area **outside** the *eiruv*[N] that is **like** the size of **the city of Ḥadasha in Judea, which has fifty residents.** Carrying within the *eiruv* is permitted, but it remains prohibited to carry in the area excluded from the *eiruv*. The reason for this requirement is to ensure that the laws of *eiruv* will not be forgotten. This is **the statement of Rabbi Yehuda. Rabbi Shimon says:** The excluded area need not be so large; rather, it is sufficient to exclude **three courtyards** with **two houses** each.

גמ׳ הֵיכִי דָּמֵי עִיר שֶׁל יָחִיד וְנַעֲשֵׂית שֶׁל רַבִּים? אֲמַר רַב יְהוּדָה: כְּגוֹן דְּאִיסְקַרְתָּא דְּרֵישׁ גָּלוּתָא.

GEMARA The Gemara asks: **What are the circumstances of** a **private city** that **becomes a public** city? **Rav Yehuda said: For example, the Exilarch's village** [***de'iskarta***][L] was a small village set aside for the Exilarch's family and attendants; since it was frequented by many people, it turned into a public city.

אָמַר לֵיהּ רַב נַחְמָן: מַאי טַעְמָא? אִילֵימָא מִשּׁוּם דִּשְׁכִיחִי גַּבֵּי הַרְמָנָא מַדְכַּרִי אַהֲדָדֵי – כּוּלְּהוּ יִשְׂרָאֵל נַמִי בְּצַפְרָא דְּשַׁבְּתָא שְׁכִיחִי גַּבֵּי הֲדָדֵי! אֶלָּא אָמַר רַב נַחְמָן: כְּגוֹן דִּיסְקַרְתָּא דְּנַתְזוּאֵי.

Rav Naḥman said to him: What is the reason for bringing this example? **If you say** that **because** large numbers of people **are to be found at** the residence of **the governor** [***harmana***][L] in order to request licenses and authorizations, and **they remind each other** of the reason it is permissible to establish an *eiruv* there, and consequently they will not arrive at mistaken conclusions with regard to other places, then every city should have the same status, as **the entire Jewish people are also found together on Shabbat morning** when they come to pray. **Rather, Rav Naḥman said: For example, the village of Natzu'i**[N] was a private city belonging to a single individual before a large influx of residents turned it into a public city.

תָּנוּ רַבָּנַן: עִיר שֶׁל יָחִיד וְנַעֲשֵׂית שֶׁל רַבִּים וּרְשׁוּת הָרַבִּים עוֹבֶרֶת בְּתוֹכָהּ כֵּיצַד מְעָרְבִין אוֹתָהּ? עוֹשֶׂה לֶחִי מִכָּאן וְלֶחִי מִכָּאן, אוֹ קוֹרָה מִכָּאן וְקוֹרָה מִכָּאן, וְנוֹשֵׂא וְנוֹתֵן בָּאֶמְצַע. וְאֵין מְעָרְבִין אוֹתָהּ לַחֲצָאִין, אֶלָּא: אוֹ כּוּלָּהּ, אוֹ מָבוֹי מָבוֹי בִּפְנֵי עַצְמוֹ.

The Sages taught in a *baraita*: If **a private city becomes public, and** a bona fide **public domain passes through it, how does one establish an** ***eiruv*** **for it? He places a side post from here,** one side of the public domain, **and side post from there,** the other side; **or,** he places a cross **beam from here,** one side of the public domain, **and** another cross **beam from there,** the other side. **He may** then **carry** items **and place** them **between** these symbolic partitions, as the public domain is now considered like one of the courtyards of the city. **And one may not establish an** ***eiruv*** **for half** the city;[HB] **rather,** one may establish **either** one *eiruv* for **all of it or** separate ones for **each alleyway separately** without including the other sections of the city.

הָיְתָה שֶׁל רַבִּים וַהֲרֵי הִיא שֶׁל רַבִּים,

The *baraita* continues: If **it was** originally **a public** city, **and it** remains **a public** city,[H]

NOTES

Unless one maintains an area outside the ***eiruv*** **– אֶלָּא אִם כֵּן עָשָׂה חוּצָה לָּהּ:** This phrase is precisely translated as: Unless one maintains an area outside of it. The pronoun it can be understood as referring to the city itself. Consequently, even if the section that is not included in the *eiruv* is not part of the city itself, it can serve as the excluded area as long as it is within the city's outskirts (*Me'iri*).

The village of Natzui – דִּיסְקַרְתָּא דְנַתְזוּאֵי: Some of the commentaries explain that the owner of the city sold his houses; others explain that he rented them out. Still other commentaries are of the opinion that he completely disassociated himself from the village, but that it was still known by his name (see Ritva).

LANGUAGE

Village [*de'iskarta*] – דְּאִיסְקַרְתָּא: From the Middle Persian dastagird, meaning an inherited plot of land.

Governor [*harmana*] – הַרְמָנָא: Probably from the Parthian *kār-hramān* and related to the New Persian kār-farmā, meaning ruler. According to the version in the *Arukh*, the word is *kaharmana*.

BACKGROUND

An ***eiruv*** **for half the city – עֵירוּב לַחֲצָאִין:** An illustration of a city that has a public domain passing through it and an *eiruv* established for half of it, so that the *eiruv*, represented by the dotted line, passes through the public domain. It is understood that the residents of both sides of the city still use the common public domain.

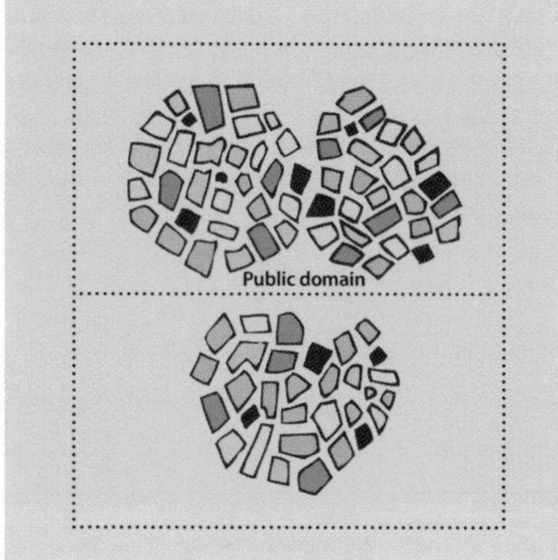

City with an *eiruv* passing through the public domain

HALAKHA

One may not establish an ***eiruv*** **for half the city – אֵין מְעָרְבִין אוֹתָהּ לַחֲצָאִין:** If a private city becomes a public city, and a public domain which is open on both sides passes through it, an *eiruv* may not be established for just half the city; it must include the entire city, or a separate *eiruv* must be established for each alleyway (*Shulḥan Arukh*, *Oraḥ Ḥayyim* 392:4).

It was originally a public city and it remains a public city – הָיְתָה שֶׁל רַבִּים וַהֲרֵי הִיא שֶׁל רַבִּים: If the public domain of the city is not open on two sides, a joining of the courtyards may be established for the entire city. This is the *halakha* even for cities that were originally public and remained public (*Shulḥan Arukh Oraḥ Ḥayyim* 392:1).

וְאֵין לָהּ אֶלָּא פֶּתַח אֶחָד – מְעָרְבִין אֶת כּוּלָּהּ.

and it has only one entrance, as it is surrounded by a wall or enclosed by houses on all sides, **one may establish an *eiruv* for all of it.**

מַאן תַּנָּא דְּמִיעַרְבָא רְשׁוּת הָרַבִּים? אָמַר רַב הוּנָא בְּרֵיהּ דְּרַב יְהוֹשֻׁעַ: רַבִּי יְהוּדָה הִיא; דְּתַנְיָא, יָתֵר עַל כֵּן אָמַר רַבִּי יְהוּדָה: מִי שֶׁיֵּשׁ לוֹ שְׁנֵי בָתִּים בִּשְׁנֵי צִידֵּי רְשׁוּת הָרַבִּים – עוֹשֶׂה לֶחִי מִכָּאן וְלֶחִי מִכָּאן, אוֹ קוֹרָה מִכָּאן וְקוֹרָה מִכָּאן, וְנוֹשֵׂא וְנוֹתֵן בָּאֶמְצַע. אָמְרוּ לוֹ: אֵין מְעָרְבִין רְשׁוּת הָרַבִּים בְּכָךְ.

The Gemara raises a question concerning this *baraita*: **Who is the *tanna*** who holds **that an *eiruv* may be established for a public domain**[N] in this manner? **Rav Huna, son of Rav Yehoshua, said: It is Rabbi Yehuda, as it was taught** in a *baraita*: **Furthermore, Rabbi Yehuda said: One who has two houses** opposite each other **on two sides of the public domain,** if he chooses, **he may** create a private domain for himself in the public domain. He may **place** a ten-handbreadth high **post from here,** on one side, **and** an additional **post from there,** the other side. This creates symbolic walls that provide the public domain with the legal status of a private domain. **Or,** one may place **a beam** extending **from here,** one end of the house, **and a beam from there,** the other end of the house, thereby creating symbolic partitions across the width of the street. In that way, one is permitted to **carry** objects **and place** them **in** the area **between** the symbolic partitions, as he would in a private domain. The Rabbis **said to him: One may not establish an *eiruv* in the public domain in that** way.

אָמַר מָר: "וְאֵין מְעָרְבִין אוֹתָהּ לַחֲצָאִין". אָמַר רַב פָּפָּא: לֹא אָמְרוּ אֶלָּא לְאָרְכָּהּ, אֲבָל לְרָחְבָּהּ – מְעָרְבִין.

The Master said in the *baraita* quoted above: **And one may not establish an *eiruv* for half** the city. **Rav Pappa said: They said** this **only** in a case where one wishes to divide the city **according to its length.** Generally, a city had a public domain that ran straight across it, from the entrance on one side of the city to the entrance on its other side. The *baraita* rules that it is prohibited to establish an *eiruv* separately for the residents of each side of the public domain. **But** if one wants to divide the city **according to its width,**[B] **he may establish an *eiruv*** for half the city. This distinction is made because in the first case the public domain that runs between the two halves is used by the residents of both halves, and therefore it joins the two into a single unit; in the second case, the residents of each half use only the half of the public domain located on their side and not the half of the public domain located on the other side.

כְּמַאן – דְּלָא כְּרַבִּי עֲקִיבָא, דְּאִי כְּרַבִּי עֲקִיבָא – הָא אָמַר רֶגֶל הַמּוּתֶּרֶת בִּמְקוֹמָהּ אוֹסֶרֶת אֲפִילּוּ שֶׁלֹּא בִּמְקוֹמָהּ!

The Gemara asks: **In accordance with whose** opinion is this *halakha*? It is **not in accordance with** the opinion of **Rabbi Akiva. As, if** it were **in accordance with** the opinion of **Rabbi Akiva, didn't he say that a foot that is permitted in** its own **place prohibits** carrying **even in a place that is not its own?** Rabbi Akiva holds the following in the case of outer and inner courtyards,[B] in which the residents of each courtyard established their own, independent *eiruv*: Since the residents of the inner courtyard, who are permitted to carry in their own courtyard, may not carry in the outer courtyard despite the fact that they have rights of passage there, it is prohibited even for the residents of the outer courtyard to carry there. By the same logic, since the residents of each half of the city are prohibited to carry in the public domain of the city's other half, despite the fact that they may travel there, it should be prohibited for everyone to carry there, and the *eiruv* should not be functional.

אֲפִילּוּ תֵּימָא רַבִּי עֲקִיבָא; עַד כָּאן לָא קָאָמַר רַבִּי עֲקִיבָא הָתָם – אֶלָּא בִּשְׁתֵּי חֲצֵירוֹת זוֹ לִפְנִים מִזּוֹ, דִּפְנִימִית לֵית לָהּ פִּיתְחָא אַחֲרִינָא. אֲבָל הָכָא – הָנֵי נָפְקִי בְּהַאי פִּיתְחָא, וְהָנֵי נָפְקִי בְּהַאי פִּיתְחָא.

The Gemara rejects this argument: **Even if you say** it is in accordance with the opinion of **Rabbi Akiva, Rabbi Akiva stated** his opinion **there only in** a case of **two courtyards, one** farther **inside** than **the other, as the inner** courtyard **has no other entrance.** Since the residents of the inner courtyard have no choice but to pass through the outer courtyard, the residents of the outer courtyard deny the residents of the inner courtyard exclusive use of their own courtyard; therefore, they can impose restrictions upon them. **But here,** in the case of two halves of the city, **these may go out through this** part of the public domain on their side of the city, leading to one **entrance** to the city, **and these may go out through this** other part of the public domain, leading to the other **entrance** to the city. Since the residents of each half do not have to use the portion of the public domain located in the other half, they do not impose any restrictions on the residents of the other half, even if they do in fact use it.

NOTES

Who is the *tanna* who holds that an *eiruv* may be established for a public domain – מַאן תַּנָּא דְּמִיעַרְבָא רְשׁוּת הָרַבִּים: Even the Rabbis concede that an *eiruv* may be established for a public domain by placing doors at the entrance or by constructing a doorway. The Gemara's question is: Which *tanna* holds that an *eiruv* can be constructed for a public domain in the manner described here (Rashba)?

BACKGROUND

A city divided according to its width – עִיר הַמְּחוּלֶּקֶת לְרָחְבָּהּ: This illustration portrays a city divided by a public domain. Nevertheless, the residents established a separate *eiruv* for each half of the city. The city has been divided along the dotted line. The public domain is thus divided between the two sides of the city, so that the inhabitants of one side of the city do not make use of the other side.

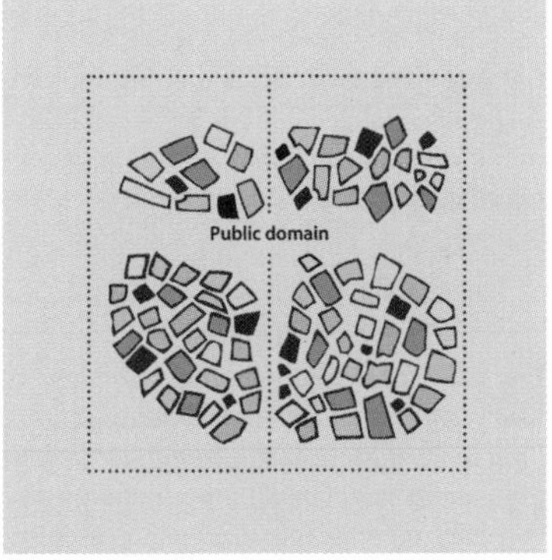

City with a public domain passing through it, divided according to its width

Outer and inner courtyards – חָצֵר חִיצוֹנָה וּפְנִימִית: An illustration of two courtyards, one within the other, in which the members of the inner courtyard must necessarily use the outer one.

Two courtyards, where only the outer one has access to the public domain

איכא דאמרי, אמר רב פפא: לא תימא לארכה הוא דלא מערבין, אבל לרחבה מערבין, אלא אפילו לרחבה נמי לא מערבין.

Some say a different version of the previous discussion. **Rav Pappa said: Do not say that it is** only if the city is divided **according to its length that one may not establish an** *eiruv* for half the city, **but** if the city is divided **according to its width, one may establish** a separate *eiruv* for each half. **Rather, even** if the city is divided **according to its width,**[H] **one may not establish an** *eiruv* for half the city.

כמאן – כרבי עקיבא! אפילו תימא רבנן; עד כאן לא קאמרי רבנן התם – אלא בשתי חצירות זו לפנים מזו, דפנימית אחדא לדשא ומשתמשא. אבל הכא – מי מצו מסלקי רשות הרבים מהכא.

The Gemara asks: **In accordance with whose** opinion is this *halakha*? It is **in accordance with** the opinion of **Rabbi Akiva.** The Gemara rejects this argument: **Even if you say** it is in accordance with the opinion of **the Rabbis,** it is possible that **the Rabbis stated** their opinion **there only** in the case of **two courtyards, one inside the other,** as the residents of **the inner** courtyard **can close the door** to the outer courtyard **and use** only their own courtyard.[N] In doing so, they impose no restrictions on the residents of the outer courtyard. **But here,** with regard to the division of a city, **are they able to move the public domain from here?** Since the residents of each half cannot be prevented from using the public domain located in the other half, even the Rabbis would agree that the *eiruv* is ineffective.

אמר מר: ״או כולה, או מבוי מבוי בפני עצמו״. מאי שנא דלחצאין דלא – דאסרי אהדדי, מבוי מבוי נמי אסרי אהדדי!

The Master said in the previously cited *baraita* that an *eiruv* must **either** be established **for all of it or for each alleyway separately.** The Gemara asks: **What is different** about an *eiruv* **for half** the city, **which is not** permissible? The residents of each half **prohibit** residents of the **other**[N] from carrying, due to the fact that all the residents may use both halves. Similarly, even if they establish a separate *eiruv* for **each alleyway,** the residents should still **prohibit** residents of the **other** from carrying, as residents of one alleyway commonly enter other alleyways as well.

הכא במאי עסקינן כגון דעבוד דקה. וכי הא דאמר רב אידי בר אבין אמר רב חסדא: אחד מבני מבוי שעשה דקה לפתחו – אינו אוסר על בני מבוי.

The Gemara answers: **With what are we dealing here?** We are dealing with a case **where** the residents **erected a partition**[HN] at the entrance to the alleyway as an indication that they do not want to be connected to the other alleyways. **And** it is **like that** which **Rav Idi bar Avin said** that **Rav Ḥisda said: One of the residents of an alleyway, who made a partition for his entrance** to the alleyway as a sign that he does not intend to carry from his house to the alleyway, **does not prohibit the** other **residents of the alleyway** from carrying there if he does not join in their *eiruv*. The reason for this is that this resident has demonstrated his desire to renounce his share of the alleyway.

״היתה של רבים והרי היא כו׳״. רבי זירא ערבה למתא דבי רבי חייא ולא שבק לה שיור. אמר ליה אביי: מאי טעמא עבד מר הכי?

It was taught in the *baraita*: If **it was** originally **a public** city **and it is** still **a public** city, and it has only one entrance to the public domain, one may establish an *eiruv* for the entire city. The Gemara relates: **Rabbi Zeira established an** *eiruv* **for Rabbi Ḥiyya's city and did not leave any section** of the city **out** of the *eiruv*. **Abaye said to him: What is the reason that the Master acted in this** manner? Why didn't you exclude a section of the city from the *eiruv*, as required in a public city?

אמר ליה: סבי דידה אמרי לי: רב חייא בר אסי מערב כולה. ואמינא: שמע מינה עיר של יחיד ונעשית של רבים היא.

Rabbi Zeira **said to** Abaye: **The** city **Elders told me** that **Rav Ḥiyya bar Asi** used to **establish an** *eiruv* for the **entire** city without excluding any section of it, **and I said** to myself: If he would establish an *eiruv* for the whole city, I can **learn from this** that it was originally **a private city and** later **becomes a public one.** Therefore, it is permitted to establish an *eiruv* for the entire city.

אמר ליה: לדידי אמרו לי הנהו סבי: ההיא אשפה הוה לה מחד גיסא, והשתא דאיפניא לה אשפה – הוה לה כשני פתחים, ואסיר. אמר ליה: לאו אדעתאי.

Abaye **said to him: Those** same **Elders told me** that the reason was different: **There was a particular garbage** dump[H] **on one side** of the public domain, which blocked one of the entrances, leaving only one entrance to the public domain. However, **now that the garbage** dump **has been cleared away, it has two entrances,**[N] **and** it is therefore **prohibited** to establish an *eiruv* for the whole city without excluding a section from the *eiruv*. Rabbi Zeira **said to him: It was not on my mind,**[N] i.e., I was unaware that this was the situation.

HALAKHA

An *eiruv* across the width of the city – עירוב לרוחב העיר: Some say that when the Sages prohibited establishing an *eiruv* for half a city that has a public domain running all the way through it, their prohibition referred only to an *eiruv* that divides the city into two halves according to its length. However, if the *eiruv* divides the city according to its width, an *eiruv* may be established if a partition is constructed between the two sides of the city. This ruling is in accordance with the first version of Rav Pappa's statement (Rema; Maharam). However, many authorities rule in accordance with the second version, as is generally accepted when the Gemara presents two versions of a statement or discussion (Rambam; *Beit Yosef*; *Shulḥan Arukh*, *Oraḥ Ḥayyim* 392:6).

Erected a partition – שעשו דקה: In a city that has a public domain passing all the way through it, the residents of the alleyways must erect partitions four handbreadths tall between them and the public domain to indicate that they have removed themselves from the city. Only then may they establish an *eiruv* for each alleyway. A partition of this kind is also effective for a resident of an alleyway who did not participate in the *eiruv*, to ensure that he does not prevent the *eiruv* from being effective for everyone else (*Shulḥan Arukh*, *Oraḥ Ḥayyim* 392:4).

Garbage in the public domain – אשפה ברשות הרבים: If a public garbage dump blocks the entrance to the public domain, the public domain is considered closed off at that end (*Shulḥan Arukh*, *Oraḥ Ḥayyim* 392:2).

NOTES

Can close the door and use only their courtyard – אחדא לדשא ומשתמשא: The residents of the inner courtyard do not actually have to lock their door, as they must pass through the outer courtyard. Indeed, they have no other means of getting to the public domain. However, since they can, in principle, close their door to the residents of the outer courtyard, they are considered a separate domain (Rashba).

Prohibit the other – אסרי אהדדי: The Ritva summarizes the opinion of several of his teachers, including the Rashba, as follows: This prohibition applies only if the residents of the different areas could establish an *eiruv* together and chose not to do so. However, if they could not establish a common *eiruv*, e.g., in the case of the residents of the part of the city that must be excluded from the *eiruv* in order for it to be valid, their right to travel through the rest of the city does not invalidate the *eiruv*.

Partition [*dakka*] – דקה: Rashi explains that the word *dakka* always refers to an entrance rather than a partition (see *Tosafot*). The Ritva explains Rashi to mean that one made a small entrance for the alleyway, which leads outside the city boundaries without passing through the common, public domain.

Two entrances – שני פתחים: The Ra'avad writes that they are considered two entrances only when they are positioned opposite one another. However, if they are not positioned opposite each other, they are considered a single entrance, and one may establish an *eiruv* there.

It was not on my mind – לאו אדעתאי: This expression appears in several contexts, but not always with the same meaning. On occasion, as in this context, it means: I erred in this matter and I was unaware of what you just mentioned. In other contexts, it connotes: The matter was done by others without my knowledge. The phrase can be used as an expression meaning: I do not agree with the question you are raising (Rashi).

בָּעֵי מִינֵּיהּ רַב אַמִּי בַּר אַדָּא הַרְפַּנָאָה מֵרַבָּה: סוּלָּם מִכָּאן וּפֶתַח מִכָּאן מַהוּ? אֲמַר לֵיהּ: הָכִי אָמַר רַב: סוּלָּם תּוֹרַת פֶּתַח עָלָיו.

Rav Ami bar Adda from Harpanya raised a dilemma before Rabba: If a public domain has **a ladder on one side,** to allow people to scale the wall that blocks it, **and an entrance on the other side,**[B] **what is** the *halakha*? Is it considered a public domain that is open on both sides? Rabba **said to him** that **Rav said as follows: A ladder has the status of an entrance,** and therefore the public domain is considered open on both sides.

אֲמַר לְהוּ רַב נַחְמָן: לָא תֵּצִיתוּ לֵיהּ, הָכִי אָמַר רַב אַדָּא אָמַר רַב: סוּלָּם תּוֹרַת פֶּתַח עָלָיו, וְתוֹרַת מְחִיצָה עָלָיו. תּוֹרַת מְחִיצָה עָלָיו – כִּדְאָמְרַן, תּוֹרַת פֶּתַח עָלָיו – בְּסוּלָּם שֶׁבֵּין שְׁתֵּי חֲצֵירוֹת, רָצוּ – אֶחָד מְעָרֵב, רָצוּ – שְׁנַיִם מְעָרְבִין.

Rav Naḥman said to them: Do not listen to him. Rav Adda said that **Rav said as follows: A ladder has the status of an entrance** in certain cases, **and it has the status of a partition** in other cases. **It has the status of a partition** in the case that **we mentioned,** where there is a ladder at the end of a public domain. In this case, the ladder is not considered an entrance and therefore the public domain is considered closed at that end. **It has the status of an entrance in** the case of a **ladder between two courtyards.** If the residents of the courtyards **wish,** they may join the two courtyards by means of the ladder and **establish one *eiruv*;** if **they wish,** the **two** courtyards may each **establish** a separate ***eiruv***.[H]

וּמִי אָמַר רַב נַחְמָן הָכִי? וְהָאָמַר רַב נַחְמָן אָמַר שְׁמוּאֵל: אַנְשֵׁי חָצֵר וְאַנְשֵׁי מִרְפֶּסֶת שֶׁשָּׁכְחוּ

The Gemara asks: **Did Rav Naḥman** actually **say this? Didn't Rav Naḥman say** that **Shmuel said:** With regard to **residents of** the ground floor of **a courtyard and residents of a balcony,** i.e., the floor above the ground floor, **who forgot**

BACKGROUND

A ladder in the public domain – סוּלָּם בִּרְשׁוּת הָרַבִּים:

Ladder at sealed end of a public domain

HALAKHA

The law of a ladder – דִּין סוּלָּם: A ladder at the entrance to a public domain is not considered an entrance. However, if it was positioned between two courtyards, the residents of the courtyards may rely on it as an entrance if they so desire, in accordance with the opinion of Rav Naḥman (*Shulḥan Arukh, Oraḥ Ḥayyim* 375:1; 392:2).

וְלֹא עֵירְבוּ, אִם יֵשׁ לִפְנֵיהֶם דַּקָּה אַרְבָּעָה – אֵינָהּ אוֹסֶרֶת, וְאִם לָאו – אוֹסֶרֶת!

and did not establish a joint *eiruv*, **if there is a partition four** handbreadths wide **in front of** the entrance to the balcony, the balcony **does not prohibit** the residents of the courtyard from carrying, as each area is considered to be independent. **And if not,** the balcony **prohibits** the residents of the courtyard from carrying in the courtyard. This indicates that a ladder between two courtyards is always considered an entrance, even when that policy leads to a stringent ruling, unless the two areas are separated by a partition.

הָכָא בְּמַאי עָסְקִינַן – בִּדְלָא גָּבוֹהַּ מִרְפֶּסֶת עֲשָׂרָה.

The Gemara answers: **With what are we dealing here? With** a case where **the balcony is not ten** handbreadths **high** from the ground. Consequently, it does not constitute a domain in its own right, and it is part of the courtyard.

וְאִי לָא גָּבוֹהַּ מִרְפֶּסֶת עֲשָׂרָה, כִּי קָא עָבֵיד דַּקָּה מַאי הָוֵי?! בִּמְגוּפֶּפֶת עַד עֶשֶׂר אַמּוֹת, דְּכֵיוָן דְּעָבֵיד דַּקָּה – אִיסְתַּלּוֹקֵי אִיסְתַּלּוֹק לֵיהּ מֵהָכָא.

The Gemara asks: **If the balcony is not ten** handbreadths **high** and is therefore part of the courtyard, **when one places a partition, what of it?** The balcony should nevertheless be considered part of the courtyard. The Gemara answers: We are dealing here **with** a balcony that is entirely **fenced off** except for a section **up to ten cubits** wide, which serves as an entrance. In that case, **since** the residents of the balcony **place a partition** at this entrance, **they** thereby **remove themselves** entirely **from** the courtyard.

אָמַר רַב יְהוּדָה, אָמַר שְׁמוּאֵל: כּוֹתֶל שֶׁרְצָפָהּ בְּסוּלָּמוֹת, אֲפִילּוּ בְּיָתֵר מֵעֶשֶׂר – תּוֹרַת מְחִיצָה עָלָיו.

Rav Yehuda said that **Shmuel said:** With regard to **a wall that one lined with ladders,**[N] **even** along a length of **more than ten** cubits, **it** still retains **the status of a partition.** The ladders do not constitute an opening that is more than ten cubits wide, which would cause the wall to be regarded as breached and would invalidate the wall as a partition.[H]

רָמֵי לֵיהּ רַב בְּרוּנָא לְרַב יְהוּדָה בְּמַעֲצַרְתָּא דְּבֵי רַב חֲנִינָא: מִי אָמַר שְׁמוּאֵל תּוֹרַת מְחִיצָה עָלָיו, וְהָאָמַר רַב נַחְמָן אָמַר שְׁמוּאֵל: אַנְשֵׁי מִרְפֶּסֶת וְאַנְשֵׁי חָצֵר שֶׁשָּׁכְחוּ וְלֹא עֵירְבוּ, אִם יֵשׁ לִפְנֵיהָ דַּקָּה אַרְבָּעָה – אֵינָהּ אוֹסֶרֶת, וְאִם לָאו – אוֹסֶרֶת!

Rav Beruna raised a contradiction to Rav Yehuda in the winepress at Rav Ḥanina's house: Did Shmuel actually **say** that such a wall **has the status of a partition? Didn't Rav Naḥman say** that **Shmuel said:** With regard to **the residents of a balcony and the residents of a courtyard who forgot and did not establish** a joint ***eiruv***, **if there is a partition** four handbreadths wide **in front** of the entrance to the balcony, the balcony **does not prohibit** the residents of the courtyard to carry; **and if not, it prohibits** the residents of the courtyard from carrying? This indicates that a ladder is considered an entrance, as the courtyard and the balcony are considered connected.

NOTES

A wall that one lined with ladders – כּוֹתֶל שֶׁרְצָפָהּ בְּסוּלָּמוֹת: As explained elsewhere, if there is a breach ten cubits wide between two courtyards, one cannot establish a separate *eiruv* for each because they are considered a single courtyard. Rather, both must establish a single, joint *eiruv*.

HALAKHA

Ladders as an entrance – סוּלָּמוֹת כְּפֶתַח: A ladder is not considered an entrance. In addition, ladders are not considered a breach if one lined more than ten cubits of a wall with ladders, as stated by Shmuel (*Shulḥan Arukh, Oraḥ Ḥayyim* 392:2).

הכא במאי עסקינן – דלא גבוה מרפסת עשרה. ואי לא גבוה מרפסת עשרה, כי עביד דקה מאי הוי? במגופפת עד עשר אמות, דכיון דעביד דקה – איסתלוקי איסתלק מהכא.

Rav Yehuda replied in the same manner as above: **With what are we dealing here?** We are dealing **with** a case where **the balcony is not ten** handbreadths **high,** and that is why it is regarded as connected to the courtyard. The Gemara asks: **If the balcony is not ten** handbreadths **high, when he places a partition, what of it?** The balcony should nevertheless be considered part of the courtyard. The Gemara answers: We are dealing here **with** a balcony that is entirely **fenced off** except for a section **up to ten cubits** wide, which serves as an entrance. In that case, **since** the residents of the balcony **place a partition** at this entrance, **they** thereby **remove themselves** entirely **from** the courtyard.

הנהו בני קקונאי דאתי לקמיה דרב יוסף, אמרו ליה: הב לן גברא דליערב לן מאתין. אמר ליה לאביי: זיל ערב להו, וחזי דלא מצווחת עלה בבי מדרשא. אזל, חזא להנהו בתי דפתיחי לנהרא, אמר: הני להוי שיור למתא.

The Gemara relates that **certain residents of** the city of **Kakunya came before Rav Yosef** and **said to him: Provide us with someone who will establish an *eiruv* for our city.** The city had originally been a public city and had turned into a private one, requiring that part of the city be excluded from the *eiruv*. Rav Yosef **said to Abaye: Go, establish an *eiruv* for them, and see** to it **that there is no outcry against it in the study hall,** i.e., make sure the *eiruv* is valid beyond any doubt. **He went** and **saw** that **certain houses opened to the river** and not to the city.[B] **He said: Let these** houses serve as **the section excluded** from the *eiruv* **for the city.**

הדר אמר: "אין מערבין את כולה" תנן, [מכלל] דאי בעי לעירובי מצי מערבי, אלא איעביד להו כווי דאי בעו לעירובי דרך חלונות מצו מערבי.

Abaye subsequently **retracted** and **said:** This cannot be done, as **we learned** in the mishna: **One may not establish an *eiruv* for all of it; by inference, if they wanted to establish an *eiruv*** for the entire city, **they would have been able to establish** such **an *eiruv*,** if not for the requirement to exclude a section of the city from the *eiruv*. However, these houses, which do not open to the city, could not have joined in an *eiruv* with the rest of the city in any case, and therefore they cannot serve as the excluded section. **Rather, I will create windows for them** between the courtyards of their houses and the rest of the city, **so that if they want to establish an *eiruv*** with the rest of the city **by way of the windows, they can establish** such **an *eiruv*,** and then these houses will be fit to serve as the excluded section.

הדר אמר: לא בעי – דהא רבה בר אבוה מערב לה לכולה מחוזא ערסייתא ערסייתא משום פירא דבי תורי, דכל חד וחד הוי שיור לחבריה, ואף על גב דאי בעו לערובי בהדי הדדי לא מצו מערבי.

He subsequently **retracted** again and **said:** This **is not necessary, as Rabba bar Avuh established an *eiruv* for the entire** city of **Meḥoza,** which was a public city that had become a private one, **neighborhood by neighborhood, due to the** fact that the neighborhoods were separated by **ditches** from which **the cattle** would feed. In other words, Rabba bar Avuh established a separate *eiruv* for each neighborhood without excluding any of them, **as** he maintained that **each one was an excluded section for the other. And although** the neighborhoods **would not have been able to establish an *eiruv*** together even **if they wanted** to, due to the ditches separating them, the neighborhoods were still able to serve as excluded areas for each other.

הדר אמר: לא דמי, התם – אי בעי לערובי דרך גגות והני לא מערבי, הילכך נעבדן כווי.

He subsequently **retracted** once again and **said:** The two cases **are not** really **comparable. There,** in Meḥoza, **if they wanted,** they could have **established** a single ***eiruv* by way of the roofs;** but **these** houses **cannot establish an *eiruv*** with the other houses of the city, and **therefore we must create windows** for them.

הדר אמר: כווי נמי לא בעי, דההוא בי תיבנא דהוה ליה למר בר פופידתא מפומבדיתא, ושויה שיור לפומבדיתא.

He subsequently **retracted** yet again and **said: Windows are also not necessary. As, that storehouse of straw**[N] **which belonged to Mar bar Pofidata from Pumbedita was designated as the section excluded from** the *eiruv* arranged for the city of **Pumbedita,** which proves that it is not necessary for the excluded section to be one that could have been included in an *eiruv* with the rest of the city.[H]

אמר: היינו דאמר לי מר "חזי דלא מצווחת עלה בבי מדרשא".

Abaye **said** to himself: **This is what the Master** meant when he **said to me: See** to it **that there is no outcry against it in the study hall.** Abaye now understood the many factors that had to be considered and how wary one must be of reaching a hasty conclusion.

BACKGROUND

The courtyards of Kakunya – החצרות בקקוניא:

Isolated courtyards of Kakunya situated along the bank of a river and detached from the rest of the city

NOTES

Storehouse of straw – בי תיבנא: Apparently, this warehouse of straw was located outside the city of Pumbedita. Nevertheless, it served as the section excluded from the *eiruv*, although it was not actually part of the city (*Me'iri*).

HALAKHA

Windows as the section excluded from a city – חלונות כשיור לעיר: The area excluded from the *eiruv* may consist of houses that do not open into the city at all. Even a warehouse of straw, which does not require an *eiruv*, may be used for this purpose, in accordance with the statement of Abaye (*Shulḥan Arukh*, *Oraḥ Ḥayyim* 392:3).

"אֶלָּא אִם כֵּן עָשָׂה חוּצָה לָהּ כְּעִיר חֲדָשָׁה". תַּנְיָא, אָמַר רַבִּי יְהוּדָה: עִיר אַחַת הָיְתָה בִּיהוּדָה וַחֲדָשָׁה שְׁמָהּ, וְהָיוּ בָהּ חֲמִשִּׁים דִּיּוּרִים אֲנָשִׁים וְנָשִׁים וָטַף, וּבָהּ הָיוּ מְשַׁעֲרִים חֲכָמִים, וְהִיא הָיְתָה שִׁיּוּר.

The mishna stated that if a public city becomes a private city, one may not establish an *eiruv* for all of it **unless he maintains** an area **outside** the *eiruv* which is like the size of **the city of Ḥadasha**[B] in Judea. **It was taught** in a *baraita* that **Rabbi Yehuda said: There was a certain city in Judea and its name was Ḥadasha, and it had fifty residents** including **men, women, and children. And the Sages would use it to measure** the size of the section that must be excluded from an *eiruv*, **and it** itself was **the excluded section** of the *eiruv* of a larger city that was adjacent to it.

אִיבַּעְיָא לְהוּ: חֲדָשָׁה מַהוּ? חֲדָשָׁה, כִּי הֵיכִי דְּאִיהִי הָוְיָא שִׁיּוּר לִגְדוֹלָה – גְּדוֹלָה נַמִי הָוְיָא שִׁיּוּר לִקְטַנָּה!

A dilemma was raised before the Sages: As for **Ḥadasha, what is** the *halakha*? Is it permissible to establish an *eiruv* for Ḥadasha itself without excluding a section of the city from the *eiruv*? The Gemara answers: With regard to **Ḥadasha, just as it was the excluded section of the larger** city, **the larger** city **was also the excluded section of the smaller** city.[H]

אֶלָּא: כְּעֵין חֲדָשָׁה מַהוּ? רַב הוּנָא וְרַב יְהוּדָה; חַד אָמַר: בָּעֲיָא שִׁיּוּר, וְחַד אָמַר: לָא בָּעֲיָא שִׁיּוּר.

Rather, the question pertains to a small city **like Ḥadasha** that stands by itself, not in proximity to a larger city: **What is the** *halakha*?[N] Does a small city require an excluded section or not? **Rav Huna and Rav Yehuda** disagreed about this issue. **One said: It requires an excluded section; and one said: It does not require an excluded section.**[H]

"רַבִּי שִׁמְעוֹן אוֹמֵר שָׁלֹשׁ חֲצֵירוֹת וכו'". אָמַר רַב חָמָא בַּר גּוּרְיָא, אָמַר רַב: הֲלָכָה כְּרַבִּי שִׁמְעוֹן. רַבִּי יִצְחָק אָמַר: אֲפִילּוּ בַּיִת אֶחָד וְחָצֵר אַחַת. חָצֵר אַחַת סָלְקָא דַּעְתָּךְ?! אֶלָּא אֵימָא: בַּיִת אֶחָד בְּחָצֵר אַחַת.

It is stated in the mishna that **Rabbi Shimon says:** The excluded area must be large enough to include at least **three courtyards** with two houses each. **Rav Ḥama bar Gurya said** that **Rav said:** The ***halakha*** **is in accordance with** the opinion of **Rabbi Shimon.** However, **Rabbi Yitzḥak said: Even one house and one courtyard** suffice.[H] The Gemara expresses surprise at the wording of this statement: **Can it enter your mind** that **one courtyard** even without a house is sufficient? **Rather,** correct it and **say** as follows: **One house in one courtyard.**

אֲמַר לֵיהּ אַבָּיֵי לְרַב יוֹסֵף: הָא דְּרַבִּי יִצְחָק גְּמָרָא אוֹ סְבָרָא? אֲמַר לֵיהּ: מַאי נָפְקָא לָן מִינַּהּ? אֲמַר לֵיהּ: גְּמָרָא גְּמוֹר זְמוֹרְתָּא תְּהֵא?!

Abaye said to Rav Yosef: Is that ruling **of Rabbi Yitzḥak** based on oral **tradition or** his own **logic?** Rav Yosef **said to him: What** practical **difference** does Rabbi Yitzḥak's source make **to us?**[N] Abaye **said to him,** quoting a well-known adage: When you **study Talmud is it** merely **a song?**; Is the material you study like the lyrics of a song that you do not understand? It is proper to investigate all aspects of the statements of the Sages, regardless of the practical ramifications.

מַתְנִי׳ מִי שֶׁהָיָה בַּמִּזְרָח וְאָמַר לִבְנוֹ "עָרֵב לִי בַּמַּעֲרָב", בַּמַּעֲרָב וְאָמַר לִבְנוֹ "עָרֵב לִי בַּמִּזְרָח", אִם יֵשׁ הֵימֶנּוּ וּלְבֵיתוֹ אַלְפַּיִם אַמָּה וּלְעֵירוּבוֹ יוֹתֵר מִכָּאן – מוּתָּר לְבֵיתוֹ וְאָסוּר לְעֵירוּבוֹ.

MISHNA **One who was to the east** of his home when Shabbat began, **and he had said to his son** before Shabbat: **Establish an *eiruv* for me to the west;** or, if he was **to the west** of his home **and he had said to his son: Establish an *eiruv* for me to the east,** the *halakha* is as follows: **If there is** a distance of **two thousand cubits from his** current location **to his house,** and the distance **to his *eiruv* is greater than this, he is permitted** to walk **to his house,** and from there he may walk two thousand cubits in every direction, **but it is prohibited** for him **to** walk to the spot where his son had deposited **his *eiruv*.**

לְעֵירוּבוֹ אַלְפַּיִם אַמָּה וּלְבֵיתוֹ יָתֵר מִכָּאן – אָסוּר לְבֵיתוֹ וּמוּתָּר לְעֵירוּבוֹ.

If the distance from one's current location **to his *eiruv* is two thousand cubits,** and the distance **to his house is greater than this, he is prohibited** from walking to his house, **and he is permitted to** walk to the spot of **his *eiruv*,** and from there he may walk two thousand cubits in every direction. In other words, with regard to the Shabbat limit, one's place of residence for Shabbat cannot be more than two thousand cubits from his physical location when Shabbat begins.[H]

BACKGROUND

Ḥadasha – חֲדָשָׁה: The small city of Ḥadasha, near Jerusalem, is mentioned in the Bible as one of the cities of the tribe of Judah. It existed during the Second Temple period as well. Judah the Maccabee's crushing defeat of Nikanor's army took place nearby.

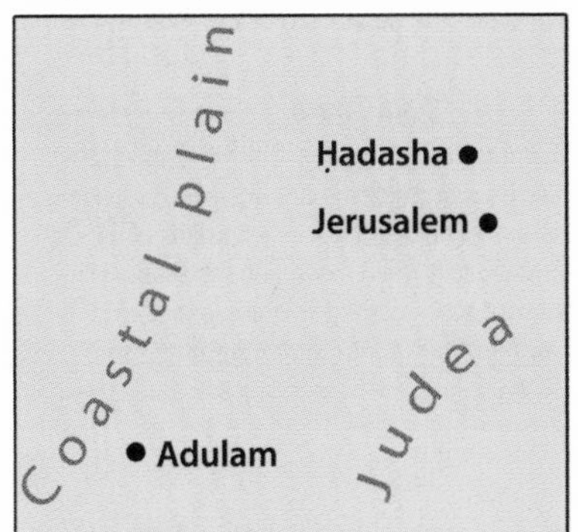

Map of Ḥadasha and surrounding area

HALAKHA

The section excluded from a city – שִׁיּוּר לְעִיר: The residents of the section of the city excluded from the *eiruv* may establish their own *eiruv*, and the rest of the city serves as the area excluded from their *eiruv* (*Shulḥan Arukh*, *Oraḥ Ḥayyim* 392:1).

It does not require an excluded section – לָא בָּעֲיָא שִׁיּוּר: A public city whose population has dwindled to the point that only fifty residents remain need not exclude a section of the city from its *eiruv*. Rather, an *eiruv* may be established for the entire city, in accordance with the following explanation of the phrase: Like Ḥadasha (*Shulḥan Arukh*, *Oraḥ Ḥayyim* 392:7).

Even one house and one courtyard suffice – אֲפִילּוּ בַּיִת אֶחָד וְחָצֵר אַחַת: The area excluded from the *eiruv* can be even a single courtyard with a single house, as stated by Rabbi Yitzḥak. Most authorities rule in accordance with his view because he is lenient, and the lenient view is generally accepted with regard to the *halakhot* of *eiruv*. Some authorities add that he was a *tanna* and could therefore disagree with Rabbi Shimon, another *tanna* (*Shulḥan Arukh*, *Oraḥ Ḥayyim* 392:1).

One who sends a person to establish an *eiruv* for him – הַשּׁוֹלֵחַ לַעֲשׂוֹת לוֹ עֵירוּב: If one is in a field at the beginning of Shabbat and had appointed an agent to establish a joining of Shabbat boundaries [*eiruv teḥumin*] for him, the following rule applies: If the *eiruv* was placed more than two thousand cubits from his current location and his house is within two thousand cubits, his *eiruv* is invalid and his Shabbat residence is in his house. If his *eiruv* is also within two thousand cubits of his present location, his Shabbat residence is at the location of his *eiruv* (*Shulḥan Arukh*, *Oraḥ Ḥayyim* 411:11).

NOTES

Like Ḥadasha, what is the *halakha* – כְּעֵין חֲדָשָׁה מַהוּ: In other words, is the city of Ḥadasha mentioned only due to the number of its residents? Or were its location and proximity to other cities also of significance (Ritva)?

What difference does Rabbi Yitzḥak's source make to us – מַאי נָפְקָא לָן מִינַּהּ: *Tosafot* explain that Rav Yosef said this because it was clear to him that the *halakha* is not in accordance with the opinion of Rabbi Yitzḥak. Consequently, there is no reason to analyze his statement. The authorities who rule in accordance with the opinion of Rabbi Yitzḥak explain the statement in the opposite manner: Since it is clear that the *halakha* is in accordance with the view of Rabbi Yitzḥak, it is not necessary to understand his reasoning (Rosh).

NOTES

The outskirts of the city – עִיבּוּרָה שֶׁל עִיר: Some explain that one placed the *eiruv* in a different city that is within two thousand cubits of his own city. According to this explanation, the mishna's point is that one gains nothing from the fact that he placed it in a city as opposed to placing it in a field (Rav Hai Gaon, cited by the *Me'iri*).

HALAKHA

***Eiruv* in the outskirts of the city – עֵירוּב בְּעִיבּוּרָה שֶׁל עִיר:** If one placed his *eiruv* inside the city where he is spending Shabbat, or even if he placed it in the outskirts of the city that are annexed to it when measuring the Shabbat limit, his *eiruv* has not accomplished anything, as stated in the mishna (*Shulḥan Arukh, Oraḥ Ḥayyim* 408:3).

הַנּוֹתֵן אֶת עֵירוּבוֹ בְּעִיבּוּרָהּ שֶׁל עִיר – לֹא עָשָׂה וְלֹא כְלוּם.

One who places his *eiruv* in the outskirts of the city,[NH] i.e., within an area of slightly more than seventy cubits surrounding the city, it is as though **he has not done anything.** The two thousand cubits of one's Shabbat limit are measured from the edge of the outskirts of the city even if there is no *eiruv*, and one therefore gains nothing from placing an *eiruv* within this area.

נְתָנוֹ חוּץ לַתְּחוּם, אֲפִילּוּ אַמָּה אַחַת

If, however, **he placed** his *eiruv* **outside the** city's **boundary, even** if he placed it only **one cubit** beyond the city,

Perek **V**
Daf **60** Amud **b**

NOTES

To the west of his son – לְמַעֲרַב בְּנוֹ: The Jerusalem Talmud's presentation of this discussion arrives at a similar conclusion, without detailing the difficulties that led to this explanation.

Within the outskirts – בְּתוֹךְ עִיבּוּרָהּ: This phrase emphasizes that if one placed his *eiruv* within the outskirts of the city that are annexed to it for the purpose of measuring the Shabbat limit, it is as though his Shabbat residence were within the city itself. However, some commentaries distinguish between the city and its outskirts when such distinctions lead to lenient conclusions (Ra'avad).

BACKGROUND

To the east of his house – לְמִזְרַח בֵּיתוֹ: The image below demonstrates that if one is located to the east of his house and the *eiruv* is to the west of his house, he must be closer to his house than to his *eiruv*.

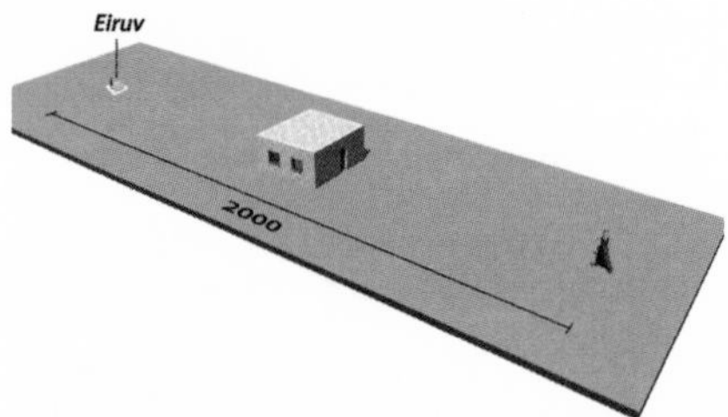

Diagram of one standing to the east as initially understood by the Gemara

In the arrangement below, it is possible for one to be positioned to the east of his house and still be closer to his eiruv.

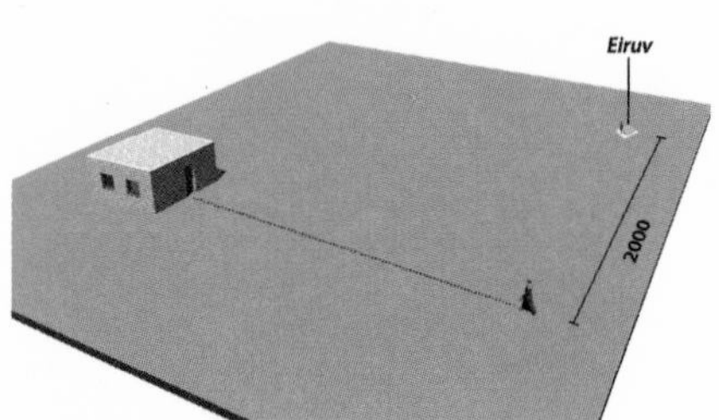

Diagram of one standing to the east according to Rava bar Rav Sheila's answer

מַה שֶּׁנִּשְׂכָּר הוּא מַפְסִיד.

what he gains in distance through his *eiruv* on one side of the city **he loses** on the other side.

גמ׳ קָא סָלְקָא דַּעְתָּךְ "לַמִּזְרָח" – לְמִזְרַח בֵּיתוֹ, "לַמַּעֲרָב" – לְמַעֲרַב בֵּיתוֹ.

GEMARA It might **enter your mind** to say that when the mishna states that one was standing **to the east,** it means that he was standing **to the east of his house** and that he had instructed his son to establish an *eiruv* to the west of his house. Similarly, when it states that he was standing **to the west,** it means that he was positioned **to the west of his house** and that he had instructed his son to establish an *eiruv* to the east of his house. In such a case, the person's house is located between him and his *eiruv*.

בִּשְׁלָמָא הֵימֶנּוּ וּלְבֵיתוֹ אַלְפַּיִם אַמָּה וּלְעֵירוּבוֹ יָתֵר מִכָּאן – מַשְׁכַּחַתְּ לַהּ דְּמָטֵי לְבֵיתֵיהּ וְלָא מָטֵי לְעֵירוּבוֹ. אֶלָּא "הֵימֶנּוּ וּלְעֵירוּבוֹ אַלְפַּיִם אַמָּה וּלְבֵיתוֹ יָתֵר מִכָּאן" הֵיכִי מַשְׁכַּחַתְּ לַהּ?

If so, the question arises: **Granted,** the mishna's case where there is a distance of **two thousand cubits from his** current location **to his house,** and the distance **to his *eiruv* is greater than this, you can find,** as it is possible **that he can reach his house** without traveling two thousand cubits **and he cannot reach his *eiruv*. But where do you find** a case where there is a distance of **two thousand cubits between him and his *eiruv*, and** the distance **to his house is greater than this?** The person's house is located between him and his *eiruv*.

אָמַר רַבִּי יִצְחָק: מִי סָבְרַתְּ "לַמִּזְרָח" – לְמִזְרַח בֵּיתוֹ, "לַמַּעֲרָב" – לְמַעֲרַב בֵּיתוֹ?! לֹא, "לַמִּזְרָח" – לְמִזְרַח בְּנוֹ, "לַמַּעֲרָב" – לְמַעֲרַב בְּנוֹ.

Rabbi Yitzḥak said: Do you think that **to the east** means that he was standing **to the east of his house, and to the west** means that he was standing **to the west of his house? No, to the east** means **to the east of his son,** who is depositing his *eiruv* for him, and **to the west means to the west of his son.**[N]

רָבָא בַּר רַב שֵׁילָא אָמַר: אֲפִילּוּ תֵּימָא לְמִזְרַח בֵּיתוֹ וּלְמַעֲרַב לְמַעֲרַב בֵּיתוֹ, כְּגוֹן דְּקָאֵי בֵּיתֵיהּ בַּאֲלַכְסוֹנָא.

Rava bar Rav Sheila said: Even if you say that **to the east** means **to the east of his house**[B] **and to the west** means **to the west of his house,** the mishna can be understood as referring to **a case where his house stood** along **a diagonal** line in relation to the person and his *eiruv*. In that case, although he is to the west of his house and the *eiruv* is located to its east, he can still be closer to his *eiruv* than he is to his house.

"הַנּוֹתֵן עֵירוּבוֹ בְּתוֹךְ עִיבּוּרָהּ וכו׳". חוּץ לַתְּחוּם סָלְקָא דַּעְתָּךְ?! אֶלָּא אֵימָא: חוּץ לְעִיבּוּרָהּ.

We learned in the mishna: **One who places his *eiruv* within the outskirts**[N] of the city has not accomplished anything. However, if he places it outside the city limits, it is effective. The Gemara expresses surprise: **Can it enter your mind** that the mishna is dealing with a case where one placed his *eiruv* **outside the** Shabbat **limit?** If the *eiruv* is outside the Shabbat limit as measured from his physical location at the onset of Shabbat, he cannot access it on Shabbat; it is therefore ineffective in establishing his Shabbat residence. **Rather,** correct it and **say** as follows: If one placed his *eiruv* **outside** the city's **outskirts,** i.e., beyond the area of slightly more than seventy cubits surrounding the city, the *eiruv* is effective in establishing his Shabbat residence at that location.

"מַה שֶּׁנִּשְׂכָּר הוּא מַפְסִיד". מַה שֶּׁנִּשְׂכָּר וְתוּ לָא?! וְהָתַנְיָא: הַנּוֹתֵן אֶת עֵירוּבוֹ בְּתוֹךְ עִיבּוּרָהּ שֶׁל עִיר – לֹא עָשָׂה וְלֹא כְלוּם. נְתָנוֹ חוּץ לְעִיבּוּרָהּ שֶׁל עִיר, אֲפִילּוּ אַמָּה אַחַת – מִשְׂתַּכֵּר אוֹתָהּ אַמָּה, וּמַפְסִיד אֶת כׇּל הָעִיר כּוּלָּהּ, מִפְּנֵי שֶׁמִּדַּת הָעִיר עוֹלָה לוֹ בְּמִדַּת הַתְּחוּם!

We learned in the next clause of the mishna concerning one who places his *eiruv* even one cubit beyond the city's boundary: **That which he gains** on one side of the city **he loses** on the other. The Gemara expresses surprise: Does that mean that only **that which he gains** on one side he loses on the other, **and no more? Wasn't it taught** in a *baraita*: With regard to **one who places his *eiruv* within the outskirts of the city, he has not done anything;**[H] if, however, **he placed it outside the outskirts of the city, even one cubit** outside, **he gains that cubit and loses the entire city because the measure of the city is included in the measure of his** Shabbat **limit?** If one's Shabbat residence had been in the city, the two thousand cubits of his Shabbat limit would have been measured from the edge of the city's outskirts; now that he has established his Shabbat residence outside the city, the city itself is included in the two thousand cubits, and he may lose far more on that side than he will gain on the other side.

לָא קַשְׁיָא; כָּאן – שֶׁכָּלְתָה מִדָּתוֹ בַּחֲצִי הָעִיר, כָּאן – שֶׁכָּלְתָה מִדָּתוֹ בְּסוֹף הָעִיר.

The Gemara answers: This is **not difficult. Here** the *baraita* is referring to a case **where his measure** of two thousand cubits **terminated in the middle of the city;** whereas **there** the mishna is referring to a case **where his measure terminated at the** far **end of the city.**[NB]

וְכִדְרַבִּי אִידִי, דְּאָמַר רַבִּי אִידִי, אָמַר רַבִּי יְהוֹשֻׁעַ בֶּן לֵוִי: הָיָה מוֹדֵד וּבָא, וְכָלְתָה מִדָּתוֹ בַּחֲצִי הָעִיר – אֵין לוֹ אֶלָּא חֲצִי הָעִיר. כָּלְתָה מִדָּתוֹ בְּסוֹף הָעִיר – נַעֲשֵׂית לוֹ הָעִיר כּוּלָּהּ כְּאַרְבַּע אַמּוֹת, וּמַשְׁלִימִין לוֹ אֶת הַשְּׁאָר.

And this is in accordance with the opinion stated by **Rabbi Idi, as Rabbi Idi said that Rabbi Yehoshua ben Levi said:** If one **was measuring** the two thousand cubits of his Shabbat limit from the location of his Shabbat residence outside the city, **and his measure terminated in the middle of the city,**[HN] **he has only half the city,** i.e., he may walk only to the end of his two thousand cubits. If, however, **his measure terminated at the** far **end of the city, the entire city is regarded as four cubits, and he completes the rest** of the Shabbat limit on the other side of the city.

אָמַר רַבִּי אִידִי: אֵין אֵלּוּ אֶלָּא דִּבְרֵי נְבִיאוּת; מַה לִּי כָּלְתָה בַּחֲצִי הָעִיר, מַה לִּי כָּלְתָה בְּסוֹף הָעִיר?!

Rabbi Idi said: These are nothing more than words of prophecy,[N] i.e., I do not see the logic behind this statement. **What** difference is it **to me** if the measure **terminated in the middle of the city, or** if it **terminated at the** far **end of the city?**

אָמַר רָבָא: תַּרְוַיְיהוּ תְּנַנְהִי: אַנְשֵׁי עִיר גְּדוֹלָה מְהַלְּכִין אֶת כׇּל עִיר קְטַנָּה,

Rava said: They are not words of prophecy, as **both** cases **were taught** in the following mishna: **The residents of a large city may walk through an entire small city** that is fully included within its Shabbat limit; the small city is considered as though it were four cubits, and the rest of the Shabbat limit is measured from the other side of the city.

Perek **V**
Daf **61** Amud **a**

וְאֵין אַנְשֵׁי עִיר קְטַנָּה מְהַלְּכִין אֶת כׇּל עִיר גְּדוֹלָה.

And the residents of a small city may not walk through an entire large city.

מַאי טַעְמָא – לָאו מִשּׁוּם דְּהָנֵי כָּלְתָה מִדָּתָן בַּחֲצִי הָעִיר, וְהָנֵי כָּלְתָה מִדָּתָן בְּסוֹף הָעִיר?

What is the reason for this difference? **Is it not because these,** the residents of the small city, **their measure** of two thousand cubits **terminated in the middle of the** large **city,** and therefore they may walk only to the end of their two thousand cubits; **and these,** the residents of the large city, **their measure** of two thousand cubits **terminated at the** far **end of the** small **city,** allowing them to walk through the entire city as though it were four cubits and complete the two thousand cubit measure of their Shabbat limit on the other side of the city?

HALAKHA

An *eiruv* outside the Shabbat limit – עֵירוּב מִחוּץ לַתְּחוּם: If one places his *eiruv* outside his Shabbat limit, it is invalid; his limit is measured either from his home or from his physical location (*Shulḥan Arukh*, *Oraḥ Ḥayyim* 408:4).

His measure terminated in the middle of the city – כָּלְתָה מִדָּתוֹ בַּחֲצִי הָעִיר: If one's Shabbat limit incorporates a city, the following distinction applies: If the entire city is within his limit, it is treated as four cubits. Consequently, he may walk anywhere in the city and still complete the rest of his two thousand cubits beyond the city. However, if his limit does not include the entire city, it is measured like regular terrain. Some say that if the entire city is not within his limit, as measured from his Shabbat residence, he is still permitted to walk throughout the city itself, as long as he does not exit it on the other side (Rema, based upon Rashi; *Shulḥan Arukh*, *Oraḥ Ḥayyim* 408:1).

NOTES

His measure terminated at the end of the city – כָּלְתָה מִדָּתוֹ בְּסוֹף הָעִיר: Even in a case where, for example, the eastern side of one's Shabbat limit includes an entire city, one is not permitted to then continue measuring the northern or southern sides of his Shabbat limit from the edge of the city. The city is treated like a four cubit strip in a single direction (Rabbeinu Yehonatan).

Terminated in the middle of the city – כָּלְתָה מִדָּתוֹ בַּחֲצִי הָעִיר: One is not permitted to deduct half the city from the two thousand cubit limit; unless the entire city is included within the two thousand cubits, the city's area is included according to its actual measurement (see *Me'iri*). The Ra'avad explains that allowing half of a city to be included in such a manner would lead to confusion and result in mistaken halakhic conclusions.

Words of prophecy – דִּבְרֵי נְבִיאוּת: See *Tosafot*, who discuss the meaning of this expression. Most commentaries, including the Rif and the Rosh, maintain that this phrase indicates a difficulty, implying that this statement is like prophecy in that it seems to have been decreed without reason. Sages are not Prophets, and they must support their statements with logical argumentation. Therefore, this statement should be rejected.

BACKGROUND

A city incorporated within his measure – הַבְלָעַת הָעִיר בְּמִדָּתוֹ: In this case, the length of the city does not count toward a person's two thousand cubits. One may add the length of the city to the end of the two thousand cubits measured from his place of residence, as indicated by the black line in the illustration below.

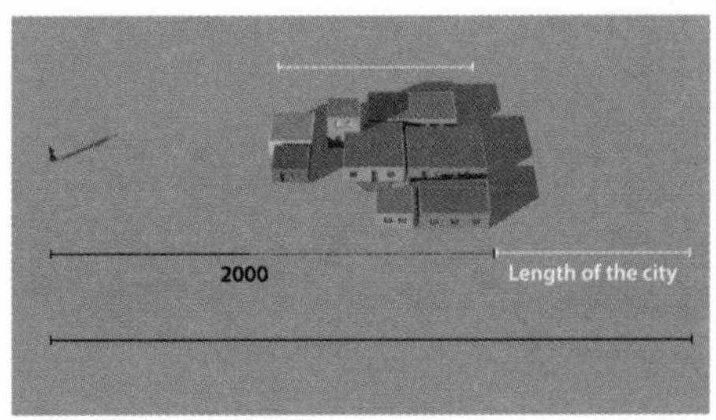

Entire city included within one's Shabbat limit

וְרַבִּי אִידִי ״אַנְשֵׁי״ ״אַנְשֵׁי״ תָּנֵי, וּמוֹקֵים לָהּ בְּנוֹתֵן, אֲבָל מוֹדֵד לֹא תְּנַן.

And Rabbi Idi, who said that Rabbi Yehoshua ben Levi's statement has no source, may hold that the mishna **teaches** the two cases with the same formulation. Just as it states: **The residents of** a large city may walk through an entire small city, it similarly states: **The residents of** a small city may walk through an entire large city. His version of the mishna did not state that the residents of a small city may not walk through an entire large city. **And he establishes** the mishna as referring **to one who placed** his *eiruv* inside the other city. Consequently, that city becomes his Shabbat residence, and he may walk anywhere in that city and an additional two thousand cubits beyond it. **But we did not learn** anything about **one who was measuring** two thousand cubits from his Shabbat residence outside the city, in which case it makes a difference whether the entire city is within his two thousand cubits or whether only part of it is within this limit.

וְלָא?! וְהָתְנַן: וְלַמּוֹדֵד שֶׁאָמְרוּ נוֹתְנִין לוֹ אַלְפַּיִם אַמָּה, שֶׁאֲפִילּוּ סוֹף מִדָּתוֹ כָּלֶה בַּמְּעָרָה!

The Gemara asks: **And** did we **not** learn in the mishna about one who was measuring? **Didn't we learn** in the mishna: **And as for one who is measuring** his Shabbat limit, **with regard to whom** the Sages **said** that **one gives him two thousand cubits,** that applies **even if the end of his measurement terminates in** the middle of **a cave?** Although a cave has the status of a private domain, he may enter only the part of the cave that is within his two thousand cubits. This case is directly parallel to the case of one whose two thousand cubits end in the middle of a city.

סוֹף הָעִיר אִיצְטְרִיכָא לֵיהּ, דְּלָא תְּנַן.

The Gemara answers: Although there is a source for the case of one whose limit ends in the middle of a city, **it was** nevertheless **necessary for** Rabbi Yehoshua ben Levi to teach the case where one's measure ends at **the** far **end of the city,** in which case the entire city is regarded as four cubits and the rest of the Shabbat limit is completed on the other side of the city, **as we did not learn** anything about such a case.

אָמַר רַב נַחְמָן: מַאן דְּתָנֵי ״אַנְשֵׁי״ לֹא מִשְׁתַּבֵּשׁ, וּמַאן דְּתָנֵי ״אֵין אַנְשֵׁי״ לֹא מִשְׁתַּבֵּשׁ.

With regard to the mishna cited above, **Rav Naḥman said: One who teaches** the following in the second clause: **The residents of** a small city may walk through an entire large city, **does not err** in his rendering of the mishna. **And one who teaches: The residents** of a small city **may not** walk through an entire large city, also **does not err.**[N] Both renderings are plausible.

מַאן דְּתָנֵי ״אַנְשֵׁי״ לֹא מִשְׁתַּבֵּשׁ – דְּמוֹקֵים לָהּ בְּנוֹתֵן, וּמַאן דְּתָנֵי ״אֵין אַנְשֵׁי״ לֹא מִשְׁתַּבֵּשׁ – דְּמוֹקֵים לָהּ בְּמוֹדֵד.

Rav Naḥman explains: **One who teaches: The residents of** a small city may walk through an entire large city, **does not err, as he establishes** the mishna as referring **to one who places** his *eiruv* inside the other city. **And one who teaches: The residents of** a small city **may not** walk through an entire large city also **does not err, as he establishes** the mishna as referring **to one who measures** his Shabbat limit and arrives at the city from the outside.

וְחַסּוֹרֵי מִחַסְּרָא וְהָכִי קָתָנֵי: אַנְשֵׁי עִיר גְּדוֹלָה מְהַלְּכִין אֶת כָּל עִיר קְטַנָּה, וְאֵין אַנְשֵׁי עִיר קְטַנָּה מְהַלְּכִין אֶת כָּל עִיר גְּדוֹלָה. בַּמֶּה דְּבָרִים אֲמוּרִים – בְּמוֹדֵד, אֲבָל מִי שֶׁהָיָה בְּעִיר גְּדוֹלָה וְהִנִּיחַ אֶת עֵירוּבוֹ בְּעִיר קְטַנָּה, הָיָה בְּעִיר קְטַנָּה וְהִנִּיחַ אֶת עֵירוּבוֹ בְּעִיר גְּדוֹלָה – מְהַלֵּךְ אֶת כּוּלָּהּ וְחוּצָה לָהּ אַלְפַּיִם אַמָּה.

And the mishna **is incomplete and it teaches the following: The residents of a large city may walk** through **an entire small city, but the residents of a small city may not walk** through **an entire large city. In what** case **is this statement said?** It was said **with regard to one who was measuring** his two thousand cubits from his Shabbat residence. **But one who was in the large city and placed his *eiruv* in the small city,** and similarly **one who was in the small city and placed his *eiruv* in the large city, he may walk** through **the entire** city in which he placed his *eiruv* **and beyond it two thousand cubits.**

אֲמַר רַב יוֹסֵף, אֲמַר רָמִי בַּר אַבָּא, אֲמַר רַב הוּנָא: עִיר שֶׁיּוֹשֶׁבֶת עַל שְׂפַת הַנַּחַל, אִם יֵשׁ לְפָנֶיהָ דַּקָּה אַרְבָּעָה – מוֹדְדִים לָהּ מִשְּׂפַת הַנַּחַל, וְאִם לָאו – אֵין מוֹדְדִין לָהּ אֶלָּא מִפֶּתַח בֵּיתוֹ.

Rav Yosef said that Rami bar Abba said that Rav Huna said: With regard to **a city located on the edge of a ravine,**[H] **if there is a barrier four** cubits high **in front of it,**[N] **one measures its** Shabbat limit **from the edge of the ravine,** as it is considered the border of the city. **And if** there **is not** a barrier four cubits high in front of it, the Shabbat limit **is measured from the entrance of** each person's **house,** as the city is not considered a permanent settlement.

NOTES

One who teaches this, and one who teaches that – מַאן דְּתָנֵי וּמַאן דְּתָנֵי: Indeed, both of these readings referred to by Rav Naḥman are recognized, ancient traditions. The text of the Jerusalem Talmud states that the residents of the small city may not walk through the entire large city, while the version of the mishna quoted in the Babylonian Talmud states that they may walk through the entire large city.

A barrier on the edge of a ravine – דַּקָּה עַל שְׂפַת הַנַּחַל: The *ge'onim* and the Rambam explained this case as referring to a city located on a riverbank that built a pier along the river's edge. Since this enables easy access to the river's water, the river itself is considered part of the city. Consequently, the city's boundary is measured from the far bank of the river. If, however, no pier was built along the river's edge, the river and the area that is between it and the houses on the edge of the city are excluded from the city's area, and the city's Shabbat limit is measured from its houses. The Rif explains the case in a similar manner.

HALAKHA

A city located on the edge of a ravine – עִיר שֶׁיּוֹשֶׁבֶת עַל שְׂפַת הַנַּחַל: In the case of a city located on the edge of a ravine that fills with water during the rainy season but is dry during the rest of the year, if the residents built a pier four cubits wide along the ravine in order to be able to use the water that flows during the rainy season, the ravine is considered part of the city. However, if they did not build such a pier, the Shabbat limit is measured from the entrance to the last houses, as in other cities. This *halakha* is in accordance with the *ge'onim* and with the Rif's explanation of the Gemara (*Shulḥan Arukh, Oraḥ Ḥayyim* 398:9).

אֲמַר לֵיהּ אַבַּיֵי: דַּקָּה אַרְבַּע אַמּוֹת אָמְרַתְּ לָן עֲלָהּ. מַאי שְׁנָא מִכָּל דַּקֵּי דְּעָלְמָא דְּאַרְבָּעָה?

Abaye said to him: You told us with regard to this case that a **barrier four cubits** high is required. **What is different** about this case that it requires a barrier that is higher **than all other barriers,** which must reach a height of only **four** handbreadths?

אֲמַר לֵיהּ: הָתָם לָא בְּעִיתָא תַּשְׁמִישְׁתָּא הָכָא בְּעִיתָא תַּשְׁמִישְׁתָּא.

He said to him: There, use of the place **is not frightening; here, use** of the place **is frightening.** Generally, partitions serve a symbolic function, and therefore it is sufficient for the partition to be four handbreadths high. In this case, however, it is frightening to stand along the edge of the ravine without a protective barrier, and therefore a barrier four cubits high must be constructed for the safety of the residents.

אֲמַר רַב יוֹסֵף: מְנָא אָמִינָא לָהּ – דְּתַנְיָא: הִתִּיר רַבִּי שֶׁיְּהוּ בְּנֵי גֶּדֶר יוֹרְדִין לְחַמְתָן, וְאֵין בְּנֵי חַמְתָן עוֹלִין לְגֶדֶר. מַאי טַעְמָא – לָאו מִשּׁוּם דְּהָנֵי עֲבוּד דַּקָּה וְהָנֵי לָא עֲבוּד דַּקָּה?

Rav Yosef said: From where do I derive to **say this** *halakha*? **As it was taught** in a *baraita*: **Rabbi** Yehuda HaNasi **permitted the residents of Geder,** situated at the top of a slope, **to descend** on Shabbat **to Ḥamtan,** situated at the bottom of the slope, but **the residents of Ḥamtan may not ascend to Geder.**[B] **What is the reason? Is it not because these,** the inhabitants of Geder, **constructed a barrier** at the lower edge of their city, **and these,** the members of Ḥamtan, **did not construct a barrier** at the upper edge of their city? Consequently, the residents of Geder measured their Shabbat limit from their barrier, and Ḥamtan was included in their two thousand cubits. The residents of Ḥamtan had to measure their Shabbat limits from their homes, and therefore Geder was not within their two thousand cubit limit.[B]

כִּי אֲתָא רַב דִּימִי, אֲמַר: טַטְרוּגֵי מְטַטְרְגֵי לְהוּ בְּנֵי גֶּדֶר לִבְנֵי חַמְתָן. וּמַאי הִתִּיר – הִתְקִין.

The Gemara relates that **when Rav Dimi came** from Eretz Yisrael to Babylonia, **he said:** This ruling was issued not due to their respective Shabbat limits, but rather because **the residents of Geder would assault** [*metatreg*][L] **the residents of Ḥamtan. And what** does it mean that Rabbi Yehuda HaNasi **permitted** the residents of Geder to descend to Ḥamtan, but not vice versa? **He instituted** this. In other words, this was not a halakhic ruling, but rather an ordinance instituted to protect the public welfare and prevent fighting.

וּמַאי שְׁנָא שַׁבָּת? דִּשְׁכִיחָא בָּהּ שִׁכְרוּת.

The Gemara asks: **What is different** about **Shabbat** that Rabbi Yehuda HaNasi instituted this ordinance only for Shabbat and not for the rest of the week? The Gemara answers: **Drunkenness is common on** Shabbat, when people eat to their heart's content. Therefore, there is a greater chance of violent behavior.

LANGUAGE

Assault [*metatreg*] – מְטַטְרֵג: Possibly from the Greek word δέδαρχα, *dedarkha*, a popular term meaning hit or struck. Other commentaries claim it comes from the Semitic-Arabic root طرق, *trq*, also meaning hit.

BACKGROUND

Geder and Ḥamtan – גֶּדֶר וְחַמְתָן: Geder was an important city in the talmudic period. It was inhabited mostly by gentiles and was one of the ten cities of the Decapolis. The town of Ḥamat Gader, or Ḥamtan, situated on the hillside below it, was named after its hot springs [*ḥamim*].

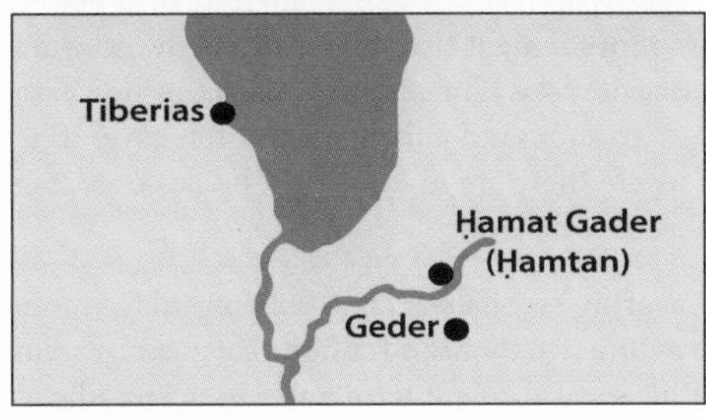

Roman bath ruins at Ḥamat Gader, and map of area surrounding Geder and Ḥamtan

Constructed a barrier – עָבַד דַּקָּה: This drawing illustrates the opinion that the residents of Geder established a barrier on the hillside, whereas their counterparts from Ḥamtan did not do so. Consequently, the residents of Geder could walk further on Shabbat than the residents of Ḥamtan.

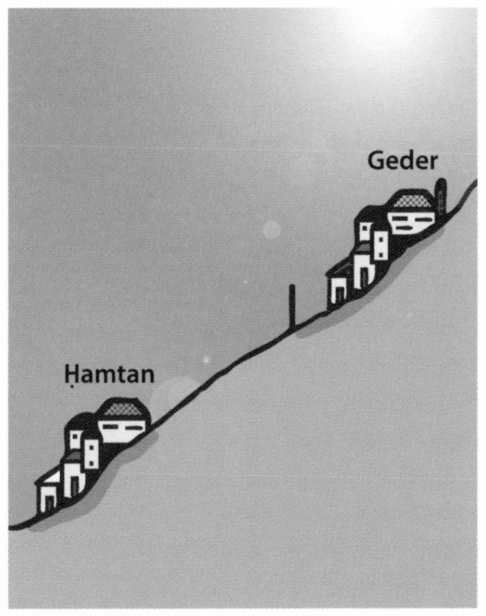

Geder, its barrier, and Ḥamtan

BACKGROUND

Geder, a city shaped like a bow – עיר העשויה כקשת: According to the explanation that Geder was a bow-shaped city, the Shabbat limit of the residents of Ḥamtan did not include all of Geder, as indicated by the dotted line. However, since the Shabbat limit of the residents of Geder was measured from the imaginary bowstring, it incorporated the entire city of Ḥamtan.

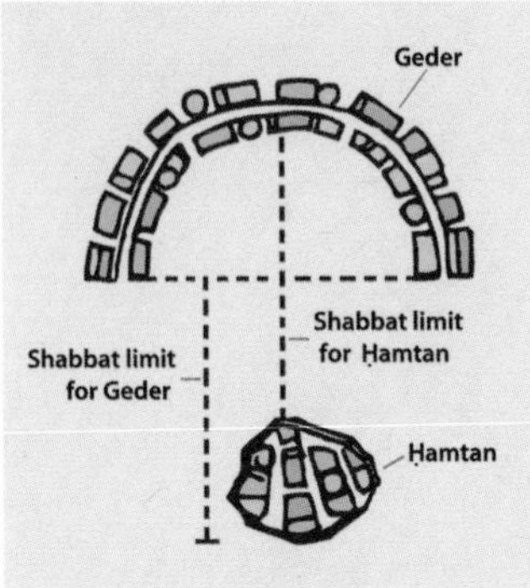

Shabbat limit of a bow-shaped city

NOTES

The inhabitants of Geder and Ḥamtan – בני גדר ובני חמתן: The Sages of the Jerusalem Talmud also disagreed about the reason for the policy permitting the residents of Geder to go to Ḥamtan but prohibiting the residents of Ḥamtan to travel to Geder. One opinion is that the policy is based on the laws of a large city near a small one. Other Sages state that Rabbi Yehuda HaNasi acted because the authorities in Geder, a city with a large gentile population, did not welcome the Jewish inhabitants of Ḥamtan. The Ra'avad explains that there was a village between the two cities, which was located closer to Geder than to Ḥamtan. The Shabbat limit of Geder included the entire village, and therefore the village was considered as though it were four cubits, and the rest of the Shabbat limit of Geder was measured from the other side of the village. Consequently, the Shabbat limit of Geder included Ḥamtan as well. However, the Shabbat limit of Ḥamtan ended in the middle of the village, and therefore the residents of Ḥamtan could travel no farther than the village.

HALAKHA

A small city and a large city – עיר קטנה ועיר גדולה: The residents of a large city, whose Shabbat limit includes an entire small city, may walk throughout the small city. The area of that city is considered as though it were only four cubits, and the rest of the Shabbat limit is then measured from the other side of the city. The residents of the small city, however, whose Shabbat limit does not incorporate the entire large city, are permitted to walk through it only until the end of their two thousand cubit limit. If they placed their *eiruv* in the large city, the large city is considered their Shabbat residence, and they may walk anywhere within the large city, and an additional two thousand cubits beyond (*Shulḥan Arukh, Oraḥ Ḥayyim* 408:1).

כי אזלי להתם נמי מטטרגי להו! כלבא בלא מתיה שב שנין לא נבח.

The Gemara asks: **When** the residents of Geder **go to** Ḥamtan, **they will assault** the residents there; of what use, then, is this ordinance? The Gemara answers, citing a popular saying: **A dog** that is **not in its place will not bark for seven years.** On its own turf, a dog barks readily, but it becomes scared in unfamiliar surroundings and remains silent. Similarly, the people of Geder are not nearly as bold when they visit Ḥamtan as they are in their own town.

השתא נמי מטטרגי בני חמתן לבני גדר! כולי האי לא כייפי להו.

The Gemara asks: If so, we should be concerned about the reverse scenario, that **now too, the residents of Ḥamtan,** in their home territory, **will** take revenge and **assault the residents of Geder.** The Gemara answers: The people of Geder **would not be submissive to such an extent.** While visiting Ḥamtan, they would not initiate fights, but they would certainly fight back if they were attacked. Consequently, the people of Ḥamtan would not dare initiate hostilities with them. Therefore, there is no concern about the safety of either group.

רב ספרא אמר: עיר העשויה כקשת הואי.

Rav Safra said: Geder **was a city shaped like a bow,**[B] whose two ends were separated by less than four thousand cubits. The empty space of the bow was viewed as though it were filled with houses, and its Shabbat limit was measured from the imaginary bowstring stretched between the two ends of the bow. Consequently, Ḥamtan was included in its Shabbat limit, and the residents of Geder were permitted to go there on Shabbat. With regard to the inhabitants of Ḥamtan, however, that same area between the ends of Geder was viewed as empty space, and therefore the houses of Geder along the arc of the bow were beyond their Shabbat limit.

רב דימי בר חיננא אמר: אנשי עיר גדולה ואנשי עיר קטנה הואי.

Rav Dimi bar Ḥinana said: The people of Geder were **residents of a large city, and** the people of Ḥamtan were **residents of a small city.** Consequently, the residents of the large city, Geder, could walk through all of Ḥamtan, the small city; but the residents of Ḥamtan could walk only through part of Geder, as explained previously.

רב כהנא מתני הכי. רב טביומי מתני הכי: רב ספרא ורב דימי בר חיננא; חד אמר: עיר העשויה כקשת הואי, וחד אמר: אנשי עיר קטנה ואנשי עיר גדולה הואי.

Rav Kahana taught it that way, as stated previously; whereas **Rav Tavyomi taught it** more concisely, in **this way: Rav Safra and Rav Dimi bar Ḥinana** disagreed about the matter. **One** of them **said:** Geder **was a city shaped like a bow; and one** of them **said:** The people of Ḥamtan **were residents of a small city and** the people of Geder **were residents of a large city.**[N]

מתני׳ אנשי עיר גדולה מהלכין את כל עיר קטנה, ואנשי עיר קטנה מהלכין את כל עיר גדולה. כיצד? מי שהיה בעיר גדולה ונתן את עירובו בעיר קטנה, בעיר קטנה ונתן את עירובו בעיר גדולה – מהלך את כולה וחוצה לה אלפים אמה.

MISHNA The residents of a large city may walk through an entire small city, and the residents of a small city may walk through an entire large city, even if part of it is located more than two thousand cubits from their city. **How so? One who was in a large city and placed his *eiruv* in a small city,** or one who was **in a small city and placed his *eiruv* in a large city, may walk** through **the entire** city in which he placed his *eiruv* **and** another **two thousand cubits beyond it,** as the entire city is considered as though it were only four cubits.[H]

רבי עקיבא אומר: אין לו אלא ממקום עירובו אלפים אמה. אמר להן רבי עקיבא: אי אתם מודים לי בנותן עירובו במערה, שאין לו אלא ממקום עירובו אלפים אמה?

Rabbi Akiva says: He has only two thousand cubits from the place of his *eiruv*, as the actual area of the city is included in the calculation. **Rabbi Akiva said to** the Rabbis: Do **you not concede to me** that **one who places his *eiruv* in a cave has only two thousand cubits from the place of his *eiruv*,** and that consequently the entire cave is not considered as merely four cubits?

אמרו לו: אימתי – בזמן שאין בה דיורין, אבל יש בה דיורין – מהלך את כולה וחוצה לה אלפים אמה. נמצא קל תוכה מעל גבה.

The Rabbis **said to him: When** does this apply? **When** the cave **has no residents. But if it has residents,** it is considered as though it were only four cubits, and **one may walk** through **all of it and** another **two thousand cubits beyond it. Consequently,** the *halakha* with regard to an *eiruv* placed **inside** a cave **is** sometimes **more lenient than** the *halakha* governing an *eiruv* placed in the area **above** the cave. If one places his *eiruv* inside a cave that has residents, he has two thousand cubits beyond the cave; if he places it above the cave, where there are no residents, he has only two thousand cubits from the place of his *eiruv*.

ולמודד שאמרו נותנין אלפים אמה – שאפילו סוף מדתו כלה במערה.

And as for one who is measuring his Shabbat limit, with regard to whom the Sages **said** that **one gives him two thousand cubits,** that measurement applies **even if the end of his measurement terminates in** the middle of **a cave.** He may not walk further into the cave, even if the cave is inhabited.

גמ׳ אָמַר רַב יְהוּדָה, אָמַר שְׁמוּאֵל: שָׁבַת בְּעִיר חֲרֵיבָה – לְרַבָּנַן מְהַלֵּךְ אֶת כּוּלָּהּ וְחוּצָה לָהּ אַלְפַּיִם אַמָּה. הִנִּיחַ אֶת עֵירוּבוֹ בְּעִיר חֲרֵיבָה – אֵין לוֹ מִמְּקוֹם עֵירוּבוֹ אֶלָּא אַלְפַּיִם אַמָּה. רַבִּי אֶלְעָזָר אוֹמֵר: אֶחָד שָׁבַת וְאֶחָד הִנִּיחַ – מְהַלֵּךְ אֶת כּוּלָּהּ וְחוּצָה לָהּ אַלְפַּיִם אַמָּה.

GEMARA **Rav Yehuda said that Shmuel said: If one established his Shabbat residence in a desolate city**[N] whose walls are still standing, **according to the Rabbis he may walk through all of it** as though it were four cubits, **and** he may walk an additional **two thousand cubits beyond it.** If, however, **he** merely **placed his** ***eiruv***[N] **in a desolate city, he has only two thousand cubits from the place of his** ***eiruv***. The Rabbis distinguish between one who establishes his Shabbat residence by actually being present in that location at the onset of Shabbat and one who does so by placing his *eiruv* there before Shabbat. **Rabbi Elazar says: Whether he established his Shabbat residence** through his physical presence **or he** merely **placed his** ***eiruv*** there, **he may walk through all of it and** another **two thousand cubits beyond it.**[H]

מֵיתִיבִי, אָמַר לָהֶן רַבִּי עֲקִיבָא: אִי אַתֶּם מוֹדִים לִי בְּנוֹתֵן אֶת עֵירוּבוֹ בִּמְעָרָה, שֶׁאֵין לוֹ מִמְּקוֹם עֵירוּבוֹ אֶלָּא אַלְפַּיִם אַמָּה? אָמְרוּ לוֹ: אֵימָתַי – בִּזְמַן שֶׁאֵין בָּהּ דִּיּוּרִין; הָא בְּאֵין בָּהּ דִּיּוּרִין – מוֹדוּ לֵיהּ!

The Gemara **raises an objection** based upon the mishna. **Rabbi Akiva said to** the Rabbis: Do **you not concede to me** that **one who places his** ***eiruv*** **in a cave has only two thousand cubits from the place of his** ***eiruv***? **They said to him: When** does this apply? **When** the cave **has no residents.** Consequently, **when it has no residents** the Rabbis **concede to** Rabbi Akiva that one has only two thousand cubits from the place of his *eiruv*. This contradicts Rabbi Elazar's assertion that, according to the Rabbis, even if one places his *eiruv* in the abandoned city, he may walk through all of it and another two thousand cubits beyond it.

מַאי "אֵין בָּהּ דִּיּוּרִין"? אֵינָהּ רְאוּיָה לְדִירָה.

The Gemara responds: **What is** the meaning of the qualification that it **has no residents?** It means that the place **is not fit for residence.** If, however, the city is suitable for habitation, it is considered like four cubits even if it is currently uninhabited.

תָּא שְׁמַע: שָׁבַת בְּעִיר, אֲפִילּוּ הִיא גְּדוֹלָה כְּאַנְטְיוֹכְיָא, בִּמְעָרָה, אֲפִילּוּ הִיא כִּמְעָרַת צִדְקִיָּהוּ מֶלֶךְ יְהוּדָה – מְהַלֵּךְ אֶת כּוּלָּהּ וְחוּצָה לָהּ אַלְפַּיִם אַמָּה. קָתָנֵי עִיר דּוּמְיָא דִּמְעָרָה, מָה מְעָרָה חֲרֵיבָה, אַף עִיר חֲרֵיבָה, וְשָׁבַת – אִין, אֲבָל הִנִּיחַ – לָא.

Come and hear another difficulty from the following *baraita*: If **one established his Shabbat residence** through his physical presence **in a city, even if it is as large as Antioch,**[B] or **in a cave, even if it is** particularly large, **like the Cave of Zedekiah, king of Judah, he may walk through all of it and** another **two thousand cubits beyond it.** The *baraita* **teaches** the case of a **city** that is **similar to** that of **a cave: Just as a cave is** presumably **desolate,** i.e., uninhabited, **so too the city** must be one that **is desolate. And** only in the case where **he established** **his Shabbat residence** through his physical presence would **yes,** this *halakha* apply; **but** if he merely **placed** his *eiruv* there, **no,** he may not measure his two thousand cubits from the edge of the city.

HALAKHA

One who establishes his Shabbat residence and one who places his ***eiruv*** **– שׁוֹבֵת וּמַנִּיחַ:** One who establishes his Shabbat residence in a desolate but inhabitable city or cave, either through his physical presence at the beginning of Shabbat or by placing an *eiruv* there before Shabbat, may walk through the entire area and two thousand cubits beyond it. If one establishes his Shabbat residence in an uninhabitable place, he may travel only two thousand cubits in all directions from that location. The *halakha* is in accordance with the Rabbis, as explained by Rava and in accordance with Rabbi Elazar, as the difficulties that were raised against him were answered. This follows the general principle that the *halakha* is in accordance with the lenient opinion with respect to the *halakhot* of *eiruv* (*Shulḥan Arukh*, *Oraḥ Ḥayyim* 408:2).

NOTES

Desolate city – עִיר חֲרֵיבָה: The terms desolate and inhabited are used in this context in their narrow sense to refer to a city that is or is not inhabited. A desolate city can be fit or unfit for habitation. Rashi explains that if the walls of a desolate city are breached, it would no longer be fit for habitation because people would be afraid of wild animals (Rabbeinu Yehonatan).

One who establishes his Shabbat residence and one who places his ***eiruv*** **– שׁוֹבֵת וּמַנִּיחַ:** Some early commentaries, including the Rashba, add that according to the opinion of Rabbi Yehuda mentioned in tractate *Eiruvin* (51b, p. 263 in Part One), one who verbally declares his Shabbat residence to be in a particular place has the same status as one who establishes his Shabbat residence through his physical presence in that location. These methods are more effective than merely placing an *eiruv* somewhere in order to establish one's Shabbat residence. Therefore, there are locations for which the following ruling applies: One who establishes his Shabbat residence by placing an *eiruv* there is able to walk only two thousand cubits from the location of his *eiruv*, but one who establishes his Shabbat residence there through physical presence or verbal declaration may walk through the entire area and an additional two thousand cubits beyond it. This is stated explicitly in the Jerusalem Talmud.

BACKGROUND

Antioch – אַנְטְיוֹכְיָא: Antioch, in the northern part of modern-day Syria, was one of the largest cities in the ancient world. Since it was built in stages, it was built in a sprawling fashion and covered a large area. At its zenith, it incorporated four adjoining cities. During the talmudic period, the city boasted a population of about six hundred thousand.

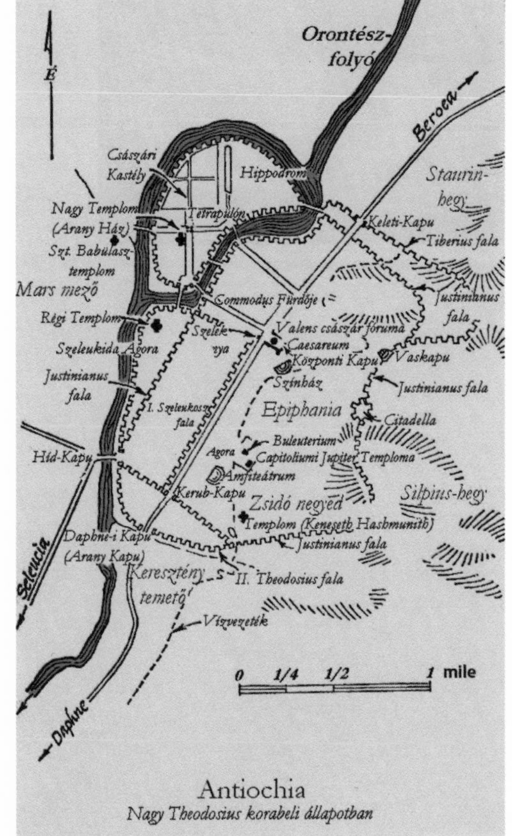

Map of Antioch during the talmudic period. The scale reveals that the area between the city walls was expansive, even without including the suburbs outside.

NOTES

An *eiruv* in a synagogue – עֵירוּב בְּבֵית כְּנֶסֶת: Rabbi Yehuda and the Rabbis disagreed above about whether or not one may establish an *eiruv* in a place from which it is prohibited to derive benefit. It is prohibited to eat or drink in a synagogue due to its sanctity. However, since the Sages permitted eating and drinking there in certain circumstances, they permitted placing an *eiruv* there as well (Rav Ya'akov Emden).

Argumentative one – פַּלְגָּאָה: The *Arukh* explains that Mar Yehuda was argumentative in that he favored opinions that were not accepted as normative *halakha*. Rashi explains that his argumentative nature was demonstrated in his habitual quarrels with his colleagues.

BACKGROUND

The Cave of Zedekiah – מְעָרַת צִדְקִיָּהוּ: Rashi here comments that Zedekiah's Cave is the cave through which King Zedekiah, the last king of the Davidic dynasty, escaped Jerusalem when the Babylonians captured the city as described in II Kings (25:4–6). In his comments on the verse, Rashi states that the cave ran from Jerusalem to the plains of Jericho, and God arranged things such that just as Zedekiah exited the eastern end of the cave, Babylonian soldiers who were hunting a deer were led by it to the cave and thus captured Zedekiah.

What is currently referred to as Zedekiah's Cave is not a natural cave but the result of quarrying, apparently beginning in the First Temple period. The cave has a maximum length of 225 m and an area of 9,000 square m. While the cave's use as a quarry during the First Temple period has yet to be supported by archaeological evidence, it is clear that the cave was used as a quarry during the Second Temple period, and it may have been the major quarry providing stone for Herod's expansion of the Temple Mount.

It is clear that the cave currently referred to as Zedekiah's Cave is not the cave mentioned in the Gemara here, both because of its size and due to the fact that it does not have an exit to the east as explained by Rashi.

What is referred to today as Zedekiah's Cave

מַנִּי? אִילֵימָא רַבִּי עֲקִיבָא – מַאי אִירְיָא חֲרֵיבָה? אֲפִילּוּ יְשִׁיבָה נַמִּי! אֶלָּא לָאו – רַבָּנַן. וְטַעְמָא; דְּשָׁבַת – אִין, אֲבָל הִנִּיחַ – לָא!

The Gemara continues clarifying the *baraita*: In accordance with **whose** opinion is this *baraita*? **If you say** it is in accordance with the opinion of **Rabbi Akiva, why** did the *baraita* **specifically** teach the case of a **desolate** city? **Even** if it was **inhabited,** the same *halakha* should **also** apply, as Rabbi Akiva holds that even if one placed his *eiruv* in an inhabited city, he has only two thousand cubits from the place of his *eiruv*. **Rather, is it not** in accordance with the opinion of **the Rabbis? And** nonetheless, **the reason is that one established his Shabbat residence** through his physical presence. In such a case, **yes,** one may walk through the entire city and another two thousand cubits beyond it. **But** if one merely **placed** his *eiruv* there, he would **not** be permitted to walk more than two thousand cubits from his *eiruv*, which would contradict the opinion of Rabbi Elazar.

לָא תֵּימָא עִיר דּוּמְיָא דִּמְעָרָה, אֶלָּא אֵימָא: מְעָרָה דּוּמְיָא דְּעִיר, מָה עִיר יְשִׁיבָה – אַף מְעָרָה יְשִׁיבָה. וְרַבִּי עֲקִיבָא הִיא, דְּאָמַר: אֵין לוֹ מִמְּקוֹם עֵירוּבוֹ אֶלָּא אַלְפַּיִם אַמָּה, וּבְשָׁבַת מוֹדֵי.

The Gemara rejects this argument and argues that the initial inference was incorrect. **Do not say** that the *baraita* is referring to **a city** that is **similar to a cave. Rather, say** that it is referring to **a cave** that is **similar to a city: Just as the city is** presumably **inhabited, so too the cave** must be one that is **inhabited.** The *baraita* is then in accordance with the opinion of **Rabbi Akiva, who said** that if one merely places his *eiruv* in the cave, **he has only two thousand cubits from the place of his *eiruv*.** However, if **one established his Shabbat residence** there through his physical presence, even Rabbi Akiva **concedes** that the entire cave is considered as though it were four cubits, and he may walk two thousand cubits beyond the cave.

וְהָא כִּמְעָרַת צִדְקִיָּהוּ קָתָנֵי! כִּמְעָרַת צִדְקִיָּהוּ – וְלָא כִּמְעָרַת צִדְקִיָּהוּ, כִּמְעָרַת צִדְקִיָּהוּ – גְּדוֹלָה, וְלָא כִּמְעָרַת צִדְקִיָּהוּ – דְּאִילּוּ הָתָם חֲרֵיבָה, וְהָכָא יְשִׁיבָה.

The Gemara asks: **Doesn't the** *baraita* **teach** that this *halakha* applies even to a cave **like the Cave of Zedekiah,**[B] which was uninhabited? The Gemara answers: The *baraita* is referring to a cave that is **like the Cave of Zedekiah** in one respect **and not like the Cave of Zedekiah** in other respects. It is **like the Cave of Zedekiah** in that the cave is as **large** as that one. **And** it is **not** exactly **like the Cave of Zedekiah, as there,** with regard to Zedekiah's cave, it was **desolate, and here** the *baraita* is referring to a cave that is **inhabited.**

מָר יְהוּדָה אַשְׁכְּחִינְהוּ לִבְנֵי מַבְרַכְתָּא דְּקָא מוֹתְבִי עֵירוּבַיְיהוּ בְּבֵי כְּנִישְׁתָּא דְּבֵי אֲגוֹבַר. אֲמַר לְהוּ: גַּוּוּ בֵּיהּ טְפֵי, כִּי הֵיכִי דְּלִישְׁתְּרֵי לְכוּ טְפֵי.

The Gemara relates that **Mar Yehuda** once **found the residents of Mavrakhta placing their *eiruvin* in the synagogue**[N] **of Beit Agovar. He said to them: Place** your *eiruv* **farther** into the synagogue, **so that more will be permitted to you,** as the Shabbat limit is measured from the spot where the *eiruv* is deposited. Mar Yehuda holds that even when an *eiruv* is placed in an inhabited city, the two thousand cubits are measured from the location of the *eiruv* rather than from the edge of the city.

אֲמַר לֵיהּ רָבָא: פַּלְגָּאָה! בְּעֵירוּבִין לֵית דְּחָשׁ לְהָא דְּרַבִּי עֲקִיבָא.

Rava said to him: Argumentative one![N] **With regard to** the *halakhot* of ***eiruv*, nobody is concerned about this** opinion of **Rabbi Akiva,** as the *halakha* is in accordance with the opinion of the Rabbis. Consequently, no matter where one places his *eiruv* in a city, the entire city is considered as though it were four cubits, and he is permitted to walk two thousand cubits beyond the edge of the city.

הדרן עלך כיצד מעברין

Summary of **Perek V**

With regard to the joining of Shabbat borders of a city and the determination of its Shabbat limit, the Gemara established several principles that apply to three areas: The essential city, the outskirts of the city, and the Shabbat boundaries of the city.

The essential city includes all contiguous residential areas in which the houses are no farther than slightly more than seventy cubits from each other. From that point, the outskirts of the city begin. Once the borders of the essential city are determined, additional areas are appended to the city on its various sides until it assumes the shape of a rectangle or square. No section of the essential city portion protrudes beyond the city boundaries. It is incorporated into the city, rendering it square. As for the measurement of the Shabbat boundaries of the city, the result is a square two thousand cubits by two thousand cubits. Accordingly, in certain places the Shabbat limit is greater than two thousand cubits, as the diagonal of the square is longer than two thousand cubits.

Since the *halakhot* of the Shabbat limits are by rabbinic law, several leniencies are applied in this measurement, including the use of estimates and assumptions even with regard to the measurement of the ground surface itself. As a result, hills and valleys are subsumed within the Shabbat limit without measurement. In the case of measurements mandated by Torah law, each and every section of the terrain must be measured.

Adjacent cities are deemed a single unit. Therefore, residents of one may walk two thousand cubits beyond the other even if that is farther than the Shabbat limit had the area been uninhabited. This is because a city incorporated within the Shabbat limit of another city is considered as merely four cubits.

Incidental to its discussion of the Shabbat limit, the Gemara also addressed certain *halakhot* of the outskirts of a city: How does a city assume the legal status of four cubits, not only with regard to traversing but also in terms of carrying inside it? Although there is no substantive link between the prohibitions of Shabbat boundaries and the prohibitions against carrying from one domain to another without a joining of courtyards, both issues deal with the needs of the community and with ensuring Shabbat observance in the city.

Introduction to **Perek VI**

After clarifying most of the issues relating to the various types of *eiruv*, the Gemara revisits the details of the halakot of the joining of courtyards and merging of alleyways.

It has been established that the residents of a courtyard must establish an *eiruv* if they wish to carry vessels from their houses into the courtyard on Shabbat. It has similarly been established that if one of the courtyard residents neglected to participate in the *eiruv*, it is prohibited for all residents of the courtyard to carry throughout the courtyard. This leads to a question of both fundamental and practical import: What is the definition of a residence in this respect? Who is classified as a resident of the courtyard or suited to be considered as living there? Is the legal status of everyone located in the courtyard, regardless of age, gender, or legal standing, that of a resident, prohibiting the residents of the courtyard from carrying in the courtyard if he fails to participate in the *eiruv*? Perhaps there are situations where one living in a courtyard e.g., a family member or visitor, is not considered a resident with regard to *eiruv*, as he is subordinate to others. The converse case must also be considered. What is the status of one whose permanent place of residence is in the courtyard, but that person is temporarily living elsewhere? Is he considered to be a resident despite his absence or not? There is also the fundamental issue of a gentile living in the courtyard; is he too considered a resident with regard to the *halakhot* of *eiruv* in terms of prohibiting the other residents from carrying if he does not participate in the *eiruv*? If so, can he establish an *eiruv*, or does this ordinance apply only to Jews?

The Gemara also discusses a different aspect of the definition of residency: Can a person who lives in a courtyard legally relinquish his rights in the courtyard or transfer his rights to others, so that he is no longer considered a resident who prohibits the other occupants from carrying? If that is indeed an option, how is it to be achieved? Must he completely renounce all rights and ownership in the courtyard, or is a partial renunciation sufficient? With regard to one who rents his house to another, at what point do his legal rights to the house cease? Is this similar to standard renunciation of one's property or not?

All the above comprise a single question: What is the definition of one who dwells in a courtyard from the perspective of the laws of *eiruv*?

In addition to this fundamental question, the Gemara addresses a series of ancillary problems with regard to the relationship between the right to use a courtyard and residence there. In the case of one who resides in one courtyard, yet passes through or carries in an adjacent courtyard on a daily basis, with or without permission, during the week or on Shabbat: When is he considered a partner to this courtyard who must participate in its *eiruv*, and when is he considered to be affiliated with a separate domain and does not prohibit members of the courtyard from carrying? Does his use of this domain join residents of the different courtyards into a partnership? Does one of the courtyards render it prohibited to carry in the other courtyard but the other courtyard does not render it prohibited to carry in the first?

These questions, which all hinge on the definition of a resident in the courtyard, are clarified both in principle and in detail in this chapter.

מתני׳ הַדָּר עִם הַנׇּכְרִי בְּחָצֵר, אוֹ עִם מִי שֶׁאֵינוֹ מוֹדֶה בָּעֵירוּב – הֲרֵי זֶה אוֹסֵר עָלָיו.

MISHNA **One who resides with a gentile in** the same **courtyard, or** one who lives in the same courtyard **with one who does not accept** the principle of ***eiruv***, even though he is not a gentile, such as a Samaritan [*Kuti*], **this** person **renders it prohibited for him** to carry from his own house into the courtyard or from the courtyard into his house, unless he rents this person's rights in the courtyard, as will be explained below.

רַבִּי אֱלִיעֶזֶר בֶּן יַעֲקֹב אוֹמֵר: לְעוֹלָם אֵינוֹ אוֹסֵר עַד שֶׁיְּהוּ שְׁנֵי יִשְׂרְאֵלִים אוֹסְרִין זֶה עַל זֶה.

Rabbi Eliezer ben Ya'akov says: Actually, the gentile **does not render it prohibited** for one to carry, **unless there are two Jews** living in the same courtyard who themselves would **prohibit one another** from carrying if there were no *eiruv*. In such a case, the presence of the gentile renders the *eiruv* ineffective. However, if only one Jew lives there, the gentile does not render it prohibited for him to carry in the courtyard.[H]

אָמַר רַבָּן גַּמְלִיאֵל: מַעֲשֶׂה בִּצְדוֹקִי אֶחָד שֶׁהָיָה דָּר עִמָּנוּ בְּמָבוֹי בִּירוּשָׁלַיִם, וְאָמַר לָנוּ אַבָּא: מַהֲרוּ וְהוֹצִיאוּ אֶת הַכֵּלִים לַמָּבוֹי עַד שֶׁלֹּא יוֹצִיא וְיֶאֱסוֹר עֲלֵיכֶם.

Rabban Gamliel said: There was **an incident involving a certain Sadducee**[N] **who lived with us in** the same **alleyway in Jerusalem,** who renounced his rights to the alleyway before Shabbat. **And Father said to us: Hurry and take out** your **utensils to the alleyway** to establish possession of it, **before he** changes his mind and **takes out** his own utensils so as to reclaim his rights, in which case **he would render it prohibited for you to** use the entire alleyway.

רַבִּי יְהוּדָה אוֹמֵר בְּלָשׁוֹן אַחֵר: מַהֲרוּ וַעֲשׂוּ צׇרְכֵיכֶם בַּמָּבוֹי, עַד שֶׁלֹּא יוֹצִיא וְיֶאֱסוֹר עֲלֵיכֶם.

Rabbi Yehuda says: Rabban Gamliel's father spoke to them **with a different formulation,** saying: **Hurry and do** whatever **you must do in the alleyway** prior to Shabbat, **before he takes out** his utensils **and renders it prohibited for you to** use the alleyway. In other words, you may not bring out utensils to the alleyway at all on Shabbat, as the institution of an *eiruv* cannot be used in the neighborhood of a Sadducee. This is because, even if he renounced his rights to the alleyway, he can always retract and reclaim them.

HALAKHA

When does a gentile render it prohibited – מָתַי אוֹסֵר גּוֹי: A gentile who shares a courtyard with a Jew renders it prohibited for the Jew to carry into the courtyard only if there are two Jews who would prohibit each other from carrying in the courtyard if there were no *eiruv*. This ruling is in accordance with the statement of Rabbi Eliezer ben Ya'akov (*Shulḥan Arukh, Oraḥ Ḥayyim* 382:1).

NOTES

A gentile, a Samaritan, and a Sadducee – נׇכְרִי כּוּתִי וּצְדוֹקִי: The mishna mentions at least three types of people who do not have the same status as Jews with regard to the laws of *eiruv*. The Gemara elaborates on each of these categories. The status of a gentile and that of a Jew is clear with regard to *eiruv*: A gentile is not obligated in any of the *halakhot* of *eiruv*, whereas all of these *halakhot* apply to a Jew. The status of a Samaritan, who is referred to by the phrase: One who does not accept the principle of an *eiruv*, in the mishna, has been disputed by the Sages over the generations. Does a Samaritan have the status of a Jew or a gentile? The mishna mentions a Sadducee, who is a full-fledged Jew but does not accept the words of the Sages. The dispute is with regard to whether his status with regard to the *halakhot* of *eiruv* is like that of a gentile, as Rabbi Yehuda states, or that of a regular Jew.

גמ׳ יְתֵיב אַבַּיֵּי בַּר אָבִין וְרַב חִינָנָא בַּר אָבִין, וִיתֵיב אַבַּיֵּי גַּבַּיְיהוּ. וְיָתְבִי וְקָאָמְרִי: בִּשְׁלָמָא רַבִּי מֵאִיר קָסָבַר: דִּירַת גּוֹי שְׁמָהּ דִּירָה, וְלָא שְׁנָא חַד וְלָא שְׁנָא תְּרֵי.

GEMARA **Abaye bar Avin and Rav Ḥinana bar Avin were sitting, and Abaye was sitting beside them, and they sat and said: Granted,** the opinion of **Rabbi Meir,** the author of the unattributed mishna, is clear, as **he holds** that **the residence of a gentile is considered a** significant **residence.** In other words, the gentile living in the courtyard is considered a resident who has a share in the courtyard. Since he cannot join in an *eiruv* with the Jew, he renders it prohibited for the Jew to carry from his house to the courtyard or from the courtyard to his house. Consequently, the case of **one** Jew living in the courtyard is **no different** from the case of **two** Jews living there. In both cases, the gentile renders it prohibited for carrying.

אֶלָּא רַבִּי אֱלִיעֶזֶר בֶּן יַעֲקֹב מַאי קָסָבַר? אִי קָסָבַר דִּירַת גּוֹי שְׁמָהּ דִּירָה – אֲפִילּוּ חַד נַמִי נִיתְסַר! וְאִי לֹא שְׁמָהּ דִּירָה – אֲפִילּוּ תְּרֵי נַמִי לָא נִיתְסַר!

But Rabbi Eliezer ben Ya'akov, what does he hold? If you say **he holds** that **the residence of a gentile is considered a** significant **residence, he should prohibit** carrying **even** when there is only **one** Jew living in the courtyard. **And if it is not considered a** significant **residence, he should not prohibit** carrying **even** when there are **two** Jews living there.

אֲמַר לְהוּ אַבַּיֵּי: וְסָבַר רַבִּי מֵאִיר דִּירַת גּוֹי שְׁמָהּ דִּירָה? וְהָתַנְיָא: חֲצֵירוֹ שֶׁל נׇכְרִי הֲרֵי הוּא כְּדִיר שֶׁל בְּהֵמָה!

Abaye said to them: Your basic premise is based on a faulty assumption. **Does Rabbi Meir** actually **hold** that **the residence of a gentile is considered a** significant **residence? Wasn't it taught** in the *Tosefta*: **The courtyard of a gentile is like the pen of an animal,**[N] i.e., just as an animal pen does not render it prohibited to carry in a courtyard, so too, the gentile's residence in itself does not impose restrictions on a Jew.

NOTES

The pen of an animal – דִּיר שֶׁל בְּהֵמָה: All of the *halakhot* of *eiruv*, like the rest of the *halakhot* of Shabbat, were given only to the Jewish people. Therefore, they do not apply to one who is not a Jew. This statement means that as a result, a gentile who lives in a certain place may be ignored for the purposes of *eiruv*, as he is not included among those to whom the *halakhot* of *eiruv* apply.

אֶלָּא דְּכוּלֵּי עָלְמָא דִּירַת גּוֹי – לָא שְׁמָהּ דִּירָה, וְהָכָא בִּגְזֵירָה שֶׁמָּא יִלְמַד מִמַּעֲשָׂיו קָא מִיפַּלְגִי,

Rather, this explanation must be rejected, and the dispute in the mishna should be understood differently: **Everyone agrees** that **the residence of gentile is not considered a** significant **residence, and here they disagree about a decree** that was issued **lest** the Jew **learn from** the gentile's **ways.** The disagreement is with regard to whether this decree is applicable only when there are two Jews living in the courtyard, or even when there is only one Jew living there.

רַבִּי אֱלִיעֶזֶר בֶּן יַעֲקֹב סָבַר: כֵּיוָן דְּגוֹי חָשׁוּד אַשְּׁפִיכוּת דָּמִים, תְּרֵי דִּשְׁכִיחִי דְּדָיְירִי – גְּזַרוּ בְּהוּ, חַד לָא שְׁכִיחַ – לָא גְּזַרוּ בֵּיהּ רַבָּנַן.

The disagreement should be understood as follows: **Rabbi Eliezer ben Ya'akov holds** that **since a gentile is suspected of bloodshed,** it is unusual for a single Jew to share a courtyard with a gentile. However, it is not unusual for two or more Jews to do so, as they will protect each other. Therefore, in the case of **two** Jews, **who commonly live** together with a gentile in the same courtyard, the Sages **issued a decree** to the effect that the gentile renders it prohibited for them to carry. This would cause great inconvenience to Jews living with gentiles and would thereby motivate the Jews to distance themselves from gentiles. In this manner, the Sages sought to prevent the Jews from learning from the gentiles' ways. However, in the case of **one** Jew, for whom **it is not common** to live together with a gentile in the same courtyard, **the Sages did not issue a decree** that the gentile renders it prohibited for him to carry, as the Sages do not issue decrees for uncommon situations.

וְרַבִּי מֵאִיר סָבַר: זִמְנִין דְּמִקְּרֵי וְדָיֵיר. וְאָמְרוּ רַבָּנַן: אֵין עֵירוּב מוֹעִיל בִּמְקוֹם גּוֹי, וְאֵין בִּיטּוּל רְשׁוּת מוֹעִיל בִּמְקוֹם גּוֹי עַד שֶׁיַּשְׂכִּיר, וְגוֹי לָא מוֹגַר.

On the other hand, **Rabbi Meir holds** that **sometimes it happens that** a single Jew **lives** together with a gentile in the same courtyard, and hence it is appropriate to issue the decree in such a case as well. **Therefore, the Sages said: An** ***eiruv*** **is not effective in a place** where **a gentile** is living, **nor is the renunciation of rights** to a courtyard in favor of the other residents **effective in a place** where **a gentile** is living. Therefore, carrying is prohibited in a courtyard in which a gentile resides, **unless** the gentile **rents** out his property to one of the Jews for the purpose of an *eiruv* regardless of the number of Jews living there.[H] **And** as **a gentile** would **not** be willing **to rent** out his property for this purpose, the living conditions will become too strained, prompting the Jew to move.

מַאי טַעְמָא? אִילֵימָא מִשּׁוּם דְּסָבַר: דִּלְמָא אָתֵי לְאַחֲזוֹקֵי בִּרְשׁוּתוֹ, הָנִיחָא לְמַאן דְּאָמַר "שְׂכִירוּת בְּרִיאָה בָּעֵינַן",

The Gemara poses a question: **What is the reason** that a gentile will not rent out his property for the purpose of an *eiruv*? **If you say** it is **because** the gentile **thinks** that **perhaps they will** later **come to take possession of his property** based on this rental, **this works out well according to the one who said** that **we require a full-fledged rental,** i.e., that rental for the purpose of an *eiruv* must be proper and valid according to all the *halakhot* of renting.

אֶלָּא לְמַאן דְּאָמַר "שְׂכִירוּת רְעוּעָה בָּעֵינַן" מַאי אִיכָּא לְמֵימַר? דְּאִתְּמַר, רַב חִסְדָּא אָמַר: שְׂכִירוּת בְּרִיאָה, וְרַב שֵׁשֶׁת אָמַר: שְׂכִירוּת רְעוּעָה.

However, according to the one who said that **we require** only **a flawed,** symbolic **rental,**[H] i.e., all that is needed is a token gesture that has the appearance of renting, **what is there to say?** The gentile would understand that it is not a real rental, and therefore he would not be wary of renting out his residence. **As it was stated** that the *amora'im* disputed this issue as follows: **Rav Ḥisda said** that we require a **full-fledged rental, and Rav Sheshet said: A flawed,** symbolic **rental** is sufficient.

מַאי רְעוּעָה, מַאי בְּרִיאָה? אִילֵימָא: בְּרִיאָה – בִּפְרוּטָה, רְעוּעָה – פָּחוֹת מִשָּׁוֶה פְּרוּטָה, מִי אִיכָּא לְמַאן דְּאָמַר מִגּוֹי בְּפָחוֹת מִשָּׁוֶה פְּרוּטָה לָא? וְהָא שְׁלַח רַבִּי יִצְחָק בְּרַבִּי יַעֲקֹב בַּר גִּיּוֹרֵי מִשְּׁמֵיהּ דְּרַבִּי יוֹחָנָן: הֱווּ יוֹדְעִין שֶׁשּׂוֹכְרִין מִן הַגּוֹי אֲפִילּוּ בְּפָחוֹת מִשָּׁוֶה פְּרוּטָה.

Having mentioned this dispute, the Gemara now clarifies its particulars: **What is a flawed** rental, and **what is a full-fledged** one? **If you say** that a **full-fledged** rental refers to a case where one gives another person **a** ***peruta*** as rent, whereas in a **flawed** rental he provides him with **less than the value of a** ***peruta*****,** this poses a difficulty. **Is there anyone who said** that renting **from a gentile for less than the value of a** ***peruta*** is **not** valid? **Didn't Rabbi Yitzḥak, son of Rabbi Ya'akov bar Giyorei, send in the name of Rabbi Yoḥanan: You should know that one may rent from a gentile even for less than the value of a** ***peruta*****?**[H]

HALAKHA

An *eiruv* in a place where there is a gentile – **עֵירוּב בִּמְקוֹם נׇכְרִי**: Neither an *eiruv* nor a renunciation of rights is effective when there is a gentile living in the courtyard. The only solution is for the gentile to rent his domain to a Jewish resident of the courtyard (*Shulḥan Arukh, Oraḥ Ḥayyim* 382:1).

Flawed rental – **שְׂכִירוּת רְעוּעָה**: The type of rental mentioned by the Sages in the context of a joining of courtyards is not the standard form of rental, as even a flawed or symbolic rental suffices (Rambam). It is not necessary to draw up a document for such a rental, and one need not explain the reason for it. This is in accordance with the opinion of Rav Sheshet, who was a greater authority than Rabbi Ḥisda and whose opinion is lenient here, as the lenient opinion is generally accepted in disputes relating to the *halakhot* of *eiruv* (*Shulḥan Arukh, Oraḥ Ḥayyim* 382:4).

Rental for less than the value of a *peruta* – **שְׂכִירוּת בְּפָחוֹת מִשָּׁוֶה פְּרוּטָה**: One may rent property from a gentile even for less than the value of a penny [*peruta*] (*Shulḥan Arukh, Oraḥ Ḥayyim* 382:5).

וְאָמַר רַבִּי חִיָּיא בַּר אַבָּא אָמַר רַבִּי יוֹחָנָן: בֶּן נֹחַ נֶהֱרָג עַל פָּחוֹת מִשָּׁוֶה פְּרוּטָה, וְלֹא נִיתַּן לְהִשָּׁבוֹן!

And Rabbi Ḥiyya bar Abba said that Rabbi Yoḥanan said: A Noahide, i.e., a gentile who stole **is executed** for his crime, according to the laws applying to Noahides, even if he stole **less than the value of a *peruta*.**[N] A Noahide is particular about his property and unwilling to waive his rights to it, even if it is of minimal value; therefore, the prohibition against stealing applies to items of any value whatsoever. **And** in the case of Noahides, the stolen item **is not returnable,**[N] as the possibility of rectification by returning a stolen object was granted only to Jews. The principle that less than the value of a *peruta* is not considered money applies to Jews alone. With regard to gentiles, it has monetary value, and therefore one may rent from a gentile with this amount.

אֶלָּא: בְּרִיאָה – בְּמוֹהַרְקֵי וְאַבּוּרְגָּנֵי, רְעוּעָה – בְּלֹא מוֹהַרְקֵי וְאַבּוּרְגָּנֵי. הָנִיחָא לְמַאן דְּאָמַר שְׂכִירוּת בְּרִיאָה בָּעֵינַן,

Rather, the distinction between a full-fledged rental and a flawed rental should be explained as follows: **A full-fledged** rental refers **to** one that is confirmed **by legal documents** [*moharkei*] and guaranteed by **officials** [*aburganei*];[L] and **a flawed** rental means one that is **not** confirmed **by legal documents and** guaranteed by **officials,** an agreement that is unenforceable in court. Based on this explanation, the Gemara reiterates what was stated earlier with regard to the gentile's concern about renting: **This works out well according to the one who said** that **we require a full-fledged rental,** as it is clear why the gentile would refuse to rent out his property.

אֶלָּא לְמַאן דְּאָמַר שְׂכִירוּת רְעוּעָה בָּעֵינַן, מַאי אִיכָּא לְמֵימַר? אֲפִילּוּ הָכִי חָשֵׁישׁ גּוֹי לִכְשָׁפִים וְלָא מוֹגַר.

But according to the one who said that **we require** only **a flawed rental, what is there to say** in this regard? Why shouldn't the gentile want to rent out his residence? The Gemara answers: **Even so, the gentile is concerned** about **witchcraft,**[N] i.e., that the procedure is used to cast a spell on him, **and** therefore he **does not rent out** his residence.

גּוּפָא: חֲצֵירוֹ שֶׁל גּוֹי הֲרֵי הוּא כְּדִיר שֶׁל בְּהֵמָה, וּמוּתָּר לְהַכְנִיס וּלְהוֹצִיא מִן חָצֵר לְבָתִּים וּמִן בָּתִּים לְחָצֵר.

The Gemara examines the ruling in the *Tosefta* cited in the previous discussion. Returning to **the matter itself: The courtyard of a gentile is like the pen of an animal, and it is permitted to carry in and carry out from the courtyard to the houses and from the houses to the courtyard,** as the *halakhot* of *eiruvin* do not apply to the residences of gentiles.

וְאִם יֵשׁ שָׁם יִשְׂרָאֵל אֶחָד – אוֹסֵר, דִּבְרֵי רַבִּי מֵאִיר.

But if there is one Jew living **there** in the same courtyard as the gentile, the gentile **renders it prohibited** for the Jew to carry from his house to the courtyard or vice versa. The Jew may carry there only if he rents the gentile's property for the duration of Shabbat. This is **the statement of Rabbi Meir.**

רַבִּי אֱלִיעֶזֶר בֶּן יַעֲקֹב אוֹמֵר: לְעוֹלָם אֵינוֹ אוֹסֵר עַד שֶׁיְּהוּ שְׁנֵי יִשְׂרְאֵלִים אוֹסְרִים זֶה עַל זֶה.

Rabbi Eliezer ben Ya'akov says: Actually, the gentile **does not render it prohibited** for the Jew to carry **unless there are two Jews** living in the same courtyard who themselves would **prohibit one another** from carrying if there were no *eiruv*, and the presence of the gentile renders the *eiruv* ineffective.

Perek **VI**
Daf **62** Amud **b**

אָמַר מָר: חֲצֵירוֹ שֶׁל גּוֹי הֲרֵי הוּא כְּדִיר שֶׁל בְּהֵמָה. וְהָא אֲנַן תְּנַן: הַדָּר עִם הַנָּכְרִי בְּחָצֵר הֲרֵי זֶה אוֹסֵר עָלָיו! –

The Gemara proceeds to analyze the *Tosefta*: **The Master said** above: **The courtyard of a gentile is like the pen of an animal,** which implies that the residence of a gentile is not considered a significant residence. **But didn't we learn** otherwise in the mishna: **One who resides with a gentile in** the same **courtyard this** person **prohibits him** from carrying? This implies that a gentile's residence is in fact of significance.

לָא קַשְׁיָא; הָא – דְּאִיתֵיהּ, הָא – דְּלֵיתֵיהּ.

The Gemara answers: **That is not difficult. This** *halakha* in the mishna is referring to a situation **where** the gentile **is present,** and therefore carrying is prohibited, whereas **that** *halakha* in the *Tosefta* refers to a situation **where he is not present,** and therefore carrying is permitted.

NOTES

Executed for less than the value of a *peruta* – נֶהֱרָג עַל פָּחוֹת מִשָּׁוֶה פְּרוּטָה: The Noahide laws are discussed in detail in tractate *Sanhedrin*. There are seven Noahide commandments that were given to all gentiles, one of which is the prohibition against stealing. Consequently, a gentile who stole is liable for punishment. The Sages had a tradition that the only punishment given for violation of the Noahide commandments is the death penalty. Therefore, a gentile who steals any amount is liable for execution (see Genesis 6:13). For Jews, the *halakhot* of theft do not apply to an object worth less than the value of a penny [*peruta*]. This is a unique stipulation based on the assumption that Jews are not particular about such a small sum, and anything worth less than a penny is not considered money. Nevertheless, the basic law of stealing applies to items of any value whatsoever.

Not returnable – לֹא נִיתַּן לְהִשָּׁבוֹן: Most commentaries explain that stolen property is not returnable because the Torah did not institute the option of returning stolen goods for gentiles. An alternate explanation is that if the stolen item is not worth a penny [*peruta*], it is not of sufficient value to be returned.

The gentile is concerned about witchcraft – נוֹכְרִי חָשֵׁישׁ לִכְשָׁפִים: Rabbeinu Yehonatan explains: When the gentile sees that the Jew is not satisfied with permission to use his residence but insists on an actual rental, he assumes that the Jew must have an ulterior motive and plans to cast a spell on him. Elsewhere, the Talmud mentions that practitioners of witchcraft find it necessary to take possession of an item that belongs to the person whom they wish to harm.

LANGUAGE

By legal documents and officials [*moharkei ve'aburganei*] – בְּמוֹהַרְקֵי וְאַבּוּרְגָּנֵי: Several explanations have been suggested for these words (see Rashi and *Tosafot*). The *Arukh* explains that *moharkei* means writing, and *aburganei* means messengers. Apparently, *moharkei* derives from the Middle Persian muhrak, meaning document, and *waborganei* comes from the Middle Persian wābarīgān, meaning validated or trustworthy.

וּמַאי קָסָבַר? אִי קָסָבַר דִּירָה בְּלֹא בְּעָלִים שְׁמָהּ דִּירָה – אֲפִילּוּ גּוֹי נַמִּי נִיתְסַר. וְאִי קָסָבַר: דִּירָה בְּלֹא בְּעָלִים לֹא שְׁמָהּ דִּירָה – אֲפִילּוּ יִשְׂרָאֵל נַמִּי לֹא נִיתְסַר!

The Gemara poses a question: **What does** Rabbi Meir **hold? If he holds** that **a residence without** its **owners is** still **considered a residence,** and it is prohibited to carry in the courtyard even when the owner is away, then **even a gentile** in absentia **should** likewise **render it prohibited** for carrying. **And if he holds** that **a residence without** its **owners is not considered a residence,** then **even a Jew** who is away **should also not render it prohibited** for carrying.

לְעוֹלָם קָסָבַר: דִּירָה בְּלֹא בְּעָלִים – לֹא שְׁמָהּ דִּירָה. וְיִשְׂרָאֵל, דְּכִי אִיתֵיהּ – אָסַר, כִּי לֵיתֵיהּ – גָּזְרוּ בֵּיהּ רַבָּנַן.

The Gemara answers: **Actually, he holds** that **a residence without** its **owners is not considered a residence, but** nevertheless, he draws a distinction between a Jew and a gentile. In the case of **a Jew, who renders it prohibited** to carry for those who dwell in the same courtyard **when** he is **present** in his residence, **the Sages decreed with regard to him** that even **when he is not present,** his residence renders it prohibited for them to carry as though he were present.

גּוֹי דְּכִי אִיתֵיהּ – גְּזֵירָה שֶׁמָּא יִלְמַד מִמַּעֲשָׂיו; כִּי אִיתֵיהּ – אָסַר, כִּי לֵיתֵיהּ – לֹא אָסַר.

However, with regard to **a gentile,** who even **when he is present** does not fundamentally render it prohibited to carry, but only due to **a rabbinic decree** that was issued **lest** the Jew **learn from** the gentile's **ways,** no further decree was necessary. Thus, **when he is present,** the gentile **renders it prohibited to** carry; but **when he is not present, he does not render it prohibited to** carry.

וְכִי לֵיתֵיהּ לֹא אָסַר?! וְהָתְנַן: הַמַּנִּיחַ אֶת בֵּיתוֹ וְהָלַךְ לוֹ לִשְׁבּוֹת בְּעִיר אַחֶרֶת, אֶחָד נָכְרִי וְאֶחָד יִשְׂרָאֵל – אוֹסֵר, דִּבְרֵי רַבִּי מֵאִיר!

The Gemara asks: **And when** the gentile **is not present, does he** really **not render it prohibited** for carrying? **Didn't we learn** elsewhere in a mishna: With regard to **one who left his house** without establishing an *eiruv* **and went to spend Shabbat in a different town, whether** he was **a gentile or a Jew, he renders it prohibited** for the other residents of his courtyard to carry objects from their houses to the courtyard and vice versa. This is **the statement of Rabbi Meir.** This indicates that according to Rabbi Meir, a gentile renders it prohibited to carry in the courtyard even if he is not present.[H]

הָתָם דְּאָתֵי בְּיוֹמֵיהּ.

The Gemara answers: **There,** it is referring to a situation **where** the person who left his house without establishing an *eiruv* intends to **return on that** same **day,** on Shabbat. Since upon his return he will render it prohibited for others to carry in the courtyard, the decree is applied even before he returns home. However, if he left his house intending to return after the conclusion of Shabbat, he does not render it prohibited to carry, in abstentia.[H]

אָמַר רַב יְהוּדָה אָמַר שְׁמוּאֵל: הֲלָכָה כְּרַבִּי אֱלִיעֶזֶר בֶּן יַעֲקֹב. וְרַב הוּנָא אָמַר: מִנְהָג כְּרַבִּי אֱלִיעֶזֶר בֶּן יַעֲקֹב. וְרַבִּי יוֹחָנָן אָמַר: נָהֲגוּ הָעָם כְּרַבִּי אֱלִיעֶזֶר בֶּן יַעֲקֹב.

Rav Yehuda said that **Shmuel said:** The *halakha* in this dispute **is in accordance with** the opinion of **Rabbi Eliezer ben Ya'akov. And Rav Huna said:** This is not an established *halakha* to be issued publicly; rather, **the custom is in accordance with** the opinion of **Rabbi Eliezer ben Ya'akov,** i.e., a Sage would rule according to his opinion for those who come to ask. **And Rabbi Yoḥanan said: The people are accustomed** to conduct themselves **in accordance with** the opinion of **Rabbi Eliezer ben Ya'akov.** Accordingly, a Sage would not issue such a ruling even to those who inquire, but if someone acts leniently in accordance with his opinion, he would not object.

אָמַר לֵיהּ אַבַּיֵי לְרַב יוֹסֵף: קַיְימָא לָן, מִשְׁנַת רַבִּי אֱלִיעֶזֶר בֶּן יַעֲקֹב קַב וְנָקִי, וְאָמַר רַב יְהוּדָה אָמַר שְׁמוּאֵל: הֲלָכָה כְּרַבִּי אֱלִיעֶזֶר בֶּן יַעֲקֹב.

Abaye said to Rav Yosef, his teacher: **We maintain** that **the teaching of Rabbi Eliezer ben Ya'akov** measures **a kav, but is clean,**[N] meaning that it is small in quantity but clear and complete, and that the *halakha* is in accordance with his opinion in all instances. Moreover, with regard to our issue, **Rav Yehuda said** that **Shmuel said:** The ***halakha* is in accordance with** the opinion of **Rabbi Eliezer ben Ya'akov,** and therefore there is no doubt about the matter.

מַהוּ לְאוֹרוּיֵי בִּמְקוֹם רַבּוֹ?

However, **what is** the *halakha* with regard to whether a disciple **may issue a ruling** according to the opinion of Rabbi Eliezer ben Ya'akov **in his teacher's place** of jurisdiction, i.e., in a place where he is the recognized authority? Although it is usually prohibited to do so, perhaps such an evident and well-known principle such as this does not fall into the category of rulings that a disciple may not issue in his teacher's territory.

HALAKHA

One who left his house on Shabbat – מִי שֶׁיָּצָא מִדִּירָתוֹ בְּשַׁבָּת: If a Jew leaves his home to spend Shabbat elsewhere without intending to return on Shabbat, he does not impose any restrictions upon his neighbors. However, a gentile does impose such restrictions, even if he is in a different town, provided he is close enough to return that day (Rambam). Others maintain that a gentile also does not impose restrictions, even if he goes to a nearby location (Rosh; *Sefer Mitzvot Gadol*; Rema; *Shulḥan Arukh, Oraḥ Ḥayyim* 371:1).

When does a gentile render it prohibited – מָתַי אוֹסֵר נָכְרִי: A gentile renders it prohibited to carry in the shared courtyard only if there are two Jews living there who would prohibit one another from carrying if there were no *eiruv*. This *halakha* is in accordance with the opinion of Rabbi Eliezer ben Ya'akov (*Shulḥan Arukh, Oraḥ Ḥayyim* 382:1).

NOTES

Measures a *kav* but is clean – קַב וְנָקִי: The statement that the teaching of Rabbi Eliezer ben Ya'akov is measured but clean appears in several places in the Talmud. The commentaries discuss whether this principle is applied in every instance or if certain distinctions should be specified. Should one apply this rule only in the case of a mishna, or can it be applied to a *baraita* as well? Is his halakhic opinion accepted in disputes with only a single authority, or even when contrary to the majority opinion? The consensus is that the opinion of Rabbi Eliezer ben Ya'akov is accepted in all instances, even in a *baraita* and even contrary to the majority opinion, except where the Gemara explicitly rules otherwise. There is an ancient tradition that statements ascribed to Rabbi Eliezer ben Ya'akov are mentioned in 102 places, the numerical value of the word *kav*, meaning measured, and that his opinion is accepted in all of these cases. Consequently, the Sages have an aphorism that his teaching is measured, *kav*, but clean (see *Yad Malakhi; Seder HaDorot*).

אָמַר לֵיהּ: אֲפִילּוּ בֵּיעֲתָא בְּכוּתְחָא בָּעוּ מִינֵּיהּ מֵרַב חִסְדָּא כָּל שְׁנֵי דְּרַב הוּנָא, וְלָא אוֹרֵי.

Rav Yosef **said to** Abaye: **Even** when **Rav Ḥisda was asked** about the permissibility of cooking **an egg in *kutaḥ*,**[B] a dairy dish, **throughout the years of Rav Huna's** life, **he refused to issue a ruling.** Rav Ḥisda was a disciple of Rav Huna, and a disciple may not issue a ruling in his teacher's place of jurisdiction about even the simplest of matters.

אָמַר לֵיהּ רַבִּי יַעֲקֹב בַּר אַבָּא לְאַבַּיֵי: כְּגוֹן מְגִלַּת תַּעֲנִית, דִּכְתִיבָא וּמַנְחָא, מַהוּ לְאוֹרוּיֵי בְּאַתְרֵיהּ דְּרַבֵּיהּ? אָמַר לֵיהּ, הָכִי אָמַר רַב יוֹסֵף: אֲפִילּוּ בֵּיעֲתָא בְּכוּתְחָא בָּעוּ מִינֵּיהּ מֵרַב חִסְדָּא כָּל שְׁנֵי דְּרַב הוּנָא וְלָא אוֹרֵי.

Rabbi Ya'akov bar Abba said to Abaye: With regard to matters **such as** those detailed in ***Megillat Ta'anit,***[N] **which is written and laid** on the shelf for all to access and offers a list of the days on which fasting is prohibited, **what is** the *halakha* concerning whether or not a disciple **may rule** about these matters **in his teacher's place** of jurisdiction? Abaye **said to him: Rav Yosef said as follows: Even when Rav Ḥisda was asked about** the permissibility of cooking **an egg in *kutaḥ* throughout the years of Rav Huna's** life, **he refused to issue a ruling.**[H]

רַב חִסְדָּא אוֹרֵי בְּכַפְרִי בִּשְׁנֵי דְּרַב הוּנָא.

The Gemara relates that **Rav Ḥisda** nonetheless **issued** halakhic **rulings in** the town of **Kafri during the years of Rav Huna's** life, as he was not actually in his teacher's place.[N]

BACKGROUND

Kutaḥ – כּוּתְחָא: *Kutaḥ* was a common seasoning used in Babylonia. It was made from milk serum, salt, and bread fermented to the point of moldiness, with the occasional addition of other spices.

NOTES

Megillat Ta'anit – מְגִלַּת תַּעֲנִית: Rashi explains that in the talmudic period this was the only portion of the Oral Law that was committed to writing. Even according to those who maintain that the Mishna was written down during the period of the *amora'im*, halakhic rulings may not be issued directly from a mishna without further analysis. Clear halakhic rulings could be found only in *Megillat Ta'anit*.

Ruling in one's teacher's place – לְהוֹרוֹת בִּמְקוֹם רַבּוֹ: The main rationale for this prohibition is the disrespect shown for the teacher when a disciple assumes the role of a ruling authority. It is similar to one who rebels against the monarchy by appropriating honor reserved for the king. For this reason, some authorities state that a student may not issue rulings in the place of his principal teacher, even if he received explicit permission from the teacher to do so.

HALAKHA

Ruling in one's teacher's place – לְהוֹרוֹת בִּמְקוֹם רַבּוֹ: A disciple is prohibited from issuing a halakhic ruling in his teacher's place. Even explicit permission from the teacher does not remove this prohibition so long as the student is within three parasangs of his teacher (Rema; *Shulḥan Arukh*, *Yoreh De'a* 242:4).

Perek **VI**
Daf **63** Amud **a**

רַב הַמְנוּנָא אוֹרֵי בְּחַרְתָּא דְּאַרְגֵּז בִּשְׁנֵי דְּרַב חִסְדָּא.

Rav Hamnuna issued halakhic **rulings in** the town of **Ḥarta De'argez**[B] **during the years of Rav Ḥisda's** life, even though Rav Ḥisda was his teacher.

רָבִינָא סָר סַכִּינָא בְּבָבֶל. אֲמַר לֵיהּ רַב אַשִׁי: מַאי טַעְמָא עֲבַד מָר הָכִי?

The Gemara relates that **Ravina** once **examined** a slaughterer's **knife in Babylonia** to check if it was fit for slaughtering,[N] during the lifetime of his teacher, Rav Ashi, who also lived in Babylonia. **Rav Ashi said to him: What is the reason** that the **Master acted in this manner?** Isn't it prohibited for a disciple to issue rulings while his teacher is still alive?[H]

אֲמַר לֵיהּ: וְהָא רַב הַמְנוּנָא אוֹרֵי בְּחַרְתָּא דְּאַרְגֵּז בִּשְׁנֵי דְּרַב חִסְדָּא. אֲמַר לֵיהּ: ״לָאו אוֹרֵי״ אִתְּמַר.

Ravina **said to him: Didn't Rav Hamnuna issue** halakhic **rulings in Ḥarta De'argez during the years of Rav Ḥisda's** life, as they were not in the same town, even though they were both located in Babylonia? Since I do not live in the same town as you, it stands to reason that I would be permitted to issue rulings as well. Rav Ashi **said to** Ravina: **It was** actually **stated** that Rav Hamnuna **did not issue** halakhic **rulings** during Rav Ḥisda's lifetime, and that is the correct tradition.

אֲמַר לֵיהּ: אִתְּמַר אוֹרֵי, וְאִתְּמַר לָא אוֹרֵי. בִּשְׁנֵי דְּרַב הוּנָא רַבֵּיהּ – הוּא דְּלָא אוֹרֵי, וְאוֹרֵי בִּשְׁנֵי דְּרַב חִסְדָּא, דְּתַלְמִיד חָבֵר דִּילֵיהּ הֲוָה. וַאֲנָא נַמִי, תַּלְמִיד חָבֵר דְּמָר אֲנָא.

Ravina **said to** Rav Ashi: In fact, **it was stated** that Rav Hamnuna **issued rulings, and it was** also stated that he **did not issue rulings,** and both traditions are correct. **During the years of** the life of **Rav Huna,** Rav Hamnuna's principal **teacher,** Rav Hamnuna **did not issue rulings** at all, **but he did issue rulings during the years of Rav Ḥisda's** life, **for** Rav Hamnuna **was** Rav Ḥisda's **disciple-colleague.**[H] **And since I, too, am the Master's disciple and colleague,** I should also be permitted to examine a slaughterer's knife when I am not in the same town.

אָמַר רָבָא: צוּרְבָא מֵרַבָּנַן חָזֵי לְנַפְשֵׁיהּ. רָבִינָא אִיקְלַע לִמְחוֹזָא, אַיְיתִי אוּשְׁפִּיזְכְנֵיהּ סַכִּינָא וְקָא מַחֲוֵי לֵיהּ. אֲמַר לֵיהּ: זִיל אַמְטְיֵיהּ לְרָבָא.

Rava said: A Torah scholar may examine a knife **for himself** and use it for slaughtering, without having to show it to the local Sage. The Gemara relates that **Ravina happened** to come **to Meḥoza,** the home town of Rava. **His host brought** out **a knife** for slaughtering **and showed** it **to him. He said to him: Go, bring it to Rava,** the town Sage, for examination.

BACKGROUND

Ḥarta De'argez – חַרְתָּא דְּאַרְגֵּז: Ḥarta De'argez was a town in Babylonia, whose builder, Argez, is the subject of various traditions. A geonic tradition places the town near Baghdad, about a parasang, or approximately 4 km, away.

NOTES

The examination of a knife – בְּדִיקַת סַכִּין: The knife utilized in ritual slaughtering must be without blemish, as an animal slaughtered with a blemished knife has the status of an unslaughtered carcass [*neveila*] and may not be eaten. Therefore, the knife must be examined before use. The Sages in tractate *Ḥullin* state that fundamentally, the slaughterer is considered trustworthy in this regard, and he is relied upon to check the knife himself. Nevertheless, out of respect for the Sages, the slaughterer must present his knife before a scholar. If the slaughterer is himself a scholar, the Sage in his town would certainly not require him to present his knife (Rosh).

HALAKHA

Examining a knife before one's teacher – בְּדִיקַת סַכִּין בִּפְנֵי רַבּוֹ: It is prohibited for a student to examine a slaughterer's knife in the presence of his teacher (*Tur*, *Yoreh De'a* 242).

Disciple-colleague – תַּלְמִיד חָבֵר: A disciple who is also his teacher's colleague may not issue a ruling in his teacher's presence if he is within three parasangs of him. If he is farther away than this, it is permitted. If the student received permission from his teacher (*Shakh*; Vilna Gaon), it is permitted for him issue a ruling even within three parasangs of his teacher (Rema). However, with regard to his principal teacher, it is prohibited in all circumstances (*Shulḥan Arukh*, *Yoreh De'a* 242:4 and in the comment of the Rema).

אֲמַר לֵיהּ: לָא סָבַר מָר הָא דְּאָמַר רָבָא צוּרְבָא מֵרַבָּנַן חָזֵי לְנַפְשֵׁיהּ! אֲמַר לֵיהּ אֲנָא מִיזְבַּן זְבִינָא.

The host **said to him: Doesn't the Master hold** in accordance with **that** which **Rava said: A Torah scholar may examine** a slaughtering knife **for himself?** In this case I am using the knife to slaughter on your behalf. Ravina **said to him:** Since **I** am only **buying** the meat **from you,** it is not considered as though I am slaughtering for myself. Rava's principle does not apply to such a case.

(סִימָן זיל״א להני״א מחלי״ף איק״א ויעק״ב)

The Gemara cites a mnemonic for the names of the Sages mentioned in the following discussion: ***Zila Lehanya*:** Rabbi Elazar from Hagronya; ***Maḥlif*:** Rav Abba bar Taḥalifa; ***Ika*:** Rav Aḥa bar Ika; **and *Ya'akov*:** Rav Aḥa bar Ya'akov.[P]

רַבִּי אֶלְעָזָר מֵהַגְרוֹנְיָא וְרַב אַבָּא בַּר תַּחֲלִיפָא אִיקְלְעוּ לְבֵי רַב אַחָא בְּרֵיהּ דְּרַב אִיקָא בְּאַתְרֵיהּ דְּרַב אַחָא בַּר יַעֲקֹב. בָּעֵי רַב אַחָא בְּרֵיהּ דְּרַב אִיקָא לְמֶיעֱבַד לְהוּ עִיגְלָא תִּילְתָּא, אַיְיתִי סַכִּינָא וְקָא מַחֲוֵי לְהוּ.

The Gemara now relates that **Rabbi Elazar from Hagronya and Rav Abba bar Taḥalifa happened** to come **to the house of Rav Aḥa, son of Rav Ika, in the place** of jurisdiction **of Rav Aḥa bar Ya'akov. Rav Aḥa, son of Rav Ika, wanted to prepare for them a third-born calf,** whose meat was considered a delicacy. **He brought** out a slaughtering **knife and showed** it **to them.**

אֲמַר לְהוּ רַב אַחָא בַּר תַּחֲלִיפָא: לָא לֵיחוּשׁ לֵיהּ לְסָבָא? אֲמַר לְהוּ רַבִּי אֶלְעָזָר מֵהַגְרוֹנְיָא, הָכִי אֲמַר רָבָא: צוּרְבָא מֵרַבָּנַן חָזֵי לְנַפְשֵׁיהּ. חָזֵי – וְאִיעֲנִישׁ רַבִּי אֶלְעָזָר מֵהַגְרוֹנְיָא.

Rav Abba bar Taḥalifa said to them: Should we not be concerned with the respect of **the Elder,** Rav Aḥa bar Ya'akov, and present the knife to him for inspection, as this is his town? **Rabbi Elazar from Hagronya said to them:** That is unnecessary, since **Rava said as follows: A Torah scholar may examine** a knife **for himself. Rabbi Elazar from Hagronya** then **inspected** the knife, **but he was** later **punished** at the hand of Heaven for disregarding the honor of the senior rabbi.

וְהָאָמַר רָבָא: צוּרְבָא מֵרַבָּנַן חָזֵי לְנַפְשֵׁיהּ! שָׁאנֵי הָתָם דְּאַתְחִילוּ בִּכְבוֹדוֹ.

The Gemara expresses surprise: What was Rabbi Elazar from Hagronya's mistake? **Didn't Rava say: A Torah scholar may examine** a slaughtering knife **for himself?** The Gemara answers: **It was different there, as they had** already **begun** to discuss the issue **of the honor** of Rav Aḥa bar Ya'akov.[H] Had the name of Rav Aḥa bar Ya'akov never arisen, they would have been permitted to examine the knife themselves. Once his name had been mentioned, however, they should have approached him with the knife. Their failure to do so is considered a display of disrespect.

וְאִי בָּעֵית אֵימָא: שָׁאנֵי רַב אַחָא בַּר יַעֲקֹב, דְּמוּפְלָג.

And if you wish, say instead: **Rav Aḥa bar Ya'akov is different, as he was illustrious** in age and wisdom, and thus deserved more honor than a regular Sage.

אָמַר רָבָא: וּלְאַפְרוֹשֵׁי מֵאִיסּוּרָא – אֲפִילּוּ בְּפָנָיו שַׁפִּיר דָּמֵי. רָבִינָא הֲוָה יָתֵיב קַמֵּיהּ דְּרַב אַשִׁי, חַזְיֵיהּ לְהַהוּא גַּבְרָא דְּקָא אָסַר לֵיהּ לַחֲמָרֵיהּ בְּצִינְתָּא בְּשַׁבְּתָא, רְמָא בֵּיהּ קָלָא וְלָא אַשְׁגַּח בֵּיהּ. אֲמַר לֵיהּ: לֶיהֱוֵי הַאי גַּבְרָא בְּשַׁמְתָּא!

Rava said: Even though it is ordinarily prohibited for a disciple to issue a halakhic ruling in his teacher's place, if he does so **in order to separate** another person **from a prohibition**[H] he is committing, **even in** his teacher's **presence it seems well,** i.e., it is permitted. The Gemara relates that **Ravina was** once **sitting before Rav Ashi** when **he saw a certain man tying his donkey to a palm tree on Shabbat,** in violation of the decree of the Sages against utilizing trees on Shabbat. **He raised his voice to him** in protest, **but** the man **paid him no attention.** Ravina then **said to** Rav Ashi: **Let this man be in excommunication** for transgressing the words of the Sages and ignoring a scholar's rebuke.

אֲמַר לֵיהּ: כִּי הַאי גַּוְונָא מִי מִתְחֲזָא כְּאַפְקָרוּתָא? אֲמַר לֵיהּ: ״אֵין חָכְמָה וְאֵין תְּבוּנָה וְאֵין עֵצָה לְנֶגֶד ה׳״, כָּל מָקוֹם שֶׁיֵּשׁ בּוֹ חִילּוּל הַשֵּׁם – אֵין חוֹלְקִין כָּבוֹד לָרַב.

Afterward, Ravina **said to** Rav Ashi: Behavior **such as this,** the way I acted in your presence just now, **does it appear like irreverent** behavior? Rav Ashi **said to him:** With regard to this it is stated: **"There is no wisdom or understanding or council against the Lord"** (Proverbs 21:30). The Sages expounded this verse as follows: **Wherever a desecration of** God's **name is involved, no respect is paid** even **to a teacher,** i.e., in such a situation one should disregard the respect due to his teacher's wisdom and understanding and object to the inappropriate behavior.

אָמַר רָבָא: בְּפָנָיו – אָסוּר, וְחַיָּיב מִיתָה, שֶׁלֹּא בְּפָנָיו – אָסוּר, וְאֵין חַיָּיב מִיתָה.

Rava said: With regard to one who issues a halakhic ruling in his teacher's location without the intention of preventing someone from violating a prohibition, the following distinction applies: **In** the teacher's actual **presence,** the disciple **is prohibited** to issue such a ruling, **and** if he does so, he **is liable** to receive the **death** penalty at the hand of Heaven. However, when he is **not in his** actual **presence,** the disciple **is** still **prohibited** to issue the ruling, **but he is not liable** to receive the **death** penalty.[H]

PERSONALITIES

Rav Aḥa bar Ya'akov – רַב אַחָא בַּר יַעֲקֹב: Rav Aḥa bar Ya'akov was a student of Rav Huna, who lived during the second generation of Babylonian *amora'im*. He lived long enough to discuss matters of *halakha* with Abaye and Rava, who were among the fourth generation of *amora'im*.

The scholars of Rav Aḥa bar Ya'akov's time admired his Torah knowledge. Rava praised him as a great person. He was similarly well known for his outstanding piety and for the miracles that were performed at his request. As the head of the town of Papunya, Rav Aḥa bar Ya'akov instituted a number of ordinances. His students included Rav Pappa and his sister's son, Rav Aḥa, son of Rav Ika. He also had a son and a grandson, the son of his daughter, both named Rav Ya'akov.

HALAKHA

They had begun to discuss the honor of Rav Aḥa bar Ya'akov – דְּאַתְחִילוּ בִּכְבוֹדוֹ: Even if a disciple is also his teacher's colleague and he is not in the presence of his teacher, he is prohibited from ruling in his teacher's place in the context of a discussion of his teacher's honor or if his teacher is elderly or an outstanding scholar. This *halakha* is in accordance with both explanations of the incident recounted in the Gemara (*Shulḥan Arukh, Yoreh De'a* 242:4).

To separate from a prohibition – לְאַפְרוֹשֵׁי מֵאִיסּוּרָא: To prevent another person from violating a prohibition, a disciple may issue a ruling even in the presence of his teacher (*Shulḥan Arukh, Yoreh De'a* 242:11).

A student who issues a ruling in his teacher's presence – תַּלְמִיד הַמּוֹרֶה בִּפְנֵי רַבּוֹ: A disciple is prohibited from issuing a ruling in his teacher's presence. One who does so is liable to be put to death at the hand of Heaven. If he is not in his teacher's presence, it is likewise prohibited, but he is not punished for this offense (*Shulḥan Arukh, Yoreh De'a* 242:4).

וְשֶׁלֹּא בְּפָנָיו לֹא? וְהָא תַּנְיָא, רַבִּי אֱלִיעֶזֶר אוֹמֵר: לֹא מֵתוּ בְּנֵי אַהֲרֹן עַד שֶׁהוֹרוּ הֲלָכָה בִּפְנֵי מֹשֶׁה רַבָּן. מַאי דְּרוּשׁ ״וְנָתְנוּ בְּנֵי אַהֲרֹן הַכֹּהֵן אֵשׁ עַל הַמִּזְבֵּחַ״ אָמְרוּ: אַף עַל פִּי שֶׁהָאֵשׁ יוֹרֶדֶת מִן הַשָּׁמַיִם – מִצְוָה לְהָבִיא מִן הַהֶדְיוֹט.

The Gemara asks: Is the disciple **not** liable to receive the death penalty if he issues his ruling **not in** the teacher's **presence? But wasn't it taught** otherwise in a *baraita*: **Rabbi Eliezer says: The sons of Aaron died**[N] **only because they issued a halakhic ruling before Moses, their teacher? What did they expound**[N] in support of their conclusion that they must bring fire inside as opposed to waiting for fire to come down from the heavens? It is stated in the Torah: **"And the sons of Aaron the priest shall put fire on the altar,** and lay the wood in order on the fire" (Leviticus 1:7), which led **them to say: Although fire descends from Heaven,** it is nonetheless **a mitzva to bring ordinary** fire.[H] Although they derived this from the verses, they were punished for ruling in the presence of their teacher.

וְתַלְמִיד אֶחָד הָיָה לוֹ לְרַבִּי אֱלִיעֶזֶר שֶׁהוֹרָה הֲלָכָה בְּפָנָיו. אָמַר רַבִּי אֱלִיעֶזֶר לְאִימָּא שָׁלוֹם אִשְׁתּוֹ: תָּמֵיהַּ אֲנִי אִם יוֹצִיא זֶה שְׁנָתוֹ. וְלֹא הוֹצִיא שְׁנָתוֹ.

It was further related that **Rabbi Eliezer had a certain disciple who issued a** halakhic **ruling in his presence. Rabbi Eliezer said to his wife, Imma Shalom: I will be surprised if this one completes his year,** i.e., if he lives until the end of the year. **And** so it was, **he did not complete his year.**

אָמְרָה לוֹ: נָבִיא אַתָּה? אָמַר לָהּ: לֹא נָבִיא אָנֹכִי וְלֹא בֶּן נָבִיא אָנֹכִי, אֶלָּא כָּךְ מְקוּבְּלַנִי: כָּל הַמּוֹרֶה הֲלָכָה בִּפְנֵי רַבּוֹ חַיָּיב מִיתָה.

His wife **said to him: Are you a prophet?** He **said to her: I am not a prophet, nor the son of a prophet, but I have received the following** tradition: **Anyone who issues a halakhic ruling in his teacher's presence is liable** to receive the **death** penalty.

וְאָמַר רַבָּה בַּר בַּר חָנָה אָמַר רַבִּי יוֹחָנָן: אוֹתוֹ תַּלְמִיד יְהוּדָה בֶּן גּוּרְיָא שְׁמוֹ, וְהָיָה רָחוֹק מִמֶּנּוּ שָׁלֹשׁ פַּרְסָאוֹת?!

And Rabba bar bar Ḥana said that **Rabbi Yoḥanan said: That disciple was named Yehuda ben Gurya, and he was three parasangs away from** Rabbi Eliezer. Apparently, one is liable for the death penalty even if he did not issue his ruling in his teacher's presence.

בְּפָנָיו הֲוָה. וְהָא רָחוֹק מִמֶּנּוּ שָׁלֹשׁ פַּרְסָאוֹת קָאָמַר! וְלִיטַעְמִיךְ שְׁמוֹ וְשֵׁם אָבִיו לָמָּה? אֶלָּא: שֶׁלֹּא תֹּאמַר מָשָׁל הָיָה.

The Gemara answers: In fact, the incident **took place in** the actual **presence** of the teacher, which is why the disciple was punished. The distance mentioned refers to the distance between the student's usual place and the teacher. The Gemara expresses surprise: **But didn't** Rabba bar bar Ḥana **say that he was three parasangs away from** his teacher? That implies that this was his distance from his teacher at the time of the ruling. The Gemara answers: **And, according to your reasoning,** that the details of the story must relate to the time of the ruling, **why** mention **his name and his father's name? Rather,** the details were given so **that you should not say it was a parable.** That is also the reason why he provided the details concerning the student's usual place. This does not contradict the fact that Yehuda ben Gurya issued his ruling in the actual presence of his teacher.

אָמַר רַבִּי חִיָּיא בַּר אַבָּא אָמַר רַבִּי יוֹחָנָן: כָּל הַמּוֹרֶה הֲלָכָה בִּפְנֵי רַבּוֹ רָאוּי לְהַכִּישׁוֹ נָחָשׁ, שֶׁנֶּאֱמַר: ״וַיַּעַן אֱלִיהוּא בֶּן בַּרַכְאֵל הַבּוּזִי וַיֹּאמַר צָעִיר אֲנִי לְיָמִים וגו׳ עַל כֵּן זָחַלְתִּי״ וּכְתִיב: ״עִם חֲמַת זוֹחֲלֵי עָפָר״.

The Gemara continues to discuss the same topic. **Rabbi Ḥiyya bar Abba said** that **Rabbi Yoḥanan said: Whoever issues a halakhic ruling in his teacher's presence is deserving of being bitten by a snake, as it is stated: "And Elihu, son of Barachel the Buzite answered and said, I am young,** and you are very old; **therefore I held back** [*zaḥalti*] and I was afraid, and did not declare my opinion to you" (Job 32:6), **and it is written: "With the venom of the crawling things of** [*zoḥalei*] **the dust"** (Deuteronomy 32:24), which refers to snakes. Elihu's statement is understood as follows: I must apologize for speaking in my teacher's presence, for one who does so is liable to be punished with the bite of a snake.

זְעֵירִי אָמַר רַבִּי חֲנִינָא: נִקְרָא חוֹטֵא, שֶׁנֶּאֱמַר: ״בְּלִבִּי צָפַנְתִּי אִמְרָתֶךָ לְמַעַן לֹא אֶחֱטָא לָךְ״.

Ze'eiri said that **Rabbi Ḥanina said:** Whoever issues a halakhic ruling in his teacher's presence **is called a sinner, as it is stated: "Your word have I hidden in my heart,**[N] **that I might not sin against You"** (Psalms 119:11). In what case would speaking one's word entail a sin? In a case where one rules on a matter of *halakha* in the presence of his teacher.

NOTES

The death of the sons of Aaron – מִיתַת בְּנֵי אַהֲרֹן: A dispute among the *tanna'im* is recorded in *Torat Kohanim* with regard to the reason for the deaths of Aaron's sons. In this context only one opinion is cited, since the *tanna'im* do not disagree about the severity of the various transgressions suggested, as they all incur the death penalty. Their dispute pertains only to that particular incident and to the nature of the sin that Aaron's sons committed.

What did they expound – מַאי דְּרוּשׁ: The Ra'avad writes that their interpretation was certainly not in accordance with the *halakha*, since this verse refers to the outer altar, rather than to the incense altar, to which they brought fire. However, the severity of their punishment was not due to their mistake; rather, it was because they ruled before their teacher.

Your word have I hidden in my heart – בְּלִבִּי צָפַנְתִּי אִמְרָתֶךָ: The connection to the topic at hand is clarified by a previous verse: "How shall a young man keep his way pure? By guarding it according to Your word" (Psalms 119:9). The verse refers to a student, or "young man," before his teacher (Maharsha).

HALAKHA

A mitzva to bring ordinary fire – מִצְוָה לְהָבִיא מִן הַהֶדְיוֹט: Even when the fire of the altar comes down from Heaven, the priests are still obligated to kindle a fire on the altar, as commanded by the Torah (Rambam *Sefer Avoda*, *Hilkhot Temidin UMusafin* 2:1).

HALAKHA

Gifts to one priest – מַתְּנוֹת לְכֹהֵן אֶחָד: A person should not give all of his gifts to a single priest or to a single pauper (*Shulḥan Arukh, Yoreh De'a* 257:9).

רַב הַמְנוּנָא רָמֵי, כְּתִיב: "בְּלִבִּי צָפַנְתִּי אִמְרָתֶךָ" וּכְתִיב: "בִּשַּׂרְתִּי צֶדֶק בְּקָהָל רָב"! לָא קַשְׁיָא: כָּאן – בִּזְמַן שֶׁעִירָא הַיָּאִירִי קַיָּים, כָּאן – בִּזְמַן שֶׁאֵין עִירָא הַיָּאִירִי קַיָּים.

Rav Hamnuna raised a contradiction between the verse previously mentioned and another verse: **It is written: "Your word have I hidden in my heart,"** implying that David did not want to reveal the words of Torah, whereas in a second verse **it is written: "I have preached righteousness in the great congregation"** (Psalms 40:10). He answered: This is **not difficult. Here,** in the verse in which David remained silent, it is referring **to the period when Ira HaYa'iri,** David's teacher, **was alive; there,** in the verse where he publicized his words, it is referring **to the period when Ira HaYa'iri was no** longer **alive.**

אָמַר רַבִּי אַבָּא בַּר זַבְדָּא: כָּל הַנּוֹתֵן מַתְּנוֹתָיו לְכֹהֵן אֶחָד – מֵבִיא רָעָב לָעוֹלָם, שֶׁנֶּאֱמַר: "עִירָא הַיָּאִירִי הָיָה כֹהֵן לְדָוִד", לְדָוִד הוּא דַּהֲוָה כֹּהֵן, לְכוּלֵּי עָלְמָא לָא? אֶלָּא שֶׁהָיָה מְשַׁגֵּר לוֹ מַתְּנוֹתָיו. וּכְתִיב בַּתְרֵיהּ: "וַיְהִי רָעָב בִּימֵי דָוִד".

Having mentioned Ira HaYa'iri, the Gemara now cites a related teaching. **Rabbi Abba bar Zavda said: Whoever gives** all **his** priestly **gifts to one priest**[H] has acted improperly and **brings famine into the world** as punishment. **As it is stated:** "And also **Ira HaYa'iri was a priest for David"** (II Samuel 20:26), which invites the question: **Was he a priest for David** alone, and **not for anyone else? Rather,** it means **that** David **would send** all **his** priestly **gifts to him** alone, i.e., he was the only priest to enjoy David's gifts. **And it is written afterward: "And there was a famine in the days of David,** three years, year after year" (II Samuel 21:1).

רַבִּי אֱלִיעֶזֶר אוֹמֵר: מוֹרִידִין אוֹתוֹ מִגְּדוּלָּתוֹ שֶׁנֶּאֱמַר: "וַיֹּאמֶר אֶלְעָזָר הַכֹּהֵן אֶל אַנְשֵׁי הַצָּבָא וגו'". אַף עַל גַּב דַּאֲמַר לְהוּ: לַאֲחִי אַבָּא צִוָּה וְאוֹתִי לֹא צִוָּה – אֲפִילּוּ הָכִי אִיעֲנַשׁ.

Rabbi Eliezer says: Anyone who rules in his teacher's presence **is lowered from his** position of **greatness, as it is stated: "And Elazar the priest said to the men of war** who went to battle: This is the statute of the Torah which the Lord commanded Moses" (Numbers 31:21). **Although** Elazar **said to** the soldiers: God commanded this statute **to** my **father's brother, while to me He did not command** it, **even so he was punished** for speaking in this manner in the presence of his teacher, Moses.

דִּכְתִיב: "וְלִפְנֵי אֶלְעָזָר הַכֹּהֵן יַעֲמֹד" – וְלָא אַשְׁכְּחַן דְּאִיצְטְרִיךְ לֵיהּ יְהוֹשֻׁעַ.

What was his punishment? **As it is written** that God had told Moses with regard to Joshua: **"And he shall stand before Elazar the priest,** who shall inquire for him by the judgment of the Urim before the Lord: at his word shall they go out, and at his word they shall come in, both he, and all the children of Israel with him, even all the congregation" (Numbers 27:21). Elazar was originally awarded a place of great honor. **But we do not find** in the Bible **that Joshua** ever **had need of him.** It is never stated that Joshua made use of the Urim through Elazar, which shows that Elazar never achieved the greatness promised him.

אָמַר רַבִּי לֵוִי: כָּל דְּמוֹתִיב מִלְּתָא קַמֵּיהּ רַבֵּיהּ – אָזֵיל לִשְׁאוֹל בְּלֹא וָלָד, שֶׁנֶּאֱמַר: "וַיַּעַן יְהוֹשֻׁעַ בִּן נוּן מְשָׁרֵת מֹשֶׁה מִבְּחוּרָיו וַיֹּאמַר אֲדֹנִי מֹשֶׁה כְּלָאֵם"

With regard to this same issue, **Rabbi Levi said: Whoever answers a word in the presence of his teacher will go down to the netherworld childless, as it is stated: "And Joshua bin Nun, the minister of Moses from his youth, answered and said: My lord Moses, shut them in"** (Numbers 11:28). Since he spoke to his teacher out of turn, he was punished by remaining childless.

Perek **VI**
Daf **63** Amud **b**

וּכְתִיב: "נוֹן בְּנוֹ יְהוֹשֻׁעַ בְּנוֹ".

And it is written at the end of the list of the descendants of Ephraim: **"Non his son, Joshua his son"** (I Chronicles 7:27), which implies that Joshua himself had no children.

וּפְלִיגָא דְּרַבִּי אַבָּא בַּר פַּפָּא, דְּאָמַר רַבִּי אַבָּא בַּר פַּפָּא: לֹא נֶעֱנַשׁ יְהוֹשֻׁעַ אֶלָּא בִּשְׁבִיל שֶׁבִּיטֵּל אֶת יִשְׂרָאֵל לַיְלָה אַחַת מִפְּרִיָּה וּרְבִיָּה,

And this tradition **differs from** the following statement of **Rabbi Abba bar Pappa, for Rabbi Abba bar Pappa said: Joshua was punished** to remain childless **only because he had prevented the Jewish people from** fulfilling the commandment of **being fruitful and multiplying for one night.** Therefore, he was punished measure-for-measure by not having children himself.

שֶׁנֶּאֱמַר: "וַיְהִי בִּהְיוֹת יְהוֹשֻׁעַ בִּירִיחוֹ וַיִּשָּׂא עֵינָיו וַיַּרְא וגו'" וּכְתִיב: "וַיֹּאמֶר (לוֹ) כִּי אֲנִי שַׂר צְבָא ה' עַתָּה בָאתִי וגו'".

As it is stated: "And it came to pass when Joshua was by Jericho that he lifted up his eyes and looked, and, behold, a man stood over against him with his sword drawn in his hand" (Joshua 5:13), **and it is written** further: **"And he said: No, but I am captain of the host of the Lord, I am now come"** (Joshua 5:14). The man, an angel, came to demand something of Joshua and to rebuke him.

אָמַר לוֹ: אֶמֶשׁ בִּיטַּלְתֶּם תָּמִיד שֶׁל בֵּין הָעַרְבַּיִם, וְעַכְשָׁיו בִּיטַּלְתֶּם תַּלְמוּד תּוֹרָה. עַל אֵיזֶה מֵהֶן בָּאתָ? אָמַר לוֹ: עַתָּה בָאתִי.

The angel **said to him: Last night,** due to your preparations for war, **you neglected the daily evening offering, and now,** tonight, **you are neglecting Torah study.** Joshua asked him: **For which of** these sins **have you come** specially to reprove me? He **said to him: "I am now come,"** i.e., the fact that I did not come last night, but waited until now, shows that the sin of neglecting Torah study is the more severe one.

מִיָּד "וַיֵּלֶךְ יְהוֹשֻׁעַ בַּלַּיְלָה הַהוּא בְּתוֹךְ הָעֵמֶק". וְאָמַר רַבִּי יוֹחָנָן: מְלַמֵּד שֶׁהָלַךְ בְּעוֹמְקָהּ שֶׁל הֲלָכָה.

Joshua **immediately** acted to rectify the matter by deciding that he must devote more time to learning Torah, as it is stated: **"And Joshua walked that night in the midst of the valley**[N] [*ha'emek*]" (Joshua 8:13). **And Rabbi Yoḥanan said:** This **teaches that he walked** all night **in the depth** [*be'omeka*] **of** ***halakha***, thereby atoning for his previous neglect of Torah study.

וּגְמִירִי: דְּכָל זְמַן שֶׁאָרוֹן וּשְׁכִינָה שְׁרוּיִין שֶׁלֹּא בִּמְקוֹמָן – אֲסוּרִין בְּתַשְׁמִישׁ הַמִּטָּה.

And they learned as a tradition that **any time that the Ark and the Divine Presence are not resting in their** proper **places,** the entire Jewish people **are prohibited** from engaging **in marital relations.** Owing to the nation's preoccupation with war, the Ark was not restored to its rightful place in the Tabernacle. Since Joshua did not attend to this state of affairs, he was responsible for the people's neglect of the commandment to be fruitful and multiply,[N] for which he was punished by remaining childless.

אֲמַר רַבִּי שְׁמוּאֵל בַּר אִינְיָא מִשְּׁמֵיהּ דְּרַב: גָּדוֹל תַּלְמוּד תּוֹרָה יוֹתֵר מֵהַקְרָבַת תְּמִידִין, דַּאֲמַר לֵיהּ: עַתָּה בָאתִי.

The Gemara now cites a further teaching in this regard: **Rabbi Shmuel bar Inya said in the name of Rav: Torah study is greater than the offering of daily** sacrifices, as the angel **said to** Joshua: **"I am now come,"** i.e., on account of the second sin, demonstrating that neglect of Torah study is a more serious offense than neglect of the daily offerings.

אָמַר רַב בְּרוּנָא אָמַר רַב: כָּל הַיָּשֵׁן בְּקִילְעָא שֶׁאִישׁ וְאִשְׁתּוֹ שְׁרוּיִין בָּהּ – עָלָיו הַכָּתוּב אוֹמֵר: "נְשֵׁי עַמִּי תְּגָרְשׁוּן מִבֵּית תַּעֲנוּגֶיהָ".

With regard to the neglect of the commandment of procreation, **Rav Beruna said** that **Rav said: Whoever sleeps in a chamber in which a husband and wife are resting,** thus thwarting their intimacy, **the verse says about him: "The women of my people you cast out from their pleasant houses"** (Micah 2:9), and his punishment is detailed in that chapter.

וְאָמַר רַב יוֹסֵף: אֲפִילּוּ בְּאִשְׁתּוֹ נִדָּה.

And Rav Yosef said: This applies not only to a woman who is ritually pure and permitted to her husband, but **even in** the case of a man **whose wife is menstruating,**[N] for even then, although she is prohibited to him, they are more comfortable being alone together.

רָבָא אָמַר: אִם אִשְׁתּוֹ נִדָּה הִיא – תָּבֹא עָלָיו בְּרָכָה. וְלָא הִיא, דְּעַד הָאִידָּנָא מַאן נָטְרֵיהּ.

Rava said: If his wife is menstruating, may a blessing come upon the person sleeping in the room, for he protects the couple from the possibility of sin. The Gemara rejects this: **But that is not so,** i.e., this argument is invalid, **for who protected** the husband **until now?** In other words, there is no need for concern in this case, and hence one must refrain from behavior that causes distress to the couple.

הַהוּא מְבוֹאָה דַּהֲוָה דָּיֵיר בָּהּ לַחְמָן בַּר רִיסְתַּק, אֲמַרוּ לֵיהּ: אוֹגַר לָן רְשׁוּתָךְ. לָא אוֹגַר לְהוּ.

The Gemara returns to the issue of renting out domains for the purpose of an *eiruv*. The Gemara relates that **there was a certain alleyway in which** the gentile, **Laḥman bar Ristak, lived.** His Jewish neighbors **said to him: Rent us your domain,**[N] i.e., your right to use the alleyway, so that it will not render it prohibited for us to carry. **He would not rent** it **to them,** and therefore they could not carry in the alleyway on Shabbat.

NOTES

And Joshua walked…in the midst of the valley – וַיֵּלֶךְ...בְּתוֹךְ הָעֵמֶק: Parallel versions of this discussion cite a different verse: "But Joshua lodged that night among the people" (Joshua 8:9). Apparently, both verses together teach that he was deeply involved in the study of *halakha* that night. It should be noted that this did not actually occur immediately after the angel spoke, but later, before the war against Ai. The Maharsha adds that the idea that the angel came to reprove Joshua for neglecting the Torah is explicitly supported by verses that follow the passage where Joshua reads the Torah before the people (see Joshua 8).

The neglect of the commandment to be fruitful and multiply – בִּיטּוּל פְּרִיָּה וּרְבִיָּה: The early authorities ask: How do we know that Joshua was not punished for neglecting the daily offering or for the neglect of the Torah? They answer that God metes out punishment based on the principle of measure for measure. Since Joshua had no children, he must have been punished for causing the nation to neglect the commandment to be fruitful and multiply (*Tosafot*).

In the case of a man whose wife is menstruating – בְּאִשְׁתּוֹ נִדָּה: Even though such a couple may not engage in relations, the presence of a stranger still prevents them from discussing private matters. In addition, a woman desires to be close to her husband (Rabbeinu Yehonatan).

Rent us your domain – אוֹגַר לָן רְשׁוּתָךְ: The Rif adds an exchange in which the Jewish residents requested of Laḥman bar Ristak: Renounce your domain in our favor; and he refused to do so. Rabbeinu Yehonatan explains that even though the renunciation of rights is ineffective in the case of a gentile, they wanted to test whether he would be willing to compromise.

אָתוּ אֲמַרוּ לֵיהּ לְאַבַּיֵי; אֲמַר לְהוּ: זִילוּ בַּטִּילוּ רְשׁוּתַיְיכוּ לְגַבֵּי חַד, הֲוָה לֵיהּ יָחִיד בִּמְקוֹם גּוֹי, וְיָחִיד בִּמְקוֹם גּוֹי לֹא אָסַר.

The Jewish neighbors **came** and **spoke to Abaye,** asking him how they might proceed. He **said to them: Go,** all of you, and **renounce your domains,** i.e., your rights to use the alleyway, **in favor of one** person, who will be permitted to carry in it. In this manner **it is** a case of **one individual** living **in the** same **place as a gentile. And** the *halakha* has already been established that in the case of **one individual** living **in the** same **place as a gentile,** the gentile **does not render it prohibited** for him to carry. Consequently, one person at least will be able to make use of the alleyway.[H]

אֲמַרוּ לֵיהּ: מִידֵּי הוּא טַעְמָא אֶלָּא דְּלָא שְׁכִיחַ דְּדָיְירִי – וְהָכָא הָא קָדָיְירִי!

They said to him: But isn't the reason that no restrictions are imposed when one person lives together with a gentile in the same courtyard **only that it is not common for** people **to live** with a gentile in that fashion? **But here,** many people **are** in fact **living** in the same alleyway as the gentile. In this more common situation, the Sages did impose restrictions.

אֲמַר לְהוּ: כָּל בְּטוּלֵי רְשׁוּתַיְיהוּ גַּבֵּי חַד – מִילְּתָא דְּלָא שְׁכִיחָא הִיא, וּמִילְּתָא דְּלָא שְׁכִיחָא לָא גְּזַרוּ בָּהּ רַבָּנַן.

Abaye **said to them: Any renunciation of the domains** of many people **in favor of a** single **individual is an uncommon occurrence.** The principle is that in the case of **an uncommon occurrence,**[N] **the Sages did not issue a decree** as a preventive measure. In pressing circumstances such as these, one may rely on this allowance.

אֲזַל רַב הוּנָא בְּרֵיהּ דְּרַב יְהוֹשֻׁעַ אֲמָרָהּ לִשְׁמַעְתָּא קַמֵּיהּ דְּרָבָא, אֲמַר לֵיהּ:

Rav Huna, son of Rav Yehoshua, went and **reported this** ***halakha*** **before Rava,** who **said to him:**

HALAKHA

Renunciation of one's domain in the place of a gentile – בִּיטּוּל רְשׁוּת בִּמְקוֹם נָכְרִי: If Jews living in a courtyard with a gentile renounce their domains in favor of one Jew, so that he would be considered a single individual living in a courtyard with a gentile, it is ineffective with regard to carrying on Shabbat. Their only recourse is to rent the gentile's residence, as stated by Rava (*Shulḥan Arukh, Oraḥ Ḥayyim* 382:2).

NOTES

An uncommon occurrence – מִילְּתָא דְּלָא שְׁכִיחָא: The rationale of the Sages for not applying their decrees to uncommon circumstances is based on the reason behind their decrees in general. A rabbinic decree does not address an action that is prohibited in and of itself. Rather, it is a safeguard to prevent the violation of another prohibition. Therefore, there is no reason to institute such preventive measures for unique and exceptional cases, as those situations are not common enough to potentially lead people to violate other prohibitions.

Perek **VI**
Daf **64** Amud **a**

אִם כֵּן בִּיטַּלְתָּ תּוֹרַת עֵירוּב מֵאוֹתוֹ מָבוֹי!

If so, you have abolished the halakhic **category of** ***eiruv*** **from that alleyway.** Since from a halakhic perspective it is considered as though only one person lives in that alleyway, there is no need for an *eiruv*. Consequently, when the residents carry in it without an *eiruv*, observers will mistakenly think that it is permitted to carry in an alleyway even without an *eiruv*.

דִּמְעָרְבִי. יֹאמְרוּ "עֵירוּב מוֹעִיל בִּמְקוֹם גּוֹי"! דְּמַכְרְזִינַן.

Rav Huna, son of Rav Yehoshua, replied: It is required **that they establish an** ***eiruv*** anyway, as a reminder of the laws of *eiruvin*, even though it serves no halakhic purpose. Rava retorted that this in turn results in a different problem: Observers will then **say** that **an** ***eiruv*** **is effective** even **in the place of a gentile,** even if he does not rent out his domain, which is against the *halakha*. He replied: **We make an announcement** to the effect that they are not carrying because of the *eiruv*, and that it only serves as a reminder.

אַכְרַזְתָּא לְדַרְדְּקֵי?!

Rava rejected this option as well: Can we make **an announcement for the children?** Even if it is assured that all adults present will hear the announcement, how will the children, who do not hear or understand the announcement, know the *halakha* later in life? Recalling that their fathers established an *eiruv* in this alleyway, they will think that an *eiruv* is effective even in the place of a gentile. Therefore, one cannot rely on Abaye's solution.

אֶלָּא אָמַר רָבָא: לֵיזֵיל חַד מִינַּיְיהוּ – לִיקְרַב לֵיהּ וְלִשְׁאוֹל מִינֵּיהּ דּוּכְתָּא, וְלִינַּח בֵּיהּ מִידֵּי, דַּהֲוָה לֵיהּ כִּשְׂכִירוֹ וּלְקִיטוֹ. וְאָמַר רַב יְהוּדָה אָמַר שְׁמוּאֵל: אֲפִילּוּ שְׂכִירוֹ וַאֲפִילּוּ לְקִיטוֹ – נוֹתֵן עֵירוּבוֹ וְדַיּוֹ.

Rather, Rava said that the gentile's Jewish neighbors should proceed as follows: **Let one of them go and become friendly with** the gentile, **and ask him** for permission to make use of **a place** in his domain, **and set something down there, thus becoming like** the gentile's **hired laborer or harvester. And Rav Yehuda said** that **Shmuel said:** Not only can the gentile himself rent out his domain for the purpose of an *eiruv*, but **even his hired laborer, and even his harvester,**[H] if he is a Jew, **may** rent out the space and **contribute to the** ***eiruv*** on his behalf, **and this is enough.**[H]

HALAKHA

Even his hired laborer and even his harvester – אֲפִילּוּ שְׂכִירוֹ וַאֲפִילּוּ לְקִיטוֹ: A gentile's wife, his laborer, or his harvester may rent out his residence for the purpose of an *eiruv*, even without his knowledge and despite his objections (Rosh). Other authorities rule that if he objects, not even his wife may rent it out, and certainly not his hired laborer (Rambam; see *Taz*; *Shulḥan Arukh, Oraḥ Ḥayyim* 382:11).

A gentile who does not want to rent – נָכְרִי שֶׁאֵינוֹ רוֹצֶה לְהַשְׂכִּיר: If a gentile refuses to rent out his residence for the purpose of an *eiruv*, one of the residents of the alleyway should befriend him until he grants the Jewish resident permission to place something in his domain. The Jewish resident thereby attains the status of the gentile's laborer and may rent out the gentile's residence to the Jews without the gentile's permission (Rambam; Rashba). Some commentaries say that in such a case it is not even necessary to rent the residence. It is sufficient to place the *eiruv* there (Rashi; *Tur*; Rabbeinu Yeruḥam). According to the *Baḥ*, one must be stringent in accordance with both of these opinions, while the *Shulḥan Arukh HaRav* rules in accordance with the second opinion. However, one should act in accordance with Rambam's opinion *ab initio* (*Shulḥan Arukh, Oraḥ Ḥayyim* 382:12).

אֲמַר לֵיהּ אַבָּיֵי לְרַב יוֹסֵף: הָיוּ שָׁם חֲמִשָּׁה שְׂכִירוֹ וַחֲמִשָּׁה לְקִיטוֹ מַהוּ? אֲמַר לֵיהּ: אִם אָמְרוּ שְׂכִירוֹ וּלְקִיטוֹ לְהָקֵל, יֹאמְרוּ שְׂכִירוֹ וּלְקִיטוֹ לְהַחְמִיר?

Abaye said to Rav Yosef: If there were five hired laborers or five harvesters there, what is the *halakha*? Does the presence of more than one of these, if they are all Jews, entail a stringency, such that they are all required to join in the *eiruv* or that they are all required to rent out his domain? Rav Yosef **said to him: If** the Sages **said** that the gentile's **hired laborer or harvester** stands in his place **as a leniency, would they say that his hired laborer or harvester** stands in his place **as a stringency?** This law was stated only as a leniency with regard to the laws of renting for the purpose of an *eiruv*, not in order to introduce more stringencies.

גּוּפָא, אָמַר רַב יְהוּדָה אָמַר שְׁמוּאֵל: אֲפִילּוּ שְׂכִירוֹ וַאֲפִילּוּ לְקִיטוֹ נוֹתֵן עֵירוּבוֹ וְדַיּוֹ. אָמַר רַב נַחְמָן: כַּמָּה מַעַלְיָא הָא שְׁמַעְתָּא.

The Gemara proceeds to examine the ruling cited in the course of the previous discussion. Returning to **the matter itself, Rav Yehuda said** that **Shmuel said: Even** the gentile's **hired laborer, and even his harvester, may contribute to the** ***eiruv*** in his stead, **and this is enough. Rav Naḥman said: How excellent is this** ***halakha***. Even Rav Naḥman agreed with this statement, and viewed it as correct and substantiated.

אָמַר רַב יְהוּדָה אָמַר שְׁמוּאֵל: שָׁתָה רְבִיעִית יַיִן אַל יוֹרֶה. אֲמַר רַב נַחְמָן: לָא מַעַלְיָא הָא שְׁמַעְתָּא; דְּהָא אֲנָא, כָּל כַּמָּה דְּלָא שָׁתֵינָא רְבִיעֲתָא דְּחַמְרָא – לָא צִילָא דַּעֲתַאי.

However, Rav Naḥman did not give his approval to all of Rav Yehuda's rulings, as **Rav Yehuda said** that **Shmuel said: If one drank a quarter-*log* of wine, he may not issue a** halakhic **ruling,**[N] as the wine is liable to confuse his thinking.[H] With regard to this second statement, **Rav Naḥman said: This** ***halakha*** **is not excellent, as** concerning **myself, as long as I have not drunk a quarter-*log* of wine, my mind is not clear.** It is only after drinking wine that I can issue appropriate rulings.

אֲמַר לֵיהּ רָבָא: מַאי טַעְמָא אֲמַר מָר הָכִי? הָאָמַר רַבִּי אַחָא בַּר חֲנִינָא: מַאי דִּכְתִיב: ״וְרוֹעֶה זוֹנוֹת יְאַבֵּד הוֹן״ כֹּל הָאוֹמֵר: ״שְׁמוּעָה זוֹ נָאָה וְזוֹ אֵינָהּ נָאָה״ – מְאַבֵּד הוֹנָהּ שֶׁל תּוֹרָה! אֲמַר לֵיהּ: הָדְרִי בִּי.

Rava said to Rav Naḥman: **What is the reason** that **the Master said this,** making a statement that praises one *halakha* and disparages another? **Didn't Rabbi Aḥa bar Ḥanina say: What is** the meaning of that **which is written: "But he who keeps company with prostitutes [*zonot*] wastes his fortune"** (Proverbs 29:3)? It alludes to the following: **Anyone who says: This teaching is pleasant [*zo na'a*]**[N] **but this is not pleasant, loses the fortune of Torah.** It is not in keeping with the honor of Torah to make such evaluations. Rav Naḥman **said to him: I retract,** and I will no longer make such comments concerning words of Torah.

אָמַר רַבָּה בַּר רַב הוּנָא: שָׁתוּי אַל יִתְפַּלֵּל, וְאִם הִתְפַּלֵּל – תְּפִלָּתוֹ תְּפִלָּה. שִׁיכּוֹר אַל יִתְפַּלֵּל, וְאִם הִתְפַּלֵּל – תְּפִלָּתוֹ תּוֹעֵבָה.

On the topic of drinking wine, **Rabba bar Rav Huna said: One who has drunk** wine **must not pray, but if he** nonetheless **prayed, his prayer is a prayer,** i.e., he has fulfilled his obligation. On the other hand, **one who is intoxicated** with wine **must not pray, and if he prayed, his prayer is an abomination.**[H]

הֵיכִי דָּמֵי שָׁתוּי וְהֵיכִי דָּמֵי שִׁיכּוֹר? כִּי הָא דְּרַבִּי אַבָּא בַּר שׁוּמְנִי וְרַב מְנַשְּׁיָא בַּר יִרְמְיָה מִגִּיפְתִּי, הָווּ קָא מִפַּטְרִי מֵהֲדָדֵי אַמַּעַבְרָא דִּנְהַר יוֹפְטִי. אָמְרוּ: כָּל חַד מִינַּן לֵימָא מִילְּתָא דְּלָא שְׁמִיעַ לְחַבְרֵיהּ. דְּאָמַר מָרִי בַּר רַב הוּנָא: לֹא יִפָּטֵר אָדָם מֵחֲבֵירוֹ אֶלָּא מִתּוֹךְ דְּבַר הֲלָכָה, שֶׁמִּתּוֹךְ כָּךְ זוֹכְרוֹ.

The Gemara poses a question: **What are the circumstances** in which a person is considered **one who has drunk** wine; **and what are the circumstances** in which a person is considered **one who is intoxicated** with wine? The Gemara answers that one can learn this from **the following** event: **As Rabbi Abba bar Shumni and Rav Menashya bar Yirmeya from Gifti were taking leave of each other at the ford of the Yofti River, they said: Let each one of us say something that his fellow** scholar **has not** yet **heard,**[N] **for Mari bar Rav Huna said: A person must take leave of his fellow only in the midst of** a discussion **of a matter of** ***halakha*****, as due to this he will remember him.**

HALAKHA

One who has drunk should not issue a ruling – שָׁתוּי אַל יוֹרֶה: One who drinks wine should be careful not to issue halakhic rulings, even with regard to something straightforward, unless it is clear and well known to all (*Shulḥan Arukh, Yoreh De'a* 242:13, in the comment of the Rema).

One who has drunk or become intoxicated with regard to prayer – שָׁתוּי וְשִׁיכּוֹר בִּתְפִלָּה: One who has drunk alchohol, i.e., one who drinks a quarter-*log* of wine, is prohibited to pray. However, if he does pray, his prayer is valid. If one prays while intoxicated, his prayer is an abomination. An intoxicated person is defined as one who cannot speak properly in the presence of the king. He is obligated to pray again after he becomes sober. If the time for the prayer passes, he must make restitution in the following prayer, like one who omitted a prayer by mistake (*Shulḥan Arukh, Oraḥ Ḥayyim* 99:1).

NOTES

If one drank a quarter-*log* of wine, he may not issue a ruling – שָׁתָה רְבִיעִית יַיִן אַל יוֹרֶה: Proof for this principle may be adduced from the warning issued to the priests: "Do not drink wine or strong drink, you, nor your sons with you…that you may teach the children of Israel all the statutes which God has spoken to them by the hand of Moses" (Leviticus 10:9–11; Rashi).

This teaching is pleasant – שְׁמוּעָה זוֹ נָאָה: In his commentary on the book of Proverbs, Rashi explains this statement based on the fact that this is the only verse where the Hebrew word for prostitutes, *zonot*, is written plene, with a double *vav*. Consequently, the word hints to the Hebrew phrase *zu na'ot*, meaning this is pleasant. In the *Me'iri* the metaphor is explained as follows: Just as each woman is beautiful in a unique way, with some people finding her beautiful while others do not, so too is the case with *halakhot*. Therefore, a Sage should not explicitly declare that he finds a particular teaching pleasant or unpleasant. Although a Sage may reject an opinion when determining the *halakha*, he never states that the teaching is fundamentally flawed. Rather, he explains that for various reasons, it must be rejected.

Something that his fellow has not heard – מִילְּתָא דְּלָא שְׁמִיעַ לְחַבְרֵיהּ: The requirement that one may take leave of his colleague only in the midst of a matter of *halakha* can be fulfilled without stating a novel law. However, if one wishes that his colleague remember him, it is better that he say something completely new, so that the other person will recall him when he thinks about that law (Rif).

פָּתַח חַד וְאָמַר: הֵיכִי דָּמֵי שָׁתוּי וְהֵיכִי דָּמֵי שִׁיכּוֹר? שָׁתוּי – כֹּל שֶׁיָּכוֹל לְדַבֵּר לִפְנֵי הַמֶּלֶךְ, שִׁיכּוֹר – כֹּל שֶׁאֵינוֹ יָכוֹל לְדַבֵּר לִפְנֵי הַמֶּלֶךְ.

One of them **opened** the discussion **and said: What are the circumstances** where a person is considered **one who has drunk** wine, **and what are the circumstances** where a person is considered **one who is intoxicated** with wine? **One who has drunk** wine refers to **anyone** who has drunk wine but whose mind remains clear enough **that he is able to talk in the presence of a king. One who is intoxicated** refers to **anyone** who is so disoriented by the wine he has drunk **that he is not able to talk in the presence of a king.**

פָּתַח אִידָךְ וְאָמַר: הַמַּחֲזִיק בְּנִכְסֵי הַגֵּר מַה יַּעֲשֶׂה וְיִתְקַיְּימוּ בְּיָדוֹ – יִקַּח בָּהֶן סֵפֶר תּוֹרָה. אָמַר רַב שֵׁשֶׁת: אֲפִילּוּ

The other one then **opened** a different discussion **and said:** With regard to **one who took possession of a convert's property, what should he do so that it remain in his hands?**[N] The property of a convert who died without children is regarded as ownerless, and is acquired by the first person to perform a valid act of acquisition upon it. Since in this case the one who took possession of the property did not acquire it through his own labor, his ownership is tenuous, and he is liable to lose it unless he uses it for the purpose of a mitzva. One in this situation **should buy a Torah scroll with** part of the revenue, and by the merit of this act, he will retain the rest. **Rav Sheshet said: Even**

NOTES

What should he do so that it remain in his hands – מַה יַּעֲשֶׂה וְיִתְקַיְּימוּ בְּיָדוֹ: One must bear in mind that his success is not only the result of his own efforts. Indeed, whoever merits great wealth is liable to fall prey to pride and forget God. Therefore, the Sages counseled him to use part of his fortune to purchase a Torah scroll, which will remind him of his faith in God and his fear of him (*Me'iri*).

Perek **VI**
Daf **64** Amud **b**

בַּעַל בְּנִכְסֵי אִשְׁתּוֹ.

a husband who acquired rights **to his wife's property** that she had brought into the marriage as her dowry should use part of the profits for the acquisition of a Torah scroll.

רָבָא אָמַר: אֲפִילּוּ עֲבַד עִיסְקָא וְרָוַוח. רַב פַּפָּא אָמַר: אֲפִילּוּ מָצָא מְצִיאָה. אָמַר רַב נַחְמָן בַּר יִצְחָק: אֲפִילּוּ כָּתַב בְּהוּ תְּפִילִּין.

Rava said: Even if he entered into a business venture and made a large **profit,** he should act in a similar manner. **Rav Pappa said: Even if he found a lost article,** he should do the same. **Rav Naḥman bar Yitzḥak said:** He need not use the money to commission the writing of a Torah scroll, as **even if** he **wrote** a set of **phylacteries with it,**[N] this, too, is a mitzva whose merit will enable him to retain the rest of the money.

וְאָמַר רַב חָנִין וְאִיתֵימָא רַבִּי חֲנִינָא: מַאי קְרָאָה, דִּכְתִיב: ״וַיִּדַּר יִשְׂרָאֵל נֶדֶר וגו׳״.

Rav Ḥanin said, and some say it was **Rabbi Ḥanina** who said: **What is the verse** that alludes to this? **As it is written: "And Israel vowed a vow** to the Lord and said: If You will indeed deliver this people into my hand, then I will consecrate their cities" (Numbers 21:2), which shows that one who wishes to succeed should sanctify a portion of his earnings for Heaven.

אָמַר רָמִי בַּר אַבָּא: דֶּרֶךְ מִיל, וְשֵׁינָה כָּל שֶׁהוּא מְפִיגִין אֶת הַיַּיִן. אָמַר רַב נַחְמָן אָמַר רַבָּה בַּר אֲבוּהּ: לֹא שָׁנוּ אֶלָּא שֶׁשָּׁתָה כְּדֵי רְבִיעִית, אֲבָל שָׁתָה יוֹתֵר מֵרְבִיעִית – כׇּל שֶׁכֵּן שֶׁדֶּרֶךְ טוֹרַדְתּוֹ וְשֵׁינָה מְשַׁכַּרְתּוֹ.

The Gemara now cites additional teachings relating to the drinking of wine. **Rami bar Abba said:** Walking a **path of a *mil*,**[B] **and** similarly, **sleeping** even **a minimal amount,** will **dispel the** effect of **wine** that one has drunk. **Rav Naḥman said** that **Rabba bar Avuh said: They only taught** this with regard to one **who has drunk a quarter-*log*** of wine, **but** with regard to **one who has drunk more than a quarter-*log*,** this advice is not useful. In that case, walking a **path** of such a distance **will preoccupy** and exhaust **him all the more, and** a small amount **of sleep will** further **intoxicate him.**

וְדֶרֶךְ מִיל מְפִיגָה הַיַּיִן?! וְהָתַנְיָא: מַעֲשֶׂה בְּרַבָּן גַּמְלִיאֵל שֶׁהָיָה רוֹכֵב עַל הַחֲמוֹר, וְהָיָה מְהַלֵּךְ מֵעַכּוֹ לִכְזִיב, וְהָיָה רַבִּי אֶילְעַאי מְהַלֵּךְ אַחֲרָיו. מָצָא גְּלוּסְקִין בַּדֶּרֶךְ, אָמַר לוֹ: אֶילְעַאי, טוֹל גְּלוּסְקִין מִן הַדֶּרֶךְ. מָצָא גּוֹי אֶחָד, אָמַר לוֹ: מַבְגַּאי, טוֹל גְּלוּסְקִין הַלָּלוּ מֵאֶילְעַאי!

The Gemara poses a question: **Does** walking **a path of** only **a *mil* dispel the** effects of **wine? Wasn't it taught** in a *baraita*: **There was an incident involving Rabban Gamliel, who was riding a donkey and traveling from Akko to Keziv,**[B] **and** his student **Rabbi Elai was walking behind him.** Rabban Gamliel **found** some **fine loaves** of bread **on the road, and he said to** his student: **Elai, take the loaves from the road.** Further along the way, Rabban Gamliel **encountered a certain gentile** and **said to him: Mavgai, take these loaves from Elai.**

NOTES

Even if he wrote a set of phylacteries with it – אֲפִילּוּ כָּתַב בְּהוּ תְּפִילִּין: Some authorities explain this phrase differently: Even if he earned money by writing texts for phylacteries. The Sages frowned upon the idea of scribes who reap large gains by writing the texts for phylacteries and *mezuzot*. Therefore, one who earned a considerable sum in this manner should use it to purchase a Torah scroll (Maharsha).

BACKGROUND

A path of a *mil* – דֶּרֶךְ מִיל: The authorities disagree about the length of the *mil* mentioned by the Sages. According to the various opinions, a *mil* measures 960–1,200 m.

From Akko to Keziv – מֵעַכּוֹ לִכְזִיב:

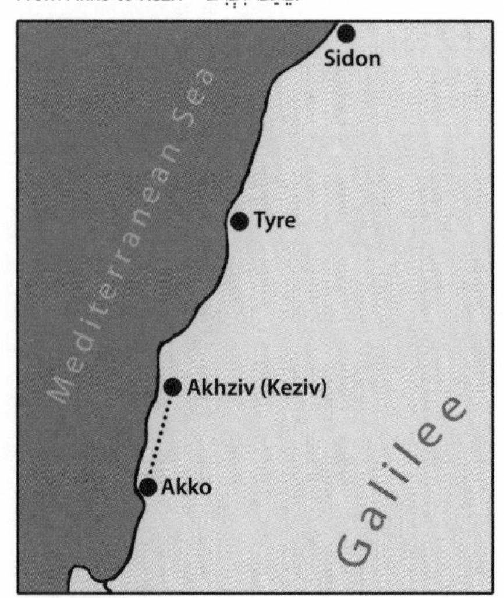

Map showing the city of Akko and the town of Akhziv (Keziv) along the northern coast of Eretz Yisrael

נִיטְפַּל לוֹ רַבִּי אֶילְעַאי, אָמַר לוֹ: מֵהֵיכָן אַתָּה? אָמַר לוֹ: מֵעֲיָירוֹת שֶׁל בּוּרְגָּנִין, וּמַה שְּׁמֶךָ? מַבְגַּאי שְׁמֵנִי. כְּלוּם הִיכִּירְךָ רַבָּן גַּמְלִיאֵל מֵעוֹלָם? אָמַר לוֹ: לָאו.

Elai joined the gentile **and said to him: Where are you from?** He **said to him: From the** nearby **towns of guardsmen.** He asked: **And what is your name?** The gentile replied: **My name is Mavgai.** He then inquired: **Has Rabban Gamliel ever met you before,** seeing as he knows your name? He **said to him: No.**

בְּאוֹתָהּ שָׁעָה לָמַדְנוּ שֶׁכִּוֵּון רַבָּן גַּמְלִיאֵל בְּרוּחַ הַקּוֹדֶשׁ. וּשְׁלֹשָׁה דְּבָרִים לָמַדְנוּ בְּאוֹתָהּ שָׁעָה: לָמַדְנוּ שֶׁאֵין מַעֲבִירִין עַל הָאוֹכָלִין,

The Gemara interrupts the story in order to comment: **At that time we learned that Rabban Gamliel divined** the gentile's name **by way of divine inspiration** that rested upon him. **And at that time we** also **learned three matters** of *halakha* from Rabban Gamliel's behavior: **We learned that one may not pass by food,** i.e., if a person sees food lying on the ground, he must stop and pick it up.

וְלָמַדְנוּ שֶׁהוֹלְכִין אַחֲרֵי רוֹב עוֹבְרֵי דְרָכִים, וְלָמַדְנוּ שֶׁחֲמֵצוֹ שֶׁל גּוֹי אַחַר הַפֶּסַח מוּתָּר בַּהֲנָאָה.

We also **learned that we follow the majority of travelers.** Since the area was populated mostly by gentiles, Rabban Gamliel assumed that the loaf belonged to a gentile, and was consequently prohibited to be eaten by a Jew. Therefore, he ordered that it be given to a gentile. And **we** further **learned that** with regard to **leavened bread belonging to a gentile,**[H] **it is permitted** to **benefit**[N] from this food **after Passover.** The incident recounted above occurred not long after the festival of Passover. By giving the loaf to the gentile instead of burning it in accordance with the *halakhot* of leavened bread that remains after Passover, Rabban Gamliel gained a certain benefit from it in the form of the gentile's gratitude. This benefit is regarded as having monetary value.

כֵּיוָן שֶׁהִגִּיעַ לִכְזִיב בָּא אֶחָד לִישָּׁאֵל עַל נִדְרוֹ, אָמַר לָזֶה שֶׁעִמּוֹ: כְּלוּם שָׁתִינוּ רְבִיעִית יַיִן הָאִיטַלְקִי? אָמַר לוֹ: הֵן. אִם כֵּן יְטַיֵּיל אַחֲרֵינוּ עַד שֶׁיָּפִיג יֵינֵנוּ.

The Gemara resumes the narrative: **When** Rabban Gamliel **arrived in Keziv,** a person **came** before him **to request** that he dissolve **his vow.** Rabban Gamliel **said to the one who was with him,** i.e., Rabbi Elai: **Did we drink a quarter-***log* **of Italian wine** earlier? He **said to him: Yes.** Rabban Gamliel replied: **If so, let him journey after us until** the effect of **our wine is dispelled,** after which we may consider his issue.

וְטִיֵּיל אַחֲרֵיהֶן שְׁלֹשָׁה מִילִין, עַד שֶׁהִגִּיעַ לְסוּלְמָא שֶׁל צוֹר. כֵּיוָן שֶׁהִגִּיעַ לְסוּלְמָא דְּצוֹר יָרַד רַבָּן גַּמְלִיאֵל מִן הַחֲמוֹר, וְנִתְעַטֵּף וְיָשַׁב, וְהִתִּיר לוֹ נִדְרוֹ.

And that person **journeyed after them** for **three** ***mil*****, until** Rabban Gamliel **arrived at the Ladder of Tyre. When he arrived at the Ladder of Tyre, Rabban Gamliel alighted from his donkey and wrapped himself** in his shawl in the customary manner of a judge, who wraps himself in a shawl in order to sit in awe at the time of judgment, **and he sat and dissolved his vow.**

וְהַרְבֵּה דְּבָרִים לָמַדְנוּ בְּאוֹתָהּ שָׁעָה: לָמַדְנוּ שֶׁרְבִיעִית יַיִן הָאִיטַלְקִי מְשַׁכֵּר, וְלָמַדְנוּ: שִׁיכּוֹר אַל יוֹרֶה, וְלָמַדְנוּ שֶׁדֶּרֶךְ מְפִיגָה אֶת הַיַּיִן, וְלָמַדְנוּ שֶׁאֵין מְפִירִין נְדָרִים לֹא רָכוּב וְלֹא מְהַלֵּךְ וְלֹא עוֹמֵד אֶלָּא יוֹשֵׁב.

The Gemara continues: **At that time we learned many matters** of *halakha* from Rabban Gamliel's conduct. **We learned that a quarter-***log* **of Italian wine intoxicates, and we learned** that **one who is intoxicated may not issue a** halakhic **ruling, and we learned that** walking on **a path dispels** the effect **of wine, and** lastly **we learned that one may not annul vows** when he is **either mounted** on an animal, **or walking,** or even **standing, but** only when he is **sitting.**

קָתָנֵי מִיהַת שְׁלֹשָׁה מִילִין! שָׁאנֵי יַיִן הָאִיטַלְקִי – דִּמְשַׁכֵּר טְפֵי.

In any event, the *baraita* **is teaching** that Rabban Gamliel found it necessary to walk **three** ***mil*** in order to become sober after drinking wine. The Gemara resolves the contradiction. **Italian wine is different** in that **it is more intoxicating,** therefore more extended activity is required in order to dispel its effects.

וְהָאָמַר רַב נַחְמָן אָמַר רַבָּה בַּר אֲבוּהּ: לֹא שָׁנוּ אֶלָּא שֶׁשָּׁתָה רְבִיעִית, אֲבָל שָׁתָה יוֹתֵר מֵרְבִיעִית – כׇּל שֶׁכֵּן דֶּרֶךְ טוֹרַדְתּוֹ וְשֵׁינָה מְשַׁכַּרְתּוֹ!

The Gemara poses a question: **But didn't Rav Naḥman say** that **Rabba bar Avuh said: They taught** this **only** with regard to one **who has drunk a quarter-***log* of wine, **but** with regard to **one who has drunk more than a quarter-***log***, walking** that distance **will preoccupy** and exhaust **him all the more, and** a small amount of **sleep** will further **intoxicate him?** If Italian wine is more intoxicating than other wine, shouldn't a quarter-*log* be considered like a larger quantity of other wine?

רָכוּב שָׁאנֵי. הַשְׁתָּא דְּאָתֵית לְהָכִי – לְרָמֵי בַּר אַבָּא נַמִי לָא קַשְׁיָא, רָכוּב שָׁאנֵי.

The Gemara answers: Being **mounted** on an animal **is different** from walking; since he is not on foot it is not such a tiring activity. Accordingly, riding three *mil* will not exhaust him; rather, it will dispel the effect of the wine. The Gemara adds: **Now that you have arrived at this** conclusion, **according to Rami bar Abba,** who says that walking one *mil* is sufficient, **it is also not difficult,** as he too can say that **riding is different** from walking. Since one is not on foot, the effects of the wine are not dispelled as quickly. Therefore, three *mil* is necessary.[H]

HALAKHA

Leavened bread belonging to a gentile – **חָמֵץ שֶׁל גּוֹי**: One is permitted to derive benefit from and even eat leavened bread that belonged to a gentile, even if it was in his possession during Passover (*Shulḥan Arukh, Oraḥ Ḥayyim* 448:1).

Dispelling the effects of wine – **הֲפָגַת הַיַּיִן**: The effects of drinking up to a quarter-*log* of wine can be dispelled by walking a *mil* or by sleeping for any duration. If one drinks more than a quarter-*log*, a small amount of sleep (*Magen Avraham*, based on the Rambam) causes him to become even more intoxicated. Riding three *mil* serves to dispel the effects of the wine, as demonstrated by the incident involving Rabban Gamliel (*Shulḥan Arukh, Oraḥ Ḥayyim* 99:2).

NOTES

Permitted to benefit – **מוּתָּר בַּהֲנָאָה**: The proof is based on the accepted principle that any gift provides benefit to the giver as well as to the recipient, because a gift obligates, or at least prompts, the receiving party to reciprocate. Therefore, one who bestows a gift also benefits from it to a certain extent.

NOTES

An opening enabling the dissolution of vows – פֶּתַח בִּנְדָרִים: The Sages derived from the Torah that a person may abrogate the obligations imposed by his vows by having them annulled by a Sage or a court. Tractate *Nedarim* discusses at great length the various methods of abrogating vows. One of the disputes on this matter concerns the question of whether a Sage may annul a vow if the one who took the vow merely expresses regret for making it, or whether the Sage must find an entrance, i.e., a special reason, to annul it. An example of an entrance is a scenario in which the person would certainly not have taken the vow had he known its ramifications. The laws of entrances for vows are complex, and not all special reasons are accepted as valid grounds for annulment of the vow. For example, one may not use the entrance found by Rabban Gamliel, which focuses on the prohibition engendered by the vow itself.

Jewish women are practiced in witchcraft – בְּנוֹת יִשְׂרָאֵל פְּרוּצוֹת בִּכְשָׁפִים: This statement does not mean that Jewish women alone practiced witchcraft, but rather that they, too, practiced the art (*Ge'on Ya'akov*).

אִינִי?! וְהָאָמַר רַב נַחְמָן: מְפִירִין נְדָרִים בֵּין מְהַלֵּךְ בֵּין עוֹמֵד וּבֵין רָכוּב!

The Gemara poses a question with regard to one of the details of the story: **Is that so,** that Rabban Gamliel was required to alight from his donkey in order to annul the vow? **But didn't Rav Naḥman say: One may annul vows walking, standing, or mounted?** Why, then, did Rabban Gamliel dismount his donkey?

תַּנָּאֵי הִיא, דְּאִיכָּא לְמַאן דְּאָמַר פּוֹתְחִין בַּחֲרָטָה

The Gemara answers: **This is** a dispute between ***tanna'im*****, as there is** an authority **who says** that **one** may **open** the possibility for dissolution of a vow[N] **by means of regret** alone.[H] In other words, there is no need to search for a special reason in order to dissolve a person's vow; it is enough to ascertain that he regrets making it. This can be done easily, even while walking, standing, or riding.

וְאִיכָּא לְמַאן דְּאָמַר אֵין פּוֹתְחִין בַּחֲרָטָה.

And there is another authority **who says** that **one** may **not open** the possibility for dissolution of a vow **by means of regret** alone. Rather, one must find an opening, i.e., a particular reason to dissolve the vow in question, which requires a thorough analysis of the circumstances of the vow. This task must be performed free of distractions, which means one must be seated (*Tosafot*).[H]

דְּאָמַר רַבָּה בַּר בַּר חָנָה אָמַר רַבִּי יוֹחָנָן: מַאי פָּתַח לֵיהּ רַבָּן גַּמְלִיאֵל לְהַהוּא גַּבְרָא – ״יֵשׁ בּוֹטֶה כְּמַדְקְרוֹת חָרֶב וּלְשׁוֹן חֲכָמִים מַרְפֵּא״, כָּל הַבּוֹטֶה רָאוּי לְדוֹקְרוֹ בַּחֶרֶב, אֶלָּא שֶׁלְּשׁוֹן חֲכָמִים מַרְפֵּא.

As Rabba bar bar Ḥana said that **Rabbi Yoḥanan said:** With **what did Rabban Gamliel open** the possibility for dissolving his vow **for that man,** i.e., what opening did he find for him? Rabban Gamliel cited the verse: **"There is one who utters like the piercings of a sword; but the tongue of the wise is health"** (Proverbs 12:18) and explained it as follows: **Whoever utters** a vow **deserves to be pierced**[H] **by a sword,** as he might fail to fulfill it. Therefore, one should not vow at all. Had you known that whoever vows is liable to be executed, would you have vowed? **Rather, it is the tongue of the wise that heals,** as when a Sage dissolves a vow, he dissolves it retroactively, and it is as though one had never taken the vow.

אָמַר מָר: וְאֵין מַעֲבִירִין עַל הָאוֹכָלִין. אָמַר רַבִּי יוֹחָנָן מִשּׁוּם רַבִּי שִׁמְעוֹן בֶּן יוֹחַאי: לֹא שָׁנוּ אֶלָּא בַּדּוֹרוֹת הָרִאשׁוֹנִים, שֶׁאֵין בְּנוֹת יִשְׂרָאֵל פְּרוּצוֹת בִּכְשָׁפִים. אֲבָל בַּדּוֹרוֹת הָאַחֲרוֹנִים, שֶׁבְּנוֹת יִשְׂרָאֵל פְּרוּצוֹת בִּכְשָׁפִים – מַעֲבִירִין.

The Gemara continues with its analysis of the *baraita*. **The Master said** previously: One of the *halakhot* learned from the incident involving Rabban Gamliel was that **one may not pass by food;** rather, one must treat the food with respect and pick it up.[H] **Rabbi Yoḥanan said in the name of Rabbi Shimon bar Yoḥai: They taught** this ruling **only in the early generations, when Jewish women were not accustomed to using witchcraft. However, in the later generations, when Jewish women are accustomed to using witchcraft,**[N] **one may pass by** food, as a spell might have been cast on the bread, and one must not put himself in unnecessary danger.

תָּנָא: שְׁלֵימִין – מַעֲבִירִין, פְּתִיתִין – אֵין מַעֲבִירִין. אֲמַר לֵיהּ רַב אַסִי לְרַב אַשִׁי: וְאַפְּתִיתִין לָא עָבְדָן? וְהָכְתִיב: ״וַתְּחַלֶּלְנָה אוֹתִי אֶל עַמִּי בְּשַׁעֲלֵי שְׂעוֹרִים וּבִפְתוֹתֵי לֶחֶם״! דְּשָׁקְלֵי בְּאַגְרַיְיהוּ.

A Sage **taught:** If the loaves are **whole, one** may **pass** them **by,** as they might have been placed there for the purposes of witchcraft; however, if they are in **pieces, one** may **not pass** them **by,** because bread in pieces is not used for witchcraft. **Rav Asi said to Rav Ashi:** Do they **not perform** magic with **pieces** of bread? **Isn't it written** in the verse that deals with witchcraft: **"And you have profaned Me among My people for handfuls of barley and for pieces of bread"** (Ezekiel 13:19)? The Gemara answers: The verse does not mean that they used pieces of bread in their witchcraft, but rather that **they took** such pieces **as their wages.**

אָמַר רַב שֵׁשֶׁת מִשּׁוּם רַבִּי אֶלְעָזָר בֶּן עֲזַרְיָה:

Rav Sheshet said in the name of Rabbi Elazar ben Azarya:

HALAKHA

Open by means of regret alone – פּוֹתְחִין בַּחֲרָטָה: If one makes a vow and later regrets the content of the vow, it may be dissolved based solely on his regret. An opening for the dissolution of vows is required in a case where one regrets not the vow itself, but the fact that he accepted the matter upon himself in the form of a vow (*Tosafot*). Other commentaries teach that even if one regrets the vow itself, it is necessary to find an opening and a reason to dissolve the vow, as regret alone is insufficient (Rashi; Rambam *Sefer Hafla'a, Hilkhot Shevuot* 6:1; *Shulḥan Arukh, Yoreh De'a* 228:7).

Annulling a vow while sitting – הֲפָרַת נְדָרִים בִּישִׁיבָה: The annulment of a vow that a person regrets completely may be performed even while standing. However, if one does not entirely regret the vow, and it is therefore necessary to find an opening in order to annul it, this must be done while sitting. Fundamentally, the *halakha* does not require the one who took the vow to stand during this procedure, but it is customary for him to do so (*Shulḥan Arukh, Yoreh De'a* 228:4).

Whoever utters a vow deserves to be pierced – כָּל הַבּוֹטֶה רָאוּי לְדוֹקְרוֹ: One who makes a vow is considered a sinner and a wicked person, even if he fulfills it. It is proper for a person not to vow at all (*Shulḥan Arukh, Yoreh De'a* 203:1).

Passing by food – הַעֲבָרָה עַל אוֹכָלִין: It is prohibited to pass bread or any other edible food and allow it to be wasted. One certainly may not actively throw away food. If the amount of food is less than an olive-bulk, there is no prohibition involved, but it is still not proper do so (*Shulḥan Arukh, Oraḥ Ḥayyim* 180:4).

יָכוֹל אֲנִי לִפְטוֹר אֶת כׇּל הָעוֹלָם כּוּלּוֹ מִן הַדִּין מִיּוֹם שֶׁחָרַב בֵּית הַמִּקְדָּשׁ וְעַד עַכְשָׁיו, שֶׁנֶּאֱמַר: ״לָכֵן שִׁמְעִי נָא זֹאת עֲנִיָּה וּשְׁכֻרַת וְלֹא מִיָּיִן״.

I can make an argument that **exempts the entire world from judgment, from the day that the Temple was destroyed until now. As it is stated: "Therefore, hear now this, you afflicted and drunken, but not from wine"** (Isaiah 51:21), which teaches that in the wake of the destruction of the Temple, all Jews are considered intoxicated and are not responsible for any sins they commit.

מֵיתִיבִי: שִׁיכּוֹר מִקָּחוֹ מִקָּח וּמִמְכָּרוֹ מִמְכָּר, עָבַר עֲבֵירָה שֶׁיֵּשׁ בָּהּ מִיתָה – מְמִיתִין אוֹתוֹ, מַלְקוּת – מַלְקִין אוֹתוֹ, כְּלָלוֹ שֶׁל דָּבָר: הֲרֵי הוּא כְּפִיקֵּחַ לְכׇל דְּבָרָיו, אֶלָּא שֶׁפָּטוּר מִן הַתְּפִלָּה.

The Gemara **raises an objection** to this argument from the following *baraita*: With regard to one who is **intoxicated, his acquisition is a** binding **acquisition**; that is, he cannot retract the transaction when he is sober, **and** similarly, **his sale is a** binding **sale.** Moreover, **if he committed a transgression for which** he is liable to receive the **death** penalty, **he is executed;** and if the offense is punishable by **lashes, he is flogged. The principle is** that **he is like a sober person in all matters, except that he is exempt from prayer.** Therefore, even if the people of Israel are considered drunk, they are nonetheless responsible for their actions.

מַאי ״יְכוֹלַנִי לִפְטוֹר״ דְּקָאָמַר – נַמִי מִדִּין תְּפִלָּה.

The Gemara answers that even Rabbi Elazar ben Azarya did not mean that they should be exempt from liability for all their sins. Rather, **what is** the meaning of **his statement: I can exempt?** He, **too,** meant that he could exempt them **from the judgment of prayer,** i.e., Jews cannot be held liable for praying without the proper intentions.

אָמַר רַבִּי חֲנִינָא: לֹא שָׁנוּ אֶלָּא שֶׁלֹּא הִגִּיעַ לְשִׁכְרוּתוֹ שֶׁל לוֹט, אֲבָל הִגִּיעַ לְשִׁכְרוּתוֹ שֶׁל לוֹט – פָּטוּר מִכּוּלָּם.

Rabbi Ḥanina said: They taught that an intoxicated person is responsible for all his actions **only** in a case where **he did not reach the** state of **intoxication of Lot; however, if he reached the** state of **intoxication of Lot,** so that he is altogether unaware of his actions, **he is exempt from all** liability.[NH]

אָמַר רַבִּי חֲנִינָא: כׇּל הַמֵּפִיק מָגֵן בִּשְׁעַת גַּאֲוָה סוֹגְרִין וְחוֹתְמִין צָרוֹת בַּעֲדוֹ שֶׁנֶּאֱמַר: ״גַּאֲוָה אֲפִיקֵי מָגִנִּים סָגוּר חוֹתָם צָר״.

Rabbi Ḥanina said: Whoever passes a shield over himself **at a time of arrogance,**[N] i.e., whoever suppresses his evil inclination as though it were covered with a shield when he is arrogant, e.g., when he is intoxicated or the like (Rabbeinu Ḥananel), **troubles will be closed and sealed from him, as it is stated: "The channels of [*afikei*] his scales are his pride, closed together as with a tight [*tzar*] seal"** (Job 41:7). The verse is interpreted homiletically: When at a time of arrogance a person passes a shield [*mapik*] over his evil inclination, his troubles [*tzarot*] will be closed and sealed before him.

מַאי מַשְׁמַע דְּהַאי אָפִיק לִישָּׁנָא דְּעַבּוֹרֵי הוּא, דִּכְתִיב: ״אַחַי בָּגְדוּ כְמוֹ נָחַל כַּאֲפִיק נְחָלִים יַעֲבוֹרוּ״.

The Gemara poses a question: **From where may it be inferred that** the meaning of **this** word ***afik*** **is a formulation** denoting **passing [*aborei*]?** The Gemara answers: **As it is written: "My brothers have dealt deceitfully like a wadi, like the channel [*afik*] of brooks that pass by [*ya'avoru*]"** (Job 6:15). This implies that the term *afik* is synonymous with the verb *ya'avoru*, which refers to something that travels and passes by.

רַבִּי יוֹחָנָן אָמַר: כׇּל שֶׁאֵינוֹ מֵפִיק אִתְּמַר.

Rabbi Yoḥanan said: This is not the correct interpretation; rather, **it was stated** that **whoever does not** cover, but **draws out [*mapik*]** a shield at a time of arrogance, troubles will be closed and sealed from him. In other words, a person must draw his weapons and shield in order to fight his evil inclination when it tries to overpower him (Rabbeinu Ḥananel).

מַאי מַשְׁמַע דְּהַאי מַפִּיק לִישָּׁנָא דְּגַלּוֹיֵי הוּא, דִּכְתִיב: ״וַיֵּרָאוּ אֲפִיקֵי מַיִם וַיִּגָּלוּ מוֹסְדוֹת תֵּבֵל״.

The Gemara poses a question: **From where may it be inferred that this word *mapik* is a formulation** denoting **revealing?** The Gemara answers: **As it is written: "The channels of [*afikei*] waters were seen, and the foundations of the world were laid bare"** (Psalms 18:16).

NOTES

The level of responsibility of an intoxicated person – **אַחְרָיוּתוֹ שֶׁל שִׁיכּוֹר**: Although one's clarity of mind is impaired when he is intoxicated, one may nevertheless be legally responsible for his actions, as he need not be fully mentally competent to incur legal responsibility. Were this not the case, there would be no way of fully determining one's obligations and responsibilities in any situation, for people are often not fully competent and aware at various times, even when sober. However, if a person is as drunk as Lot, so that not only is his reasoning impaired, but he is also rendered completely unable to make conscious decisions, he is considered compelled by forces beyond his control and is entirely lacking legal competence.

Whoever passes a shield over himself at a time of arrogance – **הַמֵּפִיק מָגֵן בִּשְׁעַת גַּאֲוָה**: See Rashi, who explains this slightly differently. Ritva interprets Rashi to mean that the word *magen*, literally meaning shield, is a general term for prayer. This interpretation is based either on the fact that the first blessing of the *Amida* prayer ends with the phrase: Shield of Abraham, or on the concept that prayer serves as a shield in times of trouble. The Ra'avad explains that the words: Time of arrogance, refer to the time of sleep. According to his explanation, the Sage who says that the word *mapik* means to pass by teaches that one should sleep as much as necessary until he wakes up of his own accord. The other opinion, that *mapik* means to reveal, indicates that one should rest for only a short time so that his sobriety is restored, after which he should pray. Therefore, the discussion concerns the question of whether one should make the effort to pray even when tired, or if it is better for him to first sleep briefly.

HALAKHA

The level of responsibility of an intoxicated person – **אַחְרָיוּתוֹ שֶׁל שִׁיכּוֹר**: The legal status of an intoxicated person is that of a competent person in almost all respects: His commercial transactions are valid, as are his acts of marriage and divorce. If he commits a transgression, he is punished for it, even by lashes or by execution. The only exception is that he is exempt from prayer. However, if one is as drunk as Lot, he has the status of an imbecile, whose actions are of no consequence (*Shulḥan Arukh*, *Even HaEzer* 44:3, *Ḥoshen Mishpat* 235:22).

מִכְּדִי, קְרָאֵי מַשְׁמַע בֵּין לְמָר וּבֵין לְמָר, מַאי בֵּינַיְיהוּ? אִיכָּא בֵּינַיְיהוּ דְּרַב שֵׁשֶׁת. דְּרַב שֵׁשֶׁת מָסַר שִׁינְתֵיהּ לְשַׁמָּעֵיהּ, מָר אִית לֵיהּ דְּרַב שֵׁשֶׁת, וּמָר לֵית לֵיהּ דְּרַב שֵׁשֶׁת.

The Gemara asks: **Now, since the verses may be interpreted both in accordance with** the opinion **of this Master and in accordance with** the opinion of the other **Master, what is** the practical difference **between them?** The Gemara answers: **The** practical difference **between them is** with regard to the following practice of **Rav Sheshet, as Rav Sheshet gave** the responsibility for monitoring **his sleep to his attendant,** instructing the attendant to wake him when the time for prayer arrived. One **Sage,** Rabbi Ḥanina, **is of** the opinion that the practice of **Rav Sheshet** is correct, as Rabbi Ḥanina maintains that if one is in great need of sleep, it is better to nap for a while and then wake up with renewed vigor. **And one Sage,** Rabbi Yoḥanan, **is not of** the opinion that the practice of **Rav Sheshet** is correct. He holds that a person must marshal his strength and pray, rather than succumb to the need for sleep.

אָמַר רַב חִיָּיא בַּר אַשִׁי אָמַר רַב: כֹּל שֶׁאֵין דַּעְתּוֹ מְיוּשֶּׁבֶת עָלָיו – אַל יִתְפַּלֵּל. מִשּׁוּם שֶׁנֶּאֱמַר: ״בַּצַּר אַל יוֹרֶה״. רַבִּי חֲנִינָא בְּיוֹמָא דְּרָתַח לָא מְצַלֵּי. אָמַר: ״בַּצַּר אַל יוֹרֶה״ כְּתִיב. מָר עוּקְבָא בְּיוֹמָא דְּשׁוּתָא לָא הֲוָה נָפֵיק לְבֵי דִּינָא.

Rav Ḥiyya bar Ashi said that **Rav said: Anyone whose mind is unsettled should not pray, as it is stated: When distressed, one should not issue decisions.**[N] The Gemara relates that **Rabbi Ḥanina, on a day that he was angry,** would **not pray,** as **he said that it is written: When distressed, one should not issue decisions.** The Gemara similarly relates that **Mar Ukva, on a day of a south wind, would not venture out to the court,** for this hot and harsh wind would disturb his usual clarity of mind.

אָמַר רַב נַחְמָן בַּר יִצְחָק: הִלְכְתָא בָּעֲיָא צִילּוּתָא כְּיוֹמָא דְּאִסְתָּנָא. אָמַר אַבַּיֵי: אִי אָמְרָה לִי אֵם קְרֵיב כּוּתְחָא – לָא תְּנָאִי.

Rav Naḥman bar Yitzḥak said: The study of ***halakha*** **requires clarity,** as on **a day** when **a north wind** blows and clears the skies. **Abaye said** similarly that **if my stepmother says to me: Bring** me a dish of ***kutaḥ*****, I can no** longer **study** Torah in my usual fashion, as even a simple task such as this troubles me and distracts me from my Torah study.

אָמַר רָבָא: אִי קָרַצְתַּן כִּינָּה – לָא תְּנָאִי. מָר בְּרֵיהּ דְּרָבִינָא עֲבַדָה לֵיהּ אִמֵּיהּ שִׁבְעָה מָנֵי לְשִׁבְעָה יוֹמֵי.

Similarly, **Rava said: If I am bitten by a louse, I can no** longer **learn** in my usual manner. The Gemara relates that **the mother of Mar, son of Ravina, would prepare seven garments for him for the seven days** of the week, so that he would not be bitten by the lice found in old clothes (Rabbeinu Ḥananel).

אֲמַר רַב יְהוּדָה: לָא אִיבְרִי לֵילְיָא אֶלָּא לְשֵׁינְתָא. אָמַר רַבִּי שִׁמְעוֹן בֶּן לָקִישׁ: לָא אִיבְרִי סִיהֲרָא אֶלָּא לְגִירְסָא. אָמְרִי לֵיהּ לְרַבִּי זֵירָא: מְחַדְּדָן שְׁמַעֲתָךְ! אֲמַר לְהוּ: דִּימָמֵי נִינְהוּ.

Rav Yehuda said: Night was created only for sleep.[N] **Rabbi Shimon ben Lakish said: The moon was created only for** Torah **study** by its light.[H] When people **said to Rabbi Zeira: Your teachings are** exceedingly **sharp, he said to them: They were** formulated **during the daytime** hours. This teaches that Torah study during the day is most beneficial to clarity of the mind.

אֲמַרָה לֵיהּ בְּרַתֵּיהּ דְּרַב חִסְדָּא לְרַב חִסְדָּא: לָא בָּעֵי מָר מֵינָם פּוּרְתָּא? אֲמַר לַהּ: הָשְׁתָּא אָתוּ יוֹמֵי דַּאֲרִיכֵי וְקַטִּינֵי, וְנֵינוּם טוּבָא.

Rav Ḥisda's daughter said to her father, **Rav Ḥisda,** who would spend his nights in study: **Doesn't the Master wish to sleep a little?** He **said to her: Days that are long** in quantity **but short** in the opportunity to study Torah and perform mitzvot **will soon arrive, and we will sleep a lot.** After I die, there will be more than enough time for sleep.

אֲמַר רַב נַחְמָן בַּר יִצְחָק: אֲנַן פּוֹעֲלֵי דִּימָמֵי אֲנַן. רַב אַחָא בַּר יַעֲקֹב יָזֵיף וּפָרַע.

Rav Naḥman bar Yitzḥak said: We, Torah scholars, **are day workers,** as our study is performed primarily during the day. The Gemara relates that **Rav Aḥa bar Ya'akov** would **borrow and repay,**[H] i.e., if for some reason he neglected to study during the day, he would use the night hours to compensate for the missed time.

NOTES

When distressed, one should not issue decisions – בַּצַּר אַל יוֹרֶה: See *Tosafot* on this point. Rashi's comments are accurate in that this verse actually comes from the book of Ben Sira (7:10), and it is from there that the Sages quoted this phrase. Although categorized as one of the apocryphal works that may not be read, the Sages themselves stated that the worthy aphorisms contained in the book of Ben Sira may be cited in his name and expounded. It is occasionally cited in the Gemara in the same manner as the books of the Bible.

Night was created only for sleep – לָא אִיבְרִי לֵילְיָא אֶלָּא לְשֵׁינְתָא: Some deduce from here that one should not sleep during the day, but rather dedicate daylight hours entirely to Torah study, as implied by the ensuing tale involving Rav Ḥisda (*Ein Ya'akov*).

HALAKHA

Torah study at night – לִימּוּד בַּלַּיְלָה: It is appropriate that one be more vigilant in studying Torah at night than he is during the day, as that is the way to merit the crown of Torah (*Shulḥan Arukh, Oraḥ Ḥayyim* 238:1, *Yoreh De'a* 246:23).

Borrow and repay – יָזֵיף וּפָרַע: If one has a fixed schedule for study each day, and one day he has to attend to some other matter so that he is unable to complete his usual schedule, he should complete his study at night. The rationale is that the schedule is considered a kind of vow. Therefore, when one accepts such a schedule upon himself, it is proper to say that he is not accepting it as a vow (*Magen Avraham*; *Shulḥan Arukh, Oraḥ Ḥayyim* 238:2).

אָמַר רַבִּי אֶלְעָזָר: הַבָּא מִן הַדֶּרֶךְ אַל יִתְפַּלֵּל שְׁלֹשָׁה יָמִים, שֶׁנֶּאֱמַר: ״וָאֶקְבְּצֵם אֶל הַנָּהָר הַבָּא אֶל אַהֲוָא וַנַּחֲנֶה שָׁם יָמִים שְׁלֹשָׁה וָאָבִינָה בָעָם וגו׳״.

Rabbi Elazar said: One who returns home **from a journey should not pray for three days** while recovering from the hardship of being on the road, **as it is stated: "And I gathered them together at the river that runs to Aḥava, and we encamped there for three days, and I inspected the people"** (Ezra 8:15), after which it is stated: "Then I proclaimed a fast there, at the river of Aḥava, that we might afflict ourselves before our God, to seek of Him a safe journey for us" (Ezra 8:21), which teaches that they rested three days before praying.

אֲבוּהּ דִּשְׁמוּאֵל, כִּי אָתֵי בְּאוֹרְחָא לָא מְצַלֵּי תְּלָתָא יוֹמֵי. שְׁמוּאֵל לָא מְצַלֵּי בְּבֵיתָא דְּאִית בֵּיהּ שִׁיכְרָא. רַב פַּפָּא לָא מְצַלֵּי בְּבֵיתָא דְּאִית בֵּיהּ הַרְסָנָא.

The Gemara relates that **Shmuel's father, when he would return** home **from his journey, would not pray** for **three days,** as he would have to rest from his journey. **Shmuel** himself **would not pray in a house that contained an alcoholic beverage,** as the scent of the alcohol would disturb his concentration during prayer. Similarly, **Rav Pappa would not pray in a house that contained small** fried **fish,** due to their smell.[H]

אָמַר רַבִּי חֲנִינָא: כָּל הַמִּתְפַּתֶּה בְּיֵינוֹ יֵשׁ בּוֹ מִדַּעַת קוֹנוֹ, שֶׁנֶּאֱמַר: ״וַיָּרַח ה׳ אֶת רֵיחַ הַנִּיחֹחַ וגו׳״.

Rabbi Ḥanina said: Whoever is appeased by his wine,[N] i.e., whoever becomes more relaxed after drinking, **has in him** an element of **the mind-set of his Creator,** who acted in a similar fashion, **as it is stated: "And the Lord smelled the sweet savor,** and the Lord said in His heart, I will not again curse the ground any more for man's sake" (Genesis 8:21). As it were, God acted more favorably toward His creatures after He was appeased with the smell of the burnt offerings. Smell can be as potent as drinking or eating itself.

אָמַר רַבִּי חִיָּיא: כָּל הַמִּתְיַישֵּׁב בְּיֵינוֹ – יֵשׁ בּוֹ דַּעַת שִׁבְעִים זְקֵנִים, יַיִן נִיתַּן בְּשִׁבְעִים אוֹתִיּוֹת, וְסוֹד נִיתַּן בְּשִׁבְעִים אוֹתִיּוֹת, נִכְנַס יַיִן יָצָא סוֹד.

Rabbi Ḥiyya said: Anyone who remains settled of mind **after** drinking **wine,** and does not become intoxicated, **has** an element of **the mind-set of seventy Elders.** The allusion is: **Wine** [*yayin* spelled *yod, yod, nun*] **was given in seventy letters,** as the numerological value of the letters comprising the word is seventy, as *yod* equals ten and *nun* equals fifty. Similarly, the word **secret** [***sod*** spelled *samekh, vav, dalet*] **was given in seventy letters,** as *samekh* equals sixty, *vav* equals six, and *dalet* equals four. Typically, when **wine entered** the body, **a secret emerged.** Whoever does not reveal secrets when he drinks is clearly blessed with a firm mind, like that of seventy Elders.

אָמַר רַבִּי חָנִין: לֹא נִבְרָא יַיִן אֶלָּא לְנַחֵם אֲבֵלִים וּלְשַׁלֵּם שָׂכָר לָרְשָׁעִים, שֶׁנֶּאֱמַר: ״תְּנוּ שֵׁכָר לְאוֹבֵד וגו׳״.

Rabbi Ḥanin said: Wine was created only in order to comfort mourners in their distress, **and to reward the wicked** in this world so they will have no reward left in the World-to-Come, **as it is stated: "Give strong drink to him that is ready to perish,** and wine to the bitter of soul. Let him drink, and forget his poverty, and remember his misery no more" (Proverbs 31:6). "Him that is ready to perish" refers to the wicked, who will perish from the world, while "the bitter of soul" denotes mourners.[N]

אָמַר רַבִּי חָנִין בַּר פַּפָּא: כֹּל שֶׁאֵין יַיִן נִשְׁפָּךְ בְּתוֹךְ בֵּיתוֹ כַּמַּיִם – אֵינוֹ בִּכְלַל בְּרָכָה, שֶׁנֶּאֱמַר: ״וּבֵרַךְ אֶת לַחְמְךָ וְאֶת מֵימֶיךָ״. מַה לֶּחֶם שֶׁנִּיקָּח בְּכֶסֶף מַעֲשֵׂר – אַף מַיִם שֶׁנִּיקָּח בְּכֶסֶף מַעֲשֵׂר. וּמַאי נִיהוּ – יַיִן, וְקָא קָרֵי לֵיהּ מַיִם.

Rabbi Ḥanin bar Pappa said: Anyone in whose house wine does not flow like water is not yet **included** in the Torah's **blessing, as it is stated: "And He shall bless your bread and your water"** (Exodus 23:25). The water mentioned in this verse actually refers to wine, as learned in the following manner: **Just as bread** is something **that may be purchased with** second-**tithe money,** i.e., one is permitted to buy bread with money used to redeem second-tithe, **so** too the word **water** in the verse is referring to a liquid **that may be purchased with** second-**tithe money. And what is that?** It is **wine,** as one may buy wine with second-tithe money, but one may not buy water; **and** nevertheless the verse **calls it "water."**

HALAKHA

Disturbances during prayer – הַטְרָדָה בִּתְפִלָּה: The early Sages said that one should not pray in a place where there is something that will disturb his concentration, or when he is tired or angry. Nowadays, people are not particular about such situations, because they do not concentrate properly during prayer in any case (*Shulḥan Arukh, Oraḥ Ḥayyim* 98:2).

NOTES

Whoever is appeased by his wine – הַמִּתְפַּתֶּה בְּיֵינוֹ: This principle does not apply only to wine. Rather, one who welcomes another person's overtures of friendship, especially when the person wishes to honor him in some way and draw closer to him, has an element of his Creator's mind-set.

The purpose for which wine was created – לְשֵׁם מַה נִּבְרָא יַיִן: Since the Sages state in several places that wine can cause much harm and lead people to sin, it was necessary to explain that it nonetheless serves a purpose in the world (*Ein Ya'akov*).

BACKGROUND

A Jew and a gentile living in the inner courtyard, while a single Jew lived in the outer one – יִשְׂרָאֵל וְגוֹי בִּפְנִימִית וְיִשְׂרָאֵל בַּחִיצוֹנָה:

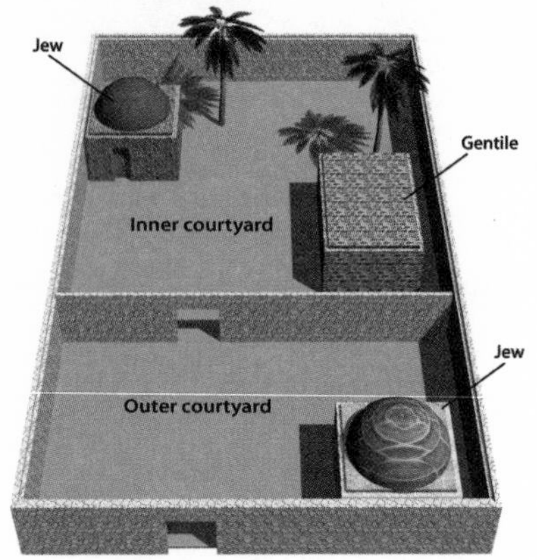

Courtyard shared by a Jew and a gentile within another courtyard in which a single Jew resides

Lecture [*pirka*] – פִּירְקָא: A *pirka* or *perek*, literally meaning chapter, is the term used to describe the regular lectures given by the *amora'im*. The lesson was an orderly explanation of a chapter of Mishna, and the *amora* giving the lecture included opinions of earlier *amora'im* and a discussion of his own opinion. The location of these lectures was also called *pirka*. Therefore, the Gemara indicates that Rabba and Rav Yosef sat at the end of the *pirka*, i.e. in the back seats, far from Rav Sheshet.

אִי נִשְׁפָּךְ בְּבֵיתוֹ כַּמַּיִם – אִיכָּא בְּרָכָה, וְאִי לָא – לָא.

This teaches that **if** wine **flows in** a person's **house like water, there is a blessing, but if not,** there is **no** blessing.

אָמַר רַבִּי אֶילְעַאי: בִּשְׁלֹשָׁה דְּבָרִים אָדָם נִיכָּר: בְּכוֹסוֹ, וּבְכִיסוֹ, וּבְכַעְסוֹ, וְאָמְרִי לַהּ: אַף בְּשַׂחֲקוֹ.

Rabbi Elai said: In three matters a person's true character is **ascertained; in his cup,** i.e., his behavior when he drinks; **in his pocket,** i.e., his conduct in his financial dealings with other people; **and in his anger.**[N] **And some say:** A person **also** reveals his real nature **in his laughter.**

אָמַר רַב יְהוּדָה אָמַר רַב: יִשְׂרָאֵל וְגוֹי בִּפְנִימִית, וְיִשְׂרָאֵל בַּחִיצוֹנָה, בָּא מַעֲשֶׂה לִפְנֵי רַבִּי וְאָסַר, וְלִפְנֵי רַבִּי חִיָּיא וְאָסַר,

The Gemara returns to the topic of *eiruvin*: **Rav Yehuda said** that **Rav said:** It once happened that there were two courtyards, one within the other,[H] with **a Jew and a gentile** living in the **inner** courtyard, **while** a single **Jew** lived **in the outer one.**[B] The **case came before Rabbi** Yehuda HaNasi for a decision as to whether carrying in the outer courtyard could be permitted without renting from the gentile, **and he prohibited** it. The case then came before **Rabbi Ḥiyya, and he** too **prohibited** it.

יָתֵיב רַבָּה וְרַב יוֹסֵף בְּשִׁילְהֵי פִּירְקֵיהּ דְּרַב שֵׁשֶׁת, וְיָתֵיב רַב שֵׁשֶׁת וְקָאָמַר: כְּמַאן אֲמָרָהּ רַב לִשְׁמַעְתֵּיהּ – כְּרַבִּי מֵאִיר. כְּרַכֵּישׁ רַבָּה רֵישֵׁיהּ.

Rabba and Rav Yosef were sitting at the end of Rav Sheshet's lecture,[B] **and Rav Sheshet sat and said: In accordance with whose** opinion **did Rav say** this **ruling of his,** with regard to the residents of two courtyards? It was **in accordance with** the opinion of **Rabbi Meir,** who maintains that a gentile renders it prohibited for even a single Jew who resides with him to carry in the courtyard, and therefore it is necessary for the Jew to rent from him. **Rabba nodded his head** in agreement with this explanation.

אָמַר רַב יוֹסֵף: תְּרֵי גַּבְרֵי רַבְרְבֵי כְּרַבָּנַן לִיטְעוּ בְּהַאי מִילְּתָא?! אִי כְּרַבִּי מֵאִיר – לָמָּה לִי יִשְׂרָאֵל בַּחִיצוֹנָה?

Rav Yosef said: Would two great men like these **Sages,** Rabba and Rav Sheshet, **err in such a matter? If** this ruling is **in accordance with** the opinion of **Rabbi Meir, why do I** need to state that there is **a Jew in the outer** courtyard? According to Rabbi Meir, even a single Jew who resides with a gentile may not carry in his courtyard, whether or not another Jew is present.

וְכִי תֵּימָא: מַעֲשֶׂה שֶׁהָיָה כָּךְ הָיָה – וְהָא בְּעוֹ מִינֵּיהּ מֵרַב: פְּנִימִי בִּמְקוֹמוֹ מַהוּ? וְאָמַר לָהֶן: מוּתָּר.

And even **if you say** that indeed this is the *halakha*, that the Jew in the outer courtyard is of no consequence, and that he is only mentioned because **the incident that took place, took place in this way,** and those who came to ask the question provided all the details without knowing whether they were relevant, this is still difficult. **Wasn't a dilemma raised before Rav** himself with regard to this very issue: **What is the** *halakha* governing a Jew living in **the inner** courtyard[H] **with regard to his** own **place?** Can he carry in the inner courtyard? **And he said to them: It is permitted** for him to carry[N] there. Therefore, according to Rav, a gentile does not render it prohibited for a single Jew to carry, which is actually contrary to Rabbi Meir's opinion.

NOTES

In his cup, in his pocket, and in his anger – בְּכוֹסוֹ, וּבְכִיסוֹ, וּבְכַעְסוֹ: The *Arukh* explains that the phrase his pocket refers to one's behavior when he becomes wealthy. An alternative explanation of the phrase his anger is that it refers to whether one can refrain from getting angry in the first place (Maharsha).

Inner courtyard…it is permitted to carry – פְּנִימִי...מוּתָּר: Since it is the Jew in the inner courtyard who shares a courtyard with the gentile, rather than the Jew in the outer courtyard, it is not clear why the prohibition should apply only to the latter. The Rashba explains that without the presence of the Jew in the outer courtyard, the Jew in the inner courtyard would not have been prohibited to carry, as he would be a single Jew living together with a gentile a case discussed at the beginning of this chapter. In this situation, the prohibiting factor is the Jew in the outer courtyard, and therefore the prohibition is applied to him.

HALAKHA

Two courtyards, one within the other – חֲצֵרוֹת זוֹ לִפְנִים מִזּוֹ: If there are two courtyards, one within the other, and a Jew and a gentile reside together in the inner one, and a single Jew resides the outer one, the gentile renders it prohibited for the Jews to carry from one courtyard to the other unless they rent his space from him. This ruling is in accordance with the opinion of Rabbi Yehuda HaNasi and Rabbi Ḥiyya. Similarly, if a Jew and a gentile share the outer courtyard, and a single Jew resides in the inner courtyard, the gentile renders it prohibited for the Jews to carry from one courtyard to the other, in accordance with the statement of Rav (*Shulḥan Arukh, Oraḥ Ḥayyim* 382:17).

A Jew in the inner courtyard – פְּנִימִי בִּמְקוֹמוֹ: If a Jew and a gentile reside in the inner courtyard, and a single Jew resides in the outer one, the Jewish resident of the inner courtyard may carry in his courtyard without an *eiruv* and without having to rent from the gentile. This ruling is in accordance with the statement of Rav (*Shulḥan Arukh, Oraḥ Ḥayyim* 382:17; see *Magen Avraham* and Rambam *Sefer Zemanim, Hilkhot Eiruvin* 2:11).

וְאֶלָּא מַאי – כְּרַבִּי אֱלִיעֶזֶר בֶּן יַעֲקֹב? הָאָמַר: עַד שֶׁיְּהוּ שְׁנֵי יִשְׂרְאֵלִים אוֹסְרִין זֶה עַל זֶה!

The Gemara raises a difficulty: **Rather, what** else can you say? Can you say that he ruled **in accordance with** the opinion of **Rabbi Eliezer ben Ya'akov? Didn't** Rabbi Eliezer ben Ya'akov **say:** The gentile does not render it prohibited to carry **unless there are two Jews** living in the same courtyard who themselves render it **prohibited for one another** to carry without an *eiruv*? In this case they do not render it prohibited for each other to carry without an *eiruv*, as they do not live in the same courtyard.

אֶלָּא כְּרַבִּי עֲקִיבָא, דְּאָמַר רֶגֶל הַמּוּתֶּרֶת בִּמְקוֹמָהּ – אוֹסֶרֶת שֶׁלֹּא בִּמְקוֹמָהּ,

Rather, you might say that he ruled **in accordance with** the opinion of **Rabbi Akiva, who said:** The **foot** of one **who is permitted in his** own **place** nonetheless **renders it prohibited not in its own place.** The Jew in the inner courtyard is permitted to carry in his own courtyard. However, in order to leave his courtyard, he passes through the outer one, in which it is prohibited for him to carry. Therefore, he renders it prohibited for the resident of the outer courtyard as well.

לָמָּה לִי גּוֹי אֲפִילּוּ יִשְׂרָאֵל נַמִי!

But if that is the case, the following difficulty arises: According to this opinion, **why do I need a gentile** in the inner courtyard? **The** single **Jew** living in the inner courtyard **would also** suffice to render it prohibited for the resident of the outer courtyard to carry in his own courtyard, even if no gentiles were present at all.

אָמַר רַב הוּנָא בְּרֵיהּ דְּרַב יְהוֹשֻׁעַ: לְעוֹלָם כְּרַבִּי אֱלִיעֶזֶר בֶּן יַעֲקֹב וּכְרַבִּי עֲקִיבָא. וְהָכָא בְּמַאי עָסְקִינַן – כְּגוֹן שֶׁעֵירְבוּ. וְטַעְמָא – דְּאִיכָּא גּוֹי דְּאָסַר, אֲבָל לֵיכָּא גּוֹי – לָא אָסַר.

Rav Huna, son of Rav Yehoshua, said that Rav's ruling should be understood as follows: **Actually,** Rav ruled **in accordance with** the opinion of **Rabbi Eliezer ben Ya'akov** with regard to a gentile, **and in accordance with** the opinion of **Rabbi Akiva** with regard to a foot that renders it prohibited to carry. **And with what we are dealing here?** This is a case **where** the two Jews **established an** ***eiruv*** with one another. **And the reason** that Rav prohibited carrying in the outer courtyard is **that there is a gentile who renders it prohibited** to carry, **but if there is no gentile, it is not prohibited,** as the Jews established an *eiruv* with one another, and therefore they are permitted to carry.

בְּעָא מִינֵּיהּ רַבִּי אֱלִיעֶזֶר מֵרַב: יִשְׂרָאֵל וְגוֹי בַּחִיצוֹנָה, וְיִשְׂרָאֵל בַּפְּנִימִית מַהוּ? הָתָם טַעְמָא – מִשּׁוּם דִּשְׁכִיחַ דְּדָיֵיר, דְּמִירְתַת גּוֹי וְסָבַר: הַשְׁתָּא אָתֵי יִשְׂרָאֵל, וְאָמַר לִי: יִשְׂרָאֵל דַּהֲוָה גַּבָּךְ הֵיכָא?

The Gemara relates that **Rabbi Eliezer raised a dilemma before Rav** as follows: If **a Jew and a gentile** live together **in the outer** courtyard, **and a Jew** lives alone **in the inner one, what is** the *halakha*? May they carry in the outer courtyard without renting from the gentile? One could argue as follows: **There,** in the case where the Jew and the gentile share the inner courtyard, **the reason** the Sages prohibited carrying is **because it is common** for a Jew and a gentile **to live** together in such a fashion. Ordinarily a single Jew would not live together in the same courtyard as a gentile, for fear that the gentile might kill him. However, here, the Jew living in the inner courtyard believes **that** the **gentile would be afraid** to kill him, **as** the gentile **thinks** to himself: **Now,** were I to kill my neighbor, the **Jew** living in the outer courtyard **might come and say to me:** The **Jew who used to** live **by you, where is** he? The gentile would not be able to offer as an excuse that the Jew left, for the other Jew from outer courtyard would know whether or not he passed through his courtyard. Therefore, since that living arrangement is common, the decree applies, and the gentile's residence in the courtyard renders it prohibited to carry there.

אֲבָל הָכָא – אָמֵינָא לֵיהּ: נְפַק אֲזַל לֵיהּ.

However, here, where the gentile lives in the outer courtyard, he is not afraid of killing his Jewish neighbor, as he says to himself: If the other Jew comes to question me, **I will say to him: He went out** and **went** on **his** way; I do not know where he went. In this case, the gentile would not be concerned that the Jew from the inner courtyard might question his story. Since it is uncommon for a Jew and a gentile to live together in such a fashion, the Sages did not issue a decree that the gentile's residence renders the courtyard prohibited for carrying.

אוֹ דִּילְמָא: הָכָא נַמִי מִירְתַת, דְּסָבַר: הַשְׁתָּא אָתֵי יִשְׂרָאֵל וְחָזֵי לִי?

Or perhaps one would say that **here, too,** the gentile **would be afraid** to kill his Jewish neighbor, **as he thinks** to himself: **Now,** were I to kill my neighbor, **the Jew** living in the inner courtyard **might come** at any moment **and see me** in the act of killing his friend. Since the gentile does not know when the resident of the inner courtyard will pass through the outer courtyard, there is a chance his crime might be witnessed. In that case, it would not be uncommon for a Jew and a gentile to live together in such a fashion, and the Sages' decree that the gentile's residence renders carrying prohibited would apply.

HALAKHA

A tenant and a landlord – שׂוֹכֵר וּמַשְׂכִּיר: The Gemara discusses a situation where a gentile rents out his house to another gentile. If the landlord still maintains a measure of control over the tenant's quarters and their use, or if he can remove the tenant whenever he wishes, it is permitted to rent the space from him for the purpose of an *eiruv*. If not, one may rent only from the tenant, as stated by Rabbi Yehuda HaNasi (*Shulḥan Arukh*, *Oraḥ Ḥayyim* 382:18).

אָמַר לֵיהּ: ״תֵּן לְחָכָם וְיֶחְכַּם עוֹד״.

Rav **said to** Rabbi Eliezer the following verse: **"Give to a wise man, and he will be yet wiser"** (Proverbs 9:9), i.e., it is proper to be stringent even in such a case. Consequently, carrying is prohibited in the outer courtyard unless the Jews rent from the gentile.

רֵישׁ לָקִישׁ וְתַלְמִידֵי דְּרַבִּי חֲנִינָא אִיקְלְעוּ לְהַהוּא פּוּנְדָּק, וְלָא הֲוָה שׂוֹכֵר וַהֲוָה מַשְׂכִּיר.

The Gemara relates that **Reish Lakish and the students of Rabbi Ḥanina happened** to come on Shabbat **to a certain inn** that had at least three permanent residents, two Jews and a gentile who rented their quarters from the gentile innkeeper. Although **the** gentile **tenant was not** present[N] on that Shabbat, the gentile **landlord was** present. Concerned that the gentile tenant might return during Shabbat and render it prohibited for them to carry, Rabbi Ḥanina's students wondered whether the gentile landlord can rent out the gentile's room again for the purpose of an *eiruv*.

אָמְרוּ: מַהוּ לְמֵיגַר מִינֵּיהּ? כָּל הֵיכָא דְּלָא מָצֵי מְסַלֵּיק לֵיהּ – לָא תִּיבְּעֵי לָךְ דְּלָא אָגְרִינָא. כִּי תִּיבְּעוּ – הֵיכָא דְּמָצֵי מְסַלֵּיק לֵיהּ,

They said: What is the *halakha* with regard **to renting from him?** The Gemara clarifies: **Anywhere that** the landlord **cannot remove** the tenant, **you** need **not raise the dilemma, for they** clearly **cannot rent** it from him. If the landlord is unable to expel the tenant, the residence temporarily belongs completely to the tenant, and only he can rent it out. **Where you** need to **raise the dilemma** is with regard to a situation **where he can remove him.**[H]

מַאי? כֵּיוָן דְּמָצֵי מְסַלֵּיק – אָגְרִינָא, אוֹ דִּילְמָא הָשְׁתָּא מִיהָא הָא לָא סַלְּקֵיהּ!

What is the *halakha*? Does one say that **since** the landlord **can remove** the tenant, **they can rent** the residence from him, as the landlord retains a measure of control over it, and therefore he can rent it out again for the purpose of an *eiruv*? **Or perhaps now, in any case he has not** actually **removed him,** which means the residence is still entirely under the tenant's jurisdiction?

אָמַר לָהֶן רֵישׁ לָקִישׁ: נִשְׂכּוֹר, וְלִכְשֶׁנַּגִּיעַ אֵצֶל רַבּוֹתֵינוּ שֶׁבַּדָּרוֹם נִשְׁאַל לָהֶן. אָתוּ שָׁיְילוּ לְרַבִּי אָפֵס, אָמַר לָהֶן: יָפֶה עֲשִׂיתֶם שֶׁשְּׂכַרְתֶּם.

Reish Lakish said to them: Let us rent it now, as the principle is that one may act leniently in a case of doubt involving a rabbinic prohibition, **and when we arrive at our Sages in the South we shall ask**[N] **them** whether we acted properly. Later **they came and asked Rabbi Afes,** who **said to them: You acted well when you rented** it from the landlord.

רַבִּי חֲנִינָא בַּר יוֹסֵף וְרַבִּי חִיָּיא בַּר אַבָּא וְרַבִּי אַסִי אִיקְלַעוּ לְהַהוּא פּוּנְדָּק, דַּאֲתָא גּוֹי מָרֵי דְּפוּנְדָּק בְּשַׁבְּתָא. אֲמַרוּ: מַהוּ לְמֵיגַר מִינֵּיהּ? שׂוֹכֵר כִּמְעָרֵב דָּמֵי, מַה מְעָרֵב מִבְּעוֹד יוֹם – אַף שׂוֹכֵר מִבְּעוֹד יוֹם,

The Gemara relates a similar incident: **Rabbi Ḥanina bar Yosef and Rabbi Ḥiyya bar Abba and Rabbi Asi happened** to come **to a certain inn, and the gentile innkeeper,** who was absent when Shabbat began, **came on Shabbat. They said: What is** the *halakha* with regard **to renting from him** now? The Gemara explains the two sides of the question: **Is renting** from a gentile **like making an** ***eiruv***? If so, **just as one who establishes an** ***eiruv*** may do so only **while it is still day, so too, one who rents** a gentile's property must do so **while it is still day.**

אוֹ דִּילְמָא: שׂוֹכֵר כִּמְבַטֵּל רְשׁוּת דָּמֵי, מַה מְבַטֵּל רְשׁוּת – וַאֲפִילּוּ בְּשַׁבָּת, אַף שׂוֹכֵר – וַאֲפִילּוּ בְּשַׁבָּת?

Or perhaps one who rents from a gentile **is like one who renounces** rights to his **domain; just as one who renounces** rights to his **domain** may do so **even on Shabbat** itself, **so too, one who rents** a gentile's property may do so **even on Shabbat.** In that case, they would be able to rent from the gentile in exchange for something of value, even on Shabbat itself.

רַבִּי חֲנִינָא בַּר יוֹסֵף אָמַר: נִשְׂכּוֹר, וְרַבִּי אַסִי אָמַר: לֹא נִשְׂכּוֹר. אָמַר לְהוּ רַבִּי חִיָּיא בַּר אַבָּא: נִסְמוֹךְ עַל דִּבְרֵי זָקֵן, וְנִשְׂכּוֹר. אָתוּ שָׁיְילוּ לֵיהּ לְרַבִּי יוֹחָנָן, אָמַר לָהֶן:

Rabbi Ḥanina bar Yosef said: Let us rent, while **Rabbi Asi said: Let us not rent. Rabbi Ḥiyya bar Abba said to them: Let us rely** now **on the words of** the **Elder,** Rabbi Ḥanina bar Yosef, **and rent.** Later **they came and asked Rabbi Yoḥanan** about the matter, and **he said to them:**

NOTES

The tenant was not present – לָא הֲוָה שׂוֹכֵר: Why didn't Reish Lakish and the students of Rabbi Ḥanina establish an *eiruv* among themselves, and then wait and see whether the gentile would return? If the gentile ultimately did not return during Shabbat, there would have been no problem. If he did arrive, they could have proceeded to rent from him. The Rashba explains that both Reish Lakish and his student Rabbi Ḥanina shared the doubts with regard to the ruling of Rabbi Ḥanina bar Yosef and his colleagues as to whether or not it is permitted to rent on Shabbat itself, as recounted in the next story.

Let us rent and ask – נִשְׂכּוֹר וְנִשְׁאַל: The Ritva explains that in this situation they relied on the principle that the *halakha* is lenient in cases of uncertainty with regard to the *halakhot* of *eiruvin*. Alternatively, they relied on the principle that where a rabbinic prohibition is involved, one is permitted to act first and clarify the *halakha* afterward (Rav Ya'akov Emden).

יָפֶה עֲשִׂיתֶם שֶׁשְּׂכַרְתֶּם. תָּהוּ בָּהּ נְהַרְדָּעֵי, וּמִי אֲמַר רַבִּי יוֹחָנָן הָכִי?! וְהָאֲמַר רַבִּי יוֹחָנָן: שׂוֹכֵר כִּמְעָרֵב דָּמֵי. מַאי לָאו: מַה מְּעָרֵב מִבְּעוֹד יוֹם – אַף שׂוֹכֵר מִבְּעוֹד יוֹם!

You acted well when you rented.[NH] The Sages **of Neharde'a wondered** at this teaching: **Did Rabbi Yoḥanan** actually **say this? Didn't Rabbi Yoḥanan say** just the opposite: **Renting** from a gentile **is like establishing an *eiruv*? What, is he not** to be understood as imposing a stringency: **Just as one** who **establishes an *eiruv*** may do so only **while it is still day, so too, one** who **rents** a gentile's property must do so **while it is still day?**

לֹא, מַה מְּעָרֵב, וַאֲפִילּוּ בִּפְחוֹת מִשָּׁוֶה פְּרוּטָה – אַף שׂוֹכֵר בִּפְחוֹת מִשָּׁוֶה פְּרוּטָה. וּמַה מְּעָרֵב – אֲפִילּוּ שְׂכִירוֹ וּלְקִיטוֹ, אַף שׂוֹכֵר – אֲפִילּוּ שְׂכִירוֹ וּלְקִיטוֹ.

The Gemara rejects this argument: **No,** his statement was intended as a leniency: **Just as one who establishes an *eiruv*** may do so **even with less than the value of a *peruta*, so too, one who rents** a gentile's property may rent it for **less than the value of a *peruta*. And just as** the **one who establishes an *eiruv*** need not be the owner himself, but **even his hired laborer or harvester** may do so, **so** too, **one who rents** a gentile's property need not rent from the landlord himself, **but** may rent **even** from **his hired laborer or harvester** who are acting on his behalf.

וּמַה מְּעָרֵב, חֲמִשָּׁה שֶׁשְּׁרוּיִן בְּחָצֵר אַחַת – אֶחָד מְעָרֵב עַל יְדֵי כּוּלָּן, שׂוֹכֵר נַמִי, חֲמִשָּׁה שֶׁשְּׁרוּיִן בְּחָצֵר אַחַת – אֶחָד שׂוֹכֵר עַל יְדֵי כּוּלָּן.

And similarly, **just as** with regard to **one who establishes an *eiruv***, the *halakha* is that if **five** people **live in the same courtyard, one** of them may **establish an *eiruv*** with the residents of a different courtyard **on behalf of them all, so** too, with regard to **one who rents** a gentile's property; if **five** people **live in the same courtyard** together with a gentile, **one** of them may **rent** the gentile's property **on behalf of them all.**[H]

תָּהֵי בָּהּ רַבִּי אֶלְעָזָר, אֲמַר רַבִּי זֵירָא: מַאי תָּהֲיָיא דְּרַבִּי אֶלְעָזָר? אֲמַר רַב שֵׁשֶׁת: גַּבְרָא רַבָּה כְּרַבִּי זֵירָא לָא יָדַע מַאי תָּהֲיָיא דְּרַבִּי אֶלְעָזָר? קָא קַשְׁיָא לֵיהּ דִּשְׁמוּאֵל רַבֵּיהּ.

Rabbi Elazar wondered[N] at Rabbi Yoḥanan's ruling that the Sages had acted well when they rented the gentile's property on Shabbat and then they renounced their rights to that one, so that at least it would be permitted to use the courtyard. **Rabbi Zeira said: What** was the reason for **Rabbi Elazar's wonder? Rav Sheshet said:** Can it be that **such a great person as Rabbi Zeira did not know what** was the source **of Rabbi Elazar's wonder? He had difficulty with** a statement **of his teacher, Shmuel.**

דְּאָמַר שְׁמוּאֵל: כָּל מָקוֹם שֶׁאוֹסְרִין וּמְעָרְבִין – מְבַטְּלִין. מְעָרְבִין וְאֵין אוֹסְרִין, אוֹסְרִין וְאֵין מְעָרְבִין – אֵין מְבַטְּלִין.

As Shmuel said: With regard to **any place where** the residents **render it prohibited for** each other to carry **but** where **they** may **establish a** joint ***eiruv*** if they so desire, in order to permit carrying, each may **renounce** his property rights for the other if they failed to establish an *eiruv* before Shabbat. However, in a place **where** the residents may **establish an *eiruv*** together **but they do not render it prohibited** for each other for carrying, or where **they render it prohibited for** each other for carrying **but they** may **not establish an *eiruv*** together, in such situations **they** may **not renounce** their property rights for each other.

כָּל מָקוֹם שֶׁאוֹסְרִין וּמְעָרְבִין – מְבַטְּלִין, כְּגוֹן שְׁתֵּי חֲצֵירוֹת זוֹ לִפְנִים מִזּוֹ.

The Gemara clarifies the above teaching: With regard to **any place where** the residents render it **prohibited** for each other to carry **but** where **they** may **establish an *eiruv*, they may renounce** their rights for each other, **such as** in the case of **two courtyards, one within the other.** The residents of the two courtyards render each other prohibited to carry between the courtyards, but they may establish a joint *eiruv* in order to permit carrying. In such a case, the residents may renounce their property rights for each other if they failed to establish an *eiruv* before Shabbat.

מְעָרְבִין וְאֵין אוֹסְרִין – אֵין מְבַטְּלִין, כְּגוֹן שְׁתֵּי חֲצֵירוֹת וּפֶתַח אֶחָד בֵּינֵיהֶן,

In a place **where** the residents may **establish an *eiruv*** together **but they do not render** each other **prohibited** to carry, **they** may **not renounce** their property rights for each other, in a case **where two courtyards** both opening to an alleyway **that have a single opening between them.** Even though the two courtyards may establish a joint *eiruv* and be considered a single courtyard, they do not render it prohibited for each other to carry if they did not do so, because neither needs to make use of the other. Consequently, there is no option of renouncing rights in favor of the other courtyard.

NOTES

You acted well when you rented – יָפֶה עֲשִׂיתֶם שֶׁשְּׂכַרְתֶּם: In the Jerusalem Talmud a slightly different version of this story is recounted, where it is added that Reish Lakish stated: You did not act well when you rented. According to one opinion cited there, Rabbi Yoḥanan and Reish Lakish disputed this issue, and others say that Reish Lakish said to them that they acted improperly, because even though they had to rent the property they were not allowed to carry.

Wondered – תָּהֵי בָּהּ: This phrase denotes puzzlement and consideration. Sometimes the Sage in question provides the reason for his reaction, as in the case of the Sages of Neharde'a. On other occasions, as in the case of Rabbi Elazar, the Sage does not elaborate the reason for his wonder at a particular ruling.

HALAKHA

Renting on Shabbat for the purpose of an *eiruv* – שְׂכִירוּת לְעֵירוּב בְּשַׁבָּת: If a gentile who resides in a courtyard arrives there on Shabbat, one may rent from him for the purpose of an *eiruv* even on Shabbat, as stated by Rabbi Yoḥanan (*Shulḥan Arukh, Oraḥ Ḥayyim* 383).

One may rent on behalf of them all – אֶחָד שׂוֹכֵר עַל יְדֵי כּוּלָּן: If several people live in one courtyard, one of them may rent from the gentile on behalf of them all (*Shulḥan Arukh, Oraḥ Ḥayyim* 382:9).

NOTES

Where the gentile arrived on the previous day – דַּאֲתָא מֵאֶתְמוֹל: In fact, the gentile might have arrived the day before but refused to rent out his residence. Nevertheless, this is assumed to be an unlikely scenario. In addition, if the gentile refused to rent his property the day before, it is as though he arrived on Shabbat. In any case, the novel aspect of Shmuel's teaching certainly does not refer to such an uncommon case (Ritva).

אוֹסְרִין וְאֵין מְעָרְבִין – אֵין מְבַטְּלִין, לְאַתּוֹיֵי מַאי? לָאו לְאַתּוֹיֵי גּוֹי.

In a place **where they render** each other **prohibited** from carrying **but they** may **not establish an** ***eiruv*** together, **what** does this come **to include?** In reference to which case did Shmuel make this statement? **Wasn't it** meant to **include a gentile** who shares a courtyard with two Jews? The Jewish residents of the courtyard render each other prohibited from carrying in such a case, but they may not establish an *eiruv* due to the presence of the gentile.

וְאִי דַּאֲתָא מֵאֶתְמוֹל – לוֹגַר מֵאֶתְמוֹל!

The Gemara further analyzes the case: **Now, if** it is referring to a situation **where** the gentile **arrived on the previous day,**[N] i.e., before Shabbat, **let him rent** the property from the gentile **on the previous day.** Before Shabbat, both options were available: They could have either established an *eiruv* or one Jew could have renounced his rights in favor of the other. Therefore, it would not have been considered a situation in which they render each other prohibited to carry but cannot establish an *eiruv*.

Perek **VI**
Daf **66** Amud **b**

BACKGROUND

A ruin between houses – חוּרְבָּה בֵּין בָּתִּים: When a ruin is located between two houses, the residents of both houses may use it, because it is shared to a certain extent by both of them.

Ruin between two houses

אֶלָּא לָאו דַּאֲתָא בְּשַׁבְּתָא, וְקָתָנֵי: אוֹסְרִין וְאֵין מְעָרְבִין – אֵין מְבַטְּלִין, שְׁמַע מִינַּהּ.

Rather, is it not referring to a case where the gentile **arrived on Shabbat, and** Shmuel **is teaching:** In a place **where they render** each other **prohibited** from carrying **but they** may **not establish an** ***eiruv*** **together,** in such a situation **they** may **not renounce** their rights for each other. Therefore, you can **learn from this** that if the gentile arrived on Shabbat, they cannot rent his property and then renounce their rights to one of them. This explains Rabbi Elazar's surprise at Rabbi Yoḥanan's ruling, as it appears to contradict this teaching of Shmuel, his first teacher.

אָמַר רַב יוֹסֵף: לָא שְׁמִיעַ לִי הָא שְׁמַעְתָּא. אֲמַר לֵיהּ אַבָּיֵי: אַתְּ אָמַרְתְּ נִיהֲלַן, וְאַהָא אָמַרְתְּ נִיהֲלַן; דְּאָמַר שְׁמוּאֵל: אֵין בִּיטּוּל רְשׁוּת מֵחָצֵר לְחָצֵר,

Rav Yosef said: I have not heard this ***halakha*** of Shmuel's with regard to two courtyards situated one within the other, that the residents of the inner courtyard may renounce their rights to the outer courtyard in favor of the residents of that courtyard. **Abaye said to him: You** yourself **told** it **to us.** Rav Yosef forgot his studies due to illness, so his student Abaye would remind him of his own teachings. Abaye continued: **And it was with regard to this** that **you told** it **to us. As Shmuel said: There is no renunciation of rights from one courtyard to another.** In other words, while one may renounce his rights to his own courtyard for the other residents of that courtyard, he may not renounce his rights to another courtyard for the residents of that courtyard.

וְאֵין בִּיטּוּל רְשׁוּת בְּחוּרְבָּה.

Likewise, **there is no renunciation of** property **rights in a ruin.** If a ruin was shared by two houses,[B] neither can renounce its rights to the ruin in favor of the other. The Sages instituted renunciation of rights only with regard to a courtyard, as that is the typical case.

וְאָמַרְתְּ לַן עֲלַהּ: כִּי אָמַר שְׁמוּאֵל "אֵין בִּיטּוּל רְשׁוּת מֵחָצֵר לְחָצֵר" – לָא אֲמָרַן אֶלָּא שְׁתֵּי חֲצֵירוֹת וּפֶתַח אֶחָד בֵּינֵיהֶן. אֲבָל זוֹ לִפְנִים מִזּוֹ, מִתּוֹךְ שֶׁאוֹסְרִין זֶה עַל זֶה – מְבַטְּלִין.

And you said to us with regard to this matter: **When Shmuel said that there is no renouncing of rights from one courtyard to another, we said** this **only** with regard to a case of **two courtyards,** one alongside the other and each opening into an alleyway, **that have a single opening between them. However,** if the two courtyards were situated **one within the other, since** the residents of the courtyards **render each other prohibited** from carrying, **they** may also **renounce** their rights in favor of each other.

אֲמַר לֵיהּ: אֲנָא אָמֵינָא מִשְּׁמֵיהּ דִּשְׁמוּאֵל הָכִי? וְהָאָמַר שְׁמוּאֵל: אֵין לָנוּ בְּעֵירוּבִין אֶלָּא כִּלְשׁוֹן מִשְׁנָתֵנוּ "אַנְשֵׁי חָצֵר" וְלֹא אַנְשֵׁי חֲצֵירוֹת!

Rav Yosef **said to** Abaye in surprise: **I said that in the name of Shmuel? Didn't Shmuel say: We may** be lenient with regard to the laws of ***eiruvin*** **only in accordance with the wording of the mishna,** which states that the **residents of a courtyard,** in the singular, may renounce their rights, **but not the residents of courtyards** in the plural. Therefore, the option of renouncing rights does not apply to two courtyards.

אֲמַר לֵיהּ: כִּי אָמְרַתְּ לַן "אֵין לָנוּ בְּעֵירוּבִין אֶלָּא כִּלְשׁוֹן מִשְׁנָתֵנוּ" – אַהָא אָמְרַתְּ לַן: שֶׁהַמָּבוֹי לַחֲצֵירוֹת כֶּחָצֵר לַבָּתִּים.

Abaye **said to him: When you told us** this ruling of Shmuel's that **we may** be lenient with regard to the laws of ***eiruvin*** **only in accordance with** the wording of **the mishna, you said it to us with regard to the following** mishna, which states: **That an alleyway in relation to its courtyards is like a courtyard in relation to its houses.** Shmuel inferred from this that there must be at least two courtyards with two houses each that open into an alleyway in order to permit carrying there by means of a side post or a cross beam.

גּוּפָא, אָמַר שְׁמוּאֵל: אֵין בִּיטּוּל רְשׁוּת מֵחָצֵר לְחָצֵר, וְאֵין בִּיטּוּל רְשׁוּת בְּחוּרְבָּה. וְרַבִּי יוֹחָנָן אָמַר: יֵשׁ בִּיטּוּל רְשׁוּת מֵחָצֵר לְחָצֵר, וְיֵשׁ בִּיטּוּל רְשׁוּת בְּחוּרְבָּה.

The Gemara examines the ruling of Shmuel that was cited in the previous discussion. Returning to **the matter itself, Shmuel said: There is no renunciation of rights from one courtyard to another, and there is no renunciation of rights in a ruin. But Rabbi Yoḥanan** disagreed and **said: There is renunciation of rights from one courtyard to another,**[H] **and there is renunciation of rights in a ruin.**[H]

וּצְרִיכָא, דְּאִי אַשְׁמְעִינַן מֵחָצֵר לְחָצֵר – בְּהָא קָאָמַר שְׁמוּאֵל, מִשּׁוּם דְּהָא תַּשְׁמִישְׁתָּא לְחוּד וְהָא תַּשְׁמִישְׁתָּא לְחוּד. אֲבָל חוּרְבָּה, דְּתַשְׁמִישְׁתָּא חֲדָא לְתַרְוַיְיהוּ – אֵימָא מוֹדֵי לֵיהּ לְרַבִּי יוֹחָנָן.

The Gemara comments: It is **necessary** to explain that Shmuel and Rabbi Yoḥanan disagreed with regard to both cases, as neither case could have been learned from the other. **As, if it had taught** only that there is no renunciation of rights **from one courtyard to another,** one could have said that it is only **with regard to this** case that **Shmuel said** that there is no renunciation of rights, **because the use** of the one courtyard stands **alone and the use** of the other courtyard stands **alone.** Each courtyard is not used by the residents of the other courtyard, and therefore there is no renunciation of rights from one courtyard to the other. **However,** with regard to **a ruin, where there is one** common **use for both** neighbors, as the residents of both houses use it, **I would say** that he **concedes to Rabbi Yoḥanan.**

וְכִי אִתְּמַר בְּהָא – בְּהָא קָאָמַר רַבִּי יוֹחָנָן, אֲבָל בְּהַךְ מוֹדֵי לֵיהּ לִשְׁמוּאֵל – צְרִיכָא.

And conversely, **if it was stated** only **with regard to** the case of a ruin, one could have said that it is only **with regard to this** case that **Rabbi Yoḥanan stated** his position, **but with regard to the other** case, renouncing rights from one courtyard to another, perhaps **he concedes to Shmuel.** Therefore, it is **necessary** to teach both cases.[N]

אָמַר אַבָּיֵי: הָא דְּאָמַר שְׁמוּאֵל אֵין בִּיטּוּל רְשׁוּת מֵחָצֵר לְחָצֵר – לָא אֲמָרַן אֶלָּא בִּשְׁתֵּי חֲצֵירוֹת וּפֶתַח אֶחָד בֵּינֵיהֶן, אֲבָל שְׁתֵּי חֲצֵירוֹת זוֹ לִפְנִים מִזּוֹ, מִתּוֹךְ שֶׁאוֹסְרִין – מְבַטְּלִין.

Abaye said: With regard to **that which Shmuel said,** that **there is no renunciation of rights from one courtyard to another, we said** this **only** with regard **to two courtyards,** one alongside the other and each opening into an alleyway, **that have a single opening between them. However,** if there were **two courtyards, one within the other, since** the residents **render** each other **prohibited** to carry, **they may** also **renounce** their rights in favor of each other.

רָבָא אָמַר: אֲפִילּוּ שְׁתֵּי חֲצֵירוֹת זוֹ לִפְנִים מִזּוֹ – פְּעָמִים מְבַטְּלִין, וּפְעָמִים אֵין מְבַטְּלִין. כֵּיצַד? נָתְנוּ עֵירוּבָן בַּחִיצוֹנָה, וְשָׁכַח אֶחָד, בֵּין מִן הַפְּנִימִית וּבֵין מִן הַחִיצוֹנָה, וְלֹא עֵירֵב – שְׁתֵּיהֶן אֲסוּרוֹת.

Rava said: Even in the case of **two courtyards, one within the other, sometimes** the residents may **renounce** their rights in favor of each other, **and sometimes they** may **not renounce** them.[N] **How so?** If the residents of the two courtyards **placed their *eiruv* in the outer** courtyard, **and one** person **forgot** to do so, **whether** he was a resident **of the inner** courtyard **or of the outer** courtyard, **and** he therefore **did not establish an *eiruv*** with the others, then it is **prohibited** to carry in **both** courtyards. The person who neglected to establish an *eiruv* renders it prohibited for the residents of both courtyards to carry, because the *eiruv* for both courtyards is located in the outer one, and it is prohibited to carry there without an *eiruv* due to the right of passage of the residents of the inner courtyard through the outer courtyard. Therefore, there is no effective *eiruv* at all, not even for the residents of the inner courtyard.

HALAKHA

Renunciation of rights from one courtyard to another – בִּיטּוּל רְשׁוּת מֵחָצֵר לְחָצֵר: One courtyard may renounce its rights to another courtyard, in accordance with the opinion of Rabbi Yoḥanan, as the *halakha* is ruled in accordance with his opinion when he disagrees with Shmuel (*Shulḥan Arukh, Oraḥ Ḥayyim* 381:2).

Renunciation of rights in a ruin – בִּיטּוּל רְשׁוּת בְּחוּרְבָּה: Rights may be renounced in a ruin, as the *halakha* is ruled in accordance with Rabbi Yoḥanan's opinion when he disagrees with Shmuel (*Shulḥan Arukh, Oraḥ Ḥayyim* 381:3).

NOTES

Renouncing rights in favor of a different courtyard or a ruin – בִּיטּוּל רְשׁוּת לְחָצֵר אַחֶרֶת וּלְחוּרְבָּה: The point of the discussion, expressed in the phrase: It is necessary, is that the laws governing the renunciation of rights are not simply repeated in the case of two courtyards and the case of a ruin. Rather, the rationale for the idea that renunciation cannot be performed in a ruin is that a ruin is not the center of a person's activity and is therefore not necessary for him on Shabbat. In this way, a ruin is similar to a different courtyard, and therefore the same principles apply to it (*Ge'on Ya'akov*). The Maharsha adds that this discussion is relevant only to Rava's approach, because according to Abaye, there is a clearly evident difference between the renunciation of rights from one courtyard to another and the renunciation of rights from a house to a ruin.

Renouncing rights from one courtyard to another – בִּיטּוּל מֵחָצֵר לְחָצֵר: Most of the early commentaries explain that Rava's comments with regard to the *halakhot* of courtyards were only stated in accordance with Shmuel's opinion. Consequently, despite the fact that Abaye and Rava discuss Shmuel's ruling, this entire discussion is not in accordance with the *halakha*, as the *halakha* is generally in accordance with Rabbi Yoḥanan's opinion in disputes with Shmuel. Since Rava himself rules in accordance with Rabbi Yoḥanan, it is somewhat surprising that he analyzes Shmuel's approach at such length. The Ra'avad explains that Rava's comments can be understood in a manner that accords with the *halakha*. He maintains that Rava's statements, which assume that one may not renounce his rights from one courtyard to another, is not to be understood as a general halakhic ruling. Rather, Rava holds that there are cases where such renunciation may not be done. He maintains the following principle: One may renounce rights in favor of a different courtyard in the case where he is permitted to carry in the courtyard where he lives. However, if he is not permitted to carry in the courtyard where he lives, he may not renounce rights in favor of a different courtyard, since the presence of the residents of his own courtyard renders it prohibited for him to carry there (*Me'iri*; Ritva).

נָתְנוּ עֵירוּבָן בַּפְּנִימִית, וְשָׁכַח אֶחָד מִן הַפְּנִימִית וְלֹא עֵירֵב – שְׁתֵּיהֶן אֲסוּרוֹת.

However, if the residents of the two courtyards **placed their *eiruv* in the inner** courtyard, the following distinction applies: **If** a resident **of the inner** courtyard **forgot and did not establish an *eiruv*, both** courtyards are **prohibited.** In that case, it is prohibited to carry in the inner courtyard itself, due to the one who did not join in the *eiruv*. Since the inner courtyard is prohibited, it also renders the outer one prohibited, as the residents of the inner courtyard must pass through it.

שָׁכַח אֶחָד מִן הַחִיצוֹנָה וְלֹא עֵירֵב – פְּנִימִית מוּתֶּרֶת, וְחִיצוֹנָה אֲסוּרָה.

On the other hand, **if a** resident **of the outer** courtyard **forgot and did not establish an *eiruv*,** it is **permitted** to carry in **the inner** courtyard **and** it is **prohibited** to carry in **the outer** courtyard. The residents of the inner courtyard have an *eiruv*, as they established an *eiruv* together, and therefore they may carry in their courtyard. The residents of the outer courtyard do not render it prohibited for them to carry, as they do not have the right to pass through the inner courtyard, and the inhabitants of the latter could bar their entrance to the inner courtyard by locking their doors.

נָתְנוּ עֵירוּבָן בַּחִיצוֹנָה, וְשָׁכַח אֶחָד בֵּין מִן הַפְּנִימִית וּבֵין מִן הַחִיצוֹנָה וְלֹא עֵירֵב – שְׁתֵּיהֶן אֲסוּרוֹת; הַאי בַּר פְּנִימִית לְמַאן נִבְטֵיל? לִיבְטֵיל לִבְנֵי פְּנִימִית – לֵיתָא לְעֵרוּבַיְיהוּ גַּבַּיְיהוּ, לִיבְטֵיל לִבְנֵי חִיצוֹנָה – אֵין בִּטּוּל רְשׁוּת מֵחָצֵר לְחָצֵר,

The Gemara explains why the residents of these courtyards cannot avail themselves of the option of renunciation: If the residents of the two courtyards **placed their *eiruv* in the outer** courtyard, **and one** person **forgot** to do so, **whether** he was a resident **of the inner** courtyard **or of the outer** courtyard, **and** he therefore **did not establish an *eiruv*** with the others, then it is **prohibited** to carry in **both** courtyards, and the person who forgot to join in the *eiruv* cannot renounce his rights to the courtyard. The reason for this is as follows: **That resident of the inner** courtyard who forgot to place his *eiruv*, **in favor of whom can he renounce** his rights? **Let him renounce** them **in favor of the residents of the inner** courtyard,[N] yet that is ineffective, as **their *eiruv* is not with them** but in the outer courtyard. Consequently, they would remain without an *eiruv*, which means they would render it prohibited to carry in the outer courtyard. **Let him renounce** them **in favor of the residents of the outer** courtyard, but that too is ineffective, as Shmuel ruled that **there is no renunciation of rights from one courtyard to another.**

הַאי בַּר חִיצוֹנָה לְמַאן נִבְטֵיל? לִיבְטֵיל לִבְנֵי חִיצוֹנָה – אִיכָּא פְּנִימִית דְּאָסְרָה עֲלַיְיהוּ, לִיבְטֵיל לִבְנֵי פְּנִימִית – אֵין בִּיטּוּל רְשׁוּת מֵחָצֵר לְחָצֵר.

Similarly, **that resident of the outer** courtyard who forgot to place his *eiruv*, **in favor of whom can he renounce** his rights? **Let him renounce** them **in favor of the residents of the outer** courtyard, but **there is** still **the inner** courtyard **that renders them prohibited** from carrying. **Let him renounce** them **in favor of the residents of the inner** courtyard, but **there is no renunciation of rights from one courtyard to another.** Therefore, the mechanism of permitting carrying by means of renunciation cannot be applied in these cases.

נָתְנוּ עֵירוּבָן בַּפְּנִימִית וְשָׁכַח אֶחָד מִן הַפְּנִימִית וְלֹא עֵירֵב – שְׁתֵּיהֶן אֲסוּרוֹת; הַאי בַּר פְּנִימִית לְמַאן נִבְטֵיל? לִיבְטֵיל לִבְנֵי הַפְּנִימִית – אִיכָּא חִיצוֹנָה דְּאָסְרָה עֲלַיְיהוּ, לִיבְטֵיל לִבְנֵי חִיצוֹנָה – אֵין בִּיטּוּל רְשׁוּת מֵחָצֵר לְחָצֵר.

Likewise, if the residents of the two courtyards **placed their *eiruv* in the inner** courtyard, **and a** resident **of the inner** courtyard **forgot** to do so **and did not establish an *eiruv*,** it is **prohibited** to carry in **both** courtyards. The reason is as follows: **That resident of the inner** courtyard who forgot to place his *eiruv*, **in favor of whom can he renounce** his rights? **Let him renounce** them **in favor of the residents of the inner** courtyard, yet **there is** still **the outer** courtyard **that renders them prohibited** from carrying, as the *eiruv* shared by the courtyards is in essence a valid *eiruv*, which gives the residents of the outer courtyard the right to enter the inner one. **Let him renounce** them **in favor of the residents of the outer** courtyard, but that is ineffective, as Shmuel maintains that **there is no renunciation of rights from one courtyard to another.** In that case, since the inner courtyard is prohibited, it renders it prohibited to carry in the outer one as well.

NOTES

Let him renounce them in favor of the residents of the inner courtyard – לִיבְטֵיל לִבְנֵי פְּנִימִית: Apparently, the other residents of the inner courtyard may all renounce their rights in favor of the one who did not establish an *eiruv* and then lock the courtyard door to the residents of the outer courtyard, and they would thereby be permitted to carry in their own courtyard. By the same token, the residents of the outer courtyard may renounce their rights for the residents of the inner one. The Rashba and the Ritva claim that such a method would indeed be effective in practice. However, the Gemara does not mention this method, as it is not common for the majority to renounce their rights in favor of an individual.

שָׁכַח אֶחָד מִן הַחִיצוֹנָה וְלֹא עֵירֵב – וַדַּאי פְּנִימִית מוּתֶּרֶת, דְּאָחֲדָא דַּשָּׁא וּמִשְׁתַּמְּשָׁא, וְחִיצוֹנָה אֲסוּרָה.

But if a resident **of the outer** courtyard **forgot and did not establish an** ***eiruv***, it is **certainly permitted** to carry in the **inner** courtyard, as its residents **can close the door** between the two courtyards, thereby preventing the residents of the outer courtyard from entering, **and** they can then **use** their courtyard on their own. **However,** it is still **prohibited** to carry in **the outer** courtyard.

אֲמַר לֵיהּ רַב הוּנָא בְּרֵיהּ דְּרַב יְהוֹשֻׁעַ לְרָבָא: וְכִי שָׁכַח אֶחָד מִן הַפְּנִימִית וְלֹא עֵירֵב, אַמַּאי שְׁתֵּיהֶן אֲסוּרוֹת? לְבַטֵּיל בַּר פְּנִימִית לִבְנֵי פְּנִימִית, וְתֵיתֵי חִיצוֹנָה וְתִשְׁתְּרֵי בַּהֲדַיְיהוּ!

Rav Huna, son of Rav Yehoshua, said to Rava: And if a resident **of the inner** courtyard **forgot and did not establish an** ***eiruv***, **why** is it **prohibited** to carry in **both** courtyards? **Let the resident of the inner** courtyard who forgot to establish an *eiruv* **renounce** his rights **in favor of the** other **residents of the inner courtyard, and** then **let** the residents of **the outer** courtyard, who had established an *eiruv* with the inner one, **come and be permitted** to carry together **with them.**

כְּמַאן – כְּרַבִּי אֱלִיעֶזֶר, דְּאָמַר: אֵינוֹ צָרִיךְ לְבַטֵּל רְשׁוּת לְכׇל אֶחָד וְאֶחָד. כִּי קָאָמִינָא – לְרַבָּנַן, דְּאָמְרִי: צָרִיךְ לְבַטֵּל לְכׇל אֶחָד וְאֶחָד.

Rava replied: **In accordance with whose** opinion do you make this suggestion? It is **in accordance with** the opinion of **Rabbi Eliezer, who said: It is not necessary to renounce** one's **rights in favor of each and every** resident. Rather, it is enough for a person to renounce his rights in favor of a single person, as once he no longer has any rights in the courtyard, he can no longer render it prohibited to carry there. According to this approach, a resident of the inner courtyard may indeed renounce his rights in favor of the other residents of his courtyard. The outer courtyard would then be rendered permitted together with the inner courtyard. However, **when I spoke,** it was **in accordance with the** opinion of **the Rabbis, who say: It is necessary to renounce** one's rights **in favor of each and every** resident. Therefore, in order to render the outer courtyard permitted, it would be necessary for the person who forgot to establish the *eiruv* to renounce his rights in favor of the residents of the outer courtyard as well. However, he may not do so, as one may not renounce rights from one courtyard to another. Therefore, the outer courtyard may not be rendered permitted in this manner.

רַב חִסְדָּא וְרַב שֵׁשֶׁת כִּי פָּגְעִי בַּהֲדֵי הֲדָדֵי, רַב חִסְדָּא מִרְתַּעָן שִׂיפְווֹתֵיהּ מִמַּתְנְיָיתָא דְּרַב שֵׁשֶׁת, וְרַב שֵׁשֶׁת מִרְתַּע כּוּלֵּיהּ גּוּפֵיהּ מִפִּלְפּוּלֵיהּ דְּרַב חִסְדָּא.

The Gemara relates that **when Rav Ḥisda and Rav Sheshet would meet each other, Rav Ḥisda's lips would tremble**[N] **from the teachings of Rav Sheshet.** Rav Sheshet's fluency and expertise were such that Rav Ḥisda would be filled with awe in his presence. For his part, **Rav Sheshet's entire body would shake from Rav Ḥisda's sharpness,** i.e., from his brilliant, analytical mind.

בְּעָא מִינֵּיהּ רַב חִסְדָּא מֵרַב שֵׁשֶׁת: שְׁנֵי בָתִּים מִשְּׁנֵי צִידֵּי רְשׁוּת הָרַבִּים, וּבָאוּ גּוֹיִם וְהִקִּיפוּם מְחִיצָּה בְּשַׁבָּת, מַהוּ?

Rav Ḥisda raised a dilemma before Rav Sheshet: If there were **two** unconnected **houses on two sides of a public domain,**[N] **and gentiles came and enclosed them** in **a partition on Shabbat,**[H] **what** is the *halakha*?[B] By erecting the fence, the gentiles nullified the public domain between the two houses, turning it into a private domain. Consequently, carrying from one house to the other is permitted by Torah law. The question is: Is it possible to render it permitted to carry even by rabbinic law? Can one resident renounce his rights to the area between the houses and thereby allow the other to carry there?

אַלִּיבָּא דְּמַאן דְּאָמַר ״אֵין בִּיטּוּל רְשׁוּת מֵחָצֵר לְחָצֵר״ – לָא תִּיבְּעֵי לָךְ. הַשְׁתָּא דְּאִי בָּעוּ לְעָרוֹבֵי מֵאֶתְמוֹל – מָצוּ מְעָרְבִי, אָמְרַתְּ: אֵין בִּיטּוּל רְשׁוּת מֵחָצֵר לְחָצֵר, הָכָא, דְּאִי בָּעוּ לְעָרוֹבֵי מֵאֶתְמוֹל – לָא מָצוּ מְעָרְבִי, לֹא כׇּל שֶׁכֵּן?!

The Gemara clarifies the question: **In accordance with** the opinion **of the one who said** that **there is no renouncing of rights from one courtyard to another, you have no dilemma,** as carrying is certainly prohibited. **Now, if** in a case **where had they wanted to establish an** ***eiruv*** **yesterday they could have established an** ***eiruv***, e.g., in a case of two adjacent courtyards with an entranceway between them, **you say** that **there is no renouncing of rights from one courtyard to another,** then **here,** in a case of two houses situated on opposite sides of a public domain, **where had they wanted to establish an** ***eiruv*** **yesterday they could not have established an** ***eiruv***, because of the public domain between the houses, **all the more so** is it **not** clear that there is no renouncing of rights?

NOTES

Rav Ḥisda's lips would tremble – רַב חִסְדָּא מִרְתַּעָן שִׂיפְווֹתֵיהּ: Rabbeinu Ḥananel and Rashi explain that Rav Ḥisda was afraid that Rav Sheshet might ask him questions about the content of the *mishnayot* he had mastered, as Rav Sheshet was famous for his breadth of knowledge. Rav Sheshet, on the other hand, would tremble in awe at the force of Rav Ḥisda's intellect and his penetrating questions.

Two houses on two sides of a public domain – שְׁנֵי בָתִּים מִשְּׁנֵי צִידֵּי רְשׁוּת הָרַבִּים: Rav Ḥisda's question is directly related to the previous discussions. The key issue is the connection between the possibility of establishing an *eiruv* and the permissibility of renouncing rights. This may be inferred from the question's answer: Where there was no possibility of establishing an *eiruv* before Shabbat, one is likewise prohibited to renounce his rights on Shabbat.

HALAKHA

Enclosed them in a partition on Shabbat – הִקִּיפוּם מְחִיצָּה בְּשַׁבָּת: The principle is that a partition erected on Shabbat, even intentionally and even by a Jew, is considered a partition according to Torah law. If it was erected by gentiles, as in this case, it may be relied upon even according to rabbinic law.

BACKGROUND

Houses surrounded by a partition – בָּתִּים שֶׁהִקִּיפוּם מְחִיצָּה: The Gemara asks whether or not the residents of the two houses are considered to be residing in a single courtyard with regard to the *halakhot* of *eiruv*.

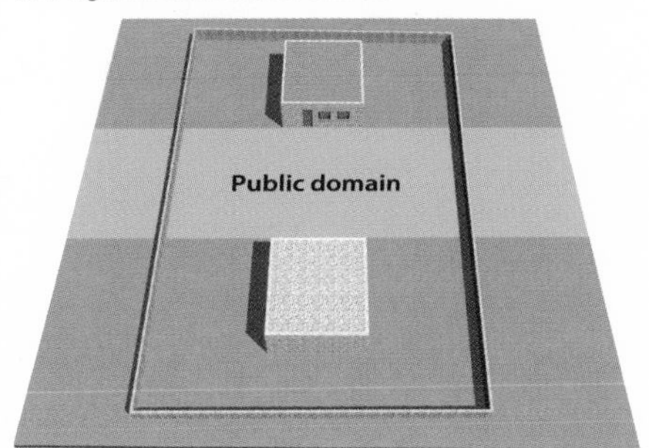

Two houses on opposite sides of a public domain, surrounded by a fence

כִּי תִּיבָּעֵי לָךְ – אַלִּיבָּא דְּמַאן דְּאָמַר יֵשׁ בִּיטּוּל רְשׁוּת מֵחָצֵר לְחָצֵר. הָתָם, דְּאִי בָּעוּ לְעָרוּבֵי מֵאֶתְמוֹל מָצוּ מְעָרְבִי – בַּטּוּלֵי נַמִּי מָצֵי מְבַטֵּל. אֲבָל הָכָא, דְּלָא מָצוּ מְעָרְבִי מֵאֶתְמוֹל – בַּטּוּלֵי נַמִּי לָא מָצֵי מְבַטֵּל.

Where you have a dilemma is in accordance with the opinion of **the one who said** that **there is renouncing of rights from one courtyard to another,** and the two sides of the question are as follows: Perhaps **there, where had they wanted to establish an *eiruv* yesterday they could have established an *eiruv*** then, **they can also renounce** rights now. **But here, where they could not have established an *eiruv* yesterday** even had they wanted to, **one** may **not renounce rights** now **either.**

אוֹ דִּילְמָא לָא שְׁנָא? אֲמַר לֵיהּ: אֵין מְבַטְּלִין.

Or perhaps there is **no difference** between the two cases. Since renunciation of rights is possible under the current circumstances, yesterday's situation is not taken into account. Rav Sheshet **said to** Rav Ḥisda: In such a case, **one** may **not renounce** his rights.[H]

מֵת גּוֹי בְּשַׁבָּת, מַהוּ?

Rav Ḥisda posed a similar question: If two Jews and a gentile shared a courtyard, and no steps had been taken prior to Shabbat to render it permitted to carry in the courtyard, **and the gentile died**[N] **on Shabbat,**[H] **what is** the *halakha*? Since the gentile died, he no longer imposes restrictions on carrying in the courtyard. May one Jew now renounce his rights in favor of the other and thereby render it permitted for him to carry in the courtyard?

אַלִּיבָּא דְּמַאן דְּאָמַר שׂוֹכְרִין – לָא תִּיבָּעֵי לָךְ, הָשְׁתָּא תַּרְתֵּי עָבְדִינַן, חֲדָא מִיבַּעְיָא?!

The Gemara clarifies the question: **In accordance with** the opinion of **the one who said** that **one** may **rent** from a gentile who arrives on Shabbat, **you have no dilemma. Now** that **we** may **perform two** actions, both rent and renounce rights, as the Jewish neighbors may rent from the gentile and subsequently each could renounce his rights in favor of the other, **is it necessary** to state that we may perform **one** action? Each Jew may certainly renounce his rights in favor of the other.

אֶלָּא כִּי תִּיבָּעֵי לָךְ – אַלִּיבָּא דְּמַאן דְּאָמַר אֵין שׂוֹכְרִין. תַּרְתֵּי הוּא דְּלָא עָבְדִינַן, הָא חֲדָא – עָבְדִינַן. אוֹ דִּילְמָא: לָא שְׁנָא? אֲמַר לֵיהּ: אֲנִי אוֹמֵר מְבַטְּלִין, וְהַמְנוּנָא אָמַר: אֵין מְבַטְּלִין.

Rather, there is a dilemma in accordance with the opinion of **the one who said** that **they** may **not rent** from the gentile in such a case. The two sides of the question are as follows: Perhaps **it is two** actions **that we** may **not perform,** rent and renounce; **however, one** action alone **we** may **perform; or perhaps** there is **no difference** between one action and two. Rav Sheshet **said to** Rav Ḥisda: **I say** that in such a case **one** may **renounce** his rights, **while** Rav **Hamnuna said** that **one** may **not renounce** his rights.

אָמַר רַב יְהוּדָה, אָמַר שְׁמוּאֵל: גּוֹי שֶׁיֵּשׁ לוֹ פֶּתַח אַרְבָּעָה עַל אַרְבָּעָה פָּתוּחַ לַבִּקְעָה, אֲפִילּוּ מַכְנִיס וּמוֹצִיא גְּמַלִּים וּקְרוֹנוֹת כָּל הַיּוֹם כּוּלּוֹ דֶּרֶךְ מָבוֹי – אֵין אוֹסֵר עַל בְּנֵי מָבוֹי.

Rav Yehuda said that **Shmuel said:** With regard to **a gentile who** lives in a courtyard that opens into an alleyway in which many Jews reside, and he **has** another **entrance**[H] on the other side of the courtyard, even one that is only **four by four** handbreadths in size, that **opens into a valley,**[B] then in such a case, **even if all day long he brings camels and wagons in and out** of his courtyard **by way of the alleyway,** so that it is evident that he uses the alleyway, **he** nonetheless **does not render it prohibited for the residents of the alleyway** to carry. He is not considered a resident of the alleyway alongside them, as the entrance from the field is viewed as the true entrance to his courtyard.

מַאי טַעְמָא? בְּפִיתְחָא דִּמְיַחַד לֵיהּ, בְּהַהוּא נִיחָא לֵיהּ.

What is the reason that his small entrance from the field is considered his main entrance? Because **the entrance that is exclusively his is preferable to him.** Despite its small size, the gentile views the entrance from the field as his main entrance, while he uses the one that opens into the alleyway only when it is convenient.

אִיבַּעְיָא לְהוּ: פָּתוּחַ לְקַרְפֵּף, מַהוּ? אֲמַר רַב נַחְמָן בַּר אַמִי מִשְּׁמֵיהּ דְּאוּלְפָּנָא:

Based on this assumption, **a dilemma was raised before** the Sages: If the gentile's courtyard opens into an alleyway in which Jews reside, and it also has an entrance that **opens into an enclosure**[N] rather than into a valley, **what is** the *halakha*? Which entrance is considered his primary entrance? **Rav Naḥman bar Ami said, citing a tradition [*mishmei de'ulpana*]**[N] he received from his teachers:

HALAKHA

Two houses that they enclosed in a partition on Shabbat – שְׁנֵי בָתִּים שֶׁהִקִּיפוּם בְּשַׁבָּת: If two houses on opposite sides of a public domain were enclosed in a partition constructed by gentiles on Shabbat, then one of the residents may not renounce his rights to the enclosed area in favor of the other. This ruling is in accordance with the opinion of Rav Sheshet (*Shulḥan Arukh, Oraḥ Ḥayyim* 381:5).

The gentile died on Shabbat – מֵת גּוֹי בְּשַׁבָּת: If the sole gentile resident of a courtyard died on Shabbat, one of the Jewish residents may then renounce his rights in favor of the others in order to render it permitted to carry in the shared courtyard (*Shulḥan Arukh, Oraḥ Ḥayyim* 383).

A gentile who has another entrance – גּוֹי שֶׁיֵּשׁ לוֹ פֶּתַח: If a gentile lives in a courtyard with two entrances, one that opens into an alleyway and a second one, even a very small one, that opens into a field or an enclosure larger than two *beit se'a*, then he does not impose restrictions on the Jewish residents of the alleyway. This ruling is in accordance with the statements of Shmuel, Rabba, and Rav Yosef (*Shulḥan Arukh, Oraḥ Ḥayyim* 389).

BACKGROUND

A courtyard that opens into a valley – חָצֵר הַפְּתוּחָה לַבִּקְעָה:

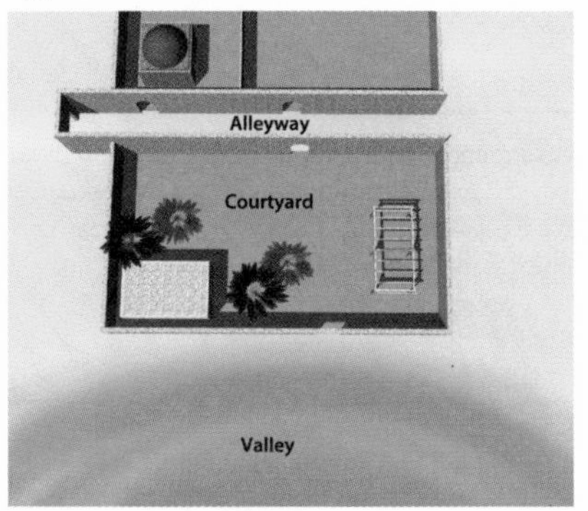

Courtyard open to an alleyway on one side and a valley on the other

NOTES

The gentile died – מֵת גּוֹי: This question posed by Rav Ḥisda is also related to the previous one. May one renounce rights to a courtyard on Shabbat only if there had been an option of establishing an *eiruv* the day before, or is it possible to change the status of the courtyard even when it had been impossible to establish an *eiruv*? The rationale of Rav Sheshet's answer to this question is based on the difference between this case and the previous one. Rav Sheshet is lenient either because the residents of the courtyard could have rented from the gentile the day before (Rashi) or because the gentile was not present the day before to render it prohibited to carry, as he arrived only on Shabbat (*Tosafot*). The common denominator in these explanations is that the option of establishing an *eiruv* was available the day before.

Opens into an enclosure – פָּתוּחַ לְקַרְפֵּף: Ritva explains that in this context, the enclosure itself opens into a valley on the other side.

Citing a tradition [*mishmei de'ulpana*] – מִשְּׁמֵיהּ דְּאוּלְפָּנָא: This expression is similar to another expression in which a tradition is cited [*mishmei detalmuda*]. In other words, Rav Naḥman bar Ami was in possession of a tradition, but the name of the original Sage who stated it had been forgotten. Consequently, it was known simply as a tradition from the Sages.

אֲפִילּוּ פָּתוּחַ לַקַּרְפֵּף.

Even if it **opens into an enclosure,**[NB] this is considered its main entrance, rather than the one that opens into the alleyway.

רַבָּה וְרַב יוֹסֵף דְּאָמְרִי תַּרְוַיְיהוּ: גּוֹי בֵּית סָאתַיִם – אוֹסֵר, יוֹתֵר מִבֵּית סָאתַיִם – אֵינוֹ אוֹסֵר.

It is **Rabba and Rav Yosef who both say:** The *halakha* in such a case depends on the identity of the owner of the courtyard. With regard to a courtyard owned by **a gentile,** if the enclosure behind his courtyard is the size of **two *beit se'a*** or less, **he renders it prohibited** for the Jewish residents of the alleyway to carry. An enclosure of this size is not large enough for all the gentile's needs, and therefore his main entrance is the one that opens into the alleyway. However, if the enclosure is **greater than** the size of **two *beit se'a*, he does not render it prohibited** for the residents of the alleyway to carry, as such an enclosure is sufficient for all his needs.

וְיִשְׂרָאֵל, בֵּית סָאתַיִם – אֵינוֹ אוֹסֵר,

On the other hand, with regard to a courtyard owned by **a Jew,** if the enclosure is the size of **two *beit se'a*** or less, **he does not render it prohibited** for the other residents of the alleyway to carry, even if he did not join in an *eiruv* with them. Because he has the option of carrying in such an enclosure on Shabbat, he would not carry in the alleyway, as it is more convenient for him to carry in a place that belongs exclusively to him.

יוֹתֵר מִבֵּית סָאתַיִם – אוֹסֵר.

However, if the enclosure is **greater than** the size of **two *beit se'a*,** in which case it is prohibited to carry there, the Jew would carry only by way of the alleyway. Therefore, **he renders it prohibited** for his fellow residents of the alleyway to carry unless he establishes an *eiruv* with them.[H]

בְּעָא מִינֵּיהּ רָבָא בַּר חַקְלַאי מֵרַב הוּנָא: פָּתוּחַ לְקַרְפֵּף, מַהוּ? אֲמַר לֵיהּ: הֲרֵי אָמְרוּ, בֵּית סָאתַיִם – אוֹסֵר, יוֹתֵר מִבֵּית סָאתַיִם – אֵינוֹ אוֹסֵר.

With regard to this issue, **Rava bar Ḥaklai raised a dilemma before Rav Huna:** If the gentile's courtyard opens into an alleyway, and it also has an entrance that **opens into an enclosure, what is** the *halakha*? He **said to him: They have** already **said** that if the enclosure is the size of **two *beit se'a*** or less, the gentile **renders it prohibited** for the Jewish residents of the alleyway to carry; however, if it is **more than two *beit se'a*, he does not render it prohibited** for them to carry.

אָמַר עוּלָּא, אָמַר רַבִּי יוֹחָנָן: קַרְפֵּף יוֹתֵר מִבֵּית סָאתַיִם שֶׁלֹּא הוּקַּף לְדִירָה, וַאֲפִילּוּ כּוֹר וַאֲפִילּוּ כּוֹרַיִים – הַזּוֹרֵק לְתוֹכוֹ חַיָּיב. מַאי טַעְמָא? מְחִיצָה הִיא, אֶלָּא שֶׁמְּחוּסֶּרֶת דִּיּוֹרִין.

Ulla said that **Rabbi Yoḥanan said:** With regard to **an enclosure greater than** the size of **two *beit se'a***[H] **that was not** originally **surrounded** by a fence **for** the purpose of **residence, even** if it is as large as a field that produces a crop of one ***kor*, and even two *kor*,** one who inadvertently **throws** an object **into it** from the public domain **is liable** to bring a sin-offering, like one who throws into a private domain. **What is the reason** for this? It is because the partition of an enclosure **is a** valid **partition.** Consequently, the enclosure is considered a private domain by Torah law, **except that it is lacking residents,** and therefore the Sages did not permit one to carry inside it as in a proper private domain.

מְתִיב רַב הוּנָא בַּר חִינָּנָא: סֶלַע שֶׁבַּיָּם, גָּבוֹהַּ עֲשָׂרָה וְרוֹחַב אַרְבָּעָה – אֵין מְטַלְטְלִין לֹא מִן תּוֹכוֹ לַיָּם, וְלֹא מִן הַיָּם לְתוֹכוֹ. פָּחוֹת מִכָּאן – מְטַלְטְלִין. עַד כַּמָּה – עַד בֵּית סָאתַיִם.

Rav Huna bar Ḥinnana raised an objection from the following *baraita*: With regard to **a rock** protruding from **the sea** that is **ten** handbreadths **high and four** handbreadths **wide, one** may **not carry from it to the sea or from the sea to it** on Shabbat. The rock has the status of a private domain, while the sea is a *karmelit*, and it is prohibited to carry from a private domain into a *karmelit* or vice versa on Shabbat. If the rock **is smaller than this,** either in height or width, so that it is no longer considered a private domain, **one** may **carry** to or from it. **How large** may the rock be? It may be **up to** the size of **two *beit se'a*.**

אַהַיָּיא? אִילֵימָא אַסֵּיפָא – בֵּית סָאתַיִם, טְפֵי לָא?! וְהָא מִכַּרְמְלִית לְכַרְמְלִית קָא מְטַלְטֵל!

The Gemara attempts to clarify the meaning of this *baraita*: **To which** part of the *baraita* is the clause: Up to the size of two *beit se'a*, referring? **If you say** it is referring **to the latter clause,** can it be that with regard to a rock that is less than ten handbreadths high, the *halakha* is that carrying is permitted if the rock is up to the size of **two *beit se'a*,** but **no more** than that? **Wouldn't he be carrying from one *karmelit* to another,** which is certainly permitted?

NOTES

Opens into an enclosure – פָּתוּחַ לְקַרְפֵּף: The Ra'avad holds that if the courtyard has a spacious entrance that opens into an enclosure, there is no distinction between large and small enclosures. The discussion in this context refers to a small entrance, i.e., one that is four by four handbreadths. Most commentaries disagree with this view and maintain that four by four handbreadths merely refers to the minimal size of an entrance, but that the same *halakha* applies to entrances of any size (Rashba; Ritva).

BACKGROUND

A courtyard that opens into an enclosure – חָצֵר פְּתוּחָה לְקַרְפֵּף:

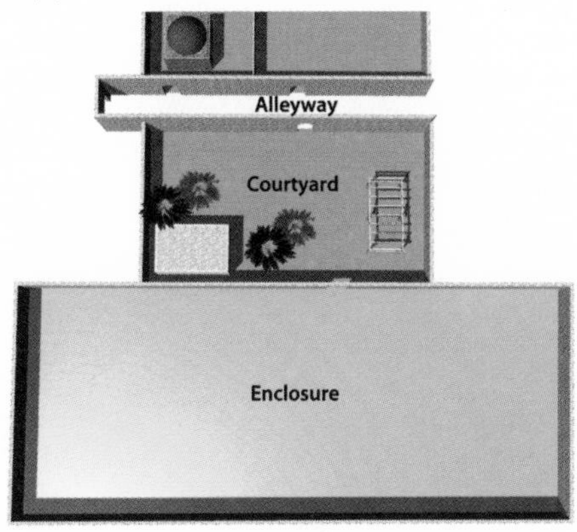

Courtyard that opens into an alleyway on one side and an enclosure on the other

HALAKHA

A Jew who has a different entrance – יִשְׂרָאֵל שֶׁיֵּשׁ לוֹ פֶּתַח אַחֵר: With regard to a Jew residing in an alleyway who did not establish an *eiruv* with the other residents of the alleyway, the *halakha* is as follows: If his courtyard has an entrance, even one that is only four by four handbreadths, i.e., a small entrance, that opens into an enclosure smaller than two *beit se'a* that was not enclosed for the purpose of residence, then he does not render it prohibited for the other residents of the alleyway to carry. However, if the enclosure is larger than two *beit se'a*, he renders it prohibited to carry in the alleyway. Had the enclosure been enclosed for the purpose of residence, he does not render it prohibited for the others to carry in the alleyway (Rashi as cited in the *Tur*; Rambam). Other commentaries state that if the enclosure was enclosed for the purpose of residence, even if it is larger than two *beit se'a*, he renders it prohibited for them to carry (*Tosafot*). The later authorities rule in accordance with the first opinion, which was adopted by most authorities (*Mishna Berura*, citing *Beit Yosef*; *Shulḥan Arukh*, *Oraḥ Ḥayyim* 389).

An enclosure greater than two *beit se'a* – קַרְפֵּף יוֹתֵר מִבֵּית סָאתַיִם: If one throws an object from a public domain into an enclosure that is larger than the size of two *beit se'a*, even if it had not been enclosed for residence, he is liable (Rambam *Sefer Zemanim*, *Hilkhot Shabbat* 16:1).

NOTES

They said and they said – הֵן אָמְרוּ וְהֵן אָמְרוּ: This expression is used in the Gemara to explain special stringencies and leniencies that apply to rabbinic decrees. Since it was the Sages who issued these decrees, they may occasionally adjust one of them due to special circumstances.

Carrying within the rock is common – תּוֹכוֹ שְׁכִיחַ: According to Rabbeinu Tam and the authorities that rule in accordance with his opinion, this principle applies to all enclosures and not only the case of a rock island at sea. Consequently, it is permitted to carry from any enclosure to a *karmelit*. Despite the general ruling, it may still be asserted that carrying within an enclosure is more common than carrying from an enclosure to an adjacent *karmelit* (Rashba).

HALAKHA

A rock in the sea – סֶלַע שֶׁבַּיָּם: It is prohibited to carry on a rock that forms an island in the sea if its area is larger than two *beit se'a*. However, it is permitted to carry from it to the sea, as stated by Rav Ashi. Whether or not it is also permitted to carry from an enclosure larger than two *beit se'a* to a *karmelit* is a matter of dispute. The Rambam and the Ra'avad hold that it is prohibited (*Maggid Mishne*), while *Tosafot* and Rashba rule that it is permitted to carry from an enclosure to an adjacent *karmelit* even on dry land. In the *Shulḥan Arukh*, the ruling is in accordance with the second opinion (Rambam *Sefer Zemanim*, *Hilkhot Shabbat* 16:2; *Shulḥan Arukh*, *Oraḥ Ḥayyim* 346:3).

אֶלָּא לָאו אַרֵישָׁא, וְהָכִי קָאָמַר: סֶלַע שֶׁבַּיָּם, גָּבוֹהַּ עֲשָׂרָה וְרוֹחַב אַרְבָּעָה – אֵין מְטַלְטְלִין לֹא מִתּוֹכוֹ לַיָּם וְלֹא מִן הַיָּם לְתוֹכוֹ. וְעַד כַּמָּה – עַד בֵּית סָאתַיִם. הָא יָתֵר מִבֵּית סָאתַיִם – מְטַלְטְלִין. אַלְמָא כַּרְמְלִית הִיא. תְּיוּבְתָּא דְּרַבִּי יוֹחָנָן!

Rather, is it not referring **to the first clause** of the *baraita*, **and this is** what **it is saying:** With regard to **a rock** protruding from **the sea** that is **ten** handbreadths **high and four** handbreadths **wide, one may not carry from it to the sea or from the sea to it,** as it has the status of a private domain. **And how large** may it be for this prohibition to apply? **Up to** the size of **two *beit se'a*. But** if the rock is **greater than** the size of **two *beit se'a*, one** may **carry. Apparently, it is a *karmelit*** in all respects, and not just as a stringency. This appears to be **a conclusive refutation of** the opinion of **Rabbi Yoḥanan.**

אָמַר רָבָא: מַאן דְּלָא יָדַע תָּרוֹצֵי מַתְנְיָיתָא, תְּיוּבְתָּא מוֹתֵיב לֵיהּ לְרַבִּי יוֹחָנָן?! לְעוֹלָם אַרֵישָׁא, וְהָכִי קָאָמַר: הָא בְּתוֹכוֹ – מְטַלְטְלִין. וְעַד כַּמָּה – עַד בֵּית סָאתַיִם.

Rava said: Only **one who does not know how to explain *mishnayot*** raises such **refutations against Rabbi Yoḥanan,** one of the greatest Sages of his generation. Rather, the *baraita* is to be understood as follows: **Actually,** the final words of the *baraita* refer **to the first clause, and this is** what **it is saying:** With regard to a rock protruding from the sea that is ten handbreadths high and four handbreadths wide, one may not carry from it to the sea or from the sea to it, **but within it,** on the rock itself, **one** may **carry,** as it is considered a private domain. And **how large** may the rock be and remain permitted? **Up to two *beit se'a*.**

רַב אַשִׁי אָמַר: לְעוֹלָם אַרֵישָׁא, הֵן אָמְרוּ וְהֵן אָמְרוּ.

Rav Ashi said that the *baraita* may be explained differently, yet still in a manner that does not refute the words of Rabbi Yoḥanan: **Actually,** the final words of the *baraita* refer **to the first clause,** as stated by Rav Huna bar Ḥanina. However, one may not infer from them a principle with regard to enclosures, as **they said** that the *halakha* is stringent in one case, **and they said**[N] that the *halakha* should be lenient in a different case, i.e., the same Sages who were stringent in one case were lenient in the another.

הֵן אָמְרוּ: קַרְפֵּף יָתֵר מִבֵּית סָאתַיִם שֶׁלֹּא הוּקַּף לְדִירָה אֵין מְטַלְטְלִין בּוֹ אֶלָּא בְּאַרְבַּע אַמּוֹת, וְהֵן אָמְרוּ: אֵין מְטַלְטְלִין מֵרְשׁוּת הַיָּחִיד לְכַרְמְלִית.

How so? **They said** that in the case of **an enclosure greater than** the size of **two *beit se'a* that was not** originally **enclosed** with a fence **for** the purpose of residence, **one** may **carry only** a distance of **four cubits,** as it has the status of a *karmelit* in this regard. **And they** also **said** that **one** may **not carry from a private domain to a *karmelit*.** Both of these *halakhot* are decrees of the Sages.

בֵּית סָאתַיִם דִּשְׁרֵי לְטַלְטוֹלֵי בְּכוּלֵּיהּ – אָסְרִי רַבָּנַן לְטַלְטוֹלֵי, לֹא מִן הַיָּם לְתוֹכוֹ וְלֹא מִתּוֹכוֹ לַיָּם. מַאי טַעְמָא? רְשׁוּת הַיָּחִיד גְּמוּרָה הִיא.

Therefore, the Sages developed the following principles: With regard to a rock that is no larger than **two *beit se'a*,** so **that it is permitted to carry on all of it, the Sages prohibited carrying from the sea to it and from it to the sea. What is the reason** for this? It is that the rock **is a full-fledged private domain,** and they did not permit one to carry from a private domain to a *karmelit* or vice versa.

יָתֵר מִבֵּית סָאתַיִם דְּאָסוּר לְטַלְטוֹלֵי בְּכוּלֵּיהּ – שָׁרוּ רַבָּנַן לְטַלְטוֹלֵי מִתּוֹכוֹ לַיָּם וּמִן הַיָּם לְתוֹכוֹ. מַאי טַעְמָא? דִּלְמָא אָמְרִי רְשׁוּת הַיָּחִיד גְּמוּרָה הִיא וְאָתֵי לְטַלְטוֹלֵי בְּכוּלֵּיהּ.

However, if it is **larger than** the size of **two *beit se'a*,** so **that it is prohibited to carry on all of it** by rabbinic decree, **the Sages permitted carrying from the sea to it and from it to the sea.**[H] **What is the reason** for this? It is because the Sages were concerned that **perhaps** people would **say** that **it is a proper private domain, and they would come to carry on all of it.** Were the Sages to prohibit carrying from the rock to the sea, people would think that it is a full-fledged private domain, and they would carry on it. Since all these decrees are rabbinic in nature, the Sages permitted carrying from a private domain to a *karmelit* in this case in order to prevent people from violating a different rabbinic decree, which prohibits carrying in an enclosure that is greater than the size of two *beit se'a*. However, no general conclusion may be inferred from this that an enclosure larger than two *beit se'a* is not a private domain by Torah law.

וּמַאי שְׁנָא? תּוֹכוֹ – שְׁכִיחַ, מִתּוֹכוֹ לַיָּם וּמִן הַיָּם לְתוֹכוֹ – לֹא שְׁכִיחַ.

The Gemara asks: **And what is the difference** between the decrees that caused the Sages to choose to uphold the one decree and not the other? The Gemara answers: The difference is that carrying **within** the rock **is common,**[N] whereas carrying **from it to the sea and from the sea to it is not common.** The Sages permitted carrying in the less likely scenario in order to reinforce the decree against carrying within the rock, the more common situation.

הַהוּא יָנוֹקָא דְּאִשְׁתַּפִּיךְ חַמִּימֵיהּ, אֲמַר לְהוּ רַבָּה: נַיְיתוּ לֵיהּ חַמִּימֵי מִגּוֹ בֵּיתַאי. אֲמַר לֵיהּ אַבָּיֵי: וְהָא לָא עָרְבִינַן!

The Gemara now relates that there was once **a certain baby whose warm water,** which had been prepared for his Shabbat circumcision, **spilled. Rabba said to them: Let them bring warm water for him from my house. Abaye said to him: But we did not establish an *eiruv*** in the courtyard, so it is prohibited to carry the water.

אֲמַר לֵיהּ: נִסְמוֹךְ אַשִּׁיתּוּף. אֲמַר לֵיהּ: הָא לָא שָׁתְפִינַן! נֵימְרוּ לֵיהּ לְגוֹי לֵיתֵי לֵיהּ.

Rabba **said to him: Let us rely on the merging** of alleyways, which may serve in place of a joining of courtyards in pressing circumstances such as these. Abaye **said to him: But we did not establish a merging** of alleyways either. Rabba replied: If so, **let them instruct a gentile**[N] **to bring** the warm water **for him,** even though it is generally prohibited to instruct a gentile to perform labor for a Jew that involves a desecration of Shabbat.[H]

אֲמַר אַבָּיֵי: בְּעֵי לְאוֹתְבֵיהּ לְמָר וְלָא שְׁבַקַן רַב יוֹסֵף, דְּאָמַר רַב [יוֹסֵף אָמַר רַב] כָּהֲנָא: כִּי הָוֵינַן בֵּי רַב יְהוּדָה, הֲוָה אָמַר לָן: בִּדְאוֹרַיְיתָא – מוֹתְבִינַן תְּיוּבְתָּא וַהֲדַר עָבְדִינַן מַעֲשֶׂה, בִּדְרַבָּנַן – עָבְדִינַן מַעֲשֶׂה וַהֲדַר מוֹתְבִינַן תְּיוּבְתָּא.

Abaye said: I wanted to raise an objection against the Master, Rabba, **but Rav Yosef would not let me** do so, as **Rav Yosef said** that **Rav Kahana said: When we were in Rav Yehuda's house, he would say to us** when we were presented with a halakhic difficulty: With regard to **a Torah law, we** first **raise objections and then we perform an act,** i.e., if someone has an objection to a proposed action, we must first clarify the matter and only then may we proceed. However, **with regard to rabbinic laws, we** first **perform an act and then we raise objections.**

לְבָתַר הָכִי אֲמַר לֵיהּ: מַאי בָּעֵית לְאוֹתְבֵיהּ לְמָר? אֲמַר [לֵיהּ: דְּתַנְיָא,] הַזָּאָה שְׁבוּת וַאֲמִירָה לְגוֹי שְׁבוּת,

Afterward, when they had brought the water, Rav Yosef **said to** Abaye: **What objection did you wish to raise against the Master,** Rabba? He **said to him: As it was taught** in a ***baraita*: Sprinkling** the water of purification on an impure person on Shabbat is not prohibited by Torah law; rather, it is only **a rabbinic decree**[N] to enhance the character of Shabbat as a day of rest. **And telling a gentile** to perform a Shabbat labor on behalf of a Jew is likewise only **a rabbinic decree.**

NOTES

Let them instruct a gentile – נֵימְרוּ לֵיהּ לְגוֹי: Despite the fact that it is generally prohibited to instruct a gentile to perform work for Jews on Shabbat, the commandment of circumcision is important enough to override the *halakhot* of Shabbat. Therefore, in this case of a rabbinic prohibition, e.g., telling a gentile to perform a prohibited labor, it is proper to violate the rabbinic decree in order to fulfill this mitzva.

Sprinkling is a rabbinic decree – הַזָּאָה שְׁבוּת: Abaye gave the example of sprinkling, as that is a case where the activity is required for the sake of a mitzva. Furthermore, the purposeful neglect of this mitzva causes the individual to incur *karet*, as in the case of the Pascal lamb. In the case of sprinkling, the Sages nonetheless reinforced their rulings and did not permit the violation of the rabbinic prohibition. In the case discussed here, where one would not be abrogating the mitzva of circumcision entirely, but merely postponing it, it is certainly possible to insist on observance of the rabbinic prohibition (Rosh).

HALAKHA

Instructing a gentile – אֲמִירָה לְגוֹי: For the sake of a circumcision, one is permitted to instruct a gentile to perform an action on Shabbat that is prohibited by rabbinic law. This ruling is in accordance with Rabba, as explained by Rav Yosef (*Shulḥan Arukh, Oraḥ Ḥayyim* 331:6).

Perek **VI**
Daf **68** Amud **a**

מָה הַזָּאָה שְׁבוּת וְאֵינָהּ דּוֹחָה אֶת הַשַּׁבָּת, אַף אֲמִירָה לְגוֹי – שְׁבוּת וְאֵינָהּ דּוֹחָה אֶת הַשַּׁבָּת!

Just as sprinkling the water of purification is prohibited by **rabbinic decree and does not override Shabbat,** even for the purpose of a mitzva, **so too, telling a gentile** to perform a prohibited labor Shabbat is prohibited by **rabbinic decree and does not override Shabbat.** How, then, could Rabba suggest that they instruct a gentile and thus transgress a rabbinic decree?

אֲמַר לֵיהּ: וְלָא שָׁנֵי לָךְ בֵּין שְׁבוּת דְּאִית בֵּיהּ מַעֲשֶׂה לִשְׁבוּת דְּלֵית בֵּיהּ מַעֲשֶׂה? דְּהָא מָר לָא אֲמַר לְגוֹי "זִיל אַחֵים".

Rav Yosef **said to him: But do you not differentiate between a rabbinic decree that involves an action and a rabbinic decree that does not involve an action?**[N] **As the Master,** Rabba, **did not say to the gentile: Go and heat** water on Shabbat, but only told him to transfer something from one domain to another, which does not involve an action and is therefore less severe.

אֲמַר לֵיהּ רַבָּה בַּר רַב חָנָן לְאַבָּיֵי: מְבוֹאָה דְּאִית בֵּיהּ תְּרֵי גַּבְרֵי רַבְרְבֵי כְּרַבָּנַן לָא לֶיהֱוֵי בֵּיהּ לֹא עֵירוּב וְלֹא שִׁיתּוּף?! אֲמַר לֵיהּ: מַאי נַעֲבֵיד? מָר לָאו אוֹרְחֵיהּ, אֲנָא טְרִידְנָא בְּגִירְסַאי, אִינְהוּ לָא מַשְׁגְּחִי.

Upon hearing of this incident and the ensuing discussion, **Rabba bar Rav Ḥanan said to Abaye: In an alleyway that contains two such great people as the Sages** Rabba and Abaye, is it possible that **there could be neither an *eiruv* nor a merging** of alleyways? Abaye **said to him: What should we do?** As for **the Master,** Rabba, **it is not his manner** to go and collect for the *eiruv* from all the residents of the alleyway. As for **myself, I am busy with my studies** and do not have time to take care of this issue. And **they,** the other residents of the alleyway, **do not attend to** such matters.

וְאִי אַקְנִי לְהוּ פִּיתָּא בְּסַלָּא – כֵּיוָן דְּאִי בָּעוּ לַהּ מִינַּאי, וְלָא אֶפְשָׁר לְיִתְבַהּ נְהַלַיְיהוּ – בָּטֵיל שִׁיתּוּף.

And if I were to transfer to the residents of the alleyway a share of the **bread in** my **basket,** so as to allow them to join a merging of alleyways, **since if they would want** to take it **from me it would be impossible** for me **to give it to them** because I am poor and need the small amount of bread that I can afford for myself, the **merging** of alleyways would therefore **be invalid.**

NOTES

A rabbinic decree that involves an action and a rabbinic decree that does not involve an action – שְׁבוּת דְּאִית בֵּיהּ מַעֲשֶׂה לִשְׁבוּת דְּלֵית בֵּיהּ מַעֲשֶׂה: There are two readings of this passage and two different explanations. The version here reads: As the Master did not say to the gentile: Go and heat. According to this reading, there is a difference between a labor that involves an action, such as the heating of water, and a labor that does not involve a creative action, such as carrying from one domain to another.

The other reading (*Ba'al Halakhot Gedolot*, Rabbeinu Ḥananel) does not include the above sentence. According to that reading, the key difference is between an act performed by the Jew himself, e.g., sprinkling, and telling a gentile to perform a prohibited act, which involves no action at all. Some commentaries explain that bringing water relies on two leniencies: The first is that he is speaking and not performing an action, and the second is that this type of carrying is prohibited not by Torah law but by rabbinic decree. The Sages did not impose a prohibition in a case prohibited by a combination of two rabbinic decrees, in cases where suffering is involved (Ra'avad).

HALAKHA

One who requests wine from a merging of alleyways – הַמְבַקֵּשׁ יַיִן מִן הַשִּׁתּוּף: If one of the residents of the alleyway wished to take from the food designated for the merging of the alleyways, and the other residents refused to allow him to do so, the merging of alleyways is invalid (*Shulḥan Arukh, Oraḥ Ḥayyim* 366:5).

Partnership in a courtyard – הַשִּׁתּוּף בְּחָצֵר: The owner of stored food may transfer ownership of a small amount of food to each of the residents of a courtyard or an alleyway. The residents may then establish an *eiruv* with this food, even though each person's portion is not identified or distinct, because the principle of retroactive selection is applied. This ruling is in accordance with the opinion of Beit Hillel (*Tur, Oraḥ Ḥayyim* 387).

Entrances for removing a corpse – פְּתָחִים לְהוֹצָאַת הַמֵּת: If there is a corpse in a house with many entrances, all of the entrances are ritually impure, either because the house is like a sealed grave (Rambam) or because the impurity will eventually exit through one of the entrances (Rashi). If one of the entrances is opened, that entrance alone is impure, while the others remain pure. Similarly, if one decided to remove the corpse through one of the entrances, that entrance alone is impure. This type of designation is effective even if the matter was decided only after the person had died, in accordance with the opinion of Beit Hillel (Rambam *Sefer Tahara, Hilkhot Tumat Met* 7:2).

NOTES

If a corpse is in a house, and the house has many entrances – הַמֵּת בַּבַּיִת וְלוֹ פְּתָחִים הַרְבֵּה: According to the Rambam's Commentary on the Mishna, this *halakha* applies only if all the entrances are closed. In that case, the entire house is considered like a grave, which imparts ritual impurity to all its surroundings. When one entrance is open, the house no longer has the status of a sealed grave, and only the open entrance is ritually impure. Rashi and Rav Shimshon of Saens explain that the impurity under discussion is that which is contracted by objects located in the space of the entrances. Consequently, regardless of whether all of the entrances are closed or open, the same *halakha* applies: They are all considered impure until it becomes clear which entrance will be used for the removal of the corpse.

A certain baby whose warm water spilled – הַהוּא יָנוּקָא דְּאִישְׁתַּפּוּךְ חַמִּימֵיהּ: The commentaries dispute the details of this incident. Is it referring to a baby who had not yet been circumcised, and they wished to heat water so they could wash and circumcise him at the proper time? Or is it referring to a baby who had already been circumcised, in which case the water was required only for his health and comfort? If the latter explanation is correct, questions arise whether or not they merely wished to increase the amount of water for the baby, in which case warming the water is not crucial, and whether or not they sought to perform a labor that is prohibited by Torah law, i.e., bringing water.

דְּתַנְיָא: אֶחָד מִבְּנֵי מָבוֹי שֶׁבִּיקֵּשׁ יַיִן וָשֶׁמֶן וְלֹא נָתְנוּ לוֹ – בָּטֵל הַשִּׁתּוּף.

As it was taught in a *baraita*: If **one of the residents of an alleyway requested wine or oil** from the merging of alleyways, **and they did not give him** any, **the merging** of alleyways **is invalid.** This is because it has become evident that he is not considered a true partner in it.[H]

וְנַקְנֵי לְהוּ מָר רְבִיעְתָּא דְּחַלָּא בְּחָבִיתָא! תַּנְיָא: אֵין מִשְׁתַּתְּפִין בְּאוֹצָר.

Rabba bar Rav Ḥanin further asked: **But let the Master transfer to them a quarter-*log* of vinegar in** one of his **barrels;** certainly even Abaye could afford to provide such a small amount of vinegar for the rest of the residents. Abaye replied: **It was taught** in a *baraita*: **One may not use** food in a **storeroom for a merging** of alleyways, as it is not clear which specific portion of the food is being set aside for that purpose.[H] The same *halakha* would apply to an unspecified quarter-*log* of vinegar in a barrel.

וְהָא תַּנְיָא: מִשְׁתַּתְּפִין! אָמַר רַב אוֹשַׁעְיָא: לָא קַשְׁיָא; הָא – בֵּית שַׁמַּאי, הָא – בֵּית הִלֵּל.

Rabba bar Rav Ḥanin raised a difficulty. **Wasn't it taught** in a different *baraita*: **One may use** stored food **for a merging** of alleyways? **Rav Oshaya said:** This is **not difficult. This** source, the *baraita* that states that one may not use stored food for a merging of alleyways, is in accordance with the opinion of **Beit Shammai.** And **that** source, the *baraita* that states that it is permitted to do so, is in accordance with the opinion of **Beit Hillel.** Beit Shammai and Beit Hillel disagree about whether or not to apply the principle of retroactive clarification.

דִּתְנַן: הַמֵּת בַּבַּיִת וְלוֹ פְּתָחִים הַרְבֵּה – כּוּלָּן טְמֵאִין.

As we learned in a mishna: If **a corpse is in a house,** and the house **has many entrances,**[N] **they are all ritually impure.** It is currently unknown through which entrance the corpse will be removed from the house, and any of the entrances might be used for this purpose. Therefore, they all contract impurity imparted by a corpse in a tent as though the corpse had already passed through each of them.

נִפְתַּח אֶחָד מֵהֶן – הוּא טָמֵא וְכוּלָּן טְהוֹרִין. חִישֵּׁב לְהוֹצִיאוֹ בְּאֶחָד מֵהֶן, אוֹ בַּחַלּוֹן שֶׁיֵּשׁ בּוֹ אַרְבָּעָה עַל אַרְבָּעָה – מַצִּיל עַל כׇּל הַפְּתָחִים כּוּלָּן.

However, if only **one of them was open, that** particular entrance **is ritually impure,** as the corpse will certainly be removed through it, **while all of the others are ritually pure.** If **one decided** from the outset **to remove** the corpse **through one of** the entrances, **or through a window that is four by four** handbreadths in size, **it saves all of the** other **entrances** from contracting impurity.

בֵּית שַׁמַּאי אוֹמְרִים: וְהוּא שֶׁחִישֵּׁב עַד שֶׁלֹּא יָמוּת הַמֵּת. וּבֵית הִלֵּל אוֹמְרִים: אַף מִשֶּׁיָּמוּת הַמֵּת.

Beit Shammai say: This applies only **if he had decided** on an entrance **before the person died,** so that the entrance through which his body would be removed was already determined at the time of death. **But Beit Hillel say:** This applies **even** if he decided the matter only **after the person had died,** as the principle of retroactive selection is invoked and the entrance through which the deceased will be removed has been retroactively established. The same dispute applies to a merging of alleyways with an unspecified portion of stored food, and it revolves around whether it can be retroactively established that a specific portion had been set aside for the merging of alleyways.[H]

הַהוּא יָנוּקָא דְּאִישְׁתַּפּוּךְ חַמִּימֵיהּ, אָמַר לְהוּ רָבָא: נִישַׁיְּילַהּ לְאִימֵּיהּ, אִי צְרִיכָא נַחֵים לֵיהּ גּוֹי אַגַּב אִימֵּיהּ.

The Gemara relates another story about **a certain baby whose warm water,** which had been prepared for his Shabbat circumcision, **spilled.**[N] **Rava said to** those who had brought the matter to his attention: **Let us ask the** baby's **mother. If** the warm water is **necessary** for her health, **let a gentile heat** water **for** the baby **indirectly, through his mother.** In other words, the water may be heated for the mother, as a woman after childbirth is regarded as being in a life-threatening situation.

אֲמַר לֵיהּ רַב מְשַׁרְשְׁיָא לְרָבָא: אִימֵּיהּ קָא אָכְלָה תַּמְרֵי! אֲמַר לֵיהּ: אֵימוּר, תּוּנְבָא בְּעָלְמָא הוּא דְּנָקֵט לַהּ.

Rav Mesharshiya said to Rava: The baby's **mother** is healthy enough that **she is eating dates.** Certainly her condition is not precarious enough to necessitate the heating of water. Rava **said to him:** It is possible to **say** that **it was merely a ravenous hunger that had seized her,** and she is unaware of what she is eating, but in fact she is still dangerously ill.

הַהוּא יָנוֹקָא דְּאִישְׁתְּפוּךְ חַמִּימֵיהּ, אֲמַר לְהוּ רָבָא: פַּנּוּ לִי מָאנַי מִבֵּי גַבְרֵי לְבֵי נָשֵׁי, וְאֵיזִיל וְאֵיתִיב הָתָם וְאִיבְטִיל לְהוּ הָא חָצֵר.

The Gemara relates yet another similar incident: There was once **a certain baby whose warm water,** which had been prepared for his Shabbat circumcision, **spilled. Rava,** who had water in his courtyard but had not established a joint *eiruv* with the adjacent courtyard where the baby was located, **said to** those who asked him about the matter: **Clear away my belongings from the men's chamber,** which opens directly into my courtyard, **to the** inner **women's chamber,** which does not. Rava was concerned that he would come to carry his belongings into the courtyard, which would be prohibited once he had renounced his rights to it. **And I will go and sit there,** in the women's chamber, **and I will renounce** my rights to **this courtyard in favor of** the residents of the baby's courtyard, so that they will be able to transfer the warm water from one courtyard to the other.[B]

אֲמַר לֵיהּ רָבִינָא לְרָבָא: וְהָאָמַר שְׁמוּאֵל אֵין בִּיטּוּל רְשׁוּת מֵחָצֵר לְחָצֵר! אֲמַר לֵיהּ: אֲנָא כְּרַבִּי יוֹחָנָן סְבִירָא לִי, דְּאָמַר: יֵשׁ בִּיטּוּל מֵחָצֵר לְחָצֵר.

Ravina said to Rava: Didn't Shmuel say: There is no renunciation of rights from one courtyard to another. How, then, can you renounce your rights to your courtyard in this manner? Rava **said to him: I hold in accordance with** the opinion of **Rabbi Yoḥanan, who said: There is renouncing of rights from one courtyard to another.**

וְאִי לָא סָבַר לַהּ מָר כִּשְׁמוּאֵל,

Ravina then asked Rava: **But if the Master does not hold in accordance with** the opinion of **Shmuel,**

BACKGROUND

Rava's courtyard – חֲצֵרוֹ שֶׁל רָבָא: Rava would generally reside in his room, the men's chamber, which opened onto the courtyard. In order to transfer hot water from his courtyard to the one where the baby was located, he needed to renounce his rights to the courtyard in favor of the residents of the baby's courtyard.

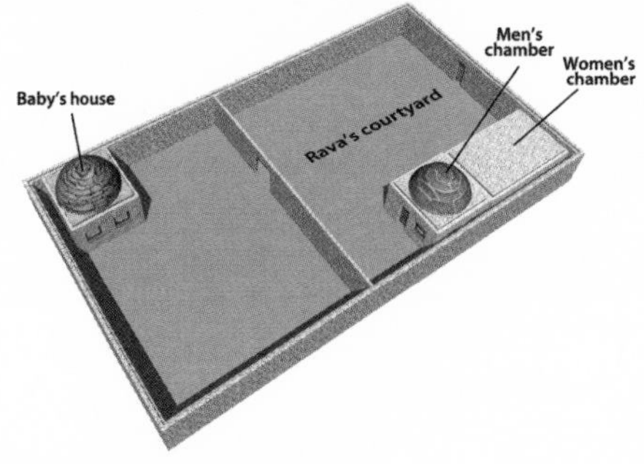

Rava's courtyard

Perek **VI**
Daf **68** Amud **b**

יָתֵיב מָר בְּדוּכְתֵּיהּ, וְנִבְטֵיל לְהוּ לְדִידְהוּ, וְנִיהַדְרוּ אִינְהוּ וְנִבְטְלוּ לֵיהּ לְמָר. דְּהָא אָמַר רַב: מְבַטְּלִין וְחוֹזְרִין וּמְבַטְּלִין!

let the Master remain in his place, i.e., in the men's chamber, **and renounce** his rights to his courtyard **in favor** of the residents of the baby's courtyard, so that they may transfer the water from one courtyard to the other. **And then,** after the water has been moved, **let them renounce** their rights **in favor of the Master,** so that he may once again carry in his courtyard. **As Rav said:** If two people who live in the same courtyard forgot to establish an *eiruv*, one person **may renounce** his rights in favor of the other when he needs it, **and** the second person **may then renounce**[H] his rights in favor of the first when he needs it.

אֲנָא בְּהָא כִּשְׁמוּאֵל סְבִירָא לִי, דְּאָמַר: אֵין מְבַטְּלִין וְחוֹזְרִין וּמְבַטְּלִין.

Rava replied: **In this** regard, **I hold in accordance with** the opinion of **Shmuel, who said: One** person may **not renounce** his rights in favor of the other **and then** subsequently have the second person **renounce** his rights in favor of the first.

וְלָאו חַד טַעְמָא הוּא? מַאי טַעְמָא אֵין מְבַטְּלִין וְחוֹזְרִין וּמְבַטְּלִין – לָאו מִשּׁוּם דְּכֵיוָן דְּבַטְּלֵיהּ לִרְשׁוּתֵיהּ, אִסְתַּלֵּק לֵיהּ מֵהָכָא לְגַמְרֵי, וַהֲוָה לֵיהּ כְּבֶן חָצֵר אַחֶרֶת, וְאֵין בִּיטּוּל רְשׁוּת מֵחָצֵר לְחָצֵר. מָר נַמִי – לָא נִבְטֵיל!

Ravina raised a difficulty: **Isn't the reason** for both *halakhot* **one** and the same? **What is the reason** that **one** may **not renounce** his rights in favor of the other **and then** subsequently have the other **renounce** his rights in favor of the first? **Is it not because** it is assumed that **since he renounced his rights** to the courtyard, it is as if he has **completely removed himself from here, and he** is now considered **like the resident of a different courtyard,** and Shmuel holds that **there is no renouncing of rights from one courtyard to another?** If so, **the Master should** likewise **not renounce** his rights to his courtyard. If you accept Shmuel's opinion with regard to subsequent renouncing, you should likewise accept his opinion with regard to renunciation of rights from one courtyard to another.

הָתָם הַיְינוּ טַעְמָא כִּי הֵיכִי דְּלָא לֶיהֱוֵי מִלְּתָא דְּרַבָּנַן כְּחוּכָא וְאִיטְלוּלָא.

Rava responded: That is not Shmuel's reason for prohibiting subsequent renunciations. **There, this is the rationale** for his opinion: **So that the words of the Sages should not be** a subject **of laughter and mockery.**[N] If it is permitted for one person to renounce his rights in favor of another and then for the second person to renounce his rights in favor of the first, the Sages' enactment will lose all meaning.

HALAKHA

One may renounce and the second person may then renounce – מְבַטְּלִין וְחוֹזְרִין וּמְבַטְּלִין: One may renounce his rights in favor of another resident of his courtyard, and then the other resident may subsequently renounce his rights in favor of the first. This ruling is in accordance with the opinion of Rav Ashi and the statement of Rav, since the *halakha* accords with Rav when he disagrees with Shmuel in matters of ritual law (*Shulḥan Arukh*, *Oraḥ Ḥayyim* 381:7).

NOTES

Laughter and mockery – חוּכָא וְאִיטְלוּלָא: The concern that the words of the Sages might be the target of ridicule appears in several contexts, usually when they rule in a manner that directly contradicts a previous ruling. Such an obvious retraction makes it seem that the original ruling was not sufficiently established and renders the whole process laughable.

NOTES

Subsequent renunciation and removal from one's domain – בִּיטּוּל חוֹזֵר וְסִילּוּק רְשׁוּת: The fact that the Gemara reconciles the statements of Rav and Shmuel with the opinions of both Rabbi Eliezer and the Rabbis implies that everyone agrees there is no renunciation of rights from one courtyard to another. However, it is also possible to explain that both sides do not allow renunciation in this case, not because those who renounce their rights and remove themselves from their domain are considered like residents of a different courtyard, but because they assume the legal status of a gentile, who can never renounce rights (*Me'iri*; Ritva).

גּוּפָא, רַב אָמַר: מְבַטְּלִין וְחוֹזְרִין וּמְבַטְּלִין, וּשְׁמוּאֵל אָמַר: אֵין מְבַטְּלִין וְחוֹזְרִין וּמְבַטְּלִין.

The Gemara proceeds to examine in greater detail the issue raised in the previous discussion. Returning to **the matter itself, Rav said:** If two people who live in the same courtyard forgot to establish an *eiruv*, one **may renounce** his rights in favor of the other, **and then** the second person **may renounce** his rights in favor of the first. **And Shmuel said: One** may **not renounce** his rights in favor of the other **and then** subsequently have the second person **renounce** his rights in favor of the first.

לֵימָא רַב וּשְׁמוּאֵל בִּפְלוּגְתָּא דְּרַבָּנַן וְרַבִּי אֱלִיעֶזֶר קָא מִיפַּלְגִי;

The Gemara suggests: **Let us say** that **Rav and Shmuel disagree about the** same point of **dispute as the Rabbis and Rabbi Eliezer.** Elsewhere it is taught that Rabbi Eliezer and the Rabbis disagree with regard to the *halakha* in a case where one of the residents of a courtyard forgot to join in the *eiruv*, but subsequently renounced his rights to the courtyard on Shabbat. The dispute revolves around the status of this resident's house. Rabbi Eliezer holds that it is prohibited for him to carry in and out of his house, while the other residents of the courtyard are permitted to do so. However, the Rabbis hold that the other residents are prohibited from carrying in and out of his house as well.

דְּרַב דְּאָמַר כְּרַבָּנַן וּשְׁמוּאֵל דְּאָמַר כְּרַבִּי אֱלִיעֶזֶר!

The suggestion is **that Rav stated** his ruling **in accordance with** the opinion of **the Rabbis,** who hold that even one who renounces his rights to his courtyard does not renounce his rights to his house. As he has not completely removed himself from the courtyard, the other residents may later go back and renounce their rights in his favor. **And Shmuel stated** his ruling **in accordance with** the opinion of **Rabbi Eliezer.** He maintains that this resident has completely removed himself from the courtyard. Therefore, there is no possibility of others subsequently renouncing their rights in his favor, as he is no longer considered a resident of the courtyard.

אָמַר לָךְ רַב: אֲנָא דַּאֲמַרִי – אֲפִילּוּ לְרַבִּי אֱלִיעֶזֶר, עַד כָּאן לָא קָאָמַר רַבִּי אֱלִיעֶזֶר הָתָם "הַמְבַטֵּל רְשׁוּת חֲצֵירוֹ רְשׁוּת בֵּיתוֹ בִּיטֵּל" – מִשּׁוּם דְּבַבַּיִת בְּלֹא חָצֵר לָא דָּיְירִי אֱינָשֵׁי, אֲבָל לְעִנְיַן אִיסְתַּלּוֹקֵי – מִי אָמַר?

The Gemara rejects this comparison: **Rav** could have **said to you: What I said is even in accordance with** the opinion of **Rabbi Eliezer. Rabbi Eliezer stated** his opinion **there,** that **one who renounces his rights to his courtyard** also **renounces his rights to his house, only because people do not live in a house without a courtyard,** and therefore it is evident that he has renounced his rights to his house as well. **However, with regard to** whether or not the person himself is considered entirely **removed** from the courtyard to the extent that the others would be unable to then renounce their rights in his favor, **did he state** this? According to this explanation, it is possible that Rav's opinion concurs with Rabbi Eliezer's statement.

וּשְׁמוּאֵל אָמַר: אֲנָא דַּאֲמַרִי – אֲפִילּוּ כְּרַבָּנַן; עַד כָּאן לָא קָאָמְרִי רַבָּנַן הָתָם – אֶלָּא מַאי דְּבָטֵיל – בָּטֵיל, וּדְלָא בָּטֵיל לָא בָּטֵיל. אֲבָל מַאי דְּבָטֵיל – מִיהָא אִיסְתַּלַּק לְגַמְרֵי.

And Shmuel could have **said: What I said is even in accordance with** the opinion of **the Rabbis. The Rabbis stated** their opinion **only there,** where they ruled: **That which he has renounced,** i.e., his rights to his courtyard, **is renounced; and** that which **he has not renounced,** i.e., his rights in his house, **is not renounced. However,** from **that which he has renounced, he has removed himself completely.** Consequently, all agree that one who renounces his rights to his courtyard is no longer considered a resident of that place.[N]

אָמַר רַב אַחָא בַּר חָנָא, אָמַר רַב שֵׁשֶׁת: כְּתַנָּאֵי; מִי שֶׁנָּתַן רְשׁוּתוֹ וְהוֹצִיא, בֵּין בְּשׁוֹגֵג בֵּין בְּמֵזִיד – אוֹסֵר, דִּבְרֵי רַבִּי מֵאִיר. רַבִּי יְהוּדָה אוֹמֵר: בְּמֵזִיד – אוֹסֵר, בְּשׁוֹגֵג – אֵינוֹ אוֹסֵר.

Rav Aḥa bar Ḥana said that **Rav Sheshet said:** This dispute between Rav and Shmuel is **like** an earlier dispute between *tanna'im*. We learned elsewhere in a mishna: If **one gave** away **his rights** to his share of the courtyard to the other residents of the courtyard by renouncing them after having forgotten to establish an *eiruv* with the other residents on the previous day, **and then he carried** something **out** from his house into the courtyard, **whether** he did so **unwittingly,** forgetting that he had renounced his rights, **or intentionally, he** once again **renders** carrying **prohibited** for all the residents of the courtyard, as his action cancels his renunciation. This is **the statement of Rabbi Meir. Rabbi Yehuda says:** If he did so **intentionally, he renders** carrying **prohibited** for the other residents; but if he did it **unwittingly, he does not render** carrying **prohibited** for them.

מַאי לָאו, בְּהָא קָמִיפַּלְגִי, דְּמָר סָבַר: מְבַטְּלִין וְחוֹזְרִין וּמְבַטְּלִין, וּמָר סָבַר אֵין מְבַטְּלִין וְחוֹזְרִין וּמְבַטְּלִין.

What, is it not that they disagree with regard to **this: One Sage,** Rabbi Meir, **holds** that a person who renounces his rights does not remove himself completely from his domain, and therefore **one** person may **renounce** his rights in favor of another, **and** the second person may **then renounce** his rights in favor of the first. As a result, even an inadvertent act of carrying serves to cancel the renunciation. And **one Sage,** Rabbi Yehuda, **holds** that one who renounces his rights removes himself completely from his domain, and therefore one person **may not renounce** his rights in favor of another **and then** subsequently have the second person **renounce** his rights in favor of the first. In that case, only an intentional act of carrying can cancel the renunciation.

אָמַר רַב אַחָא בַּר תַּחֲלִיפָא מִשְּׁמֵיהּ דְּרָבָא: לֹא, דְּכוּלֵּי עָלְמָא: אֵין מְבַטְּלִין וְחוֹזְרִין וּמְבַטְּלִין. וְהָכָא בְּקָנְסוּ שׁוֹגֵג אַטּוּ מֵזִיד קָא מִיפַּלְגִי; מָר סָבַר: קָנְסוּ שׁוֹגֵג אַטּוּ מֵזִיד, וּמָר סָבַר: לֹא קָנְסוּ שׁוֹגֵג אַטּוּ מֵזִיד.

Rav Aḥa bar Taḥalifa said in the name of Rava: No, everyone agrees that a person who renounces his rights removes himself completely from his domain, and therefore one person **may not renounce** his rights in favor of another **and then** subsequently have the second person **renounce** his rights in favor of the first. **And here, they disagree** with regard to the question: Did the Sages **penalize** an **unwitting** offender **due to** an **intentional** offender? **One Sage,** Rabbi Meir, who states that the resident always renders carrying prohibited for the others, **holds** that **they penalized** an **unwitting** offender **due to** an **intentional** offender. **And one Sage,** Rabbi Yehuda, who states that the resident renders carrying prohibited for the others only if he acted intentionally, **holds** that **they did not penalize** an **unwitting** offender **due to** an **intentional** offender.

רַב אַשִׁי אָמַר: רַב וּשְׁמוּאֵל בִּפְלוּגְתָּא דְּרַבִּי אֱלִיעֶזֶר וְרַבָּנַן קָא מִיפַּלְגִי.

Rav Ashi, disagreeing with the Gemara's refutation, **said: Rav and Shmuel disagree in the** same **dispute as** do **Rabbi Eliezer and the Rabbis.**

"אָמַר רַבָּן גַּמְלִיאֵל: מַעֲשֶׂה בִּצְדוֹקִי אֶחָד שֶׁהָיָה דָּר עִמָּנוּ". צְדוֹקִי מַאן דְּכַר שְׁמֵיהּ?!

It was stated in the mishna that **Rabban Gamliel said:** There was **an incident involving a certain Sadducee who lived with us** in the same alleyway in Jerusalem, who renounced his rights in the alleyway before Shabbat. The mishna then continues with a discussion about how and whether the alleyway may be used on Shabbat. The Gemara first poses a question: **A Sadducee; who mentioned his name?**[N] The mishna had thus far spoken only of a gentile, so why does Rabban Gamliel invoke an incident involving a Sadducee?

חַסּוּרֵי מִיחַסְּרָא, וְהָכִי קָתָנֵי: צְדוֹקִי הֲרֵי הוּא כְּגוֹי וְרַבָּן גַּמְלִיאֵל אוֹמֵר: צְדוֹקִי אֵינוֹ כְּגוֹי וְאָמַר רַבָּן גַּמְלִיאֵל: מַעֲשֶׂה בִּצְדוֹקִי אֶחָד שֶׁהָיָה דָּר עִמָּנוּ בְּמָבוֹי בִּירוּשָׁלַיִם, וְאָמַר לָנוּ אַבָּא: מַהֲרוּ וְהוֹצִיאוּ אֶת הַכֵּלִים לַמָּבוֹי, עַד שֶׁלֹּא יוֹצִיא וְיֶאֱסֹר עֲלֵיכֶם.

The Gemara answers: The mishna **is incomplete.** It is missing an important element, **and this** is what **it is teaching:** The legal status of **a Sadducee is like** that of **a gentile, and Rabban Gamliel says:** The legal status of a **Sadducee**[H] **is not like** that of **a gentile. And Rabban Gamliel** further **said:** There was **an incident involving a certain Sadducee who lived with us in** the same **alleyway in Jerusalem,** who renounced his rights in the alleyway before Shabbat, **and Father said to us: Hurry and take out** your **utensils to the alleyway** to establish possession of it **before** he changes his mind and **takes out** his utensils, in which case **he would render it prohibited for you** to use the entire alleyway.

וְהָתַנְיָא: הַדָּר עִם הַנָּכְרִי צְדוֹקִי וּבַיְתוֹסִי הֲרֵי אֵלּוּ אוֹסְרִין עָלָיו, (רַבָּן גַּמְלִיאֵל אוֹמֵר: צְדוֹקִי וּבַיְתוֹסִי אֵינָן אוֹסְרִין.) וּמַעֲשֶׂה בִּצְדוֹקִי אֶחָד שֶׁהָיָה דָּר עִם רַבָּן גַּמְלִיאֵל בְּמָבוֹי בִּירוּשָׁלַיִם, וְאָמַר לָהֶם רַבָּן גַּמְלִיאֵל לְבָנָיו: "בָּנַי מַהֲרוּ וְהוֹצִיאוּ מַה שֶּׁאַתֶּם מוֹצִיאִין, וְהַכְנִיסוּ מַה שֶּׁאַתֶּם מַכְנִיסִין, עַד שֶׁלֹּא יוֹצִיא הַתּוֹעֵב הַזֶּה וְיֶאֱסֹר עֲלֵיכֶם, שֶׁהֲרֵי בִּיטֵּל רְשׁוּתוֹ לָכֶם", דִּבְרֵי רַבִּי מֵאִיר.

And similarly, **wasn't it taught** in a *baraita* that the status of a Sadducee is a matter of dispute between *tanna'im*: If **one lives with a gentile, a Sadducee, or a Boethusian** in the same alleyway, **they render** carrying **prohibited** for **him. Rabban Gamliel says: A Sadducee or a Boethusian do not prohibit** one from carrying. There was **an incident involving a certain Sadducee who lived with Rabban Gamliel in** the same **alleyway in Jerusalem,** and he renounced his rights to the alleyway before Shabbat. **Rabban Gamliel said to his sons: Hurry and take out** those utensils **that you wish to take out, and bring in** those utensils **that you wish to bring in, before that loathsome** person retracts his renunciation and **takes out** his utensils **and prohibits you** from using the alleyway, **as he renounced his rights in your favor;** this is **the statement of Rabbi Meir.**

רַבִּי יְהוּדָה אוֹמֵר בְּלָשׁוֹן אַחֶרֶת: מַהֲרוּ וַעֲשׂוּ צוֹרְכֵיכֶם בַּמָּבוֹי עַד שֶׁלֹּא תֶּחְשַׁךְ וְיֶאֱסֹר עֲלֵיכֶם.

Rabbi Yehuda says: Rabban Gamliel spoke to them **with a different formulation,** saying: **Hurry and do whatever you must do in the alleyway** prior to Shabbat, **before night falls and he prohibits you** from using the alleyway.[N]

NOTES

Who mentioned his name – מַאן דְּכַר שְׁמֵיהּ: There is a general assumption that the statements of different Sages in a mishna are related to each other in some way. Therefore, if there is an opinion that mentions an unrelated issue without even a prior hint to it, the question arises: Who mentioned this? Whose previous mention of this issue led to its emergence as a topic of discussion?

The dispute between Rabbi Meir and Rabbi Yehuda – מַחְלוֹקֶת רַבִּי מֵאִיר וְרַבִּי יְהוּדָה: It is explained in the Jerusalem Talmud that even Rabbi Yehuda agrees that a Sadducee may renounce his rights to a courtyard, and that he differs from a gentile in this regard. However, one must distinguish between the renunciation of a Jew and that of a Sadducee. The renunciation of a Jew is complete and fully reliable, while that of a Sadducee is not a complete renunciation, since he retroactively cancels it when he retracts his decision, as ruled by several major authorities (Rambam; see Rashba).

HALAKHA

The legal status of a Sadducee – דִּין צְדוֹקִי: The legal status of a is not have the legal status of a gentile. Therefore, he may renounce his rights to a courtyard, in accordance with the opinion of Rabban Gamliel (Rosh) and one version of the opinion of Rabbi Yehuda. However, he may not participate in an *eiruv*, because he does not accept the principle of *eiruv* (*Shulḥan Arukh, Oraḥ Ḥayyim* 385:1).

אָמַר מָר: "הוֹצִיאוּ מַה שֶּׁאַתֶּם מוֹצִיאִין וְהַכְנִיסוּ מַה שֶּׁאַתֶּם מַכְנִיסִין עַד שֶׁלֹּא יוֹצִיא הַתּוֹעֵב הַזֶּה וְיֶאֱסֹר עֲלֵיכֶם". לְמֵימְרָא דְּכִי מַפְּקִי אִינְהוּ, וַהֲדַר מַפֵּיק אִיהוּ לָא אָסַר?!

The Gemara proceeds to analyze this *baraita*. **The Master said** previously: **Take out** those utensils **that you wish to take out, and bring in** those utensils **that you wish to bring in, before that loathsome** person **takes out** his utensils **and prohibits you** from using the alleyway. The Gemara poses a question: **Is that to say that,** according to Rabbi Meir, **if they took out** their utensils **and then** afterward the gentile or Sadducee **took out his** utensils on Shabbat, **he does not render** carrying **prohibited** for them?

Perek **VI**
Daf **69** Amud **a**

NOTES

Where the residents of the alleyway had taken possession – שֶׁהֶחְזִיקוּ בְּנֵי מָבוֹי: The establishment of possession [*ḥazaka*] in this context is different from the meaning of the term in other talmudic contexts. In general, *ḥazaka* refers to the acquisition of a domain or a certain right over property. In this context, however, the *ḥazaka* is merely symbolic. Nevertheless, their use of the alleyway is considered a kind of acquisition for these purposes alone (see *Me'iri*).

HALAKHA

One gave away his rights and then carried – נָתַן רְשׁוּתוֹ וְהוֹצִיא: With regard to a person who renounced his rights and subsequently carried something into the alleyway, if he did so inadvertently, his act of renunciation does not render carrying prohibited for the residents of the alleyway. However, if he did so intentionally, his action renders it prohibited to carry, as stated by Rabbi Yehuda, since the *halakha* is in accordance with his opinion in disputes with Rabbi Meir. If the residents of the alleyway had already taken possession of the alleyway, he can no longer reconsider, in accordance with the statement of Rabbi Yehuda in the *baraita* (*Shulḥan Arukh*, *Oraḥ Ḥayyim* 381:1).

וְהָתְנַן: מִי שֶׁנָּתַן רְשׁוּתוֹ וְהוֹצִיא, בֵּין בְּשׁוֹגֵג בֵּין בְּמֵזִיד – אוֹסֵר, דִּבְרֵי רַבִּי מֵאִיר!

But didn't we learn elsewhere in the mishna: If **one gave** away **his rights** in his courtyard to the other residents of the courtyard, renouncing them after having forgotten to establish an *eiruv* with them the previous day, and then **he carried** something **out** from his house into the courtyard, **whether unwittingly or intentionally, he** again **renders it prohibited** for all the residents of the courtyard to carry; this is **the statement of Rabbi Meir.** This indicates that according to Rabbi Meir, even if the resident carried something into the courtyard on Shabbat itself, he cancels his renunciation, contrary to Rabbi Meir's own statement in the mishna with regard to a Sadducee.

אָמַר רַב יוֹסֵף: אֵימָא: "אֵינוֹ אוֹסֵר". אַבָּיֵי אָמַר: לָא קַשְׁיָא; כָּאן – שֶׁהֶחְזִיקוּ בְּנֵי מָבוֹי בַּמָּבוֹי, כָּאן – שֶׁלֹּא הֶחְזִיקוּ בְּנֵי מָבוֹי בַּמָּבוֹי.

Rav Yosef said: Say that Rabbi Meir's statement should read instead: **He does not render it prohibited. Abaye said:** It is **not difficult,** as the contradiction between the two teachings of Rabbi Meir can be resolved as follows: **Here,** where the Sadducee cannot cancel his renunciation, it refers to a case **where the residents of the alleyway had** already **taken possession**[N] **of the alleyway** before he brought out his vessels; whereas **here,** where the Jew cancels his renunciation, it refers to a case **where the residents of the alleyway had not taken possession of the alleyway** prior to his act of carrying.

וְהָתַנְיָא: עַד שֶׁלֹּא נָתַן רְשׁוּתוֹ, הוֹצִיא בֵּין בְּשׁוֹגֵג בֵּין בְּמֵזִיד – יָכוֹל לְבַטֵּל, דִּבְרֵי רַבִּי מֵאִיר. רַבִּי יְהוּדָה אוֹמֵר: בְּשׁוֹגֵג – יָכוֹל לְבַטֵּל, בְּמֵזִיד – אֵינוֹ יָכוֹל לְבַטֵּל.

And similarly, **it was taught** in a *baraita*: With regard to one who failed to join in an *eiruv* with the other residents of his alleyway, **if he carried** something from his house into the alleyway **before he gave** away, i.e., renounced, **his rights** in the alleyway, **whether unwittingly or intentionally, he can** still **renounce** his rights; this is **the statement of Rabbi Meir. Rabbi Yehuda says:** If he **unwittingly** carried from his house into the alleyway, **he can** still **renounce** his rights, but if he did so **intentionally, he cannot renounce** them, for one who publicly transgresses the words of the Sages and intentionally desecrates Shabbat has the status of a gentile.

מִי שֶׁנָּתַן רְשׁוּתוֹ – וְהוֹצִיא, בֵּין בְּשׁוֹגֵג בֵּין בְּמֵזִיד – אוֹסֵר, דִּבְרֵי רַבִּי מֵאִיר. רַבִּי יְהוּדָה אוֹמֵר: בְּמֵזִיד – אוֹסֵר, בְּשׁוֹגֵג – אֵינוֹ אוֹסֵר. בַּמֶּה דְּבָרִים אֲמוּרִים – בְּשֶׁלֹּא הֶחְזִיקוּ בְּנֵי מָבוֹי בַּמָּבוֹי, אֲבָל הֶחְזִיקוּ בְּנֵי מָבוֹי בַּמָּבוֹי – בֵּין בְּשׁוֹגֵג וּבֵין בְּמֵזִיד אֵינוֹ אוֹסֵר.

However, if **one** already **gave** away, i.e., renounced, **his rights** in the alleyway, and then **he carried**[H] something from his house into the alleyway, **whether unwittingly or intentionally, he renders prohibited** all the residents' use of the alleyway, for his action cancels his renunciation; these are **the words of Rabbi Meir. Rabbi Yehuda says:** If he did it **intentionally, he renders** carrying **prohibited;** but if he carried **inadvertently, he does not render** carrying **prohibited. In what** case **is this statement said?** In a case **where the residents of the alleyway had not** already **taken possession of the alleyway. But if the residents of the alleyway had** already **taken possession of the alleyway** before he carried something into the alleyway, all agree that **whether** he did it **unwittingly or intentionally, he does not render prohibited** their use of the alleyway.

אָמַר מָר: "רַבִּי יְהוּדָה אוֹמֵר בִּלְשׁוֹן אַחֶרֶת: מַהֲרוּ וַעֲשׂוּ צָרְכֵיכֶם בַּמָּבוֹי עַד שֶׁלֹּא תֶּחְשַׁךְ וְיֶאֱסֹר עֲלֵיכֶם". אַלְמָא: גּוֹי הוּא. וְהָא אֲנַן "עַד שֶׁלֹּא יוֹצִיא" תְּנַן:

The Master said above in the *baraita*: **Rabbi Yehuda says:** Rabban Gamliel spoke to them **with a different formulation,** saying: **Hurry, and do whatever you must do in the alleyway** prior to Shabbat, **before night falls, and he will render prohibited your** use of the alleyway. **It is apparent** from this statement that a Sadducee **is** considered **a gentile,** whose renunciation of his rights in an alleyway is ineffective. **But didn't we learn** in the mishna that according to Rabbi Yehuda, he said: Hurry, and do whatever you have to do **before he takes out** [*yotzi*] his vessels and renders prohibited your use of the alleyway, which implies that until then they may in fact use the alleyway; that is, his renunciation is effective?

אֵימָא ״עַד שֶׁלֹּא יוֹצִיא הַיּוֹם״. וְאִיבָּעֵית אֵימָא: לָא קַשְׁיָא; כָּאן – בְּמוּמָר לְחַלֵּל שַׁבָּתוֹת בִּצְנָעָא, כָּאן – בְּמוּמָר לְחַלֵּל שַׁבָּתוֹת בְּפַרְהֶסְיָא.

The Gemara answers: **Say** that the mishna should read as follows: Hurry, and do whatever you have to do **before the day goes out** [*yotzi hayom*], i.e., before the end of Friday. **And if you wish, say:** It is **not difficult. Here,** where the mishna implies that a Sadducee may renounce his rights in an alleyway, it refers **to an apostate** of the kind **who desecrates Shabbat in private; here,** where the *baraita* implies that a Sadducee may not renounce his rights in an alleyway, it refers **to an apostate who desecrates Shabbat in public** [*befarhesya*].[L] Such a person is likened to a gentile in all regards, and therefore he may not renounce his rights in the alleyway.

כְּמַאן אָזְלָא הָא דְּתַנְיָא: מוּמָר וְגִילּוּי פָּנִים – הֲרֵי זֶה אֵינוֹ מְבַטֵּל רְשׁוּת. גִּילּוּי פָּנִים מוּמָר הָוֵי?!

The Gemara comments: **In accordance with which** *tanna* **is** the ruling **that was taught** in the following *baraita*: **An apostate or a brazen-faced** person **may not renounce his rights** in favor of his neighbors. Before discussing the *halakha* itself, the Gemara wonders at the phrase **brazen-faced** person. It would appear to mean an impudent person who acts against the Torah in a brazen manner, but **is** not such a one **an apostate?** Why then are the two listed separately?

אֶלָּא מוּמָר בְּגִילּוּי פָּנִים אֵינוֹ יָכוֹל לְבַטֵּל רְשׁוּת, כְּמַאן – כְּרַבִּי יְהוּדָה.

Rather, read the *baraita* as follows: **A brazen-faced apostate,** i.e., one who publicly displays his deviation from Torah, **may not renounce his rights** in favor of his neighbors. **In accordance with whose** opinion was this stated? It is **in accordance with** the opinion of **Rabbi Yehuda.**

הַהוּא דִּנְפַק בְּחוּמַרְתָּא דְּמִדּוּשָׁא, כֵּיוָן דְּחַזְיֵיהּ לְרַבִּי יְהוּדָה נְשִׂיאָה כַּסְיֵיהּ. אֲמַר: כְּגוֹן זֶה מְבַטֵּל רְשׁוּת לְרַבִּי יְהוּדָה.

The Gemara now relates that **a certain** person **went out with a coral ring**[N] into the public domain, and it is prohibited to do so on Shabbat. **When he saw Rabbi Yehuda Nesia**[P] approaching, **he** quickly **covered it.** Although he was desecrating the Shabbat, he did not want the Sage to see it. Rabbi Yehuda Nesia **said:** A person **such as this,** who is careful not to desecrate Shabbat in public, **may renounce his rights** in his courtyard **according to** the opinion of **Rabbi Yehuda.**

אָמַר רַב הוּנָא: אֵיזֶהוּ יִשְׂרָאֵל מוּמָר – זֶה הַמְחַלֵּל שַׁבָּתוֹת בְּפַרְהֶסְיָא. אֲמַר לֵיהּ רַב נַחְמָן: כְּמַאן? אִי כְּרַבִּי מֵאִיר דְּאָמַר חָשׁוּד לְדָבָר אֶחָד חָשׁוּד לְכָל הַתּוֹרָה כּוּלָּהּ – אֲפִילּוּ בְּאֶחָד מִכָּל אִיסּוּרִין שֶׁבַּתּוֹרָה נָמֵי!

In connection with the preceding discussion with regard to one who does not conform to Torah law, **Rav Huna said: Who is an apostate Jew?** This is **one who desecrates Shabbat in public. Rav Naḥman said to him: In accordance with** whose opinion did you say this? **If** he said this **in accordance with** the opinion of **Rabbi Meir,** who **said: One who is suspected of** transgressing **one matter,**[N] i.e., someone who is known to have committed one transgression, **is suspected of** transgressing **the entire Torah,** he should be considered an apostate **even** if he transgresses **one of all the** other **prohibitions of the Torah as well,** and not necessarily one as severe as Shabbat desecration.

אִי כְּרַבָּנַן – הָאָמְרִי חָשׁוּד לְדָבָר אֶחָד לָא הָוֵי חָשׁוּד לְכָל הַתּוֹרָה כּוּלָּהּ,

If he said this **in accordance with** the opinion of **the Rabbis,** it is difficult. **Didn't they say:** One who is **suspected of** transgressing **one matter is not suspected of** transgressing **the entire Torah,**

LANGUAGE

In public [*befarhesya*] – בְּפַרְהֶסְיָא: From the Greek παρρησία, *parèsiya*, meaning free, open, or unbridled speech. The Sages used this word to refer to anything performed in public for all to see.

NOTES

A certain person went out with a coral ring – הַהוּא דִּנְפַק בְּחוּמַרְתָּא דְּמִדּוּשָׁא: There are several variant readings of this passage. The reading in the Gemara describes a person who did this on only one occasion, despite the fact that he acted with full intention. Other variant readings indicate that the person would habitually act in this manner. Nevertheless, one can learn from this story about the criteria for one who qualifies as a brazen-faced apostate. The story indicates that even with regard to one who sins in public, if he is ashamed to do so in front of a great Torah authority to the extent that he will avoid passing before him, he is not considered a public sinner.

One who is suspected of transgressing one matter – חָשׁוּד לְדָבָר אֶחָד: This refers to a person who is known to commit a particular transgression, as a person is not disqualified based on suspicions alone. The word suspected is used in this context because the relevant issue is whether this transgression is sufficient grounds for suspecting him of transgressing the entire Torah, or whether he is unreliable only with regard to committing this particular transgression.

PERSONALITIES

Rabbi Yehuda Nesia – רַבִּי יְהוּדָה נְשִׂיאָה: Rabbi Yehuda Nesia was the son of Rabban Gamliel, who was the son of Rabbi Yehuda HaNasi. He was called Nesia to differentiate him from his illustrious grandfather, the editor of the Mishna. One of the earliest *amora'im* in Eretz Yisrael, he was a colleague of Rabbi Yehuda HaNasi's great students. His own students included Rabbi Yoḥanan and Reish Lakish.

Rabbi Yehuda Nesia's court enacted various decrees. It was considered the great Torah center in the Jewish world, to the extent that even the great *amora* Rav deferred to its authority.

Rabbi Yehuda Nesia served as *nasi* for many years and was probably the last *nasi* to have outstanding Torah knowledge and to serve as the head of the Sanhedrin. In his honor, he, like his grandfather, is sometimes referred to simply as Rabbi (especially in the Jerusalem Talmud). He was succeeded as *nasi*, but not as head of the Sanhedrin, by his son, Rabban Gamliel.

Perek **VI**
Daf **69** Amud **b**

עַד דְּהָוֵי מוּמָר לַעֲבוֹדָה זָרָה!

unless he is an apostate with regard to idolatry. As long as he has not worshipped idols, his transgression of a single prohibition does not put him under suspicion of transgressing the rest of the Torah.

אָמַר רַב נַחְמָן בַּר יִצְחָק: לִיתֵּן רְשׁוּת וּלְבַטֵּל רְשׁוּת. וְכִדְתַנְיָא: יִשְׂרָאֵל מוּמָר מְשַׁמֵּר שַׁבָּתוֹ בַּשּׁוּק – מְבַטֵּל רְשׁוּת, שֶׁאֵינוֹ מְשַׁמֵּר שַׁבָּתוֹ בַּשּׁוּק – אֵינוֹ מְבַטֵּל רְשׁוּת.

Rav Naḥman bar Yitzḥak said: Rav Huna was not attempting to offer a broad definition of an apostate, but was rather referring to the specific issue of **giving away rights or renouncing rights** in a domain with regard to the *halakhot* of *eiruvin*. **And as it was taught** in the following *Tosefta*: **An apostate Jew,** if **he observes his Shabbat in the marketplace,** i.e., in public, **he may renounce** his **rights** in a domain like a regular Jew, but if he **does not observe his Shabbat in the marketplace, he may not renounce** his **rights** in a domain, as he is no longer considered a Jew in this regard.[H]

HALAKHA

A Jew who may not renounce his rights – יִשְׂרָאֵל שֶׁאֵינוֹ נוֹתֵן רְשׁוּת: A Jew who is an apostate with regard to idolatry or who desecrates Shabbat in public, even if he violates only rabbinic prohibitions (*Ba'al Halakhot Gedolot*; Rashi; *Tosafot*; Rosh), has the legal status of a gentile, and he may not renounce his rights in a courtyard, but rather he must rent it out. If the person desecrates Shabbat only in private, even if he performs labors prohibited by the Torah, he is considered a Jew with regard to such renunciation, in accordance with the *baraita* in the Gemara (*Shulḥan Arukh*, *Oraḥ Ḥayyim* 385:3).

מִפְּנֵי שֶׁאָמְרוּ: יִשְׂרָאֵל נוֹטֵל רְשׁוּת וְנוֹתֵן רְשׁוּת, וּבְגוֹי עַד שֶׁיַּשְׂכִּיר. כֵּיצַד? אוֹמֵר לוֹ: רְשׁוּתִי קְנוּיָה לְךָ, רְשׁוּתִי מְבוּטֶּלֶת לְךָ – קָנָה, וְאֵין צָרִיךְ לִזְכּוֹת.

This distinction is significant **due to** the fact **that** the Sages **said: A Jew may receive rights and give** away **rights** in a domain through a mere statement of renunciation, **but with regard to a gentile** it is not so, as he may not transfer his rights to others or renounce them in a domain **unless he** actually **rents** it **out. How so?** A Jew **may say to** his fellow: **May my rights** in this domain **be acquired by you,** or **May my rights** in this domain **be renounced to you,** and his fellow thereby **acquires** those rights, **and it is not necessary that he take possession of it** through a formal mode of acquisition.[H]

רַב אַשִׁי אָמַר: הַאי תַּנָּא הוּא, דַּחֲמִירָא עֲלֵיהּ שַׁבָּת כַּעֲבוֹדָה זָרָה,

Rav Ashi said: Rav Huna's statement that a Jew who desecrates Shabbat in public is an apostate is indeed a general statement, as he is no longer considered a Jew in any sense. In accordance with the opinion of which *tanna* did he make that statement? **It** is in accordance with the opinion of **this** ***tanna*****, for whom Shabbat is as severe as idolatry,** and therefore one who desecrates Shabbat is treated like an idol worshipper.

כִּדְתַנְיָא ״מִכֶּם״ – וְלֹא כּוּלְּכֶם, פְּרָט לְמוּמָר. ״מִכֶּם״ – בָּכֶם חִלַּקְתִּי, וְלֹא בָּאוּמּוֹת.

As it was taught in a *baraita* with regard to the verse: "Speak to the children of Israel and say to them: When any man of you brings an offering to the Lord, you shall bring your offering of the cattle, of the herd, or of the flock" (Leviticus 1:2). The *baraita* expounds: **"Of you,"** i.e., some of you, but **not all of you** may bring an offering – **to the exclusion of an apostate. "Of you"** additionally serves to emphasize that **among you,** the children of Israel, **I distinguish** between those who observe the Torah and are fit to bring an offering, and those who are not fit, **but not among the nations,** i.e., in regard to the other nations, even those who do not fulfill the precepts binding upon them may offer their sacrifices.

״מִן הַבְּהֵמָה״ – לְהָבִיא בְּנֵי אָדָם הַדּוֹמִין לַבְּהֵמָה. מִכָּאן אָמְרוּ: מְקַבְּלִין קָרְבָּנוֹת מִפּוֹשְׁעֵי יִשְׂרָאֵל כְּדֵי שֶׁיַּחְזְרוּ בִּתְשׁוּבָה, חוּץ מִן הַמּוּמָר וְהַמְנַסֵּךְ יַיִן וְהַמְחַלֵּל שַׁבָּתוֹת בְּפַרְהֶסְיָא.

"Of the cattle" is expounded as follows: **To include people who are similar to animals**[N] in their disdain for the proper behavior of man, i.e., that the wicked too may offer sacrifices. **From here** the Sages **stated: We accept** voluntary **sacrifices from Jewish transgressors,**[N] **in order** to enable them **to repent,**[N] **apart from the apostate, one who pours wine libations** as part of idol worship, **and one who desecrates Shabbat in public,** from whom we do not accept sacrifices without their complete repentance.[H]

הָא גּוּפָא קַשְׁיָא: אָמְרַתְּ ״מִכֶּם״ וְלֹא כּוּלְּכֶם – לְהוֹצִיא אֶת הַמּוּמָר, וַהֲדַר תָּנֵי: מְקַבְּלִין קָרְבָּנוֹת מִפּוֹשְׁעֵי יִשְׂרָאֵל! הָא לָא קַשְׁיָא, רֵישָׁא – בְּמוּמָר לְכָל הַתּוֹרָה כּוּלָּהּ, מְצִיעֲתָא – בְּמוּמָר לְדָבָר אֶחָד.

The Gemara expresses surprise: **This** ***baraita*** **itself is difficult,** i.e., it contains an internal contradiction: **You** first **said: "Of you," but not all of you, to the exclusion of an apostate; and then you taught: We accept sacrifices from Jewish transgressors.** The Gemara answers: **This is not difficult,** as it can be explained as follows: **The first clause** refers **to an apostate with regard to the entire Torah,** whose sacrifices are not accepted, whereas **the middle clause** speaks **of an apostate with regard to one matter** alone, whose sacrifices are indeed accepted.

אֵימָא סֵיפָא: חוּץ מִן הַמּוּמָר וְהַמְנַסֵּךְ יַיִן. הַאי מוּמָר הֵיכִי דָמֵי? אִי מוּמָר לְכָל הַתּוֹרָה – הַיְינוּ רֵישָׁא! אִי לְדָבָר אֶחָד – קַשְׁיָא מְצִיעֲתָא!

The Gemara raises a difficulty: If so, **say** an explanation of **the last clause** of the mishna: **Apart from the apostate and one who pours wine libations** to idolatry, and one who desecrates Shabbat in public. **This apostate, what are the circumstances** indicating his status? **If** it refers to **an apostate with regard to the entire Torah, this is** the same as **the first clause.** And **if** it refers to **an apostate with regard to** only **one thing, the middle clause** of the *baraita* is **difficult,** for it states that we accept sacrifices from such an apostate.

אֶלָּא לָאו הָכִי קָאָמַר: חוּץ מִן הַמּוּמָר לְנַסֵּךְ וּלְחַלֵּל שַׁבָּתוֹת בְּפַרְהֶסְיָא. אַלְמָא: עֲבוֹדָה זָרָה וְשַׁבָּת כִּי הֲדָדֵי נִינְהוּ. שְׁמַע מִינָּהּ.

Rather, is it not true **that this is** what **it is saying: Apart from the apostate with regard to pouring wine libations** to idolatry **and desecrating Shabbat in public?** Although they transgress only one matter, this transgression is so serious that they are considered apostates with regard to the entire Torah. **It is apparent** from here that **idolatry and Shabbat are equivalent,** which indicates that there is a *tanna* who considers public Shabbat desecration as severe a transgression as idolatry. The Gemara concludes: Indeed, **learn from this** that it is so.[N]

HALAKHA

The method of renunciation – כֵּיצַד מְבַטְּלִין: One who renounces his rights in his domain says: May my rights in this domain be renounced to you, or: May my rights in this domain be acquired by you. He need not perform a formal act of acquisition (*Shulḥan Arukh, Oraḥ Ḥayyim* 380:1).

Sacrifices of Jewish transgressors – קָרְבָּנוֹת מִפּוֹשְׁעֵי יִשְׂרָאֵל: Sacrifices are not accepted from one who is an apostate with regard to the entire Torah, to idolatry, or to Shabbat observance. If one is an apostate with regard to any other transgression, his sacrifices are accepted. However, sacrifices are not accepted for the transgression he habitually performs until he repents (Rambam *Sefer Avoda, Hilkhot Ma'aseh HaKorbanot* 3:4).

NOTES

Who are similar to animals – הַדּוֹמִין לַבְּהֵמָה: See Rashi, who explains here that their similarity to animals lies in their inability to recognize their Creator. Elsewhere, however, he explains that their similarity to animals lies in their failure to perform mitzvot.

Jewish transgressors – פּוֹשְׁעֵי יִשְׂרָאֵל: This expression is referring exclusively to those who transgress intentionally and not to those who act unwittingly, as only one who acts with full intent and knowledge of his actions is referred to as a transgressor. Elsewhere, the Gemara demonstrates that in the Bible, the word *poshe'a* means one who rebels. Therefore, the phrase transgressors [*poshim*] of Israel is synonymous with apostates, with regard to either one matter or to the entire Torah (Rashi).

In order to enable them to repent – כְּדֵי שֶׁיַּחְזְרוּ בִּתְשׁוּבָה: As the ruling is a Torah edict, this is not necessarily the underlying reason behind the *halakha*. The Sages, however, are suggesting a reason why the verses lend themselves to such an interpretation, for a person who is an apostate with regard to one particular matter can easily repent, which is not the case for one who is an apostate with regard to the entire Torah (*Tosafot*).

An apostate and a sacrifice – מוּמָר וְקָרְבָּן: In summary, there are several *halakhot* with regard to the sacrifices of an apostate. If one is an apostate with regard to the entire Torah or to other serious transgressions, such as idolatry and, according to one opinion, Shabbat observance, then his sacrifices are not accepted. If, however, one is an apostate with regard to only one matter, he may bring sacrifices, including sin-offerings for transgressions committed unwittingly, with the exception of the transgression that he commits willfully.

מתני׳ אַנְשֵׁי חָצֵר שֶׁשָּׁכַח אֶחָד מֵהֶן וְלֹא עֵירֵב – בֵּיתוֹ אָסוּר מִלְּהַכְנִיס וּמִלְּהוֹצִיא לוֹ וְלָהֶם. וְשֶׁלָּהֶם מוּתָּרִין לוֹ וְלָהֶם. נָתְנוּ לוֹ רְשׁוּתָן – הוּא מוּתָּר וְהֵן אֲסוּרִין.

MISHNA **If one of the residents of a courtyard forgot and did not participate in an** ***eiruv***[H] with the other residents before Shabbat, and on Shabbat he renounced his rights in the courtyard to the other residents, **his house is prohibited** both **to him,** who forgot to establish an *eiruv*, **and to them,** the other residents, **to bring in** objects from the courtyard to his house **or to take** them **out** from his house into the courtyard. **But their** houses **are permitted** both **to him and to them,** for taking objects out into the courtyard and for bringing them in. **If they gave** away **their rights** in the courtyard **to him,**[H] i.e., if they renounced their rights in his favor, **he is permitted** to carry from his house into the courtyard, **but they are prohibited** from doing so.

הָיוּ שְׁנַיִם – אוֹסְרִין זֶה עַל זֶה. שֶׁאֶחָד נוֹתֵן רְשׁוּת וְנוֹטֵל רְשׁוּת, שְׁנַיִם נוֹתְנִין רְשׁוּת וְאֵין נוֹטְלִין רְשׁוּת.

If two residents of the courtyard forgot to establish an *eiruv*, and the others renounced their rights in the courtyard in their favor, **they prohibit one another.** In this scenario, the courtyard would belong to both of them, but each individual house remains the domain of its owner. It would therefore be prohibited for each of these residents to carry into the courtyard. **For one** resident **may give away and receive rights** in a domain, whereas **two** residents **may** only **give away rights** in a domain, **but they may not receive rights** in a domain. Since they did not establish an *eiruv*, it is unreasonable for the other residents of the courtyard to give away their rights in the domain, as the two who are prohibited because they did not participate in the *eiruv* render it prohibited for each other to carry.

מֵאֵימָתַי נוֹתְנִין רְשׁוּת? בֵּית שַׁמַּאי אוֹמְרִים: מִבְּעוֹד יוֹם, בֵּית הִלֵּל אוֹמְרִים: מִשֶּׁחֲשֵׁיכָה. מִי שֶׁנָּתַן רְשׁוּתוֹ וְהוֹצִיא, בֵּין בְּשׁוֹגֵג בֵּין בְּמֵזִיד – הֲרֵי זֶה אוֹסֵר, דִּבְרֵי רַבִּי מֵאִיר. רַבִּי יְהוּדָה אוֹמֵר: בְּמֵזִיד – אוֹסֵר, בְּשׁוֹגֵג – אֵינוֹ אוֹסֵר.

The mishna poses a general question: **When may one give** away **rights** in a domain? **Beit Shammai say: While it is still day,** i.e., before the onset of Shabbat; **and Beit Hillel say: Even after nightfall,** when it is already Shabbat.[H] The mishna cites another dispute: If **one gave away his rights** in his courtyard to the other residents of the courtyard, renouncing them after having forgotten to establish an *eiruv* with them the previous day, **and** then **he carried** something **out** from his house into the courtyard – **whether unwittingly,** forgetting that he had renounced his rights, **or intentionally, he** renders carrying **prohibited** for all the residents of the courtyard, for his action cancels his renunciation; this is **the statement of Rabbi Meir. Rabbi Yehuda says:** If he acted **intentionally, he** renders carrying **prohibited;** but if he acted **unwittingly, he does not** render carrying **prohibited.**

גמ׳ בֵּיתוֹ הוּא דְּאָסוּר, הָא חֲצֵירוֹ – שַׁרְיָא.

GEMARA The Gemara first analyzes the language of the mishna. It states: It is prohibited to bring in objects from the courtyard to his house and to take them out from his house into the courtyard. It can be inferred from this that **it is carrying** to and from **his house** that **is prohibited, but carrying** to and from **his** share of the **courtyard is permitted** to the other residents of the courtyard.

הֵיכִי דָּמֵי? אִי דְּבַטֵּיל – בֵּיתוֹ אַמַּאי אָסוּר? אִי דְּלָא בָּטֵיל – חֲצֵירוֹ אַמַּאי שַׁרְיָא? הָכָא בְּמַאי עָסְקִינַן – כְּגוֹן שֶׁבִּיטֵּל רְשׁוּת חֲצֵירוֹ, וְלֹא בִּיטֵּל רְשׁוּת בֵּיתוֹ. וְקָא סָבְרִי רַבָּנַן: הַמְבַטֵּל רְשׁוּת חֲצֵירוֹ – רְשׁוּת בֵּיתוֹ לֹא בִּיטֵּל, דְּדָיֵיר אִינִישׁ בְּבַיִת בְּלֹא חָצֵר.

The Gemara asks: **What are the circumstances** where this ruling applies? **If** the resident who forgot to establish an *eiruv* **renounced** his rights, **why is his house** rendered **prohibited?** And **if he did not renounce** his rights, **why is his courtyard permitted?** The Gemara explains: **With what are we dealing here?** We are dealing **with** a special case, **where he renounced his rights in his courtyard** to the others **but did not renounce his rights in his house** to them. **And the Rabbis hold that one who renounces his rights in his courtyard has not renounced his rights in his house,** as it is common **for people to reside in a house without a courtyard.**

״וְשֶׁלָּהֶן מוּתָּר לוֹ וְלָהֶן״, מַאי טַעְמָא? דְּהָוֵי אוֹרֵחַ לְגַבַּיְיהוּ.

The Gemara proceeds in its analysis of the mishna: It states that carrying in and out of **their** houses **is permitted for him and for them.** The Gemara poses a question: **What is the reason** that their houses are permitted to him? The Gemara answers: **For he is** regarded **like a guest of theirs,** i.e., he is subordinate to them and may carry wherever they may do so.

HALAKHA

If one…forgot and did not participate in an *eiruv* – שָׁכַח...וְלֹא עֵירֵב: If one resident of a courtyard forgot to establish an *eiruv*, he may renounce his rights in the courtyard in favor of the other residents. If one renounced his rights without specifying which rights he is renouncing, he has only renounced his rights in the courtyard, but not those in his house. Consequently, they are all permitted to transfer objects from their houses into the courtyard, but they are prohibited from doing so from his house into the courtyard, as stated by the Rabbis. If one renounced all of his rights in their favor, they may all carry from any of the houses into the courtyard (*Shulḥan Arukh, Oraḥ Ḥayyim* 380:1–2).

If they gave away their rights to him – נָתְנוּ לוֹ רְשׁוּתָם: If the majority renounced their rights in the courtyard in favor of the one who did not establish an *eiruv*, he is permitted to carry from his house into the courtyard, while they are prohibited from doing so. He is also prohibited from carrying from their houses into the courtyard, unless they explicitly included their houses in the renunciation (Rema; *Shulḥan Arukh, Oraḥ Ḥayyim* 380:4).

When may one give away rights in a domain – מָתַי נוֹתְנִים רְשׁוּת: One may renounce his rights in a domain even after nightfall, in accordance with the opinion of Beit Hillel (*Shulḥan Arukh, Oraḥ Ḥayyim* 380:1).

NOTES

It was not permitted – **לָא הֲוָה לֵיהּ שַׁרְיוּתָא**: As explained in the Gemara, even if the residents of the courtyard specified that they are renouncing their rights in favor of one person on the condition that he renounce his rights to the other, this is invalid. The rationale is that since the person failed to establish an *eiruv*, it is as though he is completely absent and is living in a different place entirely, so that he has no rights in the courtyard it whatsoever.

HALAKHA

Renunciation in favor of two – **בִּיטּוּל לְרַבִּים**: Rights in a domain may not be renounced in favor of two people who did not establish an *eiruv*, as although two may renounce their rights, they may not acquire rights. Even if the residents of the courtyard told one of the two to acquire their rights provided that he transfer them to the other person, this is ineffective (*Shulḥan Arukh*, *Oraḥ Ḥayyim* 380:4).

"נָתְנוּ לוֹ רְשׁוּתָן – הוּא מוּתָּר וְהֵן אֲסוּרִין". וְנֶהֱוֵי אִינְהוּ לְגַבֵּיהּ כִּי אוֹרְחִין! חַד לְגַבֵּי חֲמִשָּׁה – הָוֵי אוֹרֵחַ, חֲמִשָּׁה לְגַבֵּי חַד – לָא הָוֵי אוֹרֵחַ.

We learned in the mishna: If the other residents **gave** away **their rights** in the courtyard **to him, he is permitted** to carry from his house into the courtyard, **but they are prohibited** from doing so. The Gemara asks: **But let them,** the ones who renounced their rights in the courtyard, **be** regarded as **guests of his,** which would enable them to carry as well. The Gemara answers: **One vis-à-vis five is** considered **a guest,** whereas **five** or more **vis-à-vis one are not** ordinarily viewed as **guests.**

שְׁמַע מִינַּהּ: מְבַטְּלִין וְחוֹזְרִין וּמְבַטְּלִין!

The Gemara attempts to draw another inference from the wording of the mishna: Shall we not **learn from this,** from the order of events in the mishna, that **one may renounce** his rights in favor of another when he needs it, **and then** the latter **may renounce** his rights in favor of the former when he needs it? For the mishna first describes a case in which the one who forgot to establish an *eiruv* renounces his rights in favor of the others, at which stage they may use the courtyard, and then afterward recounts that the other residents renounce their rights in favor of the one who forgot to establish an *eiruv*, leaving it permitted for him and prohibited for them.

הָכִי קָאָמַר: נָתְנוּ לוֹ רְשׁוּתָן מֵעִיקָּרָא, הוּא מוּתָּר וְהֵן אֲסוּרִין.

The Gemara answers: No proof can be brought from here, for **this is** what the mishna **is saying: If they gave away their rights** in the courtyard **to him at the outset,** it is **permitted** for **him and** it is **prohibited for them.** In other words, this is not a continuation of the previous clause, but a separate case.

הָיוּ שְׁנַיִם – אוֹסְרִין זֶה עַל זֶה. פְּשִׁיטָא! לָא צְרִיכָא דַּהֲדַר חַד מִינַּיְיהוּ וּבָטֵיל לֵיהּ לְחַבְרֵיהּ. מַהוּ דְּתֵימָא: לִישְׁתְּרֵי, קָא מַשְׁמַע לָן: דְּכֵיוָן דִּבְעִידָּנָא דְּבָטֵיל לָא הֲוָה לֵיהּ שַׁרְיוּתָא בְּהַאי חָצֵר.

We learned in the mishna: **If two** residents of a courtyard forgot to establish an *eiruv*, and the others renounced their rights in the courtyard in their favor, **they** render **one another prohibited** from carrying. The Gemara raises a difficulty: Isn't this **obvious?** What novel teaching is stated here? The Gemara answers: **No,** this ruling **is necessary** in a case where the others renounced their rights in the courtyard in favor of the pair, and **one of them then renounced** his rights **in favor of the other. Lest you say let it** now **be permitted** for him to carry, the mishna **teaches us** that **since at the time of his renunciation** it was **not permitted**[N] for him to carry **in that courtyard,** he may not renounce his rights either. Therefore, his renunciation is ineffective, and they are both prohibited from carrying.[H]

"שֶׁאֶחָד נוֹתֵן רְשׁוּת". הָא תּוּ לָמָּה לִי? אִי נוֹתֵן – תְּנֵינָא, אִי נוֹטֵל – תְּנֵינָא!

The mishna explains: **For one** resident **may give away** and receive **rights** in a domain. The Gemara poses a question: **Why do I need this further** explanation? This ruling can be deduced from the previous cases: **If** the mishna wishes to teach the *halakha* with regard to **giving** away rights, **we** already **learned** that one person may give away his rights in a domain, and **if** it wishes to teach the *halakha* with regard to **receiving** rights, **we** already **learned** it as well, so why the repetition?

סֵיפָא אִיצְטְרִיכָא לֵיהּ: שְׁנַיִם נוֹתְנִין רְשׁוּת. הָא נַמִּי פְּשִׁיטָא! מַהוּ דְּתֵימָא:

The Gemara answers: **He needed** it due to the ruling in **the latter clause,** which includes the novel teaching that **two** residents **may give away rights** in a domain. The Gemara again wonders: But **this** *halakha* **as well,** that even multiple residents may give away their rights in a domain, is **obvious.** The Gemara answers: This was stated **lest you say:**

Perek **VI**
Daf **70** Amud **a**

לִיגְזַר דִּילְמָא אָתֵי לְבַטּוּלֵי לְהוּ – קָא מַשְׁמַע לָן.

Let us issue a decree that two residents may not give away their rights in a domain, **lest** people **come to renounce** their rights **in favor** of two residents as well. People might assume that just as two may give away their rights to one, so too may one give away his rights to two. The mishna therefore **teaches us** that we do not issue such a decree.

״וְאֵין נוֹטְלִין רְשׁוּת״. לָמָּה לִי? לָא צְרִיכָא, אַף עַל גַּב דְּאָמְרִי לֵיהּ ״קְנִי עַל מְנָת לְהַקְנוֹת״.

We learned in the mishna: **But two may not receive rights** in a domain. The Gemara poses a question: **Why do I** need to say this? Isn't it superfluous? The Gemara answers: **No,** it is **necessary** to teach that rights may not be acquired **even if** the other residents of the courtyard **say to** one of the two who did not establish an *eiruv*: **Acquire** our rights in the courtyard **on condition that you transfer** them in turn to your friend, the other one who did not establish an *eiruv*. The mishna teaches that he does not become their agent and cannot transfer the rights to the other person, as he himself cannot receive such rights under these circumstances.

בְּעָא מִינֵּיהּ אַבָּיֵי מֵרַבָּה: חֲמִשָּׁה שֶׁשְּׁרוּיִין בְּחָצֵר אַחַת, וְשָׁכַח אֶחָד מֵהֶן וְלֹא עֵירֵב, כְּשֶׁהוּא מְבַטֵּל רְשׁוּתוֹ, צָרִיךְ לְבַטֵּל לְכָל אֶחָד וְאֶחָד, אוֹ לֹא? אֲמַר לֵיהּ: צָרִיךְ לְבַטֵּל לְכָל אֶחָד וְאֶחָד.

Abaye raised a dilemma before Rabba: If **five** people **live in the same courtyard, and one of them forgot to join in an** ***eiruv*****, when he renounces his rights** in the courtyard, **must he renounce** them **in favor of each and every one** of the others **or not?** Rabba **said to him: He must renounce** his rights **in favor of each and every one.**[H]

אֵיתִיבֵיהּ: אֶחָד שֶׁלֹּא עֵירֵב – נוֹתֵן רְשׁוּתוֹ לְאֶחָד שֶׁעֵירֵב, שְׁנַיִם שֶׁעֵירְבוּ – נוֹתְנִין רְשׁוּתָן לְאֶחָד שֶׁלֹּא עֵירֵב, וּשְׁנַיִם שֶׁלֹּא עֵירְבוּ – נוֹתְנִין רְשׁוּתָן לִשְׁנַיִם שֶׁעֵירְבוּ, אוֹ לְאֶחָד שֶׁלֹּא עֵירֵב.

Abaye **raised an objection** from the following *baraita*: **One** resident of a courtyard **who did not establish an** ***eiruv*** **may renounce his rights** in the courtyard **in favor of one who did establish an** ***eiruv*****. Two** courtyard residents **who established an** ***eiruv*** **may** also **renounce their rights** in the courtyard **in favor of one who did not establish an** ***eiruv*****. And** similarly, **two** courtyard residents **who did not establish an** ***eiruv*** **may renounce their rights** in the courtyard **in favor of two** residents **who did establish an** ***eiruv*** **or in favor of one** resident **who did not establish an** ***eiruv*****.**

אֲבָל לֹא אֶחָד שֶׁעֵירֵב נוֹתֵן רְשׁוּתוֹ לְאֶחָד שֶׁלֹּא עֵירֵב. וְאֵין שְׁנַיִם שֶׁעֵירְבוּ נוֹתְנִין רְשׁוּתָן לִשְׁנַיִם שֶׁלֹּא עֵירְבוּ, וְאֵין שְׁנַיִם שֶׁלֹּא עֵירְבוּ נוֹתְנִין רְשׁוּתָן לִשְׁנַיִם שֶׁלֹּא עֵירְבוּ.

But one courtyard resident **who did establish an** ***eiruv*** **may not renounce his rights** in the courtyard **in favor of one** resident **who did not establish an** ***eiruv*****, nor may two** residents **who established an** ***eiruv*** **renounce their rights** in the courtyard **in favor of two** other residents **who did not establish an** ***eiruv*****, nor may two** residents **who did not establish an** ***eiruv*** **renounce their rights** in the courtyard **in favor of two** residents **who did not establish an** ***eiruv*****.**[H]

קָתָנֵי מִיהַת רֵישָׁא: ״אֶחָד שֶׁלֹּא עֵירֵב נוֹתֵן רְשׁוּתוֹ לְאֶחָד שֶׁעֵירֵב״. הֵיכִי דָּמֵי? אִי דְּלֵיכָּא אַחֲרִינָא בַּהֲדֵיהּ – בַּהֲדֵי מַאן עֵירֵב?

In any event the first clause is teaching: One resident of a courtyard **who did not establish an** ***eiruv*** **may renounce his rights** in the courtyard **in favor of one who did establish an** ***eiruv*****. What are the circumstances** surrounding this case? **If there is no other** resident **with him,** i.e., if there were only two people living in the courtyard, **with whom did he,** the other resident, **establish an** ***eiruv*****?** He could not have established an *eiruv* on his own.

אֶלָּא פְּשִׁיטָא – דְּאִיכָּא אַחֲרִינָא בַּהֲדֵיהּ. וְקָתָנֵי: לְאֶחָד שֶׁעֵירֵב!

Rather, it is **obvious that there is another** resident **with him,** apart from the one who failed to establish an *eiruv*, **and** yet **it states:** He may renounce his rights in the courtyard **in favor of one who did establish an** ***eiruv*****,** which implies that it is enough for him to renounce his rights in favor of one of the residents. He does not have to renounce his rights in favor of all of them.

וְרַבָּה – הָכָא בְּמַאי עָסְקִינַן – דַּהֲוָה וּמִית.

The Gemara now asks: **And** how does **Rabba** understand this teaching? The Gemara answers: Rabba can say as follows: **With what are we dealing here?** This is a special case, **where there was** another person in the courtyard with whom he established the *eiruv*, **but** that person **died**[N] in the meantime, leaving only one who established an *eiruv*, to whom the one who did not establish an *eiruv* may renounce his rights.

אִי דַּהֲוָה וּמִית – אֵימָא סֵיפָא: אֲבָל אֵין אֶחָד שֶׁעֵירֵב נוֹתֵן רְשׁוּתוֹ לְאֶחָד שֶׁלֹּא עֵירֵב. וְאִי דַּהֲוָה וּמִית – אַמַּאי לָא?

The Gemara raises a difficulty: **If** it indeed refers to a case **where there was** another person, **but he died, say** an explanation for **the latter clause** of the *baraita*: **But one** courtyard resident **who did establish an** ***eiruv*** **may not renounce his rights in favor of one who did not establish an** ***eiruv*****. Now if** it refers to a case **where there was** at first another person **but he died, why** may the one courtyard resident **not** renounce his rights in the courtyard? Now there is only one other person present in the courtyard.

HALAKHA

He must renounce his rights in favor of each and every one – צָרִיךְ לְבַטֵּל לְכָל אֶחָד וְאֶחָד: When one renounces his rights in a certain domain to a group of people, he must do so in respect to each and every one of them by saying: My rights are renounced to you and you (Rambam). Other authorities rule that it is enough if he says: My rights are renounced to all of you (*Tur*), in accordance with the opinion of Rabba (*Shulḥan Arukh, Oraḥ Ḥayyim* 380:1).

An individual and a group with regard to renunciation – יָחִיד וְרַבִּים בְּבִיטּוּל: A group of people who established an *eiruv* can renounce their rights in favor of another group who also established an *eiruv*, but neither they nor an individual may do so in favor of a group that did not establish an *eiruv*. If the group renounces its rights in favor of an individual, or if an individual does so for another individual, the renouncing party is entirely prohibited from carrying in the courtyard and is not considered in this regard like a guest, who is subordinate to his host and may carry wherever the latter may (*Shulḥan Arukh, Oraḥ Ḥayyim* 380:4).

NOTES

Where there was another person, but that person died – דַּהֲוָה וּמִית: Because of the difficulties presented by the *halakhot* of inheritance, i.e., even if the resident dies, his heir could be considered a resident of the courtyard, as discussed later in the Gemara, Rashi felt it necessary to explain that this case in the Gemara is one with special circumstances: The Sages are discussing members of a convoy who camped and surrounded their camp with a fence. As these members do not possess an actual residence that can be inherited, but are merely staying in this place, there is no issue of the inheritor being a factor in this ruling. The Ritva offers an alternative explanation, which suggests that the dead person is a convert who has no heirs. Consequently, the difficulty does not arise. Most commentaries (*Tosafot*; Rashba; Rosh; Ritva) agree that an heir does not render carrying prohibited in a place where he is not currently residing. Therefore, although there was an heir, he is located elsewhere and does not impose any restrictions on the residents.

אֶלָּא פְּשִׁיטָא דְּאִיתֵיהּ, וּמִדְּסֵיפָא אִיתֵיהּ, רֵישָׁא נַמִי אִיתֵיהּ!

Rather, it is **obvious that there is** another person present, with whom the *eiruv* was established. **And since the latter clause** of the *baraita* deals with a case **where there is** another person present, **the first clause** of the *baraita* must also be dealing with a case **where there is** another person present.

מִידֵּי אִירְיָא?! הָא כִּדְאִיתָא וְהָא כִּדְאִיתָא!

The Gemara rejects this proof: **Is this** necessarily **the designation in both** cases? Must the two clauses necessarily be dealing with the same case? **This** case **as it is, and this** case **as it is,** i.e., each clause deals with a unique set of circumstances, which need not accord with each other.

תֵּדַע, דְּקָתָנֵי סֵיפָא דְּרֵישָׁא: וּשְׁנַיִם שֶׁלֹּא עֵירְבוּ נוֹתְנִין רְשׁוּתָן לִשְׁנַיִם שֶׁעֵירְבוּ. לִשְׁנַיִם - אִין, לְאֶחָד - לָא.

The Gemara adds: **Know** that this *baraita* does not only deal with one state of affairs, **for the last** part **of the first clause teaches: And two** courtyard residents **who did not establish an *eiruv* may renounce their rights** in the courtyard **in favor of two** residents **who did establish an *eiruv*.** It can be inferred from this that **in favor of two** residents, **yes,** they may renounce their rights, but **in favor of one, no,** they may not. This clearly indicates that they must renounce their rights in the courtyard in favor of both of them.

וְאַבָּיֵי אָמַר: מַאי "לִשְׁנַיִם" - לְאֶחָד מִשְּׁנַיִם. אִי הָכִי לִיתְנֵי: לְאֶחָד שֶׁעֵירֵב, אוֹ לְאֶחָד שֶׁלֹּא עֵירֵב! קַשְׁיָא.

And Abaye can **say: What** is the meaning of **in favor of two? In favor of one of the two,** for this is as effective as renouncing their rights in favor of both of them. The Gemara raises a difficulty: **If so, let it teach** that the two courtyard residents who did not establish an *eiruv* may renounce their rights in the courtyard **in favor of one** resident **who established an *eiruv* or in favor of one** resident **who did not establish an *eiruv*,** from which one would understand that there are two present, for otherwise there could be no *eiruv*. The Gemara concludes: This is indeed **difficult** according to Abaye's opinion, although it does not completely refute his opinion.

"אֶחָד שֶׁלֹּא עֵירֵב נוֹתֵן רְשׁוּתוֹ לְאֶחָד שֶׁעֵירֵב". לְאַבָּיֵי - דְּאִיתֵיהּ, וְקָא מַשְׁמַע לַן: דְּאֵין צָרִיךְ לְבַטֵּל רְשׁוּת לְכָל אֶחָד וְאֶחָד. לְרַבָּה - דַּהֲוָה וּמִית, וְלָא גָּזוּר זִימְנִין דְּאִיתֵיהּ.

The Gemara now explains the need for each clause of the *baraita*. The *baraita* opens: **One** resident of a courtyard **who did not establish an *eiruv* may renounce his rights in favor of one who did establish an *eiruv*. According to Abaye,** this refers **to** a case **where there is** another person present, **and it teaches us** that **he need not renounce his rights** in the courtyard **in favor of each and every one** of the others. **According to Rabba,** this refers to a case **where there was** another person in the courtyard, with whom he established the *eiruv*, **but** that person **died** in the meantime, **and** the novel teaching is that the Sages **did not issue a decree** due to the concern that **sometimes** that other person **is** still **present.**

"וּשְׁנַיִם שֶׁעֵירְבוּ נוֹתְנִין רְשׁוּתָן לְאֶחָד שֶׁלֹּא עֵירֵב". פְּשִׁיטָא! מַהוּ דְּתֵימָא: כֵּיוָן דְּלָא עֵירֵב - לִיקְנְסֵיהּ, קָא מַשְׁמַע לַן.

The *baraita* continues:[N] **Two** courtyard residents **who established an *eiruv* may renounce their rights** in the courtyard **in favor of one who did not establish an *eiruv*.** The Gemara poses a question: Isn't this **obvious?** What new *halakha* is being taught here? The Gemara answers: **Lest you say** that **since he did not establish an *eiruv*, we should penalize him** by insisting that he renounce his rights in their favor and not the reverse, therefore the *baraita* **teaches us** that it is permitted even for the ones who established an *eiruv* to renounce their rights in his favor.

"וּשְׁנַיִם שֶׁלֹּא עֵירְבוּ נוֹתְנִין רְשׁוּתָן לִשְׁנַיִם שֶׁעֵירְבוּ". לְרַבָּה - תָּנָא סֵיפָא לְגַלּוּיֵי רֵישָׁא, לְאַבָּיֵי - שְׁנַיִם שֶׁלֹּא עֵירְבוּ אִיצְטְרִיכָא לֵיהּ. סָלְקָא דַּעְתָּךְ אָמֵינָא: לִגְזַר דִּלְמָא אָתֵי לְבַטּוֹלֵי לְהוּ, קָא מַשְׁמַע לַן.

It was further taught in the *baraita*: **And** similarly, **two** courtyard residents **who did not establish an *eiruv* may renounce their rights** in the courtyard **in favor of two** residents **who established an *eiruv*. According to Rabba,** the *baraita* **taught the latter clause to shed light on the first clause.**[N] As the latter clause teaches that one must renounce rights to every resident in the courtyard, the first clause must refer to the case where the additional resident passed away, for otherwise, he would not be able to renounce his rights to only one of the residents of the courtyard. **According to Abaye,** it was **necessary** for the mishna to teach the *halakha* in the case of **two who did not establish an *eiruv*.** For **it could enter your mind to say** that **we should issue a decree** determining that the two residents who did not establish an *eiruv* may not renounce their rights in favor of the two residents who established an *eiruv*, **lest** the two who established an *eiruv* **come to renounce** their rights **in favor of** the two who did not. The *baraita*, therefore, **teaches us** that we do not issue such a decree.

NOTES

The language of the *baraita* – לְשׁוֹן הַבָּרַיְיתָא: It is clear that this *baraita* is repetitive and not every repetition has halakhic implications. However, since *tanna'im*, when they repeat themselves, usually introduce certain stylistic adjustments, when such adjustments are absent, the Gemara inquires as to the reason for the repetition (Maharsha).

Taught the latter clause to shed light on the first clause – תָּנָא סֵיפָא לְגַלּוּיֵי רֵישָׁא: This expression is utilized with regard to both *mishnayot* and biblical verses. It means that although the phrase in question serves no particular purpose in and of itself, it is necessary in terms of the overall context, for it would otherwise be possible to explain some other statement in a completely different manner. Therefore, this additional section functions to ensure that a different statement is properly understood.

"אוֹ לְאֶחָד שֶׁלֹּא עֵירֵב". לָמָּה לִי? מַהוּ דְּתֵימָא: הָנֵי מִילֵּי – הֵיכָא דְּמִקְצָתָן עֵירְבוּ וּמִקְצָתָן לֹא עֵירְבוּ, אֲבָל הֵיכָא דְּכוּלָּן לֹא עֵירְבוּ – לִיקְנְסִינְהוּ כְּדֵי שֶׁלֹּא תִּשְׁתַּכַּח תּוֹרַת עֵירוּב, קָא מַשְׁמַע לַן.

The *baraita* continues: **Or** they may renounce their rights **in favor of one who did not establish an *eiruv*.** The Gemara poses a question: **Why do I** need this addition? The Gemara explains: **Lest you say** that **these** permissive **rulings** with regard to renunciation **apply only** in a case **where some of** the residents **established an *eiruv* and some of them did not establish an *eiruv*. But** in a case **where none of** the residents **established an *eiruv*, we should penalize them** by not allowing renunciation, **so that the** halakhic **category of *eiruv* should not be forgotten** by those who come after them. The *baraita*, therefore, **teaches us** that we are not concerned about this.

"אֲבָל אֵין אֶחָד שֶׁעֵירֵב נוֹתֵן רְשׁוּתוֹ לְאֶחָד שֶׁלֹּא עֵירֵב". לְאַבָּיֵי – תָּנָא סֵיפָא לְגַלּוֹיֵי רֵישָׁא, לְרַבָּה – אַיְּידֵי דְּתָנָא רֵישָׁא, תָּנָא נַמִי סֵיפָא.

We further learned in the *baraita*: **But one** courtyard resident **who did establish an *eiruv* may not renounce his rights** in the courtyard **in favor of one who did not establish an *eiruv*. According to Abaye,** the *baraita* **taught the latter clause to shed light on the first clause,** for Abaye proves from here that a person may renounce his rights to one of the two courtyard residents, and need not renounce his rights to both of them. **According to Rabba, since** the *baraita* **taught the first clause** in a certain style, **it also taught the latter clause** in that same style, but no halakhic conclusion can be garnered from here.

"וְאֵין שְׁנַיִם שֶׁעֵירְבוּ נוֹתְנִין רְשׁוּתָן לִשְׁנַיִם שֶׁלֹּא עֵירְבוּ". הָא, תּוּ לָמָּה לִי? לָא צְרִיכָא, דְּבַטֵּיל לֵיהּ חַד מִינַּיְיהוּ לְחַבְרֵיהּ. מַהוּ דְּתֵימָא: לִשְׁתְּרֵי לֵיהּ, קָא מַשְׁמַע לַן, כֵּיוָן דִּבְעִידָּנָא דְּבַטֵּיל לָא הֲוָה לֵיהּ שְׁרִיוּתָא בְּהָא חָצֵר – לָא.

The *baraita* further states: **Nor may two** residents **who established an *eiruv* renounce their rights** in the courtyard **in favor of two** other residents **who did not establish an *eiruv*.** The Gemara raises a difficulty: **Why do I** need **this further** matter? Isn't this statement superfluous? The Gemara answers: **No,** it is **necessary** for the case **where one of** the two who did not establish an *eiruv* subsequently **renounced** his rights **in favor of his fellow** resident. **Lest you say** that **it should** now **be permitted** to carry, as there is only one person left who has any rights in the courtyard and failed to establish an *eiruv*, therefore it **teaches us** that **since at the time of his renunciation he was not permitted in that courtyard,** he may **not** renounce his rights in it, and therefore carrying is prohibited for both.

"וְאֵין שְׁנַיִם שֶׁלֹּא עֵירְבוּ נוֹתְנִין רְשׁוּתָן לִשְׁנַיִם שֶׁלֹּא עֵירְבוּ". הָא, תּוּ לָמָּה לִי? לָא צְרִיכָא, דְּאָמְרִי "קְנֵי עַל מְנָת לְהַקְנוֹת".

The *baraita* concludes: **Nor may two** residents **who did not establish an *eiruv* renounce their rights** in the courtyard **in favor of two** residents **who did not establish an *eiruv*.** The Gemara poses the question: **Why do I** need **this additional** matter? Isn't it superfluous? The Gemara answers: **No,** it is **necessary** for the case **where** the other courtyard residents **said** to one of the first two who did not establish an *eiruv*: **Acquire** our rights in the courtyard **on condition that you transfer** them in turn to your friend, the other one who did not establish an *eiruv*. They attempted to appoint one of them as an agent to transfer the collective rights to the other. The *baraita* teaches us that this method is ineffective.

בְּעָא מִינֵּיהּ רָבָא מֵרַב נַחְמָן: יוֹרֵשׁ, מַהוּ שֶׁיְּבַטֵּל רְשׁוּת?

Rava raised a dilemma before Rav Naḥman: With regard to **an heir, what is** the *halakha* regarding whether **he** may **renounce rights** in a courtyard? If a person who had forgotten to establish an *eiruv* died on Shabbat, may his heir renounce his rights in his stead?

Perek **VI**
Daf **70** Amud **b**

הֵיכָא דְּאִי בָּעֵי לְעָרוֹבֵי מֵאֶתְמוֹל מָצֵי מְעָרֵב – בַּטּוֹלֵי נַמִי מָצֵי מְבַטֵּל. אֲבָל הַאי, כֵּיוָן דְּאִי בָּעֵי לְעָרוֹבֵי מֵאֶתְמוֹל – לָא מָצֵי מְעָרֵב – לָא מָצֵי מְבַטֵּל,

The Gemara explains the two sides of the question: On the one hand, perhaps only in a case **where,** if the person **wanted to establish an *eiruv* on the previous day he could have established an *eiruv*,** he **can also** renounce his rights on Shabbat. **But this** heir, **since,** if **he wanted to establish an *eiruv* the previous day he could not have established an *eiruv*,** as he was not then a resident of the courtyard, therefore, today **he cannot renounce** his rights either.

אוֹ דִּלְמָא: יוֹרֵשׁ כַּרְעֵיהּ דַּאֲבוּהּ הוּא?

Or perhaps an heir is like **his father's foot,** i.e., he is considered an extension of his father and substitutes for him in all regards, which means that just as his father could have renounced his rights, so can he.[N]

אֲמַר לֵיהּ: אֲנִי אוֹמֵר מְבַטֵּל, וְהָנֵי דְּבֵי שְׁמוּאֵל תָּנוּ: אֵין מְבַטֵּל. אֵיתִיבֵיהּ: זֶה הַכְּלָל, כֹּל שֶׁמּוּתָּר לְמִקְצָת שַׁבָּת – הוּתַּר לְכָל הַשַּׁבָּת, וְכָל שֶׁנֶּאֱסַר לְמִקְצָת שַׁבָּת – נֶאֱסַר לְכָל הַשַּׁבָּת, חוּץ מִמְּבַטֵּל רְשׁוּת.

Rav Naḥman **said to him: I** myself **say** that an heir **can** indeed **renounce** rights in a courtyard,[H] **while those** scholars of **the school of Shmuel taught: He cannot renounce** rights in a courtyard. Rava **raised an objection to** Rav Naḥman from the following *baraita*: **This is the principle: Anything that is permitted for part of Shabbat is permitted for all of Shabbat, and anything that is prohibited for part of Shabbat is prohibited for all of Shabbat, apart from one who renounces his rights** in a courtyard, for renunciation can provide an allowance halfway through Shabbat.

״כֹּל שֶׁהוּתַּר לְמִקְצָת שַׁבָּת מוּתָּר לְכָל הַשַּׁבָּת״ – כְּגוֹן עֵירֵב דֶּרֶךְ הַפֶּתַח וְנִסְתַּם הַפֶּתַח, עֵירֵב דֶּרֶךְ חַלּוֹן וְנִסְתַּם חַלּוֹן.

The Gemara now explains each element of the *baraita*: **Anything that is permitted for part of Shabbat is permitted for all of Shabbat. For example,** if an *eiruv* **was established** between two adjacent courtyards that are connected **via an opening** between them, **and** that **opening was closed up** on Shabbat, the *eiruv* is valid. Alternately, if **an** *eiruv* **was established** between the two courtyards that are connected **via a window** opening from one to the other, **and** that **window was closed up** on Shabbat, the *eiruv* is valid. As carrying from one courtyard to another was permitted at the beginning of Shabbat, it is permitted throughout Shabbat.

״זֶה הַכְּלָל״ – לְאַתּוֹיֵי מָבוֹי שֶׁנִּיטְּלוּ קוֹרוֹתָיו אוֹ לְחָיָיו.

The Gemara comments: The words **this is the principle** come **to include** the case of **an alleyway whose** cross **beams or side posts were removed** on Shabbat, teaching that one may nonetheless use the alleyway, as it had been permitted at the outset of Shabbat.

״כֹּל שֶׁנֶּאֱסַר לְמִקְצָת שַׁבָּת – נֶאֱסַר לְכָל הַשַּׁבָּת כּוּלָּהּ״ – כְּגוֹן שְׁנֵי בָתִּים בִּשְׁנֵי צִידֵּי רְשׁוּת הָרַבִּים, וְהִקִּיפוּם גּוֹיִם מְחִיצָה בַּשַּׁבָּת.

The Gemara continues its explanation of the *baraita*: **Anything that is prohibited for part of Shabbat is prohibited for all of Shabbat. For example,** if there were **two houses on two sides of a public domain, which gentiles enclosed with a wall on Shabbat,** the enclosed area remains prohibited. Even though a partition of this kind is considered a proper one with regard to Shabbat domains, it is prohibited to carry objects from either house into the enclosed area, even if the owner of the first house renounces his rights in the area in favor of the owner of the second house, as they could not have established an *eiruv* between them before Shabbat.

״זֶה הַכְּלָל״ לְאַתּוֹיֵי מַאי? לְאַתּוֹיֵי מֵת גּוֹי בַּשַּׁבָּת.

The Gemara asks: **What** do the words **this is the principle** come **to include** in this part of the *baraita*? The Gemara answers: It comes **to include** the case of **a gentile** resident of the courtyard who **died on Shabbat** without having rented out his domain to a Jew for the purpose of an *eiruv*. In this case, the Jewish neighbors are prohibited from carrying in the courtyard. Because it was prohibited to establish an *eiruv* the previous day, carrying in the courtyard continues to be prohibited on Shabbat, even though the gentile is now deceased.

וְקָתָנֵי ״חוּץ מִמְּבַטֵּל רְשׁוּת״, אִיהוּ – אִין, יוֹרֵשׁ – לָא!

And the *baraita* **teaches: Apart from one who renounces his rights** in a courtyard, which teaches that a person may renounce his rights in a courtyard even on Shabbat, despite the fact that the courtyard was prohibited prior to his renunciation. The Gemara infers: **He** himself, i.e., the original owner, **yes,** he may renounce his rights even on Shabbat, but with regard to his **heir, no,**[N] he may not renounce his rights on Shabbat, which contradicts Rav Naḥman's opinion.

אֵימָא חוּץ מִתּוֹרַת בִּיטּוּל רְשׁוּת.

Rav Naḥman replied: **Say** that the *baraita* must be understood as follows: **Apart from** anyone who falls **into the** halakhic **category of one who renounces his rights** in a domain. In other words, the *baraita* is not referring to a particular person who renounces his rights, but rather to the category of renunciation in general, which includes an heir.

NOTES

Renunciation of rights by an heir – בִּיטּוּל רְשׁוּת יוֹרֵשׁ: This discussion implies that the key issue is the status of the heir. It is possible to view the heir as receiving the domain and rights of the deceased at the time of the latter's death. Consequently, there is a defined break between them, as in a commercial transaction, where the act of acquisition divides the moment of the seller's ownership from that of the buyer. On the other hand, the heir can be viewed as a continuation of and stand-in for the deceased. As such, he already held potential ownership of the deceased's property even before the latter's passing. According to this understanding, the passing of the deceased merely actualizes the heir's rights, for he and the deceased are considered a single legal entity.

He, yes, his heir, no – אִיהוּ אִין, יוֹרֵשׁ לָא: Many versions of the Talmud omit these words. Although Rashi's explanation of the Gemara matches these words, nevertheless, his comments indicate that he too did not have this reading in front of him. See *Tosafot*, who question Rashi's explanation. Rabbeinu Ḥananel teaches the text in a completely different manner: These words are an objection to the opinion of Shmuel, and the conclusions that he deduces from the text are the opposite of Rashi's. However, this interpretation is not without difficulties of its own, as it is unusual for the Gemara to object to both sides of an argument without stating this explicitly (Rashba). One commentary understands the phrase in a manner similar to Rashi: Since the Gemara explains the *baraita* as speaking of a person who passes away, with the phrase: And the gentile died on Shabbat, it suggests that the phrase: Apart from one who renounces his rights, refers only to one who nullifies his own domain, but not to a person who was the heir of one who passed away (Rabbi Eliezer Meir Horowitz).

HALAKHA

An heir can renounce rights in a domain – יוֹרֵשׁ מְבַטֵּל רְשׁוּת: An heir can also renounce rights in a domain, in accordance with the opinion of Rav Naḥman (*Shulḥan Arukh, Oraḥ Ḥayyim* 381:6).

אֵיתִיבֵיהּ: אֶחָד מִבְּנֵי חָצֵר שֶׁמֵּת, וְהִנִּיחַ רְשׁוּתוֹ לְאֶחָד מִן הַשּׁוּק, מִבְּעוֹד יוֹם – אוֹסֵר, מִשֶּׁחֲשֵׁיכָה – אֵינוֹ אוֹסֵר.

Rava **raised a** further **objection to** the opinion of Rav Naḥman from a different *baraita*: If **a resident of a courtyard died**[H] **and left his domain,** the use of his house, **to one from the marketplace,** i.e., a non-resident of the courtyard, the following distinction applies: If he died **while it was still day,** i.e., before Shabbat, the one from the marketplace renders carrying **prohibited,** for it is assumed that he received his portion before the onset of Shabbat and should have joined in an *eiruv* with the others. Since he failed to establish an *eiruv* with the other residents of the courtyard, he renders carrying prohibited in the entire courtyard. If, however, he died **after nightfall, he does not** render carrying **prohibited,** for so long as it was permitted to carry for part of Shabbat it remains permitted for the entirety of Shabbat.

וְאֶחָד מִן הַשּׁוּק שֶׁמֵּת וְהִנִּיחַ רְשׁוּתוֹ לְאֶחָד מִבְּנֵי חָצֵר, מִבְּעוֹד יוֹם – אֵינוֹ אוֹסֵר, מִשֶּׁחֲשֵׁיכָה – אוֹסֵר.

And alternatively, if **one from the marketplace** who owned a residence in the courtyard but did not dwell there **died and left his domain to a resident of the courtyard** who does live there and usually joins in an *eiruv* with his neighbors, the following distinction applies: If the person from the marketplace died **while it was still day,** i.e., before Shabbat, the courtyard resident **does not** render carrying **prohibited,** as when he establishes his *eiruv* it includes his new residence as well. If, however, the person from the marketplace died **after nightfall** without having established an *eiruv*, the deceased renders carrying **prohibited.** As this residence was prohibited at the beginning of Shabbat, it can no longer be permitted on that Shabbat.[H]

אַמַּאי אוֹסֵר? נִיבְטִיל! מַאי "אוֹסֵר" נַמִי דְּקָתָנֵי – עַד שֶׁיְּבַטֵּל.

Rava's question is based on the first case discussed in the *baraita*: According to Rav Naḥman, **why does** the heir render carrying **prohibited** in this case? **Let him renounce** his rights in the courtyard to the other residents, as Rav Naḥman maintains that an heir may renounce rights. Rav Naḥman replied: **What is** the meaning of the word **prohibits that** the *baraita* **teaches** here? It means he renders carrying prohibited **until he renounces** his rights, i.e., although there is no way of rectifying the situation by means of an *eiruv*, it can be corrected by way of renunciation.

תָּא שְׁמַע: יִשְׂרָאֵל וְגֵר שְׁרוּיִין בִּמְגוּרָה אַחַת, וּמֵת גֵּר מִבְּעוֹד יוֹם,

Come and **hear** a different proof challenging Rav Naḥman's opinion, from the following *baraita*: If **a Jew and a convert were living in a single residency**[N] comprised of several rooms, **and the convert died** childless **while it was still day,** such a convert has no heirs, and therefore the first to take possession of his property acquires it.

Perek **VI**
Daf **71** Amud **a**

אַף עַל פִּי שֶׁהֶחֱזִיק יִשְׂרָאֵל אַחֵר בִּנְכָסָיו – אוֹסֵר. מִשֶּׁחֲשֵׁיכָה, אַף עַל פִּי שֶׁלֹּא הֶחֱזִיק יִשְׂרָאֵל אַחֵר – אֵינוֹ אוֹסֵר.

In such a case, **even though a different Jew took possession of** the convert's **property,** the one who acquires it renders carrying **prohibited.** If, however, he died **after nightfall, even though a different Jew did not take possession of** his property, **it,** i.e., carrying, **is not prohibited,** for carrying had already been permitted on that Shabbat.

הָא גּוּפָא קַשְׁיָא! אָמְרַתְּ "מִבְּעוֹד יוֹם אַף עַל פִּי שֶׁהֶחֱזִיק", וְלֹא מִיבַּעְיָא כִּי לֹא הֶחֱזִיק?! אַדְּרַבָּה, כִּי לֹא הֶחֱזִיק לֹא אָסַר!

The Gemara raises a difficulty: The *baraita* **itself is difficult. You** first **said:** If the convert died **while it was still day, even though a different Jew took possession of** his property, the latter renders carrying prohibited, which implies that **it is not necessary** to say so **where** another Jew **did not take possession of** the property, for in such a case it is certainly prohibited. But this is incorrect. **On the contrary,** in a case **where** a different person **did not take possession of** the property, **it is** certainly **not prohibited,** for in such a case the convert's property is ownerless and there is nobody to render carrying in the courtyard prohibited.

אָמַר רַב פַּפָּא: אֵימָא, "אַף עַל פִּי שֶׁלֹּא הֶחֱזִיק". וְהָא "אַף עַל פִּי שֶׁהֶחֱזִיק" קָתָנֵי!

Rav Pappa said: Say that the *baraita* should read as follows: **Even though** a different Jew **did not take possession of** it. The Gemara raises a difficulty: How can it be corrected in this manner? **But doesn't it teach: Even though he took possession of** it?

HALAKHA

If a resident of a courtyard died – אֶחָד מִבְּנֵי חָצֵר שֶׁמֵּת: With regard to one of the residents of a courtyard who died before he could establish an *eiruv*, and he left his portion to someone who was not a resident of the courtyard, the following distinctions apply: If he died before Shabbat and his heir arrived on Shabbat, the heir renders carrying prohibited. However, if he died on Shabbat after having established an *eiruv*, the heir may not impose any restrictions on the residents. If he had not established an *eiruv*, the heir imposes restrictions only when he arrives (*Shulḥan Arukh, Oraḥ Ḥayyim* 371:4).

One who inherited part of a courtyard – יוֹרֵשׁ חֵלֶק בְּחָצֵר: In the case of a person who owned a residence in a courtyard but did not dwell there, and who left his property to a resident of that courtyard, the *halakha* is as follows: If he died before Shabbat, the heir does not render carrying prohibited, for the *eiruv* that he established before Shabbat includes the portion he has inherited as well. However, if the person died after nightfall, then the heir does render carrying prohibited, because his *eiruv* is ineffective in such a case (*Shulḥan Arukh, Oraḥ Ḥayyim* 371:3).

NOTES

A Jew and a convert…in a single residency – יִשְׂרָאֵל וְגֵר...בִּמְגוּרָה אַחַת: The early commentaries point out that this case clearly refers to a legal acquisition of ownership [*ḥazaka*] rather than an inheritance (see Ritva). According to the Ra'avad, who maintains that an heir has rights because it is considered as though the deceased renounced his rights in his favor before Shabbat, one who acquires property that was ownerless is similarly like one who acquires from a person who renounced his rights to others.

הָכִי קָאָמַר: אַף עַל פִּי שֶׁלֹּא הֶחֱזִיק מִבְּעוֹד יוֹם אֶלָּא מִשֶּׁחֲשֵׁיכָה, כֵּיוָן דַּהֲוָה לֵיהּ לְהַחֲזִיק מִבְּעוֹד יוֹם – אוֹסֵר. מִשֶּׁחֲשֵׁיכָה, אַף עַל פִּי שֶׁלֹּא הֶחֱזִיק יִשְׂרָאֵל אַחֵר – אֵינוֹ אוֹסֵר.

The Gemara answers: **This is** what the *baraita* **is saying:** If the convert died while it was still day, then **even though** a different Jew **did not take possession of** the property **while it was still day but** only **after nightfall, since he had** the possibility **of taking possession** of it **while it was still day,** the person who acquires it renders carrying **prohibited.** If, however, the convert died **after nightfall, even though a different Jew did not take possession of** his property, **it does not render** it **prohibited**[N] to carry.

"אַף עַל פִּי שֶׁלֹּא הֶחֱזִיק יִשְׂרָאֵל אַחֵר" וְלָא מִיבַּעְיָא כִּי הֶחֱזִיק?! אַדְּרַבָּה, כִּי הֶחֱזִיק אָסַר!

The Gemara now considers the next clause of the *baraita*, which states: If the convert died after nightfall, **even though a different Jew did not take possession of** his property, carrying is not prohibited. This implies that **it is not necessary** to say so **where** another Jew **did take possession of** the property, for in such a case it is certainly not prohibited. But, **on the contrary, where** a different person **takes possession of** the property, **he** renders carrying **prohibited.**

אָמַר רַב פַּפָּא: אֵימָא, "אַף עַל פִּי שֶׁהֶחֱזִיק". וְהָא "אַף עַל פִּי שֶׁלֹּא הֶחֱזִיק" קָתָנֵי! הָכִי קָאָמַר: אַף עַל פִּי שֶׁהֶחֱזִיק מִשֶּׁחֲשֵׁיכָה, כֵּיוָן דְּלָא הֲוָה לֵיהּ לְהַחֲזִיק מִבְּעוֹד יוֹם – אֵינוֹ אוֹסֵר.

Rav Pappa said: Say that the *baraita* should read as follows: **Even though** a different Jew **took possession of** it. The Gemara raises a difficulty: **But didn't** the *baraita* **teach: Even though he did not take possession of** it? The Gemara explains: **This is** what the *baraita* **is saying:** If the convert died after nightfall, **even though** a different Jew **took possession of** his property **after nightfall, since he did not have** the possibility **of taking possession** of it **while it was still day, he does not** render carrying **prohibited.**[H]

קָתָנֵי מִיהַת רֵישָׁא "אוֹסֵר", אַמַּאי אוֹסֵר? נִיבְטֵל!

After explaining the *baraita*, the Gemara proceeds to clarify the issue at hand: **In any event, the first clause is teaching** that the person who acquires the convert's property **renders** carrying **prohibited;** but **why does he render** carrying **prohibited? Let him renounce** his rights in the domain like an heir. The implication then is that he does not have the option of renunciation, in contrast to the opinion of Rav Naḥman.

מַאי "אוֹסֵר" דְּקָתָנֵי, עַד שֶׁיְּבַטֵּל.

Rav Naḥman replied: **What is** the meaning of the word **prohibits that it teaches** here? It means he renders carrying prohibited **until he renounces** his rights, but renunciation is effective.

רַבִּי יוֹחָנָן אָמַר: מַתְנִיתִין מַנִּי בֵּית שַׁמַּאי הִיא, דְּאָמְרִי: אֵין בִּיטּוּל רְשׁוּת בְּשַׁבָּת. דִּתְנַן: מֵאֵימָתַי נוֹתְנִין רְשׁוּת? בֵּית שַׁמַּאי אוֹמְרִים: מִבְּעוֹד יוֹם. וּבֵית הִלֵּל אוֹמְרִים: מִשֶּׁתֶּחְשַׁךְ.

Rabbi Yoḥanan said: Who is the *tanna* of the problematic ***baraitot*** that imply that an heir cannot renounce rights, and from which objections were brought against Rav Naḥman? **It is Beit Shammai, who say** that **there is no renunciation of rights on Shabbat** at all, even for the owner of the property. **As we learned** in the mishna: **When may one give away rights** in a domain? **Beit Shammai say: While it is still day. And Beit Hillel say:** Even **after nightfall.**

אָמַר עוּלָּא: מַאי טַעְמָא דְּבֵית הִלֵּל – נַעֲשָׂה כְּאוֹמֵר "כַּלֵּךְ אֵצֶל יָפוֹת".

With regard to this dispute itself, **Ulla said: What is the reason of Beit Hillel**[N] that one may renounce rights even after nightfall? This should be considered an act of acquisition, which is prohibited on Shabbat. He explains: **It is comparable to one who says: Turn toward the high-quality ones.**[N] If a person sets aside *teruma* from another person's produce without the latter's knowledge, and when the owner finds out he says: Why did you set aside this produce? Turn toward the high-quality ones, i.e., you should have gone to find better produce to use as *teruma,* then the *teruma* that was separated is considered *teruma,* provided there was indeed quality produce in that place. The reason is that the owner has demonstrated his retroactive acquiescence to the other person's setting aside of *teruma*. Therefore, the latter is considered his agent for this purpose. The same applies to our issue. If a person intended to permit both himself and others to carry in a courtyard by means of establishing an *eiruv* but forgot to do so, by renouncing his rights after nightfall, he retroactively makes plain his desire that his domain should be mingled with that of his neighbors. What he then does on Shabbat is not a complete action, but merely a demonstration of his intentions.

אָמַר אַבָּיֵי: מֵת גּוֹי בְּשַׁבָּת מַאי "כַּלֵּךְ אֵצֶל יָפוֹת" אִיכָּא?

Abaye said: This explanation is unsatisfactory, as when **a gentile dies on Shabbat, what** connection **is there to** the concept: **Turn toward the high-quality ones?** When a gentile dies on Shabbat, his Jewish neighbors may renounce their rights in the courtyard to each other and thus render carrying in the courtyard permitted, even though such renunciation would have been ineffective prior to his passing. Consequently, it cannot be said that it works retroactively.

NOTES

After nightfall…it does not render it prohibited – מִשֶּׁחֲשֵׁיכָה...אֵינוֹ אוֹסֵר: The Ritva explains that even if the convert died without previously establishing an *eiruv*, carrying is not prohibited, as his death is considered a general renunciation of his rights in the domain.

The reason of Beit Hillel – טַעַם בֵּית הִלֵּל: Some commentaries point out that Ulla's explanation in this context disagrees with Rabbi Yoḥanan's opinion with regard to an heir, and maintains that even according to Beit Hillel, an heir may not renounce his rights in a domain. He states that Beit Hillel's reason for permitting the renunciation of rights is that the owner's intentions have been clarified retroactively, and this is not possible in the case of an heir (Rashash).

Turn toward the high-quality ones – כַּלֵּךְ אֵצֶל יָפוֹת: Just as one who says, Turn toward the high-quality ones, reveals his intention of giving from the very best quality produce, so too, one who renounces his rights indicates that he did not mean to prevent the residents of the courtyard from carrying, but, on the contrary, he wished to completely renounce his rights in the courtyard in their favor (*Me'iri*).

HALAKHA

A different Jew and a convert – יִשְׂרָאֵל וְגֵר: With regard to the case of a convert and a different Jew who shared a courtyard and established an *eiruv* together, the following distinction applies: If the convert died before Shabbat and a different Jew took possession of his property, even after nightfall, that Jew renders carrying in the courtyard prohibited. However, if the convert passed away on Shabbat, carrying is not prohibited, as it had previously been permitted for part of Shabbat (*Shulḥan Arukh, Oraḥ Ḥayyim* 371:5).

אֶלָּא, הָכָא בְּהָא קָמִיפַּלְגִי; בֵּית שַׁמַּאי סָבְרִי: בִּיטּוּל רְשׁוּת מִיקְנָא רְשׁוּתָא הוּא, וּמִיקְנָא רְשׁוּתָא בְּשַׁבָּת – אָסוּר. וּבֵית הִלֵּל סָבְרִי: אִסְתַּלּוֹקֵי רְשׁוּתָא בְּעָלְמָא הוּא, וְאִסְתַּלּוֹקֵי רְשׁוּתָא בְּשַׁבָּת שַׁפִּיר דָּמֵי.

Rather, the Gemara rejects Ulla's explanation and states that **here they disagree over the following: Beit Shammai hold** that **renunciation of a domain is** equivalent to **acquisition of a domain, and acquisition of a domain is prohibited on Shabbat. And Beit Hillel hold** that **it is merely withdrawal from a domain, and withdrawal from a domain seems well on Shabbat,** i.e., it is permitted. As such, there is no reason to prohibit renunciation as a form of acquisition, which is prohibited as a part of a decree against conducting commerce on Shabbat.

מתני׳ בַּעַל הַבַּיִת שֶׁהָיָה שׁוּתָּף לִשְׁכֵנָיו, לָזֶה בְּיַיִן וְלָזֶה בְּיַיִן – אֵינָן צְרִיכִין לְעָרֵב.

MISHNA If a **homeowner was in partnership with his neighbors, with this one in wine and with that** one **in wine,**[N] **they need not establish an** ***eiruv,*** for due to their authentic partnership they are considered to be one household, and no further partnership is required.

לָזֶה בְּיַיִן וְלָזֶה בְּשֶׁמֶן צְרִיכִין לְעָרֵב. רַבִּי שִׁמְעוֹן אוֹמֵר: אֶחָד זֶה וְאֶחָד זֶה – אֵינָן צְרִיכִין לְעָרֵב.

If, however, he was in partnership **with this** one **in wine and with that** one **in oil, they must establish an** ***eiruv.*** As they are not partners in the same item, they are not all considered one partnership. **Rabbi Shimon says:** In **both this** case **and that** case, i.e., even if he partners with his neighbors in different items, **they need not establish an** ***eiruv.***[NH]

גמ׳ אָמַר רַב: וּבִכְלִי אֶחָד. אָמַר רָבָא: דַּיְקָא נַמִי, דְּקָתָנֵי ״לָזֶה בְּיַיִן וְלָזֶה בְּשֶׁמֶן – צְרִיכִין לְעָרֵב״. אִי אָמְרַתְּ בִּשְׁלָמָא רֵישָׁא בִּכְלִי אֶחָד וְסֵיפָא בִּשְׁנֵי כֵלִים – שַׁפִּיר. אֶלָּא אִי אָמְרַתְּ רֵישָׁא בִּשְׁנֵי כֵלִים וְסֵיפָא בִּשְׁנֵי כֵלִים, מָה לִי יַיִן וְיַיִן מָה לִי יַיִן וָשֶׁמֶן?!

GEMARA Rav said: The *halakha* that one who is in partnership in wine with both his neighbors need not establish an *eiruv* applies only if their wine is **in one vessel. Rava said:** The language of the mishna **is also precise, as it teaches:** If he was in partnership **with this one in wine and with the** other **one in oil, they must establish an** ***eiruv.*** **Granted, if you say** that **the first clause** of the mishna deals **with one vessel, and the latter clause** deals **with two vessels,** one of wine and one of oil, **it is well. But, if you say** that **the first clause** of the mishna speaks **of two vessels, and the latter clause** also speaks **of two vessels, what** difference is it **to me** if it is **wine and wine or wine and oil?** The *halakha* should be the same in both cases.

אֲמַר לֵיהּ אַבָּיֵי: יַיִן וְיַיִן – רָאוּי לְעָרֵב, יַיִן וָשֶׁמֶן – אֵין רָאוּי לְעָרֵב.

Abaye said to him: This is no proof, and the first clause can be referring to a case where the wine was in separate vessels as well. The difference is that **wine and wine is suitable for mixing** together, and therefore can be considered a single unit even if divided into two containers. **Wine and oil,** however, **are not suitable for mixing.**

״רַבִּי שִׁמְעוֹן אוֹמֵר: אֶחָד זֶה וְאֶחָד זֶה אֵין צְרִיכִין לְעָרֵב״. וַאֲפִילּוּ לָזֶה בְּיַיִן וְלָזֶה בְּשֶׁמֶן?! אָמַר רַבָּה: הָכָא בְּמַאי עָסְקִינַן – בְּחָצֵר שֶׁבֵּין שְׁנֵי מְבוֹאוֹת. וְרַבִּי שִׁמְעוֹן לְטַעְמֵיהּ;

We learned in the mishna: **Rabbi Shimon says:** In **both this** case, where they are partners in wine alone, **and that** case, where the partnerships are in wine and oil, **they need not establish an** ***eiruv.*** The Gemara poses a question: Did he say this **even if** the partnership is **with this one in wine and with the other one in oil?** But these are not suitable for mixing. **Rabba said: With what are we dealing here?** We are dealing **with a courtyard** positioned **between two alleyways, and Rabbi Shimon** follows **his** usual line of **reasoning.**

דִּתְנַן, אָמַר רַבִּי שִׁמְעוֹן: לְמָה הַדָּבָר דּוֹמֶה – לְשָׁלֹשׁ חֲצֵירוֹת הַפְּתוּחוֹת זוֹ לָזוֹ וּפְתוּחוֹת לִרְשׁוּת הָרַבִּים, עֵירְבוּ שְׁתַּיִם הַחִיצוֹנוֹת עִם הָאֶמְצָעִית – הִיא מוּתֶּרֶת עִמָּהֶן וְהֵן מוּתָּרוֹת עִמָּהּ, וּשְׁתַּיִם הַחִיצוֹנוֹת אֲסוּרוֹת זוֹ עִם זוֹ.

As we learned in a mishna: **Rabbi Shimon said: To what is this matter comparable?** It is comparable **to** the case of **three courtyards that open into one another and** also **open into a public domain. If the two outer** courtyards each **established an** ***eiruv*** **with the middle one, it is permitted** for residents of the middle one to carry **with** the two outer ones, **and it is permitted** for residents of the two outer ones to carry **with** the middle one. **However, it is prohibited** for the residents of **the two outer** courtyards to carry **with each other,** as they did not establish an *eiruv* with each other. This teaches that the residents of one courtyard can establish an *eiruv* with a courtyard on each side, and need not choose between them. Here too, the residents of the courtyard can participate in an *eiruv* with both alleyways, one by means of wine and the other by means of oil.

אֲמַר לֵיהּ אַבָּיֵי: מִי דָּמֵי? הָתָם קָתָנֵי ״שְׁתַּיִם הַחִיצוֹנוֹת אֲסוּרוֹת״, הָכָא קָתָנֵי ״אֵין צְרִיכִין לְעָרֵב״ כְּלָל!

Abaye said to him: Are the cases really **comparable? There it teaches: It is prohibited** for the residents of **the two outer** courtyards to carry with each other, whereas **here it teaches: They need not establish an** ***eiruv,*** indicating that it is permitted for residents of all three domains to carry with each other.

NOTES

With this one in wine and with that one in wine – **לָזֶה בְּיַיִן וְלָזֶה בְּיַיִן**: The Rashash writes that if the homeowner maintains separate partnerships in wine with each neighbor, the three of them are not partners together at all. By stating in the Gemara that all the wine must be in a single vessel, Rav emphasizes the need for all of it to be placed in one location at least, so that theirs should be considered an actual partnership.

Rabbi Shimon's opinion – **שִׁיטַת רַבִּי שִׁמְעוֹן**: One explanation of Rabbi Shimon's statement is that his criteria are applicable only with regard to the *halakhot* of *eiruv*, such that the residents of a courtyard may establish one *eiruv* with one alleyway and a second *eiruv* with another alleyway. Other commentaries, however, explain that Rabbi Shimon was speaking of the criteria for general commercial partnerships as well as the *halakhot* of *eiruv* (see Rabbeinu Yehonatan).

HALAKHA

An *eiruv* between partners – **עֵירוּב בֵּין שׁוּתָּפִים**: One who participated in a partnership in wine with each of his neighbors need not establish an *eiruv*. Even if his partnership with one was in wine and the other one was in oil, he need not establish an *eiruv*, so long as both the wine and the oil were stored in a single vessel (*Tur*). This ruling follows the opinion of Rabbi Shimon, as the *halakha* follows the lenient opinion with regard to *eiruvin* (*Beit Yosef*). Alternatively (*Bayit Ḥadash*), even the first *tanna* would agree that he need not establish an *eiruv* in this case, as he disagreed in the case of wine and oil only because they are usually not stored in one vessel (*Shulḥan Arukh, Oraḥ Ḥayyim* 386:3 in Rema).

מַאי "אֵין צְרִיכִין לְעָרֵב" – שְׁכֵנִים בַּהֲדֵי בַּעַל הַבַּיִת, אֲבָל שְׁכֵנִים בַּהֲדֵי הֲדָדֵי – צְרִיכִין לְעָרֵב.

The Gemara explains: **What is** the subject of the phrase **they need not establish an *eiruv*?** It refers to the **neighbors together with the homeowner,** i.e., the residents of the courtyards that open into each of the alleyways with the resident of the courtyard in the middle. **But** with regard to **the neighbors with each other,** i.e., if the residents of the two alleyways wish to be permitted to carry with each other, **they must establish an *eiruv*** and place it in the middle courtyard.

Perek **VI**
Daf **71** Amud **b**

וְרַב יוֹסֵף אָמַר: רַבִּי שִׁמְעוֹן וְרַבָּנַן בִּפְלוּגְתָּא דְּרַבִּי יוֹחָנָן בֶּן נוּרִי וְרַבָּנַן קָא מִיפַּלְגִי; דִּתְנַן: שֶׁמֶן שֶׁצָּף עַל גַּבֵּי יַיִן, וְנָגַע טְבוּל יוֹם בַּשֶּׁמֶן – לֹא פָּסַל אֶלָּא שֶׁמֶן בִּלְבַד. וְרַבִּי יוֹחָנָן בֶּן נוּרִי אוֹמֵר: שְׁנֵיהֶן חִיבּוּרִין זֶה לָזֶה.

And Rav Yosef said: In fact we are dealing here with a single alleyway, and **Rabbi Shimon and the Rabbis disagree about the** same point of **dispute between Rabbi Yoḥanan ben Nuri and the Rabbis. As we learned** in a mishna: If *teruma* **oil was floating on the surface of wine,**[H] **and one who immersed during the day,**[B] **touched the oil, he disqualified only the oil alone.** However, he did not disqualify the wine, because it is considered separate from the oil. Only the oil is disqualified, and it does not render other items ritually impure. **And Rabbi Yoḥanan ben Nuri says: They are both connected to each other** and are considered as one, so the wine is also ritually impure.

רַבָּנַן – כְּרַבָּנַן, וְרַבִּי שִׁמְעוֹן – כְּרַבִּי יוֹחָנָן בֶּן נוּרִי.

The Gemara explains: **The** opinion of the **Rabbis** in our mishna **is in accordance with** the opinion of **the Rabbis** in the other mishna, who maintain that wine and oil are not connected and therefore cannot be used together in an *eiruv*, **and** the opinion of **Rabbi Shimon is in accordance with** the opinion of **Rabbi Yoḥanan ben Nuri,** who holds that wine and oil are connected, and may be used together in an *eiruv*.[N]

תַּנְיָא, רַבִּי אֱלִיעֶזֶר בֶּן תַּדַּאי אוֹמֵר: אֶחָד זֶה וְאֶחָד זֶה – צְרִיכִין לְעָרֵב. וַאֲפִילּוּ לָזֶה בְּיַיִן וְלָזֶה בְּיַיִן?!

It was taught in a *baraita*: **Rabbi Eliezer ben Taddai says:** In **both this** case, of wine and wine, **and that** case, of wine and oil, **they must establish an *eiruv*.** The Gemara expresses wonder: Did he say this **even** if the partnership is **with this one in wine and** also **with the** other **one in wine?** Why should these partnerships not be sufficient to consider the items merged?

אָמַר רַבָּה: זֶה בָּא בְּלָגִינוֹ וְשָׁפַךְ, וְזֶה בָּא בְּלָגִינוֹ וְשָׁפַךְ – כּוּלֵּי עָלְמָא לָא פְּלִיגִי דְּהָוֵי עֵירוּב.

Rabba said: If they partnered in the following manner, such that **this one came with his** wine-filled **jug and poured** its contents into a barrel, **and the** other **one came with his jug and poured** his wine into that same barrel, **everyone agrees that it is a** valid ***eiruv***, even if they did not act specifically for that purpose.

כִּי פְּלִיגִי – כְּגוֹן שֶׁלָּקְחוּ חָבִית שֶׁל יַיִן בְּשׁוּתָּפוּת. רַבִּי אֱלִיעֶזֶר בֶּן תַּדַּאי סָבַר: אֵין בְּרֵירָה, וְרַבָּנַן סָבְרִי: יֵשׁ בְּרֵירָה.

Where they disagree is in the case **where they bought a barrel of wine in partnership. Rabbi Eliezer ben Taddai holds: There is no** principle of **retroactive clarification,** i.e., there is no halakhic assumption that the undetermined halakhic status of items can be retroactively clarified. Consequently, after the wine is consumed, it is not possible to clarify retroactively which portion of the wine belonged to each person. Therefore, they cannot each be said to own a particular part of the wine, which renders it unfit for an *eiruv*. **But the Rabbis hold that there is retroactive clarification,** and therefore they may rely on this partnership to establish an *eiruv*.

רַב יוֹסֵף אָמַר: רַבִּי אֱלִיעֶזֶר בֶּן תַּדַּאי וְרַבָּנַן בְּסוֹמְכִין עַל שִׁיתּוּף בִּמְקוֹם עֵירוּב קָמִיפַּלְגִי.

Rav Yosef said that this dispute should be understood differently, as **Rabbi Eliezer ben Taddai and the Rabbis disagree about** whether one may **rely on a merging** of an alleyway **instead of an *eiruv***, i.e., whether the merging of an alleyway to permit carrying in the alleyway, exempts the courtyards that open into the alleyway from having to establish an *eiruv* for the purpose of carrying from one courtyard to the other.

דְּמָר סָבַר: אֵין סוֹמְכִין, וּמָר סָבַר: סוֹמְכִין.

As one Sage, Rabbi Eliezer ben Taddai, **holds** that one **may not rely** on it in that case, as carrying in the courtyards requires specifically an *eiruv*, and the merging of alleyways is insufficient. **And one Sage,** i.e., the Rabbis, **maintains** that one **may rely** on and use the merging of alleyways to permit carrying between the courtyards as well.

אָמַר רַב יוֹסֵף: מְנָא אָמִינָא לַהּ – דְּאָמַר רַב יְהוּדָה, אָמַר רַב: הֲלָכָה כְּרַבִּי מֵאִיר. וְאָמַר רַב בְּרוּנָא, אָמַר רַב: הֲלָכָה כְּרַבִּי אֱלִיעֶזֶר בֶּן תַּדַּאי. מַאי טַעְמָא – לָאו מִשּׁוּם דְּחַד טַעְמָא הוּא?

Rav Yosef said: From where do I say this, that this is the subject of their dispute? **As Rav Yehuda said** that **Rav said: The *halakha* is in accordance with** the opinion of **Rabbi Meir,**[N] which will be detailed later, that one may not rely on a merging of alleyways instead of an *eiruv*. **And Rav Beruna said** that **Rav said: The *halakha* is in accordance with** the opinion of **Rabbi Eliezer ben Taddai,** that in both cases they must establish an *eiruv*. **What is the reason** he ruled in this manner? **Is it not because the rationale** for both rulings is **one** and the same?

HALAKHA

Oil was floating on the surface of wine – שֶׁמֶן שֶׁצָּף עַל גַּבֵּי יַיִן: If a ritually impure person who immersed during the day but retains vestigial impurity until nightfall touched oil floating on wine, the wine is not disqualified (Rambam *Sefer Tahara, Hilkhot Tumat Okhalin* 8:3).

BACKGROUND

One who immersed during the day – טְבוּל יוֹם: When one who became ritually impure immerses himself, a vestigial impurity remains until sunset. During this interval he renders liquids with which he comes into contact ritually impure. However, those liquids do not render other items ritually impure.

NOTES

Wine and oil – יַיִן וְשֶׁמֶן: In the Jerusalem Talmud it is explained that Rabbi Shimon's rationale is that even wine and oil can in fact be mixed together in a single utensil, as they are both used in the making of *anigron*, a type of drink.

Rabbi Eliezer ben Taddai and Rabbi Meir – רַבִּי אֱלִיעֶזֶר בֶּן תַּדַּאי וְרַבִּי מֵאִיר: In the Jerusalem Talmud, it is assumed that the opinions of Rabbi Eliezer ben Taddai and Rabbi Meir are based on the same principle. The issue discussed there is whether the guiding principle is Rabbi Meir's opinion with regard to a partnership and a joining of courtyards [*eiruv*], or Rabbi Meir's opinion that one may not establish an *eiruv* for a person without his knowledge. In the case here, the people have a commercial partnership that is not for the purpose of an *eiruv* of a courtyard or an alleyway, and therefore the partnership does not serve as an *eiruv*.

אֲמַר לֵיהּ אַבַּיֵי: וְאִי חַד טַעְמָא, תַּרְתֵּי הִילְכְתָא לָמָּה לִי?! הָא קָא מַשְׁמַע לָן: דְּלָא עָבְדִינַן כִּתְרֵי חוּמְרֵי בְּעֵירוּבִין.

Abaye said to him: But if it is one reason, why do I need **two rulings?** On the contrary, it would be enough to rule in one case, from which we could infer the other as well. Rav Yosef replied: There is nevertheless a reason for both rulings, as **this** comes to **teach us that we do not act in accordance with two stringencies** of one *tanna* **in** matters of ***eiruv***.[N] Had Rav ruled only in accordance with Rabbi Meir, we would have known only that the *halakha* is in accordance with his opinion with regard to one specific detail of the case. He therefore ruled in accordance with two Sages: Rabbi Eliezer ben Taddai with regard to a merging of alleyways with wine, and Rabbi Meir with regard to a merging of alleyways with bread. Each is stringent with regard to a different detail of the case.

מַאי רַבִּי מֵאִיר וּמַאי רַבָּנַן? דְּתַנְיָא: מְעָרְבִין בַּחֲצֵירוֹת בַּפַּת. וְאִם רָצוּ לְעָרֵב בַּיַּיִן – אֵין מְעָרְבִין. מִשְׁתַּתְּפִין בַּמָּבוֹי בַּיַּיִן, וְאִם רָצוּ לְהִשְׁתַּתֵּף בַּפַּת – מִשְׁתַּתְּפִין.

Having mentioned Rabbi Meir, the Gemara now asks: **What** is the statement of **Rabbi Meir, and what** is the statement of **the Rabbis? As it was taught** in the following *baraita*: **One may establish an *eiruv* with bread between courtyards** that open to one another, **but if one wanted to establish an *eiruv* with wine, one** may **not establish an *eiruv*** in that manner.[H] **One may merge** the courtyards that open **into an alleyway with wine, and if one wanted to establish a merging** of alleyways **with bread, one** may **merge** the courtyards of alleyways in this manner.[H]

מְעָרְבִין בַּחֲצֵירוֹת וּמִשְׁתַּתְּפִין בַּמָּבוֹי, שֶׁלֹּא לְשַׁכֵּחַ תּוֹרַת עֵירוּב מִן הַתִּינוֹקוֹת שֶׁיֹּאמְרוּ ״אֲבוֹתֵינוּ לֹא עֵירְבוּ״, דִּבְרֵי רַבִּי מֵאִיר. וַחֲכָמִים אוֹמְרִים: אוֹ מְעָרְבִין, אוֹ מִשְׁתַּתְּפִין.

Why **does one establish an *eiruv* between courtyards and** also **merge** the courtyards that open **into an alleyway?** It is so **as not to cause the** halakhic **category of *eiruv* to be forgotten by the children, as** if a merging of alleyways alone were used, the children would later **say: Our fathers never established an *eiruv*.** Therefore, an *eiruv* is established for educational purposes; this is **the statement of Rabbi Meir.**[H] **And the Rabbis say:** One may **either establish an *eiruv* or merge** alleyways.

פְּלִיגִי בָּהּ רַבִּי נַחוּמִי וְרַבָּה; חַד אָמַר: בַּפַּת, דְּכוּלֵּי עָלְמָא לָא פְּלִיגִי דִּבְחֲדָא סַגִּי. כִּי פְּלִיגִי – בַּיַּיִן.

Rabbi Naḥumi and Rabba disagreed about this issue. **One** of them **said:** In the case **of bread,** which may be used both for an *eiruv* and for a merging of alleyways, **everyone agrees that one,** either an *eiruv* or a merging of alleyways, **is enough. When they disagree** in the case **of wine,** which may be used only for a merging of alleyways but not for an *eiruv*, Rabbi Meir maintains that an *eiruv* is also necessary, while the Rabbis maintain that it is not required.

NOTES

In accordance with two stringencies in matters of *eiruv* – **כִּתְרֵי חוּמְרֵי בְּעֵירוּבִין**: Rashi explains that it was necessary for Rav to rule in accordance with two *tanna'im*, because two stringencies of a single Sage in *eiruvin* are not accepted. Consequently, he had to find a second Sage who was stringent with regard to relying on a merging of the alleyways instead of an *eiruv*. Rabbi Eliezer Meir Horowitz explains that had Rav merely ruled that the *halakha* is in accordance with the opinion of Rabbi Meir, the assumption would have been that this is true with regard to only one of the stringencies of the case but not both. Therefore, Rav had to rule in accordance with Rabbi Eliezer ben Taddai as well.

The Ra'avad explains that the principle of not adopting two stringencies means that if a stringency in *halakhot* of *eiruvin* is accepted in accordance with the opinion one *tanna*, and there is a similar opinion of another *tanna* phrased slightly differently or referring to a somewhat different case, then there is no presumption that the same *halakha* applies in both cases, unless there is an explicit tradition to that effect.

With regard to the two stringencies, the Ritva explains that Rabbi Eliezer ben Taddai is referring only to a case where the partnership between the neighbors was merely a commercial one, while Rabbi Meir is stringent even if the partnership was established unequivocally for the purpose of an *eiruv*.

HALAKHA

With what may one establish an *eiruv* between courtyards – **בַּמֶּה מְעָרְבִים בַּחֲצֵרוֹת**: Bread, rather than wine, is used for establishing an *eiruv*, in accordance with the opinion of Rabbi Yehuda (*Shulḥan Arukh, Oraḥ Ḥayyim* 366:1).

With what may one establish a merging of alleyways – **בַּמֶּה מִשְׁתַּתְּפִים**: Either bread or wine may be utilized for the merging of alleyways (*Shulḥan Arukh, Oraḥ Ḥayyim* 386:4).

An *eiruv* and a merging of alleyways – **עֵירוּב וְשִׁיתּוּף**: If a merging of alleyways was established with bread, there is no need to establish an *eiruv* for the courtyards. However, if a merging of alleyways was established with wine, an *eiruv* must also be established for the courtyards, as the *halakha* is in accordance with the opinion of Rabbi Meir, as interpreted by the first explanation of the Gemara. This ruling is either due to the ruling of the Gemara or because Rabba explicitly stated (67b) that one may rely upon this merging of alleyways (Vilna Gaon). Some commentaries say that it is permitted to rely on the merging of alleyways to permit carrying between the courtyards via the opening between them only if each courtyard had already established its own internal *eiruv* but had not established an *eiruv* between the two courtyards (Rashi). The Rema maintains that one is permitted to rely on a merging of alleyways instead of an *eiruv* even if it is established with wine. He explains that in modern times all the residents contribute wine to the merging, and therefore it is considered to be both an *eiruv* and a merging of alleyways. (*Shulḥan Arukh, Oraḥ Ḥayyim* 387).

Perek **VI**
Daf **72** Amud **a**

וְחַד אָמַר: בַּיַּיִן, דְּכוּלֵּי עָלְמָא לָא פְּלִיגִי דְּבָעֵינַן תַּרְתֵּי, כִּי פְּלִיגִי – בַּפַּת.

And one said: In the case **of wine, everyone agrees that two are required,** both a merging of alleyways and a joining of courtyards. **When they disagree** is in a case where an *eiruv* was established **with bread:** Rabbi Meir maintains that both a merging of alleyways and a joining of courtyards are required, whereas the Rabbis say that one is sufficient.

מֵיתִיבִי: וַחֲכָמִים אוֹמְרִים אוֹ מְעָרְבִין אוֹ מִשְׁתַּתְּפִין. מַאי לָאו – אוֹ מְעָרְבִין בֶּחָצֵר בַּפַּת, אוֹ מִשְׁתַּתְּפִין בַּמָּבוֹי בַּיַּיִן!

The Gemara **raises an objection** from the *baraita* itself. **And the Rabbis say:** One may **either establish an *eiruv* or a merging** of alleyways. **What, does it not** mean that one **either establishes an *eiruv* in the courtyard with bread or a merging in the alleyway with wine,** which indicates that they also disagreed in a case where a merging of alleyways was established with wine?

אָמַר רַב גִּידֵּל, אָמַר רַב, הָכִי קָאָמַר: אוֹ מְעָרְבִין בֶּחָצֵר בְּפַת, וּמוּתָּרִין כָּאן וְכָאן. אוֹ מִשְׁתַּתְּפִין בַּמָּבוֹי בְּפַת, וּמוּתָּרִין כָּאן וְכָאן.

Rav Giddel said that Rav said that the Rabbis were **saying as follows:** One may **either establish an** ***eiruv*** **in the courtyard with bread, and** it would **be** rendered **permitted** to carry both **here,** in the courtyard, **and there,** in the alleyway, **or** one may **establish a merging** of alleyways **in the alleyway with bread, and** it would **be** rendered **permitted** to carry both **here,** in the courtyard, **and there,** in the alleyway.

אָמַר רַב יְהוּדָה, אָמַר רַב: הֲלָכָה כְּרַבִּי מֵאִיר. וְרַב הוּנָא אָמַר: מִנְהָג כְּרַבִּי מֵאִיר. וְרַבִּי יוֹחָנָן אָמַר: נָהֲגוּ הָעָם כְּרַבִּי מֵאִיר.

Rav Yehuda said that Rav said: The ***halakha*** **is in accordance with** the opinion of **Rabbi Meir. And Rav Huna said:** No clear halakhic ruling was issued in his favor, but **the custom is in accordance with** the opinion of **Rabbi Meir.** Therefore, if someone asks, he should be instructed to act accordingly. **And Rabbi Yoḥanan said:** It is not even a custom established by the Sages. Rather, **the people were accustomed**[N] to act **in accordance with** the opinion of **Rabbi Meir,** and we do not tell them they have acted inappropriately.

מתני׳ חֲמִשָּׁה חֲבוּרוֹת שֶׁשָּׁבְתוּ בִּטְרַקְלִין אֶחָד, בֵּית שַׁמַּאי אוֹמְרִים: עֵירוּב לְכׇל חֲבוּרָה וַחֲבוּרָה. וּבֵית הִלֵּל אוֹמְרִים: עֵירוּב אֶחָד לְכוּלָּן.

MISHNA With regard to **five groups** of people **who spent Shabbat in one hall** [***teraklin***][NHLB] that was subdivided by partitions into separate rooms,[B] each of which had a separate entrance to a courtyard that was shared with other houses, **Beit Shammai say: An** ***eiruv*** is required **for each and every group,** i.e., each group must contribute separately to the *eiruv* of the courtyard, as each is considered a different house. **And Beit Hillel say: One** ***eiruv*** suffices **for all of them,** as the partitions do not render the different sections separate houses.

וּמוֹדִים בִּזְמַן שֶׁמִּקְצָתָן שְׁרוּיִין בַּחֲדָרִים אוֹ בַּעֲלִיּוֹת, שֶׁהֵן צְרִיכִין עֵירוּב לְכׇל חֲבוּרָה וַחֲבוּרָה.

And Beit Hillel **concede** that **when some of them occupy** separate **rooms or upper stories, they require** a separate ***eiruv*** **for each and every group,** and the fact that they are in the same building does not render them one unified group.

גמ׳ אָמַר רַב נַחְמָן: מַחְלוֹקֶת בִּמְסִיפָס, אֲבָל בִּמְחִיצָה עֲשָׂרָה – דִּבְרֵי הַכֹּל עֵירוּב לְכׇל חֲבוּרָה וַחֲבוּרָה. אִיכָּא דְּאָמְרִי, אָמַר רַב נַחְמָן: אַף בִּמְסִיפָס מַחְלוֹקֶת.

GEMARA **Rav Naḥman said: The dispute** applies only where they divided the hall **with a partition of pegs** [***mesifas***].[L] **However,** if they divided it **with a** sturdy **partition ten** handbreadths high, **all agree** that a separate contribution to the ***eiruv*** is required **for each and every group,** as this certainly divides the hall into separate living quarters. **Some say** a different version of the previous passage, according to which **Rav Naḥman said** as follows: **Even** where they merely divided the room **with a partition of pegs,**[N] there is a **dispute** about whether this is considered a full-fledged partition.[N]

פְּלִיגִי בָּהּ רַבִּי חִיָּיא וְרַבִּי שִׁמְעוֹן בְּרַבִּי; חַד אָמַר: מַחְלוֹקֶת בִּמְחִיצוֹת הַמַּגִּיעוֹת לַתִּקְרָה, אֲבָל מְחִיצוֹת שֶׁאֵין מַגִּיעוֹת לַתִּקְרָה – דִּבְרֵי הַכֹּל עֵירוּב אֶחָד לְכוּלָּן. וְחַד אָמַר: מַחְלוֹקֶת בִּמְחִיצוֹת שֶׁאֵין מַגִּיעוֹת לַתִּקְרָה, אֲבָל מְחִיצוֹת הַמַּגִּיעוֹת לַתִּקְרָה – דִּבְרֵי הַכֹּל צְרִיכִין עֵירוּב לְכׇל חֲבוּרָה וַחֲבוּרָה.

The Gemara relates that **Rabbi Ḥiyya and Rabbi Shimon, son of** Rabbi Yehuda HaNasi, **disagreed about** this issue. **One of them said:** This **dispute is with regard to partitions that reach the ceiling, but** with regard to **partitions that do not reach the ceiling, all agree** that **one** ***eiruv*** suffices **for all of them,** as the partitions do not turn the compartments into separate houses. **And one said:** This **dispute is with regard to partitions that do not reach the ceiling, but** with regard to **partitions that reach the ceiling, all agree** that the compartments are considered separate living quarters, and **they require** a separate contribution to the ***eiruv*** **for each and every group.**

NOTES

The ***halakha*****…the custom…the people were accustomed – הֲלָכָה...מִנְהָג...נָהֲגוּ הָעָם:** Rashi clarifies the differences between these levels of halakhic protocol. The difference between an established *halakha* and a custom is not merely the extent to which they are publicized, but the degree of certainty of each ruling. A *halakha* is binding at all times, which is why it is made public knowledge. On the other hand, a custom is not discussed in public lectures, because the policy is not sufficiently clear to the Sages, even though they are inclined to accept it. The meaning of the statement that the people had the custom is that the Sages refrained from interfering in the matter and allowed people to act as they wished.

Groups…in one hall – אֶחָד חֲבוּרוֹת...בִּטְרַקְלִין: Several commentaries maintain that this is a special case in which there is an undivided second story above the hall, which allows the subdivisions in the hall to be considered a single unit (Ra'avad; Rabbeinu Yehonatan). The Rashba objects to this explanation on the grounds that it adds a critical detail that is not mentioned in the mishna.

Even where they divided the room with a partition of pegs – אַף בִּמְסִיפָס: The commentaries questioned this version of Rav Naḥman's statement, as it sheds light only on the opinion of Beit Shammai, which is not accepted as *halakha*. This is unusual and would typically elicit a comment from the Gemara. One answer is that even this version of Rav Naḥman's statement teaches something relevant to the opinion of Beit Hillel, who concede that if some of them were staying in separate chambers, all the groups must contribute separately to the *eiruv*; including those whose room was divided by a partition of pegs (Rabbi Elazar Moshe Horowitz).

The size of the partitions – גּוֹדֶל הַמְּחִיצוֹת: In the Jerusalem Talmud, an anonymous opinion is cited that the disagreement is about whether a partition ten handbreadths high is considered a valid partition.

HALAKHA

Groups who spent Shabbat in one hall – חֲבוּרוֹת שֶׁשָּׁבְתוּ בִּטְרַקְלִין אֶחָד: With regard to several groups of people located in one large hall that is subdivided by partitions into separate rooms, if the partitions reach the ceiling, each group must contribute separately to the *eiruv*. If the partitions do not reach the ceiling, they may make a joint contribution to the *eiruv* (*Shulḥan Arukh*, *Oraḥ Ḥayyim* 370:3).

LANGUAGE

Hall [*teraklin*] – טְרַקְלִין: From the Greek τρίκλινον, *triklinon*, originally meaning a room containing three beds for reclining. Over time it came to refer to any hall or large guest room.

Partition of pegs [*mesifas*] – מְסִיפָס: Probably related to the Greek root μέσος, *mesos*, meaning middle or connoting something positioned between other items. Some authorities are of the opinion that it derives from the Greek μεσοπόρος, *mesoporos*, meaning a hollow object, which is consistent with the explanation of the *ge'onim* that a *mesifas* is a wall with many windows (Rabbi Binyamin Musafya). Others maintain that it derives from the Latin word sepes, meaning fence or partition, or from the Greek αἱμασιά, *aimasia*.

BACKGROUND

Hall – טְרַקְלִין:

Replica of a Roman hall from the mishnaic period

Five groups…in one hall – חָמֵשׁ חֲבוּרוֹת בִּטְרַקְלִין:

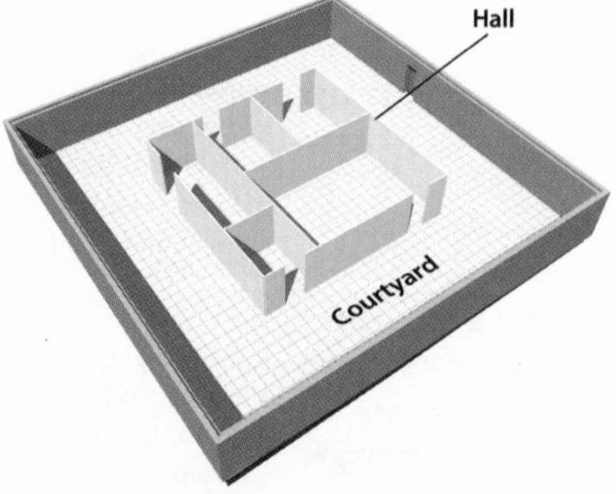

Hall divided into five rooms by means of internal partitions

מֵיתִיבִי, אָמַר רַבִּי יְהוּדָה הַסַּבָּר: לֹא נֶחְלְקוּ בֵּית שַׁמַּאי וּבֵית הִלֵּל עַל מְחִיצוֹת הַמַּגִּיעוֹת לַתִּקְרָה – שֶׁצְּרִיכִין עֵירוּב לְכָל חֲבוּרָה וַחֲבוּרָה. עַל מַה נֶחְלְקוּ – עַל מְחִיצוֹת שֶׁאֵין מַגִּיעוֹת לַתִּקְרָה. שֶׁבֵּית שַׁמַּאי אוֹמְרִים: עֵירוּב לְכָל חֲבוּרָה וַחֲבוּרָה, וּבֵית הִלֵּל אוֹמְרִים: עֵירוּב אֶחָד לְכוּלָּן.

The Gemara **raises an objection** based on the following *baraita*: **Rabbi Yehuda the Keen** [*hasabbar*],[N] who was known by this name due to his sharp mind, **said: Beit Shammai and Beit Hillel did not disagree about partitions that reach the ceiling,** as all agree that **they require** a separate contribution to the ***eiruv* for each and every group. With regard to what did they disagree?** With regard to **partitions that do not reach the ceiling, as Beit Shammai say:** A separate contribution to the ***eiruv*** is required **for each and every group, and Beit Hillel say: One** contribution to the ***eiruv*** suffices **for all of them.**

לְמַאן דְּאָמַר בִּמְחִיצוֹת הַמַּגִּיעוֹת לַתִּקְרָה מַחֲלוֹקֶת – תְּיוּבְתָּא! וּלְמַאן דְּאָמַר בִּמְחִיצוֹת שֶׁאֵין מַגִּיעוֹת לַתִּקְרָה מַחֲלוֹקֶת – סַיַּיעְתָּא. לְהָךְ לִישָּׁנָא דְּאָמַר רַב נַחְמָן מַחֲלוֹקֶת בִּמְסִיפָס – תְּיוּבְתָּא!

According to the one who said that it was with regard to **partitions that reach the ceiling** that there was a **dispute,** this *baraita* offers a **conclusive refutation. And according to the one who said** that it was with regard to **partitions that do not reach the ceiling** that there was a **dispute,** the *baraita* offers **support.** With regard **to that version** which holds that **Rav Naḥman said:** The **dispute** applies only where they divided the hall **with a *mesifas,*** this *baraita* is **a conclusive refutation.**

לְהָךְ לִישָּׁנָא דְּאָמַר רַב נַחְמָן אַף בִּמְסִיפָס מַחֲלוֹקֶת – לֵימָא תֶּיהֱוֵי תְּיוּבְתָּא?!

However, the following issue needs further clarification: With regard **to that version** which holds that **Rav Naḥman said:** The **dispute** applies **even** where the hall was divided **with a *mesifas,* shall we say** that Rabbi Yehuda the Keen's statement **is a** conclusive **refutation?** That is to say, does it imply that all agree that in the case of a *mesifas,* one *eiruv* suffices for them all?

אָמַר לָךְ רַב נַחְמָן: פְּלִיגִי בִּמְחִיצָה, וְהוּא הַדִּין בִּמְסִיפָס. וְהַאי דְּקָא מִיפַּלְגִי בִּמְחִיצָה – לְהוֹדִיעֲךָ כֹּחָן דְּבֵית הִלֵּל.

Rav Naḥman could have **said to you: They** explicitly **disagreed about a partition, and the same is true of a partition of pegs. And** the fact **that they disagree with regard to a partition** rather than a partition of pegs is **to convey to you the far-reaching nature of** the opinion of **Beit Hillel.** Even where the compartments are divided by full-fledged partitions, Beit Hillel remain of the opinion that one contribution to the *eiruv* suffices for all of them, as the partitions do not turn them into separate residences.

וְלִיפַּלְגֵי בִּמְסִיפָס לְהוֹדִיעֲךָ כֹּחָן דְּבֵית שַׁמַּאי! כֹּחַ דְּהֶיתֵּרָא עֲדִיף.

The Gemara asks: If they disagreed in both cases, **let them disagree** in the *baraita* **about a *mesifas,*** and thereby **inform you of the strength of Beit Shammai.** They are stringent and require a separate contribution to the *eiruv* for each and every group, even in the case of a *mesifas.* The Gemara answers: It is **preferable** for the *tanna* to teach us **the strength of a permissive** ruling.[N] If a *tanna* can formulate a dispute in a manner that emphasizes the strength of the more lenient position, he will do so.

אָמַר רַב נַחְמָן, אָמַר רַב: הֲלָכָה כְּרַבִּי יְהוּדָה הַסַּבָּר.

Rav Naḥman said that Rav said: The *halakha* is in accordance with the statement of **Rabbi Yehuda the Keen,** that all agree that where the partitions reach the ceiling, a separate contribution to the *eiruv* is required for each group, and that they disagree only about partitions that do not reach the ceiling.

אָמַר רַב נַחְמָן בַּר יִצְחָק: מַתְנִיתִין נַמִי דַּיְקָא: דְּקָתָנֵי "וּמוֹדִים בִּזְמַן שֶׁמִּקְצָתָן שְׁרוּיִין בַּחֲדָרִים וּבַעֲלִיּוֹת שֶׁצְּרִיכִין עֵירוּב לְכָל חֲבוּרָה וַחֲבוּרָה". מַאי חֲדָרִים וּמַאי עֲלִיּוֹת? אִילֵּימָא חֲדָרִים – חֲדָרִים מַמָּשׁ וַעֲלִיּוֹת – עֲלִיּוֹת מַמָּשׁ, פְּשִׁיטָא! אֶלָּא לָאו: כְּעֵין חֲדָרִים, כְּעֵין עֲלִיּוֹת. וּמַאי נִיהוּ – מְחִיצוֹת הַמַּגִּיעוֹת לַתִּקְרָה, שְׁמַע מִינָּהּ.

Rav Naḥman bar Yitzḥak said: The mishna is also precise according to this view, **as it teaches: And** Beit Hillel **concede** that **when some of them occupy** separate **rooms or upper stories, they require a** separate ***eiruv* for each and every group. What** is the meaning of the word **rooms, and what** is the meaning of the term **upper stories? If you say** that the word **rooms** refers to **actual rooms and** the term **upper stories** refers to **actual upper stories,** i.e., they were separate from the beginning and are not subdivisions of a larger room, it is **obvious,** as this is the *halakha* governing the case of many people residing in the same courtyard. **Rather, doesn't it** mean that they are **similar to rooms and similar to upper stories? And what** are **these** partitions? They are **partitions that reach the ceiling;** and even though they are not actual rooms or upper stories, they are considered like rooms and upper stories. The Gemara concludes: Indeed, **learn from this** that this is the case.

NOTES

Rabbi Yehuda the Keen [*hasabbar*] – רַבִּי יְהוּדָה הַסַּבָּר: See *Tosafot,* who follow Rabbeinu Ḥananel's version, which reads *hasabbakh,* an artisan who makes lace clothing [*sevakhot*] for women. Alternatively, he may have been called *hasakhakh,* after his hometown Sekhakha. Rav Ya'akov Emden points out that it is unlikely that one Sage would be singled out for his sharp intellect.

It is preferable to teach us the strength of a permissive ruling – כֹּחַ דְּהֶיתֵּרָא עֲדִיף: The basis for this statement is that a *tanna* sometimes has to decide between formulating a dispute in a manner that emphasizes the strength of the stringent position or that of the more lenient position. In such cases, the Sages said that it is preferable to teach the strength of the permissive position. The rationale is that the stringent position is occasionally the consequence of uncertainty and caution, and therefore nothing is added by demonstrating its scope. On the other hand, the lenient opinion must be based on a solid foundation and therefore should be explicated (Rashi).

תָּנָא: בַּמֶּה דְּבָרִים אֲמוּרִים – כְּשֶׁמּוֹלִיכִין אֶת עֵירוּבָן לְמָקוֹם אַחֵר, אֲבָל אִם הָיָה עֵירוּבָן בָּא אֶצְלָן – דִּבְרֵי הַכֹּל עֵירוּב אֶחָד לְכוּלָּן.

It was taught in a *baraita*: **In what** case is **this statement,** that Beit Shammai require a separate contribution to the *eiruv* from each group, **said?** It is in a case **where** the groups in the hall **bring their** ***eiruv*** **elsewhere**[H] in the courtyard, i.e., to a different house. **But if their** ***eiruv*** **was coming to them,** i.e., if the other members of the courtyard brought their contributions and established the *eiruv* in that hall, **all agree** that **one** contribution to the ***eiruv*** suffices **for all of them.** The fact that the *eiruv* is placed in this house renders all of its residents members of a single unit.

כְּמַאן אָזְלָא הָא דְּתַנְיָא: חֲמִשָּׁה שֶׁגָּבוּ אֶת עֵירוּבָן, כְּשֶׁמּוֹלִיכִין אֶת עֵירוּבָן לְמָקוֹם אַחֵר עֵירוּב אֶחָד לְכוּלָּן. כְּמַאן – כְּבֵית הִלֵּל.

The Gemara comments: **In accordance with whose** opinion **is** the ruling **that was taught** in the following *baraita*: With regard to **five** people **who** live in the same courtyard and **collected their** ***eiruv***,[H] **when they take their** ***eiruv*** **elsewhere** in the courtyard, **one** contribution to the ***eiruv*** suffices **for all of them. In accordance with whose** opinion is this ruling? **In accordance with** the opinion of **Beit Hillel.**

וְאִיכָּא דְּאָמְרִי: בַּמֶּה דְּבָרִים אֲמוּרִים – כְּשֶׁהָיָה עֵירוּב בָּא אֶצְלָן, אֲבָל אִם הָיוּ מוֹלִיכִין אֶת עֵירוּבָן לְמָקוֹם אַחֵר – דִּבְרֵי הַכֹּל צְרִיכִין עֵירוּב לְכָל חֲבוּרָה וַחֲבוּרָה.

And some say a different version of the previous passage: **In what** case is **this statement,** that Beit Hillel require only one contribution for all the groups together, **said?** It is in a case **where the** ***eiruv*** **was coming to them. But if** the groups in the hall **were bringing their** ***eiruv*** **elsewhere** in the courtyard, **all agree** that a separate contribution to the ***eiruv*** **is required for each and every one of them.**

כְּמַאן אָזְלָא הָא דְּתַנְיָא: חֲמִשָּׁה שֶׁגָּבוּ אֶת עֵירוּבָן, כְּשֶׁמּוֹלִיכִין אֶת עֵירוּבָן לְמָקוֹם אַחֵר עֵירוּב אֶחָד לְכוּלָּן, כְּמַאן – דְּלָא כְּחַד.

If so, **in accordance with whose** opinion **is** the ruling **that was taught** in the *baraita*: With regard to **five** people **who** live in the same courtyard and **collected their** ***eiruv***, **when they take their** ***eiruv*** **elsewhere** in the courtyard, **one** contribution to the ***eiruv*** suffices **for all of them. In accordance with whose** opinion is this ruling? It is **not in accordance with** either **one** of them.

מתני׳ הָאַחִין שֶׁהָיוּ אוֹכְלִין עַל שֻׁלְחַן אֲבִיהֶם וִישֵׁנִים בְּבָתֵּיהֶם – צְרִיכִין עֵירוּב לְכָל אֶחָד וְאֶחָד. לְפִיכָךְ אִם שָׁכַח אֶחָד מֵהֶם וְלֹא עֵירֵב – מְבַטֵּל אֶת רְשׁוּתוֹ.

MISHNA In the case of **brothers who were eating at their father's table and sleeping in their** own **houses** in the same courtyard, a separate contribution to the ***eiruv*** **is required for each and every one** of them.[H] **Therefore, if one of them forgot and did not** contribute to the ***eiruv***, **he** must **renounce his rights** in the courtyard in order to render carrying in the courtyard permitted to the rest of the courtyard's residents.

אֵימָתַי – בִּזְמַן שֶׁמּוֹלִיכִין עֵירוּבָן בְּמָקוֹם אַחֵר. אֲבָל אִם הָיָה עֵירוּב בָּא אֶצְלָן, אוֹ שֶׁאֵין עִמָּהֶן דִּיּוּרִין בֶּחָצֵר – אֵינָן צְרִיכִין לְעָרֵב.

When do they state this *halakha*? They state it **when they take their** ***eiruv*** **elsewhere** in the courtyard, i.e., to the house of one of the other residents. **But if the** ***eiruv*** **was coming to them,** i.e., if it was placed in their father's house, **or if there are no** other **residents with** the brothers and their father **in the courtyard, they are not required to establish an** ***eiruv***, as they are considered like a single individual living in a courtyard.

גמ׳ שְׁמַע מִינָּהּ: מְקוֹם לִינָה גּוֹרֵם! אָמַר רַב יְהוּדָה, אָמַר רַב: בִּמְקַבְּלֵי פְרָס שָׁנוּ.

GEMARA The Gemara comments on the statement in the mishna that a separate contribution to the *eiruv* must be made by each of the brothers if they sleep in their own houses: **Learn from it** that one's **place of sleep determines** the location of his residence. The Gemara rejects this conclusion. **Rav Yehuda said that Rav said: They taught** this mishna **with regard to** brothers who **receive a portion**[N] from their father. The mishna is not referring to brothers who actually eat at their father's table,[N] but rather to brothers whose father supplies them with food that they eat in their own homes.

תָּנוּ רַבָּנַן: מִי שֶׁיֵּשׁ לוֹ בֵּית שַׁעַר אַכְסַדְרָה וּמִרְפֶּסֶת בַּחֲצַר חֲבֵירוֹ – הֲרֵי זֶה אֵין אוֹסֵר עָלָיו. (אֶת) בֵּית הַתֶּבֶן (וְאֶת) בֵּית הַבָּקָר בֵּית הָעֵצִים וּבֵית הָאוֹצָרוֹת – הֲרֵי זֶה אוֹסֵר עָלָיו. רַבִּי יְהוּדָה אוֹמֵר: אֵינוֹ אוֹסֵר אֶלָּא מְקוֹם דִּירָה בִּלְבַד.

The Sages taught in a *baraita*: **One who has a gatehouse,**[H] **porch,** or **balcony in his friend's courtyard does not render** the owner of the courtyard **prohibited** from carrying there without an *eiruv*, as these locations are not considered residences. However, if he has a **storeroom of straw, a cattle shed, a woodshed, or a storehouse** in his friend's courtyard, **he renders it prohibit** for his friend to carry there without an *eiruv*. **Rabbi Yehuda says: Only a place of** actual **dwelling renders** carrying **prohibited,** but a building that is not designated for residence does not render carrying without an *eiruv* prohibited for another resident of the courtyard.

HALAKHA

Where the groups bring their eiruv elsewhere – שֶׁמּוֹלִיכִין אֶת עֵירוּבָן לְמָקוֹם אַחֵר: If there are several groups of people in one house and the *eiruv* of the courtyard is placed in that house, the various groups do not need to contribute to the *eiruv* (*Shulḥan Arukh, Oraḥ Ḥayyim* 370:3).

Five who collected their ***eiruv*** – חֲמִשָּׁה שֶׁגָּבוּ אֶת עֵירוּבָן: Several people who establish an *eiruv* together are considered like one person. Therefore, they require only one *eiruv* in order to join a different courtyard (Rambam *Sefer Zemanim, Hilkhot Eiruvin* 4:4).

Brothers in their father's courtyard – אַחִים בַּחֲצַר אֲבִיהֶם: Brothers who sleep in their own houses in the same courtyard must each contribute to the *eiruv*, even if they receive their food from their father (*Shulḥan Arukh, Oraḥ Ḥayyim* 370:5).

A gatehouse, etc. – בֵּית שַׁעַר וכו׳: If one lives in a gatehouse, porch, or balcony in another person's courtyard, it neither renders others prohibited from carrying, nor is he required to participate in an *eiruv*. However, a barn, a storeroom of straw, a cattle shed, and a woodshed are suitable for residence. Therefore, one who lives there renders carrying prohibited for others unless he participates in an *eiruv*, in accordance with the first *tanna* in the *baraita* (*Shulḥan Arukh, Oraḥ Ḥayyim* 370:1).

NOTES

Who receive a portion – מְקַבְּלֵי פְּרָס: In the Jerusalem Talmud the question is asked: If the sons eat at their father's table, or even if they receive a portion from him, the food that he provides for all of them should be considered an *eiruv* due to the fact that it is owned jointly by all of them. Consequently, no further *eiruv* should be necessary. It answers that the case in question is where the father provides food to each of his sons separately, and therefore none of it is jointly owned.

Eat at their father's table – אוֹכְלִין עַל שֻׁלְחַן אֲבִיהֶם: The Rambam explains that these brothers eat at their own tables, but occasionally they eat at their father's table as a favor to them or as payment for work they do for him, and that itself is enough for them to be considered residents of his house to a certain degree.

אָמַר רַבִּי יְהוּדָה: מַעֲשֶׂה בְּבֶן נַפָּחָא שֶׁהָיוּ לוֹ חָמֵשׁ חֲצֵרוֹת בְּאוּשָׁא, וּבָא מַעֲשֶׂה לִפְנֵי חֲכָמִים, וְאָמְרוּ: אֵינוֹ אוֹסֵר אֶלָּא בֵּית דִּירָה בִּלְבַד.

Rabbi Yehuda said: There was an incident with ben Nappaḥa, who had houses in **five courtyards in Usha,** only one of which served as his own residence. **And the case came before the Sages** to decide whether an *eiruv* must be made for all of them, **and they said: Only a house of residence renders** carrying **prohibited.**

בֵּית דִּירָה סָלְקָא דַעְתָּךְ?! אֶלָּא אֵימָא: מְקוֹם דִּירָה.

The Gemara expresses surprise at the wording of the *baraita*: **Does it enter your mind** that the correct reading is **a house of residence?** He has a house in each of the five courtyards. **Rather, say: A place of residence,** i.e., it is prohibited to carry in the place where he actually lives, but nowhere else.

מַאי מְקוֹם דִּירָה? רַב אָמַר:

The Gemara asks: **What is** considered one's **place of residence? Rav said:**

Perek **VI**
Daf **73** Amud **a**

מְקוֹם פִּיתָּא, וּשְׁמוּאֵל אָמַר: מְקוֹם לִינָה.

The place where he eats his **bread,**[H] **and Shmuel said:** His **place of sleep.**[N]

מֵיתִיבִי: הָרוֹעִים וְהַקַּיָּיצִין וְהַבּוּרְגָּנִין וְשׁוֹמְרֵי פֵירוֹת, בִּזְמַן שֶׁדַּרְכָּן לָלִין בָּעִיר – הֲרֵי הֵן כְּאַנְשֵׁי הָעִיר, בִּזְמַן שֶׁדַּרְכָּן לָלִין בַּשָּׂדֶה – יֵשׁ לָהֶם אַלְפַּיִם לְכָל רוּחַ!

The Gemara **raises an objection** to Rav's opinion from a *baraita*: With regard to **shepherds; fig watchmen,**[H] who guard figs spread out in the field; **guardsmen** who sit in small guardhouses; **and produce watchmen; when they customarily sleep in the city** in addition to eating there, **they are like the residents of the city** with regard to their Shabbat limit, even though they were in the field when Shabbat began. However, **when they customarily sleep in the field,** even though they eat in the town, **they have** only **two thousand** cubits **in each direction** from the places where they sleep. This seems to contradict the opinion of Rav, who maintains that a person's place of dwelling is determined by where he eats, not by where he sleeps.

הָתָם אֲנַן סָהֲדֵי דְּאִי מַמְטוּ לְהוּ רִיפְתָּא הָתָם – טְפֵי נִיחָא לְהוּ.

The Gemara answers: **There,** in the case of the people in the field, **we are witnesses,** i.e., it is clearly evident, **that if** people would **bring them bread there,** to the place where they sleep, **it would be more convenient for them.** Fundamentally, however, a person's dwelling place is determined by where he eats, rather than where he sleeps.

אָמַר רַב יוֹסֵף: לָא שְׁמִיעַ לִי הָא שְׁמַעְתָּא. אֲמַר לֵיהּ אַבָּיֵי: אַתְּ אֲמַרְתְּ נִיהֲלַן, וְאַהָא אֲמַרְתְּ נִיהֲלַן: הָאַחִין שֶׁהָיוּ אוֹכְלִין עַל שֻׁלְחַן אֲבִיהֶן וִישֵׁנִים בְּבָתֵּיהֶן – צְרִיכִין עֵירוּב לְכׇל אֶחָד וְאֶחָד. וְאָמְרִינַן לָךְ: שְׁמַע מִינָּהּ – מְקוֹם לִינָה גּוֹרֵם. וְאָמְרַתְּ לַן עֲלַהּ, אָמַר רַב יְהוּדָה, אָמַר רַב: בִּמְקַבְּלֵי פְרָס שָׁנוּ.

Rav Yosef said: I have not heard this *halakha* stated by Rav. An illness had caused Rav Yosef to forget his studies. His student, **Abaye, said to him: You** yourself **said it to us, and it was with regard to this that you said it to us:** With regard to **brothers who were eating at their father's table and sleeping in their** own **houses** in the same courtyard, a separate contribution to the ***eiruv* is required for each and every one** of them. **And we said to you:** Can one **learn from** here that a person's **place of sleep determines** the location of his Shabbat residence? **And you said to us in this regard** that **Rav Yehuda said** that **Rav said: They taught** this mishna **with regard to** brothers **who receive a portion** from their father and are therefore considered as though they eat at his table, whereas in actual fact they eat their meals in their own homes.

תָּנוּ רַבָּנַן: מִי שֶׁיֵּשׁ לוֹ חָמֵשׁ נָשִׁים מְקַבְּלוֹת פְּרָס מִבַּעְלֵיהֶן, וַחֲמִשָּׁה עֲבָדִים מְקַבְּלִין פְּרָס מֵרַבֵּיהֶן, רַבִּי יְהוּדָה בֶּן בְּתֵירָה מַתִּיר בְּנָשִׁים וְאוֹסֵר בַּעֲבָדִים.

The Sages taught in a *baraita*: With regard to **one who has five wives** who **receive a portion from their husband** while each living in her own quarters in the courtyard, **and five slaves** who **receive a portion**[H] **from their master** while living in their own lodgings in the courtyard, **Rabbi Yehuda ben Beteira permits in** the case of **the wives,** i.e., they do not each have to contribute separately to the *eiruv*, as they are all considered to be residing with their husband. **And he prohibits in** the case of **the slaves,** meaning that he holds that as they live in separate houses, each is considered as residing on his own.

רַבִּי יְהוּדָה בֶּן בָּבָא מַתִּיר בַּעֲבָדִים וְאוֹסֵר בְּנָשִׁים.

Rabbi Yehuda ben Bava permits in the case of **the slaves,** as a slave necessarily follows his master, **and he prohibits in** the case of **the wives,** as each woman is significant in her own right, and is not totally dependent on her husband.[N]

HALAKHA

A place of a residence – מְקוֹם דִּירָה: With regard to the *halakhot* of an *eiruv*, a person's place of residence is defined as the location where he eats, rather than where he sleeps. The *halakha* is generally in accordance with the opinion of Rav in ritual matters as opposed to the opinion of Shmuel (*Shulḥan Arukh, Oraḥ Ḥayyim* 370:5).

Shepherds, fig watchmen – הָרוֹעִים וְהַקַּיָּיצִים: If shepherds, fig-watchmen, and people with similar jobs sleep in the town, they are considered to be residents of the town and must participate in its *eiruv*, even if they eat in the field. However, if they sleep in the field, the field is considered their place of residence (*Tur, Oraḥ Ḥayyim* 409).

Wives and slaves who receive a portion – נָשִׁים וַעֲבָדִים הַמְקַבְּלִים פְּרָס: Wives and slaves who are supported by their husbands or masters do not render carrying prohibited, even if they do not contribute to the *eiruv*. This is in accordance with the lenient opinions of both Rabbi Yehuda ben Beteira and Rabbi Yehuda ben Bava, since the *halakha* is in accordance with the lenient opinion with regard to *eiruv* (*Shulḥan Arukh, Oraḥ Ḥayyim* 370:6).

NOTES

The place of bread and the place of sleep – מְקוֹם פַּת וּמְקוֹם לִינָה: The Ritva explains that this dispute applies only to cases where there is no other method of determining an individual's place of residence. However, as the Gemara's discussion indicates, the essential criterion is the location one views as his primary residence.

Wives and slaves – נָשִׁים וַעֲבָדִים: The Ra'avad explains that slaves are the property of their master and therefore cannot establish a separate place of residence, which is not the case with regard to women. However, the legal status of the wives of one man can be viewed as that of a single person, because in certain areas of *halakha*, e.g., levirate marriage, anything done to one affects all of them.

Most early commentaries rule in accordance with the opinion of Rabbi Yehuda ben Bava, since Rav, who clarifies his opinion, presumably agrees with him. Although the Rambam followed the lenient ruling of both Sages, he is not to be understood as having accepted two mutually exclusive opinions. Rather, he accepts the arguments of both Sages that for different reasons, the status of wives and slaves is equivalent to that of their husband and master respectively (Rosh).

אָמַר רַב: מַאי טַעְמָא דְּרַבִּי יְהוּדָה בֶּן בָּבָא, דִּכְתִיב: ״וְדָנִיֵּאל בִּתְרַע מַלְכָּא״.

Rav said: What is the rationale for the opinion **of Rabbi Yehuda ben Bava? As it is written: "But Daniel was in the gate of the king"** (Daniel 2:49). The verse refers to Daniel's function rather than to an actual location, indicating that wherever Daniel went, it was as though he was in the king's gate. The same applies to any slave vis-à-vis his master.

פְּשִׁיטָא, בֵּן אֵצֶל אָבִיו – כִּדְאָמְרַן. אִשָּׁה אֵצֶל בַּעְלָהּ וְעֶבֶד אֵצֶל רַבּוֹ – פְּלוּגְתָּא דְּרַבִּי יְהוּדָה בֶּן בְּתֵירָה וְרַבִּי יְהוּדָה בֶּן בָּבָא. תַּלְמִיד אֵצֶל רַבּוֹ מַאי?

The Gemara proceeds to clarify various aspects of this issue, starting with a summary of what has already been stated. The *halakha* is **obvious** in the case of **a son with his father, as we stated** it above the mishna. **A wife with her husband and a slave with his master** are subject to the **dispute** between **Rabbi Yehuda ben Beteira and Rabbi Yehuda ben Bava.** With regard to **a student** who lives **with his master** in the same courtyard and receives his sustenance from him, **what** is his status with regard to *eiruv*?

תָּא שְׁמַע: דְּרַב בֵּי רַבִּי חִיָּיא אָמַר: אֵין אָנוּ צְרִיכִין לְעָרֵב, שֶׁהֲרֵי אָנוּ סוֹמְכִין עַל שׁוּלְחָנוֹ שֶׁל רַבִּי חִיָּיא. וְרַבִּי חִיָּיא בֵּי רַבִּי אָמַר: אֵין אָנוּ צְרִיכִין לְעָרֵב, שֶׁהֲרֵי אָנוּ סוֹמְכִין עַל שׁוּלְחָנוֹ שֶׁל רַבִּי.

Come and **hear** a resolution to this question: **As Rav,** when he was **in the school of Rabbi Ḥiyya, said: We do not need to establish an *eiruv*, as we are dependent upon the table of Rabbi Ḥiyya. And** similarly, **Rabbi Ḥiyya** himself, when he was **in the school of Rabbi** Yehuda HaNasi, **said: We do not need to establish an *eiruv*, as we are dependent upon the table of Rabbi** Yehuda HaNasi.[NH]

בְּעָא מִינֵּיהּ אַבַּיֵי מֵרַבָּה: חֲמִשָּׁה שֶׁגָּבוּ אֶת עֵירוּבָן, כְּשֶׁמּוֹלִיכִין אֶת עֵירוּבָן לְמָקוֹם אַחֵר, עֵירוּב אֶחָד לְכוּלָּן, אוֹ צְרִיכִין עֵירוּב לְכָל אֶחָד וְאֶחָד? אֲמַר לֵיהּ: עֵירוּב אֶחָד לְכוּלָּן.

Abaye raised a dilemma before Rabba: With regard to **five** people **who** live in the same courtyard and **collected their *eiruv*, when they take their *eiruv* elsewhere** in order to merge their courtyard with a different one, is **one** contribution to the ***eiruv*** sufficient **for all of them, or do they need** a separate contribution to the ***eiruv* for each and every one** of them? Rabba **said to him: One** contribution to the ***eiruv*** suffices **for all of them.**

וְהָא אַחִין, דְּכִי גָּבוּ דָּמוּ, וְקָתָנֵי: ״צְרִיכִין עֵירוּב לְכָל אֶחָד וְאֶחָד״! הָכָא בְּמַאי עָסְקִינַן – כְּגוֹן דְּאִיכָּא דִּיּוּרִין בַּהֲדַיְיהוּ, דְּמִגּוֹ דְּהָנֵי אָסְרִי – הָנֵי נַמִי אָסְרִי.

Abaye asked: **But** in the case of **brothers, who are comparable** to people **who collected** their *eiruv*, the mishna nonetheless **teaches: They require** a separate ***eiruv* for each and every one** of them. Rabba responded: **With what are we dealing here?** We are dealing with a case **where there are** other **residents,** in addition to the father and his sons, living **with them.** In that case, **since these** additional residents **render** carrying in the same courtyard **prohibited** unless they join in an *eiruv*, **those** brothers **also render it prohibited** for one another to carry in the other courtyard unless each of them contributes to the *eiruv*.

הָכִי נַמִי מִסְתַּבְּרָא, דְּקָתָנֵי: אֵימָתַי – בִּזְמַן שֶׁמּוֹלִיכִין אֶת עֵירוּבָן בְּמָקוֹם אַחֵר, אֲבָל אִם הָיָה עֵירוּבָן בָּא אֶצְלָם, אוֹ שֶׁאֵין דִּיּוּרִין עִמָּהֶן בֶּחָצֵר – אֵין צְרִיכִין לְעָרֵב, שְׁמַע מִינָּהּ.

The Gemara comments: **So too, it is reasonable** to understand, as the mishna **teaches: When** do they state this *halakha*? **When they bring their *eiruv* elsewhere** in the courtyard. **But if their *eiruv* was coming to them, or if there are no** other **residents with them in the courtyard, they do not need to establish an *eiruv*,** as they are considered like a single individual living in a courtyard. **Learn from this** that the preceding ruling refers to a situation where they shared the courtyard with other residents.

בְּעָא מִינֵּיהּ רַב חִיָּיא בַּר אָבִין מֵרַב שֵׁשֶׁת: בְּנֵי בֵּי רַב דְּאָכְלִי נַהֲמָא בְּבָאגָא, וְאָתוּ וּבָיְיתִי בְּבֵי רַב, כִּי מָשְׁחִינַן לְהוּ תְּחוּמָא, מִבֵּי רַב מָשְׁחִינַן לְהוּ, אוֹ מִבָּאגָא מָשְׁחִינַן לְהוּ? אֲמַר לֵיהּ: מָשְׁחִינַן מִבֵּי רַב.

The Gemara addresses a similar issue with regard to a joining of Shabbat boundaries: **Rav Ḥiyya bar Avin raised a dilemma before Rav Sheshet:** With regard to **students in their master's house who eat** their **bread in** their houses **in the field** [*baga*][L] **and** then **come and sleep in** their **master's house, when we measure** their Shabbat **limit for them, do we measure** it **for them from** their **master's house,** where they sleep, **or do we measure** it **for them from the field,** where they eat? **He said to him: We measure** it **from** their **master's house.**[H]

וַהֲרֵי נוֹתֵן אֶת עֵירוּבוֹ בְּתוֹךְ אַלְפַּיִם אַמָּה וְאָתֵי וּבָיֵית בְּבֵיתֵיהּ דְּמָשְׁחִינַן לֵיהּ תְּחוּמָא מֵעֵירוּבֵיהּ!

Rav Ḥiyya bar Avin asked: **But** in the case of **one who deposits his *eiruv*,** which establishes the location of his meal, **within two thousand cubits, and** then **goes** back **and sleeps in his house, we measure his** Shabbat **limit from his *eiruv*.** This implies that the determining factor is where he eats, rather than where he sleeps.

NOTES

A student and his master – תַּלְמִיד וְרַבּוֹ: The Rashba explains that a student who eats in his master's home is considered subordinate to him, in accordance with the principle that students are like one's children, as indicated by the biblical expression, the sons of the prophets.

HALAKHA

Students in their master's house – תַּלְמִידִים בְּבֵית רַבָּם: Students who eat at their master's table do not have to make their own contribution to the *eiruv* (*Shulḥan Arukh, Oraḥ Ḥayyim* 370:6).

From where do we measure the boundary of students – מֵהֵיכָן מוֹדְדִים תְּחוּם לַתַּלְמִידִים: The Shabbat limit for students who sleep in their master's house is measured from the master's home, even if they eat elsewhere (*Shulḥan Arukh, Oraḥ Ḥayyim* 409:7).

LANGUAGE

Field [*baga*] – בָּאגָא: From the Persian bāγ, meaning a garden. Its meaning in Aramaic connotes an open, rural space.

בְּהַהוּא אֲנַן סַהֲדֵי, וּבְהָדָא אֲנַן סַהֲדֵי. בְּהַהוּא אֲנַן סַהֲדֵי דְּאִי מִיתְדַּר לֵיהּ הָתָם – נִיחָא לֵיהּ. וּבְהָדָא אֲנַן סַהֲדֵי דְּאִי מַיְיתוּ לְהוּ רִיפְתָּא לְבֵי רַב – נִיחָא לְהוּ טְפֵי.

The Gemara answers: **In that** case **we are witnesses, and in this** case **we are witnesses,** i.e., in both cases the person's intentions regarding his place of residence are clearly evident. **In that** case, where the person deposits his *eiruv*, **we are witnesses that if he** could **reside there,** at the site of his *eiruv*, **it would be better for him,** i.e., if he could spend the night there he would do so, since he wishes to continue from that place onward on the following day. **And in this** case of the students in their master's house, **we are witnesses that if** people **would bring them bread in their master's house,** enabling them to eat there, **it would be better for them.** Consequently, it is considered their place of residence.

בָּעֵי רָמִי בַּר חָמָא מֵרַב חִסְדָּא: אָב וּבְנוֹ, הָרַב וְתַלְמִידוֹ, כְּרַבִּים דָּמוּ, אוֹ כִּיחִידִים דָּמוּ? צְרִיכִין עֵירוּב, אוֹ אֵין צְרִיכִין עֵירוּב? מָבוֹי שֶׁלָּהֶן נִיתָּר בְּלֶחִי וְקוֹרָה, אוֹ אֵין נִיתָּר בְּלֶחִי וְקוֹרָה?

Rami bar Ḥama raised a dilemma before Rav Ḥisda: With regard to **a father and his son, or a master and his student, are they considered as many** people **or as individuals?** The practical import of the question is as follows: If they lived together in a courtyard that was within another courtyard, are they considered as many people, who **require an** *eiruv* in order to render it permitted to carry in the outer courtyard, **or do they not require an** *eiruv*, as they are treated as an individual, who does not render carrying in the outer courtyard prohibited? Is **their alleyway** rendered **permitted** for carrying **through a side post and** a cross **beam,** like one that has multiple residents, **or is it not** rendered **permitted** for carrying **through a side post and** a cross **beam?**

אֲמַר לֵיהּ, תְּנִיתוּהָ: אָב וּבְנוֹ, הָרַב וְתַלְמִידוֹ, בִּזְמַן שֶׁאֵין עִמָּהֶן דִּיּוּרִין – הֲרֵי הֵן כִּיחִידִים, וְאֵין צְרִיכִין לְעָרֵב. וּמָבוֹי שֶׁלָּהֶן נִיתָּר בְּלֶחִי וְקוֹרָה.

Rav Ḥisda **said to him: You have** already **learned this** in the following *baraita*: With regard to **a father and his son**[H] or **a master and his student, when there are no** other **residents with them, they are** considered **like individuals, and they do not need to establish an** *eiruv*, **and their alleyway** becomes **permitted** for carrying **through a side post and** a cross **beam** without a merging of alleyways.

מתני׳ חָמֵשׁ חֲצֵירוֹת פְּתוּחוֹת זוֹ לָזוֹ וּפְתוּחוֹת לַמָּבוֹי, עֵירְבוּ בַּחֲצֵירוֹת וְלֹא נִשְׁתַּתְּפוּ בַּמָּבוֹי – מוּתָּרִין בַּחֲצֵירוֹת וַאֲסוּרִין בַּמָּבוֹי.

MISHNA If **five courtyards**[B] **open into one another and** also **open into an alleyway,** the following distinctions apply: If the residents of the courtyard **established an** *eiruv* **in the courtyards**[N] **and did not merge the** courtyards that open into the **alleyway, they are permitted** to carry **in the courtyards and they are prohibited** to carry **in the alleyway.** The *eiruv* they established cannot also serve as a merging of the courtyards that open into the alleyway.

HALAKHA

A father and his son – אָב וּבְנוֹ: A father and son are considered separate individuals, even if the son eats at his father's table. Therefore, they are required to establish an *eiruv*, and their alleyway may be rendered permitted for carrying by means of a side post and a cross beam (*Shulḥan Arukh, Oraḥ Ḥayyim* 363:26).

BACKGROUND

Five courtyards – חָמֵשׁ חֲצֵרוֹת:

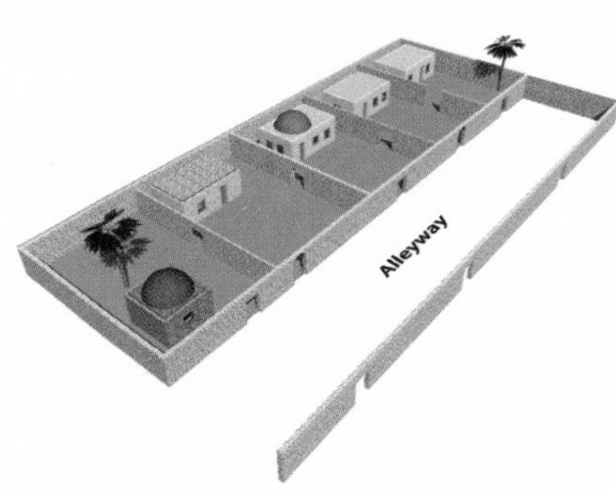

Five courtyards along one side of an alleyway, with openings both to each other and to the alleyway

NOTES

Established an *eiruv* in the courtyards – עֵירְבוּ בַּחֲצֵירוֹת: Some commentaries explain that this does not mean that the residents of the courtyards established a joint *eiruv* for all the courtyards, but that each courtyard established an *eiruv* for itself (Rabbi Ovadya Bartenura; *Penei Moshe*; *Korban HaEida*). This explanation is supported somewhat by the Jerusalem Talmud (*Yefeh Einayim*).

Perek **VI**
Daf **73** Amud **b**

וְאִם נִשְׁתַּתְּפוּ בַּמָּבוֹי – מוּתָּרִין כָּאן וְכָאן.

And if they merged the courtyards of **the alleyway, they are permitted** to carry both **here,** in the alleyway, and **there,** in the courtyards.

עֵירְבוּ בַּחֲצֵירוֹת וְנִשְׁתַּתְּפוּ בַּמָּבוֹי, וְשָׁכַח אֶחָד מִבְּנֵי חָצֵר וְלֹא עֵירֵב – מוּתָּרִין כָּאן וְכָאן.

If **they established an** *eiruv* **in the courtyards** and also **merged** the courtyards of **the alleyway, and one of the residents of the courtyard forgot and did not** contribute to the ***eiruv***[N] in his courtyard, but did participate in the merging of the courtyards in the alleyway, **they are permitted** both **here and there,** as the merging of courtyards in the alleyway serves as an effective *eiruv* for the courtyards as well.[H]

NOTES

Forgot and did not contribute to the *eiruv* – שָׁכַח...וְלֹא עֵירֵב: Most agree that this principle applies only if an individual forgot to participate in establishing an *eiruv* for his courtyard, but not if the residents of an entire courtyard forgot to establish an *eiruv* (Ritva).

HALAKHA

Forgot and did not contribute to the *eiruv* – שָׁכַח וְלֹא עֵירֵב: If each of the courtyards opening into an alleyway established its own *eiruv*, and subsequently, the residents of all of the courtyards joined in a merging of the alleyway, and a resident of one of the courtyards forgot to join in the *eiruv* for his courtyard, he has not lost out, as the merging of the alleyway serves as an *eiruv* as well. However, if one of the residents of the alleyway forgot to join in the merging of the alleyway, all the residents may carry in their own courtyards but are prohibited from carrying in the alleyway (Rambam *Sefer Zemanim*, *Hilkhot Eiruvin* 5:13).

מִבְּנֵי מָבוֹי וְלֹא נִשְׁתַּתֵּף – מוּתָּרִין בַּחֲצֵירוֹת וַאֲסוּרִין בַּמָּבוֹי, שֶׁהַמָּבוֹי לַחֲצֵירוֹת כְּחָצֵר לַבָּתִּים.

However, if one **of the residents of the alleyway** forgot **and did not** participate in the **merging** of courtyards that open into the alleyway, **they are permitted** to carry **in the courtyards and prohibited** from carrying **in the alleyway,** as the principle is: **An alleyway is to its courtyards**[N] **as a courtyard is to** its **houses.**[H]

גמ׳ מַנִּי? רַבִּי מֵאִיר הִיא, דְּאָמַר: בָּעֵינַן עֵירוּב וּבָעֵינַן שִׁיתּוּף.

GEMARA The Gemara asks: In accordance with **whose** opinion is this mishna? The Gemara answers: **It** is in accordance with the opinion of **Rabbi Meir, who said: We require an *eiruv* and we** also **require a merging** of the courtyards in an alleyway, and one is not sufficient without the other.

אֵימָא מְצִיעֲתָא: ״וְאִם נִשְׁתַּתְּפוּ בַּמָּבוֹי – מוּתָּרִין כָּאן וְכָאן״, אֲתָאן לְרַבָּנַן, דְּאָמְרִי: בַּחֲדָא סַגְיָא!

The Gemara asks: If so, say the **middle clause** of the mishna: **And if they merged** the courtyards **in the alleyway, they are permitted** to carry both **here and there. We have arrived at** the opinion of **the Rabbis, who say** that **one is enough,** and one does not need both an *eiruv* and a merging of alleyways.

הָא לָא קַשְׁיָא; וְאִם נִשְׁתַּתְּפוּ נַמִּי קָאָמַר.

The Gemara responds: **That is not difficult,** as the mishna **stated** as follows: **And if they also merged** the courtyards in the alleyway, they are permitted to carry in the courtyards and in the alleyway.

אֵימָא סֵיפָא: עֵירְבוּ בַּחֲצֵירוֹת וְנִשְׁתַּתְּפוּ בַּמָּבוֹי, וְשָׁכַח אֶחָד מִבְּנֵי חָצֵר וְלֹא עֵירֵב – מוּתָּרִים כָּאן וְכָאן. הֵיכִי דָּמֵי? אִי דְּלָא בַּטֵּיל – אַמַּאי מוּתָּרִים? אֶלָּא פְּשִׁיטָא – דְּבַטֵּיל, אֵימָא סֵיפָא: שָׁכַח אֶחָד מִבְּנֵי מָבוֹי וְלֹא נִשְׁתַּתְּפוּ – מוּתָּרִין בַּחֲצֵירוֹת, וַאֲסוּרִין בַּמָּבוֹי. וְאִי דְּבַטֵּיל – אַמַּאי אֲסוּרִין בַּמָּבוֹי?

The Gemara asks: **Say the latter clause** of the mishna: If **they established an *eiruv* in the courtyards** and also **merged** the courtyards **in the alleyway, and one of the residents of the courtyard forgot and did not** contribute to the ***eiruv*** in his courtyard but did participate in the merging of the alleyway, **they are permitted** to carry both **here and there. What are the circumstances? If** the person who forgot **did not renounce** his rights to the courtyard in favor of the others, **why are they permitted** to carry? **Rather,** it is **obvious that he did renounce** those rights. But if so, **say the last clause** of the mishna: If **one of the members of the alleyway forgot and did not** participate in the **merging** of the alleyway, **they are permitted** to carry **in the courtyards and prohibited** from carrying **in the alleyway. But if he renounced** his rights, **why are they prohibited** from carrying **in the alleyway?**

וְכִי תֵּימָא: קָסָבַר רַבִּי מֵאִיר אֵין בִּיטּוּל רְשׁוּת בַּמָּבוֹי – וְהָא תַּנְיָא: שֶׁהֲרֵי בִּיטֵּל לָכֶם רְשׁוּתוֹ, דִּבְרֵי רַבִּי מֵאִיר!

And if you say that **Rabbi Meir holds** that **renunciation of rights is not** effective **in an alleyway,** that answer is insufficient. **Wasn't it taught** in a *baraita* with regard to an alleyway: **As he renounced his rights in your favor;** this is **the statement of Rabbi Meir?** This indicates that Rabbi Meir accepts the principle of renunciation of rights in an alleyway.

אֶלָּא פְּשִׁיטָא – דְּלָא בַּטֵּיל. וּמִדְּסֵיפָא דְּלָא בַּטֵּיל – רֵישָׁא נַמִּי דְּלָא בַּטֵּיל. רֵישָׁא וְסֵיפָא רַבִּי מֵאִיר, מְצִיעֲתָא רַבָּנַן!

Rather, it is **obvious** that the person who forgot to participate in the merging of alleyways **did not renounce** his rights. **And from the** fact that **the last clause** of the mishna is referring to a case **where he did not renounce** his rights, it can be inferred that **the first clause** is **also** referring to a case **where he did not renounce** his rights. This would indicate that if they carried out a merging of alleyways, it also serves as an *eiruv*, even when one of them forgot to contribute to the *eiruv* and also failed to renounce his rights in the courtyard. This is in accordance with the opinion of the Rabbis, which leads to the puzzling conclusion that the **first and last clauses** of the mishna are in accordance with the opinion of **Rabbi Meir,** while the **middle clause** is in accordance with the opinion of **the Rabbis.**

כּוּלָּהּ רַבִּי מֵאִיר הִיא, וְטַעְמָא מַאי אָמַר רַבִּי מֵאִיר בָּעֵינַן עֵירוּב וּבָעֵינַן שִׁיתּוּף – שֶׁלֹּא לְשַׁכֵּחַ תּוֹרַת עֵירוּב מִן הַתִּינוֹקוֹת. וְהָכָא, כֵּיוָן דְּרוּבָּהּ עֵירְבוּ – לָא מִשְׁתַּכְחָא.

The Gemara answers: In fact, **it is all** in accordance with the opinion of **Rabbi Meir. And what is the reason** that **Rabbi Meir said we require an *eiruv* and we** also **require a merging** of alleyways? It was only so **as not to cause the** halakhic **category of *eiruv* to be forgotten by the children.** If people would only merge courtyards, the *halakha* of establishing an *eiruv* for a courtyard would gradually be forgotten. **And here,** where only one person forgot to contribute to the *eiruv*, **since most of** them **established an *eiruv*** for the courtyards, the *halakha* of an *eiruv* **will not be forgotten.** Therefore, there is room to be lenient after the fact and to permit carrying in both places.

אָמַר רַב יְהוּדָה: רַב לָא תָּנֵי ״פְּתוּחוֹת זוֹ לָזוֹ״. וְכֵן אָמַר רַב כָּהֲנָא: רַב לָא תָּנֵי ״פְּתוּחוֹת זוֹ לָזוֹ״. אִיכָּא דְּאָמְרִי: רַב כָּהֲנָא גּוּפֵיהּ לָא תָּנֵי ״פְּתוּחוֹת זוֹ לָזוֹ״.

Rav Yehuda said: Rav did not teach the mishna as stating that the five courtyards **open into one another,** but rather that each courtyard opens into the alleyway, and each established its own *eiruv*. **And so too, Rav Kahana said: Rav did not teach** the mishna as stating that the courtyards **open into one another. Some say** that **Rav Kahana himself did not teach** the mishna as stating that the courtyards **open into one another.**

NOTES

An alleyway is to its courtyards – הַמָּבוֹי לַחֲצֵירוֹת: In many respects, the *halakhot* of courtyards and those applicable to alleyways are the same. In addition, according to Rabbi Shimon, whose opinion is accepted as *halakha*, one is permitted to carry objects that were in a courtyard when Shabbat began into an alleyway, even without an *eiruv*. Nevertheless, it is important to emphasize that just as one may not carry from one's house into a courtyard without an *eiruv*, one may not carry these items from the courtyard to an alleyway without a merging of alleyways. The mishna introduces this *halakha* here because this is the first time that it explicitly addresses the *halakhot* of an alleyway (*Tosafot Yom Tov*).

HALAKHA

An alleyway is to its courtyards as a courtyard is to its houses – הַמָּבוֹי לַחֲצֵירוֹת כְּחָצֵר לַבָּתִּים: If the residents of one courtyard forgot to join in the merging of the alleyway with the rest of the courtyards, they may renounce their rights in the alleyway in favor of the residents of the other courtyards or vice versa, as an alleyway in relation to its courtyards is like a courtyard in relation to its houses (*Shulḥan Arukh*, *Oraḥ Ḥayyim* 391:1).

אֲמַר לֵיהּ אַבַּיֵי לְרַב יוֹסֵף: מַאי טַעְמָא דְּלָא תָּנֵי ״פְּתוּחוֹת זוֹ לָזוֹ״? קָסָבַר: כֹּל שִׁיתּוּף שֶׁאֵין מַכְנִיסוֹ וּמוֹצִיאוֹ דֶּרֶךְ פְּתָחִים בַּמָּבוֹי – לָאו שְׁמֵיהּ שִׁיתּוּף.

Abaye said to Rav Yosef: What is the reason he did not teach the mishna as stating that the five courtyards **open into one another?** Rav Yosef replied: Because **he holds** that **any merging** of alleyways **that is not brought in and taken out by way of the entrances** that open **into the alleyway,** i.e., which is not brought from each courtyard into the alleyway and then taken from the alleyway into the courtyard where it will be deposited, **is not considered** a valid **merging** of the alleyway. If the food used for the merging of alleyways is transferred directly from one courtyard to another, it seems as though it is being used to establish an *eiruv*. It is therefore ineffective as a merging of alleyways. Here too, if the courtyards open into one another, the merging of alleyways is invalid, due to a concern that the residents of the courtyard will transfer the food directly from one courtyard to another.

אֵיתִיבֵיהּ: בַּעַל הַבַּיִת שֶׁהָיָה שׁוּתָּף לִשְׁכֵנָיו, לָזֶה בְּיַיִן וְלָזֶה בְּיַיִן – אֵין צְרִיכִין לְעָרֵב! הָתָם דְּאַפְקֵיהּ וְעַיְילֵיהּ.

He raised an objection to him based upon the following mishna: **A homeowner who was a partner of his neighbors, with this one in wine and with that one in wine, they do not need to establish an** ***eiruv***. This indicates that it is not actually necessary to transfer the food used for the merging of alleyways from one place to another. For example, it is sufficient to have a jointly owned barrel of wine in one courtyard even if it did not pass through the alleyway. The Gemara rejects this proof and explains the mishna as follows: **There,** it is referring to a case **where they took** the wine **out** into the alleyway and subsequently **brought it in** to the courtyard where it was to be kept.

(אֵיתִיבֵיהּ:) כֵּיצַד מִשְׁתַּתְּפִין בַּמָּבוֹי וכו׳! הָתָם נַמִי, דְּאַפְקֵיהּ וְעַיְילֵיהּ.

He raised another **objection to him** from a different mishna: **How does one merge** courtyards that open **into alleyways?** The mishna continues and says that it is sufficient for one person to acquire the food used for the merging on behalf of all the other residents of the alleyway. This indicates that the food does not need to pass through all the courtyards in the alleyway. The Gemara rejects this proof as well: **There too,** it is referring to a case **where they** first **took** the food **out** from each of the courtyards into the alleyway **and** from there **brought it into** the courtyard where it was to be deposited.

מַתְקִיף לַהּ רַבָּה בַּר חָנָן: אֶלָּא מֵעַתָּה הִקְנָה לוֹ פַּת בְּסַלּוֹ, הָכִי נַמִי דְּלָא הָוֵי שִׁיתּוּף? וְכִי תֵּימָא הָכִי נַמִי – וְהָא אָמַר רַב יְהוּדָה, אָמַר רַב: בְּנֵי חֲבוּרָה שֶׁהָיוּ מְסוּבִּין וְקָדַשׁ עֲלֵיהֶן הַיּוֹם, הַפַּת שֶׁעַל שֻׁלְחָן סוֹמְכִים עָלֶיהָ מִשּׁוּם עֵירוּב, וְאָמְרִי לַהּ: מִשּׁוּם שִׁיתּוּף.

Rabba bar Ḥanan strongly objects to this: However, if that **is so,** if **he transferred ownership of bread in his basket to** another person, **so too, it would not be** considered a valid **merging. And if you say** that **this is** indeed **so, didn't Rav Yehuda say that Rav said:** With regard to **members of a group who were dining** together on Shabbat eve, **and the day became sanctified for them,** i.e., Shabbat began while they were eating, **they may rely upon the bread on the table as an** ***eiruv*** for the courtyard, **and some say, as a merging** of the alleyway.[N]

וְאָמַר רַבָּה: לָא פְּלִיגִי, כָּאן – בִּמְסוּבִּין בַּבַּיִת, כָּאן – בִּמְסוּבִּין בֶּחָצֵר.

And Rabba said: The two versions **do not disagree** with each other regarding whether the bread counts as an *eiruv* or as a merging of the alleyway. **Here,** where they can use it as an *eiruv*, it is referring to a case **where they were dining in a house,** since food deposited inside a house can serve as an *eiruv* for the courtyard. **There,** it is referring to a case **where they were dining in a courtyard,** and therefore they may rely on the bread as a merging of the alleyway. This proves that even Rav agrees that it is not necessary to take the food used to merge an alleyway into the alleyway itself and then bring it back to the courtyard.

אֶלָּא, טַעְמָא דְּרַב, דְּקָא סָבַר: אֵין מָבוֹי נִיתָּר בְּלֶחִי וְקוֹרָה עַד שֶׁיְּהוּ בָּתִּים וַחֲצֵירוֹת פְּתוּחִים לְתוֹכוֹ.

Rather, we must retract the previous explanation and say that **the reason Rav** did not teach the mishna as stating that the courtyards opened into one another is **that he holds** that **an alleyway cannot** be **rendered permitted** for carrying **through a side post and** a cross **beam unless there are houses and courtyards opening into it.**[N] If, however, the courtyards open into one another, they are considered like a single courtyard, in which case they cannot be rendered permitted for carrying through a side post or a cross beam, and the merging of the alleyway is ineffective.

גּוּפָא, אָמַר רַב: אֵין מָבוֹי נִיתָּר בְּלֶחִי וְקוֹרָה

The Gemara now examines **the matter itself** cited in the previous discussion. **Rav said: An alleyway cannot** become **permitted** for carrying **through a side post and** a cross **beam,**

NOTES

They may rely upon the bread on the table as an *eiruv*, and some say, as a merging of the alleyway – סוֹמְכִין עָלֶיהָ מִשּׁוּם עֵירוּב וְאָמְרִי לַהּ מִשּׁוּם שִׁיתּוּף: Some authorities understand from this that if the meal was conducted in a house, the bread can be utilized only for the *eiruv*, and if the meal was conducted in a courtyard, the bread can serve only as a merging of alleyways. However, as indicated by the Jerusalem Talmud, most commentaries hold that the statement that they can rely on the bread as an *eiruv* if they were in a house merely emphasizes that they can use the bread even for this purpose, but it is effective as a merging of alleyways as well (see Ritva).

Houses and courtyards opening into it – בָּתִּים וַחֲצֵירוֹת פְּתוּחִים לְתוֹכוֹ: The Ra'avad explains that these two criteria, houses and courtyards, are unrelated. In other words, Rav rules that it is only necessary for the alleyway to have two courtyards and two houses connected to it, even if each courtyard contains only one house.

BACKGROUND

A vineyard path – שְׁבִיל שֶׁל כְּרָמִים:

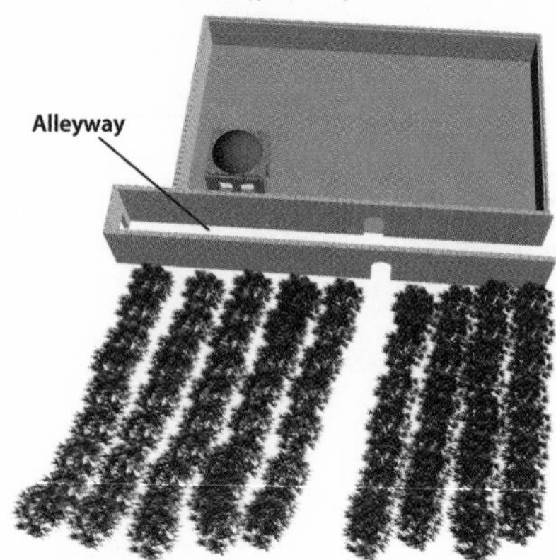

Illustration of an alleyway opening to a courtyard that includes one house, as well as a vineyard path opening into the alleyway

NOTES

Rabbi Yoḥanan followed his regular line of reasoning – וְאָזְדָא רַבִּי יוֹחָנָן לְטַעְמֵיהּ: *Tosafot* discuss the relationship between Rabbi Yoḥanan's ruling that the *halakha* is in accordance with the opinion of Rabbi Shimon, and his ruling that an alleyway connected to a ruin can be rendered permitted for carrying through a side post or a cross beam. Apparently, there is no direct link between these two rulings, as Shmuel also rules in accordance with the opinion of Rabbi Shimon, but he does not accept Rabbi Yoḥanan's opinion in the case of a ruin. Rav holds that the Sages issued a decree to prevent one from carrying from one courtyard to another. Therefore, since it is prohibited to carry in a ruin, one may not carry within an alleyway that is attached to a ruin. Although Shmuel does not agree that the Sages issued such a decree, he nevertheless maintains that a ruin is not of sufficient importance to grant an area the status of an alleyway that can be rendered permitted for carrying through a side post or cross beam.

עַד שֶׁיְּהוּ בָּתִּים וַחֲצֵירוֹת פְּתוּחִין לְתוֹכוֹ. וּשְׁמוּאֵל אָמַר: אֲפִילּוּ בַּיִת אֶחָד וְחָצֵר אַחַת. וְרַבִּי יוֹחָנָן אָמַר: אֲפִילּוּ חוּרְבָּה.

unless there are houses and courtyards opening into it. This formulation implies that there must be at least two courtyards, each of which contains at least two houses. In the absence of these conditions, however, it is not considered an alleyway that can be permitted by means of a side post or a cross beam. **And Shmuel said: Even one house** without a courtyard **and one courtyard** with just one house is enough. **And Rabbi Yoḥanan said: Even a ruin** and a courtyard with a house suffice for a side post or a cross beam to render carrying in an alleyway permitted.

אֲמַר לֵיהּ אַבַּיֵי לְרַב יוֹסֵף: אָמַר רַבִּי יוֹחָנָן אֲפִילּוּ בִּשְׁבִיל שֶׁל כְּרָמִים? אֲמַר לֵיהּ: לֹא אָמַר רַבִּי יוֹחָנָן אֶלָּא בְּחוּרְבָּה, דַּחֲזִי לְדִירָה. אֲבָל שְׁבִיל שֶׁל כְּרָמִים דְּלָא חֲזִי לְדִירָה – לָא.

Abaye said to Rav Yosef: Did **Rabbi Yoḥanan say** that **even a vineyard path**[B] and a courtyard with a house suffice to allow a side post or a cross beam to render carrying in the alleyway permitted? **He said to him: Rabbi Yoḥanan said** his ruling **only** in the case of **a ruin, which is fit** to serve **as a residence. However, a vineyard path, which is not fit** to serve **as a residence,** is **not** sufficient.

אָמַר רַב הוּנָא בַּר חִינָּנָא: וְאָזְדָא רַבִּי יוֹחָנָן לְטַעְמֵיהּ, דִּתְנַן, (אָמַר רַבִּי שִׁמְעוֹן:) אֶחָד גַּגּוֹת, וְאֶחָד קַרְפֵּיפוֹת, וְאֶחָד חֲצֵרוֹת – רְשׁוּת אַחַת הֵן לְכֵלִים שֶׁשָּׁבְתוּ לְתוֹכָן, וְלֹא לְכֵלִים שֶׁשָּׁבְתוּ בְּתוֹךְ הַבַּיִת.

Rav Huna bar Ḥinnana said: And Rabbi Yoḥanan followed his regular line of **reasoning**[N] in this regard, **as we learned** in a mishna that **Rabbi Shimon said: Roofs, enclosures, and courtyards are all** considered **one domain with regard to vessels that rested inside them** at the beginning of Shabbat. Therefore, it is permitted to carry vessels that were in one of these areas at the beginning of Shabbat to any of the other areas. However, they are **not** considered the same domain **with regard to vessels that rested inside the house** at the beginning of Shabbat. If the homeowners did not join the courtyard by means of an *eiruv*, it is prohibited to carry vessels from their houses to the roof, enclosure, or courtyard.

וְאָמַר רַב: הֲלָכָה כְּרַבִּי שִׁמְעוֹן, וְהוּא שֶׁלֹּא עֵירְבוּ, אֲבָל עֵירְבוּ – גָּזְרִינַן דִּילְמָא אָתֵי לְאַפּוֹקֵי מָאנֵי דְּבָתִּים לְחָצֵר.

And Rav said: The halakha is in accordance with the opinion of **Rabbi Shimon. And this is** only in a case **where** the residents of the courtyards **did not establish an** ***eiruv*** for each courtyard, so that they may only carry the vessels left in the courtyards, but they may not take out vessels from their houses into their courtyards. **However, if they established an** ***eiruv*** for each courtyard, **we decree** against carrying even vessels that were in the courtyard when Shabbat began, **lest they come to take out objects** from their **houses to the courtyard.** This would lead to the mistake of carrying those objects from one courtyard to another, which is prohibited.

וּשְׁמוּאֵל אָמַר: בֵּין עֵירְבוּ וּבֵין לֹא עֵירְבוּ. וְכֵן אֲמַר רַבִּי יוֹחָנָן: הֲלָכָה כְּרַבִּי שִׁמְעוֹן, בֵּין עֵירְבוּ וּבֵין לֹא עֵירְבוּ. אַלְמָא: לָא גָּזְרִינַן דִּילְמָא אָתֵי לְאַפּוֹקֵי מָאנֵי דְּבָתִּים לְחָצֵר. הָכָא נַמִי: לָא גָּזְרִינַן דִּילְמָא אָתֵי לְאַפּוֹקֵי מָאנֵי דְּחָצֵר לְחוּרְבָּה.

And Shmuel said: The *halakha* is in accordance with the opinion of Rabbi Shimon, **whether** the residents of the courtyards **established an** ***eiruv*** for each courtyard **or whether they did not establish an** ***eiruv*** for each courtyard. **And so too, Rabbi Yoḥanan said: The** ***halakha*** **is in accordance with** the opinion of **Rabbi Shimon, whether they established an** ***eiruv*** for each courtyard **or whether they did not establish an** ***eiruv*** for each courtyard. **Apparently,** Rabbi Yoḥanan maintains that **we do not decree** against carrying vessels that began Shabbat in the courtyard **lest they come to take out objects from** their **houses to the courtyard. Here too,** with regard to an alleyway that contains a ruin, **we do not decree** against carrying in the alleyway **lest they come to take out objects from the courtyard to the ruin** by carrying it through the alleyway. Although the ruin is not included in the *eiruv*, as it has no residents, and one may not carry objects into it, Rabbi Yoḥanan is not concerned that one might come to carry in this prohibited manner.

יְתֵיב רַב בְּרוּנָא, וְקָאָמַר לְהָא שְׁמַעְתָּא, אֲמַר לֵיהּ רַבִּי אֶלְעָזָר בַּר בֵּי רַב: אֲמַר שְׁמוּאֵל הָכִי?! אֲמַר לֵיהּ: אִין. אֲמַר לֵיהּ: אַחְוֵי לִי אוּשְׁפִּיזֵיהּ, אַחְוְיֵהּ לֵיהּ. אֲתָא לְקַמֵּיהּ דִּשְׁמוּאֵל, אֲמַר לֵיהּ: אֲמַר מָר הָכִי? אֲמַר לֵיהּ: אִין.

Rav Beruna sat and recited this ***halakha*** stated by Shmuel, that an alleyway containing one house and one courtyard can be rendered permitted for carrying by means of a side post or a cross beam. **Rabbi Elazar, a student of a Torah academy, said to him: Did Shmuel** really **say this?** Rav Beruna **said to him: Yes,** he did. **He said to him: Show me his lodging** and I will go and ask him myself, and **he showed him.** Rabbi Elazar **came before Shmuel** and **said to him:** Did **the Master** actually **say this?** Shmuel **said to him: Yes,** I did.

וְהָא מָר הוּא דְּאָמַר: אֵין לָנוּ בְּעֵירוּבִין אֶלָּא כִּלְשׁוֹן מִשְׁנָתֵינוּ, שֶׁהַמָּבוֹי לַחֲצֵירוֹת כֶּחָצֵר לַבָּתִּים! אִישְׁתִּיק.

Rabbi Elazar raised the following objection: **Wasn't it the Master** himself who **said** concerning a different issue: **With regard to** the *halakhot* of ***eiruv*****, we have only the wording of our mishna.** The mishna states **that an alleyway is to** its **courtyards like a courtyard is to** its **houses,** which indicates that an alleyway must have at least two courtyards in order to be considered an alleyway and be rendered permitted for carrying through a side post or cross beam. Shmuel **was silent**[N] and did not answer him.

קִבְּלָהּ מִינֵּיהּ, אוֹ לֹא קִבְּלָהּ מִינֵּיהּ? תָּא שְׁמַע: דְּהַהוּא מְבוֹאָה דַּהֲוָה דָּיֵיר בֵּיהּ אִיבוּת בַּר אִיהִי, עֲבַד לֵיהּ לֶחְיָיא וּשְׁרָא לֵיהּ שְׁמוּאֵל.

The Gemara asks: Did Shmuel's silence indicate that he **accepted** Rabbi Elazar's objection and retracted his statement, **or did he not accept it from him?** The Gemara attempts to bring a proof from the following incident. **Come and hear:** There was **a certain alleyway that Ivut bar Ihi lived in,** which contained only one house and one courtyard. **He erected a side post for it, and Shmuel permitted him** to carry in it.

NOTES

Shmuel was silent – אִישְׁתִּיק: This is not the only instance when a Sage failed to respond to an objection raised against his opinion. However, the meaning of such silence is not always evident. It might be a result of the Sage's inability to answer, or he may have thought that the question lacked substance and was unworthy of a response. *Tosafot* gauge the reply according to the relationship between the two parties. If the questioner is merely a student, the silence should be taken as a dismissal, but if he is a colleague or a peer, it as a sign that the Sage could not find an answer. Nevertheless, even if the Sage was unable to think of a reply, this does not necessarily imply a retraction on his part. The difficulty is sometimes not that severe, and despite the objection, the ruling stands. In our case, it is also possible that Shmuel retracted his other ruling rather than this one.

Perek **VI**
Daf **74** Amud **b**

אֲתָא רַב עָנָן שַׁדְיֵיהּ. אֲמַר: מְבוֹאָה דְּדָיֵירְנָא בֵּיהּ וְאָתֵינָא מִשְּׁמֵיהּ דְּמָר שְׁמוּאֵל, נֵיתֵי רַב עָנָן בַּר רַב נִישַׁדְיֵיהּ מִן?! שְׁמַע מִינָּהּ: לֹא קִיבְּלָהּ מִינֵּיהּ.

Following Shmuel's death, **Rav Anan came and threw** the side post down, thus indicating to Ivut bar Ihi that it is prohibited to carry in the alleyway, as a side post is effective only for an alleyway that has at least two courtyards containing at least two houses each. Ivut bar Ihi **said** with resentment: **The alleyway in which I have been living and walking** based on a ruling **in the name of Master Shmuel, shall Rav Anan bar Rav come** now and **throw** its side post away **from** me? The Gemara comments: **Learn from** the fact that this side post remained intact throughout Shmuel's lifetime that he **did not accept** Rabbi Elazar's objection.

לְעוֹלָם אֵימָא לָךְ: קִיבְּלָהּ מִינָּהּ, וְהָכָא – חַזָּנָא הוּא דַּהֲוָה אָכֵיל נַהֲמָא בְּבֵיתֵיהּ, וְאָתֵי בָּיֵית בְּבֵי כְּנִישְׁתָּא.

The Gemara rejects this proof. **Actually, you can say** that Shmuel **accepted** Rabbi Elazar's objection and retracted his opinion,[N] **and here there was** a synagogue **attendant** [*ḥazzana*][NB] **who would eat bread in his** own **house** that was located elsewhere, **but** would **come and sleep in the synagogue,** which was open to the alleyway.

וְאִיבוּת בַּר אִיהִי סָבַר: מְקוֹם פִּיתָּא גָּרֵים, וּשְׁמוּאֵל לְטַעְמֵיהּ, דְּאָמַר: מְקוֹם לִינָה גָּרֵים.

And Ivut bar Ihi holds that **the place** where a person eats his **bread determines** his place of residence. Therefore, he did not consider the synagogue a residence, as the attendant would eat elsewhere, and Ivut bar Ihi thought that Shmuel had permitted him to set up a side post for his alleyway even though he lived there by himself. In fact, however, this was not the case, as **Shmuel followed his** regular line of **reasoning, as he said: The place** where a person **sleeps determines** his place of residence. Since the attendant would sleep in the synagogue, it was considered a residence. Consequently, the alleyway contained two houses and courtyards, and could be made permitted for carrying by means of a side post or a cross beam.

BACKGROUND

A synagogue attendant [*ḥazzana*] – חַזָּנָא: In the talmudic period, the word *ḥazzan* referred to an attendant, especially a synagogue attendant. The attendant was charged with various synagogue-related duties, including the care of the children who came to study there, and occasionally with protecting the synagogue from thieves.

NOTES

Did Shmuel retract – הַאִם חָזַר בּוֹ שְׁמוּאֵל: In the Babylonian Talmud, the proof that Shmuel did not retract his statement is successfully rejected without it being proven that he accepted Rabbi Elazar's objection. In the Jerusalem Talmud, however, it is simply stated that Rav and Shmuel both agree that it is permitted to carry in an alleyway only if the alleyway is connected to houses and courtyards.

A synagogue attendant – חַזָּנָא בֵּית הַכְּנֶסֶת: Rashi implies that this attendant lived in the synagogue during Shmuel's lifetime, before moving away when Shmuel died. Ivut bar Avin thought that this was of no consequence, because in his opinion the factor that determines a person's place of residence is the location where he eats, while Shmuel maintained that one's place of residence is determined by where one sleeps. Nevertheless, since the *halakha* is in accordance with the opinion of Rav, even if the attendant continued living there, this would not have affected the status of the alleyway, as Rav rules that one's place of residence is where one eats. Therefore, Ivut bar Avin was the only resident of the alleyway. Consequently, carrying could not be permitted through the construction of a side post or cross beam (Rashba).

BACKGROUND

An alleyway, one side of which was occupied by a gentile and one side of which was occupied by a Jew – **מָבוֹי שֶׁצִּידּוֹ אֶחָד גּוֹי וְצִידּוֹ אֶחָד יִשְׂרָאֵל**: According to Rashi's explanation, the two adjacent Jewish courtyards are linked by means of a window.

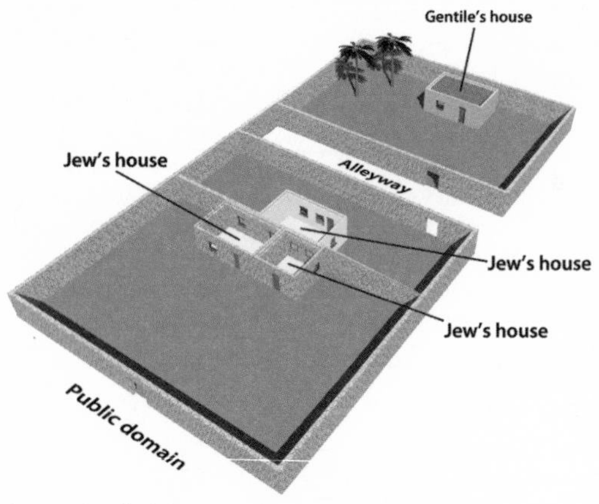

Case as explained by Rashi

According to *Tosafot*'s explanation, the alleyway is connected to several courtyards of Jews as well as one belonging to a gentile.

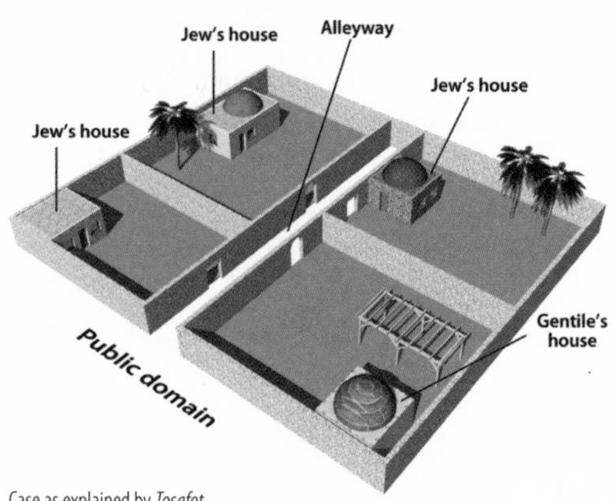

Case as explained by *Tosafot*.

אָמַר רַב יְהוּדָה, אָמַר רַב: מָבוֹי שֶׁצִּידּוֹ אֶחָד גּוֹי וְצִידּוֹ אֶחָד יִשְׂרָאֵל – אֵין מְעָרְבִין אוֹתוֹ דֶּרֶךְ חַלּוֹנוֹת, לְהַתִּירוֹ דֶּרֶךְ פְּתָחִים לַמָּבוֹי.

Rav Yehuda said that Rav said: With regard to **an alleyway, one side of which** was occupied by **a gentile**[NH] **and one side of which** was occupied by **a Jew,**[B] and the house of the Jew was connected to the houses of other Jews via windows but not via doors, and those other houses open directly into the public domain, the residents of the houses on the side of the alleyway where the Jews live **may not establish an *eiruv* through the windows**[N] in order **to render** it **permitted** for the residents of the other houses to carry **through the doors** of the house leading **to the alleyway.**

אֲמַר לֵיהּ אַבָּיֵי לְרַב יוֹסֵף: אָמַר רַב אֲפִילּוּ בְּחָצֵר? אֲמַר לֵיהּ: אִין. דְּאִי לָא אָמַר מַאי?

Abaye said to Rav Yosef: Did **Rav say** this **even with regard to a courtyard,** one side of which was occupied by a gentile and the other side of which was occupied by a Jew whose house was connected through windows to the houses of other Jews? **He said to him: Yes,** as even **if he did not say** so, **what** would be the difference? It is the exact same principle.[H]

הֲוָה אָמֵינָא: טַעְמָא דְּרַב מִשּׁוּם דְּקָסָבַר אֵין מָבוֹי נִיתָּר בְּלֶחִי וְקוֹרָה, עַד שֶׁיְּהוּ בָּתִּים וַחֲצֵירוֹת פְּתוּחִין לְתוֹכוֹ.

Abaye responded: **I would have said** that **the rationale for** the opinion of **Rav is because he holds** that **an alleyway cannot be rendered permitted** for carrying within it **with a side post** and a cross **beam unless there are houses and courtyards opening into it.**

וְתַרְתֵּי לָמָּה לִי? צְרִיכָא, דְּאִי מֵהַהִיא

Rav Yosef said: If that were the reason, **why would I need two** rulings regarding the same issue? Rav already stated that an alleyway can be rendered permitted for carrying within it only if it has houses and courtyards opening into it. Abaye explained that both rulings are **necessary. As, if** Rav had taught this *halakha* only **from that** general ruling,

NOTES

An alleyway, one side of which was occupied by a gentile – **מָבוֹי שֶׁצִּידּוֹ אֶחָד גּוֹי**: Some of the *ge'onim* suggested the following explanation of this case, and the Rambam may have agreed with this interpretation: There were several Jewish courtyards on one side of the alleyway, in addition to one courtyard of a gentile. The Jewish residents of the alleyway wanted to establish an *eiruv* together via their windows so that their courtyards would be considered a single residence. This would give them the status of a single individual living in the same place that a gentile lives, and they would not have to rent the gentile's share in the alleyway in order to be permitted to carry there. Rav ruled that they cannot be considered like an individual in this manner, and they would have to rent the gentile's share of the alleyway (*Me'iri*).

Through the windows – **דֶּרֶךְ חַלּוֹנוֹת**: Rashi explains that the same principle applies if they wished to do so through the doors, and Rav was merely using a typical example. The Ri, in *Tosafot*, explains that Rav specifically meant windows, because if the houses were linked by doorways, the Jew would continue living next to the gentile without concern for his safety even if he would not establish an *eiruv* with the other Jews. Consequently, there is no reason to prohibit the Jews living there from establishing an *eiruv* (Maharsha, citing *Mordekhai*).

HALAKHA

An alleyway, one side of which was occupied by a gentile – **מָבוֹי שֶׁצִּידּוֹ אֶחָד גּוֹי**: If an alleyway has a gentile living on one side and Jews living on the other, the Jews may not establish an *eiruv* utilizing common windows to render it permitted to carry through the doors of the Jew whose house is adjacent to and opens into the alleyway. If the courtyards of the Jews are linked by doors, it is permitted to establish an *eiruv* (*Tosafot*; Rosh), although some prohibit establishing an *eiruv* even in such a case (Rambam *Sefer Zemanim, Hilkhot Eiruvin* 5:18; *Shulḥan Arukh, Oraḥ Ḥayyim* 390:1).

A courtyard occupied by a gentile – **חָצֵר שֶׁיֵּשׁ בּוֹ גּוֹי**: If one side of a courtyard was occupied by a gentile, and the Jewish residents established an *eiruv* by way of the windows that linked their houses, it is prohibited for them to carry into the courtyard, as stated by Rav Yosef (*Shulḥan Arukh, Oraḥ Ḥayyim* 382:19).

הֲוָה אָמִינָא: דִּירַת גּוֹי – שְׁמָהּ דִּירָה. קָא מַשְׁמַע לַן: דִּירַת גּוֹי לָא שְׁמָהּ דִּירָה. וְאִי מֵהָכָא – הֲוָה אָמִינָא: לָא יָדַעְנָא בָּתִּים כַּמָּה, קָא מַשְׁמַע לַן: בָּתִּים תְּרֵין.

I would have said that **the residence of a gentile is considered a residence** with regard to defining an area as an alleyway. Therefore, he **teaches us that the** legal **status of the residence of a gentile is not considered a** full-fledged **residence** in this regard. **And if** Rav had taught this *halakha* only **from** the ruling **here,** with regard to gentiles, **I would have said** that **I do not know how many houses there** are. Therefore, he **teaches us** that there must be at least **two houses** and two courtyards.

הַשְׁתָּא דְּאָמַר רַב אֲפִילּוּ חָצֵר, טַעְמָא דְּרַב דְּקָא סָבַר: אָסוּר לַעֲשׂוֹת יָחִיד בִּמְקוֹם גּוֹי.

Now that Rav has **said** that this *halakha* applies **even** to **a courtyard,** this implies that **the reason for** the opinion of **Rav is that he holds: It is prohibited for an individual to establish** his home **in the place** where **a gentile** resides. Consequently, he is prohibited from establishing an *eiruv*, so that the difficulties of living there will force him to move.

אֲמַר רַב יוֹסֵף: אִי הָכִי, הַיְינוּ דִּשְׁמַעְנָא לֵיהּ לְרַבִּי טַבְלָא, דַּאֲמַר: גּוֹי גּוֹי תְּרֵי זִימְנֵי, וְלָא יָדַעְנָא מַאי אֲמַר.

Rav Yosef said: If so, this is why **I heard Rabbi Tavla say: A gentile, a gentile, two times**[N] while teaching this subject, even though **I did not understand** then **what he** meant to **say.** Now I realize that he was speaking about both an alleyway and a courtyard.

מתני׳ שְׁתֵּי חֲצֵירוֹת זוֹ לִפְנִים מִזּוֹ, עֵירְבָה הַפְּנִימִית וְלֹא עֵירְבָה הַחִיצוֹנָה – הַפְּנִימִית מוּתֶּרֶת, וְהַחִיצוֹנָה אֲסוּרָה.

MISHNA With regard to **two courtyards, one** of which was **within the other,**[H] and the outer one opened into the public domain, the following distinctions apply: If **the inner** courtyard **established an** ***eiruv*** for itself **and the outer** one **did not establish an** ***eiruv,*** carrying in **the inner one is permitted and** carrying in **the outer one is prohibited.**

הַחִיצוֹנָה וְלֹא הַפְּנִימִית – שְׁתֵּיהֶן אֲסוּרוֹת. עֵירְבָה זוֹ לְעַצְמָהּ וְזוֹ לְעַצְמָהּ – זוֹ מוּתֶּרֶת בִּפְנֵי עַצְמָהּ, וְזוֹ מוּתֶּרֶת בִּפְנֵי עַצְמָהּ.

If **the outer** courtyard established an *eiruv* **and the inner** one did **not,** carrying in **both** is **prohibited,** as the residents of the inner courtyard pass through the outer one, and are considered to a certain extent as residents of the courtyard who did not participate in the *eiruv*. If **this** courtyard **established an** ***eiruv*** **for itself, and that** courtyard also **established an** ***eiruv*** **for itself,** but they did not establish a joint *eiruv* with one another, **this one is permitted by itself, and that one is permitted by itself,** but they may not carry from one to the other.

רַבִּי עֲקִיבָא אוֹסֵר הַחִיצוֹנָה, שֶׁדְּרִיסַת הָרֶגֶל אוֹסַרְתָּהּ. וַחֲכָמִים אוֹמְרִים: אֵין דְּרִיסַת הָרֶגֶל אוֹסַרְתָּהּ.

Rabbi Akiva prohibits carrying in **the outer one** even in such a case, **as the** right of **entry** to the outer courtyard enjoyed by the residents of the inner courtyard **renders it prohibited. And the Rabbis** disagree and **say:** The right of **entry** enjoyed by the residents of the inner courtyard **does not render it prohibited.** Since the residents of the inner courtyard do not use the outer one other than to pass through it, and they are permitted to carry in their own courtyard, they do not render it prohibited to carry in the outer courtyard.

שָׁכַח אֶחָד מִן הַחִיצוֹנָה וְלֹא עֵירֵב – הַפְּנִימִית מוּתֶּרֶת, וְהַחִיצוֹנָה אֲסוּרָה. מִן הַפְּנִימִית וְלֹא עֵירֵב – שְׁתֵּיהֶן אֲסוּרוֹת.

If **one** resident **of the outer** courtyard **forgot and did not** contribute to the ***eiruv,*** carrying in **the inner** courtyard **is permitted and** in **the outer one is prohibited.** If one resident **of the inner** courtyard **forgot and did not** contribute to the ***eiruv,*** **they are both prohibited,** as the right of way enjoyed by the members of the inner courtyard through the outer courtyard renders the outer one prohibited as well.

נָתְנוּ עֵירוּבָן בְּמָקוֹם אֶחָד, וְשָׁכַח אֶחָד בֵּין מִן הַפְּנִימִית בֵּין מִן הַחִיצוֹנָה וְלֹא עֵירֵב – שְׁתֵּיהֶן אֲסוּרוֹת. וְאִם הָיוּ שֶׁל יְחִידִים – אֵינָן צְרִיכִין לְעָרֵב.

If the residents of both courtyards **put their** ***eiruv*** **in one place, and one** person, **whether** he was **from the inner** courtyard **or from the outer one, forgot and did not** contribute to the ***eiruv,*** **they are both prohibited** for carrying within them, as the two courtyards are treated as one. **And if** the courtyards belonged **to individuals,**[H] i.e., if only one person lived in each courtyard, **they are not required to establish an** ***eiruv,*** as this requirement applies only to a courtyard occupied by multiple residents.

NOTES

A gentile, a gentile, two times – **גּוֹי גּוֹי תְּרֵי זִימְנֵי:** Several explanations have been suggested for this expression. Later commentaries debate the implications for this discussion of Rashi's two explanations. Rabbeinu Ḥananel explains that two statements were issued in the name of Rav: The first is that the place where a gentile lives is not halakhically considered a residence. The second is that it is prohibited to live on one's own in the same courtyard as a gentile. According to this explanation, Rav Yosef did indeed hear two rulings regarding a gentile. Since he heard only that word, he was unaware of the precise topic of each teaching.

HALAKHA

Two courtyards, one within the other – **שְׁתֵּי חֲצֵירוֹת זוֹ לִפְנִים מִזּוֹ:** If there were two courtyards, one located inside the other, and the residents of each made their own *eiruv*, they are permitted to carry only within their courtyard. If the residents of the inner courtyard made an *eiruv* but the residents of the outer courtyard did not, or if one of the residents of the outer one forgot to participate in the *eiruv*, the people living in the inner courtyard are permitted to carry, but those living in the outer one are prohibited from carrying. If the residents of the outer courtyard made an *eiruv* but the residents of the inner one did not, or if one of the residents of the inner courtyard forgot to participate in the *eiruv*, it is prohibited to carry in both courtyards. The residents of the inner courtyard, who may not carry in their own courtyard, render carrying in the outer one prohibited as well (*Shulḥan Arukh, Oraḥ Ḥayyim* 378:2).

Individuals – **יְחִידִים:** If two courtyards, one positioned within the other, are each occupied by a single individual, the residents are not required to establish an *eiruv* (*Shulḥan Arukh, Oraḥ Ḥayyim* 378:4).

NOTES

The foot of one who is prohibited does not render it prohibited – רֶגֶל הָאֲסוּרָה אֵינָהּ אוֹסֶרֶת: The commentaries question how Rabbi Yannai, according to Rav Dimi, derived this view of the Rabbis, as the only opinion explicitly mentioned in the mishna that a foot does not prohibit in a different place relates to a foot that is permitted in its own place. Some explain that this view is derived based on an inference from the statement of the Rabbis recorded in the mishna. Since they said: A right of entry does not render it prohibited to carry, as opposed to stating simply: It does not render it prohibited to carry, the indication is that according to the Rabbis, a right of entry never renders it prohibited to carry (Rashba; Ritva).

גמ׳ כִּי אֲתָא רַב דִּימִי, אָמַר רַבִּי יַנַּאי: זוֹ דִּבְרֵי רַבִּי עֲקִיבָא, דְּאָמַר: אֲפִילּוּ רֶגֶל הַמּוּתֶּרֶת בִּמְקוֹמָהּ – אוֹסֶרֶת שֶׁלֹּא בִּמְקוֹמָהּ. אֲבָל חֲכָמִים אוֹמְרִים: כְּשֵׁם שֶׁרֶגֶל הַמּוּתֶּרֶת אֵינָהּ אוֹסֶרֶת – כָּךְ רֶגֶל הָאֲסוּרָה אֵינָהּ אוֹסֶרֶת.

GEMARA **When Rav Dimi came** from Eretz Yisrael to Babylonia **he said** in the name of **Rabbi Yannai: This** mishna, which states that if the residents of the outer courtyard established an eiruv but the residents of the inner one did not, they are both prohibited from carrying, is **the statement of Rabbi Akiva, who said: Even** the **foot** of one **who is permitted in its** own **place,** i.e., even someone from a courtyard in which he is permitted to carry, **renders** it **prohibited when** he is **not in its** own **place.** If he enjoys the right of entry to another courtyard he is considered like a resident of that courtyard as well, and if he does not participate in the *eiruv*, no one in that courtyard may carry. **However, the Rabbis say: Just as** the **foot** of one **who is permitted** in its own place **does not render** it **prohibited** to carry in another courtyard, **so** too, the **foot** of one **who is prohibited** in his place **does not render** it **prohibited** to carry in another courtyard.[N] Consequently, if only the residents of the outer courtyard established an *eiruv*, the residents of the inner one do not render it prohibited to carry in the outer courtyard.

תְּנַן: עֵירְבָה חִיצוֹנָה וְלֹא פְּנִימִית – שְׁתֵּיהֶן אֲסוּרוֹת. מַנִּי? אִילֵימָא רַבִּי עֲקִיבָא – מַאי אִירְיָא רֶגֶל אֲסוּרָה? אֲפִילּוּ רֶגֶל מוּתֶּרֶת נַמִּי! אֶלָּא לָאו – רַבָּנַן.

We learned in the mishna: If the residents of **the outer** courtyard **established an *eiruv* and** the residents of **the inner** courtyard did **not, they are both prohibited. Whose** opinion is this? **If you say** it is that of **Rabbi Akiva, why** discuss **particularly** the case of **a foot that is prohibited,** i.e., a case where the inner courtyard did not establish an *eiruv*? According to Rabbi Akiva, **even a foot that is permitted also** renders it prohibited to carry. Therefore, even if the residents of the inner courtyard had established an *eiruv*, they would still render it prohibited to carry in the outer courtyard. **Rather, is it not** in accordance with the opinion of **the Rabbis?** This would indicate that the Rabbis agree that one who may not carry in his own courtyard does, in fact, render it prohibited to carry in a different courtyard through which he has right of entry, contrary to Rabbi Yannai's claim.

לְעוֹלָם רַבִּי עֲקִיבָא, וְ״לֹא זוֹ אַף זוֹ״ קָתָנֵי.

The Gemara rejects this argument: **Actually,** this part of the mishna is in accordance with the opinion of **Rabbi Akiva,** and **he teaches** the mishna employing the style: **Not** only **this** but **also that.** In other words, he begins by teaching the *halakha* in a relatively straightforward case and then proceeds to a more complicated example. Consequently, the mishna should be understood as follows: Not only is it prohibited to carry in both courtyards if the residents of the outer courtyard established an *eiruv* and the residents of the inner one did not, but even if the residents of both courtyards established separate *eiruvin*, it remains prohibited to carry in the outer one.

תְּנַן: עֵירְבָה זוֹ לְעַצְמָהּ וְזוֹ לְעַצְמָהּ – זוֹ מוּתֶּרֶת בִּפְנֵי עַצְמָהּ, וְזוֹ מוּתֶּרֶת בִּפְנֵי עַצְמָהּ. טַעְמָא – דְּעֵירְבָה, הָא לֹא עֵירְבָה – שְׁתֵּיהֶן אֲסוּרוֹת.

The Gemara continues: **We learned** in the mishna: If **this** courtyard **established an *eiruv* for itself, and that** courtyard also **established an *eiruv* for itself,** but the two courtyards did not establish a joint *eiruv* with one another, **this one is permitted by itself, and that one is permitted by itself,** but it is prohibited to carry from one courtyard to the other. **The reason** both courtyards are permitted by themselves is that the residents of the inner courtyard **established an *eiruv*.** By inference, if they **did not establish an *eiruv*** carrying in **both would be prohibited.**

וְהָא הַאי תַּנָּא, דְּאָמַר: רֶגֶל הַמּוּתֶּרֶת אֵינָהּ אוֹסֶרֶת, רֶגֶל הָאֲסוּרָה אוֹסֶרֶת, מַנִּי הָא? אִילֵימָא רַבִּי עֲקִיבָא הִיא – אֲפִילּוּ רֶגֶל הַמּוּתֶּרֶת נַמִּי! אֶלָּא לָאו – רַבָּנַן הִיא. וְעוֹד, מִדְּסֵיפָא רַבִּי עֲקִיבָא – רֵישָׁא לָאו רַבִּי עֲקִיבָא!

But this *tanna*, who said that the **foot** of one **who is permitted** in his own place **does not** render it **prohibited** to carry, while the **foot** of one **who is prohibited** in its own place **does** render it **prohibited** to carry, **who is this *tanna*? If you say** it is **Rabbi Akiva,** there is a difficulty, as he holds that **even** the **foot** of one **who is permitted** in its own place **also** renders it prohibited to carry in a different place. **Rather, is it not** the opinion of **the Rabbis,** which indicates that the Rabbis agree that the foot of one who is prohibited in its own place does, in fact, render it prohibited to carry in a different place, in contrast to the statement of Rabbi Yannai? **And furthermore, from the fact that the latter clause** that follows immediately states the opinion of **Rabbi Akiva,** it is clear that **the first clause,** with which Rabbi Akiva disagrees, **is not** in accordance with the opinion of **Rabbi Akiva.**

כּוּלָּהּ רַבִּי עֲקִיבָא הִיא, וְחַסּוּרֵי מִיחַסְּרָא, וְהָכִי קָתָנֵי: עֵירְבָה זוֹ לְעַצְמָהּ וְזוֹ לְעַצְמָהּ – זוֹ מוּתֶּרֶת בִּפְנֵי עַצְמָהּ, וְזוֹ מוּתֶּרֶת בִּפְנֵי עַצְמָהּ. בַּמֶּה דְּבָרִים אֲמוּרִים – שֶׁעָשְׂתָה דַּקָּה, אֲבָל לֹא עָשְׂתָה דַּקָּה – חִיצוֹנָה אֲסוּרָה, דִּבְרֵי רַבִּי עֲקִיבָא. שֶׁרַבִּי עֲקִיבָא אוֹסֵר אֶת הַחִיצוֹנָה, מִפְּנֵי שֶׁדְּרִיסַת הָרֶגֶל אוֹסֶרֶת, וַחֲכָמִים אוֹמְרִים: אֵין דְּרִיסַת הָרֶגֶל אוֹסֶרֶת.

The Gemara responds: The **entire** mishna in accordance with the opinion of **Rabbi Akiva, and it is incomplete and teaches the following: If this** courtyard **established an *eiruv* for itself, and that** courtyard also **established an *eiruv* for itself,** but they did not establish a joint *eiruv* with one another, **this one is permitted by itself, and that one is permitted by itself,** but they may not carry from one to the other. **In what** case **is this statement said?** In a case **where** the inner courtyard **constructed** a small **partition** at its entrance. **However, if it did not construct a partition, the outer** courtyard **is prohibited.** This is **the statement of Rabbi Akiva, as Rabbi Akiva prohibits** carrying in **the outer** courtyard **because the** right of **entry** enjoyed by the members of the inner courtyard **renders** it **prohibited** to carry. **And the Rabbis say: The** right of **entry** enjoyed by the members of the inner courtyard **does not render** it **prohibited** to carry.

מְתִיב רַב בֵּיבָי בַּר אַבַּיֵי: וְאִם הָיוּ שֶׁל יְחִידִים – אֵין צְרִיכִין לְעָרֵב. הָא שֶׁל רַבִּים – צְרִיכִין לְעָרֵב. אַלְמָא: רֶגֶל הַמּוּתֶּרֶת בִּמְקוֹמָהּ – אֵינָהּ אוֹסֶרֶת, רֶגֶל הָאֲסוּרָה – אוֹסֶרֶת.

Rav Beivai bar Abaye raised an objection based upon the final clause of the mishna: **And if** the courtyards belonged **to individuals,** i.e., if only one person lived in each courtyard, **they are not required to establish an *eiruv*. Doesn't** this indicate that if they belong **to many** people jointly, **they need to establish an *eiruv*? Apparently,** the **foot** of one **who is permitted in his own place does not render** it **prohibited,** but the **foot** of one **who is prohibited** in his own place does **render** it **prohibited.** This contradicts Rabbi Yannai's understanding of Rabbi Akiva's opinion.

וְעוֹד מְתִיב רָבִינָא: שָׁכַח אֶחָד מִן הַחִיצוֹנָה וְלֹא עֵירֵב – הַפְּנִימִית מוּתֶּרֶת, וְחִיצוֹנָה אֲסוּרָה. שָׁכַח אֶחָד מִן הַפְּנִימִית וְלֹא עֵירֵב – שְׁתֵּיהֶן אֲסוּרוֹת. טַעְמָא דְּשָׁכַח, הָא לֹא שָׁכַח – שְׁתֵּיהֶן מוּתָּרוֹת. אַלְמָא: רֶגֶל הַמּוּתֶּרֶת – אֵינָהּ אוֹסֶרֶת, רֶגֶל הָאֲסוּרָה – אוֹסֶרֶת.

And Ravina raised a further objection from the mishna: If **one** resident **of the outer** courtyard **forgot and did not** contribute to the ***eiruv*****, the inner** courtyard **is permitted** for carrying **and the outer one is prohibited.** If **one** resident **of the inner** courtyard **forgot and did not** contribute to the ***eiruv*****, both** courtyards **are prohibited,** as the right of way enjoyed by the members of the inner courtyard through the outer courtyard renders the outer one prohibited as well. **The reason is that** one of the residents **forgot** to contribute to the *eiruv*. **But if he did not forget,** and each courtyard established its own valid *eiruv*, **both of them** would be **permitted. Apparently,** the **foot** of one **who is permitted in his** own **place does not render** it **prohibited** to carry, but the **foot** of one **who is prohibited** in his own place does **render** it **prohibited** to carry. This cannot be in accordance with the opinion of Rabbi Akiva, as he holds that even the foot of one who is permitted in his own place renders it prohibited to carry elsewhere. Rather, it must be the opinion of the Rabbis, which proves that even they agree that the foot of one who is prohibited in his own place does render a different courtyard prohibited.

אֶלָּא, כִּי אֲתָא רָבִין, אֲמַר רַבִּי יַנַּאי: שָׁלֹשׁ מַחֲלוֹקוֹת בַּדָּבָר: תַּנָּא קַמָּא סָבַר: רֶגֶל הַמּוּתֶּרֶת – אֵינָהּ אוֹסֶרֶת, רֶגֶל הָאֲסוּרָה – אוֹסֶרֶת. רַבִּי עֲקִיבָא סָבַר: אֲפִילּוּ רֶגֶל הַמּוּתֶּרֶת – אוֹסֶרֶת. וְרַבָּנַן בַּתְרָאֵי סָבְרִי: כְּשֵׁם שֶׁרֶגֶל מוּתֶּרֶת אֵינָהּ אוֹסֶרֶת – כָּךְ רֶגֶל הָאֲסוּרָה אֵינָהּ אוֹסֶרֶת.

Rather, this version must be rejected, and **when Ravin came** from Eretz Yisrael to Babylonia he cited a different version. **Rabbi Yannai said: There are three disputes with regard to** this **matter. The first *tanna* holds** that the **foot** of one **who is permitted in his** own **place does not render** it **prohibited** to carry elsewhere, but the **foot** of one **who is prohibited** in his own place does **render** it **prohibited** to carry. **Rabbi Akiva holds** that **even** the **foot** of one **who is permitted** in his own place **renders** it **prohibited** to carry in a different place. **And the latter Rabbis hold** that **just as** the **foot** of one **who is permitted in his** own **place does not render** it **prohibited** to carry, **so** too, the **foot** of one **who is prohibited does not render** it **prohibited** to carry. This explanation resolves all of the difficulties posed earlier.

״נָתְנוּ עֵירוּבָן בְּמָקוֹם אֶחָד וְשָׁכַח אֶחָד בֵּין מִן הַפְּנִימִית וכו׳״: מַאי מָקוֹם אֶחָד?

It was stated in the mishna: If the residents of both courtyards **put their *eiruv* in one place, and one** person, **whether** he was **from the inner** courtyard or from the outer one, **forgot** and did not contribute to the *eiruv*, it is prohibited to carry in both courtyards. The Gemara asks: **What is** the meaning of **one place?** Is the *halakha* different if the two courtyards established their *eiruv* in one place or in different places?

(סִימָן: חִיצוֹנָה עַצְמָהּ בְּבַיִת יְחִידָאָה רָבִינָא דְּלָא מַשְׁכַּח בִּפְנִים.)

Before continuing, the Gemara provides **a mnemonic** for the ensuing discussion: **Outer; for itself; in the house of an individual; Ravina; where the inner one did not forget.**[N]

NOTES

A mnemonic: Outer; for itself; in the house of an individual; Ravina; where the inner one did not forget – סִימָן: חִיצוֹנָה עַצְמָהּ בְּבַיִת יְחִידָאָה רָבִינָא דְּלָא מַשְׁכַּח בִּפְנִים: The author of the *Ge'on Ya'akov* explains this mnemonic as a reference to the difficulties the Gemara has already raised against Rav Dimi's statement in the name of Rabbi Yannai: If the inhabitants of the outer courtyard established an *eiruv*; if the residents of each courtyard established an *eiruv* for themselves; Rav Beivai's question with regard to individuals; and Ravina's objection concerning a resident of the inner courtyard who forgot to establish an *eiruv*.

אָמַר רַב יְהוּדָה, אָמַר רַב: חִיצוֹנָה, וּמַאי קָרוּ לַהּ ״מָקוֹם אֶחָד״ – מָקוֹם הַמְיוּחָד לִשְׁתֵּיהֶן.

Rav Yehuda said that Rav said: The mishna is referring to a case when the residents of both courtyards established their *eiruv* in **the outer** courtyard. **And why did they call it one** [*eḥad*] **place?**[N] Because it is a place that is **designated** [*meyuḥad*] **for** the residents of **both** courtyards, as the members of the inner one also pass through the outer courtyard. Therefore, if a member of the outer courtyard forgot to contribute to the *eiruv*, the inner courtyard is also prohibited. Since the *eiruv* of the inner courtyard is located in the outer courtyard, the residents of the inner courtyard cannot separate themselves from the outer one. However, if the *eiruv* was deposited in the inner courtyard and a member of the outer courtyard forgot to contribute to the *eiruv*, carrying in the inner courtyard is permitted, because in that situation they can separate themselves from the outer courtyard.

NOTES

One place is referring to the outer courtyard – מָקוֹם אֶחָד חִיצוֹנָה: The reason the mishna did not explicitly state that they placed the *eiruv* in the outer courtyard is that one might have thought that the reason it was invalid is that it was left in the courtyard itself rather than in one of the houses. Therefore, the mishna used the phrase one place, to indicate that the *eiruv* was left in a safe location (*Shoshanim LeDavid*).

Perek **VI**
Daf **75** Amud **b**

תַּנְיָא נַמִי הָכִי: נָתְנוּ עֵירוּבָן בַּחִיצוֹנָה, וְשָׁכַח אֶחָד בֵּין מִן הַחִיצוֹנָה וּבֵין מִן הַפְּנִימִית וְלֹא עֵירֵב – שְׁתֵּיהֶן אֲסוּרוֹת. נָתְנוּ עֵירוּבָן בַּפְּנִימִית, וְשָׁכַח אֶחָד מִן הַפְּנִימִית וְלֹא עֵירֵב – שְׁתֵּיהֶן אֲסוּרוֹת. מִן הַחִיצוֹנָה וְלֹא עֵירֵב – שְׁתֵּיהֶן אֲסוּרוֹת, דִּבְרֵי רַבִּי עֲקִיבָא. וַחֲכָמִים אוֹמְרִים: בָּזוֹ פְּנִימִית מוּתֶּרֶת וְחִיצוֹנָה אֲסוּרָה.

That was also taught in a *baraita*: If **they placed their *eiruv* in the outer** courtyard,[H] **and one** person **forgot** to contribute to the ***eiruv***, **whether he is** a resident **of the outer** courtyard **or of the inner** one, **they are both prohibited. If they put their *eiruv* in the inner** courtyard, **and one** resident **of the inner** courtyard **forgot** to contribute to the ***eiruv***, **they are both prohibited.** Similarly, if one of the residents **of the outer** courtyard **did not** contribute to the ***eiruv***, **they are both prohibited.** This is **the statement of Rabbi Akiva. And the Rabbis** disagree and **say: In this** case, where the *eiruv* was deposited in the inner courtyard and the person who forgot to contribute to the *eiruv* was a resident of the outer one, the **inner** courtyard **is permitted and the outer one is prohibited.**

אֲמַר לֵיהּ רַבָּה בַּר חָנָן לְאַבָּיֵי: מַאי שְׁנָא לְרַבָּנַן דְּאָמְרִי פְּנִימִית מוּתֶּרֶת – מִשּׁוּם דְּאָחֲדָא דַּשָּׁא וּמִשְׁתַּמְשָׁא. לְרַבִּי עֲקִיבָא נַמִי: תֵּיחַד דַּשָּׁא וְתִשְׁתַּמֵּשׁ! אֲמַר לֵיהּ: עֵירוּב מַרְגִּילָהּ.

Rabba bar Ḥanan said to Abaye: What is different according to the Rabbis, who say that the **inner** courtyard **is permitted?** It is **because** the residents of the inner courtyard can **shut the door** of their courtyard to the members of the outer one **and use** the inner courtyard on their own. But if so, **according to Rabbi Akiva as well, let** the residents of the inner courtyard **shut the door** of their courtyard to the members of the outer one **and use** their courtyard on their own. Abaye **said to him:** If the *eiruv* of the outer courtyard was not placed in the inner courtyard, your argument would be valid. But the fact that **the *eiruv*** is deposited in the inner courtyard **accustoms** the residents of the outer courtyard to enter it.

לְרַבָּנַן נַמִי עֵירוּב מַרְגִּילָהּ! דְּאָמְרָה: לְתַקּוֹנֵי שִׁיתַּפְתִּיךְ וְלָא לְעַוּוֹתֵי.

The Gemara asks: If so, **according to the Rabbis as well** we should say that the placement of the ***eiruv*** in the inner courtyard **accustoms** the residents of the outer courtyard to enter it. The Gemara answers: The reasoning of the Rabbis is **that** the members of the inner courtyard can **say** to the members of the outer one: **We joined with you** in a single *eiruv* **to** our **benefit, and not to** our **detriment.**[N] Since one of your residents forgot to contribute to the *eiruv*, we no longer acquiesce to this partnership.

לְרַבִּי עֲקִיבָא נַמִי, תֵּימָא: לְתַקּוֹנֵי שִׁיתַּפְתִּיךְ וְלָא לְעַוּוֹתֵי! דַּאֲמָרָה לַהּ: מְבַטְּלִינַן לָךְ רְשׁוּתִי. וְרַבָּנַן – אֵין בִּיטּוּל רְשׁוּת מֵחָצֵר לְחָצֵר.

The Gemara asks: **According to Rabbi Akiva as well, let** the residents of the inner courtyard **say** to the residents of the outer courtyard: **We joined with you to** our **benefit and not to** our **detriment.** The Gemara answers that according to Rabbi Akiva, the case is **that** the residents of the outer courtyard **said** to the residents of the inner courtyard: **We renounce our rights in your favor,** in which case the inhabitants of the inner courtyard are permitted to carry in their own courtyard. Consequently, his ruling that the inner courtyard is also prohibited applies only before the residents of the outer courtyard renounce their rights. **And the Rabbis** hold that **there is no renunciation of rights from courtyard to courtyard.**

HALAKHA

If they placed their *eiruv* in the outer courtyard – נָתְנוּ עֵירוּבָן בַּחִיצוֹנָה: If the residents of two courtyards, one inside the other, established a joint *eiruv* and placed it in the outer courtyard, but one of the residents forgot to participate in the *eiruv*, the residents of both courtyards are prohibited from carrying. When the *eiruv* is placed in the inner courtyard, the following distinction applies: If a resident of the outer courtyard forgot to contribute to the *eiruv*, the residents of the inner one are permitted to carry and those of the outer courtyard are prohibited from carrying. If the one who forgot to contribute was a resident of the inner courtyard, the inhabitants of both courtyards are prohibited from carrying, in accordance with the opinion of the Rabbis (*Shulḥan Arukh, Oraḥ Ḥayyim* 378:3).

NOTES

To our benefit and not to our detriment – לְתַקּוֹנֵי שִׁיתַּפְתִּיךְ וְלָא לְעַוּוֹתֵי: A similar expression is found in the context of the *halakhot* of agents: I sent you for my benefit, but not for my detriment. The rationale is that an agent, or in this case an *eiruv*, is appointed to benefit the one who sent him or who established the *eiruv*. If the mission causes harm, the one who sent the messenger can say that he did not appoint him as his agent for such an eventuality, thus nullifying the agency entirely. This claim is acceptable only where the agent improperly overstepped the bounds of his agency. Similarly, in this case, since a member of the courtyard failed to join the *eiruv*, the *eiruv* itself can be canceled.

לֵימָא שְׁמוּאֵל וְרַבִּי יוֹחָנָן בִּפְלוּגְתָּא דְּרַבָּנַן וְרַבִּי עֲקִיבָא קָא מִיפַּלְגִי; דִּשְׁמוּאֵל אָמַר כְּרַבָּנַן, וְרַבִּי יוֹחָנָן דְּאָמַר כְּרַבִּי עֲקִיבָא?

The Gemara asks: **Let us say that Shmuel and Rabbi Yoḥanan,** who disagree about whether there is renunciation of rights from one courtyard to another, **disagree about the** same point that was the subject of a **disagreement between the Rabbis and Rabbi Akiva. As Shmuel said** that there is no renunciation of rights from one courtyard to another, **in accordance with** the opinion of **the Rabbis, and Rabbi Yoḥanan said** that such renunciation is valid, **in accordance with** the opinion of **Rabbi Akiva.**

אָמַר לָךְ שְׁמוּאֵל: אֲנָא דְּאָמְרִי אֲפִילּוּ לְרַבִּי עֲקִיבָא; עַד כָּאן לָא קָאָמַר רַבִּי עֲקִיבָא הָכָא – אֶלָּא בִּשְׁתֵּי חֲצֵירוֹת זוֹ לִפְנִים מִזּוֹ, דְּאָסְרָן אַהֲדָדֵי. אֲבָל הָתָם – מִי קָא אָסְרָן אַהֲדָדֵי?

The Gemara responds: **Shmuel** could have **said to you: What I said is even in accordance with** the opinion of **Rabbi Akiva. Rabbi Akiva stated** his opinion that there is renunciation of rights from one courtyard to another **only here, with regard to two courtyards, one within the other, which render each other prohibited. However, there,** where they disagree about two adjacent courtyards, **do** the courtyards **render each other prohibited?** Consequently, even Rabbi Akiva would agree that there is no renunciation of rights from one courtyard to another.

וְרַבִּי יוֹחָנָן אָמַר: אֲנָא דְּאָמְרִי אֲפִילּוּ לְרַבָּנַן; עַד כָּאן לָא קָאָמְרִי רַבָּנַן הָכָא – אֶלָּא דְּאָמְרָה לַהּ: אַדְּמְבַטְּלַתְּ לִי – קָא אָסְרַתְּ עֲלַאי. אֲבָל הָתָם – מִי קָאָסְרַתְּ עֲלַהּ?

And Rabbi Yoḥanan could have **said: What I said is even in accordance with** the opinion of **the Rabbis. The Rabbis stated** their opinion that there is no renunciation of rights from one courtyard to another **only** in the case **here, as** the residents of the inner courtyard **said to** the residents of the outer courtyard: **Until you renounce** your rights **in our favor, you render** it **prohibited** for **us** to carry, and therefore, we will have no connection with you and forgo both the renunciation and the prohibition. **But there, does** one courtyard **prohibit** the other? Since it does not, even the Rabbis would agree that there is renunciation from one courtyard to another.

״וְאִם הָיוּ שֶׁל יְחִידִים וְכוּ׳. אָמַר רַב יוֹסֵף, תָּנֵי רַבִּי: הָיוּ שְׁלֹשָׁה – אֲסוּרִין.

We learned in the mishna: **And if** the courtyards belonged **to individuals,** i.e., if only one person lived in each courtyard, they are not required to establish an *eiruv*. **Rav Yosef said: Rabbi** Yehuda HaNasi **teaches** that if **there were three** people living in the two courtyards, whether two people lived in the outer courtyard and one person in the inner one, or two people lived in the inner courtyard and one person lived in the outer one, **they are prohibited**[N] from carrying without an *eiruv*.

אֲמַר לְהוּ רַב בֵּיבַי: לָא תְּצַיְּתוּ לֵיהּ, אֲנָא אָמְרִיתָהּ נִיהֲלָהּ, וּמִשְּׁמֵיהּ דְּרַב אַדָּא בַּר אַהֲבָה אָמְרִיתָהּ נִיהֲלָהּ: הוֹאִיל וַאֲנִי קוֹרֵא בָּהֶן רַבִּים בַּחִיצוֹנָה. אֲמַר רַב יוֹסֵף: מָרֵיהּ דְּאַבְרָהָם! רַבִּים בְּרַבִּי אִיחֲלַף לִי.

Rav Beivai said to the Sages: **Do not listen to him,** as he is mistaken. **I told it to him, and I told it to him in the name of Rav Adda bar Ahava,** not Rabbi Yehuda HaNasi, but due to his illness Rav Yosef forgot this detail. And the reason that the residents of both courtyards are prohibited from carrying if two people are living in the outer courtyard is that **since I call them many in the outer** courtyard, the Sages issued a decree prohibiting carrying, due to a case in which there are two people living in the inner courtyard. When he heard this, **Rav Yosef said** in astonishment: **Master of Abraham! I mistook** the word **Rabbi for** the word **many** [*rabbim*]. He now realized that he had mistakenly understood this ruling as attributed to Rabbi Yehuda HaNasi rather than a *halakha* regarding many, an error that led to his inaccurate version of the teaching.

וּשְׁמוּאֵל אָמַר: לְעוֹלָם מוּתָּרוֹת, עַד שֶׁיְּהוּ שְׁנַיִם בַּפְּנִימִית וְאֶחָד בַּחִיצוֹנָה.

And Shmuel said: Actually, they are permitted, unless there are two people living **in the inner** courtyard[H] **and one in the outer one.**

אָמַר רַבִּי אֶלְעָזָר: וְגוֹי הֲרֵי הוּא כְּרַבִּים. מַאי שְׁנָא יִשְׂרָאֵל דְּלָא אָסַר – דְּמַאן דְּיָדַע – יָדַע, וּמַאן דְּלָא יָדַע – סָבַר: עֵירוּבֵי עֵירֵב. גּוֹי נַמִי, אָמְרִינַן: דְּיָדַע – יָדַע, דְּלָא יָדַע – סָבַר: אֲגִירֵי אוֹגַר!

Rabbi Elazar said: And a gentile is considered **like many,**[H] i.e., if a gentile lives in the inner courtyard, the gentile's right of way in the outer courtyard renders it prohibited to carry there. The Gemara asks: **What is different** about **an** individual **Jew** living in the inner courtyard, that **he does not prohibit** the resident of the outer courtyard? **Because one who knows** that only one person lives there **knows** this fact, **and one who does not know** this **thinks** that **an *eiruv* has been established.** If so, in the case of a **gentile also, we** should **say that** one **who knows** that only one person lives there **knows,** and one **who does not know** this **thinks** that the Jew must have **rented** the domain from the gentile.

NOTES

If there were three people living in the two courtyards, they are prohibited – הָיוּ שְׁלֹשָׁה אֲסוּרִין: Rabbeinu Ḥananel, the Rif, and others explain this discussion differently. According to their understanding, the statement: If there were three they are prohibited, refers to three courtyards, one within the other, with a single person living in each. The meaning of this statement is that despite the mishna's principle that individuals do not render carrying prohibited, in such a case they do, because the members of the inner courtyards must pass through the outer one. This causes the outer courtyard to be treated as a courtyard inhabited by many people, where it is prohibited to carry without an *eiruv*. According to this explanation, Shmuel disagrees completely with Rav Adda bar Ahava, who prohibits carrying only in a case where two people live in the same courtyard.

HALAKHA

Two in the inner courtyard – שְׁנַיִם בַּפְּנִימִית: If two individuals reside in two separate courtyards, one within the other, they are permitted to carry without an *eiruv*. However, if there are two people living in the inner courtyard, an *eiruv* is required. This ruling is in accordance with the opinion of Shmuel, whose opinion is accepted over the opinion of Rav Adda bar Ahava (*Shulḥan Arukh, Oraḥ Ḥayyim* 378:5).

A gentile is considered like many – גּוֹי הֲרֵי הוּא כְּרַבִּים: If a Jew and a gentile live in an inner courtyard and a Jew lives in the outer one, the residents of the inner courtyard render it prohibited for the Jew living in the outer courtyard to carry. The same applies even if the gentile lives alone in the inner courtyard while the two Jews occupy the outer courtyard (Rashi; *Tosafot*). The Rambam prohibits carrying in the latter case even if there is only one Jew residing in the outer courtyard (*Shulḥan Arukh, Oraḥ Ḥayyim* 382:17).

NOTES

Gatehouse – **בֵּית שַׁעַר**: The term gatehouse in this context is not used in the same way it is used in other contexts. In general, a gatehouse is a structure made for the watchman who guards the gate, and it is not considered a place of a residence in its own right (see *Tosafot*). The Gemara here indicates that even a place that serves as a passageway only on Shabbat is considered a gatehouse with regard to the *halakhot* of an *eiruv*. An example is a house between two courtyards through which people pass in order to place an *eiruv* (*Me'iri*).

HALAKHA

The outer house of the innermost one – **חִיצוֹן שֶׁל פְּנִימִי**: If there are several houses, one within the other, only the two inner ones are required to establish an *eiruv*, because the others are considered gatehouses. This ruling is in accordance with the opinion of Rabbi Yoḥanan, as the *halakha* follows his view rather than the opinion of Shmuel (*Shulḥan Arukh, Oraḥ Ḥayyim* 370:7).

BACKGROUND

Two courtyards that have three houses between them – **שְׁתֵּי חֲצֵירוֹת וּשְׁלֹשָׁה בָּתִּים בֵּינֵיהֶן**:

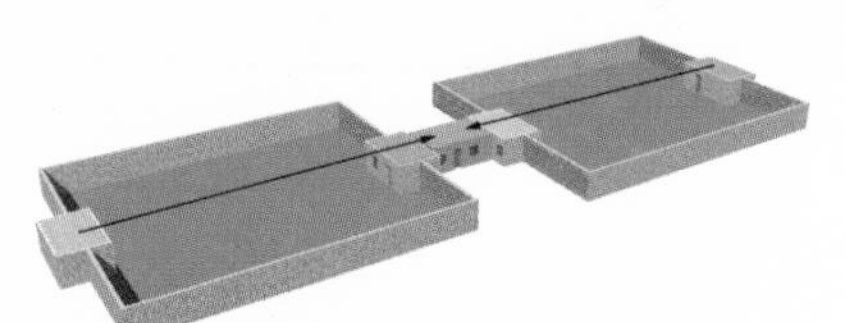

Residents of each courtyard place their *eiruv* in the middle house, as indicated by the arrows. Each of the houses that is adjacent to both the middle house and the courtyard is considered to be a gatehouse.

סְתָם גּוֹי אִי אִיתָא – דְּאוֹגַר מִיפְעָא פָּעֵי.

The Gemara answers: This is not so, as **a typical gentile, if he** had **rented** out his domain, **he would chatter** about it, and everyone would know. If he has not talked about it, everyone will assume that he did not rent out his domain.

אָמַר רַב יְהוּדָה, אָמַר שְׁמוּאֵל: עֲשָׂרָה בָּתִּים זֶה לִפְנִים מִזֶּה – פְּנִימִי נוֹתֵן אֶת עֵירוּבוֹ, וְדַיּוֹ.

Rav Yehuda said that **Shmuel said:** If there are **ten houses, one within the other,** so that the person living in the innermost house must pass through all the rest in order to reach the courtyard, **the innermost one** alone **contributes to the *eiruv*** for the courtyard, **and it is enough.** The residents of the other houses are considered as living in the gatehouse and corridor of the innermost one, and therefore they do not have to contribute to the *eiruv*.

וְרַבִּי יוֹחָנָן אָמַר: אֲפִילּוּ חִיצוֹן. חִיצוֹן, בֵּית שַׁעַר הוּא! חִיצוֹן שֶׁל פְּנִימִי.

And Rabbi Yoḥanan said: Even the **outer one** must contribute to the *eiruv*. The Gemara asks: The **outer** residence **is a gatehouse**[N] in relation to the inner ones, so why should it have to contribute to the *eiruv*? The Gemara answers that Rabbi Yoḥanan was referring to the **outer** house **of** the **innermost one.**[H] In other words, even the second-to-last house, the outer one only in relation to the innermost house, must contribute to the *eiruv*, as it is not viewed as a gatehouse.

בְּמַאי קָמִיפַּלְגִי? מָר סָבַר: בֵּית שַׁעַר דְּיָחִיד שְׁמֵיהּ בֵּית שַׁעַר, וּמָר סָבַר: לָא שְׁמֵיהּ בֵּית שַׁעַר.

The Gemara explains: **With regard to what** principle **do they disagree? One Sage,** Shmuel, **holds** that **the gatehouse of an individual is considered a gatehouse,** and therefore the ninth house, i.e., the second innermost is also a gatehouse, as it serves as a passageway for the individual living in the innermost house, **and one Sage,** Rabbi Yoḥanan, **holds** that the gatehouse of an individual **is not considered a gatehouse,** and therefore the ninth house must also contribute to the *eiruv*.

אָמַר רַב נַחְמָן, אָמַר רַבָּה בַּר אֲבוּהּ, אָמַר רַב: שְׁתֵּי חֲצֵירוֹת וּשְׁלֹשָׁה בָּתִּים בֵּינֵיהֶן, זֶה בָּא דֶּרֶךְ זֶה וְנוֹתֵן עֵירוּבוֹ בְּזֶה, וְזֶה בָּא דֶּרֶךְ זֶה וְנוֹתֵן עֵירוּבוֹ בְּזֶה –

Rav Naḥman said that **Rabba bar Avuh said** that **Rav said:** With regard to **two courtyards** that have **three houses between them,**[B] and a resident of **this** courtyard **comes through this** house that opens to his courtyard **and places his *eiruv* in that** middle house, **and** a resident of **this** other courtyard **comes through this** house that opens to his courtyard **and places his *eiruv* in that** middle house,

Perek **VI**
Daf **76** Amud **a**

HALAKHA

Need not contribute bread for the *eiruv* – **וְאֵין צָרִיךְ לִיתֵּן אֶת הַפַּת**: If two courtyards were separated by three houses that opened into one another, the residents of one courtyard may pass through the house nearest to it and place their *eiruv* in the middle house, and the residents of the other courtyard may do the same. None of the three houses has to contribute to the *eiruv*, as the outer houses are considered gatehouses while the middle house is the one in which the *eiruv* is placed (*Shulḥan Arukh, Oraḥ Ḥayyim* 379:1).

Two courtyards and two houses – **שְׁתֵּי חֲצֵרוֹת וּשְׁנֵי בָתִּים**: If two courtyards are separated by two houses and the residents of each courtyard placed their *eiruv* in the house closest to the other courtyard, the *eiruvin* are not valid, as each has placed its *eiruv* in the other courtyard's gatehouse (*Shulḥan Arukh, Oraḥ Ḥayyim* 379:2).

זֶה נַעֲשֶׂה בֵּית שַׁעַר לָזֶה, וְזֶה נַעֲשֶׂה בֵּית שַׁעַר לָזֶה. אֶמְצָעִי הָוֵה לֵיהּ בֵּית שֶׁמַּנִּיחִין בּוֹ עֵירוּב, וְאֵין צָרִיךְ לִיתֵּן אֶת הַפַּת.

this outer house **becomes a gatehouse to this** courtyard, **and that** outer house **becomes a gatehouse to that** courtyard, and therefore the residents of the outer houses need not contribute to the *eiruv*. **The middle** house between them **is the house in which the *eiruv* is placed,** and therefore its residents **need not contribute bread** for the *eiruv*.[H]

בָּדֵיק לְהוּ רַחֲבָה לְרַבָּנַן: שְׁתֵּי חֲצֵרוֹת וּשְׁנֵי בָתִּים בֵּינֵיהֶם, זֶה בָּא דֶּרֶךְ זֶה וְנָתַן עֵירוּבוֹ בָּזֶה, וְזֶה בָּא דֶּרֶךְ זֶה וְנָתַן עֵירוּבוֹ בָּזֶה, קָנוּ עֵירוּב, אוֹ לָא? מִי מְשַׁוֵּית לְהוּ לְגַבֵּי דְּהַאי בַּיִת וּלְגַבֵּי דְּהַאי בֵּית שַׁעַר [וּלְגַבֵּי דְּהַאי בֵּית שַׁעַר וּלְגַבֵּי דְּהַאי בַּיִת]

The Sage **Raḥava tested the** other **Sages:** If there were **two courtyards and two houses**[H] **between them,** and a resident of **this** courtyard **came through this** house that opens to his courtyard **and placed his *eiruv* in that** house farther from his courtyard, **and** a resident of **this** other courtyard **came through this** house that opens to his courtyard **and placed his *eiruv* in that** house that opens to the other courtyard, did **they acquire the *eiruv* or not,** i.e., are the two *eiruvin* valid? **Do you render it a house with regard to this** courtyard, whose *eiruv* was placed there, **and a gatehouse with regard to that** one who passed through it in order to place his *eiruv* in the other house? **And** similarly, do you render the other house **a gatehouse with regard to this** one **and a house with regard to that** one?

אָמְרוּ לֵיהּ: שְׁנֵיהֶן לֹא קָנוּ עֵירוּב; מַה נַּפְשָׁךְ: אִי בֵּית שַׁעַר מְשַׁוֵּית לֵיהּ, הַנּוֹתֵן אֶת עֵירוּבוֹ בְּבֵית שַׁעַר, אַכְסַדְרָה, וּמִרְפֶּסֶת – אֵינוֹ עֵירוּב. אִי בַּיִת מְשַׁוֵּית לֵיהּ, קָא מְטַלְטֵל לְבַיִת דְּלָא מְעָרֵב לֵיהּ.

The Sages **said to** Raḥava: **Neither** of them **has acquired** his *eiruv*. **Whichever way you** look at it, it is difficult: **If you consider** either house **a gatehouse,** the *halakha* with regard to **one who places his *eiruv* in a gatehouse, a porch, or a balcony,** is that **it is not a** valid ***eiruv*.** And **if you consider** either one **a house, he would be carrying into a house for which he is not establishing an *eiruv*.** Since the assumption that benefits one of them harms the other, and there is no way to establish firmly the status of these houses, the residents of both courtyards fail to acquire their *eiruv*.

וּמַאי שְׁנָא מִדְּרָבָא? דְּאָמַר רָבָא: אָמְרוּ לוֹ שְׁנַיִם צֵא וְעָרֵב עָלֵינוּ, לְאֶחָד עֵירֵב עָלָיו מִבְּעוֹד יוֹם וּלְאֶחָד עֵירֵב עָלָיו בֵּין הַשְּׁמָשׁוֹת, זֶה שֶׁעֵירֵב עָלָיו מִבְּעוֹד יוֹם נֶאֱכַל עֵירוּבוֹ בֵּין הַשְּׁמָשׁוֹת, וְזֶה שֶׁעֵירֵב עָלָיו בֵּין הַשְּׁמָשׁוֹת נֶאֱכַל עֵירוּבוֹ מִשֶּׁתֶּחְשַׁךְ – שְׁנֵיהֶם קָנוּ עֵירוּב!

Raḥava asked: **What** makes this case **different from** the ruling of **Rava? As Rava said:** In the case of **two** people who **said to** one person: **Go and establish an *eiruv*** of Shabbat limits **for** each of **us,** and **he established an *eiruv* for one** of them **while it was still day, and he established an *eiruv*** for the other **one during twilight,** and **the *eiruv* of the one for whom he established an *eiruv* while it was still day was eaten during twilight, and the *eiruv* of the one for whom he established an *eiruv* during twilight**[H] **was eaten after nightfall, both of them have acquired their *eiruv*.** Twilight is of doubtful status as to whether it is considered day or night. If it is night, any *eiruv* established at that time is invalid, and if it is day, any *eiruv* eaten at that time is invalid. Rava nonetheless ruled leniently, despite the fact that two contradictory assumptions are involved, in keeping with the principle that in cases of doubt relating to an *eiruv*, the *halakha* is lenient. Consequently, with regard to the one whose *eiruv* was eaten during twilight, it is considered as though it was already night, and therefore his *eiruv* had already taken effect while it was still day before it was eaten. Conversely, with regard to the one whose *eiruv* was established during twilight, that period of time is viewed as day, and therefore his *eiruv* is valid as well.

הָכִי הָשְׁתָּא?! הָתָם – סָפֵק יְמָמָא סָפֵק לֵילְיָא – לָא מִינְכְּרָא מִילְּתָא. אֲבָל הָכָא, אִי דִּלְגַבֵּי דְּהַאי בַּיִת – לְגַבֵּי דְּהַאי בַּיִת, אִי לְגַבֵּי דְּהַאי בֵּית שַׁעַר – לְגַבֵּי דְּהַאי נַמִי בֵּית שַׁעַר.

The Sages respond: **How can** these cases **be compared? There,** where there is **uncertainty** whether it is **day** and **uncertainty** whether it is **night, the matter is not noticeable,** as no one sees exactly when each *eiruv* was established. **But here,** where the houses are clearly distinguishable, **if with regard to this** one, who placed his *eiruv* there, it is **a house,** then **with regard to that** one, who passed through it, it should also be regarded as **a house.** And **if, with regard to this** one, who passed through it, it is **a gatehouse,** then **with regard to that** one, who placed his *eiruv* there, it should **also** be considered **a gatehouse.** Therefore, neither of them acquires his *eiruv*.[N]

הדרן עלך הדר

HALAKHA

An *eiruv* during twilight – עֵירוּב בֵּין הַשְּׁמָשׁוֹת: If an agent established an *eiruv* for one person before sunset and for another during twilight, and the *eiruv* of the former was eaten during twilight, and the *eiruv* of the latter was eaten after nightfall, both *eiruvin* are valid, as with regard to the *halakhot* of *eiruv* the ruling is lenient (*Shulḥan Arukh, Oraḥ Ḥayyim* 379:1).

NOTES

Uncertainties with regard to an *eiruv* – סְפֵקוֹת בְּעֵירוּב: Some commentaries suggest the following explanation as to the difference between the case in which *eiruvin* were placed in two houses, in which case neither one is valid, and the case of one *eiruv* that was established during twilight and another that was established during the day and eaten during twilight, in which case both are considered valid: In the case of the houses, since a house is a particular location, it cannot legally be a gatehouse and a house at the same time. Twilight, however, is not a single unit of time. It is possible that the earlier part of twilight is day, while the end of twilight is night. Consequently, it is possible that the *eiruv* that was established during twilight was established during the day, while the other *eiruv* was eaten at night. Therefore, there is no necessary contradiction between the two possibilities. Even according to Rashi's explanation that the key point is a matter of appearances, the exact moment of twilight when day becomes night is not evident to all. On the other hand, this is not the case with regard to houses (see Ritva; Rav Tzvi Hirsch Ḥayyot).

Summary of **Perek VI**

The questions dealing with the basic definition of residence, which were analyzed and resolved in the chapter, can be divided into several categories. One resolution is that a gentile living in a courtyard prohibits all the other members of the courtyard from carrying, not because he is obligated to observe the *halakhot* of *eiruv* or included in an *eiruv* that is established, but for other reasons. Consequently, since he can neither participate in an *eiruv* nor can others include him in their *eiruv*, in order to establish an *eiruv* in that courtyard, the Jews in the courtyard must rent the gentile's domain for the purposes of the *eiruv*.

Another related matter discussed in this chapter was the renunciation of rights over one's property. The resident of a courtyard can relinquish his rights to use the courtyard on Shabbat. Once he has removed himself from that courtyard, he assumes the status of a guest. As his rights were transferred to others, he no longer prohibits the residents of the courtyard from carrying. The Gemara clarified when and how this renunciation can be performed.

In addition, ancillary members of a residence do not have to participate in a joining of the courtyards and a merging of the alleyways, as the *eiruv* of the homeowner is on their behalf as well. As a result, children, slaves, students, and partners do not require a separate *eiruv* of their own. It is sufficient that they live in the same courtyard or house as the homeowner.

With regard to courtyards so close to each other that the residents of one have the right to use or pass through the other, or if a sort of partnership exists between them, the Sages disputed in what cases the members of one courtyard prohibit the members of the other from carrying. The halakhic conclusion was that only in a case where the courtyards are not considered a single unit, and those who pass through the courtyard are prohibited from carrying in their own courtyard according to the *halakhot* of *eiruv*, do they prohibit the residents of the courtyard through which they pass or to which they are tied from carrying.

Introduction to **Perek VII**

At the end of the sixth chapter, the Gemara discussed several problems involving two adjacent courtyards each utilized by the residents of the other. The fundamental question is whether, under what circumstances, and in what manner they are considered one courtyard rather than two. This inquiry is pursued from a different perspective in this chapter, specifically with regard to determining the status of the area between the courtyards. The Gemara analyzes the requisite conditions for a partition between two courtyards to be considered as a barrier that separates them, as opposed to the circumstances under which the partition is considered nonexistent. In general, what types of partitions effectively divide courtyards?

There are, of course, some unambiguous cases, e.g., a tall, sealed partition between two domains, which is a clear, conspicuous barrier, or, in contrast, a flimsy, easily dismantled partition. However, there are many intermediate cases, each of which requires elucidation and analysis. Under what circumstances is the partition negated despite the fact that its remnants, or some indication that there was a partition, are still extant? What is the ruling of an intact partition that enables passage between the courtyards via an entrance, a window, or a ladder? Does an entrance of this kind negate the barrier, rendering the two courtyards a single unit in every sense, or do they retain the status of two courtyards?

These clarifications relate mainly to courtyards and houses for which an *eiruv* was established; however, it is also necessary to analyze the details of the practical factors of the merging of courtyards that open into a common alleyway. How is the placement of the meal common to the residents of the courtyards, which, for all intents and purposes, is the essence of the *eiruv*, accomplished? This question refers both to the amount of food as well as the type of food required. Another issue is the manner in which an *eiruv* is acquired. Must it always be acquired in the same manner, with each partner to the *eiruv* contributing a certain amount of actual food, after which all the food is collected as a shared meal, or are there ways to simplify the process, by allowing for partial funding of the meal, or by appointing an agent to acquire it on one's behalf? These issues are the primary focus of this chapter.

Courtyard surrounded by various types of partitions. The barrier on the right is a ditch, on the left are piles of straw, and on the third side of the courtyard there is a wall with a window.

מתני׳ חַלּוֹן שֶׁבֵּין שְׁתֵּי חֲצֵירוֹת, אַרְבָּעָה עַל אַרְבָּעָה בְּתוֹךְ עֲשָׂרָה – מְעָרְבִין שְׁנַיִם. וְאִם רָצוּ – מְעָרְבִין אֶחָד.

MISHNA If there is **a window** in a wall that separates **between two courtyards,**[H] and the window measures **four by four** handbreadths and is **within ten** handbreadths of the ground, the inhabitants of the courtyards **establish two *eiruvin*,** one for each courtyard. **And if they desire, they** may **establish one *eiruv*,** thereby merging the two courtyards, as they may be considered as one due to the window.

פָּחוֹת מֵאַרְבָּעָה עַל אַרְבָּעָה, אוֹ לְמַעְלָה מֵעֲשָׂרָה – מְעָרְבִין שְׁנַיִם וְאֵין מְעָרְבִין אֶחָד.

However, if the window measures **less than four by four** handbreadths, or if it is **above ten** handbreadths from the ground, it is no longer considered a valid opening, and the two courtyards cannot be considered a single courtyard. Therefore, the residents **establish two *eiruvin*, but they** may **not establish one *eiruv*.**

גמ׳ לֵימָא תְּנַן סְתָמָא כְּרַבָּן שִׁמְעוֹן בֶּן גַּמְלִיאֵל, דְּאָמַר: כֹּל פָּחוֹת מֵאַרְבָּעָה כְּלָבוּד דָּמֵי!

GEMARA With regard to the mishna's determination that the size of the window must be four by four handbreadths, the Gemara asks: **Let us say** that **we learned** an **unattributed** mishna **in accordance with** the previously cited opinion of **Rabban Shimon ben Gamliel, who said: Any** gap **less than four** handbreadths **is considered *lavud*,** i.e., two objects are considered connected if the space between them is less than four handbreadths. That would explain why the window must be four handbreadths in size, as otherwise it would be considered as though it were sealed, based on the principle of *lavud*.

אֲפִילּוּ תֵּימָא כְּרַבָּנַן. עַד כָּאן לָא פְּלִיגִי רַבָּנַן עֲלֵיהּ דְּרַבָּן שִׁמְעוֹן בֶּן גַּמְלִיאֵל – אֶלָּא לְעִנְיַן לְבוּדִין, אֲבָל לְעִנְיַן פִּתְחָא – אֲפִילּוּ רַבָּנַן מוֹדוּ, דְּאִי אִיכָּא אַרְבָּעָה עַל אַרְבָּעָה– חֲשִׁיב, וְאִי לָא – לָא חֲשִׁיב.

The Gemara rejects this suggestion: **Even if you say** that the mishna is **in accordance with** the opinion of **the Rabbis** that only gaps of less than three handbreadths are included in the principle of *lavud*, **the Rabbis disagreed with Rabban Shimon ben Gamliel only with regard to** the *halakhot* of *lavud*, i.e., what is considered connected. **But with regard to an opening, even the Rabbis agree that if there is** an opening of **four by four** handbreadths, it is **significant, and if not, it is not significant.**

״פָּחוֹת מֵאַרְבָּעָה וכו׳״. פְּשִׁיטָא! כֵּיוָן דְּאָמַר אַרְבָּעָה עַל אַרְבָּעָה בְּתוֹךְ עֲשָׂרָה – מִמֵּילָא אֲנָא יָדַעְנָא דְּפָחוֹת מֵאַרְבָּעָה וּלְמַעְלָה מֵעֲשָׂרָה לֹא!

It was taught in the mishna: If the window is **less than four** by four handbreadths, or above ten handbreadths from the ground, the residents of each courtyard must establish a separate *eiruv*. The Gemara objects: **This** is **obvious. Since** the mishna **stated** in the previous clause that if the window is **four by four** handbreadths and **within ten** handbreadths from the ground, they establish one *eiruv*, **from this** *halakha* **itself I know**[N] that if the window is **less than four** by four handbreadths **or above ten** handbreadths, they may **not** establish one *eiruv*. Why was it necessary to teach this in the mishna?

הָא קָא מַשְׁמַע לָן: טַעְמָא דְּכוּלֵּיהּ לְמַעְלָה מֵעֲשָׂרָה, אֲבָל מִקְצָתוֹ בְּתוֹךְ עֲשָׂרָה – מְעָרְבִין שְׁנַיִם. וְאִם רָצוּ – מְעָרְבִין אֶחָד.

The Gemara answers: It **teaches us this** matter: **The reason** is specifically that **the entire** window is **above ten** handbreadths; **however,** if **part of it is within ten** handbreadths of the ground, **they establish two *eiruvin*, and if they desire, they** may **establish one *eiruv*.**

תָּנֵינָא לְהָא, דְּתָנוּ רַבָּנַן: כּוּלּוֹ לְמַעְלָה מֵעֲשָׂרָה וּמִקְצָתוֹ בְּתוֹךְ עֲשָׂרָה, כּוּלּוֹ בְּתוֹךְ עֲשָׂרָה וּמִקְצָתוֹ לְמַעְלָה מֵעֲשָׂרָה – מְעָרְבִין שְׁנַיִם. וְאִם רָצוּ – מְעָרְבִין אֶחָד.

The Gemara comments: According to this explanation, **we** already **learned** in the mishna **that** which **the Sages taught** in a *baraita*: If nearly **all of** the window **is above ten** handbreadths **and** only a small **part of it is within ten** handbreadths, or if nearly **all of it is within ten** handbreadths **and** only a small **part of it is above ten** handbreadths, **they establish two *eiruvin*, and if they desire, they** may **establish one *eiruv*.**

הָשְׁתָּא כּוּלּוֹ לְמַעְלָה מֵעֲשָׂרָה וּמִקְצָתוֹ בְּתוֹךְ עֲשָׂרָה אָמְרַתְּ ״מְעָרְבִין שְׁנַיִם וְאִם רָצוּ מְעָרְבִין אֶחָד״ כּוּלּוֹ בְּתוֹךְ עֲשָׂרָה וּמִקְצָתוֹ לְמַעְלָה מֵעֲשָׂרָה מִיבַּעְיָא?!

The essential meaning of this *baraita* is clear, but the Gemara raises a question with regard to its formulation: **Now,** if nearly **all of it is above ten** handbreadths **and** only a small **part of it is within ten** handbreadths, **you said** that **they establish two *eiruvin*, and if they desire, they** may **establish one *eiruv*,** i.e., the window has the status of an opening and therefore the two courtyards may establish a joint *eiruv*, then **is it necessary** to state the *halakha* governing the case where almost **all of it is within ten and** only a small **part of it is above ten?**

HALAKHA

A window between two courtyards – חַלּוֹן שֶׁבֵּין שְׁתֵּי חֲצֵירוֹת: If a window in a wall that separates two courtyards is four by four handbreadths, and at least part of the window is within ten handbreadths of the ground, the two courtyards may establish one *eiruv*. If the window does not meet these criteria, then the residents of each courtyard must establish their own *eiruv* (*Shulḥan Arukh, Oraḥ Ḥayyim* 372:4).

NOTES

From this *halakha* itself I know – מִמֵּילָא אֲנָא יָדַעְנָא: The commentaries note that this is an unusual question, as the Gemara does not generally inquire why something that could have been deduced by implication was taught explicitly. However, in this context, the question is uniquely relevant: The notion that a window above ten handbreadths can serve the purpose of an *eiruv* is unacceptable, since even if an entire wall were no higher than ten handbreadths, as Rashi explains, it would be considered a partition. The single window it contains is certainly insignificant, and therefore the Gemara saw fit to raise the question (Maharsha).

NOTES

A circular window must have a circumference of twenty-four – חַלּוֹן עָגוֹל צָרִיךְ שֶׁיְּהֵא בְּהֶיקֵּפוֹ עֶשְׂרִים וְאַרְבָּעָה: The Gemara below completely rejects Rabbi Yoḥanan's opinion as based on mistaken assumptions; nevertheless, there have been various attempts to explain it. Some suggest that Rabbi Yoḥanan was aware that his measurement was inexact, but because it is easy to err in this regard, he added to the amount so that the window will comfortably include the measure of four handbreadths (*Ge'on Ya'akov*).

זו וְאֵין צָרִיךְ לוֹמַר זוֹ קָתָנֵי.

The Gemara answers that indeed, this *baraita* **teaches** employing the style: **This, and it is unnecessary to say that,** moving from the more difficult and novel case to the easier, more straightforward one.

אָמַר רַבִּי יוֹחָנָן: חַלּוֹן עָגוֹל צָרִיךְ שֶׁיְּהֵא בְּהֶיקֵּפוֹ עֶשְׂרִים וְאַרְבָּעָה טְפָחִים, וּשְׁנַיִם וּמַשֶּׁהוּ מֵהֶן בְּתוֹךְ עֲשָׂרָה, שֶׁאִם יְרַבְּעֶנּוּ נִמְצָא מַשֶּׁהוּ בְּתוֹךְ עֲשָׂרָה.

Rabbi Yoḥanan said: A circular window must have a circumference of twenty-four[N] **handbreadths, with two and a bit of them within ten** handbreadths of the ground, **so that when he squares** the window, i.e., if he forms the shape of a square inside it, it measures four by four handbreadths, and **a bit of it is then within ten** handbreadths of the ground.

מִכְּדֵי כֹּל שֶׁיֵּשׁ בְּהֶיקֵּפוֹ שְׁלֹשָׁה טְפָחִים – יֵשׁ בּוֹ בְּרוֹחְבּוֹ טֶפַח, בִּתְרֵיסַר סַגְיָא!

The Gemara poses a question with regard to this calculation: **Now, since** there is a general principle that **any** circle **with a circumference of three handbreadths is one handbreadth in diameter,** then according to this formula, a window with a circumference **of twelve** handbreadths, meaning that it has a diameter of four handbreadths, should be **sufficient** to create a window of four by four.

BACKGROUND

A circle and a square – עִיגּוּל וְרִיבּוּעַ: This diagram presents *Tosafot*'s proof that the area of a square circumscribed by a circle is exactly half of the area of a square circumscribing a circle. The four small squares formed by the lines within the circle demonstrate that the inner square is comprised of four triangles, each of which measures half a small square.

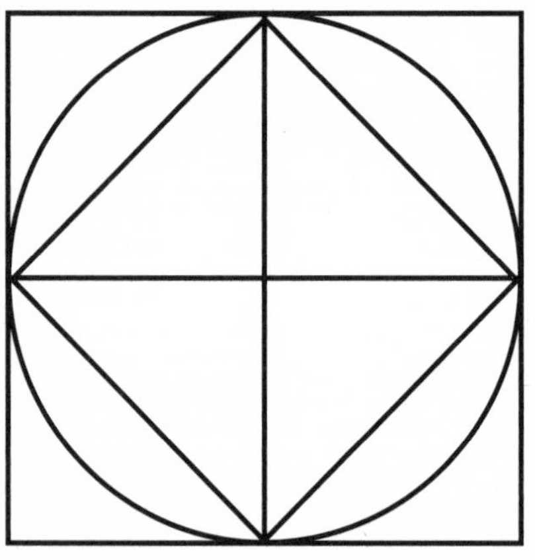

Ratio between a square circumscribed by a circle and a square circumscribing the same circle

הָנֵי מִילֵּי – בְּעִיגּוּלָא, אֲבָל בְּרִיבּוּעָא בָּעֵינַן טְפֵי.

This measurement **applies** only **to a circle** and the ratio between its circumference and diameter, **but with regard to a square** that must fit entirely within that circle, **we require** a circle with a **larger** circumference. In order for a square of four by four handbreadths to be entirely contained within a circle, the circumference of the circle must measure more than twelve handbreadths

מִכְּדֵי, כַּמָּה מְרוּבָּע יָתֵר עַל הָעִגּוּל – רְבִיעַ, בְּשִׁיתְּסַר סַגְיָא!

The Gemara asks: **Now, how much larger is a square than a circle?** It is larger by **one quarter.** If so, a circle **with** a circumference of **sixteen** handbreadths at most should **suffice.**

הָנֵי מִילֵּי – עִיגּוּלָא דְּנָפֵיק מִגּוֹ רִיבּוּעָא, אֲבָל רִיבּוּעָא דְּנָפֵיק מִגּוֹ עִיגּוּלָא – בָּעֵינַן טְפֵי. מַאי טַעְמָא – מִשּׁוּם מוֹרְשָׁא דְּקַרְנָתָא.

The Gemara answers: **This** statement that a square is larger than a circle by a quarter **applies** only **to a circle circumscribed by a square, but** with regard to **a square circumscribed by a circle,**[B] **we require more,** and the difference between the square and the circle is greater. **What is the reason** for this? It is **due to the projection of the corners** of the square, as the distance from the center of the square to its corners is greater than the distance from the center to its sides.

מִכְּדֵי, כָּל אַמְּתָא בְּרִיבּוּעַ אַמְּתָא וּתְרֵי חוּמְשֵׁי בַּאֲלַכְסוֹנָא, בְּשִׁיבְסַר נְכֵי חוּמְשָׁא סַגְיָא!

The Gemara further objects: **Since every cubit in** the side of **a square** is **a cubit and two-fifths in the diagonal,** a square of four by four handbreadths has a diagonal of five and three-fifths handbreadths. And since the diameter of a circle equals the diagonal of the square that it encompasses, the circle circumscribing a square of four by four handbreadths has a diameter of five and three-fifths handbreadths. If that measure is multiplied by three to arrive at the circumference of that circle, the result is that a circle with a circumference of **seventeen handbreadths minus a fifth is sufficient** to circumscribe a square of four by four handbreadths. Why, then, does Rabbi Yoḥanan say that a circular window[H] must have a circumference of twenty-four handbreadths?

HALAKHA

A circular window – חַלּוֹן עָגוֹל: If a circular window between two courtyards is large enough to circumscribe a square four by four handbreadths in size, and part of the window is within ten handbreadths of the ground, the two courtyards may establish one *eiruv*. The circumference of such a window is roughly sixteen and four-fifths handbreadths (Rambam *Sefer Zemanim*, *Hilkhot Eiruvin* 3:2).

רַבִּי יוֹחָנָן אָמַר כִּי דַּיָּינֵי דְּקֵיסָרִי, וְאָמְרִי לַהּ כְּרַבָּנַן דְּקֵיסָרִי, דְּאָמְרִי: עִיגּוּלָא מִגּוֹ רִיבּוּעָא – רִיבְעָא, רִיבּוּעָא מִגּוֹ עִיגּוּלָא – פַּלְגָא.

The Gemara answers: **Rabbi Yoḥanan spoke in accordance with** the opinion of **the judges of Caesarea,**[N] **and some say in accordance with** the opinion of **the Sages of Caesarea, who say: A circle** that is circumscribed **within a square** is smaller than it by **one quarter;** with regard to **a square** that is circumscribed **within a circle,** the difference between them is equal to **half** the square. According to this explanation, Rabbi Yoḥanan calculated as follows: Since a square of four by four handbreadths has a perimeter of sixteen handbreadths, the circumference of the circle that encompasses it must be fifty percent larger, or twenty-four handbreadths.

"פָּחוֹת מֵאַרְבָּעָה עַל אַרְבָּעָה וכו׳". אָמַר רַב נַחְמָן: לֹא שָׁנוּ אֶלָּא חַלּוֹן שֶׁבֵּין שְׁתֵּי חֲצֵירוֹת, אֲבָל חַלּוֹן שֶׁבֵּין שְׁנֵי בָתִּים – אֲפִילּוּ לְמַעְלָה מֵעֲשָׂרָה נָמֵי, אִם רָצוּ לְעָרֵב – מְעָרְבִין אֶחָד. מַאי טַעְמָא – בֵּיתָא כְּמַאן דְּמָלֵי דָּמֵי.

It was taught in the mishna: If a window is **less than four by four** handbreadths, or if it is above ten handbreadths from the ground, the residents of the two courtyards may not establish one joint *eiruv* but must instead establish two independent ones. **Rav Naḥman said: They taught** this *halakha* of a window within ten handbreadths of the ground **only** with regard to **a window between two courtyards. But** with regard to **a window between two houses,**[H] **even** if it is **above ten** handbreadths **as well, if they wish to establish an *eiruv*, they establish one *eiruv*. What is the reason** for this *halakha*? It is that **a house is considered as though it** were **filled,**[N] and therefore there is no difference between below and above ten handbreadths with regard to a window in a house.

אֵיתִיבֵיהּ רָבָא לְרַב נַחְמָן: אֶחָד לִי חַלּוֹן שֶׁבֵּין שְׁתֵּי חֲצֵירוֹת, וְאֶחָד לִי חַלּוֹן שֶׁבֵּין שְׁנֵי בָתִּים, וְאֶחָד לִי חַלּוֹן שֶׁבֵּין שְׁתֵּי עֲלִיּוֹת, וְאֶחָד לִי חַלּוֹן שֶׁבֵּין שְׁנֵי גַּגִּין, וְאֶחָד לִי חַלּוֹן שֶׁבֵּין שְׁנֵי חֲדָרִים – כּוּלָּן אַרְבָּעָה עַל אַרְבָּעָה בְּתוֹךְ עֲשָׂרָה!

Rava raised an objection to the opinion of **Rav Naḥman** from that which was taught in a *baraita*: **A window between two courtyards, and a window between two houses, and a window between two attics, and a window between two roofs, and a window between two rooms are all one and the same to me; they all** must be **four by four** handbreadths and **within ten** handbreadths from the ground. This directly contradicts Rav Naḥman's opinion.

HALAKHA

A window between two houses – **חַלּוֹן שֶׁבֵּין שְׁנֵי בָתִּים**: If a window between two houses is four by four handbreadths in size, the residents of the two houses may establish one *eiruv*, even if the window is higher than ten handbreadths from the ground (*Shulḥan Arukh*, *Oraḥ Ḥayyim* 372:5).

NOTES

A house is considered as though it were filled – **בֵּיתָא כְּמַאן דְּמָלֵי**: The presence of chairs and benches in a house always makes it possible to put them against a wall and access even a high window from inside the house. Although it is more difficult to reach an opening in the middle of a house, it is nevertheless possible, which explains the discussion in the Gemara with regard to an opening in the ceiling of one home that is in the floor of the home above (Rabbeinu Yehonatan; *Me'iri*).

NOTES

The opinion of Rabbi Yoḥanan and the judges of Caesarea – **שִׁיטַת רַבִּי יוֹחָנָן וְדַיָּינֵי דְּקֵיסָרִי**: All the commentaries struggle to explain this opinion, which seems entirely inaccurate. A wide variety of answers has been offered. *Tosafot*, following the *ge'onim*, attempt to explain the opinion of the judges of Caesarea, but they are unable to account for Rabbi Yoḥanan's statement, which, according to their understanding is even more puzzling. The Ra'avad suggests that the judges of Caesarea and Rabbi Yoḥanan knew that in truth the ratios cited by the Gemara are inaccurate, and that the precise measurements are larger: The ratio is not 1:4, but roughly 1:4.14, and approximately 1:3.1413 rather than 1:3. Indeed, according to this, a square window four handbreadths wide requires a circle of more than seventeen and a half handbreadths in circumference to encompass it, which is why they added to the measure to reach the correct amount. However, this too has been challenged, as it was unnecessary to increase the circumference to such an extent. Rashba and Ritva explain that the judges of Caesarea calculated according to this shape:

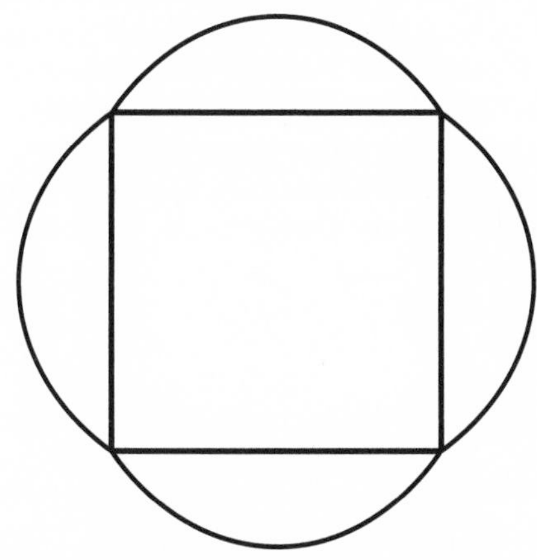

Calculation of the judges of Caesarea according to the Rashba

However, the Rashba maintains that they erred by calculating the circumference of the circle according to this approximation. According to the Ritva, from the outset Rabbi Yoḥanan's statement referred to a window of such a shape. In the comment of the *Baḥ* on the Rif it is explained that Rabbi Yoḥanan intended that the window should be a particular shape, a square within a square, as depicted here:

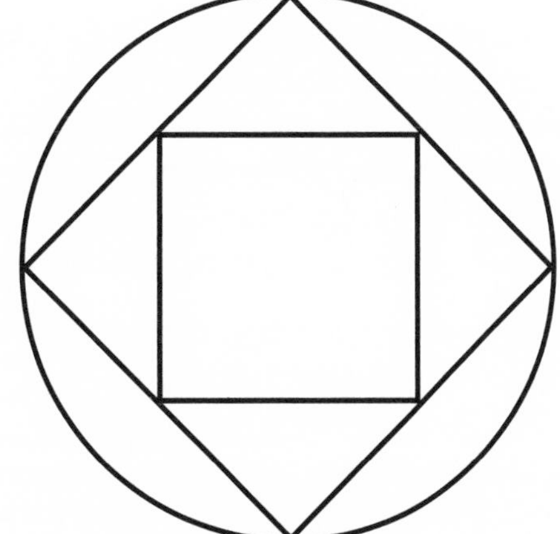

Rabbi Yoḥanan's opinion according to *Baḥ*

In that case, the calculation is correct, based on the formula of the Sages: For its area to be four by four handbreadths, its circumference must measure twenty-four handbreadths. Some commentaries explain the statements of both the judges of Caesarea and Rabbi Yoḥanan with regard to the areas of the circle and the square as follows: Only within a circle whose area is twenty-four square handbreadths can one insert a window of four by four, which is correct according to the formula of the Sages (Rabbi Neḥemya Beirakh).

תַּרְגּוּמָא אַחֲצֵירוֹת. וְהָא "אֶחָד לִי" קָתָנֵי! תַּרְגּוּמָא אַאַרְבָּעָה עַל אַרְבָּעָה.

The Gemara answers: **Explain** that this *halakha* of ten handbreadths mentioned in the *baraita* is referring only to **courtyards.** The Gemara objects: **Doesn't** the *baraita* **teach: Are all one and the same to me,** indicating that they are all equal in this regard? Rather, **explain** that they are all equal in that the window must be the size of **four by four** handbreadths, but not that all must be within ten handbreadths of the ground.

בְּעָא מִינֵּיהּ רַבִּי אַבָּא מֵרַב נַחְמָן: לוּל הַפָּתוּחַ מִן בַּיִת לַעֲלִיָּיה, צָרִיךְ סוּלָּם קָבוּעַ לְהַתִּירוֹ, אוֹ אֵין צָרִיךְ סוּלָּם קָבוּעַ לְהַתִּירוֹ?

Rabbi Abba raised a dilemma before Rav Naḥman: With regard to **an aperture that opens from** the ceiling of **a house** occupied by one person **to an attic** occupied by another,[H] **must a permanent ladder** be positioned in the opening **to render** carrying from one level to the other **permitted** by turning the two into a single residence? **Or, is a permanent ladder not necessary to render it permitted?**

כִּי אָמְרִינַן בֵּיתָא כְּמַאן דְּמָלֵי דָּמֵי – הָנֵי מִילֵּי מִן הַצַּד, אֲבָל בָּאֶמְצַע – לֹא. אוֹ דִּילְמָא לָא שְׁנָא?

The Gemara clarifies the two sides of the question: **When we say** that **a house is considered as though it** were **filled,** does **this apply** only to a window positioned **on the side, but not** to a window **in the middle?** In that case, the opening would not be viewed as near the full part of the house, and a permanent ladder would be required. **Or perhaps there is no difference,** and since the house is considered filled, no ladder is necessary.

אֲמַר לֵיהּ: אֵינוֹ צָרִיךְ. סָבוּר מִינָּהּ: סוּלָּם קָבוּעַ הוּא דְּאֵינוֹ צָרִיךְ, הָא סוּלָּם עֲרַאי – צָרִיךְ. אִיתְּמַר, אָמַר רַב יוֹסֵף בַּר מַנְיוּמִי, אָמַר רַב נַחְמָן: אֶחָד סוּלָּם קָבוּעַ וְאֶחָד סוּלָּם עֲרַאי – אֵינוֹ צָרִיךְ.

Rav Naḥman **said to him: It is not necessary.** The Sages **understood from** this response that he meant that **a permanent ladder is not required, but a temporary ladder is required.** However, **it is stated** in this regard: **Rav Yosef bar Manyumi said** that **Rav Naḥman said: Neither a permanent ladder nor a temporary ladder is required,** as the fact that the opening is located within the house is sufficient to render it permitted to carry from the house to the attic.

מתני׳ כּוֹתֶל שֶׁבֵּין שְׁתֵּי חֲצֵירוֹת, גָּבוֹהַּ עֲשָׂרָה וְרוֹחַב אַרְבָּעָה – מְעָרְבִין שְׁנַיִם, וְאֵין מְעָרְבִין אֶחָד.

MISHNA If **a wall between two courtyards**[H] **is ten** handbreadths **high and four** handbreadths **wide,** the residents of the courtyard **establish two *eiruvin*,** a separate one for each courtyard, **but they** may **not establish one *eiruv*.**

הָיוּ בְּרֹאשׁוֹ פֵּירוֹת – אֵלּוּ עוֹלִין מִכָּאן וְאוֹכְלִין, וְאֵלּוּ עוֹלִין מִכָּאן וְאוֹכְלִין, וּבִלְבַד שֶׁלֹּא יוֹרִידוּ לְמַטָּן.

If there was produce on top of the wall, **these** residents of one courtyard **may ascend from this side and eat** from it, **and those** residents of the other courtyard **may ascend from that side and eat** from it, **provided that they do not lower** the produce **down** from on top of the wall to one of the courtyards.

נִפְרְצָה הַכּוֹתֶל, עַד עֶשֶׂר אַמּוֹת – מְעָרְבִין שְׁנַיִם, וְאִם רָצוּ – מְעָרְבִין אֶחָד, מִפְּנֵי שֶׁהוּא כְּפֶתַח. יוֹתֵר מִכָּאן – מְעָרְבִין אֶחָד, וְאֵין מְעָרְבִין שְׁנַיִם.

If the wall was breached,[H] the following distinction applies: If the breach was **up to ten cubits** wide, **they establish two *eiruvin*, and if they desire, they** may **establish one *eiruv*, as it is similar to an entrance,** like any opening less than ten cubits wide. If the breach was **more than this, they establish one *eiruv*, and they** may **not establish two,** as a breach of this size nullifies the partition and joins the two courtyards into a single domain.

גמ׳ אֵין בּוֹ אַרְבָּעָה מַאי? אָמַר רַב: אֲוִיר שְׁתֵּי רְשׁוּיוֹת שׁוֹלֶטֶת בּוֹ, לֹא יָזִיז בּוֹ אֲפִילּוּ מְלֹא נִימָא.

GEMARA The Gemara asks: If this wall **is not four** handbreadths in width, **what** is the *halakha*? **Rav said:** In this case, **the air of two domains controls it.** Since the wall is not broad enough to be regarded a domain of its own, the top of the wall is seen as belonging to both courtyards and is then prohibited to both of them. Accordingly, **one may not move** anything **on** top of the wall, **even as much as a hair's breadth.**[N]

HALAKHA

An aperture between a house and an attic – לוּל בֵּין בַּיִת וַעֲלִיָּיה: If there is an aperture between a home on the first floor and a home on the second floor that is four by four handbreadths in size, even if there is no ladder, permanent or temporary, between the first floor and the second floor, the residents of the two floors may establish one *eiruv*, in accordance with the opinion of Rav Naḥman (*Shulḥan Arukh*, *Oraḥ Ḥayyim* 372:5).

A wall between two courtyards – כּוֹתֶל שֶׁבֵּין שְׁתֵּי חֲצֵירוֹת: If a wall ten handbreadths high and four handbreadths wide separates two courtyards, the residents of both courtyards must each establish their own *eiruv* (*Shulḥan Arukh*, *Oraḥ Ḥayyim* 372:6).

If the wall was breached – נִפְרְצָה הַכּוֹתֶל: If a wall between courtyards was breached and the breach is larger than ten cubits wide, then the two courtyards are considered a single courtyard, and their respective residents must establish a joint *eiruv*. However, if the breach is less than ten cubits wide and neither courtyard was fully breached into the other (Rabbeinu Yehonatan), the breach is considered an entrance, and the residents of the two courtyards may choose to establish an independent *eiruv* for each area, or one *eiruv* together (*Shulḥan Arukh*, *Oraḥ Ḥayyim* 372:7).

NOTES

One may not move anything on top of the wall, even as much as a hair's breadth – לֹא יָזִיז בּוֹ אֲפִילּוּ מְלֹא נִימָא: This is ostensibly more stringent than the prohibition against moving something in the public domain, which is a Torah law (see Rashi). However, since here each and every handbreadth of the wall is part of two different domains, even the slightest movement of an object is regarded as carrying it from one domain to another. Therefore, it is prohibited to move an object even by a hair's breadth, and one who does so is liable (Rabbeinu Yehonatan).

וְרַבִּי יוֹחָנָן אָמַר: אֵלּוּ מַעֲלִין מִכָּאן וְאוֹכְלִין, וְאֵלּוּ מַעֲלִין מִכָּאן וְאוֹכְלִין.

And Rabbi Yoḥanan said: These residents of one courtyard **may raise** food **from** their courtyard to the top of the wall **and eat** it there, and they may lower the food from the wall to the courtyard; **and those** residents of the other courtyard **may raise** food **from** their courtyard **and eat** it there, and they may lower the food from the wall to the courtyard. This is because the wall is considered nonexistent, and its domain is viewed as part of the two courtyards.

תְּנַן: אֵלּוּ עוֹלִין מִכָּאן וְאוֹכְלִין, וְאֵלּוּ עוֹלִין מִכָּאן וְאוֹכְלִין. עוֹלִין – אִין, מַעֲלִין – לָא!

We learned in the mishna: If there was produce on top of the wall, **these** residents of one courtyard **may ascend from this side and eat** from it, **and those** residents of the other courtyard **may ascend from that side and eat** from it. The Gemara infers from this: To **ascend, yes,** it is permitted, but to **raise** food from the courtyard to the top of the wall, **no,** it is not permitted. This presents a challenge to Rabbi Yoḥanan's opinion.

הָכִי קָאָמַר: יֵשׁ בּוֹ אַרְבָּעָה עַל אַרְבָּעָה, עוֹלִין – אִין, מַעֲלִין – לָא. אֵין בּוֹ אַרְבָּעָה עַל אַרְבָּעָה – מַעֲלִין נַמִי.

The Gemara answers that **this is what** the mishna **is saying:** If the top of the wall between the two courtyards **is four by four** handbreadths, then to **ascend, yes,** it is permitted. However, to **raise** food, **no,** it is prohibited, because in that case the top of the wall is considered a domain in its own right. But if **it is not four by four** handbreadths, it is an exempt domain, and therefore **they may raise** their food onto the wall **as well.**[H]

וְאָזְדָא רַבִּי יוֹחָנָן לְטַעְמֵיהּ, דִּכִי אֲתָא רַב דִּימִי, אָמַר רַבִּי יוֹחָנָן: מָקוֹם שֶׁאֵין בּוֹ אַרְבָּעָה עַל אַרְבָּעָה – מוּתָּר לִבְנֵי רְשׁוּת הָרַבִּים וְלִבְנֵי רְשׁוּת הַיָּחִיד לְכַתֵּף עָלָיו, וּבִלְבַד שֶׁלֹּא יַחֲלִיפוּ.

And Rabbi Yoḥanan followed his line of **reasoning** in this regard, **as when Rav Dimi came** from Eretz Yisrael to Babylonia, he said that **Rabbi Yoḥanan said:** With regard to **a place that does not have** an area of **four by four** handbreadths and is situated between a public and a private domain, **it is permissible for** both **the people in the public domain and for the people in the private domain to** adjust the burden on their **shoulders upon it, provided they do not exchange** objects between them from one domain to the other domain. This demonstrates that in the case of an exempt domain, Rabbi Yoḥanan was not concerned that one might carry from one domain to another, and permitted members of both domains to use it.

וְרַב לֵית לֵיהּ דְּרַב דִּימִי?! אִי בִּרְשׁוּיוֹת דְּאוֹרַיְיתָא – הָכִי נַמִי.

The Gemara asks: **And** does **Rav,** who prohibits carrying in that case even as much as a hair's breadth, **not accept** the opinion **of Rav Dimi** in this matter? The Gemara answers: **If** this referred **to** an exempt domain situated between two **domains by Torah law,** i.e., between a public and a private domain, **so too,** Rav would agree that the members of both domains may adjust their burdens there.

הָכָא בְּמַאי עָסְקִינַן – בִּרְשׁוּיוֹת דְּרַבָּנַן, וַחֲכָמִים עָשׂוּ חִיזּוּק לְדִבְרֵיהֶם יוֹתֵר מִשֶּׁל תּוֹרָה.

However, **with what are we dealing here,** in the case of the wall? We are dealing **with domains by rabbinic law, and the Sages reinforced their statements**[HN] even **more than those of the Torah.** Due to their severity, Torah laws are generally observed. Therefore, there is no need to impose decrees and enactments in order to preserve them. The same is not true of rabbinic decrees; if people ignore the preventive measures, they might come to violate the entire enactment.

אָמַר רַבָּה, (אָמַר) רַב הוּנָא, אָמַר רַב נַחְמָן: כּוֹתֶל שֶׁבֵּין שְׁתֵּי חֲצֵירוֹת, צִידּוֹ אֶחָד גָּבוֹהַּ עֲשָׂרָה טְפָחִים וְצִידּוֹ אֶחָד שָׁוֶה לָאָרֶץ – נוֹתְנִין אוֹתוֹ לָזֶה שֶׁשָּׁוֶה לָאָרֶץ,

Rabba said that **Rav Huna said** that **Rav Naḥman said:** With regard to **a wall that is between two courtyards,** and **one side** facing one courtyard is **ten handbreadths high, and the other side is level with the ground** of the second courtyard,[HB] i.e., the second courtyard is built on a higher plane, so that the wall is less than ten handbreadths above its floor, in this case the Sages **grant** the use of the top of the wall on Shabbat only **to the** courtyard in which the wall is **level with the ground.**

מִשּׁוּם דְּהָוֵה לָזֶה תַּשְׁמִישׁוֹ בְּנַחַת וְלָזֶה תַּשְׁמִישׁוֹ בְּקָשֶׁה, וְכׇל לָזֶה בְּנַחַת וְלָזֶה בְּקָשֶׁה – נוֹתְנִין אוֹתוֹ לָזֶה שֶׁתַּשְׁמִישׁוֹ בְּנַחַת.

The reason is **because the use of** the wall **is convenient for one** side, i.e., the higher courtyard, **but difficult for the other** side. The wall can be used more conveniently by the residents of the higher courtyard. **And** the principle is that in **any** case with regard to Shabbat where an action is **convenient for one** party **and difficult for another,** the Sages **grant it to the one for whom its use is convenient.**

HALAKHA

A wall between courtyards – כּוֹתֶל שֶׁבֵּין חֲצֵירוֹת: If there is a wall between two courtyards, the residents of both courtyards may carry food to the top of the wall and eat it there, provided that the wall is less than four handbreadths wide. However, if it is four handbreadths wide, they may not bring food there that was in the house when Shabbat began, in accordance with the opinion of Rabbi Yoḥanan (*Shulḥan Arukh, Oraḥ Ḥayyim* 372:6).

Reinforced their statements – עָשׂוּ חִיזּוּק לְדִבְרֵיהֶם: The authorities disagree over whether or not objects may be transferred from one rabbinic domain to another by way of an exempt domain. Some prohibit this based on the Gemara here (Ra'avad; Rabbi Zeraḥya HaLevi; Rashba; Rosh). However, others permit it, asserting that there is no need to differentiate between the *halakhot* of the Torah and those of the Sages, and a decree is not issued to prevent the violation of another decree (Rif; Rambam; *Shulḥan Arukh, Oraḥ Ḥayyim* 346:1).

A wall that is level with the ground on one side – כּוֹתֶל הַשָּׁוֶה לָאָרֶץ בְּצִידּוֹ הָאֶחָד: If a wall four handbreadths wide is ten handbreadths above the ground of the courtyard on one side, but less than ten handbreadths above the ground of the courtyard on the other side (Rashi), the right of use is granted to the residents of the courtyard for which the wall is closer to the ground. Utensils that were in the house at the onset of Shabbat may also be placed on it. If the wall is less than four handbreadths wide, both courtyards may make use of it (*Shulḥan Arukh, Oraḥ Ḥayyim* 372:6).

NOTES

The Sages reinforced their statements – חֲכָמִים עָשׂוּ חִיזּוּק לְדִבְרֵיהֶם: This does not mean that the Sages reinforced their statements to the extent that they are more stringent than those of the Torah itself. Rather, with respect to several of their decrees, they issued more enactments and preventive measures than the Torah requires. Some write that the Sages reinforced their decrees only in matters involving prohibitions, but not in monetary matters. Additionally, they did not reinforce the *halakha* in unusual cases (*Tosafot*).

BACKGROUND

A wall higher on one side – כּוֹתֶל גָּבוֹהַּ מִצַּד אֶחָד: The image below depicts a wall ten handbreadths high on the side facing one courtyard, but almost level with the ground of the adjacent, higher courtyard.

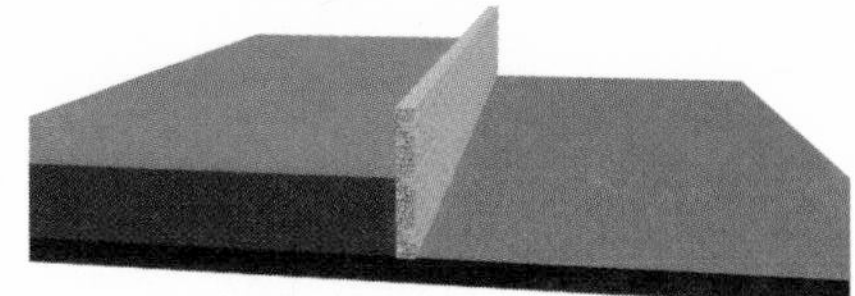

Wall between two courtyards on different levels

BACKGROUND

A ditch between courtyards – חָרִיץ שֶׁבֵּין חֲצֵירוֹת: This illustration demonstrates how a ditch can be ten handbreadths deep in one courtyard, but much shallower with respect to the adjacent, lower courtyard.

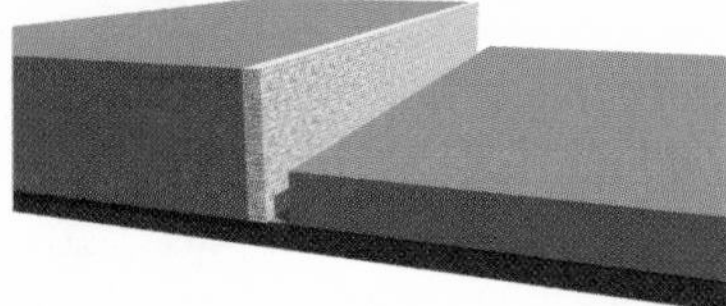

Ditch between courtyards

A basin next to a wall – סֵפֶל סָמוּךְ לְכוֹתֶל:

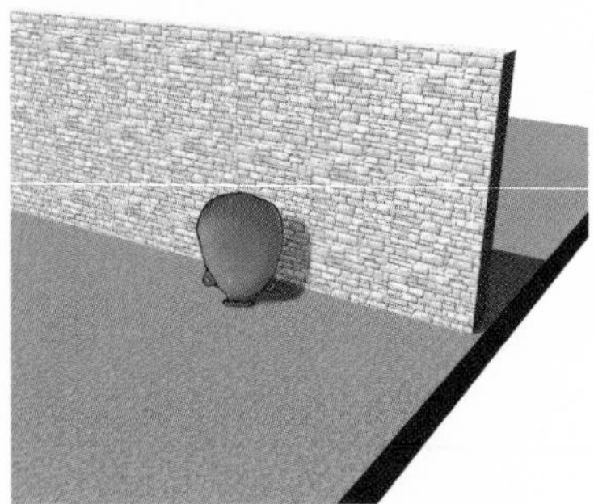

Basin with a rim placed next to a wall in order to diminish the wall's height to less than ten handbreadths

NOTES

If the diminished section is less than four handbreadths wide at the top – מִיעוּט פָּחוֹת מֵאַרְבָּעָה בְּרֹאשׁוֹ: The rationale is that if one diminishes the wall by creating a slightly elevated area at the bottom of the wall, since it is less than four handbreadths wide it is very difficult to use. This is because its purpose is for standing upon, and it is difficult to stand on such a narrow platform. However, when one removes a layer at the top, it is suitable for use, because it is convenient to stand on the ground near the wall (Rashba).

A diminished section fit for use – מִיעוּט שֶׁרָאוּי לְהִשְׁתַּמֵּשׁ בּוֹ: Generally, a place that is mostly breached into a prohibited area is itself prohibited. That is not the case here, because there is a noticeable difference between the section from which the layer has been removed and the rest of the wall. Where such a difference exists, it is not considered fully breached into a prohibited domain (Ritva).

אָמַר רַב שֵׁיזְבִי, אָמַר רַב נַחְמָן: חָרִיץ שֶׁבֵּין שְׁתֵּי חֲצֵירוֹת, צִידּוֹ אֶחָד עָמוֹק עֲשָׂרָה וְצִידּוֹ אֶחָד שָׁוֶה לָאָרֶץ – נוֹתְנִין אוֹתוֹ לָזֶה שֶׁשָּׁוֶה לָאָרֶץ, מִשּׁוּם דַּהֲוָה לֵיהּ לָזֶה תַּשְׁמִישׁוֹ בְּנַחַת וְלָזֶה תַּשְׁמִישׁוֹ בְּקָשֶׁה וכו׳.

Similarly, **Rav Sheizvi said** that **Rav Naḥman said:** In the case of **a ditch between two courtyards,**[BH] **one side of which is ten** handbreadths **deep, and the other side of which is level with the ground** of the second courtyard, i.e., is less than ten handbreadths below it, the Sages **grant** the use of the ditch **to the** courtyard in which the ditch is **level with the ground.** This is **because it is** a case in which **the use of** the ditch **is convenient for one** side, where it is close to level with the ground, **and difficult for the other,** where the ditch is ten handbreadths deep, and whenever use of an item is convenient for one party and inconvenient for another, it is granted to the one for whom it is convenient.

וּצְרִיכִי, דְּאִי אַשְׁמְעִינַן כּוֹתֶל – מִשּׁוּם דִּבְגוֹבְהָא מִשְׁתַּמְּשִׁי אִינָשֵׁי, אֲבָל חָרִיץ – בְּעוּמְקָא לָא מִשְׁתַּמְּשִׁי אִינָשֵׁי, אֵימָא לָא.

The Gemara comments: **And** it was **necessary** to cite both of these cases, as it would not have been possible to learn one from the other, **since, had** Rav Naḥman **taught us** only the case **with regard to a wall,** one could have said that the *halakha* applies only in that case, **because people use an elevated** surface. Even for the residents of the lower courtyard, it is relatively easy to use this wall. **However,** with regard to **a ditch, people do not use a deep** surface, as it is troublesome to bend down and place an item in a ditch. In that case, one might **say** that it may **not** be used by the residents of either courtyard.

וְאִי אַשְׁמְעִינַן בְּחָרִיץ – מִשּׁוּם דְּלָא בְּעִיתָא תַּשְׁמִישְׁתָּא, אֲבָל כּוֹתֶל דִּבְעִיתָא תַּשְׁמִישְׁתָּא – אֵימָא לָא, צְרִיכָא.

And likewise, **had he taught us** only the case **with regard to a ditch,** one could have said that the *halakha* applies only in that case, **because its use does not cause worry,** as anything placed in the ditch is protected. **However,** with regard to **a wall, the use of which causes worry** that the objects placed there are liable to fall, one might **say** that it may **not** be used by the residents of either courtyard. Therefore, it was **necessary** to state both of these rulings.

בָּא לְמַעֲטוֹ, אִם יֵשׁ בְּמִיעוּטוֹ אַרְבָּעָה – מוּתָּר לְהִשְׁתַּמֵּשׁ בְּכָל הַכּוֹתֶל כּוּלּוֹ, וְאִם לָאו – אֵין מִשְׁתַּמֵּשׁ אֶלָּא כְּנֶגֶד הַמִּיעוּט.

With regard to a wall between two courtyards, the Gemara states: If **one comes to diminish** the height of the wall[H] by placing a stone next to it, or by building a platform in order to permit its use or to utilize it as a passageway to another courtyard, the following distinction applies: **If the diminished** section **is** at least **four handbreadths** wide, **it is permitted to use the entire wall.** This area has the status of an entrance and the two courtyards are considered one, which renders the entire wall permitted. **However, if** the diminished section is **not** at least four handbreadths wide, **one** may **use only the** area of the wall **opposite** the **diminished** section, but no more.

מַה נַּפְשָׁךְ? אִי אַהֲנֵי מִיעוּטָא – בְּכוּלֵּיהּ כּוֹתֶל לִישְׁתַּמֵּשׁ, אִי לָא אַהֲנֵי – אֲפִילּוּ כְּנֶגֶד הַמִּיעוּט נָמֵי לָא! אָמַר רָבִינָא: כְּגוֹן שֶׁעָקַר חוּלְיָא מֵרֹאשׁוֹ.

The Gemara challenges this ruling: **Whichever way you** look at it, this ruling is difficult. **If the diminishing was effective, although** it extends less than four handbreadths, **let him use** the entire **wall;** and **if** the diminishing **was not effective, even** the area **corresponding to the diminished** section should **also not** be permitted for use, as this section is insignificant. **Ravina said:** Here, it refers to a case **where one removed a segment** of stone **from the top**[N] of the wall.[H] Since the wall is actually less than ten handbreadths high along that section, it is fit for use as is an opening in the wall.[N]

אָמַר רַב יְחִיאֵל: כָּפָה סֵפֶל – מְמַעֵט.

Rav Yeḥiel said: If **one overturned a basin** and placed it next to a wall,[B] such that the wall is no longer ten handbreadths high, **it** effectively **diminishes** the height of the wall.[H]

HALAKHA

A ditch between two courtyards – חָרִיץ שֶׁבֵּין שְׁתֵּי חֲצֵירוֹת: If a ditch runs between two courtyards, and on one side the ground level of the courtyard is ten handbreadths above the bottom of the ditch, while on the other side the ground level of the courtyard is far less that ten handbreadths above the bottom of the ditch, then the residents of the second courtyard may utilize the ditch, in accordance with the conclusion of the Gemara (Rambam *Sefer Zemanim, Hilkhot Eiruvin* 3:15).

Diminishing the height of a wall – מִיעוּט כּוֹתֶל: The height of a wall between courtyards may be diminished to below ten handbreadths by constructing a platform four handbreadths wide and four handbreadths long. This permits the use of the entire wall. However, the platform is not considered a passageway between the courtyards unless it reaches the top of the wall (*Tosafot*; Rosh; *Shulḥan Arukh, Oraḥ Ḥayyim* 372:9).

One removed a segment from the top of the wall – עָקַר חוּלְיָא מֵרֹאשׁוֹ: If one removes a segment of brick or stone four handbreadths wide from the top of the wall, thereby diminishing its height to less than ten handbreadths, it is considered an opening. The two courtyards may then establish a joining of courtyards. In addition, it is permitted to use the entire wall on Shabbat. If the removed segment is less than four handbreadths wide, only the section of wall where the height was diminished may be used. Even if one did not diminish the height of the wall through its entire thickness, but diminished a section measuring four by four handbreadths, then the residents of the side where the height was diminished may use the entire wall (*Shulḥan Arukh, Oraḥ Ḥayyim* 372:8).

Diminishing the height by means of a basin – מִיעוּט סֵפֶל: If a basin measuring four by four handbreadths is placed next to a wall, thereby diminishing the height of the wall, it is permitted to use the area opposite the diminished section, provided the basin is securely attached to the ground with clay. This ruling is in accordance with the conclusion of the Gemara. Some authorities rule that this section is effective in rendering the entire wall permitted for use, as in the case of a ladder (*Taz*; Vilna Gaon; *Shulḥan Arukh HaRav*; *Shulḥan Arukh, Oraḥ Ḥayyim* 372:10).

וְאַמַּאי? דָּבָר הַנִּיטָּל בְּשַׁבָּת הוּא, וְדָבָר הַנִּיטָּל בְּשַׁבָּת אֵינוֹ מְמַעֵט! לָא צְרִיכָא, דְּחַבְּרֵיהּ בְּאַרְעָא.

The Gemara asks: **And why** should this be so? Isn't this basin **an item that may be moved on Shabbat,** i.e., something that one is permitted to handle? **And** the principle is that **an item that may be moved on Shabbat does not diminish** a wall. Since it can be removed at any moment on Shabbat, such an object cannot be viewed as a permanent part of the wall. The Gemara answers: **No, it is necessary;** this basin can be considered a permanent part of the wall in a case **where he attached** the basin **to the ground** by covering it with soil. The basin may then not be moved on Shabbat due to the prohibition of handling soil.

וְכִי חַבְּרֵיהּ בְּאַרְעָא מַאי הָוֵי? וְהָא תַּנְיָא: פַּגָּה שֶׁהִטְמִינָהּ בְּתֶבֶן, וַחֲרָרָה שֶׁהִטְמִינָהּ בְּגֶחָלִים, אִם מְגוּלָּה מִקְצָתָהּ – נִטֶּלֶת בְּשַׁבָּת!

The Gemara challenges this explanation: **And if one attached** the basin **to the ground, what of it? Wasn't it taught** in a *baraita*: With regard to **an unripe** fig **that one buried in straw** intended for kindling, so that it would ripen, **or a cake that one buried in coals** before Shabbat, and the coals were extinguished, **if part of** either one **is visible, it may be moved on Shabbat.** This is not prohibited, although as a result one will move the straw or the coals, which are set aside.

הָכָא בְּמַאי עָסְקִינַן – דְּאִית לֵיהּ אוֹגְנַיִים.

The Gemara explains: **With what are we dealing here?** We are dealing **with** a case where the top of the basin **has a rim** that is fully buried in the ground, so that removing the basin will dislodge the earth under which it is buried in a manner similar to digging, which is prohibited on Shabbat.

וְכִי אִית לֵיהּ אוֹגְנַיִים מַאי הָוֵי? וְהָתְנַן: הַטּוֹמֵן לֶפֶת וּצְנוֹן תַּחַת הַגֶּפֶן, בִּזְמַן

The Gemara further challenges this explanation: **And if** the basin **has a rim, what of it? Didn't we learn** in a mishna: With regard to **one who buries a turnip**[N] **or a radish** in the ground **beneath a vine** for safekeeping, **when**

NOTES

One who buries a turnip – הַטּוֹמֵן לֶפֶת: In the Jerusalem Talmud it is explained that this refers to whole bundles of turnips. In that case, hiding them in soil is not considered sowing, nor does it resemble sowing. Therefore, there is no concern in that regard.

Perek **VII**
Daf **77** Amud **b**

שֶׁמִּקְצָת עָלָיו מְגוּלִּין – אֵינוֹ חוֹשֵׁשׁ לֹא מִשּׁוּם כִּלְאַיִם וְלֹא מִשּׁוּם מַעֲשֵׂר, וְלֹא מִשּׁוּם שְׁבִיעִית, וְנִיטָּלִין בְּשַׁבָּת.

some of the leaves of the turnip or radish **are showing, he need not be concerned due to diverse kinds,**[H] i.e., that he violated the prohibition of planting food crops in a vineyard, as he did not intend to commit an act of planting; **nor due to tithes,** i.e., there is no concern lest the turnip or radish grew further, in which case he would be obligated to tithe it; **nor due to** the prohibition against working the land during **the Sabbatical Year,**[H] and similarly, he need not be concerned that they grew further and that the additional growth is prohibited as produce that grew during the Sabbatical Year. **And** therefore, the turnip or radish **may be taken** from the ground **on Shabbat.**[H] Even if most of the turnip or radish is underground, it is permitted to pull it from the ground on Shabbat. If so, in the case described in the mishna here, even if the basin buried in the ground has a rim, it should nevertheless be permitted to move it.

לָא צְרִיכָא, דְּבָעֵי מָרָא וַחֲצִינָא.

The Gemara answers: **No,** Rabbi Yeḥiel's ruling **is necessary** in a case where the basin was so firmly attached to the ground **that one would need a hoe** [*mara*][L] **or a spade** to remove it, as this action would certainly involve the digging, which is prohibited on Shabbat. Therefore, since the basin cannot be removed on Shabbat, it is considered fixed in its place and effectively diminishes the height of the wall.

״סוּלָּם הַמִּצְרִי – אֵינוֹ מְמַעֵט, וְהַצּוֹרִי – מְמַעֵט״. הֵיכִי דָּמֵי סוּלָּם הַמִּצְרִי? אָמְרִי דְּבֵי רַבִּי יַנַּאי: כֹּל שֶׁאֵין לוֹ אַרְבָּעָה חֲווּקִים.

It was taught in a *baraita*: **An Egyptian ladder,**[B] which is small, **does not diminish** the height of a wall, whereas **a** larger, **Tyrian** ladder effectively **diminishes** its height.[H] The Gemara asks: **What are the circumstances** of **an Egyptian ladder;** i.e., what characterizes it? **The** scholars of the **school of Rabbi Yannai said: Any** ladder **that does not have four rungs.**

LANGUAGE

Hoe [*mara*] – מָרָא: Some maintain that this word is from the Greek μάρρον, *marron*, or from the Latin marra, meaning hoe. However, it is likely that the word is originally of Semitic origin and subsequently spread to Europe.

BACKGROUND

Ladder – סוּלָּם: The wooden stairs pictured below are also termed a ladder by the Sages. The Romans too did not distinguish between a ladder of this type and one fashioned from isolated rungs.

Illustration of a Roman ladder from the talmudic period

HALAKHA

A buried turnip with regard to diverse kinds – לֶפֶת טְמוּנָה מִשּׁוּם כִּלְאַיִם: If one buries a turnip in a vineyard for safekeeping and leaves some of its leaves showing, he need not be concerned with regard to the prohibition against planting diverse kinds in a vineyard (*Shulḥan Arukh, Yoreh De'a* 297:11).

A buried turnip with regard to the Sabbatical Year – לֶפֶת טְמוּנָה מִשּׁוּם שְׁבִיעִית: One does not violate the prohibition against planting if he buries a turnip in the ground for safekeeping during the Sabbatical Year (Rambam *Sefer Zera'im, Hilkhot Shemitta VeYovel* 1:15).

May be taken from the ground on Shabbat – נִיטָּלִין בְּשַׁבָּת: If a turnip was buried in the ground for safekeeping with some of its leaves showing, it is permitted to remove it from the ground on Shabbat. This is not considered handling a set-aside object (*Shulḥan Arukh, Oraḥ Ḥayyim* 311:8).

Tyrian and Egyptian ladders – סוּלָּם צוֹרִי וּמִצְרִי: A ladder that does not have four rungs, such as an Egyptian ladder, does not diminish the height of a wall against which it is placed, unless the ladder is extremely heavy (*Tosafot*; Vilna Gaon; *Shulḥan Arukh, Oraḥ Ḥayyim* 372:8).

BACKGROUND

A platform above another platform – אִיצְטַבָּא עַל גַּב אִיצְטַבָּא:

Platform above another platform built adjacent to a wall

A ladder whose rungs are disconnected – סוּלָּם שֶׁשְּׁלִיבוֹתָיו פּוֹרְחוֹת: According to *Tosafot*, this is the ladder with disconnected rungs referred to in the Gemara.

Depiction of ladder from the talmudic period according to *Tosafot*

According to Rashi, the image below depicts the ladder with disconnected rungs. The lowest rung measures four handbreadths, and the gap between it and the second rung is less than three handbreadths.

Ladder with disconnected rungs according to Rashi

אֲמַר לֵיהּ רַב אַחָא בְּרֵיהּ דְּרָבָא לְרַב אַשִׁי: מַאי טַעְמָא דְּסוּלָּם הַמִּצְרִי דְּלָא מְמַעֵט? אֲמַר לֵיהּ: לָא שְׁמִיעַ לָךְ הָא דְּאָמַר רַב אַחָא בַּר אַדָּא, אָמַר רַב הַמְנוּנָא, אָמַר רַב: מִשּׁוּם דַּהֲוָה לֵיהּ דָּבָר שֶׁנִּיטַּל בַּשַּׁבָּת, וְכָל דָּבָר שֶׁנִּיטָּל בַּשַּׁבָּת – אֵינוֹ מְמַעֵט.

Rav Aḥa, son of Rava, said to Rav Ashi: What is the reason that **an Egyptian ladder does not diminish** the height of a wall? He **said to him: Did you not hear** that which **Rav Aḥa bar Adda said** that **Rav Hamnuna said** that **Rav said:** It is **because it is an object that may be moved on Shabbat,** i.e., it is not set-aside [*muktze*], **and** the principle is that **any object that may be moved on Shabbat does not diminish** the height of a wall, as it cannot be considered a permanent part of the wall.

הָכִי, אֲפִילּוּ צוֹרִי נַמִי! הָתָם כּוֹבְדוֹ קוֹבְעוֹ.

The Gemara objects: **If so,** this should apply **even** to **a Tyrian** ladder **as well,** as a large ladder is also not set-aside and may be handled on Shabbat. The Gemara answers: **There,** in the case of a Tyrian ladder, **its heaviness establishes it** as part of the wall.[N] Even though one is permitted to move it, since due to its weight it is not moved easily, it effectively diminishes the height of the wall.

אָמַר אַבַּיֵי: כּוֹתֶל שֶׁבֵּין שְׁתֵּי חֲצֵירוֹת גָּבוֹהַּ עֲשָׂרָה טְפָחִים, וְהִנִּיחַ סוּלָּם רָחָב אַרְבָּעָה מִכָּאן וְסוּלָּם רָחָב אַרְבָּעָה מִכָּאן, וְאֵין בֵּין זֶה לָזֶה שְׁלֹשָׁה טְפָחִים – מְמַעֵט, שְׁלֹשָׁה – אֵינוֹ מְמַעֵט.

Abaye said: If **a wall between two courtyards** is **ten handbreadths high, and one placed a ladder four** handbreadths **wide** against the wall **on one side,** in one courtyard, **and** another **ladder four** handbreadths **wide on the other side,**[H] in the other courtyard, **and there are less than three handbreadths between them,** i.e., the two ladders on the opposite sides of the wall are within three handbreadths of each other, even if they are not directly opposite each other, this **diminishes** the height of the wall. The pair of ladders is regarded as a valid passageway between the two courtyards. However, if the gap between the two ladders is **three** handbreadths or more, this **does not diminish** the height of the wall.

וְלָא אֲמַרַן אֶלָּא דְּלָא הָוֵי כּוֹתֶל אַרְבָּעָה, אֲבָל הָוֵי כּוֹתֶל אַרְבָּעָה – אֲפִילּוּ מוּפְלָג טוּבָא נַמִי.

And we only said this qualification if the **wall was less than four** handbreadths wide. However, **if the wall was** at least **four** handbreadths wide, then **even** if one ladder was **greatly distanced** from the other, this **likewise** renders it permitted. Since it is possible to walk along the thickness of the wall, the pair of ladders constitutes a passageway between the two courtyards.

אָמַר רַב בֵּיבָי בַּר אַבַּיֵי: בָּנָה אִיצְטַבָּא עַל גַּב אִיצְטַבָּא, אִם יֵשׁ בָּאִיצְטַבָּא הַתַּחְתּוֹנָה אַרְבָּעָה – מְמַעֵט. אִי נַמִי, אֵין בַּתַּחְתּוֹנָה אַרְבָּעָה וְיֵשׁ בָּעֶלְיוֹנָה אַרְבָּעָה, וְאֵין בֵּין זֶה לָזֶה שְׁלֹשָׁה – מְמַעֵט.

Rav Beivai bar Abaye said: If one built a wooden **platform** next to the wall **above** another **platform,**[BHN] then **if the lower platform is four** handbreadths wide, **it diminishes** the height of the wall to below ten handbreadths. **Alternatively,** if **the lower** one **is not four** handbreadths wide, **but the upper** one **is four** handbreadths wide, **and there is** a gap of **less than three** handbreadths **between them, it diminishes** the height of the wall, as the two platforms are considered as one.

וְאָמַר רַב נַחְמָן, אָמַר רַבָּה בַּר אֲבוּהּ: סוּלָּם שֶׁשְּׁלִיבוֹתָיו פּוֹרְחוֹת, אִם יֵשׁ בַּשְּׁלִיבָה הַתַּחְתּוֹנָה אַרְבָּעָה – מְמַעֵט, אִי נַמִי, אֵין בַּשְּׁלִיבָה הַתַּחְתּוֹנָה אַרְבָּעָה וְיֵשׁ בַּשְּׁלִיבָה הָעֶלְיוֹנָה אַרְבָּעָה, וְאֵין בֵּין זֶה לָזֶה שְׁלֹשָׁה – מְמַעֵט.

And Rav Naḥman said that **Rabba bar Avuh said:** In the case of **a ladder whose rungs are disconnected,**[BHN] **if the bottom rung is four** handbreadths wide, **it diminishes** the height of the wall. **Alternatively,** if **the bottom rung is not four** handbreadths wide, **but the upper rung is four** handbreadths wide, **and there is** a gap of **less than three** handbreadths **between them, it diminishes** the height of the wall, because the principle of *lavud* joins the two rungs together.

HALAKHA

Ladders on both sides – סוּלָּמוֹת מִשְּׁנֵי צְדָדִים: If ladders four handbreadths wide are placed against a wall on both sides, then if the wall itself is four handbreadths wide, they effectively diminish the height of the wall, even if the ladders are separated by more than three handbreadths. However, if the wall is less than four handbreadths wide, they effectively diminish the height of the wall only when they are separated by less than three handbreadths (*Shulḥan Arukh, Oraḥ Ḥayyim* 372:8).

A platform above another platform – אִיצְטַבָּא עַל גַּב אִיצְטַבָּא: If one constructs a platform above another platform next to a wall and the lower one is four by four handbreadths, or the upper one is four by four handbreadths and is separated from the lower one by less than three handbreadths, then they diminish the height of the wall (*Shulḥan Arukh, Oraḥ Ḥayyim* 311:11).

A ladder whose rungs are disconnected – סוּלָּם שֶׁשְּׁלִיבוֹתָיו פּוֹרְחוֹת: If a ladder's rungs are disconnected, and the lowest rung of the ladder is four handbreadths wide, and the gap between the rungs is smaller than three handbreadths, then the ladder diminishes the height of the wall (Rambam *Sefer Zemanim, Hilkhot Eiruvin* 3:5).

NOTES

Its heaviness establishes it as part of the wall – כּוֹבְדוֹ קוֹבְעוֹ: Some commentaries explain that an extremely heavy object may not be moved on Shabbat, because it is considered as though it were set-aside and therefore may not be handled (Ra'avad).

A platform above another platform – אִיצְטַבָּא עַל גַּב אִיצְטַבָּא: With regard to a platform and a ladder, the commentaries disagree as to whether or not a width of four handbreadths is also required so that the area upon which one can stand measures a minimum four by four handbreadths. With regard to the statement of Rav Beivai bar Abaye concerning a platform, and that of Rav Naḥman concerning a ladder, despite the fact that they are very similar, there is no need to demonstrate why both are necessary, since two different scholars may teach similar points (Ritva).

A ladder whose rungs are disconnected – סוּלָּם שֶׁשְּׁלִיבוֹתָיו פּוֹרְחוֹת: See *Tosafot*, who explain the word disconnected [*porḥot*] differently. They write that this refers to a ladder made from isolated platforms, each one separated from the other by empty space. According to their explanation, the word *porḥot*, which literally means flying, refers to these unconnected steps of the ladder. In contrast, Rabbeinu Ḥananel says that this ladder is fashioned similarly to stairs, as Rashi explains with regard to all ladders. The *Arukh* states that this phrase refers to a ladder in which the wooden bars on the sides of its rungs are particularly distant from one another.

וְאָמַר רַב נַחְמָן, אָמַר רַבָּה בַּר אֲבוּהּ:

And Rav Naḥman said that Rabba bar Avuh said:

Perek **VII**
Daf **78** Amud **a**

זִיז הַיּוֹצֵא מִן הַכּוֹתֶל אַרְבָּעָה עַל אַרְבָּעָה, וְהִנִּיחַ עָלָיו סוּלָּם כׇּל שֶׁהוּא – מִיעֲטוֹ.

If **a projection four by four** handbreadths in area **extends from a wall,**[H] **and one placed a ladder of any** width **against it,** if the rungs of the ladder are less than three handbreadths apart, **he has diminished**[N] the height of the wall by means of this ladder and projection.

וְלָא אֲמַרַן אֶלָּא דְּאוֹתְבֵיהּ עֲלֵיהּ, אֲבָל אוֹתְבֵיהּ בַּהֲדֵיהּ – אַרְווֹחֵי אַרְוְחֵיהּ.

The Gemara qualifies this statement: **And we said** this **only** in a case **where one placed** the ladder directly **against** the projection, so that the ladder serves as a passage to it. **However, if he placed it adjacent to** the projection, **he has** merely **widened** the projection, while the ladder remains separate from it. Consequently, the projection does not have any connection to the ground, and a projection that is not within three handbreadths of the ground does not diminish the height of a wall.

וְאָמַר רַב נַחְמָן, אָמַר רַבָּה בַּר אֲבוּהּ: כּוֹתֶל תִּשְׁעָה עָשָׂר – צָרִיךְ זִיז אֶחָד לְהַתִּירוֹ.

And Rav Naḥman said that Rabba bar Avuh said: If **a wall** between two courtyards is **nineteen** handbreadths high, **it requires one projection to** render the use of the wall **permitted.** If there is a single projection in the middle of the wall, with a ladder of any width resting against it, it is considered a passageway between the courtyards, as the projection is within ten handbreadths of the top of the wall.

כּוֹתֶל עֶשְׂרִים – צָרִיךְ שְׁנֵי זִיזִים לְהַתִּירוֹ. אָמַר רַב חִסְדָּא: וְהוּא שֶׁהֶעֱמִידָן זֶה שֶׁלֹּא כְּנֶגֶד זֶה.

However, if **the wall** is **twenty** handbreadths high, it **requires two projections**[HN] **to** render the use of the wall **permitted,** one within ten handbreadths of the ground, and the other within ten handbreadths of the top of the wall. **Rav Ḥisda said: And this** applies only **where he positioned** the projections **not** directly **one above the other,** so that it is possible to use a ladder to climb from one projection to the other.

אָמַר רַב הוּנָא: עַמּוּד בִּרְשׁוּת הָרַבִּים, גָּבוֹהַּ עֲשָׂרָה וְרָחָב אַרְבָּעָה, וְנָעַץ בּוֹ יָתֵד כׇּל שֶׁהוּא – מִיעֲטוֹ.

Rav Huna said: If **a pillar in the public domain** is **ten** handbreadths **high and four** handbreadths **wide,** so that it is considered a private domain,[H] **and one drove a stake of any** size **into** the top **of it,**[N] **he has diminished its** area. The usable area is now less than four handbreadths, and therefore the pillar is no longer considered a private domain.

אָמַר רַב אַדָּא בַּר אַהֲבָה: וּבְגָבוֹהַּ שְׁלֹשָׁה. אַבַּיֵּי וְרָבָא דְּאָמְרִי תַּרְוַיְיהוּ: אַף עַל פִּי שֶׁאֵין גָּבוֹהַּ שְׁלֹשָׁה.

Rav Adda bar Ahava said: This applies only if the stake is at least **three** handbreadths **high.** If it is less than three handbreadths high, it is considered part of the top of the pillar, based on the principle of *lavud*. This is in contrast to **Abaye and Rava, who both say: Even if** the stake is **not three** handbreadths **high,** the pillar is no longer considered a private domain.

HALAKHA

If a projection extends from a wall – זִיז הַיּוֹצֵא מִן הַכּוֹתֶל: If a projection measuring four by four handbreadths extends from a wall, and a ladder is placed against it, this diminishes the height of the wall. However, the height is not effectively diminished if one places the ladder adjacent to the projection (*Shulḥan Arukh*, *Oraḥ Ḥayyim* 372:12).

Projections in a high wall – זִיזִים בְּכוֹתֶל גָּבוֹהַּ: If a wall is nineteen handbreadths high and has a single projection in the middle of it, its height may be diminished by means of a ladder. However, if the height of the wall is twenty handbreadths, it requires two projections, one within ten handbreadths of the ground and another within ten handbreadths of the top of the wall. Additionally, the projections may not be placed directly above one other (*Shulḥan Arukh*, *Oraḥ Ḥayyim* 372:12).

A pillar as a private domain – עַמּוּד רְשׁוּת הַיָּחִיד: A pillar standing in the public domain that is ten handbreadths high and four handbreadths square has the status of a private domain. However, if one drove a stake into it that is three handbreadths tall, he has diminished its height (Ra'avad). It seems that the Rambam had a different version of the text, as he understands that the stake was inserted into the side of the pillar, and that the height of the pillar is measured from the location of the stake (*Maggid Mishne*; Rambam *Sefer Zemanim*, *Hilkhot Shabbat* 14:9).

NOTES

Diminishing by means of a projection – מִיעוּט זִיז: Some explain this differently from Rashi: If a projection extends from a wall and a person places a ladder on it, it is no longer convenient to use the projection; it is as though its size were reduced. If, however, he positioned the ladder adjacent to the projection, then it is as though he has enlarged the projection, and it is certainly suitable for use (Rashba).

Two projections – שְׁנֵי זִיזִים: Some explain that these projections are effective without a ladder, and they diminish the height of the wall because they can be used to scale the wall. However, since these projections are not very close to one another, they must be slightly tilted in order to allow one to use them to climb the wall, and they are not considered similar to an upright ladder (Ra'avad; Rashba).

Drove a stake into the pillar – נָעַץ יָתֵד בְּעַמּוּד: The Rambam understands this case completely differently, and Rabbeinu Ḥananel seems to interpret it similarly, though he had a different version of the text. Rather than explaining that the stake was driven into the top of a pillar, he understands that the stake was inserted into its side, giving the stake the status of a projection in a wall. Therefore, the stake effectively diminishes the height of the wall. The dispute concerns the size of the stake required to diminish the height of the wall. One opinion maintains that it must be three handbreadths in size so that it can be used for climbing, while Rav Ashi holds, according to Rabbeinu Ḥananel's version of the text, that even a stake of less than three handbreadths serves to diminish its height, because it can be utilized for hanging items (see *Maggid Mishne*).

מַאי טַעְמָא – לָא מִשְׁתַּמֵּשׁ לֵיהּ.

What is the reason for the opinion of Abaye and Rava? It is that the pillar **is no longer** fit to be **used,** as a surface of four by four handbreadths is suitable for use only when it is level. If it has even a small projection, it is no longer usable.

רַב אַשִׁי אָמַר: אֲפִילּוּ שֶׁגָּבוֹהַּ שְׁלֹשָׁה, מַאי טַעְמָא – אֶפְשָׁר דְּתָלֵיהּ בֵּיהּ מִידֵּי.

Rav Ashi said: Even a stake three handbreadths **high** does not diminish the area of the pillar. **What is the reason** for this? It is that **it is possible to hang an item on it. Although** it is no longer possible to rest objects on top of the pillar, it is still useful in some way.

אֲמַר לֵיהּ רַב אַחָא בְּרֵיהּ דְּרָבָא לְרַב אַשִׁי: מִלְאוֹ כּוּלּוֹ בִּיתֵדוֹת מַהוּ?

Rav Aḥa, son of Rava, said to Rav Ashi: According to your opinion, if **he filled it entirely with stakes,**[B] i.e., if he drove so many stakes into the top of the post that it was completely filled, **what is the** *halakha*?

אֲמַר לֵיהּ: לָא שְׁמִיעַ לָךְ הָא דְּאָמַר רַבִּי יוֹחָנָן: בּוֹר וְחוּלְיָיתָהּ מִצְטָרֵף לַעֲשָׂרָה?

Rav Ashi **said to him: Did you not hear that** which **Rabbi Yoḥanan said?** He said that **a pit and its embankment** of stone around the edge **join** together to complete the measure of **ten** handbreadths. Similarly, the width of the embankment joins with the diameter of the pit to complete the measure of four by four handbreadths necessary to define the pit as a private domain.

וְאַמַּאי? הָא לָא מִשְׁתַּמֵּשׁ לֵיהּ! אֶלָּא מַאי אִית לָךְ לְמֵימַר – דְּמַנַּח מִידֵּי וּמִשְׁתַּמֵּשׁ. הָכָא נַמִי – דְּמַנַּח מִידֵּי וּמִשְׁתַּמֵּשׁ.

There, too, one can raise the question: **But why? He cannot use** the embankment, as most of the area is the empty space of the pit. **Rather, what have you to say,** i.e., how can you solve this problem? The solution is **that he places an item,** e.g., a board, over the mouth of the pit, **and** then he can make **use** of it. **Here, too, he places an item** over the stakes **and** can make **use** of the pillar.

אָמַר רַב יְהוּדָה, אָמַר שְׁמוּאֵל: כּוֹתֶל עֲשָׂרָה – צָרִיךְ סוּלָּם אַרְבָּעָה עָשָׂר לְהַתִּירוֹ. רַב יוֹסֵף אָמַר: אֲפִילּוּ שְׁלֹשָׁה עָשָׂר וּמַשֶּׁהוּ.

Rav Yehuda said that **Shmuel said:** If **a wall** is **ten** handbreadths high, **it requires a ladder fourteen** handbreadths high, so that one can place the ladder at a diagonal against the wall. The ladder then functions as a passageway and thereby renders the use of the wall **permitted. Rav Yosef said: Even** a ladder with a height of **thirteen** handbreadths **and a bit** is enough, as it is sufficient if the ladder reaches within one handbreadth of the top of the wall.

אַבָּיֵי אָמַר: אֲפִילּוּ אַחַד עָשָׂר וּמַשֶּׁהוּ.

Abaye said: Even a ladder that is only **eleven** handbreadths **and a bit** suffices, as the ladder will still reach a height of over seven handbreadths, i.e., within three handbreadths of the top of the wall.

רַב הוּנָא בְּרֵיהּ דְּרַב יְהוֹשֻׁעַ אָמַר: אֲפִילּוּ שִׁבְעָה וּמַשֶּׁהוּ.

Rav Huna, son of Rav Yehoshua, said: Even if the ladder is only **seven** handbreadths **and a bit**[BH] it is sufficient, as he can stand the ladder upright against the wall. Since it will reach within three handbreadths of the top of the wall, the principle of *lavud* applies. Therefore, even a ladder placed in this manner is considered a valid passageway between the two courtyards.

אָמַר רַב: סוּלָּם זָקוּף מְמַעֵט, גְּמָרָא, וְלָא יָדַעְנָא מַאי טַעְמָא.

Similarly, **Rav said: An upright ladder** effectively **diminishes** the height of a wall, as it creates a passageway. I received this teaching as **a tradition, but I do not know what the reason is,** as people do not generally climb ladders positioned in this manner.

אָמַר שְׁמוּאֵל: וְלָא יָדַע אַבָּא טַעְמָא דְּהָא מִלְּתָא?! מִידֵּי דַּהֲוָה אַאִיצְטַבָּא עַל גַּבֵּי אִיצְטַבָּא.

Shmuel said: Does Abba, i.e., Rav, actually **not know the reason for this matter?** The reason here is **just as it is** in the case of **a platform above** another **platform.** Even though it is not easy to climb, since it provides steps that can be climbed, albeit with difficulty, it is considered a valid passageway.

אָמַר רַבָּה, אָמַר רַבִּי חִיָּיא: דְּקָלִים שֶׁבְּבָבֶל אֵינָן צְרִיכִין קֶבַע. מַאי טַעְמָא – כְּבֵידָן קוֹבַעְתָּן.

Rabba said that **Rabbi Ḥiyya said:** The trunks of **palm trees in Babylonia** that were placed next to a wall between two courtyards so that people could climb on them and pass from one courtyard to another **do not need to be established** permanently and attached to the ground; rather, they serve to diminish the wall as they are. **What is the reason** for this? It is that **their heaviness establishes them** as connected to the ground. Although it is permitted to handle them, nevertheless, since their weight makes them difficult to move, they are considered fixed in place.

BACKGROUND

He filled it entirely with stakes – מִלְאוֹ כּוּלּוֹ בִּיתֵדוֹת: The image below illustrates a pillar entirely filled with stakes. It also shows, by means of the tallest stake, how a stake of this kind makes it inconvenient to place items on the pillar. This depiction is based on Rashi's explanation. According to the Rambam (see Notes), the stake is inserted into the side of the pillar, and as a result the height of the pillar is considered diminished.

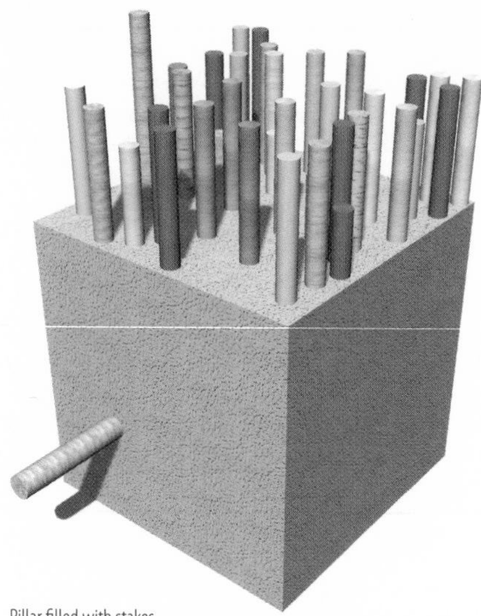

Pillar filled with stakes

The height of the ladder – גּוֹבַהּ הַסּוּלָּם: Based on the context and on mathematical calculations, the explanation of *Tosafot* seems correct: The ladder is placed at a 45° angle so that the distance of its foot from the wall and the height of its top against the wall are equal. This is especially reasonable if the ladder resembles stairs, rather than a modern one with rungs.

The image below demonstrates that a ladder fourteen handbreadths in height would reach the top of the wall, which is ten handbreadths high. A ladder thirteen handbreadths high would reach above a height of nine handbreadths on the wall, and even one eleven handbreadths high would reach higher than seven handbreadths.

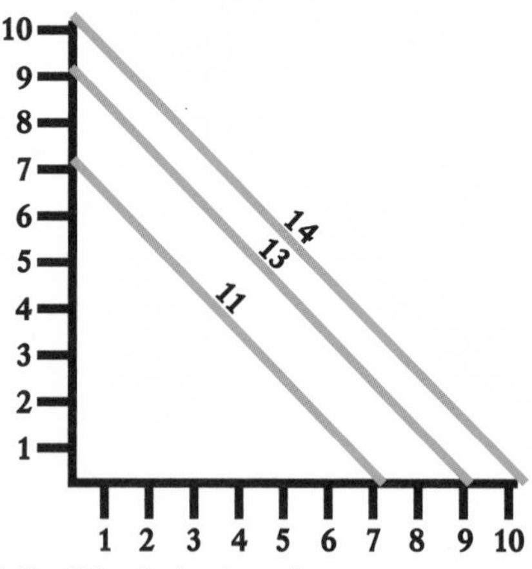

Ladders of different lengths against a wall

HALAKHA

The size of the ladder – גּוֹדֶל הַסּוּלָּם: A ladder that is a bit more than seven handbreadths tall is sufficient to diminish the height of a wall that is ten handbreadths high. This ruling is in accordance with the opinion of Rav Huna, son of Rabbi Yehoshua, who is the latest authority cited in the Gemara and who rules in accordance with the opinion of Rav (*Maggid Mishne*; *Shulḥan Arukh*, *Oraḥ Ḥayyim* 372:8).

וְרַב יוֹסֵף אָמַר רַבִּי אוֹשַׁעְיָא: סוּלָּמוֹת שֶׁבְּבָבֶל אֵינָן צְרִיכִין קֶבַע, מַאי טַעְמָא – כְּבֵידָן קוֹבַעְתָּן.	**And** similarly, **Rav Yosef** said that **Rabbi Oshaya said: Ladders in Babylonia do not need** to be **established** and fixed permanently in place. **What is the reason** for this? It is that **their heaviness establishes them,**[H] as the ladders in Babylonia were typically large and heavy.
מַאן דְּאָמַר סוּלָּמוֹת – כׇּל שֶׁכֵּן דְּקָלִים, וּמַאן דְּאָמַר דְּקָלִים – אֲבָל סוּלָּמוֹת – לָא.	The Gemara comments: With regard to **the one who said** that Babylonian **ladders** do not need to be fixed in place, **all the more so** would he agree that the trunks of **palm trees,** which are placed there from the outset for this purpose, are considered fixed, as both are extremely heavy and also designed to remain in place. On the other hand, **the one who said** that the trunks of **palm trees** need not be fixed permanently in the ground, spoke only with regard to palm trees. **However,** as for **ladders, no,** they are not considered fixed in place. A ladder, even a heavy one, is designed to be moved from place to place.
בְּעָא מִינֵּיהּ רַב יוֹסֵף מֵרַבָּה: סוּלָּם מִכָּאן וְסוּלָּם מִכָּאן וְקַשִּׁין בָּאֶמְצַע, מַהוּ?	**Rav Yosef raised a dilemma before Rabba:** If there is a narrow **ladder** measuring less than two handbreadths wide **on one** side, **and** a similarly narrow **ladder on the other** side, **and** there are rungs of woven **straw in the middle** between them[B] which would not support a person's weight, **what is** the *halakha*? Are the two ladders considered a single unit, forming a ladder four handbreadths wide, which serves to diminish the height of a wall?
אֲמַר לֵיהּ: אֵין כַּף הָרֶגֶל עוֹלָה בָּהֶן.	Rabba **said to him: The sole of the foot cannot** climb **upon them.** A person usually places his foot in the middle of a ladder. Since the middle of this ladder is made of straw, then although it appears to be four handbreadths wide, it is not fit for use and does not diminish the height of the wall.
קַשִּׁין מִכָּאן וְקַשִּׁין מִכָּאן וְסוּלָּם בָּאֶמְצַע, מַהוּ? אֲמַר לֵיהּ: הֲרֵי כַּף הָרֶגֶל עוֹלָה בָּהֶן.	Rav Yosef continued to ask: And what if there were rungs of **straw on one** side **and** rungs of **straw on the other** side, **and a** narrow **ladder**[HN] less than four handbreadths wide **in the middle,**[B] and their combined width is four handbreadths? **What is** the *halakha* in this case? Rabba **said to him: The sole of the foot can** climb **upon them,** and the ladder appears to be four handbreadths wide. Therefore, it serves to diminish the height of the wall.

HALAKHA

Their heaviness establishes them – כְּבֵידָן קוֹבַעְתָּן: Heavy ladders and stumps of palm trees that are placed next to a wall serve to diminish its height. Even though it is permissible to move them, their weight establishes them as fixed in place (Rambam *Sefer Zemanim*, *Hilkhot Eiruvin* 3:7).

Rungs of straw…and a narrow ladder – סוּלָּם וְקַשִּׁים: If there are two ladders alongside one another, each of which is less than two handbreadths wide, and one connects them with straw rungs, they do not serve to diminish the height of the wall. However, a ladder less than four handbreadths wide that one increased to the size of four handbreadths by attaching straw rungs on each side effectively diminishes the height of the wall (*Shulḥan Arukh*, *Oraḥ Ḥayyim* 372:13).

NOTES

Rungs of straw…and a narrow ladder – סוּלָּם וְקַשִּׁים: Some commentaries interpret this case in an entirely different manner, explaining that there is a straw partition separating two courtyards, with ladders leaning against it from both sides. Rav Yosef asked whether these ladders can be considered a passageway, to which Rabba replied that since one cannot climb the ladders due to the instability of the straw partition, they are insignificant. Rav Yosef then inquired as to the ruling in a case where the ladders are leaning on a section of the partition made of stable material, while the rest of the partition is made of straw. Rabba answered that in that case the ladders are effective, since it is possible to climb them (*ge'onim*; Ra'avad).

BACKGROUND

Rungs of woven straw in the middle between them – קַשִּׁין בָּאֶמְצַע: The image below shows two narrow ladders held together by rungs of straw or another weak material, which would not support a person's weight. This illustration is in accordance with Rashi's explanation.

Ladders held together by rungs of straw

Straw rungs on each side and a ladder in the middle – קַשִּׁין מִכָּאן וּמִכָּאן וְסוּלָּם בָּאֶמְצַע: The image below depicts a narrow ladder with weak additions made of straw added to its rungs, which would not support a person's weight (in accordance with the explanation of Rashi).

Ladder with straw rungs added on either side

חָקַק לְהַשְׁלִים בְּכוֹתֶל, בְּכַמָּה? אֲמַר לֵיהּ: בַּעֲשָׂרָה.

Rav Yosef further asked: If the ladder resting against the wall was less than four handbreadths wide, and **one dug out** grooves **in the wall**[H] as extensions of the rungs of the ladder **to complete** the measure,[NB] **how** high must this hollowed-out section be to consider the ladder a valid passageway between the two courtyards? Rabba **said to him:** If it is **ten** handbreadths high and four handbreadths wide, it is considered a passageway.

אֲמַר לֵיהּ: חֲקָקוֹ כּוּלּוֹ בְּכוֹתֶל, בְּכַמָּה? אֲמַר לֵיהּ: מְלֹא קוֹמָתוֹ. וּמַאי שְׁנָא? אֲמַר לֵיהּ: הָתָם – מִסְתַּלַּק לֵיהּ, הָכָא לָא מִסְתַּלַּק לֵיהּ.

Rav Yosef **said to him:** If there was no ladder, and **one dug out the entire** ladder **in the wall,** so that all the steps are grooves in the wall, **how much** must he hollow out? Rabba **said to him:** Those steps must reach **the full height of** the wall. Rav Yosef asked: **And what is the difference** in this case? Why must the steps reach higher in this case than in the case where the hollowed-out section was merely an extension of an existing ladder? Rabba **said to him: There,** where there is a ladder, **it is easy to climb** to the top of the wall; however, **here,** where there are only grooves in the wall, **it is not easy to climb.** If one cannot reach the top of the wall, the steps are not considered a passageway between the courtyards.

בְּעָא מִינֵּיהּ רַב יוֹסֵף מֵרַבָּה: עֲשָׂאוֹ לְאִילָן סוּלָּם, מַהוּ?

Rav Yosef raised a dilemma before Rabba: If one designated a tree as a ladder, what is the *halakha*? Given that it is prohibited to climb a tree on Shabbat, if a tree stands next to a wall and it is easy to climb, is it considered with regard to the *halakhot* of Shabbat as an opening in the wall that can serve as a passageway between the two courtyards?

תִּיבְּעֵי לְרַבִּי, תִּיבְּעֵי לְרַבָּנַן;

Let the dilemma be raised according **to** the opinion of **Rabbi** Yehuda HaNasi, who maintains that a joining of Shabbat boundaries [*eiruv teḥumin*] placed in a tree is valid; and **let the dilemma be raised** according **to** the opinion of **the Rabbis,** who disagree.

תִּיבְּעֵי לְרַבִּי: עַד כָּאן לָא קָאָמַר רַבִּי הָתָם "כָּל דָּבָר שֶׁהוּא מִשּׁוּם שְׁבוּת לֹא גָּזְרוּ עָלָיו" הָנֵי מִילֵּי – בֵּין הַשְּׁמָשׁוֹת, אֲבָל כּוּלֵּי יוֹמָא – לָא.

The Gemara elaborates: **Let the dilemma be raised** according **to** the previously stated opinion of **Rabbi** Yehuda HaNasi. **Rabbi** Yehuda HaNasi **only stated there** that with regard to **anything that is** prohibited on Shabbat **due to a rabbinic decree** [*shevut*], the Sages **did not prohibit** it during twilight. Therefore, in Rabbi Yehuda HaNasi's opinion, it is permitted to use an *eiruv* that was deposited in a tree, as the use of a tree is prohibited on Shabbat by rabbinic decree. However, **this applies only** in that case, as the *eiruv* takes effect **during the twilight period.** Since there is doubt with regard to whether that period is considered day or night, the decree is not in force, and the *eiruv* is therefore valid. **However,** in this case, where the opening must be valid for **the entire day,** Rabbi Yehuda HaNasi would **not** rule that the decree does not apply. Since it is prohibited by rabbinic decree to climb a tree on Shabbat, a tree cannot be considered a valid passageway.

אוֹ דִּילְמָא: אֲפִילּוּ לְרַבָּנַן, פִּיתְחָא הוּא, וְאַרְיָא הוּא דִּרְבִיעַ עֲלֵיהּ.

Or perhaps it may be argued that **even according to** the opinion of **the Rabbis,** this tree is considered an opening. They may have said that a joining of Shabbat boundaries placed in a tree is not valid only because the *eiruv* must actually be accessible during twilight, and in that case it is not, due to the rabbinic decree. However, in this case, where it is not necessary to make actual use of the tree, they would agree that a tree that serves as a ladder **is a valid entrance, but a lion crouches upon it.** Just as a lion crouching at an opening does not thereby nullify its status as an entrance, although in practice no one can pass through it, so too, in the case of the tree, the prohibition against climbing it does not nullify its status as a passageway.

עֲשָׂאוֹ לַאֲשֵׁירָה סוּלָּם, מַהוּ? תִּיבְּעֵי לְרַבִּי יְהוּדָה, תִּיבְּעֵי לְרַבָּנַן;

Rav Yosef further inquired: **If one designated a tree worshipped as part of idolatrous rites** [*asheira*],[N] from which it is forbidden to derive benefit, **as a ladder, what is** the *halakha*? Is it considered a valid passageway in the wall with regard to the *halakhot* of Shabbat? Here, too, **let the dilemma be raised** according **to** the opinion of **Rabbi Yehuda,** and **let the dilemma be raised** according **to** the opinion of **the Rabbis.**

HALAKHA

One dug out grooves in the wall – חָקַק הַכּוֹתֶל: If one hollowed out grooves in a wall in order to complete the measure of a narrow ladder to four handbreadths wide, the grooves are required only up to a height of ten handbreadths. However, if one hollowed out an entire ladder in a wall, then the steps, which must be four handbreadths wide, must reach the top of the wall (*Shulḥan Arukh, Oraḥ Ḥayyim* 372:14).

NOTES

Dug it out to complete the measure – חֲקָקוֹ לְהַשְׁלִים: Some interpret this case differently: The ladder is four handbreadths wide, but very short, and it is completed by hollowing out additional rungs in the wall above the ladder to a height of within ten handbreadths of the top of the wall (Rashba; *Me'iri*). Rabbeinu Ḥananel explains that the phrase dug out to complete indicates that there is a hole in the wall that one sought to widen to a measure of four by four handbreadths so that it may serve as a window. According to this explanation, Rabba's answer is that if one hollowed out a space of four handbreadths within ten handbreadths of the ground, it is sufficient. However, if one wishes to hollow out a proper entrance in the wall, it must reach the full height of a person. The reason is that since he has decided to make an entrance, it must be one through which people can pass.

Asheira – **אֲשֵׁרָה:** The assumption is that this tree is no longer growing, but has fully dried out or has been uprooted from its place. Otherwise, two questions are relevant here, since it is both an *asheira* and a tree that may not be climbed on Shabbat.

BACKGROUND

Dug out in the wall to complete the measure – חָקַק לְהַשְׁלִים בְּכוֹתֶל: The illustration below depicts grooves hollowed out in a wall to complete the required width of a narrow ladder.

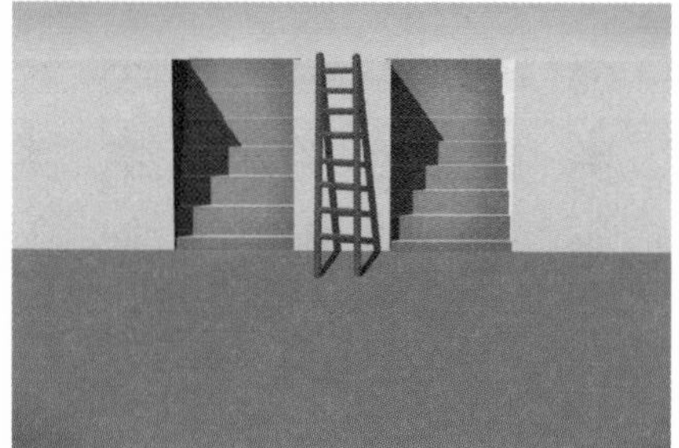

Grooves dug out on either side of a ladder

תיבעי לרבי יהודה: עד כאן לא קאמר רבי יהודה התם דמותר לקנות בית באיסורי הנאה – אלא התם, דבתר דקנה ליה עירוב לא ניחא ליה דלינטר.

The Gemara elaborates: **Let the dilemma be raised** according **to the** previously stated opinion of **Rabbi Yehuda. Rabbi Yehuda only stated there** that **it is permitted to acquire,** i.e., make use of, **a house** for the purposes of establishing an *eiruv* even if it is among the **items** from which it is **prohibited to** derive **benefit,** such as a grave. This statement applies only **there,** with regard to acquiring an *eiruv* in that location, **since after the *eiruv* has acquired** a place of residence **for him, it is not important to him that it is guarded.** He requires the grave only for the moment of the acquisition of the *eiruv*, and what happens to it afterward is of no consequence to him. However, here, since one desires the continued presence of the ladder, it is possible that even Rabbi Yehuda would agree that one may not rely on an *asheira*, as one may not climb and make use of it, since it is prohibited to derive benefit from it.

או דילמא: אפילו לרבנן פיתחא הוא, ואריא דרביע עליה?

Or perhaps it may be argued that **even** though according **to the** opinion of **the Rabbis** it is prohibited to use a grave to acquire an *eiruv*, here they would agree that the *asheira* **is an opening, but a lion crouches upon it,**[N] and this does not nullify its status as an opening.

אמר ליה: אילן מותר, ואשירה אסורה. מתקיף לה רב חסדא: אדרבה, אילן שאיסור שבת גורם לו – ניתסר,

Rabba **said to him: A tree is permitted** for use as a ladder, **but an *asheira* is prohibited. Rav Ḥisda strongly objects to this: On the contrary, a tree,** with regard to **which a Shabbat prohibition causes it** to be prohibited, **should be prohibited,** so that it will not be said that a Shabbat prohibition has been disregarded in a case involving the *halakhot* of Shabbat.

אשירה שאיסור דבר אחר גורם לו – לא ניתסר.

And the converse is also true: **An *asheira*,** with regard to **which something else,** a *halakha* unrelated to the *halakhot* of Shabbat, **causes it** to be prohibited, **should not be prohibited.** Rather, it should be considered an opening with regard to Shabbat.

איתמר נמי, כי אתא רבין, אמר רבי אלעזר, ואמרי לה אמר רבי אבהו, אמר רבי יוחנן: כל שאיסור שבת גרם לו – אסור, כל שאיסור דבר אחר גרם לו – מותר.

Indeed, **it was also stated: When Ravin came** from Eretz Yisrael to Babylonia, he said that **Rabbi Elazar said, and some say** that **Rabbi Abbahu said** that **Rabbi Yoḥanan said: Anything** with regard to **which a prohibition of Shabbat causes it** to be prohibited **is prohibited;** and conversely, **anything** with regard to **which something else causes it** to be prohibited **is permitted.**

רב נחמן בר יצחק מתני הכי: אילן – פלוגתא דרבי ורבנן, אשירה – פלוגתא דרבי יהודה ורבנן.

However, in contrast to Rav Yosef, **Rav Naḥman bar Yitzḥak taught as follows:** These questions are indeed dependent on the known disputes. Whether **a tree** serving as a ladder constitutes a valid opening **is** the subject of **a dispute** between **Rabbi** Yehuda HaNasi **and the Rabbis;** Rabbi Yehuda HaNasi permits it and the Rabbis prohibit it. The debate with regard to whether or not **an *asheira*** is considered an opening **is** the subject of **a dispute** between **Rabbi Yehuda,** who permits using items from which it is prohibited to derive benefit for the sake of an *eiruv*, **and the Rabbis,** who prohibit making an *eiruv* with such items.[H]

מתני׳ חריץ שבין שתי חצירות, עמוק עשרה ורוחב ארבעה – מערבין שנים, ואין מערבין אחד, אפילו מלא קש או תבן. מלא עפר או צרורות מערבין אחד, ואין מערבין שנים.

MISHNA With regard to **a ditch between** two **courtyards**[H] that is **ten** handbreadths **deep and four** handbreadths **wide,** it is considered a full-fledged partition, and the residents of the courtyard **establish two *eiruvin*,** one for each courtyard, **but they** may **not establish one *eiruv*. Even** if the ditch is **filled** with **straw or hay,** it is not regarded as sealed and is therefore not nullified. However, if the ditch is **filled with dirt or pebbles,** the residents **establish one *eiruv*, but they** may **not establish two *eiruvin*,** as the ditch is nullified and considered nonexistent.

נתן עליו נסר שרחב ארבעה טפחים, וכן שתי גזוזטראות זו כנגד זו – מערבין שנים, ואם רצו – מערבין אחד. פחות מכאן – מערבין שנים, ואין מערבין אחד.

If **one placed a board four handbreadths wide across** the ditch[H] so that he could cross it, **and similarly,** if **two balconies** [*gezuztraot*][HL] in two different courtyards are **opposite one another,** and one placed a board four handbreadths wide between them, the residents of the courtyards or balconies **establish two *eiruvin*, and if they desire, they** may **establish one,** as the board serves as an opening and a passageway between them. If the width of the plank is **less than** four handbreadths, the residents **establish two *eiruvin*, but they** may **not establish one *eiruv*.**

NOTES

A lion crouches upon it – אַרְיָא דִּרְבִיעַ עֲלֵיהּ: It was clear to those asking the question that a lion actually crouching in an entrance would not nullify its status as an entrance. Therefore, the question here is whether the prohibition involved in climbing a tree affects its status as a passageway, or whether this is considered an external factor, similar to a lion crouching at an entrance. According to Rabba, the prohibition to use a tree on Shabbat is an external factor, as the tree itself is not prohibited, and the prohibition to use it can be viewed as secondary. However, the prohibition to derive benefit from an *asheira* affects the status of the tree itself to the extent that it is considered as though the tree were not there at all. Rav Ḥisda maintains that since the prohibition with regard to an *asheira* does not belong to the category of Shabbat laws, it does not affect the tree's status as an opening with regard to Shabbat. By contrast, a Shabbat prohibition does nullify a tree's status as an entrance, at least for the day of Shabbat itself (see *Me'iri*).

HALAKHA

A tree and an *asheira* – עֵץ וַאֲשֵׁרָה: If one fashioned a ladder for a wall out of a living tree, this effectively diminishes the height of the wall and permits the use of the wall on Shabbat. However, the height of a wall may not be diminished by means of an *asheira*, in accordance with Rabba's opinion. The Rosh issues the opposite ruling, i.e., that a tree is prohibited but one is permitted to utilize a dried *asheira*, in accordance with the opinion of Rabbi Yoḥanan. Most of the later authorities agree with the first opinion, since Rabbi Naḥman bar Yitzḥak, a later Sage, adopts that interpretation. Furthermore, that approach can also bring this passage in the Gemara in line with a discussion of the same topic elsewhere in the Talmud (Vilna Gaon; *Eliya Rabba*; *Shulḥan Arukh, Oraḥ Ḥayyim* 372:15).

A ditch between two courtyards – חָרִיץ שֶׁבֵּין שְׁתֵּי חֲצֵירוֹת: If a ditch ten handbreadths deep and four handbreadths wide separates two courtyards, the residents of each courtyard must establish a separate *eiruv*, even if the ditch is filled with straw and hay. However, if the ditch is filled with dirt, it is nullified, and the residents of the two courtyards establish one *eiruv* (*Shulḥan Arukh, Oraḥ Ḥayyim* 372:16).

A board across a ditch – נֶסֶר עַל חָרִיץ: If a board four handbreadths wide is placed across a ditch that separates two courtyards, it is considered a passageway between the courtyards, and the residents of the two courtyards may establish one joint *eiruv* if they wish. The same applies if the residents sealed the ditch along a length of four handbreadths with material that would render it nullified (Rema, based on Ritva and *Beit Yosef*; *Shulḥan Arukh, Oraḥ Ḥayyim* 372:17).

Two balconies – שְׁתֵּי גְּזוּזְטְרָאוֹת: If a plank four handbreadths wide is placed between two balconies that face each other, the residents of the two balconies may establish a single *eiruv* (*Shulḥan Arukh, Oraḥ Ḥayyim* 373:1).

LANGUAGE

Balcony [*gezuztra*] – גְּזוּזְטְרָא: From the Greek ἐξώστρα, *exostra*, meaning a balcony or area that protrudes from a building.

HALAKHA

A house that one filled – בַּיִת שֶׁמִּילְּאוֹ: If one filled a house with straw and hay that he subsequently nullified, it is as though the house were nonexistent. Therefore, the ritual impurity imparted by a corpse found inside is not contained by the house; rather, it extends in all directions (Rambam *Sefer Tahara, Hilkhot Tumat Met* 7:6).

גמ׳ וְתֶבֶן לָא חָיֵיץ? וְהָא אֲנַן תְּנַן: מַתְבֵּן שֶׁבֵּין שְׁתֵּי חֲצֵירוֹת, גָּבוֹהַּ עֲשָׂרָה טְפָחִים – מְעָרְבִין שְׁנַיִם, וְאֵין מְעָרְבִין אֶחָד.

GEMARA The Gemara wonders: Does **hay not** constitute **a** proper **filling** to seal the ditch? **Didn't we learn** in the following mishna: With regard to **a haystack ten handbreadths high** that stands **between two courtyards,** the residents of the two courtyards **establish two** ***eiruvin*****, but they** may **not establish one** ***eiruv*****.** This indicates that hay can create a valid partition.

אָמַר אַבָּיֵי: לְעִנְיַן מְחִיצָה – כּוּלֵּי עָלְמָא לָא פְּלִיגִי דְּהָוְיָא מְחִיצָה, אֲבָל לְעִנְיַן חֲצִיצָה, אִי בַּטְלֵיהּ – חָיֵיץ, וְאִי לָא בַּטְלֵיהּ – לָא חָיֵיץ.

Abaye said that the matter should be understood as follows: **With regard to a partition, everyone agrees that** hay **is a partition** and that it divides between the courtyards as long as it is placed there. **But with regard to filling** the ditch so that it is considered sealed, one must distinguish between two cases: **If one** explicitly **nullified** the hay and decided to leave it there, **it fills** and seals the ditch; **however, if he did not nullify it** but intends to remove the hay from the ditch, **it does not fill** it, and the ditch is not considered sealed.

״מָלֵא עָפָר״. וַאֲפִילּוּ בִּסְתָמָא? וְהָתְנַן: בַּיִת שֶׁמִּילְּאָהוּ תֶּבֶן אוֹ צְרוֹרוֹת וּבִיטְּלוֹ – בָּטֵל.

It is written in the mishna: If the ditch is **filled with dirt** or pebbles, it is considered sealed. The Gemara asks: Does this apply **even if one did not specify** his intention to leave it there? **Didn't we learn** in a mishna with regard to the ritual impurity of a corpse: If there is **a house that one filled**[H] **with hay or pebbles, and he nullified** the hay or pebbles and decided to leave them in the house, then the house (Rambam) **is nullified** and is no longer considered a house with partitions? Generally, a house containing a corpse is ritually impure on the inside but does not impart impurity to the surrounding area. However, in this case, the house is considered an enclosed grave that imparts ritual impurity to its surroundings.

בִּיטְּלוֹ – אִין,

And one can infer from the mishna: **If he nullified** the hay or pebbles, **yes,** the house is nullified and considered sealed.

Perek **VII**
Daf **79** Amud **a**

לֹא בִּיטְּלוֹ – לָא. אָמַר רַב הוּנָא: מַאן תְּנָא אֳהָלוֹת – רַבִּי יוֹסֵי הִיא.

However, if **he did not nullify it, no,** the house retains the status of a house, although it is filled with hay. **Rav Huna said: Who** is the *tanna* who **taught** tractate ***Oholot*****? It is Rabbi Yosei,** and the *tanna* of the mishna does not accept his opinion.

אִי רַבִּי יוֹסֵי – אִיפְּכָא שָׁמְעִינַן לֵיהּ. דְּתַנְיָא: רַבִּי יוֹסֵי אוֹמֵר: תֶּבֶן וְאֵין עָתִיד לְפַנּוֹתוֹ – הֲרֵי הוּא כִּסְתָם עָפָר וּבָטֵל, עָפָר וְעָתִיד לְפַנּוֹתוֹ – הֲרֵי הוּא כִּסְתָם תֶּבֶן וְלָא בְּטִיל!

The Gemara asks: **If** that mishna is in accordance with the opinion of **Rabbi Yosei,** there is a difficulty, since **we heard him** say **the opposite, as it was taught** in the *Tosefta* that **Rabbi Yosei says:** In a case where there is a house full of **hay and** the owner **does not intend to remove, it is considered as though** it were filled with **indeterminate dirt, and it is** therefore **nullified.** However, if the house was full of **dirt** that **he intends to remove, it is considered as though** it were filled with **indeterminate hay, and it is** therefore **not nullified.** Apparently, the decisive factor for Rabbi Yosei is not the specific material in the house, but whether or not the owner intends to remove it.

אֶלָּא אָמַר רַב אַסִי: מַאן תְּנָא עֵירוּבִין – רַבִּי יוֹסֵי הִיא.

Rather, Rav Asi said: Who is the *tanna* who **taught** tractate *Eiruvin*? **It is Rabbi Yosei,** who does not accept the opinion of the *tanna* of tractate *Oholot*.

רַב הוּנָא בְּרֵיהּ דְּרַב יְהוֹשֻׁעַ אָמַר: טוּמְאָה אַשַּׁבָּת קָרָמֵית?! הַנַּח אִיסּוּר שַׁבָּת, דַּאֲפִילּוּ אַרְנְקֵי נָמֵי מְבַטֵּל אִינִישׁ.

Rav Huna, son of Rav Yehoshua, said: Are you raising a contradiction between the *halakhot* of ritual **impurity** and the *halakhot* of **Shabbat?** These two areas of *halakha* cannot be compared. **Leave** aside the **prohibition of Shabbat.** With regard to Shabbat, **a person nullifies even a pouch** full of money. The pouch may not be moved on Shabbat and is therefore considered fixed in place. However, hay, which may be moved even on Shabbat, is not considered to be fixed in the ditch. With regard to ritual impurity, by contrast, the nullification must be permanent.

רַב אַשִׁי אָמַר: בַּיִת אַחָרִיץ קָא רָמֵית? בִּשְׁלָמָא חָרִיץ – לְמִיטַּיְּימֵיהּ קָאֵי. אֶלָּא בַּיִת לְמִיטַּיְּימֵיהּ קָאֵי?!

Rav Ashi said: And are you raising a contradiction between the *halakha* that governs **a house** and that which governs **a ditch? Granted** in the case of **a ditch,** it typically **stands to be** permanently **filled.** As there is no doubt that one's intention is to fill the ditch, the assumption is that anything placed inside a ditch will remain there. **However,** does **a house stand to be** permanently **filled?** Of course it does not. Presumably, the hay and dirt will be removed. Consequently, additional proof is necessary in order to conclude that the owner of the house intends to seal it permanently.

נָתַן עָלָיו נֶסֶר שֶׁרוֹחַב אַרְבָּעָה. אָמַר רָבָא: לֹא שָׁנוּ אֶלָּא שֶׁנָּתַן לְרָחְבּוֹ, אֲבָל לְאָרְכּוֹ – אֲפִילּוּ כׇּל שֶׁהוּא נַמִי, שֶׁהֲרֵי מִיעֲטוֹ מֵאַרְבָּעָה.

The mishna states: If **one placed a plank that is four** handbreadths **wide** across a ditch that separates two courtyards, the plank is considered an entrance. **Rava said: They taught** this *halakha* **only** in a case **where one placed** the plank **along the width** of the ditch. **But** if one positioned a plank **along its length,**[HB] **even** if the plank is of **minimum** width, it is **also** considered an entrance and reduces the ditch, **as he reduced** the opening **to less than four** handbreadths. The ditch was originally only four handbreadths wide. Therefore, if one places a plank of any width along its length, it becomes less than four handbreadths wide and no longer constitutes a partition.

״וְכֵן שְׁתֵּי גְזוּזְטְרָאוֹת זוֹ כְּנֶגֶד זוֹ״. אָמַר רָבָא: הָא דְּאָמְרַתְּ זוֹ כְּנֶגֶד זוֹ – אִין, זוֹ שֶׁלֹּא כְּנֶגֶד זוֹ – לָא. וְזוֹ לְמַעְלָה מִזּוֹ, נַמִי, לָא אֲמַרַן אֶלָּא שֶׁיֵּשׁ בֵּין זֶה לָזֶה שְׁלֹשָׁה טְפָחִים, אֲבָל אֵין בֵּין זֶה לָזֶה שְׁלֹשָׁה – גְּזוּזְטְרָא עֲקוּמָּה הִיא.

The mishna continues: **And similarly,** if **two balconies**[B] are **opposite each other,**[H] and one placed a plank four handbreadths wide between them, the residents of the two courtyards may establish a single *eiruv*, as the plank is considered an entrance from one courtyard to the other. **Rava said: That which you said:** If the two balconies are **opposite each other, yes,** carrying between them is permitted by means of a plank; by inference, if they are **not opposite each other, no,** carrying is not permitted in this manner, **and** in a case where **one** balcony **is above the other as well,** it is prohibited, as it is not an entrance because it is too dangerous to walk from one to the other by means of the plank. **We said** the prohibition in these cases **only where there is** a disparity of at least **three** handbreadths **between this** balcony and **that** balcony. **However,** if **there is** a difference of **less than three** handbreadths **between this** balcony and **that** balcony, **it** is considered a single **crooked balcony.** Two balconies separated by a gap of less than three handbreadths are considered joined, based on the principle of *lavud*.

מתני׳ מַתְבֵּן שֶׁבֵּין שְׁתֵּי חֲצֵירוֹת גָּבוֹהַּ עֲשָׂרָה טְפָחִים – מְעָרְבִין שְׁנַיִם, וְאֵין מְעָרְבִין אֶחָד. אֵלּוּ מַאֲכִילִין מִכָּאן, וְאֵלּוּ מַאֲכִילִין מִכָּאן. נִתְמַעֵט הַתֶּבֶן מֵעֲשָׂרָה טְפָחִים – מְעָרְבִין אֶחָד, וְאֵין מְעָרְבִין שְׁנַיִם.

MISHNA With regard to **a haystack that is** positioned **between two courtyards**[H] and is **ten handbreadths high,** it has the status of a partition, **and** therefore the residents of the courtyards may **establish two *eiruvin*, and they** may **not establish one *eiruv*. These,** the inhabitants of one courtyard, may **feed** their animals **from here,**[N] from one side of the haystack, **and those,** the inhabitants of the other courtyard, may **feed** their animals **from there,** from the other side of the haystack. There is no concern that the haystack might become too small to serve as a partition. If the height of **the hay was reduced** to less **than ten handbreadths** across its entire length, its legal status is no longer that of a partition. Consequently, the residents of both courtyards **establish one *eiruv*, and they do not establish two *eiruvin*.**

BACKGROUND

A plank placed along its width or its length – נֶסֶר לְרׇחְבּוֹ וּלְאׇרְכּוֹ: A plank placed across the width of the ditch forms an entrance that links the two courtyards on either side of the ditch. A plank placed lengthwise across the ditch does not join the two courtyards, but reduces the ditch to less than four handbreadths in width, and consequently forms a kind of entrance as well.

One plank placed across a ditch and one plank placed along its length

Two balconies – שְׁתֵּי גְזוּזְטְרָאוֹת:

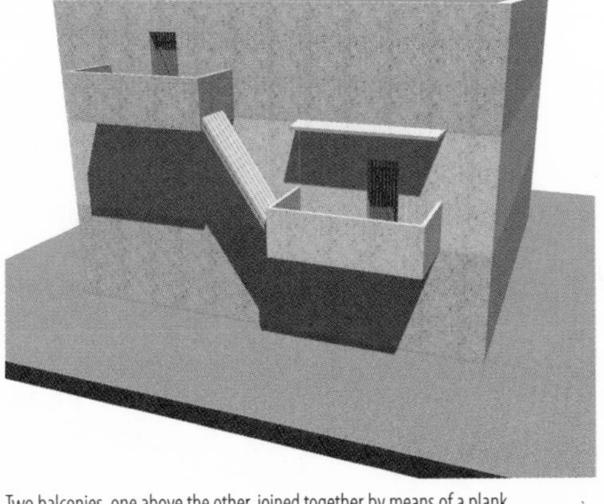

Two balconies, one above the other, joined together by means of a plank

HALAKHA

A plank along its length – נֶסֶר לְאוֹרְכּוֹ: With regard to a person who places a plank along the length of the ditch, even a plank of minimal width, if the width of the ditch is thereby reduced to less than four handbreadths, the plank is considered an entrance. If the plank is longer than ten cubits, it has the status of a breach in a wall, and therefore the inhabitants on both sides of the ditch may establish only one *eiruv* (Rambam *Sefer Zemanim, Hilkhot Eiruvin* 3:14; *Shulḥan Arukh, Oraḥ Ḥayyim* 372:17).

Balconies opposite each other – גְּזוּזְטְרָאוֹת זוֹ כְּנֶגֶד זוֹ: With regard to a case of two balconies that face each other, or a case of one balcony positioned above the other on the same wall, if the balconies are separated by a gap of more than three handbreadths in height, they cannot be joined by means of a plank. If the difference in height is less than three handbreadths, it is considered a single crooked balcony and is permitted, as stated by Rava (*Shulḥan Arukh, Oraḥ Ḥayyim* 373:1).

A haystack that is between two courtyards – מַתְבֵּן שֶׁבֵּין שְׁתֵּי חֲצֵירוֹת: If a haystack between two courtyards is ten handbreadths high, the residents establish two *eiruvin*. If the haystack was reduced to less than ten handbreadths in height before Shabbat, the residents of both courtyards establish one *eiruv*. The Rosh maintains that the same *halakha* is in effect if the haystack was reduced on Shabbat itself.

It is prohibited to remove hay from a haystack ten handbreadths high on Shabbat to feed one's animal, and it is likewise prohibited to position an animal near the haystack. However, it is permitted to stand in front of the animal so that it will go there of its own accord. If the haystack is positioned between two houses, it is permitted to feed one's animal from it, even by hand (*Shulḥan Arukh, Oraḥ Ḥayyim* 372:19).

NOTES

These may feed from here – אֵלּוּ מַאֲכִילִין מִכָּאן: The Rosh explains that this statement of the mishna is referring only to a weekday. The mishna is teaching that even though the hay is required for a partition on Shabbat, the residents need not be concerned about this eventuality on a weekday. Rather, they may feed their animals from the haystack. This interpretation explains why the Gemara does not cite a proof or an objection from the mishna with regard to the statement of Rav Huna, as the *tanna* does not deal with the issue feeding an animal on Shabbat at all. However, in the Jerusalem Talmud an explanation is stated that is completely at odds with the above interpretation: It is indeed permitted to feed an animal on Shabbat, and contrary to the opinion of Rav Huna, one is even permitted to place hay into a basket and give it to his animal, as can be inferred from the phrase: They may feed.

NOTES

One does not put hay into his basket – לֹא יִתֵּן לְתוֹךְ קוּפָּתוֹ: Rashi offers two reasons why it is prohibited to remove hay manually from the partition. Some commentaries explain that the rationale for this prohibition is that one would thereby break the partition, as the hay serves as a fence between the courtyards. Consequently, if he removes enough of the hay to nullify its status as a partition, this is tantamount to performing the labor of dismantling on Shabbat and is prohibited by rabbinic decree (Rashba).

Pit [*gov*] of hay – גּוֹב שֶׁל תֶּבֶן: Rabbeinu Ḥananel, the *Arukh*, the Ra'avad, and others read this word as *giv*, a pile of straw comprised of bundles tied together. This explanation is closer to the case described in the mishna.

HALAKHA

Where an animal may be positioned on Shabbat – הֵיכָן מַעֲמִיד בְּהֵמָה בְּשַׁבָּת: A person may position his animal on a patch of grass on Shabbat so that it may graze there, but he may not place the animal on set-aside objects (*Shulḥan Arukh*, *Oraḥ Ḥayyim* 324:13).

גמ׳ אָמַר רַב הוּנָא: וּבִלְבַד שֶׁלֹּא יִתֵּן לְתוֹךְ קוּפָּתוֹ וְיַאֲכִיל.

GEMARA With regard to the mishna's statement that the inhabitants of the two courtyards are permitted to place their animals next to the haystack and feed them, **Rav Huna said: And** this is the *halakha* **provided that one does not** actually **put** hay **into his basket**[N] **and feed** his animals. In that case, there is concern that one might inadvertently reduce the height of the partition to less than ten handbreadths, which would constitute a breach between the courtyards and invalidate both *eiruvin*.

וּלְאוֹקְמֵי שָׁרֵי? וְהָאָמַר רַב הוּנָא, אָמַר רַבִּי חֲנִינָא: מַעֲמִיד אָדָם אֶת בְּהֶמְתּוֹ עַל גַּבֵּי עֲשָׂבִים בְּשַׁבָּת, וְאֵין מַעֲמִיד אָדָם אֶת בְּהֶמְתּוֹ עַל גַּבֵּי מוּקְצֶה בְּשַׁבָּת!

The Gemara asks: **And** if the actual handling of the hay is prohibited, is it **permitted to stand** one's animal next to the haystack and let it eat? **Didn't Rav Huna say** that **Rabbi Ḥanina said: A person may stand his animal on** a patch of **grass on Shabbat,** as he will certainly be careful not to pull out grass for the animal, due to the severity of the Torah prohibition involved. However, **a person may not stand his animal on set-aside** items **on Shabbat.**[H] As the prohibition of set-aside is rabbinic in origin, he might forget and move the set-aside objects himself. The same reasoning should apply in the case of the haystack. If it is prohibited by rabbinic decree to remove hay from the stack manually, it should likewise be prohibited to position one's animal alongside the stack.

דְּקָאֵים לַהּ בְּאַפָּהּ וְאָזְלָה וְאָכְלָה.

The Gemara answers: The mishna is not referring to a case where one directly brings the animal and places it alongside the haystack. Rather, it is dealing with a situation **where one stands in front of** the animal so that it cannot go elsewhere, **and it goes and eats** from the haystack of its own accord. In that case, the rabbinic decree does not apply.

וְלֹא יִתֵּן לְתוֹךְ קוּפָּתוֹ תֶּבֶן? וְהָתַנְיָא: בַּיִת שֶׁבֵּין שְׁתֵּי חֲצֵירוֹת וּמִילְאָהוּ תֶּבֶן – מְעָרְבִין שְׁנַיִם, וְאֵין מְעָרְבִין אֶחָד. זֶה נוֹתֵן לְתוֹךְ קוּפָּתוֹ וְיַאֲכִיל, וְזֶה נוֹתֵן לְתוֹךְ קוּפָּתוֹ וְיַאֲכִיל. נִתְמַעֵט הַתֶּבֶן מֵעֲשָׂרָה טְפָחִים – שְׁנֵיהֶם אֲסוּרִים.

The Gemara asks a question with regard to Rav Huna's statement itself: **And may one not put hay into his basket** and feed his animal? **Wasn't it taught** in a *baraita*: In the case of **a house that is** positioned **between two courtyards and** the residents **filled it with hay,** they **establish two *eiruvin*, but** they **do not establish one *eiruv*,** as the hay is considered a partition that divides the house. The resident of **this** courtyard **puts** hay **into his basket and feeds** his animal, **and** The resident of **that** courtyard **puts** hay **into his basket and feeds** his animal. **If the hay was reduced** to a height less **than ten handbreadths,** it is **prohibited** for residents of **both** to carry in their respective courtyards.

כֵּיצַד הוּא עוֹשֶׂה? נוֹעֵל אֶת בֵּיתוֹ וּמְבַטֵּל אֶת רְשׁוּתוֹ, הוּא אָסוּר וַחֲבֵירוֹ מוּתָּר.

How, then, **does** the resident of one of the courtyards **act** if he seeks to permit use of the other courtyard to its resident? He **locks his house and renounces his right** to carry in the courtyard in favor of the other person. Consequently, **it is prohibited** for him to carry from his house into the courtyard, **and it is permitted** for **the other** resident to do so.

וְכֵן אַתָּה אוֹמֵר בְּגוֹב שֶׁל תֶּבֶן שֶׁבֵּין שְׁנֵי תְחוּמֵי שַׁבָּת. קָתָנֵי מִיהַת: זֶה נוֹתֵן לְתוֹךְ קוּפָּתוֹ וְיַאֲכִיל, וְזֶה נוֹתֵן לְתוֹךְ קוּפָּתוֹ וְיַאֲכִיל!

And you say likewise with regard to a **pit** [*gov*] **of hay**[N] **that is** positioned **between two Shabbat limits.** The residents of each area may feed their animals from the common hay, as there is no concern lest the animals go beyond the limit. **In any case,** the *baraita* **teaches:** The resident of **this** courtyard **puts** hay **into his basket and feeds** his animal, **and** the resident of **that** courtyard **puts** hay **into his basket and feeds** his animal. This *halakha* poses a difficulty to Rav Huna's opinion.

אָמְרִי: בַּיִת כֵּיוָן דְּאִיכָּא (מְחִיצוֹת וְ)תִקְרָה כִּי מִיפַּחִית – מִינְכְּרָא לֵיהּ מִלְּתָא. הָכָא – לָא מִינְכְּרָא לֵיהּ מִלְּתָא.

The Gemara answers: **We** can **say** that in the case of **a house, since it has walls and a ceiling, when** the height of the haystack **is reduced the matter is conspicuous.** The height disparity between the haystack and the ceiling is obvious. Consequently, when the haystack is reduced to less than ten handbreadths, people will stop carrying in the courtyard. **Here,** however, with regard to the hay in the pit, the difference in height **is not conspicuous.** The height of the hay in the pit could become diminished to the extent that the partition is nullified without anyone noticing.

"נִתְמַעֵט הַתֶּבֶן מֵעֲשָׂרָה טְפָחִים שְׁנֵיהֶן אֲסוּרִין". הָא עֲשָׂרָה – שָׁרֵי, וְאַף עַל גַּב דְּמִידְלְיָא תִּקְרָה טוּבָא. שְׁמַע מִינָּהּ: מְחִיצּוֹת שֶׁאֵין מַגִּיעוֹת לַתִּקְרָה – שְׁמָן מְחִיצּוֹת!

It is stated in the *baraita*: **If the hay was reduced** to less **than ten handbreadths** it is **prohibited** to carry in **both** courtyards. The Gemara infers from the phrasing of the *baraita*: If the hay was at least **ten** handbreadths high, it is **permitted** to carry there, even though the **ceiling is much higher** than the hay. **Conclude from it** that the legal **status of** ten-handbreadth **partitions that do not reach the ceiling is that of** standard **partitions,** which was the subject of a dispute elsewhere. Apparently, this *baraita* proves that they have the status of partitions in all respects.

אָמַר אַבַּיֵי: הָכָא בְּבַיִת שְׁלֹשָׁה עָשָׂר חָסֵר מַשֶּׁהוּ עָסְקִינַן, וְתֶבֶן עֲשָׂרָה.

Abaye said: Here, we are dealing with the case of a **house** that is **slightly less than thirteen** handbreadths high **and the hay** is **ten** handbreadths high. The haystack is less than three handbreadths from the ceiling, and based on the principle of *lavud*, they are considered joined as though the partitions reach the ceiling.

וְרַב הוּנָא בְּרֵיהּ דְּרַב יְהוֹשֻׁעַ אָמַר: אֲפִילּוּ תֵּימָא בְּבַיִת עֲשָׂרָה

And Rav Huna, son of Rav Yehoshua, said: Even if **you say** that the *baraita* is dealing **with a house ten** handbreadths high,

Perek **VII**
Daf **79** Amud **b**

וְתֶבֶן שִׁבְעָה וּמַשֶּׁהוּ. דְּכָל פָּחוֹת מִשְּׁלֹשָׁה כְּלָבוּד דָּמֵי.

and the hay in the house is **slightly more than seven** handbreadths high it is considered a full-fledged partition that reaches the ceiling, as objects separated by **any** gap of **less than three** handbreadths **are considered joined,** based on the principle of *lavud*.

בִּשְׁלָמָא לְאַבַּיֵי – הַיְינוּ דְּקָתָנֵי "מֵעֲשָׂרָה". אֶלָּא לְרַב הוּנָא בְּרֵיהּ דְּרַב יְהוֹשֻׁעַ, מַאי מֵעֲשָׂרָה?

The Gemara comments. **Granted, according to** the opinion of **Abaye, that is why** the *baraita* **teaches:** If the height of the haystack was reduced to less **than ten** handbreadths. **However, according to Rav Huna, son of Rav Yehoshua, what is** the meaning of: Less **than ten?** Even at the outset it was never as high as ten handbreadths.

מִתּוֹרַת עֲשָׂרָה.

The Gemara answers: It means that it was reduced to less **than the law of ten** handbreadths. As long as the hay is slightly more than seven handbreadths high, it is regarded as ten handbreadths high, in accordance with the principle of *lavud*. Once its height is reduced to less than seven handbreadths, the *halakha* of a partition ten handbreadths high is no longer in effect.

"שְׁנֵיהֶן אֲסוּרִין". שְׁמַע מִינָּהּ: דִּיּוּרִין הַבָּאִין בְּשַׁבָּת אֲסוּרִין.

The same *baraita* taught that if the height of the hay was reduced to less than ten handbreadths, it is **prohibited** to carry in **both.** The Gemara comments: Should we **learn from this** that **residents who arrive on Shabbat prohibit** the other residents from carrying? At the onset of Shabbat, both sets of residents were permitted to use the hay and the house, but once the hay was reduced on Shabbat it is as though new residents had been added to each of the courtyards, and it is prohibited for all of them to carry. Why not say that since at the beginning of Shabbat it was permitted to carry in the domain, they are permitted to do so for its duration?

דִּלְמָא דְּאִימְּעַט מֵאֶתְמוֹל.

The Gemara rejects this contention: **Perhaps** the *baraita* is referring to a case **where** the hay **was** already **reduced on the previous day,** before Shabbat began. In that case, it was never permitted to carry at all.

"כֵּיצַד הוּא עוֹשֶׂה? נוֹעֵל אֶת בֵּיתוֹ וּמְבַטֵּל רְשׁוּתוֹ". תַּרְתֵּי?! הָכִי קָאָמַר: אוֹ נוֹעֵל אֶת בֵּיתוֹ, אוֹ מְבַטֵּל אֶת רְשׁוּתוֹ.

The *baraita* continues: **How,** then, **does** the resident of one of the courtyards **act** if he seeks to permit use of the other courtyard to its resident? He **locks his house and renounces his right** to carry in the courtyard in favor of the other person. The Gemara is surprised by this ruling: Does he require these **two** steps? One should suffice. The Gemara answers: **This is what** the *tanna* of the *baraita* **is saying: Either he locks his house or he renounces his right** to the courtyard.

וְאִיבָּעֵית אֵימָא: לְעוֹלָם תַּרְתֵּי, כֵּיוָן דְּדָשׁ בֵּיהּ – אָתֵי לְטַלְטוּלֵי.

And if you wish, say a different explanation instead. **Actually, both** actions are required in this case, even though one of them would ordinarily suffice. The reason is: **Since he is accustomed to** using the courtyard, **he will come to carry.** Consequently, the Sages were stringent with a person in this position and obligated him to implement an additional change so that he will not forget and come to carry when it is prohibited.

״הוּא אָסוּר וַחֲבֵירוֹ מוּתָּר״. פְּשִׁיטָא! לָא צְרִיכָא דַּהֲדַר אִידָּךְ וּבָטֵיל לֵיהּ לְחַבְרֵיהּ. וְהָא קָא מַשְׁמַע לָן: דְּאֵין מְבַטְּלִין וְחוֹזְרִין וּמְבַטְּלִין.

It was taught in the *baraita*: If one locks his house and renounces his rights to the courtyard, **it is prohibited** for him to carry, **and it is permitted** for **the other** person to carry. The Gemara raises a difficulty: Isn't this **obvious?** Why was it necessary to state this *halakha*? The Gemara answers: **It was necessary only** in a case **where the other** person **then renounced** his right in favor **of the first** person. **And** the *baraita* **teaches us that** one **may not renounce** his rights in favor of the other, **and then** have the latter **renounce** his own rights in favor of the former.

״וְכֵן אַתָּה אוֹמֵר בְּגוֹב שֶׁל תֶּבֶן שֶׁבֵּין שְׁנֵי תְחוּמֵי שַׁבָּת״. פְּשִׁיטָא! לָא צְרִיכָא לְרַבִּי עֲקִיבָא דְּאָמַר: תְּחוּמִין דְּאוֹרַיְיתָא. מַהוּ דְּתֵימָא: לִיגְזוֹר דִּלְמָא אָתֵי לְאִיחְלוּפֵי – קָא מַשְׁמַע לָן.

It was further taught in the *baraita*: **And you** can **say likewise with regard to a pit of hay that** is situated **between two Shabbat limits.** The inhabitants of each area may feed their animals from the common hay. The Gemara raises a difficulty: Isn't this **obvious?** The same principle that is in effect with regard to a haystack between courtyards should apply here as well. The Gemara answers: **It was necessary** to state this *halakha* only **according to** the opinion of **Rabbi Akiva, who said** that the principle of Shabbat **boundaries** is **by Torah law. Lest you say** that **let us issue a decree** and prohibit it, **lest** people **come to exchange**[N] objects from one boundary to another, which would violate a Torah prohibition; therefore, the *baraita* **teaches us** that no distinction is made between the cases, and no decree of this kind is issued.

מתני׳ כֵּיצַד מִשְׁתַּתְּפִין בַּמָּבוֹי? מַנִּיחַ אֶת הֶחָבִית, וְאוֹמֵר: הֲרֵי זוֹ לְכָל בְּנֵי מָבוֹי. וּמְזַכֶּה לָהֶן עַל יְדֵי בְּנוֹ וּבִתּוֹ הַגְּדוֹלִים, וְעַל יְדֵי עַבְדּוֹ וְשִׁפְחָתוֹ הָעִבְרִים, וְעַל יְדֵי אִשְׁתּוֹ.

MISHNA **How does one merge** the courtyards that open **into the alleyway,** if a person wishes to act on behalf of all the residents of the alleyway? **He places a barrel**[N] filled with his own food **and says: This is for all the residents of the alleyway.** For this gift to be acquired by the others, someone must accept it on their behalf, **and** the *tanna* therefore teaches that **he** may **confer possession**[N] **to them** even **by means of his adult son or daughter, and** likewise **by means of his Hebrew slave or maidservant,** whom he does not own, **and by means of his wife.** These people may acquire the *eiruv* on behalf of all the residents of the alleyway.

אֲבָל אֵינוֹ מְזַכֶּה לֹא עַל יְדֵי בְּנוֹ וּבִתּוֹ הַקְּטַנִּים, וְלֹא עַל יְדֵי עַבְדּוֹ וְשִׁפְחָתוֹ הַכְּנַעֲנִים, מִפְּנֵי שֶׁיָּדָן כְּיָדוֹ.

However, he may **not confer possession by means of his minor son or daughter, nor by means of his Canaanite slave or maidservant,**[H] **because** they cannot effect acquisition, as ownership of objects that come into **their possession is as** if those objects came into **his possession.** Consequently, the master or father cannot confer possession to the slave or minor respectively on behalf of others as their acquisition is ineffective and the object remains in his own possession.

גמ׳ אָמַר רַב יְהוּדָה: חָבִית שֶׁל שִׁיתּוּפֵי מְבוֹאוֹת – צָרִיךְ לְהַגְבִּיהַּ מִן הַקַּרְקַע טֶפַח.

GEMARA **Rav Yehuda said:** With regard to **a barrel for the merging of alleyways,** the one acquiring it on behalf of the alleyway's residents **must raise** it **a handbreadth**[N] **from the ground,** as he must perform a valid act of acquisition on their behalf.[H]

אָמַר רָבָא: הָנֵי תַּרְתֵּי מִילֵּי סָבֵי דְּפוּמְבְּדִיתָא אָמְרִינְהוּ. חֲדָא – הָא. אִידָּךְ: הַמְקַדֵּשׁ, אִם טָעַם מְלֹא לוּגְמָיו – יָצָא, וְאִם לָאו – לֹא יָצָא.

Rava said: The elders of Pumbedita, Rav Yehuda and his students, **stated these two matters. One** was **this** mentioned above with regard to lifting the barrel; and **the other** was: With regard to **one who recites *kiddush*** over wine on Shabbat or a Festival, **if he tasted a mouthful** of wine, **he fulfilled** his obligation;[H] **however, if** he did **not** taste a mouthful, **he did not fulfill** his obligation.

אָמַר רַב חֲבִיבָא: הָא נַמִי סָבֵי דְּפוּמְבְּדִיתָא אָמְרִינְהוּ. דְּאָמַר רַב יְהוּדָה, אָמַר שְׁמוּאֵל: עוֹשִׂין מְדוּרָה לַחַיָּה בַּשַּׁבָּת.

Rav Ḥaviva said: In addition to the aforementioned pair of teachings, **the elders of Pumbedita stated this too, as Rav Yehuda said** that **Shmuel said: One builds a fire for a woman in childbirth on Shabbat.**

NOTES

Lest people come to exchange – דִּלְמָא אָתֵי לְאִיחְלוּפֵי: The concern is not that people might transfer objects from one Shabbat limit to another, for even according to Rabbi Akiva the Torah prohibits only walking beyond the boundary, not transferring of objects without leaving one's boundary. Instead, the worry is that they might forget, exchange objects, and end up walking beyond their Shabbat limit.

He places a barrel – מַנִּיחַ אֶת הֶחָבִית: There is no obligation to use a barrel specifically. The mishna uses the example of a barrel simply because people would typically establish a merging of alleyways with wine, which is kept in a barrel.

Conferring possession – זִיכּוּי: This conferral of possession must be achieved by parties legally capable of performing acquisitions in general. One method of acquisition is the lifting of the object to be acquired by the one acquiring it or receiving it as a gift [. The acquisition must be performed by means of another person because one cannot transfer rights to others by mere speech. In addition, any act of acquisition, including the donation of a gift, requires two sides, representing the original owner and the new owner. In this case, too, someone who is not the giver must acquire the gift on behalf of the receivers.

Raise it a handbreadth – לְהַגְבִּיהַּ...טֶפַח: Most commentaries understand this lifting of the object as a form of acquisition. However, some *ge'onim* explain that the barrel used for the merging the alleyway must remain a handbreadth higher than the other barrels, as a sign that it is the barrel of the merging (Rambam *Sefer Zemanim, Hilkhot Eiruvin* 1:17; see Rabbeinu Yehonatan).

HALAKHA

By means of whom may one confer possession – עַל יְדֵי מִי זוֹכִים: One may transfer possession of an *eiruv* to others by means of his wife, or his adult children, or by means of his Jewish servant or maidservant, even if they are minors and even if they eat from his table. As they can acquire possessions for themselves, they may do so on behalf of others as well. However, one may not transfer possession by means of his minor children, who have no right of acquisition, nor by means of a Canaanite slave, who has no right of acquisition either, as his hand is considered like his master's hand with regard to acquisition (Rif; Rambam *Sefer Zemanim, Hilkhot Eiruvin* 1:20; Ran).

Some authorities maintain that one may not transfer possession by means of his adult children if they eat at his table, i.e., if he supports them financially, or by means of his wife if he supports her, or by means of his daughter who has not reached maturity, as the Sages decreed that all their earnings belongs to their father or husband. The reason is that these people have no right of acquisition themselves (Rav Shimshon of Saens, who rules in accordance with Rabbi Yehuda in monetary matters). However, he may transfer possession by means of his minor children who are not supported by him. One should be stringent in accordance with both opinions *ab initio* (*Tur*). Nevertheless, after the fact, the lenient opinion with regard to an *eiruv* is accepted (Rema; *Shulḥan Arukh, Oraḥ Ḥayyim* 366:10).

How the possession of an *eiruv* is conferred to others – כֵּיצַד מְזַכֶּה עֵירוּב: One may place a barrel of wine for a merging of alleyways or bread for a joining of courtyards, lift it a handbreadth, and thereby transfer its possession to the residents of the courtyard or alleyway and all those who live with them. There is no need to inform them before Shabbat that one is transferring possession on their behalf (Rema; *Shulḥan Arukh, Oraḥ Ḥayyim* 366:9).

The obligation of *kiddush* – חוֹבַת קִידּוּשׁ: One who recited *kiddush* over wine and drank a mouthful, i.e., most of a quarter of a *log*, has fulfilled his obligation with regard to *kiddush* (*Shulḥan Arukh, Oraḥ Ḥayyim* 271:13).

סְבוּר מִינָּהּ: לַחַיָּה – אִין, לַחוֹלֶה – לָא. בִּימוֹת הַגְּשָׁמִים – אִין, בִּימוֹת הַחַמָּה – לָא.

The Gemara comments that the Sages **thought** to infer **from here: For a woman in childbirth, yes,** one builds a fire, due to her highly precarious state; **for a sick person, no,** one does not build a fire. Likewise, **in the rainy season,** when the danger of catching cold is ever present, **yes,** one builds a fire; **in the summer, no,** one may not.

אִיתְּמַר, אָמַר רַב חִיָּיא בַּר אָבִין, אָמַר שְׁמוּאֵל: הִקִּיז דָּם וְנִצְטַנֵּן – עוֹשִׂין לוֹ מְדוּרָה בַּשַּׁבָּת, וַאֲפִילּוּ בִּתְקוּפַת תַּמּוּז.

The Gemara adds that which **was stated: Rav Ḥiyya bar Avin said** that **Shmuel said:** With regard to one who **let blood and caught cold, one builds a fire for him on Shabbat, even during the season of Tammuz,** i.e., the summer. Clearly, Rav Yehuda's ruling is limited neither to a woman in childbirth nor to the rainy season.

אָמַר אַמֵימָר: הָא נַמִי סָבֵי דְּפוּמְבְּדִיתָא אָמְרִינְהוּ. דְּאִיתְּמַר: אֵיזוֹ הִיא אֲשֵׁירָה סְתָם?

Ameimar said: This too was stated by the elders of Pumbedita, as it was stated that the *amora'im* disagreed with regard to **which** tree **is presumed** to be **a tree designated for idolatry** [*asheira*],[N] even though no one actually saw it worshipped.

אָמַר רַב: כֹּל שֶׁכּוֹמָרִין שׁוֹמְרִין אוֹתָהּ,

Rav said: It is any tree **that** idolatrous **priests guard.**

NOTES

Asheira – אֲשֵׁירָה: The *asheira* that is mentioned in the Torah several times was worshipped as an idol. This is the "*asheira* of Moses," i.e., the tree that appears in the Torah. However, little is known about a plain *asheira*. Is it a tree dedicated by idolatrous priests, or an idol?

Perek **VII**
Daf **80** Amud **a**

וְאֵין טוֹעֲמִין מִפֵּירוֹתֶיהָ.

and whose fruit they do not taste. This tree is evidently consecrated to the cult.

וּשְׁמוּאֵל אָמַר: כְּגוֹן דְּאָמְרִי "הָנֵי תַּמְרֵי לְשִׁיכְרָא דְּבֵי נִצְרְפֵי דְּשָׁתוּ לֵיהּ בְּיוֹם חַגָּם". (אֲמַר אַמֵימָר,) וַאֲמַרוּ לִי סָבֵי דְּפוּמְבְּדִיתָא: הִלְכְתָא כְּוָותֵיהּ דִּשְׁמוּאֵל.

And Shmuel said: For example, if they say: These dates are for the beer of the temple of Nitzrefei,[L] **which they drink on the day of their festival,**[N] then this is enough to establish the tree as an *asheira*.[H] **Ameimar said: And the elders of Pumbedita said to me** with regard to this issue: The ***halakha* is in accordance with** the opinion of **Shmuel.**

מֵיתִיבִי: כֵּיצַד מִשְׁתַּתְּפִין בַּמָּבוֹי – מְבִיאִים חָבִית שֶׁל יַיִן וְשֶׁל שֶׁמֶן וְשֶׁל תְּמָרִים וְשֶׁל גְּרוֹגָרוֹת וְשֶׁל שְׁאָר מִינֵי פֵּירוֹת,

The Gemara returns to Rav Yehuda's ruling that the barrel used for merging the alleyway must be raised a handbreadth from the ground. The Gemara **raises an objection** from a *baraita*: **How does one merge an alleyway? One brings a barrel of wine, or oil, or dates, or dried figs, or any other type of produce** for merging the alleyway.

אִם מִשֶּׁלּוֹ – צָרִיךְ לְזַכּוֹת, וְאִם מִשֶּׁלָּהֶן – צָרִיךְ לְהוֹדִיעַ. וּמַגְבִּיהַּ מִן הַקַּרְקַע מַשֶּׁהוּ! מַאי "מַשֶּׁהוּ" נַמִי דְּקָאָמַר – טֶפַח.

If one contributed a barrel **of his own, he must confer possession** to all the other residents by means of another person who acquires it on their behalf. **And if** the barrel **is theirs, he must** at least **inform** them that he is merging the alleyway. **And** the one acquiring it on behalf of the others **raises** the barrel **a minimal amount from the ground.** Apparently, the barrel need not be raised a handbreadth. The Gemara answers: Here **too, what is** this **minimal amount of which** the *tanna* of the *baraita* **spoke?** This expression means **a handbreadth,** but no less.

אִיתְּמַר, שִׁיתּוּפֵי מְבוֹאוֹת, רַב אָמַר: אֵין צָרִיךְ לְזַכּוֹת, וּשְׁמוּאֵל אָמַר: צָרִיךְ לְזַכּוֹת. עֵירוּבֵי תְחוּמִין, רַב אָמַר: צָרִיךְ לְזַכּוֹת. וּשְׁמוּאֵל אָמַר: אֵין צָרִיךְ לְזַכּוֹת.

It is stated that the *amora'im* disagreed with regard to the acquisition of a **merging of alleyways. Rav said: It is not necessary to confer possession** of the food used in merging the alleyway to all the residents of the alleyway; **and Shmuel said: It is necessary to confer possession** to them. They likewise disagreed with regard to a **joining of** Shabbat **boundaries,** but the opinions are reversed. **Rav said: It is necessary to confer possession** of the food to all those who wish to be included in the *eiruv*, **and Shmuel said: It is not necessary to confer possession** to them.

בִּשְׁלָמָא לִשְׁמוּאֵל – הָכָא – תְּנַן, וְהָכָא – לָא תְּנַן. אֶלָּא לְרַב, מַאי טַעְמָא?

The Gemara raises a difficulty: **Granted, according to** the opinion of **Shmuel,** his reasoning is clear, as **here,** with regard to a merging of the alleyways, **we learned** in the mishna that he must confer possession, **whereas there,** with regard to a joining of Shabbat boundaries, **we did not learn** that this is the *halakha*. **However, according to Rav, what is the reason** that he differentiates between the cases in this manner?

LANGUAGE

The temple of Nitzrefei – בֵּי נִצְרְפֵי: The source of this word is unclear. Apparently, it is a deliberate corruption of *bei nisrafei*, the place of burning [*sereifa*], where the Persian fire-worship was conducted. This would be in accordance with the requirement of *halakha* that the names of idolatry must be corrupted and mispronounced.

NOTES

Which they drink on the day of their festival – דְּשָׁתוּ לֵיהּ בְּיוֹם חַגָּם: Shmuel maintains that any tree consecrated for the purposes of a cult, even if it itself is not worshipped, is nonetheless considered an *asheira*, at least by rabbinic decree. Rav's opinion is included in the opinion of Shmuel, as the fact that the priests tend to the tree without deriving benefit from it proves that it is worshipped as a god to a certain extent.

HALAKHA

Asheira – אֲשֵׁירָה: The category of *asheira* includes a tree used by priests in the preparation of a drink for their idolatrous festival. This *halakha* also extends to a tree under which they sit without deriving benefit from its fruit (*Shakh*), in accordance with Shmuel's stringent opinion (*Shulḥan Arukh*, *Yoreh De'a* 142:12).

תַּנָּאֵי הִיא; דְּאָמַר רַב יְהוּדָה, אָמַר רַב: מַעֲשֶׂה בְּכַלָּתוֹ שֶׁל רַבִּי אוֹשַׁעְיָא שֶׁהָלְכָה לְבֵית הַמֶּרְחָץ וְחָשְׁכָה לָהּ, וְעֵירְבָה לָהּ חֲמוֹתָהּ.

The Gemara answers: **This is** the subject of a dispute between **the** ***tanna'im*****, as Rav Yehuda said** that **Rav said:** There was **an incident involving** the **daughter-in-law of Rabbi Oshaya, who went** before Shabbat **to the bathhouse,** which was located beyond the Shabbat boundary, **and it grew dark** before **she** was able to return, **and her mother-in-law established a joining** of Shabbat boundaries for her so that she could return home.

וּבָא מַעֲשֶׂה לִפְנֵי רַבִּי חִיָּיא, וְאָסַר. אָמַר לוֹ רַבִּי יִשְׁמָעֵאל בְּרַבִּי יוֹסֵי: בַּבְלַאי! כׇּל כָּךְ אַתָּה מַחְמִיר בְּעֵירוּבִין?! כָּךְ אָמַר אַבָּא: כֹּל שֶׁיֵּשׁ לְךָ לְהָקֵל בְּעֵירוּבִין – הָקֵל.

And the incident came before Rabbi Ḥiyya for a ruling as to whether the *eiruv* is valid, **and he** ruled that it was not valid and **prohibited** her return. **Rabbi Yishmael, son of Rabbi Yosei, said to him: Babylonian, are you so stringent with regard to an** ***eiruv*****?** **This** is what my **father said: Any** case **where you have** the ability **to be lenient with regard to an** ***eiruv*****, be lenient.**

וְאִבַּעְיָא לְהוּ: מִשֶּׁל חֲמוֹתָהּ עֵירְבָה לָהּ, וּמִשּׁוּם דְּלָא זִיכְּתָה לָהּ, אוֹ דִּילְמָא: מִשֶּׁלָּהּ עֵירְבָה לָהּ, וּמִשּׁוּם דְּשֶׁלֹּא מִדַּעְתָּהּ?

And a dilemma was raised before the Sages: Did the mother-in-law **establish the** ***eiruv*** **for** her daughter-in-law **with the mother-in-law's** food, and Rabbi Ḥiyya prohibited it **because she did not confer possession to her,** i.e., she merely prepared the *eiruv* but did not confer possession of the food, and an *eiruv* of this kind is not effective? **Or perhaps she established the** ***eiruv*** **for her with the** daughter-in-law's **own** food, but the *eiruv* was invalid **because** it was prepared **without her knowledge?**

אֲמַר לְהֶן הַהוּא מֵרַבָּנַן וְרַבִּי יַעֲקֹב שְׁמֵיהּ: לְדִידִי מִיפָּרְשָׁא לִי מִינֵּיהּ דְּרַבִּי יוֹחָנָן: מִשֶּׁל חֲמוֹתָהּ עֵירְבָה, וּמִשּׁוּם דְּלָא זִיכְּתָה לָהּ.

One of the Sages, named Rabbi Ya'akov, said to them: It was personally **explained to me by Rabbi Yoḥanan** that the mother-in-law **established the** ***eiruv*** **for her with the mother-in-law's** food, **and** Rabbi Ḥiyya prohibited it **because she did not confer possession** of the food **to her.**

אֲמַר לֵיהּ רַבִּי זֵירָא לְרַבִּי יַעֲקֹב (בְּרֵיהּ) דְּבַת יַעֲקֹב: כִּי מָטֵית הָתָם, אַקִּיף וְזִיל לְסוּלָּמָא דְּצוֹר, וּבְעָא מִינֵּיהּ מֵרַב יַעֲקֹב בַּר אִידִי.

Rabbi Zeira said to Rabbi Ya'akov, son of the daughter of Ya'akov: When you go there, to Eretz Yisrael, **take a roundabout** route, i.e., do not travel by the shortest path, **and go to the Ladder of Tyre**[B] **and raise** this **dilemma before Rav Ya'akov bar Idi.**

בְּעָא מִינֵּיהּ: מִשֶּׁל חֲמוֹתָהּ עֵירְבָה, וּמִשּׁוּם דְּלָא זִיכְּתָה לָהּ, אוֹ דִּלְמָא: מִשֶּׁלָּהּ עֵירְבָה, וּמִשּׁוּם דְּשֶׁלֹּא מִדַּעְתָּהּ?

Rabbi Ya'akov did so and **raised a dilemma before him:** With regard to that incident, did the mother-in-law **establish the** ***eiruv*** **for** her daughter-in-law **from the mother-in-law's** food, **and** Rabbi Ḥiyya prohibited it **because she did not confer possession** of the food **to her? Or perhaps she established the** ***eiruv*** **for her with** the daughter-in-law's **own** food, but the *eiruv* was invalidated **because** it was prepared **without her knowledge?**

אֲמַר לֵיהּ: מִשֶּׁל חֲמוֹתָהּ עֵירְבָה לָהּ, וּמִשּׁוּם דְּלָא זִיכְּתָה לָהּ.

Rav Ya'akov bar Idi **said to him:** The mother-in-law **established the** ***eiruv*** **for her with the mother-in-law's** food, and Rabbi Ḥiyya prohibited it **because she did not confer possession** of the food **to her.** Like his master and uncle, Rabbi Ḥiyya, Rav also maintains that possession of the food must be conferred upon those who wish to be included in a joining of Shabbat boundaries.[N]

אָמַר רַב נַחְמָן, נְקִטִינַן: אֶחָד עֵירוּבֵי תְחוּמִין, וְאֶחָד עֵירוּבֵי חֲצֵירוֹת, אֶחָד שִׁיתּוּפֵי מְבוֹאוֹת – צָרִיךְ לְזַכּוֹת. בָּעֵי רַב נַחְמָן: עֵירוּבֵי תַבְשִׁילִין, צָרִיךְ לְזַכּוֹת, אוֹ אֵין צָרִיךְ לְזַכּוֹת?

Rav Naḥman said: We hold based on tradition that with regard to **all of them, joining of** Shabbat **boundaries,**[H] **joining of courtyards,**[H] **and merging of alleyways,**[H] **it is necessary to confer possession.** After issuing this statement, **Rav Naḥman raised a dilemma** concerning an issue that was not sufficiently clear to him: With regard to **a joining of cooked foods** [***eiruv tavshilin***],[N] which must be prepared in order to permit cooking for Shabbat on a Festival that occurs on a Friday, **is it necessary to confer possession, or is it not necessary to confer possession?**

BACKGROUND

Take a roundabout route…go to the Ladder of Tyre – אַקִּיף...לְסוּלָּמָא דְּצוֹר: The map depicts the two routes by means of which Rabbi Ya'akov could have reached Eretz Yisrael. One possible route would have taken him north, via Antioch. However, the shortest route is south, by way of Damascus, through the Golan to the Lower Galilee. It is also possible to travel to the coast and scale the hills known as the Ladder of Tyre before descending southward along the coast to Acre, and from there inland to Tiberias. This is a longer route to Eretz Yisrael.

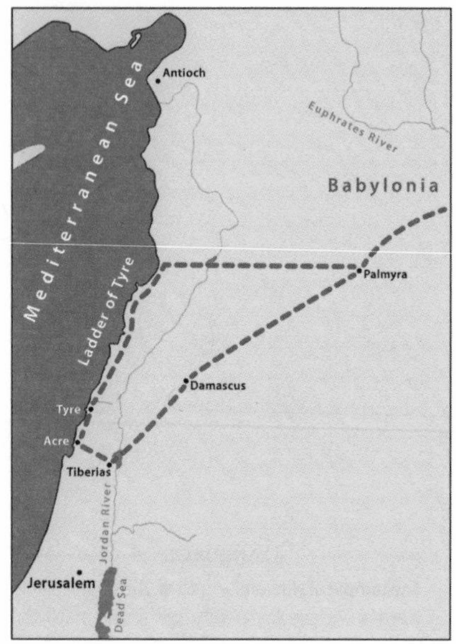

Different routes to Eretz Yisrael

NOTES

Rav's opinion with regard to conferring possession – שִׁיטַת רַב בִּזְכִיָּה: Rashi and *Tosafot* question Rav's position, which apparently does not coincide with the content of the mishna and no fully acceptable proof is provided for it. Several commentaries explain that Rav distinguishes between a merging of alleyways and a joining of courtyards, which do not necessitate transfer of possession to others, and a joining of Shabbat boundaries, where transferring possession is required. The reason for this difference is that in the cases of an *eiruv* and a merging of alleyways the one transferring possession and the recipient are linked, as they reside in the same place and share the *eiruv* with the other inhabitants. As the recipient receives the possession and benefit of the *eiruv* himself, it stands to reason that he can acquire it on behalf of others as well. However, this is not the case with regard to a joining of boundaries, as the one transferring possession gains no benefit from the fact that another person can accompany him beyond the Shabbat limit. Consequently, if no one else receives possession, he cannot acquire it on behalf of another (Rashba; Ritva).

A joining of cooked foods [*eiruv tavshilin*] – עֵירוּב תַּבְשִׁילִין: On a Festival that occurs on a Friday, it is prohibited to cook food for the upcoming Shabbat *ab initio*. To circumvent this prohibition, one may prepare a joining of cooked foods [*eiruv tavshilin*]. This is done by setting aside bread and a cooked dish before the Festival and reserving them for Shabbat. One may then cook other food for Shabbat on the Festival, in addition to these foods.

HALAKHA

Conferring possession for a joining of Shabbat boundaries – זִיכּוּי בְּעֵירוּב תְּחוּמִין: If the food used for a joining of boundaries belongs to one of the residents alone, he must transfer possession to all his neighbors by means of another person, in accordance with Rav Naḥman because he is a later authority (*Shulḥan Arukh, Oraḥ Ḥayyim* 413:1).

Transferring possession for a joining of courtyards – זִיכּוּי בְּעֵירוּב חֲצֵרוֹת: It is necessary to transfer possession of the food used for a joining of courtyards to the other residents of the courtyards (*Shulḥan Arukh, Oraḥ Ḥayyim* 366:9).

Transferring possession for a merging of alleyways – זִיכּוּי בְּשִׁיתּוּף מְבוֹאוֹת: It is necessary to transfer possession of the food used for a merging of alleyways to the other residents of the alleyways. The *halakha* of an alleyway in this regard is the same as that of a courtyard, in accordance with the opinion of Rav Naḥman (*Shulḥan Arukh, Oraḥ Ḥayyim* 386:3).

אֲמַר רַב יוֹסֵף: וּמַאי תִּיבָּעֵי לֵיהּ? לָא שְׁמִיעַ לֵיהּ הָא דְּאָמַר רַב נַחְמָן בַּר רַב אַדָּא אָמַר שְׁמוּאֵל: עֵירוּבֵי תַבְשִׁילִין צָרִיךְ לְזַכּוֹת?! אֲמַר לֵיהּ אַבַּיֵי: פְּשִׁיטָא דְּלָא שְׁמִיעַ לֵיהּ, דְּאִי שְׁמִיעַ לֵיהּ – מַאי תִּיבָּעֵי לֵיהּ?

Rav Yosef said: What is his dilemma? Did **he not hear that** which **Rav Naḥman bar Rav Adda said** that **Shmuel said:** With regard to **a joining of cooked foods, it is necessary to confer possession?**[H] **Abaye said to** Rav Yosef: It is **obvious that he did not hear** that ruling, **as had he heard it, why would he have raised this dilemma?**

אֲמַר לֵיהּ: אַטּוּ עֵירוּבֵי תְחוּמִין מִי לָא אֲמַר שְׁמוּאֵל "אֵין צָרִיךְ לְזַכּוֹת", וַאֲמַר אִיהוּ "צָרִיךְ לְזַכּוֹת"?

Rav Yosef **said to him: Didn't Shmuel say,** with regard to a **joining of** Shabbat **boundaries,** that **it is not necessary to confer possession, and** Rav Naḥman nonetheless **said** that **it is necessary to confer possession?** Perhaps here too Rav Naḥman did not accept Shmuel's ruling.

הָכִי הָשְׁתָּא?! בִּשְׁלָמָא הָתָם – פְּלִיגִי רַב וּשְׁמוּאֵל, וְקָא מַשְׁמַע לַן כְּחוּמְרִין דְּמָר וְכִי חוּמְרִין דְּמָר, אֲבָל הָכָא, אִי אִיתָא דִּשְׁמִיעַ לֵיהּ – מִי אִיכָּא דְּמַאן דְּפָלֵיג?

Abaye replied: **How can you compare** the two cases? **Granted, there,** with regard to a merging of alleyways and a joining of Shabbat boundaries, **Rav and Shmuel disagree, and** Rav Naḥman **teaches us** that the *halakha* is in accordance **with the stringency of** this **master and the stringency of** that **master,**[N] i.e., his ruling is based on both opinions. **However, here,** with regard to a joining of cooked foods, **if it is so,** if **he** actually **heard** Shmuel's ruling, **is there anyone who disputes** it? If one of his teachers issued an uncontested ruling, it is presumably an established *halakha*.

הַהוּא טוּרְזִינָא דַּהֲוָה בְּשִׁיבָבוּתֵיהּ דְּרַבִּי זֵירָא, אֲמַרוּ לֵיהּ אוֹגִיר לָן רְשׁוּתָךְ. לָא אוֹגִיר לְהוּ. אֲתוּ לְקַמֵּיהּ דְּרַבִּי זֵירָא, אֲמַרוּ לֵיהּ: מַהוּ לְמֵיגַר מִדְּבֵיתְהוּ?

A certain gentile **superintendent** [*turzina*][L] **lived in Rabbi Zeira's neighborhood.** The neighbors **said to him: Rent your domain to us** so that we may carry on Shabbat. However, **he would not rent** it **to them. They came before Rabbi Zeira and asked him: What is** the *halakha* if we seek **to rent** the domain **from his wife** without her husband's knowledge?

אֲמַר לְהוּ: הָכִי אֲמַר רֵישׁ לָקִישׁ מִשְּׁמֵיהּ דְּגַבְרָא רַבָּה, וּמַנּוּ – רַבִּי חֲנִינָא: אִשְׁתּוֹ שֶׁל אָדָם מְעָרֶבֶת שֶׁלֹּא מִדַּעְתּוֹ.

Rabbi Zeira **said to them: Reish Lakish said as follows in the name of a great man, and who is** this great man? It is **Rabbi Ḥanina.** He stated: **A man's wife may establish an *eiruv* without his knowledge.**[H] According to this principle, the superintendent's wife could indeed rent out the domain without his knowledge.

הַהוּא טוּרְזִינָא דַּהֲוָה בְּשִׁיבָבוּתֵיהּ דְּרַב יְהוּדָה בַּר אוֹשַׁעְיָא, אָמְרִי לֵיהּ: אוֹגַר לָן רְשׁוּתָךְ. לָא אוֹגַר לְהוּ. אָתוּ לְקַמֵּיהּ דְּרַב יְהוּדָה בַּר אוֹשַׁעְיָא, אָמְרִי לֵיהּ: מַהוּ לְמֵיגַר מִדְּבֵיתְהוּ? לָא הֲוָה בִּידֵיהּ, אָתוּ לְקַמֵּיהּ דְּרַב מַתָּנָה – לָא הֲוָה בִּידֵיהּ. אָתוּ לְקַמֵּיהּ דְּרַב יְהוּדָה, אֲמַר לְהוּ, הָכִי אֲמַר שְׁמוּאֵל: אִשְׁתּוֹ שֶׁל אָדָם מְעָרֶבֶת שֶׁלֹּא מִדַּעְתּוֹ.

The Gemara relates a similar incident: **A certain superintendent lived in the neighborhood of Rav Yehuda bar Oshaya.** The neighbors **said to him: Rent your domain to us** so that we may establish an *eiruv* and carry on Shabbat, but **he would not rent it to them. They came before Rav Yehuda bar Oshaya** and **said to him: What is** the *halakha* if we seek **to rent** it **from his wife? He did not have** a ready answer **at hand. They** subsequently **came before Rav Mattana,** and **he** too **did not have** an answer **at hand. They came before Rav Yehuda,** who **said to them** that **Shmuel said as follows: A man's wife may establish an *eiruv* without his knowledge,** and the same applies to renting out his property.

מֵיתִיבִי: נָשִׁים שֶׁעֵירְבוּ וְנִשְׁתַּתְּפוּ שֶׁלֹּא מִדַּעַת בַּעֲלֵיהֶן – אֵין עֵירוּבָן עֵירוּב, וְאֵין שִׁיתּוּפָן שִׁיתּוּף!

The Gemara **raises an objection** from a *baraita*: **Women who joined** the courtyards **or merged the alleyways without the knowledge of their husbands, their *eiruv* is not a valid *eiruv*, and their merging** of alleyways **is not a** valid **merging.** How can Shmuel rule against an explicit *baraita*?

לָא קַשְׁיָא; הָא – דַּאֲסַר, הָא – דְּלָא אֲסַר.

The Gemara answers: This is **not difficult.** In **this** case, where Shmuel said that a wife may establish an *eiruv* without her husband's knowledge, he was referring to a situation where the husband **would prohibit**[N] his neighbors from carrying if he did not join their *eiruv*, and the *halakha* is therefore lenient, as a wife may establish an *eiruv* on his behalf. However, in **that** case, the *baraita*, which states that his wife may not establish an *eiruv* without his knowledge, is referring to a situation where **he would not prohibit** his neighbors from carrying.

HALAKHA

Conferring possession of a joining of cooked foods – זִיכּוּי בְּעֵירוּב תַּבְשִׁילִין: It is necessary to transfer possession of a joining of cooked foods to all those who will benefit from the *eiruv*, in accordance with the opinion of Shmuel (*Shulḥan Arukh, Oraḥ Ḥayyim* 527:10).

A man's wife may establish an *eiruv* without his knowledge – אִשְׁתּוֹ שֶׁל אָדָם מְעָרֶבֶת שֶׁלֹּא מִדַּעְתּוֹ: With regard to a man who would impose restrictions on the other residents of his courtyard or alleyway, his wife may establish an *eiruv* without his knowledge and even against his will. Some commentaries state that she may establish the *eiruv* only without his knowledge, but not against his will (Rambam *Sefer Zemanim, Hilkhot Eiruvin* 2:12). If he is located in a place that would not prevent establishment of the *eiruv*, but he is accustomed to joining in an *eiruv* with the other residents, his wife may establish an *eiruv* without his knowledge. However, if he is not accustomed to participating with them and would not impose restrictions, then although she may establish an *eiruv* without his knowledge, she may not do so against his will (*Shulḥan Arukh, Oraḥ Ḥayyim* 367:1).

NOTES

With the stringency of this master and the stringency of that master – כְּחוּמְרִין דְּמָר וְכִי חוּמְרִין דְּמָר: In general, the Sages applied the verse: "And the fool walks in darkness" (Ecclesiastes 2:14) to one who acts in accordance with the stringencies of both sides of a debate. However, that principle does not apply to this case, as Rav and Shmuel provide different and not necessarily contradictory reasons. In this case, it is possible to accept both opinions (Ritva).

In this case he would prohibit – הָא דַּאֲסַר: Apparently, the Rambam interprets the phrase: In this case he would prohibit, as referring to a situation where he states that he does not wish to participate in the *eiruv*. In that case, it is prohibited for his wife to establish an *eiruv* for him without his knowledge. The phrase: In that case he would not prohibit, refers to a situation where he did not indicate his preference.

LANGUAGE

Superintendent [*turzina*] – טוּרְזִינָא: The source and meaning of this word are unclear. Some authorities maintain that it refers to the person who guards the clothes in the royal chambers. Other linguists explain that it derives from the Persian tirzan, or tabarozan, meaning military men, archers, or swordsmen. It possibly refers to a military appointment.

הָכִי נַמִי מִסְתַּבְּרָא, דְּאִם כֵּן – קַשְׁיָא דִּשְׁמוּאֵל אַדִּשְׁמוּאֵל; דְּאָמַר שְׁמוּאֵל: אֶחָד מִבְּנֵי מָבוֹי שֶׁרָגִיל לְהִשְׁתַּתֵּף עִם בְּנֵי מָבוֹי, וְלֹא נִשְׁתַּתֵּף – בְּנֵי הַמָּבוֹי נִכְנָסִין לְתוֹךְ בֵּיתוֹ וְנוֹטְלִין שִׁיתּוּפָן מִמֶּנּוּ בְּעַל כָּרְחוֹ.

The Gemara adds: **So too, it is reasonable** that this is the correct interpretation, **as if** you do not say **this,** there is **a contradiction between** this ruling **of Shmuel and** another ruling **of Shmuel. As Shmuel said:** With regard to **one of the residents of an alleyway who was accustomed to join in a merging of alleyways**[H] **with the** other **residents of** the **alleyway, but** one Shabbat **he did not join in a merging** of alleyways with them, **the** other **residents of the alleyway** may **enter his house and take** his contribution to **their merging of alleyways from him** even **against his will.**

רָגִיל – אִין, שֶׁאֵין רָגִיל – לָא. שְׁמַע מִינַּהּ.

The Gemara infers: If he was **accustomed** to join in their merging of the alleyway, **yes,** they may enter his house to collect his contribution, but if he was **not accustomed** to do so, **no,** they may not do so. Clearly, it is not possible in all cases to compel a person to participate in a merging of alleyways against his will. The Gemara concludes: Indeed, **conclude from it** that it is so.

לֵימָא מְסַיַּיע לֵיהּ: כּוֹפִין אוֹתוֹ לַעֲשׂוֹת לֶחִי וְקוֹרָה לַמָּבוֹי.

The Gemara suggests: **Let us say** that the following *baraita* **supports him.** The residents of an alleyway may **compel** anyone who lives in the alleyway **to erect a side post**[H] **and a cross beam for the alleyway.** This teaching indicates that with regard to these Shabbat enactments, a person's wishes are not taken into account; rather, others may act on his behalf even against his will.

HALAKHA

One…who was accustomed to join in a merging of alleyways – מִי שֶׁרָגִיל לְהִשְׁתַּתֵּף: With regard to a resident of an alleyway who is accustomed to participating in merging the alleyway with the other residents of his alleyway, but who does not impose restrictions upon them, or one who does impose restrictions but is unaccustomed to participate, and yet he now desires to participate in this merging, the other residents may collect his contribution from him even against his will (*Shulḥan Arukh, Oraḥ Ḥayyim* 367:1).

Compel to erect a side post – כּוֹפִין לַעֲשׂוֹת לֶחִי: All residents of an alleyway may be forced to erect a side post and a cross beam for the alleyway (*Shulḥan Arukh, Ḥoshen Mishpat* 162:1).

Perek **VII**
Daf **80** Amud **b**

שָׁאנֵי הָתָם דְּלֵיכָּא מְחִיצוֹת.

The Gemara answers: **It is different there, as there are no partitions.** That alley is breached, and it is therefore fitting to compel its residents to establish some sort of partition, if only for the sake of protection. However, if there are partitions, one is not obligated to join in a merging of alleyways.

לִישָּׁנָא אַחֲרִינָא: מִצַּד שָׁאנֵי.

Another version of this explanation: **From the side it is different,**[NH] i.e., the preparation of an *eiruv* does not involve an adjustment to the alleyway itself, but rather it is a side issue. Consequently, an individual cannot be forced to participate in its preparation (*Meir Netiv*).

אִתְּמַר, רַב חִיָּיא בַּר אַשִׁי אָמַר: עוֹשִׂין לֶחִי אֲשֵׁירָה. וְרַבִּי שִׁמְעוֹן בֶּן לָקִישׁ אָמַר: עוֹשִׂין קוֹרָה אֲשֵׁירָה.

It is stated that the *amora'im* disputed this issue. **Rav Ḥiyya bar Ashi said: One** may **build a side post** from the wood of **an *asheira*.** Although it is prohibited to benefit from the tree and it must be burned, setting up a side post is a mitzva, and mitzvot were not given for benefit, i.e., the fulfillment of a mitzva is not in itself considered a benefit. **And Rabbi Shimon ben Lakish said: One** may **build a** cross **beam** from the wood of **an *asheira*.**[H]

מַאן דְּאָמַר קוֹרָה – כׇּל שֶׁכֵּן לֶחִי, וּמַאן דְּאָמַר לֶחִי – אֲבָל קוֹרָה לֹא, כְּתוּתֵי מִכְתַּת שִׁיעוּרֵיהּ.

The Gemara clarifies their opinions: With regard to **the one who said** that one may build **a cross beam** from the wood of an *asheira*, Rabbi Shimon ben Lakish, **all the more so** he would permit **a side post** to be prepared from an *asheira*. **And the one who said** that one may build a **side post** from an *asheira*, Rav Ḥiyya bar Ashi, spoke only of a side post; **but** as for **a cross beam, no,** he did not permit one to build it from an *asheira*. The reason is that an *asheira* must be burned, and it is therefore as though **its size has** already **been crushed.** Consequently, a cross beam, which must be at least a handbreadth in size, may not be prepared from an *asheira*. With regard to a side post, by contrast, a minimum width suffices, which means that even wood from an *asheira* is fit, despite the fact that it is viewed as burned.

מתני׳ נִתְמַעֵט הָאוֹכֶל – מוֹסִיף וּמְזַכֶּה, וְאֵין צָרִיךְ לְהוֹדִיעַ. נִתּוֹסְפוּ עֲלֵיהֶן – מוֹסִיף וּמְזַכֶּה, וְצָרִיךְ לְהוֹדִיעַ.

MISHNA **If the food** in the barrel for the merging of the alleyway **diminished** and was less than the requisite measure, **one** may **add** a little of his own **and confer possession** to the others, **and he need not inform** them of his addition. However, if new residents **were added to** the residents of the alleyway, **he may add** food on behalf of those residents **and confer possession** to them, **and he must inform** the new residents of their inclusion in the merging of alleyways.

NOTES

From the side [*mitzad*] it is different – מִצַּד שָׁאנֵי: This phrase is unclear, and the commentaries sought to explain it. Some commentaries rely on variant readings of the text that omit the phrase. The Vilna Gaon and the author of the *Noda Bihuda* read: In the court [the abbreviation of *beveit din*, *beit*, *beit*, *dalet*] it is different, i.e., there is a difference between neighbors coercing each other of their own accord, and the coercion of a court order.

Other authorities maintain that the phrase: From the side is different, is referring to carrying from the side. In other words, if the alleyway had a side post or a cross beam, the full prohibition of carrying would not be in effect, as it would be considered carrying from the side, i.e., in an unusual manner. It is therefore necessary to coerce each person to contribute to the adjustment of the alleyway (*Mekom Shmuel*).

Alternatively, the word *mitzad* may be derived from *metzuda*, a fortress (see I Chronicles 11:7). As the alleyway has partitions and is closed off like a fortress, one is forced to erect a side post or a cross beam as well (Rabbi A. Z. Margaliyot).

Yet other commentaries explain that the phrase: From the side, is referring to the adjustment of a merging of alleyways, which is not part of the alleyway itself, and therefore one is not compelled to participate. The same cannot be said with regard to the adjustment of a side post or a cross beam, which does affect the alleyway itself (*Sefer Yehoshua*; Responsa *Meir Netiv*).

HALAKHA

From the side it is different – מִן הַצַּד שָׁאנֵי: One who is not accustomed to participating in an *eiruv* cannot be compelled to join an *eiruv* against his will. However, he may be coerced by the court to do so. According to the Vilna Gaon and other authorities, the source for that *halakha* is this passage in the Gemara, due to the variant reading: In the court, it is different (*Shulḥan Arukh, Oraḥ Ḥayyim* 367:1).

A side post and a cross beam from an *asheira* – לֶחִי וְקוֹרָה מֵאֲשֵׁרָה: A side post may be built from the wood of an *asheira*, but a cross beam may not, as the latter must be of a particular length and width, in accordance with the opinion of Rabbi Ḥiyya bar Ashi (*Shulḥan Arukh, Oraḥ Ḥayyim* 363:8, 16).

כַּמָּה הוּא שִׁיעוּרָן? בִּזְמַן שֶׁהֵן מְרוּבִּין – מְזוֹן שְׁתֵּי סְעוּדוֹת לְכוּלָּם, בִּזְמַן שֶׁהֵן מוּעָטִין – כַּגְּרוֹגֶרֶת לְכָל אֶחָד וְאֶחָד.

What is the measure of food required for a merging of the alleyways? **When** the residents of the alley **are numerous, food for two meals** is sufficient **for all of them; when they are few,** less than a certain number, **a dried fig-bulk for each and every one of them** is enough.[H]

אָמַר רַבִּי יוֹסֵי: בַּמֶּה דְּבָרִים אֲמוּרִים – בִּתְחִילַּת עֵירוּב, אֲבָל בִּשְׁיָרֵי עֵירוּב – כָּל שֶׁהוּא.

Rabbi Yosei said: In what case **is this statement said?** It is said **with regard to the beginning of an *eiruv*,** when it is initially established. **However, with regard to the remnants of an *eiruv*,** e.g., if the *eiruv* decreased in size on Shabbat, it remains valid if even **any amount** remains.[H]

וְלֹא אָמְרוּ לְעָרֵב בַּחֲצֵירוֹת אֶלָּא כְּדֵי שֶׁלֹּא לְשַׁכֵּחַ אֶת הַתִּינוֹקוֹת.

And in general **they said** that it is necessary **to join the courtyards,**[H] even though a merging of the alleyways was already in place, **only so that** the halakhic category of *eiruv* **will not be forgotten by the children,** i.e., so that the next generation should be aware that an *eiruv* can be established for a courtyard, for otherwise they would be entirely unaware of this halakhic category.

גמ׳ בְּמַאי עָסְקִינַן? אִילֵימָא בְּמִין אֶחָד – מַאי אִירְיָא נִתְמַעֵט, אֲפִילּוּ כָּלָה נַמִי!

GEMARA The mishna stated: If the food in the barrel for the merging of the alleyway diminished and was less than the requisite measure, one may add to it without informing the others. The Gemara poses a question: **With what** case **are we dealing** here? **If you say** that he added **the same type** of food that had initially been used for the merging of the alleyway, **why specify** this particular case where the food **decreased**[H] in measure? **Even if** the food **was** entirely **finished,** he should **likewise** not be obligated to inform them.

אֶלָּא בִּשְׁנֵי מִינִין – אֲפִילּוּ נִתְמַעֵט נַמִי לֹא, דְּתַנְיָא: כָּלָה הָאוֹכֶל, מִמִּין אֶחָד – אֵין צָרִיךְ לְהוֹדִיעַ, מִשְּׁנֵי מִינִים – צָרִיךְ לְהוֹדִיעַ!

Rather, perhaps it is referring **to two types** of food, i.e., one added a different kind of food that had not been used beforehand. If so, **even if** it only **decreased** in measure, **no,** he should **also** not be permitted to add to the merging of the alleyway without informing them. **As it was taught** in a *baraita*: **If the food** of a merging of the alleyway **was** entirely **finished,** and he added **the same type** of food to it, **he need not inform** the other residents; however, if the amount he added was **from two types** of food, i.e., if the added food was different from the original, **he must inform** them. The Gemara assumes that the same *halakha* is in effect even if the food of the merging of the alleyway only decreased in measure.

אִיבָּעֵית אֵימָא: מִמִּין אֶחָד, וְאִיבָּעֵית אֵימָא: מִשְּׁנֵי מִינִין. אִיבָּעֵית אֵימָא מִמִּין אֶחָד, מַאי נִתְמַעֵט – נִתְמַטְמֵט.

The Gemara answers: **If you wish, say** that the mishna is referring to a case where his addition was **from the same kind** of food, **and if you wish, say** instead that it was **from two kinds.** The Gemara clarifies the previous statement: **If you wish, say** that it is referring to a case where his addition was **from the same kind** of food, and **what** is the meaning of **decreased?** It means that the food entirely **crumbled away,** so that nothing at all remained.

וְאִיבָּעֵית אֵימָא מִשְּׁנֵי מִינִין – כָּלָה שָׁאנֵי.

And if you wish, say instead that the mishna is referring to a case where his addition was **from two kinds** of food, for if the *eiruv* **was** entirely **finished,** the *halakha* **is different.**[N] That is to say, the *halakha* of the *baraita* that he must inform the others is in effect only if the food was entirely finished, but if any of it remains there is no need to inform them of his addition, and he may confer possession of even a different kind of food.

NOTES

If the *eiruv* was finished, the *halakha* is different – כָּלָה שָׁאנֵי: The Ritva maintains that finished does not mean completely finished, as in that case it cannot be likened to food that has merely decreased. Rather, it means that it has been so greatly reduced from its original amount that it is virtually finished.

HALAKHA

The measure of an *eiruv* at the beginning – שִׁיעוּר עֵירוּב בַּתְּחִילָּה: What is the initial amount of food required for an *eiruv*? If there are numerous residents participating, there must be enough food for two meals for all of them. If there were few participants, the amount of a dried fig-bulk for each of them is sufficient (*Shulḥan Arukh, Oraḥ Ḥayyim* 368:4).

The measure of the remnants of an *eiruv* – שִׁיעוּר בִּשְׁיָרֵי עֵירוּב: With regard to food of an *eiruv* that decreased to less than the required amount after Shabbat began, if any part of it remains, it is a valid *eiruv*, even for another Shabbat. However, the consensus among the later commentaries is that one should not rely on an *eiruv* of this kind (*Be'er Heitev; Shulḥan Arukh, Oraḥ Ḥayyim* 367:4).

To join the courtyards – עֵירוּב בַּחֲצֵירוֹת: In places where everyone participates in the merging of an alleyway, they should nonetheless establish an *eiruv* for their courtyards, so that the *halakha* of *eiruv* will not be forgotten by their children (*Shulḥan Arukh, Oraḥ Ḥayyim* 387:1).

If an *eiruv* decreased – נִתְמַעֵט הָעֵירוּב: When the food of an *eiruv* is reduced to less than the required amount, the following rules apply: If one adds the same type of food to it, he is not obligated to inform the other residents. If he added a different type of food, he must inform the other participants if the food was entirely finished. However, if the food only decreased in amount, he is not required to inform them. These *halakhot* apply only if he prepared the *eiruv* from their food. However, if he transferred possession of his own food to them, he need not inform them in any of these cases (Rashi; *Shulḥan Arukh, Oraḥ Ḥayyim* 368:2).

״נִיתּוֹסְפוּ עֲלֵיהֶן מוֹסִיף וּמְזַכֶּה וכו׳״. אָמַר רַב שֵׁיזְבִי, אָמַר רַב חִסְדָּא, זֹאת אוֹמֶרֶת: חֲלוּקִין עָלָיו חֲבֵירָיו עַל רַבִּי יְהוּדָה.

We learned in the mishna: If other residents **were added**[H] **to** the residents of the alleyway, **he may add** food for those residents **and confer possession** to them, but he must inform the new residents of their inclusion in the merging of the alleyway. **Rav Sheizvi said** that **Rav Ḥisda said: That is to say,** i.e., we can infer from the mishna, that **Rabbi Yehuda's colleagues disagree with him.**

דִּתְנַן, אָמַר רַבִּי יְהוּדָה: בַּמֶּה דְּבָרִים אֲמוּרִים – בְּעֵירוּבֵי תְחוּמִין, אֲבָל בְּעֵירוּבֵי חֲצֵירוֹת – מְעָרְבִין בֵּין לָדַעַת וּבֵין שֶׁלֹּא לָדַעַת. פְּשִׁיטָא דַּחֲלוּקִין!

As we learned in a mishna that **Rabbi Yehuda said: In what** case **is this statement,** that an *eiruv* may be established for a person only with his knowledge, **said?** It is said **with regard to a joining of** Shabbat **boundaries; however, with regard to a joining of courtyards, one** may **establish an** ***eiruv*** for another person either **with his knowledge or without his knowledge.** Rabbi Yehuda's opinion conflicts with that of the *tanna* of the mishna, who does not permit a person to be included in a joining of courtyards without his knowledge. The Gemara is surprised at this statement: **It is obvious** that **they disagree;** why did Rav Ḥisda find it necessary to teach us something so evident?

מַהוּ דְּתֵימָא: הָנֵי מִילֵּי – בְּחָצֵר שֶׁבֵּין שְׁנֵי מְבוֹאוֹת, אֲבָל חָצֵר שֶׁל מָבוֹי אֶחָד – אֵימָא לָא, קָמַשְׁמַע לָן. ״כַּמָּה הוּא שִׁיעוּרוֹ וכו׳״.

The Gemara answers: It was nonetheless necessary, **lest you say** that **this** ruling, i.e., that he must inform them, **applies only to a courtyard that is** situated **between two alleyways,** in which case the residents of the courtyard may join in a merging of alleyways with whichever alleyway they prefer. Consequently, he must inform them with which alleyway he prepared the merging, in case they preferred to join the other alleyway. **However,** with regard to **a courtyard** that opens into only **one alleyway,** the merging of the alleyway only benefits them and does not harm them in any way, and you might therefore **say no,** that even the *tanna* of the mishna concedes that it is not necessary to inform them. Rav Ḥisda therefore **teaches us** that the *tanna* of the mishna maintains that he must inform them in all cases, contrary to the opinion of Rabbi Yehuda.

כַּמָּה הוּא מְרוּבִּין? אָמַר רַב יְהוּדָה, אָמַר שְׁמוּאֵל: שְׁמוֹנֶה עֶשְׂרֵה בְּנֵי אָדָם. שְׁמוֹנֶה עֶשְׂרֵה וְתוּ לָא? אֵימָא: מִשְּׁמוֹנֶה עֶשְׂרֵה וְאֵילָךְ.

The mishna continues: **What is the measure** of food required for a merging of the alleyways? It then specifies different amounts when the residents of the alley are numerous and when they are few. The Gemara asks: **How many are numerous,** and how many are considered few?[H] **Rav Yehuda said** that **Shmuel said: Eighteen people** are considered numerous. The Gemara registers surprise: **Eighteen and no more?**[N] The Gemara answers: **Say: From eighteen upward.**

וּמַאי שְׁמוֹנֶה עֶשְׂרֵה דְּנָקַט? אָמַר רַב יִצְחָק בְּרֵיהּ דְּרַב יְהוּדָה: לְדִידִי מִיפָּרְשָׁא לִי מִינֵּיהּ דְּאַבָּא, כֹּל שֶׁאִילּוּ מְחַלְּקוֹ לִמְזוֹן שְׁתֵּי סְעוּדוֹת בֵּינֵיהֶן וְאֵין מַגַּעַת גְּרוֹגֶרֶת לְכָל אֶחָד וְאֶחָד – הֵן הֵן מְרוּבִּין, וְסַגִּי בִּמְזוֹן שְׁתֵּי סְעוּדוֹת. וְאִי לָא (הֵן הֵן) מוּעָטִין נִינְהוּ.

The Gemara asks: **And what is** the significance of the number **eighteen that he cited?** Why this figure in particular? The Gemara answers that **Rav Yitzḥak, son of Rav Yehuda, said: It was explained to me** personally **by my father,** Rav Yehuda: **Any** case where, **if** one were to **divide** the food **of two meals between them and it does not amount to** the measure of **a dried fig for each and every one of them, these are the very ones** the *tanna* called **numerous, and** in this case **food for two meals suffices** for all of them. **And if not, these are the very ones** the *tanna* termed **few,** which means food in the measure of a dried fig is required for each of them.

וְאַגַּב אוֹרְחֵיהּ קָא מַשְׁמַע לָן דִּשְׁתֵּי סְעוּדוֹת הָוְיָין שְׁמוֹנֶה עֶשְׂרֵה גְּרוֹגָרוֹת.

And Rav Yehuda **incidentally teaches us that** food for **two meals consists of** a measure equal to **eighteen dried figs.** Consequently, if there were numerous residents in the alley, then eighteen dried figs, which is food sufficient for two meals, is enough for them.

מתני׳ בַּכֹּל מְעָרְבִין וּמִשְׁתַּתְּפִין, חוּץ מִן הַמַּיִם וּמִן הַמֶּלַח, דִּבְרֵי רַבִּי אֱלִיעֶזֶר. רַבִּי יְהוֹשֻׁעַ אוֹמֵר: כִּכָּר הוּא עֵירוּב, אֲפִילּוּ מַאֲפֶה סְאָה וְהוּא פְּרוּסָה – אֵין מְעָרְבִין בָּהּ. כִּכָּר כְּאִיסָּר וְהוּא שָׁלֵם – מְעָרְבִין בּוֹ.

MISHNA **One** may **join** courtyards **and merge** alleyways **with all** types of food, **except for water and salt,** as they are not considered foods. This is **the statement of Rabbi Eliezer. Rabbi Yehoshua says** that a different limitation applies: A whole **loaf** may be used for **an** ***eiruv.*** With regard to **a baked** product even the size **of a** ***se'a,*** **if it** consists of **pieces, one** may **not join** courtyards **with it.** However, with regard to **a loaf,** even one the size of **an** ***issar,***[LB] **if it is whole, one** may **join** courtyards **with it.**[H]

HALAKHA

If residents were added – נִיתּוֹסְפוּ דַּיָּירִים: If a person included more residents in an *eiruv* of courtyards, he is required to inform them, even if he prepared the *eiruv* from his own food (*Magen Avraham*), especially if they have the option of participating in an *eiruv* in a different place (*Shulḥan Arukh, Oraḥ Ḥayyim* 368:2).

Numerous and few – מְרוּבִּין וּמוּעָטִין: With regard to the food of an *eiruv*, numerous means eighteen people or more, in accordance with the opinion of Shmuel (*Shulḥan Arukh, Oraḥ Ḥayyim* 368:3).

With a loaf but not with a broken piece – בְּכִכָּר וְלֹא בִּפְרוּסָה: An *eiruv* must be prepared from a whole loaf of bread, even a small one. A broken piece may not be used, even if it is large. The Rema explains that each person provides a small amount of flour with which they bake a single loaf, in accordance with the Ra'avad and the *Maggid Mishne*. This is the prevalent custom.

According to the Rosh and the *Mordekhai*, if one person transfers possession of the *eiruv* to all the rest, he may even use a broken piece (*Shulḥan Arukh HaRav; Shulḥan Arukh, Oraḥ Ḥayyim* 366:6).

NOTES

Eighteen and no more – שְׁמוֹנֶה עֶשְׂרֵה וְתוּ לָא: This question is surprising, as it is well known that whenever the Sages established a measure as a particular number they mean from that number upwards. However, in this context it perhaps they permitted using food for two meals in merging alleyways only if there are eighteen people participating, which would be slightly less than a dried fig-bulk per person. However, if there were more than eighteen people, perhaps a larger amount would be required. Consequently, the question is appropriate (Rashba).

LANGUAGE

Issar – אִיסָּר: From the Greek ἀσσάριον, *assariyon*, meaning a Roman *issar* coin.

BACKGROUND

Issar – אִיסָּר: A small coin typically made of copper. Its standard value was eight *perutot*.

Roman *issar* from the time of Tiberius Caesar

גמ׳ תָּנֵינָא חֲדָא זִימְנָא: ״בַּכֹּל מְעָרְבִין וּמִשְׁתַּתְּפִין חוּץ מִן הַמַּיִם וְהַמֶּלַח״!

GEMARA With regard to the mishna's ruling concerning the foods which may or may not be used for an *eiruv* and to merge alleyways, the Gemara poses a question: This ruling is apparently superfluous, as we have already **learned** it **once** before in another mishna: **One** may **establish an *eiruv* and a merging of alleyways with all** kinds of food, **except for water and salt.**

אָמַר רַבָּה: לְאַפּוֹקֵי מִדְּרַבִּי יְהוֹשֻׁעַ, דְּאָמַר: כִּכָּר אִין, מִידֵּי אַחֲרִינָא לָא – קָמַשְׁמַע לָן ״בַּכֹּל״.

Rabba said: This addition comes **to exclude** the opinion of **Rabbi Yehoshua** in the mishna, who **said** that **a loaf, yes,** it may be used for an *eiruv*; but **anything else, no,** other foods may not be used. Therefore, the mishna **teaches us** that an *eiruv* may be established **with all** kinds of food, not only bread.

אֵיתִיבֵיהּ אַבַּיֵי: בַּכֹּל מְעָרְבִין עֵירוּבֵי חֲצֵירוֹת וּבַכֹּל מִשְׁתַּתְּפִין שִׁיתּוּפֵי מְבוֹאוֹת, וְלֹא אָמְרוּ לְעָרֵב בַּפַּת אֶלָּא בְּחָצֵר בִּלְבַד. מַאן שָׁמְעַתְּ לֵיהּ דְּאָמַר: פַּת אִין מִידֵּי אַחֲרִינָא לָא – רַבִּי יְהוֹשֻׁעַ, וְקָתָנֵי: בַּכֹּל!

Abaye raised an objection from a *baraita*: **One** may **establish a joining of courtyards with all** kinds of food, **and** likewise **one may establish a merging of alleyways with all** kinds of food. **They said** that **one** must **establish an *eiruv* with bread only with regard to** an *eiruv* of **a courtyard. Who did you hear that said** that **bread, yes,** it may be used for an *eiruv*, but **anything else, no,** it may not be used? It was **Rabbi Yehoshua, and** yet the *baraita* **teaches: With all** kinds of food. This proves that the phrase: One may establish an *eiruv* with all kinds of food, does not necessarily exclude Rabbi Yehoshua's opinion.

אֶלָּא אָמַר רַבָּה בַּר בַּר חָנָה: לְאַפּוֹקֵי מִדְּרַבִּי יְהוֹשֻׁעַ, דְּאָמַר: שְׁלֵימָה אִין, פְּרוּסָה לָא – קָמַשְׁמַע לָן ״בַּכֹּל״.

Rather, Rabba bar bar Ḥana said: It comes **to exclude** a different aspect of the opinion of **Rabbi Yehoshua, as** Rabbi Yehoshua **said: A whole** loaf, **yes,** it is fit to be used as an *eiruv*, but **a broken** loaf, **no,** it is not suitable for this purpose. The mishna therefore **teaches us** that one may prepare an *eiruv* **with all** kinds of bread, even a broken loaf.

וּפְרוּסָה מַאי טַעְמָא לָא? אָמַר רַבִּי יוֹסֵי בֶּן שָׁאוּל, אָמַר רַבִּי: מִשּׁוּם אֵיבָה.

The Gemara analyzes Rabbi Yehoshua's position itself: **And** with regard to a **broken** loaf of bread, **what is the reason** that it may **not** be used for an *eiruv*? **Rabbi Yosei ben Shaul said** that **Rabbi** Yehuda HaNasi **said:** The reason is **due to** potential **enmity** between neighbors. To avoid a situation where one person says to the other: You contributed a mere slice of bread, while I donated an entire loaf, the Sages instituted that each person should provide a whole loaf.

אֲמַר לֵיהּ רַב אַחָא בְּרֵיהּ דְּרָבָא לְרַב אַשִׁי: עֵירְבוּ כּוּלָּן בִּפְרוּסוֹת, מַהוּ? אֲמַר לֵיהּ: שֶׁמָּא יַחֲזוֹר דָּבָר לְקִלְקוּלוֹ.

Rav Aḥa, son of Rava, said to Rav Ashi: If **they all established** the ***eiruv* with broken** loaves of bread, **what is the** *halakha*? In this case there is no cause for enmity. Rav Ashi **said to him:** There is nonetheless a concern **lest the problem recur,** as one of them might give an entire loaf and proceed to complain about his neighbor who donated only a partial loaf.

אָמַר רַבִּי יוֹחָנָן בֶּן שָׁאוּל: נִיטְּלָה הֵימֶנָּה כְּדֵי חַלָּתָהּ וּכְדֵי דִּימּוּעָהּ – מְעָרְבִין לוֹ בָּהּ.

A portion of dough, known as *ḥalla*, must be set aside and given to the priests. If *ḥalla* was not set aside from the dough, it must be separated from the baked bread. Moreover, if one part *teruma* fell into a hundred parts non-sacred produce, a proportionate amount must be removed from the mixture and given to a priest, after which the remainder may be eaten. **Rabbi Yoḥanan ben Shaul said: If one removed from** the loaf **as much as** must be set aside for **its *ḥalla*, or as much as** must be separated **from a mixture**[N] of *teruma* and non-sacred produce, **he** may **establish an *eiruv* with** that loaf. The reason is that in this case people would not complain that he did not give a whole loaf, as they would assume the loaf had a small part missing because *ḥalla* had been separated from it, or because *teruma* had fallen into the dough, which necessitated the separation of a certain portion. However, if more than this amount was missing, people would suspect him of eating from the *eiruv*.

וְהָתַנְיָא: כְּדֵי דִּימּוּעָהּ – מְעָרְבִין לוֹ בָּהּ, כְּדֵי חַלָּתָהּ – אֵין מְעָרְבִין לוֹ בָּהּ!

The Gemara raises a difficulty: **Wasn't it was taught** otherwise in a *baraita*: If a loaf was missing **as much as** must be removed **from a mixture** of *teruma* and non-sacred produce, **one may establish an *eiruv* with it,** but if it was missing **as much as** must be removed for **its *ḥalla*, one may not establish an *eiruv* with it?**[N]

NOTES

Mixture [*dimua*] – דִּימּוּעַ: This term means mixtures in general, but the Sages typically used it in reference to *teruma* that became intermingled with regular produce. If *teruma*, or anything that has the sanctity of *teruma*, such as *ḥalla*, became mixed with regular produce, if the mixture does not contain more than one part *teruma* to one hundred parts non-sacred produce, one may separate one one-hundredth of the mixture, and the rest is permitted to be eaten by non-priests.

As much as must be removed for its *ḥalla* and as much as must be removed from a mixture – כְּדֵי חַלָּתָהּ וּכְדֵי דִּימּוּעָהּ: Some commentaries explain that the missing portion was actually removed from the loaf as *ḥalla* or as the portion removed from a mixture of *teruma* and non-sacred produce. However, if it were removed for any other reason, the loaf is not suitable for an *eiruv*. Most commentaries maintain that if the portion removed was the amount of *ḥalla* or the amount removed from the mixture, even if the portion was used for a different purpose, the loaf is fit for an *eiruv*, as people do not know why it is missing (Rosh; see *Tosafot*).

לָא קַשְׁיָא; הָא – בְּחַלַּת נַחְתּוֹם, הָא – בְּחַלַּת בַּעַל הַבַּיִת.

The Gemara answers: This is **not difficult,** as the two sources are not dealing with the same amounts. In **this** case, where the *tanna* permitted a loaf that was missing the amount that must be removed for *ḥalla,* he is referring **to a baker's *ḥalla,*** which is a smaller amount and is therefore not considered a significant reduction of the loaf. However, in **that** case, where the *tanna* did not permit a loaf that was lacking the amount that must be removed for *ḥalla,* it is referring **to an** ordinary **homeowner's *ḥalla.***[NH] This *ḥalla* portion is larger in size, and consequently the loaf may not be used for an *eiruv* if it is missing such a large amount.[N]

דִּתְנַן: שִׁיעוּר חַלָּה אֶחָד מֵעֶשְׂרִים וְאַרְבָּעָה, הָעוֹשֶׂה עִיסָּה לְעַצְמוֹ וְעִיסָּה לְמִשְׁתֵּה בְנוֹ, אֶחָד מֵעֶשְׂרִים וְאַרְבָּעָה. נַחְתּוֹם שֶׁהוּא עוֹשֶׂה לִמְכּוֹר בַּשּׁוּק, וְכֵן הָאִשָּׁה שֶׁעָשְׂתָה לִמְכּוֹר בַּשּׁוּק – אֶחָד מֵאַרְבָּעִים וּשְׁמוֹנָה.

The Gemara explains that this is **as we learned** in a mishna: **The measure of *ḥalla*** fixed by the Sages is **one twenty-fourth** of the dough. Consequently, **one who prepares dough for himself or dough for his son's wedding feast,** the measure for *ḥalla* is **one twenty-fourth.** However, **a baker who prepares** dough **for sale in the market, and likewise a woman who prepares** dough **for sale in the market,** is required to separate only **one forty-eighth** of the dough, as the Sages were lenient with those who sell their wares so that they should not suffer loss.[H]

אָמַר רַב חִסְדָּא: תְּפָרָהּ בְּקֵיסָם – מְעָרְבִין לוֹ בָּהּ. וְהָא תַּנְיָא: אֵין מְעָרְבִין לוֹ בָּהּ! לָא קַשְׁיָא; הָא – דִּידִיעַ תִּיפְרָהּ, הָא – דְּלָא יְדִיעַ תִּיפְרָהּ.

Rav Ḥisda said: With regard to **one who connected** the two portions of a broken loaf **with a wood chip,**[NH] **one** may **establish an *eiruv* with it,** as it looks whole. The Gemara raises a difficulty: **But wasn't it taught** in a *baraita* with regard to a case of this kind that **one** may **not establish an *eiruv* with it?** The Gemara answers: This is **not difficult,** as in **this** case, where it may not be used for an *eiruv,* we are dealing with a situation **where the seam is conspicuous;** however, in **that** case, where it may be used for an *eiruv,* the reference is to a situation **where the seam is not conspicuous.**

אָמַר רַבִּי זֵירָא, אָמַר שְׁמוּאֵל: מְעָרְבִין בְּפַת אוֹרֶז וּבְפַת דּוֹחַן. אָמַר מָר עוּקְבָא: לְדִידִי מִיפָּרְשָׁא לִי מִינֵּיהּ דְּמָר שְׁמוּאֵל, בְּפַת אוֹרֶז – מְעָרְבִין, וּבְפַת דּוֹחַן – אֵין מְעָרְבִין.

Rabbi Zeira said that **Shmuel said: One** may **establish an *eiruv*** even **with rice bread or with millet bread. Mar Ukva said:** This ruling **was explained to me by Mar Shmuel** himself. **With rice bread one** may **establish an *eiruv,* but with millet bread one** may **not establish an *eiruv,*** as it is difficult to bake edible bread out of millet.

אָמַר רַב חִיָּיא בַּר אָבִין, אָמַר רַב: מְעָרְבִין בְּפַת עֲדָשִׁים. אִינִי?! וְהָא הַהִיא דַּהֲוַאי בִּשְׁנֵי דְּמָר שְׁמוּאֵל, וְשַׁדְיֵיהּ לְכַלְבֵּיהּ וְלָא אֲכָלָהּ!

Rav Ḥiyya bar Avin said that **Rav said: One** may **establish an *eiruv* with lentil bread.**[H] The Gemara raises a difficulty: **Is that so?** Is such bread edible? **But there was that** lentil bread **in the days of Mar Shmuel, which he threw to his dog, and** even **it would not eat it.** Clearly, lentil bread is not fit for human consumption.

הַהִיא דִּשְׁאָר מִינִים הֲוָיָא, דִּכְתִיב: "וְאַתָּה קַח לְךָ חִטִּין וּשְׂעוֹרִים וּפוֹל וַעֲדָשִׁים וְדוֹחַן וְכוּסְּמִים" וגו׳.

The Gemara answers: **That** bread which the dog refused to eat **was** a mixture of **various types** of grain. It was baked in order to discover the taste of a bread of mixed ingredients and was similar to that which the prophet Ezekiel was commanded to eat, **as it is written: "Take you for yourself wheat, and barley, and beans, and lentils, and millet, and spelt,** and put them in one vessel, and make them for yourself into bread" (Ezekiel 4:9). This bread is unfit for human consumption, as even a dog at times will not eat it. However, bread prepared from lentils alone is edible.

רַב פַּפָּא אָמַר: הַהִיא צְלוּיָה בְּצוֹאַת הָאָדָם הֲוַאי, דִּכְתִיב: "וְהִיא בְּגֶלְלֵי צֵאַת הָאָדָם תְּעֻגֶנָה לְעֵינֵיהֶם".

Rav Pappa said: That bread of Ezekiel's **was roasted in human excrement, as it is written:** "And you shall eat it as barley cakes, **and you shall bake it with human excrement, in their sight"** (Ezekiel 4:12).

מַאי "וְעֻגַת שְׂעֹרִים תֹּאכְלֶנָּה"? אָמַר רַב חִסְדָּא: לְשִׁיעוּרִים. רַב פַּפָּא אָמַר: עֲרִיבָתָהּ כַּעֲרִיבַת שְׂעוֹרִים, וְלֹא כַּעֲרִיבַת חִטִּים.

Having mentioned this verse, the Gemara asks a related question: **What is** the meaning of: **"And you shall eat it as barley [*seorim*] cakes"? Rav Ḥisda said:** The verse means that he should eat it **in** small **measures [*leshiurim*],** not as a satisfying meal. **Rav Pappa said: Its preparation** must be **like the preparation of barley** bread, coarse bread with regard to which one invests little effort, **and not like the preparation of wheat** bread.

NOTES

A baker's dough and a homeowner's dough – עִיסַּת נַחְתּוֹם וְעִיסַּת בַּעַל הַבַּיִת: In the Jerusalem Talmud a dispute is cited concerning the rationale for this distinction. One opinion stated there is that a homeowner is required to give more because the dough he prepares is smaller. Were he to separate one forty-eighth of his dough, the measure that a baker is obligated to separate, this would not constitute a proper gift, which is not the case with the baker's large batches of dough. Another opinion is that a homeowner is stingy with regard to the dough he sets aside. Therefore, the Sages ruled that he should give more, in hope that he would not give less (see Rambam and Rav Shimshon of Saens).

Its *ḥalla* and its mixture of *teruma* and non-sacred produce – חַלָּתָהּ וְדִימּוּעָהּ: A difficulty remains: A baker's *ḥalla* is one forty-eighth of the dough, while the mixture of *teruma* is one one-hundredth. If the amount of a baker's *ḥalla* is permitted, all the more so the amount of the mixture of *teruma* should be permitted. The Ra'avad answers that the reference here is not to a mixture of *teruma* in its usual sense. Rather, it is referring to a case where one forgot to separate regular *teruma* from the produce, a mistake they intend to rectify. The average gift of regular *teruma* is one-fiftieth, which is very close to the measure of a baker's *ḥalla*.

Connected with a chip – תְּפָרָהּ בְּקֵיסָם: In other talmudic sources the Sages do not consider a connection of this kind as attached, because in those cases the attachment is required by *halakha*. In our context, a whole loaf is required only for the sake of appearances, and it is therefore permitted, as long as the seam is inconspicuous (Rav Ya'akov Emden).

HALAKHA

A baker's dough and a homeowner's dough – עִיסַּת נַחְתּוֹם וְעִיסַּת בַּעַל הַבַּיִת: If a loaf is missing a piece the size of a portion that is generally removed as baker's *ḥalla*, it may be still be used for an *eiruv*. This rule applies even if that amount had not been removed as *ḥalla* (Rosh), since the neighbors will think that the missing part is *ḥalla* and no enmity will result (*Magen Avraham*; *Shulḥan Arukh, Oraḥ Ḥayyim* 366:6).

The measure of *ḥalla* – שִׁיעוּר חַלָּה: By Torah law, there is no fixed measure for *ḥalla*. Nevertheless, the Sages determined that it must constitute one twenty-fourth of the dough. They were lenient with regard to a baker, due to the potential loss (*Taz*) or due to the thickness of his dough (Rambam *Sefer Zera'im, Hilkhot Bikkurim* 5:2). Consequently, they required him to separate only one forty-eighth of the dough (*Shulḥan Arukh, Yoreh De'a* 322:1).

Connected with a chip – תְּפָרָהּ בְּקֵיסָם: If one connected the portions of a broken loaf with a wooden chip and the seam is inconspicuous, the loaf may be used for an *eiruv* (*Shulḥan Arukh, Oraḥ Ḥayyim* 366:6).

Rice, lentil, and millet bread – פַּת אוֹרֶז עֲדָשִׁים וְדוֹחַן: An *eiruv* may be prepared with rice bread, in accordance with Shmuel's opinion, and with lentil bread, as stated by Rav, but not with millet bread, as per the statement of Mar Ukva in the name of Shmuel (*Shulḥan Arukh, Oraḥ Ḥayyim* 366:8).

מתני׳ נוֹתֵן אָדָם מָעָה לַחֶנְוָנִי וְלַנַּחְתּוֹם כְּדֵי שֶׁיִּזַּכֶּה לוֹ עֵירוּב, דִּבְרֵי רַבִּי אֱלִיעֶזֶר.

MISHNA **A person** may **give a** ***ma'a*** coin **to a grocer or a baker,** if they live in the same alleyway or courtyard, **so that** the grocer or baker **will confer upon him possession** of wine or bread **for** a merging of the alleyway or **an** ***eiruv*,** if other residents come to them to purchase these products for that purpose. This is **the statement of Rabbi Eliezer.**

וַחֲכָמִים אוֹמְרִים: לֹא זָכוּ לוֹ מְעוֹתָיו.

And the Rabbis say: His money did not confer possession on him,[H] as the transfer of money alone is not a valid mode of acquisition and cannot confer possession. One must perform a valid mode of acquisition, e.g., pulling an article into one's possession, to transfer ownership.

HALAKHA

Acquiring an *eiruv* with money – קְנִיַּית עֵירוּב בְּמָעוֹת: If a person gives money to a storeowner or a baker to transfer possession of an *eiruv* to him, the money does not transfer possession and the *eiruv* is invalid, in accordance with the opinion of the Rabbis. However, if he appointed the baker as his agent for establishing the *eiruv*, the *eiruv* is valid (*Shulḥan Arukh HaRav*, based on the Rosh and the *Tur*; *Shulḥan Arukh, Oraḥ Ḥayyim* 369:1).

וּמוֹדִים בִּשְׁאָר כָּל הָאָדָם שֶׁזָּכוּ לוֹ מְעוֹתָיו, שֶׁאֵין מְעָרְבִין לָאָדָם אֶלָּא מִדַּעְתּוֹ.

And the Rabbis **concede with regard to all** other **people,** apart from grocers and bakers, **that** if one gave them money for the food of an *eiruv*, **his money confers possession upon him, as one** may **establish an** ***eiruv*** **for a person only with his knowledge**[NH] and at his bidding. With regard to a grocer or baker, the person giving the money does not intend to appoint the grocer or the baker as his agent and the money itself does not effect an acquisition, and consequently, he did not accomplish anything. With regard to anyone else, however, there is no doubt that he must have intended to appoint him his agent, and his act is effective.[N]

אָמַר רַבִּי יְהוּדָה: בַּמֶּה דְּבָרִים אֲמוּרִים – בְּעֵירוּבֵי תְחוּמִין, אֲבָל בְּעֵירוּבֵי חֲצֵירוֹת – מְעָרְבִין לְדַעְתּוֹ וְשֶׁלֹּא לְדַעְתּוֹ, לְפִי שֶׁזָּכִין לָאָדָם שֶׁלֹּא בְּפָנָיו וְאֵין חָבִין לָאָדָם שֶׁלֹּא בְּפָנָיו.

Rabbi Yehuda said: In what case is this statement said? It is said **with regard to a joining of** Shabbat **boundaries, but with regard to a joining of courtyards, one** may **establish an** ***eiruv*** for a person either **with his knowledge or without his knowledge.**[H] The reason is **because one may act for a person's benefit in his absence, but one may not act to a person's disadvantage in his absence.** As a participant in a joining of courtyards benefits from his inclusion in the *eiruv*, his consent is not required. However, with regard to a joining of Shabbat boundaries, although it enables one to go farther in one direction, he loses the option of traveling in the opposite direction. When an action is to a person's disadvantage, or if it entails both benefits and disadvantages, one may act on that person's behalf only if he has been explicitly appointed his agent.

גמ׳ מַאי טַעְמָא דְּרַבִּי אֱלִיעֶזֶר? הָא לָא מָשַׁךְ!

GEMARA The Gemara poses a question: **What is the reason for Rabbi Eliezer's** opinion that one who gave money to a grocer or a baker has acquired possession of the food for the *eiruv*? This ruling is difficult, as **he did not** perform a transaction by **pulling** the food into his possession, and one can acquire an object only by performing a valid act of acquisition.

אָמַר רַב נַחְמָן, אָמַר רַבָּה בַּר אֲבוּהּ: עֲשָׂאוֹ רַבִּי אֱלִיעֶזֶר כְּאַרְבָּעָה פְּרָקִים בַּשָּׁנָה. דִּתְנַן: בְּאַרְבָּעָה פְּרָקִים אֵלּוּ מַשְׁחִיטִין אֶת הַטַּבָּח בְּעַל כׇּרְחוֹ, אֲפִילּוּ שׁוֹר שָׁוֶה אֶלֶף דִּינָר וְאֵין לַלּוֹקֵחַ אֶלָּא דִּינָר אֶחָד – כּוֹפִין אוֹתוֹ לִשְׁחוֹט.

Rav Naḥman said that **Rabba bar Abbahu said: Rabbi Eliezer established** this acquisition so that it should be **like the four times**[N] **during the year** that the payment of money effects acquisition, **as we learned** in a mishna: **On these four times** every year, on the eves of Passover, *Shavuot*, Rosh HaShana, and the Eighth Day of Assembly, one who paid for meat may **force the butcher to slaughter**[H] an animal against his will. **Even** if his **ox** was **worth a thousand dinar, and the customer has** paid for **only one dinar's** worth of meat, the customer may **force** the butcher **to slaughter** it, so that the buyer can receive his meat. The reason is that on these four occasions everyone buys meat, and therefore the butcher who promised to supply the customer with meat must give it to him, even if this causes the butcher a considerable loss.

NOTES

As one may establish an *eiruv* for a person only with his knowledge – שֶׁאֵין מְעָרְבִין לָאָדָם אֶלָּא מִדַּעְתּוֹ: According to Rashi and other commentaries, the expression: As one may establish an *eiruv* for a person only with his knowledge, is referring to the previous statement of the mishna. The phrase explains why the money does not effect the transfer of possession to the one who gave the money to the storeowner. The Rosh, however, claims that the mishna is referring to a case of purchase, rather than to a case where another confers possession upon him. Consequently, the phrase: As one may establish an *eiruv* for a person only with his knowledge, does not clarify the previous statement; rather, it stands on its own.

The subject of the mishna – עִנְיָנָהּ שֶׁל הַמִּשְׁנָה: The mishna apparently deals with a joining of courtyards. However, some authorities maintain that with regard to a joining of courtyards, the transfer of the money should establish a valid *eiruv*, either because the storeowner himself is located in the courtyard or because everyone agrees, according to this approach, that a joining of courtyards is a benefit and not a disadvantage. Therefore, these commentaries explain the mishna as referring only to a joining of Shabbat boundaries (see Rashba).

Four times – אַרְבָּעָה פְּרָקִים: These are four dates on which everyone holds large feasts. Any purchase of meat is evidently for this purpose and cannot be postponed to another occasion (see Rashi in tractate *Ḥullin*). Consequently, the butcher must slaughter the ox, even if he will entail a financial loss.

HALAKHA

As one may establish an *eiruv* for a person only with his knowledge – שֶׁאֵין מְעָרְבִין לָאָדָם אֶלָּא מִדַּעְתּוֹ: One may establish a joining of Shabbat boundaries for someone only with his knowledge, as stated by Rabbi Yehuda (*Shulḥan Arukh, Oraḥ Ḥayyim* 414:1).

A joining of courtyards without his knowledge – עֵירוּבֵי חֲצֵירוֹת שֶׁלֹּא לְדַעַת: There is no need to inform the people on whose behalf a joining of courtyards is established, because it is regarded as a benefit for them, in accordance with the opinion of Rabbi Yehuda. This *halakha* applies to a merging of alleyways as well (*Shulḥan Arukh, Oraḥ Ḥayyim* 366:10 in the comment of the Rema, and 392:8).

One may force the butcher to slaughter – מַשְׁחִיטִין אֶת הַטַּבָּח: On the four dates listed in the mishna, a butcher must slaughter an animal even for a buyer who wishes to purchase only a small amount, and the transaction is effected by the payment. Some authorities maintain that the *halakha* is the same with regard to one who purchases wine for *kiddush*, that his payment effects the transaction (Rema, based on the Maharil; *Shulḥan Arukh, Ḥoshen Mishpat* 199:3).

לְפִיכָךְ, אִם מֵת – מֵת לַלּוֹקֵחַ. מֵת לַלּוֹקֵחַ?! הָא לֹא מָשַׁךְ! אָמַר רַב הוּנָא: בְּשֶׁמָּשַׁךְ.

Therefore, if the ox **died, it died at the buyer's** expense. That is to say, he must bear the loss and is not entitled to get his dinar back. The Gemara asks: Why is this so? The customer **did not pull** the ox into his possession. As he did not perform an act of acquisition, he has not acquired any part of the ox, and his dinar should therefore be restored to him.[N] **Rav Huna said:** We are dealing here with a case **where he did pull** the ox into his possession.

אִי הָכִי, אֵימָא סֵיפָא: בִּשְׁאָר יְמוֹת הַשָּׁנָה אֵינוֹ כֵּן; לְפִיכָךְ, אִם מֵת – מֵת לַמּוֹכֵר. אַמַּאי? הָא מָשַׁךְ!

The Gemara raises a difficulty: **If so, say the latter clause** of that mishna as follows: With regard to **the rest of the days of the year, it is not so. Therefore, if** the animal **died, it died at the seller's** expense. If, as Rav Huna claims, the mishna is referring to a case where the purchaser had already pulled the animal into his possession, **why** must the seller suffer the loss? Since the customer **pulled** it into his possession and has acquired it, the ox died in his possession.

אֲמַר רַבִּי שְׁמוּאֵל בַּר יִצְחָק: לְעוֹלָם בְּשֶׁלֹּא מָשַׁךְ, הָכָא בְּמַאי עָסְקִינַן – בְּשֶׁזִּיכָּה לוֹ עַל יְדֵי אַחֵר.

Rabbi Shmuel bar Yitzḥak said: Actually, the mishna is referring to a case **where** the customer **did not pull** the animal into his possession. **With what are we dealing here?** We are dealing **with** a case **where** the butcher **conferred possession upon** his customer **by means of another** person, i.e., the butcher conferred possession upon the customer by instructing another person to acquire a dinar's worth of the ox's meat on his behalf, without having obtained his consent.

בְּאַרְבָּעָה פְּרָקִים אֵלּוּ, דִּזְכוּת הוּא לוֹ – זָכִין לוֹ שֶׁלֹּא בְּפָנָיו, בִּשְׁאָר יְמוֹת הַשָּׁנָה דְּחוֹב הוּא לוֹ – אֵין חָבִין לוֹ אֶלָּא בְּפָנָיו.

Consequently, **at these four times, when it is for his benefit,** as everyone wishes to buy meat on these days, **one may act for his benefit in his absence,** and the acquisition is valid. With regard to **the rest of the days of the year, when it is to his disadvantage,** as it obligates him in payment and he might have no interest in this purchase, **one may act to his disadvantage only in his presence.**

וְרַב אִילָא אָמַר רַבִּי יוֹחָנָן: בְּאַרְבָּעָה פְּרָקִים אֵלּוּ הֶעֱמִידוּ חֲכָמִים דִּבְרֵיהֶן עַל דִּבְרֵי תוֹרָה. דְּאָמַר רַבִּי יוֹחָנָן: דְּבַר תּוֹרָה מָעוֹת קוֹנוֹת,

And Rav Ila said that **Rabbi Yoḥanan said: At these four times, the Sages based their statement on Torah law,** i.e., they ruled in accordance with Torah law. **As Rabbi Yoḥanan said: By Torah law,** the payment of **money** is an effective act of acquisition, which **acquires** movable property. Merchandise that is purchased with money is immediately transferred to the ownership of the buyer.

וּמִפְּנֵי מָה אָמְרוּ ״מְשִׁיכָה קוֹנָה״ – גְּזֵירָה שֶׁמָּא יֹאמַר לוֹ: נִשְׂרְפוּ חִיטֶּיךָ בַּעֲלִיָּיה.

And why, then, **did** the Sages **say** that the mode of acquisition of **pulling,** not monetary payment, **acquires** movable goods? It is **a decree** issued by the Sages, **lest** the seller **say to** a buyer who has already paid for his merchandise: **Your wheat was burned in the upper story** of my house, and you have lost everything. According to Torah law, once the buyer pays, he owns the merchandise wherever it is located. As this state of affairs can lead to fraud, the Sages instituted that only an act of physical transfer of the item purchased can finalize the sale. On these four occasions, however, the Sages ordained that Torah law remains in effect. Rabbi Eliezer maintains that this enactment applies to an *eiruv* as well.

״וּמוֹדִים בִּשְׁאָר כׇּל הָאָדָם כו׳״. מַאן שְׁאָר כׇּל אָדָם? אָמַר רַב: בַּעַל הַבַּיִת.

The mishna stated: The Rabbis **concede with regard to all** other **people** that if he gave them money for food for an *eiruv*, his money confers possession upon him. The Gemara asks: **Who is** included among **all** other **people? Rav said:** The reference is to **an** ordinary **homeowner,**[H] not a merchant, who was asked by someone to receive possession of food for an *eiruv* on his behalf, by means of the money that he provided.

וְכֵן אָמַר שְׁמוּאֵל: בַּעַל הַבַּיִת. דְּאָמַר שְׁמוּאֵל: לֹא שָׁנוּ אֶלָּא נַחְתּוֹם, אֲבָל בַּעַל הַבַּיִת – קוֹנֶה. וְאָמַר שְׁמוּאֵל: לֹא שָׁנוּ אֶלָּא מָעָה, אֲבָל כְּלִי – קוֹנֶה.

And likewise, Shmuel said: The reference is to **an** ordinary **homeowner. As Shmuel said: They taught** this *halakha* **only** with regard to **a baker, but an** ordinary **homeowner** may **acquire** the food on behalf of another person. **And Shmuel** also **said: They taught** this *halakha* **only** in a case where he gave him **a** *ma'a*, **but** if he gave him **a utensil, he acquires**[H] the food for the *eiruv* by the mode of acquisition known as exchange. By handing over the utensil in exchange for the food of the *eiruv*, he acquires that food wherever it is located. However, one cannot perform the mode of acquisition of exchange with money.

NOTES

Acquisition and pulling – קִנְיָן וּמְשִׁיכָה: In general, the transfer of money is not a valid mode of acquisition according to *halakha*. In other words, the money paid by a buyer does not transfer to him the actual ownership of the object he seeks to purchase. Consequently, both the seller and the buyer may renege on the deal, although it is considered improper to do so. In addition, the seller bears responsibility if something happens to the object. The transfer of money merely obligates the seller either to return the money or hand over the object, whichever he prefers. In contrast, the act of pulling the object into one's possession, or one of the other modes of acquisition, results in the full transfer of ownership from seller to buyer. According to Torah law, the object now belongs to the purchaser. This means that even if the purchaser has not yet paid for it, the outstanding payment is considered a debt, while the item itself belongs to him.

HALAKHA

If he gave a *ma'a* to a homeowner – נָתַן מָעָה לְבַעַל הַבַּיִת: With regard to one who gave a *ma'a* to a homeowner to establish an *eiruv* for him, if he said to the homeowner: Confer possession upon me, even if he did not explicitly appoint him as his agent, his intention was certainly to appoint him his agent. Consequently, he acquires the *eiruv*, in accordance with the opinion of Rav and Shmuel (*Shulḥan Arukh, Oraḥ Ḥayyim* 369:1).

But if he gave him a utensil, he acquires – כְּלִי קוֹנֶה: If a person gave a utensil to a baker, even if he said: Confer possession upon me, he establishes the *eiruv* by means of the form of acquisition known as exchange, in accordance with the opinion of Shmuel (*Shulḥan Arukh, Oraḥ Ḥayyim* 369:1).

וְאָמַר שְׁמוּאֵל: לֹא שָׁנוּ אֶלָּא דְּאָמַר לוֹ ״זְכֵה לִי״, אֲבָל אָמַר ״עָרֵב לִי״ – שָׁלִיחַ שַׁוְיֵהּ, וְקָנֵי.

And Shmuel further **said: They taught** this *halakha* **only** in a case **where he said to** the grocer or baker: **Confer possession upon me; but if he said** to him: **Establish an *eiruv* on my behalf,**[H] he clearly intended to **appoint him** his **agent** to establish an *eiruv* on his behalf, **and** therefore the *eiruv* **is acquired** by means of his agency.

״אָמַר רַבִּי יְהוּדָה בַּמֶּה דְּבָרִים אֲמוּרִים וכו׳״. אָמַר רַב יְהוּדָה, אָמַר שְׁמוּאֵל: הֲלָכָה כְּרַבִּי יְהוּדָה. וְלֹא עוֹד, אֶלָּא: כָּל מָקוֹם שֶׁשָּׁנָה רַבִּי יְהוּדָה בְּעֵירוּבִין – הֲלָכָה כְּמוֹתוֹ.

We learned in the mishna: **Rabbi Yehuda said: In what** case **is this statement,** that one may establish an *eiruv* only with a person's knowledge, **said?** This *halakha* applies to a joining of Shabbat boundaries, but not a joining of courtyards. **Rav Yehuda said** that **Shmuel said:** The ***halakha* is in accordance with** the opinion of **Rabbi Yehuda** in this regard, **and not only that, but any place where Rabbi Yehuda taught** a *halakha* **with regard to *eiruvin*,** the ***halakha* is in accordance with his** opinion.

אֲמַר לֵיהּ רַב חָנָא בַּגְדָּתָאָה לְרַב יְהוּדָה: אָמַר שְׁמוּאֵל אֲפִילּוּ בְּמָבוֹי שֶׁנִּיטְּלוּ קוֹרוֹתָיו אוֹ לְחָיָיו?!

Rav Ḥana from Baghdad said to Rav Yehuda: Did **Shmuel state** this ruling **even with regard to an alleyway whose** cross **beam or side post was removed** during Shabbat? Rabbi Yehuda maintains that it is permitted to carry in this alleyway on that same Shabbat.

אֲמַר לֵיהּ: בְּעֵירוּבִין אָמַרְתִּי לָךְ, וְלֹא בִּמְחִיצוֹת.

He said to him: I spoke to you with regard to the acquisition of ***eiruvin*, and not with regard to partitions.** The *halakhot* of partitions are not considered part of the *halakhot* of *eiruvin*, as they touch upon several areas of *halakha*, only one of which is the issue of an *eiruv*. With regard to partitions, the *halakha* is not in accordance with Rabbi Yehuda.

אֲמַר לֵיהּ רַב אַחָא בְּרֵיהּ דְּרָבָא לְרַב אַשִׁי: הֲלָכָה מִכְּלָל דִּפְלִיגִי? וְהָאָמַר רַבִּי יְהוֹשֻׁעַ בֶּן לֵוִי: כָּל מָקוֹם שֶׁאָמַר רַבִּי יְהוּדָה ״אֵימָתַי״ וּ״בַמֶּה״ בְּמִשְׁנָתֵנוּ – אֵינוֹ אֶלָּא לְפָרֵשׁ דִּבְרֵי חֲכָמִים!

Rav Aḥa, son of Rava, said to Rav Ashi: As it is stated that the ***halakha*** is in accordance with Rabbi Yehuda, this proves **by inference that there is a dispute** concerning this issue. **But didn't Rabbi Yehoshua ben Levi say: Any place where Rabbi Yehuda says when, or in what** case is this, **in the Mishna,** he intends **only to explain the** earlier **statement of the Rabbis,** not to disagree with them. Why, then, did Shmuel say that the *halakha* is in accordance with the opinion of Rabbi Yehuda, when according to Rabbi Yehoshua ben Levi he is merely clarifying the opinion of the Rabbis, and there is no dispute between them?

וְלָא פְּלִיגִי?! וְהָא אֲנַן תְּנַן: נִתּוֹסְפוּ עֲלֵיהֶן – מוֹסִיף וּמְזַכֶּה וְצָרִיךְ לְהוֹדִיעַ!

Before addressing this question, the Gemara expresses surprise over the claim itself: **And** do Rabbi Yehuda and the Sages **not dispute** this issue? **Didn't we learn** in an earlier mishna: If new residents **were added to** the original residents of the alleyway, **he may add** to the *eiruv* for those residents **and confer possession** on them, **and he must inform** the new residents of their inclusion in the merging of alleyways. Apparently, this *tanna* maintains that one must inform them even with regard to a joining of courtyards. This ruling contradicts the opinion of Rabbi Yehuda, which proves that there is at least one Sage who does not accept his opinion.

הָתָם בְּחָצֵר שֶׁבֵּין שְׁנֵי מְבוֹאוֹת.

The Gemara answers: **There,** the mishna is referring **to a courtyard** situated **between two alleyways,**[H] in which case the residents of the courtyard may join a merging with whichever alleyway they prefer. As their participation in the merging involves a certain disadvantage, for perhaps the residents of the courtyard would not want to establish a merging of alleyways with one alleyway and lose out on a potential merging with the other, it is necessary to inform them.

וְהָאָמַר רַב שֵׁיזְבִי, אָמַר רַב חִסְדָּא: זֹאת אוֹמֶרֶת חֲלוּקִין עָלָיו חֲבֵירָיו עַל רַבִּי יְהוּדָה!

The Gemara raises a further difficulty: **Didn't Rav Sheizvi say** that **Rav Ḥisda said** with regard to that same mishna: **That is to say** that **Rabbi Yehuda's colleagues disagree with him** over the need to inform the other residents about the *eiruv*? This statement indicates that at least some Sages hold that the matter is in dispute, and not everyone agrees with Rabbi Yehuda.

אֶלָּא

Rather, the Gemara resolves both difficulties together:

HALAKHA

If he said: Establish an *eiruv* on my behalf – אָמַר עָרֵב לִי: If one said to a baker or anyone else: Establish an *eiruv* on my behalf, and gave him money for this purpose, he has appointed him his agent for the *eiruv*, and the baker acquires the *eiruv* for him (*Shulḥan Arukh, Oraḥ Ḥayyim* 369:1).

A courtyard between two alleyways – חָצֵר שֶׁבֵּין שְׁנֵי מְבוֹאוֹת: With regard to a courtyard situated between two alleyways, one who transfers possession of a merging to the residents must inform them before he does so, as they might prefer to participate in a merging of alleyways with the other alleyway (*Shulḥan Arukh, Oraḥ Ḥayyim* 368:2).

גַּבְרָא אַגַּבְרָא קָא רָמֵית?! מָר סָבַר: פְּלִיגִי, וּמָר סָבַר: לָא פְּלִיגִי.

Are you raising a contradiction between the opinion of **one person and** that of **another?**[N] In other words, a difficulty cannot be raised from the statement of one *amora* against those of another. **One Sage,** Shmuel, **maintains** that Rabbi Yehuda and the Sages **disagree, and one** other **Sage,** Rabbi Yehoshua ben Levi, **maintains** that they **do not disagree.**

גּוּפָא, אָמַר רַבִּי יְהוֹשֻׁעַ בֶּן לֵוִי: כָּל מָקוֹם שֶׁאָמַר רַבִּי יְהוּדָה, "אֵימָתַי" וּ"בַמֶּה" בְּמִשְׁנָתֵינוּ – אֵינוֹ אֶלָּא לְפָרֵשׁ דִּבְרֵי חֲכָמִים. וְרַבִּי יוֹחָנָן אָמַר: "אֵימָתַי" – לְפָרֵשׁ, וּ"בַמֶּה" – לַחֲלוֹק.

The Gemara analyzes the statement of Rabbi Yehoshua ben Levi cited in the course of the previous discussion. With regard to **the matter itself: Rabbi Yehoshua ben Levi said** that **any place where Rabbi Yehuda says when, or in what** case **are these, in the Mishna, he** intends **only to explain the** earlier **statement of the Rabbis,** not to disagree with them. **And Rabbi Yoḥanan said:** The term **when** indicates that Rabbi Yehuda comes **to explain,** but the phrase **in what** case is this, indicates that he intends **to disagree.**

וְ"אֵימָתַי" לְפָרֵשׁ הוּא? וְהָא תְּנַן: וְאֵלּוּ הֵן הַפְּסוּלִים: הַמְשַׂחֵק בְּקוּבְיָא, וּמַלְוֶה בְּרִיבִּית, וּמַפְרִיחֵי יוֹנִים, וְסוֹחֲרֵי שְׁבִיעִית.

The Gemara raises a difficulty: **Is** the word **when** invariably a sign that Rabbi Yehuda merely seeks **to explain? Didn't we learn** in a mishna: **The following** people **are disqualified**[NH] by the Sages from giving testimony, as they are people who commit transgressions for profit: **One who plays with dice** [*kubiyya*][LB] for money,[B] **and one who lends** money **at interest, and those who fly pigeons,** i.e., people who arrange competitions between pigeons while placing wagers on which bird will fly faster. The reason for their disqualification is that those who play games of chance do not fully relinquish ownership of their gambling money, as they expect to win their bet. Consequently, one who accepts money in such circumstances has effectively taken something that the giver has not wholeheartedly handed over, and he is therefore like a robber, at least by rabbinic decree. The list of those disqualified from giving testimony includes **merchants** who trade in the produce **of the Sabbatical Year,** which may be eaten but may not be sold as an object of commerce.

אָמַר רַבִּי יְהוּדָה: אֵימָתַי – בִּזְמַן שֶׁאֵין לוֹ אוּמָּנוּת אֶלָּא הִיא, אֲבָל יֵשׁ לוֹ אוּמָּנוּת שֶׁלֹּא הִיא – הֲרֵי זֶה כָּשֵׁר.

Rabbi Yehuda said: When is this so? **When he has no occupation other than this** one, **but if he has a** worthy **occupation other than this,** although he also earns money by these means, **this** person **is qualified** to give testimony. Rabbi Yehuda maintains that one who earns money by means of games of chance is not a criminal or a robber. Rather, the reason why these people are disqualified from giving testimony is because they are not occupied in the constructive development of the world. As they earn their money without effort, they do not care about the monetary losses of others. Consequently, if they have any other occupation, they are valid witnesses.

וְתָנֵי עֲלָהּ בְּבָרַיְיתָא: וַחֲכָמִים אוֹמְרִים: בֵּין שֶׁאֵין לוֹ אוּמָּנוּת אֶלָּא הִיא, וּבֵין שֶׁיֵּשׁ לוֹ אוּמָּנוּת שֶׁלֹּא הִיא – הֲרֵי זֶה פָּסוּל!

The Gemara resumes its difficulty: According to the above principle with regard to statements introduced with the term when, Rabbi Yehuda's statement should be understood merely as an explanation of the previous opinion. However, a ***baraita*** **was taught about** the mishna: **And the Rabbis say: Whether he has no occupation other than this** one, **or whether he has a** fitting **occupation other than this, this** person **is disqualified** from giving testimony. Apparently, Rabbi Yehuda is disagreeing rather than explaining, even though he introduced his statement with the term when.

הַהִיא דְּרַבִּי יְהוּדָה אָמַר רַבִּי טַרְפוֹן הִיא;

The Gemara answers: **That** opinion in the *baraita,* with regard to those disqualified from providing testimony, is not the opinion of the Rabbis of the mishna. Rather, **it is** that **of Rabbi Yehuda,** who maintained that **Rabbi Tarfon said** this opinion. The Rabbis of the mishna, however, agree with Rabbi Yehuda in this regard, and his statement serves to explain their position.

NOTES

Are you raising a contradiction between one person and another – גַּבְרָא אַגַּבְרָא קָא רָמֵית: This expression indicates that the contradiction involves a dispute between two *amora'im*, which does not pose a problem. Indeed, it is possible to raise a difficulty against the opinion of an *amora* only from a statement of a *tanna*, as an *amora* may not dispute a *tanna*. However, he may take issue with another *amora*.

The following people are disqualified – אֵלּוּ הֵן הַפְּסוּלִים: There are various reasons for disqualifying a person from giving testimony. Some people are disqualified because they are relatives of the litigants or due to their personal interest in the matter, while others are disqualified as sinners. The Torah excludes the testimony of a wicked witness. The Sages list the witnesses disqualified by rabbinic law in a mishna in tractate *Sanhedrin*. Although those listed in the mishna are not criminals according to the Torah's standards, nevertheless, as they are suspected of committing a transgression due to greed for prohibited gain, they will similarly testify falsely for a bribe or due to some other financial incentive.

HALAKHA

Those who are disqualified from giving testimony – הַפְּסוּלִין לְעֵדוּת: The following people are disqualified from giving testimony because their credibility is suspect: Moneylenders for interest, pigeon-racers, traders in Sabbatical Year produce, and gamblers if they have no other occupation. Some authorities disqualify gamblers even if only a small portion of their income is from dice playing (Rambam *Sefer Shofetim, Hilkhot Edut* 10:4; 12:1), while others disqualify them only if their entire livelihood is based on gambling (Rashi; *Tur*; *Shulḥan Arukh*, *Ḥoshen Mishpat* 34:16).

LANGUAGE

Dice [*kubiyya*] – קוּבִּיָּה: From the Greek κυβεία, *kubèya*, a game of chance played with dice.

BACKGROUND

Dice – קוּבִּיָּה:

Roman dice used for games of chance

Games of dice – מִשְׂחֲקֵי קוּבִּיָּה:

Roman sketch depicting dice playing, from the talmudic period

דְּתַנְיָא, אָמַר רַבִּי יְהוּדָה מִשּׁוּם רַבִּי טַרְפוֹן: לְעוֹלָם אֵין אֶחָד מֵהֶן נָזִיר, לְפִי שֶׁאֵין נְזִירוּת אֶלָּא לְהַפְלָאָה.

As it was taught in a *baraita* with regard to naziriteship: **Rabbi Yehuda said in the name of Rabbi Tarfon:** In a case where two people accepted a bet, with each undertaking to become a nazirite if he lost the wager, and a doubt arose as to who won, **neither one** of them **can possibly be a nazirite, as there is no** acceptance of **naziriteship without** clear and definitive **pronunciation.**[N] A vow of naziriteship is only binding if it was expressly pronounced, i.e., if it was clear from the outset that the person intended to become a nazirite.

אַלְמָא: כֵּיוָן דִּמְסַפְּקָא לֵיהּ אִי נָזִיר אִי לָא נָזִיר הוּא – לָא מְשַׁעְבֵּיד נַפְשֵׁיהּ, הָכָא נָמֵי: כֵּיוָן דְּלָא יָדַע אִי קָנֵי אִי לָא קָנֵי – לָא גָּמַר וּמַקְנֶה.

Consequently, it can be inferred that **since he is in doubt** as to **whether he is a nazirite or he is not a nazirite, he does not submit himself** to and accept his vow of naziriteship. **Here, too,** Rabbi Yehuda disqualifies those who play games of chance from delivering testimony due to the fact that they are robbers. **Since** the player **does not know whether he will** win and **acquire** the money **or whether he will** lose and **not acquire** it, **he does not fully transfer ownership** of the money with which he plays to others, which means that the one who gains from these games receives money that was not wholeheartedly given to him. He is therefore likened to a robber, at least on the rabbinic level, which disqualifies him from giving testimony.

הדרן עלך חלון

NOTES

Distinct utterance and a stipulation of surety – הַפְלָאָה וְאַסְמַכְתָּא: According to Rabbi Yehuda, who cites Rabbi Tarfon, the flaw that applies to a naziriteship made conditional on a wager is equally relevant to games of chance. The assumption is that a stipulation of surety does not effect acquisition, i.e., a person does not wholeheartedly transfer possession of an object to another unless he's certain of his obligation. Since his stipulation that he will pay if he loses was based on his certainty that he will win, he does not commit himself to pay. Consequently, this is not a legal acquisition, just as an analogous unclear condition does not result in halakhic naziriteship.

Summary of **Perek VII**

The Gemara resolved the problems relating to the definition of the boundaries that demarcate between two courtyards by dividing the cases into three categories.

Any partition created by a ten-handbreadth height disparity either above or below the surface of the courtyard is considered a full-fledged barrier. Each courtyard on either side of a partition is a separate domain, whose residents establish their own *eiruv*.

If the barrier is lower than ten handbreadths, or if there is a breach wider than ten cubits, the two courtyards are considered a single unit, and the residents establish one *eiruv* together, as residents of one large courtyard. If the barrier was properly erected but includes an entrance, whether an actual passageway or merely a window large enough to transfer objects, the residents of the courtyards may opt to establish a single *eiruv* as residents of one courtyard, or to establish a separate *eiruv* in each of the courtyards. In the latter case, they may not carry into the other courtyard.

Regarding the second issue, the manner in which the merging of courtyards that open into an alleyway is accomplished in practice, the consensus was that all types of *eiruv*, i.e., courtyards, alleyways, and Shabbat boundaries, can be established with anything characterized as food. However, the Sages instituted that the joining of courtyards should be performed only with a whole loaf of bread, to preclude quarrels between the residents.

As for the manner of participation in an *eiruv*, the Gemara concluded that it is not necessary for each member to contribute his portion in person, as one may acquire the *eiruv* through an agent acting on his behalf. Similarly, a person may acquire an *eiruv* on behalf of others. The principle is that any *eiruv* that is exclusively for the benefit and convenience of its participants, e.g., the joining of courtyards and the merging of alleyways, can be acquired on behalf of another even without his knowledge, as long as he is eventually informed that it was established. In the case of the joining of Shabbat boundaries, in contrast, since that *eiruv* involves a degree of loss as it prevents walking beyond the city limits in the opposite direction, the consent of the other party is required for its acquisition.

Introduction to **Perek VIII**

In this chapter the discussion of details of the partnership of *eiruv* continues from the previous chapter, although its main focus is on two different matters.

The first matter is completing the definition of the essence of a residence. While the location and the boundaries of a residence as well as the manner in which one resides in a residence have already been addressed, some matters remain that require clarification. Once the structure has been classified as a residence, there are additional, adjacent areas beyond the residence proper to which the residents have access and which they have the right to use. Although the residents do not necessarily own the adjacent areas, the question with regard to the *halakhot* of Shabbat is to what degree the residents have the right to utilize that adjacent area and under what circumstances those rights are revoked, either because the residents were never entitled to make use of that area or because the rights of others take precedence over theirs.

In continuation of the discussion concerning what constitutes a residence, an additional question arises: Is every structure in which people reside considered a residence, or are there places that by their very nature are not considered residences as far as the *halakhot* of *eiruv* are concerned? Examples include places that are not fit for residence, dwellings that belong to others, and uninhabited dwellings whose owners are not present. Are all of these considered residences in terms of the *halakhot* of *eiruv*?

The other matter addressed in this chapter is the use of water on Shabbat, within the constraints of the *halakhot* of boundaries and of moving objects on Shabbat. Typically, the legal status of any body of water is that of a *karmelit*; however, since there are bodies in which the water is not stationary, e.g., rivers, streams, and canals, special guidelines are necessary in some cases. Water is needed for drinking and washing, and waste water must be poured out. The *halakhot* of Shabbat in general, and of *eiruv* in particular, pose problems as to how those needs can be met without violating prohibitions by Torah or rabbinic law.

מתני׳ כֵּיצַד מִשְׁתַּתְּפִין בִּתְחוּמִין? מַנִּיחַ אֶת הֶחָבִית, וְאוֹמֵר: הֲרֵי זֶה לְכָל בְּנֵי עִירִי לְכָל מִי שֶׁיֵּלֵךְ לְבֵית הָאֵבֶל אוֹ לְבֵית הַמִּשְׁתֶּה. וְכָל שֶׁקִּיבֵּל עָלָיו, מִבְּעוֹד יוֹם – מוּתָּר, מִשֶּׁתֶּחְשַׁךְ – אָסוּר, שֶׁאֵין מְעָרְבִין מִשֶּׁתֶּחְשַׁךְ.

MISHNA **How does one participate in** the joining of Shabbat **boundaries?** One who wishes to establish a joining of Shabbat boundaries for himself and others **places a barrel** of food in the location he designates as their place of residence, **and says: This is for all the residents of my town, for anyone who** wishes to **go** on Shabbat **to a house of mourning or to a house of** a wedding **feast**[N] situated beyond the Shabbat limit. **Anyone who accepted upon himself while it was still day,** i.e., before the onset of Shabbat, that he will rely on the *eiruv*, **is permitted** to rely upon it; but if one did so only **after nightfall,** he is **prohibited** to rely upon it, as the principle is that **one may not establish an *eiruv* after nightfall.**

גמ׳ אָמַר רַב יוֹסֵף: אֵין מְעָרְבִין אֶלָּא לִדְבַר מִצְוָה. מַאי קָא מַשְׁמַע לַן? תְּנֵינָא: לְכָל מִי שֶׁיֵּלֵךְ לְבֵית הָאֵבֶל אוֹ לְבֵית הַמִּשְׁתֶּה!

GEMARA **Rav Yosef said: One may establish a joining** of Shabbat boundaries **only for the purpose of a mitzva,**[NH] i.e., to enable the fulfillment of a religious obligation, but not for an optional activity. The Gemara asks: **What** novel element **is he teaching us** by this? **We** explicitly **learned** this idea in the mishna from the phrase: **For anyone who** wishes to **go** on Shabbat **to a house of mourning or to a house of** a wedding **feast.** This mishna indicates that an *eiruv* may be established only for the purpose of a mitzva, e.g., in order to comfort mourners or to celebrate a wedding, but not for any other reason.

מַהוּ דְּתֵימָא: אוֹרְחָא דְּמִלְּתָא קָתָנֵי, קָא מַשְׁמַע לַן.

The Gemara answers: This teaching is necessary, **lest you say** that the mishna merely **teaches the usual case.** Generally, a group of people would establish an *eiruv* in order to walk beyond the Shabbat limit only for a special purpose, such as a wedding, but one might be permitted to establish an *eiruv* even for an optional activity as well. Rav Yosef therefore **teaches us** that an *eiruv* may indeed be established only for the purpose of a mitzva.

״וְכָל שֶׁקִּיבֵּל עָלָיו מִבְּעוֹד יוֹם״ – שְׁמַעְתְּ מִינַּהּ: אֵין בְּרֵירָה. דְּאִי יֵשׁ בְּרֵירָה – תִּיגְּלֵי מִילְּתָא לְמַפְרֵעַ דְּמִבְּעוֹד יוֹם הֲוָה נִיחָא לֵיהּ!

We learned in the mishna: **Anyone who accepted upon himself while it was still day** that he will rely upon the *eiruv*[N] is permitted to rely upon it on Shabbat. The Gemara comments: Apparently, **learn from here** that **there is no** halakhic principle of retroactive **clarification.** That is to say, there is no halakhic assumption that an uncertain state of affairs can be retroactively clarified. A later statement or action cannot retroactively clarify one's earlier intentions as though he had explicitly stated those intentions at the outset. For **if there is** a halakhic principle of retroactive **clarification, the** *eiruv* should be effective even if one relied upon it only after nightfall, as **it is retroactively revealed that he wanted** the *eiruv* **while it was still day.**

אָמַר רַב אָשֵׁי: ״הוֹדִיעוּהוּ״ וְ״לֹא הוֹדִיעוּהוּ״ קָתָנֵי.

Rav Ashi said that the mishna **teaches:** While it was still day. This phrase does not require one to make the decision to rely on the *eiruv* before Shabbat. Rather, the criterion for using the *eiruv* on Shabbat is whether **they informed him or they did not inform him**[H] of the existence of the *eiruv* prior to Shabbat. In other words, if one knew about the *eiruv* while it was still day, he may rely on it, even if he decided to use it only after the onset of Shabbat, as the halakhic principle of retroactive clarification is accepted. However, if one was unaware of the existence of the *eiruv* when it came into effect at the onset of Shabbat, the matter cannot be retroactively clarified.

אָמַר רַב אַסִי: קָטָן בֶּן שֵׁשׁ יוֹצֵא בְּעֵירוּב אִמּוֹ. מֵיתִיבִי: קָטָן שֶׁצָּרִיךְ לְאִמּוֹ – יוֹצֵא בְּעֵירוּב אִמּוֹ. וְשֶׁאֵין צָרִיךְ לְאִמּוֹ – אֵין יוֹצֵא בְּעֵירוּב אִמּוֹ.

Rav Asi said: A six-year-old child may go out by means **of his mother's *eiruv*.**[H] As he is subordinate to her, he is included in her *eiruv* and does not require his own *eiruv*. **The Gemara raises an objection** from a *baraita*: **A child who needs his mother may go out by** means **of his mother's *eiruv*, but one who does not need his mother may not go out by** means **of his mother's *eiruv*.**

וּתְנַן נַמִי גַּבֵּי סוּכָּה כִּי הַאי גַּוְונָא: קָטָן שֶׁאֵין צָרִיךְ לְאִמּוֹ – חַיָּיב בְּסוּכָּה.

And we also learned a similar *halakha* in a mishna **with regard to a *sukka*: A child who does not need his mother is obligated in** the mitzva of ***sukka*** by rabbinical law, so that he will be trained in the observance of mitzvot.[H]

NOTES

To a house of mourning or to a house of a wedding feast – לְבֵית הָאֵבֶל אוֹ לְבֵית הַמִּשְׁתֶּה: The mishna mentions a house of mourning before a house of a wedding feast, in accordance with the verse "It is better to go to the house of mourning than to go to the house of feasting" (Ecclesiastes 7:2; Ritva).

A joining of Shabbat boundaries only for the purpose of a mitzva – עֵירוּב לִדְבַר מִצְוָה: Some commentaries claim that the limitation of an *eiruv* for the purpose of a mitzva applies only to one who acquires an *eiruv* by placing bread at the place in question. However, one may establish an *eiruv* even for a voluntary matter if he does so by means of his physical presence (Rabbeinu Yehonatan).

Who accepted upon himself while it was still day that he will rely upon the *eiruv* – שֶׁקִּיבֵּל עָלָיו מִבְּעוֹד יוֹם: The Ra'avad explains that this entire discussion concerns one who establishes an *eiruv* for another individual. The Gemara initially assumed that the other person must accept and acquire the *eiruv*. Rav Ashi rejects this approach, as he maintains that it is enough to inform the recipient that the *eiruv* exists, as his mere knowledge of the *eiruv* is sufficient to enable him to be included in it retroactively.

HALAKHA

A joining of Shabbat boundaries only for the purpose of a mitzva – עֵירוּב לִדְבַר מִצְוָה: One may establish an joining of Shabbat boundaries only for the purpose of a mitzva, e.g., to celebrate a wedding, to go to a mourner's house, to greet one's master or student, or to run from danger. Nonetheless, if one establishes an *eiruv* for an everyday purpose, the *eiruv* is valid (*Tur*, citing the Rambam; *Shulḥan Arukh, Oraḥ Ḥayyim* 415:1).

They informed him or they did not inform him – הוֹדִיעוּהוּ וְלֹא הוֹדִיעוּהוּ: If one is informed about an *eiruv* of Shabbat limits while it is still day, the *eiruv* is valid even if he accepted it only after nightfall. If he was not informed about the existence of the *eiruv* prior to the onset of Shabbat, he may not rely on it, even if he so desires (*Shulḥan Arukh, Oraḥ Ḥayyim* 413:1).

May go out by means of his mother's *eiruv* – יוֹצֵא בְּעֵירוּב אִמּוֹ: A child up to and including the age of six may use his mother's *eiruv*, without contributing two meals toward the *eiruv*. The *halakha* is in accordance with the opinion of Rav Asi (Rif; Rambam; *Sefer Mitzvot Gadol*; *Sefer Mitzvot Katan*). However, other sources indicate that a five-year-old child who does not need his mother may not rely on her *eiruv* (*Shulḥan Arukh, Oraḥ Ḥayyim* 414:2).

A minor with regard to a *sukka* – קָטָן לְעִנְיַן סוּכָּה: The Sages obligate parents to educate their young children in the observance of mitzvot. This duty pertains to minors from the age of five or six. Some authorities maintain that the obligation begins when the child is six years old, in accordance with the opinion of Rav Asi (Vilna Gaon; *Shulḥan Arukh, Oraḥ Ḥayyim* 640:2).

NOTES

And does not call Mother – וְאֵינוֹ קוֹרֵא אִימָּא: Rashi explains in tractate *Sukka* that this definition of a young child is referring to one who cries Mother, Mother for as long as he remains awake, whereas one who does not need his mother calls out to her only from time to time.

וְהָוֵינַן בָּהּ: וְאֵיזֶהוּ קָטָן שֶׁאֵין צָרִיךְ לְאִמּוֹ? אָמְרִי דְּבֵי רַבִּי יַנַּאי: כֹּל שֶׁנִּפְנֶה וְאֵין אִמּוֹ מְקַנַּחְתּוֹ.

And we discussed this mishna and raised a question: **But who is the child who does not need his mother? The** Sages of the **school of Rabbi Yannai said:** This is referring to **any** child **who defecates and his mother does not wipe him.** A child who can clean himself is considered sufficiently mature for the purposes of the *halakha* of *sukka*.

רַבִּי שִׁמְעוֹן בֶּן לָקִישׁ אָמַר: כֹּל שֶׁנֵּיעוֹר וְאֵינוֹ קוֹרֵא "אִימָּא". אִימָּא סָלְקָא דַּעְתָּךְ? גְּדוֹלִים נַמִי קָרוּ! אֶלָּא אֵימָא: כֹּל שֶׁנֵּיעוֹר מִשְּׁנָתוֹ וְאֵינוֹ קוֹרֵא "אִימָּא אִימָּא".

Rabbi Shimon ben Lakish said: Any child **who wakens** from sleep **and does not call: Mother,**[N] is obligated in the mitzva of *sukka*. The Gemara expresses surprise at this statement: **Can it enter your mind** that every child who cries: **Mother** is considered to be one who needs his mother? Much **older** children **also call** out to their mothers for assistance when they awaken. **Rather, say** that the *halakha* includes **any** child **who wakens from sleep and does not** persistently **call: Mother, Mother.** A minor who arises only when his mother comes is classified as one who needs his mother.

וְכַמָּה, כְּבַר אַרְבַּע כְּבַר חָמֵשׁ!

The Gemara continues. The Sages who discussed the mishna asked: **And** at **what** age is a child no longer considered to be in need of his mother? Such a child is **one about four** years **old** or **about five** years **old,** as some children become independent of their mothers earlier than others. This poses a difficulty to the opinion of Rav Asi, who maintains that even a six-year-old child is considered to be in need of his mother, and may go out by means of his mother's *eiruv*.

Perek **VIII**
Daf **82** Amud **b**

אָמַר רַב יְהוֹשֻׁעַ בְּרֵיהּ דְּרַב אִידִי: כִּי קָאָמַר רַב אַסִי – כְּגוֹן שֶׁעֵירֵב עָלָיו אָבִיו לַצָּפוֹן, וְאִמּוֹ לַדָּרוֹם. דַּאֲפִילּוּ בַּר שֵׁשׁ נַמִי, בְּצַוְותָא דְּאִמֵּיהּ נִיחָא לֵיהּ.

Rav Yehoshua, son of Rav Idi, said in answer: **When Rav Asi said** that this child may go out by means of his mother's *eiruv*, he was referring to a case **where his father established an *eiruv* on his behalf to the north, and his mother** prepared an *eiruv* on his behalf **to the south, as even a six-year-old prefers the company of his mother** to that of his father. However, Rav Asi agrees that if they did not both establish an *eiruv* for him he is not subordinate to his mother.

מֵיתִיבִי: קָטָן שֶׁצָּרִיךְ לְאִמּוֹ – יוֹצֵא בְּעֵירוּב אִמּוֹ, עַד בֶּן שֵׁשׁ. תְּיוּבְתָּא דְּרַב יְהוֹשֻׁעַ בַּר רַב אִידִי! תְּיוּבְתָּא.

The Gemara raises an objection from a *baraita*: **A child who needs his mother may go out by** means of **his mother's *eiruv*** that she established for herself. Until what age may he do so? He can be **up to the age of six.** This *baraita* **is a conclusive refutation of** the opinion of **Rav Yehoshua bar Rav Idi,** who maintains that a six-year-old may go out by means of his mother's *eiruv* only if she established an *eiruv* on his behalf as well? The Gemara concludes: This is indeed **a conclusive refutation.**

לֵימָא תֶּיהֱוֵי תְּיוּבְתֵּיהּ דְּרַב אַסִי?! אָמַר לָךְ רַב אַסִי: "עַד" וְעַד בִּכְלָל.

The Gemara comments: **Let us say** that this **is** also **a refutation of** the opinion of **Rav Asi,** as here it states: Until the age of six, which indicates that he can be up to, but not including, six years old, whereas Rav Asi maintains that even a six-year-old is included in this *halakha*. The Gemara states: **Rav Asi** can **say to you** that when the *baraita* states: **Up to** the age of six, it means **up to and including** six years old.

לֵימָא תֶּיהֱוֵי תְּיוּבְתֵּיהּ דְּרַבִּי יַנַּאי וְרֵישׁ לָקִישׁ?! לָא קַשְׁיָא; הָא – דְּאִיתֵיהּ אֲבוּהִי בְּמָתָא, הָא – דְּלָא אִיתֵיהּ אֲבוּהִי בְּמָתָא.

The Gemara comments: **Let us say** that this **is** also **a refutation of** the opinion of **Rabbi Yannai and Reish Lakish,** who maintain that a child in need of his mother is one who is up to age four or five. The Gemara explains: This is **not difficult. Here** Rabbi Yannai and Reish Lakish are referring to a situation **when** the child's **father is in town.** As the child can go out with his father, he is no longer in need of his mother, even though he is younger than six. In contrast, **there** the *baraita* is referring to a case **when his father is not in town.** The child therefore needs his mother until he reaches the age of six.

תָּנוּ רַבָּנַן: מְעָרֵב אָדָם עַל יְדֵי בְּנוֹ וּבִתּוֹ הַקְּטַנִּים, עַל יְדֵי עַבְדּוֹ וְשִׁפְחָתוֹ הַכְּנַעֲנִים, בֵּין לְדַעְתָּן בֵּין שֶׁלֹּא לְדַעְתָּן אֲבָל אֵינוֹ מְעָרֵב לֹא עַל יְדֵי עַבְדּוֹ וְשִׁפְחָתוֹ הָעִבְרִים, [וְלֹא] עַל יְדֵי בְּנוֹ וּבִתּוֹ הַגְּדוֹלִים, וְלֹא עַל יְדֵי אִשְׁתּוֹ, אֶלָּא מִדַּעְתָּם.

Our Sages taught in a *baraita*: **A person may establish an *eiruv* on behalf of his minor son or daughter, and on behalf of his Canaanite servant or maidservant, either with their knowledge or without their knowledge. However, he may not establish an *eiruv*, neither on behalf of his Hebrew servant or maidservant, nor on behalf of his adult son or daughter, nor on behalf of his wife, except with their knowledge.**

תַּנְיָא אִידָךְ: לֹא יְעָרֵב אָדָם עַל יְדֵי בְּנוֹ וּבִתּוֹ הַגְּדוֹלִים וְעַל יְדֵי עַבְדּוֹ וְשִׁפְחָתוֹ הָעִבְרִים, וְלֹא עַל יְדֵי אִשְׁתּוֹ, אֶלָּא מִדַּעְתָּן. אֲבָל מְעָרֵב הוּא עַל יְדֵי עַבְדּוֹ וְשִׁפְחָתוֹ הַכְּנַעֲנִים, וְעַל יְדֵי בְּנוֹ וּבִתּוֹ הַקְּטַנִּים, בֵּין לְדַעְתָּן וּבֵין שֶׁלֹּא לְדַעְתָּן – מִפְּנֵי שֶׁיָּדָן כְּיָדוֹ.

It was taught in another *baraita*: **A person may establish an *eiruv* on behalf of his adult son or daughter, and on behalf of his Hebrew servant or maidservant, and on behalf of his wife, only with their knowledge. However, he may establish an *eiruv* on behalf of his Canaanite servant or maidservant, and on behalf of his minor son or daughter, either with their knowledge or without their knowledge, as their hand is like his hand,** i.e., their status and the domain in which they are located are determined by his status and domain.

וְכוּלָּן שֶׁעֵירְבוּ, וְעֵירֵב עֲלֵיהֶם רַבָּן – יוֹצְאִין בְּשֶׁל רַבָּן, חוּץ מִן הָאִשָּׁה, מִפְּנֵי שֶׁיְּכוֹלָה לִמְחוֹת.

And all of these who established an *eiruv* for themselves, **and** at the same time **their master established an *eiruv* for them** in a different direction, **they may go out** by means of **their master's** ***eiruv*, except for a wife, because she can object** by saying that she does not want her husband's *eiruv*.

אִשָּׁה מַאי שְׁנָא? אָמַר רַבָּה: אִשָּׁה וְכָל דְּדָמֵי לָהּ.

The Gemara begins its analysis of the *baraitot* by posing a question: **A wife,** in **what** way **is** she **different** from an adult son or daughter? Why can't they object? They are also of age and under their own authority. **Rabba said:** The reference is not only to a wife; the *tanna* is speaking of **a wife and all who are similar to her** in this regard, such as a Hebrew servant or an adult son.

אָמַר מָר: חוּץ מִן הָאִשָּׁה, מִפְּנֵי שֶׁיְּכוֹלָה לִמְחוֹת. טַעְמָא: דְּמָחֵי, הָא סְתָמָא – נָפְקָא בְּדִבַעְלָהּ. הָא קָתָנֵי רֵישָׁא: "אֶלָּא מִדַּעְתָּם", מַאי לָאו דְּאָמְרִי אִין!

The Master said in the *baraita*: These people may go out by means of their master's *eiruv*, **except for a wife, because she can object.** The Gemara infers: **The reason is due to** the fact **that she objected, but** if he established an *eiruv* and she **did not specify** her feelings about it one way or another, **she may go out by** means of **her husband's** *eiruv*. The Gemara raises an objection: **Doesn't the first clause** of the *baraita* **state** that he may establish an *eiruv* **only with their knowledge? What,** is this **not** referring to a case where he asked them whether or not they want this *eiruv*, and **they said yes?** It can be inferred from here that if his wife did not say anything, she may not use the *eiruv*.

לָא, מַאי "אֶלָּא מִדַּעְתָּם", דְּאִשְׁתִּיקוּ. לְאַפּוּקֵי הֵיכָא דְּאָמְרִי "לָא".

The Gemara rejects this argument: **No; what is** the meaning of the phrase: **Only with their knowledge?** It means **that they were silent** and said nothing in protest. This comes **to exclude** a case **where they said no.** If, however, they did not object, they may go out by means of the *eiruv* of the head of the family.

הָא "וְכוּלָּן שֶׁעֵירְבוּ וְעֵירֵב עֲלֵיהֶן רַבָּן יוֹצְאִין בְּשֶׁל רַבָּן" וּסְתָמָא הוּא, וְקָתָנֵי חוּץ מִן הָאִשָּׁה, דְּלָא נָפְקִי!

The Gemara raises an objection: **Wasn't** it taught in that same *baraita*: **And** with regard to **all of these who established an** ***eiruv*** for themselves, **and their master established an *eiruv* for them** in a different direction, **they may go out by** means of **their master's** ***eiruv*. And that is** referring to a situation when they **did not specify** their feelings, as it does not state that they objected, **and** yet the *baraita* **states: Except for a wife, who may not go out** by means of her husband's *eiruv*. The *baraita* clearly indicates that even if she did not object, the husband's *eiruv* is ineffective for his wife.

אָמַר רָבָא: כֵּיוָן שֶׁעֵירְבוּ – אֵין לְךָ מִיחוּי גָּדוֹל מִזֶּה.

Rava said: Since they established an *eiruv* in a different direction, **you have no protest greater than this.** They need not register any other objection, as their actions prove that they do not wish to be part of their master's *eiruv*.[H]

HALAKHA

For whom may an *eiruv* be established with his knowledge – לְמִי מְעָרְבִין מִדַּעְתּוֹ: An *eiruv* cannot be established for an adult, including one's wife, adult child, and Jewish servant and maidservant, without that person's knowledge. If they raise an objection or establish an *eiruv* in a different direction, they may not use his *eiruv*. However, if they remain silent, it is as though they gave their consent. One may establish an *eiruv* for his minor children without their knowledge, to educate them in mitzvot (*Magen Avraham*). One may also establish an *eiruv* for his gentile servant and maidservant, and his *eiruv* includes them even if they raise an objection (*Shulḥan Arukh, Oraḥ Ḥayyim* 414:1).

מתני׳ כַּמָּה הוּא שִׁיעוּרוֹ? מְזוֹן שְׁתֵּי סְעוּדוֹת לְכָל אֶחָד וְאֶחָד, מְזוֹנוֹ לַחוֹל וְלֹא לַשַּׁבָּת, דִּבְרֵי רַבִּי מֵאִיר. רַבִּי יְהוּדָה אוֹמֵר: לַשַּׁבָּת וְלֹא לַחוֹל. וְזֶה וָזֶה מִתְכַּוְּונִים לְהָקֵל.

MISHNA **What is the measure** for an joining of Shabbat boundaries? It consists of a quantity of **food** sufficient for **two meals for each and every one** of those included in the *eiruv*.[NH] The *tanna'im* disagree with regard to the size of these two meals. It is referring to **one's food** that he eats **on a weekday and not on Shabbat;** this is **the statement of Rabbi Meir. Rabbi Yehuda says:** It is referring to the amount he eats **on Shabbat and not on a weekday. And** both **this** Sage, Rabbi Meir, **and that** Sage, Rabbi Yehuda, **intended to be lenient,**[N] as Rabbi Meir maintains that people eat more food on Shabbat, whereas Rabbi Yehuda believes that they consume more on a weekday.

רַבִּי יוֹחָנָן בֶּן בְּרוֹקָה אוֹמֵר: מִכִּכָּר בְּפוּנְדְּיוֹן מֵאַרְבַּע סְאִין בְּסֶלַע. רַבִּי שִׁמְעוֹן אוֹמֵר: שְׁתֵּי יָדוֹת לְכִכָּר מִשָּׁלֹשׁ לְקַב.

Rabbi Yoḥanan ben Beroka says: Food for two meals is the size **of a loaf** bought **with a *pundeyon*,**[LB] which is one-forty-eighth of a *sela*, **when four *se'a*** of wheat are sold **for a *sela*.**[NB] **Rabbi Shimon says:** Food for two meals is **two** of three **parts of a loaf, when three** loaves are prepared **from a *kav*** of wheat. In other words, the measure is two-thirds of a loaf the size of one-third of a *kav*.

חֶצְיָהּ לַבַּיִת הַמְנוּגָּע, וַחֲצִי חֶצְיָהּ לִפְסוֹל אֶת הַגְּוִיָּה.

Having discussed measures with regard to a loaf of bread, the mishna states that **half** of this loaf is the amount called a half [*peras*], a measure relevant **for the** *halakhot* **of a leprous house.**[H] If one enters a house afflicted with leprosy and remains there long enough to eat this amount of food, the clothes he is wearing become ritually impure. **And half of its half,** a quarter of this loaf, is the amount of ritually impure food that **disqualifies the body.**[NH] In other words, impure food of this amount imparts ritual impurity to the body of the eater, and disqualifies him by rabbinic law from eating *teruma*.

גמ׳ וְכַמָּה מְזוֹן שְׁתֵּי סְעוּדוֹת? אָמַר רַבִּי יְהוּדָה, אָמַר רַב: תַּרְתֵּי רִיפְתָּא אִיכַּרְיָיתָא. רַב אַדָּא בַּר אַהֲבָה אָמַר: תַּרְתֵּי רִיפְתָּא נְהַר פַּפִּיתָא.

GEMARA The Gemara asks: **And how much is food for two meals** according to the measures of Rabbi Yehuda and Rabbi Meir? **Rabbi Yehuda said** that **Rav said: Two farmers'** [*ikaryata*][N] **loaves of bread. Rav Adda bar Ahava said: Two** standard **loaves of bread** baked in the region of **the Pappa River.**

LANGUAGE

Pundeyon – **פּוּנְדְּיוֹן:** From the Latin dupondium, a coin worth two *issar*.

BACKGROUND

Pundeyon – **פּוּנְדְּיוֹן:** A copper coin worth two *issar*.

Pundeyon from the talmudic period

Money and produce – כְּסָפִים וּתְבוּאָה: This table lists the various coins and the amounts of wheat or loaves of bread that can be bought with them, in accordance with the opinion of Rabbi Yoḥanan ben Beroka.

Amount of money	Purchase
1 *sela*	4 *se'a*
1 *dinar*	1 *se'a*
24 *ma'a*	4 *se'a*
48 *pundeyon*	48 or 96 loaves

NOTES

Food for two meals with regard to an *eiruv* – מְזוֹן שְׁתֵּי סְעוּדוֹת בְּעֵירוּב: As one must eat three meals on Shabbat, why is food for two meals enough with regard to an *eiruv*? Some commentaries explain that for the purpose of establishing a place of residence, one need only deposit food sufficient for him to eat on an ordinary weekday. In talmudic times, it was customary to eat only two meals on a weekday (*Tosafot Yom Tov*).

Intended to be lenient – מִתְכַּוְּונִים לְהָקֵל: In the Jerusalem Talmud, as well as in the Rambam and Rashi elsewhere, it is explained that according to Rabbi Meir, one who eats the well-seasoned food typically eaten on Shabbat and has much food available will consume a large quantity of bread with his meal. Rabbi Yehuda, in contrast, claims that one eats less bread if he has an abundance of other foods.

When four *se'a* are sold for a *sela* – מֵאַרְבַּע סְאִין בְּסֶלַע: Although the calculation would be easier had Rabbi Yoḥanan ben Beroka said one *se'a* for a *dinar*, he preferred to cite a common example, as storeowners would generally purchase four *se'a* at once (*Ge'on Ya'akov*).

Disqualification of the body – פְּסוּל הַגְּוִיָּה: According to Torah law, ritually impure food of any level of impurity cannot impart impurity to a person. In fact, one can become ritually impure only as a result of contact with a primary source of impurity or from impure utensils. However, an early rabbinic decree established that the consumption of ritually impure foods defiles one's body. This level of impurity is not severe enough for him to impart impurity to other people, but he does defile any *teruma* with which he comes into contact. This *teruma* must subsequently be burned.

Farmers [*ikaryata*] – אִיכַּרְיָיתָא: Rashi explains that these farmers are herdsmen. He associates the word *ikar* with *kar*, one meaning of which is sheep (Rav Ya'akov Emden). Some commentaries understand *ikaryata* as a reference to a particular place (*Arukh*).

HALAKHA

The measure for a joining of Shabbat boundaries – שִׁיעוּר עֵירוּב תְּחוּמִין: An *eiruv* of Shabbat boundaries must consist of food sufficient for two meals for each person included in the *eiruv*. The measure for two meals is an amount of bread equal in volume to six egg-bulks (Rambam, in accordance with Rabbi Yoḥanan ben Beroka; Vilna Gaon). Some authorities rule that the amount must be equal to the volume of at least eight egg-bulks (Rema). This measure applies to both an average person and a gluttonous one. However, an elderly or sick person requires less food (*Shulḥan Arukh, Oraḥ Ḥayyim* 409:7).

Half for a leprous house – חֶצְיָהּ לַבַּיִת הַמְנוּגָּע: If one enters a leprous house and remains there long enough to eat food equal in volume to that of three egg-bulks, which is half the amount of food required for two meals, his clothing contracts ritual impurity (Rambam *Sefer Tahara, Hilkhot Tumat Tzara'at* 17:6).

Half of its half disqualifies the body – חֲצִי חֶצְיָהּ לִפְסוֹל אֶת הַגְּוִיָּה: Ritually impure food in the amount of half a *peras*, equivalent in volume to approximately an egg-bulk and one half, imparts impurity to a person (Rambam *Sefer Tahara, Hilkhot Tumat Okhalin* 4:1).

אָמַר לֵיהּ רַב יוֹסֵף לְרַב יוֹסֵף בְּרֵיהּ דְּרָבָא: אֲבוּךְ כְּמַאן סְבִירָא לֵיהּ? כְּרַבִּי מֵאִיר סְבִירָא לֵיהּ. אֲנָא נַמִּי כְּרַבִּי מֵאִיר סְבִירָא לֵיהּ, דְּאִי כְּרַבִּי יְהוּדָה – קַשְׁיָא הָא דְּאָמְרִי אֱינָשֵׁי "רַוְוחָא לִבְסִימָא שְׁכִיחַ".

Rav Yosef said to Rav Yosef, son of Rava: Your father, in accordance with whose opinion **does he hold,** that of Rabbi Yehuda or Rabbi Meir? He replied: **He holds in accordance with** the opinion of **Rabbi Meir.** Rav Yosef added: **I too agree with** the ruling of **Rabbi Meir, because if** the *halakha* is **in accordance with Rabbi Yehuda, a difficulty** would arise **from the popular saying: There** is always **room for sweets.** It is generally accepted that one dining on delicacies eats more, and therefore, the amount of food in Shabbat meals is greater than that of weekdays, as they include more sweet foods.

"רַבִּי יוֹחָנָן בֶּן בְּרוֹקָה אוֹמֵר". תָּנָא: וּקְרוֹבִים דִּבְרֵיהֶן לִהְיוֹת שָׁוִין. מִי דָּמֵי?! דְּרַבִּי יוֹחָנָן – אַרְבַּע סְעוּדָתָא לְקַבָּא, דְּרַבִּי שִׁמְעוֹן – תְּשַׁע סְעוּדָתָא לְקַבָּא!

We learned in the mishna that **Rabbi Yoḥanan ben Beroka says** that one measure is the amount of food for two meals, while Rabbi Shimon established a different amount. A Sage **taught** in the *Tosefta*: **And their statements are close to being identical.** The Gemara expresses surprise at this: **Are they** really **identical?** According to the opinion **of Rabbi Yoḥanan** there are **four meals to a *kav*.** He maintains that food for two meals is equivalent to a loaf that can be purchased with a *pundeyon*, which is one-forty-eighth of a *sela*, when four *se'a* are bought for a *sela*. As there are twenty-four *kav* in four *se'a*, a loaf purchased with a *pundeyon* is half of a *kav*. This means that each meal is a quarter of a *kav*, or that there are four meals in a *kav*. In contrast, according to the opinion **of Rabbi Shimon,** there are **nine meals to a *kav*.** Rabbi Shimon maintains that food for two meals is two-thirds of a loaf equal in size to one-third of a *kav*. By this calculation, one meal is one-third of a loaf that itself is one-third of a *kav* in size, which amounts to nine meals in a *kav*.

אָמַר רַב חִסְדָּא: צֵא מֵהֶן שְׁלִישׁ לַחֶנְוָנִי.

Rav Ḥisda said in explanation of Rabbi Yoḥanan ben Beroka's opinion: **Deduct one-third for the grocer's** markup, as he takes one-third as profit. This adds one half to the total cost.

וְאַכַּתֵּי לְמָר – תִּשְׁעָה, וּלְמָר – שִׁית!

The Gemara asks: Even after allowing for this adjustment, it **remains** the case that **according to** this **Sage,** Rabbi Shimon, there are **nine** meals to a *kav*, **whereas according to** the other **Sage,** Rabbi Yoḥanan, although it suffices for more than four meals, there are only **six** meals to a *kav*. According to the measure of Rabbi Yoḥanan ben Beroka, each meal is two-thirds of a quarter *kav*, i.e., one sixth of a *kav*, which still leaves a considerable discrepancy between their measures.

[אֶלָּא כְּאִידָךְ] דְּרַב חִסְדָּא, דְּאָמַר: צֵא מֵהֶן מֶחֱצָה לַחֶנְוָנִי.

Rather, we must explain **in accordance with** that **other** statement **of Rav Ḥisda, as he said: Deduct one half for the grocer's** markup. If the calculation is based on the assumption that the grocer takes half the sum as profit, the two measures are indeed close.

וְאַכַּתֵּי, לְמָר – תֵּשַׁע, וּלְמָר – תְּמָנֵי! הַיְינוּ דְּקָאָמַר "וּקְרוֹבִים דִּבְרֵיהֶם לִהְיוֹת שָׁוִין".

The Gemara asks: **But** it **remains** the case that **according to** this **Sage,** there are **nine** meals to a *kav*, whereas **according to** the other **Sage,** there are only **eight** meals to a *kav*, as each meal is one half of a quarter *kav*, or one-eighth of a *kav*. The Gemara answers: **This is** the meaning of **that which was stated** in the *Tosefta*: **And their rulings are close to being identical.** Although their measures are not exactly the same, there is no great difference between them.

קַשְׁיָא דְּרַב חִסְדָּא אַדְּרַב חִסְדָּא! לָא קַשְׁיָא; הָא – דְּקָא יָהֵיב בַּעַל הַבַּיִת צִיבֵי, הָא – דְּלָא יָהֵיב בַּעַל הַבַּיִת צִיבֵי.

The Gemara comments: Nonetheless, there is **a contradiction between** one statement of **Rav Ḥisda and** the other statement of **Rav Ḥisda** concerning the size of the grocer's profit. The Gemara answers: This is **not difficult,** as in **this** case, **the homeowner provides the wood** for baking bread, and the grocer therefore marks up the price by one-third as compensation for his efforts. Whereas in **that** case, **the homeowner does not provide the wood;** the grocer is entitled to reimbursement for the cost of the wood in addition to the work of baking, and consequently he marks up the price by one half.

"חֶצְיָיהּ לַבַּיִת הַמְנוּגָּע וַחֲצִי חֶצְיָיהּ לִפְסוֹל אֶת הַגְּוִיָּיה".

We learned in the mishna that the time it takes to eat **half** the loaf is the time it takes **for** the clothes of one who entered **a leprous house** to become ritually impure, and **half of its half,** of the loaf, is the amount of ritually impure food that **disqualifies the body** from eating *teruma*.

HALAKHA

Half of one half of its half contracts the ritual impurity of foods – חֲצִי חֲצִי חֶצְיָהּ לְטַמֵּא טוּמְאַת אוֹכָלִין: Food that is the volume of an egg without its shell is susceptible to contract ritual impurity of foods, in accordance with the opinion of the Rabbis (Rambam *Sefer Tahara, Hilkhot Tumat Okhalin* 4:1).

LANGUAGE

Measure [*modya*] – מוֹדְיָא: From the Greek μόδιος, *modios*, a dry measure.

תָּנָא: וַחֲצִי חֲצִי חֶצְיָהּ לְטַמֵּא טוּמְאַת אוֹכָלִין. וְתַנָּא דִּידַן, מַאי טַעְמָא לָא תָּנֵי טוּמְאַת אוֹכָלִין? מִשּׁוּם דְּלָא שָׁווּ שִׁיעוּרַיְיהוּ לַהֲדָדֵי.

A Sage **taught** in the *Tosefta*: **And half of one half of its half,**[N] one-eighth of this loaf, is the minimum measure of food that **contracts the** ritual **impurity of foods.**[H] The Gemara asks: **And our *tanna*,** in the mishna, for **what reason** did **he did not teach** the measure of **the impurity of foods?** The Gemara answers: He did not state this *halakha* **because their measures are not** precisely **identical.** The measure for the impurity of foods is not exactly half the amount of ritually impure food that disqualifies one from eating *teruma*.

דְּתַנְיָא: כַּמָּה שִׁיעוּר חֲצִי פְּרָס – שְׁתֵּי בֵיצִים חָסֵר קִימְעָא, דִּבְרֵי רַבִּי יְהוּדָה. רַבִּי יוֹסֵי אוֹמֵר: שְׁתֵּי בֵיצִים שׁוֹחֲקוֹת. שִׁיעֵר רַבִּי שְׁתֵּי בֵיצִים וְעוֹד. כַּמָּה וְעוֹד? אֶחָד מֵעֶשְׂרִים בַּבֵּיצָה.

As it was taught in a *baraita*: **How much is half a *peras*? Two eggs minus a little;** this is **the statement of Rabbi Yehuda. Rabbi Yosei says: Two large eggs,** slightly larger ones than average. **Rabbi** Yehuda HaNasi **measured** the amount of half a *peras* after calculating the number of *kav* in the *se'a* brought before him, and found it to be **a little more than two eggs.**[N] The *tanna* asks: **How much is this little more? One-twentieth of an egg.**

וְאִילּוּ גַּבֵּי טוּמְאַת אוֹכָלִין תַּנְיָא: רַבִּי נָתָן וְרַבִּי דּוֹסָא אָמְרוּ: כַּבֵּיצָה שֶׁאָמְרוּ – כָּמוֹהָ וְכִקְלִיפָּתָהּ, וַחֲכָמִים אוֹמְרִים: כָּמוֹהָ בְּלֹא קְלִיפָּתָהּ.

In contrast, concerning the impurity of foods, it was taught in a *baraita*: **Rabbi Natan and Rabbi Dosa said** that the measure of **an egg-bulk, which** the Sages **said** is the amount that contracts the impurity of foods, is **equivalent to it,** i.e., the egg, **and its shell. And the Rabbis say:** It is **equivalent to it without its shell.**[N] These amounts are not precisely half of any of the measurements given for half a *peras*.

אָמַר רַפְרָם בַּר פַּפָּא, אָמַר רַב חִסְדָּא: זוֹ דִּבְרֵי רַבִּי יְהוּדָה וְרַבִּי יוֹסֵי, אֲבָל חֲכָמִים אוֹמְרִים: כְּבֵיצָה וּמֶחֱצָה שׁוֹחֲקוֹת. וּמַאן חֲכָמִים – רַבִּי יוֹחָנָן בֶּן בְּרוֹקָה.

As for the issue itself, **Rafram bar Pappa said** that **Rav Ḥisda said: This** *baraita* that clarifies the measure of half a *peras* is in accordance with **the statements of Rabbi Yehuda and Rabbi Yosei,** a measure that is identical to that of Rabbi Shimon in the mishna. **But the Rabbis say: One and one half large egg-bulks. And who are** these **Rabbis? Rabbi Yoḥanan ben Beroka.**

פְּשִׁיטָא! שׁוֹחֲקוֹת אֲתָא לְאַשְׁמוּעִינַן.

The Gemara registers surprise: This is **obvious,** as Rabbi Yoḥanan ben Beroka maintains that half a loaf is three egg-bulks, half of which is an egg-bulk and one half. The Gemara explains: The novel aspect of this teaching is not the amount itself; rather, **he came to teach us** that the measurement is performed with **large eggs.**

כִּי אֲתָא רַב דִּימִי, אֲמַר: שִׁיגֵּר בּוֹנְיוֹס לְרַבִּי מוֹדְיָא דְּקוֹנְדִּיס דְּמִן נַאוּסָא, וְשִׁיעֵר רַבִּי מָאתָן וּשְׁבַע עֶשְׂרֵה בֵּיעִין.

The Gemara relates that **when Rav Dimi came** from Eretz Yisrael to Babylonia, **he said:** A person named **Bonyos sent Rabbi** Yehuda HaNasi **a measure** [*modya*][L] **of a *se'a* from** a place called **Na'usa,** where they had a tradition that it was an ancient and accurate measure (Ritva). **And Rabbi** Yehuda HaNasi **measured** it and found it contained **217 eggs.**

הָא סְאָה דְּהֵיכָא? אִי דְּמִדְבָּרִית – מֵאָה אַרְבָּעִים וְאַרְבַּע הָוְיָא,

The Gemara asks: **This *se'a*, from where** is it, i.e., on what measure is it based? **If** it is based on **the wilderness** *se'a*, the standard measure used by Moses in the wilderness, which is the basis for all the Torah's measurements of volume, the difficulty is that a *se'a* is composed of six *kav*, where each *kav* is equivalent to four *log* and each *log* is equivalent to six egg-bulks. This means that a *se'a* **is** equivalent to a total of **144** egg-bulks.

NOTES

And half of one half of its half – וַחֲצִי חֲצִי חֶצְיָהּ: The early commentaries discuss the question of whether or not the measure for the impurity of foods is linked to the measure of a loaf of bread and half-a-loaf [*peras*]. Some commentaries accept this connection (Rashi, *Tosafot*, and others). Other authorities maintain that all the Sages agree that the minimum amount required for food to be susceptible to ritual impurity is the volume of an egg, even according to Rabbi Yoḥanan ben Beroka, as a different reason is offered for this minimum amount. In that case, there is no connection between the two measures (Ritva). Even so, this issue remains problematic: If the Ritva is correct, and there is no connection between the two, why does the Gemara inquire into the reason that the *tanna* did not teach this amount (*Baḥ*)? One answer is that even though it would not have been accurate according to Rabbi Yoḥanan ben Beroka's ruling, it would have been reasonable to expect the mishna to continue in accordance with the opinion of Rabbi Shimon and the others (Rashi).

A little more than two eggs – שְׁתֵּי בֵיצִים וְעוֹד: Some commentaries explain that this additional amount is referring to both egg-bulks together. In other words, one-fortieth of an egg-bulk is added to each egg-bulk (see Rashi). However, it is more likely that the excess amount of one-twentieth is added to each egg-bulk. Consequently, the amount for two egg-bulks is one-tenth of an egg-bulk, as implied by Rashi's calculation (Ritva).

An egg-bulk without the egg's shell – כַּבֵּיצָה בְּלִי קְלִיפָּתָהּ: Food is susceptible to ritual impurity when it consists of the measure of food eaten in one sitting. Since this measure was established as an egg-bulk, it must refer to the edible part of an egg, which excludes its shell (*Me'iri*).

וְאִי דִירוּשַׁלְמִית – מֵאָה שִׁבְעִים וְשָׁלֹשׁ הָוְיָא.

And if it is **the Jerusalem** *se'a*, then the *se'a* **is** only **173** egg-bulks, as they enlarged the measures in Jerusalem by adding a fifth to the measures of the wilderness.

וְאִי דְּצִיפּוֹרִית – מָאתַיִם וְשֶׁבַע הָוְיָין!

And if it is a *se'a* **of Tzippori,** as the measures were once again increased in Tzippori, where another fifth was added to the Jerusalem measure,[B] the *se'a* **is 207** egg-bulks.[B] The *se'a* measured by Rabbi Yehuda HaNasi does not correspond to any of these measures of a *se'a*.

לְעוֹלָם דְּצִיפּוֹרִית, אַיְיתִי חַלְּתָא שְׁדֵי עֲלַיְיהוּ.

The Gemara answers: **Actually,** this measure is based **on the** *se'a* **of Tzippori,** but you must **bring** the amount of **the *ḥalla*** given to a priest, **and add it to them.** That is to say, although this measure is slightly larger than a *se'a*, if it is used for flour and you deduct the amount due as *ḥalla*, you are left with exactly one *se'a*, or 207 egg-bulks.

חַלְּתָא כַּמָּה הָוְיָין – תְּמָנֵי, אַכַּתִּי בָּצַר לֵיהּ?!

The Gemara raises an objection: The amount of ***ḥalla*, how many** egg-bulks **is it?** Approximately **eight** egg-bulks, one-twenty-fourth of 207.[H] Yet in that case, **it remains less** than 217 egg-bulks, for even if we were to add another eight egg-bulks for *ḥalla* to the 207 egg-bulks, we would have only 215 egg-bulks, almost 216 to be more precise, which is still less than 217.

אֶלָּא: אַיְיתִי וְעוֹדוֹת דְּרַבִּי שְׁדֵי עֲלַיְיהוּ.

Rather, you must **bring** the **excess** amounts of **Rabbi** Yehuda HaNasi, the little more he included in his measure, **and add** these **to them.** In Rabbi Yehuda HaNasi's calculations, he did not factor in the *ḥalla* that had to be separated. Instead, the egg-bulks he used to measure the *se'a* were small egg-bulks. Consequently, one-twentieth of an egg-bulk must be added for each egg-bulk. Since one-twentieth of 207 egg-bulks is roughly ten, the total amount equals 217 egg-bulks.

אִי הָכִי, הָוֵי לֵיהּ טְפֵי! כֵּיוָן דְּלָא הָוֵי כְּבֵיצָה – לָא חָשֵׁיב לֵיהּ.

The Gemara raises an objection: **If so, it is** still slightly **more** than 217 egg-bulks, by seven-twentieths of an egg-bulk, to be precise. The Gemara answers: **Since it is not** more than 217 egg-bulks by a whole **egg, he did not count it.**

תָּנוּ רַבָּנַן: סְאָה יְרוּשַׁלְמִית יְתֵירָה עַל מִדְבָּרִית שְׁתוּת, וְשֶׁל צִיפּוֹרִית יְתֵירָה עַל יְרוּשַׁלְמִית שְׁתוּת. נִמְצֵאת שֶׁל צִיפּוֹרִית יְתֵירָה עַל מִדְבָּרִית שְׁלִישׁ.

The Sages taught in a *baraita*: **A Jerusalem *se'a* is larger than a wilderness *se'a* by one-sixth, and that of Tzippori is larger than a Jerusalem *se'a* by one-sixth. Consequently,** a ***se'a* of Tzippori is larger than a wilderness *se'a* by one-third.**

שְׁלִישׁ דְּמַאן? אִילֵימָא שְׁלִישׁ דְּמִדְבָּרִית, מִכְּדֵי שְׁלִישׁ דְּמִדְבָּרִית כַּמָּה הָוֵי – אַרְבְּעִין וּתְמָנְיָא, וְאִילּוּ עוֹדְפָא – שִׁיתִּין וּתְלָת!

The Gemara inquires: **One-third of which** measurement? **If you say** it means **one-third of a wilderness** *se'a*, **now** you must consider: **One-third of a wilderness** *se'a*, **how much is it? Forty-eight** egg-bulks, and **yet the difference** between the wilderness *se'a* and the Tzippori *se'a* is **sixty-three** egg-bulks. As stated above, a Tzippori *se'a* is 207 egg-bulks, whereas a wilderness *se'a* is only 144 egg-bulks.

וְאֶלָּא שְׁלִישׁ דִּירוּשַׁלְמִית, שְׁלִישׁ דִּידַהּ כַּמָּה הָוֵי – חַמְשִׁין וּתְמָנְיָא, נְכֵי תִּילְתָּא. וְאִילּוּ עוֹדְפָא שִׁתִּין וּתְלָת! וְאֶלָּא דְּצִיפּוֹרִי שְׁלִישׁ דִּידַהּ כַּמָּה הָוֵי – שִׁבְעִין נְכֵי חֲדָא, וְאִילּוּ עוֹדְפָא – שִׁשִּׁים וְשָׁלֹשׁ!

But rather, this one-third mentioned in the *baraita* is referring to **one-third of a Jerusalem** *se'a*, which is 173 egg-bulks, as stated above. The Gemara again examines the calculation: **One-third of that** *se'a*, **how much is it? Fifty-eight less one-third,** and **yet the difference** between the wilderness and the Tzippori *se'a* is **sixty-three. Rather,** you must say that it is referring to one-third of a **Tzippori** *se'a*. **One-third of that** *se'a*, **how much is it? Seventy less one-third,** and **yet the difference** between the wilderness *se'a* and the Tzippori *se'a* is **sixty-three** egg-bulks. The difference between the measures is not exactly one-third according to any of the known *se'a* measurements.

אֶלָּא אָמַר רַבִּי יִרְמְיָה, הָכִי קָאָמַר: נִמְצֵאת סְאָה שֶׁל צִיפּוֹרִי יְתֵירָה עַל מִדְבָּרִית קָרוֹב לִשְׁלִישׁ שֶׁלָּהּ, וּשְׁלִישׁ שֶׁלָּהּ קָרוֹב לְמֶחֱצָה דְּמִדְבָּרִית.

Rather, Rabbi Yirmeya said that **this is** what the *tanna* **is saying: Consequently, a *se'a* of Tzippori is larger than a wilderness *se'a*** by sixty-three egg-bulks, which is **close to one-third of** a Tzippori *se'a* of sixty-nine egg-bulks. **And one-third of it,** sixty-nine egg-bulks, **is close to half of a wilderness** *se'a* of seventy-two egg-bulks.

BACKGROUND

The changing measurements – **הַמִּדּוֹת וְשִׁנּוּיָין**: The three measures mentioned here are from three different periods in Jewish history. The wilderness *se'a* is the biblical measure for calculating measurements required by Torah law, which is the basis for the calculation of measures and weights. The Jerusalem measure was used in the Second Temple period, and the Tzippori *se'a* was established when the center of Torah and political activity moved there after the destruction of the Temple.

It should be kept in mind that these differences do not pertain to the basic measure of an egg-bulk but rather to the other measures. This is because an egg is a rough natural measure of volume, independent of human convention. This is the reason it was adopted as a standard, and later adjustments did not tamper with the measure of the egg-bulk but only with conventional measures such as the *log*, the *kav*, and the *se'a* (*ge'onim*).

The various measurements – **הַמִּדּוֹת הַשּׁוֹנוֹת**:

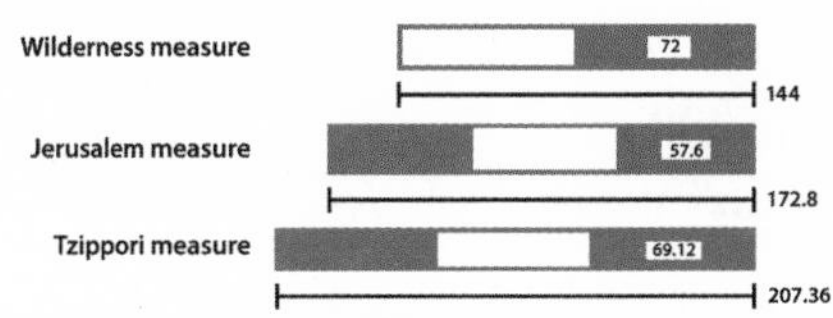

Wilderness, Jerusalem, and Tzippori measures in egg-bulks, without Rabbi Yehuda HaNasi's additions, placed on a uniform scale

HALAKHA

Dough from which *ḥalla* is separated – **עִיסָּה לְהַפְרִישׁ מִמֶּנָּה חַלָּה**: *Ḥalla* must be separated from dough that has the volume of at least 43⅕ egg-bulks. This amount is measured with a mound of flour that has been flattened on top (Rashba). In practice, *ḥalla* is separated without a blessing from dough containing 1.25 kg of flour. It is separated with a blessing from dough that contains 1.75 kg of flour. *Ḥalla* is not separated from dough that contains less than 1.25 kg of flour (*Shulḥan Arukh, Yoreh De'a* 324:1).

מַתְקִיף לָהּ רָבִינָא: מִידֵּי ״קָרוֹב״ ״קָרוֹב״ קָתָנֵי?! אֶלָּא אָמַר רָבִינָא, הָכִי קָאָמַר: נִמְצֵאת שְׁלִישׁ שֶׁל צִיפּוֹרִי בְּוְעוֹדִיּוֹת שֶׁל רַבִּי, יְתֵירָה עַל מֶחֱצָה שֶׁל מִדְבָּרִית שְׁלִישׁ בֵּיצָה.

Ravina raised an objection to the opinion of Rabbi Yirmeya: **Does** the *baraita* **state** either: **Close** to one-third of a Tzippori *se'a* or: **Close** to half of a wilderness *se'a*? The wording of the *baraita* indicates an exact amount. **Rather, Ravina said** that **this is** what the *tanna* **is saying: Consequently, one-third of a Tzippori** *se'a* together **with the excess** amounts **of Rabbi** Yehuda HaNasi[N] **is greater than half** of a **wilderness** *se'a* of seventy-two egg-bulks by only **one-third of an egg.**[N] In other words, a Tzippori *se'a* of 207 egg-bulks added to the excess amounts of Rabbi Yehuda HaNasi of one-twentieth of an egg-bulk for each egg-bulk amounts to a total of 217 egg-bulks, one-third of which is seventy-two and one-third egg-bulks.

תָּנוּ רַבָּנַן: ״רֵאשִׁית עֲרִיסוֹתֵיכֶם״ –

Our Sages taught a *baraita*: The verse states: "You shall set apart a cake of **the first of your dough** as a gift; like the gift of the threshing floor, so shall you set it apart" (Numbers 15:20).

NOTES

The excess amounts of Rabbi Yehuda HaNasi – וְעוֹדִיּוֹת שֶׁל רַבִּי: Some commentaries explain that this measurement sent by Bonyos was indeed that of a Tzippori *se'a*, as it was a large measure calculated with outsized eggs (*Me'iri*).

One-third of the Tzippori *se'a* and half of the wilderness *se'a* – שְׁלִישׁ צִיפּוֹרִית וּמַחֲצִית מִדְבָּרִית: Although the final sum is accurate, the wording of the *baraita* remains difficult (see *Tosafot*). However, it can in fact be explained in a straightforward manner: One-third of the large Tzippori measure of 217 egg-bulks is the difference between the Tzippori and the wilderness measurements, which is 143 egg-bulks plus one-third of an egg-bulk. This interpretation fits the wording of the *baraita* precisely.

כְּדֵי עִיסּוֹתֵיכֶם. וְכַמָּה עִיסּוֹתֵיכֶם – כְּדֵי עִיסַּת הַמִּדְבָּר. וְכַמָּה עִיסַּת הַמִּדְבָּר –

What is the quantity of dough from which *ḥalla* must be separated? **The amount of "your dough." And how much is "your dough"?** This amount is left unspecified by the verse. The Gemara answers: It is **as the amount of the dough of the wilderness.** The Gemara again asks: **And how much is the dough of the wilderness?**

דִּכְתִיב: ״וְהָעוֹמֶר עֲשִׂירִית הָאֵיפָה הוּא״. מִכָּאן אָמְרוּ: שִׁבְעָה רְבָעִים קֶמַח וְעוֹד חַיֶּיבֶת בְּחַלָּה, שֶׁהֵן שִׁשָּׁה שֶׁל יְרוּשַׁלְמִית, שֶׁהֵן חֲמִשָּׁה שֶׁל צִיפּוֹרִי.

The Gemara responds: The Torah states that the manna, the dough of the wilderness, was "an *omer* a head" (Exodus 16:16). A later verse elaborates on that measure, **as it is written: "And an *omer* is the tenth part of an *eifa*"** (Exodus 16:36). An *eifa* is three *se'a*, which are eighteen *kav* or seventy-two *log*. An *omer* is one-tenth of this measure. **From here,** this calculation, Sages **said** that dough prepared from **seven quarters** of a *kav* of **flour and more is obligated in *ḥalla*. This is equal to six** quarter-*kav* of the **Jerusalem** measure, **which is five** quarter-*kav* of the **Tzippori** measure.

מִכָּאן אָמְרוּ: הָאוֹכֵל כְּמִדָּה זוֹ, הֲרֵי זֶה בָּרִיא וּמְבוֹרָךְ, יָתֵר עַל כֵּן – רַעַבְתָן, פָּחוֹת מִכָּאן – מְקוּלְקָל בְּמֵעָיו.

From here the Sages also **said: One who eats roughly this amount** each day, **is healthy,** as he is able to eat a proper meal; **and** he is also **blessed,** as he is not a glutton who requires more. One who eats **more than this** is **a glutton,** while one who eats **less than this has damaged bowels** and must see to his health.

מתני׳ אַנְשֵׁי חָצֵר וְאַנְשֵׁי מִרְפֶּסֶת שֶׁשָּׁכְחוּ וְלֹא עֵירְבוּ, כֹּל שֶׁגָּבוֹהַּ עֲשָׂרָה טְפָחִים – לַמִּרְפֶּסֶת, פָּחוֹת מִכָּאן – לֶחָצֵר.

MISHNA If both **the residents of** houses that open directly into **a courtyard and the residents of** apartments that open onto **a balcony**[N] from which stairs lead down to that courtyard[B] **forgot and did not establish an *eiruv***[NH] between them, **anything** in the courtyard **that is ten handbreadths high,** e.g., a mound or a post, is part **of the balcony.** The residents of the apartments open to the balcony may transfer objects to and from their apartments onto the mound or post. Any post or mound that is **lower than this** height is part **of the courtyard.**

NOTES

The residents of a courtyard and…a balcony – אַנְשֵׁי חָצֵר וְאַנְשֵׁי מִרְפֶּסֶת: This chapter began with a discussion of the *halakhot* governing the joining of Shabbat limits, a natural extension of the previous chapters, which focused on the required measures for merging courtyards that open into an alleyway and a joining of houses in a courtyard. Now, however, the mishna returns to the main topic of these chapters, the *halakhot* of the joining of courtyards.

Forgot and did not establish an *eiruv* – שָׁכְחוּ וְלֹא עֵירְבוּ: Rashi and most commentaries explain that the residents of the courtyard and the balcony established separate *eiruvin*. However, Rabbi Zeraḥya HaLevi maintains that the same *halakha* applies even if they did not establish an *eiruv* at all. *Tosafot Yom Tov* adduces proof for Rashi's explanation from the phrase: Forgot and did not establish an *eiruv*. The seeming redundancy of this double expression indicates that the inhabitants prepared some sort of *eiruv*, albeit not a complete one. Had they established no *eiruv* at all, the mishna would simply have stated that they did not establish an *eiruv*.

BACKGROUND

A balcony with stairs leading to a courtyard – מִרְפֶּסֶת עִם גִּישָׁה לְחָצֵר: The residents on the upper story access the balcony and the courtyard via stairs.

Balcony with stairs leading to a courtyard with a post ten handbreadths high

HALAKHA

The residents of a courtyard and the residents of a balcony forgot and did not establish an *eiruv* – אַנְשֵׁי חָצֵר וְאַנְשֵׁי מִרְפֶּסֶת שֶׁשָּׁכְחוּ וְלֹא עֵירְבוּ: With regard to a mound or a post that is located in a courtyard and belongs to both to the courtyard and the balcony, both of whose residents did not establish a joint *eiruv*, if the mound or post is not ten handbreadths high, the residents of the courtyard render it prohibited for the residents of the balcony to carry any utensil that was located in the house when Shabbat began and vice versa. If the post is four handbreadths away from the house, some commentaries state that it belongs to both groups because the inhabitants of the balcony can use it by throwing objects onto it (*Magen Avraham*, citing the *Beit Yosef*). Other authorities maintain that if the post stands at a distance of four handbreadths from the balcony or if it is lower than ten handbreadths from the balcony, it may be used exclusively by the residents of the courtyard (*Tur* and other authorities; *Shulḥan Arukh HaRav*). If the post is ten handbreadths higher than the courtyard but within ten handbreadths of the height of the balcony, and the post is within four handbreadths of the balcony, use of the post is granted to the residents of the balcony (*Shulḥan Arukh*, *Oraḥ Ḥayyim* 375:2).

חוּלְיַית הַבּוֹר וְהַסֶּלַע גְּבוֹהִים עֲשָׂרָה טְפָחִים – לַמִּרְפֶּסֶת, פָּחוֹת מִכָּאן – לֶחָצֵר.

A similar *halakha* applies to **an embankment** that surrounds **a cistern or a rock:** If the embankments that surround a cistern or rock are **ten handbreadths high,** they belong **to the balcony;** if they are **lower than this,** they may be used only **by** the inhabitants of **the courtyard.**

בַּמֶּה דְּבָרִים אֲמוּרִים – בִּסְמוּכָה, אֲבָל בְּמוּפְלֶגֶת – אֲפִילּוּ גְּבוֹהָה עֲשָׂרָה טְפָחִים לֶחָצֵר. וְאֵיזוֹ הִיא סְמוּכָה – כֹּל שֶׁאֵינָהּ רְחוֹקָה אַרְבָּעָה טְפָחִים.

In what case **are these matters,** the *halakha* that anything higher than ten handbreadths belongs to the balcony, **stated?** When the mound or embankment is **near** the balcony. **But in** a case where the embankment or mound is **distant** from it, **even** if it is **ten handbreadths high,** the right to use the embankment or mound goes **to** the members of **the courtyard. And what is** considered **near? Anything that is not four handbreadths removed** from the balcony.

גמ׳ פְּשִׁיטָא; לָזֶה בְּפֶתַח וְלָזֶה בְּפֶתַח – הַיְינוּ חַלּוֹן שֶׁבֵּין שְׁתֵּי חֲצֵירוֹת.

GEMARA The Gemara comments: It is **obvious** that if the residents of two courtyards established separate *eiruvin*, and the residents of both courtyards have convenient access to a certain area, the residents of **this** courtyard **through an entrance, and** the residents of **that** courtyard **through** another **entrance, this is** similar to the case of **a window between two courtyards.** If the residents did not establish a joint *eiruv*, the use of this window is prohibited to the residents of both courtyards.

לָזֶה בִּזְרִיקָה וְלָזֶה בִּזְרִיקָה – הַיְינוּ כּוֹתֶל שֶׁבֵּין שְׁתֵּי חֲצֵירוֹת. לָזֶה בְּשִׁלְשׁוּל וְלָזֶה בְּשִׁלְשׁוּל – הַיְינוּ חָרִיץ שֶׁבֵּין שְׁתֵּי חֲצֵירוֹת.

It is similarly obvious that if a place can be used by the residents **of this** courtyard only **by throwing** an object onto it **and** by the residents **of that** courtyard only **by throwing,** but it cannot be conveniently used by either set of residents, then **this is** equivalent to the case of **a wall between two courtyards.** If there is a wall between two courtyards, it may not be used by either courtyard. Likewise, if a place can be used by the residents **of this** courtyard only **by lowering** an object down to it **and** by the residents **of that** courtyard **by** a similar act of **lowering, this is** comparable to the *halakha* of **a ditch between two courtyards,** which may not be used by the residents of either courtyard.

לָזֶה בְּפֶתַח וְלָזֶה בִּזְרִיקָה – הַיְינוּ דְּרַבָּה בַּר רַב הוּנָא אָמַר רַב נַחְמָן. לָזֶה בְּפֶתַח וְלָזֶה בְּשִׁלְשׁוּל – הַיְינוּ דְּרַב שֵׁיזְבִי אָמַר רַב נַחְמָן.

It is likewise obvious that in a place that can be conveniently used by the residents **of this** courtyard **through an entrance but** can be used by the residents of **that** courtyard only **by throwing** an object onto it, **this is** governed by the ruling **of Rabba bar Rav Huna,** who said that **Rav Naḥman said:** This place may be used only by those who have access to the area by way of an entrance. Likewise, a place that can be conveniently used by the residents **of this** courtyard **through an entrance but** can be used by the residents **of that** courtyard only **by lowering** an object down to it, **this is** governed by the ruling **of Rav Sheizvi,** who said **that Rav Naḥman said:** This place may be used only by those who have convenient access to it.

לָזֶה בְּשִׁלְשׁוּל וְלָזֶה בִּזְרִיקָה מַאי?

The ruling in each of the aforementioned cases is clear. **What** is the *halakha* concerning a place that can be used by the residents **of this** courtyard only **by lowering** an object down to it **and by** the residents **of that** courtyard only **by throwing**[H] an object on top of it? In other words, if an area is lower than one courtyard but higher than the other, so that neither set of residents has convenient access to it, which of them is entitled to use it?[N]

אָמַר רַב: שְׁנֵיהֶן אֲסוּרִין. וּשְׁמוּאֵל אָמַר: נוֹתְנִין אוֹתוֹ לָזֶה שֶׁבְּשִׁלְשׁוּל, שֶׁלָּזֶה תַּשְׁמִישׁוֹ בְּנַחַת וְלָזֶה תַּשְׁמִישׁוֹ בְּקָשֶׁה. וְכׇל דָּבָר שֶׁתַּשְׁמִישׁוֹ לָזֶה בְּנַחַת וְלָזֶה בְּקָשֶׁה – נוֹתְנִים אוֹתוֹ לָזֶה שֶׁתַּשְׁמִישׁוֹ בְּנַחַת.

Rav said: It is **prohibited** for **both** sets of residents to use it. As the use of the area is equally inconvenient to the residents of both courtyards, they retain equal rights to it and render it prohibited for the other group to use. **And Shmuel said:** The use of the area **is granted to those who** can reach it **by lowering, as** it is relatively easy **for them** to lower objects to it, and therefore **its use is** more **convenient;** whereas **for the others,** who must throw onto it, **its use is** more **demanding. And** there is a principle concerning Shabbat: **Anything whose use is convenient for one** party **and** more **demanding for another** party, **one provides it to that** one **whose use** of it **is convenient.**

תְּנַן: אַנְשֵׁי חָצֵר וְאַנְשֵׁי מִרְפֶּסֶת שֶׁשָּׁכְחוּ וְלֹא עֵירְבוּ, כֹּל שֶׁגָּבוֹהַּ עֲשָׂרָה טְפָחִים – לַמִּרְפֶּסֶת, פָּחוֹת מִכָּאן – לֶחָצֵר.

In order to decide between these two opinions, the Gemara attempts to adduce a proof from the mishna: If **the residents of** houses that open directly into **a courtyard and the residents of** apartments that open onto **a balcony** from which stairs lead down to that courtyard **forgot and did not establish an** *eiruv* between them, **anything** in the courtyard **that is ten handbreadths high** belongs **to the balcony,** while anything that is **less than this** height belongs **to the courtyard.**

HALAKHA

This by lowering and…that by throwing – לָזֶה בְּשִׁלְשׁוּל וְלָזֶה בִּזְרִיקָה: When a mound or a post in a courtyard can be used by two separate groups of people, one group by lowering items down to it and the other group by throwing items onto it, both groups are prohibited to use it, as the *halakha* is in accordance with the opinion of Rav with regard to cases involving prohibitions (*Maggid Mishne*; Rambam *Sefer Zemanim*, *Hilkhot Eiruvin* 3:16).

NOTES

Throwing and lowering – זְרִיקָה וְשִׁלְשׁוּל: Apparently, this discussion pertains to a post ten handbreadths high, at roughly the height of the average person's hand when he is standing. If so, why does Shmuel consider lowering an object down to it more convenient than throwing an object onto it? One explanation is that it is easier to lower a heavy item than to throw it, even onto a low level (Rabbeinu Yehonatan).

קָא סָלְקָא דַּעְתָּךְ, מַאי מִרְפֶּסֶת –

The Gemara first explains: **It might have entered your mind** to say: **What is** the meaning of the **balcony** mentioned in the mishna?

Perek **VIII**
Daf **84** Amud **a**

NOTES

The difficulty raised against Rav – הַקּוּשְׁיָה עַל רַב: A similar question appears in the Jerusalem Talmud, in which the difficulty is resolved by claiming that the dispute between Rav and Shmuel is limited to a case where the distances for lowering and throwing are equal. Consequently, if the post is closer to the balcony and within three handbreadths of it, and the post is higher than ten handbreadths from the courtyard, Rav would concede that its use is reserved exclusively for the residents of the balcony.

A post in a courtyard – עַמּוּד בְּחָצֵר: Some commentaries accept the explanation in the Jerusalem Talmud that the residents of both the courtyard and the balcony have the right to use the post on weekdays. However, if the post belongs exclusively to one group of residents, the other group cannot impose restrictions upon them, even if its use is more convenient for the other group than for its owners.

HALAKHA

Those who live in the balcony – אוֹתָן הַדָּרִין בְּמִרְפֶּסֶת: With regard to the use of a mound or post in a courtyard, the same *halakha* applies to the residents of a balcony as to those who live in the upper story, in accordance with the opinion of Rav Huna. That is, if the mound or post is ten handbreadths high, the right to use it belongs solely to the residents of the balcony or upper story (*Shulḥan Arukh, Oraḥ Ḥayyim* 375:2).

בְּנֵי עֲלִיָּיה וּמַאי קָרוּ לָהּ מִרְפֶּסֶת – דְּקָסָלְקִי בְּמִרְפֶּסֶת. אַלְמָא: כֹּל לָזֶה בְּשִׁלְשׁוּל וְלָזֶה בִּזְרִיקָה – נוֹתְנִין אוֹתוֹ לָזֶה שֶׁבְּשִׁלְשׁוּל!

It is referring to **the residents of an upper story** above the balcony; **and** if so, **why do we call** the upper story **a balcony?** Because the residents of the upper story **ascend** and descend to and from their apartments **by** way of **the balcony. From here** the Gemara infers: With regard to **any** place **that** can be used **by one** set of residents only **by lowering** an object down to it **and by another** set of residents only **by throwing** an object on top of it, **we grant** Shabbat use of **it to those who** can use it **by lowering**, as the residents of the upper story who use the area ten handbreadths high do so by means of lowering. Apparently, the mishna supports Shmuel and presents a difficulty to Rav.[N]

כִּדְאָמַר רַב הוּנָא: לְאוֹתָן הַדָּרִים בְּמִרְפֶּסֶת. הָכִי נַמִי: לְאוֹתָן הַדָּרִין בְּמִרְפֶּסֶת.

The Gemara rejects this argument: **As Rav Huna said** with regard to a different issue discussed in a subsequent mishna, that the *tanna* is referring **to those who live in** apartments that open directly onto **the balcony** rather than those who live in an upper story; **here too,** the *tanna* is speaking **of those who live in** apartments that open directly onto **the balcony.**[H] In this case, the use of an area ten handbreadths high is convenient for the residents of the balcony, as it is on their level; whereas its use is relatively inconvenient for the residents of the courtyard. Consequently, the right to use this area is granted to the residents of the balcony.

אִי הָכִי, אֵימָא סֵיפָא: פָּחוֹת מִכָּאן – לֶחָצֵר, אַמַּאי? לָזֶה בְּפֶתַח וְלָזֶה בְּפֶתַח הוּא!

The Gemara raises an objection: **If so, say the next clause** of the mishna: Anything that is **lower than this,** i.e., lower than ten handbreadths, its use belongs **to the courtyard.** But **why** should this be the *halakha*? This is similar to a case of residents of two courtyards who have equally convenient access to a certain area. The residents **of this** courtyard access the area **through** one **entrance, and** the residents **of that** courtyard access the area **through** another **entrance.** In our case, the use of the area is equally convenient for the inhabitants of both the balcony and the courtyard; why should the latter be granted exclusive right of use?[N]

מַאי לֶחָצֵר – אַף לֶחָצֵר, וּשְׁנֵיהֶן אֲסוּרִין.

The Gemara answers: **What is** the meaning of the phrase **to the courtyard?** It means **also to the courtyard.** In other words, even the residents of the courtyard can make use of this mound or post, **and** therefore residents of **both** the courtyard and the balcony **are prohibited.** If residents of two domains can conveniently use a single area and they did not establish an *eiruv* between their domains, they are all prohibited to carry in that area.

הָכִי נַמִי מִסְתַּבְּרָא, מִדְּקָתָנֵי סֵיפָא: בַּמֶּה דְּבָרִים אֲמוּרִים – בִּסְמוּכָה, אֲבָל בְּמוּפְלֶגֶת, אֲפִילּוּ גְּבוֹהָ עֲשָׂרָה טְפָחִים – לֶחָצֵר. מַאי לֶחָצֵר? אִילֵימָא לֶחָצֵר וְשָׁרֵי; אַמַּאי? רְשׁוּתָא דְּתַרְוַיְיהוּ הוּא!

The Gemara comments: **So too, it is reasonable** to explain the mishna in this manner, **as it was taught in the latter clause** of the mishna: **In what case is this statement said? When** the mound or embankment is **near** the balcony; **but in** a case where it is **distant** from it, **even** if it is **ten handbreadths high,** its use belongs **to the courtyard. What,** then, **is** the meaning of the phrase **to the courtyard** in this context? **If you say** it means **to the** residents of **courtyard, and** therefore the use of the mound or embankment **is permitted** to them, **why** should this be so? **It is the domain of** the residents of **both** the courtyard and the balcony, as the mound or embankment is positioned near enough to the balcony for its residents to use it as well.

אֶלָּא מַאי לֶחָצֵר – אַף לֶחָצֵר, וּשְׁנֵיהֶן אֲסוּרִין. הָכִי נַמִי, מַאי לֶחָצֵר – אַף לֶחָצֵר, וּשְׁנֵיהֶן אֲסוּרִין, שְׁמַע מִינַּהּ.

Rather, what is the meaning of the phrase **to the courtyard?** It means **also to the courtyard. And,** consequently, as the residents of both the courtyard and the balcony can use it, **both are prohibited** to carry there on Shabbat. **Here too,** in the earlier part of the mishna, **what is** the meaning of the clause **to the courtyard?** It likewise means **also to the courtyard, and** therefore **both** sets of residents are **prohibited** to carry. The Gemara concludes: Indeed, **learn from this** that this is the correct interpretation of this phrase.

תְּנַן: חוּלְיַית הַבּוֹר וְהַסֶּלַע שֶׁהֵן גְּבוֹהִין עֲשָׂרָה – לַמִּרְפֶּסֶת, פָּחוֹת מִכָּאן – לֶחָצֵר. אָמַר רַב הוּנָא: לְאוֹתָן הַדָּרִים בַּמִּרְפֶּסֶת.

The Gemara attempts to adduce further proof from the mishna to resolve the dispute between Rav and Shmuel. **We learned** in the mishna: **The embankments** that surround **a cistern or a rock that are ten handbreadths high** may be used **by the balcony;** if they are **lower than that** height, the right to use them belongs **to the courtyard.**[H] The Gemara assumes that the phrase to the balcony is referring to the residents of an upper story, who access their apartments through the balcony. The mishna indicates that if one set of residents can make use of a place by lowering and another set of residents can use it by throwing, the use of the place is granted to those who lower their objects, in accordance with the opinion of Shmuel and contrary to the opinion of Rav. The Gemara answers: **Rav Huna said** that the phrase to the balcony is to be understood here literally as referring **to those who live in** apartments that open directly onto **the balcony.**

תֵּינַח סֶלַע, בּוֹר מַאי אִיכָּא לְמֵימַר?

The Gemara asks: **Granted,** in the case of **a rock,** the residents of the balcony can use it conveniently, as its surface is more or less level with the balcony itself. But with regard to **a cistern, what can be said?** The water in the cistern is lower than the balcony and can be reached only by lowering a bucket down to it. How, then, can it be argued that the cistern is conveniently used by the residents of the balcony but not by the residents of the courtyard?

אָמַר רַב יִצְחָק בְּרֵיהּ דְּרַב יְהוּדָה: הָכָא בְּבוֹר מְלֵאָה מַיִם עָסְקִינַן. וְהָא חָסְרָא!

Rav Yitzḥak, son of Rav Yehuda, said: We are dealing here with a cistern full of water, as the water can be drawn from the cistern's upper portion, near the balcony. The Gemara raises an objection: **But doesn't** the cistern gradually **lose** its water as the liquid near the surface is drawn out? Although the water might at first reach the balcony, the water level gradually recedes. Eventually, the only way to reach the water will be by lowering a bucket into the cistern.

כֵּיוָן דְּכִי מַלְיָא שָׁרְיָא, כִּי חָסְרָא – נַמִי שָׁרְיָא. אַדְּרַבָּה, כֵּיוָן דְּכִי חָסְרָא אֲסִירָא, כִּי מַלְיָא נַמִי אֲסִירָא!

The Gemara answers: **Since** it **is permitted** to draw water from the cistern **when** it is **full,**[N] **it is likewise permitted** even **when it is lacking.** The Gemara counters this argument: **On the contrary,** you should say that **since** the cistern **is prohibited when it is lacking, it should likewise be prohibited** even **when it is full.**

אֶלָּא אָמַר אַבַּיֵי: הָכָא בְּבוֹר מְלֵיאָה פֵּירוֹת עָסְקִינַן. וְהָא חַסְרֵי!

Rather, Abaye said: Here we are dealing with a cistern full of produce, as the upper produce is near the balcony. The Gemara raises an objection: **But doesn't** the amount of produce also **diminish,** as the produce is removed, increasing the distance between the pile and the balcony?

בְּטִיבְלָא.

The Gemara answers: This teaching is referring **to untithed produce,** which one may not tithe on Shabbat. Since this produce may not be used, the height of the pile will remain constant for the duration of Shabbat.

דַּיְקָא נַמִי, דְּקָתָנֵי דּוּמְיָא דְּסֶלַע, שְׁמַע מִינָּהּ.

The Gemara comments: The language of the mishna **is also precise, as it teaches** the *halakha* of an embankment of a cistern **together with** that of **a rock.** Just as in the case of the rock only the upper surface is used, so too, in the case of the embankment of the cistern, the mishna is referring to the use of the surface of the cistern and not its contents. The Gemara concludes: Indeed, **learn from this** that this is the correct explanation.

וְלָמָּה לִי לְמִיתְנָא בּוֹר, וְלָמָּה לִי לְמִיתְנָא סֶלַע? צְרִיכָא, דְּאִי אַשְׁמְעִינַן סֶלַע – דְּלֵיכָּא לְמִיגְזַר, אֲבָל בּוֹר – לִיגְזוֹר, זִמְנִין דְּמַלְיָא פֵּירוֹת מְתוּקָּנִין – צְרִיכָא.

The Gemara asks: **But** if this is indeed correct, and the cistern and rock are similar in all respects, **why do I need** the *tanna* **to state** the case of **a cistern, and why do I need** him **to state** the case of **a rock** as well? The Gemara answers: **It was necessary** to teach both cases. **As had** the mishna **taught us** only about **a rock,** one might have said that only a rock may be used by the residents of the balcony, **as there is no** need **to decree** in case its height is diminished. **But** with regard to **a cistern,** perhaps **we should decree** and prohibit its use, as **at times it might be filled with tithed produce,** which may be removed and eaten, thereby diminishing its height. It was therefore **necessary** to teach us that this is not a concern, and a cistern, as well as a rock, may be used by the residents of the balcony.

HALAKHA

A cistern in a courtyard – בּוֹר שֶׁבֶּחָצֵר: If a cistern in a courtyard full of water is located ten handbreadths above the floor of the courtyard and near the balcony, the residents of both the balcony and the courtyard are prohibited to make use of it. If it is full of non-tithed produce or anything else that may not be moved on Shabbat, it may be used by the residents of the courtyard (Rambam *Sefer Zemanim, Hilkhot Eiruvin* 4:18).

NOTES

It is permitted when full – מַלְיָא שָׁרְיָא: The argument that a cistern permitted at the beginning of Shabbat remains permitted the entire day is based on the established principle that anything permitted at the onset of Shabbat is permitted throughout Shabbat. However, this principle does not apply to this particular situation, due to the fact that it is foreseeable that the waters of the cistern will recede over the course of Shabbat, as it is there to be used. Consequently, the Gemara counters with the opposite claim: As it will be prohibited over the course of time, it should be prohibited from the beginning of Shabbat (Ritva).

HALAKHA

Walls and ledges – כְּתָלִים וְזִיזִים: If the residents of a courtyard and the residents of an upper story did not establish an *eiruv* together, any ledges positioned within ten handbreadths of the ground are available exclusively to the inhabitants of the courtyard; ledges within ten handbreadths of the upper story may be utilized exclusively by the inhabitants of the upper story. Any ledges in the middle are prohibited to both groups (*Shulḥan Arukh*, *Oraḥ Ḥayyim* 375:4).

NOTES

Above and below ten – לְמַעְלָה וּלְמַטָּה מֵעֲשָׂרָה: The phrases above ten and below ten can be understood in one of two ways. Above ten can mean ten handbreadths above the ground, or it can refer to the uppermost ten handbreadths of the post, and the meaning of below ten will be affected accordingly. The difficulty posed to Shmuel from the expression above ten is based on the assumption that the expression is referring to the uppermost ten handbreadths. Rabbi Naḥman's response indicates that the phrases above ten and below ten always mean above or below ten handbreadths from the ground, respectively (see the Ritva).

תָּא שְׁמַע: אַנְשֵׁי חָצֵר וְאַנְשֵׁי עֲלִיָּיה שֶׁשָּׁכְחוּ וְלֹא עֵירְבוּ – אַנְשֵׁי חָצֵר מִשְׁתַּמְּשִׁין בַּעֲשָׂרָה הַתַּחְתּוֹנִים, וְאַנְשֵׁי עֲלִיָּיה מִשְׁתַּמְּשִׁין בַּעֲשָׂרָה הָעֶלְיוֹנִים. כֵּיצַד? זִיז יוֹצֵא מִן הַכּוֹתֶל, לְמַטָּה מֵעֲשָׂרָה – לֶחָצֵר, לְמַעְלָה מֵעֲשָׂרָה – לָעֲלִיָּיה.

Returning to the dispute between Rav and Shmuel, the Gemara suggests a different proof: **Come** and **hear** a *baraita*: **If the residents of** houses opening directly into **a courtyard and the residents of** apartments in **an upper story forgot and did not establish** an *eiruv* together, **the residents of the courtyard may use the lower ten** handbreadths of the wall near them, **and the residents of the upper story may use the upper ten** handbreadths adjacent to them. **How so?** If a **ledge protrudes from the wall below ten** handbreadths from the ground, its use is **for** the residents **of the courtyard;** but if it protrudes **above ten** handbreadths, its use is **for** the residents **of the upper story.**

הָא דְּבֵינֵי בֵּינֵי – אָסוּר!

The Gemara infers: **Consequently,** a ledge situated **between** this **and between** the other, i.e., in-between the courtyard and the upper story, **is prohibited.**[H] This middle area has the status of a place that can be used by one set of residents by lowering and by another set of residents by throwing, and yet they are both prohibited, in accordance with the opinion of Rav and in opposition to the opinion of Shmuel.

אָמַר רַב נַחְמָן: הָכָא בְּכוֹתֶל תִּשְׁעָה עָשָׂר עָסְקִינַן, וְזִיז יוֹצֵא מִמֶּנּוּ. לְמַטָּה מֵעֲשָׂרָה – לָזֶה בְּפֶתַח וְלָזֶה בְּשִׁלְשׁוּל, לְמַעְלָה מֵעֲשָׂרָה – לָזֶה בְּפֶתַח וְלָזֶה בִּזְרִיקָה.

Rav Naḥman said: No proof can be adduced from this teaching, as **here we are dealing with a wall of nineteen** handbreadths **that has a protruding ledge.** If the ledge protrudes **below ten** handbreadths from the ground, **for this** set of residents, those of the courtyard, it can be used **as an entrance, and for that** set of residents, those of the upper story, it can be used only **by lowering.** If the ledge protrudes **above ten** handbreadths, **for this** set of residents, those in the balcony, it can be accessed **as an entrance, and for that** set of residents, those of the courtyard, it can be used only **by throwing.** In this case, there is no middle area between the ten-handbreadths available to each set of residents. Consequently, this case cannot serve as a proof with regard to the dispute between Rav and Shmuel.[N]

Perek **VIII**
Daf **84** Amud **b**

NOTES

Within ten…they render it prohibited for one another – דִּבְגוֹ עֲשָׂרָה...אָסְרָן אַהֲדָדֵי: Abaye introduces an additional consideration. The status of a cistern beneath two domains situated within ten handbreadths of one another is not determined by the difficulty or ease of their use. Rather, the two domains are treated as one, even if one of them can access the water of the cistern only with great difficulty. For instance, even if the lower of two balconies requires both lowering and throwing to use the cistern, they are considered a single domain in this regard, due to their proximity.

תָּא שְׁמַע: שְׁתֵּי גְּזוּזְטְרָאוֹת זוֹ לְמַעְלָה מִזּוֹ, עָשׂוּ לָעֶלְיוֹנָה וְלֹא עָשׂוּ לַתַּחְתּוֹנָה – שְׁתֵּיהֶן אֲסוּרוֹת עַד שֶׁיְּעָרְבוּ!

The Gemara attempts to cite yet another proof to resolve the dispute between Rav and Shmuel. **Come** and **hear** a mishna: If a balcony extends over a body of water, and the residents of the balcony cut out a hole in the floor and constructed a partition ten handbreadths high around the hole, water may be drawn through the hole on Shabbat. If there are **two balconies** of this kind, **one above the other,** and **they erected** a partition **for the upper** balcony **but they did not erect** one **for the lower one, they are both prohibited** from drawing water, **unless they establish an** *eiruv* between them. This mishna apparently is referring to a case where the residents of the upper balcony draw water by lowering their buckets down, whereas the residents of the lower balcony hoist their bucket to the upper one and draw water from there, i.e., one balcony draws the water by lowering and the other by throwing. The mishna rules that they are both prohibited, in accordance with the opinion of Rav and contrary to the opinion of Shmuel.

אָמַר רַב אַדָּא בַּר אַהֲבָה: בְּבָאִין בְּנֵי תַחְתּוֹנָה דֶּרֶךְ עֶלְיוֹנָה לְמַלְּאוֹת.

Rav Adda bar Ahava said: Here we are dealing with a case **where the residents** of the **lower** balcony **go up to the upper** balcony by means of a ladder **to draw** their water from there. Since they themselves are located in the upper balcony when they draw their water, both sets of residents gain access to their water by lowering.

אַבָּיֵי אָמַר: כְּגוֹן דְּקָיְימִין בְּתוֹךְ עֲשָׂרָה דַּהֲדָדֵי. וְלָא מִיבַּעְיָא קָאָמַר; לָא מִיבַּעְיָא עָשׂוּ לַתַּחְתּוֹנָה וְלֹא עָשׂוּ לָעֶלְיוֹנָה – דַּאֲסִירִי, דְּכֵיוָן דִּבְגוֹ עֲשָׂרָה דַּהֲדָדֵי קָיְימִין אָסְרָן אַהֲדָדֵי.

Abaye said: Here we are dealing with a case, **where** the two balconies **are situated within ten** handbreadths **of each other, and the** *tanna* **was speaking** in the style of: **There is no need.** In other words, the mishna should be understood in the following manner: **There is no need** to say that if **they erect** a partition **for the lower** balcony **but they did not erect** one **for the upper one, they are** both **prohibited** to draw water. The reason is **that since they are positioned within ten** handbreadths **of each other, they** render it **prohibited for one another** anyway.[N]

אֶלָּא אֲפִילּוּ עָשׂוּ לָעֶלְיוֹנָה וְלֹא עָשׂוּ לַתַּחְתּוֹנָה, סָלְקָא דַּעְתָּךְ אָמִינָא כֵּיוָן דִּלְזֶה בְּנַחַת וְלָזֶה בְּקָשֶׁה – לֵיתְבֵיהּ לָזֶה שֶׁתַּשְׁמִישׁוֹ בְּנַחַת, קָא מַשְׁמַע לַן: כֵּיוָן דִּבְגוֹ עֲשָׂרָה קַיְימִין – אָסְרָן אַהֲדָדֵי.

Rather, the *halakha* is the same **even** if **they established** a partition for the **upper** balcony **and they did not establish** a partition **for the lower** one, despite the fact that **it might have entered your mind to say** the following: **Since for this,** the residents of the upper balcony, its use **is convenient, while for that** lower balcony, its use **is demanding,** as the lower balcony can draw water only by hoisting its bucket upward, the use of the hole **should** therefore **be granted to the one whose use is convenient.** This reasoning would render the hole permitted to the upper balcony and prohibited to the lower balcony. To counter this hypothetical argument, the mishna **teaches us** that **since** the upper and lower balconies **are located within ten** handbreadths of each other, they render it **prohibited for one another.**

כִּי הָא דְּאָמַר רַב נַחְמָן, אָמַר שְׁמוּאֵל: גַּג הַסָּמוּךְ לִרְשׁוּת הָרַבִּים – צָרִיךְ סוּלָּם קָבוּעַ לְהַתִּירוֹ. סוּלָּם קָבוּעַ – אִין, סוּלָּם עֲרַאי – לָא. מַאי טַעְמָא – לָאו מִשּׁוּם דְּכֵיוָן דִּבְתוֹךְ עֲשָׂרָה דַּהֲדָדֵי קַיְימִי אָסְרָן אַהֲדָדֵי?

This is **similar to** a teaching **that Rav Naḥman said** that **Shmuel said:** In the case of **a roof that is adjacent to a public domain,**[N] **there must be a fixed ladder** from the courtyard to the roof **to permit** the use of the roof to the residents of the courtyard. The Gemara infers: If there is **a fixed ladder, yes,** the residents of the courtyard may use the roof; if there is merely **a temporary ladder, no,** they are prohibited to use it. **What is the reason** for this distinction? Is it **not** that since the balcony and the public domain **are situated within ten** handbreadths **of each other,** the residents of both render it **prohibited for one another,** in accordance with the opinion of Abaye? Since the residents of the balcony are located within ten handbreadths of the public domain, the presence of people in the public domain renders the use of the roof prohibited for the inhabitants of the balcony. The only way for the members of the balcony to be permitted to use the roof is by means of a fixed ladder that has the status of a proper door.

מַתְקִיף לַהּ רַב פַּפָּא: וְדִילְמָא כְּשֶׁרַבִּים מַכְתְּפִין עָלָיו בְּכוּמְתָא וְסוּדְרָא!

Rav Pappa strongly **objected to this** argument, claiming that this proof can be refuted: **But perhaps** this applies only to a roof upon which **many people place their hats** [*kumta*][L] **and shawls** when they are in need of rest.[N] Even if the people in the public domain are not situated within ten handbreadths of the roof, they can still use it conveniently if they wish to place light objects upon it on a temporary basis. If there was not a fixed ladder, the residents of the courtyard would not be permitted to use the roof, as it serves the public domain as well. Consequently, no proof can be adduced from here either. In summary, no compelling proof has been found either for Rav's opinion or for Shmuel's opinion.

אָמַר רַב יְהוּדָה, אָמַר שְׁמוּאֵל:

Rav Yehuda said that **Shmuel said:**

NOTES

A roof that is adjacent to a public domain – גַּג הַסָּמוּךְ לִרְשׁוּת הָרַבִּים: According to the *Me'iri*, there is no balcony in this case at all. Rather, the roof of the house is lower than the public domain by less than ten handbreadths, which is why it is available to the people in the public domain. See *Tosafot*, who cite a slightly different explanation.

Hats and shawls – כּוּמְתָא וְסוּדְרָא: In contrast to Rashi, some commentaries explain that this does not refer exclusively to hats and shawls. Rather, it means that even if the members of the public domain use it solely for hats and shawls and nothing else, they are still considered to be utilizing this area. Consequently, it can indeed be said that the roof is an adjunct of the public domain (*Me'iri*).

LANGUAGE

Hat [*kumta*] – כּוּמְתָא: Seemingly related to the Arabic قبعة, *qubba'ah*, meaning a cap or a hat. The *ge'onim* explain that *kumta* means a soft hat that lies flat on the head.

Perek **VIII**
Daf **85** Amud **a**

בּוֹר שֶׁבֵּין שְׁתֵּי חֲצֵירוֹת, מוּפְלֶגֶת מִכּוֹתֶל זֶה אַרְבָּעָה וּמִכּוֹתֶל זֶה אַרְבָּעָה – זֶה מוֹצִיא זִיז כָּל שֶׁהוּא וּמְמַלֵּא, וְזֶה מוֹצִיא זִיז כָּל שֶׁהוּא וּמְמַלֵּא. וְרַב יְהוּדָה דִּידֵיהּ אָמַר: אֲפִילּוּ קָנֶה.

If **a cistern** in a small alleyway **between two courtyards is separated** by **four** handbreadths **from the wall** of one courtyard **and** by **four** handbreadths **from the wall** of another courtyard, the resident of **this** courtyard **may extend a ledge of minimal size**[B] from his window in the direction of the cistern, as a sign that he is not using the domain of the other, **and he may** subsequently proceed to **draw** water from the cistern through the window. **And the** resident of the **other** courtyard **may** likewise **extend a ledge of minimal size and draw** water from the cistern through his widow. **And Rav Yehuda himself said:** An actual ledge is unnecessary, as it is enough **even** if one merely extends **a** simple **reed.**[N]

NOTES

Even a reed – אֲפִילּוּ קָנֶה: Various explanations have been offered for the pertinent difference between a ledge and a reed. Some commentaries say that a ledge is something large and noticeable, as opposed to a reed, which is extremely thin and barely visible (Rashba). Others state that a ledge indicates something solid and stable, whereas a reed is an easily moveable object (Ritva).

BACKGROUND

A cistern between two courtyards – בּוֹר שֶׁבֵּין שְׁתֵּי חֲצֵירוֹת: The Gemara is describing a cistern located between the walls of two adjacent houses. The walls form a small street between the houses. Ledges protrude below each window in order to permit the drawing of water from the cistern, as indicated in the image below.

Cistern between two courtyards

NOTES

This ruling of Rav Yehuda – **הָא דְּרַב יְהוּדָה:** Abaye is saying that Rabbi Yehuda's statement was not intended to conflict with the ruling of his teacher, Shmuel. Rather, Rabbi Yehuda merely explains and elucidates Shmuel's opinion. Indeed, Shmuel himself spoke of a ledge of minimum size. The phrase of minimum size can indicate either the smallest possible ledge or a specific size that is not particularly large. Rabbi Yehuda therefore stated that Shmuel's expression, of minimum size, does not necessarily refer to a ledge, and the ledge need not be of any defined size. Consequently, even a reed is sufficient (Rashba).

Prohibited…by way of the air – **אוֹסֵר...דֶּרֶךְ אֲוִיר:** Rav's opinion is not clarified by his statement concerning the *halakhot* applicable to ruins, as that statement can be explained in accordance with Shmuel's ruling. However, his explanation to Rabbi Elazar (85b) indicates that in his opinion, one whose only option is to use airspace does not impose restrictions on another person.

HALAKHA

Does not render it prohibited by way of the air – **אֵין אוֹסֵר דֶּרֶךְ אֲוִיר:** In the case of a cistern between two courtyards, even if it is four handbreadths away from the wall of each courtyard, the residents of both courtyards may draw water from it, despite the lack of a ledge. In addition, they do not render it prohibited for each other to utilize the cistern (Rambam), provided that they draw the water by way of the windows (Rema, based on Rashi and the *Maggid Mishne*). Some authorities maintain that if the cistern is within four handbreadths of the courtyards, the residents of both courtyards are prohibited from drawing its water (Rashi; *Shulḥan Arukh, Oraḥ Ḥayyim* 376:2).

Two houses with three ruins – **שְׁנֵי בָתִּים וְשָׁלֹשׁ חוּרְבוֹת:** With regard to two houses separated by three ruins, the residents of each house are permitted to use the ruin adjacent to their house by throwing objects into it through their windows (Rashi), and the middle ruin is permitted to both of them (*Shulḥan Arukh, Oraḥ Ḥayyim* 376:3).

אֲמַר לֵיהּ אַבַּיֵי לְרַב יוֹסֵף: הָא דְּרַב יְהוּדָה – דִּשְׁמוּאֵל הִיא. דְּאִי דְּרַב הָא אָמַר: אֵין אָדָם אוֹסֵר עַל חֲבֵירוֹ דֶּרֶךְ אֲוִיר.

Abaye said to Rav Yosef: This ruling **of Rav Yehuda,**[N] that some minimal sort of adjustment is required, **is** in accordance with the opinion of his teacher, **Shmuel. Since if** he holds in accordance with the opinion **of** his other teacher, **Rav,** this would present a difficulty, **as didn't** Rav **say: One person does not render it prohibited for another person** to perform an action **by way of the air,**[NH] if the place he is using is four handbreadths away from him? Consequently, not even a reed is required.

וְדִשְׁמוּאֵל מֵהֵיכָא? אִילֵימָא מֵהָא דְּאָמַר רַב נַחְמָן, אָמַר שְׁמוּאֵל: גַּג הַסָּמוּךְ לִרְשׁוּת הָרַבִּים – צָרִיךְ סוּלָּם קָבוּעַ לְהַתִּירוֹ. דִּילְמָא כִּדְרַב פַּפָּא!

The Gemara asks: **And from where** is it ascertained that this is the opinion **of Shmuel? If you say** we learn it **from that** teaching **which Rav Naḥman said** that **Shmuel said:** With regard to a low **roof adjacent to a public domain, there must be a fixed ladder** from the courtyard to the roof in order **to permit** the use of the roof to the residents of the courtyard, it might be inferred from here that the people in the public domain render it prohibited to use the roof because they can use it through the air, by throwing. However, this proof is inconclusive. **Perhaps,** this *halakha* can be understood **in accordance with the opinion of Rav Pappa:** Here we are dealing with a roof upon which people in the public domain place their hats and shawls when in need of rest. That would mean that this *halakha* does not involve use of the airspace at all.

אֶלָּא מֵהָא: זֶה מוֹצִיא זִיז כָּל שֶׁהוּא וּמְמַלֵּא, וְזֶה מוֹצִיא זִיז כָּל שֶׁהוּא וּמְמַלֵּא. טַעְמָא – דְּאַפֵּיק, הָא לָא אַפֵּיק – אָמְרִינַן: אָדָם אוֹסֵר עַל חֲבֵירוֹ דֶּרֶךְ אֲוִיר.

Rather, Shmuel's opinion is learned **from this** statement: **This** one, the resident of one courtyard, **may extend a ledge of minimal size and draw** water from the cistern through his window; **and the** resident of the **other** courtyard **may** also **extend a ledge of minimal size and draw** water through his window. **The reason** for this *halakha* **is that one extended** a ledge, **but if he did not extend** a ledge, **we say** that **one person renders it prohibited for another person by way of the air.** One resident would be prohibited to draw water from the cistern due to the other resident, who has equal access to the water in the cistern by way of the air.

וּדְרַב מֵהֵיכָא? אִילֵימָא מֵהָא – שְׁתֵּי גְּזוּזְטְרָאוֹת זוֹ לְמַעְלָה מִזּוֹ, עָשׂוּ מְחִיצָה לָעֶלְיוֹנָה וְלֹא עָשׂוּ מְחִיצָה לַתַּחְתּוֹנָה – שְׁתֵּיהֶן אֲסוּרוֹת עַד שֶׁיְּעָרְבוּ.

The Gemara asks: **And from where** is the opinion **of Rav** learned, that one person does not render it prohibited for another by way of the air? **If you say** it is derived **from that** which was taught in a mishna: If **two balconies** extend over a body of water, **one above the other,** and the residents **erected a partition for the upper** balcony **but they did not erect a partition for the lower one,** residents of **both** balconies **are prohibited** to draw water, **unless they established an** *eiruv* together.

וְאָמַר רַב הוּנָא, אָמַר רַב: לֹא שָׁנוּ אֶלָּא בִּסְמוּכָה, אֲבָל בְּמוּפְלֶגֶת אַרְבָּעָה – עֶלְיוֹנָה מוּתֶּרֶת וְתַחְתּוֹנָה אֲסוּרָה.

The Gemara continues. **And Rav Huna said** that **Rav said: They taught** that the residents of one balcony render it prohibited for the residents of the other balcony to draw water **only when** one balcony **is near** the other, i.e., horizontally within four handbreadths. **But** if each balcony is **four** handbreadths **removed** from the other, so that each can use the other only by means of the air, **the upper** balcony **is permitted** to draw water, **while the lower one is prohibited** to do so. This teaching indicates that one person does not render it prohibited for use by another by way of the air.

דִּלְמָא שָׁאנֵי הָכָא, דְּכֵיוָן דְּלָזֶה בִּזְרִיקָה וְשִׁלְשׁוּל, וְלָזֶה בְּשִׁלְשׁוּל לְחוּדֵיהּ – כְּלָזֶה בִּזְרִיקָה וְלָזֶה בְּפֶתַח דָּמֵי.

However, this proof is inconclusive, as **perhaps it is different here, since for the** residents of **this** lower balcony, their use of the area is relatively inconvenient, as they can use it only **by** way of **hoisting and lowering.** The residents of the lower balcony must hoist the bucket from the lower balcony to the upper one before lowering it from there to draw water; **whereas for** the residents of **the other one,** i.e., the upper balcony, use of the water is convenient, as they can utilize it **by** way of **lowering alone.** Consequently, this case **is similar to** that of an area that can be used by the residents of **one** courtyard only **by throwing and** by the residents of **another** courtyard **as an entrance.** Since it is easier for the upper balcony to draw water, the lower balcony does not render it prohibited for the upper balcony in this particular case.

אֶלָּא מֵהָא, דְּאָמַר רַב נַחְמָן, אָמַר רַבָּה בַּר אֲבוּהּ, אָמַר רַב: שְׁנֵי בָתִּים וְשָׁלֹשׁ חוּרְבוֹת בֵּינֵיהֶם – זֶה מִשְׁתַּמֵּשׁ בְּסָמוּךְ שֶׁלּוֹ עַל יְדֵי זְרִיקָה, וְזֶה מִשְׁתַּמֵּשׁ בְּסָמוּךְ שֶׁלּוֹ עַל יְדֵי זְרִיקָה,

Rather, we can learn that this is the opinion of Rav **from that** teaching, **which Rav Naḥman said** that **Rabba bar Avuh said** that **Rav said:** If there are **two houses with three ruins**[H] **between them,** the resident of **this** house **may use** the ruin **adjacent to him by means of throwing** into the ruin through his windows that open out to that ruin, **and the** resident of **the other** house **may use** the ruin **adjacent to him by means of throwing** through his windows,

וְהָאֶמְצָעִי – אָסוּר.

and the middle ruin **is prohibited** to both of them.

יָתֵיב רַב בְּרוּנָא וְקָאָמַר לְהָא שְׁמַעְתָּא. אֲמַר לֵיהּ רַבִּי אֱלִיעֶזֶר בַּר בֵּי רַב: אָמַר רַב הָכִי? אֲמַר לֵיהּ: אִין. אַחְוֵי לִי אוּשְׁפִּיזֵיהּ. אַחְוֵי לֵיהּ. אֲתָא לְקַמֵּיהּ דְּרַב, אֲמַר לֵיהּ: אָמַר מָר הָכִי? אֲמַר לֵיהּ: אִין.

Rav Beruna sat and stated this ***halakha*** in the name of Rav. **Rabbi Elazar, a student of the Torah academy, said to him: Did Rav** actually **say this?** Rav Beruna **said to him: Yes,** he did. He said to him: **Show me his** place of **lodging,** and I will go and ask him myself. **He showed him** where Rav lived. Rabbi Elazar **came before Rav** and **said to him:** Did **the Master** actually **say this? He said to him: Yes,** I did.

אֲמַר לֵיהּ: וְהָא מָר הוּא דַּאֲמַר: לָזֶה בְּשִׁלְשׁוּל וְלָזֶה בִּזְרִיקָה – שְׁנֵיהֶן אֲסוּרִין!

Rabbi Elazar then **said to** Rav: Since you prohibit using the middle ruin, you evidently maintain that one person renders it prohibited for another by way of the air. That being the case, it must be that you permit the resident of each house to use the adjacent ruin because one's use of the ruin, while not convenient for him, is more convenient than the other person's usage. **But wasn't it the Master** himself who **said:** With regard to a place that can be used by the residents of **the one** courtyard only **by lowering** an object down to it **and** by the residents of **another** courtyard only **by throwing** an object on top of it, so that neither courtyard has convenient access to it, **both** sets of residents **are prohibited** from using it, although lowering an object is more convenient than throwing it?

אֲמַר לֵיהּ: מִי סָבְרַתְּ דְּקָיְימִי כְּשׁוּרָה? לָא! דְּקָיְימִי כַּחֲצוּבָה.

Rav **said to him: Do you think that** we are dealing with a case of three ruins **positioned** alongside each other **in** a straight **line? No. They are** arranged in the form **of a tripod,**[N] i.e. in a triangular form. In other words, two of the ruins, each adjacent to one of the houses, are located next to each other; the third is positioned adjacent to one side of the other two, near both houses. The middle ruin is prohibited to the residents of both houses because both houses have equally inconvenient but direct access to it. However, each of the other ruins is permitted to the resident of the adjacent house, as he has direct access to it, while the resident of the other house can reach it only through the air of the ruin nearest to him, and Rav maintains that one person does not render it prohibited for use by another by way of the air.

אֲמַר לֵיהּ רַב פַּפָּא לְרָבָא: לֵימָא שְׁמוּאֵל לֵית לֵיהּ דְּרַב דִּימִי. דְּכִי אֲתָא רַב דִּימִי, אָמַר רַבִּי יוֹחָנָן: מָקוֹם שֶׁאֵין בּוֹ אַרְבַּע עַל אַרְבַּע – מוּתָּר לִבְנֵי רְשׁוּת הָרַבִּים וְלִבְנֵי רְשׁוּת הַיָּחִיד לְכַתֵּף עָלָיו, וּבִלְבַד שֶׁלֹּא יַחֲלִיפוּ.

Rav Pappa said to Rava: Let us say that **Shmuel,** who maintains that one renders it prohibited for another by way of the air, **does not agree with** the opinion **of Rav Dimi. When Rav Dimi came** from Eretz Yisrael to Babylonia, he said that **Rabbi Yoḥanan said: A place less than four by four** handbreadths in size is an exempt domain with respect to carrying on Shabbat. Consequently, if this place is located between a public domain and a private domain, **it is permitted for** both **the people in the public domain and the people in the private domain to adjust** the burden **on their shoulders in it, as long as they do not exchange** objects with each other by way of the exempt domain. According to Shmuel's opinion this should be prohibited due to the air of a different domain.

הָתָם רְשׁוּיוֹת דְּאוֹרַיְיתָא, הָכָא רְשׁוּיוֹת דְּרַבָּנַן, וַחֲכָמִים עָשׂוּ חִיזּוּק לְדִבְרֵיהֶם יוֹתֵר מִשֶּׁל תּוֹרָה.

Rava replied: **There,** Rabbi Yoḥanan is dealing **with** an exempt domain situated between a public domain and a private domain, the two existing **domains by Torah law.** In that case, the Sages did not prohibit the use of the place due to the air. By contrast, **here,** with regard to the air between private domains, we are dealing **with domains** between which carrying is prohibited **by rabbinic law, and the Sages reinforced their statements** even **more than those of the Torah;**[N] they added preventive measures in order to safeguard their decrees. Consequently, according to Shmuel, the Sages indeed decreed that one renders it prohibited for another by way of the air.

NOTES

In the form of a tripod – דְּקָיְימִי כַּחֲצוּבָה: The image below shows two houses with three ruins between them in a triangular form. Each house is close to one ruin and relatively far from another, while the use of the third ruin is equally inconvenient for both houses.

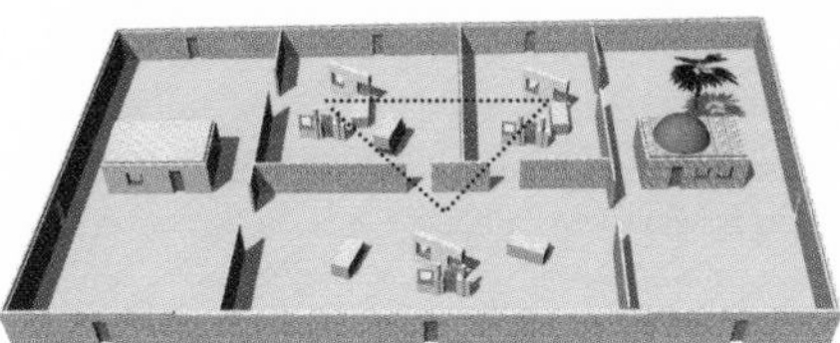

Arrangement of houses and ruins according to Rashi

The commentaries dispute the exact positioning of these houses and ruins:

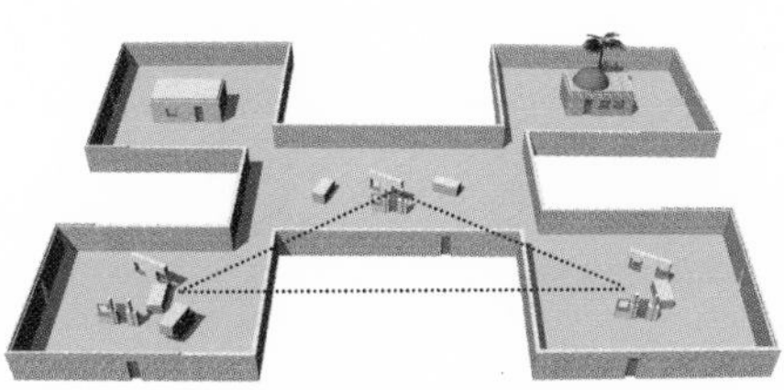

Arrangement according to Rabbi Zeraḥya HaLevi

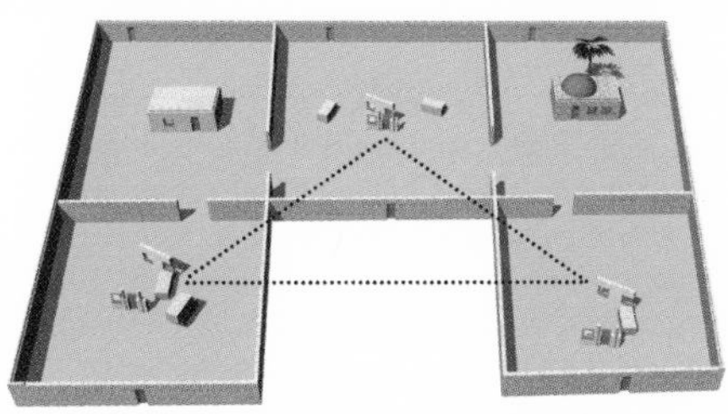

Arrangement according to Rabbeinu Yeruḥam and possibly Rabbeinu Ḥananel

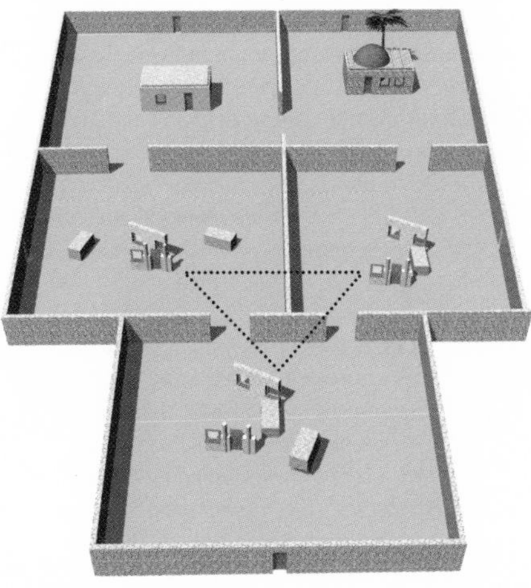

Arrangement according to the *Me'iri* and the Ritva

Domains from the Torah and from the Sages – רְשׁוּיוֹת דְּאוֹרַיְיתָא וּדְרַבָּנַן: This is problematic, as Rav himself stated, in reference to a wall between two courtyards, that the Sages reinforced their rulings more than those of the Torah. By saying so, he appears to contradict himself. The Rashba answers that Rav only prohibited two courtyards that actually use their shared wall, but not if airspace alone is involved.

אֲמַר לֵיהּ רָבִינָא לְרָבָא: מִי אָמַר רַב הָכִי? וְהָא אִיתְּמַר, שְׁנֵי בָתִּים מִשְּׁנֵי צִידֵּי רְשׁוּת הָרַבִּים, רַבָּה בַּר רַב הוּנָא אָמַר רַב: אָסוּר לִזְרוֹק מִזֶּה לָזֶה. וּשְׁמוּאֵל אָמַר: מוּתָּר לִזְרוֹק מִזֶּה לָזֶה!

Ravina said to Rava: But did Rav actually **say this,** that one person does not render it prohibited for use by another by way of the air? **But wasn't it stated** that *amora'im* disagreed with regard to **two houses** belonging to one person that stood **on two** opposite **sides of a public domain.**[H] **Rabba bar Rav Huna** said that **Rav said:** It is **prohibited to throw** an object **from one** house **to the other; and Shmuel said** that it is **permitted to throw from one to the other.** Rav apparently forbade the act of throwing due to the prohibited air of the public domain that lies between the two houses.

אֲמַר לֵיהּ: לָאו מִי אוֹקִימְנָא – דְּמִדְּלִי חַד וּמִתַּתִּי חַד, זִימְנִין דְּמִגַּנְדַּר וְנָפֵיל וְאָתֵי לְאִיתוּיֵי.

Rava **said to him: Wasn't it established that one** house was relatively **higher and the** other **one** was **lower** than the first? Rav prohibited throwing from one domain to the other, not due to the air of the public domain, but rather due to the difficulty of throwing from a low place to a higher one, as the thrown object **might sometimes roll and fall** back into the public domain **and** people might **come to pick it up**[N] and carry it from the public domain to the private domain. It was for this reason that Rav prohibited throwing an object from one house to another.

מתני׳ הַנּוֹתֵן אֶת עֵירוּבוֹ בְּבֵית שַׁעַר, אַכְסַדְרָה, וּמִרְפֶּסֶת – אֵינוֹ עֵירוּב. וְהַדָּר שָׁם – אֵינוֹ אוֹסֵר עָלָיו.

MISHNA With regard to **one who placed his** ***eiruv*** of courtyards **in a gatehouse**[H] or in **a portico,** a roofed structure without walls or with incomplete walls, **or** one who deposited it in **a balcony,** this **is not** a valid ***eiruv.*** **And one who resides there,**[H] in any of these structures, **does not render it prohibited** for the homeowner and the other residents of the courtyard to carry, even if he did not contribute to the *eiruv.*

בֵּית הַתֶּבֶן, וּבֵית הַבָּקָר, וּבֵית הָעֵצִים, וּבֵית הָאוֹצָרוֹת – הֲרֵי זֶה עֵירוּב, וְהַדָּר שָׁם אוֹסֵר, רַבִּי יְהוּדָה אוֹמֵר: אִם יֵשׁ שָׁם תְּפִיסַת יָד שֶׁל בַּעַל הַבַּיִת – אֵינוֹ אוֹסֵר.

If, however, one deposited his *eiruv* in **a hay shed or** in **a cowshed or** in **a woodshed or** in **a storehouse, this is** a valid ***eiruv,*** as it is located in a properly guarded place. **And one who resides there** with permission, if he neglected to contribute to the *eiruv,* he **renders it prohibited** for the homeowner and the other residents of the courtyard to carry. **Rabbi Yehuda says: If the homeowner has there,** in the hay shed or the other places listed above, **a right of usage,** i.e., if he is entitled to use all or part of the area for his own purposes, then the one who lives there **does not render it prohibited** for the homeowner, as the area is considered the homeowner's quarters, and the person living there is classified as a member of his household.

גמ׳ אָמַר רַב יְהוּדָה, בְּרֵיהּ דְּרַב שְׁמוּאֵל בַּר שֵׁילַת: כָּל מָקוֹם שֶׁאָמְרוּ הַדָּר שָׁם אֵינוֹ אוֹסֵר – הַנּוֹתֵן אֶת עֵירוּבוֹ אֵינוֹ עֵירוּב, חוּץ מִבֵּית שַׁעַר דְּיָחִיד. וְכָל מָקוֹם שֶׁאָמְרוּ חֲכָמִים אֵין מַנִּיחִין בּוֹ עֵירוּב – מַנִּיחִין בּוֹ שִׁיתּוּף, חוּץ מֵאֲוִיר מָבוֹי.

GEMARA **Rav Yehuda, son of Rav Shmuel bar Sheilat, said: Any place** with regard to **which** the Sages **said** that **one who resides there does not render it prohibited** for the other residents of the courtyard to carry, **one who places his** ***eiruv*** there, his **is not** a valid ***eiruv,*** **except for a gatehouse** that belongs **to an individual.**[N] If a structure is used as a passageway by only one person, he does not render it prohibited for the other residents of the courtyard, and an *eiruv* placed there is a valid *eiruv.* **And any place** with regard to **which the Sages said** that **a joining** of courtyards **may not be placed there, a merging** of alleyways **may be placed there, except for** the **airspace** of an **alleyway,** which is not inside one of the courtyards.[H]

מַאי קָא מַשְׁמַע לָן? תְּנֵינָא: הַנּוֹתֵן אֶת עֵירוּבוֹ בְּבֵית שַׁעַר, אַכְסַדְרָה, וּמִרְפֶּסֶת – אֵינוֹ עֵירוּב. עֵירוּב – הוּא דְּלָא הָוֵי, הָא שִׁיתּוּף – הָוֵי!

The Gemara asks: **What is he teaching us** by this? **We have** already **learned** this in the mishna: With regard to **one who placed his** ***eiruv*** **in a gatehouse** or in **an portico** or in **a balcony, it is not** a valid ***eiruv.*** It can be inferred from the mishna that **an** ***eiruv,*** **it is not, a merging** of the alleyway, it **is.** What, then, is novel in this statement?

בֵּית שַׁעַר דְּיָחִיד וַאֲוִיר דְּמָבוֹי אִיצְטְרִיכָא לֵיהּ, דְּלָא תְּנַן. תַּנְיָא נַמִי הָכִי: הַנּוֹתֵן אֶת עֵירוּבוֹ בְּבֵית שַׁעַר אַכְסַדְרָה וּמִרְפֶּסֶת, וּבְחָצֵר וּבְמָבוֹי – הֲרֵי זֶה עֵירוּב. וְהָתְנַן: אֵין זֶה עֵירוּב! אֵימָא: הֲרֵי זֶה שִׁיתּוּף.

The Gemara answers: **It was necessary for him** to teach the *halakha* of **a gatehouse** that belongs **to an individual and** the *halakha* of **the airspace of an alleyway, which we did not learn** in the mishna. **This was also taught** in a *baraita*: **One who placed his** ***eiruv*** **in a gatehouse,** or in **a portico, or in a balcony, or in a courtyard, or in an alleyway, this is** a valid ***eiruv.*** **But didn't we learn** in the mishna that this **is not an** ***eiruv***? Rather, you must **say** that the *baraita* should read: **This is** a valid **merging** of the alleyway.

HALAKHA

Two houses on two sides of a public domain – שְׁנֵי בָּתִּים מִשְּׁנֵי צִידֵּי רְשׁוּת הָרַבִּים: If two houses on opposite sides of a public domain belong to the same person, or if an *eiruv* was established between them, it is permitted to throw from one house to the other, provided that one throws above ten handbreadths from the ground and the two houses are equal in height. If they are not of the same height, it is prohibited. However, it is permitted to throw an earthenware vessel or any other breakable item. If the houses are on opposite sides of a *karmelit*, it is permitted to throw from one to the other under all circumstances (*Shulḥan Arukh, Oraḥ Ḥayyim* 353:1).

His ***eiruv*** **in a gatehouse – עֵירוּבוֹ בְּבֵית שַׁעַר:** If one places his *eiruv* in a gatehouse, in a portico or on a balcony, it is not a valid *eiruv*, as an *eiruv* may be placed only in a house suitable for a residence (*Shulḥan Arukh, Oraḥ Ḥayyim* 366:3).

One who resides in a gatehouse – הַדָּר בְּבֵית שַׁעַר: One who resides in a gatehouse, portico, or balcony does not impose restrictions upon the other residents of the courtyard. However, if he lives in a cowshed, woodshed, hay shed, or storehouse, he does impose restrictions upon the other residents of the courtyard (*Shulḥan Arukh, Oraḥ Ḥayyim* 370:1).

The appropriate locations for placement of a merging of the alleyway – הַמָּקוֹם הָרָאוּי לְהַנָּחַת שִׁיתּוּף: A merging of the alleyway may be deposited even in places unsuitable for an *eiruv*, provided that the location is protected; however, it may not be deposited in the airspace of the alleyway (*Shulḥan Arukh, Oraḥ Ḥayyim* 386:1).

NOTES

And people might come to pick it up – וְאָתֵי לְאִיתוּיֵי: The fact that the object fell from a private domain into the public domain is not in itself an issue of concern. As the person from whom the object fell undoubtedly did not intend to transfer the object into the public domain, this would be considered an act performed unawares, which is certainly not a transgression. However, if one forgot and brought the object back into the private domain, this would be considered an intentional act and would constitute a transgression.

A gatehouse that belongs to an individual – בֵּית שַׁעַר דְּיָחִיד: The exact opposite is stated in the Jerusalem Talmud, that the gatehouse of an individual is not considered a place of residence, and it therefore neither renders it prohibited for the other residents of the courtyard nor serves as a suitable location for an *eiruv*. Conversely, a gatehouse owned by a group of people has the full status of a residence, which means that an *eiruv* may be placed there and one who lives there imposes restrictions on carrying upon the other residents of the courtyard. The reason is apparently that a gatehouse owned by an individual is of no consequence. Therefore, the status of the resident there is negated in favor of the owner of the house. This is not the case with regard to a gatehouse owned by a group of inhabitants, who impose restrictions on each other in any event.

שִׁיתּוּף בְּמָבוֹי לָא מִינְטַר? אֵימָא בֶּחָצֵר שֶׁבַּמָּבוֹי.

The Gemara raises a difficulty: But if one places the food of the **merging** of the alleyway **in the alleyway** itself, it is **not** properly **guarded,** which means that it is as though he has not placed the merging of the alleyway there at all. Rather, you must **say** that the *baraita* should read: If he placed his merging of the alleyway **in a courtyard in the alleyway,** it is valid.

אָמַר רַב יְהוּדָה, אָמַר שְׁמוּאֵל: בְּנֵי חֲבוּרָה שֶׁהָיוּ מְסוּבִּין וְקָדַשׁ עֲלֵיהֶן הַיּוֹם, פַּת שֶׁעַל הַשֻּׁלְחָן סוֹמְכִין עֲלֵיהֶן מִשּׁוּם עֵירוּב. וְאָמְרִי לָהּ: מִשּׁוּם שִׁיתּוּף.

Rav Yehuda said that **Shmuel said:** If there were **a group** of people **who were dining** together on Shabbat eve, **and the day became sanctified for them,** i.e., Shabbat began while they were eating, **they may rely upon the bread on the table for an *eiruv*** of courtyards, so that they are all permitted to carry in the courtyard.[H] **And some say** they may rely on the bread **for a merging** of the alleyway.

אָמַר רַבָּה: וְלָא פְּלִיגִי; כָּאן – בִּמְסוּבִּין בַּבַּיִת, כָּאן – בִּמְסוּבִּין בֶּחָצֵר.

Rabba said: The two versions **do not disagree** with regard to whether the bread counts as an *eiruv* or a merging of the alleyway. Rather, **here,** the teaching that states it can be used as an *eiruv*, is referring to a case **where** they are **dining in the house,** as food deposited in a house can be used as an *eiruv* for the courtyard. By contrast, **there** it is referring to a situation **where** they are **dining in the courtyard,** and they may therefore rely on the bread only as a merging of the alleyway but not as an *eiruv*.

אֲמַר לֵיהּ אַבָּיֵי לְרַבָּה, תַּנְיָא דִּמְסַיַּיע לָךְ: עֵירוּבֵי חֲצֵירוֹת בֶּחָצֵר, וְשִׁיתּוּפֵי מְבוֹאוֹת בַּמָּבוֹי. וְהָוֵינַן בָּהּ: עֵירוּבֵי חֲצֵירוֹת בֶּחָצֵר? וְהָתְנַן: הַנּוֹתֵן אֶת עֵירוּבוֹ בְּבֵית שַׁעַר, אַכְסַדְרָה, וּמִרְפֶּסֶת אֵינוֹ עֵירוּב! אֵימָא: עֵירוּבֵי חֲצֵירוֹת – בַּבַּיִת שֶׁבֶּחָצֵר, שִׁיתּוּפֵי מְבוֹאוֹת – בֶּחָצֵר שֶׁבַּמָּבוֹי.

Abaye said to Rabba: A *baraita* **was taught that supports you. Joinings of courtyards** are deposited **in a courtyard, and mergings of alleyways** are placed **in an alleyway. And we discussed** this *baraita* and raised a difficulty: How can it be that ***eiruvin* of courtyards** are deposited **in a courtyard? But didn't we learn** in the mishna: If **one deposited his *eiruv* in a gatehouse,** or in **a portico, or** in **a balcony it is not a** valid ***eiruv*?** The mishna clearly indicates that the *eiruv* may not be deposited in the airspace of a courtyard. Rather, you must **say** that the *baraita* should read as follows: ***Eiruvin* of a courtyard** are placed **in a house in** that **courtyard;** whereas **mergings of alleyways** are placed **in a courtyard** that opens **into** that **alleyway.**

״רַבִּי יְהוּדָה אוֹמֵר אִם יֵשׁ שָׁם תְּפִיסַת יָד״ וכו׳. הֵיכִי דָּמֵי תְּפִיסַת יָד? כְּגוֹן חֲצֵירוֹ שֶׁל בּוֹנְיָיס.

We learned in the mishna that **Rabbi Yehuda says: If** the homeowner **has there,** in the hay shed or one of the other places listed, **a right of usage,** the person living there does not render the courtyard prohibited. The Gemara asks: **What are the circumstances of a right of usage?** The Gemara answers: **For example, the courtyard of** a man named **Bonyas,** an extremely wealthy individual who allowed various people to take up residence on his property, and he kept some of his many possessions in the living quarters assigned to those people. As he retained the right to remove his articles from their apartments, those areas continued to be regarded as quarters belonging to Bonyas and the people living there were deemed members of his household.

בֶּן בּוֹנְיָיס אֲתָא לְקַמֵּיהּ דְּרַבִּי, אֲמַר לְהוּ: פַּנּוּ מָקוֹם לְבֶן מֵאָה מָנֶה. אֲתָא אִינִישׁ אַחֲרִינָא, אֲמַר לְהוּ:

The Gemara relates another incident involving Bonyas and his wealth: The **son of Bonyas came before Rabbi** Yehuda HaNasi. Realizing from his visitor's clothing that he was dealing with a wealthy individual, Rabbi Yehuda HaNasi **said to** his attendants: **Make way for one** who possesses **one hundred *maneh*,** i.e., one hundred times one hundred *zuz*, as one of this status deserves to be honored in accordance with his riches. Later, **another person came** before him, and Rabbi Yehuda HaNasi once again turned to his attendants and **said to them:**

HALAKHA

Members of a group who establish an *eiruv* – בְּנֵי חֲבוּרָה שֶׁמְּעָרְבִין: If a group of people are dining together when Shabbat begins, they may use the bread on the table as an *eiruv*. This option is available only if they are dining in a house, but not if they are eating in the courtyard (*Shulḥan Arukh, Oraḥ Ḥayyim* 366:11).

פַּנּוּ מָקוֹם לְבֶן מָאתַיִם מָנֶה. אָמַר לְפָנָיו רַבִּי יִשְׁמָעֵאל בְּרַבִּי יוֹסֵי: רַבִּי, אָבִיו שֶׁל זֶה יֵשׁ לוֹ אֶלֶף סְפִינוֹת בַּיָּם וּכְנֶגְדָּן אֶלֶף עֲיָירוֹת בַּיַּבָּשָׁה! אָמַר לוֹ: לִכְשֶׁתַּגִּיעַ אֵצֶל אָבִיו אֱמוֹר לוֹ: אַל תְּשַׁגְּרֵהוּ בְּכֵלִים הַלָּלוּ לְפָנַי.

Make way even more **for one** who possesses **two hundred *maneh*. Rabbi Yishmael, son of Rabbi Yosei, said before him: My teacher,** Bonyas, **father of this one, has a thousand ships out at sea and, corresponding to them, a thousand towns on land.** He should be granted pride of place due to his exorbitant wealth. Rabbi Yehuda HaNasi **said to him: When you reach** his **father, tell him: Do not send him to me in these garments.** Dress him in accordance with his wealth and status, so that he will be honored accordingly.

רַבִּי מְכַבֵּד עֲשִׁירִים, רַבִּי עֲקִיבָא מְכַבֵּד עֲשִׁירִים. כִּדְדָרַשׁ רָבָא בַּר מָרִי: ״יֵשֵׁב עוֹלָם לִפְנֵי אֱלֹהִים חֶסֶד וֶאֱמֶת מַן יִנְצְרֻהוּ״, אֵימָתַי יֵשֵׁב עוֹלָם לִפְנֵי אֱלֹהִים – בִּזְמַן שֶׁחֶסֶד וֶאֱמֶת מַן יִנְצְרֻהוּ.

In explanation of this story, the Gemara comments: **Rabbi** Yehuda HaNasi would **honor the wealthy,**[N] and **Rabbi Akiva would** likewise **honor the wealthy, in accordance with Rava bar Mari's interpretation** of the verse: **"May he be enthroned before God forever; appoint mercy and truth, that they may preserve him"** (Psalms 61:8). **When may he be enthroned before God forever? When he appoints** [*man*] **mercy and truth that they may preserve him.**[N] Rava bar Mari explains the word *man* as referring to portions of food and interprets the verse as follows: If one provides food to others, he deserves to be enthroned before God, to be shown honor and respect. Consequently, it is proper to honor the wealthy who bestow such kindnesses.

רַבָּה בַּר בַּר חָנָה אָמַר: כְּגוֹן יָתֵד שֶׁל מַחֲרֵישָׁה,

Rabba bar bar Ḥana said: What is considered a right of usage? **For example,** if the homeowner stores **the pin of a plough** in his tenant's quarters. The tenant is prohibited to remove this pin from his residence on Shabbat due to its being set aside from use [*muktze*], and the homeowner therefore enjoys a fixed right of usage there.

אָמַר רַב נַחְמָן, תָּנָא דְּבֵי שְׁמוּאֵל: דָּבָר הַנִּיטָּל בַּשַּׁבָּת – אוֹסֵר, דָּבָר שֶׁאֵינוֹ נִיטָּל בַּשַּׁבָּת – אֵינוֹ אוֹסֵר.

Rav Naḥman said: A Sage **of the school of Shmuel taught** the following *baraita*: If the homeowner stores **an object that can be moved on Shabbat** with his tenant, the tenant's residence **renders** the other residence **prohibited**[H] if he neglected to join the *eiruv*. This is not considered a right of usage. If the **object** being stored is one **that cannot be moved on Shabbat,** the tenant's residence **does not render it prohibited for** them to use the courtyard.

תַּנְיָא נַמִי הָכִי: יֵשׁ לוֹ טֶבֶל, יֵשׁ לוֹ עֲשָׁשִׁית, וְכָל דָּבָר שֶׁאֵינוֹ נִיטָּל בַּשַּׁבָּת – אֵינוֹ אוֹסֵר.

The Gemara adds: **So too, it was taught** in a *baraita* that if the tenant **has untithed produce** that may not be moved on Shabbat; or if **he has lumps** of glass or iron; **or anything** else **that may not be moved on Shabbat** that the homeowner deposited with him, the tenant **does not render it prohibited for** the other residents to use the courtyard.

מתני׳ הַמַּנִּיחַ בֵּיתוֹ וְהָלַךְ לִשְׁבּוֹת בְּעִיר אַחֶרֶת, אֶחָד נׇכְרִי וְאֶחָד יִשְׂרָאֵל – הֲרֵי זֶה אוֹסֵר, דִּבְרֵי רַבִּי מֵאִיר. רַבִּי יְהוּדָה אוֹמֵר: אֵינוֹ אוֹסֵר.

MISHNA One who leaves his house,[H] which is located in a shared courtyard, **and goes to spend Shabbat in a different town, whether** he is **a gentile or a Jew, he renders it prohibited** for the other residents to use the courtyard as though he were still at home; this is **the statement of Rabbi Meir.**[N] **Rabbi Yehuda says: He does not render it prohibited for** them, as he left behind him an empty residence.

רַבִּי יוֹסֵי אוֹמֵר: נׇכְרִי – אוֹסֵר, יִשְׂרָאֵל – אֵינוֹ אוֹסֵר, שֶׁאֵין דֶּרֶךְ יִשְׂרָאֵל לָבֹא בַּשַּׁבָּת.

Rabbi Yosei says: A gentile renders it prohibited but **a Jew does not render it prohibited,** as **it is not the manner of a Jew to come** home **on Shabbat.** A Jew will not return home, therefore his empty residence does not render it prohibited. By contrast, a gentile might return over the course of Shabbat. Therefore, he is not considered to have fully uprooted himself from his house, and he renders it prohibited.

רַבִּי שִׁמְעוֹן אוֹמֵר: אֲפִילּוּ הִנִּיחַ בֵּיתוֹ וְהָלַךְ לִשְׁבּוֹת אֵצֶל בִּתּוֹ בְּאוֹתָהּ הָעִיר – אֵינוֹ אוֹסֵר, שֶׁכְּבָר הִסִּיעַ מִלִּבּוֹ.

Rabbi Shimon says: Even if the Jew **left his house and went to spend Shabbat with his daughter** who lived **in the same town, he does not render it prohibited.** Although he can return home at any time, it is assumed **that he has already removed from his mind** any thought of going back there and has established his Shabbat residence away from his home.

NOTES

Rabbi Yehuda HaNasi would honor the wealthy – רַבִּי מְכַבֵּד עֲשִׁירִים: One rather fanciful interpretation of this passage is that Rabbi Yehuda HaNasi would honor the wealthy so that others would learn from him. As a result, he too would be honored for his wealth rather than for his Torah studies, as he did not want to derive personal benefit from the honor of the Torah (Maharil, citing the Maharam).

Appoint mercy and truth that they may preserve him – חֶסֶד וֶאֱמֶת מַן יִנְצְרֻהוּ: Several explanations have been offered for this homiletic interpretation. Some commentaries explain that it is referring to wealthy people who give charity and offer kindness and assistance, thereby contributing to the betterment of the world. Others teach that the wealth of these people is preserved because they must use it for kindness and truth, and consequently, they deserve to be honored (*Arukh*). Yet other commentaries explain that the verse "May he be enthroned before God [*Elohim*] forever" is referring to great people and judges, who are also termed *elohim*. This is in recognition of the fact that the wealthy are granted a seat before the leaders of the generation because they perform acts of kindness and maintain the orderly operation of the world (Maharsha). In addition, it would be impossible for the Sages to sit before God and occupy themselves with Torah unless there were wealthy people busy doing mitzvot and attending to the needs of the community (Rabbi Zvi Hirsch Chajes).

Rabbi Meir's opinion – שִׁיטַת רַבִּי מֵאִיר: According to most commentaries, Rabbi Meir maintains that an empty residence is like any residence occupied by people and renders it prohibited for other residents to use the courtyard. In the Jerusalem Talmud, however, Rabbi Meir's reasoning is explained that there is always a chance that one might return to his home. Indeed, even a Jew in a different city can establish an *eiruv* and come home on Shabbat.

HALAKHA

An object that can be moved…renders it prohibited – דָּבָר הַנִּיטָּל...אוֹסֵר: If a homeowner permanently stores his items in the living quarters of his residents, the residents do not impose restrictions upon him. This *halakha* applies only to items that cannot be moved on Shabbat, either due to their weight or due to prohibition. In addition, this ruling pertains only to houses that belong to the homeowner. However, if the homeowner does not actually own these houses but merely possesses rights to them, the residents restrict each other (*Beit Yosef*, based on the Rambam). Some authorities state that if there are other residents in the courtyard, these residents impose restrictions even if the homeowner has access to his properties (Rema, based on Rabbeinu Yehonatan; *Shulḥan Arukh*, *Oraḥ Ḥayyim* 370:2).

One who leaves his house – הַמַּנִּיחַ בֵּיתוֹ: A Jew who leaves his home to spend Shabbat elsewhere and has no plans to return does not impose restrictions on the other residents of his courtyard. The *halakha* is in accordance with Rabbi Shimon's opinion, as Rav ruled in accordance with him in the Gemara. As for a gentile, if he went to a place from which he can return home on Shabbat, he imposes restrictions; he does not impose restrictions if he is more than a day's travel away from his home (Rambam). Rabbi Yosei's opinion is accepted as the *halakha*, as the halakha is ruled in his favor in disputes with Rabbi Yehuda. Additionally, he is supported by Rabbi Meir's opinion (*Maggid Mishne*). Some commentaries teach that even a gentile who left for a nearby place does not render it prohibited for other residents to carry. This ruling is in accordance with Rabbi Yehuda, as the *halakha* is in accordance with the lenient opinion in the *halakhot* of *eiruv* (Rosh; *Mordekhai*; *Sefer Mitzvot Gedolot*; Rema; *Shulḥan Arukh*, *Oraḥ Ḥayyim* 371:1).

גמ׳ אָמַר רַב: הֲלָכָה כְּרַבִּי שִׁמְעוֹן. וְדַוְקָא בִּתּוֹ, אֲבָל בְּנוֹ – לָא. דְּאָמְרִי אִינָשֵׁי: נְבַח בָּךְ כַּלְבָּא – עוּל, נְבַח בָּךְ גּוּרְיְיתָא – פּוּק:

GEMARA **Rav said: The *halakha* is in accordance with** the opinion of **Rabbi Shimon.** The Gemara comments: **And** this is the *halakha* **only** if one went to **his daughter's** house; **but** if he went to **his son's** house, **no,** this is not the *halakha*. One cannot be sure that he will be able to stay at his son's house, for his daughter-in-law might object to his presence and force him to return home. **As people say: If a dog barks at you, enter; if a female dog barks at you, leave.** In other words, the objections of a female, such as one's daughter-in-law, who will certainly not be opposed by her husband, are more powerful than those of a male, such as one's son-in-law.

מתני׳ בּוֹר שֶׁבֵּין שְׁתֵּי חֲצֵירוֹת אֵין מְמַלְּאִין מִמֶּנּוּ בְּשַׁבָּת, אֶלָּא אִם כֵּן עָשׂוּ לוֹ מְחִיצָה גָּבוֹהַּ עֲשָׂרָה טְפָחִים, בֵּין מִלְּמַטָּה, בֵּין מִתּוֹךְ אוֹגְנוֹ.

MISHNA In the case of **a cistern that is** located **between two courtyards,** situated partly in each courtyard,[B] **one may not draw** water **from it on Shabbat,** lest the residents of one courtyard draw water from the domain of the other courtyard, **unless a partition ten handbreadths high was erected for it** as a separation between the domains. This partition is effective **whether** it is **below,** in the water, **or whether it is within the** airspace of the cistern below the **rim,** above the surface of the water.

רַבָּן שִׁמְעוֹן בֶּן גַּמְלִיאֵל אוֹמֵר, בֵּית שַׁמַּאי אוֹמְרִים: מִלְּמַטָּה, וּבֵית הִלֵּל אוֹמְרִים: מִלְּמַעְלָה. אָמַר רַבִּי יְהוּדָה: לֹא תְּהֵא מְחִיצָה גְּדוֹלָה מִן הַכּוֹתֶל שֶׁבֵּינֵיהֶם.

Rabban Shimon ben Gamliel said:[N] This is the subject of an early dispute of *tanna'im*, as **Beit Shammai said** that the partition, which permits drawing water, must be placed **below; and Beit Hillel said** it should be positioned **above. Rabbi Yehuda said: A partition is no better than the wall between them.** A wall dividing the two courtyards passes over the cistern, therefore it is not necessary to erect an additional partition in the cistern's airspace.

גמ׳ אָמַר רַב הוּנָא: לְמַטָּה – לְמַטָּה מַמָּשׁ, לְמַעְלָה – לְמַעְלָה מַמָּשׁ. וְזֶה וָזֶה בַּבּוֹר. וְרַב יְהוּדָה אָמַר: לְמַטָּה – לְמַטָּה מִן הַמַּיִם, לְמַעְלָה – לְמַעְלָה מִן הַמַּיִם.

GEMARA **Rav Huna said:** When Beit Shammai said **below,** they meant **actually below,** near the water; the partition need not touch the water itself. When Beit Hillel said **above,** they meant **actually above,** higher than the water and near the rim of the cistern. **And both of these** are within the airspace of the **cistern. And Rav Yehuda said: Below** means **below the water,** so that part of the partition is inside the water; whereas **above** means **above the water,** in such a manner that the partition does not come into contact with the water.[B]

אֲמַר לֵיהּ רַבָּה בַּר רַב חָנָן לְאַבָּיֵי: הָא דְּאָמַר רַב יְהוּדָה "לְמַטָּה – לְמַטָּה מִן הַמַּיִם" מַאי שְׁנָא לְמַטָּה מַמָּשׁ דְּלָא – דְּעָרִיבִי מַיָּא, לְמַטָּה מִן הַמַּיִם נַמִי – הָא עָרִיבִי מַיָּא!

Rabba bar Rav Ḥanan said to Abaye: With regard to **that** which **Rav Yehuda said: Below** means **below the water, what is different** about a case where the partition is **actually below,**[N] in the airspace cistern near the water, that led Rav Yehuda to say that one may **not** draw water in that case? It is **because** he was concerned lest **the water** of the two courtyards **become intermingled** beneath the partition. In a case where the partition is located **below the water,** near the bottom of the cistern, **as well, won't the water** of the two courtyards **become intermingled** above it?

BACKGROUND

A cistern between courtyards – בּוֹר שֶׁבֵּין חֲצֵירוֹת:

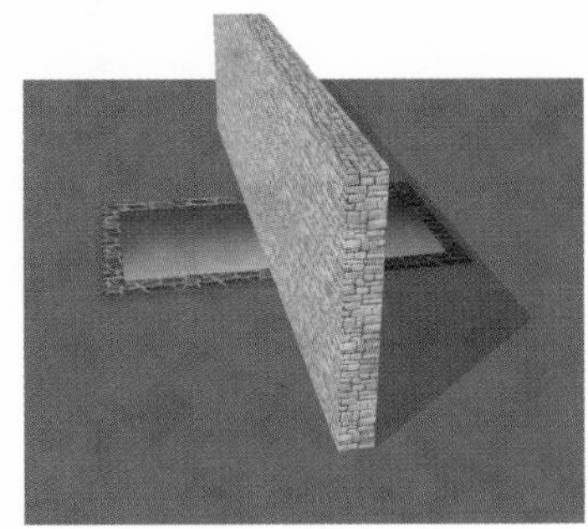

Cistern located under a wall that separates two courtyards

NOTES

Rabban Shimon ben Gamliel's opinion – שִׁיטַת רַבָּן שִׁמְעוֹן בֶּן גַּמְלִיאֵל: Some commentaries explain that Rabban Shimon ben Gamliel accepts the ruling of the first *tanna*. He merely adds that this issue is the subject of a dispute between earlier *tanna'im*. Other authorities maintain that Rabban Shimon ben Gamliel disagrees with the first *tanna*, as he is of the opinion that the partition must be placed either below or above.

Actually below – לְמַטָּה מַמָּשׁ: The expression actually below does not seem to fit the context, as the partition is placed above the water, in the depths of the cistern. One explanation is that Rav Huna never heard the statement of the younger Rav Yehuda. Consequently, Rav Huna's statement must be understood as referring to the mishna itself, in which case the phrase actually below means that it is not enough for the partition to descend slightly below the edge of the cistern, but it must actually lie below its rim (Ritva). The *Me'iri* explains the phrase actually below literally, as he maintains that the partition must be placed right on the floor of the cistern, even if it is not visible from above at all.

BACKGROUND

Above and below – לְמַעְלָה וּלְמַטָּה: In the image below, which reflects Rav Huna's view, the upper partition is situated far above the level of the water, while the lower partition is positioned close to the water.

Cross section of a water cistern, in accordance with Rav Huna's view

In this image, reflecting Rav Yehuda's new wording of the conclusion as explained by Abaye, the lower partition is submerged, although it partly protrudes above the water level. A section of the upper partition also remains underwater.

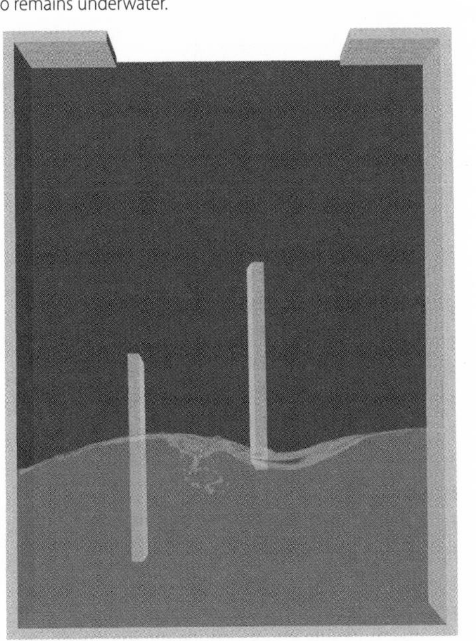

Cross section of a water cistern, in accordance with Rav Yehuda's view

HALAKHA

A partition above a cistern – מְחִיצָה שֶׁעַל הַבּוֹר: It is prohibited to draw water from a cistern located between two courtyards, unless a partition ten handbreadths high is constructed over it. At least a handbreadth of this partition must be submerged beneath the water, with another handbreadth protruding above the water. It does not matter whether most of it is above or below the level of the water. The *halakha* is in accordance with Rabbi Yehuda's position, as his opinion is the focus of the Gemara's analysis (Rif; Rosh; Rambam; *Shulḥan Arukh, Oraḥ Ḥayyim* 376:1).

אֲמַר לֵיהּ: לָא שְׁמִיעַ לָךְ הָא דְּאָמַר רַב יְהוּדָה אָמַר רַב, וּמָטוּ בָּהּ מִשּׁוּם רַבִּי חִיָּיא: צָרִיךְ שֶׁיֵּרָאוּ רָאשֵׁן שֶׁל קָנִים לְמַעְלָה מִן הַמַּיִם טֶפַח.

Abaye **said to him: Didn't you hear that which Rav Yehuda said** that **Rav said, and some arrived at** this statement **in the name of Rabbi Ḥiyya: The tops of the reeds** of the partition **must be visible a handbreadth above** the surface of **the water?** This will ensure that there is a full partition between the two sides of the cistern.

וְתוּ, הָא דְּאָמַר רַב יְהוּדָה: ״לְמַעְלָה – לְמַעְלָה מִן הַמַּיִם״, מַאי שְׁנָא לְמַעְלָה מַמָּשׁ דְּלָא – דְּעָרְבִי מַיָּא, לְמַעְלָה מִן הַמַּיִם נַמִי – הָא עָרְבִי מַיָּא! אֲמַר לֵיהּ: לָא שְׁמִיעַ לָךְ הָא דְּתָנֵי יַעֲקֹב קַרְחִינָאָה: צָרִיךְ שֶׁיַּשְׁקִיעַ רָאשֵׁי קָנִים בַּמַּיִם טֶפַח.

And Rabba bar Rav Ḥanan **further** asked: With regard to **that** which **Rav Yehuda said: Above** means **above the water,** we can inquire: **What is different** about a case where the partition is **actually above,** i.e., near the rim of the cistern that led Rav Yehuda to say that one may **not** draw water in that case? It is **because** he was concerned lest **the water** of the two courtyards **become intermingled** beneath the partition. However, even if the partition is **above the water** below the rim of the cistern, **the water** of the two courtyards will **also become intermingled** beneath it. Abaye **said to him: Haven't you heard that which Ya'akov from Karḥina taught: The ends of the reeds** of a partition **must be immersed** at least **a handbreadth** into the **water,** so that they divide the water in the cistern?[H]

וְאֶלָּא הָא דְּאָמַר רַב יְהוּדָה: קוֹרָה אַרְבַּע מַתֶּרֶת בְּחוּרְבָּה, וְרַב נַחְמָן אָמַר רַבָּה בַּר אֲבוּהּ:

But the Gemara raises a further question. **Rav Yehuda said:** If there is a cross **beam of four** handbreadths, it **permits** one to carry underneath it **in a ruin.** If a crossbeam four handbreadths wide is laid across the walls of a ruin, its edges are viewed as though they descended to the ground on each side, thereby forming partitions that permit one to carry under the cross beam. **And Rav Naḥman said** that **Rabba bar Avuh said:**

Perek **VIII**
Daf **86** Amud **b**

HALAKHA

A cross beam in water – קוֹרָה בַּמַּיִם: A cross beam four handbreadths wide that is placed over the opening of a cistern permits the residents of both courtyards to draw from it, as stated by Rabbi Naḥman (*Shulḥan Arukh, Oraḥ Ḥayyim* 376:1).

NOTES

The Sages were lenient with regard to water – קַל הוּא שֶׁהֵקֵילוּ בַּמַּיִם: According to the Ra'avad, the rationale for this leniency is that water generally rises more than ten handbreadths above the ground level of the place where it is found. Consequently, the *halakhot* of domains and boundaries do not apply to the water itself. Other commentaries explain that as it is common for houses and courtyards to be constructed over cisterns of this type, the Sages were not stringent in this regard (Rashba). Yet other commentaries point out that the usual objection to suspended partitions, the concern that goats might break through, does not apply in this context. Even if the water contains fish, their breaking through from one side to the other would not be noticeable, as they are covered by the water (*Me'iri*).

קוֹרָה אַרְבָּעָה מַתֶּרֶת בַּמַּיִם,

A cross **beam of four** handbreadths laid across a cistern located between two courtyards **permits** one to draw **water**[H] from that cistern.

הָא קָא אָזֵיל דְּלִי לְאִידָךְ גִּיסָא וּמַיְיתִי! קִים לְהוּ לְרַבָּנַן דְּאֵין דְּלִי מְהַלֵּךְ יוֹתֵר מֵאַרְבָּעָה טְפָחִים. תַּחַת קוֹרָה.

With this in mind, the following difficulty arises: The **bucket** he uses to draw the water **might drift** under the cross **beam to the other side** of the cistern **and bring** water from the other courtyard. The Gemara answers: **The Sages have established that a bucket does not drift more than four handbreadths** from the point where it was lowered, and it will therefore stay on its original side of the partition.

מִיהָא הָא עָרְבִי מַיָּא! אֶלָּא: מִשּׁוּם דְּקַל הוּא שֶׁהֵקֵילוּ חֲכָמִים בַּמַּיִם. כִּדְבָעָא מִינֵּיהּ רַבִּי טַבְלָא מֵרַב: מְחִיצָה תְּלוּיָה, מַהוּ שֶׁתַּתִּיר בְּחוּרְבָּה? אֲמַר לֵיהּ: אֵין מְחִיצָה תְּלוּיָה מַתֶּרֶת אֶלָּא בַּמַּיִם, קַל הוּא שֶׁהֵקֵילוּ חֲכָמִים בַּמַּיִם.

The Gemara raises a difficulty: **Nonetheless, the water becomes intermingled under the** cross **beam,** and consequently the bucket will bring up water from the other courtyard. **Rather,** it must be that the reason for the leniency is not that the cross beam actually prevents the flow of the water, but **because the Sages were lenient with regard to water.**[N] They allowed a partition suspended above the water to be considered as though it blocked the flow of the water. **As Rav Tavla asked of Rav:** With regard to **a suspended partition, does it permit** carrying **in a ruin?** Do we say that the remnants of the walls suspended in the air are considered as though they descended to the ground and closed off the area, thereby rendering it a private domain? Rav **said to him: A suspended partition** of this kind **permits** carrying **only** in the case **of water,** as **the Sages were lenient with regard to water.**

״אָמַר רַבִּי יְהוּדָה: לֹא תְּהֵא מְחִיצָה״. אָמַר רַבָּה בַּר בַּר חָנָה, אָמַר רַבִּי יוֹחָנָן: רַבִּי יְהוּדָה בְּשִׁיטַת רַבִּי יוֹסֵי אֲמָרָהּ, דְּאָמַר: מְחִיצָה תְּלוּיָה מַתֶּרֶת אֲפִילּוּ בַּיַּבָּשָׁה.

The mishna teaches: **Rabbi Yehuda said:** There is no need for a partition in the cistern, as **a partition** inside a cistern **is no** better than the wall above it. **Rabba bar bar Ḥana said** that **Rabbi Yoḥanan said: Rabbi Yehuda stated this in accordance with the opinion of Rabbi Yosei, who said: A suspended partition permits** carrying **even on land,** as it is considered as though it descended to the ground and sealed off the area. Accordingly, there is no need to erect a partition inside the airspace of a cistern.

דִּתְנַן: הַמְשַׁלְשֵׁל דְּפָנוֹת מִלְמַעְלָה לְמַטָּה בִּזְמַן שֶׁגְּבוֹהוֹת מִן הָאָרֶץ שְׁלֹשָׁה טְפָחִים – פְּסוּלָה, מִמַּטָּה לְמַעְלָה, אִם גְּבוֹהוֹת עֲשָׂרָה טְפָחִים – כְּשֵׁירָה.

As we learned in a mishna: **One who lowers** *sukka* **walls from above** going **downward, when** the walls **are three handbreadths higher than the ground,** the *sukka* **is invalid,** as they are not considered partitions;[H] but if he constructed walls **from below** going **upward, if they are ten handbreadths high** the *sukka* **is valid,** even if they do not reach the roofing.

רַבִּי יוֹסֵי אוֹמֵר: כְּשֵׁם שֶׁמִּלְמַטָּה לְמַעְלָה עֲשָׂרָה כָּךְ מִלְמַעְלָה לְמַטָּה עֲשָׂרָה.

Rabbi Yosei, however, **says: Just as** with regard to walls constructed **from below** going **upward, ten** handbreadths suffice, **so** too, in the case of walls built **from above** going **downward, ten** handbreadths are enough for it to be considered a whole wall, even if it more than three handbreadths above the ground. Similarly, Rabbi Yehuda maintains that a partition suspended above a cistern is considered as though it descended and sealed off the area.

וְלָא הִיא, לָא רַבִּי יְהוּדָה סָבַר לַהּ כְּרַבִּי יוֹסֵי, וְלָא רַבִּי יוֹסֵי סָבַר לַהּ כְּרַבִּי יְהוּדָה.

The Gemara rejects this argument: **But this is not so,**[N] for we can distinguish between the two opinions and claim that **neither Rabbi Yehuda holds** in accordance **with Rabbi Yosei, nor does Rabbi Yosei hold** in accordance **with Rabbi Yehuda.**

רַבִּי יְהוּדָה לָא סָבַר לַהּ כְּרַבִּי יוֹסֵי; עַד כָּאן לָא קָאָמַר רַבִּי יְהוּדָה – אֶלָּא בְּעֵירוּבֵי חֲצֵירוֹת דְּרַבָּנַן, אֲבָל סוּכָּה דְּאוֹרַיְיתָא – לָא.

The Gemara elaborates: **Rabbi Yehuda does not** necessarily **hold** in accordance **with Rabbi Yosei,** as a distinction can be made between the two cases. **Rabbi Yehuda stated** his opinion **only with regard to the joining of courtyards,** which are required **by rabbinic law, but** in the case of **a** ***sukka*****, which** is required **by Torah law, no,** he did not say that we can rely on suspended partitions.

וְלָא רַבִּי יוֹסֵי סָבַר לַהּ כְּרַבִּי יְהוּדָה; עַד כָּאן לָא קָאָמַר רַבִּי יוֹסֵי – אֶלָּא בְּסוּכָּה דְּאִיסּוּר עֲשֵׂה הוּא, אֲבָל שַׁבָּת דְּאִיסּוּר סְקִילָה הוּא – לָא אָמַר.

And conversely, **Rabbi Yosei does not** necessarily **hold** in accordance **with Rabbi Yehuda,** as **Rabbi Yosei stated** his opinion **only with regard to a** ***sukka*****,** which **is a prohibition** stated in the Torah **from a positive commandment.**[N] The prohibition is not written as a negative commandment, but it can be inferred from a positive commandment. Neglect of the positive commandment of *sukka* is not punishable by the court, therefore we are not stringent in this regard. **But** with regard to **Shabbat,** which is **a prohibition** punishable **by stoning,** Rabbi Yosei **did not state** his opinion. Consequently, Rabbi Yosei might agree that we must be very stringent with regard to all *halakhot* of Shabbat, even those that are rabbinic in origin.

וְאִם תֹּאמַר: אוֹתוֹ מַעֲשֶׂה שֶׁנַּעֲשָׂה בְּצִיפּוֹרִי עַל פִּי מִי נַעֲשָׂה? לֹא עַל פִּי רַבִּי יוֹסֵי אֶלָּא עַל פִּי רַבִּי יִשְׁמָעֵאל בְּרַבִּי יוֹסֵי נַעֲשָׂה.

And if you ask: That incident, which occurred in Tzippori,[N] when they relied on suspended partitions on land for Shabbat, **on whose authority was it performed?** It was done **not on the authority of Rabbi Yosei, but** rather **it was performed on the authority of Rabbi Yishmael, son of Rabbi Yosei,** who maintains that a suspended partition renders it permitted to carry even if it is over land and even on Shabbat.

דְּכִי אֲתָא רַב דִּימִי, אָמַר: פַּעַם אַחַת שָׁכְחוּ וְלֹא הֵבִיאוּ סֵפֶר תּוֹרָה מִבְּעוֹד יוֹם, לְמָחָר פָּרְסוּ סָדִין עַל הָעַמּוּדִים, וְהֵבִיאוּ סֵפֶר תּוֹרָה, וְקָרְאוּ בּוֹ.

The incident transpired in the following manner. **As when Rav Dimi came** from Eretz Yisrael to Babylonia, **he said:** It **once** happened that the people **forgot and did not bring a Torah scroll** to the synagogue on Friday **while it was still day,** which meant they were left without a scroll from which to read on Shabbat. **On the following day,** Shabbat, **they spread a sheet over the pillars**[B] positioned between the house where the scroll was kept and the synagogue, thereby forming a corridor with partitions suspended on each side. **And** in this manner **they brought the Torah scroll** to the synagogue **and read from it.**[B]

HALAKHA

Hanging walls – דְּפָנוֹת מְשׁוּלְשָׁלוֹת: If one hangs walls from above, so that they end three handbreadths above the ground, these walls do not have the status of a partition, as stated by the anonymous opinion in the mishna. As for partitions ten handbreadths in height, they are considered walls in every regard, even if they do not reach the roof (*Shulḥan Arukh, Oraḥ Ḥayyim* 630:9).

BACKGROUND

A sheet on pillars – סָדִין עַל גַּבֵּי עַמּוּדִים: The sheet serves as a suspended partition that forms a kind of closed corridor in the area over which it is spread. According to many commentaries, these sheets were spread over only a single row of pillars, as a result of which they merely formed a partition but not a covering.

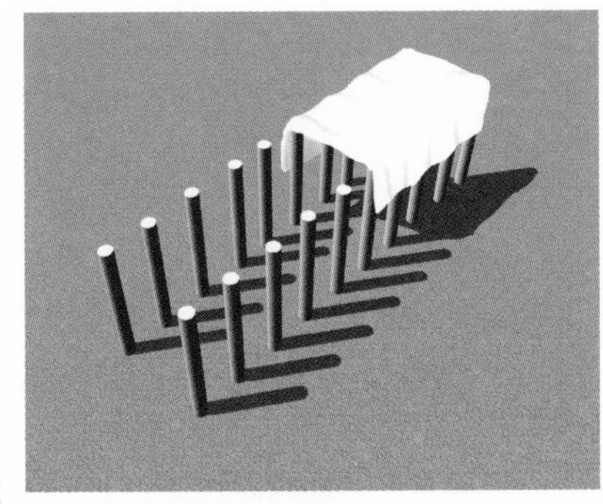

Sheet spread over a double row of pillars

The synagogue and a Torah scroll – בֵּית הַכְּנֶסֶת וְסֵפֶר תּוֹרָה: Synagogues in the talmudic period were not inside the towns but generally located outside of the towns' boundaries. Occasionally they were even at some distance from the towns. Apparently, this was so that several towns could share a single synagogue. As the synagogue was sometimes left unattended, Torah scrolls were not left in the synagogue's sanctuary. Rather, the scrolls were placed in a portable ark and locked in a room adjacent to the sanctuary, or placed in the inhabited house closest to the synagogue, from which they could be brought to the synagogue when necessary.

NOTES

But this is not so – וְלָא הִיא: Some commentaries maintain that the Gemara's wording indicates that this is not merely a possible rejection, as in that case it would have stated: And perhaps it is not so. Rather, this is a definitive rejection based on a tradition concerning the respective opinions of Rabbi Yehuda and Rabbi Yosei (*Ge'on Ya'akov*).

Sukka **is a prohibition from a positive commandment – סוּכָּה דְּאִיסּוּר עֲשֵׂה:** This claim, which differentiates between a prohibition inferred from a positive commandment and one punishable by stoning, cannot be taken literally, especially with regard to the joining of courtyards, which is rabbinic in origin. It is unreasonable to assume that Rabbi Yosei is of the opinion that a hanging partition is invalid on Shabbat. If a hanging partition has the legal status of a partition, it must be classified as a partition in all cases. The correct conclusion is that Rabbi Yosei maintains that although a suspended partition is considered a partition according to Torah law, the Sages ruled that one should not rely on this partition for the stringent *halakhot* of Shabbat (Ritva).

That incident which occurred in Tzippori – אוֹתוֹ מַעֲשֶׂה שֶׁנַּעֲשָׂה בְּצִיפּוֹרִי: The *ge'onim* teach that this incident did not take place inside a courtyard, but in the public domain or on the margins of the public domain. The Ritva and the *Me'iri*, who cite similar explanations, explicitly state that this partition was actually constructed and used to permit carrying in the public domain. See Rashi's explanation of this incident.

HALAKHA

A temporary tent on Shabbat – אֹהֶל עֲרַאי בְּשַׁבָּת: One may not erect even a temporary tent, *ab initio*, on Shabbat (*Shulḥan Arukh, Oraḥ Ḥayyim* 315:1).

פָּרְסוּ?! לְכַתְּחִילָּה מִי שָׁרֵי? וְהָא הַכֹּל מוֹדִים שֶׁאֵין עוֹשִׂין אֹהֶל עֲרַאי בְּשַׁבָּת!

The Gemara expresses surprise at the wording of this account: Did they actually **spread** sheets on Shabbat? **Is it permitted** to do so ***ab initio*? But doesn't everyone agree that one may not erect a temporary tent on Shabbat *ab initio*?**[H] Spreading sheets over pillars is considered constructing a temporary tent.

אֶלָּא: מָצְאוּ סְדִינִין פְּרוּסִין עַל הָעַמּוּדִים, וְהֵבִיאוּ סֵפֶר תּוֹרָה, וְקָרְאוּ בּוֹ.

Rather, what happened was that **they found sheets spread over the pillars,** which they used as partitions, **and** in this manner **they brought the Torah scroll** to the synagogue **and read from it.**

אָמַר רַבָּה: רַבִּי יְהוּדָה וְרַבִּי חֲנַנְיָא בֶּן עֲקַבְיָא אָמְרוּ דָּבָר אֶחָד. רַבִּי יְהוּדָה – הָא דַּאֲמַרַן. רַבִּי חֲנַנְיָא בֶּן עֲקַבְיָא (דִּתְנַן,) רַבִּי חֲנַנְיָא בֶּן עֲקַבְיָא אוֹמֵר: גְּזוּזְטְרָא שֶׁיֵּשׁ בָּהּ אַרְבַּע אַמּוֹת עַל אַרְבַּע אַמּוֹת –

Rabba said: Rabbi Yehuda and Rabbi Ḥananya ben Akavya said the same thing. Both were very lenient with regard to the *halakha* of a partition over water. The ruling of **Rabbi Yehuda is that which we** just **said,** that the wall of the courtyard permits a cistern. The ruling of **Rabbi Ḥananya ben Akavya is as we learned: Rabbi Ḥananya ben Akavya says:** In the case of a **balcony that contains four cubits by four cubits,** which is suspended over water,

Perek **VIII**
Daf **87** Amud **a**

BACKGROUND

One may carve in it a hole and draw through it – חוֹקֵק בָּהּ וּמְמַלֵּא: A balcony with a hole in its center is depicted below. In this case, the balcony itself is at least four by four cubits, with a hole in its center of four by four handbreadths. All the measurements in the diagram are in handbreadths. If the floor of the balcony is considered to be folded along the lines in the image, it forms a virtual shaft under the hole through which it is permitted to draw water.

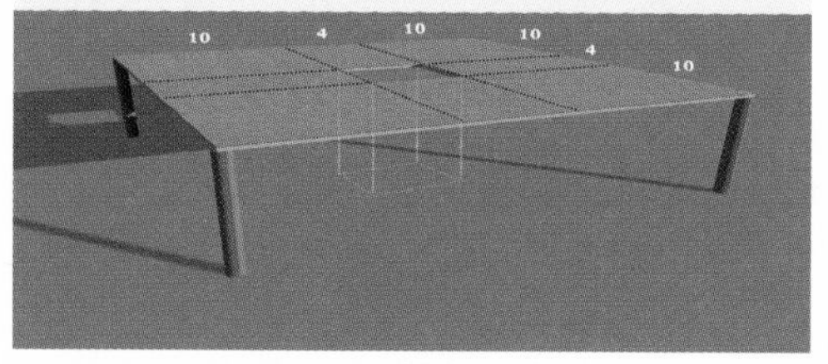

Balcony with a hole in its center and a virtual shaft

A balcony near a wall – גְּזוּזְטְרָא סְמוּכָה לַכּוֹתֶל: In the image below, the balcony is positioned within three handbreadths of the wall. The balcony is four cubits long and slightly more than eleven handbreadths wide. An area of slightly more than one handbreadth deep and four handbreadths wide is cut into the balcony near the building's wall. If the sections of the balcony were folded downward along the broken lines, they would form partitions of ten handbreadths in height on each side of the hole cut out of the floor of the balcony. Four cubits is twenty-four handbreadths, which suffices for ten handbreadths on each side, minus four handbreadths for the hole. The width of the balcony, which is slightly more than eleven handbreadths, is enough to cut slightly more than one handbreadth into the balcony and for ten handbreadths to be virtually folded so as to enclose the hole from the side parallel to the building's wall.

Balcony near a wall

חוֹקֵק בָּהּ אַרְבַּע עַל אַרְבַּע וּמְמַלֵּא.

one may carve in it a hole of **four by four** handbreadths **and draw** water through it.[B] Even if there are no actual partitions around the hole, the section surrounding the hole is considered as though it were bent downward and formed partitions ten handbreadths high on all sides. Consequently, it is permitted to draw water through the hole.

אֲמַר לֵיהּ אַבָּיֵי: וְדִילְמָא לָא הִיא; עַד כָּאן לָא קָאָמַר רַבִּי יְהוּדָה הָתָם – אֶלָּא דְּקָאָמַר: ״גּוֹד אַחֵית מְחִיצָּתָא״, אֲבָל כּוֹף וְגוֹד – לָא.

Abaye said to him: But perhaps that is not so, as we can distinguish between the opinions. It is possible that **Rabbi Yehuda stated** his opinion **only there,** with regard to the wall of the courtyard and the cistern, **as he said** that we rely on the halakhic principle of **extend and lower the partition.** The partition above the cistern is considered as though it descended to the bottom. **But** the principle of **bend** the partition **and extend** it downward, as suggested by Rabbi Ḥananya ben Akavya, **no,** he does not accept this principle.

וְעַד כָּאן לָא קָאָמַר רַבִּי חֲנַנְיָא בֶּן עֲקַבְיָא הָתָם – אֶלָּא בְּיַמָּהּ שֶׁל טְבֶרְיָא, הוֹאִיל וְיֵשׁ לָהּ אוֹגְנִים, וַעֲיָירוֹת וְקַרְפִּיפוֹת מַקִּיפוֹת אוֹתָהּ, אֲבָל בִּשְׁאָר מֵימוֹת – לָא.

And we can likewise say that **Rabbi Ḥananya ben Akavya stated** his opinion **only there,** in the case of the balcony, **with regard to the Sea of Tiberias,** i.e., the Sea of Galilee, **since it has** clearly defined **banks** around it, **and towns and enclosures surround it** on all sides. The Sea of Galilee is surrounded by clear boundaries on all sides and is therefore somewhat similar to a private domain in appearance. Consequently, even a minor adjustment is sufficient. **However, with regard to other waters, no,** Rabbi Ḥananya ben Akavya did not permit this practice.

אָמַר אַבָּיֵי: וּלְדִבְרֵי רַבִּי חֲנַנְיָא בֶּן עֲקַבְיָא, הָיְתָה סְמוּכָה לַכּוֹתֶל בִּפְחוֹת מִשְּׁלֹשָׁה טְפָחִים – צָרִיךְ שֶׁיְּהֵא אוֹרְכָּהּ אַרְבַּע אַמּוֹת וְרוֹחְבָּהּ אַחַד עָשָׂר וּמַשֶּׁהוּ.

Abaye said: And according to the statement of Rabbi Ḥananya ben Akavya, if the balcony **was less than three handbreadths** away **from the wall,** it is permitted to draw water from it in the following circumstances: **Its length must be four cubits, and its width** must be **eleven** handbreadths **and** any **amount.** By carving out a hole of slightly more than one handbreadth by four handbreadths on the side near the wall, alongside the other three handbreadths, one creates a hole of four handbreadths by four handbreadths. This hole is surrounded by partitions ten handbreadths high on each side. How so? The wall itself is one partition. The four-cubit length is viewed as bent down on both sides of the hole, forming two partitions of ten handbreadths; the remaining ten handbreadths of the width is seen as though it were bent down, which creates a partition on the fourth side of the balcony.[B]

הָיְתָה זְקוּפָה – צָרִיךְ שֶׁיְּהֵא גּוֹבְהָהּ עֲשָׂרָה טְפָחִים, וְרוֹחְבָּהּ שִׁשָּׁה טְפָחִים וּשְׁנֵי מַשֶּׁהוּיִין.

If the balcony **was upright,**[N] i.e., it had upright partitions on all sides (Rabbeinu Ḥananel),[B] **the height** of these partitions **must be ten handbreadths, and the width** of the balcony must be **six handbreadths and two** minimal **amounts.** This leaves slightly more than a handbreadth on each side of the hole of four handbreadths, on which he can stand.[B]

אָמַר רַב הוּנָא בְּרֵיהּ דְּרַב יְהוֹשֻׁעַ: הָיְתָה עוֹמֶדֶת בְּקֶרֶן זָוִית – צָרִיךְ שֶׁיְּהֵא גּוֹבְהָהּ עֲשָׂרָה טְפָחִים, וְרוֹחְבָּהּ שְׁנֵי טְפָחִים וּשְׁנֵי מַשֶּׁהוּיִין.

Rav Huna, son of Rav Yehoshua, said: If it **was positioned in a corner**[N] between two walls (Rabbeinu Ḥananel),[B] **the height** of the partition **must be ten handbreadths, and the** requisite **width** of the balcony must be **two handbreadths and two** minimal **amounts.** As he is able to stand, he is provided with actual partitions.[B]

וְאֶלָּא הָא דְּתַנְיָא, רַבִּי חֲנַנְיָא בֶּן עֲקַבְיָא אוֹמֵר: גְּזוּזְטְרָא שֶׁיֵּשׁ בָּהּ אַרְבַּע אַמּוֹת עַל אַרְבַּע אַמּוֹת – חוֹקֵק בָּהּ אַרְבָּעָה עַל אַרְבָּעָה וּמְמַלֵּא, הֵיכִי מַשְׁכַּחַתְ לַהּ?

The Gemara asks: **However,** with regard to **that which is taught** in a *baraita* that **Rabbi Ḥananya ben Akavya said:** If **a balcony** that **has** an area of **four cubits by four cubits** is suspended above water, **one carves in it** a hole of **four by four** handbreadths **and** then **draws** water through it, under **what circumstances** can a balcony with these dimensions **be found?**

דַּעֲבִידָא כִּי אָסִיתָא.

The Gemara answers: It is necessary in the case of a balcony **that is built in the shape of a mortar,** where the balcony is positioned over the water on its own pillars and far removed from any wall. In that case, all of the partitions must be constructed from its floor space. And the balcony must be four cubits by four cubits in size.

NOTES

Upright balcony – גְּזוּזְטְרָא זְקוּפָה: According to Rashi, this balcony has no floor and consists only of a partition positioned upright at a distance of four handbreadths from the wall. The ends of the balcony are viewed as though they are bent toward the wall, which creates a space of four by four handbreadths in the middle, surrounded by the wall on one side and the actual partition of the balcony on the opposite side. The other two partitions are formed by application of the principle of *lavud*.

Rabbeinu Ḥananel and other commentaries maintain that the term upright balcony is referring to a regular balcony with partitions ten handbreadths high on each side, enclosing a space of more than six by six handbreadths. In the center of the balcony there is a hole, four by four handbreadths in size. This leaves more than one handbreadth on each side for one's feet. It is necessary for there to be more than a handbreadth due to the height and the danger involved.

If it was positioned in a corner – הָיְתָה עוֹמֶדֶת בְּקֶרֶן זָוִית: According to Rashi, this case is referring to an upright board ten handbreadths high and slightly more than two handbreadths wide, positioned opposite the corner. This forms a space of four handbreadths in the middle, as the wall is a partition from two sides, while the other two partitions are formed with this board by means of the principle of *lavud*.

Rabbeinu Ḥananel explains that we are dealing with an upright balcony that closes off the corner between two walls in a triangular shape. The height of the third partition is ten handbreadths, while the floor need be only two handbreadths alongside the walls, so that it forms an area suitable for standing.

BACKGROUND

Upright balcony – גְּזוּזְטְרָא זְקוּפָה: The image below illustrates Rabbeinu Ḥananel's interpretation. He explains that the discussion in the Gemara is referring to a balcony enclosed by partitions ten handbreadths in height. Consequently, the partition must be ten handbreadths high, while the requisite width of the porch is six handbreadths on all sides, leaving slightly more than one handbreadth on each side of the hole.

Upright balcony according to Rabbeinu Ḥananel

Upright balcony – גְּזוּזְטְרָא זְקוּפָה: Rashi's explanation is illustrated by this picture of a balcony that consists of a lone wooden board, ten handbreadths high and six handbreadths wide. This board is viewed as though it were bent inward by a handbreadth on each side, along the dotted lines. It forms a space four handbreadths long, between the broken lines, and four handbreadths wide, closed in by folding the board toward the wall. The board is considered to be joined to the wall by means of *lavud*.

Upright balcony according to Rashi

A balcony in a corner – גְּזוּזְטְרָא בְּקֶרֶן זָוִית: According to Rabbeinu Ḥananel, this case pertains to a triangular porch situated in a corner between two walls. It has a partition of ten handbreadths, and a floor that need be only two handbreadths along the walls, upon which one can stand while drawing water from below.

Balcony in a corner according to Rabbeinu Ḥananel

A balcony in a corner – גְּזוּזְטְרָא בְּקֶרֶן זָוִית: According to Rashi, it is sufficient if the corner porch is a post ten handbreadths high and two handbreadths wide. If this post is positioned within three handbreadths of one of the walls, it forms a partition ten handbreadths high and four handbreadths wide on one side. If it is within four handbreadths of the other wall, one handbreadth of the post is viewed as though it were bent toward that wall, forming another partition of four handbreadths. In this manner, the hole is surrounded on all sides.

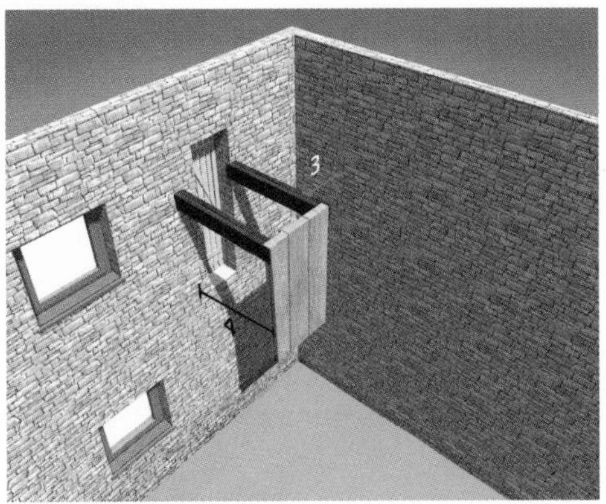

Balcony in a corner according to Rashi

מתני׳ אַמַּת הַמַּיִם שֶׁהִיא עוֹבֶרֶת בֶּחָצֵר – אֵין מְמַלְּאִין הֵימֶנָּה בְּשַׁבָּת, אֶלָּא אִם כֵּן עָשׂוּ לָהּ מְחִיצָּה גָּבוֹהַּ עֲשָׂרָה טְפָחִים בַּכְּנִיסָה וּבַיְּצִיאָה. רַבִּי יְהוּדָה אוֹמֵר: כּוֹתֶל שֶׁעַל גַּבָּהּ תִּידּוֹן מִשּׁוּם מְחִיצָּה.

MISHNA With regard to **a water channel**[N] **that passes through a courtyard,**[H] the residents **may not draw** water **from it on Shabbat, unless they erected for it a partition ten handbreadths high at the entrance and at the exit** of the courtyard. **Rabbi Yehuda says:** There is no need for a special partition, as the **wall that** runs **on top of it,** i.e., the courtyard wall, **is considered as a partition.**

אָמַר רַבִּי יְהוּדָה: מַעֲשֶׂה בְּאַמָּה שֶׁל אָבֵל שֶׁהָיוּ מְמַלְּאִין מִמֶּנָּה עַל פִּי זְקֵנִים בַּשַּׁבָּת. אָמְרוּ לוֹ: מִפְּנֵי שֶׁלֹּא הָיָה בָּהּ כַּשִּׁיעוּר.

Rabbi Yehuda said: There was **an incident involving a** water **channel** that passed through the courtyards **of** the town of **Avel,** from **which** the residents **would draw** water **from it on Shabbat by the authority of the Elders,** relying on the courtyard wall suspended above it. **They said to him:** It is **due to** the fact that channel **was not of the size** that requires a partition, i.e., it was less than ten handbreadths deep or less than ten handbreadths wide, it was permitted to draw water from it even without a partition.

גמ׳ תָּנוּ רַבָּנַן: עָשׂוּ לָהּ בַּכְּנִיסָה וְלֹא עָשׂוּ לָהּ בַּיְּצִיאָה, עָשׂוּ לָהּ בַּיְּצִיאָה וְלֹא עָשׂוּ לָהּ בַּכְּנִיסָה – אֵין מְמַלְּאִין הֵימֶנָּה בַּשַּׁבָּת, אֶלָּא אִם כֵּן עָשׂוּ לָהּ מְחִיצָּה עֲשָׂרָה טְפָחִים בַּיְּצִיאָה וּבַכְּנִיסָה. רַבִּי יְהוּדָה אוֹמֵר: כּוֹתֶל שֶׁעַל גַּבָּהּ תִּידּוֹן מִשּׁוּם מְחִיצָּה.

GEMARA **The Sages taught** in a *baraita*: If **they erected** a partition **for** the water channel **at the entrance but they did not erect** one **for it at the exit,** or if **they erected** a partition **for it at the exit but they did not erect** one **for it at the entrance, one may not draw** water **from it on Shabbat, unless they erected for it a partition ten handbreadths** high both **at the exit and at the entrance. Rabbi Yehuda says: The wall** that runs **on top of it,** i.e., the courtyard wall, **is considered as a partition.** Therefore, there is no need for a special partition.

אָמַר רַבִּי יְהוּדָה: מַעֲשֶׂה בְּאַמַּת הַמַּיִם שֶׁהָיְתָה בָּאָה מֵאָבֵל לְצִפּוֹרִי, וְהָיוּ מְמַלְּאִין הֵימֶנָּה בַּשַּׁבָּת עַל פִּי הַזְּקֵנִים.

Rabbi Yehuda said: There was **an incident involving the water channel that went from Avel to Tzippori,**[B] **and** the residents **would draw** water **from it on Shabbat by the authority of the Elders,** without any additional partition.

אָמְרוּ לוֹ: מִשָּׁם רְאָיָה?! מִפְּנֵי שֶׁלֹּא הָיְתָה עֲמוּקָּה עֲשָׂרָה טְפָחִים וְרוֹחְבָּהּ אַרְבָּעָה.

They said to him: Are you trying to bring **a proof from there?** That was either **due to** the fact that the channel **was not ten handbreadths deep or** because it was not **four** handbreadths **wide.** It lacked the requisite measure to be considered a domain in its own right. Everyone agrees that it is permitted to draw water from it even without an additional partition.

תַּנְיָא אִידָךְ: אַמַּת הַמַּיִם הָעוֹבֶרֶת בֵּין הַחַלּוֹנוֹת, פָּחוֹת מִשְּׁלֹשָׁה – מְשַׁלְשֵׁל דְּלִי וּמְמַלֵּא, שְׁלֹשָׁה – אֵין מְשַׁלְשֵׁל דְּלִי וּמְמַלֵּא. רַבָּן שִׁמְעוֹן בֶּן גַּמְלִיאֵל אוֹמֵר: פָּחוֹת מֵאַרְבָּעָה – מְשַׁלְשֵׁל דְּלִי וּמְמַלֵּא. אַרְבָּעָה – אֵין מְשַׁלְשֵׁל דְּלִי וּמְמַלֵּא.

It was taught in another *baraita*: With regard to **a water channel that passes between the windows**[BH] of two houses, if it is **less than three** handbreadths, **one may lower a bucket** from the window **and draw** water from it; however, if it is **three** handbreadths, **one may not lower a bucket and draw** water from it. **Rabban Shimon ben Gamliel says:** If it is **less than four** handbreadths, **one may lower a bucket and draw** water from it; but if it is at least **four** handbreadths, **one may not lower a bucket and draw** water.

בְּמַאי עָסְקִינַן? אִילֵימָא בְּאַמַּת הַמַּיִם גּוּפָהּ, וְאֶלָּא הָא דְּכִי אֲתָא רַב דִּימִי, אָמַר רַבִּי יוֹחָנָן: אֵין כַּרְמְלִית פְּחוּתָה מֵאַרְבָּעָה –

With regard to these measures of three and four handbreadths, the Gemara asks: **With what are we dealing** here? **If you say** this *halakha* is referring **to the water channel itself,** that it was three or four handbreadths wide, this presents a difficulty, **for when Rav Dimi came** from Eretz Yisrael to Babylonia, he said that **Rabbi Yoḥanan said: A** ***karmelit*** **cannot be less than four** handbreadths wide. The *karmelit* is an intermediate domain established by the Sages, whose status is between a public and a private domain. Any open area that is not a public thoroughfare, e.g., a field, sea, river, alleyway, or a lane, is classified as a *karmelit*. It is prohibited to carry an article four cubits within a *karmelit*, or to transfer an object from a private domain or a public domain to a *karmelit*, or vice versa. One who draws water through a window from a water channel into a house has carried from a *karmelit* to a private domain. Consequently, if the *tanna'im* of the *baraita* dispute the width of the channel, they are in effect disagreeing about the minimal size of a *karmelit*.

לֵימָא כְּתַנָּאֵי אֲמָרָהּ לִשְׁמַעְתֵּיהּ?

The Gemara resumes its question: **Let us say,** then, that **the teaching that** Rav Dimi **cited,** that a *karmelit* cannot be less than four handbreadths wide, was actually the subject of a dispute of ***tanna'im*** and not a unanimous *halakha*.

NOTES

A water channel and an inlet – אַמַּת מַיִם וּלְשׁוֹן יָם: The early commentaries ask: In the beginning of the tractate, the Sages stated that if an inlet entered a courtyard and the courtyard wall passed above it, it is permitted to use the water. Why doesn't the same principle apply to a water channel? The Rashba answers that since the water in the channel, as opposed to the water in an inlet, flows in and out of the courtyard, it does not become part of the courtyard.

BACKGROUND

Avel and Tzippori – אָבֵל וְצִפּוֹרִי: The water channel mentioned by Rabbi Yehuda ran for several kilometers from the town of Avel before joining the water supply of Tzippori, a relatively large city.

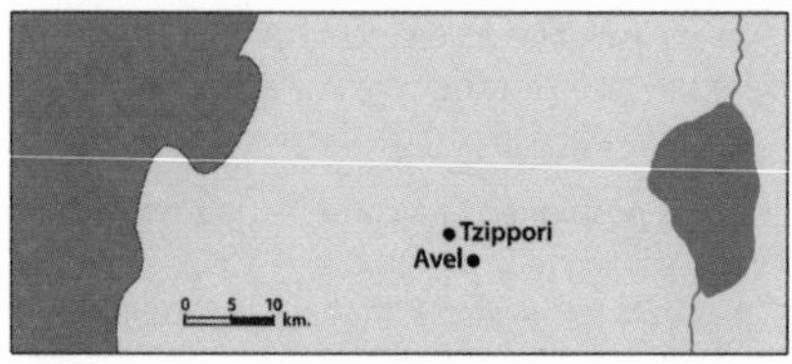

Map showing the relative locations of the towns of Avel and Tzippori

A water channel that passes between the windows – אַמַּת הַמַּיִם הָעוֹבֶרֶת בֵּין הַחַלּוֹנוֹת:

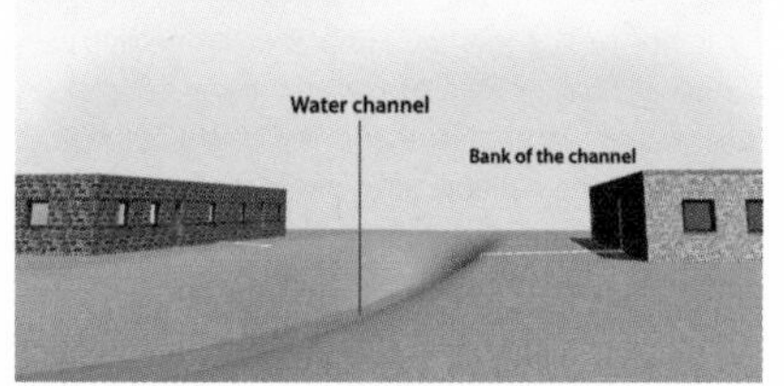

Water channel that passes between the windows of two houses

HALAKHA

A water channel in a courtyard – אַמַּת הַמַּיִם בְּחָצֵר: If a water channel ten handbreadths deep and four handbreadths wide passes through a courtyard, it is permitted to draw water from it only if a partition ten handbreadths high has been erected at its entrance and at its exit. A channel of smaller dimensions shares the status of the domain in which it is located (*Shulḥan Arukh, Oraḥ Ḥayyim* 356:1).

A water channel that passes between the windows – אַמַּת הַמַּיִם הָעוֹבֶרֶת בֵּין הַחַלּוֹנוֹת: If a water channel ten handbreadths deep and four handbreadths wide has partitions at both ends, each constructed from two parts, the partitions have the legal status of solid partitions if they are within three handbreadths of each other, and it is therefore permitted to draw water from the channel. If a water channel does not have such partitions, the residents may not draw water from the channel, in accordance with Ravina's explanation of the *baraita* (*Shulḥan Arukh, Oraḥ Ḥayyim* 356:1).

אֶלָּא בַּאֲגַפֶּיהָ, וּלְהַחֲלִיף.

The Gemara rejects the previous explanation. **Rather,** the measure of three or four handbreadths is referring not to the channel itself but **to the banks** of the channel, **and** it is stated **with regard to** an act of **exchange.** The dispute here does not concern the measure of a *karmelit*, but the measure of an exempt domain. It is permitted to transfer the empty bucket from the window, which is a private domain, by way of the channel's banks, which are exempt domains, to the water channel, which is a *karmelit*, and back again with the full bucket.

וְהָא כִּי אֲתָא רַב דִּימִי, אָמַר רַבִּי יוֹחָנָן: מָקוֹם שֶׁאֵין בּוֹ אַרְבָּעָה עַל אַרְבָּעָה – מוּתָּר לִבְנֵי רְשׁוּת הַיָּחִיד וְלִבְנֵי רְשׁוּת הָרַבִּים לְכַתֵּף עָלָיו, וּבִלְבַד שֶׁלֹּא יַחֲלִיפוּ!

The Gemara raises a difficulty: **But when Rav Dimi came** from Eretz Yisrael to Babylonia, **he said** that **Rabbi Yoḥanan said: A place that does not have** an area of **four by four** handbreadths is an **exempt domain.** Consequently, if this place is situated between a public domain and a private domain, **it is permitted for** both **the people of the private domain and for the people of the public domain to** adjust the burdens on their **shoulders on it, provided** that **they do not exchange** objects between them via the exempt domain. How, then, can the bucket be transferred from the window to the channel, and vice versa, by means of the banks?

הָתָם רְשׁוּיוֹת דְּאוֹרַיְיתָא,

The Gemara answers: **There,** Rav Dimi is referring to **domains by Torah law,** i.e., this *halakha* involves the transfer of objects from a private domain to a public domain via an exempt domain. The Sages forbade this activity, so that people would not transfer objects directly from the private domain to the public domain.

Perek **VIII**
Daf **87** Amud **b**

הָכָא רְשׁוּיוֹת דְּרַבָּנַן.

However, **here,** Rav Dimi is referring to **domains by rabbinic law.** As the transfer of objects from a private domain to a *karmelit* is prohibited only by rabbinic decree, the Sages did not prohibit this transfer when it is accomplished by way of an exempt domain.

וְהָא רַבִּי יוֹחָנָן בִּרְשׁוּיוֹת דְּרַבָּנַן נַמִּי אָמַר, (דְּתַנְיָא:) כּוֹתֶל שֶׁבֵּין שְׁתֵּי חֲצֵירוֹת גָּבוֹהַּ עֲשָׂרָה טְפָחִים וְרוֹחַב אַרְבָּעָה – מְעָרְבִין שְׁנַיִם, וְאֵין מְעָרְבִין אֶחָד.

The Gemara raises a difficulty: **But Rabbi Yoḥanan said** that transferring objects from one domain to another by way of an exempt domain is prohibited **even in** the case of **domains** that apply **by rabbinic law. As we learned** in a mishna: In the case of **a wall that is between two courtyards,** if it is **ten handbreadths high and four** handbreadths **wide,** the residents **establish two *eiruvin*,** a separate one for each courtyard, **but they do not establish one** joint ***eiruv*.**

הָיוּ בְּרֹאשׁוֹ פֵּירוֹת – אֵלּוּ עוֹלִין מִכָּאן וְאוֹכְלִין, וְאֵלּוּ עוֹלִין מִכָּאן וְאוֹכְלִין.

If there was produce on top of the wall, **these,** the residents of one courtyard, **may ascend from this** side **and eat** them, **and those,** the residents of the other courtyard, **may ascend from the other** side **and eat** them, provided that they do not bring the produce down from the top of the wall to the courtyards.

נִפְרַץ הַכּוֹתֶל, עַד עֶשֶׂר אַמּוֹת – מְעָרְבִין שְׁנַיִם, וְאִם רָצוּ – מְעָרְבִין אֶחָד, מִפְּנֵי שֶׁהוּא כַּפֶּתַח. יוֹתֵר מִכָּאן – מְעָרְבִין אֶחָד וְאֵין מְעָרְבִין שְׁנַיִם.

If **the wall is breached,** a distinction applies: If the breach is **up to ten cubits** wide, **they may establish two *eiruvin*, and if they wish, they may establish one *eiruv*, for it is like an entrance.** This breach is similar to any opening of less than ten cubits. If the breach is **more than this, they may establish one *eiruv*, but they may not establish two *eiruvin*.** A breach of this size nullifies the partition, as the two courtyards merge into a single domain.

וְהָוֵינַן בָּהּ: אֵין בּוֹ אַרְבָּעָה מַאי? אָמַר רַב: אֲוִיר שְׁתֵּי רְשׁוּיוֹת שׁוֹלֶטֶת בּוֹ, וְלֹא יָזִיז בּוֹ מְלֹא נִימָא.

And we discussed this mishna and raised a question: If this wall **is not four** handbreadths thick, **what is the** *halakha*? **Rav said:** In that case, **the air of two domains controls it.** As the wall is not broad enough to be considered a domain of its own, its top belongs to both courtyards, and it is therefore prohibited to both of them. Accordingly, **one may not move** anything **on** top of the wall even as much as **a hairsbreadth.**

NOTES

Let it be like the cavities of a *karmelit* – תֶּיהֱוֵי כִּי חוֹרֵי כַּרְמְלִית: Rabbeinu Ḥananel explains that essentially the Gemara is asking why the status of the windows of the house is not determined by that of the water channel. The water channel is a *karmelit*; therefore, the windows should be considered the cavities of a *karmelit*, and drawing water from the channel through the windows should be permitted. The answer given is that the *halakha* governing the cavities of a *karmelit* applies only to cavities that are adjacent to the *karmelit*, whereas here the windows are far from the *karmelit*. Consequently, it does not determine their status.

Where one fashioned outlets – דַּעֲבַד לָהּ נִיפְקֵי: According to some commentaries, Ravina is saying that when the *baraita* speaks of a water channel that passes between windows, it is not referring to the windows of the houses that are adjacent to the channel. Rather, the Gemara is speaking of the openings through which the channel passes (Rabbi Zeraḥya HaLevi).

BACKGROUND

Fashioned outlets for the water channel – עֲבַד לָהּ נִיפְקֵי:

Water channel with a gap in the partition to enable water flow

וְרַבִּי יוֹחָנָן אָמַר: אֵלּוּ מַעֲלִין מִכָּאן וְאוֹכְלִין, וְאֵלּוּ מַעֲלִין מִכָּאן וְאוֹכְלִין.

And Rabbi Yoḥanan disagreed and **said: These,** the residents of one courtyard, **may carry up** their food **from** their courtyard to the top of the wall **and eat** it there, **and those,** the residents of the other courtyard, **may** likewise **carry up** their food **from** their courtyard **and eat** it there. The entire top of the wall has the status of an exempt domain that can be combined with either courtyard, provided that the residents of the different courtyards do not exchange food between them.

וְאָזְדָא רַבִּי יוֹחָנָן לְטַעְמֵיהּ, דְּכִי אֲתָא רַב דִּימִי, אָמַר רַבִּי יוֹחָנָן: מָקוֹם שֶׁאֵין בּוֹ אַרְבָּעָה עַל אַרְבָּעָה – מוּתָּר לִבְנֵי רְשׁוּת הָרַבִּים וְלִבְנֵי רְשׁוּת הַיָּחִיד לְכַתֵּף עָלָיו, וּבִלְבַד שֶׁלֹּא יַחֲלִיפוּ!

And Rabbi Yoḥanan follows his regular line of **argument** here, **for when Rav Dimi came** from Eretz Yisrael to Babylonia, **he said** that **Rabbi Yoḥanan said: A place that contains less than four by four** handbreadths is an exempt domain. Consequently, if this place is located between a public domain and a private domain, **it is permitted for the people of the private domain and for the people of the public domain to load** their burdens **onto their shoulders in it, as long as they do not exchange** objects with each other by way of the exempt domain. Apparently, Rabbi Yoḥanan prohibited exchanging articles between two domains, even if they are rabbinic domains.

הַהִיא זְעֵירִי אֲמָרָהּ. וְלִזְעֵירִי קַשְׁיָא הָא!

The Gemara answers: **That** ruling concerning a wall between two courtyards, **Ze'eiri stated it** in the name of Rabbi Yoḥanan. Rav Dimi transmitted a different tradition of Rabbi Yoḥanan's opinion. The Gemara raises a difficulty: Nonetheless, **this** *halakha* concerning a water channel between two windows **is difficult according to Ze'eiri.**

מוֹקִים לָהּ בְּאַמַּת הַמַּיִם גּוּפַהּ. וְרַב דִּימִי תַּנָּאֵי הִיא.

The Gemara answers: Ze'eiri **explains** that the measures mentioned in the *baraita* are referring **to the water channel itself.** That is to say, the dispute between Rabban Shimon ben Gamliel and the Sages does not concern the width of the banks of the channel but the width of the channel itself, as they dispute the basic parameters of a *karmelit.* **And** Ze'eiri maintains that the teaching of **Rav Dimi,** that a *karmelit* can be no less than four handbreadths wide, **is** in fact the subject of a dispute between ***tanna'im.***

וְתֶיהֱוֵי כִּי חוֹרֵי כַּרְמְלִית!

The Gemara raises a difficulty: **And let** the water channel that passes through the courtyard **be** treated at least **like the cavities of a *karmelit,***[N] even if it is not wide enough to be considered a *karmelit* on its own. Just as the cavities in the wall of a private domain are considered a private domain even if they do not include the prescribed measure of a private domain, the water channel passing through the courtyard should likewise be considered as a cavity of the larger water channel in the street. It should therefore have the status of a *karmelit.*

אַבָּיֵי בַּר אָבִין וְרַב חֲנִינָא בַּר אָבִין דְּאָמְרִי תַּרְוַיְיהוּ: אֵין חוֹרִין לְכַרְמְלִית.

The Gemara answers: **Abaye bar Avin and Rav Ḥanina bar Avin both said: There is no** category of **cavities for a *karmelit.*** As a *karmelit* is only a rabbinic in origin, the *halakha* is not so stringent with regard to this domain. Consequently, a *karmelit* does not annex nearby cavities.

רַב אָשֵׁי אָמַר: אֲפִילּוּ תֵּימָא יֵשׁ חוֹרִין לְכַרְמְלִית – הָנֵי מִילֵּי בִּסְמוּכָה, הָכָא בְּמוּפְלֶגֶת.

Rav Ashi said: You can **even say** that in general **there are holes for** a ***karmelit,*** but **this applies only to** holes that are **adjacent** to the *karmelit,* and are therefore nullified by it. **Here, however,** we are dealing with a water channel **that is** far **removed** from the *karmelit.* Therefore, it does not assume the status of the *karmelit.*

רָבִינָא אָמַר: כְּגוֹן דַּעֲבַד לָהּ נִיפְקֵי אַפּוּמָּהּ.

Ravina said a different explanation of the dispute between Rabban Shimon ben Gamliel and the Rabbis: The measures of three and four handbreadths refer neither to the width of the water trench nor to the width of its banks. Rather, we are dealing with a case **where one fashioned outlets**[N] **for** the water channel[B] **at its ends,** i.e., one formed gaps in the partitions to allow the water to flow.

וְאָזְדוּ רַבָּנַן לְטַעְמַיְיהוּ, וְרַבִּי שִׁמְעוֹן בֶּן גַּמְלִיאֵל לְטַעְמֵיהּ.

And the Rabbis follow their regular line of **argument,** that the principle of *lavud* applies only to a gap less than three handbreadths wide. An opening less than three handbreadths is therefore considered completely closed, while one of four is not viewed as closed. **And Rabban Shimon ben Gamliel follows his** regular line of **argument,** that the principle of *lavud* applies even to a gap of four handbreadths.

מתני׳ גְּזוּזְטְרָא שֶׁהִיא לְמַעְלָה מִן הַמַּיִם – אֵין מְמַלְּאִין הֵימֶנָּה בְּשַׁבָּת, אֶלָּא אִם כֵּן עָשׂוּ לָהּ מְחִיצָּה גְּבוֹהָה עֲשָׂרָה טְפָחִים, בֵּין מִלְּמַעְלָה בֵּין מִלְּמַטָּה.

MISHNA With regard to **a balcony that** extends **over** a body of **water,**[H] if a hole was opened in the floor, its residents **may not draw** water **from** it through the hole **on Shabbat, unless they erected for it a partition ten handbreadths high** around the hole. It is permitted to draw water by means of that partition, **whether** it is positioned **above** the balcony, in which case the partition is seen as descending downward, **or** whether it is placed **below** the balcony.[N]

וְכֵן שְׁתֵּי גְּזוּזְטְרָאוֹת זוֹ לְמַעְלָה מִזּוֹ, עָשׂוּ לָעֶלְיוֹנָה וְלֹא עָשׂוּ לַתַּחְתּוֹנָה – שְׁתֵּיהֶן אֲסוּרוֹת עַד שֶׁיְּעָרְבוּ.

And likewise, with regard to **two** such **balconies, one above the other,**[H] if **they erected** a partition **for the upper balcony but they did not erect** one **for the lower one,**[B] the residents **are both prohibited** from drawing water through the upper one, **unless they establish an** ***eiruv*** between them.

גמ׳ מַתְנִיתִין דְּלֹא כַּחֲנַנְיָא בֶּן עֲקַבְיָא. דְּתַנְיָא, חֲנַנְיָא בֶּן עֲקַבְיָא אוֹמֵר: גְּזוּזְטְרָא שֶׁיֵּשׁ בָּהּ אַרְבַּע עַל אַרְבַּע אַמּוֹת – חוֹקֵק בָּהּ אַרְבָּעָה עַל אַרְבָּעָה וּמְמַלֵּא.

GEMARA The Gemara comments: **The mishna is not in accordance with** the opinion **of Ḥananya ben Akavya, as it was taught** in a *baraita* that **Ḥananya ben Akavya says: If a balcony that contains four** cubits **by four cubits** is suspended above water, **one may carve out** a hole of **four** handbreadths **by four** handbreadths **in it and draw** water through it. The section of the floor surrounding the hole is considered as though it bent downward and formed a partition ten handbreadths high on all sides. Consequently, no other partition is necessary.

אָמַר רַבִּי יוֹחָנָן מִשּׁוּם רַבִּי יוֹסֵי בֶּן זִימְרָא: לֹא הִתִּיר רַבִּי חֲנַנְיָא בֶּן עֲקַבְיָא אֶלָּא בְּיַמָּהּ שֶׁל טְבֶרְיָא, הוֹאִיל וְיֵשׁ לָהּ אוֹגָנִים, וַעֲיָירוֹת וְקַרְפֵּיפוֹת מַקִּיפוֹת אוֹתָהּ. אֲבָל בִּשְׁאָר מֵימוֹת לֹא.

Rabbi Yoḥanan said in the name of Rabbi Yosei ben Zimra: Rabbi Ḥananya ben Akavya permitted a balcony that is not surrounded by partitions **only in** the case of **the Sea of Tiberias,** the Sea of Galilee, **as it has** clearly defined **banks** that are visible on all sides, **and towns and enclosures surround it.** It is therefore considered part of an inhabited area. **But with regard to other waters,** such as larger seas, **no,** he did not permit them.

תָּנוּ רַבָּנַן: שְׁלֹשָׁה דְּבָרִים הִתִּיר רַבִּי חֲנַנְיָא בֶּן עֲקַבְיָא לְאַנְשֵׁי טְבֶרְיָא: מְמַלְּאִין מַיִם מִגְּזוּזְטְרָא בְּשַׁבָּת, וְטוֹמְנִין בְּעָצָה, וּמִסְתַּפְּגִין בַּאֲלוּנְטִית.

Our Sages taught a *baraita*: **Rabbi Ḥananya ben Akavya permitted three activities to the inhabitants of Tiberias: They may draw water** from the sea **through** a hole cut out of **a balcony on Shabbat, and they may insulate** produce **in the pods** of legumes,[N] **and they may dry themselves** on Shabbat **with a towel** [*aluntit*].[L]

מְמַלְּאִין מַיִם מִגְּזוּזְטְרָא בְּשַׁבָּת – הָא דַּאֲמָרַן. וְטוֹמְנִין בְּעָצָה מַאי הִיא? דְּתַנְיָא: הִשְׁכִּים לְהָבִיא פְּסוֹלֶת, אִם בִּשְׁבִיל שֶׁיֵּשׁ עָלָיו טַל – הֲרֵי הוּא בְּ״כִי יוּתַּן״,

The Gemara clarifies this *baraita*: **They may draw water through** a hole cut out of **a balcony on Shabbat** is the *halakha* **that we stated** above. **And they may insulate** produce **in the pods** of legumes; **what is this** *halakha*? **As it was taught** in a *baraita*: If one **rose early** in the morning **to bring residue** from the field, e.g., the straw of wheat or the stalks or pods of legumes, in order to store his produce in them, the following distinction applies: **If** he rose early **because** the residue still **has dew on it,** and he wants to use this moisture for his produce, **this** instance **is considered** to be in the following category: **If** any water **be put.** Food or produce can contract ritual impurity only if it has come into contact with a liquid, either directly through the action of its owner, or without his direct intervention but with his approval. This is derived from the verse: "But if any water be put on the seed, and any part of their carcass falls on it, it shall be unclean to you" (Leviticus 11:38). Returning to our issue, if this person rose early because the residue still has dew on it, the produce he stores in it is rendered susceptible to ritual impurity, as it has come into contact with the dew with its owner's approval.

וְאִם בִּשְׁבִיל שֶׁלֹּא יְבַטֵּל מִמְּלַאכְתּוֹ – אֵינוֹ בְּ״כִי יוּתַּן״. וּסְתָם

And if one rose early only **in order not to neglect his** usual **work,** this **is not considered** an instance of **if it be put,** as it was not his intention to place the dew on the produce. Unintended contact with a liquid does not render food susceptible to ritual impurity. **And normally,** unless they specify otherwise,

HALAKHA

A balcony above water – גְּזוּזְטְרָא מֵעַל מַיִם: With regard to a balcony that extends over water, which has an entrance opening onto it from the house, it is only permitted to draw water from a hole in the middle of the balcony if it is enclosed by a partition ten handbreadths high, either above or below the balcony (*Shulḥan Arukh*, *Oraḥ Ḥayyim* 355:1).

Balconies one above the other – גְּזוּזְטְרָאוֹת זוֹ מֵעַל זוֹ: With regard to two balconies that extend over water, one above the other, which are not within ten handbreadths of each other, if the residents of the balconies jointly established a partition for the upper one but they did not establish one for the lower one at all, the residents of both balconies are prohibited to draw water through the holes in either balcony unless they establish a joint *eiruv* (*Shulḥan Arukh*, *Oraḥ Ḥayyim* 355:1).

NOTES

A partition above and below – מְחִיצָּה לְמַעְלָה וּלְמַטָּה: The commentaries explain that the word above means they erected a partition beneath the balcony itself, while the word below indicates that they erected it inside the water (*Tosafot*; Ritva).

Insulating in the pods of legumes – טְמִינָה בְּעָצָה: Several commentaries explain that this *halakha* includes the act of insulating hot food inside the refuse of straw and stubble to preserve its heat. The mishna prohibits insulating food inside moist straw on Shabbat, as this might add heat to the food. Rabbi Ḥananya ben Akavya states that it is permitted to insulate food in the dry legume pods owned by the inhabitants of Tiberias on Shabbat, as they do not want the pods to be moist. Consequently, there is no cause for concern (Rabbeinu Ḥananel; *ge'onim*).

BACKGROUND

The partitions of a balcony – מְחִיצוֹת גְּזוּזְטְרָא: The image below is of a balcony with partitions built on top of it. In order to permit drawing water on Shabbat through the balcony, one could build the partitions on the bottom of the balcony, as portrayed in this image by the translucent partitions.

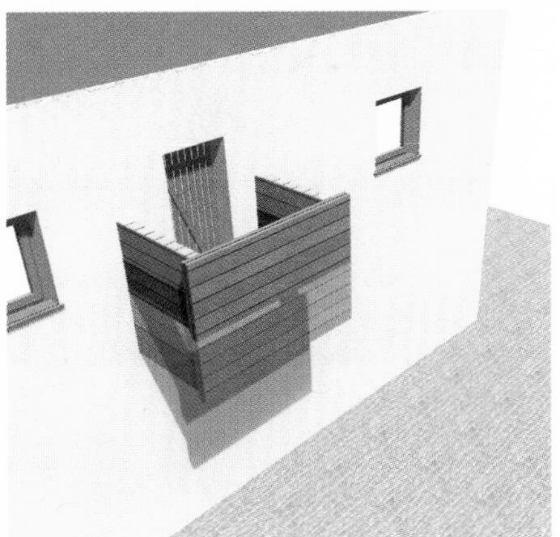

Balcony enclosed by partitions

LANGUAGE

Towel [*aluntit*] – אֲלוּנְטִית: From the Greek λέντιον, *lentiyon*, or from the Latin linteum, a linen towel.

אַנְשֵׁי טְבֶרְיָא כְּמִי שֶׁלֹּא יְבַטֵּל מִמְּלַאכְתּוֹ דָּמֵי.

the inhabitants of Tiberias are considered **like one** who does so in order **not to neglect his** usual **work.** Most of them are ordinary laborers. It can be assumed that if they rose early to bring home straw or stalks in which to store their produce, they did so only to save work time.

וּמִסְתַּפְּגִין בַּאֲלוּנְטִית מַאי הִיא? דְּתַנְיָא: מִסְתַּפֵּג אָדָם בַּאֲלוּנְטִית וּמַנִּיחָהּ בַּחַלּוֹן, וְלֹא יִמְסְרֶנָּה לְאוֹלַיְירִין, מִפְּנֵי שֶׁחֲשׁוּדִין עַל אוֹתוֹ דָּבָר. רַבִּי שִׁמְעוֹן אוֹמֵר: אַף מְבִיאָהּ בְּיָדוֹ לְתוֹךְ בֵּיתוֹ.

The Gemara turns to the third activity that Rabbi Ḥananya ben Akavya permitted for the inhabitants of Tiberias: **And they may dry themselves with a towel. What is** this *halakha*? **As it was taught** in a *baraita*: **A person** who washed himself in cold water on Shabbat or a Festival **may dry himself with a towel**[H] **and place it on a window,** as there is no concern that he perform the prohibited labor of wringing out the towel. **And he may not give** the towel **to the bathhouse attendants** [*olayerin*][L] **because they are suspected with regard to that matter,** as they might wring out the towel before giving it to other bathers. Furthermore, one may not bring the towel home because if he does so, he might forget and wring it out. **Rabbi Shimon said: He may even bring** the towel **in his hand to his house,** as there is no concern lest he wring it.

אָמַר רַבָּה בַּר רַב הוּנָא: לֹא שָׁנוּ אֶלָּא לְמַלְאוֹת, אֲבָל לִשְׁפּוֹךְ – אָסוּר.

Rabba bar Rav Huna: They taught the leniency of partitions surrounding a hole in a balcony **only** with regard **to drawing** water through the hole; **but to pour** waste water down the hole, it is **prohibited.**

מַתְקִיף לָהּ רַב שֵׁיזְבִי: וְכִי מָה בֵּין זֶה לְעוּקָה?

Rav Sheizvi raised an objection against this *halakha*: **And what is** the difference **between this** case of a hole in the balcony **and** that of **a pit** [*uka*][L] used in a courtyard for waste water? The Sages rule in the next mishna below that one who digs a pit with a capacity of two *se'a* in a small courtyard that is less than four cubits may pour waste water into the courtyard on Shabbat, even if the pit was full before Shabbat. He need not be concerned that this will cause water to flow out of the courtyard into the public domain on Shabbat.

הָנֵי תָּיְימִי, וְהָנֵי לָא תָּיְימִי.

The Gemara answers: **These** waters, which are poured out into the courtyard, **are** likely to be **absorbed** into the ground, and it is therefore uncertain that the water will indeed leave the courtyard. **But these,** the water poured through the hole into the body of water under the balcony, **will not be absorbed.** Therefore, one knows with certainty that the water will flow out beyond the permitted boundary.

אִיכָּא דְּאָמְרִי, אָמַר רַבָּה בַּר רַב הוּנָא: לָא תֵּימָא לְמַלְאוֹת הוּא דְּשָׁרֵי, לִשְׁפּוֹךְ אָסוּר, אֶלָּא, לִשְׁפּוֹךְ נַמִי שָׁרֵי. אֲמַר רַב שֵׁיזְבִי: פְּשִׁיטָא! הַיְינוּ עוּקָה! מַהוּ דְּתֵימָא: הָנֵי תָּיְימִי, וְהָנֵי לָא תָּיְימִי, קָא מַשְׁמַע לָן.

Some say that **Rabba bar Rav Huna** actually **said: You should not say that it is** only **drawing** water through the hole in the balcony **that is permitted,** while **pouring** waste water through it **is prohibited; rather, pouring** waste water through the hole **is also permitted.**[H] **Rav Sheizvi said:** This is **obvious,** as **this is** exactly the same as the *halakha* of the **pit** discussed in the next mishna. The Gemara rejects this argument: It is necessary to specify both *halakhot*, **lest you say** there is a difference between the cases, as **these,** the water poured in the courtyard, **are** likely to be **absorbed** into the ground, **whereas these,** the water poured through the hole in the balcony, **will not be absorbed.** Rabba bar Rav Huna therefore **teaches us** that we do not distinguish between the two cases.

״וְכֵן שְׁתֵּי גְּזוּזְטְרָאוֹת זוֹ וכו׳״ אָמַר רַב הוּנָא, אָמַר רַב: לֹא שָׁנוּ אֶלָּא בִּסְמוּכָה, אֲבָל בִּמוּפְלֶגֶת – עֶלְיוֹנָה מוּתֶּרֶת.

We learned in the mishna: **And likewise,** if there are **two balconies, one** above the other, and a partition is erected for the upper balcony but is not erected for the lower one, it is prohibited for residents of both balconies to draw water through the upper one, unless they establish a joint *eiruv* between them. **Rav Huna said** that **Rav said: They taught** that one balcony renders it prohibited for residents of the other **only where** the one balcony **is near** the other, i.e., horizontally within four handbreadths. **But** if each balcony is **separated** by four handbreadths from the other,[H] so that the residents of each balcony can use the other only by means of the air, the residents of **the upper** balcony **are permitted** to draw water, while the residents of the lower one are prohibited from doing so.

HALAKHA

He may dry himself with a towel – מִסְתַּפֵּג בַּאֲלוּנְטִית: It is permitted to dry oneself with a towel on Shabbat, and even to bring it home. However, one may not give it to the bathhouse attendants because it is suspected that they will wring it out (*Shulḥan Arukh, Oraḥ Ḥayyim* 301:48).

Pouring is also permitted – לִשְׁפּוֹךְ נַמִי שָׁרֵי: It is permitted to pour waste water through a hole in a balcony, just as it is permitted to draw water through it. The *halakha* is in accordance with the second version of Rabba bar Rav Huna's teaching in the Gemara (*Shulḥan Arukh, Oraḥ Ḥayyim* 355:1).

Balconies separated from one another – גְּזוּזְטְרָאוֹת מוּפְלָגוֹת זוֹ מִזּוֹ: With regard to two adjacent balconies more than four handbreadths apart, the residents of the upper balcony are permitted to draw water. They are not prohibited from doing so by the lower one, in accordance with Rav (*Shulḥan Arukh, Oraḥ Ḥayyim* 355:5).

LANGUAGE

Bathhouse attendants [*olayerin*] – אוֹלַיְירִין: From the Latin olearius, which means a bathhouse attendant, or one who watches over the clothes at a bathhouse.

Pit [*uka*] – עוּקָה: A pit or a hole. The *Arukh* maintains that it is referring to a particular type of round hole. Others explain *uka* as an alternate form of *ḥuka*, a hollowed-out [*ḥakuka*] space.

וְרַב לְטַעְמֵיהּ, דְּאָמַר רַב: אֵין אָדָם אוֹסֵר עַל חֲבֵירוֹ דֶּרֶךְ אֲוִיר.

And Rav follows **his** regular line of **argument** here, **as Rav said: One person does not impose restrictions upon another person by way of the air.** Since the lower balcony is far from the higher one, it does not prohibit it, although it can make use of it by means of the vacant airspace between them, albeit with difficulty.

אָמַר רַבָּה, אָמַר רַבִּי חִיָּיא וְרַב יוֹסֵף, אָמַר רַבִּי אוֹשַׁעְיָא: יֵשׁ גָּזֵל בַּשַּׁבָּת, וְחוּרְבָּה מַחֲזִיר לַבְּעָלִים.

Rabba said that **Rabbi Ḥiyya said, and Rav Yosef said** that **Rabbi Oshaya said:** The *halakha* of **stealing applies to Shabbat** domains, **and a ruin must be returned to its owner.**

הָא גּוּפָא קַשְׁיָא! אָמְרַתְּ "יֵשׁ גָּזֵל בַּשַּׁבָּת" אַלְמָא קַנְיָא. "וְחוּרְבָּה מַחֲזִיר לַבְּעָלִים" אַלְמָא: לָא קַנְיָא!

The Gemara registers surprise: **This** ruling **itself is difficult,** i.e., it is self-contradictory. **You** first **said** that the *halakha* of **stealing applies to Shabbat** domains, which at this point is understood by the Gemara as referring to the following case: A person's house adjoins the ruin of another, and he observes that the ruin has been left deserted by its owner. If this person uses the ruin during the week, on Shabbat he may treat it as though it were his own, by carrying objects from his own house into the ruin and vice versa. **From here** we can infer that a stolen place **is acquired** for the purpose of Shabbat domains, although it does not belong to the person for other purposes. However, you subsequently said that **a ruin must be returned to its owner,** and **from here** we can infer that a ruin **is not acquired** for the purpose of Shabbat domains by the person who used it during the week, and therefore he may not carry objects from his own house into the ruin.

הָכִי קָאָמַר: יֵשׁ דִּין גָּזֵל בַּשַּׁבָּת. כֵּיצַד – דְּחוּרְבָּה מַחֲזִיר לַבְּעָלִים.

The Gemara answers: We should not understand this statement as suggested above, but rather **this is** what Rabbi Ḥiyya and Rabbi Oshaya **are saying: The *halakha* of** returning **stolen** property **applies to Shabbat**[N] domains. **How so?** This means **that a ruin must be returned to its owner.** In other words, one who uses a ruin during the week does not acquire it even for the purpose of Shabbat domains.

אָמַר רַבָּה: וּמוֹתְבִינַן אַשְׁמַעְתִּין: וְכֵן שְׁתֵּי גְּזוּזְטְרָאוֹת זוֹ לְמַעְלָה מִזּוֹ וכו׳. וְאִי אָמְרַתְּ יֵשׁ דִּין גָּזֵל בַּשַּׁבָּת, אַמַּאי אֲסוּרוֹת?

Rabba said: And we ourselves **raised an objection** against **our** own **teaching,** as we learned in the mishna. **And likewise,** if there are **two balconies, one above the other,** they prohibit one another. **But if you say** that **the *halakha*** against **stealing applies on Shabbat,** which means one may not use the domain of another, and he acquires no rights to it if he does so, **why** are the two balconies **prohibited** from using it. The lower one has no right to make use of the upper one.

אָמַר רַב שֵׁשֶׁת: הָכָא בְּמַאי עָסְקִינַן – כְּגוֹן שֶׁעָשׂוּ מְחִיצָה בְּשׁוּתָּפוּת.

Rav Sheshet said: We are dealing here with a situation **where, for example,** the residents of the upper balcony and the residents of the lower balcony **jointly erected a partition**[H] for the upper balcony. Consequently, the residents of the lower balcony share the right to use it with the residents of the upper one.

אִי הָכִי, כִּי עָשׂוּ לַתַּחְתּוֹנָה נָמִי!

The Gemara raises a difficulty: **If so,** in a case **where they erected** a separate partition **for the lower** balcony, the residents of the upper balcony should **likewise** be prohibited to use it. As the residents of the lower one are partners in the upper one, they should prohibit its residents from using it.

כֵּיוָן דְּעָשׂוּ לַתַּחְתּוֹנָה – גִּלּוּי גַּלֵּי דַּעְתָּהּ דַּאֲנָא בַּהֲדָךְ לָא נִיחָא לִי.

The Gemara answers: **Since they erected** a separate partition **for the lower** balcony, **they** each thereby **revealed their intention** to the residents of the upper balcony **that: It is not my wish to be** partners **with you.** Consequently, they no longer prohibit the residents of the upper balcony from using it.

מתני׳ חָצֵר שֶׁהִיא פְּחוּתָה מֵאַרְבַּע אַמּוֹת, אֵין שׁוֹפְכִין בְּתוֹכָהּ מַיִם בַּשַּׁבָּת אֶלָּא אִם כֵּן עָשׂוּ לָהּ עוּקָה מַחֲזֶקֶת סָאתַיִם מִן הַנֶּקֶב וּלְמַטָּה.

MISHNA With regard to **a courtyard that is less than four cubits** by four cubits in area, **one may not pour** waste **water into it on Shabbat, unless a pit**[H] **was fashioned** to receive the water, and the pit **holds two *se'a*** in volume **from its edge below.**

בֵּין מִבַּחוּץ בֵּין מִבִּפְנִים, אֶלָּא שֶׁמִּבַּחוּץ צָרִיךְ לִקְמוֹר, מִבִּפְנִים אֵין צָרִיךְ לִקְמוֹר.

This *halakha* applies **whether** the pit was fashioned **outside** the courtyard **or** whether it was dug **inside** the courtyard itself. The **only** difference is as follows: **If the pit was dug outside** in the adjoining public domain, **it is necessary to arch over it,**[N] so that the water will not flow into the public domain. If it was dug **inside** the courtyard, **it is not necessary to arch over** it.

NOTES

The *halakha* of stolen property applies to Shabbat – יֵשׁ דִּין גָּזֵל בַּשַּׁבָּת: Although there is broad consensus among the commentaries as to the basic meaning of this statement, they differ with regard to the details. One explanation is that one who stole a ruin and changed it by building it up has acquired the ruin in terms of Shabbat boundaries. Nevertheless, the ruin must be returned to its owner in its current state. The Gemara's response is that the *halakhot* of theft in general do indeed apply on Shabbat. However, in the case of a ruin, as one has not acquired it by changing it, he has no rights to it (Rabbeinu Ḥananel).

The *ge'onim* explain that this phrase: The *halakha* of stolen property applies to Shabbat, is referring to one who stole a place on Shabbat. He has acquired it in terms of Shabbat boundaries and may use it. Conversely, the following phrase: A ruin must be returned to its owner, means that if a stolen ruin was restored to its rightful owner on Shabbat, it is considered returned, and it belongs to the original owner even with regard to the boundaries of Shabbat.

It is necessary to arch over it – צָרִיךְ לִקְמוֹר: Some commentaries add that if an arched cover is fashioned over it, the place has the status of the cavities of a public domain (Ra'avad). The Rambam states that this cover is only required to be arched for the sake of appearances, to separate the pit from the public domain. The *Darkei Moshe* explains that the cover is arched so the pit will not be left uncovered in the public domain. See Rashi and *Tosafot*, who cite the Rashbam.

HALAKHA

Jointly erected a partition – שֶׁעָשׂוּ מְחִיצָה בְּשׁוּתָּפוּת: If the residents of two adjacent balconies erect a partition together in one of the balconies in order to permit the drawing of water, they are nonetheless both prohibited from doing so, unless they establish a joint *eiruv*. If the inhabitants of one balcony erect a partition on their own, they are permitted to draw water, even if the other balcony does not have a partition and even if the occupants of the second balcony generally use the first one (*Magen Avraham*). If they jointly erect partitions for both balconies, they no longer prohibit one another, in accordance with Rav Sheshet (*Shulḥan Arukh*, *Oraḥ Ḥayyim* 355:5).

A courtyard and a pit – חָצֵר וְעוּקָה: In the case of a courtyard less than four by four cubits in area that is adjacent to a public domain, it is permitted to pour waste water into it on Shabbat only if a pit with the capacity of two *se'a* were dug in the courtyard to receive the water, or if this pit were dug outside the courtyard and covered with boards (*Shulḥan Arukh*, *Oraḥ Ḥayyim* 357:1).

רַבִּי אֱלִיעֶזֶר בֶּן יַעֲקֹב אוֹמֵר: בִּיב שֶׁהוּא קָמוּר אַרְבַּע אַמּוֹת בִּרְשׁוּת הָרַבִּים – שׁוֹפְכִים לְתוֹכוֹ מַיִם בַּשַּׁבָּת. וַחֲכָמִים אוֹמְרִים: אֲפִילּוּ גַּג אוֹ חָצֵר מֵאָה אַמָּה לֹא יִשְׁפּוֹךְ עַל פִּי הַבִּיב, אֲבָל שׁוֹפֵךְ הוּא לַגַּג וְהַמַּיִם יוֹרְדִין לַבִּיב.

Rabbi Eliezer ben Ya'akov says: In the case of a drainage **ditch whose** first **four cubits are arched over**[H] **in the public domain, one may pour** waste **water into it on Shabbat. And the Rabbis say: Even if a roof or a courtyard is a hundred cubits** in area, **one may not pour** water directly **onto the mouth of the** drainage **ditch. However, he may pour** it **upon the roof,** from which **the water spills into the drain** of its own accord.

הֶחָצֵר וְהָאַכְסַדְרָה מִצְטָרְפִין לְאַרְבַּע אַמּוֹת. וְכֵן שְׁתֵּי דְּיוֹטָאוֹת זוֹ כְּנֶגֶד זוֹ, מִקְצָתָן עָשׂוּ עוּקָה, וּמִקְצָתָן לֹא עָשׂוּ עוּקָה, אֶת שֶׁעָשׂוּ עוּקָה – מוּתָּרִין, אֶת שֶׁלֹּא עָשׂוּ עוּקָה – אֲסוּרִין.

A courtyard and a portico, a roofed but unwalled structure in front of a house, **combine for the four cubits** by virtue of which it is permitted to pour water even into a courtyard that lacks a pit. **And likewise,** with regard to **two upper stories [*deyotaot*],**[L] **one opposite the other** in the same small courtyard, if the residents of **one** of them **fashioned a pit**[H] in the courtyard, **and** the residents of **the other did not fashion a pit, those who fashioned a pit are permitted** to pour their waste water into the courtyard, whereas **those who did not fashion a pit are prohibited** to do so.

גמ׳ מַאי טַעְמָא? אָמַר רַבָּה: מִפְּנֵי שֶׁאָדָם עָשׂוּי לְהִסְתַּפֵּק סָאתַיִם מַיִם בְּכׇל יוֹם, בְּאַרְבַּע אַמּוֹת – אָדָם רוֹצֶה לְזַלְּפָן,

GEMARA The Gemara asks: **What is the reason** that a courtyard four by four cubits in area does not require a pit? **Rabba said: Because a person ordinarily uses two *se'a* of water a day,** and with regard to a courtyard **of** at least **four cubits** by four cubits, **a person wants to sprinkle** the water on the ground to prevent any dust from rising. Consequently, even if in practice the water does flow out of the courtyard, this effect is not necessarily his intention.

HALAKHA

Arched drainage ditch – בִּיב קָמוּר: If four cubits of a ditch are arched over in the public domain, it is permitted to pour waste water into the drainage ditch in a courtyard on Shabbat, even if the water will flow outside. This *halakha* is in accordance with Rabbi Eliezer ben Ya'akov (*Tosafot*; *Shulḥan Arukh, Oraḥ Ḥayyim* 357:2).

Two upper stories and a pit – שְׁתֵּי דְּיוֹטָאוֹת וְעוּקָה: In the case of a small courtyard less than four by four cubits in area and containing two upper stories, and the residents of only one of the stories dug a pit, if the residents established an *eiruv*, the residents of both stories are permitted to pour waste water into the pit. However, if they did not establish an *eiruv* together, the residents who dug a pit may pour into the pit, although the water will run down from it into the courtyard; but the residents of the other story, who did not establish an *eiruv*, are prohibited to pour even inside their house (*Shulḥan Arukh, Oraḥ Ḥayyim* 377:1).

LANGUAGE

Upper stories [*deyotaot*] – דְּיוֹטָאוֹת: From the Greek δίαιτα, *diaita*, a residence or a collection of rooms, among other meanings.

Perek **VIII**
Daf **88** Amud **b**

פָּחוֹת מֵאַרְבַּע – שׁוֹפְכָן. אִי דַּעֲבִיד עוּקָה – שְׁרֵי, אִי לָא – אָסוּר.

But if the courtyard is **less than four cubits** by four cubits in area, **one** simply **pours** the water out, as the place is not fit for sprinkling. Therefore, **if one fashioned a pit, it is permitted** to pour out water; but if **not, it is prohibited** to do so, as one certainly intends for the water to flow outside.

רַבִּי זֵירָא אָמַר: אַרְבַּע אַמּוֹת – תָּיְימִי, פָּחוֹת מֵאַרְבַּע אַמּוֹת – לָא תָּיְימִי.

Rabbi Zeira offered a different reason and **said:** In a courtyard of **four cubits** by four cubits,[H] the water is likely to be **absorbed** into the ground. If it is **less than four cubits** in size, the water **will not be absorbed** but will flow out.

מַאי בֵּינַיְיהוּ? אָמַר אַבָּיֵי: אֲרִיךְ וְקָטִין אִיכָּא בֵּינַיְיהוּ.

The Gemara asks: **What is** the practical **difference between** these two explanations? **Abaye said: There is** a difference **between them** with regard to a **long and narrow**[N] courtyard. As the area of this courtyard is also sixteen square cubits, it likewise absorbs the water. Rabbi Zeira would therefore rule that it does not require a pit. However, as this courtyard is not in need of sprinkling, it requires a pit according to Rabba.

תְּנַן: חָצֵר וְאַכְסַדְרָה מִצְטָרְפִין לְאַרְבַּע אַמּוֹת. בִּשְׁלָמָא לְרַבִּי זֵירָא – נִיחָא, אֶלָּא לְרַבָּה קַשְׁיָא!

We learned in the mishna: **A courtyard and a portico combine for the** requisite **four cubits,** permitted the pouring of water into a courtyard that lacks a pit. The Gemara asks: **Granted, according to** the opinion of **Rabbi Zeira,** this **works out well,** as the total area is large enough to absorb the water. **However, according to Rabba it is difficult,** for when the courtyard is joined with the portico it is no longer in the shape of a square, and it is therefore unfit for sprinkling.

תַּרְגְּמָא רַבִּי זֵירָא אַלִּיבָּא דְּרַבָּה: בְּאַכְסַדְרָה מְהַלֶּכֶת עַל פְּנֵי כׇל הֶחָצֵר כּוּלָּהּ.

Rabbi Zeira explained the mishna **in accordance with** the opinion of **Rabba,** by saying that it is referring **to a portico that extends along the entire courtyard,**[B] so that it adds to its width alone. Consequently, the courtyard and the portico together form a square of four by four cubits, an area that is fit for sprinkling.

HALAKHA

A courtyard four by four – חָצֵר אַרְבַּע עַל אַרְבַּע: If a courtyard is long and narrow, i.e., sixteen square cubits in area, but not four by four cubits, it is permitted to pour into it as much water as one wishes. The *halakha* is in accordance with Rabbi Zeira, as he accepts the ruling of Rabbi Eliezer ben Ya'akov, whose teachings are clear and precise (*Shulḥan Arukh, Oraḥ Ḥayyim* 357:1).

NOTES

Long and narrow – אֲרִיךְ וְקָטִין: Rabbeinu Ḥananel and the Ra'avad maintain that this dispute is referring to a courtyard four cubits long but less than four cubits wide. The early commentaries question their opinion: How is it possible for water to be absorbed in a place whose length is four cubits but whose width is of a minimal size? Notwithstanding this objection, the Gemara's comparison with Rabbi Eliezer ben Ya'akov's opinion concerning a drainage ditch, which is certainly less than four by four cubits in size, supports this interpretation (see Ritva).

BACKGROUND

Portico that extends along the entire courtyard – אַכְסַדְרָה מְהַלֶּכֶת עַל פְּנֵי כׇל הֶחָצֵר כּוּלָּהּ: The portico of this courtyard extends along the entire width of the courtyard. Consequently, the courtyard and portico together form a square.

Portico extending along the entire width of a courtyard

תָּא שְׁמַע: חָצֵר שֶׁאֵין בָּהּ אַרְבַּע עַל אַרְבַּע אַמּוֹת – אֵין שׁוֹפְכִין לְתוֹכָהּ מַיִם בְּשַׁבָּת. בִּשְׁלָמָא לְרַבָּה – נִיחָא, אֶלָּא לְרַבִּי זֵירָא קַשְׁיָא!

The Gemara suggests: **Come and hear** a *baraita* that can decide this dispute. With regard to **a courtyard that is not four cubits by four cubits** in area, **one may not pour water into it on Shabbat.** The Gemara assumes that the *baraita*, which teaches that one may pour water only into a courtyard that it is four by four cubits, is precise in its wording. **Granted, according to Rabba,** this **works out well,** as he maintains that it is prohibited to pour water into a long and narrow courtyard. **However, according to Rabbi Zeira,** who maintains that the critical factor is the area of the courtyard, this is **difficult.**

אָמַר לָךְ רַבִּי זֵירָא: הָא מַנִּי – רַבָּנַן הִיא, וּמַתְנִיתִין רַבִּי אֱלִיעֶזֶר בֶּן יַעֲקֹב הִיא.

The Gemara answers that **Rabbi Zeira** can **say to you:** In accordance with **whose** opinion is **this** *baraita*? **It is** in accordance with the opinion of **the Rabbis** at the end of the mishna, who maintain that the area of the courtyard is of no importance, **whereas our** unattributed **mishna is** in accordance with the opinion of **Rabbi Eliezer ben Ya'akov,** according to whom the area is the decisive factor.

וּמַאי דּוּחְקֵיהּ דְּרַבִּי זֵירָא לְאוֹקְמָהּ לְמַתְנִיתִין כְּרַבִּי אֱלִיעֶזֶר בֶּן יַעֲקֹב? אָמַר רָבָא: מַתְנִיתִין קַשִׁיתֵיהּ; מַאי אִירְיָא דְּתָנֵי ״חָצֵר שֶׁהִיא פְּחוּתָה״ לִיתְנֵי ״חָצֵר שֶׁאֵין בָּהּ אַרְבַּע אַמּוֹת עַל אַרְבַּע אַמּוֹת״!

The Gemara asks: **And what forced Rabbi Zeira to establish the mishna in accordance with** the opinion of **Rabbi Eliezer ben Ya'akov?**[N] **Rava said: The mishna was difficult for him. Why** did the *tanna* **specifically teach** his ruling with respect to **a courtyard that is less** than four cubits, from which it can be inferred that if it has an area of four by four cubits it is permitted to pour water, even if it is not square in shape? **Let** the mishna **teach: A courtyard that is not four cubits by four cubits,** i.e., one that is not square shaped, even if it includes an area of sixteen square cubits.

אֶלָּא לָאו – שְׁמַע מִינָּהּ דְּרַבִּי אֱלִיעֶזֶר בֶּן יַעֲקֹב הִיא, שְׁמַע מִינָּהּ.

Rather, shouldn't one conclude from this argument that the unattributed section of the mishna is in accordance with the opinion **of Rabbi Eliezer ben Ya'akov?** The Gemara summarizes: Indeed, **conclude from this** that it is so.

וְהָא מִדְּסֵיפָא רַבִּי אֱלִיעֶזֶר בֶּן יַעֲקֹב, רֵישָׁא לָאו רַבִּי אֱלִיעֶזֶר בֶּן יַעֲקֹב!

The Gemara raises a difficulty with this conclusion: **But from** the fact that **a latter clause** of the mishna explicitly cites the opinion of **Rabbi Eliezer ben Ya'akov,** it can be inferred that **the first clause** does **not** represent the opinion of **Rabbi Eliezer ben Ya'akov.**

כּוּלָּהּ רַבִּי אֱלִיעֶזֶר בֶּן יַעֲקֹב הִיא, וְחַסּוֹרֵי מִיחַסְּרָא וְהָכִי קָתָנֵי: חָצֵר שֶׁהִיא פְּחוּתָה מֵאַרְבַּע אַמּוֹת – אֵין שׁוֹפְכִין לְתוֹכָהּ מַיִם בְּשַׁבָּת, הָא אַרְבַּע אַמּוֹת – שׁוֹפְכִין, שֶׁרַבִּי אֱלִיעֶזֶר בֶּן יַעֲקֹב אוֹמֵר: בִּיב הַקָּמוּר אַרְבַּע אַמּוֹת בִּרְשׁוּת הָרַבִּים שׁוֹפְכִין לְתוֹכוֹ מַיִם בְּשַׁבָּת.

The Gemara rejects this argument: In fact, **the entire** mishna is in accordance with the opinion of **Rabbi Eliezer ben Ya'akov, and** as for its problematic style, the mishna **is incomplete and it teaches the following:** With regard to **a courtyard that is less than four cubits** in area, **one may not pour** waste **water into it on Shabbat. Consequently,** if it is **four cubits** in area, **one may pour** water into it, **as Rabbi Eliezer ben Ya'akov says:** If the first **four cubits of a** drainage **ditch were arched over in the public domain, one may pour** waste **water into it on Shabbat.**

״רַבִּי אֱלִיעֶזֶר בֶּן יַעֲקֹב אוֹמֵר: בִּיב הַקָּמוּר״.

We learned in the mishna that **Rabbi Eliezer ben Ya'akov says:** If the first four cubits of a drainage **ditch were arched over** in the public domain, it is permitted to pour waste water into it on Shabbat. However, the Rabbis say: One may pour water only upon the roof, from which it will spill into the drain of its own accord.

מַתְנִיתִין דְּלָא כַּחֲנַנְיָא. דְּתַנְיָא, חֲנַנְיָא אוֹמֵר: אֲפִילּוּ גַּג מֵאָה אַמָּה – לֹא יִשְׁפּוֹךְ, לְפִי שֶׁאֵין הַגַּג עָשׂוּי לִבְלוֹעַ אֶלָּא לְקַלֵּחַ.

The Gemara comments: **The mishna** was **not** taught **in accordance with** the opinion of **Ḥananya. For it was taught** in a *baraita* that **Ḥananya says: Even** with regard to **a roof one hundred cubits** in area, **one may not pour** water onto it, **because a roof is not apt to absorb** the water. **Rather, it** causes it **to run off.** Consequently, pouring water onto this roof is equivalent to pouring it directly outside.

תָּנָא: בַּמֶּה דְּבָרִים אֲמוּרִים – בִּימוֹת הַחַמָּה, אֲבָל בִּימוֹת הַגְּשָׁמִים – שׁוֹפֵךְ וְשׁוֹנֶה וְאֵינוֹ נִמְנַע. מַאי טַעְמָא? אָמַר רָבָא: אָדָם רוֹצֶה שֶׁיִּבָּלְעוּ מַיִם בִּמְקוֹמָן.

A *tanna* **taught: In what** case **is this statement,** that a pit is required, **said?**[N] **In the summer, but in the rainy season,**[H] **one may pour and repeat, and** he need **not hold back. What is the reason? Rava said: A person is** equally **willing for the water to be absorbed on the spot,** i.e., as there is abundant water in the courtyard during the rainy season, it will remain muddy in any case, and he therefore does not care whether the added waste water remains in the courtyard or if it flows out.

NOTES

To establish the mishna in accordance with Rabbi Eliezer ben Ya'akov – **לְאוֹקְמָהּ לְמַתְנִיתִין כְּרַבִּי אֱלִיעֶזֶר בֶּן יַעֲקֹב:** The Gemara's question is difficult to understand: There is a principle that the words of Rabbi Eliezer ben Ya'akov are clear and precise, and his opinion is therefore always accepted as the *halakha*. This should be sufficient reason to explain the mishna in accordance with his ruling. Apparently, this principle does not necessarily apply when Rabbi Eliezer ben Ya'akov maintains a sole dissenting opinion against the majority. Consequently, a different reason was required for establishing the mishna in accordance with Rabbi Eliezer ben Ya'akov, as the Gemara proceeds to explain (Ritva).

In what case is this statement said – **בַּמֶּה דְּבָרִים אֲמוּרִים:** The Ra'avad explains that the expression used here, in what case is this statement said, is referring to the entire mishna, which is why it appears at the end of the mishna. His interpretation incorporates the explanations of both Rashi and Rabbeinu Tam, who dispute the meaning of this phrase in this context (see *Tosafot*).

HALAKHA

In the rainy season – **בִּימוֹת הַגְּשָׁמִים:** It is permitted to pour as much water as one wishes into his courtyard in the rainy season, even a *kor* or two, which is thirty and sixty times more than a *se'a*, respectively. This leniency applies even if the courtyard is not four by four cubits, as stated in the *baraita*. This is in accordance with Abaye, whose ruling is accepted in the final conclusion of the Gemara (*Shulḥan Arukh, Oraḥ Ḥayyim* 357:1).

אֲמַר לֵיהּ אַבַּיֵי: וַהֲרֵי שׁוֹפְכִין, דְּאָדָם רוֹצֶה שֶׁיִּבָּלְעוּ, וְקָתָנֵי "לֹא יִשְׁפּוֹךְ"!

Abaye said to him: With regard to **waste** water poured into a drainage ditch, **that a person wants it to be absorbed** in the ditch itself, rather than flow out, **and** yet the mishna **teaches** that **one may not pour** water into the ditch.

אֲמַר לֵיהּ: הָתָם לְמַאי נֵיחוּשׁ לַהּ? אִי מִשּׁוּם קִלְקוּל חֲצֵירוֹ – הָא מִיקַּלְקְלָא וְקַיְימָא, וְאִי מִשּׁוּם גְּזֵירָה שֶׁמָּא יֹאמְרוּ צִינּוֹרוֹ שֶׁל פְּלוֹנִי מְקַלֵּחַ מַיִם – סְתָם צִינּוֹרוֹת מְקַלְּחִים הֵם.

Rava **said to him: There,** during the rainy season, there is no reason to prohibit the practice, for **with regard to what need we be concerned? If** you say he wants the water to flow out into the public domain **because** he is concerned about **spoiling** and sullying **his courtyard,** it is **already spoiled** by the rainwater. **And if** you say it should be prohibited **due to a decree lest** people **say** that **so-and-so's gutter is flowing with water** on Shabbat, which might lead them to think he is watering his garden or violating some other prohibition, and they might act likewise even in the summer, this is not a relevant concern. As **gutters ordinarily flow** with water in the rainy season, people do not entertain this suspicion.

אָמַר רַב נַחְמָן: בִּימוֹת הַגְּשָׁמִים, עוּקָה מַחֲזֶקֶת סָאתַיִם – נוֹתְנִין לוֹ סָאתַיִם, מַחֲזֶקֶת סְאָה – נוֹתְנִין לוֹ סְאָה. בִּימוֹת הַחַמָּה, מַחֲזֶקֶת סָאתַיִם – נוֹתְנִין לוֹ סָאתַיִם, סְאָה – אֵין נוֹתְנִין לוֹ כׇּל עִיקָּר.

Rav Naḥman said: In the rainy season, with regard to **a pit that holds two *se'a*, we grant him** permission to pour **two *se'a*** of water into it. If it **holds** only **one *se'a*, we grant him one *se'a*.** However, **in the summer,** if the pit has a capacity of **two *se'a*, we grant him two *se'a***; if it holds only **one *se'a*, we do not grant him** permission to pour any water **at all.**

בִּימוֹת הַחַמָּה נָמֵי, מַחֲזֶקֶת סְאָה נֵיתִיב לֵיהּ סְאָה! גְּזֵירָה דִּלְמָא אָתֵי לִיתֵּן לֵיהּ סָאתַיִם. אִי הָכִי, בִּימוֹת הַגְּשָׁמִים נָמֵי לִיגְזוֹר!

The Gemara raises a difficulty: **In the hot season as well,** if the pit **holds one *se'a*, let us grant him one *se'a*,** for if he pours only this amount of water, it will not flow out into the public domain. The Gemara answers: This is prohibited due to **a decree lest he come to put two *se'a* into it.** The Gemara asks: **If so, in the rainy season let us also apply the** same **preventive measure.**

הָתָם מַאי נֵיחוּשׁ לַהּ? אִי מִשּׁוּם קִילְקוּל – הָא מִיקַּלְקְלָא וְקַיְימָא, אִי מִשּׁוּם גְּזֵירָה שֶׁמָּא יֹאמְרוּ צִינּוֹרוֹ שֶׁל פְּלוֹנִי מְקַלֵּחַ מַיִם – סְתָם צִינּוֹרוֹת מְקַלְּחִין הֵן.

The Gemara answers: **There,** in the rainy season, there is no reason to prohibit the practice, for if one pours more water into a pit than it can take, **about what need we be concerned? If** you say he wants the waste water to flow out into the public domain **because** he is concerned about **spoiling** his courtyard, **it is already spoiled** by the rainwater. **If** you say it should be prohibited due to **a decree lest** people **say** that **so-and-so's gutter is flowing with water** on Shabbat, **gutters ordinarily gush** with water in the rainy season, as stated above.

אָמַר אַבַּיֵי: הִילְכָּךְ, אֲפִילּוּ כּוֹר וַאֲפִילּוּ כּוֹרַיִים.

Abaye said: Therefore, in accordance with this reasoning, one can pour **even a *kor* and even two *kor***[N] of waste water into a small pit. As all gutters flow with water in the rainy season, there is no cause for any concern.

"וְכֵן שְׁתֵּי דְיוֹטָאוֹת זוֹ כְּנֶגֶד זוֹ". אָמַר רָבָא: אֲפִילּוּ עֵירְבוּ.

We learned in the mishna: **And likewise,** with regard to **two upper stories, one opposite the other** in the same courtyard, the residents of the one who dug a pit in the courtyard may pour water into it, while the residents of the other one who did not dig a pit in the courtyard are prohibited from doing so. **Rava said:** This *halakha* applies **even if** the residents of the two upper stories **established an *eiruv*** together.

אֲמַר (לֵיהּ) אַבַּיֵי: מַאי טַעְמָא? אִילֵּימָא מִשּׁוּם נְפִישָׁא דְּמַיָּא – וְהָתַנְיָא: אַחַת לִי עוּקָה וְאַחַת לִי גִּיסְטְרָא בְּרֵיכָה וַעֲרֵיבָה, אַף עַל פִּי שֶׁנִּתְמַלְּאוּ מַיִם מֵעֶרֶב שַׁבָּת – שׁוֹפְכִין לְתוֹכָן מַיִם בְּשַׁבָּת!

Abaye said to him: What is the reason for this ruling? **If you say** it is **due to the increase** in the amount **of water,** as two upper stories pour out more water than one, **wasn't it taught** in a *baraita*: **The same** *halakha* applies to **a pit, and the same** applies to **a cracked** earthenware **vessel** used as a receptacle for water, or a small **pond, or a basin: Even though they were** already **filled with water on Shabbat eve, one may pour water into them on Shabbat.** It is evident from here that as long as the pit is the requisite size, there is no concern about the amount of water that will flow out from it.

אֶלָּא אִי אִיתְּמַר – הָכִי אִיתְּמַר: אָמַר רָבָא:

Rather, if it was stated it was stated as follows. Rava said:

NOTES

Even a *kor* and even two *kor* – אֲפִילּוּ כּוֹר וַאֲפִילּוּ כּוֹרַיִים: Some commentaries explain that the Sages instituted a fixed enactment that the residents always require a pit with a capacity of two *se'a*, without differentiating between the various cases (*Me'iri*). One explanation is that as an ordinary person uses two *se'a* on a daily basis, according to Rabba, the use of more than this amount is rare, and the accepted principle is that the Sages did not apply their decrees to uncommon cases.

לֹא שָׁנוּ אֶלָּא שֶׁלֹּא עֵירְבוּ, אֲבָל עֵירְבוּ – מוּתָּרִין.

They taught this *halakha* **only** with regard to a case **where** the residents of the two upper stories **did not establish an *eiruv*** together, **but if they established a** joint ***eiruv*, they are** all **permitted** to pour water into the courtyard.[H]

וְכִי לֹא עֵירְבוּ מַאי טַעְמָא לֹא? אָמַר רַב אַשִׁי: גְּזֵירָה דִילְמָא אָתֵי לְאַפּוֹקֵי מִמָּאנֵי דְּבָתִּים לְהָתָם.

The Gemara asks: **And where they did not establish an *eiruv*,**[N] **what is the reason** that the residents who did not dig a pit may **not** pour water into the courtyard? **Rav Ashi said:** It is **a decree, lest** people **come to take out vessels** filled with water **from** their **houses into** the courtyard, to pour into the pit. In the absence of an *eiruv*, this practice is prohibited.

הדרן עלך כיצד משתתפין

HALAKHA

If they established an *eiruv* or if they did not establish an *eiruv* – עֵירְבוּ וְלֹא עֵירְבוּ: With regard to the residents of two houses who live opposite one another, and whose houses face a single courtyard less than four cubits by four cubits in area, if they did not establish an *eiruv*, and only one of the houses dug a pit, the members of that household are permitted to pour into it, while the inhabitants of the other are prohibited from doing so. If they did establish an *eiruv*, they are all permitted to use the pit (*Shulḥan Arukh*, *Oraḥ Ḥayyim* 377:1).

NOTES

Two residents who did not establish an *eiruv* – שְׁתֵּי דִּיוֹטוֹת שֶׁלֹּא עֵירְבוּ: Why aren't the residents of the house who established an *eiruv* also prohibited from pouring water? The others who failed to establish an *eiruv* should impose restrictions upon all the residents of the courtyard. One answer is that this is a case of indirect pouring into the pit, by way of the upper story, and the Sages did not extend their decree to such a case (Rosh).

Summary of **Perek VIII**

In addition to the *halakhot* of merging and joining cited again in this chapter, constituting a review and summary of matters discussed in the previous chapter, additional issues were elucidated. Emerging from the *halakhot* discussed in this chapter was the fact that the definition of residence in the context of the *halakhot* of *eiruv* differs from its definition in other areas of *halakha*. A principle governing the *halakhot* of *eiruv* is that the legal status of one who does not actually live in a given residence, even if he owns it, is not that of a resident; therefore, his status cannot impinge on the rights of the other residents of the courtyard. Furthermore, one who resides in a residence owned by another is not deemed a full-fledged resident if the owner maintains legal rights providing him access. The owner is deemed the primary resident for the purposes of the *eiruv*.

Similarly, the legal status of a place that serves as a passageway for several residences, e.g., a gatehouse or a balcony, is not that of a residence, and one who resides there is not deemed a resident.

While the concept of a residence may be restricted in one sense, it is expanded in the sense that a residence is not merely a place in which one has actual proprietary rights to reside. Any place adjacent to a residence to which tenants have access, and, in the formulation of the Sages, its use is convenient, is considered part of the residence. Based upon this principle, there was a discussion with regard to areas whose use is convenient for the residents of two separate residences or is inconvenient for residents of both.

As for the use of water on Shabbat, many of the *halakhot* are based on the principle: The Sages were lenient with regard to water. The primary reason for this leniency is due to the fact that it is difficult to determine boundaries with regard to water the way that one does with regard to land, as in water the boundaries are not discernible. In addition, water lacks the stability of land, as it is often in motion. Consequently, its passage from one spot is not observable nor is its position constant. Therefore, the Sages were lenient in several areas related to water, e.g., considering a partition suspended above the water's surface as if it extended down below the water's surface, thereby effectively creating partitions within the water and dividing it into distinct domains. Similar ordinances obviating the need for actual partitions in the water were also discussed.

With regard to pouring out waste water on Shabbat, it was determined that as long as a person does not pour the water from his domain directly into the public domain, but rather does so indirectly via a pit or a drainage ditch, it is permitted. Although the Sages ruled stringently in most cases involving indirectly carrying out objects on Shabbat, they ruled leniently with regard to water and its usage.

Introduction to **Perek IX**

To this point, tractate *Eiruvin* has primarily addressed the problem of establishing an *eiruv*, i.e., how it is possible to combine residences, courtyards, and alleyways into one domain enabling the transfer of objects from one to another? It has also addressed the manner in which it is possible to expand the Shabbat limit, extending the distance that one is permitted to walk on Shabbat. However, some very fundamental issues require elucidation. What is the *halakha* when no *eiruv* was established at all or where the *eiruv* was breached? Only by means of clarification of these points can the nature of the relationship between the various secondary Shabbat domains, in both Torah and rabbinic law, be understood. The *halakhot* of the four primary Shabbat domains were fully elucidated in tractate *Shabbat*, leaving the status of the various forms of the private domain in need of clarification.

Indeed, the primary focus of this chapter is the discussion of the relationship between various types of private domains, e.g., courtyards, rooftops, alleyways, and enclosures, when no *eiruv* has been established between them. Is each of these areas considered an independent unit requiring an *eiruv* to unite them? Or are they all components of one overriding domain and it is permitted to transfer objects from one to the other without establishing an *eiruv*? In other words, what is the criterion for distinguishing private domains from one another? Is it the existence of a partition between them; is it the fact that they have different owners; or is it the fact that they are utilized in different ways?

Another issue is that all of the *halakhot* relating to partitions or the lack thereof were addressed from the perspective of the *halakhot* of *eiruv*. However, when the partitions are removed, when the courtyard is breached, or when one domain is completely open into a second domain, what is the halakhic status in that case? Does the domain that opens into another domain lose its independent status, or has its status merely been altered? Is the change in status dependent solely on the existence of the partitions, or are the use of the courtyard and the function it serves also significant factors?

These problems and others that arise from them constitute the crux of the discussions in this chapter.

מתני׳ כָּל גַּגּוֹת הָעִיר רְשׁוּת אַחַת, וּבִלְבַד שֶׁלֹּא יְהֵא גַּג גָּבוֹהַּ עֲשָׂרָה אוֹ נָמוּךְ עֲשָׂרָה, דִּבְרֵי רַבִּי מֵאִיר. וַחֲכָמִים אוֹמְרִים: כָּל אֶחָד וְאֶחָד רְשׁוּת בִּפְנֵי עַצְמוֹ.

MISHNA All the roofs of the city[B] are considered **one domain.** It is permitted to carry from one roof to another, even if the residents of the houses did not establish an *eiruv* between them. The Sages did not prohibit carrying between roofs, as it is rare to transfer an item from one roof to another. However, it is only permitted to transfer objects between roofs **provided that** one **roof is neither ten** handbreadths **higher nor ten** handbreadths **lower** than the adjacent roof. This is **the statement of Rabbi Meir. And the Rabbis say: Each and every one** of the roofs is **a domain in and of itself.** It is permitted to carry from one to the other only if the residents of both houses established an *eiruv*.

רַבִּי שִׁמְעוֹן אוֹמֵר: אֶחָד גַּגּוֹת וְאֶחָד חֲצֵירוֹת וְאֶחָד קַרְפֵּיפוֹת – רְשׁוּת אַחַת הֵן לְכֵלִים שֶׁשָּׁבְתוּ לְתוֹכָן, וְלֹא לְכֵלִים שֶׁשָּׁבְתוּ בְּתוֹךְ הַבַּיִת.

Rabbi Shimon says: Roofs, courtyards, and enclosures[NH] **are all one domain with regard to vessels that were inside them** when **Shabbat** began, and one may therefore carry from one of these areas to another. However, they are **not** one domain **with regard to vessels that were inside the house** when **Shabbat** began and were later taken into one of the above domains. A vessel that was inside the house when Shabbat began and subsequently carried to one of these areas may be carried from one roof, courtyard, or enclosure to another only if an *eiruv* had been established between the domains.

גמ׳ יְתֵיב אַבָּיֵי בַּר אָבִין וְרַבִּי חֲנִינָא בַּר אָבִין, וִיתֵיב אַבָּיֵי גַּבַּיְיהוּ, וְיָתְבִי וְקָאָמְרִי: בִּשְׁלָמָא רַבָּנַן סָבְרִי: כְּשֵׁם שֶׁדִּיּוּרִין חֲלוּקִין לְמַטָּה – כָּךְ דִּיּוּרִין חֲלוּקִין לְמַעְלָה.

GEMARA Abaye bar Avin and Rabbi Ḥanina bar Avin were sitting, and Abaye was sitting beside them, and they sat and said: Granted, the Rabbis maintain: Just as residents are divided into separate domains **below,** and they may not carry from house to house without an *eiruv*, **so are residents divided** into separate domains **above,** on the rooftops, and it is prohibited to carry from one roof to another without an *eiruv*.

אֶלָּא רַבִּי מֵאִיר מַאי קָסָבַר? אִי קָסָבַר כְּשֵׁם שֶׁדִּיּוּרִין חֲלוּקִין לְמַטָּה כָּךְ דִּיּוּרִין חֲלוּקִין לְמַעְלָה – אַמַּאי רְשׁוּת אַחַת הֵן? וְאִי קָסָבַר אֵין חֲלוּקִין, דְּכׇל לְמַעְלָה מֵעֲשָׂרָה רְשׁוּת אַחַת הִיא – אֲפִילּוּ גַּג גָּבוֹהַּ עֲשָׂרָה וְנָמוּךְ עֲשָׂרָה נָמֵי!

However, Rabbi Meir, what does he maintain; what is the rationale for his opinion? **If he maintains** that **just as residents are divided** into separate domains **below, so are residents divided** into separate domains **above, why,** in his opinion, **are they** considered **one domain? And if he maintains** that **they are not divided** into separate domains, **as any** place **above ten** handbreadths off the ground **is** considered **one domain, even** if **a roof** is **ten** handbreadths **higher or ten** handbreadths **lower** than the adjacent roof, it should **likewise** be permitted to carry from one roof to the other.

אָמַר לְהוּ אַבָּיֵי: לָא שְׁמִיעַ לְכוּ הָא דְּאָמַר רַב יִצְחָק בַּר אַבְדִּימִי, אוֹמֵר הָיָה רַבִּי מֵאִיר: כׇּל מָקוֹם שֶׁאַתָּה מוֹצֵא שְׁתֵּי רְשׁוּיוֹת וְהֵן רְשׁוּת אַחַת, כְּגוֹן עַמּוּד בִּרְשׁוּת הַיָּחִיד גָּבוֹהַּ עֲשָׂרָה וְרָחָב אַרְבָּעָה – אָסוּר לְכַתֵּף עָלָיו, גְּזֵירָה מִשּׁוּם תֵּל בִּרְשׁוּת הָרַבִּים. הָכִי נָמֵי – גְּזֵירָה מִשּׁוּם תֵּל בִּרְשׁוּת הָרַבִּים.

Abaye said to them: Have **you not heard that which Rav Yitzḥak bar Avdimi said** that **Rabbi Meir would say: Any place that you find two domains,** i.e., places set apart from each other by disparity in height or by boundaries, **and** yet **they are** halakhically **one domain,**[N] **for example, a pillar ten** handbreadths **high and four** handbreadths **wide** situated **in a private domain,** it is **prohibited to adjust** a burden on one's **shoulders upon it,** by rabbinic **decree, due to** the concern lest he come to do the same thing on **a mound in the public domain.** The legal status of a mound ten handbreadths high and four handbreadths wide located in a public domain is that of a private domain. In that case, it is prohibited by Torah law to transfer an object from the public domain to the mound. **Here too,** in the case of roofs, Rabbi Meir prohibited transferring objects between roofs with a height disparity of ten handbreadths, by rabbinic **decree, due to** the concern lest one come to transfer an object from the public domain to **a mound in a public domain.**

סָבוּר מִינָּהּ: אֲפִילּוּ מַכְתֶּשֶׁת וַאֲפִילּוּ גִּיגִית.

Abaye and Ḥanina bar Avin **understood** by inference **from this** ruling that in the opinion of Rabbi Meir, it would be prohibited to adjust one's burden **even** on **a mortar and even** on **a vat** that were overturned in a private domain and that are large enough to constitute private domains in their own right.

BACKGROUND

The roofs of the city – גַּגּוֹת הָעִיר: According to Rabbi Meir, all roofs that are roughly equal in height are considered one domain, excluding one that is ten handbreadths higher or lower than the others.

Roof ten handbreadths higher than the rest of the roofs

NOTES

A courtyard and an enclosure – חָצֵר וְקַרְפֵּף: Rashi distinguishes between a courtyard and an enclosure in terms of ownership; a courtyard is typically shared by many houses, while an enclosure is owned by a single individual. This explanation has been questioned by other commentaries. Rashi adds that a courtyard is subject to frequent use, and people regularly carry objects in it, whereas an enclosure is designed for specific purposes, e.g., as a garden, and it is rarely an area where objects are carried from one place to another (see Maharsha and others).

Two domains and one domain – שְׁתֵּי רְשׁוּיוֹת וּרְשׁוּת אַחַת: The commentaries explain that Rabbi Meir issued this decree only with regard to a private domain such as a courtyard, but not a roofed private domain, as it has nothing in common with a public domain. Other authorities maintain, contrary to Rashi's opinion, that Rabbi Meir's decree applies only if the two private domains belong to different people who did not establish an *eiruv*, as the prohibition against carrying from one domain to another is similar to that of carrying into the public domain. However, Rabbi Meir did not extend his decree to two private domains that belong to the same individual (Ritva).

HALAKHA

Roofs, courtyards, and enclosures – גַּגִּין חֲצֵירוֹת וְקַרְפֵּיפוֹת: With regard to rooftops, courtyards, and enclosures owned by several different people who each established his own *eiruv* but did not establish an *eiruv* together, it is nonetheless permitted to carry from one to another any utensils that were located in one of them when Shabbat began. However, those utensils that were inside the house when Shabbat commenced may only be carried into a courtyard whose inhabitants established an *eiruv* together, in accordance with the opinion of Rabbi Shimon (*Shulḥan Arukh*, *Oraḥ Ḥayyim* 372:1).

NOTES

Base of a millstone – אַמַּת הָרֵחַיִם:

Millstone marking the summit of Møllehøj, the highest natural point in Denmark

Rabbi Meir's opinion – שִׁיטַת רַבִּי מֵאִיר: According to Rav Yehuda's explanation of Rabbi Meir's opinion, in any place other than an actual house, the Sages issued a decree that prohibits carrying, based not on ownership but rather on the designation and the use of the domain. Consequently, all courtyards are considered a single domain in this regard, even if they belong to different people. The same applies to all roofs and enclosures. It is not permitted, however, to carry from one type of domain to another (see *Me'iri* and Ritva).

אֲמַר לְהוּ אַבַּיֵי, הָכִי אָמַר מָר: לֹא אָמַר רַבִּי מֵאִיר אֶלָּא עַמּוּד וְאַמַּת הָרֵיחַיִם, הוֹאִיל וְאָדָם קוֹבֵעַ לָהֶן מָקוֹם.

Abaye said to them: The Master, Rabba, **said as follows: Rabbi Meir spoke only** in the case of **a pillar or the** raised **base of a millstone.**[N] **Since a person fixes a place for them** they are comparable to a mound in a public domain in that they are rarely moved. However, the Sages did not issue a decree in the case of portable objects.

וַהֲרֵי כּוֹתֶל שֶׁבֵּין שְׁתֵּי חֲצֵירוֹת דְּקָבוּעַ, וְאָמַר רַב יְהוּדָה: כְּשֶׁתִּימְצֵי לוֹמַר לְדִבְרֵי רַבִּי מֵאִיר: גַּגִּין רְשׁוּת לְעַצְמָן, חֲצֵירוֹת רְשׁוּת לְעַצְמָן, קַרְפֵּיפוֹת רְשׁוּת לְעַצְמָן.

The Gemara raises a difficulty. There is the case of **a wall that is between two courtyards, which** is **fixed, and** nevertheless **Rav Yehuda said: When** you analyze the matter, **you will find** that **according to Rabbi Meir** all **roofs** form a single **domain in and of themselves,** and likewise all **courtyards** form a single **domain in and of themselves,** and all **enclosures** form a single **domain in and of themselves.**[N] It is permitted to carry from one courtyard to another, although it is not permitted to carry from a courtyard to a roof.

מַאי לָאו – דְּשָׁרֵי לְטַלְטוּלֵי דֶּרֶךְ כּוֹתֶל!

What, is it not that it is permitted to move objects from one courtyard to another **via a** dividing **wall,** even though it is ten handbreadths high? This poses a difficulty to the opinion of Rabbi Meir, who prohibits the transfer of an object from one place to a place ten handbreadths higher or lower.

אָמַר רַב הוּנָא בַּר יְהוּדָה, אָמַר רַב שֵׁשֶׁת: לֹא, לְהַכְנִיס וּלְהוֹצִיא דֶּרֶךְ פְּתָחִים.

Rav Huna bar Yehuda said that **Rav Sheshet said: No,** that explanation is incorrect, as Rav Yehuda meant to say that according to Rabbi Meir it is permitted **to carry in and carry out** between one courtyard and another, or from one enclosure to another, **via the openings** between them. However, Rabbi Meir concedes that one may not transfer objects over the wall that separates the two domains, as the wall is considered a domain in and of itself.

״וַחֲכָמִים אוֹמְרִים כָּל אֶחָד וְאֶחָד רְשׁוּת בִּפְנֵי עַצְמוֹ״. אִיתְּמַר, רַב אָמַר: אֵין מְטַלְטְלִין בּוֹ אֶלָּא בְּאַרְבַּע אַמּוֹת, וּשְׁמוּאֵל אָמַר: מוּתָּר לְטַלְטֵל בְּכוּלּוֹ.

We learned in the mishna: **And the Rabbis say** that **each and every one** of the roofs **is a domain in and of itself. It was stated** that *amora'im* disagreed about the following issue. **Rav said:** According to the Rabbis, **one may move** objects on each roof **only within four cubits.** As, according to the Rabbis, the legal status of roofs is like that of courtyards, in that it is prohibited to carry from one roof to another, and each roof is fully open to a domain into which carrying is prohibited. Therefore, it is also prohibited to carry objects farther than four cubits on each roof. **And Shmuel said: It is permitted to move** objects throughout each **entire** roof.

בִּמְחִיצוֹת הַנִּיכָּרוֹת – דְּכוּלֵּי עָלְמָא לָא פְּלִיגִי. כִּי פְּלִיגִי – בִּמְחִיצוֹת שֶׁאֵינָן נִיכָּרוֹת.

The Gemara comments: **With regard to partitions that are conspicuous,** i.e., detached houses whose walls are distinct, **everyone agrees** that it is permitted to carry throughout each roof. **Where they disagree** is **with regard to partitions that are not conspicuous,** i.e., attached houses, which appear as though they share a common roof although they are owned by different people.

רַב אָמַר: אֵין מְטַלְטְלִין בּוֹ אֶלָּא בְּאַרְבַּע אַמּוֹת, לֹא אָמַר גּוּד אַסִּיק מְחִיצָּתָא, וּשְׁמוּאֵל אָמַר: מוּתָּר לְטַלְטֵל בְּכוּלּוֹ, דְּאָמַר גּוּד אַסִּיק מְחִיצָּתָא.

Rav said: One may carry on each roof **only within four cubits.** Rav **does not state** the principle: **Extend and raise the partitions** between the houses below, which states that the walls of the houses are considered to extend upward and create partitions between the roofs. **And Shmuel said:** It is **permitted to carry throughout** each **entire** roof, **as he states** the principle: **Extend and raise the partitions.**

תְּנַן, וַחֲכָמִים אוֹמְרִים: כָּל אֶחָד וְאֶחָד

The Gemara asks a question based on that which **we learned** in the mishna: And **the Rabbis say** that **each and every one** of the roofs

Perek **IX**
Daf **89** Amud **b**

רְשׁוּת לְעַצְמוֹ, בִּשְׁלָמָא לִשְׁמוּאֵל – נִיחָא, אֶלָּא לְרַב – קַשְׁיָא!

is **a domain in and of itself.** This indicates that each roof constitutes a discrete domain, and one may carry throughout this entire domain. **Granted according to** the opinion of **Shmuel,** this works out **well, but according to** the opinion of **Rav,** it is **difficult.**

אָמְרִי בֵּי רַב מִשְּׁמֵיהּ דְּרַב: שֶׁלֹּא יְטַלְטֵל שְׁתֵּי אַמּוֹת בְּגַג זֶה וּשְׁתֵּי אַמּוֹת בְּגַג זֶה.

The Gemara answers that the Sages of the **school of Rav said in the name of Rav:** The ruling in the mishna is not a leniency permitting one to carry throughout the entire roof; rather, it is a stringency, ruling **that one may not move** an object **two cubits on this roof and two cubits on that roof.** The *tanna* rules that even the allowance to carry within four cubits is restricted to a single roof.

וְהָא אָמַר רַבִּי אֶלְעָזָר, כִּי הֲוֵינַן בְּבָבֶל הֲוָה אָמְרִינַן, בֵּי רַב מִשְּׁמֵיהּ דְּרַב אָמְרוּ: אֵין מְטַלְטְלִין בּוֹ אֶלָּא בְּאַרְבַּע אַמּוֹת, וְהָנֵי דְּבֵי שְׁמוּאֵל תָּנוּ: אֵין לָהֶן אֶלָּא גַּגָּן.

The Gemara raises a difficulty. **But didn't Rabbi Elazar say: When we were in Babylonia we** would **say** that the Sages of **the school of Rav said in the name of Rav: One may move** an object **on** each roof **only within four cubits, and those** Sages of **the school of Shmuel taught**[N] a *baraita* in accordance with their opinion: **They have only their** own **roof.**

מַאי "אֵין לָהֶן אֶלָּא גַּגָּן" – לָאו דִּשְׁרוּ לְטַלְטוֹלֵי בְּכוּלֵּיהּ? וּמִי אַלִּימָא מִמַּתְנִיתִין, דְּאוֹקִימְנָא שֶׁלֹּא יְטַלְטֵל שְׁתֵּי אַמּוֹת בְּגַג זֶה וּשְׁתֵּי אַמּוֹת בְּגַג זֶה – הָכִי נַמִי: שְׁתֵּי אַמּוֹת בְּגַג זֶה וּשְׁתֵּי אַמּוֹת בְּגַג זֶה.

The Gemara seeks to clarify this *baraita*. **What is** the meaning of the statement: **They have only their** own **roof? Is it not that they are permitted to move** an object **throughout** each **entire** roof? This *baraita* poses a difficulty to Rav. The Gemara rejects this contention: **And is** this *baraita* any **stronger** a proof **than our mishna, which we established** as a stringency, **that one may not move** an object **two cubits on this roof and two cubits on that roof? So too,** this *baraita* is teaching that one may not carry **two cubits on this roof and two cubits on that roof.**[N]

אֲמַר רַב יוֹסֵף: לָא שְׁמִיעַ לִי הָא שְׁמַעְתָּא. אֲמַר לֵיהּ אַבָּיֵי: אַתְּ אֲמַרְתְּ נִיהֲלַן, וְאַהָא אֲמַרְתְּ נִיהֲלַן: גַּג גָּדוֹל הַסָּמוּךְ לְקָטָן – הַגָּדוֹל מוּתָּר וְהַקָּטָן אָסוּר.

Rav Yosef said, after an illness had caused him to forget his knowledge: **I have not heard this *halakha*** of Shmuel's with regard to roofs. His student **Abaye said to him: You** yourself **said it to us, and it was about this** that **you said it to us:** With regard to **a large roof that is adjacent to a small one,**[B] carrying on **the large** one **is permitted,** as its partitions are distinct where it extends beyond the small one, **and** carrying on **the small one is prohibited,** as it is breached along its entire length into the other roof, onto which it is prohibited to carry.[N]

וַאֲמַרְתְּ לַן עֲלַהּ, אָמַר רַב יְהוּדָה, אָמַר שְׁמוּאֵל: לֹא שָׁנוּ אֶלָּא שֶׁיֵּשׁ דִּיּוּרִין עַל זֶה וְדִיּוּרִין עַל זֶה, דַּהֲוָיָא לַהּ הָא דְּקָטָן מְחִיצָה נִדְרֶסֶת.

And you said to us about it: Rav Yehuda said that **Shmuel said: They only taught** this *halakha* in a case **where there are residents on this** roof **and residents on that** roof, as the extended, virtual partition **of the small** roof is considered **a trampled partition.** The residents trample this virtual partition as they move from one roof to the other, and the entire length of the small roof is considered breached into the large one.

אֲבָל אֵין דִּיּוּרִין עַל זֶה וְעַל זֶה – שְׁנֵיהֶן מוּתָּרִין.

However, if **there are no residents on this** roof **and** none **on that** one, carrying on **both** roofs is **permitted.** Presumably, Shmuel's reasoning is that in this case the walls of the houses below extend upward and form partitions between the roofs, in accordance with the principle: Extend and raise the partitions.

אֲמַר לֵיהּ: אֲנָא הָכִי אָמְרִי לְכוּ: לֹא שָׁנוּ אֶלָּא שֶׁיֵּשׁ מְחִיצָה עַל זֶה וּמְחִיצָה עַל זֶה, דְּגָדוֹל מִשְׁתְּרֵי בְּגִיפּוּפֵי, וְקָטָן נִפְרָץ בִּמְלוֹאוֹ. אֲבָל אֵין מְחִיצָה לֹא עַל זֶה וְלֹא עַל זֶה – שְׁנֵיהֶן אֲסוּרִין.

Rav Yosef **said to him:** I remember it now. **I said to you as follows: They taught** this *halakha*, that carrying is prohibited on the small roof, **only** with regard to a case **where there was an** actual **partition on** all sides of **this** roof **and an** actual **partition on** all sides of **that** roof, not only between the two roofs. In **that** case, carrying on **the large** roof **is permitted by** means of **the remnants** of the partition on either side of the opening, **and** carrying on the **small** roof **is** prohibited because it is **fully breached** into the larger one. **However, if there is no partition, neither on** all sides of **this** roof **nor on** all sides of **that** roof, carrying on **both of them is prohibited.**

וְהָא דִּיּוּרִין אֲמַרְתְּ לַן! אִי אָמְרִי לְכוּ דִּיּוּרִין – הָכִי אָמְרִי לְכוּ: לֹא שָׁנוּ אֶלָּא שֶׁיֵּשׁ מְחִיצָה רְאוּיָה לְדִירָה עַל זֶה וּמְחִיצָה רְאוּיָה לְדִירָה עַל זֶה, דְּגָדוֹל מִשְׁתְּרֵי בְּגִיפּוּפֵי וְקָטָן נִפְרָץ בִּמְלוֹאוֹ.

Abaye raised a difficulty: **But didn't you speak to us** of **residents?** Rav Yosef replied: **If I spoke to you** of **residents, this** is what **I said to you: They taught** this *halakha*, that carrying is prohibited on the small roof, **only** in a case **where there is an** actual **partition** that renders the area **fit for residence on** all sides of **this** roof, **and an** actual **partition** that renders the area fit **for residence on** all sides of **that** roof, as carrying on **the large** roof **is permitted by** means of **the remnants** of the partition on either side of the opening, **and** carrying on the **small** roof **is** prohibited because it is **fully breached** into the larger one.

NOTES

And those of the school of Shmuel taught – וְהָנֵי דְּבֵי שְׁמוּאֵל תָּנוּ: This *baraita*, which was taught in the school of Shmuel, was not well known and is less authoritative than a mishna or even of a well-documented *Tosefta*. Therefore, the Gemara did not cite the fact that despite the fact that he was an *amora*, Rav's status is that of a *tanna*, and therefore he may disagree with a *baraita*, because that answer is used only as a last resort, when no other explanation is available (Ritva).

Two cubits on that roof – שְׁתֵּי אַמּוֹת בְּגַג זֶה: The Gemara might have answered this question simply by stating that both the mishna and *baraita* refer to a situation where the partitions are conspicuous, as in that case Rav agrees with Shmuel. Nevertheless, the Gemara chose to provide an answer in keeping with the question itself, rather than introduce a special set of circumstances (*Me'iri*).

A large roof and a small roof – גַּג גָּדוֹל וְגַג קָטָן: In the Jerusalem Talmud a question is raised with regard to Rav's opinion: As Rav maintains that it is permitted to carry only four cubits on any roof, the fact that carrying on the small roof is prohibited apparently means that it is prohibited to carry even four cubits. However, this level of stringency is not applied even to a public domain. The answer offered in the Jerusalem Talmud, similar to the resolution that appears in our Gemara, is that this statement means that it is prohibited to carry even less than four cubits into the area of the large roof.

BACKGROUND

A large roof that is adjacent to a small one – גַּג גָּדוֹל הַסָּמוּךְ לְקָטָן:

Large roof adjacent to small roof

BACKGROUND

If he built an upper story and a partition – בָּנָה עֲלִיָּה וְדַקָּה: The illustration is of an upper story constructed above one of the houses, with a partition [*dakka*] in front of it. This upper story and partition establish the person's dwelling upon the roof, as a result of which it is permitted to carry on the adjacent roofs as well.

Upper story and partition

NOTES

A small partition [*dakka*] that permits and prohibits – דַּקָּה לְהֵיתֵר וּלְאִסּוּר: The commentaries dispute the meaning of the word *dakka*. Rashi maintains that it connotes an entrance, while Rabbeinu Ḥananel explains that it is a shelf. *Tosafot* and other commentaries explain that it means a partition. In addition, the commentaries dispute the correct version of the text. Some authorities adopt Rabbeinu Ḥananel's reading and explain that if one erects a partition that separates his roof from the others, those other roofs may be used by their owners, as he no longer imposes restrictions upon them. However, if it is possible that he built this partition to provide himself with a vantage point from which he could survey his garden, there is no longer any proof that he completely isolated himself from all the other roofs. Therefore, the existence of the partition does not render it permitted for them to carry there because of him (*Me'iri*; Ritva).

אֲבָל יֵשׁ מְחִיצָה רְאוּיָה לְדִירָה עַל הַגָּדוֹל, וְאֵין רְאוּיָה לְדִירָה עַל הַקָּטָן – אֲפִילּוּ קָטָן שָׁרֵי לִבְנֵי גָּדוֹל. מַאי טַעְמָא – כֵּיוָן דְּלָא עֲבוּד מְחִיצָה – סַלּוּקֵי סַלִּיקוּ נַפְשַׁיְיהוּ מֵהָכָא.

However, if **there is a partition** that renders the area fit **for a residence on** all sides of **the large roof, but** there is **no** partition that renders the area fit for **a residence on the small** roof, carrying **even** on **the small** roof **is permitted for the residents of the large** roof. **What is the reason** for this? **Since** the residents of the small roof **did not erect a partition** around their roof, **they** thereby **removed themselves from here** and transferred the right to their domain to the residents of the large roof.

כְּהָא דְּאָמַר רַב נַחְמָן: עָשָׂה סוּלָּם קָבוּעַ לְגַגּוֹ – הוּתַּר בְּכׇל הַגַּגִּין כּוּלָּן.

This is **in accordance with that which Rav Naḥman said:** If one **affixed a permanent ladder to his roof,** while the owners of the neighboring roofs did not do so, it **is permitted for him to** carry on **all the roofs.** The failure of the other owners to erect a ladder indicates that they relinquished the right to their roofs to the one who affixed the permanent ladder.

אָמַר אַבָּיֵי: בָּנָה עֲלִיָּיה עַל גַּבֵּי בֵּיתוֹ וְעָשָׂה לְפָנֶיהָ דַּקָּה אַרְבַּע – הוּתַּר בְּכׇל הַגַּגִּין כּוּלָּן.

Abaye said: If a person **built an upper story atop his house,** by surrounding the roof with walls, **and erected before its** entrance **a small partition** [*dakka*] **four** cubits high that opens to other roofs, **it is permitted** for him **to** carry on **all the roofs.** His construction of the partition is indicative of his plans to utilize the other roofs, while the failure of the other owners to do so indicates that they conceded use of their roofs to him.[B]

אָמַר רָבָא: פְּעָמִים שֶׁהַדַּקָּה לְאִיסּוּר. הֵיכִי דָּמֵי – דַּעֲבִידָא לְהָדֵי תַּרְבִּיצָא דְּבֵיתֵיהּ, דְּאָמַר

Rava said: Sometimes the small partition leads **to prohibition.**[N] **What are the circumstances** of this case? It is a case **where** the partition **was erected** facing **toward the garden of his house** and the sides facing the other roofs were sealed. The reason is **that** through his actions **he said**

Perek **IX**
Daf **90** Amud **a**

LANGUAGE

Garden [*tarbitza*] – תַּרְבִּיצָא: Courtyard or garden. Some linguists claim that the word is Persian in origin, but it is more likely of Semitic origin, in the form of the Akkadian word *tarbāṣu*.

NOTES

A *karmelit* and a private domain – כַּרְמְלִית וּרְשׁוּת הַיָּחִיד: *Tosafot* explain this: The adjacent pillar is the *karmelit*, while the roof of the house is the private domain, which is the opposite of Rashi's undertanding. Rabbeinu Ḥananel explains it this way as well.

BACKGROUND

A house and a portico – בַּיִת וְאַכְסַדְרָה: The image displays the differences between a house and a portico and the ease of transferring objects from the roof of the portico to the roof of the house.

House with adjoining portico

לְנַטּוּרֵי תַּרְבִּיצָא הוּא דַּעֲבִידָא.

that he built the upper story **to protect the garden** [*tarbitza*],[L] not to access the roofs.

בָּעֵי רָמֵי בַּר חָמָא: שְׁתֵּי אַמּוֹת בַּגַּג וּשְׁתֵּי אַמּוֹת בָּעַמּוּד מַהוּ? אָמַר רַבָּה: מַאי קָא מִיבַּעְיָא לֵיהּ? כַּרְמְלִית וּרְשׁוּת הַיָּחִיד קָא מִיבַּעְיָא לֵיהּ?!

Rami bar Ḥama raised a dilemma: According to Rav, who holds that one may carry only within four cubits on each roof, if he carries an object **two cubits on a roof and** another **two cubits on a pillar** ten handbreadths high and four handbreadths wide adjacent to the roof, **what is the** *halakha*? **Rabba said:** With regard to **what** matter **is he raising a dilemma?** Is it with regard to **a *karmelit* and a private domain**[N] that **he is raising a dilemma?** The roof is a *karmelit* and the pillar is a private domain; certainly carrying from one to the other is prohibited.

וְרָמֵי בַּר חָמָא אַגַּב חוּרְפֵּיהּ לָא עַיֵּין בַּהּ, אֶלָּא הָכִי קָמִיבַּעְיָא לֵיהּ: שְׁתֵּי אַמּוֹת בַּגַּג, וּשְׁתֵּי אַמּוֹת בְּאַכְסַדְרָה מַהוּ?

The Gemara explains that this was not in fact the dilemma, **and Rami bar Ḥama, due to his keen** mind, **did not analyze** the dilemma carefully and was imprecise in its formulation. **Rather, this is** the **dilemma he is raising:** If one carries an object **two cubits on the roof** of a house, **and** another **two cubits on** the slanted roof of **a portico,**[B] a roofed structure without walls, before a house belonging to someone else, **what is** the *halakha*?

מִי אָמְרִינַן: כֵּיוָן דְּלָא הַאי חֲזִי לְדִירָה, וְלָא הַאי חֲזִי לְדִירָה – חֲדָא רְשׁוּתָא הִיא. אוֹ דִּילְמָא: כֵּיוָן דְּמִגַּג לְגַג אָסִיר, מִגַּג לְאַכְסַדְרָה נַמֵי אָסִיר?

The Gemara elaborates on Rami bar Ḥama's dilemma: **Do we say** that **since neither this** roof **is fit for residence, nor is this** portico roof **fit for residence,** it **is** regarded as **one domain,** and therefore carrying between them is permitted? **Or perhaps since** carrying **from a roof to** another **roof is prohibited,** carrying **from a roof to a portico is likewise prohibited,** as the latter is also a domain in and of itself.

בָּעֵי רַב בֵּיבָי בַּר אַבַּיֵי: שְׁתֵּי אַמּוֹת בַּגַּג וּשְׁתֵּי אַמּוֹת בְּחוּרְבָּה מַהוּ?

Rav Beivai bar Abaye raised a similar **dilemma:** If one carries **two cubits on the roof** of a house **and** another **two cubits** on the roof **of a ruin** belonging to someone else, one side of which was completely open to a public domain, **what is** the *halakha*?

אָמַר רַב כָּהֲנָא: לָאו הַיְינוּ דְּרָמִי בַּר חָמָא? אֲמַר רַב בֵּיבָי בַּר אַבַּיֵי: וְכִי מְאַחֵר אֲתָאי וּנְצָאי?! אַכְסַדְרָה – לָא חַזְיָא לְדִירָה, וְחוּרְבָּה – חַזְיָא לְדִירָה.

Rav Kahana said: Is that not precisely the same dilemma raised **by Rami bar Ḥama** with regard to a portico? **Rav Beivai bar Abaye said: And did I come late** [*me'aḥer*] merely **to quarrel,**[N] and meddle in other people's questions? That is not the case, as the two dilemmas are not identical. **A portico is not fit for residence, while a ruin is fit for residence.** Therefore, the *halakha* might differ in each case.

וְכִי מֵאַחַר דְּחַזְיָא לְדִירָה, מַאי קָמִיבַּעְיָא לֵיהּ? אִם תִּימְצֵי לוֹמַר קָאָמַר; אִם תִּימְצֵי לוֹמַר אַכְסַדְרָה לָא חַזְיָא לְדִירָה – חוּרְבָּה חַזְיָא לְדִירָה, אוֹ דִּילְמָא הַשְׁתָּא מִיהָא לֵית בָּהּ דִּיוּרִין? תֵּיקוּ.

The Gemara is surprised by this explanation: **And now that it is fit for residence, what dilemma is he raising?** The situation is comparable to the case of two standard roofs. The Gemara answers: Rav Beivai was unaware of the resolution to the dilemma raised by Rami bar Ḥama, and therefore, **he states** the dilemma employing the style: **If you say. If you say** that **a portico is not fit for residence,** and therefore carrying is permitted, it can be argued that as **a ruin is fit for residence,** the legal status of its roof should be like that of a standard roof. **Or perhaps** that is not the case, as **now in any event there are no residents in** the ruin, and therefore its roof is not comparable to a standard roof. No resolution was found for these dilemmas, and they **stand** unresolved.

גַּגִּין הַשָּׁוִין לְרַבִּי מֵאִיר, וְגַג יְחִידִי לְרַבָּנַן, רַב אָמַר: מוּתָּר לְטַלְטֵל בְּכוּלּוֹ, וּשְׁמוּאֵל אָמַר: אֵין מְטַלְטְלִין בּוֹ אֶלָּא בְּאַרְבַּע.

The Gemara discusses a different question. With regard to **roofs that are level,** i.e., with a height disparity of less than ten handbreadths, **according to** the opinion of **Rabbi Meir, or an isolated roof** that does not border other roofs, **according to** the opinion of **the Rabbis, Rav said: It is permitted to move** an object **throughout the entire** roof; **and Shmuel said: One may move** an object **in it only within four** cubits.

רַב אָמַר: מוּתָּר לְטַלְטֵל בְּכוּלּוֹ, קַשְׁיָא דְּרַב אַדְּרַב! הָתָם – לָא מִינְכְּרָא מְחִיצָּתָא, הָכָא מִינְכְּרָא מְחִיצָּתָא. וּשְׁמוּאֵל אָמַר: אֵין מְטַלְטְלִין בּוֹ אֶלָּא בְּאַרְבַּע אַמּוֹת,

The Gemara seeks to clarify the conflicting opinions. **Rav said** that **it is permitted to move** objects **throughout the entire** roof. This is **difficult,** as there is an apparent contradiction between one statement **of Rav and** another statement **of Rav.** With regard to level roofs, Rav said that according to the Rabbis one may carry on each roof only within four cubits. The Gemara answers: **There,** in the case of a roof among roofs, **the** inner **partitions** between the houses **are not conspicuous,** and therefore, are not taken into consideration. **Here,** however, **the** outer **partitions** of a single house or group of houses **are conspicuous,** meaning that they are considered to extend upward and delineate the edge of the roof.

וּשְׁמוּאֵל אָמַר: אֵין מְטַלְטְלִין בּוֹ אֶלָּא בְּאַרְבַּע אַמּוֹת קַשְׁיָא דִּשְׁמוּאֵל אַדִּשְׁמוּאֵל! הָתָם – לָא הָוֵי יוֹתֵר מִבֵּית סָאתַיִם, הָכָא – הָוֵי יוֹתֵר מִבֵּית סָאתַיִם. וְהָנֵי מְחִיצוֹת לְמַטָּה עֲבִידָן, לְמַעְלָה לָא עֲבִידָן, וַהֲוָה כְּקַרְפֵּף יָתֵר מִבֵּית סָאתַיִם שֶׁלֹּא הוּקַּף לְדִירָה, וְכָל קַרְפֵּף יוֹתֵר מִבֵּית סָאתַיִם שֶׁלֹּא הוּקַּף לְדִירָה – אֵין מְטַלְטְלִין בּוֹ אֶלָּא בְּאַרְבַּע.

The Gemara returns to discuss Shmuel's ruling. **And Shmuel said: One may carry only within four** cubits. Once again, it is **difficult,** as there is an apparent contradiction between one statement **of Shmuel and** another statement **of Shmuel,** who said that in the case of level roofs, according to the Rabbis one may carry throughout each separate roof. The Gemara answers: **There,** the area of the roof **is no greater than two** ***beit se'a***; whereas **here,** the area **is greater than two** ***beit se'a*****. And these partitions** of the house **were erected** for use **below** as partitions for the residence itself; **they were not erected to** serve as partitions for use on the roof **above.** Consequently, even if the walls are viewed as extending upward so that they constitute surrounding partitions for the roof, the legal status of the roof is **like** that of **an enclosure greater than two** ***beit se'a*** **that was not enclosed** from the outset for the purpose of **residence; and** the principle is that with regard to **any enclosure greater than two** ***beit se'a*** **that was not enclosed** from the outset **for** the purpose of **residence, one may move** an object **in it only within four cubits.**[N]

אִיתְּמַר; סְפִינָה, רַב אָמַר: מוּתָּר לְטַלְטֵל בְּכוּלָּהּ, וּשְׁמוּאֵל אָמַר: אֵין מְטַלְטְלִין בָּהּ אֶלָּא בְּאַרְבַּע. רַב אָמַר: מוּתָּר לְטַלְטֵל בְּכוּלָּהּ,

It was further **stated** that these same *amora'im* disagreed with regard to a large **ship. Rav said: It is permitted to move** an object **throughout** the entire ship, as it is all one domain; **and Shmuel said: One may move** an object **in it only within four** cubits. The Gemara proceeds to clarify their respective opinions. **Rav said: It is permitted to move** an object **throughout** the boat,

NOTES

And did I come late [*me'aḥer*] merely to quarrel – וְכִי מְאַחֵר אֲתָאי וּנְצָאי: There are several explanations of this obscure phrase (see Rashi). The *Me'iri* explains that Rav Beivai bar Abaye said: Are you treating me as though I came late to the study hall, missed the lesson, and am now disagreeing for no reason? Some commentaries omit the phrase: And did, transforming the rhetorical question of Rav Beivai bar Abaye into a statement, saying that he came to instigate a gratuitous quarrel (Rabbeinu Ḥananel). Following this version of the text, the *Me'iri* understands *me'aḥer* differently: He is younger than me and yet he comes to pick a fight with me.

The opinions of Rav and Shmuel with regard to level roofs – שִׁיטַת רַב וּשְׁמוּאֵל בְּגַגִּין הַשָּׁוִין: The early commentaries struggled to account for the Gemara's statement with regard to contradictions in the rulings of both Rav and Shmuel. Rashi explains, in a forced explanation, that according to Rav the case involves an added structure built next to an isolated roof, which could be considered grounds for prohibition (see Ritva). With regard to the contradiction between Shmuel's statements, since the Gemara already established that even Rav agrees in the case of visible partitions, the focus on Shmuel must serve to underscore the difficulty, as it is doubly difficult according to his approach (see *Ge'on Ya'akov*).

דְּהָא אִיכָּא מְחִיצָתָא. וּשְׁמוּאֵל אָמַר: אֵין מְטַלְטְלִין בָּהּ אֶלָּא בְּאַרְבַּע אַמּוֹת – מְחִיצוֹת לְהַבְרִיחַ מַיִם עֲשׂוּיוֹת.

as there are partitions. **And Shmuel said: One may move** an object **in it only within four cubits,** as **the partitions** of the ship are not considered full-fledged partitions; they **are erected** only **to keep water out,**[N] not to render it a residence.

אֲמַר לֵיהּ רַב חִיָּיא בַּר יוֹסֵף לִשְׁמוּאֵל: הִילְכְתָא כְּוָותָךְ, אוֹ הִילְכְתָא כְּרַב? אֲמַר לֵיהּ: הִילְכְתָא כְּרַב.

Rav Ḥiyya bar Yosef said to Shmuel: Is **the** ***halakha*** **in accordance with your** opinion[N] **or** is **the** ***halakha*** **in accordance with** the opinion of **Rav?** Shmuel **said to him: The** ***halakha*** **is in accordance with** the opinion **of Rav,** as his rationale is more convincing.[H]

אָמַר רַב גִּידֵּל, אָמַר רַב חִיָּיא בַּר יוֹסֵף: וּמוֹדֶה רַב שֶׁאִם כְּפָאָהּ עַל פִּיהָ – שֶׁאֵין מְטַלְטְלִין בָּהּ אֶלָּא בְּאַרְבַּע אַמּוֹת. כְּפָאָהּ לְמַאי? אִילֵימָא לָדוּר תַּחְתֶּיהָ – מַאי שְׁנָא מִגַּג יְחִידִי?

Rav Giddel said that **Rav Ḥiyya bar Yosef said: And Rav concedes that if one overturned** the ship **onto its mouth,**[H] and it is more than ten handbreadths high, **that one may move** an object **on it only within four cubits.** The Gemara asks: **For what** purpose **was** the ship **overturned? If you say** it was overturned so **that** one may **reside beneath it, what is the difference** between it and **an isolated roof?** The legal status of the overturned ship should in every sense be that of a house, and therefore it should be permitted to carry throughout the entire ship.

אֶלָּא שֶׁכְּפָאָהּ לְזוּפְתָהּ.

Rather, it must be **that he overturned it to tar it,** i.e., to add a fresh coat to its underside. In that case, the boat certainly does not serve as a residence, and its sides are not considered full-fledged partitions.

רַב אַשִׁי מַתְנֵי לָהּ אַסְּפִינָה, וְרַב אַחָא בְּרֵיהּ דְּרָבָא מַתְנֵי לָהּ אַאַכְסַדְרָא. דְּאִיתְּמַר: אַכְסַדְרָה בְּבִקְעָה, רַב אָמַר: מוּתָּר לְטַלְטֵל בְּכוּלָּהּ, וּשְׁמוּאֵל אָמַר: אֵין מְטַלְטְלִין בָּהּ אֶלָּא בְּאַרְבַּע.

Rav Ashi teaches Shmuel's acceptance of Rav's opposing view (Ritva) with regard **to a ship,** as stated above; **and Rav Aḥa, son of Rava, teaches it** with regard **to a portico,**[N] **as it was stated** that *amora'im* disagreed with regard to **a portico** located **in a field.**[H] A portico has a roof and either incomplete walls or no walls. Consequently, in the case of a portico located in a valley, which is a *karmelit*, it remains to be determined whether or not it is permitted to carry in it. **Rav said: It is permitted to move** an object **throughout the entire** portico, as it is a private domain. **And Shmuel said: One may move** an object **in it only within four** cubits.

רַב אָמַר: מוּתָּר לְטַלְטֵל בְּכוּלָּהּ – אָמְרִינַן: "פִּי תִקְרָה יוֹרֵד וְסוֹתֵם". וּשְׁמוּאֵל אָמַר: אֵין מְטַלְטְלִין בָּהּ אֶלָּא בְּאַרְבַּע – לָא אָמְרִינַן: "פִּי תִקְרָה יוֹרֵד וְסוֹתֵם".

The Gemara elaborates. **Rav said: It is permitted to move** an object **throughout the entire** portico, as **we say: The edge of the roof descends** to the ground **and seals** the portico on all sides, rendering it a private domain. **And Shmuel said: One may move** an object **in it only within four** cubits, as **we do not say: The edge of the roof descends** to the ground **and seals** the portico.

וְרַב אַלִּיבָּא דְּרַבִּי מֵאִיר, לִיטַלְטְלִי מִגַּג לְחָצֵר! גְּזֵירָה מִשּׁוּם דְּרַב יִצְחָק בַּר אַבְדִּימִי.

The Gemara asks: **But** according to **Rav's** statement **in accordance with** the opinion **of Rabbi Meir** that one is permitted to carry from one roof to another if they are level, it should also be permitted **to carry from a roof to a courtyard.** Why then does Rabbi Meir rule that roofs and courtyards are separate domains and that carrying between them is prohibited? The Gemara answers: It is prohibited because Rabbi Meir issued **a decree, due to** the opinion **of Rav Yitzḥak bar Avdimi.** As stated previously, Rav Yitzḥak bar Avdimi rules that one may not transfer objects between two halakhically equivalent but physically distinct domains ten or more handbreadths high. This is a decree lest one standing in a public domain adjust a burden on a mound ten handbreadths high and four handbreadths wide, which is a private domain, an act prohibited by Torah law.

וּשְׁמוּאֵל אַלִּיבָּא דְּרַבָּנַן, נִיטַלְטֵל מִגַּג לְקַרְפֵּף! אָמַר רָבָא בַּר עוּלָּא: גְּזֵירָה שֶׁמָּא יִפְחַת הַגַּג.

The Gemara continues: **And** according to **Shmuel's** statement **in accordance with** the opinion **of the Rabbis** that the legal status of an isolated roof greater than two *beit se'a* is that of a *karmelit*, it should be permitted **to move** an object **from** an isolated **roof to an enclosure** within four cubits of the roof, as the legal status of the enclosure is also that of a *karmelit*. Why then do the Rabbis rule that roofs and enclosures are separate domains and carrying from one to the other is prohibited? **Rava bar Ulla said:** It is prohibited because the Rabbis issued **a decree lest the** area of the **roof diminish**[N] to less than two *beit se'a*, in which case it would assume the status of a private domain, as it is prohibited to carry between a private domain and an enclosure.

NOTES

The partitions are erected to keep water out – מְחִיצוֹת לְהַבְרִיחַ מַיִם: Apparently, Shmuel's rationale is not that the sides of a boat are designed solely in order to keep water out, and that consequently they cannot serve as a residence. Instead, Shmuel maintains that their primary function is to support the ship, while their use for a residence is a secondary one. However, some commentaries explain that Rabbi Zeira prohibits carrying in the entire boat, even if the boat is smaller than two *beit se'a*. This ruling is also in accordance with Shmuel's opinion that the partitions are not used for a residence at all (*Ge'on Ya'akov*).

Is the *halakha* in accordance with your opinion – הִילְכְתָא כְּוָותָךְ: Although the Sages frequently disagreed with each other, and each held firm to his own principles, occasionally one Sage would rule in favor of the Sage with whom he disagreed if he concluded that the other's reasoning was more convincing. In some cases, the Sage would completely retract his opinion. In other cases, despite the fact that he still considered his own opinion the correct one, he deemed the rationale behind the opposing opinion more compelling.

Portico – אַכְסַדְרָה: According to Rashi, the portico mentioned here is open on all sides, as it consists merely of four posts and a roof. *Tosafot*, by contrast, maintain that this portico, like all others mentioned by the Sages, is closed on three sides and entirely open on the fourth side.

Lest the area of the roof diminish – שֶׁמָּא יִפְחַת הַגַּג: The *Me'iri* explains that the height of the roof might decrease to the point that it is no longer a private domain, for example if dirt piled up around the outside of the house within ten handbreadths of the roof. This explains why this difference is not immediately visible, as those living in the house might not notice the change. Conversely, the decreased partitions of an enclosure are visible to all. See *Tosafot*, who suggest a very different explanation.

HALAKHA

Moving objects on a boat – טִלְטוּל בִּסְפִינָה: It is permitted to carry on a boat, even if it is more than two *beit se'a*, as it is considered to be enclosed for the purpose of residence. The *halakha* is in accordance with the opinion of Rav, as even Shmuel agrees with him in this case (*Shulḥan Arukh, Oraḥ Ḥayyim* 362:4).

An overturned ship – סְפִינָה הֲפוּכָה: If a boat is overturned, enabling one to live beneath it, it is permitted to carry even on the underside of the boat, which then serves as the roof of this house, as in a private domain. However, if it is overturned for it to be tarred, and its area is greater than two *beit se'a*, one may carry only four cubits beneath it (Rashi; *Shulḥan Arukh, Oraḥ Ḥayyim* 362:4).

A portico in a field – אַכְסַדְרָה בְּבִקְעָה: It is permitted to carry in a portico with three walls and a roof that is located in a field, based on application of the principle: The edge of the roof descends and seals, to the fourth side (Rambam *Sefer Zemanim, Hilkhot Shabbat* 17:35).

אִי הָכִי, מִקַּרְפֵּף לְקַרְפֵּף נַמִּי לֹא יְטַלְטֵל, דִּילְמָא מִיפַּחִית וְאָתֵי לְטַלְטוּלֵי! הָתָם, אִי מִיפְּחִית – מִינְכְּרָא לֵיהּ מִילְּתָא, הָכָא, אִי מִיפְּחִית – לָא מִינְכְּרָא מִילְּתָא.

The Gemara asks: **If so, one should also not** be permitted to **move** an object **from one enclosure to** another **enclosure,** due to the concern that **perhaps** the area of one of the enclosures will **diminish** and become a private domain, **and he** will **come** to **move** an object from one to the other as before. The Gemara answers: **There, if** the enclosure **is diminished, the matter is conspicuous,** as its walls are clearly visible. **Here,** however, **if** the roof **is diminished, the matter is not conspicuous,** as the roof does not have walls.

אָמַר רַב יְהוּדָה: כְּשֶׁתִּמְצָא לוֹמַר, לְדִבְרֵי רַבִּי מֵאִיר: גַּגִּין רְשׁוּת לְעַצְמָן, חֲצֵירוֹת רְשׁוּת לְעַצְמָן,

Rav Yehuda said: After careful analysis, **you will find** that you can say that **according to the statement of Rabbi Meir, roofs are a domain in and of themselves,** and one may carry from one roof to another; and likewise **courtyards are** considered **a domain in and of themselves,** and one may likewise carry from one courtyard to another.

Perek **IX**
Daf **91** Amud **a**

קַרְפֵּיפוֹת רְשׁוּת לְעַצְמָן. לְדִבְרֵי חֲכָמִים: גַּגִּין וַחֲצֵירוֹת רְשׁוּת אַחַת, קַרְפֵּיפוֹת רְשׁוּת אַחַת הֵן. לְדִבְרֵי רַבִּי שִׁמְעוֹן: כּוּלָּן רְשׁוּת אַחַת הֵן.

Similarly, **enclosures are a domain in and of themselves,** and one is therefore permitted to carry from one enclosure to another. **According to the statement of the Rabbis, roofs and courtyards** constitute **one domain,** and therefore, one may carry even from a roof to a courtyard; however, **enclosures are one** discrete **domain. According to the statement of Rabbi Shimon, all of them,** roofs, courtyards, and enclosures, **are one domain,** and therefore it is permitted to carry between any of them.[N]

תַּנְיָא כְּוָותֵיהּ דְּרַב, תַּנְיָא כְּוָותֵיהּ דְּרַב יְהוּדָה. תַּנְיָא כְּוָותֵיהּ דְּרַב: כׇּל גַּגּוֹת הָעִיר רְשׁוּת אַחַת הֵן, וְאָסוּר לְהַעֲלוֹת וּלְהוֹרִיד מִן הַגַּגִּין לֶחָצֵר וּמִן הֶחָצֵר לַגַּגִּין, וְכֵלִים שֶׁשָּׁבְתוּ בְּחָצֵר – מוּתָּר לְטַלְטְלָן בֶּחָצֵר. בַּגַּגִּין – מוּתָּר לְטַלְטְלָן בַּגַּגִּין, וּבִלְבַד שֶׁלֹּא יְהֵא גַּג גָּבוֹהַּ עֲשָׂרָה אוֹ נָמוּךְ עֲשָׂרָה, דִּבְרֵי רַבִּי מֵאִיר. וַחֲכָמִים אוֹמְרִים: כׇּל אֶחָד וְאֶחָד רְשׁוּת לְעַצְמוֹ, וְאֵין מְטַלְטְלִין בּוֹ אֶלָּא בְּאַרְבַּע.

The Gemara comments: A *baraita* **was taught in accordance with** the opinion of **Rav,** and a *baraita* **was taught in accordance with** the opinion of **Rav Yehuda.** The Gemara elaborates. A *baraita* **was taught in accordance with** the opinion of **Rav,** that according to the Rabbis one may carry only four cubits on each roof: **All the roofs of a city are one domain, and it is prohibited to carry** objects **up or carry** them **down, from the roofs to the courtyard or from the courtyard to the roofs. And** with regard to **vessels that were inside a courtyard** when **Shabbat** began, **it is permitted to carry them in the courtyard** even if an *eiruv* was not established, and it is likewise permitted to carry them from that courtyard to other courtyards. With regard to vessels that were **on the roofs** when **Shabbat** began, **it is permitted to carry them on the roofs, provided that one roof is neither ten** handbreadths **higher nor ten** handbreadths **lower** than the other. This is **the statement of Rabbi Meir. And the Rabbis say: Each and every one of** the roofs **is a domain in and of itself, and one may move** objects **on** each roof **only within four** cubits.

תַּנְיָא כְּוָותֵיהּ דְּרַב יְהוּדָה: אָמַר רַבִּי: כְּשֶׁהָיִינוּ לוֹמְדִים תּוֹרָה אֵצֶל רַבִּי שִׁמְעוֹן בִּתְקוֹעַ, הָיִינוּ מַעֲלִין שֶׁמֶן וַאֲלוּנְטִית מִגַּג לְגַג, וּמִגַּג לֶחָצֵר, וּמֵחָצֵר לְחָצֵר, וּמֵחָצֵר לְקַרְפֵּף, וּמִקַּרְפֵּף לְקַרְפֵּף אַחֵר, עַד שֶׁהָיִינוּ מַגִּיעִין אֵצֶל הַמַּעְיָין שֶׁהָיִינוּ רוֹחֲצִין בּוֹ.

Likewise, a *baraita* **was taught in accordance with Rav Yehuda's** interpretation of the opinion of Rabbi Shimon. **Rabbi** Yehuda HaNasi **said: When we were studying Torah with Rabbi Shimon in Tekoa,**[B] **we would carry oil** for smearing **and a towel** for drying **from roof to roof, and from roof to courtyard, and from courtyard to courtyard, and from courtyard to enclosure, and from enclosure to enclosure,** to refrain from carrying in a prohibited place, **until we reached the spring in which we would bathe.**

אָמַר רַבִּי יְהוּדָה: מַעֲשֶׂה בִּשְׁעַת הַסַּכָּנָה וְהָיִינוּ מַעֲלִין תּוֹרָה מֵחָצֵר לְגַג, וּמִגַּג לֶחָצֵר, וּמֵחָצֵר לְקַרְפֵּף, לִקְרוֹת בּוֹ.

And similarly, **Rabbi Yehuda said:** There was **an incident during a time of danger,** when decrees were issued that banned religious observance, **and we would carry a Torah scroll from courtyard to roof, and from roof to courtyard, and from courtyard to enclosure, to read from it.**

אָמְרוּ לוֹ: אֵין שְׁעַת הַסַּכָּנָה רְאָיָה.

The Sages **said to him:** The *halakha* cannot be determined from that incident, as an incident occurring during **a time of danger is no proof.** At a time of danger it is permitted to carry even in places where carrying is ordinarily prohibited by rabbinic law.

NOTES

The opinion of the Rabbis with regard to moving objects – שִׁיטַת חֲכָמִים בְּטִלְטוּל: It is unclear from the formulation of the *baraita* in this context, with regard to the opinions of Rabbi Yehuda HaNasi and Rabbi Yehuda, whether or not the latter agrees with Rabbi Shimon. The more precise version of the text indicates, as stated in the Jerusalem Talmud, that there are in fact four opinions: The first is that of the Rabbis, who maintain that each roof is considered a domain in its own right. The second opinion is Rabbi Meir's. He rules that all level roofs form a single domain, but it is one that is discrete from courtyards and enclosures. Rabbi Yehuda offers a third opinion. He teaches that roofs and courtyards are one domain, while enclosures constitute an independent domain. The fourth opinion is that of Rabbi Shimon, who considers all these areas a single domain.

BACKGROUND

Tekoa – תְּקוֹעַ: There are at least two cities in Israel called Tekoa, one in Judea and the other in the Galilee. Based on the time period, the city mentioned in this context is probably the Galilean Tekoa.

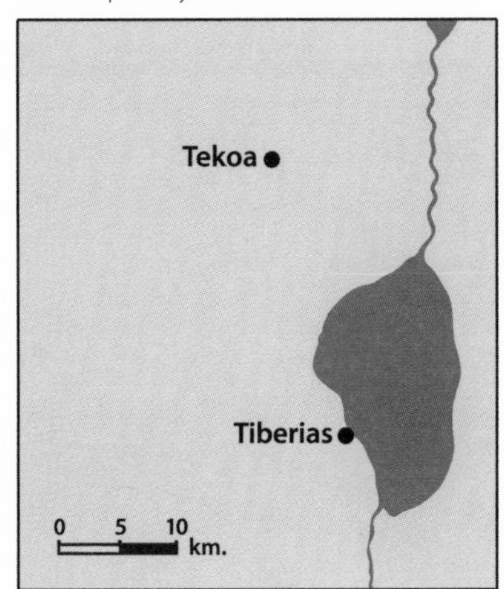

Tekoa in the Galilee

HALAKHA

The *halakha* is in accordance with the opinion of Rabbi Shimon – הֲלָכָה כְּרַבִּי שִׁמְעוֹן: The *halakha* is ruled in accordance with the opinion of Rabbi Shimon. It is permitted to carry from courtyards to roofs and to enclosures, even if the residents of each courtyard establish a separate *eiruv*, as the *halakha* is in accordance with the opinion of Rabbi Yoḥanan in disputes with Rav. In addition, Shmuel also agrees with him (*Shulḥan Arukh, Oraḥ Ḥayyim* 372:1).

NOTES

Who whispered to you – מִי לְחָשְׁךָ: *Tosafot* point out that this expression also appears in the halakhic midrash. Other commentaries note that it is also featured in various aggadic midrash. As for its meaning in this context, several commentaries explain, in the wake of Rabbeinu Tam's interpretation, that the question: Who whispered to you, was posed by Rabbi Yoḥanan to Shmuel. He asked him who informed him of this *halakha*. Apparently, as stated elsewhere, this is not Shmuel's own opinion. Nevertheless, he cited the *halakha* correctly. Indeed, in the Jerusalem Talmud it is stated that Shmuel is of the opinion that in a place where they established an *eiruv* it is prohibited to carry anything from one courtyard to another, including utensils from the courtyard in which they established an *eiruv* (see Maharsha; Rabbi Eliezer Meir Horowitz).

Rabbi Shimon conforms to his standard reasoning – רַבִּי שִׁמְעוֹן לְטַעְמֵיהּ: The *halakha* stated in the mishna with regard to the three courtyards challenges the opinion that Rabbi Shimon ruled leniently where they did not establish an *eiruv*. The answer is that in the case of three courtyards each person knows which utensils are his and which belong to his neighbor. Consequently, he knows which utensils it is permitted to carry. However, in this case some of the utensils are prohibited, while others are permitted, even though they came from the same place. As there is no obvious difference between them, the residents might mistakenly carry the prohibited objects (Ritva).

"רַבִּי שִׁמְעוֹן אוֹמֵר אֶחָד גַּגִּין" וכו'.

Rabbi Shimon says: Roofs, courtyards, and enclosures are **all** one domain with regard to vessels that were inside them when Shabbat began, and one may therefore carry from one of these areas to the other. However, they are not one domain with regard to vessels that were inside the house when Shabbat began.

אָמַר רַב: הֲלָכָה כְּרַבִּי שִׁמְעוֹן, וְהוּא, שֶׁלֹּא עֵירְבוּ, אֲבָל עֵירְבוּ – לֹא, דְּגָזְרִינַן דִּילְמָא אָתֵי לְאַפּוֹקֵי מָאנֵי דְּבָתִּים לְחָצֵר.

Rav said: The *halakha* is in accordance with the opinion of **Rabbi Shimon,**[H] **provided that** the residents of each courtyard **did not establish** a separate ***eiruv*** for themselves, as in that case they may not move objects from their houses into the courtyard. **However, if they established** a separate ***eiruv*** for each courtyard, without establishing an *eiruv* between the various courtyards, **no,** that is not the *halakha*, **as we issue a decree lest one come to take out vessels** from one **of the houses to the courtyard,** an action that is fundamentally permitted, and subsequently proceed to carry them out to a different courtyard with which an *eiruv* had not been established, which everyone agrees is prohibited.

וּשְׁמוּאֵל אָמַר: בֵּין עֵירְבוּ, בֵּין שֶׁלֹּא עֵירְבוּ. וְכֵן אָמַר רַבִּי יוֹחָנָן: מִי לְחָשְׁךָ בֵּין עֵירְבוּ וּבֵין שֶׁלֹּא עֵירְבוּ?

And Shmuel said: The *halakha* is in accordance with Rabbi Shimon, **whether they established an *eiruv* or whether they did not establish an *eiruv*. And similarly Rabbi Yoḥanan said: Who whispered to you,**[N] who told you that there is a difference **whether they established an *eiruv* or whether they did not establish an *eiruv*?**

מַתְקִיף לַהּ רַב חִסְדָּא: לִשְׁמוּאֵל וּלְרַבִּי יוֹחָנָן, יֹאמְרוּ: שְׁנֵי כֵלִים בְּחָצֵר אַחַת, זֶה מוּתָּר וְזֶה אָסוּר!

Rav Ḥisda strongly objects to this ruling. **According to Shmuel and according to Rabbi Yoḥanan,** people **will say** with regard to **two vessels** located **in the same courtyard,** one of which was in the courtyard when Shabbat began while the other was in the house, that moving **this** one, which was in the courtyard at the start of Shabbat, to another courtyard is **permitted, while** moving **that one,** which was in the house at the start of Shabbat, to another courtyard, is **prohibited.**

רַבִּי שִׁמְעוֹן לְטַעְמֵיהּ דְּלָא גָּזַר. דִּתְנַן, אָמַר רַבִּי שִׁמְעוֹן: לְמָה הַדָּבָר דּוֹמֶה – לְשָׁלֹשׁ חֲצֵירוֹת הַפְּתוּחוֹת זוֹ לָזוֹ וּפְתוּחוֹת לִרְשׁוּת הָרַבִּים, וְעֵירְבוּ שְׁתֵּי הַחִיצוֹנוֹת עִם הָאֶמְצָעִית, הִיא מוּתֶּרֶת עִמָּהֶן וְהֵן מוּתָּרוֹת עִמָּהּ, וּשְׁתֵּי הַחִיצוֹנוֹת אֲסוּרִין זוֹ עִם זוֹ.

The Gemara answers: In this regard, **Rabbi Shimon** conforms **to his** standard **reasoning,**[N] **as he did not issue a decree** due to these concerns. **As we learned** in a mishna, **Rabbi Shimon said: To what is this matter comparable?** It is comparable **to three courtyards that are open into each other, and that are** also **open into a public domain.** If **the two outer** courtyards each **established an *eiruv* with the middle one,** it is **permitted** for the residents of the middle one to carry **into** the two outer ones, **and they,** the residents of the two outer ones, **are permitted** to carry **into it, but** for the residents of **the two outer** courtyards it is **prohibited** to carry **into each other,** as they did not establish an *eiruv* together.

וְלָא גָּזַר דִּילְמָא אָתֵי לְאַפּוֹקֵי מָאנֵי דְּהָא חָצֵר לְהָא חָצֵר – הָכִי נַמִי לָא גָּזְרִינַן דִּילְמָא אָתֵי לְאַפּוֹקֵי מָאנֵי דְּבָתִּים לְחָצֵר.

And in that case Rabbi Shimon **did not issue a decree** prohibiting one to carry objects from the middle courtyard to one of the outer ones **lest one come to take out vessels from this** outer **courtyard to that** outer **courtyard,** despite the fact that both sets of vessels are located in the middle courtyard. **Here too, we do not issue a decree lest one come to take out utensils** from one **of the houses to the courtyard,** and carry them to a different courtyard.

מֵתִיב רַב שֵׁשֶׁת, רַבִּי שִׁמְעוֹן אוֹמֵר: אֶחָד גַּגּוֹת, אֶחָד חֲצֵירוֹת, וְאֶחָד קַרְפֵּיפוֹת – רְשׁוּת אַחַת הֵן לְכֵלִים שֶׁשָּׁבְתוּ בְּתוֹכָן, וְלֹא לְכֵלִים שֶׁשָּׁבְתוּ בְּתוֹךְ הַבַּיִת. אִי אָמְרַתְּ בִּשְׁלָמָא דְּעֵירְבוּ – הַיְינוּ דְּמַשְׁכַּחַתְּ לַהּ מָאנֵי דְּבָתִּים בְּחָצֵר.

Rav Sheshet raised an objection. We learned in the mishna that **Rabbi Shimon says: Roofs, courtyards, and enclosures are all one domain with regard to vessels that were inside them** when **Shabbat** began. **But** they are **not** one domain **with regard to vessels that were inside the house** when **Shabbat** began. **Granted, if you say** that it is dealing with a case where the residents of the courtyards **established an *eiruv*, that is how you find vessels** that were taken **from the house in the courtyard.** Because those vessels were in the house at the beginning of Shabbat, they may not be moved to a different courtyard.

אֶלָּא אִי אָמְרַתְּ בְּשֶׁלֹּא עֵירְבוּ – הֵיכִי מַשְׁכַּחַתְּ לַהּ מָאנֵי דְּבָתִּים בְּחָצֵר? הוּא מוֹתִיב לַהּ וְהוּא מְפָרֵק לַהּ: בְּכוּמְתָּא וְסוּדְרָא.

However, if you say it is referring to a case **where they did not establish an *eiruv*,** under **what** circumstances can the case of **vessels from the house in the courtyard** be found? This poses a difficulty for Rav. Rav Sheshet **raised the objection, and he resolved it:** It refers **to** the case of **a hat or a shawl,** which one wore in the house and subsequently went out to the courtyard and placed it there. In this manner, it is possible that objects taken from the house can be found in the courtyard, even if an *eiruv* was not established.

תָּא שְׁמַע: אַנְשֵׁי חָצֵר וְאַנְשֵׁי מִרְפֶּסֶת שֶׁשָּׁכְחוּ וְלֹא עֵירְבוּ, כֹּל שֶׁגָּבוֹהַּ עֲשָׂרָה טְפָחִים – לַמִּרְפֶּסֶת, פָּחוֹת מִכָּאן – לֶחָצֵר. בַּמֶּה דְּבָרִים אֲמוּרִים – שֶׁהָיוּ אֵלּוּ שֶׁל רַבִּים וְאֵלּוּ שֶׁל רַבִּים, וְעֵירְבוּ אֵלּוּ לְעַצְמָן וְאֵלּוּ לְעַצְמָן, אוֹ שֶׁל יְחִידִים שֶׁאֵין צְרִיכִין לְעָרֵב.

Come and hear proof from a *baraita*: With regard to **the residents of** houses that open directly into **a courtyard and the residents of** upper stories that open onto **a balcony** from which stairs lead down to that courtyard, **who forgot and did not establish an** ***eiruv*** between them, **anything ten handbreadths high** in the courtyard, e.g., a mound or a pillar, is attributed **to the balcony** in terms of its use on Shabbat. The residents of the balcony may move objects between the mound or pillar and their apartments. Anything **lower than that** is attributed **to the courtyard. In what** case **is this statement,** that it is prohibited for the residents of the courtyard to carry to the balcony and vice versa, **stated?** It is in a case **where** the residents of the courtyard **were many, and** the residents of the balcony were **many, and these established an** ***eiruv*** **for themselves, and those established an** ***eiruv*** **for themselves; or** if the courtyard and the balcony were occupied by **individuals who need not establish an** ***eiruv*** for themselves.

אֲבָל הָיוּ שֶׁל רַבִּים, וְשָׁכְחוּ וְלֹא עֵירְבוּ – גַּג וְחָצֵר וְאַכְסַדְרָה וּמִרְפֶּסֶת כּוּלָּן רְשׁוּת אַחַת הֵן.

However, if the residents of the courtyard and the balcony **were many, and they forgot and did not establish an** ***eiruv*** for their courtyard or balcony, in that case **roof, and courtyard, and portico, and balcony are all one domain,** and it is permitted to carry from one to another any vessels that were located in any one of them when Shabbat began.

טַעְמָא – דְּלֹא עֵירְבוּ, הָא עֵירְבוּ – לֹא! הָא מַנִּי – רַבָּנַן הִיא.

The Gemara infers: **The reason** that carrying between them is permitted is **that they did not** each **establish** their own ***eiruv***; however, if **they** each **established** their own ***eiruv***, **no,** it is prohibited to carry between them. This inference supports Rav and poses a difficulty for Shmuel. The Gemara answers: **Whose** opinion is represented by **this** *baraita*? **It is** that of **the Rabbis,**[N] who maintain that roofs and courtyards form a single domain, contrary to the opinion of Rabbi Shimon. The Rabbis indeed issued a decree that carrying is prohibited if each group established a separate *eiruv*.

דַּיְקָא נַמִי, דְּלָא קָתָנֵי קַרְפֵּף וּמָבוֹי, שְׁמַע מִינָּהּ.

The Gemara comments: The language of the *baraita* **is also precise, as it is not teaching** the cases of **an enclosure and an alleyway,** in accordance with the opinion of Rabbi Shimon, but only the cases of a roof and a courtyard, in accordance with the opinion of the Rabbis. The Gemara concludes: Indeed, **learn from here** that this is the correct understanding.

תָּא שְׁמַע: חָמֵשׁ חֲצֵירוֹת הַפְּתוּחוֹת זוֹ לָזוֹ וּפְתוּחוֹת לַמָּבוֹי, וְשָׁכְחוּ כּוּלָּם וְלֹא עֵירְבוּ – אָסוּר לְהַכְנִיס וּלְהוֹצִיא מֵחָצֵר לַמָּבוֹי, וּמִן הַמָּבוֹי לֶחָצֵר. וְכֵלִים שֶׁשָּׁבְתוּ בֶּחָצֵר – מוּתָּר לְטַלְטְלָן בֶּחָצֵר, וּבַמָּבוֹי – אָסוּר.

Come and **hear** from another *baraita*: With regard to **five courtyards that are open to each other**[N] **and** are also **open to an alleyway, and** the residents of **all** the courtyards **forgot and did not establish an** ***eiruv***, **it is prohibited to carry in or carry out, from a courtyard to the alleyway or from the alleyway to a courtyard. And** with regard to **vessels that were in the courtyard** when **Shabbat** began, **it is permitted to carry them in the courtyard, but in the alleyway it is prohibited** to carry them.

וְרַבִּי שִׁמְעוֹן מַתִּיר. שֶׁהָיָה רַבִּי שִׁמְעוֹן אוֹמֵר: כָּל זְמַן שֶׁהֵן שֶׁל רַבִּים וְשָׁכְחוּ וְלֹא עֵירְבוּ, גַּג וְחָצֵר וְאַכְסַדְרָה וּמִרְפֶּסֶת וְקַרְפֵּף וּמָבוֹי – כּוּלָּן רְשׁוּת אַחַת הֵן.

And Rabbi Shimon permits doing so, **as Rabbi Shimon would say: Whenever** the courtyards **are** in the possession **of many** people, **and they forgot and did not establish an** ***eiruv***, the **roof, and courtyard, and portico, and balcony, and enclosure, and alleyway are all one domain.** These areas are all classified as private domains, and therefore, it is permitted to carry from one to the other.

טַעְמָא – דְּלֹא עֵירְבוּ, הָא עֵירְבוּ – לֹא! מַאי לֹא עֵירְבוּ – לֹא עֵירְבוּ חֲצֵירוֹת בַּהֲדֵי הֲדָדֵי, הָא חָצֵר וּבָתִּים – עֵירְבוּ.

The Gemara infers: **The reason** that carrying between them is permitted is **that they did not** each **establish** their own ***eiruv***; however, if **they** each **established** their own ***eiruv***, **no,** it is prohibited to carry between them. This inference supports Rav and poses a difficulty for Shmuel. The Gemara answers: **What is** the meaning of the phrase: **They did not establish an** ***eiruv***? It means that the residents of the **courtyards did not establish an** ***eiruv*** **with each other; however, the** residents of each **courtyard established an** ***eiruv*** with the residents of **the houses** inside it, and it is nevertheless permitted to carry between them, in accordance with the opinion of Shmuel.

NOTES

Whose opinion is this? It is that of the Rabbis – הָא מַנִּי רַבָּנַן הִיא: It can be proven that the Rabbis indeed issued a decree in a case where they established an *eiruv*, because they issued a decree in the case of three courtyards that open into one another, as they disagree with Rabbi Shimon in this matter as well (Ritva).

Courtyards that are open to each other – חֲצֵירוֹת הַפְּתוּחוֹת זוֹ לָזוֹ: It was necessary to state that the courtyards open into each other according to the opinion of Rabbi Meir; he maintains that one may not carry from one courtyard to another over a wall ten handbreadths high, as in his opinion, a roof constitutes a domain in and of itself. Therefore, this discussion must refer to a case where there are openings between the courtyards (Ra'avad).

NOTES

But doesn't it state they did not establish an *eiruv* – וְהָא לֹא עֵירְבוּ קָתָנֵי: Rabbeinu Ḥananel explains this difficulty as follows. The expression: Established an *eiruv*, refers specifically to the joining of the houses inside a courtyard, as the joining of separate courtyards that open into an alleyway is called a merging of an alleyway. The ensuing response is also based on a linguistic consideration: Although the term *eiruv* usually denotes the joining of households through a courtyard, this is not its exclusive meaning, as it can also refer to the merging of several courtyards.

The superfluous teaching – מִשְׁנָה יְתֵירָא: Although inferences cannot be drawn from seemingly redundant phrases in a mishna, and certainly not from those of *baraitot*, in the manner that they are drawn from verses in the Bible, occasionally concepts or *halakhot* are inferred from superfluous expressions in a mishna. This is especially true with regard to obvious repetitions in adjacent sentences, as in this case.

וְהָא "לֹא עֵירְבוּ" קָתָנֵי! מַאי לֹא עֵירְבוּ – לֹא נִשְׁתַּתְּפוּ.

The Gemara raises a difficulty. **But doesn't** the *baraita* **state: They did not establish an *eiruv*,**[N] indicating that they did not establish any *eiruv* at all, either with the residents of the other courtyard or within each courtyard? The Gemara rejects this argument. **What** is the meaning of: **They did not establish an *eiruv*?** It means that **they did not merge** the courtyards facing the alleyway.

וְאִיבָּעֵית אֵימָא: רַבִּי שִׁמְעוֹן לְדִבְרֵיהֶם דְּרַבָּנַן קָאָמַר לְהוּ; לְדִידִי לָא שְׁנָא עֵירְבוּ וְלָא שְׁנָא לֹא עֵירְבוּ, אֶלָּא לְדִידְכוּ – אוֹדוּ לִי מִיהַת דְּהֵיכָא דְּלֹא עֵירְבוּ רְשׁוּת אַחַת הִיא.

And if you wish, say instead: **Rabbi Shimon is speaking to the Rabbis in accordance with their** own **opinion,** not enumerating the leniencies inherent in his own ruling. His statement should therefore be understood as follows: **According to my own** opinion, **there is no difference** if **they established an *eiruv* and there is no difference** if **they did not establish an *eiruv*. However, according to your** opinion, **agree with me at least that** in a case **where they did not establish an *eiruv* it is** all considered **one domain.**

וְאָמְרוּ לֵיהּ רַבָּנַן: לֹא, שְׁתֵּי רְשׁוּיוֹת הֵן.

And the Rabbis said to him: No, although we agree with you in the cases of a roof, courtyard, portico, and balcony, in the cases of an enclosure and an alleyway we disagree, as **they are two domains** and therefore it is prohibited to carry from one to the other.

אָמַר מָר: וּבַמָּבוֹי אָסוּר. לֵימָא מְסַיַּיע לֵיהּ לְרַבִּי זֵירָא אָמַר רַב, דְּאָמַר רַבִּי זֵירָא, אָמַר רַב: מָבוֹי שֶׁלֹּא נִשְׁתַּתְּפוּ בּוֹ – אֵין מְטַלְטְלִין אֶלָּא בְּאַרְבַּע אַמּוֹת! אֵימָא: וְלַמָּבוֹי אָסוּר.

The Master said above in the *baraita*: Vessels that were in a courtyard at the start of Shabbat may be carried within the courtyard, **but in the alleyway it is prohibited.** The Gemara asks: **Let us say** that this **supports that** which **Rabbi Zeira said** that **Rav said, as Rabbi Zeira said** that **Rav said:** In **an alleyway in which they did not merge** the courtyards facing it, **one may carry only within four cubits.** The Gemara rejects this suggestion. **Say** that the *baraita* means: **But to an alleyway it is prohibited,** i.e., it is prohibited to carry from the courtyard to the alleyway; however, within the alleyway itself it is permitted to carry.

הַיְינוּ רֵישָׁא! מִשְׁנָה יְתֵירָא אִיצְטְרִיכָא לֵיהּ, מַהוּ דְּתֵימָא: כִּי פְּלִיגִי רַבָּנַן עֲלֵיהּ דְּרַבִּי שִׁמְעוֹן – הָנֵי מִילֵּי הֵיכָא דְּעֵירְבוּ, אֲבָל הֵיכָא דְּלֹא עֵירְבוּ – מוֹדוּ לֵיהּ, קָא מַשְׁמַע לָן.

The Gemara raises a difficulty. If so, **that is** identical to **the first clause** of the *baraita*. The *tanna* would not have taught the very same thing twice. The Gemara answers: **The** apparently **superfluous teaching**[N] **was necessary, lest you say: When the Rabbis disagree with Rabbi Shimon, it is only** in a case **where they established an *eiruv*, but** in a case **where they did not establish an *eiruv*,** the Rabbis **concede to** Rabbi Meir that it is all considered one domain and carrying is permitted. The *baraita* therefore **teaches us** that the Rabbis disagree with Rabbi Shimon in both cases, as they prohibit carrying in the alleyway even if the residents did not establish an *eiruv*.

אָמַר לֵיהּ רָבִינָא לְרַב אַשִׁי:

Ravina said to Rav Ashi:

Perek **IX**
Daf **92** Amud **a**

מִי אָמַר רַבִּי יוֹחָנָן הָכִי? וְהָא אָמַר רַבִּי יוֹחָנָן: הֲלָכָה כִּסְתַם מִשְׁנָה. וּתְנַן: כּוֹתֶל שֶׁבֵּין שְׁתֵּי חֲצֵירוֹת, גָּבוֹהַּ עֲשָׂרָה וְרוֹחַב אַרְבָּעָה – מְעָרְבִין שְׁנַיִם וְאֵין מְעָרְבִין אֶחָד. הָיוּ בְּרֹאשׁוֹ פֵּירוֹת – אֵלּוּ עוֹלִין מִכָּאן וְאוֹכְלִים, וְאֵלּוּ עוֹלִין מִכָּאן וְאוֹכְלִים, וּבִלְבַד שֶׁלֹּא יוֹרִידוּ לְמַטָּה!

Did Rabbi Yoḥanan actually **say this,** that the *halakha* is in accordance with Rabbi Shimon's opinion that all courtyards constitute a single domain, even if each courtyard established an independent *eiruv*? **But didn't Rabbi Yoḥanan say** that **the *halakha* is in accordance with an unattributed mishna, and we learned:** With regard to **a wall between two courtyards, ten** handbreadths **high and four** handbreadths **wide, they establish two *eiruvin*,** one for each courtyard, **but they do not establish one *eiruv*.** If **there was fruit atop** the wall, **these,** the residents of one courtyard, **may ascend from here and eat** it, **and those,** the residents of the other courtyard, **may ascend from there and eat** it, **provided that they do not take** the fruit **down** from atop the wall to the courtyards. According to Rabbi Yoḥanan, all the courtyards are considered a single domain. Why may they not bring the fruit down?

מַאי "לְמַטָּה" – לְמַטָּה לַבָּתִּים. וְהָא תָּנֵי רַבִּי חִיָּיא: וּבִלְבַד שֶׁלֹּא יְהֵא זֶה עוֹמֵד בִּמְקוֹמוֹ וְאוֹכֵל, וְזֶה עוֹמֵד בִּמְקוֹמוֹ וְאוֹכֵל!

The Gemara answers: **What is** the meaning of the word **down** in this context? It means **down to the houses;** however, it is indeed permitted to bring the fruit down to the courtyards. The Gemara raises a difficulty: **But didn't Rabbi Ḥiyya** explicitly **teach** in a *Tosefta*: **Provided that neither will this** one **stand** below **in his place** in his courtyard **and eat, nor** will **that** one **stand in his place** in his courtyard **and eat?**

אֲמַר לֵיהּ: וְכִי רַבִּי לֹא שְׁנָאָהּ, רַבִּי חִיָּיא מִנַּיִן לוֹ?!

Rav Ashi **said to** Ravina: No proof can be cited from this *baraita* of Rabbi Ḥiyya with regard to the mishna. **If Rabbi** Yehuda HaNasi **did not** explicitly **teach it**[N] in this manner, **from where does** his student **Rabbi Ḥiyya** know it? If a *halakha* is not taught by the mishna itself, it should not be distorted to have it correspond with a *Tosefta*.

אִתְּמַר, שְׁתֵּי חֲצֵירוֹת וְחוּרְבָּה אַחַת בֵּינֵיהֶם, אַחַת עֵירְבָה וְאַחַת לֹא עֵירְבָה. אָמַר רַב הוּנָא: נוֹתְנִין אוֹתָהּ לָזוֹ שֶׁלֹּא עֵירְבָה, אֲבָל לְשֶׁעֵירְבָה – לֹא, דִּילְמָא אָתֵי לְאַפּוֹקֵי מָאנֵי דְּבָתִּים לַחוּרְבָּה.

It was stated that *amora'im* dispute the following case: If there were **two courtyards and** there was **one ruin**[N] **between them,** and the residents of **one** courtyard **established an** *eiruv* for themselves, while the residents of **the other** courtyard **did not establish an** *eiruv* for themselves, **Rav Huna said:** The Sages **confer** the right to utilize the ruin **to** the residents of **that** courtyard **that did not establish an** *eiruv;* **however, to** the residents of the courtyard **that established an** *eiruv,* **no,** they do not confer the right to utilize the ruin. It is prohibited due to a decree, **lest people come to take out vessels** from one **of the houses to the ruin,** which is prohibited, as no *eiruv* was established with the ruin itself. However, this concern does not extend to the courtyard whose residents did not establish an *eiruv*. They are not permitted to move objects from their houses to the courtyard, and therefore there is no reason to issue a decree prohibiting the carrying of objects from the courtyard to the ruin.

וְחִיָּיא בַּר רַב אָמַר: אַף לְשֶׁעֵירְבָה, וּשְׁתֵּיהֶן אֲסוּרוֹת. וְאִם תֹּאמַר שְׁתֵּיהֶן מוּתָּרוֹת, מִפְּנֵי מָה אֵין נוֹתְנִין חָצֵר שֶׁלֹּא עֵירְבָה לְחָצֵר שֶׁעֵירְבָה –

And Ḥiyya bar Rav disagreed with Rav Huna and **said:** Rights to the ruin are conferred **to** the residents of the courtyard **that established an** *eiruv,* and consequently, it is **prohibited** for residents of **both** courtyards to carry objects. **And if you say** that it should be **permitted** for residents of **both** to move articles to the ruin, that is incorrect. As if that were so, **for what** reason did the Sages **not confer** the right to carry in **the courtyard that did not establish an** *eiruv,* **to the** residents of the **courtyard that established an** *eiruv*? If there is no cause for concern, it should always be permitted to the residents of a courtyard that established an *eiruv* to carry from their courtyard to a different courtyard whose residents did not establish an *eiruv*.

הָתָם כֵּיוָן דְּמִינְטְרִי מָאנֵי דְּבָתִּים בֶּחָצֵר אָתֵי לְאַפּוֹקֵי, הָכָא בַּחוּרְבָּה כֵּיוָן דְּלָא מִינְטְרִי מָאנֵי דְּחָצֵר בַּחוּרְבָּה – לָא אָתֵי לְאַפּוֹקֵי.

The Gemara refutes this contention: **There,** in the case of courtyards, **since the vessels from the houses are protected in the courtyard** as well, there is a concern lest people **come to take them out** from the house to the courtyard, where they could be confused with those vessels already in the courtyard, and they might come to move those objects into the other courtyard. **Here,** in the case of **a ruin, since the vessels from the courtyard are not protected in the ruin,** there is **no** concern lest people **come to take out** the vessels from the courtyard into the ruin. Therefore, it is possible that residents of both courtyards would be permitted to utilize the ruin.

אִיכָּא דְּאָמְרִי, חִיָּיא בַּר רַב אָמַר: אַף לְשֶׁעֵירְבָה, וּשְׁתֵּיהֶן מוּתָּרוֹת. וְאִם תֹּאמַר: שְׁתֵּיהֶן אֲסוּרוֹת – לְפִי שֶׁאֵין נוֹתְנִים חָצֵר שֶׁלֹּא עֵירְבָה לְחָצֵר שֶׁעֵירְבָה. הָתָם כֵּיוָן דְּמִינְטְרִי מָאנֵי דְּבָתִּים בֶּחָצֵר לָא שָׁרוּ בְּהוּ רַבָּנַן, דְּאָתֵי לְאַפּוֹקֵי, אֲבָל בְּחוּרְבָּה – לָא מִינְטְרִי.

Some say a different version of the previous discussion. **Ḥiyya bar Rav** disagreed with Rav Huna and **said:** The ruin belongs **even to** the residents of the courtyard **that established an** *eiruv,* **and** it is **permitted** for residents of **both** to carry in the ruin. **And if you say** they should **both** be **prohibited** to do so in accordance with the argument presented above, **that** the Sages **do not confer** the right to carry in **the courtyard that did not establish an** *eiruv* **to the** residents of the **courtyard that established an** *eiruv*, this proof can be refuted. **There, since the vessels from the houses are protected in the courtyard, the Sages did not permit** carrying **them,** due to the concern **lest** people **come to take them out** from the house to the courtyard and from there to the other courtyard. **However, in** the case of **a ruin,** the vessels **are not protected** in the ruin, and therefore, there is no cause for concern.

NOTES

If Rabbi Yehuda HaNasi did not teach it – **וְכִי רַבִּי לֹא שְׁנָאָהּ:** It is evident that this principle is not absolute, for otherwise there would be no point in studying *baraitot* and comparing them to the Mishna, which is one of the primary modes of analysis in the Gemara. This principle simply means that nothing can be learned from a *baraita* that contradicts the plain meaning of a mishna or that leads to a conclusion not found in a mishna, as in that case it cannot be viewed as an elucidation and explanation of the mishna. Rather, it represents Rabbi Ḥiyya's own opinion (see *Tosafot Yevamot*).

Two courtyards and one ruin – **שְׁתֵּי חֲצֵירוֹת וְחוּרְבָּה אַחַת:** This entire discussion is based on Rav's opinion that Rabbi Shimon's statement applies only to a courtyard whose residents did not establish an *eiruv*. Rabbi Huna, Rav's student, and Ḥiyya, Rav's son, disagree about his opinion. Rashi maintains that Ḥiyya received a tradition from his father that the ruin is permitted even to the residents of the courtyard who did not establish an *eiruv*, but he could not decide whether in practice it should be prohibited or permitted for both courtyards to use the ruin.

The Ra'avad explains that this entire discussion with regard to a ruin applies only if it belongs equally to both courtyards. However, if it belongs only to the residents of one of the courtyards, the inhabitants of the other courtyard have nothing to do with it.

מתני׳ גַּג גָּדוֹל סָמוּךְ לְקָטָן – הַגָּדוֹל מוּתָּר וְהַקָּטָן אָסוּר. חָצֵר גְּדוֹלָה שֶׁנִּפְרְצָה לִקְטַנָּה – גְּדוֹלָה מוּתֶּרֶת וּקְטַנָּה אֲסוּרָה, מִפְּנֵי שֶׁהִיא כְּפִתְחָהּ שֶׁל גְּדוֹלָה.

MISHNA If **a large roof** was **adjacent to a small roof,**[H] and the boundary between them was no wider than ten cubits, use of **the large one is permitted,** i.e., one may bring objects up to the roof from the house below and carry them on the roof, **and** use of **the small one is prohibited.** A similar *halakha* applies to **a large courtyard that was breached into a small** one,[H] in a manner that one entire side of the small courtyard was breached, but the breach was less than ten cubits; it is **permitted** for the residents of **the large** courtyard to carry, **but** it is **prohibited** for the residents of **the small one** to do so. The rationale for this difference is **because** in that case, the legal status of the breach **is like** that of **the entrance of the large** courtyard. As the breach in the wall of the larger courtyard is surrounded on both sides by the remaining portions of that wall, and the breach is no greater than ten cubits wide, its legal status is like that of an entrance in the wall of the courtyard, and therefore it is permitted to carry in the large courtyard. With regard to the small courtyard, however, since one entire side of the small courtyard was breached, there remains no partition whatsoever on that side and carrying in that courtyard is therefore prohibited.

גמ׳ לָמָּה לֵיהּ לְמִיתְנֵי תַּרְתֵּי?

GEMARA The Gemara poses a question: **Why does** the mishna **teach** the same *halakha* **twice?** Why is it necessary to repeat the ruling with regard to both roofs and courtyards when the cases are apparently identical?

לְרַב קָתָנֵי גַּג דּוּמְיָא דְּחָצֵר; מַה חָצֵר מִנְכַּרָא מְחִיצָּתָא – אַף גַּג נַמִי מִנְכַּרָא מְחִיצָּתָא.

The Gemara answers: **According to** the opinion of **Rav,** with regard to the lenient ruling that the residents may carry on a roof, the repetition comes to **teach** the *halakha* of **a roof similar to** that of **a courtyard: Just as a courtyard, its partitions are conspicuous, so too a roof, its** extended **partitions,** based on the principle: Extend and raise the walls of the house, must be **conspicuous**[H] for it to be permitted for the residents to carry on their account. In other words, the roof must not extend beyond the walls of the house.

וְלִשְׁמוּאֵל גַּג דּוּמְיָא דְּחָצֵר; מַה חָצֵר דְּקָא דָּרְסִי לָהּ רַבִּים – אַף גַּג נַמִי דְּקָא דָּרְסִי לֵיהּ רַבִּים.

Whereas **according to** the opinion of **Shmuel,** the repetition should be understood in the opposite manner, as it comes to teach the *halakha* of **a roof similar to** that of **a courtyard: Just as a courtyard** is a place **where multitudes tread, so too, the roof** is a place **where multitudes tread.** However, if it is not used by many people, even the small roof is permitted, as the principle: Extend and raise the walls of the house, is applied to the wall between the houses, despite the fact that the partition is not conspicuous.

יְתֵיב רַבָּה וְרַבִּי זֵירָא וְרַבָּה בַּר רַב חָנָן, וִיתֵיב אַבַּיֵי גַּבַּייהוּ, וְיָתְבִי וְקָאָמְרִי: שְׁמַע מִינָּהּ מִמַּתְנִיתִין: דִּיּוּרֵי גְדוֹלָה בִּקְטַנָּה, וְאֵין דִּיּוּרֵי קְטַנָּה בִּגְדוֹלָה.

Rabba, Rabbi Zeira, and Rabba bar Rav Ḥanan were sitting, and Abaye was sitting beside them, and they sat and said: Learn from the mishna that the rights of **the residents of the large** courtyard extend **into the small one,**[N] **but** the rights of **the residents of the small** courtyard do **not** extend **into the large one.**

כֵּיצַד? גְּפָנִים בִּגְדוֹלָה – אָסוּר לִזְרוֹעַ אֶת הַקְּטַנָּה, וְאִם זָרַע – זְרָעִין אֲסוּרִין.

How so? If there are **vines in the large** courtyard,[H] **it is prohibited to sow** crops **in the small one,**[N] even at a distance of four cubits, due to the prohibition against planting other food crops in a vineyard. **And if he sowed** crops, **the seeds are prohibited.** As the small courtyard is considered part of the large one, the vines in the larger courtyard render the seeds in the smaller courtyard prohibited.

HALAKHA

Large and small roofs – גַּג גָּדוֹל וְקָטָן: If a wall that separates a small roof from a larger roof is completely breached before Shabbat, it is prohibited to carry any utensils that were inside the house when Shabbat began up to the small roof. However, it is permitted to carry these utensils to the larger roof. Even if the wall is breached on Shabbat, since it was permitted at the beginning of Shabbat it remains permitted throughout the day (*Beit Yosef*; *Shulḥan Arukh, Oraḥ Ḥayyim* 374:4).

A large courtyard that was breached into a small one – חָצֵר גְּדוֹלָה שֶׁנִּפְרְצָה לִקְטַנָּה: If the entire length of a wall separating a small courtyard from an adjacent larger one is breached, and the breach is less than ten cubits long, it is permitted to carry utensils from the house into the larger courtyard if they establish an *eiruv* there, but residents of the small courtyard may not carry from the house into the small courtyard. If the breached wall is more than ten cubits long, it is also prohibited to carry into the larger courtyard (*Shulḥan Arukh, Oraḥ Ḥayyim* 374:3).

A roof, its partitions must be conspicuous – גַּג נַמִי מִנְכַּרָא מְחִיצָּתָא: It is permitted to utilize a large roof when the wall separating it from an adjacent smaller roof was breached, only if the walls of the house below are visible on the roof as well. If not, the status of the roof is that of a *karmelit*. This is in accordance with the opinion of Rav and contrary to the opinion of Shmuel (*Shulḥan Arukh, Oraḥ Ḥayyim* 374:4).

Vines in the large courtyard – גְּפָנִים בִּגְדוֹלָה: If vines are growing in a large courtyard, it is prohibited to sow seeds in a smaller courtyard that opens into it. Any seeds sown there are prohibited, although the vines remain permitted, in accordance with the conclusion inferred from the mishna (*Shulḥan Arukh, Yoreh De'a* 296:49).

NOTES

The residents of the large one into the small one – דִּיּוּרֵי גְדוֹלָה בִּקְטַנָּה: The Ritva maintains that the principle is that the larger courtyard is considered as though it spread out and enveloped the smaller one. However, the residents of the smaller one are not considered residents of the larger courtyard. This is in accordance with Rashi's later version of the text as opposed to his explanation in this context.

Vines in the large one and seeds in the small one – גְּפָנִים בִּגְדוֹלָה וּזְרָעִים בִּקְטַנָּה: Generally, both the seeds and the vines that are planted together in a vineyard are prohibited, due to the violation of planting diverse kinds in a vineyard. However, in this case the vines were planted first, in an entirely permissible manner. Consequently, the seeds planted in the other courtyard cannot render them prohibited, and the seeds alone are prohibited due to the vines.

גְּפָנִים מוּתָּרִין. גְּפָנִים בַּקְּטַנָּה – מוּתָּר לִזְרוֹעַ אֶת הַגְּדוֹלָה.

The vines, however, **are permitted,** as the small courtyard does not extend into and impact upon the large one. The converse is also true: If there are **vines in the small** courtyard, **it is permitted to sow** other crops **in the large one**[N] *ab initio*, even if they are not planted four cubits away from the vines, because the vines are not considered to be located in the larger courtyard, and therefore there is no prohibition whatsoever.

אִשָּׁה בַּגְּדוֹלָה וְגֵט בַּקְּטַנָּה – מִתְגָּרֶשֶׁת. אִשָּׁה בַּקְּטַנָּה וְגֵט בַּגְּדוֹלָה – אֵינָהּ מִתְגָּרֶשֶׁת.

Likewise, if there were two adjacent courtyards, and **a wife,** who owned both courtyards, was standing **in the large** courtyard, **and** her husband threw her **a bill of divorce** into **the small** courtyard, **she is divorced.** Her presence in the larger courtyard extends to the smaller one, and she is therefore considered to be standing in the small courtyard. If, however, **the wife was in the small** courtyard **and the bill of divorce** was thrown into **the large one, she is not divorced.**

צִבּוּר בַּגְּדוֹלָה וּשְׁלִיחַ צִבּוּר בַּקְּטַנָּה – יוֹצְאִין יְדֵי חוֹבָתָן. צִיבּוּר בַּקְּטַנָּה וּשְׁלִיחַ צִבּוּר בַּגְּדוֹלָה – אֵין יוֹצְאִין יְדֵי חוֹבָתָן.

Likewise, with regard to communal prayer, if the **congregation** was **in the large** courtyard, **and the prayer leader** was **in the small one,**[H] **they fulfill their obligation** through his prayer, as the congregation is considered to be in the small one as well. However, if **the congregation** was **in the small** courtyard, **and the prayer leader** was **in the large one, they do not fulfill their obligation.**

תִּשְׁעָה בַּגְּדוֹלָה וְיָחִיד בַּקְּטַנָּה – מִצְטָרְפִין. תִּשְׁעָה בַּקְּטַנָּה וְאֶחָד בַּגְּדוֹלָה – אֵין מִצְטָרְפִין.

The same principle applies to a prayer quorum: If there were **nine** men **in the large** courtyard **and one** man **in the small one,**[H] **they join** together to form the necessary quorum of ten, as the small courtyard is subsumed within the large one, and the individual is considered to be in the large courtyard. However, if there were **nine** men **in the small** courtyard **and one in the large one, they do not join** together.

צוֹאָה בַּגְּדוֹלָה – אָסוּר לִקְרוֹת קְרִיאַת שְׁמַע בַּקְּטַנָּה. צוֹאָה בַּקְּטַנָּה – מוּתָּר לִקְרוֹת קְרִיאַת שְׁמַע בַּגְּדוֹלָה.

Furthermore, if there was **excrement in the large** courtyard,[H] **it is prohibited to recite *Shema* in the small one,** as the excrement is considered to be in the small courtyard as well, and it is prohibited to recite *Shema* in the presence of excrement. If, however, there was **excrement in the small** courtyard, **it is permitted to recite *Shema* in the large one.**[N]

אֲמַר לְהוּ אַבַּיֵי: אִם כֵּן מָצִינוּ מְחִיצָה לְאִיסּוּר, שֶׁאִילְמָלֵי אֵין מְחִיצָה – מַרְחִיק אַרְבַּע אַמּוֹת וְזוֹרֵעַ. וְאִילּוּ הָשְׁתָּא אֲסוּרָה!

Abaye said to them: If so, we have found a partition that causes **prohibition.**[N] According to these principles, the existence of a partition renders sowing crops prohibited; in the absence of a partition sowing the crops would have been permitted due to their distance from the vines. Ostensibly, this is a counterintuitive conclusion. **As, were there no partition** at all, it would be sufficient to **distance** oneself **four cubits** from the vine **and sow** the crop, **whereas now** that the area is divided into two courtyards by means of a partition, **it is prohibited** to sow the crop in the entire small courtyard.

NOTES

It is permitted to sow in the large one – מוּתָּר לִזְרוֹעַ אֶת הַגְּדוֹלָה: This is a surprising statement, as, in general, the principle is that the seeds are considered as though they were situated between the vines. Even if the planted seeds do not render the vines prohibited, what reason could there be for permitting this act *ab initio*? The Ra'avad explains that when the Gemara states that it is permitted to sow, this does not mean that it is entirely permitted to maintain the seeds for an unlimited length of time and one is not required to uproot them. Rather, he may maintain them until the grapes begin to ripen, at which point he must uproot the seedlings before they too reach a fully ripened state. See Rashi, who addresses this difficulty, as well as *Tosafot*, who suggest a different answer.

Small and large courtyards – חָצֵר קְטַנָּה וּגְדוֹלָה: A careful analysis of these cases reveals that at least two fundamental principles are at play. According to Rashi, for example, from the perspective of the smaller courtyard, it is considered as though there were a partition between the domains, which is why it is permitted to sow in the larger courtyard. However, in another sense, the status of the smaller courtyard is negated by that of the larger one. In fact, the smaller one is subsumed within the larger one, as though it were merely its entrance. Furthermore, one additional principle must be taken into account, as the larger courtyard is not invariably considered the main section with the smaller one considered its entrance, as in some cases the situation is reversed. For example, in the case of a woman and her bill of divorce, the guiding principle is that the bill of divorce must enter the woman's domain. The same is true with regard to a prayer leader, and when nine people praying are separated from the tenth (see *Ge'on Ya'akov*).

A partition that causes prohibition – מְחִיצָה לְאִיסּוּר: It is, of course, possible for a prohibition to take effect due to the presence of a partition. For example, the domains of Shabbat are based on partitions and the prohibitions that result from them. The meaning of this claim in this context, however, is that the existence of the partition causes two items to be deemed closer together than they actually are, rendering them prohibited. This is problematic, because the essence of a partition is for separation, while here it apparently brings two items together.

HALAKHA

If the congregation was in the large courtyard, and the prayer leader was in the small one – צִבּוּר בַּגְּדוֹלָה וּשְׁלִיחַ צִבּוּר בַּקְּטַנָּה: If a congregation is located in a large courtyard, which is not separated by a wall from a smaller courtyard, and the prayer leader is in the smaller one, the congregants fulfill their prayer obligation through his prayers. However, if the community is in the smaller courtyard and the prayer leader in the larger one, they do not fulfill their prayer obligation by means of his prayers (*Shulḥan Arukh, Oraḥ Ḥayyim* 55:17).

If there were nine in the large courtyard and one in the small one – תִּשְׁעָה בַּגְּדוֹלָה וְיָחִיד בַּקְּטַנָּה: If there are nine people praying in the larger courtyard and one person in the smaller one, they together constitute a quorum. However, if nine are in the smaller one and one in the larger one, they do not constitute a quorum (*Shulḥan Arukh, Oraḥ Ḥayyim* 55:16).

Excrement in the large courtyard – צוֹאָה בַּגְּדוֹלָה: If there is excrement or any other filth in a large courtyard, it is prohibited to recite *Shema* in an adjacent smaller one. Conversely, if there is excrement in the smaller one, it is permitted to recite *Shema* in the larger courtyard, provided that there is no foul odor there (*Shulḥan Arukh, Oraḥ Ḥayyim* 79:3).

BACKGROUND

Even its protrusions – הִשְׁוָה אֶת גִּיפּוּפֶיהָ: In the image, the partition that separates the smaller courtyard from the larger one is fully breached, while the larger protrudes to the sides of the smaller one. If, however, one were to build partitions opposite the smaller courtyard, as portrayed here by the translucent partitions, the two courtyards would be considered entirely merged, and it would be prohibited to carry in both. This constitutes a partition that renders it prohibited to carry, according to Abaye.

Partitions opposite the smaller courtyard

אמר ליה רבי זירא לאביי: ולא מצינו מחיצה לאיסור?! והא תנן: חצר גדולה שנפרצה לקטנה – גדולה מותרת וקטנה אסורה, מפני שהיא כפתחה של גדולה.

Rabbi Zeira said to Abaye: And didn't we find a partition that causes **prohibition? But didn't we learn** in the mishna: With regard to **a large courtyard that was breached into a small** one, it is **permitted** for the residents of **the large** courtyard to carry, **but** it is **prohibited** for the residents of **the small one** to do so. That is **because** in that case, the legal status of the breach **is like** that of **the entrance of the large** courtyard.

ואילו השוה את גיפופיה – גדולה נמי אסורה!

And if he were to even its protrusions[B] by constructing partitions in the larger courtyard so that the large courtyard no longer protruded beyond the smaller one, carrying in **the large** courtyard would **also be prohibited,** as it would now be completely breached into the smaller courtyard. Apparently, in this case, construction of additional partitions causes prohibition.

אמר ליה: התם סילוק מחיצות הוא.

Abaye **said to** Rabbi Zeira: The two cases are not comparable, as **there,** adding partitions in order to even the protrusions is not considered establishment of partitions. On the contrary, **it is** effectively **the removal of partitions.** These partitions are designed to negate the original partitions of the courtyard.

אמר ליה רבא לאביי: ולא מצינו מחיצה לאיסור? והא אתמר:

Rava said to Abaye: And didn't we find a partition that causes **prohibition? But wasn't it stated:**

Perek **IX**
Daf **93** Amud **a**

BACKGROUND

Evened the doorposts – הִשְׁוָה פַּצִּימֶיהָ: The illustration depicts a portico that has doorposts. The doorposts, which support the roof, are in each corner, while the existing partitions are on the outer sides of the doorposts (A). If a second set of partitions were to be constructed on the inside of the doorposts (B), the doorposts would no longer be considered valid partitions.

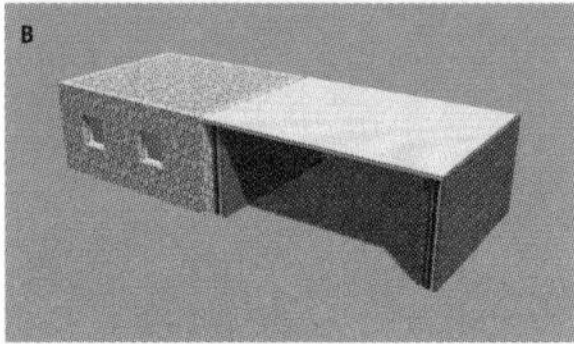

Porticos with different sets of partitions

A house, half of which is roofed – בַּיִת שֶׁחֶצְיוֹ מְקוֹרֶה: The structure has a roof covering half of its area, underneath which vines have been planted. In the other, unroofed section, other crops are planted. In accordance with the principle: The edge of the roof descends and seals, it is as though the two sections of the structure are separated by a full-fledged partition. However, if a roof was subsequently erected over the unroofed side the building, the entire area would be considered a single room, and the other crops would be prohibited.

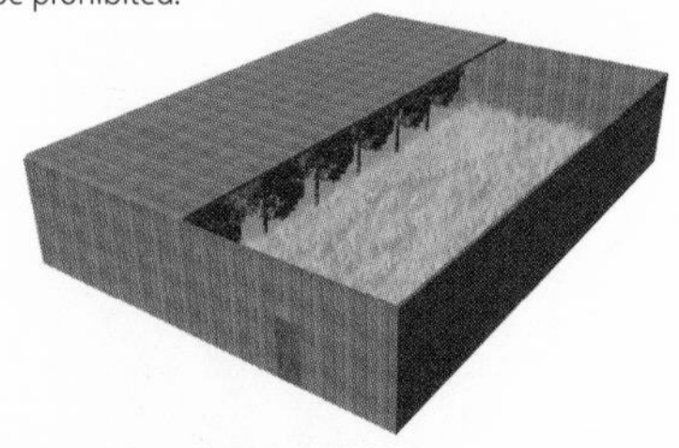

Structure with a roof covering half of its area

סיכך על גבי אכסדרה שיש לה פצימין – כשירה, ואילו השוה פצימיה – פסולה!

If one **placed roofing on top of a portico that has doorposts,**[NH] i.e., a portico with two parallel walls that are valid for a *sukka*, as well as posts in the corners supporting the portico and protruding like doorposts, which are considered as sealing the other two sides of the portico, it is a **valid** *sukka*. However, **if he evened the doorposts**[BN] by constructing walls adjacent to the existing walls, obscuring the posts so that they do not protrude, the *sukka* is **invalid.** This teaching indicates that the creation of a partition can cause prohibition.

אמר ליה אביי: לדידי – כשירה, לדידך – סילוק מחיצות היא.

Abaye said to him: In my opinion, with regard to that case of a portico, the *sukka* is **valid.** However, even **according to your opinion,** this **is** another instance of **the removal of partitions.** Evening the doorposts does not render the *sukka* invalid through the establishment of new partitions, but because it negates the original partitions of the *sukka*.

אמר ליה רבה בר רב חנן לאביי: ולא מצינו מחיצה לאיסור? והתניא: בית שחציו מקורה וחציו אינו מקורה, גפנים כאן – מותר לזרוע כאן.

Rabba bar Rav Ḥanan said to Abaye: And didn't we find that **a partition** causes **prohibition? But wasn't it taught** in a *baraita*: With regard to **a house, half of which is roofed**[BH] **and half unroofed,** if there are **vines here,** under the roofed section of the house, **it is permitted to sow** crops **there,** in the open section. The reason is that it is as though the edge of the roof descends to the ground and forms a partition between the two sections of the house.

NOTES

A portico that has doorposts – אַכְסַדְרָה שֶׁיֵּשׁ לָהּ פַּצִּימִין: Rashi in tractate *Sukka* and *Tosafot* here explain that the Gemara is referring to a portico with doorposts positioned within three handbreadths of each other, which means that the principle of *lavud* is in effect.

He evened the doorposts – הִשְׁוָה פַּצִּימֶיהָ: According to Rashi, he built a partition inside, obscuring the doorposts. The Rambam maintains that the doorposts are regarded as removed only if there is a double partition completely obscuring them on all sides.

HALAKHA

A portico that has doorposts – אַכְסַדְרָה שֶׁיֵּשׁ לָהּ פַּצִּימִין: If one placed roofing atop a portico with doorposts, the *sukka* is valid whether the doorposts are visible from the inside or from the outside. This *halakha* is in accordance with the Rambam's ruling, not with Rashi's interpretation. Some authorities dispute this *halakha*, claiming that one may not build a *sukka* in this manner *ab initio* (*Shulḥan Arukh, Oraḥ Ḥayyim* 630:8, and in the comment of the Rema).

A house, half of which is roofed – בַּיִת שֶׁחֶצְיוֹ מְקוֹרֶה: If a structure has a roof over one half of its area, while the other half is unroofed, it is permitted to sow other seeds beneath the roof even if vines were planted in the unroofed section, or vice versa. However, if one extended the roof to cover the entire structure, it is prohibited to sow a second species of plants (Rambam *Sefer Zera'im, Hilkhot Kilayim* 7:18).

וְאִילּוּ הִשְׁוָה אֶת קֵרוּיוֹ – אָסוּר! אֲמַר לֵיהּ: הָתָם סִילּוּק מְחִיצּוֹת הוּא.

And if he evened its roofing, by extending the roof to cover the entire house, it would be **prohibited** to sow other crops there. It is evident that the very placement of a partition, in this case a roof, causes prohibition. Abaye **said to him: There** too **it is** an instance of **the removal of partitions.** It is prohibited to sow not due to the added roofing; rather, it is prohibited due to the negation of the imaginary partition.

שְׁלַח לֵיהּ רָבָא לְאַבַּיֵי בְּיַד רַב שְׁמַעְיָה בַּר זְעֵירָא: וְלֹא מָצִינוּ מְחִיצָּה לְאִיסּוּר? וְהָתַנְיָא: יֵשׁ בִּמְחִיצּוֹת הַכֶּרֶם לְהָקֵל וּלְהַחְמִיר; כֵּיצַד? כֶּרֶם הַנָּטוּעַ עַד עִיקַּר מְחִיצָּה – זוֹרֵעַ מֵעִיקַּר מְחִיצָּה וְאֵילָךְ, שֶׁאִילּוּ אֵין שָׁם מְחִיצָּה מַרְחִיק אַרְבַּע אַמּוֹת וְזוֹרֵעַ, וְזֶה הוּא מְחִיצּוֹת הַכֶּרֶם לְהָקֵל.

Rava sent a different proof to **Abaye by means of Rav Shemaya bar Ze'eira,** with regard to the same issue. **And didn't we find a partition** causes **prohibition? But wasn't it taught** in a *baraita*: **There is** an element **in the partitions of a vineyard** that causes **leniency** with regard to diverse kinds of seeds **and** an element that causes **stringency.**[H] **How so?** With regard to **a vineyard that is planted until the** very **base of a partition, one sows** crops **from the base of** the other side of **the partition onward.** This is a leniency, **as were there no partition there,** he would be required to **distance** himself **four cubits** from the last vine **and** only then **sow** there. **And this is** an element in **partitions of a vineyard** that causes **leniency.**

וּלְהַחְמִיר כֵּיצַד? הָיָה מָשׁוּךְ מִן הַכּוֹתֶל אַחַת עֶשְׂרֵה אַמָּה – לֹא יָבִיא זֶרַע לְשָׁם, שֶׁאִילְמָלֵי אֵין מְחִיצָּה – מַרְחִיק אַרְבַּע אַמּוֹת וְזוֹרֵעַ, וְזוֹהִי מְחִיצּוֹת הַכֶּרֶם לְהַחְמִיר!

And as for an element in partitions that causes **stringency, how so?** If the vineyard **was distanced eleven cubits from a wall, one may not bring** the **seeds** of other crops **there,** between the vineyard and the wall, and sow that area. This is a stringency, **as were there no partition,** it would suffice to **distance** himself **four cubits** from the last vine, **and sow** there. **This is** an element of **partitions in a vineyard** that causes **stringency,** a clear situation of a partition that causes prohibition.

אֲמַר לֵיהּ: וְלִיטַעְמִיךְ, אוֹתְבַן מִמַּתְנִיתִין, דִּתְנַן: קׇרַחַת הַכֶּרֶם, בֵּית שַׁמַּאי אוֹמְרִים: עֶשְׂרִים וְאַרְבַּע אַמּוֹת, וּבֵית הִלֵּל אוֹמְרִים: שֵׁשׁ עֶשְׂרֵה אַמָּה. מְחוֹל הַכֶּרֶם, בֵּית שַׁמַּאי אוֹמְרִים: שֵׁשׁ עֶשְׂרֵה אַמָּה, וּבֵית הִלֵּל אוֹמְרִים: שְׁתֵּים עֶשְׂרֵה אַמָּה.

Abaye **said to him: And according to your reasoning** that this presents a difficulty, **raise an objection against our** opinion **from a mishna,** rather than a less authoritative *baraita*, **as we learned** in a mishna: With regard to **a clearing in a vineyard,**[H] **Beit Shammai say:** Its measure is **twenty-four cubits, and Beit Hillel say: Sixteen cubits.** With regard to **the perimeter of a vineyard, Beit Shammai say: Sixteen cubits, and Beit Hillel say: Twelve cubits.**

וְאֵיזוֹ הִיא קׇרַחַת הַכֶּרֶם – כֶּרֶם שֶׁחָרַב אֶמְצָעִיתוֹ. אִם אֵין שָׁם שֵׁשׁ עֶשְׂרֵה אַמָּה – לֹא יָבִיא זֶרַע לְשָׁם, הָיוּ שָׁם שֵׁשׁ עֶשְׂרֵה אַמָּה – נוֹתֵן לוֹ כְּדֵי עֲבוֹדָתוֹ, וְזוֹרֵעַ אֶת הַמּוֹתָר.

The mishna explains: **And what is a clearing in a vineyard?** It is referring to **a vineyard whose middle** section **was laid bare** of vines. If **there are not sixteen cubits** across in the clearing, **one may not bring** foreign **seeds** and sow them **there,** due to the Torah prohibition against sowing other crops in a vineyard (Deuteronomy 22:9). If **there were sixteen cubits** across in the clearing, **one provides** the vineyard with **its** requisite **work** area, i.e., four cubits along either side of the vines are left unsown to facilitate cultivation of the vines, **and he sows the rest** of the cleared area with foreign crops.

אֵי זוֹ הִיא מְחוֹל הַכֶּרֶם – בֵּין הַכֶּרֶם לַגָּדֵר. שֶׁאִם אֵין שָׁם שְׁתֵּים עֶשְׂרֵה אַמָּה – לֹא יָבִיא זֶרַע לְשָׁם, הָיוּ שָׁם שְׁתֵּים עֶשְׂרֵה אַמָּה – נוֹתֵן לוֹ כְּדֵי עֲבוֹדָתוֹ וְזוֹרֵעַ אֶת הַמּוֹתָר.

The mishna continues: **What is the perimeter of a vineyard?** It is the vacant area **between the vineyard and the fence** surrounding it. If **there are not twelve cubits** in that area, **one may not bring** foreign **seeds** and sow them **there.** If **there are twelve cubits** in that area, **he provides** the vineyard with **its** requisite **work area,** four cubits, **and he sows the rest.** However, were the vineyard not surrounded by a fence, all he would need to do is distance himself four cubits from the last vine. It is clear from this *halakha* that the partition causes prohibition.

אֶלָּא הָתָם לָאו הַיְינוּ טַעְמָא – דְּכָל אַרְבַּע אַמּוֹת לְגַבֵּי כֶּרֶם – עֲבוֹדַת הַכֶּרֶם, לְגַבֵּי גָּדֵר – כֵּיוָן דְּלָא מִזְדַּרְעָן – אַפְקוּרֵי מַפְקַר לְהוּ. דְּבֵינֵי בֵּינֵי, אִי אִיכָּא אַרְבַּע – חֲשִׁיבָן, וְאִי לָא – לָא חֲשִׁיבָן.

Rather, the objection was not raised from there because **there, isn't this the reason** that the partition is not considered to cause prohibition? It is **because the entire** area of **four cubits alongside a vineyard is** considered **the vineyard's work area,** and is therefore an actual part of it. Likewise, with regard to the four cubits **alongside the fence** surrounding the vineyard, **since they cannot** easily **be sown**[N] due to the wall, **he renounces ownership over** the area. With regard to the space **in between, if it is four** cubits, **it is** deemed **significant** in its own right, **and if not, it is not significant** and is nullified relative to the rest, and it is prohibited to sow there. A similar reasoning applies to the *baraita*. The stringency is not due to the fact that the partition causes prohibition, but because the partition impedes cultivation of the vineyard.

HALAKHA

The partitions of a vineyard as a leniency and as a stringency – מְחִיצּוֹת הַכֶּרֶם לְהָקֵל וּלְהַחְמִיר: If a full-fledged partition, ten handbreadths high, separates a vineyard from the adjacent land, it is permitted to sow other crops on the other side. If there is a gap of less than twelve cubits between the vineyard and the partition, which is the measure of the perimeter of a vineyard, it is prohibited to sow there (Rambam *Sefer Zera'im, Hilkhot Kilayim* 7:13).

A clearing in a vineyard – קׇרַחַת הַכֶּרֶם: If there is a clearing free of vines inside a vineyard sixteen by sixteen cubits in size, it is permitted to sow crops there four cubits from the vines. The *halakha* is in accordance with the opinion of Beit Hillel (Rambam *Sefer Zera'im, Hilkhot Kilayim* 7:11).

NOTES

They cannot easily be sown – לָא מִזְדַּרְעָן: This area is generally left unsown, either because the plow would loosen the earth, or because the crops themselves would undermine the fence and ruin it (Rashash).

BACKGROUND

Protruding enclosures – **קַרְפֵּיפוֹת מְגוּפָּפִים**: Three enclosures in a row, with the middle one fully open into the outer two, which extend beyond it.

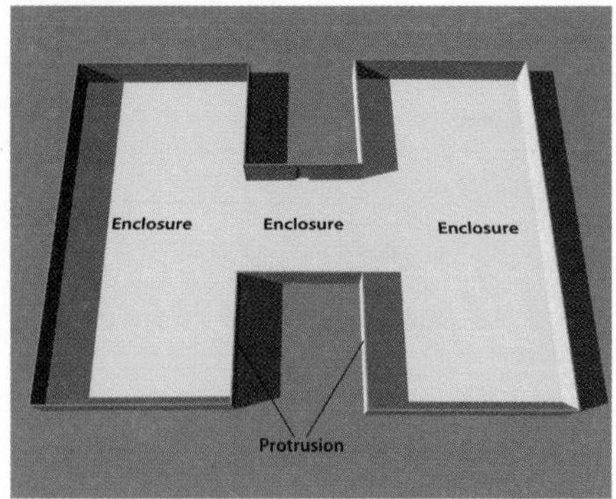

Outer enclosures extending beyond the inner one

The middle enclosure protruded – **אֶמְצָעִי מְגוּפָּף**: Here the middle enclosure extends beyond the two outer ones, which open into it.

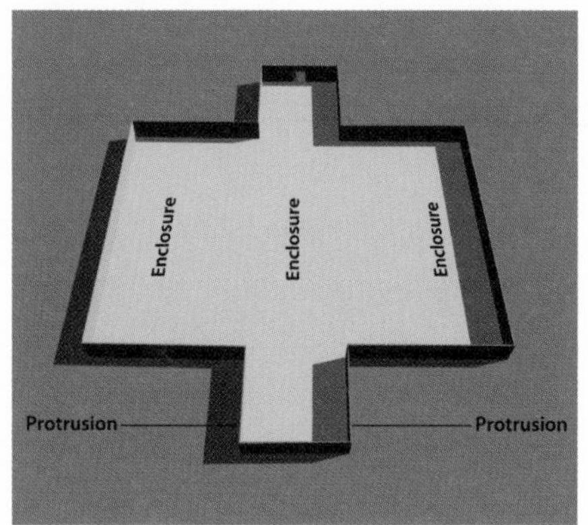

Middle enclosure extending beyond the outer two

HALAKHA

Three enclosures and there are individuals in them – **שְׁלֹשָׁה קַרְפֵּיפוֹת וִיחִידִים בָּהֶם**: Three enclosures in a row are considered a single domain. This *halakha* is in effect only if the middle enclosure is narrower than the outer enclosures and its opening into those enclosures is less than ten cubits. The Ritva adds another condition: The wall separating the enclosures must not be a side post that is even with the entrance on the inside and visible on the outside. In addition, there can be only one person in each of them. Some authorities state that the residents of the enclosures receive only two *beit se'a*, as the statement: One provides them with all the space that they require, refers only to the middle enclosure (Rashi; *Tur*). If the middle enclosure is wider than the others, and the other two are fully breached into it, the residents of the outer enclosures are each provided an area of two *beit se'a* (*Shulḥan Arukh, Oraḥ Ḥayyim* 360:3).

Two in one of the enclosures – **שְׁנַיִם בְּאַחַד הַקַּרְפֵּיפִים**: If there were two people in one of these enclosures, and a single person or two people in the middle one, whether they were all situated in the middle one or one of the outer ones, they are considered like members of a caravan, and are provided with all the space they require in the middle enclosure (*Magen Avraham*; *Shulḥan Arukh, Oraḥ Ḥayyim* 360:3).

אָמַר רַב יְהוּדָה: שְׁלֹשָׁה קַרְפֵּיפוֹת זֶה בְּצַד זֶה, וּשְׁנַיִם הַחִיצוֹנִים מְגוּפָּפִים וְהָאֶמְצָעִי אֵינוֹ מְגוּפָּף, וְיָחִיד בָּזֶה וְיָחִיד בָּזֶה נַעֲשֶׂה כְּשַׁיָּירָא וְנוֹתְנִין לָהֶן כׇּל צוֹרְכָּן וַדַּאי.

Rav Yehuda said: If there are **three enclosures alongside one another, and the two outer** ones **protrude,** i.e., they are wider than the middle one, so that there are partitions on both sides of the breach between them and the middle enclosure, **and the middle one does not protrude,** and there are no partitions between it and the outer enclosures, as it is totally breached, **and there is one** person **in this** one **and one** person **in that** one and yet another person in the third enclosure,[B] the people in the enclosures are considered as though they are all living in one large enclosure.[H] Consequently, the legal status of the group **becomes like** that of a **caravan, and one provides them** with **all** the space **that they require.** In other words, they may use the entire enclosure even if it is very large, just as there are no limits to the size of the enclosed area in which members of a caravan may carry.

אֶמְצָעִי מְגוּפָּף וּשְׁנַיִם הַחִיצוֹנִים אֵינָן מְגוּפָּפִין, וְיָחִיד בָּזֶה וְיָחִיד זֶה [וְיָחִיד בָּזֶה] אֵין נוֹתְנִין לָהֶם אֶלָּא בֵּית שֵׁשׁ,

However, if the **middle** enclosure **protruded, and the two outer ones did not protrude,** i.e., they were narrower than the middle enclosure, so that their entire width was breached into it,[B] **and there is one** person **in this** one **and one** person **in that** one and yet another in the third, **one provides them only** an area of **six *beit se'a*,** in accordance with the *halakha* of individuals in a field, who may enclose an area of only two *beit se'a* per person. As the middle enclosure is larger than the two outer ones, it determines their status, in accordance with the principle stated above, not the other way around. Consequently, the person in the middle enclosure is regarded as though he established residence in only one of the outer enclosures, constituting a group of no more than two, which does not have the legal status of a caravan.

אִיבַּעְיָא לְהוּ: אֶחָד בָּזֶה וְאֶחָד בָּזֶה וּשְׁנַיִם בָּאֶמְצָעִי מַהוּ? אִי לְהָכָא נָפְקִי תְּלָתָא הָווּ, וְאִי לְהָכָא נָפְקִי תְּלָתָא הָווּ.

Based on these assumptions, **a dilemma was raised before** the Sages: If there is **one** person **in this** outer enclosure, **and one person in the other** outer enclosure, **and two** people **in the middle** enclosure,[H] **what is** the *halakha*? Is the ruling that **if** the pair **exit to here,** one of the outer enclosures, **they are three** people in one place, **and if they exit to there,** the other outer enclosure, **they are three** people in one place, and three people are considered a caravan and provided with all the space they require, as stated above?

אוֹ דִּילְמָא: חַד לְהָכָא נָפֵיק, וְחַד לְהָכָא נָפֵיק.

Or perhaps, as **one may exit to here**[N] **and the other may exit to there,** in which case there would be no more than two people in each enclosure, they are provided with only two *beit se'a* per person.

וְאִם תִּימְצֵי לוֹמַר: חַד לְהָכָא נָפֵיק וְחַד לְהָכָא נָפֵיק; שְׁנַיִם בָּזֶה וּשְׁנַיִם בָּזֶה, וְאֶחָד בָּאֶמְצָעִי מַהוּ? הָכָא וַדַּאי, אִי לְהָכָא נָפֵיק תְּלָתָא הָווּ, וְאִי לְהָכָא נָפֵיק תְּלָתָא הָווּ, אוֹ דִּילְמָא: אֵימַר לְהָכָא נָפֵיק, וְאֵימַר לְהָכָא נָפֵיק?

And if you say that **one may exit to here and one may exit to there,** if there were **two** people **in this** outer enclosure, **and two** people **in that** outer enclosure, **and one** person **in the middle** enclosure, **what** is the *halakha*? Is the ruling that **here, certainly, if he exits to here they are three, and if he exits to there they are** likewise **three,** and consequently they should be provided with all the space they require in any case? **Or perhaps,** in this case too there is uncertainty, as **say** that he might **exit to here, and say** that **he** might **exit to there.** As the direction in which he will leave his enclosure is undetermined, they should be provided with only two *beit se'a* each.

וְהִלְכְתָא: בְּעָיָין לְקוּלָּא.

These dilemmas were essentially left unresolved, **but the *halakha* is** that **these dilemmas** are decided **leniently,**[N] **and** they are provided with all the space they require in these cases.

אָמַר רַב חִסְדָּא:

Rav Ḥisda said:

NOTES

Perhaps one may exit to here – **דִּילְמָא חַד לְהָכָא נָפֵיק**: This is a distinct possibility, because it stands to reason that they would each seek a larger area in which to live. Therefore, they are each likely to move in different directions.

But the *halakha* is that these dilemmas are decided leniently – **וְהִלְכְתָא בְּעָיָין לְקוּלָּא**: The later commentaries are puzzled by this statement: As these dilemmas involve a rabbinic prohibition, the *halakha* would be lenient in any case. One explanation is that according to the Rambam's principle that in cases where the Gemara presents two alternatives, introducing the second with the phrase: If you wish, say instead, the *halakha* is in accordance with the latter opinion, the first case should be prohibited. Therefore, it was necessary to specify that the ruling is lenient in all these cases, even the first one (see *Beit Yitzḥak*; Rashash).

גידוד חֲמִשָּׁה וּמְחִיצָה חֲמִשָּׁה אֵין מִצְטָרְפִין, עַד שֶׁיְּהֵא אוֹ כּוּלּוֹ בְּגִידוּד אוֹ כּוּלּוֹ בִּמְחִיצָה.

An embankment, a height disparity between two surfaces **of five** handbreadths, **and** an additional **partition of five**[H] handbreadths **do not join** together to form a partition of ten handbreadths, the minimum height for a partition to enclose a private domain.[B] It is regarded as a partition of ten handbreadths **only if** the barrier **is** composed **entirely of the embankment or if it is** composed **entirely of a partition.**

מֵיתִיבִי: שְׁתֵּי חֲצֵירוֹת זוֹ לְמַעְלָה מִזּוֹ, וְעֶלְיוֹנָה גְּבוֹהָה מִן הַתַּחְתּוֹנָה עֲשָׂרָה טְפָחִים, אוֹ שֶׁיֵּשׁ בָּהּ גִּידוּד חֲמִשָּׁה וּמְחִיצָה חֲמִשָּׁה – מְעָרְבִין שְׁנַיִם וְאֵין מְעָרְבִין אֶחָד. פָּחוֹת מִכָּאן – מְעָרְבִין אֶחָד וְאֵין מְעָרְבִין שְׁנַיִם!

The Gemara raises an objection from a *baraita*: If there were **two courtyards, one above the other, and** the **upper one was ten handbreadths higher than the lower one, or if it had an embankment of five** handbreadths **and a partition** of **five** handbreadths, the two courtyards are considered separate domains **and they establish two *eiruvin*,** one for each courtyard, **and they do not establish one *eiruv*.** If the height disparity was **less than** ten handbreadths, the two areas are considered a single domain, and **they establish one *eiruv* and they do not establish two *eiruvin*.**

אָמַר (רַב:) מוֹדֶה רַב חִסְדָּא בַּתַּחְתּוֹנָה, הוֹאִיל וְרוֹאָה פְּנֵי עֲשָׂרָה. אִי הָכִי, תַּחְתּוֹנָה תְּעָרֵב שְׁנַיִם וְלֹא תְּעָרֵב אֶחָד, עֶלְיוֹנָה לֹא תְּעָרֵב לֹא אֶחָד וְלֹא שְׁנַיִם!

Rav said: Rav Ḥisda concedes that an embankment and a partition combine **with regard to the lower** courtyard, **since it faces a wall of ten,** i.e., there is a full partition of ten handbreadths before its residents. The Gemara raises a difficulty: **If so,** according to this reasoning, the residents of the **lower** courtyard, from whose perspective there is a valid partition, should **establish two *eiruvin*,** i.e., an independent *eiruv*, **and do not establish one *eiruv*** together with the upper courtyard, while the residents of **the upper** courtyard **establish neither one *eiruv* nor two.** The residents of the upper courtyard neither establish an *eiruv* on their own, as it is breached into the lower one, nor can they establish an *eiruv* together with the lower courtyard, because the latter is separated from it.[N]

אָמַר רַבָּה בַּר עוּלָּא: כְּגוֹן שֶׁהָיְתָה עֶלְיוֹנָה מְגוּפֶּפֶת עַד עֶשֶׂר אַמּוֹת.

Rabba bar Ulla said: The *baraita* is referring to a case **where** the **upper** courtyard had full-fledged ten-handbreadth-high walls that **protruded** on both sides of the section of the partition that was merely five handbreadths high, a protrusion that extended **up to ten cubits.**[B] In this case, the upper courtyard is properly enclosed by a partition ten handbreadths high, while the section that is only five handbreadths high is deemed an entrance. Consequently, even the residents of the upper courtyard can establish an *eiruv* on their own. But the two courtyards cannot be merged by a single *eiruv*, because the lower courtyard is enclosed by a partition from which there is no entrance to the upper courtyard.

אִי הָכִי, אֵימָא סֵיפָא: פָּחוֹת מִכָּאן – מְעָרְבִין אֶחָד וְאֵין מְעָרְבִין שְׁנַיִם. אִי בָּעֵיָא – חַד תְּעָרֵב, אִי בָּעֵיָא – תְּרֵי תְּעָרֵב!

The Gemara raises a difficulty: **If so, say the latter clause** of that same *baraita*: If the height disparity was **less than** ten handbreadths, **they** are considered a single domain, and the residents therefore **establish one *eiruv*, but they do not establish two *eiruvin*.** According to the explanation suggested above, that there is a partition ten handbreadths high between the courtyards with an entrance of sorts between them, **if they wish, they establish one *eiruv*,** and **if they wish, they establish two *eiruvin*.** That is the *halakha* in a case of two courtyards with an entrance between them.

אָמַר רַבָּה בְּרֵיהּ דְּרָבָא: כְּגוֹן שֶׁנִּפְרְצָה הַתַּחְתּוֹנָה בִּמְלוֹאָהּ לָעֶלְיוֹנָה.

Rabba, son of Rava, said: The *baraita* refers to a case **where the lower** courtyard **was fully breached into the upper one,** i.e., the gap in the wall spanned the entire width of the lower courtyard. In that case, the residents of the lower courtyard establish a joint *eiruv* with the upper courtyard; however, they may not establish an *eiruv* of their own, in accordance with the mishna in which we learned that if a large courtyard is breached into a smaller one, it is permitted for the residents of the large courtyard to carry, but it is prohibited for the residents of the small one to do so.

HALAKHA

An embankment of five and a partition of five – גִּידוּד חֲמִשָּׁה וּמְחִיצָה חֲמִשָּׁה: An embankment five handbreadths high and a wall that is five handbreadths high combine to form a valid partition ten handbreadths in height (*Shulḥan Arukh, Oraḥ Ḥayyim* 362:2).

BACKGROUND

An embankment…and a partition – גִּידוּד...וּמְחִיצָה: The partition between the upper and lower courtyards is partly a constructed wall and partly an embankment, which in this case is the height disparity between the courtyards.

A protrusion that extended up to ten cubits – מְגוּפֶּפֶת עַד עֶשֶׂר אַמּוֹת: The upper courtyard is enclosed by a partition ten handbreadths high, while the section that is five handbreadths high is deemed an entrance, provided that it is not wider than ten cubits.

NOTES

Rav Ḥisda's opinion with regard to an embankment – שִׁיטַת רַב חִסְדָּא בְּגִידוּד: Apparently, Rav Ḥisda maintains that the status of a barrier consisting of an embankment five handbreadths high and a wall five handbreadths high is not that of a partition at all. Indeed, this seems to be the reasoning of the Gemara at the outset. As the discussion continues, however, it becomes evident that this partition is a valid one, especially after the Gemara states that Rav Ḥisda agrees in the case of the lower courtyard. The reason that Rav Ḥisda disagrees with regard to the upper courtyard is due to the concern that one might arrive at the mistaken conclusion that a partition five handbreadths high is sufficient, as that is all that the residents of the upper courtyard can see (Ritva).

NOTES

Has the master taught anything – תָּנֵי מָר מִידֵּי: This style of questioning originates with a certain idea or basic assumption that seems to be particularly reasonable, in this case that the embankment and the partition combine to form a partition of ten handbreadths. Consequently, if the Sage did not teach anything in this regard, he evidently accepts the basic assumption. In these cases, the absence of comment indicates that the more novel approach is rejected (Rosh).

Residents who arrive on Shabbat – דִּיוּרִין הַבָּאִין בְּשַׁבָּת: Although the cases of residents who arrive on Shabbat and partitions that are removed on Shabbat are apparently identical, there is a difference between them. If courtyard partitions that face the public domain are removed, the area is no longer a private domain. Consequently, the principle: Since it was permitted it was permitted, is not in effect as it is in the case of residents who arrive, even though it also involves ruined partitions. The rationale for this difference is that the destruction of partitions between courtyards does not affect the status of the courtyard, as it remains a private domain. It merely adds new residents to the courtyard, which affects the *halakhot* of *eiruv*. As a result, the principle: Since it was permitted it was permitted, is in effect.

אִי הָכִי, תַּחְתּוֹנָה – חַד תְּעָרֵב תְּרֵי לֹא תְּעָרֵב. עֶלְיוֹנָה, אִי בָּעְיָא – תְּרֵי תְּעָרֵב, אִי בָּעְיָא – חַד תְּעָרֵב!

The Gemara raises a difficulty: **If so,** the *halakha* should be that the residents of the **lower** courtyard **establish one *eiruv*** together with the upper one, but they **do not establish two *eiruvin*,** i.e., the residents cannot establish an independent *eiruv* for their courtyard. However, with regard to **the upper one, if** its residents **wish,** they **establish one *eiruv*** together with the lower courtyard, and **if** they **wish,** they **establish two *eiruvin*.** The residents of the upper courtyard can establish an independent *eiruv* for their courtyard, as the larger courtyard renders it prohibited for the residents of the smaller courtyard to carry, but not vice versa.

אִין הָכִי נַמִי. וְכִי קָתָנֵי: ״פָּחוֹת מִכָּאן מְעָרְבִין אֶחָד וְאֵין מְעָרְבִין שְׁנַיִם״ – אַתַּחְתּוֹנָה.

The Gemara answers: **Yes, it is indeed so;** that is the *halakha*. **And when** the *baraita* **teaches:** If the height disparity was **less than** ten handbreadths, the residents **establish one *eiruv*, but they do not establish two *eiruvin*,** this statement is not referring to both courtyards, but only **to the lower** one.

דָּרַשׁ מָרֵימָר: גִּידּוּד חֲמִשָּׁה וּמְחִיצָה חֲמִשָּׁה מִצְטָרְפִין. אַשְׁכְּחֵיהּ רָבִינָא לְרַב אַחָא בְּרֵיהּ דְּרָבָא אֲמַר לֵיהּ: תָּנֵי מָר מִידֵּי בִּמְחִיצָה? אֲמַר לֵיהּ: לָא. וְהִלְכְתָא: גִּידּוּד חֲמִשָּׁה וּמְחִיצָה חֲמִשָּׁה – מִצְטָרְפִין.

Mareimar taught: An embankment of five handbreadths **and an** additional **partition of five** handbreadths above it **combine** to form a partition of ten handbreadths. **Ravina met Rav Aḥa, son of Rava,** and **said to him:** Has **the Master taught anything**[N] **with regard to** this **partition,** whether it is effective or not? **He said to him: No.** The Gemara concludes: The ***halakha*** is that **an embankment of five** handbreadths **and a partition of five** handbreadths **combine** to form an effective partition of ten handbreadths.

בָּעֵי רַב הוֹשַׁעְיָא: דִּיוּרִין הַבָּאִין בְּשַׁבָּת מַהוּ שֶׁיַּאַסְרוּ?

Rav Hoshaya raised a dilemma: What is the ruling with regard to **residents who arrive on Shabbat,**[N] i.e., who join the residents of a courtyard on Shabbat, e.g., if the wall between two courtyards collapsed on Shabbat so that new residents arrive in one courtyard from the other. Had these people arrived before Shabbat they would have rendered it prohibited for the residents to carry in the courtyard unless they participated with the original residents in their *eiruv*. **Do** these residents **render it prohibited** for the original residents to carry in the courtyard, even if they arrive on Shabbat itself?

אָמַר רַב חִסְדָּא: תָּא שְׁמַע, חָצֵר גְּדוֹלָה שֶׁנִּפְרְצָה לִקְטַנָּה – הַגְּדוֹלָה מוּתֶּרֶת וְהַקְּטַנָּה אֲסוּרָה, מִפְּנֵי שֶׁהִיא כְּפִתְחָהּ שֶׁל גְּדוֹלָה. אֲמַר רַבָּה: אֵימַר מִבְּעוֹד יוֹם נִפְרְצָה.

Rav Ḥisda said: Come and **hear** a resolution to the dilemma from the mishna: With regard to **a large courtyard that was breached into a small** courtyard, it is **permitted** for the residents of **the large** courtyard to carry, but it is **prohibited** for the residents of **the small** one to do so. It is permitted to carry in the large courtyard **because** the breach **is** regarded **like the entrance of the large** courtyard. Apparently, even if the breach occurred on Shabbat, it is prohibited for the residents of the small courtyard to carry. **Rabba said: Say** that the mishna is dealing with a case where **it was breached while it was still day,** i.e., on Friday. However, there is no prohibition if the breach occurred on Shabbat itself.

אֲמַר לֵיהּ אַבַּיֵי: לָא תֵּימָא מָר ״אֵימַר״ אֶלָּא ״וַדַּאי מִבְּעוֹד יוֹם נִפְרְצָה״. דְּהָא מָר הוּא דַּאֲמַר: בְּעַי מִינֵּיהּ מֵרַב הוּנָא, וּבְעַי מִינֵּיהּ מֵרַב יְהוּדָה: עֵירֵב דֶּרֶךְ הַפֶּתַח וְנִסְתַּם הַפֶּתַח, עֵירֵב דֶּרֶךְ חַלּוֹן וְנִסְתַּם הַחַלּוֹן, מַהוּ? וְאָמַר לִי: שַׁבָּת, כֵּיוָן שֶׁהוּתְּרָה – הוּתְּרָה.

Abaye said to him: The Master should not state: Say, indicating that it is possible to explain the mishna in this manner. **Rather,** the mishna is **certainly** referring to a case where the courtyard **was breached while it was still day. As Master,** you **are the one who said: I raised a dilemma before Rav Huna, and I raised a dilemma before Rav Yehuda:** If one **established an *eiruv*** to join one courtyard to another **via** a certain **opening, and that opening was sealed** on Shabbat, or if one established an *eiruv* **via** a certain **window, and that window was sealed** on Shabbat, **what is** the *halakha*? May one continue to rely on this *eiruv* and carry from one courtyard to the other via other entrances? **And he said to me: Once** it **was permitted** to carry from courtyard to courtyard at the onset of **Shabbat, it was permitted** and remains so until the conclusion of Shabbat. According to this principle, if a breach that adds residents occurs on Shabbat, the breach does not render prohibited activities that were permitted when Shabbat began.

אִתְּמַר, כּוֹתֶל שֶׁבֵּין שְׁתֵּי חֲצֵירוֹת שֶׁנָּפַל, רַב אָמַר: אֵין מְטַלְטְלִין בּוֹ אֶלָּא בְּאַרְבַּע אַמּוֹת,

It is stated that *amora'im* disagreed: With regard to **a wall between two courtyards,** whose residents did not establish a joint *eiruv*, **that collapsed** on Shabbat, **Rav said: One may carry in** the joint courtyard **only within four cubits,** as carrying in each courtyard is prohibited due to the other, because they did not establish an *eiruv* together. Rav does not accept the principle that an activity that was permitted at the start of Shabbat remains permitted until the conclusion of Shabbat.

וּשְׁמוּאֵל אָמַר:

And Shmuel said:

זֶה מְטַלְטֵל עַד עִיקַּר מְחִיצָה, וְזֶה מְטַלְטֵל עַד עִיקַּר מְחִיצָה.

This one may carry to the base of the former **partition, and that** one **may** likewise **carry to the base of the partition,** as he maintains that since it was permitted at the beginning of Shabbat, it remains permitted until the conclusion of Shabbat.

וְהָא דְּרַב לָאו בְּפֵירוּשׁ אִתְּמַר, אֶלָּא מִכְּלָלָא אִתְּמַר. דְּרַב וּשְׁמוּאֵל הֲווֹ יָתְבִי בְּהַהוּא חָצֵר, נְפַל גּוּדָא דְּבֵינֵי בֵּינֵי. אֲמַר לְהוּ שְׁמוּאֵל: שְׁקוּלוּ גְּלִימָא נְגִידוּ בַּהּ.

The Gemara comments: **And this** ruling **of Rav was not stated explicitly; rather, it was stated by inference;** i.e., it was inferred by his students from another one of his teachings. As once **Rav and Shmuel were sitting in a certain courtyard** on Shabbat, and **the wall between** the two courtyards **fell.**[H] **Shmuel said to** the people around him: **Take a cloak** and **suspend it on** the remnant of the partition.

אַהְדְּרִינְהוּ רַב לְאַפֵּיהּ. אֲמַר לְהוּ שְׁמוּאֵל: אִי קָפֵיד אַבָּא – שְׁקוּלוּ (הֵימְנֵיהּ) וּקְטַרוּ בַּהּ.

Rav turned his face away,[N] displaying his displeasure with Shmuel's opinion, as Rav maintained it was prohibited to carry a cloak in this courtyard. **Shmuel said to them** in a humorous vein: **If Abba,** Rav, **is particular, take his belt**[N] and **tie it** to the cloak, to secure it to the partition.

וְלִשְׁמוּאֵל לָמָּה לִי הָא? הָא אָמַר: זֶה מְטַלְטֵל עַד עִיקַּר מְחִיצָה, וְזֶה מְטַלְטֵל עַד עִיקַּר מְחִיצָה!

The Gemara asks: **And according to Shmuel, why was it necessary** to suspend the cloak? He himself **said:** If a wall between two courtyards collapsed on Shabbat, **this** one **may carry to the base of the** former **partition, and that** one **may** likewise **carry to the base of the partition.**

שְׁמוּאֵל עֲבֵיד לִצְנִיעוּתָא בְּעָלְמָא.

The Gemara answers: **Shmuel** did not **do** so to render it permitted to carry in the courtyard. He did so **merely for** the purpose of **privacy,** as he did not want the residents of the other courtyard to see into his own courtyard.

וְרַב, אִי סְבִירָא לֵיהּ דַּאֲסִיר – לֵימָא לֵיהּ! אַתְרֵיהּ דִּשְׁמוּאֵל הֲוָה.

The Gemara asks: **And Rav, if he maintains that** in this case carrying is **prohibited, he should have said** so **to him** explicitly. The Gemara answers: **It was Shmuel's place.**[N] Rav did not want to disagree with his colleague in his jurisdiction, as he accepted the opinion of the local authority.

אִי הָכִי, מַאי טַעְמָא אַהְדְּרִינְהוּ לְאַפֵּיהּ? דְּלָא נֵימְרוּ כִּשְׁמוּאֵל סְבִירָא לֵיהּ, (וַהֲדַר בֵּיהּ מִשְּׁמַעְתֵּיהּ.)

The Gemara asks: **If so,** if he accepted the jurisdiction of the local rabbinic authority, **why did he turn his face away?** The Gemara answers: He acted in this manner so **that** people would **not say** that **he holds in accordance with** the opinion of **Shmuel, and that he retracted his** opinion with regard to this ***halakha.***

מתני׳ חָצֵר שֶׁנִּפְרְצָה לִרְשׁוּת הָרַבִּים, הַמַּכְנִיס מִתּוֹכָהּ לִרְשׁוּת הַיָּחִיד אוֹ מֵרְשׁוּת הַיָּחִיד לְתוֹכָהּ – חַיָּיב, דִּבְרֵי רַבִּי אֱלִיעֶזֶר.

MISHNA With regard to **a courtyard that was breached into the public domain,**[NH] and the breach was more than ten cubits wide, so that it cannot be considered an entrance, **one who carries** an object **from inside** the courtyard **into the private domain, or from the private domain into it, is liable,** as it ceases to be a private domain and is subsumed into the public domain. This is **the statement of Rabbi Eliezer.**

וַחֲכָמִים אוֹמְרִים: מִתּוֹכָהּ לִרְשׁוּת הָרַבִּים אוֹ מֵרְשׁוּת הָרַבִּים לְתוֹכָהּ – פָּטוּר, מִפְּנֵי שֶׁהִיא כְּכַרְמְלִית.

And the Rabbis disagree and **say:** One who carries **from inside** the courtyard **into the public domain,**[N] **or from the public domain into it, is exempt, because its** legal status **is like** that of **a *karmelit*.** Although it ceases to be a private domain, it does not become a full-fledged public domain.

NOTES

Rav turned his face away – אַהְדְּרִינְהוּ רַב לְאַפֵּיהּ: According to Rav, this case involves two prohibitions, and he maintains that placing the cloak in place of a fallen partition creates a full-fledged partition (*Tosafot*). Consequently, one who erects a partition of this kind on Shabbat performs the prohibited labor of building. Shmuel, in contrast, maintains that its legal status is not that of a partition, and therefore its construction does not violate the prohibition against building (Rabbeinu Yehonatan; *Tosafot*).

Take his belt – שְׁקוּלוּ הֵימְנֵיהּ: This comment was certainly spoken in jest. Some commentaries explain that Shmuel is pointing out that if Rav feels that a partition consisting of a cloak is not sturdy enough, he should use his belt to tighten it.

Shmuel's place – אַתְרֵיהּ דִּשְׁמוּאֵל: Although it is improper to defer to a Torah authority in a case involving a Torah prohibition, since this incident involves a rabbinic prohibition, one may remain silent in deference to the local Torah scholar (*Me'iri*). Furthermore, as no definitive halakhic ruling was reached, it is not considered a mistake contrary to an explicit teaching of a mishna. Therefore, there is no reason to rule against the local scholar (Ritva).

A courtyard that was breached into the public domain – חָצֵר שֶׁנִּפְרְצָה לִרְשׁוּת הָרַבִּים: The early commentaries ask: As the Sages said that by Torah law the legal status of any area surrounded by three partitions is that of a private domain, how can this be the topic of a dispute between the Rabbis and Rabbi Eliezer in the mishna? The Ra'avad resolves this apparent contradiction by pointing out that three partitions are effective by Torah law only if there is some sort of barrier on the fourth side as well, either by means of a conspicuous marker in its construction or by a difference in height. Alternatively, if one of the partitions collapses, it can be assumed that they are all removed, which leaves the courtyard bereft of proper partitions and surrounded by mere protrusions (*Ge'on Ya'akov*).

From inside the courtyard into the public domain – מִתּוֹכָהּ לִרְשׁוּת הָרַבִּים: The difference in phrasing between Rabbi Eliezer and the Rabbis, where Rabbi Eliezer speaks about carrying out into or in from a private domain, while the Rabbis refer to carrying out into or in from a public domain, is deliberate and serves as a point of emphasis. Rabbi Eliezer is underscoring the point that the status of this courtyard is not that of a private domain at all, and therefore one who carries an object into it is liable. In contrast, had the Rabbis merely exempted one who carries an article from a private domain, this would have created the impression that they consider the courtyard a private domain, and consequently their ruling was stringent as a precaution. To avoid this erroneous conclusion, they emphasize that the courtyard is a full-fledged *karmelit*, even when this entails a leniency (*Tosafot*; Ritva).

HALAKHA

A wall between courtyards that fell – כּוֹתֶל שֶׁבֵּין חֲצֵרוֹת שֶׁנָּפַל: With regard to a wall between two courtyards that collapses after the residents of each courtyard established an independent *eiruv*, if the wall collapses on Shabbat, it is permitted to carry throughout the courtyard up to where the wall once stood, as though it had not fallen. The *halakha* is in accordance with the opinion of Shmuel, who acted upon his own ruling. In addition, the *halakha* is in accordance with the principle that something permitted at the onset of Shabbat remains permitted throughout Shabbat (*Shulḥan Arukh, Oraḥ Ḥayyim* 374:2).

A courtyard that was breached into the public domain – חָצֵר שֶׁנִּפְרְצָה לִרְשׁוּת הָרַבִּים: It is prohibited to carry in a courtyard that was breached into the public domain, as its legal status is that of a *karmelit*. It is also prohibited to carry from this courtyard into a private or a public domain and vice versa. The same *halakha* applies to carrying from the place where the wall stood into the public or private domains. The *halakha* is in accordance with the majority opinion of the Rabbis (*Shulḥan Arukh, Oraḥ Ḥayyim* 361:2).

גמ׳ וְרַבִּי אֱלִיעֶזֶר, מִשּׁוּם דְּנִפְרְצָה לִרְשׁוּת הָרַבִּים הָוְיָא לָהּ רְשׁוּת הָרַבִּים?! אִין, רַבִּי אֱלִיעֶזֶר לְטַעְמֵיהּ.

GEMARA The Gemara asks: **And** according to **Rabbi Eliezer, due to** the fact that the courtyard **was breached into the public domain,** does **it become the public domain?** The Gemara answers: **Yes,** as in this regard the opinion of **Rabbi Eliezer** conforms **to his** standard line of **reasoning.**

דְּתַנְיָא, רַבִּי יְהוּדָה אוֹמֵר מִשּׁוּם רַבִּי אֱלִיעֶזֶר: רַבִּים שֶׁבָּרְרוּ דֶּרֶךְ לְעַצְמָן – מַה שֶּׁבָּרְרוּ בָּרְרוּ.

As it was taught in a *baraita* that **Rabbi Yehuda said in the name of Rabbi Eliezer:** In a situation where the **multitudes selected a path for themselves** in a field, or between fields, the path **that they selected, they selected,** and they retain the right to traverse this path even if the place belongs to an individual. Here too, as the partition of the courtyard was breached to the extent that the public can enter, its status is that of a public domain.

אִינִי?! וְהָאָמַר רַב גִּידֵּל, אָמַר רַב: וְהוּא שֶׁאָבְדָה לָהֶן דֶּרֶךְ בְּאוֹתוֹ שָׂדֶה.

The Gemara expresses surprise at this opinion: **Is that so? But didn't Rav Giddel say** that **Rav said: And this** applies only **if they had misplaced a path in that field.** Generally speaking, the public does not have the right to establish a path wherever it chooses. The *baraita* is referring to a case where a public path used to run through that field, but it fell into disuse, and no one remembers its precise course. In this case the public may once again select a path through the field.

וְכִי תֵּימָא: הָכָא נַמִי כְּגוֹן שֶׁאָבְדָה לָהּ דֶּרֶךְ בְּאוֹתָהּ חָצֵר – וְהָאָמַר רַבִּי חֲנִינָא: עַד מְקוֹם מְחִיצָּה מַחֲלוֹקֶת!

And if you say: Here too, the mishna is dealing with a case **where** the public **misplaced a path in that courtyard.** They do not remember the exact position of the partition that once separated the courtyard and the public domain. The public claims that the residents of the courtyard appropriated that part of their domain. It is only this area that Rabbi Eliezer says is considered a public domain. The Gemara asks: **But didn't Rabbi Ḥanina say:** The **dispute** between Rabbi Eliezer and the Rabbis is with regard to the entire courtyard **to** [*ad*] **the place of** the fallen **partition,** not only the small section that might have been a public path.

אֵימָא: עַל מְקוֹם מְחִיצָּה מַחֲלוֹקֶת.

The Gemara rejects this argument: **Say** that Rabbi Ḥanina stated that Rabbi Eliezer and the Rabbis **disagree over** [*al*] **the place of** the **partition,** i.e., the dispute does not concern the entire courtyard, but only the former location of the partition, where a public path might once have passed.

וְאִיבָּעֵית אֵימָא: בְּצִידֵּי רְשׁוּת הָרַבִּים קָמִיפַּלְגִי; דְּרַבִּי אֱלִיעֶזֶר סָבַר: צִידֵּי רְשׁוּת הָרַבִּים – כִּרְשׁוּת הָרַבִּים דָּמוּ, וְרַבָּנַן סָבְרִי: צִידֵּי רְשׁוּת הָרַבִּים – לָאו כִּרְשׁוּת הָרַבִּים דָּמוּ.

And if you wish, say instead that the mishna is dealing with a case where the location of the original partition is known, and the *tanna'im* **disagree with regard to** the legal status of **the sides of a public domain. As Rabbi Eliezer maintains** that **the sides of a public domain are considered like a public domain,** i.e., the areas adjacent to the public domain are subsumed into the public domain. The same applies to the place of the partition that once separated the courtyard and the public domain but was breached. **And the Rabbis maintain** that **the sides of a public domain are not considered like a public domain.**

וְלִיפְלוֹג בְּצִידֵּי רְשׁוּת הָרַבִּים בְּעָלְמָא! אִי אִיפְלִיגוּ בְּצִידֵּי רְשׁוּת הָרַבִּים בְּעָלְמָא – הֲוָה אָמְרִינַן: כִּי פְּלִיגִי רַבָּנַן עֲלֵיהּ דְּרַבִּי אֱלִיעֶזֶר – הָנֵי מִילֵּי הֵיכָא דְּאִיכָּא חִיפּוּפֵי, אֲבָל הֵיכָא דְּלֵיכָּא חִיפּוּפֵי – אֵימָא מוֹדוּ לֵיהּ, קָא מַשְׁמַע לָן.

The Gemara asks: If so, **let them disagree with regard to the sides of a public domain in general;** why did they disagree about this particular case? The Gemara answers: **Had they disagreed with regard to the sides of a public domain in general, we would have said: When do the Rabbis disagree with Rabbi Eliezer? This** dispute **applies only where there are stakes**[B] alongside the houses, which interfere with the use of the sides of the public domain. **However, where there are no** such **stakes, say** that **they concede to him** that the sides of a public domain are considered like a public domain. By formulating the dispute with regard to a courtyard that was breached into the public domain, the mishna is **teaching us** that they disagree in all cases.

וְהָא ״מִתּוֹכָהּ״ קָאָמַר!

The Gemara raises a difficulty: **But didn't** Rabbi Eliezer **say** with regard to a courtyard that was breached into the public domain, that one who carries an object **from inside** the courtyard into the private domain is liable? Apparently, he is liable if he carries an article into the private domain from anywhere in the courtyard, not only from the area adjacent to the public domain, as the entire courtyard is considered a public domain.

BACKGROUND

Stakes – חִיפּוּפֵי:

House with stakes on the side facing the public domain, to prevent carriages and crowds of people from approaching the walls of the house

דְּאָמוּר רַבָּנַן ״מִתּוֹכָהּ״, אָמַר אִיהוּ נָמֵי ״מִתּוֹכָהּ״.

The Gemara answers: **As the Rabbis said: From inside** the courtyard, Rabbi Eliezer **also said: From inside** the courtyard. No conclusion can be inferred from his use of the term, as he was referring only to the section adjacent to the public domain.

וְרַבָּנַן, אָמַר רַבִּי אֱלִיעֶזֶר צִידֵּי רְשׁוּת הָרַבִּים, וּמְהַדְּרוּ לֵיהּ אִינְהוּ ״מִתּוֹכָהּ״?!

The Gemara asks: **But,** if that is the case, the statement of **the Rabbis** is difficult. **Rabbi Eliezer said** that the legal status of **the sides of the public domain** is like that of a public domain, **and they replied to him** by referring to: **From inside** the entire courtyard? They appear to be addressing two different cases.

הָכִי קָאָמְרִי לֵיהּ רַבָּנַן לְרַבִּי אֱלִיעֶזֶר: מִי לָא קָא מוֹדֵית לַן הֵיכָא דְּטִילְטֵל מִתּוֹכָהּ לִרְשׁוּת הָרַבִּים, וּמֵרְשׁוּת הָרַבִּים לְתוֹכָהּ דְּפָטוּר – מִפְּנֵי שֶׁהִיא כַּרְמְלִית, צִידֵּי נָמֵי לָא שְׁנָא.

The Gemara answers: **This is what the Rabbis are saying to Rabbi Eliezer: Don't you concede to us** with regard to a case **where he carried** an object **from inside** the courtyard **to the public domain, or from the public domain to** the courtyard, **that** he is **exempt, because** the courtyard **is** considered **like a** ***karmelit*****? The sides** of the public domain are **no different,** and should have the status of a *karmelit* **as well.**

וְרַבִּי אֱלִיעֶזֶר – הָתָם לָא קָא דָּרְסִי לַהּ רַבִּים, הָכָא – קָא דָּרְסִי לַהּ רַבִּים.

And how does **Rabbi Eliezer** counter this argument? **There, the public does not tread on** the courtyard; **here,** the **public treads on** the edge of the courtyard adjacent to the public domain, and therefore its status is that of a public domain in every sense.

מתני׳ חָצֵר שֶׁנִּפְרְצָה לִרְשׁוּת הָרַבִּים מִשְּׁתֵּי רוּחוֹתֶיהָ, וְכֵן בַּיִת שֶׁנִּפְרַץ מִשְּׁתֵּי רוּחוֹתָיו, וְכֵן מָבוֹי שֶׁנִּטְּלוּ קוֹרוֹתָיו אוֹ לְחָיָיו – מוּתָּרִים בְּאוֹתוֹ שַׁבָּת, וַאֲסוּרִים לֶעָתִיד לָבֹא, דִּבְרֵי רַבִּי יְהוּדָה.

MISHNA With regard to **a courtyard that was breached** on Shabbat **into a public domain from two of its sides, and likewise** with regard to **a house that was breached from two of its sides, and likewise** with regard to **an alleyway whose** cross **beams or side posts were removed** on Shabbat, the residents of that domain **are permitted** to carry there **on that Shabbat,**[N] **but are prohibited** from doing so **in the future.** This is **the statement of Rabbi Yehuda.**

רַבִּי יוֹסֵי אוֹמֵר: אִם מוּתָּרִין לְאוֹתוֹ שַׁבָּת – מוּתָּרִין לֶעָתִיד לָבֹא, וְאִם אֲסוּרִין לֶעָתִיד לָבֹא – אֲסוּרִין לְאוֹתוֹ שַׁבָּת.

Rabbi Yosei says: This cannot be the *halakha*, as **if they are permitted** to carry there **on that Shabbat, they are** likewise **permitted** to do so **in the future, and if they are prohibited** from carrying there **in the future, they are** also **prohibited** from carrying there **on that Shabbat.**

גמ׳ בְּמַאי עָסְקִינַן? אִילֵימָא בְּעֶשֶׂר – מַאי שְׁנָא מֵרוּחַ אַחַת – דְּאָמַר ״פִּיתְחָא הוּא״, מִשְּׁתֵּי רוּחוֹת נָמֵי פִּיתְחָא הוּא! אֶלָּא בְּיָתֵר מֵעֶשֶׂר – אִי הָכִי אֲפִילּוּ מֵרוּחַ אַחַת נָמֵי!

GEMARA The Gemara poses a question: **With what case are we dealing? If you say** the mishna is referring to a case **where** the breach was up to **ten** cubits wide, in **what** way **is** a breach **on** only **one side different?**[N] It is due to the fact **that we say: It is an entrance** rather than a breach, and carrying is therefore permitted. If so, if it was breached **on two sides as well,** say: **It is an entrance,** and there are entrances on two sides of the courtyard. **Rather,** the mishna is certainly dealing **with** a breach that is **greater than ten** cubits. **If so,** it should be prohibited to carry **even** if the courtyard was breached **on** only **one side,** as a breach that size negates all the partitions.

אָמַר רַב: לְעוֹלָם בְּעֶשֶׂר,

Rav said: Actually, the mishna is dealing **with** a breach that is no wider than **ten** cubits,

NOTES

Permitted on that Shabbat – מוּתָּרִים בְּאוֹתוֹ שַׁבָּת: Some commentaries explain that Rabbi Yehuda conforms with his standard line of reasoning here. By Torah law, two partitions create a private domain. As the Torah permits one to carry in this courtyard and house, there is no need to completely refrain from using them for one Shabbat, as the Sages permitted using the courtyard in exigent circumstances (see *Tosafot*; Rashash; and others).

In what way is a breach on one side different – מַאי שְׁנָא מֵרוּחַ אַחַת: The early commentaries ask: Perhaps this refers to a situation where a courtyard or house was breached on opposite sides, as in that case everyone agrees that the principle: The edge of the roof descends to the ground and seals the opening is not in effect and therefore it is prohibited to carry. *Tosafot* and other commentaries explain that since the mishna does not specify which walls collapsed, it can be assumed that the same *halakha* applies regardless of which sides were affected. Other authorities claim that it makes no difference according to Rabbi Yehuda, as he permits carrying even if the breaches are on opposite sides (see *Me'iri* and Ritva).

וּכְגוֹן שֶׁנִּפְרְצָה בְּקֶרֶן זָוִית, דְּפִיתְחָא בְּקֶרֶן זָוִית לָא עָבְדִי אִינָשֵׁי.

and with a case **where** the courtyard **was breached in a corner,** so that it is breached on two sides.[H] Although the opening is no more than ten cubits wide, it cannot be considered an entrance, **as people do not build an entrance in a corner.**[N] It is therefore clear that this is a breach that negates the partition.

״וְכֵן בַּיִת שֶׁנִּפְרַץ מִשְּׁתֵּי רוּחוֹתָיו״. מַאי שְׁנָא מֵרוּחַ אַחַת – דְּאָמְרִינַן ״פִּי תִקְרָה יוֹרֵד וְסוֹתֵם״, מִשְּׁתֵּי רוּחוֹת נַמִי, לֵימָא ״פִּי תִקְרָה יוֹרֵד וְסוֹתֵם״!

We learned in the mishna: **And likewise,** with regard to **a house that was breached** on Shabbat **from two of its sides**[H] into a public domain, the residents are permitted to carry in the house on that Shabbat, but not a future Shabbat. The Gemara asks: In **what** way **is** a breach **on one side different?** The difference is due to the fact **that we say: The edge of the roof descends and seals** the house, as if there were a full-fledged partition there. **So too,** when it is breached **on two sides, let us say: The edge of the roof descends and seals.**

אָמְרִי דְּבֵי רַב מִשְּׁמֵיהּ דְּרַב: כְּגוֹן שֶׁנִּפְרַץ בְּקֶרֶן זָוִית, וְקֵירוּיוֹ בַּאֲלַכְסוֹן, דְּלֵיכָּא לְמֵימַר ״פִּי תִקְרָה יוֹרֵד וְסוֹתֵם״.

The Gemara answers: **The** Sages of the **school of Rav said in the name of Rav:** The mishna is referring to a case **where** the house **was breached in a corner,**[B] **and its roofing was inclined,**[NB] as in that case, **one cannot say: The edge of the roof descends and seals,** as the edge of an inclined roof does not appear to be the beginning of a partition.

וּשְׁמוּאֵל אָמַר: אֲפִילּוּ בְּיָתֵר מֵעֶשֶׂר. אִי הָכִי, מֵרוּחַ אַחַת נַמִי!

And Shmuel said: The mishna is referring to a breach that is **even wider than ten** cubits. The Gemara asks: **If so,** why did the mishna cite a case where it is breached from two sides? It should be prohibited to carry there **even** if it were breached **from one side.**

מִשּׁוּם בַּיִת.

The Gemara answers: The reason that it is prohibited only if it is breached from two sides is **due to** the fact that it is **a house.** In the case of a courtyard, the same *halakha* would apply even if it were breached on only one side. However, the mishna sought to teach the *halakha* of a house as well, in which case, it is prohibited to carry only if it is breached on two sides. If it is breached on one side, the edge of the roof descends and seals, and carrying is permitted.

וּבַיִת גּוּפֵיהּ תִּקְשֵׁי, מַאי שְׁנָא מֵרוּחַ אַחַת – דְּאָמְרִי ״פִּי תִקְרָה יוֹרֵד וְסוֹתֵם״, מִשְּׁתֵּי רוּחוֹת נַמִי נֵימָא ״פִּי תִקְרָה יוֹרֵד וְסוֹתֵם״!

The Gemara asks: **But** the *halakha* of **a house itself should pose a difficulty** according to this explanation. In **what** way **is** a breach **on one side different?** It is due to the fact **that we say: The edge of the roof descends and seals** the house, as if there were a full-fledged partition there. **So too,** when it is breached **on two sides, let us say: The edge of the roof descends and seals.**

HALAKHA

The courtyard was breached in a corner on two sides – חָצֵר שֶׁנִּפְרְצָה בְּקֶרֶן זָוִית: It is prohibited to carry in a courtyard that was breached in a corner, even if the breach was narrower than ten cubits wide, in accordance with Rav's explanation of the mishna (*Shulḥan Arukh*, *Oraḥ Ḥayyim* 361:2).

A house that was breached from two sides – בַּיִת שֶׁנִּפְרַץ מִשְּׁתֵּי רוּחוֹתָיו: With regard to a house that was breached in a corner with a breach less than ten cubits, if the ceiling also partially collapsed such that the breach runs diagonally across as explained by *Tosafot*, or if the roof was inclined as explained by Rashi, it is considered breached and it is prohibited to carry there. This ruling is in accordance with the opinion of Rav (*Shulḥan Arukh*, *Oraḥ Ḥayyim* 361:2).

NOTES

An entrance in a corner – פִּתְחָא בְּקֶרֶן זָוִית: *Tosafot* explain that people do not generally consider a corner breach an entrance. If, however, they decided to construct the form of a doorway in a corner, it certainly assumes the status of an entrance, as indicated by the Gemara elsewhere.

Its roofing was inclined – קֵירוּיוֹ בַּאֲלַכְסוֹן: The Ra'avad maintains that if the roof was breached diagonally as explained by *Tosafot*, the edge of the roof descends and seals. However, if the roof was intact when a section of the partition fell, the principle: The edge of the roof descends and seals, does not apply, because in that case, the edge of the roof is not positioned above the walls.

BACKGROUND

The house was breached in a corner – בַּיִת שֶׁנִּפְרַץ בְּקֶרֶן זָוִית: The house in the image below is breached at a corner, while its roof above is also breached at an angle. According to Shmuel, the principle: The edge of the ceiling descends and seals, is not applicable to this case. This illustration follows the interpretation of *Tosafot*.

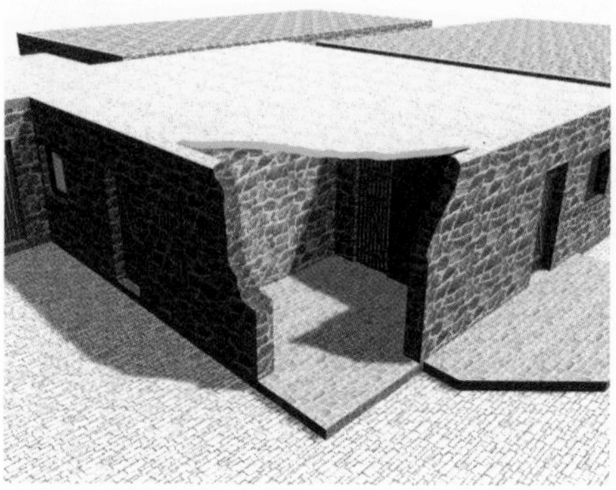
Breach in the corner according to *Tosafot*

Its roofing was inclined – קֵירוּי בַּאֲלַכְסוֹן: The house in the image below, with an inclined roof, is breached at a corner. This illustration follows Rashi's interpretation.

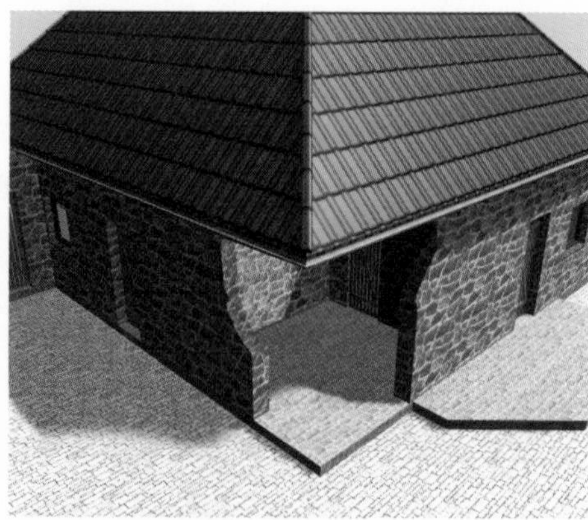
Breach in the corner according to Rashi

וְתוּ: מִי אִית לֵיהּ לִשְׁמוּאֵל פִּי תִקְרָה יוֹרֵד וְסוֹתֵם? וְהָא אִתְּמַר, אַכְסַדְרָה בְּבִקְעָה; רַב אָמַר: מוּתָּר לְטַלְטֵל בְּכוּלָּהּ, וּשְׁמוּאֵל אָמַר: אֵין מְטַלְטְלִין בָּהּ אֶלָּא בְּאַרְבַּע אַמּוֹת!

And furthermore: Is Shmuel of the opinion that there is a principle: **The edge of a roof descends and seals? But wasn't it stated** that there is an amoraic dispute with regard to a portico located **in a valley,** which has the status of a *karmelit.* **Rav said:** It **is permitted to carry in the entire** portico, as he maintains that the edge of the roof of the portico descends and seals, rendering it a private domain. **And Shmuel said: One may carry only within four cubits.** Apparently, Shmuel does not accept the principle: The edge of a roof descends and seals.

הָא לָא קַשְׁיָא, כִּי לֵית לֵיהּ – בְּאַרְבַּע, אֲבָל בְּשָׁלֹשׁ – אִית לֵיהּ.

The Gemara answers: **This is not a difficulty. Where** Shmuel **is not of** the opinion that this principle is applied, it is **with regard to** a structure where walls on all **four** sides[N] are formed in that manner. **However, with regard to** a structure where only **three** sides are formed in that manner and the fourth side is an actual wall, **he is of** the opinion that the principle is applied.

מִכׇּל מָקוֹם קַשְׁיָא!

The Gemara comments: **In any case,** this is **difficult.** Although the contradiction between the two statements of Shmuel was resolved, the question remains: Why do we not apply the principle: The edge of a roof descends and seals, to two sides of the house?

כִּדְאָמְרִי בֵּי רַב מִשְּׁמֵיהּ דְּרַב: כְּגוֹן שֶׁנִּפְרַץ בְּקֶרֶן זָוִית וְקֵירוּיוֹ בַּאֲלַכְסוֹן, הָכָא נַמִי: כְּגוֹן שֶׁנִּפְרַץ בְּקֶרֶן זָוִית וְקֵירוּיוֹ בְּאַרְבַּע.

The Gemara answers: The reason is **as the** Sages of the **school of Rav said in the name of Rav:** The mishna is referring to a case **where** the house **was breached in a corner, and its roofing was inclined,** as in that case, one cannot say: The roof of the house descends and seals. **Here too,** Shmuel's opinion can be explained in a similar manner: The mishna is dealing with a case **where** the house **was breached in a corner, and its roof is** at a distance **of** at least **four** handbreadths from the breach,[B] and is uneven. In that case, the principle: The edge of a roof descends and seals, would have to be applied to four corners, and Shmuel is of the opinion that it may not be applied in that case.

שְׁמוּאֵל לָא אָמַר כְּרַב – אֲלַכְסוֹן לָא קָתָנֵי. וְרַב לָא אָמַר כִּשְׁמוּאֵל – אִם כֵּן הָוְיָא לַיהּ אַכְסַדְרָה, וְרַב לְטַעְמֵיהּ, דְּאָמַר: אַכְסַדְרָה מוּתָּר לְטַלְטֵל בְּכוּלָּהּ.

The Gemara explains: **Shmuel did not say** his explanation of the mishna **in accordance with** the opinion of **Rav,** as the mishna **does not teach** that the roof was **slanted,** which is the crux of Rav's explanation. **And Rav did not say** his explanation of the mishna **in accordance with** the opinion of **Shmuel,** as **if so,** even if the roof was breached on several sides, **its** legal status **would be** that of **a portico, and Rav** conforms **to his** standard line of **reasoning, as he said:** With regard to **a portico, it is permitted to carry throughout the entire** portico.

דְּאִיתְּמַר, אַכְסַדְרָה בְּבִקְעָה, רַב אָמַר: מוּתָּר לְטַלְטֵל בְּכוּלָּהּ, וּשְׁמוּאֵל אָמַר: אֵין מְטַלְטְלִין בָּהּ אֶלָּא בְּאַרְבַּע אַמּוֹת.

The Gemara proceeds to cite the dispute between Rav and Shmuel in a more comprehensive manner. **As it was stated** that **Rav said:** It **is permitted to carry in the entire** portico as it is considered sealed. **And Shmuel said: One may carry only within four cubits.** As the portico does not have actual partitions it is subsumed into the field, and shares its status of a *karmelit.*

רַב אָמַר: מוּתָּר לְטַלְטֵל בְּכוּלָּהּ, אָמְרִינַן ״פִּי תִקְרָה יוֹרֵד וְסוֹתֵם״, וּשְׁמוּאֵל אָמַר: אֵין מְטַלְטְלִין בָּהּ אֶלָּא בְּאַרְבַּע אַמּוֹת, לָא אָמְרִינַן ״פִּי תִקְרָה יוֹרֵד וְסוֹתֵם״.

The Gemara elaborates on their respective opinions. **Rav said:** It **is permitted to carry in the entire** portico, as he maintains that **we say: The edge of the roof descends and seals** the portico to form a partition. As there is a roof over the portico, it is considered sealed with partitions on all four sides. **And Shmuel said: One may carry only within four cubits,** as **we do not say: The edge of the ceiling descends and seals.**

בְּעֶשֶׂר כּוּלֵּי עָלְמָא לָא פְּלִיגִי, כִּי פְּלִיגִי – בְּיָתֵר מֵעֶשֶׂר.

The Gemara elaborates further: If the openings on the sides of the portico are no wider than **ten** cubits, **everyone agrees** that they are considered sealed, as the status of even an unroofed breach of ten cubits or less is that of an entrance, and one is permitted to carry throughout the entire domain. **They disagree** only in a case **where** the openings are **more than ten** cubits wide.

וְאִיכָּא דְּאָמְרִי: בְּיָתֵר – כּוּלֵּי עָלְמָא לָא פְּלִיגִי, כִּי פְּלִיגִי – בְּעֶשֶׂר.

And some say: On the contrary, if the openings are **more** than ten cubits wide, **everyone agrees** that they are considered breaches, and the principle: The edge of the roof descends and seals, is not applied. **They disagree** only in a case **where** the openings are no wider than **ten** cubits.

וְהָא דְּאָמַר רַב יְהוּדָה:

And that which Rav Yehuda said:

NOTES

Where Shmuel is not of the opinion that this principle is applied, it is with regard to a structure where walls on all four sides – כִּי לֵית לֵיהּ בְּאַרְבַּע: The text in the Gemara is in accordance with Rashi's reading. This reading is the subject of a fundamental dispute between Rashi and *Tosafot*, here and elsewhere, with regard to the definition of the term *akhsadra*, translated here as portico. Rashi maintains that an *akhsadra* located in a valley consists of only four posts and no partitions, whereas *Tosafot* and most commentaries explain that an *akhsadra* has three walls and is open on only one side. Consequently, according to *Tosafot*, the correct version of Shmuel's statement is: Where Shmuel is not of the opinion that this principle is applied, it is with regard to a structure where there are walls on three sides. In other words, if there are only three partitions, Shmuel does not accept the principle that the edge of the roof descends and seals. However, if there are four partitions, three of which were properly constructed while the fourth has protrusions or side posts, Shmuel concedes to Rav that the principle is applied. The entire discussion is subject to two different explanations, in accordance with these two approaches.

BACKGROUND

A roof that collapsed at a distance of at least four handbreadths from the breach – גג שֶׁנָּפַל קֵירוּיוֹ בְּאַרְבַּע: The house in the image below is breached in the corner, while the roof collapsed unevenly in a manner that is four handbreadths away from the walls. It is necessary, therefore, to complete not only one wall but four, by means of the edge of the roof, as indicated by the dotted lines.

Collapsed roof at a distance of four handbreadths from the breach

קוֹרָה אַרְבָּעָה מַתִּיר בְּחוּרְבָּה. וְרַב נַחְמָן אָמַר רַבָּה בַּר אֲבוּהּ: קוֹרָה אַרְבָּעָה מַתִּיר בְּמַיִם. מַנִּי?

A cross **beam four** handbreadths wide **renders** carrying **in a ruin** that is breached into a public domain **permitted,** as the edge of the cross beam is considered to descend and seal the breach. **And** that which **Rav Naḥman said** that **Rabba bar Avuh said: A cross beam four** handbreadths wide **renders** carrying **in water permitted** like a partition. In accordance with **whose** opinion were these rulings stated?

לְהָךְ לִישָּׁנָא דְּאָמְרַתְּ בְּעֶשֶׂר לָא פְּלִיגִי – בְּעֶשֶׂר, וְדִבְרֵי הַכֹּל. לְהָךְ לִישָּׁנָא דְּאָמְרַתְּ בְּעֶשֶׂר פְּלִיגִי – כְּרַב.

The Gemara explains: **According to this version that you stated,** that Rav and Shmuel **agree with regard to** an opening no wider than **ten** cubits, here it is referring **to** a cross beam that is no longer than **ten** cubits, **and everyone,** both Rav and Shmuel, **agrees** with these rulings. **According to that** other **version that you stated,** that **they disagree with regard to** an opening no wider than **ten** cubits, these rulings are **in accordance with** the opinion of **Rav** alone.

לֵימָא אַבָּיֵי וְרָבָא בִּפְלוּגְתָּא דְּרַב וּשְׁמוּאֵל קָמִיפַּלְגִי; דְּאִיתְּמַר: סִיכֵּךְ עַל גַּבֵּי אַכְסַדְרָה שֶׁיֵּשׁ לָהּ פַּצִּימִין – כְּשֵׁירָה. אֵין לָהּ פַּצִּימִין, אַבָּיֵי אָמַר: כְּשֵׁירָה, וְרָבָא אָמַר: פְּסוּלָה.

The Gemara suggests: **Let us say** that **Abaye and Rava are disagreeing with regard to the** point that was the subject of a **dispute between Rav and Shmuel. As it was stated:** If one **placed roofing on top of a portico**[B] **that has doorposts,** i.e., pillars that form the beginnings of partitions, **it is a valid *sukka*.** If, however, he placed the roofing atop a portico that **has no doorposts,** there is a dispute. **Abaye said: It is a valid *sukka*. And Rava said: It is invalid.**

אַבָּיֵי אָמַר: כְּשֵׁירָה – אָמַר: ״פִּי תִקְרָה יוֹרֵד וְסוֹתֵם״. וְרָבָא אָמַר: פְּסוּלָה – לֹא אָמַר ״פִּי תִקְרָה יוֹרֵד וְסוֹתֵם״. לֵימָא אַבָּיֵי כְּרַב, וְרָבָא כִּשְׁמוּאֵל!

The Gemara elaborates: **Abaye said: It is valid.** As **he said: The edge of a roof descends and seals.** Since the portico is roofed, it is considered to have partitions as well. **And Rava said: It is invalid,** as **he did not say: The edge of a roof descends and seals. Let us say** that **Abaye** holds **in accordance with** the opinion of **Rav, and Rava** holds **in accordance with** the opinion of **Shmuel?**

אַלִּיבָּא דִּשְׁמוּאֵל כּוּלֵּי עָלְמָא לָא פְּלִיגִי, כִּי פְּלִיגִי – אַלִּיבָּא דְּרַב. אַבָּיֵי, כְּרַב. וְרָבָא, עַד כָּאן לָא קָאָמַר רַב הָתָם – אֶלָּא דְּהָנֵי מְחִיצוֹת לְאַכְסַדְרָה עֲבִידִי. אֲבָל הָכָא, דְּהָנֵי מְחִיצוֹת לָאו לְסוּכָּה עֲבִידִי – לָא.

The Gemara answers: **According to** the opinion of **Shmuel, everyone,** including Abaye, **agrees**[N] that this *sukka* is invalid. **Where they disagree** is **according to** the opinion of **Rav. Abaye** holds **in accordance with** the opinion of **Rav** in a straightforward manner. **And Rava** claims: **Rav stated** his opinion, that the edge of the portico descends and seals, **only there, where those partitions** formed by the roof **were built for the portico,**[N] and they are therefore viewed as sealing it. **However here, where these partitions were not built for** the mitzva of ***sukka*, no,** even Rav would agree that the partitions are not sufficiently significant to utilize for the purpose of this mitzva.

״רַבִּי יוֹסֵי אוֹמֵר אִם מוּתָּרִין״. אִיבַּעְיָא לְהוּ: רַבִּי יוֹסֵי לֶאֱסוֹר אוֹ לְהַתִּיר?

We learned in the mishna: **Rabbi Yosei says: If they are permitted** to carry there on that Shabbat, they are likewise permitted to do so in the future, and if they are prohibited from carrying there in the future, they are also prohibited from carrying there on that Shabbat **A dilemma was raised before** the Sages: Did **Rabbi Yosei** intend **to prohibit** carrying even on that Shabbat, **or to permit** carrying even in the future?

אָמַר רַב שֵׁשֶׁת: לֶאֱסוֹר. וְכֵן אָמַר רַבִּי יוֹחָנָן: לֶאֱסוֹר. תַּנְיָא נָמֵי הָכִי, אָמַר רַבִּי יוֹסֵי: כְּשֵׁם שֶׁאֲסוּרִין לֶעָתִיד לָבֹא, כָּךְ אֲסוּרִין לְאוֹתוֹ שַׁבָּת.

Rav Sheshet said: His intention was **to prohibit** carrying even on that Shabbat. **And similarly, Rabbi Yoḥanan said:** His intention was **to prohibit** carrying even on that Shabbat. **This** opinion **was also taught** in a *baraita*: **Rabbi Yosei said: Just as they are prohibited** from carrying **in the future, so are they prohibited** from carrying **on that Shabbat.**

אִיתְּמַר, רַב חִיָּיא בַּר יוֹסֵף אָמַר: הֲלָכָה כְּרַבִּי יוֹסֵי. וּשְׁמוּאֵל אָמַר: הֲלָכָה כְּרַבִּי יְהוּדָה.

It was stated: Rav Ḥiyya bar Yosef said that the ***halakha* is in accordance with** the opinion of **Rabbi Yosei,**[H] **while Shmuel said** that the ***halakha* is in accordance with** the opinion of **Rabbi Yehuda.**

BACKGROUND

If one placed roofing on top of a portico – סִכֵּךְ עַל גַּבֵּי אַכְסַדְרָה: As explained elsewhere, this refers to a situation similar to the illustration below: The house is U-shaped with a portico along the inner walls. The roofing is placed over the indented section. The question is whether or not the external walls of the portico can be considered partitions for the *sukka*.

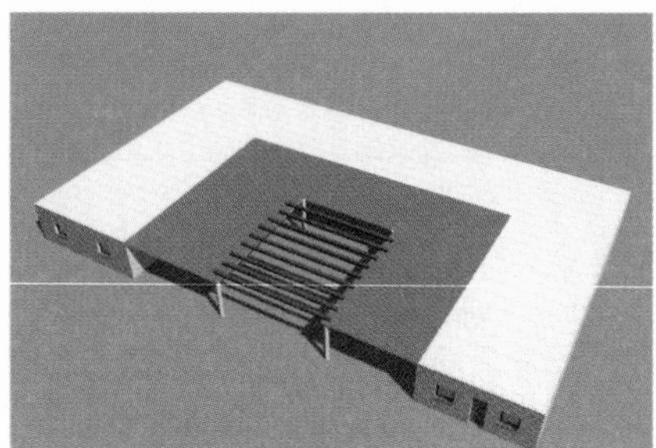

Portico along the inner walls of a house

NOTES

According to Shmuel everyone agrees – אַלִּיבָּא דִּשְׁמוּאֵל...לָא פְּלִיגִי: Rashi explains that Abaye concedes that Shmuel invalidates the *sukka* in this case. The Ritva questions Rashi's approach and amends it slightly. Rabbeinu Ḥananel explains that the phrase: According to Shmuel everyone agrees, means that as the *halakha* is not in accordance with his opinion, the two *amora'im* certainly did not discuss his ruling.

Partitions were built for the portico – מְחִיצוֹת לְאַכְסַדְרָה עֲבִידִי: Rashi explains that the partitions must be built for the purpose of the mitzva of *sukka*. This is puzzling, as the generally accepted *halakha* is that the walls of a *sukka* need not be constructed for the sake of the mitzva. In tractate *Sukka*, Rashi says that the roof of the portico is in any case built for its inner area, as the edge of this roof seals the portico from the inside. In the case of a *sukka*, however, as the edge of the portico roof is on the outside, it cannot create external partitions for the *sukka* as well.

HALAKHA

The *halakha* is in accordance with the opinion of Rabbi Yosei – הֲלָכָה כְּרַבִּי יוֹסֵי: Rabbi Yosei's statement in the mishna is intended as a prohibition, and his opinion is accepted as the *halakha*. Furthermore, the *halakha* is in accordance with Rav in disputes with Shmuel with regard to prohibitions. Consequently, if the partition is removed it is prohibited to carry even on that Shabbat (*Shulḥan Arukh, Oraḥ Ḥayyim* 361:2).

וּמִי אָמַר שְׁמוּאֵל הָכִי? וְהָתְנַן, אָמַר רַבִּי יְהוּדָה: בַּמֶּה דְּבָרִים אֲמוּרִים – בְּעֵירוּבֵי תְחוּמִין, אֲבָל בְּעֵירוּבֵי חֲצֵירוֹת – מְעָרְבִין בֵּין לָדַעַת בֵּין שֶׁלֹּא לָדַעַת, לְפִי שֶׁזָּכִין לְאָדָם שֶׁלֹּא בְּפָנָיו וְאֵין חָבִין שֶׁלֹּא בְּפָנָיו.

The Gemara expresses surprise: **But did Shmuel** really **say this? Didn't we learn** in a mishna that **Rabbi Yehuda said: In what** case **are these matters**, that an *eiruv* may be established for a person only with his knowledge, **stated?** It is **with regard to a joining of** Shabbat **boundaries, but with regard to a joining of courtyards, one may establish an** *eiruv* for another person **both with his knowledge and without his knowledge, because one may act in a person's interest** even when **not in his presence, but one may act to his disadvantage only in his presence.** One may take unilateral action on another's behalf when it is to that other person's benefit. However, if it is to that person's disadvantage, or when the action entails both benefits and disadvantages, he may act on the other person's behalf only if he was explicitly appointed as his agent. A joining of courtyards is always to a person's benefit, and therefore it can be established even without his knowledge. However, with regard to a joining of Shabbat boundaries, any distance that a person gains in one direction he forfeits in the opposite direction. Consequently, this type of *eiruv* may be established only with his knowledge.

וְאָמַר רַב יְהוּדָה, אָמַר שְׁמוּאֵל: הֲלָכָה כְּרַבִּי יְהוּדָה. וְלֹא עוֹד אֶלָּא, כָּל מָקוֹם שֶׁשָּׁנָה רַבִּי יְהוּדָה בְּעֵירוּבִין – הֲלָכָה כְּמוֹתוֹ.

And Rav Yehuda said that **Shmuel said:** The ***halakha* is in accordance with** the opinion of **Rabbi Yehuda. And furthermore, anyplace where Rabbi Yehuda taught with regard to** the *halakhot* of ***eiruv*, the *halakha* is in accordance with his** opinion.

וְאָמַר לֵיהּ רַב חָנָא בַּגְדָּתָאָה לְרַב יְהוּדָה: אָמַר שְׁמוּאֵל אֲפִילּוּ בְּמָבוֹי שֶׁנִּיטַּל קוֹרָתוֹ אוֹ לֶחָיָיו? וְאָמַר לֵיהּ: בְּעֵירוּבִין אָמַרְתִּי לָךְ, וְלֹא בִּמְחִיצּוֹת.

And Rav Ḥana of Baghdad said to Rav Yehuda: Did **Shmuel state** this ruling **even with regard to an alleyway whose** cross **beam or side post was removed** during Shabbat? **And** Rav Yehuda **said to him: I spoke to you with regard to** the acquisition of **an *eiruv*, and not with regard to partitions.** The Gemara asks: How, then, could Shmuel rule that the *halakha* is in accordance with the opinion of Rabbi Yehuda in this case, after explicitly stating that the *halakha* is not in accordance with his opinion in the case of fallen partitions?

אָמַר רַב עָנָן: לְדִידִי מִיפָּרְשָׁא לִי מִינֵּיהּ דִּשְׁמוּאֵל, כָּאן – שֶׁנִּפְרְצָה לְכַרְמְלִית, כָּאן – שֶׁנִּפְרְצָה לִרְשׁוּת הָרַבִּים.

Rav Anan said: This matter **was explained to me** personally **by Shmuel** himself: **Here,** where Shmuel rules in accordance with the opinion of Rabbi Yehuda, it is in a case **where** the courtyard **was breached into a *karmelit*.**[N] In that case the *halakha* is lenient, as there is no concern lest one transgress a Torah prohibition. **There,** where Shmuel states that the *halakha* is not in accordance with the opinion of Rabbi Yehuda, it is in a case **where** the courtyard **was breached into a public domain,** and the *halakha* is therefore stringent, due to the concern lest one transgress a Torah prohibition.

מתני׳ הַבּוֹנֶה עֲלִיָּיה עַל גַּבֵּי שְׁנֵי בָתִּים, וְכֵן גְּשָׁרִים הַמְפוּלָּשִׁים – מְטַלְטְלִין תַּחְתֵּיהֶן בְּשַׁבָּת, דִּבְרֵי רַבִּי יְהוּדָה. וַחֲכָמִים אוֹסְרִין.

MISHNA With regard to **one who builds an upper story atop two houses**[B] on opposite sides of a public domain that passes beneath it, **and likewise bridges with a thoroughfare** beneath them[B] that rest on walls on opposite sides of a public domain, **one** may **carry beneath** the upper story and beneath the bridge **on Shabbat.** This is **the statement of Rabbi Yehuda,** who maintains that these areas are considered private domains.[N] **And the Rabbis prohibit** carrying in these areas.

וְעוֹד אָמַר רַבִּי יְהוּדָה: מְעָרְבִין לְמָבוֹי הַמְפוּלָּשׁ, וַחֲכָמִים אוֹסְרִין.

And furthermore, Rabbi Yehuda said: One may **establish an** *eiruv* even **for an alleyway that is open** at both ends,[H] with no need for any additional measures, **and the Rabbis prohibit** doing so.

NOTES

Where the courtyard was breached into a *karmelit* – שֶׁנִּפְרְצָה לְכַרְמְלִית: The *Me'iri* explains that Shmuel was stringent with regard to a case where the courtyard was breached into a *karmelit*, in accordance with the principle: One type found a similar type and was revived, i.e., when the measure of each of two items is less than the measure that renders an action prohibited and the two items are combined, resulting in a measure that renders an action prohibited, the prohibition takes effect, rendering the entire entity prohibited. However, if the courtyard was breached into the public domain, it is not prohibited to carry in the domain, as it is completely set apart from the courtyard.

Rabbi Yehuda's opinion with regard to an upper story – שִׁיטַת רַבִּי יְהוּדָה בַּעֲלִיָּיה: In the Jerusalem Talmud as well as in the *Tosefta*, the explanation is given that the decisive factor is the presence of a roof, as everyone agrees that carrying within a roofed domain is not prohibited by Torah law, but rather by rabbinic decree. Consequently, even the Rabbis, who dispute Rabbi Yehuda's opinion, rule that carrying is prohibited by rabbinic law.

BACKGROUND

An upper story atop two houses – עֲלִיָּיה שֶׁעַל שְׁנֵי בָתִּים: According to Rabbi Yehuda, an upper story constructed above two houses on either side of a street has the status of an alleyway in its own right, as there is a private domain on both sides. If the principle: The edge of a roof descends and seals, is in effect, it is as though the lower edge of the upper story descends to the ground and closes off the area between the houses from all sides.

Upper story above two houses

Bridges over an underpass – גְּשָׁרִים הַמְפוּלָּשִׁים: Below is a view of the Roman bridge in Ourense, Spain, that traverses the Miño River. On the right-hand side, a street can be seen running below the bridge.

Roman bridge in Ourense, Spain, with a public domain running under it

HALAKHA

An alleyway that is open at both ends – מָבוֹי הַמְפוּלָּשׁ: An alleyway that opens at both ends into a public domain or a *karmelit* cannot be rendered fit for carrying within it by means of a side post or a cross beam. Instead, the form of a doorway must be constructed at one end and a side post or a cross beam placed at the other end, as the *halakha* is in accordance with the majority opinion of the Rabbis, and contrary to the opinion of Rabbi Yehuda (*Shulḥan Arukh*, *Oraḥ Ḥayyim* 364:1).

גמ׳ אֲמַר רַבָּה: לָא תֵּימָא הַיְינוּ טַעְמָא דְּרַבִּי יְהוּדָה מִשּׁוּם דְּקָא סָבַר שְׁתֵּי מְחִיצוֹת דְּאוֹרַיְיתָא, אֶלָּא מִשּׁוּם דְּקָסָבַר: ״פִּי תִקְרָה יוֹרֵד וְסוֹתֵם״.

GEMARA **Rabba said: Do not say this is Rabbi Yehuda's reason;**[N] **that he maintains** that **by Torah law two partitions** constitute a private domain, i.e., the areas beneath the upper story and the bridge are considered private domains, as each has two partitions, one on each side of the public domain. Rather, the reason for Rabbi Yehuda's opinion is **because he maintains** that **the edge of a roof descends and seals.** The edges of the upper story and the bridge are considered to seal the areas beneath them.

אֵיתִיבֵיהּ אַבַּיֵי: יָתֵר עַל כֵּן אָמַר רַבִּי יְהוּדָה: מִי שֶׁיֵּשׁ לוֹ שְׁנֵי בָתִּים מִשְּׁנֵי צִידֵּי רְשׁוּת הָרַבִּים – עוֹשֶׂה לֶחִי מִכָּאן וְלֶחִי מִכָּאן, אוֹ קוֹרָה מִכָּאן וְקוֹרָה מִכָּאן, וְנוֹשֵׂא וְנוֹתֵן בָּאֶמְצַע. אָמְרוּ לוֹ: אֵין מְעָרְבִין רְשׁוּת הָרַבִּים בְּכָךְ!

Abaye raised an objection to Rabba from a *baraita*: **Furthermore, Rabbi Yehuda said:** With regard to **one who has two houses on two sides of a public domain** and seeks to carry from one house to the other on Shabbat via the public domain, **he places a side post from here,** adjacent to one of the houses, **and** another **side post from there,** adjacent to the other house, **or** he places **a** cross **beam from here and** another cross **beam from there, and he may** subsequently **carry** objects **and place** them **in the middle** of the area, as he transformed it into a private domain. His colleagues **said to him: One cannot establish an *eiruv*** to transform a **public domain** into a private domain **in this manner.** Clearly, the rationale for Rabbi Yehuda's opinion in that case is not that the edge of the roof descends and seals, as the area is not covered. Rather, he apparently holds that by Torah law, two walls suffice to form a private domain.

אָמַר לֵיהּ: מֵהַהִיא – אִין, מֵהָא – לֵיכָּא לְמִשְׁמַע מִינָּהּ.

Rabba **said to him: From that** *baraita*, **yes,** it is indeed possible to arrive at this conclusion. But **from this,** the mishna, **nothing can be learned from this** source, as there could be a different reason for Rabbi Yehuda's opinion.

אֲמַר רַב אַשִׁי: מַתְנִיתִין נַמִּי דַּיְקָא, מִדְּקָתָנֵי ״וְעוֹד אָמַר רַבִּי יְהוּדָה מְעָרְבִין בְּמָבוֹי הַמְפוּלָּשׁ וַחֲכָמִים אוֹסְרִין״.

Rav Ashi said: The mishna is also precise in its wording, as it indicates that the rationale for Rabbi Yehuda's opinion is that the edge of a roof descends and seals. **As the mishna teaches: And furthermore, Rabbi Yehuda said:** One may **establish an *eiruv*** even **for an alleyway that is open** at both ends, **and the Rabbis prohibit** doing so.

אִי אָמְרַתְּ בִּשְׁלָמָא מִשּׁוּם דְּקָא סָבַר ״פִּי תִקְרָה יוֹרֵד וְסוֹתֵם״ – הַיְינוּ דְּקָתָנֵי ״וְעוֹד״,

Granted, if you say that the reason for Rabbi Yehuda's leniency with regard to carrying beneath an upper story and a bridge is **that he maintains** that **the edge of a roof descends and seals, that is** why the mishna **states: And furthermore,** to introduce the ruling for an alleyway. In other words, the *tanna* of our mishna is saying that the ruling applies not only to a roofed area, but also to an unroofed alleyway, despite the fact that the reason there is that two partitions suffice to create a private domain by Torah law.

אֶלָּא אִי אָמְרַתְּ מִשּׁוּם דְּקָא סָבַר שְׁתֵּי מְחִיצוֹת דְּאוֹרַיְיתָא – מַאי ״וְעוֹד״? שְׁמַע מִינָּהּ.

However, if you say that Rabbi Yehuda permitted the first case as well **because he maintains** that **by Torah law two partitions** suffice to create a private domain, **what** is the need for the introduction: **And furthermore?** The rationale for the second ruling is no different from the rationale for the first. The Gemara concludes: Indeed, **learn from here** that this is correct.

הדרן עלך כל גגות

NOTES

Do not say this is Rabbi Yehuda's reason – **לָא תֵּימָא הַיְינוּ טַעְמָא דְּרַבִּי יְהוּדָה**: There is a practical difference between the two rationales for Rabbi Yehuda's opinion. If the rationale is the principle that two partitions can create a private domain by Torah law, two side posts or cross beams are required to render it permitted to carry in the domain by rabbinic law. However, if the rationale is the principle: The edge of the roof descends and seals, no additional steps are necessary to render it permitted to carry there (*Ge'on Ya'akov*).

Summary of **Perek IX**

In this chapter, the *halakhot* of limits and partitions were elucidated, with some fundamental differences of opinion surrounding the roots of these principles. Ultimately the halakhic conclusion was that those ordinances and decrees cited in tractate *Eiruvin* that established that one may not move objects from house to house and from courtyard to courtyard without an *eiruv* apply only to those objects that were in the house at the onset of the Shabbat. All private domains other than the house proper are considered a single domain. The fact that one area differs from another in its use, specifications, or ownership has no impact on the legal status domains. Therefore, all the adjacent courtyards, adjacent rooftops, and adjacent enclosures are considered one domain, and it is permitted to freely move objects from one to the other provided that the object was in that domain at the onset of the Shabbat.

Another issue involved partitions that were destroyed, causing a change in the definition of the courtyards. Primarily, the issues addressed here pertained to courtyards that were breached and now open into each other, especially if the breach created a situation where one courtyard is completely open to the other. Had these two courtyards, and for all intents and purposes rooftops as well, not been equal in size, and the situation were one of a smaller courtyard opening into a larger courtyard, the independent status of the smaller courtyard would have been negated, creating a complex relationship between the two courtyards. On the basis of this, the relationship of a large courtyard to a smaller neighbor and that of a small courtyard to its larger neighbor were determined.

Another matter that was elucidated with regard to partitions was the relationship between two parallel principles: First, that the determining factor in the *halakhot* of Shabbat is the existence of a partition or lack thereof during Shabbat itself; and second, that once it is permitted to carry in a domain on Shabbat it remains permitted. The halakhic conclusion was that where the matter is not dependent on the presence or absence of partitions, but rather on the residents and the residence, the latter principle prevails and once carrying is permitted it remains permitted. In cases where the matter depends on partitions, the former principle prevails and carrying is permitted only as long as the partitions are intact.

Introduction to **Perek X**

The *halakhot* of *eiruv* comprise merely one halakhic category that falls under the rubric of rabbinic decrees issued to prevent performance of labor prohibited by Torah law and to enhance the character of Shabbat as a day of rest. The final chapter of tractate *Eiruvin* goes beyond the limited realm of the *halakhot* of *eiruv* and addresses additional decrees issued to achieve those objectives. However, it does not address all such decrees, but primarily those that in one sense or another relate to the prohibitions against moving objects on Shabbat.

The key question of concern is: To what degree must moving objects be prohibited within the confines of a single domain or within the confines of those domains established by rabbinic law, in order to prevent one from moving objects in a manner absolutely prohibited by Torah law? With regard to all rabbinic ordinances and decrees, the question arises: To what extent should application of these preventive measures be expanded in order to prevent one from performing a full-fledged prohibited labor on Shabbat? In what cases is it appropriate to enact preventive measures, and in what cases are they superfluous? Or, under what circumstances are the Sages less than insistent that people abide by these measures? As all these prohibitions are rabbinic ordinances and decrees, a fine line distinguishes the permitted from the prohibited. There is no fixed principle applicable in every case, and these decrees are not Torah decrees with regard to which there can be no flexibility. There were areas in which the Sages were concerned, ruled stringently, and issued decrees, and there were other areas where they ruled leniently and did not issue decrees.

In general, the Sages adopted one approach with regard to the Temple precincts and consecrated items, as they were careful to avoid implementation of their decrees in the Temple and with regard to all other sacred matters. This is the rationale for the principle: There are no rabbinic decrees in the Temple, which is in effect almost universally. In any event, here too there is a plethora of issues that arise: In what cases did the Sages completely suspend their decree and in what cases were they lenient in applying certain aspects of the decree while maintaining the fundamental prohibition? Clarification of these matters is the primary focus of this chapter.

מתני׳ הַמּוֹצֵא תְּפִילִּין – מַכְנִיסָן זוּג זוּג. רַבָּן גַּמְלִיאֵל אוֹמֵר: שְׁנַיִם שְׁנַיִם. בַּמֶּה דְּבָרִים אֲמוּרִים – בִּישָׁנוֹת, אֲבָל בַּחֲדָשׁוֹת – פָּטוּר.

MISHNA **One who finds phylacteries**[NH] outside the city on Shabbat, where they are in danger of becoming lost or damaged, **brings them in** to his house **pair** by **pair** by donning them in the manner in which they are typically donned for the mitzva. **Rabban Gamliel says:** He brings them in **two** pairs by **two** pairs. **In what case is this statement** that one is permitted to carry phylacteries inside **said?** It is **with regard to old** phylacteries, which have already been used and are designated for the mitzva. **However, with regard to new** ones, as it is unclear whether they are phylacteries or merely amulets in the form of phylacteries, he is **exempt** from performing the task.

מְצָאָן צְבָתִים אוֹ כְּרִיכוֹת – מַחְשִׁיךְ עֲלֵיהֶן וּמְבִיאָן.

If **one finds** phylacteries **tied in bundles or in wrapped piles,** in which case he is unable to carry them in pairs, **he** sits there and **waits with them until dark,**[N] guarding them until the conclusion of Shabbat, **and** then **brings them in** to his house.

NOTES

One who finds phylacteries – הַמּוֹצֵא תְּפִילִּין: According to most *tanna'im* and *amora'im*, phylacteries are not donned on Shabbat. Nevertheless, since all the Sages agree that one who walks in the public domain donning phylacteries in the appropriate manner is not liable and doing so is prohibited only by rabbinic law, the Sages did not impose their decree in a case where a sacred object might be profaned.

He waits with them until dark – מַחְשִׁיךְ עֲלֵיהֶן: The question arises: Why shouldn't one do the same in the case of new phylacteries? Since he cannot carry them with him, shouldn't he wait until the conclusion of Shabbat when their identity can be determined? *Tosafot* explain that with regard to phylacteries that are certainly sacred, the Sages were stringent and required him to wait. However, they did not require him to do so in a case of uncertainty.

HALAKHA

One who finds phylacteries – הַמּוֹצֵא תְּפִילִּין: If one finds phylacteries on Shabbat that were discarded or left unguarded, he dons them one pair at a time in the typical manner and brings them into the town. If it is dangerous to do so due to a government decree against donning phylacteries, he covers them and only then proceeds on his way (Rambam *Sefer Zemanim*, *Hilkhot Shabbat* 19:23; *Shulḥan Arukh*, *Oraḥ Ḥayyim* 301:42).

וּבַסַּכָּנָה מְכַסָּן וְהוֹלֵךְ לוֹ.

And in a time of **danger,** when it is dangerous to tarry outside town, **he covers** the phylacteries **and proceeds on his** way.

רַבִּי שִׁמְעוֹן אוֹמֵר: נוֹתְנָן לַחֲבֵירוֹ, וַחֲבֵירוֹ לַחֲבֵירוֹ, עַד שֶׁמַּגִּיעַ לֶחָצֵר הַחִיצוֹנָה.

Rabbi Shimon says that there is an alternative method of transferring the phylacteries: **One gives them to another** who is less than four cubits from him, **and the other** passes them **to another, until** the phylacteries **reach the outermost courtyard** of the city. Since carrying less than four cubits in a public domain is not prohibited by Torah law, in this case, the Sages permitted carrying in that manner due to the sanctity of the phylacteries.[H]

וְכֵן בְּנוֹ – נוֹתְנוֹ לַחֲבֵירוֹ, וַחֲבֵירוֹ לַחֲבֵירוֹ, אֲפִילּוּ מֵאָה. רַבִּי יְהוּדָה אוֹמֵר: נוֹתֵן אָדָם חָבִית לַחֲבֵירוֹ, וַחֲבֵירוֹ לַחֲבֵירוֹ אֲפִילּוּ חוּץ לַתְּחוּם. אָמְרוּ לוֹ: לֹא תְּהַלֵּךְ זוֹ יוֹתֵר מֵרַגְלֵי בְעָלֶיהָ.

And similarly, with regard to **one's son** who was born in a field and may not be carried on Shabbat, since that is akin to carrying a burden in the public domain: **One gives him to another, and the other** passes him **to another, even** if it requires **a hundred** people. **Rabbi Yehuda says: A person** may even **give a barrel to another,**[N] **and the other** may pass it **to another,** and in that way **even** take it **beyond the** Shabbat **limit,** provided that no one person carries it more than four cubits. **They said to him: This** barrel may **not go a greater** distance **than the feet of its owner,** i.e., it may not be carried any farther than its owner may walk.[H]

גמ׳ זוּג אֶחָד – אִין, טְפֵי – לָא. לֵימָא תְּנַן סְתָמָא דְּלָא כְּרַבִּי מֵאִיר.

GEMARA We learned in the mishna that a person who finds phylacteries in a field may carry them by pairs, indicating that **one pair, yes,** it may be carried; however, **more** than one pair, **no,** they may not be carried. The Gemara asks: **Let us say** that **we learned the unattributed** mishna **not in accordance with** the opinion of **Rabbi Meir,**[N] despite the principle that an unattributed mishna usually reflects Rabbi Meir's opinion.

דְּאִי כְּרַבִּי מֵאִיר – הָאָמַר: לוֹבֵשׁ כָּל מַה שֶּׁיָּכוֹל לִלְבּוֹשׁ, וְעוֹטֵף כָּל מַה שֶּׁיָּכוֹל לַעֲטוֹף. דִּתְנַן: וּלְשָׁם מוֹצִיא כָּל כְּלֵי תַשְׁמִישׁוֹ, וְלוֹבֵשׁ כָּל מַה שֶּׁיָּכוֹל לִלְבּוֹשׁ, וְעוֹטֵף כָּל מַה שֶּׁיָּכוֹל לַעֲטוֹף!

As, if you say that the mishna is **in accordance with** the opinion of **Rabbi Meir, didn't** Rabbi Meir **say:** In order to rescue items from a fire, one is permitted to remove items from his house by wearing them, and **he dons all** the clothes **that he can wear, and wraps** himself **in all** items in **which he can wrap** himself. **As we learned** in a mishna: **And one removes all the utensils to** the courtyard adjacent to the fire, **and dons all** the garments **that he can wear, and wraps** himself in **all** the items in **which he can wrap** himself in order to rescue his property.

HALAKHA

Carrying phylacteries – טִלְטוּל תְּפִילִּין: If one finds pairs of phylacteries outside the city on Shabbat, and there are too many to bring them in one pair at a time before dark, he must remain with them until the conclusion of Shabbat. If he is concerned about bandits, he may move them less than four cubits at a time. Alternatively, he may pass them to another person, who passes them to another person, and so forth (*Shulḥan Arukh*, *Oraḥ Ḥayyim* 301:42).

Carrying a barrel – טִלְטוּל חָבִית: One may pass a barrel to another person, who passes it to yet another person in the public domain, provided no single person carries it four cubits, and it is passed beyond the Shabbat boundary. This ruling is in accordance with the opinion of Rabbi Yehuda. The Rambam, however, rules in accordance with Rav Ashi's opinion that Rabbi Yehuda stated his opinion only with regard to ownerless objects. Still other authorities prohibit carrying in this manner in accordance with the opinion of the first *tanna*, who prohibits doing so even in the case of phylacteries (Rabbi Zeraḥya HaLevi; *Maggid Mishne*). The Rema is inclined to be lenient, in accordance with the first opinion that the *halakha* accords with the opinion of Rabbi Yehuda (Rambam *Sefer Zemanim*, *Hilkhot Shabbat* 19:23; *Shulḥan Arukh*, *Oraḥ Ḥayyim* 349:3).

NOTES

A person may give a barrel to another – נוֹתֵן אָדָם חָבִית לַחֲבֵירוֹ: Some commentaries explain that the Gemara is referring to the case of a sick, thirsty person situated at a distance, to whom water had to be transported. Indeed, even Rabbi Yehuda permitted doing so only in order to fulfill a mitzva (Rabbeinu Yehonatan).

Let us say we learned…not in accordance with the opinion of Rabbi Meir – לֵימָא...דְּלָא כְּרַבִּי מֵאִיר: See *Tosafot*, who address this issue. The Ritva explains that the Sages who discussed this issue were unfamiliar with the *baraita* that ascribes the opposite viewpoint to Rabbi Meir. It was not unusual for *amora'im* to be unfamiliar with certain *baraitot*.

וְהַהִיא סְתָמָא, מִמַּאי דְּרַבִּי מֵאִיר הִיא, דְּקָתָנֵי עֲלַהּ: לוֹבֵשׁ וּמוֹצִיא, וּפוֹשֵׁט וְלוֹבֵשׁ וּמוֹצִיא וּפוֹשֵׁט, אֲפִילּוּ כׇּל הַיּוֹם כּוּלּוֹ, דִּבְרֵי רַבִּי מֵאִיר.

The Gemara asks: **And from where** do we know that **this unattributed** mishna with regard to Shabbat **is** a reflection of the opinion of **Rabbi Meir? As it teaches with regard to** that mishna: If there are many garments there, one **dons** a garment, and **takes** it **out** to a safe place, **and removes** it there, **and returns** to the fire, **and dons** another garment, **and takes** it **out and removes** it. **And** he may do so **even all day long;** this is **the statement of Rabbi Meir.** Apparently, according to Rabbi Meir, one may don only one garment at a time.

אָמַר רָבָא: אֲפִילּוּ תֵּימָא רַבִּי מֵאִיר. הָתָם – דֶּרֶךְ מַלְבּוּשׁוֹ – כַּחוֹל שַׁוְיֵהּ רַבָּנַן, וְהָכָא דֶּרֶךְ מַלְבּוּשׁוֹ – כַּחוֹל שָׁוְיָהּ רַבָּנַן.

In answer to the question, **Rava said: Even if you say** that the mishna is in accordance with the opinion of **Rabbi Meir,** there is a distinction between the cases. **There,** if he dons the clothes in **the manner that he** typically **wears them, the Sages rendered** the legal status of wearing garments on Shabbat **like** the status of wearing garments during the **week** and permitted him to remove clothes from his house by wearing them in that manner. **And here,** too, if he dons phylacteries in **the manner that he** typically **dons them, the Sages rendered** the legal status of donning phylacteries on Shabbat **like** the status of donning phylacteries during the **week.**

הָתָם דִּבְחוֹל כַּמָּה דְּבָעֵי לָבֵישׁ – לְעִנְיַן הַצָּלָה נַמִּי שָׁרוּ לֵיהּ רַבָּנַן. הָכָא דִּבְחוֹל נַמִּי, זוּג אֶחָד – אִין, טְפֵי – לָא, לְעִנְיַן הַצָּלָה נַמִּי: זוּג אֶחָד – אִין, טְפֵי לָא.

Consequently, **there, where during the week he** may **wear as many** clothes **as he wishes, with regard to rescue** from a fire **the Sages likewise permitted him** to wear as many clothes as he wishes. However, **here,** in the case of phylacteries, **even during the week,** donning **one pair, yes,** one may do so, but donning **more** than one pair, **no,** he may not do so. Therefore, **with regard to rescue as well,** the Sages said: Donning **one pair, yes,** one may do so; however, donning **more** than one pair, **no,** he may not.

"רַבָּן גַּמְלִיאֵל אוֹמֵר שְׁנַיִם שְׁנַיִם". מַאי קָסָבַר? אִי קָסָבַר שַׁבָּת זְמַן תְּפִילִּין הוּא – זוּג אֶחָד – אִין, טְפֵי – לָא.

We learned in the mishna that **Rabban Gamliel says:** He brings the phylacteries in **two** pairs **by two** pairs. The Gemara asks: **What does he hold?** What is the rationale for this *halakha*? **If he holds** that **Shabbat is a time for phylacteries,** and one is permitted or even obligated to don phylacteries on Shabbat, then the ruling should be: Donning **one pair, yes,** this is permitted; donning **more, no,** it is prohibited. It should be prohibited to wear more than one pair as there is room to don only one set of phylacteries on one's head.

וְאִי קָסָבַר שַׁבָּת לָאו זְמַן תְּפִילִּין הוּא, וּמִשּׁוּם הַצָּלָה דֶּרֶךְ מַלְבּוּשׁ שָׁרוּ לֵיהּ רַבָּנַן – אֲפִילּוּ טְפֵי נַמִּי!

And if he holds that **Shabbat is not a time for phylacteries, and** it was only **due to** the fact that **rescue** was permitted only in the **manner** that one typically wears **clothing** that **the Sages permitted him** to don phylacteries, he should **likewise** be permitted to don **even more** than two pairs. He should be permitted to don as many pairs of phylacteries as possible, not only two.

לְעוֹלָם קָסָבַר: שַׁבָּת לָאו זְמַן תְּפִילִּין הוּא, וְכִי שָׁרוּ רַבָּנַן לְעִנְיַן הַצָּלָה – דֶּרֶךְ מַלְבּוּשׁ בִּמְקוֹם תְּפִילִּין.

The Gemara answers: **Actually, he holds** that **Shabbat is not a time for phylacteries, and when the Sages permitted** one to don phylacteries **for the purpose of rescue,** it was only by donning them in the **manner** that one typically wears **clothing,** i.e., in the appropriate **place** for **phylacteries.** He may not don them anywhere else on his body, as in that case he is considered to be carrying, not wearing them.

אִי הָכִי, זוּג אֶחָד נַמִּי – אִין, טְפֵי – לָא! אָמַר רַב שְׁמוּאֵל בַּר רַב יִצְחָק: מָקוֹם יֵשׁ בָּרֹאשׁ לְהַנִּיחַ בּוֹ שְׁתֵּי תְפִילִּין.

The Gemara raises a difficulty: **If so,** then **one pair, yes,** it should be permitted, but **more, no,** it should not be permitted, as the second pair is necessarily positioned out of place. **Rav Shmuel bar Rav Yitzḥak said: There is room on** one's **head**[N] **to place two phylacteries.** One can place two phylacteries on his head and don them both in the proper manner.

הָנִיחָא דְּרֹאשׁ, דְּיַד מַאי אִיכָּא לְמֵימַר?

The Gemara asks: **It works out well** with regard to donning two phylacteries **of the head,** as there is room; however, with regard to the phylacteries **of the arm, what is there to say?** How can one wear two phylacteries on his arm simultaneously?

כִּדְרַב הוּנָא; דְּאָמַר רַב הוּנָא: פְּעָמִים שֶׁאָדָם בָּא מִן הַשָּׂדֶה וַחֲבִילָתוֹ עַל רֹאשׁוֹ, וּמְסַלְּקָן מֵרֹאשׁוֹ וְקוֹשְׁרָן בִּזְרוֹעוֹ.

The Gemara answers that even when one dons two phylacteries on his arm, he is regarded as donning them in the typical manner, **in accordance with** the opinion of **Rav Huna. As Rav Huna said: Sometimes a person comes from the field with his bundle on his head,** and in order not to crush the phylacteries, he **removes them from his head and binds them on his arm.** This indicates that there is room for additional phylacteries on his arm.

NOTES

There is room on one's head – מָקוֹם יֵשׁ בָּרֹאשׁ: It is evident from this discussion that phylacteries must be a certain size. Otherwise, the concept of sufficient room for phylacteries is moot. There is a dispute as to whether the size mentioned in *Tosafot* represents the average or the minimum size. For many generations, Jews who were scrupulous in the fulfillment of mitzvot adopted the custom to don two pairs of phylacteries due to uncertainty; one set was configured in accordance with Rashi's opinion and the other was in accordance with Rabbeinu Tam. Many Sephardic and other Jews adopted the custom of placing these two pairs of phylacteries on the head at the same time, relying on this passage in the Gemara.

אֵימַר דְּאָמַר רַב הוּנָא שֶׁלֹּא יִנְהַג בָּהֶן דֶּרֶךְ בִּזָּיוֹן, רָאוּי מִי אָמַר?

The Gemara rejects this: **Say that Rav Huna said** that one may remove the phylacteries from his head and tie them on his arm **so that he will not** come to **treat** them **in a degrading manner** by placing a bundle on top of them. However, **did he say** that the spot on his arm is **fit** for two phylacteries? Can proof be cited from here that one may don additional phylacteries on his arm *ab initio*?

אֶלָּא כִּדְאָמַר רַב שְׁמוּאֵל בַּר רַב יִצְחָק: מָקוֹם יֵשׁ בָּרֹאשׁ שֶׁרָאוּי לְהַנִּיחַ בּוֹ שְׁתֵּי תְפִילִּין. הָכָא נַמִי: מָקוֹם יֵשׁ בַּיָּד שֶׁרָאוּי לְהַנִּיחַ בּוֹ שְׁתֵּי תְפִילִּין.

Rather, it is **in accordance with** that which **Rav Shmuel bar Rav Yitzḥak said: There is room on** one's **head to place two phylacteries. Here, too, there is room on the arm to place two phylacteries.**

תָּנָא דְּבֵי מְנַשֶּׁה: "עַל יָדֶךָ" – זוֹ קִיבּוֹרֶת, "בֵּין עֵינֶיךָ" – זוֹ קָדְקֹד. הֵיכָא? אָמְרִי דְּבֵי רַבִּי יַנַּאי: מָקוֹם שֶׁמּוֹחוֹ שֶׁל תִּינוֹק רוֹפֵס.

The Gemara comments: **The school of Menashe taught** the following. The verse states: "And you shall bind them for a sign on your arm, and they shall be as frontlets between your eyes" (Deuteronomy 6:8). **"On your arm," this is the biceps** muscle of the arm;[H] **"between your eyes," this is the crown** of the head. The Gemara asks: **Where** exactly on the crown of the head? **The school of Rabbi Yannai say:** Phylacteries are placed on **the spot where a baby's head is soft** after birth.[H]

לֵימָא בִּדְרַב שְׁמוּאֵל בַּר רַב יִצְחָק קָמִיפַּלְגִי; דְּתַנָּא קַמָּא לֵית לֵיהּ דְּרַב שְׁמוּאֵל בַּר רַב יִצְחָק, וְרַבָּן גַּמְלִיאֵל אִית לֵיהּ דְּרַב שְׁמוּאֵל בַּר רַב יִצְחָק!

The Gemara asks: **Let us say that** the *tanna'im* of the mishna **disagree about** the principle of **Rav Shmuel bar Rav Yitzḥak,** such **that the first *tanna* is not** of the opinion that the ruling is in accordance with the opinion of **Rav Shmuel bar Rav Yitzḥak** that there is room on one's head for two phylacteries, **while Rabban Gamliel is of** the opinion that the ruling is in accordance with the opinion of **Rav Shmuel bar Rav Yitzḥak,** and therefore one is permitted to bring in two pairs of phylacteries at a time.

לָא, דְּכוּלֵּי עָלְמָא אִית לְהוּ דְּרַב שְׁמוּאֵל בַּר רַב יִצְחָק. וְהָכָא בְּ"שַׁבָּת זְמַן תְּפִילִּין" קָמִיפַּלְגִי. דְּתַנָּא קַמָּא סָבַר: שַׁבָּת זְמַן תְּפִילִּין הוּא,

The Gemara rejects this: **No, everyone is** of the opinion of **Rav Shmuel bar Rav Yitzḥak, and here they disagree with regard to** whether or not **Shabbat is a time for phylacteries.**[N] **The first *tanna* holds** that **Shabbat is a time for phylacteries.** Although one may don one pair of phylacteries, he may not add to the mitzva by donning an extra pair. If he does so, it is tantamount to carrying a prohibited burden.

וְרַבָּן גַּמְלִיאֵל סָבַר: שַׁבָּת לָאו זְמַן תְּפִילִּין הוּא.

And Rabban Gamliel holds that **Shabbat is not a time for phylacteries.** Consequently, one may don more than one pair, as the day itself is not at all suitable for donning phylacteries. When he dons the second pair, he is not adding to the mitzva. With regard to rescuing them, the phylacteries have the legal status of an ornament that he is permitted to don, provided that he dons no more than two pairs.

וְאִיבָּעֵית אֵימָא: דְּכוּלֵּי עָלְמָא – שַׁבָּת זְמַן תְּפִילִּין הוּא. וְהָכָא בְּ"מִצְוֹת צְרִיכוֹת כַּוָּונָה" קָמִיפַּלְגִי. תַּנָּא קַמָּא סָבַר: לָצֵאת בָּעֵי כַּוָּונָה,

And if you wish, say instead that the dispute should be understood as follows. **Everyone agrees that Shabbat is a time for phylacteries, and here they disagree with regard to** whether or not fulfillment of **mitzvot requires intent. The first *tanna* holds: To fulfill** a mitzva one **needs intent.**[N] Therefore, if one dons phylacteries without intent to fulfill the mitzva, no mitzva is performed, and he is merely carrying a burden. However, if he has intent to fulfill the mitzva, he may don no more than one pair. If he does so, he violates the prohibition against adding to mitzvot.

וְרַבָּן גַּמְלִיאֵל סָבַר: לָא בָּעֵי כַּוָּונָה.

And Rabban Gamliel holds: In order to fulfill a mitzva, **one does not need intent.** Therefore, if one dons two pairs of phylacteries he fulfills his obligation with one of them, but does not violate the prohibition against adding to mitzvot with the other. In order to do so, he would require specific intent to fulfill a second mitzva with the additional pair.

HALAKHA

The place of the phylacteries of the arm – מְקוֹם תְּפִילִּין שֶׁל יָד: The phylacteries of the arm is placed on the lower slope of the biceps, the muscle between the elbow and the armpit. While the entire biceps is suitable for phylacteries, the custom is to place it closer to the elbow, rather than the armpit, so that it is opposite the heart (Rambam *Sefer Ahava, Hilkhot Tefillin UMezuza VeSefer Torah* 4:2; *Shulḥan Arukh HaRav*; *Shulḥan Arukh, Oraḥ Ḥayyim* 27:1).

The place of the phylacteries of the head – מְקוֹם תְּפִילִּין שֶׁל רֹאשׁ: The phylacteries of the head are placed on the crown of the head between the eyes, anywhere from the beginning of the hairline back to the place where an infant's head is soft. This area is large enough to hold two sets of phylacteries (Rambam *Sefer Ahava, Hilkhot Tefillin UMezuza VeSefer Torah* 4:1; *Shulḥan Arukh, Oraḥ Ḥayyim* 27:9).

NOTES

Shabbat is a time for phylacteries – שַׁבָּת זְמַן תְּפִילִּין: In the Jerusalem Talmud it is stated that it was clear to Rabban Gamliel that Shabbat is not a time for phylacteries, which is why he permitted donning two pairs, whereas the first *tanna* maintains that the matter remains undetermined. Therefore, he was reluctant to permit bringing in more than one pair at a time.

To fulfill a mitzva one needs intent – לָצֵאת בָּעֵי כַּוָּונָה: The correct version of the Gemara according to most commentaries (Rashi, Rabbeinu Ḥananel, *Me'iri*, Ritva, and others) is the opposite of the version that appears here. The first *tanna* maintains that intent is not required in order to fulfill a mitzva. Therefore, one may not don two pairs of phylacteries, because he will perforce fulfill the obligation and violate the prohibition against adding to mitzvot. On the other hand, Rabban Gamliel maintains that intent is required to fulfill a mitzva, and therefore one may don an additional pair.

NOTES

One who sleeps in a *sukka* on the Eighth Day of Assembly – הַיָּשֵׁן בִּשְׁמִינִי בַּסּוּכָּה: Why doesn't the *tanna* state that one who eats in a *sukka* on the Eighth Day of Assembly receives lashes as well? One answer is that since a person recites the blessing: To dwell in the *sukka*, before eating throughout the festival of *Sukkot*, the fact that he does not do so on the Eighth Day of Assembly indicates his lack of intention to perform a full mitzva. However, as no blessing is recited when sleeping in the *sukka*, his intention is not evident when he sleeps there (*Shem MiShimon*). The nature of the lashes mentioned in this context is a matter of dispute. Some authorities maintain that these lashes are imposed by the Torah for the violation of the prohibition against adding to mitzvot, while other authorities claim that they are by rabbinic law due to the transgression of a rabbinic enactment (see Rambam and the commentaries on his work).

וְאִיבָּעֵית אֵימָא: דְּכוּלֵּי עָלְמָא לָצֵאת לָא בָּעֵי כַּוָּונָה. וְהָכָא, לַעֲבוֹר מִשּׁוּם ״בַּל תּוֹסִיף״ קָמִיפַּלְגִי. דְּתַנָּא קַמָּא סָבַר: לַעֲבוֹר מִשּׁוּם ״בַּל תּוֹסִיף״ – לָא בָּעֵי כַּוָּונָה, וְרַבָּן גַּמְלִיאֵל סָבַר: לַעֲבוֹר מִשּׁוּם ״בַּל תּוֹסִיף״ – בָּעֵי כַּוָּונָה.

And if you wish, say instead that **everyone agrees** that **to fulfill** a mitzva **one does not need intent, and here they disagree with regard to** the condition needed **to violate** the prohibition: **Do not add** to mitzvot of the Torah. **As the first *tanna* holds** that **one does not need intent to violate** the prohibition: **Do not add** to mitzvot. One who dons another pair of phylacteries transgresses the prohibition against adding to mitzvot even if he does not don them with the intention of fulfilling the mitzva. **And Rabban Gamliel holds** that in order **to violate** the prohibition: **Do not add** to mitzvot, **one needs intent** to perform a mitzva. Since in this case one's intention is merely to move the phylacteries to a safer place, he may don a second pair.

וְאִיבָּעֵית אֵימָא: אִי דִּסְבִירָא לַן דְּשַׁבָּת זְמַן תְּפִילִּין – דְּכוּלֵּי עָלְמָא לָא לַעֲבוֹר בָּעֵי כַּוָּונָה, וְלָא לָצֵאת בָּעֵי כַּוָּונָה.

And if you wish, say instead that the dispute may be explained as follows. **If we were to maintain** that **Shabbat is** a fit **time for** donning **phylacteries, everyone** would **agree** that **one does not need intent to violate** the prohibition against adding to mitzvot, **nor does one need intent to fulfill** a mitzva. In this case, one's intention has no bearing on his action.

וְהָכָא בְּ״לַעֲבוֹר שֶׁלֹּא בִּזְמַנּוֹ״ קָמִיפַּלְגִי. תַּנָּא קַמָּא סָבַר: לָא בָּעֵי כַּוָּונָה, וְרַבָּן גַּמְלִיאֵל סָבַר: ״לַעֲבוֹר שֶׁלֹּא בִּזְמַנּוֹ״ בָּעֵי כַּוָּונָה.

However, here, they disagree with regard to the condition for **violating** the prohibition against adding to a mitzva **not in its** proper **time,** i.e., when a mitzva is performed not at its prescribed time. **The first *tanna* holds** that if the act of a mitzva is performed not in its proper time, **one does not need intent;** that is, even if one does not intend to perform the mitzva he nonetheless violates the prohibition against adding to mitzvot by his action alone. Consequently, in this case, a person may not don more than one pair of phylacteries. **And Rabban Gamliel holds that to violate** the prohibition against adding to a mitzva **not in its** proper **time, one needs intent** to fulfill the mitzva. Without such intent one does not violate the prohibition, and therefore in this case he may don a second pair of phylacteries.

אִי הָכִי, לְרַבִּי מֵאִיר זוּג אֶחָד נָמֵי לָא.

With regard to this last explanation the Gemara asks: **If so, according to** the opinion of **Rabbi Meir** one should **not even** don **one pair** of phylacteries. According to Rabbi Meir's opinion, one who does so violates the prohibition against adding to mitzvot merely by donning one pair, since he is fulfilling the mitzva of phylacteries at a time when he is not commanded to do so.

וְעוֹד: הַיָּשֵׁן בִּשְׁמִינִי בַּסּוּכָּה יִלְקֶה. אֶלָּא מְחַוַּורְתָּא כִּדְשַׁנֵּינַן מֵעִיקָּרָא.

And furthermore, according to this opinion, **one who sleeps in a *sukka* on the Eighth Day** of Assembly[N] **should be flogged** for violating the prohibition against adding to mitzvot, as he adds to the mitzva of: "You shall dwell in booths for seven days" (Leviticus 23:42). Yet the Sages instituted that outside of Eretz Yisrael, Jews must observe *Sukkot* for eight days, even though one who sleeps in a *sukka* on the eighth night outside of Eretz Yisrael transgresses a Torah law. **Rather, it is clear as we originally answered,** i.e., you must accept one of the other explanations.

וּמַאן שָׁמְעַתְּ לֵיהּ שַׁבָּת זְמַן תְּפִילִּין – רַבִּי עֲקִיבָא. דְּתַנְיָא: ״וְשָׁמַרְתָּ אֶת הַחֻקָּה הַזֹּאת לְמוֹעֲדָהּ מִיָּמִים יָמִימָה״ – יָמִים וְלֹא לֵילוֹת. ״מִיָּמִים״ – וְלֹא כׇּל יָמִים, פְּרָט לְשַׁבָּתוֹת וְיָמִים טוֹבִים, דִּבְרֵי רַבִּי יוֹסֵי הַגְּלִילִי.

Since the topic of phylacteries was discussed, the Gemara continues to explore this issue. **Whom did you hear** who said that **Shabbat is** a fit **time for** donning **phylacteries?** It is **Rabbi Akiva, as it was taught** in a *baraita* with regard to the end of the section in the Torah beginning with: "Sanctify all firstborns to me" (Exodus 13:2), which deals with the mitzvot of the Paschal lamb and phylacteries: **"And you shall observe this ordinance in its season from year [*miyamim*] to year"** (Exodus 13:10), which indicates that these mitzvot apply during the **days [*yamim*] and not** during the **nights.** Furthermore, the letter *mem* in **"from year" [*miyamim*]** teaches: **But not** on **all days;** this **excludes Shabbat and Festivals,** on which phylacteries are not worn. This is **the statement of Rabbi Yosei HaGelili.**

רַבִּי עֲקִיבָא אוֹמֵר: לֹא נֶאֱמַר חוּקָּה זוֹ אֶלָּא לְעִנְיַן פֶּסַח בִּלְבַד.

Rabbi Akiva says: This ordinance is stated only with regard to the Paschal lamb, and it does not refer to phylacteries at all. According to Rabbi Akiva, there is no reason to refrain from donning phylacteries on Shabbat and Festivals.

וְאֶלָּא הָא דִּתְנַן: הַפֶּסַח וְהַמִּילָה מִצְוֹת עֲשֵׂה, לֵימָא דְּלָא כְּרַבִּי עֲקִיבָא; דְּאִי רַבִּי עֲקִיבָא – כֵּיוָן דְּמוֹקֵי לָהּ בַּפֶּסַח, לָאו נַמִי אִיכָּא, כִּדְרַבִּי אָבִין אָמַר רַבִּי אֶילְעַאי; דְּאָמַר רַבִּי אָבִין, אָמַר רַבִּי אֶילְעַאי: כָּל מָקוֹם שֶׁנֶּאֱמַר ״הִשָּׁמֶר״ ״פֶּן״ וְ״אַל״ אֵינוֹ אֶלָּא בְּלֹא תַעֲשֶׂה.

The Gemara asks: **But** with regard to **that** which **we learned** in a mishna that **the Paschal lamb**[H] **and circumcision**[H] **are positive mitzvot, let us say that** this statement is **not in accordance with** the opinion of **Rabbi Akiva.** The reason for this claim is **that if** you say this teaching is in accordance with the opinion of **Rabbi Akiva, since he establishes** this verse as referring **to the Paschal** lamb, this would mean that in failure to bring this offering there **is also** the violation of **a negative** mitzva, **in accordance with** the principle **that Rabbi Avin** said that **Rabbi Elai said. As Rabbi Avin said** that **Rabbi Elai said: Any place** where **it is stated: Observe, lest, or do not,**[N] this means **nothing other than a negative** mitzva, as these are negative terms. Consequently, the verse "You shall observe this ordinance," which refers to the Paschal lamb, constitutes a negative mitzva.

אֲפִילּוּ תֵּימָא רַבִּי עֲקִיבָא: ״הִשָּׁמֶר״ דְּלָאו – לָאו, ״הִשָּׁמֵר״ דַּעֲשֵׂה – עֲשֵׂה.

The Gemara rejects this: **Even if you say** that **Rabbi Akiva** holds that no negative mitzva applies to the Paschal lamb, it is not difficult, as an additional principle must be taken into account. Although it is true that the term **observe with regard to a negative** mitzva indicates the presence of another **negative** mitzva; that same term **observe** with regard to **a positive** mitzva has the force of **a positive** mitzva, as the Torah is warning adherents to take special care in the observance of a mitzva. The word observe in connection with the Paschal lamb is an example of this type of positive mitzva.

וְסָבַר רַבִּי עֲקִיבָא שַׁבָּת זְמַן תְּפִילִּין הוּא? וְהָתַנְיָא, רַבִּי עֲקִיבָא אוֹמֵר: יָכוֹל יַנִּיחַ אָדָם תְּפִילִּין בְּשַׁבָּתוֹת וְיָמִים טוֹבִים – תַּלְמוּד לוֹמַר: ״וְהָיָה לְךָ לְאוֹת עַל יָדְךָ״ – מִי שֶׁצְּרִיכִין אוֹת, יָצְאוּ אֵלּוּ שֶׁהֵן גּוּפָן אוֹת.

The Gemara returns to the issue at hand: **And** does **Rabbi Akiva** really **hold that Shabbat is a time for** donning **phylacteries? Wasn't it taught** in a *baraita* that **Rabbi Akiva says:** I **might** have thought that **a person should don phylacteries on *Shabbatot* and Festivals.**[H] Therefore, **the verse states: "And it shall be for a sign for you on your arm,** and for a remembrance between your eyes, so that God's law shall be in your mouth; for with a strong arm God brought you out of Egypt" (Exodus 13:9). The obligation to don phylacteries applies when Jews **require a sign** to assert their Judaism and their status as the Chosen People, i.e., during the week, **excluding** Shabbat and Festivals, **as they are themselves signs**[N] of Israel's status as the Chosen People and a remembrance of the exodus from Egypt. Consequently, no further sign is required on these days. This teaching proves that Rabbi Akiva maintains that Shabbat is not a fit time for donning phylacteries.

אֶלָּא, הַאי תַּנָּא הוּא: דְּתַנְיָא, הַנֵּיעוֹר בַּלַּיְלָה, רָצָה – חוֹלֵץ, רָצָה – מַנִּיחַ, דִּבְרֵי רַבִּי נָתָן. יוֹנָתָן הַקִּיטוֹנִי אוֹמֵר: אֵין מַנִּיחִין תְּפִילִּין בַּלַּיְלָה. מִדְּלַיְלָה לְתַנָּא קַמָּא זְמַן תְּפִילִּין – שַׁבָּת נַמִי זְמַן תְּפִילִּין.

Rather, it is this *tanna*, Rabbi Natan, who maintains that Shabbat is not a fit time for donning phylacteries, **as it was taught** in a *baraita*: With regard to **one who is awake at night, if he wishes he** may **remove** his phylacteries, and **if he wishes he** may continue to **don** them, and he need not worry about violating the prohibition against adding to mitzvot. This is **the statement of Rabbi Natan. Yonatan HaKitoni**[L] **says:** One **may not don phylacteries at night. From** the fact **that according to the first *tanna*,** Rabbi Natan, **night is** a fit **time for phylacteries,** it may be inferred that **Shabbat, too, is a time for** donning **phylacteries,** as Rabbi Natan evidently does not accept Rabbi Yosei HaGelili's limitation based on the phrase: From year to year.

דִּילְמָא סְבִירָא לֵיהּ: לַיְלָה זְמַן תְּפִילִּין הוּא, שַׁבָּת – לָאו זְמַן תְּפִילִּין הוּא. דְּהָא שָׁמְעִינַן לֵיהּ לְרַבִּי עֲקִיבָא, דַּאֲמַר: לַיְלָה זְמַן תְּפִילִּין הוּא, שַׁבָּת לָאו זְמַן תְּפִילִּין הוּא.

The Gemara rejects this contention: This is not a conclusive proof, as **perhaps he holds** that although **night is** a fit **time for phylacteries, Shabbat is not** a fit **time for phylacteries. As we** have **heard that Rabbi Akiva said** that **night is a time for phylacteries,**[H] because he does not accept the limitation of "from days to days," and yet he maintains that **Shabbat is not a time for phylacteries,** as no sign is required on Shabbat. It is therefore possible that Rabbi Natan holds the same opinion.

HALAKHA

The Paschal lamb as a positive mitzva – פֶּסַח מִצְוַת עֲשֵׂה: The sacrifice of the Paschal lamb is a positive mitzva and one who intentionally neglects this obligation is liable to receive *karet*. However, if one unwittingly fails to fulfill this mitzva, he does not bring a sin-offering, as he has not violated a prohibition (Rambam *Sefer Korbanot, Hilkhot Korban Pesaḥ* 1:1–2).

Circumcision as a positive mitzva – מִילָה מִצְוַת עֲשֵׂה: Circumcision is a positive mitzva, and one who intentionally refrains from circumcising himself is liable to receive *karet*. However, one does not bring a sin-offering for unwitting failure to fulfill this mitzva as he did not violate a prohibition (Rambam *Sefer Ahava, Hilkhot Tefillin UMezuza VeSefer Torah* 4:1; *Shulḥan Arukh, Yoreh De'a* 260:1).

Phylacteries on *Shabbatot* and Festivals – תְּפִילִּין בְּשַׁבָּתוֹת וְיָמִים טוֹבִים: Not only is there no obligation to don phylacteries on Shabbat and Festivals, it is prohibited to do so, as this is a sign of disrespect of the sacred day. The early commentaries dispute whether one dons phylacteries on the intermediate days of a Festival. Some commentaries argue that the prohibition of donning phylacteries on Shabbat and Festivals is a function of the prohibition against performing work, while other authorities connect this issue to the sanctity of the day. Since the kabbalistic tradition is not to don phylacteries on the intermediate days of a Festival, all Sephardic and Hassidic communities follow suit. This is also the prevailing custom in Eretz Yisrael (*Shulḥan Arukh, Oraḥ Ḥayyim* 31:1–2).

Phylacteries at night – תְּפִילִּין בַּלַּיְלָה: One does not don phylacteries at night, as he might fall asleep while donning them and treat them disrespectfully. This prohibition is only by rabbinic law, as the *halakha* is in accordance with Rabbi Akiva, who maintains that night is a fit time for phylacteries. The Rambam holds that the prohibition against donning phylacteries at night is by Torah law, as indicated by the discussion here. Nevertheless, all authorities agree that if one donned phylacteries during the day, he need not remove them after nightfall; however, a public ruling is not issued to that effect (*Shulḥan Arukh, Oraḥ Ḥayyim* 30:2).

LANGUAGE

Yonatan HaKitoni – יוֹנָתָן הַקִּיטוֹנִי: According to this reading of the name, this individual was probably given his name due to his profession as a maker of beds or some other item related to the bedroom [*kiton*]. According to an alternative reading, *HaKatroni*, the name refers to the town of Katron in the territory of Zebulun.

NOTES

Observe, lest, or do not – ״הִשָּׁמֶר״ ״פֶּן״ וְ״אַל״: The biblical word *lo*, you shall not, clearly indicates a prohibition. The Sages added that the word *al*, do not, also refers to a negative commandment. *Tosafot* explain that there is a dispute among the Sages with regard to the word *hishamer*, observe, in all of its forms. Some authorities maintain that the term observe always means that one should refrain from a particular action. According to this opinion, all forms of observance connote that whoever does not perform a particular mitzva has violated a prohibition. The discussion in the Gemara reveals that some Sages distinguish between the term observe in the context of a positive mitzva and its association with a prohibition.

As they are themselves signs – שֶׁהֵן גּוּפָן אוֹת: There are different opinions with regard to the nature of Shabbat and Festivals as signs. Some commentaries maintain that the mitzva to sanctify these days serves as a sign of Israel's uniqueness. Others teach that the main feature of their nature as signs is the avoidance of labor on these days. Yet other commentaries explain that the signs are the special mitzvot of these days, e.g., the *sukka* on *Sukkot* and the prohibition against eating leaven on Passover.

HALAKHA

Women and phylacteries – נָשִׁים וּתְפִילִּין: A woman is not permitted to don phylacteries even if she wishes to be stringent upon herself. One reason is that women are not careful regarding the purity of their bodies (*Magen Avraham*). This ruling is based on the statement in the Jerusalem Talmud and the *Pesikta* that the Sages objected to the conduct of Michal, daughter of Saul (*Shulḥan Arukh, Oraḥ Ḥayyim* 38:3, and in the comment of the Rema).

אֶלָּא הַאי תַּנָּא הוּא, דְּתַנְיָא: מִיכַל בַּת כּוּשִׁי הָיְתָה מַנַּחַת תְּפִילִּין וְלֹא מִיחוּ בָּהּ חֲכָמִים. וְאִשְׁתּוֹ שֶׁל יוֹנָה הָיְתָה עוֹלָה לָרֶגֶל וְלֹא מִיחוּ בָּהּ חֲכָמִים. מִדְּלָא מִיחוּ בָּהּ חֲכָמִים – אַלְמָא קָסָבְרִי מִצְוַת עֲשֵׂה שֶׁלֹּא הַזְּמַן גְּרָמָא הִיא.

Rather, we must say that **it is this *tanna*** who maintains that Shabbat is a time for phylacteries, **as it was taught** in a *baraita*: **Michal, daughter of Kushi,**[N] King Saul, **would don phylacteries, and the Sages did not protest against her** behavior, as she was permitted to do so.[H] **And** similarly, **Jonah's wife**[N] **would undertake the Festival pilgrimage and the Sages did not protest against her** practice. **From the fact that the Sages did not protest against** Michal's donning phylacteries, **it is apparent that these** Sages **hold** that phylacteries **is a positive mitzva not bound by time,**[N] i.e., it is a mitzva whose performance is mandated at all times, including nights and Shabbat. There is an accepted principle that women are obligated in all positive mitzvot not bound by time.

וְדִילְמָא סָבַר לַהּ

The Gemara rejects this contention: **But perhaps** that *tanna* **holds**

NOTES

Michal, daughter of Kushi – מִיכַל בַּת כּוּשִׁי: Parallel sources read: Michal, daughter of Saul. Kushi is another name for Saul, based on the Gemara's interpretation of the verse: "Concerning Kush a Benjamite" (Psalms 7:1). The incident discussed here is not mentioned in the Bible; rather, it is a rabbinic tradition.

Michal and Jonah's wife – מִיכַל וְאֵשֶׁת יוֹנָה: In the Jerusalem Talmud and the *Pesikta* it is related that Jonah's wife was sent home, and that the Sages did object to the actions of Michal, daughter of Saul. Some commentaries explain that Jonah's wife was sent home because the kings of Israel established guards to prevent people from undertaking the pilgrimage to Jerusalem because it was in Judea. Since Jonah was from Gat HaḤefer in the north, the Sages ruled that Jonah's wife was not required to endanger herself for something from which she was exempt (Rabbi Zvi Hirsch Chajes).

A positive mitzva not bound by time – מִצְוַת עֲשֵׂה שֶׁלֹּא הַזְּמַן גְּרָמָא: The commentaries point out that if donning phylacteries is not a time-bound mitzva, women should be obligated to don them just as men are. However, even according to the opinion that donning phylacteries is not a time-bound mitzva, the Sages decreed that women should not observe it, due to the concern that they will be unable to take proper care of the phylacteries or maintain their sanctity. The Sages have the power to abrogate the practice of mitzvot by instructing individuals to refrain from performing them (Ritva).

Perek **X**
Daf **96** Amud **b**

NOTES

It is optional for women to place their hands – נָשִׁים סוֹמְכוֹת רְשׁוּת: This statement can be understood in several ways. The commentaries and authorities debate whether women transgress the prohibition against adding to the mitzvot by observing a mitzva that they are not obligated to perform, or whether there is no prohibition whatsoever in those cases. If the woman's intent is not to fulfill the mitzva but simply to perform it, there are no grounds for concern (Ritva). However, in this context, the discussion concerns mitzvot that the Sages permitted women to perform even when there is a certain measure of prohibition involved. For example, it could be argued in the case of placing one's hands on a sacrifice that it should be prohibited for women to do so, as they would be guilty of misusing the sacrifice. Consequently, the issue is similar to that of women donning phylacteries on Shabbat (see *Tosafot*, *Ḥullin* 85a).

Fulfillment of mitzvot in which women are not obligated – קִיּוּם מִצְוֹת שֶׁבָּהֶן נָשִׁים פְּטוּרוֹת: It could be argued that since women may don phylacteries on weekdays if they choose, they may don them on Shabbat as well, as in rescuing phylacteries the Sages permitted wearing on Shabbat anything that one wears on a weekday (Ritva).

כְּרַבִּי יוֹסֵי, דְּאָמַר: נָשִׁים סוֹמְכוֹת רְשׁוּת.

in accordance with the opinion of **Rabbi Yosei, who said:** It is **optional** for **women** to **place** their hands[N] on the head of a sacrificial animal before it is slaughtered. Although only men have this obligation, women may perform that rite if they wish. Similarly, women may perform other mitzvot that they have no obligation to fulfill.[N]

דְּאִי לָא תֵּימָא הָכִי – אִשְׁתּוֹ שֶׁל יוֹנָה הָיְתָה עוֹלָה לָרֶגֶל וְלֹא מִיחוּ בָּהּ. מִי אִיכָּא לְמַאן דְּאָמַר רֶגֶל לָאו מִצְוַת עֲשֵׂה שֶׁהַזְּמַן גְּרָמָא הוּא? אֶלָּא: קָסָבַר רְשׁוּת, הָכָא נַמִי: רְשׁוּת.

As, if you do not say so, that this *tanna* holds in accordance with the opinion of Rabbi Yosei, the *baraita* states that **Jonah's wife would ascend** to Jerusalem for **the Festival pilgrimage and** the Sages **did not reprimand her. Is there anyone who says** that the mitzva of **Festival** pilgrimage **is not a time-bound positive mitzva** and that women are obligated to fulfill it? **Rather, he holds** that she did not embark on the pilgrimage as an obligation, but that it was **optional; here, too,** with regard to phylacteries, it is **optional.** Consequently, no proof can be cited from this *baraita* as to whether or not Shabbat is a fit time for phylacteries.

אֶלָּא הַאי תַּנָּא הִיא, דְּתַנְיָא: הַמּוֹצֵא תְּפִילִּין – מַכְנִיסָן זוּג זוּג, אֶחָד הָאִישׁ וְאֶחָד הָאִשָּׁה, אֶחָד חֲדָשׁוֹת וְאֶחָד יְשָׁנוֹת, דִּבְרֵי רַבִּי מֵאִיר. רַבִּי יְהוּדָה אוֹסֵר בַּחֲדָשׁוֹת וּמַתִּיר בִּישָׁנוֹת.

Rather, who is the *tanna* who maintains that Shabbat is a time for phylacteries? **It is this *tanna*** who taught the *halakha*, **as it was taught** in the *Tosefta*: **One who finds phylacteries brings them in pair** by **pair, whether** the finder is **a man or whether** she is **a woman,** and **whether** the phylacteries are **new or whether** they are **old.** This is **the statement of Rabbi Meir. Rabbi Yehuda prohibits** bringing in **new** phylacteries since they might merely be amulets in the form of phylacteries, **but** he **permits** bringing in **old** ones, which are certainly valid phylacteries.

עַד כָּאן לָא פְּלִיגִי אֶלָּא בַּחֲדָשׁוֹת וִישָׁנוֹת, אֲבָל בְּאִשָּׁה – לָא פְּלִיגִי. שְׁמַע מִינַּהּ: מִצְוַת עֲשֵׂה שֶׁלֹּא הַזְּמַן גְּרָמָא הוּא, וְכׇל מִצְוַת עֲשֵׂה שֶׁאֵין הַזְּמַן גְּרָמָא נָשִׁים חַיָּיבוֹת.

Analysis of this *Tosefta* indicates that Rabbi Meir and Rabbi Yehuda **disagree only with regard to** the issue of **new** phylacteries **and old ones; however, with regard to a woman** bringing in the phylacteries, **they do not disagree** that it is permitted. **Learn from it** that this *tanna* maintains that donning phylacteries **is a positive mitzva not bound by time, and** since **women are obligated in every positive mitzva not bound by time,** a woman may don these phylacteries and walk into the town.

וְדִילְמָא סָבַר לָהּ כְּרַבִּי יוֹסֵי, דְּאָמַר: נָשִׁים סוֹמְכוֹת רְשׁוּת? לָא סָלְקָא דַּעְתָּךְ, דְּלָא רַבִּי מֵאִיר סָבַר לָהּ כְּרַבִּי יוֹסֵי, וְלָא רַבִּי יְהוּדָה סָבַר לָהּ כְּרַבִּי יוֹסֵי.

The Gemara attempts to refute this. **But perhaps** that *tanna* **holds in accordance with** the opinion of **Rabbi Yosei, who said:** It is **optional** for **women** to **place** their hands on the head of a sacrificial animal before it is slaughtered. Here too, perhaps it is optional for women to don phylacteries. The Gemara answers: **This cannot enter your mind, as neither Rabbi Meir holds in accordance with** the opinion of **Rabbi Yosei, nor does Rabbi Yehuda hold in accordance with** the opinion of **Rabbi Yosei,** as the Gemara proceeds to prove.

לָא רַבִּי מֵאִיר סָבַר לָהּ כְּרַבִּי יוֹסֵי דִּתְנַן: אֵין מְעַכְּבִין אֶת הַתִּינוֹקוֹת מִלִּתְקוֹעַ. הָא נָשִׁים – מְעַכְּבִין. וּסְתָם מַתְנִיתִין רַבִּי מֵאִיר.

Neither Rabbi Meir holds in accordance with the opinion of **Rabbi Yosei, as we learned** in a mishna: **One** need **not prevent children from sounding**[H] the *shofar* on Rosh HaShana. Although there is an element of prohibition in sounding the *shofar* when there is no obligation to do so, since the children will one day be obligated to sound the *shofar*, one need not prevent them from doing so and learning. It may be inferred from here that **one must prevent women** from sounding the *shofar*. **And an unattributed mishna** is in accordance with the opinion of **Rabbi Meir,** indicating that according to Rabbi Meir, a woman does not even have the option of performing a time-bound positive mitzva.

וְלָא רַבִּי יְהוּדָה סָבַר לָהּ כְּרַבִּי יוֹסֵי דְּתַנְיָא: ״דַּבֵּר אֶל בְּנֵי יִשְׂרָאֵל וְסָמַךְ״ בְּנֵי יִשְׂרָאֵל סוֹמְכִין וְאֵין בְּנוֹת יִשְׂרָאֵל סוֹמְכוֹת. רַבִּי יוֹסֵי וְרַבִּי שִׁמְעוֹן אוֹמְרִים: נָשִׁים סוֹמְכוֹת רְשׁוּת.

Nor does Rabbi Yehuda hold in accordance with the opinion of **Rabbi Yosei, as it was taught** in the *Sifra*, the halakhic *midrash* on Leviticus. The verse states: **"Speak to the sons of Israel… and he shall place** his hands on the head of the burnt-offering" (Leviticus 1:2–4). By inference, **the sons of Israel place** their hands, **but the daughters of Israel do not place** their hands.[H] **Rabbi Yosei and Rabbi Shimon say:** It is **optional** for **women** to **place** their hands on the head of a sacrificial animal before it is slaughtered.

וּסְתָם סִיפְרָא מַנִּי – רַבִּי יְהוּדָה.

And who is the author of **an unattributed** ***Sifra*****?** It is **Rabbi Yehuda.**[N] This teaching proves that Rabbi Yehuda maintains that women do not have the option of placing their hands on a sacrifice. Neither Rabbi Meir nor Rabbi Yehuda accepts Rabbi Yosei's opinion that it is optional for women to perform time-bound positive mitzvot; therefore, the *tanna* who cited their opinions that a woman may bring in phylacteries on Shabbat maintains that the mitzva of phylacteries is not time-bound and is in effect even on Shabbat, which is why even women are obligated.

אָמַר רַבִּי אֶלְעָזָר: הַמּוֹצֵא תְּכֵלֶת בַּשּׁוּק, לְשׁוֹנוֹת – פְּסוּלוֹת, חוּטִין – כְּשֵׁרִין.

Rabbi Elazar said: With regard to **one who one finds** fabric dyed **sky blue**[H] **in the marketplace,**[N] if he found **strips** of combed and dyed wool **they are unfit** for use as ritual fringes. The sky blue threads used in ritual fringes must be spun and dyed for the purpose of the mitzva, and these strips might have been dyed for a different purpose. However, if one found sky blue **threads, they are fit** for use in ritual fringes, as it can be assumed they were prepared for that purpose.

מַאי שְׁנָא לְשׁוֹנוֹת – דְּאָמַר: אַדַּעְתָּא דִּגְלִימָא צָבְעִינְהוּ. חוּטִין נַמִּי, נֵימָא: אַדַּעְתָּא דִּגְלִימָא טָוְינְהוּ. בִּשְׁזוּרִים.

The Gemara asks: **What is different** about **strips** that renders them unfit? It is because Rabbi Elazar **said: One dyed** the strips **with the intent** to use them **for a cloak.** If so, with regard to **threads as well, let us say: One spun them with the intent** to use them **for a cloak.** In that case, they too would be deemed unfit. The Gemara answers: Here, it is referring to threads that are **twisted,** which are not typically used for weaving.

שְׁזוּרִים נַמִּי, נֵימָא: אַדַּעְתָּא דְּשִׁיפְתָּא דִּגְלִימָא עַיְּיפִינְהוּ. בִּמְוּפְסָקִין, דִּכְוּלֵּי הַאי וַדַּאי לָא טָרְחִי אֱינָשֵׁי.

The Gemara asks: With regard to **twisted** threads **as well, let us say** that **one twisted them with the intent** of attaching them to **the hem of a cloak** as ornamentation. The Gemara answers: It is referring to twisted threads **that were cut** into short strings suitable for use as ritual fringes, **as people certainly do not exert** themselves and fashion fringes of a cloak to resemble ritual fringes.

אָמַר רָבָא: וְכִי אָדָם טוֹרֵחַ לַעֲשׂוֹת קָמֵיעַ כְּמִין תְּפִילִּין? דִּתְנַן: בַּמֶּה דְּבָרִים אֲמוּרִים – בִּיְשָׁנוֹת, אֲבָל בַּחֲדָשׁוֹת – פָּטוּר.

Rava said: The assertion that people do not exert themselves is problematic, **as** by the same token, **does a person exert** himself **to fashion an amulet in the form of phylacteries?** Nevertheless, the Sages were concerned that an object that appears to be phylacteries might actually be a different object. **As we learned** in a mishna: **In what** case **is this statement** that one is permitted to carry phylacteries inside on Shabbat **said?** It is **with regard to old** phylacteries. **However, with regard to new** ones, **he is exempt** from the obligation to bring them in, as it is possible that they are not phylacteries but amulets in the form of phylacteries. Similarly, there should be concern lest people fashion items similar to objects used for a mitzva, even if exertion is involved.

HALAKHA

One need not prevent children from sounding – אֵין מְעַכְּבִין אֶת הַתִּינוֹקוֹת מִלִּתְקוֹעַ: One is not obligated to prevent children who have not reached the age of education from sounding a *shofar* on Shabbat. However, if they have reached the age of five or six years old, one must stop them from doing so. An adult is permitted to teach a child to sound the *shofar* on Rosh HaShana, even if it coincides with Shabbat, whether or not the child has reached the age of education (Rambam). According to the Ra'avad, if the child has reached the age of education one can assist him even on Shabbat; however, if he has not reached that age, one may not teach him on Shabbat, and one need not prevent him from sounding the *shofar* on the Festival (Rambam *Sefer Zemanim, Hilkhot Shofar VeSukka VeLulav* 2:7). The author of the *Tur* writes that if a child has not reached the age of education, he is encouraged to sound the *shofar*. If he has reached it, he is not told to sound the *shofar*, but if he attempts to do so, one need not stop him (*Tur, Oraḥ Ḥayyim* 588).

The daughters of Israel do not place their hands – אֵין בְּנוֹת יִשְׂרָאֵל סוֹמְכוֹת: Women do not place their hands on a sacrifice, as stated by the mishna in tractate *Menaḥot* (Rambam *Sefer Avoda, Hilkhot Ma'aseh HaKorbanot* 3:8).

One who finds fabric dyed sky blue – הַמּוֹצֵא תְּכֵלֶת: If a person finds strips of fabric dyed sky blue, or even cut threads, they are invalid for use as ritual fringes. However, if he finds twisted threads, they are valid, in accordance with the opinion of Rabbi Eliezer (Rambam *Sefer Ahava, Hilkhot Tzitzit* 2:7).

NOTES

The author of an unattributed *Sifra*…is Rabbi Yehuda – סְתָם סִפְרָא...רַבִּי יְהוּדָה: There is a difference between the assertion that an unattributed *Sifra* reflects Rabbi Yehuda's opinion, and similar statements that a certain Sage edited a rabbinic text. A Sage who edited a book is not required to agree with everything the volume contains. According to Rambam, the *Sifra*, also known as *Torat Kohanim*, was edited by Rav and not by Rabbi Yehuda. However, the statement that an unattributed *Sifra* reflects Rabbi Yehuda's opinion indicates that although he did not edit the *Sifra*, the unattributed teaching is in accordance with his opinion (see *Baḥ* and Rashash).

One who finds fabric dyed sky blue in the marketplace – הַמּוֹצֵא תְּכֵלֶת בַּשּׁוּק: In tractate *Menaḥot*, the Sages explain that not every blue-dyed wool is considered dyed sky blue, and there are many signs for determining the nature of the dye used to color the wool. Even if the wool threads were certainly dyed with sky blue dye, it is still possible that they were dyed improperly as several factors can invalidate the wool used for the mitzva of ritual fringes. For example, the wool would be invalidated if the dye upon it was used only as a test (see *Tosafot* and *Me'iri*).

אמר רבי זירא לאהבה בריה, פוק תני להו: המוצא תכלת בשוק, לשונות – פסולין, חוטין מופסקין – כשירין, לפי שאין אדם טורח.

Rabbi Zeira said to his son Ahava: Go out and teach this *baraita* **to** the Sages. With regard to **one who finds** fabric dyed **sky blue in the marketplace,** if he finds **strips, they are unfit** for use in ritual fringes; however, if he finds **threads cut** into short strings, **they are fit** for use in ritual fringes **because a person does not exert** himself. Apparently, that is the reason for the *halakha*.

אמר רבא: ומשום דתני לה אהבה בריה דרבי זירא כיפי תלא לה? והתנן: במה דברים אמורים – בישנות, אבל בחדשות – פטור.

Rava said: And because Ahava, son of Rabbi Zeira, taught this *halakha*, **has he hung** ornamental **rings on** that line of reasoning, i.e., does that constitute an absolute proof? The difficulty posed by Rava from the mishna is not resolved by the *baraita*, **as we learned: In what** case **is this statement** that one is permitted to carry phylacteries inside **said?** It is **with regard to old** phylacteries. **However, with regard to new** ones, **he is exempt.** Apparently, there is concern lest one exert himself to fashion an object similar to one used in a mitzva.

אלא אמר רבא: טרח ולא טרח – תנאי היא,

Rather, Rava said: The sources are not contradictory, as the question of whether one **exerts** himself **or does not exert** himself **is** the subject of a dispute between ***tanna'im***. Some hold that one exerts himself as indicated by the mishna with regard to phylacteries, whereas others hold that one does not exert himself as stated with regard to sky blue dye.

דתניא: המוצא תפילין – מכניסן זוג זוג, אחד האיש ואחד האשה,

As it was taught in the *Tosefta*: **One who finds phylacteries** in a field **brings them in** to the town **pair** by **pair, whether** the finder is **a man or a woman,**

Perek **X**
Daf **97** Amud **a**

NOTES

New and old phylacteries – תפילין חדשות וישנות: In the Jerusalem Talmud it is stated that the concern with regard to new phylacteries is unrelated to their status as phylacteries. Rather, the issue is whether or not they have been examined. Since it is possible that they are not valid phylacteries, they may not be carried on Shabbat.

Straps that are tied – רצועות ומקושרות: The Rif explains that in the final analysis Rabbi Yehuda prohibits carrying new phylacteries not due to the prohibition against making a knot, but due to the concern that they might be amulets. If it only has straps, the phylacteries might be amulets; on the other hand, if the straps have actually been tied, it can be assumed that they are not amulets, as no one would go to the trouble of tying knots for amulets. The Rambam's ruling indicates that he explains this in a similar manner (Ramban).

HALAKHA

New and old phylacteries – תפילין חדשות וישנות: New phylacteries may not be carried on Shabbat, even if they have straps, unless the straps have been knotted (*Shulḥan Arukh, Oraḥ Ḥayyim* 301:42).

אחד חדשות ואחד ישנות, דברי רבי מאיר. רבי יהודה אוסר בחדשות ומתיר בישנות. אלמא, מר סבר: טרח איניש, ומר סבר לא טרח איניש.

and **whether** the phylacteries are **new or old;** this is **the statement of Rabbi Meir. Rabbi Yehuda prohibits** carrying **new** phylacteries **but permits** carrying **old ones.**[NH] **Apparently,** one **Sage,** Rabbi Yehuda, **holds** that **a person exerts** himself to fashion an amulet that looks like phylacteries, **and** one **Sage,** Rabbi Meir, **holds** that **a person does not exert** himself for this purpose, and therefore something that has the appearance of phylacteries must be phylacteries.

(שיצ״י עצב״י סימן). והשתא דתני אבוה דשמואל בר רב יצחק: אלו הן ישנות – כל שיש בהן רצועות ומקושרות, חדשות – יש בהן רצועות ולא מקושרות. דכולי עלמא לא טרח איניש.

Shin, yod, tzadi, yod, ayin, tzadi, beit, yod is a **mnemonic** for the statements that follow. The Gemara adds: **And now that the father of Shmuel bar Rav Yitzḥak has taught** that **these are** deemed **old** phylacteries: **Any that have straps that** are permanently **tied**[N] in the manner of phylacteries, and **new** phylacteries are those **that have straps that are not tied,** the conclusion is **that everyone agrees** that **a person exerts** himself to fashion an amulet similar to phylacteries or string-like ritual fringes. They disagree with regard to new phylacteries that are not tied properly and cannot be donned in a manner typical of a weekday. The reason is that tying a permanent knot on Shabbat is prohibited by Torah law. Therefore, these phylacteries may not be donned, and Rabbi Zeira's opinion is accepted.

וליענבינהו מיענב. אמר רב חסדא, זאת אומרת: עניבה פסולה בתפילין.

The Gemara asks a question with regard to Rabbi Yehuda's opinion that new phylacteries may not be brought into town because they lack a permanent knot: Why must one tie the phylacteries with a knot? **Let him** simply **tie a bow,** which is not prohibited on Shabbat, and place the phylacteries on his head and arm in that manner. **Rav Ḥisda said: That is to say** that **a bow is invalid for phylacteries,** as a proper knot is required.

אביי אמר: רבי יהודה לטעמיה, דאמר: עניבה קשירה מעלייתא היא.

Abaye said: This is not the correct interpretation. Rather, **Rabbi Yehuda** conforms to **his** standard line of **reasoning, as he said: A bow is a full-fledged knot,** and it is prohibited to tie it on Shabbat by Torah law.

טעמא דעניבה קשירה מעלייתא היא, הא לאו הכי – עניב להו? והאמר רב יהודה בריה דרב שמואל בר שילת משמיה דרב: קשר של תפילין הלכה למשה מסיני הוא. ואמר רב נחמן: ונוייהן לבר.

The Gemara asks: **The reason** that it is prohibited to tie a bow is **that a bow is a full-fledged knot. If that were not so,** one could **tie** the phylacteries **with a bow. But didn't Rav Yehuda, son of Rav Shmuel bar Sheilat, say in the name of Rav:** The form of the permanent **knot of phylacteries**[B] **is a** ***halakha*** **transmitted to Moses from Sinai; and Rav Naḥman said: And their decorative** side, the side of the knot where the shape of the letter appears, must face **outward.**[N] Apparently, a bow does not suffice for phylacteries, as an actual knot is required.

דעניב להו כעין קשירה דידהו.

The Gemara rejects this contention: It is referring to a case **where one tied a bow similar** in form **to a** permanent **knot,** without actually tying a permanent knot.

אמר רב חסדא, אמר רב: הלוקח תפילין ממי שאינו מומחה – בודק שתים של יד ואחת של ראש, או שתים של ראש ואחת של יד.

Rav Ḥisda said that **Rav said: One who purchases** a large quantity **of phylacteries from one who is not an expert,** i.e., a person who has not proven to be a reliable manufacturer of phylacteries, the purchaser **examines two** phylacteries **of the arm and one of the head, or two of the head and one of the arm,** to see if they are valid and the individual reliable. If the three phylacteries are found to be valid upon examination, the seller is considered an expert and the rest of the phylacteries are presumed valid as well.

מה נפשך; אי מחד גברא קא זבין – לבדוק או שלש של יד או שלש של ראש.

The Gemara asks: **Whichever way you look at it,** this ruling is problematic: **If** the buyer **purchased** all of the phylacteries **from one person,** who acquired them from somebody else, **let him examine three** phylacteries **of the arm or three of the head,** in accordance with the principle that presumptive status is established after three instances.

אי מתרי תלתא גברי זבין – כל חד וחד ליבעי בדיקה. לעולם מחד גברא זבין, ובעינן דמיתמחי בשל יד ובשל ראש.

If he purchased the phylacteries **from two** or **three people, each and every one** of the phylacteries **should require examination.**[H] The presumptive status of one pair of phylacteries does not apply to the others, as they might have been produced by a different person. The Gemara answers: **Actually,** this refers to a case where the buyer **bought** the phylacteries **from one person, and we require** that the seller prove himself **to be an expert with regard to** both the phylactery **of the arm and** the phylactery **of the head.**

איני? והא תני רבה בר שמואל: בתפילין בודק שלש של יד ושל ראש. מאי לאו או שלש של יד, או שלש של ראש? לא, שלש, מהן של יד מהן של ראש.

The Gemara asks: **Is that so? Didn't Rabba bar Shmuel teach** that **with** regard to **phylacteries one examines three of the arm and** three **of the head? What, is it not** that he examines **either three** phylacteries **of the arm or three of the head?** The Gemara rejects this explanation: **No,** it means that he examines **three** phylacteries in total, **among them** phylacteries **of the arm and among them** phylacteries **of the head,** as stated by Rav Ḥisda in the name of Rav.

והתני רב כהנא: בתפילין בודק שתים של יד ושל ראש. הא מני רבי היא, דאמר: בתרי זימני הוי חזקה.

The Gemara asks: **But didn't Rav Kahana teach** that **with** regard to **phylacteries one examines two of the arm and** two **of the head?** This statement certainly contradicts Rav's opinion. The Gemara explains: In accordance with **whose** opinion **is this** ***halakha***? **It is** the opinion of **Rabbi** Yehuda HaNasi, **who said: Presumptive status is** established[N] **by two times.** Although most Sages maintain that it takes three instances to establish a presumptive status, Rabbi Yehuda HaNasi rules that two cases suffice. Consequently, in the case of phylacteries, it is sufficient to examine two.

BACKGROUND

Knot of phylacteries – **קשר של תפילין**: The pictures show the letter *shin* on the head phylactery itself, the knot of the head phylactery according to the Ashkenazic custom, which is tied in the shape of the letter *dalet*, and the knot of the arm phylactery, which is tied in the shape of the letter *yod*. Together these spell out the Hebrew word *Shadai*, which is one of God's names.

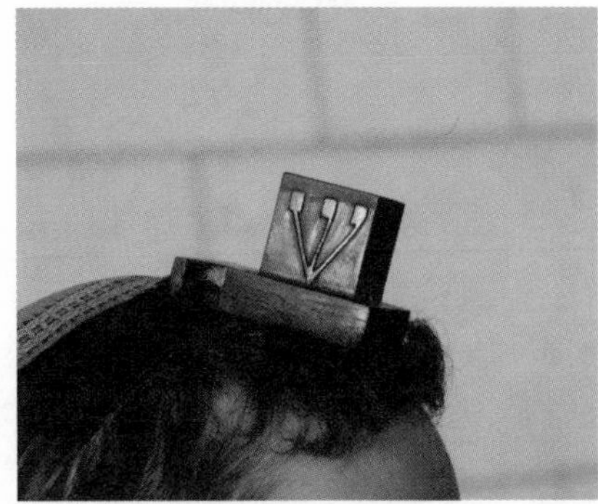

Letter *shin* on head phylactery

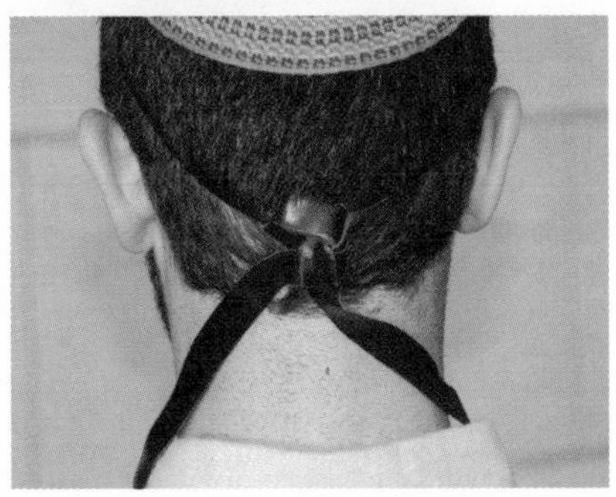

Head phylactery, with knot in the shape of a *dalet*

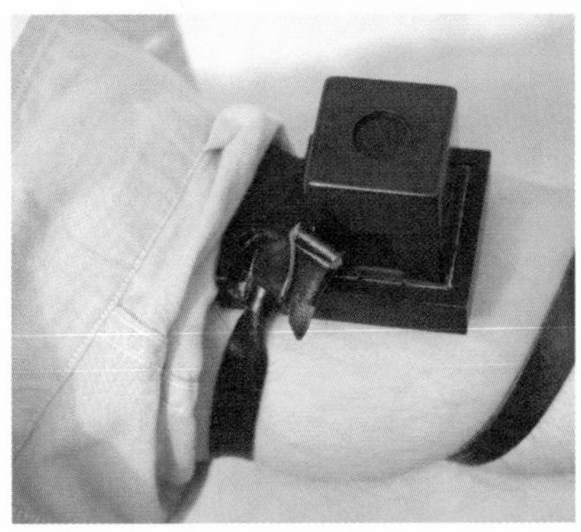

Arm phylactery, with knot in the shape of a *yod*

HALAKHA

Examination of phylacteries – **בדיקת תפילין**: One who buys phylacteries from a person who has not been established as an expert must examine them. If he checked three phylacteries of the head and the arm and found them to be valid, all the other phylacteries are presumed to be valid as well. If he bought them in bundles he must examine each and every bundle, as stated by Rav (Rambam *Sefer Ahava, Hilkhot Tefillin UMezuza VeSefer Torah* 2:10; *Shulḥan Arukh, Oraḥ Ḥayyim* 39:9).

NOTES

Their decorative side must face outward – **נוייהן לבר**: This statement has been explained in several ways. Some commentaries state that it refers to the raised letter *shin* on the phylactery of the head, which should not be contained inside the phylactery box, but must be visible on the outside, as taught by Rashi. Other authorities explain that this means the *shin* must be raised rather than carved into the phylactery. Yet other commentaries maintain that the reference is to the *halakha* that the parchments must be written on the better quality side of the hide (*Me'iri*).

The establishment of a presumptive status – **קביעת חזקה**: This dispute regarding the laws of a presumptive status appears in several places in the Talmud. The Rabbis maintain that something that recurs three times has a presumptive status, i.e., it forms an established status quo. An example of this is the *halakha* of an ox that gored three times, at which point its owner is considered forewarned and must pay full damages if the animal causes further harm. By contrast, Rabbi Yehuda HaNasi maintains that a simple repetition is enough to create a presumptive status. In this context, three consecutive examinations that reveal valid phylacteries are enough to establish a reliable presumptive status that all of the phylacteries are valid. This status can only be annulled by evidence to the contrary.

LANGUAGE

Pairs [*zuvei*] – זווי: Related to the Greek ζεῦγος, *zeugos*, meaning a yoke, and by extension, a pair.

Bandits [*listim*] – לִסְטִים: From the Greek ληστής, *lestès*, meaning thief or bandit. The written form was corrupted slightly to *listim* instead of *listis*.

BACKGROUND

Wrapped piles – כְּרִיכוֹת: A pile of phylacteries wrapped and placed together, as opposed to bundles of phylacteries placed in pairs.

Pile of phylacteries

HALAKHA

Any instance that were he to bring them in pair by pair – כֹּל שֶׁאִילּוּ מַכְנִיסָן זוּג זוּג: If one finds a large pile of phylacteries outside and is unable to bring them all in by nightfall in pairs, he may not carry any of them. Instead, he must wait alongside them and guard them until nightfall (Rambam *Sefer Zemanim*, *Hilkhot Shabbat* 19:23; *Shulḥan Arukh*, *Oraḥ Ḥayyim* 301:42).

Danger – סַכָּנָה: If it is dangerous to walk in public with phylacteries on one's head due to bandits, one may carry them in increments of less than four cubits each, or pass them to another who then passes the phylacteries to another until the phylacteries reach a private domain. In this case the *halakha* is not in accordance with the first *tanna*, but with the lenient opinion of Rabbi Shimon (*Beit Yosef*). Furthermore, Rabbi Yehuda permits one to carry in this manner even for an optional purpose (Rambam *Sefer Zemanim*, *Hilkhot Shabbat* 19:24; *Shulḥan Arukh*, *Oraḥ Ḥayyim* 301:42, and in the comment of the Vilna Gaon).

אִי רַבִּי, אֵימָא סֵיפָא: וְכֵן בַּצְּבָת הַשֵּׁנִי, וְכֵן בַּצְּבָת הַשְּׁלִישִׁי. וְאִי רַבִּי – שְׁלִישִׁי מִי אִית לֵיהּ?

The Gemara asks: **If** this ruling is in accordance with the opinion of **Rabbi** Yehuda HaNasi, **say the latter clause** of that same *baraita* as follows: **And** he must **likewise** examine **the second bundle** of phylacteries, **and likewise the third bundle. And if it is** in accordance with **Rabbi** Yehuda HaNasi's opinion, **is he of** the opinion that **a third** examination is necessary? Rabbi Yehuda HaNasi does not require a third examination to establish a presumptive status, as he maintains that the examination of two bundles suffices.

מוֹדֶה רַבִּי בִּצְבָתִים, דְּמִתְּרֵי תְּלָתָא גַּבְרֵי זָבֵין. אִי הָכִי, אֲפִילּוּ רְבִיעִי נָמֵי, וַאֲפִילּוּ חֲמִישִׁי נָמֵי.

The Gemara answers: **Rabbi** Yehuda HaNasi **concedes with regard to bundles, as one buys** them **from two** or **three** different **people.** It can be assumed that the various bundles of phylacteries were not all manufactured by the same person. Consequently, the validity of one bundle does not establish a presumption with regard to another. The Gemara asks: **If so, even** the **fourth** bundle must be examined **as well, and even** the **fifth as well.** If the bundles were bought from different manufacturers, every one of them requires examination, not only the third.

אִין הָכִי נָמֵי, וְהַאי דְּקָתָנֵי שְׁלִישִׁי – לְאַפּוֹקֵי מֵחֲזָקֵיהּ, וּלְעוֹלָם אֲפִילּוּ רְבִיעִי וַחֲמִישִׁי נָמֵי.

The Gemara answers: **Yes, it is indeed so;** this is how one must proceed. **And** the reason **that** Rabbi Yehuda HaNasi **teaches three** bundles rather than four or five is **to exclude** the third bundle **from its presumptive status.** By stating that the third bundle must be examined, Rabbi Yehuda HaNasi indicates that in this case two examinations do not establish a presumption; rather, all of the bundles must be checked. **And actually, even** the **fourth and fifth** bundles require examination **as well.**

״מְצָאָן צְבָתִים אוֹ כְּרִיכוֹת וכו׳״ מַאי צְבָתִים, וּמַאי כְּרִיכוֹת? אָמַר רַב יְהוּדָה, אָמַר רַב: הֵן הֵן צְבָתִים, הֵן הֵן כְּרִיכוֹת. צְבָתִים זְוָוֵי זְוָוֵי, כְּרִיכוֹת דִּכְרִיכָן טוּבָא.

It was stated in the mishna that if **one finds** phylacteries **tied in bundles or in wrapped piles,** he sits there and waits with them until dark and then brings them in. The Gemara asks: **What is** the meaning of **bundles** in this context, **and what is** meant by **wrapped piles? Rav Yehuda said** that **Rav said:** The same types of objects **are called bundles, and they are** also called **wrapped piles,** i.e., both contain more than one pair of phylacteries. **Bundles** consist of many pairs of phylacteries arranged **in pairs** [*zuvei*][L] of a head phylactery with an arm phylactery, whereas **wrapped piles**[B] indicates **that many** phylacteries **are wrapped together** in no particular arrangement.

״מַחְשִׁיךְ עֲלֵיהֶן וּמְבִיאָן״. וְאַמַּאי? לְעַיְּילִינְהוּ זוּג זוּג. אָמַר רַב יִצְחָק בְּרֵיהּ דְּרַב יְהוּדָה: לְדִידִי מִיפָּרְשָׁא לֵיהּ מִינֵּיהּ דְּאַבָּא: כֹּל שֶׁאִילּוּ מַכְנִיסָן זוּג זוּג וְכָלוֹת קוֹדֶם שְׁקִיעַת הַחַמָּה – מַכְנִיסָן זוּג זוּג, וְאִי לֹא – מַחְשִׁיךְ עֲלֵיהֶן וּמְבִיאָן.

We learned in the mishna that one sits there and **waits with them until dark and** then **brings them** in. The Gemara asks: **And why** must he do that? **Let him bring them in pair** by **pair. Rav Yitzḥak, son of Rav Yehuda, said:** This matter **was explained to me** personally **by** my **father** as follows: **Any** instance where there are few enough phylacteries **that were he to bring them in pair** by **pair**[H] **he would finish before sunset, he brings them** in **pair** by **pair. But if not,** i.e., if there are so many pairs of phylacteries that were he to bring them in one pair at a time he would not bring them all in before sunset, **he waits** there **with** all of **them until dark and** then **brings them** in.

״וּבְסַכָּנָה מְכַסָּן וְהוֹלֵךְ״. וְהָתַנְיָא: וּבְסַכָּנָה מוֹלִיכָן פָּחוֹת פָּחוֹת מֵאַרְבַּע אַמּוֹת. אָמַר רַב: לָא קַשְׁיָא; הָא – בְּסַכָּנַת גּוֹיִם, הָא – בְּסַכָּנַת לִסְטִים.

It was stated in the mishna that **in** a time of **danger**[H] one **covers** the phylacteries **and proceeds on his** way. The Gemara asks: **Wasn't it taught** in a different *baraita*: **And in** a time of **danger he carries them less than four cubits** at a time? The Gemara answers that **Rav said:** It is **not difficult.** In **this** mishna, which states that the finder covers the phylacteries, it is referring **to the danger** posed **by gentiles,** where the gentile authorities decreed against donning phylacteries and the finder is afraid to be seen carrying them. However, in **that** *baraita*, which teaches that one may carry them less than four cubits at a time, it is dealing **with the danger** posed **by bandits** [***listim***].[L] In that case he is afraid to remain there until dark, but he is not worried about taking the phylacteries with him. Consequently, he may carry them less than four cubits at a time.

אָמַר לֵיהּ אַבָּיֵי: בְּמַאי אוֹקִימְתָּא לְמַתְנִיתִין – בְּסַכָּנַת גּוֹיִם, אֵימָא סֵיפָא; רַבִּי שִׁמְעוֹן אוֹמֵר: נוֹתְנָן לַחֲבֵירוֹ, וַחֲבֵירוֹ לַחֲבֵירוֹ. כׇּל שֶׁכֵּן דְּאַוְושָׁא מִילְּתָא.

Abaye said to him: In what manner **did you establish our mishna as** dealing **with the danger** posed **by gentiles? Say the latter clause** of the mishna as follows: **Rabbi Shimon says** that **one gives them to another and the other** passes them **to another.** In that case, **all the more so** will **the matter be conspicuous,** and they should fear the decree issued by the gentiles.

חַסּוּרֵי מִיחַסְּרָא, וְהָכִי קָתָנֵי: בַּמֶּה דְּבָרִים אֲמוּרִים – בְּסַכָּנַת גּוֹיִם אֲבָל בְּסַכָּנַת לִיסְטִים – מוֹלִיכָן פָּחוֹת פָּחוֹת מֵאַרְבַּע אַמּוֹת.

The Gemara answers: The mishna **is incomplete and is teaching the following: In what case is this statement** that the finder covers the phylacteries **said?** It is where the concern is **danger** posed by **gentiles. However,** where the concern is **danger** posed by **bandits, one carries them less than four cubits at a time.** In that case Rabbi Shimon disagrees, maintaining that it is preferable that many people carry the phylacteries.

"רַבִּי שִׁמְעוֹן אוֹמֵר נוֹתְנָן לַחֲבֵירוֹ וכו׳". בְּמַאי קָמִיפַּלְגִי? מָר סָבַר: פָּחוֹת מֵאַרְבַּע אַמּוֹת עָדִיף, דְּאִי אָמְרַתְּ נוֹתְנָן לַחֲבֵירוֹ וַחֲבֵירוֹ לַחֲבֵירוֹ – אַוְושָׁא מִלְּתָא דְּשַׁבָּת.

It is stated in the mishna that **Rabbi Shimon says: One gives them to another** and the other passes them to another. The Gemara asks: **With regard to what** principle do **they disagree?** One **Sage,** the first *tanna,* **holds** that having one person carrying the phylacteries **less than four cubits** at a time **is preferable, as if you say** that the finder **gives them to another, and** the **other** passes them **to another, Shabbat** desecration **will be noticeable,**[N] thereby demeaning Shabbat's character as a sacred day of rest.

וּמָר סָבַר: נוֹתְנָן לַחֲבֵירוֹ עָדִיף, דְּאִי אָמְרַתְּ מוֹלִיכָן פָּחוֹת מֵאַרְבַּע אַמּוֹת – זִימְנִין דְּלָאו אַדַּעְתֵּיהּ, וְאָתֵי לְאַתּוֹיֵינְהוּ אַרְבַּע אַמּוֹת בִּרְשׁוּת הָרַבִּים.

And the other **Sage,** Rabbi Shimon, **holds** that the solution that **one gives** the phylacteries **to another is preferable, as if you say** that the finder **carries them less than four cubits** at a time, **sometimes it is not in his thoughts and** will unwittingly **come to carry** the phylacteries **four cubits in the public domain.** That is unlikely if there are numerous people together.

"וְכֵן בְּנוֹ". בְּנוֹ מַאי בָּעֵי הָתָם? דְּבֵי מְנַשֶּׁה תָּנָא: בְּשֶׁיְּלָדַתּוֹ אִמּוֹ בַּשָּׂדֶה.

It was stated in the mishna: **And the same** is true with regard to **one's son.** The Gemara is surprised: **What is his son doing there**[N] in the field necessitating his retrieval in this way? **The school of Menashe taught:** It is referring to a case **where his mother gave birth to him in a field,**[N] and he must be brought to town.

וּמַאי אֲפִילּוּ הֵן מֵאָה – דְּאַף עַל גַּב דְּקַשְׁיָא לֵיהּ יָדָא, אֲפִילּוּ הָכִי – הָא עֲדִיפָא.

And what may be inferred from the mishna's ruling that the baby is passed from one person to the next, **even** if it requires **a hundred** people? This teaches **that although it is difficult for** the child to be passed from **hand** to hand, **even so, this** method of transporting him **is preferable** to his being carried by one person less than four cubits at a time.

"רַבִּי יְהוּדָה אוֹמֵר נוֹתֵן אָדָם חָבִית". וְלֵית לֵיהּ לְרַבִּי יְהוּדָה הָא דִּתְנַן: הַבְּהֵמָה וְהַכֵּלִים כְּרַגְלֵי הַבְּעָלִים?

It was stated in the mishna that **Rabbi Yehuda says: A person gives a barrel to another,** and the other may pass it to another, and in that way they may take it even beyond the Shabbat limit. The Gemara asks: **And is Rabbi Yehuda not of the opinion** of that **which we learned** in a mishna: The distance that **an animal and vessels** may be taken **is like** the distance that **the feet of the owners** may go with regard to Shabbat limits?

אָמַר רֵישׁ לָקִישׁ מִשּׁוּם לֵוִי סָבָא: הָכָא בְּמַאי עָסְקִינַן – בִּמְעָרֶה מֵחָבִית לְחָבִית. וְרַבִּי יְהוּדָה לְטַעְמֵיהּ, דְּאָמַר: מַיִם אֵין בָּהֶם מַמָּשׁ.

Reish Lakish said in the name of Levi the Elder: With what are we dealing here? We are dealing **with** a case where **one pours** the water **from one barrel to** another **barrel** so that only the water, rather than the barrel itself, is taken beyond the limit. **And Rabbi Yehuda** follows **his** usual **reasoning, as he said: Water has no substance,** i.e., it is not significant enough for its transfer beyond the Shabbat limit to be prohibited.

דִּתְנַן: רַבִּי יְהוּדָה פּוֹטֵר בַּמַּיִם, מִפְּנֵי שֶׁאֵין בָּהֶן מַמָּשׁ.

As we learned in a mishna that discusses a dispute on this issue: If one person adds flour for dough while another adds the water, the Rabbis say that the dough may only be taken as far as both owners are permitted to go, whereas **Rabbi Yehuda exempts water** from any limit **due to** the fact that **it has no substance.**[N]

NOTES

Shabbat desecration will be noticeable – אַוְושָׁא מִלְּתָא דְּשַׁבָּת: Some commentaries explained the problem as follows: Although this does not constitute a prohibition, the concern is that a person ignorant in *halakha* might think they are desecrating Shabbat (Rabbeinu Yehonatan).

What is his son doing there – בְּנוֹ מַאי בָּעֵי הָתָם: In other words, the case being discussed must certainly be some sort of an emergency, as one does not generally carry a child in this method. The Gemara therefore asks how the child got there (Ritva).

Where his mother gave birth to him in a field – בְּשֶׁיְּלָדַתּוֹ אִמּוֹ בַּשָּׂדֶה: The explanation in the Jerusalem Talmud is that this refers to a baby whose life would be threatened were it to remain outside the town. Nevertheless, the Sages insisted that the situation should be addressed without performing labor prohibited on Shabbat if possible.

The commentaries on the Babylonian Talmud and the halakhic authorities disagree with this interpretation. They maintain that if the baby's life is threatened or if it requires first aid, Shabbat prohibitions may certainly be violated. Rather, it is referring to a case where bringing the baby to town would permit better care for the child, although the baby would not be in danger if left where it is (see Ritva).

Water…has no substance – מַיִם...אֵין בָּהֶם מַמָּשׁ: The initial assumption is surprising: How can water in dough be comparable to water in its pure unadulterated form? The Ritva suggests that even water in dough is discernible. That is because dough can only be prepared with water, which facilitates its preparation, and an ingredient that facilitates preparation of that food cannot be nullified.

NOTES

The barrel is nullified relative to the water – בָּטְלָה חָבִית לְגַבֵּי מַיִם: Since all authorities agree that with regard to carrying on Shabbat the barrel is nullified relative to the water, why do they disagree here? The Ra'avad answers that although that is certainly the case as far as the Torah prohibition is concerned, carrying the barrel is prohibited by rabbinic decree.

Threshold – אִיסְקוּפָּה: Some commentaries explain that this term refers to a kind of couch placed at the entrance to a house (*Agur* by Rabbi Shmuel Jama).

HALAKHA

A sacred book on a threshold – סֵפֶר עַל הָאִיסְקוּפָּה: If one is sitting on a threshold with a book in scroll form in his hand, and one end of the scroll rolls out of his hand into the public domain, he may roll it back toward himself (*Shulḥan Arukh*, *Oraḥ Ḥayyim* 352:1).

וּמַאי ״לֹא תְהַלֵּךְ זוֹ״ – לֹא יְהַלֵּךְ מַה שֶּׁבְּזוֹ יוֹתֵר מֵרַגְלֵי הַבְּעָלִים.

And what, then, is the meaning of the Rabbis' statement in the mishna: **This** may **not go** farther than the feet of the owners may go, which apparently refers to the barrel? It means: **That which is in this** barrel may **not go farther than the feet of the owners** may go.

אֵימַר דְּשָׁמְעַתְּ לֵיהּ לְרַבִּי יְהוּדָה הֵיכָא דְּבָלִיעַן בְּעִיסָּה, הֵיכָא דְּאִיתַנְהוּ בְּעֵינַיְיהוּ מִי שָׁמְעַתְּ לֵיהּ? הַשְׁתָּא בִּקְדֵירָה אָמַר רַבִּי יְהוּדָה לָא בָּטְלִי, בְּעֵינַיְיהוּ בָּטְלִי? דְּתַנְיָא, רַבִּי יְהוּדָה אוֹמֵר: מַיִם וּמֶלַח בְּטֵלִין בְּעִיסָּה, וְאֵין בְּטֵלִין בִּקְדֵירָה, מִפְּנֵי רוֹטְבָהּ.

The Gemara rejects this explanation. **Say that you heard Rabbi Yehuda** express **his** opinion that water has no substance in a case **where it is absorbed in dough;** but in a case **where it is in its pure, unadulterated** state **did you hear him** say so? **Now,** if with regard to water **in a pot** of cooked food **Rabbi Yehuda said** that it **is not nullified,** would it be **nullified when it is in its pure, unadulterated** state? That is clearly not the case, **as it was taught** in a *baraita* that **Rabbi Yehuda says: Water and salt are nullified in dough,** as they are absorbed into it and are not independently discernible. However, **they are not nullified in a pot** of cooked food, **because** the water and salt are discernible in **its gravy.**

אֶלָּא אָמַר רָבָא: הָכָא בְּחָבִית שֶׁקָּנְתָה שְׁבִיתָה, וּמַיִם שֶׁלֹּא קָנוּ שְׁבִיתָה עָסְקִינַן, דְּבָטְלָה חָבִית לְגַבֵּי מַיִם.

Rather, Rava rejected this explanation and **said: Here, we are dealing with a barrel** that belonged to a particular individual who **acquired residence** at the start of Shabbat in a specific location, **and water that did not** remain in one place, i.e., spring or river water, and that does not belong to any individual who **acquired residence.** In that case, **the barrel is nullified relative to the water,**[N] since the barrel is designated to hold the water.

כִּדְתְנַן: הַמּוֹצִיא הַחַי בְּמִטָּה – פָּטוּר אַף עַל הַמִּטָּה, מִפְּנֵי שֶׁהַמִּטָּה טְפֵילָה לוֹ.

As we learned in a mishna: **One who carries out a living person on a bed** from one domain to another on Shabbat **is exempt even for** carrying out **the bed, due to** the fact **that the bed is secondary to** the person. He is exempt for carrying out the living person because a living being carries itself, i.e., the person being carried lightens the load and thereby assists those bearing him.

הַמּוֹצִיא אוֹכָלִין פָּחוֹת מִכַּשִּׁיעוּר בִּכְלִי – פָּטוּר אַף עַל הַכְּלִי, מִפְּנֵי שֶׁהַכְּלִי טָפֵל לוֹ.

Similarly, **one who carries out** an amount of **food, less than the measure** that determines liability for carrying out food on Shabbat, **in a vessel is exempt, even for** carrying out **the vessel, due to** the fact **that the vessel is secondary to** the food inside it. By the same reasoning, the barrel should be nullified relative to the water it contains.

מְתִיב רַב יוֹסֵף, רַבִּי יְהוּדָה אוֹמֵר: בְּשַׁיָּירָא נוֹתֵן אָדָם חָבִית לַחֲבֵירוֹ, וַחֲבֵירוֹ לַחֲבֵירוֹ. בְּשַׁיָּירָא – אִין, שֶׁלֹּא בְּשַׁיָּירָא – לָא. אֶלָּא אָמַר רַב יוֹסֵף: כִּי תְּנַן נָמֵי בְּמַתְנִיתִין – בְּשַׁיָּירָא תְּנַן.

Rav Yosef raised an objection from the following *baraita*. **Rabbi Yehuda says:** If members of a **caravan** camped in a field wish to drink, one **person gives a barrel to another, and the other** passes it **to another.** By inference: **In a caravan, yes,** it is permitted to do so due to exigent circumstances; however, in a case **that** is **not a caravan, no,** it is prohibited. **Rather, Rav Yosef said: When we learned** the case **in the mishna as well, we learned** it with regard **to a caravan.** The Sages were lenient in the case of a caravan due to the lack of water.

אַבָּיֵי אָמַר: בְּשַׁיָּירָא – אֲפִילּוּ חָבִית שֶׁקָּנְתָה שְׁבִיתָה וּמַיִם שֶׁקָּנוּ שְׁבִיתָה. שֶׁלֹּא בְּשַׁיָּירָא – חָבִית שֶׁקָּנְתָה שְׁבִיתָה וּמַיִם שֶׁלֹּא קָנוּ שְׁבִיתָה.

Abaye said that this explanation is unnecessary: **In a caravan, even** if **the barrel acquired residence and the water acquired residence,** it is permitted to move them. If one is **not in a caravan,** if **the barrel acquired residence and the water did not acquire residence,** it is prohibited to move them.

רַב אַשִׁי אָמַר: הָכָא בְּחָבִית דְּהֶפְקֵר עָסְקִינַן, וּמַיִם דְּהֶפְקֵר עָסְקִינַן. וּמַאן אָמְרוּ לוֹ – רַבִּי יוֹחָנָן בֶּן נוּרִי הִיא, דְּאָמַר: חֶפְצֵי הֶפְקֵר קוֹנִין שְׁבִיתָה. וּמַאי לֹא תְהַלֵּךְ זוֹ יוֹתֵר מֵרַגְלֵי הַבְּעָלִים – לֹא יְהַלְּכוּ אֵלּוּ יוֹתֵר מִכֵּלִים שֶׁיֵּשׁ לָהֶם בְּעָלִים.

Rav Ashi said: Here, we are dealing with an ownerless barrel and ownerless water, neither of which acquired residence as they do not belong to anyone. **And who** is the *tanna* about whom it says in the mishna that **they said to** Rabbi Yehuda that it may not go farther than the feet of its owners may go? **It is Rabbi Yoḥanan ben Nuri,** who, consistent with his approach, **said** that **ownerless objects acquire residence** where they were located when Shabbat began, and it is prohibited to move them beyond their limit. **And what** is the meaning of the statement: **This** may **not go farther than the feet of its owners** may go, as it has no owner? It means that the barrel and water may **not go farther than vessels that have owners,** i.e., they may not be moved beyond their limit.

מתני׳ הָיָה קוֹרֵא בַּסֵּפֶר עַל הָאִיסְקוּפָּה, וְנִתְגַּלְגֵּל הַסֵּפֶר מִיָּדוֹ, גּוֹלְלוֹ אֶצְלוֹ.

MISHNA One who **was reading** a sacred **book** in scroll form on Shabbat **on** an elevated, wide **threshold,**[NH] **and the book rolled from his hand**[B] into the public domain, **he** may **roll it** back **to himself,** since one of its ends remains in his hand.

BACKGROUND

The book rolled from his hand – נִתְגַּלְגֵּל הַסֵּפֶר מִיָּדוֹ:

Person sitting on a threshold with one end of a scroll in his hand, while the other end has rolled away from him

הָיָה קוֹרֵא בְּרֹאשׁ הַגַּג וְנִתְגַּלְגֵּל הַסֵּפֶר מִיָּדוֹ, עַד שֶׁלֹּא הִגִּיעַ לַעֲשָׂרָה טְפָחִים – גּוֹלְלוֹ אֶצְלוֹ, מִשֶּׁהִגִּיעַ לַעֲשָׂרָה טְפָחִים – הוֹפְכוֹ עַל הַכְּתָב.

If he was **reading on top the roof,** which is a full-fledged private domain, **and the book rolled from his hand, as long as** the edge of the book **did not reach** within **ten handbreadths** above the public domain, the book is still in its own domain, and he may **roll it** back **to himself.** However, **once the book has reached** within **ten handbreadths** above the public domain, it is prohibited to roll the book back to oneself. In that case, **he** may only **turn it** over **onto the** side with **writing,** so that the writing of the book will be facedown and not exposed and degraded.

רַבִּי יְהוּדָה אוֹמֵר: אֲפִילּוּ אֵין מְסוּלָּק מִן הָאָרֶץ אֶלָּא כִּמְלֹא מַחַט – גּוֹלְלוֹ אֶצְלוֹ. רַבִּי שִׁמְעוֹן אוֹמֵר: אֲפִילּוּ בָּאָרֶץ עַצְמוֹ – גּוֹלְלוֹ אֶצְלוֹ, שֶׁאֵין לְךָ דָּבָר מִשּׁוּם שְׁבוּת עוֹמֵד בִּפְנֵי כִּתְבֵי הַקּוֹדֶשׁ.

Rabbi Yehuda says: Even if the scroll **is removed only a needle breadth from the ground, he rolls it** back **to himself. Rabbi Shimon says: Even if** the scroll is **on the ground itself, he rolls it** back **to himself, as you have nothing** that was instituted **as a rabbinic decree** to enhance the character of Shabbat as a day of **rest** that **stands** as an impediment **before** the rescue of **sacred writings.**

גמ׳ הַאי אִיסְקוּפָּה הֵיכִי דָּמֵי? אִילֵימָא אִיסְקוּפָּה רְשׁוּת הַיָּחִיד, וְקַמָּה רְשׁוּת הָרַבִּים, וְלָא גָּזְרִינַן דִּילְמָא נָפֵיל וְאָתֵי לְאַתּוֹיֵי,

GEMARA The Gemara questions the first clause of the mishna: **What are the circumstances of this threshold? If you say** it is referring to a **threshold** that is **a private domain, and** there is **a public domain before it, and** the mishna teaches that **we do not issue a decree lest** the entire scroll **fall** from one's hand **and he come to bring it** from a public to a private domain,

Perek **X**
Daf **98** Amud **a**

מַנִּי רַבִּי שִׁמְעוֹן הִיא, דְּאָמַר: כָּל דָּבָר שֶׁהוּא מִשּׁוּם שְׁבוּת אֵינוֹ עוֹמֵד בִּפְנֵי כִּתְבֵי הַקּוֹדֶשׁ. אֵימָא סֵיפָא, רַבִּי יְהוּדָה אוֹמֵר: אֲפִילּוּ אֵין מְסוּלָּק מִן הָאָרֶץ אֶלָּא מְלֹא הַחוּט – גּוֹלְלוֹ אֶצְלוֹ. רַבִּי שִׁמְעוֹן אוֹמֵר: אֲפִילּוּ בָּאָרֶץ עַצְמָהּ – גּוֹלְלוֹ אֶצְלוֹ.

who is the *tanna* of the mishna? **It is Rabbi Shimon, who said: Anything that** is prohibited on Shabbat and its prohibition is not by Torah law, but rather **is due to** a **rabbinic decree** issued to enhance the character of Shabbat as a day of rest **stands** as an impediment **before** the rescue of **sacred writings.** But if it is the opinion of Rabbi Shimon, **say the latter clause** of the mishna as follows: **Rabbi Yehuda says: Even if** the scroll **is removed only a needle breadth from the ground, he rolls it** back **to himself;** and **Rabbi Shimon says: Even if** the scroll is **on the ground itself, he rolls it** back **to himself.**

רֵישָׁא וְסֵיפָא רַבִּי שִׁמְעוֹן, מְצִיעֲתָא רַבִּי יְהוּדָה? אָמַר רַב יְהוּדָה: אִין, רֵישָׁא וְסֵיפָא רַבִּי שִׁמְעוֹן, מְצִיעֲתָא רַבִּי יְהוּדָה.

Is it possible that the *tanna* cited in **the first clause** of the mishna is Rabbi Shimon, as claimed above, while it is explicitly stated that **the last clause** represents the opinion of **Rabbi Shimon,**[N] and yet its **middle clause** reflects the opinion of **Rabbi Yehuda? Rav Yehuda said: Yes,** that is the correct, albeit unconventional, explanation. **The first and last clauses** are in accordance with the opinion of **Rabbi Shimon,** while **the middle clause** of the mishna reflects the opinion of **Rabbi Yehuda.**

רַבָּה אָמַר: הָכָא בְּאִיסְקוּפָּה הַנִּדְרֶסֶת עָסְקִינַן, וּמִשּׁוּם בִּזְיוֹן כִּתְבֵי הַקֹּדֶשׁ שָׁרוּ רַבָּנַן.

Rabba said that the mishna may be understood differently. **Here, we are dealing with a threshold that is trodden upon** by the public, **and due to** the potential **degradation of the sacred writings the Sages permitted** one to violate the rabbinic decree.[N] It would be disgraceful if people were to trample over sacred writings.

אֵיתִיבֵיהּ אַבָּיֵי: תּוֹךְ אַרְבַּע אַמּוֹת גּוֹלְלוֹ אֶצְלוֹ, חוּץ לְאַרְבַּע – הוֹפְכוֹ עַל הַכְּתָב. וְאִי אָמְרַתְּ בְּאִיסְקוּפָּה נִדְרֶסֶת עָסְקִינַן, מָה לִי תּוֹךְ אַרְבַּע אַמּוֹת מָה לִי חוּץ לְאַרְבַּע אַמּוֹת?

Abaye raised an objection to his explanation: It was taught that if the scroll rolled **within four cubits, he rolls it** back **to himself;** if it rolled **beyond four cubits, he turns it over onto** its **writing. And if you say we are dealing with a threshold that is trodden on** by the public, **what** difference is there **to me** whether it remained **within four cubits** and **what** difference is there **to me** if it rolled **beyond four cubits?** Since the prohibition is a rabbinic decree, not a Torah prohibition, why isn't one permitted to move the scroll in both cases to prevent the degradation of the sacred writings?

אֶלָּא אָמַר אַבָּיֵי: הָכָא בְּאִיסְקוּפָּה כַּרְמְלִית עָסְקִינַן, וּרְשׁוּת הָרַבִּים עוֹבֶרֶת לְפָנֶיהָ.

Rather, Abaye said: Here, we are dealing with a threshold that is a ***karmelit,*** as the threshold is four handbreadths wide but is less than ten handbreadths high. Furthermore, on one side of the *karmelit* there is a private domain, **and a public domain passes before it.**

NOTES

Is it possible that the *tanna* cited in the first clause is Rabbi Shimon, while it is explicitly stated that the last clause represents the opinion of Rabbi Shimon – רֵישָׁא וְסֵיפָא רַבִּי שִׁמְעוֹן: Although this question appears often in the Talmud, it bears a different meaning in this context. The question is usually raised in a case where two statements are quoted without attribution. Here, Rabbi Shimon is explicitly cited as the author of the last clause of the mishna. The Ritva explains that the difficulty here stems from the fact that Rabbi Shimon's name is omitted from the first clause.

Sacred writings and other scrolls – כִּתְבֵי הַקֹּדֶשׁ וּשְׁאָר סְפָרִים: *Tosafot* ask: If the concern is that one might carry, why is there a difference between sacred writings and other scrolls? Apparently, the Sages were lenient only with regard to sacred writings, as they distinguished between carrying four cubits and less than four cubits (Ritva).

תּוֹךְ אַרְבַּע אַמּוֹת, דְּאִי נָפֵיל וּמַיְיתִי לֵיהּ לָא אָתֵי לִידֵי חִיּוּב חַטָּאת – שָׁרוּ לֵיהּ רַבָּנַן.

The reason for the different rulings is as follows: If the scroll rolled **within four cubits,** even **if** the entire scroll **falls** out of the one's hand **and he brings it** back, **he** cannot **incur liability** to bring **a sin-offering,** as the prohibition against carrying from a public domain to a *karmelit* is a rabbinic decree. Consequently, **the Sages permitted him** to roll it back to himself, as there is no danger of transgressing a Torah prohibition.

חוּץ לְאַרְבַּע אַמּוֹת, דְּאִי מַיְיתִי לֵיהּ אָתֵי לִידֵי חִיּוּב חַטָּאת – לָא שָׁרוּ לֵיהּ רַבָּנַן.

However, if it rolled **beyond four cubits, so that if he brings it** back **he incurs liability** to bring **a sin-offering,** as carrying an object four cubits in the public domain is prohibited by Torah law, **the Sages did not permit him** to roll it back. In this case, if he forgot and carried the scroll instead of rolling it, he would be violating a severe prohibition.

אִי הָכִי, תּוֹךְ אַרְבַּע אַמּוֹת נַמִי, נִגְזַר דִּילְמָא מְעַיֵּיל מֵרְשׁוּת הָרַבִּים לִרְשׁוּת הַיָּחִיד. וְכִי תֵּימָא: כֵּיוָן דְּמַפְסֶקֶת כַּרְמְלִית לֵית לָן בָּהּ – וְהָאָמַר רָבָא: הַמַּעֲבִיר חֵפֶץ מִתְּחִלַּת אַרְבַּע לְסוֹף אַרְבַּע, וְהֶעֱבִירוֹ דֶּרֶךְ עָלָיו – חַיָּיב.

The Gemara asks: **If so, let us likewise issue a decree** in the case where the scroll remained **within four cubits, lest he bring** the scroll **in from the public domain to the private domain,** i.e., to his house. **And lest you say: Since a** ***karmelit*** **separates** the public and private domains **we have no** problem **with it,** as nothing is directly carried from one domain to the other, **didn't Rava say: One who carries an object from the beginning of four** cubits **to the end of four** cubits in the public domain, **and he carried it by way of** the airspace **above his head,**[H] he **is liable,** **even though** the object remained more than ten handbreadths off the ground and passed from the beginning to the end of four cubits by way of an exempt zone? Here, too, one should be liable for carrying the scroll from the public domain to a private domain by way of a *karmelit.*

הָכָא בְּמַאי עָסְקִינַן – בְּאִיסְקוּפָּה אֲרוּכָּה אַדְּהָכִי וְהָכִי מִידְכַּר.

The Gemara answers: **With what are we dealing here?** We are dealing **with an extended threshold.**[HN] Consequently, **in the meantime,** while he is carrying the scroll along the length of the threshold, **he will remember** not to bring it into the private domain.

וְאִיבָּעֵית אֵימָא: לְעוֹלָם בְּאִסְקוּפָּה שֶׁאֵינָהּ אֲרוּכָּה, וּסְתָם כִּתְבֵי הַקֹּדֶשׁ עִיּוּנֵי מְעַיֵּין בְּהוּ וּמַנַּח לְהוּ. וְלֵיחוּשׁ דִּילְמָא מְעַיֵּין בְּהוּ בִּרְשׁוּת הָרַבִּים, וְעָיֵיל לְהוּ בְּהֶדְיָא לִרְשׁוּת הַיָּחִיד.

And if you wish, say instead: **Actually,** it is referring **to a threshold that is not extended;** however, **ordinarily one peruses sacred writings and** then **puts them** in their place. Consequently, there is no concern that he might pass directly from the public to the private domain, as he will pause on the threshold to read the scroll. The Gemara asks: According to this explanation too, **let us be concerned lest he** pause to **peruse** the scroll **in the public domain, and** subsequently **carry it directly into the private domain** without pausing in the *karmelit.*

הָא מַנִּי בֶּן עַזַּאי הִיא, דְּאָמַר: מְהַלֵּךְ כְּעוֹמֵד דָּמֵי. וְדִילְמָא זָרֵיק לְהוּ מִזְרָק, דְּאָמַר רַבִּי יוֹחָנָן: מוֹדֶה בֶּן עַזַּאי בְּזוֹרֵק?

The Gemara answers: In accordance with **whose** opinion is **this** mishna? **It is** the opinion of **Ben Azzai, who said** that **walking is considered like standing.** Consequently, one who passes through the *karmelit* is considered to have paused and stood there. Therefore, the object was not transferred directly from the public domain to the private domain, as he paused in the *karmelit.* The Gemara asks: **But** what of the concern **lest he throw** the scrolls inside, rather than carry them by hand, **as Rabbi Yoḥanan said: Ben Azzai concedes** that **one who throws** an object from the public domain to a private domain by way of an exempt domain is liable?

אָמַר רַב אַחָא בַּר אַהֲבָה: זֹאת אוֹמֶרֶת: אֵין מְזָרְקִין כִּתְבֵי הַקּוֹדֶשׁ.

The Gemara answers that **Rav Aḥa bar Ahava said: That is to say** that **one does not throw sacred writings,**[H] as this is demeaning to them. Consequently, there is no concern that one might throw the scrolls rather than carry them by hand.

״הָיָה קוֹרֵא בְּרֹאשׁ הַגַּג וכו׳״. וּמִי שָׁרֵי? וְהָתַנְיָא: כּוֹתְבֵי סְפָרִים תְּפִילִּין וּמְזוּזוֹת לֹא הִתִּירוּ לָהֶן לַהֲפֹךְ יְרִיעָה עַל פָּנֶיהָ, אֶלָּא פּוֹרֵס עָלֶיהָ אֶת הַבֶּגֶד.

It was stated in the mishna: If **one was reading on top of the roof,**[B] which is a full-fledged private domain, and the scroll rolled from his hand, as long as the edge of the scroll did not reach ten handbreadths above the public domain, he may roll it back to himself. However, once the scroll reached within ten handbreadths above the public domain, it is prohibited to roll it back. In that case, he should turn it over, so that the writing of the scroll will be facedown and not be exposed and degraded. The Gemara asks: **And is it permitted** to do so? **Wasn't it taught** in a *baraita* that with regard to **writers of scrolls, phylacteries, and** ***mezuzot*** who interrupt their work, the Sages **did not permit them to turn the sheet** of parchment **facedown**[H] lest it become soiled? **Rather, one spreads a cloth over it** in a respectful manner.

HALAKHA

He carried it…above his head – **הֶעֱבִירוֹ דֶּרֶךְ עָלָיו**: One who carries an object four cubits in the public domain by carrying it above his head is liable, in accordance with Rava's opinion (Rambam *Sefer Zemanim, Hilkhot Shabbat* 12:14).

An extended threshold – **אִיסְקוּפָּה אֲרוּכָּה**: With regard to one who is reading a scroll while sitting on a threshold and one end of it rolls out of his hand, if the other end remains in his hand he may roll it back to himself even if it rolled beyond four cubits. This ruling is in accordance with the opinion of Rabba, as Abaye's answer with regard to a long threshold is rejected due to the fact that the Sages do not distinguish between different cases in the application of their decrees. The second resolution is based on the opinion of Ben Azzai, which is not accepted as *halakha* (Vilna Gaon). However, this ruling applies only to sacred writings, not to other scrolls (Rema, based on the Rashba). Other later commentaries rule leniently in all cases involving scrolls (*Nehar Shalom*; Vilna Gaon; *Shulḥan Arukh, Oraḥ Ḥayyim* 352:1).

One does not throw sacred writings – **אֵין מְזָרְקִין כִּתְבֵי הַקֹּדֶשׁ**: It is prohibited to throw the sacred writings that are in the Bible, and that prohibition applies to other sacred books as well (*Shulḥan Arukh, Yoreh De'a* 282:5).

Turn the sheet facedown – **לַהֲפֹךְ יְרִיעָה**: A scribe is not permitted to turn the parchment of a Torah scroll facedown onto its writing. Instead, he spreads a cloth over it. It is also prohibited to turn over other sacred writings (*Baḥ*; *Shulḥan Arukh, Yoreh De'a* 277).

NOTES

An extended threshold – **אִיסְקוּפָּה אֲרוּכָּה**: Rabbi Zeraḥya HaLevi rules that the *halakha* is not in accordance with this resolution because elsewhere the accepted *halakha* is that there is no distinction between the cases, and that the decree applies even if there is no concern that one might violate a prohibition. Other commentaries explain that since this is an unlikely circumstance, the Sages were lenient in deference to the sacred writings (*Ge'on Ya'akov*).

BACKGROUND

Reading on top of the roof – **קוֹרֵא בְּרֹאשׁ הַגַּג**: In this illustration, a scroll has rolled down from a rooftop toward the public domain along a vertical rather than inclined wall.

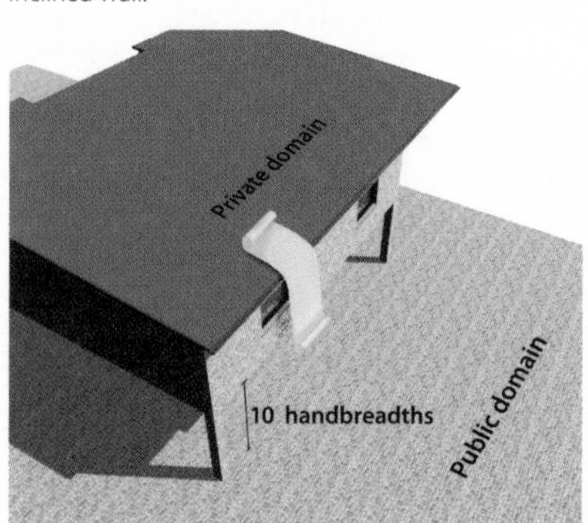

Scroll that has rolled down from a rooftop

הָתָם אֶפְשָׁר, הָכָא לָא אֶפְשָׁר. וְאִי לָא אַפֵּיךְ, אִיכָּא בִּזְיוֹן כִּתְבֵי הַקּוֹדֶשׁ טְפֵי.

The Gemara answers: **There,** with regard to scribes, **it is possible** to cover the parchment respectfully; **here, it is not possible**[N] to do so. **And if he does not turn** the scroll **over, it will be more degrading to the sacred writings.** Consequently, although this is not an ideal solution, it is preferable to turn it over rather than leave the scroll exposed.

״הוֹפְכוֹ עַל הַכְּתָב״. וְהָא לָא נָח. [אֲמַר רָבָא:] בְּכוֹתֶל מְשׁוּפָּע

The mishna states: Once the scroll has reached within ten handbreadths above the public domain, it is prohibited to roll it back to oneself, and **one turns it over onto the writing.** The Gemara asks: **But** why is this prohibited? Since the scroll **did not** come to **rest** in the public domain, rolling it back to oneself should not be prohibited. **Rava said:** This teaching is referring **to an inclined wall.** Although the scroll did not reach the ground, it came to rest within the confines of the public domain.

[אֲמַר לֵיהּ אַבַּיֵי:] בְּמַאי אוֹקֵימְתָּא לְמַתְנִיתִין – בְּכוֹתֶל מְשׁוּפָּע, אֵימָא סֵיפָא: רַבִּי יְהוּדָה אוֹמֵר: אֲפִילּוּ אֵינוֹ מְסוּלָּק מִן הָאָרֶץ אֶלָּא מְלֹא הַחוּט – גּוֹלְלוֹ אֶצְלוֹ. וְהָא נָח לֵיהּ.

Abaye said to him: In what manner **did you establish** that **the mishna** is referring **to** the case of **an inclined wall? Say the latter clause** of the mishna as follows: **Rabbi Yehuda says: Even** if the scroll **is removed only a needle breadth from the ground, he rolls it** back **to himself. But didn't** the scroll come to **rest** in the public domain? It shouldn't matter whether or not the scroll is in contact with the ground.

חַסּוּרֵי מִיחַסְּרָא וְהָכִי קָתָנֵי: בַּמֶּה דְּבָרִים אֲמוּרִים – בְּכוֹתֶל מְשׁוּפָּע, אֲבָל

The Gemara answers: The mishna **is incomplete and is teaching the following: In what** case **is this statement said?** It is said **in the** case of **an inclined wall. However,**

NOTES

Here it is not possible – הָכָא לָא אֶפְשָׁר: Rashi explains that it is not possible because there is no large cloth available with which to cover it. The Ritva explains that covering the scroll is not an option, as one may not place a cloth on the scroll if the scroll itself was unintentionally rolled to a location where it may not be placed.

Perek **X**
Daf **98** Amud **b**

בְּכוֹתֶל שֶׁאֵינוֹ מְשׁוּפָּע, לְמַעְלָה מִשְּׁלֹשָׁה – גּוֹלְלוֹ אֶצְלוֹ, לְמַטָּה מִשְּׁלֹשָׁה – הוֹפְכוֹ עַל הַכְּתָב.

with regard to a wall that is not inclined, the following distinction applies: If the end of the scroll is **three** handbreadths **above** the ground, **he** may **roll it** back **to himself;** but if it is **below three** handbreadths from the ground, it is considered as though the scroll is on the ground, and **he must** therefore **turn it** facedown **onto the writing.**

״רַבִּי יְהוּדָה אוֹמֵר אֲפִילּוּ אֵינוֹ מְסוּלָּק מִן הָאָרֶץ וכו׳״. דְּבָעֵינַן הַנָּחָה עַל גַּבֵּי מַשֶּׁהוּ.

It was stated in the mishna that **Rabbi Yehuda says: Even** if the scroll **is removed only** a needle breadth **from the ground,** one rolls it back to himself. The Gemara explains: Rabbi Yehuda maintains **that** in order for an object to be deemed at rest, **we require** that it **rest atop something.** Consequently, a scroll that is not actually touching the ground is not considered resting and may be rolled back.

וְאֶלָּא הָא דְּאָמַר רָבָא: תּוֹךְ שְׁלֹשָׁה לְרַבָּנַן צָרִיךְ הַנָּחָה, לֵימָא כְּתַנָּאֵי אֲמָרָהּ לִשְׁמַעְתֵּיהּ?

The Gemara asks: **But** consider **that** which **Rava said** with regard to an object located **within three** handbreadths of the ground.[H] Rava said that according **to** the opinion of **the Rabbis,** who disagree with Rabbi Akiva and claim that something in the air is not considered to be at rest, nevertheless, for one to incur liability **it is necessary** for the object to **rest** on a surface. **Let us say** that **he stated his *halakha* in accordance with** only one of **the *tanna'im*,**[N] but not in accordance with all of them. This is an unacceptable conclusion.

אֶלָּא כּוּלָּהּ רַבִּי יְהוּדָה הִיא, וְחַסּוּרֵי מִיחַסְּרָא, וְהָכִי קָתָנֵי: בַּמֶּה דְּבָרִים אֲמוּרִים – בְּכוֹתֶל מְשׁוּפָּע, אֲבָל בְּכוֹתֶל שֶׁאֵינוֹ מְשׁוּפָּע – אֲפִילּוּ פָּחוֹת מִשְּׁלֹשָׁה טְפָחִים גּוֹלְלוֹ אֶצְלוֹ. שֶׁרַבִּי יְהוּדָה אוֹמֵר: אֲפִילּוּ אֵינוֹ מְסוּלָּק מִן הָאָרֶץ אֶלָּא מְלֹא הַחוּט – גּוֹלְלוֹ אֶצְלוֹ.

Rather, the Gemara rejects the previous explanation in favor of the following one: The mishna **is all** in accordance with **Rabbi Yehuda, and it is incomplete and is teaching** the following: **In what** case **is this statement** that once the end of the scroll is within ten handbreadths of the ground it may not be rolled back **said?** It was said in the case of **an inclined wall.**[H] **But with regard to a wall that is not inclined, even** if the end of the scroll is **less than three handbreadths** from the ground, **one** may **roll it** back **to himself, as Rabbi Yehuda says: Even** if the scroll **is removed only a needle breadth from the ground, he rolls it** back **to himself.**

HALAKHA

Placement within three handbreadths – הֲנָחָה תּוֹךְ שְׁלֹשָׁה: For an object to be considered at rest with regard to the *halakhot* of Shabbat, it must rest atop a surface. This requirement applies even if it is hanging within three handbreadths of the ground, in accordance with the opinion of Rava (Rambam *Sefer Zemanim*, *Hilkhot Shabbat* 13:16).

An inclined wall – כּוֹתֶל מְשׁוּפָּע: If one end of a scroll rolls off a roof and rests on the incline of a wall ten handbreadths above the ground, it is permitted to roll it back. If it is less than ten handbreadths off the ground, one must turn it facedown (*Shulḥan Arukh*, *Oraḥ Ḥayyim* 352:2).

NOTES

Let us say he stated his *halakha* in accordance with one of the *tanna'im* – לֵימָא כְּתַנָּאֵי אֲמָרָהּ לִשְׁמַעְתֵּיהּ: This expression bears an unusual meaning in this context. In this case, it is clear that this matter is indeed a tannaitic dispute. However, according to the first presentation of the issue, Rava's opinion is a minority opinion contrary to the majority opinion. After the Gemara implements several corrections, Rava's statement is taken to mean that there is no dispute in the mishna, as the Rabbis did not disagree with Rabbi Yehuda with regard to this principle (Ritva).

NOTES

Fragile utensils – כֵּלִים הַנִּשְׁבָּרִים: Another reason that it is permitted to place fragile utensils on a ledge is that a person is very careful that they should not fall. Consequently, there is no concern that one might carry them out into the public domain (Rabbeinu Yehonatan).

Two ledges – שְׁנֵי זִיזִים: The Gemara does not explain why the ruling with regard to two ledges is more stringent than the ruling with regard to one ledge. The Rambam and other commentaries explain that in this case one domain renders the other prohibited. If the lower and upper ledges are each four by four handbreadths in size, each owner of a ledge retains his own domain, provided that the two ledges are not too close to each other (see *Ge'on Ya'akov*). However, if the lower ledge is four by four handbreadths , while the upper one is smaller, the entire domain of the wall up to the sky belongs to the owner of the lower ledge, and the upper ledge may not be used (Rashba). The Rambam rules differently, but it is unclear whether he does so due to a different reading of the text, or because he does not distinguish between these cases.

BACKGROUND

A ledge in front of a window – זִיז שֶׁלִּפְנֵי הַחַלּוֹן: The *ge'onim* define the difference between a ledge and a balcony as follows: A balcony is an outwardly protruding section of a house, with walls, while a ledge is a protrusion from a house, beneath which there are partitions.

Window with a ledge in front of it

LANGUAGE

Small cups [*kitoniyot*] – קִיתוֹנִיּוֹת: From the Greek κώθων, *kothon*, meaning earthenware drinking vessel.

מַאי טַעְמָא – דְּבָעֵינַן הֲנָחָה עַל גַּבֵּי מַשֶּׁהוּ.

What is the reason for this ruling? The reasoning is that for an object to be considered at rest, **we require** that it **rest atop some** surface. Consequently, if the scroll is not actually touching the ground, it is not considered at rest, even if it is less than three handbreadths from the ground.

מתני׳ זִיז שֶׁלִּפְנֵי חַלּוֹן – נוֹתְנִין עָלָיו וְנוֹטְלִין מִמֶּנּוּ בְּשַׁבָּת.

MISHNA With regard to **a ledge in front of a window,** that is ten handbreadths high and four handbreadths wide, **one** may **place** objects **upon it or remove** them **from it on Shabbat** via the window.

גמ׳ הַאי זִיז דְּמַפֵּיק לְהֵיכָא? אִילֵימָא דְּמַפֵּיק לִרְשׁוּת הָרַבִּים – לֵיחוּשׁ דִּילְמָא נָפֵיל, וְאָתֵי לְאֵיתוּיֵי! אֶלָּא דְּמַפֵּיק לִרְשׁוּת הַיָּחִיד – פְּשִׁיטָא!

GEMARA The Gemara clarifies: **This ledge, to where does it protrude? If you say** that the ledge **protrudes into a public domain,** one should be prohibited to place an object on it, as **we should be concerned lest** the object **fall and he** will forget and **come to bring it in** from the public domain to a private domain. **Rather,** it must be **that** the ledge **protrudes into a private domain;** but if so, it is **obvious** that it is permitted to place objects on it and to remove them.

אָמַר אַבַּיֵי: לְעוֹלָם דְּמַפֵּיק לִרְשׁוּת הָרַבִּים, וּמַאי נוֹתְנִין עָלָיו דְּקָתָנֵי – כֵּלִים הַנִּשְׁבָּרִים.

Abaye said: Actually, the mishna is dealing with a case **where it protrudes into a public domain, and what** is the meaning of **that** which **it teaches: One** may **place** objects **upon it?** This refers to **fragile utensils,**[N] which would break instantly if they fell. Consequently, there is no concern that one might then bring them in from the public domain to the private domain.

תַּנְיָא נַמִי הָכִי: זִיז שֶׁלִּפְנֵי הַחַלּוֹן הַיּוֹצֵא לִרְשׁוּת הָרַבִּים – נוֹתְנִין עָלָיו קְעָרוֹת וְכוֹסוֹת קִיתוֹנִיּוֹת וּצְלוֹחִיּוֹת.

The Gemara comments: **That was also taught** in a *baraita*: With regard to **a ledge in front of a window**[BH] **that protrudes into a public domain, one** may **place on it bowls, cups, small cups [*kitoniyot*],**[L] **and saucers.** All of these utensils are made of fragile glass or earthenware, which supports Abaye's opinion.

וּמִשְׁתַּמֵּשׁ בְּכָל הַכּוֹתֶל עַד עֲשָׂרָה הַתַּחְתּוֹנִים. וְאִם יֵשׁ זִיז אַחֵר לְמַטָּה מִמֶּנּוּ מִשְׁתַּמֵּשׁ בּוֹ, וּבָעֶלְיוֹן אֵין מִשְׁתַּמֵּשׁ בּוֹ אֶלָּא כְּנֶגֶד חַלּוֹנוֹ.

The *baraita* continues: **And one** may **use** this ledge along the **entire** length of **the wall,** if the ledge spans its length, whether in close proximity to the window or removed from it, **until the lower ten** handbreadths of the wall, but not if the ledge is lower than that. **And if there is one** other **ledge below it** but still ten handbreadths above the ground, **one** may **use** the lower ledge along the entire length of the wall; **but with regard to the upper** ledge, **one** may **use it only opposite his window.**[NH]

הַאי זִיז הֵיכִי דָּמֵי אִי דְּלֵית בֵּיהּ אַרְבָּעָה מָקוֹם פָּטוּר הוּא, וַאֲפִילּוּ כְּנֶגֶד חַלּוֹנוֹ נַמִי לֹא יִשְׁתַּמֵּשׁ. וְאִי אִית בֵּיהּ אַרְבָּעָה – בְּכוּלֵּי הַכּוֹתֶל לִישְׁתַּמֵּשׁ!

The Gemara asks: **This** upper **ledge, what are its circumstances? If it is not four** handbreadths deep, although **it is an exempt domain** with regard to the *halakhot* of Shabbat, which means it does not pose a problem in itself, **one should** nonetheless **not** be permitted to **use** it **even opposite his window,** as anything placed on this narrow ledge is likely to fall. Consequently, it is as though he has thrown the object directly to the ground. **And if it is four** handbreadths deep, **let him use** the ledge along the **entire** length of the ledge along **the wall.**

אָמַר אַבַּיֵי: תַּחְתּוֹן – דְּאִית בֵּיהּ אַרְבָּעָה, וְעֶלְיוֹן – לֵית בֵּיהּ אַרְבָּעָה, וְחַלּוֹן מַשְׁלִימָתוֹ לְאַרְבָּעָה. כְּנֶגֶד חַלּוֹן – מִשְׁתַּמֵּשׁ, דְּחוֹרֵי חַלּוֹן הוּא, דְּהַאי גִּיסָא וּדְהַאי גִּיסָא – אָסוּר.

Abaye said: We are dealing with a case where **the lower** ledge **is four** handbreadths deep **and the upper** ledge **is not four** handbreadths deep, but the **windowsill** on the inside **completes it to** form a surface **four** handbreadths deep. Accordingly, **one** may **use** the part of the upper ledge **opposite the window, as it is** considered **an extension of the window,** but the parts **to this side or to that side** of the window are **prohibited,** as they are less than four handbreadths deep.

HALAKHA

A ledge in front of a window – זִיז שֶׁלִּפְנֵי חַלּוֹן: One may place fragile utensils on a window ledge four by four handbreadths in size (Rashi). According to the Rambam, one may do so even if the ledge is less than four by four handbreadths, provided that it protrudes from a wall ten handbreadths above the public domain, as stated in the mishna, in accordance with Abaye's explanation (*Shulḥan Arukh, Oraḥ Ḥayyim* 353:2).

Two ledges – שְׁנֵי זִיזִים: With regard to two window ledges owned by different people on the same wall, if the upper ledge is four by four handbreadths, the lower ledge serves to render the use of the upper ledge prohibited to its owner, even if it is smaller than four by four handbreadths (*Magen Avraham, Oraḥ Ḥayyim* 353:2, based on the *Maggid Mishne* on Rambam *Sefer Zemanim, Hilkhot Shabbat* 15:4). However, if both ledges are smaller than four by four handbreadths in size, both may be used. If the lower ledge is four by four handbreadths and the upper one is less than four by four handbreadths, one may use only the section of the upper one that is opposite his window, as stated by Abaye (*Shulḥan Arukh, Oraḥ Ḥayyim* 353:2).

מתני׳ עוֹמֵד אָדָם בִּרְשׁוּת הַיָּחִיד וּמְטַלְטֵל בִּרְשׁוּת הָרַבִּים, בִּרְשׁוּת הָרַבִּים וּמְטַלְטֵל בִּרְשׁוּת הַיָּחִיד, וּבִלְבַד שֶׁלֹּא יוֹצִיא חוּץ מֵאַרְבַּע אַמּוֹת.

MISHNA A person may **stand in a private domain and move** objects that are **in a public domain,** as there is no concern that he might mistakenly bring them into the private domain. Similarly, one may stand **in a public domain and move** objects **in a private domain, provided that he does not carry** them **beyond four cubits** in the public domain, which is prohibited on Shabbat.[H]

לֹא יַעֲמוֹד אָדָם בִּרְשׁוּת הַיָּחִיד וְיַשְׁתִּין בִּרְשׁוּת הָרַבִּים, בִּרְשׁוּת הָרַבִּים וְיַשְׁתִּין בִּרְשׁוּת הַיָּחִיד, וְכֵן לֹא יָרוֹק.

However, **a person** may **not stand in a private domain and urinate into a public domain,** nor may one stand **in a public domain and urinate into a private domain. And likewise, one** may **not spit** in such a manner that the spittle passes from a private domain to a public domain or vice versa.[H]

רַבִּי יְהוּדָה אוֹמֵר: אַף מִשֶּׁנִּתְלַשׁ רוּקּוֹ בְּפִיו לֹא יְהַלֵּךְ אַרְבַּע אַמּוֹת, עַד שֶׁיָּרוֹק.

Rabbi Yehuda says: Even once a person's **spittle is gathered in his mouth,**[H] **he** may **not walk four cubits** in the public domain **until he spits** it out, for he would be carrying the accumulated spittle in his mouth, which is akin to carrying any other object.

גמ׳ מַתְנֵי לֵיהּ רַב חִינָּנָא בַּר שְׁלֶמְיָא לְחִיָּיא בַּר רַב קַמֵּיהּ דְּרַב: לֹא יַעֲמוֹד אָדָם בִּרְשׁוּת הַיָּחִיד וּמְטַלְטֵל בִּרְשׁוּת הָרַבִּים. אֲמַר לֵיהּ: שְׁבַקְתְּ רַבָּנַן וַעֲבַדְתְּ כְּרַבִּי מֵאִיר!

GEMARA **Rav Ḥinnana bar Shelamiya would teach** this mishna **to Ḥiyya bar Rav before Rav** as follows: **A person** may **not stand in a private domain and move** objects that are **in a public domain. Rav said to him:** Have **you abandoned** the majority opinion of **the Rabbis**[N] **and followed** the solitary dissenting opinion of **Rabbi Meir,** who is stringent in this regard?

HALAKHA

Moving objects in a different domain – טִלְטוּל בִּרְשׁוּת אַחֶרֶת: One may stand in one domain and move objects that are in another domain, provided that he does not carry them four cubits in the public domain. However, one may not move any objects he needs, as he might inadvertently draw them to him. According to the Rambam, one is permitted to stand in one domain and move even utensils he needs, with the exception of utensils used for drinking, in another domain (*Shulḥan Arukh, Oraḥ Ḥayyim* 350:1).

Spitting into a different domain – יְרִיקָה לִרְשׁוּת אַחֶרֶת: It is prohibited to stand in a public domain and spit or urinate into a private domain or vice versa. The same *halakha* applies to a *karmelit* (Rosh; *Shulḥan Arukh, Oraḥ Ḥayyim* 350:2).

Once a person's spittle is gathered in his mouth – מִשֶּׁנִּתְלַשׁ רוּקּוֹ בְּפִיו: Once a person has gathered spittle in his mouth, he may not walk four cubits in the public domain or move from one domain to another until after removing the spittle, as the Rabbis did not disagree with Rabbi Yehuda in this regard (*Tur*). The later commentaries rule likewise (*Eliya Rabba*; *Shulḥan Arukh, Oraḥ Ḥayyim* 350:3).

NOTES

Have you abandoned the Rabbis – שְׁבַקְתְּ רַבָּנַן: The Ritva explains that Rav Ḥinnana bar Shelamiya sought to be more stringent than the basic *halakha* of the mishna. Rav replied that this stringency itself is a matter of dispute between *tanna'im*, and the *halakha* is not in accordance with the stringent ruling.

Perek **X**
Daf **99** Amud **a**

הוּא סָבַר: מִדְּסֵיפָא רַבִּי מֵאִיר – רֵישָׁא נַמִי רַבִּי מֵאִיר, וְלָא הִיא: סֵיפָא רַבִּי מֵאִיר, וְרֵישָׁא רַבָּנַן.

The Gemara explains: Rav Ḥinnana **maintains that from the** fact that **the latter clause** of the mishna, was taught in accordance with the opinion of **Rabbi Meir,** it can be inferred that **the first clause** was **likewise** taught in accordance with the opinion of **Rabbi Meir. But** in fact **that is not so: The latter clause** is in accordance with the opinion of **Rabbi Meir, while the first clause** is in accordance with that of **the Rabbis.**

״וּבִלְבַד שֶׁלֹּא יוֹצִיא חוּץ״. הָא הוֹצִיא – חַיָּיב חַטָּאת. לֵימָא מְסַיַּיע לֵיהּ לְרָבָא, דְּאָמַר רָבָא: הַמַּעֲבִיר חֵפֶץ מִתְּחִילַּת אַרְבַּע לְסוֹף אַרְבַּע, וְהֶעֱבִירוֹ דֶּרֶךְ עָלָיו – חַיָּיב.

We learned in the mishna: One may move objects in a public domain when he is standing in a private domain, **provided that he does not carry** them **beyond** four cubits in the public domain. The Gemara infers: This teaching indicates that if **he carried** them beyond four cubits, **he is liable** to bring **a sin-offering.** The Gemara asks: **Let us say** that **this** ruling **supports** the opinion of **Rava, as Rava said:** With regard to **one who carries an object** in a public domain **from the beginning of four** cubits **to the end of** those **four** cubits, even if he **carried it above his head,** i.e., he lifted the object above his head so that it passed through an exempt place, **he is** nonetheless **liable** for carrying four cubits in a public domain. Here, too, although he is standing in an elevated private domain and carries the object at that elevated height, he is still liable.

מִי קָתָנֵי ״אִם הוֹצִיא חַיָּיב חַטָּאת״, דִּילְמָא, אִם הוֹצִיא – פָּטוּר אֲבָל אָסוּר.

The Gemara rejects this contention: **Is** the mishna **teaching** that **if he carried** the object beyond four cubits **he is liable** to bring **a sin-offering? Perhaps** the mishna means: **If he carried** the object beyond four cubits, he is **exempt** from bringing a sin-offering, **but it is** nevertheless **prohibited** by rabbinic decree to do so.

אִיכָּא דְּאָמְרִי: הָא הוֹצִיא – פָּטוּר אֲבָל אָסוּר. לֵימָא תֶּיהֱוֵי תְּיוּבְתֵּיהּ דְּרָבָא, דְּאָמַר רָבָא: הַמַּעֲבִיר מִתְּחִילַּת אַרְבַּע לְסוֹף אַרְבַּע וְהֶעֱבִירוֹ דֶּרֶךְ עָלָיו – חַיָּיב! מִי קָתָנֵי, "הוֹצִיא פָּטוּר אֲבָל אָסוּר"? דִּילְמָא: אִם הוֹצִיא – חַיָּיב חַטָּאת.

Some say a different version of the previous discussion: The Gemara's initial inference was actually that if **he carried** the object beyond four cubits he is **exempt** from bringing a sin-offering, **but it is prohibited** by rabbinic decree to do so. The Gemara asks: If so, **let us say** that this **is a conclusive refutation of Rava's** opinion, **as Rava said:** With regard to **one who carries** an object in a public domain **from the beginning of four** cubits **to the end of** those **four** cubits, even if he **carried it above his head, he is liable.** The Gemara rejects this suggestion: **Is** the mishna **teaching** that **if he took** it beyond four cubits he is **exempt, but it is prohibited** to do so? **Perhaps** the *tanna* means that **if he carried** it beyond four cubits, he is **liable** to bring **a sin-offering.**

"לֹא יַעֲמוֹד אָדָם בִּרְשׁוּת הַיָּחִיד וכו'" אָמַר רַב יוֹסֵף: הִשְׁתִּין וְרָק – חַיָּיב חַטָּאת.

The mishna states: **A person** may **not stand in a private domain** and urinate or spit into the public domain. **Rav Yosef said: One who urinated or spat** in this manner is **liable** to bring **a sin-offering.**[NH]

וְהָא בָּעֵינַן עֲקִירָה וְהַנָּחָה מֵעַל גַּבֵּי מְקוֹם אַרְבָּעָה, וְלֵיכָּא!

The Gemara raises a difficulty: **But** for an act of carrying to be considered a prohibited Shabbat labor that entails liability, **we require** that the **lifting and placing** of the object be performed **from atop an area four** by four handbreadths, the minimal size of significance with regard to the *halakhot* of carrying on Shabbat. **And** that is **not** the case here, as one's mouth, which produces the spittle, is not four by four handbreadths in size.

מַחְשַׁבְתּוֹ מְשַׁוְיָא לֵיהּ מָקוֹם. דְּאִי לָא תֵּימָא הָכִי, הָא דְּאָמַר רָבָא: זָרַק וְנָח בְּפִי הַכֶּלֶב אוֹ בְּפִי הַכִּבְשָׁן – חַיָּיב חַטָּאת. וְהָא בָּעֵינַן הַנָּחָה עַל גַּבֵּי מְקוֹם אַרְבָּעָה – וְלֵיכָּא!

The Gemara answers: One's **intent renders it an area**[N] of significance, i.e., as one certainly considers his mouth a significant area, it is regarded as four by four handbreadths in size. **As, if you do not say so,** that the size of an area is not the sole criterion, but that a person's thoughts can also establish a place as significant, there is a difficulty with **that** which **Rava said:** If **a person threw** an object **and it landed in the mouth of a dog**[H] **or in the mouth of a furnace,** he is **liable** to bring a **sin-offering. But don't we require** that the object be **placed on an area of four** by four handbreadths? **And** that is **not** the case here.

אֶלָּא: מַחְשַׁבְתּוֹ מְשַׁוְיָא לֵיהּ מָקוֹם, הָכִי נַמִי מַחֲשָׁבָה מְשַׁוְיָא לָהּ מָקוֹם.

Rather, the person's **intent** to throw the object into the dog's mouth **renders it an area** of significance. **Here too, his intent renders** his own mouth a significant **area.**

בָּעֵי רָבָא: הוּא בִּרְשׁוּת הַיָּחִיד, וּפִי אַמָּה בִּרְשׁוּת הָרַבִּים מַהוּ? בָּתַר עֲקִירָה אָזְלִינַן, אוֹ בָּתַר יְצִיאָה אָזְלִינַן? תֵּיקוּ.

Rava raised a dilemma: If **one** is standing **in a private domain, and the opening of his** male **member is in the public domain,**[H] and he urinates, **what is** the *halakha*? How should this case be regarded? Do **we follow** the domain where the urine is **uprooted** from the body, i.e., the bladder, which is in the private domain? **Or do we follow the** point of the urine's actual **emission** from the body, and since the urine leaves his body through the opening of his member in the public domain, no prohibition has been violated? Since this dilemma was not resolved, the Gemara concludes: **Let it stand** unresolved.

"וְכֵן לֹא יָרוֹק. רַבִּי יְהוּדָה אוֹמֵר" וכו'. אַף עַל גַּב דְּלָא הָפֵיךְ בָּהּ?

The mishna states: **And likewise, one** may **not spit** from one domain to another. **Rabbi Yehuda says:** Once a person's spittle is gathered in his mouth, he may not walk four cubits in the public domain until he removes it. The Gemara asks: Does this teaching mean that it is prohibited to do so **even if he has not turned** the spittle **over** in his mouth,[H] i.e., after he has dredged up the saliva but before he has rolled it around in his mouth in preparation to spit it out?

וְהָתְנַן: הָיָה אוֹכֵל דְּבֵילָה בְּיָדַיִם מְסוֹאָבוֹת, וְהִכְנִיס יָדוֹ לְתוֹךְ פִּיו לִיטּוֹל צְרוֹר, רַבִּי מֵאִיר מְטַמֵּא,

Didn't we learn in a mishna the *halakha* of one who **was eating a dried fig** of *teruma* **with unwashed hands?** By Torah law, only food that has come into contact with a liquid is susceptible to ritual impurity, and no liquid had ever fallen on this fig. The significance of the fact that his hands are unwashed is that by rabbinic law, unwashed hands have second degree ritually impurity status and therefore invalidate *teruma*. If this person **inserted his hand into his mouth to remove a pebble, Rabbi Meir deems** the dried fig **impure,** as it had been rendered liable to contract impurity by the spittle in the person's mouth, and it subsequently became impure when it was touched by his unwashed hand.

NOTES

One who urinated or spat is liable to bring a sin-offering – הִשְׁתִּין וְרָק חַיָּיב חַטָּאת: This issue also depends on the tannaitic dispute with regard to a prohibited labor performed on Shabbat not for its own sake. In this case, one who spits into a different domain does not specifically desire that spittle come to rest in a particular spot, merely that it should leave his mouth. The Ritva states that those who maintain that one is exempt for a prohibited labor performed on Shabbat not for its own sake would apply the same ruling in this case as well.

One's intent renders it an area – מַחְשַׁבְתּוֹ מְשַׁוְיָא לֵיהּ מָקוֹם: The Rosh explains that the principle that his intent renders it an area of significance applies only if he has a particular reason why the object should be uprooted from an area less than four by four handbreadths in size, or why it should come to rest in an area of that size. However, intent alone cannot establish an area as being one of significance.

HALAKHA

Spitting from one domain to another – רָק מֵרְשׁוּת לִרְשׁוּת: One who stands in a private domain and spits or urinates into a public domain, or vice versa, is liable to bring a sin-offering, in accordance with the opinion of Rav Yosef (Rambam *Sefer Zemanim*, *Hilkhot Shabbat* 13:3).

Landed in the mouth of a dog – נָח בְּפִי הַכֶּלֶב: If one throws an object from a private domain, intending it to land in a dog's mouth or in the mouth of a furnace in a public domain, he is liable to bring a sin-offering if his intent is fulfilled (Rambam *Sefer Zemanim*, *Hilkhot Shabbat* 13:13).

The opening of his member is in a different domain – פִּי אַמָּה בִּרְשׁוּת אַחֶרֶת: If one is standing in one domain while the opening of his member is in a different domain, and he urinates, he is exempt from bringing a sin-offering; however, it is prohibited to do so, as this question was left unresolved by the Gemara (Rambam *Sefer Zemanim*, *Hilkhot Shabbat* 13:3).

Spittle that he turned over – רוֹק שֶׁהֲפַךְ בּוֹ: If one inserts a ritually impure hand into his mouth, and touches food that is not susceptible to contract ritual impurity, and there is spittle in his mouth that he had turned over, the food is rendered liable to become ritual impure by the spittle, and is subsequently rendered impure by his hands. However, if he had not turned the spittle over in his mouth, the food remains ritually pure, in accordance with the opinion of Rabbi Yehuda (Rambam *Sefer Tahara*, *Hilkhot Tumat Okhalin* 15:7).

As spittle that has not been turned over is not considered detached from one's mouth, the prohibition against spitting into a different domain on Shabbat is applied only to spittle that one has turned over in his mouth (*Shulḥan Arukh*, *Oraḥ Ḥayyim* 350:3).

וְרַבִּי יוֹסֵי מְטַהֵר. רַבִּי יְהוּדָה אוֹמֵר: הִיפֵּךְ בָּהּ – טָמֵא, לֹא הִיפֵּךְ בָּהּ – טָהוֹר!

And Rabbi Yosei deems the fig **ritually pure,** as he maintains that spittle which is still in one's mouth is not considered liquid that renders food liable to contract impurity; the spittle does so only after it has left the mouth. **Rabbi Yehuda says** that there is a distinction between the cases: If **he turned** the spittle **over** in his mouth, it is like spittle that has been detached from its place, and it therefore its legal status is that of a liquid, which means the fig is **impure.** However, if **he** had **not** yet **turned** the spittle **over** in his mouth, the fig is **pure.** This indicates that according to Rabbi Yehuda, spittle that has not yet been turned over in one's mouth is not considered detached.

אָמַר רַבִּי יוֹחָנָן: מוּחְלֶפֶת הַשִּׁיטָה.

Rabbi Yoḥanan said: The attribution of the **opinions is reversed,** as the opinion attributed to Rabbi Yehuda is actually that of a different *tanna*, while Rabbi Yehuda himself maintains that the fig is ritually impure in either case.

רֵישׁ לָקִישׁ אָמַר: לְעוֹלָם לֹא תַּחֲלִיף, וְהָכָא בְּמַאי עָסְקִינַן – בְּכִיחוֹ.

Reish Lakish said: Actually, do not reverse the opinions, **and** the apparent contradiction can be reconciled in accordance with the original version of the text: **With what we are dealing here** in the mishna? We are dealing **with his phlegm** that is expelled through coughing.

וְהָתַנְיָא, רַבִּי יְהוּדָה אוֹמֵר: כִּיחוֹ וְנִתְלַשׁ. מַאי לָאו – רוֹק וְנִתְלַשׁ! לֹא, כִּיחוֹ וְנִתְלַשׁ. וְהָא תַּנְיָא רַבִּי יְהוּדָה אוֹמֵר: כִּיחוֹ שֶׁנִּתְלַשׁ, וְכֵן רוּקּוֹ שֶׁנִּתְלַשׁ, לֹא יְהַלֵּךְ אַרְבַּע אַמּוֹת עַד שֶׁיָּרוֹק! אֶלָּא מְחַוַּורְתָּא כִּדְשַׁנֵּינַן מֵעִיקָּרָא.

The Gemara raises a difficulty against this resolution. **Wasn't it taught** in a *baraita* that **Rabbi Yehuda says: If one's phlegm was detached,** he may not walk four cubits in the public domain with it in his mouth? **What, is it not** the case that this *halakha* refers to **spittle that was detached?** The Gemara rejects this contention: **No,** this ruling applies only to **one's phlegm that was detached.** The Gemara raises a difficulty: **Wasn't it taught** in a *baraita* that **Rabbi Yehuda says: If one's phlegm was detached, and likewise,** if **his spittle was detached, he** may **not walk four cubits** in the public domain **before he spits** it out, even if he has not yet turned it over. **Rather, it is clear as we originally answered,** that the opinions in the mishna with regard to spittle and ritual impurity must be reversed.

אָמַר רֵישׁ לָקִישׁ: כִּיחַ בִּפְנֵי רַבּוֹ חַיָּיב מִיתָה, שֶׁנֶּאֱמַר: "כׇּל מְשַׂנְאַי אָהֲבוּ מָוֶת", אַל תִּקְרֵי "לִמְשַׂנְאַי" אֶלָּא "לְמַשְׂנִיאַי".

Having mentioned phlegm, the Gemara cites a related teaching: **Reish Lakish said:** One who expelled **phlegm in front of his master** has acted in a disrespectful manner and is **liable for** the punishment of **death** at the hand of Heaven,[H] **as it is stated: "All they who hate Me[N] love death"** (Proverbs 8:36). **Do not read it** as: **"They who hate** [*mesanai*] **Me"; rather,** read it as: **"Those who make themselves hateful** [*masniai*] **to Me,"** i.e., those who make themselves hateful by such a discharge.

וְהָא מֵינַס אָנֵיס! כִּיחַ וָרָק קָאָמְרִינַן.

The Gemara expresses surprise at this ruling: **But doesn't he** do so **involuntarily,** as no one coughs and emits phlegm by choice; why should this be considered a transgression? The Gemara answers: **We are speaking** here of someone who had **phlegm** in his mouth **and spat** it out, i.e., one who had the opportunity to leave his master's presence and spit outside.

מתני׳ לֹא יַעֲמוֹד אָדָם בִּרְשׁוּת הַיָּחִיד וְיִשְׁתֶּה בִּרְשׁוּת הָרַבִּים, בִּרְשׁוּת הָרַבִּים וְיִשְׁתֶּה בִּרְשׁוּת הַיָּחִיד, אֶלָּא אִם כֵּן הִכְנִיס רֹאשׁוֹ וְרוּבּוֹ לַמָּקוֹם שֶׁהוּא שׁוֹתֶה. וְכֵן בְּגַת.

MISHNA A person may **stand in a private domain** and extend his head **and drink in a public domain,** and he may stand **in a public domain and drink in a private domain,**[H] **only if he brings his head and most of his** body **into the domain** in which he drinks. **And the same** applies **in a winepress,** as will be explained in the Gemara.

גמ׳ רֵישָׁא רַבָּנַן וְסֵיפָא רַבִּי מֵאִיר!

GEMARA The Gemara registers surprise at the mishna: It would seem that **the first clause,** i.e., the previous mishna, is in accordance with the opinion of **the Rabbis,** who maintain that a person located in one domain is permitted to move objects in another domain, **whereas the latter clause,** i.e., this mishna, is in accordance with the opinion of **Rabbi Meir,** who maintains that it is prohibited for a person in one domain to move objects in a different domain.

אָמַר רַב יוֹסֵף: בַּחֲפֵיצִין שֶׁצְּרִיכִין לוֹ, וְדִבְרֵי הַכֹּל.

Rav Yosef said: This mishna is referring **to objects that one needs,**[N] **and** the ruling is accepted by **all.** In this case, even the Rabbis concede that it is prohibited to move objects in another domain, lest one absent-mindedly draw the objects to him and thereby violate a Torah prohibition.

HALAKHA

One who expelled phlegm and spittle in front of his master – כִּחַ וְרָק בִּפְנֵי רַבּוֹ: One who expectorates phlegm or spittle in front of his master is considered to have acted in a disrespectful manner and will be punished by Heaven. For the same reason, one must be careful not to expel phlegm or spittle during prayer (*Shulḥan Arukh, Yoreh De'a* 242:29).

Drinking in a different domain – לִשְׁתּוֹת בִּרְשׁוּת אַחֶרֶת: It is prohibited for one to stand in a private domain and drink in a public domain or vice versa, as he might draw the water to him (Rashi). The Rambam maintains that this *halakha* applies only if he drinks from quality utensils. The *Mishna Berura*, based on *Eliya Rabba*, rules in accordance with the first opinion that it is always prohibited (*Shulḥan Arukh, Oraḥ Ḥayyim* 350:1).

NOTES

All they who hate Me – כׇּל מְשַׂנְאַי: According to the interpretation of Reish Lakish, the verse does not refer to those who hate God or to those who are hated by Him. Rather, it speaks of those who cause people to hate Him, i.e., those who desecrate the name of Heaven. This idea is applied to scholars who act or dress inappropriately, as such behavior leads others to disrespect the Torah. In this case, it refers to those who make themselves hateful to their masters, as the fear of one's master should be like the fear of Heaven.

Objects that one needs – חֲפֵיצִין הַצְּרִיכִין לוֹ: According to Rashi, anything a person requires, including water, is included in the category of objects that he needs. However, the Rambam maintains that only especially attractive utensils are considered objects that one needs. Therefore, one need not be concerned about drinking water in a different domain.

אִיבַּעְיָא לְהוּ: כַּרְמְלִית מַאי? אָמַר אַבָּיֵי: הִיא הִיא. אָמַר רָבָא: הִיא גּוּפָא גְּזֵירָה, וַאֲנַן נֵיקוּם וְנִגְזוֹר גְּזֵירָה לִגְזֵירָה?!

A dilemma was raised before the Sages: If one of the domains is a ***karmelit*****, what is** the *halakha*? **Abaye said: This** case **is equal to that** case, i.e., in this situation a *karmelit* is governed by the same *halakha* that applies to a domain defined by Torah law. Just as the Sages prohibited one in the private domain from drinking from the public domain and vice versa, so too, they prohibited one in a *karmelit* from drinking in the same manner. **Rava said:** How can you say so? The prohibition against carrying to or from a *karmelit* is **itself** a rabbinic **decree. And will we** then **proceed to issue a decree to** prevent violation of another **decree?**

אָמַר אַבָּיֵי: מְנָא אָמֵינָא לַהּ – מִדְּקָתָנֵי:

Abaye said in explanation of his opinion: **From where do I say that** *halakha*? **From** the fact **that it is taught** in the mishna:

וְכֵן בַּגַּת.

And the same applies **in a winepress.** This winepress cannot be a private domain, as the first clause of the mishna already dealt with a private domain. The winepress must therefore be a *karmelit*, which proves that it is prohibited to drink from a *karmelit* while standing in a public domain.

וְרָבָא אָמַר: לְעִנְיַן מַעֲשֵׂר. וְכֵן אָמַר רַב שֵׁשֶׁת: "וְכֵן בַּגַּת" – לְעִנְיַן מַעֲשֵׂר.

And Rava said: This proof is not conclusive, as the words: The same applies in a winepress, do not refer to Shabbat but **to the matter of** the *halakhot* of **tithes,** as explained below. **And similarly, Rav Sheshet said** that the statement that **the same** applies **in a winepress** refers **to the matter of tithes.**

דִּתְנַן: שׁוֹתִין עַל הַגַּת בֵּין בְּחַמִּין וּבֵין בְּצוֹנֵן וּפָטוּר, דִּבְרֵי רַבִּי מֵאִיר. רַבִּי אֱלִיעֶזֶר בַּר צָדוֹק מְחַיֵּיב.

The Gemara clarifies this statement. **As we learned** in a mishna: **One** may **drink** grape juice directly **on the winepress**[H] *ab initio* without tithing, **whether** the juice was diluted **with hot** water, even though he will then be unable to return the leftover wine to the press, as it would ruin all the wine in the press, **or whether** the juice was diluted **with cold** water, in which case he could return the leftover wine without ruining the rest, **and he is exempt.** Drinking that way is considered incidental drinking, and anything that is not a fixed meal is exempt from tithing. That is the **statement of Rabbi Meir.** This is the **statement of Rabbi Meir. Rabbi Eliezer bar Tzadok deems** one **obligated** to tithe in both cases.

וַחֲכָמִים אוֹמְרִים: עַל הַחַמִּין – חַיָּיב, וְעַל הַצּוֹנֵן – פָּטוּר, מִפְּנֵי שֶׁמַּחֲזִיר אֶת הַמּוֹתָר.

And the Rabbis say: There is a distinction between these two cases. When the juice is diluted **with hot** water, since one cannot return what is left of the juice to the press, **he is obligated** to tithe it, as this drinking is like fixed drinking for which one is obligated to tithe. However, when the juice is diluted **with cold** water, **he is exempt** from tithing it, **because he** can **return the leftover** juice to the press. Therefore, it is considered incidental drinking, which is exempt from tithing. The teaching of the mishna: The same applies to a winepress, is in accordance with the opinion of Rabbi Meir, as it teaches that that the leniency to drink without separating tithes applies only if the drinker's head and most of his body are in the winepress.

מתני׳ קוֹלֵט אָדָם מִן הַמַּזְחֵילָה לְמַטָּה מֵעֲשָׂרָה טְפָחִים, וּמִן הַצִּינּוֹר מִכׇּל מָקוֹם שׁוֹתֶה.

MISHNA A person standing in a public domain on Shabbat may **catch** water in a vessel **from a gutter** running along the side of a roof, if it is **less than ten handbreadths** off the ground, which is part of the public domain. **And from a pipe**[HBN] that protrudes from the roof, **one** may **drink in any manner,** i.e., not only by catching the water in a vessel, but even by pressing his mouth directly against the spout.

HALAKHA

One may drink on the winepress – שׁוֹתִים עַל הַגַּת: One who drinks wine directly from a winepress is not required to separate tithes, as this is considered incidental drinking. However, if he diluted it with hot water it is considered fixed drinking, in accordance with the opinion of the Rabbis, which is the intermediate opinion between the two other rulings (Rambam *Sefer Zera'im, Hilkhot Ma'aserot* 5:16).

A gutter and a pipe – מַזְחֵילָה וְצִינּוֹר: With regard to a gutter that is within three handbreadths of a roof, it is prohibited to stand in the public domain and press one's mouth or a vessel to the gutter. However, it is permitted to collect the water as it pours down. If the pipe or gutter extends three handbreadths beyond the roof, it is permitted to press one's mouth or a vessel against it, as long as the gutter is not four by four handbreadths in size (*Shulḥan Arukh, Oraḥ Ḥayyim* 351:1).

BACKGROUND

A gutter and a pipe – מַזְחֵילָה וְצִינּוֹר: A gutter is fashioned out of the wall itself. It catches rainwater falling from the roof and pours it out.

Gutter

A pipe is a spout connected to a house that collects water from the roof. It differs from the gutter in that it protrudes from the wall and is typically made of earthenware or metal.

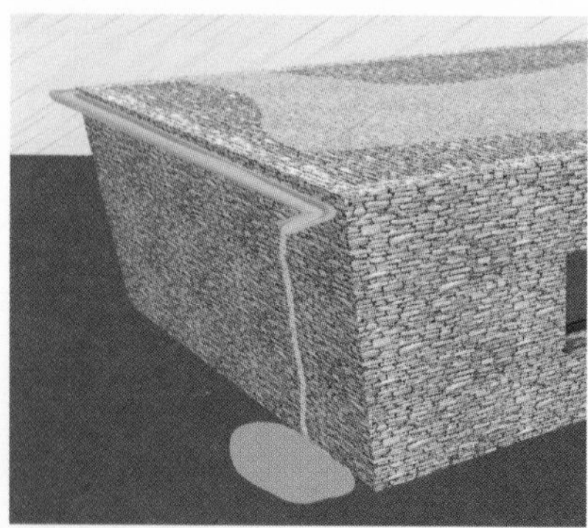

Pipe

NOTES

A gutter and a pipe – מַזְחֵילָה וְצִינּוֹר: There are many variant readings, and therefore many different conclusions, with regard to these *halakhot*. One widespread version of the text reads: A person may catch from a gutter above ten handbreadths. This is explained as referring to a gutter precisely thirteen handbreadths tall. It is evident from the continuation of the discussion in the Gemara, and especially from the two *baraitot* it cites, that a wide variety of readings are possible. Different versions can be found in the commentaries of the Rif, Rabbeinu Ḥananel, the Rambam, the Rashba, the Ra'avad, and others.

גמ׳ קולֵט – אִין, אֲבָל מְצָרֵף – לָא. מַאי טַעְמָא? אָמַר רַב נַחְמָן: הָכָא בְּמַזְחִילָה פָּחוֹת מִשְּׁלֹשָׁה סָמוּךְ לַגַּג עָסְקִינַן, דְּכָל פָּחוֹת מִשְּׁלֹשָׁה סָמוּךְ לַגַּג כַּגַּג דָּמֵי.

GEMARA A careful reading of the mishna indicates that to **catch, yes,** one may catch the water from a distance, **but** to **press** his hand or mouth to the gutter, **no,** that is prohibited. The Gemara asks: **What is the reason** for this distinction? **Rav Naḥman said: Here, we are dealing with a gutter within three** handbreadths **of the roof,** and the *halakha* is in accordance with the principle that **anything within three** handbreadths **of a roof is considered like the roof** itself, based on the principle of *lavud,* according to which two solid surfaces are considered joined if there is a gap of less than three handbreadths between them. Since the roof of the house is a private domain, one would be carrying from a private domain to a public domain, which is prohibited.

תַּנְיָא נַמִי הָכִי: עוֹמֵד אָדָם בִּרְשׁוּת הַיָּחִיד וּמַגְבִּיהַּ יָדוֹ לְמַעְלָה מֵעֲשָׂרָה טְפָחִים לְפָחוֹת מִשְּׁלֹשָׁה סָמוּךְ לַגַּג, וְקוֹלֵט, וּבִלְבַד שֶׁלֹּא יְצָרֵף.

That ruling, that there is a distinction between catching water falling from a gutter and pressing one's hand or mouth to it, **was also taught** in a *baraita*: **A person** may **stand in a private domain and raise his hand above ten handbreadths,** until it is **within three** handbreadths **of the roof, and catch** any water falling from his neighbor's roof in a vessel, **provided that he does not press** his hand or mouth to the roof.

תַּנְיָא אִידָךְ: לֹא יַעֲמוֹד אָדָם בִּרְשׁוּת הַיָּחִיד וְיַגְבִּיהַּ יָדוֹ לְמַעְלָה מֵעֲשָׂרָה טְפָחִים לְפָחוֹת מִשְּׁלֹשָׁה סָמוּךְ לַגַּג וִיצָרֵף, אֲבָל קוֹלֵט הוּא וְשׁוֹתֶה.

It was likewise **taught** in **another** *baraita*: **A person** may **not stand in a private domain and raise his hand above ten handbreadths, to within three** handbreadths **of the roof, and press** his hand to the gutter, **but he** may **catch** water falling from the gutter **and drink.**

מִן הַצִּינּוֹר מִכׇּל מָקוֹם שׁוֹתֶה. תָּנָא: אִם יֵשׁ בַּצִּינּוֹר אַרְבָּעָה עַל אַרְבָּעָה – אָסוּר, מִפְּנֵי שֶׁהוּא כְּמוֹצִיא מֵרְשׁוּת לִרְשׁוּת.

It was stated in the mishna: **But from a pipe one** may **drink in any manner,** as it protrudes more than three handbreadths from the roof. A Sage **taught** in the *Tosefta*: **If the pipe** itself **is four by four** handbreadths wide, **it is prohibited** to stand in the public domain and press one's hand or mouth to the water, **because he is like** one who **carries from one domain to** another **domain,** as the pipe is considered a domain in its own right.

מתני׳ בּוֹר בִּרְשׁוּת הָרַבִּים וְחוּלְיָיתוֹ גְּבוֹהָהּ עֲשָׂרָה טְפָחִים – חַלּוֹן שֶׁעַל גַּבָּיו מְמַלְּאִין הֵימֶנּוּ בְּשַׁבָּת.

MISHNA With regard to **a cistern in a public domain, with an embankment ten handbreadths high,** i.e., the embankment constitutes a private domain by itself, if there is **a window above** the cistern,[B] i.e., the window of an adjacent house is situated above the cistern, **one** may **draw** water **from** the cistern **on Shabbat** through the window, as it is permitted to carry from one private domain to another.

אַשְׁפָּה בִּרְשׁוּת הָרַבִּים גְּבוֹהָה עֲשָׂרָה טְפָחִים – חַלּוֹן שֶׁעַל גַּבָּיו שׁוֹפְכִין לְתוֹכָהּ מַיִם בְּשַׁבָּת.

Similarly, with regard to **a garbage dump in a public domain** that is **ten handbreadths high,** which means it has the status of a private domain, if there is **a window above** the pile of refuse that abuts the garbage dump, **one** may **throw water** from the window **onto** the dump **on Shabbat,** as it is permitted to carry from one private domain to another.

גמ׳ בְּמַאי עָסְקִינַן? אִילֵימָא בִּסְמוּכָה – לָמָּה לִי חוּלְיָא עֲשָׂרָה?

GEMARA The Gemara asks: **With what are we dealing** here? **If you say** we are dealing **with** a cistern that is **adjacent** to the wall of the house, i.e. the cistern and wall are separated by less than four handbreadths, **why do I** need the cistern's **embankment** to be **ten** handbreadths high? Presumably the cistern is ten handbreadths deep, which makes it a private domain, and as it is too close to the house for the public domain to pass between them, one should be permitted to draw water from the cistern through the window, regardless of the height of the embankment.

אָמַר רַב הוּנָא: הָכָא בְּמַאי עָסְקִינַן – בִּמוּפְלֶגֶת מִן הַכּוֹתֶל אַרְבָּעָה.

Rav Huna said: With what we are dealing here? With a case where the cistern or garbage dump is **four** handbreadths **removed from the wall** of the house, i.e., a public domain separates the house from the cistern or heap. It is prohibited to carry from one private domain to another by way of a public domain. However, if the cistern's embankment is ten handbreadths high, the one drawing the water transfers it by way of an area that is more than ten handbreadths above the public domain, which is an exempt domain.

BACKGROUND

A cistern near a window – בּוֹר לְיַד חַלּוֹן: The image illustrates a cistern with an embankment, i.e., the stone wall surrounding the mouth of the cistern, in a public domain. There is a window in the house above the cistern.

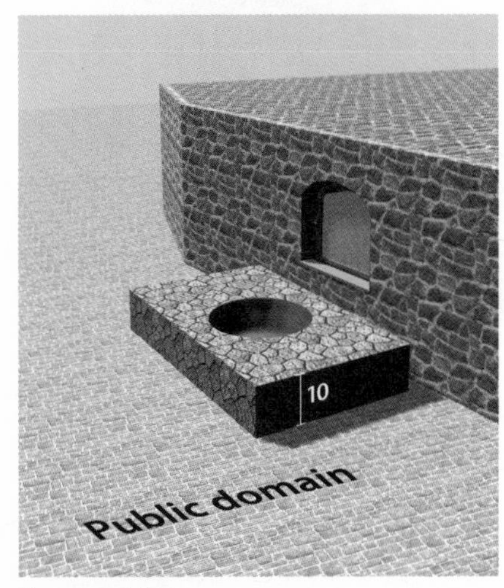

Cistern near a window

וְטַעְמָא – דְּאִיכָּא חוּלְיָא עֲשָׂרָה, הָא לֵיכָּא חוּלְיָא עֲשָׂרָה – קָא מְטַלְטֵל מֵרְשׁוּת הַיָּחִיד לִרְשׁוּת הַיָּחִיד דֶּרֶךְ רְשׁוּת הָרַבִּים.

And the reason that drawing the water is permitted is **that there is an embankment of ten** handbreadths; but **if there is no embankment of ten** handbreadths, it is prohibited, as this would involve **moving** objects **from one private domain to another by way of the public domain.**[H]

וְרַבִּי יוֹחָנָן אָמַר: אֲפִילּוּ תֵּימָא בִּסְמוּכָה, הָא קָא מַשְׁמַע לָן: דְּבוֹר וְחוּלְיָיתוֹ מִצְטָרְפִין לַעֲשָׂרָה.

And Rabbi Yoḥanan said: The above explanation is unnecessary. **Even** if **you say** that we are dealing **with** a cistern that is **adjacent** to the wall of the house, the mishna comes to **teach us that a cistern and its embankment combine to** complete the **ten** handbreadths required for a private domain, and it is not necessary that the embankment itself reach a height of ten handbreadths.

״אַשְׁפָּה בִּרְשׁוּת הָרַבִּים וכו׳״. וְלָא חָיְישִׁינַן שֶׁמָּא תִּנָּטֵל אַשְׁפָּה?

The mishna states: With regard to **a garbage dump in a public domain** that is ten handbreadths high, if there is a window above the heap, one may throw water from the window onto the heap on Shabbat. The Gemara asks: **Aren't we concerned that the** entire **garbage dump** or part of it **might be removed,** turning the area into a public domain, and people will continue to throw water onto it on Shabbat?[H]

וְהָא רָבִין בַּר רַב אַדָּא אָמַר רַבִּי יִצְחָק: מַעֲשֶׂה בְּמָבוֹי אֶחָד שֶׁצִּידּוֹ אֶחָד כָּלֶה לַיָּם וְצִידּוֹ אֶחָד כָּלֶה לָאַשְׁפָּה, וּבָא מַעֲשֶׂה לִפְנֵי רַבִּי וְלֹא אָמַר בּוֹ לֹא אִיסּוּר וְלֹא הֶיתֵּר.

But didn't Ravin bar Rav Adda say that **Rav Yitzḥak said: An incident** occurred **involving a certain alleyway, one of whose sides terminated in the sea,** which closed it off on one side, **and the other side** of which **terminated in a garbage dump. And the incident came before Rabbi** Yehuda HaNasi for his ruling as to whether the alleyway has the status of an alleyway closed on both sides, **and he did not say** anything **about it, either prohibition or permission.**[N]

הֶיתֵּר לֹא אָמַר בּוֹ – דְּחָיְישִׁינַן שֶׁמָּא תִּנָּטֵל אַשְׁפָּה וְיַעֲלֶה הַיָּם שִׂירְטוֹן.

The Gemara clarifies: Rabbi Yehuda HaNasi **did not say about it** that carrying in the alleyway is **permitted, as we are concerned lest the garbage dump be removed** from its present spot, leaving one side of the alleyway open, **and** we are likewise concerned that perhaps **the sea will throw up sediment** and recede. These sedimentary deposits will intervene between the end of the alleyway and the sea, thereby depriving the alleyway of one its partitions.

אִיסּוּר לֹא אָמַר בּוֹ – דְּהָא קַיָּימִין מְחִיצוֹת.

Similarly, **he did not say about it** that carrying in the alleyway was **prohibited, as** its **partitions,** the sea and the garbage dump, indeed **exist,** and it was certainly permitted at that time to carry in the alleyway. Apparently, there is indeed a concern that a garbage dump might be removed; why, then, does the same concern not apply to the case in the mishna?

לָא קַשְׁיָא; הָא – דְּיָחִיד, הָא – דְּרַבִּים.

The Gemara answers: This is **not difficult.** In **this** case, with regard to the alleyway between the garbage dump and the sea, we are concerned, as we are dealing **with a private** garbage dump, whose owner might change his mind and remove it; whereas in **that** case, i.e., the case in the mishna, it is referring **to a public** heap, which will certainly remain fixed in place.

מתני׳ אִילָן שֶׁהָיָה מֵיסֵךְ עַל הָאָרֶץ, אִם אֵין גּוֹפוֹ גָּבוֹהַּ מִן הָאָרֶץ שְׁלֹשָׁה טְפָחִים – מְטַלְטְלִים תַּחְתָּיו.

MISHNA With regard to **a tree that was hanging over**[H] **the ground,**[B] i.e., its branches hung down on all sides like a tent so that it threw a shadow on the ground, **if** the tips of **its branches are no higher than three handbreadths from the ground, one** may **carry under it.** This applies even if the tree is planted in a public domain, as the branches form partitions which turn the enclosed area into a private domain.

שָׁרָשָׁיו גְּבוֹהִים מִן הָאָרֶץ שְׁלֹשָׁה טְפָחִים – לֹא יֵשֵׁב עֲלֵיהֶן.

If **its roots** were **three handbreadths higher than the ground, one** may **not sit on them,** as it is prohibited to use a tree on Shabbat. Any part of a tree that is three handbreadths above the ground has the status of a tree with regard to this prohibition.

גמ׳ אָמַר רַבִּי הוּנָא בְּרֵיהּ דְּרַב יְהוֹשֻׁעַ: אֵין מְטַלְטְלִין בּוֹ יָתֵר מִבֵּית סָאתַיִם. מַאי טַעְמָא?

GEMARA Rav Huna, son of Rav Yehoshua, said: One may **not move** objects in the area **under** the tree if it is **more than two *beit se'a*. What is the reason** for this prohibition?

HALAKHA

Drawing water from a cistern – שְׁאִיבָה מִבּוֹר: It is permitted to draw water into a private domain from a cistern in the public domain by way of a window ten handbreadths high (*Magen Avraham*), if the cistern is within four handbreadths of the private domain. However, if the cistern is more than four handbreadths away, it is permitted to draw water from it only if the embankment of the cistern itself is ten handbreadths high. This ruling is in accordance with the statement in the mishna as explained by Rav Huna, as even Rabbi Yoḥanan does not disagree with him (*Shulḥan Arukh, Oraḥ Ḥayyim* 354:1).

Throwing into a garbage dump – זְרִיקָה לָאַשְׁפָּה: It is permitted to throw objects onto a garbage dump that has the dimensions of a private domain but is located in the public domain, from a private domain located within four handbreadths of the heap. However, if the heap is privately owned, it is prohibited to throw into it, as the heap might be removed. If the pile is not a garbage dump, one may not throw objects there, as the owner might change his mind and remove the pile (Rema, citing the *Maggid Mishne* and the Rashba; *Shulḥan Arukh, Oraḥ Ḥayyim* 354:2).

A tree that was hanging over – אִילָן שֶׁהָיָה מֵיסֵךְ: The space formed under a tree that has large hanging branches is considered partitioned off. Therefore, one is permitted to carry beneath it as he would in a private domain, if the following conditions are met: The tips of its branches are no higher than three handbreadths from the ground; its branches are at least ten handbreadths high at the spot where they join the tree; and the branches are tied so that they cannot move in the wind. This ruling is in accordance with the *halakha* stated in the mishna, as explained by Rav Huna, son of Rav Yehoshua (*Shulḥan Arukh, Oraḥ Ḥayyim* 362:1).

NOTES

He did not say anything about it, either prohibition or permission – לֹא אָמַר בּוֹ לֹא אִיסּוּר וְלֹא הֶיתֵּר: Since Rabbi Yehuda HaNasi did not expressly permit carrying in the alleyway, one must treat the alleyway as though carrying is prohibited there. Rabbi Yehuda HaNasi's noncommittal response reflects the fact that the prohibition against carrying in the alleyway is merely due to the concern over a possible future change, not because there is any problem with the domain as it currently stands.

BACKGROUND

A tree that was hanging over the ground – אִילָן שֶׁהָיָה מֵיסֵךְ עַל הָאָרֶץ: The image shows a tree with branches hanging down on its sides, forming a kind of canopy that encloses the area surrounding the trunk.

Tree with hanging branches

מִשּׁוּם דְּהָוֵי דִּירָה שֶׁתַּשְׁמִישָׁהּ לָאֲוִיר, וְכָל דִּירָה שֶׁתַּשְׁמִישָׁהּ לָאֲוִיר – אֵין מְטַלְטְלִין בָּהּ יָתֵר מִבֵּית סָאתַיִם.

This was prohibited **because it is a dwelling that serves** only **the air,** i.e., it is used only by someone guarding the fields or the like. It is not used as permanent living quarters, despite its partitions. **And** the rule with respect to **any dwelling that serves** only **the air** is that **it is not permitted to carry in it** if its area is **more than two** ***beit se'a.*** As it is not a proper place of residence, the Sages treated it as an enclosure.

״שָׁרָשָׁיו גְּבוֹהִין מִן הָאָרֶץ וכו׳״. אִיתְּמַר, שָׁרְשֵׁי אִילָן הַבָּאִין מִלְמַעְלָה מִשְּׁלֹשָׁה לְתוֹךְ שְׁלֹשָׁה, רַבָּה אָמַר: מוּתָּר לְהִשְׁתַּמֵּשׁ בָּהֶן, רַב שֵׁשֶׁת אָמַר: אָסוּר לְהִשְׁתַּמֵּשׁ בָּהֶן.

The mishna states: If **the roots** of the tree are three handbreadths **above the ground,** one may not sit on them on Shabbat.[H] **It was stated** that *amora'im* disagreed with regard to **the roots of a tree that** rise up[B] and then bend and **come** down **from above,**[H] from a height of **three** handbreadths **to within three** handbreadths of the ground. **Rabba said: It is permitted to use them,** and **Rav Sheshet said: It is prohibited to use them.**

רַבָּה אָמַר מוּתָּר לְהִשְׁתַּמֵּשׁ בָּהֶן – דְּכָל פָּחוֹת מִשְּׁלֹשָׁה דְּאַרְעָא – אַרְעָא הִיא. רַב שֵׁשֶׁת אָמַר: אָסוּר לְהִשְׁתַּמֵּשׁ בָּהֶן, דְּכֵיוָן דְּמִכֹּחַ אִיסּוּר קָאָתֵי – אֲסוּרִין.

The Gemara clarifies the rationale of each opinion. **Rabba said** that **it is permitted to use them,** as **anything less than three** handbreadths **from the ground is** considered as **the ground. Rav Sheshet said: It is prohibited to use them; since they come from a prohibited source, they are prohibited.** The section of the tree from which they grow is prohibited. Therefore, these roots should likewise be prohibited.

דְּדָמוּ כִּמְשׁוּנִיתָא, דְּסָלְקִין לְעֵילָּא – אֲסוּרִין, דְּנָחְתִּין לְתַתַּאי – שָׁרוּ. לְצִדְדִין – פְּלוּגְתָּא דְּרַבָּה וְרַב שֵׁשֶׁת.

The Gemara proceeds to qualify the dispute: With regard to ascending and descending roots **that resemble** a rocky **crag, those that rise upward are** certainly **prohibited** according to all opinions; those that **fall downward are permitted** according to everyone. It is the roots that branch out **to the sides** that are the subject of the **dispute between Rabba and Rav Sheshet.** Rav Sheshet prohibits using them, while Rabba is lenient.

וְכֵן אַנִּיגְרָא, וְכֵן בְּקֶרֶן זָוִית.

And likewise, Rabba and Rav Sheshet disagree about **a tree that grows in a ditch**[B] that has elevated roots, some of which are concealed by the banks of the ditch. The *amora'im* dispute whether the roots concealed by the banks are considered part of the ground. **And likewise,** in the case of a tree that grows **in a corner**[B] between two walls, they disagree as to whether the section between the walls is considered part of the ground.

HALAKHA

The use of roots – שִׁימּוּשׁ בְּשָׁרָשִׁים: It is prohibited to use tree roots that are more than three handbreadths above the ground. However, one may use roots that are within three handbreadths of the ground (*Shulḥan Arukh, Oraḥ Ḥayyim* 336:2).

Roots of a tree that come from above – שָׁרְשֵׁי אִילָן הַבָּאִין מִלְמַעְלָה: With regard to roots of a tree that are connected to the tree above three handbreadths, it is permitted to sit on the part of the root that lies below three handbreadths. The *halakha* is in accordance with the opinion of Rabba, as Rav Yosef ruled in this manner (*Shulḥan Arukh, Oraḥ Ḥayyim* 336:2).

BACKGROUND

Roots of a tree that rise up – שָׁרְשֵׁי אִילָן הַבָּאִין מִלְמַעְלָה:

Roots above three handbreadths that bend to within three handbreadths

A tree that grows in a ditch – אַנִּיגְרָא: The height of a tree planted in a ditch can be measured either from the bottom of the ditch or from its banks.

Tree growing in a ditch

A tree in a corner – אִילָן בְּקֶרֶן זָוִית: There is a dispute with regard to a tree growing in a corner as to whether the three handbreadths are measured from the ground or from the top of the walls.

Tree growing in a corner

הַהוּא דִּיקְלָא דַּהֲוָה לְאַבַּיֵי וַהֲוָה סָלֵיק בְּאִיפּוּמָא. אֲתָא לְקַמֵּיהּ דְּרַב יוֹסֵף וּשְׁרָא לֵיהּ.

The Gemara relates that **Abaye had a certain palm tree** that grew in his house and **that projected through an opening in the roof.**[B] **He came before Rav Yosef** to ask him about it, **and he permitted him** to use the first three handbreadths of the palm tree above the roof, as the tree's lower part is treated as though it were in the ground.

אָמַר רַב אַחָא בַּר תַּחֲלִיפָא: דִּשְׁרָא לָךְ – כְּרַבָּה שְׁרָא לָךְ.

Rav Aḥa bar Taḥlifa said to Abaye: **He who permitted** it **to you, permitted it to you** in accordance with the opinion of **Rabba,** who maintains that a section of a tree concealed from view in at least two directions is considered as though it were underground. Consequently, the first three handbreadths above that section may be used on Shabbat, as they have the status of the ground.

פְּשִׁיטָא! מַהוּ דְּתֵימָא: אֲפִילּוּ לְרַב שֵׁשֶׁת, בֵּיתָא כְּמַאן דְּמָלֵי דָּמֵי, וְלִישְׁתַּמֵּשׁ בְּפָחוֹת מִשְּׁלֹשָׁה סָמוּךְ לַגַּג, קָא מַשְׁמַע לָן.

The Gemara expresses surprise: This is **obvious.** What novel element is Rav Aḥa bar Taḥlifa teaching us? The Gemara answers: It is necessary, **lest you say** that in this case it should be permitted **even according to Rav Sheshet,** as **the house is considered full,** i.e., it is as though it were filled with earth, **and** this would mean it is permitted **to use** the section **less than three** handbreadths **from the roof.** Rav Aḥa bar Taḥlifa therefore **teaches us** that Rav Sheshet is stringent even in this case.

תְּנַן: "שָׁרָשָׁיו גְּבוֹהִין מִן הָאָרֶץ שְׁלֹשָׁה טְפָחִים – לֹא יֵשֵׁב עֲלֵיהֶם". הֵיכִי דָּמֵי? אִי דְּלָא הָדְרִי כָּיְפִי – פְּשִׁיטָא! אֶלָּא לָאו – אַף עַל גַּב דְּהָדְרִי כָּיְפִי!

The Gemara attempts to adduce proof from the mishna, in which **we learned:** If **the roots** of the tree are **three handbreadths above the ground, one** may **not sit on them. What are the circumstances** of this case? **If** the situation is **that** the roots **do not bend over again,** this is **obvious,** as anything higher than three handbreadths is part of the tree. **Rather, doesn't** it mean that one may not sit on them **even though they bend back** downward to within three handbreadths of the ground? The mishna apparently indicates that if parts of the roots are more than three handbreadths above the ground, it is prohibited to use them along the rest of their entire length, as maintained by Rav Sheshet, contrary to Rabba.

לֹא, לְעוֹלָם דְּלָא הָדְרִי כָּיְפִי. וְהָא קָא מַשְׁמַע לָן: אַף עַל גַּב דְּצִידּוֹ אֶחָד שָׁוֶה לָאָרֶץ.

The Gemara rejects this contention: **No, actually** the mishna is referring to a case **where they do not bend back** downward, **and** the *tanna* comes to **teach us** the following: **Although** on **one side** of the tree the roots are **level with the ground,** nevertheless, it is prohibited to sit on them, as the roots on the other sides are more than three handbreadths above the ground.

תָּנוּ רַבָּנַן: שָׁרְשֵׁי אִילָן שֶׁגְּבוֹהִין מִן הָאָרֶץ שְׁלֹשָׁה טְפָחִים. אוֹ שֶׁיֵּשׁ חָלָל תַּחְתֵּיהֶן שְׁלֹשָׁה טְפָחִים, אַף עַל פִּי שֶׁצִּידּוֹ אֶחָד שָׁוֶה לָאָרֶץ – הֲרֵי זֶה לֹא יֵשֵׁב עֲלֵיהֶן, לְפִי שֶׁאֵין עוֹלִין בָּאִילָן, וְאֵין נִתְלִין בָּאִילָן, וְאֵין נִשְׁעָנִין בָּאִילָן,

The Sages taught in a *baraita*: With regard to **roots of a tree that are three handbreadths above the ground, or if there is** a hollow **space beneath them** of **three handbreadths, although** on **one side** of the tree the roots **are level with the ground, one** may **not sit on them**[H] **because** of the following rule: **One** may **not climb a tree, nor** may **one hang from a tree** by one's hands, **nor** may **one** even **lean against a tree** on Shabbat.[HN]

וְלֹא יַעֲלֶה בָּאִילָן מִבְּעוֹד יוֹם וְיֵשֵׁב שָׁם כָּל הַיּוֹם כּוּלּוֹ, אֶחָד אִילָן וְאֶחָד כָּל הַבְּהֵמָה. אֲבָל בּוֹר שִׁיחַ וּמְעָרָה וְגָדֵר מְטַפֵּס וְעוֹלֶה מְטַפֵּס וְיוֹרֵד, וַאֲפִילּוּ הֵן מֵאָה אַמָּה.

And similarly, **one** may **not climb a tree** on Friday **while it is still day and sit there the entire day** of Shabbat. This constitutes the use of the tree itself, not merely climbing it, and it is therefore prohibited. This *halakha* applies **both to a tree and** to **all animals;** one may not climb upon them, hang from them, or lean against them. **However,** the prohibition is not due to the effort involved in climbing, as is evident from the case of **a cistern, ditch, cave, or a fence. One** may **climb up** and **climb down** them, **even if they are a hundred cubits** deep.

תָּנֵי חֲדָא: אִם עָלָה – מוּתָּר לֵירֵד, וְתָנֵי חֲדָא: אָסוּר לֵירֵד. לָא קַשְׁיָא; כָּאן – מִבְּעוֹד יוֹם, כָּאן – מִשֶּׁחָשֵׁיכָה.

The Gemara comments: **It was taught** in **one** *baraita*: **If one climbed up** a tree, he is **permitted to climb down; and it was taught** in **one** other *baraita* that he is **prohibited to climb down.** The Gemara resolves this apparent contradiction: This is **not difficult. Here,** where it is permitted to descend, one climbed up on Friday, **while it was still day; there,** where it is prohibited to descend, one climbed up on Shabbat **after nightfall.**

וְאִיבָּעֵית אֵימָא: הָא וְהָא מִשֶּׁחָשֵׁיכָה, וְלָא קַשְׁיָא; כָּאן – בְּשׁוֹגֵג, כָּאן – בְּמֵזִיד.

And if you wish, say instead that **both** *baraitot* are referring to a case where one climbed up the tree **after nightfall. But** even so, it is **not difficult: Here,** it is permitted to descend, as one climbed up the tree **unwittingly; there,** it is prohibited to descend, as the *baraita* is dealing with one who climbed **intentionally.**

BACKGROUND

A tree projecting through an opening in the roof – אִילָן בַּאֲרוּבָּה:

Palm tree growing in a house and protruding through an opening in the roof

HALAKHA

Roots that have a hollow space beneath them – שָׁרָשִׁים שֶׁיֵּשׁ חָלָל תַּחְתֵּיהֶם: It is prohibited to use roots that have a hollow space of three handbreadths beneath them, even if they are level with the ground on one side. However, if they are level with the ground on both sides, it is permitted (Vilna Gaon, based on Rabba; *Shulḥan Arukh, Oraḥ Ḥayyim* 336:2).

The use of a tree – שִׁימּוּשׁ בְּאִילָן: It is prohibited to climb a tree on Shabbat, lean against it, hang from one its branches, or utilize it in any other manner (*Shulḥan Arukh, Oraḥ Ḥayyim* 336:1).

NOTES

The prohibition against using a tree – אִיסּוּר שִׁימּוּשׁ בְּאִילָן: The prohibition against using a tree, by either climbing on it, leaning against it, or hanging from one of its branches, is not due to the exertion involved. In fact, it is permitted to climb a tall fence or descend a deep cistern. Rather, using a tree is prohibited because one might pluck the fruit of the tree or cut off a branch, thereby transgressing the prohibited labor of reaping. The same logic applies to the prohibition against riding an animal on Shabbat. One might mistakenly pull off a branch to use as a riding crop.

וְאִיבָּעֵית אֵימָא: הָא וְהָא בְּשׁוֹגֵג, וְהָכָא בְּקָנְסוּ שׁוֹגֵג אַטּוּ מֵזִיד קָמִיפַּלְגִי; מָר סָבַר: קָנְסִינַן, וּמָר סָבַר: לָא קָנְסִינַן.

And if you wish, say instead that **both** *baraitot* are referring to a case where one climbed up **unwittingly, and they disagree about** whether or not the Sages **penalized** an **unwitting** offender **due to an intentional** offender. One **Sage,** who ruled that it is prohibited to descend, **maintains** that **they penalized** an unwitting sinner to prevent others from climbing up on purpose and descending. Therefore, one may not come down even if he ascended by mistake. **And** one **Sage,** who ruled that it is permitted, **maintains** that **they did not penalize** the unwitting sinner in this manner.[H]

אָמַר רַב הוּנָא בְּרֵיהּ דְּרַב יְהוֹשֻׁעַ: כְּתַנָּאֵי, הַנִּיתָּנִין בְּמַתָּנָה אַחַת שֶׁנִּתְעָרְבוּ בְּנִיתָּנִין מַתָּנָה אַחַת – יִנָּתְנוּ בְּמַתָּנָה אַחַת. מַתַּן אַרְבַּע בְּמַתַּן אַרְבַּע – יִנָּתְנוּ בְּמַתַּן אַרְבַּע.

Rav Huna, son of Rav Yehoshua, said: This dispute between the two *baraitot* is **parallel to the** dispute of the ***tanna'im,*** who disagreed with regard to a different matter. The blood of certain sacrifices, e.g., the firstborn and tithe offerings, is sprinkled once on the altar, while the blood of other sacrifices, e.g., burnt-offerings, is sprinkled four times. They require two sprinklings that are four, i.e., two sprinklings on opposite corners, so that the blood falls on all four sides. If the blood of sacrifices **that require** only **one sprinkling becomes intermingled with** the blood of other sacrifices that **require** only **one sprinkling,** the mixture **will be sprinkled once.** Likewise, if the blood of sacrifices that require **four sprinklings** becomes intermingled **with** the blood of other sacrifices that require **four sprinklings,** the mixture **will be sprinkled four times.**

מַתַּן אַרְבַּע בְּמַתַּן אַחַת – רַבִּי אֱלִיעֶזֶר אוֹמֵר: יִנָּתְנוּ בְּמַתַּן אַרְבַּע, וְרַבִּי יְהוֹשֻׁעַ אוֹמֵר: יִנָּתְנוּ בְּמַתָּנָה אַחַת.

If, however, the blood of a sacrifice that requires **four sprinklings** becomes intermingled **with** the blood of a sacrifice that requires only **one sprinkling,** the *tanna'im* disagree: **Rabbi Eliezer says:** The mixture of blood **is sprinkled four times. And Rabbi Yehoshua says:** It **is sprinkled once,** and this suffices for the atonement of the sacrifice.[H]

אָמַר לוֹ רַבִּי אֱלִיעֶזֶר: הֲרֵי הוּא עוֹבֵר עַל ״בַּל תִּגְרַע״! אָמַר לוֹ רַבִּי יְהוֹשֻׁעַ: הֲרֵי הוּא עוֹבֵר בְּ״בַל תּוֹסִיף״!

Rabbi Eliezer said to Rabbi Yehoshua: If one sprinkles the blood only once, **he transgresses** the prohibition **"you shall not diminish,"** which prohibits the omission of any elements of the performance of a mitzva, as he has not sprinkled the blood of the burnt-offering in the proper manner. **Rabbi Yehoshua said to** Rabbi Eliezer: According to your ruling, that one must sprinkle the blood four times, **he transgresses** the prohibition: **Do not add** (Deuteronomy 13:1), which prohibits the addition of elements to a mitzva, as he sprinkles the blood of the firstborn animal more times than necessary.

אָמַר רַבִּי אֱלִיעֶזֶר: לֹא אָמְרוּ אֶלָּא כְּשֶׁהוּא בְּעַצְמוֹ. אָמַר לוֹ רַבִּי יְהוֹשֻׁעַ: לֹא נֶאֱמַר ״בַּל תִּגְרַע״ אֶלָּא כְּשֶׁהוּא בְּעַצְמוֹ.

Rabbi Eliezer said to Rabbi Yehoshua: **They said** the prohibition against adding to the mitzvot **only where** the blood stands **by itself,** not when it is part of a mixture. **Rabbi Yehoshua said** to Rabbi Eliezer: Likewise, the prohibition: **Do not diminish, was stated only** in a case **where** the blood stands **by itself.**

וְעוֹד אָמַר רַבִּי יְהוֹשֻׁעַ: כְּשֶׁנָּתַתָּ – עָבַרְתָּ עַל ״בַּל תּוֹסִיף״ וְעָשִׂיתָ מַעֲשֶׂה בְּיָדְךָ, כְּשֶׁלֹּא נָתַתָּ – עָבַרְתָּ עַל ״בַּל תִּגְרַע״ וְלֹא עָשִׂיתָ מַעֲשֶׂה בְּיָדְךָ.

And Rabbi Yehoshua further said in defense of his position: **When you sprinkle** four times, **you have transgressed** the prohibition: **Do not add,** with regard to one of the sacrifices, **and you** also **performed an action with your** own **hand,** i.e., you transgress the Torah's command by means of a positive act. By contrast, **when you do not sprinkle** four times, even if **you have transgressed** the prohibition: **Do not diminish, you did not perform** the **action**[N] **with your** own **hand.** If one is forced to deviate from the commands of the Torah, it is better to do so in a passive manner.

לְרַבִּי אֱלִיעֶזֶר, דְּאָמַר הָתָם: קוּם עֲשֵׂה עָדִיף – הָכִי נַמִי יֵרֵד. לְרַבִּי יְהוֹשֻׁעַ דְּאָמַר הָתָם שֵׁב וְאַל תַּעֲשֶׂה עֲדִיף – הָכִי נַמִי לֹא יֵרֵד.

Rav Huna, son of Rav Yehoshua, sought to argue the following: **According to Rabbi Eliezer, who said there,** with regard to sacrifices, that if both alternatives involve the violation of a prohibition **it is preferable to stand and take action,** i.e., perform a positive action, **here too,** one should **climb down** from the tree, as it is better to perform a single positive transgression by climbing down rather than commit a passive transgression throughout the entire Shabbat by remaining on the tree. By contrast, **according to Rabbi Yehoshua,** who **said** with regard to sacrifices that **it is preferable to sit and not take action, here too,** one should **not descend** from the tree.

HALAKHA

One who is situated on a tree on Shabbat – הַמָּצוּי עַל הָאִילָן בְּשַׁבָּת: In the case of one who climbed up a tree on Shabbat, if he did so intentionally, it is prohibited for him to climb down until nightfall. However, if acted unwittingly he is permitted to descend. If he went up on Friday, he may descend after nightfall in either case. The most lenient ruling is accepted here, as no conclusion was reached in the Gemara's discussion. In addition, the *halakha* is lenient with regard to an uncertainty that involves a rabbinic prohibition.

Some authorities state that if one ascended Friday intentionally, with the intention of staying there in a prohibited manner on Shabbat, he is prohibited from coming down (*Tur*). The Rema claims these *halakhot* apply only to a person. It is certainly prohibited to remove on Shabbat in any manner an object that has been placed on a tree before Shabbat (*Shulḥan Arukh, Oraḥ Ḥayyim* 336:1).

Mixtures of blood – תַּעֲרוֹבוֹת דָּמִים: When the blood of different sacrifices becomes intermingled, the following rules apply: If the blood of a sacrifice that requires a single sprinkling becomes intermingled with the blood of another sacrifice that requires a single sprinkling, the mixture is sprinkled once. If the blood of a sacrifice that requires four sprinklings becomes mixed with the blood of another sacrifice that requires four sprinklings, it is sprinkled four times. If the blood of a sacrifice that requires one sprinkling becomes intermingled with the blood of a sacrifice that requires four sprinklings, it is sprinkled only once, as the *halakha* is in accordance with the opinion of Rabbi Yehoshua as opposed to that of Rabbi Eliezer (Rambam *Sefer Avoda, Hilkhot Pesulei HaMukdashin* 2:11).

NOTES

You did not perform the action – לֹא עָשִׂיתָ מַעֲשֶׂה: This rationale is offered in several talmudic discussions, as the Sages have the authority to uproot Torah obligations by instructing one to sit and refrain from acting. In addition to the fact that refraining from doing something does not constitute an actual transgression, the Torah is far more stringent with regard to negative commandments than positive ones. Consequently, it is preferable to sin by failing to perform a positive commandment. *Tosafot* add that the rule that a positive command sets aside a negative one does not apply to sacrifices (see Ritva).

דִּילְמָא לָא הִיא, עַד כָּאן לָא קָאָמַר רַבִּי אֱלִיעֶזֶר הָתָם קוּם עֲשֵׂה עָדִיף אֶלָּא דְּקָא עָבֵיד מִצְוָה, אֲבָל הָכָא דְּלָא עָבֵיד מִצְוָה – הָכִי נַמִי לָא יֵרֵד.

The Gemara refutes this comparison: **Perhaps that is not** the case, as the two *halakhot* are not identical. **Rabbi Eliezer** might have **stated** his opinion that **it is preferable to stand and take action only** in the case dealt with **there, where one performs a mitzva** with respect to the additional sprinklings of the burnt-offering. **However, here,** where **one performs no mitzva** whatsoever by descending, **indeed, he** should **not descend.**

וְאִי נַמִי, עַד כָּאן לָא קָאָמַר רַבִּי יְהוֹשֻׁעַ הָתָם שֵׁב וְאַל תַּעֲשֶׂה עָדִיף – אֶלָּא

Alternatively, the comparison can be rejected in a different fashion: **Rabbi Yehoshua** may have **stated** his opinion that **it is preferable to sit and not take action only** in the case dealt with **there,**

Perek **X**
Daf **100** Amud **b**

דְּלָא קָא עָבֵיד אִיסּוּרָא, אֲבָל הָכָא דְּקָא עָבֵיד אִיסּוּרָא – הָכִי נַמִי דְּיֵרֵד.

where one does not commit a transgression by refraining from action. **However, here, where one commits a transgression** every additional moment he remains in the tree, **indeed, he** should **descend** from it.

תָּנֵי חֲדָא: אֶחָד אִילָן לַח וְאֶחָד אִילָן יָבֵשׁ. וְתַנְיָא אִידָּךְ: בַּמֶּה דְּבָרִים אֲמוּרִים – בְּלַח, אֲבָל בְּיָבֵשׁ – מוּתָּר.

The Gemara cites an apparent contradiction: **It was taught** in **one** *baraita* that **both a green tree and a dry tree** are included in the prohibition against climbing a tree,[H] whereas **it was taught** in **another** *baraita*: **In what** case **are these matters,** that one may not climb a tree, **stated? With regard to a green** tree. **But in** the case of **a dry** one, **it is permitted** to climb it.

אָמַר רַב יְהוּדָה: לָא קַשְׁיָא; כָּאן – בְּשֶׁגִּזְעוֹ מַחֲלִיף, כָּאן – בְּשֶׁאֵין גִּזְעוֹ מַחֲלִיף.

Rav Yehuda said: It is **not difficult. Here,** the *baraita* that includes a dry tree in the prohibition is referring to a tree whose **stump sends out new** shoots when cut; whereas **there,** the *baraita* that excludes a dry tree from the prohibition is referring to one whose **stump does not send out new** shoots.

גִּזְעוֹ מַחֲלִיף יָבֵשׁ קָרֵית לֵיהּ? אֶלָּא: לָא קַשְׁיָא; כָּאן – בִּימוֹת הַחַמָּה, כָּאן – בִּימוֹת הַגְּשָׁמִים.

The Gemara expresses surprise at this answer: **You call** a tree whose **stump sends out new** shoots **dry?** This tree is not dry at all. **Rather,** it is **not difficult,** as both *baraitot* deal with a dry tree whose stump will not send out any new shoots. However, **here,** the *baraita* that permits climbing a dry tree, is referring **to the summer,** when it is evident that the tree is dead; whereas **there,** the *baraita* that prohibits climbing the tree is referring **to the rainy season,** when many trees shed their leaves and it is not obvious which remain alive and which are dead.

בִּימוֹת הַחַמָּה הָא נָתְרִי פֵּירֵי! בִּדְלֵיכָּא פֵּירֵי. וְהָא קָא נָתְרִי קִינְסֵי! בִּגְדוּדָא.

The Gemara raises a difficulty: **In the summer, the fruit** of the previous year left on the dry tree **will fall off** when he climbs it, and climbing the tree should therefore be prohibited lest he come to pick the fruit. The Gemara answers: We are dealing here with a case **where there is no fruit** on the tree. The Gemara asks: **But small branches will fall off** when he climbs the tree, and once again this should be prohibited in case he comes to break them off. The Gemara answers: We are dealing here **with a tree that has** already **been stripped** of all its small branches.

אִינִי?! וְהָא רַב אִיקְלַע לְאַפְסְטַיָא, וַאֲסַר בִּגְדוּדָא! רַב בִּקְעָה מָצָא, וְגָדַר בָּהּ גָּדֵר.

The Gemara asks: **Is that** really **so? But Rav arrived at** a place called **Apsetaya and prohibited** its residents from climbing even **a tree that had** already **been stripped of** all **its branches.** The Gemara answers: In truth, no prohibition was involved, but **Rav found** an unguarded **field,** i.e., a place where transgression was widespread, **and fenced it in.** He added a stringency as a safeguard and prohibited an action that was fundamentally permitted.

אָמַר רָמִי בַּר אַבָּא, אָמַר רַב אַסִי: אָסוּר לְאָדָם שֶׁיְּהַלֵּךְ עַל גַּבֵּי עֲשָׂבִים בְּשַׁבָּת, מִשּׁוּם שֶׁנֶּאֱמַר: ״וְאָץ בְּרַגְלַיִם חוֹטֵא״.

Rami bar Abba said that **Rav Asi said: It is prohibited for a person to walk on grass on Shabbat, due to** the fact **that it is stated: "And he who hastens with his feet sins"** (Proverbs 19:2). This verse teaches that mere walking occasionally involves a sin, e.g., on Shabbat, when one might uproot the grass on which he walks.

HALAKHA

Green and dry trees – אִילָן לַח וְיָבֵשׁ: It is prohibited to use any tree on Shabbat, even a dry one whose leaves have shriveled up. This *halakha* is in accordance with Rav (*Shulḥan Arukh, Oraḥ Ḥayyim* 336:1).

תָּנֵי חֲדָא: מוּתָּר לֵילֵךְ עַל גַּבֵּי עֲשָׂבִים בַּשַּׁבָּת, וְתַנְיָא אִידָךְ: אָסוּר. לָא קַשְׁיָא; הָא – בְּלַחִים, הָא – בִּיבֵשִׁים.

The Gemara cites another apparent contradiction: **It was taught in one** *baraita* that **it is permitted to walk on grass on Shabbat,**[H] **and it was taught** in **another** *baraita* that **it is prohibited** to do so. The Gemara answers: This is **not difficult. This** *baraita* is referring **to green** grass, which one might uproot, thereby transgressing the prohibition against reaping on Shabbat. **That** other *baraita* is referring **to dry** grass, which has already been cut off from its source of life, and therefore the prohibition of reaping is no longer in effect.

וְאִי בָּעֵית אֵימָא: הָא וְהָא בְּלַחִים, וְלָא קַשְׁיָא; כָּאן – בִּימוֹת הַחַמָּה, כָּאן – בִּימוֹת הַגְּשָׁמִים.

And if you wish, say instead that **both** *baraitot* are referring **to green** grass, **and** yet **there is no difficulty: Here,** the *baraita* that prohibits walking on grass is referring **to the summer,** when the grass includes seeds that might be dislodged by one's feet, whereas **there,** the *baraita* that permits doing so is referring **to the rainy season,** when this problem does not exist.

וְאִיבָּעֵית אֵימָא: הָא וְהָא בִּימוֹת הַחַמָּה, וְלָא קַשְׁיָא; הָא – דְּסַיֵּים מְסָאנֵיהּ, הָא – דְּלָא סַיֵּים מְסָאנֵיהּ.

And if you wish, say instead that **both** *baraitot* are referring **to the summer, and** it is **not difficult: This** *baraita*, which permits walking on grass, is referring to a case **where one is wearing his shoes,** whereas **that** other *baraita*, which prohibits it, deals with a situation **where one is not wearing his shoes,** as the grass might get entangled between his toes and be uprooted.

וְאִיבָּעֵית אֵימָא: הָא וְהָא דְּסַיֵּים מְסָאנֵיהּ, וְלָא קַשְׁיָא; הָא – דְּאִית לֵיהּ עוּקְצֵי, הָא דְּלֵית לֵיהּ עוּקְצֵי.

And if you wish, say instead that **both** *baraitot* are referring to a case **where one is wearing his shoes, and** nevertheless this is **not difficult: This** *baraita* prohibits walking on grass, as it involves a case **where** one's shoe **has a spike**[N] on which the grass might get caught and be uprooted, whereas **that** other *baraita* permits it, because it deals a case **where** one's shoe **does not have a spike.**

וְאִיבָּעֵית אֵימָא: הָא וְהָא דְּאִית לֵיהּ עוּקְצֵי, הָא – דְּאִית לֵיהּ שְׁרָכָא, הָא – דְּלֵית לֵיהּ שְׁרָכָא.

And if you wish, say instead that **both** are referring to a case **where** the shoe **has a spike,** and it is not difficult: **This** *baraita*, which prohibits walking on grass, is referring to a case **where** the grass is **long and entangled,**[N] and it can easily get caught on the shoe, whereas **that** other *baraita* is referring to a case **where** the grass **is not long and entangled.**

וְהָאִידָּנָא דְּקַיְימָא לַן כְּרַבִּי שִׁמְעוֹן – כּוּלְּהוּ שָׁרֵי.

The Gemara concludes: **And now, when we maintain** that the *halakha* is **in accordance with the opinion** of **Rabbi Shimon,** who maintains that there is no liability for a prohibited act committed unwittingly during the performance of a permitted act, **all of these** scenarios **are permitted,** as here too, one's intention is merely to walk and not to uproot grass on Shabbat.

וְאָמַר רָמִי בַּר חָמָא, אָמַר רַב אַסִי: אָסוּר לְאָדָם שֶׁיָּכוֹף אִשְׁתּוֹ לִדְבַר מִצְוָה, שֶׁנֶּאֱמַר: ״וְאָץ בְּרַגְלַיִם חוֹטֵא״.

The Gemara cites another *halakha* derived from the verse mentioned in the previous discussion. **Rami bar Ḥama said** that **Rav Asi said: It is prohibited for a man to force his wife in the** conjugal **mitzva,**[HN] i.e., sexual relations, **as it is stated: "And he who hastens with his feet sins"** (Proverbs 19:2). The term his feet is understood here as a euphemism for intercourse.

וְאָמַר רַבִּי יְהוֹשֻׁעַ בֶּן לֵוִי: כָּל הַכּוֹפֶה אִשְׁתּוֹ לִדְבַר מִצְוָה – הָוְיָין לוֹ בָּנִים שֶׁאֵינָן מְהוּגָּנִין. אָמַר רַב אִיקָא בַּר חִינָּנָא: מַאי קְרָאָה ״גַּם בְּלֹא דַעַת נֶפֶשׁ לֹא טוֹב״.

And Rabbi Yehoshua ben Levi said: Anyone who forces his wife to perform **the** conjugal **mitzva will have unworthy children** as a consequence. **Rav Ika bar Ḥinnana said: What is the verse** that alludes to this? **"Also, that the soul without knowledge is not good"** (Proverbs 19:2). If intercourse takes place without the woman's knowledge, i.e., consent, the soul of the offspring will not be good.

תַּנְיָא נַמִי הָכִי: ״גַּם בְּלֹא דַעַת נֶפֶשׁ לֹא טוֹב״ – זֶה הַכּוֹפֶה אִשְׁתּוֹ לִדְבַר מִצְוָה. ״וְאָץ בְּרַגְלַיִם חוֹטֵא״ – זֶה הַבּוֹעֵל וְשׁוֹנֶה.

That was also taught in a *baraita*: **"Also, without knowledge the soul is not good"; this is one who forces his wife to** perform **the** conjugal **mitzva. "And he who hastens with his feet sins"; this is one who has intercourse** with his wife **and repeats** the act in a manner that causes her pain or distress.

אִינִי?! וְהָאָמַר רָבָא: הָרוֹצֶה לַעֲשׂוֹת כָּל בָּנָיו זְכָרִים – יִבְעוֹל וְיִשְׁנֶה! לָא קַשְׁיָא; כָּאן – לְדַעַת, כָּאן – שֶׁלֹּא לְדַעַת.

The Gemara is surprised by this teaching: **Is that so? But didn't Rava say: One who wants all his children to be males** should **have intercourse** with his wife **and repeat** the act? The Gemara answers: This is **not difficult: Here,** where Rava issued this advice, he was referring to a husband who acts **with** his wife's **consent. There,** the *baraita* that condemns this behavior is referring to one who proceeds **without** her **consent.**

HALAKHA

Walking on grass – הֲלִיכָה עַל גַּבֵּי עֲשָׂבִים: It is permitted to walk on grass on Shabbat, whether it is green or dry, as the *halakha* is in accordance with Rabbi Shimon's opinion that anything one does not intend to do is permitted (*Shulḥan Arukh, Oraḥ Ḥayyim* 336:3).

Forcing one's wife into the conjugal mitzva – לִכְפּוֹת אִשְׁתּוֹ לִדְבַר מִצְוָה: It is prohibited to force one's wife to have sexual intercourse. The Sages speak of the harm this practice inflicts upon the offspring of such relations (*Shulḥan Arukh, Oraḥ Ḥayyim* 240:10 and *Even HaEzer* 25:2).

NOTES

Where one's shoe has a spike – דְּאִית לֵיהּ עוּקְצֵי: Rabbeinu Ḥananel explains that this refers to vegetation that has prickles and thorns, which become entangled in people's feet.

Long and entangled – שְׁרָכָא: Some commentaries explain that this refers to plant roots, while other authorities maintain that it means broad leaves resting on the ground (*ge'onim*).

In the conjugal mitzva – לִדְבַר מִצְוָה: Throughout this discussion, the Gemara refers to conjugal relations as a mitzva. This terminology teaches that while fulfilling a mitzva, one must be sensitive to his wife's wishes and dignity (Rav Ya'akov Emden; *Ge'on Ya'akov*).

אָמַר רַבִּי שְׁמוּאֵל בַּר נַחְמָנִי, אָמַר רַבִּי יוֹחָנָן: כָּל אִשָּׁה שֶׁתּוֹבַעַת בַּעְלָהּ לִדְבַר מִצְוָה – הָוְיָין לָהּ בָּנִים שֶׁאֲפִילּוּ בְּדוֹרוֹ שֶׁל מֹשֶׁה לֹא הָיוּ כְּמוֹתָן. דְּאִילּוּ בְּדוֹרוֹ שֶׁל מֹשֶׁה כְּתִיב: "הָבוּ לָכֶם אֲנָשִׁים חֲכָמִים וּנְבוֹנִים וִידוּעִים לְשִׁבְטֵיכֶם", וּכְתִיב: "וָאֶקַּח אֶת רָאשֵׁי שִׁבְטֵיכֶם אֲנָשִׁים חֲכָמִים וִידוּעִים", וְאִילּוּ נְבוֹנִים לָא אַשְׁכַּח.

Apropos relations between husband and wife, the Gemara cites that **Rav Shmuel bar Naḥmani said that Rabbi Yoḥanan said: Any woman who demands of her husband that** he fulfill his conjugal **mitzva will have sons the likes of whom did not exist even in Moses' generation. With regard to Moses' generation, it is written: "Get you, wise men, and understanding, and well-known from each one of your tribes, and I will make them head over you"** (Deuteronomy 1:13), **and it is** later **written: "So I took the heads of your tribes, wise men, and well-known,** and made them heads over you" (Deuteronomy 1:15). **However,** men possessing **understanding,** which is a more lofty quality than wisdom,[N] Moses **could not find** any of these.

וְאִילּוּ גַּבֵּי לֵאָה כְּתִיב: "וַתֵּצֵא לֵאָה לִקְרָאתוֹ וַתֹּאמֶר אֵלַי תָּבוֹא כִּי שָׂכוֹר שְׂכַרְתִּיךָ", וּכְתִיב: "וּמִבְּנֵי יִשָּׂשכָר יוֹדְעֵי בִינָה לָעִתִּים לָדַעַת מַה יַּעֲשֶׂה יִשְׂרָאֵל רָאשֵׁיהֶם מָאתַיִם וְכָל אֲחֵיהֶם עַל פִּיהֶם".

While with regard to Leah, it is written: "And Leah went out to meet him, and said, You must come in to me, for indeed I have hired you with my son's mandrakes" (Genesis 30:16). Her reward for demanding that Jacob fulfill the conjugal mitzva with her was the birth of Issachar, **and it is written: "And of the children of Issachar, men who had understanding of the times, to know what Israel ought to do; the heads of them were two hundred, and all their brethren were at their commandment"** (1 Chronicles 12:33).

אִינִי?! וְהָאָמַר רַב יִצְחָק בַּר אַבְדִּימִי: עֶשֶׂר קְלָלוֹת נִתְקַלְּלָה חַוָּה, דִּכְתִיב:

The Gemara poses a question: **Is that so?** Is it proper for a woman to demand her conjugal rights from her husband? **But didn't Rav Yitzḥak bar Avdimi say: Eve was cursed with ten curses,** due to the sin of the Tree of Knowledge, as **it is written:** "To the woman He said, I will greatly multiply your pain and your travail; in sorrow you shall bring forth children; and yet your desire shall be to your husband, and he shall rule over you" (Genesis 3:16)?

"אֶל הָאִשָּׁה אָמַר הַרְבָּה אַרְבֶּה" – אֵלּוּ שְׁנֵי טִפֵּי דָמִים, אַחַת דַּם נִדָּה, וְאַחַת דַּם בְּתוּלִים. "עִצְּבוֹנֵךְ" – זֶה צַעַר גִּידּוּל בָּנִים. "וְהֵרוֹנֵךְ" – זֶה צַעַר הָעִיבּוּר. "בְּעֶצֶב תֵּלְדִי בָנִים" – כְּמַשְׁמָעוֹ.

Rav Yitzḥak bar Avdimi **proceeds to** explain this verse. **"To the woman He said: I will greatly multiply [*harba arbe*]"; these are** the **two drops of blood** unique to a woman, which cause her suffering, **one the blood of menstruation and** the other **one the blood of virginity. "Your pain"; this is the pain of raising children. "And your travail"; this is the pain of pregnancy. "In sorrow you shall bring forth children"; in accordance with its** plain **meaning,** i.e., the pain of childbirth.

"וְאֶל אִישֵׁךְ תְּשׁוּקָתֵךְ" – מְלַמֵּד שֶׁהָאִשָּׁה מִשְׁתּוֹקֶקֶת עַל בַּעְלָהּ בְּשָׁעָה שֶׁיּוֹצֵא לַדֶּרֶךְ. "וְהוּא יִמְשָׁל בָּךְ" – מְלַמֵּד שֶׁהָאִשָּׁה תּוֹבַעַת בַּלֵּב, וְהָאִישׁ תּוֹבֵעַ בַּפֶּה, זוֹ הִיא מִדָּה טוֹבָה בַּנָּשִׁים!

"And yet your desire shall be to your husband" teaches that the woman desires her husband, e.g., **when he sets out on the road; "and he shall rule over you" teaches that the woman demands** her husband **in** her **heart** but is too shy to voice her desire, **but the man demands** his wife **verbally.** Rav Yitzḥak bar Avdimi adds: **This is a good trait in women,**[N] that they refrain from formulating their desire verbally. Apparently, it is improper for a woman to demand her conjugal rights from her husband.

כִּי קָאָמְרִינַן – דִּמְרַצְיָא אַרְצוּיֵי קַמֵּיהּ.

The Gemara answers: **When we say** that a woman who demands her conjugal rights from her husband is praiseworthy, it does not mean she should voice her desires explicitly. Rather, it means **that she** should **make herself pleasing to him,**[H] and he will understand what she wants on his own.

הָנֵי שֶׁבַע הָוְיָין! כִּי אֲתָא רַב דִּימִי, אֲמַר: עֲטוּפָה כְּאָבֵל, וּמְנוּדָּה מִכָּל אָדָם, וַחֲבוּשָׁה בְּבֵית הָאֲסוּרִין.

The Gemara analyzes the above statement with regard to Eve's ten curses: Are they in fact ten? **They are** only **seven. When Rav Dimi came** from Eretz Yisrael to Babylonia, **he said** that the other curses are: A woman is **wrapped like a mourner,** i.e., she must cover her head; and she is **ostracized from all people and incarcerated within a prison,** as she typically spends all her time in the house.

מַאי מְנוּדָּה מִכָּל אָדָם? אִילֵּימָא מִשּׁוּם דַּאֲסִיר לָהּ יִיחוּד – אִיהוּ נַמִי אֲסִיר לֵיהּ יִיחוּד! אֶלָּא דַּאֲסִירָא לְבֵי תְּרֵי.

The Gemara asks: **What is the meaning of ostracized from all people? If you say** this is **because it is forbidden for her to seclude herself** with a man, **it is also forbidden** for a man **to seclude himself** with women. **Rather,** it means **that it is forbidden** for her **to** marry **two** men, whereas a man can marry two women.

בְּמַתְנִיתָא תָּנָא: מְגַדֶּלֶת שֵׂעָר כְּלִילִית, וְיוֹשֶׁבֶת וּמַשְׁתֶּנֶת מַיִם כִּבְהֵמָה, וְנַעֲשֵׂית כַּר לְבַעְלָהּ.

It was taught in a *baraita* that the three additional curses are: **She grows** her **hair** long **like Lilit,** a demon; **she sits and urinates, like an animal; and serves as a pillow for her husband** during relations.

NOTES

Wise and understanding – **חָכָם וְנָבוֹן**: In general, a wise man is one who comprehends an idea that is explained to him, while a man of understanding can infer one idea from another.

A good trait in women – **מִדָּה טוֹבָה בַּנָּשִׁים**: If shyness is a good trait, why does the Torah consider this a curse? One answer is that despite the fact that it is a laudable trait, the inability to formulate a demand verbally can lead to frustration, so it is a curse as well (Ramban).

HALAKHA

That she should make herself pleasing to him – **דִּמְרַצְיָא אַרְצוּיֵי קַמֵּיהּ**: Although it is inappropriate for a woman to demand her conjugal rights verbally, she is certainly permitted to make herself pleasing to her husband and allude to her desire. Once a woman has expressed her desire, it is a mitzva for her husband to initiate relations with her, even beyond his general conjugal obligation (*Shulḥan Arukh, Oraḥ Ḥayyim* 240:1).

וְאִידָךְ – הָנֵי, שֶׁבַח הוּא לָהּ.

And why doesn't **the other** Sage include these curses? The Gemara answers: He maintains that **these are praise for her,** not pain, either because they are modest practices, e.g., urinating in a seated position, or because they add to her comfort, e.g., her bottom position during relations.

דְּאָמַר רַבִּי חִיָּיא: מַאי דִּכְתִיב "מַלְּפֵנוּ מִבַּהֲמוֹת אָרֶץ וּמֵעוֹף הַשָּׁמַיִם יְחַכְּמֵנוּ", "מַלְּפֵנוּ מִבַּהֲמוֹת" – זוֹ פְּרֵידָה שֶׁכּוֹרַעַת וּמַשְׁתֶּנֶת מַיִם. "וּמֵעוֹף הַשָּׁמַיִם יְחַכְּמֵנוּ" – זֶה תַּרְנְגוֹל שֶׁמְּפַיֵּיס וְאַחַר כָּךְ בּוֹעֵל.

As Rabbi Ḥiyya said: What is the meaning of **that which is written: "Who teaches us by the beasts of the earth, and makes us wiser by the birds of the sky"** (Job 35:11)? He explains: **"Who teaches us by the beasts of the earth"; this is the female mule, which crouches and urinates** and from which we learn modesty. **"And makes us wiser by the birds of the sky"; this is the rooster, which** first **cajoles** the hen **and then mates** with it.

אָמַר רַבִּי יוֹחָנָן: אִילְמָלֵא לֹא נִיתְּנָה תּוֹרָה – הָיִינוּ לְמֵידִין צְנִיעוּת מֵחָתוּל, וְגָזֵל מִנְּמָלָה, וַעֲרָיוֹת מִיּוֹנָה. דֶּרֶךְ אֶרֶץ מִתַּרְנְגוֹל – שֶׁמְּפַיֵּיס וְאַחַר כָּךְ בּוֹעֵל.

Similarly, **Rabbi Yoḥanan said: Even if the Torah had not been given, we would** nonetheless **have learned modesty from the cat,** which covers its excrement, **and** that **stealing** is objectionable **from the ant,** which does not take grain from another ant, **and forbidden relations from the dove,**[B] which is faithful to its partner, **and proper relations from the rooster,**[B] **which** first **appeases** the hen **and then mates** with it.

וּמַאי מְפַיֵּיס לָהּ? אָמַר רַב יְהוּדָה, אָמַר רַב, הָכִי קָאָמַר לָהּ: זַבִּינְנָא לִיךְ זִיגָא דְּמָטוּ לִיךְ עַד כַּרְעִיךְ. לְבָתַר הָכִי אָמַר לָהּ: לִישַּׁמְטֵתִּיהּ לְכַרְבַּלְתֵּיהּ דְּהַהוּא תַּרְנְגוֹלָא, אִי אִית לֵיהּ וְלָא זַבִּינְנָא לִיךְ.

What does the rooster do to **appease** the hen?[N] **Rav Yehuda said** that **Rav said:** Prior to mating, it spreads its wings as if to **say this: I will buy you a coat that will reach** down to **your feet. After** mating, the rooster bends its head as if to **say this: May the crest of this rooster fall off if he has** the wherewithal **and does not buy you one.** I simply have no money to do so.

Perek **X**
Daf **101** Amud **a**

מתני׳ הַדֶּלֶת שֶׁבַּמּוּקְצֶה, וַחֲדָקִים שֶׁבַּפִּרְצָה, וּמַחְצָלוֹת – אֵין נוֹעֲלִין בָּהֶן אֶלָּא אִם כֵּן גְּבוֹהִים מִן הָאָרֶץ.

MISHNA With regard to **the door to a rear court,**[H] i.e., a door that opens from a house to the courtyard situated behind it, which is typically not a proper door but merely a wooden board without hinges that closes off the doorway; **and** likewise **bundles of thorns** that seal **a breach; and** reed **mats, one** may **not close** an opening **with them** on Shabbat. This would be considered building or completing a building, **unless they** remain **above the ground** even when they are open.

גמ׳ וּרְמִינְהוּ: דֶּלֶת הַנִּגְרֶרֶת, וּמַחְצֶלֶת הַנִּגְרֶרֶת, וְקַנְקַן הַנִּגְרָר, בִּזְמַן שֶׁקְּשׁוּרִין וּתְלוּיִין – נוֹעֲלִין בָּהֶן בַּשַּׁבָּת, וְאֵין צָרִיךְ לוֹמַר בְּיוֹם טוֹב!

GEMARA And the Gemara **raises a contradiction** from a *baraita*: With regard to **a door, or a mat, or a lattice** [*kankan*][L] **that drag** along the ground and are used for closing up openings, **when they are tied and suspended** in place **one** may **close** an opening **with them on Shabbat; and needless to say** this is permitted **on a Festival.** According to the *baraita*, the critical factor is apparently that they must be tied and suspended, not that they have to be held up above the ground.

אָמַר אַבָּיֵי: בְּשֶׁיֵּשׁ לָהֶם צִיר. רָבָא אָמַר: בְּשֶׁהָיָה לָהֶן צִיר.

Abaye said: The *baraita* is referring **to** ones **that have a hinge.**[N] As they are considered proper doors, closing them does not appear like building. **Rava said:** The *baraita* is referring even **to** doors **that** once **had a hinge,** even though they no longer have one. These partitions also bear the clear form of a door, and therefore one's action does not have the appearance of building.

מֵיתִיבִי: דֶּלֶת הַנִּגְרֶרֶת, וּמַחְצֶלֶת הַנִּגְרֶרֶת, וְקַנְקַן הַנִּגְרָר, בִּזְמַן שֶׁקְּשׁוּרִין וּתְלוּיִין וּגְבוֹהִים מִן הָאָרֶץ אֲפִילּוּ מְלֹא נִימָא – נוֹעֲלִין בָּהֶן, וְאִם לָאו – אֵין נוֹעֲלִין בָּהֶן.

The Gemara **raises an objection** from another *baraita*: With regard to **a door, or a mat, or a lattice that drag** along the ground, **when they are tied and suspended** in place **and** they are held **above the ground even by** as little as **a hairbreadth, one** may **close** an opening **with them. However, if** they are **not** raised in this manner, **one** may **not close** an opening **with them.** Clearly, these doors must indeed be raised above the ground as well.

BACKGROUND

Forbidden relations from the dove – עֲרָיוֹת מִיּוֹנָה: After a male and female dove copulate they remain faithful to one another. If one of them disappears, the other usually does not breed during that season.

Proper relations from the rooster – דֶּרֶךְ אֶרֶץ מִתַּרְנְגוֹל: There are mating rituals unique to various animal species. The Gemara offers an explanation of the mating ritual of chickens. Indeed, the very nature of mating rituals is to appease, as roosters will not engage in sexual intercourse without the prior performance of the ritual.

NOTES

What does the rooster do to appease the hen – מַאי מְפַיֵּיס לָהּ: The Gemara asks this question in order to teach the proper way for a man to behave in this situation (Rav Ya'akov Emden).

HALAKHA

The door to a rear court – הַדֶּלֶת שֶׁבַּמּוּקְצֶה: With regard to a door to a rear court or a door built from woven thorns used to seal a breach, if they have a hinge, one may use them to close an opening on Shabbat. However, if they never had a hinge, one may use them only if they are held above the ground. This ruling is in accordance with Rava's explanation of the mishna (*Shulḥan Arukh, Oraḥ Ḥayyim* 313:3).

LANGUAGE

Lattice [*kankan*] – קַנְקַן: Most commentaries associate *kankan* with its common meaning, the blade of a plough. The Ra'avad maintains that it refers to the wooden handle into which the plough blade is inserted. However, the parallel discussion in the Jerusalem Talmud uses the word *kankal*, with the Hebrew letters *nun* and *lamed* transposed. From the Greek κιγκλίς, *kinklis*, a net or an item crafted into a lattice. Accordingly, *kankan* in this context refers to a wooden lattice or some other material used to close a door.

NOTES

To ones that have a hinge – בְּשֶׁיֵּשׁ לָהֶם צִיר: Why is a hinge effective for these doors but not for a widowed door? One answer is that it is unusual to construct parts of a house from mats and lattices and the like, and therefore the addition of a hinge establishes any one of those items as a door. However, it is not uncommon to install a single plank as a permanent feature of a house, which is why a hinge alone is not effective in rendering it a door (*Turei Zahav*).

אַבַּיֵי מְתָרֵץ לְטַעְמֵיהּ, וְרָבָא מְתָרֵץ לְטַעְמֵיהּ. אַבַּיֵי מְתָרֵץ לְטַעְמֵיהּ: אוֹ שֶׁיֵּשׁ לָהֶן צִיר, אוֹ שֶׁגְּבוֹהִין מִן הָאָרֶץ. רָבָא מְתָרֵץ לְטַעְמֵיהּ: כְּשֶׁהָיָה לָהֶן צִיר, אוֹ שֶׁגְּבוֹהִין מִן הָאָרֶץ.

The Gemara answers: **Abaye reconciles** the objection **in accordance with his reasoning, and Rava reconciles** the objection **in accordance with his reasoning.** The Gemara elaborates: **Abaye reconciles** the objection **in accordance with his reasoning** by adding to the *baraita*: They must **either have a hinge or** be held **above the ground. Rava** likewise **reconciles** the objection **in accordance with his reasoning,** as he reads: They must **have had a hinge or** else be held **above the ground.**

תָּנוּ רַבָּנַן: סוּכֵּי קוֹצִים וַחֲבִילִין שֶׁהִתְקִינָן לְפִירְצָה שֶׁבֶּחָצֵר, בִּזְמַן שֶׁקְּשׁוּרִין וּתְלוּיִין – נוֹעֲלִין בָּהֶן בַּשַּׁבָּת, וְאֵין צָרִיךְ לוֹמַר בְּיוֹם טוֹב.

The Sages taught a *baraita*: With regard to **branches of thorn bushes or bundles** of wood **that were arranged** so that they sealed off a **breach in a courtyard, when they are tied and suspended** in place, **one** may **close** an opening **with them on Shabbat; and needless to say,** this is permitted **on a Festival.**

תָּנֵי רַבִּי חִיָּיא: דֶּלֶת אַלְמָנָה הַנִּגְרֶרֶת – אֵין נוֹעֲלִין בָּהּ. הֵיכִי דָּמֵי דֶּלֶת אַלְמָנָה – אִיכָּא דְּאָמְרִי: דְּחַד שִׁיפָא, וְאִיכָּא דְּאָמְרִי: דְּלֵית לֵיהּ גִּשְׁמָה.

Rabbi Ḥiyya taught a *baraita*: With regard to **a widowed door**[NH] **that drags** along the ground, **one** may **not close** an opening **with it.** The Gemara asks: **What are the circumstances** of **a widowed door? Some say** it refers to a door built **from a single plank,** which does not look like a door, **and others say** it is **a door that does not have a lower doorsill** (*ge'onim*) and that touches the ground when closed.

אָמַר רַב יְהוּדָה: הַאי מְדוּרְתָא, מִמַּעְלָה לְמַטָּה שָׁרֵי – מִמַּטָּה לְמַעְלָה – אָסִיר.

With regard to activities that are prohibited because of their similarity to building, the Gemara cites a teaching that **Rav Yehuda said:** When arranging a pile of wood for **a fire** on a Festival, if the logs are arranged **from the top down,** i.e., the upper logs are temporarily suspended in the air while the lower logs are inserted below them, **it is permitted.** However, if the wood is placed from **the bottom up, it is prohibited,** as the arrangement of wood in the regular manner is a form of building.

וְכֵן בֵּיעֲתָא, וְכֵן קִידְרָא, וְכֵן פּוּרְיָא, וְכֵן חָבִיתָא.

And the same applies to **eggs** that are to be arranged in a pile, **and the same** applies to **a cauldron** that is to be set down on a fire by means of supports, **and the same** applies to a **bed** that will be placed on its frame, **and the same** applies to **barrels** arranged in a cellar. In all these cases, the part that goes on top must be temporarily suspended in the air while the lower section is inserted beneath it.[H]

אֲמַר לֵיהּ הַהוּא מִינָא לְרַבִּי יְהוֹשֻׁעַ בֶּן חֲנַנְיָה: חַדְקָאָה! דִּכְתִיב בְּכוּ: "טוֹבָם כְּחֵדֶק". אֲמַר לֵיהּ: שַׁטְיָא, שְׁפִיל לְסֵיפֵיהּ דִּקְרָא, דִּכְתִיב: "יָשָׁר מִמְּסוּכָה". וְאֶלָּא מַאי – "טוֹבָם כְּחֵדֶק" – כְּשֵׁם שֶׁחֲדָקִים הַלָּלוּ מְגִינִּין עַל הַפִּירְצָה, כָּךְ טוֹבִים שֶׁבָּנוּ מְגִינִּים עָלֵינוּ. דָּבָר אַחֵר: "טוֹבָם כְּחֵדֶק" – שֶׁמְּהַדְּקִין אֶת הָרְשָׁעִים לַגֵּיהִנָּם, שֶׁנֶּאֱמַר: "קוּמִי וָדוֹשִׁי בַת צִיּוֹן כִּי קַרְנֵךְ אָשִׂים בַּרְזֶל וּפַרְסוֹתַיִךְ אָשִׂים נְחוּשָׁה וַהֲדִיקּוֹת עַמִּים רַבִּים וגו'".

With regard to bundles of thorns used to seal a breach, the Gemara cites a related incident: **A certain heretic** once **said to Rabbi Yehoshua ben Ḥananya: Man of thorns! For it says about you: "The best of them is as a brier"**[N] (Micah 7:4), which indicates that even Israel's best are merely thorns. **He said to him: Fool, go down to the end of the verse: "The most upright is worse than a thorn hedge,"** a derogatory expression meant as praise. **Rather, what is** the meaning of **the best of them is as a brier?** It means that **just as these thorns protect a breach, so the best among us protect us. Alternatively: The best of them is as a brier** [*ḥedek*] means **that they grind** [*mehaddekin*] **the nations of the world into Gehenna, as it is stated: "Arise and thresh, O daughter of Zion, for I will make your horn iron, and I will make your hoofs brass, and you shall beat in pieces** [*vahadikot*] **many peoples;** and you shall devote their gain to God, and their substance to the God of the whole earth" (Micah 4:13).

מתני׳ לֹא יַעֲמוֹד אָדָם בִּרְשׁוּת הַיָּחִיד וְיִפְתַּח בִּרְשׁוּת הָרַבִּים, בִּרְשׁוּת הָרַבִּים וְיִפְתַּח בִּרְשׁוּת הַיָּחִיד, אֶלָּא אִם כֵּן עָשָׂה מְחִיצָה גְּבוֹהָה עֲשָׂרָה טְפָחִים, דִּבְרֵי רַבִּי מֵאִיר.

MISHNA **A person** may **not stand in the private domain and open** a door located **in the public domain** with a key, lest he inadvertently transfer the key from one domain to the other. Likewise, one may not stand **in the public domain and open** a door **in the private domain** with a key, **unless** in the latter case **he erected a partition ten handbreadths high** around the door and stands inside it. This is **the statement of Rabbi Meir.**

אָמְרוּ לוֹ: מַעֲשֶׂה בְּשׁוּק שֶׁל פַּטָּמִים שֶׁהָיָה בִּירוּשָׁלַיִם שֶׁהָיוּ נוֹעֲלִין וּמַנִּיחִין אֶת הַמַּפְתֵּחַ בַּחַלּוֹן שֶׁעַל גַּבֵּי הַפֶּתַח. רַבִּי יוֹסֵי אוֹמֵר: שׁוּק שֶׁל צַמָּרִים הָיָה.

The Rabbis **said to him:** There was **an incident at the poultry dealers' market in Jerusalem,** where they would fatten fowl for slaughter (Rabbeinu Ḥananel), **and they would lock** the doors to their shops **and place**[H] **the key in the window that was over the door,**[B] which was more than ten handbreadths off the ground, and nobody was concerned about the possible violation of any prohibition. **Rabbi Yosei says:** That place **was a market of wool dealers.**

NOTES

A widowed door – דֶּלֶת אַלְמָנָה: Most commentaries explain that a widowed door is one that is missing a significant component, like a woman who has lost her husband (Ritva). Others maintain that it means the door of a widow. A widowed woman has nobody to assist her; consequently, her doors are usually attached incorrectly (Rashash).

The best of them is as a brier – טוֹבָם כְּחֵדֶק: This verse compares the leaders of Israel to thorns in a positive light, in that they protect the people. The rationale for this unusual metaphor is that it is the job of the leaders to reprove the people and set them on the correct path (*Me'iri*).

HALAKHA

A widowed door – דֶּלֶת אַלְמָנָה: It is prohibited to close an opening with a door built from a single plank or one that does not have a lower doorsill. The *halakha* is in accordance with the stringencies of both explanations of a widowed door (*Shulḥan Arukh, Oraḥ Ḥayyim* 313:4).

A fire, an egg, a cauldron – מְדוּרְתָא, בֵּיעֲתָא, קִידְרָא: On a Festival, it is prohibited to arrange firewood or other items in the manner that they are typically arranged, from the bottom up. Instead, one must arrange them in an unusual fashion, e.g., place one log, then place another beneath it, and so on (*Shulḥan Arukh, Oraḥ Ḥayyim* 502:1).

Lock and place – נוֹעֲלִין וּמַנִּיחִין: It is permitted to stand in a public domain and lock a door in a private domain, as the *halakha* rejects Rabbi Meir's opinion in favor of the ruling of the Rabbis (*Shulḥan Arukh, Oraḥ Ḥayyim* 350:1).

BACKGROUND

A door and a window – פֶּתַח וְחַלּוֹן: The window in this image is clearly visible above the door. The discussion concerning how to use a door key without removing it from one domain to another is referring to a window of this type.

Synagogue door from the talmudic period, Bar'am National Park, Israel

גמ׳ וְרַבָּנַן, אָמַר רַבִּי מֵאִיר רְשׁוּת הָרַבִּים – וּמְהַדְּרוּ אִינְהוּ כַּרְמְלִית? דְּאָמַר רַבָּה בַּר בַּר חָנָה, אָמַר רַבִּי יוֹחָנָן: יְרוּשָׁלַיִם, אִלְמָלֵא דַּלְתוֹתֶיהָ נִנְעָלוֹת בַּלַּיְלָה – חַיָּיבִין עָלֶיהָ מִשּׁוּם רְשׁוּת הָרַבִּים.

GEMARA The Gemara asks: **And** those **Rabbis,** who cited the case of the poultry dealers of Jerusalem to rebut Rabbi Meir's opinion, **Rabbi Meir spoke** to them about unlocking a door in a private domain while standing **in the public domain, and they responded** with an incident involving **a** ***karmelit*****. As Rabba bar bar Ḥana said** that **Rabbi Yoḥanan said:** With regard to **Jerusalem, were it not** for the fact that **its doors are locked at night, one would be liable for** carrying in **it** on Shabbat, **because** its thoroughfares have the status of **the public domain.** However, since Jerusalem's doors are typically locked, it is considered one large *karmelit,* which is subject to rabbinic prohibitions. How, then, could a proof be cited from the markets of Jerusalem with regard to the transfer of objects between a public domain and a private domain, which is prohibited by Torah law?

אָמַר רַב פַּפָּא: כָּאן – קוֹדֶם שֶׁנִּפְרְצוּ בָּהּ פְּרָצוֹת. כָּאן – לְאַחַר שֶׁנִּפְרְצוּ בָּהּ פְּרָצוֹת.

Rav Pappa said: Here, the Rabbis considered Jerusalem a *karmelit* during the period **before breaches were made in its** walls. Its doors did not turn it into a public domain, as they were locked. Whereas **there,** Rabbi Meir is referring to the time **after breaches had been made in** the walls, and it therefore acquired the status of a public domain.

רָבָא אָמַר: סֵיפָא אֲתָאן לְשַׁעֲרֵי גִינָּה. וְהָכִי קָאָמַר: וְכֵן לֹא יַעֲמוֹד בִּרְשׁוּת הַיָּחִיד וְיִפְתַּח בְּכַרְמְלִית, בְּכַרְמְלִית וְיִפְתַּח בִּרְשׁוּת הַיָּחִיד,

Rava said: In the latter clause of the mishna **we came to** a different issue,[N] i.e., the final section of the mishna is not designed to counter Rabbi Meir's statement with regard to the public domain. Rather, it refers **to the gates of a garden** with an area greater than two *beit se'a* in size, whose legal status is that of a *karmelit.* Consequently, the mishna **is saying as follows: And likewise,** one may **not stand in the private domain and open** a door **in a** ***karmelit*****;** neither may one stand **in a** ***karmelit*** **and open** a door **in the private domain,**

NOTES

In the latter clause we came to a different issue – **סֵיפָא אֲתָאן:** Rava does not necessarily maintain that the mishna is missing a section, as it is possible that Rabbi Meir stated one *halakha,* while the Rabbis taught a related *halakha.* Indeed, some commentaries assert that according to this opinion there is no dispute between them at all (see Rabbi Zeraḥya HaLevi; *Ge'on Ya'akov*).

אֶלָּא אִם כֵּן עָשָׂה מְחִיצָה גְּבוֹהָה עֲשָׂרָה טְפָחִים, דִּבְרֵי רַבִּי מֵאִיר. אָמְרוּ לוֹ: מַעֲשֶׂה בְּשׁוּק שֶׁל פַּטָּמִים שֶׁהָיָה בִּירוּשָׁלַיִם, שֶׁהָיוּ נוֹעֲלִין וּמַנִּיחִין אֶת הַמַּפְתֵּחַ בַּחַלּוֹן שֶׁעַל גַּבֵּי הַפֶּתַח. רַבִּי יוֹסֵי אוֹמֵר: שׁוּק שֶׁל צַמָּרִים הָיָה.

unless he erected a partition ten handbreadths high around the door and stands inside it; this is **the statement of Rabbi Meir.** The Rabbis **said to him: An incident** occurred **at the poultry dealers' market in Jerusalem, as they would lock** the doors to their shops **and place the key in a window that was over the door,** which was higher than ten handbreadths. **Rabbi Yosei says:** That place **was a market of wool dealers.**

תָּנוּ רַבָּנַן: פִּתְחֵי שַׁעֲרֵי גִינָּה, בִּזְמַן שֶׁיֵּשׁ לָהֶן בֵּית שַׁעַר מִבִּפְנִים – פּוֹתֵחַ וְנוֹעֵל מִבִּפְנִים. מִבַּחוּץ – פּוֹתֵחַ וְנוֹעֵל מִבַּחוּץ. מִכָּאן וּמִכָּאן – פּוֹתֵחַ וְנוֹעֵל כָּאן וְכָאן. אֵין לָהֶן לֹא לְכָאן וְלֹא לְכָאן – אֲסוּרִין כָּאן וְכָאן.

The Sages taught a *baraita*: With regard to **the entrances of garden gates** that open into a public domain, **when they have a gatehouse**[N] **on the inside,** which is a private domain, **one** may **open and close** them **from within.** This is because the lock, which is four handbreadths wide and ten handbreadths high, also constitutes a private domain. Consequently, the key may be passed from the gatehouse to the lock. However, they may not be opened or closed from without, as the key may not be passed from the public domain to the private domain of the lock. If the gatehouse is **on the outside, one** may **open and close** the doors **from without,** as once again both the lock and the gatehouse are private domains. They may not, however, be opened from within, as the key may not be passed from the garden, which is a *karmelit,* to the lock. If they have a gatehouse **from here,** from within, **and there,** from without, **one** may **open and close** the doors **here and there.** If **they do not have** a gatehouse; **neither here nor there, it is prohibited** to open or close the doors **here and there,** as one may not carry the key either in the public domain or in the garden.

וְכֵן חֲנוּיוֹת הַפְּתוּחוֹת לִרְשׁוּת הָרַבִּים, בִּזְמַן שֶׁהַמַּנְעוּל לְמַטָּה מֵעֲשָׂרָה – מֵבִיא מַפְתֵּחַ מֵעֶרֶב שַׁבָּת וּמַנִּיחוֹ בָּאִיסְקוּפָּה, לְמָחָר פּוֹתֵחַ וְנוֹעֵל וּמַחֲזִירוֹ לָאִיסְקוּפָּה.

And likewise, this is the *halakha* with regard to **stores that open into the public domain: When the lock is below ten** handbreadths off the ground, it is in the public domain. In that case, **one** may **bring a key on Shabbat eve and place it on the threshold,** whose legal status is that of a *karmelit,* and **the following day he** may **open and close** the door **and return** the key **to the threshold.**

NOTES

When they have a gatehouse – **שֶׁיֵּשׁ לָהֶן בֵּית שַׁעַר:** The distinction between a gatehouse on the inside and a gatehouse on the outside and all these other details are not necessary for establishing the *halakha* (Ritva). Nevertheless, as it is not unusual for a gatehouse to be on either side of a doorway, the Gemara addresses all the various situations.

וּבִזְמַן שֶׁהַמַּנְעוּל לְמַעְלָה מֵעֲשָׂרָה – מֵבִיא מַפְתֵּחַ מֵעֶרֶב שַׁבָּת, וּמַנִּיחוֹ בַּמַּנְעוּל, לְמָחָר פּוֹתֵחַ וְנוֹעֵל וּמַחֲזִירוֹ לִמְקוֹמוֹ, דִּבְרֵי רַבִּי מֵאִיר.

And when the lock is above ten handbreadths off the ground, one may **bring a key on Shabbat eve and place it in the lock.** And **the following day he** may **open and close** the door **and return** the key **to its place** on top of the lock. This is **the statement of Rabbi Meir.**

וַחֲכָמִים אוֹמְרִים: אַף בִּזְמַן שֶׁהַמַּנְעוּל לְמַעְלָה מֵעֲשָׂרָה טְפָחִים – מֵבִיא מַפְתֵּחַ מֵעֶרֶב שַׁבָּת, וּמַנִּיחוֹ בָּאִיסְקוּפָּה, לְמָחָר פּוֹתֵחַ וְנוֹעֵל וּמַחֲזִירוֹ לִמְקוֹמוֹ, אוֹ בַּחַלּוֹן שֶׁעַל גַּבֵּי הַפֶּתַח.

And the Rabbis say: Even when the lock is above ten handbreadths off the ground, **one** may **bring a key on Shabbat eve and place it on the threshold,** and **the following day he** may **open and close** the door **and return** the key **to its place** on the threshold **or in the window that is above the door.**

אִם יֵשׁ בַּחַלּוֹן אַרְבָּעָה עַל אַרְבָּעָה – אָסוּר, מִפְּנֵי שֶׁהוּא כְּמוֹצִיא מֵרְשׁוּת לִרְשׁוּת.

However, **if the window is four by four** handbreadths and ten handbreadths above the ground, its status is that of a private domain, **and it is** therefore **prohibited** to place the key in the window, **because** it would be **as though one is transferring** the key **from** one **domain,** a *karmelit*, **to** another private **domain.**

מִדְּקָאָמַר וְכֵן חֲנוּיוֹת – מִכְּלָל דְּבְאִיסְקוּפַּת כַּרְמְלִית עָסְקִינַן. הַאי מַנְעוּל הֵיכִי דָּמֵי? אִי דְּלֵית בֵּיהּ אַרְבָּעָה – מְקוֹם פְּטוּר הוּא,

The Gemara infers: **From** the fact that **it is stated** in the *baraita*: **And similarly, stores,** this proves **by inference that we are dealing with a threshold** that is **a *karmelit*,** as it would otherwise be prohibited to transfer the key from the threshold to the lock. If so, with regard to **this lock, what are the circumstances? If there is not** an area of **four** by four handbreadths **in it,** it does not have the status of a prohibited domain at all, and **it is an exempt domain.**

וְאִי אִית בֵּיהּ אַרְבָּעָה – בְּהָא לֵימָא רַבָּנַן: אַף בִּזְמַן שֶׁהַמַּנְעוּל לְמַעְלָה מֵעֲשָׂרָה מֵבִיא מַפְתֵּחַ מֵעֶרֶב שַׁבָּת, וּמַנִּיחוֹ בָּאִיסְקוּפָּה, לְמָחָר פּוֹתֵחַ וְנוֹעֵל בּוֹ וּמַחֲזִירוֹ לָאִיסְקוּפָּה, אוֹ לַחֲלוֹן שֶׁעַל גַּבֵּי הַפֶּתַח? וְהָא קָא מְטַלְטֵל מִכַּרְמְלִית לִרְשׁוּת הַיָּחִיד!

And if it is four by four handbreadths, and therefore a private domain, **would the Rabbis say in that** case: **Even when the lock is above ten handbreadths** off the ground, **he** may **bring a key on Shabbat eve and place it in the threshold,** and **the following day he** may **open and close** the door **and return** the key **to the threshold or to a window above the door? Isn't he moving** an object **from a *karmelit* to the private domain?**

אָמַר אַבַּיֵי: לְעוֹלָם דְּאֵין בּוֹ אַרְבָּעָה, וְיֵשׁ בּוֹ לָחוֹק וּלְהַשְׁלִימוֹ לְאַרְבָּעָה.

Abaye said: Actually, the lock **is not four** by four handbreadths, **but there is** enough space in the door surrounding it **to carve out** a hole that would **complete** its area to the requisite **four** handbreadths.

וּבְהָא פְּלִיגִי; דְּרַבִּי מֵאִיר סָבַר: חוֹקְקִין לְהַשְׁלִים, וְרַבָּנַן סָבְרִי: אֵין חוֹקְקִין לְהַשְׁלִים.

And this is their **dispute: Rabbi Meir,** who conforms to his standard line of reasoning, **maintains** that **one carves out** the space **to complete** it to four handbreadths. In other words, if a small opening is located in a place large enough for it to be widened, the place is viewed as though it had already been carved out, providing the opening with the larger dimensions. **And the Rabbis** conform to their standard line of reasoning, as they **maintain** that **one does not carve out** the space **to complete** it to four handbreadths. Consequently, the lock in its present condition is not large enough to constitute a place of significance, and it is therefore regarded as an exempt place.

אָמַר רַב בֵּיבָי בַּר אַבַּיֵי: שְׁמַע מִינָּהּ מֵהָא מַתְנִיתָא תְּלָת; שְׁמַע מִינָּהּ: חוֹקְקִין לְהַשְׁלִים, וּשְׁמַע מִינָּהּ: הֲדַר בֵּיהּ רַבִּי מֵאִיר מִשַּׁעֲרֵי גִינָּה,

Rav Beivai bar Abaye said: Learn from this *baraita* three *halakhot*: Learn from it that according to Rabbi Meir, **we carve out to complete**[N] the necessary dimensions. **And** further **learn from it** that **Rabbi Meir retracted** his ruling with regard to **garden gates.** According to Rava, Rabbi Meir prohibited a man standing in a *karmelit* from opening a door in a private domain, and yet here he permits a similar case.

וְשָׁמְעַתְּ מִינָּהּ: מִדְּרַבָּנַן אִיתָא לְדְרַב דִּימִי. דְּכִי אֲתָא רַב דִּימִי, אָמַר רַבִּי יוֹחָנָן: מָקוֹם שֶׁאֵין בּוֹ אַרְבָּעָה עַל אַרְבָּעָה – מוּתָּר לִבְנֵי רְשׁוּת הָרַבִּים וְלִבְנֵי רְשׁוּת הַיָּחִיד לְכַתֵּף עָלָיו, וּבִלְבַד שֶׁלֹּא יַחֲלִיפוּ.

And learn from the statement of **the Rabbis** that the ruling of **Rav Dimi is accepted. As when Rav Dimi came** to Babylonia from Eretz Israel, he said that **Rabbi Yoḥanan said: A place** with an area **that is less than four by four** handbreadths and that is set apart from the surrounding area is an exempt domain with regard to carrying on Shabbat. Consequently, if the domain is located between a public domain and a private domain, **it is permitted for** both **the people in the public domain and for the people in the private domain to adjust** the burden **onto their shoulders, provided that they do not exchange** objects with one another. This ruling, that it is prohibited to exchange articles, is supported by the position of the Rabbis that it is prohibited to transfer the key from the threshold, which is a *karmelit*, via the lock, an exempt domain, to the private domain of the window, as one may not transfer an object from one prohibited domain to another, even via an exempt domain.

NOTES

Learn from it that we carve out to complete – שְׁמַע מִינָּהּ חוֹקְקִין לְהַשְׁלִים: Although Rabbi Meir's opinion with regard to carving out to complete the requisite dimensions is well known, the Gemara felt it was necessary to stress that this is indeed his opinion, since he never explicitly formulated his position in these terms. Moreover, there is a novel element to this discussion, as it teaches that Rabbi Meir maintains it is possible to carve out a space to complete dimensions even with regard to an object such as a door, not only a building (Ritva).

מתני׳ נֶגֶר שֶׁיֵּשׁ בְּרֹאשׁוֹ גְּלוֹסְטְרָא, רַבִּי אֱלִיעֶזֶר אוֹסֵר, וְרַבִּי יוֹסֵי מַתִּיר.

MISHNA With regard to **a bolt** that secures a door in place **and** that **has** a thick **knob [*gelustera*]**[L] **at its end,**[BHN] a useful implement for a variety of purposes, the *tanna'im* disagree whether the bolt has the status of a vessel, and one may therefore close the door with it, or whether it is considered a cross beam, which would mean that doing so is classified as building. **Rabbi Eliezer prohibits** its use, **and Rabbi Yosei permits** it.

אָמַר רַבִּי אֱלִיעֶזֶר: מַעֲשֶׂה בִּכְנֶסֶת שֶׁבִּטְבֶרְיָא שֶׁהָיוּ נוֹהֲגִין בּוֹ הֶיתֵּר, עַד שֶׁבָּא רַבָּן גַּמְלִיאֵל וְהַזְּקֵנִים וְאָסְרוּ לָהֶן. רַבִּי יוֹסֵי אוֹמֵר: אִיסּוּר נָהֲגוּ בּוֹ, וּבָא רַבָּן גַּמְלִיאֵל וְהַזְּקֵנִים וְהִתִּירוּ לָהֶן.

Rabbi Eliezer said: An incident occurred **in a synagogue in Tiberias, where they were accustomed** to treat use of this bolt as **permitted, until Rabban Gamliel and the Elders came and prohibited** it to **them. Rabbi Yosei says** that the opposite was the case: At first **they were accustomed** to treat use of this bolt as **prohibited, and Rabban Gamliel and the Elders came and permitted** it to **them.**

גמ׳ בְּנִיטָּל בְּאִגְדוֹ – כּוּלֵּי עָלְמָא לָא פְּלִיגִי, כִּי פְּלִיגִי –

GEMARA The Gemara narrows the dispute: **If** the bolt **can be moved by the rope** with which it is attached to the door, **everyone agrees** that it is considered part of the door, and one may secure the door with it. **When** Rabbi Yosei and Rabbi Eliezer **disagree,**

NOTES

A bolt and a knob – **נֶגֶר וּגְלוֹסְטְרָא**: Rashi and other commentaries explain that this refers to a bolt placed in the bottom of a door. It keeps the door closed when it is inserted into a hole in the threshold. Other authorities assert that it is a bar inserted through rings to hold two doors together (Rambam). Rashi, as well as the *Me'iri* and others, state that the knob is the thick part of the bolt that can also be used for pounding and is therefore a kind of utensil. The Rambam explains that the end of the bolt has a special part shaped like a pomegranate or a square, which signifies that this bar is no longer a cross beam but has been changed into a permanent utensil. Still other commentaries claim that the knob is a kind of key, located on the thin end of the bolt (Rabbi Zeraḥya HaLevi).

BACKGROUND

A bolt that has a knob at its end – **נֶגֶר שֶׁיֵּשׁ בְּרֹאשׁוֹ גְּלוֹסְטְרָא**:

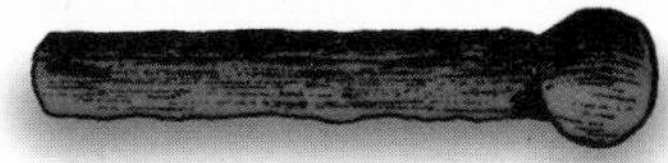

Illustration of a bolt with a knob at its end, which allows it to be used as a kind of vessel

LANGUAGE

Knob [*gelustera*] – **גְּלוֹסְטְרָא**: From the Greek κλεῖστρον, *kleistron*, or the Latin claustrum, meaning lock. In this context, it probably refers to the thick end of the bolt, which can be used for locking.

HALAKHA

A bolt that has a knob at its end – **נֶגֶר שֶׁיֵּשׁ בְּרֹאשׁוֹ גְּלוֹסְטְרָא**: It is permitted to use a bolt with a knob at its end to close a door on Shabbat, in accordance with the opinion of Rabbi Yosei. However, it must be attached to the door in some fashion (*Shulḥan Arukh*, *Oraḥ Ḥayyim* 313:1).

בְּשֶׁאֵינוֹ נִיטָּל בְּאִיגְדוֹ – דְּמָר סָבַר: כֵּיוָן דְּיֵשׁ בְּרֹאשׁוֹ גְּלוֹסְטְרָא – תּוֹרַת כְּלִי עָלָיו, וּמָר סָבַר: כֵּיוָן דְּאֵינוֹ נִיטָּל בְּאִיגְדוֹ – לֹא.

it is **in** a case **where it cannot be picked up by its rope,** as it is too thin to bear the weight of the bolt. **As this Sage,** Rabbi Yosei, **maintains: Since it has a knob at its end, it has the status of a vessel,**[N] and one is therefore permitted to secure the door with it. **And this Sage,** Rabbi Eliezer, **maintains: Since it cannot be picked up by its rope, no,** it is not considered a proper vessel merely because of the knob, and consequently, its use is prohibited on Shabbat.

מתני׳ נֶגֶר הַנִּגְרָר – נוֹעֲלִין בּוֹ בַּמִּקְדָּשׁ, אֲבָל לֹא בַּמְּדִינָה.

MISHNA With regard to **a bolt that** is attached to the door, but owing to the length of the rope, it does not hang from the door but **drags**[H] along the ground, **one** may **lock** a door **with it in the Temple** on Shabbat, as this is prohibited only by rabbinic decree, issued to enhance the character of Shabbat as a day of rest, and rabbinic decrees are not in effect in the Temple. **However,** one may **not** lock a door with this bolt **in the country** outside the Temple.

וְהַמּוּנָּח – כָּאן וְכָאן אָסוּר. רַבִּי יְהוּדָה אוֹמֵר: הַמּוּנָּח – מוּתָּר בַּמִּקְדָּשׁ, וְהַנִּגְרָר – בַּמְּדִינָה.

And with regard to **one that** is not tied at all but **rests** entirely on the ground, it **is prohibited in both** places, in and outside the Temple, as the use of this bolt is considered building.[N] **Rabbi Yehuda says: One that rests** entirely on the ground **is permitted in the Temple, and one that drags** along the ground is permitted even **in** the rest of **the country.**

גמ׳ תָּנוּ רַבָּנַן: אֵיזֶהוּ נֶגֶר הַנִּגְרָר שֶׁנּוֹעֲלִין בַּמִּקְדָּשׁ אֲבָל לֹא בַּמְּדִינָה – כֹּל שֶׁקָּשׁוּר וְתָלוּי, וְרֹאשׁוֹ אֶחָד מַגִּיעַ לָאָרֶץ. רַבִּי יְהוּדָה אוֹמֵר זֶה – אַף בַּמְּדִינָה מוּתָּר, אֶלָּא אֵיזֶהוּ נֶגֶר שֶׁנּוֹעֲלִין בַּמִּקְדָּשׁ אֲבָל לֹא בַּמְּדִינָה – כֹּל שֶׁאֵינוֹ לֹא קָשׁוּר וְלֹא תָלוּי, וְשׁוֹמְטוֹ וּמַנִּיחוֹ בְּקֶרֶן זָוִית.

GEMARA **The Sages taught** in a *baraita*: **Which is the bolt that drags** along the ground **with which one** may **lock** a door on Shabbat **in the Temple but not in the** rest of the **country? Any that is tied** to the door **and suspended** from it, **while one end** of the bolt **reaches the ground. Rabbi Yehuda says:** This type of bolt **is permitted even in** the rest of **the country. Rather, which is** the **bolt with which one** may **lock** a door **in the Temple but not in** the rest of **the country? Any that is neither tied** to the door **nor suspended** from it, **but which one removes** after use **and places in a corner.**

NOTES

It has the status of a utensil – **תּוֹרַת כְּלִי עָלָיו**: In the Jerusalem Talmud, it is explained that the dispute is whether the bolt is nullified by the knob at its end and is therefore considered a utensil, or whether it is not nullified, which would mean that the bolt itself does not have the status of a utensil. Consequently, using it would be considered building.

One that rests and one that drags – **הַמּוּנָּח וְהַנִּגְרָר**: *Tosafot* explain that the use of a bar that rests entirely on the ground does not constitute building. Rather, the dispute concerns whether or not one may move the bar. If it has the status of a utensil, one may move the bar, but if its status is not that of a utensil, it is considered set-aside [*muktze*] and may not be moved on Shabbat.

HALAKHA

A bolt that drags – **נֶגֶר הַנִּגְרָר**: If a bolt that does not have a knob at its end is attached to a door, it is permitted to lock the door with it, even if it rests entirely on the ground. However, if it was attached to the bar that locks the door, it must be tied with a rope with which it can be picked up (*Shulḥan Arukh*, *Oraḥ Ḥayyim* 313:1).

BACKGROUND

Pressed bolt – **נִקְמָז**: The *ge'onim* explain that this refers to a bolt suspended on a small hook. It descends by itself when removed from the hook, thereby locking the door. The bolt in the image is permitted for use on Shabbat, as it is like a utensil and is properly affixed in place. The pressed bolt discussed in the Gemara is similar in design, only it is made from a plain piece of wood and nails.

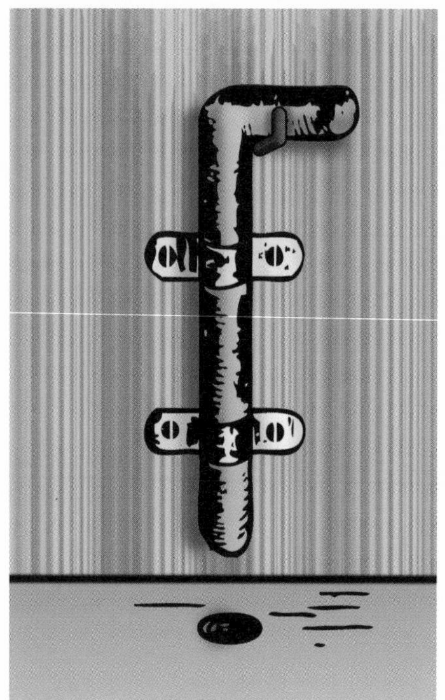

Pressed bolt, according to the *ge'onim*

HALAKHA

A certain cross beam – **הַהוּא שָׁרִיתָא**: Although a utensil may be extremely large and heavy, it does not lose its status as a utensil, provided that it can be moved on Shabbat. This *halakha* is in accordance with what is implied by the incidents reported in the Gemara with regard to a cross beam and a mortar (*Shulḥan Arukh*, *Oraḥ Ḥayyim* 308:2).

אָמַר רַב יְהוּדָה, אָמַר שְׁמוּאֵל: הֲלָכָה כְּרַבִּי יְהוּדָה בִּנְגָרָר.

Rav Yehuda said that **Shmuel said: The *halakha* is in accordance with** the opinion of **Rabbi Yehuda with regard to** a bolt **that is dragged.**[N] It is permitted to use this bolt on Shabbat even outside the Temple, but it is prohibited to use a bolt that rests on the ground, even in the Temple.

אָמַר רָבָא: וְהוּא שֶׁקָּשׁוּר בַּדֶּלֶת. אִינִי?! וְהָא רַבִּי טַבְלָא אִיקְּלַע לִמְחוֹזָא, וַחֲזָא לְהָהוּא דַּהֲוָה תָּלֵי בְּעִיבְרָא דְּדַשָּׁא, וְלָא אָמַר לְהוּ וְלָא מִידֵּי! הַהוּא נִיטָּל בְּאִיגְדּוֹ הֲוָה.

Rava said: And that is the case only **if** the bolt **is tied to the door** itself. The Gemara is surprised by this ruling: **Is that** really **so? But didn't Rabbi Tavla happen** to come **to Meḥoza and he saw a certain** bolt **that was suspended from the side of the door, and he did not say anything to** the people there with regard to a prohibition? The Gemara rejects this contention: **That** bolt **was one that could be picked up by its rope.** Everyone agrees that a bolt of this kind may be used for locking a door on Shabbat even if it is not tied to the door itself.

רַב אַוְיָא אִיקְּלַע לִנְהַרְדְּעָא, חַזְיֵיהּ לְהָהוּא גַּבְרָא דַּהֲוָה קָא קָטֵיר בְּגֶמִי, אֲמַר: דֵּין לָא נִטְרוֹק.

The Gemara relates that **Rav Avya** once **happened** to come **to Neharde'a and saw a certain person tying** a bolt to a door **with a reed. He said: This** door may **not be locked** on Shabbat, as the bolt is not adequately fastened to it.

בָּעֵי רַבִּי זֵירָא: נִקְמָז מַהוּ? אָמַר רַב יוֹסֵף: מַאי תִּיבְּעֵי לֵיהּ? לָא שְׁמִיעַ לֵיהּ הָא דְּתַנְיָא: נִשְׁמַט – אָסוּר, נִקְמָז – מוּתָּר. וְרַבִּי יְהוּדָה אוֹמֵר: נִקְמָז אַף עַל פִּי שֶׁאֵינוֹ נִשְׁמָט – אָסוּר.

Rabbi Zeira raised the following **dilemma:** If the bolt **was pressed**[BN] into the ground through a hole in the threshold, **what is the** *halakha*? Is the use of this bolt considered building? **Rav Yosef said: What is** Rabbi Zeira's **dilemma?** Has **he not heard that which was taught** in the *Tosefta*: If the bolt **was** altogether **detached** from the rope to which it had been tied, **it is prohibited;** but **if it was pressed** into the ground, **it is permitted; and Rabbi Yehuda said:** If it **was pressed** into the ground, **even though it was not** entirely **detached** from its rope, **it is prohibited?**

וְאָמַר רַב יְהוּדָה, אָמַר שְׁמוּאֵל: הֲלָכָה כְּרַבִּי יְהוּדָה בְּנִקְמָז. וְטַעְמָא מַאי? אָמַר אַבַּיֵי: מִשּׁוּם דְּמֶיחְזֵי כְּבוֹנֶה.

And Rav Yehuda said that **Shmuel said: The *halakha* is in accordance with** the opinion of **Rabbi Yehuda with regard to** a bolt **that was pressed** into the ground. The Gemara asks: **And what is the reason** that the Sages prohibited the use of a bolt **that was pressed** into the ground? **Abaye said:** They prohibited its use **because it appears like building,** as the bolt enters all the way into the ground.

בְּעָא מִינֵּיהּ רַב נְחוּמֵי בַּר זְכַרְיָה מֵאַבַּיֵי: עָשָׂה לוֹ בֵּית יָד, מַהוּ? אָמַר לֵיהּ: בּוּכְנָא קָאָמַרְתְּ. אִיתְּמַר, אָמַר רַב נְחוּמֵי בַּר אַדָּא: עָשָׂה לוֹ בֵּית יָד – מוּתָּר.

Rav Neḥumei bar Zekharya raised a dilemma before Abaye: If **one produced a handle for** the bolt in order to hold it, but it was not tied to the door, **what is** the *halakha*? Abaye **said to him: A pestle, you say?** If it has a handle it is a proper utensil, which may be freely used according to all opinions. This teaching **was stated** also in the form of a direct statement: **Rav Neḥumei bar Adda said:** If **he produced a handle for** the bolt, **it is permitted.**

הַהוּא שָׁרִיתָא דַּהֲוָה בֵּי רַבִּי פְּדָת, דַּהֲוָה מַדְלוּ לַהּ בֵּי עַשְׂרָה וְשָׁדוּ לַהּ אַדַּשָּׁא, וְלָא אָמַר לְהוּ וְלָא מִידֵּי. אָמַר: תּוֹרַת כְּלִי עָלֶיהָ.

The Gemara relates that **there was a certain** cross **beam**[H] **in the house of Rabbi Pedat that** was so heavy it took **ten** people **to lift it, and they would place it against the door** at night in order to secure it. **And** Rabbi Pedat **did not say anything to them** with regard to a possible prohibition. **He said:** I permit it because **it has the status of a utensil.** It appears like a utensil and it serves a distinct purpose; therefore, it may be used on Shabbat.

NOTES

The *halakha* is in accordance with Rabbi Yehuda with regard to a bolt that is dragged – **הֲלָכָה כְּרַבִּי יְהוּדָה בִּנְגָרָר**: This appears unnecessary, as *halakhot* related to the Temple are not practical and are considered a *halakha* for messianic times. Why then was it necessary to rule that the *halakha* is not in accordance with the opinion of Rabbi Yehuda with regard to the Temple? One answer is that in exigent circumstances or for the purpose of a mitzva, it is at times necessary to override a rabbinic decree, even in modern times outside the Temple. Consequently, a ruling was issued with regard to the Temple as well (Rav Ya'akov Emden).

Pressed [*nikmaz*] – **נִקְמָז**: One explanation is that a pressed bolt is one that is suspended by a small hook protruding from the door. When the hook is turned, the bolt falls from its place, either opening or closing the door. The word *nikmaz* is related to *nikmatz*, an object held by means of something else (Rav Hai Gaon).

הַהִיא אָסִיתָא דַּהֲוַת בֵּי מָר שְׁמוּאֵל, דַּהֲוָה מַחֲזֶקֶת אַדְרִיבָא, שְׁרָא מָר שְׁמוּאֵל לְמִישְׁדְּיֵיהּ אַדַּשָּׁא, אֲמַר: תּוֹרַת כְּלִי עָלֶיהָ.

The Gemara further relates that **there was a certain mortar in the house of Mar Shmuel that had a capacity of an** ***adriva***,[L] which is equal to half a *kor*. **Mar Shmuel permitted** them **to place it against the door** to secure it. He **said: It** falls into the halakhic **category of a utensil,** and it may therefore be used to secure the door, as this is not regarded as building.

שְׁלַח לֵיהּ רָמֵי בַּר יְחֶזְקֵאל לְרַב עַמְרָם: נֵימָא לָן מָר מֵהָנֵין מִילֵּי מַעַלְיָיתָא דְּאָמְרַתְּ לָן מִשְּׁמֵיהּ דְּרַב אַסִי בְּכֵיפֵי דְּאַרְבָא! שְׁלַח לֵיהּ, הָכִי אֲמַר רַב אַסִי: הָנֵי כֵּיפֵי דְּאַרְבָא, בִּזְמַן שֶׁיֵּשׁ בָּהֶן טֶפַח, אִי נַמִי, אֵין בָּהֶן טֶפַח וְאֵין בֵּין זֶה לָזֶה שְׁלֹשָׁה – לְמָחָר מֵבִיא מַחֲצֶלֶת וּפוֹרֵס עֲלֵיהֶן.

Rami bar Yeḥezkel sent a request **to Rav Amram: Let the Master tell us** some **of those outstanding matters that you told us in the name of Rav Asi** with regard to **the arches of a boat**[BH] upon which mats are draped as protection against the elements. Rav Amram **sent** back **to him** that **Rav Asi said as follows:** With regard to **the arches of a boat, when they are a handbreadth** wide, or **even if they are not a handbreadth** wide **but there is less than three** handbreadths **between them,** in which case the intervening space is regarded as filled in based on the principle of *lavud*, **on the following day,** i.e., on Shabbat, **one** may **bring a mat and spread** it **over them.**

מַאי טַעְמָא – מוֹסִיף עַל אֹהֶל עֲרַאי הוּא, וְשַׁפִּיר דָּמֵי.

What is the reason for this leniency? The reason is that **this is** considered **adding to a temporary tent,** and therefore one may **well** spread a mat over the arches. They themselves constitute a tent. Therefore, one who spreads a mat over them is merely adding to the temporary tent.

הָנְהוּ דִּכְרֵי דַּהֲווּ לֵיהּ לְרַב הוּנָא, דְּבִימָמָא בְּעוּ טוּלָּא וּבְלֵילְיָא בְּעוּ אֲוִירָא. אֲתָא לְקַמֵּיהּ דְּרַב.

The Gemara further relates that **Rav Huna had certain rams that required shade during the day and required air at night.** He therefore sought a way for the pen to be covered by day but not at night, even on Shabbat. **He came before Rav** to seek his advice.

אָמַר לֵיהּ: זִיל כְּרוֹךְ בּוּדְיָיא, וְשַׁיֵּיר בָּהּ טֶפַח. לְמָחָר פְּשׁוֹטָהּ, וּמוֹסִיף עַל אֹהֶל עֲרַאי הוּא, וְשַׁפִּיר דָּמֵי.

Rav **said to him: Go, roll up** the **mats** [***budeya***][L] that were spread out there for shade, but **leave** one **handbreadth** covered. **On the following day, unroll** the entire mat, which is considered **adding to a temporary tent** and **which is permitted.**

אָמַר רַב מִשּׁוּם רַבִּי חִיָּיא: וִילוֹן מוּתָּר לְנוֹטְתוֹ וּמוּתָּר לְפוֹרְקוֹ בְּשַׁבָּת.

Rav said in the name of Rabbi Ḥiyya: With regard to **a curtain** put up for privacy, **one is permitted to spread it out, and one is** also **permitted to dismantle it on Shabbat.**[H] As it is not a tent but merely a temporary wall, akin to a door, one does not violate a prohibition if it is not fixed firmly in place.

כִּילַּת חֲתָנִים מוּתָּר לְפוֹרְקָהּ וְלִנְטוֹתָהּ בְּשַׁבָּת. אָמַר רַב שֵׁשֶׁת בְּרֵיהּ דְּרַב אִידִי: לָא אֲמַרַן אֶלָּא שֶׁאֵין בְּגַגָּהּ טֶפַח, אֲבָל יֵשׁ בְּגַגָּהּ טֶפַח – אָסוּר.

With regard to **a bridal canopy,**[BHN] a curtain that is suspended over a bed and inclines outward in both directions, **it is permitted** both **to dismantle it and to spread it on Shabbat. Rav Sheshet, son of Rav Idi, said: We said** that this is permitted **only where** the curtain extends over the bed and falls on both sides in such a manner that **the top** of the curtain, the apex of the canopy, **is less than a handbreadth** wide. **However, if its top is a handbreadth** wide, i.e., if the curtain does not rise to a sharp point but extends horizontally for a handbreadth, after which it falls to the side, this handbreadth is regarded as a tent and is therefore **prohibited.**

HALAKHA

The arches of a boat – כֵּיפֵי דְּאַרְבָא: If one spread a covering at least one handbreadth wide over posts on Friday, he may spread it out as much as he wants on Shabbat. Spreading it is considered adding to a temporary tent, as asserted by Rav (*Shulḥan Arukh, Oraḥ Ḥayyim* 315:2).

A curtain on Shabbat – וִילוֹן בְּשַׁבָּת: Curtains and other partitions used only for the purpose of modesty, as opposed to walls of a building, may be set up and spread out even on Shabbat, as they are not considered proper tents (Rashi). Since they move in the wind and people can pass through them, they are not considered even legal partitions (*Magen Avraham*; *Shulḥan Arukh, Oraḥ Ḥayyim* 315:1, and in the comment of the Rema).

A bridal canopy – כִּילַּת חֲתָנִים: On Shabbat, it is permitted to spread and dismantle a canopy whose roof is less than a handbreadth wide and does not reach a width of one handbreadth within three handbreadths of its roof. Since a canopy is prepared to be used in this manner, no construction is involved, as stated by Rav and Rav Sheshet, son of Rabbi Idi. However, that reading of the Gemara: And its incline is less than a handbreadth, is rejected (*Tosafot*; *Maggid Mishne*), even though the Rosh and the *Tur*, based on Rashi's explanation, accept it (*Shulḥan Arukh, Oraḥ Ḥayyim* 315:11).

LANGUAGE

***Adriva* – אַדְרִיבָא:** Some linguists read *ardava*, the form that appears in the *Arukh* and a relatively reliable Vatican manuscript. The word might be of Old Persian origin, with Aramaic having borrowed it at an earlier stage, given the fact that it already appears in Aramaic documents from Elephantine (c. fifth century BCE). It refers to a measurement of fifteen *se'a*, which is more than 130 ℓ.

Mats [*budeya*] – בּוּדְיָא: Some suggest that it should be read as *buriya*, which means mat in several Semitic languages, ranging from ancient Babylonian to modern Arabic.

BACKGROUND

The arches of a boat – כֵּיפֵי דְּאַרְבָא:

Boat with arches upon which mats would occasionally be draped to provide protection from the sun and rain

Bridal canopy – כִּילַּת חֲתָנִים: According to *Tosafot*, this tall and narrow canopy is suspended by means of a single side post positioned over the center of a bed.

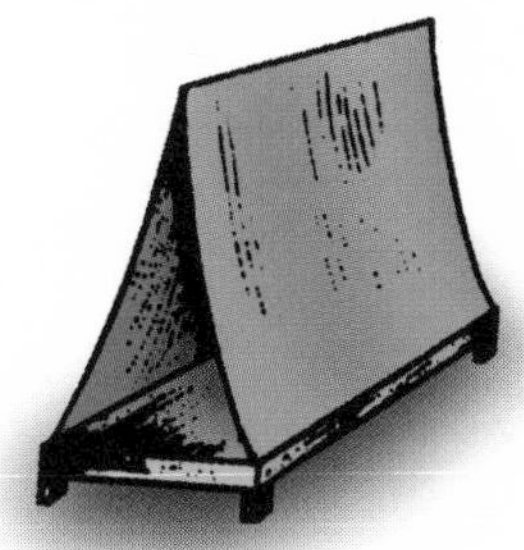

Bridal canopy as explained by *Tosafot* and accepted as *halakha*

Rashi accepts the following reading: And its incline does not extend a handbreadth. Therefore, in this context, the Gemara is referring to a series of small canopies that extend across the entire bed.

Bridal canopy as explained by Rashi

NOTES

A bridal canopy – כִּילַּת חֲתָנִים: An ordinary canopy, one not designed for decorative purposes, consists of four side posts over which the canopy is spread. That canopy has a wide roof, and therefore one who sets it up has erected a tent. However, the canopy discussed in this context is primarily for decorative purposes.

וְכִי אֵין בְּגַגָּהּ טֶפַח לָא אֲמַרַן אֶלָּא שֶׁאֵין בְּפָחוֹת מִשְּׁלֹשָׁה סָמוּךְ לְגַג טֶפַח, אֲבָל יֵשׁ בְּפָחוֹת מִשְּׁלֹשָׁה סָמוּךְ לְגַג טֶפַח – אָסוּר.

And even where its horizontal **top is not a handbreadth** wide, **we said** this leniency **only if** its width **is less than a handbreadth within three** handbreadths **from** its **top. However, if** its width **is a handbreadth within three** handbreadths **from** its **top,** this handbreadth is considered a tent and it is therefore **prohibited** to spread it on Shabbat.

וְכִי אֵין בְּפָחוֹת מִשְּׁלֹשָׁה סָמוּךְ לְגַג טֶפַח נַמִי, לָא אֲמַרַן אֶלָּא שֶׁאֵין

And even **where it is less than a handbreadth** wide **within three** handbreadths **of** its **top, we said** this leniency **only where**

Perek **X**
Daf **102** Amud **b**

בְּשִׁיפּוּעָהּ טֶפַח, אֲבָל יֵשׁ בְּשִׁיפּוּעָהּ טֶפַח – שִׁיפּוּעֵי אֹהָלִים כְּאֹהָלִים דָּמוּ.

its incline does not extend a handbreadth from the center to each side. **However, if its incline extends a handbreadth** from the center to the side, the *halakha* is that **the inclines of tents are considered like tents,** and it is therefore prohibited to suspend them.

וְאָמַר רַב שֵׁישָׁא בְּרֵיהּ דְּרַב אִידִי: סַיְינָא שָׁרֵי. וְהָתַנְיָא: אָסוּר! לָא קַשְׁיָא; הָא – דְּאִית בֵּיהּ טֶפַח, הָא – דְּלֵית בֵּיהּ טֶפַח.

And Rav Sheisha, son of Rav Idi, said: With regard to a stiff **felt hat** [*sayna*],[L] **it is permitted** to wear it on Shabbat. The Gemara raises a difficulty: **But wasn't it taught** in a *baraita* that wearing this hat **is prohibited?** The Gemara answers: It is **not difficult. This** *baraita,* which prohibits wearing a felt hat, is referring to a case **where** the hat extends **a handbreadth** from the person's head and is therefore regarded as a tent; whereas **that** statement by Rav Sheisha, who permits doing so, is referring to a case **where it does not** extend **a handbreadth** from one's head.

אֶלָּא מֵעַתָּה שַׁרְבֵּיב בִּגְלִימֵיהּ טֶפַח הָכִי נַמִי דְּאָסוּר!

The Gemara is surprised at this answer: **But if that is so,** one who **pulled his cloak a handbreadth** beyond his head, **is it also prohibited** for him to do so? This is unreasonable, as it is an article of clothing, not a tent.

אֶלָּא לָא קַשְׁיָא; הָא – דְּמִיהֲדַק, הָא – דְּלָא מִיהֲדַק.

Rather, the previous explanation must be rejected, as the issue with regard to a felt hat is not whether it is considered a tent, but whether there is concern that one might come to carry it in the public domain if it falls from his head. This is **not difficult; this** statement of Rav Sheisha, which permits it, is referring to a case **where** the hat **fits snugly**[N] on his head. There is no concern lest the hat fall and one will come to carry it; therefore it is permitted to wear it. Conversely, **that** *baraita,* which prohibits wearing this hat, is referring to a case **where it does not fit snugly** on his head. It is therefore liable to fall, and one might come to carry it in the public domain.[H]

מתני׳ מַחֲזִירִין צִיר הַתַּחְתּוֹן בַּמִּקְדָּשׁ, אֲבָל לֹא בַּמְּדִינָה. וְהָעֶלְיוֹן – כָּאן וְכָאן אָסוּר. רַבִּי יְהוּדָה אוֹמֵר: הָעֶלְיוֹן בַּמִּקְדָּשׁ, וְהַתַּחְתּוֹן בַּמְּדִינָה.

MISHNA **One** may **restore** the **lower hinge pin** of the door of a carriage, box, or cupboard that becomes dislocated to its place on Shabbat **in the Temple,** as this action is prohibited by rabbinic decree, which is not in effect in the Temple; **but** it may **not** be restored to its place **in** the rest of **the country. And** restoring **the upper** hinge pin **is prohibited in both** places, as this is considered building, a labor prohibited by Torah law, which applies everywhere.[NBH] **Rabbi Yehuda says:** Restoring **the upper** hinge pin to its place is permitted **in the Temple, while** one may restore **the lower one** to its place even **in** the rest of **the country.**

LANGUAGE

Felt hat [*sayna*] – סַיְינָא: Of unclear origin. Some have suggested that it is related to the Middle Iranian word sāyag (shadow) and refers to the welcome protection from the sun that the head covering provides.

NOTES

Rather…where the hat fits snugly – אֶלָּא...הָא דְּמִיהֲדַק: There are two opinions with regard to the halakhic ruling in this case, largely based on the question of whether the version of the Gemara is: Rather, this is not difficult, or whether the version of the Gemara is: This is not difficult. The difference between the two opinions hinges on the unique meaning of the word rather in the Talmud. This word indicates that the previous answer has been rejected, and the Gemara is suggesting a new interpretation. The version of Rashi and the commentaries who agree with him includes the word rather. They maintain that the Gemara rejects the notion that wearing a felt hat is prohibited as a tent due to the difficulty presented by the case of a cloak. Consequently, there must be a different reason for the prohibition, i.e., that it might fall and one will come to carry it. By contrast, although in the version of Rabbeinu Ḥananel and other authorities the word rather is included, they explain that the new answer does not reject the previous one but it is an extension of that opinion. The hat is indeed prohibited as a tent, but there is a distinction between a soft hat that does not fit snugly on the head, which has a brim that folds, and a stiff hat that has the status of a tent.

One may restore a hinge pin – מַחֲזִירִין צִיר: The reason for the prohibition against restoring an upper hinge is a matter of dispute. Rashi rules that its restoration is a violation of the primary category of the prohibited labor of building, or at least a subcategory of this prohibited labor. However, in the Jerusalem Talmud, as well in *Tosafot*, it is maintained that this act constitutes only the violation of a rabbinic prohibition. Nevertheless, there is a difference between a lenient rabbinic prohibition and a stringent one, as there are types of rabbinic prohibitions that the Sages did not permit even in the Temple.

BACKGROUND

Upper and lower hinges – צִיר עֶלְיוֹן וְתַחְתּוֹן: In talmudic times, there were no hinges in the entrance doorjamb. Instead, there were strong pegs in the top and bottom of the door, which were placed in corresponding holes in the lintel and doorsill, allowing the door to swing open and close.

Door with its two hinges

HALAKHA

Hat – כּוֹבַע: A hat with a brim a handbreadth wide that does not fold over may not be worn on Shabbat even in the house, as it is considered a tent, in accordance with the opinion of Rabbeinu Ḥananel and others. The custom nowadays is to be lenient with respect to hats, as their brims are not considered stiff. This custom relies on Rashi's opinion that a hat does not constitute a tent. Consequently, no objection is raised against those who are lenient in this regard (*Mishna Berura*, citing *Eliya Rabba*). As for a hat whose brim is less than a handbreadth wide, some authorities prohibit wearing it, as it might be blown off one's head by the wind and he might carry it in a public domain. However, if it fits snugly on one's head or if it is tied with a strap, it is permitted to wear it, in accordance with Rashi's explanation (*Shulḥan Arukh, Oraḥ Ḥayyim* 301:40–41).

Restoring a hinge pin – הַחְזָרַת צִיר: If the lower hinge pin of a carriage, box, or cupboard comes slightly loose, one may push it back in. If it comes out entirely, one may not put it back on Shabbat, lest he bang it in forcefully. One may not restore the upper hinge pin, even by means of pushing (*Tur*). In the Temple, one may restore the lower hinge pin to its place, even if it came out entirely (Rambam *Sefer Zemanim, Hilkhot Shabbat* 22:25; *Shulḥan Arukh, Oraḥ Ḥayyim* 313:2).

גמ׳ תָּנוּ רַבָּנַן: צִיר דֶּלֶת שִׁידָּה תֵּיבָה וּמִגְדָּל, בַּמִּקְדָּשׁ – מַחֲזִירִין, בַּמְּדִינָה – דּוֹחֲקִין. וְהָעֶלְיוֹן – כָּאן וְכָאן לֹא יַחֲזִיר, גְּזֵרָה שֶׁמָּא יִתְקַע. וְאִם תָּקַע – חַיָּיב חַטָּאת.

GEMARA **The Sages taught** a *baraita*: With regard to the lower **hinge pin of the door of a carriage, box, or cupboard, one** may **restore** it to its place **in the Temple; in the** rest of the **country one** may only push it **back** into place, provided that it did not come out of its socket entirely. As for **the upper** hinge, **one** may **not restore** it **in either** place. This is prohibited as **a preventive measure, lest** one come to **bang** it in forcefully, thereby performing an actual labor prohibited by Torah law. **And if he** actually **banged** it in, **he is liable** to bring **a sin-offering,** as his action is considered building.

שֶׁל בּוֹר וְשֶׁל דּוּת וְשֶׁל יָצִיעַ – לֹא יַחֲזִיר, וְאִם הֶחֱזִיר – חַיָּיב חַטָּאת.

With regard to the hinge pin of the door of **a pit, cistern, or an extension** to a building, **one** may **not restore** it to its place at all. **And if** one **restored** it to its place, **he is liable** to bring **a sin-offering.** The above distinction applies only to movable utensils, whereas anything attached to the ground may certainly not be fixed in place, as this is regarded as prohibited building.

מתני׳ מַחֲזִירִין רְטִיָּה בַּמִּקְדָּשׁ, אֲבָל לֹא בַּמְּדִינָה. אִם בַּתְּחִילָּה – כָּאן וְכָאן אָסוּר.

MISHNA **One** may **return** to its place **a bandage** that became detached from a wound on Shabbat **in the Temple.** In the Temple, this is not prohibited as a preventive measure, lest one come to spread the ointment and thereby perform the prohibited labor of smoothing. **However,** one may **not** return a bandage to its place **in the** rest of **the country. If** one sought to apply the bandage **for the first time** to an untreated wound on Shabbat, **it is prohibited in both** places.

גמ׳ תָּנוּ רַבָּנַן: רְטִיָּה שֶׁפָּרְשָׁה מֵעַל גַּבֵּי מַכָּה – מַחֲזִירִין בַּשַּׁבָּת. רַבִּי יְהוּדָה אוֹמֵר: הוּחְלְקָה לְמַטָּה – דּוֹחֲקָהּ לְמַעְלָה, לְמַעְלָה – דּוֹחֲקָהּ לְמַטָּה. וּמְגַלֶּה מִקְצָת הָרְטִיָּה וּמְקַנֵּחַ פִּי הַמַּכָּה, וְחוֹזֵר וּמְגַלֶּה מִקְצָת רְטִיָּה, וּמְקַנֵּחַ פִּי הַמַּכָּה.

GEMARA **The Sages taught** a *baraita*: With regard **to a bandage that became detached from a wound, one** may **return** it to its place **on Shabbat** in all cases. **Rabbi Yehuda says:** If **it slipped downward, one** may **push it upward;** if it slipped **upward, one** may **push it** downward. **One** may also **uncover part of the bandage and clean the opening of the wound** on one side, **and then uncover another part of the bandage** on the other side **and clean the opening of the wound** on that side.[H]

וּרְטִיָּה עַצְמָהּ לֹא יְקַנֵּחַ, מִפְּנֵי שֶׁהוּא מְמָרֵחַ. וְאִם מֵירַח – חַיָּיב חַטָּאת.

However, **one** may **not clean the bandage itself, because** that would involve **spreading** the ointment, which is a subcategory of the prohibited labor of smoothing, **and if one spread** the ointment **he is liable** to bring **a sin-offering.** Actually restoring a bandage that was completely detached from the wound is prohibited in all cases.

אָמַר רַב יְהוּדָה, אָמַר שְׁמוּאֵל: הֲלָכָה כְּרַבִּי יְהוּדָה. אָמַר רַב חִסְדָּא: לֹא שָׁנוּ אֶלָּא שֶׁפֵּירְשָׁה עַל גַּבֵּי כְּלִי, אֲבָל פֵּירְשָׁה עַל גַּבֵּי קַרְקַע – דִּבְרֵי הַכֹּל אָסוּר!

Rav Yehuda said that **Shmuel said: The *halakha* is in accordance with** the opinion of **Rabbi Yehuda. Rav Ḥisda said:** The Sages **taught** that it is permitted to restore the bandage to the wound **only where it became detached** and fell **onto a utensil,** in which case one may immediately pick it up and replace it. **However,** if **it became detached** and fell **onto the ground, everyone agrees it is prohibited,** as this is considered as though one were bandaging the wound for the first time.[H]

אֲמַר מָר בַּר רַב אָשֵׁי: הֲוָה קָאֵימְנָא קַמֵּיהּ אַבָּא! נָפְלָה לֵיהּ אַבֵּי סָדְיָא וְקָא מַהֲדַר לֵיהּ. אָמֵינָא לֵיהּ: לָא סָבַר לַהּ מָר לְהָא דְּאָמַר רַב חִסְדָּא: מַחֲלוֹקֶת – שֶׁפֵּירְשָׁה עַל גַּבֵּי כְּלִי, אֲבָל פֵּירְשָׁה עַל גַּבֵּי קַרְקַע – אָסוּר. וְאָמַר שְׁמוּאֵל: הֲלָכָה כְּרַבִּי יְהוּדָה!

Mar bar Rav Ashi said: I was standing before Father, and his bandage **fell onto a pillow and he replaced it. I said to him: Doesn't the Master hold that which Rav Ḥisda said: The dispute** is restricted to a case **where** the bandage **became detached** and fell **onto a utensil, but if it became detached** and fell **onto the ground,** everyone agrees that **it is prohibited; and** furthermore, **Shmuel said: The *halakha* is in accordance with** the opinion of **Rabbi Yehuda,** that it is prohibited to replace even a bandage that fell onto a utensil?

אֲמַר לִי: לָא שְׁמִיעַ לִי. כְּלוֹמַר: לָא סְבִירָא לִי.

He said to me: I did not hear this teaching;[N] **that is to say, I do not agree** with Rav Ḥisda's interpretation that the dispute is only in a case where the bandage fell onto a utensil. Rather, they disagree even if it fell onto the ground, and the *halakha* is that the bandage may be restored to the wound.

HALAKHA

Uncovering a bandage – מְגַלֶּה רְטִיָּה: It is permitted to uncover a bandage and clean part of the wound, and then uncover a different part of the bandage to clean a different section of the wound, in accordance with Rabbi Yehuda (*Shulḥan Arukh, Oraḥ Ḥayyim* 328:26).

Restoring a bandage – הַחְזָרַת רְטִיָּה: It is prohibited to remove a bandage from a wound on Shabbat. If one did so intentionally, he is prohibited to restore it (*Magen Avraham*, citing the *Beit Yosef*). If the bandage fell onto a utensil, one may restore it. If it fell onto the ground, one may not restore it to the wound, in accordance with the respective opinions of Rashi and the Rif (*Shulḥan Arukh, Oraḥ Ḥayyim* 328:25).

NOTES

I did not hear this teaching – לָא שְׁמִיעַ לִי: The authorities dispute the subject of Rav Ashi's comment that he did not hear this teaching. According to the rule that the *halakha* follows the latter authority, Rav Ashi's statement should be accepted, yet it is unclear which opinion he was rejecting. Did he reject Shmuel's ruling that the *halakha* is in accordance with Rabbi Yehuda, or Rav Ḥisda's comment that the dispute pertains only to a case where the bandage fell onto a utensil, or does he reject both opinions? The Rif, for example, maintains that Rav Ashi rejected both statements. Consequently, he rules that the *halakha* is in accordance with the unattributed *baraita*. Rashi, by contrast, claims that Rav Ashi merely rejects Rabbi Ḥisda's position, as he contends that the dispute pertains only to a case where it fell onto the ground, but if it fell on a utensil, even Rabbi Yehuda agrees that it is permitted to replace the bandage.

LANGUAGE

String [*nima*] – נִימָא: From the Greek νῆμα, *nèma*, a thread or a string.

BACKGROUND

Harp – כִּנּוֹר: In antiquity, harps and lyres were closely related. Below is an image of a reconstructed ancient lyre resembling the ones that existed in the talmudic period. The strings of the lyre are tied to the buttons that protrude along its edge.

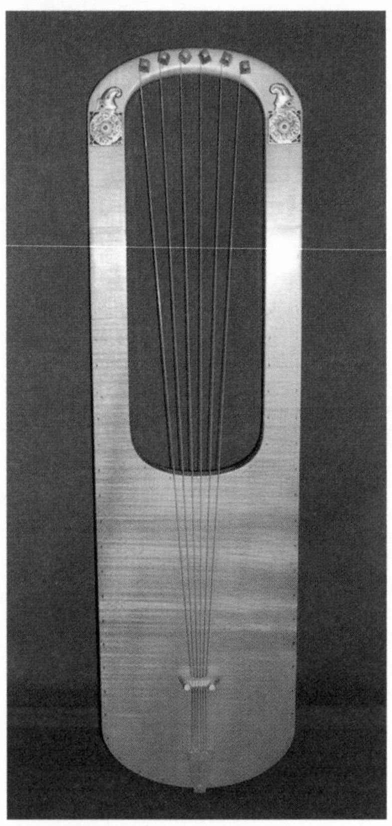

A reconstructed lyre from the sixth or seventh century

HALAKHA

A string in the Temple – נִימָא בַּמִּקְדָּשׁ: It is permitted to tie a temporary knot for the purpose of a mitzva. One may tie a broken harp string in the Temple but not outside of it. However, it is prohibited to tie a knot in the first instance, even in the Temple (Rambam *Sefer Zemanim*, *Hilkhot Shabbat* 10:6).

מתני׳ קוֹשְׁרִין נִימָא בַּמִּקְדָּשׁ, אֲבָל לֹא בַּמְּדִינָה. וְאִם בַּתְּחִילָּה – כָּאן וְכָאן אָסוּר.

MISHNA One may **tie up** on Shabbat **a string** [*nima*][L] that came loose from a harp[B] used **in the Temple,**[H] **but not in** the rest of **the country. And** tying the string to the harp for **the first time is prohibited** both **here and there.**

גמ׳ וּרְמִינְהוּ: נִימַת כִּנּוֹר שֶׁנִּפְסְקָה – לֹא הָיָה קוֹשְׁרָהּ, אֶלָּא עוֹנְבָהּ! לָא קַשְׁיָא; הָא – רַבָּנַן, וְהָא – רַבִּי אֱלִיעֶזֶר.

GEMARA And the Gemara **raises a contradiction** from a *baraita*: If **a harp string broke, one would not tie it up** with a knot, **but fashion a bow.** This teaching indicates that tying up a harp string is prohibited even in the Temple. The Gemara answers: It is **not difficult; this** *baraita*, which prohibits tying, was taught **in accordance with** the opinion of **the Rabbis; and that** mishna is in accordance with the opinion of **Rabbi Eliezer.**

לְרַבִּי אֱלִיעֶזֶר דְּאָמַר: ״מַכְשִׁירֵי מִצְוָה דּוֹחִין אֶת הַשַּׁבָּת״ – קוֹשְׁרָהּ, לְרַבָּנַן דְּאָמְרִי אֵין דּוֹחִין – עוֹנְבָהּ,

The Gemara clarifies this answer: **According to Rabbi Eliezer, who said** that **the preparations** that enable the performance **of a mitzva override** the prohibitions of **Shabbat,** one may **tie** even the broken harp string, as this is for the purpose of the mitzva of accompanying the Temple service with music. However, **according to the Rabbis, who say** that preparations for a mitzva **do not override** Shabbat prohibitions, **one** may only **fashion a bow.**

אִי רַבִּי אֱלִיעֶזֶר – אֲפִילּוּ לְכַתְּחִילָּה נַמִּי!

The Gemara raises a difficulty: **If** in fact the mishna is in accordance with the opinion of **Rabbi Eliezer,** who permits facilitating performance of a mitzva even when it involves desecration of Shabbat, **even** in a case where the string did not break and one is tying it **for the first time,** this **too** should be permitted, as he is acting for the purpose of a mitzva.

אֶלָּא, לָא קַשְׁיָא; הָא רַבִּי יְהוּדָה, וְהָא – רַבָּנַן.

Rather, the Gemara provides a different resolution of the contradiction: It is **not difficult. This,** the mishna that permits tying the broken string, was taught in accordance with the opinion of **Rabbi Yehuda,** who maintains that making a bow is considered tying, and there is no difference between the two actions; **and that,** the *baraita* that prohibits it, is in accordance with the opinion of **the Rabbis,** who rule that fashioning a bow is not prohibited by Torah law, and therefore it is permitted to fashion a bow.

וְרַבִּי יְהוּדָה אַלִּיבָּא דְּמַאן?

The Gemara asks: **And Rabbi Yehuda, in accordance with whose** opinion did he express his view?

Perek **X**
Daf **103** Amud **a**

אִי אַלִּיבָּא דְּרַבִּי אֱלִיעֶזֶר קָאָמַר – אֲפִילּוּ לְכַתְּחִילָּה נַמִּי!

If he stated his ruling **in accordance with** the opinion **of Rabbi Eliezer,** why did he permit tying a bow only after the fact? It should **also** be permitted **even *ab initio*,** as Rabbi Eliezer maintains that preparations required for the performance of a mitzva override the prohibitions of Shabbat.

אֶלָּא לָא קַשְׁיָא; הָא – רַבִּי שִׁמְעוֹן, הָא – רַבָּנַן. דְּתַנְיָא: בֶּן לֵוִי שֶׁנִּפְסְקָה לוֹ נִימָא בַּכִּנּוֹר – קוֹשְׁרָהּ, רַבִּי שִׁמְעוֹן אוֹמֵר: עוֹנְבָהּ.

Rather, the Gemara rejects the previous explanation: It is **not difficult; this** *baraita* that deems tying prohibited is according to the opinion of **Rabbi Shimon,** while **that** mishna that rules that tying is permitted, is according to the opinion of **the Rabbis. As it was taught** in a *baraita*: If **a string of the Levite's harp was severed** on Shabbat, **he** may **tie it** with a knot; **Rabbi Shimon says: He** may only **form a bow.** The Rabbis permit the preparations for a mitzva that could not have been performed before Shabbat, whereas Rabbi Shimon is stringent and prohibits even those preparations.

רַבִּי שִׁמְעוֹן בֶּן אֶלְעָזָר אוֹמֵר: אַף הִיא אֵינָהּ מַשְׁמַעַת אֶת הַקּוֹל, אֶלָּא מְשַׁלְשֵׁל מִלְּמַטָּה וְכוֹרֵךְ מִלְּמַעְלָה, אוֹ מְשַׁלְשֵׁל מִלְּמַעְלָה וְכוֹרֵךְ מִלְּמַטָּה.

The Gemara continues its citation of the *baraita*. **Rabbi Shimon ben Elazar says: Even** if he ties a knot or a bow, the harp **will not issue the** proper **sound,** and he would therefore be committing a transgression without performing the mitzva in a fitting manner. **Rather, he unwinds** the string **from the lower** knob and **winds it around the upper** one, **or he unwinds** the string **from the upper** knob **and winds it around the lower** one,[B] before tightening the string until it produces the proper note.

וְאִיבָּעֵית אֵימָא: הָא וְהָא רַבָּנַן, וְלָא קַשְׁיָא; כָּאן – בְּאֶמְצַע, כָּאן – מִן הַצַּד.

And if you wish, say instead that **both** sources were taught in accordance with the opinion of **the Rabbis,** who permit preparations for a mitzva that could not have been performed the day before, **and** even so it is **not difficult; here,** the mishna permits tying in a case where the string was severed **in the middle,** in which case the sound would be affected if the string were reconnected with a bow, whereas **there,** the *baraita* is referring to a string that was severed **on the side**[N] near the end of the string, which can be fixed with a bow.

וְאִיבָּעֵית אֵימָא: הָא וְהָא בְּאֶמְצַע, מָר סָבַר: גָּזְרִינַן, וּמָר סָבַר: לָא גָּזְרִינַן.

And if you wish, say instead that **both** sources are referring to a case where the string snapped **in the middle,** and the issue at hand is subject to a dispute between Rabbi Shimon and the Rabbis: **One Sage,** Rabbi Shimon, **maintains** in the *baraita* that it is prohibited even to tie a knot in the middle, **as a decree,** lest one unnecessarily tie a knot on the side as well. **And** the other **Sage,** the Rabbis, **maintains** in the mishna that **we do not issue a decree** of this kind.

מתני׳ חוֹתְכִין יַבֶּלֶת בַּמִּקְדָּשׁ, אֲבָל לֹא בַּמְּדִינָה. וְאִם בִּכְלִי – כָּאן וְכָאן אָסוּר.

MISHNA

A wart is an example of a blemish that temporarily disqualifies a priest from performing the Temple service, and disqualifies an animal from being offered on the altar; they regain their fitness once the wart is removed. Consequently, on Shabbat **one** may **cut off a wart** by hand **in the Temple,** as this constitutes a preparatory act required for the sacrificial service. **However,** he may **not** cut off a wart **in** the rest of **the country. And if** he seeks to cut off the wart **with an instrument, it is prohibited in both** places.[H]

גמ׳ וּרְמִינְהוּ הַרְכָּבוֹ וַהֲבָאָתוֹ מִחוּץ לַתְּחוּם וַחֲתִיכַת יַבַּלְתּוֹ אֵין דּוֹחִין, רַבִּי אֱלִיעֶזֶר אוֹמֵר: דּוֹחִין!

GEMARA

And the Gemara **raises a contradiction** from another mishna: When Passover eve occurs on Shabbat, the acts of **carrying** a Paschal lamb[N] on one's shoulders, **bringing it** to the Temple **from outside the** Shabbat **boundary,**[H] **and cutting off its wart** to render it fit for the altar, **do not override** the prohibitions of Shabbat. **Rabbi Eliezer,** conforming to his standard opinion, **says: They override** the Shabbat prohibitions. The mishna in *Eiruvin* apparently contradicts the opinion of these Sages.

רַבִּי אֶלְעָזָר וְרַבִּי יוֹסֵי (בֶּן) חֲנִינָא; חַד אָמַר: הָא וְהָא בְּלַחָה, וְלָא קַשְׁיָא; כָּאן – בַּיָּד, כָּאן – בִּכְלִי,

Rabbi Elazar and Rabbi Yosei ben Ḥanina suggested different resolutions to this difficulty: **One said** that **both** sources are referring to **a moist** wart, **and** it is **not difficult. Here,** the mishna permits removing the wart **by hand.** It is prohibited by rabbinic decree, as that is not the usual manner of performing the procedure. Whereas **there,** the mishna prohibits removal of the wart **with an instrument** by Torah law.

וְחַד אָמַר: הָא וְהָא בַּיָּד, וְלָא קַשְׁיָא; הָא – בְּלַחָה, הָא – בִּיבֵשָׁה.

And the other **one said** that in **both** cases the wart is removed **by hand, and** it is **not difficult. There,** the mishna prohibits the removal of **a moist** wart, whereas **here,** the mishna is referring to **a dry** wart, the removal of which does not constitute a prohibited labor.

וּלְמַאן דְּאָמַר "הָא – בַּיָּד, הָא – בִּכְלִי" מַאי טַעְמָא לָא אָמַר הָא – בְּלַחָה, הָא – בִּיבֵשָׁה? אָמַר לָךְ: יְבֵשָׁה אֲפִילּוּ בִּכְלִי נָמֵי שָׁרֵי. מַאי טַעְמָא – אִיפְּרוּכֵי אִיפַּרְכָא.

The Gemara raises a difficulty: **And according to the one who said: This** is referring to removal **by hand,** and **that** is referring to removal **with an instrument; what is the reason that he did not say,** as did his colleague: **This is referring to a moist** wart and **that** is referring **to a dry** one? The Gemara answers: **He can say to you** that with regard to **a dry** wart, **it is permitted** to remove it **even with an instrument. What is the reason?** As **it crumbles** on its own, cutting it is like cutting off dead skin.

BACKGROUND

Unwinding and winding – מְשַׁלְשֵׁל וְכוֹרֵךְ: The image below shows how a broken string can be unwound. As every string has a surplus at each end, if it breaks near one end it can be unwound at the other end. Another method is to knot the torn string, as was done for the second string from the left. Pictured is an endongo, which is considered the national musical instrument of the Baganda people of Uganda.

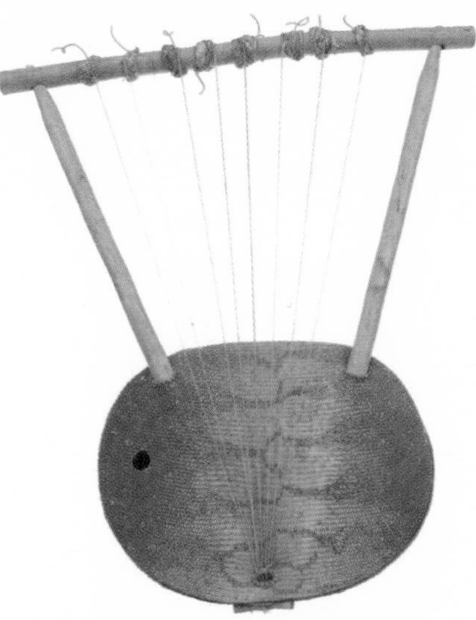

Endongo

NOTES

In the middle…on the side – בְּאֶמְצַע...מִן הַצַּד: Some commentaries suggest a different explanation: Tying in the middle is permitted, because one will certainly not leave a harp string tied in that manner; he will undoubtedly untie it the following day. Consequently, it is a temporary knot. Tying on the side, however, is prohibited, as the sound is less adversely affected and he might therefore leave it tied as it is; this would establish it as a permanent knot prohibited by Torah law (Rabbeinu Yehonatan; Rabbi Ovadya Bartenura).

Carrying a Paschal lamb – הַרְכָּבוֹ: As the Paschal sacrifice can be a kid goat or a lamb less than a year old, it is sometimes necessary to carry the animal. These animals are often so delicate that they cannot walk a great distance on their own, and their owners must therefore bear them on their shoulders.

HALAKHA

Cutting off a wart – חֲתִיכַת יַבֶּלֶת: It is prohibited to cut off a wart on Shabbat, whether by hand or with an instrument and whether the wart is dry or moist. If one cuts off a moist wart with an instrument, he is liable (*Maggid Mishne*; *Be'er Heitev*), but he is exempt if he removes it manually or if it is dry. In the Temple, it is permitted to cut off a moist wart by hand, and a dry one even with an instrument (Rambam *Sefer Zemanim, Hilkhot Shabbat* 9:8).

Carrying a Paschal lamb…bringing it from outside the Shabbat boundary – הַרְכָּבוֹ וַהֲבָאָתוֹ מִחוּץ לַתְּחוּם: It is prohibited to carry the Paschal lamb on one's shoulders in the public domain on Shabbat, or to bring it from beyond the Shabbat boundary, as these tasks can be performed before Shabbat (Rambam *Sefer Korbanot, Hilkhot Korban Pesaḥ* 1:18).

ולמאן דאמר "הא – בלחה, והא – ביבישה" מאי טעמא לא אמר "הא – ביד, הא – בכלי"?! אמר לך: בכלי – הא תנן: אם בכלי – כאן וכאן אסור.

And according to the one who said: This is referring **to a moist** wart and **that** is referring **to a dry** one, **what is the reason that he did not say,** like the other Sage: **This** is referring to removal **by hand** and **that** is referring to removal **with an instrument?** The Gemara answers: **He** can **say to you** that **with regard to an instrument, we** explicitly **learned** in the mishna: **If** he wishes to cut off the wart **with an instrument, it is prohibited in both** places. Consequently, it is unnecessary to teach again that it is prohibited to remove a wart with an instrument.

ואידך: הא דקתני התם – משום דקא בעי איפלוגי רבי אליעזר ורבנן.

And the other Sage, how does he respond to this contention? He can say that the other mishna **teaches this** *halakha* **there because it wants** to record **the dispute** between **Rabbi Eliezer and the Rabbis** on this issue, i.e., to inform us that Rabbi Eliezer disagrees and permits cutting off the wart even with an instrument.

ואידך: דומיא דהרכיבו והבאתו מחוץ לתחום קתני, דרבנן.

And the other Sage, how does he counter this reasoning? He can say that the *tanna* **teaches** the case of the wart **parallel to** the cases of **carrying** the animal **and bringing it** to the Temple **from outside the** Shabbat **boundary,** activities **that are** prohibited **by rabbinic law.** Consequently, the ruling involving a wart is also referring to cutting that is prohibited by rabbinic law, i.e., cutting by hand, not with an instrument.

ואידך: הרכיבו דלא כרבי נתן, דאמר: החי נושא את עצמו. הבאתו מחוץ לתחום כרבי עקיבא, דאמר: תחומין דאורייתא.

And the other Sage maintains that these cases also involve Torah prohibitions. How so? With regard to **carrying** the animal, the mishna was taught **not in accordance with** the opinion of **Rabbi Natan, who said: A living being carries itself,** which means that carrying an animal on one's shoulders is not considered carrying by Torah law, and is prohibited by rabbinic law.[N] If we do not accept this opinion, one who carries the Paschal lamb transgresses the Torah prohibition against carrying an object four cubits in the public domain. As for the case of **bringing** the animal **from outside the** Shabbat **boundary,** the mishna was taught **in accordance with** the opinion of **Rabbi Akiva, who said:** Bringing an animal from outside the Shabbat **boundaries** is prohibited **by Torah law.**

מתיב רב יוסף, אמר רבי אליעזר: קל וחומר ומה שחיטה שהיא משום מלאכה – דוחה את השבת, אלו שמשום שבות – אינו דין שידחו את השבת?

Rav Yosef raised an objection against this explanation from a mishna. **Rabbi Eliezer said** that this *halakha* is **an** ***a fortiori*** **inference: If slaughtering** the Paschal lamb, **which is** prohibited **due to** the fact that it is **a prohibited labor** by Torah law, nonetheless **overrides Shabbat** in the Temple, with regard to **these** actions, i.e., carrying the animal, bringing it from outside the Shabbat boundary, and cutting off its wart, which are prohibited **due to rabbinic decree, isn't it right that they** should **override Shabbat?** Evidently, the previous explanation must be rejected, as there too the mishna is referring to rabbinic prohibitions.

אלא אמר רב יוסף: הא והא – ביד, ושבות מקדש במקדש – התירו, שבות דמקדש במדינה – לא התירו.

Rather, Rav Yosef said: Both sources are referring to a case where the wart is removed **by hand,** an activity that constitutes a rabbinic prohibition, **and** the contradiction can be resolved as follows: To transgress **a rabbinic decree** relating to **the Temple within** the confines of **the Temple** itself, **they permitted** doing so. However, to transgress **a rabbinic decree** relating **to the Temple, in the country, they did not permit** doing so. Consequently, although these procedures involving the Paschal lamb are prohibited due to rabbinic decree and are indeed related to the Temple service, since they are performed outside the Temple, the Sages did not permit their performance.

יתיב אביי וקאמר להא שמעתא. איתיביה רב ספרא לאביי: היה קורא בספר על האסקופה, ונתגלגל הספר מידו – גוללו אצלו. והא הכא, דשבות דמקדש במדינה הוא ולא גזרינן דילמא נפיל ואתי לאיתויי!

Abaye sat with the scholars **and recited this** ***halakha*** in the name of Rav Yosef. **Rav Safra raised an objection to** the opinion cited by **Abaye** from a mishna: If **one was reading a scroll** of the Bible while sitting **on the threshold** of his house, **and the scroll rolled out of his hand,** i.e., while he was holding one end, the scroll rolled open into the public domain, **he** may **roll** the scroll back **to himself. And here, isn't it a rabbinic decree** involving a sacred scroll, which due to its sanctity should have the legal status of a rabbinic decree relating **to the Temple** with regard to an incident that occurred **in the country. And** yet **we do not issue a decree** prohibiting one to roll the scroll back to himself, **lest** the scroll **fall and he will** forget and **come to bring it in** from the public domain to a private domain. Apparently, the Sages did not impose a rabbinic prohibition with regard to matters relating to the Temple, even outside the Temple compound.

NOTES

Carrying the animal and bringing it – הרכיבו והבאתו: The Gemara's discussion is based on the assumption that these are rabbinic prohibitions. Indeed, most authorities rule that the Shabbat boundary is a rabbinic ordinance. With regard to carrying a lamb on one's shoulders, the Gemara accepts the principle of Rabbi Natan: A living being carries itself, and consequently carrying the lamb is not considered carrying a burden by Torah law. The Gemara suggests that these cases involve Torah prohibitions, in an effort to resolve the difficulty.

וְלָא אוֹקִימְנָא בְּאִסְקוּפָּה כַּרְמְלִית, וּרְשׁוּת הָרַבִּים עוֹבֶרֶת לְפָנֶיהָ! דְּכֵיוָן דְּאִיגְּדוֹ בְּיָדוֹ – אֲפִילּוּ שְׁבוּת נַמִּי לֵיכָּא.

Abaye refutes this contention: **Didn't we** already **establish** this mishna as referring **to a threshold** that is **a *karmelit*,** e.g., one that is four handbreadths wide but less than ten handbreadths high, **and before which the public domain passes? As he holds** one end of the scroll **in his hand, it is not** prohibited **even** by **rabbinic decree.** The reason is that even if the scroll fell from his hand and rolled into the public domain, and he were to carry it back from the public domain to the *karmelit,* he would not transgress a Torah prohibition.

אִיתִיבֵיהּ: מְשַׁלְשְׁלִין אֶת הַפֶּסַח לַתַּנּוּר עִם חֲשֵׁיכָה. וְהָא הָכָא, דִּשְׁבוּת דְּמִקְדָּשׁ בִּמְדִינָה וְלָא גָּזְרִינַן שֶׁמָּא יַחְתֶּה בְּגֶחָלִים!

Rav Safra **raised an objection** from a different mishna: **One** may **lower the Paschal** lamb **into the oven**[H] on Shabbat eve **just before nightfall,** after its blood is sprinkled and it is brought outside the Temple for roasting. **But here** we are dealing **with** a violation of **a rabbinic decree** relating **to the Temple** that occurred **in the country,** and yet **we do not issue** a decree against lowering the sacrifice into the oven at that late hour **lest** one **rake the coals** to hasten the cooking. Once again, the mishna indicates that the Sages did not issue a rabbinic decree prohibiting an action related to the Temple service, even outside the Temple.

אִישְׁתִּיק. כִּי אֲתָא לְקַמֵּיהּ דְּרַב יוֹסֵף, אֲמַר לֵיהּ: הָכִי אֲמַר לִי רַב סָפְרָא. אֲמַר לֵיהּ: מַאי טַעְמָא לָא תְּשַׁנֵּי לֵיהּ: בְּנֵי חֲבוּרָה זְרִיזִין הֵן?

Abaye **was silent** and did not answer. **When he came before Rav Yosef, he said to him: This is what Rav Safra said to me,** contrary to your approach. Rav Yosef **said to him: What is the reason** that **you didn't answer him: Members of a group** who joined together to prepare and partake of a single Paschal lamb, which, like all sacrifices, requires careful attention, **are** certainly **vigilant**[N] and exacting in the performance of this mitzva. Consequently, there is less concern that they might commit a transgression than with regard to people in other circumstances. However, other rabbinic decrees relating to the Temple remain in effect outside the Temple.

וְאַבָּיֵי, כֹּהֲנִים זְרִיזִין הֵן – אָמְרִינַן, בְּנֵי חֲבוּרָה זְרִיזִין הֵן – לָא אָמְרִינַן.

The Gemara comments: **And** as for **Abaye,** why did he not accept this reasoning? He maintains that **we say** that only **priests are vigilant,**[N] as they are constantly involved in the Temple service, and they will therefore not mistakenly commit a transgression. However, that **members of a group** of people who join together for a single Paschal lamb **are vigilant, we do not say.** As they are not accustomed to that level of watchfulness, they might forget.

רָבָא אָמַר: רַבִּי אֱלִיעֶזֶר הִיא, דְּאָמַר מַכְשִׁירֵי מִצְוָה דּוֹחִין אֶת הַשַּׁבָּת. וּמוֹדֶה רַבִּי אֱלִיעֶזֶר, דְּכַמָּה דְּאֶפְשָׁר לְשַׁנּוֹיֵי – מְשַׁנֵּינַן.

Rava stated a different resolution of the contradiction between the two *mishnayot:* The mishna which permits the cutting of a wart, **is** according **to Rabbi Eliezer, who said** that the **preparations** for the performance **of a mitzva override** the prohibitions of **Shabbat,** and it is therefore permitted to cut the wart by hand. **And** if you say that in that case one should be permitted to do so with an instrument as well, **Rabbi Eliezer concedes** that **as much as it is possible to alter** the manner in which a procedure is performed to prevent violation of a Torah prohibition, **we alter** it, to emphasize that the day is Shabbat.

Perek **X**
Daf **103** Amud **b**

מַאי הִיא? דְּתַנְיָא: כֹּהֵן שֶׁעָלְתָה בּוֹ יַבֶּלֶת – חֲבֵירוֹ חוֹתְכָהּ לוֹ בְּשִׁינָּיו. בְּשִׁינָּיו – אִין, בִּכְלִי – לָא. חֲבֵירוֹ – אִין, אִיהוּ – לָא.

What is the source for this idea? **As it was taught** in a *baraita:* If a **priest grew a wart,** which temporarily disqualifies him from performing the service, **his fellow** priest may **cut it off for him** on Shabbat **with his teeth.** The Gemara infers: **With his teeth, yes,** this is permitted; but **with an instrument, no,** he may not do so. Likewise, for **his fellow** priest, **yes,** he may cut off his wart; but **he** himself, **no,** he may not cut off his own wart.

HALAKHA

One may lower the Paschal lamb into the oven – מְשַׁלְשְׁלִין אֶת הַפֶּסַח לַתַּנּוּר: It is permitted to lower the Paschal sacrifice, a kid goat or a whole lamb, into an oven on Shabbat eve just before nightfall, even though the oven is not sealed with clay, a requirement when roasting other animals. The rationale is that the members of the group who joined together to partake of a single Paschal sacrifice are vigilant in the performance of *mitzvot* and will not rake the coals (Rambam *Sefer Zemanim, Hilkhot Shabbat* 3:15).

NOTES

Members of a group are vigilant – בְּנֵי חֲבוּרָה זְרִיזִין הֵן: It can be assumed that every group includes at least one scholar, who instructs them how they must treat the sacrifice and who can also be relied upon to ensure that they do not transgress other prohibitions (Rashash).

Priests are vigilant – כֹּהֲנִים זְרִיזִין הֵן: Rashi suggests various reasons for this. One explanation is that priests were typically learned in Torah and served as teachers in Israel, as it states: "They shall teach Jacob Your judgments" (Deuteronomy 33:10). In addition, as they were numerous, they would remind each other not to make mistakes.

מַנִּי? אִילֵימָא רַבָּנַן וּבַמִּקְדָּשׁ, כֵּיוָן דְּאָמְרִי רַבָּנַן בְּעָלְמָא מִשּׁוּם שְׁבוּת – הָכָא מָה לִּי הוּא מָה לִּי חֲבֵירוֹ?

The Gemara inquires: According to **whose** opinion was this *baraita* taught? **If you say** it is in accordance with the opinion of **the Rabbis, and** the leniency is based on the principle that a rabbinic prohibition does not apply **in the Temple, since the Rabbis say in general** that biting off even one's own nails or wart, and certainly those of another, is prohibited **due to rabbinic decree,** then in this case **here, what is** the difference **to me** whether it is the priest **himself** who cuts off the wart, or **what is** the difference **to me** whether it is **another** priest who cuts it off?

אֶלָּא לָאו רַבִּי אֱלִיעֶזֶר, דְּאָמַר בְּעָלְמָא חַיָּיב חַטָּאת, וְהָכָא – אַף עַל גַּב דְּמַכְשִׁירֵי מִצְוָה דּוֹחִין אֶת הַשַּׁבָּת – כַּמָּה דְּאֶפְשָׁר לְשַׁנּוֹיֵי מְשַׁנֵּינַן.

Rather, wasn't it taught in accordance with the opinion of **Rabbi Eliezer,** who **said** that **in general** one **is liable to** bring **a sin-offering** for biting off his own nails or wart? **And here, even though** he maintains that **preparations** for a **mitzva override** the prohibitions of **Shabbat,** and it should therefore be permitted for him to cut off his own wart with an instrument, nevertheless, **as much as it is possible to alter** the procedure so that it does not entail the violation of a Torah prohibition, **one alters,** and biting off another person's wart is prohibited due to rabbinic decree, not Torah law.

לֹא, לְעוֹלָם רַבָּנַן, וְאִי עָלְתָה בִּכְרֵיסוֹ – הָכִי נָמֵי.

The Gemara rejects this contention: **No,** this is not necessarily the case. **Actually,** this *baraita* can be explained in accordance with the opinion of the Rabbis, **and if** the wart **grew on his abdomen,** or anywhere else easily removable by hand, **so too,** it is clear that according to the Rabbis there is no difference between himself and his fellow priest, and he may remove it himself.

הָכָא בְּמַאי עָסְקִינַן – כְּגוֹן שֶׁעָלְתָה לוֹ נְשִׁיכָה בְּגַבּוֹ וּבְאַצִּילֵי יָדָיו, דְּאִיהוּ לָא מָצֵי שָׁקֵיל לַהּ.

However, **here, we are dealing with** a case **where,** the priest **received a bite** that developed into a wart **on his back**[N] **or on his elbow,** from **where he** himself **cannot remove it,** but someone else can.

וְאִי רַבָּנַן, נִשְׁקְלֵיהּ נִיהֲלֵיהּ בְּיָד, וְתִפְשׁוֹט דְּרַבִּי אֶלְעָזָר. דְּאָמַר רַבִּי אֶלְעָזָר: מַחְלוֹקֶת בְּיָד, אֲבָל בִּכְלִי – דִּבְרֵי הַכֹּל – חַיָּיב!

The Gemara asks: **But if** the *baraita* reflects the opinion of **the Rabbis,** the other priest should be permitted to **remove** the wart **from him by hand,** rather than with an instrument, **and** therefore one should **resolve** the dilemma in accordance with the teaching of **Rabbi Elazar, as Rabbi Elazar said: The dispute** between the Rabbis and Rabbi Eliezer with regard to the removal of one's nails is limited to one who removed them **by hand, but** if he removed them **with an instrument, everyone agrees** that **he is liable** to bring a sin-offering.

וְלִיטַעְמִיךְ, לְרַבִּי אֱלִיעֶזֶר נָמֵי: לִישְׁקְלֵיהּ נִיהֲלֵיהּ בְּיָד! הָאִי מַאי? אִי אָמְרַתְּ בִּשְׁלָמָא רַבִּי אֱלִיעֶזֶר – הַיְינוּ דִּגְזַר יָד אַטּוּ כְּלִי. אֶלָּא אִי אָמְרַתְּ רַבָּנַן הִיא – נִשְׁקְלֵיהּ נִיהֲלֵיהּ בְּיָד, וְתוּ לָא מִידֵּי.

The Gemara rejects this argument: **And according to your reasoning, Rabbi Eliezer** should **also** agree **that he** should be permitted to **remove it for him by hand.** The Gemara expresses surprise at this comment: **What is** the nature of **this** contention? **Granted, if you say** that it was taught in accordance with **Rabbi Eliezer, this is** why removing the wart **by hand was decreed** prohibited **due to** a preventive measure, lest he remove it with **an instrument,** as he maintains that removing a wart with an instrument is prohibited by the Torah. **However, if you say it** is according to the opinion of **the Rabbis,**[N] **he** should be permitted to **remove it for him by hand. And nothing more** need be said,[N] as it is clear that the *baraita* was taught in accordance with the opinion of Rabbi Eliezer.

מתני׳ כֹּהֵן שֶׁלָּקָה בְּאֶצְבָּעוֹ – כּוֹרֵךְ עָלֶיהָ גֶּמִי בַּמִּקְדָּשׁ, אֲבָל לֹא בַּמְּדִינָה. אִם לְהוֹצִיא דָּם – כָּאן וְכָאן אָסוּר.

MISHNA With regard to **a priest who was injured on his finger** on Shabbat, **he** may temporarily **wrap it with a reed**[B] so that his wound is not visible while he is serving in the Temple.[H] This leniency applies **in the Temple, but not in the country,** as it also heals the wound, and medical treatment is prohibited on Shabbat due to rabbinic decree.[H] **If** his intention **is to draw blood** from the wound or to absorb blood, **it is prohibited in both** places.

גמ׳ אָמַר רַב יְהוּדָה בְּרֵיהּ דְּרַבִּי חִיָּיא: לֹא שָׁנוּ אֶלָּא גֶּמִי, אֲבָל צִלְצוֹל קָטָן – הָוֵי יִתּוּר בְּגָדִים.

GEMARA Rav Yehuda, son of Rabbi Ḥiyya, said: They taught that **only a reed** is permitted. **However, a small sash is** prohibited, as it would be **considered an extra garment,**[H] and it is prohibited for a priest to add to the priestly garments prescribed by the Torah.

NOTES

Received a bite on his back – שֶׁעָלְתָה לוֹ נְשִׁיכָה בְּגַבּוֹ: This response is puzzling for two reasons: First, the connection between a bite and a wart is unclear, and second, there is an apparent difficulty in identifying the parts of the body where one's hands cannot reach. Some commentaries explain that it means that one cannot reach his back with his teeth. The Rashash maintains that the individual in question is suffering from a bite in addition to his wart, and is unable to reach his back with his hand due to the pain.

If you say it is the Rabbis – אִי אָמְרַתְּ רַבָּנַן הִיא: The Gemara's difficulty is unclear; see Rashi and *Tosafot*. The Maharshal explains: If it is the opinion of the Rabbis, the other priest could have removed the wart by hand. Rather, the Rabbis evidently prohibit its removal by hand as well, which indicates that they agree with Rabbi Eliezer's opinion that a sin-offering must be brought even for the manual removal of a wart. This proves Rabbi Elazar's claim that the dispute concerns removal by hand, which Rabbi Eliezer prohibits.

And nothing more need be said – וְתוּ לָא מִידֵּי: In several places, Rashi explains this expression as follows: If this approach is accepted, there is no room for any further objections or discussion, as the matter is perfectly clear.

BACKGROUND

Reed – גֶּמִי: The reed referred to in this context is probably an umbrella term for objects produced from the papyrus sedge plant, *Cyperus papyrus* L. This plant, which grows in streams and swamps, was used in various industries. Its outer, harder section was used in the weaving of mats, while paper was manufactured from its inner part in ancient Egypt and other countries. These soft inner parts were also converted into strips with which objects could be tied, and occasionally as a bandage for a wound, as in this case.

Papyrus sedge

HALAKHA

Wrapping with a reed in the Temple – כְּרִיכַת גֶּמִי בַּמִּקְדָּשׁ: A priest who hurt his finger may wrap a reed around it. However, it is prohibited if his intention is to draw blood (Rambam *Sefer Avoda*, *Hilkhot Kelei HaMikdash* 10:9).

A reed on a wound – גֶּמִי עַל פֶּצַע: It is prohibited to place a reed on a wound on Shabbat, because it heals the wound (*Shulḥan Arukh*, *Oraḥ Ḥayyim* 328:24, and in the comment of the Rema).

An extra garment – יִתּוּר בְּגָדִים: It is prohibited for a priest to add to the priestly garments he is commanded to wear in the Torah. In a place on his body where he dons the priestly garments, even one extra thread is considered an interposition. If a piece of cloth is not in a place where the priest wears the garments, it is considered an interposition only if it is at least three by three fingerbreadths. However, a small sash interposes in either case, as it is considered more significant than a nondescript piece of cloth (Rambam *Sefer Avoda*, *Hilkhot Kelei HaMikdash* 10:6–8).

וְרַבִּי יוֹחָנָן אָמַר: לֹא אָמְרוּ יִתּוּר בְּגָדִים אֶלָּא בִּמְקוֹם בְּגָדִים, אֲבָל שֶׁלֹּא בִּמְקוֹם בְּגָדִים – לָא הָוֵי יִתּוּר בְּגָדִים.

And Rabbi Yoḥanan said: They said that donning an **extra garment** is prohibited **only** if it is worn **in a place** on the priest's body where the priestly **garments** are worn. **But in a place** where those **garments** are **not** worn, e.g., on his hand or the like, a sash that is tied there **is not considered an extra garment.**

וְתֵיפוֹק לֵיהּ מִשּׁוּם חֲצִיצָה! בִּשְׂמֹאל,

The Gemara asks: **And let him derive** that both the reed and the sash are prohibited **as an interposition.** As the reed and sash interpose between the priest's hand and the holy vessel, they should invalidate the service.[N] The Gemara rejects this contention: Perhaps the wound is **on** the priest's **left** hand, while the entire service is performed exclusively with his right hand. Consequently, a bandage on his left hand is not an interposition.

אִי נָמֵי: בְּיָמִין, וְשֶׁלֹּא בִּמְקוֹם עֲבוֹדָה.

Alternatively, it is possible that the wound is **on** the priest's **right** hand, **but not in a place** used in the **service,** which means the bandage does not interpose between his hand and the holy vessels used in the Temple service.

וּפְלִיגָא דְּרָבָא, דְּאָמַר רָבָא, אָמַר רַב חִסְדָּא: בִּמְקוֹם בְּגָדִים – אֲפִילּוּ נִימָא אַחַת חוֹצֶצֶת, שֶׁלֹּא בִּמְקוֹם בְּגָדִים – שָׁלֹשׁ עַל שָׁלֹשׁ חוֹצְצוֹת, פָּחוֹת מִשָּׁלֹשׁ עַל שָׁלֹשׁ – אֵינָן חוֹצְצוֹת.

And this conclusion **disputes** the opinion **of Rava, as Rava said** that **Rav Ḥisda said: In a place** on the priest's body where the priestly **garments** are worn, **even one** extra **thread interposes** and is prohibited, whereas **in a place** where the priestly **garments** are **not** worn, if the fabric was **three** fingerbreadths **by three** fingerbreadths, **it interposes,** but if it was **less than three** fingerbreadths **by three** fingerbreadths, **it does not interpose.**

אַדְּרַבִּי יוֹחָנָן וַדַּאי פְּלִיגָא, אַדְּרַב יְהוּדָה בְּרֵיהּ דְּרַבִּי חִיָּיא מִי נֵימָא פְּלִיגָא?

The Gemara comments: This teaching **certainly disagrees with** the opinion **of Rabbi Yoḥanan,** as he maintains that the prohibition against interpositions does not apply at all in a place on the priest's body where the priestly garments are not worn. However, **shall we say that it** also **disagrees with** the opinion **of Rav Yehuda, son of Rabbi Ḥiyya,** who prohibits even a sash smaller than three by three fingerbreadths?

שָׁאנֵי צִלְצוֹל קָטָן דַּחֲשִׁיב.

The Gemara answers: Nothing can be proven from here, as **a small sash is different, since it is significant,** and it is therefore considered a garment even if it is less than three by three fingerbreadths.

לִישָּׁנָא אַחֲרִינָא, אָמְרִי לָהּ, אָמַר רַב יְהוּדָה בְּרֵיהּ דְּרַבִּי חִיָּיא: לֹא שָׁנוּ אֶלָּא גֶּמִי, אֲבָל צִלְצוֹל קָטָן – חוֹצֵץ.

According to **another version, they reported** this dispute as follows: **Rav Yehuda, son of Rabbi Ḥiyya, said** that **they taught** this leniency **only** with regard to **a reed, but** that **a small sash interposes.**

וְרַבִּי יוֹחָנָן אָמַר: לֹא אָמְרוּ חֲצִיצָה בְּפָחוֹת מִשָּׁלֹשׁ עַל שָׁלֹשׁ אֶלָּא בִּמְקוֹם בְּגָדִים, אֲבָל שֶׁלֹּא בִּמְקוֹם בְּגָדִים,

And Rabbi Yoḥanan said: They said that there is **interposition with regard to** an article that is **less than three by three** fingerbreadths **only in a place** where the priestly **garments** are worn. **However, in a place** where the priestly **garments** are **not** worn, the following distinction applies:

Perek **X**
Daf **104** Amud **a**

שָׁלֹשׁ עַל שָׁלֹשׁ – חוֹצְצוֹת, פָּחוֹת מִשָּׁלֹשׁ – אֵין חוֹצְצוֹת. וְהַיְינוּ דְּרָבָא אָמַר רַב חִסְדָּא.

If the fabric was **three** fingerbreadths **by three** fingerbreadths, **it interposes;** but if it was **less than three** fingerbreadths by three fingerbreadths, **it does not interpose. And this is** the same teaching that **Rava** said that **Rav Ḥisda said.**

לֵימָא פְּלִיגָא דְּרַב יְהוּדָה בְּרֵיהּ דְּרַבִּי חִיָּיא? שָׁאנֵי צִלְצוֹל קָטָן דַּחֲשִׁיב.

The Gemara suggests: **Let us say that this disagrees with** the opinion of **Rav Yehuda, son of Rav Ḥisda,** who prohibits a sash even smaller than three fingerbreadths by three fingerbreadths. The Gemara rejects this contention: This is not necessarily so, as **a small sash is different, since it is significant.** It is therefore like a garment, even if it is smaller than three fingerbreadths by three fingerbreadths.

וּלְרַבִּי יוֹחָנָן, אַדְּאַשְׁמְעִינַן גֶּמִי, לִישְׁמְעִינַן צִלְצוֹל קָטָן

The Gemara raises a question: **And according to** the opinion of **Rabbi Yoḥanan: Rather than teaching us** the *halakha* with regard to a **reed, let** the mishna **teach us** that a priest may wrap his wounded finger with **a small sash,** as that does not constitute an interposition.

NOTES

Interposition and an extra garment – **חֲצִיצָה וְיִתּוּר בְּגָדִים:** Although the Gemara is apparently discussing these two issues simultaneously, they are not identical. Interposition means that an object intervenes between the priest and his service, or between the priest and his garments. Consequently, if the interposition is not in a place where clothes are worn or is not in a place used in the service, such as the back of the hand, the prohibition of interposition is not in effect. However, an extra garment is prohibited in its own right, either based on the prohibition: "You shall not add" (Deuteronomy 4:2), or because it is equivalent to the absence of a priestly garment, which invalidates the service (Jerusalem Talmud). In this case, the guiding principle is not the particular location involved, but the nature of the extra garment (see *Ge'on Ya'akov*).

מִילְּתָא אַגַּב אוֹרְחֵיהּ קָא מַשְׁמַע לַן, דִּגְמִי מַסֵּי.

The Gemara explains: The *tanna* **teaches us** another **matter in passing, that a reed heals.** However, as far as a priest involved in the service in concerned, there is no concern with regard to this prohibition either, as it is also a rabbinic decree that is not in effect in the Temple.

מתני׳ בּוֹזְקִין מֶלַח עַל גַּבֵּי כֶבֶשׁ בִּשְׁבִיל שֶׁלֹּא יַחֲלִיקוּ, וּמְמַלְּאִין מִבּוֹר הַגּוֹלָה וּמִבּוֹר הַגָּדוֹל בְּגַלְגַּל בְּשַׁבָּת, וּמִבְּאֵר הֶקֵר בְּיוֹם טוֹב.

MISHNA **One** may **scatter**[N] **salt** on Shabbat **on the ramp**[H] that leads to the altar **so that** the priests will **not slip** on their way up. **And** likewise, **one** may **draw water from the Cistern of the Exiles**[NB] **and from the Great Cistern,**[N] which were located in the Temple, **by** means of **the wheel**[B] designed for drawing water, even **on Shabbat. And** one may draw water **from the Heker Well** only **on a Festival.**

גמ׳ רָמֵי לֵיהּ רַב אִיקָא מִפַּשְׁרוֹנְיָא לְרָבָא, תְּנַן: בּוֹזְקִין מֶלַח עַל גַּבֵּי הַכֶּבֶשׁ בִּשְׁבִיל שֶׁלֹּא יַחֲלִיקוּ. בַּמִּקְדָּשׁ – אִין, בַּמְּדִינָה – לָא. וּרְמִינְהִי: חָצֵר שֶׁנִּתְקַלְקְלָה בְּמֵימֵי גְשָׁמִים – מֵבִיא תֶּבֶן וּמְרַדֶּה בָּהּ!

GEMARA **Rav Ika from Pashronya raised a contradiction before Rava: We learned** in the mishna: **One** may **scatter salt** on Shabbat **on the ramp** that leads to the altar, **so that** the priests will **not slip,** from which it can be inferred: **In the Temple, yes,** it is permitted to do so, but outside the Temple, **in** the rest of **the country, no,** it is prohibited to scatter salt on a ramp. **And** he **raised** his **contradiction** from a *baraita*: With regard to **a courtyard that was damaged** on Shabbat **by rainwater,**[H] so that it became difficult to cross, **one** may **bring straw and scatter it about** to absorb the water. Apparently, an action of this kind is permitted even outside the Temple.

שָׁאנֵי תֶּבֶן דְּלָא מְבַטֵּיל לֵיהּ.

The Gemara answers: **Straw is different, as one does not negate it;** rather, he intends to remove it once the water has been absorbed. He is therefore permitted to scatter the straw in the courtyard, just as it is permitted to put it in any other place. However, it is prohibited to scatter objects that one intends to leave in place, such as salt, as this appears as though he is adding to the ground and building.

אֲמַר לֵיהּ רַב אַחָא בְּרֵיהּ דְּרָבָא לְרַב אַשִׁי: הַאי מֶלַח הֵיכִי דָּמֵי? אִי דִּמְבַטְּלֵיהּ – קָא מוֹסִיף אַבִּנְיָן (וּכְתִיב: ״הַכֹּל בִּכְתָב מִיַּד ה׳ עָלַי הִשְׂכִּיל״),

Rav Aḥa, son of Rava, said to Rav Ashi: This salt, what are the circumstances? If one negates it vis-à-vis the ramp so that it becomes part of the ramp, **he** effectively **adds to the structure**[N] of the Temple, **and it states** with regard to the Temple: **"All this do I give you in writing as God has made me wise by His hand upon me,** even all the works of this pattern" (1 Chronicles 28:19). This verse indicates that all the details of the Temple structure were determined through prophecy and may not be changed in any way, even on a weekday.

וְאִי דְּלָא קָא מְבַטְּלֵיהּ – קָא הָוְיָא חֲצִיצָה!

And if he does not negate the salt vis-à-vis the ramp, **it** would **constitute an interposition** between the feet of the priests and the altar. This would mean that they would not be walking on the ramp during their service, and consequently they would not be performing the service as required by the Torah.

בְּהוֹלָכַת אֵבָרִים לַכֶּבֶשׁ, דְּלָאו עֲבוֹדָה הִיא.

The Gemara answers: In fact, he does not negate the salt. However, he scatters it **when the limbs** of the sacrifice **are brought up the ramp,** a procedure **that is not** considered part of the **Temple service** subject to disqualification due to interposition, as it is merely preparation for the burning of the limbs.

וְלָאו? וְהָא כְּתִיב: ״וְהִקְרִיב הַכֹּהֵן אֶת הַכֹּל וְהִקְטִיר הַמִּזְבֵּחָה״, וְאָמַר מָר: זוֹ הוֹלָכַת אֵבָרִים לַכֶּבֶשׁ! אֶלָּא אֵימָא: בְּהוֹלָכַת עֵצִים לַמַּעֲרָכָה, דְּלָאו עֲבוֹדָה הִיא.

The Gemara asks: **And** is this **not** a service? **But isn't it written: "And the priest shall offer it whole and make it smoke upon the altar"** (Leviticus 1:13), **and the Master said** in explanation: **This** is referring to **bringing the limbs to** the top of **the ramp.** Evidently, this too is a service written in the Torah. **Rather, say** that he scatters the salt **when the wood is brought** up the ramp **to the arrangement** of wood on the altar, a procedure **that is not a service.**

NOTES

Scatter – בּוֹזְקִין: Rashi explains the word as break, i.e., to crush large chunks of salt. The Rambam in his Commentary on the Mishna states that it means to throw repeatedly.

Cistern of the Exiles [*hagola*] – בּוֹר הַגּוֹלָה: Some commentaries vocalize this word without the definite article *ha*, as *gula*, meaning a bowl, as in the verse: "With a bowl [*gula*] upon the top if it" (Zechariah 4:2).

The Great Cistern – בּוֹר הַגָּדוֹל: The Rambam explains that the Great Cistern was located outside the Temple confines, but because of a certain incident the Sages permitted drawing water from it, similar to the Heker Well on a Festival (Rambam's Commentary on the Mishna).

Adds to the structure – מוֹסִיף אַבִּנְיָן: The First Temple was built by the word of God as received by prophecy. The Second Temple was constructed partly on the model of the First Temple, and partly in accordance with the prophecies of Ezekiel. Consequently, a special set of conditions must be met in order to make changes. For example, only the Great Sanhedrin may enlarge the Temple courtyards, and only by means of a special ceremony. Otherwise, even the smallest addition is prohibited.

BACKGROUND

Cistern of the Exiles – בּוֹר הַגּוֹלָה: The image below depicts three of the northern chambers in the Temple. The Parhedrin Chamber is to the right, with the yellow roof. On its left is the Exile Chamber, with the blue roof, which contained both the Cistern of the Exiles and the Great Cistern. Alongside them, with the red roof, is the Hewn Chamber, which housed the Sanhedrin.

Three northern chambers in the Temple

Wheel – גַּלְגַּל: The image below is of an ancient Roman well at Gonio Fortress in Adjara, near Turkey, with a wheel for drawing water. It is possible that the wheel in the Temple resembled this one.

Ancient well at Gonio Fortress in Adjara with a wheel for drawing water

HALAKHA

Salt on the ramp – מֶלַח עַל גַּבֵּי כֶּבֶשׁ: One may scatter salt on the ramp of the altar on Shabbat so that priests will not slip on it. This is permitted only when the priests are bringing wood to the arrangement of wood on the altar, but not when they are carrying items that are an integral part of the Temple service (Rambam *Sefer Avoda, Hilkhot Temidin UMusafin* 6:3).

A courtyard that was damaged by rainwater – חָצֵר שֶׁנִּתְקַלְקְלָה בְּמֵימֵי גְשָׁמִים: It is permitted to scatter straw on Shabbat in a courtyard that was damaged by rainwater, as this does not constitute building. However, one must alter his usual weekday manner of doing so, by scattering the straw with the bottom of a broken basket (*Shulḥan Arukh, Oraḥ Ḥayyim* 313:10).

דָּרַשׁ רָבָא: חָצֵר שֶׁנִּתְקַלְקְלָה בְּמֵימֵי גְשָׁמִים – מֵבִיא תֶּבֶן וּמְרַדֶּה בָּהּ. אֲמַר לֵיהּ רַב פַּפָּא לְרָבָא, וְהָתַנְיָא: כְּשֶׁהוּא מְרַדֶּה – אֵינוֹ מְרַדֶּה לֹא בְּסַל וְלֹא בְּקוּפָּה אֶלָּא בְּשׁוּלֵי קוּפָּה!

Rava taught: In a **courtyard that was damaged** on Shabbat **by rainwater, one** may **bring straw and scatter it about** to make it easier to walk across. **Rav Pappa said to Rava: But wasn't it taught** in a *baraita*: **When one scatters** the straw, **he** must **not scatter** it either **with a** small **basket or with a** large **basket, but** only **with the bottom of a** broken **basket,** i.e., he must scatter the straw in a manner different from that of an ordinary weekday. Rava, however, indicates that he may scatter the straw in the usual fashion.

הֲדַר אוֹקִים רָבָא אָמוֹרָא עֲלֵיהּ וְדָרַשׁ: דְּבָרִים שֶׁאָמַרְתִּי לִפְנֵיכֶם טָעוּת הֵן בְּיָדִי, בְּרַם כָּךְ אָמְרוּ מִשּׁוּם רַבִּי אֱלִיעֶזֶר: וּכְשֶׁהוּא מְרַדֶּה אֵינוֹ מְרַדֶּה לֹא בְּסַל וְלֹא בַּקּוּפָּה אֶלָּא בְּשׁוּלֵי קוּפָּה.

Rava then appointed an ***amora*** **before him** to publicize his teaching, **and taught: The statement I issued before you was a mistake of mine. However,** in fact **they said in the name of Rabbi Eliezer** as follows: **And when one scatters** the straw, **he** must **not scatter** it either **with a** small **basket or with a** large **basket, but** only **with the bottom of a** broken **basket.**

״מְמַלְּאִין מִבּוֹר הַגּוֹלָה״. עוּלָּא אִיקְּלַע לְבֵי רַב מְנַשֶּׁה, אֲתָא הַהוּא גַּבְרָא טְרַף אַבָּבָא. אֲמַר: מַאן הַאי? לִיתְחַל גּוּפֵיהּ, דְּקָא מְחִיל לֵיהּ לְשַׁבְּתָא.

We learned in the mishna: **One** may **draw** water **from the Cistern of the Exiles** by means of a wheel. The Gemara relates: **Ulla happened** to come **to the house of Rav Menashe** when **a certain man came and knocked at the door. Ulla said: Who is that? May his body be desecrated, as he desecrates Shabbat**[N] by producing a sound.

אֲמַר לֵיהּ רַבָּה: לֹא אָסְרוּ אֶלָּא קוֹל שֶׁל שִׁיר. אֵיתִיבֵיהּ אַבַּיֵּי: מַעֲלִין בִּדְיוֹפֵי, וּמַטִּיפִין מִיאַרַק לַחוֹלֶה בַּשַּׁבָּת.

Rabba said to him: The Sages **prohibited only a** pleasant **musical sound** on Shabbat, not the rasping sound of knocking on a door.[H] **Abaye raised an objection to** Rabba from a *baraita*: **One** may **draw up** wine from a barrel **with a siphon** [***diyofei***],[L] **and one** may **drip** water from a vessel that releases water in drops [***miarak***],[LB] **for an ill** person **on Shabbat.**

לַחוֹלֶה – אִין, לַבָּרִיא – לָא. הֵיכִי דָּמֵי? לָאו דְּנִים וְקָא בָּעֵי דְּלִיתְעַר? שְׁמַע מִינָּהּ: אוֹלוּדֵי קָלָא אֲסִיר!

The Gemara infers: **For an ill** person, **yes,** this is permitted, but **for a healthy** person, **no,** one may not do so, **what are the circumstances?** Is it **not** the case **that he is dozing off and they wish to waken him,** and as they do not want to alarm him due to his illness, they do it by means of the sound of water poured from a vessel? **And** one can **learn from here** that **it is prohibited to produce a sound** on Shabbat, even one that is unpleasant, as the Sages permitted this only for an ill person.

לָא, דְּתִיר וְקָא בָּעֵי דְּלֵינִים, דְּמִשְׁתַּמַּע כִּי קָלָא דְּזַמְזוּמֵי.

The Gemara rejects this contention: **No,** it is referring to an ill person **who is awake and whom they want to have fall asleep,** and to this end they let water fall in drops, producing **a sound that is heard as melodious.**

אֵיתִיבֵיהּ: הַמְשַׁמֵּר פֵּירוֹתָיו מִפְּנֵי הָעוֹפוֹת וּדְלָעָיו מִפְּנֵי הַחַיָּה – מְשַׁמֵּר כְּדַרְכּוֹ בַּשַּׁבָּת, וּבִלְבַד שֶׁלֹּא יְסַפֵּק וְלֹא יְטַפֵּחַ וְלֹא יְרַקֵּד כְּדֶרֶךְ שֶׁהֵן עוֹשִׂין בַּחוֹל.

Abaye **raised** another **objection to** Rabba from a *baraita*: **One who is guarding his produce**[H] **from birds or his gourds from beasts** may **guard** them, **in the manner that he** typically does so, **on Shabbat,** as his guarding does not entail a prohibited labor, **provided that he neither claps, nor slaps** his hands against his body, **nor dances** and produces noise with his feet, **in the manner that is performed on weekdays** to chase away birds and animals.

מַאי טַעְמָא – לָאו דְּקָמוֹלִיד קָלָא, וְכָל אוֹלוּדֵי קָלָא אֲסִיר! אָמַר רַב אַחָא בַּר יַעֲקֹב: גְּזֵירָה שֶׁמָּא יִטּוֹל צְרוֹר.

The Gemara asks: **What is the reason** that these activities are prohibited? Is it **not because he is producing a sound** on Shabbat, **and any production of a sound is prohibited? Rav Aḥa bar Ya'akov said:** This is not the reason. Rather, it is a **decree** issued by the Sages, **lest** while acting in his usual weekday fashion **he** mistakenly **picks up a pebble** to throw at the birds, thereby handling an object that is set-aside.

NOTES

As he desecrates Shabbat – דְּקָא מְחִיל לֵיהּ לְשַׁבְּתָא: The *amora'im* of Eretz Yisrael were especially particular with regard to this prohibition. It is related that Rabbi Ilai spent the entire night outside his home because he did not want to knock on his door on Shabbat.

LANGUAGE

Siphon [*diyofei*] – דְּיוֹפֵי: Probably from the Greek διαβήτης, *diabetès*, meaning a siphon or an instrument for extracting liquid from a utensil by means of differences in height.

A vessel that releases water in drops [*miarak*] – מִיאַרַק: The *Arukh* reads *miadak*, from an Arabic term meaning an object that produces a sound or a rattle.

BACKGROUND

A vessel that releases water in drops [*miarak*] – מִיאַרַק: Based on the descriptions in the Gemara and the responsa of the *ge'onim*, this refers to an instrument very narrow at one end but wide and perforated at the other. When one presses his finger on the narrow end, the water stays inside, but once he releases his finger, the water drips slowly from the utensil. In order to produce a noise, the vessel is positioned so that its water drips onto a metal platter.

Miarak

HALAKHA

Producing a noise on Shabbat – הַשְׁמָעַת קוֹל בְּשַׁבָּת: It is prohibited to play an instrument on Shabbat. It is even prohibited to knock on a door if this is done in a rhythmic fashion, although it is otherwise permitted. The *halakha* is in accordance with Rava, because even Rabbi Aḥa bar Ya'akov accepts his approach, and Ameimar sought to act likewise (Rif). The Rema rules that one may not knock with an instrument designed to produce a sound, such as a door knocker. Others teach that if he performs a different action and the sound is produced of its own accord, this is permitted if it is not with the intention to produce a sound (Vilna Gaon, based on the Jerusalem Talmud; *Shulḥan Arukh, Oraḥ Ḥayyim* 338:1).

Guarding his produce – מְשַׁמֵּר פֵּירוֹתָיו: It is permitted to guard fruit and other produce to protect them from birds and animals on Shabbat, provided that one does not clap or slap his hands in the manner that he would during the week, lest he continue to conduct himself in the manner that he would during the week and pick up a stone to throw at them, which is prohibited in the public domain. The *Magen Avraham* rules that perhaps today it is unnecessary to be so stringent with regard to this matter, as actual public domains are rare (*Shulḥan Arukh, Oraḥ Ḥayyim* 338:4).

BACKGROUND

Play with nuts – מִשְׂחָק בֶּאֱגוֹזִים: The game is played by leaning a wooden board against a wall and rolling nuts down it. The player whose nut hits the other nuts wins them all. Variations of this game were played in Rashi's time and are played nowadays as well.

Game played with nuts

Wheel pump – גַּלְגַּל שְׁאִיבָה: The image depicts a sophisticated wheel pump, resembling ones found in Alexandria and Rome. Wheels of this type, powered by animals or a person, served as both bucket and pump by creating a powerful, steady jet of water for watering fields. It is possible that the wheel in Meḥoza and even the one used in the Temple looked like this machine.

Wheel pump

וְאֶלָּא הָא דְּאָמַר רַב יְהוּדָה אָמַר רַב: נָשִׁים הַמְשַׂחֲקוֹת בֶּאֱגוֹזִים – אָסוּר. מַאי טַעְמָא – לָאו דְּקָא מוֹלִיד קָלָא, וְכָל אוֹלוּדֵי קָלָא אֲסִיר?

The Gemara asks: **However,** with regard to **that which Rav Yehuda said** that **Rav said: Women who play with nuts**[BN] by rolling them on the ground until they collide with each other, it is **prohibited** for them to do so; **what is the reason** for this prohibition? Is it **not because** knocking nuts together **produces a sound, and any production of a sound is prohibited?**

לָא, דִּלְמָא אָתֵי לְאַשְׁווּיֵי גּוּמוֹת.

The Gemara rejects this contention: **No,** it is prohibited because **perhaps they will come to level the holes.** As small holes in the ground will interfere with their game, they might level them out and seal them up on Shabbat, which is prohibited as building.

דְּאִי לָא תֵּימָא הָכִי – הָא דְּאָמַר רַב יְהוּדָה: נָשִׁים מְשַׂחֲקוֹת בְּתַפּוּחִים אָסוּר, הָתָם מַאי אוֹלוּדֵי קָלָא אִיכָּא? אֶלָּא: דִּילְמָא אָתֵי לְאַשְׁווּיֵי גּוּמוֹת.

For if you do not say that **this** is the reason, there is a difficulty with **that** which **Rav Yehuda said: Women who play with apples,** this is **prohibited,**[H] as **what production of a sound is involved there?** Apples do not produce a sound when they collide with each other. **Rather,** the reason is that **they will perhaps come to level holes,** and the same reasoning applies to nuts.

תְּנַן: מְמַלְּאִין מִבּוֹר הַגּוֹלָה וּמִבּוֹר הַגָּדוֹל בְּגַלְגַּל בְּשַׁבָּת. בַּמִּקְדָּשׁ – אִין, בַּמְּדִינָה – לָא. מַאי טַעְמָא – לָאו מִשּׁוּם דְּאוֹלוּדֵי קָלָא וַאֲסִיר

We learned in the mishna: **One** may **draw water from the Cistern of the Exiles and from the Great Cistern by** means of **the wheel on Shabbat.**[BH] From this it can be inferred: **In the Temple, yes,** it is permitted to do so; but outside the Temple **in** the rest of **the country, no,** it is prohibited to draw water from cisterns. **What is the reason** for this? Is it **not because he is producing a sound, and** that **is prohibited** on Shabbat?

לֹא, גְּזֵירָה שֶׁמָּא יְמַלֵּא לְגִינָּתוֹ וּלְחוּרְבָּתוֹ.

The Gemara again rejects this contention: **No,** it is **a decree** issued by the Sages, **lest he draw** water **for his garden and for his ruin.** As the wheel draws up large quantities of water, once he starts to use it, he might draw water for his garden as well and thereby transgress the prohibition against watering on Shabbat, a subcategory of a prohibited labor.

אַמֵימָר שְׁרָא לְמִימְלָא בְּגִילְגְּלָא בִּמְחוֹזָא, אָמַר: מַאי טַעְמָא גָּזְרוּ רַבָּנַן – שֶׁמָּא יְמַלֵּא לְגִינָּתוֹ וּלְחוּרְבָּתוֹ, הָכָא לָא גִּינָּה אִיכָּא וְלָא חוּרְבָּה אִיכָּא.

The Gemara relates that **Ameimar permitted** people **to draw** water on Shabbat **by** means of **a wheel in Meḥoza, as he said: What is the reason the Sages decreed** that this is prohibited? They did so **lest one draw** water **for his garden and for his ruin.** However, **here** in Meḥoza **there are neither gardens nor ruins.** Meḥoza was entirely built up and lacked gardens or empty areas for sowing, and consequently, there was no concern that people might transgress.

כֵּיוָן דְּקָא חֲזָא דְּקָא

However, **once he saw that**

NOTES

Women who play with nuts – נָשִׁים הַמְשַׂחֲקוֹת בֶּאֱגוֹזִים: The reason this *halakha* was stated twice, with regard to both nuts and apples, is that after Rabbi Yehuda stated the first ruling, which specified nuts, in the name of his master Rav, he realized that it is possible to misconstrue the reason as being due to the sound produced. Consequently, he issued a similar ruling of his own concerning apples, which don't produce a sound when they collide (*Ge'on Ya'akov*). In addition, the winner of this game of nuts would not keep her winnings, as otherwise the game would violate the prohibition against engaging in commerce on Shabbat (Rashash; see Rema).

HALAKHA

Playing with nuts and apples – מִשְׂחָק בֶּאֱגוֹזִים וּבְתַפּוּחִים: One may not play games of nuts and apples on Shabbat that might lead him to level holes in the ground. However, if the game is played on a smooth table, it is permitted (*Shulḥan Arukh, Oraḥ Ḥayyim* 338:5, and in the comment of the Rema).

Drawing water with a wheel – שְׁאִיבָה בְּגַלְגַּל: It is prohibited to draw water by means of a wheel, lest one draw water for his garden. Consequently, if it is in a courtyard that is entirely paved it is permitted. The Rambam rules in accordance with Ameimar, as the latter did not reconsider his basic position, but merely took into account the special circumstances of Meḥoza (*Maggid Mishne*). The *Tosafot Rosh* claims that the Sages only prohibited using large wheels that draw water in great quantities, whereas small wheels are always permitted for use (*Shulḥan Arukh, Oraḥ Ḥayyim* 338:6).

תָּרוּ בָּהּ כִּיתְנָא, אֲסַר לְהוּ.

they were soaking flax in the water, **he prohibited them** from drawing water by means of a wheel, so that they should not draw water for prohibited purposes.

"וּמִבְּאֵר הַקֵּר". מַאי בְּאֵר הַקֵּר? אָמַר שְׁמוּאֵל: בּוֹר שֶׁהִקְּרוּ עָלֶיהָ דְּבָרִים וְהִתִּירוּהָ.

We learned in the mishna that water may be drawn on a Festival **from the Heker Well.** The Gemara asks: **What is the Heker Well? Shmuel said:** It is **a cistern with regard to which they advanced** [*hikru*] **arguments and permitted** drawing water from **it** on a Festival, by proving that the Torah permits doing so.

מֵיתִיבִי: לֹא כָּל הַבּוֹרוֹת הַקֵּרוֹת הִתִּירוּ, אֶלָּא זוֹ בִּלְבַד. וְאִי אָמְרַתְּ "שֶׁהִקְּרוּ דְּבָרִים עָלֶיהָ" מַאי "זוֹ בִּלְבַד"?

The Gemara **raises an objection** from a *baraita*: **They did not permit all Heker wells, but only this one. And if you say** it was named because it is a cistern **with regard to which they put forward arguments** and permitted it, **what is** the meaning of Heker wells in the plural, and what does **only this one** mean? If it was named because of a particular announcement, how could other wells, about which no announcement was issued, bear the same name?

אֶלָּא אָמַר רַב נַחְמָן בַּר יִצְחָק: בְּאֵר מַיִם חַיִּים, שֶׁנֶּאֱמַר: "כְּהָקִיר בַּיִר מֵימֶיהָ וגו׳".

Rather, Rav Naḥman bar Yitzḥak said: The term Heker well denotes **a well of living water, as it is stated: "As a well keeps its water fresh** [*hakir*], so she keeps fresh her wickedness" (Jeremiah 6:7), i.e., it is a well of spring water.

גּוּפָא: לֹא כָּל הַבּוֹרוֹת הַקֵּרוֹת הִתִּירוּ, אֶלָּא זוֹ בִּלְבַד. וּכְשֶׁעָלוּ בְּנֵי הַגּוֹלָה חָנוּ עָלֶיהָ, וּנְבִיאִים שֶׁבֵּינֵיהֶן הִתִּירוּ לָהֶן. וְלֹא נְבִיאִים שֶׁבֵּינֵיהֶן, אֶלָּא מִנְהַג אֲבוֹתָם בִּידֵיהֶם.

Returning to **the matter itself,** the Gemara cites the above *baraita* in full: **They did not permit all Heker wells, but only this one. And when the exiles ascended** from Babylonia, **they encamped by it, and the prophets among them,** Haggai, Zechariah, and Malachi, **permitted it to them. And it was not** really **the prophets among them** who permitted them to draw water from this well on a Festival, **but** rather, it was **a customary practice**[N] that was handed down **to them from their forefathers,** a practice the prophets permitted them to continue.

מתני׳ שֶׁרֶץ שֶׁנִּמְצָא בַּמִּקְדָּשׁ – כֹּהֵן מוֹצִיאוֹ בְּהֶמְיָינוֹ, שֶׁלֹּא לְשַׁהוֹת אֶת הַטּוּמְאָה, דִּבְרֵי רַבִּי יוֹחָנָן בֶּן בְּרוֹקָה. רַבִּי יְהוּדָה אוֹמֵר: בִּצְבָת שֶׁל עֵץ, שֶׁלֹּא לְרַבּוֹת אֶת הַטּוּמְאָה.

MISHNA With regard to the carcass of **a creeping animal,** of one of the eight species of reptile or rodent listed in Leviticus 11:29–30, one of the primary sources of ritual impurity **that is found in the Temple,**[H] **a priest** should **carry it out** on Shabbat **in his girdle,** which was one of the priestly garments. Although the girdle will be defiled by the carcass of the creeping animal, this is the best way to proceed, **so as not to delay** the removal of **the impurity** from the Temple. This is **the statement of Rabbi Yoḥanan ben Beroka. Rabbi Yehuda says:** The creeping animal carcass should be removed **with wooden prongs, so as not to increase the impurity,** as a wooden prong is not susceptible to impurity.

מֵהֵיכָן מוֹצִיאִין אוֹתוֹ – מִן הַהֵיכָל, וּמִן הָאוּלָם, וּמִבֵּין הָאוּלָם וְלַמִּזְבֵּחַ, דִּבְרֵי רַבִּי שִׁמְעוֹן בֶּן נַנָּס.

It is obvious that on a weekday the creeping animal carcass is removed from wherever it is found in the Temple, but **from where does one remove it** on Shabbat? **From the Sanctuary, from the Entrance Hall, and from** the area in the courtyard **between the Entrance Hall and the altar,** the most sanctified precincts of the Temple. However, it need not be removed from the rest of the courtyard.[BN] This is **the statement of Rabbi Shimon ben Nannas.**

BACKGROUND

The Temple and its courtyards – הַמִּקְדָּשׁ וַעֲזָרוֹתָיו: The image illustrates the primary sections of the Temple: The Sanctuary, the Entrance Hall, the area between the Entrance Hall and the altar, and the various courtyards.

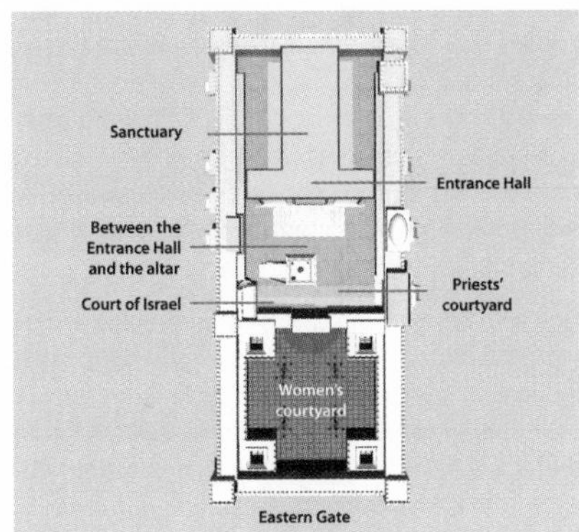

Main sections of the Temple

HALAKHA

The carcass of a creeping animal that is found in the Temple – שֶׁרֶץ שֶׁנִּמְצָא בַּמִּקְדָּשׁ: If a creeping animal carcass is found in the Temple, a priest removes it with wooden tongs, even though the impurity will remain there longer while the tongs are brought than if the priest carried it out in his girdle, as the *halakha* is in accordance with Rabbi Yehuda (Rambam *Sefer Avoda, Hilkhot Biat HaMikdash* 3:20).

NOTES

It was not the prophets…but a customary practice – לֹא נְבִיאִים אֶלָּא מִנְהַג: It was not the prophets among them, Haggai, Zechariah and Malachi, who permitted the people to draw water from the Heker Well. Rather, they relied on a custom of their ancestors. This expression is based on the well-known saying: The Jewish people are holy; if they are not prophets, they are the sons of prophets (Rav Ya'akov Emden).

From the Sanctuary and from the courtyard – מִן הַהֵיכָל וּמִן הָעֲזָרָה: With regard to the severity of the sin, there is no difference between the Sanctuary and the courtyard, as a ritually impure person who knowingly enters either of them is subject to the punishment of *karet*. However, Rabbi Shimon ben Nannas maintains that greater respect is granted to the Sanctuary than the courtyard, due to the honor of the Divine Presence (*Ge'on Ya'akov*).

רַבִּי עֲקִיבָא אוֹמֵר: כָּל מָקוֹם שֶׁחַיָּיבִין עַל זְדוֹנוֹ כָּרֵת וְעַל שִׁגְגָתוֹ חַטָּאת, מִשָּׁם מוֹצִיאִין אוֹתוֹ. וּשְׁאָר כָּל הַמְּקוֹמוֹת – כּוֹפִין עָלָיו פְּסַכְתֵּר.

Rabbi Akiva says: Any place where one is liable to be punished with *karet* if he **intentionally** enters there in a state of ritual impurity, **and** is liable to bring a **sin-offering** if he does so **unwittingly, from there one** must **remove it.** This includes the entire area of the Temple courtyard. **And** as for **the rest of the places** in the Temple, **one covers** the creeping animal carcass **with a bowl** [*pesakhter*][L] and leaves it there until the conclusion of Shabbat.[NH]

רַבִּי שִׁמְעוֹן אוֹמֵר: מָקוֹם שֶׁהִתִּירוּ לְךָ חֲכָמִים – מִשֶּׁלְּךָ נָתְנוּ לְךָ. שֶׁלֹּא הִתִּירוּ לְךָ אֶלָּא מִשּׁוּם שְׁבוּת.

Rabbi Shimon says that this is the principle: **Wherever the Sages permitted** something **to you, they granted you** only **from your own, as they permitted to you only** activities that are prohibited **due to rabbinic decree,** not labors prohibited by Torah law.

גמ׳ אָמַר רַב טָבִי בַּר קִיסְנָא, אָמַר שְׁמוּאֵל: הַמַּכְנִיס טְמֵא שֶׁרֶץ לַמִּקְדָּשׁ – חַיָּיב. שֶׁרֶץ עַצְמוֹ – פָּטוּר. מַאי טַעְמָא? אָמַר קְרָא: ״מִזָּכָר וְעַד נְקֵבָה תְּשַׁלֵּחוּ״ – מִי שֶׁיֵּשׁ לוֹ טׇהֳרָה בְּמִקְוֶה, יָצָא שֶׁרֶץ שֶׁאֵין לוֹ טׇהֳרָה.

GEMARA **Rav Tavi bar Kisna said** that **Shmuel said:** With regard to **one who brings into the Temple** an object that was **defiled by a creeping animal** carcass, **he is liable,** but if he brings in the carcass of **a creeping animal**[N] **itself, he is exempt. What is the reason** for this distinction? **The verse said: "Both male and female shall you put out,** without the camp shall you put them; that they defile not their camp, in the midst whereof I dwell" (Numbers 5:3). This verse teaches that the obligation to send out of the camp applies only to **one who has** the option of **purification in a ritual bath,** i.e., the male and female mentioned by the Torah; this **excludes** the carcass of **a creeping animal, which has no purification.** Consequently, one who brings the carcass of a creeping animal into the Temple is exempt, as he did not transgress the Torah's commandment to send away the impure.

לֵימָא מְסַיֵּיע לֵיהּ: ״מִזָּכָר עַד נְקֵבָה תְּשַׁלֵּחוּ״ פְּרָט לִכְלִי חֶרֶשׂ, דִּבְרֵי רַבִּי יוֹסֵי הַגְּלִילִי. מַאי טַעְמָא – לָאו מִשּׁוּם דְּלֵית לֵיהּ טׇהֳרָה בְּמִקְוֶה?

The Gemara suggests: **Let us say** that a *baraita* **supports him: "Both male and female shall you put out"; this excludes an earthenware vessel.** This is **the statement of Rabbi Yosei HaGelili. What is the reason** for this? Is it **not because** an earthenware vessel **does not have purification in a ritual bath,**[H] in accordance with the opinion of Rav Tavi bar Kisna?

לֹא, מִי שֶׁנַּעֲשָׂה אָב הַטּוּמְאָה – יָצָא כְּלִי חֶרֶס שֶׁאֵינוֹ נַעֲשֶׂה אָב הַטּוּמְאָה.

The Gemara rejects this contention: **No,** the reason is that only **something that can become a primary source of ritual impurity,** i.e., a human being or a metal utensil, must be sent out of the camp. This **excludes an earthenware vessel, which cannot become a primary source of ritual impurity.**[H]

לֵימָא כְּתַנָּאֵי: שֶׁרֶץ שֶׁנִּמְצָא בַּמִּקְדָּשׁ – כֹּהֵן מוֹצִיאוֹ בְּהֶמְיָינוֹ, שֶׁלֹּא לְשַׁהוֹת אֶת הַטּוּמְאָה, דִּבְרֵי רַבִּי יוֹחָנָן בֶּן בְּרוֹקָה. רַבִּי יְהוּדָה אוֹמֵר: בִּצְבָת שֶׁל עֵץ מוֹצִיאוֹ, שֶׁלֹּא לְרַבּוֹת אֶת הַטּוּמְאָה.

The Gemara suggests: **Let us say** that this issue, whether or not there is liability for bringing a creeping animal carcass into the Temple, is **parallel to** a dispute between *tanna'im*, as we learned in the mishna: With regard to **a creeping animal** carcass **that is found in the Temple, a priest** should **carry it out** on Shabbat **in his girdle, so as not to delay** the removal of **the impurity.** This is **the statement of Rabbi Yoḥanan ben Beroka. Rabbi Yehuda says: He** should **remove it with wooden prongs, so as not to increase the impurity.**

מַאי לָאו בְּהָא קָא מִיפַּלְגִי: דְּמַאן דְּאָמַר שֶׁלֹּא לְשַׁהוֹת – קָסָבַר: הַמַּכְנִיס שֶׁרֶץ לַמִּקְדָּשׁ – חַיָּיב, וּמַאן דְּאָמַר שֶׁלֹּא לְרַבּוֹת – קָסָבַר: הַמַּכְנִיס שֶׁרֶץ לַמִּקְדָּשׁ – פָּטוּר!

What, isn't it the case **that this** is the matter with regard to which the two *tanna'im* **disagree: The one who said** we should **not delay** the removal of the impurity **maintains** that **one who brings a creeping animal** carcass **into the Temple is liable,** and therefore every effort must be made to remove it immediately. **And the one who said** we should **not increase impurity maintains** that **one who brings a creeping animal** carcass **into the Temple is exempt.** As no special command is in effect, the correct procedure is to prevent any additional impurity.

לֹא, דְּכוּלֵּי עָלְמָא חַיָּיב, וְהָכָא בְּהָא קָא מִיפַּלְגִי; מָר סָבַר: שְׁהוּיֵי טוּמְאָה עָדִיף, וּמָר סָבַר אַפּוּשֵׁי טוּמְאָה עָדִיף.

The Gemara rejects this explanation: **No, everyone agrees** that one who brings a creeping animal carcass itself into the Temple **is liable, and here, this** is the matter with regard to which **they disagree: The** one **Sage,** Rabbi Yoḥanan ben Beroka, **holds: Delaying** removal of the **impurity**[N] is the consideration that **takes precedence.** Consequently, it is permitted even to defile the priestly garments to prevent any delay in the removal of the impurity from the holy place. **Whereas the** other **Sage,** Rabbi Yehuda, **holds: Increasing impurity** is the consideration that **takes precedence,** and therefore the impurity should be removed only by means of wooden prongs.

LANGUAGE

Bowl [*pesakhter*] – **פְּסַכְתֵּר:** From the Greek ψυκτήρ, *psuktèr*, a kind of copper pot.

NOTES

Impurity in the Temple – טוּמְאָה בַּמִּקְדָּשׁ: The issue is not the propriety of bringing impurity into the Temple. Rather, the question is whether the obligation to remove impurity from the Temple precinct, a positive commandment, applies even to an object that cannot be purified in a ritual bath, or to an article that cannot become a primary source of ritual impurity. The verse: "both male and female you shall put out" (Numbers 5:3) is referring to people suffering from gonorrhea [*zavim*], a primary source of ritual impurity. Accordingly, the question concerns the extent of the commandment, and what is not included in the mitzva.

One who brings…the carcass of a creeping animal – הַמַּכְנִיס...שֶׁרֶץ: It is important to note that the one who brought in the creeping animal did not touch it, for otherwise he would be impure and prohibited from entering the Temple. Indeed, this is why the cited example involves a creeping animal carcass, because one who carries the carcass of other animals is defiled by carrying it, even if he does not touch it, whereas one who carries a creeping animal without touching it is not thereby rendered impure (*Tosafot*).

Delaying removal of the impurity – שְׁהוּיֵי טוּמְאָה: In the Jerusalem Talmud this discussion is linked to the dispute between Rabbi Eliezer and Rabbi Yehoshua with regard to intermingled blood. Apparently, the issue here is the relationship between two mitzvot, the commandment to "put out of the camp" (Numbers 5:2) anything impure and "they shall not defile their camp" (Numbers 5:3), the prohibition against defiling sacred places and objects. The question of which of these mitzvot takes precedence forms the basis of the dispute between Rabbi Yoḥanan ben Beroka and Rabbi Yehuda.

HALAKHA

Removal of a creeping animal carcass on Shabbat – הוֹצָאַת שֶׁרֶץ בְּשַׁבָּת: If a creeping animal carcass is found in the Temple on Shabbat, it must be removed from any place where one would be subject to the punishment of *karet* if he intentionally entered that place while impure. If it is found in other places in the Temple, it must be covered with a bowl until after Shabbat, in accordance with the opinion of Rabbi Akiva, contrary to the opinion of Rabbi Shimon (Rambam *Sefer Avoda, Hilkhot Biat HaMikdash* 3:20).

The purification of an earthenware vessel – טׇהֳרַת כְּלִי חֶרֶס: An earthenware vessel that contracts ritual impurity cannot be purified in a ritual bath. The impurity remains in effect until the vessel is broken (Rambam *Sefer Tahara, Hilkhot Mikvaot* 1:3).

The impurity of an earthenware vessel – טוּמְאַת כְּלִי חֶרֶס: An earthenware vessel cannot become a primary source of ritual impurity. Even if it were to come into contact with a corpse, which has the highest level of impurity, it would be impure only to the first degree and would not render people or utensils impure, by Torah law (Rambam *Sefer Tahara, Hilkhot Tumat Met* 5:6).

אֶלָּא כְּהָנֵי תַּנָּאֵי, דִּתְנַן: מֵהֵיכָן מוֹצִיאִין אוֹתוֹ כו׳?

Rather, the Gemara suggests that this issue is the subject of a dispute between **these *tanna'im*, as we learned** in that same mishna: **From where does one remove** the creeping animal carcass? Rabbi Shimon ben Nannas and Rabbi Akiva disagree whether it is removed only from the Sanctuary, the Entrance Hall, and the area of the courtyard between the Entrance Hall and the altar, or from the entire area of the courtyard as well.

מַאי לָאו בְּהָא קָא מִיפַּלְגִי; דְּמַאן דְּאָמַר מֵעֲזָרָה – לָא, קָסָבַר: הַמַּכְנִיס שֶׁרֶץ לַמִּקְדָּשׁ פָּטוּר, וּמַאן דְּאָמַר מִכּוּלָּהּ עֲזָרָה – קָסָבַר: חַיָּיב.

Isn't it the case **that** the two *tanna'im* **disagree about the following: The one who said** we do **not** remove it **from the** Temple **courtyard maintains** that **one who brings a creeping animal** carcass **into the Temple**[H] **is exempt,** and there is therefore no obligation to remove it from the courtyard on Shabbat. **And the one who said that** it must be removed **from the entire courtyard maintains** that one who brings a creeping animal carcass into the Temple **is liable.**

HALAKHA

One who brings a creeping animal carcass into the Temple – הַמַּכְנִיס שֶׁרֶץ לַמִּקְדָּשׁ: One who intentionally brings a creeping animal carcass into the Temple is subject to the punishment of *karet*. Even according to the second approach in the Gemara, which states that this opinion is not unanimous, Rabbi Akiva's opinion is accepted as *halakha* (Rambam *Sefer Avoda, Hilkhot Biat HaMikdash* 3:16).

אָמַר רַבִּי יוֹחָנָן: וּשְׁנֵיהֶם מִקְרָא אֶחָד דָּרְשׁוּ: ״וַיָּבֹאוּ הַכֹּהֲנִים לִפְנִימָה בֵּית ה׳ לְטַהֵר וַיּוֹצִיאוּ אֵת כׇּל הַטּוּמְאָה אֲשֶׁר מָצְאוּ בְּהֵיכַל ה׳ לַחֲצַר בֵּית ה׳ וַיְקַבְּלוּ הַלְוִיִּם לְהוֹצִיא לְנַחַל קִדְרוֹן חוּצָה״.

Rabbi Yoḥanan said: Both of them, Rabbi Shimon ben Nannas and Rabbi Akiva, **derived their opinions from the same verse: "And the priests went into the inner part of the House of God, to cleanse it, and they brought out all the impurity that they found in the Temple of God into the courtyard of the House of God. And the Levites took it, to carry it out to the brook of Kidron"** (II Chronicles 29:16).[N]

מָר סָבַר: מִדְּאִשְׁתַּנֵּי בָּעֲזָרָה בַּלְוִיִּם – טוּמְאָה בָּעֲזָרָה לֵיכָּא.

One Sage, Rabbi Shimon Ben Nannas, **maintains: As there was a change** from the priests who removed the ritual impurity from the inner part of the Temple to **the Levites,** who took over **in the courtyard,** this indicates that **there is no** obligation to remove **impurity in the courtyard,** and consequently the priests are not required to do so.

וּמָר סָבַר: עַד הֵיכָא דְּלָא אֶפְשָׁר בַּלְוִיִּם – מַפְּקִי כֹּהֲנִים, הָשְׁתָּא דְּאֶפְשָׁר בַּלְוִיִּם – תּוּ לָא מְטַמְּאִי כֹּהֲנִים.

And one **Sage,** Rabbi Akiva, **maintains: Up to where it is impossible** for the task to be performed **by the Levites,** as it is prohibited for Levites to enter the Sanctuary, **the priests took it out.** However, **now** in the courtyard, **where it is possible** for the ritual impurity to be removed **by the Levites, the priests no longer render themselves ritually impure,** as they are prohibited from maintaining contact with ritual impurity for any longer than necessary. That is to say, the Levites removed it from any place where they were permitted to enter.

תָּנוּ רַבָּנַן: הַכֹּל נִכְנָסִין בַּהֵיכָל לִבְנוֹת לְתַקֵּן וּלְהוֹצִיא אֶת הַטּוּמְאָה, וּמִצְוָה בְּכֹהֲנִים. אִם אֵין שָׁם כֹּהֲנִים – נִכְנָסִין לְוִיִּם, אֵין שָׁם לְוִיִּם – נִכְנָסִין יִשְׂרְאֵלִים. וְאִידִי וְאִידִי טְהוֹרִין – אִין, טְמֵאִין – לָא.

The Sages taught in a *baraita*: It is permitted for **everyone** to **enter the Sanctuary to build, to repair, or to remove impurity** from inside. However, wherever possible, **the mitzva is** for these tasks to be performed **by priests.**[B] **If no priests are available, Levites enter; if no Levites are available, Israelites enter. In both** cases, if **they are** ritually **pure, yes,** they may enter, but if **they are impure, no,** they may not enter the holy place.[H]

אָמַר רַב הוּנָא: רַב כָּהֲנָא מְסַיֵּיעַ כָּהֲנֵי, דְּתָנֵי רַב כָּהֲנָא: מִתּוֹךְ שֶׁנֶּאֱמַר: ״אַךְ אֶל הַפָּרֹכֶת לֹא יָבֹא״ יָכוֹל לֹא יְהוּ כֹּהֲנִים בַּעֲלֵי מוּמִין נִכְנָסִין בֵּין הָאוּלָם וְלַמִּזְבֵּחַ לַעֲשׂוֹת רִיקּוּעֵי פַּחִים –

Rav Huna said: Rav Kahana, who was a priest, **supports priests**[N] by emphasizing their special sanctity. **As Rav Kahana taught** in a *baraita*: **Since it is stated** with regard to a priest who has a physical blemish, **"Only he shall not go in unto the veil,** nor come near to the altar, because he has a blemish, that he profane not My holy places; for I am the Lord who sanctifies them" (Leviticus 21:23), **I might** have thought that **priests with blemishes** may **not enter** the area **between the Entrance Hall and the altar to manufacture beaten plates**[N] of gold for the Holy of Holies.

תַּלְמוּד לוֹמַר: ״אַךְ״ – חִלֵּק. מִצְוָה בִּתְמִימִים, אֵין שָׁם תְּמִימִים – נִכְנָסִין בַּעֲלֵי מוּמִין. מִצְוָה בִּטְהוֹרִין, אֵין שָׁם טְהוֹרִין – נִכְנָסִין טְמֵאִין. אִידִי וְאִידִי, כֹּהֲנִים – אִין, יִשְׂרְאֵלִים – לָא.

Therefore **the verse teaches "only"** as an expression of exclusion, which means that there is **a distinction** here: Although the **mitzva** should be performed with **unblemished** priests *ab initio*, **if no unblemished** priests **are available, blemished ones** may **enter.** Likewise, it is the duty of ritually **pure** priests; **if no pure** priests **are available, impure ones** may **enter.**[H] **In both** cases, if they are **priests, yes,** they may enter, but if they are **Israelites, no,** they may not enter the holy place. According to Rav Kahana, ritually impure priests take precedence over ritually pure Israelites.

NOTES

Impurity in the Sanctuary – טוּמְאָה שֶׁבַּהֵיכָל: According to some commentaries, this was an impurity imparted by a corpse itself, as priests are specifically prohibited from contracting impurity by touching a corpse (*Ge'on Ya'akov*).

Supports priests – מְסַיֵּיעַ כָּהֲנֵי: Rashi explains that in several places, Rav Kahana cites teachings that elevate the status of priests above that of the rest of the people.

Beaten plates – רִיקּוּעֵי פַּחִים: The inside of the Holy of Holies was entirely overlaid with gold plates. To lay these golden plates, it was necessary in practice to allow artisans, either priests or others, to enter, despite the fact that the High Priest alone was permitted to enter the Holy of Holies, and then only on Yom Kippur.

BACKGROUND

Sanctuary repairs – תִּיקּוּן הַהֵיכָל: This discussion concerning those suitable to enter the Sanctuary to build and to perform repairs had numerous practical ramifications, especially when the Temple was rebuilt by Herod. While the overall structure, particularly the large outer framework, was built relatively quickly, it took many years, some even say generations, before all the work was completed, as they wanted the work on the Temple itself to be performed by priests.

HALAKHA

Who enters the Sanctuary to perform repairs – מִי נִכְנָס לְהֵיכָל לְתַקֵּן: When it is necessary to perform repairs in the Sanctuary, the mitzva should be performed by ritually pure, unblemished priests. If no unblemished priests can do the repairs, blemished ones are allowed to enter. If there are no priests available, Levites enter, and if there are no Levites, Israelites enter. If no one is pure, then ritually impure people may enter to perform the repairs (Rambam *Sefer Avoda, Hilkhot Beit HaBeḥira* 7:23).

Impure and blemished – טָמֵא וּבַעַל מוּם: If it is necessary to allow either an impure priest or a blemished one to enter to perform repairs in the Sanctuary, it is preferable that a blemished priest enter rather than an impure one. This ruling is based on the conclusion elsewhere that communal impurity is only suspended, not freely permitted. Consequently, a pure, blemished priest takes precedence (*Kesef Mishne*). According to an alternative reading, the Rambam reversed the opinions, and ruled in accordance with Rav, contrary to his disciple Rabbi Elazar (*Mishne LeMelekh*, in accordance with *Mabit*; Rambam *Sefer Avoda, Hilkhot Beit HaBeḥira* 7:23).

NOTES

The statement of Rabbi Shimon – דִּבְרֵי רַבִּי שִׁמְעוֹן: Rabbi Ovadya Bartenura explains that Rabbi Shimon sought to clarify why he is so stringent in the case of the broken harp string, despite his leniency with regard to one outside the Shabbat boundary. His explanation is that the Sages permit only activities prohibited by rabbinic decree, as: From your own they grant you. Consequently, they were lenient in the case of boundaries, where the surveyors' measurements allow for a certain leeway, but they were stringent in a case involving a Torah prohibition.

The conclusion of the tractate – סִיּוּם הַמַּסֶּכֶת: The Maharsha adds that although the Gemara suggests particular sources for Rabbi Shimon's statement, his teaching basically applies to the entire tractate, according to all opinions. In other words, the guiding principle of rabbinic prohibitions and the leniencies granted by the Sages with respect to their own stringencies, pertain to all the *halakhot* of *eiruvin*. Likewise, in the *Tosefta* and the Jerusalem Talmud, the concluding statement is: Tongs are formed with tongs, i.e., one set of tongs can be used to produce many tongs. Analogously, all rabbinic decrees intended to enhance the character of Shabbat as a day of rest were derived from the basic principle of rest.

אִיבַּעְיָא לְהוּ: טָמֵא וּבַעַל מוּם אֵיזוֹ מֵהֶן נִכְנָס? רַב חִיָּיא בַּר אַשִׁי אָמַר רַב: טָמֵא נִכְנָס, דְּהָא אִישְׁתְּרֵי בַּעֲבוֹדַת צִיבּוּר. רַבִּי אֶלְעָזָר אוֹמֵר: בַּעַל מוּם נִכְנָס, דְּהָא אִישְׁתְּרֵי בַּאֲכִילַת קָדָשִׁים.

A dilemma was raised before the Sages: If one priest is ritually **impure and** another **has a blemish, which of them** should **enter** to perform repairs? **Rav Ḥiyya bar Ashi said** that **Rav said:** The **impure one** should **enter, as he is permitted** to participate **in communal service.** If the entire community is ritually impure, even impure priests may perform the service, whereas blemished priests may not serve under any circumstances. **Rabbi Elazar says:** The **one with the blemish** should **enter, as he is permitted to eat consecrated foods,** which indicates that he retains the sanctity of the priesthood despite his blemish. The Gemara leaves this question unresolved.

״רַבִּי שִׁמְעוֹן אוֹמֵר וכו׳״. רַבִּי שִׁמְעוֹן הֵיכָא קָאֵי? הָתָם קָאֵי, דִּתְנַן: מִי שֶׁהֶחְשִׁיךְ חוּץ לַתְּחוּם, אֲפִילּוּ אַמָּה אַחַת לֹא יִכָּנֵס. רַבִּי שִׁמְעוֹן אוֹמֵר: אֲפִילּוּ חֲמֵשׁ עֶשְׂרֵה אַמָּה יִכָּנֵס, לְפִי שֶׁאֵין הַמָּשׁוֹחוֹת מְמַצְּעִין אֶת הַמִּדּוֹת מִפְּנֵי הַטּוֹעִים.

We learned in the mishna that **Rabbi Shimon says:** Wherever the Sages permitted an action to you, they granted you only from your own. The Gemara asks: With regard to **Rabbi Shimon, on the basis of what** mishna did he formulate this principle? The Gemara answers: He taught this principle **on the basis** of the mishna **there, as we learned:** With regard to **one** for **whom it grew dark** while he was **outside the** Shabbat **limit, even** if he was only **one cubit** outside the limit **he** may **not enter** the town. **Rabbi Shimon says: Even** if he was **fifteen cubits** outside the limit, **he** may **enter** the town, **because** when **the surveyors** mark the Shabbat limit, they **do not measure precisely.** Rather they position the boundary mark within the two-thousand-cubit limit, **because of those who err.**

דְּקָאָמַר תַּנָּא קַמָּא לֹא יִכָּנֵס, וְאָמַר לֵיהּ רַבִּי שִׁמְעוֹן יִכָּנֵס.

With regard to **that which the first *tanna* said,** i.e., that **he** may **not enter, Rabbi Shimon said to** the *tanna*: **He** may **enter.** His reason, as stated, is that the limit does in fact extend that far, as any area the Sages granted to a person was actually permitted to him by Torah law.

״שֶׁלֹּא הִתִּירוּ לָךְ אֶלָּא מִשּׁוּם שְׁבוּת״. הֵיכָא קָאֵי? הָתָם קָאֵי, דְּקָאָמַר תַּנָּא קַמָּא: קוֹשְׁרָהּ, וְאָמַר לֵיהּ רַבִּי שִׁמְעוֹן: עוֹנְבָהּ.

Rabbi Shimon further said: **As they permitted to you only** activities prohibited **due to rabbinic decree,** but not actions prohibited by Torah law. The Gemara asks: **On the basis of what** teaching did he formulate this principle? The Gemara answers: He taught it **on the basis** of the mishna **there, where the first *tanna* said** with regard to a harp string in the Temple that broke on Shabbat, that **one** may **tie it** with a knot, **and Rabbi Shimon said: He** may **form** only **a bow.**[N]

עֲנִיבָה דְּלָא אָתֵי לִידֵי חִיּוּב חַטָּאת – שָׁרוּ לֵיהּ רַבָּנַן, קְשִׁירָה דְּאָתֵי לִידֵי חִיּוּב חַטָּאת – לֹא שָׁרוּ לֵיהּ רַבָּנַן.

The reason why only **forming a bow** is permitted, is **that it cannot lead to liability for a sin-offering,** as forming a bow cannot constitute a violation of the category of the prohibited labor of tying. Consequently, **the Sages permitted it.** However, with regard to **tying** a knot, **which can lead to liability for a sin-offering** when performed outside the Temple, **the Sages did not permit it,** as Rabbi Shimon maintains that the Sages permitted only activities whose prohibition involves a rabbinic decree.[N]

הדרן עלך המוצא תפילין
וסליקא לה מסכת עירובין

Summary of **Perek X**

Several aspects of the rabbinic decrees designed to preserve the integrity of Shabbat as a day of rest were discussed in this chapter. Essentially, what are the limits of rabbinic decrees? Under what circumstances do the Sages insist on full compliance and when are they more flexible? The prohibited labor of carrying out is an inferior labor, as, in contrast to the other primary categories of prohibited labor, no apparent change has been engendered in the object, and the lines demarcating the boundaries between the various domains of Shabbat are similarly not always apparent. Consequently, numerous rabbinic decrees were issued in an attempt to limit the possibility that one will transfer objects from one domain to another. The Sages prohibited transfer of objects from domain to domain even when it is accomplished through an intermediate domain, unless it was performed while observing numerous precautionary measures.

Indeed, the principle established by Rabbi Shimon was, in a certain sense, the key to all of the halakhic issues discussed in this chapter; it applied to the rabbinic decrees issued to preserve the character of Shabbat as a day of rest: Wherever the Sages permitted you to perform a certain action, they merely gave you from that which was yours. As it was the Sages who issued these decrees, they, at times, permitted the performance of actions similar to those they prohibited for various reasons.

Therefore, the Sages employed extensive leniency with regard to matters associated with sacred items, e.g., sacred writings, phylacteries, and the like. This approach was especially conspicuous with regard to the Temple precincts. There, many of the decrees issued by the Sages were not in effect, either due to the diligence of the priests and their meticulousness in the performance of mitzvot, in contrast to the general public, whose lack of attention could lead to failure in those matters, or due to the fact that stringency within the Temple precincts with regard to one matter could lead to laxity with regard to other mitzvot of the Temple that are Torah obligations.

Nevertheless, not everything permitted by Torah law was actually performed within the Temple precincts. The suspension of decrees was implemented only for matters that were essential and with regard to which there was no danger that a Torah prohibition would be violated. Just as the Sages were lenient in applying decrees issued to preserve Shabbat as a day of rest within the Temple precincts, so too were they lenient with regard to other rabbinic decrees and stringencies there, limiting their decrees only to cases where there was concern lest even the priests in the Temple come to violate a Torah prohibition.

Index of **Background**

Index of **Background**

Index of **Language**

Index of **Personalities**

Image **Credits**

תלמוד בבלי

— מהדורת נאה —

עירובין ב

הוצאת קורן ירושלים

— מהדורת נאה —

מסכת עירובין ב

COMMENTARY BY

Rabbi Adin Even-Israel
(Steinsaltz)

EDITOR-IN-CHIEF

Rabbi Dr Tzvi Hersh Weinreb

EXECUTIVE EDITOR

Rabbi Joshua Schreier

•

SHEFA FOUNDATION
KOREN PUBLISHERS JERUSALEM

כמאן — [א]כרב יוסף, ואליבא דר' יוסי בר יהודה. לא, כרבה ואליבא דר' יהודה.§ "ר"מ אומר: כל שיכול לערב כו'".§ הא תנינא חדא זימנא: *ספק, ר"מ ורבי יהודה אומרים: הרי זה חמר גמל! אמר רב ששת: לא תימא טעמא דר"מ ספק עירב ספק לא עירב, הוא דהוי חמר גמל; אבל ודאי לא עירב — לא הוי חמר גמל, אלא: אפילו ודאי לא עירב — הוי חמר גמל. דהא הכא ודאי לא עירב, וקא הוי חמר גמל.§

מתני' [ב]מי שיצא חוץ לתחום — אפילו אמה אחת לא יכנס. *ר"א אומר: שתים — יכנס, שלש — לא יכנס.§ **גמ'** א"ר חנינא: רגלו אחת בתוך התחום ורגלו אחת חוץ לתחום — לא יכנס, דכתיב: °"אם תשיב משבת רגלך", "רגלך" כתיב. (ישעיהו נח) והתניא: רגלו אחת בתוך התחום ורגלו אחת חוץ לתחום — יכנס! הא מני — אחרים היא. דתניא, אחרים אומרים: למקום שרובו הוא *נזקר. איכא דאמרי, אמר ר' חנינא: [ג]רגלו אחת בתוך התחום ורגלו אחת חוץ לתחום — יכנס, דכתיב: °"אם תשיב משבת רגלך", "רגליך" קרינן. והתניא: לא יכנס! הוא דאמר כאחרים, דתניא: למקום שרובו הוא נזקר.§ "ר"א אומר: שתים — יכנס, שלש — לא יכנס".§ והתניא, ר"א אומר: אחת — יכנס, שתים — לא יכנס! לא קשיא; הא — דעקר חדא וקם אתרתי, הא — דעקר תרתי וקם אתלת. והתניא, ר"א אומר: אפילו אמה אחת לא יכנס! כי תניא ההיא — למודד. *דתנן: ולמודד שאמרו נותנין לו אלפים אמה — אפילו סוף מדתו כלה במערה.§

מתני' *[ד]מי שהחשיך חוץ לתחום — אפילו אמה אחת לא יכנס. ר"ש אומר: אפילו חמש עשרה אמות יכנס, שאין המשוחות ממצין את המדות מפני הטועין.§ **גמ'** תנא: מפני טועי המדה.§

הדרן עלך מי שהוציאוהו

כיצד [ה]מעברין את הערים? בית נכנס בית יוצא, פגום נכנס פגום יוצא. היו שם גדודיות גבוהות עשרה טפחים, וגשרים

רש"י

כמאן. בעינן החזיק בדרך ו"לין פה". וללישנא אחרינא הכי גרסינן: כמאן דסגי ליה בהכי, ואע"ג דלא אמר שביתתי במקום פלוני — כרב יוסף אליבא דרבי יוסי בר' יהודה? לא, כרבה ואליבא דרבי (יוסי ברבי) יהודה. וה"פ: כמאן הוי — כרב יוסף ואליבא דרבי יוסי בר' יהודה, דלא בעי אלא להחזיק, והאי נמי החזיק ולא אמר. ומשני: לא, דאמר עסקינן, וכרבה אליבא דר' יהודה דבעי תרתי. והוא הדין נמי לרב יוסף ואליבא דרבי יהודה, אלא אליבא דרבה עדיפא ליה לאוקמי משום דרבה, ורב יוסף הילכתא כרבה, לבר מתלת: שדה, ענין, ומחצה: ספק. בפרק "בכל מערבין" (לעיל דף לה.): נתגלגל חוץ לתחום, נשרף, מבעוד יום — אינו עירוב, משחשיכה — הרי זה עירוב. ספק מבעוד יום ספק משחשיכה, ר' מאיר ור' יהודה אומרים כו' אלמא: כל ספיקא חמר גמל הוא. ומתני' נמי ספיקא הוא. וללישנא בתרא הכי קשיא ליה: תנינא חדא זימנא לר"מ דהיכא דעירב במקום שאינו עירוב, הוה חמר גמל: לא תימא. התם הוא דספק עירב וקנה שם שביתה, וספק לא עירב וקנה בביתו הוא דהוי חמר גמל. אבל היכא דודאי לא עירב, כגון חוזר זה שהיה לו לערב בפת שקרוב לביתו היה. ל"א: שהיה לו לומר "שביתתי במקום פלוני" לא הוי חמר גמל, דאין כאן ספק אלא לגמרי נתכוון לביתו, ויהא כאנשי עירו: אלא אפילו ודאי לא עירב. שלא אמר שביתתי לשם — נמי מחזקינן ליה בספק, משום גלויי דעתא. וללישנא בתרא דפרשינן, דרבי מאיר עשיר משוי ליה, ואפילו הכי הוי חמר גמל ולא כבני עירו — ש"מ דאפילו במקום שאין ספק, כגון נתגלגל חוץ לתחום מבעוד יום, דודאי לאו עירוב הוא — אפילו הכי לרבי מאיר חמר גמל הוא, דסילק עצמו בכוונתו מאלפים של צד שני לביתו. והאי סתמא דקתני התם מבעוד יום אינו עירוב, דמשמע והרי הוא כבני עירו — ר' יהודה היא. והא דלא עריב להו ותני בהדי סיפא, דקתני "הרי זה חמר גמל" — משום דר' יהודה בסיפא מודה לר' מאיר, אבל ברישא — כבני עירו שוי להו. ורישא ר' יהודה היא: **מתני'** מי שיצא חוץ לתחום. במזיד. ומדעת שלא לשם מצוה: שתים יכנס. משום הבלעת תחומין, כדאמרינן בפירקין (לעיל דף מה.): ר' אליעזר לטעמיה, דאמר: והוא באמצען: **גמ'** ה"ג: הא מני אחרים היא: למקום שרובו שם הוא נזקר. ורובו בתוך התחום הוא: נזקר. כלומר: בתר רובו שדינן ליה. וכיון דלא הויא אלא רגלו אחת חוץ לתחום — עדיין רובו בתוך התחום, הילכך, יכנס: הוא דאמר. ר' חנינא: מתני' דעקר חדא. שיצא מן האחת ועומד בשניה, והכי קאמר: אם בשתים עומד — יכנס. וברייתא דקתני שתים לא יכנס — שיצא מכל השתים: למודד. שחשכה לו, ואמר שביתתי במקומי, ומודד אלפים פסיעות בינוניות אולי יכנס לתחום העיר. וכלו אלפים שלו אמה אחת חוץ לתחום — לא יכנס, שאפילו האלפים מוליכות אותו לתוכו — אינו מותר לצאת מאלפים, כדתנן: ולמודד שאמרו נותנין לו אלפים — אפילו סוף מדתו כלה במערה לא יהלך להלן מאלפים, דכיון שמדד אלפים לבד מקום שביתתו שהן ארבע — אינו יכול לעבור חוץ לאלפים: **מתני'** מי שהחשיך. שהוא בא בדרך, וחשכה לו חוץ לתחום: אפילו חמש עשרה אמה כו'. לאו דווקא ט"ו אמה: המשוחות. מודדי התחומין לעיירות, ועושין סימן לתוך התחום: אינן ממצין את המדות. להציב הסימן בסוף אלפים, אלא כונסין אותן לתוך אלפים: מפני הטועין. מפני טועי המדה, שאין מכירין את הסימן, ופעמים הולכין להלן ממנו וחוזרין, ולאו אדעתייהו. ל"א, ולא שמעתיו: דדוקא ט"ו נקט, וטועי המדה הן המשוחות הקובעין התחומין, ואמרינן לקמן ב"כיצד מעברין" (דף נז:): אין מודדין אלא בחבל של חמשים אמה. ארבעים חבלים יש לאלפים, וכל חבל וחבל מתמעט שני אחיזות שזה תופס מכאן וזה תופס מכאן, והאחיזה טפח וחצי אצבע — הרי פ' טפחים ומ' אצבעות, העולין ליו"ד טפחים, הרי תשעים טפחים שהן חמש עשרה אמות:

הדרן עלך מי שהוציאוהו

כיצד מעברין. מפרש בגמרא לשון אשה עוברה, דתנן לקמן*: הנותן עירובו בעיבורה של עיר, אלמא: יש עיבור לעיר. ומפרש השתא כיצד יש לה עיבור: בית נכנס ובית יוצא או פגום נכנס ופגום יוצא או היו גדודיות כו' מוציאין המדה כנגדו. כלומר: כשבא לציין סימן תחום העיר, ובא למדוד אלפים חוצה לה, אם הוה מחיצתה שור איגר, שאינה חומה חלקה אלא בתים סמוכין ומחוברין ויש בית נכנס לתוך העיר, יותר מחבירו, ונראית כניסתו פגומה מבחוץ, ויש בית בולט ויוצא לחוץ יותר מחבירו, או פגום נכנס או פגום יוצא, שהיתה עיר מוקפת חומה ויש מגדלין עגולין בולטין בחומה, פעמים שבולטין בפנים פעמים שבולטין בחוץ. או שהיו שם לאחת הקרנות של עיר גדודיות — שברי חומה של חרבות בתים, וישנן בתוך שבעים אמה ושירים לעיר, כדמפרש לקמן*: או

תוספות

כמאן כרב יוסף ואליבא דרבי יוסי. פירש הקונטרס: דמאע"פ דייק, דמשמע דמוחזק מלקנות שביתה. ואם כן לא אמר אי נמי הכי דייק אי בעי תרתי דהחזיק וגם אמירה — א"כ לימא הילכתא כרבי יהודה, דבין לרב יוסף ובין לרבה לרבי יהודה בעי תרתי.

תנינא חדא זימנא. דכל ספיקא לר"מ חמר גמל הוא, ומתניתין נמי ספיקא הוא. וקשה: דמההיא היכא הויא שמעינן דהוי הכא ספק לרבי מאיר. ואומר ר"י: דפריך דהוה ליה למיתני כל שיכול וכו' ספק וממילא ידענא דהוי חמר גמל. ומשני: דה"א דהיכא דודאי לא עירב כי הכא — לא הוי חמר גמל. דאפילו אם הוה תנן ספק, הוה מפרשינן: ספק אם חשוב בכך עני כשאר בא בדרך, אם לאו. ולכך לא קנה עירוב, דודאי עני אמרו שמערב ברגליו במקום פלוני, ולא בספק עני ודינו כודאי עשיר, ויהיה כבני עירו — קא משמע לן:

כי תניא ההיא למודד. שאפילו כלה מדתו במערה — לא יכנס אמה אחת יותר. ופ"ה לא נראה. והא דלא קאמר: כי תניא להחשיך אמה חוץ לתחום לא יכנס — דמילתא דפשיטא הוא דאין לו לצאת חוץ לתחומו. אבל בכלה למערה איצטריך לאשמועינן.

הדרן עלך מי שהוציאוהו

כיצד מעברין פגום נכנס. פי' ר"ח: פגום נכנס — בנין העשוי כעין שובך, כדאמרי' ב"זה בורר" (סנהדרין דף כה:) גבי מפריחי יונים: משישברו את פגמיהם. ומיהו, שובך ממש אין מתעבר עם העיר, כדאמרינן בגמ'*: [דף נה:]

עין משפט נר מצוה

[שייך לע"א]

[צ"ל דמוחזק וכ"ה בדפוס ויניציא משנת רפ"ח]

עא א מיי' פ"ז מהלכ' עירובין הלכה ח' טוש"ע א"ח סימן ת"י סעיף ב:

עב ב מיי' פכ"ז מהל' שבת הלכה יא סמג לאוין סו טוש"ע א"ח סי' תה סעיף א:

עג ג מיי' שם טוש"ע שם סעיף ב:

עד ד מיי' שם טוש"ע שם סעיף ג:

א ה מיי' פכ"ח מהל' שבת הלכה ו סמג שם טור ש"ע א"ח סי' שצח סעיף ו:

רבינו חננאל

יוסף אליבא דר' יוסי ב"ר יהודה. ר' מאיר אומר כל מי שיש לערב ולא עירב הרי זה חמר גמל הא תו למה לי תנינא ספק ר' מאיר ור' יהודה אומרים הרי זה חמר גמל ופרקינן אצטריך סד"א התם דהוא ספק אמרי חמר גמל אבל הכא דודאי לא עירב לא אלא הרי הוא כבני העיר [קמ"ל] כיון שיצא לילך והחזיק בדרך עקר רשותיה מן העיר ובמקום שרצה לילך לא קנה שביתה דהא לא עירב בפת ולאו עני הוא דקתני (כמחזיק) [החזיק] הלכך לא יזוז ממקומו. מי שיצא חוץ לתחום אפי' אמה אחת כו' איכא דאמר א"ר חנניא רגלו אחת בתוך התחום והאחרת חוץ לתחום יכנס. שנאמר אם תשיב משבת רגלך רגליך קרינן. והתניא לא יכנס ההיא אחרים היא דא' למקום שכלו (ט"ז): פיסקא ר' אליעזר אומר ב' יכנס ג' לא יכנס והתניא ר' אליעזר אומר א' יכנס ב' לא יכנס. ופרקינן הא דקתני אחת יכנס ב' לא יכנס כגון שיצא אמה אחת ועומד בשניה יכנס אבל אם מצא שתים ועומד בשלישית לא יכנס ומתני' נמי הכי קתני ב' פי' אם עומד בשתים יכנס עומד בשלש לא יכנס והא דתניא אפילו אמה אחת לא יכנס במודד כלומר אין לו להוסיף על מדתו. כדתנן ולמודד שאמרו נותנין לו אלפים ומודד:

הדרן עלך מי שהוציאוהו

כיצד מעברין את הערים פגים נכנס פגים יוצא כו'.

מסורות הש"ס

[לעיל לה.]

[לעיל מה.]

ס"א נזדקר

לקמן סא.

לקמן קה.

[לקמן או גשרים כו' הד"א. רש"ל]

[דף ס.]

וּגְשָׁרִים וּנְפָשׁוֹת שֶׁיֵּשׁ בָּהֶן בֵּית דִּירָה — מוֹצִיאִין אֶת הַמִּדָּה כְּנֶגְדָּן, וְעוֹשִׂין(א) אוֹתָהּ כְּמִין טַבְלָא מְרוּבַּעַת, כְּדֵי שֶׁיְּהֵא נִשְׂכָּר אֶת הַזָּוִיּוֹת.§ **גמ'** רַב וּשְׁמוּאֵל: חַד תָּנֵי "מְעַבְּרִין", וְחַד תָּנֵי "מְאַבְּרִין". מַאן דְּתָנֵי "מְאַבְּרִין" — *אֵבֶר אֵבֶר. וּמַאן דְּתָנֵי "מְעַבְּרִין" — כְּאִשָּׁה עוּבָּרָה. °מְעָרַת הַמַּכְפֵּלָה, רַב וּשְׁמוּאֵל; חַד אָמַר: *שְׁנֵי בָתִּים זֶה לִפְנִים מִזֶּה, וְחַד אָמַר: בַּיִת וַעֲלִיָּיה עַל גַּבָּיו. בִּשְׁלָמָא לְמַאן דְּאָמַר זֶה עַל גַּב זֶה — הַיְינוּ מַכְפֵּלָה. אֶלָּא לְמַאן דְּאָמַר שְׁנֵי בָתִּים זֶה לִפְנִים מִזֶּה, מַאי מַכְפֵּלָה? שֶׁכְּפוּלָה בְּזוּגוֹת. °"מַמְרֵא קִרְיַת אַרְבַּע", *א"ר יִצְחָק: קִרְיַת הָאַרְבַּע זוּגוֹת: אָדָם וְחַוָּה, אַבְרָהָם וְשָׂרָה, יִצְחָק וְרִבְקָה, יַעֲקֹב וְלֵאָה. °"וַיְהִי בִּימֵי אַמְרָפֶל", רַב וּשְׁמוּאֵל; חַד אָמַר: נִמְרוֹד שְׁמוֹ, וְלָמָּה נִקְרָא שְׁמוֹ אַמְרָפֶל — שֶׁאָמַר וְהִפִּיל לְאַבְרָהָם אָבִינוּ בְּתוֹךְ כִּבְשַׁן הָאֵשׁ. וְחַד אָמַר: אַמְרָפֶל שְׁמוֹ, וְלָמָּה נִקְרָא שְׁמוֹ נִמְרוֹד — *שֶׁהִמְרִיד אֶת כָּל הָעוֹלָם כּוּלּוֹ עָלָיו בְּמַלְכוּתוֹ. °"וַיָּקָם מֶלֶךְ חָדָשׁ עַל מִצְרָיִם" *רַב וּשְׁמוּאֵל; חַד אָמַר: חָדָשׁ מַמָּשׁ, וְחַד אָמַר: שֶׁנִּתְחַדְּשׁוּ גְּזֵירוֹתָיו. מ"ד חָדָשׁ מַמָּשׁ — דִּכְתִיב "חָדָשׁ", וּמַאן דְּאָמַר שֶׁנִּתְחַדְּשׁוּ גְּזֵירוֹתָיו — מִדְּלָא כְּתִיב "וַיָּמָת וַיִּמְלוֹךְ". וּלְמַאן דְּאָמַר שֶׁנִּתְחַדְּשׁוּ גְּזֵירוֹתָיו, הָא כְּתִיב: °"אֲשֶׁר לֹא יָדַע אֶת יוֹסֵף"! מַאי "אֲשֶׁר לֹא יָדַע אֶת יוֹסֵף" — דַּהֲוָה דָּמֵי כְּמַאן דְּלָא יָדַע לֵיהּ לְיוֹסֵף כְּלָל.§ (סִימָן שְׁמוֹנֶה עֶשְׂרֵה וּשְׁנֵים עָשָׂר לָמַדְנוּ *כְּדָוִד וְיָבֵן).§ א"ר יוֹחָנָן: י"ח יָמִים גִּידַּלְתִּי אֵצֶל רַבִּי אוֹשַׁעְיָא בְּרִיבִּי, וְלֹא לָמַדְתִּי מִמֶּנּוּ אֶלָּא דָּבָר אֶחָד בְּמִשְׁנָתֵינוּ: כֵּיצַד מְאַבְּרִין אֶת הֶעָרִים — בְּאָלֶף. אִינִי?! וְהָאָמַר רַבִּי יוֹחָנָן: י"ב תַּלְמִידִים הָיוּ לוֹ לְרַבִּי אוֹשַׁעְיָא בְּרִיבִּי, וְי"ח יָמִים גִּידַּלְתִּי בֵּינֵיהֶן, וְלָמַדְתִּי לֵב כָּל אֶחָד וְאֶחָד וְחָכְמַת כָּל אֶחָד וְאֶחָד! לֵב כָּל אֶחָד וְאֶחָד וְחָכְמַת כָּל אֶחָד וְאֶחָד — גְּמַר, גְּמָרָא — לָא גְּמַר. אִיבָּעֵית אֵימָא: מִנַּיְיהוּ דִּידְהוּ — גְּמַר, מִינֵּיהּ דִּידֵיהּ — לָא גְּמַר. וְאִב"א: דָּבָר אֶחָד *בְּמִשְׁנָתֵינוּ קָאָמַר. וְא"ר יוֹחָנָן: כְּשֶׁהָיִינוּ לוֹמְדִין תּוֹרָה אֵצֶל ר' אוֹשַׁעְיָא, הָיִינוּ יוֹשְׁבִין אַרְבָּעָה אַרְבָּעָה בָּאַמָּה. אָמַר רַבִּי: כְּשֶׁהָיִינוּ לוֹמְדִין תּוֹרָה אֵצֶל רַבִּי אֶלְעָזָר בֶּן שַׁמּוּעַ, הָיִינוּ יוֹשְׁבִין שִׁשָּׁה שִׁשָּׁה בָּאַמָּה. א"ר יוֹחָנָן: *רַבִּי אוֹשַׁעְיָא בְּרִיבִּי בְּדוֹרוֹ — כְּר' מֵאִיר בְּדוֹרוֹ, מָה רַבִּי מֵאִיר בְּדוֹרוֹ *לֹא יָכְלוּ חֲבֵירָיו לַעֲמוֹד עַל סוֹף דַּעְתּוֹ — אַף רַבִּי אוֹשַׁעְיָא לֹא יָכְלוּ חֲבֵירָיו לַעֲמוֹד עַל סוֹף דַּעְתּוֹ. אָמַר ר' יוֹחָנָן: לִבָּן שֶׁל רִאשׁוֹנִים כְּפִתְחוֹ שֶׁל אוּלָם, וְשֶׁל אַחֲרוֹנִים כְּפִתְחוֹ שֶׁל הֵיכָל, וְאָנוּ כִּמְלֹא נֶקֶב מַחַט סִידְקִית. רִאשׁוֹנִים — ר"ע, אַחֲרוֹנִים — ר"א בֶּן שַׁמּוּעַ. אִיכָּא דְּאָמְרִי: רִאשׁוֹנִים — ר' אֶלְעָזָר בֶּן שַׁמּוּעַ, אַחֲרוֹנִים — ר' אוֹשַׁעְיָא בְּרִיבִּי, וְאָנוּ כִּמְלֹא נֶקֶב מַחַט סִידְקִית. אָמַר אַבַּיֵי: וַאֲנַן כִּי סִיכְתָּא בְּגוּדָא לִגְמָרָא. אָמַר רָבָא: וַאֲנַן כִּי אֶצְבַּעְתָּא בְּקִירָא לִסְבָרָא. אָמַר רַב אַשִׁי: אֲנַן כִּי אֶצְבַּעְתָּא בְּבֵירָא לְשִׁכְחָה. אָמַר רַב יְהוּדָה, אָמַר רַב: בְּנֵי יְהוּדָה שֶׁהִקְפִּידוּ עַל לְשׁוֹנָם — נִתְקַיְּימָה תּוֹרָתָם בְּיָדָם, בְּנֵי גָלִיל שֶׁלֹּא הִקְפִּידוּ עַל לְשׁוֹנָם — לֹא נִתְקַיְּימָה תּוֹרָתָם בְּיָדָם. מִידֵּי בְּקְפִידָא תַּלְיָא מִילְּתָא? אֶלָּא בְּנֵי יְהוּדָה דְּדָיְיקֵי לִישָּׁנָא, וּמִתְנַחֵי לְהוּ סִימָנָא — נִתְקַיְּימָה תּוֹרָתָן בְּיָדָן, בְּנֵי גָלִיל דְּלָא דָּיְיקֵי לִישָּׁנָא וְלָא מִתְנַחֵי לְהוּ סִימָנָא — לֹא נִתְקַיְּימָה תּוֹרָתָן בְּיָדָם. *בְּנֵי יְהוּדָה גָּמְרוּ מֵחַד רַבָּה — נִתְקַיְּימָה תּוֹרָתָן בְּיָדָם, בְּנֵי גָלִיל דְּלָא גָּמְרִי מֵחַד רַבָּה — לֹא נִתְקַיְּימָה תּוֹרָתָן בְּיָדָם. רָבִינָא אָמַר: בְּנֵי יְהוּדָה דְּגַלּוּ מַסֶּכְתָּא — נִתְקַיְּימָה תּוֹרָתָן בְּיָדָם, בְּנֵי גָלִיל דְּלָא גַּלּוּ מַסֶּכְתָּא — לֹא נִתְקַיְּימָה תּוֹרָתָן בְּיָדָם. דָּוִד גַּלֵּי מַסֶּכְתָּא, *שָׁאוּל לָא גַּלֵּי מַסֶּכְתָּא. דָּוִד דְּגַלֵּי מַסֶּכְתָּא כְּתִיב בֵּיהּ: °"יְרֵאֶיךָ יִרְאוּנִי וְיִשְׂמָחוּ", שָׁאוּל דְּלָא גַּלֵּי מַסֶּכְתָּא כְּתִיב בֵּיהּ: (*°"אֶל כָּל) אֲשֶׁר יִפְנֶה יַרְשִׁיעַ".

(* נ"ל ובכל)

(בראשית כג; שם לה; שם יד; שמות א; שם; תהלים קיט; ש"א יד; תורה אור)

רש"י

אוֹ גְּשָׁרִים אוֹ נְפָשׁוֹת. כְּעֵין שֶׁעוֹשִׂין עַל הַקֶּבֶר: מוֹצִיאִין אֶת הַמִּדָּה כְּנֶגְדָּן. אִם בְּלִיטוֹת הַלָּלוּ אֵצֶל קֶרֶן מִזְרָחִית צְפוֹנִית — רוֹאִין כְּאִילּוּ יֵשׁ בְּלִיטָה אַחֶרֶת כְּנֶגְדָּהּ בְּקֶרֶן מִזְרָחִית דְּרוֹמִית, וְחוּט מָתוּחַ מִזּוֹ לָזוֹ וּמוֹדֵד מִן הַחוּט וְלַחוּץ, כְּדֵי שֶׁיְּהֵא הַתְּחוּם שָׁוֶה לִשְׁתֵּי קְרָנוֹת וְלֹא יְהֵא כָּאן קָצָר וְכָאן אָרוֹךְ: וְעוֹשִׂין אוֹתָן. אֶת הַתְּחוּמִין מְרוּבָּעִין כְּדֵי שֶׁיְּהֵא אֲלָפַיִם לַצְּדָדִין כְּבָאֶמְצַע. וְלֹא עֲגוּלִּין שֶׁיְּהֵא לָהֶן אַלְפַּיִם בְּאֶמְצָעָן וּבַצְּדָדִין הֵן מִתְמַעֲטִין כְּדֶרֶךְ כָּל עִגּוּל. וּבְעִיר מְרוּבַּעַת עָסְקִינַן, שֶׁאֵין בָּהּ אֶלָּא אַלְפַּיִם עַל אַלְפַּיִם, דְּהָווּ נַמִי תְּחוּמִין מְרוּבָּעִים. וְאִם אֵינָהּ מְרוּבַּעַת כְּגוֹן שֶׁהָיְתָה יְתֵירָה עַל אַלְפַּיִם לְאׇרְכָּהּ אוֹ פְּחוּתָה מֵאַלְפַּיִם —(ב) לָא הָווּ מְרוּבָּעִין, דִּתְחוּמִין מְרוּבָּעִין לָאו דַּוְוקָא שֶׁיְּהֵא אׇרְכָּן כְּרׇחְבָּן, שֶׁהֲרֵי רׇחְבָּן לְמִדַּת הָעִיר הִיא — אִם קְטַנָּה אִם גְּדוֹלָה, וְאׇרְכָּן אַלְפַּיִם. אֶלָּא מְרוּבָּעִין דְּקָתָנֵי — לְמַעוּטֵי עֲגוּלִּין, כְּדֵי שֶׁיְּהֵא נִשְׂכָּר אֶת הַזָּוִיּוֹת: **גמ'** חַד תָּנֵי מְאַבְּרִין. בְּאָלֶף: אֵבֶר אֵבֶר. שֶׁמּוֹסִיפִין לָהּ אֵבָרִים, שֶׁאִם יֵשׁ אֵבֶר שֶׁיּוֹצֵא מִן הָעִיר בְּקֶרֶן מִזְרָחִית דְּרוֹמִית — רוֹאִין כְּאִילּוּ אֵבֶר גַּם בְּקֶרֶן מִזְרָחִית צְפוֹנִית וּמוֹדְדִין מִשָּׁם: מְעָרַת הַמַּכְפֵּלָה. מִשּׁוּם דִּפְלִיגֵי בְּמַשְׁמָעוּת לְשׁוֹן מַכְפֵּלָה נָקַט לָהּ הָכָא. מִשּׁוּם דִּפְלִיגֵי נַמִי בְּלִישָּׁנָא דְּמַתְנִיתִין. וְכֵן בְּאַמְרָפֶל, וְכֵן בְּמֶלֶךְ חָדָשׁ: שְׁנֵי בָתִּים. הָיוּ בָּהּ זֶה לִפְנִים מִזֶּה:

בית פנימי	בית חילון	פתח מערה

בַּיִת וַעֲלִיָּה. הָוֵי כְּפוּלָה בִּשְׁתֵּי תִּקְרוֹת, אֲבָל שְׁנֵי בָתִּים לֹא שַׁיָּיךְ בְּהוּ לְשׁוֹן כְּפוּלָה: שֶׁכְּפוּלָה בְּזוּגוֹת. שֶׁנִּקְבְּרוּ כּוּלָּן אִישׁ וְאִשְׁתּוֹ, דְּהַיְינוּ זוּג זוּג. דִּכְתִיב (בראשית מט): "שָׁמָּה קָבְרוּ אֶת אַבְרָהָם וְאֵת שָׂרָה" וְגוֹמֵר: עָלָיו. כְּלַפֵּי מַעְלָה אֶלָּא שֶׁכִּינּוּ חֲכָמִים בִּלְשׁוֹנָם: מִדְּלָא כְּתִיב וַיָּמָת. זֶה וַיִּמְלוֹךְ פְּלוֹנִי תַּחְתָּיו: אוֹשַׁעְיָא בְּרִיבִּי. אָדָם גָּדוֹל בְּדוֹרוֹ וְכָל הֵיכִי דְּקָרֵי בְּרִיבִּי הָכִי פֵּירוּשׁוֹ: לֵב כָּל אֶחָד וְאֶחָד. כַּמָּה הָיָה מְחוּדָּד, כְּלוֹמַר: בְּכוּלָּן הִכַּרְתִּי מַה חֲרִיפוּת יֵשׁ מִזֶּה לָזֶה: וְחָכְמַת כָּל אֶחָד וְאֶחָד. כַּמָּה זֶה חָכָם מִזֶּה, וְכַמָּה לָמַד יוֹתֵר מִמֶּנּוּ: אִיבָּעֵית אֵימָא. בְּמִשְׁנָתֵינוּ לֹא לָמַד אֶלָּא דָּבָר אֶחָד, אֲבָל בָּרַיְיתוֹת וּגְמָרוֹת גְּמַר טוּבָא: שִׁשָּׁה בָּאַמָּה. שֶׁהָיִינוּ מִתְקָרְבִין לִשְׁמוֹעַ מִפִּיו וְדוֹחֲקִין זֶה אֶת זֶה: ר"מ לֹא עָמְדוּ חֲבֵירָיו עַל סוֹף דַּעְתּוֹ. כִּדְאָמְרִינַן בְּפֶרֶק קַמָּא (דף יג:) שֶׁהָיָה אוֹמֵר עַל טָמֵא טָהוֹר וּמַרְאֶה פָּנִים: פֶּתַח אוּלָם. רׇחְבּוֹ כ' וְשֶׁל הֵיכָל י': סִדְקִית. מַחַט שֶׁתּוֹפְרִין בָּהּ סִדְקֵי בְּגָדִים, וְהוּא דַּק בְּיוֹתֵר: כְּסִיכְתָּא בְּגוּדָא לִגְמָרָא. כְּיָתֵד שֶׁתּוֹקְעִין אוֹתוֹ בַּכּוֹתֶל בְּנֶקֶב צַר, וְנִכְנָס בְּדוֹחַק, כָּךְ אֵין יְכוֹלִין אָנוּ לְהָבִין מַה שֶּׁאָנוּ שׁוֹמְעִין, כִּי אִם מְעַט וּבְקוֹשִׁי: כְּאֶצְבַּע בְּקִירָא. בְּשַׁעֲוָה קָשָׁה, שֶׁאֵין הָאֶצְבַּע יָכוֹל לִיכָּנֵס בְּתוֹכָהּ, אֶלָּא מְדַבֵּק מְעַט: כְּאֶצְבַּע בְּבִירָה לְשִׁכְחָה. כְּשֵׁם שֶׁהָאֶצְבַּע נוֹחַ לִיכָּנֵס בְּפִי הַבּוֹר, כָּךְ אָנוּ מְהִירִין לְשִׁכּוֹחַ: שֶׁהִקְפִּידוּ עַל לְשׁוֹנָם. לְדַבֵּר בְּלָשׁוֹן נַח וְלֹא בְּלָשׁוֹן מְגוּנֶּה, כִּדְאָמְרִינַן לְקַמָּן בִּבְנֵי גָלִיל: דְּדָיְיקֵי לִישָּׁנָא. לַחֲזֵר בְּאוֹתוֹ לָשׁוֹן שֶׁהָיוּ שׁוֹמְעִין מֵרַבָּן וְע"י שֶׁהָיוּ שׁוֹמְעִין ע"פ שְׁמוּעָה אַחַר שְׁמוּעָה הָיוּ נוֹתְנִין בָּהֶן סִימָן זוֹ אַחַר זוֹ, וּמִתּוֹךְ כָּךְ שֶׁהָיוּ מְדַקְדְּקִים בַּלָּשׁוֹן — יוֹדְעִין לְהָנִיחַ סִימָנִין נָאִין, וְאֵינָן מִשְׁתַּכְּחִין מֵהֶן: וּמִתְנַחֵי. וּמַנִּיחִין סִימָנִין: לָא גָּמְרֵי מֵחַד רַבָּה. וְהָיוּ שׁוֹמְעִין מִזֶּה בְּלָשׁוֹן זֶה וּמִזֶּה בְּלָשׁוֹן אַחֵר, אַע"פ שֶׁשְּׁנֵיהֶם אֶחָד — שִׁינּוּי לָשׁוֹן מְבַלְבְּלָן וּמְשַׁכְּחָן: דְּגַלּוּ מַסֶּכְתָּא. לִמְּדוּ לַאֲחֵרִים, כָּךְ שָׁמַעְתִּי. ל"א: מְפָרְשִׁין שְׁמוּעוֹתֵיהֶן וּמְדַקְדְּקִים בְּטַעְמוֹ שֶׁל דָּבָר עַד שֶׁמִּתְיַישֵּׁב בְּלִבָּן: יְרֵאוּנִי וְיִשְׂמָחוּ. לְפִי שֶׁשְּׁמוּעוֹתָיו מְכוּוָּנוֹת, לְאִיסּוּר אִיסּוּר וּלְהֶיתֵּר הֶיתֵּר: דָּוִד דְּגַלֵּי מַסֶּכְתָּא. כִּדְאָמַר בִּבְרָכוֹת (דף ז.) שֶׁהָיָה יָגֵעַ בַּתּוֹרָה וּמוֹרֶה הוֹרָאוֹת. כִּדְאָמַר: יָדַי מְלוּכְלָכוֹת בְּדָם וְשָׁפִיר וְשִׁלְיָא. וְאוֹמֵר: מְפִיבֹשֶׁת רַבִּי יָפֶה דַּנְתָּ יָפֶה זִכִּיתָ כו', וְאָמְרִינַן נַמִי בְּמוֹעֵד קָטָן (דף טז:) "עֲדִינוֹ הָעֶצְנִי יוֹשֵׁב בַּשֶּׁבֶת תַּחְכְּמֹנִי" זֶה דָּוִד כו':

תוספות

וגשרים ונפשות שיש בהן בית דירה. הא דקתני "שיש להן בית דירה" לא קאי אנפשות, כדמוכח בברייתא דנפשות גופיה סתמא לדירת שומר קבר עביד, הלכך אף ע"ג דלא דייר בה — דירה היא, דנפש בנין שעל הקבר, כדפ"ה בגמרא. אלא אגשרים קאי, דגשר וקבר ובית הכנסת וכל הנהו דקתני בגמ' בברייתא שיש להם בית דירה — לאו לבית דירה עביד, ואי לית ביה בית דירה — לאו דירה הוא. בערוך מפרש: נפש = ציון. כדאמרינן בירושלמי, אמר רשב"ג: אין עושין נפשות לצדיקי', אלא דבריהם הם זכרונם. וכן הביא מפ"ב דשקלים (דף ג:):

לא למדתי ממנו כו'. והא דאמר בפרק "הבא על יבמתו" (יבמות דף נז.), בעי מיניה רבי יוחנן מרבי אושעיא: פצוע דכא כהן כו' — לא באותן י"ח ימים היה:

כי אצבעתא בבירא לשכחא. ור"ח גרס "בביזרי". פירש: כשוקע אצבעו בזרעונים, כמו בחרדל וכיוצא בו, נראה כמו גומא. וכשמסיר אצבעו — חוזרת ומתמלאת הגומא מיד. כך אנו, כשאנו מסיימין המסכתא ומתחילין האחרת — מיד שוכחין הראשונה:

דגמרי מחד רבה. לגמרא רב אחד עדיף, שלא יבלבל לשונס יחד. אבל למיסבר — אמרינן בפ"ק דע"ז (דף יט.): כל הלומד תורה לפני רב אחד אינו רואה סימן ברכה לעולם:

רבינו חננאל

פי' פגים בניין כמו שובך כדאמרינן (סנהדרין כה) במפריחי יונים (מי ששברו) [משישברו] את פגמיהן כגון שובך של יונים עשוי בניין עומד. ירושלמי בית נכנס מוציאין אותו כנגד העיר פגום יוצא מוציאין את העיר כנגדו. רב תני מעברין מלשון אשה עוברה. שמואל תני מאברין מוסיפין לה אבר. רב תני עד שיאותו לאורו כדכתיב אך בזאת נאותה לכם. שמואל תני יעותו כדכתיב לדעת לעות את יעף דבר. (תני רב) [רב תני] אידיהם כדכתי' כי קרוב יום אידם שמואל אמר עידיהם כדכתיב ועדיהם המה שעתידים לבייש עובדיהן. כתיב ומשה יקח את האהל כמה היה רחוק מיל והיה כל מבקש משה אין כתיב אלא כל מבקש ה' מיכן כל המקביל פני רבו כמקביל פני השכינה. רב אמר כתיב ויאמר אליהו התשבי וגו' והלא אליהו טירונין של נביאים היה אלא מלמד שכל עמידות שעמד לפני אחיה השילוני כאילו עמד לפני השכינה. ויבא אהרן וכל זקני ישראל לאכל לחם עם חותן משה לפני האלהים וכי לפני האלהים אכלו. אלא מלמד שכל המקבל פני חבירו כאלו מקבל פני שכינה. מערת המכפלה רב ושמואל חד א' ב' בתים זה לפנים מזה וחד אמר בית ועליה קרית ארבע ד' זוגות אדם וחוה אברהם ושרה יצחק ורבקה יעקב ולאה א"ר יוחנן י"ב תלמידים היו לר' אושעי' (ב"ר) [בריבי] וששה חדשים גדלתי אצלו ולמדתי (מכל) [לב כל] אחד ואחד וחכמת כל אחד ואחד ולא למדתי ממנו אלא דבר אחד במשנתנו כיצד מאברין [באל"ף] והיינו יושבין ד' באמה ור' אושעי' היה בדורו כר' מאיר בדורו ולא עמדו חבריהם על סוף דעתם. א"ר יוחנן לבן של ראשונים והם ר' עקיבא (וחכמים אומרים) כפתחו של אולם מ' אמה לבן של אחרונים והוא רבי אלעזר בן שמוע כפתחו של היכל כ' אמה ואנו לבינו כמלוא נקב מחט סדקית. פי' מחט דק מאד כסיכתא בגודא לגמרא. פי' היתד בכותל שאינו לא מעלה ולא מוריד. כך אנו בגמרא. ואמר רבא ואנו לסברא כאצבעתא בקירה פי' (רב) [רק] כשמניח אצבעו בתוכו נעשה גומא וכשמגביה מפעפע ועולה ומתמלאת הגומא כאלו לא נשקעה בתוכה אצבע ולא היתה גומא בתוכו אמר רב אשי ולשכחה כאצבעתא (בבירא) [בביזרא]. פי' כמו ששוקע אצבע בזירעונים כמו חרדל וכיוצא בו נראה כאלו עשה גומא וכאשר מרים אצבעו חוזרת ומתמלאת את הגומא מיד. כך אנו כשמשלימים מסכת ומתחילין אחרת מיד שוכחים הראשונה: אמר רב יהודה אמר רב בני יהודה שמקפידים על לשונם ומחתי סימן וגמרי מחד רבה ודייקי לישנא נתקיימה תלמודן בידן. ולא עוד אלא דגלו מסכתא כדכתיב ביה יראיך יראוני וישמחו. אבל בני גליל דלא קפדי אלשונם ולא גמירי מחד רבה ולא דקו (לשונם) [בלשונם] ולא נתקיימה תלמודם בידם ולא גלו מסכת נמי כשאול דכתיב ביה ובכל אשר יפנה

מסורת הש"ס

[פי' שבולטין מן החומה אבר אבר כאבריו של אדם שבולטין מן האדם ערוך]

[סוטה יג.]

[פסחים נד: חגיגה יג.]

סוטה יא.

[בכפוס וניליגה בדורו לבן וכן עיקר]

[ברכות יט. וש"נ]

[עי' תוס' ב"ב נט. ד"ה החוטו]

*[לעיל יג:]

הגהות הב"ח

(א) במשנה ועושין אותן כמין טבלא: (ב) רש"י ד"ה ועושין כו' או פתוחה מאלפים לרוחבה לא הוו:

ס"א ואב"א

[ז"ל רש"י בגיטין נט. ד"ה שאול גדול בתורה היה אלא שלא לימד לאחרים כדאמרינן בעירובין שאול לא גלי מסכתא וכו']

ב א טוש"ע א"ח סי' קע סעיף ג:

עלת נקפת בכד. כלי שדולין בו יין מן הכד. והא דאמר בפרק "כל כתבי" (שבת דף קיט.) גבי רב יוסף מוקר שבי, ובפרק "יש נוחלין" (ב"ב דף קלג:) גבי יוסף בן יועזר: זבני בתליסר עיליתא דדינרי – מפרש ר"ת: דעיליתא הוא כלי כמו עלת דהכא, ולא כמו שפי' בקונט' שם עליות, וגוזמא קאמר:

גבר פום דין חי. פי' רבינו חננאל: אושפיזכנא, תרגום איש – גבר, ופי – פום, זה – דין, נא – חי, "אל תאכלו ממנו נא" מתרגמינן: "כד חי" (שמות יב):

משיירין פיאה בקערה ואין משיירין פיאה באילפס. *בפרק "בן עזאי" קתני: משיירין פיאה במעשה קדירה, ואין משיירין פיאה במעשה אילפס. פירוש: במעשה קדירה נראה כרעבתן אם אינו משייר, אבל במעשה אילפס – אינו נראה כרעבתן אם אינו משייר: תנו

[ג] כמס' ד"א פ' הנכנס פ"ו. משיירין פיאה במעשה אילפס ואין משיירין במעשה קדירה פירוש במעשה אילפס נראה כרעבתן אם אינו משייר אבל במעשה קדירה אינו נראה כרעבתן אם אינו משייר גירס רש"ל:

יַרְשִׁיעַ". *וְאָמַר ר' יוֹחָנָן: מִנַּיִן שֶׁמָּחַל לוֹ הקב"ה עַל אוֹתוֹ עָוֹן – שֶׁנֶּאֱמַר: °"מָחָר אַתָּה וּבָנֶיךָ עִמִּי" (ש"א כח) – עִמִּי בִּמְחִיצָתִי. א"ר אַבָּא: אִי אִיכָּא דְּמַשְׁאִיל לְהוּ לִבְנֵי יְהוּדָה דְּדַיְיקִי לִשָּׁנֵי: "מְאַבְּרִין" תְּנַן, אוֹ "מְעַבְּרִין" תְּנַן? "אַכּוּזוֹ" תְּנַן, אוֹ "עַכּוּזוֹ" תְּנַן? יָדְעִי. שְׁאֵילִינְהוּ, וְאָמְרִי לֵיהּ: אִיכָּא דְּתָנֵי "מְאַבְּרִין", וְאִיכָּא דְּתָנֵי "מְעַבְּרִין". אִיכָּא דְּתָנֵי "אַכּוּזוֹ", וְאִיכָּא דְּתָנֵי "עַכּוּזוֹ". בְּנֵי יְהוּדָה דַּיְיקִי לִישָּׁנָא מַאי הִיא? דְּהַהוּא בַּר יְהוּדָה דַּאֲמַר לְהוּ: טַלִּית יֵשׁ לִי לִמְכּוֹר. אָמְרוּ לֵיהּ: מַאי גַּוְון טַלִּיתְךָ? אֲמַר לְהוּ: כִּתְרָדִין עֲלֵי אֲדָמָה. בְּנֵי גָלִיל דְּלָא דַּיְיקִי לִישָּׁנָא מַאי הִיא? (דְּתַנְיָא:) דְּהַהוּא בַּר גָּלִילָא [דַּהֲוָה קָאָזֵיל] וַאֲמַר לְהוּ: אַמַּר לְמַאן, אַמַּר לְמַאן? אָמְרוּ לֵיהּ: גְּלִילָאָה שׁוֹטֶה, חֲמַר לְמִירְכַּב, אוֹ חֲמַר לְמִישְׁתֵּי, עֲמַר לְמִילְבַּשׁ, אוֹ אִימַּר לְאִיתְכְּסָאָה? הַהִיא אִיתְּתָא דְּבָעְיָא לְמֵימַר לַחֲבֶרְתָּהּ "תָּאִי דְּאוֹכְלִיךְ חֶלְבָּא", אָמְרָה לָהּ: שְׁלוֹכְתִּי, תּוֹכְלִיךְ לָבְיָא. הַהִיא אִתְּתָא דְּאָתְיָא לְקַמֵּיהּ דְּדַיָּינָא, אָמְרָה לֵיהּ: מָרִי כִּירִי, תַּפְלָא הֲוֵית לִי וּגְנָבוּךְ מִין. וּכְדוּ הֲוַות[א] דְּכַד שָׁדְרוּ לָךְ עִילָוֵיהּ – לָא מָטֵי כַּרְעִיךְ אַאַרְעָא. אַמְהֲתָא דְּבֵי רַבִּי, כִּי הֲוָה מִשְׁתַּעְיָא בִּלְשׁוֹן חָכְמָה, אָמְרָה הָכִי: עֶלֶת נָקְפַתְּ בַּכַּד, יִדְאוּן נִישְׁרַיָּא לְקִינֵּיהוֹן. וְכַד הֲוָה בָּעֵי דְּלֵיתְבוּן, הֲוָה אֲמַרָה לְהוּ: יַעֲדֵי בָּתַר חֲבֶרְתָּהּ מִינָּהּ, וְתִתְקְפֵי עֶלֶת בַּכַּד כְּאִילְפָא דְּאָזְלָא בְּיַמָּא. רַבִּי יוֹסֵי בַּר אַסְיָין, כִּי הֲוָה מִשְׁתָּעֵי בִּלְשׁוֹן חָכְמָה, אֲמַר: עֲשׂוּ לִי שׁוֹר בְּמִשְׁפָּט בְּטוּר מִסְכֵּן. וְכַד הֲוָה שָׁאֵיל בְּאוּשְׁפִּיזָא, אֲמַר הָכִי: גְּבַר פּוּם דֵּין חַי, מַה זוֹ טוֹבָה יֵשׁ? רַבִּי אַבָּהוּ, כִּי הֲוָה מִשְׁתָּעֵי בִּלְשׁוֹן חָכְמָה, הֲוָה אֲמַר הָכִי: אַתְרִיגוּ [א] לְפֶחָמִין, אַרְקִיעוּ לְזָהֳבִין, וַעֲשׂוּ לִי שְׁנֵי מַגִּידֵי בַּעֲלָטָה. אִיכָּא דְּאָמְרִי: וְיַעֲשׂוּ לִי בָּהֶן שְׁנֵי מַגִּידֵי בַּעֲלָטָה. אָמְרוּ לֵיהּ רַבָּנַן לְרַבִּי אַבָּהוּ: הַצְפִּינֵנוּ הֵיכָן רַבִּי אֶלְעַאי צָפוּן: אָמַר לָהֶן: עָלַץ בְּנַעֲרָה אַהֲרוֹנִית אַחֲרוֹנִית עֵירָנִית וְהִנְעִירַתּוּ. אָמְרִי לָהּ: אִשָּׁה, וְאָמְרִי לָהּ: מַסֶּכְתָּא. אָמְרִי לֵיהּ לְרַבִּי אֶלְעַאי: הַצְפִּינֵנוּ הֵיכָן רַבִּי אַבָּהוּ [צָפוּן]! אָמַר לָהֶן: נִתְיָיעֵץ בַּמַּכְתִּיר, וְהִנְגִּיב לִמְפִיבֹשֶׁת. *אָמַר רַבִּי יְהוֹשֻׁעַ בֶּן חֲנַנְיָה: מִיָּמַי לֹא נִצְּחַנִי אָדָם חוּץ מֵאִשָּׁה(ב) תִּינוֹק וְתִינוֹקֶת. אִשָּׁה מַאי הִיא? פַּעַם אַחַת נִתְאָרַחְתִּי אֵצֶל אַכְסַנְיָא אַחַת, עָשְׂתָה לִי פּוֹלִין. בְּיוֹם רִאשׁוֹן אֲכַלְתִּים וְלֹא שִׁיַּירְתִּי מֵהֶן כְּלוּם. שְׁנִיָּיה וְלֹא שִׁיַּירְתִּי מֵהֶן כְּלוּם. בְּיוֹם שְׁלִישִׁי הִקְדִּיחָתַן בְּמֶלַח. כֵּיוָן שֶׁטָּעַמְתִּי – מָשַׁכְתִּי יָדַי מֵהֶן. אָמְרָה לִי: רַבִּי, מִפְּנֵי מָה אֵינְךָ סוֹעֵד? אָמַרְתִּי לָהּ: כְּבָר סָעַדְתִּי מִבְּעוֹד יוֹם. אָמְרָה לִי: הָיָה לְךָ לִמְשׁוֹךְ יָדֶיךָ מִן הַפַּת. אָמְרָה לִי: רַבִּי, שֶׁמָּא [ב] לֹא הִנַּחְתָּ פֵּאָה בָּרִאשׁוֹנִים? וְלֹא כָּךְ אָמְרוּ חֲכָמִים: אאֵין מְשַׁיְּירִין פֵּאָה בָּאִלְפָּס, אֲבָל מְשַׁיְּירִין פֵּאָה בַּקְּעָרָה. תִּינוֹקֶת מַאי הִיא? פַּעַם אַחַת הָיִיתִי מְהַלֵּךְ בַּדֶּרֶךְ, וְהָיְתָה דֶּרֶךְ עוֹבֶרֶת בַּשָּׂדֶה וְהָיִיתִי מְהַלֵּךְ בָּהּ. אָמְרָה לִי תִּינוֹקֶת אַחַת: רַבִּי, לֹא שָׂדֶה הִיא זוֹ? אָמַרְתִּי לָהּ: לֹא, דֶּרֶךְ כְּבוּשָׁה הִיא. אָמְרָה לִי: לִיסְטִים כְּמוֹתְךָ כְּבָשׁוּהָ. תִּינוֹק מַאי הִיא? פַּעַם אַחַת הָיִיתִי מְהַלֵּךְ בַּדֶּרֶךְ, וְרָאִיתִי תִּינוֹק יוֹשֵׁב עַל פָּרָשַׁת דְּרָכִים. וְאָמַרְתִּי לוֹ: בְּאֵיזֶה דֶּרֶךְ נֵלֵךְ לָעִיר? אָמַר לִי: זוֹ קְצָרָה וַאֲרוּכָּה, וְזוֹ אֲרוּכָּה וּקְצָרָה. וְהָלַכְתִּי בִּקְצָרָה וַאֲרוּכָּה, כֵּיוָן שֶׁהִגַּעְתִּי לָעִיר מָצָאתִי שֶׁמַּקִּיפִין אוֹתָהּ גַּנּוֹת וּפַרְדֵּיסִין, חָזַרְתִּי לַאֲחוֹרַי. אָמַרְתִּי לוֹ: בְּנִי, הֲלֹא אָמַרְתָּ לִי קְצָרָה! אָמַר לִי: וְלֹא אָמַרְתִּי לְךָ אֲרוּכָּה?! נְשַׁקְתִּיו עַל רֹאשׁוֹ, וְאָמַרְתִּי לוֹ: אַשְׁרֵיכֶם יִשְׂרָאֵל שֶׁכּוּלְּכֶם חֲכָמִים גְּדוֹלִים אַתֶּם, מִגְּדוֹלְכֶם וְעַד קְטַנְכֶם. § רַבִּי יוֹסֵי הַגְּלִילִי הֲוָה קָא אָזֵיל בְּאוֹרְחָא, אַשְׁכְּחַהּ לִבְרוּרְיָה, אֲמַר לָהּ: בְּאֵיזוֹ דֶּרֶךְ נֵלֵךְ לְלוֹד? אָמְרָה לֵיהּ: גְּלִילִי שׁוֹטֶה, לֹא כָּךְ אָמְרוּ חֲכָמִים *אַל תַּרְבֶּה שִׂיחָה עִם הָאִשָּׁה; הָיָה לְךָ לוֹמַר: בְּאֵיזֶה לְלוֹד. בְּרוּרְיָה אַשְׁכַּחְתֵּיהּ לְהַהוּא תַּלְמִידָא דַּהֲוָה קָא גָּרֵיס בְּלַחִישָׁה, בָּטְשָׁה

יַרְשִׁיעַ. לֹא הָיָה זוֹכֶה לְהוֹרוֹת כַּהֲלָכָה: עַל אוֹתוֹ עָוֹן. עֲוֹן דְּנוֹב עִיר הַכֹּהֲנִים: אַתָּה וּבָנֶיךָ עִמִּי. שְׁמוּאֵל קָאָמַר לְשָׁאוּל, כְּשֶׁהֶעֱלָהוּ ע"י בַּעֲלַת אוֹב: אַכּוּזוֹ תְּנַן אוֹ עַכּוּזוֹ. בִּבְכוֹרוֹת (דף מ.) גַּבֵּי מוּמִין תְּנַן, שֶׁאֵין לוֹ אֶלָּא בֵּיצָה אַחַת – הֲרֵי זֶה מוּם. ר' עֲקִיבָא אוֹמֵר: מוֹשִׁיבִין אוֹתוֹ עַל עַכּוּזוֹ וּמְמַעֵךְ, אִם יֵשׁ בֵּיצָה אַחֶרֶת – סוֹפָהּ לָצֵאת. אַכּוּזוֹ = עַגְבוֹתָיו, וְכֵן עַכּוּזוֹ: יָדְעִי. הָיוּ יוֹדְעִין: כִּתְרָדִין עֲלֵי אֲדָמָה. יְרַקְרֶקֶת הָיְתָה, כְּצֶבַע יֶרֶק הָאָרֶץ: אַמַּר לְמַאן. מְדַבֵּר בְּשָׂפָה רָפָה, וְלֹא פֵּירֵשׁ הָאוֹת, וְאֵינוֹ נִיכָּר אִם עֲמַר אִם חֲמַר אִם אִימַּר: עֲמַר לְמִילְבַּשׁ. לַעֲשׂוֹת בְּגָדִים: אִימַּר לְאִיתְכְּסָאָה. שֶׂה לִשְׁחוֹט: תָּא דְּאוֹכְלִיךְ חֲלָבָא. הָיְתָה רוֹצָה לוֹמַר בּוֹאִי וְאוֹכְלִיךְ חָלָב, וְאֵינָהּ מְפָרֶשֶׁת לַחְתּוֹךְ תֵּיבוֹת זוֹ מִזּוֹ וּלְהַשְׁמִיעַ כָּל תֵּיבָה וְתֵיבָה, וּמִצְטָרְפוֹת שְׁתֵּי תֵּיבוֹת כְּאַחַת [וּמְגַמְגֶּמֶת הַתֵּיבוֹת וְאוֹמֶרֶת תֹּאכְלִיךְ לָבְיָא]. וְאוֹמֶרֶת נַמִּי "שְׁלוֹכְתִּי" בְּכ"ף, וְהָיְתָה רוֹצָה לוֹמַר "שְׁלוֹבְתִּי" בְּב' כְּמוֹ "מְשׁוּלָּבוֹת", כְּלוֹמַר: חֲבֶרְתִּי: תּוֹכְלִיךְ לָבְיָא. קְלָלָה, מַשְׁמַע שֶׁתֹּאכְלֵךְ לָבִיא: מָרִי כִּירִי. וְרוֹצָה לוֹמַר "קִירִי", וְהוּא אָדוֹן, וְאָמְרָה "כִּירִי", וְהוּא עֶבֶד: תַּפְלָא הֲוַת לִי. רוֹצָה לוֹמַר טַבְלָא הֲוַת לִי, וְאָמְרָה תַּפְלָא וְהִיא קוֹרָה: וּגְנַבוּךְ מִין.(ג) רוֹצָה לוֹמַר גְּנָבוּהָ מִמֶּנִּי, וְאָמְרָה גְּנַבוּךְ מִין, דְּמַשְׁמַע שֶׁגְּנָבוּ אֶת הַדַּיָּן: וּכְדוּ הֲוַת דְּכִי שְׁדַרוּ לָךְ עִילָוֵיהּ לָא מַטְיָין כַּרְעִיךְ אַאַרְעָא. גְּדוֹלָה הָיְתָה כ"כ שֶׁאִם מוֹתְחִין אוֹתְךָ עָלֶיהָ לֹא הָיוּ רַגְלֶיךָ נוֹגְעוֹת בָּאָרֶץ. וַהֲרֵי שְׁטוּיוֹת הַרְבֵּה. "וּכְדוּ" מַשְׁמַע עַכְשָׁיו, וּבָעֲיָא לוֹמַר וּכְדַן הֲוַת. וְעוֹד שֶׁהָיְתָה מַזְכֶּרֶת תְּלִיָּיה בַּדַּיָּן וְאוֹמֶרֶת: אִם תּוֹלִין אוֹתְךָ עָלֶיהָ כו': עֶלֶת. שֵׁם כְּלִי שֶׁדּוֹלִין בּוֹ יַיִן מִן הֶחָבִית וּמְמַלְּאִין הַכּוֹסוֹת: נָקְפַתְּ בַּכַּד. מְנַקֶּפֶת בֶּחָבִית, כְּלוֹמַר: כְּבָר כָּלָה הַיַּיִן, נוֹגֵעַ בְּתַחְתִּית הֶחָבִית: יִדְאוּן נִישְׁרַיָּא לְקִינֵּיהוֹן. יֵלְכוּ תַּלְמִידִים לְבָתֵּיהֶם. כְּלוֹמַר: יִפְסְקוּ סְעוּדָתָן, [שֶׁאֵין עוֹד יַיִן]. (אוֹ) יַעֲדֵי בָּתַר חֲבֶרְתָּהּ מִינָּהּ. נָסִיר מְגוּפַת חָבִית הָאַחֶרֶת וְנִמְזוֹג עוֹד: וְתִתְקְפֵי עֶלֶת בַּכַּד. תְּהֵא צָפָה עֶלֶת בַּכַּד בְּרֵיוַח: כְּאִילְפָא בְּיַמָּא. כָּאֳנִיָּה הַצָּפָה בַּיָּם. "תִּתְקְפֵי" כְּמוֹ "אַקְפוּ יְדַיְיכוּ" בַּחֲגִיגָה (דף טז:), וּכְמוֹ "קָפָא תְּהוֹמָא" דְּסוּכָּה (דף נג.) – צָף הַתְּהוֹם וְעָלָה: בִּלְשׁוֹן חָכְמָה. שֶׁלֹּא יָבִינוּ הָאֲחֵרִים: שׁוֹר מִשְׁפָּט. תּוֹרְדִין – תּוֹר דִּין. שׁוֹר = תּוֹר, מִשְׁפָּט = דִּין: בְּטוּר מִסְכֵּן. הַר דַּל, חַרְדָּל: מְשַׁיֵּיל בְּאוּשְׁפִּיזָא. שׁוֹאֵל עוֹבְרֵי דְּרָכִים בְּעִנְיַן אוּשְׁפִּיזְכְנֵי: גְּבַר פּוּם דֵּין חַי. אִישׁ פִּי זוֹ חַי, "אוּשׁ" – כְּמוֹ אִישׁ, "פּוּם" – כְּמוֹ פִּי, "דֵּין" – כְּמוֹ זֶה: מַה זוֹ טוֹבָה יֵשׁ. כְּלוֹמַר: כַּמָּה טוֹב לוֹ: אַתְרִיגוּ לְפֶחָמִין אַרְקִיעוּ לְזָהֳבִין. הַבְעִירוּ אֶת הַפֶּחָמִין לִהְיוֹת אֲדוּמִּין כְּאֶתְרוֹג. שֶׁיִּשְׁטְחוּ גֶּחָלִים הַלּוֹחֲשׁוֹת עַל פִּי הַכִּירָה לְהִתְחַמֵּם כְּנֶגְדָּן: אַרְקִיעוּ. שִׁטְחוּ כְּמוֹ רָקִיעַ: לְזָהֳבִין. גֶּחָלִים לוֹחֲשׁוֹת, אֲדוּמּוֹת כַּזָּהָב: מַגִּידֵי בַּעֲלָטָה. תַּרְנְגוֹלִין, הַמּוֹדִיעִין עוֹנוֹת הַלַּיְלָה: בָּהֶן. עַל הַפֶּחָמִין: הַצְפִּינֵנוּ. הַרְאֵנוּ, לְשׁוֹן "צוֹפִיָּה הֲלִיכוֹת בֵּיתָהּ" (משלי לא): צָפוּן. הָוֵה מִתְחַבֵּא, דְּלֹא הָיוּ יוֹדְעִים הַתַּלְמִידִים לְהֵיכָן הָיָה, וְהָיוּ שׁוֹאֲלִים מִמֶּנּוּ: עָלַץ בְּנַעֲרָה אַהֲרוֹנִית אַחֲרוֹנִית עֵירָנִית וְהִנְעִירַתּוּ. שָׂמַח הַלַּיְלָה בְּנַעֲרָה אַהֲרוֹנִית וְעַכְשָׁיו הוּא יָשֵׁן: אָמְרִי לָהּ אִשָּׁה. אַהֲרוֹנִית – בַּת כֹּהֵן, אַחֲרוֹנִית – מֵתָה אִשְׁתּוֹ רִאשׁוֹנָה וְזוֹ אַחֲרוֹנָה: עֵירָנִית. בַּעֲלַת חֵן וַחֲרִיפָה כְּאָדָם עֵר, וְהִנְעִירַתּוּ לֹא הָיָה יָכוֹל לִישׁוֹן: מַסֶּכְתָּא. אַהֲרוֹנִית מְסַדֵּר קָדָשִׁים, עֲבוֹדַת אַהֲרֹן. אַחֲרוֹנִית – סִיֵּים אַחֶרֶת וְהִתְחִיל בְּזוֹ, עֵירָנִית – עֲמוּקָּה וַחֲמוּרָה וּמְעוֹרֶרֶת לוֹמְדֶיהָ: נִתְיָיעֵץ בַּמַּכְתִּיר. נָטַל רְשׁוּת מִנָּשִׂיא, "מַכְתִּיר" ע"ש שֶׁנּוֹתֵן רְשׁוּת לִסְמוֹךְ וְלִקְרוֹתוֹ רַבִּי, וּמֵאָז וָהָלְאָה הוּא כָּשֵׁר לִהְיוֹת מוּכְתָּר לִיקָּרֵא רַבִּי מוּמְחֶה לָרַבִּים. וְאִם טָעָה לֹא יְשַׁלֵּם: וְהִנְגִּיב. וְהִדְרִים, הָלַךְ לוֹ לִדְרוֹם: לִמְפִיבֹשֶׁת. לִפְנֵי זִקְנֵי דָרוֹם שֶׁהֵן חֲכָמִים מְאֹד. ע"ש שֶׁהָיָה מְפִיבֹשֶׁת *אָדָם גָּדוֹל קָרֵי לְהוּ הָכִי: לֹא נִצְּחַנִי אָדָם. בִּדְבָרִים: הִקְדִּיחָתַן. שְׂרָפַתּוּ, כְּמוֹ "כִּי אֵשׁ קָדְחָה" (דברים לב). כְּלוֹמַר: נָתְנָה בּוֹ מֶלַח יוֹתֵר מִדַּאי: אֵין מְשַׁיְּירִין פֵּאָה בָּאִלְפָּס. כְּשֶׁהַשַּׁמָּשׁ מְעָרֶה מִן הָאִלְפָּס לְתוֹךְ הַקְּעָרָה – אֵין דֶּרֶךְ לְהָנִיחַ בָּאִלְפָּס כְּלוּם לְצוֹרְכוֹ, אֲבָל כָּל אֶחָד מַנִּיחַ פֵּאָה בַּקְּעָרָה וּמַחֲזִירָהּ לַשַּׁמָּשׁ, וְהוּא מַאֲכַל שַׁמָּשׁ: פָּרָשַׁת דְּרָכִים. דֶּרֶךְ פּוֹרֵשׁ לְכָאן וּלְכָאן: אֲרוּכָּה. שֶׁמַּאֲרִיךְ הַדֶּרֶךְ: וּקְצָרָה. שֶׁמּוֹלִיא מְבוֹי הָעִיר פָּנוּי לִיכָּנֵס: בָּטְשָׁה

רבינו חננאל

יפנה ירשיע: פי' (עבו זו) [עכוזו] בית הירכים בית העגבות מקום החלחולת והוא משנה בבכורות פ"ג [החלחולת] גוואן כוליתן של מין צבע כולית זו כתרדין עלי אדמה פי' דמות כרתן. אמר למאן אמר למן כו'. א"ל שוטה פרש דבריך לומר [חמר] למרכב או חמר יין או עמר למלבוש כלומר היתה לשונם ערלה: ההיא דהות בעיא למימר לחברתה שכינתיתא אי ספי לך חלבא וא' לה שלוכתיתא איספי לך לבא ואיתתא אחריתא אמרה לדיין מרי כירא תפלה הות לי וגנבוך. אני וברי הואי כד הוה שדרו לך עליה ולא מטו כרעיך ארעא. פי' אדוני קורה היתה לי וגנבוה ממני והיתה קומתה כמו קומתך. ואלו היו מרבצין אותך עליה לא היו מגיעין רגליך לארץ. פי' עלת נקפת בכד כלומר [כלי] שמוציאין בו היין נגע בתחתית החבית ולא נשאר יין בחבית יבעון נשרייא לקיניהון אתערו בתר חברתא מינה. פי' ילכו התלמידים לאהליהם או תוסר מגופת החבית אחרת וישארו במשתה היין. פעמים היה משיב להם יבעון נשרייא לקיניהון כלומר ילכו לבתיהן. ופעמים היה אומר להם תוסר מגופת חבית אחרת ותשוט (הובא) בחבית כספינה בלב ים. שור משפט תרגום שור תור. ותרגום משפט דין נמצא שור משפט תרגומו תור דין. חרדל תרגומו (סוד) [טור] מסכן. נמצא הלשון תרדין בחרדל. גבר דין. חי פירושו אושפיזיכנא [תרגום] איש גבר (תרגום) פי פום. תרגום זה דין. תרגום אל תאכלו ממנו נא (חי מה) [כד חי] טיבו יש כפשוטו. התריגו (לפני חמין) [לפחמין]. ארקיעו לרהבין פי' הטריגו. (הכי פחמין). [לפחמין] שיברו אותן מלשון טטרוגי מטטרגי להו הרקיע לזהבין. פי' אותן להיות לוחשות כמראה הזהב. ועשו לי בהן ב' עופות והם (שבו) נקראו כך שהן מגידין בעלטה העיתות איזה עת מן הלילה היא: הצפינני היכן ר' אילעאי צפון פי' הראני מלשון צופה. היכן ר' אלעא טמון. עלץ בנערה אהרונית עירונית אחרונית. יש שאומר (שרוה) [שמח] שנשא אשה כהנת מזרע אהרן והיא מבנות הכפרים כדגרסינן בתלמוד [בפרק] המביא ביו"ט [דף לג] מאי הרניות. אמר רב יהודה עירניות. אמר אביי צעי חקלייתא. אחרונית והיא אשתו אחרונה שכבר נשא ראשונה וזו אחרונה ויש אומרים שמח ששנא מסכתא מתורת כהנים כגון שחיטת קדשים וכיוצא בה עירוניות כלומר משנה חיצונה. אחרוניות שגורה באחרית ימיו: נתייעץ במכתיר. נשא עצה מראש ישיבה והנגיב והלך לארץ הנגב אצל חכמי דרום. משיירין פיאה באילפס ואין משיירין פאה בקערה. פשוטה היא: ברוריה (בנושא) [בטשא] בההוא תלמוד דהוה גריס בלחישה אמר

הגהות הב"ח

(א) גמ' וכדו הות דכי שדרו: (ב) שם חוץ מאשה ותינוק' ותינוק אשה מאי: (ג) רש"י ד"ה וגנבוך מין כמו מנאי ר"ל גנבוה ממני:

הגהות הגר"א

[א] גמרא לפחמין. רשום קו עליו ונ"ב לבהמין. (וכ"ה בירושל' ספ"ב למעשרות ע"ש): [ב] שמא לא הנחת פיאה בראשונים. נ"ל שמא הנחת פיאה על ראשונים: [ג] הגהה זו מוקפת בעגולים:

רב נסים גאון

כיצד מעברין. **אכוזו** תנן או עכוזו תנן מחוי כלפי מה ששנינו בבכורות בפרק אלו מומין (דף מ) ר' עקיבה אומר מושיבין אותו על עכוזו:

ברכות יב: | ש"א כח | רש"ל | [מס' ד"א פ"ו] | אבות פ"א מ"ה [נדרים כ.] | [ברכות ז.]

בְּמַשְׁה בֵּיהּ, אָמְרָה לֵיהּ: לֹא כָּךְ כָּתוּב: °"עֲרוּכָה בַכֹּל וּשְׁמֻרָה", ^א^אִם עֲרוּכָה בְּרמ"ח אֵבָרִים שֶׁלְּךָ — מִשְׁתַּמֶּרֶת, וְאִם לָאו — אֵינָהּ מִשְׁתַּמֶּרֶת. תָּנָא: תַּלְמִיד אֶחָד הָיָה לְרַבִּי אֱלִיעֶזֶר* שֶׁהָיָה שׁוֹנֶה בְּלַחַשׁ, לְאַחַר ג' שָׁנִים שָׁכַח תַּלְמוּדוֹ. תָּנָא: תַּלְמִיד אֶחָד הָיָה לוֹ לְרַבִּי אֱלִיעֶזֶר שֶׁנִּתְחַיֵּיב בִּשְׂרֵיפָה לַמָּקוֹם. אָמְרוּ: הַנִּיחוּ לוֹ, אָדָם גָּדוֹל שִׁמֵּשׁ. א"ל שְׁמוּאֵל לְרַב יְהוּדָה: *שִׁינָּנָא, פְּתַח פּוּמָיךְ קְרֵי, פְּתַח פּוּמָיךְ תְּנֵי, כִּי הֵיכִי דְּתִתְקַיֵּים בִּיךְ וְתוֹרִיךְ חַיֵּי. שֶׁנֶּאֱמַר: °"כִּי חַיִּים הֵם לְמֹצְאֵיהֶם וּלְכָל בְּשָׂרוֹ מַרְפֵּא", אַל תִּקְרֵי "לְמֹצְאֵיהֶם" אֶלָּא "לְמוֹצִיאֵיהֶם בַּפֶּה". א"ל שְׁמוּאֵל לְרַב יְהוּדָה: שִׁינָּנָא, חֲטוֹף וֶאֱכוֹל, חֲטוֹף וְאִישְׁתֵּי, דְּעָלְמָא דְּאָזְלִינַן מִינֵּיהּ כְּהִלּוּלָא דָּמֵי. °א"ל רַב לְרַב הַמְנוּנָא: *בְּנִי, אִם יֵשׁ לְךָ — הֵיטֵב לָךְ, שֶׁאֵין בִּשְׁאוֹל תַּעֲנוּג וְאֵין לַמָּוֶת הִתְמַהְמֵהַּ. וְאִם תֹּאמַר אַנִּיחַ לְבָנַי — חוֹק בִּשְׁאוֹל מִי יַגִּיד לָךְ. בְּנֵי הָאָדָם דּוֹמִים לְעִשְׂבֵי הַשָּׂדֶה, הַלָּלוּ נוֹצְצִין וְהַלָּלוּ נוֹבְלִין. *א"ר יְהוֹשֻׁעַ בֶּן לֵוִי: הַמְהַלֵּךְ בַּדֶּרֶךְ וְאֵין עִמּוֹ לְוָיָה — יַעֲסוֹק בַּתּוֹרָה, שֶׁנֶּאֱמַר: °"כִּי לִוְיַת חֵן *הֵם". °חָשׁ בְּרֹאשׁוֹ — יַעֲסוֹק בַּתּוֹרָה, שֶׁנֶּאֱמַר: "כִּי לִוְיַת חֵן הֵם לְרֹאשֶׁךָ". חָשׁ בִּגְרוֹנוֹ — יַעֲסוֹק בַּתּוֹרָה, שֶׁנֶּאֱמַר: "וַעֲנָקִים לְגַרְגְּרוֹתֶיךָ". חָשׁ בְּמֵעָיו — יַעֲסוֹק בַּתּוֹרָה, שֶׁנֶּאֱמַר: "רִפְאוּת תְּהִי לְשָׁרֶּךָ". חָשׁ בְּעַצְמוֹתָיו — יַעֲסוֹק בַּתּוֹרָה, שֶׁנֶּאֱמַר: "וְשִׁקּוּי לְעַצְמוֹתֶיךָ". חָשׁ בְּכָל גּוּפוֹ — יַעֲסוֹק בַּתּוֹרָה, שֶׁנֶּאֱמַר: "וּלְכָל בְּשָׂרוֹ מַרְפֵּא". אָמַר רַב יְהוּדָה בְּרַ' חִיָּיא: בֹּא וּרְאֵה שֶׁלֹּא כְּמִדַּת הקב"ה מִדַּת בָּשָׂר וָדָם. מִדַּת בָּשָׂר וָדָם, אָדָם נוֹתֵן סַם לַחֲבֵירוֹ — לָזֶה יָפֶה וְלָזֶה קָשֶׁה. אֲבָל הקב"ה אֵינוֹ כֵּן, נָתַן תּוֹרָה לְיִשְׂרָאֵל — סַם חַיִּים לְכָל גּוּפוֹ, שֶׁנֶּאֱמַר: "וּלְכָל בְּשָׂרוֹ מַרְפֵּא". א"ר אַמִי: מ"ד: °"כִּי נָעִים כִּי תִשְׁמְרֵם בְּבִטְנֶךָ יִכֹּנוּ יַחְדָּיו עַל שְׂפָתֶיךָ", אֵימָתַי ד"ת נְעִי' — בִּזְמַן שֶׁתִּשְׁמְרֵם בְּבִטְנֶךָ, וְאֵימָתַי תִּשְׁמְרֵם בְּבִטְנֶךָ — בִּזְמַן שֶׁיִּכּוֹנוּ יַחְדָּו עַל שְׂפָתֶיךָ. ר' זֵירָא אָמַר, מֵהָכָא: °"שִׂמְחָה לָאִישׁ בְּמַעֲנֵה פִיו וְדָבָר בְּעִתּוֹ מַה טּוֹב", אֵימָתַי "שִׂמְחָה לָאִישׁ" — בִּזְמַן שֶׁמַּעֲנֶה בְּפִיו. ל"א: אֵימָתַי שִׂמְחָה לָאִישׁ בְּמַעֲנֵה פִּיו — בִּזְמַן שֶׁדָּבָר בְּעִתּוֹ מַה טּוֹב. ר' יִצְחָק אָמַר, מֵהָכָא: °"כִּי קָרוֹב אֵלֶיךָ הַדָּבָר מְאֹד בְּפִיךָ וּבִלְבָבְךָ לַעֲשׂוֹתוֹ", אֵימָתַי קָרוֹב אֵלֶיךָ — בִּזְמַן שֶׁבְּפִיךָ וּבִלְבָבְךָ לַעֲשׂוֹתוֹ. רָבָא אָמַר, מֵהָכָא: °"תַּאֲוַת לִבּוֹ נָתַתָּה לּוֹ וַאֲרֶשֶׁת שְׂפָתָיו בַּל מָנַעְתָּ סֶּלָה", אֵימָתַי תַּאֲוַת לִבּוֹ נָתַתָּה לּוֹ — בִּזְמַן שֶׁאֲרֶשֶׁת שְׂפָתָיו בַּל מָנַעְתָּ סֶּלָה. רָבָא רָמֵי: כְּתִיב: "תַּאֲוַת לִבּוֹ נָתַתָּה לּוֹ", וּכְתִיב: "וַאֲרֶשֶׁת שְׂפָתָיו בַּל מָנַעְתָּ סֶּלָה"! זָכָה — תַּאֲוַת לִבּוֹ נָתַתָּה לּוֹ, לֹא זָכָה — וַאֲרֶשֶׁת שְׂפָתָיו בַּל מָנַעְתָּ סֶּלָה. תָּנָא דְּבֵי ר"א בֶּן יַעֲקֹב: כָּל מָקוֹם שֶׁנֶּאֱמַר "נֶצַח" "סֶלָה" "וָעֶד" — אֵין לוֹ הֶפְסֵק עוֹלָמִית. "נֶצַח" — דִּכְתִיב: °"כִּי לֹא לְעוֹלָם אָרִיב וְלֹא לָנֶצַח אֶקְּצוֹף". "סֶלָה" — דִּכְתִיב: °"כַּאֲשֶׁר שָׁמַעְנוּ כֵּן רָאִינוּ בְּעִיר ה' צְבָאוֹת בְּעִיר אֱלֹהֵינוּ אֱלֹהִים יְכוֹנְנֶהָ עַד עוֹלָם סֶלָה". "וָעֶד" — דִּכְתִיב: °"ה' יִמְלֹךְ לְעוֹלָם וָעֶד". §(סִימָן עֲנָקִים לְחָיָיו לוּחוֹת חָרוּת).§ א"ר (*אֱלִיעֶזֶר), מַאי דִּכְתִיב: °"וַעֲנָקִים לְגַרְגְּרוֹתֶיךָ" — אִם מֵשִׂים אָדָם עַצְמוֹ כַּעֲנָק זֶה שֶׁרָף עַל הַצַּוָּאר, וְנִרְאֶה וְאֵינוֹ נִרְאֶה — תַּלְמוּדוֹ מִתְקַיֵּים בְּיָדוֹ, וְאִם לָאו — אֵין תַּלְמוּדוֹ מִתְקַיֵּים בְּיָדוֹ. וְאָמַר ר"א, מַאי דִּכְתִיב: °"לְחָיָו כַּעֲרוּגַת הַבֹּשֶׂם" — ^ב^אִם מֵשִׂים אָדָם עַצְמוֹ כַּעֲרוּגָה זוֹ שֶׁהַכֹּל דָּשִׁין בָּהּ, וּכְבוֹשֶׂם זֶה שֶׁהַכֹּל מִתְבַּשְּׂמִין בָּהּ — תַּלְמוּדוֹ מִתְקַיֵּים, וְאִם לָאו — אֵין תַּלְמוּדוֹ מִתְקַיֵּים. וְא"ר (*אֱלִיעֶזֶר,) מ"ד: °"לוּחוֹת אֶבֶן" — אִם אָדָם מֵשִׂים עַצְמוֹ אֶת לְחָיָיו כְּאֶבֶן זוֹ שֶׁאֵינָהּ נִמְחֵית — תַּלְמוּדוֹ מִתְקַיֵּים בְּיָדוֹ, וְאִם לָאו — אֵין תַּלְמוּדוֹ מִתְקַיֵּים בְּיָדוֹ. וְא"ר (*אֱלִיעֶזֶר), מַאי דִּכְתִיב: °"חָרוּת עַל הַלֻּחֹת" — אִלְמָלֵי לֹא נִשְׁתַּבְּרוּ לוּחוֹת הָרִאשׁוֹנוֹת לֹא נִשְׁתַּכְּחָה תּוֹרָה מִיִּשְׂרָאֵל. רַב אַחָא בַּר יַעֲקֹב אָמַר: *אֵין כָּל אוּמָּה וְלָשׁוֹן שׁוֹלֶטֶת בָּהֶן, שֶׁנֶּאֱמַר: "חָרוּת", אַל תִּקְרֵי "חָרוּת" אֶלָּא "חֵירוּת". אָמַר רַב מַתְנָה, מַאי דִּכְתִיב: °"וּמִמִּדְבָּר מַתָּנָה" — אִם מֵשִׂים אָדָם עַצְמוֹ כְּמִדְבָּר זֶה שֶׁהַכֹּל דָּשִׁין בּוֹ — תַּלְמוּדוֹ מִתְקַיֵּים בְּיָדוֹ, וְאִם לָאו — אֵין תַּלְמוּדוֹ מִתְקַיֵּים בְּיָדוֹ. *רָבָא בְּרֵיהּ דְּרַב יוֹסֵף בַּר חָמָא הֲוָה לֵיהּ מִלְּתָא לְרַב יוֹסֵף בַּהֲדֵיהּ, כִּי מְטָא מַעֲלֵי יוֹמָא דְּכִיפּוּרֵי אָמַר: אֵיזִיל וַאֲפַיְּיסֵיהּ. אֲזַל, אַשְׁכְּחֵיהּ לְשַׁמָּעֵיהּ דְּקָא מָזֵיג לֵיהּ כָּסָא. אֲמַר: הַב לִי וְאִימְזְגֵיהּ אֲנָא. יְהַב לֵיהּ, מַזְגֵיהּ. כִּדְטַעֲמֵיהּ אֲמַר: *)דָּמֵי הַאי מְזִיגָא לִמְזִיגָא דְּרָבָא בְּרֵיהּ דְּרַב יוֹסֵף בַּר חָמָא. א"ל: אֲנָא הוּא. *א"ל: *לָא תֵּתִיב אַכַּרְעָיךְ עַד דִּמְפָרַשְׁתְּ לִי הָנֵי קְרָאֵי, מַאי דִּכְתִיב: "וּמִמִּדְבָּר מַתָּנָה וּמִמַּתָּנָה נַחֲלִיאֵל וּמִנַּחֲלִיאֵל בָּמוֹת וּמִבָּמוֹת הַגַּיְא". א"ל: ^ג^אִם אָדָם מֵשִׂים עַצְמוֹ כְּמִדְבָּר זֶה שֶׁהַכֹּל דָּשִׁין בּוֹ — תּוֹרָה נִיתְּנָה לוֹ בְּמַתָּנָה. וְכֵיוָן שֶׁנִּיתְּנָה לוֹ בְּמַתָּנָה — נְחָלוֹ אֵל, שֶׁנֶּאֱמַר: "וּמִמַּתָּנָה נַחֲלִיאֵל". וְכֵיוָן שֶׁנְּחָלוֹ אֵל — עוֹלֶה לִגְדוּלָּה, שֶׁנֶּאֱמַר: "וּמִנַּחֲלִיאֵל בָּמוֹת". וְאִם מֵגִיס לִבּוֹ — הַקָּדוֹשׁ בָּרוּךְ הוּא מַשְׁפִּילוֹ, שֶׁנֶּאֱמַר: "וּמִבָּמוֹת הַגַּיְא". וְאִם חוֹזֵר בּוֹ — הקב"ה מַגְבִּיהוֹ, שֶׁנֶּאֱמַר: °"כָּל גֶּיא יִנָּשֵׂא". אָמַר רַב הוּנָא, מ"ד: °"חַיָּתְךָ יָשְׁבוּ בָהּ תָּכִין בְּטוֹבָתְךָ לֶעָנִי אֱלֹהִים" — ^ג^אִם אָדָם מֵשִׂים עַצְמוֹ כְּחַיָּה זוֹ שֶׁדּוֹרֶסֶת וְאוֹכֶלֶת, וְאִיכָּא דְּאָמְרִי: שֶׁמַּסְרַחַת וְאוֹכֶלֶת — תַּלְמוּדוֹ מִתְקַיֵּים בְּיָדוֹ, וְאִם לָאו — אֵין תַּלְמוּדוֹ מִתְקַיֵּים בְּיָדוֹ. וְאִם עוֹשֶׂה כֵּן — הקב"ה עוֹשֶׂה לוֹ סְעוּדָה בְּעַצְמוֹ, שֶׁנֶּאֱמַר: "תָּכִין בְּטוֹבָתְךָ לֶעָנִי אֱלֹהִים". א"ר חִיָּיא בַּר אַבָּא, א"ר יוֹחָנָן: מַאי דִּכְתִיב: °"נֹצֵר תְּאֵנָה יֹאכַל פִּרְיָהּ", לָמָּה נִמְשְׁלוּ דִּבְרֵי תוֹרָה כִּתְאֵנָה — מַה תְּאֵנָה זוֹ כָּל

*) [עתוס' שבת עז. ד"ה לאמר]

רש"י

בְּמַשְׁה בֵּיהּ. בָּעֲטָה בּוֹ: תּוֹרִיךְ חַיֵּי. שֶׁתַּאֲרִיךְ יָמִים: חֲטוֹף אֱכוֹל. אִם יֵשׁ לְךָ מָמוֹן לְהִתְהַנּוֹת עַצְמְךָ, אַל תַּמְתִּין עַד לְמָחָר שֶׁמָּא תָּמוּת וְשׁוּב אֵין לְךָ הֲנָאָה: דְּעָלְמָא דְּאָזְלִינַן מִינֵּיהּ. גָּרְסִינַן: כְּהִלּוּלָא דָּמֵי. הַיּוֹם יֶשְׁנוֹ וּלְמָחָר אֵינֶנּוּ, דּוֹמֶה לַחוּפָּה שֶׁהוֹלֶכֶת מַהֵר: אִם יֵשׁ לְךָ. מָמוֹן: וְאֵין לַמָּוֶת הִתְמַהְמֵהַּ. עִיכּוּב, כִּי פִּתְאוֹם תּוֹרָה אוֹר הָאָדָם מֵת: חוֹק. מָזוֹן: מִי יַגִּיד לָךְ. אִם נִשְׁאַר בְּיָדָם, שֶׁמָּא יְאַבְּדוּהוּ: הַלָּלוּ נוֹצְצִין. כְּלוֹמַר: כְּשֶׁהֵן גְּדֵלִין גְּדֵילָה פַּרְנָסָתָן וְעׇשְׁרָן עִמָּהֶן, וְאֵינְךָ צָרִיךְ לְהִדָּאֵג עֲלֵיהֶן: וְהַלָּלוּ נוֹבְלִין. מֵתִים, לְשׁוֹן "וְהֶעָלֶה נָבֵל": יָפֶה. לְחוֹלִי זֶה וְקָשֶׁה לְחוֹלִי זֶה, יָפֶה לַלֵּב וְרַע לָעֵינַיִם: שֶׁתִּשְׁמְרֵם בְּבִטְנֶךָ. שֶׁהֵן שְׁמוּרִים בְּיָדְךָ, שֶׁאֵין מִשְׁתַּכְּחִין מִמְּךָ: יִכֹּנוּ יַחַד. שֶׁאַתָּה סוֹדְרָן וּמוֹצִיאָן בַּפֶּה, וְלֹא בְּגִימְגּוּם וּבִלְחִישָׁה: אֵימָתַי שִׂמְחָה וְכוּ' בִּזְמַן. שֶׁיּוֹדֵעַ לִדְרוֹשׁ הִלְכוֹת חַג בֶּחָג. ד"א: אֵימָתַי שִׂמְחָה לָאִישׁ, אֵימָתַי אָדָם שָׂמֵחַ בְּתַלְמוּדוֹ - בִּזְמַן שֶׁיֵּשׁ לוֹ מַעֲנֶה כְּשֶׁשּׁוֹאֲלִין מִמֶּנּוּ דְּבַר הֲלָכָה: שֶׁאֲרֶשֶׁת. סְפִירַת שְׂפָתָיו בַּל תִּמְנַע סֶלָה, כְּשֶׁנָּתַתָּ בּוֹ דַּעַת לְהוֹצִיא בִּשְׂפָתָיו: זָכָה. אִם יֵשׁ לוֹ מַזָּל טוֹב תַּאֲוַת לִבּוֹ נָתַתָּ לוֹ, שֶׁבְּעוֹד שֶׁהוּא מִתְאַוֶּה בָּאָה לוֹ תַּאֲוָתוֹ עַד שֶׁלֹּא יִשְׁאָלֶנָּה: לֹא זָכָה. צָרִיךְ(א) לְהִתְמַקְמֵק וּלְהִצְטַעֵר: כִּי לֹא לְעוֹלָם אָרִיב וְלֹא לָנֶצַח אֶקְצוֹף. אַלְמָא: "לָנֶצַח" לְשׁוֹן עוֹלָם הוּא, מִדְּסָמִיךְ לֵיהּ. וְכֵן "עַד עוֹלָם סֶלָה" - אַלְמָא: "סֶלָה" לְשׁוֹן לְעוֹלָם מַשְׁמַע: שֶׁרָף לַצַּוָּאר. שֶׁאֵינוֹ מְגוּמְגָּם בְּדוֹחַק סְבִיב הַצַּוָּאר, אֶלָּא שֶׁרָפוּי בְּרֶיוַח, כָּךְ הוּא נָעִים וּמְרוּצֶּה לַבְּרִיּוֹת: וְנִרְאֶה וְאֵינוֹ נִרְאֶה. כְּשֶׁמַּגְבִּיהַּ צַוָּארוֹ נִרְאֶה מִתַּחַת זְקָנוֹ, וְרוֹב פְּעָמִים שֶׁמְּכוּסֶּה וּזְקָנוֹ מְכַסֶּה אוֹתוֹ. כָּךְ, אִם תַּלְמִיד חָכָם הוּא אֵינוֹ רוֹדֵף לָצֵאת וְלָבֹא בַּשּׁוּק, אֶלָּא יוֹשֵׁב וּמְחַזֵּר עַל תַּלְמוּדוֹ – מִתְקַיֵּים בְּיָדוֹ: שֶׁהַכֹּל דָּשִׁין אוֹתוֹ. שֶׁאֵין לוֹ גַּסּוּת(ב): שֶׁהַכֹּל מִתְבַּשְּׂמִין מִמֶּנּוּ. שֶׁמְּלַמֵּד תּוֹרָה לַתַּלְמִידִים: כְּאֶבֶן זוֹ שֶׁאֵינָהּ נִמְחֵית. מִפְּנֵי דְּרִיסַת רַגְלֵי בְּנֵי אָדָם, כָּךְ לְחָיָיו אֵינָן נִלְאִין מִלְּחַזֵּר עַל לִמּוּדוֹ וּלְלַמֵּד לַאֲחֵרִים: לֹא נִשְׁתַּכְּחָה. "חָרוּת" מַשְׁמַע חָקוּק, וְאֵינוֹ נִמְחָק לְעוֹלָם. עַל יְדֵי הַלּוּחוֹת הָיְתָה תּוֹרָה חֲקוּקָה לְיִשְׂרָאֵל מֵהִשְׁתַּכֵּחַ מֵהֶן עוֹלָמִית: עַל הַלּוּחוֹת. בִּשְׁבִיל הַלּוּחוֹת הָיוּ בְּנֵי יִשְׂרָאֵל בְּנֵי חוֹרִין: מִמִּדְבָּר מַתָּנָה. אִם כַּמִּדְבָּר הוּא תּוֹרָה נְתוּנָה לוֹ בְּמַתָּנָה, וְלֹא יִשְׁכַּח: מִילְּתָא. כַּעַס: אֵמַר. רָבָא, אֵיזִיל אֲפַיְּיסֵיהּ לְרַב יוֹסֵף: מָזוּג. בְּמַיִם: רַב יוֹסֵף סַגֵּי נְהוֹר הֲוָה, וְלֹא הָיָה רוֹאֵהוּ, וְהִכִּירוֹ בְּטַעַם הַיַּיִן שֶׁהוּא מְזָגוֹ. לְפִי שֶׁהָיָה מַכִּיר רַב יוֹסֵף בְּמִזְגּוֹ שֶׁל רָבָא מִתְּחִילָּה, שֶׁהָיָה בָּקִי לִיתֵּן מַיִם בְּמִדָּה: כָּל גֶּיא יִנָּשֵׂא. אַף עַל גַּב דְּלָאו גַּבֵּי הָנֵי קְרָאֵי כְּתִיב, דָּרְשֵׁי לֵיהּ דְּמִי שֶׁבָּא לִידֵי גֵּיא, שֶׁהוּשְׁפַּל – חוֹזֵר וּמִתְנַשֵּׂא: שֶׁדּוֹרֶסֶת וְאוֹכֶלֶת. מִיָּד לְאַחַר הֲרִיגָתָהּ, שֶׁאֵינוֹ מַקְפִּיד עַל תַּעֲנוּגִים, אֶלָּא אוֹכֵל בָּשָׂר בְּלֹא תַּבְלִין, וְכֵן שְׁאָר עִינּוּגִין: שֶׁמַּסְרַחַת. בְּטִיט. הַיְינוּ מִי שֶׁאֵינוֹ הוֹלֵךְ אַחַר גַּבְהוּת לָקוּץ בְּמַאֲכָלוֹ אִם לֹא נִתְבַּשֵּׁל כׇּל צׇרְכּוֹ. ל"א: שֶׁדּוֹרֶסֶת וְאוֹכֶלֶת – לְאַחַר הֲרִיגָתָהּ אוֹכֶלֶת מִיָּד, כָּךְ תַּלְמִיד חָכָם מְחַזֵּר עַל תַּלְמוּדוֹ מִיָּד כְּשֶׁמְּקַבְּלוֹ מֵרַבּוֹ, מַסְרַחַת – מְנַבֵּל עַצְמוֹ עַל דִּבְרֵי תוֹרָה. לָשׁוֹן זֶה נִרְאֶה בְּעֵינַי, לְפִי שֶׁמָּצִינוּ בְּכׇל הַתַּלְמוּד *שֶׁדֶּרֶךְ תַּלְמִידֵי חֲכָמִים לְהַקְפִּיד עַל מַאֲכָלָן דֶּרֶךְ גְּדוּלָּה וְכָבוֹד, וְעַל מַלְבּוּשֵׁיהֶן, כִּדְכְתִיב (משלי ח) *"וְלִמְשַׂנְאַי אָהֲבוּ מָוֶת": לֶעָנִי. לָזֶה שֶׁשָּׂם עַצְמוֹ כְּעָנִי. וּלְלִישָּׁנָא בַּתְרָא – שֶׁשָּׂם עַצְמוֹ כְּעָנִי לְחַזֵּר עָלֶיהָ: תְּאֵנָה. אִילָן: כׇּל

עין משפט נר מצוה

ג א מיי' פ"ג מהלכות ת"ת הלכה יב סמג עשין יב טוש"ע י"ד סי' רמו סעיף כב:
ד ב מיי' שם הלכה ט:
ה ג מיי' וסמג שם טוש"ע שם סעיף כא:

מסורת הש"ס

ש"ב כג | משלי ד | ס"א בן יעקב | [ברכות לו. וש"נ ועי' בחגיגה טו: מ"ש שם על לידו פירוש על שיננא] | שם א | כל זה עד נובלין מס' בן סירא | סוטה מו: | בסי' איתא וגו' ומילת הם ליתא | שם כב | שם טו | דברים ל | תהלים כא | ישעיהו נז | תהלים מח | [נ"ל אלעזר] | שמות טו | שיר ה | [נ"ל אלעזר] | שמות לא | [נ"ל אלעזר] | שם לב | [ע"ז ה. ע"ש] | במדבר כא | נדרים נה. ע"ש | [קידושין לו: וש"נ] | *[עמ"ש תוס' נזיר כב: ד"ה אמר וכו' פי' דקך מילתא] | ישעיה מ | תהלים סח | משלי כז | [שבת קיד.] | נ"ל כל משנאי | משלי א

הגהות הב"ח

(א) רש"י ד"ה לא זכה צריך (להתמקמק) תז"מ ונ"ב ס"א להתמהמה [וכ"ה בע"י]: (ב) ד"ה שהכל דשין וכו' גסות הרוח הס"ד:

גליון הש"ס

גמ' א"ל רב לרב המנונא. עיין לקמן דף סג ע"א תד"ה רב המנונא: שם תא בראשו יעסוק בתורה. עי' תורת חיים שבועות דף טו ע"ב ד"ה אסור להתרפאות:

רבינו חננאל

אמרה ליה כתיב ערוכה בכל ושמורה אם ערוכה ברמ"ח אברים נשמרת בלב ואם לאו אינה נשמרת. א"ל רב שמואל לרב יהודה שיננא פתח פומך קרי ותני כי היכי דתוריך חיי שנאמר כי חיים הם למוצאיהם בפיו. תנא תלמיד היה לר' אליעזר שנתחייב שרפה למקום ואמרו (המקום) הניחו לו אדם גדול שימש. כתיב נעים כי תשמרם בבטנך אימתי דברי תורה נעימים בשעה שתשמרם בבטנך. כיצד בעת שיכונו יחדו על שפתיו. כתיב שמחה לאיש במענה פיו אימתי בעת שדבר בעתו מה טוב. ר' יצחק אמר מהכא כי קרוב אליך הדבר מאד בשעה שבפיך ובלבבך לעשותו. תאות לבו נתתה לו אם זכה ואם לא זכה ארשת שפתיו בל מנעת סלה. תנא כל מקום שנאמר לנצח כגון ולא לנצח אקצוף. סלה כגון אלהים יכוננה עד עולם סלה. ועד כגון ה' ימלוך לעולם ועד אין להם הפסק לעולם. כתיב חיתך

רב נסים גאון

רבא הויא ליה מילתא לרב יוסף בהדיה. תמצא פירוש הדברים שאירעו ביניהן בפרק הנודר מן הירק בנדרים (דף נה) (מר שמואל מר) [בר מר שמואל] פקיד דליתנון תליסר אלפי זוזי לרבא מן אללתא דנהר פניא שלחה רבא לקמיה דרב יוסף אללתא היכי מיקריא אמר רב יוסף ושוין בנודר מן התבואה שאינו אסור אלא בה' המינים אמר ליה אביי מי דמי (הכו אקלא) [תבואה לא] משמע אלא ה' המינין אללתא כל מילי (דשמעא) [משמע] אהדרוה לקמיה (דר' אבא) [דרבא] אמר להון הדא לא איבעיא לי דאללתא כל מילי משמע הדא היא דאיבעיא לי שכר בתים ושכר ספינות מאי מי אמרינן כיון דפחתן לאו אללתא היא או דלמא כיון דלא ידיע פחתיהו כי אללתא היא אמרוה קמיה דרב יוסף וכי מאחר דלא צריך לן אמאי שלח לן איקפד רב יוסף שמע רבא ואתא לקמיה ביומא דכיפורי:

כמאן

ו א מיי' פ"ד מהלכות ת"ת הלכה ד טוש"ע י"ד סי' רמו סעיף י:
ז ב מיי' פ"ו מהלכות ת"ת הלכה ה טוש"ע י"ד סי' רמב סעיף יז:
ח ג טוש"ע א"ח סי' קנה סעיף א:

כָּל זְמַן שֶׁאָדָם מְמַשְׁמֵשׁ בָּהּ מוֹצֵא בָּהּ תְּאֵנִים — אַף דִּבְרֵי תוֹרָה כָּל זְמַן שֶׁאָדָם הוֹגֶה בָּהֶן — מוֹצֵא בָּהֶן טַעַם. א"ר שְׁמוּאֵל בַּר נַחְמָנִי: מַאי דִּכְתִיב: °"אַיֶּלֶת אֲהָבִים וְיַעֲלַת חֵן וגו'" לָמָּה נִמְשְׁלוּ דִּבְרֵי תוֹרָה לְאַיֶּלֶת? לוֹמַר לָךְ: *מָה אַיָּלָה רַחְמָהּ צַר וַחֲבִיבָה עַל בּוֹעֲלָהּ כָּל שָׁעָה וְשָׁעָה כְּשָׁעָה רִאשׁוֹנָה — אַף דִּבְרֵי תוֹרָה חֲבִיבִין עַל לוֹמְדֵיהֶן כָּל שָׁעָה וְשָׁעָה כְּשָׁעָה רִאשׁוֹנָה. "וְיַעֲלַת חֵן" — שֶׁמַּעֲלַת חֵן עַל לוֹמְדֶיהָ. "דַּדֶּיהָ יְרַוֻּךָ בְכָל עֵת", לָמָּה נִמְשְׁלוּ דִּבְרֵי תוֹרָה כַּדַּד? מָה דַּד זֶה כָּל זְמַן שֶׁהַתִּינוֹק מְמַשְׁמֵשׁ בּוֹ מוֹצֵא בּוֹ חָלָב — אַף דִּבְרֵי תוֹרָה, כָּל זְמַן שֶׁאָדָם הוֹגֶה בָּהֶן — מוֹצֵא בָּהֶן טַעַם. "בְּאַהֲבָתָהּ תִּשְׁגֶּה תָמִיד" — כְּגוֹן רַבִּי *אֱלִיעֶזֶר בֶּן פְּדָת. אָמְרוּ עָלָיו עַל רַבִּי (*אֱלִיעֶזֶר) שֶׁהָיָה יוֹשֵׁב וְעוֹסֵק בַּתּוֹרָה בַּשּׁוּק הַתַּחְתּוֹן שֶׁל צִיפּוֹרִי, וּסְדִינוֹ מוּטָּל בַּשּׁוּק הָעֶלְיוֹן שֶׁל צִיפּוֹרִי. (*תַּנְיָא,) א"ר יִצְחָק בֶּן אֶלְעָזָר: פַּעַם אַחַת בָּא אָדָם לִיטְּלוֹ וּמָצָא בּוֹ שָׂרָף. תָּנָא דְּבֵי רַב עָנָן, מַאי דִּכְתִיב: °"רוֹכְבֵי אֲתוֹנוֹת צְחוֹרוֹת יוֹשְׁבֵי עַל מִדִּין [וְהוֹלְכֵי עַל דֶּרֶךְ שִׂיחוּ]", "רוֹכְבֵי אֲתוֹנוֹת" — אֵלּוּ תַּלְמִידֵי חֲכָמִים שֶׁמְּהַלְּכִין מֵעִיר לְעִיר וּמִמְּדִינָה לִמְדִינָה לִלְמוֹד (בּוֹ) תּוֹרָה. "צְחוֹרוֹת" — שֶׁעוֹשִׂין אוֹתָהּ כַּצָּהֳרַיִם. "יוֹשְׁבֵי עַל מִדִּין" — שֶׁדָּנִין דִּין אֱמֶת *לַאֲמִיתּוֹ. "וְהוֹלְכֵי" — אֵלּוּ בַּעֲלֵי מִקְרָא. "עַל דֶּרֶךְ" — אֵלּוּ בַּעֲלֵי מִשְׁנָה. "שִׂיחוּ" — אֵלּוּ בַּעֲלֵי תַלְמוּד, שֶׁכָּל שִׂיחָתָן דִּבְרֵי תוֹרָה. *אָמַר רַב שֵׁיזְבִי מִשּׁוּם רַבִּי אֶלְעָזָר בֶּן עֲזַרְיָה, מַאי דִּכְתִיב: °"לֹא יַחֲרוֹךְ רְמִיָּה צֵידוֹ" — לֹא יִחְיֶה וְלֹא יַאֲרִיךְ יָמִים צַיָּיד הָרַמַּאי. רַב שֵׁשֶׁת אָמַר: צַיָּיד הָרַמַּאי יַחֲרוֹךְ? כִּי אֲתָא רַב דִּימִי, אֲמַר: מָשָׁל לְצַיָּיד שֶׁצָּד צִפֳּרִים, אִם רִאשׁוֹן רִאשׁוֹן מְשַׁבֵּר כְּנָפָיו — מִשְׁתַּמֵּר, וְאִם לָאו — אֵין מִשְׁתַּמֵּר. אָמַר (*רַבָּה), אָמַר רַב סְחוֹרָה, אָמַר רַב הוּנָא, *מַאי דִּכְתִיב: °"הוֹן מֵהֶבֶל יִמְעָט וְקוֹבֵץ עַל יָד יַרְבֶּה", אִם עוֹשֶׂה אָדָם תּוֹרָתוֹ חֲבִילוֹת חֲבִילוֹת — מִתְמַעֵט, וְאִם לָאו — קוֹבֵץ עַל יָד יַרְבֶּה. אָמַר *רַבָּה: יָדְעִי רַבָּנַן לְהָא מִלְּתָא וְעָבְרִי עֲלַהּ. אָמַר רַב נַחְמָן בַּר יִצְחָק: אֲנָא *עֲבַדְתַּהּ, וְאִיקַּיַּים בִּידַאי.§ ת"ר: כֵּיצַד סֵדֶר מִשְׁנָה? מֹשֶׁה לָמַד מִפִּי הַגְּבוּרָה, נִכְנַס אַהֲרֹן וְשָׁנָה לוֹ מֹשֶׁה פִּירְקוֹ. נִסְתַּלֵּק אַהֲרֹן וְיָשַׁב לִשְׂמֹאל מֹשֶׁה. נִכְנְסוּ בָּנָיו וְשָׁנָה לָהֶן מֹשֶׁה פִּירְקָן, נִסְתַּלְּקוּ בָּנָיו, אֶלְעָזָר יָשַׁב לִימִין מֹשֶׁה וְאִיתָמָר לִשְׂמֹאל אַהֲרֹן. רַבִּי יְהוּדָה אוֹמֵר: לְעוֹלָם אַהֲרֹן לִימִין מֹשֶׁה חוֹזֵר. נִכְנְסוּ זְקֵנִים וְשָׁנָה לָהֶן מֹשֶׁה פִּירְקָן, נִסְתַּלְּקוּ זְקֵנִים, נִכְנְסוּ כָּל הָעָם וְשָׁנָה לָהֶן מֹשֶׁה פִּירְקָן. נִמְצְאוּ בְּיַד אַהֲרֹן אַרְבָּעָה, בְּיַד בָּנָיו שְׁלֹשָׁה, וּבְיַד הַזְּקֵנִים שְׁנַיִם, וּבְיַד כָּל הָעָם אֶחָד. נִסְתַּלֵּק מֹשֶׁה, וְשָׁנָה לָהֶן אַהֲרֹן פִּירְקוֹ. נִסְתַּלֵּק אַהֲרֹן, שָׁנוּ לָהֶן בָּנָיו פִּירְקָן. נִסְתַּלְּקוּ בָּנָיו, שָׁנוּ לָהֶן זְקֵנִים פִּירְקָן. נִמְצָא בְּיַד הַכֹּל אַרְבָּעָה. מִכָּאן א"ר אֱלִיעֶזֶר: חַיָּיב אָדָם לִשְׁנוֹת לְתַלְמִידוֹ אַרְבָּעָה פְּעָמִים. וְקַל וָחוֹמֶר, וּמָה אַהֲרֹן שֶׁלָּמַד מִפִּי מֹשֶׁה, וּמֹשֶׁה מִפִּי הַגְּבוּרָה — כָּךְ, הֶדְיוֹט מִפִּי הֶדְיוֹט — עַל אַחַת כַּמָּה וְכַמָּה. ר"ע אוֹמֵר: אמִנַּיִן שֶׁחַיָּיב אָדָם לִשְׁנוֹת לְתַלְמִידוֹ עַד שֶׁיִּלְמְדֶנּוּ — שֶׁנֶּאֱמַר: °"וְלַמְּדָהּ אֶת בְּנֵי יִשְׂרָאֵל". וּמִנַּיִן עַד שֶׁתְּהֵא סְדוּרָה בְּפִיהֶם — שֶׁנֶּאֱמַר: "שִׂימָהּ בְּפִיהֶם". וּמִנַּיִן שֶׁחַיָּיב לְהַרְאוֹת לוֹ פָּנִים — שֶׁנֶּאֱמַר: °"וְאֵלֶּה הַמִּשְׁפָּטִים אֲשֶׁר תָּשִׂים לִפְנֵיהֶם". *(א) וְלִיגְמְרוּ כּוּלְּהוּ מִמֹּשֶׁה! כְּדֵי לַחֲלוֹק כָּבוֹד לְאַהֲרֹן וּבָנָיו, וְכָבוֹד לַזְּקֵנִים. וְנֵיעוּל אַהֲרֹן וְנִיגְמַר מִמֹּשֶׁה, וְלֵיעַיְּילוּ בָּנָיו וְלִיגְמְרוּ מֵאַהֲרֹן, וְלֵיעַיְּילוּ זְקֵנִים וְלֵילְפוּ מִבָּנָיו, וְלֵיזְלוּ וְלִיגְמְרִינְהוּ לְכוּלְּהוּ יִשְׂרָאֵל! כֵּיוָן דְּמֹשֶׁה מִפִּי הַגְּבוּרָה גָּמַר — מִסְתַּיְּיעָא מִלְּתֵיהּ. אָמַר מָר, רַבִּי יְהוּדָה אוֹמֵר: לְעוֹלָם אַהֲרֹן לִימִין מֹשֶׁה חוֹזֵר. כְּמַאן אָזְלָא הָא *דְּתַנְיָא: בשְׁלֹשָׁה שֶׁהָיוּ מְהַלְּכִין בַּדֶּרֶךְ — הָרַב בָּאֶמְצַע, וְגָדוֹל בִּימִינוֹ, וְקָטָן בִּשְׂמֹאלוֹ. לֵימָא רַבִּי יְהוּדָה הִיא וְלָא רַבָּנַן! אֲפִילּוּ תֵּימָא רַבָּנַן, מִשּׁוּם טִירְחָא דְּאַהֲרֹן. רַבִּי פְּרִידָא הֲוָה לֵיהּ הַהוּא תַּלְמִידָא דַּהֲוָה תָּנֵי לֵיהּ אַרְבַּע מְאָה זִימְנֵי וְגָמַר. יוֹמָא חַד בָּעְיוּהּ לְמִלְּתָא דְּמִצְוָה, תְּנָא לֵיהּ וְלָא גָּמַר. א"ל: הָאִידָּנָא מַאי שְׁנָא? א"ל: מִדְּהַהִיא שַׁעְתָּא דְּא"ל לְמָר אִיכָּא מִילְּתָא דְּמִצְוָה — אַסְּחַאי לְדַעְתַּאי, וְכָל שַׁעְתָּא אָמִינָא, הַשְׁתָּא קָאֵי מָר, הַשְׁתָּא קָאֵי מָר. א"ל: הַב דַּעְתִּיךְ וְאַתְנֵי לָךְ. הֲדַר תְּנָא לֵיהּ ד' מְאָה זִימְנֵי [אַחֲרִינֵי], נְפָקָא בַּת קָלָא וְא"ל: נִיחָא לָךְ *דְּלִיסְפּוּ לָךְ ד' מְאָה שְׁנֵי, אוֹ דְּתִיזְכּוּ אַתְּ וְדָרָךְ לְעָלְמָא דְּאָתֵי? אֲמַר: דְּנִיזְכּוּ אֲנָא וְדָרַיי לְעָלְמָא דְּאָתֵי. אָמַר לָהֶן הקב"ה: תְּנוּ לוֹ זוֹ וָזוֹ. אָמַר רַב חִסְדָּא: *אֵין תּוֹרָה נִקְנֵית אֶלָּא בְּסִימָנִין, שֶׁנֶּאֱמַר: "שִׂימָהּ בְּפִיהֶם", אַל תִּקְרֵי "שִׂימָהּ" אֶלָּא "סִימָנָהּ". שַׁמְעַהּ רַב תַּחְלִיפָא מִמַּעַרְבָא, אֲזַל אַמְרַהּ קַמֵּיהּ דְּר' אַבָּהוּ, אֲמַר: אַתּוּן מֵהָתָם מַתְנִיתוּ לַהּ, אֲנַן מֵהָכָא מַתְנֵינַן לַהּ: °"הַצִּיבִי לָךְ צִיּוּנִים שִׂמִי לָךְ וגו'" עֲשׂוּ צִיּוּנִים לַתּוֹרָה. וּמַאי מַשְׁמַע דְּהַאי צִיּוּן לִישָּׁנָא דְּסִימָנָא הוּא — דִּכְתִיב: °"וְרָאָה עֶצֶם אָדָם וּבָנָה אֶצְלוֹ צִיּוּן". ר' *אֱלִיעֶזֶר אֲמַר, מֵהָכָא: °"אֱמוֹר לַחָכְמָה אֲחוֹתִי אָתְּ וּמוֹדָע לַבִּינָה תִקְרָא" — געֲשֵׂה מוֹדָעִים לַתּוֹרָה. רָבָא אָמַר: עֲשֵׂה מוֹעֲדִים לַתּוֹרָה. וְהַיְינוּ

כָּל זְמַן שֶׁמְּמַשְׁמֵשׁ בָּהּ מוֹצֵא בָהּ תְּאֵנִים. שֶׁאֵינָן מִתְבַּשְּׁלִין בְּבַת אַחַת, אֶלָּא הַיּוֹם מְעַט וּלְמָחָר מְעַט, וְכָל שָׁעָה רָאוּי לֶאֱכוֹל מֵהֶן: שֶׁמַּעֲלַת חֵן עַל לוֹמְדֶיהָ. שֶׁהַכֹּל מְנַשְּׂאִין אוֹתוֹ, וְתוֹרָתוֹ נוֹתֶנֶת לוֹ חֵן: בְּאַהֲבָתָהּ תִּשְׁגֶּה תָּמִיד. בִּשְׁבִיל אַהֲבָתָהּ תַּעֲשֶׂה עַצְמְךָ שׁוֹגֶה וָפֶתִי, לְהַנִּיחַ עֲסָקֶיךָ וְלָרוּץ לִדְבַר הֲלָכָה: לֹא יַחֲרוֹךְ. נוֹטָרִיקוֹן דָּרֵישׁ לֵיהּ לֹא יִחְיֶה וְלֹא יַאֲרִיךְ: צַיָּיד רַמַּאי. שֶׁמַּרְבֶּה בְּגִירְסָא וְאֵינוֹ מְחַזֵּר עָלֶיהָ: וְרַב שֵׁשֶׁת אָמַר. אֵין זֶה רַמַּאי אֶלָּא שׁוֹטֶה, וְהַקּוֹבֵץ עַל יָד הוּא הָרַמַּאי וְעָרוּם בַּדָּבָר, וְהוּא יַחֲרוֹךְ, כְּלוֹמַר: יִתְקַיֵּים בְּיָדוֹ, כְּצַיָּיד הָרַמַּאי שֶׁמְּשַׁבֵּר גַּף רִאשׁוֹן רִאשׁוֹן כְּשֶׁהוּא לוֹכְדוֹ שֶׁלֹּא יִבְרַח, הוּא חוֹרֵךְ עוֹפוֹת וְאוֹכְלָן. וְקָרָא אַתְּמוּהֵי מְתַמַּהּ: לֹא יַחֲרוֹךְ? לֹא יִצְלֶה וְיֹאכַל? אֲנָא עֲבַדְתַּהּ וְקַיֵּימְתִּיהָ. לְקַבֵּץ עַל יָד, וְחָזַרְתִּי עָלֶיהָ עַד שֶׁהֶחֱזַקְתִּי בָּהּ, וְאַחַ"כ חָזַרְתִּי וְשָׁמַעְתִּי אַחֶרֶת: כֵּיצַד סֵדֶר הַמִּשְׁנָה. כֵּיצַד לָמְדוּ יִשְׂרָאֵל תּוֹרָה שֶׁבְּעַל פֶּה: נִכְנַס אַהֲרֹן. וְיָשַׁב לִפְנֵי מֹשֶׁה, כִּדְכְתִיב (ישעיהו ל): "וְהָיוּ עֵינֶיךָ רוֹאוֹת אֶת מוֹרֶיךָ", וְכֵן כּוּלָּם, בִּשְׁעַת שְׁמוּעָתָן(ג) כּוּלָּן יוֹשְׁבִין לְפָנָיו: יָשַׁב לִשְׂמֹאל מֹשֶׁה. דְּתַנְיָא: *הַמְהַלֵּךְ לִימִין רַבּוֹ הֲרֵי זֶה בּוּר, וְכָל שֶׁכֵּן יוֹשֵׁב בִּזְמַן שֶׁאֵין שֵׁנִי לֵישֵׁב בִּשְׂמֹאל: וְשָׁנָה לָהֶן פִּירְקָן. אוֹתוֹ פֶּרֶק עַצְמוֹ שֶׁשָּׁנָה לְאַהֲרֹן: אַהֲרֹן לִימִין מֹשֶׁה חוֹזֵר. אַחֲרֵי שֶׁשָּׁמְעוּ בָּנָיו, וְיֵשׁ שֵׁנִי לֵישֵׁב בִּשְׂמֹאל מֹשֶׁה — כָּבוֹד הוּא לְאַהֲרֹן וּלְמֹשֶׁה לִהְיוֹת אַהֲרֹן שֶׁהוּא גָּדוֹל בָּא וְיוֹשֵׁב בְּיָמִין: וּמָה אַהֲרֹן שֶׁשָּׁמַע מִמֹּשֶׁה כו'. וּמִסְתַּיְּיעָא מִילְּתָא לְהִתְקַיֵּים בְּלִבּוֹ לְהָבִין מַהֵר, אַפ"ה שָׁמַע ד' פְּעָמִים: לְהַרְאוֹת לוֹ פָּנִים. לְלַמְּדוֹ, לָתֵת טַעַם בִּדְבָרָיו בְּכָל אֲשֶׁר יוּכַל, וְלֹא יֹאמַר: כָּךְ שָׁמַעְתִּי, הָבֵן אַתָּה הַטַּעַם מֵעַצְמְךָ. וַחֲבֵירוֹ בְּפֶרֶק רִאשׁוֹן (דף יג:): שֶׁהָיָה אוֹמֵר עַל טָמֵא טָהוֹר, וּמַרְאֶה לוֹ פָּנִים: אֲשֶׁר תָּשִׂים לִפְנֵיהֶם. וְלֹא כְּתִיב: "אֲשֶׁר תְּלַמְּדֵם" — צָרִיךְ אַתָּה לְסַדֵּר וְלָשׂוּם לִפְנֵיהֶם טַעַם הַמְיַישֵּׁב תַּלְמוּדָם: וְלֵיעַיְּילוּ כּוּלָּן(ג) בְּרֵישָׁא וְלֵילְפוּ מִמֹּשֶׁה. ד' זִימְנִין: וְלֵיעַיְּילוּ בָּנָיו וְלֵילְפוּ מֵאַהֲרֹן. ד' זִימְנִין, וְכֵן כּוּלָּן: מִשּׁוּם טִרְחָא דְּאַהֲרֹן. דְּמִתְּחִילָּה דְּיָחִיד הֲוָה לָא סַגִּי דְּלָאו לִשְׂמֹאל יָתִיב, וְכִי הֲדוּר עַיְּילוּ אִיכָּא טִרְחָא לְאוֹקוּמֵיהּ וּלְאַהֲדוּרֵיהּ לְיָמִין(ד): ד' מְאָה זִימְנֵי. כָּל פִּירְקָא, מִקַּמֵּי דְּלִיגְמַר: בָּעְיוּהּ. לְר' פְּרִידָא לְמִלְּתָא דְּמִצְוָה:(ה) נְפַק בָּהּ קוֹל וַאֲמַר. לְר' פְּרִידָא: סִימָנִין. סִימָנֵי הַשְּׁמוּעוֹת זוֹ אַחַר זוֹ, וְסִימָנֵי חֲכָמִים כְּדֶרֶךְ שֶׁיֵּשׁ בַּתַּלְמוּד(ו) *וְתָשִׂים גִּירְסָא דְּסִמָּנֶיהָ בְּפִיהֶם: עֲשׂוּ מוֹעֵד לַתּוֹרָה. קִבְעוּ עִתִּים(ז) לְתַלְמִידֵיכֶם, שֶׁיֵּדְעוּ עֵת לָבֹא וְלִשְׁנוֹת: וְהַיְינוּ

תנו לו זו וזו. והא דאמר בפרק בתרא דמגילה (דף כז:) שאלו תלמידיו את ר' פרידא: במה הארכת ימים? אמר להן: מעולם לא קדמני אדם לבית המדרש, הא והא גרמא לו. אי נמי: באותה שעה לא ידע שאמר ליה הקב"ה תנו לו זו וזו, עד לאחר שחי ארבע מאות שנה:

*אם היה בית אחד יוצא כמין פגום. נראה דפגום אחד נמי רואין כאילו היה פגום אחר כנגדו, ומותחין חוט עליהן. ולא שמותחו בחוט באלכסון מן הפגום עד ראש הא' של העיר, דהא רחבה מן הצד האחד רואין אותה כאילו שוה, ועגולה כאילו היתה מרובעת השתא פריך שפיר, השתא פגום אחד כו':

רבינו חננאל

ישבו בה וגו' אם משים אדם את עצמו כחיה זו שדורסת ואוכלת ואמרי שמסרחת ואוכלת ישבו כלומר תלמודו מתקיים בידו וכיון שתלמודו מתקיים בידו הקב"ה מכין סעודתו שנא' תכין בטובתך לעני אלהים: נוצר תאנה יאכל פריה. מה תאנה כ"ז שממשמש בה מוצא בה תאנים טובות אף ד"ת כו'. כיוצא בו א"ר יוחנן אילת אהבים ויעלת חן וגו' באהבתה תשגה תמיד כגון ר' אלעזר בן פדת שהיה עוסק בתורה בשוק התחתון של צפורי וסדינו מוטל בשוק העליון כלומר היתה דעתו בתורה ושכח סדינו בשוק. תנא בא אדם ליטלו מצא בו נחש שרף: רוכבי אתונות צחורות אלו ת"ח שעוסקים בתורה ומבררין כצהרים. יושבי על מדין שיושבים ודנין דין אמת לאמתו והולכי אלו בעלי מקרא. דרך אלו בעלי משנה. שיחו שכל שיחתן ד"ת. כתיב לא יחרוך רמיה צידו כלומר אם לא יחרוך כנפי העוף רמיה צידו (כלומר אם יחרך כנפי העוף רמיה צידו) יעיפו ממנו כך גם ד"ת אם לא יחזיק בהם בטוב יעיפו מידו לא יחיה ולא יאריך ימים. כיוצא בו הון מהבל ימעט אם משים אדם תורתו חבילות חבילות ימעט ואם קובץ על יד ומחזיקם ירבה. א' רבא הא מלתא גמירי לה רבנן ועברי עלה: ת"ר כיצד סדר המשנה משה רבינו למד מפי הגבורה. בא אהרן שנה לו משה פרקו נסתלק אהרן וישב לו משמאל משה. נכנסו בני אהרן שנה להן פרקו. נסתלקו אלעזר שב לימין משה. איתמר ישב לשמאל אהרן. ר' יהודה א' אהרן לימין משה הוה חוזר *) נכנסו כל העם שנה להן פרקן נמצא ביד אהרן ארבע. מיכן א"ר אלעזר בן עזריה חייב אדם לשנות לתלמידו ד' פעמים ק"ו ומה אהרן שלמד מפי משה ומשה למד מפי הגבורה [למד] ד' פעמים הלומד מהדיוט עאכו"כ. ר"ע אומר חייב אדם לשנות לתלמידו עד שילמד שנא' ולמדה את בני ישראל ומניין שחייב לסדרה בפיו שנא' שימה בפיהם. ומניין שחייב להראות לו פנים כדי לבא בלבו שנאמר ואלה המשפטים אשר תשים לפניהם. אין תורה נקנית אלא בסימנים שנאמר שימה בפיהם. סמנה בסימנין. כיוצא בו הציבי לך ציונים עשו ציונים לתורה. ר' אלעזר אומר ומודע לבינה תקרא עשה מיודעין לתורה. רבא אמר עשה (מודיעין) [מועדין] לתורה. ר' פרידא היה מתני ת' זימני לתלמידיה כו'. תניא כשמהלכין בדרך באמצע מהלך הרב והגדול מימינו והקטן משמאלו וכן מצינו במלאכים שבאו אל אאע"ה מיכאל באמצע גבריאל מימינו ורפאל משמאלו. כתיב

*) נראה לחסר בדברי רבינו נכנסו זקנים ושנה להם משה פרקן וכו'.

[יומא כט.] [חולין נח.] [נ"ל אלעזר] [נ"ל אלעזר] [ליתא בילקוט וכן מוכרח] [עי' תוס' שבת י. ד"ה דין] ע"ז יט. ע"ש [נ"ל רבא] [שם. ע"ש] [נ"ל רבא] [נ"ל עבידתיה עי' תוס' ע"ז יט. ד"ה אנא] [נ"ל ומשים] [שייך לדף נה.] דברים לא שמות כא עיין בע"י ותמצא שם גירסות שונות בזה הענין יומא לז. מס' ד"א פ"ג [נ"ל דליספוב] [עי' שבת קד. סימנין עשה בתורה] ירמיהו לא יחזקאל לט [נ"ל אלעזר] משלי ז משלי ה שופטים ה משלי יב משלי יג

הגהות הב"ח

(א) גמ' אשר תשים לפניהם וליעיילו כולן ולילפו כולהו ממשה: (ב) רש"י ד"ה נכנס אהרן וכו' בשעת שמיעתן היו יושבין: (ג) ד"ה וליעיילו כולן. מריש"א ויעסו לכולן ארבע פעמים הס"ד ואח"כ מ"ה וליעול אהרן ולילף ממשה ד' זמנין וליעיילו בניו כנ"ל והוא ד"א: (ד) ד"ה משום טרחא וכו' לימין משה הס"ד: (ה) ד"ה בעיוה וכו' למצוה בשוקא הס"ד: (ו) ד"ה סימנין וכו' שיש בהש"ס הס"ד ואחר כך מ"ה שימה גירסא וסימניה בפיהם: (ז) ד"ה עשו וכו' עתים לתורה לתלמידיכם:

וְהַיְינוּ דְּאָמַר(א) אַבְדִּימִי בַּר חָמָא בַּר דּוֹסָא, מַאי דִּכְתִיב: °"לֹא בַשָּׁמַיִם הִיא וְלֹא מֵעֵבֶר לַיָּם הִיא", "לֹא בַשָּׁמַיִם הִיא" – שֶׁאִם בַּשָּׁמַיִם הִיא אַתָּה צָרִיךְ לַעֲלוֹת אַחֲרֶיהָ, וְאִם מֵעֵבֶר לַיָּם הִיא – אַתָּה צָרִיךְ לַעֲבוֹר אַחֲרֶיהָ. *רָבָא אָמַר: "לֹא בַשָּׁמַיִם הִיא" – אלֹא תִּמָּצֵא בְּמִי שֶׁמַּגְבִּיהַּ דַּעְתּוֹ עָלֶיהָ כַּשָּׁמַיִם, וְלֹא תִּמָּצֵא בְּמִי שֶׁמַּרְחִיב דַּעְתּוֹ עָלֶיהָ כַּיָּם. רַבִּי *יוֹחָנָן אָמַר: "לֹא בַשָּׁמַיִם הִיא" – לֹא תִּמָּצֵא בְּגַסֵּי רוּחַ, "וְלֹא מֵעֵבֶר לַיָּם הִיא" – לֹא תִּמָּצֵא לֹא בְּסַחֲרָנִים וְלֹא בְּתַגָּרִים.§ תָּנוּ רַבָּנַן: *כֵּיצַד מְעַבְּרִין אֶת הֶעָרִים? אֲרוּכָּה – כְּמוֹת שֶׁהִיא, בעֲגוּלָּה – עוֹשִׂין לָהּ זָוִיּוֹת. מְרוּבַּעַת – אֵין עוֹשִׂין לָהּ זָוִיּוֹת. גהָיְתָה רְחָבָה מִצַּד אֶחָד וּקְצָרָה מִצַּד אַחֵר – רוֹאִין אוֹתָהּ כְּאִילּוּ הִיא שָׁוָה. הָיָה בַּיִת אֶחָד יוֹצֵא כְּמִין פְּגוּם, אוֹ שְׁנֵי בָתִּים יוֹצְאִין כְּמִין שְׁנֵי פְּגוּמִין – רוֹאִין אוֹתָן כְּאִילּוּ חוּט מָתוּחַ עֲלֵיהֶן, וּמוֹדֵד מִמֶּנּוּ וּלְהַלָּן אַלְפַּיִם אַמָּה. הָיְתָה עֲשׂוּיָה כְּמִין קֶשֶׁת אוֹ כְּמִין *גַּאם – רוֹאִין אוֹתָהּ כְּאִילּוּ הִיא מְלֵאָה בָּתִּים וַחֲצֵירוֹת, וּמוֹדֵד מִמֶּנּוּ וּלְהַלָּן אַלְפַּיִם אַמָּה. אָמַר מָר: אֲרוּכָּה – כְּמוֹת שֶׁהִיא, פְּשִׁיטָא! לָא צְרִיכָא, דדַּאֲרִיכָא וְקַטִינָא, מַהוּ דְּתֵימָא: לִיתֵּן לָהּ פּוּתְיָא (ג)אַאוּרְכָּהּ, קמ"ל. "מְרוּבַּעַת – אֵין עוֹשִׂין לָהּ זָוִיּוֹת", פְּשִׁיטָא! לָא צְרִיכָא, דִּמְרַבְּעָא וְלָא מְרַבְּעָא בְּרִיבּוּעַ עוֹלָם. מַהוּ דְּתֵימָא: לִירַבְּעָא בְּרִיבּוּעַ עוֹלָם, קָא מַשְׁמַע לָן. "הָיָה בַּיִת אֶחָד יוֹצֵא כְּמִין פְּגוּם, אוֹ שְׁנֵי בָתִּים יוֹצְאִין כְּמִין שְׁנֵי פְּגוּמִין", הָשְׁתָּא בַּיִת אֶחָד אָמַרְתְּ, שְׁנֵי בָתִּים מִיבַּעְיָא?! לָא צְרִיכָא, מִשְּׁתֵּי רוּחוֹת. מַהוּ דְּתֵימָא: מֵרוּחַ אַחַת – אָמְרִינַן, מִשְּׁתֵּי רוּחוֹת – לָא אָמְרִינַן, קָא מַשְׁמַע לָן. "הָיְתָה עֲשׂוּיָה כְּמִין קֶשֶׁת אוֹ כְּמִין גַּאם – רוֹאִין אוֹתָהּ כְּאִילּוּ הִיא מְלֵאָה בָּתִּים וַחֲצֵירוֹת, וּמוֹדֵד מִמֶּנָּה וּלְהַלָּן אַלְפַּיִם אַמָּה". *אָמַר רַב הוּנָא: העִיר הָעֲשׂוּיָה כַּקֶּשֶׁת, אִם יֵשׁ בֵּין שְׁנֵי רָאשֶׁיהָ פָּחוֹת מֵאַרְבַּעַת אֲלָפִים אַמָּה – מוֹדְדִין לָהּ מִן הַיֶּתֶר, וְאִם לָאו – מוֹדְדִין לָהּ מִן הַקֶּשֶׁת. וּמִי אָמַר רַב הוּנָא הָכִי? וְהָאָמַר רַב הוּנָא: וחוֹמַת הָעִיר שֶׁנִּפְרְצָה בְּמֵאָה וְאַרְבָּעִים וְאַחַת וּשְׁלִישׁ! אָמַר רַבָּה בַּר עוּלָּא: לָא קַשְׁיָא; כָּאן – בְּרוּחַ אַחַת, כָּאן – זמִשְּׁתֵּי רוּחוֹת. וּמַאי קמ"ל – דְּנוֹתְנִין קַרְפֵּף לָזוֹ וְקַרְפֵּף לָזוֹ? הָא אֲמָרָהּ רַב הוּנָא חֲדָא זִימְנָא! דִּתְנַן: נוֹתְנִין

רש"י

וְהַיְינוּ דְּאָמַר רַב אַבְדִּימִי. הָא דַּאֲמַרַן דְּצָרִיךְ לִטְרוֹחַ וּלְהַעֲמִיד סִימָנִין וּלְהַעֲרִים בְּתַחְבּוּלוֹת כְּדֵי שֶׁתִּתְקַיֵּים הַתּוֹרָה בְּלוֹמְדֶיהָ – הַיְינוּ דְּר' אַבְדִּימִי דִּמְפָרֵשׁ דְּיוּקָא דִּקְרָא, שֶׁאִם בַּשָּׁמַיִם הִיא צָרִיךְ אַתָּה לַעֲלוֹת אַחֲרֶיהָ: סַחֲרָנִין. מְחַזְּרִין בָּעֲיָירוֹת: תַּגָּרִין.[א] בְּעִירָן בִּמְקוֹמָן, אֶלָּא נִרְאֶה וְאֵינוֹ נִרְאֶה כִּדְאָמַר לְעֵיל*[ב]: אֲרוּכָּה כְּמוֹת שֶׁהִיא. לְקַמָּן מְפָרֵשׁ: עֲגוּלָּה עוֹשִׂין לָהּ זָוִיּוֹת. כְּשֶׁבָּא לִמְדּוֹד תְּחוּמִין לְקְלוֹטֶיהָ לֹא יִמְדּוֹד לָהּ מֵהַחוֹמָה, אֶלָּא יוֹסִיף לָהּ רִיבּוּעַ. כְּלוֹמַר: יַרְחִיק מִן הַחוֹמָה כְּדֵי רִיבּוּעַ, דְּהָא מְרַבִּינַן פֵּיאוֹת לְכָל מִילֵּי דְּשַׁבָּת, וְאַחַ"כ יִמְדּוֹד תְּחוּמֵי הַקְּרָנוֹת. שֶׁאִם בָּא לָצֵאת דֶּרֶךְ קֶרֶן הָעִיר – יִשְׂתַּכֵּר בַּהֲלִיכָתוֹ רְבִיעַ, דִּמְרוּבָּע יוֹתֵר עַל הָעִגּוּל רְבִיעַ: מְרוּבַּעַת אֵין עוֹשִׂין לָהּ זָוִיּוֹת. לְקַמָּן מְפָרֵשׁ: הָיְתָה רְחָבָה מִצַּד זֶה וּקְצָרָה מִצַּד זֶה רוֹאִין אוֹתָהּ כְּאִילּוּ הִיא שָׁוָה. כְּשֶׁבָּא לִמְדּוֹד הַתְּחוּמִין לַמַּעֲרָב אֵצֶל קֶרֶן מַעֲרָבִית דְּרוֹמִית אֵינוֹ מוֹדֵד מִן הַחוֹמָה, אֶלָּא מַרְחִיק וּמוֹשֵׁךְ לַמַּעֲרָב עַד כְּנֶגֶד חוּדָּהּ שֶׁל קֶרֶן מַעֲרָבִית צְפוֹנִית הַנִּמְשֶׁכֶת וְיוֹצֵא' לַמַּעֲרָב, וּמוֹדֵד. וְכֵן לְקֶרֶן דְּרוֹמִית מִזְרָחִית: הָיָה בַּיִת אֶחָד בּוֹלֵט. מְחוֹמַת הָעִיר לְאַחַת הַצְּדָדִין, כְּשֶׁבָּא לִמְדּוֹד תְּחוּם צָפוֹן אֵצֶל קֶרֶן מַעֲרָבִית צְפוֹנִית, (ג)כְּשֶׁבָּא לְמָקוֹם שֶׁאֵין הַבַּיִת בּוֹלֵט שָׁם מַרְחִיק מִן הַחוֹמָה עַד כְּנֶגֶד מָקוֹם שֶׁכָּלָה בְּלִיטַת הַבַּיִת לְקֶרֶן מִזְרָחִית צְפוֹנִית, כְּאִילּוּ חוּט מָתוּחַ מְכוּוָּן וְהוֹלֵךְ כְּנֶגְדּוֹ מִמָּקוֹם שֶׁכָּלָה הַבַּיִת עַד כְּנֶגֶד קֶרֶן צְפוֹנִית מַעֲרָבִית, וּמוֹדֵד מִן הַחוּט וְלַצָּפוֹן אַלְפַּיִם: שְׁנֵי בָתִּים כְּמִין שְׁתֵּי פְּגוּמִין. קס"ד לְרוּחַ אַחַת, וְקָאָמַר: רוֹאִין כְּאִילּוּ חוּט מָתוּחַ מִזֶּה לָזֶה. וּלְקַמָּן פָּרֵיךְ: הָשְׁתָּא בַּיִת אֶחָד אָמַרְתְּ רוֹאִין שְׁנֵי בָתִּים מִיבַּעְיָא: הָיְתָה עֲשׂוּיָה כְּמִין קֶשֶׁת. שֶׁאֵין הַבָּתִּים בִּמְקוֹם חֲלַל הַקֶּשֶׁת: אוֹ כְּמִין גַּאם. גִּימֶל יְוָונִי, עָשׂוּי כְּמִין כַּף *כְּפוּפָה שֶׁלָּנוּ**): רוֹאִין אוֹתָהּ כְּאִילּוּ הִיא מְלֵאָה בָּתִּים. כְּשֶׁבָּא לִמְדּוֹד תְּחוּמִין מִן הַצָּפוֹן – מוֹדֵד מִן הַיֶּתֶר, כְּאִילּוּ הָיְתָה מוּקֶּפֶת בָּתִּים, וְהַדָּר בַּקֶּשֶׁת לֹא יַתְחִיל לִמְדּוֹד מִבֵּיתוֹ וְלַצָּפוֹן אַלְפַּיִם, אֶלָּא כָּל הָעִיר עַד הַיֶּתֶר חֲשׁוּבָה לוֹ כְּד' אַמּוֹת. וְכֵן הָעֲשׂוּיָה כְּמִין גַּאם הַיּוֹצֵא מִן הַמִּזְרָח לַמַּעֲרָב: אע"פ שֶׁאֵין בָּתִּים בַּמַּעֲרָב – רוֹאִין כְּאִילּוּ מָלֵא כָּל הֶחָלָל בָּתִּים, וְכֵן מִן הַדָּרוֹם לַצָּפוֹן. וְהַיּוֹצֵא מִבֵּיתוֹ אֵין חֲלַל הֶחָלָק שֶׁל עִיר עוֹלֶה לוֹ מִן הַמִּדָּה: אֲרוּכָּה כְּמוֹת שֶׁהִיא פְּשִׁיטָא. וְכִי תַּעֲלֶה עַל דַּעְתְּךָ שֶׁיְּקַצְּרֶנָּה: דַּאֲרִיכָא וְקַטִינָא. קְצָרָה בְּרָחְבָּהּ: מַהוּ דְּתֵימָא. יַרְחִיבֶנָּה לַמִּזְרָח וְלַמַּעֲרָב עַד שֶׁתְּהֵא מְרוּבַּעַת יָפֶה: קמ"ל. כְּמוֹת שֶׁהִיא מַנִּיחִין אוֹתָהּ, שֶׁהֲרֵי יֵשׁ לָהּ פֵּיאוֹת: דִּמְרַבְּעָא אֲבָל לָא מְרַבְּעָא בְּרִיבּוּעוֹ שֶׁל עוֹלָם. שֶׁיְּהֵא צְפוֹנָהּ לִצְפוֹן עוֹלָם וּדְרוֹמָהּ לִדְרוֹם עוֹלָם, אֶלָּא עוֹמֶדֶת בַּאֲלַכְסוֹן: לָא צְרִיכָא לְב' רוּחוֹת. אֶחָד לַצָּפוֹן וְא' לַדָּרוֹם: בֵּין ב' רָאשֶׁיהָ. הַיְינוּ אוֹרֶךְ מְקוֹם הַיֶּתֶר: פָּחוֹת מִד' אֲלָפִים. שֶׁתְּחוּם רֹאשָׁהּ זֶה נִבְלָע בְּתוֹךְ תְּחוּם רֹאשָׁהּ הָאַחֵר, נַעֲשֵׂית עִיר אַחַת, וּמוֹדְדִין לָהּ מִן הַיֶּתֶר וְרוֹאִין כְּאִילּוּ הִיא מְלֵיאָה בָּתִּים. וְאִם יוֹתֵר – אֵין מְקָרְבִין אוֹתָהּ לִהְיוֹת אַחַת, וּמוֹדְדִין לָהּ מִן הַקֶּשֶׁת לְכָל אֶחָד מִפֶּתַח בֵּיתוֹ, וַחֲלַל הָעִיר הֶחָלָק שֶׁאֵין בּוֹ בָּתִּים – מִן הַמִּדָּה הוּא: חוֹמַת הָעִיר שֶׁנִּפְרְצָה שִׁיעוּרָהּ בְּקמ"א וּשְׁלִישׁ. אִם רוֹחַב פִּירְצָה קמ"א אַמּוֹת וּשְׁלִישׁ, דְּהַיְינוּ שִׁיעוּר ב' קַרְפֵּיפוֹת שֶׁל שִׁבְעִים אַמָּה וְשִׁירַיִים, וְנַעֲשׂוּ כְּב' עֲיָירוֹת לִהְיוֹת אַחַת וְהַיּוֹצֵא מִזּוֹ לָזוֹ לָלֶכֶת דֶּרֶךְ זוֹ חוּצָה לָהּ – אֵין עוֹלָה לוֹ מִדַּת הָעִיר מִן הַמִּנְיָן. אַלְמָא: בְּיוֹתֵר מִקמ"א וּשְׁלִישׁ הָוְיָא הַבְדָּלָה: כָּאן בְּרוּחַ אַחַת. עִיר הָעֲשׂוּיָה כַּקֶּשֶׁת אֵינָהּ מוּבְדֶּלֶת אֶלָּא מֵרוּחַ אַחַת, הִלְכָּךְ, עַד דְּהָוֵי ד' אֲלָפִים: וְהָא. דְּחוֹמַת הָעִיר שֶׁנִּפְרְצָה בִּשְׁתֵּי רוּחוֹתֶיהָ זוֹ כְּנֶגֶד זוֹ קָאָמַר. הִלְכָּךְ, כִּשְׁתֵּי עֲיָירוֹת נִינְהוּ, וּכְגוֹן שֶׁאֵין יִשּׁוּב בַּחֲלַל הָעִיר כְּנֶגֶד *בֵּית הַפְּרָצוֹת: וּמַאי קמ"ל. אִי בְּב' רוּחוֹת, דְּוַדַּאי כְּב' עֲיָירוֹת הֵן – אַמַּאי אַשְׁמוּעִי' רַב קַרְפֵּף לָזוֹ וְקַרְפֵּף לָזוֹ? דִּשְׁתֵּי עֲיָירוֹת הַסְּמוּכוֹת זוֹ לָזוֹ נוֹתְנִין קַרְפֵּף שֶׁל שִׁבְעִים אַמָּה וְשִׁירַיִים לְכָל אַחַת לִהְיוֹת כְּעִיר אַחַת, כְּדֵי לְחַבְּרָם ע"י קַרְפֵּיפוֹת הַלָּלוּ לַעֲשׂוֹתָן כְּעִיר אַחַת, וְאע"פ שֶׁאֵין בִּנְיָן בֵּין הַקַּרְפֵּיפוֹת וְגַם הַקַּרְפֵּיפוֹת עַצְמָן אֵינָן מוּקָּפוֹת מְחִיצָּה אֶלָּא שִׁיעוּר קַרְפֵּף קָאָמַר: נוֹתְנִין

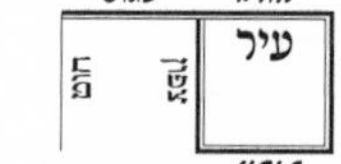

**) [ועי' רש"י פסחים ח: ורש"י זבחים נג: סא: ד"ה כמין גמא] *) [נ"ל בין]

עיר | מזרח | דרום | צפון | מערב | פגוס | קשת | פנוי חבל | כמין גאם | אלכסון | חומה | יתר | אלפיסאמה | יתרעלד' אלפים

תוספות

עיר העשויה בקשת. הא דלא נקט רב הונא מלתיה אשני פגומין – משום דהתם פגום הוי תוך שבעים אמה ושיריים מעיקר העיר, וכיון דהוי תוך עיבור העיר – אפי' יש בין פגומין יותר מד' אלפים, רואין כאילו חוט מתוח עליהם. ואפילו יש פגומין הרבה זה אחר זה, כל אחד תוך ע' אמה ושיריים של חבירו בשני ראשי העיר – שמא יש לחלק, דגבי פגומין שאינם מעיקר העיר אפילו אין שם הבלעת תחומין מעברין אותן עם העיר, לפי שבטל אגב העיר. אבל ב' ראשי הקשת שהם מעיקר העיר – אין מבטלין אגב העיר, ולכך בעי שיהא שם הבלעת תחומין. ומיהו, נראה לר"י דאין לחלק בין שני פגומין לעיר העשויה כקשת. וכן פר"ח. והא דלא נקט רב הונא מילתיה על שני פגומין – משום דברייתא לא איירי בשני פגומין מרוח אחת, אלא בפגום אחד: **פחות** מד' אלפים מודדין מן היתר. רבה בר רב הונא בעי נמי בסמוך שגם בין יתר לקשת לא יהא יותר מאלפים, משום דבעי שיהו תחומין מובלעין מכל לד. אבל לרבא בריה דרבה בר רב הונא, דאמר מודדין מן היתר ואפי' יותר מאלפים בין יתר לקשת – משום דאי בעי הדר אתי ליה דרך בתים, ולא חש שיהו מובלעין רק מלד אחד – נראה דהוא הדין נמי לדידיה אם אין בין יתר לקשת אלא אלפים, דמודדין לו מן היתר. אפי' יש יותר מד' אלפים בין שני ראשי הקשת. דהא מצי אתי דרך היתר(ד) מראש האחד לראש האחר, כיון דהיתר מובלע תוך הקשת: ואם

רבינו חננאל

כתיב לא בשמים היא לא תמצא תורה במי שמגביה דעתו עליה כשמים ולא מעבר לים היא במי שמרחיב דעתו עליה כים ר' יוחנן אמר כו'. ת"ר כיצד (מערבין) [מעברין] את הערים ארוכה כמות שהיא מהו דתימא מעביד (תותיה) [פותיא] כאורכיה (כי) [כדי] שתתרבע קמ"ל דלא. עגולה עושין לה זוויות פי' מרבעה ונותן זויות. מרובעות אין עושין לה זויות. כלומר אם אינה נתונה בריבועה בריבועו של עולם צפון העיר לצפון העולם ודרומה לדרום העולם. מהו דתימא מרבעה בריבועו של עולם קמ"ל דלא צריכינן כולי האי היתה זו העיר רחבה מצד אחד אלף אמה ומצד אחד שכנגדו חמש מאות אמה כגון שהיה הצד המזרחי אלף אמה רחבו והמערבי ת"ק אמה רחבו נותנין גם לצד מערבי כרחבו מחוץ ת"ק אמה אחרים להשוות הצדדין כדי למדוד אלפים אמה מחוץ אלף אמה מכל צד היה בית אחד יוצא מן העיר כמין פגים או ב' בתים כמין ב' פגימין יוצאין אחד למזרח ואחד לצפון רואין כאילו חוט מתוח עליהן ומוציאין גבול העיר למזרח וגבול העיר לצפון כנגד החוט המתוח מזה ומזה ומודד מן החוט ולהלן אלפים אמה. היתה העיר עשויה כמין קשת או כמין (טם) [גאם] רואין אותה העיר כאילו היא מלאה בתים וחצרות וכאילו הן מרובעות הקשת כמין טבלא מרובעת וכן הגם ומודד מהן ולהלן אלפים אמה. אמר רב הונא עיר העשויה בקשת

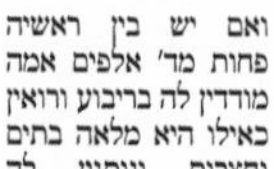

כמין גם ואלו הבתים | קשת | יתר

ואם יש בין ראשיה פחות מד' אלפים אמה מודדין לה בריבוע ורואין כאילו היא מלאה בתים וחצרות ונותנין לה אלפים אמה תחום מן היתר ולחוץ ואם לאו מודדין מן הקשת. פי' כגון מקום העיר שעשוי כקשת מזרחו והיתר הוא מערבי וב' ראשי הקשת חשובות כמין ב' פיגמין אחד בולט לצפון ואחד בולט לדרום וצריכין למתוח חוט משוה עולה עד נגד מקום החץ. (ואין) [אם] היתר פחות מארבעת אלפים אמה. נמצא המתוח מן הצפון לדרום ע"ג הקשת פחות מד' אלפים כמדת היתר והדרין במקום החץ מהלכין כלפי הדרום פחות מאלפים אמה וכן לצפון אבל אם הם ד' אלפים אמה יצאו מתורת פגימה שלם וכן בשני ראשיה כיון שיש בין ביניהם ב' תחומין נסתלקה מהן תורת פגום ואין מודדין אלא מן היתר (וכעשבי) [וכיושבי] שדות הן חשובין שמודדין להם מפתח בתיהן. ואקשינן ומי אמר רב הונא הכי כי אין נפרדין אלו מאלו עד שיהיה ביניהן מקום חרב בלי ישוב ד' אלפים אמה והא איהו הוא דאמר חומת העיר שנפרצה במאה וארבעים ואחת אמה ושליש עדיין דינה כדין עיר אחת שאפי' ב' עיירות הן כשתתן קרפף לזו שהן כל קרפף ע' אמה ושיריים והקרפפיות מערבות אותן וכאחת הן חשובות יתר מיכן לא. ופרקינן זו חומת העיר שנפרצה פרצתה מב' רוחות זו כנגד זו שנחלקו לשתים. לפיכך אמר רב הונא אם פרצה כנגד קרפף לזו וקרפף לזו ועדיין בחזקתן עומדות אם יתר מיכן נחלקו אבל בעיר העשויה כקשת שאינה חריבה אלא מרוח אחת בלבד והקשת עומד בישובו אי הוו אלפים אמה אין לא לא. ואקשינן ומאי אתא רב הונא לאשמועינן בחומת העיר שנפרצה כי אם יש בפרצותיה [מאה וארבעים ואחת] אמה ושליש שהן כדי (שני) [שהן] קרפיפות עשאן הקרפיף להיותן אחת אלא *) משום דקודם עיר [אחת] היתה ולכן מתירין אותה עכשיו בזה השיעור אבל ב' עיירות שלא היתה בהן היתר אין מתירין אותן בב' קרפיפות ואי אשמעינן בב' עיירות שנותנין קרפיף לזו וקרפיף לזו משום דרחיקא תשמישתיהו אבל

עין משפט נר מצוה

ט א מיי' פ"ג מהל' ת"ת הלכה ח:
י ב מיי' פכ"ח מהל' שבת הלכה ו סמג לאוין סו טוש"ע א"ח סי' שלח סעיף ב:
יא ג מיי' שם הל' ח טוש"ע שם ס"ד:
יב ד מיי' שם הלכה ו טוש"ע שם ס"א:
יג ה מיי' שם הל' ח טוש"ע שם ס"ד:
יד ו ז מיי' שם הל' ה טוש"ע שם סעיף ז בהג"ה וברא"ש סי' ד:

מסורת הש"ס

[דף נג.]
[גיר' השאלתות פ' תולדות סי' יט ר' יוחנן]
[גיר' השאלתות שם רבא]
[תוספתא פ"ד ע"ש]
[בערוך ערך גם פי' כמין ד' הפוך]
[לקמן נז:]
נ"ל הפוכה ר"ל כף פשוטה או פתוחה ך שהיא הפוכה L עי' ב"מ כח.

גליון הש"ס

גמ' לא תמצא במי שמגביה דעתו. עיין תענית דף ז ע"א תוס' ד"ה אף דברי תורה:

הגהות הב"ח

(א) גמ' והיינו דאמר רבי אבדימי: (ב) שם ליתן לה פותיא כאורכה: (ג) רש"י ד"ה היה בית אחד בולט כו' מערבית צפונית (כשבא למקום) תא"מ ונ"ב ס"א אין זה: (ד) תוס' ד"ה פחות וכו' דהא מצי אתי דרך היתר: כזה:

הגהות מהר"ב רנשבורג [א] רש"י ד"ה תגרין. בעירן במקומן. ר"ל שלא תמצא התורה לא בסחרנים ולא בתגרים אלא במי שמשים עצמו נראה ואינו נראה: [ב] בא"ד כדאמר לעיל. דף נד. ויעוש"ה ברש"י ד"ה נראה ואינו נראה ודו"ק:

*נותנין קרפף לעיר, דברי רבי מאיר. וחכמים אומרים: לא אמרו קרפף אלא בין שתי עיירות. ואיתמר, רב הונא אמר: קרפף לזו וקרפף לזו. וחייא בר רב אמר: אין נותנין אלא קרפף אחד לשניהם. צריכא, דאי אשמעינן הכא – משום דהוה ליה צד היתר מעיקרא, אבל התם – אימא לא. ואי אשמעינן התם – משום דדחיקא תשמישתייהו, אבל הכא דלא דחיקא תשמישתייהו – אימא לא, צריכא. וכמה הוי בין יתר לקשת? רבה בר רב הונא אמר: אלפים אמה. רבא בריה דרבה בר רב הונא אמר: אאפילו יתר מאלפים אמה. אמר אביי: *כוותיה דרבא בריה דרבה בר רב הונא מסתברא, דאי בעי – הדר אתי דרך בתים.§ "היו שם גדודיות גבוהות עשרה טפחים כו'".§ מאי גדודיות? אמר רב יהודה: בשלש מחיצות שאין עליהן תקרה. איבעיא להו: שתי מחיצות ויש עליהן תקרה מהו? ת"ש: *גאלו שמתעברין עמה: נפש שיש בה ארבע אמות על ארבע אמות, והגשר והקבר שיש בהן בית דירה, ובית הכנסת שיש בה בית דירה לחזן, ובית עבודה זרה שיש בה בית דירה לכומרים, והאורוות והאוצרות שבשדות ויש בהן בית דירה, והבורגנין שבתוכה, והבית שבים – הרי אלו מתעברין עמה. ואלו שאין מתעברין עמה: נפש שנפרצה משתי רוחותיה אילך ואילך, והגשר והקבר שאין להן בית דירה, ובית הכנסת שאין לה בית דירה לחזן, ובית עבודה זרה שאין לה בית דירה לכומרים, והאורוות והאוצרות שבשדות שאין להן בית דירה, ובור ושיח ומערה וגדר ושובך שבתוכה, והבית שבספינה – אין אלו מתעברין עמה. קתני מיהת: נפש שנפרצה משתי רוחותיה אילך ואילך. מאי לאו – דאיכא תקרה? לא, דדליכא תקרה. בית שבים למאי חזי? אמר רב פפא: בית שעשוי לפנות בו כלים שבספינה. ומערה אין מתעברת עמה? והתני רבי חייא: מערה מתעברת עמה! אמר אביי: הכשיש בנין על פיה. ותיפוק ליה משום בנין גופיה! לא צריכא, להשלים. אמר רב הונא: ויושבי צריפין אין מודדין להן אלא מפתח בתיהן. מתיב רב חסדא: °"ויחנו על הירדן מבית הישימות" (במדבר לג), *ואמר רבה בר בר חנה, (אמר רבי יוחנן): לדידי חזי לי ההוא אתרא, והוי תלתא פרסי *על תלתא פרסי. ותניא: כשהן נפנין – אין נפנין לא לפניהם ולא לצדיהן, אלא לאחריהן. אמר ליה רבא: דגלי מדבר קאמרת? כיון דכתיב בהו: °"על פי ה' יחנו ועל פי ה' יסעו" (שם ט) – כמאן דקביע להו דמי. אמר רב חיננא בר רב כהנא, אמר רב אשי: זאם יש שם שלש חצירות של שני בתים – הוקבעו. אמר רב יהודה, אמר רב: יושבי צריפין והולכי מדברות – *חייהן אינן חיים, ונשיהן ובניהן אינן שלהן. תניא נמי הכי, אליעזר איש בירייא אומר: יושבי צריפין כיושבי קברים, *ועל בנותיהם הוא אומר: °"ארור שוכב עם כל בהמה" (דברים כז). מאי טעמא? עולא אמר: שאין להן מרחצאות. ורבי יוחנן אמר: מפני שמרגישין זה לזה בטבילה. מאי בינייהו? איכא בינייהו נהרא דסמיך לביתא. אמר רב הונא: כל עיר שאין בה ירק – אין תלמיד חכם רשאי לדור בה. למימרא דירק מעליא? והתניא: *שלשה *מרבין את הזבל, וכופפין את הקומה, ונוטלין אחד מחמש מאות ממאור עיניו של אדם, ואלו הן:

פת

רש"י

נותנין קרפף לעיר. כשבא למדוד התחומין, מניח לעיר אויר של שבעים אמה ושיריים שהוא כעיר, לבד התחום: אלא לב' עיירות. לחברן על ידי קרפף שביניהן: ואיתמר רב הונא אמר כו'. ולקמן מפרש בפירקא פלוגתייהו: אי אשמעינן. בחומת העיר שנפרצה, התם קאמר רב הונא קרפף לזו ולזו לחברן – משום דהוה להו צד היתר מעיקרא, שהיו כבר עיר אחת: דדחיקא תשמישתייהו. ב' עיירות ממש דחיקא תשמישתייהו בחד קרפף, הלכך, קרפף מיחשב לכל חד כעיר גופה, וכיון דצריך לה והוי כעיר, כי מחברי ב' הקרפיפות – כאילו העיירות מחוברות דמו: אבל הכא. דעיר אחת היא, ומעיקרא כי מחברי קודם שנפרצה הויא כולה מלאה, והוי סגיא לה בלאו האי אויר – השתא נמי לא ניתיב האי אוירא לתשמישן, קמ"ל: וכמה. יהא אויר החלק מן היתר לקשת דאמרו מודדין לה מן היתר כי ליכא ארבעת אלפים בין ב' ראשיה: אלפים. אבל יותר מאלפים, כיון דמכי נפק מביתו הולך לו תחום שלם מקמי דלימטי ליתר – לא משחינן ליה מן היתר: דאי בעי הדר אתי. למקום היתר דרך הבתים סביב הקשת יכול להלך עד שמגיע לאחד מן הראשין, ומשם יכול להלך לראשו האחר, שהרי תחומיהן נבלעין זה בזה. וכיון דביתר יכול להלך למקום היתר – תו לא חסר ליה אורך החלק לשווי' כשתי עיירות, ורואין אותה כאילו היא מלאה בתים וחצירות: שאין עליהן תקרה. וכל שכן אם מקורות הן מזו לזו בגג דהוו להו דירה מעלייתא: נפש. בנין על הקבר. וסתמא לדירת שומר הקבר עביד, הלכך, אע"ג דלא דייר ביה בית דירה הוא: והקבר. בית הקברות: ובית הכנסת. סתם ביהכ"נ לאו לדירה עביד, הלכך, אי לית ביה דירה לחזן הכנסת – לאו דירה היא: ובית עבודה זרה. נמי לאו לדירה עביד: והאורוות. אורוות סוסים: אוצרות. לתבואה ולשמן וליין לאו לדירה נינהו: והבורגנין שבתוכה. בתוך השדה: והבית שבים. באיי הים, בתוך ע' אמה ושיריים לעיר: בור ושיח. בבבא קמא (דף נ:) מפרש מאי בור ומאי שיח: שבתוכה. שבשדה: בית שבספינה. לא קביע ליה דוכתא, פעמים שהוא בתוך שבעים לעיר, ופעמים שאינו: ותיפוק ליה משום בנין. אם יש בנין על פיה מאי אהניא מערה? בלאו מערה נמי מבנין משחינן: להשלים. אם אין הבנין ראוי לדירה, כגון שאין בו ד' על ד' – מהניא ליה מערה לאשלומי: צריפין. דירה של הוצין וערבה, ואינו קבע. הלכך, אפילו יש הרבה במקום אחד כשיעור – מהלך מאה אמה, אין חשובין עיר להיות כארבע אמות, וכל אחד ואחד מודד מפתח ביתו אלפים לכל רוח, אם בא לצאת: ויחנו על הירדן. במחנה ישראל כתיב: אין נפנין לא לפניהן. חוץ לענן, שמא ילך הענן והארון שם: ולא לצידיהן. חוץ לענן, שאין יודעין אנה יפנה הענן לעבור: אלא לאחוריהן. חוץ לענן, דודאי לא יחזור הענן לאחוריו. אלמא: המהלך בראש והולך לנקביו חוזר לאחוריו שלש פרסאות, וישראל במדבר יושבי אהלים היו, שאינן קבועין, ואפילו הכי מהלכין את כל המחנה כארבע אמות: כיון דכתיב על פי ה' יחנו. חשובה היא חנייתן להיות נידונת קבע: ג' חצירות של ב' בתים. קבועין, של אבן או של עץ, בהכי חשיבי עיר וקובעת את כולן. וכדתנן לקמן (דף נט.): ר' שמעון אומר: שלש חצירות של ב' ב' בתים: ומהלכי מדברות. ונשותיהן עמהן: ויושבי צריפין. נמי אנשי מקנה הן, וחונין בו חדש או חדשים עד שכלה המרעה לבהמות, ונוסעין משם ונקבעין במקום אחר: אינן שלהן. לקמן מפרש טעמא: כיושבי קברות. כמתים, לפי שמחוסרין הנאה הן, ולוקין ברוחות בזרם ובמטר: מ"ט. חשודין בנותיהן: שאין להן מרחצאות. והולכין במקום רחוק לרחוץ, ונשותיהן נזקקות למנאפין, לפי שהעיר עזובה מאין איש: בטבילה. שאין להן מקוואות, והולכות הנשים לטבול במקום רחוק, וקוראה לחברתה ומרגישין השכנים. ויש רשע רודף אחריהן. ומתייחד עמהן ותנן (קידושין דף פ:): לא יתייחד אדם עם שתי נשים: נהרא. ראוי לטבילה ולא למרחץ, הרגש טבילה ליכא, דהא סמוך לה. אבל טעמא דמשום מרחצאות – איכא: אין תלמיד חכם כו'. לפי שהירק טוב למאכל, ונלקח בזול, ויכול לעסוק בתורה: וכופפין גרסינן:

פת

תוספות

*ואם לאו מודדין לה מן הקשת. לא מן הקשת ממש, אלא ממקום שמתקצר בפנים ואין שם ד' אלפים, דלא גרע מאילו ניטל אותו של מעלה. ור"ח פירש: עיר העשויה כקשת – שאין מתקצר והולך:

נפש שיש בו ד' אמות. גבי נפש הזכיר ד' אמות, ולא דירה – משום דסתמיה עשוי לדירה, כדפ"ה. וגבי גשר וקבר הזכיר דירה. ומה שלא הזכיר ד' אמות – לאו משום דסתמייהו ד' אמות, דהא קבר סתמא לא הוי ד' אמות. אלא כיון שהזכיר בית דירה – כאילו הזכיר ד' אמות, דפחות מד' אמות לא הוי דירה:

לא צריכא להשלים. פי' בקונטרס: שהבנין לא הוי ד' אמות על ד' אמות, והמערה משלימה לד' אמות. ונראה לר"י: דצריך שיהא בנין רוב ד' אמות. ועוד יש לפרש: להשלים – דיש בבנין ד' אמות, וקאמר שמשלימה למערה לצרפה לבנין, ואין מתחילין למדוד אלא מסוף המערה:

כל עיר שאין בה ירק. פי': לפי שניקח בזול, ויכול לעסוק בתורה. והא דאמר בפ' "תולין" (שבת דף קמ:) בר בי רב לא ליכול ירקא משום דגריר – משמע שגורם לו להוציא הרבה באכילת לחם – התם מיירי בירק חי, אבל מבושל טוב ומשביע בדבר קל:

כאן

עין משפט נר מצוה

[שייך לעמוד הקודם]

טו א מיי' פכ"ח מהל' שבת הלכה ח טוש"ע א"ח סי' שנ"ח סעיף ד בהג"ה:

טז ב ג ד ה מיי' שם הלכה ז טוש"ע שם סעיף ו:

יז ו ז מיי' שם הל' י טוש"ע שם סעיף י:

מסורת הש"ס

לקמן נז. | [לקמן נז:] | [תוספ' פ"ד] | [יומא עה: ע"ש ושם ליתא אמר רבי יוחנן] | ד"א זוטא פ"י | [פסחים מט:] | [נ"ל שלשה דברים מרבין כו'] | [ביומא ליתא על תלתא פרסי ועי' מהרש"א בח"א מיהו בסוטה לד. וכמה גובהן וכו' משמע כלאיתא הכא וכ"א ברש"י ברכות נד: ד"ה מחנה ישראל וכו' ואמר רבה בב"ח לדידי חזי לי ההוא דוכתא והוי תלתא פרסי אורכא ותלתא פרסי פותיא] | פסחים מב.

רבינו חננאל

אבל בחומת העיר דלא דחיקא תשמישתיה אימא אפי' יתר מיכן מותר קמ"ל: כמה יהא בין יתר לקשת ומודדין לה מן היתר ונחלקו בזה השיעור ואסקה אביי כמ"ד אפי' יתר מאלפים. (ואי מסברת כוותיה) [דמסתברא כוותיה] דאי בעי מקיף ואתי דרך בתים שסביבות הקשת עד שמגיע אל ראש היתר ומהלך עם היתר כיון שהוא פחות מד' אלפים אמה עד שמגיע לראשו האחרת לפיכך אפי' יש בין יתר לקשת יותר מאלפים אמה לא חיישינן אלא מותר ורואין אמצע הקשת וחוצה לה בריבוע כאילו מלא כולו בתים וחצרות ומודדין [התחום] משם (אלפים אמה) ולהלן אלפים אמה (התחום): היו שם (ב') גדודיות י"ט מאי גדודיות אמר רב יהודה ג' מחיצות אע"פ שאין (לו שם ולהלן אלפים אמה) עליהן תקרה: איבעיא להו ב' מחיצות יש עליהן תקרה מאי [ולא] איפשיטא (א"ל) [אלו] שמתעברין עם העיר נפש. פי' קיקביל מקאבר שיש בה ד' אמות על ד' אמות והגשר והקבר שיש בהן בית דירה ובית הכנסת שיש בה בית דירה (לחול) [לחזן] בית ע"ז שיש בה [בית דירה] לכומרים ואורוות ואוצרות שיש בהן בית דירה והבורגנין שבתוכה והבית שבים ואלו (שלו אין) [שאין] מתעברות עמה. [נפש שנפרצה וכו']: בית שבים חזי לפנות לתוכו כלי ספינה ומערה שיש בנין על פיה מתעברת עם העיר. אמר רב הונא יושבי צריפין שהן כהולכי מדברות [מודדין להם] מפתח אהליהם (להם) והכתיב ויחנו על הירדן מבית הישימות עד אבל השטים. ואמר רב הונא ג' פרסי מקום מחנה ישראל ותנא אין מפנין לצידיהן ולא לפניהן אלא לאחוריהן. ופריק רבה (ב') [שאני] דגלי מדבר כיון דכתיב ע"פ ה' יחנו ע"פ ה' יסעו. כמאן דקביעי דמו ומן הבתים החיצונים מודדין להם. ואם יש שם בתוך יושבי צריפין ג' חצרות של ב' בתים הוקבעו ומן החיצון מודדין להם. אמר רב הונא יושבי צריפין והולכי מדבריות חייהן אינם חיים כו'.
אמר

יח א מיי' פכ"ח מה' שבת הלכה ז טוש"ע סי' שלח סעיף ג:
יט ב מיי' פי"ג ופי"ב מהל' קה"ח:
כ ג מיי' פ"ט שם הל' ד סמג עשין מו טור א"ח סי' תכח:
כא ד מיי' שם הל' ב טור א"ח שם:

תורה אור

פת קיבר, ושכר חדש, וירק! לא קשיא; הא — בתומי וכרתי, הא — בשאר ירקי. כדתניא: שום — ירק, כרישין — חצי ירק, נראה צנון — נראה סם חיים. והא תניא: נראה צנון — נראה סם המות! לא קשיא; כאן — בעלין, כאן — באמהות; כאן — בימות החמה, כאן — בימות הגשמים. אמר רב יהודה, אמר רב: כל עיר שיש בה מעלות ומורדות — אדם ובהמה שבה מתים בחצי ימיהן. מתים ס"ד? אלא אימא: מזקינים בחצי ימיהן. אמר רב הונא בריה דרב יהושע: הני *מולייתא *דבי בירי ודבי נרש אזקנון. תנו רבנן: *[א]בא לרבעה — מרבעה בריבוע עולם, נותן צפונה לצפון עולם ודרומה לדרום עולם. וסימניך: *עגלה בצפון ועקרב בדרום. רבי יוסי אומר: אם אינו יודע לרבעה בריבוע של עולם — מרבעה כמין התקופה. כיצד? [ב]חמה יוצאה ביום ארוך ושוקעת ביום ארוך — זה הוא פני צפון, חמה יוצאה ביום קצר ושוקעת ביום קצר — זה הוא פני דרום. תקופת ניסן ותקופת תשרי — חמה יוצאה בחצי מזרח ושוקעת בחצי מערב, שנאמר: °"הולך אל דרום וסובב אל צפון". *"הולך אל דרום" — ביום, "וסובב אל צפון" — בלילה. "סובב סובב הולך הרוח" — אלו פני מזרח ופני מערב, פעמים מהלכתן ופעמים מסבבתן. אמר רב משרשיא: ליתנהו להני כללי. דתניא: לא יצאה חמה מעולם מקרן מזרחית צפונית ושקעה בקרן מערבית צפונית, ולא יצאה חמה מקרן מזרחית דרומית ושקעה בקרן מערבית דרומית. אמר שמואל: [ג]אין תקופת ניסן נופלת אלא בארבעה רבעי היום, או בתחלת היום, או בתחלת הלילה, או בחצי היום, או בחצי הלילה. ואין תקופת תמוז נופלת אלא או באחת ומחצה, או בשבע ומחצה, בין ביום ובין בלילה. ואין תקופת תשרי נופלת אלא או בשלש שעות, או בתשע שעות, בין ביום ובין בלילה. ואין תקופת טבת נופלת אלא או בארבע ומחצה, או בעשר ומחצה, בין ביום ובין בלילה. [ד]ואין בין תקופה לתקופה אלא תשעים ואחד יום ושבע שעות ומחצה. ואין תקופה מושכת מחברתה אלא חצי שעה. ואמר שמואל: אין לך תקופת ניסן שנופלת בצדק שאינה משברת את האילנות, ואין לך תקופת טבת שנופלת בצדק שאינה מייבשת את הזרעים, והוא דאיתליד לבנה או בלבנה או בצדק.§ תנו

קהלת א

פת קיבר. שנודר' בלע"ז: תומי וכרתי. לא מעלו, כך שמעתי. ונראה בעיני: תומי וכרתי מעלי, והכי תניא (ב"ק דף פב.): חמשה דברים נאמרו בשום: משביע, משחין, ומצהיל הפנים, ומרבה את הזרע, והורג כינה שבמעים. וכרישין נמי תניא בברכות (דף מד:) דיפין לבני מעים: שום ירק. אני שמעתי לגנאי, ואני אומר: לשבח: עלין. — קשין. אמהות — יפין. אמהות שרשין: בימות החמה. יפין, שמלגנין את הגוף. בימות הגשמים קשין: מזקינין. מפני הטורח: בי בירי ובי נרש. ב' עיירות, ויש בין זו לזו מעלות ומורדות, והן מולייתא: אזקנון. הזקינוני: בריבוע של עולם. כדמפרש ואזיל: נותן צפונה לצפון עולם ודרומה לדרום עולם. ולא במלכסונו של עולם: וסימניך. אם אינך יודע לכוין צפון ודרום: עגלה בצפון ועקרב בדרום. מזלות הן: אם אינו יודע לרבעה בריבוע של עולם. שאינו מכיר במזלות הללו: מרבעה כמין התקופה. לפי הילוך סיבוב החמה ניכר איזו רוח דרומית ואיזו רוח צפונית: חמה יוצאה ביום ארוך. אותו רוח שאתה רואה שחמה יוצאה ביום ארוך של ימי תקופת תמוז[א] יוצאה בצידו האחד ושוקעת באותו רוח עצמו בצידו האחר: זהו פני צפון. לפי שהחמה לעולם ביום ממזרח לדרום מהלכת, כדאמר קרא (קהלת א): "הולך אל דרום", והליכת החמה ביום היא, אבל בלילה אינו הולך, אלא סובב מחוץ לכיפה. וביום הארוך עומדת בקרן מזרחית צפונית, ומהלכת מזרח דרום ומערב, ושוקעת בקרן צפונית מערבית, ובלילה סובבת פני צפון, ולמחרת היום נקצר מעט ואינה יוצאה בקרן אלא נמשכת מן הקרן ולמזרח מעט, ויוצאה. ובערב שוקעת בתוך המערב, משוך מן הקרן מעט. ובלילה סובבת אותו מעט וכל הצפון, ומעט במזרח יותר מליל של אמש. וכן בכל יום, עד שיוצאה בתקופת תשרי באמצע המזרח ושוקעת באמצע המערב, לפיכך היום והלילה שוין. ועדיין בכל יום נמשכת לצד דרום ויוצאה, ובשקיעתה נמשכת לצד דרום ושוקעת עד שיוצאה ביום בתקופת טבת בקרן מזרחית דרומית, ומהלכת דרום לבדו ושוקעת בקרן מערבית דרומית, והיינו דקאמר: חמה יוצאה ביום קצר ושוקעת ביום קצר — זהו פני דרום: פני מזרח ומערב פעמים מהלכתן. ביום, בימים הארוכין: פעמים מסבבתן בלילה בימי תקופת טבת: ליתנהו להני כללי. דאמרן לעיל חמה יוצאה ביום ארוך כו' או בתחלת היום או בתחלת הלילה כו'. לפי שהמאורות נתלו בתחילת ליל רביעי בשבת ובחדש ניסן. וימות החמה שס"ה ימים ושש שעות, חשוב אותן כולם בשביעית — וישאר בידך יום ורביע. נמצאת תקופת ניסן בשנה הבאה בחצי ליל חמישי, לשנה השלישית בתחלת יום ו' ובשנה הרביעית בחצי יום שבת, וכן לעולם יום ורביע בין תקופת שנה לתקופת שנה הבאה, ולעולם הן כלות בא' מן הרביעיות הללו: ואין תקופת תמוז נופלת אלא באחת ומחצה או בשבע ומחצה או ביום או בלילה. שכשתקופת ניסן נופלת בתחילת היום אותה של תמוז בשבעה ומחצה ביום. וכשתקופת ניסן בחצי היום — של תמוז בא' ומחצה בלילה, לפי שז' שעות ומחצה יש בין תקופה לתקופה, שבאותו יום שזו נופלת, אלא נמשכת להלן משעה שנפלה זו ז' שעות ומחצה, שהן ל' שעות לד' התקופות, דהיינו יום ורביע. ולפי זה החשבון אותה של תשרי נופלת או בג' או בט' אם נפלה תקופת תמוז בא' ומחצה — של תשרי נופלת בט' ואם של תמוז בז' ומחצה — של תשרי בג', וכן כולם. וזהו סימן אזג"י ואט"ד, כשתקופת ניסן בא' של תמוז בז' ומחצה, ושל תשרי בג' ושל טבת בי' ומחצה. ושנה שניה של ניסן בחצי היום, דהיינו בו' שעות ושל תמוז בא' ומחצה, ושל תשרי בט' ושל טבת בד' ומחצה ביום: ואין בין תקופה לתקופה כו'. כדפרישית. חשוב צ"א יום כולן שביעיות תמימות הן, וז' שעות ומחצה היא נמשכת אחריהן, שימי התקופות כך הם צ"א יום וז' שעות ומחצה הם, שהן רביע של שס"ה ורביע: ואין תקופה מושכת מחברתה אלא חצי שעה.[ב] סימן לחניו אז"ח גי"ח וא"ח טד"ח, שמוש השעות כל"ש צמח"ן הוא סידורן והילוכן. תחלת ליל א' בשבת משמש כוכב ואחריו לבנה ואחריו שבתי, צדק, מאדים, חמה, נוגה. הרי ז' שעות. וחוזרים חלילה, נמצא שעה ראשונה ליום א' בשבת — חמה, ואחריו נוגה ועוד כל"ש צמח"ן. תמצא סימני שעות ראשונות של ימות השבוע חל"מ ככנ"ש, ימים וסימני שעות ראשונות של כל לילי השבוע כככ"ש חל"מ. ור' שבתי דטל"ו הרופא ז"ל פירשו היטב בספר חכמוני שלו למה נסדרו הכוכבים בענין זה, וכיון דאין בין תקופה לתקופה אלא ז' שעות ומחצה, נמצא שאם נפלה תקופת ניסן בתחלת כוכב, תקופת תמוז יפול בחצי כוכב, תשרי בראש לבנה, טבת בחצי לבנה. וכן כולם, כשתוליא ז' שעות ומחצה אחר נפילתה של זו, תגיע לאותה שעה עצמה, אלא שנמשכת חצי שעה לאחריה: והני מילי דאיתליד. מולד לבנה של ניסן או של טבת בשעת לבנה, או בשעת צדק: המרבע

כאן בעלין כאן באמהות כאן בימות החמה כאן בימות הגשמים. פ"ה: דעלין קשין, ואמהות יפין. אמהות שרשין, בימות החמה יפין שמלגנין הגוף, בימות הגשמים קשין. משמע לפירושו דעלין לעולם קשין, ואפי' אמהות אינן יפין אלא בימות החמה. ותימה: דבפרק קמא דע"ז (דף יא.) אמר גבי אנטונינוס ורבי שלא פסקו מעל שלחנם לא צנון ולא חזרת לא בימות החמה ולא בימות הגשמים! ונראה לפרש: דכאן בימות החמה וכאן בימות הגשמים — כלומר, עלין ואמהות חד מעלי בימות החמה, וחד מעלי בימות הגשמים. ואית ספרים דגרסי: ואיבעית אימא הא והא בעלין אבל(ג) באמהות לעולם מעלו:

ואין בין תקופה לתקופה אלא צ"א יום ושבע שעות ומחצה. וקשה לר"י: דאם יש לעולם בין ביום קצר ובין ביום ארוך י"ב שעות ביום וי"ב שעות בלילה, אם כן אין התקופות שוות, ולעולם האחת ארוכה מהאחרת. שאם תפול תקופת ניסן בתחלת ליל ד' — תפול תקופת תמוז בז' שעות ומחצה בלילה ותקופת תשרי בג' שעות ביום, הרי במקום ז' שעות ומחצה הקטנות שבליל תמוז שלא נפלה תקופת תמוז בתחלת לילה אנו משלימין לה(ד) צ"א יום וז' שעות ומחצה בלילי תשרי שהן בינוניות, וגם בז' ומחצה שבסוף תקופת ניסן העודפות על צ"א היו קצרות ובתקופת תמוז היו בינוניות, ואם נאמר שהשעות לעולם שוות וביום ארוך ובלילה ארוך י"ח שעות ובלילה קצר ו' או להפך — לא משכחת הא דאמרת אין תקופת ניסן נופלת אלא כו' אין תקופת תמוז נופלת אלא כו' [וכן שארי התקופות כולן]. וגם לא משכחת הא דאמרינן בפרק "מפנין" בסופו (שבת דף קכט:) דתלתא בשבתא ומעלי שבתא קאי מאדים *בזוגי, ובשאר יומי לא קאי. ולפי זה משכחת לה נמי דבשאר יומי קאי, ובהאי לא קאי: פלגא

[ע' תוס' חולין קכז. ד"ה הגין]

פסחים לד.

ב"ב כה:

[גירסת הערוך מליאתא ופירוש רכסים גבוהים] [תוספ' פ"ד]

[* לפנינו הגירסא זווי והיא היא עיין בערוך ערך זוו א']

הגהות הב"ח

(א) רש"י ד"ה חמה וכו' תקופת תמוז בצידו כצ"ל ותיבת יוצאה נמחק: (ב) ד"ה ואין תקופה מושכת מחברתה אלא חצי שעה (סימן וכו' טד"ח) תא"מ ונ"ב נ"ל הגה"ה: (ג) תוס' ד"ה כאן וכו' אבל אמהות כצ"ל ואות ב' נמחק: (ד) ד"ה ואין בין וכו' אנו משלימין לה כצ"א יום וכו' וגם ז' ומחצה שבסוף תקופת תשרי העודפות על צ"א יהיו קצרות ובתקופת טבת יהיו בינוניות נ"ב ר"ל כשתקופת תשרי נופלת בשלש שעות ביום תפול תקופת טבת בעשר ומחצה ביום ואז היום קצר ומשלימין אותם הז' שעות ומחצה בימים בינונים:

רבינו חננאל

אמר רב הונא בריה דרב יהושע (אתא דנרש ודבי בארי) [הני מוליאתא דנרש ודבי בארי] פי' מיליאתה דביקים גבוהי' אזקנון: ת"ר הבא לרבעה מרבעה בריבוע העולם. נותן צפונה לצפון העולם והרוצה לכוון צפון העולם יראה מקום העגלה בשמים והוא צפון העולם וכנגדה עקרב בדרום והמכין (וארבע) [ומרבע] העיר המקום שהוא תחת העגלה הוא הצפון ושתחת עקרב הוא הדרום. וכשנותן ימינו לדרום ושמאלו לצפון לפניו מזרח ואחריו מערב. בא ר' יוסי ואמר הין כן הוא כי עגלה בצפון ועקרב בדרום מיהו לאו כל אדם יכול לכוון כיון זה בקביעות הכוכבים. אלא נוח לו לרבעה בסביבות התקופה כיצד מקום שהחמה זורחת בו בתקופת תמוז והוא חלון פעמון והולך וסובב לאחוריו ומהלך כל היום המזרח והדרום ועולה ושוקעת כנגדו במערב זהו פני צפון ומקום שהחמה זורחת בו בתקופת טבת מחלון בילגה והולך ויורד מערב זה פני דרום. תקופת ניסן ותקופת תשרי חמה יוצאה באמצע מזרח ושוקעת באמצע בתקופת ניסן וזורחת מחלון תעלומה והולך וסובב בקרן צפונית חלון אחר חלון עד שמגיע לחלון בילגה תשרי סובב בקרן דרומית כמימי אקיאנוס בין קצות השמים לקצת הארץ כו' לפיכך היום והלילה שוין נמצאת שחמה עולה וזורחת מתקופת ניסן עד תקופת תמוז מאמצע הרקיע ולצפון מהלכת רחת כנגד הנשאר מן המזרח כולו ובמערב עד שמגיע כנגד המקום שזרחה ממנו ושוקעת בו וכן בכל יום ויום עד תקופת תמוז. בתקופת תמוז זורחת בקרן מזרחית צפונית ומהלכת ביום מזרחו וקעת בקרן מערבית צפונית עד טבת. ומתקופת טבת חוזרת החמה ועולה כנגד הדרום בכל יום ויום עד שחוזרת בתקופת תשרי באמצע המזרח עולה והולכת בכל יום עד שחוזרת בתקופת ית דרומית ושוקעת בקרן דרומית מערבית נמצא החמה מהלכת מזרח ומערב פעמים ביום ופעמים בלילה אבל בדרום לעולם מהלכת ביום ובצפון לעולם בלילה ולא נראית לעולם ביום ברוח צפונית דרומית וזהו שכתב (צפון בלילה) [הולך אל דרום] הולך אל דרום ביום וסובב אל צפון וכו' סובב הולך הרוח כו' (ופני) [זהו פני מזרח וכו'] מזרח ומערב שפעמים מהלכתן זו דרך זו השמועה ובעלי כוכבים טוענין עליהם ובא רב משרשיא ודחה דברי רבי יוסי ואומר ליתנהו להני כללי מעולם לא יצאה חמה מקרן מזרחית צפונית ולא שקעה בקרן מערבית צפונית וכן לא זרחה מקרן מזרחית דרומית. ולא שקעה בקרן מערבית דרומית. תלמוד ארץ ישראל א"ר יוסי מי שאין יכול לכוון את הרוחות ילמד מן התקופה ממקום שהחמה זורחת בתקופת תמוז עד מקום שזורחת בתקופת טבת. אלו פני מזרח. ומקומות שהיא שוקעת בתקופת תמוז אלו פני מערב והשאר פני צפון ודרום כדכתיב הולך אל דרום וסובב אל צפון. ניחא בשלה ובבית עולמים לדמיה יגיעות יגעו הנביאים לעשות המזרחי להיות החמה מצומצמת בין בתקופת טבת ותקופת תמוז. ז' שמות נקרא שער סוד שער התווך. שער החרסית. שער איתון. שער חדש. שער העליון. שער היסוד כו' ומפורשים כולם. אמר שמואל אין תקופת ניסן נופלת אלא בארבעה רבעי היום או בתחלת היום או בתחלת הלילה או בחצי היום או בחצי הלילה [(בא) ב'] ומחצה או בז' ומחצה] ואין תקופת תשרי נופלת אלא בג' [בט'] ואין תקופת ניסן בתחלת היום או ב' ומחצה [אלא בה' ומחצה או בז'] כדי שתפול תקופת תמוז בז' שעות. ותקופת תשרי ותקופת טבת בו' שעות

כב א מיי' פכ"ח מהל' שבת הלכה ו ז סמג לאוין סו טוש"ע א"ח סי' שצט סעיף י:
כג ב מיי' פי"ג מהל' שמיטה ויובל הל' ב סמג עשין קכה:

*תָּנוּ רַבָּנַן: אהַמְרַבֵּעַ אֶת הָעִיר – עוֹשֶׂה אוֹתָהּ כְּמִין טַבְלָא מְרוּבַּעַת, וְחוֹזֵר וּמְרַבֵּעַ אֶת הַתְּחוּמִין, וְעוֹשֶׂה אוֹתָן כְּמִין טַבְלָא מְרוּבַּעַת. וּכְשֶׁהוּא מוֹדֵד – לֹא יִמְדּוֹד מֵאֶמְצַע הַקֶּרֶן אַלְפַּיִם אַמָּה, מִפְּנֵי שֶׁהוּא מַפְסִיד אֶת הַזָּוִיּוֹת. אֶלָּא מֵבִיא טַבְלָא מְרוּבַּעַת שֶׁהִיא אַלְפַּיִם אַמָּה עַל אַלְפַּיִם אַמָּה, וּמַנִּיחָהּ בַּקֶּרֶן בַּאֲלַכְסוֹנָהּ, נִמְצֵאת הָעִיר מִשְׂתַּכֶּרֶת אַרְבַּע מֵאוֹת אַמּוֹת לְכָאן וְאַרְבַּע מֵאוֹת אַמּוֹת לְכָאן, נִמְצְאוּ תְּחוּמִין מִשְׂתַּכְּרִין ח' מֵאוֹת אַמּוֹת לְכָאן וּשְׁמוֹנֶה מֵאוֹת לְכָאן, נִמְצְאוּ הָעִיר וּתְחוּמִין מִשְׂתַּכְּרִין אֶלֶף וּמָאתַיִם לְכָאן וְאֶלֶף וּמָאתַיִם לְכָאן. אָמַר אַבַּיֵי: וּמַשְׁכַּחַתְּ לָהּ בְּמָתָא דַּהֲוָיָא תְּרֵי אַלְפֵי אַתְּרֵי אַלְפֵי. תַּנְיָא, *אָמַר רַבִּי אֱלִיעֶזֶר בְּרַבִּי יוֹסֵי: בתְּחוּם עָרֵי לְוִיִּם אַלְפַּיִם אַמָּה, צֵא מֵהֶן אֶלֶף אַמָּה מִגְרָשׁ – נִמְצָא מִגְרָשׁ רָבִיעַ, וְהַשְּׁאָר שָׂדוֹת וּכְרָמִים. מְנָא הָנֵי מִילֵּי? אָמַר רָבָא, דְּאָמַר קְרָא: °"מִקִּיר הָעִיר וָחוּצָה אֶלֶף אַמָּה סָבִיב", אָמְרָה תּוֹרָה: סַבֵּב אֶת הָעִיר בְּאֶלֶף, נִמְצָא מִגְרָשׁ רָבִיעַ. רָבִיעַ?! פַּלְגָּא הָוֵי! אָמַר רָבָא: בַּר אַדָּא מְשׁוֹחָאָה אַסְבְּרָהּ לִי, מַשְׁכַּחַתְּ לָהּ בְּמָתָא דַּהֲוָיָא תְּרֵי אַלְפֵי אַתְּרֵי אַלְפֵי. תְּחוּם כַּמָּה הָוְיָא – שִׁיתְסַר, קְרָנוֹת כַּמָּה הָוְיָין – שִׁיתְסַר. דַּל תְּמַנְיָא דִּתְחוּמִין, וְאַרְבָּעָה דְּקְרָנוֹת, כַּמָּה הָוֵי – תְּרֵיסַר. נִמְצָא מִגְרָשׁ רְבִיעַ? טְפֵי מִתִּלְתָּא נִינְהוּ! אַיְיתֵי אַרְבָּעָה דְּמָתָא שְׁדֵי עֲלַיְיהוּ, אַכַּתִּי תִּילְתָּא הָוֵי! מִי סָבְרַתְּ בְּרִיבּוּעָא קָאָמַר? בְּעִיגּוּלָא קָאָמַר. *כַּמָּה מְרוּבָּע יָתֵר עַל הָעִגּוּל – רָבִיעַ, דַּל רָבִיעַ מִינַּיְיהוּ – פְּשׁוּ לְהוּ תִּשְׁעָה, וְתִשְׁעָה מִתְּלָתִין וְשִׁיתָּא רִיבְעָא, הָוֵי. אַבַּיֵי אָמַר: מַשְׁכַּחַתְּ לָהּ נַמִי בְּמָתָא דַּהֲוָיָא אַלְפָּא בְּאַלְפָּא. תְּחוּמִין כַּמָּה הָווּ – תְּמַנְיָא, קְרָנוֹת כַּמָּה הָוֵי – שִׁיתְסַר, דַּל

תורה אור: במדבר לה

הַמְרַבֵּעַ עִיר. עֲגוּלָּה: עוֹשִׂין לָהּ כְּמִין טַבְלָא מְרוּבַּעַת. לְקַמָּן מוֹקֵי לָהּ בְּמָתָא דַּהֲוָיָא תְּרֵי אַלְפֵי אַתְּרֵי אַלְפֵי בְּעִיגּוּלָא, שֶׁכְּשֶׁאַתָּה מוֹסִיף רִיבּוּעַ עָלֶיהָ הֲרֵי הִיא כְּמִין טַבְלָא מְרוּבַּעַת אוֹרְכָּהּ כְּרׇחְבָּהּ וּתְחוּמֶיהָ כְּמִין טַבְלָא מְרוּבַּעַת – אוֹרְכָּן כְּרׇחְבָּן, רׇחְבָּן לְמִדַּת הָעִיר עַל פְּנֵי חוֹמָתָהּ שֶׁהִיא אַלְפַּיִם, וְכֵן אוֹרְכָּן לְהַלָּן מִן הָעִיר אַלְפַּיִם. וְהַיְינוּ דְּקָאָמַר חוֹזֵר וּמְרַבֵּעַ אֶת הַתְּחוּמִין, כְּלוֹמַר: חוֹזֵר וּמוֹדֵד לָהּ תְּחוּמֶיהָ, וְעַל כׇּרְחָךְ מְרוּבָּעִין הֵן: וּכְשֶׁהוּא מוֹדֵד. תְּחוּמֵי הָעִיר לְאַחַר שֶׁרִיבְּעָהּ, לֹא יִמְדּוֹד מֵאֶמְצַע קֶרֶן זָוִית שֶׁל עִיר כְּנֶגְדּוֹ בַּאֲלַכְסוֹן אַלְפַּיִם לְכׇל קֶרֶן וְקֶרֶן לִמְתּוֹחַ חוּט מִתְּחוּם קֶרֶן זֶה לִתְחוּם קֶרֶן זֶה: מִפְּנֵי שֶׁמַּפְסִיד אֶת הַזָּוִיּוֹת. לְכׇל קֶרֶן וְקֶרֶן מַפְסִיד מַה שֶּׁאֲלַכְסוֹן שֶׁל אַלְפַּיִם עַל אַלְפַּיִם עוֹדֵף עַל רִיבּוּעַ, וּכְשֶׁמּוֹתֵחַ הַחוּט לֹא תִּמְצָא בְּאוֹרֶךְ הַתְּחוּמִין מִן הָעִיר וָהָלְאָה לְכׇל צַד אֶלָּא אֶלֶף וְתכ"ח אַמּוֹת. כֵּיצַד? תֵּן

טבלא מתחום אלפים במלוי זויות
אלכסון אורך שני אלפים ות"ת
טבל' של אלף ותכח מקרן אלכסון אורך אלפים
תחום אלפים
עיר ב"א בעיג'
טבלא ריבוע העיר

תְּחוּמִין שֶׁל אֶלֶף וְתכ"ח אוֹרֶךְ לְכׇל צַד כְּנֶגֶד הָעִיר אַתָּה צָרִיךְ לָתֵת טַבְלָא שֶׁל אֶלֶף וְתכ"ח(א) עַל אֶלֶף וְתכ"ח לְכׇל קֶרֶן לְמַלְּאוֹת פְּגִימָתָן שֶׁל אוֹרֶךְ בְּרִיבּוּעַ, שֶׁיְּהוּ הַתְּחוּמִין מְרוּבָּעִין, שֶׁהֲרֵי רִיבּוּעַ פֵּיאוֹת לְכׇל שׁוֹבְתֵי שַׁבָּת. וְתִמְצָא בַּאֲלַכְסוֹנוֹ שֶׁל טַבְלָא מְכוּוָּן כְּנֶגֶד אֲלַכְסוֹן קֶרֶן הָעִיר אַלְפַּיִם, דְּקַיְימָא לָן כׇּל אַמְּתָא בְּרִיבּוּעַ אַמְּתָא וּתְרֵי חוּמְשֵׁי בַּאֲלַכְסוֹנָא. טַבְלָא שֶׁל אֶלֶף וְתכ"ח עַל אֶלֶף וְתכ"ח אֲלַכְסוֹן שֶׁלָּהּ עוֹדֵף אַלְפַּיִם וְתתכ"ו חוּמְשִׁין, שֶׁהֵן תקע"ב אַמָּה פָּחוֹת ד' חוּמְשִׁין. תֵּן עַל אֶלֶף וְתכ"ח – הֲרֵי אַלְפַּיִם. נִמְצָא כְּשֶׁמָּדַדְתָּ מֵאֶמְצַע קֶרֶן הָעִיר בַּאֲלַכְסוֹן אַלְפַּיִם – קִיפַּרְתָּ אֶת הַתְּחוּם, וְאֵינָן אֶלָּא אֶלֶף וְתכ"ח. וְכׇל כָּךְ לָמָּה – מִפְּנֵי שֶׁהִפְסַדְתָּ אֶת הַזָּוִיּוֹת, שֶׁהָיִיתָ צָרִיךְ לִמְדּוֹד אַלְפַּיִם וַאֲלַכְסוֹנָן מֵאֶמְצַע קֶרֶן הָעִיר, וְלִמְתּוֹחַ חוּט אַחַר כֵּן מִתְּחוּם קֶרֶן לִתְחוּם קֶרֶן, וְתִמְצָא מִן הַחוּט וְלָעִיר עַל פְּנֵי כׇּל הָעִיר לְכׇל צַד אַלְפַּיִם אַמָּה. כֵּיצַד? תֵּן אַלְפַּיִם תְּחוּם כְּנֶגֶד הָעִיר לְאַרְבַּע רוּחוֹתֶיהָ, תִּמְצָא פְּגִימַת אַלְפַּיִם עַל אַלְפַּיִם לְכׇל קֶרֶן, וַעֲדַיִין אַתָּה צָרִיךְ לִמְתּוֹחַ חוּט כְּמִין גַּאם לְהַשְׁווֹת תְּחוּמֵי הַקְּרָנוֹת לִתְחוּמֵי הָעִיר, וְתִמְצָא לְכׇל קֶרֶן טַבְלָא שֶׁל אַלְפַּיִם עַל אַלְפַּיִם, וּמְכַוֵּין אֲלַכְסוֹנָהּ כְּנֶגֶד אֲלַכְסוֹן קֶרֶן הָעִיר. וּמַהוּ אֲלַכְסוֹנָהּ – אַלְפַּיִם וְת"ת אַמָּה, שֶׁכָּךְ עוֹלֶה חֶשְׁבּוֹן ד' אֲלָפִים חוּמְשִׁין לְח' מֵאוֹת אַמָּה. לְפִיכָךְ, הַבָּא לִמְדּוֹד תְּחוּמֵי הָעִיר מֵבִיא טַבְלָא – רוֹאֶה כְּאִילּוּ הֵבִיא טַבְלָא שֶׁהִיא אַלְפַּיִם עַל אַלְפַּיִם, וּמַנִּיחָהּ כְּנֶגֶד הָעִיר בַּאֲלַכְסוֹן, אֲלַכְסוֹן שֶׁל טַבְלָא כְּנֶגֶד אֲלַכְסוֹן שֶׁל קֶרֶן. כְּלוֹמַר: מוֹדֵד אַלְפַּיִם וְח' מֵאוֹת כְּנֶגֶד הַקֶּרֶן בַּאֲלַכְסוֹן, וְאַחַר כָּךְ מוֹתֵחַ חוּט מִתְּחוּם קֶרֶן לִתְחוּם קֶרֶן: נִמְצָא הָעִיר מִשְׂתַּכֶּרֶת. כַּמָּה שֶׁרִבַּעְנוּהָ ד' מֵאוֹת אַמָּה לְכׇל קֶרֶן וְקֶרֶן. שֶׁכְּשֶׁהָיְתָה עֲגוּלָּה לֹא הָיָה לָהּ אֲלַכְסוֹן, וְעַכְשָׁיו שֶׁרִיבַּעְנוּהָ נָתַנּוּ לָהּ אֲלַכְסוֹן, וְהַיּוֹצֵא דֶּרֶךְ הַקֶּרֶן מִשְׂתַּכֵּר ת' אַמָּה לְקֶרֶן זוֹ, וְת' אַמָּה לְקֶרֶן זוֹ: נִמְצְאוּ תְּחוּמֵי הַקְּרָנוֹת מִשְׂתַּכְּרִין. כַּמָּה שֶׁנָּתַנּוּ טַבְלָא בַּאֲלַכְסוֹן כְּנֶגֶד הַקֶּרֶן, ח' מֵאוֹת לְכׇל קֶרֶן: צֵא מֵהֶן. סְבִיב הָעִיר אֶלֶף אַמָּה לְמִגְרָשׁ, שֶׁאֵין נוֹטְעִין וְלֹא זוֹרְעִין שָׁם, אֶלָּא מַנִּיחִין אוֹתוֹ לְנוֹי הָעִיר, כְּדִמְתַרְגֵּם רְוָוחֵי קִרְוַיָּא: נִמְצָא מִגְרָשׁ רְבִיעִי. לְקַמָּן מְפָרֵשׁ: וְהַשְּׁאָר. שְׁאָר הַתְּחוּם שָׂדוֹת וּכְרָמִים וְחוּץ לַתְּחוּם לֹא הָיָה לָהֶן כְּלוּם: מְנָהֲנֵי מִילֵּי. דְּמִגְרָשׁ אֶלֶף אַמָּה: מִקִּיר הָעִיר וְגוֹ'. רֵישָׁא דִּקְרָא "וּמִגְרְשֵׁי הֶעָרִים אֲשֶׁר תִּתְּנוּ": בַּר אַדָּא. שֵׁם הָאִישׁ: מְשׁוֹחָאָה. מְצַיֵּין תְּחוּמֵי הָעִיר: תְּחוּמִין כַּמָּה הָווּ שִׁיתְסַר. י"ו רְבָעִין שֶׁל אֶלֶף עַל אֶלֶף יֵשׁ בָּהֶן. כֵּיצַד? אַלְפַּיִם עַל אַלְפַּיִם לְכׇל צַד חֲלוֹקֵם שְׁתִי וָעֵרֶב – הֲרֵי ד' רְבָעִין שֶׁל אֶלֶף עַל אֶלֶף, וְכֵן לְכׇל רוּחַ שֶׁל עִיר: קְרָנוֹת כַּמָּה הָווּ. תְּחוּמֵי הַקְּרָנוֹת שֶׁל תְּחוּמִין נַמִי שִׁיתְסַר נִינְהוּ, שֶׁהֲרֵי לְכׇל קֶרֶן יֵשׁ טַבְלָא שֶׁל אַלְפַּיִם עַל אַלְפַּיִם, כִּדְפָרְשִׁינַן לְעֵיל: דַּל. לְצוֹרֶךְ מִגְרָשׁ: ח' דִּתְחוּמִין וְד' דְּקְרָנוֹת. דְּהָא אָמַרְתְּ סַבֵּב אֶת הָעִיר בְּאֶלֶף, הֲרֵי לְכׇל הַתְּחוּם אַלְפַּיִם עַל פְּנֵי הָעִיר בְּאוֹרֶךְ וּבְרוֹחַב אֶלֶף לְהַלָּן מִן הָעִיר. וְכֵיוָן שֶׁנָּתַתָּ אֶלֶף בְּלִיטַת מִגְרָשׁ לְד' רוּחוֹת, צָרִיךְ אַתָּה לִיתֵּן לְכׇל קֶרֶן טַבְלָא שֶׁל אֶלֶף עַל אֶלֶף, הָא אַרְבָּעָה מִן הַקְּרָנוֹת לְמִגְרָשׁ, הָא תְּרֵיסַר לְצוֹרֶךְ מִגְרָשׁ כּוּלָּן אֶלֶף עַל אֶלֶף: נִמְצָא מִגְרָשׁ רְבִיעַ. בִּתְמִיָּה: אַיְיתֵי אַרְבָּעָה דְּמָתָא שְׁדֵי עֲלַיְיהוּ. דִּתְלָתִין וּתְרֵין, וְהָווּ לְהוּ תְּלָתִין וְשִׁית. דְּהָא דְּקָתָנֵי מִגְרָשׁ רְבִיעַ – אַכּוּלָּהּ מִילְּתָא קָאֵי, רְבִיעַ הַחֶשְׁבּוֹן כּוּלּוֹ שֶׁל עִיר וּתְחוּמִין וּקְרָנוֹת: כַּמָּה מְרוּבָּע יוֹתֵר עַל הָעִגּוּל רְבִיעַ דַּל רִיבְעָא מִינֵּיהּ כו'. אִי חָשַׁבְתְּ בְּעִיר מְרוּבַּעַת, וַעֲבַדְתְּ מִגְרָשׁ סָבִיב נַמִי בְּרִיבּוּעַ, לְפִיכָךְ עָלָה חֶשְׁבּוֹן הָעִיר וּמִגְרָשֶׁיהָ ד' אֲלָפִים עַל ד' אֲלָפִים מְרוּבָּעִין שֶׁהֵן י"ו רְבָעִין שֶׁל אֶלֶף עַל אֶלֶף, וּמֵהֶן ג' חֲלָקִים לְמִגְרָשׁ, וְהַיְינוּ תְּרֵיסַר וְחֵלֶק הָרְבִיעִי לָעִיר. וְאַנַן בְּמָתָא עֲגוּלְּתָא עָסְקִינַן, כִּדְמוֹקְמִינַן לְקַמָּן. וּמִכׇּל מָקוֹם אָנוּ מוֹסִיפִין עָלֶיהָ לָתֵת לַלְוִיִּם רִיבּוּעָא עִמָּהּ, וְקַרְנוֹתֶיהָ וּתְחוּמִין אַלְפַּיִם לְכׇל רוּחַ, הֲרֵי חֵלֶק הַלְוִיִּם סַךְ הַכֹּל ו' אֲלָפִים שֶׁהֵן תְּלָתִין וְשִׁית רְבָעִין שֶׁל אֶלֶף עַל אֶלֶף וְהָעִיר בְּאֶמְצָעִיתָן עֲגוּלָּה אַלְפַּיִם, וּמִגְרָשֶׁיהָ סָבִיב לָהּ אֶלֶף רוֹחַב. נִמְצֵאת עִיר וּמִגְרָשֶׁיהָ ד' אֲלָפִים עַל ד' אֲלָפִים עֲגוּלִּין. וְאִם הָיוּ ד' עַל ד' מְרוּבָּעִין – הָווּ שִׁיתְסַר, הַשְׁתָּא דַּעֲגוּלִּין – דַּל רִיבְעָא, הָווּ תְּרֵיסַר. וּמֵהֶן ג' חֲלָקִים לְמִגְרָשׁ וְהָרְבִיעִי לָעִיר, דְּהָווּ לְהוּ ט' מִגְרָשִׁין וְט' מִתְּלָתִין וְשִׁית הַנִּיתָּנִין לַלְוִיִּם רִיבְעָא הָוֵי: מַשְׁכַּחַתְּ לָהּ נַמִי בְּמָתָא דַּהֲוָיָא אַלְפָּא בְּאַלְפָּא. וְלֹא תַּחְשׁוֹב הָעִיר עֲלֵיהֶן, אֶלָּא נִמְצָא מִגְרָשׁ רְבִיעַ הַתְּחוּמִין וּקְרָנוֹת קָאֵי: תְּחוּמִין כַּמָּה הָווּ תְּמַנְיָא. רְבָעִין שֶׁל אֶלֶף עַל אֶלֶף, שֶׁהֲרֵי תְּחוּם לְכׇל צַד אַלְפַּיִם אוֹרֶךְ לְהַלָּן מִן הָעִיר וְאֶלֶף רוֹחַב עַל פְּנֵי הָעִיר, וּקְרָנוֹת שִׁיתְסַר – דְּכֵיוָן דְּאוֹרֶךְ הַתְּחוּמִין מְשׁוּכִין אַלְפַּיִם לְכׇל צַד, אַתָּה צָרִיךְ לְמַלְּאוֹת פְּגָם לְכׇל קֶרֶן בְּטַבְלָא אַלְפַּיִם עַל אַלְפַּיִם:
דַּל

פלגא הוי. פירוש: מגרש דתחומין הוי פלגא דתחומין. ולא רצה לדקדק ולהקשות דמגרש דתחומין והקרנות כך וכך הוי מתחומין וקרנות, משום דפעמים הוי תלתא או רביע או חומש מן התחומין ומן הקרנות, לפי מה שהעיר גדולה או קטנה:

משכחת לה במתא. הקשה השר מקוצי: דמשכחת לה מגרש רביע דתחומין וקרנות במתא דהוי ח' אלפים על ח' אלפים ומגרש הוי ל"ו ותחומין וקרנות ומתא הוו קמ"ד פעמים אלף על אלף! וי"ל: דערי מקלט אינן גדולים כל כך, כדאמר בפרק "אלו הן הגולין" (מכות דף י.): ערים הללו אין עושין אותם לא גדולות ולא קטנות. ומהר"י אומר: שמתרץ האמת, דהשתא קמ"ל דמגרש אינו מרובע כדמסיק. ולרבינא קמ"ל דאין מגרש לקרנות. ולרב אשי דאין מגרש אלא לקרנות, אבל בכה"ג לא היה משמיענו שום חידוש:

כמה מרובע יתר על העגול רביע. ואור"י: דהא רביע – בין בהיקף בין בגוף הקרקע, כדאמר הכא נמצא מגרש רביע. וכן משמע גבי ים שעשה שלמה (לעיל דף יד:), ועל ההיקף יש להוכיח בהדיא כדפ"ה, דכל שברחבו טפח יש בהיקפו ג' טפחים, ובטפח מרובע יש בהיקפו ד' טפחים, ועל הקרקע שבפנים יש להוכיח נמי, שאם תקיף טפח עגול סביב בחוטין דקין עד הנקודה האמצעי' שבעגול, ותחתוך מן הנקודה ולמטה כל החוטין לב' ותפשטם, יהיה העליון ארוך ג' טפחים והאחרים מתקצרים והולכים עד הנקודה שהוא חצי טפח מן החוט העליון. תחתוך שוב כל החוטין לשנים ושים הארוך בצד הקצר – נמצא הרבוע אורכו טפח וחצי ורחבו חצי טפח, דהיינו שלש חתיכות של חצי טפח על חצי טפח. ובטפח מרובע יש ד' חלקים של חצי טפח על חצי טפח:

עיגול טפח
ג' טפחים
טפח וחצי

אביי אמר משכחת. ואם תאמר: לפי מה דמוקי לה לקמן במתא עגולה קשה דתחומין הוו טפי כמו שאנו מרבעין העיר, ולא הוי מגרש רביע מהם[א]! ויש לומר: דלא קאמר מגרש רביע אלא מתחומין שבחוץ לריבוע העיר:
מאי

רבינו חננאל

שעות. ושנה אחרת ואט"ד [סי' ועי' בר"ש"י]. אמר שמואל אין בין תקופה לתקופה אלא ז' שעות ומחצה ואין תקופה מושכת מחברתה אלא חצי שעה. אלו כולן פשוטות הן. ואמר שמואל אין לך תקופת ניסן שנופלת בצדק שאינה משברת את האילנות ואין תקופת טבת נופלת בצדק שמייבשת האילנו' והוא דאתייליד לבנה או בלבנה או בצדק: ת"ר המרבע את העיר עושה אותה כמין טבלא מרובעת המרבע תחומין עושין אותן כמין טבלא מרובעת. כשהוא מודד לא ימדוד מאמצע הקרן מפני שמפסיד הזויות אלא מביא טבלא שהיא אלפים על אלפים ומניחה כנגד הקרן באלכסון נמצאת העיר משתכרת הזויות. ת' אמה לכאן ות' אמה לכאן נמצאו תחומין משתכרין ת"ת אמה לכאן ות"ת אמה לכאן נמצאת העיר ותחומיה משתכרין אלף ומאתים אמה לכאן ואלף ומאתים אמה לכאן. אמר אביי משכחת לה במאתא דהיא אלפים אמה על אלפים אמה. פי' זו העיר שהעמדנוה אלפים על אלפים עגולה היא וכבר אמרנו למעלה שצריך למדידת תחומין פיאות לפיכך צריכין להוסיף על אלפים אמה הללו העודף המרובע על העיגול והוא כדמסיקנא לה בסיפא דשמעתא דאמרינן הכי כל אמתא בריבוע אמתא ותרין חומשי באלכסונא הלכך נמצא באלפים על אלפים עודף ד' אלפים חומשין שהוא ת"ת אמה. נמצא עודף בעיר שהיא אלפים על אלפים ת"ת אמה. ובמזרח בתחומין שהן אלפים על אלפים ת"ת אחרונות וכן במערב נמצא העודף אלפים אמה ות' אמה כשתחלקם נמצא חציים אלף ומאתים אמה תופסת על אלפים לתחום המזרח ואלף ומאתים לתחום המערב נמצא התחום חוץ לעיר ג' אלפים ומאתים אמה. תניא ר' אליעזר בנו של ריה"ג אמר תחום ערי לוים אלפים. צא מהן אלף אמה מגרש והשאר לשדות וכרמים. נמצא מגרש רביע. ואקשינן מכדי תחום כמה הוי אלפים כשתוציא ותסבב העיר באלף נשארו אלף אחרות הנה החצי איך שנה מגרש רביע *) אלפים אמה אורך ברוחב אלף וכן בצפון וכן במערב וכן בדרום. נמצאו בד' צדדי העיר ט"ז אלף אורך ברוחב אלף וצריך למלאות הקרנות אלפים אורך ברוחב אלפים על כל זוית וזוית נמצאו ד' קרנות עוד ט"ז אלף אמה באורך ורוחב אלף אמה ושיעור המגרש סביבות העיר אלף רוחב. וכיון שהעיר היא אלפים על אלפים נמצאו בד' צדדי העיר אלפים אמה אורך ברוחב אלף שמונת אלפים אמה אורך ברוחב אלף. גם יש לה למלאות הקרנות בד' זוויותיה אלף על אלף בכל זוית שהן ד' אלפים אמה נמצא מגרש בסבוב העיר כולה עם הקרנות י"ב אלף אמה. ותחום העיר וקרנותיה הויין (י"ב ש"ב) [ל"ב אלפים] אמה הנה י"ב אלף שהן מגרש לגבי ל"ב של תחומין טפי מתלתא הויין ופרקינן אייתי ארבע דמתא. כלומר תוך העיר אלפים על אלפים עושין ד' אלפים אורך ברוחב אלף אמה הוסיף אותם בכלל ל"ב אמה נמצאו הכל [ששה ושלשים] אלפים אמה ואכתי י"ב אלף משלשה ושלשים אלף שליש הן איך שנינו נמצא מגרש רביע. ופרקינן מי סברת האי מגרש בריבועא הוא בעיגולא הוא פחות שליש. ואיכא למימר מתא נמי עיגולא היא והכי קאמר רחמנא מקיר העיר וחוצה וגו' צריך סביבות העיר כולה אלף אמה ולגבי תחומין יהבינן לה פאות כר' חנינא דתני זה יהיה לכם כזה יהיו כל שובתי שבת. אבל לגבי מגרש לא יהבינן ליה פיאות הלכך הסר מהן יתרון שמעדף המרובע על העיגול וכמה הוא היתרון רביע נמצא רביע י"ב אלף ג' אלפים כשתפחות מי"ב אלף ג' אלפים נמצא המגרש ט' אלפים אמה. והתחומין עם העיר והקרנות הן ל"ו אלף אמה נמצאות ט' אלפים אמה מל"ו אלף רביע שלהן וזוהי ששנינו נמצא מגרש רביע. אמר אביי משכחת

*) הדבר פשוט דחסר בדברי רבינו וצ"ל ומשכחת לה במתא דהוי תרי אלפי על תרי אלפי ונמצא דהתחומין הם אלפים אמה אורך ברוחב אלפים וכן בצפון וכו'.

[תוס' פ"ד]

[תוספ' סוף ערכין ע"ש סוטה כז: ע"ש]

[לעיל יד: ושם נסמן]

הגהות הב"ח

(א) רש"י ד"ה מפני שמפסיד וכו' לתת טבלא של אלף ותכ"ח וד' חומשין על אלף ותכ"ח וד' חומשין לכל קרן [וכ"ה בדפוס ווינציא]:

הגהות הגר"א

[א] תוס' ד"ה אביי אמר משכחת כו' ולא הוי מגרש רביע מהם. וי"ל וכו' נ"ב ודוחק אבל גמ' קאמר בעיר אלף ורביע וגמ' לא חשש לדקדק:

כד א מיי' פכ"ח מהל' שבת הלכה ה סמג לאוין סו טוש"ע א"ח סי' שצח סעיף ה:

כה ב מיי' שם הלכה ה טוש"ע שם ס"ז:

דל אַרְבַּע דִּתְחוּמִין וְאַרְבַּע דְּקְרָנוֹת, כַּמָּה הָוֵי — תְּמַנְיָא. תִּילְתָּא הָווּ! מִי סָבְרַתְּ בְּרִבּוּעָא קָאָמַר? בְּעִיגּוּלָא קָאָמַר. כַּמָּה מְרוּבָּע יָתֵר עַל הָעִגּוּל — רָבִיעַ, דַּל רָבִיעַ — פְּשׁוּ לָהּ שִׁיתָּא, וְשִׁיתָּא מִכ"ד רִיבְעָא הָוֵי. רָבִינָא אָמַר: מַאי רָבִיעַ — רָבִיעַ דִּתְחוּמִין. רַב אַשִׁי אָמַר: מַאי רָבִיעַ — רָבִיעַ דְּקְרָנוֹת. אֲמַר לֵיהּ רָבִינָא לְרַב אַשִׁי: וְהָא "סָבִיב" כְּתִיב! מַאי "סָבִיב" — סָבִיב דִּקְרָנוֹת. דְּאִי לָא תֵּימָא הָכִי, גַּבֵּי עוֹלָה דִּכְתִיב: °"וְזָרְקוּ (בְּנֵי אַהֲרֹן) אֶת הַדָּם עַל הַמִּזְבֵּחַ סָבִיב" ה"נ סָבִיב מַמָּשׁ? אֶלָּא מַאי סָבִיב — סָבִיב דִּקְרָנוֹת, ה"נ: מַאי סָבִיב — סָבִיב דִּקְרָנוֹת. א"ל רַב חֲבִיבִי מְחוֹזְנָאָה לְרַב אַשִׁי: וְהָא אִיכָּא מוֹרְשָׁא דְּקַרְנָתָא! בְּמָתָא עִיגּוּלְתָּא. וְהָא רִיבְּעוּהָ! אֵימוֹר דְּאָמְרִינַן: חָזֵינַן כְּמַאן דִּמְרַבְּעָא, רִבּוּעֵי וַדַּאי מִי מְרַבְּעֲנָא? אֲמַר לֵיהּ רַב חֲנִילַאי מְחוֹזְנָאָה לְרַב אַשִׁי: מִכְּדִי, *כַּמָּה מְרוּבָּע יָתֵר עַל הָעִגּוּל — רָבִיעַ, הָנֵי תְּמַנֵי מְאָה שִׁית מְאָה וְשִׁיתִּין וְשִׁבְעָה נְכֵי תִּילְתָּא הָוֵי! אֲמַר לֵיהּ: ה"מ בְּעִיגּוּלָא מִגּוֹ רִבּוּעַ, אֲבָל בַּאֲלַכְסוֹנָא — בָּעֵינָא טְפֵי. דְּאָמַר מָר: *כָּל אַמְּתָא בְּרִיבּוּעַ — אַמְּתָא וּתְרֵי חוּמְשֵׁי בַּאֲלַכְסוֹנָא.§

מתני' **נוֹתְנִין קַרְפֵּף לָעִיר, דִּבְרֵי רַבִּי מֵאִיר. וַחֲכ"א: לֹא אָמְרוּ קַרְפֵּף אֶלָּא בֵּין שְׁתֵּי עֲיָירוֹת, אִם יֵשׁ לָזוֹ שִׁבְעִים אַמָּה וְשִׁירַיִים וְלָזוֹ שִׁבְעִים אַמָּה וְשִׁירַיִים — עוֹשֶׂה קַרְפֵּף אֶת שְׁתֵּיהֶן לִהְיוֹת אֶחָד. וְכֵן ג' כְּפָרִים *הַמְשׁוּלָּשִׁין, אִם יֵשׁ בֵּין שְׁנַיִם חִיצוֹנִים מֵאָה וְאַרְבָּעִים וְאַחַת וּשְׁלִישׁ — עָשָׂה אֶמְצָעִי אֶת שְׁלָשְׁתָּן לִהְיוֹת אֶחָד.§

גמ' מְנָא הָנֵי מִילֵּי? אָמַר רָבָא, דְּאָמַר קְרָא: °"מִקִּיר הָעִיר וָחוּצָה", אָמְרָה תּוֹרָה: תֵּן חוּצָה וְאַחַר כָּךְ מְדוֹד.§ "וַחֲכ"א לֹא אָמְרוּ וכו'".§ אִיתְּמַר, *רַב הוּנָא אָמַר: נוֹתְנִין קַרְפֵּף לָזוֹ וְקַרְפֵּף לָזוֹ. חִיָּיא בַּר רַב אָמַר: קַרְפֵּף [א'] לִשְׁתֵּיהֶן. תְּנַן, וַחֲכָמִים אוֹמְרִים: לֹא אָמְרוּ קַרְפֵּף אֶלָּא בֵּין ב' עֲיָירוֹת. תְּיוּבְתָּא דְּרַב הוּנָא! אָמַר לָךְ רַב הוּנָא: מַאי קַרְפֵּף — תּוֹרַת קַרְפֵּף. וּלְעוֹלָם קַרְפֵּף לָזוֹ וְקַרְפֵּף לָזוֹ. ה"נ מִסְתַּבְּרָא, מִדְּקָתָנֵי סֵיפָא: אִם יֵשׁ לָזוֹ ע' אַמָּה וְשִׁירַיִים וְלָזוֹ ע' אַמָּה וְשִׁירַיִים — עוֹשֶׂה קַרְפֵּף(א) לִשְׁתֵּיהֶן לִהְיוֹת אֶחָד. שְׁמַע מִינַּהּ. לֵימָא תֶּיהֱוֵי תְּיוּבְתֵּיהּ דְּחִיָּיא בַּר רַב! אָמַר לָךְ חִיָּיא בַּר רַב:

הָא

ויקרא א | במדבר לה | [לעיל נה.] | ב"ב קב.

רש"י

דל. לְאוֹרֶךְ מִגְרָשׁ ד' מִן הַתְּחוּמִין, שֶׁהֲרֵי אֶלֶף לְכָל צַד לְהַלָּן(ב) הָעִיר וְעַל פְּנֵי הָעִיר אֶלֶף הוּא דְּהָוֵי כְּמִדַּת הָעִיר, הֲרֵי אֶלֶף עַל אֶלֶף מִגְרָשׁ לְכָל צַד, וְכֵן לַקְּרָנוֹת – הָא תְּמַנְיָא: כַּמָּה מְרוּבָּע יָתֵר כו'. לְפִי שֶׁחִשַּׁבְתָּ בְּעִיר מְרוּבַּעַת, הוֹלַכְתָּ עַל כָּרְחָךְ לָתֵת מִגְרָשֶׁיהָ בְּרִיבּוּעַ סָבִיב, לְפִיכָךְ עָלוּ לִשְׁמוֹנָה אֲלָפִים. חֲשׁוֹב הָעִיר עֲגוּלָּה וּמִגְרָשֶׁי' עֲגוּלִּין, וַהֲרֵי הֵן ג' אֲלָפִים עַל ג' אֲלָפִים עֲגוּלִּין. וְאִילּוּ הָיוּ מְרוּבָּעִין – הָווּ ט', ח' לְמִגְרָשׁ וְהַתְּשִׁיעִי לָעִיר. עַכְשָׁיו שֶׁהַכֹּל עָגוֹל – נִתְמַעֵט רְבִיעַ הָעִיר וּרְבִיעַ הַמִּגְרָשׁ: וּפָשׁוּ לְהוּ שִׁיתָּא מִגְרָשׁ וְשִׁיתָּא מִכ"ד. הַנִּיתָּנִין לַלְוִיִּם לְבַד הָעִיר, רִיבְעָה הָוֵי שֶׁאַע"פ שֶׁיִּשּׁוּב הָעִיר עֲגוּלָּה, וּמִגְרָשֶׁיהָ עֲגוּלִּין – מ"מ לְעִנְיַן חֵלֶק הַלְוִיִּם וּלְעִנְיַן תְּחוּמֵי שַׁבָּת אָנוּ מוֹסִיפִין לָהֶם רִיבּוּעַ, וְנוֹתְנִין לָהּ תְּחוּמִין אֶלֶף רוֹחַב לְמִדַּת הָעִיר לְכָל צַד, וְהָאוֹרֶךְ אֲלָפַיִם וְקַרְנוֹתֵיהֶן לְמַלְּאוֹת פְּגָמֵיהֶן אֲלָפַיִם עַל אֲלָפַיִם, הֲרֵי סַךְ הַכֹּל ה' אֲלָפִים עַל ה' אֲלָפִים מְרוּבָּעִין. אֲלָפַיִם תְּחוּם לְכָאן וּלְכָאן, וְהָעִיר אֶלֶף בֵּינְתַיִם. דְּהָווּ לְהוּ תְּחוּמִין תְּמַנְיָא, וּקְרָנוֹת שִׁיתְּסַר. נִמְצָא מִגְרָשׁ רְבִיעַ הַתְּחוּמִין וְהַקְּרָנוֹת: **רָבִינָא אָמַר.** לְעוֹלָם כִּדְמֵעִיקָּרָא בְּמָתָא מְרַבְּעָתָא, וּבִתְרֵי אַלְפֵי אַתְּרֵי אַלְפֵי דְּהָווּ לְהוּ תְּחוּמִין שִׁיתְּסַר וּקְרָנוֹת שִׁיתְּסַר, וּמִגְרָשׁ מִנַּיְיהוּ תְּרֵיסַר. וּמַאי רְבִיעַ דְּקָתָנֵי – בִּתְחוּמִין דְּקָאָמַר: נִמְצָא מִגְרָשׁ דִּתְחוּמִין רְבִיעַ דִּתְחוּמִין, וּקְרָנוֹת דְּמִגְרָשׁ דִּתְחוּמִין תְּמַנְיָא, כִּדְאָמְרִינַן מֵעִיקָּרָא, וְהוּא רִיבְעָא דִּתְלָתִין וּתְרֵין: **רַב אַשִׁי.** נָמֵי כְּרָבִינָא מוֹקֵי לָהּ בְּמָתָא מְרַבְּעָתָא, דִּתְרֵי אַלְפֵי אַתְּרֵי אַלְפֵי. וּמַאי נִמְצָא מִגְרָשׁ רְבִיעַ דְּקָתָנֵי – ה"ק: מִגְרָשׁ דִּקְרָנוֹת הָוֵי רְבִיעַ דִּקְרָנוֹת, דְּשִׁיתְּסַר דִּקְרָנוֹת הָוֵי רְבִיעַ הַמִּגְרָשׁ: **וְהָא** סָבִיב כְּתִיב. בִּקְרָא, גַּבֵּי מִגְרָשׁ, וְתַנָּא כִּי רְהָטָא דִּקְרָא נָקַט וְתָנָא: ל"א: רַב אַשִׁי ס"ל דְּאֵין נוֹתְנִין מִגְרָשׁ אֶלָּא לְקַרְנוֹת הָעִיר אֶלֶף עַל אֶלֶף, הִלְכָּךְ, לְעוֹלָם בֵּין הָעִיר גְּדוֹלָה בֵּין הָעִיר קְטַנָּה מִגְרָשׁ שֶׁלָּהּ רְבִיעַ, [דִּלְעוֹלָם] הַקְּרָנוֹת שִׁיתְּסַר וּמִגְרָשׁ ד': **וְהָא אִיכָּא מוֹרְשָׁא** דִּקְרָנוֹת. לְמַאי דַּאֲמַרַן לְעֵיל כַּמָּה מְרוּבָּע יוֹתֵר כו' דִּמְדַדִּינַן מִגְרָשׁ בְּעִיגּוּלָא, וְקַשְׁיָא לֵיהּ לְרַב חֲבִיבָא: כֵּיוָן דְּתַנְיָא מְרַבֵּעַ אֶת הָעִיר – הֲרֵי הִיא מְרוּבַּעַת, וְכִי יָהֲבָא מִגְרָשׁ בְּעִיגּוּל אֶלֶף סָבִיב לָהּ – נִמְצְאוּ קַרְנוֹת הָעִיר אוֹכְלִין בְּתוֹךְ הַמִּגְרָשׁ, וְאֵין כְּנֶגֶד הַקְּרָנוֹת אֶלֶף מִגְרָשׁ: **בְּמָתָא עֲגוּלְתָּא.** דְּלֵית לָהּ מוֹרְשָׁא דְּקַרְנָתָא: **אֵימוֹר דְּאָמְרִינַן** חַזְיֵיהּ **כְּמַאן דִּמְרַבְּעָא.** לְעִנְיַן לְהוֹסִיף לָהּ תְּחוּמִין, בֵּין לְהִילּוּךְ שַׁבָּת בֵּין לְעִנְיַן נְתִינַת לְוִיִּם. אֲבָל רִבּוּעֵי וַדַּאי לָא מְרַבַּעְנָא, כְּלוּם הוֹסַפְנוּ בָּתִּים בְּתוֹסֶפֶת רִיבּוּעָא, שֶׁיְּמַעֲטוּ אֶת נוֹי הַמִּגְרָשׁ: **הָנֵי ח' מֵאוֹת.** בִּתְמִיָּה: דְּקָתָנֵי לְעֵיל נִמְצְאוּ תְּחוּמִין מִשְׂתַּכְּרִין בְּמַה שֶּׁהִנַּחְנוּ טַבְלָא בַּאֲלַכְסוֹן ח' מֵאוֹת אַמָּה, וַהֲלֹא אֵין עוֹדֵף הָאֲלַכְסוֹן אֶלָּא מִפְּנֵי הָרִיבּוּעַ, דְּדָבָר עָגוֹל אֵין לוֹ אֲלַכְסוֹן, וְהַמְּרוּבָּע יֵשׁ לוֹ אֲלַכְסוֹן. וְכַמָּה מְרוּבָּע יוֹתֵר עַל הָעִגּוּל – רְבִיעַ, וּרְבִיעָא הַיְיתוּ עֲלָהּ מִלְּבַר, שֶׁהוּא חֵלֶק שְׁלִישִׁי מִלְּגָו: **וְהָנֵי שִׁית מְאָה וְשִׁיתִּין וְשִׁבְעָה נְכֵי תִּילְתָּא דְּאַמְּתָא הָווּ.** דְּהַיְינוּ תִּילְתָּא דַּאֲלָפַיִם: **ה"מ.** הוּא דִּרְבִיעַ יוֹתֵר עָלָיו וְתוּ לָא – ה"מ בְּעִיגּוּלָא דְּנָפֵיק מִגּוֹ רִיבּוּעַ. כִּי אָמְרִינַן רְבִיעַ – ה"מ בְּעָלְמָא, כָּל הֵיכָא דְּאַיְירֵי בְּעִגּוּל הַנַּעֲשֶׂה מִתּוֹךְ הַמְּרוּבָּע, זֶה הָרִיבּוּעַ יוֹתֵר עַל הָעִגּוּל שֶׁאָנוּ עוֹסְקִין בְּמִדַּת הֶחָלָל כּוּלּוֹ כַּמָּה נִשְׂכָּר כָּל הֶחָלָל בְּתוֹסֶפֶת זוֹ בֵּין בְּהֶיקֵּיפוֹ בֵּין בַּחֲלָלוֹ – לֹא נִשְׂכָּר אֶלָּא רְבִיעַ. שֶׁהֲרֵי עִיר עֲגוּלָּה אֲלָפַיִם, הֶקֵּיפָהּ ו' אֲלָפִים, כְּדְיָלְפִינַן בְּפ"ק (דף יד:) מ"וְקָו שְׁלֹשִׁים בָּאַמָּה יָסוֹב אוֹתוֹ" וגו' וְעִיר מְרוּבַּעַת הֶיקֵּיפָהּ ח' אֲלָפִים. וְכֵן לְמִדַּת חֲלָלָהּ, אִם בָּאתָ לַחֲלֵק הַתּוֹסֶפֶת לְפִי חֶשְׁבּוֹן לְכָל הָעִיר – לֹא רָבְתָה הַמִּדָּה עַל מַה שֶּׁבַּתְּחִילָּה אֶלָּא רְבִיעַ. דְּהָכִי קִים לְהוּ לְרַבָּנַן שֶׁהַמְּרוּבָּע יוֹתֵר עַל הָעִגּוּל רְבִיעַ: **אֲבָל בַּאֲלַכְסוֹנָא.** כְּלוֹמַר: אֲבָל כָּאן שֶׁאָנוּ עוֹסְקִין לֵידַע כַּמָּה נִיתּוֹסֵף הִילּוּךְ הָאֲלַכְסוֹן בִּשְׁבִיל רִבּוּעַ זֶה שֶׁהוֹסַפְנוּ – אִיכָּא טְפֵי מֵרְבִיעַ. לְפִי שֶׁכָּל הָרִבּוּעַ הַזֶּה שֶׁהוֹסַפְתָּ נִתְּנוּ לְקַרְנוֹתֶיהָ, וְלֹא נִשְׂתַּכְּרוּ בּוֹ אֶמְצָעֵי הָעִיר כְּלוּם. שֶׁמִּתְּחִילָּה אֲלָפַיִם וְעַכְשָׁיו אֲלָפַיִם, וְהַשָּׂכָר הַזֶּה רוּבּוֹ לְחוּדָּן שֶׁל קְרָנוֹת וּמִיעוּטוֹ לִסְמוֹךְ לָהֶן מִכָּאן וּמִכָּאן, לְפִי הָאֲלַכְסוֹן יוֹתֵר עַל הָרִבּוּעַ: **מתני'** נוֹתְנִין קַרְפֵּף לָעִיר. כְּשֶׁבָּא לִמְדּוֹד הַתְּחוּמִין אֵין מוֹדְדִין מִן הַחוֹמָה, אֶלָּא מַרְחִיק ע' אַמָּה וְשִׁירַיִים כַּחֲצַר הַמִּשְׁכָּן, וּמַתְחִיל לִמְדּוֹד: קמ"א **וּשְׁלִישׁ אַמָּה.** הַיְינוּ ב' קַרְפֵּיפוֹת: **לִהְיוֹת אַחַת.** וְהַיּוֹצֵא לָלֶכֶת דֶּרֶךְ חֲבֶרְתָּהּ חוּלָּה לָהּ מוֹדֵד מֵחוֹמַת חֲבֶרְתָּהּ וָאֵילָךְ: **וְכֵן ג' כְּפָרִים הַמְשׁוּלָּשִׁין.** מְפָרֵשׁ בַּגְּמָרָא: **גמ'** תֵּן חוּצָה. קַרְפֵּף:

הָא

[לעיל יד: וש"נ] | [לקמן עו: סוכה ח. ב"ב קא:] | [עי' תוספות בכורות לט. ד"ה שיהו משולשין] | [לעיל נה:]

תוספות

מאי רביע רביע דתחומא. קסבר דאין מגרש לקרנות, ורב אשי סבר: דאדרבה אין מגרש אלא לקרנות ולא לתחומין. (ומה שפרש"י דרב אשי איירי במתא דתרי אלפי – לא נהירא, דבכל עיר בקרנות הוי מגרש רביע): **כל** אמתא בריבוע אמתא ותרי חומשי באלכסונא. ואין החשבון מכוון. שאם תחתוך טבלא של עשר על עשר שתי וערב, יהיו בה ד' טבלאות של ה' על ה'. ועשה ריבוע בפנים שילך באלכסון של ארבע טבלאות, תמצא בריבוע הפנימי נ' אמות על אמה, שהרי הוא חציו

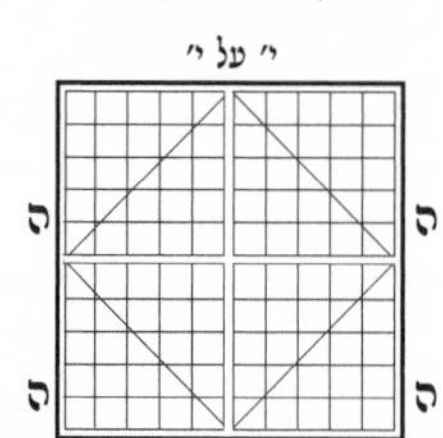

של חילון שהוא ק'. ואם אין באלכסון של ה' אלא(ג) כמו שעולה בחשבון אמתא ותרי חומשי באלכסונא – אז לא היה לו להיות בריבוע הפנימי אלא מ"ט אמות על אמה, כדין ז' על ז'. והאלכסון נמי של ריבוע הפנימי לא היה לו להיות עשר, אלא ט' אמות וד' חומשין. אלא יש מעט יותר מאמתא ותרי חומשי באלכסונא: **רב** הונא אמר נותנין קרפף לזו וקרפף לזו. נראה לר"י: דדוקא בשתי עיירות נותנין קרפף לזו וקרפף לזו לרבנן, דכמו שלר"מ עיר דוקא דהא קרא קדריש – ה"ה לרבנן דב' עיירות דוקא. אבל עיר ובית אין נותנין להם שני קרפיפות. אלא דוקא אם הוא תוך שבעים אמה ושיריים לעיר מתעברת לעיר. וכן אם יש בית אחר תוך ע' אמות ושיריים לאותו בית של עיר אחת – יכולין לעשות בורגנין כמו שירצו, כדאמר ב"עושין פסין" (לעיל דף כא.): אתיתו מברניש לבי כנישתא דדניאל דהוו תלתא פרסי כו', אמאי סמכיתו אבורגנין. כי נפק(ד) אחוי ליה מתוותא דמבלען בתוך ע' אמה ושיריים. והשתא אתי שפיר הא דבשמעתא דא"ל רב ספרא לרבא הני בני אקטיספון דמשחו להו תחומא מהאי גיסא דארדשיר – הא מפסקא דיגלת דהוו טפי מקמ"א אמות ושליש. השתא מזכיר שליש וקמ"א אמה, דהוי ב' קרפיפות – משום דאיירי בב' עיירות. וגבי רבא נקט דאחוי ליה אטמהתא דשורא דמבלען תוך תחום בשבעים אמה ושיריים – דלחבר לעיר צריך שיהיה תוך ע' אמה ושיריים. ונראה דאפי' בית ובית בלא עיר נותנים להם קרפף אחת לשתיהן. דאי לא תימא הכי – עיר שאין לה חומה במה יתחברו כאחת, אם לא ע"י שמובלעים יחד תוך ע' אמה ושיריים? דאין סברא להצריך שיגעו זה לזה. ולפ"ז, לרב חייא בר רב דאמר קרפף אחד(ה) לשתיהן – לאו דוקא הא דקאמרי רבנן ב' עיירות – דהוא הדין בית ובית, אלא אגב דנקט ר' מאיר עיר אחת נקטי רבנן ב' עיירות. והא דתניא בריש

סוכה

רבינו חננאל

משכחת לה נמי במתא דהיא אלפא אאלפא כו' אביי נמי על הדרך הראשונה שחשבנו א' לשמועה. מיהו אביי לא חשב חשבון מדידת העיר בכלל אלא התחום והקרנות בלבד. וכך פירושו העיר היא אלף על אלף תחומיה מכל צד אלפים ארך ברוחב אלף כמדת העיר נמצאו תחומיה בד' רוחות אלפים על אלף לכל רוח שמונת אלפים אמה אבל הקרנות הן בכל קרן אלפים על אלפים. כיון שבמזרח אלפים ובצפון אלפים צריך טבלא אלפים על אלפים למלאות מקום הקרנות מד' זווית הלכך קרנות כולהו כמה הוו ט"ז אלף נמצאו הקרנות והתחום כ"ד אלפים אמה ומגרש סביבות העיר ד' אלפים אמה ומן הקרנות ד' אלפים נמצא הכל ח' אלפים (בסר) [חסר] מהן (הרביע) [הריבוע] אלפים אמה נשארו ו' אלפים נמצאו ו' אלפים (כ"ד) [מכ"ד] אלף של תחומין ושל קרנות [ריבעא הוי]. רבינא אמר מאי רביע דתחומין רבינא דברי אביי [קמפרש]. וה"ק לא תימ' דאביי דאמר משכחת לה במתא דהיא אלפא אאלפא בהדי אלפא במתא קאמר *) אלא בר ממתא. ומאי רביע. רביע דתחומין הוא דקאמר. בא רבא לפרק דרך אחרת וא' האי דקתני נמצא מגרש רביע רביע דקרנות כי לעולם הקרנות הן י"ו אלף ומגרש הקרנות אלף מכל קרן שהן ד' אלפים נמצא לעולם מגרש הקרנות (רביעם) [רביע]. והאי דכתיב אלף אמה סביב דקרנות כדכתיב וזרקו את הדם על המזבח סביב. והוא סביב הקרנות ואחרי שהשלימו פי' דברי ר' אליעזר בר' יוסי הגלילי חזרו להקשות על הא דתניא נמצאת העיר משתכרת ת' אמה לכאן ות' אמה לכאן. והא איכא מורשא מורשא דקרנתא דעדיפי טפי מהאי שיעורא כדאמרינן בכל אתרא בעינן טפי משום מורשא דקרנתא. ודחינן הכא במאי עסקינן במתא עגילתא ואקשינן והא (דבעינן ד') [ריבעוה]. ופרקינן אימור דאמרינן כו'. אלא הוספנו על זו העיר זה השיעור. ואקשינן מכדי עגילא הוא כדקאמרת ואוספינן עלה כדי ריבועא מאבראי שיהא הוא ורבועו ד' כמה (מארבעה) [מרובע] יתר על העיגול רביע. כשתחשוב רביע של אלפים להיות הן ורבוען ד' כגון אלף וחמש מאות תוסיף עליהן ת"ק נמצאו הן ורבוען ד' חלקים כל חלק ת"ק נשארו מן האלפים ת"ק וריבועם (ת"ק) [דת"ק] מאבראי (קס"ד פחות שליש הכל קס"ז. ות"ק תרס"ז ועל זה הדרך רביע ת"ק הנשארים מן האלפים קס"ו פחות) [קס"ז פחות שליש] נמצאו הכל אלפים ושש מאות וששים ושבע אמה פחות שליש אמה ופרקינן בריבוע הכי נמי אבל בהלוכה בעינן טפי דאמר מר כל אמתא בריבועא אמתא ותרי חומשי באלכסונא וכיון דהכי מסקנא דשמעתא פרישנא מרישא על הדין אורחא דפרקינן ומוקמינן לה: **מתני'** נותנין קרפף לעיר כו'. אתמר ב' עיירות קרובות זו לזו מערבה כנגד מזרחה של חברתה. רב הונא אמר נותנין קרפף לזו וקרפף לזו. פי' נותנין לכל אחד [שבעים אמה] ושירים. שהן בית סאתים ואם אין בין ב' עיירות הללו יתר מזה השיעור נחשבות שתיהן עיר אחת וכל אחת נותנין לו תחומה לזו במזרח חברתה ולזו במערב חברתה מחוץ לעיר הקרובה לה במאה וארבעים אמה ואחת ושליש אלפים אמה. וחייא בר רב אמר אין נותנין אלא קרפף אחד לשתיהן. ואקשינן לרב הונא ממתניתין דתנן וחכ"א אין נותנין תורת קרפף אלא לשתי עיירות ופריק הכי קתני אין נותנין קרפף אלא לשתי עיירות ולעולם שתי קרפיפות לשתיהן הכי נמי מסתברא

מדקתני

*) [דברי רבינו אלו כמו שהם הם משולל הבנה ואולי ט"ס יש בכאן ואי"ה בסוף המסכת יבא ביאור על זה].

הגהות הב"ח

(א) גמ' ולזו שבעים אמה ושיריים עושה קרפף את שתיהן להיות אחת ש"מ: (ב) רש"י ד"ה דל לאורך וכו' להלן מן העיר: (ג) תוס' ד"ה כל אמתא וכו' ואם אין באלכסון של ה' אלא שבע אמות כמו שעולה: (ד) ד"ה רב הונא וכו' אבורגנין כו' נפק ואחוי ליה הני מתוותא דמיבלען וכו' מהאי גיסא לארדשיר כו' הא וכו' השתא מזכיר רב ספרא קמ"א אמה ושליש דהוי ב' וכו' אטמהתא דשורא דמיבלען בתוך ע' אמה ושיריים כצ"ל ותיבת תחום נמחק: (ה) בא"ד דאמר קרפף אחד לשניהם הא דקאמרי רבנן שתי עיירות לאו דוקא דהוא הדין בית:

הא מני — ר' מאיר היא. אי רבי מאיר היא, הא תני ליה רישא: נותנין קרפף לעיר דברי רבי מאיר! צריכא, דאי מההיא הוה אמינא: חד לחדא, וחד לתרתי, קמ"ל דלתרתי תרי יהבינן להו. ואי אשמעינן הכא — משום דדחיקא תשמישתייהו, אבל התם דלא דחיקא תשמישתייהו — אימא לא, צריכא. תנן: וכן שלשה כפרים המשולשין, אם יש בין שנים החיצונים מאה וארבעים ואחת אמה ושליש — עושה אמצעי את שלשתן להיות אחד. טעמא דאיכא אמצעי, הא ליכא אמצעי — לא. תיובתא דרב הונא! אמר לך רב הונא: הא אתמר עלה, אמר *רבה אמר רב אידי, א"ר חנינא: לא משולשין ממש, אאלא רואין: כל שאילו מטיל אמצעי ביניהן ויהיו משולשין, ואין בין זה לזה אלא ק"מ אמה ואחת ושליש — עשה אמצעי את שלשתן להיות אחד. א"ל רבא לאביי: כמה יהא בין חיצון לאמצעי? א"ל: באלפים אמה. והא את הוא דאמרת: *כוותיה דרבא בריה דרבה בר רב הונא מסתברא, דאמר: יותר מאלפים אמה! הכי השתא! התם — איכא בתים, הכא — ליכא בתים. ואמר ליה רבא לאביי: כמה יהא בין חיצון לחיצון? כמה יהא?! מאי נפקא לך מינה? גכל שאילו מכנים אמצעי ביניהן ואין בין זה לזה אלא מאה וארבעים ואחת ושליש. ואפילו ד' אלפים אמה?! א"ל: אין. והאמר רב הונא: *עיר העשויה כקשת, אם יש בין ב' ראשיה פחות מארבעת אלפים אמה — מודדין לה מן היתר, ואם לאו — מודדין לה מן הקשת! א"ל: התם — ליכא למימר "מלי", הכא — איכא למימר "מלי". א"ל רב ספרא לרבא: הרי בני אקיסטפון דמשחינן להו תחומא מהאי גיסא דארדשיר, ובני תחומא דארדשיר משחינן להו תחומא מהאי גיסא דאקיסטפון, הא איכא דגלת דמפסקא יתר ממאה וארבעים ואחת ושליש! נפק אחוי ליה הנך *אטמהתא דשורא, דמבלעי בדגלת בע' אמה ושיריים.§

מתני' דאין מודדין אלא בחבל של נ' אמה, לא פחות ולא יותר. הולא ימדוד אלא כנגד לבו. והיה מודד והגיע לגיא או לגדר — מבליעו וחוזר למדתו. *הגיע להר — מבליעו וחוזר למדתו, ובלבד

הא מני ר"מ היא. הך סיפא סתמא היא, ולאו מסקנא דמלתא דרבנן היא: ואי מהא. מסיפא דמיירי בשתי עיירות התם הוא דקאמר ר"מ דאף על גב דאיכא קרפף לכל חדא אמרינן חדא היא: משום דדחיקא תשמישתייהו. דהואיל וקרובות אין להן נויי העיר בב' קרפיפות עד דאיכא טפי, הלכך, עשה קרפף את שתיהן להיות אחת. אבל חדא דלא דחיקא תשמישתיה, שאין עיר אחרת סמוכה לה ויש לה אויר הרבה: אימא לא. ניתיב לה קרפף כלל, קמ"ל: טעמא דאיכא אמצעי. דהשתא אין בין עיר לעיר אלא קרפף אחד: לא משולשין ממש. בשורה אחת, אלא שלישי עומד מרחוק כנגד בין שני החיצונים*: כל שאילו מטיל אמצעי ביניהן. כלומר: הא דקתני במתניתין אם יש בין ב' החיצונים קמ"א — לא כדס"ד מעיקרא שאין ביניהן יותר, אלא מתניתין דמרחקי מהדדי טובא, וה"ק: אם יש אויר בין ב' החיצונים כדי להתמלאות אמצעי ולעמוד אויר הנשאר בין אמצעי ולחיצונים מכאן ומכאן על קמ"א לכאן, ומאה וארבעים ואחת לכאן — דהיינו ב' קרפיפות לשניהן, רואין כאילו הוא נתון ביניהן והרי כולן אחת. והיוצא מאחת מהן לילך דרך אחת מחברותיה מודד מחומת חברתה. אבל אם רבה אויר יותר מכאן — לא אמרינן רואין: וכמה. יהא רחוק אמצעי מהן דאמרינן רואין: אלפים. הואיל ויכול לבוא מזו לזו בלא עירוב, אמרי' רואין: והא את הוא דאמרת. לעיל (דף נה:) גבי עיר שעשויה כקשת, דאפילו יש בין יתר לקשת יותר מאלפים — הרי היא אחת, ומודדין לה מן היתר: איכא בתים. בקשת, והרי הדר בקשת יכול לבוא לראשיה דרך בתי הקשת: הכא. בין אמצעי לחיצונים: ואפילו טובא. ובלבד שיהא שיעור באמצעי למלאות כדאמרינן: ליכא למימר מליוה. מלא האויר שביניהן, דאין לך במה למלאותו: **מתני'** לא פחות ולא יותר. בגמ' מפרש טעמא: ולא ימדוד אלא כנגד לבו. קבעו לו חכמים מקום לשום כנגדו ראש החבל, שלא יתן זה כנגד צוארו וזה כנגד רגליו והחבל מתקצר, והתחומין מתמעטין: מבליעו. אם אינו רחב נ' אמה משפתו לשפתו מלמעלה, אע"פ שיש במדרונו הילוך יותר מאלפים — אין אומרים תעלה מדת מדרונו למדת התחום, אלא יעמוד זה על שפתו מכאן וזה על שפתו מכאן ויבליע מדרונו בחבל אחד: לגדר. חומת אבנים שנפלה ונעשה גל גבוה ומשופע, ובני אדם מהלכין עליו: וחוזר למדתו. בגמרא מפרש דמדקתני "חוזר למדתו" — משמע שאם היה רוחבו כנגד העיר יותר מחמשים, ואינו יכול להבליעו בחבל, ובאחד מראשיו שלא כנגד העיר יכול להבליעו — הולך ומבליעו שם ומודד והולך שם משפתו והלאה עד כנגד מקום שכלה בו שם רוחב הגיא כנגד העיר, וחוזר למדתו כנגד העיר ומשלים למדת תחומין:

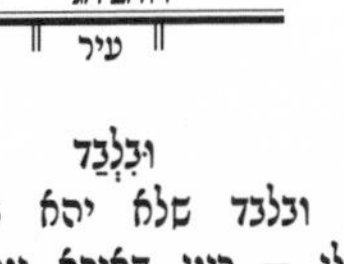

כזה לופה
רוחב הגי'
עיר

ובלבד

סוכה (דף ג:) בית שאין בו ד' אמות על ד' אמות אין עושין אותו עיבור בין ב' עיירות, ק"ק: מאי נפקא מינה מאותו בית, דבלא"ה נותנין קרפף לעיר! ואי משום שע"י הבית יוכל ללכת יותר — א"כ מה היה לו להזכיר ב' עיירות? אלא הל"ל אין עושין אותו עיבור לעיר! ואומר רשב"ס: דגרסינן התם "אין עושין אותו עיבור לעיר". ועי"ל: דנקט ב' עיירות — משום דאז רגילות לעשות בורגנין ללכת מזו לזו, כשרחוקין יותר מד' אלפים, שאין יכולין לבא ע"י עירוב. ואור"ת: דהלכה כרב הונא, דאמר קרפף לזו וקרפף לזו, דגדול היה בחכמה ובמנין מחייא בר רב דזוטר מיניה טובא, כדמוכח בסוף פרק "יש" בערכין (דף טז:) שהיה רב הונא מוכיחו. והנהו אמוראי דקאמרי: לאו משולשין ממש — סברי כרב הונא, דלחייא בר רב יכול להיות משולשין ממש. ורב ספרא דקאמר הא מפסקת דיגלת דהוה יותר מקמ"א ושליש, משמע דאי לאו טפי שפיר עבדי — והיינו כרב הונא. ועוד, אפי' לחייא בר רב הא משני סיפא דמתני' דקתני לזו ע' אמה ושירייס ולזו ע' אמה ושירייס כר"מ, והוי מחלוקת ואח"כ סתם — וא"כ לדידיה הוה הלכה כר"מ:

הא ליכא אמצעי לא תיובתא דרב הונא. וא"ת: לחייא בר רב נמי קשה, דהא אוקי סיפא כר"מ ולא בעי אמצעי! וי"ל: דלדידיה איכא לפרש דהך סיפא דג' כפרים אתיא כרבנן, ובא להשמיענו דעושים בורגנין הרבה זה אחר זה, כל אחד תוך ע' אמה ושירייס של חבירו, ליחשב הכל אחד, כמו שכאן עושה אמצעי שלשתן להיות אחד:

אלא כל שאילו מטיל כו'. ובין ב' החיצונות היינו בין החיצונות לאמצעית, ויש קמ"א ושליש לכאן וקמ"א ושליש לכאן כמו שפ"ה. וא"ת: מעיקרא נמי דקא ס"ד משולשין ממש, יפרש נמי כן דבין אמצעית לחיצונות קאמר, ולא יקשה לרב הונא! וי"ל: דבמשולשין ממש אין שייך לפרש כן, דא"כ לא ה"ל למתני בין ב' החיצונות, אלא הל"ל: אם יש בין זה לזה קמ"א ושליש. אבל כי לא איירי במשולשין ממש לא מצי למתני בין זה לזה, כיון שאין האמצעי שם ביניהן. ונראה דלחייא בר רב נמי צ"ל דלאו משולשין ממש, דאי משולשין ממש קאמר — אמאי נקט בין שנים החיצונות קמ"א אמה ושליש, וכולל אויר שמכאן ומכאן בבת אחת? הל"ל אם יש בין זה לזה ע' אמה ושירייס. ואם כן דמודה חייא בר רב למסקנא זו, אין ראייה מכאן דהלכה כרב הונא:

התם ליכא למימר מלי. פי': התם לבני אמצעי הקשת, אין מודדין להם מן היתר. וליכא למימר: מלי בענין זה כאילו בתיהם שבקשת נתונים ביתר, דא"כ מפסידין לצד אחר. דאם הוי היתר למזרח מפסידין למערב. וה"נ לא אמרינן מלי להיות רואין בני אמצעית כאילו עומדין בין החיצונות, למדוד להם משם אלפים. ודוקא לחיצונה דאמר מלי, כשבאין בני חיצונה זו לילך דרך חיצונה האחרת, שמודדין לכל אחת מפתח חברתה. וה"נ בני ראש קשת האחד שבאו לילך לצד ראש הקשת האחר דאמר מלי, ומודדין להם אלפים מראש הקשת האחר, אפילו יש בין שני ראשי הקשת יותר מארבע אלפים, ובלבד שלא יהא בין יתר לקשת יותר מאלפים כמו בין אמצעית לחיצונות דהכא, דלא שרי אלא עד אלפים. ועי"ל: דהתם לא אמרי' מלי — כיון דאיכא יותר מאלפים, דאביי לטעמיה דאמר כוותיה דרבא בריה דרבה בר רב הונא מסתברא, וביתר מאלפים לא אמרינן מלי. הכא איכא למימר מלי, דאוקימנא דליכא אלא אלפים בין האמצעית לחיצונה. ועוד י"ל: דהתם ליכא למימר מלי — כיון דהאויר שביתר אין יכול להחזיק בני הקשת, והוא הדין הכא אם היה אמצעית גדולה יותר מן האויר שבין ב' החיצונות, דליכא למימר מלי:

ובידו

כו א ב ג מיי' פכ"ח מהל' שבת הל' ה טוש"ע א"ח סי' שלח סעי' ח:
כז ד מיי' פכ"ח מהל' שבת הלכה יא סמג לאוין פו טוש"ע א"ח סי' שלט סעיף א:
כח ה מיי' שם טוש"ע שם סעיף ג:
כט ו מיי' שם טוש"ע שם סעיף ה:

רבינו חננאל

מדקתני סיפא *) אם יש בין שנים החיצונים [ק"מ] אמה [ואחת] ושליש כו' [נימא] תהוי תיובתא סיפא לחייא בר רב ודחינן הכי סיפא ר"מ היא **) מדקתני נותנין שלשה כפרים המשולשין פירוש השרויין כמין קשת שנים זה כנגד זה והשלישי ממוצע בין שתיהן עולה למעלה מהן אם יש בין שנים החיצונים כו' דייקינן מינה טעמא דאיכא אמצעי והוא שלישי לפיכך צריך כדי ב' קרפיפות מכלל דלשני כפרים לא יהבינן להו אלא קרפף אחד תיובתיה דרב הונא ודחי ולאו אמר רבא לא משולשין ממש אלא כל שאילו מכנים אמצעי לבניהן ואין בין זה לזה [אלא] ק"מ אמה ואחת ושליש ויראו כשהן משולשין עשה האמצעי שלשתן להיות כאחד. א"ל רבא לאביי כמה יהא בין חיצון לאמצעי א"ל אלפים. והא את הוא דאמרת בעיר העשויה כקשת כרבה בר רב הונא מסתברא אפילו יתר מאלפים [ומשני] הכי השתא התם בעיר העשוי' כקשת איכא מן (הראש) [הקשת] עד מקום החץ בתים הכא ליכא בתים. ועוד א"ל כמה יהא בין שנים החיצונים א"ל כל שאילו מכנים האמצעי ביניהן ואין ביניהן אלא ממאה וארבעים אמה ואחת ושליש ולמטה נמצא הדבר תלוי באמצעי אם הוא משוך הרבה או מעט הכל לפי (במשך) [משך] האמצעי. איני והאמר רב הונא עיר העשויה כקשת [וכו' התם] ליכא למימר מליא כי מקום החץ אינו ממלא אבל הכא בכפר האמצעי איכא למימר מלייה א"ל רב ספרא לרבא הני איקטיספון וארדשיר דאינון תרתי אתרא וסמיכא להדדי ודיגלת מפסקא להו בינייהו דהוא יתר מק"מ אמה ואחת ושליש היכי משחינן לבני איקטיספון תחומא אאידך גיסא דארדשיר ולבני ארדשיר מאידך גיסא דאקטיספון נפק אחוי ליה הנהו אטמהתא דמיבלען בדיגלת בתוך שבעים אמה ושיריים. פי' אטמהתא ירכות בניין כמו מערות ועומדין בתוך המים כאילו עיבור להטמתוותא: **מתני'** אין מודדין אלא בחבל של חמשים אמה.

*) [לכאורה נראה דט"ס הוא וצ"ל מדקתני סיפא אם יש לזו ע' אמה ושירייס וכו']. **) [נראה דצ"ל מדקתני וכן שלשה כפרים וכו'].

כזה * * *
[בק"ד רבא ובכ"י רב אדא]
[לעיל נה:]
[שם.]
[פי' ירכיות של חומה ערוך]
[ירושל' ל"ג]

מסורת הש"ס

עין משפט נר מצוה

ובלבד שלא יצא חוץ לתחום. *אם אינו יכול להבליעו – בזו אמר רבי דוסתאי בר ינאי משום ר' מאיר: שמעתי שמקדרין בהרים.§ גמ' מנא הני מילי? אמר רב יהודה, אמר רב: דאמר קרא: °"ארך החצר מאה באמה ורוחב חמשים בחמשים", אמרה תורה: בחבל של חמשים אמה מדוד. *האי מיבעי ליה *ליטול חמשים ולסבב חמשים! א"כ לימא קרא: "חמשים חמשים", מאי "חמשים בחמשים" – שמעת מינה תרתי.§ "לא פחות ולא יותר".§ תנא: לא פחות – מפני שמרבה, ולא יותר – מפני שממעט. א"ר *אסי: אין מודדין אלא בחבל של אפסקימא. מאי *אפסקימא? א"ר אבא: נרגילא. מאי נרגילא? א"ר יעקב: דיקלא דחד נברא. איכא דאמרי: מאי אפסקימא? רבי אבא אמר: נרגילא, רבי יעקב אמר: דיקלא דחד נברא. תניא, אמר רבי יהושע בן חנניא: אין לך שיפה למדידה יותר משלשלאות של ברזל, אבל מה נעשה שהרי אמרה תורה: °"ובידו חבל מדה". והכתיב: °"וביד האיש קנה המדה"! ההוא לתרעי. תני רב יוסף: שלשה חבלים הם: של *מגג, של נצר, ושל פשתן. של מגג – לפרה, *דתנן: [א]כפתוה בחבל המגג ונתנוה על גב מערכתה. של נצרים – לסוטה, *דתנן: [ב]ואח"כ מביא חבל המצרי וקושרו למעלה מדדיה. [ג]של פשתן – למדידה.§ "היה מודד והגיע".§ מדתני "חוזר למידתו" – מכלל דאם אינו יכול להבליעו, הולך למקום שיכול להבליעו, ומבליעו, וצופה כנגד מידתו וחוזר. תנינא להא, דתנו רבנן: *[ד]היה מודד והגיע המידה לגיא, אם יכול להבליעו בחבל של חמשים אמה – מבליעו, ואם לאו – הולך למקום שיכול להבליעו, ומבליעו, וצופה וחוזר למידתו. אם היה גיא מעוקם – מקדיר ועולה, מקדיר ויורד. הגיע לכותל – אין אומרים יקוב הכותל, אלא אומדו והולך לו. והא אנן תנן: מבליעו וחוזר למידתו! התם ניחא תשמישתא, הכא לא ניחא תשמישתא. אמר רב יהודה,[א] אמר שמואל: [ה]לא שנו אלא שאין חוט המשקולת יורד כנגדו, אבל

שמות כז | לעיל כג: | זכריה ב | יחזקאל מ

רש"י

ובלבד שלא יצא חוץ לתחום. שאם היה רחבו של גיא כנגד העיר יוצא חוץ לתחום, וזה הלך והבליעו שלא כנגד העיר ומודד משפתו ולהלן, לא ימדוד אלא עד כדי השלמת התחומין, וצופה כנגד מקום שמדתו כלה כנגד העיר בתוך הגיא, ויציין סימני התחום אבל לא ימדוד, וילך חוץ לתחום עד כנגד מקום תכלית שפת הגיא שכנגד העיר לידע כמה אמות יצא, וכמנין אותן אמות יחזור ויכנס לתוך הגיא ויציין. משום גזירה, שהרואה אותו מודד והולך שם יאמר שמידת התחומין ע"כ. ל"א: שלא יצא חוץ לתחום, אם היה ארוך וראשיו יוצאין חוץ לתחומי העיר ואין יכול להבליעו בחבל כנגד התחומין מפני רחבו, ויכול להבליעו שלא כנגד התחומין – לא יצא להבליעו שם, גזירה שמא יאמרו מדת תחומין של לידי העיר באה לכאן: בזו א"ר דוסתאי בר' ינאי. בזו למעוטי ערי מקלט ועגלה ערופה, דאין מקדרין בהן, כדמפרש בגמ' [לקמן:]: מקדרין. נוקבין. רואין כאלו נוקבין אותן ומודדין דרך הנקב, למעט מדת מדרונו. כדאמר בגמ' שמודדין אותו בחבל של ד"א, והתחתון מניח את החבל כנגד לבו והעליון כנגד מרגלותיו, ומתמעט מדרונו של כל ד"א חצי קומת אדם: גמ' מפני שמרבה. כשהחבל קצר יכול למותחו ומאריך המדה, והתורה אמרה בחבל של נ' אמה ימדוד: מפני שמתמעט. שכובדו מכפילו, ומתקצר באמצעיתו: נברא. סיב שגדל ומתגלגל סביב הדקל, כעין ויגל"א של גפנים: ובידו חבל מדה. במשכן של יחזקאל: וביד האיש קנה המדה. במשכן של יחזקאל: בדתרעי. למדוד רוחב השערים: מגג. יונ"ק בלע"ז. לפי שאינה מקבלת טומאה, שיהו כל מעשה פרה בטהרה: נצרים. ערבה קלופה. ל"א: נורי דקל, והוא סיב. הך דרב יוסף פליג אדרב אסי: הולך למקום כו'. כדפירשתי לעיל: ואם היה גיא מעוקם. שהיה מדרונו משופע ונוח להילוך – מקדר ועולה, כדפירשתי תחתון כנגד לבו כו' כך שמעתי, וקשה לי בה לקמן. ובתוספתא [פ"ד ה"ג]: ואם היה גיא מעוקם ואינו יכול להבליעו – מקדר וכו' וה"ק: אם היה גיא מתעקם והולך וסובב את העיר, וכשהוא מודד תחום מערב אינו יכול להבליעו בחבל של נ' אמה ברוח מערבית, עד שהוא מתעקם לצפון הוא מתחיל להשוות – אותה הבלעה אינה מועלת למדת תחום מערב, ומקדר ועולה: בדניחא תשמישתיה. נוח להילוך קצת, כגון מתלקט עשרה מתוך ארבעה, התם קתני: מבליעו אם יכול, ואם לאו – מקדר: הכא. בכותל זקוף יותר מדאי, דכיון דלא חזי להילוך אין גובה שיפועו עולה למדת התחום: לא שנו. דמקדר אלא דניחא תשמישתיה, שמעוקם כל כך שאין חוט המשקולת יורד כנגדו שכשמניח חוט משקולת הבנאים אצל שפתו והיא יורדת לעומקו מנקפת בשיפועו, ומעכבת המדרון מלירד כנגדו אלא מרחיקו מלמטה. כנגדו – משמע מכוון, ולקמן [ע"ב] מפרש דעד ד' אמות קרי ליה יורד כנגדו, שירחיק השיפוע את המשקולת לקרקעיתו ד"א מכנגד שפתו העליונה: אבל

תוספות

ובידו חבל מדה. פ"ה: במשכן של יחזקאל. *ור"ת כתב דההוא בספר זכריה, אבל "וביד האיש קנה המדה" הוא ביחזקאל: ההוא בדתרעי. וההוא דכתיב: מדד את רוח הקדים חמש מאות קנים בקנה המדה סביב וכן כתיב בד' רוחות, מפרש ר"י: דבחבל מדה היו מודדין ה' מאות קנים: בחבל המגג. אע"ג דשום חבל אינו מקבל טומאה, דבעינן טווי וארוג, כדאמר בפ' "במה אשה" (שבת דף סד.) – משום מעלה דפרה בעי' ממין שאין מקבל טומאה. *הגיע להר מבליעו. וא"ת: אמאי לא כייל להו בהדי הדדי, הגיע להר או לגדר – מבליעו? וי"ל: משום סיפא, דתני: שמעתי שמקדרין בהרים. לכך תני הר בפני עצמו, אע"ג דקידור שייך נמי בגיא וגדר. ואם נאמר דגיא וגדר שוין לגמרי, והר חלוק קצת מהן – הוה ניחא: ובלבד שלא יצא חוץ לתחום. רש"י פירש בלשון ראשון: שאם היה רחבו של גיא כנגד העיר, יוצא חוץ לתחום והולך להבליעו שלא כנגד העיר – לא ימדוד וילך חוץ לתחום עד כנגד תכלית שפת הגיא שכנגד העיר, וכמנין אמות שילא יחזור ויכנס לתוך הגיא ויציין – שלא יאמרו מידת תחומין באה לכאן כדמפרש בגמ' (לקמן:). ואין נראה, דבלאו הכי אי אפשר למדוד בענין זה שאם יחזור לתוך גיא ויציין במקום שכלות מנין אמות שיצא – הרי הוא מציין חוץ לתחום, שאותן אמות שיצא היו במישור ואותן אמות שנכנסו לתוך הגיא הן בשיפוע. ואי אפשר לומר שיתן חבל בגיא משפתו אל שפתו וכנגד אמות שיצא ימדוד על החבל וישים שם חוט המשקולת – דהא כיון דגיא רחב יותר מנ' אמה, אמרו חכמים שאין חבל מועיל שם, דהא אפילו ע"י כלונסין אין מועיל למתוח עליהם חבל של נ' אמה מזה לזה, אלא ילך למקום שיכוין ויבליע או יקדר: ואם אין יכול להבליעו. פי': אלא א"כ יצא חוץ לתחום, או שהיה גיא מעוקם, כדקתני בברייתא בגמ' [ע"ב]: ואם היה גיא מעוקם. פי' הקונטרס בלשון ראשון: שהיה מדרונו משופע ונוח להלוך – מקדרין. כך שמעתי, וקשה לי בה. ולא פירש מה קשיא ליה בה. ואומר ר"י, דקשה ליה משום דבסמוך קאמר עלה: לא שנו, כלומר, דמקדרין בגיא מעוקם – אלא שאין חוט המשקולת יורד כנגדו, אבל אם חוט המשקולת יורד כנגדו – מודדו מדידה יפה. פירוש: מדלג כל השיפוע, ואינו מודד אלא המישור שבתוך הגיא. וא"כ, הא דקתני מבליעו – היכי משכחת לה? כל זמן שאין חוט המשקולת יורד כנגדו – אכתי הוה מעוקם ומקדר ואינו מבליעו, וכי החוט יורד כנגדו – אין צריך להבליעו, אלא מודדו מדידה יפה ומדלג כל השיפוע. ומיהו, לפי' זה מצינו למימר ד"לא שנו" לא קאי אגיא מעוקם דמקדר כדפ"ה. אלא ה"פ: ל"ש דמבליעו או היכא דאינו יכול להבליעו דמקדרין – אלא שאין החוט יורד כנגדו. ואע"ג דאוקימנא דמבליעו היכא דניחא תשמישתא – בגיא מעוקם דניחא תשמישתא טפי, מקדרין. ומיהו, מדקתני בתוספתא אם היה גיא מעוקם ואינו יכול להבליעו – נ"ל כלשון שני של הקו', שהגיא מתעקם והולך סביב העיר, ואם יבלע מצד אחד יכול לטעות שצריך להיות נופה והולך כמה פעמים: אין אומרים יקוב את הכותל. פירוש: שיעמיד כלונסות ארוכין מכאן ומכאן, וימתח החבל מזה לזה להבליעו. אלא הקילו חכמים לסמוך על אמידה בעלמא, ואומדו בלבו והולך לו. כדמוקי לה בדלא ניחא תשמישתיה, וטורח לעלות על גביו. ומיהו, אם זקוף יותר מדאי עד שחוט יורד כנגדו, אפילו אמידה אין צריך, ומדלג כל שיפוע הכותל, כדאמר שמואל בסמוך גבי גיא. ודוקא גבי כותל והר הקילו היכא דלא ניחא תשמישו דאומדין – משום דצריך לעלות על גביו כשרוצה להבליע, וטירחא דמילתא טובא. אבל גבי גיא (מעוקם) לעולם מבליע אף על גב דלא ניחא תשמישתא, כל זמן שאין החוט יורד כנגדו, כדאמר שמואל – משום דאין טורח להבליע כולי האי: איכא

עין משפט נר מצוה

רש"ל גרס ור"ת כתב הגורס בשמועה זו ובידו חבל מדה הוא קרא הכתוב בספר זכריה אבל וביד האיש קנה המדה הוא ביחזקאל והגי' הנכונה פתיל פשתים בידו והכתיב וקנה המדה:

ל א מיי' פ"ג מהלכות פרה הלכה ב סמג עשין רלב:

[שלשה דיבורים אלו הגיע ובלבד ואם שייכין למתניתין]

לא ב מיי' פ"ג מהל' סוטה הלכה יא:

לב ג מיי' פכ"ח מהל' שבת הלכה יא סמג לאוין סו טוש"ע א"ח סי' שצט סעיף א:

לג ד ה מיי' שם הלכה יב יג טוש"ע שם סעיף ד ה:

מסורת הש"ס

לעיל לה:

[ע' תוס' לעיל כג: ד"ה פשטיה דקרא]

[גי' הערוך רבי אמי]

[גירסת הערוך אפקימא יש מפרשין חבל שעושין אותו מן קליפת אילן של אגוז עכ"ל ופי' שכתב הערוך היינו ע"כ לאיכא דאמרי מאי אפקימא וכו']

פי' מין גמי

פרה פ"ג מ"ט

סוטה ז:

[תוספתא פ"ד]

רבינו חננאל

מנ"ל אמר רב יהודה דאמר קרא אורך החצר מאה באמה ורחב חמשים בחמשים. אמרה תורה בחבל של חמשים אמה מדוד. ואקשינן האי קרא מיבעי לי ליטול חמשים ממאה של אורך וסבבם בחמשים האחרות כדי שיבא שבעים אמה ושיריים על שבעים אמה ושיריים ודחי א"כ נימא קרא חמשים חמשים ומאי בחמשים שמעינן מינה תרתי: לא פחות ולא יותר. תנא פחות מפני כשנמתח נמתח הרבה ומוסיף המדה. ואם הוא יתר מחמשים אמה אינו נמתח הרבה וממעט במדת התחום: ירושלמי. מדת התחום [ארבעים] חבלים לא פחות שהוא נמתח ונשבר ולא יותר שהוא נקמט ויפסיד. הגורס בשמועה זו ובידו חבל מדה. הוא הכתוב בס' זכריה (ב') אבל וביד איש קנה המדה ביחזקאל הוא והגירסא נכונה והכתיב ופתיל פשתים בידו וקנה המדה והוא עומד בשער. ביחזקאל (מ'). ההוא לתרעי פי' הקנה למוד בו מדת השער. חבל של אפסקמא. יש מי שאומר גוזל הנר ודקלא דחד נבארא זליף. א) פי' מקדרין חותכין כדגרסינן איזהו עור לבב כל שקרוע כנגד הלב ב). וקדור כמין ארובה ועיקרו מגדדין מלשון גודו אילנא. תני רב יוסף ג' חבלים [הן] של מגג לקשור בו את הפרה כדתנן בחבל של מגג כו' והוא חלקו. של נצרים לסוטה דתנן ואח"כ מביא חבל של מצרי וקושר למעלה מדדיה. חבל של פשתן למדידת התחום: מתני' היה מודד והגיע לגיא או לגדר כו' תנינא להא דת"ר היה מודד והגיע מדידה לגיא אם יכול להבליעו בחבל של חמשים אמה מבליעו כלומר מעביר החבל על גביו ואם לאו הולך למקום שפתח הגיא צר ומבליעו שם וצופה וחוזר למדתו. אם היה גיא מעוקם מקדיר ויורד. הגיע לכותל אין אומרים יקדיר את הכותל אלא אומדו והולך לו. ואי ניחא תשמישתיה מודד מדידה יפה. אמר רב יהודה אמר שמואל לא שנו שאין חוט משקולת יורד כנגדו אבל

א) [מתיבת פי' מקדרין עד תיבת גודו אילנא שייך למטה אחר תיבת מקדיר ויורד]. ב) עיין בערוך ערך קד א'.

הגהות הגר"א

[א] גמ' אר"י אמר שמואל ל"ש אלא כו'. נ"ב כאן ג' [illegible] לשמואל. ולישנא בתרא לרב יוסף. ולישנא בתרא דרבה. ראשונה בקידור לבד ואחרונה בהבלעה לבד [illegible]

[illegible] לקידור והבלעה] לגיא לבד וכו' אע"ג למפרע אבל רש"י לא כתב כן אלא מילתא דרבא בקידור ובהבלעה [*דהר [illegible] [*רש"י] וכן בעומקו של גיא חולק גם [*כן] רש"י (ושאר פוסקים) [*שמפרש] רק בהבלעה:

* כ"ה בכי"ק שעל גליון הגמ' שלו

לד א ב ג מיי' פכ"ח מהל' שבת הל' טו טז טוש"ע א"ח סי' שצ"ט סעיף ז:

לה ד מיי' פ"ט מהל' רוצח הלכה ד סמג עשין עח:

לו ה מיי' פכ"ח מהל' שבת הלכה יז סמג לאוין סו טוש"ע א"ח סי' שצ"ט סעיף ד וסעיף ז:

לז ו מיי' שם הלכה יט טוש"ע שם סעיף יא:

רבינו חננאל

אבל חוט המשקולת יורד כנגדו מודדו מדידה יפה. וכמה עומק של גיא. אמר רב יוסף אלפים והוא דאמר כאחרים דתניא אחרים אומרים אפילו עמוק אלפים ורחב נ' מבליעו. וחב"א עמוק ק' ורחב נ' מבליעו ואם לאו אין מבליעו איכא דאמרי [אמר] רב יוסף אפילו (יורד) [יותר] מאלפים א"ל אביי כמאן לא כרבנן ולא כאחרים ושנינן כי אמר רב יוסף בשאין חוט המשקולת יורד כנגדו וכי חוט המשקולת יורד כנגדו מודדו מדידה יפה עד כמה אמר אביי עד ד"א: **ירושלמי** כיצד מודדין את הנחל צר מלמעלה ורחב מלמטה עד נ' אמה אתה רואה אותו כאילו רואה עפר או צרורות. ואם לאו אתה רואה כאלו מטרפס ועולה מטרפס ויורד. היה הנחל מעוקם ר' חסדאי א' נוטל מצופות ומשער בה בעיניו במישור וחוזר ועושה כן בהר. הגיע להר מבליעו וחוזר למדתו. אמר רבא לא שנו אלא בהר המתלקט עשרה מתוך ה' מפני שעולה כמין גבשושית יתר משיעור שליש ואין החבל נמתח. אבל הר המתלקט י' טפחים מתוך (ד') [ה'] אמות. נוח הוא למדידה מודדו מדידה יפה כי גבשושית (שלישי) [שליש] כי הא דתניא [בזבחים פ"ג] כל כבשי כבשים ג' אמות לאמה חוץ מכבשו של מזבח שהוא מתוך שלש ומחצה ואצבע וחצי אצבע *) ובלבד שלא יצא חוץ לתחום. מאי כדי שלא יבואו לטעות הרואים ויאמרו מדת תחומין באה לכאן. ואם אינו יכול להבליעו מקדר ביצד מקדר תנא התחתון כנגד לבו ועליון כנגד מרגלותיו אמר אביי נקטינן אין מודדין אלא בחבל של ד' אמות. אמר רב נחמן אמר רבה בר אבוה אין מקדרין לא בעגלה ערופה ולא בערי מקלט מפני שהן של תורה: **מתני'** אין מודדין אלא מן המומחה

*) [עיין בגמ' הגי' ושליש אצבע וע"ש בתוס']

[מסכת דירושל' אמתני' דלאמר ההדיוט מריבה אין שומעין משמע כפרש"י תו"ע] [עיין תוספות תלמיש שלתה דברי תו"ע]

איכא דאמרי א"ר יוסף אפילו יותר מאלפים. ומסיק רב יוסף: כשהחוט יורד כנגדו איירי. ולפי המסקנא זו לא קאי רב יוסף אהבלעה כדאמר עד השתא. דהא אמרינן לעיל דמודדו מדידה יפה, אלא אדרב יהודה קאי, דאמר כשהחוט יורד כנגדו מודדו מדידה יפה. וקמ"ל, דאפילו יותר מאלפים מודדו מדידה יפה:

וכי אין חוט המשקולת יורד כנגדו עד כמה אמר אבימי עד ד"א. פי' רבינו שמואל: ואין חילוק בין עמוק נ' לק' או אלף או אלפים, אע"פ שב' אמות שיפוע של דבר מועט נוח להשתמש יותר מארבע אמות שיפוע של דבר גדול:

אבל מתלקט י' מתוך ה' מודדו מדידה יפה. [האי מודדו מדידה יפה] דהכא לא פ"ה כההיא דלעיל שמדלג כל השיפוע, אלא אדרבה: אין מבליע ואין מקדר, אלא מודד כל השיפוע דקרקע חלקה דמיא. ונראה דס"ה בגיא וגדר אם מתלקט י' מתוך ה', דקרקע חלקה דמי. והשתא איכא ד' דינים בכותל והר: דאם מתלקט י' מתוך ה' – מודד כקרקע חלקה, ואם מתלקט י' מתוך ד' – מבליע, ואם אין יכול להבליע – מקדר, ואי לא ניחא תשמישי' – אומדו והולך לו. ואם חוט יורד כנגדו – מדלג כל השיפוע. ובגיא אין חילוק בין ניחא תשמישי' ללא ניחא תשמישי', כדפרישית. ולהאי לישנא דרבא לא ידענא מאי קורין "ניחא תשמיש" ומאי קורין "לא ניחא תשמיש". אבל בלשון אחרון דרבא דאמר מתלקט י' מתוך ה' מבליעו – והיינו ניחא תשמישתא. ובמתלקט י' מתוך ד' אומדו והולך לו. והיינו "לא ניחא תשמישתא". ולפ"ז הלשון "אין בכותל והר" כי אם שלשה דינים: מתלקט י' מתוך ה' – מבליעו, ומתוך ד' – אומדו, וחוט יורד כנגדו – מדלג כל השיפוע. כך סוגיא זו מפורשת לפי שיטת הקונטרס. ור"ת מפרש: דחוט המשקולת קרי לכל דבר משופע וחלק שאין בו מורד ועיכוב שיוכל אדם לעמוד שם, והיינו משקולת. ותרגומא "יתמרהו בשרד" (ישעיה מד) – "ימסר במתקלא". אפי' יהא משופע בשיפוע הרבה נקרא משקולת, הואיל והוא משופע וחלק ביותר. וה"פ: לא שנו אלא שאין חוט המשקולת יורד כנגדו, פי': שאין בחוט המשקולת שיוכל אדם לרדת בו ולעלות, דהואיל דלא חזי להילוך – הקילו בו להבליעו. אבל חוט המשקולת יורד כנגדו, שיש בו מורד לירד ולעלות – לא הקילו להבליעו אלא מודדו מדידה יפה לגמרי, כי היא דלקמן דמן הדין בכ"מ היא(ה) למדוד כל השיפוע כדאמרינן לקמן: אין מקדרין לא בערי מקלט כו', אלא שבתחומין הקילו להבליעו כשאין חוט המשקולת יורד' כנגדו. וכמה עומקו של גיא דמבליעין – א"ר יוסף: אלפים, אבל מאלפים ואילך – לא, דכיון דהוי כתחום שבת – אין להקל בו. התם כשאין חוט המשקולת יורד כנגדו. א"ר יוסף קאי אמתניתין, כשאין (מודד ג) חוט המשקולת יורד כנגדו, ולכך מבליעין אפי' ביותר מאלפים. ורבנן ואחרים כשחוט המשקולת יורד כנגדו, דחזי להילוך. ואפ"ה מבליעין לגמר עד ק' אמה ולמר עד אלפים. ולהאי לישנא בתרא דרב יוסף הא דמפליג רב יהודה לעיל בחוט המשקולת יורד כנגדו – היינו ביותר מק' לרבנן, או ביותר מאלפים לאחרים, "עד כמה", פי': עד כמה יהיה הגיא שמבליעין – עד ד', אבל פחות מד' – הוי כקרקע חלקה, ומודד הכל. אבל מתלקט י' מתוך ארבע – אומדו והולך לו. פי' ר"ת: דלדוקא בהר שעשוי בידי שמים הקילו להיות אומדו, אבל גיא שעשוי בידי אדם כדרך שעושין גיאות ועמקים סביבות העיר לחוזק – לא הקילו להיות אומדו, אלא אפילו אין חוט המשקולת יורד כנגדו, דלא חזי להילוך – מבליעו, וכן גדר. ורבינו שמואל גרס לעיל בברייתא: הגיע לכותל יעוד את הכותל, והכי איתא בתוספתא (פ"ד), פי': יעוד כל שיפוע הכותל. ומוקי לה בדניחא תשמישתא, והיינו במתלקט י' מתוך ה'. ומתניתין דמבליעו – היינו במתלקט מתוך ד'. והכי נמי מוקי לה רבא בלישנא קמא. והא דקאמר התם בדניחא כו' – היינו משום דברייתא גופא מייתי אגב גררא. ושייך שפיר לישנא התם: לא שנו דמבליע אלא כשאין חוט המשקולת יורד כנגדו, כיון דאיכא ד"א לא בעלי וצריך להבליע. אבל חוט המשקולת יורד כנגדו, כיון דאין בשיפוע ד"א, ועוד, דלאוקימנא מתניתין בדלא ניחא תשמישתא – מדלג השיפוע ומודדו מדידה יפה. וכמה עומקו של גיא דלא בטלי ד"א ומבליע – אמר רבי יוסף: אלפים, אבל טפי מאלפים, אפילו ארבע אמות אויר או יותר – מדלג כל השיפוע. ומידת חכמים כך הוא, דפחות מארבע אמות לא חשיבי, ואפילו בפחות מק' וד' אמות או יותר חשיבי עד אלפים. טפי לא חשיבי. איתיביה אביי: עמוק ק' מבליעו, ואם לאו – אין מבליעו, אלא מדלג כל השיפוע. הוא דאמר כאחרים. איכא דאמרי, אמר רב יוסף: אפילו ביותר מאלפים לא בטלי ארבע אמות, ומבליע. ה"ג: התם כשחוט יורד כנגדו. פירוש: דרבנן ודאחרים דפחות מארבע חשיבי עד ק' לרבנן, או עד אלפים לאחרים. הכא כשאין חוט כו', דד' אמות חשיבי ולא בטלי אפילו ביותר מאלפים:

אין מודדין אלא מן המומחה. פי' ר"ת: דרך ישרה ומכוונת כנגד העיר. ו"מומחה" מלשון "ומחה על כתף ים כנרת" (במדבר לד). שלא ילך לצדי העיר למדוד שם אלפים, לפי שפעמים יש שם קרקע חלקה ונוח למדוד, ואחרי כן יהיה לופה ובא לו כנגד העיר, ולופה כנגד מידתו – אין לו לעשות כן, משום דפעמים יש כנגד העיר הרים וגאיות שיש לו להבליע או לקדר:

למקום

אֲבָל חוּט הַמִּשְׁקוֹלֶת יוֹרֵד כְּנֶגְדּוֹ – מוֹדְדוֹ מְדִידָה יָפָה. וְכַמָּה עוֹמְקוֹ שֶׁל גַּיְא? אָמַר רַב יוֹסֵף: אַלְפַּיִם. אֵיתִיבֵיהּ אַבַּיֵי: עָמוֹק ק' וְרוֹחַב נ' מַבְלִיעוֹ, וְאִם לָאו – אֵין מַבְלִיעוֹ. הוּא דְּאָמַר כַּאֲחֵרִים; דְּתַנְיָא, אֲחֵרִים אוֹמְרִים: אֲפִילּוּ עָמוֹק אַלְפַּיִם וְרוֹחַב נ' מַבְלִיעוֹ. אִיכָּא דְּאָמְרִי, אָמַר רַב יוֹסֵף: אֲפִילּוּ יָתֵר מֵאַלְפַּיִם. כְּמַאן? דְּלָא כְּת"ק וְלָא כַּאֲחֵרִים! הָתָם – שֶׁאֵין חוּט הַמִּשְׁקוֹלֶת יוֹרֵד כְּנֶגְדּוֹ, הָכָא – בְּחוּט הַמִּשְׁקוֹלֶת יוֹרֵד כְּנֶגְדּוֹ. וְכִי אֵין חוּט הַמִּשְׁקוֹלֶת יוֹרֵד כְּנֶגְדּוֹ עַד כַּמָּה? אָמַר אֲבִימִי: ד'. וְכֵן תָּנֵי רָמִי בַּר יְחֶזְקֵאל: ד'.§ "הִגִּיעַ לָהָר, מַבְלִיעוֹ, וְחוֹזֵר לְמִידָּתוֹ".§ אָמַר רָבָא: לֹא שָׁנוּ אֶלָּא בְּהַר הַמִּתְלַקֵּט י' מִתּוֹךְ ד', אֲבָל בְּהַר הַמִּתְלַקֵּט י' מִתּוֹךְ ה' – מוֹדְדוֹ מְדִידָה יָפָה. רַב הוּנָא בְּרֵיהּ דְּרַב נָתָן מַתְנֵי לְקוּלָּא; אָמַר רָבָא: [א]לֹא שָׁנוּ אֶלָּא בְּהַר הַמִּתְלַקֵּט עֲשָׂרָה מִתּוֹךְ חָמֵשׁ, אֲבָל בְּהַר הַמִּתְלַקֵּט עֲשָׂרָה מִתּוֹךְ ד' – אוֹמְדוֹ וְהוֹלֵךְ לוֹ.§ "וּבִלְבַד שֶׁלֹּא יֵצֵא חוּץ לַתְּחוּם".§ מַאי טַעְמָא? אָמַר רַב כָּהֲנָא: גְּזֵירָה שֶׁמָּא יֹאמְרוּ "מִדַּת תְּחוּמִין בָּאָה לְכָאן".§ "אִם אֵינוֹ יָכוֹל לְהַבְלִיעוֹ".§ תָּנוּ רַבָּנַן: [ב]כֵּיצַד מְקַדְּרִין? תַּחְתּוֹן כְּנֶגֶד לִבּוֹ, עֶלְיוֹן כְּנֶגֶד מַרְגְּלוֹתָיו. אָמַר אַבַּיֵי, *נְקִיטִינַן: [ג]אֵין מְקַדְּרִין אֶלָּא בְּחֶבֶל שֶׁל אַרְבַּע אַמּוֹת. *אָמַר ר"נ, אָמַר רַבָּה בַּר אֲבוּהּ, (א)(נְקִיטִינַן): אֵין מְקַדְּרִין [ד]לֹא בְּעֶגְלָה עֲרוּפָה וְלֹא בְּעָרֵי מִקְלָט, מִפְּנֵי שֶׁהֵן שֶׁל תּוֹרָה.§

מתני' [ה]אֵין מוֹדְדִין אֶלָּא מִן הַמּוּמְחֶה. רִיבָּה לְמָקוֹם א' וּמִיעֵט לְמָקוֹם אַחֵר – שׁוֹמְעִין לְמָקוֹם שֶׁרִיבָּה. רִיבָּה לְאֶחָד וּמִיעֵט לְאֶחָד – שׁוֹמְעִין לַמְרוּבֶּה. *וַאֲפִילּוּ עֶבֶד אֲפִילּוּ שִׁפְחָה נֶאֱמָנִין לוֹמַר "עַד כָּאן תְּחוּם שַׁבָּת". שֶׁלֹּא אָמְרוּ חֲכָמִים אֶת הַדָּבָר לְהַחְמִיר, אֶלָּא לְהָקֵל.

גמ'

אֲבָל אִם הָיָה חוּט הַמִּשְׁקוֹלֶת יוֹרֵד כְּנֶגְדּוֹ. שְׂפָתוֹ זְקוּפָה מְאֹד, שֶׁאֵין מִתְרַחֶקֶת שְׂפַת תַּחְתִּיתוֹ מִכְּנֶגֶד שְׂפַת גּוֹבְהוֹ. ד"א אֵין(ג) מִידַּת מִדְרוֹנוֹ מְמַעֵט מִידַּת הַתְּחוּם ע"י קִידּוּר, אֶלָּא נִכְנָס לְתוֹכוֹ וּמוֹדֵד קַרְקָעִיתוֹ מְדִידָה יָפָה כְּקַרְקַע חֲלָקָה, וְיוֹצֵא לִשְׂפָתוֹ וּמַשְׁלִים מִדָּתוֹ וְהוֹלֵךְ: כַּמָּה עוֹמְקוֹ שֶׁל גַּיְא. דְּנֵימָא מַבְלִיעוֹ כְּשֶׁהוּא רָחָב נ': אַלְפַּיִם. אֲבָל יוֹתֵר מִכָּאן, אַף עַל פִּי שֶׁיָּכוֹל לְהַבְלִיעוֹ – אֵינוֹ מַבְלִיעוֹ אֶלָּא מְקַדֵּר: הָתָם כְּשֶׁאֵין חוּט הַמִּשְׁקוֹלֶת יוֹרֵד כְּנֶגְדּוֹ. פְּלוּגְתָּא דת"ק וַאֲחֵרִים – הִלְכָּךְ, כֵּיוָן דַּחֲזֵי לְהִילּוּךְ קְצָת – חָזְיָינַן בֵּיהּ לְחוּמְרָא: עַד כַּמָּה. יִתְרַחֵק הַמִּשְׁקוֹלֶת מִכְּנֶגְדּוֹ, דְּקָרֵי לֵיהּ אֵין יוֹרֵד, וְנַחְמִיר בֵּיהּ: בְּמִתְלַקֵּט י' מִתּוֹךְ ד'. הַבָּא לִלְקוֹט כַּמָּה הוּא מַגְבִּיהַּ וְהוֹלֵךְ – מוֹצֵא י' טְפָחִים גּוֹבַהּ קוֹדֶם שֶׁיַּגִּיעַ לְהִילּוּךְ ד"א. אֲבָל מִתּוֹךְ חָמֵשׁ – כְּקַרְקַע חֲלָקָה דָּמֵי, וּמוֹדְדוֹ מְדִידָה יָפָה, וְאֵין כָּאן לֹא הַבְלָעָה וְלֹא קִידּוּר: מַתְנֵי לְקוּלָּא. בְּהַר מְשׁוּפָּע הוּא דְּבָעֵינַן הַבְלָעָה אוֹ קִידּוּר, אֲבָל בְּזָקוּף – אוֹמֵד בְּעָלְמָא: שֶׁלֹּא יֵצֵא חוּץ לַתְּחוּם. הָא פָּרְשִׁינַן לְעֵיל: בְּעָרֵי מִקְלָט. בִּתְחוּם עָרֵי מִקְלָט לִקְלוֹט, דִּתְנַן (מכות דף יא:): כְּשֵׁם שֶׁהָעִיר קוֹלֶטֶת, כָּךְ תְּחוּמָהּ קוֹלֶטֶת: בְּעֶגְלָה עֲרוּפָה. כְּשֶׁמּוֹדְדִין לֵידַע אֵיזוֹ הִיא קְרוֹבָה אֶל הֶחָלָל: מִפְּנֵי שֶׁמְּדִידָתָן מִן הַתּוֹרָה. הִלְכָּךְ, (ג)לָא מְשַׁעֲרִינַן בְּהוּ מִידֵּי, אֶלָּא מוֹדְדִין הָרִים וְגֵאָיוֹת כְּקַרְקַע חֲלָקָה:

מתני' ה"ג: אֵין מוֹדְדִין אֶלָּא מוּמְחֶה. בָּקִי בִּמְדִידָה: רִיבָּה בְּמָקוֹם אֶחָד וּמִיעֵט בְּמָקוֹם אַחֵר. שֶׁנִּמְצְאוּ סִימָנֵי תְּחוּם קֶרֶן זֶה אֲרוּכִּין וּדְלוּטִין מִכְּנֶגֶד סִימָנֵי תְּחוּם קֶרֶן שֶׁכְּנֶגְדּוֹ: שׁוֹמְעִין לְמָקוֹם שֶׁרִיבָּה. (וּמַה) וּמוֹצִיאִין מִידָּה הַקְּצָרָה כְּנֶגְדָּהּ, מִפְּנֵי שֶׁלֹּא מָתַח מִתְּחִילָּה הַחֶבֶל כָּל צָרְכּוֹ וְנִתְקַצֵּר, וְצָרִיךְ לְמוֹתְחוֹ בְּכָל כֹּחוֹ וְהָכִי תַּנְיָא נַמֵּי בְּתוֹסֶפְתָּא [פ"ד]: רִיבָּה לְא' וּמִיעֵט לְאֶחָד. מְפָרֵשׁ בַּגְּמָ': שֶׁלֹּא אָמְרוּ חֲכָמִים כו'. כְּשֶׁגָּזְרוּ שֶׁלֹּא לָצֵאת חוּץ לִתְחוּם לֹא אָמְרוּ לְהַחְמִיר בִּתְחוּמִין, אֶלָּא לְהָקֵל בִּתְחוּמִין:

גמ'

[עי' פירש"י לעיל ה. ד"ה והאמר ר"נ]

לעיל לה:

[עי' תוס' לקמן נט. ד"ה ריבה]

[נט.] [עי' תוס' לקמן נט. ד"ה אפילו]

הגהות הב"ח

(א) גמ' אמר רבה בר אבוה (נקיטינן) תא"מ ונ"ב ס"א אין זה וכן באלפס: (ב) רש"י ד"ה ורבנן כו' כל"ל: (ג) רש"י ד"ה אבל אם וכו' ד' אמות אין מדרונו ממעט מידת וכו' ונשר דף ל' דם: (ג) ד"ה מפני וכו' ה"ל מכין להם כ"ע: שם אין מקדרין לא בעגלה ערופה מפני שהן של תורה. (ד) תוס' ד"ה אבל וכו' ותרגומא יתמרהו בשרד. (ה) בא"ד בכל מקום היה ראוי למדוד:

גמ' למקום שריבה — אין, למקום שמיעט — לא?! אימא: אאף למקום שריבה.§ "ריבה לאחד ומיעט לאחד כו'".§ הא תו למה לי? היינו הך! הכי קאמר: בריבה אחד ומיעט אחד — שומעין לזה שריבה. אמר אביי: גובלבד שלא ירבה יותר ממדת העיר באלכסונא.§ "שלא אמרו חכמים את הדבר להחמיר, אלא להקל".§ והתניא: לא אמרו חכמים את הדבר להקל, אלא להחמיר! אמר רבינא: לא להקל על דברי תורה, אלא להחמיר על דברי תורה, *ותחומין דרבנן.§ [לעיל נח:]

מתני' *דעיר של יחיד ונעשית של רבים — מערבין את כולה. ושל רבים ונעשית של יחיד — אין מערבין את כולה, אא"כ עשה חוצה לה כעיר חדשה שביהודה, שיש בה חמשים דיורין, דברי רבי יהודה. ר"ש אומר: ג' חצירות של שני בתים.§ גמ' היכי דמי עיר של יחיד ונעשית של רבים? אמר רב יהודה: כגון *דאיסקרתא' דריש גלותא. א"ל ר"נ: מ"ט? אילימא משום דשכיחי גבי *הרמנא מדכרי אהדדי — כולהו ישראל נמי בצפרא דשבתא שכיחי גבי הדדי! אלא אמר רב נחמן: כגון דיסקרתא דנתזואי. ת"ר: עיר של יחיד ונעשית של רבים ורה"ר עוברת בתוכה כיצד מערבין אותה? עושה לחי מכאן ולחי מכאן, או קורה מכאן וקורה מכאן, ונושא ונותן באמצע. הואין מערבין אותה לחצאין, אלא: או כולה, או מבוי מבוי בפני עצמו. והיתה של רבים והרי היא של רבים, ואין

רש"י

גמ' למקום שמיעט לא. בתמיה: והלא יש בכלל מאתים מנה: היינו הך. דהיינו חדא, היינו למקום א': ה"ק ריבה א' ומיעט א'. שמדדום שני בני אדם, זה מיעט וזה ריבה: שלא ירבה יותר ממדת העיר באלכסונא. דאפי' ריבה שיעור גדול, דליכא למיתלי במתיחת החבל — תלינן ביה בטעות האלכסון. דאמרינן: זה היה בקי במדידה, והניח טבלא של תחומין כנגד הקרן באלכסון, כדאמרן (דף נו:) וזה מדד אלפים מאמצע הקרן, והפסיד את הזויות כל אלכסון של אלפים. אבל אם ריבה יותר מכך — אין לנו במה לתלות. ולבי מגמגם בלשון: לא להקל על דברי תורה. כל מה שגזרו חכמים בתחומין — להחמיר על דברי תורה באו, דמדאורייתא לא מתסרי מידי, ואינהו גזור. הלכך, אזלינן בהו לקולא, דהא תחומין עצמן מדרבנן: מתני' עיר של יחיד. שלא היו נכנסין בה תמיד ס' רבוא של בני אדם, ולא חשיבא רה"ר, דלא דמיא לדגלי מדבר: ונעשית של רבים. שנתוספו בה דיורין, או נקבעו בה שווקים: מערבין את כולה. כבתחלה, ואין מבואותיה צריכין תיקון, שהרי היא כחצר אחת. וכגון שאין בה רה"ר גמורה של ט"ז אמה. ואם יש בה — מפרש בגמרא תקנתא לרה"ר שבתוכה: ושל רבים שנעשית של יחיד. רבותא אשמועינן דאע"ג דנעשית של יחיד — אין מערבין את כולה, הואיל ותחלתה של רבים, דדילמא הדרא ומתעבדא של רבים ואתו לערובה כולה, ואסור לערב עיר של רבים בלא שיור. ואע"ג דאין בה רה"ר גמורה, שלא תשתכח תורת רה"ר. וההוא שיור הוי היכרא דטעמא משום עירוב הוא: אא"כ עשה חוצה לה. שיור, שלא עירבו עם שאר העיר, אלא לבדן: כעיר חדשה. כך שמה*: גמ' מ"ט. תלו טעמא בה דלא משכחת עיר של יחיד ונעשית של רבים אחריתי: משום דשכיחי רבים גבי הרמנא. אצל המושל, דהיינו ריש גלותא, ליטול רשות לדון ולהתיר בכורות ולסמוך: מדכרי אהדדי. דלא אתו למישרי של רבים, והרי היא של רבים: בצפרא דשבתא שכיחי אהדדי. לשמוע דרשה: אלא א"ר נחמן. כל עיר של יחיד ונעשית של רבים שריא: כגון דיסקרתא דנתזואי. כרך של אותו האיש: ורה"ר עוברת בתוכה. של ט"ז אמה רוחב: לחי מכאן ולחי מכאן. לראשי רה"ר. ובעיירות שאין להם חומה עסקינן, שראשי רה"ר מפולשין. ובשל רבים. והרי היא של רבים, לא שרו רבנן להא תקנתא, דכל מבואותיה המפולשין הוו כרה"ר, ובעו תקנתא מדרבנן דמיחלפי ברה"ר אבל בעיר של יחיד מוכחא מילתיה: ואין מערבין אותה לחצאין. דכיון דמעיקרא חדא היא — אסרי הני אהני, והויא כמבוי ששכח אחד מן החצירות ולא נשתתפה בו, דאסרה אכולהו: או מבוי מבוי. ולקמן פריך: השתא נמי ליסרו אהדדי:

תוספות

למקום שריבה אין למקום שמיעט לא. פ"ה: והלא יש בכלל מאתים מנה. ותימה: דמאי קשיא? דודאי אין שומעין למקום שמיעט, אלא הולכין עד מקום המרובה. ועוד: לישנא דמשני אף למקום שריבה — לא אתי שפיר. דלמקום שריבה דוקא הוא ולא אף למקום שריבה. ונראה לפרש: דהולכין למקום שריבה — משמע ליה דאף במקום שמיעט מצד שני, מאותו רוח מוליאין המדה עד כנגד מקום שריבה. ומתמי': נהי דאזלינן (א) ממקום שריבה עד מקום שציין ואומר דשפיר ציין, למקום שמיעט נמי אית לן למימר דשפיר ציין? ויש לתלות בהבלעה ובקידורין ובמדידה יפה שמודדין בהר המתלקט י' מתוך ה' ולא נתלה בטעות! ומשני: אף למקום שריבה, וכ"ש דאזלינן נמי אחר מקום שמיעט להחמיר. גירס' ר"ח: ובלבד שלא ירבה ממדתו ואלכסון. ולא גריס "באלכסון" אלא גרסינן "ואלכסון". ומיירי שמדדו שניהן מצד אחד. ולא הוי דומיא דרישא, והכי פירושו: דאם האחרון הרחיק ציון שלו יותר מן הראשון כמדת העיר ואלכסון, אין לנו לומר שטעה, אלא יש לנו לומר שהראשון קיצר ציון שלו לעיר בקרן מערבית דרומית, כי באותה שעה לא היו בעיר אלא ב' וג' בתים בקרן מזרחית לפונית ומדד משם, וזה מדד אחר שנתיישבה העיר ולא טעה:

אפילו עבד אפי' שפחה נאמנים כו'. וא"ת: והא אפי' עד אחד אינו נאמן, כדתניא בפרק ב' דכתובות (ד' כח.): אלו נאמנים להעיד בגודלן מה שראו בקוטנן: זהו כתב ידו של אבא, ועד כאן היינו מהלכין בשבת. ומוקי לה בגמרא — והוא דיש גדול עמו. משמע דגדול בפני עצמו לא מהימן! וי"ל: דה"נ איירי בגדול עמו, ולא חש כאן לפרש, הואיל וכבר פי' שם. ועוד י"ל: דהא דקאמר התם והוא דגדול עמו — לא קאי אכולהו. דע"כ לא קאי אאיש פלוני שהיה יוצא מבית הספר לאכול בתרומתו, דמוקי לה בתרומה דרבנן וסגי בגדול לחוד, דהא אין מעלין מתרומה דרבנן ליוחסין:

ותחומין דרבנן. משמע אי הוה דאורייתא — לא מהימני. ואע"ג דמעשה בכל יום שמאמינין לנשים בשחיטה וניקור ולתרום חלה — היינו משום דהוי בידה קודם שנעשית השחיטה, הוי בידה לשחוט. אבל תחומין — לא הוי כלל בידה. ולהכי נאמן קטן טפי בבדיקת חמץ מבתחומין, שאינו נאמן בקוטנו לומר: ע"כ היינו מהלכין, משום דבדיקת חמץ בידו. והא דקאמר *גבי בדיקת חמץ נשים ועבדים דהימנוהו רבנן בדרבנן, משמע דאי הוי דאורייתא — לא הימנוס, אע"ג דבידו! היינו משום דבדיקת חמץ צריך דקדוק וטורח גדול, לפיכך יש לחוש לעצלות הנשים טפי ממקום אחר. וכן משמע בירושלמי, דאיכא מ"ד דנשים אינן נאמנות בבדיקת חמץ מפני שהן עצלות, ובודקות כל שהוא*:

עיר של יחיד. פי' בקונט': שלא נכנסין בו תמיד ס' רבוא, ולא חשיב רה"ר, דלא דמי לדגלי מדבר. ונעשית של רבים — שניתוספו בה דיורין, או נקבעו שווקין, אז מערבין את כולה כבתחלתה. ואין מבואותיה צריכין תיקון שהרי היא כחצר אחת, כגון שאין בה רה"ר גמורה של ט"ז אמה. ואם יש בה — מפרש בגמרא: תקנתא לרה"ר שבתוכה. ע"כ לשון הקונטרס. והדין עמו, דודאי מתני' לא איירי ברה"ר גמורה, מדלא קתני: ורה"ר עוברת בתוכה, כדקתני בברייתא בגמרא. ואתיא מתני' נמי כרבנן דלית להו תקנתא דר' יהודה לערב רה"ר. ומיהו, בגמרא נמי לא איירי ברחב ט"ז אמה, דטפי מי"ג אמה ושליש לא הוי שרי ר' יהודה בלחי וקורה, כדפירשנו בפ"ק (דף ו.*). אלא י"ל: ורה"ר עוברת בתוכה — שאינו רחב ט"ז אמה, אלא יש רה"ר רחב ט"ז אמה מכאן ומכאן, ובוקעין דרך העיר מזו לזו, והוי רה"ר אף לתוכה דליכא ט"ז אמה, כמו בין העמודין דפ"ק דשבת (דף ז.) כדפירשנו בפ"ק (דף ו:). *כמאן דלא כר"ע. וא"ת: ולרבנן, לארכה נמי יערבו לחצאין, שיערבו מצד א' כל מבוי ומבוי בפני עצמו וליתיב כולה רה"ר לצד השני, דהשתא בני כל מבוי ומבוי מותרין כל אחד וא' במקומו ולא יאסרו שלא במקומן! וי"ל: דלא דמי, דשני חצירות זו לפנים מזו — רגל הפנימי המותרת במקומה אינה אוסרת שלא במקומה על החיצונה, דאחדא לדשא ומשתמשא ומסתלקא מלהשתמש בחיצונה. דעיקר תשמיש דחצר החיצונה לבני חיצונה היא, והויא פנימית בחיצונה שלא במקומה. אבל הכא, אף ע"ג דכל מבוי ומבוי מותר כל אחד ואחד במקומו — מודו רבנן דאסרי רה"ר על צד האחד, דהא מקומן הוא דרה"ר הוי להני כמו להני. ולרחבה דמערבין מדמי השתא לב' חצירות משום דיש לאלו רה"ר ופתח, וכן לאלו, ואין צריכין להשתמש בני פתח זה בצד פתח האחר. ובדאיכא דאמרי קאמר אפי' לרחבה אין מערבין, דלא מצי להסתלק מר"ה כלל, אע"ג דאית להו רה"ר כנגדו:

שער
מבוי | ר"ה | מבוי
דפנימית

עין משפט נר מצוה

לח א מיי' פכ"ח מהל' שבת הל' י"ז טוש"ע א"ח סימן שנ"ט סעיף ח:
לט ב ג מיי' שם טוש"ע שם סעיף ט:
מ ד מיי' פ"ה מהלכות עירובין הלכה יט סמג עשין א טוש"ע א"ח סי' שצ"ב סעיף א:
מא ה מיי' שם הלכה כד טוש"ע שם סעיף ד:
מב ו מיי' שם הל' יט טוש"ע שם סעיף א:

בערוך הגי' דסקרתא וכ"ה בר"ח וכן הגיה ה"ר יעב"ץ ז"ל

[שייך לעיל נח: במשנה]

[עי' שם תוס' ד"ה והוא]

רבינו חננאל

פירוש מקום ישרה מלשון ומחה [על כתף ים כנרת (במדבר ל"ד)]. ריבה למקום אחד ומיעט למקום אחר כו' אוקימנא שומעין למקום שמיעט ואף למקום שריבה. וכן ריבה אחד ומיעט אחד שומעין לזה שריבה ובלבד שלא ירבה יתר (מדירת) [ממדת] העיר ואלכסונה. אפילו עבד ואפילו שפחה נאמנין והתניא לא אמרו חכמים בדבר להקל אלא להחמיר אוקמא רבינא לא אמרו חכמים בדבר להקל על דברי תורה אלא להחמיר על דברי תורה ותחומין דרבנן כיוצא בו בנדה סוף פרק הרואה כתם א' רבינא לא אמרו להקל על ד"ת אלא להחמיר על ד"ת וכתמים עצמן מדרבנן: מתני' עיר של יחיד שנעשית של (יחיד) [רבים] מערבין את כולה [היכי דמי] עיר של יחיד ונעשית של רבים כגון דיסקרתא דריש גלותא ומקשינן אמאי התירו להו לערב כולן אי נימא דשכיחי כולהו קהרמנא פי' השלטון של מקום ומדכרי הדדי ומערבי ולא אתו למסמך חד (מחבריה) [אחבריה] אי הכי אפילו עיר של רבים ונעשית של יחיד נמי ליערבו דהא כולהו ישראל שכיחי גבי הדדי בצפרא בשבתא בעידן צלותא ומדכרי אהדדי. אלא אמר רב נחמן כגון דיסקרתא דאתי אזואר [דנתזואי]. פי' שם אדם: ת"ר עיר של יחיד ונעשית של רבים ורשה"ר עוברת כו' עד ואין מערבין אותה לחצאין אלא או

מסורת הש"ס

[לעיל לו. סוטה ל:]

[גיר' הערוך קהרמנא פי' השלטון של מקום]

הגהות הב"ח

(א) תוס' ד"ה למקום וכו' נהי דאזלינן למקום שריבה עד מקום שציין ואמרינן דשפיר:

[עי' רש"י קדושין עו. ד"ה אף מי וכו' הוסיף רש"י לבאר כדכתיב לנן וחלקה (יהושע טו)]

[ועי' תוס' לעיל לח: ד"ה כאן ותוס' פסחים ד: ד"ה הימנוהו]

[בד"ה וכו']

שייך לע"ב

מג א ב מיי' פ"ה מהל' עירובין הלכה כב טוש"ע א"ח סימן שצ"ב ס"ו בהג"ה:
מד ג ד מיי' שם הלכה כב טוש"ע שם סעיף ...:
מה ה ו מיי' שם הל' כב טוש"ע שם סעיף ב:
מו ז מיי' פ"ג שם הל' ג סמג עשין א' טוש"ע שם סי' שעא ס"ח:
מז ח מיי' שם פ"ד הלכה טז טוש"ע שם סעיף ג:

וְאֵין לָהּ אֶלָּא פֶּתַח אֶחָד — מְעָרְבִין אֶת כּוּלָּהּ, מַאן תַּנָּא דְּמִיעַרְבָא רה"ר? אָמַר רַב הוּנָא בְּרֵיהּ דְּרַב יְהוֹשֻׁעַ: רַבִּי יְהוּדָה הִיא; *דְּתַנְיָא, יָתֵר עַל כֵּן א"ר יְהוּדָה: מִי שֶׁיֵּשׁ לוֹ שְׁנֵי בָתִּים בִּשְׁנֵי צִידֵּי רה"ר — עוֹשֶׂה לֶחִי מִכָּאן וְלֶחִי מִכָּאן, אוֹ קוֹרָה מִכָּאן וְקוֹרָה מִכָּאן, וְנוֹשֵׂא וְנוֹתֵן בָּאֶמְצַע. אָמְרוּ לוֹ: אֵין מְעָרְבִין רה"ר בְּכָךְ. אָמַר מָר: "וְאֵין מְעָרְבִין אוֹתָהּ לַחֲצָאִין". אָמַר רַב פַּפָּא: [א]לֹא אָמְרוּ אֶלָּא לְאָרְכָּהּ, אֲבָל לְרָחְבָּהּ — מְעָרְבִין. כְּמַאן — דְּלָא כְּר"ע, דְּאִי כְּר"ע — *הָא אָמַר רֶגֶל הַמּוּתֶּרֶת בִּמְקוֹמָהּ אוֹסֶרֶת *אֲפִי' שֶׁלֹּא בִּמְקוֹמָהּ! אֲפִי' תֵּימָא ר' עֲקִיבָא; עַד כָּאן לָא קָאָמַר רַבִּי עֲקִיבָא הָתָם — אֶלָּא בִּשְׁתֵּי חֲצֵירוֹת זוֹ לִפְנִים מִזּוֹ, דִּפְנִימִית לֵית לָהּ פִּיתְחָא אַחֲרִינָא. אֲבָל הָכָא — [ב]הָנֵי נָפְקִי בְּהַאי פִּיתְחָא, וְהָנֵי נָפְקִי בְּהַאי פִּיתְחָא. אִיכָּא דְּאָמְרִי, אָמַר רַב פַּפָּא: לָא תֵּימָא לְאָרְכָּהּ הוּא דְּלָא מְעָרְבִין, אֲבָל לְרָחְבָּהּ מְעָרְבִין, אֶלָּא אֲפִילּוּ לְרָחְבָּהּ נַמִי לָא מְעָרְבִין. כְּמַאן — כְּר"ע! אֲפִילּוּ תֵּימָא רַבָּנַן; עַד כָּאן לָא קָאָמְרִי רַבָּנַן הָתָם — אֶלָּא בִּשְׁתֵּי חֲצֵירוֹת זוֹ לִפְנִים מִזּוֹ, דִּפְנִימִית אַחֲדָא לְדַשָּׁא וּמִשְׁתַּמְּשָׁא. אֲבָל הָכָא — מִי מָצוּ מְסַלְּקִי רה"ר מֵהָכָא. אָמַר מָר: "אוֹ כּוּלָּהּ, אוֹ מָבוֹי מָבוֹי בִּפְנֵי עַצְמוֹ". מ"ש דְּלַחֲצָאִין דְּלָא — דְּאָסְרִי אַהֲדָדֵי, מָבוֹי מָבוֹי נַמִי אָסְרִי אַהֲדָדֵי! הב"ע [ג]כְּגוֹן דַּעֲבוּד דַּקָּה. וְכִי הָא דְּאָמַר רַב אִידִי בַּר אָבִין אָמַר רַב חִסְדָּא: [ד]אֶחָד מִבְּנֵי מָבוֹי שֶׁעָשָׂה דַּקָּה לְפִתְחוֹ — אֵינוֹ אוֹסֵר עַל בְּנֵי מָבוֹי.§ "הָיְתָה שֶׁל רַבִּים וַהֲרֵי הִיא כו'".§ רַבִּי זֵירָא עַרְבָהּ לְמָתָא דְּבֵי רַבִּי חִיָּיא וְלָא שְׁבַק לָהּ שִׁיּוּר. א"ל אַבַּיֵי: מַאי טַעְמָא עֲבַד מָר הָכִי? אֲמַר לֵיהּ: סָבֵי דִידָהּ אָמְרִי לִי: רַב חִיָּיא בַּר אַסִּי מְעָרֵב כּוּלָּהּ. וְאָמִינָא: ש"מ עִיר שֶׁל יָחִיד וְנַעֲשֵׂית שֶׁל רַבִּים הִיא. א"ל: לְדִידִי אֲמַרוּ לִי הָנְהוּ סָבֵי: [ה]הַהִיא אַשְׁפָּה הֲוָה לָהּ מֵחַד גִּיסָא, וְהָשְׁתָּא דְּאִיפַּנְיָא לָהּ אַשְׁפָּה — הֲוָה לָהּ כִּשְׁנֵי פְתָחִים, וַאֲסִיר. א"ל: *לָאו אַדַּעֲתַאי. בָּעֵי מִינֵּיהּ רַב אַמִּי בַּר אַדָּא הַרְפָּנָאָה מֵרַבָּה: סוּלָּם מִכָּאן וּפֶתַח מִכָּאן מַהוּ? א"ל: הָכִי אֲמַר רַב: סוּלָּם תּוֹרַת פֶּתַח עָלָיו. אֲמַר לְהוּ רַב נַחְמָן: לָא תַּצִּיתוּ לֵיהּ, הָכִי אֲמַר(א) רַב אַדָּא אֲמַר רַב: סוּלָּם תּוֹרַת פֶּתַח עָלָיו, וְתוֹרַת מְחִיצָּה עָלָיו. [ו]תּוֹרַת מְחִיצָּה עָלָיו — כְּדַאֲמַרַן, [ז]תּוֹרַת פֶּתַח עָלָיו — בְּסוּלָּם שֶׁבֵּין שְׁתֵּי חֲצֵירוֹת, רָצוּ — אֶחָד מְעָרֵב, רָצוּ — שְׁנַיִם מְעָרְבִין. וּמִי אָמַר רַב נַחְמָן הָכִי? וְהָאָמַר רַב נַחְמָן אָמַר שְׁמוּאֵל: [ח]אַנְשֵׁי חָצֵר וְאַנְשֵׁי מִרְפֶּסֶת שֶׁשָּׁכְחוּ וְלֹא

לעיל ו. יב: כב. לקמן נה. שבת ו. קיז.

[לקמן סה: עה.]

בדפוס ויניציה ליתא מלת אפי' וגם רש"י ל"ג לה

[ברכות כו. ושם נסמן]

וְאֵין לָהּ אֶלָּא פֶּתַח א'. וְלָאו מְפוּלֶּשֶׁת הִיא, וְלָא דָּמֵי לְדִגְלֵי מִדְבָּר: אֶלָּא לְאוֹרְכָּהּ. דֶּרֶךְ עֲיָירוֹת לִהְיוֹת פִּתְחֵי פִּילוּשֵׁיהֶן לְאוֹרְכָּם, ורה"ר עוֹבֶרֶת מִפֶּתַח לְפֶתַח וַחֲלוּקָה לְאוֹרְכָּהּ. הִלְכָּךְ, אֵין בְּנֵי עֵבֶר הַלָּז רַשָּׁאִין לְעָרֵב לְבַדָּן, וּבְנֵי עֵבֶר הַלָּז לְבַדָּן מִשּׁוּם דְּהָנֵי וְהָנֵי דָּרְסִי בְּהַךְ רה"ר, וְיוֹצְאִין וְנִכְנָסִין דֶּרֶךְ פְּתָחִים לְכָאן וּלְכָאן, ורה"ר זוֹ מְחַבַּרְתָּם שֶׁכּוּלָּם מְעוֹרָבִין בָּהּ, וְאָסְרֵי אַהֲדָדֵי: אֲבָל לְרָחְבָּהּ. בְּנֵי שְׁנֵי הָעֲבָרִים לָרֹאשׁ הָאֶחָד לְבַד, וּבְנֵי שְׁנֵי הָעֲבָרִים לָרֹאשׁ הַשֵּׁנִי לְבַד – מְעָרְבִין, שֶׁהֲרֵי יְכוֹלִין לְהִסְתַּלֵּק אֵלּוּ מֵאֵלּוּ וְלֹא יְהֵא דֶּרֶךְ לְאֵלּוּ עַל אֵלּוּ, וּבוֹרְרִין לָהֶן אֵלּוּ פֶּתַח שֶׁאֶצְלָן וְאֵלּוּ פֶּתַח שֶׁאֶצְלָן: פְּלוּגְתָּא דְּרַבָּנַן ור"ע בְּפֶרֶק "הַדָּר" (לקמן דף עה.): רֶגֶל הַמּוּתֶּרֶת בִּמְקוֹמָהּ אוֹסֶרֶת שֶׁלֹּא בִּמְקוֹמָהּ. כְּגוֹן ב' חֲצֵירוֹת זוֹ לִפְנִים מִזּוֹ, וְהַחִיצוֹנָה פְּתוּחָה לִרה"ר וְהַפְּנִימִית אֵין לָהּ פֶּתַח לִרה"ר, אֶלָּא יוֹצֵאת דֶּרֶךְ חִיצוֹנָה. וְלָא מִיבַּעְיָא הֵיכָא דְּעֵירְבוּ דִּיּוּרִין שֶׁבַּחִיצוֹנָה לְבַדָּן, וּבְנֵי פְּנִימִית לֹא עֵירְבוּ בֵּינֵיהֶן לְבַדָּן לִהְיוֹת מוּתָּרִין בְּתַשְׁמִישׁ חָצֵר לְעַצְמוֹ – דַּהֲוָיָא רֶגֶל הָאֲסוּרָה בִּמְקוֹמָהּ דְּאָסְרָה דְּרִיסַת הָרֶגֶל דִּידְהוּ אַחִיצוֹנָה, אֲפִי' לְרַבָּנַן. דְּכֵיוָן דְּבֶחָצֵר דְּגוּפַיְיהוּ אָסְרֵי, לֵיכָּא לְמִכְפְּיִנְהוּ לְמֵיחַד דַּשָּׁא דִּידְהוּ, וְיִמְחֲלוּ עַל דְּרִיסַת הָרֶגֶל שֶׁיֵּשׁ לָהֶן עַל הַחִיצוֹנָה. אֶלָּא אֲפִילּוּ עֵירְבוּ זוֹ לְעַצְמָהּ וְזוֹ לְעַצְמָהּ, דַּהֲוָיָא פְּנִימִית מוּתֶּרֶת בִּמְקוֹמָהּ – פָּלֵיג ר"ע, וְאוֹמֵר: דְּרִיסַת הָרֶגֶל דִּידָהּ אָסְרָה אַחִיצוֹנָה, וּפְנִימִית מוּתֶּרֶת וְחִיצוֹנָה אֲסוּרָה. וְהָכִי נַמִי נִיתָּסְרוּ אַהֲדָדֵי: דִּפְנִימִית אַחְדָא דַּשָּׁא וּמִשְׁתַּמְּשָׁא. דְּכֵיוָן דְּמוּתֶּרֶת בִּמְקוֹמָהּ, כְּגוֹן זוֹ כּוֹפִין עַל מִדַּת סְדוֹם שֶׁלֹּא יְהֵא לָהּ הַיּוֹם דְּרִיסַת הָרֶגֶל עַל הַחִיצוֹנָה, אֶלָּא תִּסְגּוֹר דֶּלֶת שֶׁבֵּינֵיהֶן וְתִשְׁתַּמֵּשׁ בִּמְקוֹמָהּ: אֲבָל הָכָא. הֲרֵי רְשׁוּת הָרַבִּים שֶׁל אֵלּוּ וְשֶׁל אֵלּוּ אֶחָד הוּא, שֶׁאֵין בּוֹ חִילּוּק בְּאֶמְצַע אוֹרְכּוֹ וְלֹא רֶמֶז שֶׁל מְחִיצָּה, לוֹמַר: תִּיחוּד דַּשָּׁא וְתִשְׁתַּמֵּשׁ אֶת כּוּלָּהּ בִּמְקוֹמָהּ, וְהֵיכִי מָצֵית לְסַלֵּק הָנֵי מֵהָנֵי: מָבוֹי נַמִי אָסְרִי אַהֲדָדֵי. דְּכֵיוָן דְּמֵעִיקָּרָא שֶׁל יָחִיד הֲוָה, וְהָיוּ מְעָרְבִין אֶת כּוּלָּהּ וְהוּרְגְּלוּ לִהְיוֹת אֶחָד – אָסְרִי אַהֲדָדֵי. וַאֲפִי' אִיכָּא לֶחִי אוֹ קוֹרָה לַמָּבוֹי – לָא מְהַנֵּי: דְּעָבוּד דַּקָּה. פֶּתַח נָמוּךְ בְּרֹאשׁ כָּל מָבוֹי, דְּגָלוּ אַדַּעְתַּיְיהוּ לְאִסְתַּלּוּקֵי כָּל חַד מֵחַבְרֵיהּ: לְפִתְחוֹ. לְפֶתַח חֲצֵירוֹ: אֵינוֹ אוֹסֵר עַל הַמָּבוֹי. אִם לֹא נִשְׁתַּתֵּף עִמָּהֶן, דְּגַלֵּי אַדַּעְתֵּיהּ דְּאִסְתַּלַּק: וְלֹא שָׁבַק לָהּ שִׁיּוּר. וְעִיר שֶׁל רַבִּים וַהֲרֵי הִיא שֶׁל רַבִּים הֲוָה, מִדְּקָאָמַר לֵיהּ עִיר שֶׁל יָחִיד וְנַעֲשֵׂית שֶׁל רַבִּים(ב) אַלְמָא: הַהִיא שַׁעְתָּא דְּרַבִּים הֲוָה, וְאָמְרוּ לֵיהּ אִינְהוּ: מֵעִיקָּרָא נַמִי דְּרַבִּים הֲוָה, אֶלָּא אַשְׁפָּה הֲוָה לָהּ שֶׁסּוֹתֵם אֶחָד *[סַגֵּי לָהּ] מִפְּתָחֶיהָ, וְלֹא הָיָה לָהּ אֶלָּא פֶּתַח אֶחָד. וְאָמַר לְעֵיל דַּאֲפִי' שֶׁל רַבִּים בְּהָכִי הֲוָה סַגֵּי לֵיהּ: סוּלָּם. שֶׁעוֹלִין וְיוֹרְדִין בּוֹ חוּץ לְחוֹמָתָהּ: תּוֹרַת מְחִיצָּה עָלָיו. כְּלוֹמַר: אֵינוֹ מְבַטֵּל אֶת הַסְּתִימָה לִהְיוֹת כְּפֶתַח: בְּסוּלָּם שֶׁבֵּין ב' חֲצֵירוֹת. וְאֵין בֵּינֵיהֶן פֶּתַח, וְזֶה הַסּוּלָּם רָחָב ד' בֵּינֵיהֶן – הֲרֵי הוּא כִּשְׁתֵּי חֲצֵירוֹת וּפֶתַח בֵּינֵיהֶן, דְּאָמְרִינַן בְּפ' "חַלּוֹן" (לקמן דף עו.): רָצוּ – מְעָרְבִין אֶחָד, עֵירוּב אֶחָד לִשְׁתֵּיהֶן וְיִשְׁתַּמְּשׁוּ זוֹ בָּזוֹ דֶּרֶךְ גּוֹבַהּ הַכּוֹתֶל, וְדֶרֶךְ נְקָבִים וּסְדָקִין. דְּאִי לָא הֲוֵי פֶּתַח – אֵין מְעָרְבִין אֶחָד, וְלָא מָצוּ לְאִשְׁתַּמּוּשֵׁי דֶּרֶךְ חוֹרִין וּסְדָקִין: רָצוּ שְׁנַיִם מְעָרְבִין. שְׁנֵי עֵירוּבִין, אֵלּוּ לְעַצְמָן בְּנֵי בָּתִּים שֶׁל חָצֵר(ג) שֶׁלֹּא יֶאֶסְרוּ זֶה עַל זֶה לְהוֹצִיא מִבָּתֵּיהֶן שֶׁהֵן רְשׁוּת הַמְיוּחֶדֶת לְכָל אֶחָד לְתוֹךְ הֶחָצֵר שֶׁהוּא רְשׁוּת כּוּלָּן, וְאֵלּוּ לְעַצְמָן וְלֹא יִשְׁתַּמְּשׁוּ זוֹ בָּזוֹ: וּמִי אָמַר ר"נ הָכִי. דְּתוֹרַת מְחִיצָּה עָלָיו לְקוּלָּא: מִרְפֶּסֶת. אלדוי"ר בְּלַעַ"ז. דִּיּוּרֵי עֲלִיּוֹת סְמוּכוֹת זוֹ לָזוֹ וּפְתוּחוֹת לֶחָצֵר וְעוֹשִׂין מִרְפֶּסֶת עַל פְּנֵי אוֹרֶךְ עֲלִיּוֹת, וּפוֹתְחִין לָהּ פִּתְחֵי כּוּלָּן וְעוֹלִין וְיוֹרְדִין דֶּרֶךְ סוּלָּם שֶׁל מִרְפֶּסֶת לֶחָצֵר וּדְרִיסַת רַגְלֵיהֶן וִילִיאָתָן לִרְשׁוּת הָרַבִּים דֶּרֶךְ הֶחָצֵר הָוְיָא. לְפִיכָךְ, אִם אֵינָן מְעָרְבִין עִם הַדִּיּוּרִין הַתַּחְתּוֹנִים – אוֹסְרִים אֵלּוּ עַל אֵלּוּ לְהוֹצִיא כְּלֵי הַבָּתִּים לֶחָצֵר: וְלֹא

רש"ל

דפנימית אחדא דשא ומשתמשא. ומה שפי' בקונט': שלא יהא לה דריסת הרגל על החיצונה – לאו דוקא, דליכא קפידא בדריסת הרגל, דא"כ היתה מסתלקת לגמרי מרה"ר, דהא דרך חיצונה נפקא. ואין לנו לסלקה מרה"ר, כדאמרי' הכא: מי מצי מסלקי להו רה"ר מהכא? אלא תיחוד דשא מלהשתמש בחיצונה קאמר. וכן עשיית דקה דשמעתין – לענין תשמיש לא לענין הילוך: אבל הכא מי מצי מסלקי כו'. פי': דוקא פנימית אחדא דשא מלהשתמש בחיצונה שאינה מקומה, דעיקר חיצונה לבני חיצונה, אבל רה"ר, הוי להני כמו להני. ובחנם פ"ה דברה"ר אין חילוק באמצע ארכו, ולא רמז מחיצה, לומר תיחוד דשא ותשמש: מבוי מבוי נמי אסרי אהדדי. פי' בקונט': כיון דמעיקרא של יחיד הואי, והיו מערבין את כולה והורגלו להיות אחד – אסרי אהדדי. ואפי' איכא לחי או קורה למבוי – לא מהני. וקשה לר"י, דאמר בפ"ק (דף יד:): עושה לחי לחצי מבוי – יש לו חצי מבוי. אלמא משתרי חצי מבוי בפני עצמו אע"פ שהורגלו לערב כל המבוי יחד! ומיהו, איכא לאוקמא לההיא בדליכא חצירות פתוחות למבוי מן הלחי ולהלן: דעבוד דקה. מחיצה גבוה ד' (ס"א י') טפחים, כגון איצטבא בפני המבוי. ובקונט' פירש: פתח נמוך בראש כל מבוי. וכפירושו נראה, מדאמר בריש "כל גגות" (לקמן דף פט:): בנה עלייה ע"ג ביתו ועשה לפניה דקה – הותר בכל הגגין כולן, ולא יתכן לפרש שם אלא לשון פתח. ומיהו בסוף פירקין *פ"ה: דקה – מחיצה. ולא שבק לה שיור. משמע דאי שבק לה שיור הוה עביד שפיר, ולא הוה פריך ליה אביי מידי. וא"כ משמע כפי הקונט' דפי' במתני' דשל רבים והרי היא של רבים מהני ליה שיור. וכן משמע לקמן (דף ס.) גבי מחוזא: דמהני ליה שיור אע"ג דהיא של רבים כדמשמע בפ"ק (דף ו:), ומעיקרא נמי היתה של רבים. דאי של יחיד – לא היתה צריכה שיור. והא דנקט במתני' של רבים ונעשית של יחיד, לאשמועינ' דאע"ג דנעשית של יחיד – בעיא שיור*: בעא מיניה כו' מרבה. לא גרס "מרבה בר אבוה", דעליו לא היה אומר רב נחמן לא תציתו ליה, דרבו היה: תורת פתח עליו בסול' שבין ב' חצירות. תורת מחיצה עליו להקל היה יכול למנות נמי בסולם שבין ב' חצירות, כגון שרצפו בסולמות: דליערב

[דף סא. ד"ה אם יש לפניה דקה]

[ועי' תוס' לעיל כו. ד"ה מערבין]

הגהות הב"ח

(א) גמ' אמר רב אדא כו' אהבה אמר רב סולם תורת פתח: (ב) רש"י ד"ה ולא שביק וכו' ונעשית של רבים היא אלמא וכו' ואמר ליה איהו מעיקרא: (ג) ד"ה רצו וכו' של חצר זו שלא:

רבינו חננאל

או כולה או מבוי מבוי בפני עצמו ואם היתה של רבים והרי היא של רבים ואין לה אלא פתח אחד מערבין את כולה. הא דתניא אין מערבין אותה לחצאין אמר רב פפא לא שנו אלא לארכה רה"ר מפסקתה אבל לרחבה מערבין אותה לחצאין דהא לא מפסקתה בה רה"ר רב פפא דאמר כמאן דלא כר' עקיבא דאמר בב' חצרות זו לפנים מזו ועירבה זו לעצמה וזו לעצמה כי החיצונה אסורה שדריסת רגל הפנימית אוסרתה ודחינן אפי' תימא ר' עקיבא עד כאן לא קאמר ר' עקיבא אלא בב' חצרות זו לפנים מזו דפנימית לית לה פתחא אחרינא וכמאן בהא חצר דמי. אבל הכא בעיר שעירבו לחצאין הני נפקי בהא פתחא והני נפקי בפתחא אחריתי. איכא דאמרי אמר רב פפא כיון דרה"ר מפסקתה אפילו לרחבה אין מערבין אותה. נימא כר' עקיבא אמרה אפי' תימא רבנן עד כאן לא קאמרי רבנן בב' חצרות זו לפנים מזו אלא דפנימי' אחדא לדשא ומשתמשא אבל הכא מי מצי מסלקי רה"ר מהכא כיון דדרסי רבים לה אסרי לה אלא אי כולה אי מבוי מבוי בפני עצמו. ואסיקנא כגון דעביד דקה. פירוש כגון אצטבא בפני המבוי. וכדרב חסדא דאמר אחד מבני מבוי שעשה דקה על פתחו אינו אוסר על בני מבוי שכבר סילק עצמו מן המבוי כך מבוי אחד שעשה דקה לאותו מבוי אינו אוסר על מבואות אחרות. היתה עיר של רבים והרי היא של רבים ואין לה אלא פתח אחד מערבין את כולה. עיר של ר' חייא עיר של רבים ונעשית של יחיד הואי ועירבה ר' חייא לכולא ולא שבק שיורא א"ל אביי אמאי עבד מר הכי א"ל דאמרו סבי דהוו בה רב חייא בר אשי הוה מערב לכולא ואמינא ש"מ עיר של יחיד ונעשית של רבים *) של יחיד היא. א"ל לדידי אמרו לי סבי אשפה הוה לה מחד גיסא והשתא דאיפנאי הוו להו כב' פתחים ואסור. א"ל לאו אדעתאי. אמר רב נחמן אמר רב סולם מיכן ופתח מיכן תורת פתח עליו ותורת מחיצה עליו. תורת מחיצה עליו דלא בעי שיור. ש"מ דכל היכא [דאיכא] ב' פתחים לא מערבין לה עד דעבדין לה שיור. טעמא דשיור כדי שיזכרו בו כי העירוב הוא שהתיר את הטלטול לפיכך [צריך שיעור] כדי להיות מוכיח על העירוב. תורת פתח עליו בכותל שבין

*) [נראה דצ"ל וחזרה ונעשית של יחיד הוא].

רב נסים גאון

כמאן דלא כר' עקיבא דאי ר' עקיבא האמר רגל המותרת במקומה אוסרת שלא במקומה החיצונה שדריסת הרגל אוסרתה ובגמרא גרסי זו דברי רבי עקיבא דאמר אפי' רגל המותרת במקומה אוסרת שלא במקומה: עיקר דברי רבי עקיבא בפרק הדר עם הגוי (דף סב) דתנן רבי עקיבא אוסר את סליק כיצד מעברין

ולא עירבו, אם יש לפניהם דקה ארבעה — אינה אוסרת, ואם לאו — אוסרת! הכא במאי עסקינן — בדלא גבוה מרפסת עשרה. ואי לא גבוה מרפסת עשרה, כי קא עביד דקה מאי הוי?! במגופפת עד עשר אמות, דכיון דעביד דקה — איסתלוקי איסתלוק ליה מהכא. אמר רב יהודה, אמר שמואל: [א]כותל שרצפה בסולמות, אפילו ביתר מעשר — תורת מחיצה עליו. רמי ליה רב ברונא לרב יהודה במעצרתא דבי רב חנינא: מי אמר שמואל תורת מחיצה עליו, והאמר רב נחמן אמר שמואל: אנשי מרפסת ואנשי חצר ששכחו ולא עירבו, אם יש לפניה דקה ארבעה — אינה אוסרת, ואם לאו — אוסרת! הכא במאי עסקינן — דלא גבוה מרפסת עשרה. ואי לא גבוה מרפסת עשרה, כי עביד דקה מאי הוי? במגופפת עד עשר אמות, דכיון דעביד דקה — איסתלוקי איסתלק מהכא. הנהו בני קקונאי דאתי לקמיה דרב יוסף, אמרו ליה: הב לן גברא דליערב לן מאתין. א"ל לאביי: זיל ערב להו, *וחזי דלא מצווח' עלה בבי מדרשא. אזל, חזא להנהו בתי דפתיחי לנהרא, אמר: הני להוי שיור למתא. הדר אמר: "אין מערבין את כולה" תנן, [מכלל] דאי בעי לעירובי מצי מערבי, אלא איעביד להו כווי דאי בעו לעירובי דרך חלונות מצו מערבי. הדר אמר: לא בעי — *דהא רבה בר אבוה מערב לה לכולה מחוזא ערסייתא ערסייתא משום פירא דבי תורי, דכל חד וחד הוי שיור לחבריה, ואע"ג דאי בעו לערובי בהדי הדדי לא מצו מערבי. הדר אמר: לא דמי, התם — אי בעי לערובי דרך גגות והני לא מערבי, הילכך נעבדן כווי. הדר אמר: [ב]כווי נמי לא בעי, דההוא בי תיבנא דהו"ל למר בר פופידתא מפומבדיתא, ושויה שיור לפומבדיתא. אמר: היינו דאמר לי מר "חזי דלא מצווחת עלה בבי מדרשא".§ "אלא א"כ עשה חוצה לה כעיר חדשה".§ תניא, א"ר יהודה: עיר אחת היתה ביהודה וחדשה שמה, והיו בה נ' דיורים אנשים ונשים וטף, ובה היו משערים חכמים, והיא היתה שיור. איבעיא להו: חדשה מהו? [ג]חדשה, כי היכי דאיהי הויא שיור לגדולה — גדולה נמי הויא שיור לקטנה! אלא: כעין חדשה מהו? רב הונא ורב יהודה; חד אמר: בעיא שיור, וחד אמר: [ד]לא בעיא שיור.§ "ר"ש אומר ג' חצירות וכו'".§ *אמר רב חמא בר גוריא, אמר רב: הלכה כר"ש. רבי יצחק אמר: אפי' בית אחד וחצר אחת. חצר אחת ס"ד?! אלא אימא: [ה]בית אחד בחצר אחת. אמר ליה אביי לרב יוסף: הא דרבי יצחק גמרא או סברא? *אמר ליה: מאי נפקא לן מינה? אמר ליה: גמרא גמור וזמורתא תהא?!§

מתני' [ו]מי שהיה במזרח ואמר לבנו "ערב לי במערב", במערב ואמר לבנו "ערב לי במזרח", אם יש הימנו ולביתו אלפים אמה ולעירובו יותר מכאן — מותר לביתו ואסור לעירובו. לעירובו אלפים אמה ולביתו יתר מכאן — אסור לביתו ומותר לעירובו. [ז]הנותן את עירובו בעיבורה של עיר — לא עשה ולא כלום. נתנו חוץ לתחום, אפילו אמה אחת מה

רש"י

ולא עירבו. בני מרפסת עם בני חצר אלא אלו לבדן ואלו לבדן: אם יש לפניהם. לפני המרפסת, לרגלי הכבש בתחלת עלייתה: דקה. פתח קטן, גובה ארבעה, אין אוסרין בני מרפסת על בני החצר, דהא איסתלק להו: ואם לאו אוסרת. אלמא: תורת פתח עליו, ואפילו לחומרא: בדלא גבוה י'. דליכא למימר תורת מחיצה עליה: כי עביד דקה לפניה מאי הוי. הרי כל המרפסת סביבותיה נמוכה ופתוחה לחצר, והרי הן כשתי חצירות שאין כותל ביניהן: מגופפת. מוקפת מחיצה סביב, אלא שנשאר לפניה י' אמות כדין פתח בלא היקף. דאי עבוד התם דקה — סלוק נפשייהו, ואי לא ע"כ לחומרא נמי פתח הוא, הואיל דלא גבוה י': שרצפו. זקף סולם אצל סולם: תורת מחיצה עליו. ואין מבטלין המחיצה למהוי כנפרץ הכותל יותר מעשר, דאמר לקמן: מערבין אחד ואין מערבין שנים. אלא, רצו אחד מערבין ולקולא, והוי כפתח רצו שניהם מערבין, דלחומרא לא אמרינן דליבטליה למחיצה, דכל בעירובין להקל: ומי אמר שמואל. דלא מבטלא סולם למחיצה לחומרא: ואי לאו אוסרת. אלמא: אע"ג דגבוה מרפסת י' אתי סולם ומבטיל ליה: בדלא גבוה כו'. דבלא סולם נמי בטלה: דליערב מאתין. ועיר של רבים ונעשית של יחיד הואי, ובעיא שיור: דפתיחי לנהרא. פתחיהן אחורי העיר לנהר, ולא היה להם פתח פתוח לעיר: דאי בעו לערובי. הנך דמשיירי, מצו מערבי: איעביד להו כווי. חלונות שיש בהן ד' על ד' לצד העיר, דאי בעו הוו מצו מערבי, ואעבדינהו שיור למתא דלא ליערבו בהדייהו: ערסייתא ערסייתא. שכונות שכונות, ולא היו מערבין כל העיר כאחת: פירא דבי תורי.

גומא גדולה שמטמינים שם גרעיני תמרים למאכל בהמה. והיו אותן גומות מבדילות בין השכונות מתחת, ובכל שכונה היו מבואות הרבה, ומערבין יחד. ולא היו מתקנין לה לחיים, משום דעיר של רבים ונעשית של יחיד הויא, וכל חד וחד הוי שיור לחבריה, דאי לא הוי שיור — היכי מצו לערבי מבואות הרבה שבכל שכונה יחד. בכל עיר של רבים ונעשית של יחיד כל חד וחד באנפי נפשיה בעו עירובי, ובעי לחי וקורה בכל עיירות של רבים: ואף על גב דאי בעו לערובי לא מצי מערבי. משום פירא דמפסיק, ואין יכולין להלך משכונה לשכונה, והוי(א) חריץ שבין שתי חצירות, דאמרינן לקמן (דף עח.): מערבין שנים ואין מערבין אחד: דרך גגות. שהיו להם דיוטאות עוברות מגגי שכונה זו לגגי שכונה זו: דההוא בי תבנא כו'. ואמרינן לקמן: הלכה כר"ש דלא בעי נ' דיורין לשיור: ובה שיערו חכמים. שיורי עיירות. והיא עצמה היתה שיור לעיר גדולה הסמוכה לה: חדשה מהו. לעירובי באנפה נפשה, כולה בלא שיור: כעין חדשה. עיר קטנה אחרת של נ' דיורין ואינה סמוכה לגדולה: חצר אחת ס"ד. חצר בלא בית מי הוי דירה! בית אחד בחצר להם דיוטאות עוברות מגגי שכונה זו לגגי שכונה זו: דההוא בי תבנא כו'. ואמרינן לקמן: הלכה כר"ש דלא בעי נ' דיורין לשיור: ובה שיערו חכמים. שיורי עיירות. והיא עצמה היתה שיור לעיר גדולה הסמוכה לה: חדשה מהו. לעירובי באנפה נפשה, כולה בלא שיור: כעין חדשה. עיר קטנה אחרת של נ' דיורין ואינה סמוכה לגדולה: חצר אחת ס"ד. חצר בלא בית מי הוי דירה! בית אחד בחצר אחת. חצר ובית לתוכה סגי להיות שיור: **מתני'** מי שהיה במזרח. בשדה, וקדש עליו שם היום: ואמר לבנו. לערב מבעוד יום למערב: ולעירובו יותר מכאן. שנתן לו העירוב מביתו והלאה: מותר לביתו. לדין ביתו, כלומר: למנות שביתתו מביתו כאילו לא עירב: ואסור לעירובו. לדין עירובו, למנות שביתתו מעירובו. דכיון דקידש עליו היום רחוק מעירובו יותר מאלפים, נמצא שאינו יכול להלך וליטלו, שהרי אין עירובו קונה לו אלא אלפים לכל רוח. וכיון דאינו עירוב — הוי ליה שביתתו בביתו, שהרי בתחום ביתו הוה. ואע"ג דאוקמי' בשילהי "מי שהוציאוהו" *דאי מוקמת ליה באידך גיסא דאילן קם ליה כו' אלמא: אמר שביתתי רחוק מאלפים, ה"ז לא יזוז ממקומו — הני מילי בבא בדרך, דכיון דבמקום פלוני לא יכול לקנות דרחוק מאלפים הוה, ובמקום רגליו לא הוה ניחא ליה דליקני ליה — אין לו שביתה כלל, לפיכך לא יזוז ממקומו, אבל בעומד בביתו ועירב במקום שאינו עירוב — יש לו שביתה בביתו, דמסתמא בביתו ניחא ליה למיקני בשאין עירובו עירוב. כדתנן בפרק "בכל מערבין" (לעיל דף לה.) גבי נתגלגל חוץ לתחום ספק מבעוד יום ספק משחשיכה — ה"ז חמר גמל, ולא קתני לא יזוז ממקומו. שמעינן מינה דאם אינו עירוב יש לו שביתה בביתו: אסור לביתו. לדין ביתו, למנות מביתו אלפים לכל רוח: בעיבורה של עיר. באחד מן הבתים העומדין בתוך שבעים אמה ושירים: לא עשה ולא כלום. שהרי בלא עירוב נמי יש לו מן העיר אלפים לכל רוח, וכל העיר לו כארבע אמות: נתנו חוץ לתחום. מפרש בגמרא: חוץ לעיבורה של עיר: מה

תוספות

דליערב לן מאתין. מה שפי' בקונט' דעיר של רבים ונעשית של יחיד הואי – לאו דוקא לאפוקי והרי היא של רבים, אלא לאפוקי של יחיד ונעשית של רבים.

ושויה שיור לפומבדיתא. בהדי שיור דג' חצירות של שני בתים בעינן, והלכה כר"ש:

היינו דאמר (*ליה) חזי דלא מצווחא. שאם היה מזקיקם לעשות כווי על חנם, היו סותרין את בתיהם:

וחדשה שמה. בספר יהושע (טו) היא כתובה בנחלת יהודה:

גמרא. שהיה לו קבלה משום תנא, או סברא שמסברא היה אומר שכן נראה, אף על פי שאין שום תנא סובר כן. ולא לפסוק הלכה בא, אלא שכך היו דברים נראים. וקאמר: מאי נפקא לן מינה, כלומר: הא פסקינן לעיל כרבי שמעון! ומשני: גמרא גמור כו' – מ"מ יש לנו לחקור ולידע אם גמרא או סברא:

כאן

עין משפט נר מצוה

מח א מיי' פ"ה מהל' עירובין הלכה כב סמג שם טוש"ע א"ח סי' שלב סעיף ב:
מט ב שם סעיף ג:
נ ג שם סעיף א.
נא ד שם סעיף ז:
נב ה שם סעיף א:
נג ו מיי' פ"ו מהלכות עירובין הלכה ה טוש"ע א"ח סי' תיא:
נד ז מיי' שם הלכה ה טוש"ע א"ח סי' תה סעיף ג:

רבינו חננאל

ב' חצרות רצה אחד מערב רצו שנים מערבין. ומי אמר רב נחמן הכי והאמר רב נחמן אמר רב אנשי חצר ואנשי מרפסת ששכחו ולא עירבו אם יש לפניה דקה ארבעה אינה אוסרת ודחינן הכא במ"ע בדלא גבוהה עשרה אי הכי כי עביד דקה מאי הוי ופרקינן במגופפת פירוש מוקפת כמו מעקה עד עשר אמות כיון דעבוד בה דקה סלוקי מסלקי בני מרפסת נפשייהו מהתם. אמר רב יהודה אמר שמואל כותל שרצפו בסולמות אפילו ביתר מעשר תורת מחיצה עליו. ומקשינן ומי אמר שמואל הכי והא אמר רב נחמן אנשי חצר ואנשי מרפסת ששכחו ולא עירבו כו' פי' הא דאמר שמואל כותל שבין ב' חצרות שרצפו בסולמות ביתר מי' אמות במשכא שיכולין י' בני אדם באחד לעלות ולירד באחד לא חיישינן לסולמות הללו אלא תורת מחיצה שם. ההוא בני קקוניא דאמרו לרב יוסף הב לן גברא דמערב לן וא"ל לאביי זיל ערוב להן אזל חזא להנהו (והני) [בתי] דלא פתיחי (במתא) [למתא] ולא מצו מערבי לא הוי שיור אלא אעבד להו חלונות בהדי מתא דאי בעו מערבי דרך חלונות הדר אמר לא צריכי חלונות דהא רבה בר אבוה מערב לכולא מחוזא ערסתא ערסתא. פי' שכונות שכונות משום פירא (דכי) [דבי] תורי דהוה מפסקתה בינייהו כל ערסתא הוי שיור לאחריתי ואע"ג (מאי) [דאי] בעי לערובי לא מצי לערובי [הדר אמר התם אי בעי לאערובי] דרך גגות מצו מערבי הכא לא מצו מערבי אלא דרך חלונות ולא היא דהא ההוא בי תיבנא דהוה ליה למר (לבר) [בר] מפומבדיתא והוא הוה שיור לכולא מתא. ואמר אביי היינו דאמר לי רב יוסף זיל עריב להו וחזי (מאי צווית עלי) [דלא צווחת עלה] בבי מדרשא. תניא א"ר יהודה עיר אחת היתה ביהודה וחדשה היה שמה והיו בה נ' דיורין אנשים ונשים וטף ובה היו משערין חכמים והיתה שיור. ואיבעיא לן כי היכי דהוי היא שיור לגדולה גדולה נמי הוי שיור לדידה ומערבין לה' או לה רב הונא ורב יהודה חד אמר הויא שיור וחד אמר לא הויא שיור: ר' שמעון אומר שלש חצרות כו'. אמרינן משמיה דרב הלכה כר' שמעון רבי יצחק אמר אפילו בית אחד בחצר אחד הוי שיור והא דר' יצחק גמרא היא: **מתני'** מי שהיה במזרח יאמר לבנו לערב כו' קס"ד

הגהות הב"ח

(א) רש"י ד"ה ואע"ג כו' לשכונה והוי כחריץ:

[ע"ז עב:]
לעיל כו.
[לעיל מו. מט:]
[שבת קו: וש"נ]
[דף נ:]

נה א מיי' פ"ו מהלכות עירובין הלכה ה טוש"ע סי' תח סעיף ד:
נו ב מיי' שם הלכה ג טוש"ע שם סעיף א:
נז ג מיי' שם ופכ"ז מהל' שבת הלכה ח סמג עשין ח טוש"ע שם סעיף א:

מה שנשכר הוא מפסיד.§ גמ' קא סלקא דעתך "למזרח" – למזרח ביתו, "למערב" – למערב ביתו. בשלמא הימנו ולביתו אלפים אמה ולעירובו יתר מכאן – משכחת לה דמטי לביתיה ולא מטי לעירובו. אלא "הימנו ולעירובו אלפים אמה ולביתו יתר מכאן" היכי משכחת לה? א"ר יצחק: מי סברת "למזרח" – למזרח ביתו, "למערב" – למערב ביתו?! לא, "למזרח" – למזרח בנו, "למערב" – למערב בנו. *רבא בר רב שילא אמר: אפי' תימא למזרח למזרח ביתו ולמערב למערב ביתו, כגון דקאי ביתיה באלכסונא.§ "הנותן עירובו בתוך עיבורה וכו'".§ חוץ לתחום [א]ס"ד?! אלא אימא: חוץ לעיבורה.§ "מה שנשכר הוא מפסיד".§ מה שנשכר ותו לא?! והתניא: הנותן את עירובו בתוך עיבורה של עיר – לא עשה ולא כלום. נתנו חוץ לעיבורה של עיר, אפילו אמה אחת – משתכר אותה אמה, ומפסיד את כל העיר כולה, מפני שמדת העיר עולה לו במדת התחום! לא קשיא; [ב]כאן – שכלתה מדתו בחצי העיר, כאן – שכלתה מדתו בסוף העיר. וכדר' אידי, דאמר רבי אידי, א"ר יהושע בן לוי: *[ג]היה מודד ובא, וכלתה מדתו בחצי העיר – אין לו אלא חצי העיר. כלתה מדתו בסוף העיר – נעשית לו העיר כולה כד' אמות, ומשלימין לו את השאר. א"ר אידי: *אין אלו אלא דברי נביאות; מה לי כלתה בחצי העיר, מה לי כלתה בסוף העיר?! אמר רבא: תרווייהו תננהי; *אנשי עיר גדולה מהלכין את כל עיר קטנה, ואין

רש"י

מה שנשכר. לרוח זה נפסד לרוח שכנגדה. שהרי מנה מן העירוב אלפים לכל רוח, ואם נתנו בסוף אלף למזרח – נמצא שכלות אלפים של מזרח בסוף ג' אלפים לעיר, ונשתכר אלף. ואלפים של מערב כלות בסוף אלף של מערב העיר, והפסיד האלף. וקמ"ל דאין העיר עולה לו מן החשבון האלפים של מערב, אלא כולה כד"א: גמ' למזרח ביתו. ואמר לבנו לערב לו במערב ביתו, נמצא שביתו עומד[א] בינו לבין עירובו. והיכי תני "ממנו ולעירובו אלפים ולביתו יותר מכאן", הא ודאי עירובו מרחיק טפי: דמטי לביתיה. שהיה יכול לילך לביתו בלא עירוב, אבל לעירוביה לא הוה מטי: באלכסונא. בינו לבין עירובו משוך עירובו למערב יותר מביתו ואעפ"כ פעמים שהאלכסון רב, והרי ביתו רחוק ממנו יותר מעירובו: י"ג רבה

חוץ לתחום ס"ד. הא לא הוי עירוב: משתכר אותה אמה. לרוח העירוב, והפסיד מדת כל העיר לרוח שכנגדה. שכשימדוד אלפים מעירובו לצד העיר – תעלה לו מדת העיר מן החשבון: שכלתה מדתו בחצי העיר. אם היתה עיר גדולה, או שהרחיק עירובו מן העיר עד שאין כל העיר נבלעת במדת אלפים של עירוב – תעלה לו העיר מן החשבון, ומפסידה. ואם היתה כל העיר נבלעת באלפים של עירובו – הויא לה כולה כארבע אמות: היה מודד ובא. שבת חוץ לעיר, ולא היה יודע שיש עיר סמוך לו. ותנן בפרק "מי שהוציאוהו" (לעיל דף מה.) הואיל ולא היתה כוונתו לכך – לא יכנס לעיר אלא עד אלפים ממקום שביתתו. והתחיל למנות אלפים פסיעות בינוניות וכלתה מדתו כו' והוא הדין נמי לנותן עירובו חוץ לעיר וקנה שביתה: א"ר אידי אין אלו אלא דברי נביאות. כמתנבא מפני הגבורה, שאינו נותן טעם לדבריו אמרן רבי יהושע בן לוי לדברים הללו. ואי לאו דגמיר להו מרביה לא הוה אמר כי האי מילתא בלא טעמא: אמר רבא. ומאי נביאותיה? תרווייהו תנינהי במתני' דאנשי עיר גדולה שהיתה להן עיר קטנה בתוך אלפים, ויוצאין מעירן והולכין לילך דרך הקטנה מהלכין את כל העיר הקטנה הסמוכה להן, ועל כרחך ה"ק: מהלכין את כולה כד' אמות, ומשלימין מדתן חוצה לה. דאי ס"ד מדת העיר סליק להו – מאי אתא לאשמועינן?! פשיטא דעד אלפים יכול להלך*:

לעיל מב: ע"ש
ב"ב יב. בכורות מה.
[לקמן סא.]
[יכול להלך ואין אנשי כו' הד"א. רש"ל]

תוספות

כאן שכלתה מדתו בסוף העיר. תימה: ולרבנן, דאמרי בפרק "מי שהוציאוהו" (לעיל דף מה.) בישן בדרך שיש לו ח' על ח', ומסתמא דה"ה לנותן עירובו, כיון דקיס לן דנותן עירובו יש לו ד' אמות כמו שבת, הוא נשכר ד' אמות. שאם נתן עירובו למזרח העיר ד' אמות חוץ לעיבורה של עיר – הרי הולך למזרח ח' אמות ואלפים, ולמערב אלפים פחות ד' אמות מה שהעיר נחשב לו! וי"ל: דלר"א דאמר והוא באמצען, או לרבי יהודה דאמר בורר לו ד' אמות בכל רוח שירצה מה שנשכר הוא מפסיד, שנשכר ד' אמות במקום העירוב ומפסיד ד' אמות העיר דמונין לו העיר כד' אמות. וא"ת: לרמי בר חמא דמספקא ליה בסוף "מי שהוציאוהו" (לעיל דף נב.) בנותן עירובו אם יש לו ד' אמות, תפשוט מהכא, דאי אין לו ד' אמות – א"כ מפסיד יותר ממה שנשכר, שאם נותן עירוב ארבע אמות חוץ לעיבורה של עיר לצד מזרח, נשכר ד' אמות לצד מזרח ומפסיד ח' אמות לצד מערב דמונין לו ד"א שחוץ לעיבורה של עיר והעיר ד' אמות! ואומר ר"י: דלרמי בר חמא[ב], אם נותן עירובו אין לו ד"א, גם העיר אם מובלעת תוך תחום העירוב נחשבת לו כמשהו, ואין מפסיד כלום במשך העיר. דהאמר בס"פ דהנותן עירובו בתוך העיר או בתוך מערה שיש בה דיורין – יש לו אלפים חוצה לה, ואמאי יש לו אלפים שלימות? כיון דנחשבה כד' אמות, ונאמר שהנותן עירובו אין לו ד' אמות. אלא ודאי ס"ל שאם אין לו ד' אמות – העיר נחשבת לו כמשהו. וא"ת: ולר"א דאמר והוא באמצען, כשנתן עירובו באמה אחרונה של עיבור העיר לצד מזרח – יהיה לו לצד מזרח ב' אמות ואלפים, ולצד מערב אלפים פחות ב' אמות, דהעיר נחשבת לו כד' אמות. ולעירוב נותן ב' אמות וב' אמות שניות של עיר יעלו לחשבון אלפים, ואמאי תנן: המניח עירובו בעיבורה של עיר לא עשה ולא כלום? וי"ל: כשעומד תוך המחילות או במקום שנחשב כד"א – אין חילוק בין עומד באמצע לעומד בסוף, דאפי' עומד בסופו כאילו עומד באמצעו, ואין נותנין חוצה לה כלום. דהא במי שהוציאוהו חוץ לתחום ונתנוהו בדיר או בסהר – מהלך את כולה ולא חוצה לה, ואפי' הוא עומד בסופה: אין אלו אלא דברי נביאות. אומר ר"י: דבכ"מ שאומר אין אלו אלא דברי נביאות – הוי לשבח, כלומר: אין חכמה כזו שמבין לחלק כל כך סברא מועטת, וברוח הקדש אמר. דהכי משמע בפ"ק דבבא בתרא (דף יב.) גבי מנת בכרס אני מוכר לך, סומכוס אומר: לא יפחות לו מג' קבין. א"ר יוסי: אין אלו אלא דברי נביאות. ומייתי עלה: מיום שחרב בית המקדש נטלה נבואה מן הנביאים ונתנה לחכמים. משמע לשבח קאמר. ובפ'[ג] "אלו מומין" (בכורות דף מה.) דאשכחן דלא הוי לשבח, לא קאמר בהאי לישנא, אלא "עשו דבריהם כדברי נביאות", פי': לאומרם בלא טעם. דפריך: אי אבר הוא – באהל נמי ליטמא. והכא נמי הוי לשבח, כההוא דב"ב. וקאמר רבא: תרווייהו תננהי, ומאי קמ"ל ריב"ל? ומסיק: דסוף העיר איצטריכא ליה לריב"ל לאשמעינן, דלא תנן. אבל אין לפרש דרב אידי קורא אותן דברי נביאות לומר שאין נראה לחלק בדבר, ורבא קאמר תרווייהו תננהי ושפיר חילק ריב"ל. אע"ג דבפרק "בהמה המקשה" (חולין דף עא:) גבי הא דאמר רבה כשם שטומאה בלועה כו', קאמר: תרווייהו תננהי, והתם הוי פירושו מאי קמ"ל רבה? מדקא משני: כי קאמר רבה – כגון שבלע ב' טבעות. מ"מ אשכחן נמי בפרק "אין מעמידין"* תרווייהו תננהי דלא להקשות מאי קמ"ל קאתי, אלא להביא סייעתא לדבריו. גבי הא דקאמר*) (רבא) (המקדש**) (בשור) הנסקל כו'. מ"מ, הכא משמע דרבא בא להקשות מאי קמ"ל ריב"ל, מדמסיק סוף העיר איצטריכא ליה. ומיהו, רבינו שמואל לא גרס "איצטריך" אלא סוף העיר לא תנן. ודוחק הוא, שמוחק הספרים. ועוד: לא מצינו למימר דר' אידי לא סבר[ד] כר' יהושע, דהא לא מתרצא מתני' ובריתא אלא כר' יהושע, כדאמר לעיל. ומהר"י אומר: דמתני' ובריתא איירי בלן בה, ולהכי כי כלתה מדתו בסוף העיר – כל העיר נחשבת לו כד' אמות למנין אלפים. דהא אפילו כלתה מדתו בחצי העיר בלן בה, נחשבת לו כד' אמות להלך את כולה. כדמשמע ב"הדר" (לקמן דף עג.), דקאמר: והרי נותן עירובו בסוף אלפים וקאתי וביית בביתיה. אלמא: בלן בה, אפילו כלו אלפים שלו בתחילת העיר – נעשית כל העיר כד' אמות, וכן בפרק "בכל מערבין" (לעיל דף לח:) דקאמר: מי סברת דמנח ליה בסוף אלפים לכאן. ופירש רש"י: דכל העיר נעשית לו כד' אמות, כיון דלן בה. ור' אידי לא מתמה אלא אר' יהושע, דאמר אפילו במודד כשכלתה מדתו בסוף העיר – כל העיר נעשית לו כד' אמות. ולהכי מתמה: כיון [ה]כשכלתה מדתו בחצי העיר אין לו אלא חצי העיר, ולא נעשית לו כד' אמות אפילו להלך את כולה, כי כלתה בסוף העיר נמי אין נעשית כל העיר כד' אמות להשלים לו את השאר. והשתא אתי שפיר מאי דפריך לעיל מה שנשכר ותו לא, והתניא כו'. ולא פריך ממתני' והתנן ולמודד שאמרו כו'. דלגבי מודד הוה ידע דיש לחלק בין כלתה מדתו בחצי העיר לכלתה בסוף העיר. ולהכי פריך מנותן דהוה לן בה. ומשני: דבלן בה נמי יש לחלק, דבכלתה מדתו בחצי העיר נהי דנעשית לו כד' אמות שיכול להלך כל העיר, לענין שיוכל לצאת לצד אחר של עיר – לא נעשית לו כד' אמות. ולספרים דגרסי נמי סוף העיר איצטריכא ליה דלא תנן – אתי שפיר. אף על גב דסוף העיר נמי תנן, דאם לא כן תיקשה ממתניתין אברייתא, כדאקשי לעיל – מ"מ במודד איצטריכא ליה, דהא לא שמעי' ממתניתין, כדפירשתי:
*) [צ"ל רב] **) [צ"ל בפרק שור]

[ע"ז דף לד:]

רבינו חננאל

קס"ד מזרח [מזרח] ביתו ומערב מערב ביתו בשלמא לביתו אלפים לעירובו יתר מיכן משכחת לה כגון דעירב ואנח עירובו למזרח ביתו ואתי ממערב ביתו דמטא לביתו ולא מטא לעירוביה אלא לעירובו אלפים אמה ולביתו יתר מיכן היכי משכחת לה ופריק ר' יצחק מתני' דקתני מזרח ביתו מזרח בנו הוא ולא ידע היכא מנח בנו עירוב וחשיך ליה יומא בדוכתא *) האי דיניה דמטי לביתיה ולא מטי לעירוביה. רבה בר בר שילא אמר אפילו תימא מזרח ביתו ומערב ביתו וכגון דקאי ביתו באלכסון פי' כגון שנתן עירובו במזרח ביתו מן הצד נמצא ממקום רגליו עד עירובו אלפים אמה מכוונות וביתו עומד בקרן זוית לעירובו כשמניח הדרך הנכון מוטה ללכת לביתו נמצא מהלך באלכסון ועודף עליו יתרון האלכסון כולו שהוא בכל אמה שני חומשי אמה כדקיימא לן כל אמתא בריבועא אמתא ותרי חומשי באלכסונא. וזהו שאמר לעירובו אלפים אמה ולביתו יתר מיכן אסור לביתו ומותר לעירובו שכבר עקר שביתתו מביתו אבל אם ביתו בתוך אלפים אמה עומד אע"פ שעירב (לנו) [לו] בנו לא נעקרה שביתתו מביתו אלא מותר לביתו ובטל עירובו: הנותן עירובו בעיבורה של עיר שהיא בתוך שבעים אמה ושיריים לא עשה כלום שהעיבור מכלל העיר הוא חשוב וכאילו עירובו בתוך העיר הוא וכמו מי שלא נתן עירוב כלל דמי. נתנו לעירוב חוץ לתחום (בין) [כיון] שאין יכול להלך לעירוב בשבת אינו עירוב שנמצא הוא במקום אחד ועירובו במקום אחר ותריצ' אלא אימא חוץ לעיבורה של עיר. מה שנשכר הוא מפסיד פי' הנותן עירובו במזרחו של עיר מחוץ לעיבורה אלף אמה נשתכר אלף אמה שיש (לך) [לו] לילך במזרחה של עיר שלשת אלפים אמה אלף אמה שהן מן העיר ועד עירובו ומעירובו ולהלן אלפים אמה והפסיד ממערבה של עיר אלף אמה שאין לו רשות לילך במערבה של עיר אלא אלף אמה בלבד ואקשינן איני והא תניא נתנו חוץ לעיבורה של עיר אפי' אמה אחת נשכר אותה אמה והפסיד את העיר כולה מפני שמדת העיר עולה למדת התחום. ופרקי' לא קשיא משנתינו כגון שכלתה מדתו בסוף העיר כגון שנתן העירוב חוץ לעיבורה של עיר באלף אמה והעיר היתה כולה אלף אמה. נמצא ממקום עירוב עד סוף העיר אלפים אמה שהן מן העירוב עד עיבורה של עיר ואלף אמה מדת העיר וכריב"ל דאמר היה מודד ובא והגיע מדתו בסוף העיר נעשית כל העיר כד' אמות ומשלימין תשלום אלפים אמה מחוץ לעיר שהן אלף אמה נמצא מה שנשכר במזרח הפסיד כנגדו במערב ולא הפסיד מכלל העיר כלום. ובריתא כגון שכלתה מדתו בחצי העיר אין לו אלא חצי העיר. נמצא (זה) שהפסיד חצי העיר ואלפים אמה שמן הצד האחד ולא נשתכר באותו הצד שנתן עירובו אלא אלף אמה בלבד ואע"ג דא"ר אידי אין אלו אלא דברי נביאות שאינן נשמעין הימנו אלא כגזירה מה לי כלתה מדתו בחצי העיר ומה לי כלתה בסוף העיר הא אמר רבא כריב"ל ומסייע ליה ממשנתנו נמצא מקיים דבריו ולפיכך אמר תרווייהו תננהי אנשי עיר גדולה מהלכין את כל עיר קטנה מפני שהיא קטנה וכלתה מדתו בסוף העיר. אבל בעיר שהיא גדולה בני עיר קטנה שכלתה מדתו בחצי העיר אין מהלכין כל עיר גדולה

*) לשון זה אין בו ביאור ואולי צ"ל דמשכחת להו דהיינו דמטא לעירוביה ולא מטא לביתיה וצ"ע.

הגהות הב"ח

(א) רש"י ד"ה למזרח ביתו וכו' עומד בינו לבין עירובו כזה:

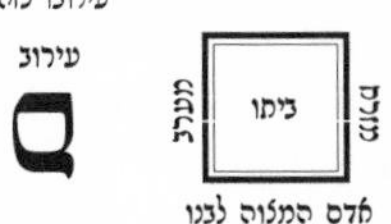

אדם המלוה לבנו

(ב) תוס' ד"ה כאן וכו' ולרמי בר חמא לאס: (ג) ד"ה אין אלו וכו' ובפרק מומין אלו לאו הוי: (ד) בא"ד לא סבר לה כר' יהושע ב"ל דהא לא כנ"ל וכן בסמוך: (ה) בא"ד ולהכי מתמה כיון דכשכלתה:

ואין אנשי עיר קטנה מהלכין את כל עיר גדולה. מאי טעמא – לאו משום דהני כלתה מדתן בחצי העיר, והני כלתה מדתן בסוף העיר? ורבי אידי "אנשי" "אנשי" תני, ומוקים לה בנותן, אבל מודד לא תנן. ולא?! והתנן: ולמודד שאמרו נותנין לו אלפים אמה, שאפילו סוף מדתו כלה במערה! סוף העיר איצטריכא ליה, דלא תנן. אמר רב נחמן: מאן דתני "אנשי" לא משתבש, ומאן דתני "אין אנשי" לא משתבש. מאן דתני "אנשי" לא משתבש – דמוקים לה בנותן, ומאן דתני "אין אנשי" לא משתבש – דמוקים לה במודד. וחסורי מחסרא והכי קתני: אנשי עיר גדולה מהלכין את כל עיר קטנה, ואין אנשי עיר קטנה מהלכין את כל עיר גדולה. במה דברים אמורים – במודד, אבל מי שהיה בעיר גדולה והניח את עירובו בעיר קטנה, היה בעיר קטנה והניח את עירובו בעיר גדולה – מהלך את כולה וחוצה לה אלפים אמה. אמר רב יוסף, אמר רמי בר אבא, אמר רב הונא: [א]עיר שיושבת על שפת הנחל, אם יש לפניה דקה ארבעה – מודדים לה משפת הנחל, ואם לאו – אין מודדין לה אלא מפתח ביתו. אמר ליה אביי: [ב]דקה ארבע אמות אמרת לן עלה. מאי שנא מכל דקי דעלמא דארבעה? א"ל: התם לא בעיתא תשמישתא, הכא בעיתא תשמישתא. אמר רב יוסף: מנא אמינא לה – דתניא: *התיר ר' שיהו בני גדר יורדין לחמתן, ואין בני חמתן עולין לגדר. מאי טעמא – לאו משום דהני עבוד דקה והני לא עבוד דקה? כי אתא רב דימי, אמר: טטרוגי מטטרגי להו בני גדר לבני חמתן. ומאי התיר – התקין. ומאי שנא שבת? דשכיחא בה שכרות. כי אזלי להתם נמי מטטרגי להו! כלבא בלא *מתיה שב שנין לא נבח. השתא נמי מטטרגי בני חמתן לבני גדר! כולי האי לא כייפי להו. רב ספרא אמר: עיר העשויה כקשת הואי. רב דימי בר חיננא אמר: אנשי עיר גדולה ואנשי עיר קטנה הואי. רב כהנא מתני הכי. רב טביומי מתני הכי: רב ספרא ורב דימי בר חיננא; חד אמר: עיר העשויה כקשת הואי, וחד אמר: אנשי עיר קטנה ואנשי עיר גדולה הואי.§ מתני' *אנשי עיר גדולה מהלכין את כל עיר קטנה, *ואנשי עיר קטנה מהלכין את כל עיר גדולה. כיצד? מי שהיה בעיר גדולה ונתן את עירובו בעיר קטנה, בעיר קטנה ונתן את עירובו בעיר גדולה – מהלך את כולה וחוצה לה אלפים אמה. רבי עקיבא אומר: אין לו אלא ממקום עירובו אלפים אמה. אמר *להן ר"ע: אי אתם מודים לי בנותן עירובו *במערה, שאין לו אלא ממקום עירובו אלפים אמה? אמרו לו: אימתי – בזמן שאין בה דיורין, אבל יש בה דיורין – מהלך את כולה וחוצה לה אלפים אמה. נמצא קל תוכה מעל גבה. *ולמודד שאמרו נותנין אלפים אמה – *)שאפילו סוף מדתו כלה במערה.§

גמ'

*) [לעיל נב: איתא אפילו ובכרי"ף איתא ואפילו]

רש"י

ואין אנשי עיר קטנה מהלכין את הגדולה. כולה כד' אמות, לפי שהעיר עולה להו במדת התחומין: ור' אידי. דאמר דברי נבואה הן אנשי אנשי דקתני במתני' בתרווייהו תני מהלכין, ומוקי לה בנותן עירובו בעיר, כדמפרש במתניתין: כיצד מי שהיה בעיר גדולה ונתן עירובו בעיר קטנה הסמוכה לה בתוך אלפים, מהלך את כולה, שעירוב קונה לו כל העיר כד"א, כאילו שבת הוא שם. ורבא תני: "אין אנשי", כדאמר לקמן מאן דתני "אין אנשי" לא משתבש: אבל מודד. מחוץ לעיר ובא לעיר, לא תנן מידי חלוק בין כלתה בחצייה לכלתה בסופה: ולמודד. ממקום שביתתו או ממקום עירובו, שאמרו ליתן לו אלפים – אפילו סוף מדת אלפים כלה במערה – לא יכנס מאלפים והלאה. אלמא: כלתה מדתו בחצי העיר תנן דעולה לו מדת העיר, ומאי נפקותיה: סוף העיר איצטריכא ליה. לרבי יהושע בן לוי, לאשמועינן דהיכא דכלתה מדתו בסוף העיר הויא כל העיר כד' אמות, דלא תנן לה: מוקי לה בנותן. כדקתני במתני' בהדיא: ומאן דתני אין אנשי עיר קטנה כו' לא משתבש מוקי לה במודד. אנשי עיר גדולה שיוצאין מעירן לעיר קטנה הנבלעת כולה בתוך אלפים שלהן, כגון שרחוקה מעירן אלף והיא עצמה אלף, מהלכין את כולה כד' אמות ומשלימין אלף חוצה לה. ואין אנשי עיר קטנה מהלכין את כל עיר גדולה הרחוקה מעירן אלף והיא עצמה אלפים הואיל ואין כולה נבלעת באלפים שלהן – עולה להן במדת התחום, ואין נכנסין לה אלא באלף ומתניתין דמפרשא וחזיא בנותן עירובו – חסורי מיחסרא כו': שפת הנחל. עמוק: אם יש לפניה דקה. מחיצה ארבע אמות גובה על פני העיר כולה משפת הנחל, מודד משפת הנחל שהיא כלה שם כשאר עיירות: ואם לאו. כיון דבעיתא תשמישתייהו – לא הוי ישוב קבוע, והוו להו כיושבי צריפין, ואין מונין לכל אחד אלא מפתח ביתו: דקה ד"א אמרת לן. בגינותא. והשתא בעינן מינך טעמא מאי שנא מכל דקי דעלמא, דסגי להו בגובה ארבעה טפחים, כדאמרן לעיל גבי מרפסת שלפניה דקה ד' כו': לאו משום דעבוד דקה כו'. גדר וחמתן יושבין בהר בשיפוע, גדר למעלה וחמתן למטה. הואיל ושתיהן יושבות בשיפוע צריכות שתיהן דקה בשיפולן. וקס"ד שהיו שתיהן מובלעות זו כולה בתוך אלפים של חברתה. וקתני בני גדר יורדים לחמתן כו' לאו משום דבני גדר עבוד דקה, לפיכך כל יושביה כשרוצין לילך לחמתן מתחילין למנות ולמדוד מחומתה לצד חמתן כשאר עיירות והרי חמתן כולה מובלעת בתחומן. והני בני חמתן לא עבוד דקה לשיפולה, לפיכך לא הויא עיר ומודדין לכל אחד מפתח ביתו. ואלו שבגובהן הקרובין בתוך אלפים לגדר, וכולה מובלעת בתחומין – נכנסין לה לכולה. אבל(א) אם היו יושבין בשיפוליה – אין עולין לה: מטטרגי להו בני גדר לחמתן. מכין והורגין היו בני גדר לבני חמתן: כי הוו אזלי. בני גדר לחמתן נמי מטטרגי להו בני גדר לבני חמתן: כולי האי ודאי לא כייפו להו. בני גדר, דאפילו בלא מתייהו(ב) ליטטרגו להו בני חמתן: עיר העשויה כקשת הואי. חמתן, ובין ב' ראשיה יותר מד' אלפים. דאמרינן בריש פרקין: מודדין לה מן הקשת כל אחד מפתח ביתו, ויתר שלה לצד גדר. הלכך, יורדין בני גדר לחמתן, שהרי מודדין לגדר מחומתה, וכל חמתן מובלעת בתחומה. ובני חמתן היושבים בקשת ומודדין להן מן הקשת כלה תחומין בראשיה של גדר, ואין יכולין ליכנס לה: גדר – עיר גדולה, וכשעולין בני חמתן לגדר, כלתה מדתן בחצי העיר. וחמתן עיר קטנה, וכשיורדין לה בני גדר, כלתה מידתן בסוף העיר. והכי קאמר ר' שיהו בני גדר יורדין לחמתן להיות להן כולה כד' אמות, ומשלימין להן את השאר. אבל גדר עולה לבני חמתן במדת התחום: רב כהנא מתני הכי. מפרש בהדיא מר אמר הא ומר אמר הא: מתני' את כל עיר קטנה. לבד מדת תחומין: נמצא קל תוכה. משום דיורין: מעל גבה. שאין שם דיורין, ואילו נתנו על גבה – לא היו לו אלא אלפים ממקום עירובו: ולמודד שאמרו כו'. ואע"פ שחלוקין חכמים על ר' עקיבא בנותן עירובו בעיר, לומר שכל העיר לו כארבע אמות – מודין הן בבא מעיר אחרת או ממקום שביתתו, וכלתה מדתו של אלפים פסיעות בינוניות אפי' במערה [שיש בה] דיורין, שאינו נכנס להלן ממדתו כלום:

גדר | דקה | חמתן

תוספות

ועוד התיר רבי. רבינו שמואל ל"ג "ועוד", דהאי "ועוד" אמילתא דלעיל מיניה קאי. והכי איתא בתוספתא דמכילתין: מעשה ברועה זקן שבא לפני רבי, ואמר לו: זכור הייתי שהיו בני מגדל יורדין לחמתן עד החלר החיצונה הסמוכה לגשר ועוד, והדר קאמר שהתיר רבי שיהו בני גדר כו'. ומיהו, יש תוספתא שכתוב בה בתר עדותו דרועה "התיר רבי שיהו בני מגדל יורדין לחמתן עד החלר החיצונה הסמוכה לעיר". ונראה הספר דגרס "ועוד התיר ר' שיהו בני גדר כו'", כיון דמיירי לעיל במה שהתיר רבי לבני מגדל על פי עדותו של רועה. ובפי' ר"ח כתוב: "ועוד זאת התיר רבי":

עיר העשויה כקשת הואי. פירש בקונטרס: חמתן, ובין שני ראשיה יותר מד' אלפים, דאמר לעיל מודדין לה מן הקשת וכלה תחומן של בני הקשת בראש של גדר, ואין יכולין ליכנס בה, אבל בני גדר יורדין לחמתן דמודדין לגדר מחומתן וכל חמתן מובלעת בתחומיהן. ופירושו תמוה, דאי בני הקשת מובלעין בתחומן של גדר – א"כ גם הם מותרין לעלות לגדר. ואם בבני ראשי הקשת קאמר דמובלעין בתחום גדר – אכתי כל היכא דשרי להני שרי להני, דבני ראשי הקשת ובני גדר באין מזה לזה, ואותן שבאמצע הקשת ובני גדר תרווייהו אסרי בהדדי. ונראה כפי' *ר"ת: דגדר עיר העשויה כקשת הואי, ולא היה בין ראשיה ארבעה אלפים ומודדין לה מן היתר, לפיכך באין לחמתן. אבל בני חמתן אינן יכולין לעלות לגדר לאמצע הקשת, ואפשר שאף מחמתן לראשי הקשת של גדר היה יותר מאלפים, ואף שם לא היו יכולין לילך:

לית

גדר | אלפים | חמתן | גדר | חמתן

רבינו חננאל

גדולה ור' אידי בין אנשי עיר קטנה בין אנשי עיר גדולה מהלכין כולה קתני [ומוקים] לה למתני' בנותן את עירובו שהנותן את עירובו בעיר נעשית לו כל העיר כד' אמות ויש לו חוץ לעיר אלפים אמה לכל רוח אבל הנותן עירובו חוץ לעיר ומודד ובא בתוך העיר (ואין) [אין] לו חוץ מן המקום שכלתה מדתו (לעשר) [לעירוב] אפילו אמה אחת לא שנא בחצי העיר ולא שנא בסוף העיר. והא דתנן למודד נותנין לו אלפים אמה שאפי' מדתו (כולה) [כלה] במערה אצטריך (מתני') [ריב"ל] לאשמעינן סוף העיר שהוא דינו כסוף המערה ורב נחמן נמי לא פליג עליה אלא טעמא דמתני' קא מפרש ואמר מאן דתני בתרווייהו מהלכין כל העיר לא משתבש דמוקי לה בנותן ומאן דתני אין מהלכין מוקי לה במודד כמו שאמרנו ואסיקנא חסורי מחסרא והכי קתני אנשי העיר הגדולה מהלכין כל עיר קטנה [ואין אנשי קטנה] מהלכין כל עיר הגדולה בד"א במודד אבל בנותן מי שהיה מעיר גדולה ונתן עירובו [בעיר קטנה בעיר קטנה ונתן עירובו] בעיר הגדולה מהלכין כולה וחוצה לה אלפים אמה. והא דר' אידי לא בריר טעמא. אמר רב יוסף אמר רמי בר אבא אמר רב הונא עיר שיושבת על שפת הנחל אם יש לפניה דקה בתוך הנחל ארבע מודדין לה אלפים אמה מן הנחל ולהלן (שם נחל) [שהנחל] כיון שמשתמשים בו כאילו מן העיר הוא. ואם לא עשו לפניה דקה אין מודדין להן אלא מפתח בתיהן ומאי שנא דכל דקה בעלמא ד' טפחים והאי (דקאמר) [קאמר] רב יוסף ד' אמות ופרקי' כיון דבעיתא תשמישתה שהיא על הנחל אם היא רחבה ד' אמות אין ואי לא לא אמר רב יוסף מנא אמינא דמאן דאית ליה דקה לפניה מדקה ולהלן משחינן לה תחומא דתניא ועוד זאת התיר רבי (כשהיו) [שיהו] בני גדר יורדין לחמתן ואין בני חמתן יורדין לגדר מ"ט לאו משום דהוו בני גדר עיר היושבת על שפת הנחל ועביד דקה והיה בין גדר לחמתן יותר מאלפים אמה ובני גדר דעבדו דקה מדדו להם אלפים אמה מחוץ לנחל וכלתה מדתן לחמתן ובני חמתן כלתה מדתן עד הנחל ולא יכלי לבוא בגדר דהא לא עשובני חמתן דקה. כי אתא רב דימי אמר (להו) [לאו] משום האי טעמא לא הוו אתו בני חמתן לגדר אלא משום דהוו בני גדר פריצים והוו מטטרגי לבני חמתן. פי' מריבין עמהן ומכין אותן. ובשבת דשכיחה שכרות התקין להו ר' שלא יהיו באין בני חמתן לגדר. רב ספרא אמר גדר עיר העשויה כקשת הואי ומדדו לה (כמין) [מן] היתר *) ולפיכך באין לחמתן אבל בני חמתן אינן יכולין לעלות על עיר גדר שהיא יושבת במקום החץ וממקום הקשת עד היתר אלפים אמה ולפיכך לא היו באין אליהן. רב דימי אמר גדר עיר גדולה היתה וחמתן עיר קטנה ותנן אנשי עיר גדולה מהלכין כל העיר קטנה וכו':

אמר

*) פי' שלא היה בין ראשיה ארבעת אלפים וכמו שכתבו התוס' ונראה שלדברי רבינו אלו כוונת התוס' בד"ה עיר וכמו שגרס רש"ל ורש"א ר"ח תחת ר"ת.

עין משפט נר מצוה

נח א ב מיי' פכ"ח מהל' שבת הל' ט סמג לאוין סה טוש"ע א"ח סי' שצח סעיף ט:

מסורת הש"ס

[תוספ' פ"ד]

[נ"ל מתא ועי' שבת קמה:]

[לעיל ס:]

לעיל ובירושל' ובכרי"ף ועוד אי' ואין אנשי ועי' בפ"מ על הירושלמי

[נ"ל להם]

[גיר' ירושלמי והרא"ש על פי המערה]

[לעיל נב:]

הגהות הב"ח

(א) רש"י ד"ה לאו משום וכו' אבל היושבין בשפולה כצ"ל ותיבת אם היו נמחק: (ב) ד"ה כולי האי וכו' בלא מתייהו (ליטטרגי) תא"מ ונ"ב נ"ל להגיה לא טטרגו פי' אפי' כשבני גדר באים לחמתן לא כייפו לבני חמתן שיהא מכים להם בני חמתן וק"ל:

גמ' אָמַר רַב יְהוּדָה, אָמַר שְׁמוּאֵל: שָׁבַת בְּעִיר חֲרֵיבָה — לְרַבָּנַן מְהַלֵּךְ אֶת כּוּלָּהּ וְחוּצָה לָהּ אַלְפַּיִם אַמָּה. הִנִּיחַ אֶת עֵירוּבוֹ בְּעִיר חֲרֵיבָה — אֵין לוֹ מִמְּקוֹם עֵירוּבוֹ אֶלָּא אַלְפַּיִם אַמָּה. ר"א אוֹמֵר: [א]אֶחָד שָׁבַת וְאֶחָד הִנִּיחַ — מְהַלֵּךְ אֶת כּוּלָּהּ וְחוּצָה לָהּ אַלְפַּיִם אַמָּה. מֵיתִיבִי, אָמַר לָהֶן ר"ע: אִי אַתֶּם מוֹדִים לִי בְּנוֹתֵן אֶת עֵירוּבוֹ בִּמְעָרָה, שֶׁאֵין לוֹ מִמְּקוֹם עֵירוּבוֹ אֶלָּא אַלְפַּיִם אַמָּה? אָמְרוּ לוֹ: אֵימָתַי — בִּזְמַן שֶׁאֵין בָּהּ דִּיּוּרִין, הָא בְּאֵין בָּהּ דִּיּוּרִין — מוֹדוּ לֵיהּ! מַאי "אֵין בָּהּ דִּיּוּרִין"? אֵינָהּ רְאוּיָה לְדִירָה. תָּא שְׁמַע: [ב]שָׁבַת בָּעִיר, אֲפִי' הִיא גְּדוֹלָה כְּאַנְטִיוֹכְיָא, בִּמְעָרָה, אֲפִילּוּ הִיא כִּמְעָרַת צִדְקִיָּהוּ מֶלֶךְ יְהוּדָה — מְהַלֵּךְ אֶת כּוּלָּהּ וְחוּצָה לָהּ אַלְפַּיִם אַמָּה. קָתָנֵי עִיר דּוּמְיָא דִּמְעָרָה, מַה מְּעָרָה חֲרֵיבָה, אַף עִיר חֲרֵיבָה, וְשָׁבַת — אִין, אֲבָל הִנִּיחַ — לָא. מַנִּי? אִילֵימָא רַבִּי עֲקִיבָא — מַאי אִירְיָא חֲרֵיבָה? אֲפִילּוּ יְשִׁיבָה נַמִי! אֶלָּא לָאו — רַבָּנַן. וְטַעְמָא; דְּשָׁבַת — אִין, אֲבָל הִנִּיחַ — לָא! לָא תֵּימָא עִיר דּוּמְיָא דִּמְעָרָה, אֶלָּא אֵימָא: מְעָרָה דּוּמְיָא דְּעִיר, מַה עִיר יְשִׁיבָה — אַף מְעָרָה יְשִׁיבָה. וְרַבִּי עֲקִיבָא הִיא, דְּאָמַר: אֵין לוֹ מִמְּקוֹם עֵירוּבוֹ אֶלָּא אַלְפַּיִם אַמָּה, וּבְשָׁבַת מוֹדֵי. וְהָא כִּמְעָרַת צִדְקִיָּהוּ קָתָנֵי! כִּמְעָרַת צִדְקִיָּהוּ — וְלֹא כִּמְעָרַת צִדְקִיָּהוּ, כִּמְעָרַת צִדְקִיָּהוּ — גְּדוֹלָה, וְלֹא כִּמְעָרַת צִדְקִיָּהוּ — דְּאִילּוּ הָתָם חֲרֵיבָה, וְהָכָא יְשִׁיבָה. מָר יְהוּדָה אַשְׁכְּחִינְהוּ לִבְנֵי מַבְרַכְתָּא דְּקָא מוֹתְבִי עֵירוּבַיְיהוּ בְּבֵי כְּנִישְׁתָּא דְּבֵי אַגּוֹבַר. אֲמַר לְהוּ: גַּוּוּ בֵּיהּ טְפֵי, כִּי הֵיכִי דְּלִישְׁתְּרֵי לְכוּ טְפֵי. אֲמַר לֵיהּ רָבָא: *פַּלְגָּאָה! בְּעֵירוּבִין [ג]לֵית דְּחָשׁ לְהָא דְּרַבִּי עֲקִיבָא.§

הדרן עלך כיצד מעברין

הַדָּר עִם הַנָּכְרִי בְּחָצֵר, אוֹ עִם *מִי שֶׁאֵינוֹ מוֹדֶה בָּעֵירוּב — הֲרֵי זֶה אוֹסֵר עָלָיו. *ר' אֱלִיעֶזֶר בֶּן יַעֲקֹב אוֹמֵר: [ד]לְעוֹלָם אֵינוֹ אוֹסֵר עַד שֶׁיְּהוּ שְׁנֵי יִשְׂרְאֵלִים אוֹסְרִין זֶה עַל זֶה. אָמַר ר"ג: מַעֲשֶׂה בִּצְדוֹקִי אֶחָד שֶׁהָיָה דָּר עִמָּנוּ בְּמָבוֹי בִּירוּשָׁלַיִם, וְאָמַר לָנוּ אַבָּא: מַהֲרוּ וְהוֹצִיאוּ אֶת הַכֵּלִים לַמָּבוֹי עַד שֶׁלֹּא יוֹצִיא וְיֶאֱסֹר עֲלֵיכֶם. רַבִּי יְהוּדָה אוֹמֵר בְּלָשׁוֹן אַחֵר: מַהֲרוּ וַעֲשׂוּ צָרְכֵיכֶם בַּמָּבוֹי, עַד שֶׁלֹּא יוֹצִיא וְיֶאֱסֹר עֲלֵיכֶם.§ גמ'

רש"י

גמ' בְּעִיר חֲרֵיבָה. מִדִּיּוּרֶיהָ, אֲבָל מְחִיצוֹתֶיהָ קַיָּימוֹת סָבִיב לָהּ: לְרַבָּנַן מְהַלֵּךְ אֶת כּוּלָּהּ. דְּהָא שָׁבַת בַּאֲוִיר מְחִיצוֹת, וְהוּא הַדִּין לְר"ע. וְהָא דְּנָקַט רַבָּנַן — מִשּׁוּם הַמַּנִּיחַ עֵירוּבוֹ, דְּבָעֵי לְמִיתְנֵי חִילּוּק בֵּין חֲרֵיבָה לִישִׁיבָה, וּלְר"ע אֲפִי' בִּישִׁיבָה אֵין לוֹ מִמְּקוֹם עֵירוּבוֹ אֶלָּא אַלְפַּיִם: הִנִּיחַ עֵירוּבוֹ בְּעִיר חֲרֵיבָה כו'. דְּכִי אָמוּר רַבָּנַן כָּל הָעִיר לוֹ כְּד' אַמּוֹת — בִּמְיוּשֶּׁבֶת, כִּדְתְנַן בְּהֶדְיָא: אֵימָתַי — בִּזְמַן שֶׁאֵין בָּהּ דִּיּוּרִין, אַלְמָא: בַּחֲרֵיבָה מוֹדוּ: ה"ג: הָא בְּאֵין בָּהּ דִּיּוּרִין מוֹדִין לֵיהּ: אֵינָהּ רְאוּיָה לְדִירָה. שֶׁנָּפְלוּ מְחִיצוֹתֶיהָ: מְעָרַת צִדְקִיָּהוּ. גְּדוֹלָה הָיְתָה, וְהִיא שֶׁיָּצָא בָּהּ צִדְקִיָּהוּ לַיְלָה מִירוּשָׁלַיִם לִבְרוֹחַ מִפְּנֵי הַכַּשְׂדִּים, כִּדְכְתִיב בְּיִרְמְיָה (נב): "וַתִּבָּקַע הָעִיר" וגו': אַף עִיר חֲרֵיבָה. וְעַל כָּרְחָךְ חֲרֵיבָה מִדִּיּוּרִין וְלֹא מֵחוֹמָה, דְּאִי מֵחוֹמָה — לָא הָוֵי תָּנֵי מְהַלֵּךְ אֶת כּוּלָּהּ, כֵּיוָן דְּלֹא שָׁבַת בַּאֲוִיר מְחִיצוֹת. (וה"ה ר' עֲקִיבָא) וְאע"ג דְּיֵשׁ (א) חוֹמָה, קָתָנֵי שָׁבַת וְלָא קָתָנֵי הִנִּיחַ: מַנִּי. הָא דְּלָא תָּנֵי הִנִּיחַ: אִי נֵימָא ר"ע. דְּלֵית לֵיהּ בְּהִנִּיחַ מְהַלֵּךְ אֶת כּוּלָּהּ, אַמַּאי תָּנֵי עִיר דּוּמְיָא דִּמְעָרָה, לְמֵימַר דְּבַחֲרֵיבָה קָאֵי: אֲפִי' יְשִׁיבָה נַמִי. הִנִּיחַ לְר"ע לָא, וְהָא לֵיכָּא לְמֵימַר דְּהָא דְּנָקַט חֲרֵיבָה מִשּׁוּם שָׁבַת נָקַט לְמֵימַר אע"ג דְּהִיא חֲרֵיבָה, הֵיכָא דְּשָׁבַת מְהַלֵּךְ אֶת כּוּלָּהּ הָא מַאי אִירְיָא עִיר? אֲפִילּוּ תֵּל וְנֶקַע וְקָמָה קְלוּרָה וְשִׁיבּוֹלִין מַקִּיפוֹת אוֹתָהּ אֲמַרַן בְּפִרְקִין קַמָּא (דף טו.) מְהַלֵּךְ אֶת כּוּלָּהּ: אֶלָּא לָאו רַבָּנַן. וּשְׁמַע מִינָּהּ: בַּחֲרֵיבָה מוֹדוּ. דְּהָא עַל כָּרְחָךְ הָא דְּנָקַט חֲרֵיבָה מִשּׁוּם שִׁיוּרָא דְּשַׁיֵּיר וְלָא תָּנָא "הִנִּיחַ" נָקַט לָהּ: אַף מְעָרָה יְשִׁיבָה. וְלַאַשְׁמוּעִינַן דַּאֲפ"ה שָׁבַת — אִין, הִנִּיחַ — לָא, כְּר"ע: וְהָא כִּמְעָרַת צִדְקִיָּהוּ קָתָנֵי. *וְאֵין שָׁם דִּיּוּרִין [דָּרִין] דְּהָא שֶׁל מֶלֶךְ הָיְתָה. א"נ: הַשְׁתָּא לֵית בָּהּ דִּיּוּרִין: בְּבֵי כְּנִישְׁתָּא דְּבֵי אַגּוֹבַר. בֵּית הַכְּנֶסֶת גָּדוֹל הָיָה, וְכוּלּוֹ מוּבְלָע בְּאַלְפַּיִם שֶׁל תְּחוּם מַבְרַכְתָּא. וְהֵם לֹא הָיוּ חוֹשְׁשִׁין לְהוֹלִיךְ הָעֵירוּב עַד סוֹפוֹ וּלְהַנִּיחוֹ שָׁם, דִּסְבִירָא לְהוּ כְּרַבָּנַן דְּכֵיוָן דְּמוּנָּח בַּאֲוִיר מְחִיצוֹת — מְהַלְּכִין אֶת כּוּלּוֹ וְחוּצָה לוֹ אַלְפַּיִם: גַּוּוּ בֵּיהּ טְפֵי. הַעֲמִיקוּ עוֹד לְהַעֲמִיד הָעֵירוּב עַד סוֹפוֹ וּלְהַנִּיחוֹ שָׁם: כִּי הֵיכִי דְּלִישְׁתְּרוּ לְכוּ טְפֵי. דְּהָא מִמְּקוֹם הָעֵירוּב בָּעֵיתוּ לְמְדּוֹד: פַּלְגָּאָה. חוֹלֵק עַל חֲכָמִים אַתָּה: בְּעֵירוּבִין לֵית דְּחָשׁ לְהָא דְּר' עֲקִיבָא. דְּקַיְ"ל הֲלָכָה כְּדִבְרֵי הַמֵּיקֵל בְּעֵירוּב:

הדרן עלך כיצד מעברין

הַדָּר עִם הַנָּכְרִי אוֹ עִם מִי שֶׁאֵינוֹ מוֹדֶה בָּעֵירוּב. כּוּתִי, כִּדְאָמַר בְּפֶרֶק "בַּכֹּל מְעָרְבִין" (דף לא:): אוֹסֵר עָלָיו. לְטַלְטֵל מִבֵּיתוֹ לֶחָצֵר עַד שֶׁיִּשְׂכּוֹר הֵימֶנּוּ רְשׁוּת שֶׁיֵּשׁ לוֹ בֶּחָצֵר: עַד שֶׁיְּהוּ ב' יִשְׂרְאֵלִים. דָּרִין בְּב' בָּתִּים, וְאוֹסְרִין זֶה עַל זֶה, וּבָאִין לְעָרֵב בֵּינֵיהֶן — הַנָּכְרִי אוֹסֵר עֲלֵיהֶן, אֲבָל עַל הַיָּחִיד אֵינוֹ אוֹסֵר, וּבַגְּמָרָא מְפָרֵשׁ טַעְמָא: מַעֲשֶׂה בִּצְדוֹקִי אֶחָד. קָסָבַר ר"ג צְדוֹקִי אֵינוֹ כְּנָכְרִי. וְלָא דָּמֵי לְכוּתִי, דְּגֵרֵי אֲרָיוֹת הֵן וְאֵינָם גֵּרִים גְּמוּרִים. אֲבָל צְדוֹקִי יִשְׂרָאֵל הוּא וְנֶהְפַּךְ לְמִינוּת וְאֵינוֹ מוֹדֶה בַּתּוֹרָה שֶׁבְּעַל פֶּה. כֵּיוָן דְּיִשְׂרָאֵל הוּא — יָכוֹל לְבַטֵּל רְשׁוּתוֹ בְּלֹא שׁוּם שְׂכִירוּת:

מַעֲשֶׂה בִּצְדוֹקִי שֶׁהָיָה דָּר עִמָּנוּ בַּמָּבוֹי. *וּבִיטַּלְנוּ רְשׁוּתוֹ: וְאָמַר לָנוּ אַבָּא מַהֲרוּ וְהוֹצִיאוּ כְּלֵיכֶם לַמָּבוֹי. וְהַחֲזִיקוּ בּוֹ כֵּיוָן דְּקָדַשׁ הַיּוֹם מִיָּד, כְּדֵי שֶׁלֹּא יַחֲזוֹר בּוֹ: עַד שֶׁלֹּא יוֹצִיא. כֵּלָיו תְּחִילָּה, וְיַחֲזוֹר וְיַחֲזִיק בִּרְשׁוּתוֹ וְיֶאֱסוֹר עֲלֵיכֶם. וש"מ דְּאֵינוֹ כְּנָכְרִי, דְּאִי אַגִּירוּ מִינֵּיהּ — הֵיכִי מָצֵי לְמֶהְדַּר? אע"ג דְּמַפֵּיק לָא אָסַר, דְּהָא נָקֵיט דָּמֵי: מַהֲרוּ וַעֲשׂוּ צָרְכֵיכֶם בַּמָּבוֹי. מִבְּעוֹד יוֹם, דִּבְשַׁבָּת לֹא מְהַנֵּי לְכוּ הַאי בִּיטּוּל, שֶׁמָּא יוֹצִיא וְיֶאֱסוֹר עֲלֵיכֶם. דְּקָסָבַר ר' יְהוּדָה: אע"ג דְּהֶחֱזִיקוּ בְּנֵי מָבוֹי בַּמָּבוֹי תְּחִילָּה — מָצֵי לְאַהֲדוּרֵי בֵּיהּ: גְּמָרָא

תוספות

לית דחש להא דר' עקיבא. דקיימא לן כדברי המיקל בעירוב כדפי' בקונט' ותחומין דרבנן, כדפי' בפ' "מי שהוציאוהו" (לעיל דף מו.).

הדרן עלך כיצד מעברין

הדר. ר' אליעזר בן יעקב אומר עד שיהו ב' ישראלים אוסרים כו'. משמע דאתרוייהו קאי ר"א בן יעקב, אנכרי ואכותי. ובגמ' מפרש דטעמא דראב"י דכיון דנכרי חשוד אשפיכות דמים, בתרי דשכיחי דדיירי – גזרו בהו רבנן שמא ילמד ממעשיו כו'. וא"ת: והרי כותים דלא חשידי אשפיכות דמים ולא ארביעה, כדמוכח פ"ק דמס' ע"ג (דף טו:) שמעמידין בהמה בפונדקאות של כותים ומתיחדין עמהם, א"כ שכיחי דדיירי, ונגזור בחד! ואין לומר דר"א בן יעקב סבר דכותים גרי אריות הן וחשידי, דהא אפילו למ"ד גרי אריות הן לא חשידי, מדפריך התם בע"ז עלה מברייתא דאסרו למכור בהמה דקה לכותים, ורוצה להוכיח מתוך כך דטעמא משום דאתי לזבוני לגוי ולא משום דחשידי, ואמאי? דלמא בכותים גרי אריות או גרי אמת הן פליגי. ואומר ר"י: דעיקר תקנה משום גוי איתקן, שמא ילמד ממעשיו, ולא משום לדוקי וכותי. ואגב שאסרו בגוי אסרו נמי בכותי. וכיון שלא נאסר אלא ע"י נכרי – לא החמיר בהן יותר מן הנכרי:

אמר רבן גמליאל מעשה בצדוקי א' כו'. קסבר: לדוקי אינו כנכרי, כדמפרש בגמ'. ופי' בקונטרס: אבל בכותי מודה דהרי הוא כנכרי, משום דגרי אריות הן. ואע"ג דת"ק דאסר כותי היינו רבי מאיר, כדאמר בגמ', ושמעינן ליה דקסבר גרי אמת הן בפרק "ד' וה'" (ב"ק דף לח:), ואפ"ה אסר בכותי. מ"מ הוצרך בקונטרס לפרש טעמא דר"ג משום גרי אריות. דת"ק ניחא דלא מפליג בין לדוקי לכותי, ואסר לדוקי אע"ג דישראל גמור הוא, וה"ה בכותי. אבל לר"ג, דמפליג בין לדוקי לכותי – ע"כ לריך לומר משום דלדוקי ישראל גמור הוא, וכותי עו"ג גמור, דגרי אריות הן. ומיהו, קשיא לר"י: דמשמע בהדיא בפ"ק דגיטין (דף י.) דר"ג סבר ליה דכותים גרי אמת הן, דמכשיר גט שסני עדיו כותים, ואמר נמי בפ"ק דחולין (דף ה:) דר"ג ובית דינו נמנו אשחיטת כותים ואסרוה. ומפרש התם טעמא – משום דסבירא להו כר"מ דגזר על יינם, לפי שנמלא להם דמות יונה, וחייש למיעוט. ש"מ דגרי אמת הן. דאי גרי אריות הן – לא היה לריך למיגזר עליהן, ומאליהן קמיתסרי. ובקונטרס פירש דההיא רבן גמליאל בנו של ר' יהודה הנשיא. אבל תימה, דבכל מקום רגיל לקרותו או רבן גמליאל בר רבי, או רבן גמליאל בנו של ר"י הנשיא. ועוד: דלא יתכן, דר"מ דהוה קודם רבן גמליאל בר רבי גזר על יינם, דרבנן, ושבק שחיטה דאורייתא, שהולרך ר"ג ב"ר לגזור עליה?! ועוד: דאין סברא כלל דאם גזר על יינם משום יין נסך שתהא שחיטתם מותרת, כיון שנחשבו כמומרי' לע"ז דהא אמרינן בפ"ק דחולין (דף ה.) מומר לע"ז אסור לאכול

רבינו חננאל

אמר רב יהודה אמר שמואל שבת בעיר חריבה לרבנן מהלך את כולה וחוצה לה אלפים אמה והנותן עירובו בעיר החריבה אין לו אלא ממקום עירובו אלפים אמה. רבי (אליעזר) [אלעזר] אומר בין השובת בין הנותן מהלך את כולה וחוצה לה אלפים אמה. ואקשינן לר' אליעזר תנן אמר להן ר' עקיבא אין אתם מודים לי בנותן את עירובו כו' וחריבה לית בה דיורין (ובחוצה) [ובחריבה] מיהת מודו ליה לר' עקיבא שאין לו אלא ממקום עירובו אלפים אמה. והיאך א"ר אליעזר בין שובת בין נותן מהלך את כולה וחוצה לה אלפים אמה. ופריק לא תימא שאין בה דיורין שהיא חריבה אלא אימא שאינה ראויה לדירה נותן לה ממקום עירובו אלפים אמה והחריבה ראויה לדירה היא. ת"ש שבת בעיר גדולה ואפי' היא כאנטוכיא במערה ואפי' כמערת צדקיהו מהלך את כולה וחוצה לה אלפים אמה וכו' ואקשינן טעמא דשבת הא נותן לא והיאך אמר ר' אליעזר לא שנא שובת ולא שנא נותן מהלך את כולה וחוצה לה אלפים אמה. ופריק לא תימא עיר חריבה דומיא דמערה אלא אימא מערה ישיבה דומיא דעיר ור' עקיבא היא דאמר אין לו אלא ממקום עירובו אלפים אמה ובשובת מודה שמהלך את כולה וחוצה לה אלפים: מר יהודה אשכח לבני מברכתא דהוו מותבי עירובא בכנישתא דאבי גבר. אמר להו נמי אחיתו ליה כלומר הכניסוהו כלפי התחום כי היכי דנשתרו לכו טפי בתחומא כר' עקיבא דאמר אין נותן לו ממקום עירובו אלא אלפים אמה. אמר רבא לרב יהודה פלגאה. פי' בעל מחלוקת לית דחש לה לדר' עקיבא אלא בי כנישתא כולה דלהון היא ומחוץ לכנישתא משחינן להו תחומא דאמר מר הלכה כדברי המקיל בעירובין:

הדרן עלך פרק כיצד מעברין

פרק ו הדר עם הגוי בחצר הרי זה אוסר עליו. ר' אליעזר בן יעקב אומר לעולם אינו אוסר עד שיהו שנים ישראלים כו'.

עין משפט נר מצוה

נט א ב ג מיי' פ"ו מהל' עירובין הל' ד סמג עשין א טוש"ע א"ח סי' תח סעיף ב:

א ד מיי' פ"ב מהלכות עירובין הל' ט סמג עשין א טור ש"ע א"ח סי' שפב סעיף א:

מסורת הש"ס / הגהות הב"ח

רש"ל ורש"א מ"ז

הגהות הב"ח: (א) רש"י ד"ה אף העיר וכו' ואע"ג דיש לה חומה:

בס"י ליתא: שאין בה דיורין דהא

[בקידושין נח. קרי רבה על מר יהודה פלגאה פרש"י קנטר רגיל לחלוק על חביריו]

[לעיל לח:]

[במשנה שבמשניות גרס דברי ר"מ]

[נ"ל וביטל לנו]

גמ' יְתִיב אַבַּיֵי בַּר אָבִין וְרַב חִינָּנָא בַּר אָבִין,
ויתיב אַבַּיֵי גַּבַּיְיהוּ. וְיָתְבִי וְקָאָמְרִי: בִּשְׁלָמָא
ר"מ קָסָבַר: *דִּירַת גּוֹי שְׁמָהּ דִּירָה,
וְלָא שְׁנָא חַד וְלָא שְׁנָא תְּרֵי. אֶלָּא ר' אֱלִיעֶזֶר
בֶּן יַעֲקֹב מַאי קָסָבַר? אִי קָסָבַר דִּירַת גּוֹי
שְׁמָהּ דִּירָה — אֲפִילּוּ חַד נַמִי נִיתְסַר!
וְאִי לֹא שְׁמָהּ דִּירָה — אֲפִי' תְּרֵי נַמִי לָא נִיתְסַר!
אֲמַר לְהוּ אַבַּיֵי: וְסָבַר רַבִּי מֵאִיר דִּירַת גּוֹי
שְׁמָהּ דִּירָה? וְהָתַנְיָא: *חֲצֵירוֹ שֶׁל נָכְרִי
הֲרֵי הוּא כְּדִיר שֶׁל בְּהֵמָה! אֶלָּא דְּכ"ע דִּירַת
גּוֹי — לֹא שְׁמָהּ דִּירָה, וְהָכָא בִּגְזֵירָה *שֶׁמָּא
יִלְמַד מִמַּעֲשָׂיו קָא מִיפַּלְגִי, ר' אֱלִיעֶזֶר בֶּן יַעֲקֹב
סָבַר: כֵּיוָן דְּגוֹי *חָשׁוּד אַשְּׁפִיכוּת
דָּמִים, תְּרֵי דִּשְׁכִיחִי דְּדָיְירִי — גָּזְרוּ בְּהוּ, חַד
לָא שְׁכִיחַ — לָא גָּזְרוּ בֵּיהּ רַבָּנַן. וְר"מ סָבַר:
זִמְנִין דְּמִקְּרֵי וְדָיֵיר. וְאָמְרוּ רַבָּנַן: [א]אֵין עֵרוּב
מוֹעִיל בִּמְקוֹם גּוֹי, וְאֵין בִּיטּוּל רְשׁוּת מוֹעִיל
בִּמְקוֹם גּוֹי עַד שֶׁיַּשְׂכִּיר, וְגוֹי לֹא מוּגַר.
מ"ט? אִילֵימָא מִשּׁוּם דְּסָבַר: דִּלְמָא אָתֵי
לְאַחֲזוּקֵי בִּרְשׁוּתוֹ, הָנִיחָא לְמ"ד "שְׂכִירוּת
בְּרִיאָה בָּעֵינַן", אֶלָּא לְמ"ד "שְׂכִירוּת רְעוּעָה
בָּעֵינַן" מַאי אִיכָּא לְמֵימַר? דְּאִתְּמַר, רַב חִסְדָּא
אָמַר: שְׂכִירוּת בְּרִיאָה, וְרַב שֵׁשֶׁת אָמַר:
[ב]שְׂכִירוּת רְעוּעָה. מַאי רְעוּעָה, מַאי בְּרִיאָה?
אִילֵימָא: בְּרִיאָה — בִּפְרוּטָה, רְעוּעָה — פָּחוֹת
מִשָּׁוֶה פְּרוּטָה, מִי אִיכָּא לְמַאן דְּאָמַר מִגּוֹי
בְּפָחוֹת מִשָּׁוֶה פְּרוּטָה לֹא? וְהָא שָׁלַח רַבִּי
יִצְחָק בְּרַבִּי יַעֲקֹב בַּר גִּיּוֹרֵי מִשְּׁמֵיהּ דְּרַבִּי
יוֹחָנָן: [ג]הֱווּ יוֹדְעִין שֶׁשּׂוֹכְרִין מִן הַגּוֹי אֲפִילּוּ
בְּפָחוֹת מִשָּׁוֶה פְּרוּטָה. *וְאָמַר רַבִּי חִיָּיא
בַּר אַבָּא א"ר יוֹחָנָן: בֶּן נֹחַ נֶהֱרָג עַל
פָּחוֹת מִשָּׁוֶה פְּרוּטָה, וְלֹא נִיתָּן לְהִשָּׁבוֹן! אֶלָּא:
בְּרִיאָה — בְּמוֹהַרְקֵי וְאַבּוּרְגְּנֵי, רְעוּעָה — בְּלֹא
מוֹהַרְקֵי וְאַבּוּרְגְּנֵי. הָנִיחָא לְמ"ד שְׂכִירוּת בְּרִיאָה
בָּעֵינַן, אֶלָּא לְמ"ד שְׂכִירוּת רְעוּעָה בָּעֵינַן, מַאי
אִיכָּא לְמֵימַר? אֲפִי' הָכִי חָשֵׁישׁ גּוֹי לִכְשָׁפִים
וְלָא מוּגַר. גּוּפָא: חֲצֵירוֹ שֶׁל גּוֹי הֲרֵי
הוּא כְּדִיר שֶׁל בְּהֵמָה, *וּמוּתָּר לְהַכְנִיס וּלְהוֹצִיא
מִן חָצֵר לְבָתִּים וּמִן בָּתִּים לְחָצֵר. וְאִם יֵשׁ
שָׁם יִשְׂרָאֵל אֶחָד — אוֹסֵר, *דִּבְרֵי רַבִּי מֵאִיר. רַבִּי
אֱלִיעֶזֶר בֶּן יַעֲקֹב אוֹמֵר: לְעוֹלָם אֵינוֹ אוֹסֵר
עַד שֶׁיְּהוּ שְׁנֵי יִשְׂרְאֵלִים אוֹסְרִים זֶה עַל זֶה.

רש"י

גמ' לֹא שְׁנָא חַד. יִשְׂרָאֵל יְחִידִי דָּר עִמּוֹ: שְׁמָהּ דִּירָה. וְיֵשׁ לוֹ רְשׁוּת בֶּחָצֵר, וְנִמְצָא יִשְׂרָאֵל הַמּוֹצִיא לֶחָצֵר מִבֵּיתוֹ שֶׁהוּא מְיוּחָד לוֹ, מוֹצִיא מֵרְשׁוּת לִרְשׁוּת – וְרַבָּנַן גָּזְרוּ שֶׁלֹּא לְהוֹצִיא מֵרְשׁוּת לִרְשׁוּת בְּלֹא עֵירוּב, דִּלְמָא אָתֵי לְאַפּוּקֵי מֵרה"י לְרה"ר: הֲרֵי הוּא כְּדִיר שֶׁל בְּהֵמָה. וְאֵין לוֹ כֹּחַ לֶאֱסוֹר. וְר"מ קָאָמַר לָהּ לְקַמָּן כִּבְרַיְיתָא בִּשְׁמַעְתִּין, וּרְמִינַן מַתְנִי' עֲלָהּ וּמוֹקְמִינַן בִּדְלֵיתֵיהּ. וְיִשְׂרָאֵל אֲפִי' כִּי לֵיתֵיהּ אוֹסֵר. אַלְמָא: דִּירַת נָכְרִי לָאו שְׁמָהּ דִּירָה: אֶלָּא דְּכ"ע לָאו שְׁמָהּ דִּירָה. אֶלָּא מִשּׁוּם גְּזֵרָה שֶׁמָּא יִלְמוֹד יִשְׂרָאֵל מַעֲשָׂיו שֶׁל נָכְרִי הִטְרִיחוּהוּ וְהִפְסִידוּהוּ חֲכָמִים לְיִשְׂרָאֵל הַדָּר עִמּוֹ, כְּדֵי שֶׁיִּקְשֶׁה בְּעֵינָיו לִיתֵּן שָׂכָר בְּכָל שַׁבָּת וְשַׁבָּת, וְיֵצֵא מִשָּׁם. וּבְהָהִיא גְּזֵרָה פְּלִיגֵי ר"מ וְר"א בֶּן יַעֲקֹב אִי גָּזְרִינַן לֵיהּ עַל יִשְׂרָאֵל יָחִיד הַדָּר עִם הַנָּכְרִי אוֹ לָא: ר"א סָבַר כֵּיוָן דְּגוֹי חָשׁוּד עַל שְׁפִיכוּת דָּמִים. לָא שְׁכִיחַ יְחִידִי דְּדָיֵיר בַּהֲדֵיהּ וּמִילְּתָא דְּלָא שְׁכִיחָא לָא גְּזוּר בָּהּ רַבָּנַן וְר"מ סָבַר יְחִידִי נַמִי זִימְנִין דְּדָיֵיר וּמשׁ"ה אֲמוּר רַבָּנַן אֵין עֵירוּב מוֹעִיל כו': וְגוֹי לֹא מוּגַר. לֹא יְהֵא רוֹצֶה *לְשְׂכּוֹר וְיֵצֵא יִשְׂרָאֵל זֶה מִשָּׁם: מַאי טַעְמָא. לָא מוּגַר נָכְרִי: בְּרִיאָה. חֲזָקָה, שֶׁיִּתְנֶה יִשְׂרָאֵל עִמּוֹ לְמַלְאוֹת כָּל הַמָּבוֹי כֵּלִים אִם יִרְצֶה: בֶּן נֹחַ נֶהֱרָג עַל הַגָּזֵל. דְּהִיא מִז' מִצְוֹת, כִּדְאָמַר בְּ"ד' מִיתוֹת" בְּסַנְהֶדְרִין (דף נו.) וְאָמַר אַזְהָרָה שֶׁלָּהֶן זוֹ הִיא מִיתָתָן וְאַשְׁמוּעִינַן ר' יוֹחָנָן דְּנָכְרִי לָא מָחֵיל אֲפִילּוּ אַפָּחוֹת מִשָּׁוֶה פְּרוּטָה וְהָוֵי גָּזֵל לְדִידְהוּ: לֹא נִיתָּן לְהִישָּׁבוֹן. דְּגַבֵּי יִשְׂרָאֵל כְּתִיב: *"וְהֵשִׁיב אֶת הַגְּזֵלָה" אֲבָל בְּנָכְרִי לָא כְּתִיב הַשָּׁבָה, הִלְכָּךְ, כֵּיוָן שֶׁעָבַר נֶהֱרָג, וְאֵינוֹ מְשַׁלֵּם: בְּמוֹהַרְקֵי וְאַבּוּרְגְּנֵי. לְמַלְאוֹת הֶחָצֵר בְּסַפְסָלִין וְקָתֶידְרָאוֹת אִם יִרְצֶה: חֲצֵירוֹ שֶׁל גּוֹי. אַע"ג שֶׁפְּתַחִים הַרְבֵּה פְּתוּחִין לְתוֹכָהּ בָּתִּים הַרְבֵּה, אֵין רְשׁוּת נָכְרִי חֲלוּקָה לְהֵיחָשֵׁב רְשׁוּת לְכָל אֶחָד וְאֶחָד לְבַדּוֹ. דְּדִירַת נָכְרִי לָא שְׁמָהּ דִּירָה. וְיִשְׂרָאֵל שֶׁאֵינוֹ דָּר עִמָּהֶן, שֶׁנִּכְנָס לְאֶחָד מִן הַבָּתִּים בְּשַׁבָּת – מוּתָּר לְהוֹצִיא מִן הַבָּתִּים לֶחָצֵר וְלָא הָוֵי מוֹצִיא מֵרְשׁוּת הַמְיוּחֶדֶת לְנָכְרִי זֶה לִרְשׁוּת שֶׁהִיא לְכוּלָּן: וְאִם יֵשׁ שָׁם יִשְׂרָאֵל אֶחָד. דָּר עִמָּהֶן, אוֹסֵר עַל כֹּל יִשְׂרָאֵל לְהוֹצִיא מִן הַבָּתִּים לֶחָצֵר, מִפְּנֵי שֶׁהִיא כַּחֲצֵירוֹ: ר"א בֶּן יַעֲקֹב אוֹמֵר[(א)] עַד שֶׁיְּהוּ שְׁנֵי יִשְׂרְאֵלִים. דָּרִין בִּשְׁנֵי בָּתִּים, וְאוֹסְרִין זֶה עַל זֶה, רְשׁוּת הַנָּכְרִי חֲלוּקָה מֵהֶן, וְאוֹסֵר הַנָּכְרִי עַל בָּתֵּיהֶם וְהֵן אוֹסְרִין עַל בָּתֵּי הַנָּכְרִים מִלְּהוֹצִיא לֶחָצֵר, דְּשָׁוְיוּהּ רַבָּנַן לְדִירַת נָכְרִי דִּירָה, כִּדְאָמַר לְעֵיל. אֲבָל בְּיִשְׂרָאֵל יְחִידִי לָא שָׁוְיוּהּ רַבָּנַן לְדִירַת נָכְרִי דִּירָה, וְלָא הָוֵה אוֹסֵר עַל בֵּיתוֹ שֶׁל יִשְׂרָאֵל וְלָא יִשְׂרָאֵל אוֹסֵר עַל בֵּיתוֹ, שֶׁאֵין חִילּוּק רְשׁוּת בְּנָכְרִי: אָמַר

תוספות

לאכול משחיטתו. אלא ודאי ר"ג דיבנה הוה, ותחלה גזר על שחיטה דאורייתא ושבק סתם יינס דרבנן. ואע"ג דר"ג קודם דר' מאיר הוה – תלי אותו בדר"מ, משום דפשיטא לן בכל דוכתא דחייש ר"מ למיעוט. ולספרים נמי דגרסי הכא רשב"ג, הא שמעינן ליה בפ"ק דחולין (דף ד.) דס"ל כותים גירי אמת הן גבי מלת כותי מותרת, דקתני, רשב"ג אומר: כל מצוה שהחזיקו בה כותים, יותר מדקדקין בה מישראל. ועוד: דאם כן מה חדשו ר' אמי ור' אסי* במה שעשאום נכרים גמורים לבטל רשות וליתן רשות והלא כך היו מעולם לכ"ע! דליכא למימר דמעיקרא גזור ולא קבלו מינייהו. דלענין שחיטה ויין נסך הוא דקאמר התם גזור ולא קבלו מינייהו ונראה לר"י: דבין לדוקי ובין כותי* לדירה אינם כנכרים ומה שלא הוסיף כותי בחסורי מחסרא בגמ' ר"ג אומר לדוקים וכותים אינם כנכרים, היינו משום שלא בא המתרץ אלא לתקן שלא יקשה לדוקי מאן דכר שמיה. ועוד י"ל: דאפילו ר"ג עלמו לא הזכיר בדבריו כשחלק על תנא קמא אלא לדוקי לבדו – לפי שלא הביא ראייה אלא מלדוקי. וא"ת: אי גרס רשב"ג היכי פסקינן בגמרא כר"א בן יעקב? ור' יוחנן נמי דקאמר נהגו כר"א בן יעקב*, הא ר' יוחנן נמי אמר הלכה כרשב"ג במשנתינו! וי"ל: דלא פסקינן בגמרא כר"א בן יעקב אלא על עיקר דבריו, דלא אסר בחד ישראל עד שיהו שנים. אבל בהא דסבר ליה כת"ק דכותים כנכרים – לא פסקינן כוותיה, ואפשר דבהא הלכה כרשב"ג דאינן כנכרים. ועוד: דהאידנא לא נפקא לן מידי לענין כותים – לבסוף *כשעשאום נכרים גמורים:

חצירו של נכרי הרי הוא כדיר של בהמה. ואם יש בתים הרבה של נכרים פתוחין בחלר – מותר לישראל להכנים ולהוציא לשם מאחר שאין ישראל דר שם:

ונכרים לא מוגר. וא"ת: ומעיקרא דס"ד דטעמא משום דדירת נכרי שמה דירה, מ"ט דעירוב לא מהני ושכירות מהני? וי"ל: דעירוב וביטול בדין הוא דלא מהני, שאין הנכרי מכיר בהן, אבל יודע הוא שישראל קונה רשותו בשכירות. אבל השתא דאסיקנא שהוא כדיר של בהמה, ומן הדין לא בעי מידי, לריך הוא לפרש מ"ט תקינו רבנן שכירות טפי מעירוב וביטול:

בן נח נהרג על פחות משוה פרוטה ולא ניתן להשבון. פירש בקונטרס: דגבי ישראל כתיב: "והשיב את הגזלה אשר גזל", אבל בנכרי לא כתיב. הלכך, כיון שעבר – נהרג ואין משלם. משמע מתוך פירושו דאפילו בגזל מנכרי חבירו לא מיחייב בהשבה. ולא יתכן לומר כן, לפי אותה שיטה דפרק בתרא דעבודה זרה (דף עא:) דבעי למידק דמשיכה בנכרי קונה, דאי אינה קונה – אמאי נהרג? אבל בהא דנהרג על שוה פרוטה לא קשיא ליה, דבדין הוא שיהרג אע"ג דלא קני ביה משיכה – כיון דהוי ממון חשוב. אבל בפחות משוה פרוטה, דלאו ממון הוא, ובמשיכה נמי לא קני אמאי נהרג? ואי בגוזל מנכרי איירי – א"כ אפי' בפחות משוה פרוטה ממון חשוב הוא לגבי נכרי, דלא מחיל על פחות משוה פרוטה, ובדין הוא שיהרג. אף על גב דלא קני ליה – כיון דחשיב ממון לגביה כמו שוה פרוטה לישראל. וכל הגזלנים דמיחייבי על הגזילה אע"ג דלא קנו ליה. אבל מהא דנהרג על גזל פחות משוה פרוטה מישראל דייק שפיר, כדפרשתי. ומשמע ליה דאיירי בגוזל מישראל, מדקתני ולא ניתן להשבון, כלומר, דאינו חייב להחזיר ובגוזל מנכרי היה חייב, כיון דקפיד. ולא כפ"ה דפטר[(ב)] בגוזל מן הנכרי משום דלא כתיבא ביה "השבה". ומשום קס ליה בדרבה מיניה לא מיפטר, דלא שייך גבי נכרי. דהא נטלו לסטין כסותו ב"הגוזל" בתרא (ב"ק דף קיד.), משמע דלא קנו אלא ביאוש, ומוקמינן בלסטים נכרי. ועוד: דאפילו בישראל אי הוי בעין חייב להחזיר ולא אמרינן קים ליה בדרבה מיניה כדמוכח בפרק "בן סורר" (סנהדרין דף עב.) גבי בא במחתרת. ומשני: דהא דמיחייב מיתה – משום דמלער לישראל. כלומר, שהוא חשוב ממון ביד נכרי, דאין סברא לומר שאם ליערו בשום ענין שיתחייב מיתה. ומאי "לא ניתן להשבון" – כלומר, כיון דלא קניא במשיכה, א"כ כל היכא דאיתיה – של ישראל הוא. דאי משום דמייאש – זימנין דלא מייאש. ומפרש: "שאינו בתורת השבון" – כלומר, אם אכלו שאינו בעין לא מיחייב ליתן דמיו אבל כל זמן שהוא בעין ודאי חייב להחזיר. אבל אין לפרש: "אינו בתורת השבון" לענין שיפטר בהשבתו ממיתה כמו ישראל ממלקות, דהוי בכך ניתק לעשה דאם כן דחק בחנם להעמידה בישראל ומשום דמלערינא דלוקמה בגזול מנכרי: **מוהרקי** ואבורגני. פירוש "מוהרקי" – כתיבה וחותמות, כמו "מוהרקייהו דהני בטפסא דמלכא מנח" בסוף "החולץ" (יבמות דף מו:). ואבורגני *שלוחים ור"ח פירש מוהרקי ואבורגני כמו בניין: ורבי

עין משפט נר מצוה

ב א מיי' פ"ב מהל' עירובין הלכה י טוש"ע א"ח סי' שפ"ב ס"א.
ג ב מיי' שם הלכה יב טוש"ע שם ס"ד.
ד ג מיי' שם טוש"ע שם ס"ה.

מסורת הש"ס

[לקמן עה.] [תוספ' פ"ה] [כ"מ עה.] [ע"ז כב.] [נ"ל להשכיר] (ויקרא ה) ע"ז עה. יבמות מז: [תוספתא פ"ה] [בתוספ' ליתא דברי ר"מ] [חולין ו.] גי' מהרש"א לדידיה [כתובות עז.] [חולין ו.]

הגהות הב"ח

(א) רש"י ד"ה ר"א בן יעקב אומר לעולם אינו אוסר עד שיהו וכו' דירה ולא הוא אוסר: (ב) תום' ד"ה בן נח וכו' ולא כפ"ה דפטר אף בגוזל מן הגוי וכו' דלא שייך גבי גוי דהא גזלו לסטים את כסותו:

[וכ"פ הערוך בשם רב האי גאון שבלשון פרסי נקרא אבורגני שלוחים גם בערך מהרק כתב פי' זה בשם ר' נסים וגם על מוהרקי פי' כתיבה וחתימה ורבינו גרשום פי' כלי הבית]

רבינו חננאל

סוגיא דשמעתא דירת גוי לא שמה דירה ובגזירה שמא ילמד ממעשיו פליגי. ר"א בן יעקב סבר (כגון) [כיון] דחשיד אשפיכות דמים תרי דשכיחי דדיירי בהדי גוים גזרו בהו רבנן איסור עד שיערבו*) חד ישראל בהדי גוי דלא שכיח דדייר אי מקרי דדיירי לא גזרו ביה רבנן. ור' מאיר זמנין דחד נמי דייר ואמור רבנן אין עירוב ולא ביטול רשות מועיל בהדי גוי עד שישכיר וגוי אינו משכיר לישראל ואע"ג דלא בעינן שכירות בריאה כמו מוהרקי ואבורגני כגון בנין אלא אפי' שכירות רעועה דיי לן אפילו הכי גוי לא משכיר לישראל דחייש לכשפים ודכולי עלמא שכירות בפחות משוה פרוטה מן הגוי הויא שכירות דקיי"ל בן נח נהרג על פחות משוה פרוטה ולא ניתן להישבון פי' בן נח נהרג על הגזל שאזהרתן זו היא מיתתן ואם יגזול בן נח פחות משוה פרוטה נהרג עליה וישראל אין חייבין עליה שאין ישראל חייבין אלא מפרוטה ולמעלה לפיכך לא ניתן להישבון שהתורה הזהירה והשיב את הגזלה אשר גזל ואם אין גזלה אין השבה: **גופה** חצרו של גוי הרי הוא כדיר של בהמה מותר להכנים מתוכה לבתים ומן הבתים לתוכה ואם יש שם ישראל אוסר דברי ר' מאיר אוקימנא בזמן דליכא ההוא גוי בחצר ולא חיישינן דלמא אתי ואי במקום קרוב הוא דיכול למיתא ביומיה חיישינן ולא שרי ר' מאיר ר' אלעזר בן יעקב אומר לעולם אינו אוסר עד שיהיו שני ישראלים אוסרין זה על זה תנא

*) [לכאורה צ"ל עד שיסכרו ממנו].

רב נסים גאון

פרק ששי בן נח נהרג על פחות משוה פרוטה משכחת לה בסנהדרין בפרק ארבע מיתות (דף נו) תנו רבנן ז' מצות נצטוו בני נח דינים וברכת השם וע"ז וגילוי עריות שפיכות דמים וגזל ואבר מן החי ואמרו אחר זה על שבע מצות בן נח נהרג ואמרו עוד אזהרה שלהן זו היא מיתתן ואמרו פחות משוה פרוטה כיון דלאו בני מחילה נינהו גזל מעליא הוא ולפיכך אם בן נח גזל פחות משוה פרוטה נהרג ומה שאמרו ולא ניתן להישבון כלומר אפילו השיב את הגזילה לגזול אינו נפטר מן המיתה אלא נהרג מכל מקום שכבר חייב מיתה ובמס' ע"ז בפ' השוכר את הפועל (דף עב)

עין משפט נר מצוה

ה א ב מיי' פ"ד מהל' עירובין הלכה יג סמג עשין א טור ש"ע א"ח סימן שעא ס"א:
ו ג מיי' פ"ב שם הלכה ט סמג שם טוש"ע א"ח סימן שפב סעיף א:
[דף מו.]
ז ד מיי' פ"ה מהלכות ת"ת הלכה ב סמג עשין יג טור ש"ע י"ד סימן רמב ס"ד [וברב אלפס שבועות פ"ו דף שטז: ובפ"ז שם דף שיז.]

אמר מר: חצירו של גוי הרי הוא כדיר של בהמה. והא אנן תנן: הדר עם הנכרי בחצר הרי זה אוסר עליו! — לא קשיא; הא — דאיתיה, הא — דליתיה. ומאי קסבר? אי קסבר דירה בלא בעלים שמה דירה — אפי' גוי נמי ניתסר. ואי קסבר: דירה בלא בעלים לא שמה דירה — אפילו ישראל נמי לא ניתסר! לעולם קסבר: [א]דירה בלא בעלים — לא שמה דירה. וישראל, דכי איתיה — אסר, כי ליתיה — גזרו ביה רבנן. גוי דכי איתיה — גזירה *שמא ילמד ממעשיו; כי איתיה — אסר, כי ליתיה — לא אסר. וכי ליתיה לא אסר?! והתנן: *המניח את ביתו והלך לו לשבות בעיר אחרת, אחד נכרי ואחד ישראל — אוסר, דברי רבי מאיר! [ב]התם דאתי ביומיה. אמר רב יהודה אמר שמואל: *[ג]הלכה כרבי אליעזר בן יעקב. ורב הונא אמר: מנהג כרבי אליעזר בן יעקב. ור' יוחנן אמר: נהגו העם כר' אליעזר בן יעקב. א"ל אביי לרב יוסף: קי"ל, *משנת רבי אליעזר בן יעקב קב ונקי, ואמר רב יהודה אמר שמואל: הלכה כרבי אליעזר בן יעקב. מהו לאורויי במקום רבו? א"ל: *[ד]אפילו ביעתא בכותחא(א) בעו מיניה מרב חסדא כל שני דרב הונא, ולא(ב) אורי. א"ל ר' יעקב בר אבא לאביי: כגון מגלת תענית, דכתיבא ומנחא, מהו לאורויי באתריה דרביה? א"ל, הכי א"ר יוסף: אפי' ביעתא בכותחא(ג) בעו מיניה מרב חסדא כל שני דרב הונא(ד) ולא אורי. רב חסדא אורי בכפרי בשני דרב הונא.

רב

רש"י

אמר מר הרי הוא כדיר של בהמה. דנכרי לא אסר מידי, וכי דייר ישראל גביה קאמר ר' מאיר דישראל(ה) אוסר על ביתו של נכרי. אבל נכרי אינו אוסר על ביתו של ישראל, והתנן כו': הא דליתיה. לנכרי לא אסר, ואם יש שם ישראל אחר — אוסר על ביתו של נכרי, ואפי' ליתא לישראל: (ו)ה"ג: לעולם קסבר דירה בלא בעלים לאו שמה דירה. וישראל דכי איתיה אסר — משום דירה, דדירת ישראל שמה דירה: כי ליתיה גזרו רבנן. משום כי איתיה. אבל נכרי, דאפילו כי איתיה לאו שמה דירה, אלא משום שמא ילמד כו': דאתי ביומיה. שהלך למקום קרוב, ויבא בו ביום. ואי שרית להו קודם שיבא — מטלטלי נמי אחר שיבא, ולא מסקי אדעתייהו: ל"א: הכי גרסינן: ואם יש שם ישראל אחר, שדר ישראל עם ישראל אחר בבית א' — הרי זה הנכרי אוסר עליו. דהכי שכיח דדייר. ורישא דקתני הרי הוא כדיר של בהמה — בישראל הדר יחידי עמו, דלא שכיח דדייר. ואתא ר' אליעזר למימר עד שיהו דרין בשני בתים. ומשום הכי מותבינן לר"מ: וביחידי לא אסר, והתנן כו' ואי אפשר לומר כן, דהא משנינן הא דאיתיה הא דליתיה. וכיון דבליתיה מוקמינן לה, כי יש שם ישראל אחר דר עם חבירו בבית מאי טעמא אסר נכרי? ועוד, דבתוספ' (פ"ה) הכי גרסינן: ואם יש שם ישראל אחר — הרי זה אוסר, מפני שהוא כחבירו. ואי האי אוסר בנכרי קאמר — מאי "מפני שהוא כחבירו"? ועוד, הא טעמא משום שמא ילמד הוא: הלכה. דדרשינן לה בפירקא ברבים: מנהג. בפירקא לא דרשינן, אבל אורויי מורינן לה בבא *לישאל. ומאן דאמר נהגו — אורויי נמי לא מורינן, אבל אי עבדי — לא מחינן בידייהו: קיימא לן. ביבמות פ' "החולץ" בסופיה (דף מט:): משנת ר' אליעזר בן יעקב קב ונקי. כלומר: במקומות מועטין מוזכר במשנה, אבל נקי הוא — דהלכה כמותו בכל מקום. והכא אמר שמואל דהלכה כמותו, ומשמע דפשיטא לן דהכי הילכתא: מהו לאורויי תלמיד במקום רבו. כיון דלא תליא בסברא ומילתא פשיטא היא — שרי, או דילמא חוצפא הוא: ביעתא. ביצה לאוכלה: בכותח. שיש בו ניסיובי דחלבא. דמילתא פשיטא הוא: בעו מיניה מרב חסדא. אם מותר אם אסור, ולנסותו היה מתכוין, אם יורה במקום רבו: ולא אורי. בשני דרב הונא רביה: כגון מגלת תענית דכתיבא ומנחא. אלו ימים אסורין להתענות. להכי נקט מגלת תענית שלא היתה דבר הלכה כתובה בימיהן אפילו אות אחת חוץ ממגלת תענית. ולהכי קרי לה מגלה: בכפרי. שם מקום, ולא היה מקומו של רב הונא. ומקומו בפומבדיתא, ושתיהן בבבל:

חרפא

תוספות

ורבי יוחנן אמר נהגו העם כר' אליעזר בן יעקב. במסכת תענית בפ' "שלשה פרקים" (דף כו:) מפרש דהלכה דרשינן בפרקא, ומנהגא בפרקא לא דרשינן, אבל אורויי מורינן. ומ"ד נהגו — אורויי נמי לא מורינן, אבל אי עבדי — לא מחינן בידייהו. ואע"ג דבכל דוכתא קיימא לן כר' יוחנן לגבי שמואל — בהא קי"ל כשמואל, דאמר הלכה אפילו בפירקא דריש לה, דקי"ל: הלכה כדברי המיקל בעירוב, כדפסיק ריב"ל לעיל. *וקי"ל כוותיה לגבי ר"י. ואפי' כביעתא בכותחא חשבי ליה אביי ורב יוסף להא דראב"י. ורבא נמי מודה לאביי גבי עובדא *דהמן בר ריסתק, אי לא משום דביטלא תורת עירוב מאותו מבוי. ואומר ר"י דאותן ישראלים הדרים יחידים בכרכים המוקפים חומה שיש להם מחילות גמורות, ודלתותיהן נעולות בלילה — שרי לטלטל בכולה בשבת, כיון דליכא ישראל אחר דאסר עליה(ז):

מהו לאורויי במקום רביה. אומר ר"י: כל הני הוראות — כגון שבא מעשה לפניו ומורה לעשות כן. אבל אם שואלין לתלמיד הלכה כדברי מי, יכול לומר כל מה שבדעתו, ובלבד שלא יורה על מעשה שבא:

אפילו ביעתא בכותחא. מפרש בערוך: *דלאו בסתם ביצים איירי, דאותן אין צריכין היתר, דאין לך עם הארץ שלא ידע שמותרות בחלב, אלא כששוחט את התרנגולת ומצא בה ביצים גמורות שמותר לאוכלן בחלב. כדתניא בפ"ק דביצה (דף ו:). ואם תאמר: אמאי מותר לאוכלן בחלב, מ"ש מבילת נבילה דאסרינן אפי' כמוה נמכרת בשוק, כדתנן במס' עדיות (פ"ה מ"א)! ותירץ בהלכות גדולות: דגבי איסור נבילה דאורייתא — החמירו, אבל בבשר עוף בחלב דרבנן — הקילו. ואם תאמר: אם כן, מאי "אפילו" דקאמרינן אפילו ביעתא בכותחא, דאטו מי פשיט היתר טפי משאר דברים? הא פלוגתא היא, דלמ"ד בשר עוף בחלב דאורייתא — אסירי, מידי דהוה אבילת נבילה! ואומר ר"י: דלהכי קאמר "אפי'", שאע"פ שכל העולם נוהגין בו היתר. ובפ"ק דביצה (דף ו:) נמי פשיטא ליה להתלמוד דשרייא, גבי הא דאמר רב: ביצה עם יציאתה נגמרה. דקאמרינן: למאי, אילימא דשרי לאוכלה בחלב — הא במעי אמו אסורה, והא תניא: השוחט את התרנגולת כו'. משמע דפשיטא ליה דלא הוה פליג רב. ולפירוש רבינו תם אתי שפיר, שפי' דבבילת נבילה החמירו — משום דנבילה דבר האסור הוא, אבל בבשר בחלב לא החמירו, דכל חד וחד באפי נפשיה שרי*:

כגון מגלת תענית. פירש בקונטרס: דכתיבא ומנחא אלין ימים האסורין להתענות. וה"ה לומר הכי דלפרושי מאיסורא שרי במקום רביה, כדאמרינן לקמן: "אין חכמה ואין תבונה כו'". אלא בימים המותרים איירי, אי שרי לאורויי. וכי ההוא דמקלתן הוו דלא למספד בהון, דמורי הי מינייהו שרי ולפניו אסור ולאחריו מותר. ובזמן שהיה מגלת תענית נוהגת קאמרינן, כי האידנא בטלה מגלת תענית, כדפסיק בפ"ק דר"ה (דף יט:):

רב חסדא אורי בכפרי בשני דרב הונא. כדמפרש הקונטרס, שלא היה שם מקומו של רב הונא ובפומבדיתא היתה מקומו. ונ"ל דתלמיד חבר דרב הונא הוה, כמו רב המנונא דאורי בחרתא דארגז בשני דרב חסדא, דמפרש בסמוך משום דתלמיד חבר דיליה היה. *אבל תלמיד גמור אין יכול להורות אפילו שלא במקום רביה, כדאמרינן בשני דרב הונא לא אורי רב המנונא בחרתא דארגז, אע"פ שהיה מקומו של רב הונא בפומבדיתא, ואפילו רחוק ממנו שלש פרסאות או אפילו טפי — אסור, ואינו חייב מיתה. דפריך עלה מאותו תלמיד שנתחייב מיתה על שהורה ברחוק שלש פרסאות מר"א. אבל אם לא נתחייב מיתה — לא הוה קשיא מידי, אפילו איכא איסורא במילתיה. ורבינא דשר סכינא בבבל — משמע שהיה רחוק הרבה מרב אשי, והיה אסור שם אם היה תלמידו גמור כו'. והא דאמרינן בפ"ק דסנהדרין (דף ה:) תנחום בריה דר' אמי איקלע *) לאתרא, דרש להו מותר ללתות חטין בפסח. אמרו ליה: לאו ר' מני דמן צור איכא הכא? ותנא: תלמיד לא יורה הלכה במקום רבו, אא"כ רחוק ממנו שלש פרסאות כנגד מחנה ישראל. צריך לומר דתלמיד חבר הוה, ומש"ה חוץ לג' פרסאות שרי. והא דאמרינן: בפניו אסור וחייב מיתה, כל תוך שלש פרסאות חשיב בפניו, כדמשמע באותו תלמיד שהורה לפני ר"א, דאם היה תוך שלש פרסאות בדין היה חייב מיתה. ומסתמא נמי לא בפניו ממש היה. וכן בני אהרן מסתמא לא הורו בפני משה ממש. ועיקר שיעור דגמרינן שלש פרסאות כנגד מחנה ישראל — מבני אהרן גמרינן לה, והתם חייבי מיתה הוו. ואומר ר"י: דווקא בדבר שנראה חידוש לשואל, ואפילו ביעתא בכותחא ומגלת תענית בכי האי גוונא איירי, ולא נקטינהו אלא לאשמועינן דאפילו בהני שהתלמיד בעצמו יודע שאינו טועה — אסור להורות. אבל דבר שהשואל יודע שידוע מנהגו של דבר זה, כגון נותן טעם לפגם וכיוצא בו, דכשמורה לו היתר אין דומה לו דבר חידוש — שרי. ורבינא דשר סכינא בבבל — כעין דבר חידוש הוא, שנוטל שררה כדאמרינן (חולין דף יח.): לא אמרו להראות סכין לחכם אלא מפני כבודו של חכם:

*) [לפנינו הגי' לחתר]

רב

רבינו חננאל

תנא *) אכסנאי לעולם אינו אוסר אמר רב יהודה אמר שמואל הלכה כר' אליעזר בן יעקב רב הונא א' מנהג כר' אליעזר בן יעקב ר' יוחנן אמר נהגו העם כר' אליעזר בן יעקב א"ל אביי לרב יוסף כיון דאמר הלכה כר' אליעזר בן יעקב וקי"ל משנת ר' אליעזר קב ונקי כלומר מעט ומנוקה ואין צריך לנפותו ולנקותו מהו לאורויי קמיה רביה א"ל ביעתא בכותחא בעי מינה דרב חסדא בשני דרב הונא רביה. פי' השוחט תרנגולת ומצא בה ביצים גמורות מותרות לאוכלן בכותח שיש בו ניסיובי דחלבא דלאו כבשר הן. או דלמא כבשר הן ואסור ולא פשיט לי כלומר אסור להורות אפי' כמו זה הדבר שהוא ברור בפני מרב חסדא בשני דרב הונא ולא אורי ליה בפסחים בפרק ואלו עוברין בפסח (דף מב) גרסי כי כותח הבבלי יש בו קומניתא דאומא ומילחא ונסיובי והביצה מותרת לאכלה בחלב שאינה בכלל בשר ואפילו אם שחט עופות ומצא בתוכן ביצים מותרות לאכלן בחלב ובלבד שתהא הביצה גמורה כמו שאמרו (ביצה דף ו) השוחט את התרנגולת ומצא בה ביצים גמורות מותר לאכלן בחלב ונמנע רב חסדא בימי רב הונא מלהורות

*) [בירושלמי בפירקין הל' ב' וע"ש דאית תנא תני לאוסר לאחר ל' יום ע"ש היטב].

[וע"ע תוספות ביצה דף ו: ד"ה ביצים]

רב נסים גאון

אמרו ומאי לא ניתן להישבון אינו בתורת הישבון כי זה שכתוב בתורה (ויקרא ה) והשיב את הגזלה לישראל נאמר ולא לבני נח: **אמר** רב יהודה אמר שמואל הלכה כרבי אליעזר בן יעקב ורב הונא אמר מנהג כר' אליעזר בן יעקב ורבי יוחנן אמר נהגו העם כר' אליעזר בן יעקב ובמס' תעניות בפרק בשלשה פרקים (דף כו) פירשוה מאן דאמר הלכה דרשי' לה בפירקא ומאן דאמר מנהג לא דרשינן כי אתו לקמן מורינן להו ומאן דאמר נהגו אפילו אורויי נמי לא מורינן להו ואי עבוד לא מהדרינן להו: **אמר** ליה ביעתא בכותחא בעי מיניה

מסורת הש"ס

[לקמן סב:]
[פסחים קמח]
[לעיל עא: ב"מ עא.]
לעיל מז. לקמן פו.
[עי' תוספות בכורות כג: ד"ה משנת]
יבמות מט: ס. [גיטין סז. בכורות כג:]
[כתובות ס:]
[כלאי' תענית כו:]

הגהות הב"ח

(א) גמ' ביעתא בכותחא בעי מיניה מרב חסדא וכו': (ב) שם ולא אורי לי אמר ליה וכו': (ג) שם בכותחא בעי מיניה מרב חסדא וכו': (ד) שם ולא אורי לי רב חסדא: (ה) רש"י ד"ה אמר מר וכו' דישראל הוא דאוסר על ביתו: (ו) ד"ה ה"ג וד"ה וישראל וד"ה כי ליתיה הכל דיבור אחד: (ז) תום' סד"ה ורבי יוחנן וכו' ישראל אחר דאסר עליה תוספות שנ"ץ ואפי' הרבה בעלי בתים דרים בבית אחד אינם אוסרים זע"ז אא"כ דרים בשני בתים הס"ד ונ"ב ועיין באשר"י ועיין בתוספו' דף עד בד"ה מבוי שלנו:

גליון הש"ס

תום' ד"ה ר"ח אורי וכו'. אבל תלמיד גמור. עי' בס' בני חייא בלקוטים שבסוף הספר:

רב הַמְנוּנָא אוֹרֵי בְּחַרְתָּא דְּאַרְגַּז בִּשְׁנֵי דְּרַב חִסְדָּא. רָבִינָא *סָר סַכִּינָא בְּבָבֶל. א"ל רַב אַשִׁי: אמַאי טַעְמָא עֲבַד מָר הָכִי? א"ל: וְהָא רַב הַמְנוּנָא אוֹרֵי בְּחַרְתָּא דְּאַרְגַּז בִּשְׁנֵי דְּרַב חִסְדָּא. אֲמַר לֵיהּ: "לָאו אוֹרֵי" אִתְּמַר. אֲמַר לֵיהּ: אִתְּמַר אוֹרֵי, וְאִתְּמַר לָא אוֹרֵי. בִּשְׁנֵי דְּרַב הוּנָא רַבֵּיהּ — הוּא דְּלָא אוֹרֵי, וְאוֹרֵי בִּשְׁנֵי דְּרַב חִסְדָּא, בדְּתַלְמִיד חָבֵר דִּילֵיהּ הֲוָה. וַאֲנָא נַמִי, תַּלְמִיד חָבֵר דְּמָר אֲנָא. אָמַר רָבָא: °צוּרְבָא מֵרַבָּנַן חָזֵי לְנַפְשֵׁיהּ. רָבִינָא אִיקְּלַע לִמְחוֹזָא, אַיְיתִי אוּשְׁפִּיזְכְנֵיהּ סַכִּינָא וְקָא מַחֲוֵי לֵיהּ. אֲמַר לֵיהּ: זִיל אַמְטְיֵיהּ לְרָבָא. אֲמַר לֵיהּ: לָא סָבַר(א) מָר הָא דְּאָמַר רָבָא צוּרְבָא מֵרַבָּנַן חָזֵי לְנַפְשֵׁיהּ! אֲמַר לֵיהּ: אֲנָא מִיזְבַּן זְבִינָא. (סִימָן זיל"א (ב)להני"א מחלי"ף איק"א ויעק"ב) רַבִּי אֶלְעָזָר מֵהַגְרוֹנְיָא וְרַב *אַבָּא בַּר תַּחֲלִיפָא אִיקְּלְעוּ לְבֵי רַב אַחָא בְּרֵיהּ דְּרַב אִיקָא בְּאַתְרֵיהּ דְּרַב אַחָא בַּר יַעֲקֹב. בָּעֵי רַב אַחָא בְּרֵיהּ דְּרַב אִיקָא לְמֶיעְבַּד לְהוּ עִיגְלָא תִּילְתָּא, אַיְיתִי סַכִּינָא וְקָא מַחֲוֵי לְהוּ. אֲמַר לְהוּ רַב אַחָא בַּר תַּחֲלִיפָא: לָא לֵיחוּשׁ לֵיהּ לְסָבָא? אֲמַר לְהוּ ר"א מֵהַגְרוֹנְיָא, הָכִי אֲמַר רָבָא: צוּרְבָא מֵרַבָּנַן חָזֵי לְנַפְשֵׁיהּ. חָזֵי — וְאִיעֲנִישׁ רַבִּי אֶלְעָזָר מֵהַגְרוֹנְיָא. וְהָאָמַר רָבָא: צוּרְבָא מֵרַבָּנַן חָזֵי לְנַפְשֵׁיהּ! שָׁאנֵי הָתָם גדְּאַתְחִילוּ בִּכְבוֹדוֹ. וְאִי בָּעֵית אֵימָא: שָׁאנֵי רַב אַחָא בַּר יַעֲקֹב, דדְּמוּפְלָג. אָמַר רָבָא: הוּלְאַפְרוֹשֵׁי מֵאִיסּוּרָא — אֲפִילּוּ בְּפָנָיו שַׁפִּיר דָּמֵי. רָבִינָא הֲוָה יָתֵיב קַמֵּיהּ דְּרַב אַשִׁי, חַזְיֵיהּ לְהַהוּא גַּבְרָא דְּקָא *אָסַר לֵיהּ לַחֲמָרֵיהּ בְּצִינְתָּא בְּשַׁבְּתָא, רְמָא בֵּיהּ קָלָא וְלָא אַשְׁגַּח בֵּיהּ. א"ל: לֶיהֱוֵי הַאי גַּבְרָא בְּשַׁמְתָּא! א"ל: כִּי הַאי גַּוְונָא מִי מִתְחֲזֵא כְּאַפְקְרוּתָא? אֲמַר לֵיהּ: °"אֵין חָכְמָה וְאֵין תְּבוּנָה וְאֵין עֵצָה לְנֶגֶד ה'", *כָּל מָקוֹם שֶׁיֵּשׁ בּוֹ חִילּוּל הַשֵּׁם — אֵין חוֹלְקִין כָּבוֹד לָרַב. אֲמַר רָבָא: ובְּפָנָיו — אָסוּר, וְחַיָּיב מִיתָה, שֶׁלֹּא בְּפָנָיו — אָסוּר, וְאֵין חַיָּיב מִיתָה. וְשֶׁלֹּא בְּפָנָיו לָא? וְהָא תַּנְיָא, *ר"א(ג) אוֹמֵר: לֹא מֵתוּ בְּנֵי אַהֲרֹן עַד שֶׁהוֹרוּ הֲלָכָה בִּפְנֵי מֹשֶׁה רַבָּן. מַאי דָּרוּשׁ °"וְנָתְנוּ בְּנֵי אַהֲרֹן הַכֹּהֵן אֵשׁ עַל הַמִּזְבֵּחַ" אָמְרוּ: *אַף עַל פִּי שֶׁהָאֵשׁ יוֹרֶדֶת מִן הַשָּׁמַיִם — מִצְוָה לְהָבִיא מִן הַהֶדְיוֹט. וְתַלְמִיד אֶחָד הָיָה לוֹ לְרַבִּי אֱלִיעֶזֶר שֶׁהוֹרָה הֲלָכָה בְּפָנָיו. א"ר אֱלִיעֶזֶר לְאִימָּא שָׁלוֹם אִשְׁתּוֹ: תְּמֵיהַּ אֲנִי אִם יוֹצִיא זֶה שְׁנָתוֹ. וְלֹא הוֹצִיא שְׁנָתוֹ. אָמְרָה לוֹ: נָבִיא אַתָּה? אָמַר לָהּ: לֹא נָבִיא אָנֹכִי וְלֹא בֶּן נָבִיא אָנֹכִי, אֶלָּא כָּךְ מְקוּבְּלַנִי: *כָּל הַמּוֹרֶה הֲלָכָה בִּפְנֵי רַבּוֹ חַיָּיב מִיתָה. וְאָמַר רַבָּה בַּר בַּר חָנָה אָמַר רַבִּי יוֹחָנָן: אוֹתוֹ תַּלְמִיד יְהוּדָה בֶּן גּוּרְיָא שְׁמוֹ, וְהָיָה רָחוֹק מִמֶּנּוּ שָׁלֹשׁ פַּרְסָאוֹת?! בְּפָנָיו הֲוָה. וְהָא רָחוֹק מִמֶּנּוּ שָׁלֹשׁ פַּרְסָאוֹת קָאָמַר! וְלִיטַעְמִיךְ *שְׁמוֹ וְשֵׁם אָבִיו לָמָּה? אֶלָּא: שֶׁלֹּא תֹּאמַר מָשָׁל הָיָה. אָמַר ר' חִיָּיא בַּר אַבָּא אָמַר רַבִּי יוֹחָנָן: כָּל הַמּוֹרֶה הֲלָכָה בִּפְנֵי רַבּוֹ רָאוּי לְהַכִּישׁוֹ נָחָשׁ, שֶׁנֶּאֱמַר: °"וַיַּעַן אֱלִיהוּא בֶּן בַּרַכְאֵל הַבּוּזִי וַיֹּאמַר צָעִיר אֲנִי לְיָמִים וגו' עַל כֵּן זָחַלְתִּי"(ד) וּכְתִיב: °"עִם חֲמַת זֹחֲלֵי עָפָר". זְעֵירִי אָמַר רַבִּי חֲנִינָא: נִקְרָא חוֹטֵא, שֶׁנֶּאֱמַר: °"בְּלִבִּי צָפַנְתִּי אִמְרָתֶךָ לְמַעַן לֹא אֶחֱטָא לָךְ". רַב הַמְנוּנָא רָמֵי, כְּתִיב: "בְּלִבִּי צָפַנְתִּי אִמְרָתֶךָ" וּכְתִיב: °"בִּשַּׂרְתִּי צֶדֶק בְּקָהָל רָב"! לָא קַשְׁיָא: כָּאן — בִּזְמַן שֶׁעִירָא הַיָּאִירִי קַיָּים, כָּאן — בִּזְמַן שֶׁאֵין עִירָא הַיָּאִירִי קַיָּים. אָמַר רַבִּי אַבָּא בַּר *זַבְדָּא: חכָּל הַנּוֹתֵן מַתְּנוֹתָיו לְכֹהֵן אֶחָד — מֵבִיא רָעָב לָעוֹלָם, שֶׁנֶּאֱמַר: °"עִירָא הַיָּאִירִי הָיָה כֹהֵן לְדָוִד",(ה) לְדָוִד הוּא דַּהֲוָה כֹּהֵן, לְכוּ"ע לָא? אֶלָּא שֶׁהָיָה מְשַׁגֵּר לוֹ מַתְּנוֹתָיו. וּכְתִיב בַּתְרֵיהּ: "וַיְהִי רָעָב בִּימֵי דָוִד". ר' *אֱלִיעֶזֶר אוֹמֵר: מוֹרִידִין אוֹתוֹ מִגְּדוּלָּתוֹ שֶׁנֶּאֱמַר: °"וַיֹּאמֶר אֶלְעָזָר הַכֹּהֵן אֶל אַנְשֵׁי הַצָּבָא וגו'". אע"ג דַּאֲמַר לְהוּ: לַאֲחִי אַבָּא צִוָּה וְאוֹתִי לֹא צִוָּה — אפ"ה אִיעֲנַשׁ. דִּכְתִיב: °"וְלִפְנֵי אֶלְעָזָר הַכֹּהֵן יַעֲמֹד" — °וְלָא אַשְׁכְּחַן דְּאִיצְטְרִיךְ לֵיהּ יְהוֹשֻׁעַ. א"ר לֵוִי: כָּל דְּמוֹתִיב מִלָּה קַמֵּיהּ רַבֵּיהּ — אָזֵיל לִשְׁאוֹל בְּלָא וָלָד, שֶׁנֶּאֱמַר: °"וַיַּעַן יְהוֹשֻׁעַ בִּן נוּן מְשָׁרֵת מֹשֶׁה מִבְּחוּרָיו וַיֹּאמַר אֲדֹנִי מֹשֶׁה כְּלָאֵם" וּכְתִיב

(מסורת הפסוקים בגליון: משלי כא; ויקרא א; איוב לב; דברים לב; תהלים קיט; שם מ; ש"ב כ; במדבר לא; שם כז; שם יא)

רש"י

חרתא. שם העיר: דארגז. שם האיש שבנאה, והוה אמגושי. כך ראיתי בתשובת הגאונים: סר סכינא. בדק סכין לטבח. ולא אמרו *להראות סכין לחכם אלא מפני כבודו של חכם, ונמלא רבינא נוטל לו עטרת כבוד העיר, ורב אשי רבו במתא מחסיא הוה, והיא מבבל: *דהא רב המנונא אורי בחרתא דארגז. הואיל ולא היה רבו דר בה, אע"פ שהיתה בבבל. ואני לא הוריתי במתא מחסיא שהיא מקומך: תלמיד חבר. חכם כמותו, אלא שלמד ממנו דבר אחד או יותר: לנפשיה. בודק סכין לשחוט בו הוא עצמו בהמה שלו, ואין צריך להראות לרבו: למחוזא. אתריה דרבא: אנא מיזבן זבינא. כי אכילנא מהאי בישרא בדמי, אנא זבין לה מינך. הלכך, לאו לנפשאי, אלא כשאר טבחא הוית לי: עגלא תילתא. גדל שליש, ואז הוא עומד בעיקר טעם בשרו, כדתנן (ב"מ דף סח.): ומגדלין אותן עד שיהו משולשין. ואמרינן נמי (שם דף סט.) מותר שליש — בשכרך. אלמא: אורחיה עד שליש. ל"א: שלישי לבטן(ו) וקשה לי: הא דאמר בעלמא (סנהדרין דף סה:) רב חנינא ורב אושעיא הוו עסקי בספר יצירה, וכל מעלי שבתא אברי להו עגלא תילתא, דהתם מאי שלישי לבטן איכא? הא לא היה בבטן מעולם: לא ליחוש לסבא. לרב אחא בר יעקב. ובתמיה קאמר: דאתחילו בכבודו. מאחר שנאמר לו דניחוש לסבא והתחילו לדבר בכבודו, לא היה לו לזלזל בדבר: ואב"א שאני רב אחא בר יעקב דמפליג. הרבה מאד. היה זקן וחכם: ולאפרושי מאיסורא. ראה תלמיד אדם רוצה לעבור עבירה ורבו שם ושותק — מותר לתלמיד לקפוץ ולגעור: בצינתא. בדקל, ואין משתמשין באילן משום שבות: אמר ליה. רבינא לרב אשי, הא מילתא דעבידנא קמך השתא מי הויא אפקירותא חולפה או לא: אין חכמה וגו'. אין תורת חכמה ותבונה ויועץ עומדת כנגד חילול השם: בפניו אסור. להורות וחייב מיתה בידי שמים והא דרבא לאו לאפרושי מאיסור קאי אלא על הבא לישאל: בפניו הוה. והאי דקתני: רחוק ממנו — שהיה רחוק מקומו ממקום רבו שלש פרסאות. ומיהו, כי אורי — קמיה אורי: והא רחוק ממנו קאמר. ואי הוראה לאו רחוק ממנו הוה, מאי אתא ר' יוחנן לאשמועינן: צפנתי אמרתך. כנסתי דברי מלהורות, במקום שאהא חוטא עליהן: צדק. דברי תורה: עירא היאירי. רבו הוה, כדכתיב: "היה כהן לדוד" — רב לדוד: מורידין אותו מגדולתו. לעיל קאי אדזעירי. במורה הלכה בפני רבו: את אחי אבא צוה. דחלק כבוד למשה, דכתיב: "אשר צוה ה' את משה" והורה הלכות גיעול "אך את הזהב": איענש. לירד מגדולה שפסקו לו מקמי הכי: דכתיב ולפני אלעזר הכהן יעמוד ושאל לו. שהיה עתיד יהושע להיות צריך לישאל דבר הלכה מאלעזר: ולא אשכחן. לאחר מיתת משה דאיצטריך ליה יהושע לאלעזר לשאול כלום: מותיב. משיב דבר מורה הלכה: לשאול. למיתה: כלאם. ראויים הם לכך, דהוי ליה כמורה הלכה:

תוספות

רב המנונא אורי בחרתא דארגז. תרי רב המנונא הוו, חד שהיה תלמידו של רב חסדא כדמשמע הכא, ובפרק קמא דקדושין (דף כה.), גבי סבי דנזוניא דאמר ליה רב חסדא לרב המנונא זיל לנעינהו. ועוד היה אחר שהיה תלמידו של רב, כדלעיל בפרק "כילד מעברין" (דף נד.), דאמר ליה רב לרב המנונא: ברי מדאית לך אוטיב לך:

מאי דרוש ונתנו בני אהרן הכהן אש על המזבח אע"פ שהאש יורדת מן השמים מצוה להביא מן ההדיוט. לכאורה משמע שהקטרת שהקטירו — על מזבח החיצון היה, והוראת שעה היתה, כדאשכחנא בקטרת של נשיאים, כדאמרינן בשילהי "התכלת" (מנחות דף נ:). דאי על מזבח הפנימי הקטירו — מאי שייכא אותה דרשה לשם? והא לא היה יורד אש על מזבח הפנימי לשם קטרת! דהא קי"ל בפרק "אמר להן הממונה" (יומא דף לג.) דמערכה שניה שעל מזבח החיצון לקטרת. מיהו ב"תורת כהנים" משמע שלבית קדשי הקדשים נכנסו להקטיר, ולשם נשרפו, וצ"ע:

כל הנותן מתנותיו לכהן אחד כו'. הא דקרי ליה עירא היאירי, אף על פי שהיה כהן — שמא אביו מאהרן ואמו ממנשה, כדאמר במגילה (דף יב:): אביו מבנימין ואמו מיהודה. ופשטיה דקרא כהן לדוד — לאו כהן ממש הוא, אלא שר. כמו דאמר "ובני דוד כהנים היו" (שמואל ב ח):

מביא רעב לעולם. ואף על גב דכתיב:(ז) "על שאול ועל בית הדמים" — הא והא גרם, וסמוכין קדרש: מיד

עין משפט נר מצוה

ח א טור יו"ד סי' רמב:
ט ב ג ד טוש"ע שם סעיף ד בהג"ה:
י ה מיי' פ"ה מהל' ת"ת ה"ג וטוש"ע שם סעי' יא:
יא ו מיי' שם הלכה ב וטוש"ע שם ס"ד:
יב ז מיי' פ"ב מהלכות תמידין הלכה א סמג עשין קכא:
יג ח טוש"ע י"ד סימן רנז סעיף ט:

רבינו חננאל

רבו: רבינא סאר סכינא פי' בדק הסכין לטבח בבבל כדגרסי' האי טבחא דלא סאיר סכיניה קמי חכם כו' והוא מלשון פוקד תרגום מסער א"ל רב אשי אמאי עבדת הכי כלומר אנא רבך א"ל רבינא הא רב חסדא אורי בכפרי בשני דרב הונא ורב המנונא אורי בארגז פי' שם מקום בשני דרב חסדא. א"ל רב אשי לא הורה איתמר [א"ל איתמר אורו וכו']. איתמר דאורי רב המנונא בשני דרב חסדא מ"ט תלמיד חבר הוא גבי רב חסדא אנא נמי גבי מר תלמיד חבר אנא. פי' מופלג גדול בחכמה מופלג משאר חכמים: אמר רבא ת"ח שרוצה לשחוט בביתו מה שיאכל רואה הסכין ובודקו אבל לבודקו לטבח שישחט ויקנה ממנו לא. אמר רבה ולאפרושי מאיסורא אפילו בפני רבו שפיר דמי כי הא דרבינא הוה יתיב קמיה דרב אשי חזא לההוא גברא דהוה אסיר חמרא בצינתא. פי' בדקל. כדתנן ציני הר הברזל כשירות והוא אילני תמרים היה קושר בו החמור בשבת א"ל רבינא ליהוי ההוא גברא בשמתא א"ל רבינא לרב אשי כי האי גוונא מתחזי כאפקירותא אי לא א"ל לא אין חכמה ואין עצה ואין תבונה לנגד ה' כל מקום שיש חלול השם אין חולקין כבוד לרב. אמר רב בפניו אסור וחייב מיתה שלא בפניו אסור ואינו חייב מיתה ולא מתו ב' בני אהרן אלא מפני שהורו הלכה בפני משה רבן. ותלמיד היה לו לר' אליעזר ויהודה בן גודיא היה שמו שהורה הלכה בפני רבו ולא הוציא שנתו. וא"ר אליעזר כל תלמיד המורה הלכה בפני רבו

רב נסים גאון

מלהורות אפי' הביצה בחלב שהיתר גמור הוא לאכלה: רבינא סר סכינא בבבל. בדק הסכין של שחיטה שמא יהיה בה פגם ותרגום פוקד מסער וכן דרכו של לשון חכמים שמחסרין את העי"ן והחי"ת ואמרו סר

מסורת הש"ס

[חולין י:]
נ"ל והא
[פי' כמו סער עי' ערוך ערך סר ב]
[אחא]
[גיר' הערוך ע' צני קטר פי' היה קושר חמורו בדקל]
[ברכות יט:] שבועות ל: סנהדרין פב.
[יומא נג.]
יומא כח:
ברכות לא:
[כ"ב טו.]
[גי' ע"י והרא"ש א"ר אבא בר כהנא כל המשגר וכו']
[נ"ל אלעזר]

גליון הש"ס

גמרא צורבא מרבנן חזי לנפשיה. עיין בכורות דף לא ע"א תוס' ד"ה דהא. ובר"ש סוף פ"ב דנגעים: שם ולא אשכחן דאצטריך ליה יהושע. עי' סנהדרין דף טז. תוס' ד"ה מה תחלתה:

הגהות הב"ח

(א) גמ' לא סבר לה מר: (ב) שם סימן זיל"א מהניא: (ג) שם והא תניא ראב"י אומר לא מתו בני אהרן אלא על שהורו הלכה: (ד) שם על כן זחלתי ואירא וכתיב התם עם חמת זחלי: (ה) שם כהן לדוד וכי לדוד הוא דהוה כהן לכולי עלמא לא הוה כהן אלא שהיה: (ו) רש"י ד"ה עגלא תילתא וכו' ל"א שלישי לבטן. נ"ב עיין בשבת דף יא: (ז) תוס' ד"ה מביא וכו' דכתיב אל שאול ואל בית:

וּכְתִיב: °"נוּן בְּנוֹ יְהוֹשֻׁעַ בְּנוֹ". וּפְלִיגָא דְּר' אַבָּא בַּר פַּפָּא, דְּאָמַר ר' אַבָּא בַּר פַּפָּא: לֹא נֶעֱנַשׁ יְהוֹשֻׁעַ אֶלָּא בִּשְׁבִיל שֶׁבִּיטֵּל אֶת יִשְׂרָאֵל לַיְלָה אַחַת מִפְּרִיָּה וּרְבִיָּה, שֶׁנֶּאֱמַר: °"וַיְהִי בִּהְיוֹת יְהוֹשֻׁעַ בִּירִיחוֹ וַיִּשָּׂא עֵינָיו וַיַּרְא וגו'" וּכְתִיב: "וַיֹּאמֶר (*לוֹ) כִּי אֲנִי שַׂר צְבָא ה' עַתָּה בָאתִי וגו'". *אָמַר לוֹ: אֶמֶשׁ בִּיטַּלְתֶּם תָּמִיד שֶׁל בֵּין הָעַרְבַּיִם, וְעַכְשָׁיו בִּיטַּלְתֶּם(א) תַּלְמוּד תּוֹרָה. עַל אֵיזֶה מֵהֶן בָּאתָ? אָמַר לוֹ: עַתָּה בָּאתִי. מִיָּד °"וַיֵּלֶךְ(א) יְהוֹשֻׁעַ בַּלַּיְלָה הַהוּא בְּתוֹךְ הָעֵמֶק". וְאָמַר רַבִּי יוֹחָנָן: מְלַמֵּד שֶׁהָלַךְ בְּעוֹמְקָהּ שֶׁל הֲלָכָה. וּגְמִירִי: דְּכָל זְמַן שֶׁאָרוֹן וּשְׁכִינָה שְׁרוּיִין שֶׁלֹּא בִּמְקוֹמָן — אֲסוּרִין בְּתַשְׁמִישׁ הַמִּטָּה. *א"ר שְׁמוּאֵל בַּר *אִינְיָא מִשְּׁמֵיהּ דְּרַב: גָּדוֹל תַּלְמוּד תּוֹרָה יוֹתֵר מֵהַקְרָבַת תְּמִידִין, דְּאָמַר לֵיהּ: עַתָּה בָּאתִי. אָמַר רַב בְּרוֹנָא אָמַר רַב: כָּל הַיָּשֵׁן בְּקִילְעָא שֶׁאִישׁ וְאִשְׁתּוֹ שְׁרוּיִין בָּהּ — עָלָיו הַכָּתוּב אוֹמֵר: °"נְשֵׁי עַמִּי תְּגָרְשׁוּן מִבֵּית תַּעֲנוּגֶיהָ". וְאָמַר(ב) רַב יוֹסֵף: אֲפִי' בְּאִשְׁתּוֹ נִדָּה. רָבָא אָמַר: אִם אִשְׁתּוֹ נִדָּה הִיא — תָּבֹא עָלָיו בְּרָכָה. וְלֹא הִיא, דְּעַד הָאִידָּנָא מַאן נָטְרֵיהּ. הַהוּא מְבוֹאָה דַּהֲוָה דָּיֵיר בָּהּ לַחְמָן בַּר רִיסְתָּק, אֲמַרוּ לֵיהּ: אוֹגַר לָן רְשׁוּתָךְ. אלָא אוֹגַר לְהוּ. אָתוּ אֲמַרוּ לֵיהּ לְאַבָּיֵי; אֲמַר לְהוּ: זִילוּ בַּטִּילוּ רְשׁוּתַיְיכוּ לְגַבֵּי חַד, הֲוָה לֵיהּ יָחִיד בִּמְקוֹם גּוֹי, וְיָחִיד בִּמְקוֹם גּוֹי לֹא אָסַר. אֲמַרוּ לֵיהּ: מִידֵּי הוּא טַעְמָא אֶלָּא דְּלָא שְׁכִיחַ דְּדָיְירִי — וְהָכָא הָא קָדָיְירִי! אֲמַר לְהוּ: כָּל בְּטוּלֵי רְשׁוּתַיְיהוּ גַּבֵּי חַד — מִילְּתָא דְּלָא שְׁכִיחָא הִיא, *וּמִילְּתָא דְּלָא שְׁכִיחָא לָא גְּזַרוּ בָּהּ רַבָּנַן. אֲזַל רַב הוּנָא בְּרֵיהּ דְּרַב יְהוֹשֻׁעַ אֲמָרָהּ לִשְׁמַעְתָּא קַמֵּיהּ דְּרָבָא, אֲמַר לֵיהּ: אִם

רש"י

וּכְתִיב נוּן בְּנוֹ יְהוֹשֻׁעַ בְּנוֹ. וּבָתַר יְהוֹשֻׁעַ לָא חָשֵׁיב בֵּן: לֹא נֶעֱנַשׁ יְהוֹשֻׁעַ. לִהְיוֹת עֲרִירִי, אֶלָּא שֶׁבִּיטֵּל כו': וַיְהִי בִּהְיוֹת יְהוֹשֻׁעַ וגו'. מִדִּכְתִיב: "וְחַרְבּוֹ שְׁלוּפָה בְּיָדוֹ" מִכְּלָל דִּלְפוּרְעָנוּת בָּא. "וְעַתָּה בָּאתִי" דְּקָאָמַר לֵיהּ, הָכִי קָאָ"ל: עַל עֲבֵירָה שֶׁל עַכְשָׁיו בָּאתִי. וּמִדְּאִיצְטְרִיךְ לְמֵימַר עַל שֶׁל עַכְשָׁיו — מִכְּלָל דְּאִכָּא אַחֲרִיתִי, וּמַאי הִיא? הָכִי קָאָמַר לֵיהּ: אֶמֶשׁ בִּיטַּלְתֶּם תָּמִיד שֶׁל בֵּין הָעַרְבַּיִם, בָּעֶרֶב בִּיטַּלְתֶּם הַתָּמִיד, וְעַכְשָׁיו שֶׁחֲשֵׁיכָה אַתֶּם מְבַטְּלִים תַּלְמוּד תּוֹרָה, לְפִי שֶׁהָיוּ עֲסוּקִים בַּמִּלְחָמָה בַּיּוֹם לֹא הָיָה לָהֶן עֵת לַעֲסוֹק בַּתּוֹרָה אֶלָּא בַּלַּיְלָה. וְהַדָּבָר מוֹכִיחַ שֶׁעַל עִסְקֵי תַּלְמוּד תּוֹרָה הוֹכִיחוֹ, מִדִּכְתִיב קְרָא אַחֲרִינָא בַּמִּלְחָמָה שֶׁל עַי שֶׁהָיְתָה אַחֲרֶיהָ: "וַיֵּלֶךְ יְהוֹשֻׁעַ בַּלַּיְלָה הַהוּא בְּתוֹךְ הָעֵמֶק" וְאָמַר ר' יוֹחָנָן: מְלַמֵּד שֶׁלָּן בְּעוֹמְקָהּ שֶׁל הֲלָכָה: וּגְמִירִי דְּכָל זְמַן שֶׁאָרוֹן וּשְׁכִינָה שְׁרוּיִין שֶׁלֹּא בִּמְקוֹמָן כו'. וְאוֹתוֹ לַיְלָה שֶׁהוֹכִיחָם הַמַּלְאָךְ הָיוּ מְבַטְּלִים ת"ת, בִּשְׁבִיל שֶׁהָיוּ אוֹרְבִין עַל הָעִיר וְלֹא הֶחֱזִירוּ בָּעֶרֶב אֶת אָרוֹן לִמְקוֹמוֹ בַּגִּלְגָּל וְהוּא הַלַּיְלָה שֶׁבִּיטְּלוּ מִפְּרִיָּה וּרְבִיָּה: בְּקִילְעָא. בְּחֶדֶר: נְשֵׁי עַמִּי תְּגָרְשׁוּן. שֶׁבּוֹשִׁין הֵן מִמֶּנּוּ: לַחְמָן בַּר רִיסְתַּק. כָּךְ שְׁמוֹ: בַּטִּילוּ רְשׁוּתַיְיכוּ. דְּמָבוֹי לְגַבֵּי חַד מִינַּיְיכוּ, וְאַף עַל גַּב דְּאִינְהוּ אֲסוּרִים לְהוֹצִיא מֵחַצְרוֹתֵיהֶם לַמָּבוֹי, כִּדְתְנַן: *נָתְנוּ לוֹ רְשׁוּתָן — הוּא מוּתָּר וְהֵן אֲסוּרִין אַהֲנֵי לֵיהּ מִיהָא לְטַלְטֵל בְּכָל הַמָּבוֹי כֵּלִים שֶׁשָּׁבְתוּ בְּתוֹכוֹ, וְכֵלִים שֶׁשָּׁבְתוּ בְּבֵית הַיָּחִיד שֶׁבִּטְּלוּ רְשׁוּתָן אֶצְלוֹ. דְּאִי לָאו הָכִי(ג) אֲסִירֵי לְטַלְטוּלֵי בֵּיהּ כִּדְאָמְרִינַן בְּמַסֶּכֶת שַׁבָּת בְּפֶרֶק "ר"א אוֹמֵר": אִם לֹא הֵבִיא כְּלִי (דף קל:): דִּמְעָרְבִי

תוספות

מיד *וילך יהושע בלילה ההוא בתוך העמק. גרסינן. וגרסינן נמי: מלמד שהלך "בעומקה של הלכה כו'". ובמלחמת עי כתיב בפרשה אחרונה "וילן" אבל התם כתיב "בתוך העם", והא דקאמר מיד – לאו לאלתר הוה, אלא כשהופנה הלך בעומקה של הלכה. אבל לבתר מעשה דמלאך טובא הוה:

כל זמן שארון ושכינה שלא במקומן ישראל אסורין בתשמיש המטה. תימה לר"י: דגבי עובדא של אוריה החתי היה ארון שלא במקומו, דכתיב: *"(הנה) הארון וישראל [ויהודה] (חונים) [יושבים] בסוכות ואדוני יואב ועבדי אדוני על פני השדה חונים ואני [וגו'] (אשכב) [ולשכב] עם אשתי", דמשמע שהיו אחרים מותרים בתשה"מ, אלא שאוריה החתי היה מחמיר על עצמו לפי שהיו ישראל בצרה, דהא קאמר ליה דוד: "(לך) רד לביתך". ועוד קאמרינן בפרק "חלק" (סנהדרין דף קז.) גבי דוד שהפך משכבו של לילה למשכבו של יום, ונתעלמה ממנו הלכה זו כו'. משמע: בלילה היה מותר. ואומר ר"י: דשני ארונות היו, אחד שבו שברי הלוחות מונחים, ואותו היו מוליכין במלחמות, כדתניא בספרי: "וארון ברית ה' נוסע לפניהם יומם" – זה שיוצא עמהם(ד) במחנה, והוא ארון עץ שעשה משה בעלותו לסיני, כדכתיב בלוחות אחרונות במשנה תורה: "ועשית לך ארון עץ", ותחלה שם בו גם לוחות אחרונות, כדכתיב: "ואשים את הלוחות בארון אשר עשיתי", עד שנעשה ארון של זהב שעשה בצלאל, ואז נתנו בו לוחות אחרונות, כדכתיב: "ונתת אל הארון את העדות אשר אתן אליך". וכן עשה, כדכתיב בויקהל. ובההוא איירי הכא שהיו נאסרין בתשמיש המטה כשלא היה במקומו, ואותו לא היו רגילין (ה)להוליך במלחמה. כדכתיב בשילה: °"מי יצילנו מיד האלהים האדירים האלה כי לא היתה כזאת מתמול שלשום", שלא היו רגילין להוליכו, ואז כשהוליכוהו לקו וגלה כדמפרש רש"י התם. ומה שהיה עמהן במלחמת יהושע – ע"פ הדיבור היה עושה הכל. והא דדרשינן בפ"ק דב"ב (דף יד.): "אין בארון רק כו'", מלמד שהלוחות ושברי לוחות מונחים בארון – היינו ארון שעשה בצלאל כדמשמע התם – זה היה בבית עולמים, דבשלמה כתיב האי קרא. ואפילו למאן דדריש מ"אשר שברת ושמתם בארון" – היינו בבנין הבית שהיתה מונחת עדי עד. ובירושלמי איכא פלוגתא בפרק "משוח מלחמה" דיש מי שאומרים ארון אחד היה, *[וקאמר התם קרא מסייע ליה לרבי יהודה. פירוש: שאומר שני ארונות היו, "הארון וישראל יושבים בסוכות", והלא ארון בציון היה, מאי עבדין ליה רבנן שאומרים ארון אחד היה]? אלא שהיה בקירוי עד שלא נבנה בית הבחירה. פירוש: דבסוכות דקאמרינן לא שהיה עמהם במלחמה, אלא כלומר שהיה בקירוי של חול שאינו בית המקדש. אע"פ שבכך לא היו נאסרין בתשמיש המטה וגם אוריה עצמו היה נשוי בת שבע – אם כן לא היה מחמיר על עצמו לפרוש מן האשה בשביל שאינו במקדש, מ"מ כיון דאיכא תרתי לריעותא דישראל היו במלחמה יושבין בסוכות וגם ארון אינו במקדש – היה רוצה להחמיר על עצמו. ואי הוה גריס בירושלמי שהיה שלא פירוש אלא בתוך היריעה – ניחא טפי, דלישנא דקירוי לא משמע שיהא חול. לחמן בר ריסתק. ר"ח גריס "המן": בטילו רשותייכו לגבי חד מינייכו. פירש בקונטרס: אע"ג דאינהו אסירי להוציא מחצרותיהן למבוי, כדתנן: נתנו לו רשותן – הוא מותר והן אסורין, אהני להו מיהו לטלטל בכל המבוי כלים ששבתו בתוכו, וכלים ששבתו בבית היחיד שבטלו רשותם אצלו. דאי לאו הכי הוו אסירי לטלטולי ביה, כדאמרינן במסכת שבת פרק "ר"א אומר אם לא הביא" (דף קל:), דמבוי שלא נשתתפו בו(ו) עירובי חצירות עם הבתים – אין מטלטלין בו אלא בארבע אמות, לא עירבו חצירות עם הבתים – מותר לטלטל בכולו, דכשעירבו חצירות עם הבתים שכיחי מאני דבתים בחצר, וגזרינן דלמא אתי לאפוקינהו מחצר למבוי, לפיכך אסור לטלטל במבוי אלא בד' אמות. אבל בשלא עירבו, דלא שכיחי מאני דבתים בחצר – ליכא למיגזר. דאי משום דלמא אתי לטלטולי כלים ששבתו בחצר למבוי – רב לטעמיה, דאמר לקמן (דף מט.) הלכה כר"ש דאמר חצר וקרפף ומבוי רשות אחת הן, והוא שלא עירבו, כדפירש התם בקונטרס. °וקשיא לר"י: דמסתמא הני דשמעתין היו מערבין חצירות עם הבתים, ורשות המבוי לבדו היו מבטלין. דאי לא היו מערבין – א"כ היו מפסידין כל החצירות, שלא היו יכולין להוציא להן מן הבתים, וטוב היה להם שיהו מותרין בחצירות ויאסרו כולם במבוי, ממה שהיו כולן אסורין בחצירות ובמבוי בשביל האחד שהיה מותר. וכיון שהיו מערבין בחצירות – א"כ לא יתכן מה שפירש בקונטרס דאהני ביטול זה לטלטל בכל המבוי כלים ששבתו בתוכו, וכלים ששבתו בבית היחיד, דהא כיון דעירבו חצירות עם הבתים – אין מטלטלין בו אלא בד'. ועוד: דקי"ל כוותיה דר"י דאמר לקמן (שם) הלכה כר"ש דאמר קרפף וחצר רשות אחת הן בין עירבו בין לא עירבו, ולא קי"ל כההיא דרב דשבת. וא"כ, מתחילה נמי היה מותר לטלטל בכולו. ומיהו, לגבי בית היחיד ודאי מהני ביטול, ואפי' לשתף בתי האחרים מהני לענין שהיחיד שביטלו רשותן אצלו יכול להוציא כלי בתיהן למבוי, שהעירוב עושה אותן כבית אחד. וגם אם החצירות פתוחות זו לזו ועירבו יכול היחיד להוציא מכל הבתים והחצירות למבוי, שנעשין הכל אחד על ידי עירוב, ומכל מקום יחיד במקום נכרי לא חשיב ע"י עירוב, שאם כן – לא היה צריך לעולם לשכור. ואין לומר: כיון שעל ידי ביטול משתרי לא היה צריך לשכור עוד כי ודאי יצטרכו, שהביטול אינו מתיר אלא ליחיד אבל השאר אסורין, שאם יוציאו – הרי הן מחזיקין ברשותן שיש להם במבוי קודם הביטול, ובטל הביטול בכך, והוו להו מרובין במקום נכרי. ואם תאמר: כיון שכל החצירות נעשות אחת, גם בתיהם כמו כן נעשין אחד על ידי עירוב. כשיבטלו המבוי לאחד למה יהיו הם אסורין? וכי אם שנים דרים בבית אחד ובטלו בני החצר רשותן לאחד מהשנים, וכי לבדו יהא מותר להוציא מן הבית לחצר וחבירו הדר עמו יהא אסור, ולא יועיל הביטול לו? זה אינו קשיא כלום, כי אם נראה נוכל לומר: אין הכי נמי. מיהו, לא צריכין למימר הכי. כי אפי' אם נאמר שא"א שיהא זה אסור וזה מותר, אלא לשניהם מועיל הביטול בשוה, אע"פ שלא ביטלו אלא לאחד – יש ליתן טעם גדול בדבר, כי שנים בבית אחד כאיש אחד דמו, וגם לענין להיות יחיד במקום נכרי. אבל ע"י עירוב אין נעשין יחיד במקום נכרי, וה"ה לענין ביטול, לומר שכמו שיועיל הביטול לאותן שביטלו(ז) יועיל לו לחביריו שלא יחשבו כאיש אחד. ועוד: דאי אפשר לומר כאן להתיר לכולן מכח

עין משפט נר מצוה

[עי' תוספות מגילה ג. ד"ה וילן וכו' ע"ש]

יד א מיי' פ"ב מהל' עירובין הלכה י סמג עשין א טוש"ע א"ח סי' שפב סעיף ב:

[שמואל ב יא]

[גיר' ע"י א"ל]

רבינו חננאל

חייב מיתה וראוי להכישו נחש כו' ונקרא חוטא שנאמר בלבי צפנתי אמרתך למען לא אחטא לך: כל המשגר את מתנותיו לכהן אחד מביא רעב לעולם שנא' וגם עירא היאירי היה כהן לדוד: ר' אלעזר אומר המורה הלכה בפני רבו מורידין אותו מגדולתו שנאמר ויאמר אלעזר הכהן אל אנשי הצבא הבאים למלחמה זאת חקת כו'. כל דמותיב מלה באנפי רביה אזל לשאול בלא ולד שנאמר ויען יהושע בן נון משרת משה כו'. כלאם הטיל עליהן צרכי צבור והן כלין מאליהן וכתיב נון בנו יהושע בנו. ופליגא דר' אבא דאמר לא נענש יהושע אלא על שביטל ישראל מפריה ורביה שנאמר ויהי בהיות יהושע ביריחו וישא עיניו וירא והנה איש עומד לנגדו כו' מפני שנתעצל ולא הקים המשכן בו ביום. וגמירי כל זמן שארון ושכינה שרויין שלא במקומן ישראל אסורין בתשמיש המטה: גדול תלמוד תורה מהקרבת תמידין כו'. כל הלן בקילעא שאיש ואשתו שרויין בה עליו הכתוב אומר נשי עמי תגרשון מבית תענוגיה. ואפילו אשתו נדה. (איירי) [אורי] אביי בההוא מבואה דהוה דייר בה המן בר (רפתק) [רסתק] ולא בעו לאוגורי להו רשותא (ליבטליה) [דליבטליה] כולהו בני מבואה רשותייהו גבי חד דליהוי ישראל אחד בהדי גוי דלא אסר' ואמר בטלי רבים רשותייהו גבי חד מילתא דלא שכיחא היא ומילתא דלא שכיחא לא גזרו בה רבנן.

רב נסים גאון

סכינא כלומר סער סכינא ואומרין שותא כלומר שעותא ושודא במקום שוחדא וכאלה רבות ובפרק הכל שוחטין (חולין יז) אמרו אמר רב חסדא מניין לבדיקת סכין מן התורה שנאמר (ש"א יד) ושחטתם בזה ואכלתם פשיטא דכי נקבה טרפה בעיא בדיקה בדיקת חכם קאמרינן כו' ואמרינן האי טבחא דלא סר סכינא משמתינן ליה והתם במסכתא דיום טוב בפרק (אין צדין דף כח) אמרו איבעיא להו מהו להראות סכין לחכם ביום טוב רב מרי בריה דרב ביסנא שארי ורבנן אסרי אמר רב יוסף ות"ח רואה לעצמו ומשאילה לאחרים:

מסורת הש"ס

תורה אור

ד"ה א ז

יהושע ה

[נ"ל לא]

סנהדרין מד. מגילה ג.

שם ח

[מגילה שם: ע"ש סנהדרין שם:]

[גיר' ע"י אויא]

מיכה ב

[לקמן סט:]

[ביצה ב: יח. יבמות לח. כתובות נו: קדושין כח: גיטין ה. מד. נזיר נה. ב"מ מו: מז. בכורו' ג. נדה לב.]

[ש"א ד]

רש"ל

הגהות הב"ח

(א) גמ' תלמוד תורה א"ל על איזה מהן באת א"ל עתה באתי (מיד וילך וכו' של הלכה) תא"מ ונ"ב ס"א מיד וילן יהושע בלילה ההוא בתוך העם וכתיב בתוך העמק מלמד שלן בעומקה של הלכה: (ב) שם ואמר רב יוסף לא נצרכה אלא אפי' באשתו: (ג) רש"י ד"ה בטילו כו' לאו הכי הוו אסירי: (ד) תוס' ד"ה כל זמן וכו' לפניהם יומם זהו שיוצא עמהם למלחמה והוא ארון עץ: (ה) בא"ד ואותו לא היו רגילין להוליכו למלחמה כו' כדמפרש התם כצ"ל ותיבת רש"י נמחק: (ו) ד"ה בטילו וכו' במבוי שלא נשתתפו בו עירבו חצירות: (ז) בא"ד שכמו שיועיל הבטול לאותו שבטלו לו יועיל לחביריו שלא יחשבו אלא כאיש א':

גליון הש"ס תוס' ד"ה בטילו וקשיא לר"י דמסתמא הני בשמעתין היו מערבין ע"ח. לא ידעתי למאי הוצרכו לאריכות זו ולמה לא הקשו בחזקה דממ"נ אם לא עירבו בלאו ביטול היה מותר כלים ששבתו במבוי ובעירבו גם ביטול לא מהני ולע"ג:

דמערבי. ביניהן אף על גב דלא מהני: דמכרזינן. הוו יודעין שאין עירובנו מועיל כלום, ואין אנו מוציאין מחצרותינו למבוי. ומה שאנו מטלטלין בתוכו – בשביל שרה"י היא: אכרזתא לדרדקי. וכי הכרזה זו מועיל לדורות הבאין, שיראו אותן מטלטלין כאן ולא שמעו בהכרזה: ליקריב לגביה. ישתדל עם הנכרי עד שיהא אוהבו, וישאיל לו הנכרי מקום בחצרו לאתנוחי ביה מידי. דכיון דהשתא דייר ישראל בחצר הנכרי, הוה ליה האי ישראל כשכירו ולקיטו של נכרי: ואמר רב יהודה אפילו שכירו ולקיטו. של נכרי, אם ישראל הוא – נותן עירובו עם בני מבוי ודיו. שכיר – לעבודת כל השנה, ולקיטו – לימות הקציר והאסיף: היו שם. בבית הנכרי: חמשה שכירים ולקיטין. דרין בחדרים ועליות, שאילו היתה רשות שלהן היו צריכין ליתן כולן בעירוב, כדתנן *במתניתין:(ב) ומודין בזמן שמקצתן שרויין בחדרים כו' והשתא דרשותא דנכרי(ג), מהו ליתן כולן בעירוב, אם שכח האחד ולא נתן אוסר על בני מבוי. מי אמרינן כי היכי דשוינהו ליה לשכיר וללקיט כבעלים להקל, ולהתיר עירובו במבוי זה – הוו נמי בעלים להחמיר, או דלמא לקולא שוינהו רבנן כבעלים, אבל לחומרא לא, דכל בעירובין להקל, והני דירה ודאי לאו דידהו היא: מאי טעמא אמר מר הכי. זו נאה וזו אינה נאה(ד): הונה. כבודה של תורה, וסופה להשתכח ממנו: רועה זונות. נוטריקון: זו נאה וארעה, ואעסוק בה, כדי שתתקיים בידי: הדרי בי. לא אוסיף עוד: המחזיק בנכסי הגר. מידי דתמיהה היא, ותווהי בה אינשי. לפי שבאו לו בלא יגיעה, לפיכך אין מתקיימין, אם לא על ידי מצוה: יקח בהן ס"ת. במקצתם, ובשכר אלו יתקיימו האחרים בידו: בעל

[לקמן עב.]

[כתובות י: נזיר לח. ועי' תוס' סנהדרין מב. ד"ה העוסקים]

[במשלי פירש רש"י שאין זונות במקרא מלא אלא זה בלבד לכך דרשו כך]

[גי' ע"י דרבה בר שומני]

[נ"ל מדיפתי]

תורה אור

אם כן ביטלת תורת עירוב מאותו מבוי! דמערבי. יאמרו "עירוב מועיל במקום גוי"! דמכרזינן. אכרזתא לדרדקי?! – אלא אמר רבא: אליזיל חד מינייהו – ליקרב ליה ולשאול מיניה דוכתא, ולינח ביה מידי, דהוה ליה כשכירו ולקיטו. ואמר רב יהודה אמר שמואל: אפילו שכירו ואפילו לקיטו – בנותן עירובו ודיו. אמר ליה אביי לרב יוסף: היו שם חמשה שכירו וה' לקיטו מהו? אמר ליה: אם אמרו שכירו ולקיטו להקל, גיאמרו שכירו ולקיטו להחמיר? גופא, אמר רב יהודה אמר שמואל: אפילו שכירו ואפי' לקיטו נותן עירובו ודיו. אמר רב נחמן: כמה מעליא הא שמעתא. אמר רב יהודה אמר שמואל: *דשתה רביעית יין אל יורה. אמר רב נחמן: לא מעליא הא שמעתא; דהא אנא, כל כמה דלא שתינא רביעתא דחמרא – לא צילא דעתאי. אמר ליה רבא: מאי טעמא אמר מר הכי? האמר ר' אחא בר חנינא: מאי דכתיב: "ורועה *זונות יאבד הון" (משלי כט) כל האומר: "שמועה זו נאה וזו אינה נאה" – מאבד הונה של תורה! אמר ליה: הדרי בי. אמר רבה בר רב הונא: השתוי אל יתפלל, ואם התפלל – תפלתו תפלה. שיכור אל יתפלל, ואם התפלל – תפלתו תועבה. היכי דמי שתוי והיכי דמי שיכור? כי הא *דרבי אבא בר שומני ורב מנשיא בר ירמיה *מגיפתי, הוו קא מפטרי מהדדי אמעברא דנהר יופטי. אמרו: כל חד מינן לימא מילתא דלא שמיע לחבריה. *)דאמר מרי בר רב הונא: לא יפטר אדם מחבירו אלא מתוך דבר הלכה, שמתוך כך זוכרו. פתח חד ואמר: היכי דמי שתוי והיכי דמי שיכור? שתוי – כל שיכול לדבר לפני המלך, שיכור – כל שאינו יכול לדבר לפני המלך. פתח אידך ואמר: המחזיק בנכסי הגר מה יעשה ויתקיימו בידו – יקח בהן ספר תורה. אמר רב ששת: אפילו בעל

*) ברכות לא. ע"ש שנ"ל מרי בר בריה דרב הונא בריה דר' ירמיה בר אבא

מכח שהביטול יועיל לכולן כשנים הדרים בבית אחד – שא"כ אין כאן ביטול כלל, שכמו שמתחילה היתה רשות לכולן – ה"נ תהא עתה לכולן והרי הם כבתחילה מרובין במקום נכרים. ועוד: דבהדיא אמר(א) דצריך לבטל לכל אחד מאותן שעירבו, למאן דאית ליה לעיל בענין רעה מבטל. ואידך נמי מודה שאם פירש בהדיא שאינו מבטל רק לאחד – שלא ביטל לאחרים, אע"פ שעירבו עם זה שביטל לו. וא"ת: כיון שעל ידי עירוב שהניחו כל החצירות יחד היה מתיר לכולן, הא דפריך רבא א"כ ביטלת תורת עירוב מאותו מבוי, ומשני: דמערבי מעיקרא – נמי דווקא ע"י עירוב היה מתיר, כדי לעשות תקנה לכולן שהיחיד היה מוציא כלי בתיהן למבוי כדפרישית. וי"ל: דרבא סבר שבא להתיר כלים ששבתו בבית היחיד בלא עירוב החצירות, ולא היה יודע שפתוחות זו לזו. ולפי מה שהיה סבור שלא היו פתוחות זו לזו, מה שהיה מקשה ביטלת תורת עירוב מאותו מבוי – בשיתוף איירי, דקרי ליה עירוב:

אם כן ביטלת תורת עירוב מאותו מבוי. אומר ר"י: שבא מעשה לפני רש"י בחופה אחת ששכחו ולא עירבו, והוצרכו להוציא מבית לבית, והתיר להם ע"י שביטלו רשותם לאחד. ואומר ר"י: דאם יועיל ביטול מבית לבית – א"כ יהו מותרין כולן לטלטל מזו לזו, גם אותן שביטלו להם. שאע"פ שהמבטל רשות חצירו אסור להוציא מביתו לחצר – התם הוא, שיש להם חלק בחצר, ונראה כחוזר ומחזיק ברשותו אפי' למ"ד לעיל בפ"ב (דף כו.): רשות ביתו ביטל. אבל הכא, כשביטלו כל השכונות רשותם לאחד – איסתרו כולהו, דאין דומה כלל כחוזר ומחזיק ברשותו כשמטלטל מביתו לבית חבירו, ולא דמי למוציא מביתו לחצר שיש לו בחצר חלק. וכיון דמיסתרו כולהו על ידי ביטול – אין לביטול להועיל כאן, דא"כ ביטלת תורת עירוב מאותו מבוי, שלא יחושו לעשות עוד עירוב כיון דמישתרו כולהו בביטול. ומיהו, אור"י: דאם יש חדרים בבית – יכול לבטל כל הבית בלא החדרים, שיהא עכשיו אסור להוציא מן החדר לבית כמו מבית לחצר, ואין שייך כאן ביטלת תורת עירוב – שהרי ישתכר בעירוב יותר מן הביטול. ודווקא לרבי יוחנן דאמר לקמן: יש ביטול רשות מחצר לחצר, אבל לשמואל דאמר לקמן (דף סו.): אין ביטול רשות מחצר לחצר – ה"ה מבית לבית, דהא תשמישתיה לחוד(ה). ומיהו, כר"י קי"ל. ונראה דאין ראיה מכאן לחלוק על הוראת רש"י דשפיר דמי דחוזר בו מביטולו כשנוטל כליו והכניסם לתוך בית חבירו, וחזר והחזירם לביתו שהיא רשות המיוחדת לו – נראה כחוזר בו מביטולו. וכיון שמפסיד בדבר – לא ביטלת תורת עירוב. ור"ת היה מדקדק מהא דאפליגו ר"י ושמואל לענין ביטול רשות מחצר לחצר, ולענין ביטול רשות בחורבה – משמע דמבית לבית אסור לכ"ע, מדלא איירו ביה. וכדפרישית, שאם התרת – תתיר לכולן, וכיון דשרית לכולהו – יבא לטלטל בלא ביטול. ועוד הביא ראיה מההוא ינוקא דלקמן (דף סז:), דאשתפיך חמימיה, שהתיר לומר לנכרי למייתי ליה חמין מגו ביתיה (דרבא) [נ"ל: דרבה], אע"ג דלא עירבו – מדלא מצאו תקנה בענין אחר. ואמאי? ליבטלו כולהו רשותייהו לההוא ביתא דהוה ביה תינוק. דמסתמא כר"י סבירא להו, דאמר: יש ביטול רשות מחצר לחצר, כדאמר רבא בההוא שמעתא: אנא כר"י סבירא לי. אלא ודאי אפי' ר"י מודה דאין ביטול רשות מבית לבית. ואומר ר"י: דאין משם ראיה, דעל כרחך הוו התם חצירות ומבוי, כדאמרינן התם והא לא עירבנו, והא לא שיתפנו. והיו יכולין להביא חמין ע"י ביטול דרך חצירות ומבוי לבית שהיה בו קטן, ומה שלא עשו כן משום שלא היו בעלים התם:

שתה רביעית יין אל יורה. יש ספרים שכתוב בהן: אל יתפלל. ולא יתכן כלל, דא"כ מאי קאמר רב נחמן: לא מעליא הא שמעתא, דהא אנא [כל] כמה דלא שתינא רביעתא לא צילא דעתאי. מה ענין צילותא אצל תפלה? אלא "אל יורה" גרסינן ברוב ספרים, וכן אמר ר"ח. וא"ת: ומאי קאמר ר"נ לא מעליא הא שמעתתא, הא פלוגתא דתנאי היא בכריתות בפרק "אמרו לו" (דף יג:) כדדריש התם: "ולהבדיל ולהורות" וא"יין ושכר אל תשת" קאי, דמוקמינן ליה התם ברביעית. ועוד קשה: דהא ר"נ גופיה קאמר לקמן בשמעתין דרך מיל ושינה כל שהוא מפיגין את היין, כששתה רביעית. ש"מ: דאסור. ומיהו, ההיא איכא לאוקומא כגון דלא רמא ביה מיא, והכא דרמא ביה מיא כר"א בכריתות (דף יג:), *(דתנן) התם, ר"א אומר: אם נתן לתוכו מים כל שהוא – פטור, ורב נמי פסיק התם הלכה כר"א. אבל מ"מ קשיא, דלא הוי ליה למימר לא מעליא הא שמעתא כיון דאיכא רבנן דפליגי עליה דר"א התם, ואסרי אע"פ שנתן בו מים:

[נ"ל דתניא]

שיכור אל יתפלל ואם התפלל תפלתו תועבה. ולא יצא, כיון שאינו יכול לדבר לפני המלך, וצריך לחזור ולהתפלל. וכן ההיא דברכות (דף כג:) שהיה מתפלל ונמצא צואה כנגדו, דמסיק: כיון שחטא, אע"פ שהתפלל – תפלתו תועבה, וצריך לחזור ולהתפלל. וצ"ע אם יש להשוות ברכות לתפלה לענין צואה ושיכור. וע"כ לאו לכל מילי דמיין, דהא שתוי אל יתפלל עד שיפיג יינו, ואפי' ביין מזוג אל יתפלל ביותר מרביעית, דאפי' ר"א דכריתות (דף יג:) לא שרי ביותר מרביעית. ואפי' לענין הוראה, כדאמרינן התם. ופשיטא דשתוי מברך ברכת המזון וכל הברכות כולן, כדאמ' בירושלמי דברכות, דמפיק ליה מ"ואכלת ושבעת וברכת" – ואפי' מדומדם. ומיהו, משום מי רגלים פשיטא דא"צ לחזור ולברך. אפי' א"ת דמשוינן ברכות לתפלה בצואה תניא, ומי רגלים לא חמירי כמו צואה, דהא אמר בסוף פ' "מי שמתו" (ברכות דף כה.) לא אסרה תורה אלא כנגד עמוד בלבד, הא נפול לארעא שרי. ורבנן הוא דגזרו בהו, וכי גזרו בהו – בודאן, אבל בספקן לא גזרו בהו רבנן:

שכיוון

עין משפט נר מצוה

טו א ב מיי' פ"ב מהל' עירובין הלכה יב טוש"ע א"ח סי' שפ"ב סעיף יא יב:

טז ג שם סעיף טז:

יז ד מיי' פ"א מהלכות ביאת מקדש הלכה ג סמג לאוין ס [טוש"ע י"ד סימן רמב סעיף יג בהג"ה]

יח ה מיי' פ"ד מהל' תפלה הלכה יז סמג לאוין ס טוש"ע א"ח סי' צ"ט סעי' א [וברב אלפס ברכות פרק ה דף כו: וברא"ש שם סימן ט]:

רבינו חננאל

ודחאה רבא ואמר א"כ בטלת תורת עירוב מאותו מבוי וא"ל דמערבי יאמרו עירוב מועיל במקום גוי דמכרזינן בשביל שלא רצה להשכיר. וכי אכרזתא לדרדקי. אלא אמר רבא ניזיל חד מינייהו ויתקרב להחוא גוי ונישול מיניה ונותיב מידי בביתיה דהוה ליה שכירי ולקיטי ואמר רב יהודה אמר שמואל אפילו שכירו ואפילו לקיטו נותן עירובו ודיו. ואם יש לו ה' שכירי ולקיטי נותן אחד מהן ודיו כי לא אמרו שכירו ולקיטו להחמיר אלא להקל. אמר רב נחמן כמה מעליא הא שמעתא: **אמר** רב יהודה אמר שמואל השותה רביעית אל יורה אמר רב נחמן לאו מעליא הא שמעתא דאנא כמה לא שתינא רביעתא דחמרא לא צילא דעתאי. א"ל רבה והא כל האומר שמועה [זו] נאה היא וזו אינ' נאה מאבד הונה של תורה שנאמר ורועה זונות יאבד הון ויאבד הונה של תורה א"ל הדרי בי אמר רב הונא שתוי אל יתפלל ואם התפלל תפלתו (תועבה) [תפלה שיכור אל יתפלל ואם התפלל תפלתו תועבה]. רבה בר שימני ורב מנשיא בר ירמיה אמרי לא נפטר אלא מתוך דבר הלכה שמתוך כך זוכרו פתח חד ואמר המחזיק בנכסי גר מה יעשה ויתקיימו בידו יקח מהן ספר תורה ואפי'

גליון הש"ס

גמ' אפילו שכירו ואפילו לקיטו נותן עירובו ודיו. עי' לקמן דף ע ע"א תוספו' ד"ה יורש מהו שיבטל. ולקמן דף עב ע"א תוס' ד"ה ומודין: **שם** אמר ליה הדרי בי. בב"מ דף סה ע"א: **שם** שיכור אל יתפלל. עי' ברכות דף לא ע"א: **תוס'** ד"ה בטילו רשותייכו וכו' ועוד דבהדיא אמר. לעיל דף כו ע"ב:

הגהות הב"ח

(א) תוס' ד"ה בטילו. ועוד דבהדיא אמר לעיל בפ' שני דצריך לבטל: (ב) רש"י ד"ה חמשה וכו' כדתנן במתני'. נ"ב דף עב וע"ש בתוספות בד"ה ומודין: (ג) בא"ד דגוי היא מהו וכו ואם שכח וכו' דכל בעירובין להקל. נ"ב לקמן דף פ ע"א: (ד) ד"ה מ"ט וכו' נ"ה הס"ד ואחר כך מ"ה רועה זונות וכו' בידי הס"ד ואח"כ מ"ה הונה כבודה וכו' ממנו הס"ד ואח"כ מ"ה הדרי: (ה) תוס' ד"ה א"כ וכו' דהא תשמישתיה לחוד והא תשמישתיה לחוד ומיהו:

גמרא

בַּעַל בְּנִכְסֵי אִשְׁתּוֹ. רָבָא אָמַר: אֲפִילּוּ עֲבַד עִיסְקָא וְרָוַוח. רַב פַּפָּא אָמַר: אֲפִי' מָצָא מְצִיאָה. אָמַר רַב נַחְמָן בַּר יִצְחָק: אֲפִילּוּ כָּתַב בְּהוּ תְּפִילִּין. וְאָמַר רַב חָנִין וְאִיתֵימָא ר' חֲנִינָא: מַאי קְרָאָה, דִּכְתִיב: °"וַיִּדַּר יִשְׂרָאֵל נֶדֶר וגו'". *אָמַר רָמִי בַּר אַבָּא אדֶּרֶךְ מִיל, וְשֵׁינָה כָּל שֶׁהוּא מְפִיגִין אֶת הַיַּיִן. אָמַר רַב נַחְמָן אָמַר רַבָּה בַּר אֲבוּהּ: בלֹא שָׁנוּ אֶלָּא שֶׁשָּׁתָה כְּדֵי רְבִיעִית, אֲבָל שָׁתָה יוֹתֵר מֵרְבִיעִית – כָּל שֶׁכֵּן שֶׁדֶּרֶךְ טוֹרַדְתּוֹ וְשֵׁינָה מְשַׁכַּרְתּוֹ. וְדֶרֶךְ מִיל מְפִיגָה הַיַּיִן?! וְהָתַנְיָא: *מַעֲשֶׂה בְּר"ג שֶׁהָיָה רוֹכֵב עַל הַחֲמוֹר, וְהָיָה מְהַלֵּךְ מֵעַכּוֹ לִכְזִיב, וְהָיָה רַבִּי אֶילְעַאי מְהַלֵּךְ אַחֲרָיו. מָצָא גְּלוּסְקִין בַּדֶּרֶךְ, אָמַר לוֹ: אֶילְעַאי, טוֹל גְּלוּסְקִין מִן הַדֶּרֶךְ. מָצָא גּוֹי אֶחָד, אָמַר לוֹ: מַבְגַּאי, טוֹל גְּלוּסְקִין הַלָּלוּ מֵאֶילְעַאי! נִיטְפַּל לוֹ ר' אֶילְעַאי, אָמַר לוֹ: מֵהֵיכָן אַתָּה? אָמַר לוֹ: מֵעֲיָירוֹת שֶׁל בּוּרְגָּנִין, וּמַה שִּׁמְךָ? מַבְגַּאי – שְׁמֵנִי. – כְּלוּם הִיכִּירְךָ רַבָּן גַּמְלִיאֵל מֵעוֹלָם? אָמַר לוֹ: לָאו. בְּאוֹתָהּ שָׁעָה לָמַדְנוּ שֶׁכִּוֵּון רַבָּן גַּמְלִיאֵל בְּרוּחַ הַקּוֹדֶשׁ. וּשְׁלֹשָׁה דְּבָרִים לָמַדְנוּ בְּאוֹתָהּ שָׁעָה: לָמַדְנוּ *גשֶׁאֵין מַעֲבִירִין עַל הָאוֹכָלִין, וְלָמַדְנוּ שֶׁהוֹלְכִין אַחֲרֵי רוֹב עוֹבְרֵי דְרָכִים, וְלָמַדְנוּ *דשֶׁחֲמֵצוֹ שֶׁל גּוֹי אַחַר הַפֶּסַח מוּתָּר בַּהֲנָאָה. כֵּיוָן שֶׁהִגִּיעַ לִכְזִיב בָּא אֶחָד לִישָּׁאֵל עַל נִדְרוֹ, אָמַר לָזֶה שֶׁעִמּוֹ: כְּלוּם שָׁתִינוּ רְבִיעִית יַיִן הָאִיטַלְקִי? אָמַר לוֹ: הֵן. אִם כֵּן יְטַיֵּיל אַחֲרֵינוּ עַד שֶׁיָּפִיג יֵינֵינוּ. וְטִיֵּיל אַחֲרֵיהֶן ג' מִילִין, עַד שֶׁהִגִּיעַ לְסוּלָּמָא שֶׁל צוֹר. כֵּיוָן שֶׁהִגִּיעַ לְסוּלָּמָא דְּצוֹר *יָרַד ר"ג מִן הַחֲמוֹר, וְנִתְעַטֵּף וְיָשַׁב, וְהִתִּיר לוֹ נִדְרוֹ. וְהַרְבֵּה דְּבָרִים לָמַדְנוּ בְּאוֹתָהּ שָׁעָה: לָמַדְנוּ שֶׁרְבִיעִית יַיִן הָאִיטַלְקִי מְשַׁכֵּר, וְלָמַדְנוּ: שִׁיכּוֹר אַל יוֹרֶה, וְלָמַדְנוּ שֶׁדֶּרֶךְ מְפִיגָה אֶת הַיַּיִן, וְלָמַדְנוּ השֶׁאֵין מְפִירִין נְדָרִים לֹא רָכוּב וְלֹא מְהַלֵּךְ וְלֹא עוֹמֵד אֶלָּא יוֹשֵׁב. קָתָנֵי מִיהַת שְׁלֹשָׁה מִילִין! שָׁאנֵי יַיִן הָאִיטַלְקִי – דִּמְשַׁכֵּר טְפֵי. וְהָאָמַר רַב נַחְמָן אָמַר רַבָּה בַּר אֲבוּהּ: לֹא שָׁנוּ אֶלָּא שֶׁשָּׁתָה רְבִיעִית, אֲבָל שָׁתָה יוֹתֵר מֵרְבִיעִית – כָּל שֶׁכֵּן דֶּרֶךְ טוֹרַדְתּוֹ וְשֵׁינָה מְשַׁכַּרְתּוֹ! רָכוּב שָׁאנֵי. הַשְׁתָּא דְּאָתֵית לְהָכִי – לְרָמִי בַּר אַבָּא נַמִי לָא קַשְׁיָא, רָכוּב שָׁאנֵי. אִינִי?! וְהָאָמַר *רַב נַחְמָן: ומְפִירִין נְדָרִים בֵּין מְהַלֵּךְ בֵּין עוֹמֵד וּבֵין רָכוּב! תַּנָּאֵי הִיא, דְּאִיכָּא לְמַאן דְּאָמַר זפּוֹתְחִין בַּחֲרָטָה וְאִיכָּא לְמַאן דְּאָמַר אֵין פּוֹתְחִין בַּחֲרָטָה. *דְּאָמַר רַבָּה בַּר בַּר חָנָה א"ר יוֹחָנָן: מַאי פָּתַח לֵיהּ רַבָּן גַּמְלִיאֵל לְהַהוּא גַּבְרָא – °"יֵשׁ בּוֹטֶה כְּמַדְקְרוֹת חָרֶב וּלְשׁוֹן חֲכָמִים מַרְפֵּא", חכָּל הַבּוֹטֶה רָאוּי לְדוֹקְרוֹ בַּחֶרֶב, אֶלָּא שֶׁלְּשׁוֹן חֲכָמִים מַרְפֵּא. אָמַר מָר: וְאֵין מַעֲבִירִין עַל הָאוֹכָלִין. אָמַר רַבִּי יוֹחָנָן מִשּׁוּם רַבִּי שִׁמְעוֹן בֶּן יוֹחַאי: לֹא שָׁנוּ אֶלָּא בַּדּוֹרוֹת הָרִאשׁוֹנִים, שֶׁאֵין בְּנוֹת יִשְׂרָאֵל פְּרוּצוֹת בִּכְשָׁפִים. אֲבָל בַּדּוֹרוֹת הָאַחֲרוֹנִים, שֶׁבְּנוֹת יִשְׂרָאֵל פְּרוּצוֹת בִּכְשָׁפִים – מַעֲבִירִין. תָּנָא: שְׁלֵימִין – מַעֲבִירִין, פְּתִיתִין – אֵין מַעֲבִירִין. אֲמַר לֵיהּ רַב אַסִּי לְרַב אָשֵׁי: וּפְתִיתִין לָא עָבְדָן? וְהָכְתִיב: °"וַתְּחַלֶּלְנָה אוֹתִי אֶל עַמִּי בְּשַׁעֲלֵי שְׂעוֹרִים וּבִפְתוֹתֵי לֶחֶם"! דְּשָׁקְלִי בְּאַגְרַיְיהוּ. אָמַר רַב שֵׁשֶׁת מִשּׁוּם רַבִּי אֶלְעָזָר בֶּן עֲזַרְיָה: יָכוֹל

רש"י

בַּעַל בְּנִכְסֵי אִשְׁתּוֹ. בָּעֵי לְמֶיעֱבַד בְּהוּ מִצְוָה, דְּמִילְּתָא דְּתָווּהוּ בָּהּ אֱינָשֵׁי נָמֵי הִיא, וְשָׁלְטָא בְּהוּ עֵינָא בִּישָׁא: אֲפִילּוּ כּוֹתֵב בְּהוּ תְּפִילִּין. נָמֵי מִיקַּיְימוּ בִּידֵיהּ: מַאי קְרָאָה. דְּעַל יְדֵי דַּעֲבַד בְּהוּ מִצְוָה מִיקַּיְימִי בִּידֵיהּ, דִּכְתִיב: "וַיִּדַּר יִשְׂרָאֵל וגו' וְהַחֲרַמְתִּי" לְשׁוֹן הֶקְדֵּשׁ, וְעַל יְדֵי כָּךְ נִשְׁמַעַת תְּפִלָּתָם וְנָפְלוּ בְּיָדָם: וְשֵׁינָה כָּל שֶׁהוּא. אוֹ זוֹ אוֹ זוֹ: נִיטְפַּל לוֹ ר' אֶלְעַאי. נִתְקָרֵב אֵצֶל הַנָּכְרִי: מַבְגַּאי שְׁמֵנִי. כָּךְ שְׁמִי: אֵין מַעֲבִירִין עַל הָאוֹכָלִין. הַמּוֹצֵא אוֹכָלִין בַּדֶּרֶךְ – אֵינוֹ רַשַּׁאי לַעֲבוֹר עֲלֵיהֶן וּלְהַנִּיחָן שָׁם: שֶׁהוֹלְכִין אַחֲרֵי רוֹב עוֹבְרֵי דְרָכִים. מִדְּלָא שְׁרָא לֵיהּ לְר' אֶלְעַאי לְמֵיכְלִינְהוּ, דְּאַחְזְקִינְהוּ בְּחֶזְקַת פִּיתָּן שֶׁל נָכְרִים, שֶׁרוֹב עוֹבְרֵי דְרָכִים נָכְרִים הֵן: שֶׁחֲמֵצוֹ שֶׁל נָכְרִי. שֶׁאַחַר הַפֶּסַח הָיָה: מוּתָּר בַּהֲנָאָה. כְּגוֹן הָכָא, דְּאִיכָּא טוֹבַת הֲנָאָה לְנָכְרִי: לָזֶה שֶׁעִמּוֹ. לְר' אֶלְעַאי: לְסוּלָּמָא שֶׁל צוֹר. מַעֲלוֹת הַר גָּבוֹהַּ: אֲבָל יוֹתֵר מֵרְבִיעִית כו'. וְכֵיוָן דְּיַיִן הָאִיטַלְקִי הֲוָה, וּמְשַׁכֵּר טְפֵי – הֲוָה לֵיהּ כְּיוֹתֵר מֵרְבִיעִית: רָכוּב שָׁאנֵי. דְּאֵין לוֹ טוֹרַח הַדֶּרֶךְ: לְרָמִי בַּר אַבָּא נַמִי. דְּאָמַר: דֶּרֶךְ מִיל, וְהָכָא תָּנֵי: שָׁלֹשׁ מִילִין – לָא תִּיקְשֵׁי, דְּרָכוּב שָׁאנֵי, דְּאֵין לוֹ טוֹרַח וּלְפִיכָךְ אֵין מְפִיגוֹ כָּל כָּךְ: תַּנָּאֵי הִיא. בְּמַסֶּכֶת נְדָרִים: פּוֹתְחִין בַּחֲרָטָה. צָרִיךְ לֶחָכָם לִמְצוֹא פֶּתַח לַשּׁוֹאֵל שֶׁיְּהֵא לוֹ פִּתְחוֹן פֶּה לוֹמַר: לְדַעַת כֵּן לֹא נָדַרְתִּי, וְאִלּוּ הָיִיתִי יוֹדֵעַ שֶׁכֵּן הוּא לֹא הָיִיתִי נוֹדֵר. וְנִמְצָא נֶדֶר נֶעֱקָר מֵאֵלָיו: אֵין פּוֹתְחִין. אֵין צָרִיךְ לִפְתּוֹחַ לוֹ בַּחֲרָטָה, אֶלָּא הֶחָכָם עוֹקְרוֹ אַע"פ שֶׁאֵינוֹ מוֹצֵא לוֹ טַעַם עֲקִירָה. רַבָּן גַּמְלִיאֵל סָבַר כְּמַאן דְּאָמַר פּוֹתְחִין, לְפִיכָךְ הוּצְרַךְ יִשּׁוּב הַדַּעַת לַחֲשׁוֹב אֵיזֶה פֶּתַח יִמְצָא לוֹ: כָּל הַבּוֹטֶה. הַנּוֹדֵר נֶדֶר: רָאוּי לְדוֹקְרוֹ. דִּלְמָא לֹא מְקַיֵּים לֵיהּ, וְהַיְינוּ פֶּתַח, דְּקָאָמַר לֵיהּ: אִילּוּ הָיִיתָ יוֹדֵעַ שֶׁאָסוּר לִנְדּוֹר, וְחַיָּיב מִיתָה אַתָּה עָלָיו, כְּלוּם הָיִיתָ נוֹדֵר? וְאָמַר לֵיהּ הָאִיךְ: לֹא: אֶלָּא לְשׁוֹן חֲכָמִים מַרְפֵּא. שֶׁמַּתִּירִין לוֹ נִדְרוֹ: פְּתִיתִין אֵין מַעֲבִירִין עֲלֵיהֶן. אֶלָּא נוֹטְלִין אוֹתָן, דְּלֵיכָּא לְמֵיחַשׁ לִכְשָׁפִים: וּפְתִיתִין לָא עָבְדָן. כְּשָׁפִים: דְּשָׁקְלָן בְּאַגְרַיְיהוּ. פְּתִיתֵי לֶחֶם לַעֲשׂוֹת כְּשָׁפִים מִדְּבָרִים אֲחֵרִים. וְהָכִי קָאָמַר נָבִיא: בִּשְׁבִיל פִּיתּוֹתֵי לֶחֶם שֶׁנּוֹתְנִים לָכֶן בִּשְׂכַרְכֶן חִילַּלְתֶּן אֶת שְׁמִי בְּתוֹךְ עַמִּי, שֶׁהֱיִיתֶן עוֹשׂוֹת בָּהֶן כְּשָׁפִים לִנְבִיאֵי הַבַּעַל לְהַטְעוֹת אֶת עַמִּי: יָכוֹלְנִי

תוספות

שכוון רבן גמליאל ברוח הקדש. אע"פ שהיה שם זה רגיל באומות, כדאמרינן בפרק שני דמכות (דף יא.): תמן אמרין שכם נסיב מבגאי גזר, מכל מקום חשיב ליה כוונה ברוח הקדש. והיא דסוף יבמות (דף קכב:) שאמר ליה יפה כוונת, שאריה שמי כך קורין אותי בעירי, לא שכוון אותו האיש ברוח הקדש, שלא קראו אריה אלא על שם כחו:

שהולכין אחר רוב עוברי דרכים. כדפירש בקונטרס: מדלא שרי ליה לר' אלעאי למכלינהו – דאחזקינהו בחזקת פתן של נכרים, שרוב עוברי דרכים נכרים הם. דאם היינו תולין בשל ישראל – היה מותר, אף על פי שאחר הפסח היה בסמוך דישראל יש לומר דאחר הפסח נעשה:

ולמדנו שחמצו של נכרי אחר הפסח מותר בהנאה. מדנתנו לנכרי, דאיכא טובת הנאה דנכרי כדפירש בקונטרס. דאי ס"ל דאסור בהנאה – היה לו לאסור מספק, דשמא בפסח נעשה. וא"ת: והיאך נתן ר"ג והא דריש ר"י בסוף פ"ק דע"ז (דף כ.): לא תחנם – לא תתן להם מתנת חנם! ואע"ג דלנכרי המכירו שרי אפילו לר"י, דהא מוקמינן כר"י ההוא דשולח אדם ירך לנכרי בפסחים בפרק "כל שעה" (דף כב.). ותניא בתוספתא [דע"ז פ"ג]: דאם היה שכינו – מותר, מפני שהוא כמוכרו לו. מ"מ, הכא הא אמרינן שלא היה מכירו רבן גמליאל מעולם! ויש לומר דשמא לא סבר לה ר"ג להא דר"י. אי נמי: כיון שהיה הנכרי מתלוה עמהן בדרך – שרי, דחשיב כמוכרו לו. והא דתניא ב"הניזקין" (גיטין דף סא.): מפרנסין עניי נכרים עם עניי ישראל מפני דרכי שלום – ההיא נמי שרי משום דרכי שלום:

פותחין בחרטה. פי' בקונטרס: צריך לחכם למצוא פתח לשואל. שיהא לו פתחון פה לומר: על דעת כן לא נדרתי, ואילו הייתי יודע שכן לא הייתי נודר, ונמצא נדר נעקר מאליו. אין פותחין – אין צריך לפתוח לו בחרטה, אלא החכם עוקר אע"פ שאינו מוצא לו טעם עקירה. ר"ג סבר כמ"ד פותחין, לפיכך הוצרך יישוב הדעת לחשב איזה פתח ימצא לו, ע"כ לשון הקונטרס. וקשיא לר"ת: דהא רב נחמן גופיה שמעינן ליה בהדיא בפרק "ד' נדרים" (דף כב:) דאמר: הלכה פותחין בחרטה, ונזקקין ל"אלהי ישראל". ובפ' "נערה המאורסה" (שם דף עז:) נמי קאמר רב נחמן: הלכה, נשאלין לנדרים מעומד, יחיד, ובלילה. ופריך עלה מהא דר"ג. וכתוב בכל הספרים: ר"ג סבר אין פותחין בחרטה, למיעקר נדרא בעינן ובעי לעיוני, להכי ישב. ורב נחמן סבר: פותחין בחרטה, ואפילו מעומד. אלא שיש ספרים שהגיהו איפכא, על פי פירוש הקונטרס דהכא בשמעתא. ועוד: דאמר בסוף "אלו מותרין" (שם כ.): בשלמא מחמירין עליו – דלא פתחינן ליה בחרטה. משמע דאין פותחין היא חומרא. ועוד אמר בריש "ד' נדרים" (דף כא:) דרב הונא סבר פותחין בחרטה, מההוא דאתא לקמיה ואמר ליה "לבך עלך". ורבה בר בר חנה דאמר ליה להההוא דאתא: אלו אתו י' בני אדם שיפייסוך, קסבר: אין פותחין בחרטה. מפרש ר"ת: פותחין בחרטה – היינו ששואלין אותו אם הוא מתחרט על מה שנדר, שאומר לו: "כדו תהית", או "לבך עלך", או "בעית נדר" (שם), ושרינן ליה בהכי. ור"ג סבר: אין פותחין להתיר לו בחרטה לחוד, שמתחרט בו על מה שנדר, אלא צריך למצוא פתח לנדרו, כגון שאומר לו: אילו באו עשרה בני אדם שיפייסוך, וכדפתח ר"ג לההוא טייעא ששואלין אותו אדעתא דהכי נדרת, שצריך לטרוח הרבה ולחשוב באיזה ענין ימצאו לו פתח לנדרו: **כל** הבוטה ראוי לדוקרו בחרב. בפרק "ד' נדרים" (דף כב.) אמר דלא פתחינן ליה בהא, דמתוך יראה יאמר אדעתא דהא לא נדר, אף על פי שמשקר. ועוד: פסקינן התם הלכה פותחין בחרטה:

רבינו חננאל

[בעל] בנכסי אשתו. רבא אמר אפי' עבד עיסקא ורווח ואפי' מצא מציאה. רב נחמן בר יצחק אמר אפילו (מצא תפילין) [כותב בהו תפלין] דיו א"ר יוחנן מהאי קרא שנאמר וידר ישראל נדר לה' ויאמר אם נתון תתן את העם הזה בידי והחרמתי את עריהם: **אמר** חייא בר אבא דרך מיל ושינה כל שהוא מפיגין את היין ולא שנו אלא ששתה כדי רביעית אבל יותר מרביעית כ"ש שדרך משכרתו ושינה טרדתו. ואקשינן דרך מיל מפיגה את היין והתניא מעשה ברבן גמליאל שהיה מהלך מעכו לכזיב והיה רבי אלעאי מחמר אחריו כו' עד הרבה דברים למדנו מאותו מעשה למדנו שרביעית יין האיטלקי משכר ולמדנו שהשכור אל יורה ולמדנו שאין מפירין נדרים לא רכוב ולא מהלך ולא עומד אלא יושב. קתני מיהא וטייל אחריהן שלשה מילין ודחינן שאני יין האיטלקי דמשכר טפי כו'. א"ר יוחנן מאי פתח ליה רבן גמליאל לההוא גברא יש בוטה כמדקרות חרב כל בוטה ראוי לדוקרו בחרב אלא לשון חכמים מרפא: **אין** מעבירין על האוכלין. א"ר יוחנן לא שנו אלא בדורות הראשונים שלא היו בנות ישראל פרוצות בכשפים. אבל בדורות האחרונים שבנות ישראל פרוצות בכשפים מעבירין עליהן. תנא שלימים מעבירין עליהן פתיתין אין מעבירין עליהן פי' אין עושין כשפנות בפתיתין איני והכתיב ותחללנה אותי אל עמי בשעלי שעורים ובפתותי לחם וגו' מכלל דעבדי בפתיתין ופרקינן התם בפתיתין דהוו שקלן באגרייהו:

עין משפט נר מצוה

יט א ב מיי' פ"א מהל' ביאת מקדש הלכה ופ"ד מהלכות תפלה הלכה יז סמג עשין ק ולאוין ס טוש"ע א"ח סימן צט סעיף ב:
כ ג טוש"ע א"ח סי' קפ סעיף ד:
כא ד מיי' פ"ד מהלכות חמץ ומצה הלכה ב סמג עשין נט טוש"ע א"ח סימן תמח סעיף א:
כב ה טוש"ע י"ד סי' רכח סעיף ד:
כג ו מיי' פ"ו מהלכות שבועות הלכה ו סמג לאוין רלח טוש"ע י"ד שם סעיף ג:
כד ז מיי' שם הלכה י טוש"ע שם סעיף ז:
כה ח מיי' פי"ג מהל' נדרים הלכה כה טוש"ע י"ד סי' רג סע"א:

מסורת הש"ס

תורה אור; במדבר כא; תענית יז: סנהדרין כב: ע"ש בגה"ל רב אחא; [תוספתא פסחים פ"ב] ועי' בירושלמי ע"ז פ"א הלכה ט ובויקרא רבה סוף פ' בחקותי; [ב"מ כג.]; פסחים כח.; נדרים עז.; [שם:] [ע"ש]; שם כב.; משלי יב; יחזקאל יג

גליון הש"ס

גמרא ולמדנו שיכור אל יורה. עיין בסנהדרין דף מב ע"א תוספות ד"ה והעוסקים: רש"י ד"ה מסר

מאי קראה וכו' ועי"כ נשמעת תפלתם. עיין חולין דף ב ע"ב תוספות ד"ה אבל אמר. ועיין תשובת מהר"ם פאדוואה ס"ס עט: בעין משפט אות ג' טוש"ע א"ח סימן קפ. ליתא שם מזה והובאה במ"א סי' קעא ס"ק א':

רב נסים גאון

לא קשיא הא כמאן דאמר פותחין בחרטה והא כמאן דאמר אין פותחין בחרטה זו חלוקה בין רב אסי ורב הונא רב אסי היה סובר אין פותחים בחרטה ורב הונא חלק עליו ואמר פותחים בחרטה ואיתא במסכת נדרים (דף כא) בפרק ארבעה נדרים התירו חכמים.

תורה אור

*יָכוֹל אֲנִי לִפְטוֹר אֶת כׇּל הָעוֹלָם כּוּלּוֹ מִן הַדִּין מִיּוֹם שֶׁחָרַב בֵּית הַמִּקְדָּשׁ וְעַד עַכְשָׁיו, שֶׁנֶּאֱמַר: °"לָכֵן שִׁמְעִי נָא זֹאת עֲנִיָּה וּשְׁכֻרַת וְלֹא מִיָּיִן". מֵיתִיבִי: *אשִׁיכּוֹר מִקָּחוֹ מִקָּח וּמִמְכָּרוֹ מִמְכָּר, עָבַר עֲבֵירָה שֶׁיֵּשׁ בָּהּ מִיתָה — מְמִיתִין אוֹתוֹ, מַלְקוּת — מַלְקִין אוֹתוֹ, כְּלָלוֹ שֶׁל דָּבָר: הֲרֵי הוּא כְּפִיקֵּחַ לְכׇל דְּבָרָיו, אֶלָּא שֶׁפָּטוּר מִן הַתְּפִלָּה. מַאי "יְכוֹלְנִי לִפְטוֹר" דְּקָאָמַר — נַמִי מִדִּין תְּפִלָּה. אָמַר רַבִּי חֲנִינָא: בל"ש אֶלָּא שֶׁלֹּא הִגִּיעַ לְשִׁכְרוּתוֹ שֶׁל לוֹט, אֲבָל הִגִּיעַ לְשִׁכְרוּתוֹ שֶׁל לוֹט — פָּטוּר מִכּוּלָּם.§ א"ר חֲנִינָא: כׇּל הַמַּפִּיק מָגֵן בִּשְׁעַת גַּאֲוָה סוֹגְרִין וְחוֹתְמִין צָרוֹת בַּעֲדוֹ שֶׁנֶּאֱמַר: °"גַּאֲוָה אֲפִיקֵי מָגִנִּים סָגוּר חוֹתָם צָר". מַאי מַשְׁמַע דְּהַאי אָפִיק לִישָּׁנָא דְּעַבּוֹרֵי הוּא, דִּכְתִיב: °"אַחַי בָּגְדוּ כְמוֹ נָחַל כַּאֲפִיק נְחָלִים יַעֲבֹרוּ". ר' יוֹחָנָן אָמַר: כׇּל שֶׁאֵינוֹ מַפִּיק אִתְּמַר. מַאי מַשְׁמַע דְּהַאי מַפִּיק לִישָּׁנָא דְּגַלּוֹיֵי הוּא, דִּכְתִיב: °"וַיֵּרָאוּ אֲפִיקֵי מַיִם וַיִּגָּלוּ מוֹסְדוֹת תֵּבֵל". מִכְּדִי, קְרָאֵי מַשְׁמַע בֵּין לְמָר וּבֵין לְמָר, *מַאי בֵּינַיְיהוּ? אִיכָּא בֵּינַיְיהוּ דְּרַב שֵׁשֶׁת. דְּרַב שֵׁשֶׁת מָסַר שִׁינְתֵיהּ לְשַׁמָּעֵיהּ, מָר אִית לֵיהּ דְּרַב שֵׁשֶׁת, וּמָר לֵית לֵיהּ דְּרַב שֵׁשֶׁת. אָמַר רַב חִיָּיא בַּר אַשִׁי אָמַר רַב: כׇּל שֶׁאֵין דַּעְתּוֹ מְיוּשֶּׁבֶת עָלָיו — אַל יִתְפַּלֵּל. מִשּׁוּם שֶׁנֶּא': "בַּצַּר אַל יוֹרֶה". רַבִּי חֲנִינָא בְּיוֹמָא דְּרָתַח לָא מְצַלֵּי. אָמַר: "בַּצַּר אַל יוֹרֶה" כְּתִיב. מָר עוּקְבָא בְּיוֹמָא דְּשׁוּתָא לָא הֲוָה נָפֵיק לְבֵי דִינָא. *אָמַר רַב נַחְמָן בַּר יִצְחָק: הִלְכְתָא בָּעֲיָא צִילּוּתָא כְּיוֹמָא דְּאִסְתַּנָּא. אָמַר אַבָּיֵי: אִי *אָמְרָה לִי אֵם קְרִיב כּוּתְחָא — לָא תְּנַאי. אָמַר *רָבָא: אִי קְרַצְתַּן כִּינָּה — לָא תְּנַאי. מָר בְּרֵיהּ דְּרָבִינָא עֲבַדָה לֵיהּ אִמֵּיהּ ז' *מָנֵי לְז' יוֹמֵי. אָמַר רַב יְהוּדָה: לָא אִיבְרִי לֵילְיָא אֶלָּא לְשֵׁינְתָא. א"ר שִׁמְעוֹן בֶּן לָקִישׁ: גלָא אִיבְרִי סִיהֲרָא אֶלָּא לִגְירְסָא. אָמְרִי לֵיהּ לְר' זֵירָא: מְחַדְּדָן שְׁמַעְתָּךְ! אֲמַר לְהוּ: דִּימָמֵי נִינְהוּ. אֲמַרָה לֵיהּ *בְּרַתֵּיהּ דְּרַב חִסְדָּא לְרַב חִסְדָּא: לָא בָּעֵי מָר מֵינַם פּוּרְתָּא? אָמַר לַהּ: הָשְׁתָּא אָתוּ יוֹמֵי דַּאֲרִיכֵי וְקַטִּינֵי, וְנֵינוּם טוּבָא. אָמַר רַב נַחְמָן בַּר יִצְחָק: אֲנַן פּוֹעֲלֵי דִימָמֵי אֲנַן. רַב אַחָא בַּר יַעֲקֹב דיָזִיף וּפָרַע. אָמַר ר"א: הַבָּא מִן הַדֶּרֶךְ אַל יִתְפַּלֵּל שְׁלֹשָׁה יָמִים, שֶׁנֶּאֱמַר: °"וָאֶקְבְּצֵם אֶל הַנָּהָר הַבָּא אֶל *אַהֲוָא וַנַּחֲנֶה שָׁם יָמִים שְׁלֹשָׁה וָאָבִינָה בָּעָם וגו'". אֲבוּהּ דִּשְׁמוּאֵל, כִּי אָתֵי בְּאוֹרְחָא לָא מְצַלֵּי תְּלָתָא יוֹמֵי. השְׁמוּאֵל לָא מְצַלֵּי בְּבֵיתָא דְּאִית בֵּיהּ שִׁיכְרָא. רַב פַּפָּא לָא מְצַלֵּי בְּבֵיתָא דְּאִית בֵּיהּ הַרְסָנָא. א"ר חֲנִינָא: כׇּל הַמִּתְפַּתֶּה בְּיֵינוֹ יֵשׁ בּוֹ מִדַּעַת קוֹנוֹ, שֶׁנֶּאֱמַר: °"וַיָּרַח ה' אֶת רֵיחַ הַנִּיחֹחַ וגו'". אָמַר ר' חִיָּיא: כׇּל הַמִּתְיַישֵּׁב בְּיֵינוֹ — יֵשׁ בּוֹ דַּעַת ע' זְקֵנִים, *יַיִן נִיתַּן בְּע' אוֹתִיּוֹת, וְסוֹד נִיתַּן בְּע' אוֹתִיּוֹת, נִכְנַס יַיִן יָצָא סוֹד. *)א"ר חָנִין: לֹא נִבְרָא יַיִן(א) אֶלָּא לְנַחֵם אֲבֵלִים וּלְשַׁלֵּם שָׂכָר לָרְשָׁעִים, שֶׁנֶּא': °"תְּנוּ שֵׁכָר לְאוֹבֵד וגו'" א"ר חָנִין בַּר פַּפָּא: כׇּל שֶׁאֵין יַיִן נִשְׁפָּךְ בְּתוֹךְ בֵּיתוֹ כַּמַּיִם — אֵינוֹ בִּכְלַל בְּרָכָה, שֶׁנֶּא': °"וּבֵרַךְ אֶת לַחְמְךָ וְאֶת מֵימֶיךָ". מַה לֶּחֶם שֶׁנִּיקָּח בְּכֶסֶף מַעֲשֵׂר — אַף מַיִם שֶׁנִּיקָּח בְּכֶסֶף מַעֲשֵׂר. וּמַאי נִיהוּ — יַיִן, וְקָא קָרֵי לֵיהּ מַיִם.

אִי

*) סנהדרין ע.

ישעיהו נא | איוב מא | שם ו | תהלים יח | עזרא ח | בראשית ח | משלי לא | שמות כג

רש"י

יְכוֹלְנִי לִפְטוֹר. לִטְעוֹן עַל כׇּל יִשְׂרָאֵל לִפְנֵי הקב"ה דָּבָר שֶׁיִּפָּטְרוּ כּוּלָּן מִדִּינָא לע"ל לוֹמַר שֶׁהֵן(ב) שִׁיכּוֹרִים וְאֵין נִתְפָּשִׂין עַל עֲוֹנָם: מִדִּין תְּפִלָּה. אִם דָּנִין אוֹתָן עַל שֶׁלֹּא הָיוּ מִתְפַּלְּלִין בְּכַוָּונָה, יָכוֹל אֲנִי לְפוֹטְרָן: הַמַּפִּיק מָגֵן. הַמַּעֲבִיר תְּפִלַּת "מָגֵן אַבְרָהָם", שֶׁאֵינוֹ אוֹמְרָהּ: בִּשְׁעַת גַּאֲוָה. בִּשְׁעַת שִׁיכְרוּת אֵינוֹ מִתְפַּלֵּל: סוֹגְרִין וְחוֹתְמִין צָרוֹת בַּעֲדוֹ. שֶׁלֹּא יָבֹאוּ עָלָיו: שֶׁאֵינוֹ מַפִּיק אִיתְּמַר. דְּהַאי מַפִּיק — לִישָּׁנָא דְּגַלּוּיֵי הוּא, וְה"ק: כׇּל שֶׁאֵינוֹ מְגַלֶּה תְּפִלָּה בִּשְׁעַת שִׁיכְרוּת, כְּלוֹמַר: שֶׁאֵינוֹ מִתְפַּלֵּל: אֲפִיקֵי מַיִם. גִּילּוּיֵי הַיָּם, כִּדְכְתִיב: "וַיִּגָּלוּ מוֹסְדוֹת": מָסַר שִׁינְתֵיהּ לְשַׁמָּעֵיהּ. אָמַר לוֹ: הַנִּיחֵנִי לִישַׁן מְעַט, וּכְשֶׁיַּגִּיעַ זְמַן תְּפִלָּה הַקִּיצֵנִי. ר' חֲנִינָא דְּאָמַר אַעְבּוּרֵי בָּעֵי — לֵית לֵיהּ דְּרַב שֵׁשֶׁת, וְאָסוּר לְהִתְפַּלֵּל עַד שֶׁיֵּעוֹר מֵאֵלָיו: בַּצַּר אַל יוֹרֶה. בָּדַקְתִּי אַחַר הַמִּקְרָא זֶה, וְאֵינוֹ בְּכׇל הַכְּתוּבִים. וְשֶׁמָּא בְּסֵפֶר בֶּן סִירָא הוּא: יוֹמָא דְּשׁוּתָא. רוּחַ דְּרוֹמִית מְנַשֶּׁבֶת בּוֹ(ג) וַחֲזָקָה: צִלּוּתָא. דַּעַת נְלוֹלָה: כְּיוֹמָא דְּאִיסְתְּנָא. כְּשֶׁמְּנַשֶּׁבֶת רוּחַ צְפוֹנִית יוֹם אוֹרָה הוּא, וְנוֹחַ לַכֹּל. כִּדְאָמַר בִּיבָמוֹת בְּפֶרֶק "הֶעָרֵל" (דף עב.): מִפְּנֵי מָה לֹא מָלוּ יִשְׂרָאֵל בַּמִּדְבָּר — מִפְּנֵי שֶׁלֹּא נָשְׁבָה בָּהֶן רוּחַ צְפוֹנִית. אֲבָל בְּיוֹמָא דְּשׁוּתָא אָמַר הָתָם: לָא מְהַלִּינַן בֵּיהּ, וְלָא מְסוֹכְרִינַן בֵּיהּ: קְרִיב כּוּתְחָא. אֲפִי' לִיוּוּי עֲבוֹדָה קַלָּה הָיְתָה מְבַטֶּלֶת אוֹתִי: לָא תְּנַאי. לֹא הָיִיתִי שׁוֹנֶה כְּמוֹ שֶׁשָּׁנִיתִי: יוֹמֵי דַּאֲרִיכֵי. יָמִים שֶׁהוּא בַּקָּצֵר אֲרִיכֵי לִישַׁן, וְקַטִּינֵי לַעֲסוֹק בַּתּוֹרָה וּבַמִּצְוֹת: וְנֵינוּם טוּבָא. וְנִישַׁן הַרְבֵּה: יָזִיף וּפָרַע. הָיָה קוֹבֵעַ לוֹ לִשְׁנוֹת כָּךְ וְכָךְ פְּרָקִים בַּיּוֹם, וְהָיָה רָגִיל לַעֲסוֹק בַּיּוֹם. וּפְעָמִים שֶׁהָיָה טָרוּד בִּמְזוֹנוֹתָיו בַּיּוֹם, וּפוֹרֵעַ קְבִיעוּת עִתּוֹ בַּלַּיְלָה: אַל יִתְפַּלֵּל ג' יָמִים. שֶׁאֵין דַּעְתּוֹ מְיוּשֶּׁבֶת עָלָיו מִפְּנֵי טוֹרַח הַדֶּרֶךְ: וַנַּחֲנֶה שָׁם יָמִים שְׁלֹשָׁה. וַהֲדַר "וָאָבִינָה", מִכְּלָל דְּעַד הָשְׁתָּא לָא הֲוָיָא בִּינָה: דְּאִית בֵּיהּ שִׁיכְרָא. רֵיחַ הַשֵּׁכָר מְשַׁכְּרָתוֹ: דְּאִית בֵּיהּ הַרְסָנָא. מִשּׁוּם רֵיחָא: הַמִּתְפַּתֶּה בְּיַיִן. שֶׁמְּפַיְּיסִין אוֹתוֹ עַל דָּבָר, וּמִתְרַצֶּה כְּשֶׁטּוֹב לִבּוֹ בַּיַּיִן: רֵיחַ הַנִּיחוֹחַ. וַאֲמָרַן לְעֵיל(ד) דְּרֵיחָא דּוּמְיָא דְּמִשְׁתְּיָיא הוּא. וּכְתִיב: "וַיֹּאמֶר אֶל לִבּוֹ לֹא אוֹסִיף" וגו' דְּאִירְצֵי: הַמִּתְיַישֵּׁב בְּיֵינוֹ. שֶׁשּׁוֹתֶה יַיִן וְאֵין דַּעְתּוֹ מִטָּרֶפֶת: נִיתַּן בְּשִׁבְעִים אוֹתִיּוֹת. כָּךְ חֶשְׁבּוֹנוֹ בְּגִימַטְרִיָּא: יָצָא סוֹד. וְזֶה, הוֹאִיל וְלֹא יָצָא סוֹדוֹ — שָׁקוּל הוּא כְּסַנְהֶדְרִין שֶׁל ע': לְשַׁלֵּם בּוֹ שָׂכָר לָרְשָׁעִים. שֶׁשּׁוֹתִין וּשְׂמֵחִין וּמְקַבְּלִין עוֹלָמָן בְּחַיֵּיהֶם: לְאוֹבֵד. רָשָׁע: אֵינוֹ בִּכְלַל הַבְּרָכָה. לֹא הִגִּיעַ לְסוֹף בְּרָכָה גְמוּרָה, וַאֲפִילּוּ הוּא עָשִׁיר בִּדְבָרִים אֲחֵרִים: שֶׁנִּיקָּח בְּכֶסֶף מַעֲשֵׂר. שֶׁמּוּתָּר לְלוֹקְחוֹ בְּכֶסֶף מע"ש בִּירוּשָׁלַיִם. הַכֹּל נִיקָּח בְּכֶסֶף מַעֲשֵׂר חוּץ מִן הַמַּיִם וּמֶלַח, בְּפֶרֶק "בַּכֹּל מְעָרְבִין" (לעיל דף כו:):

אִם

תוספות

מסר שינתיה לשמעיה. פי' בקונט': לרבי חנינא דאמר איעבורי בעי — לית ליה דרב ששת, ואסור להתפלל עד שיעור מאליו. ואומר ר"י: דאפי' עובר זמן תפלה לא יתפלל, דשכור או שתוי חשבינן ליה עד שיעור מאליו. ומיהו, אין נראה דהלכה כרב ששת. *ור"ח פי' בענין אחר, וז"ל: אמר ר' חנינא, כל המפיק מגן בשעת גאוה, פי': כל המעביר מגן, ומכסה יצרו בשעת גאוה, כלומר: בעת שמתגבר עליו טומן אותו שלא יתגבר — סוגרין וחותמין צרות בעדו. לשון מפיק כ"אפיק נחלים יעבורו" (איוב ו). ר' יוחנן אמר: כל שאינו מפיק איתמר. כלומר: כל מי שאינו מכסה ומעביר, אלא מגלהו ומפיק מגן, ויוצא להלחם כנגדו ולכובשו. וזו הגאוה היא עת שכרותו של אדם. רבי חנינא סבר לכובשו בשינה כדי להעבירו ולהפיגו טפי עדיפא, ור' יוחנן אמר חיישינן שמא ישתקע בשינה וימנע מן התפלה, אלא לגלותו כדי להתעסק בדרך וכיוצא בה כדי להפיגו ואחר כך יתפלל טפי עדיף:

בצר אל יורה. פירש בקונטרס: בדקתי אחר מקרא זה ואינו בכל הכתובים. ושמא בספר בן סירא הוא. ומצינו בכמה מקומות שמביא התלמוד מקראות הכתובים בספר בן סירא, כדאשכחן ב"החובל" (ב"ק צב:): "כל עוף למינהו ישכון ובן אדם לדומה לו". *וכן "סלסלה ותרוממך ובנדיבים תושיבך", ואמרינן בירושלמי דברכות שהוא כתוב בספר בן סירא. ורבינו שמואל פירש: ששמע רבינו קלונימוס שכן דורש בירושלמי: כל המיצר אל יורה, דכתיב "שמעי נא זאת ענייה ושכורת ולא מיין". והכי איתא בירושל' בריש פרק "אין עומדין": הבא מן הדרך אסור להתפלל, מזה הטעם דכתיב: "שמעי נא זאת וכו'" וגם רבי זריקא ורבי יוחנן בשם ר' אליעזר בנו של ר' יוסי הגלילי אומר המיצר אסור להתפלל — לא מסתברא אלא מן הדין קרא "שמעי נא זאת" ועתה מדמה צרה לשכרות. ובשכרות כתיב "להבדיל ולהורות" כדדרש בכריתות (דף יג:). ומהאי טעמא אל יתפלל, דהוי שכור מתוך שטרוד בצרתו ובכעסו. ור"ת מפרש, דמהאי קרא קדרים: "היערוך שועך לא בצר" (איוב לו), כלומר: בשעת צרה אל תערוך תפלתך, כשיש טירוד. ובכמה מקומות רגיל התלמוד לקצר המקרא, כגון "ונתן הכסף וקם לו"*. ומיהו, קצת קשה: "בצר אל יורה" דהוה ליה למימר אל יתפלל:

אלא לשינתא. כמו לילי תקופת תמוז: **וקרי** ליה בלשון מים. פשטא דקרא מים ממש, דכתיב בסיפיה דקרא "והסירותי מחלה מקרבך" ע"י שיברך המים, כדאשכחן גבי רפואות מי מרה: "כל המחלה אשר שמתי במצרים לא אשים עליך", וכתיב נמי (מלכים ב ב): "רפאתי למים האלה".

עין משפט נר מצוה

[כל זה איתא בערוך ערך פק ד]

כו א ב מיי' פ"ד מהל' אישות הל' יח [ופ"א מהלכות נזירות דין יב] ופרק כט מהל' מכירה הלכה יח סמג עשין פב טור ש"ע אה"ע סימן מד סעיף ג וטוש"ע ח"מ סימן רלה סעיף כב:

כז ג מיי' פ"ג מהלכות ת"ת הלכה יג טוש"ע א"ח סי' רל"ח סעיף א וטוש"ע י"ד סימן רמו סעיף כג:

כח ד טוש"ע א"ח סי' רלח סעיף ב:

כט ה טוש"ע א"ח סי' לח סעיף ב:

רבינו חננאל

מיום שחרב ביהמ"ק כתיב שמעי נא זאת ענייה ושכורת ולא מיין מכאן אמר יכול אני לפטור את העולם מיום שחרב ביהמ"ק מדין תפלה דקי"ל שכור אל יתפלל. (והא) דתניא שכור מקחו מקח וממכרו ממכר עבר עבירה שיש בה מיתה ממיתין אותו מלקות מלקין אותו כללו של דבר הרי (הן) [הוא] כפיקח לכל דבריו אלא שפטור מן התפלה. והני מילי שלא הגיע לשכרותו של לוט. אבל הגיע לשכרותו של לוט פטור מכלום: **אמר** רבי חנינא כל המפיק מגן בשעת גאוה. פי' כל המעביר מגן ומכסה יצרו בשעת גאוה כלומר בעת שמתגבר עליו טומן אותו שלא יתגבר סוגרין וחותמין צרות בעדו. לשון מפיק כאפיק נחלים יעבורו. ר' יוחנן אמר כל שאינו מפיק איתמר. כלומר כל מי שאינו מעביר ומכסה אלא מגלהו ומפיק מגן לנגדו להלחם כנגדו ולכבשו וזו הגאוה היא עת שכרותו של אדם. רבי חנינא סבר לכבשו בשינה כדי להעבירו ולהפיגו טפי עדיף ור' יוחנן אמר חיישינן שמא ישתקע בשינה (זימנן) [וימנע] מן התפלה אלא לגלותו כדי להתעסק בדרך וכיוצא בה להפיגו ואח"כ יתפלל טפי עדיף ואמרינן מכדי קראי משמעי כר' חנינא וכר' יוחנן במאי פליגי בדרב ששת דהוה מסר שינתיה לשמעיה ומזהירו כדי להקיצו בשעת התפלה ר' חנינא אית ליה דרב ששת. ר' יוחנן לית ליה דרב ששת חייש דילמא משתקע בשינה. אמר רב כל שאין דעתו מיושבת עליו אל יתפלל שנאמר בצר אל יורה. ר' חנינא כל יומא דהוה רתח לא הוה מצלי אמר בצר אל יורה כתיב. מר עוקבא ביומא דשותא. פי' יום עבים לא הוה נפיק לדינא.

אמר צריכא הילכתא צילותא כיומא איסתנא פי' יום שמנשבת בו רוח צפונית: **אמר** אביי אי אמרה לי אם קריב כותחא לא גרסי פי' אילו היתה מעסקת אותו לתשמיש הבית והיתה נטרחת דעתו לא הוינא יכול למיגרס. ורבא אמר אי קרצתי כינה לא גרסי כלומר אילו היה הכינים נושכין אותו לא הוינא יכול למיגרס ולפיכך עשתה לו אמו למר בר רבנא ז' חלוקים להחליף בכל יום חלוק מפני הכינים. כל הגורס ביום שמעתתיה מחדדן כר' זירא. ר' אחא הוה ישן ביום והיה ניעור בלילה וגרים. א"ר אלעזר הבא מדרך אל יתפלל ג' ימים שנאמר ואקבצם אל הנהר הבא אל אחוה ונחנה שם ימים שלשה וגו'. אבוה דשמואל כל כי הוה אתא מאורחא תלתא יומי לא הוה מתפלל. שמואל לא הוה מצלי בביתא דאית בה שיכרא. א"ר חנינא כל המתפתה ביינו יש בו מדעת קונו שנאמר וירח ה' את ריח הניחוח. אמר רב כל שדעתו מיושבת עליו ביינו יש בו מדעת שבעים זקנים מ"ט יין עולה ע' וסוד עולה ע' נכנס יין יצא סוד. לא נברא יין אלא לנחם בו אבלים ולשלם שכר לרשעים שנאמר תנו שכר לאובד ויין למרי נפש ופליגא דר' חנינא בר פפא דאמר כל בית שאין יין נשפך בתוכו כמים אינו בכלל ברכה שנאמר וברך את לחמך ואת מימיך. מה לחם הניקח בכסף מעשר אף הני מים דניקחים בכסף מעשר ומאי ניהו יין וקרי להן מים

מסורת הש"ס

עי' אדר"נ פט"ז ד"ה רשב"י אמר

[תוספתא תרומות פ"ג]

[גיר' ע"י במאי פליגי בדר' ששת]

מגילה כח: ע"ש

[קדושין לא: וש"נ]

גי' ע"י רבינא

גי' ע"י לבושי

גי' ע"י אמרין לה בנתיה וכו' אמר להו

[נ"ל אהוא]

[סנהדרין לח. ע"ש בתוספות ד"ה נכנס]

הגהות הב"ח

(א) גמרא לא נברא יין בעוה"ז אלא לנחם: (ב) רש"י ד"ה יכולני וכו' לומר שהן (שיכורין) תז"מ ונ"ב ס"א שוגגין: (ג) ד"ה יומא דשותא וכו' בו בחזקה: (ד) ד"ה ריח הניחוח ואמרן לעיל. נ"ב היינו מה שפי' דריח השכר משכרתו:

גליון הש"ס

תום' ד"ה בצר. ובנדיבים תושיבך וכן כתובות דף קי ע"ב נדה דף טז ע"ב מדרש ב"ר פ"ח:

ל א מיי' פ"ב מהלכות עירובין הלכה יא סמג עשין א טוש"ע א"ח סימן שפב סעיף יז:
לא ב מיי' שם:
לב ג מיי' וטוש"ע שם:
לג ד ה מיי' שם הלכה יד וטוש"ע שם סעיף יח:

אִי נִשְׁפַּךְ בְּבֵיתוֹ כַּמַּיִם – אִיכָּא בְּרָכָה, וְאִי לָא – לָא. א"ר אֶילְעַאי: *בִּשְׁלֹשָׁה דְּבָרִים אָדָם נִיכָּר: בְּכוֹסוֹ, וּבְכִיסוֹ, וּבְכַעֲסוֹ, וְאָמְרִי לַהּ: אַף בְּשַׂחֲקוֹ.§ אָמַר רַב יְהוּדָה אָמַר רַב: יִשְׂרָאֵל וְגוֹי בַּפְּנִימִית, וְיִשְׂרָאֵל בַּחִיצוֹנָה, בָּא מַעֲשֶׂה לִפְנֵי רַבִּי [א]וְאָסַר, וְלִפְנֵי ר' חִיָּיא וְאָסַר, יָתוּב רַבָּה וְרַב יוֹסֵף בְּשִׁילְהֵי פִּירְקֵיהּ דְּרַב שֵׁשֶׁת, וְיָתֵיב רַב שֵׁשֶׁת וְקָאָמַר: כְּמַאן אֲמָרָהּ רַב לִשְׁמַעְתֵּיהּ – כְּר' מֵאִיר. כַּרְכֵּישׁ רַבָּה רֵישֵׁיהּ. אָמַר רַב יוֹסֵף: *תְּרֵי גַּבְרֵי רַבְרְבֵי כְּרַבָּנַן לִיטְעוּ בְּהַאי מִילְּתָא?! אִי כְּרַבִּי מֵאִיר – לָמָּה לִי יִשְׂרָאֵל בַּחִיצוֹנָה? וְכִי תֵּימָא: *מַעֲשֶׂה שֶׁהָיָה כָּךְ הָיָה – וְהָא בָּעוּ מִינֵּיהּ מֵרַב: פְּנִימִי בִּמְקוֹמוֹ מַהוּ? וַאֲמַר לְהֶן: [ב]מוּתָּר. וְאֶלָּא מַאי – כְּר"א בֶּן יַעֲקֹב? הָאָמַר: עַד שֶׁיְּהוּ שְׁנֵי יִשְׂרְאֵלִים אוֹסְרִין זֶה עַל זֶה! *אֶלָּא כְּר"ע, דְּאָמַר רֶגֶל הַמּוּתֶּרֶת בִּמְקוֹמָהּ – אוֹסֶרֶת שֶׁלֹּא בִּמְקוֹמָהּ, לָמָּה לִי גּוֹי אֲפִילּוּ יִשְׂרָאֵל נַמִי! אָמַר רַב הוּנָא בְּרֵיהּ דְּרַב יְהוֹשֻׁעַ: לְעוֹלָם כְּר' אֱלִיעֶזֶר בֶּן יַעֲקֹב וּכְרַבִּי עֲקִיבָא. וְהָכָא בְּמַאי עָסְקִינַן – כְּגוֹן שֶׁעֵירְבוּ. וְטַעְמָא – דְּאִיכָּא גּוֹי דְּאָסִיר, אֲבָל לֵיכָּא גּוֹי – לָא אָסִיר. בְּעָא מִינֵּיהּ רַבִּי *אֱלִיעֶזֶר מֵרַב: יִשְׂרָאֵל וְגוֹי בַּחִיצוֹנָה, וְיִשְׂרָאֵל בַּפְּנִימִית מַהוּ? הָתָם טַעְמָא – מִשּׁוּם דִּשְׁכִיחַ דְּדָיֵיר, דְּמִירְתַת גּוֹי וְסָבַר: הַשְׁתָּא אָתֵי יִשְׂרָאֵל, וְאָמַר לִי: יִשְׂרָאֵל דַּהֲוָה גַּבָּךְ הֵיכָא? אֲבָל הָכָא – אָמֵינָא לֵיהּ: נְפַק אֲזַל לֵיהּ. [ג]אוֹ דִילְמָא: ה"נ מִירְתַת, דְּסָבַר: הַשְׁתָּא אָתֵי יִשְׂרָאֵל וְחָזֵי לִי? א"ל: °"תֵּן לְחָכָם וְיֶחְכַּם עוֹד". ר"ל וְתַלְמִידֵי דְּרַבִּי חֲנִינָא אִיקְלְעוּ לְהַהוּא פּוּנְדָּק, וְלָא הֲוָה שׂוֹכֵר וַהֲוָה מַשְׂכִּיר. אָמְרוּ: מַהוּ לְמֵיגַר מִינֵּיהּ? [ד]כָּל הֵיכָא דְּלָא מָצֵי מְסַלֵּיק לֵיהּ – לָא תִּיבָּעֵי לָךְ דְּלָא אָגְרִינָא. כִּי תִּיבָּעוּ – הֵיכָא דְּמָצֵי מְסַלֵּיק לֵיהּ, מַאי? כֵּיוָן דְּמָצֵי מְסַלֵּיק – אָגְרִינָא, אוֹ דִילְמָא הַשְׁתָּא מִיהָא הָא לָא סַלְּקֵיהּ! אָמַר לְהֶן רֵישׁ לָקִישׁ: נִשְׂכּוֹר, וְלִכְשֶׁנַּגִּיעַ אֵצֶל רַבּוֹתֵינוּ שֶׁבַּדָּרוֹם נִשְׁאַל לָהֶן. אָתוּ שַׁיְילוּ לְר' אָפֵס, אֲמַר לְהֶן: [ה]יָפֶה עֲשִׂיתֶם שֶׁשְּׂכַרְתֶּם. רַבִּי חֲנִינָא בַּר יוֹסֵף וְר' חִיָּיא בַּר אַבָּא וְר' אַסִּי אִיקְלַעוּ לְהַהוּא פּוּנְדָּק, דַּאֲתָא גּוֹי מָרֵי דְּפוּנְדָּק בְּשַׁבְּתָא. אֲמַרוּ: מַהוּ לְמֵיגַר מִינֵּיהּ? שׂוֹכֵר כִּמְעָרֵב דָּמֵי, מַה מְּעָרֵב מִבְּעוֹד יוֹם – אַף שׂוֹכֵר מִבְּעוֹד יוֹם, אוֹ דִילְמָא: שׂוֹכֵר כִּמְבַטֵּל רְשׁוּת דָּמֵי, מַה מְּבַטֵּל רְשׁוּת – וַאֲפִילּוּ בַּשַּׁבָּת, אַף שׂוֹכֵר – וַאֲפִילּוּ בַּשַּׁבָּת? רַבִּי חֲנִינָא בַּר יוֹסֵף אָמַר: נִשְׂכּוֹר, וְר' אַסִּי אָמַר: לֹא נִשְׂכּוֹר. אָמַר לְהוּ ר' חִיָּיא בַּר אַבָּא: נִסְמוֹךְ עַל דִּבְרֵי זָקֵן, וְנִשְׂכּוֹר. אָתוּ שַׁיְילוּ לֵיהּ לְרַבִּי יוֹחָנָן, אָמַר לְהֶן: יָפֶה

תורה אור: מִשְׁלֵי ט

רש"י

אם נִשְׁפַּךְ בְּבֵיתוֹ כַּמַּיִם. הָוֵי בִּכְלָל בְּרָכָה, וְאִי לָא – לָא: אָדָם נִיכָּר. אִם הָגוּן הוּא: בְּכוֹסוֹ. אִם דַּעְתּוֹ מְיוּשֶּׁבֶת עָלָיו בְּיֵינוֹ: בְּכִיסוֹ. כְּשֶׁנּוֹשֵׂא וְנוֹתֵן עִם בְּנֵי אָדָם, אִם בֶּאֱמוּנָה הוּא עוֹשֶׂה: בְּכַעֲסוֹ. שֶׁאֵינוֹ קַפְּדָן יוֹתֵר מִדַּאי: יִשְׂרָאֵל וְגוֹי בַּפְּנִימִית. שְׁתֵּי חֲצֵירוֹת זוֹ לִפְנִים מִזּוֹ, וְהָיָה לוֹ לְגוֹי פְּנִימִית דְּרִיסַת הָרֶגֶל עַל גַּב חִיצוֹנָה: וְאָסַר. בַּחִיצוֹנָה, עַד שֶׁיַּשְׂכִּיר: בְּשִׁילְהֵי פִּירְקֵיהּ. לְאַחַר שֶׁסִּיֵּים הַדְּרָשָׁה: כְּר"מ. דְּלָא בָּעֵי שְׁנֵי יִשְׂרְאֵלִים אוֹסְרִין זֶה עַל זֶה: כַּרְכֵּישׁ רַבָּה רֵישֵׁיהּ. הוֹדָה לִדְבָרָיו: לָמָּה לִי יִשְׂרָאֵל בַּחִיצוֹנָה. דְּבָעֵינַן שְׁנֵי יִשְׂרְאֵלִים: פְּנִימִי בִּמְקוֹמוֹ. בֶּחָצֵר הַפְּנִימִית: מַהוּ. לְהוֹצִיא מִבֵּיתוֹ לֶחָצֵר: אָמַר לָהֶם מוּתָּר. אַלְמָא: לֹא אָסַר אֶלָּא בַּחִיצוֹנָה, שֶׁרְשׁוּת שְׁנֵי יִשְׂרְאֵלִים שׁוֹלֶטֶת בָּהּ: אוֹסְרִים זֶה עַל זֶה. וְהָנֵי לָאו אוֹסְרִים זֶה עַל זֶה נִינְהוּ, דְּהָא אָמְרֵי רַבָּנַן בְּשִׁילְהֵי פִּירְקִין רֶגֶל הַמּוּתֶּרֶת בִּמְקוֹמָהּ אֵינָהּ אוֹסֶרֶת שֶׁלֹּא בִּמְקוֹמָהּ מִשּׁוּם דְּרִיסַת הָרֶגֶל, וְאַף עַל פִּי שֶׁלֹּא עֵירְבָה עִמָּהּ: וְאֶלָּא. רַב כְּר"ע ס"ל, וְהָווּ לְהוּ שְׁנֵי יִשְׂרְאֵלִים אוֹסְרִין זֶה עַל זֶה, הִלְכָּךְ, אָסַר נָכְרִי עֲלַיְיהוּ. לָמָּה לִי מִשּׁוּם נָכְרִי? יִשְׂרָאֵל פְּנִימִי לְחוּדֵיהּ נַמִי אָסַר עַל חִיצוֹן: לְעוֹלָם כְּר"א[א]. מִשּׁוּם הָכִי פְּנִימִי בִּמְקוֹמוֹ מוּתָּר, וְחִיצוֹן אָסוּר מִשּׁוּם דְּרִיסַת הָרֶגֶל דִּפְנִימִי כְּר"ע, וְכֵיוָן דְּאָסַר עֲלֵיהּ הָווּ לְהוּ בַּחִיצוֹנָה שְׁנֵי יִשְׂרְאֵלִים אוֹסְרִין זֶה עַל זֶה – וּמַהֲנֵי נָכְרִי לְבַטֵּל אֶת עֵירוּבָן אֲפִילּוּ עֵירְבוּ. וְאִי לֵיכָּא נָכְרִי, כִּי עֵירְבוּ – שָׁרֵי: דְּמִירְתַת נָכְרִי. לַהֲרוֹג אֶת יִשְׂרָאֵל הַדָּר עִמּוֹ בַּפְּנִימִית, דְּסָבַר: אָתֵי יִשְׂרָאֵל דְּחִיצוֹנָה וְתָבַע לֵיהּ מִינֵּיהּ, וְלָא מָצֵינוּ לְמֵימַר לֵיהּ נְפַק אָזֵיל לֵיהּ לְבָרָאֵי. דְּאָמַר לִי: אִי הֲוָה נָפֵיק – אֲנָא חֲזָא לֵיהּ: תֵּן לְחָכָם וְיֶחְכַּם עוֹד. כִּי הֵיכִי דְּהָתָם אָסוּר, הָכָא נַמִי אָסוּר: אִיקְלַעוּ לְהַהוּא פּוּנְדָּק. דְּהָווּ דָּיְירֵי בֵּיהּ בְּהַהוּא חָצֵר תְּרֵי יִשְׂרְאֵלִים וְחַד נָכְרִי שֶׁשָּׂכַר אֶת דִּירָתוֹ מֵחֲבֵירוֹ נָכְרִי, וְאוֹתוֹ שַׁבָּת לֹא הָיָה שָׁם אוֹתוֹ נָכְרִי הַשּׂוֹכֵר, אֶלָּא נָכְרִי הַמַּשְׂכִּיר, וְהָיוּ יְרֵאִים שֶׁמָּא יָבֹא נָכְרִי בַּשַּׁבָּת:[ב] פּוּנְדָּק. יֵשׁ בּוֹ חֲדָרִים פְּתוּחִין לֶחָצֵר, וְהָאַכְסְנָאִים נִכְנָסִים בָּהֶן, וְאוֹסְרִין זֶה עַל זֶה בַּשַּׁבָּת: הֵיכָא דְּלָא מָצֵי מְסַלֵּיק לֵיהּ. מַשְׂכִּיר לַשּׂוֹכֵר עַד זְמַנּוֹ: לָא תִּיבָּעֵי לָךְ. דְּוַדַּאי [לָאו] בִּרְשׁוּתֵיהּ הוּא, וְלָא מָצֵינַן לְמֵיגַר מִינֵּיהּ: נִשְׂכּוֹר. דְּסָפֵק דִּבְרֵיהֶם לְהָקֵל: דַּאֲתָא גּוֹי בַּשַּׁבָּת. דְּמֵאֶתְמוֹל שַׁפִּיר מָצוּ לְעָרוּבֵי דִּיּוּרִין דְּיִשְׂרָאֵל דַּהֲווּ בֵּיהּ, מִשּׁוּם דְּנָכְרִי לָא אָסַר עֲלַיְיהוּ הֵיכָא דְּלֵיתֵיהּ[ג] וְלָא עֵירְבוּ מֵאֶתְמוֹל וְלָא הֲווּ (מָצֵי) מְטַלְטְלֵי בֶּחָצֵר, כִּי אֲתָא נָכְרִי אָמְרֵי: מַהוּ לְמֵיגַר מִינֵּיהּ, וַהֲדַר נְבַטֵּל רְשׁוּת לְגַבֵּי חַד, וְהַהוּא מִיהוּ לִישְׁתְּרֵי לְהוֹצִיא: מַה מְּבַטֵּל רְשׁוּת אֲפִילּוּ בַּשַּׁבָּת. כִּדְתְנַן בְּמַתְנִיתִין: *)בֵּית הִלֵּל אוֹמְרִים מִשֶּׁתֶּחְשַׁךְ כו':

*) [לקמן סט:]

תוספות

התם טעמא מאי משום דשכיח דדייר. וא"ת: כיון דשכיח, אם כן פנימי במקומו אמאי מותר? דע"כ לא שרי ראב"י יחיד במקום נכרי אלא משום דלא שכיח דדייר! וי"ל: כיון דרוב פעמים חד לא שכיח, לא פלוג רבנן ושרו בכולהו. וא"ת: א"כ מאי קמיבעיא ליה, אבל הכא אמינא כו' – נהי דלא שכיח, מ"מ ליתסר, דלא פלוג רבנן בכל תרי במקום נכרי! וי"ל: דלחומרא לא אמר דלא פלוג:

ריש לקיש ותלמידי ר' חנינא. כאן מוכיח כדברי ר"ת. דר"ל גברא רבה הוה קודם שבא לפני רבי יוחנן, דהאי עובדא הוה סמוך לפטירתו של רבי, כיון דשיילוה לרבי אפס דר' אפס לא היה אחר רבי אלא שתי שנים ומחצה, כדאיתא בכתובות בסוף "הנושא" (דף קג:). וכן משמע בפ' "הבע"י" (יבמות נז.) גבי שמעתא דקהל גרים אקרי קהל*: איקלעו להוא פונדק. פי' בקונטרס: והיו יראין שמא יבא נכרי בשבת. רוצה לומר: דאם לא היה בא – לא היה אוסר, והיינו כרבי יהודה, דתנן בפרק "כיצד משתתפין" (לקמן דף פו.): המניח ביתו והלך לשבות בעיר אחרת – אחד ישראל ואחד נכרי אוסר(ד). רבי יהודה אומר: אינו אוסר כו'. ואע"ג דפסקינן לעיל בפרק "מי שהוציאוהו" (דף מז.) דהלכה כר"ש, דאמר: אפילו הניח את ביתו והלך לשבות אצל בתו באותה העיר – אינו אוסר, לא בא ר"ש להחמיר בנכרי יותר מרבי יהודה, אלא לגמרי בא להקל ולהתיר בישראל טפי מרבי יהודה, דאפילו באותה העיר שרי, שכבר הסיח מדעתו. ועוד, דקיימא לן כדברי המיקל בעירוב. ואע"ג דרבי יוחנן לית ליה(ה) דלגמרי קאמר הנהו כללי דפרק "מי שהוציאוהו" (שם דף מו:) דר' יהודה ור"ש הלכה כרבי יהודה אפי' בעירוב, מדבעי למידק דרב לית ליה הני כללי מדאשכחנא דפסיק כר"ש בההיא דעירוב – מ"מ קיימא לן כרבי יהושע בן לוי לגבי ר' יוחנן, דקאמר: הלכה כדברי המיקל בעירוב, כמו שרגיל ר"ת לדקדק ממגילה פרק בתרא (דף כז.) גבי "ואת (ו)הבית הגדול שרף באש"*):

דלא הוה שוכר. לא היה שם אפי' אחד מבני ביתו. דהא אמרינן לקמן(ז) דשוכר אפי' משכירו ולקיטו ואשתו נמי אם היתה שם היתה יכולה להשכיר, °כדמשמע לקמן(ח) גבי ההוא טורזינא:

דאתא נכרי בשבתא. פירש בקונטרס: ומאתמול לא הוו מצו לאיערובי דיורין מישראל דהוו ביה, משום דנכרי אסר עלייהו אע"ג דליתיה. ודבריו תמוהים, שפירש סוגיא זו דלא כהלכתא, דקיימא לן דאין נכרי אוסר אלא היכא דאיתיה כדפירשתי לעיל [ד"ה איקלעו]. וכדפי' נמי בקונט' בההיא עובדא דלעיל. ובפי' רש"י אחרים מצאתי: דמאתמול שפיר מצו לאיערובי דיורין דישראל דהוו ביה, משום דנכרי לא אסר עלייהו היכא דליתיה. אמרו: מהו למיגר מיניה והדר נבטל רשותא לגבי דחד, דההוא יהא מותר להוציא. עד כאן לשון הקונטרס. והדין עמו שפירש דבעי ביטול אחר שכירות, כדמוכח כולה שמעתא דבעי תרתי, שכירות וביטול. ואף על פי שעירבו – לא משתרי בשכירות לחודיה, דמיד כשבא הנכרי בטל ליה עירוב. וכי הדר שכרו – אין העירוב חוזר לקדמותו. אף על גב דבספינות אמר במסכת שבת (דף קא:): ספינות קשורות זו בזו – מערבין ומטלטלין מזו לזו. נפסקו – נאסרו. חזרו ונתקשרו – חזרו להתירן הראשון – שאני הכא, דמתחילה כשעשה העירוב אין סופו להתקיים כל השבת, שעתיד הנכרי לבא. אבל התם – אין הספינות עומדות להפסק. ואף על גב דהיכא דשכח אחד מבני חצר ולא עירב אין עירובו בטל, אלא מבטל היחיד רשותו לאותן שעירבו, ומותרין להכניס ולהוציא – שאני התם לא דחזו

*) [ועי' תוספות חולין לז. ד"ה אמר רבה וכו' דר"ת עצמו חזר ודחה ראיה זו ועמ"ש במגילה כז. בתוס' ד"ה כותיה]

[ועי' תוס' כתובות קג: ד"ה אותו היום ותוס' יבמות נז. ד"ה לאו]

[וע"ע תוס' ב"מ פה. ד"ה לא הדרת ותוס' יבמות נז. ד"ה אתה]

[לקמן סט:]

[חולין קז:]

[פסחים פג: ר"ה יד: כתובות ז. כז. קדושין עו. ב"ב קנה: ע"ז לח.]

[לעיל נט: לקמן עה.]

[ר"ה זוטא פ"ה ע"ש]

רבינו חננאל

מים אלמא (איקנו) [אם נשפך] כמים אין אי לא לא. אמר רבי אלעאי בג' דברים אדם ניכר בכוסו בשעה שמתגבר עליו יינו אם יכול לכובשו. בכיסו כשמתעשר אם דעתו זחה עליו. בכעסו אם מושל בכעסו לבלתי הסיתו ואמרי לה אף בשוחקו: אמר רב יהודה אמר רב ישראל וגוי בפנימית וישראל בחיצונה אוקימנא כשעירבו הפנימית עם החיצונה ואסרום ר' ור' חייא כר' אליעזר [בן יעקב] דאמר אין אוסר עד שיהו שני ישראל אוסרין זה על זה וכיון דעירבו הויין להו הפנימית והחיצונה כחדא ואינון תרי ישראל וחד גוי וכר' עקיבא דאמר רגל המותרת במקומה אוסרת שלא במקומה. בעי מיניה ר' אליעזר מרב ישראל וגוי בחיצונה וישראל בפנימית מהו משתכח דדיירי בהדי גוי כה"ג אי לא מהו דתימא התם הוא דישראל וגוי בפנימית אפשר (דיירי יו"ג) [דשכיחי דדיירי] גוי מרתת למיקטליה לישראל סבר אי אמרין לי' ישראל דהוה בהדך איכן הוא ישראל וגוי בפנימית איך קלקלתיה (ומירתתו) [ומיראתו] לא קטיל ליה אבל הכא אי אמרין לי' ישראל דהוה הכא היכן הוא א"ל נפק אזל ליה לעלמא וכיון דלא מרתת קטיל ליה הלכך משום הא לא דאיר ישראל בהדיה ואי דאיר ישראל בהדיה לא חיישינן או דלמא הכא נמי מירתת סבר דלמא כד קטילנא ליה נפיק מן הפנימית ומשכח ליה בידי א"ל תן לחכם ויחכם עוד כלומר זו כמו זו ושתיהן אסורות. ריש לקיש ותלמידיה דר' חנינא איקלעו לההוא פונדק דלא הוה שוכר גוי התם משכיר כו'. פי' ההוא פונדק הוה משכיר מצי מסלק לכל מי דהוה דייר בההוא פונדק מיהו השתא לא סלקיה מהו דתימא כיון דמצי מסליק להו אגרינן מן המשכיר דרשותיה הוא או דלמא כיון דלא סלקי' לא. אמר ר"ל נשכור ולכשנלך אצל רבותינו שבדרום נשאל איתו שיילוה לר' אפס א"ל יפה עשיתם ששכרתם וכן ר' חמא ב"ר יוסף ור' חייא בר אבא ור' אסא אקלעו לפונדק ולא הוה ביה גוי ואתא גוי בשבת ומיבעי להו שוכר כי מערב דמי מה מערב מבעו"י אין משחשכה לא אף שוכר כותיה או דלמא שוכר כמבטל רשות דמי מה ביטול רשות אפילו בשבת דתנן בית הלל אומרים אפילו משתחשך אף שוכר בשבת שרי אמר להו רבי חמא נשכור סמכו על דבריו ושכרו ואתו ושיילוה לרבי יוחנן ואמר להו

הגהות הב"ח

(א) רש"י ד"ה לעולם כר"א ב"י משום הכי: (ב) ד"ה איקלעו וכו' שמא יבא הנעו"ג בשבת. לישנא אחרינא פונדק יש בו: (ג) ד"ה דאתא עו"ג וכו' היכא דליתיה (ולא עירבו מאתמול ולא הוו מטלטלי בחצר) תא"מ ונ"ב ס"א אין זה וכן מוכח בתוספו' דלא גרסי ליה גם בס"א מצאתי וז"ל דעו"ג לא אסר עלייהו היכא דליתיה ועירבו מאתמול והוי מצי מטלטלי בחצר: (ד) תוס' ד"ה איקלעו וכו' וא' גוי אוסר דברי ר' מאיר ר' יהודה אומר: (ה) בא"ד ואע"ג דרבי יוחנן לית ליה הלכה כדברי המיקל בעירוב דלגמרי קאמר: (ו) בא"ד גבי ואת כל בית גדול שרף: (ז) ד"ה דלא וכו' אמרינן לקמן. נ"ב דף ס"ו ע"א: (ח) בא"ד כדמשמע לקמן. נ"ב פ' חלון דף פ ע"א:

רב נסים גאון

ואלא כר' עקיבא דאמר רגל המותרת במקומה אוסרת שלא במקומה דברי ר' עקיבא במקומה זה הפרק:

גליון הש"ס

גמ' א"ל תן לחכם ויחכם עוד. בכ"ק דף קיז ע"ב: תוס' ד"ה דלא הוי שוכר וכו' כדמשמע לקמן. דף פ ע"א ועי' בתוספות ד"ה אתו לקמיה וכו' ע"ב:

אִיָּפֶה עֲשִׂיתֶם שֶׁשְּׂכַרְתֶּם. תָּהוּ בָּהּ נְהַרְדָּעֵי, וּמִי אָ"ר יוֹחָנָן הָכִי?! וְהָאָ"ר יוֹחָנָן: שׂוֹכֵר כִּמְעָרֵב דָּמֵי. מַאי לָאו: מַה מְּעָרֵב מִבְּעוֹד יוֹם — אַף שׂוֹכֵר מִבְּעוֹד יוֹם! לֹא, מַה מְּעָרֵב, וַאֲפִילּוּ בְּפָחוֹת מִשָּׁוֶה פְּרוּטָה — אַף שׂוֹכֵר בְּפָחוֹת מִשָּׁוֶה פְּרוּטָה. וּמַה מְּעָרֵב — אֲפִילּוּ שְׂכִירוֹ וּלְקִיטוֹ, אַף שׂוֹכֵר — אֲפִילּוּ שְׂכִירוֹ וּלְקִיטוֹ. וּמַה מְּעָרֵב, חֲמִשָּׁה שֶׁשְּׁרוּיִן בְּחָצֵר אַחַת — אֶחָד מְעָרֵב ע"י כּוּלָּן, שׂוֹכֵר נַמִי, בחֲמִשָּׁה שֶׁשְּׁרוּיִן בְּחָצֵר אַחַת — אֶחָד שׂוֹכֵר ע"י כּוּלָּן. תָּהֵי בָּהּ רַבִּי אֶלְעָזָר, אֲמַר רַבִּי זֵירָא: מַאי תְּהָיָיא דְּר"א? אֲמַר רַב שֵׁשֶׁת: גַּבְרָא רַבָּה כְּרַבִּי זֵירָא לָא יָדַע מַאי תְּהָיָיא דְּר"א? קָא קַשְׁיָא לֵיהּ דִּשְׁמוּאֵל רַבֵּיהּ. דְּאָמַר שְׁמוּאֵל: כָּל מָקוֹם שֶׁאוֹסְרִין וּמְעָרְבִין — מְבַטְּלִין. מְעָרְבִין וְאֵין אוֹסְרִין, אוֹסְרִין וְאֵין מְעָרְבִין — אֵין מְבַטְּלִין. כָּל מָקוֹם שֶׁאוֹסְרִין וּמְעָרְבִין — מְבַטְּלִין, כְּגוֹן(א) ב' חֲצֵירוֹת זוֹ לִפְנִים מִזּוֹ. מְעָרְבִין וְאֵין אוֹסְרִין — אֵין מְבַטְּלִין, כְּגוֹן(ב) ב' חֲצֵירוֹת וּפֶתַח א' בֵּינֵיהֶן, אוֹסְרִין וְאֵין מְעָרְבִין — אֵין מְבַטְּלִין, לְאַתּוּיֵי מַאי? לָאו לְאַתּוּיֵי גּוֹי וְאִי דַּאֲתָא מֵאֶתְמוֹל — לוֹגֵר מֵאֶתְמוֹל! אֶלָּא

רש"י

לֹא מַה מְּעָרֵב אֲפִילּוּ בְּפָחוֹת כו'. דִּלְקוּלָּא אַקְשִׁינְהוּ רַבִּי יוֹחָנָן וְלֹא לְחוּמְרָא, דְּכָל בְּעֵירוּבִין לְהָקֵל: וּמַה מְּעָרֵב אֲפִילּוּ שְׂכִירוֹ וּלְקִיטוֹ. דְּנָכְרִי, אִם יִשְׂרָאֵל הוּא כִּדְאָמַר לְעֵיל (דף סד.): נוֹתֵן עֵירוּבוֹ וְדַיּוֹ: אַף שׂוֹכֵר אֲפִי' שְׂכִירוֹ וּלְקִיטוֹ. דְּנָכְרִי, עִם נָכְרִי הוּא, מַשְׂכִּיר רְשׁוּת אֲדוֹנָיו לְדִיּוּרֵי הֶחָצֵר: אֶחָד מְעָרֵב ע"י כּוּלָּן. כְּגוֹן ב' חֲצֵירוֹת וּפֶתַח בֵּינֵיהֶן, וּבָאוּ לְעָרֵב זוֹ עִם זוֹ — אֶחָד מוֹלִיךְ עֵירוּבָהּ שֶׁל זוֹ לְתוֹךְ שֶׁל זוֹ וְהָוֵי שָׁלִיחַ לַחֲבֵירָיו, כִּדְתַנְיָא בְּהַאי פִּירְקָא (דף עב:): חֲמִשָּׁה שֶׁגָּבוּ אֶת עֵירוּבָן, כְּשֶׁהֵן מוֹלִיכִין אוֹתוֹ לְמָקוֹם אַחֵר — אֶחָד מוֹלִיךְ ע"י כּוּלָּן: חֲמִשָּׁה. יִשְׂרָאֵל שֶׁשְּׁרוּיִין עִם הַנָּכְרִי בְּחָצֵר אַחַת, אֶחָד מֵהֶן שׂוֹכֵר מִן הַנָּכְרִי בִּשְׁבִיל כּוּלָּן: תָּהֵי בָּהּ ר"א. בְּהָא מִילְּתָא דַּאֲמָרַן לְעֵיל שֶׁשְּׂכָרוֹ מִן הַנָּכְרִי וְאַח"כ בִּיטְּלוֹ. וְתָהֵי — לְשׁוֹן מֵרִיחַ, כְּמוֹ "בַּת תְּיָהָא" דְּמַסֶּ' ע"ז (דף סו:) כְּלוֹמַר: מְעַיֵּין וּמְחַשֵּׁב לָדַעַת טַעֲמוֹ שֶׁל דָּבָר: כָּל מָקוֹם שֶׁאוֹסְרִין. זֶה עַל זֶה בְּלֹא עֵירוּב, וְאִם הָיוּ רוֹצִין לְעָרֵב יְכוֹלִין לְעָרֵב: מְבַטְּלִין. אִם שָׁכְחוּ וְלֹא עֵירְבוּ — מְבַטְּלִין רְשׁוּתָן לְאֶחָד מֵהֶן, וְהָוֵי כּוּלָּהּ חָצֵר דִּידֵיהּ, וּתְהֵא מוּתֶּרֶת לְטַלְטֵל בְּכוּלָּהּ, וּבִלְבַד שֶׁלֹּא יוֹצִיאוּ מִן הַבָּתִּים לֶחָצֵר אֶלָּא מִבֵּיתוֹ שֶׁל אוֹתוֹ יָחִיד בִּלְבָד: כָּל מָקוֹם לְאַתּוּיֵי שְׁתֵּי חֲצֵירוֹת זוֹ לִפְנִים מִזּוֹ. דְּהֵיכָא דְּלֹא עֵירְבָה פְּנִימִית לְעַצְמָהּ אָסְרָה אַחִיצוֹנָה. אֲפִי' לְרַבָּנַן דִּפְלִיגִי עֲלֵיהּ דְּר"ע מוֹדוּ דְּרֶגֶל הָאוֹסֶרֶת בִּמְקוֹמָהּ אוֹסֶרֶת שֶׁלֹּא בִּמְקוֹמָהּ, כְּגוֹן בַּחִיצוֹנָה מִשּׁוּם דְּרִיסַת הָרֶגֶל שֶׁיֵּשׁ לָהּ עָלֶיהָ. וְאִם רָצְתָה לְעָרֵב עִמָּהּ — מְעָרְבִין. וְאִם שָׁכְחוּ וְלֹא עֵירְבוּ — מְבַטְּלִין בְּנֵי פְּנִימִית רְשׁוּתָן לִבְנֵי חִיצוֹנָה, אוֹתוֹ דְּרִיסַת הָרֶגֶל שֶׁיֵּשׁ לָהּ עָלֶיהָ: שְׁתֵּי חֲצֵירוֹת. פְּתוּחוֹת לְמָבוֹי אוֹ לִרְשׁוּת הָרַבִּים וּפֶתַח בֵּינֵיהֶן — מְעָרְבִין אִם רוֹצִין, וְאִם לֹא עֵירְבוּ זוֹ עִם זוֹ — זוֹ מוּתֶּרֶת לְעַצְמָהּ וְזוֹ מוּתֶּרֶת לְעַצְמָהּ: אֵין מְבַטְּלִין. אִם הוּצְרְכוּ לְטַלְטֵל מִזּוֹ לָזוֹ, אֵין מְבַטְּלִין רְשׁוּת שֶׁל זוֹ לָזוֹ, דְּלָא תַּקּוּן רַבָּנַן בִּיטּוּל רְשׁוּת אֶלָּא הֵיכָא דְּאָסְרִי עֲלַיְיהוּ: לָאו לְאַתּוּיֵי גּוֹי. שֶׁדָּר עִם שְׁנֵי יִשְׂרְאֵלִים בֶּחָצֵר, שֶׁאוֹסְרִין אוֹתָן שְׁנֵי יִשְׂרְאֵלִים זֶה עַל זֶה, וְאֵין יְכוֹלִין לְעָרֵב בִּשְׁבִיל הַנָּכְרִי, וְקָאָמְרִינַן דְּאֵין מְבַטְּלִין: וְאִי אֲתָא גּוֹי מֵאֶתְמוֹל. אַמַּאי קָרֵי לְהוּ אוֹסְרִין, וְאֵין מְעָרְבִין, הָא מָצוּ לְעֵירוּבֵי וּלְמֵיגַר: אֶלָּא

תוספות

דחזו כולהו לאיערובי מאתמול, לפיכך אין בטל העירוב שלהן כלל. וגם אין שייך לומר כלל "שבת הואיל והותרה הותרה" ולא יתבטל עירוב שלהן כשיבא הנכרי בשבת. וזה אין נראה לפרש כלל, דכאן לא עירבו, ולפיכך לא סגי בשכירות לחוד בלא ביטול. דהא על כרחך היו יכולין לערב כאן כדפרישית לעיל דהלכה כר' יהודה, דנכרי כי ליתיה לא אסר. וכיון שהיה מועיל(ג) באותו עירוב, מנא ליה שלא עירבו ועשו שכירות וביטול, דקשיא ליה לקמן דשמואל רביה דאמר אוסרין ואין מערבין – אין מבטלין. ובסוף שמעתא דקאמר למ"ד שוכרין לא תיבעי לך תרתי עבדינן שכירות וביטול. דלמא הכא הוא דעירבו ולא עשו אלא שכירות לחוד! על כן נראה כפירוש הקונטרס, דאפילו עירבו – בטל העירוב לגמרי מיכן, כיון שבא הנכרי. *ואם תאמר: ולמה להו הכא תרתי, שכירות וביטול? בביטול לחודיה סגי, כיון דבטלי רשותייהו לגבי חד – הוה ליה יחיד במקום נכרי, כדאמר לעיל* גבי עובדא דהמן בר רסתק. דקיימא לן כראב"י יחיד במקום נכרי שרי. ואע"ג דמסיק רבא דלא מהני ביטול לעשותו יחיד במקום נכרי, משום דא"כ בטלת תורת עירוב מאותו מבוי – ה"מ בנכרי שאינו רוצה להשכיר, דלא אפשר להו לערב. אבל הכא שהוא מתרצה להשכיר, ובשבת אחרת יוכלו לערב להתיר לכולן, אלא היום שבא הנכרי בשבת לא אפשר – מועיל ביטול לעשות יחיד במקום נכרי, דאין שייך כאן לומר בטלת תורת עירוב! וי"ל: כיון שאם לא היה מתרצה להשכיר לא היה מועיל ביטול, משום דא"כ ביטלת תורת עירוב – אין לחלק בין לשאינו מתרצה, דאטו אמירת הנכרי תגרום הביטול, שיועיל כשיאמר אתרצה לכם להשכיר, או לא יועיל כשיאמר לא אתרצה לכם. ועוד י"ל: דהני אמוראי סבירא להו כר"מ, דאמר אסור יחיד במקום נכרי. ור' יוחנן דבסמוך נמי לטעמיה, דאמר: *נהגו העם כר"א בן יעקב, אבל אורויי לא מורינן. אבל אנן סבירא לן ודאי כרבי אליעזר בן יעקב, דהא אביי ורבא קיימי כוותיה בעובדא דהמן בר רסתק:

הגה"ה

(ד) *ה"ג כי לא אמרי' שבת הואיל והותרה הותרה אלא במקום שיכול לעמוד ולהתקיים כל השבת כגון עירב דרך הפתח(ה) ונסתם או ניטלה קורתו או לחיו ומכאן יש להוכיח היכא שא' מבני חצר אחת היה גוסס בשעת העירוב וערבו עמו שבטל העירוב הואיל ורוב גוססים למיתה אינו ראוי להתקיים כל השבת ע"כ לשון הגה"ה בשם רבי מאיר מרוטנבורג ז"ל.

*איקלעו להההוא פונדק כו'. פירש בקונטרס: היו שם הרבה בתים של ישראלים שהיו אוסרים זה על זה. ויש פירושים שמוגה בהם: פונדק יש בו חדרים הרבה פתוחין לחצר, והאכסנאים נכנסין בהן ואוסרין זה על זה. וגם זה אמת, דכי האי גוונא נמי אסרי כמו חבורה ששבתה בטרקלין: יפה עשיתם ששכרתם. רבינו חננאל פסק כר' יוחנן אע"ג דשמואל פליג עליה בסמוך, דקסבר דכל מקום שאוסרין *אין מערבין ואין מבטלין, דבכל דוכתא קיימא לן כר' יוחנן לגבי שמואל וכדברי המיקל בעירוב. ואומר ר"י: דלקמן בפירקין (דף ע:) דייק ברייתא כשמואל, דתניא: כל שנאסר למקצת שבת – נאסר לכל השבת כולה, כגון שני בתים בשני צידי רשות הרבים והקיפום נכרים מחילה בשבת. זה הכלל לאתויי מת נכרי בשבת דאין מבטלין, ולקמן(ו) בסוף שמעתא אמרינן דמת נכרי בשבת אליבא דמ"ד שוכרין – לא תיבעי לך, השתא תרתי עבדינן, חדא מיבעיא. ש"מ: לא מיתוקמא ההיא ברייתא כר' יוחנן דאמר שוכרין. ודוחק לומר דלאתויי מת נכרי בשבת איירי דלא ביטלו, דלא משתרו כשמת הנכרי אע"פ שעירבו מע"ש, אבל ביטול מהני. שהרי הקיפום נכרים מחילה איירי אפי' ע"י ביטול, כדאמרינן בסוף שמעתא דאין מבטלין. ודומיא דהכי קאמר לאתויי מת נכרי בשבת דאין מבטלין. ואפי' את"ל שר' יוחנן היה מעמיד זה הכלל דברייתא לאתויי מילתא אחריתי, מ"מ מדנקט סתמא דהתלמוד הכי – שמע מינה דהכי הלכתא: יפה עשיתם ששכרתם. לא דמי למקח וממכר ליאסר בשבת. דלא הוי אלא כמתנה בעלמא שאין עושין אלא להתיר טלטול: מערב אפי' שכירו ולקיטו. פירוש: כדאמר שמואל לעיל אפי' שכירו ולקיטו של נכרי נותן עירובו ודיו. ואם תאמר: דהכא אליבא דר' יוחנן קיימא, וירושלמי משמע דלית ליה לרבי יוחנן האי סברא. דקאמר ר' יוחנן התם: ישראל ונכרי שהיו דרים בבית אחד – צריך ישראל לבטל והנכרי להשכיר! ויש לומר(ז): דהתם שניהם שותפים בבית ישראל ונכרי, דלא הוי כשכירו ולקיטו דהכא. ועוד יש לחלק: דאם ייחד הנכרי לישראל שהוא שכירו ולקיטו חדר אחד שלא יוכל הנכרי להשתמש בו, דהוי השתא הנכרי מסולק מישראל ואין יכול לסלק הישראל – בכה"ג לא אמרינן נותן עירובו ודיו, ובכי האי גוונא איכא לאוקמי ההיא דירושלמי: כל מקום שאוסרין ומערבין מבטלין. האי כללא לאו דוקא בכל מקום, דהרי חורבה שאמר שמואל בסמוך: אין ביטול רשות בחורבה. ואפי' בחצר מסיק רבא לקמן* אליבא דשמואל דאפי' ב' חצירות זו לפנים מזו, פעמים מבטלין ופעמים אין מבטלין. ומה שמפרש כאן כגון שתי חצירות זו לפנים מזו – היינו לאביי ורבא לאותו ענין שמפרש לקמן. והוה מצי למימר: כגון אנשי חצר ששכח אחד מהם ולא עירב, אבל הא – מתניתין היא לקמן* ולא אצטריך ליה לאשמעינן האי:

ואי דאתא מאתמול לוגר מאתמול. דאם אין הנכרי רוצה להשכיר – מה יכול ביטול להועיל? אע"ג דשמואל אית ליה לעיל* הלכה כראב"י דשרי יחיד במקום נכרי, הא אמרינן לעיל* דאין הביטול עושהו יחיד במקום נכרי – משום דא"כ בטלת תורת עירוב מאותו מבוי, ואפילו מתרצה היום להשכיר או שמת. ועל זה קאמרינן דאין מבטלין, משום דמאתמול לא היו יכולים לערב לפי שלא נתרצה להם מאתמול להשכיר, אכתי מערבין קרינא ביה, דכיון דאם היה אתמול מתרצה היו יכולין לערב, וכששכרו היום ממנו או שמת – יכולין לבטל שפיר: אלא

[לעיל דף סב:] [עי' לעיל] [עמוד ב] [דף סט:] [דף סב:] [דף סד.] [דף סב:]

ע"ל ואין מערבין אין מבטלין כו'

עין משפט נר מצוה

לד א מיי' שם הל"ב וסמג שם טור שו"ע או"ח סימן שפג:

לה ב מיי' שם הלכה י וסמג שם טור שו"ע או"ח סימן שפב סעיף ט:

רבינו חננאל

יפה עשיתם ששכרתם. איני והא"ר יוחנן שוכר כמערב דמי מאי לאו מערב מבעו"י אף שוכר מבעו"י ודחינן לא שוכר כמערב מה מערב אפי' בפחות משוה פרוטה אף שוכר אפילו בפחות משוה פרוטה. מה מערב אפילו שכירו ולקיטו אף שוכר כך. ומה מערב ה' שגבו את עירובן אחד מוליך ע"י כולן אף שוכר ה' ששרויין בחצר אחת [אחד] שוכר ע"י כולן. תהי בה ר' אלעזר בהא דר' יוחנן שעשה השוכר כמבטל רשות. וא' מה מבטל רשות אפי' בשבת כדתנן בה"א אפי' משתחשך אף שוכר מגוי משתחשך אי הכי קשיא דשמואל דאמר כל מקום שאוסרין ומערבין מבטלין כגון ב' חצירות זו לפנים מזו אוסרין בני הפנימיות על החיצונה ויש לערב זה מזה ומותרין לפיכך כיון שהעירוב מתירן אם שכח אחד מהן ולא עירב יכול לבטל רשותו מזו לזו אבל במקום (שאין מערבין) [שמערבין] ואין אוסרין כגון ב' חצירות ופתח ביניהן כדתנן בכותל אחד שבין ב' חצירות נפרץ הכותל עד י' אמות מותר מפני שהוא כפתח (ואין) [ואם] סותמין אותו מערבין שנים כל חצר בפני עצמה ואינה אוסרת זו על זו ואם רצו ופתחוהו מערבין אחד כגון אלו אין מבטלין מזו לזו. וכן חצר שאוסרין הדרין בה ואין מערבין בה. פי' אין בה היתר בעירוב כגון דדאיר בה גוי. ואמר שמואל כל מקום שאוסרין ואין מערבין כענין שאמרנו אין מבטלין. חצר שאוסרין (בה) ואין מערבין בה היכי דמי לאו דדאיר בה גוי ואי הוה גוי מאתמול הוה למיגר מיניה מבעו"י אלא לאו דאתא גוי בשבת וקא' אוסרין ואין מבטלין והאי ביטול שכירות הוא דהא כבר אמר בתחילת פרקין אין עירוב מועיל במקום גוי. ואין ביטול רשות מועלת במקום גוי עד שישכיר ש"מ. ואע"ג דתהי בה ר' אלעזר הלכתא כר' יוחנן דקיימא לן שמואל ור' יוחנן

הגהות הב"ח

(א) גמרא ב' חצירות זו לפנים מזו כזה:

מבוי
חיצונה
פנימית

(ב) שם שתי חצירות ופתח א' ביניהן כזה:

מבוי
חצר | חצר
פתח

(ג) תוס' ד"ה לאתא וכו' כיון שהיה מועיל כאן עירוב מנא לי': (ד) בא"ד ה"ה כי לא אמרינן כל"ל ותיבת ה"ג נמחק: (ה) בא"ד כגון עירב דרך פתח. נ"ב ע"ל דף ע ע"ב: (ו) ד"ה יפה וכו' לקמן בסוף שמעתא. נ"ב ס"ז ע"א: (ז) ד"ה מערב כו' וי"ל דהתם מיירי כשניהם שותפים:

לו א מיי' פ"ב מהלכות עירובין הל"ה סמג עשין א טור ש"ע או"ח סימן שפ סעיף ב:
לז ב מיי' שם טוש"ע שם סעיף ג:

אֶלָּא לָאו דַּאֲתָא בְּשַׁבְּתָא, וְקָתָנֵי: אוֹסְרִין וְאֵין מְעָרְבִין — אֵין מְבַטְּלִין, שְׁמַע מִינָּהּ. *אָמַר רַב יוֹסֵף: לָא שְׁמִיעַ לִי הָא שְׁמַעְתָּא. *אֲמַר לֵיהּ אַבַּיֵי: אַתְּ אֲמַרְתְּ נִיהֲלַן, וְאַהָא אֲמַרְתְּ נִיהֲלַן; דְּאָמַר *שְׁמוּאֵל: אֵין בִּיטּוּל רְשׁוּת מֵחָצֵר לְחָצֵר, וְאֵין בִּיטּוּל רְשׁוּת בְּחוּרְבָּה. וְאָמְרַתְּ לַן עֲלָהּ: כִּי אָמַר שְׁמוּאֵל "אֵין בִּיטּוּל רְשׁוּת מֵחָצֵר לְחָצֵר" — לָא אֲמָרַן אֶלָּא שְׁתֵּי חֲצֵירוֹת וּפֶתַח אֶחָד בֵּינֵיהֶן. אֲבָל זוֹ לִפְנִים מִזּוֹ, מִתּוֹךְ שֶׁאוֹסְרִין זֶה עַל זֶה — מְבַטְּלִין. א"ל: אֲנָא אֲמִינָא מִשְּׁמֵיהּ דִּשְׁמוּאֵל הָכִי? *וְהָאָמַר שְׁמוּאֵל: אֵין לָנוּ בְּעֵירוּבִין אֶלָּא כִּלְשׁוֹן מִשְׁנָתֵנוּ "אַנְשֵׁי חָצֵר" וְלֹא אַנְשֵׁי חֲצֵירוֹת! אֲמַר לֵיהּ: כִּי אָמְרַתְּ לַן "אֵין לָנוּ בְּעֵירוּבִין אֶלָּא כִּלְשׁוֹן מִשְׁנָתֵנוּ" — אַהָא אָמְרַתְּ לַן: *שֶׁהַמָּבוֹי לַחֲצֵירוֹת כְּחָצֵר לַבָּתִּים. גּוּפָא, אָמַר שְׁמוּאֵל: אֵין בִּיטּוּל רְשׁוּת מֵחָצֵר לְחָצֵר, וְאֵין בִּיטּוּל רְשׁוּת בְּחוּרְבָּה. וְרַבִּי יוֹחָנָן אָמַר: אוְיֵשׁ בִּיטּוּל רְשׁוּת מֵחָצֵר לְחָצֵר, בוְיֵשׁ בִּיטּוּל רְשׁוּת בְּחוּרְבָּה. וּצְרִיכָא, דְּאִי אַשְׁמְעִינַן מֵחָצֵר לְחָצֵר — בְּהָא קָאָמַר שְׁמוּאֵל, מִשּׁוּם דְּהָא תַּשְׁמִישְׁתָּא לְחוּד וְהָא תַּשְׁמִישְׁתָּא לְחוּד. אֲבָל חוּרְבָּה, דְּתַשְׁמִישְׁתָּא חֲדָא לְתַרְוַויְיהוּ — אֵימָא מוֹדֵי לֵיהּ לְרַבִּי יוֹחָנָן. וְכִי אִתְּמַר בְּהָא — בְּהָא קָאָמַר רַבִּי יוֹחָנָן, אֲבָל בְּהָךְ מוֹדֵי לֵיהּ לִשְׁמוּאֵל — צְרִיכָא. אָמַר אַבַּיֵי: הָא דְּאָמַר שְׁמוּאֵל אֵין בִּיטּוּל רְשׁוּת מֵחָצֵר לְחָצֵר — לָא אֲמָרַן אֶלָּא בִּשְׁתֵּי חֲצֵירוֹת וּפֶתַח אֶחָד בֵּינֵיהֶן, אֲבָל ב' חֲצֵירוֹת זוֹ לִפְנִים מִזּוֹ, מִתּוֹךְ שֶׁאוֹסְרִין — מְבַטְּלִין. רָבָא אָמַר: אֲפִילּוּ שְׁתֵּי חֲצֵירוֹת זוֹ לִפְנִים מִזּוֹ — פְּעָמִים מְבַטְּלִין, וּפְעָמִים אֵין מְבַטְּלִין. כֵּיצַד? נָתְנוּ עֵירוּבָן *בַּחִיצוֹנָה, וְשָׁכַח אֶחָד, בֵּין מִן הַפְּנִימִית וּבֵין מִן הַחִיצוֹנָה, וְלֹא עֵירֵב — שְׁתֵּיהֶן אֲסוּרוֹת. נָתְנוּ עֵירוּבָן בַּפְּנִימִית, וְשָׁכַח אֶחָד מִן הַפְּנִימִית וְלֹא עֵירֵב — שְׁתֵּיהֶן אֲסוּרוֹת. שָׁכַח אֶחָד מִן הַחִיצוֹנָה וְלֹא עֵירֵב — פְּנִימִית מוּתֶּרֶת, וְחִיצוֹנָה אֲסוּרָה. נָתְנוּ עֵירוּבָן בַּחִיצוֹנָה, וְשָׁכַח אֶחָד בֵּין מִן הַפְּנִימִית וּבֵין מִן הַחִיצוֹנָה וְלֹא עֵירֵב — שְׁתֵּיהֶן אֲסוּרוֹת; הַאי בַּר פְּנִימִית לְמַאן נִיבְטִיל? לִיבְטִיל לִבְנֵי פְּנִימִית — לֵיתָא לְעֵרוּבַיְיהוּ גַּבַּיְיהוּ, לִיבְטִיל לִבְנֵי חִיצוֹנָה — אֵין בִּטּוּל רְשׁוּת מֵחָצֵר לְחָצֵר, הַאי בַּר חִיצוֹנָה לְמַאן נִבְטִיל? לִיבְטִיל לִבְנֵי חִיצוֹנָה — אִיכָּא פְּנִימִית דְּאָסְרָה עֲלַיְיהוּ, לִיבְטִיל לִבְנֵי פְּנִימִית — אֵין בִּיטּוּל רְשׁוּת מֵחָצֵר לְחָצֵר. נָתְנוּ עֵירוּבָן בַּפְּנִימִית וְשָׁכַח אֶחָד מִן הַפְּנִימִית וְלֹא עֵירֵב — שְׁתֵּיהֶן אֲסוּרוֹת; הַאי בַּר פְּנִימִית לְמַאן נִבְטִיל? לִיבְטִיל לִבְנֵי הַפְּנִימִית — אִיכָּא חִיצוֹנָה דְּאָסְרָה עֲלַיְיהוּ, לִיבְטִיל לִבְנֵי חִיצוֹנָה — אֵין בִּיטּוּל רְשׁוּת מֵחָצֵר לְחָצֵר.

שָׁכַח

*) עי' בתשו' הגאון ח"צ סימן י"ד פירוש לדברי תוס' אלו.

אֶלָּא לָאו דַּאֲתָא בְּשַׁבְּתָא. אַלְמָא: בִּיטּוּל רְשׁוּת לָא תַּקּוּן אֶלָּא הֵיכָא דַּחֲזוּ לְעָרוּבֵי מֵאֶתְמוֹל: הָא שְׁמַעְתָּא. דִּשְׁמוּאֵל, דְּאָמַר בִּשְׁתֵּי חֲצֵירוֹת זוֹ לִפְנִים מִזּוֹ שֶׁיּוּכַל לְבַטֵּל דְּרִיסַת רַגְלָם לַחִיצוֹנָה: אַתְּ אֲמַרְתְּ נִיהֲלַן. רַב יוֹסֵף חָלָה וְשָׁכַח תַּלְמוּדוֹ, וְקָא מַדְכַּר לֵיהּ אַבַּיֵי תַּלְמִידוֹ: אֵין בִּיטּוּל רְשׁוּת בְּחוּרְבָּה. בַּיִת מִכָּאן וּבַיִת מִכָּאן וְחוּרְבָּה בֵּינֵיהֶן, וּב' הַבָּתִּים פְּתוּחִים לָהּ, וְאָסוּר לְהִשְׁתַּמֵּשׁ בָּהּ אא"כ עֵירְבוּ — אֵין מְבַטְּלִין רְשׁוּתָן זֶה לָזֶה לְהַתִּיר אֶת הָאֶחָד לְהַכְנִיס וּלְהוֹצִיא מִבֵּיתוֹ לְחוּרְבָּה. דְּלָא שָׁרוּ רַבָּנַן בִּיטּוּל רְשׁוּת אֶלָּא בְּחָצֵר שֶׁלִּפְנֵי הַבַּיִת, דְּאַקִּילוּ בָּהּ רַבָּנַן, דְּהָוֵי עִיקַּר תַּשְׁמִישְׁתַּיְיהוּ הָתָם: מִתּוֹךְ שֶׁאוֹסְרִין. בְּנֵי פְּנִימִית עַל בְּנֵי חִיצוֹנָה מִשּׁוּם דְּרִיסַת הָרֶגֶל — מְבַטְּלִין לָהֶם דְּרִיסַת רַגְלָם אִם לֹא עֵירְבוּ בְּנֵי פְּנִימִית אֲפִילּוּ לְעַצְמָהּ, דַּהֲוָיָא רֶגֶל אֲסוּרָה בִּמְקוֹמָהּ וְאוֹסֶרֶת שֶׁלֹּא בִּמְקוֹמָהּ עַד שֶׁתִּבָּטֵל: אֲנָא אֲמִינָא מִשְּׁמֵיהּ דִּשְׁמוּאֵל הָכִי. בִּתְמִיָּה: וְהָאָמַר שְׁמוּאֵל אֵין לָנוּ בְּעֵירוּבִין. לְהוֹסִיף הֵיתֵּר: אֶלָּא כִּלְשׁוֹן מִשְׁנָתֵנוּ. וּבְמִשְׁנָתֵנוּ (דף סט:) תְּנַן: אַנְשֵׁי חָצֵר שֶׁשָּׁכַח אֶחָד מֵהֶם כו' נָתְנוּ לוֹ רְשׁוּתָן כו', אַלְמָא: בַּחֲדָא חָצֵר תְּנַן בִּיטּוּל, וְלֹא בִּשְׁתֵּי חֲצֵרוֹת. וְהַאי סִיּוּמָא דְּאַנְשֵׁי חָצֵר וְלֹא אַנְשֵׁי חֲצֵירוֹת — לָאו שְׁמוּאֵל קָאָמַר לַהּ, אֶלָּא רַב יוֹסֵף קָא דָּיֵיק לָהּ מִמִּילְּתָא דִּשְׁמוּאֵל: שֶׁהַמָּבוֹי לַחֲצֵירוֹת כֶּחָצֵר לַבָּתִּים. בְּמַתְנִיתִין דְּפִירְקִין הִיא* וְקָא דָּיֵיק שְׁמוּאֵל בְּלִישָּׁנָא דַּחֲצֵירוֹת וּבָתִּים. וְיָלֵיף מִינֵּיהּ לְקַמָּן* דְּלָא מִיקְּרֵי מָבוֹי לִהְיוֹת נִיתָּר בְּלֶחִי וְקוֹרָה עַד שֶׁיִּהְיוּ בָּתִּים וַחֲצֵירוֹת פְּתוּחִין לְתוֹכוֹ, שְׁתֵּי חֲצֵירוֹת לְמָבוֹי וּשְׁנֵי בָּתִּים לְחָצֵר: אֲבָל חוּרְבָּא דַּחֲדָא תַּשְׁמִישְׁתָּא לְתַרְוַיְיהוּ. וְאָסְרֵי אַהֲדָדֵי, אֵימָא לִיבְטְלוּ: מִתּוֹךְ שֶׁאוֹסְרִין. אִם לֹא עֵירְבָה פְּנִימִית לְעַצְמָהּ, דַּהֲוָיָא רֶגֶל הָאֲסוּרָה בִּמְקוֹמָהּ — אֲפִי' רַבָּנַן מוֹדוּ דְּאוֹסֶרֶת שֶׁלֹּא בִּמְקוֹמָהּ: מְבַטְּלִין. דְּרִיסַת רַגְלָם לַחִיצוֹנָה וּמוּתָּרִין בְּנֵי חִיצוֹנָה לְעַצְמָן: וּפְעָמִים אֵין מְבַטְּלִין. וְאע"ג דְּאוֹסְרִין: נָתְנוּ אֶת עֵירוּבָן בַּחִיצוֹנָה. כֵּן דֶּרֶךְ כְּשֶׁמְּעָרְבִין שְׁתֵּי חֲצֵירוֹת יַחַד, אוֹתוֹ עֵירוּב שֶׁעֵירְבוּ חָצֵר זֶה לְעַצְמָהּ לְהַתִּיר דִּיּוּרִין שֶׁבְּתוֹכָהּ — מוֹלִיכִין לְתוֹךְ חֲבֶירְתָּהּ, וְאֵין עוֹשִׂין עֵירוּב אַחֵר: שְׁתֵּיהֶן אֲסוּרוֹת. וְלָא מְהַנֵּי לְהוּ בִּיטּוּל וְטַעְמָא מְפָרֵשׁ לְקַמָּן וְאָזֵיל: נָתְנוּ עֵירוּבָן בַּפְּנִימִית. בְּנֵי חִיצוֹנָה מוֹלִיכִין עֵירוּב שֶׁבֵּינֵיהֶן(א) הַמַּתִּירָן לַחֲצֵירָן, וּנְתָנוּהוּ לְתוֹךְ הַפְּנִימִית: שְׁתֵּיהֶן אֲסוּרוֹת. וְאֵין בִּיטּוּל מוֹעִיל: פְּנִימִית מוּתֶּרֶת. עַל יְדֵי בִּיטּוּל שֶׁבִּיטְּלוּ לָהֶן אוֹתָן בְּנֵי חִיצוֹנָה שֶׁנָּתְנוּ עֵירוּבָן לְתוֹכָהּ, וְהִרְגִּילָה עֵירוּבָן לְהֵיחָשֵׁב כְּדִיוּרֵי פְּנִימִית, וְאוֹסְרִין עֲלֵיהֶם, מִשּׁוּם דַּהֲוָיָא רֶגֶל הָאֲסוּרָה בִּמְקוֹמָהּ בִּשְׁבִיל הַהוּא דְּשָׁכַח וְלֹא עֵירֵב, וְאוֹסֶרֶת שֶׁלֹּא בִּמְקוֹמָהּ, הוֹאִיל וְהִרְגִּילָה הָעֵירוּב שָׁם. וּמוֹדֶה שְׁמוּאֵל בְּהָא דִּמְבַטְּלִין אוֹתוֹ הָרֶגֶל שֶׁהִרְגִּילוּ עֵירוּבָן לְתוֹךְ הַפְּנִימִית, וּמִשְׁתַּרְיָא פְּנִימִית לְעַצְמָהּ: הַאי בַּר פְּנִימִית. שֶׁשָּׁכַח וְלֹא נָתַן בָּעֵירוּב, לְמַאן נִיבְטִיל: לִיבְטִיל לִבְנֵי פְּנִימִית. רְשׁוּת חֲצֵירוֹ, דְּתֶיהֱוֵי פְּנִימִית מִיהָא שָׁרְיָא לְעַצְמָהּ. וְחִיצוֹנָה תֵּיאָסֵר מִפְּנֵי דְּרִיסַת רַגְלוֹ שֶׁל זֶה שֶׁאֲסוּרָה בִּמְקוֹמָהּ: לֵיתָא לְעֵירוּבַיְיהוּ גַּבַּיְיהוּ. וְלִכְשֶׁיִּבָּדְלוּ מִן הַחִיצוֹנָה — הֲרֵי הֵן בְּלֹא עֵירוּב, וְכוּלָּן אוֹסְרִין זֶה עַל זֶה: לִבְטִיל. נַמִי דְּרִיסַת רַגְלוֹ לִבְנֵי חִיצוֹנָה, וּרְשׁוּתוֹ לִבְנֵי חִיצוֹנָה, דְּאִסְתַּלַּק לֵיהּ לְגַמְרֵי וַהֲרֵי כּוּלָּן מוּתָּרִין: אֵין בִּיטּוּל רְשׁוּת. מִבֶּן חָצֵר זוֹ לְבֶן חָצֵר אַחֶרֶת לִשְׁמוּאֵל, וְאע"ג דְּאָסַר עֲלַיְיהוּ. וְאִי קַשְׁיָא: לִיבְטְלוּ בְּנֵי פְּנִימִית רְשׁוּת חֲצֵירָן לְגַבֵּי הַאי דְּלָא עֵירֵב, וִיהֵא הוּא רֶגֶל הַמּוּתָּר בִּמְקוֹמוֹ, דְּהָא יָחִיד הוּא וְאֵינוֹ אוֹסֵר עַל חִיצוֹנָה, וְתִשְׁתְּרֵי חִיצוֹנָה! לָאו מִילְּתָא הִיא, דְּהָא דְּכֵיוָן דְּבָטְלֵי רְשׁוּתַיְיהוּ לְגַבֵּיהּ — הָוֵי לְהוּ אִינְהוּ רֶגֶל הָאֲסוּרָה בִּמְקוֹמָהּ, כְּדִתְנַן:* נָתְנוּ לוֹ רְשׁוּתָן הוּא מוּתָּר וְהֵן אֲסוּרִין. וְאָסְרֵי הַחִיצוֹנָה. וְאע"ג דְּעֵירְבוּ בַּהֲדָהּ — הָא בְּטֵיל עֵירוּבַיְיהוּ מִכִּי אִיסְתַּלְּקוּ לְהוּ מֵרְשׁוּתָא דִּפְנִימִית. וְנִהְי דְּאֵין לָהֶן רְשׁוּת לְהוֹצִיא מִבָּתֵּיהֶן לְחָצֵר — מ"מ דְּרִיסַת הָרֶגֶל יֵשׁ לָהֶן בַּפְּנִימִית וּבַחִיצוֹנָה. וְא"ת: יְבַטְּלוּ אַף דְּרִיסַת רַגְלָם לַחִיצוֹנָה! אֵין בִּיטּוּל רְשׁוּת מֵחָצֵר לְחָצֵר: אִיכָּא פְּנִימִית דְּאָסְרָה עֲלַהּ. שֶׁהֲרֵי בָּטַל הָעֵירוּב בִּשְׁבִיל זֶה, וְהָוֵי לַהּ פְּנִימִית רֶגֶל הָאֲסוּרָה בִּמְקוֹמָהּ, דְּלֵיתֵיהּ לְעֵירוּבָהּ גַּבָּהּ: לִיבְטִיל לִבְנֵי פְּנִימִית. אַף לִבְנֵי פְּנִימִית: הַאי בַּר פְּנִימִית לְמַאן נִיבַּטֵּיל כו' אִיכָּא חִיצוֹנָה דְּאָסְרָה עֲלַהּ. שֶׁעֵירוּב מַרְגִּילָהּ לְתוֹכָהּ: אֵין בִּיטּוּל רְשׁוּת מֵחָצֵר לְחָצֵר. כְּלוֹמַר: אֵין בִּיטּוּל רְשׁוּת מִבֶּן חָצֵר זוֹ לְבֶן חָצֵר אַחֶרֶת. כֵּיוָן דִּפְנִימִית אֲסוּרָה — חִיצוֹנָה נַמִי אֲסוּרָה מִפְּנֵי רֶגֶל הָאֲסוּרָה בִּמְקוֹמָהּ שֶׁאוֹסֶרֶת עָלֶיהָ. וְעוֹד, שֶׁאֵין עֵירוּבָהּ אֶצְלָהּ:

שָׁכַח

אלא לאו דאתא בשבתא. להכי חשיב אין מערבין, אפי' עירבו מאתמול, לפי שאין הנכרי אוסר כי ליתיה, כרבי יהודה. מכל מקום כשבא הנכרי – נתבטל העירוב לגמרי, ושוב אינו חוזר למקומו אע"פ שחזרו ושכרו ממנו "אוסרין ואין מערבין" קרינא ביה:

שהמבוי לחצירות כחצר לבתים. דייקינן מינה בסוף פירקין(ב) דאין מבוי ניתר בלחי וקורה, עד שיהו בתים וחצירות פתוחים לתוכו: שתי חצירות למבוי, ושני בתים לחצר. ומיהו, בההוא שמעתא קאמר שמואל: אפילו בית אחד וחצר אחת *)וחד מינייהו באחריתא:

כיצד נתנו עירובן בחיצונה כו' שתיהן אסורות. וא"ת: אביי היכי פליג עליה ואמר יש בטול מחצר לחצר? הא בהדיא תנא הכי לקמן(ג) בסוף פירקין! וי"ל: דאביי הוה מפרש שתיהן אסורות – עד שיבטל:

נתנו עירובן בחיצונה כו' האי בר פנימית למאן ניבטיל. הא פשיטא לן דכולן יכולין לבטל אצלו, (ד)דהוא מותר למקומן. ורבא לא איירי אלא בשריותא דהנך דעירבו.

ליבטיל לבני פנימית ליתא לעירובייהו גבייהו. דכיון שאין יכול לבטל לבני חיצונה משום שאין ביטול רשות מחצר לחצר – לא מצי שקלי בני פנימית לעירובייהו בחיצונה, דאסרי עלייהו. ולא דמי להא דאמרינן ב"מי שהוציאוהו" (לעיל דף מח:): רשות אחת משתמש לשתי רשויות, ואין שתי רשויות משתמשות לרשות אחת, מפרש ר"ת: דכשנתנה אמצעית עירובה בזו ובזו – מותרת עם שתיהן, ושתיהן אסורות עמה. דהתם כל חיצונה וחיצונה לעצמה מותרת במקומה, אבל הכא, דבני חיצונה נמי(ה) אסרי במקומן, מפני הפנימית שלא עירבו דאוסרת עליהם – אתו אינהו נמי ואסרי אצירן נמי לבני הפנימית, כמו שעירבו עמהם ובטל עירובן:

שכח

רבינו חננאל

הלכה כר' יוחנן מסקנא דשמעתין כל פונדק או חצר כיוצא בו דמשכיר יכול לסלוקי הני דדיירי ביה בכל אימת [שרוצה] שוכר ישראל מן המשכיר וקני ליה רשותא ושרי להו לכולהו ישראל דדיירי התם לעירובי ולטלטולי ושוכרין אפי' בשבת אי לא הוה גוי התם מבעו"י כר' יוחנן ואי לא הוה יכיל לסלוקינהו צריך לשכור מן הדיירין. הא דאמר שמואל אין לנו בעירובין אלא כלשון משנתנו ואמרינן לה בה דתנן אנשי חצר ששכח אחד מהן ולא עירב כו' ש"מ דבחצר אחת יכולין לבטל אבל בב' חצרות זו לפנים מזו ולא עירב אין יכול לבטל דהא חצר שנינו ולא חצירות ודחינן לא כי אמרה שמואל אהא אמרה דתנן שהמבוי לחצירות כחצר לבתים. פי' בעינן במבוי חצירות להתירו בלחי וקורה. אבל אם אין במבוי אלא חצר אחת לא בלשון משנתנו דתני חצירות: גופה אמר שמואל אין ביטול רשות מחצר לחצר ואין ביטול רשות בחורבה. ור' יוחנן א' יש ביטול רשות מחצר לחצר ויש ביטול רשות בחורבה. וקיימא לן כר' יוחנן. וכי פליגי בב' חצירות ופתח א' בינהן אבל בב' חצירות זו לפנים מזו מתוך שאוסרין זו על זו מבטלין. בא רבא ואמר אפילו ב' חצירות זו לפני' מזו פעמי' מבטלין ופעמים אין מבטלין. כיצד נתנו עירובן בחיצונה כו': נשאר לי לכתוב בכאן פירוש הא דאמר רבא פעמים מבטלין ופעמים אין מבטלין כיצד כו' ושכח אחד בין מן הפנימית בין מן החיצונה ולא עירב שתיהן אסורות *) בהא מבטלין בפנימית למאן יבטל בא לפני פנימית ליתיה לעירוב גבייהו יבטל לבני החיצונה אין מבטלין מחצר לחצר. דברי אביי ורבא לפרושי טעמא דשמואל אינון. ויש מי שאומר דאשקליה ותרו אביי ורבא לתרוצי טעמא דשמואל ש"מ דהלכתא כוותיה. מיהו אנן קבלינן הלכתא כהני כולהו שמעתא כר' יוחנן דאפילו ב' חצירות שיש בכל אחת מהן כמה בתים וכמה דיורין ופתח א' בינהן כשם שמבטל אחד מבני חצר רשותו לבני חצירו כך יש לו לבטל אפילו מחצר לחצר אחרת דהא רב חסדא ורב ששת אליבא דר' יוחנן בעו

*) נ"לה לנ"ל אסורות ואין מבטלין דבר פנימית למאן יבטל וכו'.

[לעיל ו: וש"נ] [שם] [לקמן סז. סח. עה:] לקמן עד. [לקמן עג.] [דף עג.] [דף עד.] [לקמן עה:] [לקמן דף סט:]

הגהות הב"ח

(א) רש"י ד"ה נתנו עירובן וכו' שבינייהן המתירין: (ב) תוס' ד"ה שהמבוי וכו' בסוף פירקין נ"ב ראה דף עד ע"ב: (ג) ד"ה כיצד וכו' בהדיא תנן הכי לקמן. נ"ב ריש דף עה: (ד) ד"ה נתנו וכו' לבטל אצלו ויהא הוא מותר במקומו ורבא לא איירי: (ה) ד"ה ליבטיל וכו' חיצונה נמי אסרי במקומן:

גליון הש"ס

גמ' ור"י אמר יש ביטול רשות מחצר לחצר. ע"ל סד ע"א תוספות ד"ה אם כן:

שכח אחד מן החיצונה ולא עירב – ודאי פנימית מותרת, דאחדא דשא ומשתמשא, וחיצונה אסורה. אמר ליה רב הונא בריה דרב יהושע לרבא: וכי שכח אחד מן הפנימית ולא עירב, אמאי שתיהן אסורות? לבטיל בר פנימית לבני פנימית, ותיתי חיצונה ותשתרי בהדייהו! כמאן – כרבי אליעזר, דאמר: אינו צריך לבטל רשות לכל אחד ואחד. כי קאמינא – לרבנן, דאמרי: צריך לבטל לכל אחד ואחד. § רב חסדא ורב ששת כי פגעי בהדי הדדי, רב חסדא מרתען שיפוותיה ממתנייתא דרב ששת, ורב ששת *מרתע כוליה גופיה מפלפוליה דרב חסדא. בעא מיניה רב חסדא מרב ששת: שני בתים משני צידי רשות הרבים, ובאו גוים והקיפום מחיצה בשבת, מהו? אליבא דמאן דאמר *"אין ביטול רשות מחצר לחצר" – לא תיבעי לך. השתא דאי בעו לערובי מאתמול – מצו מערבי, אמרת: אין ביטול רשות מחצר לחצר, הכא, דאי בעו לערובי מאתמול – לא מצו מערבי, לא כל שכן?! כי תיבעי לך – אליבא דמאן דאמר *יש ביטול רשות מחצר לחצר. התם, דאי בעו לערובי מאתמול מצו מערבי – בטולי נמי מצי מבטל. אבל הכא, דלא מצו מערבי מאתמול – בטולי נמי לא מצי מבטל. או דילמא לא שנא? אמר ליה: [א]אין מבטלין. מת גוי בשבת, מהו? אליבא דמאן דאמר שוכרין – לא תיבעי לך, השתא תרתי עבדינן, חדא מיבעיא?! אלא כי תיבעי לך – אליבא דמ"ד אין שוכרין. תרתי הוא דלא עבדינן, הא חדא – עבדינן. או דילמא: לא שנא? אמר ליה: [ב]אני אומר מבטלין, והמנונא אמר: אין מבטלין. § אמר רב יהודה, אמר שמואל: [ג]גוי שיש לו פתח ארבעה על ארבעה פתוח לבקעה, אפילו מכנים ומוציא גמלים וקרונות כל היום כולו דרך מבוי – אין אוסר על בני מבוי. מ"ט? בפיתחא דמיחד ליה, בההוא ניחא ליה. איבעיא להו: פתוח לקרפף, מהו? א"ר נחמן בר אמי משמיה דאולפנא: אפילו

רש"י

שכח אחד מן החיצונה ולא עירב. בהא מודי שמואל דמבטלי בני חיצונה לבני פנימית אותו רשות שבא להן לתוכן ע"י הרגל עירובן, משום דאמר לה: לתקוני שתפתיך ולא לעוותי. והכי מפרש לה בסוף פירקין. והא דבעינן ביטול – אליבא דרבי עקיבא אמרה רבא למילתיה. דאי לרבנן – בלאו ביטול נמי אמרה לה פנימית הכי, ועקרה לה לעירוב משום דמעוותי בה. אבל ר"ע אמר דבעיא לבטולי בשילהי פירקין. וכי שכח בן פנימית – ליכא למימר הכי דליבטל לבני פנימית ותיחוד דשא ותשמש(א) דלא מצי למימר לתקוני שתפתיך ולא לעוותי – שהרי תחילת העיוות ע"י בן פנימי בא: כמאן כר' אליעזר. רבא קא מהדר ליה לרב הונא: כמאן קאמרת למילתך – כר"א, דאמר: אינו צריך כו' בשילהי "עושין פסין" אוקימנא הכי: ממתנייתא דרב ששת. שהיו משניות סדורות לו, ויירא רב חסדא שלא יקשה לו ממשנה על משנה, ויאמר לו לתרצן: מפלפוליה. חריף וסבר היה ביותר, ועמוק בשאלותיו: והקיפום. סתמו רה"ר מכאן ומכאן, ונשאר לפני ב' הבתים כעין חצר שהבתים פתוחות לה: מהו. שיבטל זה רשותו לזה, ויהא מותר להוציא מביתו לכאן. דהא קי"ל בפירקא תנינא (דף כ.): כל מחיצות הנעשות בשבת, בין בשוגג בין במזיד – שמה מחיצה, וכ"ש הכא דנכרים עבדוה: אליבא דמאן דאמר אין ביטול רשות מחצר לחצר. ואוקימנא טעמא משום דאין אוסרין(ב) ואין מבטלין, ואע"ג דאי בעו לערובי הוו מערבי – אלמא: תרתי בעינן, אוסרין ומערבין: לא תיבעי לך. דכ"ש דהכא לא הא ולא הא, דלא הוו אוסרין זה על זה אתמול, ולא תורת עירוב היתה לכאן: כי תיבעי לך אליבא דמאן דאמר יש ביטול. ואע"ג דאין אוסרין, מאי? מי אמרינן: התם הוא דאי בעו לערובי הוו מערבי, ואע"ג דתרתי ליכא – חדא מיהא איכא, אבל הכא דאפילו חדא ליכא – לא. או דילמא: מדההא לא קפיד האי נמי לא קפיד: אין מבטלין. דחדא מיהא בעינן: מת גוי בשבת. הא נמי בעא מיניה: שני ישראלים ונכרי הדרים בחצר, ולא שכרו ולא עירבו, ומת נכרי בשבת, מהו לבטל זה לזה: אליבא דמ"ד. לעיל בפירקין (דף סה:) היכא דאתי נכרי בשבת שוכרין ואח"כ מבטלין – לא תיבעי לך: השתא תרתי עבדינן. שכירות וביטול, חדא מיבעיא: אני אומר מבטלין. ולא דמיא להיא דלעיל. דהכא, אי בעי מיגר וערובי מאתמול – מצי עבדי: והמנונא אמר אין מבטלין. כיון דאי בעו ערובי מאתמול לא מצי עבדי בלא שכירות – אין ביטול אלא במקום עירוב: בההוא ניחא ליה. משום דאיכא אוירא טפי ממבוי: דאולפנא. ששמע מרבו ורבו מרבו:

תוספות

שכח אחד מבני חיצונה ולא עירב עמהן. בהא מודה שמואל דמבטלין בני חיצונה לבני הפנימית אותו רשות שיש להן בתוכן על ידי הרגל עירובן, משום דאמרה: לתקוני שתפתיך ולא לעוותי. והכי מפרש בשילהי פירקין. והא דבעיא ביטול – אליבא דר"ע אמר רבא למילתיה, דאי לרבנן – בלא ביטול נמי אמרי לה לפנימית הכי, ועקרה לעירוב' משום דמעוותי לה. אבל ר' עקיבא(ג), דבעי לבטולי בשילהי פירקין, וכי שכח אחד מן הפנימית ליכא למימר הכי לבטל לבני פנימית ותיחוד דשא ותשמש – דלא מצי למימר לתקוני שתפתיך ולא לעוותי דבעיא ביטול, שהרי תחילת [העיוות] ע"י בן הפנימית הוא בא, כל זה לשון הקונט'. וא"ת: ורבא מנא ליה דשמואל מוקי לה כר"ע דבעי' ביטול? דלמא כרבנן דסברו לקמן בלא ביטול! וי"ל: משום דשמעינן ליה לשמואל דאמר אוסרין ומערבין ומבטלין ב' חצירות זו לפנים מזו, ולא מתוקם אלא(ד) בהכי. וא"ת: וכי שכח אחד מבני פנימית ולא עירב ומבטל לבני פנימית, אמאי אתיא חיצונה ואסרה עלייהו משום עירוב המרגילה לתוכה? הא אמר לעיל בפרק "מי שהוציאוהו" (דף מח:) דלא אמרו דיורין להחמיר! י"ל: דההיא דלעיל ליכא שום פשיעותה, אבל הכא – הפנימית פשעה ועותה את עצמה:

כמאן כר' אליעזר כו'. לעיל במתניתין: כשנתנו עירובן בחיצונה ושכח א' מן החיצונה ולא עירב – לא מצי למיפרך הכי – דלימא דמצי מבטל בן חיצונה לבני החיצונה, ותיתי פנימית ותשתרי בהדייהו. דהכא ליכא דיורי חיצונה בפנימית אלא ע"י עירוב המרגילה, לא חשיב ביטולי רשות מחצר לחצר, כיון דמאיליהן משתרו בני חיצונה ע"י שמבטל בן פנימי לבני פנימית(ה) כרא"י, דאמר אין צריך לבטל רשות לכל אחד וא'. אבל לעיל, דפנימית אוסרת החיצונה ע"י דריסת הרגל שלה, אע"ג דא"צ לבטל לכל אחד ואחד – חשיב ליה ביטול רשות מחצר לחצר:

אני אומר מבטלין. פי' בקונטרס: דלא דמיא להיא דלעיל היכא דאתא נכרי בשבתא(ו). דהכא, אי בעו מיגר ועירובי מאתמול – מצו עבדי. ורב המנונא אמר אין מבטלין, כיון דאי בעו לערובי מאתמול – לא מצו מערבי בלא שכירות, אין ביטול אלא במקום עירוב, עד כאן לשון הקונט'. ותימה: דלעיל (דף סו.) פשיטא לן היכא דאתא נכרי מאתמול דמבטלין ואוסרין ומערבין קרינן ביה, דאמר לעיל: ואי דאתא נכרי מאתמול – לוגר מאתמול! י"ל: דסוגיא דלעיל כרב ששת, דאמר הכא דמבטלין. ומיהו, קשה: דמשמע הכא דפשיטא לן אפי' לרב ששת דתרתי לא עבדינן, ודוקא מת הוא דמבטלין. אבל לא מת, דבעי תרתי שכירות וביטול – לא עבדינן. ולעיל פשיטא לן בדאתא מאתמול דבשבת שוכרין ומבטלין, ודוקא באתא בשבת קאמר שמואל דאין מבטלין. ונראה לפרש דהכא באתא בשבת ומת בשבת איירי. וכן משמע הלשון, דקאמר: כי תיבעי לך – אליבא דמאן דאמר אין שוכרין, תרתי הוא דלא עבדינן, ובאתא נכרי בשבת נחלקו. ועל זה מיבעיא ליה: כשמת, אי עבדינן חדא אי לא. וא"ת: כי לא מת נמי תסגי בחדא בביטול לחודיה, דהוה יחיד במקום נכרי! וי"ל: כדפי' לעיל, דלא משתרי בביטול לחודיה כשמתרצה הנכרי לשכור. כיון דאם לא היה מתרצה לא היה מותר, משום דאם כן בטלת תורת עירוב. אי נמי: רב חסדא כר' מאיר סבירא ליה, דאסר יחיד במקום נכרי. ומיהו, לפי טעם זה אחרון לא יתכן לומר(ז) אליבא דמאן דאמר אין שוכרין, דקאמר *(אני אומר מבטלין) היינו שמואל. דממה נפשך לשמואל סגי בביטול. דאיהו קאמר הלכה כראב"י, וקאמר שמואל לעיל דאין מבטלין, ש"מ דאפי' חדא לא עבדינן לשמואל. אלא היינו ר' אסי, דאמר לעיל לא נשכור: אני אומר מבטלין. אף על גב דבשני בתים אין מבטלין, התם ליכא לא אוסרין ולא מערבין, שהיא רה"ר מבעוד יום. אבל הכא – אוסרין איכא וגם מערבין עד שיבא הנכרי. א"נ: גבי שני בתים לא היה לו כח מבעוד יום לעשות אותו ביטול שעושה עכשיו, אבל הכא – מבעוד יום היה בו כח לבטל: וישראל

מסורת הש"ס

[גיר' הערוך מרתת]

[לעיל סו. לקמן סח. עה:]

[שם]

עין משפט נר מצוה

לח א מיי' פ"ב מהל' עירובין הלכה ז טוש"ע או"ח סי' שפא סעיף ה:

לט ב מיי' שם הל' יג וסמג שם טוש"ע או"ח סי' שפב:

מ ג מיי' פ"ה מהל' עירובין הלכה יז טוש"ע או"ח סי' שפט:

רבינו חננאל

ופשטי. רב חסדא כי הוה פגע ברב ששת הוה (מתרען) [מרתען] שפוותיה. כלומר הוה מתיירא ממנו שמא ישאלנו ממתנייתא דהוו בידיה. ורב ששת הוה (מיתרע) [מרתע] כוליה גופיה מפלפוליה דרב חסדא שמא ישאלהו. בעא מיניה רב חסדא מרב ששת ב' חצירות בב' צידי רה"ר והקיפום גוים מחיצה בשבת. אליבא דר' יוחנן דאמר יש ביטול מחצר לחצר מהו מחדא לחברתה הוא דאמר דכיון דאיבעי לעירובי מאתמול הוה מצי מערב בטולי השתא מצי בטיל אבל הכא בהקיפום גוים מחיצות בשבת דאיבעי לעירובי מאתמול לא מצי מערבי בטולי השתא נמי לא מצי מבטלי או דלמא לא שנא א"ל אין מבטלין. תוב בעא מיניה מת גוי בשבת מהו אליבא דר' יוחנן לא תיבעי לך השתא שוכרין ומבטלין עבדי להו בשבת להני תרתי חדא אי מבטלין אי לא מיבעיא. כי תבעי לך אליבא דשמואל דאמר אין שוכרין מאי תרתי הוא דלא עבדי אבל הכא בחצר דהוו בה דיורין ישראלים הרבה וגוי ואסר עלייהו גוי ולא עירבו דהא אין עירוב מועיל במקום גוי בשבת ונסתלקה רשותו ונשתיירו ישראל מהו שיבטל אחד רשותו ויהא האחד מותר לטלטל. א"ל (אביי) [רב ששת] אני אומר מבטלין והמנונא אמר אין מבטלין: **אמר** רב יהודה אמר שמואל גוי שיש לו אפי' פתח ד' טפחים על ד' טפחים פתוח מחצירו לבקעה כבר סילק רשותו מכל המבוי ואפילו הוא מכנים ומוציא גמלים וקרונות כל היום דרך מבוי אינו אוסר על בני המבוי. אלא כעובר דרך הוא חשוב במבוי מ"ט בההוא פתחא דמיחד לו טפי ניחא ליה ולא תימא לבקעה ממש אלא אפי' לקרפף אם פתח וסילק רשותו

גליון הש"ס

גמ' כי קאמינא לרבנן דאמרי צריך לבטל. עי' לקמן סח ע"ב תוס' ד"ה רב אשי:

רש"ל מ"ז ועי' רש"ל

רב נסים גאון

כמאן כר' אליעזר דאמר אין צריך לבטל רשות לכל אחד ואחד אנא כי קא קאמינא כרבנן עיקר דבריו של ר' אליעזר בסוף פרק עושין פסין (דף כו:) דתנן אמר ר' אילעאי שמעתי מר' אליעזר שאפי' היא כבית כור וכן שמעתי ממנו אנשי חצר ששכח אחד מהן ולא עירב ביתו אסור מלהכנים ומלהוציא לו ולהם ופרקינן לא קשיא הא ר' אליעזר הא רבנן כשתמצא לומר לדברי ר' אליעזר המבטל רשות חצירו רשות ביתו נמי ביטל לרבנן המבטל רשות חצירו רשות ביתו לא ביטל:

הגהות הב"ח

(א) רש"י ד"ה שכח וכו' ותיחוד דשא ותשמש. נ"ב ס"א ותבטל חיצונ' לפנימית רשותה: (ב) ד"ה אליבא וכו' דאין אוסרין אין מבטלין: (ג) תוס' ד"ה שכח וכו' אבל ר' עקיבא אמר בשילהי פירקין דבעי לבטולו וכי שכח: (ד) בא"ד ולא מתוקם אלא כר' עקיבא וא"ת: (ה) ד"ה כמאן וכו' לבני פנימית לר' אליעזר דאמר: (ו) ד"ה אני אומר וכו' דלעיל היכא דאתא עו"ג בשבתא. נ"ב וקשה לי לפ"ז דתוספות היו מפרשים מה שפירש רש"י יל"ד דהא דלעיל פי' היינו על היכא דאתא עו"ג בשבתא דא"כ ה"ל לתרץ בקיצור משום דהתם תרתי והכא חדא כסברת בעל איבעיא בעצמו דהאי פשיט למותר [ע"כ נראה דמה שפירש רש"י] ולא דמי להיא דלעיל קאי [אהיכא דבאו עו"ג והקיפוה מחיצה בשבת דאין מבטלין דהתם ג"כ אינו אלא חדא וכעין] שהקשו התוס' לקמן בדיבור שאחר זה ועל זה תירץ רש"י דהכא אי בעי מיגר ועירובי מאתמול מצי עבדי ר"ל דרש"י פי' ג"כ היכא דאתא עו"ג בשבת והא דקאמר אי בעי מיגר ועירובי מאתמול פי' אי הוה בא העו"ג מאתמול מה שאין כן לעיל דמאתמול לא הוה מחילה כלל וכעין זה כתבו התוס' לעיל דף סו בד"ה ואי דאתא וכו' דאף על גב דלא רצה העו"ג להשכיר מאתמול אכתי מערבין קרינא ביה דאם היה רוצה העו"ג היו יכולין לערב ה"ה הכא נמי משום [דאי הוה בא העו"ג מאתמול היו יכולין להשכיר ולערב מצי מיגר ועירובי מאתמול קרינא ביה]: (ז) בא"ד לא יתכן לומר כי תבעי לך אליבא דמאן דאמר אין שוכרין דהיינו שמואל כצ"ל ותיבת דקאמר אני אומר מבטלין נמחק:

עין משפט נר מצוה

מא א מיי' פ"ה מהל' עירובין הלכה י"ז טוש"ע א"ח סימן שפג:
מב ב מיי' פ"ה מהל' שבת הלכה ח טוש"ע א"ח סי' שמ סעיף א:
מג ג ד מיי' שם הל' ב:
מד ה מיי' פ"א מהל' עירובין הלכה כ ופ"ה שם הלכה יא סמג עשין ח טוש"ע א"ח סי' שפז:
מה ו מיי' פ"ו מהלכות שבת הלכה י ופ"ב מה' מילה הלכה ט סמג לאוין סה ועשין כח טוש"ע א"ח סי' שלא סעיף ו וסי' שכה סעיף יז וטוש"ע יו"ד סי' רסו סעיף ה:

גמרא

אפי' פתוח לקרפף. רבה ורב יוסף דאמרי תרוייהו: [א]גוי בית סאתים – אוסר, יותר מבית סאתים – אינו אוסר. וישראל, בית סאתים – אינו אוסר, יותר מבית סאתים – אוסר. בעא מיניה רבא בר חקלאי מרב הונא: פתוח לקרפף, מהו? א"ל: הרי אמרו, בית סאתים – אוסר, יותר מבית סאתים – אינו אוסר. *אמר עולא, אמר רבי יוחנן: [ב]קרפף יותר מבית סאתים שלא הוקף לדירה, ואפילו כור ואפילו כוריים – הזורק לתוכו חייב. מ"ט? מחיצה היא, אלא שמחוסרת דיורין. מתיב רב הונא בר חיננא: [ג]סלע שבים, גבוה עשרה ורוחב ארבעה – אין מטלטלין לא מן תוכו לים, ולא מן הים לתוכו. פחות מכאן – מטלטלין. עד כמה – עד בית סאתים. אהייא? אילימא אסיפא – בית סאתים, טפי לא?! והא מכרמלית לכרמלית קא מטלטל! אלא לאו ארישא, והכי קאמר: סלע שבים, גבוה עשרה ורוחב ד' – אין מטלטלין לא מתוכו לים ולא מן הים לתוכו. ועד כמה – עד בית סאתים. הא יתר מבית סאתים – מטלטלין. אלמא כרמלית היא. תיובתא דר' יוחנן! אמר רבא: מאן דלא ידע תרוצי מתנייתא, תיובתא מותיב ליה לרבי יוחנן?! לעולם ארישא, והכי קאמר: הא בתוכו – מטלטלין. ועד כמה – עד בית סאתים. רב אשי אמר: [ד]לעולם ארישא, הן אמרו והן אמרו. הן אמרו: קרפף יתר מבית סאתים שלא הוקף לדירה אין מטלטלין בו אלא בד' אמות, והן אמרו: אין מטלטלין מרשות היחיד לכרמלית. בית סאתים דשרי לטלטולי בכוליה – אסרי רבנן לטלטולי, לא מן הים לתוכו ולא מתוכו לים. מ"ט? רה"י גמורה היא. יתר מבית סאתים דאסור לטלטולי בכוליה – שרו רבנן לטלטולי מתוכו לים ומן הים לתוכו. מ"ט? דלמא אמרי רה"י גמורה היא ואתי לטלטולי בכוליה. ומאי שנא? תוכו – שכיח, מתוכו לים ומן הים לתוכו – לא שכיח. § ההוא ינוקא דאשתפיך חמימיה, אמר להו רבה: נייתו ליה חמימי מגו ביתאי. א"ל אביי: והא לא ערבינן! א"ל: [ה]נסמוך אשיתוף. א"ל: הא לא שתפינן! [ו]נימרו ליה לגוי ליתי ליה. אמר אביי: בעי לאותביה למר ולא שבקן רב יוסף, דאמר רב [יוסף אמר רב] כהנא: כי הוינן בי רב יהודה, הוה אמר לן: בדאורייתא – מותבינן תיובתא והדר עבדינן מעשה, בדרבנן – עבדינן מעשה והדר מותבינן תיובתא. לבתר הכי אמר ליה: מאי בעית לאותביה למר? אמר [ליה: דתניא,] הזאה שבות *ואמירה לגוי שבות,

מה

רש"י

אפי' פתוח לקרפף. ניחא ליה ביה טפי דאיכא אוירא טפי ממבוי ואינו אוסר על בני מבוי: גוי בית סאתים אוסר. אם היה לו פתח לקרפף בית סאתים ופתח למבוי עדיין אוסר על בני מבוי דאוירא דקרפף לא נפיש אבל אם יותר מבית סאתים נפיש אוירא ובההיא ניחא ליה ואינו אוסר: ישראל. שיש לו פתח לקרפף ופתח למבוי ושכח ולא עירב במבוי אם קרפף בית סאתים הוא שראוי להשתמש בו אינו אוסר על בני מבוי ואע"ג דלגבי נכרי חשיב זוטרא, לגבי ישראל נפיש. דהא בשבת ליכא הוצאת משאות יתירין וסגי בהכי ונפיש אוירא ממבוי אבל יותר מבית סאתים דכרמלית הוא כגון שלא הוקף לדירה כיון דאסיר ליה לאישתמושי לא ניחא ליה ביה ואוסר על בני מבוי: פתוח לקרפף מהו. אנכרי קאי ואמילתיה דרב יהודה: הזורק לתוכו. מרה"ר: חייב. חטאת ואע"ג דלענין איסור טלטול שויוה רבנן כרמלית שאסרו לטלטל בתוכו אלא בד' מדאורייתא רה"י גמורה היא דמחיצה היא אלא שמחוסרת דיורין ומש"ה אסרי רבנן לטלטולי: ים. כרמלית הוא: אין מטלטלין לא מתוכו לים. אפי' בד' אמות משום דכל גבוה עשרה ורוחב ד' הוי רה"י: פחות מכאן. שאינו גבוה עשרה, כרמלית היא כים, ומטלטלין מזה לזה תוך ד' אמות: עד כמה. יהא רחב סלע: עד בית סאתים. אבל טפי לא. ולקמיה מפרש אהייא קאי: אי נימא אסיפא. אפחות מעשרה תרוייהו כרמלית נינהו לא שנא רחב ולא שנא קצר: הא יותר מבית סאתים. בטל תורת רה"י מיניה והוי כרמלית אפי' לקולא ואף על גב דגבוה עשרה: לעולם ארישא. ולאו אמתוכו לים קאי אלא אדיוקא קאי והכי קא דייק: הא בתוכו מטלטלין דהא רה"י היא, עד כמה – עד בית סאתים אבל טפי לא דשויוה רבנן ככרמלית לענין טלטול משום דמחוסר דירה ומיחלף ברה"ר מיהו לענין מתוכו לים רה"י היא: רב אשי אמר לעולם ארישא. ולאו אדיוקא קאי ואפי' לענין מתוכו לים נמי כרמלית שויוה ושרי. מיהו לר' יוחנן לא תיקשי דודאי לענין חיובא מדאורייתא רה"י היא ומאי טעמא שרו רבנן לטלטולי מיניה לכרמלית, משום דאיסור טלטול מרשות היחיד לכרמלית מדרבנן הוא דהם אמרו זאת והם אמרו עוד איסור אחר וראו שאין שניהם עומדים כאן וביטלו זה מפני זה וכדמפרש: הם אמרו קרפף יותר מבית סאתים אין מטלטלין בו. דשויוה כרמלית לענין טלטול משום דמיחלף ברה"ר ומיהו אסור לטלטל מרה"ר לתוכו ומתוכו לרה"ר כדר' יוחנן דמדאורייתא רה"י היא: והם אמרו אין מטלטלין מרה"י לכרמלית. משום דלא ליתי לטלטולי מרה"י לרה"ר ובהאי רה"י שהיא ביותר מבית סאתים לא גזור מאי טעמא בית סאתים דשרי לטלטולי בכוליה כי אסרינן ליה לטלטולי מיניה לכרמלית לא אתיא מיניה חורבה אבל טפי מבית סאתים אי אסרת מתוכו לים תוך ד' אמות אתי למימר רה"י גמורה היא אפי' מדרבנן ומטלטלי בכוליה ומיעקרא אידך תקנתא דרבנן ובטלו הא מקמי הא: ומאי שנא. דאלים הך תקנתא טפי מהך השתא נמי קא מטלטלי מרשות היחיד לכרמלית: תוכו שכיח. וכי שרי ליה לטלטולי בגוויה חזו ליה עלמא ומיחלף ברה"ר: מתוכו לים לא שכיח. ולא גזרו רבנן במילתא דלא שכיחא ואע"ג דבשאר רה"י לכרמלית גזור רבנן הנהו שכיחן אבל הני תרתי כחדא יותר מבית סאתים ומתוכו לכרמלית לא שכיח: דאישתפוך חמימיה. שהיו רוצין למולו והחמו לו חמין מבערב ונשפכו היום: מגו ביתאי. מביתיה דרבה והתינוק היה בבית אחר באותה חצר: נסמוך אשיתוף. דמבוי דתנן (לקמן עג.) במתני' אם נשתתפו במבוי מותר כאן וכאן במבוי ובחצירות אף על פי שלא עירבו: בדאורייתא מותבינן תיובתא. באיסור של תורה וחכם מורה בו היתר ויש בתלמידים שיודע להשיב ישיב קודם מעשה שלא נעבור על דברי תורה אבל בדרבנן כגון עירובי חצירות שבקינן לחכם לעשות כהוראתו: והדר מותבינן. ליה ללמוד אם יפה הורה: הזאה. על הטמא איכא אסורה בשבת אלא משום שבות:

תוספות

וישראל בית סאתים אינו אוסר כו'. אומר ר"י: דאם הוקף לדירה – אפי' בית סאתים אוסר. דכיון שהוקף לדירה, הוה כביתו ואינו עומד (א) במקום אויר של מבוי, ואוסר עדיין פתח הפתוח למבוי. ובקונט' לא פירש כן, דאדרבה פירש: יותר מבית סאתים דוקא כשלא הוקף לדירה, אבל הוקף לדירה – אינו אוסר: ומאי טעמא דלמא אמרי רה"י גמורה היא. מכאן התיר ר"ת בגינה אחת יתירה מבית סאתים שלא הוקפה לדירה לטלטל מתוכה לחוץ, הואיל ולא היתה רה"ר גמורה, כגון סרטיא ופלטיא עוברת לפניה. והתיר להטמין המפתח בתוך הגינה אע"פ שעומד בחוץ ונותן בתוך הגינה, או ליטול מתוכה לחוץ. ואין לחלק בין סלע דהתם, משום דלא שכיח, שהרי כל עיקר גזירה זו שלא יבא לטלטל בכולו והאי טעמא שייך נמי הכא. ועוד יש לדקדק מהא דתניא בפ"ק דשבת (דף ו.): ארבע רשויות לשבת, ואם היה אסור לטלטל משאר כרמלית לקרפף יותר מבית סאתים – משכחת להו חמשה: והא לא ערבינן כו'. קודם מילה היה, כדפירש בקונט'. וכן משמע, מדמדמה הך אמירה להזאה, שהיא משום מצוה לעשות פסח. אבל לאחר מילה ומשום סכנה, על זה לא היה אומר: והא לא ערבינן, דפקוח נפש הזריז הרי זה משובח, כדאמרינן פרק בתרא דיומא (דף פד:): נסמוך אשיתוף. דמבוי. פירש בקונט', דתנן במתני': אם נשתתפו במבוי – מותרין כאן וכאן, ולא היה לו להביא מאותה משנה, דלקמן (ב) בתלמוד מוקמינן לה כולה כר"מ דבעינן עירוב ובעינן שיתוף, ואם נשתתפו נמי קאמר. אלא היה לו להביא ראיה מהא דתניא לקמן בפירקין (דף עא:): וחכמים אומרים מערבין או משתתפין. ואע"ג דפסיק רב לקמן (ג) הלכה כר"מ דבעי תרתי – סבר לה כר' יוחנן דאמר נהגו כר"מ, אבל לכתחלה לא עבדינן כוותיה. אי נמי: סבר כמאן דאמר (ד): בפת כולי עלמא לא פליגי דבחדא סגי, ונסמוך אשיתוף דקאמר – היינו אם נשתתפו בפת:

לשבות

רבינו חננאל

מכל המבוי. רבה ורב יוסף דאמרי תרוייהו גוי בית סאתים אוסר יותר מבית סאתים אינו אוסר. פי' פתח ד' על ד' פתוח לקרפף אם יש בו בית סאתים עדיין אוסר [על] בני המבוי שלא סילק רשותו [יותר מב' סאתים אינו] (ואינו) אוסר. וכן סוגיא דשמעתא. לפי' שיירא שחנו ושבתו בקרפף שיש בו כמה סאין ושבת גוי עמהן ההוא (גוי) בית סאתים ששבת עליו אסר לישראל ששבתו עמו לטלטל בו אבל בשאר המקום כולו אינו אוסר. ישראל שלא עירבו בית סאתים אינו אוסר כי בלא עירוב מותר בו אבל יותר מבית סאתים שאין לו [לטלטל] אלא ע"י [עירוב] אוסר אא"כ ביטל רשותו כר' יוחנן דאמר יש ביטול ברחבה. אמר עולא א"ר יוחנן (א"ר) קרפף יותר מבית סאתים שלא הוקף לדירה אפי' כור ואפי' כורים הזורק מרה"ר לתוכו חייב מחיצה היא אלא שמחוסרת דיורין. ומותבינן עלה מהא סלע שבים גבוה י' ורחב ד' טפחים אין מטלטלין לא מתוכו לים ולא מן הים לתוכו. פחות מכאן מטלטלין עד בית סאתים. האי בית סאתים דקתני *) אפחות מכאן בית סאתים הוא דמטלטלין הא יתר מבית סאתים לא. והא פחות מי' טפחים כרמלית הוא. והים כרמלית הוא מכרמלית לכרמלית הוא ואפי' יתר מהאי שרי אלא לאו ארישא והכי קתני סלע שבים גבוה י' ורחב ד' אין מטלטלין לא מתוכו לים ולא מן הים לתוכו. ועד כמה עד בית סאתים. כלומר שהוא כרה"י הא יתר מבית סאתים מטלטלין אלמא כרמלית היא. והאי סלע שבים כי קרפף יתר מבית סאתים שלא הוקף לדירה הוא וקתני דמטלטלין מן הים לתוכו אלמא כרמלית היא. ותיובתא דר' יוחנן תיובתא ודחי רבא לעולם אין מטלטלין לא מתוכו לים ולא מן הים לתוכו. [וה"ק] בתוכו הוא דמטלטלין עד בית סאתים רב אשי אמר לעולם ארישא והן אמרו קרפף יותר מבית סאתים שלא הוקף לדירה אין מטלטלין בו אלא בד' אמות. והן אמרו אין מטלטלין מרה"י לכרמלית בית סאתים דשרי לטלטולי בכוליה אסרו רבנן לטלטולי מתוכו לים ומן הים לתוכו מ"ט דילמא אמרי רה"י הוא ואתי לטלטולי בכוליה. ומ"ש תוכו שכיח ולפיכך אסרו. מתוכו לים ומן הים לתוכו דלא שכיח לא גזרו ביה רבנן: ההוא ינוקא דאישתפוך המים שחיממו לו למול עליהן א' להן רבה נייתו ליה מיא חמימי מגו ביתו. והא לא ערבינן. א"ל נסמוך על שיתוף שבמבוי אמר ליה לית לן שיתופי מבוי אמר להו לגוי וייתי

*) נ"ל דקתני אפחות מכאן קאי אפחות מכאן וכו'.

הגהות הב"ח

(א) תוס' ד"ה וישראל וכו'. במקום אויר (של מבוי). תא"מ ונ"ב בתשב"ץ אין זה: (ב) ד"ה נסמוך וכו' משנה לקמן. נ"ב דף עג ע"ב: (ג) בא"ד דפסיק רב לקמן. נ"ב ריש דף עה ע"ב: (ד) בא"ד סבר כמאן דאמר. נ"ב סוף דף עה ע"ב:

גליון הש"ס

גמ' נימרו ליה לגוי. עי' לעיל דף סד ע"ב תוס' ד"ה א"כ:

מסורת הש"ס

שבת דף ז.
[שבת קנ. וש"נ]

מה הזאה שבות ואינה דוחה את השבת, אף אמירה לגוי – שבות ואינה דוחה את השבת! א"ל: ולא שני לך בין שבות דאית ביה מעשה לשבות דלית ביה מעשה?(א) דהא מר לא אמר לגוי "זיל אחים". א"ל רבה בר רב חנן לאביי: מבואה דאית ביה תרי גברי רברבי כרבנן לא ליהוי ביה לא עירוב ולא שיתוף?! א"ל: מאי נעביד? מר לאו אורחיה, אנא טרידנא בגירסאי, אינהו לא משגחי. ואי אקני להו פיתא בסלא – כיון דאי בעו לה מינאי, ולא אפשר ליתבה נהלייהו – בטיל שיתוף. דתניא: [א]אחד מבני מבוי שביקש יין ושמן ולא נתנו לו – בטל השיתוף. ונקני להו מר רביעתא דחלא בחביתא! תניא: אין משתתפין באוצר. והא תניא: [ב]משתתפין! אמר רב אושעיא: ל"ק; הא – ב"ש, הא – [ג]ב"ה. *דתנן: [ד]המת בבית ולו פתחים הרבה – כולן טמאין. נפתח אחד מהן – הוא טמא וכולן טהורין. חישב להוציאו באחד מהן, או בחלון שיש בו ארבעה על ארבעה – מציל על כל הפתחים כולן. בית שמאי אומרים: והוא שחישב עד שלא ימות המת. וב"ה אומרים: [ה]אף משימות המת. ההוא ינוקא דאישתפוך חמימיה, אמר להו רבא: נישיילה לאימיה, אי צריכא *נחים ליה גוי אגב אימיה. אמר ליה רב משרשיא לרבא: אימיה קא אכלה תמרי! א"ל: אימור, תונבא בעלמא הוא דנקט לה. ההוא ינוקא דאישתפוך חמימיה, אמר להו רבא: פנו לי מאני מבי גברי לבי נשי, ואיזיל ואיתיב התם ואיבטיל להו הא חצר. א"ל רבינא לרבא: *והאמר שמואל אין ביטול רשות מחצר לחצר! אמר ליה: *אנא כר' יוחנן סבירא לי, דאמר: יש ביטול מחצר לחצר. ואי לא סבר לה מר כשמואל, ניתיב

רש"י

מה הזאה שבות ואינה דוחה שבת. ואפי' במקום מצוה, כגון לשחוט פסחו, כדתנן בפסחים בפרק "אלו דברים" (דף סה:): תרי גברי רברבי כרבנן. כגון אתה ורבה דדיירינו ביה: מר. רבה אין כבודו לחזר על בני המבוי ולגבות השיתוף: אינהו. שאר בני מבוי לא משגחי: אקני להו. משלי ריפתא בסלא בדיבורא, דליכא טרחא, ויהו כולן זוכין בו לשם שיתוף: כיון דאי בעו מינאי. אם אחד מהן היה צריך לאכול מן השיתוף, והיה שואלו ממני – אין יכולת בידי לוותר משלי בכל שבת(ב) לכך נמצא שאין בלבי להיות בו חלק גמור, ובטל השיתוף: שביקש יין ושמן. משל שיתוף: רביעתא דחלא. חומץ: בחביתא. באחת מחביותיך, דמידי דלית ביה קפידא הוא, ועיקר שיתוף ביין, כדאמר בהאי פירקא (דף עא:) ויניח החבית בחצר ויסמוך על רביעית שבה לשום שיתוף לאורך כל השנה כולה, שמניחין שיתוף בחצר: אין משתתפין באוצר. בדבר האצור, כגון חבית של יין או פירות המכונסין – אין סומכין על מה שבתוכן, משום דאין ברירה איזהו של שיתוף, וכי מסתפק ממנו איכא למימר אזל ליה שיתוף: כולן טמאין. כל הכלים הנתונין בעובי האסקופה טמאין, ואע"פ שאינס באהל המת – מפני שאין אנו יודעין באיזו פתח יוציאנו. ופתח שעתיד לצאת בו מיטמא מיד. וטעמא ליכא, אלא הלכות טומאה הכי גמירי לה. ואפי' חלונות של טפח על טפח טמאין, דכיון דכולן סתומין – לא מוכחא מילתא בהי מפיק ליה: נפתח אחד מהן. ודאי בההוא מפיק ליה: פחות מד' על ד' אינו חשיב להציל על השאר: עד שלא ימות. דלא נחתא להו טומאה אשאר פתחים. אבל משימות המת – כבר נטמאו הכלים, ולא אמרינן הוברר הדבר דמעיקרא נמי דעתיה לאפוקי בהאי פיתחא, אלא נחתא להו טומאה, ואפי' כלים הבאין (ג)(לשאר פתחים) שם לאחר מחשבה טמאים, דכיון דנחתא להו טומאה תו לא סלקא מינייהו במחשבה, עד דעביד להו מעשה ממש – דפתח ליה להאי, ומהני לטהר את האחרים מכאן ולהבא. כדקתני לעיל: נפתח אחד מהן כו': וב"ה אומרים אף משימות המת. דאמרינן יש ברירה, דמאתמול דעתיה בהאי פיתחא, ולא נחתא טומאה לאחריני, ואפי' כלים דקודם מחשבה טהורין: נישיילה לאימיה אם צריכה. לצורכה חמין, נחים ליה נכרי אגב אימיה. דקי"ל *חיה אחר שבעה, אפי' אמרה צריכה אני – אין מחללין עליה את השבת, אבל עושין לה ע"י ארמאי: הא אכלה תמרי. כלומר: הא חזינן דאינה צריכה חמין לשתות, דהא נוגן נמי אכלה: תונבא. אשדורדיש"ן ואוכלת ואינה יודעת מה: פנו לי מאני. בחצירו של רבא היו חמין, והתינוק נשפכו חמיו בחצר אחרת ופתח ביניהן, ולא עירבו שתי חצירות יחד, ולרבא היו בביתו חדרים פנימיים שאינן פתוחין לחצר והן לצניעות, והנשים יושבות שם ובי גברי הוה פתוח לחצר, ותנן* במתני': המבטל רשות חצירו אסור להוציא מביתו לחצר, דהא לאו דידיה הוא. הלכך, פינה כליו מבי גברי כדי שלא יבא להוציא משם לחצר, והלך וישב בחדרים הפנימיים, וביטל רשות חצרו לבני חצר האחרת, ויביאו חמין מחצירו לחצירן: ניתיב

בי נשי / בי נשי	בי גבר'	חמין	פתח	חצר	בית של קטן

תוספות

לשבות דלית ביה מעשה. וא"ת: דההוא ינוקא דלקמן דאמר להו רבא: נשיילה לאימיה אי צריכא – ניחיימוה ליה אגב אימיה כי לא צריכא נמי, וכי לא היה נכרי בכל העיר שיאמרו לו שיחם בשביל הקטן למולו? ובפ"ק דגיטין (דף ח. ד"ה אע"ג) פירשתי.

כיון דאי בעו מינאי ולא יהיבנא להו. צריך ליזהר כשאדם עושה עירוב שלא יערב בדבר שהוא מקפיד עליו, כגון אותן דברים שתיקן לכבוד שבת, או(ד) אם יש לו ככר נאה שקורין גשטי"ל או פשטיד"א וכיוצא בהן. דאי בעו ליה מיניה ולא יהיב להו – בטל עירוב: **ונקני** להו מר רביעתא דחלא בחביתא. לכאורה משמע לצורך שיתוף מבוי קאמר, דלעירובי חצירות בעי פת. אע"ג דאמר לקמן בפרק "חלון" (דף פא.): מאן שמעת ליה דאמר פת אין מידי אחרינא לא, ר' יהושע. הא קי"ל כר' יהושע לגבי ר"א דפליג עליה התם. ולקמן בפירקא*: בין ר"מ בין רבנן סבירא להו דעירובי חצירות אינו אלא בפת, ולכאורה כולהו אמוראי דההיא שמעתא הכי אית להו. ואור"י: דנ"ל דההיא חביתא דחלא דהכא בחצר הוה ולא בבית, דהא אמר לקמן בפרק "כיצד משתתפין" (דף פה:) דעירובי חצירות בבית שבחצר, ושיתופי מבואות בחצר שבמבוי, ותרוייהו דוקא *כמו שאפרש לקמן(ה). וכן ההיא דבעל הבית שהיה שותף עם שכיניו לזה ביין כו' – איירי כגון דמונח בחצר:

תניא אין משתתפין באוצר. וא"ת: ואביי כב"ש, דהא כב"ש מסיק לה. וי"ל: דאביי לא חשיב הא דקאמר רב אושעיא הא ב"ש הא ב"ה, וקסבר אביי: לא נחלקו ב"ש וב"ה בדבר זה – דכמה פלוגתא דתנאי ואמוראי אשכחן לענין ברירה. ועוד אומר ר"י: דאביי הוה מוקים כולהו אליביה, ולמפרע כולן טמאין, דאין ברירה. והוה מפרש (*כרבה) דמסיק במסכת ביצה (דף י. ולז:) לטהר את הפתחים מכאן ולהבא:

אמר רב אושעיא לא קשיא כו'. הקשה ר"ת: דהכא מוקי רב אושעיא פלוגתייהו בברירה, ובפ"ק דביצה (דף י.) וגם בסוף ביצה (דף לז:) מסיק רב אושעיא דפליגי לטהר את הפתחים מכאן ולהבא. דכיון דנחתא להו טומאה – לא נפקא לב"ש אלא בשינוי מעשה, ולב"ה סגי במחשבה(ו). ואור"ת: דרב אושעיא לחוד, ורבי אושעיא לחוד. דהכא גרס בכל הספרים "רב אושעיא" והתם גרסינן "רבי אושעיא". ומצינו רב אושעיא שהיה באמוראים אחרונים בתר ההיא שמעתא דפ' בתרא דביצה (דף לח:) גבי ליבטיל מים ומלח גבי עיסה, דקאמר רב(ז) אושעיא דשפיר עביד, דאחיכו עליה. וביבמות בריש "כיצד" (דף יח:) על מילתיה דרב אושעיא דאמר חלוק היה ר"ש אף בראשונה, אמר: *מתיב ר' אושעיא. ובפרק "כל הגט" (גיטין דף כה.) בעא מיניה רב אושעיא מרב יהודה, וה"ר מנחם מיונ"י פי': דלא פליגי הכא בברירה אלא לטהר את הפתחים מכאן ולהבא, כדאמר בביצה. וה"ק: הא ב"ש דלא מהניא מחשבה לטהר את הפתחים – ה"נ לא מהני לענין עירוב. ואע"פ שמזכה להו, כיון דמתחילה לא הונח בחבית לשם עירוב. ולב"ה דמהניא מחשבה התם – מהני נמי הכא. והא דתנן לקמן* בעל הבית שהיה שותף עם שכניו, והא דתנן נמי ב"כיצד משתתפין" (לקמן דף פב.) מניח את החבית כו' – כב"ה דלא בעו הנחה לשם עירוב. וניחא השתא דשבק שאר פלוגתייהו דתנאי, דפליגי לענין ברירה בהלוקח יין מבין הכותים ובשאר מקומות. ואף על גב דקאי השתא אביי כב"ש – לא היה חושש לכך להשיבו, דבלאו הכי היה יכול להקשות להו וליקני להו רביעתא דחלא במנא. אלא לא היה חושש לטרוח כל כך לערב. ואין זו סברא תמוה כל כך אם אינו מועיל זכוי לב"ש אם לא הונח בכלי לשם עירוב, דהא בסוף פירקין(ח) נמי פרכינן: אלא מעתה הקנה לו פת בסלו, ה"נ דלא הוי שיתוף? פירוש(ט): ולא יועיל שיתוף משום דלא אפקי ועיילי דרך פתחים למבוי. מיהו, זה קשיא: דאדפריך מברייתא דתניא משתתפין באוצר, הוה ליה למיפרך ממתני' דבעה"ב שהיה שותף עם שכיניו, וכמה משניות דלא בעו הנחה בכלי לשם עירוב. ועוד קשיא: דמה ענין מחשבה לטהר את הפתחים למחשבה דעירוב? **אי** צריכה ניחממו ליה אגב אימיה. פירשנו בפרק קמא דגיטין (דף ח. ד"ה אע"ג): אנא

מסורת הש"ס: ביצה דף י. ודף לז: אהלות פ"ז מ"ג | [ע' תוס' ב"ק פ: ד"ה אומר לגוי ותוספות גיטין ח: ד"ה אע"ג ותוס' מנחות סד. ד"ה שחים] | [לעיל סו: וכס נסמן] | [לקמן עה.] | [שבת קכט.] | דף עה: | [נ"ל כרבי אושעיא] ועיין ביצה י. | [שם יע. ושם] | [דף עה.]

עין משפט נר מצוה: מו א מיי' פ"ה מהלכות עירובין הלכה כ סמג עשין א טוש"ע או"ח סי' שסו סעיף ה: מז ב ג מיי' שם הל' ג וסמג שם טור או"ח סי' שפו: מח ד מיי' פ"ז מהל' טומאת מת הלכה ב סמג עשין רלג:

רבינו חננאל

וייתי להו אמר אביי בעי לאותובי למר והא הזאה שבות היא. ואמירה לגוי שבות היא. מה הזאה אינה דוחה את השבת אף אמירה לגוי לא תדחה את השבת. א' לי ולא שני לך בין שבות דאית ביה מעשה כגון הזאה לשבות דלית ביה מעשה כגון אמירה לגוי. ואי מקנה להו חד ריפתא לבני מבוי ובעי ליה חד מינייהו ולא יהבי ליה בטל השיתוף דתניא אחד מבני מבוי שביקש יין ושמן ולא נתנו לו בטל השיתוף. תנא אין משתתפין באוצר אוקימנא לב"ש דלית להו ברירה והא דתניא משתתפין באוצר כב"ה דאית להו ברירה. דתנן המת בבית ולו פתחים הרבה כולן טמאין נפתח אחד מהן הוא טמא וכולן טהורים חישב להוציאו באחד מהן או בחלון שיש בו ד' על ד' הציל על פתחין כולן בש"א יחשוב עד שלא ימות המת. ובה"א אף משמת המת ש"מ לב"ה אית להו ברירה. ואע"פ שאחרי שמת חישב להוציאו באחד מהן נתברר כי הוא שהיה מוכן להוציאו ממנו. וההוא ינוקא דאשתפוך בשבת אותן המים החמין שהיו מוכנים לקטן למול אותו עליהן אמר רבא ישאלו לאמו. כלומר אם מרגשת בעצמה חולי שצריכה מים חמים נחים ליה לקטן גוי אגב אמיה ואקשינן ליה לרבא והא חזינן לאמיה דקא אכלה קמן תמרי כמו הבריאים ואמר להו לא סמכינן אהאי דקא אכלה קמן [תמרי] תנבא הוא דנקיט לה כלומר קור החזיק בה ואוכלת בלא תיקון דעת ואי אמרה צריכנא מים חמין מחמין לה. (רב) [רבא] היו לו ב' חצרות באחת היה יושב הוא ובני אדם יוצאין ובאין אצלו ובני אדם אחרים עוד יש להן בתים באותה חצר ששוכנים בהן. ואחד מבני חצר בא למול את בנו בשבת. ואישפכן חמימי. אמר להו רבא הכינו לי כלים לישב עליהן בחצרי האחרת שהנשים יושבות בה ואלך ואשב שם ואבטל להם רשותי מזו החצר ויטול החמין שלי וימול עליהן הקטן. א"ל רבינא לרבא והאמר שמואל אין מבטלין מחצר לחצר א"ל כר' יוחנן סבירא לי דא' מבטלין רשות מחצר לחצר א"ל ואי לא סבירא לך כשמואל

הגהות הב"ח

(א) גמ' דלית ביה מעשה (דהא מר וכו' אחים) תא"מ ונ"ב ס"א לא גרסי ליה וכן מוכח בתוספו' בד"ה לשבות: (ב) רש"י ד"ה כיון וכו' לוותר משלי בכל שבת כל כך נמנא: (ג) ד"ה עד שלא וכו' כלים הבאין (לשאר פתחים) תא"מ ונ"ב ס"א נמחק והגה"ה היא: (ד) תוס' ד"ה כיון וכו' לכבוד שבת או ככר נאה כצ"ל ותיבות אם יש לו נמחק: (ה) ד"ה ונקני כו' כמו שאפרש לקמן. נ"ב בדף ע"ב בד"ה בפת: (ו) ד"ה אמר ר' הושעיא וכו' סגי במחשבה (ואור"ת וכו' באמוראין) תא"מ ונ"ב ס"א ואומר ר"ת דרב הושעיא לחוד ורב אושעיא לחוד דהכא גרסינן בכל הספרים רב הושעיא והתם גרסינן רב אושעיא ומצינו רב הושעיא שהיה באמוראים: (ז) בא"ד דקאמר רבי הושעיא דשפיר וכו' מתיב רבי הושעיא וכו' בעא מינה ר' הושעיא: (ח) בא"ד בסוף פרקין. נ"ב סוף דף עג: (ט) בא"ד פי' דלא יועיל וכו' קשה לפירוש זה לאדפריך:

גליון הש"ס רש"י ד"ה פנו לי מאני וכו'. הלכך פונה כליו. ע' לקמן דף עט ע"ב תוס' ד"ה ואיבעית אימא: **תוס'** ד"ה וניקני ליה וכו' כמו שאפרש לקמן דף עא ע"ב בתוס' ד"ה בפת:

ניתיב מר בדוכתיה, וניבטיל להו לדידהו, וניהדרו אינהו וניבטלו ליה למר. דהא אמר רב: *מבטלין וחוזרין ומבטלין! אנא בהא כשמואל סבירא לי, דאמר: *אין מבטלין וחוזרין ומבטלין. ולאו חד טעמא הוא? מ"ט אין מבטלין וחוזרין ומבטלין — לאו משום דכיון דבטליה לרשותיה, אסתלק ליה מהכא לגמרי, והוה ליה כבן חצר אחרת, ואין ביטול רשות מחצר לחצר. מר נמי — לא ניבטיל! התם היינו טעמא כי היכי דלא ליהוי מלתא דרבנן כחוכא *ואטלולא. גופא, רב אמר: מבטלין וחוזרין ומבטלין, ושמואל אמר: אין מבטלין וחוזרין ומבטלין. לימא רב ושמואל בפלוגתא דרבנן ור' אליעזר קא מיפלגי; דרב דאמר כרבנן ושמואל דאמר כר"א! אמר לך רב: אנא דאמרי — אפי' לרבי אליעזר, עד כאן לא קאמר רבי אליעזר התם "המבטל רשות חצירו רשות ביתו ביטל" — משום *דבבית בלא חצר לא דיירי אינשי, אבל לענין איסתלוקי — מי אמר? ושמואל אמר: אנא דאמרי — אפילו כרבנן; עד כאן לא קאמרי רבנן התם — אלא מאי דבטיל — בטיל, ודלא בטיל לא בטיל. אבל מאי דבטיל — מיהא איסתלק לגמרי. אמר רב אחא בר חנא, אמר רב ששת: כתנאי; *מי שנתן רשותו והוציא, בין בשוגג בין במזיד — אוסר, דברי ר"מ. רבי יהודה אומר: במזיד — אוסר, בשוגג — אינו אוסר. מאי לאו, בהא קמיפלגי, דמר סבר: מבטלין וחוזרין ומבטלין, ומר סבר אין מבטלין וחוזרין ומבטלין. אמר רב אחא בר תחליפא משמיה דרבא: לא, דכ"ע: אין מבטלין וחוזרין ומבטלין. והכא *בקנסו שוגג אטו מזיד קא מיפלגי; מ"ס: קנסו שוגג אטו מזיד, ומר סבר: לא קנסו שוגג אטו מזיד. רב אשי אמר: רב ושמואל בפלוגתא דר"א ורבנן קא מיפלגי.§ "אמר רבן גמליאל: מעשה בצדוקי אחד שהיה דר עמנו".§ צדוקי מאן דכר שמיה?! חסורי מיחסרא, והכי קתני: צדוקי הרי הוא כגוי ורבן גמליאל אומר: צדוקי אינו כגוי ואמר רבן גמליאל: מעשה בצדוקי אחד שהיה דר עמנו במבוי בירושלים, ואמר לנו אבא: מהרו והוציאו את הכלים למבוי, עד שלא יוציא ויאסר עליכם. והתניא: הדר עם הנכרי צדוקי וביתוסי הרי אלו אוסרין עליו, (רבן גמליאל אומר: צדוקי וביתוסי אינן אוסרין.) ומעשה בצדוקי אחד שהיה דר עם רבן גמליאל במבוי בירושלים, ואמר להם רבן גמליאל לבניו: "בני מהרו והוציאו מה שאתם מוציאין, והכניסו מה שאתם מכניסין, עד שלא יוציא התועב הזה ויאסר עליכם, *שהרי ביטל רשותו לכם", דברי רבי מאיר. רבי יהודה אומר בלשון אחרת: מהרו ועשו צורכיכם במבוי עד שלא תחשך ויאסר עליכם. אמר מר: "הוציאו מה שאתם מוציאין והכניסו מה שאתם מכניסין עד שלא יוציא התועב הזה ויאסר עליכם". למימרא דכי מפקי אינהו, והדר מפיק איהו לא אסר והתנן

רש"י

ניתיב מר אדוכתיה. דמדקאמרת פנו לי מאני — גלית אדעתך דמאחר שתבטל רשותך אין לך היום היתר בחצר, והיינו כשמואל דאמר לקמן: אין מבטלין וחוזרין ומבטלין. דאי לאו כשמואל סבירא לך — ליתיב מר אדוכתיה, ובטל להם רשות חצרך שעה אחת עד שיקחו החמין. ויחזרו הם ויבטלו לך אותו הרשות ויחזירו לך חצרך: דהא אמר רב מבטלין וחוזרין ומבטלין. שנים הדרין בחצר אחת ולא עירבו, מבטל זה רשותו לזה עד שיעשה צרכיו, ויחזור זה ויבטל לזה: מר נמי לא ליבטיל. דהא מחצר לחצר הוא: התם. דאין חוזרין ומבטלין, טעמא לאו משום דה"ל כבן חצר אחרת, אלא משום דלא ליהוי מילי דרבנן: כחוכא. שחוק: ואטלולא. ליצנות: רב דאמר כרבנן. דאמרי במתני':* ביתו אסור להכניס ולהוציא לו ולהם. דאמרי: המבטל רשות חצירו לא ביטל רשות ביתו, אלמא: לא מסתלק ליה לגמרי, ולא הוה ליה כבן חצר אחרת: ושמואל כרבי אליעזר. דאמר בפרק "עושין פסין" (לעיל דף כו:): ביתו מותר להכניס ולהוציא להם, מאחר שביטל רשותו, דרשות ביתו נמי ביטל: אבל לענין איסתלוקי. לשוויה נפשיה כבן חצר אחרת, דלא לימני למהדר וקבולי רשותיה — מי אמר: אבל מאי דבטיל מיהא איסתלק לגמרי. מן החצר שביטל בפירוש — ודאי איסתלק, וה"ל כבן חצר אחרת: מי שנתן רשותו. לבני חצר, מפני ששכח ולא עירב, ולאחר שביטל הוציא מביתו לחצר — אוסר על בני חצר, דהדר שקליה לרשותיה: ר"מ. דאמר אפילו בשוגג הדרא ליה רשותיה, סבר: לא מסולק הוא, וגבי ביטול נמי חוזרין ומבטלין, והדרא ליה: לא דכ"ע אין חוזרין ומבטלין. דאיסתלק ליה, ובדין הוא דבשוגג לא הדרא ליה. אלא ר"מ קניס שוגג אטו מזיד, ובמזיד כולהו מודו דאף על גב דאיסתלק ליה, כיון דהדר — הדר, דהא לא זבניה. וכגון שלא החזיקו בני מבוי במבוי לאחר ביטול, קודם חזרה: צדוקי מאן דכר שמיה. מי קאמר ת"ק דבעי למיגר, דפליג רבן גמליאל ואמר דיכול לבטל: הרי הוא כגוי. דאינו יכול לבטל בלא שכירות: והוציאו את הכלים. והחזיקו במבוי, ושוב לא יוכל לחזור מביטולו. וכשקדש היום עסקינן, דחזקה דמבעוד יום לא מוכחא: והתניא. בניחותא, דפליגי רבנן בצדוקי: עד שלא יוציא. כליו במבוי, ויחזור ויטול את רשותו: ועשו צורכיכם. מבעוד יום עד שלא תחשך. קסבר ר' יהודה דלא פליג רבן גמליאל אלא צדוקי כנכרי ס"ל, ואין יכול לבטל. ולקמן* פריך, והתנן לרבי יהודה עד שלא יוציא. אלמא: לר' יהודה אליבא דרבן גמליאל יכול הוא לבטל. ובהא הוא דפליג רבי יהודה, דקסבר: לאחר חזקה נמי יכול לחזור בו: אימא

תוספות

אנא דאמרי אפילו כרבנן. הוה מצי למימר טעמא דלעיל דלא ליהוו מילי דרבנן חוכא ואטלולא.

קנסו שוגג אטו מזיד. לא שייך לקנסו שוגג אטו מזיד דעלמא, דהכא לא קנסי' לדידיה מידי, דבלאו הכי הוה אסיר, אלא כלומר: גזרו שוגג אטו מזיד:

רב אשי אמר רב ושמואל בפלוגתא דרבי אליעזר כו'. לית ליה לרב אשי הא דאמר רבא לעיל* אליבא דשמואל פעמים מבטלין ופעמים אין מבטלין, דהא מסיק לעיל*: כי קאמר — לרבנן, והכא לרב אשי הוה שמואל כרבי אליעזר:

אמר רבן גמליאל מעשה בצדוקי כו'. פירשתי במשנתנו:

והתניא. בניחותא ומייתי סיועא דפליגי רבנן בצדוקי, אבל מכל מקום בברייתא זו צ"ל חסורי מיחסרא, שלא יהא מעשה לסתור. ואינו נראה כלל לחלק, משום דמתני' סתמא קתני, אבל בברייתא מסיים בה: דברי ר"מ, שהיה שונה דברי רבותיו: **והוציאו** מה שאתם מוציאין והכניסו מה כו'. פירוש: או הכניסו, דבחד מינייהו הוי חזקה כשעושה דבר שהיה נאסר בלא ביטול. והא דקתני בסמוך: מי שנתן רשותו והוציא, בין בשוגג בין במזיד אוסר — לאו דוקא הוציא, אלא אפילו הכניס.

למימרא דכי מפקי אינהו כו'. מתוך הלשון משמע דמסיק אדעתיה שפיר לחלק בין מפיק אינהו והדר מפיק איהו, למפיק איהו ברישא. ותימה: דאם כן מאי קא קשיא ליה? הא איכא לאוקומי מתני' דמי שנתן רשותו כו' — כגון דמפיק איהו ברישא, כדמשני אביי: כאן שהחזיקו? ואין לומר דמי שנתן רשותו והוציא משמע ליה בכל ענין שהוציא, אפילו דמפקי ליה אינהו ברישא — דהא כי משני רב יוסף: אימא אינו אוסר, ע"כ לאו בכל ענין קתני, דהא בעי למימר כי מפיק איהו ברישא אוסר! ומפרש ר"י: דמי שנתן רשותו משמע ליה שנגמרה לגמרי מתנתו, דהיינו כי החזיקו, דאפקי אינהו ברישא, מדלא קתני "מי שביטל", דמשמע אמירה בעלמא כדקתני לעיל שהרי ביטל (א)לכם רשותו. ואביי דמוקי לה בשלא החזיקו — קא סבר דשייך למיתני "מי שנתן" אף על גב דאיירי בלא החזיקו. ומייתי סייעתא מברייתא דקתני "מי שנתן", וקתני סיפא: בד"א — בשלא החזיקו. אבל להא לא אצטריכא ליה לאביי לאתויי ראיה לחלק בין החזיקו ללא החזיקו, דמברייתא דלעיל שמעי' ליה, דקתני מהרו והוציאו כו' עד שלא יוציא הוא כו', ומאי אולמיה דהא מהאי: והא

עין משפט נר מצוה

מט א מיי' פ"ב מהל' עירובין הלכה ה סמג עשין א טוש"ע או"ח סי' שפא סעיף ז:
נ ב מיי' שם הלכה טז וסמג שם טוש"ע או"ח סי' שפה סעיף א:

רבינו חננאל

כשמואל לא צריכא לאיסתלוקי מחצר לחצר. נינח מר אדוכתיה וניבטל להו רשותיה ונשקלו חמימיה ונהדרו אינהו ונבטלו רשותייהו למר ולישתרי למר לאשתמושי בחצר כרב דאמר מבטלין מהני להני ותוב הדרי הני ומבטלי להני. א"ל בהא כשמואל סבירא לי דאמר אין חוזרין ומבטלין. א"ל ולאו הדא היא טעמא דשמואל בקמייתא דסבר כיון דבטיל רשותיה אסתליק ליה מההיא חצר והוה ליה בן חצר אחרת. ומשום הכי אין חוזרין ומבטלין ליה דאין מבטלין מחצר לחצר. א"ל לאו מהאי טעמא אלא משום דלא מהוויין מילי דרבנן כחוכא ואטלולא. כלומר כמו שחוק אלו מבטלין להן וחוזרין אחרי שעה ומבטלין אלו לאלו: **גופא** רב אמר מבטלין וחוזרין ומבטלין. ושמואל אמר אין מבטלין וחוזרין ומבטלין. נימא רב דאמר כר' אליעזר דתנן וכן שמעתי מר' אליעזר אנשי חצר ששכח א' מהן ולא עירב [ביתו] אסור להכנים ולהוציאו לו אבל הן מותרין ומקשינן והא תנן אסור לו ולהן. ופרקינן הא מתני' ר' אליעזר היא וסבר המבטל רשות חצרו רשות ביתו נמי ביטל ושמואל דאמר כרבנן דתנן הכא אנשי חצר ששכח אחד מהם ולא עירב ביתו אסור כו'. ואוקימנא כשביטל רשותו וקתני ביתו אסור לו ולהם ש"מ המבטל רשות חצירו רשות ביתו לא ביטל כו'. ורב מוקים לטעמי' אפילו כרבנן ושמואל אנא דאמרי אפילו לר' אליעזר כו' ואתא רב ששת לאוקומי לרב כר' מאיר דאמר מי שנתן רשותו והוציא בין בשוגג בין במזיד הרי זה אוסר. דייק כיון דבשוגג אוסר על בני החצר ש"מ דלא נסתלקה רשותו ואם יבטלו החצר לגביה חזרה רשותו אליו והותר בכל ושמואל אמר כר' יהודה דאמר בשוגג אינו אוסר. ונדחה ואסקה רב אשי דרב ושמואל בפלוגתא דר' אליעזר ורבנן פליגי ודברי רבי אליעזר מפורשין בסוף פ' עושין פסין לביראות: **ירושלמי** שלהם מותרין לו ולהם שביטלו רשותו (מהם) [מהו] שתחזור חלילה. תלמידי דרב משמיה דרב אמרי חוזרות חלילה *) הוא מותר והן אסורין פתר לה לצדדין הא מתניתא כו': **אר"ג** מעשה בצדוקי אחד כו'. אוקימנא חסורי מחסרא והכי קתני צדוקי אינו כגוי ר"ג אומר **) הרי הוא כגוי ואר"ג מעשה בצדוקי כו' עד והתניא הדר עם הגוי וצדוקי הרי אלו אוסרין עליו. ומעשה בצדוקי אחד שהיה דר עם ר"ג במבוי בירושלים. ואר"ג לבני מבוי מהרו והוציאו מה שתרצו להכנים שלא יוציאו (התועבה הזה) [התועב] ויאסר עליכם שהרי ביטל לכם רשות דברי ר"מ ואקשינן עלה ואי מפקי בני מבוי והדר מפיק הצדוקי מי לא אסר והתנן מי שנתן רשותו והוציא בין בשוגג בין במזיד אוסר דברי ר"מ. ודחי רב יוסף תני במתנית' אינו אוסר דברי ר"מ ופירק אביי פירוק אחר ואמר מתניתא בשלא החזיקו בני המבוי במבוי לפיכך אע"ג דביטל רשותו אם הוציא אוסר. אבל המבטל רשותו וקדמו בני המבוי והחזיקו במבוי אע"פ שהוציא אח"כ לא

*) [חסר כאן וכ"ה בירושלמי שמואל אמר אין חוזרות חלילה מתניתין פליגא על שמואל שלהן מותרין וכו' והתניא נתנו לו רשותן הוא מותר וכו']. **) [לפי הגהת מסוגיית הש"ס ז"ל להיפך דת"ק סבר לצדוקי ה"ה כגוי ור"ג סבר דלאו כגוי. וצ"ע].

הגהות הב"ח

(א) תוס' ד"ה למימר וכו' כדקתני לעיל שהרי בטל רשותו לכם ואביי:

גליון הש"ס

גמ' רב אמר מבטל וחוזרין ומבטלין. עי' לקמן דף עט ע"ב תוס' ד"ה וכו' קמ"ל:

מסורת הש"ס

[לקמן סט:] [לקמן עט:] (לקמן דף סט:) [גי' הערוך וטלולא] [לעיל כו:] [לקמן סט] [שבת ג: וש"נ] (לקמן דף עג:) [דף סו:] [דף סז.]

והתנן: *מי שנתן רשותו והוציא, בין בשוגג בין במזיד — אוסר, דברי רבי מאיר! אמר רב יוסף: אימא: "אינו אוסר". אביי אמר: לא קשיא; כאן — שהחזיקו בני מבוי במבוי, כאן — שלא החזיקו בני מבוי במבוי. והתניא: עד שלא נתן רשותו, הוציא בין בשוגג בין במזיד — יכול לבטל, דברי רבי מאיר. רבי יהודה אומר: בשוגג — יכול לבטל, במזיד — אינו יכול לבטל. מי שנתן רשותו — והוציא, בין בשוגג בין במזיד — אוסר, דברי רבי מאיר. רבי יהודה אומר: [א]במזיד — אוסר, בשוגג — אינו אוסר. במה דברים אמורים — בשלא החזיקו בני מבוי במבוי, אבל החזיקו בני מבוי במבוי — בין בשוגג ובין במזיד אינו אוסר.§ אמר מר: "ר' יהודה אומר בלשון אחרת: מהרו ועשו צורכיכם במבוי עד שלא תחשך ויאסר עליכם". אלמא: גוי הוא. והא אנן "עד שלא יוציא" תנן! אימא "עד שלא(א) יוציא היום". ואיבעית אימא: לא קשיא; כאן — במומר לחלל שבתות בצנעא, כאן — במומר לחלל שבתות בפרהסיא. כמאן אזלא הא דתניא: מומר וגילוי פנים — הרי זה אינו מבטל רשות. גילוי פנים מומר הוי?! אלא: מומר בגילוי פנים אינו יכול לבטל רשות, כמאן — כר' יהודה. ההוא (ב)דנפק בחומרתא דמדושא, כיון דחזייה לר' יהודה נשיאה כסייה. אמר: כגון זה מבטל רשות לר' יהודה.§ אמר רב הונא: איזהו ישראל מומר — זה המחלל שבתות בפרהסיא. א"ל רב נחמן: כמאן? אי כר"מ דאמר* חשוד לדבר א' חשוד לכל התורה כולה — אפ' בא' מכל איסורין שבתורה נמי! אי כרבנן — האמרי חשוד לדבר א' לא הוי חשוד לכל התורה כולה, עד

רש"י

אימא אינו אוסר. לר"מ: **והתניא.** בניחותא: **עד שלא נתן כו'.** אישראל שלא עירב קאי: **יכול לבטל.** אע"ג דמומר הוא לחלל שבת, יכול לבטל: **במזיד אין יכול לבטל.** קסבר ר' יהודה: מחלל שבת אין יכול לבטל בלא שכירות: **אוסר.** דהדר שקליה לרשותיה, ובשוגג נמי קנסו שוגג אטו מזיד: **במה דברים אמורים.** ר"מ קאמר לה. דאילו ר' יהודה ללישנא דמתני' קאמר דלא מהניא חזקה, וללישנא דברייתא דקאמר ר' יהודה עד שלא תחשך — טעמא לאו משום דלא מהניא חזקה הוא, אלא משום דקסבר הרי הוא כנכרי. וגבי ישראל שביטל איכא למימר דאפי' לר' יהודה מהניא חזקה, ובמה דברים אמורים — דברי הכל הוא: **והא אנן תנן.** לר' יהודה, "עד שלא יוציא". אלמא: מהני ביטול כל כמה דלא הדר ביה, ובחזקה הוא דפליג, דקסבר לא מהניא: **ואיבעית אימא.** מתני' דמשמע דלוקי מבטל — במומר לחלל בצנעא: **גילוי פנים.** חצוף: **מומר הוי.** בתמיה, וכי משום גילוי פנים חשיב ליה מומר: **מומר בגילוי פנים.** בפרהסיא: **כר' יהודה.** דלר"מ מומר לחלל שבת בפרהסיא מבטל: **בחומרתא דמדושא.** טבעת שחותמה ממין אחר, ואמרי' במסכת שבת (דף נט:): היא של אלמוג וחותמה של מתכת — אסור לצאת בה. חומרתא חותם. מדושא — לא אתפרש, ובדקתי במס' שבת ולא נשנית שם לענין שבת אלא לענין טומאה. ואומר אני: חומרתא דמדושא — קשר של בושם, אחד ממיני הבשמים. וכי האי גוונא אמרי' בשבת (דף סב:) דאין יוצאין בחומרתא דפילון, וחייב עליו חטאת משום דמשאוי הוא, ואינו תכשיט אדם: **כגון זה.** שמחלל שבת בצנעא: **איזהו ישראל מומר.** דחשבינן ליה מומר לכל מילי: **ר' מאיר ורבנן.** במס' בכורות בפר' "עד כמה" (דף ל:): עד

תוספות

והא תנן מי שנתן רשות כו'. הא דפריך אברייתא טפי מאמתני', משום דבברייתא מסיים בה דברי ר"מ.

הוציא בין בשוגג בין במזיד יכול לבטל. פירש בקונט': אע"ג דמומר הוא לחלל שבת — יכול לבטל. ר' יהודה אומר: במזיד אינו יכול לבטל, קסבר: מומר לחלל שבת אינו יכול לבטל בלא שכירות. ומדתולה טעם בקונטרס משום מומר, צריך לומר דבפרהסיא קאמר, כדמסיק דדוקא בפרהסיא לר' יהודה אינו יכול לבטל רשות, ואפ"ה לר"מ מבטל רשות. ובסמוך נמי, דקאמר מומר בגילוי פנים אינו מבטל רשות, כמאן — כר' יהודה. פירש בקונט': דלר"מ במומר לחלל שבת בפרהסיא מבטל. ותימה: דבמתני' קתני לדוקי הרי הוא כנכרי, כדמסיק לעיל. ומשמע בריש פירקין דרישא דמתני' ר"מ! וי"ל: דודאי כולה מתניתא עד ר' יהודה ר"מ קתני לה: כדמסיים בה בברייתא דברי ר"מ, דר"מ שונה דברי רבותיו, דברי חכמים ודברי ר"ג, ואפשר דסבר כר"ג דאמר לדוקי אינו כנכרי. (ג)ועוד: מדפליגי ר"מ ור' יהודה אליבא דר"ג, משמע נמי דכר"ג סבירא ליה. ומיהו, לא משמע כלל לפרש ברייתא זו מטעם מומר. חדא, דלמה ליה למנקט "הוציא"? הוה ליה למימר שחילל שבת, בכל מלאכה שחילל! ועוד: דמשמע דמשום דהוציא בשבת זו, דקתני "עד שלא נתן רשותו הוציא". ועוד: דמשמע סתם הוציא — בכל ענין, בין בצנעא בין בפרהסיא. כמו "מי שנתן רשותו והוציא" דסיפא. ומפרש ר"י: דהכא לאו מטעם מומר קאמר. דמומר לא שייך אלא באדם הרגיל לחלל שבתות ואינו נזהר כלל. אבל הכא — לא ברגיל איירי, אלא שבמקרה בעלמא אירע כך שהוציא, שהיה דחוק לפי שעה, ואם בשבת שעברה עשה כן, אפי' במזיד — לא היה מזיק כלום אפי' לר' יהודה, דלאו מומר הוא, כדפירשתי. אלא דוקא בשבת זו, דמאחר שהחזיק ברשותו — אינו יכול לבטל, כמו החזיק אחר ביטול דאין יכול עוד לבטל. ור"מ סבר דיכול לבטל, משום דלא חשיב מחזיק, כיון שאחר הנתינה לא החזיק:

כאן במומר לחלל שבתות בפרהסיא. לפירוש הקונט' שהוציא במזיד דלעיל חשיב מומר אפי' במילי דרבנן, וכן משמע, מדלא משני: הא והא בפרהסיא, הא — בדאורייתא, הא — בדרבנן. ותימה: דהא סתם לדוקי אינו נזהר כלל במילי דרבנן אפי' בפרהסיא, וכותים נמי שהיו מבטלים ונותנים רשות קודם שגזרו עליהם ר' אמי ור' אסי בפ"ק דחולין (דף ו:) — הא סתם כותים אינם מאמינים בדברי חכמים ואפי' בפרהסיא, ולא מזדהרי! וי"ל: שרגילים הם ליזהר, לפי שיראים מחכמים, כדאשכחן בנדה פרק "בנות כותים" (דף לג:*): אע"פ שצדוקים אנו — מתיראין אנו מפני הפרושים.

כיון דחזיה לר' יהודה נשיאה כסייה. וא"ת: והא ר' יהודה נשיאה גופיה נפק בחומרתא דמדושא, כדאמרי' במועד קטן בפרק "מי שהפך" (דף יב:)! ותירץ ר"ח: דהאי גברא דהכא נפק ברשות הרבים, והתם בחצר. ותימה: אפי' בחצר משמע התם דאסור, דקאמר על ר' אמי דאיקפד. מאי טעמא איקפד? אי משום חומרתא דמדושא — והא תניא השירים והנזמים והטבעות הרי הן ככל הכלים הניטלין בחצר, ואמר עלה דההיא ברייתא בסוף פרק "כירה" (שבת דף מו:), אמר עולא: מאי טעמא — הואיל ואיכא תורת כלי עליהן. ומדנקט טעמא דתורת כלי — משמע דאסור להתקשט בהם בחצר, דלא חזו בשבת, ואפ"ה שרי לצורך גופו ולצורך מקומו כמו כל דבר שיש תורת כלי עליו. אע"פ שמלאכתו לאיסור. כדאמר בפרק "במה אשה" (שם דף סד:): כל מקום שאסרו חכמים לצאת בו לרה"ר — אסור לצאת בו לחצר, חוץ מכבול ופאה נכרית. ואור"י: דודאי שירים ונזמים וטבעות אסור להתקשט בהם בחצר, שמא יצא בהן לרה"ר. וברשות הרבים אסור, דילמא שליף ומחוי, ולא חשיב גזירה לגזירה. אבל חומרתא דמדושא אינו תכשיט כלל, ואפי' הוציאה באצבעו לחצר ליכא איסור משום תכשיט, דלאו תכשיט הוא, אלא איסור טלטול בעלמא הוא דאיכא, כלשון ראשון שפירש בקונט': טבעת(ד) שחותמה ממין אחר, ולא כלשון ב' שפירש קשר של בשמים. וכן(ה) במועד קטן (דף יב:) דמדמה להו לשירים ונזמים וטבעות. ור' יהודה נשיאה לצורך גופו ולצורך מקומו אפקינהו, כגון לטייל בהם את התינוק או שאר עניינים. ומשום הכי קאמר מ"ט איקפד — דאיסור טלטול ליכא, שהרי יש עליה תורת כלי, כדתניא: השירים והנזמים שהם כשאר כלים שמלאכתן לאיסור, שניטלין לצורך גופן. וכיון דאיסור טלטול ליכא, איסור תכשיט פשיטא דליכא — דאינו עשוי לתכשיט, אלא כמו עץ בעלמא שעשוי לחתום בה חותמות. ור"ת מפרש: דתרווייהו נפקי לרה"ר, ר' יהודה נשיאה באצבעותיו, וההוא גברא בקומצו. ואם היה מותר לטלטל — היה יכול להתקשט בו לרה"ר, שתכשיט הוא, ולא שייך למגזר באיש(ו) שליף ומחוי. לכך לא הוצרך להביא ראיה אלא על הטלטול, דלא חשיב כחתיכה של מתכת או של עץ דעלמא. ומיהו, קשה לר"י: דזה היה יכול לדקדק מן מתני' דפ' "במה אשה יוצאה" (שבת דף נז.). דתנן: בטבעת שאין עליה חותם — לא תצא, ואם יצאה — אינה חייבת חטאת. ש"מ דחשיב ראויות לתכשיט. ועוד: דלישנא דנפק לא משמע בקומצו:

אי כר"מ אפי' בא' מכל איסורין נמי. וה"נ תניא בהדיא בבכורות בפ' "עד כמה" (ד' ל.): נחשד לדבר אחד — נחשד לכל התורה כולה, דברי ר"מ. ותימה: דבפ' "זה בורר" (סנהדרין דף כז.) גבי פלוגתא דאביי ורבא דאוכל נבלות להכעיס, ורבא אמר כשר, בעי לאוקמי רבא כר' יוסי דאמר: הוזם בדיני

עין משפט נר מצוה

נא א מיי' פ"ב מהלכות עירובין הלכה ו וסמג שם טוש"ע או"ח סי' שפא סעיף א:

רבינו חננאל

לא אסר. וכדתניא אם עד שלא נתן רשותו והוציא בין בשוגג בין במזיד יכול לבטל רשותו דברי ר' מאיר. ר' יהודה אמר בשוגג יכול לבטל. אבל אם הוציא במזיד לאסור עליהן אין יכול לבטל. מי שנתן רשותו והוציא (אחר) בין שוגג בין מזיד אוסר דברי ר' מאיר. ר' יהודה א' מזיד אוסר שוגג אינו אוסר. בד"א בשלא החזיקו בני המבוי במבוי. אבל אם הוציאו הכלים שלהם והחזיקו בני המבוי במבוי אע"ג שהוציא הוא בין בשוגג בין במזיד אין אוסר. אמר מר רבי יהודה אומר בלשון אחרת מהרו ועשו צורכיכם במבוי עד שלא תחשך ויאסר עליכם אלמא גוי הוא ואין ביטול רשות מועיל במקום גוי עד שישכיר. והא אנן תנן במתני' עד שלא יוציא ויאסור עליכם אלמא לאו גוי הוא ובביטול סגי ליה. אלא אם יוציא יאסר. ופרקינן מאי שלא יוציא דקתני במתני' שלא יוציא היום. כר' יהודה דקתני עד שלא תחשך. איבעית אימא לא קשיא הא דקתני ר' יהודה הצדוקי אינו מבטל אלא הרי הוא כגוי המחלל שבתות בפרהסיא והאי במומר דמחלל שבתות בצנעא והא דתניא מומר בגלוי פנים אינו מבטל רשותו כר' יהודה: **ההוא** מומר דנפק בחומרתא דמדושא *) אקפד ר' אמי אמר רב יוסף מ"ט אקפד והתניא השירים והנזמים והטבעות הרי הן ככלים המטלטלין בחצר וזה המומר נפיק בה בשבת ברה"ר. בהדי דחזייה לר' יהודה נשיאה כסייה להאי חומרתא כלומר נתבייש ממנו. אמר כגון זה שאינו מחלל שבת בגילוי פנים יכול לבטל רשות לר' יהודה. אמר רב הונא איזהו ישראל מומר זה המחלל שבת

*) דברי רבינו מסולא הבנה ונראה לחסר וצ"ל [וא"ת הא ר"י נשיאה גופא נפיק בחומרתא דמדושא כדאמרינן במו"ק ד' י"ב וי"ל דהתם מיירי בחצר וכמו דמסיק שם איקפד ר' אמי וכו']. כצ"ל וכן משמע בתו' כאן בד"ה כיון דהי' לפניהם הגי' כן בד' רבינו.

רב נסים גאון

כמאן אי כר' מאיר דאמר מומר לדבר אחד הוי מומר לכל התורה כולה אפילו אחד מכל איסורין שבתורה נמי ואי כרבנן הא אמרי חשוד לדבר אחד לא נחשד לכל התורה הא דר' מאיר משכחת לה בתוספתא דמאי (פרק ב) דתניא עם הארץ שקיבל עליו כל דברי חבירות ונחשד על דבר אחד נחשד על כולם דברי ר' מאיר ואיתא להא ברייתא בגמ' דבכורות בפרק עד כמה ישראל חייבין להטפל בבכור (דף ל) ודברי חכמים עד דהוי מומר לעבודת כוכבים אתניהו נמי בתוספתא בכורות (פרק ג) דתניא חשוד על עבודת כוכבים חשוד על כל המצות שבתורה ולא למפרע אלא מיכן ולהבא שנא' (במדבר טו) למן היום אשר צוה ה' והלאה:

מסורת הש"ס

[לקמן עמוד ב]

בכורות דף ל.

[נע"ש דהתם איתא אע"פ שבני צדוקים הן מתייראות מן הפרושים ולכן נ"ל כדאשכחן ביומא פרק א' דף יט: דשם איתא בלשון זה]

הגהות הב"ח

(א) גמ' אימא עד שלא יצא היום: (ב) שם ההוא גברא דנפק בחומרתא: (ג) תוס' ד"ה הוציא וכו' אינו כנכרי וכו"ג (ועוד מדפליגי) תא"מ ונ"ב ס"א ומדפליגי: (ד) ד"ה כיון וכו' טבעת של עץ שחותמה ממין אחר: (ה) בא"ד וכן משמע במועד קטן דמדמה: (ו) בא"ד ולא שייך למגזר באיש דילמא שליף:

עד דהוי מומר לעבודה זרה! אמר רב נחמן בר יצחק: ליתן רשות ולבטל רשות. *וכדתניא: [א]ישראל מומר משמר שבתו בשוק – מבטל רשות, שאינו משמר שבתו בשוק – אינו מבטל רשות. מפני שאמרו: ישראל נוטל רשות ונותן רשות, ובגוי עד שישכיר. כיצד? [ב]אומר לו: רשותי קנויה לך, רשותי מבוטלת לך – קנה, ואין צריך לזכות. רב אשי אמר: האי תנא הוא, דחמירא עליה שבת כע"ז, כדתניא* °"מכם" – ולא כולכם, פרט למומר. "מכם" – בכם חלקתי, ולא באומות. "מן הבהמה" – להביא בני אדם הדומין לבהמה. מכאן אמרו: [ג]מקבלין קרבנות מפושעי ישראל כדי שיחזרו בתשובה, חוץ מן המומר והמנסך יין והמחלל שבתות בפרהסיא. הא גופא קשיא: אמרת "מכם" ולא כולכם – להוציא את המומר, והדר תני: מקבלין קרבנות מפושעי ישראל! הא לא קשיא, רישא – במומר לכל התורה כולה, מציעתא – במומר לדבר אחד. אימא סיפא: חוץ מן המומר והמנסך יין. האי מומר היכי דמי? אי מומר לכל התורה – היינו רישא! אי לדבר אחד – קשיא מציעתא! אלא לאו הכי קאמר: חוץ מן המומר לנסך ולחלל שבתות בפרהסיא. אלמא: ע"ז ושבת כי הדדי נינהו. שמע מינה. §

מתני' *[ד]אנשי חצר ששכח אחד מהן ולא עירב – ביתו אסור מלהכנים ומלהוציא לו ולהם. ושלהם מותרין לו ולהם. [ה]נתנו לו רשותן – הוא מותר והן אסורין. היו שנים – אוסרין זה על זה. שאחד נותן רשות ונוטל רשות, שנים נותנין רשות ואין נוטלין רשות. מאימתי נותנין רשות? ב"ש אומרים: מבעוד יום, וב"ה אומרים: [ו]משחשיכה. מי שנתן רשותו והוציא, בין בשוגג בין במזיד – ה"ז אוסר, דברי ר' מאיר. ר' יהודה אומר: במזיד – אוסר, בשוגג – אינו אוסר. §

גמ' ביתו הוא דאסור, הא חצירו – שריא. היכי דמי? אי דבטיל – ביתו אמאי אסור? אי דלא בטיל – חצירו אמאי שריא? הכא במאי עסקינן – כגון שביטל רשות חצירו, ולא ביטל רשות ביתו. וקא סברי רבנן: *[ז]המבטל רשות חצירו – רשות ביתו לא ביטל, דדייר איניש בבית בלא חצר. "ושלהן מותר לו ולהן", מאי טעמא? דהוי אורח לגבייהו. § "נתנו לו רשותן – הוא מותר והן אסורין". § ונהוי אינהו לגביה כי אורחין! חד לגבי חמשה – הוי אורח, חמשה לגבי חד – לא הוי אורח. ש"מ: *מבטלין וחוזרין ומבטלין! הכי קאמר: נתנו לו רשותן מעיקרא, הוא מותר והן אסורין. § היו שנים – אוסרין זה על זה. § פשיטא! לא צריכא דהדר חד מינייהו ובטיל ליה לחבריה. מהו דתימא: לישתרי, קמ"ל: דכיון דבעידנא דבטיל לא הוה ליה שריותא בהאי חצר. § "שאחד נותן רשות". § הא תו למה לי? אי נותן – תנינא, אי נוטל – תנינא! סיפא איצטריכא ליה: שנים נותנין רשות. הא נמי פשיטא! מהו דתימא: ליגזר

תורה אור

עד דהוי מומר לע"ג. דההוא ודאי חשוד לכל מילי. דאמר מר: חמורה ע"ג שכל המודה בה ככופר בכל התורה כולה, דכתיב: "וכי תשגו ולא תעשו את כל המצות האלה" ובע"ג משתעי קרא, בהוריות (דף ח.): אמר רב נחמן. איזהו ישראל מומר דקאמר רב הונא לעיל – לענין ביטול רשות קאמר: בשוק. בפרהסיא, ואע"ג דמחלל בצנעא: כיצד. אישראל קאי: רשותי קנויה לך. או רשותי מבוטלת לך: לזכות. בקנין סודר: רב אשי אמר. לעולם מומר דקאמר רב הונא – לכל מילי קחשיב ליה מומר, וכרבנן ס"ל. והאי תנא הוא, דאלימא ליה שבת כע"ג: אדם כי יקריב מכם פרט למומר. דאין מקבלין קרבנות ד"מכם" משמע מקצתכם: מכם. מדכתיב האי מיעוטא גבי ישראל, ולא כתיב כי יקריב מן האדם קרבן – ש"מ בישראל הוא דחלק ומיעט מומר: ולא באומות. שמקבלין קרבן מכולם. כדתניא: "איש" מה ת"ל "איש איש" לרבות את הנכרים שנודרין נדרים ונדבות כישראל, ב"הכל שוחטין" (חולין דף יג:): להביא בני אדם הדומין לבהמה. רשעים, שעשו עצמן כבהמה שאינה מכרת את בוראה – מקבלין מהן קרבן: מקבלין קרבנות. של נדבה מפושעי ישראל, דהאי קרא בנדרים ונדבות משתעי, דכתיב "כי יקריב": כדי שיחזרו בתשובה. דאי דחינן להו בידים, תו לא הדרי: והמנסך את היין. לע"ג: אלא לאו הכי קאמר. מקבלין קרבנות מפושעי ישראל המומרים לדבר אחד: חוץ מן המומר לנסך את היין או לחלל שבת. דכמומר לכל התורה דמי, דאימעיט ליה "מכם" ולא כולכם: **מתני'** ביתו אסור להכנים ולהוציא. מביתו לחצר, בין הוא בין שאר בני החצר. ובגמרא מפרש כשביטל להן רשות שהיה לו בחצר, ולא ביטל להן רשות ביתו. הלכך, הוה ליה רשות ביתו רשות דידיה, וחצר רשותא דידהו: ושלהם. בתים שלהן מותרין להוציא מהן לחצר, בין הוא בין הן, דהא בתים שלהן וחצר רשות אחת הן: נתנו לו. הם רשות חצרן: הוא מותר. להוציא מביתו לחצר: והן אסורין. אפי' מביתו לחצר ואע"ג דרשות אחת הן ובגמרא מפרש טעמא: היו שנים. ששכחו ולא עירבו, ושאר בני חצר בטלו להן רשותן – שניהן אוסרין זה על זה, מפני שהוא של שניהן. והבתים מיוחדין, כל בית לבעליו, ואין מוציא מרשות המיוחדת לו לרשות שלו ושל חבירו: הרי זה אוסר. דמיהדר ומשקל רשותא הוא וחזר בו מביטולו: **גמ'** הא חצירו. רשות שהיתה לו בחצירו, שריא לבני החצר ומותר להן להוציא מבתיהן לחצר, כדקתני מתניתין להדיא: אי דבטיל. רשותו לבני חצר: ביתו אמאי אסור. הרי נתן להן ביתו ונסתלק: ואי דלא בטיל. מידי, רשות חצירו מאן שרייה: וקסברי רבנן. תנא דמתני' דסתמא היא, ופליגא אדר' אליעזר דאמר בפרק "עושין פסין" (לעיל דף כו:): ביתו אסור להכניס ולהוציא לו, אבל להם מותר. המבטל רשות חצירו – רשות ביתו ביטל: דהוי אורח לגבייהו. כיון דמביתו לא מפיק, אע"ג דמשתמש בחצר – לא מיהדר ומשקל רשותיה הוא, אלא כשאר אורחין: והן אסורין. אפי' מביתו לחצר, דכיון דמשתמשי בחצר אע"ג דלאו מבית דידהו מפקי הוה ליה משקל רשותא דחמשה לגבי חד לא דמו לאורחין: חמשה. לאו דוקא: שמע מינה מבטלין כו'. דמשמע נתנו לו רשות – ארישא קאי, דקתני: ושלהן מותר לו ולהן, דבטל להם רשותו חזרו הם ונתנו לו רשותן – הוא מותר: היו שנים. ששכחו ולא עירבו עם השאר, ובטלו להן חבריהן רשותן – אוסרין שניהן זה על זה: פשיטא. דאי הוו תרוייהו לחודייהו מעיקרא הוו אסרי אהדדי: לא צריכא דהדר חד ובטיל לחבריה. רשות עצמו, ואת חלקו ברשות שבטלו להן חבריהן: מהו דתימא לישתרו. דהוו להו כחמשה ששרויין בחצר ולא עירבו, דמבטלי רשותא לחד מינייהו: קמ"ל. דלא דמי. דאילו התם כל חד וחד מבטל ליה רשותיה. אבל הכא, כיון דשאר בני חצר לאו להאי דפייש לחודיה בטלי, אלא לתרוייהו, כי הדר חד ומבטל לאידך – רשותא דידיה מצי לבטולי, רשותא דאקני ליה חבריה – לא מצי לבטולי. דכיון דבעידנא דבטלי להו הנך קמאי רשותייהו, אפ"ה לא הוה להאי מבטל שריותא בהאי חצר, משום דאסרי אהדדי – אשתכח דבטול דקמאי לא אהני, וכי הדר מבטל האי – לא מצי לאקנויי רשותא דידהו, דהא לא קנייה: נותן תנינא. ושלהם מותר לו ולהן. ואי לאו דבטיל(א) ליה, אמאי משתרו: נוטל תנינא. נתנו לו, אלמא: יחיד נוטל רשות: ליגזר

בדיני ממונות – כשר בדיני נפשות. ומשני: דרבא אפי' כר"מ, דאמר עד זומם פסול לכל התורה כולה. דע"כ לא קאמר ר"מ התם אלא גבי עד זומם דממון, דרע לשמים ולבריות. אבל הכא, דרע לשמים ולא לבריות – לא שמע מיניה דלית ליה לר"מ חשוד לאחד מכל האסורין להוי חשוד לכל התורה כולה לרבא. דלא אמר מקילתא לחמירתא אלא בעד זומם דממון דווקא, דרע לשמים ורע לבריות. ומיהו, לאביי דהתם ניחא, וקיי"ל כוותיה. וי"ל: דאפי' לרבא חשוד לדבר אחד, דרע לשמים ולא לבריות – חשוד לכל התורה כולה. בכיולא בה דרע לשמים ולא לבריות, אפי' מקילתא לחמירתא. וחשוד לדבר אחד דרע לשמים ורע לבריות – חשוד לכל התורה כולה, אפילו רע לשמים ורע לבריות:

ושלהם מותר לו ולהן. דהוי אורח לגבייהו. פירש ר"ח: דאמר בירושלמי*: אכסנאי אינו אוסר לעולם. ואומר ר"י: דלא דמי להכא כלל, דהתם איירי(ב) כגון הבא לדור במבוי לשם אכסנאות, ולא לקבוע עצמו. דהכי איתא התם: אית תנא תני *קסדור אוסר מיד, ואכסנאי לאחר שלשים. ואית תנא תני: קסדור אוסר לאחר שלשים, ואכסנאי אינו אוסר לעולם. מ"ד קסדור אוסר מיד – ברגיל, ואכסנאי לאחר שלשים – בשאינו רגיל. מ"ד קסדור לאחר שלשים – כאלין דעלין ברשות, ואכסנאי אינו אוסר לעולם – כאלין דלא עלין ברשות:

בעא

(הפרקין הל' ב)

[צ"ל גרס קסדור וכ"ה בירושלמי]

נב א מיי' פ"ב מהלכות עירובין הלכה יו סמג עשין א טוש"ע או"ח סי' שפה סעיף ג:

נג ב מיי' וסמג שם טוש"ע או"ח סי' שפ סעיף א:

נד ג מיי' פ"ג מהלכות מעשה קרבנות הלכה ד וסמג עשין קפג:

נה ד מיי' פ"ב מהלכות עירובין הלכה א סמג עשין א טוש"ע או"ח סי' שפ סעיף א:

נו ה מיי' שם הלכה ג טוש"ע שם סעיף ד:

נז ו ז מיי' שם הל' ב טוש"ע שם סעיף א:

רבינו חננאל

בפרהסיא וא"ל רב נחמן אי לר' מאיר אפילו עבר על אחת מכל המצות שבתורה מומר הוי אי לרבנן עד דהוי מומר לע"ז. ואמר רב אשי כי האי תנא הוא דאמר דחמיר ליה שבת כע"ז. דתניא אדם כי יקריב מכם קרבן לה' מכם ולא כלכם להוציא את המומר לכל התורה כולה שאין מקבלין ממנו קרבן. מכם בכם חלקתי ולא באו"ה ש"מ (באומות העולם) שאין מקבלין קרבנות מפושעי ישראל שעברו על מקצת מצות כדי שיחזרו בתשובה חוץ מן המומר לנסך יין לע"ז ולחלל שבתות בפרהסיא שאלו כמומר לכל התורה כולה הן לפיכך אין מקבלין מהן. כיוצא בו ישראל מומר שמשמר שבתו בשוק ואינו מחלל אלא בסתר מבטל רשות. ושאינו משמר שבתו בשוק אלא מחלל בגילוי פנים אינו מבטל רשות מפני שאמרו ישראל מבטל רשות ונותן רשות. ובאוה"ע עד שישכיר. כיצד אמר לו רשותי קנויה לך. רשותי מבוטלת לך קנה ואין צריך לזכות: **מתני'** אנשי חצר ששכח אחד מהן ולא עירב ביתו אסור להכנים ולהוציא כו' אוקימנא בשביטל רשותו בחצר. וקסברו רבנן המבטל רשות חצרו רשות ביתו לא ביטל. לפיכך ביתו אסור. שלהן מותרין לו ולהן כלומר בתיהן מותרין לו ולהן. כיון דביטל רשותו הוה ליה אכסנאי לגבייהו: **ירושלמי** אכסנאי אינו אוסר לעולם נתנו לו רשותם הוא מותר דהא נתנו לו רשותם אבל הן אסורין דליכא למימר דאכסנאין אינון לגבייהו דחמשה גבי חד לא הוו אורחין ומקום שמואל למתניתין הכי לא תימא דאינון דבטלו להון רשותהו הדרו אינהו ונתנו לו רשותם דשמעינן מינה דמבטלין וחוזרין ומבטלין אלא הכי קתני

(תוספ' פ"ה) ע"ז דף סד: חולין דף ו.

חולין דף ה.

לעיל דף כו.

[לעיל כו:]

[לעיל סח:]

הגהות הב"ח

(א) רש"י ד"ה נותן וכו' דבטיל להו אמאי: (ב) תום' ד"ה ושלהם וכו' דהתם איירי בעו"ג הבא. נ"ב כ"ה בסה"א ובאשר"י ובטור סי' שפ"ד:

ומבטלין אלא הכי קתני מתני' נתנו לו הם רשותם מעיקרא והוא לא נתן להם הוא מותר והן אסורין. היו שנים אוסרין זה על זה פי' היו ב' שלא עירבו ונתנו להם כל בני החצר רשותם אלו שנים כל חד מהן אוסר על חבירו אע"פ שאח"כ חזר האחד ונתן רשותו לחבירו כיון דבעידנא דבטילי להו כל בני החצר להני תרי לא הות שריותא לחצר דהא חד אסר על חבריה לא מיבטיל. והא מיפריש הכי *) בחיצונה דתניא ואין שנים שעירבו נותנין רשות לשנים שלא עירבו דהדר חד מינייהו ובטיל ליה לחבריה מהו דתימא נישתרי ליה קמ"ל **) שלא עירבו ואע"ג דאמרי להו קני ע"מ להקנות:

*) פי' בברייתא לקמן דף ע'. **) נראה דצ"ל ואין שנים שלא עירבו נותנים רשותם לשנים שלא עירבו ואע"ג וכו'.

ליגְזַר דִּילְמָא אָתֵי לְבַטּוּלֵי לְהוּ – קמ"ל.§ "וְאֵין נוֹטְלִין רְשׁוּת".§ לָמָּה לִי? לָא צְרִיכָא, [א]אַף עַל גַּב דְּאָמְרִי לֵיהּ "קְנֵי עַל מְנָת לְהַקְנוֹת". בְּעָא מִינֵּיהּ אַבַּיֵּי מֵרַבָּה: חֲמִשָּׁה שֶׁשְּׁרוּיִין בְּחָצֵר אַחַת, וְשָׁכַח אֶחָד מֵהֶן וְלֹא עֵירֵב, כְּשֶׁהוּא מְבַטֵּל רְשׁוּתוֹ, צָרִיךְ לְבַטֵּל לְכָל אֶחָד וְאֶחָד, אוֹ לֹא? א"ל: *[ב]צָרִיךְ לְבַטֵּל לְכָל אֶחָד וְאֶחָד. אֵיתִיבֵיהּ: [ג]אֶחָד שֶׁלֹּא עֵירֵב – נוֹתֵן רְשׁוּתוֹ לְאֶחָד שֶׁעֵירֵב, שְׁנַיִם שֶׁעֵירְבוּ – נוֹתְנִין רְשׁוּתָן לְאֶחָד שֶׁלֹּא עֵירֵב, וּשְׁנַיִם שֶׁלֹּא עֵירְבוּ – נוֹתְנִין רְשׁוּתָן לִשְׁנַיִם שֶׁעֵירְבוּ, אוֹ לְאֶחָד שֶׁלֹּא עֵירֵב. אֲבָל לֹא אֶחָד שֶׁעֵירֵב נוֹתֵן רְשׁוּתוֹ לְאֶחָד שֶׁלֹּא עֵירֵב. וְאֵין שְׁנַיִם שֶׁעֵירְבוּ נוֹתְנִין רְשׁוּתָן לִשְׁנַיִם שֶׁלֹּא עֵירְבוּ, וְאֵין שְׁנַיִם שֶׁלֹּא עֵירְבוּ נוֹתְנִין רְשׁוּתָן לִשְׁנַיִם שֶׁלֹּא עֵירְבוּ. קָתָנֵי מִיהַת רֵישָׁא: "אֶחָד שֶׁלֹּא עֵירֵב נוֹתֵן רְשׁוּתוֹ לְאֶחָד שֶׁעֵירֵב". ה"ד? אִי דְּלֵיכָּא אַחֲרִינָא בַּהֲדֵיהּ – בַּהֲדֵי מַאן עֵירֵב? אֶלָּא פְּשִׁיטָא – דְּאִיכָּא אַחֲרִינָא בַּהֲדֵיהּ. וְקָתָנֵי: לְאֶחָד שֶׁעֵירֵב! וְרַבָּה – הָכָא בְּמַאי עָסְקִינַן – דַּהֲוָה וּמִית. אִי דַּהֲוָה וּמִית – אֵימָא סֵיפָא: אֲבָל אֵין אֶחָד שֶׁעֵירֵב נוֹתֵן רְשׁוּתוֹ לְאֶחָד שֶׁלֹּא עֵירֵב. וְאִי דַּהֲוָה וּמִית – אַמַּאי לָא? אֶלָּא פְּשִׁיטָא דְּאִיתֵיהּ, וּמִדְּסֵיפָא אִיתֵיהּ, רֵישָׁא נַמִי אִיתֵיהּ! מִידֵּי אִירְיָא?! הָא כִּדְאִיתָא וְהָא כִּדְאִיתָא! תֵּדַע, דְּקָתָנֵי סֵיפָא דְּרֵישָׁא: וּשְׁנַיִם שֶׁלֹּא עֵירְבוּ נוֹתְנִין רְשׁוּתָן לִשְׁנַיִם שֶׁעֵירְבוּ. לִשְׁנַיִם – אִין, לְאֶחָד – לָא. וְאַבַּיֵּי אָמַר: מַאי "לְב'" – לְאֶחָד מִב'. אִי הָכִי לִיתְנֵי: לְאֶחָד שֶׁעֵירֵב, אוֹ לְאֶחָד שֶׁלֹּא עֵירֵב! קַשְׁיָא. "אֶחָד שֶׁלֹּא עֵירֵב נוֹתֵן רְשׁוּתוֹ לְאֶחָד שֶׁעֵירֵב". לְאַבַּיֵּי – דְּאִיתֵיהּ, וְקמ"ל: דְּאֵין צָרִיךְ לְבַטֵּל רְשׁוּת לְכָל אֶחָד וְאֶחָד. לְרַבָּה – דַּהֲוָה וּמִית, וְלָא גָּזוּר זִימְנִין דְּאִיתֵיהּ. "וּשְׁנַיִם שֶׁעֵירְבוּ נוֹתְנִין רְשׁוּתָן לְאֶחָד שֶׁלֹּא עֵירֵב". פְּשִׁיטָא! מַהוּ דְּתֵימָא: כֵּיוָן דְּלֹא עֵירֵב – לִיקַנְסֵיהּ, קמ"ל. "וּב' שֶׁלֹּא עֵירְבוּ נוֹתְנִין רְשׁוּתָן לִשְׁנַיִם שֶׁעֵירְבוּ". לְרַבָּה – תָּנָא סֵיפָא לְגַלּוּיֵי[א] רֵישָׁא, לְאַבַּיֵּי – ב' שֶׁלֹּא עֵירְבוּ אִיצְטְרִיכָא לֵיהּ. סד"א: לִגְזַר דִּלְמָא אָתֵי לְבַטּוּלֵי לְהוּ, קמ"ל. "אוֹ לְאֶחָד שֶׁלֹּא עֵירֵב". לָמָּה לִי? מַהוּ דְּתֵימָא: הָנֵי מִילֵּי – הֵיכָא דִּמְקְצָתָן עֵירְבוּ וּמִקְצָתָן לֹא עֵירְבוּ, אֲבָל הֵיכָא דְּכוּלָּן לֹא עֵירְבוּ – לִיקַנְסִינְהוּ כְּדֵי שֶׁלֹּא תִּשְׁתַּכַּח תּוֹרַת עֵירוּב, קמ"ל. "אֲבָל אֵין אֶחָד שֶׁעֵירֵב נוֹתֵן רְשׁוּתוֹ לְאֶחָד שֶׁלֹּא עֵירֵב". לְאַבַּיֵּי – תָּנָא סֵיפָא לְגַלּוּיֵי רֵישָׁא, לְרַבָּה – אַיְּדֵי דְּתָנָא רֵישָׁא, תָּנָא נַמִי סֵיפָא. "וְאֵין שְׁנַיִם שֶׁעֵירְבוּ נוֹתְנִין רְשׁוּתָן לִשְׁנַיִם שֶׁלֹּא עֵירְבוּ". הָא, תּוּ לָמָּה לִי? לָא צְרִיכָא, דְּבַטֵּיל לֵיהּ חַד מִינַּיְיהוּ לְחַבְרֵיהּ. מַהוּ דְּתֵימָא: לִשְׁתְּרֵי לֵיהּ, קמ"ל, כֵּיוָן דִּבְעִידָּנָא דְּבַטֵּיל לָא הֲוָה לֵיהּ שַׁרְיוּתָא בְּהַאי חָצֵר – לָא. "וְאֵין שְׁנַיִם שֶׁלֹּא עֵירְבוּ נוֹתְנִין רְשׁוּתָן לִשְׁנַיִם שֶׁלֹּא עֵירְבוּ". הָא, תּוּ לָמָּה לִי?[ב] לָא צְרִיכָא, דְּאָמְרִי "קְנֵי עַל מְנָת לְהַקְנוֹת". בְּעָא מִינֵּיהּ רָבָא מֵרַב נַחְמָן: יוֹרֵשׁ, מַהוּ שֶׁיְּבַטֵּל רְשׁוּת? הֵיכָא

ליגזר. דאי מבטלי אינהו ליחיד, אתו למימר נמי: יחיד מבטל לשנים: ואין נוטלין רשות למה לי. הא תנא ליה: היו שנים – אוסרין זה על זה: לא צריכא. משנה יתירה, לאשמועינן דאפי' אמרו ליה קמאי קני על מנת להקנות, והדר איהו ובטיל לחבריה – לא מישתרי האי בתרא. דמהו דתימא שליחא שוינהו, קא משמע לן כיון דלא קנה איהו לאישתרויי, לא מצי לאקנויי: אחד שלא עירב כו'. כגון ג' דיורין בחצר, השנים עירבו והשלישי לא עירב. מבטל לאחד מן המעורבין, ומותר. דהאי בהדי חבריה עירב. אלמא: אין צריך לבטל אלא לאחד, דכולהו הוו כחד: ושנים שלא עירבו נותנין רשותן לשנים. הדרים עמהן ועירבו, או ליחיד שלישי הדר עמהן ולא עירב לא הוא ולא הן: אבל אין אחד שעירב. עם אחר, נותן רשותו ליחיד שלישי שדר עמהן ולא עירב דכי בטיל ליה איהו רשותיה – אכתי איכא חבריה דאסר עליה: לשנים שלא עירבו. כדאמרינן לעיל: שנים אין נוטלין רשות: דהוה ומית. ועל כרחך דרבה בשיירא שחנתה בבקעה והקיפוה חצר, ונטו שם איש אהלו מוקי לה. דכי מת אין ליורשיו שם כלום דאי בחצר ממש – הא איכא יורשין, וכיון דאילו הוה אבוהון קיים הוה אסר – אינהו נמי אסרי: תדע. מרישא דהוה ומית עסקינן דאי איתיה, צריך להאי לבטוליה ליה: סיפא דרישא. מרישא דמתניתא עד אבל כו' חדא בבא היא, הלכך, סיפא דההיא קרי ליה סיפא דרישא: לאחד לא. דצריך לבטל לכל אחד ואחד: אי הכי ליתני לאחד שעירב. כדתנא ברישא ואנא ידענא דתרי נינהו דאין עירוב בלא שנים: או לאחד שלא עירב. סיפא דההיא היא, דהכי תנא: לשנים שעירבו או לא' שלא עירב: אחד שלא עירב כו'. השתא מפרש לה לכולה, אמאי איצטריך למיתנייהו לכולהו: ולא גזרינן כו'. כלומר: אי קשיא כיון דמית, פשיטא דמבטל ליה להאי דפייש, דהא קתני לה סיפא דאפי' שנים מבטלין ליחיד: ושנים שעירבו כו'. פשיטא דהכא ליכא למגזר דלמא אתי יחיד לבטולי להו. דאי מבטל להו – שפיר דמי, דהא עירבו. וכיון דאורי ביחיד דמצי לבטולי – מה לי חד מה לי תרי: כיון דלא עירב ליקנסיה. דמרישא לא נפקא לן, דרישא איירי דהאי דלא עירב בטיל להנך דעירבו: תנא הך סיפא לגלויי רישא. דבדהוה ומית עסקינן. רישא דקתני לאחד שעירב, דאילו איתיה לאידך בעי לבטולי ליה, כדקתני בהך סיפא: ולאביי. דמתרץ הך סיפא מאי לשנים – לאחד משנים, למה לי דתנייה? הא תנא ליה רישא דיחיד מבטל לאחד משנים, מה לי חד מבטל מה לי תרין מבטלין: הני מילי כו'. דכל הני בטולין דלעיל איכא מקצתייהו דעירבו: תורת עירוב. תורת עירוב מן התינוקות הבאים אחרי כן: לאביי תנא הך סיפא. דלא איצטריך, דהא פשיטא דאיכא חד דלא בטיל ליה רשותיה אלא להכי תנייה – לאשמועינן דכולה מתניתא בדאיתנהו לתרווייהו המעורבין עסקינן, ואפילו הכי קתני רישא דרישא אחד שלא עירב נותן רשותו לאחד שעירב דאין צריך לבטל רשותיה לכל אחד ואחד ואיהו לא אסר אחבריה: איידי דתנא רישא. "אחד שלא עירב נותן רשותו לאחד שעירב" תנא הך סיפא דאיפכא לא ולעולם רישא בדהוה ומית וסיפא בדאיתנהו: הא תו למה לי. פשיטא דאסרי אהדדי: הכי גרסינן: כיון דבעידנא דבטיל להו הנך כו'. ולעיל פרישנא לה: קני על מנת להקנות. ממשנה יתירה נפקא לן. דאי לאו הכי לא איצטריך למיתנייה, ולעיל פרישנא לה: יורש. ששכח אביו ולא עירב, ומת בשבת, ולא ביטל רשותו. מהו שיבטל היורש: היכא

בעא מיניה אביי מרבה כו'. לא שמיע ליה ברייתא דלעיל דסוף פ"ב (דף כו:): כשהוא מבטל רשותו – אין צריך לבטל לכל אחד. ומשמע התם דפלוגתא היא דר"א ורבנן, וההוא ברייתא כר"א. ואין לומר דלרבנן מיבעיא ליה ופשט ליה, דצריך לבטל – דאם כן מאי פריך מברייתא דבסמוך?

הכא במאי עסקינן דהוה ומית. פירש רש"י: דעל כרחך דרבה בשיירא שחנתה בבקעה והקיפוה חצר, ונטו בה איש אהלו מוקי לה, דכי מת אין ליורשיו שם כלום. דאי בחצר ממש – איכא יורשין, וכיון דאילו הוה אבוהון קיים הוה אסר – אינהו נמי אסרי. ובחנם דחק, דאין היורש אוסר אלא א"כ הולך לדור שם, דלעיל בפ' "מי שהוציאוהו" (דף מז.) פסקינן כר"ש, דתנן לקמן פרק "כיצד משתתפין" (דף פו.), ר"ש אומר: אפי' הניח את ביתו והלך לשבות אצל בתו באותה העיר – אינו אוסר, שכבר הסיח מלבו. ומיהו, אי בעו לאוקומי כר"מ, דאמר כשהלך לשבות בעיר אחרת א' נכרי ואחד ישראל – אוסר. וקאמרינן נמי לקמן בפירקין (דף עג:): בית התבן ובית הבקר ובית העצים ובית האוצרות הרי זה אוסר עליו – צריך לאוקומי בשיירא שחנתה בבקעה. א"נ: כגון שזה עצמו שעירב הוא יורש: יורש מהו שיבטל. בשלא עירב האב מיירי, כדפי' בקונט', דאם עירב – הא תני לקמן (עמוד ב'): א' מבני חצר שמת והניח רשותו לאחד מן השוק, מבעוד יום – אינו אוסר. ואיירי כגון שבא היורש לדור שם בשבת, דאם לא כן – לא בעי ביטול, דהוי כמו בית התבן ובית הבקר דלא אסר. כדאמר רבי יהודה לקמן בפירקין (עג:) דאינו אוסר אלא מקום דירה. ור"ש דפסיק פרק "מי שהוציאוהו" (לעיל מז.) כוותיה קאמר, דאפילו הלך לשבות אצל בתו באותה העיר אינו אוסר. ומיהו, אם היה היורש דר באותה חצר – שמא היה אוסר להם בית אביו כשירש בשבת, אע"פ שלא בא לדור שם, אפילו עירב עם חביריו בערב שבת – אפילו הכי בעי ביטול, ולא מהני עירובן לגבי אותה חצר שירש בשבת

נח א טוש"ע א"ח סי' שפ סעיף ד:
נט ב מיי' פ"ב מהל' עירובין הלכה ב טוש"ע שם סעיף א:
ס ג מיי' שם הלכה ג טוש"ע שם סעיף ד:

רבינו חננאל

בעא מיניה אביי מרבה ה' ששרויין בחצר אחת ושכח אחד מהם ולא עירב כשהוא מבטל צריך לבטל רשות לכל אחד ואחד אי לא א"ל צריך לבטל רשות לכל אחד ואחד איתיביה אחד שלא עירב נותן רשותו לאחד שעירב. היכי דמי אי ליכא אחריני בהדיה [בהדי] מאן מערב דקתני לאחד שעירב אלא פשיטא דאיכא אחרינא ועירב בהדיה [ותירץ רבה דבתר] (ובתר) הכי מת. ואקשינן אימא סיפא אבל אין אחד שעירב נותן רשותו לאחד שלא עירב ואי איהו דעריב בהדיה מת והשתא ליכ' אחרינא בהדיה אמאי לא אלא פשיטא דאיתיה ואסר עליה ומדסיפא איתיה רישא נמי איתיה ודחי רבא מידי איריא סיפא איתיה רישא ליתיה תדע דבעינן לכל חד וחד דקתני סיפא דרישא ושנים שלא עירבו נותנין רשותן לשנים שעירבו [מאי לאו] שנים ממש. ש"מ בעינן ביטול רשות לכל אחד ואחד ודחי אביי מאי לשנים דקתני אחד (לשנים) [משנים] ואקשינן אי הכי ליתני לאחד שעירב או לאחד שלא עירב דמשמע דאיכא אחריני בהדיה ואפי' הכי בחד סגי ליה אלא מדלא קתני הכי אלא קתני לשנים שעירבו לשנים שעירבו ממש הוא שמעינן מינה דבעינן ביטול לכל חד וחד ונדחה אביי בקושיא פי' להא מתניתא פסקא פסקה פשוטה היא

לעיל כו:

הגהות הב"ח

(א) גמ' סיפא לגלויי רישא כצ"ל וכן בסמוך: (ב) שם לא צריכא דאע"ג דאמרי קני:

עין משפט
נר מצוה

סא א מיי' פ"ב מהל' עירובין הלכה ב סמג עשין א טוש"ע א"ח סי' שפא סעיף ו:
סב ב מיי' שם הל' ז וסמג שם טוש"ע א"ח סי' שעא סעיף ד:
סג ג מיי' שם וטוש"ע שם סעיף ג:

הֵיכָא דְּאִי בָּעֵי לְעָרוּבֵי מֵאֶתְמוֹל מָצֵי מְעָרֵב — בַּטּוּלֵי נַמִּי מָצֵי מְבַטֵּל. אֲבָל הַאי, כֵּיוָן דְּאִי בָּעֵי לְעָרוּבֵי מֵאֶתְמוֹל — לָא מָצֵי מְעָרֵב — לָא מָצֵי מְבַטֵּל, אוֹ דִּלְמָא: יוֹרֵשׁ כְּרַעֵיהּ דַּאֲבוּהּ הוּא? א"ל: [א]אֲנִי אוֹמֵר מְבַטֵּל, וְהָנֵי דְּבֵי שְׁמוּאֵל תָּנוּ: אֵין מְבַטֵּל. אֵיתִיבֵיהּ: זֶה הַכְּלָל, כֹּל שֶׁמּוּתָּר לְמִקְצָת שַׁבָּת — הוּתַּר לְכָל הַשַּׁבָּת, וְכֹל שֶׁנֶּאֱסַר לְמִקְצָת שַׁבָּת — נֶאֱסַר לְכָל הַשַּׁבָּת, חוּץ מִמְּבַטֵּל רְשׁוּת. "כֹּל שֶׁהוּתַּר לְמִקְצָת שַׁבָּת מוּתָּר לְכָל הַשַּׁבָּת" — כְּגוֹן עֵירֵב דֶּרֶךְ הַפֶּתַח וְנִסְתַּם הַפֶּתַח, עֵירֵב דֶּרֶךְ חַלּוֹן וְנִסְתַּם חַלּוֹן. "זֶה הַכְּלָל" — לְאַתּוֹיֵי מָבוֹי שֶׁנִּיטְּלוּ קוֹרוֹתָיו אוֹ לְחָיָיו. "כֹּל שֶׁנֶּאֱסַר לְמִקְצָת שַׁבָּת — נֶאֱסַר לְכָל הַשַּׁבָּת כּוּלָּהּ" — כְּגוֹן שְׁנֵי בָתִּים בִּשְׁנֵי צִידֵּי רה"ר, וְהִקִּיפוּם גּוֹיִם מְחִיצָה בַּשַּׁבָּת. "זֶה הַכְּלָל" לְאַתּוֹיֵי מַאי? לְאַתּוֹיֵי מֵת גּוֹי בַּשַּׁבָּת. וְקָתָנֵי "חוּץ מִמְּבַטֵּל רְשׁוּת", (א)אִיהוּ — אִין, יוֹרֵשׁ — לָא! אֵימָא חוּץ מִתּוֹרַת בִּיטּוּל רְשׁוּת. אֵיתִיבֵיהּ: [ב]אֶחָד מִבְּנֵי חָצֵר שֶׁמֵּת, וְהִנִּיחַ רְשׁוּתוֹ לְאֶחָד מִן הַשּׁוּק, מִבְּעוֹד יוֹם — אוֹסֵר, מִשֶּׁחֲשֵׁיכָה — אֵינוֹ אוֹסֵר. [ג]וְאֶחָד מִן הַשּׁוּק שֶׁמֵּת וְהִנִּיחַ רְשׁוּתוֹ לְאֶחָד מִבְּנֵי חָצֵר, מִבְּעוֹד יוֹם — אֵינוֹ אוֹסֵר, מִשֶּׁחֲשֵׁיכָה — אוֹסֵר. אַמַּאי אוֹסֵר? נִיבְטִיל! מַאי "אוֹסֵר" נַמִּי דְּקָתָנֵי — עַד שֶׁיְּבַטֵּל. תָּא שְׁמַע: יִשְׂרָאֵל וְגֵר שֶׁרוּיִין בִּמְגוּרָה אַחַת, וּמֵת גֵּר מִבְּעוֹד יוֹם, אע"פ

היכא דאי בעי לערובי כו'. כְּלוֹמַר: אָבִיו שֶׁהָיָה אֶתְמוֹל רָאוּי לְעָרֵב, הָיָה יָכוֹל לְבַטֵּל: **אבל האי דלא מצי לערובי אתמול.** דְּלֹא הָיָה לוֹ חֵלֶק בָּהּ – לֹא: **כל שהותר למקצת שבת כו'.** מְפָרֵשׁ לָהּ וְאָזֵיל: ה"ג: כְּגוֹן עֵירֵב דֶּרֶךְ הַפֶּתַח כו' זֶה הַכְּלָל לְאַתּוֹיֵי מָבוֹי שֶׁנִּיטְּלָה קוֹרָתוֹ אוֹ לְחָיָיו: **עירב דרך הפתח.** שְׁתֵּי חֲצֵירוֹת וּפֶתַח א' בֵּינֵיהֶם, וְעֵירְבוּ ע"י אוֹתוֹ פֶּתַח. וּבַשַּׁבָּת נָפְלָה כְּנֶגְדּוֹ מַפּוֹלֶת, וְנִסְתַּם — מוּתָּרִים לְהִשְׁתַּמֵּשׁ מִזּוֹ לְזוֹ ע"י זְרִיקָה וְדֶרֶךְ חוֹרִין קְטַנִּים. דְּאע"ג דְּאֵין עֵירוּב בֵּין ב' חֲצֵירוֹת בְּלֹא פֶּתַח, כְּדִתְנַן (לקמן עו.) בְּחַלּוֹן שֶׁבֵּין ב' חֲצֵירוֹת הָכָא – שַׁבָּת הוֹאִיל וְהוּתְּרָה הוּתְּרָה: **זה הכלל** לְאַתּוֹיֵי מָבוֹי שֶׁנִּיטְּלָה קוֹרָתוֹ אוֹ לְחָיָיו. בַּשַּׁבָּת, אע"ג דְּאִשְׁתַּקּוּל מְחִיצּוֹת דִּידֵיהּ – שָׁרֵי, הוֹאִיל וְאִישְׁתְּרֵי בֵּין הַשְּׁמָשׁוֹת. וּמֵרֵישָׁא לָא שָׁמְעִינַן לַהּ. דְּהָתָם אִיתְנְהוּ לִמְחִיצּוֹת אֲבָל הָכָא לֹא. וְהָכִי אָמְרִינַן לַהּ בְּשִׁילְהֵי פִּירְקָא קַמָּא (דף יז:): **והקיפום גוים מחיצה.** דַּאֲסוּרִין לְבַטֵּל זֶה לָזֶה כְּדֵי שֶׁיִּשְׁתַּמֵּשׁ בָּהּ אֶחָד מֵהֶן, דְּהוֹאִיל וְאִי הֲווּ בָּעוּ עָרוּבֵי מֵאֶתְמוֹל – לָא מָצוּ מְעָרְבִי. אֲבָל אִי לָא הֲוָה הָתָם אֶלָּא חַד בַּיִת – שָׁרֵי, דִּמְחִיצָּה הַנַּעֲשֵׂית בַּשַּׁבָּת – מְחִיצָּה הִיא: **זה הכלל.** דְּרֵישָׁא נַמִּי קָאֵי אַסֵּיפָא, לְאַתּוֹיֵי מֵת נָכְרִי בַּשַּׁבָּת. דְּכֵיוָן דְּאִי בָּעוּ לְעָרוּבֵי מֵאֶתְמוֹל לָא מָצוּ מְעָרְבִי – הַשְׁתָּא נַמִּי לָא מְבַטְּלֵי. וּמֵרֵישָׁא דְּסֵיפָא לָא שָׁמְעִינַן לַהּ, אִי לָא תָּנֵי' בְּ"זֶה הַכְּלָל", דְּהָתָם לָא מָצוּ לְעָרוּבֵי מֵאֶתְמוֹל כְּלָל, אֲבָל הָכָא מָצוּ לְעָרוּבֵי ע"י שְׂכִירוּת: **חוץ מן המבטל רשות.** שֶׁשָּׁכַח וְלֹא עֵירֵב. שֶׁאַף ע"פ שֶׁנֶּאֱסַר לְמִקְצָת שַׁבָּת, יֵשׁ לוֹ תַּקָּנָה בַּשַּׁבָּת. וּמִדְּלָא קָתָנֵי חוּץ מִשֶּׁבִּיטֵּל רְשׁוּת וְיוֹרֵשׁ – שְׁמַע מִינַּהּ: יוֹרֵשׁ לֹא: **אימא חוץ מתורת ביטול רשות.** וְיוֹרֵשׁ בִּכְלָל דְּכַרְעֵיהּ דַּאֲבוּהּ הוּא, וְתוֹרַת בִּיטּוּל נוֹהֶגֶת בּוֹ: **מבעוד יום.** שֶׁעֲדַיִין לֹא קָנָה עֵירוּבוֹ שֶׁל רִאשׁוֹן, הֲרֵי זֶה מִן הַשּׁוּק אוֹסֵר, וְאע"פ שֶׁאֵינוֹ דָּר כָּאן. כִּדְתַנְיָא לְקַמָּן בְּהַאי פִּירְקָא: [דף עב:] *מִי שֶׁיֵּשׁ לוֹ בֵּית הַתֶּבֶן וּבֵית הַבָּקָר בַּחֲצַר חֲבֵירוֹ – אוֹסֵר עָלָיו: **משחשיכה אינו אוסר עליו.** שֶׁהֲרֵי הוּתַּר לְמִקְצָת שַׁבָּת: **ואחד מן השוק.** שֶׁהָיָה לוֹ בֵּית דִּירָה בְּחָצֵר זוֹ: **מבעוד יום אינו אוסר.** שֶׁהֲרֵי יְעָרֵב זֶה עִם שְׁכֵנָיו: **משחשיכה.** דְּאֵינוֹ יָכוֹל לְעָרֵב – אוֹסֵר. וְאִי יוֹרֵשׁ מְבַטֵּל רְשׁוּת – אַמַּאי אוֹסֵר: **ישראל וגר** גָּרְסִינַן. גֵּר שֶׁמֵּת וְאֵין לוֹ יוֹרְשִׁין, הַמַּחֲזִיק בִּנְכָסָיו זָכָה בָּהֶן: **מגורה.** גּוֹרֶן הוּא, וְחָלוּק בַּחֲדָרִים, וְהָיָה לְכָל אֶחָד פִּתְחוֹ בֶּחָצֵר, וְאוֹסְרִין זֶה עַל זֶה: אע"פ

בשבת. כדתניא לקמן בשמעתין: אחד מן השוק שמת והניח רשותו לאחד מבני חצר, מבעוד יום – אינו אוסר. פי': לפי שבן חצר מערב עם חביריו. משחשיכה – אוסר. פי': דלא מהני עירוב לענין אותו חצר שירש בשבת. ומיהו, הא לא אפשר לומר דמיירי כשהיה היורש דר עם אביו – דאם כן, אי בעו לאיערובי מאתמול מצו מערבין קרינן ביה, דאם נותן פת משלו הוי עירוב, אף ע"פ שלא זיכה לאביו. כדאמר לעיל פרק "מי שהוציאוהו" (דף מט:): חמשה שגבו את עירובן, כשהן מוליכין את עירובן למקום אחר – א' מוליכו ע"י כולן. דאם לקח הפת משלו ונתן בחצר של שיתוף – מועיל לכולם, כדפירש התם בקונטרס: דשליחות דכולהו קעביד, הואיל ועירבו יחד. ועוד, תניא לקמן בפירקין*: חמשה חבורות ששבתו בטרקלין, ב"ה אומר: עירוב אחד לכולם. אע"פ שיש לחלק, דהתם כולם שוים בבית זה כמו זה ואין זה, טפל לזה, אבל הכא שהבן טפל לאביו אם נתן הבן פת אינו מועיל – מ"מ אינו דומה כלל לחלק. ומהא דאמר לעיל (דף סד.): אפילו שכירו ולקיטו נותן את עירובו – אין ראיה לכאן, דלמא הני מילי בנכרי, אבל בישראל – לא: [דף עב.]

אבל האי כיון דאי בעי לערובי מאתמול לא מצי לערב. אפילו למ"ד לעיל (דף סז.): מבטלין, גבי מת נכרי בשבת – יכול להיות דאין מבטלין. כיון דהתם הוא דאותו רשות שהוא מבטל עכשיו היה לו כח לבטל מאתמול, אלא שלא היה מועיל מפני הנכרי דאוסר. אבל הכא, האי רשות דמבטל השתא – אין לו כח לבטל מאתמול אלא משעה שירש, והוי כב' בתים בשני צידי רה"ר דאין מבטלין, דלא היה בידו רשות זה מאתמול. ולמאן דאמר לעיל נמי אין מבטלין – יכול להיות דזה מבטל, כדאמר יורש כרעיה דאבוה הוא:

לאתויי מת נכרי בשבת. פירש בקונטרס: כיון דאי בעו לערובי מאתמול לא מצו מערבי – השתא נמי לא מצו מבטלי. ומרישא דסיפא לא שמעינן ליה, אי לא אתי בזה הכלל. דהתם לא מצו מערבי מאתמול כלל, אבל הכא מצו מערבי ע"י שכירות. משמע מתוך פירושו דאיירי דאתא נכרי מערב שבת, ובעי למימר דאין מבטלין כשמת, וכ"ש דאם לא מת. דבעי תרתי, שכירות וביטול. ולא יתכן לפי מה שפיר' לעיל(ב), דהתם כולי עלמא מודו דמבטלין גבי מת נכרי בשבת מהו אלא בדאתא נכרי בשבת איירי הכא. ואי לאו "זה הכלל" הוי אמינא דהכא מבטל, כיון דהאי רשותא דקמבטל הוי בידו מאתמול, ולא דמי לב' בתים: **וקתני** חוץ ממבטל רשות. פי' בקונטרס: דפריך לר"נ, דאמר דמבטלין, מדלא קתני חוץ ממבטל רשות ויורש, שמע מינה: יורש לא. ודבר תימה הוא, מה דיוק הוא זה? ור"ח פירש: דפריך לשמואל, דאמר אין מבטלין. וזה לשונו: זה הכלל, כל שנאסר למקצת שבת. כגון שני בתים בשני צידי רה"ר, חוץ ממבטל רשות אע"פ שנאסר למקצת שבת, משעה שביטל רשותו הותרה שאר שבת. לא שנא הוא, ל"ש יורש. מדקתני חוץ מן המבטל רשות, דייקי מיניה: כל מי שיש לו רשות עכשיו יכול לבטל. ופריק לה לברייתא הכי: חוץ מתורת ביטול, דכי איתא לאוסר מעיקרא והשתא בטל רשות – הותרה לשאר שבת. לאפוקי יורש, דלא הוי ליה רשות הכא בעידנא דקדש היום, ולא הוי ליה לערובי. דלא איתמר תורת ביטול אלא היכא דליכא עירוב, ומאן דלא יכול לערובי – לא יכול לבטל רשותו, עכ"ל. אע"פ שהקושיות אחרות לר"נ – אין לחוש אם זאת לשמואל. ורבינו חננאל בעצמו פירש(ג) דמותבינן לר"נ, משמע מתוך פירושו דחוץ ממבטל רשות קאי אשני בתים משני צידי רשות הרבים והקיפום נכרים מחיצות בשבת, שמועיל שם ביטול. והיכא דלא ביטלו זה לזה קאמר דנאסר לכל השבת כולה. וקשה: דאם כן מאי נאסר למקצת שבת דקאמר? ונראה לומר לפירושו דאיירי בעירבו, וכיון שלא חל העירוב בתחילת השבת – תו לא חייל כשבאו אחרי כן והקיפום בשבת. וכן מת נכרי בשבת איירי כשעירבו מערב שבת ובטל עירובן מפני הנכרי, דכשמת תו לא חייל. אבל ביטול מועיל בתרוייהו, כדקתני "חוץ ממבטל רשות". ומדמהני(ד) ביטול ב' בתים, אע"פ שלא היה לו כח לבטל רשות של חצר זה מאתמול, דרה"ר היה – כל שכן יורש, דיש לו כח לבטל. וקשה לדבי שמואל דאמרי אין מבטלין. והוא הדין דהוה מצי למיפרך מהך ברייתא לרב חסדא ורב ששת, דאמרי לעיל אין מבטלין גבי ב' בתים. ונראה דלמאי דמשני "אימא חוץ מתורת ביטול" – לא קאי אב' בתים, אלא אבני חצר ששכח אחד מהן ולא עירב, שיכול לבטל רשות באמצע השבת. ומיהו, אם נאמר לפי המסקנא כן גם לדברי המקשה לחוק על חנם, לומר דקאי אב' בתים, דבלאו הכי יכול להקשות כמו שפירש ר"ח, דחוץ ממבטל רשות דמשמע דכל מי שיש לו רשות עכשיו יכול לבטל: **אחד** מבני חצר שמת והניח רשותו לא' מן השוק מבעוד יום אוסר כו'. הך ברייתא איירי בהכי דבן חצר מערב עם חבריו, אבל בן השוק אין מערב עמהם אפי' כשירש מבעוד יום. ולא משום שלא יוכל לערב עמהן לפי שאינו דר שם, דמסתמא לא גרע בהכי לענין עירוב וביטול רשות, כיון דאסר עלייהו, כדקתני מבעוד יום אוסר. אלא אורחא דמילתא היא, דבן חצר רגיל לערב עם חבריו שהוא צריך להשתמש בחצר, כיון שהוא דר שם. אבל אותו שבשוק אין יכול לערב לפי שאינו רגיל להשתמש. וקסבר האי תנא כמ"ד לקמן בפירקין (דף עב:): בית התבן ובית הבקר – הרי זה אוסר עליו:

תא שמע ישראל וגר כו'. קסבר רבא דמכח הגר חשיב כמו יורש, דהוי כרעיה דאבוה. דאי לאו הכי – לא קשה מידי לרב נחמן: כלך

רבינו חננאל

בעא מיניה רבא מרב נחמן יורש מהו שיבטל רשות כגון שמת אביו בשבת מאי יורש כרעא דאבוה הוא ומבטל או לא א"ל אני אומר מבטל והני דבי שמואל תנא אין מבטל ומותבינן לתנא דבי שמואל מהא דתניא זה הכלל כל שהותר מקצת שבת כגון שעירבו דרך הפתח ונסתם הפתח או דרך חלון ונסתם החלון מותר כל השבת כולה וזה הכלל למה לי לאתויי מבוי שניטלה קורתו או לחייו שמותרין בשבת כולה זה הכלל כל שנאסר למקצת שבת כגון ב' בתים בב' צידי רה"ר *) אע"פ שנאסר במקצת שבת משעה שביטל רשותו הותרה שאר שבת ל"ש הוא ל"ש יורש. מדקתני חוץ מן המבטל רשות דייקינן מינה כל מי שיש לו רשות עכשיו יכול לבטל ופריק תני לברייתא הכי חוץ מתורת ביטול דבר איתיה לאוסר מעיקרא והשתא בטיל רשותי' הותרה מקצת שבת ולאפוקי יורש דלא הוה ליה רשותא הכא בעידנא דקדש היום ולא הוה ליה לערובי דלא אתמר תורת ביטול אלא היכא דליכא עירוב ומאן דלא יכול לערוב לא יכול לבטל רשותיה. תוב אהדרינן ומותבינן לרב נחמן אחד מבני חצר שמת כו' עד אחד מן השוק שמת והניח רשותו לאחד מבני החצר מת מבע"י בע"ש וזכה בן החצר בנכסיו אינו אוסר שכבר עירב עם בני החצר [גם] הוא. מת משחשיכה אוסר שכבר נאסר במקצת שבת ואמאי אוסר אי אמרת יורש מבטל יבטל השתא ונשתרו ופריק רב נחמן מאן אוסר נמי דקתני עד שיבטל אבל אם (לא) ביטל הותרו בני החצר לטלטל: ת"ש וגוי ששבתו במגורה. פי' בדירה אחת מלשון לגור בארץ וי"א מלשון נהרסו ממגורות כי הוביש דגן. ומת הגר

*) [חסר כאן וצ"ל חוץ ממבטל רשות אע"פ שנאסר וכו' וכן העתיקו התוס' בד"ה וקתני לשון רבינו:]

הגהות הב"ח

(א) גמ' חוץ ממבטל רשות (איהו אין יורש לא) תא"מ ונ"ב ס"א אין זה והכי מוכח בתוספות: (ב) תוס' ד"ה לאתויי וכו' לפי מה שפירשתי לעיל נ"ב ד' סז בד"ה אומר אני ולפי מה שכתבתי לעיל י"ל דגם דברי רש"י כאן הם נכונים דרש"י ז"ל פי' ג"כ בבא הגוי בשבת ואפ"ה מקרי מצו לעירובי על ידי שכירות אי הוה בא הגוי מאתמול מש"כ בב' בתים וע' לעיל: (ג) ד"ה וקתני וכו' ורבינו חננאל עצמו פי' דתוב מותבינן לר"נ: (ד) בא"ד ומדמהני ביטול בשני בתים:

אע"פ שֶׁהֶחֱזִיק יִשְׂרָאֵל אַחֵר בִּנְכָסָיו — אוֹסֵר. מִשֶּׁחֲשֵׁיכָה, אע"פ שֶׁלֹּא הֶחֱזִיק יִשְׂרָאֵל אַחֵר — אֵינוֹ אוֹסֵר. הָא גּוּפָא קַשְׁיָא! אָמְרַתְּ "מִבְּעוֹד יוֹם אע"פ שֶׁהֶחֱזִיק", וְלָא מִיבָּעֲיָא כִּי לֹא הֶחֱזִיק?! אַדְּרַבָּה, כִּי לֹא הֶחֱזִיק לֹא אָסַר! אָמַר רַב פַּפָּא: אֵימָא, "אע"פ שֶׁלֹּא הֶחֱזִיק". וְהָא "אע"פ שֶׁהֶחֱזִיק" קָתָנֵי! ה"ק: [א]אע"פ שֶׁלֹּא הֶחֱזִיק מִבְּעוֹד יוֹם אֶלָּא מִשֶּׁחֲשֵׁיכָה, כֵּיוָן דַּהֲוָה לֵיהּ לְהַחֲזִיק מִבְּעוֹד יוֹם — אוֹסֵר. מִשֶּׁחֲשֵׁיכָה, אע"פ שֶׁלֹּא הֶחֱזִיק יִשְׂרָאֵל אַחֵר — אֵינוֹ אוֹסֵר. "אע"פ שֶׁלֹּא הֶחֱזִיק יִשְׂרָאֵל אַחֵר" וְלָא מִיבָּעֲיָא כִּי הֶחֱזִיק?! אַדְּרַבָּה, כִּי הֶחֱזִיק אָסַר! אָמַר רַב פַּפָּא: אֵימָא, "אע"פ שֶׁהֶחֱזִיק". וְהָא "אע"פ שֶׁלֹּא הֶחֱזִיק" קָתָנֵי! ה"ק: [ב]אע"פ שֶׁהֶחֱזִיק מִשֶּׁחֲשֵׁיכָה, כֵּיוָן דְּלָא הֲוָה לֵיהּ לְהַחֲזִיק מִבְּעוֹד יוֹם — אֵינוֹ אוֹסֵר. קָתָנֵי מִיהַת רֵישָׁא "אוֹסֵר", אַמַּאי אוֹסֵר? נִיבְטֵל! מַאי "אוֹסֵר" דְּקָתָנֵי, [ג]עַד שֶׁיְּבַטֵּל. ר' יוֹחָנָן אָמַר: מַתְנִי' מַנִּי ב"ש הִיא, דְּאָמְרִי: אֵין בִּיטּוּל רְשׁוּת בַּשַּׁבָּת. דִּתְנַן: מֵאֵימָתַי נוֹתְנִין רְשׁוּת? ב"ש אוֹמְרִים: מִבְּעוֹד יוֹם. וּב"ה אוֹמְרִים: מִשֶּׁתֶּחְשַׁךְ. אָמַר עוּלָּא: מ"ט דְּב"ה — נַעֲשָׂה כְּאוֹמֵר *"כַּלֵּךְ אֵצֶל יָפוֹת". אָמַר אַבָּיֵי: מֵת גּוֹי בַּשַּׁבָּת מַאי "כַּלֵּךְ אֵצֶל יָפוֹת" אִיכָּא? אֶלָּא, הָכָא בְּהָא קָמִיפַּלְגִי; דב"ש סָבְרִי: בִּיטּוּל רְשׁוּת מִיקְנָא רְשׁוּתָא הוּא, וּמִיקְנָא רְשׁוּתָא בַּשַּׁבָּת — אָסוּר. וּב"ה סָבְרִי: אִסְתַּלּוּקֵי רְשׁוּתָא בְּעָלְמָא הוּא, וְאִסְתַּלּוּקֵי רְשׁוּתָא בַּשַּׁבָּת שַׁפִּיר דָּמֵי.§

מתני' **[ד]בַּעַל הַבַּיִת שֶׁהָיָה שׁוּתָּף לִשְׁכֵנָיו, לָזֶה בְּיַיִן וְלָזֶה בְּיַיִן — אֵינָן צְרִיכִין לְעָרֵב. לָזֶה בְּיַיִן וְלָזֶה בְּשֶׁמֶן [ה]צְרִיכִין לְעָרֵב. ר"ש אוֹמֵר: אֶחָד זֶה וְאֶחָד זֶה — אֵינָן צְרִיכִין לְעָרֵב.§

גמ' אָמַר רַב: [ו]וּבִכְלִי אֶחָד. אָמַר רָבָא: דַּיְקָא נַמִּי, דְּקָתָנֵי "לָזֶה בְּיַיִן וְלָזֶה בְּשֶׁמֶן — צְרִיכִין לְעָרֵב". אִי אָמְרַתְּ בִּשְׁלָמָא רֵישָׁא בִּכְלִי אֶחָד וְסֵיפָא בִּשְׁנֵי כֵלִים — שַׁפִּיר. אֶלָּא אִי אָמְרַתְּ רֵישָׁא בִּשְׁנֵי כֵלִים וְסֵיפָא בִּשְׁנֵי כֵלִים, מַה לִּי יַיִן וְיַיִן מַה לִּי יַיִן וְשֶׁמֶן?! א"ל אַבָּיֵי: יַיִן וְיַיִן — רָאוּי לְעָרֵב, יַיִן וְשֶׁמֶן — אֵין רָאוּי לְעָרֵב. "ר"ש אוֹמֵר: אֶחָד זֶה וְאֶחָד זֶה אֵין צְרִיכִין לְעָרֵב".§ וַאֲפִילּוּ לָזֶה בְּיַיִן וְלָזֶה בְּשֶׁמֶן?! אָמַר רַבָּה: הָכָא בְּמַאי עָסְקִינַן — בְּחָצֵר שֶׁבֵּין שְׁנֵי מְבוֹאוֹת. *וְר"ש לְטַעֲמֵיהּ; (א)דִּתְנַן, אָמַר ר"ש: לְמָה הַדָּבָר דּוֹמֶה — לְשָׁלֹשׁ חֲצֵירוֹת הַפְּתוּחוֹת זוֹ לָזוֹ וּפְתוּחוֹת לִרה"ר, עֵירְבוּ שְׁתַּיִם הַחִיצוֹנוֹת עִם הָאֶמְצָעִית — הִיא מוּתֶּרֶת עִמָּהֶן וְהֵן מוּתָּרוֹת עִמָּהּ, וּשְׁתַּיִם הַחִיצוֹנוֹת אֲסוּרוֹת זוֹ עִם זוֹ. א"ל אַבָּיֵי: מִי דָּמֵי? הָתָם קָתָנֵי "שְׁתַּיִם הַחִיצוֹנוֹת אֲסוּרוֹת", הָכָא קָתָנֵי "אֵין צְרִיכִין לְעָרֵב" כְּלָל! מַאי "אֵין צְרִיכִין לְעָרֵב" — שְׁכֵנִים בַּהֲדֵי בַּעַל הַבַּיִת, אֲבָל שְׁכֵנִים בַּהֲדֵי הֲדָדֵי — צְרִיכִין לְעָרֵב.

וְרַב

רש"י

אע"פ שֶׁהֶחֱזִיק כו'. לְקַמָּן פָּרֵיךְ: מַאי אע"פ שֶׁהֶחֱזִיק כו': **אוֹסֵר.** הַמַּחֲזִיק עַל הַדָּר: **מִשֶּׁחֲשֵׁיכָה.** שֶׁכְּבָר קָנָה עֵירוּב: **אע"פ.** פָּרֵיךְ לְקַמָּן: כִּי לֹא הֶחֱזִיק הֲוָה לֵיהּ זֶה דָּר יָחִיד, וְלֵיכָּא דְּאָסַר עֲלֵיהּ. וְהַאי דְּאָסַר מִשּׁוּם דְּהֶחֱזִיק הוּא, וְהָכִי אִיבָּעֵי לֵיהּ לְמִיתְנֵי: אִם הֶחֱזִיק יִשְׂרָאֵל אַחֵר בִּנְכָסָיו – אוֹסֵר(ב): **אע"פ שֶׁלֹּא הֶחֱזִיק.** מִבְּעוֹד יוֹם מִיָּד, וְהִמְתִּין עַד שֶׁחֲשֵׁיכָה, וְאִיכָּא הֶיתֵּר לְמִקְצָת שַׁבָּת – אוֹסֵר. כִּדְמְפָרֵשׁ לְקַמָּן, הוֹאִיל וְהָיָה לוֹ כֹּחַ לְהַחֲזִיק בָּהּ מִבְּעוֹד יוֹם אִם יִרְצֶה – נִמְצֵאת רְשׁוּת זוֹ תְּלוּיָה וְעוֹמֶדֶת, וְלֹא הָיָה הוּתַּר לְמִקְצָת שַׁבָּת: **ה"ק כו'.** וְחַסּוּרֵי מִיחַסְּרָא. וְהַאי "אע"פ" – אַשֶּׁלֹּא הֶחֱזִיק קָאֵי. וְהַאי הֶחֱזִיק דְּקָתָנֵי – הָיָה לוֹ לְהַחֲזִיק קָאָמַר: **אֵימָא אַף אע"פ שֶׁהֶחֱזִיק.** אֵינוֹ אוֹסֵר, הוֹאִיל וְהוּתַּר לְמִקְצָת שַׁבָּת: **ה"ק.** חַסּוּרֵי מִיחַסְּרָא' וְהַאי אע"פ אַשֶּׁהֶחֱזִיק קָאֵי. וְשֶׁלֹּא הֶחֱזִיק דְּקָתָנֵי – ה"ק: וְלֹא הָיָה לוֹ לְהַחֲזִיק מִבְּעוֹד יוֹם, שֶׁלֹּא הָיְתָה רְשׁוּת זוֹ תְּלוּיָה בֵּין הַשְּׁמָשׁוֹת אֶלָּא מוּחְזֶקֶת לַגֵּר, אִם הָיָה זֶה בָּא לְהַחֲזִיק – לֹא הָיָה יָכוֹל, הֶיתֵּר הָיָה בָּהּ לְמִקְצָת שַׁבָּת וְאֵינוֹ אוֹסֵר: **ר' יוֹחָנָן אָמַר.** הָנֵי תַּרְתֵּי מַתְנִיתָא בַּתְרַיְיתָא דְּאָמְרִי יוֹרֵשׁ אוֹסֵר – ב"ש הִיא: **כַּלֵּךְ אֵצֶל יָפוֹת.** גַּבֵּי תּוֹרֵם אֶת שֶׁל חֲבֵירוֹ שֶׁלֹּא מִדַּעַת תַּנְיָא (ב"מ דף כב.): בָּא בַּעַל הַבַּיִת וּמְצָאוֹ שֶׁהוּא תּוֹרֵם, וְאָמַר לוֹ "כַּלֵּךְ אֵצֶל יָפוֹת", אִם יֵשׁ לוֹ יָפוֹת מֵהֶן – תְּרוּמָתוֹ תְּרוּמָה, דְּגַלֵּי אַדַּעְתֵּיהּ דְּנִיחָא לֵיהּ, וְאָמְרִינַן כְּמַאן דְּשַׁוְיֵיהּ שָׁלִיחַ מֵעִיקָּרָא דָּמֵי. ה"נ: כֵּיוָן דְּבַטֵּיל הָשְׁתָּא – גַּלֵּי דַּעְתֵּיהּ דְּמֵעִיקָּרָא בְּשָׁרְיוּתָא נִיחָא לֵיהּ, אֶלָּא שֶׁשָּׁכַח וְלֹא עֵירֵב, וְלָא הֲוָה לֵיהּ אַקְנוּיֵי רְשׁוּתָא בְּשַׁבָּת: **וּמִיקְנָא רְשׁוּתָא בַּשַּׁבָּת אָסוּר.** דְּדָמֵי לְמִקָּח וּמִמְכָּר: **מתני' שֶׁהָיָה שׁוּתָּף עִם שְׁכֵנָיו.** שֶׁבַּמָּבוֹי, לְשֵׁם שׁוּתָּפוּת בְּעָלְמָא, וְלֹא לְשֵׁם שִׁיתּוּף: **לָזֶה בְּיַיִן וְלָזֶה בְּיַיִן כו'.** בַּגְּמָרָא מוֹקֵי לָהּ בִּכְלִי א': **לָזֶה בְּיַיִן וְלָזֶה בְּשֶׁמֶן.** אֵין זֶה שִׁיתּוּף וְאֵין יָכוֹל לִסְמוֹךְ עָלָיו – שֶׁהֲרֵי חָלוּק בִּשְׁנֵי כֵלִים: **גמ' אָמַר רַב וּבִכְלִי אֶחָד.** שֶׁכּוּלָּן הָיָה שׁוּתָּפוּתָן בִּכְלִי אֶחָד. אֲבָל בִּשְׁנֵי כֵלִים – לֹא. וְאַע"ג דְּאָמְרִי ב"ה בְּפֶרֶק "מִי שֶׁהוֹצִיאוּהוּ" (לעיל דף מט.): עֵירוּב הַנָּתוּן בִּשְׁנֵי כֵלִים – כָּשֵׁר. הָתָם הוּא דְּמֵעִיקָּרָא לְשֵׁם עֵירוּב גַּבּוּ וּמַלְיוּהּ לְמָנָא וְאַיְיתַר. אֲבָל הָכָא, דְּלָאו לְשֵׁם שִׁיתּוּף הֲוָה, בִּכְלִי א' – אִין, בְּב' כֵלִים – לָא: **יַיִן וְיַיִן רָאוּי לְעָרֵב.** הִלְכָּךְ, אע"פ דְּלָא עָרְבֵיהּ – סָמְכִינַן עֲלֵיהּ: **וַאֲפִי' לָזֶה בְּיַיִן וְלָזֶה בְּשֶׁמֶן.** בִּתְמִיהָ: הָא לָא חֲזֵי לְעֵירוּבֵי: **שֶׁבֵּין ב' מְבוֹאוֹת.** וְלָא בְּשִׁיתּוּף דְּמָבוֹי אֶחָד קָאָמַר, אֶלָּא עִם זֶה נִשְׁתַּתְּפָה בְּיַיִן, וְעִם זֶה בְּשֶׁמֶן, וּשְׁנֵי עֵירוּבִין הֵן: **וְר"ש לְטַעֲמֵיהּ.** דְּאָמַר: חָצֵר אַחַת יְכוֹלָה לְעָרֵב ב' עֵירוּבִין עִם ב' מְבוֹאוֹת, וְאַע"פ שֶׁלֹּא שִׁיתְּפוּ ב' הַמְּבוֹאוֹת יַחַד. ה"נ, אַע"פ שֶׁאֵין הַשִּׁיתּוּף מְחוּבָּר יַחַד, וְלֹא הוּתְּרוּ מְבוֹאוֹת זֶה עִם זֶה – הִיא מוּתֶּרֶת עִם שְׁנֵיהֶם, וְלָא גָּזְרִינַן דִּילְמָא אָתֵי לְאַפּוּקֵי כֵּלִים שֶׁשָּׁבְתוּ בְּמָבוֹי זֶה לְמָבוֹי זֶה דֶּרֶךְ חָצֵר זוֹ: **לָמָּה הַדָּבָר דּוֹמֶה.** בְּפ' "מִי שֶׁהוֹצִיאוּהוּ" וּלְרַבָּנַן דְּמַתְנִי', אִם נִשְׁתַּתְּפָה בְּיַיִן וּבִכְלִי א' – הֲווּ לְהוּ ב' הַמְּבוֹאוֹת כְּמִי שֶׁנִּשְׁתַּתְּפוּ יַחַד, וְשַׁפִּיר דָּמֵי. אֲבָל לָזֶה בְּיַיִן וְלָזֶה בְּשֶׁמֶן, דִּתְרֵי עֵירוּבֵי נִינְהוּ, כֵּיוָן דְּב' הַמְּבוֹאוֹת אֲסוּרִין זֶה עִם זֶה – הִיא נַמִּי אֲסוּרָה עִמָּהֶן, וּשְׁנֵיהֶן אֲסוּרִין עִמָּהּ, כִּדְקָתָנֵי בְּפֶרֶק "מִי שֶׁהוֹצִיאוּהוּ": **שְׁכֵנִים בַּהֲדֵי הֲדָדֵי.** אִם רוֹצִין בְּנֵי מָבוֹי זֶה לְהִשְׁתַּמֵּשׁ בָּזֶה – צְרִיכִין לְעָרֵב וְלָתֵת כּוּלָּן פַּת בֶּחָצֵר זוֹ(ג) וְאִית דִּמְפָרְשִׁי מַתְנִי' מִילֵּי מִילֵּי קָתָנֵי, וְר"ש לָאו אַמִּילְּתַיְיהוּ קָאֵי, דְּאִילּוּ רַבָּנַן בְּחָצֵר שֶׁבֵּין ב' מְבוֹאוֹת אֲפִי' לָזֶה בְּיַיִן וְלָזֶה בְּיַיִן לֹא. זוֹ פֵּירַשְׁתִּי, וְרִאשׁוֹן נִרְאֶה בְּעֵינַי:

וְרַב

תוספות

כלך אצל יפות. פי' רש"י: דכשיש לו יפות מהן, גלי דעתיה דניחא ליה, והוי כמאן דשויה שליח מעיקרא דמי. ואין להקשות לפירושו מהא דמוקי לה בריש "אלו מציאות" (ב"מ דף כב.) כגון דשויה שליח, דנהי דשויה שליח לתרום – לא שויה שליח לתרום מן היפות. ועל זה מפרש בקונטרס: כמאן דשויה שליח לתרום מן היפות דמי, כיון דנמצא יפות מהן:

ומקני רשותא בשבת אסור. תימה דבגיטין בריש "הזורק" (דף עז:) גבי ההוא שכיב מרע אמר דליקני לה דוכתא דמנח ביה גיטא, ותיזל איהי ותיחד ותפתח ושבת היתה כדאיתא התם! וי"ל:(ד) דשכיב מרע התירו, *שלא תטרף דעתו עליו. ואין לומר דדוקא קנין שאינו צריך הוא דשרי, כי ההיא [דפרק "מי שמת"] (ב"ק קנו:) דבלא קנין קני, כדאמר התם, דאין הלכה כר' אלעזר. דהא משמע [התם] דאי הוה הלכה כר' אלעזר – כ"ש דהוה ניחא טפי, שהיו צריכין להתיר. והכי נמי איכא למיחש למיטרף דעת אם לא היה יכול לגרשה כרצונו. תדע, דאף בלא קנין איכא איסורא לגרש בשבת, כדתניא* בתוספתא דאין מקדשין ואין מגרשין בשבת. אלא ודאי בשכיב מרע דוקא התירו, שלא תטרוף דעתו, שירא שימות בשבת, ואינו רוצה להמתין עד החול. וה"ה דהתירו נמי קנין. *וכן פסק רבינו שמואל דאפי' מתנת שכיב מרע במקצת, דבעיא קנין – קונין ממנו בשבת:

אי אמרת בשלמא רישא בכלי אחד כו'. והוא הדין יין ויין בב' כלים, אלא אורחא דמלתא נקט. ועוד: דלא הוצרך התנא לפרש, דסתם יין ושמן בב' כלים. אע"ג דשרו ב"ה בפרק "מי שהוציאוהו" (לעיל דף מט.) עירוב הנתון בשני כלים – כי מלייה למנא ואייתר – ה"מ כי גבו לשם עירוב, כדפי' בקונטרס. אבל הכא, דלאו לשם שתוף, בכלי א' – אין, בשני כלים – לא:

יין ושמן אין ראוי לערב. אף ע"ג דכל האוכלין מצטרפין למזון ב' סעודות לעירוב וה"ה משקין – היינו כשנשתתפו לשם עירוב:

בחצר שבין ב' מבואות כו'. לא בעי לאוקומי בג' חצירות ממש כאידך משנה, דעירובי חצירות בעי פת בין לר"מ בין לרבנן דלקמן בסמוך, ואין רוצה להעמיד מתני' כמ"ד(ה) ביין, ופליג אר"מ ורבנן:

ור' שמעון לטעמיה. דלא גזר, לרב ששת דמוקי לה לעיל בפרק "מי שהוציאוהו" (דף מח.) שנתנו(ו) שתים עירובן באמצעית, ובב' בתים – הכא אפי' בבית א' ובשני כלים כב' בתים דמו – כיון דלא עביד לשם שיתוף(ז). דממה נפשך תרוייהו הכא בחצר קיימי, דשיתופי מבואות בחצר שבמבוי.

רבינו חננאל

מבע"י אע"פ שלא בא ישראל והחזיק בחלקו של גר מבע"י אלא משחשיכה כיון דהוה ליה להחזיק מבע"י אע"פ שלא הוחזק מבע"י אלא משחשיכה אוסר. מת הגר משחשיכה ובא ישראל אחר והחזיק כיון דלא הוה ליה להחזיק מבע"י אינו אוסר. קתני מיהת רישא אוסר אמאי יבטל רשותו ופרקינן הכי נמי קאמר אוסר עד שיבטל ר' יוחנן אמר הני מתנייתא דדייקי אין ביטול רשות בשבת [ב"ש היא] דתנן מאימתי נתינת רשות בש"א מבע"י קסברי ביטול רשות מקנא רשותא הוא ומקנא רשותא בשבת אסירי. ובה"א אפי' משתחשך קסברי ביטול רשות איסתלוקי הוא ואיסתלוקי בשבת שפיר דמי: **ירושלמי** רב חסדאי אמר י' ישראלין הדרין בבית אחד כל אחד ואחד צריך לבטל רשותו וכן עשרה גוים הדרים בבית אחד צריך להשכיר כל אחד רשותו ור' יסא בשם ר' יוחנן אמר ישראל וגוי שדרין בבית אחד הלכה ישראל צריך לבטל רשותו וגוי צריך להשכיר ואסיקנא [אפי'] באגוז ואפילו בתמרה. ומעשה באשתו של פרסי (א"ר) [אחד] שהשכירה חצרה בלא דעת בעלה ושרא ר' שמואל סברין למימר אפי' שמשו ולקיטו: **מתני'** בעל הבית שהיה שותף לשכיניו לזה ביין ולזה ביין אינן צריכין אוקימנא בזמן שהיין של שניהם הוא בכלי אחד ובא אביי ודחה ואמר אפי' בשני כלים הואיל וראויין לערבן אין צריכין עירוב אחר ולא דמי ליין ושמן שהיין והשמן אין ראויין לערבן ר' שמעון אומר אפי' לזה ביין ולזה בשמן אינן צריכין לערב אוקמה רבה בחצר שבין ב' מבואות וכגון שיש לחצר עם זו המבוי האחר שותפות בשמן ורבי שמעון לטעמיה דאמר בני החצר מותרין עם זה המבוי. דתנן אמר רבי שמעון למה הדבר דומה לג' חצרות שפתוחות זו לזו כו' ודחי אביי מי דמי התם קתני ב' החיצונות אסורות זו עם זו הכא קתני אין צריכין לערב כלומר אין צריכין עירוב אחר. מכלל שכולן מותרות הן ושני ליה מאי אין צריכין לערב שכינין ובעל הבית. אבל השכינין החיצונין בהדי הדדי צריכין לערב דקתני במתני':

עין משפט נר מצוה

סד א ב ג מיי' פ"ב מהל' עירובין הל' ח טוש"ע או"ח סימן שפ"א סעיף ה:

סה ד ה ו מיי' פ"ה מהל' עירובין הל' א טור א"ח סי' שפו וש"ע סי' שפו סעיף ג בהג"ה:

שלא תטרף דעתו עליו. כדאמרינן פ' מי שמת קונין מש"מ ואפילו בשבת ולא לחוש לדברי ר"א פי' דבעי קנין אלא שלא תטרוף דעתו ואין לומר כו' כל רש"ל

[וכב"ב קנו: ד"ה קונין הביאו שתוספתא זאת היא בביצה אבל לפנינו ליתא]

[ועי' תוס' ביצה יז. ד"ה מ"ט וקד לו: ד"ה והא מנוה ותוס' גיטין עז: ד"ה ותיזל ותוס' ב"ב קנו: ד"ה קונין]

מסורת הש"ס

[ב"מ כב.]

לקמן עג:

לעיל מה: לקמן נא.

גליון הש"ס

מתני' בעל הבית שהיה שותף. עיין לעיל דף מט ע"א תד"ה ר' שמעון. תוס' ד"ה ור"ש לטעמיה וכו' בחצר שבמבוי. לקמן דף פה ע"ב:

הגהות הב"ח

(א) גמ' ור"ש לטעמיה דלא גזר דתנן אמר ר"ש: (ב) רש"י ד"ה אע"פ פריך לקמן וכו' ישראל אחר בנכסיו אוסר ואם לא החזיק ישראל אחר בנכסיו אינו אוסר הס"ד: (ג) ד"ה שכנים וכו' ולתת כולן פת בחצר זו זו פירשתי ואית דמפרשי וכו' דלאו לרבנן וכו' ולזה ביין לא ולראשון נראה בעיני: (ד) תוס' ד"ה ומקני וכו' וי"ל דבשכיב מרע: (ה) ד"ה בחצר וכו' מתני' כמ"ד לקמן ביין כ"ב בפ' חלון דאין דף פא דפליג אר' יהושע ועי"ל בדף כו': (ו) ד"ה ור' שמעון וכו' שנתנו שתים החיצונות עירובן: (ז) בא"ד לשם שתוף ועוד דממה נפשך כ"ב כלומר אפי' אי עביד לשם שתוף לא נפקא לן מידי דממה נפשך תרווייהו בחצר קיימא לשיתופי מבואות בחצר אחד חשוב כבית אחד דדוקא בעירובי חצירות שהוא בבית שבחצר איכא לחלק בין בית אחד לשני בתים אבל הכא ליכא לחלק:

רב נסים גאון

אמר רבא מאי טעמייהו דבית הלל נעשה כאומר לו לך אצל יפות בירור זה (בתוספות) [בתוספתא] תרומות (פרק א) כיצד אמרו תורם שלא מדעת תרומתו תרומה הרי שירד לתוך שדה חברו ולקט ותרם שלא ברשות אם חושש משום גזל אין תרומתו תרומה ומניין הוא יודע אם חושש משום גזל אם לאו הרי שבא בעל הבית ומצאו ואמר לו כלך אצל יפות אם נמצאו יפות מהן תרומתו תרומה ואם לאו אין תרומתו תרומה ומשכחת לה בגמ' בפרק האיש מקדש במסכת קידושין (דף נב) ואיתא נמי בפרק אלו מציאות (בבא מציעא דף כב):

מתני'

סו א מיי' פ"ח מהל' טומאת אוכלין הלכה ג:
סז ב מיי' פ"א מהל' עירובין הלכה ח סמג עשין א טוש"ע א"ח סי' שסו סעיף א:
סח ג מיי' שם סמג שם טוש"ע א"ח סי' שפו סעיף ד ה ו:
סט ד מיי' שם הלכה יט סמג שם טוש"ע א"ח סי' שפז:
ע ה מיי' שם טוש"ע א"ח שם:

וְרַב יוֹסֵף אָמַר: רַבִּי שִׁמְעוֹן וְרַבָּנַן בִּפְלוּגְתָּא דְּרַבִּי יוֹחָנָן בֶּן נוּרִי וְרַבָּנַן קָא מִיפַּלְגִי; *דִּתְנַן: אשֶׁמֶן שֶׁצָּף עַל גַּבֵּי יַיִן, וְנָגַע טְבוּל יוֹם בַּשֶּׁמֶן – לֹא פָּסַל אֶלָּא שֶׁמֶן בִּלְבַד. וְרַבִּי יוֹחָנָן בֶּן נוּרִי אוֹמֵר: שְׁנֵיהֶן חִיבּוּרִין זֶה לָזֶה. רַבָּנַן – כְּרַבָּנַן, וְרַבִּי שִׁמְעוֹן – כְּר"י בֶּן נוּרִי. תַּנְיָא, ר"א בֶּן תַּדַּאי אוֹמֵר: אֶחָד זֶה וְאֶחָד זֶה – צְרִיכִין לְעָרֵב, וַאֲפִילוּ לָזֶה בְּיַיִן וְלָזֶה בְּיַיִן?! אָמַר רַבָּה: זֶה בָּא בְּלָגִינוֹ וְשָׁפַךְ, וְזֶה בָּא בְּלָגִינוֹ וְשָׁפַךְ – כּוּלֵּי עָלְמָא לָא פְּלִיגִי דְּהָוֵי עֵירוּב. כִּי פְּלִיגִי – כְּגוֹן שֶׁלָּקְחוּ חָבִית שֶׁל יַיִן בְּשׁוּתָּפוּת. ר"א בֶּן תַּדַּאי סָבַר: *אֵין בְּרֵירָה, וְרַבָּנַן סָבְרִי: יֵשׁ בְּרֵירָה. רַב יוֹסֵף אָמַר: ר"א בֶּן תַּדַּאי וְרַבָּנַן בְּסוֹמְכִין עַל שִׁיתּוּף בִּמְקוֹם עֵירוּב קָמִיפַּלְגִי. דְּמָר סָבַר: אֵין סוֹמְכִין, וּמָר סָבַר: סוֹמְכִין. אָמַר רַב יוֹסֵף: מְנָא אָמִינָא לַהּ – דְּאָמַר רַב יְהוּדָה, אָמַר רַב: הֲלָכָה כְּר"מ. וְאָמַר רַב בְּרוֹנָא, אָמַר רַב: הֲלָכָה כְּר"א בֶּן תַּדַּאי. מ"ט – לָאו מִשּׁוּם דְּחַד טַעְמָא הוּא? א"ל אַבַּיֵי: וְאִי חַד טַעְמָא, תַּרְתֵּי הִילְכְתָא לָמָּה לִי?! הָא קמ"ל: דְּלָא עָבְדִינַן כְּתְרֵי חוּמְרֵי בְּעֵירוּבִין. מַאי ר"מ וּמַאי רַבָּנַן? דְּתַנְיָא: במְעָרְבִין בַּחֲצֵירוֹת בַּפַּת. וְאִם רָצוּ לְעָרֵב בְּיַיִן – אֵין מְעָרְבִין. גמִשְׁתַּתְּפִין בַּמָּבוֹי בְּיַיִן, וְאִם רָצוּ לְהִשְׁתַּתֵּף בַּפַּת – מִשְׁתַּתְּפִין. דמְעָרְבִין בַּחֲצֵירוֹת וּמִשְׁתַּתְּפִין בַּמָּבוֹי, שֶׁלֹּא לְשַׁכַּח תּוֹרַת עֵירוּב מִן הַתִּינוֹקוֹת שֶׁיֹּאמְרוּ "אֲבוֹתֵינוּ לֹא עֵירְבוּ", דִּבְרֵי ר"מ. וַחכ"א: אוֹ מְעָרְבִין, אוֹ מִשְׁתַּתְּפִין. פְּלִיגִי בָּהּ ר'(א) נַחוּמִי וְרַבָּה; חַד אָמַר: הבַּפַּת, דְּכוּלֵּי עָלְמָא לָא פְּלִיגִי דְּבַחֲדָא סַגֵּי. כִּי פְּלִיגִי – בְּיַיִן.
וְחַד

רש"י

וְרַב יוֹסֵף אָמַר. לְעוֹלָם בְּמָבוֹי אֶחָד כִּדְמֵעִיקָּרָא, וּדְקָאָמְרַתְּ לְר"ש הֵיכִי הָוֵי חַד עֵירוּב ר"ש כְּר' יוֹחָנָן ס"ל: שֶׁמֶן שֶׁצָּף כו'. וְשֶׁל תְּרוּמָה הֵן: וַאֲפִי' לָזֶה בְּיַיִן וְלָזֶה בְּיַיִן. בִּתְמִיָּה: זֶה בָּא בְּלָגִינוֹ וְשָׁפַךְ. וְכֵן זֶה עַד שֶׁמִּלְּאוּ חָבִית. וַאֲפִי' שֶׁלֹּא לְשֵׁם שִׁיתּוּף עָשׂוּ מִתְּחִילָּה – סוֹמְכִין עָלָיו, שֶׁהֲרֵי הֵבִיא כָּל אֶחָד יַיִן. אֲבָל לָקְחוּ חָבִית יַיִן בְּשׁוּתָּפוּת, ס"ל לְבֶן תַּדַּאי אֵין בְּרֵירָה, וְהָוֵי לְהוּ כְּמִי שֶׁנִּשְׁתַּתְּפוּ בְּמָעוֹת שֶׁלֹּא הוּבְרַר יַיִן לְכָל אֶחָד וְא': בְּסוֹמְכִין אַשִּׁיתּוּף בִּמְקוֹם עֵירוּב קָמִיפַּלְגִי. וּבֶן תַּדַּאי מוֹדֶה דְּמָבוֹי מוּתָּר, וּבַחֲצֵירוֹת פְּלִיגִי. רַבָּנַן סָבְרִי: כֵּיוָן דְּנִשְׁתַּתְּפוּ בַּמָּבוֹי – אֵין צְרִיכִין לְעָרֵב חֲצֵירוֹת זוֹ עִם זוֹ, וּמוּתָּרִין לְהוֹצִיא מִזּוֹ לָזוֹ דֶּרֶךְ פְּתָחִים שֶׁבֵּינֵיהֶם, שֶׁהֲרֵי שִׁיתּוּף הַמָּבוֹי שֶׁהֵן פְּתוּחוֹת בּוֹ מְחַבְּרָן, וְסוֹמְכִין עַל שִׁיתּוּף הַמָּבוֹי תַּחַת עֵירוּב שֶׁל חָצֵר. וּבֶן תַּדַּאי סָבַר: אֵין סוֹמְכִין: מְנָא אָמִינָא לַהּ. דִּבְהָכִי פְּלִיגִי: הֲלָכָה כְּר"מ. דְּאֵין סוֹמְכִין עַל שִׁיתּוּף בִּמְקוֹם עֵירוּב: מ"ט. ס"ל לְרַב בְּתַרְוַיְיהוּ, לָאו מִשּׁוּם דְּתַרְוַיְיהוּ חֲדָא מִלְּתָא וְחַד טַעְמָא אָמְרֵי: וְאִי חַד טַעְמָא הוּא תַּרְתֵּי הִילְכְתָא לָמָּה לֵיהּ. לְרַב לְמֵימַר בְּתַרְוַיְיהוּ? בִּשְׁלָמָא הֲלָכָה כְּר"מ – אִיצְטְרִיךְ, דְּאִי מִדְּר"א, הֲוָה אָמִינָא: טַעְמָא דְּר"א לָאו מִשּׁוּם דְּאֵין סוֹמְכִין עַל שִׁיתּוּף, אֶלָּא מִשּׁוּם דְּקָסָבַר אֵין מְעָרְבִין בַּחֲצֵירוֹת בְּיַיִן, כִּדְקָאָמַר ר"מ לְקַמָּן. וְהַאי שִׁיתּוּף דְּבֶן תַּדַּאי דְּיַיִן הוּא, כִּדְקָתָנֵי מַתְנִי': לָזֶה בְּיַיִן וְלָזֶה בְּיַיִן – הִלְכָּךְ, לָא סָמְכִינַן עֲלֵיהּ בַּחֲצֵירוֹת. אֲבָל הֵיכָא דְּנִשְׁתַּתְּפוּ בְּפַת – סוֹמְכִין, קמ"ל הֲלָכָה כְּר"מ, דְּאוֹקְמָא רַב גִּידֵּל אָמַר רַב לְקַמָּן בְּנִשְׁתַּתְּפוּ בְּפַת, וַאֲפ"ה אָסַר ר"מ. אֶלָּא כֵּיוָן דְּאָמַר הֲלָכָה כְּר"מ, דַּאֲפִי' בְּפַת לָא סָמְכִינַן עֲלֵיהּ – הֲלָכָה כְּר"א ל"ל: הָא קמ"ל דְּלָא עָבְדִינַן כִּתְרֵי חוּמְרֵי בְּעֵירוּבִין. מִדְּאִיצְטְרִיךְ לֵיהּ לְרַב לְמֵימַר הֲלָכָה כְּבֶן תַּדַּאי, אַשְׁמְעִינַן דְּלָא עָבְדִינַן כִּתְרֵי חוּמְרֵי דְּחַד תַּנָּא בְּעֵירוּבִין וְר"מ תְּרֵי חוּמְרֵי אָמַר: אֵין סוֹמְכִין בַּחֲצֵירוֹת עַל שִׁיתּוּף מָבוֹי, בֵּין שֶׁנִּשְׁתַּתְּפוּ בְּפַת וּבֵין שֶׁנִּשְׁתַּתְּפוּ בְּיַיִן. וּפְלִיגִי רַבָּנַן עֲלֵיהּ בְּפַת, וּמוֹדוּ לֵיהּ בְּשֶׁנִּשְׁתַּתְּפוּ בְּיַיִן. וְרַבָּנַן דְּמַתְנִי' דְּהָכָא אוֹקִימְנָא דַּאֲפִילוּ בְּנִשְׁתַּתְּפוּ בְּיַיִן אָמְרֵי דְּסוֹמְכִין, אִשְׁתַּכַּח דְּמַחְמִיר(ב) תְּרֵי חוּמְרֵי. וְרַב ס"ל כְּוָותֵיהּ בְּתַרְוַיְיהוּ, וְלָא מָצֵי לְאַקְבּוּעֵי הִלְכְתָא כְּוָותֵיהּ בִּתְרֵי חוּמְרֵי. הִלְכָּךְ, אַשְׁמְעִינַן הֲלָכָה כְּבֶן תַּדַּאי בַּחֲדָא מִינַּיְיהוּ דְּאֵין סוֹמְכִין בַּחֲצֵירוֹת עַל שִׁיתּוּף הַמָּבוֹי בְּיַיִן, וְכִי הָדוּר אִיפְלוּג ר"מ וְרַבָּנַן בְּפַת – אַשְׁמְעִינַן הֲלָכָה כְּר"מ: וְאִם רָצוּ לְעָרֵב בְּיַיִן אֵין מְעָרְבִין. דְּעֵירוּב מִשּׁוּם דִּירָה הוּא, לְעָרֵב דִּירָתָן לַעֲשׂוֹתָן אַחַת. כִּדְאָמַר בְּפ' "מִי שֶׁהוֹצִיאוּהוּ" (לעיל דף מט.) וְדִירָתוֹ שֶׁל אָדָם אֵינוֹ נִמְשָׁךְ אַחַר הַיַּיִן, אֶלָּא אַחַר פִּיתּוֹ: וּמִשְׁתַּתְּפִין בַּמָּבוֹי בְּיַיִן. דְּשִׁיתּוּף דְּמָבוֹי אֵינוֹ אֶלָּא לְשַׁתֵּף רְשׁוּת הַחֲצֵירוֹת שֶׁבַּמָּבוֹי, וְלֹא רְשׁוּת הַבָּתִּים. וְחָצֵר לָאו בֵּית דִּירָה הוּא וְכ"ש פַּת דַּחֲשִׁיב טְפֵי: מְעָרְבִין בַּחֲצֵירוֹת. הַפְּתוּחוֹת מִזּוֹ לָזוֹ, אַע"פ שֶׁעֵירְבוּ דֶּרֶךְ פִּתְחֵיהֶן – צְרִיכִין לְהִשְׁתַּתֵּף בַּמָּבוֹי לְהַתִּיר הַמָּבוֹי. וְאִם לָאו – חֲצֵירוֹת מוּתָּרוֹת מִזּוֹ לָזוֹ, וּמָבוֹי אָסוּר דְּאֵין סוֹמְכִין עַל עֵירוּב בִּמְקוֹם שִׁיתּוּף, וְלֹא עַל שִׁיתּוּף בִּמְקוֹם עֵירוּב הֵיכָא דְּלֹא עֵירְבוּ בְּנֵי חָצֵר לְעַצְמָן, שֶׁאִם יִסְמְכוּ עַל זֶה – תּוֹרַת עֵירוּב יִשְׁתַּכַּח. אֲבָל עֵירְבָה כָּל חָצֵר לְעַצְמָהּ וְנִשְׁתַּתְּפוּ כּוּלָּם בַּמָּבוֹי, אַע"פ שֶׁלֹּא עֵירְבוּ חֲצֵירוֹת זוֹ עִם זוֹ – שִׁיתּוּף הַמָּבוֹי מְחַבְּרָן, וּמְטַלְטְלִין מִזּוֹ לָזוֹ בֵּין דֶּרֶךְ הַמָּבוֹי בֵּין דֶּרֶךְ פְּתָחִים. דִּתְנַן: שֶׁהַמָּבוֹי לַחֲצֵירוֹת כַּחֲצֵירוֹת לַבָּתִּים, מַה עֵירוּב הֶחָצֵר מְשַׁוֵּי לַבָּתִּים חֲדָא, אַף שִׁיתּוּף הַמָּבוֹי מְשַׁוֵּי חֲצֵירוֹת חֲדָא: דְּבַחֲדָא סַגְיָא. דְּהָא פַּת חֲזֵי הָכָא וְהָכָא, וּבֵין לְמָר וּבֵין לְמָר סוֹמְכִין עַל שִׁיתּוּף בִּמְקוֹם עֵירוּב: כִּי פְּלִיגִי בְּיַיִן. כְּשֶׁנִּשְׁתַּתְּפוּ בְּיַיִן בַּמָּבוֹי, דְּלְר"מ לָא סָמְכִינַן עֲלֵיהּ בְּעֵירוּבֵי חֲצֵירוֹת, דְּאֵין מְעָרְבִין לַחֲצֵירוֹת בְּיַיִן וּלְרַבָּנַן שָׁרֵי, וְאַע"ג דְּיַיִן בְּחָצֵר לָא חֲזֵי מִגּוֹ דַּחֲזֵי לְמִלְּתֵיהּ בְּשִׁיתּוּף, סָמְכִינַן עֲלֵיהּ בְּחָצֵר. דְּמוֹדֵית לָן דְּסוֹמְכִין עַל שִׁיתּוּף בִּמְקוֹם עֵירוּב, וְתַרְוַיְיהוּ אִית לְהוּ דְּסוֹמְכִין בְּמָבוֹי עַל עֵירוּבֵי חֲצֵירוֹת, שֶׁהוּא לְעוֹלָם שֶׁל פַּת:
וְחַד

תוספות

שמן שצף על גבי יין כו'. השתא משמע דשמן חשיב משקה, מדקאמר ר' יוחנן בן נורי: שניהם מחוברין. דאי חשיב אוכל – כיון דטבול יום אינו אלא פוסל, לא הדר שמן ומטמא ליין. דאין סברא לומר דפליגי רבנן ור"י בן נורי בהכי, אם יכול להבדיל זה מזה או לא. ועוד: דתניא בפ"ק דפסחים (דף יז.): הדם והמים והשמן והיין משקה בי מדבחיא כו'. וקרא דחגי(ב) נמי "ואל היין ואל השמן" מוכח דהוי משקה. ועוד תנן התם (דף יד.), הוסיף ר"ע: מימיהן של כהנים לא נמנעו מלהדליק את השמן שנפסל בטבול יום [בנר שנטמא בטמא מת, אע"פ שמוסיפין טומאה על טומאתו]. וקאמר בגמרא, קסבר ר"ע: טומאת משקין לטמא אחרים – דאורייתא. והקשה ר"ת: מההיא דאמרינן ב"הקומץ רבה" (מנחות דף לא.) ר"מ אומר: שמן טבול יום – תחילה לעולם, וחכ"א: אף הדבש. ר"ש שזורי אומר: יין. ומסיק: יין דוקא, ולא שמן. ומשמע התם דהלכה כר"ש שזורי! ואומר ר"ת: דהתם בקרוש איירי, כדתקני רישא במסכת טהרות (פ"ג מ"א)*: השמן והחלב והמקפה של גריסין, בזמן שהן לחין – הרי הן ראשון, קרשו – הרי הן שניים. פי': דהוי אוכל. ר"מ אומר: שמן תחלה לעולם. כלומר: לעולם, אפי' קרש. *ולא כמו שפירש בקונט' במנחות: לעולם – בין נטמא באב הטומאה, בין נטמא בולד הטומאה: **רבי** אלעזר בן תדאי אומר אין ברירה. אין זה כעין ברירות דבכל דוכתא, כדפי' בקונט', דהוו להו כאילו נשתתפו במעות שלא הוברר יין לכל אחד ואחד:

דלא עבדינן כתרי חומרי בעירוב. כך היא גירס' הקונטרס. ור"ת גריס: דעבדינן כתרי חומרי בעירוב. כלומר: הכא עבדינן כתרי חומרי. ומיהו, לשון "בעירוב" לא יתכן כל כך, דמשמע בכל עירוב: **משתתפין** במבוי ביין. משמע קצת דלכתחלה ביין מצוה יותר מבפת, מדלא תניא דומיא דרישא משתתפין במבוי בפת, ואם רצו להשתתף ביין – משתתפין. ושמא ביין מינכר טפי שהוא שיתוף. ומיהו, בכל דבר מהני, כדתנן בפרק "בכל מערבין(ג) ומשתתפין" (לעיל דף כו:). ובפ' "חלון" (לקמן דף פ.) נמי תניא: כיצד משתתפין במבוי – מביאין חבית של יין ושל שמן ושל תמרים ושל גרוגרות וכל מיני פירות: **בפת** כ"ע לא פליגי דבחד סגי. משום דבפת סגי הכא והכא. ופירש בקונטרס: דבין למר ובין למר סומכין במבוי על עירובי חצירות, שהוא לעולם בפת(ד). ולפיכך הא דקתני מערבין בחצירות ומשתתפין במבוי – לא בעי למימר דאחר שעירבו בחצירות יהיו עדיין זקוק להשתתף במבוי, אלא כלומר: מערבין בחצירות בפת, אע"פ שנשתתפו במבוי ביין. ואין הלשון משמע כן. ועוד, תנן לקמן בפירקין (דף עג:): ה' חצירות הפתוחות זו לזו ופתוחות למבוי, עירבו בחצירות ולא נשתתפו במבוי – מותרין בחצירות ואסורין במבוי. וקאמר בגמרא: מני – ר"מ היא, דאמר: בעינן עירוב ובעינן שיתוף. מיהו, איכא לאוקמי ההוא סוגיא כמ"ד בפת פליגי. ומ"ד בפת ל"פ – סבר לה כרב דלא תני פתוחות זו לזו. ור"י מפרש: דאשיתוף דפת קאי, דכיון דסגי ביין. והם דתקו לעשות בפת ואלמוה טפי – מועיל אף לחצירות. ועוד: שהשיתוף לכל הבתים והחצירות, שכולם משתתפין יחד. אבל עירובי חצירות דפת – אין לו להועיל כל כך במבוי, ולפי מה שפירש שאפי' למ"ד בפת לא פליגי – מודה הוא דבעירובי חצירות דפת פליגי, אם מועיל למבוי. *[אומר ר"י: דמצינו לפרש תרי חומרי בעירובין דלעיל, דאי אמר הלכה כר"א בן תדאי – לא הוה ידעינן מאי טעמיה, ואי אמרינן הלכה כר"מ – הוה אמינא בחדא, בהא דאין סומכין על עירוב במקום שיתוף, כדמשמע לישנא דר"מ דאמר מערבין בחצירות ומשתתפין במבוי, דמשמע דאף ע"פ שעירבו – צריכין עדיין להשתתף, אבל על שיתוף במקום עירוב – סומכין, קמ"ל הלכה כר"א בן תדאי, דאין סומכין על שיתוף במקום עירוב, דמסתמא בא לגלות דהלכה כר"מ לגמרי. ומיהו, פי' הקונטרס דלעיל גבי תרי חומרי – ניחא טפי]. וא"ת: כשעירבו בחצירות בפת, והניחו עירובן בבית אחד מן החצירות למה לא יועיל לכ"ע למבוי? אי משום דתניא ב"כילד משתתפין" (לקמן דף פה:): עירובי חצרות בבית שבחצר, ושיתופי מבואות בחצר שבמבוי, והאי כיון דאנחיה בבית לא שמיה שיתוף אלא עירוב – הא פירש בקונטרס לקמן בפירקין* גבי כאן במסובין בבית כאן במסובין בחצר, דהא דאמרינן שיתופי מבואות בחצר שבמבוי – וכ"ש(ה) שבביתו דף עג:
וכן

[לפנינו ליתא האי לישנא]
[עי' תוס' מנחות לג. ד"ה אומא כו' שביארו יותר ע"ש]

רבינו חננאל

רב יוסף אמר ר"ש ורבנן בהא פליגי דתנן שמן שצף ע"פ (המים) [היין] ונגע טבול יום בשמן לא פסל אלא שמן. ר' יוחנן בן נורי אמר שניהן חיבורין זה לזה. רבנן כת"ק. ור' שמעון כר' יוחנן בן נורי ודבריו פשוטין הן. תניא בעה"ב שהיה שותף לזה ביין [ולזה ביין] (אין) צריכין לערב. אמר רבה זה בא בלגינו ושפך וזה בא בלגינו ושפך כ"ע לא פליגי דהוו עירוב דהא ידיע חמרא דכל חד וחד כי פליגי כגון שלקחו חבית בשותפות רבנן סברי יש ברירה ואלעזר בן תדאי סבר אין ברירה ולא נקרא עירוב אלא דהוו ידיע ונתערב עכשיו ורב יוסף אמר כגון ששתפו במבוי בזה היין (ובסמוכין) [ובסומכין] (בעו) לעירוב בשיתוף פליגי רבנן סברי סומכין. ואלעזר בן תדאי סבר אין סומכין אלא צריכין עירוב אחר. אמר רב יוסף מנא אמינא לה דאמר רב יהודה אמר רב הלכה כר' מאיר דתניא מערבין לחצרות בפת ואם רצו לערב ביין אין מערבין שאין עירוב ביין משתתפין במבוי ביין ואם רצו להשתתף ביין משתתפין מערבין בחצרות ומשתתפין במבוי כדי שלא תשתכח תורת עירוב דברי ר' מאיר. ש"מ דאע"ג דנשתתפו במבוי מערבין ואין סומכין על עירוב במקום שיתוף. ורב ברונא אמר רב הלכה כאלעזר בן תדאי לאו משום דאלעזר בן תדאי ור' מאיר תרווייהו טעמא חדא נינהו ודחינן ואי חדא טעמא נינהו תרתי הלכתא למה לי ושנינן הא קמ"ל דאלעזר בן תדאי כר' מאיר סבירא ליה ועבדינן כתרי חומרי בעירובין. וחכ"א מערבין או משתתפין אוקמוה משמיה דרב הכי קתני או מערבין בחצרות בפת או שבת אחד מהן ולא נשתתף ובטיל רשותו לר' מאיר אית ליה ביטול ומותרין כאן וכאן או

מסורת הש"ס

שבת ה: ק. טבול יום פ"ב מ"ה ושם איתא ריב"נ אומר שניהם חיבור ובשבת ה' מחוברין וכן הגיה הגאון יעב"ץ ז"ל כאן.
[לעיל לו: ש"נ]

הגהות הב"ח

(א) גמ' פליגי בה רב רחומי ורבה בר יוסף חד אמר בפת: (ב) רש"י ד"ה הא קמ"ל וכו' אישתכח דמחמיר ר"מ תרי: (ג) תוס' ד"ה משתתפין וכו' כדתנן בפרק בכל מערבין בכל מערבין ומשתתפין: (ד) ד"ה בפת וכו' לעולם בפת ולפירושו הא דקתני: (ה) בא"ד וכ"ש שבבית וכן:

וְחַד אָמַר: בַּיַּיִן, דְּכוּ"ע לָא פְּלִיגִי דְּבָעֵינַן תַּרְתֵּי, כִּי פְּלִיגִי — בַּפַּת. מֵיתִיבִי: וַחֲכָמִים אוֹמְרִים אוֹ מְעָרְבִין אוֹ מִשְׁתַּתְּפִין. מַאי לָאו — אוֹ מְעָרְבִין בֶּחָצֵר בַּפַּת, אוֹ מִשְׁתַּתְּפִין בַּמָּבוֹי בַּיַּיִן! אָמַר רַב גִּידֵּל, אָמַר רַב, ה"ק: אוֹ מְעָרְבִין בֶּחָצֵר בַּפַּת, וּמוּתָּרִין כָּאן וְכָאן. אוֹ מִשְׁתַּתְּפִין בַּמָּבוֹי בַּפַּת, וּמוּתָּרִין כָּאן וְכָאן. אָמַר רַב יְהוּדָה, אָמַר רַב: הֲלָכָה כְּרַבִּי מֵאִיר. וְרַב הוּנָא אָמַר: מִנְהָג כְּר"מ. וְרַבִּי יוֹחָנָן אָמַר: נָהֲגוּ הָעָם כְּרַבִּי מֵאִיר.§

מתני' חֲמִשָּׁה חֲבוּרוֹת שֶׁשָּׁבְתוּ בִּטְרַקְלִין אֶחָד, ב"ש אוֹמְרִים: עֵירוּב לְכָל חֲבוּרָה וַחֲבוּרָה. וּב"ה אוֹמְרִים: [א]עֵירוּב אֶחָד לְכוּלָּן. וּמוֹדִים בִּזְמַן שֶׁמִּקְצָתָן שְׁרוּיִין בַּחֲדָרִים אוֹ בַּעֲלִיּוֹת, שֶׁהֵן צְרִיכִין עֵירוּב לְכָל חֲבוּרָה וַחֲבוּרָה.§

גמ' אָמַר רַב נַחְמָן: מַחֲלוֹקֶת *בִּמְסִיפָס, אֲבָל בִּמְחִיצָה עֲשָׂרָה — דִּבְרֵי הַכֹּל עֵירוּב לְכָל חֲבוּרָה וַחֲבוּרָה. אִיכָּא דְּאָמְרִי, אָמַר ר"נ: אַף בִּמְסִיפָס מַחֲלוֹקֶת. פְּלִיגִי בָּהּ רַבִּי חִיָּיא וְרַבִּי שִׁמְעוֹן בְּרַבִּי; חַד אָמַר: מַחֲלוֹקֶת *בִּמְחִיצוֹת הַמַּגִּיעוֹת לַתִּקְרָה, אֲבָל מְחִיצוֹת שֶׁאֵין מַגִּיעוֹת לַתִּקְרָה — דִּבְרֵי הַכֹּל עֵירוּב אֶחָד לְכוּלָּן. וְחַד אָמַר: מַחֲלוֹקֶת *בִּמְחִיצוֹת שֶׁאֵין מַגִּיעוֹת לַתִּקְרָה, [ב]אֲבָל מְחִיצוֹת הַמַּגִּיעוֹת לַתִּקְרָה — דִּבְרֵי הַכֹּל צְרִיכִין עֵירוּב לְכָל חֲבוּרָה וַחֲבוּרָה.

מֵיתִיבִי

וְחַד אָמַר בַּיַּיִן. אֲפִי' רַבָּנַן מוֹדוּ דְּלָא סָמְכִינַן עֲלֵיהּ בֶּחָצֵר דְּלָא אָמְרִי' מִגּוֹ: כִּי פְּלִיגִי בַּפַּת. וּפְלִיגִי בֵּין בְּשִׁיתּוּף בֵּין בְּעֵירוּב. דְּלְר' מֵאִיר אֵין סוֹמְכִין עַל זֶה בִּמְקוֹם זֶה: מַאי לָאו כו'. וְקַשְׁיָא לְמַאן דְּאָמַר בַּיַּיִן לָא פְּלִיגִי: אוֹ מִשְׁתַּתְּפִין בַּמָּבוֹי בַּפַּת. דְּמִשְׁתַּתְּפִין דּוּמְיָא דִּמְעָרְבִין קָתָנֵי: הִלְכְתָא וּמִנְהָג וְנָהֲגוּ, בְּפֶרֶק בַּתְרָא דְּתַעֲנִית (דף כו:) מְפוֹרָשׁ: הֲלָכָה — דָּרְשִׁינַן בְּפִירְקָא, הֲלָכָה כְּרַבִּי מֵאִיר. מִנְהָג — מִדְרַשׁ לָא דָּרְשִׁינַן אוֹרוּיֵי מוֹרֵינַן לְיָחִיד הַבָּא לִימָּלֵךְ. נָהֲגוּ — אוֹרוּיֵי נַמִי לָא מוֹרֵינַן, וְאִי עֲבוּד — לָא מָחֵינַן בְּהוּ: **מתני'** בִּטְרַקְלִין אֶחָד. וְחִלְּקוּהוּ לַחֲמִשָּׁה, וְכוּלָּן יֵשׁ לָהֶן פֶּתַח מִן הַטְּרַקְלִין לֶחָצֵר וְצָרִיךְ לְעָרֵב עִם שְׁאָר בְּנֵי חָצֵר: ב"ש אוֹמְרִים. רְשׁוּיוֹתֵיהֶן חֲלוּקִין, וְצָרִיךְ לְכָל חֲבוּרָה לִיתֵּן פַּת בְּעֵירוּב הֶחָצֵר, דְּהָווּ לְהוּ כְּה' בָּתִּים וְה"ה דְּאִם בָּאוּ לְהוֹצִיא מֵרְשׁוּת זוֹ לָזוֹ — צְרִיכִין עֵירוּב בֵּינֵיהֶן: וּב"ה אוֹמְרִים. אֵין מְחִיצָּה זוֹ חִילּוּק רְשׁוּת, דִּמְחִיצָּה שְׁפָלָה הִיא, כִּדְמְפָרֵשׁ בַּגְּמָ'. הִלְכָּךְ: עֵירוּב אֶחָד לְכוּלָּן. וּבְתוֹךְ הַטְּרַקְלִין נַמִי מוֹצִיאִין מִזּוֹ לָזוֹ בְּלֹא עֵירוּב, שֶׁהַטְּרַקְלִין מְחַבְּרָן. וְכֵיוָן דְּבֵינֵיהֶן א"צ עֵירוּב — נַעֲשֶׂה אֶחָד מֵהֶן שָׁלִיחַ לְכוּלָּן. דְּאָמְרִי' לְקַמָּן: חֲמִשָּׁה שֶׁגָּבוּ אֶת עֵירוּבָן, כְּלוֹמַר: שֶׁשְּׁרוּיִין בַּחֲמִשָּׁה בָּתִּים בֶּחָצֵר, וְעֵירְבוּ בֵּינֵיהֶן וְהָווּ לְהוּ חֲדָא, וְאִם בָּאִין לְעָרֵב עִם אֲחֵרִים — עֵירוּב אֶחָד לְכוּלָּן: וּמוֹדִין כְּשֶׁמִּקְצָתָן שְׁרוּיִין כו'. דְּהָווּ לְהוּ כְּה' בָּתִּים וְלָא דָּמוּ לְה' שֶׁגָּבוּ אֶת עֵירוּבָן — שֶׁהֲרֵי לֹא עֵירְבוּ בֵּינֵיהֶן: **גמ'** מַחֲלוֹקֶת. בְּשֶׁרְשׁוּיוֹתֵיהֶן חֲלוּקוֹת בִּמְסִיפָס = מְחִיצָּה נְמוּכָה שֶׁל חֲתִיכוֹת עֵצִים, דְּהָתָם לְבֵית הִלֵּל בַּיִת אֶחָד הוּא, וְדָמוּ לְה' שֶׁגָּבוּ אֶת עֵירוּבָן דְּהָנֵי נַמִי כְּמִי שֶׁעֵירְבוּ דָּמִי: אַף בִּמְסִיפָס מַחֲלוֹקֶת. דְּלָא תֵּימָא בֵּית שַׁמַּאי בִּמְחִיצָּה עֲשָׂרָה הוּא דְּאָסְרִי, וּבִמְסִיפָס מוֹדוּ. אֶלָּא: אֲפִילּוּ בִּמְסִיפָס נַמִי אָסְרִי: פְּלִיגִי בָּהּ. אַמַּתְנִיתִין קָאֵי: מַחֲלוֹקֶת. בֵּית שַׁמַּאי וּבֵית הִלֵּל כו': אֲבָל מְחִיצוֹת שֶׁאֵין מַגִּיעוֹת לַתִּקְרָה. אֲפִילּוּ הֵן עֲשָׂרָה — דִּבְרֵי הַכֹּל עֵירוּב אֶחָד לְכוּלָּן וּפְלִיגִי אַתַּרְוַיְיהוּ לִישָּׁנֵי דְּרַב נַחְמָן. דְּהָא[(א)] לִישָּׁנָא קַמָּא קָאָמַר דְּבִמְחִיצָּה עֲשָׂרָה מוֹדוּ דַּחֲלוּק הָוֵי, וְהָכָא אָמְרִינַן: אֲפִילּוּ בְּמַגִּיעוֹת לַתִּקְרָה פְּלִיגֵי. וּלְלִישָּׁנָא בָּתְרָא קָאָמַר דְּבִמְסִיפָס נַמִי פְּלִיגִי, וְאָסְרִי בֵּית שַׁמַּאי. וְהָכָא אָמְרִי דַּאֲפִילּוּ בִּמְחִיצּוֹת עֲשָׂרָה לֹא אָסְרוּ, אֶלָּא בִּמְחִיצּוֹת הַמַּגִּיעוֹת לַתִּקְרָה:

הַסַּפָּר

וכן פירש בריש סוכה (דף ג:). ואע"פ שפירש כאן בקונטרס דלכ"ע סומכין במבוי על עירובי חלירות שהיא לעולם בפת — מכל מקום למ"ד בפת פליגי, קשה: דלמה לא יועיל עירוב החלירות למבוי? כיון שתורתו נמי להניח בבית, דאטו השם גורם שנקרא עירוב שיש לו להועיל לחלירות ולא למבוי? ולמאן דאמר ביין נמי פליגי, ומפרש ברייתא דבסמוך או משתתפין במבוי ביין ומותרין כאן וכאן, אבל עירובי חלירות ביין — לא מהני, ואמאי? כיון דשיתוף מהני, לא תקראנו "עירוב", אלא תקראנו "שיתוף"! דתימה הוא לומר דמה שקראהו "עירוב" — לבטל תורת שיתוף מעליו. ודוחק ר"י לפירוש הקונט': שבתחילת העירוב לא עירבו אלא בני חלר אחת יחד, או שתי חלירות יחד, ולא היו סבורים שכל בני המבוי ישתתפו יחד. נמלא שלא נתנו עירובן לשם שיתוף, ולכך, כשניתוספו עליהם כל בני המבוי — אין לחושבו שיתוף, כיון שהראשונים לא היו שם ולא ידעו מעולם שעליהם ניתוספו כל האחרים. ונראה לר"י: דכולה מלתא דוקא עירובי חלירות בבית שבחלר, ושיתופי מבואות דוקא בחלר שבמבוי ולא בבית. משום דבחלר מינכר טפי לשם שיתוף, דשייכא טפי למבוי וקרובים תשמישם דמבוי זה לזה. והשתא הא דקאמר לקמן במסובין בבית: בפת שעל השולחן סומכין משום עירוב — לאו אף משום עירוב קאמר, אלא משום עירוב דוקא ולא משום שיתוף. והא דאמר בריש סוכה (דף ג.): בית שאין בו ארבע על ארבע — אין מניחין בו עירובי חלירות, אבל מניחין בו שיתופי מבואות דלא גרע מחלר שבמבוי. ומשמע דכל שכן אם היה בית גמור, שהיו מניחין בו שיתופין! אור"י: דודאי בית גמור גרע לענין שיתוף, והא דנקט[(ב)] בהא דלא גרע — שלא תאמר כי היכי דיולאין מכלל בתים לענין עירוב, יולאין נמי מכלל חלר לענין שיתוף לפי שיש מחילות מפסיקות וחלר בעי ד' אמות, ובהאי בית ליכא ד' אמות. והשתא, הך דבעל הבית שהיה שותף לשכיניו לזה ביין, והיא נמי דלעיל (דף סח.) דליקני מר רביעתא דחלא — לריך לומר דבחלר היה אותו חבית דבשיתופי מבואות איירי. דאילו עירובי חלירות — בעי פת. ובירושלמי משמע כפי' הקונט' דכ"ש בית, דאמר בפ' "מי שהוליאוהו": עירוב לריך בית, שיתוף מהו שילטרך בית? מלתא דשמואל אמרה: שיתוף לריך בית. ומסיק רבי אבהו[(ג)] בשם רבי יוחנן: נותנו בין באויר דחלר, ובין באויר דמבוי.

משמע בהדיא דכ"ש בית: **נהגו** העם כר' מאיר. בפרק בתרא דתענית (דף כו:) מפרש: דאורויי לא מורינן כוותיה, ואי עבדינן — לא מחינן בידייהו. וא"ת: מה מחאה שייך כאן אם מחמירין כר"מ, לעשות עירוב ושיתוף? וי"ל: דלא הוי ברכה לבטלה. אי נמי: אם נמנעים על כך להביא סכין וחמין לצורך מילה. אי נמי: לכי הא דאמר ב"מי שהוליאוהו" (לעיל דף מט.) גבי חלר שבין שני מבואות והיא רגילה באחד אם עירב רגיל לעלמו, וזה שאינו רגיל לא עירב, והיא נמי לא עירבה — דוחה אותה אלל מי שאינה רגילה, דכופין על מדת סדום. והשתא, אם עירב מי שאינו רגיל ולא שיתף, והם דוחין אותה אלל מי שאינו רגיל כר"מ דבעי שיתוף — לא מחינן בהו. אי נמי: אם עירבה עם שניהם ולא שיתפה אלא עם האחד, דלרבנן הוו להו עירבה עם שניהם, אסורה עם שניהם ולר"מ עם אותו ששיתפה עמו — מותרת, דעם האחר לא נשתתפה, ואין עירוב מועיל במקום שיתוף: **ומודין** כשמקצתן שרויין בחדרים ועליות שהן צריכין עירוב לכל חבורה וחבורה. והני חדרים ועליות איירי כגון שכל אחד פתוח לחלר, כדפירש בקונט' דהנך ה' חבורות ששבתו בטרקלין כולהו יש להן פתח מן הטרקלין לחלר. דאם לא היה לכל אחד פתח לחלר — הוה אמרינן פנימי נותן עירובו ודיו, או שני הפנימיים לר' יוחנן דסוף פרקין גבי עשרה בתים זה לפנים מזה. ומיהו, אם יש לאדם סופר או מלמד בביתו, או כעין אותן [הבחורים] הבאין ללמוד תורה ושרויין כל א' בחדר או בעלייה בפני עצמו, אע"פ שחלוקין מבעל הבית בפתו — אין אוסרין עליו, ולא בעו עירוב בין יש להם פתח לרה"ר בין אין להם פתח לרה"ר דלא מיבעיא אם כולם אוכלין במקום אחד, אף ע"פ שכל אחד ישן בחדרו — קי"ל כמאן דאמר לקמן (דף עג.): מקום פיתא גורם אלא אפילו לשמואל, דאמר מקום לינה גורם. או אפילו אוכלין וישנים כל אחד בחדרו — אין אוסרין זה על זה, כיון שכולם משתמשין בתוך הבית בכל עיסקי תשמישתיה באפייה ובבישול ובכל דבר — חשיבי כולהו כאילו אוכלים וישנים במקום אחד. אע"פ שיש להם פתח לגד רה"ר — הכל נקראים על שם בעל הבית. ועוד: דאין משאיל להם רשותו לאסור עליו, ולא זה על זה, ומאי לסלוקינהו, והוה ליה כה' שכירים וה' לקיטים דלא אמרי' להחמיר. כדאמרינן לעיל (דף סו.) דאחד נותן עירובו ודיו, ואפי' שרויין בחדרים ובעליות. דאם בשרויין כולם בבית — בזה לא הוה מספקא אביי, דקאמר: מהו. דאפילו היה הבית שלהם לא היו אוסרין זה על זה. וכיון דגבי נכרי דדירתו לא שמה דירה לא אסרי אלא חשיבי כולהו כחד — כל שכן גבי ישראל, דדירתו שמה דירה דבטלה דירתם גבי דירתו של בע"ה. ולא דמי למקצתן שרויין בחדרים ובעליות דהכא — שיש כח לזה כמו לזה. ואע"פ שהקילו בנכרי טפי מבישראל, דכי מושיל דוכתא לישראל אחר, דישראל נותן עירובו ודיו, ואע"פ שאין הנכרי רוצה להשכיר ובע"כ של נכרי, וכה"ג בביתו של ישראל לא שרי — התם נמי טעמא משום דדירת נכרי לא חשיב כ"כ, אבל מכל מקום יש ללמוד מדלא אסרי חמשה שכירים זה על זה גבי נכרי, כל שכן גבי ישראל, כדפרישית: **במחיצות** המגיעות לתקרה. והא דקתני מתני' דמודים היכא דמקצתן שרויין בחדרים ובעליות — לא דמי, דהכא איירי במחילות עראי, כגון יריעות שמפסיקין עד התקרה:

רבי

עא א ב מיי' פ"ד מהל' עירובין הל' ז סמג עשין א טוש"ע א"ח סי' שע סעיף ג:

רבינו חננאל

או משתתפין במבוי ביין ושכח אחד מבני חצר ולא עירב מותרין כאן וכאן ואסיקנא לכ"ע עירובי חצרות בפת דאין סומכין על עירוב במקום שיתוף דאמר רב יהודה אמר רב הלכה כר' מאיר ורב ברונא אמר רב הלכה כאלעזר בן תדאי: **מתני'** חמש חבורות ששבתו בטרקלין אחד. פי' בירה אחת כו'. אוקמיה רב נחמן מחלוקת ב"ש ובית הלל [בששבתו בבירה אחת] חלוקין וחלוקין במסיפס פי' פיסקא דארזי אבל אם הם חלוקים במחיצה י' טפחים ד"ה עירוב לכל חבורה איכא דאמרי אמר רב נחמן אף במסיפס מחלוקת פליגי בה ר' חייא ור' שמעון ב"ר חד אמר מחלוקת במחיצות שאין מגיעות לתקרה כו'.

הגהות הב"ח

(א) רש"י ד"ה אבל וכו' דהא ללישנא קמא: (ב) תד"ה בפת כו' והא דנקט בהא לישנא דלא גרע: (ג) בא"ד בשם ר"י שיתוף נותנו בין כו':

[...פירש גאון מסיפס כותל ...לול שיש בו חלונות. ערוך]

[...׳ רש"ל ורש"א בד"ה אבל]

[לקמן עט.]

מֵיתִיבִי, אָמַר רַבִּי יְהוּדָה הַסַּבָּר: לֹא נֶחְלְקוּ ב"ש וב"ה עַל מְחִיצוֹת הַמַּגִּיעוֹת לַתִּקְרָה — שֶׁצְּרִיכִין עֵירוּב לְכָל חֲבוּרָה וַחֲבוּרָה. °עַל מַה נֶחְלְקוּ — עַל מְחִיצוֹת שֶׁאֵין מַגִּיעוֹת לַתִּקְרָה. שֶׁבֵּית שַׁמַּאי אוֹמְרִים: עֵירוּב לְכָל חֲבוּרָה וַחֲבוּרָה, וּב"ה אוֹמְרִים: עֵירוּב א' לְכוּלָּן. לְמַאן דְּאָמַר בִּמְחִיצוֹת הַמַּגִּיעוֹת לַתִּקְרָה מַחֲלוֹקֶת — תְּיוּבְתָּא! וּלְמַאן דְּאָמַר בִּמְחִיצוֹת שֶׁאֵין מַגִּיעוֹת לַתִּקְרָה מַחֲלוֹקֶת — סִיַּיעְתָּא. לְהָךְ לִישָּׁנָא דְּאָמַר רַב נַחְמָן מַחֲלוֹקֶת בִּמְסִיפָס — תְּיוּבְתָּא! לְהָךְ לִישָּׁנָא דְּאָמַר רַב נַחְמָן אַף בִּמְסִיפָס מַחֲלוֹקֶת — לֵימָא תֶּהֱוֵי תְּיוּבְתָּא?! אָמַר לָךְ רַב נַחְמָן: פְּלִיגִי בִּמְחִיצָה, וְהוּא הַדִּין בִּמְסִיפָס. וְהַאי דְּקָא מִיפַּלְגִי בִּמְחִיצָה — לְהוֹדִיעֲךָ כֹּחָן דְּב"ה. וְלִיפַּלְגֵי בִּמְסִיפָס לְהוֹדִיעֲךָ כֹּחָן דְּב"ש! *כֹּחַ דְּהֶיתֵּרָא עֲדִיף. אָמַר רַב נַחְמָן, אָמַר רַב: הֲלָכָה כְּרַבִּי יְהוּדָה הַסַּבָּר. °אָמַר רַב נַחְמָן בַּר יִצְחָק: מַתְנִיתִין נַמִי דַּיְקָא: דְּקָתָנֵי "וּמוֹדִים בִּזְמַן שֶׁמִּקְצָתָן שְׁרוּיִין בַּחֲדָרִים וּבַעֲלִיּוֹת שֶׁצְּרִיכִין עֵירוּב לְכָל חֲבוּרָה וַחֲבוּרָה". מַאי חֲדָרִים וּמַאי עֲלִיּוֹת? אִילֵימָא חֲדָרִים — חֲדָרִים מַמָּשׁ וַעֲלִיּוֹת — עֲלִיּוֹת מַמָּשׁ, פְּשִׁיטָא! אֶלָּא לָאו: כְּעֵין חֲדָרִים, כְּעֵין עֲלִיּוֹת. וּמַאי נִיהוּ — מְחִיצוֹת הַמַּגִּיעוֹת לַתִּקְרָה, שְׁמַע מִינַּהּ. תָּנָא: [א]בַּמֶּה דְּבָרִים אֲמוּרִים — כְּשֶׁמּוֹלִיכִין אֶת עֵירוּבָן לְמָקוֹם אַחֵר, אֲבָל אִם הָיָה עֵירוּבָן בָּא אֶצְלָן — דִּבְרֵי הַכֹּל עֵירוּב אֶחָד לְכוּלָּן. כְּמַאן אָזְלָא הָא *דְּתַנְיָא: [ב]חֲמִשָּׁה שֶׁגָּבוּ אֶת עֵירוּבָן, כְּשֶׁמּוֹלִיכִין אֶת עֵירוּבָן לְמָקוֹם אַחֵר *עֵירוּב אֶחָד לְכוּלָּן. כְּמַאן — כְּבֵית הִלֵּל. וְאִיכָּא דְּאָמְרִי: בַּמֶּה דְּבָרִים אֲמוּרִים — כְּשֶׁהָיָה עֵירוּב בָּא אֶצְלָן, אֲבָל אִם הָיוּ מוֹלִיכִין אֶת עֵירוּבָן לְמָקוֹם אַחֵר — דִּבְרֵי הַכֹּל צְרִיכִין עֵירוּב לְכָל חֲבוּרָה וַחֲבוּרָה. כְּמַאן אָזְלָא הָא דְּתַנְיָא: חֲמִשָּׁה שֶׁגָּבוּ אֶת עֵירוּבָן, כְּשֶׁמּוֹלִיכִין אֶת עֵירוּבָן לְמָקוֹם אַחֵר עֵירוּב אֶחָד לְכוּלָּן, כְּמַאן — דְּלָא כְּחַד.§ **מתני'** [ג]הָאַחִין שֶׁהָיוּ אוֹכְלִין עַל שֻׁלְחַן אֲבִיהֶם וִישֵׁנִים בְּבָתֵּיהֶם — צְרִיכִין עֵירוּב לְכָל אֶחָד וְאֶחָד. לְפִיכָךְ אִם שָׁכַח אֶחָד מֵהֶם וְלֹא עֵירֵב — מְבַטֵּל אֶת רְשׁוּתוֹ. אֵימָתַי — בִּזְמַן שֶׁמּוֹלִיכִין עֵירוּבָן בְּמָקוֹם אַחֵר. אֲבָל אִם הָיָה עֵירוּב בָּא אֶצְלָן, אוֹ שֶׁאֵין עִמָּהֶן דִּיּוּרִין בֶּחָצֵר — אֵינָן צְרִיכִין לְעָרֵב.§ **גמ'** ש"מ: *מְקוֹם לִינָה גּוֹרֵם! אָמַר רַב יְהוּדָה, אָמַר רַב: [ד]בִּמְקַבְּלֵי פְּרָס שָׁנוּ. ת"ר: מִי שֶׁיֵּשׁ לוֹ בֵּית שַׁעַר אַכְסַדְרָה וּמִרְפֶּסֶת בַּחֲצַר חֲבֵירוֹ — הֲרֵי זֶה אֵין אוֹסֵר עָלָיו. (אֶת) °בֵּית הַתֶּבֶן (וְאֶת) בֵּית הַבָּקָר בֵּית הָעֵצִים וּבֵית הָאוֹצָרוֹת — הֲרֵי זֶה אוֹסֵר עָלָיו. רַבִּי יְהוּדָה אוֹמֵר: [ה]אֵינוֹ אוֹסֵר אֶלָּא מְקוֹם דִּירָה בִּלְבַד. *אָמַר רַבִּי יְהוּדָה: מַעֲשֶׂה בְּבֶן *נַפָּחָא שֶׁהָיוּ לוֹ חָמֵשׁ חֲצֵרוֹת בְּאוּשָׁא, וּבָא מַעֲשֶׂה לִפְנֵי חֲכָמִים, וְאָמְרוּ: אֵינוֹ אוֹסֵר אֶלָּא בֵּית דִּירָה בִּלְבַד. בֵּית דִּירָה סַלְקָא דַּעְתָּךְ?! אֶלָּא אֵימָא: מְקוֹם דִּירָה. מַאי מְקוֹם דִּירָה? רַב אָמַר:

מְקוֹם

רש"י

הַסַּבָּר. עַל שֵׁם חוּרְפֵיהּ קָרֵי לֵיהּ הָכִי: לְהָךְ לִישָּׁנָא דְּאָמַר רַב נַחְמָן מַחֲלוֹקֶת בִּמְסִיפָס. אֲבָל בִּמְחִיצּוֹת מוֹדוּ ב"ה — תְּיוּבְתָּא, דְּהָא בְּהֶדְיָא קָתָנֵי דְּבִמְחִיצּוֹת(א) שָׁרוּ: אֶלָּא לְלִישָּׁנָא בָּתְרָא דְּקָאָמַר דְּבִמְסִיפָס נַמִי אָסְרִי ב"ש מִי לֵימָא דְּתֶהֱוֵי הָא תְּיוּבְתֵּיהּ, דְּקָתָנֵי בִּמְחִיצּוֹת הוּא דִּפְלִיגִי הָא בִּמְסִיפָס מוֹדוּ: הֲלָכָה כְּרַבִּי יְהוּדָה. דְּבִמְחִיצּוֹת הַמַּגִּיעוֹת לַתִּקְרָה מוֹדוּ: חֲדָרִים מַמָּשׁ. שֶׁלֹּא הָיוּ מְחוּבָּרִין מֵעוֹלָם: בַּמֶּה דְּבָרִים אֲמוּרִים. דְּאָסְרִי ב"ש — כְּשֶׁהֵם מוֹלִיכִין הָעֵירוּב בְּאֶחָד מִשְּׁאָר בָּתֵּי הֶחָצֵר: אֲבָל אִם הָיוּ. שְׁאָר בְּנֵי הֶחָצֵר מְבִיאִין פִּיתָּן לַטְּרַקְלִין — דִּבְרֵי הַכֹּל כו' וְהַאי תַּנָּא, מִדְּקָא מַפְלִיג בֵּין מָקוֹם אַחֵר לְבָא אֶצְלָן — סְבִירָא לֵיהּ טַעֲמַיְיהוּ דְּב"ש וּבֵית הִלֵּל לָאו בִּמְחִיצּוֹת פְּלִיגִי, אֶלָּא אֲפִי' לְבֵית שַׁמַּאי נַמִי טְרַקְלִין מְחַבְּרָן וְאֵין צָרִיךְ עֵירוּב בֵּינַיְיהוּ, וְהָווּ לְהוּ כַּחֲמִשָּׁה שֶׁגָּבוּ אֶת עֵירוּבָן, וּסְבִירָא לְהוּ דַּחֲמִשָּׁה שֶׁעֵירְבוּ אֶת חֲצֵירָן וּבָאִין לְעָרֵב עִם חָצֵר אַחֶרֶת, אִם מוֹלִיכִין שָׁם אֶת עֵירוּבָן — אֵין א' מֵהֶן שָׁלִיחַ לְכוּלָּן, אֶלָּא כּוּלָּן צְרִיכִין לִיתֵּן פַּת. וְאִם עֵירוּב בָּא בְּבֵית א' מֵהֶן — כּוּלָּן שָׁוִין שָׁם. וְהָנָךְ דִּטְרַקְלִין נַמִי, כֵּיוָן דִּרְשׁוּת אַחַת הִיא — לְהָנֵי דָּמוּ. דְּאִי לְבֵית שַׁמַּאי רְשׁוּיוֹת חֲלוּקוֹת הֵן, וְהֵן לֹא עֵירְבוּ, כִּי עֵירוּב בָּא אֶצְלָן — מַאי הָוֵי: שֶׁגָּבוּ אֶת עֵירוּבָן. שֶׁדָּרִין בְּחָצֵר וְעֵירְבוּ אֶת חֲצֵירָן: וְאִיכָּא דְּאָמְרִי כו'. וּבְהָא פְּלִיגִי, דְּב"ש סָבְרִי: אע"פ שֶׁרְשׁוּת אַחַת הִיא, וְדָמֵי לַחֲמִשָּׁה שֶׁעֵירְבוּ וְעֵירוּב בָּא אֶצְלָן — אֲפִילּוּ הָכִי כּוּלְּהוּ בָּעֵי לְעָרוּבֵי וּב"ה סָבְרִי כֵּיוָן דְּעֵירוּב בָּא אֶצְלָן — לֹא:§ **מתני'** הַשּׁוּתָפִין. לֹא גָּרְסִינַן: וִישֵׁנִים בְּבָתֵּיהֶם. וְהֵם וַאֲבִיהֶם וַאֲחֵרִים דָּרִין בְּחָצֵר אַחַת: שֶׁצְּרִיכִין עֵירוּב לְכָל אֶחָד וְאֶחָד. אִם רוֹצִין לְעָרֵב עִם שְׁאָר בְּנֵי הֶחָצֵר, וְטַעֲמָא מְפָרֵשׁ בַּגְּמָרָא: מְבַטֵּל אֶת רְשׁוּתוֹ. צָרִיךְ לְבַטֵּל אֶת רְשׁוּתוֹ: אֵימָתַי בִּזְמַן שֶׁמּוֹלִיכִין אֶת עֵירוּבָן. לִיתְּנוֹ בְּאֶחָד מִבָּתֵּי שְׁאָר בְּנֵי הֶחָצֵר, דְּהוֹאִיל וְהוּזְקְקוּ לְעֵירוּב אָמְרִינַן בַּגְּמָרָא: מִגּוֹ דִּשְׁאָר דִּיּוּרִין אָסְרֵי — אִינְהוּ נַמִי אָסְרֵי, וּצְרִיכִין כּוּלָּן לִיתֵּן פַּת הוֹאִיל וַחֲלוּקִין דִּיּוּרֵיהֶן בְּלִינָה. וּמְקַבְּלֵי פְּרָס הֵן, כִּדְמוּקֵי בַּגְּמָ' שֶׁאֵין אוֹכְלִין בְּבֵית אֲבִיהֶן מַמָּשׁ: אֲבָל אִם הָיָה. עֵירוּב כָּל הֶחָצֵר בָּא לְבֵית אֲבִיהֶן, שֶׁלֹּא הוּזְקְקוּ לְעֵירוּב, דְּאָמְרִינַן בְּ"מִי שֶׁהוֹצִיאוּהוּ" (לעיל דף מט.): בַּיִת שֶׁמַּנִּיחִין בּוֹ עֵירוּב — אֵין צָרִיךְ לִיתֵּן אֶת הַפַּת, וְהֵם כּוּלָּם נִמְשָׁכִין בּוֹ: אוֹ שֶׁאֵין עִמָּהֶן דִּיּוּרִין אֲחֵרִים. שֶׁאֵין דִּיּוּרִין מַזְקִיקִין אוֹתָן לְעֵירוּב: אֵין צְרִיכִין לְעָרֵב. דִּכְיְחִידִים הֵן: **גמ'** שָׁמְעַתְּ מִינַּהּ מְקוֹם לִינָה גּוֹרֵם. דְּאִי הָווּ יְשֵׁנִים בְּבֵית אֲבִיהֶן אֲפִילּוּ מוֹלִיכִין עֵירוּבָן לְמָקוֹם אַחֵר — לָא הָווּ צְרִיכִין לְעָרוּבֵי אֶלָּא אֲבִיהֶם. וְלֵימָא תֶּיהֱוֵי תְּיוּבְתֵּיהּ דְּרַב, דְּאָמַר לְקַמָּן בִּשְׁמַעְתִּין "מְקוֹם פִּיתָּא גּוֹרֵם". וַהֲרֵי אֵלּוּ אוֹכְלִין בְּבֵית אֲבִיהֶם וְחָשְׁבִינַן לְהוּ חֲלוּקִין: בִּמְקַבְּלֵי פְּרָס. הוֹלָכָה מִבֵּית אֲבִיהֶם, וְאֵין אוֹכְלִין עַל שׁוּלְחָנוֹ מַמָּשׁ:

מְקוֹם

תוספות

רבי יהודה הסבר. רבינו חננאל גרים: *הסבך. פירוש: (ב) גדיל לסבכה, כעין מצנפת וכובע, כמו "שבכים מעשה שבכה" (מלכים א ז). א"נ: על שם עירו, דבספר יהושע (טו) כמו כן כתיב "מדין *וסככה": **כח** דהיתרא עדיף ליה. לא שייך הכא למיפרך ליפלגו בתרוייהו, כדפריך בריש ביצה (*דף ב:) דהתם כדי להודיע כחן דבית הלל דאוסרין הוה ליה לאשמעי' בתרוייהו, משום דכח דהיתרא עדיף דב"ש לא חשיבי ליה כ"כ, דב"ש במקום ב"ה אינה משנה: **אמר** ר"נ אמר רב הלכה כרבי יהודה. אע"ג דאותבי' מינה לל"ק דר"נ(ג), אתיא כלישנא בתרא: **אבל** אם היה עירוב בא אצלן דברי הכל עירוב אחד לכולן. וא"ת: טעמא דב"ש אתא לאשמעינן?! דלב"ה לא איצטריך, דאפילו מוליכין עירובן אמר עירוב אחד לכולן. וכי האי גוונא פריך במס' שבת בפ' "ר"א דמילה" (ד' קלה.). וי"ל: דלב"ה נמי נפקא מינה, דכעין חדרים ועליות דדווקא במוליכין עירובן קאמר דמודו שצריכין עירוב לכל חבורה וחבורה אבל בעירוב בא אצלן עירוב אחד לכולן דכעין חדרים ועליות לב"ה כמו מחיצות שאין מגיעות לתקרה לב"ש. ומיהו, בחדרים ועליות ממש — אין נראה לחלק בין מוליכין עירובן לעירוב בא אצלן, מדפשיט ליה כ"כ להתלמוד, דקאמר אילימא חדרים ועליות ממש — פשיטא: **כמאן** כבית הלל. וליכא למימר דאתיא כב"ש, וברייתא באין עמהם דיורין כדאוקמינן לה לקמן. אבל במתניתין — כשיש עמהן דיורין, דמיגו דהני אסרי אהדדי — הני נמי אסרי. דהיכי דמי הני דיורין? אי בחצר קיימי — מ"מ כל הטרקלין חשיב כחדא, ומטלטלין זה עם זה בכל הטרקלין בלא עירוב כשיש דיורין בחצר כמו שאין דיורין בחצר. ואי בעו ביניהם עירוב — כשיש עמהן דיורין בחצר — הכי נמי ליבעי כשאין עמהן דיורין. דמה ענין דיורין בחצר לגבי הטרקלין? ומיהו, ה"מ למימר: כגון שיש בטרקלין דמתניתין חדרים ועליות גמורין שאין להם פתח בחצר, אלא יוצאין דרך טרקלין. דמיגו דהני אסרי — הנך ה' חבורות נמי אסרי. אבל לא משמע ליה לאוקמי מתניתין בהכי, ועוד: דדילמא בהא הוו מודו ב"ה: **במקבלי** פרס שנו. ואע"פ דמקום פיתא ולינה בבתיהם — אהני מה שאוכלים מצל אביהם דאם היה עירוב בא אצלם, או שאין עמהם דיורין — אין צריכין לערב: **מי** שיש לו בית שער אינו אוסר עליו. אע"פ שדרין בו, כדתנן לקמן בפרק "כיצד משתתפין" (דף פה:). ואם תאמר: אי בבית שער דבית — תיפוק ליה משום בית דאסר על בני החצר אע"פ שאין דרין בו, מידי דהוה אבית התבן! וי"ל: כגון שנתן בעל הבית עירובו. וקמ"ל דהדר בבית שער לא בעי לערב, דלא אסר:

ודניאל

עין משפט נר מצוה

[ע' בערוך ערך סבך]

[לפנינו בקרא כתיב וסככה בב' כפי"ן]

[ע' תוס' שם ד"ה ונפלוג בתרוייהו]

עב א מיי' פ"ד מהל' עירובין הל"ב טוש"ע א"ח סי' שע סעיף ג:

עג ב מיי' שם הל' ד:

עד ג ד מיי' שם הל' ו סמג עשין א טוש"ע א"ח שם סעיף ה:

עה ה מיי' שם הל' ח טוש"ע שם סעיף א:

רבינו חננאל

מיתיבי א"ר יהודה הסכך פי' גדיל סבכה *) על שם עירו לא נחלקו ב"ש וב"ה על מחיצות המגיעות לתקרה שצריכין עירוב לכל חבורה וחבורה על מה נחלקו על מחיצות שאינן מגיעות לתקרה שב"ש אומרים עירוב לכל חבורה וחבורה וב"ה אומרים עירוב אחד לכולן. אמר רב נחמן בר יצחק מתני' נמי דיקא דקתני מודין בזמן שמקצתן שרוין בחדרים או בעליות שצריכין עירוב לכל חבורה וחבורה ואוקימנא כעין חדרין וכעין עליות ומאי נינהו מחיצות המגיעות לתקרה. תנא בד"א במוליכין עירובן למקום אחד. אבל אם היה עירובן בא אצלן דברי הכל עירוב אחד לכולן והא דתניא ה' שגבו את עירובן כשמוליכין אותו במקום אחד אחד מוליך ע"י כולן כמאן כב"ה: **מתני'** האחין שהיו אוכלין על שלחן אביהן כו' אוקימנא במקבלי פרס שנו. פי' לאו אוכלין על שלחן אביהן ממש אלא מקבלין פרס משלחן אביהן ואוכלין אותו בבתיהן שנמצאת אכילה ושינה בבתיהן: ת"ר מי שיש לו בית שער אכסדרה ומרפסת בחצר חבירו הרי זה אינו אוסר עליו כו' עד ובא מעשה לפני חכמים ולא אסרו אלא מקום בית דירה כו' דירה בלבד. מאי מקום בית דירה רב אמר

*) לפי גי' הב"ח בדברי התוס' ד"ה רבי נראה דצ"ל בדברי רבינו ר"י הסכך פי' גדול סבכה א"נ הסכך גרסינן על שם עירו.

הגהות הב"ח

(א) רש"י ד"ה להך לישנא וכו' במחיצות עשרה מודו: (ב) תוס' ד"ה ר' יהודה וכו' פירוש גודל סבכה וכו' כמו שבכים מעשה שבכה אי נמי הסכך גרסינן על שם וכו' מדין וסככה הס"ד: (ג) ד"ה אמר וכו' דרב נחמן הא אתיא:

גליון הש"ס

גמ' על מה נחלקו על מחיצות שאין מגיעות לתקרה. עיין לקמן דף עט ע"א תד"ה ש"מ: **שם** אמר רב נחמן בר יצחק מתני' נמי דיקא. עיין לעיל דף מג ע"ב תד"ה יתיב. ולעיל דף יח ע"ב תד"ה מתקיף: **שם** אמר ר"י אמר רב במקבלי פרס. עיין לקמן דף עט ע"ב תוס' ד"ה וע"י אשתו: **שם** בית התבן. עיין לקמן דף פה ע"ב תוס' ד"ה בית התבן ולעיל דף ע ע"א תוס' ד"ה הב"ע:

מסורת הש"ס

[ברכות ס. וש"נ ועי' פי' על זה ברש"י דביצה ב ד"ה דהיתרא]

לעיל מט: ע"ש

[ע' רש"י לעיל סו. ד"ה אחד מערב]

[לקמן עג. עד:]

[תוס' פ"ה]

[שם אית נשיא]

מקום פיתא. שהוא אוכל שם: קייצין. שומרי תאנים המשטוחים בשדה ליבשן לקציעות: בזמן שדרכן ללין בעיר. במקום שאוכלין, אע"פ שקדש עליהן היום בשדה – יש להן מן העיר אלפים לכל רוח, וכל העיר להן כד' אמות: בזמן שדרכן ללין בשדה. אע"פ שאוכלין בעיר – אין מודדין להן אלא מן השדה: תורה אור

*[א]מקום פיתא, ושמואל אמר: מקום לינה. מיתיבי: [ב]הרועים והקייצין והבורגנין ושומרי פירות, בזמן שדרכן ללין בעיר — הרי הן כאנשי העיר, בזמן שדרכן ללין בשדה — יש להם אלפים לכל רוח! התם אנן סהדי דאי ממטו להו ריפתא התם — טפי ניחא להו. *אמר רב יוסף: לא שמיע לי הא שמעתא. *אמר ליה אביי: את אמרת ניהלן, ואהא אמרת ניהלן: האחין שהיו אוכלין על שלחן אביהן וישנים בבתיהן — צריכין עירוב לכל אחד ואחד. ואמרינן לך: שמע מינה — מקום לינה גורם. ואמרת לן עלה, אמר רב יהודה, אמר רב: במקבלי פרס שנו. תנו רבנן: [ג]מי שיש לו חמש נשים מקבלות פרס מבעליהן, וחמשה עבדים מקבלין פרס מרביהן, רבי יהודה בן בתירה מתיר בנשים ואוסר בעבדים. °רבי יהודה בן בבא מתיר בעבדים ואוסר בנשים. אמר רב: מאי טעמא דרבי יהודה בן בבא, דכתיב: °"ודניאל בתרע מלכא". פשיטא, בן אצל אביו — כדאמרן. אשה אצל בעלה ועבד אצל רבו — פלוגתא דרבי יהודה בן בתירה ורבי יהודה בן בבא. תלמיד אצל רבו מאי? ת"ש: דרב בי רבי חייא אמר: [ד]אין אנו צריכין לערב, שהרי אנו סומכין על שולחנו של רבי חייא. ורבי חייא בי רבי אמר: אין אנו צריכין לערב, שהרי אנו סומכין על שולחנו של רבי. בעא מיניה אביי מרבה: חמשה שגבו את עירובן, כשמוליכין את עירובן למקום אחר, עירוב אחד לכולן, או צריכין עירוב לכל אחד ואחד? אמר ליה: עירוב אחד לכולן. והא אחין, דכי גבו דמו, וקתני: "צריכין עירוב לכל אחד ואחד"! הכא במאי עסקינן — כגון דאיכא דיורין בהדייהו, דמגו דהני אסרי — הני נמי אסרי. הכי נמי מסתברא, דקתני: אימתי — בזמן שמוליכין את עירובן במקום אחר, אבל אם היה עירובן בא אצלם, או שאין דיורין עמהן בחצר — אין צריכין לערב, שמע מינה. בעא מיניה רב חייא בר אבין מרב ששת: בני בי רב דאכלי נהמא בבאגא, ואתו ובייתי בבי רב, כי משחינן להו תחומא, מבי רב משחינן להו, או מבאגא משחינן להו? אמר ליה: [ה]משחינן מבי רב. והרי נותן את עירובו בתוך אלפים אמה ואתי וביית בביתיה דמשחינן ליה תחומא מעירוביה!(א) בההוא אנן סהדי, ובהדא אנן סהדי. בההוא אנן סהדי דאי מיתדר ליה התם — ניחא ליה. ובהדא אנן סהדי דאי מייתו להו ריפתא לבי רב — ניחא להו טפי. בעי רמי בר חמא מרב חסדא: אב ובנו, הרב ותלמידו, כרבים דמו, או כיחידים דמו? צריכין עירוב, או אין צריכין עירוב? מבוי שלהן ניתר בלחי וקורה, או אין ניתר בלחי וקורה? א"ל, תניתוה: [ו]אב ובנו, הרב ותלמידו, בזמן שאין עמהן דיורין — הרי הן כיחידים, ואין צריכין לערב. [ז]ומבוי שלהן ניתר בלחי וקורה. § **מתני'** חמש חצירות פתוחות זו לזו ופתוחות למבוי, עירבו בחצירות ולא נשתתפו במבוי — מותרין בחצירות ואסורין במבוי. ואם

[לקמן עד:] ה"ג: דאי ממטו להו ריפתא להתם טפי ניחא להו. הואיל וצריכין לשמור שהרי ישנים שם כל הלילה: לא שמיע לי הא שמעתא. דאמר רב: מקום פיתא גורם. רב יוסף חלה ושכח תלמודו, [נדרים מא.] *והיה אביי תלמידו מזכירו: מקבלות פרס. וכל אחת יש לה דירה לבדה עמו בחצר: אוסר בעבדים. [לעיל י. וש"נ] שאינן נמשכין אחריו: [שם] בתרע מלכא. בכ"מ שהוא – חשיב ליה בתרע מלכא: תלמיד אצל רבו. דר עמו בחצר, ומקבל פרס הימנו, מאי: דרב בי ר' חייא. כשהיה מקבל פרס מבי ר' חייא: למקום אחר. לחצר אחרת. אביי לא שמיע ליה ההיא מתניתא דתניא לעיל [דף עב:] ה' שגבו את עירובן. אי נמי: שמיע ליה, ומיבעיא ליה הלכתא מאי? משום דאוקימנא לה בפלוגתא: והא אחין. דמתניתין, כגבו את עירובן דמי. דהא קתני אם אין עמהן דיורין — אין צריכין לערב: הכא במאי עסקינן דאיכא דיורין בהדייהו. ומוליכין דמתניתין — אפי' בחצר שלהן קאמר, שמערבין עם דיורין שעמהן: דמגו דהני אסרי. והזקיקוהו לעירוב — הני נמי אסרי איש על אחיו. אבל שתי חצירות ופתח ביניהם, וגבו אלו עירובן לעצמן והותרה חצירן, ואלו לעצמן והותרה חצירן, או שדרין באחת מהן אב ובניו בלא דיורין אחרים, ובאו לערב זו עם זו — הואיל ואין אוסר עליהן וליכא מגו — אחד נעשה שליח לכולן. דיקא נמי דטעמא משום מגו, דקתני: או שאין עמהן כו' הא יש עמהן, דאיכא מגו — צריכין. וטעמא דרישא משום דיורין הוא: בבאגא. בית אושפיזא בבקעה: בייתי. לנים: בבי רב. בית המדרש, ובתוך אלפים אמה הוא: מבאגא משחינן להו. אלפים לכל רוח, ולא מבי רב, דבתר פיתא אזלינן. או דילמא: מקום לינה גורם: בההיא אנן סהדי. הואיל והוא צריך ללכת מחר לאותה הרוח, אי הוה ליה הלילה הזה בית דירה ללון במקום עירוב – טפי הוה ניחא ליה: ה"ג: דאי מייתי ליה ריפתא לבי רב טפי ניחא ליה: האב ובנו הרב ותלמידו כרבים דמו. לענין שתי חצירות זו לפנים מזו, ודריסת רגל הפנימית על החיצונה. ותנן במתניתין [לקמן עה.] אם היו של יחידים, שיחיד דר בפנימית, דהויא רגל המותרת במקומה – אינה אוסרת שלא במקומה. ואם של רבים, ולא עירבה פנימית לעצמה דהויא רגל האסורה במקומה – אוסרת על החיצונה, אפי' עירבה חיצונה לעצמה: צריכין עירוב. כשאין דיורין אחרים עמהן: ניתר בלחי וקורה. דקי"ל אין מבוי ניתר בלחי וקורה עד שיהו בתים וחצירות פתוחים לתוכו. ואת"ל הני כיחידים דמו – הכא מי חשבינן שתי חצירות אחת של אב ואחת של בן כחדא חצר, ולא מישתרי מבוי דידהו: ומבוי שלהן ניתר בלחי וקורה. לערב חצירות ואע"ג דאין צריכין – מ"מ פתוחות לו: **מתני'** (חמש חצירות פתוחות זו לזו) עירבו בחצירות. אף מזו לזו: ואסורין במבוי. דאין סומכין על עירוב במקום שיתוף: ואם

ודניאל בתרע מלכא. פי' ר"ח: וסימנך בבא – שער, תרע – שער. פי': רבי יהודה בן בבא הוא מתיר בעבדים. ובבא ותרע הכל שער. נראה דמייתי קרא לסימן ולטעם לדבריו: **בעא** מיניה אביי מרבה חמשה שגבו עירובן כו'. ואע"ג דאביי ידע להאי ברייתא דלעיל, דהא בסוף פרק "מי שהוציאוהו" (לעיל דף מט:) פריך מינה לרבה, דקאמר ליה לדידך קשה, לשמואל קשה גבי עירוב משום קנין – לא שאל כאן לרבה אלא כדי להקשות לו ממתניתין:

כרבים דמו או כיחידים דמו. פי' בקונטרס: לענין ב' חצירות זו לפנים מזו, דתנן בסוף פירקין: ואם היו של יחידים – אין צריכין לערב. ומיבעיא ליה אם אב ובנו דרים בפנימית, אי חשיבי כיחידים או כרבים. תימה לר"י: דממתני' שמעינן ליה, דמוכחא דאין אב ובנו אוסרים זה על זה. וכיון דלא אסרי – אם כן הויא לה רגל המותרת במקומה, ואינה אוסרת שלא במקומה. דהיא טעמא דיחידים אין צריכין לערב. וי"ל: דמקבלי פרס מיבעיא ליה, ומספקא ליה אי מתני' בסמוכין על שלחן אביהם ממש, והתם הוא דאין צריכין לערב כשאין עמהם דיורין, דאהני קצת מה שסמוכים בפת אע"ג דמקום לינה גורם, אבל מקבלי פרס, אע"ג דאין עמהם דיורין – צריכין לערב, או דילמא: מתניתין במקבלי פרס, כדאוקמא רב, דאמר התם: מקום פיתא גורם. ומייתי ראייה מברייתא, דסתם האב ובנו הרב ותלמידו מקבלי פרס נינהו, כיון שישנים בבתיהם, היכא דלא קתני בהדיא אוכלין על שלחן אביהן. ומיהו, לא משמע כלל לומר כן. ונראה לר"י: דמיבעיא ליה בדליכא בכל המבוי אלא אב ובנו, או הרב ותלמידו. דבתים וחצירות שלהם פתוחין למבוי. וכיון שכל המבוי שלהם – משתכחת תורת עירוב. וקמיבעיא ליה נמי, דאם תימצי לומר אין צריכין לערב – מבוי שלהם ניתר בלחי וקורה או לא? אימא

עו א מיי' פ"ד מה' עירובין הל' ד וסמג עשין א טוש"ע א"ח סי' שע סעיף ה:
עז ב טור א"ח סי' תט בב"י:
עח ג ד מיי' שם הלכה ה ו טוש"ע שם סעיף ו:
עט ה מיי' פ"ז מהל' עירובין הלכה י טוש"ע א"ח סי' תט ס"ז:
פ ו מיי' פ"ד מהלכות עירובין הלכה ה:
פא ז טוש"ע א"ח סי' שסג סעיף כו:

הגהות הב"ח
(א) גמ' תחומא מעירוביה אמר ליה בההוא אנן סהדי:

גליון הש"ס
גמ' ר"י בן בבא מתיר בעבדים. עיין לקמן דף עט ע"ב תוס' ד"ה וע"י אשתו:

רבינו חננאל
מקום פיתא ושמואל אמר מקום לינה ומותבינן לרב מהא הרועין והקייצין והבורגנין. פי' שומרי הקייצות או שומרי הבורגנין ושומרי פירות תלושין בזמן שדרכן ללון בעיר הרי הן כאנשי העיר ויש להן אלפים אמה לכל רוח. דרכן ללון בשדה אין להן אלא אלפים אמה בלבד. פי' ממקום שקנו בו שביתה. ואפילו מדתן כלה בעיר אין להן אלא אלפים אמה בלבד ש"מ מקום לינה גורם. ודחי רב שאני התם אנן סהדי כלומר ברי לן דאי הוו ממטי להו ריפתא התם בשדה התם ניחא להו למיכרך ריפתא הלכך כאלו מקום פיתא דידהו התם בשדה היא. ת"ר מי שיש לו [חמש] נשים מקבלות פרס מבעליהן ושוכנות במקום אחד מקום פיתה ומקום לינה. וכן ה' עבדים מקבלי פרס. ר' יהודה בן בתירה מתיר בנשים שיוצאות בעירוב בעליהן ואין צריכות הן עירוב כל אחת ואחת. ואוסר בעבדים. והיה מצריכם עירוב כל אחד ואחד. ר' יהודה בן בבא מתיר בעבדים ואוסר בנשים אמר רב מ"ט דר' יהודה בן בבא דמתיר בעבדים ואוסר בנשי' משום (דמשכינים) [דשוכנים] על פתח אדוניהם וכאלו מקום אכילתם ומקום שינה שלהם שם. וסימן ודניאל בתרע מלכא כלומר דניאל בשער המלך מקבל פרס היה ופיתה ולינה בביתיה הוה וכתיב ביה ודניאל בתרע מלכא כלומר כאלו שכונתו בשער המלך היא וסימן בבא שער ותרע שער. מאן תני תרע ר' יהודה בן בבא ששמו שער כי היכי דלא תתחלק מי הוא המתיר בעבדים בין ר' יהודה בן בתירה ובין ר' יהודה בן בבא. תרע. מי ששמו שער סמך על השער וא' דניאל בתרע מלכא. וסוגיין דשמעתין כרב וכיון דאוקימנא בן אצל אביו [דמתניתין] במקבל פרס [שנו] אמרינן תלמיד אצל רבו יוצא בעירוב רבו או לא ואסיקנא רב בבית ר' חייא ור' חייא בבית רבי הא אמרי אין צריכין לערב שהרי אנו סמוכין על שלחנו: **בעא** מיניה אביי מרבה ה' שגבו עירובן כשמוליכין עירובן למקום אחד אחד מוליך ע"י כולן או כל אחד ואחד מוליך ע"י עצמו ופשט ליה אחד מוליך ע"י כולן ואקשינן עליה והא אחין כמו שגבו דמו. מדקתני סיפא אם אין עמהן דיורין אין צריכין לערב כלומר הן בלא עירוב מותרין כמו אחרים שעירבו וגיבו את עירובן וקתני צריכין עירוב לכל אחד ומשני התם גבי אחין כגון דאיכא אחריני בהדייהו מגו דהני אסרי אהני הני נמי אסרי אהני הכי נמי מסתברא דאיכא אחריני התם דשמעינן להא מסיפא דמתני' דאחין דקתני סיפא אימתי בזמן שמוליכין את עירובן למקום אחד כו' בעו מיניה מרב ששת בני בי רב דאכלי בבגא פי' בשדה ולנין בי רב מאן מודדין להן התחום. ממקום פיתה או ממקום לינה ופשט להו מבי רב שהוא ממקום לינה ואקשינן עליה והא הנותן עירובו במקום אחד ולא אזיל גוי *) התם ונותנין לו מדת התחום ממקום עירובו אע"ג דלא לן שם. ושני להו רב ששת כשיטתיה דרב לעילא התם גבי נותן עירובו אנן סהדי דאי מתדר ליה התם ניחא ליה וכאילו מקום לינה לשם הוא. הכא בבני בי רב אנן סהדי דאי איכא דמייתי להו ריפתא הכא ניחא להו שנמצא כאלו מקום פיתה ומקום לינה במקום אחד הוא ואסיקנא האב ובנו הרב ותלמידו בזמן שאין עמהן דיורין הרי הן כיחידים ואין צריכין לערב ומבוי שלהן ניתר בלחי וקורה שהרי בתים וחצרות פתוחות לתוכו: **מתני'** חמש חצרות פתוחות

*) אולי צ"ל ולא אזיל ללון שם נותנין לו כו'.

וְאִם נִשְׁתַּתְּפוּ בַּמָּבוֹי – מוּתָּרִין כָּאן וְכָאן. עֵירְבוּ בַּחֲצֵירוֹת וְנִשְׁתַּתְּפוּ בַּמָּבוֹי, וְשָׁכַח אֶחָד מִבְּנֵי חָצֵר וְלֹא עֵירֵב – מוּתָּרִין כָּאן וְכָאן. *מִבְּנֵי מָבוֹי וְלֹא נִשְׁתַּתֵּף – מוּתָּרִין בַּחֲצֵירוֹת וַאֲסוּרִין בַּמָּבוֹי, *שֶׁהַמָּבוֹי לַחֲצֵירוֹת כְּחָצֵר לַבָּתִּים.§

גמ' מַנִּי? רַבִּי מֵאִיר הִיא, דְּאָמַר: בָּעֵינַן עֵירוּב וּבָעֵינַן שִׁיתּוּף. אֵימָא מְצִיעֲתָא: "וְאִם נִשְׁתַּתְּפוּ בַּמָּבוֹי – מוּתָּרִין כָּאן וְכָאן", אֲתָאן לְרַבָּנַן, דְּאָמְרִי: בַּחֲדָא סַגְיָא! הָא ל"ק; וְאִם נִשְׁתַּתְּפוּ נַמִי קָאָמַר. אֵימָא סֵיפָא: עֵירְבוּ בַּחֲצֵירוֹת וְנִשְׁתַּתְּפוּ בַּמָּבוֹי, וְשָׁכַח אֶחָד מִבְּנֵי חָצֵר וְלֹא עֵירֵב – מוּתָּרִים כָּאן וְכָאן. הֵיכִי דָּמֵי? אִי דְּלָא בַּטֵּיל – אַמַּאי מוּתָּרִים? אֶלָּא פְּשִׁיטָא – דְּבַטֵּיל, אֵימָא סֵיפָא: שָׁכַח אֶחָד מִבְּנֵי מָבוֹי וְלֹא נִשְׁתַּתְּפוּ – מוּתָּרִין בַּחֲצֵירוֹת, וַאֲסוּרִין בַּמָּבוֹי. וְאִי דְּבַטֵּיל – אַמַּאי אֲסוּרִין בַּמָּבוֹי? וְכִי תֵּימָא: קָסָבַר רַבִּי מֵאִיר אֵין בִּיטּוּל רְשׁוּת בַּמָּבוֹי – וְהָא *תַּנְיָא: שֶׁהֲרֵי בִּיטֵּל לָכֶם רְשׁוּתוֹ, דִּבְרֵי רַבִּי מֵאִיר! אֶלָּא פְּשִׁיטָא – דְּלָא בַּטֵּיל. וּמִדְּסֵיפָא דְּלָא בַּטֵּיל – רֵישָׁא נַמִי דְּלָא בַּטֵּיל. רֵישָׁא וְסֵיפָא רַבִּי מֵאִיר, מְצִיעֲתָא רַבָּנַן! כּוּלָּהּ רַבִּי מֵאִיר הִיא, וְטַעְמָא מַאי אָמַר רַבִּי מֵאִיר בָּעֵינַן עֵירוּב וּבָעֵינַן שִׁיתּוּף – שֶׁלֹּא לְשַׁכֵּחַ תּוֹרַת עֵירוּב מִן הַתִּינוֹקוֹת. וְהָכָא, כֵּיוָן דְּרוּבָּהּ עֵירְבוּ – לָא מִשְׁתַּכְחָא. אָמַר רַב יְהוּדָה: רַב לָא תָּנֵי "פְּתוּחוֹת זוֹ לָזוֹ". וְכֵן אָמַר רַב כָּהֲנָא: רַב לָא תָּנֵי "פְּתוּחוֹת זוֹ לָזוֹ". אִיכָּא דְּאָמְרִי: רַב כָּהֲנָא גּוּפֵיהּ לָא תָּנֵי "פְּתוּחוֹת זוֹ לָזוֹ". אֲמַר לֵיהּ אַבַּיֵי לְרַב יוֹסֵף: מַאי טַעְמָא דְּלָא תָּנֵי "פְּתוּחוֹת זוֹ לָזוֹ"? קָסָבַר: כׇּל שִׁיתּוּף שֶׁאֵין מַכְנִיסוֹ וּמוֹצִיאוֹ דֶּרֶךְ פְּתָחִים בַּמָּבוֹי – לָאו שְׁמֵיהּ שִׁיתּוּף. אֵיתִיבֵיהּ: *בַּעַל הַבַּיִת שֶׁהָיָה שׁוּתָּף לִשְׁכֵנָיו, לָזֶה בְּיַיִן וְלָזֶה בְּיַיִן – אֵין צְרִיכִין לְעָרֵב! הָתָם דְּאַפְּקֵיהּ וְעַיְּילֵיהּ. (אֵיתִיבֵיהּ:) *כֵּיצַד מִשְׁתַּתְּפִין בַּמָּבוֹי וכו'! הָתָם נַמִי, דְּאַפְּקֵיהּ וְעַיְּילֵיהּ. מַתְקִיף לַהּ רַבָּה בַּר(א) חָנָן: אֶלָּא מֵעַתָּה הִקְנָה לוֹ פַּת בְּסַלּוֹ, ה"נ דְּלָא הָוֵי שִׁיתּוּף? וְכִי תֵּימָא הָכִי נַמִי – וְהָא *אָמַר רַב יְהוּדָה, אָמַר רַב: בְּנֵי חֲבוּרָה שֶׁהָיוּ מְסוּבִּין וְקָדַשׁ עֲלֵיהֶן הַיּוֹם, הַפַּת שֶׁעַל שֻׁלְחָן סוֹמְכִים עָלֶיהָ מִשּׁוּם עֵירוּב, וְאָמְרִי לַהּ: מִשּׁוּם שִׁיתּוּף. וְאָמַר רַבָּה: לָא פְּלִיגִי, כָּאן – בִּמְסוּבִּין בַּבַּיִת, כָּאן – בִּמְסוּבִּין בֶּחָצֵר. אֶלָּא, טַעְמָא דְּרַב, דְּקָא סָבַר: אֵין מָבוֹי נִיתָּר בְּלֶחִי וְקוֹרָה עַד שֶׁיְּהוּ בָּתִּים וַחֲצֵירוֹת פְּתוּחִים לְתוֹכוֹ. גּוּפָא, *אָמַר רַב: אֵין מָבוֹי נִיתָּר בְּלֶחִי וְקוֹרָה

עַד

רש"י

וְאִם נִשְׁתַּתְּפוּ כו'. בַּגְּמָרָא מְתָרֵץ לָהּ: דְּשָׁכַח אֶחָד מִבְּנֵי חָצֵר וְלֹא עֵירֵב. בַּחֲצֵירוֹ, לְהַתִּיר חֲצֵירוֹ. אֲבָל בַּשִּׁיתּוּף הָיָה לוֹ חֵלֶק: מוּתָּרִין כָּאן וְכָאן. הָשְׁתָּא מַשְׁמַע דְּסוֹמְכִין, וּבַגְּמָרָא מְתָרֵץ לָהּ: שֶׁהַמָּבוֹי לַחֲצֵירוֹת כְּחָצֵר לַבָּתִּים. כְּשֵׁם שֶׁאָסוּר לְהוֹצִיא מִן הַבָּתִּים לֶחָצֵר בְּלֹא עֵירוּב, כָּךְ אָסוּר לְהוֹצִיא מִן הֶחָצֵר לַמָּבוֹי בְּלֹא שִׁיתּוּף. וְלָא תֵּימָא דְּלָא דָּמוּ, דְּבַיִת וְחָצֵר זוֹ רְשׁוּת הַיָּחִיד וְזוֹ רְשׁוּת הָרַבִּים, אֲבָל חָצֵר וּמָבוֹי שְׁנֵיהֶן רְשׁוּיוֹת שֶׁל רַבִּים הֵן:

גמ' וְאִם נִשְׁתַּתְּפוּ נַמִי. וְאַקַּמַּיְיתָא קָאֵי וְאִם נִשְׁתַּתְּפוּ אַף בַּמָּבוֹי קָאָמַר: אַמַּאי מוּתָּרִין. בְּאוֹתָהּ חָצֵר? הָא רַבִּי מֵאִיר לֵית לֵיהּ סוֹמְכִין עַל שִׁיתּוּף: מִבְּנֵי מָבוֹי וְלֹא נִשְׁתַּתֵּף. אַחַת מִן הַחֲצֵירוֹת לֹא נִשְׁתַּתְּפָה עִם חֲבֶרְתָּהּ בַּמָּבוֹי: וְהָא תַּנְיָא. לְעֵיל(ב) בְּפִירְקִין גַּבֵּי צְדוֹקִי: רֵישָׁא נַמִי דְּלָא בַּטֵּיל. הָא דְּקָתָנֵי: שָׁכַח אֶחָד מִבְּנֵי חָצֵר – בִּדְלָא בַּטֵּיל, וְקָתָנֵי מוּתָּרִים. אַלְמָא: סוֹמְכִין עַל הַשִּׁיתּוּף: רֵישָׁא וְסֵיפָא רַבִּי מֵאִיר. רֵישָׁא קָתָנֵי: עֵירְבוּ בַּחֲצֵירוֹת וְלֹא נִשְׁתַּתְּפוּ בַּמָּבוֹי – אֲסוּרִין בַּמָּבוֹי אֶלָּא אִם כֵּן נִשְׁתַּתְּפוּ נַמִי בַּמָּבוֹי, כְּרַבִּי מֵאִיר. וְסֵיפָא קָתָנֵי: מִבְּנֵי מָבוֹי וְלֹא נִשְׁתַּתֵּף אֲסוּרִין בַּמָּבוֹי – כְּרַבִּי מֵאִיר: וּמְצִיעֲתָא. דְּקָתָנֵי: מִבְּנֵי חָצֵר וְלֹא עֵירֵב כו' כְּרַבָּנַן: כּוּלָּהּ רַבִּי מֵאִיר הִיא. וּמְצִיעֲתָא אַמַּאי סוֹמְכִין בְּנֵי אוֹתָהּ חָצֵר עַל הַשִּׁיתּוּף – מִשּׁוּם דְּרוּבָּן עֵירְבוּ, דְּטַעְמָא מַאי כו': רַב לָא תָּנֵי פְּתוּחוֹת זוֹ לָזוֹ. וְכׇל "עֵירְבוּ בַּחֲצֵירוֹת" דְּמַתְנִיתִין – עֵירְבוּ כׇּל חָצֵר לְעַצְמָהּ קָאָמַר, וּ"מוּתָּרִין בַּחֲצֵירוֹת" דְּקָתָנֵי – מוּתָּרִין בְּנֵי חָצֵר לְעַצְמָן קָאָמַר: כׇּל שִׁיתּוּף שֶׁאֵין. כׇּל אֶחָד וְאֶחָד מַכְנִיס חֶלְקוֹ דֶּרֶךְ פֶּתַח חֲצֵירוֹ לַמָּבוֹי, וְדֶרֶךְ מָבוֹי יוֹלִיכוּהוּ לֶחָצֵר שֶׁיְּהֵא מוּנָּח בּוֹ: לָאו שְׁמֵיהּ שִׁיתּוּף. שֶׁאִם יַכְנִיסוּהוּ דֶּרֶךְ פְּתָחִים שֶׁמֵּחָצֵר לֶחָצֵר – אֵין נִרְאֶה כְּשִׁיתּוּף מָבוֹי. וְהָכָא נַמִי חָיֵישׁ רַב דִּילְמָא מְעַיְּילֵי לֵיהּ דֶּרֶךְ פְּתָחִים שֶׁבֵּינֵיהֶן: אֵין צָרִיךְ לְעָרֵב. וְהָא הָכָא דְּלָקְחוּ חָבִית בְּשׁוּתָּפוּת, וְלֹא נִכְנְסָה אֶלָּא לְאוֹתָהּ חָצֵר לְבַדָּהּ: דְּאַפְּקֵיהּ וְעַיְּילֵיהּ. לֶחָבִית בְּכׇל הַחֲצֵירוֹת, וּמֵהֶן לַמָּבוֹי, וּמִשָּׁם לֶחָצֵר שֶׁהוּנַּח שָׁם, וְלֹא לְשֵׁם שִׁיתּוּף. וְשִׁינּוּיָא דְּחִיקָא הוּא, וְלָא הָוֵי מַסְקָנָא הָכִי: כֵּיצַד מִשְׁתַּתְּפִין כו'. תְּיוּבְתָּא קָא מוֹתִיב מִמַּתְנִיתִין דְּפֶרֶק "חַלּוֹן" דִּלְקַמָּן [דף עט:] דְּקָתָנֵי הָתָם: כֵּיצַד מִשְׁתַּתְּפִין בַּמָּבוֹי? מַנִּיחַ אֶת הֶחָבִית, וְאוֹמֵר: הֲרֵי זֶה לְכׇל בְּנֵי מָבוֹי, וּמְזַכֶּה לָהֶן כו' וְהָא הָכָא דְּחַד מְזַכֶּה מִדִּידֵיהּ לְכוּלְּהוּ, וְלֹא נִכְנְסָה לַחֲצֵרוֹתֵיהֶן: מְסוּבִּין בַּבַּיִת. סוֹמְכִין מִשּׁוּם עֵירוּב הֶחָצֵר, כִּדְאָמַר לְקַמָּן [פה:] עֵירוּבֵי חֲצֵירוֹת בַּבַּיִת שֶׁבֶּחָצֵר: מְסוּבִּין בֶּחָצֵר. סוֹמְכִין מִשּׁוּם שִׁיתּוּף, דְּשִׁיתּוּפֵי מְבוֹאוֹת מוּתָּר לְהָנִיחָן בֶּחָצֵר שֶׁבַּמָּבוֹי. אֲבָל מִשּׁוּם עֵירוּב לֹא, דְּבַיִת בָּעֵינַן, דְּעֵירוּב מִשּׁוּם דִּירָה, וְחָצֵר לָאו בַּר דִּירָה הוּא:

בָּתִּים

תוספות

אימא מציעתא ואם נשתתפו במבוי מותרין כאן וכאן אתיא כרבנן. ואפילו למאן דאמר לעיל [דף עא:] דבפת לא פליגי, משמע ליה ואם נשתתפו במבוי – בכל ענין, ואפילו נשתתפו במבוי ביין: **אלא** פשיטא דבטיל. ואם תאמר: למאן דאמר אין מבטלין רשות מחצר לחצר, היאך מותרין במבוי? הא אין יכול לבטל רשותו לבני חצר אחרת לרבא *דאמר לשמואל דאפילו ב' חצירות זו לפנים מזו פעמים דאין מבטלין! ויש לומר: דהא לא קשיא, שהרי במבוי נשתתף. אבל הא קשיא, היאך מועיל במבוי ביטול לרבא, דאמר בב' חצירות זו לפנים מזו דאין מבטלין? ועל כרחך יש ביטול רשות במבוי(ג), כדדייקי: שהרי ביטל להם רשותו! ויש לומר: דכיון דכולם שוין במבוי, זה כזה – יכול לבטל אף לבני חצר אחרת, שהמבוי חדא תשמישתא לתרוייהו. ולא דמי לב' חצירות דהא תשמישתא לחוד והא תשמישתא לחוד, כדאמר לעיל(ד). ולקמן (דף עט.) תניא גבי בית שבין שתי חצירות ומלאוהו תבן, דאם נתמעט התבן מעשרה טפחים – מבטלין הבית לזה ולזה, והיינו טעמא כדפרישית דאפילו לשמואל הבית לחצירות חדא תשמישתא הוא לתרוייהו: **כל** שיתוף שאין מכניסו ומוציאו דרך פתחים למבוי לאו שמיה שיתוף. פי' בקונטרס: ולהכי לא תני רב ופתוחין זו לזו, דחייש דילמא מעיילי ליה דרך פתחים שביניהם. משמע לפירושו(ה): ואם פתוחות זו לזו – לא מהני בהן שיתוף, ואפילו מעיילי ליה דרך מבוי – גזרינן דילמא לא מעיילי אלא דרך פתח החצר וסמכינן עליה. ואם תאמר: היכי משכחת ליה פלוגתא דרבי מאיר ורבנן דמערבין ומשתתפין אם לא בחצירות הפתוחות זו לזו? ומשמע התם דמהני שיתוף! ויש לומר: דאשכחן לה בשעירבו החצירות דרך חלונות, וכיון שאין פתח גמור מחצר לחצר גבוה י' ורוחב ד' – ליכא למיגזר דילמא מפקי ועיילי השיתוף שלא כדרך המבוי, כיון דמחצר לחצר לא סלקי להדיא אי ליכא פתחים אלא חלונות בעלמא: **דאפקיה** ועייליה. פירש בקונט': לאותה חבית בכל החצירות, ומהן למבוי ומשם לחצר שהונח שם, ולא לשם שיתוף. ולפירושו ה"ל למימר דעייליה ואפקיה ועייליה ובחנם דחק לומר כן, דתחילה היה בשאר חצירות ואפקיה למבוי, והדר עיילי בזה החצר: **בני** חבורה שהיו מסובין כו'. כאן לא שייך למימר דאפקיה ועייליה. דאע"ג דיכול לומר דכל חד וחד הביא פת בחצר זה [דרך מבוי] כדי לסעוד, סתמא דמלתא איירי שבעל הבית זה הזמינם לסעוד אצלו, ואע"פ שלא זיכה – סומכין על פת שבעל השלחן, דכזכו בו דמו. שאין לומר שכך אירע שפת של בעל הבית היה מונח בשאר חצירות, והובא כאן דרך מבוי – דהוצאה והכנסה זו לא מהניא מידי, כיון שלא היה קנוי פת לכל בני החבורה באותה שעה, אלא היה של בעל הבית זה, ואין הכנסה והוצאה מועלת אא"כ היה של בעל השיתוף מאותה שעה:

עד

עין משפט נר מצוה

פב א מיי' פ"ה מהל' עירובין הלכה יג סמג עשין א טור ש"ע א"ח סי' שפז:

פג ב מיי' וסמג שם טוש"ע א"ח סי' שלא סעיף א:

לעיל סו:

פד ג מיי' שם טוש"ע א"ח שם וסי' שפו סעיף ג:

פה ד מיי' פי"ז מהל' שבת הלכה ז סמג שם טוש"ע א"ח סי' שסג סעיף כו:

רבינו חננאל

פתוחות זו לזו ופתוחות למבוי עירבו בחצרות ולא נשתתפו במבוי מותרין בחצרות ואסורין במבוי מני ר' מאיר היא דאמר בעינן עירוב ובעינן נמי שיתוף אי הכי אימא מציעתא נשתתפו במבוי מותרין כאן וכאן בחצרות ובמבוי כרבנן דאמרי או מערבי או משתתפי ופריקנא אעירוב דרישא קאי והכי קתני כיון שעירבו (או נשתתפו) [ונשתתפו] נמי במבוי מותרין כאן וכאן. אי הכי אימא סיפא שכח אחד מבני חצר ולא עירב מותרין כאן וכאן. היכי דמי אי נימא כדקתני אמאי מותרין והלא אוסר עליהן דתנן שכח אחד מהן ולא עירב ביתו אסור כו' ואוקימנא בשביטל רשותו בחצר כו'. ופרקינן אלא מתני' ודאי בשביטל ומדרישא בשביטל סיפא נמי בשביטל. אימא סיפא שכח אחד מבני מבוי ולא נשתתף מותרין בחצרות ואסורין במבוי ומאחר שביטל רשותו במבוי אמאי אסורין במבוי הא שמעינן ליה לר' מאיר דאית ליה ביטול רשות במבוי דתניא בענין הצדוקי הדר עמו במבוי שהרי ביטל לכם רשותו דברי ר' מאיר אלא פשיטא דלא ביטל משום הכי אסירי במבוי. ומדסיפא לא ביטל רישא נמי לא ביטל וקתני מותרין כרבנן וכי רישא וסיפא ר' מאיר ומציעתא רבנן. ושנינן כולה ר' מאיר היא וטעמא מאי בעי ר' מאיר עירוב ושיתוף כדי שלא תשתכח תורת עירוב. הכא מציעתא דמתניתין כיון דאחד שכח ורובה עירבו לא משתכח תורת עירוב דהא רובה עירבו. אמר רב יהודה (אמר) רב לא תני במתני' פתוחות זו לזו קסבר כל שיתוף שאין מכניסין אותו דרך פתחין למבוי לאו שמיה שיתוף ואלו הן פתוחות זו לזו מכניסות אותו מזו לזו ואין מוציאין אותו למבוי אינו שיתוף לפיכך לא תנו במתני' פתוחות זו לזו ומותבינן עליה מהא בעל הבית שהיה שותף לשכיניו לזה ביין ולזה ביין וכו' ופריק כגון דאפקיה לההוא יין והדר עייליה דרך פתחין למבוי והכי נמי פריק בכיצד משתתפ[ין] במבוי כגון דאפקיה לההוא מידי דמקני להו לבני מבוי והדר עייליה דרך פתחין למבוי איני דרב אמר לא הוי שיתוף עד דמעייל ליה דרך פתחין למבוי והא רב הוא דאמר בני חבורה שהיו מסובין וקדש עליה[ן] היום פת שע"ג השלחן סומכין עליה משום עירוב ואמרי לה משום שיתוף ואמר רבה לא פליגי אי מסובין בבית סומכין עליה משום עירוב ואי מסובין בחצר סומכין עליה משום שיתוף. ופרקינן אלא היינ[ו]

מסורת הש"ס

נ"א שכח אחד

[לעיל סו:]

לעיל סח:

לעיל עא.

לקמן עט:

לקמן פה:

שבת קל: לעיל ה. [ע"ש] ג"ע] [לקמן עב:]

הגהות הב"ח

(א) גמ' מתקיף לה רבה בר רב חנן: (ב) רש"י ד"ה והא תניא לעיל נ"ב סו דף סח ע"ב: (ג) תום' ד"ה אלא וכו' כדדייקי מדת שהרי וכו': (ד) בא"ד כדאמר לעיל נ"ב דף ס[...] ע"ב: (ה) ד"ה כל וכו' משמע לפירושו דאם:

רב נסים גאון

מתני' מני ר' מאיר היא דאמר בעינן עירוב ובעינן שיתוף הא דר' מאיר ורבנן כבר מפורש בזה הפרק (דף עא) מאי ר' מאיר ומאי רבנן דתניא מערבין בחצרות בפת:

גליון הש"ס גמ' ואם נשתתפו נמי קאמר. עיין לעיל דף סז ע"ב ברש"י ד"ה נסמוך אשיתוף: **תום'** ד"ה בני. ואין הכנסה והוצאה מועלת. קשה לי דא"כ איך מקשי תחלה על מתני' דכיצד משתתפים במבוי וכו' ה"נ דאפקיה ועייליה. הא מקודם לא מהני ז[...] כיון דהחבית כולה דבעה"ב. וע"כ דעתה אחר הזיכוי מפקא ומעיילא א"כ למאי צריך לזכות ע"י בנו ובתו הא כיון דעיילא לכל חצר וחצר יקנה חצירו של כל אחד חלקו ביין ולע"ג:

עַד שֶׁיְּהוּ *בָּתִּים וַחֲצֵירוֹת פְּתוּחִין לְתוֹכוֹ. וּשְׁמוּאֵל אָמַר: אֲפִילּוּ בַּיִת אֶחָד וְחָצֵר אַחַת. וְרַבִּי יוֹחָנָן אָמַר: אֲפִילּוּ חוּרְבָּה. אֲמַר לֵיהּ אַבַּיֵי לְרַב יוֹסֵף: אָמַר רַבִּי יוֹחָנָן אֲפִילּוּ בִּשְׁבִיל שֶׁל כְּרָמִים? אֲמַר לֵיהּ: לֹא אָמַר רַבִּי יוֹחָנָן אֶלָּא בְּחוּרְבָּה, דַּחֲזֵי לְדִירָה. אֲבָל שְׁבִיל שֶׁל כְּרָמִים דְּלָא חֲזֵי לְדִירָה — לָא. אָמַר רַב הוּנָא בַּר חִינְּנָא: *וְאַזְדָּא רַבִּי יוֹחָנָן לְטַעְמֵיהּ, דִּתְנַן, *(אָמַר ר"ש:)(א) [נ"ל ר"ש אומר] אֶחָד גַּגּוֹת, וְאֶחָד קַרְפֵּיפוֹת, וְאֶחָד חֲצֵירוֹת — רְשׁוּת אַחַת הֵן לְכֵלִים שֶׁשָּׁבְתוּ לְתוֹכָן, וְלֹא לְכֵלִים שֶׁשָּׁבְתוּ בְּתוֹךְ הַבַּיִת. *וְאָמַר רַב: הֲלָכָה כְּר"ש, וְהוּא שֶׁלֹּא עֵירְבוּ, אֲבָל עֵירְבוּ — גָּזְרִינַן דִּילְמָא אָתֵי לְאַפּוֹקֵי מָאנֵי דְּבָתִּים לְחָצֵר. וּשְׁמוּאֵל אָמַר: בֵּין עֵירְבוּ וּבֵין לֹא עֵירְבוּ. וְכֵן א"ר יוֹחָנָן: הֲלָכָה כְּר"ש, בֵּין עֵירְבוּ וּבֵין לֹא עֵירְבוּ. אַלְמָא: לָא גָּזְרִינַן דִּילְמָא אָתֵי לְאַפּוֹקֵי מָאנֵי דְּבָתִּים לְחָצֵר. הָכָא נַמִי: לָא גָּזְרִינַן דִּילְמָא אָתֵי לְאַפּוֹקֵי מָאנֵי(ב) דְּחָצֵר לְחוּרְבָּה. יָתֵיב רַב בְּרוּנָא, וְקָאָמַר לְהָא שְׁמַעְתָּא, א"ל ר"א בַּר בֵּי רַב: אָמַר שְׁמוּאֵל הָכִי?! א"ל: אִין. א"ל: *אַחְוֵי לִי אוּשְׁפִּיזֵיהּ, אַחְוְיֵי לֵיהּ. אֲתָא לְקַמֵּיהּ דִּשְׁמוּאֵל, אֲמַר לֵיהּ: אָמַר מָר הָכִי? אֲמַר לֵיהּ: אִין. וְהָא מָר הוּא דְּאָמַר: *אֵין לָנוּ בְּעֵירוּבִין אֶלָּא כִּלְשׁוֹן מִשְׁנָתֵינוּ, שֶׁהַמָּבוֹי לַחֲצֵירוֹת כֶּחָצֵר לַבָּתִּים! אִישְׁתִּיק. קִבְּלָהּ מִינֵּיהּ, אוֹ לֹא קִבְּלָהּ מִינֵּיהּ? ת"ש: דְּהַהוּא מְבוֹאָה דַּהֲוָה דָּיֵיר בֵּיהּ אִיבוּת בַּר אִיהִי, עֲבַד לֵיהּ לֶחְיָא וּשְׁרָא לֵיהּ שְׁמוּאֵל, אֲתָא

[שבת קל. וש"נ] [שבת קל: לעיל כג: ועיין תוס' לקמן פט.] שם נא. [לקמן פה:] לעיל סו:

רש"י

בָּתִּים וַחֲצֵירוֹת פָּתוּחַ לְתוֹכוֹ. בָּתִּים לַחֲצֵירוֹת שְׁנֵי בָּתִּים לְכָל חָצֵר וּשְׁתֵּי חֲצֵירוֹת לְמָבוֹי. וְהָנָךְ כֵּיוָן דְּכוּלָּן פְּתוּחִים זוֹ לָזוֹ וּמְעָרְבוֹת יַחַד דֶּרֶךְ פִּתְחֵיהֶם — חֲדָא חָשֵׁיב לְהוּ. וְלֵית לֵיהּ לְרַב הָא דְּתַנְיָא לְעֵיל: אָב וּבְנוֹ מָבוֹי שֶׁלָּהֶן נִיתָּר בְּלֶחִי וְקוֹרָה. דְּכָל הֵיכָא דְּלָא בָּעֵי לְעָרוּבֵי וּמָצֵי לְעָרוּבֵי בְּלָא שִׁיתּוּף מָבוֹי — לָא מִשְׁתַּרֵי הַהוּא מָבוֹי בְּלֶחִי וְקוֹרָה, עַד שֶׁתְּהֵא שָׁם חָצֵר אַחַת שֶׁאֵינָהּ פְּתוּחָה לַחֲבֵרוֹתֶיהָ, אוֹ שְׁתֵּי שׁוּרוֹת שֶׁל חֲצֵירוֹת אַחַת לְצִידּוֹ זֶה וְאַחַת לְצִידּוֹ אַחֵר וְהַמָּבוֹי בֵּינֵיהֶן, שֶׁאֵינָן יְכוֹלוֹת לְהִתְעָרֵב אֶלָּא עַל יְדֵי מָבוֹי: בַּיִת אֶחָד וְחָצֵר אַחַת. בַּיִת בְּלֹא חָצֵר, וְחָצֵר שֶׁבַּיִת אַחֵר פָּתוּחַ לָהּ: אֲפִי' חוּרְבָּה. מִכָּאן, וְחָצֵר מִכָּאן, דְּאֵין חָצֵר בְּלֹא בַּיִת: אֲפִי' שְׁבִיל שֶׁל כְּרָמִים. פָּתוּחַ לַמָּבוֹי מִכָּאן, וְחָצֵר מִכָּאן: אֶחָד גַּגּוֹת כו'. כּוּלָּן רְשׁוּת אַחַת לְטַלְטֵל כֵּלִים שֶׁשָּׁבְתוּ בְּגַג זֶה לְגַג חֲבֵירוֹ. וְלָא אָמְרִי' כְּשֵׁם שֶׁדִּירִין חֲלוּקִין לְמַטָּה כָּךְ חֲלוּקִין לְמַעְלָה. וְכֵלִים שֶׁשָּׁבְתוּ בְּחָצֵר זוֹ מוֹצִיאִין לַחֲבֶרְתָּהּ, וְכֵן לְקַרְפֵּף, וְכֵן לְחָצֵר, וְלַקַּרְפֵּף מִן הַגַּגִּין. הוֹאִיל וְכוּלָּן רְשׁוּת שֶׁאֵינָהּ דִּירָה הִיא, וְאֵין צָרִיךְ לְעָרֵב מֵחָצֵר לְחָצֵר אֶלָּא בִּשְׁבִיל כֵּלִים שֶׁשָּׁבְתוּ בַּבַּיִת שֶׁבֶּחָצֵר זוֹ, לְהוֹצִיאָם לְחָצֵר אַחֶרֶת: הֲלָכָה כְּר"ש. שֶׁהַחֲצֵירוֹת מוֹצִיאִין מִזּוֹ לָזוֹ בְּלֹא עֵירוּב: וְהוּא שֶׁלֹּא עֵירְבוּ. בְּנֵי הַחֲצֵירוֹת כָּל אַחַת לְעַצְמָהּ, וְאָסוּר לְהוֹצִיא מִן הַבָּתִּים לֶחָצֵר. דְּכֵיוָן דְּאֵין מְצוּיִין כְּלֵי הַבַּיִת בֶּחָצֵר — לֵיכָּא לְמֵיגְזַר אִי מַפְּקַתְּ כֵּלִים שֶׁשָּׁבְתוּ בֶּחָצֵר לַחֲבֶרְתָּהּ, אָתוּ לְאַפּוֹקֵי נַמִי כֵּלִים שֶׁשָּׁבְתוּ בַּבַּיִת שֶׁהוֹצִיאָן מֵחָצֵר זוֹ, לְחָצֵר אַחֶרֶת: דִּילְמָא אָתֵי לְאַפּוֹקֵי מָאנֵי דְּבָתִּים. שֶׁבְּחָצֵר זוֹ לְחָצֵר אַחֶרֶת: הָכָא נַמִי לָא גְּזוֹר דִּילְמָא אָתֵי לְאַפּוֹקֵי מָאנֵי דְּחָצֵר לַחוּרְבָּה. דֶּרֶךְ מָבוֹי. וַהֲרֵי רְשׁוּת אַחֶרֶת הִיא, שֶׁיֵּשׁ לָהּ בְּעָלִים, וּבַמָּבוֹי לֹא נִשְׁתַּתְּפוּ, שֶׁהֲרֵי אֵינָהּ אוֹסֶרֶת. כִּדְתַנְיָא לְעֵיל בְּפִירְקִין: אֵינוֹ אוֹסֵר אֶלָּא מְקוֹם דִּירָה בִּלְבָד, דְּהַיְינוּ מְקוֹם פִּיתָּא אוֹ מְקוֹם לִינָה: לְהָא שְׁמַעְתָּא. דְּאָמַר שְׁמוּאֵל לְעֵיל אֲפִילּוּ בַּיִת וְחָצֵר: אַחְוֵי לִי אוּשְׁפִּיזֵיהּ. דְּאֵיזִיל וְאֵישַׁיְילֵיהּ לִשְׁמוּאֵל: שֶׁהַמָּבוֹי לַחֲצֵירוֹת. דָּיְיקִינַן לִישָּׁנָא דַּחֲצֵירוֹת וְלֹא חָצֵר: קִבְּלָהּ מִינֵּיהּ. שְׁמוּאֵל, וַהֲדַר בֵּיהּ לְגַבֵּי רַב, אִי לֹא:
אֲתָא

תוספות

עד שיהו בתים וחצירות פתוחים לתוכו.(ג) ומערבין יחד דרך פתחיהן חדא חשיב להו, ולית ליה לרב הא דתניא לעיל אב ובנו מבוי שלהן ניתר בלחי וקורה. דכל היכא דלא בעי עירוב, אי נמי בעו עירוב ומצי לערובי בלא שיתוף מבוי — לא משתרי ההוא מבוי בלחי וקורה עד שתהא שם חצר אחת שאינה פתוחה לחברותיה, או שתי שורות של חצירות אחת לצידו אחד ואחת לצידו אחר והמבוי ביניהם, שאינן יכולות להתערב אלא ע"י מבוי. ע"כ לשון הקונט'. וקשה לר"י: דלא מסתבר למימר דפליג רב אברייתא דלעיל דהא קי"ל בהא כרב, מדאמר רב נחמן בפ"ק (לעיל דף יב:), נקיטינן: איזהו מבוי שניתר בלחי וקורה וכו'. ופי' ר"י: דלא חשבינן בתים וחצירות דאב ובנו חדא, כיון שאין הבתים פתוחים זה לזה ולא החצירות פתוחות זו לזו אלא למבוי, דכי היכי דבעירבו ונשתתפו להיות מותרים להוציא מחצר לחצר דרך המבוי חשובות החצירות שתים, ולא משוי להו *שיתוף חדא חצר לענין בתים וחצירות פתוחים לתוכו, כיון שאין פתוחין זו לזו(ד) אלא למבוי — הכא נמי. כי במה שהם של אב ובנו אין לחושבם אחת, יותר מבשל נכרים ועירבו. דטפי מעירוב לא מהני מה שהם של אב ובנו להחשב אחת, ולהחשב המבוי כאילו אין בתים וחצירות פתוחין לתוכו. ואם תאמר: כיון דמשוי להו כחדא כשפתוחות זו לזו, *משמע דיכולין לערב יחד בלא מבוי, אם כן היכי משכחת לה שעירבו בחצירות ומותרין לרבנן כאן וכאן, ולר' מאיר אין מותרין אלא בחצירות. ובכל החצירות מיהא מותרין. וכשעירבו ונשתתפו מותרים כאן וכאן, אע"פ שסתם מבוי דמשנה וברייתא משמע שהכשירו בלחי וקורה. דלהכי לא תני פתוחות זו לזו — דבעי לאוקומי במבוי הניתר בלחי וקורה. הא כיון דבעירוב לחודיה סגי לרבנן, בין בחצירות בין במבוי — א"כ עירבו כל החצירות יחד. ומאחר שרבי מאיר אוסרו למבוי ומתירן כולן מזו לזו, שהרי אינו אוסרן אלא המבוי לבדו — אם כן פתוחות כולן זו לזו. והואיל וכן, היאך מותר המבוי בלחי וקורה לרב, שאוסר כשיכולין לערב דרך פתחיהן מזו לזו ואף על פי שלא עירבו, וכל שכן כאן שעירבו כולן יחד דרך פתחיהן עצמן בלא פתחיהן הפתוחות למבוי! ויש לומר: דמשכחת לרב כגון שעירבו חצירות זו לזו דרך סולמות, דלא חשיבי בהכי פתוחות זו לזו. דהא אמרינן ב"כיצד מעברין" (לעיל דף נט:): דסולם תורת מחיצה עליו להקל, אף בשעה שיש עליו תורת פתח להקל. ועוד יש למצוא: כגון שמערבין דרך חלונות הפתוחות מחצר לחצר בתוך עשרה, כיון דהוי כוליה חלון למעלה מארבעה טפחים — אין ראוי לאסור (ה)אפי' פתח שעשוי ליציאה וכניסה ואין פתח אחר לצאת שם אינו אוסר, כיון שיש שם דקה ד'. ואפילו אם נפסק לומר שכשהיה פתח והיה עושה לפניו דקה נראה שם הסילוק יותר מכאן, לפי שהיה כאן פתח וביטלו, אבל בחלון למעלה מד' — לא חשיב גובהו ביטול פתח (ו)כיון שלא פתח מעולם, ולא דמי לפתח המתבטל מ"מ כיון שחלון שמחצר לחצר אינו עשוי ליציאה וכניסה כמו פתח שישנו מזו לזו לא עדיף מסולם לחושבו אחת. וגם אם לא יהיה החלון למעלה מד', אלא יהיה למעלה מג', דכיון דלא מידרים — יש סברא לומר כן. ועוד: דאפי' פתח גמור(ז), כיון שאינו רגיל — אינו אוסר. כדאמרינן בפרק "מי שהוציאוהו" (לעיל דף מט.). וכיון דתורת מחיצה עליו שלא לאסור גם לענין זה שבכאן בחלון, שאין רגילות כניסה ויציאה דרך חלון כמו בפתח גמור — יהא בחלון שבין חצר לחצר(ח) (יש עליו) תורת מחיצה כמו בסולם, שלא להחשיב החצירות אחת ע"י עירוב שמערבין יחד דרך חלונותיהם מזו לזו. ולא דמו לפתחים שבין זו לזו דמשוו להו חדא, אע"פ שאין בני כל חצר וחצר רגילין בהן כמו בפתחי המבוי. כי מה שאין רגילין בהן כמו בפתחי המבוי — זה לפי שרשויות החצירות חלוקות, ואין עיקר תשמיש ודירה של כל חצר וחצר אלא לבני החצר עצמה, ולא לבני האחרת. ולהכי חשיב כרגיל, לשוינהו חדא על ידי עירוב. אבל חלון — יהא עליו תורת מחיצה דלא לשוינהו חדא ע"י חלון, כיון דלא חזי למיהוי רגיל כפתח הפתוח למבוי, אפי' היו כל החצירות של אדם אחד:

ושמואל אמר אפי' בית וחצר. פי' בקונטרס: בית בלא חצר ובית וחצר למעלה פי' באופן אחר בפ"ק (לעיל דף יב:) גבי הא דאמר ר"נ, נקיטינן: איזהו מבוי שניתר בלחי וקורה — שאורכו יתר על רחבו ובתים וחצירות פתוחין לתוכו: **הכא** נמי לא גזרינן דילמא אתי לאפוקי מאני דבתים לחורבה. תימה: מאי קאמר ואזדא ר' יוחנן לטעמיה? כי סבר כרב נמי, דאמר והוא שלא עירבו אבל עירבו גזר דילמא אתי לאפוקי מאני דבתים לחצר — מכל מקום הכא אין לו לגזור, דהא בחצר שעירבו לעצמה לא אסרינן לה לאפוקי מאני דבתים לתוכה, דילמא אתי לאפוקינהו לחצר אחרת. ה"נ(ט) כשעירבו במבוי — לא אסרי' לאפוקי מאני דבתים למבוי דילמא אתי לאפוקינהו לחורבה, דהא לא אשכחן דגזר מקום המותר דילמא אתי לאפוקי אותם כלים עצמן משם למקום האסור. ואור"י דהכי פי': דלרב כשגזר כשעירבו לאסור כלים ששבתו בחצר לאפוקינהו לחצר אחרת, אע"פ שכל החצרות רשות אחת לר"ש לכלים ששבתו בתוכה — אפי' הכי אסר רב כשעירבו, דילמא אתי לאפוקי לחצר אחרת כלים ששבתו בתוך הבית ומצויין באותה חצר. ה"נ(י) כשעירבו במבוי — היה אוסר כלים ששבתו במבוי לאפוקינהו לחורבה, דילמא אתי לאפוקי כלים ששבתו בתוך הבית לחורבה, שהם מצויין במבוי. וכיון דאסור להוציא מן המבוי לחורבה — אם כן אין לחורבה להתיר המבוי. אבל רבי יוחנן, דלא גזר — הכי נמי לא היה אוסר להוציא כלים ששבתו(כ) במבוי דילמא אתי לאפוקי מאני דבתים לחורבה, ומש"ה מהני שפיר חורבה להתיר את המבוי:
מבוי

רבינו חננאל

טעמא דרב קסבר אין מבוי ניתר בלחי וקורה אלא אם הוו בתים וחצירות פתוחות לתוכו והני כיון דפתוחות זו לזו נעשית כחצר אחת לפיכך לא הוה תני פתוחות זו לזו ושמואל אמר אפי' בית אחד ור' יוחנן אמר אפי' חורבה אם יש במבוי כיון שהיא ראויה לבית דירה ניתר בלחי וקורה אבל שביל של כרמים דלא חזי לדירה לא. וקיי"ל כר' יוחנן ואזדו לטעמייהו דתנן ר"ש אומ' אחד גגות ואחד חצירות [ואחד קרפיפות רשות אחת הן] לכלים ששבתו בתוכן כו'. אמר רב הלכה כר"ש והוא שלא עירבו אבל עירבו גזרינן דלמא אתי לאפוקי מאני דבתים לחצר. ושמואל אמר הלכתא כר' שמעון בין עירבו בין לא עירבו וכן א"ר יוחנן מי לחשך. פי' מלשון לחש כלומר (איש) [מי] השמיעך הלכתא כר"ש בין עירבו בין לא עירבו ולא גזרינן דלמא אתי לאפוקי מאני דבתים לחצר ה"נ לא גזרינן דלמא אתי לאפוקי מאני דחצר

הגהות הב"ח

(א) גמ' אחד גגות ואחד חצירות ואחד קרפיפות רשות אחת: (ב) שם לאפוקי מאני (דחצר) תז"מ ונ"ב ס"א דבתים והכי מוכח בתוס' אבל בא"י פ' כילד משתתפין תופס הגירסא דילמא אתי לאפוקי מאני דחצר לחורבה: (ג) תוס' ד"ה עד שיהיו בתים וחצירות פתוחים לתוכו והנך כיון דכולן פתוחין זו לזו ומערבין יחד: (ד) בא"ד כיון שאין פתוחין זו לזו למבוי הכא כצ"ל ותיבת אלא נמחק: (ה) בא"ד אין ראוי לאסור לאפילו: (ו) בא"ד כיון שלא היה פתח מעולם: (ז) בא"ד ועוד דאפי' פתח גמור שאינו כצ"ל. ותיבת כיון נמחק: (ח) בא"ד בחלון שבין חצר לחצר תורת מחיצה עליו כמו בסולם: (ט) ד"ה הכא נמי וכו' ה"נ כשנשתתפו במבוי לא אסרינן: (י) בא"ד הכי נמי כשנשתתפו במבוי היה אוסר: (כ) בא"ד כלים ששבתו במבוי לחורבה דילמא אתי:

גליון הש"ס

גמ' ואזדא ר"י לטעמיה. עיין לקמן דף לב ע"א תוס' ד"ה איכא דאמרי: **רש"י** ד"ה ה"נ לא גזור וכו' והרי רשות אחרת. עיין לקמן דף פה ע"א תוס' ד"ה שני בתים:

אֲתָא רַב עָנָן שַׁדְיֵהּ. אֲמַר: מְבוֹאָה דְּדָיֵירְנָא בֵּיהּ וְאָתֵינָא מִשְּׁמֵיהּ דְּמָר שְׁמוּאֵל, נֵיתֵי רַב עָנָן בַּר רַב נִישְׁדְּיֵיהּ מִן?! שְׁמַע מִינָּהּ: לָא קִיבְּלָהּ מִינֵּיהּ. לְעוֹלָם אֵימָא לָךְ: קִיבְּלָהּ מִינָּהּ, וְהָכָא — חַזָּנָא הוּא דַּהֲוָה אָכֵיל נַהֲמָא בְּבֵיתֵיהּ, וְאָתֵי בָּיֵית בְּבֵי כְּנִישְׁתָּא. וְאִיבּוּת בַּר אִיהִי סָבַר: *מְקוֹם פִּיתָּא גָּרֵים, *וּשְׁמוּאֵל לְטַעְמֵיהּ, דְּאָמַר: מְקוֹם לִינָה גָּרֵים.§ [א]אָמַר רַב יְהוּדָה, אָמַר רַב: מָבוֹי שֶׁצִּידּוֹ אֶחָד גּוֹי וְצִידּוֹ אֶחָד יִשְׂרָאֵל — אֵין מְעָרְבִין אוֹתוֹ דֶּרֶךְ חַלּוֹנוֹת, לְהַתִּירוֹ דֶּרֶךְ פְּתָחִים לַמָּבוֹי. א"ל אַבַּיֵי לְרַב יוֹסֵף: אָמַר רַב אֲפִילּוּ בֶּחָצֵר? אֲמַר לֵיהּ: [ב]אִין. דְּאִי לָא אָמַר מַאי? הֲוָה אָמִינָא: טַעְמָא דְּרַב מִשּׁוּם דְּקָסָבַר *אֵין מָבוֹי נִיתָּר בְּלֶחִי וְקוֹרָה, עַד שֶׁיְּהוּ *בָּתִּים וַחֲצֵירוֹת פְּתוּחִין לְתוֹכוֹ. וְתַרְתֵּי לָמָּה לִי? צְרִיכָא, דְּאִי מֵהַהִיא הֲוָה

מבוי שצידו אחד נכרי. פי': בתים(א) וחלירות, ולידו א' ישראל בית וחלר אין מערבין אותו דרך חלונות כו'. ולבסוף מסיק משום דאסור לעשות יחיד במקום נכרי. וקאמר: אם יש בתי ישראל אלל ביתו של ישראל פתוחין לרשות הרבים ולא למבוי, וחלונות ביניהן — אין מערבין דרך חלונות זה עם זה להוליא כליהם למבוי, דרך פתחו של זה שפתוח למבוי משום דאסור לדור יחיד במקום נכרי שלא ילמוד ממעשיו לפיכך לא יערבו אלו עמו, ולא ישתמשו אלו עמו במבוי, כדי שיהא יחיד ויירא מן הכנעני שלא יהרגנו וילא. כך פי' הקונט'. וא"ת: אפי' יערבו יחד, איך יהו מותרין להשתמש במבוי? הא אין כאן אלא חלר אחת של ישראל הפתוחה למבוי, ולא מישתרי בלחי וקורה, דחלירות של נכרי לא חשיבא דלא שמה דירה! וי"ל: דבלורת הפתח מיהו יכולין להתירו, או בפס ד' או בב' פסין משהו מכאן ומשהו מכאן. ועוד: דלמאי דמסקינן דטעמא דרב משום דאסור לעשות יחיד במקום נכרי ס"ל שפיר דדירת נכרי שמה דירה, לענין ליחשב בתים וחלירות פתוחים לתוכו, אע"פ שאין לריך בתשמיש הנכרי להתיר בשבילו בלחי וקורה. ואע"ג דנכרי אוסר עלייהו — יכולין להשכיר. או שמא אפי' שכירות אינו לריך לראב"י. ואע"פ שיש בתים של ישראל פתוחין לתוך אותו בית, כיון דלא עיילי למבוי אלא דרך אותו בית — חשיבי כולהו יחיד במקום נכרי. ועוד אור"י: דאפי' היו הרבה בתים, וכל אחד פתוח לחלר — לגבי מבוי הוי כל בני חלר אחת יחידים במקום נכרי. כמו בחלר שיש בה נכרי ובית אחד של ישראל דאינה אוסרת לראב"י, אפי' יש הרבה ישראלים באותו בית — כולהו חשיבי יחיד במקום נכרי. והא דנקט חלונות, פי' בקונט': לפי שאין דרך בני אדם לעשות פתחים גדולים מבית לבית. ור"י פי': דדוקא חלונות נקט, דאז אסור לערב. שיש לחוש שיבטח זה הדר בחלר בשכניו המשתמשין עמו, ויתייחד עם הנכרי במבוי ויזיקנו הנכרי אבל אם יש פתחים ביניהן — מותר לערב, דמרתת הנכרי טובא ולא יזיקנו, כיון שדרך פתחים יכולין לבא שם. ומביא ר"י ראייה דדוקא נקט חלונות — דהא משמע דבחלונות שבין בית לבית איירי, מדקאמר דרך פתחים למבוי — דהיינו פתח הבית ופתח החלר. דאי בחלונות מבתים לחלר איירי — לא הוה ליה למימר דרך פתחים, אלא דרך פתח למבוי, דליכא אלא פתח החלר. והשתא אי דרך פתחים נמי אסור לערב — אמאי נקט שפתוחים לבית טפי מפתוחים לחלר? אלא ודאי חלונות דווקא, כדפרישית. ולכך איירי בפתוחים לבית טפי משום דבין בית ובית דרך לעשות חלונות, כדפירש בקונט'. אבל בפתוחים לחלר — אין דרך לעשות חלונות אלא פתחים ובפתחים שרי לערב: **הוה** אמינא טעמא דרב משום דאין מבוי כו'. ולפי' זה אין להעמיד בחלר אחת נכרי וחלר אחת ישראל. דא"כ — אפי' מערבין דרך חלונות להחשב בתים פתוחים לחלר אין מבוי(ב) ניתר בלחי וקורה, דאין כאן אלא חלר אחת של ישראל. ועוד: דמאי קאמר דדירת נכרי לא שמה דירה? אפילו שמה דירה — אין מבוי(ג) ניתר בלחי וקורה, כיון דאין מערבין דרך חלונות, וליכא בחלר ישראל אלא בית אחד. אלא הוה מוקמינן לה במבוי שלידו אחד הרבה חלירות ובתים של נכרי, ולידו אחד הרבה חלירות של ישראל, ובכל חלר בית אחד אלא שפתוחים דרך חלונות בתים לכל בית שבחלר, וקמ"ל דאין מבוי זה ניתר בלחי וקורה משום דדירת נכרי לא שמה דירה. וע"י חלונות נמי אין מערבין אלא להחשיב בתים פתוחים לתוכו. והא דנקט חלונות — לאשמעינן דלא מיבעי אם יש פתחים בין כל בית ובית, שנחשבים כבית אחד כדאמר רב לעיל, וליכא שני בתים לחלר. ולא מיבעיא נמי אם לא עירבו דרך חלונות שביניהם — שאין כאן שני בתים לחלר, כיון שאין היתר תשמיש לבית החילון ולא שייך למבוי. אלא, אפילו עירבו דרך חלונות, דהשתא שייכי כולהו בתים למבוי, שיכולים להביא ע"י עירובן חפליהם למבוי ולא משוי להו עירוב נמי כחד — כיון שאין פתוחים למבוי אלא ע"י חלונות. ואפילו אם כשיש פתח בין בית לבית ראוי לחושבן אחד בלא עירוב, כשאין פתח אלא חלון — אין ראוי לחושבן א' אפילו עירבו. מ"מ, לא חשיבי בתים פתוחים לחלר כשפתוחים לבית עד שיהו שני בתים שניהם פתוחים לחלר. ועי"ל: דאם היו פתוחים בתים זה לזה דרך פתח ע"י עירוב — הוו חשיבי שני בתים פתוחים לחלר. דאע"פ דחילונה אין עיקר יליאתה דרך בתים למבוי אלא מלד א', מ"מ ע"י פתחים ועירובן נחשבים להיות מן המבוי. אבל כשאין כי אם חלונות — אין נחשבים להיות מן המבוי ע"י עירוב. ור"ת פירש: מבוי שלידו א' נכרי וכו' גם לפי *ההוה אמינא איירי בשאינו כי אם חלר אחת נכרי וחלר אחת ישראל, כמו לפי המסקנא. וע"י חלונות חשיבי שפיר שני בתים פתוחים לחלר, ואין מערבין דרך חלונות משום דדירת נכרי לא שמיה דירה, וליכא אלא חלר אחת של ישראל. והא דנקט אין מערבין דרך חלונות ולא נקט אין מערבין סתם, ואפי' יש הרבה בתים פתוחים לחלר — אתא לאשמועינן דאי הוה מבוי שני לדיו ישראל כי האי גוונא, שאין כי אם בית א' בחלר ובית א' פתוח לו דרך חלון — בתים וחלירות קרינא ביה. ואע"ג דלעיל גבי חלירות חשבינן פתוחות זו לזו כחד, ולקמן [דף עה.] נמי אמר שמואל גבי עשרה בתים זה לפנים מזה דלעשירי הוו כולהו כבית שער, ונותן הפנימי עירובו ודיו — התם לפי שאין להם פתח אחר לרה"ר וכולם יולאים דרך פתח אחד. אבל הכא, שיש להם פתח אחר לרה"ר — אסרו החלר, דחשיבי בתים. וקשה לר"י על פירושו: דמאי קאמר? אי מהכא לא ידענא בתים וחלירות כמה, אמאי לא ידענא? כיון דאין מערבין דרך חלונות נקט לאשמועינן דאי הוה לידו שני נמי ישראל דאיכא ב' חלירות וב' בתים לחלר ע"י עירוב חלונות ניתר בלחי וקורה! ולר"י אתי שפיר, שפירש דמיירי דאיכא חלירות דנכרים וישראלים טובא. ועי"ל: דה"א טעמא דרב משום דאין מבוי ניתר בלחי וקורה כו', והוה מפרשינן דאיכא טובא חלירות ובתים דנכרים ודישראלים, ואין כי אם חלר אחת של ישראל הפתוח למבוי זה, והשאר אינן פתוחות למבוי זה. וקאמר דע"י חלונות שיפתחו למבוי לא יועילו לחושבם פתוחות למבוי אלא בפתח גמור. ובמהדורא קמא פר"ת בענין אחר: מבוי שלידו אחד נכרי כו' שמבוי כולו חלירות של ישראל, אלא בראש המבוי מלד אחד נכרי ופתוח לרה"ר, ובלידו אחד ישראל כמו כן פתוח לרה"ר. (כזה) וקאמר דאין מערבין שכניו של ישראל היושבים בראש המבוי עמו דרך חלונות שביניהם כדי שיוכל ע"י עירוב להוליא כליו למבוי — דאסור לעשות יחיד במקום נכרי שהוא יחיד עמו ברה"ר. וכשלא יערבו עמו *(נכרי) יסתום פתחו לגד רה"ר, ויעשה פתחו לגד מבוי. ולדו אחד נקט לרבותא, דאע"פ שרוחב המבוי מפסיק ביניהם. וכ"ש אם שניהם בלד א' זה אלל זה ה"א טעמא דרב כו'. והוה מפרשי הכי: שלדו א' נכרי שכל חלירות שבמבוי מלד אחד נכרים, ומלד אחד ישראלים, ויש בין כל חלירות של ישראל חלונות פתוחות מזו לזו, וקאמר דאין מערבין יחד דרך חלונות כדי להכניס ולהוליא מחלרותיהן דרך פתח למבוי. דאותו עירוב לא מיבעיא דאינו מתיר להן, אלא גם המבוי עלמו שהיה מותר לטלטל בו אם לא עירבו — השתא שעירבו אין מטלטלין בו אלא בד', לפי שע"י עירוב נעשו כל החלירות אחת, ואין כאן ב' חלירות למבוי דדירת נכרי לא שמיה דירה. אבל בלא עירוב — חשיבי ב' חלירות אע"ג דפתוחות זו לזו, ודלא כפ"ה דלעיל. ואין פירוש זה כשיטה שפי' לעיל גבי מילתיה דרב, ופירוש דלעיל פירש במהדורא בתרא:
הוה

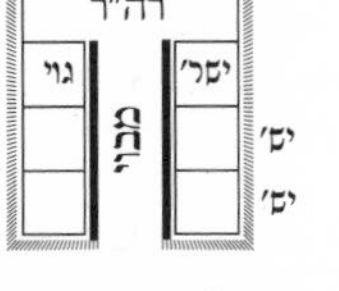

אֲתָא רַב עָנָן. לְאַחַר מוֹת שְׁמוּאֵל: שַׁדְיֵהּ. הִפִּיל הַלֶּחִי: נִשְׁדְּיֵיהּ מִן. יַשְׁלִיכֶנּוּ מִמֶּנּוּ. וּמִשּׁוּם דְּלָא הֲוָה בַּיִת אֶלָּא בַּיִת וְחָצֵר אָסַר עָלֶיהָ, כְּרַב: וְהַהוּא חַזָּנָא הֲוָה כו'. וְהַהוּא מְבוֹאָה לְהָכִי שָׁרָא לֵיהּ שְׁמוּאֵל, דְּחַזָּנָא הֲוָה אָכֵיל נַהֲמָא בְּבֵיתֵיהּ שֶׁהָיָה לוֹ בְּמָקוֹם אַחֵר: וְאָתֵי בָּיֵית בְּבֵי כְּנִישְׁתָּא. דַּהֲוָה פָּתוּחַ לְהַהוּא מְבוֹאָה, וְהָשְׁתָּא כִּי שָׁדְיֵיהּ רַב עָנָן לָא הֲוָה חַזָּנָא בָּיֵית בְּהַהוּא בֵּי כְּנִישְׁתָּא: וְאִיבּוּת בַּר אִיהִי סָבַר. דִּשְׁמוּאֵל לָאו מִשּׁוּם חַזָּנָא שַׁרְיֵיהּ, דִּמְקוֹם פִּיתָּא גּוֹרֵם, וְהָא לָא הֲוָה אָכֵיל בְּבֵי כְּנִישְׁתָּא: וּשְׁמוּאֵל לְטַעְמֵיהּ דְּאָמַר מְקוֹם לִינָה גּוֹרֵם. וְהָווּ לְהוּ שְׁתֵּי חֲצֵירוֹת: צִידּוֹ אֶחָד גּוֹי וְצִידּוֹ א' יִשְׂרָאֵל. וּמָבוֹי בֵּינֵיהֶם: אֵין מְעָרְבִין דֶּרֶךְ חַלּוֹנוֹת לְהַתִּיר דֶּרֶךְ פְּתָחִים לַמָּבוֹי. אִם יֵשׁ בָּתֵּי יִשְׂרָאֵל אֵצֶל בֵּיתוֹ שֶׁל יִשְׂרָאֵל זֶה פְּתוּחוֹת לִרְשׁוּת הָרַבִּים וְלֹא לַמָּבוֹי, וְחַלּוֹנוֹת בֵּינֵיהֶם — אֵין מְעָרְבִין זֶה עִם זֶה דֶּרֶךְ חַלּוֹנוֹתֵיהֶם לְהוֹצִיא כְּלֵיהֶם לַמָּבוֹי דֶּרֶךְ פִּתְחוֹ שֶׁל זֶה שֶׁפָּתוּחַ לַמָּבוֹי, וְטַעְמָא מְפָרֵשׁ לְקַמֵּיהּ: א"ר אֲפִילּוּ חָצֵר. יִשְׂרָאֵל וְנָכְרִי דָּרִין בָּהּ, וּבָתֵּי יִשְׂרָאֵל אֵצֶל בֵּיתוֹ שֶׁל יִשְׂרָאֵל זֶה פְּתוּחוֹת לִרה"ר, וְלֹא בֶּחָצֵר שֶׁאָסוּר לְעָרֵב דֶּרֶךְ חַלּוֹנוֹת לְהוֹצִיא כְּלֵיהֶם דֶּרֶךְ בֵּיתוֹ שֶׁל זֶה לֶחָצֵר. לְהָכִי נָקַט חַלּוֹנוֹת — שֶׁאֵין דֶּרֶךְ בְּנֵי אָדָם לַעֲשׂוֹת פְּתָחִים גְּדוֹלִים מִבַּיִת לְבַיִת: דְּאִי לָא אָמַר. אַף בֶּחָצֵר, מַאי תֵּיפּוֹק אַדַּעְתִּיךְ דְּלִשְׁתַּנֵּי חָצֵר מִמָּבוֹי: בָּתִּים וַחֲצֵירוֹת פְּתוּחִים לְתוֹכוֹ. וְהָכָא חֲדָא חָצֵר הוּא דִּפְתִיחָא לֵיהּ, דְּדִירַת נָכְרִי לָאו שְׁמָהּ דִּירָה. וְכ"ת תַּרְתֵּי ל"ל, הָא אֲמָרָהּ רַב לְעֵיל אֵין הַמָּבוֹי נִיתָּר כו':
הֲוָה

[לעיל עג.] [שם] [לעיל עג: ש"נ] [שבת קלח. וש"נ]

צ"ל מאי דמקוי טעמא דרב משום דאין מבוי ניתר איירי כו' רש"ל

[על כרחך כצ"ל]

פו א מיי' פ"ה מהל' עירובין הלכה יח טוש"ע א"ח סי' שנ סעיף א ב:
פז ב מיי' שם פ"ב הלכה טו טוש"ע א"ח סי' שפב סעיף יט כ:

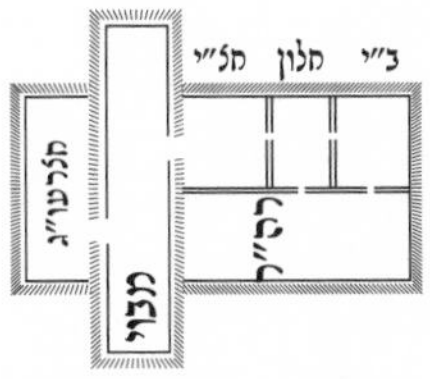

רבינו חננאל

לחורבה: אמר רב יהודה אמר רב מבוי שצדו אחד גוי וצדו אחד ישראל אין מערבין אותו דרך חלונות להתירו דרך פתחים למבוי פי' רב לטעמיה דלא הוה תני במתני' פתוחות זו לזו לפי שאם הם פתוחות כיון דמערבי הוו כלהו כחד ישראל ולגבי גוי שרי לטלטולי מיהו אסר רב משום דקסבר אסור ליעשות יחיד במקום גוי משום [הכי] קאמר רב (כי) [דכי] האי גוונא אסר במקום גוי אפי' בחצר. ולא מפני דסבר רב כיון דעירבו להו הוו להו כחצר (אחרת) [אחת] ודירת גוי לא שמיה דירה (הלכתא) [הלכך] ליכא בהאי מבוי אלא חצר אחת

הגהות הב"ח

(א) תוס' ד"ה מבוי וכו' פי' בתים וחלר ולידו: (ב) ד"ה הוה אמינא וכו' אין מבוי זה ניתר בלחי: (ג) בא"ד שמה דירה אין מבוי זה ניתר:

הוה אמינא: *דירת גוי — שמה דירה. קא משמע לן: דדירת גוי לא שמה דירה. ואי מהכא — הוה אמינא: לא ידענא בתים כמה, קא משמע לן: בתים תרין. השתא דאמר רב אפילו חצר, טעמא דרב דקא סבר: אסור לעשות יחיד במקום גוי. אמר רב יוסף: אי הכי, היינו דשמענא ליה לרבי טבלא, דאמר: *גוי גוי תרי זימני, ולא ידענא מאי אמר.§ **מתני'** אשתי חצירות זו לפנים מזו, עירבה הפנימית ולא עירבה החיצונה — הפנימית מותרת, והחיצונה אסורה. החיצונה ולא הפנימית — שתיהן אסורות. עירבה זו לעצמה וזו לעצמה — זו מותרת בפני עצמה, וזו מותרת בפני עצמה. רבי עקיבא אוסר החיצונה, שדריסת הרגל אוסרתה. וחכ"א: אין דריסת הרגל אוסרתה. בשכח אחד מן החיצונה ולא עירב — הפנימית מותרת, והחיצונה אסורה. מן הפנימית ולא עירב — שתיהן אסורות. *נתנו עירובן במקום אחד, ושכח אחד בין מן הפנימית בין מן החיצונה ולא עירב — שתיהן אסורות. גואם היו של יחידים — אינן צריכין לערב.§ **גמ'** כי אתא רב דימי, א"ר ינאי: זו דברי רבי עקיבא, דאמר: אפילו רגל המותרת במקומה — אוסרת שלא במקומה. אבל חכמים אומרים: כשם שרגל המותרת אינה אוסרת — כך רגל האסורה אינה אוסרת. תנן: עירבה חיצונה ולא פנימית — שתיהן אסורות. מני? אילימא רבי עקיבא — מאי איריא רגל אסורה? אפילו רגל מותרת נמי! אלא לאו — רבנן. לעולם ר"ע, ו"לא זו אף זו" קתני. תנן: עירבה זו לעצמה וזו לעצמה — זו מותרת בפני עצמה, וזו מותרת בפני עצמה. טעמא — דעירבה, הא לא עירבה — שתיהן אסורות. והא האי תנא, דאמר: רגל המותרת אינה אוסרת, רגל האסורה אוסרת, מני הא? אילימא ר"ע היא — אפילו רגל המותרת נמי! אלא לאו — רבנן היא. ועוד, מדסיפא רבי עקיבא — רישא לאו ר"ע! כולה רבי עקיבא היא, וחסורי מיחסרא, והכי קתני: עירבה זו לעצמה וזו לעצמה — זו מותרת בפני עצמה, וזו מותרת בפני עצמה. בד"א — שעשתה דקה, אבל לא עשתה דקה — חיצונה אסורה, דברי ר"ע. שר"ע אוסר את החיצונה, מפני שדריסת הרגל אוסרת, וחכ"א: אין דריסת הרגל אוסרת. מתיב רב ביבי בר אביי: ואם היו של יחידים — אין צריכין לערב. הא של רבים — צריכין לערב. אלמא: רגל המותרת במקומה — אינה אוסרת, רגל האסורה — אוסרת. ועוד מתיב רבינא: שכח אחד מן החיצונה ולא עירב — הפנימית מותרת, וחיצונה אסורה. שכח אחד מן הפנימית ולא עירב — שתיהן אסורות. טעמא דשכח, הא לא שכח — שתיהן מותרות. אלמא: רגל המותרת — אינה אוסרת, רגל האסורה — אוסרת. אלא, כי אתא רבין, א"ר ינאי: *ג' מחלוקות בדבר: ת"ק סבר: דרגל המותרת — אינה אוסרת, רגל האסורה — אוסרת. *)ר"ע סבר: אפילו רגל המותרת — אוסרת. ורבנן בתראי סברי: כשם שרגל מותרת אינה אוסרת — כך רגל האסורה אינה אוסרת.§ "נתנו עירובן במקום אחד ושכח אחד בין מן הפנימית וכו'": מאי מקום אחד? (סימן: חיצונה עצמה בבית יחידאה רבינא דלא משכח בפנים.) אמר רב יהודה, אמר רב: חיצונה,(א) ומאי קרו לה "מקום אחד" — מקום המיוחד לשתיהן.

תניא

*) [לעיל נט: סה.]

רש"י

הוה אמינא שמה דירה. להא מילתא, קמ"ל: ה"ג: ואי מהכא ה"א בתים לא ידענא כמה. כלומר: אי מהא ה"א נהי דבחצירות שמעינן מינה דבתרתי סגי, מדנקט לידו אחד נכרי הא תרווייהו ישראלים שרי אבל בתים לא ידענא כמה לכל חצר: קמ"ל. בתים וחצירות, סתם בתים שנים סתם חצירות שתים: אסור לעשות.(ב) לדור יחיד במקום נכרי, שלא ילמד ממעשיו. לפיכך לא יערבו אלו עמו ולא ישתמשו עמו במבוי, כדי שיהא יחיד, ויירא מן הנכרי שלא יהרגנו, ויצא: דשמענא ליה לר' טבלא דאמר. בהא מילתא דרב: נכרי נכרי תרתי זמני ולא ידענא מאי קאמר. השתא ודאי מפרש למילתיה דרב הוה. מבוי שאחד נכרי — אין מערבין אותו כולו משום דאסור לעשות יחיד במקום נכרי. לשון אחר: חד למבוי וחד לחצר: **מתני'** זו לפנים מזו. פנימית פתוחה לחיצונה, וחיצונה לרה"ר, ודריסת רגלה של פנימית על החיצונה לצאת לרשות הרבים: עירבה פנימית. לעצמה, לטלטל בחצירה: שתיהן אסורות. דהויא פנימית רגל האסורה במקומה, ואוסרת בדריסת רגלה על החיצונה: מותרת לעצמה כו'. קסברי דרגל המותרת במקומה אינה אוסרת: ר"ע סבר אף רגל המותרת אוסרת. במקום שלא עירבה שם: וחכ"א. בגמרא מפרש לה: מן הפנימית ולא עירבה שתיהן אסורות. דהויא פנימית רגל האסורה: נתנו עירובן במקום אחד. שעירבו שתיהן זו עם זו. והאי במקום אחד מפרש בגמ' שנתנוהו בחיצונה: ושכח א'. אפי' מן החיצונה ולא עירב — שתיהן אסורות. דפנימית נמי אסורה לטלטל בחצירה, משום דלא מציא למיחד דשא ולאסתלוקי מחיצונה לאשתמושי בחנפי נפשה, דהא ליתא לעירובה גבה דאותו עירוב המתירן בחצירן הוליכוהו בחיצונה: אם היו של יחידים. שאין בפנימית אלא אחד, ובחיצונה אחד — אין צריכין לערב זה עם זה משום דריסת הרגל. דכיון דיחיד הוא, והפנימית הויא רגל המותרת ואינה אוסרת, וסתמא כרבנן. ואם היו שנים — אפילו בחיצונה גזרינן דילמא אתי למישרי שנים בפנימית ואחד בחיצונה: **גמ'** אף רגל האסורה אינה אוסרת. ומתני' מותבינן ליה לקמיה: תנן חיצונה ולא פנימית שתיהן אסורות. הא עירבה נמי פנימית — תרווייהו שריין, אלמא: רגל המותרת לא אסרה: אפילו רגל המותרת נמי. דקתני סיפא גבי עירבו שתיהן כל אחת לעצמה, ר"ע אוסר את החיצונה. ומשום לאשמועינן היא גופה לא איצטריך, דמסיפא נפקא לן, דהשתא מותרת אסרה, אסורה מיבעיא: לעולם ר"ע. ולא תידוק מינה: עירבה לא אסרה, אלא היא גופה קמ"ל דרגל האסורה אוסרת. ודקא קשיא לך מסיפא נפקא — אין ה"נ, אלא הא אשמועינן ברישא והדר אמר: לא זו בלבד אסר ר"ע, דהויא רגל האסורה, אלא אף זו: עירבה זו לעצמה וזו לעצמה, דפנימית רגל המותרת היא — אפ"ה ר' עקיבא אוסר החיצונה: טעמא דעירבה. פנימית דהויא רגל המותרת: הא לא עירבה שתיהן אסורות. דרגל האסורה אוסרת. דהא ליכא למידק: הא לא עירבה חיצונה המעורבת מותרת ושאינה מעורבת אסורה, דהא פשיטא דשאינה מעורבת אסורה, דהא כבר תני לה לעיל מתני'. ואי משום היא גופה, לאשמועינן רגל המותרת אינה אוסרת — לאשמועינן רגל האסורה, וליתני: כגון עירבה חיצונה ולא פנימית חיצונה מותרת, וכל שכן האי. אלא ודאי דוקא קתני: מדסיפא רבי עקיבא. דהא רבי עקיבא אהא מילתא פליג: שעשתה דקה. פנימית עשתה דלת קטנה לפני פתחה, וסילקה דריסת רגלה מחיצונה: אין דריסת הרגל אוסרת. ואתרוייהו מילי דרבי עקיבא פליגי, ואפי' ארישא, דקתני חיצונה ולא פנימית שתיהן אסורות. ונטרוה לרבי עקיבא עד דאפסקיה למלתיה, והדר איפליגו עליה: טעמא דשכח. אחד מן הפנימית. הא לא שכח — שתיהן מותרות. והא דלא כרבי עקיבא, דאי כר"ע(ג) אי עירבו שתיהן נמי אסר על החיצונה, אלא לאו רבנן, ובשכח אסרי. אלמא: רגל האסורה אוסרת: אמר רבי יהודה אמר רב חיצונה. דאם פנימית אסורה משום שכחה דחיצונה, דליכא למימר תסתלק מינה ותשתמש — דליתיה לעירובה גבה. וחיצונה מיתסרא בשכחה דפנימית, משום רגל האסורה. אבל נתנוה בפנימית — חיצונה הוא דמיתסרא בשכחה דפנימית, משום רגל האסורה. אבל פנימית לא מיתסרא משום שכחה דחיצונה, דאחדא דשא ומשתמשא:

תניא

תוספות

הוה אמינא דירת נכרי שמה דירה. אע"ג דאמר בריש פרקין* דלכולי עלמא לא שמה דירה, הכא דלהקל להתיר המבוי להחשיב כבתים וחצירות פתוחים לתוכו — אמר שמה דירה:

מתיב רב ביבי בר אביי. ק"ק, דה"ל לאקשויי מרישא מעיקרא: אלמא רגל המותרת אינה אוסרת כו'. הא דלא מוקי בעשתה דקה — היינו משום דתיקשי: רישא וסיפא בעשתה דקה, ומציעתא ההיא דשכח אחד מן הפנימית — בלא עשתה דקה:

עד

רבינו חננאל

ורב סבר אין מבוי ניתר בלחי וקורה עד שיהו בתים וחצירות פתוחות לתוכו והאי לית ביה חצירות אלא משום דסבר רב אסור ליעשות יחיד במקום גוי אמר רב יוסף לאו היינו דשמענא ליה לר' טבלא דאמר גוי גוי ולא ידענא מאי היא. פי' דירת גוי לא שמה דירה ואסור לעשות יחיד במקום גוי: **ירושלמי** רב הונא בשם רב אין תורת חצר לגוי שאם היה שרוי בעליונה אתה מורידו *) (לסיד) [לסור]. ואין תורת דקה לגוי שאם דר בפנימית אתה מוציאו (לסוד) [לסור]. ר' (ולא) [לא] בשם ר"א יש תורת חצר לגוי שאם היה ישראל וגוי דרין בפנימית לעולם אינו אוסר עד שיהו שני ישראלים אוסרין ר' אבא בשם רב יהודה מי שיש לו דקה לפנים מביתו גבוה י' טפחים בישראל אינו אוסר בגוי אוסר מחלפה שיטתיה תמן א' בשם שמואל כותל שהקיפוה סולמות מיכן ומיכן מערבין שנים ואין מערבין אחד. א"ר יוסי ב"ר אבין תמן ע"י סולמות הן נידונין כפתחין ברם הכא דרך העליונים לירד למטה ואין דרך התחתונים לעלות למעלה:

מתני' ב' חצרות זו לפנים מזו כו'. א"ר (מינאי) [ינאי] זו דברי רבי עקיבא דאמר אפילו רגל המותרת במקומה כגון שעירבה זו לעצמה וזו לעצמה והותרה הפנימית במקומה **) אינה אוסרת את החיצונה כך רגל האסורה אינה אוסרת כלומר אפילו לא עירבה הפנימית לעצמה אינה אוסרת את החיצונה ואקשינן עליה ממתניתין תנן עירבה חיצונה ולא עירבה הפנימית שתיהן אסורות מני אי נימא ר' עקיבא מאי איריא בשלא עירבה פנימית שהיא אסורה במקומה אפי' עירבה הפנימית שהיא מותרת במקומה אוסרת החיצונה בדריסתה לה ברגלה אלא לאו רבנן היא וטעמא דהיא במקומה אסורה. הא רגל שהיא מותרת במקומה אינה אוסרת שלא במקומה ומפרק לעולם ר"ע היא והכי קתני לא זו האסורה [במקומה] בלבד היא האוסרת אלא אפי' המותרת במקומה אוסרת שלא במקומה כגון שעירבה זו לעצמה וזו לעצמה ומקשינן איני והא תנן עירבה זו לעצמה כו' טעמ' דעירבו הא לא עירבו שתיהן אסורות אלמא רגל המותרת אינה אוסרת (כמי שרגל) [אבל רגל] האסורה אוסרת. ופרקי' לעולם ר"ע היא וחסורי מחסרא והכי קתני עירבה זו לעצמה וזו לעצמה זו מותרת בפני עצמה וזו מותרת בפני עצמה. בד"א שעשתה הפנימית [דקה] וסילקה עצמה. אבל לא עשתה דקה החיצונה [אסורה] שר"ע אוסר החיצונה כי דריסת הרגל [אוסרתה] ומותבינן אסיפא דקתני אם היו של יחידים אין צריכות לערב ורבינא נמי מתיב משכח אחד מן החיצונות ולא עירב דייקינן מיניה רגל המותרת במקומה אינה אוסרת שלא במקומה רגל האסורה במקומה אוסרת שלא במקומה. ופרקינן אלא כי אתא רבין א"ר ינאי ג' מחלוקות בדבר ר' עקיבא סבר אפי' רגל המותרת במקומה אוסרת שלא במקומה. ורבנן סברי אפי' רגל האסורה במקומה אינה אוסרת שלא במקומה. והאי ת"ק דתני עירבה החיצונה ולא עירבה הפנימית כו' סבר רגל המותרת במקומה אינה אוסרת ורגל האסורה במקומה אוסרת נמי שלא במקומה: **פיסקא** נתנו עירובן במקום אחד מאי מקום אחד אמר רב החיצונה ואמאי קרי לה מקום אחד מקום המיוחד לשתיהן לפנימית ולחיצונה כי הפנימית (שלה) [יש לה] מעבר [על] החיצונה אבל החיצונה אין לה בפנימית

*) פירוש אתה מורידו לאסור על בני החצר עי' בק"ע ובפ"מ שם. **) נראה דחסר וצ"ל אוסרת שלא במקומה אבל חכ"א דכשם שרגל המותרת אינה אוסרת את החיצונה וכו'.

עין משפט נר מצוה

פח א ב מיי' פ"ד מהל' עירובין הלכה יט כ טוש"ע א"ח סי' שעח סעיף ב:

פט ג מיי' שם הלכה כב טוש"ע שם סעיף ד:

צ ד מיי' שם הלכה כג טוש"ע שם סעיף ה:

מסורת הש"ס

[לעיל סב.]

[חולין יט:]

[לעיל סו:]

[ביצה כג. יבמות נג: קידושין כג. עה: מנחות יא: יז: בכורות כו.]

הגהות הב"ח

(א) גמ' אמר רב חיצונה ואמאי קרו: (ב) רש"י ד"ה אסור לעשות יחיד כצ"ל ותיבת לדור נמחק: (ג) ד"ה טעמא דשכח וכו' דאי כרבי עקיבא אפי' עירבו:

תַּנְיָא נַמִּי הָכִי: נָתְנוּ [א]עֵירוּבָן בַּחִיצוֹנָה, וְשָׁכַח אֶחָד בֵּין מִן הַחִיצוֹנָה וּבֵין מִן הַפְּנִימִית וְלֹא עֵירֵב — שְׁתֵּיהֶן אֲסוּרוֹת. נָתְנוּ עֵירוּבָן בַּפְּנִימִית, וְשָׁכַח אֶחָד מִן הַפְּנִימִית וְלֹא עֵירֵב — שְׁתֵּיהֶן אֲסוּרוֹת. מִן הַחִיצוֹנָה וְלֹא עֵירֵב — שְׁתֵּיהֶן אֲסוּרוֹת, דִּבְרֵי רַבִּי עֲקִיבָא. וַחֲכָמִים אוֹמְרִים: [ב]בָּזוֹ פְּנִימִית מוּתֶּרֶת וְחִיצוֹנָה אֲסוּרָה. אֲמַר לֵיהּ רַבָּה בַּר חָנָן לְאַבַּיֵי: מַאי שְׁנָא לְרַבָּנַן דְּאָמְרִי פְּנִימִית מוּתֶּרֶת — מִשּׁוּם דְּאַחְדָא דַּשָּׁא וּמִשְׁתַּמְּשָׁא. לְרַבִּי עֲקִיבָא נַמִּי: תֵּיחַד דַּשָּׁא וְתִשְׁתַּמֵּשׁ! אֲמַר לֵיהּ: עֵירוּב מַרְגִּילָהּ. לְרַבָּנַן נַמִּי עֵירוּב מַרְגִּילָהּ! דְּאָמְרָה: *לְתַקּוּנֵי שִׁיתַּפְתִּיךְ וְלָא לְעַוּוֹתֵי. לר"ע נַמִּי, תֵּימָא: לְתַקּוּנֵי שִׁיתַּפְתִּיךְ וְלָא לְעַוּוֹתֵי! דַּאֲמָרָה לָהּ: מְבַטְּלִינַן לָךְ רְשׁוּתִי. וְרַבָּנַן — אֵין בִּיטּוּל רְשׁוּת מֵחָצֵר לְחָצֵר. לֵימָא *שְׁמוּאֵל וְרַבִּי יוֹחָנָן בִּפְלוּגְתָּא דְּרַבָּנַן וְר"ע קָא מִיפַּלְגִי; דִּשְׁמוּאֵל אָמַר כְּרַבָּנַן, וְרַבִּי יוֹחָנָן דְּאָמַר כר"ע? אָמַר לָךְ שְׁמוּאֵל: אֲנָא דַּאֲמַרִי אֲפִי' לְרַבִּי עֲקִיבָא; ע"כ לָא קָאָמַר ר"ע הָכָא — אֶלָּא בִּשְׁתֵּי חֲצֵירוֹת זוֹ לִפְנִים מִזּוֹ, דְּאָסְרָן אַהֲדָדֵי. אֲבָל הָתָם — מִי קָא אָסְרָן אַהֲדָדֵי? וְרַבִּי יוֹחָנָן אָמַר: אֲנָא דַּאֲמַרִי אֲפִילּוּ לְרַבָּנַן; ע"כ לָא קָאָמְרִי רַבָּנַן הָכָא — אֶלָּא דַּאֲמָרָה לָהּ: אַדְּמְבַטְּלַתְּ לִי — קָא אָסְרַתְּ עֲלַאי. אֲבָל הָתָם — מִי קָאָסְרַתְּ עֲלָהּ? § "וְאִם הָיוּ שֶׁל יְחִידִים וְכוּ'." § אֲמַר רַב יוֹסֵף, תָּנֵי רַבִּי: הָיוּ ג' — אֲסוּרִין. אֲמַר לְהוּ רַב בֵּיבָי: לָא תְּצִיתוּ לֵיהּ, אֲנָא אֲמַרִיתָהּ נִיהֲלֵהּ, וּמִשְּׁמֵיהּ דְּרַב אַדָּא בַּר אַהֲבָה אֲמַרִיתָהּ נִיהֲלֵהּ: הוֹאִיל וַאֲנִי קוֹרֵא בָּהֶן רַבִּים בַּחִיצוֹנָה. *אֲמַר רַב יוֹסֵף: מָרֵיהּ דְּאַבְרָהָם! רַבִּים בְּרַבִּי אִיחֲלַף לִי. וּשְׁמוּאֵל אָמַר: [ג]לְעוֹלָם מוּתָּרוֹת, עַד שֶׁיְּהוּ שְׁנַיִם בַּפְּנִימִית וְאֶחָד בַּחִיצוֹנָה. א"ר אֶלְעָזָר: [ד]וְגוֹי הֲרֵי הוּא כְּרַבִּים. מַאי שְׁנָא יִשְׂרָאֵל דְּלָא אָסַר — דְּמַאן דְּיָדַע — יָדַע, וּמַאן דְּלָא יָדַע — סָבַר: עֵירוּבֵי עֵירֵב. גּוֹי נַמִּי, אָמְרִינַן: דְּיָדַע — יָדַע, דְּלָא יָדַע — סָבַר: אֲגִירֵי אוֹגַר! סְתָם גּוֹי אִי אִיתָא — דְּאוֹגַר *מִיפְעָא פָּעֵי. אָמַר רַב יְהוּדָה, אָמַר שְׁמוּאֵל: י' בָּתִּים זֶה לִפְנִים מִזֶּה — פְּנִימִי נוֹתֵן אֶת עֵירוּבוֹ, וְדַיּוֹ. וְר' יוֹחָנָן אָמַר: אֲפִילּוּ חִיצוֹן. חִיצוֹן, בֵּית שַׁעַר הוּא! [ה]חִיצוֹן שֶׁל פְּנִימִי. בְּמַאי קָמִיפַּלְגִי? מָר סָבַר: בֵּית שַׁעַר דְּיָחִיד שְׁמֵיהּ בֵּית שַׁעַר, וּמ"ס: לָא שְׁמֵי' בֵּית שַׁעַר. א"ר נַחְמָן, אָמַר רַבָּה בַּר אֲבוּהּ, אָמַר רַב: [ו]ב' חֲצֵירוֹת וְג' בָּתִּים בֵּינֵיהֶן, זֶה בָּא דֶּרֶךְ זֶה וְנוֹתֵן עֵירוּבוֹ בָּזֶה, וְזֶה בָּא דֶּרֶךְ זֶה וְנוֹתֵן עֵירוּבוֹ בָּזֶה — זֶה

רש"י

תַּנְיָא נַמִּי הָכִי. כְּרַב יְהוּדָה, דְּהָא מָקוֹם אֶחָד דְּמַתְנִי' בַּחִיצוֹנָה קָאָמַר: וּבֵין מִן הַפְּנִימִית כו' שְׁתֵּיהֶן אֲסוּרוֹת. כִּדְפָרְשִׁינָן: נָתְנוּ אֶת עֵירוּבָן בַּפְּנִימִית וְשָׁכַח אֶחָד מִן הַפְּנִימִית שְׁתֵּיהֶן אֲסוּרוֹת. דְּחִיצוֹנָה מִיתַּסְרָא בִּשְׁכְחָה דִּפְנִימִית, דְּלָא מָצֵי אִסְתַּלּוּקֵי מִינָּהּ. וְעוֹד, דְּלֵיתֵיהּ לְעֵירוּבָהּ גַּבָּהּ: שְׁתֵּיהֶן אֲסוּרוֹת דִּבְרֵי ר"ע. וְלָא אָמְרִי' תִּסְתַּלֵּק פְּנִימִית מִינָּהּ כִּדְמְפָרֵשׁ לְקַמֵּיהּ. דְּעֵירוּב הַחִיצוֹנָה הַמּוּנָּח לְתוֹכָהּ מַרְגִּילָהּ שָׁם: בָּזוֹ פְּנִימִית מוּתֶּרֶת. דְּמִשּׁוּם שִׁכְחָה דְּחִיצוֹנָה לָא מִיתַּסְרָא, אֶלָּא אַחְדָא דַּשָּׁא וּמִסְתַּלְּקָא מִינָּהּ: מְבַטְּלִינַן לָךְ. וְכִי אָמַר ר"ע פְּנִימִית אֲסוּרָה עַד שֶׁתְּבַטֵּל לָהּ חִיצוֹנָה רְשׁוּת הָרֶגֶל עֵירוּבָהּ קָאָמַר: אֵין בִּיטּוּל רְשׁוּת מֵחָצֵר לְחָצֵר. וְאִי אָמְרַתְּ תֵּיסַר עֲלָהּ — מְעַוְּותָא לָהּ, הִלְכָּךְ, אָמְרָה לָהּ: לְתַקּוּנֵי שִׁיתַּפְתִּיךְ וְלָא לְעַוּוֹתֵי: שְׁמוּאֵל וְרַבִּי יוֹחָנָן. דְּאִיפְּלִגוּ לְעֵיל בְּפִרְקִין (דף סח.) בְּבִטּוּל מֵחָצֵר לְחָצֵר: דְּאָסְרַן אַהֲדָדֵי. ע"י הָרֶגֶל הָעֵירוּב וּמִתּוֹךְ שֶׁאוֹסְרִין — מְבַטְּלִין. וְכִי אָמְרִי אֲנָא בִּשְׁתֵּי חֲצֵירוֹת וּפֶתַח בֵּינֵיהֶן, וְלֹא עֵירְבוּ, וְהוּצְרְכָה זוֹ לְטַלְטֵל לִרְשׁוּת שֶׁל זוֹ — אֵין מְבַטְּלִין: אֲפִילּוּ לְרַבָּנַן. דְּרַבָּנַן נַמִּי מוֹדוּ דְּיֵשׁ בִּיטּוּל, וַאֲפִילּוּ הָכִי עִיוּוּת קָרֵי לֵיהּ: דְּאָמְרָה לָהּ. פְּנִימִית: אַדְּמְבַטְּלִית לִי. בְּעוֹד שֶׁלֹּא בִּטַּלְתָּהּ אַתְּ אוֹסֶרֶת עָלַי, הִלְכָּךְ, דַּל אַנְתְּ וְדַל בִּיטּוּלָךְ, דְּלָא בָּעֵינָא לֵיהּ: מִי קָאָסְרַתְּ. חָצֵר עַל חֲבֶרְתָּהּ בְּפֶתַח שֶׁבֵּינֵיהֶן בְּלֹא עֵירוּב; דְּאִי אָמְרַתְּ תְּבַטֵּיל לֶיהֱוֵי עִיוּוּת: אֲמַר רַב יוֹסֵף תָּנֵי רַבִּי אִם הָיוּ ג'. בֵּין ג' הַחֲצֵירוֹת אוֹסְרִין, וְלָא מִיבַּעְיָא שְׁנַיִם בַּפְּנִימִית — דְּהָוְיָא רֶגֶל הָאֲסוּרָה, אֶלָּא אֲפִי' שְׁנַיִם בַּחִיצוֹנָה אָסוּר, עַד שֶׁעֵירְבוּ שְׁתֵּיהֶן יַחַד, גְּזֵירָה מִשּׁוּם רַבִּים בַּפְּנִימִית: לָא תְּצִיתוּ לֵיהּ. (א)לְמַאי דְּתָנֵי לָהּ מִשְּׁמֵיהּ דְּרַבִּי, דְּלָאו מַתְנִי' הִיא אֶלָּא שְׁמַעֲתָא (*דְּרַב יוֹסֵף) הִיא: וַאֲנָא אֲמַרִיתָהּ נִיהֲלֵהּ מִשְּׁמֵיהּ דְּרַב אַדָּא. וּמִן הַטַּעַם הַזֶּה אֲמַרְתִּי לוֹ: הוֹאִיל וַאֲנִי קוֹרֵא רַבִּים בַּחִיצוֹנָה גָּזְרִי' מִשּׁוּם רַבִּים בַּפְּנִימִית. רַב יוֹסֵף חָלָה וְשָׁכַח תַּלְמוּדוֹ: רַבִּים בְּרַבִּי אִחֲלַף לִי. הַטַּעַם שֶׁאָמַר לִי "רַבִּים בַּחִיצוֹנָה" נִתְחַלֵּף לִי בְּרַבִּי, כְּשֶׁשָּׁכַחְתִּי הַדָּבָר בְּחָלְיִי, וְחָזַרְתִּי לְגִירְסָתִי הָרִאשׁוֹנָה נִזְכַּרְתִּי שֶׁהוּזְכַּר לִי רַבִּים בַּדָּבָר, וְסָבוּר הָיִיתִי שֶׁנֶּאֱמַר לִי בְּשֵׁם רַבִּי: הֲרֵי הוּא כְּרַבִּים. אִם דָּר נָכְרִי בַּפְּנִימִית, וּשְׁנֵי יִשְׂרְאֵלִים בַּחִיצוֹנָה — אוֹסֶרֶת דְּרִיסַת רַגְלוֹ עֲלֵיהֶן עַד שֶׁיַּשְׂכִּיר. וְאַלִּיבָּא דִּשְׁמוּאֵל אֲמָרָהּ ר"א לְמִילְּתֵיהּ. דְּאִי לְרַב אַדָּא — מַאי אִירְיָא נָכְרִי? אֲפִילּוּ יִשְׂרָאֵל נַמִּי אָסַר כִּי הָווּ שְׁנַיִם בַּחִיצוֹנָה. וְהָא לֵיכָּא לְמֵימַר דְּבְיָחִיד בַּחִיצוֹנָה אָסַר — דְּהַשְׁתָּא אֲפִילּוּ דָּר עִמּוֹ בֶּחָצֵר עַצְמָהּ, הָא קי"ל כר"א בֶּן יַעֲקֹב דְּאָמַר עַד שֶׁיְּהוּ שְׁנֵי יִשְׂרְאֵלִים אוֹסְרִין זֶה עַל זֶה. דְּרִיסַת רַגְלוֹ לֹא כָּל שֶׁכֵּן דְּלָא אָסְרָה: דְּיָדַע. שֶׁהוּא שָׁם יְחִידִי וְיָדַע שֶׁאֵין רֶגֶל הַמּוּתֶּרֶת אוֹסֶרֶת, וְלָא נָפְקָא מִינָּהּ חוּרְבָה: מִפְעָא פָּעֵי. קָלָא אִית לֵיהּ וְהָנֵי לָא אֵיגוּר, וּמַאן דְּלָא יָדַע שֶׁהוּא דָּר שָׁם יְחִידִי סָבַר דְּאֵין דְּרִיסַת הָרֶגֶל אוֹסֶרֶת. ה"נ: עֵירוּב שֶׁל פְּנִימִים וְחִיצוֹנִים מוֹעִיל בִּמְקוֹם נָכְרִי בְּלֹא שְׂכִירוּת: י' בָּתִּים זֶה לִפְנִים מִזֶּה. חִיצוֹן פָּתוּחַ לֶחָצֵר, וְכוּלָּן דְּרִיסַת רַגְלוֹ עָלָיו. וּפְנִימִי דּוֹרֵס עַל כּוּלָּן, שֶׁאֵין לוֹ יְצִיאָה אֶלָּא דֶּרֶךְ זוֹ — כּוּלָּן נַעֲשִׂין בֵּית שַׁעַר לוֹ, וְאֵינָן אוֹסְרִין עַל בְּנֵי חָצֵר אֶלָּא פְּנִימִי לְבַדּוֹ. כְּדַאֲמָרַן(ב) בְּפִירְקִין (דף עב:): וְהַדָּר שָׁם אֵינוֹ אוֹסֵר. הִלְכָּךְ, כְּשֶׁבָּאִין שְׁאָר דִּיּוּרִין הַפְּתוּחִין לֶחָצֵר וּלְעָרֵב אֶת חֲצֵירָן — פְּנִימִי זֶה נוֹתֵן פַּת. וְהַשְּׁאָר אֵין צְרִיכִין: אֲפִילּוּ חִיצוֹן. צָרִיךְ לִיתֵּן אֶת הַפַּת: חִיצוֹן שֶׁל פְּנִימִית. בֵּית הַתְּשִׁיעִי לֶחָצֵר: (ג)ג' בָּתִּים בֵּינֵיהֶן. בַּיִת זֶה פָּתוּחַ לְחָצֵר זוֹ, וְזֶה לָזוֹ, וּבַיִת אֶמְצָעִי פָּתוּחַ לְב' הַבָּתִּים: זֶה בָּא בְּדֶרֶךְ זֶה. בֶּן חָצֵר זוֹ בָּא דֶּרֶךְ בַּיִת הַפָּתוּחַ לוֹ וְנָתַן עֵירוּבוֹ בָּאֶמְצָעִי, וְעָשָׂה בַּיִת הַפָּתוּחַ לוֹ כְּבֵית שַׁעַר לַעֲבוֹר דֶּרֶךְ עָלָיו לָאֶמְצָעִי. וְכֵן בֶּן חָצֵר הָאַחֶרֶת עָשָׂה בַּיִת הַפָּתוּחַ לוֹ כְּבֵית שַׁעַר, וְעֵירֵב בָּאֶמְצָעִי חָצֵר הָאַחֶרֶת — אֵין אֶחָד מִדִּיּוּרֵי הַבָּתִּים הָאֵלֶּה צָרִיךְ לִיתֵּן פַּת. אֵלּוּ מִשּׁוּם בֵּית שַׁעַר, וְאֶמְצָעִי מִשּׁוּם בַּיִת שֶׁמַּנִּיחִין בּוֹ עֵירוּב:

תוספות

עד כאן לא קאמר ר"ע הכא אלא בב' חצירות זו לפנים מזו דאסרן אהדדי. יש ליישב הך סוגיא נמי אליבא דרבא דאמר לעיל (דף סו.) לשמואל דבשתי חצירות זו לפנים מזו — פעמים אין מבטלין אע"ג דלאסרן אהדדי דהכא קאמר דאסרן אהדדי בפסיעות בני חיצונה (ד)שהורגלו עירובן בפנימית, דשכח א' מהן ולא עירב. אבל בכל הנהו דאמר שמואל אין מבטלין מי אסרן אהדדי בפסיעה, דכי נתנו עירובן בחיצונה ושכח אחד מהן ולא עירב — אין האיסור בא ע"י שפסעו במה שהרגילו עירובן, ושכח אחד מהם ולא עירב. דבלאו הכי היה להם דריסת הרגל. ואין לתמוה היאך מתוקם לרבא שמואל כר"ע וכרבנן, הא ע"כ כר"ע דוקא ס"ל כדפי' בקונטרס לעיל! דמ"מ בעיקר פלוגתייהו דאין ביטול רשות מחצר לחצר *מוקמי נפשיה בכולהו. וא"ת: ולאביי, דאמר שתי חצירות זו לפנים מזו דמבטלין בכל ענין לשמואל (מי נימא), שמואל כר"ע ולא כרבנן. דלרבנן ב' חצירות זו לפנים מזו — אין מבטלין! וי"ל: דהוה מפרש כר' יוחנן דבסמוך, עד כאן לא קאמרי רבנן(ה) התם אלא דאמר' לה אדמבטלת לי קאסרת עלי בפסיעותא, שהרגלת עירובך ושכח אחד מהם:

ואני קורא בהם רבים בחיצונה. ויסברו שיש כמו כן שנים בפנימית ולא עירבו. אבל כשיש שנים בפנימית ועירבו — לא גזרינן אטו לא עירבו. דעירבו אטו לא עירבו לא גזרינן. אבל כשיש אחד בפנימית ולא עירבו — יסברו שהם שנים כמו בחיצונה, והרי לא עירבו. נכרי הרי הוא כרבים. אליבא דשמואל קאמר, כדפי' בקונט'. דליכא למימר דיחיד בחיצונה נמי אסר. דאפי' היה דר עמו בחצר לא אסר, דקיימא לן "כראב"י", כ"ש דריסת רגל דלא אסרה. וכן מוכחת בהדיא לעיל(ו) גבי ישראל ונכרי בפנימית, וישראל בחיצונה. דאי ליכא ישראל בפנימית אלא נכרי לחודיה — לא אסר. וא"ת: ולמה ליה למימר "הרי הוא כרבים"? אפילו לא הוו כרבים — אסר, דכיון דיש שני ישראלים בחיצונה ואוסרין זה על זה, ויש לו דריסת רגל עליהן. וי"ל: כיון דישראל לא אסר — נכרי נמי לא אסר, דאין להחמיר בנכרי יותר מבישראל, אי לאו דהוו כרבים:

ורבי יוחנן סבר בית שער דיחיד לא הוי בית שער. והא דאמר בפ' "כיצד משתתפין" (לקמן דף פה:): כל מקום שאמרו חכמים הדר שם אינו אוסר — הנותן שם עירובו אינו עירוב, חוץ מבית שער דיחיד. פי': דאף על גב דהדר שם אינו אוסר, הנותן שם עירובו הוי עירוב. אתי נמי כר' יוחנן דהתם איירי בבית שער דחצר, כדפי' שם בקונטרס, דאינו עשוי לדירה. אבל הכא(ז) — העשוי לדירה — אוסר:

אמצעי

עין משפט נר מצוה

צא א ב מיי' פ"ד מהל' עירובין הלכה כא טוש"ע א"ח סי' שעט סעיף ה:
צב ג מיי' שם הלכה כג טוש"ע שם סעיף ה:
צג ד מיי' פ"ד שם הלכה כב טוש"ע א"ח סי' שפב סעיף יז:
צד ה מיי' שם הל' ט סמג עשין א טוש"ע א"ח סי' שע סעיף ו:
צה ו מיי' שם הלכה ז סמג שם טוש"ע א"ח סי' שעט סעיף א:

מוקי נפשייהו בכולהו [רש"ל]
[לעיל סב:]

מסורת הש"ס

[קידושין מב: וש"נ]
[לעיל סו: סח.]
[שבת כב. וש"נ] רש"ל מ"ז
*[חולין קלג: עירובין ו:]

רבינו חננאל

בפנימית לא מעבר עליה ולא דריסה. תניא נמי הכי נתנו עירובן בחיצונה ושכח בין מן הפנימית [ובין] מן החיצונה ולא עירב שתיהן אסורות. נתנו את עירובן בפנימית ושכח אחד ולא עירב בין מן הפנימית בין מן החיצונית שתיהן אסורות. דברי רבי עקיבא וחכ"א בזו ששכח אחד מן החיצונית ולא עירב פנימית מותרת והחיצונה אסורה ואקשינן לרבנן מ"ש פנימית דשריא דאמרי אחדא לדשא ומשתמשא לעצמה. לר' עקיבא נמי נימא הכי אמאי תני שתיהן אסורות ודחינן סבר ר"ע [עירוב] מרגילה כלומר עירובה מכנים רגלי החיצונה בפנימית ופרקי' רבנן סברי יכולה לומר לה לתקוני שיתפתיך ולא לעוותי *) כי א' שליח לתקוני שיתפתיך ולא לעוותי. ור' עקיבא אמר לך כי האי גוונא לא מקריא עוות דאמרה לה חיצונה מבטילנא לך רשותאי וכאלו הרשות כולה לפנימית והנה (יש הן) [יש כאן] מי שלא עירב ואוסר עליה ורבנן [ס"ל] אין ביטול רשות מחצר לחצר **) כרבנן ור' יוחנן דאמר מבטלין רשות מחצר לחצר כרבי עקיבא ופרקינן לעולם רבי יוחנן (עקיבא) ואפילו לרבנן עד כאן לא קאמרי רבנן אין ביטול רשות מחצר לחצר אלא משום דאמרה להאי (מבטלת) [אדמבטלת] לי בטולי רשותיך הא (אם) [קא] אסרת עלי אבל מחצר לחצר כגון ב' חצרות ופתח ביניהן מאי קאסר עלה הלכך אפי' רבנן סברי מבטלין רשות מחצר לחצר וקיי"ל כר' יוחנן דכל היכא דפליגי רב ושמואל ור' יוחנן הלכתא כר' יוחנן: **פיסקא** ואם היו של יחידים אין צריכין לערב. אמר רב יוסף אמר רב ג' אסורין פי' אין ניתרין יחידים אלא בזמן שהן ב' חצרות ובכל חצר דר אחד. אבל בג' חצירות ובכל חצר דר אחד שנמצאו כולן ג' אסורין. ואמר רב ביבי אנא אמרתה ליה ומשמיה דרב אדא בר אהבה אמרת ליה ולא משמיה דר' ומ"ט ג' חצירות ובכל חצר שוכן יחיד אסורין הואיל ואני קורא רבים בחיצונה כי כל שלשה רבים הם ועכשיו שנמצאו דורסין אותה שלשה והן רבים אסורין [אמר רב יוסף] מארי דאברהם רבים ברבי איחלף לי. כלומר אמר לי רב ביבי רבים ונתחלף לי וקבעתי שמועה זו ברבי ושמואל אמר לעולם מותרין עד שיהו בפנימית ב' ולא עירבו לפיכך אסורין בחיצונית שהן רגל האסורה. אר"א גוי הרי הוא כרבים ואוסר ואמרינן מ"ש דישראל יחיד לא אסר דכל מאן דחזי ליה דמטלטל אמרינן אי ידע דיחיד הוא הא ידע ואי לא אמר בדעתיה האי דמטלטל משום ***) דאגר מיניה. ודחינן סתם גוי לא שתיק אלא פעי ומכריז מלשון כיולדה אפעה. כלומר צועק ואומר אנא אוגרית רשותי להאי ישראל וכיון דלא פעי ידעיה דלא אגר ואמרי מטלטל במקום גוי הוא לפיכך אסור. אמר רב יהודה אמר שמואל י' בתים זה לפנים מזה הפנימי נותן עירובו ודיו. פי' כיון שדורסין כולן [על החיצונים] כאילו רשותו הן ורשות

*) [אולי צ"ל כי אמרינן בשליח לתקוני שדרתיך ולא לעוותי]. **) [חסר כאן ונראה דצ"ל לימא שמואל דאמר דאין ביטול רשות מחצר לחצר כרבנן וכו']. ***) [חסר וצ"ל משום דעירובו עירוב גוי נמי אמרינן דידע ידע וכו' אמר דאגר מיניה].

רב נסים גאון

לימא שמואל ור' יוחנן בפלוגתא דרבי עקיבא ורבנן קא מיפלגי. והיינו חלוקתם בזה הפרק לשעבר (דף סו) אמר שמואל אין ביטול רשות מחצר לחצר:

סליק פרק הדר

הגהות הב"ח

(א) רש"י ד"ה לא תציתו ליה לרב יוסף למאי: (ב) ד"ה עשרה בתים וכו' כדאמרן בפרק כיצד כ"ג דף פה: (ג) ד"ה שתי חצירות וג' בתים ביניהן: כזה

חצר	בית	בית אמצעי והוא פתוח לשתיהן	בית וזה בית שער מחצר שאצלה לילך לבית אמצעי	חצר

(ד) תום' ד"ה עד כאן וכו' שהרגילו עירובן בפנימית ושכח אחד: (ה) בא"ד ע"כ לא קאמרי רבנן הכא אלא: (ו) ד"ה עו"ג וכו' לעיל נ"ב דף ס"ה ע"ב: (ז) ד"ה ור' יוחנן וכו' אבל הכא בית העשוי:

זֶה נַעֲשָׂה בֵּית שַׁעַר לָזֶה, וְזֶה נַעֲשָׂה בֵּית שַׁעַר לָזֶה. אֶמְצָעִי הֲוָה לֵיהּ בַּיִת שֶׁמַּנִּיחִין בּוֹ עֵירוּב, וְאֵין צָרִיךְ לִיתֵּן אֶת הַפַּת. בָּדֵיק לְהוּ רַחֲבָה לְרַבָּנַן: ב' חֲצֵרוֹת וּב' בָּתִּים בֵּינֵיהֶם, זֶה בָּא דֶּרֶךְ זֶה וְנָתַן עֵירוּבוֹ בָּזֶה, וְזֶה בָּא דֶּרֶךְ זֶה וְנָתַן עֵירוּבוֹ בָּזֶה, קָנוּ עֵירוּב, אוֹ לֹא? מִי מְשַׁוֵּי' לְהוּ לְגַבֵּי דְּהַאי בַּיִת וּלְגַבֵּי דְּהַאי בֵּית שַׁעַר [*וּלְגַבֵּי דְּהַאי בֵּית שַׁעַר וּלְגַבֵּי דְּהַאי בַּיִת] אָמְרוּ לֵיהּ: [א]שְׁנֵיהֶן לֹא קָנוּ עֵירוּב; מַה נַּפְשָׁךְ: אִי בֵּית שַׁעַר מְשַׁוֵּית לֵיהּ, *הַנּוֹתֵן אֶת עֵירוּבוֹ בְּבֵית שַׁעַר, אַכְסַדְרָה, וּמִרְפֶּסֶת — אֵינוֹ עֵירוּב. אִי בַּיִת מְשַׁוֵּית לֵיהּ, קָא מְטַלְטֵל לְבַיִת דְּלָא מְעָרֵב לֵיהּ. וּמַאי שְׁנָא *מִדְּרָבָא? *דְּאָמַר רָבָא: [ב]אָמְרוּ לוֹ שְׁנַיִם צֵא וְעָרֵב עָלֵינוּ, לְאֶחָד עֵירֵב עָלָיו מִבְּעוֹד יוֹם וּלְא' עֵירֵב עָלָיו בֵּין הַשְּׁמָשׁוֹת, זֶה שֶׁעֵירֵב עָלָיו מִבְּעוֹד יוֹם נֶאֱכַל עֵירוּבוֹ בֵּין הַשְּׁמָשׁוֹת, וְזֶה שֶׁעֵירֵב עָלָיו בֵּין הַשְּׁמָשׁוֹת נֶאֱכַל עֵירוּבוֹ מִשֶּׁתֶּחְשַׁךְ — שְׁנֵיהֶם קָנוּ עֵירוּב! הָכִי הָשְׁתָּא?! הָתָם — סְפֵק יְמָמָא סְפֵק לֵילְיָא — לָא מִינְכְּרָא מִילְּתָא. אֲבָל הָכָא, אִי דִּלְגַבֵּי דְּהַאי בַּיִת — לְגַבֵּי דְּהַאי בַּיִת, אִי לְגַבֵּי דְּהַאי בֵּית שַׁעַר — לְגַבֵּי דְּהַאי נַמִי בֵּית שַׁעַר.§

הדרן עלך הדר

*חַלּוֹן [ג]שֶׁבֵּין ב' חֲצֵירוֹת, ד' עַל ד' בְּתוֹךְ עֲשָׂרָה — מְעָרְבִין שְׁנַיִם. וְאִם רָצוּ — מְעָרְבִין א'. פָּחוֹת מִד' עַל ד', אוֹ לְמַעְלָה מִי' — מְעָרְבִין שְׁנַיִם וְאֵין מְעָרְבִין אֶחָד.§ **גמ'** לֵימָא תְּנַן סְתָמָא כְּר"ש בֶּן גַּמְלִיאֵל, *דְּאָמַר: כָּל פָּחוֹת מִד' כְּלָבוּד דָּמֵי! אֲפִי' תֵּימָא כְּרַבָּנַן. עַד כָּאן לָא פְּלִיגִי רַבָּנַן עֲלֵיהּ דְּרשב"ג — אֶלָּא לְעִנְיַן לְבוּדִין, אֲבָל לְעִנְיַן פִּתְחָא — אֲפִי' רַבָּנַן מוֹדוּ, דְּאִי אִיכָּא ד' עַל ד' — חֲשִׁיב, וְאִי לָא — לָא חֲשִׁיב.§ "פָּחוֹת מִד' וכו'".§ פְּשִׁיטָא! כֵּיוָן דְּאָמַר ד' עַל ד' בְּתוֹךְ עֲשָׂרָה — מִמֵּילָא אֲנָא יָדַעְנָא דְּפָחוֹת מִד' וּלְמַעְלָה מִי' לֹא! הָא קמ"ל: טַעְמָא דְּכוּלֵּיהּ לְמַעְלָה מִי', [ד]אֲבָל מִקְצָתוֹ בְּתוֹךְ י' — מְעָרְבִין שְׁנַיִם. וְאִם רָצוּ — מְעָרְבִין אֶחָד. תַּנְיָא לְהָא, דְּת"ר: כּוּלּוֹ לְמַעְלָה מִי' וּמִקְצָתוֹ בְּתוֹךְ עֲשָׂרָה, כּוּלּוֹ בְּתוֹךְ י' וּמִקְצָתוֹ לְמַעְלָה מִי' — מְעָרְבִין שְׁנַיִם. וְאִם רָצוּ — מְעָרְבִין אֶחָד. הַשְׁתָּא כּוּלּוֹ לְמַעְלָה מִי' וּמִקְצָתוֹ בְּתוֹךְ י' אָמְרַתְּ "מְעָרְבִין שְׁנַיִם וְאִם רָצוּ מְעָרְבִין א'" כּוּלּוֹ בְּתוֹךְ י' וּמִקְצָתוֹ לְמַעְלָה מִי' מִיבַּעְיָא?! *זוֹ וְאצ"ל זוֹ קָתָנֵי. א"ר יוֹחָנָן: חַלּוֹן עָגוֹל צָרִיךְ שֶׁיְּהֵא בְּהֶיקֵּפוֹ עֶשְׂרִים וְאַרְבָּעָה טְפָחִים, וּשְׁנַיִם וּמַשֶּׁהוּ מֵהֶן בְּתוֹךְ י', שֶׁאִם יְרַבְּעֶנּוּ נִמְצָא מַשֶּׁהוּ בְּתוֹךְ י'. מִכְּדִי *)כָּל שֶׁיֵּשׁ בְּהֶיקֵּפוֹ שְׁלֹשָׁה טְפָחִים — יֵשׁ בּוֹ בְּרוֹחְבּוֹ טֶפַח, בִּתְרֵיסַר סַגְיָא!

הָנֵי

*) [לעיל יג: וש"נ]

זֶה נַעֲשָׂה בֵּית שַׁעַר לָזֶה. כָּל בַּיִת נַעֲשָׂה בֵּית שַׁעַר לְחָצֵר שֶׁהוּא פָּתוּחַ לוֹ: בָּדֵיק. מְנַסֶּה אִם חָכְמוּ לְהָשִׁיב: שְׁתֵּי חֲצֵירוֹת וּשְׁנֵי בָּתִּים בֵּינֵיהֶן. וְאֵין בְּנֵי שְׁתֵּי הַחֲצֵירוֹת רוֹצִין לְעָרֵב זוֹ עִם זוֹ, אֶלָּא כָּל אַחַת לְעַצְמָהּ. וְכָל חָצֵר לֹא הִנִּיחָה עֵירוּבָהּ בַּבַּיִת הַפָּתוּחַ לָהּ, אֶלָּא עֲשָׂאַתּוּ בֵּית שַׁעַר, וְהִנִּיחַ עֵירוּבָהּ בַּבַּיִת הַפָּתוּחַ לַחֲבֶרְתָּהּ: מַהוּ. וַדַּאי אִי תַּרְוַיְיהוּ בֵּית שַׁעַר מְשַׁוֵּינַן — אֵין אֶחָד מֵהֶן עֵירוּב. דְּהַנּוֹתֵן אֶת עֵירוּבוֹ בְּבֵית שַׁעַר תְּנַן לְקַמָּן (פה:) דְּאֵינוֹ עֵירוּב. וְאִי תַּרְוַיְיהוּ בַּיִת גָּמוּר — אֵין אֶחָד מֵהֶן עֵירוּב, שֶׁהֲרֵי בַּיִת זֶה מַפְסִיק בֵּין חָצֵר לְעֵירוּבָהּ, וְהוּא לֹא עֵירֵב עִמָּהּ וְאֵינָהּ יְכוֹלָה לְהָבִיא עֵירוּבָהּ לְתוֹכָהּ דֶּרֶךְ בַּיִת זֶה: מִי מְשַׁוֵּינַן. לְכָל בַּיִת לְגַבֵּי חָצֵר הַסְּמוּכָה לוֹ כְּבֵית שַׁעַר, שֶׁלֹּא לֶאֱסוֹר עָלָיו וְגַבֵּי חָצֵר הָאַחֶרֶת שֶׁעֲשָׂאַתּוּ בַּיִת גָּמוּר וְהִנִּיחַ בּוֹ עֵירוּבָהּ — מְשַׁוֵּינַן לָהּ כִּי בַּיִת לְמִיקְנֵי עֵירוּבָהּ: מַה נַּפְשָׁךְ. טַעְמָא מְפָרְשִׁי וְאָזְלִי: קָא מְטַלְטֵל. כָּל חָצֵר בְּבַיִת דְּלָא מְעָרֵב לֵיהּ: שְׁנֵיהֶן קָנוּ עֵירוּב. אַלְמָא: מִשּׁוּם דְּבֵין הַשְּׁמָשׁוֹת סָפֵק הוּא, וּסְפֵק דְּדִבְרֵיהֶם לְהָקֵל, וְעֵירוּב מִדִּבְרֵיהֶם הוּא, לְגַבֵּי הַאי שֶׁנֶּאֱכַל עֵירוּבוֹ בֵּין הַשְּׁמָשׁוֹת מְשַׁוֵּינַן לֵיהּ לֵילְיָא, וְאָמְרִינַן: כְּבָר קָנָה עֵירוּב. וּלְגַבֵּי הַאי שֶׁעֵירֵב עָלָיו בֵּין הַשְּׁמָשׁוֹת מְשַׁוֵּינַן לֵיהּ יוֹם, וַעֲדַיִין הָוֵה לוֹ שָׁהוּת לִקְנוֹת שְׁבִיתָה: לָא מִינְכְּרָא מִילְּתָא. וְלָא הָווּ מִילֵּי דְּרַבָּנַן כִּי חוּכָא וְאִיטְלוּלָא. אֲבָל הָנָךְ בָּתִּים — הָא קָיְימֵי קַמָּן, וְאִי מְשַׁוֵּינַן הָכָא הָכִי וְהָכָא הָכִי — הָוְיָין מִילֵּי דְּרַבָּנַן כִּי חוּכָא וְאִיטְלוּלָא, וְלֹא נִיתֵּן פֶּה לַצְּדוֹקִים לִרְדּוֹת:

הדרן עלך הדר

חַלּוֹן שֶׁבֵּין שְׁתֵּי חֲצֵירוֹת. בְּתוֹךְ עֲשָׂרָה. מְפָרֵשׁ בַּגְּמָ' שֶׁיְּהֵא קְצָת הֵימֶנּוּ, וַאֲפִי' מַשֶּׁהוּ, בְּתוֹךְ עֲשָׂרָה לַקַּרְקַע: מְעָרְבִין שְׁנַיִם. שְׁנֵי עֵירוּבִין, אֵלּוּ לְעַצְמָן וְאֵלּוּ לְעַצְמָן. וַאֲסוּרִין זוֹ עִם זוֹ: וְאִם רָצוּ מְעָרְבִין אֶחָד. עֵירוּב אֶחָד, שֶׁיִּתְּנוּ אֵלּוּ עֵירוּבָן בָּאַחֶרֶת וִיעָרְבוּ עִמָּהֶן, וְיִהְיוּ כְּאֶחָד: פָּחוֹת מֵאַרְבַּע. לָאו פֶּתַח הָוֵי. לְמַעְלָה מֵעֲשָׂרָה נַמִי, דְּאִילּוּ כָּל הַכּוֹתֶל אֵינוֹ גָּבוֹהַּ יוֹתֵר — הָוֵי מְחִיצָה מַעַלְיָיתָא. הִלְכָּךְ, כְּשֶׁאֵין כְּלוּם מִן הֶחָלָל בְּתוֹךְ עֲשָׂרָה — לָאו פֶּתַח הוּא, וְאֵין מְעָרְבִין אֶחָד וַאֲסוּרוֹת זוֹ עִם זוֹ דֶּרֶךְ רֹאשׁ הַכּוֹתֶל, וְדֶרֶךְ אוֹתוֹ חַלּוֹן, וְדֶרֶךְ חוֹרִים וּסְדָקִים: **גמ'** רַבָּן שִׁמְעוֹן. בְּפִירְקָא קַמָּא[(א)] בַּבָּרַיְיתָא בִּגְמָרָא: הָא קַמַּשְׁמַע לָן טַעְמָא דְּכוּלֵּיהּ לְמַעְלָה מִי' כו'. דְּאִי מֵרֵישָׁא הֲוָה אָמֵינָא: כּוּלּוֹ בְּתוֹךְ י' בָּעֵינַן: וּמִקְצָתוֹ. אֲפִילּוּ מַשֶּׁהוּ: צָרִיךְ שֶׁיְּהֵא בְּהֶיקֵּפוֹ עֶשְׂרִים וְאַרְבָּעָה. דְּבְלָאו הָכִי לָא מָצֵית לְמִינְקַט בְּגַוֵּויהּ חַלּוֹן מְרוּבָּע ד' עַל ד'. כָּל חַלּוֹן עָגוֹל בְּתַחְתִּית אֶמְצָעִיתוֹ נָמוּךְ, וּמֵאֶמְצָעִיתוֹ לְכָאן וּלְכָאן הָוֵה מַגְבִּיהַּ וְהוֹלֵךְ. וְצָרִיךְ לָזֶה שֶׁיְּהוּ שְׁנֵי טְפָחִים וּמַשֶּׁהוּ אוֹרֶךְ מֵהֶקֵּיפוֹ בְּתוֹךְ י' מֵאֶמְצָעוֹ לְכָאן טֶפַח וּמֵאֶמְצָעוֹ לְכָאן טֶפַח וְעוֹד מַשֶּׁהוּ מִשּׁוּם דְּכִי מְרַבְּעִינַן לֵיהּ מַדְלִינַן לֵיהּ מִינֵּיהּ שְׁנֵי טְפָחִים מִן הַהֶיקֵּף עִגּוּל שֶׁבֵּין קֶרֶן לְקֶרֶן לְכָל צַד, דְּסַתְמִינַן לְהוּ, וּמוֹקְמִינַן לָהּ אַרִיבּוּעָא. וְנִמְצָא אוֹתוֹ מַשֶּׁהוּ הַנִּשְׁאָר בְּסוֹף י'[(ב)] עַל פְּנֵי רוֹחַב הַחַלּוֹן, כִּדְאָמַר לְקַמָּן: רִבּוּעָא מִגּוֹ עִגּוּלָא פַּלְגָא בָּעֵית לְדַלּוּיֵי, כְּלוֹמַר, חֲצִי מִדָּה הַנּוֹתֶרֶת בְּרִיבּוּעַ רִיבָּה הָעִגּוּל עָלָיו. וְהֶיקֵּף הַמְּרוּבָּע ט"ז, נִמְצָא הָעִגּוּל רִבָּה עָלָיו ח' הֲרֵי ב' טְפָחִים לְכָל צַד:

אמצעי הוה ליה בית שמניחין כו'. נראה דאפי' יתנו העירוב באחד הבתים הסמוכים לחצירות, או אפילו באחד מבתי החצירות – אלו ג' בתים אין צריכין ליתן עירוב, דנעשו כולם בית שער לאותה חצר המוליכה עירוב דרך עליהן לחצר אחרת:

שניהם קנו עירוב. מתוך פי' הקונטרס משמע דאיירי בעירובי תחומין. וקשה: דבפרק "במה מדליקין" (שבת דף לד.) משמע דלא איירי רבא בתרווייהו בעירובי חצירות ובעירובי תחומין, דמשני: לא קשיא, כאן – בעירובי חצירות, כאן – בעירובי תחומין. וא"כ, לפירוש הקונט' בעירובי חצירות לא קנו. וקשה: דא"כ מאי פריך הכא מדרבא? ונראה כפירוש רבינו חננאל: דרבא איירי בעירובי חצירות, אבל בעירובי תחומין דחמירי – לא קנו. והשתא פריך שפיר, ולשון "לא" דקאמר לא וערב עלינו – שייך אפי' בעיר, כמו "לא ושכור לנו פועלים" (ב"מ דף פג.*):

הדרן עלך הדר

לימא תנן סתמא כרשב"ג. דקס"ד, דלרבנן כיון דנג' יוצא מתורת לבוד חשוב פתח:

הא קמ"ל טעמא דכוליה למעלה. ואגב דהדר ותנא למעלה מעשרה, תנא נמי פחות מארבעה על ארבעה: ושנים ומשהו מהן בתוך י'. לא כמו שפירש בקונט': ב' טפחים ומשהו אורך מהיקפו בתוך י' מאמצעו ולכאן טפח ומאמצעו ולכאן טפח. אלא כמו שפירש ריב"ן: אלו שני טפחים ומשהו זקופים מלמטה למעלה. דחלון זה הוי שמונה טפחים על שמונה טפחים, מאחר דבעגולו כ"ד טפחים – על כרחך באמצעו ח' טפחים, דכל שבהיקפו שלשה טפחים יש ברוחבו טפח. וכשתסיר שני טפחים למטה וכן למעלה וכן משני צדדין – ישארו ד' על ד'. הלכך צריך שיהא החלון ב' טפחים ומשהו בתוך י' באורך זקיפת החלון באמצעיתו, כדי שיהא משהו מן המרובע בתוך עשרה:

ורבי

ה"מ

צו א מיי' פ"ד מהלכות עירובין הלכה יא טוש"ע א"ח סי' שע"ט סעיף ב:

צז ב מיי' פ"ו מהל' עירובין הלכה יג טור ש"ע א"ח סי' שנג סעיף ג:

א ג ד מיי' פ"ג מהל' עירובין הלכה ט טור ש"ע א"ח סי' שעב סעיף ז:

[וע"ע תוס' שבת לד. ד"ה שניהם]

רש"ל

לקמן פה: [סוכה ג.]

גיר' הרא"ש מדרבה דאמר רבה שבת לד.

[לקמן פג:]

לעיל ט. וש"נ

[ר"ה לב: לג. יבמות יג: כתובות נח. נדרים יז: הוריות ב: כריתות יז:]

הגהות הב"ח

(א) רש"י ד"ה רבן שמעון בפירקא קמא נ"ב ראש דף ט: (ב) ד"ה צריך וכו' בסוף עשרה הוא על פני:

רבינו חננאל

אחת הן. ור' יוחנן אמר אפי' חיצון של פנימי דסבר אע"ג דבבית שער הוא בית שער דפנימי לא הוי בית שער דהא איכא אחריני חוצה לו. ושמואל סבר אפי' בית שער דפנימי בית שער הוא. אמר [רב נחמן אמר רבה בר אבוה] משמיה דרב ב' חצירות ושלשה בתים ביניהן זה בעל החצר [בא] בדרך הבית שקרוב לו ובעל החצר האחר בא בדרך הבית האחר הקרוב לו ושניהן כאן ונתנו עירובן בבית האמצעי זה הבית הקרוב לה נעשה בית שער לחצר זו וזה הבית נעשה בית שער לחצר זו נמצאו ב' הבתים החיצונים בתי שער ואין צריכין עירוב. כדתנן הדר בבית שער אכסדרה ומרפסת אינו אוסר והאמצעי הוה ליה בית שמניחין בו עירוב כי בתוכו נתנו עירובן ב' חצירות וקיי"ל כל בית שמניחין בו עירוב אין צריך ליתן פת. נמצאו ג' בתים וב' חצירות יוצאין בעירוב אחד של חצר. בדיק להו רחבה לרבנן כלומר אם הן (בקיין) [בקיאי] בהלכות עירובין שתי חצירות ושתי חורבות של אחרים ביניהן זה בא מחצירו דרך החורבה הסמוכה לחצירו ונתן עירובו בחורבה [האחרת] (שכיחי צהלה). וכן בא זה מחצירו דרך החורבה הקרובה לחצירו ונתן עירובו בחורבה האחרת קנו עירוב או לא קנו עירוב ואמרו ליה לא קני עירוב ממה נפשך אי הני חורבות כל חדא הויא בית שער לחצר הסמוכה לה הנותן עירובו בבית שער אכסדרה ומרפסת אינו עירוב ואי הני חורבות בתין נינהו נמצאו כל אחד מטלטל בחורבה הסמוכה לה בבית דלא מערב דהא (של) [כל] חד מינייהו לא יהב עירוביה אלא בחורבה הסמוכה לחברתה ואמרינן מיכדי ספיקא הוא מאי שנא מדרבה דאמר א' לשנים צאו ועירב עלינו כו'. ודחינן הכי השתא התם בין השמשות ספק יום וספק לילה וספק (העירוב) [עירוב] כשר הכא אי לתרווייהו בית שער [או לתרווייהו בית] אבל לגבי האי בית שער ולגבי האי בית לא: **הדרן עלך פרק הדר**

פ"ז חלון שבין ב' חצירות ד' על ד' בתוך י' מערבין שנים ואין מערבין כו'. אוקימנא להא מתניתין אפילו לרבנן דסבירא להו דשלשה לא אמרינן בהו לבוד ותלתא סגי הכא דלהווי פתחא אי איכא (י') [ד'] טפחים הוי פתחא ואי לא לא ואוקימנא נמי דהאי חלון שיש בו ד' על ד' טפחים אי הוו הני ד"ט כולהו למעלה מי' טפחים [ומקצתן בתוך י'] אם רצו מערבין אחד. תנינא להא דתנו רבנן כולו למעלה מי' ומקצתו בתוך י' כו'. תנא [בתוספתא] באהלות פי"ג עמוד המוטל באויר אינו מביא את הטומאה תחת דופנו עד שיהא בהיקפו כ"ד טפחים ר' (אסי) [יוסי] א' כ"ה *). אין לך כ"ה טפחים שאין הארץ אוכלת טפח וכה"א ויהיו הרמונים תשעים וששה אי אפשר לומר: א"ר יוחנן [חלון] עגול צריך שיש בהיקפו כ"ד טפחים ומהן ב' טפחים ומשהו בתוך י' שאם ירבענו נמצא משהו בתוך י' ואסיקנא דר' יוחנן בדייני דקיסרי דטעו ואמרי ריבועא דנפיק מגו עיגולא פלגא אמרה לשמעתיה. פי' (בהדיא) [מכדי] דכל שיש בהיקפו ג"ט יש בו רוחב טפח מדכתיב ויעש את הים מוצק י' באמה וגו' וקו ל' באמה יסוב אותו סביב. וכבר פירשנוהו בפרק הראשון וגם פירשנוהו במסכת סוכה בפרק א בסוכה העשויה כבשן וכיון שכל מה שיש בהיקפו שלשה טפחים יש בו רוחב טפח (המרובע) [והמרובע] היוצא מן העיגול לטעמיה דדייני דקיסרי

*) חסר כאן וצ"ל שהיה ר' יוסי אומר אין לך כו' וכ"ה אומר רימונים תשעים וששה וגו' ואומר כל הרימונים מאה על השבכה סביב אי אפשר לומר מאה שהרי כבר נאמר וכו' אמור מעתה ארבעה בלועין בכותל ותשעים וששה נראה מבחוץ ע"כ.

עד

רב נסים גאון

פ"ז חלון שבין שתי חצירות לימא תנן סתמא כרבן שמעון בן גמליאל דאמר כל פחות מד' עיקר מכותל זה כו' רבן שמעון בן גמליאל אומר פחות מד' אין צריך להביא קורה אחרת ואיתא נמי (סוכה דף כב) בפרק הישן תחת המטה והיא שנויה בתוספתא דעירובין בפרק א': דברי רבן שמעון בן גמליאל בברייתא אמורה בפרק מבוי (דף יד) תנו רבנן קורה היוצאה

*הָנֵי מִילֵּי — בְּעִיגּוּלָא, אֲבָל בְּרִיבּוּעָא בָּעֵינַן טְפֵי. מִכְּדִי, *כַּמָּה מְרוּבָּע יָתֵר עַל הָעִגּוּל — רְבִיעַ, בְּשִׁיתְּסַר סַגְיָא! ה"מ — עִיגּוּלָא דְּנָפֵיק מִגּוֹ רִיבּוּעָא, אֲבָל רִיבּוּעָא דְּנָפֵיק מִגּוֹ עִיגּוּלָא — בָּעֵינַן טְפֵי. מ"ט — מִשּׁוּם מוֹרְשָׁא דְּקַרְנָתָא. *מִכְּדִי, כָּל אַמְּתָא בְּרִיבּוּעַ אַמְּתָא וּתְרֵי חוּמְשֵׁי בַּאֲלַכְסוֹנָא, ^א^בְּשִׁיבְסַר נְכֵי חוּמְשָׁא סַגְיָא! רַבִּי יוֹחָנָן אָמַר כִּי *דַּיָּינֵי דְּקֵיסָרִי, וְאָמְרִי לָהּ כְּרַבָּנַן דְּקֵיסָרִי, דְּאָמְרִי: עִיגּוּלָא מִגּוֹ רִיבּוּעָא — רִיבְעָא, רִיבּוּעָא מִגּוֹ עִיגּוּלָא — פַּלְגָא. § "פָּחוֹת מִד' עַל ד' וכו'. § אָמַר רַב נַחְמָן: ^ב^לֹא שָׁנוּ אֶלָּא חַלּוֹן שֶׁבֵּין ב' חֲצֵירוֹת, אֲבָל חַלּוֹן שֶׁבֵּין ב' בָּתִּים — אֲפִילּוּ לְמַעְלָה מֵעֲשָׂרָה נַמִי, אִם רָצוּ לְעָרֵב — מְעָרְבִין אֶחָד. מ"ט — *בֵּיתָא כְּמַאן דְּמָלֵי דָּמֵי. אֵיתִיבֵיהּ רָבָא לְרַב נַחְמָן: אֶחָד לִי חַלּוֹן שֶׁבֵּין ב' חֲצֵירוֹת, וְאֶחָד לִי חַלּוֹן שֶׁבֵּין ב' בָּתִּים, וְאֶחָד לִי חַלּוֹן שֶׁבֵּין ב' עֲלִיּוֹת, וְאֶחָד לִי חַלּוֹן שֶׁבֵּין ב' גַּגִּין, וְאֶחָד לִי חַלּוֹן שֶׁבֵּין ב' חֲדָרִים — כּוּלָּן ד' עַל ד' בְּתוֹךְ עֲשָׂרָה! תַּרְגּוּמָא אַחֲצֵירוֹת. וְהָא "אֶחָד לִי" קָתָנֵי! תַּרְגּוּמָא אַד' עַל ד'. בְּעָא מִינֵּיהּ ר' אַבָּא מֵרַב נַחְמָן: לוּל הַפָּתוּחַ מִן בַּיִת לַעֲלִיָּיה, צָרִיךְ סוּלָּם קָבוּעַ לְהַתִּירוֹ, אוֹ אֵין צָרִיךְ סוּלָּם קָבוּעַ לְהַתִּירוֹ? כִּי אָמְרִינַן בֵּיתָא כְּמַאן דְּמָלֵי דָּמֵי — הָנֵי מִילֵּי מִן הַצַּד, אֲבָל בָּאֶמְצַע — לֹא. אוֹ דִילְמָא לָא שְׁנָא? אֲמַר לֵיהּ: אֵינוֹ צָרִיךְ. סָבוּר מִינָּהּ: סוּלָּם קָבוּעַ הוּא דְּאֵינוֹ צָרִיךְ, הָא סוּלָּם עֲרַאי — צָרִיךְ. אִיתְּמַר, *אָמַר רַב יוֹסֵף בַּר מַנְיוּמִי, אָמַר רַב נַחְמָן: ^ג^אֶחָד סוּלָּם קָבוּעַ וְאֶחָד סוּלָּם עֲרַאי — אֵינוֹ צָרִיךְ. §

מתני' *^ד^כּוֹתֶל שֶׁבֵּין ב' חֲצֵירוֹת, גָּבוֹהַּ עֲשָׂרָה וְרוֹחַב אַרְבָּעָה — מְעָרְבִין שְׁנַיִם, וְאֵין מְעָרְבִין אֶחָד. הָיוּ בְּרֹאשׁוֹ פֵּירוֹת — אֵלּוּ עוֹלִין מִכָּאן וְאוֹכְלִין, וְאֵלּוּ עוֹלִין מִכָּאן וְאוֹכְלִין, וּבִלְבַד שֶׁלֹּא יוֹרִידוּ לְמַטָּן. ^ה^נִפְרְצָה הַכּוֹתֶל, עַד עֶשֶׂר אַמּוֹת — מְעָרְבִין שְׁנַיִם, וְאִם רָצוּ — מְעָרְבִין אֶחָד, מִפְּנֵי שֶׁהוּא כַּפֶּתַח. יוֹתֵר מִכָּאן — מְעָרְבִין אֶחָד, וְאֵין מְעָרְבִין שְׁנַיִם. §

גמ' אֵין בּוֹ אַרְבָּעָה מַאי? אָמַר רַב: אֲוִיר שְׁתֵּי רְשׁוּיוֹת שׁוֹלֶטֶת בּוֹ, לֹא יָזִיז בּוֹ אֲפִילּוּ מְלֹא נִימָא.

וְרַבִּי

[לעיל ח. וש"נ] [סוכה ח.] [לקמן פג. פז: ולב.]

רש"י

הָנֵי מִילֵּי בְּעִגּוּלָא. כְּדַת רוֹחַב דָּבָר עָגוֹל הָוֵי טֶפַח וְדַת רוֹחַב עִגּוּל אֵין רָחְבּוֹ אֶלָּא בְּאֶמְצָעוֹ, וַאֲנַן רוֹחַב ד' כְּדַת מְרוּבָּע בָּעֵינַן, שֶׁרָחָב בִּדְפָנוֹתָיו כְּמִדַּת אֶמְצָעוֹ: בְּשִׁיתְסַר. הֶיקֵּף סַגְיָא, ד' הֶיקֵּף לְכָל רוּחַ דִּמְרוּבָּע: ה"מ. דְּסַגֵּי בְּאַטְפּוּיֵי רִיבְעָא לְמֶיהֱוֵי שִׁיתְסַר בְּעִגּוּלָא דְּנָפֵיק מִגּוֹ רִיבּוּעָא, כְּגוֹן חַלּוֹן מְרוּבָּע ד' עַל ד' הֶקֵּיפוֹ שִׁיתְסַר. וְאִי מְעַגַּלְתְּ מִגַּוָּאֵי דְּאֵין רוֹחַב ד' אֶלָּא בְּאֶמְצָעוֹ, אִית לֵיהּ הֶיקֵּפָא תְּרֵיסַר וְטָפֵי עֲלֵיהּ מְרוּבָּע רְבִיעַ: אֲבָל. הָכָא דְּבָעֵית לְמִינְקַט רִיבּוּעַ ד' עַל ד' וְהֶיקֵּפוֹ שִׁיתְסַר, ד' לְכָל רוּחַ בְּגוֹ עִיגּוּלָא, לְבַד מַאי דְּמַדְלֵית מֵעִגּוּלָא — בָּעֵי הֶיקֵּפָא טְפֵי, כְּדֵי לְמִנְקַט בְּגַוֵּיהּ מוֹרְשֵׁי דְּרִיבּוּעָא, דְּהָוֵי ד' הֵן וַאֲלַכְסוֹנָן: מִכְּדִי כָּל אַמְּתָא כו'. וְסַגֵּי לֵיהּ לְהַאי עִגּוּלָא בְּפוּתְיָא דְּד' טְפָחִים, וַאֲלַכְסוֹנָ' בְּעִיגּוּלָא וְכָל דָּבָר עָגוֹל שָׁוֶה מִדַּת אֲלַכְסוֹנוֹ לְמִדַּת אֶמְצָעוֹ, דְּהָא אֵין לוֹ זָוִיּוֹת כַּמָּה בָּעֵי לְמֶיהֱוֵי פּוּתְיֵהּ — ד' וּתְמָנֵי חוּמְשֵׁי, דְּהָווּ לְהוּ חֲמִשָּׁה וּתְלָת חוּמְשֵׁי. וְכִי מַקַּפְתְּ לְעִיגּוּלָא דְּהַאי שִׁיעוּרָא כַּמָּה הֲוָה הֶיקֵּפָא — חֲמֵיסַר פּוּשְׁכֵי וְתִשְׁעָה חוּמְשֵׁי, דַּהֲוָה לְהוּ שִׁיבְסַר נְכֵי חוּמְשָׁא: רִיבּוּעַ מִגּוֹ עִיגּוּלָא פַּלְגָא. בָּעֵי לְמִשְׁקַל מִינֵּיהּ פַּלְגָא דְּהַאי שִׁיעוּרָא דְּפָיֵישׁ, דְּהַיְינוּ תִּילְתָּא דְּמֵעִיקָּרָא, דְּהָווּ לְהוּ תְּמַנְיָא מִכ"ד וּפָשׁוּ לְהוּ שִׁיתְסַר, דִּסְבִירָא לְהוּ דְּכָל אֲלַכְסוֹנָא הָכִי הָוֵי: ל"ש. דְּבָעֵי' תּוֹךְ עֲשָׂרָה: שֶׁבֵּין שְׁנֵי גַּגִּין. וְאַלִּיבָּא דְּרַבָּנַן, דְּאָמְרִי לְקַמָּן: כְּשֵׁם שֶׁדִּיּוּרִין חֲלוּקִין לְמַטָּה — כָּךְ חֲלוּקִין לְמַעְלָה, דְּלָא מָצֵי לְטַלְטֵל מִגַּג זֶה לְאִידָךְ בְּלֹא עֵירוּב: תַּרְגְּמָא. לְהַאי בְּתוֹךְ עֲשָׂרָה דְּקָתָנֵי, מִשּׁוּם חֲצֵירוֹת: וְהָא אֶחָד לִי קָתָנֵי. אַלְמָא: כּוּלָּן שָׁוִין: תַּרְגְּמָא. לְ"אֶחָד לִי" דְּמַשְׁמַע דְּכוּלָּן שָׁוִין — אַאַרְבָּעָה עַל אַרְבָּעָה: בַּיִת וַעֲלִיָּיה. שֶׁל שְׁנֵי בְּנֵי אָדָם: לוּל. אֲרוּבָּה בְּקַרְקָעִית הָעֲלִיָּיה, וְהָעֲלִיָּיה גְּבוֹהָה מִקַּרְקַע הַבַּיִת. מִי אָמְרִי' בֵּיתָא כְּמַאן דְּמָלֵי דָּמֵי, וְהָוֵי כְּמַאן דְּלָא גְּבוֹהַּ עֲשָׂרָה, וְאֵין צָרִיךְ סוּלָּם קָבוּעַ לִהְיוֹת שָׁם בִּמְקוֹם הַפֶּתַח לְהַתִּירָן לְעָרֵב זֶה עִם זֶה, אוֹ לָא אָמְרִינַן כְּמַאן דְּמָלֵי, וּבָעֵי סוּלָּם לְמֶיהֱוֵי כְּפֶתַח' בֵּינֵיהֶן כִּדְאָמְרִי' בְּ"כֵיצַד מְעַבְּרִין" (לעיל דף נט:) סוּלָּם תּוֹרַת פֶּתַח עָלָיו: מִן הַצַּד. בַּחַלּוֹן שֶׁבַּכּוֹתֶל: **מתני'** כּוֹתֶל שֶׁבֵּין שְׁתֵּי חֲצֵירוֹת. הַאי דְּנָקַט רוֹחַב אַרְבַּע — מִשּׁוּם סֵיפָא נָקַט לֵיהּ, דְּבָעֵי לְמִיתְנֵי הָיוּ בְּרֹאשׁוֹ פֵּירוֹת — אֵלּוּ עוֹלִין מִכָּאן וְאוֹכְלִין, וּבִלְבַד שֶׁלֹּא יוֹרִידוּ לְמַטָּה. דַּחֲשִׁיב רְשׁוּתָא בְּאַנְפֵּי נַפְשֵׁיהּ, וְלָא מִיבְטַל לֹא לְגַבֵּי הַאי וְלֹא לְגַבֵּי הַאי. אֲבָל לְעִנְיַן מֶיהֱוֵי מְחִיצָּה — בְּכָל דְּהוּ פּוּתְיָא הָוֵי סְתִימָה, וְאֵין מְעָרְבִין אֶחָד: וּבִלְבַד שֶׁלֹּא יוֹרִידוּ. כִּדְפָרֵישִׁית: יוֹתֵר מִכָּאן. הָוֵי פִּירְצָה, וְהָוֵי לְהוּ כּוּלְּהוּ כְּדִיּוּרֵי חָצֵר אַחַת. וְאִם עֵירְבָה כָּל אַחַת לְעַצְמָהּ — הָווּ לְהוּ כְּאוֹלְקִין אֶת עֵירוּבָן, וְאוֹסְרִין אֵלּוּ עַל אֵלּוּ: **גמ'** אֲוִיר ב' רְשׁוּיוֹת שׁוֹלְטוֹת בּוֹ. כֵּיוָן דְּלָא חָשִׁיב לְמֶיהֱוֵי רְשׁוּתָ' בָּטֵיל לְגַבֵּי תַּרְוַיְיהוּ, וּרְשׁוּת ב' הַחֲצֵירוֹת שׁוֹלְטוֹת בּוֹ, וְאוֹסְרִין זֶה עַל זֶה, וַאֲפִי' עַל רֹאשׁוֹ אָסוּר לְטַלְטֵל:

מַעֲלִין

תוספות

ורבי יוחנן אמר כדייני דקיסרי כו'. דקסבר, אמתא בריבועא תרי אמתא באלכסונא. וליתא להך דדייני דקיסרי, כדאמר בפ"ק דסוכה (דף ח:), דהא קא חזינא דלאו הכי הוא, שכל האורך והרוחב לא הוי אלא תרי אמה. ואע"ג דהתם מפרש שפיר מילתיה דר' יוחנן — הכא לא מצי לאוקומי אלא כדייני דקיסרי. וכי היכי דאמר התם דליתא לדייני דקיסרי — ה"נ ליתא לדרבי יוחנן דהכא. וקשה: היאך טעו דייני דקיסרי, הא קא חזינן דלאו הכי הוא! ועוד: דכי היכי דקאמר עיגולא מגו ריבועא ריבעא — דהיינו מכל הריבוע, הכי נמי הוה להו למינקט ריבועא מגו עיגולא תילתא מכל העיגול, שהוא פלגא מן הריבוע שבפנים. או הוי להו למינקט עיגולא מגו ריבועא תילתא, מן העיגול שבפנים. וי"מ: דדייני דקיסרי לא דברו אלא לענין קרקע שבתוך הריבוע והעיגול, דלענין זה דבריהם אמת. שכשתעשה ריבוע ב' אמות על ב' אמות, ותעשה עיגול בפנים ב' על ב' ועוד ריבוע בתוך העיגול — תמצא

כזה

בריבוע החיצון ארבע חתיכות אמה על אמה, ובעיגול מתוך ריבוע שלש חתיכות של אמה על אמה, דמרובע יותר על העיגול רביע ובריבוע הפנימי אין בו כי אם ב', שהרי הוא חציו של חיצון, דהיינו תילתא פחות מן העיגול. אלא שהתלמוד בסוכה ור' יוחנן דהכא[א] טעו בדבריהם, והיו סבורים שעל ההיקף אמרו. והשתא אתי שפיר מה דנקט פלגא, דהכל קאי אריבוע החיצון, כלומר: עיגולא מגו ריבועא ריבעא, כלומר: פחות רביע מריבוע החיצון. ריבועא מגו עיגולא פלגא ממה שנשאר בריבוע החיצון, על ריבוע הפנימי, דהוא נמי חציו של פנימי:

ובלבד שלא יורידו למטה. דוקא לפי שאין פתח ביניהם — שאין החצירות יכולין לערב יחד. אבל אם יש פתח בכותל זה ועירבו — מותר להוריד ולהביא לבתים מן החצר ומן הבתים מעלין על הכותל. ואתיא מתני' דלא כר"ש, דלדידיה מותר להוריד ולהביא אע"ג דלא עירבו. דאמר לקמן (דף פט.): גגות חצירות וקרפיפות רשות אחת לכלים ששבתו בתוכן — אי נמי, אפילו כר"ש אתיא. ומאי למטה — למטה לבתים. הכי איתא בריש "כל גגות" (לקמן דף פט.). וא"ת: ולרבנן אמאי אסור להוריד למטה לחצר? הא מודו רבנן דחצירות רשות לעצמן! דאמר רב יהודה בפרק "כל גגות" (לקמן דף צ:): כשתמצא לומר לדברי רבי מאיר כו', לדברי חכמים, גגות וחצירות — רשות אחת, וקרפיפות — רשות אחת. ושם פירש בקונטרס: דמותר להוציא מחצר לחצר לרבנן, והביא ראייה מברייתא, מדתניא התם: אנשי חצר ואנשי מרפסת כו'. וליכא למימר דעל גבי הכותל, כיון דלא ניחא תשמישתא חשיב כקרפף, ולהכי אסור להוריד לרבנן, דחצר וקרפף שתי רשויות הן. דא"כ, אפילו יש פתח ביניהן ועירבו — אסור להוריד למטה, דאין עירוב מועיל לקרפף, ואפילו מקרפף שלו אסור לטלטל לחצירו, כדאמרינן לעיל בפרק שני (דף כג:) גבי נזרע רובו — הרי הוא כגינה ואסור. ואם כן, מאי איריא כותל שבין שתי חצירות? אפילו יש לו כותל שלו בחצירו יהא אסור להשתמש על גביו, אי חשיב קרפף. ואומר ר"י: דודאי לא מטעם קרפף הוא דאסור, אלא משום דאסרי אהדדי. והא דשרו רבנן מחצר לחצר — היינו דוקא כשלא עירבה כל חצר לעצמה, דלא שכיחי מאני דבתים בחצר. אבל עירבה כל חצר לעצמה — גזרינן דילמא אתי לאפוקי מאני דבתים לחצר אחרת. וכן מוכחא ההיא דאנשי חצר ואנשי מרפסת בפרק "כל גגות" (לקמן דף צא:):

ורבי

עין משפט נר מצוה

ב א מיי' פ"ג מהלכות עירובין הלכה ב:
ג ב ג מיי' שם טוש"ע או"ח סי' שע"ג ס"ה:
ד ד מיי' שם הלכה ג טור ש"ע שם סעיף ו:
ה ה מיי' שם הלכה י טור ש"ע שם סעיף ז:

רבינו חננאל

ניפחת חציו הוצרך ר' יוחנן לומר (לטעותא והא) [לטעותייהו] דדייני דקיסרי צריך זה החלון שהוא עגול כ"ד טפחים היקפו שנמצא בו ח' טפחים על ח' טפחים והוא שליש היקפו כשתוציא מתוכו מרובע יפחת בסיתומין מכל צד ב"ט ואחרי כן ישאר באמצע ד"ט על (טפח) [ד' טפחים] חלל נמצא סתום מזה החלון מכל צלע מלמעלה טפחים ומלמטה טפחים נמצא באמצע ד' טפחים עכשיו כשסותם מן הצלע התחתון שהוא בתוך י' טפחים אם לא תתן לו יותר מב' טפחים בתוך הי' *) שאם יסתמו טפחים ישאר מקצת מחללו של חלון אחר שתרבענו בתוך י' טפחים רצו מערבין אחד לפיכך הוצרך ב' טפחים ומשהו שיסיימו הטפחים וישאר אותו משהו בכלל הריבוע פתוח בתוך י' האי דא' מכדי כמה יתר מרובע על העיגול רביע וכל אמתא בריבועא אמתא ותרי חומשי באלכסונא בשיבסר נכי חומשא סגי פשוטה היא. אמר רב נחמן מתני' דווקא חלון בין שתי חצירות הוא דבעינן בתוך עשרה אבל חלון שבין ב' בתים אפי' למעלה מעשרה מערבין אחד דביתא כמאן דמלי דמי. ומותיב רבא עליה מהא דתניא אחד חלון שבין ב' חצירות ואחד חלון שבין ב' בתים ואחר חלון שבין ב' עליות ואחר חלון שבין ב' גגין ואחר חלון שבין ב' (חידורין) [חדרים] כולן בתוך י' ופריק רב נחמן כי קתני אחד אחד אר' [אבל] בתוך י' לא בעינן אלא בחצירות וביוצא בהן שאין עליה תקרה אבל בית וביוצא בו אפי' לעיל מעשרה. בעא מיניה ר' אבא מרבן נחמן לול פתוח מבית ועליה צריך סולם קבוע להתירו להשתמש מזה לזה או לא. ופשט ליה אין צריך (ולא) [דלא] שנא מן הצד ולא שנא באמצע אמרינן ביתא כמאן דמלי דמי. ואסיקנא אמר רב נחמן אחד סולם קבוע ואחד סולם עראי אינו צריך: מתני' כותל שבין ב' חצירות גבוה י' ורחב ד' כו' אין בו ד' מאי אמר רב בר' רשויות משוטטות בו ואסור להוציא בו ואפי' כמלא

*) לפי סוגית לשון רבינו נראה דצ"ל שאם יסתמו טפחים לא ישאר מקצת מחללו של חלון אחר שירבענו בתוך י' לא היו יכולין לערבו כאחד לפיכך הוצרך וכו'.

מסורת הש"ס

סוכה ח.
[אהלות פי"ב מ"ו לעיל יד: וש"נ]

הגהות הגר"א

[א] תוס' ד"ה ור"י כו' להכא טעו. נ"ב וזה טעות שלא סתר אלא כהיקפו ל"ל בריבוע החיצון (כאן נמחק תיבה אחת שהוא מכפ"ק) וחד האלכסון בעיגול הוא ח' טפחים וג' חומשין ורביע חומש נמצא היקף ריבוע החיצון כ"ד טפחים וג' חומשין. ומ"ש וסגינו ומשהו ר"ל דהיקף העיגול כפירש"י אלא שפירושו לא אחד שהוא נקודה על ד' טפחים (מנוין כבי"ק בלוין שבתוס) ולא שמעתו יותר משנים הוא מעט קט שיעור גדול הקשת מע היתר והוא חצי חומש.

גיר' הרא"ש אמר רב יהודה אמר ר"י בר מניומי אמר ר"נ

גליון הש"ס

גמ' ביתא כמאן דמלי דמי. שבת דף ה ע"א:

גמרא

וְרַבִּי יוֹחָנָן אָמַר: [א]אֵלּוּ מַעֲלִין מִכָּאן וְאוֹכְלִין, וְאֵלּוּ מַעֲלִין מִכָּאן וְאוֹכְלִין. תְּנַן: אֵלּוּ עוֹלִין מִכָּאן וְאוֹכְלִין, וְאֵלּוּ עוֹלִין מִכָּאן וְאוֹכְלִין. עוֹלִין — אִין, מַעֲלִין — לָא! הָכִי קָאָמַר: יֵשׁ בּוֹ אַרְבָּעָה עַל אַרְבָּעָה, עוֹלִין — אִין, מַעֲלִין — לָא. אֵין בּוֹ אַרְבָּעָה עַל אַרְבָּעָה — מַעֲלִין נַמִי. וְאָזְדָא רַבִּי יוֹחָנָן לְטַעְמֵיהּ, *דְּכִי אֲתָא רַב דִּימִי, א"ר יוֹחָנָן: מָקוֹם שֶׁאֵין בּוֹ אַרְבָּעָה עַל אַרְבָּעָה — מוּתָּר לִבְנֵי רְשׁוּת הָרַבִּים וְלִבְנֵי רְשׁוּת הַיָּחִיד לְכַתֵּף עָלָיו, וּבִלְבַד שֶׁלֹּא יַחֲלִיפוּ. וְרַב לֵית לֵיהּ דְּרַב דִּימִי?! אִי בִּרְשׁוּיוֹת דְּאוֹרָיְיתָא — הָכִי נַמִי. הָכָא בְּמַאי עָסְקִינַן — בִּרְשׁוּיוֹת דְּרַבָּנַן, *[ב]וַחֲכָמִים עָשׂוּ חִיזּוּק לְדִבְרֵיהֶם יוֹתֵר מִשֶּׁל תּוֹרָה. אָמַר רַבָּה, (*אָמַר) רַב הוּנָא, אָמַר רַב נַחְמָן: *[ג]כּוֹתֶל שֶׁבֵּין שְׁתֵּי חֲצֵירוֹת, צִידּוֹ אֶחָד גָּבוֹהַּ עֲשָׂרָה טְפָחִים וְצִידּוֹ אֶחָד שָׁוֶה לָאָרֶץ — נוֹתְנִין אוֹתוֹ לָזֶה שֶׁשָּׁוֶה לָאָרֶץ, מִשּׁוּם דְּהָוֵה לָזֶה תַּשְׁמִישׁוֹ בְּנַחַת וְלָזֶה תַּשְׁמִישׁוֹ *בְּקָשֶׁה, וְכָל לָזֶה בְּנַחַת וְלָזֶה בְּקָשֶׁה — נוֹתְנִין אוֹתוֹ לָזֶה שֶׁתַּשְׁמִישׁוֹ בְּנַחַת. *אָמַר רַב שֵׁיזְבִי, אָמַר רַב נַחְמָן: [ד]חָרִיץ שֶׁבֵּין שְׁתֵּי חֲצֵירוֹת, צִידּוֹ אֶחָד עָמוֹק עֲשָׂרָה וְצִידּוֹ אֶחָד שָׁוֶה לָאָרֶץ — נוֹתְנִין אוֹתוֹ לָזֶה שֶׁשָּׁוֶה לָאָרֶץ, מִשּׁוּם דְּהָוֵה לֵיהּ לָזֶה תַּשְׁמִישׁוֹ בְּנַחַת וְלָזֶה תַּשְׁמִישׁוֹ בְּקָשֶׁה וכו'. וּצְרִיכִי, דְּאִי אַשְׁמְעִינַן כּוֹתֶל — מִשּׁוּם דִּבְגוֹבְהָא מִשְׁתַּמְּשִׁי אֱנָשֵׁי, אֲבָל חָרִיץ — בְּעוּמְקָא לָא מִשְׁתַּמְּשִׁי אֱנָשֵׁי, אֵימָא לָא. וְאִי אַשְׁמְעִינַן בְּחָרִיץ — מִשּׁוּם דְּלָא בְּעִיתָא תַּשְׁמִישְׁתָּא, אֲבָל כּוֹתֶל דִּבְעִיתָא תַּשְׁמִישְׁתָּא — אֵימָא לָא, צְרִיכָא. בָּא לְמַעֲטוֹ, אִם יֵשׁ בְּמִיעוּטוֹ אַרְבָּעָה — מוּתָּר לְהִשְׁתַּמֵּשׁ בְּכָל הַכּוֹתֶל כּוּלּוֹ, וְאִם לָאו — אֵין מִשְׁתַּמֵּשׁ אֶלָּא כְּנֶגֶד הַמִּיעוּט. [ה]מַה נַּפְשָׁךְ? אִי אַהֲנֵי מִעוּטָא — בְּכוּלֵּיהּ כּוֹתֶל לִישְׁתַּמֵּשׁ, אִי לָא אַהֲנֵי — אֲפִילּוּ כְּנֶגֶד הַמִּיעוּט נַמִי לָא! אָמַר רָבִינָא: [ו]כְּגוֹן שֶׁעָקַר חוּלְיָא מֵרֹאשׁוֹ. אָמַר רַב יְחִיאֵל: [ז]כָּפָה סֵפֶל — מְמַעֵט. וְאַמַּאי? דָּבָר הַנִּיטָּל בְּשַׁבָּת הוּא, וְדָבָר הַנִּיטָּל בְּשַׁבָּת אֵינוֹ מְמַעֵט! לָא צְרִיכָא, דְּחַבְּרֵיהּ בְּאַרְעָא. וְכִי חַבְּרֵיהּ בְּאַרְעָא מַאי הָוֵי? וְהָא תַּנְיָא: *פַּגָּה שֶׁהִטְמִינָהּ בַּתֶּבֶן, וַחֲרָרָה שֶׁהִטְמִינָהּ בַּגֶּחָלִים, אִם מְגוּלָּה מִקְצָתָהּ — נִטֶּלֶת בַּשַּׁבָּת! הָכָא בְּמַאי עָסְקִינַן — דְּאִית לֵיהּ אוֹגְנַיִים. וְכִי אִית לֵיהּ אוֹגְנַיִים מַאי הָוֵי? וְהָתְנַן: *הַטּוֹמֵן לֶפֶת וּצְנוֹן תַּחַת הַגֶּפֶן, בִּזְמַן שֶׁמִּקְצָת

רש"י

מַעֲלִין. מְחַלְיָן לְרֹאשׁוֹ. וְהוּא הַדִּין דְּמוֹרִידִין, דִּמְקוֹם פְּטוּר הוּא וּבָטֵיל לְכָאן וּלְכָאן לְהָקֵל: מָקוֹם שֶׁאֵין בּוֹ ד'. רוֹחַב: וְעוֹמֵד בֵּין רה"י לרה"ר. וְיֵשׁ לָנוּ הֶיכֵּר, כְּגוֹן גָּבוֹהַּ מִן הָאָרֶץ ג' וְאִילּוּ הָיָה רוֹחַב ד' – הָיָה נִקְרָא רְשׁוּת לְעַצְמוֹ. וְהָוְיָא כַּרְמְלִית וְאָסוּר לְכָאן וּלְכָאן. אֲבָל עַכְשָׁיו נִקְרָא מְקוֹם פְּטוּר, וּמוּתָּר לְכָאן וּלְכָאן לְכַתֵּף עָלָיו מַשּׂאוֹי שֶׁלָּהֶן: וּבִלְבַד שֶׁלֹּא יַחֲלִיפוּ. דְּרַבָּנַן הִיא דְּאִילּוּ חִיּוּבָא לֵיכָּא, דְּבָעֵינַן עֲקִירָה מֵרְשׁוּת זוֹ וְהַנָּחָה לִרְשׁוּת זוֹ. וְהָכָא, עֲקִירָה מֵרה"י גְּמוּרָה וְהַנָּחָה לִמְקוֹם פְּטוּר, וַעֲקִירָה מִמְּקוֹם פְּטוּר וְהַנָּחָה לרה"ר גְּמוּרָה: וְרַב לֵית לֵיהּ דְּרַב דִּימִי. בִּתְמִיָּה, וְהָא מַתְנִיתָא הִיא בְּמַסֶּכֶת שַׁבָּת בְּפ"ק [דף ו.]: עוֹמֵד אָדָם עַל הָאִסְקוּפָּה, נוֹטֵל מֵעָנִי וְנוֹתֵן לוֹ, מִבַּעַל הַבַּיִת וְנוֹתֵן לוֹ, וּבִלְבַד שֶׁלֹּא יִטּוֹל מִזֶּה וְיִתֵּן לָזֶה: רְשׁוּיוֹת דְּאוֹרָיְיתָא. כְּגוֹן רְשׁוּת רַבִּים וְיָחִיד: דְּרַבָּנַן. חֲצֵירוֹת, דִּרְשׁוּת יָחִיד וְיָחִיד הוּא, וּמִדְּרַבָּנָן הוּא דְּאָסוּר: וְצִידּוֹ אֶחָד שָׁוֶה לָאָרֶץ. כְּלוֹמַר: גָּבוֹהַּ הוּא מִן הָאַחַת, וְנָמוּךְ הוּא לַחֲבֶרְתָּהּ, כְּגוֹן שֶׁקַּרְקָעִיתָהּ שֶׁל זוֹ גְּבוֹהָה. כָּל כַּמָּה דְּלָא גָּבוֹהַּ י' קָרֵי לֵיהּ שָׁוֶה לָאָרֶץ: נוֹתְנִין אוֹתוֹ. לְהַעֲלוֹת וּלְהוֹרִיד מֵעָלָיו, וַחֲבֵירוֹ אָסוּר: חָרִיץ. עַל פְּנֵי אוֹרֶךְ הַחֲצֵירוֹת, מַבְדִּיל בֵּין זוֹ לָזוֹ, הָוֵי מְחִיצָּה מַעַלְיָיתָא: שָׁוֶה לָאָרֶץ. שֶׁאֵינוֹ עָמוֹק מִמֶּנָּה י' כְּגוֹן שֶׁקַּרְקָעִיתָהּ נָמוּךְ: אֵימָא לָא. מִשְׁתְּרֵי, דִּלְדִידֵיהּ נַמִי תַּשְׁמִישׁוֹ בְּקָשֶׁה הוּא: לָא בְּעִיתָא תַּשְׁמִישְׁתֵּיהּ. מַה שֶּׁמַּנִּיחַ בּוֹ מִשְׁתַּמֵּר: בְּעִיתָא תַּשְׁמִישְׁתֵּיהּ. שֶׁנּוֹפְלִים הַחֲפָצִים: בָּא לְמַעֵט. אַכּוֹתֶל קָאֵי. וְקס"ד שֶׁעָשָׂה תֵּל עָפָר לְמַטָּה בַּקַּרְקַע סָמוּךְ לַכּוֹתֶל, אוֹ בָּנָה אִיצְטַבָּא, אוֹ הִנִּיחַ שָׁם פַּסְפָּסִים: אִם יֵשׁ בְּמִיעוּטוֹ ד'. אוֹרֶךְ, בְּצַד מֶשֶׁךְ הַכּוֹתֶל – הָוֵי כְּפֶתַח. וְכֵיוָן דְּמִמֶּנּוּ וּלְמַעְלָה לָא גָּבוֹהַּ עֲשָׂרָה – מִשְׁתַּמֵּשׁ בְּכָל הַכּוֹתֶל, שֶׁהֲרֵי תַּשְׁמִישׁוֹ בְּנַחַת, שֶׁעוֹלֶה לוֹ דֶּרֶךְ פִּתְחוֹ: אִי אַהֲנֵי מִעוּטָא. לְמֶיהֱוֵי פִּתְחָא – כּוּלֵּיהּ שָׁרֵי: וְאִי לָא אַהֲנֵי. הָא בָּטֵיל לֵיהּ: אָמַר רָבִינָא. לָאו מִלְּמַטָּה עָסְקִינַן, דְּהָתָם וַדַּאי בְּצִיר מד' לָא מַהֲנֵי לְמִידֵי. אֶלָּא כְּגוֹן שֶׁעָקַר חוּלְיָא מֵרֹאשׁוֹ. מִגּוֹבְהוֹ שֶׁל כּוֹתֶל קָרֵי רֹאשׁוֹ, כִּדְתְנַן: הָיוּ בְּרֹאשׁוֹ פֵּירוֹת. הִלְכָּךְ: אִי הָוֵי מִעוּטָא אַרְבָּעָה אוֹרֶךְ – הָוֵי פִּיתְחָא לְכָל הַכּוֹתֶל, בְּצִיר מֵהָכָא – פִּיתְחָא הוּא דְּלָא הָוֵי, אֲבָל לְאִשְׁתַּמּוּשֵׁי בֵּיהּ שָׁרֵי דְּכֵיוָן דְּלָא גָּבוֹהַּ י' – לָא הָוֵי רְשׁוּתָא: כַּפָּה סֵפֶל. סָמוּךְ לַכּוֹתֶל, וּמִיעֵט גּוֹבְהוֹ מֵעֲשָׂרָה. כָּל הָנֵי מִיעוּטֵי כְּגוֹן דְּלֵיכָּא י' מֵרֹאשׁוֹ לְרֹאשׁ הַכּוֹתֶל: מַאי הָוֵי. אַכַּתִּי נִיטָּל בְּשַׁבָּת הוּא: פַּגָּה. תְּאֵנָה בּוֹסֶר שֶׁטּוֹמְנִין אוֹתָהּ בַּתֶּבֶן לְהִתְבַּשֵּׁל. וְתֶבֶן מוּקְצֶה הוּא וְאָסוּר לְטַלְטְלוֹ, כְּגוֹן שֶׁהִקְצָהוּ לְלִבּוֹן לְבֵנִים: וַחֲרָרָה שֶׁהִטְמִינָהּ. אֶתְמוֹל בַּגֶּחָלִים, וְעַכְשָׁיו כָּבוּ. וּמ"מ מוּקְצִין הֵן. אֲבָל לֹא כָּבוּ – לָא, דְּמִתּוֹךְ שֶׁנֶּהֱפָכִים מְכַבֶּה אֶת הַתַּחְתּוֹנוֹת וּמַבְעִיר אֶת הָעֶלְיוֹנוֹת, כִּדְאָמְרִינַן בִּכְרֵיתוֹת (דף כ.): דְּאִית לְהוּ אוֹגְנַיִים. כְּעֵין סְפָלִים שֶׁלָּנוּ דְּעַכְשָׁיו עָפָר מוּנָּח עֲלֵיהֶן וְהָוֵי מֵזִיז עָפָר מִמְּקוֹמוֹ וְדוֹמֶה לְחוֹפֵר: הַטּוֹמֵן. לְהַצְנִיעַ: מִקְצָת

תוספות

ורבי יוחנן אמר אלו מעלין כו'. פירוש: מן הבית. דמן החצר אפילו ברחב ד' – שרי, דכר"ש מוקי לה רבי יוחנן לקמן בריש "כל גגות" (דף פט.): עולין אין מעלין לא. תימה: דמאי קס"ד, וכי לא ידע דרבי יוחנן איירי באין לו ארבעה? וי"ל: דס"ד דטעמא דרבי יוחנן(א) משום דאין רגילות להשתמש שם, ולא אסרי אהדדי, והוא הדין ברוחב ד' – כיון שהוא גבוה י' ואין נח להשתמש שם, ולהכי לא פריך אלא לר' יוחנן, אבל לרב דטעמא משום דבטל הוא – לא שייך אלא באין בו ד' על ד': הכא במאי עסקינן ברשויות דרבנן. נראה דוקא כי הכא שהכל רה"י, אלא שלא עירבו. אבל מקום שאין בו ד' על ד' שבין רה"י לכרמלית – אין נראה שיחלוק רב, אלא מותר לבני רה"י ולבני כרמלית לכתף עליו. וקצת מוכח כן בפ"ק (דף ט.), דמוקי רבה הא דאמר רב: תוך הפתח, אע"פ שאין בו ד' על ד', צריך לחי אחר להתירו הפתוח לכרמלית משום דמלא מין את מינו, ולרה"ר שרי. ולא קאמר משום דעשו חיזוק. אלא ודאי אף לרב בין כרמלית לרה"י לא עשו חיזוק. ומיהו מצינו למימר: דהתם לא נקט טעמא דחיזוק, משום דאית ליה טעמא אחרינא: ברשויות דרבנן. בפרק "כילד משתתפין"(ב) מיקל רב דימי טפי משמיה דרבי יוחנן ברשויות דרבנן, ושרי אפילו להחליף כשיש בין רשות היחיד לכרמלית מקום שאין בו ד' על ד'. והא דאמר ר' יוחנן הכא אלו מעלין מכאן ואוכלין – מסיק דזעירי אמרה: כותל שבין ב' חצירות גבוה עשרה וצדו אחד שוה לארץ. לאו שוה ממש קאמר, דאם כן לאו היינו כותל, אלא הכל היא קרקעית חצר. אלא כל שאין גבוה י' שוה לארץ קרי ליה. כך פי' בקונטרס. וא"ת: לרב חסדא, דאמר בפרק "כל גגות" (לקמן דף פט:): גידוד ה' ומחיצה ה' אין מצטרפין, מאי קאמר נותנין אותו לזה ששוה לארץ? הא אין מטלטלין בעליונה אלא בד'! וי"ל: דמכל מקום נפקא מינה, דתוך ד'(ג) מיהא שרי לטלטל מן הכותל לעליונה: הטומן לפת וצנון כו'. בשלא השרישו איירי, דכשהשרישו לא היו ניטלין בשבת. וא"ת: בשלמא גבי כלאים ושביעית אצטריך לאשמועי' דלא גזרינן כשמתכוון להטמין, אטו דילמא אתי ליטע. אבל מעשר, מה שייך כאן? אפי' השריש, כיון דליכא תוספת! ואי(ד) נקטינן לענין דשרי לעשר עליו מן התלוש, או ממנו על התלוש, ולא חיישינן דילמא אתי לפרושי מן התלוש על המחובר ומן המחובר על התלוש, א"כ, הוה ליה למנקט תרומה דגבי מחובר ותלוש רגיל להזכיר תרומה בכל מקום: אין תורמין מן התלוש על המחובר; פירות ערוגה זו תלושין יהיו תרומה על פירות מחוברין. ואור"י: דרגילות הוא שמתוספין מחמת ליחלוחית הקרקע, כעין שאנו רואין שומין ובצלים שמתוספין אפילו כשמונחים בחלון. ועל אותה תוספת קאמר דאין צריך לעשר, הואיל והיו מתוקנים מקודם לכן. ודוקא נקט הטומן, אבל אם לשם נטיעה עושה – חושש משום כולם:

עין משפט נר מצוה

ו א מיי' פ"ג מהל' עירובין הלכה ד טוש"ע סי' שעב סעיף ו:
ז ב שם ובסי' שמו סעיף א:
ח ג מיי' שם הל' טו טור ש"ע שם סי' שעב סעיף ו:
ט ד מיי' שם טוש"ע שם סעיף טז:
י ה מיי' שם הלכה ט טוש"ע שם סעיף ט:
יא ו מיי' שם טוש"ע שם סעיף ח:
יב ז מיי' שם הל' יג טוש"ע שם סעיף י:

רבינו חננאל

נימא ור' יוחנן אמר אם יש בכותל ד' ויש עליו פירות עולין בני אדם מחצר זו לחצר זו ואוכלין שם ואם אין בו ד' אפי' אם אינו להעלות בו מעלין. ר' יוחנן לטעמיה דאמר מקום שאין בו ד' על ד' מותר לבני רה"ר ולבני רה"י לכתף עליו ובלבד שלא יחליפו זה מזה. ואמרינן וכי רב לית ליה אהא דר' יוחנן לעולם אית ליה וכי אית ליה לרב האי סברא ברשויות דאוריי' כגון רה"י ורה"ר אבל ברשויות דרבנן כגון זה הכותל לית ליה דסברי חכמים עשו חיזוק לדבריהם יתר משל תורה לפיכך א' אסור להזיז בו אפי' כמלא נימא. אמר רב נחמן כותל שבין ב' חצרות גבוה ורחב ד' וצדו אחד שוה לארץ *) היה לזו ששוה לארץ תשמישו בנחת ולזה שצדו גבוה י' תשמישו בקשה וכל לזה תשמישו בנחת ולזה תשמישו בקשה נותנין אותו לזה שתשמישו בנחת וכן אמר רב נחמן בחריץ שבין שתי חצרות עמוק י' ורחב ד' וצדו אחד שוה לארץ נותנין אותו לזה שתשמישו בנחת כו'. וצריכא דאי אשמעי' כותל משום דבגובהה משתמשי אינשי. פי' עומדין ומשתמשין אבל חריץ דלא שחו ומשתמשי אימא לא כו': בא למעט הכותל שגבוה מי' טפחים. אם יש במיעוטו ד' באורך הכותל על ד' מותר להשתמש בכולו. ואם לאו אינו משתמש אלא כנגד מיעוטו פי' כנגד אותו המקום שמיעט בלבד. ואמר רבינא כגון שעקר חוליא מראשו של כותל כגון זה אינו משתמש אלא במקום מיעוטו בלבד: א"ר יחיאל כפה ספל בקרקעית הכותל וחבריה בארעא הוי מיעוט ואם (היינו) [רצו] מערבין אחד. ואקשינן עליה וכי חבריה מאי הוי. והתניא פגה טמונה בתבן (והדר) [וחררה] שהטמינה בגחלים אם מקצת מגולה ניטלת בשבת. ופריק כגון דאית ליה להאי ספל אוגנים והן שפתים נשוכות לאחורי הספל ומשתקעין בעפר. אין מגולין שאינו יכול לטלטלו בשבת שהרי אוגנים משוקעין ואקשינן עליה ואפ' הכי כיון ששולי הספל מגולין הוה ליה כלי שהוא ניטל בשבת וכל דבר שניטל בשבת אינו ממעט כדתנן הטומן לפת וצנון תחת הגפן אם

*) נראה דחסר וצ"ל נותנין אותו לזה ששוה לארץ משום דהוי לזו וכו'.

מסורת הש"ס

שבת ח: לעיל ט. לקמן פה: פז. וקלח:
[לקמן פה: כתובות ט.]
[נ"ל בר וכ"ה לקמן פג:]
[לקמן פג:]
שם
[שם]
שבת קכג.
כלאים פ"ה מ"ע שבת נ: קיג.

הגהות הב"ח

(א) תוס' ד"ה עולין וכו' טעמא דר' יוחנן למשום וכו' להשתמש שם לא כצ"ל ואות א' נמחק: (ב) ד"ה ברשויות דרבנן בפרק כילד וכו': (ג) ד"ה כותל וכו' דתוך ד' אמות מיהא שרי: (ד) ד"ה הטומן וכו' ואי נקטיה לענין וכו' אתי לאפרושי מן:

שֶׁמִּקְצָת עָלִין מְגוּלִּין – אֵינוֹ חוֹשֵׁשׁ [א]לֹא מִשּׁוּם כִּלְאַיִם וְלֹא מִשּׁוּם מַעֲשֵׂר, [ב]וְלֹא מִשּׁוּם שְׁבִיעִית, [ג]וְנִיטָּלִין בַּשַּׁבָּת. לָא צְרִיכָא, דְּבָעֵי מָרָא וַחֲצִינָא.§ "סוּלָּם הַמִּצְרִי – אֵינוֹ מְמַעֵט, וְהַצּוֹרִי – מְמַעֵט".§ הֵיכִי דָּמֵי סוּלָּם הַמִּצְרִי? אָמְרִי דְּבֵי רַבִּי יַנַּאי: [ד]כֹּל שֶׁאֵין לוֹ אַרְבָּעָה חֲווֹקִים. אֲמַר לֵיהּ רַב אַחָא בְּרֵיהּ דְּרָבָא לְרַב אַשִׁי: מַאי טַעְמָא דְּסוּלָּם הַמִּצְרִי דְּלָא מְמַעֵט? אֲמַר לֵיהּ: לָא שְׁמִיעַ לָךְ הָא דְּאָמַר רַב אַחָא בַּר אַדָּא, אָמַר רַב הַמְנוּנָא, אָמַר רַב: מִשּׁוּם דַּהֲוָה לֵיהּ דָּבָר שֶׁנִּיטַּל בַּשַּׁבָּת, וְכָל דָּבָר שֶׁנִּיטָּל בַּשַּׁבָּת – אֵינוֹ מְמַעֵט. אִי הָכִי, אֲפִי' צוֹרִי נַמִי! [ה]הָתָם כּוֹבְדוֹ קוֹבְעוֹ. אָמַר אַבַּיֵי: [ו]כּוֹתֶל שֶׁבֵּין שְׁתֵּי חֲצֵירוֹת גָּבוֹהַּ עֲשָׂרָה טְפָחִים, וְהִנִּיחַ סוּלָּם רָחָב אַרְבָּעָה מִכָּאן וְסוּלָּם רָחָב אַרְבָּעָה מִכָּאן, וְאֵין בֵּין זֶה לָזֶה שְׁלֹשָׁה טְפָחִים – מְמַעֵט, שְׁלֹשָׁה – אֵינוֹ מְמַעֵט. וְלָא אֲמַרַן אֶלָּא דְּלָא הָוֵי כּוֹתֶל אַרְבָּעָה, אֲבָל הָוֵי כּוֹתֶל אַרְבָּעָה – אֲפִילּוּ מוּפְלָג טוּבָא נַמִי. אָמַר רַב בֵּיבָי בַּר אַבַּיֵי: [ז]בָּנָה אִיצְטַבָּא עַל גַּב אִיצְטַבָּא, אִם יֵשׁ בָּאִיצְטַבָּא הַתַּחְתּוֹנָה אַרְבָּעָה – מְמַעֵט. אִי נַמִי, אֵין בַּתַּחְתּוֹנָה אַרְבָּעָה וְיֵשׁ בָּעֶלְיוֹנָה אַרְבָּעָה, וְאֵין בֵּין זֶה לָזֶה שְׁלֹשָׁה – מְמַעֵט. וְאָמַר רַב נַחְמָן, אָמַר רַבָּה בַּר אֲבוּהּ: [ח]סוּלָּם שֶׁשְּׁלִיבוֹתָיו פּוֹרְחוֹת, אִם יֵשׁ בַּשְּׁלִיבָה הַתַּחְתּוֹנָה אַרְבָּעָה – מְמַעֵט, אִי נַמִי, אֵין בַּשְּׁלִיבָה הַתַּחְתּוֹנ' אַרְבָּע' וְיֵשׁ בַּשְּׁלִיבָה הָעֶלְיוֹנָה אַרְבָּעָה, וְאֵין בֵּין זֶה לָזֶה שְׁלֹשָׁה – מְמַעֵט. וְאָמַר רַב נַחְמָן, אָמַר רַבָּה בַּר אֲבוּהּ:
זיז

רש"י

מִקְצָת עָלִין מְגוּלִּין. מִשּׁוּם שַׁבָּת – נָקַט לֵיהּ דְּבָעֵי לְמִיתְנֵי: נִיטָּלִין בַּשַּׁבָּת. שֶׁנּוֹטְלָן וְאוֹחֲזָן בָּעָלִין שֶׁלָּהֶן: אֵינוֹ חוֹשֵׁשׁ. מִשּׁוּם כִּלְאֵי הַכֶּרֶם: וְלֹא מִשּׁוּם שְׁבִיעִית. אִם שָׁנָה שְׁבִיעִית הִיא: וְלֹא מִשּׁוּם מַעֲשֵׂר. לְשֶׁמָּא נִשְׁרַשׁ וְנִיתּוֹסֵף, וְאִם הָיָה חוֹשֵׁשׁ לְמַעֲשֵׂר – צָרִיךְ לְעַשֵּׂר אֶת תּוֹסַפְתּוֹ לֵיכָּא לְמֵיחַשׁ לְהָכִי דְּלֹא נִשְׁרַשׁ: מָרָא פושיי"ר: חֲצִינָא. דולדויי"א: סוּלָּם הַמִּצְרִי. הוֹאִיל וְקָטָן הוּא וְנוֹחַ לִיטְּלוֹ מִשָּׁם – אֵינוֹ מְמַעֵט: חֲווֹקִין. אישקלוניי"ש: כּוֹבְדוֹ קוֹבְעוֹ.(א) וּמִתּוֹךְ שֶׁהוּא כָּבֵד אֵין נוֹטְלִין אוֹתוֹ מִשָּׁם, וְלֹא מִשּׁוּם אִיסּוּר אֶלָּא מִשּׁוּם שֶׁקָּשֶׁה לִיטְּלוֹ: סוּלָּם רָחָב ד' מִכָּאן. בְּחָצֵר זוֹ וְכֵן בְּזוֹ וּבָהֶן עוֹלִין וְיוֹרְדִין מִזּוֹ לָזוֹ: וְאֵין בֵּין זֶה לָזֶה ג'. כְּלוֹמַר: אַפִּי' אֵינָן מְכוּוָּנִין זֶה נֶגֶד זֶה, אֲבָל אֵין מְרוּחָקִין זֶה מִכְּנֶגֶד זֶה ג' – הָווּ כִּמְכוּוָּנִין, וְהָוֵי פֶּתַח. וְאִם רָצוּ מְעָרְבִין א' אֲבָל מְרוּחָקִין זֶה מִכְּנֶגֶד זֶה ג' טְפָחִים – לָאו פֶּתַח הוּא: וְלָא אֲמַרַן. אֶלָּא בְּכוֹתֶל צַר שֶׁאֵין(ג) נוֹחַ לְהַלֵּךְ עָלָיו: אֲבָל. יֵשׁ בְּרוֹחְבּוֹ ד' – אֲפִילּוּ מוּפְלָג טוּבָא, שֶׁהֲרֵי עוֹלֶה לְרֹאשׁוֹ וּמְהַלֵּךְ בְּרֹאשׁוֹ עַד שֶׁמַּגִּיעַ לְסוּלַּם חֲבֵירוֹ: בָּנָה אִיצְטַבָּא. שֶׁל עֵץ: עַל גַּבֵּי הָאִיצְטַבָּא. סָמוּךְ לַכּוֹתֶל, וְיֵשׁ אֲוִיר מַפְסִיק בֵּין זוֹ לָזוֹ שֶׁהָיָה לָעֶלְיוֹנָה רַגְלַיִם: אִם יֵשׁ. בַּתַּחְתּוֹנָה אוֹרֶךְ ד' וּבָהּ נִתְמַעֵט גּוֹבְהוֹ שֶׁל כּוֹתֶל מִי' – מְמַעֵט. דַּל עֶלְיוֹנָה מֵהָכָא: אִי נַמִי אֵין בָּהּ ד' וְיֵשׁ בָּעֶלְיוֹנָה ד' וְאֵין בֵּין זֶה לָזֶה ג'. חָשְׁבִינַן לְהוּ כְּחַד, וְאַע"פ שֶׁהַמִּיעוּט הַזֶּה קָצָר מִלְּמַטָּה, הוֹאִיל וּמִתְמַלֵּא שִׁיעוּרוֹ מִלְמַעְלָה – שַׁפִּיר דָּמֵי. אֲבָל יֵשׁ בֵּינֵיהֶן שְׁלֹשָׁה – תְּרֵי נִינְהוּ וּמִיעוּט בַּאֲוִיר לָאו שְׁמֵיהּ מִיעוּט: שֶׁשְּׁלִיבוֹתָיו פּוֹרְחוֹת. שְׁלִיבוֹת חֲווֹקִין שקלוני"ש בְּלַעַ"ז. מַדְרֵגוֹת שֶׁלָּנוּ שֶׁקּוֹרִין גרדי"ן קָרֵי לֵיהּ נַמִי סוּלָּם. וְסוּלָּם שֶׁאֵינוֹ עָשׂוּי כְּעֵין מַדְרֵיגָה אֶלָּא כְּעֵין שְׁלִיבוֹת שֶׁלָּנוּ, שֶׁיֵּשׁ אֲוִיר בֵּין חֲווֹקֶיהָ, וְהַיְינוּ פּוֹרְחוֹת, שֶׁפּוֹרְחוֹת זוֹ עַל זוֹ וּזְקָפוֹ אֵצֶל הַכּוֹתֶל: אִם יֵשׁ בַּשְּׁלִיבָה הַתַּחְתּוֹנָה אַרְבָּעָה. וּבָהּ נִתְמַעֵט הַכּוֹתֶל מֵעֲשָׂרָה – מְמַעֵט: אִי נַמִי כו'. כִּדְפָרֵישִׁית גַּבֵּי אִיצְטַבָּא וּשְׁלִיבָה תַּחְתּוֹנָה נַמִי, כְּשֶׁאֵין מוּבְדֶּלֶת מִן הַקַּרְקַע שְׁלֹשָׁה קָאָמַר:
זיז

תוספות

מקצת עלין מגולין. משום שבת נקט לה. כך פי' בקונטרס. ופריך: כיון דכל העצ מכוסה, ואין מגולה אלא מקצת עלין – דומה לספל שיש לו אוגנים. וא"ת: והא משמע בריש "כל הכלים" (שבת דף קכג.) דלרבנן דר"א בן תדאי, דאית להו טלטול מן הצד שמיה טלטול, פוגלא מלמטה למעלה אסור, שהעצ הוא למטה, מ"ש מגנון שמקצת עלין מגולין דשרי, ולא חשיב אפי' טלטול מן הצד אע"פ שהעצ תחת העלין כולו מכוסה? וי"ל: דמ"מ קל להגביהו ולנערו מן העפר יותר מכשהוא מונח מלמטה למעלה. וא"ת: דמשמע הכא דניעור לא חשיב טלטול מן הצד, מדשרינן מקצתה מגולה אפילו לרבנן. וכמה משניות דשרו לנער, כדתנן פרק "במה טומנין" (שם מט.): *נוער את הכסוי והן נופלות, ומעות שעל גבי הכר – מנער את הכר והן נופלות, *ואבן שעל פי החבית – מטה על צידה והיא נופלת. *וא"כ, אמאי אסר רב בפרק "כירה" (שם דף מג:) גבי מת המוטל בחמה להופכו ממיטה למיטה משום דטלטול מן הצד שמיה טלטול. אע"ג דמניח אסרינן בפרק "נוטל" (שם דף קמב:) מטעם בסיס לדבר האסור – מת בשבת הוי כמו שכח. וכל דבר שדעתו ליטלו בשבת ולא להניחו בו כל השבת – אפי' מניח חשיב כשוכח, כי ההיא דנוער את הכסוי והן נופלות, אע"פ שמתכוין כיסה בדבר שאינו ניטל. ואומר ר"י: דשאני טלטול דמת, שעיקר טלטול לצורך המת עצמו, שהוא איסור. ולא דמי לכל הני שעושה הטלטול לצורך היתר ולא לצורך איסור, כמו לפת וכנון שאין צריך לטלטול עפר. וכן גבי גיזי צמר ומעות ואבן, א"צ לטלטולם. להכי לא מייתי בפרק "כירה" (שם דף מג:) גבי פלוגתא דרב ושמואל אלא ההיא דר' יהודה בן לקיש(ג) דדמיא ליה, ולא מייתי עלה פלוגתא דר"א בן תדאי ורבנן. והשתא אתי שפיר דלא תיקשי ההיא דרב דאמרי בי רב בפרק "תולין" (שם דף קמא.), דמשמע דסברי דלא שמיה טלטול – כי זה אינו נראה לומר דפליגי. ואור"י: אע"ג דקי"ל בעלמא דטלטול מן הצד לא שמיה טלטול, דבריש "כל הכלים" (שם דף קכג.) פסיק רב נחמן כר"א בן תדאי – בההוא דמת הלכה כרב דאסר, דקי"ל הלכה כרב באיסורי. ומדמסיק עלה דכולי עלמא טלטול מן הצד שמיה טלטול, פירוש ר' יהודה בן לקיש ורבנן, והוה מצי למימר לא שמיה טלטול, ולאוקמי פלוגתייהו בטלטול גמור. ואין להאריך כאן:

אי הכי אפי' צורי נמי. משמע הכא דכל סולמות ניטלין בשבת, בין מצרי ובין צורי. ותימה: דבפ"ק דביצה (דף ט:) משמע דסולם של עלייה אסור לטלטל, ולא שרי התם אלא סולם של שובך, משום דשובכו מוכיח עליו. ואפי' הטוי סולם של עלייה אסר התם ללישנא בתרא דבני ר' חייא! ועוד: דר' חייא גופיה דאסר התם – משמע בשמעתין דשרי, דס"ל סולמות של בבל צריכין קבע. ודוחק להעמיד בסולם של שובך. ואין נראה נמי להעמיד הך דשמעתין כרב חנן בר אמי, דמפרש התם *דברה"ר פליגי אבל ברה"י מותר – דלית הלכתא הכי, אלא כרב קי"ל, דאמר: כל מקום שאסרו חכמים מפני מראית העין – אפי' בחדרי חדרים אסור, וכן פסק במגילת סתרים. ואור"ת: דהכא בסולמות של בית, שדרך לטלטל מזוית לזוית. ולא דמי לסולמות של עלייה שהם גדולים, וחזו להטיח בהן גגו, וכן סולמות של שובך. וה"ר אברהם מפרש: דהתם בי"ט שמוליך הסולם ברה"ר ורואין אותו ואומר להטיח גגו הוא צריך, וכיון דאסור ברה"ר – אסור בחדרי חדרים. אבל בשבת דאין רגילות להוליכו ברה"ר – לא גזור בחצר. ולפי פירוש זה אסור לטלטל סולמות שלנו בי"ט:

אם יש באיצטבא התחתונה ארבעה ממעט. פי' בקונט': אורך ארבעה, ובה נתמעט גובהו של כותל מעשרה. ומשמע דלא בעי ד' על ד'. וכן פירש סולם שהשליבותיו פורחות – כעין סולמות שלנו, אורך החווקים יכול להיות ארבעה, שעושין כמין מקלות דקים. ותימה: דבסמוך בעינן שיגיע סולם עד ראש הכותל, דבעי סולם י"ד או ז' ומשהו. ואין לומר דהתם בדלית ביה ד' – דסתם סולם ברחב ד' איירי. אלא היכא דקאמר כל שהוא, כמו גבי זיז – דמשום זיז לא בעי רוחב ד'. וכן משמע דקאמר לקמן [דף עח.]: סולם מכאן וסולם מכאן וקשין באמצע מהו? חקק להשלים בכותל בכמה*? משמע דבעי רחב ארבעה. ודוחק לומר דהא דבעינן שיגיע לראש הכותל, ולא סגי במה שמיעטו – איירי כשיש בין זה לזה ג', ושליבה התחתונה נמי גבוה מן הארץ שלשה, דהוי מיעוט באויר ולא שמיה מיעוט. ומפרש ר"י: דהכא בעינן ארבעה על ארבעה שיהא ראוי לעמוד ולהסתכב עליו ולעלות על הכותל, ולהכי לא בעינן אלא שיתמעט הכותל מעשרה, אבל לקמן בעי שיגיע עד ראש הכותל – לא איירי ברחב ד' על ד'. וסולם ששליבות פורחות – לא כעין סולמות(ד) אלא כעין מדרגות שקורין גרד"ש, ולא כעין מדרגות של אבנים שעושין כמין סטיו לפניס מסטיו, אלא המדרגות בולטין זה על גב זה, שיש חלל ואויר בין שליבה לשליבה. וזהו ל' "פורחות" – כמו "נמלא כבש פורח על גבי אמה יסוד ואמה סובב" דפרק "קדשי קדשים" (זבחים סב:). והשליבות רחבות ארבעה על ארבעה ולהכי ממעט, ואיצטריך לאשמעינן באיצטבא ובסולם ששליבותיה פורחות, דאי אשמעינן באיצטבא – הוה אמינא דסולם שאין(ה) התחתונה ארבעה ויש בעליונה ארבעה, אפי' יש בין זה לזה שלשה – ממעט, דלא חשיב מיעוט באויר, כיון דמאחורי הסולם מחובר הכל יחד, דהוי כאיצטבא אחת. ואי אשמעינן סולם – הוה אמינא דאיצטבא אפי' אין בין זה לזה ג' הוי מיעוט באויר, דאין האיצטבא התחתונה מבטלת האויר, ולא חשיבא כסולם כל שהוא דחזי לעלייה, ומבטל האויר שתחת הזיז. ור"ת מפרש: דהא דבעי שיגיע סולם(ו) על ראש הכותל – היינו בסולם שאין קבוע. ואין נראה לר"י, דגבי לול הפתוח לעלייה מיבעיא לן לעיל* אי צריך סולם קבוע או לאו, משמע דבכל דוכתא בעינן סולם קבוע. ועוד: שאינו קבוע, כיון דניטל בשבת – אפי' מגיע עד ראש הכותל – אין לו להועיל, כמו תריך שבין שתי חצירות, דתנן לקמן*: אפי' מלא קש או תבן – מערבין שנים ואין מערבין אחד, לפי שאין קבוע שם ועתיד ליטלו:
אלא

עין משפט נר מצוה

יג א מיי' פ"ב מהל' כלאים הלכה יא טוש"ע י"ד סי' רלו סעיף יא:
יד ב מיי' פ"א מהל' שמטה ויובל הל' טו:
טו ג מיי' פכ"ה מהל' שבת הלכה טו סמג לאוין סה טור ש"ע א"ח סי' שיא סעיף ח:
טז ד ה ו מיי' פ"ג מהל' עירובין הלכה ד טוש"ע א"ח סי' שעב סעיף ח:
יז ז מיי' שם הלכה ה טור ש"ע שם סעיף יא:
יח ח מיי' פ"ג שם הלכה ה:

לפנינו הגירסא נוטל

[שבת דף קמב:]

[שם]

[דף ט.]

[שם ע"ב]

[דף עו:]

[דף עח:]

רבינו חננאל

אם היו מקצת עליו מגולין אינו חושש לא משום כלאים ולא משום [מעשר ולא משום שביעית] ונטלין בשבת ופריק לא צריכא דהספל לא יכול למישמטיה אלא עד דחפיר במרא וחצינא שאינו ניטל בשבת לפיכך ממעט בכותל: סולם המצרי שאין לו ד' חווקים אינו ממעט מפני שהוא קל וניטל בשבת וכל הניטל בשבת אינו ממעט דחייש דלמא שקיל ליה אבל סולם צורי שהוא כבד ואינו ניטל בשבת ממקום למקום ממעט מפני שהסולם ניחא תשמישתיה. אמר אביי כותל שבין ב' חצרות גבוה י' טפחים והניח סולם רחב ד' טפחים מיכן וסולם רחב ד' טפחים מיכן זה שלא כנגד זה ואין בין זה הסולם לזה הסולם ג' טפחים אמרינן כל פחות מג' טפחים כלבוד דמי וכאלו ב' הסולמות זה כנגד זה הן וממעטו ואם רצו מערבין אחד כי לשתי החצרות תשמישן בנחת הוא. והני מילי בדלא הוי רחב הכותל ד"ט אבל אי הוי ד' טפחים כמרפסת ואע"ג דמפלגי סולמות הללו זה מזה טובא כיון דהוי רוחב הכותל (ב) [ד'] טפחים נעשה כמרפסת וחצר פתוחה לתוכו ואפי' זה שלא כנגד זה והסולמות מיעטו הן. וכאילו אין שם כותל שהרי תשמיש ב' החצרות הוא. וכן אם בנה איצטבא ע"ג איצטבא אם יש באיצטבא התחתונה ד' טפחים אי נמי אין באיצטבא התחתונה ד' טפחים ואין בין איצטבא התחתונה לאיצטבא העליונה אלא (ג' טפחים) פחות מג' אמרינן כלבוד דמי וכאילו רחב האיצטבא העליונה והתחתונה ביחד הן והן ד' וממעטין את הגובה. ודברי רב נחמן נמי בהאי טעמא שייך דא' סולם ששליבותיו פורחות כלומר המדרגות המשולבות זו בזו עודפות אחת על חברתה מוצאות זו מזו אם יש בשליבה התחתונה ד' טפחים ממעטת. ואם אין בה ד' טפחים והשליבה של מעלה ממנה קרובה בפחות מג' טפחים חשבינן להם כלבודות ופריחת זו ופריחת זו מצטרפת לד' טפחים וממעט אותו הסולם בכותל ואם רצו מערבין אחד ועוד אמר ר"נ
זיז

הגהות הב"ח

(א) רש"י ד"ה כובדו קובעו דמתוך: (ב) ד"ה ולא אמרן אלא בכותל צר שאין ברחבו ד' שאין נוח להלך עליו אבל יש כצ"ל והד"א: (ג) תוס' ד"ה מקצת וכו' דר' יהודה בן לקיש ורבנן דדמיא: (ד) ד"ה אם יש וכו' לא כעין סולמות שלנו אלא כעין (ה) בא"ד הוה אמינא דסולם שאין בשליבה התחתונה: (ו) בא"ד דבעי שיגיע סולם עד ראש הכותל:

אִזִיז הַיּוֹצֵא מִן הַכּוֹתֶל ד' עַל ד', וְהִנִּיחַ עָלָיו סוּלָּם כׇּל שֶׁהוּא — מִיעֲטוֹ. וְלָא אֲמַרַן אֶלָּא דְּאוֹתְבֵיהּ עֲלֵיהּ, אֲבָל אוֹתְבֵיהּ בַּהֲדֵי' — אַרְווֹחֵי אַרְוְחֵיהּ. וְאָמַר רַב נַחְמָן, אָמַר רַבָּה בַּר אֲבוּהּ: בכּוֹתֶל תִּשְׁעָה עָשָׂר — צָרִיךְ זִיז אֶחָד לְהַתִּירוֹ. כּוֹתֶל עֶשְׂרִים — צָרִיךְ שְׁנֵי זִיזִים לְהַתִּירוֹ. אָמַר רַב חִסְדָּא: גוְהוּא שֶׁהֶעֱמִידָן זֶה שֶׁלֹּא כְּנֶגֶד זֶה. אָמַר רַב הוּנָא: דעַמּוּד בִּרה"ר, גָּבוֹהַּ עֲשָׂרָה וְרָחָב אַרְבָּעָה, וְנָעַץ בּוֹ יָתֵד כׇּל שֶׁהוּא — מִיעֲטוֹ. אָמַר רַב אַדָּא בַּר אַהֲבָה: הוּבְגָבוֹהַּ שְׁלֹשָׁה. אַבַּיֵּי וְרָבָא דְּאָמְרִי תַּרְוַיְיהוּ: אַף עַל פִּי שֶׁאֵין גָּבוֹהַּ שְׁלֹשָׁה. מַאי טַעְמָא — לָא מִשְׁתַּמֵּשׁ לֵיהּ. רַב אַשִׁי אָמַר: אֲפִילּוּ שֶׁגָּבוֹהַּ שְׁלֹשָׁה, מַאי טַעְמָא — אֶפְשָׁר דְּתָלֵי בֵּיהּ מִידֵי. אֲמַר לֵיהּ רַב אַחָא בְּרֵיהּ דְּרָבָא לְרַב אַשִׁי: מִלְאוֹ כּוּלּוֹ בִּיתֵדוֹת מַהוּ? א"ל: לָא שְׁמִיעַ לָךְ הָא *דְּאָמַר רַבִּי יוֹחָנָן: בּוֹר וְחוּלְיָיתָהּ מִצְטָרֵף לַעֲשָׂרָה? וְאַמַּאי? הָא לָא מִשְׁתַּמֵּשׁ לֵיהּ! אֶלָּא מַאי אִית לָךְ לְמֵימַר — דְּמַנַּח מִידֵי וּמִשְׁתַּמֵּשׁ. והָכָא נַמִי — דְּמַנַּח מִידֵי וּמִשְׁתַּמֵּשׁ. אָמַר רַב יְהוּדָה, אָמַר שְׁמוּאֵל: כּוֹתֶל עֲשָׂרָה — צָרִיךְ סוּלָּם אַרְבָּעָה עָשָׂר לְהַתִּירוֹ. רַב יוֹסֵף אָמַר: אֲפִילּוּ שְׁלֹשָׁה עָשָׂר וּמַשֶּׁהוּ. אַבַּיֵּי אָמַר: אֲפִילּוּ אַחַד עָשָׂר וּמַשֶּׁהוּ. רַב הוּנָא בְּרֵיהּ דְּרַב יְהוֹשֻׁעַ אָמַר: זאֲפִילּוּ שִׁבְעָה וּמַשֶּׁהוּ. אָמַר רַב: סוּלָּם זָקוּף מְמַעֵט, גְּמָרָא, וְלָא יָדַעְנָא מ"ט. אָמַר שְׁמוּאֵל: וְלָא יָדַע *אַבָּא טַעְמָא דְּהָא מִלְּתָא?! מִידֵי דַּהֲוָה אַאִיצְטַבָּא עַל גַּבֵּי אִיצְטַבָּא. אָמַר רַבָּה, אָמַר רַבִּי חִיָּיא: חדְּקָלִים שֶׁבְּבָבֶל אֵינָן צְרִיכִין קֶבַע. מַאי טַעְמָא — כְּבֵידָן קוֹבַעְתָּן. וְרַב יוֹסֵף אָמַר רַבִּי אוֹשַׁעְיָא: טסוּלָּמוֹת שֶׁבְּבָבֶל אֵינָן צְרִיכִין קֶבַע, מ"ט — כְּבֵידָן קוֹבַעְתָּן. מַאן דְּאָמַר סוּלָּמוֹת — כׇּל שֶׁכֵּן דְּקָלִים, וּמַאן דְּאָמַר דְּקָלִים — אֲבָל סוּלָּמוֹת — לָא. בְּעָא מִינֵּיהּ רַב יוֹסֵף מֵרַבָּה: סוּלָּם מִכָּאן וְסוּלָּם מִכָּאן וְקַשִּׁין בָּאֶמְצַע, מַהוּ? אֲמַר לֵיהּ: יאֵין כַּף הָרֶגֶל עוֹלָה בָּהֶן. קַשִּׁין מִכָּאן וְקַשִּׁין מִכָּאן וְסוּלָּם בָּאֶמְצַע, מַהוּ? אֲמַר לֵיהּ: כהֲרֵי כַּף הָרֶגֶל עוֹלָה בָּהֶן.

חֲקַק

רש"י

זיז היוצא מן הכותל ד' על ד'. טפחים: והניח עליו סולם כל שהוא. אפילו אין ברחבו ד' והעמידו בקרקע, וסמך ראשו בזיז – הוי כחד מיעוטא, והרי בעליון ארבעה. וכגון שאין חווקי הסולם מרוחקין שלשה: ולא אמרן אלא דאותביה עליה. סמך ראשו עליו, כדפרישית: אבל אותביה בהדיה. אצלו, וראשו נסמך לכותל: ארווחי ארווחיה. לזיז, ולא הוי האי סולם מתחתיו דרגא לזיז, ואין כאן מיעוט – שהוא מובדל מן הקרקע הרבה: צריך זיז אחד להתירו. בסולם כל שהוא, והזיז יוצא באמצעיתו, שאינו גבוה עשרה לא ממנו ולמטה, ולא ממנו ולמעלה: צריך שני זיזין. אחד קודם עשרה תחתונים, ואחד למעלה הימנו בתוך עשרה עליונים. דאי הוה גבוה עשרה – לא הוה סגי ליה בסולם כל שהוא, מידי דהוה אכותל: זה שלא כנגד זה. שיוכל לקבוע סולם שני מזה לזה: עמוד גבוה עשרה ברה"ר ורחב ד'. רה"י הוא, והנוטל ממנו והנותן על גביו – חייב. ואם נעץ בראשו יתד כל שהוא – מיעטו לרחבו מארבעה, וביטלו מתורת רה"י: יתד. קביל"א בלע"ז: ובגבוה היתד שלשה. אבל אם אינו גבוה שלשה – כגגו דעמוד חשיב, ולא ממעט: אפשר דתלי ביה מידי. וכיון דחזי לתשמישתיה דעמוד – מיניה חשיב, ולא ממעט: מלאו כולו ביתדות. לדידך, דאמרת (חד) חד תשמישתיה הוא, ולא ממעט – יתדות טובא מאי? מי אמרינן: כיון דלא משתמש בהאי רוחב – לאו רוחב הוא: בור וחולייתה. קרקע שניטלה מחפירת הבור, והקיפו בו פי הבור סביב: מצטרפת. להשלים עשרה לעומק הבור, לשוויה רה"י. וה"ה נמי דחלל הבור ועובי היקף החוליא מצטרפין להשלים ארבעה לרוחבו, לחייב הנוטל מעל גב החוליא כלום ואת הנותן על גבה. כדתנן ב"הזורק" [שבת דף צט.]: חוליית הבור והסלע, שהן גבוהין עשרה ורחבין ארבעה – הנוטל מהן והנותן על גבן חייב. ומההיא יליף ר' יוחנן לטעמיה, דאמר: מאי איריא דתני חוליית הבור והסלע – ליתני הבור והסלע. אלא הא קא משמע לן: דהבור וחולייתה מצטרפין לעשרה, וכי היכי דשמעינן מינה לגובה – שמעינן מינה נמי דמצטרפין לפותיא, דהא קתני ורוחבן ארבעה. והאי דנקט הכא לדר' יוחנן, ולא נקט מתני' – משום דבמתני' לא תני צירוף בהדיא: ואמאי. הוי גגה דחוליא רה"י? הא לא חזו ארבעה דידיה לתשמישתיה, מפני החלל שהוא מהן: אלא מאי אית לך למימר דמנח מידי. כגון דף או אבן על פיה, ומשתמש: הכא נמי. מניח דף ארבעה, או שוטח בגד על היתדות, ומשתמש עליו בנחת: סולם ארבעה עשר. שצריך למשוך רגלי הסולם ארבעה מן הכותל, לפי שאין סולם זקוף נוח לעלות: אפילו י"ג ומשהו. שכשתמשוך רגליו מן הכותל ארבעה לא יהא ראשו נמוך מן הכותל טפח, וכיון דלא הוי טפח לית לן בה: אחד עשר ומשהו. שכשתרחיק רגליו ארבעה יהא ראשו נמוך מן הכותל פחות משלשה – וכלבוד דמי: שבעה ומשהו. דס"ל כרב, דאמר לקמן: סולם זקוף ממעט, ואי זקיף ליה מגיע לפחות מג' לראש הכותל: אמר רב סולם זקוף ממעט גמרא. שמעתי מרבותי, וטעמא לא ידענא, דהא אין נוח לעלות: מידי דהוה אאיצטבא על גבי איצטבא. שהן מכוונות ואמרן לעיל* דממעטין: דקלים שבבבל. פיסקי דקלים של בבל שהניחן סמוך לכותל למעטו – אין צריך לקובען בקרקע. ואע"ג דדבר הניטל הוא, דתורת כלי עליהן דראויין למושב – אפ"ה כבידן קובען, שאין בא אדם ונוטלן, וכן סולמות: סולם. כל שהוא מכאן וסולם כל שהוא מכאן אצלו, ואין בשניהן לא בזה שני טפחים ולא בזה שני טפחים רוחב, וקבע קשין של תבואה כעין חווקין מזה לזה להשלימן לארבעה, מהו: אין כף הרגל עולה. בקשים, וספק עליית הרגלים באמצע סולם הוא, וזה אין ראוי לכך: קשין מכאן ומכאן. להשלים רוחבו לארבעה, מהו: הרי כף הרגל עולה. בסולם, וראויין הקשין לאחוז היד בהן, ולעלות בסולם:

חֲקַק

תוספות

אלא מאי אית לך למימר דמנח עליה מידי ומשתמש. אצירוף עשרה לא איצטריך לטעמא דמנח מידי, דאם הבור רחב ד' ואינו עמוק עשרה אלא ע"י צירוף חוליא – רה"י גמורה היא, ומשתמש ליה שפיר, כיון שכותלי הבור מבפנים גבוהים עשרה. וטעמא דמנח עליהן מידי – מה יש להועיל שם, כיון דאין חוליא גבוה י' מבחוץ לרה"ר. ולא קאי האי טעמא אלא היכא דאין הבור רחב ד' מבפנים אלא ע"י צירוף חוליא, והחוליא גבוה עשרה מבחוץ לרה"ר. דאע"ג דתוכו לאו רה"י הוא – על גביו רה"י, משום דאי בעי מנח עליה מידי ומשתמש. ואע"ג דרבי יוחנן לא הזכיר אלא צירוף עשרה – מכל מקום דייק ממילתיה. והא לא משתמש ליה משום דר' יוחנן אמתני' דפ' "הזורק" (שבת דף צט.) קאי, כדפירש בקונטרס דשמעינן מינה נמי צירוף ארבעה, דהא קתני ורחבן ד'. ותימה: דאמתני' דלקמן בפ' בתרא (דף צט:) דייק נמי רבי יוחנן הכי, גבי בור ברה"ר וחוליתו גבוה עשרה טפחים. וקאמר ר' יוחנן בגמ': אפילו תימא בסמוכין. והא קמ"ל – דבור וחוליתו מצטרפין לעשרה. והשתא תרתי למה לי? ואור"י: דההיא דשבת אצטריך לענין צירוף ארבעה, דלא קתני לקמן. ואי לאו ההיא דלקמן – מההיא דשבת לחוד לא הוה דייק, דהוה אמינא: דאגב סלע נקט חולית הבור, דבכל דוכתא רגיל להזכיר חוליא בהדי סלע: **צריך** סולם ארבעה עשר להתירו. פי' בקונטרס: שצריך למשוך רגלי הסולם ארבעה מן הכותל. ולא דק, דכי משיך ליה י' טפחים נמי מן הכותל, שהוא שיעור גובה הכותל – יגיע ראש הסולם לראש הכותל, דארבעה עשר הוא שיעור אלכסון של י' על י', דכל אמתא בריבועא אמתא ותרי חומשי באלכסונא. וכן פי' ר"ת: **רב** יוסף אמר י"ג ומשהו אביי אמר אפילו י"א ומשהו. וא"ת: אם תרחיק רגלי הסולם מן הכותל עשרה טפחים, וראש הסולם תסמוך לכותל – על כרחך יהיה ראש הכותל גבוה מן הסולם יותר מטפח לרב יוסף, ויותר משלשה טפחים לאביי. שהרי אם לא היה הסולם אלא י' טפחים – ממה נפשך הוה מתרחק יותר מד' טפחים, שהרי יפול הסולם לגמרי לארץ. וגם אין נראה דלרב יוסף ואביי נמי נשען ראש הסולם לראש הכותל, אלא שמקרבין רגלי הסולם יותר מלשמואל. ולאביי יהיה קרוב לזקוף, דלמה להן למינקט האי שיעורא, ולמה הזכירו רב יוסף ואביי אותו משהו? אלא נראה לר"י: דלסימנא בעלמא נקטי' הכי, דלעולם צריך להרחיק הסולם כשיעור גובה שנשען על הכותל, ושלא יהא גובה הכותל מן הסולם טפח לרב יוסף, ולאביי שלשה טפחים כשיעור לבוד, ולרב יוסף סגיא במשהו. ושלש עשרה פחות שני חומשין, שהוא אלכסון של ט' על ט'. ולאביי במשהו ועשרה טפחים פחות חומש, שהוא אלכסון ז' על ז': **אמר** שמואל לא ידע כו'. אליבא דרב קאמר, אבל שמואל גופיה סבר דסולם זקוף אינו ממעט, דהא בעי סולם י"ד: **סולמות** של בבל אין צריכין קבע. אע"ג שאין להם ד' חווקין, דכובדן קובען. ולא כמו שפירש רבינו שמואל דהיינו סולם צורי דלעיל – דאם כן לא ה"ל למימר סולמות של בבל. ועוד: דההיא דלעיל ליכא מאן דפליג, והכא אמרינן סולמות לא:

חקק

עין משפט נר מצוה

יט א ב ג מיי' פ"ג מהל' עירובין הל' ו טוש"ע סימן שע"ב סעיף יב:

כ ד ה ו מיי' פי"ד מהלכות שבת הלכה ט:

כא ז מיי' פ"ג מהל' עירובין הלכה ג טוש"ע שם סעיף ח:

כב ח ט מיי' שם הלכה ז:

כג י כ מיי' שם טור ש"ע שם סעיף יג:

מסורת הש"ס

שבת דף צט. [לקמן צט:]

[ולרב קרי הכי משום חשיבות ועי' פרש"י בחולין לח. ד"ה לאבא וכו' ומ"ש תוס' שם וכן עוד בפרש"י יבמות נז: ד"ה מודה ובתוס' שם ד"ה אמר שמואל וע"ע רש"י שבת נג. ד"ה אבא וברכות מז. ברש"י ד"ה אלו]

[דף עז:]

רבינו חננאל

זיז היוצא מן הכותל והניח עליו סולם כל שהוא כלומר אפי' אין בסולם ד' טפחים ממעט ולא אמרן אלא דאנחיה עליה דזיז אבל אשוויה אשוויה לא ממעט דאמרינן (אפתויי) [ארווחי] הוא דקא (מפתי) [מרוח] ליה לזיז פי' אם נתן הסולם בכותל עם הזיז יש לומר הזיז הרחיב ואינו ממעט דהא לא משתמש בסולם זה ע"ג הכותל אלא [משתמש] בסולם לעלות בזיז הוא נותן בעת שנתנו בצד הזיז על הכותל: אמר רב נחמן כותל י"ט טפחים גובהו זיז אחד ממעט אותו. כלומר נותנו למעלה בכותל בט' טפחים וחצי ונמצא בגובהה של כותל כט' טפחים וחצי ממועט נשארו מן הכותל ט' טפחים אחרים וחצי טפח כיון שאינן י' טפחים אינו אוסר. אבל אם גובהו של כותל כ' טפחים אינו ממעטו אלא ב' זיזין (זה) אחד (בי') [בתוך י'] טפחים והסולם ממעטו כאילו קרקע הוא עד אותו הזיז. וצריך זיז אחר (כעשרין) [בתוך עשרים]. וי"א סולם נתון על כל זיז וזיז. אמר רב חסדא והוא שהעמידן אלו זיזין זה שלא כנגד זה והסולמות עליהן. ואם היו הזיזין רחבין ד' טפחים שיכול להשתמש בהן אין צריך. אמר רב הונא עמוד ברה"ר גבוה י' ורחב ד' ונעץ בו יתד כל שהוא ממעט ונעתק מרשות היחיד ונעשה ככרמלית. ולא אמרן אלא בזמן שהיתד גבוה מן הקרקע ג' טפחים. אביי ורבא דאמרי אפי' גבוה ג' טפחים לא מידי הוא כלומר אינו ממעט. רב אשי אמר אע"פ שאינה גבוה ג' אפשר (דלית) [דתלי] ביה מידי כגון מחצלת וממעט. א"ל רב אחא בריה דרבא לרב אשי דאע"פ שאין גבוה היתד ג' טפחים חזי לאישתמושי ביה אפשר (דלית) [דתלי] ביה מידי. אם מלא לזה עמוד כולו יתדות להשתמש בו מהו. א"ל לא שמיעא לך הא דר' יוחנן בור וחוליתה מצטרפין לעשרה. אמאי והא לא קא משתמש ליה בבור כמו החוליא שהבור רחב מלמטה והחוליא צרה אלא מאי אית לך למימר דמנח מידי כגון מחצלת ומשוה הבור צר כמו החוליא ומשמש הכא נמי בעמוד שהוא מלא יתידות מנח מידי עליהו ומשתמש. כיון שאמר כי הסולמות ממעטין ומתירין לשתי החצירות לערב אחד הוצרך שמואל לומר כמה יהא גובהו של סולם שהוא ממעט בכותל ואמר כותל שגובהו י' טפחים צריך סולם י"ד טפחים גובהו פי' כיון דקי"ל כי עודף האלכסון על המרובע ב' חומשין כדגרסינן כל אמתא בריבועא אמתא ותרי חומשי באלכסונא. והסולם לעולם שאינו נסמך על הכותל לעלות בו אלא באלכסון אבל זקוף אין דרך לעלות ולפיכך אמר כותל י' צריך להיות סולם כדי גובהו של כותל וישפיעהו כלפי חוץ באלכסון ולפיכך צריך כדי גובה כל הסולם ויתרון אלכסונו וכיון שהכותל י' טפחים וכל טפח צריך יתרון למדת דאלכסון ב' חומשין נמצא שיעור הסולם י' טפחים וב' חומשין לכל טפח הרי י' טפחים ועשרין חומשין. עשרין חומשין הרי ד' טפחים נמצא גובה הסולם י"ד טפחים. רב יוסף אמר אפי' י"ג טפחים ומשהו דיי. שאין דרך להשפיעו זה כולו. ופחות מטפח לא חשיב. אביי אמר אפי' אין בסולם אלא י"א ומשהו ומעמידו בראשו של כותל בפחות מג' וכל פחות מג' כלבוד דמי וכאילו בראש הכותל הוא סמוך. הלכך בי"א ומשהו דיי לו. רב הונא בריה דרב יהושע אמר אפי' ז' ומשהו. קסבר אפי' סולם זקוף ממעט וכל פחות מג' כלבוד דמי הלכך בז' טפחים ומשהו סגיא. אמר רב סולם זקוף ממעט ולא ידענא מ"ט. והלא אין דרך בני אדם לעלות כן. וא"ל שמואל מידי דהוה אאיצטבא ע"ג איצטבא שהן זקופות וממעטות. דקלין שבבבל וסולמות שבבבל אין צריך לקבען אלא כיון שנתנו ע"ג הכותל ממעטין שכבידן קובען הואיל ואין ניטלין בשבת מפני הכובד שלהן. בעא מיניה רב יוסף מרבה סולם מיכן וסולם מיכן וקשין באמצע בין ב' הסולמות מהן. ופשט ליה אין כף הרגל עולה בהן (וממעט) [ואינו ממעט].

עוד

כד א ב מיי' פ"ג מהל' עירובין הלכה יא טוש"ע א"ח סי' שעב סעיף יד:
כה ג ד מיי' שם הלכה ח טוש"ע שם סעיף טו:
כו ה מיי' שם הלכה יב טוש"ע שם סעיף טז:
כז ו מיי' שם הלכה יג טוש"ע שם סעיף יז:
כח ז מיי' שם הלכה יד טור ש"ע א"ח סימן שעג:
כט ח מיי' פ"ז מהל' טומאת מת הלכה ו סמג עשין רלג:

חָקַק לְהַשְׁלִים בַּכּוֹתֶל, בְּכַמָּה? א"ל: [א]בַּעֲשָׂרָה. א"ל: חֲקָקוֹ כּוּלּוֹ בַּכּוֹתֶל, בְּכַמָּה? א"ל: [ב]מְלֹא קוֹמָתוֹ. וּמַאי שְׁנָא? א"ל: הָתָם — מִסְתַּלַּק לֵיהּ, הָכָא לֹא מִסְתַּלַּק לֵיהּ. בְּעָא מִינֵּיהּ רַב יוֹסֵף מֵרַבָּה: עֲשָׂאוֹ לָאִילָן סוּלָּם, מַהוּ? תִּיבָּעֵי לְרַבִּי, תִּיבָּעֵי לְרַבָּנַן; תִּיבָּעֵי לְרַבִּי: עַד כָּאן לָא קָאָמַר רַבִּי הָתָם *"כָּל דָּבָר שֶׁהוּא מִשּׁוּם שְׁבוּת לֹא גָּזְרוּ עָלָיו" ה"מ — בֵּין הַשְּׁמָשׁוֹת, אֲבָל כּוּלֵּי יוֹמָא — לֹא. אוֹ דִּילְמָא: אֲפִילּוּ לְרַבָּנַן, פִּיתְחָא הוּא, וְאַרְיָא הוּא דִּרְבִיעַ עֲלֵיהּ. עֲשָׂאוֹ לַאֲשֵׁירָה סוּלָּם, מַהוּ? תִּיבָּעֵי לְרַבִּי יְהוּדָה, תִּיבָּעֵי לְרַבָּנַן; תִּיבָּעֵי לְרַבִּי יְהוּדָה: ע"כ לָא קָאָמַר *רַבִּי יְהוּדָה הָתָם דְּמוּתָּר לִקְנוֹת בַּיִת בְּאִיסּוּרֵי הֲנָאָה — אֶלָּא הָתָם, *דְּבָתַר דְּקָנָה לֵיהּ עֵירוּב לָא נִיחָא לֵיהּ דְּלִינְטַר. אוֹ דִּילְמָא: אֲפִילּוּ לְרַבָּנַן פִּיתְחָא הוּא, וְאַרְיָא דִּרְבִיעַ עֲלֵיהּ? א"ל: [ג]אִילָן מוּתָּר, וַאֲשֵׁירָה אֲסוּרָה. מַתְקִיף לָהּ רַב חִסְדָּא: אַדְּרַבָּה, אִילָן שֶׁאִיסּוּר שַׁבָּת גּוֹרֵם לוֹ — נִיתְסַר, אֲשֵׁירָה שֶׁאִיסּוּר דָּבָר אַחֵר גּוֹרֵם לוֹ — לָא נִיתְסַר. אִיתְּמַר נַמִי, כִּי אֲתָא רָבִין, א"ר אֶלְעָזָר, וְאָמְרִי לָהּ א"ר אַבָּהוּ, א"ר יוֹחָנָן: [ד]כָּל שֶׁאִיסּוּר שַׁבָּת גָּרַם לוֹ — אָסוּר, כָּל שֶׁאִיסּוּר דָּבָר אַחֵר גָּרַם לוֹ — מוּתָּר. ר"נ בַּר יִצְחָק מַתְנֵי הָכִי: אִילָן — פְּלוּגְתָּא דְּרַבִּי וְרַבָּנַן, אֲשֵׁירָה — פְּלוּגְתָּא דְּרַבִּי יְהוּדָה וְרַבָּנַן.§

מתני' *[ה]חָרִיץ שֶׁבֵּין ב' חֲצֵירוֹת, עָמוֹק י' וְרוֹחַב ד' — מְעָרְבִין שְׁנַיִם, וְאֵין מְעָרְבִין אֶחָד, אֲפִילּוּ מָלֵא קַשׁ אוֹ תֶּבֶן. מָלֵא עָפָר אוֹ צְרוֹרוֹת *מְעָרְבִין אֶחָד, וְאֵין מְעָרְבִין שְׁנַיִם. [ו]נָתַן עָלָיו נֶסֶר שֶׁרָחָב אַרְבָּעָה טְפָחִים, [ז]וְכֵן ב' גְּזוּזְטְרָאוֹת זוֹ כְּנֶגֶד זוֹ — מְעָרְבִין שְׁנַיִם, וְאִם רָצוּ — מְעָרְבִין אֶחָד. פָּחוֹת מִכָּאן — מְעָרְבִין שְׁנַיִם, וְאֵין מְעָרְבִין אֶחָד.§

גמ' וְתֶבֶן לָא חָיֵיץ? וְהָא אֲנַן תְּנַן: *מַתְבֵּן שֶׁבֵּין שְׁתֵּי חֲצֵירוֹת, גָּבוֹהַּ עֲשָׂרָה טְפָחִים — מְעָרְבִין שְׁנַיִם, וְאֵין מְעָרְבִין אֶחָד. אָמַר אַבַּיֵי: לְעִנְיַן מְחִיצָה — כּוּלֵּי עָלְמָא לָא פְּלִיגִי דְּהָוְיָא מְחִיצָה, אֲבָל לְעִנְיַן חֲצִיצָה, אִי בַּטְלֵי' — חָיֵיץ, וְאִי לָא בַּטְלֵי' — לָא חָיֵיץ.§ "מָלֵא עָפָר".§ וַאֲפִילּוּ בִּסְתָמָא? *וְהָתְנַן: [ח]בַּיִת שֶׁמִּילְּאָהוּ תֶּבֶן אוֹ צְרוֹרוֹת וּבִיטְּלוֹ — בָּטֵל. בִּיטְּלוֹ — אִין, לא

[לעיל לב: וש"נ] [לעיל לה.] [שם] [לקמן פג:] [עי' בנוסחת הרא"ש ועי' ג"כ נוסח המשנה זו ברב אלפס וראה ג"כ בהרא"ש] [לקמן עט.] [סוכה ז. אהלות פט"ו מ"ז] [דף יט:]

תוספות

חקק להשלים בכותל בכמה. כגון שהכותל עב ובולט מצד הסולם, או שהסולם מונח בסוף הכותל בקרן זוית. ואיירי בכותל משופע. דהא רב יוסף אית ליה דסולם זקוף אינו ממעט, דבעינן שלש עשרה ומשהו, והכא רב יוסף קבעי לה: **אמר** ליה בעשרה. פירש בקונטרס: עד עשרה ישלימנו, אע"ג דגבוה כותל טובא – לית לן בה. וקשה לפירושו, דהא לא מסתלק ליה, כיון דאכתי גבוה כותל טובא. וי"ל: נהי דלא חקק בכותל אלא עד עשרה – אין לחוש אלא שיגיע הסולם עד ראש הכותל. ור"ת מפרש: בעשרה – היינו שלא ישאר מן הסולם עד ראש הכותל עשרה: **אשירה** פלוגתא דרבי יהודה ורבנן. לית ליה לרב נחמן בר יצחק סוגיא דלעיל דפ' "בכל מערבין" (דף לא.), דמשמע התם דלכולי עלמא אסור לקנות בית באיסורי הנאה. והכא קאמר דבמותר לקנות בית באיסורי הנאה פליגי:

אפילו מלא קש ומלא תבן. בקש ותבן הניטלין בשבת איירי, ולא כההיא דלעיל [דף עז.] פגה(ג) הטמונה בתבן. דהא אמר בגמרא דאפילו ארנקי מבטל אינים. וא"ת: והא אמרינן אפילו פירות מבטלין מחיצות, דאמרינן במסכת שבת בסוף "הזורק" (דף ק.): בור ברה"ר עמוק עשרה ורחב ד' מלא מים, וזרק לתוכו – חייב, מלא פירות וזרק לתוכו – פטור. מאי טעמא – מיא לא מבטלי מחיצה, פירות – מבטלי מחיצה! ואור"י: דמדאורייתא ודאי מבטלי, אבל לעירוב דרבנן הוא יש לחלק בין ניטל לשאינו ניטל. וקלת קשה, דמדמי לה בסמוך לבית שמילאהו, דהוי לענין אהל דאורייתא. ומההיא דאהל נמי תיקשי אההיא דשבת. **וכן** שתי גזוזטראות כו'. פי' בקונטר': בנותן נסר רחב ד' מזו לזו, דהוי נמי פתח. ותימה: כיון דע"י נסר רחב ד' איירי, היכי דייק בגמרא זו כנגד זו – אין, זו שלא כנגד זו – לא. אפילו מיפלגי טובא ליסתרי ע"י נסר ד', כדאמר לעיל(ד) דכי הוי כותל ד' אפילו מיפלגי טובא! ומפרש ר"ת: דלא איירי בנותן נסר מזו לזו, ודין חריץ נותן לגזוזטראות. דאם יש מזו לזו ד' – מערבין שנים ואין מערבין אחד כמו חריץ. אבל בפחות מד' – רגיל לפסוע מזו לזו כמו גבי חריץ, וכדאמר במס' שבת בפ' "הזורק" (דף ק:) גבי רקק של מים, דהיכא דלא הוי ארבעה טפחים – מפסע פסעי ליה. מש"ה, כי ליכא ד' מזו לזו – מערבין שנים, ואם רצו – מערבין אחד, אפילו היא מופלגת שלשה, כשהן זו כנגד זו. אבל זו שלא כנגד זו – אין מערבין אחד, כשמשוכות זו מזו שלשה, כדאמרינן בגמרא. [ופחות מכאן דקאמר במתניתין חוזר וקאי אנסר]: **והתנן** בית שמילאהו תבן או צרורות וביטלו בטל. כך היא הגירסא בכל הספרים, וכן פירש ר"ת. ור"י אומר דההיא משנה במסכת אהלות (פט"ו משנה ז), ואין כתוב שם תבן אלא עפר או צרורות. ולא גרס נמי התם: וביטלו בטל, והכי איתא התם: בית שמילאהו עפר או צרורות וביטלו, וכן כרי של תבואה או גל של צרורות אפילו כגלו של עכן, ואפילו טומאה בצד כלים – טומאה בוקעת ועולה טומאה בוקעת ויורדת. והתלמוד מביאה בקוצר, וכן דרך התלמוד בכמה מקומות. ואין לומר דהך דמייתי היא

רש"י

חָקַק לְהַשְׁלִים בַּכּוֹתֶל. סוּלָּם צַר, וְחָקַק בַּכּוֹתֶל מִכָּאן וּמִכָּאן כְּנֶגֶד חֲווּקֵי הַסּוּלָּם. לְהַשְׁלִים רׇחְבּוֹ בְּד': בְּכַמָּה. צָרִיךְ לְהַשְׁלִים הָרוֹחַב בְּגוֹבַהּ הַכּוֹתֶל: בַּעֲשָׂרָה. עַד עֲשָׂרָה יַשְׁלִימֶנּוּ, וְכֵיוָן דְּאִיכָּא בְּגוֹבַהּ עֲשָׂרָה רוֹחַב אַרְבָּעָה – הָוֵי בֵּיהּ שִׁיעוּר פֶּתַח וְאע"ג דְּגָבוֹהַּ כּוֹתֶל טוּבָא לֵית לָן בַּהּ: חָקַק כׇּל הַסּוּלָּם בַּכּוֹתֶל. כְּעֵין שְׁלִיבוֹת, וְרׇחְבּוֹ בְּמֶשֶׁךְ הַכּוֹתֶל אַרְבָּעָה: בְּכַמָּה. גּוֹבַהּ, צָרִיךְ לָחוֹק רוֹחַב אַרְבָּעָה: מְלֹא קוֹמָתוֹ. שֶׁל כּוֹתֶל צָרִיךְ שֶׁיְּהֵא מֶשֶׁךְ הַחֲווּקִין אַרְבָּעָה: הָתָם. כִּי אִיכָּא סוּלָּם מַגִּיעַ לְרֹאשׁ הַכּוֹתֶל – נוֹחַ לַעֲלוֹת בּוֹ. וּמִיהוּ לָא חָשֵׁיב לְמֶיהֱוֵי פֶּתַח בְּלֵיר מְרוּחָב ד'(א) הִלְכָּךְ, כִּי מְשַׁוֵּי לֵיהּ רוֹחַב אַרְבָּעָה בְּגוֹבַהּ עֲשָׂרָה – פִּיתְחָא הָוֵי. אֲבָל הָכָא – אֵין נוֹחַ לַעֲלוֹת כׇּל כָּךְ: מִסְתַּלֵּק לֵיהּ. נוֹחַ לַעֲלוֹת לָאָדָם: תִּיבָּעֵי לְרַבִּי. דְּאָמַר בְּפֶרֶק "בַּכֹּל מְעָרְבִין" [לעיל לג:]: הַנּוֹתֵן עֵירוּב תְּחוּמִין בָּאִילָן – קָנָה עֵירוּב. דְּהָתָם טַעְמָא מִשּׁוּם מִיקְנָא שְׁבִיתָה בֵּין הַשְּׁמָשׁוֹת הוּא וְדָבָר שֶׁהוּא מִשּׁוּם שְׁבוּת כְּגוֹן שִׁמּוּשׁ בִּמְחוּבָּר – לֹא גָּזְרוּ עָלָיו בֵּין הַשְּׁמָשׁוֹת. אֲבָל לְגַבֵּי עֵירוּבֵי חֲצֵירוֹת – טַעְמָא מִשּׁוּם דְּפֶתַח מְשַׁוֵּי לְהוּ חַד עַל יְדֵי עֵירוּב, וְאִי לָא חָזֵי לְתַשְׁמִישְׁתֵּיהּ כּוּלֵּי יוֹמָא – לָאו פִּתְחָא מִיקְרֵי. הִלְכָּךְ, לָא שָׁרָא לְהוּ עֵירוּבַיְיהוּ בֵּין הַשְּׁמָשׁוֹת: וְאַרְיָא רְבִיעַ עֲלֵיהּ. אִיסּוּר שְׁבוּת אוֹמֵר לָנוּ סוּרוּ. וּמִכׇּל מָקוֹם פֶּתַח (הָוֵי) שְׁמֵיהּ, וּמְשַׁוֵּי לְהוּ חַד לְהִשְׁתַּמֵּשׁ דֶּרֶךְ חוֹרִין, וְדַיּוֹ: עֲשָׂאוֹ לַאֲשֵׁירָה. אִילָן שֶׁעוֹבְדִין אוֹתוֹ, וְאָסוּר בַּהֲנָאָה. אִם תִּימְצֵי לוֹמַר בִּשְׁאָר אִילָן פֶּתַח הוּא, הָכָא דְּמַטְיָא לְהוּ הֲנָאָה עַל יָדֵיהּ מַאי: תִּיבָּעֵי לְר' יְהוּדָה. דְּאָמַר בְּפֶרֶק "בַּכֹּל מְעָרְבִין" בַּגְּמָרָא (דף לא.), רַבִּי יְהוּדָה אוֹמֵר: הַנּוֹתֵן אֶת עֵירוּבוֹ בַּקֶּבֶר – קָנָה עֵירוּב, וְאַף עַל גַּב דְּקֶבֶר אָסוּר בַּהֲנָאָה: הָכִי גָּרְסִינַן: הָתָם הוּא דְּבָתַר דְּקָנָה לֵיהּ עֵירוּב לָא נִיחָא לֵיהּ דְּלִינְטַר. לָא אִיכְפַּת לֵיהּ בִּשְׁמִירָתוֹ, וְאִישְׁתַּכַּח דְּלָא מִיתְהַנֵּי מִקִּיבְרָא אֶלָּא קְנִיַּית עֵירוּב לְחוּדֵיהּ, וְהַהִיא לָאו הֲנָאָה הִיא, כְּדִמְפָרֵשׁ הָתָם דְּאֵין מְעָרְבִין בִּתְחוּמִין אֶלָּא לִדְבַר מִצְוָה, וּמִצְוֹת לָאו לֵיהָנוֹת נִיתְּנוּ. אֲבָל עֵירוּבֵי חֲצֵירוֹת(ב) – לַהֲנָאָתוֹ הִיא, וְלָא לִדְבַר מִצְוָה, וְהָוְיָא הֲנָאָה: אוֹ דִּילְמָא. אע"ג דְּאָסוּר בַּהֲנָאָה – הָא לָא מִשְׁתַּמֵּשׁ בָּהּ מִידֵּי, וּפִיתְחָא שְׁמֵיהּ וְאַרְיָא הוּא דִּרְבִיעַ עֲלֵיהּ. וּמִכׇּל מָקוֹם הַחֲצֵירוֹת מְחוּבָּרִין: **מתני'** חָרִיץ. אָרוֹךְ הוּא, וּמַפְסִיק עַל פְּנֵי הֶחָצֵר כּוּלָּהּ: וְרוֹחַב ד'. טְפָחִים. דִּפְחוֹת מִכָּאן נוֹחַ לִפְסוֹעַ מִשְּׂפָתוֹ אֶל שְׂפָתוֹ: וַאֲפִילּוּ מָלֵא תֶּבֶן וְקַשׁ. לָאו סְתִימָה הִיא, דְּלָא מְבַטֵּיל לֵיהּ הָתָם, דְּסוֹפוֹ לִיטְּלוֹ: נָתַן עָלָיו נֶסֶר. מִשְּׂפָתוֹ לִשְׂפָתוֹ, כְּעֵין גֶּשֶׁר וְהָוֵי כְּפֶתַח: שְׁתֵּי גְּזוּזְטְרָאוֹת. נְסָרִין בּוֹלְטִין מִשְּׂפַת תִּקְרַת הָעֲלִיָּיה לִרְה"ר, וְקוֹרִין לוֹ אלדויי"ר. וְאִם יֶשְׁנָן זוֹ אֵצֶל זוֹ בִּשְׂפַתֵי עֲלִיּוֹת שֶׁל שְׁנֵי דִּיּוּרִין, וְנָתַן נֶסֶר רָחָב ד' כְּמִין גֶּשֶׁר מִזּוֹ לָזוֹ – הָוֵי נַמִי פֶּתַח: פָּחוֹת מִכָּאן. שֶׁאֵינוֹ רָחָב: **גמ'** לָא חָיֵיץ. לָא סָתֵים: וְהָתְנַן מַתְבֵּן שֶׁבֵּין שְׁתֵּי חֲצֵירוֹת כו'. גָּדִישׁ שֶׁל תֶּבֶן, וְקָתָנֵי "מְעָרְבִין שְׁנַיִם" – אַלְמָא: חָיֵיץ: לְעִנְיַן מְחִיצָה. אע"ג דְּעָתִיד לִיטְּלוֹ, כׇּל כַּמָּה דְּהָוֵי הָתָם – מְחִיצָּה הִיא, דְּהָא מַפְסִיק. מִידֵּי דַּהֲוָה אַעֲבִיטִין וְאוּכָּפוֹת וּכְלֵי בְּהֵמָה, דִּתְנַן בְּפֶרֶק קַמָּא (דף טו:) דְּמַקִּיפִין בָּהֶן: אֲבָל לְעִנְיַן חֲצִיצָה. לָחוֹץ בִּפְנֵי אֲוִיר הֶחָרִיץ, וְלִידּוֹן כְּסָתוּם, דִּמְשַׁוְּיָא לֵיהּ כְּאַרְעָא: אִי בַּטְלֵיהּ. לְהֶדְיָא, וְאָמַר: לָא שָׁקֵילְנָא לֵיהּ מֵהָכָא – בָּטֵיל, וְאִי לָא – לָא: וַאֲפִילּוּ בִּסְתָמָא. דְּלָא יָדְעִינַן אִי שָׁקֵיל אוֹ אִי לָא: בַּיִת. שֶׁטּוּמְאַת מֵת בְּתוֹכוֹ, וּמִילְּאָהוּ עָפָר אוֹ צְרוֹרוֹת וּבִיטְּלוֹ – מְבוּטָּל, וַהֲוֵי טוּמְאָה רְצוּצָה שֶׁאֵין לָהּ אֹהֶל לְעַצְמָהּ, וּבוֹקַעַת וְעוֹלָה עַד לָרָקִיעַ, וְהַמַּאֲהִיל עַד הַגַּג טָמֵא. וְכׇל טוּמְאָה שֶׁאֵין לָהּ אֹהֶל טֶפַח בּוֹקַעַת וְעוֹלָה עַד הָרָקִיעַ, כִּדְאָמַר בִּבְרָכוֹת בְּפֶרֶק "מִי שֶׁמֵּתוֹ"*. לא

רבינו חננאל

עוד שאלו חקק בכותל להשלים ד' טפחים בחלון בכמה אמר בעשרה. כלומר מכלל העשרה אמר לו חקקו כולו לכותל שהוא כעין פתח בכמה אמר לו מלא קומתו. ומ"ש דבחלון אמרת די לו בעשרה. חלון בכלל י' טפחים וזה מלא קומתו א"ל גבי חלון דאית ליה רווחא מאבראי שנכנס ויוצא מסתלק ליה מן החלון ודיו ד' טפחים בתוך י' הכא דחקק כל הכותל שויה כפתח ולא מסלק נפשיה מהכא ובעי למיעל ולמיפק בגויה. ואי איכא מלא קומתיה אין ואי לא לא. הא דבעי רב יוסף מרבה עשאו לאילן סולם מהו תיבעי לרבי דאמר כל דבר שמשום שבות כגון עליה באילן בשבת שהיא משום שבות לא גזרו עלי' בין השמשות הני מילי בין השמשות כגון העירוב אבל הכא דבעינן פיתחא כולי יומא לא. או דילמא אפי' לרבנן דפליגי עליה דר' פיתחא הוא ואריא רביע עליה. פי' האילן כמו פתח הוא כיון שיכול לעלות ולירד בו. וגזירת השבת שמנע מלעלות בו. עשאו לאשירה סולם מהו כו'. ר' יהודה דאמר אפי' בבית הקברות מפני שהוא יכול לחוץ ולוכל ואמרינן קסבר מותר לקנות בית באיסורי הנאה ורבנן פליגי עליה והוא מפורש בפרק בכל מערבין. ופשט ליה אילן מותר אשירה אסור מתקיף לה רב חסדא אדרבה איפכא מסתברא אשירה מותר אילן אסור כו' וקי"ל כוותיה דהא ר' יוחנן קאי כוותיה דאמר ר' יוחנן כל שאיסור שבת גרם לו אסור כל שאיסור דבר אחר גרם לו מותר. רב נחמן בר יצחק מתני לה בהדיא אילן פלוגתא דר' יוחנן ורבנן וקי"ל כרבנן: **מתני'** חריץ שבין ב' חצירות עמוק י' ורחב ד' מערבין שנים ואפי' מלא קש או תבן. ואסיקנא דתבן נמי חייץ והוה מחיצה מיהו לענין ביטול בחריץ אי בטליה אין ואי לא לא. ואקשינן עפר או צרורות ששנינו במשנתנו כי הן בטלין ואפי' בסתמא כלומר אע"פ שלא פירש כי ביטלם. והתניא (ב"ש לא תנן) [בית שמלאוהו תבן] או צרורות וביטלו הנה אי פריש כי ביטלו אין בסתמא

הגהות הב"ח

(א) רש"י ד"ה התם וכו' בליר מרוחב ארבעה בגובה עשרה הלכך: (ב) ד"ה הכי גרסינן וכו' אבל עירובי חצרות (להנאתו הוא) תא"מ ונ"ב ס"א לשוויא פיתחא הוא: (ג) תוס' ד"ה אפי' וכו' פגה שהטמינה בתבן: (ד) ד"ה וכן שתי וכו' כדאמר לעיל. נ"ב דף עז ע"ב:

גליון הש"ס

גמ' כל שאיסור דבר אחר גרם ליה מותר. עי' לקמן דף פ ע"ב תוד"ה אבל קורה:

רב נסים גאון

עד כאן לא קאמר רבי התם כל דבר שהוא משום שבות לא גזרו עליו בין השמשות. עיקר דברי רבי בפרק בכל מערבין (דף לג) וכבר פירשנום למעלה. תיבעי לר' יהודה תיבעי לרבנן תיבעי לר' יהודה עד כאן לא קאמר ר' יהודה דמותר לקנות בית באיסורי הנאה עיקרו בפרק בכל מערבין (דף לו) דתנן ר' יהודה אומר אפי' בבית הקברות מפני שהוא יכול לחוץ ולאכול:

שמעת

לא בִיטְּלוֹ — לָא. אָמַר רַב הוּנָא: מַאן תָּנָא אָהֳלוֹת — רַבִּי יוֹסֵי הִיא. אִי רַבִּי יוֹסֵי — אִיפְּכָא שָׁמְעִינַן לֵיהּ. דְּתַנְיָא: *רַבִּי יוֹסֵי אוֹמֵר: תֶּבֶן וְאֵין עָתִיד לְפַנּוֹתוֹ — הֲרֵי הוּא כִּסְתָם עָפָר וּבָטֵל, עָפָר וְעָתִיד לְפַנּוֹתוֹ — הֲרֵי הוּא כִּסְתָם תֶּבֶן וְלָא בְּטִיל! אֶלָּא אָמַר רַב אַסִי: מַאן תָּנָא עֵירוּבִין — רַבִּי יוֹסֵי הִיא. רַב הוּנָא בְּרֵיהּ דְּרַב יְהוֹשֻׁעַ אָמַר: טוּמְאָה אַשַּׁבָּת קָרָמֵית?! הָנַח אִיסּוּר שַׁבָּת, דַּאֲפִילּוּ אַרְנָקֵי נַמִי מְבַטֵּל אִינִישׁ. רַב אַשִׁי אָמַר: בַּיִת אַחָרִיץ קָא רָמֵית? בִּשְׁלָמָא חָרִיץ — לְמִיטַּיְימֵיהּ קָאֵי. אֶלָּא בַּיִת לְמִיטַּיְימֵיהּ קָאֵי?!§ נָתַן עָלָיו נֶסֶר שֶׁרוֹחַב ד'.§ אָמַר רָבָא: [א]לֹא שָׁנוּ אֶלָּא שֶׁנָּתַן לְרָחְבּוֹ, אֲבָל לְאָרְכּוֹ — אֲפִילּוּ כָּל שֶׁהוּא נַמִי, שֶׁהֲרֵי מִיעֲטוֹ מִד'.§ "וְכֵן שְׁתֵּי גְּזוּזְטְרָאוֹת זוֹ כְּנֶגֶד זוֹ".§ אָמַר רָבָא: [ב]הָא [(א)]דְּאָמַרְתְּ זוֹ כְּנֶגֶד זוֹ — אִין, זוֹ שֶׁלֹּא כְּנֶגֶד זוֹ — לָא. וְזוֹ לְמַעְלָה מִזּוֹ, נַמִי לָא אֲמַרַן אֶלָּא שֶׁיֵּשׁ בֵּין זֶה לָזֶה שְׁלֹשָׁה טְפָחִים, אֲבָל אֵין בֵּין זֶה לָזֶה שְׁלֹשָׁה — גְּזוּזְטְרָא עֲקוּמָּה הִיא.§

מתני' *[ג]מַתְבֵּן שֶׁבֵּין שְׁתֵּי חֲצֵירוֹת גָּבוֹהַּ עֲשָׂרָה טְפָחִים — מְעָרְבִין שְׁנַיִם, וְאֵין מְעָרְבִין אֶחָד. אֵלּוּ מַאֲכִילִין מִכָּאן, וְאֵלּוּ מַאֲכִילִין מִכָּאן. נִתְמַעֵט הַתֶּבֶן מֵעֲשָׂרָה טְפָחִים — מְעָרְבִין אֶחָד, וְאֵין מְעָרְבִין שְׁנַיִם.§ [לעיל עח:]

גמ' אָמַר רַב הוּנָא: [ד]וּבִלְבַד שֶׁלֹּא יִתֵּן לְתוֹךְ קוּפָּתוֹ וְיַאֲכִיל. וּלְאוֹקְמֵי שָׁרֵי? *וְהָאָמַר רַב הוּנָא, א"ר חֲנִינָא: [ה]מַעֲמִיד אָדָם אֶת בְּהֶמְתּוֹ עַל גַּבֵּי עֲשָׂבִים בַּשַּׁבָּת, וְאֵין מַעֲמִיד אָדָם אֶת בְּהֶמְתּוֹ עַל גַּבֵּי מוּקְצֶה בַּשַּׁבָּת! [ו]דְּקָאֵים לָהּ בְּאַפָּהּ וְאָזְלָה וְאָכְלָה. וְלֹא יִתֵּן לְתוֹךְ קוּפָּתוֹ תֶּבֶן? וְהָתַנְיָא: בַּיִת שֶׁבֵּין שְׁתֵּי חֲצֵירוֹת וּמִילְאָהוּ תֶּבֶן — מְעָרְבִין שְׁנַיִם, וְאֵין מְעָרְבִין אֶחָד. זֶה נוֹתֵן לְתוֹךְ קוּפָּתוֹ וְיַאֲכִיל, וְזֶה נוֹתֵן לְתוֹךְ קוּפָּתוֹ וְיַאֲכִיל. נִתְמַעֵט הַתֶּבֶן מִי' טְפָחִים — שְׁנֵיהֶם אֲסוּרִים. כֵּיצַד הוּא עוֹשֶׂה? נוֹעֵל אֶת בֵּיתוֹ וּמְבַטֵּל אֶת רְשׁוּתוֹ, הוּא אָסוּר וַחֲבֵירוֹ מוּתָּר. וְכֵן אַתָּה אוֹמֵר *בְּגוּב שֶׁל תֶּבֶן שֶׁבֵּין ב' תְּחוּמֵי שַׁבָּת. קָתָנֵי מִיהַת: זֶה נוֹתֵן לְתוֹךְ קוּפָּתוֹ וְיַאֲכִיל, וְזֶה נוֹתֵן לְתוֹךְ קוּפָּתוֹ וְיַאֲכִיל! אָמְרִי: בַּיִת כֵּיוָן דְּאִיכָּא (מְחִיצוֹת וְ)תִקְרָה כִּי מִיפְחִית — מִינְכְּרָא לֵיהּ מִלְּתָא. הָכָא — לָא מִינְכְּרָא לֵיהּ מִלְּתָא.§ "נִתְמַעֵט הַתֶּבֶן מֵעֲשָׂרָה טְפָחִים שְׁנֵיהֶן אֲסוּרִין".§ הָא עֲשָׂרָה — שָׁרֵי, וְאע"ג דְּמִידְּלְיָא תִקְרָה טוּבָא. שְׁמַע מִינָּהּ: *מְחִיצוֹת שֶׁאֵין מַגִּיעוֹת לַתִּקְרָה — שְׁמָן מְחִיצוֹת! אָמַר אַבָּיֵי: הָכָא בְּבַיִת שְׁלֹשָׁה עָשָׂר חָסֵר מַשֶּׁהוּ עָסְקִינַן, וְתֶבֶן עֲשָׂרָה. וְרַב הוּנָא בְּרֵיהּ דְּרַב יְהוֹשֻׁעַ אָמַר: אֲפִילּוּ תֵּימָא בְּבַיִת עֲשָׂרָה וְתֶבֶן

רש"י

לא בִיטְּלוֹ. לָא בָּטִיל, וְאֵין הַטּוּמְאָה בּוֹקַעַת לְמַעְלָה מִן הַגָּג, שֶׁיֵּשׁ לָהּ אֹהֶל לְעַצְמָהּ: רַבִּי יוֹסֵי הִיא. מִשּׁוּם דְּאַיְירֵי בָּהּ רַבִּי יוֹסֵי, כִּדְאָמְרִינַן לְקַמָּן נָקֵיט לָהּ: תֶּבֶן. מִלְּאוּהוּ תֶּבֶן, וְיוֹדְעִין אָנוּ שֶׁאֵינוֹ צָרִיךְ לוֹ, מִכָּל מָקוֹם לֹא בִּיטְּלוֹ בְּפֵירוּשׁ: הֲרֵי הוּא כִּסְתָם עָפָר. כְּעָפָר שֶׁאֵין אָנוּ יוֹדְעִין אִם עָתִיד לְפַנּוֹתוֹ אִי לֹא — דִּסְתָמֵיהּ בָּטִיל. אַלְמָא: לְר' יוֹסֵי עָפָר סְתָם בָּטִיל. סְתָם תֶּבֶן שֶׁאֵין אָנוּ יוֹדְעִין אִם יִצְטָרֵךְ לִיטְּלוֹ — לָא בָּטִיל: עָפָר. וְיוֹדְעִין אָנוּ שֶׁיְּפַנֵּהוּ, דְּלָאו סְתָמָא הוּא: הֲרֵי הוּא כִּסְתָם תֶּבֶן. שֶׁאֵין אָנוּ יוֹדְעִין אִם יְפַנֵּהוּ אִם לָאו, דִּסְתָמָא לָא בָּטִיל: הָנַח אִיסּוּר שַׁבָּת. כְּגוֹן מַתְנִי' כֵּיוָן דְּעָפָר אֵינוֹ נִיטָּל בְּשַׁבָּת — סְתָמֵיהּ בָּטִיל: אֲפִילּוּ אַרְנָקֵי. כִּיס מָלֵא מָעוֹת בָּטֵיל שָׁם. אֲבָל תֶּבֶן וְקַשׁ נִיטָּל לְמַאֲכַל בְּהֵמָה: לְמִיטַּיְימֵיהּ קָאֵי. הִלְכָּךְ, סְתָם עָפָר בָּטִיל לֵיהּ, וַאֲפִילּוּ לְרַבָּנַן: בַּיִת לְמִיטַּיְימֵיהּ קָאֵי. בִּתְמִיָּה: לא שָׁנוּ. דְּבָעֵי נֶסֶר ד': אֶלָּא שֶׁנְּתָנוֹ לְרָחְבּוֹ. אָרְכּוֹ שֶׁל דַּף לְרוֹחַב הֶחָרִיץ, מִשָּׂפָה לְשָׂפָה, כְּעֵין גֶּשֶׁר: אֲבָל לְאָרְכּוֹ. שֶׁנְּתָנוֹ לְאָרְכּוֹ שֶׁל חָרִיץ דַּף ד' אוֹרֶךְ עַל גַּבֵּי יְתֵדוֹת אֵצֶל שְׂפָתוֹ, סָתַם קְצָת רוֹחַב הֶחָרִיץ וּמִיעֲטוֹ מִד': אֲפִילּוּ כָּל שֶׁהוּא. שֶׁהָיְתָה דַּף קְצָרָה[(ב)] אֲפִילּוּ אֵינָהּ אֶלָּא כְּאֶצְבַּע — הֲרֵי מִיעֲטוֹ לְרוֹחַב הֶחָרִיץ מֵאַרְבָּעָה בְּמֶשֶׁךְ מִדַּת הַפֶּתַח, וּמַתְנִי' רָחָב ד' תְּנַן: זוֹ שֶׁלֹּא כְּנֶגֶד זוֹ. שֶׁהָיְתָה זוֹ בּוֹלֶטֶת לְרה"ר יוֹתֵר מֵחֲבֶרְתָּהּ לָא סַגֵּי לְהוּ בְּנֶסֶר אַרְבָּעָה: אֵין בֵּין זוֹ לָזוֹ ג'. אֵין רְחוֹקָה זוֹ מִזּוֹ שְׁלֹשָׁה:

מתני' מַתְבֵּן. גָּדִישׁ שֶׁל תֶּבֶן, וּמַפְסִיק עַל פְּנֵי רוֹחַב כָּל הַחֲצֵירוֹת: מַאֲכִילִין. מִן הַתֶּבֶן לִבְהֶמְתָּן, וְלָא חָיְישִׁינַן דִּילְמָא מְמַעֵיט תֶּבֶן מִי' דְּהָוְיָא לָהּ חֲדָא רְשׁוּתָא, וְאָסְרִי אַהֲדָדֵי, וְלָא מַסְּקִי אַדַּעְתַּיְיהוּ וּמְטַלְטְלִי בֶּחָצֵר. לְהָא לָא חָיְישִׁינַן, דְּהָא אֲפִילּוּ אִימְעִיט, אִי לָא הָוֵי מִיעוּט עַל פְּנֵי עֶשֶׂר אַמּוֹת וְיוֹתֵר — לָא אָסְרִי. דְּהָא עַד עֶשֶׂר פִּיתְחָא הָוֵי, וְאֵין בְּהֵמָה מְמַעֶטֶת כָּל כָּךְ בַּאֲכִילָתָהּ בְּשַׁבָּת אֶחָד: נִתְמַעֵט הַתֶּבֶן. עַל[(ג)] כָּל הֶחָצֵר — אוֹ בְּמֶשֶׁךְ י' אַמּוֹת וְעוֹד: מְעָרְבִין אֶחָד. אִם נִתְמַעֵט בְּחוֹל:

גמ' שֶׁלֹּא יִתֵּן. בְּיָדַיִם לְתוֹךְ קוּפָּתוֹ, דִּלְמָא שָׁקֵיל טוּבָא וּמְמַעֵיט לֵיהּ מֵעֲשָׂרָה, וְקָא מְטַלְטֵל בֶּחָצֵר הָאוֹסֶרֶת. וּמַאֲכִילִין דְּקָתָנֵי בְּמַתְנִי' — שֶׁהַבְּהֵמָה בָּאָה וְאוֹכֶלֶת, וְהָתָם לָא חָיְישִׁינַן לְדִלְמָא מְמַעֵיט, דִּבְהֵמָה קָלֵי קָלֵי אָכְלָה. לִישָּׁנָא אַחֲרִינָא: לֹא יִתֵּן לְתוֹךְ קוּפָּתוֹ — מִשּׁוּם דְּמוּקְצֶ' מֵאֶתְמוֹל לִמְחִיצָה זוֹ: וּלְאוֹקְמֵי. בְּהֶמְתּוֹ עַל הַתֶּבֶן כְּדֵי לֶאֱכוֹל — שָׁרֵי, וְלָא גָּזְרִינַן דִּילְמָא שָׁקֵיל בְּיָדַיִם וְסָפֵי לָהּ. אַלְמָא: חָמִיר עֲלֵיהּ אִיסּוּר דְּרַבָּנַן וְלֹא עָבַר עֲלֵיהּ: וְהָא א"ר חֲנִינָא מַעֲמִיד אָדָם אֶת בְּהֶמְתּוֹ ע"ג עֲשָׂבִים. מְחוּבָּרִים, לֶאֱכוֹל. וְלָא חָיְישִׁינַן דִּלְמָא עָקַר בְּיָדַיִם וּמַאֲכִיל לָהּ, דְּהָא חֲמִיר עֲלֵיהּ אִיסּוּר שַׁבָּת. אֲבָל אִיסּוּר מוּקְצֶה — קִיל לֵיהּ, וְחָיְישִׁינַן דִּלְמָא שָׁקֵיל בְּיָדַיִם וְסָפֵי לָהּ. ה"נ, כֵּיוָן דְּאִיסּוּרָא דְּרַבָּנַן הוּא דְּאִיכָּא — נֵיחוּשׁ: דְּקָאֵים בְּאַפָּהּ. מַתְנִי' לָאו דְּמוֹקִים לָהּ עֲלָהּ בְּיָדַיִם, אֶלָּא קָאֵי בְּאַפָּהּ שֶׁלֹּא תֵּלֵךְ בְּמָקוֹם אַחֵר, וְאִיהִי אָזְלָה וְאָכְלָה — וּכְוָלֵי הַאי לָא גְּזוּר רַבָּנַן: בַּיִת שֶׁבֵּין שְׁתֵּי חֲצֵירוֹת. וּשְׁנֵי בָּתִּים מִשְּׁתֵּי הַחֲצֵירוֹת פְּתוּחִין לוֹ: כֵּיצַד הוּא עוֹשֶׂה. לְהַתִּיר מִיהַת אֶת הָאֶחָד. נוֹעֵל אֶת בֵּיתוֹ הַפָּתוּחַ לְאוֹתוֹ בַּיִת, וּמְבַטֵּל אֶת רְשׁוּתוֹ וּלְקַמָּן [עמו' ב] פָּרֵיךְ: תַּרְתֵּי לָמָּה לִי נְעִילָה וּבִיטּוּל: הוּא אָסוּר. לְהוֹצִיא מֵאוֹתוֹ בַּיִת לֶחָצֵר שֶׁלּוֹ, שֶׁהֲרֵי בִּיטֵּל רְשׁוּתוֹ, וְכָל הַבַּיִת כְּחָצֵר אַחֶרֶת הוּא: בְּגוֹב שֶׁבֵּין שְׁנֵי תְּחוּמֵי שַׁבָּת. בּוֹר רָחָב לְהַכְנִיס בּוֹ תֶּבֶן, וְאִם בֵּין שְׁנֵי תְּחוּמִין הוּא, חֶצְיוֹ בִּתְחוּם עִיר זוֹ וְחֶצְיוֹ בִּתְחוּם עִיר זוֹ — אֵלּוּ נוֹטְלִין וְאוֹכְלִין מִתּוֹךְ תְּחוּמָן בְּיוֹם טוֹב, וְכֵן אֵלּוּ. וְאֵין חוֹשְׁשִׁין שֶׁמָּא אֵלּוּ יִקְחוּ מִן הַתְּחוּם הַשֵּׁנִי: כֵּיוָן דְּאִיכָּא תִּקְרָה. נִיכָּר שֶׁגַּג הַגָּדִישׁ מִתְרַחֵק מִן הַתִּקְרָה, וְאִי מְפַחִית מֵעֲשָׂרָה — רָמֵי אַנַּפְשֵׁיהּ וּפָרֵישׁ. וּלְלִישָּׁנָא דְּמוּקְצֶה נַמִי אֵין אָסוּר מִשּׁוּם מוּקְצֶה אֶלָּא מִי' וּלְמַטָּה, דְּכָל מֵעֲשָׂרָה וּלְמַעְלָה — לָאו *[כּוֹרַת] מְחִיצָּה הִיא. אֲבָל מַתְנִי' דְּקָאֵי מַתְבֵּן בֶּחָצֵר וְאֵין עָלָיו תִּקְרָה — לָא מִינְכְּרָא מִילְּתָא: שָׁמְעַתְּ מִינָּהּ מְחִיצוֹת. הַמַּפְסִיקוֹת בַּבַּיִת, וְאֵין מַגִּיעוֹת לַתִּקְרָה — שְׁמָן מְחִיצוֹת, וּתְיוּבְתָּא דְּמַאן דְּאָמַר בְּפֶרֶק "הַדָּר" (לעיל דף עב.) גַּבֵּי ה' חֲבוּרוֹת שֶׁשָּׁבְתוּ בִּטְרַקְלִין דִּבְמְחִיצּוֹת י' שָׁרוּ ב"ה, וּמִשּׁוּם דְּאֵין מַגִּיעוֹת לַתִּקְרָה לָא מִפַּלְגֵי דִּיוּרִין:

תוספות

היא ברייתא. דאין להביא ברייתא כיון שיכול להביא המשנה. ומה שאומר בפ"ק דסוכה (דף ז.): תבן ואין עתיד לפנותו, ועפר סתם – מחלוקת ר' יוסי ורבנן. אע"ג דבמתני' דאהלות לא איירי רבנן מידי בתבן, מ"מ מכל שכן דעפר שמעינן דבעי ביטול. והא דפשיטא ליה תבן וביטלו הוה מיעוט לרבנן – שפיר שמעינן מכל שכן דכרי דתבואה, דמהני ביטול. והא דקאמר התם, עפר סתם מחלוקת רבי יוסי ורבנן – הוה מצי למימר נמי: עפר ואין עתיד לפנותו. דבהא נמי פליגי רבנן, ואמרי: דלא בטיל אלא אם כן ביטלו ואין עתיד לפנותו לאו היינו ביטלו, כדמוכח התם. אלא משום רבי יוסי נקט עפר סתם, ולא חש להאריך ולמינקט תרוייהו:

מאן תנא אהלות ר' יוסי היא. אע"פ שלא היה יודע ברייתא זו דקא מייתי – יודע היה שרבי יוסי דיבר על ההיא משנה דאהלות. וכי האי גוונא איכא בפרק קמא דיומא (דף יד:) גבי מאן תנא תמיד – ר"ש איש המצפה היא:

הרי הוא כסתם עפר ובטל. וטומאה בוקעת ועולה, כדקתני באהלות. וא"ת: והא ר' יוסי קסבר דטומאה טמונה אינה בוקעת בפ' "העור והרוטב" (חולין דף קכה:), דקאמר ר' יוסי חבילי המטה וסריגי החלונות שפירשו על פני המת באויר, הנוגע שלא כנגד הנקב – טהור. ומוקי לה בסמוכין לו בפחות מטפח! ואומר ר"י: דמ"מ מהני ביטול, לענין שלא יבא טומאה לכלים שבצידו. והא דא"ר יוסי בפרק "הישן" (סוכה כא:): במקומו היה עומד וממלא, מפני קבר התהום – היינו דוקא בקבר, דכתיב קרא (במדבר יט): "או בקבר" שהמאהיל על הקבר טמא. אבל בעלמא קסבר ר' יוסי דאינה בוקעת וטהור:

דקאים לה באפה ואזלה. ואם תאמר: אם כן מאי איריא דנקט רב הונא שלא יתן לתוך קופתו ויאכיל? כיון דאסור אפילו להעמידה, אע"ג דלא מטלטל! וי"ל: דאי הוה נקט ליה אסור להעמיד – לא הוה ידעינן מאי טעמא, כל כמה דלא אשמעינן שאסור לטלטל. הלכך אשמעינן שאסור ליתן לתוך קופתו, משום דלמא מיפחית ולאו אדעתא וממילא ידעינן דאסור להעמיד:

וכן אתה מוצא בגוב של תבן. פירש בקונטרס: גוב = בור. ולא שייך בור גבי תבן, ויש מפרשים לשון קש וגבבא:

שמע מינה מחיצות שאין מגיעות לתקרה שמן מחיצות. בתמיה. פי': במחילות עראי כי הך. ולעיל (עב:) פסקינן כרבי יהודה הסבר, דאמר לב"ה עירוב אחד לכולן במחילות שאינן מגיעות לתקרה, והתם נמי במחילות עראי איירי, כדפי' התם(ד):

דכל

עין משפט נר מצוה

ל א מיי' פ"ג מהלכות עירובין הלכה יג טוש"ע א"ח סי' שעב סעיף יז:

לא ב מיי' שם הלכה יד טור ש"ע א"ח סי' שעג:

לב ג ד מיי' שם הלכה ג טוש"ע א"ח סי' שעב סעיף יט:

לג ה מיי' פכ"א מהל' שבת הלכה לו סמג לאוין סה טוש"ע א"ח סי' שכל סעיף יג:

לד ו מיי' שם וטוש"ע שם וסי' שעב סעיף יט:

רבינו חננאל

בסתמא לא בטיל. ופריק רב הונא מאן תנא אהלות ר' יוסי ופליג אתנא דידן איני והא ר' יוסי איפכא קתני (דתנן) [דתניא בתוספתא באהלות פ' [ט"ו] ר' יוסי אומר תבן ואין עתיד לפנותו הרי הוא כסתם עפר ובטיל. עפר (ואין עתיד) [ועתיד] לפנותו הרי הוא כסתם תבן ואינו בטל קתני מיהת הרי הוא כסתם עפר ובטל מכלל דר' יוסי סבר עפר סתם בטל אלא תנא דעירובין הוא ר' יוסי ופליג עליה תנא דאהלו' רב הונא בריה דרב יהושע א' גבי איסור שבת אפי' ארנקי בטיל וכ"ש עפר או צרורות רב אסי אמר בית אחריץ לא רמינן חריץ למטמייהו קאי הלכך סתמא בטיל אבל בית לאו למימליה קאי הלכך אי פריש דבטליה אין אי לא לא: מתני' נתן עליו נסר שרחב ד' טפחים כו' אמר רבה לא שנו שאם נתן בחריץ נסר פחות מד' טפחים מערבין שנים ואין מערבין אחד אלא בזמן שהושיט זה הנסר מזה הצד לצדו האחר של חריץ לרחבו אבל אם נתן זה הנסר לארכו של חריץ מצד אחר של חריץ אפי' פחות מד' מערבין אחד שהרי מיעט החריץ מד' טפחים לפי שרחב החריץ שנינו כי הוא [רוחב ד' ואם] נתן בו זה הנסר לארכו [הרי] מיעט רחבו מד' טפחים אמר רבא הא דתנן וכן ב' גזוזטראות זו כנגד זו מותר אבל זו שלא כנגד זו או למעלה מזו [לא] ולא אמרן [אלא] שיש ביניהן ג' טפחים אבל אין [ביניהן] ג' טפחים עמוקה היא ושרי: מתני' מתבן שבין ב' חצירות גבוה י' טפחים מערבין שנים ואין מערבין אחד. אלו מאכילין מיכן ואלו מאכילין מיכן. ואוקימנא מתבן שבין ב' חצירות גבוה י' טפחים לא שרי לכל חד וחד מינייהו אלא למיקם באפי בהמתו ממילא ואזלא ואכלה אבל ליתן תבן לתוך קופה או להעמידה על המתבן ולהאכילה אסור. ואם הוא מתבן בתוך הבית גבוה י' טפחים והבית בין שתי החיצונות זה נותן לתוך קופתו ומאכיל וזה נותן לתוך קופתו ומאכיל. ומ"ש בית דאית ליה מחיצות ותקרה כי מיפחית התבן מי' טפחים מינכרא מילתא דחזי ליה דקא מירחק מן התקרה וכיון דתתמעט מעשרה טפחים ידע דתרווייהו אסירי ואי בעי נועל פתח ביתו ומבטל רשותו והוא אסור וחבירו מותר. וכן אתה אומר בגיב של תבן. פי' תבן מעובה כמין חבילות שבין ב' תחומי שבת. דין (גבוה) [גיב של תבן] ודין מתבן שבין ב' חצירות אחד הוא ולא שרו אלא למיקם באפי בהמתו ותיזיל היא ותיכול. אבל לתת לתוך קופתו או להאכילה הוא לא (דבר) [דכר] מפחית

מסורת הש"ס

[תוספתא דאהלות פט"ו] סוכה ז.

שבת קכב.

[גי' הערוך ע' גב א' בגיב של תבן פי' תבן מעובה כמו חבילות]

רש"ל מ"ז

[לעיל עב.]

[נ"ל טורך]

הגהות הב"ח

(א) גמ' אמר רבא הא דתנן וכן שתי גזוזטראות וכו' זו כנגד זו אין זו שלא כנגד זו או זו למעלה מזו לא וזו למעלה מזו נמי: (ב) רש"י ד"ה אפילו כו' ואפילו אינה: (ג) ד"ה נתמעט התבן על פני רוחב כל החצר: (ד) תוס' סד"ה שמע וכו' כדפירש התם. נ"ב בד"ה במחילות:

גליון הש"ס

גמ' מאן תנא עירובין ר' יוסי היא. עיין לקמן דף פד ע"ב תד"ה כור מאי איכא למימר:

רב נסים גאון

שמעת מינה מחיצות שאין מגיעות לתקרה הויאן מחיצות הוויא דהא מילתא בפרק הדר עם הגוי (דף עב) פליגו בה ר' חייא ור' שמעון בר' חד אמר מחלוקת במחיצות שאין מגיעות לתקרה ויש בה עוד הדברים של ענין דיורין הבאין בשבת:

ותבן שבעה ומשהו. דכל *פחות משלשה כלבוד דמי. בשלמא לאביי — היינו דקתני "מעשרה". אלא לרב הונא בריה דרב יהושע, מאי מעשרה? מתורת עשרה.§ "שניהן אסורין".§ שמע מינה: דיורין הבאין בשבת *אסורין. דלמא דאימעט מאתמול.§ "כיצד הוא עושה? נועל את ביתו ומבטל רשותו".§ תרתי?! הכי קאמר: או נועל את ביתו, או מבטל את רשותו. ואיבעית אימא: לעולם תרתי, כיון דדש ביה — אתי לטלטולי.§ "הוא אסור וחבירו מותר".§ פשיטא! לא צריכא דהדר אידך ובטיל ליה לחבריה. והא קמ"ל: *דאין מבטלין וחוזרין ומבטלין.§ "וכן אתה אומר בגוב של תבן שבין שני תחומי שבת".§ פשיטא! לא צריכא לרע"ק *דאמר: תחומין דאורייתא. מהו דתימא: ליגזור דלמא אתי לאיחלופי — קמ"ל.§

מתני' *כיצד משתתפין במבוי? [א]מניח את החבית, ואומר: הרי זו לכל בני מבוי. ומזכה להן [ב]על ידי בנו ובתו הגדולים, וע"י עבדו ושפחתו העברים, וע"י אשתו. אבל אינו מזכה לא ע"י בנו ובתו הקטנים, ולא ע"י עבדו ושפחתו הכנענים, מפני שידן כידו.§

גמ' אמר רב יהודה: [ג]חבית של שיתופי מבואות — צריך להגביה מן הקרקע טפח. אמר רבא: הני תרתי מילי סבי דפומבדיתא אמרינהו. חדא — הא. אידך: *[ד]המקדש, אם טעם מלא לוגמיו — יצא, ואם לאו — לא יצא. אמר רב חביבא: הא נמי סבי דפומבדיתא אמרינהו. *דאמר רב יהודה, אמר שמואל: [ה]עושין מדורה לחיה בשבת. סבור מינה: לחיה — אין, לחולה — לא. בימות הגשמים — אין, בימות החמה — לא. איתמר, אמר רב חייא בר אבין, אמר שמואל: [ו]הקיז דם ונצטנן — עושין לו מדורה בשבת, ואפילו בתקופת תמוז. אמר אמימר: הא נמי סבי דפומבדיתא אמרינהו. *דאיתמר: איזו היא אשירה סתם? אמר רב: כל שכומרין שומרין אותה, ואין

רש"י

תבן שבעה ומשהו. ולקמן פריך: הא "נתמעט מעשרה" קתני: שניהן אסורין. לעיל קאי, דקתני נתמעט התבן מעשרה – אסרי אהדדי: שמע מינה דיורין הבאין בשבת. כי הכא, דאמש לא היו דיורין אלו שולטין מן התבן והלאה, ועכשיו הן שולטין בכל הבית: אסורין. ולא אמר: שבת הואיל והותרה הותרה. ופלוגתא היא בפ"ק (דף יז.)(א) גבי שיירא שחנתה בבקעה*: או נועל את ביתו. דגלי דעתיה דאסתלק מהכא, והיינו ביטוליה: ואיבעית אימא לעולם תרתי. ולענין היתר חבירו – בחדא סגי, ומיהו לדידיה בעי למיעבד הרחקה, דלא ליתי לטלטולי. והוא הדין דסבירא ליה להאי תנא בכל מבטלי רשות דבעי לנעול: לא צריכא אלא דהדר. האי מקבל רשותו, ובטיל ליה רשותיה להאי מבטל, לאחר שעשה צרכיו: פשיטא. מאי אולמיה דתחומין מחיצות, הא והא דרבנן היא: דרע"ק. במסכת סוטה בפרק "כשם" (דף כז.): מהו דתימא ניגזור דלמא אתי לאיחלופי. וליקח מתחום שאינו שלהן, וקא עברי אדאורייתא: מתני' מניח את החבית. משלו אם ירצה: ומזכה להן על ידי בנו ובתו. ואומר להן: קבלו חבית זו וזכו בה לשם כל בני מבוי: שידן כידו. ולא זכייה היא: גמ' צריך להגביה מן הקרקע. כשהוא מזכה אותה להן. דכל כמה דמנחא ברשותיה לא הויא זכייה. והכי תני לה בתוספתא (פ"ו): אם משלהן – אין צריך לזכות, ואם משלו – המשליח מגביה מן הקרקע, ואומר זכיתי *לכם: סבי דפומבדיתא. רב יהודה וישיבתו, בשילהי פ"ק דסנהדרין*: מדורה. היסק גדול: איזו היא אשירה סתם. אף על גב דלא חזינן ליה דפלחוה, מחזקינן לה בהכי:

תוספות

דכל פחות מג' כלבוד דמי. ולאביי, אע"ג דבעלמא מהני לבוד בכי האי גוונא, כדאשכחן לעיל (דף טז:) גבי חבלים – הכא לא חשיב ליה. דהא מחילות שאין מגיעות נמי לא מחשבי להו הכא:

שמע מינה דיורין הבאין בשבת אסורין. יש דיורין הבאין בשבת שאסורין – כגון ישראל וגר ששרויין *בדירה אחת, ומת גר מבעוד יום, כדאמר בפרק "הדר" (לעיל דף ע:) והכא בדיורין הבאין בשבת על ידי נפילת מחילה שבין שתי חצירות איירי, [דפליגי ביה רב ושמואל], ומיבעיא ליה לרב אושעיא בפרק "כל גגות" (לקמן דף צג.):

ואיבעית אימא לעולם תרתי. פי' בקונטרס: ולענין היתר חבירו – בחדא סגי. מיהו, לדידיה בעי למיעבד הרחקה דלא ליתי לטלטולי והוא הדין דסבירא ליה להאי תנא בכל מבטלין רשות, דצריך לנעול. וקצת תימה באנשי חצר ששכח אחד מהן ולא עירב, היאך יכנס ויצא אם לא דרך חצר, אם צריך לנעילת דלת? ושמא י"ל: דבעי נעילת דלת, ובשעה שיצטרך להיכנס ולצאת – יפתח וינעול אחר כך. וקצת נראה דדווקא הכא צריך נעילת דלת. שעד עתה הורגלו לטלטל בלא שום עירוב, שהיה תבן מפסיק, ואיכא למיחש כדאמר כיון דדש ביה, אתי לטלטולי. אבל באנשי חצר ששכח אחד מהן ולא עירב, ולא הורגל לטלטל באותה חצר אלא על ידי עירוב או ביטול רשות – הלכך לא בעי נעילת דלת. ונראה דהכא נמי לא בעו לנעילת דלת אלא שבת ראשונה שאחר המיעוט, כיון שבשבת שעברה היו מטלטלין שם בלא עירוב ובלא ביטול רשות, אבל לשבת אחרת לא יצטרכו עוד לנעול. דאין סברא שעד לעולם יהא צריך נעילה, ולא נשוה אותו לשאר ביטול בשביל שהיתה שם מחילה מפסקת פעם אחת. ולעיל בפרק "הדר" (דף סח.) דאמר להו רבא: פנו לי מאני מדי גברי לבי נשי. [ופי' שם הקונטרס: דפינה כליו, שלא יבוא להוציא משם לחצר], משמע קצת דחיישינן שמא יטלטל. ומיהו, אדרבה משמע דלא הוו בעו נעילת דלת. וגם רבא שצוה לפנות כליו משמע דווקא לפי שביטל הוצרך לפנות, שלא יוציא בשוגג ויאסור. אבל אם לא היה מבטל – לא היה צריך לא הוא ולא שאר בני החצר לפנות כלים, ולא לנעול. ומיהו, מצי למימר כמו שפי' בקונטרס: דליכא למיחש דלמא אתי לטלטולי אלא כשרואה אחרים מטלטלין. ויותר נראה הטעם דלמא יוציא ויחזיק. ונראה דאם הלכה כר' יהודה, *דאמר בשוגג אינו אוסר – אין נראה שיהא טעם שלא יוציא במזיד ויאסור, דאין לחוש שיוציא במזיד באיסור:

והא קמ"ל דאין מבטלין וחוזרין ומבטלין. ומהך ברייתא לא תיקשי לרב דאמר פ' "הדר" (לעיל דף סח:) חוזרין ומבטלין, דהוא מוקי מילתיה כתנאי כדקאמר רב ששת התם:

ומזכה להם על ידי בנו ובתו הגדולים כו'. אומר ר"ת: דלר' יוחנן, דאמר בפ"ק דב"מ (ד' יב:) גבי מציאה, לא גדול גדול ממש, והוא הדין הכא, וצריך ליזהר שלא לזכות העירוב ע"י בנו הגדול הסמוך לשלחנו, דידו כיד אביו הוא. ואע"ג דשמואל פליג עליה התם, ואומר: גדול – גדול ממש, קיימא לן כרבי יוחנן לגבי שמואל. ואין לתמוה לרבי יוחנן היאך יש יד לקטן לזכות, דהא מה נפסק אמה העבריה [נמי] קטנה היא. דלאי אתיא שערות – מאי בעיא גביה, וקתני דמזכה על ידה. ואע"ג דבעלמא אין קטן זוכה לאחרים – *שאני שיתופי מבואות דרבנן. והכי איתא בהדיא בפרק "התקבל" (גיטין דף סד:). ואם תאמר: אמה העבריה היכי זוכה? והלא היא סמוכה על שלחן רבה! ואר"ת: דבשכרה קא אכלה. ולר"י נראה: דלא מהני טעמא דסמוך על שלחן – אלא בבנו שרגיל לפרנסו, ואם לא יהיה מציאתו לאביו יש לחוש שלא יתן לו מזונות. אבל שאר בני אדם הסמוכים על שלחנו של בעל הבית – אין מציאתן שלו. ומיהו, בתו אפילו נערה, ואינה סמוכה על שלחנו – מציאתה לאביה משום איבה, ודילמא מסר לה למנוול ומוכה שחין, כדאמר בפ' "נערה" בכתובות (דף מז.) דטעמא דאיבה שייך אפילו באינה סמוכה ואפילו בנערה:

ועל ידי אשתו. בסוף נדרים (דף פח:) מוקי לה שיש לה בית באותו מבוי, דמגו דזכייה לנפשה זכייה נמי לאחריני. אבל אין לה בית – לא, דיד אשה כיד בעלה. ואם תאמר: אי במקבלת פרס – הא אינה צריכה לזכות לעצמה, כדאמר פרק "הדר" (לעיל עג.) דרבי יהודה בן בתירא מתיר בנשים ואוסר בעבדים. ואע"ג דהתם בעירוב בא אצלו, הכא נמי: כיון שהוא מזכה להם – מסתמא מניח העירוב בביתו. ואי אינה מקבלת פרס – אפילו אין לה בית נמי תזכה להם, דאין ידה כיד בעלה. וי"ל: דהכא כשנותן לה הבעל מעות למזונות. וכי האי גוונא לא חשיבא מקבלת פרס, אלא אם כן הביאה המאכל והמשתה מתוך ביתו ואוכלת. אי נמי: הכא במספקת במעשה ידיה. ולענין מציאה ולכל דבר הוי ידה כיד בעלה, דכסמוכה על שלחנו דמיא ולענין מקבלת פרס – לא דמיא. ואם תאמר: א"כ, בנו ובתו הקטנים יזכו לאחרים בעירובם כי האי גוונא על ידי מיגו כשיש להם בית באותה חצר, וכן עבדו ושפחתו הכנענים – דהא ודאי יש להם זכייה לענין עירוב, כיון שאוסרין כשיש להם חצר או בית כדאמר לעיל דאוסר בעבדים ומתיר בנשים. ולענין עירובי תחומין דאמרינן בריש "כיצד משתתפין" (לקמן דף פב.) שהרב מערב על ידם, אטו אם ליתיה לרבם נאמר שלא יוכלו לערב? סתמא דמלתא תקינו להו רבנן זיכוי לענין עירוב. ונראה לר"י: דלפי המסקנא דנדרים אתי כר' יהודה בן בבא, דמתיר בעבדים ואוסר בנשים. לעיל בפרק "הדר" [עג.] ותרווייהו מקבלי פרס, ואשתו צריכה לערב, אבל עבד אין צריך לערב:

צריך להגביה מן הקרקע טפח. מכאן אין להוכיח דהגבהה סגי בטפח* – דשאני שיתופי מבואות דרבנן. תדע, דהא לא קאתי הכא לאשמעינן דין הגבהה בכל מקום*:

אם טעם מלא לוגמיו. פירש ר"ת: דהא מלא לוגמיו לאו דווקא מלא לוגמיו, אלא ר"ל כדמפרש בפ' בתרא דיומא (דף פ.): כל שאילו מסלקו לצד אחד ונראה כמלא לוגמא, ובפ' בתרא דיומא (שם) מוכח דמלא לוגמיו נפיש מרביעית, וב"ערבי פסחים" (דף קח:) אמר דבארבע כוסות יש שיעור רביעית, וכוס של קידוש אחד. מהן והיך יטעום מלא לוגמא? הא אין בו כל כך:

רב

עין משפט נר מצוה

לה א מיי' פ"א מהלכות עירובין הלכה יז סמג עשין א טוש"ע א"ח סי' שסו סעיף ט:

[נ"ל במגורה]

לו ב מיי' שם הלכה כ וטוש"ע שם סעיף י:

לז ג מיי' שם הלכה יז וטוש"ע שם סעיף ט:

לח ד מיי' פכ"ט מהל' שבת הלכה ז סמג עשין כט טוש"ע א"ח סי' רעא סעיף יג:

לט ה ו מיי' פ"ב מהל' שבת הלכה יד סמג לאוין סה טוש"ע א"ח סי' שכח סעיף יח וסי' של סעיף ו:

רבינו חננאל

מפחית מי' טפחים כיון דליכא תקרה לא מינכרא מילת': ואוקימנא דהאי בית דאית ביה האי תיבנא גובהו י"ג טפחים חסר משהו והתבן י' טפחים (חסר משהו) דכל פחות מג' כלבוד דמי שנמצא התבן כאילו מגיע עד שמי תקרה דבעינן מחיצות המגיעות לתקרה מדקתני הוא אסור וחבירו מותר ש"מ דקסבר אין מבטלין וחוזרין ומבטלין. וכן אתה אומר בגיב של תבן שבין ב' תחומי שבת פשיטה לא צריכא לר' עקיבא דאמר תחומין דאורייתא: **מתני'** כיצד משתתפין במבוי כו' אמר רבה חבית של שיתופי מבוי צריך להגביהה מן הקרקע טפח והמקדש אם טעם מלא לוגמיו יצא. ואם לאו לא יצא. הני מילי תרי סבי דפומבדיתא אמרוה. שמואל אמר (אף) עושין מדורה לחיה בשבת סבור מינה לחיה אין לחולה לא אמר שמואל הקיז דם ונצטנן עושין לו מדורה אפי' בתקופת תמוז כו'. איזו היא אשירה אמר רב כל שהכומרים שומרין אותה

רב נסים גאון

לא צריכא לר' עקיבא דאמר תחומין דאורייתא כבר פירשנוה למעלה דעיקר דברי ר' עקיבא במס' סוטה (דף כז):

[וע"ע תוס' ב"ק כט: ד"ה אלא ותוס' כתובות לא. ד"ה לאי וד"ה נימא ותוס' קידושין כו. ד"ה אי נמי]

מסורת הש"ס

לעיל טז.

[נ"ל ומת אחד מהן ע' מהרש"א על תוס' ד"ה ש"מ]

בד"י אוסרין וכהן פי' שם ברש"י ותוס'

[לעיל סח.]

[לקמן קג. סוטה כז: וש"נ]

לעיל עג: נדרים פח: גיטין סד:

נ"ל להם

[דף יז:]

שבת קכט.

ע"ז מח.

[לעיל סט.]

הא אמרי' בפ' התקבל שאני שיתופי מבואות דרבנן וא"ת אמה וכו' כ"ל רש"ל

[קידושין כה:]

הגהות הב"ח

(א) רש"י ד"ה אסורין וכו' בפ"ק. נ"ב פלוגתא דרב הונא ור' יצחק בדף יז ע"א:

ואין טועמין מפירותיה. ושמואל אמר: [א]כגון דאמרי "הני תמרי לשיכרא דבי נצרפי דשתו ליה ביום חגם". (אמר אמימר,) ואמרו לי סבי דפומבדיתא: הלכתא כוותיה דשמואל. מיתיבי: כיצד משתתפין במבוי — מביאים חבית של יין ושל שמן ושל תמרים ושל גרוגרות ושל שאר מיני פירות, אם משלו — צריך לזכות, ואם משלהן — צריך להודיע. ומגביה מן הקרקע משהו! מאי "משהו" נמי דקאמר — טפח. איתמר, שיתופי מבואות, רב אמר: אין צריך לזכות, ושמואל אמר: צריך לזכות. עירובי תחומין, רב אמר: צריך לזכות. ושמואל אמר: אין צריך לזכות. בשלמא לשמואל — הכא — תנן, והכא — לא תנן. אלא לרב, מאי טעמא? תנאי היא; דאמר רב יהודה, אמר רב: מעשה בכלתו של רבי אושעיא שהלכה לבית המרחץ וחשכה לה, ועירבה לה חמותה. ובא מעשה לפני רבי חייא, ואסר. אמר לו רבי ישמעאל ברבי יוסי: בבלאי! כל כך אתה מחמיר בעירובין?! כך אמר אבא: כל שיש לך להקל בעירובין — הקל. ואבעיא להו: משל חמותה עירבה לה, ומשום דלא זיכתה לה, או דילמא: משלה עירבה לה, ומשום דשלא מדעתה? אמר להן ההוא מרבנן ורבי יעקב שמיה: לדידי מיפרשא לה מיניה דרבי יוחנן: משל חמותה עירבה, ומשום דלא זיכתה לה. אמר ליה רבי זירא לרבי יעקב (*בריה) דבת יעקב: כי מטית התם, אקיף וזיל לסולמא דצור, ובעי' מיניה מרב יעקב בר אידי. בעא מיניה: משל חמותה עירבה, ומשום דלא זיכתה לה, או דלמא: משלה עירבה, ומשום דשלא מדעתה? אמר ליה: משל חמותה עירבה לה, ומשום דלא זיכתה לה. אמר רב נחמן, נקטינן: [ב]אחד עירובי תחומין, (א)[ג]ואחד עירובי חצירות, [ד]אחד שיתופי מבואות — צריך לזכות. בעי רב נחמן: עירובי תבשילין, צריך לזכות, או אין צריך לזכות? אמר רב יוסף: ומאי תיבעי ליה? לא שמיע ליה הא דאמר ר"נ בר רב אדא אמר שמואל: [ה]עירובי תבשילין צריך לזכות?! אמר ליה אביי: פשיטא דלא שמיע ליה, דאי שמיע ליה — מאי תיבעי ליה? אמר ליה: אטו עירובי תחומין מי לא אמר שמואל "אין צריך לזכות", ואמר איהו "צריך לזכות"? הכי השתא?! בשלמא התם — פליגי רב ושמואל, וקא משמע לן כחומרין דמר וכי חומרין דמר, אבל הכא, אי איתא דשמיע ליה — מי איכא דמאן דפליג? ההוא טורזינא דהוה בשיבבותיה דרבי זירא, א"ל אוגיר לן רשותך. לא אוגיר להו. אתו לקמיה דר' זירא, אמרו ליה: מהו למיגר מדביתהו? אמר להו: הכי אמר ר"ל משמיה דגברא רבה, ומנו — רבי חנינא: [ו]אשתו של אדם מערבת שלא מדעתו. ההוא טורזינא דהוה בשיבבותיה דרב יהודה בר אושעיא, אמרי ליה: אוגר לן רשותך. לא אוגר להו. אתו לקמיה דרב יהודה בר אושעיא, אמרי ליה: מהו למיגר מדביתהו? לא הוה בידיה, אתו לקמיה דרב מתנה — לא הוה בידיה. אתו לקמיה דרב יהודה, אמר להו, הכי אמר שמואל: אשתו של אדם מערבת שלא מדעתו. מיתיבי: נשים שעירבו ונשתתפו שלא מדעת בעליהן — אין עירובן עירוב, ואין שיתופן שיתוף! לא קשיא; [ז]הא — דאסר, הא — דלא אסר. הכי נמי מסתברא, דאם כן — קשיא דשמואל אדשמואל; דאמר שמואל: [ח]אחד מבני מבוי שרגיל להשתתף עם בני מבוי, ולא נשתתף — בני המבוי נכנסין לתוך ביתו ונוטלין שיתופן ממנו בעל כרחו. רגיל — אין, שאין רגיל — לא. שמע מינה. לימא מסייע ליה: [ט] כופין אותו לעשות לחי וקורה למבוי. שאני

ואין טועמין מפירותיה. דאי לאו דפלחוה לא הוו פרשי מינה: נצרפי. שם ע"ז שהיתה באותה מדינה: צריך להודיע. אם חפצין בכך, שמא מקפידין בעירובין, ואמר (*בפ"ק): המקפיד על עירובו — אינו עירוב שאינו נראה באותה פת ליתן לחביריו. אבל משלו אין צריך להודיעו דזכין לו לאדם שלא בפניו: הכא תנן. בעירובי חצירות: "ומזכה להן": הכא לא תנן. בעירובי תחומין קתני לקמן (דף פב.): כיצד משתתפין בתחומין כו', ולא קתני ומזכה להן: שהלכה לבית המרחץ. מבעוד יום, חוץ לתחום עירה וחשכה לה, ואסר לה לחזור: ר' חייא בבלי היה, כדאמרינן במסכת סוכה (דף כ.): עלו ר' חייא ובניו ויסדוה: ואיבעיא להו. גרסינן: *בריה דבת יעקב. אביו לא היה הגון, לפיכך לא הזכירו: אקיף. הרבה עלי הדרך בשבילו: וזיל אסולמא דצור. דרך מסילת(ב) נור: רבי חייא קאי כרב בתחומין. וגבי חצירות טעמא דרב משום דכיון דקאסר עליה גמר ומקני, ואין צריך זכייה ואע"ג דמתני' פליגא עליה דרב — רב תנא ופליג: מי איכא למאן דפליג. מי אשכחן דפליג איניש עליה: טורזינא. נכרי היה, ממונה על כלי זיין העשויין לשמירת העיר להלחם על הפרים ודר בעיר: הא דאסר. על בני המבוי — לא בעינן דעתיה. ומתני' בדלא אסר, כגון חצר שבין שני מבואות, ורגילה עם זה ולא עם זה: הכי נמי מסתברא. דמודה שמואל היכי דלא אסר: ולא נשתתף. אינו רוצה, ומתכוין לאסור עליהן: שאני

רב אמר א"צ לזכות. דכיון דאסר עליה — גמר ומקני ליה. ובתחומין צריך לזכות, דלא אסר עליה ולא גמר ומקני, כדפירש בקונטרס. ולשמואל, במבוי צריך לזכות — דלמקני רשות הוא, דקסבר עירוב משום קנין, בפ' "מי שהוציאוהו" (לעיל דף מט.) אפילו למ"ד עירוב משום דירה — צריך לזכות כדי שיהא קונה דירה בבית חבירו. ובתחומין סבר שמואל דאין צריך לזכות, דלא קני רשות אחרים הוא. אי נמי: כיון דאין מערבין עירובי תחומין אלא לדבר מצוה — משום מצוה גמר ומקני. ועוד: כיון דעירובי תחומין אין מערבין אלא מדעתו, אמירתו כשהוא אומר "צא וערב לי" חשובה כזכייה. והשתא יש דברים שאנו מחמירין בחצירות מתחומין, דחצירות צריך לזכות לשמואל ובעי פת, ובתחומין אין צריך לזכות ואין צריך פת. ויש דברים שאנו מחמירין בתחומין טפי, דבתחומין בעי ב' סעודות לכל אחד, ובחצירות בזמן שהן מרובין סגי [במזון ב' סעודות לכולם, ובזמן שהן מועטין סגי] בגרוגרת לכל אחד, כדאמרינן *סוף פירקין. והשולח עירוב ביד חרש שוטה וקטן אינו עירוב בתחומין, ובחצירות קטן גובה את העירוב:

מעשה בכלתו כו'. פי' בקונטרס: דהאי עובדא בתחומין הוה, ואע"ג דבחצירות פליגא מתני' עליה דרב — רב תנא הוא ופליג. וקשה, דעיקר הקושיא לא היתה אלא מחצירות, ומהא לא משני מידי! וי"ל: דבעירובי חצירות היה המעשה. וכן פירש רבינו חננאל. ורב סבר כרבי ישמעאל, וקסבר רב דתנא דידן תנא בחצירות דבעינן זיכוי, כל שכן בתחומין דתחומין, לכולי עלמא בעי זכיה. ולפירוש הקונטרס דמוקי לה בתחומין — יש לומר דרבי חייא ורבי ישמעאל בר' יוסי משום אביו אזדו לטעמייהו. דר' חייא אית ליה לעיל בספ"ק *דתחומין דאורייתא, ולהכי מחמיר בהו. ור' יוסי דמיקל — לטעמיה דאמר לעיל (דף לה.): ספק עירוב — כשר:

אמר רב נחמן נקיטינן אחד עירובי תחומין ואחד שיתופי מבואות צריך לזכות. וכן הלכה. וכן פסק בשאלתות *בפרשת "ויהי בשלח" דכולם צריכין לזכות: עירובי תחומין, וחצירות, ושיתופי מבואות, ועירובי תבשילין. ואע"ג דבעי רב נחמן עירובי תבשילין מאי — הא מסיק אביי דלא שמיע ליה דשמואל, דאי שמיע ליה לא הוה מיבעיא ליה:

אתו לקמיה דרב יהודה אמר להו הכי אמר שמואל אשתו של אדם כו'. ואם תאמר: ואמאי לא מייתי מדרב יהודה, דאמר בריש "הדר" (לעיל דף סד.) משמיה דשמואל: שכירו ולקיטו של נכרי נותן עירובו ודיו, °וכל שכן אשתו. והוה מייתי מנכרי אנכרי! ויש לומר: °דאשתו אאשתו ניחא ליה לאתויי: רגיל אין שאינו רגיל לא. דרגיל אסר כמו פתח הרגיל, אבל שאינו רגיל — אינו אוסר, ונוטלים שיתופו בעל כרחו. דקאמר — היינו של בעל הבית, אבל דעת אשתו צריך. ואף על גב דאסיקנא דאשתו של אדם מערבת שלא מדעתו — אין ללמוד מכאן שתוכל לזכות לבני המבוי ולבני חצר לתת פת עבורם, נהי דבשביל עצמה יכולה ליתן שלא מדעת בעלה, אין לה כח לזכות לשכניה שלא מדעת. וצריך ליזהר שלא תזכה האשה לשכניה כשאין בעלה בעיר. ואף על גב דאם כל אחד ואחד נותן פת נראה דשרי, אפילו לא אסרי אהדדי כל זמן שלא מיחה הבעל, דמסתמא לא קפיד — מכל מקום אין לסמוך על זה לענין שתוכל לזכות לאחרים. ואם אין הבעל והאשה בעיר אלא בני ביתו — צריך לדקדק אם יכולין לערב בני ביתו בלא רשות משל בעל הבית, דהא בסמוך [עמוד ב] תנן: ניתוספו עליהן — מוסיף, וצריך להודיע וכשלה האוכל נמי, קתני דצריך להודיע ממין אחר: שאני

רבינו חננאל

ואין טועמין מפירותיה. ושמואל אמר כגון דאמרי הני תמרי לשיכרא דבי נצרפי ושתו ליה ביום אידם אמר אמימר אמרו לי סבו דפומבדיתא הלכתא כשמואל מותבינן על מאן דאמר צריך להגביה חבית של (שותפים) [שיתופי מבואות] מן הקרקע טפח והתניא כיצד משתתפין במבוי מניח אדם חבית של יין של שמן ושל תמרים ושל גרוגרות ושל שאר מיני פירות בין משלו ובין משל חבירו צריך להודיע ומגביהה מן הקרקע כל שהוא ופריק מאי כל שהוא דקתני טפח: איתמר שיתופי מבואות רב אמר אין צריך לזכות ושמואל אמר צריך לזכות. עירובי תחומין רב אמר צריך לזכות ושמואל אמר אין צריך לזכות. בשלמא לשמואל דתנן בשיתופי מבוי ומזכה להן אלא לרב דאמר בשיתופי מבוי אין צריך לזכות קשיא ליה מתני' ופריק תנאי היא. ר' חייא סבר צריך לזכות. ור' ישמעאל ב"ר יוסי אמר משום אביו אין צריך לזכות דתניא מעשה בכלתו של ר' אושעיא שהלכה למרחץ ועירבה לה חמותה משלה ולא זכתה לה ואסר לה ר' חייא ואמר לו ר' ישמעאל ב"ר יוסי בבלאי כל כך אתה מחמיר בעירובין כך אמר אבא כל שיש לך להקל בעירובין (בעירובין) הקל. וכן אמר ר' יוחנן דחמותה משל עצמה עירבה ולא זכתה לכלתה ולפיכך אסר ר' חייא. אמר רב נחמן נקטינן אחד שיתופי מבואות ואחד עירובי תחומין צריך לזכות. בעי רב נחמן עירובי תבשילין צריך לזכות או לא. ואמר רב יוסף מאי תיבעי ליה הא אמר שמואל צריך לזכות: ההוא טורזינא דלא בעא לאוגורי להו רשותיה לבני מבוי ואזלו ואגרו אינהו מדביתהו. ואמר להו ר' זירא שפיר עבידיתו דאשתו של אדם מערבת לו שלא מדעתו וכן באשתו של גוי משכרת שלא רשות בעלה. ואם בא בעלה הגוי ומיחה בטילה אותה השכירות ונאסרו וחזרו לאיסורן. וכן אמר רב יהודה בר הושעיה משמיה דשמואל אשתו של אדם מערבת לו שלא מדעתו. ואותבינן עלייהו והתניא נשים שעירבו ונשתתפו שלא מדעת בעליהן אין עירובן עירוב ואין שיתופן שיתוף. ופרקינן *) מתניתא בדלא אסר עלייהו כגון שאינו רגיל לערב עמהן וגם אינו אוסר עליהן. כלומר אינו ממחה על אשתו

*) נראה דצ"ל כאן דר' חנינא ושמואל בדלא אסר וכו' כצ"ל וכן מסיים רבינו להדיא בסוף הענין ודשמואל ודר"ח היכי שלא אסר וכו':

רב נסים גאון

ובא מעשה לפני ר' חייא ואסר אמר לו ר' ישמעאל בר' יוסי בבלאי כל כך אתה מחמיר בעירוב. ר' חייא בבלי הוה ואיתא בסוף פרק א' דמסכת סוכה (דף כ) אמר ריש לקיש הריני כפרת ר' חייא ובניו שבתחלה נשתכחה תורה מישראל עלה עזרא מבבל ויסדה חזרה ונשתכחה עלה ר' חייא הבבלי ובניו ויסדוה ובפרק ל"ו כריתות (דף ח) ר' הושעיה הוה שכיח קמיה דבר קפרא שבקיה ואתא לקמיה דר' חייא ואתה מוצא [שם] שבר קפרא שואלו בשביל ר' חייא מה בבלי אומר בדבר זה:

עין משפט נר מצוה

מ א מיי' פ"ח מהלכות ע"ז הלכה ג טוש"ע י"ד סי' קמב סעיף יב:
מא ב מיי' פ"ו מהל' עירובין הלכה יט סמג עשין א טוש"ע א"ח סי' תיג:
מב ג מיי' פ"א מהל' עירובין הלכה כ סמג שם טוש"ע א"ח סי' שסו סעיף ט:
מג ד מיי' שם טוש"ע א"ח סי' שפו סעיף ג:
מד ה מיי' פ"ו מהל' י"ט הלכה ו סמג לאוין עה טוש"ע א"ח סי' תקכז סעיף ו:
מה ו ז מיי' פ"ב מהל' עירובין הלכה יג ופ"ה הלכה ה סמג עשין א טוש"ע א"ח סי' שסו וסי' שפז סעיף יא:
מו ח מיי' פ"ה מהל' עירובין הלכה כ סמג שם טוש"ע א"ח סי' שסז:
[מו] [ב מיי' פ"א מהל' שכנים דין יב טוש"ע ח"מ ר"ס קסב ובר"ב הלכה ב"ב פ"א דף קנז: בשם התוספתא וכן הביא הרא"ש ע"ש ובתוספתא דב"ב שלפנינו ליתא]

מסורת הש"ס

[נ"ל בפ"ב דף מט.] — רש"י מ"ז — [נ"ל ברה] — [נ"ל ברה] — נ"ל בסמוך ע"ב — [דף יז:] — [סוף סי' מח וסי' נ]

הגהות הב"ח

(א) גמ' נקטינן אחד עירובי תחומין (ואחד עירובי חצירות) תא"מ ונ"ב ס"א נמחק: (ב) רש"י ד"ה וזיל אסולמא וכו' נור הס"ד ואח"כ מ"ה שהלכה לבית המרחץ מבעו"י חוץ לתחום עירה ונחשכה לה ואסר לה לחזור הס"ד:

גליון הש"ס

תוס' ד"ה מעשה כו'. [illegible] ב"א"ד לאשתו ניחא ליה לאתויי. ק"ל ממימרא דשמואל באשתו קמייתרא כיון דכבר אמר בשכירו ולקיטו מערבי' והיינו ג"כ אפי' בע"כ [illegible] מייתי ליה לעיל אההיא דלחמן בר ריסתק דלא רצה לא גזרו. וא"כ מכ"ש באשתו והיה נראה מזה ראיה גדולה לפשוט ספיקת תוס' לעיל דף ע' ד"ה יורש בסה"ד דאפשר דשכירו ולקיטו רק דגוי אבל לא דישראל דהולך שמואל לאשתו דהכא מיירי בישראל דזהו דוקא באשתו ולא בשכירו ולקיטו:

שמעת

שאני התם דליכא מחיצות.(א)[א][א] *ל"א: *מצד שאני. איתמר, רב חייא בר אשי אמר: אעושין לחי אשירה. ור' שמעון בן לקיש אמר: עושין קורה אשירה. מאן דאמר קורה – כל שכן לחי, ומאן דאמר לחי – באבל קורה לא, כתותי מכתת שיעוריה.§ **מתני'** נתמעט האוכל – מוסיף ומזכה, ואין צריך להודיע. *גנתוספו עליהן – מוסיף ומזכה, וצריך להודיע. דכמה הוא *שיעורן? בזמן שהן מרובין – מזון שתי סעודות לכולם, בזמן שהן מועטין – כגרוגרת *לכל אחד ואחד. *אמר ר' יוסי: הבמה דברים אמורים – בתחילת עירוב, אבל בשירי עירוב – כל שהוא.(ב) *וולא אמרו לערב בחצירות אלא כדי שלא לשכח את התינוקות.§ **גמ'** במאי עסקינן? אילימא במין אחד – מאי איריא נתמעט, אפילו כלה נמי! אלא בשני מינין – אפילו נתמעט נמי לא, דתניא: זכלה האוכל, ממין אחד – אין צריך להודיע, מב' מינים – צריך להודיע! איבעית אימא: ממין אחד, ואיבעית אימא: משני מינין. איבעית אימא ממין אחד, מאי נתמעט – נתמטמט. ואיבעית אימא משני מינין – חכלה שאני.§ "ניתוספו עליהן מוסיף ומזכה וכו'.§ *אמר רב שיזבי, אמר רב חסדא, זאת אומרת: חלוקין עליו חביריו על ר' יהודה. *דתנן, אמר רבי יהודה: במה דברים אמורים – בעירובי תחומין, אבל בעירובי חצירות – מערבין בין לדעת ובין שלא לדעת. פשיטא דחלוקין! מהו דתימא: הני מילי – בחצר שבין שני מבואות, אבל חצר של מבוי אחד – אימא לא, קמשמע לן.§ "כמה הוא שיעורו וכו'.§ כמה הוא מרובין? אמר רב יהודה, אמר שמואל: שמונה עשרה בני אדם. שמונה עשרה ותו לא? אימא: טמשמונה עשרה ואילך. ומאי(ג) שמונה עשרה דנקט? אמר רב יצחק בריה דרב יהודה: לדידי מיפרשא לי מניה דאבא, כל שאילו מחלקו למזון שתי סעודות ביניהן ואין מגעת גרוגרת לכל אחד ואחד – הן הן מרובין, וסגי במזון שתי סעודות. ואי לא (הן הן) מועטין נינהו. ואגב אורחיה קא משמע לן דשתי סעודות הויין שמונה עשרה גרוגרות.§ **מתני'** בכל מערבין ומשתתפין, חוץ מן המים ומן המלח, דברי ר"א. רבי יהושע אומר: ככר הוא עירוב, יאפילו מאפה סאה והוא פרוסה – אין מערבין בה. ככר *)כאיסר והוא שלם – מערבין בו.§

גמ'

*) [בסדר המשנה הגיר' באיסר עי' תי"ט ד"ה ככר]

תורה אור (דברים יג): "ואשריהם תשרפון באש"

שאני התם דליכא מחיצות. ומבוי מגולה הוא, ואינו נוח לשומרו, הילכך כופין אותו. אבל להתיר בטלטול – לעולם אימא לך דבעינן דעת: כ"ש לחי. דאין לו שיעור לרחבו ועוביו: אבל קורה. צריכה טפח לקבל אריח, ובריאה כדי לקבל אריח. והאי אשירה, כיון דבעי שריפה, דכתיב (דברים יג): "ואשריהם תשרפון באש" – שיעורה לאו שיעורא היא, דכשרופה דמיא: **מתני'** נתמעט האוכל. משיעורו. ולקמן מפרש שיעורא במתני': ואינו צריך להודיע. שהרי כולן נתרצו בתחלה: וצריך להודיע. לדיורין שניתוספו אם דעתן בעירוב, וכגון שמערב משלהן. וטעמא פרישית לעיל. ותרתי קתני: מוסיף ומזכה – אם משלו מערב, וצריך להודיע – אם משלהן מערב: מרובין ומועטין. מפרש בגמרא: שירי עירוב. שנתמעט משיעורו: כל שהוא. אין צריך להוסיף, [ורבי יוסי פליג את"ק]: לא אמרו לערב בחצרות. לאחר שנשתתפו: אלא שלא לשכח. תורת עירובי חצירות מהתינוקות הבאין, הלכך, מקילינן ביה: **גמ'** במאי עסקינן. דקתני: בנתמעט אין צריך להודיע, הא כלה לגמרי – צריך להודיע, אם בא לערב: במין אחד. שחוזר ומערב מן המין הראשון: מב' מינין. שעירב בשניה ממין אחר: צריך להודיע. וקא סלקא דעתך: והוא הדין לנתמעט: נתמטמט. כלה לגמרי: איבעית אימא מב' מינין. ודוקא נקט נתמעט, ודקא קשיא לך מברייתא – כלה שאני. דברייתא כלה דווקא נקט. אבל נתמעט, אפילו מב' מינין – אין צריך להודיע: זאת אומרת חלוקין כו'. דלא תימא האי "במה דברים אמורים" לפרושי אתי: במה דברים אמורים. דצריך דעת: בעירובי תחומין. שמא אין נוח לו לקנות כאן כדי להפסיד לרוח שכנגדה: פשיטא. דשמעינן מינה דחלוקין, דהא בעירובי חצירות נקיט ואתי, וקתני "צריך להודיע": מהו דתימא. לעולם רבי יהודה בההוא מפרש הוא, ומתני' דהכא בחצר שבין שני מבואות, דלא ידעינן בהי ניחא ליה: קמ"ל. רב שיזבי, דשמיעא ליה מרביה דבמבוי אחד עסקינן: ותו לא. בתמיה. כ"ש דטפי מהכי הוו מרובין: לדידי מיפרשא לי מיניה דאבא. דלקולא קתני. בזמן שהם מרובים, דגרוגרת דידהו הוי יותר מב' סעודות – סגי בב' סעודות, ולא בעינן גרוגרת לכל חד וחד. כשהן מועטים, דלא מטי גרוגרת דידהו לב' סעודות – סגי בגרוגרת לכל אחד, ולקולא: כל שאילו מחלק מזון ב' סעודות ביניהן ואין גרוגרת לכל א'. שיש בהן בני אדם יותר ממנין גרוגרות של שתי סעודות – מרובין נינהו. ותנן במתני' דלא בעי כגרוגרת לכל אחד, אלא: כשיש בו מזון שתי סעודות – סגי: ואי לא. שאין מניינם רב כמנין גרוגרות של שתי סעודות – לא בעי שתי סעודות, אלא כגרוגרת לכל אחד. היינו פירוש דמתניתין. ורב יהודה דנקט שמנה עשרה, ולא תנא כדאמרינן – אגב אורחיה, דבעי לפרושי מתניתין נקט הושבנא, ולאשמעינן דמזון שתי סעודות הוו שמנה עשרה גרוגרות: **מתני'** ככר. שלם: מאפה סאה. שאפה סאה בככר אחד, ונטל ממנו מעט ושווייה פרוסה – אין מערבין בה, וטעמא מפרש בגמרא: ככר. קטן, כמדת איסר: והוא שלם מערבין בו. ובלבד שיהיו שם ככרות הרבה כגרוגרת לכל אחד ואחד: גמ'

שאני התם דאיכא מחיצה. פר"ת: דין הוא דכופין אותו לעשות לחי וקורה. דמהני מחילות להתיר לטלטל בתוכו אע"פ שנעשו בעל כרחו של אדם, ולא דמי לעירוב. דבין הוה משום דירה ובין משום קנין – אין לו להועיל בעל כרחו של אדם. ובקונטרס לא פירש כן.

ובספרים דגרס שאני התם דליכא מחילות יש לפרש כן, דכי ליכא מחילות דאסור לטלטל בתוכו – דין הוא שנכוף אותו לעשות תקנה להתיר לטלטל, אבל אין לנו לכופו לעשות תקנה לטלטל מן הבתים ומן החלירות לתוכו: **אבל** קורה כתותי מכתת שיעוריה. אע"ג דלחי נמי בעי שיעור גובה, וגם רוחב משהו מיהא בעי – מכל מקום, כיון דלא בעי אלא שיעור זוטא – לא החמירו בו. וה"ר אברהם פירש: לחי, אם היה מדבק הכתיתים בכותל – הוי לחי, ובלבד שלא יהו ניטלות ברוח. ואין להקשות מהא *דפסלינן לולב של אשירה אפילו ביו"ט שני, דמשמע דכמאן דליתיה דמי, דגבי לולב של מצוה החמירו. וא"ת: דמכשרינן לעיל* סולם של אשירה, אע"ג דבעי רחב ד' ולא אמר מיכתת שיעורא כמו קורה! ואור"י: דהתם חשיב פתח, כיון דחזי לעלייה אי לאו איסורא דאשירה. אבל קורה – הצריכו חכמים שיעורא של חשיבות:

אלא בב' מינין אפילו נתמעט נמי דתניא כו'. ס"ד דכלה דנקט בברייתא – משום מין א' נקטיה, דאפילו בכלה אין צריך להודיע:

אגב אורחא קמ"ל דב' סעודות הויין י"ח גרוגרות. הקשה ר"ת, דבפרק "כילד משתתפין" (לקמן דף פב:) תנן, רבי שמעון אומר: ב' ידות לככר, משלש לקב. דהיינו שיעור שתי סעודות ה' ביצים ושליש ביצה, שהככר הוא ח' ביצים. כשתחלק י"ח גרוגרות לחמש ביצים ושליש ביצה דזה וזה הוי שיעור שתי סעודות, תמצא לכל ביצה שלש גרוגרות וג' שמינית של גרוגרות, דבחמש ביצים ושליש ביצה יש י"ו שלישי ביצה. וגרוגרת גדולה מכזית, כדמוכח בריש "המצניע" (שבת דף צא.) ובתורת כהנים קתני, ובפרק בתרא דיומא (דף פ.) דשיערו חכמים דאין בית הבליעה מחזקת יותר מכביצת תרנגולת. ובכריתות פרק "אמרו לו" (דף יד.) אמרינן גבי יש אוכל אכילה אחת כו' דאין בית הבליעה מחזיק יותר מב' זיתים. ואע"ג דפליגי תנאי לקמן אדר' שמעון – כר"ש קי"ל. דבכל דוכתי אמר כביצה לטמא טומאת אוכלין – דהיינו כר"ש, כדקתני לקמן בגמ' (דף פג.): וחצי [חצי] חציה לטמא טומאת אוכלין. ולר"ש עולה השיעור כביצה, אבל לשאר תנאי אינו כן, ואכולהו תנאי קאי כדמוכח הסוגיא לקמן! ואומר ר"י: דלכולהו תנאי הוי כביצה לטמא אוכלים. והא דקתני לקמן בברייתא וחצי חצי חציה כו', לא קאי אר"מ ואר' יהודה, אלא ארבי שמעון ור' יוחנן בן ברוקה שהזכירו שיעור ככר, תדע, דהא קתני בברייתא בגמ' כמה שיעור חצי פרס – שתי ביצים חסר קימעא דברי ר' יהודה. משמע דקאי בשיטתיה דר"ש, דחשיב חצי חציה לפסול את הגוויה בשתי ביצים. והשתא לא קשה מידי, דבשתי סעודות של עירוב לא קי"ל כר"ש אלא כר"מ, או כרבי יהודה. כדמוכח לקמן דרב יוסף ורבה כר"מ בריש "כילד משתתפין" (לקמן דף פב.). ותרתי ריפתא נמי דקאמר רב יהודה ורב אדא בר אהבה – היינו כר"מ או כר' יהודה: איתיביה

רבינו חננאל

מפני שעירבה עמהן אבל אם ממחה על ידי אשתו אוסר על בני חצר וכן קאמר שמואל כך (אסר) [דבאסר] עלייהו [אינו עירוב]. דאמר שמואל אחד מבני מבוי שרגיל ומשתתף עם בני מבוי ונמנע ולא רצה לישתתף בני מבוי נכנסין לביתו ונוטלין ממנו שיתופי מבוי על כרחו. *) קשיין אהדדי דהא הוא דאמר מדעתו אלא לאו הא דמיחה על ידה ואמר איני רוצה בזה העירוב שעירבה אשתי ודשמואל ודר' חנינא היכא דלא אסר כגון שלא מיחה. נימא מסייע ליה כופין אותו (ועושין) ועושה לחי וקורה למבוי ודחינן שאני התם דאיכא מחיצות: **פי'** נתמעט האוכל מכדי ב' סעודות מוסיף ומזכה לכל בני מבוי ואינו צריך להודיעם עכשיו כי נתמעטו והוספתי עליו וזכיתי לכם שכבר הודיעם מקודם לכן ועל אותה ידיעה הן סמוכים אין צריכין ידיעה אחרת ואוקימנא למתניתין במין אחד. ומאי נתמעט דקתני נתמוטט כלומר כלה לגמרי ואפי' הכי מוסיף ומזכה וא"צ להודיע ואיבעית אימא מתניתין בב' מינין ודוקא נתמעט ולא כלה כולו אבל כלה צריך להודיע כדתניא כלה האוכל ממין אחד אינו צריך להודיע. מב' מינין צריך להודיע. ניתוספו עליהן מוסיף ומזכה (וא"צ) [וצריך] להודיע. הא מתניתא פליגא על ר' יהודה דהא ר' יהודה בעירובי חצירות אמר מערבין לו לאדם שלא מדעתו דתנן א"ר יהודה בד"א שאין מערבין לו לאדם אלא מדעתו בעירובי תחומין אבל בעירובי חצירות מערבין לו מדעתו ושלא מדעתו שזכין לו לאדם כו'. ואוקימנא דודאי חולקין עליו חכמים. ואי מהתם הוה אמינא בחצר של ב' מבואות הוא דפליגי אבל בחצר של מבוי אחד אימא לא כמו שהוא מפורש בסוף פרק זה קמ"ל. וכמה הן מרובין משבעה עשר ואילך קי"ל שיעור העירוב מזון ב' סעודות לרבים וכ"ש למועטין. וכל עירוב שאילו בא לחלקו למי שעירב להן ואין מגיע לכל אחד ואחד כגרוגרת מזון ב' סעודות וקי"ל די"ח גרוגרות הן ב' סעודות לפי חשבון ר' יוחנן בן ברוקא שנותנין שיעור העירוב בקב. ואם הן מרובין מי"ח בני אדם ולמעלה. ואפי' הן מאה ויותר כשיעור ב' סעודות די להן העירוב ואע"פ שאין העירוב מגיע כגרוגרת אבל כשהן מועטין פחותין מי"ח בני אדם צריכין להיות עירובן כשיעור גרוגרת לכל אחד ואחד. ואם הוא פחות צריך להוסיף להיות העירוב למלאות לכל אחד ואחד כגרוגרת. א"ר יוסי בד"א שצריך למזון ב' סעודות למרובין או כגרוגרת לכל אחד ואחד למעוטין בתחלת העירוב. אבל בזמן שעירב כשיעור שנתנו חכמים לערב ונתמעט ונשתייר הימנו כל שהוא כשר: מתני' בכל מערבין ומשתתפין חוץ מן המים כו' בכל

*) נראה דל"ל רגיל אין שאינו רגיל לא. קשיין אהדדי דהא הוא דאמר דאשתו מערבת אפי' שלא מדעתו אלא לאו וכו' כל"ל.

עין משפט נר מצוה

מז א מיי' פ"ה מהל' שבת הלכה יב סמג עשין א טוש"ע א"ח סי' שסג סעיף ח:

מח ב מיי' שם הלכה יג וטוש"ע שם סעיף טז:

[שלש תיבות הללו משוללי הבנה למאד ועי' בתיקוני כלי שרת ועי' במראה הפנים בירושלמי הלכה ו' ישוב נכון על זה] [ובכ"י דפוס וויניציא משנת רפ"ח ובדפוס שאלוניקי משנת רפ"ב ליתנהו]

מט ג מיי' פ"ה מהל' עירובין הלכה ו סמג שם טוש"ע א"ח סי' שסו סעיף ב:

נ ד מיי' פ"א שם הלכה ט' סמג שם טוש"ע שם סעיף ג:

[עי' תוס' סוכה לג: ד"ה בהשירה]

[דף עח:]

נא ה מיי' פ"ה [ואינו שם ובפירושו כתב שאין כהלכה כרבי יוסי] וסמג שם טוש"ע שם סעיף ד:

נב ו מיי' פ"א שם הלכה יג וסמג שם טוש"ע שם סעיף ה:

נג ז ח מיי' שם הלכה ו וסמג שם טוש"ע א"ח סי' שסח סעיף א: [לקמן פא.]

[לעיל עג: ולקמן פא. לה.]

נד ט מיי' פ"א הלכה ט וטוש"ע שם סעיף ג:

נה י מיי' שם הלכה ח סמג עשין א טוש"ע א"ח סי' שסו סעיף ו:

מסורת הש"ס

[עי' ג"כ מ"ח ח"מ סי' לט דף קמב ע"ג]

לעיל עו:

[גירי ירושלמי ורי"ף לא]

[לקמן פא:]

בק"ד שיעורו

[בסדר המשנה ובפי' הרמב"ם הגיר' להוצאת שבת]

הגהות הב"ח

(א) גמ' דליכא מחיצות איתמר רב חייא בר אשי כצ"ל ותיבות ל"א מצד שאני נמחק: (ב) שם במשנה כל שהוא לא כצ"ל ואות ו' נמחק: (ג) שם גמ' ומאי שנא שמ"ע:

הגהות הגר"א

[א] גמ' ל"א מצד שאני. נ"ב בכ"ד שאני. ועי' בפי' הגאון על א"ח סי' שסו ס"ק י':

הגהות מהר"ב רנשבורג

[א] גמ' ל"א מצד שאני. עי' עלי תמרים סי' שעב ס"ק ... בד"ה ... ודבריו לחוקים מהחמת. והנכון כביאור הגאון מוהר"ח ווילנא זצוק"ל בא"ח סי' שסו.

המחבר שם סוף ס"א אבל כופין אותו בכ"ד לערב עמהן וכתב הגאון שם ס"ק י' וז"ל אבל כופין תוספתא וגמ' בעירובין דף ע"ב ליתא אחרינא בכ"ד שאני וכל"ל. וט"ס שם בגמ' שכתוב מלד שאני עיין שם. עכ"ל הגאון. ודברי אלהים חיים הם לפ"ד למ"ש הרב"י וטור שם סי' שסו שמקור דין זה נלמד מדברי הה"מ. כ"א מתוספתא ותלמוד ערוך הוא. וכמ"ש שם בהקדמת ככל הגאון המחבר:

גמ' לְאַפּוּקֵי מִדְּר' יְהוֹשֻׁעַ דְּאָמַר פַּת אִין מִידֵי אַחֲרִינָא לָא קָא מַשְׁמַע לָן מַתְנִי' בַּכֹּל. אֲפִילּוּ יַיִן וּפֵירוֹת. וְאִי מֵהָהִיא הֲוָה אָמִינָא: הָתָם הוּא דִּבְעֵירוּבֵי תְּחוּמִין עָסְקִינַן. וְהָתָם מוֹדֶה רַבִּי יְהוֹשֻׁעַ, דְּלֵיכָּא לְמֵיחַשׁ מִשּׁוּם אֵיבָה כִּי הָכָא בְּעֵירוּבֵי חֲצֵירוֹת דְּטַעְמָא מִשּׁוּם אֵיבָה, כִּדְלְקַמָּן. אֲבָל בְּעֵירוּבֵי חֲצֵירוֹת – אֵימָא לֹא, לְהָכִי הֲדַר תַּנְיֵיהּ גַּבֵּי חֲצֵירוֹת. לִישָּׁנָא אַחֲרִינָא גָּרְסִינַן: לְאַפּוּקֵי מִדְּר' מֵאִיר, דְּאָמַר: בְּפַת אִין, בְּמִידֵי אַחֲרִינָא לָא, בְּפ' "הַדָּר" (לעיל דף עא:), קמ"ל: בַּכֹּל, וְהִיא הִיא: אֵיתִיבֵיהּ אַבַּיֵי בַּכֹּל מְעָרְבִין עֵירוּבֵי חֲצֵירוֹת גָּרְסִינַן וּבַכֹּל מִשְׁתַּתְּפִין שִׁיתּוּפֵי מָבוֹי. בֵּין בְּפַת וּבֵין בְּיַיִן בֵּין בִּשְׁאָר פֵּירוֹת: וְלֹא אָמְרוּ לְעָרֵב בְּפַת כו'. וּבַכֹּל מְעָרְבִין דְּרֵישָׁא – הָכִי קָאָמַר: בְּכָל מִינֵי פַּת מְעָרְבִין עֵירוּבֵי חֲצֵירוֹת: מַאן שָׁמְעַתְּ לֵיהּ דְּאָמַר פַּת אִין מִידֵי *אַחֲרִינָא לֹא רַבִּי יְהוֹשֻׁעַ. וּלְלִישָּׁנָא אַחֲרִינָא ר' מֵאִיר: וְקָתָנֵי בַּכֹּל. אַפַּת. וּמַתְנִי' נַמִי, מַאי דְּבַכֹּל דְּתָנֵי אַכָּל מִילֵּי קָאָמַר, וּלְאַפּוּקֵי מֵהָא דְּר' יְהוֹשֻׁעַ אָתָא – דִּילְמָא בַּכֹּל דְּקָתָנֵי אַפַּת קָאֵי, כְּבָרַיְיתָא. וְהָכִי קָאָמַר: בְּכָל מִינֵי פַּת מְעָרְבִין בַּחֲצֵירוֹת, וּמִשְׁתַּתְּפִין בַּמָּבוֹי בְּכָל מִילֵּי – חוּץ מִמַּיִם וּמֶלַח: אֶלָּא אָמַר רַבָּה בַּר בַּר חָנָה. אִי אִיכָּא לְמֵימַר דְּאַפְּקָא מַתְנִי' מִדְּר' יְהוֹשֻׁעַ – אַסֵּיפָא דְּמִלְּתָא פְּלִיגָא, דְּאָמַר: פְּרוּסָה לֹא, קָא מַשְׁמַע לָן בַּכֹּל: מִשּׁוּם אֵיבָה. שֶׁבָּאִין לִידֵי מַחֲלוֹקֶת, שֶׁאוֹמֵר: אֲנִי נוֹתֵן שְׁלֵימָה וְאַתָּה פְּרוּסָה: לְקִלְקוּלוֹ. זֶה פָּרוּס וְזֶה שָׁלֵם: חַלָּתָהּ. אֵינוֹ חִסָּרוֹן, שֶׁזֶּהוּ תִּיקּוּנָהּ: כְּדֵי דִּימוּעָהּ. אִם נִדְמַעַת, שֶׁנָּפְלָה תְּרוּמָה בְּחוּלִּין וְעָשׂוּ מִמֶּנָּה כִּכָּר זוֹ, וְנָטְלוּ מִמֶּנָּה דִּימוּעָהּ אֶחָד מִמֵּאָה לְתַקְּנָהּ: חַלַּת נַחְתּוֹם. קְטַנָּה הִיא, וְאֵין זֶה חִסָּרוֹן: תִּפָּרָהּ בְּקֵיסָם. כִּכָּר שֶׁנִּפְרְסָה, וְתָפַר הַפְּרוּסוֹת בְּקֵיסָם וְנִרְאֵית שְׁלֵימָה: יְדִיעַ תִּיפְרָהּ. נִיכָּר מְקוֹם תְּפִירָתָהּ, וְהָוְיָא כִּפְרוּסָה: דִּשְׁאָר מִינֵי הֲוָה. מִינִין הַרְבֵּה הָיוּ מְעוֹרָבִין בָּהּ, דְּהָהִיא וַדַּאי לָאו פַּת הִיא, דִּכְתִיב גַּבֵּי יְחֶזְקֵאל: "וְאַתָּה קַח לְךָ חִטִּין" וגו' וּכְתִיב (שם כד): "לֶחֶם אֲנָשִׁים לֹא תֹאכֵל" אַלְמָא: לָאו לֶחֶם הוּא: וְעוּגַת שְׂעוֹרִים תֹּאכְלֶנָּה אָמַר רַב חִסְדָּא. הַאי שְׂעוֹרִים לָאו דַּוְוקָא, דְּהָא שְׁאָר מִינִין טוּבָא הָווּ בָּהּ, אֶלָּא לְשִׁיעוּרִין תֹּאכְלֶנָּה – בְּמִשְׁקָל, דֶּרֶךְ רְעָבוֹן וְלֹא לְשׂוֹבַע: *עֲרִיבָתָהּ כַּעֲרִיבַת שְׂעוֹרִין. מְגוּנָּה, וְלֹא יָפָה כְּתִיקּוּן עֲרִיבַת חִטִּים שֶׁמְּיַיפֶּה תִּיקּוּן הָעוּגָה עֲגוּלָּה וְנָאָה: מתני' נוֹתֵן אָדָם מָעָה לַחֶנְוָנִי. שֶׁהוּא מוֹכֵר יַיִן, וְדָר עִמּוֹ בַּמָּבוֹי: אוֹ לַנַּחְתּוֹם. מוֹכֵר כִּכָּרוֹת, וְדָר עִמּוֹ בֶּחָצֵר, שֶׁיְּזַכֶּה לוֹ בָּעֵירוּב עִם חֲבֵרָיו אִם יָבוֹאוּ בְּנֵי הַמָּבוֹי לָקַחַת מִמְּךָ כִּכָּר לָעֵירוּב אוֹ יַיִן לְשִׁיתּוּף – יְהֵא לִי חֵלֶק בּוֹ: לֹא זָכוּ לוֹ מָעוֹתָיו. שֶׁאֵין מָעוֹת קוֹנוֹת עַד שֶׁיִּמְשׁוֹךְ. וַאֲפִי' עֵירֵב הַחֶנְוָנִי הַזֶּה לְכָל הָאֲחֵרִים, וְזִיכָּה גַּם לָזֶה – אֵינוֹ עֵירוּב, שֶׁהֲרֵי לֹא נִתְכַּוֵּון לְזַכּוֹת לוֹ בְּמַתְּנַת חִנָּם כִּשְׁאָר מְזַכִּין בְּעֵירוּב אֶלָּא לִקְנוֹת הַמָּעָה וַהֲרֵי אֵינָהּ קְנוּיָה לוֹ דְּכֵיוָן דְּמָעוֹת אֵינָן קוֹנוֹת – לֹא סָמְכָה דַּעְתֵּיהּ דְּהַאי, וְלָא הָוֵי דַּעְתֵּיהּ לְאַקְנוּיֵי, וְנִמְצָא מְעָרֵב לוֹ בְּמָעוֹתָיו שֶׁלֹּא מִדַּעְתּוֹ: וּמוֹדִים

תורה אור

גמ' תָּנֵינָא חֲדָא זִימְנָא: *"בַּכֹּל מְעָרְבִין וּמִשְׁתַּתְּפִין חוּץ מִן הַמַּיִם וְהַמֶּלַח"! אָמַר רַבָּה: לְאַפּוּקֵי מִדְּרַבִּי יְהוֹשֻׁעַ, דְּאָמַר: כִּכָּר אִין, מִידֵי אַחֲרִינָא לָא – קָמַשְׁמַע לָן "בַּכֹּל". אֵיתִיבֵיהּ אַבַּיֵי: בַּכֹּל מְעָרְבִין עֵירוּבֵי חֲצֵירוֹת וּבַכֹּל מִשְׁתַּתְּפִין שִׁיתּוּפֵי מְבוֹאוֹת, וְלֹא אָמְרוּ לְעָרֵב בַּפַּת אֶלָּא בְּחָצֵר בִּלְבַד. מַאן שָׁמְעַתְּ לֵיהּ דְּאָמַר: פַּת אִין מִידֵי אַחֲרִינָא לָא – רַבִּי יְהוֹשֻׁעַ, וְקָתָנֵי: בַּכֹּל! אֶלָּא אָמַר רַבָּה בַּר בַּר חָנָה: לְאַפּוּקֵי מִדְּרַבִּי יְהוֹשֻׁעַ, דְּאָמַר: שְׁלֵימָה אִין, פְּרוּסָה לָא – קָמַשְׁמַע לָן "בַּכֹּל". וּפְרוּסָה מַאי טַעְמָא לָא? אָמַר רַבִּי יוֹסֵי בֶּן שָׁאוּל, אָמַר רַבִּי: מִשּׁוּם אֵיבָה. אֲמַר לֵיהּ רַב אַחָא בְּרֵיהּ דְּרָבָא לְרַב אַשִׁי: עֵירְבוּ כּוּלָּן בִּפְרוּסוֹת, מַהוּ? א"ל: °שֶׁמָּא יַחֲזוֹר דָּבָר לְקִלְקוּלוֹ. א"ר *יוֹחָנָן בֶּן שָׁאוּל: נִיטְּלָה הֵימֶנָּה כְּדֵי חַלָּתָהּ וּכְדֵי דִּימוּעָהּ – מְעָרְבִין לוֹ בָּהּ. וְהָתַנְיָא: כְּדֵי דִּימוּעָהּ – מְעָרְבִין לוֹ בָּהּ, כְּדֵי חַלָּתָהּ – אֵין מְעָרְבִין לוֹ בָּהּ! לָא קַשְׁיָא; הָא – [א]בְּחַלַּת נַחְתּוֹם, הָא – בְּחַלַּת בַּעַל הַבַּיִת. *דִּתְנַן: [ב]שִׁיעוּר חַלָּה אֶחָד מֵעֶשְׂרִים וְאַרְבָּעָה, הָעוֹשֶׂה עִיסָּה לְעַצְמוֹ וְעִיסָּה לְמִשְׁתֵּה בְּנוֹ, אֶחָד מֵעֶשְׂרִים וְאַרְבָּעָה. נַחְתּוֹם שֶׁהוּא עוֹשֶׂה לִמְכּוֹר בַּשּׁוּק, וְכֵן הָאִשָּׁה שֶׁעָשְׂתָה לִמְכּוֹר בַּשּׁוּק – אֶחָד מֵאַרְבָּעִים וּשְׁמוֹנָה. אָמַר רַב חִסְדָּא: [ג]תְּפָרָהּ בְּקֵיסָם – מְעָרְבִין לוֹ בָּהּ. וְהָא תַּנְיָא: אֵין מְעָרְבִין לוֹ בָּהּ! לָא קַשְׁיָא; [ד]הָא – דִּידִיעַ תִּיפְרָהּ, הָא – דְּלָא יְדִיעַ תִּיפְרָהּ. א"ר זֵירָא, אָמַר שְׁמוּאֵל: מְעָרְבִין בְּפַת אוֹרֶז וּבְפַת דּוֹחַן. אָמַר מָר עוּקְבָא: לְדִידִי מִיפַּרְשָׁא לִי מִינֵּיהּ דְּמָר שְׁמוּאֵל, [ה]בְּפַת אוֹרֶז – מְעָרְבִין, וּבְפַת דּוֹחַן – אֵין מְעָרְבִין. אָמַר רַב חִיָּיא בַּר אָבִין, אָמַר רַב: [ו]מְעָרְבִין בְּפַת עֲדָשִׁים. אִינִי?! וְהָא הַהִיא דַּהֲוַאי בִּשְׁנֵי דְּמָר שְׁמוּאֵל, וְשַׁדְיֵיהּ לְכַלְבֵּיהּ וְלָא אֲכָלָהּ! הַהִיא דִּשְׁאָר מִינִים הֲוָיָא, דִּכְתִיב: °"וְאַתָּה קַח לְךָ חִטִּין וּשְׂעוֹרִים וּפוֹל וַעֲדָשִׁים וְדוֹחַן וְכוּסְּמִים" וגו'. רַב פַּפָּא אָמַר: הַהִיא צְלוּיָה בְּצוֹאַת הָאָדָם הֲוַאי, דִּכְתִיב: °"וְהִיא בְּגֶלְלֵי צֵאַת הָאָדָם תְּעֻגֶנָּה לְעֵינֵיהֶם". מַאי "וְעוּגַת שְׂעֹרִים תֹּאכְלֶנָּה"? אָמַר רַב חִסְדָּא: לְשִׁיעוּרִים. רַב פַּפָּא אָמַר: *עֲרִיבָתָהּ *כַּעֲרִיבַת שְׂעוֹרִים, וְלֹא *כַּעֲרִיבַת חִטִּים.§

מתני' נוֹתֵן אָדָם מָעָה לַחֶנְוָנִי וְלַנַּחְתּוֹם כְּדֵי שֶׁיִּזַּכֶּה לוֹ עֵירוּב, דִּבְרֵי רַבִּי אֱלִיעֶזֶר. וַחֲכָמִים אוֹמְרִים: [ז]לֹא זָכוּ לוֹ מָעוֹתָיו. וּמוֹדִים

איתיביה אביי בכל מערבין עירובי תחומין כו'. כך היא הגירסא בספרים ישנים, וכן גרס ר"ת. ופירש ה"ר אברהם כולה סוגיא דה"ק: תנינא חדא זימנא בכל מערבין כו' משמע סתמא בין בעירובי חצירות בין בעירובי תחומין. אמר רבה, לאפוקי מר' יהושע דאמר: פת אין כו', והאי בכל מערבין – אכולהו עירובין קאי, ואכולהו פליג ר' יהושע, ואומר: פת – אין, מידי אחרינא – לא. ולהכי איצטריך תרי זימני, דאי לא הדר ותנא בבא דהכא – הוה מוקמינן ההיא דלעיל בתחומין דאיירי בהו כולי פירקא. ומילתא דר' יהושע דהכא הוה מוקמינן בחצירות. דמיירי בהו לעיל ולא מפקא ההיא דלעיל כלל מרבי יהושע דהכא. אבל השתא, דמיתניא נמי גבי מלתיה דרבי יהושע – מפקא מדידיה, דלאיפלוגי קאתי: "איתיביה אביי" פריך על מה שאמר שסבר רבי יהושע דאפילו בתחומין אין מערבין אלא בפת, והכי גרסינן בכל הספרים הישנים: בכל מערבין עירובי תחומין(א) קאמר כו' קס"ד דהאי בכל מערבין – בכל מיני פירות קאמר, מאן שמעת ליה דאמר פת אין מידי אחרינא לא – רבי יהושע, דהא אמרינן דר' אליעזר בכל מערבין בין בחצירות בין בתחומין קאמר. וקתני לה גבי תחומין(ב) בכל דבר, אלמא: תחומין בכל דבר לרבי יהושע. אלא לאפוקי מרבי יהושע כו'. אלא האי בכל מערבין – ה"ק: בכל עניני פת מערבין, בין בשלמין בין בחסרין. והשתא מיירי מתני' בכל מערבין דווקא בחצירות דאיירי בהו לעיל, ופליג על ר' יהושע דבעי שלמין בחצירות. והא דלא שני אפירכא דאביי דודאי רבי יהושע מודה דתחומין בכל דבר, ובמתניתין תנן בכל מערבין אפילו בחצירות, ור' יהושע פליג בחצירות לחודייהו – היינו משום דאי ר' אליעזר איירי בתרוייהו ור' יהושע לא פליג אלא אחצירות, הוה ליה לפרושי דאחצירות לחודייהו קאי*:

כדי חלתה וכדי דימועה מערבין לו בה. ונראה לר"י: דווקא בטבולה לחלה ובמדומע איירי דאי לא בעיא תיקון – איכא איבה אפילו בחסרון מועט. דלישנא דמתניתין משמע דשלמים לגמרי בעי. ומיהו, לשון כדי קשה, דהוה ליה למימר חלתה ודמועתה! ואור"י: דנקט כדי – לאשמועינן דאפילו נטל לשם חלה, אם הפריש יותר מכדי צורך – איכא איבה. ואם תאמר: כיון דאשמעינן כדי חלתה, דהוה אחד מארבעים ושמונה כל שכן כדי דימועה דהוה יותר ממאה! ואור"י: דס"ד דדימוע, כיון דחזי הכי לכהן – אפילו בפורתא איכא איבה:

והא ההיא דהואי בשני דמר שמואל כו'. עשו לנסות מה טעמא, לפי שצוה הקב"ה ליחזקאל לעשות:

דכתיב ואתה קח לך כו'. פ"ה: וכתיב בתריה "לחם אנשים לא תאכל", אלמא: לאו לחם הוא. והגיה ר"ת: דהאי לחם אנשים – בהברא כתיב, רחוק מפרשה זו כמה דפין. והכי פירושא: ההיא דשאר מינין הואי, דכתיב "ואתה קח לך" ולימי המצור ושעת הדחק נאכל, ולא פת הוא, אלא לנפש רעבה – דכלבא בכפניה גלליה בלע [ב"ק נב.].

לא זכו לו מעותיו. פירש הקונטרס: ואפילו עירב החנוני הזה לכל האחרים, וזכה גם לזה – אינו עירוב, שהרי לא נתכוון לזכות לו במתנת חנם כשאר מזכין בעירוב אלא לקנות המעה – והרי אינה קנויה לו. ובחנם פירש כן, דאפילו מתכוין לו להקנות לו בחנם, ואפילו זיכה לו ע"י אחר, או לקח המעה וקנה לו מן השוק – אינו עירוב, כיון שהנותן מתכוין לקנות לו מן החנוני, ואין המעה קונה לו. וכל הזכיות שעושה החנוני – שלא מדעת בעל הבית קא עביד, ואין מערבין אלא לדעתו. ולשון הקונטרס נמי מוכיח כן בסמוך:

באלבעה

עין משפט נר מצוה

נו א טור ש"ע סי' שסז סעיף ו:

נז ב מיי' פ"ה מהלכות בכורים הלכה ב סמג עשין קמא טוש"ע י"ד סי' שכב סעיף א:

נח ג ד טור ש"ע א"ח סי' שסו סעיף ו:

נט ה ו מיי' פ"א מהל' עירובין הלכה ח וטוש"ע שם סעיף ח:

ס ז מיי' פ"ו מהלכות עירובין הלכה כ סמג עשין א טור ש"ע א"ח סי' שסט:

[ועי' תוס' שבת לד. ד"ה ל"ק]

רבינו חננאל

[איתיביה אביי] בכל מערבין עירובי תחומין ובכל משתתפין שיתופי מבואות ולא אמרו לערב בפת אלא בעירובי חצירות בלבד ואוקימנא להא ברייתא (לר') [דר'] יהושע היא דקתני בתחומין ובמבואות בכל ובחצירות בפת. והני מילי בשלימה אבל בפרוסה לא. ופרוסה מ"ט לא משום איבה דאמר אמאי מייתינא אנא שלימה והאי פרוסה. ואמרינן ואי אייתו כולהו פרוסות דליכא איבה מאי ושנינן גזירה שמא יביא אחד פרוסה ואחד שלימה ויבואו לידי קלקול איבה כדאמרן. וסוגיין דשמעתין כר' יהושע דאמר שלימה אין פרוסה לא: א"ר יונתן בן שאול א"ר אם ניטלה מככר העירוב כדי חלתה כדי חלת הנחתום העושה למכור בשוק או אשה העושה למכור בשוק שהוא אחד וארבעים ושמונה בעיסה וכדי דימוע שהוא אחד ממאה ועוד. דתנן בתרומות (פ"ד מ"ז) (פ') ר"א אומר תרומה עולה באחד ומאה ר' יהושע אומר במאה ועוד. ר' יוסי בן המשולם אמר [ועוד קב למאה] סאה. שתות (לדומע) [למדמע]. ואמר בתלמוד א"י והלכה כדבריו של ר' יוסי בן המשולם נמצא המדמע סאה במאה סאה שאין הן חסר הין יתר שיעורו במאה וכשם שתרומה מדמעת כך חלה מדמעת. ואם ניטלה ממנה כזה השיעור ונשתייר בה מזון ב' סעודות מערבין לו בה. אבל אם ניטלה ממנה חלק אחד מכ"ד כדי חלת העושה עיסה לעצמו או למשתה בנו אין מערבין בה שכבר נעשית כפרוסה. וכן אם נפרסה ככר ותפרה בקיסם ונראית שלימה מערבין לו בה. אבל אם נראית פרוסה כגון דידע תפירה אין מערבין לו בה. משמיה דשמואל אמרו מערבין בפת אורז אבל לא בפת דוחן. ועוד אמרו משמו מערבין בפת עדשים. ואם היא פת עשויה ממינים הרבה כגון חטים ושעורים ופול ועדשים ודוחן וכוסמין *) ועוגת שעורים תאכלנו לשיעורין תאכלנה כלומר כשיעור כך וכך. רב פפא אמר עריכתה כעריכת שעורים ולא כעריכת חטין כדתנן אוכלין עראי מן העיסה עד שתגלגל בחטין ותטמטם בשעורין גלגלה בחטין וטימטם בשעורין האוכל ממנה חייב מיתה כיון שהיא נותנת המים מגבהת חלתה ובלבד שלא יהיה שם ה' רבעים קמח: ירושלמי מפני מה אמרו מערבין בחצרות מפני דרכי שלום ומעשה באחת שהיתה עויבה עם חבירתה ושלחה ערובה ביד בנה נטלתה וגפפתה ונשקתה אתא ואמר לאימיה אמר הכין רחמה לי מתוך כך עשו שלום הה"ד כל נתיבותיה שלום:

*) נראה דחסר כאן וצ"ל ודוחן וכוסמין אין מערבין בה: מאי ועוגת שעורים וכו' כצ"ל.

מסורת הש"ס

לעיל כו: קידושין לג.

גי' הרא"ש יונתן

חלה פ"ב מ"ז

בקד"ס הגי' בגמ' ובכס"י בכ"מ עריבתה כעריבת. וכ"ה הגהות יעב"ץ ז"ל.

הגהות הב"ח

(א) תוס' ד"ה איתיביה וכו' בכל הספרים הישנים בכל מערבין עירובי תחומין כו' קס"ד כו' ותיבת קאמר נמחק: (ב) בא"ד וקתני לה גבי תחומין למערבין בכל דבר אלמא:

גליון הש"ס

גמ' שמא יחזור דבר לקלקולו. גיטין דף ס ע"ב:

ומודים בשאר כל האדם שזכו לו מעותיו, [א]שאין מערבין לאדם אלא מדעתו. *אמר רבי יהודה: במה דברים אמורים – בעירובי תחומין, אבל בעירובי חצירות – [ב]מערבין לדעתו ושלא לדעתו, לפי *שזכין לאדם שלא בפניו ואין חבין לאדם שלא בפניו.§ **גמ'** מ"ט דר' אליעזר? הא לא משך! אמר רב נחמן, אמר רבה בר אבהו: עשאו ר"א כד' פרקים בשנה. *דתנן: [ג]בד' פרקים אלו משחיטין את הטבח בעל כרחו, אפילו שור שוה אלף דינר ואין ללוקח אלא דינר אחד – כופין אותו לשחוט. לפיכך, אם מת – מת ללוקח. מת ללוקח?! *הא לא משך! אמר רב הונא: בשמשך. אי הכי, אימא סיפא: בשאר ימות השנה אינו כן; לפיכך, אם מת – מת למוכר. אמאי? הא משך! א"ר שמואל בר יצחק: לעולם בשלא משך, הכא במאי עסקינן – בשזיכה לו על ידי אחר. בד' פרקים אלו, דזכות הוא לו – זכין לו שלא בפניו, בשאר ימות השנה דחוב הוא לו – אין חבין לו אלא בפניו. *ורב אילא אמר ר' *יוחנן: [ד]בד' פרקים אלו העמידו חכמים דבריהן על דברי תורה. *דאמר רבי יוחנן: דבר תורה מעות קונות, ומפני מה אמרו "משיכה קונה" – גזירה שמא יאמר לו: נשרפו חיטיך בעלייה.§ "ומודים בשאר כל האדם כו'.§ מאן שאר כל אדם? אמר רב: [ה]בעל הבית. וכן אמר שמואל: בעה"ב. דאמר שמואל: ל"ש אלא נחתום, אבל בעה"ב – קונה. ואמר שמואל: [ו]ל"ש אלא מעה, אבל כלי – קונה. ואמר שמואל: [ז]לא שנו אלא דאמר לו "זכה לי", אבל אמר "ערב לי" – שליח שויה, וקני.§ "א"ר יהודה בד"א וכו'.§ *אמר רב יהודה, אמר שמואל: הלכה כרבי יהודה. ולא עוד, אלא: כל מקום ששנה רבי יהודה בעירובין – הלכה כמותו. אמר ליה רב חנא בגדתאה לרב יהודה: אמר שמואל אפילו במבוי שניטלו קורותיו או לחייו?! אמר ליה: בעירובין אמרתי לך, ולא במחיצות. אמר ליה רב אחא בריה דרבא לרב אשי: *הלכה מכלל דפליגי? *והאמר ר' יהושע בן לוי: כל מקום שאמר ר' יהודה "אימתי" ו"במה" במשנתנו – אינו אלא לפרש דברי חכמים! ולא פליגי?! והא אנן תנן: *נתוספו עליהן – מוסיף ומזכה וצריך להודיע! התם [ח]בחצר שבין שני מבואות. והאמר *רב שיזבי, אמר רב חסדא: זאת אומרת חלוקין עליו חביריו על רבי יהודה! *אלא

גברא

ומודין בשאר כל אדם. מפרש בגמרא: בעל הבית שאמר לו חברו הילך מעה זו וזכה לי בעירוב והלך וזיכה לו – שקנה עירוב, דהואיל ואין בעה"ב רגיל למכור ככרות לא נתכוין זה אלא לעשותו שליח, ונעשה כאומר לו ערב לי. וגבי חנוני גופיה, אי א"ל "ערב לי" אמרינן בגמרא דקני: שאין מערבין לו לאדם אלא לדעתו. הלכך, גבי חנוני כי א"ל זכי לי – לא נתכוין אלא לקנות הימנו, ולא סמך עליו שיעשה שלוחו. ומעות אינן קונות, ולא סמכה דעתיה – נמצא מערב לו שלא לדעתו. אבל אם משך ככר והניחו אצלו לכך – שליח עשאו: עירובי תחומין. חוב הוא לו שמפסיד לצד האחר, ושמא אינו נוח לו: **גמ'** בד' פרקים. דמתרץ ר' יוחנן לקמן דהעמידו בהן חכמים דבריהם על דין תורה דמעות קונות. אף כאן, מפני תיקון שבת – העמידו דבריהם על דין תורה: בד' פרקים אלו. בפ' "אותו ואת בנו" בחולין (דף פג.): עיו"ט הראשון של פסח, ועי"ט של עצרת, וערב ר"ה. ועי"ט האחרון של חג, וערב יוה"כ בגליל: ואין ללוקח. באותו השור אלא דינר, שנתן לו דינר מבעוד יום בשוה דינר בשר: אם מת. השור אבד הלוקח מה שנתן: אינו כן. אין משחיטין אותו על כרחו, ואם רצה טבח – מחזיר לו את הדינר: בשזיכה לו. טבח ללוקח בשור זה שוה דינר ע"י אחר. שמסר השור לאחר, ואמר לו: זכה לו בו בשם פלוני. והוא לא עשאו שליח לאותו אחר הזוכה בשבילו: זכות הוא לו. להוציא מעות ולקנות בשר, שהכל דרכן בכך: חוב הוא לו. שמוציא הוצאות: דבר תורה מעות קונות. דכתיב בפודה מן ההקדש (ויקרא כז): "ונתן הכסף וקם לו" – ק"ו בלוקח מן ההדיוט: נשרפו חיטיך. שנתת לי מעות עליהן. הלכך, מוקמינן להו ברשות מוכר, כי היכי דלימסר נפשיה עלייהו וניטרח לאצולינהו: אבל כלי. קנין סודר: בעל הבית. פרישית טעמא לעיל: אלא דאמר זכה לי. דלא שוויה שליח, אלא כשאר מוכרין דעלמא, אבל אם אמר ערב לי – שליחא שוויה, וסמכא דעתיה. דקיימא לן: חזקה שליח עושה שליחותו, בפרק "בכל מערבין" (לעיל ד' לג.) הלכך, מערב לדעתיה הוא: אמר שמואל אפילו במבוי שניטלו קורותיו. בשבת, דמיקל בה ר' יהודה בפ' "כל גגות" *ואמר: מותרין לאותו שבת: בעירובין. כל היכא דאיירי בהלכות קניית עירוב:

גברא

בארבעה פרקים כו'. בפ' "אותו ואת בנו" (חולין דף פג.) מפרש: ערב יו"ט הראשון של פסח, ועיו"ט של עצרת, וערב יו"ט האחרון של חג, וערב ר"ה, ועיו"כ בגליל. והא דלא חשיב עיו"ט ראשון של חג – אומר ר"ת: משום דכו"ע טרידי בסוכה ולולב, ואין להם פנאי להרבות בשחיטה כל כך*.

לעולם בשלא משך. מלתא דרב הונא דאוקמי כשמשך אתא לפרושי דהיינו משיכה שזיכה לו ע"י אחר, ומש"ה לא קאמר אלא דלא הדר ביה כלל:

דבר תורה מעות קונות. פירש בקונטרס: דכתיב בפודה מן ההקדש: "ונתן הכסף וקם לו", וק"ו בלוקח מן ההדיוט. וריש לקיש דאמר משיכה מפורשת מן התורה ואין מעות קונות, קסבר: מהקדש לא ילפינן. דכסף קני ליה – משום דלא שייכא ביה משיכה דכל היכא דאיתיה בי גזא דרחמנא איתא. ואין נראה זה הטעם נכון כ"כ, דמ"מ נילף מהקדש שיקנה גם הכסף בהדיוט! ואומר ר"י: משום דתרתי לא מצי למקני בהדיוט, דפרק "הלוקח עובר פרתו" (בכורות דף יג:) דריש ר' יוחנן: "או קנה מיד עמיתך", הא לנכרי – במשיכה, ואם היה קונה משיכה וכסף לר"ל, אם כן, לנכרי במה? וכ"ת: הא לנכרי בכסף דקאי א"מיד עמיתך" דדריש ליה אמשיכה, מכל מקום מדנכרי בחד דוקא – ישראל נמי בחד דוקא, ובכי האי גוונא קאמר התם. ועוד מפרש ר"י: דהיינו טעמא דמעות קונות דבר תורה – דסתם קנין דקרא בכסף איירי, כדאשכחן בכמה דוכתי(א) קנין בכסף: "אוכל בכסף תשבירני" (דברים ב) "שדות בכסף יקנו" (ירמיה לב). ואף על גב דכתיב "ספר המקנה" דנפקא לן *מהתם קנין שטר – מ"מ סתם קנין דבכל דוכתין הוי בכסף. ועוד: מוכח קרא דבכסף איירי, דכתיב [ויקרא כה]: "אל תונו" ואמוכר ואלוקח קאי: **שמא** יאמר חיטיך נשרפו בעלייה. וא"ת: למה עקרו חכמים קנין כסף לגמרי, דהוי דאורייתא, היה להם לתקן דמבעי כסף ומשיכה! ותירץ ר"י: משום תקנת השוק עשו כן, שלא להצריך תרתי, משיכה ומעות. וריב"ן תירץ: דאם המשיכה לבדה לא תקנה – אם כן יאמר הלוקח למוכר נשרפו חיטיך בעלייה. ואם תאמר: א"כ, כשנתן הלוקח מעות ולא משך, יאמר לו המוכר נשרפו מעותיך בעלייה, כיון דאין המעות קונות לו! ואי לאו תירוץ ריב"ן היינו יכולין לומר דלא חיישינן להכי, משום דלא שכיח שיאחר המשיכה לאחר נתינת המעות, כיון דאין מעות קונות. אבל לפי תירוצו לא נוכל לומר כן. דאם כן, לא היה לו נמי למיחש שמא יאמר הלוקח נשרפו חיטיך בעלייה, דלא שכיח שיאחרו הכסף אחר משיכת הפירות, כיון דמשיכה לחוד לא היתה קונה. וי"ל: דמעות נוח לשמרן, ואין טורח בהצלתם כמו פירות, דאין יכול להציל אלא בטורח גדול. ועוד אומר ר"י: דגבי מעות אין שייך לומר נשרפו מעותיך בעלייה, דאפילו הוי עלייהו שומר חנם – הא אמרינן בפרק "המפקיד" (ב"מ דף מב.) דאין להם שמירה אלא בקרקע, ואי לא מותיב להו בקרקע – הוי פשיעותא לגבי נורא, כדמוכח התם גבי ההוא דאותיב זוזי בצריפתא דאורבני. וא"ת: והיכי חיישינן שמא יאמר לו נשרפו חיטיך בעלייה, הא הוי עלייהו שומר שכר ואם לא יציל ישלם. דכי היכי דגבי זוזי הוי מוכר עלייהו שומר שכר, כדמשמע בפ' "הזהב" (שם דף מט.) גבי ההוא גברא דיהיב זוזי אשומשמי, אוקירו שומשמי והדר ביה. וא"ל: שקול זוזך, ולא שקלינהו, ואגנוב. ואמר רבא: דכל כה"ג לא מיבעיא דשומר שכר לא הוי כו'. משמע: דאי לא הוה אומר ליה שקול זוזך – הוי עלייהו שומר שכר. וה"נ גבי חיטין, הוי נמי שומר שכר! ואור"י: לעולם גבי זוזי נמי לא הוי שומר שכר, והא דקאמר: לא מיבעיא דשומר שכר לא הוי, ה"פ: לא מיבעיא היכא דנותן לו שכר, וקאמר לו שקול זוזך, דסליק נפשיה מחיוב שומר שכר – אלא אפילו שומר חנם לא הוי. וכה"ג צריך לפרש באידך עובדא (שם ע"ב), דא"ל: ליהוי הנך זוזי גבך פקדון, דמשכה לי. וא"ל: הא ביתא קמך. ומסיק עלה: לא מיבעיא דשומר שכר לא הוי כו', היינו ע"כ בנותן לו שכר קאמר. ועוד י"ל דאע"ג דגבי זוזי הוי שומר שכר – היינו משום דשרי להוציאם. ואע"ג דמפקיד מעות אצל בעה"ב, תנן ב"המפקיד" (שם מג.) דלא ישתמש בהן, מ"מ מוכר ישתמש בהן כיון דדבר תורה מעות קונות – אליס כמו, ויכול להוציא. אע"ג דתקין רבנן דלא קני אלא במשיכה: ה"ג: **אמר** ר' יהושע ב"ל כל מקום ששנה רבי יהודה אימתי ובמה במשנתינו אינו אלא לפרש דברי חכמים וכ"נ כספרים דגרסי במשנתינו. דבברייתא מצינו דאימתי דרבי יהודה לחלוק בפרק "כיסוי הדם" (חולין דף פח.) גבי דם הניתז ושעל גבי הסכין, ופ"ק דגיטין (דף ז.) גבי המביא גט בספינה. ואין להאריך כאן.

[וע"ע תוס' ביצה ט. ד"ה ולא היא ותוס' סוכה מא. בד"ה שמא יגדל ותוס' גיטין ז. ד"ה אמר ותוס' שבועות מח. סד"ה נשבע ותוס' חולין פח. ד"ה רבנן]:

ואלו

סא א מיי' פ"ו מהל' עירובין הלכה יח וסמג א טוש"ע א"ח סי' תיד סעיף א:

[וע"ע תוס' ע"ג ה: ד"ה ערב]

סב ב מיי' פ"א שם הלכה כ וסמג שם טוש"ע א"ח סי' שסו סעיף י ובהג"ה וסי' שלב סעיף ח:

סג ג ד מיי' פ"ט מהל' מכירה הלכה ז סמג עשין פב טור ש"ע ח"מ סי' קלט סעיף ג:

סד ה ו ז מיי' פ"ו מהלכות עירובין הלכה כ סמג עשין א טוש"ע א"ח סי' שסט:

סה ח מיי' פ"ה שם הלכה ו טור ש"ע א"ח סי' שסח סעיף ב:

גיר' רש"ל יהודה

[קידושין כו.]

רבינו חננאל

מתני' נותן אדם מעות לחנוני או לנחתום כדי שיזכה לו עירוב דברי ר' אליעזר כו'. ואמרי' מ"ט דר' אליעזר והא לא משך אמר רב נחמן אמר רבה בר אבוה השוה ר' אליעזר מדותיו בעירובין כאותן ששנינו בשחיטת חולין (פ') (בפרק כסוי הדם) בד' פרקים אלו משחיטין את הטבח בע"כ ואסקה ר' יוחנן לעולם בשלא משך ושלא זיכה ובד' פרקים אלו העמידו דבריהן על דין תורה דדבר תורה מעות קונות. ומפני מה אמרו משיכה קונה גזירה [שמא] יאמר לו נשרפו חיטיך בעלייה ומודים חכמים לר' יהודה בשאר כל אדם שזכו לו מעותיו. מאן שאר כל אדם. אמר רב מן בעה"ב. וכן אמר שמואל בעה"ב קני דלא שנו חלוקה אלא בנחתום ולא שנו בנחתום דלא קנו אלא מעה יהיב אבל יהיב כלי קני ולא שנו אלא דאמר ליה לנחתום זכי ליה אבל אמר ערב לי קניה: **פיסקא** א"ר יהודה בד"א שאין מערבין לו אלא מדעתו בעירובי תחומין שפעמים שהיא חובה לו שאתה מתירו בצפון ואוסרו בדרום כנגד מה שהתרת והוא אין לו צורך אלא בדרום נמצאת עושה לו חובה לפיכך אין חבין לו אלא בפניו (אלא) [אבל] בעירובי חצרות אתה מתירו תוספת ואינך אוסרו בדבר לפיכך זכין לו אפילו שלא מדעתו. אמר רב יהודה אמר שמואל הלכתא כר' יהודה ולא עוד אלא כ"מ ששנה ר' יהודה בעירובין הלכה כמותו והני מילי בעירוב אבל לא במחיצות ואקשינן למה הוצרך שמואל לומר הלכה כר' יהודה מכלל דחכמים פליגי עליה בהא. והאמר ר' יהושע כל מקום ששנה ר' יהודה אימתי ובמה [אינו] אלא לפרש דברי חכמים ומתני' במה היא ודחינן ולא פליגי והתנן ניתוספו עליהן מוסיף ומזכה וצריך להודיע הלא המשנה זו לרבנן היא ושנו בעירובי חצרות צריך להודיע. ושנינן התם דקתני צריך להודיע בחצר שבין ב' מבואות שכשאתה מתירו במבוי אחד אתה אוסרו במבוי האחר. ונמצאת לו חובה. אבל חצר אחד במבוי אחד לא פליגי עליה. איני והאמר רב חסדא אתה מדחה דברי ר' יהודה. ריב"ל ור' יוחנן נמי הודה בריב"ל בהא כי כל מקום

ששנה

הגהות הב"ח

(א) תוס' ד"ה דבר וכו' בכמה דוכתי (קנין בכסף) תא"מ ונ"ב ס"א קנין כספו:

לעיל מו: פ. לקמן לה. | [גיטין יא: קידושין כג. וש"נ] | חולין פג. | [שם. ע"ש] | [בכורות יג: קידושין כו. כח:] | ב"מ מז: שם | לקמן לה. | [שבת קו: וש"נ] | [סנהדרין כד:] | [לקמן לז.] | [לעיל פ:] | [שם:] | ס"א א"ל

גַּבְרָא אַגַּבְרָא קָא רָמֵית?! מָר סָבַר: פְּלִיגִי, וּמָר סָבַר: לָא פְּלִיגִי. גּוּפָא, *א"ר יְהוֹשֻׁעַ בֶּן לֵוִי: כָּל מָקוֹם שֶׁאָמַר ר' יְהוּדָה, "אֵימָתַי" וּ"בַמֶּה" בְּמִשְׁנָתֵינוּ — אֵינוֹ אֶלָּא לְפָרֵשׁ דִּבְרֵי חֲכָמִים. וְר' יוֹחָנָן אָמַר: "אֵימָתַי" — לְפָרֵשׁ, וּ"בַמֶּה" — לַחֲלוֹק. וְ"אֵימָתַי" לְפָרֵשׁ הוּא? וְהָא תְּנַן:* [א]וְאֵלּוּ הֵן הַפְּסוּלִים: הַמְשַׂחֵק בְּקוּבְיָא, וּמַלְוֶה בְּרִבִּית, וּמַפְרִיחֵי יוֹנִים, וְסוֹחֲרֵי שְׁבִיעִית. אָמַר ר' יְהוּדָה: [ב]אֵימָתַי — בִּזְמַן שֶׁאֵין לוֹ אוּמָּנוּת אֶלָּא הִיא, אֲבָל יֵשׁ לוֹ אוּמָּנוּת שֶׁלֹּא הִיא — הֲרֵי זֶה כָּשֵׁר. וְתָנֵי עֲלָהּ בְּבָרַיְיתָא: וַחכ"א: בֵּין שֶׁאֵין לוֹ אוּמָּנוּת אֶלָּא הִיא, וּבֵין שֶׁיֵּשׁ לוֹ אוּמָּנוּת שֶׁלֹּא הִיא — הֲרֵי זֶה פָּסוּל! הַהִיא דְּרַבִּי יְהוּדָה א"ר טַרְפוֹן הִיא; *דְּתַנְיָא, א"ר יְהוּדָה מִשּׁוּם ר"ט: לְעוֹלָם אֵין אֶחָד מֵהֶן נָזִיר, לְפִי שֶׁאֵין נְזִירוּת אֶלָּא לְהַפְלָאָה. אַלְמָא: כֵּיוָן דְּמִסְפְּקָא לֵיהּ אִי נָזִיר אִי לָא נָזִיר הוּא — לָא מְשַׁעְבֵּיד נַפְשֵׁיהּ, הָכָא נַמִי: כֵּיוָן דְּלָא יָדַע אִי קָנֵי אִי לָא קָנֵי — לָא גָּמַר וּמַקְנֶה.§

הדרן עלך חלון

כֵּיצַד מִשְׁתַּתְּפִין בִּתְחוּמִין? מַנִּיחַ אֶת הֶחָבִית, וְאוֹמֵר: הֲרֵי זֶה לְכָל בְּנֵי עִירִי לְכָל מִי שֶׁיֵּלֵךְ לְבֵית הָאֵבֶל אוֹ לְבֵית הַמִּשְׁתֶּה. וְכָל שֶׁקִּיבֵּל עָלָיו, מִבְּעוֹד יוֹם — מוּתָּר, מִשֶּׁתֶּחְשַׁךְ — אָסוּר, שֶׁאֵין מְעָרְבִין מִשֶּׁתֶּחְשַׁךְ.§ **גמ'** *אָמַר רַב יוֹסֵף: [ג]אֵין מְעָרְבִין אֶלָּא לִדְבַר מִצְוָה. מַאי קמ"ל? תְּנֵינָא: לְכָל מִי שֶׁיֵּלֵךְ לְבֵית הָאֵבֶל אוֹ לְבֵית הַמִּשְׁתֶּה! מַהוּ דְּתֵימָא: אוֹרְחָא דְּמִלְּתָא קָתָנֵי, קמ"ל. "וְכָל שֶׁקִּיבֵּל עָלָיו מִבְּעוֹד יוֹם" — שְׁמַעַתְּ מִינַּהּ: אֵין בְּרֵירָה. דְּאִי יֵשׁ בְּרֵירָה — תִּיגְלֵי מִילְּתָא לְמַפְרֵעַ דְּמִבְּעוֹד יוֹם הֲוָה נִיחָא לֵיהּ! אָמַר רַב אַשִׁי: "הוֹדִיעוּהוּ" וְ"לֹא [ד]הוֹדִיעוּהוּ" קָתָנֵי. אָמַר רַב אַסִי: *[ה]קָטָן בֶּן שֵׁשׁ יוֹצֵא בְּעֵירוּב אִמּוֹ. מֵיתִיבִי: קָטָן שֶׁצָּרִיךְ לְאִמּוֹ — יוֹצֵא בְּעֵירוּב אִמּוֹ. וְשֶׁאֵין צָרִיךְ לְאִמּוֹ — אֵין יוֹצֵא בְּעֵירוּב אִמּוֹ. וּתְנַן נַמִי גַּבֵּי סוּכָּה כִּי הַאי גַּוְונָא: *[ו]קָטָן שֶׁאֵין צָרִיךְ לְאִמּוֹ — חַיָּיב בַּסּוּכָּה. וְהָוֵינַן בָּהּ: *וְאֵיזֶהוּ קָטָן שֶׁאֵין צָרִיךְ לְאִמּוֹ? אָמְרִי דְּבֵי ר' יַנַּאי: כֹּל שֶׁנִּפְנֶה וְאֵין אִמּוֹ מְקַנַּחְתּוֹ. ר"ש בֶּן לָקִישׁ אָמַר: כֹּל שֶׁנֵּיעוֹר וְאֵינוֹ קוֹרֵא "אִימָּא". אִימָּא ס"ד? גְּדוֹלִים נַמִי קָרוּ! אֶלָּא אֵימָא: כֹּל שֶׁנֵּיעוֹר מִשְּׁנָתוֹ וְאֵינוֹ קוֹרֵא "אִימָּא אִימָּא". וְכַמָּה, [ז]כְּבַר אַרְבַּע כְּבַר חָמֵשׁ! אָמַר

רש"י

גַּבְרָא אַגַּבְרָא. דר' יְהוֹשֻׁעַ בֶּן לֵוִי אַדִּשְׁמוּאֵל, שְׁמוּאֵל דְּאָמַר הֲלָכָה, סָבַר: פְּלִיגִי, וְרַבִּי יְהוֹשֻׁעַ סָבַר: לָא פְּלִיגִי: הַפְּסוּלִין. לְעֵדוּת דְּכוּלָּן גַּזְלָנִין מִדִּבְרֵיהֶן הֵן, דְּאַסְמַכְתָּא לָא קַנְיָא, וּמִגְזַל גָּזֵיל לֵיהּ: בְּקוּבְיָא. בְּעֵירָבוֹן: מַפְרִיחֵי יוֹנִים. אִי תִּיקְדְּמֵיהּ יוֹנָךְ לְיוֹנִי: סוֹחֲרֵי שְׁבִיעִית. דְּרַחֲמָנָא אָמַר: "לְאָכְלָה" וְלֹא לִסְחוֹרָה, וְזֶה שֶׁחוֹמֵד מָמוֹן לַעֲבוֹר עֲבֵירָה עַל הַמָּמוֹן — רָשָׁע הוּא, וְהַתּוֹרָה אָמְרָה: "אַל תָּשֶׁת רָשָׁע עֵד" (שמות כג): בִּזְמַן שֶׁאֵין לָהֶם אוּמָּנוּת אֶלָּא הִיא. דְּקָסָבַר ר' יְהוּדָה: אַסְמַכְתָּא שֶׁהוּא נִסְמָךְ עַל דַּעְתּוֹ שֶׁהוּא יְנַצְּחֶנּוּ, וְעַל אוֹתָהּ אַסְמַכְתָּא הוּא מַתְנֶה — קַנְיָא, וְלָאו גַּזְלָנִין נִינְהוּ. וּפְסוּלַיְיהוּ לְפִי שֶׁאֵין עֲסוּקִין בְּיִשּׁוּבוֹ שֶׁל עוֹלָם, דְּכֵיוָן דְּאֵין מַכִּירִין וּבְקִיאִין בְּטוֹרַח וְצַעַר בְּנֵי אָדָם — אֵינָן חָסִין עַל חַבְרֵיהֶן מִלְּהַפְסִידָן מָמוֹן: וַחכ"א כו'. קָא ס"ד: הַיְינוּ ת"ק דְּמַתְנִי' אַלְמָא: "אֵימָתַי" לַחֲלוֹק: הַהִיא. בָּרַיְיתָא מִשּׁוּם ר"ט הִיא, דְּאָמַר: אַסְמַכְתָּא לָא קַנְיָא. אֲבָל בְּמַתְנִיתִין לָא פָּלֵיג רַבִּי יְהוּדָה אַדְּתַנָּא קַמָּא אֶלָּא מְפָרֵשׁ לְטַעְמֵיהּ: אֵין אֶחָד מֵהֶן נָזִיר. שְׁנַיִם שֶׁיּוֹשְׁבִין וְרָאוּ אֶחָד בָּא, וְאָמַר אֶחָד מֵהֶן: הֲרֵינִי נָזִיר שֶׁזֶּה נָזִיר וְאָמַר חֲבֵירוֹ: הֲרֵינִי נָזִיר שֶׁאֵין זֶה נָזִיר: לְהַפְלָאָה. שֶׁיְּהֵא נִדְרוֹ מְפוֹרָשׁ עַל הַוַּדַּאי, וְלֹא בְּתוֹרַת סָפֵק אִי נָזִיר אוֹתוֹ הַבָּא כְּנֶגְדּוֹ: אִי קָנֵי. אִי נָצַח:

הדרן עלך חלון

כֵּיצַד מִשְׁתַּתְּפִין כו' וְכָל מִי שֶׁמְּקַבֵּל מִבְּעוֹד יוֹם. לִסְמוֹךְ עַל עֵירוּב זֶה וְלֵילֵךְ — מוּתָּר: **גמ'** אֵין מְעָרְבִין. לֹא הִתִּירוּ חֲכָמִים לָצֵאת חוּץ לַתְּחוּם ע"י עֵירוּב, אֶלָּא לִדְבַר מִצְוָה: הוֹדִיעוּהוּ מִבְּעוֹד יוֹם וְלֹא הוֹדִיעוּהוּ קָתָנֵי. הוֹדִיעוּהוּ, אע"פ שֶׁלֹּא נִתְרַצָּה מִבְּעוֹד יוֹם וְנִתְרַצָּה מִשֶּׁחֲשֵׁיכָה — אָמְרִינַן: הוּבְרַר שֶׁקּוֹדֶם זְמַן קְנִיַּית עֵירוּב דַּעְתּוֹ לְכָךְ הָיָה. לֹא הוֹדִיעוּהוּ עַד שֶׁחֲשֵׁיכָה מַאי בְּרֵירָה אִיכָּא? הָא לָא הֲוָה יָדַע דְּאִיכָּא עֵירוּב, דְּנֵימָא דַּעְתֵּיהּ עֲלֵיהּ הֲוַאי: יוֹצֵא בְּעֵירוּב אִמּוֹ. עֵירְבָה אִמּוֹ לְעַצְמָהּ, וְלֹא זִיכְּתָה לוֹ בָּעֵירוּב — מוֹלִיכַתּוֹ עִמָּהּ, דִּכְגוּפָהּ דָּמֵי דְּמִסְתַּמָּא דַּעְתָּהּ עֲלֵיהּ, דְּלָא סַגֵּי לֵיהּ בְּלָאו אִמּוֹ: וּתְנַן נַמִי גַּבֵּי סוּכָּה. כְּלוֹמַר: וְכִי תֵּימָא בֶּן שֵׁשׁ צָרִיךְ לְאִמּוֹ קָרֵי לֵיהּ — הָא לֵיכָּא לְמֵימַר, דִּתְנַן נַמִי גַּבֵּי סוּכָּה* כִּי הַאי גַּוְונָא, וּפָרְשִׁינַן הָתָם הֵי קָטָן צָרִיךְ לְאִמּוֹ: חַיָּיב בַּסּוּכָּה. מְחַנְּכִינַן לֵיהּ מִדְּרַבָּנַן: וְאֵינוֹ קוֹרֵא אִימָּא. כֵּיוָן דְּלָא קָרֵי — הַהִיא שַׁעְתָּא לָאו צָרִיךְ הוּא: וּפָרְכִינַן אִימָּא סָלְקָא דַּעְתָּךְ גָּדוֹל נַמִי קָרֵי. כְּלוֹמַר: לָא מְשַׁוֵּית לֵיהּ אֵין צָרִיךְ לְאִמּוֹ עַד שֶׁיְּהֵא נֵיעוֹר מִשְּׁנָתוֹ וְלֹא יִקְרָא אִימָּא, הָא אִי קָרָא אִימָּא צָרִיךְ לְאִמּוֹ מְשַׁוֵּית לֵיהּ — הָא אֲפִילּוּ גָּדוֹל דַּרְכּוֹ בְּכָךְ: אֶלָּא כָּל שֶׁנֵּיעוֹר מִשְּׁנָתוֹ וְאֵינוֹ קוֹרֵא אִימָּא אִימָּא. דְּלָא *נָוַח עַד דְּאָתְיָא לְקַמֵּיהּ — הָוֵי "אֵינוֹ צָרִיךְ לְאִמּוֹ": וְכַמָּה. בַּר כַּמָּה שְׁנֵי הָוֵי: כְּבַר אַרְבַּע כְּבַר חָמֵשׁ. קָרֵי לֵיהּ אֵין צָרִיךְ לְאִמּוֹ, כָּל חַד לְפוּם חוּרְפֵּיהּ. אַלְמָא: מִכִּי הָוֵי בַּר חָמֵשׁ בָּעֵי לְזַכּוּיֵיהּ, וּטְפֵי מִבַּר[(א)] ד' לָא קָרֵי לֵיהּ צָרִיךְ לְאִמּוֹ דְּלֵיפּוּק: אָמַר

תוספות

ואלו הן הפסולין. מפורש בפרק "זה בורר" (סנהדרין דף כד:):
אמר ר' יהודה אימתי[(ב)] כו' בזמן שאין לו **אומנות כו'**. אע"ג דמסקינן דפליגי רבנן עליה דרבי יהודה — הלכה כרבי יהודה. כדפסיק בפרק "זה בורר" (שם דף כו:), א"ר אבהו: הלכה כרבי יהודה. ומכאן משמע דשרי לשחוק בקוביא. דאפילו לרמי בר חמא דמפרש טעמא דמשחק בקוביא פסול משום דאסמכתא לא קניא — היינו לרבנן, אבל לר' יהודה דמכשר היכא דגמיר אומנות אחריתי — קסבר דכה"ג לאו אסמכתא היא, וטעם דלא הוי אסמכתא — כדפירש הקונטרס בפ' "זה בורר" (שם דף כד:) משום דלא דמי להאיך דב"מ (ד' קד:): אם אוביר ולא איעביד אשלם אלפא זוזי. דהתם הוי בידו, ולהכי לא גמר ומקני. דמעיקרא כי אתני — אדעתא דלא יהיב ליה[(ג)]. אסמכתא קמתני דטועה, וסבור שלא יבא לידי כך. אבל הכא לא סמיך אמידי, משום דלא ידע אי נצח או לא. ובפרק "זה בורר" (סנהדרין דף כה.) משמע גבי מפריחי יונים, דקאמר: וצריכא, דאי תנא דתולה בדעת עצמו — התם הוא דאמר קים לי בנפשאי דידענא טפי, ולהכי הוי אסמכתא. משמע היכא דבידו — הויא אסמכתא טפי. וקשה לר"ת: דבסוף "איזהו נשך" (ב"מ דף עג:) גבי האי מאן דיהיב זוזי לחבריה למזבן ליה חמרא כו', ופריך: מ"ש דאם אוביר ולא איעביד אשלם במיטבא? ומשני: התם — בידו, הכא — לאו בידו. אלמא: משום דלאו בידו הויא אסמכתא טפי! ונראה: היכא דבידו לגמרי, ולא גזים כי ההוא דאם אוביר ולא איעביד אשלם במיטבא[(ד)] — לא הויא אסמכתא. וכן היכא דאין בידו כלל, ואפילו הכי גמיר ומקני — כגון קוביא, וכה"ג. אבל היכא דבידו ולא בידו, כי ההוא חמרא דפשע ולא זבן ליה, ואע"ג דיין מצוי הרבה לקנות — מ"מ כיון דתלוי באחרים, דאם לא ירצו למכור לו ממי יקנה — הלכך לא גמר ומקני, והוי אסמכתא גמורה. ועוד פר"ת טעם אחר: דדווקא כי ההוא דאם אני חוזר בי ערבוני מחול, דפרק "הזהב" (שם דף מח:), ומי שפרע מקצת חובו והשליש את שטרו ד"גט פשוט" (ב"ב דף קסח.), וכל כה"ג חשיב אסמכתא, שאינו מתכוין אלא להסמיך חבירו על דבריו שיאמינוהו. אבל הכא — אדעתא דהכי קעבדו שירויחו או זה או זה. ואותם המשחקים באמנה — אומר ר"י: דאינו חייב לשלם, דבמה יקנה? דלמ"ד אסמכתא היא — לא קני אפילו בקנין, אלא בב"ד חשוב, כדמוכח בנדרים (דף כז:). ולמ"ד לאו אסמכתא היא — היאך יקנה בדברים בלא קנין, בשביל שנולא חבירו:

הדרן עלך חלון

כיצד משתתפין מניח את החבית. כל פירותיהן היו רגילים להניח בחבית, כדתניא לעיל [דף פ.]: מביאין את החבית של יין ושל שמן ושל גרוגרות ושל שאר כל מיני פירות:

אין מערבין אלא לדבר מצוה. לעיל, *דתנן: אם באו נכרים למזרח [דף לו:] וכו'. ומוקי לה בגמ' במרי מתא. ופי' שם בקונטרס: שצריך לצעוק לפניו — הוי נמי דבר מצוה, שהולך לצורך בני עירו, ומפקח על עסקי רבים:

שמע מינה אין ברירה. דלא מסתבר דאפילו בעירובי תחומין דרבנן אין ברירה, כדאמרינן פרק "בכל מערבין" (לעיל דף לז:): מאן האי תנא דאפילו בדרבנן לית ליה ברירה: **קטן** בן שש יוצא בעירוב אמו. אף על גב דאין מערבין אלא לדבר מצוה — מכל מקום יוצא קטן בעירוב אמו, דאי אפשר לה להניחו משום דכרוך אחריה. א"נ: בקטן נמי איכא °מצוה לחנכו:

עד

[סנהדרין כה.]
שם כד: [ר"ה כב.]
סנהדרין כה. חגיגה י. נזיר לד. לב. נדרים יט: כח.
[דף כח.]
ס"א יוצא
לעיל לו.
סוכה כח:
[ד"ה כ:]
[דף לו:]

סו א ב מיי' פ"י מהל' עדות הלכה ד ופי"ב הלכה א סמג לאוין רי"ד טוש"ע ח"מ סי' לד סעיף טז:
א ג מיי' פ"ו מהלכות עירובין הלכה ו סמג עשין א טוש"ע א"ח סי' תטו סעיף א:
ב ד מיי' שם הלכה יח וסמג שם טור ש"ע א"ח סי' תיג:
ג ה מיי' שם הלכה כא וסמג שם טוש"ע א"ח סי' תיד סעיף ב:
ד ו ז מיי' פ"ו מהלכות סוכה הלכה א סמג עשין מג טוש"ע א"ח סי' תרמ סעיף ב:

רבינו חננאל

ששנה ר' יהודה אימתי לפרש הוא. ואקשינן עליה איני והתנן בסנהדרין פרק דיני ממונות בג' זה בורר לו אחד אלו הן הפסולין המשחק בקוביא כו'. א"ר יהודה אימתי בזמן שאין לו אומנות אלא היא אבל יש לו אומנות שלא היא הרי זה כשר. וקתני בברייתא וחכ"א בין שיש לו אומנות שלא היא בין שאין לו אומנות אלא היא הרי זה פסול הנה חולקין דר' יהודה אמר כשר וחכ"א אפילו יש לו אומנות שלא היא הרי זה פסול. ופרקינן לעולם אימתי לפרש הוא והאי דקתני בברייתא וחכ"א [ר"י היא] ומפרש דברי ר' טרפון. (דתנן) [דתניא] ר' יהודה אומר משום ר' טרפון אין אחד מהן נזיר לפי שלא נתנה נזירות אלא להפלאה שנאמר איש כי יפליא (אלא) [אלמא] כיון דמספקא ליה אי נזיר הוא אי לא נזיר הוא לא ידע (דנחיל) [דנחית] ולא משעביד נפשיה הכא נמי גבי המשחק בקוביא לא ידע אי קני אי לא קני לא גמר ומקני:

הדרן עלך חלון

פ"ח **כיצד** משתתפין בתחומין מניח את החבית כו' אמר רב יוסף אין מערבין אלא לדבר מצוה כל מי שקבל עליו מבעו"י מותר. ש"מ אין ברירה אפילו בדרבנן דהא עירובי תחומין דרבנן נינהו ודלא כר' עקיבא ופריק רב אשי הודיעוהו קתני פי' הודיעוהו שצריך לערב לילך למקום פלוני כיון *) שמקבל נתברר כאלו מאתמול עירב. אמר רב יוסף קטן בן שש יוצא בעירוב אמו והא דתניא קטן יוצא בעירוב אמו

*) אולי צ"ל כיון שמקבל עליו אפילו משחשיכה נתברר וכו'.

רב נסים גאון

פ"ח **כיצד**. שמעת מינה אין ברירה אפי' בדרבנן בהרבה מקומות בתלמוד איתה להוויא דהא מילתא אבל במסכת יום טוב בפרק משילין פירות (דף לח) והכין סליקא לה מילתא כי לית ליה לר' הושעיה ברירה בדאורייתא אבל בדרבנן אית ליה דרש מר זוטרא הילכתא כר' אושעיא: ר'

הגהות הב"ח

(א) רש"י ד"ה כבר ארבע וכו' טפי מבר (ארבע) תז"מ נ"ב ס"א חמש: (ב) תוס' ד"ה אמר ר' יהודה אימתי בזמן כו' איתא כו' נמחק: (ג) בא"ד דאדעתא דלא יהיב ליה קמתני והוי אסמכתא לטועה וסבור וכו' משמע כגי מפריחי: (ד) בא"ד ולא גזים כי ההוא דאם אוביר ולא איעביד אשלם במיטבא או היכא דלאו בידו כלל ואפי' הכי גמר ומקני כגון קוביא וכה"ג באותה לא הויא אסמכתא אבל היכא דבידו ולא בידו כו'.

גליון הש"ס

תום' ד"ה קטן בן שש בתוס' ד"ה מצוה לחנכו. עי' תה"ד סימן לד:

ה א ב ג מיי' פ"ו מהלכות עירובין הלכה כא סמג עשין א טוש"ע א"ח סי' תיד סעיף א:
ו ד מיי' שם הלכה ז וסמג שם טוש"ע א"ח סי' תט סעיף ז:
ז ה מיי' פט"ז מהלכות טומאת צרעת הלכה ו:
ח ו מיי' פ"ד מהלכות טומאת אוכלין הל"א:

אָמַר רַב יְהוֹשֻׁעַ בְּרֵיהּ דְּרַב אִידִי: כִּי קָאָמַר רַב אַסִי – כְּגוֹן שֶׁעֵירֵב עָלָיו אָבִיו לַצָּפוֹן, וְאִמּוֹ לַדָּרוֹם. דַּאֲפִילּוּ בַּר שֵׁשׁ נַמִי, בְּצַוְותָא דְּאִמֵּיהּ נִיחָא לֵיהּ. מֵיתִיבִי: קָטָן שֶׁצָּרִיךְ לְאִמּוֹ – יוֹצֵא בְּעֵירוּב אִמּוֹ, עַד בֶּן שֵׁשׁ. תְּיוּבְתָּא דְּרַב יְהוֹשֻׁעַ בַּר רַב אִידִי! תְּיוּבְתָּא. לֵימָא תֶּיהֱוֵי תְּיוּבְתֵּיהּ דְּרַב אַסִי?! אָמַר לָךְ רַב אַסִי: *"עַד" וְעַד בִּכְלָל. לֵימָא תֶּיהֱוֵי תְּיוּבְתֵּיהּ דְּרַבִּי יַנַּאי וְר"ל?! ל"ק; הָא – דְּאִיתֵיהּ אֲבוּהִי בְּמָתָא, הָא – דְּלָא אִיתֵיהּ אֲבוּהִי בְּמָתָא. ת"ר: אמְעָרֵב אָדָם עַל יְדֵי בְּנוֹ וּבִתּוֹ הַקְּטַנִּים, עַל יְדֵי עַבְדּוֹ וְשִׁפְחָתוֹ הַכְּנַעֲנִים, בֵּין לְדַעְתָּן בֵּין שֶׁלֹּא לְדַעְתָּן(א) אֲבָל אֵינוֹ מְעָרֵב לֹא ע"י עַבְדּוֹ וְשִׁפְחָתוֹ הָעִבְרִים, [וְלֹא] עַל יְדֵי בְּנוֹ וּבִתּוֹ הַגְּדוֹלִים, וְלֹא עַל יְדֵי אִשְׁתּוֹ, אֶלָּא מִדַּעְתָּם. תַּנְיָא אִידָךְ: לֹא יְעָרֵב אָדָם עַל יְדֵי בְּנוֹ וּבִתּוֹ הַגְּדוֹלִים(ב) וְע"י עַבְדּוֹ וְשִׁפְחָתוֹ הָעִבְרִים, וְלֹא ע"י אִשְׁתּוֹ, אֶלָּא מִדַּעְתָּן. אֲבָל מְעָרֵב הוּא ע"י עַבְדּוֹ וְשִׁפְחָתוֹ הַכְּנַעֲנִים, וְעַל יְדֵי בְּנוֹ וּבִתּוֹ הַקְּטַנִּים, בֵּין לְדַעְתָּן וּבֵין שֶׁלֹּא לְדַעְתָּן – מִפְּנֵי שֶׁיָּדָן כְּיָדוֹ. וְכוּלָּן שֶׁעֵירְבוּ, וְעֵירֵב עֲלֵיהֶם רַבָּן – יוֹצְאִין בְּשֶׁל רַבָּן, חוּץ מִן הָאִשָּׁה, מִפְּנֵי שֶׁיְּכוֹלָה לִמְחוֹת. אִשָּׁה מַאי שְׁנָא? אָמַר רַבָּה: אִשָּׁה וְכָל דְּדָמֵי לָהּ.(ג) אָמַר מָר: חוּץ מִן הָאִשָּׁה, מִפְּנֵי שֶׁיְּכוֹלָה לִמְחוֹת. טַעְמָא: דְּמָחֵי, הָא סְתָמָא – נָפְקָא בִּדְבַעְלָהּ. הָא קָתָנֵי רֵישָׁא: "אֶלָּא מִדַּעְתָּם", מַאי לָאו דְּאָמְרִי אִין! לָא, מַאי "אֶלָּא מִדַּעְתָּם", בדְּאִשְׁתִּיקוּ. לְאַפּוֹקֵי הֵיכָא דְּאָמְרִי "לָא". הָא "וְכוּלָּן שֶׁעֵירְבוּ וְעֵירֵב עֲלֵיהֶן רַבָּן יוֹצְאִין בְּשֶׁל רַבָּן"(ד) וּסְתָמָא הוּא, וְקָתָנֵי חוּץ מִן הָאִשָּׁה, דְּלָא נָפְקִי! אָמַר רָבָא: גכֵּיוָן שֶׁעֵירְבוּ – אֵין לְךָ מִיחוּי גָּדוֹל מִזֶּה.§ **מתני'** ד*כַּמָּה הוּא שִׁיעוּרוֹ? מְזוֹן שְׁתֵּי סְעוּדוֹת לְכָל אֶחָד וְאֶחָד, מְזוֹנוֹ לַחוֹל וְלֹא לַשַּׁבָּת, דִּבְרֵי ר"מ. רַבִּי יְהוּדָה אוֹמֵר: לַשַּׁבָּת וְלֹא לַחוֹל. וְזֶה וָזֶה מִתְכַּוְּונִים לְהָקֵל. ר' יוֹחָנָן בֶּן בְּרוֹקָה אוֹמֵר: מִכִּכָּר בְּפוּנְדְּיוֹן מִד' סְאִין בְּסֶלַע. ר"ש אוֹמֵר: שְׁתֵּי יָדוֹת לְכִכָּר מִשָּׁלֹשׁ לַקַּב, החֶצְיָיהּ לַבַּיִת הַמְנוּגָּע, ווַחֲצִי חֶצְיָיהּ לִפְסוֹל אֶת הַגְּוִיָּה.§ **גמ'** וְכַמָּה מְזוֹן שְׁתֵּי סְעוּדוֹת? א"ר יְהוּדָה, אָמַר רַב: תַּרְתֵּי רִיפְתָּא *אִיכַּרְיָיתָא. רַב אַדָּא בַּר אַהֲבָה אָמַר: תַּרְתֵּי רִיפְתָּא נְהַר פַּפִּיתָא. א"ל רַב יוֹסֵף לְרַב יוֹסֵף בְּרֵיהּ(ה) דְּרָבָא: אֲבוּךְ כְּמַאן ס"ל? כְּר' מֵאִיר ס"ל. אֲנָא נַמִי כְּר"מ ס"ל, דְּאִי כְּרַבִּי יְהוּדָה – קַשְׁיָא הָא דְּאָמְרִי אֱינָשֵׁי *"רַוְוחָא לִבְסִימָא שְׁכִיחַ".§ "רַבִּי יוֹחָנָן בֶּן בְּרוֹקָה אוֹמֵר".§ תָּנָא: וּקְרוֹבִים דִּבְרֵיהֶן לִהְיוֹת שָׁוִין. מִי דָּמֵי?! דְּר"י – אַרְבַּע סְעוּדָתָא לְקַבָּא, דר"ש – תְּשַׁע סְעוּדָתָא לְקַבָּא! *א"ר חִסְדָּא: צֵא מֵהֶן שְׁלִישׁ לַחֶנְוָנִי. וְאַכַּתִּי לְמָר – תִּשְׁעָה, וּלְמָר – שִׁית! [*אֶלָּא כְּאִידָךְ] דְּרַב חִסְדָּא, דְּאָמַר: *צֵא מֵהֶן מֶחֱצָה לַחֶנְוָנִי. וְאַכַּתִּי, לְמָר – תֵּשַׁע, וּלְמָר – תְּמָנֵי! הַיְינוּ דְּקָאָמַר "וּקְרוֹבִים דִּבְרֵיהֶם לִהְיוֹת שָׁוִין". קַשְׁיָא דְּרַב חִסְדָּא אַדְּרַב חִסְדָּא! ל"ק; הָא – דְּקָא יָהֵיב בַּעַל הַבַּיִת צִיבֵי, הָא – דְּלָא יָהֵיב בַּעַל הַבַּיִת צִיבֵי.§ "חֶצְיָיהּ לְבֵית הַמְנוּגָּע וַחֲצִי חֶצְיָיהּ לִפְסוֹל אֶת הַגְּוִיָּה".§ תָּנָא

[עמוד ב]

רש"י

אָמַר רַב יְהוֹשֻׁעַ. וַדַּאי כִּדְאַמְרַתְּ בֶּן ה' אֵינוֹ יוֹצֵא עַד שֶׁיְּעָרְבוּ עָלָיו, וְרַב אַסִי נַמִי בְּשֶׁעֵירְבָה אִמּוֹ עָלָיו קָאָמַר. וְקמ"ל: דְּאִם עֵירֵב עָלָיו אָבִיו לְרוּחַ אַחֶרֶת – בָּתַר אִמּוֹ שָׁדֵינַן לֵיהּ: מֵיתִיבִי כו' עַד בֶּן שֵׁשׁ.(ו) הָא לֵיכָּא לְמֵימַר כְּשֶׁעֵרֵב עָלָיו זֶה לְכָאן וְזֶה לְכָאן, דְּהָא "עַד" קָתָנֵי. דְּמַשְׁמַע: בֶּן שָׁנָה וּבֶן שְׁתַּיִם וְשָׁלֹשׁ עַד בֶּן שֵׁשׁ – יוֹצֵא בְּעֵירוּב אִמּוֹ. וְכִי הֵיכִי דְּבֶן שָׁנָה וּבֶן שְׁתַּיִם בְּלֹא זִיכּוּי עֵירוּב קָאָמַר – בֶּן ד' וּבֶן ה' נַמִי בְּלֹא עֵירְבוּ עָלָיו קָאָמַר. וְכִי נַמִי אָמְרִינַן עַד וְלֹא עַד בִּכְלָל – הָוְיָא תְּיוּבְתָּא דְּרַב יְהוֹשֻׁעַ, דְּתָרֵיץ דְּבֶן ה' צָרִיךְ לְזַכּוֹת לוֹ תְּיוּבְתָּא: לֵימָא תֶּהֱוֵי תְּיוּבְתֵּיהּ דְּרַב אַסִי. דְּ"עַד" וְלֹא עַד בִּכְלָל מַשְׁמַע, וְאִיהוּ אָמַר: אֲפִילּוּ בֶּן שֵׁשׁ: לֵימָא תֶּהֱוֵי תְּיוּבְתֵּיהּ דְּר' יַנַּאי וּדְרֵישׁ לָקִישׁ. דִּמְפָרְשִׁי גַּבֵּי סוּכָּה בַּר אַרְבַּע וּבַר חַמְשָׁא קָרֵי לֵיהּ "אֵין צָרִיךְ לְאִמּוֹ" וְהָכָא תָּנֵי יוֹצֵא בְּעֵירוּב אִמּוֹ. וְתַנְיָא לְעֵיל דְּקָטָן שֶׁאֵינוֹ צָרִיךְ לְאִמּוֹ – אֵינוֹ יוֹצֵא בְּעֵירוּבָהּ: הָא דְּאִיתֵיהּ לַאֲבוּהּ בְּמָתָא. וְהַתִּינוֹק נִכְנָס וְיוֹצֵא עִמּוֹ – לָא קָרֵי לֵיהּ צָרִיךְ לְאִמּוֹ מִבֶּן ד' וּלְמַעְלָה. וּבָרַיְיתָא – בִּדְלֵיתֵיהּ לַאֲבוּהּ בְּמָתָא. וְרַב יְהוֹשֻׁעַ לָא מָצֵי לְשַׁנּוּיֵי הָכִי, דְּהָא כִּי אוֹתְבִינֵיהּ לְרַב אַסִי לְעֵיל: אִם אִיתָא דְּאִית לֵיהּ לְרַב יְהוֹשֻׁעַ הָא סְבָרָא – הָכִי הֲוָה מְשַׁנֵּי לֵיהּ לְדְרַב אַסִי, בִּדְלֵיתֵיהּ לַאֲבוּהּ בְּמָתָא, וְנֵימָא בִּדְלָא עֵירֵב שָׁרֵי, וְאַשְׁמְעִינַן רְבוּתָא: עַל יָדָן. בִּשְׁבִילָן: וְעֵירֵב רַבָּן עֲלֵיהֶן. לְרוּחַ אַחֶרֶת: אִשָּׁה מַאי שְׁנָא. מֵעֶבֶד עִבְרִי, וּבְנוֹ וּבִתּוֹ הַגְּדוֹלִים: הָא סְתָמָא. דְּאִישְׁתִּיקָה, וּלְרוּחַ אַחֶרֶת נַמִי לָא עֵירְבָה: **מתני'** מִתְכַּוְּונִין לְהָקֵל. ר' מֵאִיר סָבַר: בְּשַׁבָּת אָכֵיל אִינִישׁ טְפֵי, מִשּׁוּם דְּבָסִים תַּבְשִׁילֵיהּ, וְאָמְרֵי אֱינָשֵׁי: רַוְוחָא לִבְסִימָא שְׁכִיחַ. וְר' יְהוּדָה סָבַר: כֵּיוָן דִּבְשַׁבָּת סוֹעֵד שָׁלֹשׁ סְעוּדוֹת – אֵינוֹ אוֹכֵל הַרְבֵּה בְּכָל סְעוּדָה: כִּכָּר הַלָּקוּחַ מִן הַנַּחְתּוֹם בְּפוּנְדְּיוֹן כְּשֶׁנִּמְכָּרִים אַרְבַּע סְאִין בְּסֶלַע. הַשְׁתָּא ס"ד חֲצִי קַב הָוֵי שְׁתֵּי סְעוּדוֹת. כֵּיצַד: ו' מָעוֹת לְדִינָר, מָעָה שְׁתֵּי פוּנְדְּיוֹנִין – נִמְצָא דִּינָר י"ב פוּנְדְּיוֹנִין, נִמְצָא סֶלַע מ"ח פוּנְדְּיוֹנִין. וּסְאָה ו' קַבִּין, לְד' סְאִין – כ"ד קַבִּין, הֲרֵי מ"ח חֲצָאֵי קַבִּין, חֲצִי קַב לְפוּנְדְּיוֹן: ר"ש. מְמַעֵט מִשִּׁיעוּר, וְאוֹמֵר: תֵּשַׁע סְעוּדוֹת יֵשׁ לַקַּב, וְדֵי לְעֵירוּב בְּב' יָדוֹת שֶׁל כִּכָּר שֶׁל ג' כִּכָּרוֹת לַקַּב. נִמְצֵאת כִּכָּר הַשְּׁלֵימָה שְׁלִישִׁית הַקַּב, וּב' יְדוֹתֶיהָ הָווּ שְׁתֵּי סְעוּדוֹת: חֶצְיָהּ לְבֵית הַמְנוּגָּע. סְתָמָא הִיא וְהָכִי קָאָמַר: חֲצִי כִּכָּר הַשְּׁלֵימָה, שֶׁשִּׁיעֲרוּ בָּהּ אֶת הָעֵירוּב וּבֵין לְמָר בֵּין לְמָר לִשְׁהִיַּית בַּיִת הַמְנוּגָּע לְטַמֵּא בְּגָדִים – הַנִּכְנָס טָמֵא מִיָּד, דִּכְתִיב (ויקרא יד): "וְהַבָּא אֶל הַבַּיִת יִטְמָא". אֲבָל כִּבּוּס בְּגָדִים לֹא נֶאֶמְרָה בּוֹ עַד שֶׁיִּשְׁהֶה כְּדֵי אֲכִילָה דִּכְתִיב (שם): "וְהָאוֹכֵל בַּבַּיִת יְכַבֵּס אֶת בְּגָדָיו" וּמוֹקְמִינַן לָהּ בְּתוֹרַת כֹּהֲנִים לְשׁוֹהֶה כְּדֵי סְעוּדָה וְאע"פ שֶׁלֹּא אָכַל. וַחֲצִי כִּכָּר זוֹ הָוֵי כְּדֵי אֲכִילָה. אע"ג דְּלר"ש לְעִנְיַן עֵירוּבִין הָוֵי בְּכִכָּר ג' סְעוּדוֹת – הָתָם הוּא דִּבְשִׁיעוּר הָעֵירוּב נִתְכַּוְּונוּ כּוּלָּן לְהָקֵל, אֲבָל שִׁיעוּר סְעוּדָה – קִים לְהוּ לְרַבָּנָן הָכִי, וּבָעֵינַן שֶׁיִּשְׁהֶה בִּכְדֵי אֲכִילַת חֲצִי כִּכָּר זוֹ. וְהוּא פְּרָס דְּכוּלֵּיהּ הַתַּלְמוּד. עַל שֵׁם שֶׁשִּׁיעוּרָהּ בִּפְרוּסָה, כְּלוֹמַר: בַּחֲצִי כִּכָּר: לִפְסוֹל אֶת הַגְּוִיָּה. הָאוֹכֵל אוֹכָלִין טְמֵאִין כַּחֲצִי פְּרָס – נִפְסְלָה גְּוִיָּיתוֹ מִלֶּאֱכוֹל בִּתְרוּמָה. וּמִדְּרַבָּנַן הוּא, דְּאֵין אוֹכֶל מְטַמֵּא אָדָם, וְרַבָּנַן גָּזְרוּ שֶׁהָאוֹכְלוֹ יִפָּסֵל בִּתְרוּמָה עַד שֶׁיִּטְבּוֹל. כִּדְאָמַר בְּפֶרֶק בַּתְרָא דְּיוֹמָא (דף פ:): הַנַּח לְטוּמְאַת גְּוִיָּה דְּלָאו דְּאוֹרַיְיתָא: **גמ'** וְכַמָּה. לְר"מ וּלְר' יְהוּדָה קָבָעֵי: רִיפְתָּא אִיכַּרְיָיתָא. שֶׁאוֹכְלִין הָאִכָּרִים עִמָּהֶם לַשָּׂדֶה אִכָּרִים מַנְהִיגֵי שְׁוָורִים: נְהַר פַּפִּיתָא. הוּא מְקוֹם נְהַר פַּפָּא: אֲבוּךְ כְּמַאן. מֵהָנָךְ תַּנָּאֵי סְבִירָא לֵיהּ בְּעֵירוּב, כְּר' יְהוּדָה אוֹ כְּר' מֵאִיר? דְּקַיְ"ל בְּעֵירוּב לְכָל אָדָם כְּדֵי מְזוֹנוֹ, וְאִם בָּא לְשַׁעֵר בְּעַצְמוֹ – בְּאֵיזוֹ יְשַׁעֵר, בְּשַׁבָּת אוֹ בְּחוֹל: דְּאִי כְּר' יְהוּדָה קַשְׁיָא לִי הָא דְּאָמְרֵי אֱינָשֵׁי רַוְוחָא לִבְסִימָא שְׁכִיחַ. כְּלוֹמַר: הַמְּעַיִים מִתְרַוְּוחִין לְפַנּוֹת מָקוֹם לְדָבָר הַמָּתוֹק: דִּבְרֵיהֶן. דְּרַבִּי יוֹחָנָן בֶּן בְּרוֹקָא וְרַבִּי שִׁמְעוֹן: צֵא מֵהֶן שְׁלִישׁ לַחֶנְוָנִי. רַבִּי יוֹחָנָן בֶּן בְּרוֹקָה לֹא הִזְכִּיר חֲצִי קַב שֶׁשִּׁיעֵר לְךָ אֶלָּא בְּכִכָּר הַלָּקוּחַ מִן הַחֶנְוָנִי בְּפוּנְדְּיוֹן, וַהֲרֵי הַחֶנְוָנִי מִשְׂתַּכֵּר בַּחֲצִי קַב שֶׁלָּקַח בְּפוּנְדְּיוֹן שְׁלִישׁ, וּמוֹכֵר ב' שְׁלִישֵׁי חֲצִי קַב בְּפוּנְדְּיוֹן. וּבְהָךְ שְׁנֵי שְׁלִישֵׁי אַשְׁמְעִינַן רַבִּי יוֹחָנָן דְּאִיכָּא שְׁתֵּי סְעוּדוֹת – הֲרֵי בַּחֲצִי קַב שָׁלֹשׁ סְעוּדוֹת: צִיבֵי. עֵצִים לֶאֱפוֹת, אֵין הַחֶנְוָנִי מִשְׂתַּכֵּר אֶלָּא שְׁלִישׁ: וַחֲצִי

תוספות

עד ועד בכלל. לא בעי לשנויי: הא דאיתיה לאבוה במתא כו' כדמשני בסמוך – דא"כ הוי פליגי דרבי ינאי ור"ל אדרב אסי, והלכתא כרב אסי, דמייתי לה התלמוד בסוף פ' "אע"פ" (כתובות דף סה:):

הא דאיתיה לאבוה במתא כו'. לרב יהושע בריה דרב אידי לא הוי מצי לשנויי הכי, דהא לא מפליג בין איתיה לליתיה, מדלא משני הכי, וכן פירש בקונטרס:

מערב ע"י בנו ובתו הקטנים. ואור"י: דאף רבי יוחנן מודה הכא דקטן קטן ממש:

מפני שידן כידו. אעבדו ושפחתו קאי, כדאמרינן בריש "הזורק" בגיטין (דף עז:): דיד עבד קני ליה רביה:

וחצי חציה לפסול את הגברייה. והיינו שני בילים. אומר ר"ת: דפסול נכרייה גזירת קדמונים היתה, ולא מי"ח דבר – דהאוכל אוכל ראשון ואוכל שני. תדע, דבפרק בתרא דיומא (דף פ:) סלקא דעתיה דהוי דאורייתא, ובעי למדרשיה מ"ולא תטמאו בהם ונטמתם בם". ובי"ח דבר היו בקיאין. ואם היתה דאורייתא – א"כ חסר להו! ועוד: דלשון פסול נכרייה משמע דדוקא פסול הגוף, דנפסל גופו מלאכול בתרומה, וגזירה דהאוכל אוכל ראשון – פסול מגע הוא. אלא ודאי פסול נכרייה גזרו קודם י"ח דבר הרבה. ולא גזרו על מגעו שיפסל, אלא גופו מלאכול בתרומה. וגזרו על טומאת פנים אטו טומאת חוץ, שהרואה אוכל תרומה אחר שאכל אוכלין טמאין, או שתה משקין טמאים – סבור שמותר ליגע בהן גם בתוך תרומה טהורה, כמו שבתוך מעיו נוגעין זה בזה. ודווקא בשני בילים, אבל בכבילה, אף על פי שראוי לטמא אחרים – לא גזרו, דא"א שלא ישאר קצת בין השינים והחניכין או מתעכל קצת במעיו. וכיון דאפקוה מכבילה – אוקמוה אשני בילים, שהוא חצי הסעודה דבית המנוגע, ולר' יוחנן בן ברוקה אבילה ומחצה. אבל במשקין טמאין, שאינם מתעכלין ונכנס הכל במעיו – לא בעינן יותר מרביעית. אבל בי"ח דבר דהאוכל אוכל ראשון – גזרו אפילו בכבילה, ושיפסול תרומה במגע, כדמפרש טעמא בפרק קמא דשבת (דף יד.) משום דזמנין דאוכל אוכלין טמאין כו'. ואין להאריך כאן:

רבינו חננאל

עד בן שש מוקי ליה עד ועד בכלל: **ת"ר** לא יערב אדם לא ע"י בנו ובתו הגדולים ולא ע"י עבדו ושפחתו העברים ולא ע"י אשתו אלא מדעתן. ואוקימנא מאי מדעתן בשהודיען ואפילו בסתמא מערב עליהן אלא אם ימחו ויאמרו לא. אבל מערב ע"י בנו ובתו הקטנים וע"י עבדו ושפחתו הכנענים בין מדעתן ובין שלא מדעתן וכולן שעירבו ועירב רבן עליהן יוצאין בשל רבן חוץ מן האשה וכל דכוותה והן בניו הגדולים ועבדיו [ושפחותיו] העברים מפני שיכולין למחות וכיון שעירבו לעצמן אין לך מיחוי גדול מזה ואין יוצאין אלא בעירוב של עצמן: **מתני'** וכמה שיעורו מזון ב' סעודות לכל אחד ואחד מזונו לחול דברי ר' מאיר כי בשבת דכיון דקבע סעודתי' על היין אכיל טפי וכי רעבתן דמי ולא בעינן אלא (בחול) [לחול] דהוה ליה סעודה בינונית ר' יהודה אומר כסעודת השבת. דכיון דאית ליה בשבת בשר ודגים לא אכיל פת אלא פחות מסעודתו בחול. וזהו שאמרו ושניהן מתכוונין להקל. בא ר' יוחנן בן ברוקה לתת שיעור בעירוב בדבר ידוע דאמר מככר בפונדיון מד' סאין בסלע פי' שיעור סאה ו' קבין (כשהן) [שהן] כ"ד רטיל והסלע ו' דינרים (כמו) [ואם] שיהיה השער שבשוק ד' סאין בסלע נמצא סאה בדינר וחשבון הדינר שש מעה כסף והמעה ב' פונדיונות נמצאו י"ב פונדיונין בדינר וככר הוזכרנו למעלה כי סאה היא כ"ד רטלין כשתימכר סאה בדינ' (רטלה בפונדיונין) [ב' רטיל בפונדיון] נמצאת ככר של עירוב (ריטלין) [ב' רטלין בפונדיון] זהו ב' סעודות כל סעודה רטל. ר' שמעון אומר [שתי] ידות לככר מג' ככרות בקב הוי עירוב נמצא שיעור הככר רטל ושליש (ב') [וב'] ידותיה הן שיעור העירוב. תנא וקרובין דבריהן להיות שוין. אוקמה רב חסדא הא דאמר ר' יוחנן בן ברוקה בתר דאפיק מחצה מהן לחנוני. באתרא דלא יהיב בעה"ב עצים לתנור. נמצאת חצי סאה פת אפויה בדינר. נמצאת רטיל פת בפונדיון והוא ב' סעודות ולר' שמעון דאמר ב' סעודות של עירוב הן ב' ידות לככר מג' לקב נמצאו ב' ידות של זה הככר רטל פחות *) י"ב תישועין והיינו דאמר וקרובין להיות שוין. הא דא"ר יוחנן בן ברוקה ב' סעודות מד' סעודות בקב ור' שמעון דאמר ב' סעודות מתשע סעודות בקב דבריהן פשוטין הן ומתני' אליבא דר' יהושע שנויה דאמר

*) אולי צ"ל רטיל פחות תיקוע כי כל הככר מחזיק י"ב תיקועין וצ"ע.

[ברכות כו: וש"נ]

הגהות הב"ח

(א) גמ' בין שלא לדעתן מפני שידן כידו אבל אינו מערב: (ב) שם תניא אידך וכו' הגדולים ולא ע"י עבדו: (ג) שם וכל דדמי לה (אמר מר וכו' דמחי) תא"מ ונ"ב שם היא גופה קשיא אמרת מפני שיכולה למחות טעמא דמחי: (ד) שם דסתמא הוא: (ה) שם א"ל רב יוסף לרב יוסף בריה דרבה אבוך: (ו) רש"י ד"ה מיתיבי וכו' עד בן שש והכא ליכא למימר:

כתובות סד: כלים פי"ז מי"א

[שם מקום ויש מפרשים ככרין שאוכלין הרועי' ערוך ערך אכר]

מגילה ז:

[כתובות סד:]

רש"ל

רב נסים גאון

ר' יוחנן בן ברוקה אומר ככר בפונדיון מד' סאין בסלע ר' שמעון אומר ב' ידות לככר מג' לקב חציה לבית המנוגע וחצי חציה לפסול את הגויה הפונדיון הוא חלק אחד משנים עשר בדינר ואיתיה לפירוש דיליה בפ' האשה נקנית (קידושין יב) דתניא שש מעה כסף [דינר] והמעה ב' פונדיונות והסאה הוא ו' קבין והקב כ"ד ביצה וכבר פירשו הגאונים ז"ל כי שיעור הביצה משקל (י"ג *) כספים פחות שליש מכספים של ארץ ישראל יעלו בו' ביצים ק' כספים נמצא בקב משקל ת' כסף ובגמרא דבני מערבא במס' תרומות (פ"ה ה"א) אמרו כמה קבא עביד כ"ד ביעין והסלע יש בו ד' דינרין שבכל דינר י"ב פונדיונות יעלה הסלע למ"ח פונדיונות ואיתיה לפירושיה בגמ' דבכורות בפ' יש בכור לנחלה (דף נ) והלא סלע הקדש מ"ח פונדיון ובגמ' דקידושין דבני מערבא (פ"א ה"א) גרסי תני ר' חייא סלע ד' דינרין ונפקא לן ממתני' דפרק הזהב דסלע ד' דינרין דתנן (בב"מ דף נג) כמה תהא הסלע חסרה ולא יהא בה אונאה ר"מ אומר ד' איסרות מאיסר לדינר מכלל שהסלע יש בו ד' דינרין והכי אמרי בפרק האשה נקנית (ירושלמי קידושין הלכה א) חילפיי אותבוני על כיף נהרא דלא אפיקית מתניתא דר' חייא רבה מן מתני' זרקוני לנהרא אמרון ליה והא תני ר' חיי' סלעא ד' דינרין אמר לון אף אנן תנינא כמה תהא הסלע חסרה ולא יהא בה אונאה ר' מאיר אומר ד' איסרות מאיסר לדינר. חציה לבית המנוגע עיקרו מן הכתוב (ויקרא יד) והאוכל בבית יכבס את בגדיו ופירשוהו בתורת כהנים אם סופנו לרבות את אע"פ שאינו שוכב מה ת"ל

*) אולי צ"ל מז.

תָּנָא: [א]וַחֲצִי חֲצִי חֶצְיָהּ לְטַמֵּא טוּמְאַת אוֹכָלִין. [ב]וְתַנָּא דִידַן, מ"ט לָא תָּנֵי טוּמְאַת אוֹכָלִין? מִשּׁוּם דְּלָא שָׁווּ שִׁיעוּרַיְיהוּ לַהֲדָדֵי. דְּתַנְיָא: כַּמָּה שִׁיעוּר חֲצִי פְּרָס — ב' בֵּיצִים חָסֵר קִימְעָא, דִּבְרֵי רַבִּי יְהוּדָה. ר' יוֹסֵי אוֹמֵר: ב' בֵּיצִים שׂוֹחֲקוֹת. שִׁיעֵר רַבִּי ב' בֵּיצִים וְעוֹד. כַּמָּה וְעוֹד? אֶחָד מֵעֶשְׂרִים בַּבֵּיצָה. וְאִילּוּ גַּבֵּי טוּמְאַת אוֹכָלִין תַּנְיָא: רַבִּי נָתָן וְרַבִּי דּוֹסָא אָמְרוּ: כַּבֵּיצָה שֶׁאָמְרוּ — כָּמוֹהָ וּכְקְלִיפָּתָהּ, וַחכ"א: [ג]כָּמוֹהָ בְּלֹא קְלִיפָּתָהּ. אָמַר רַפְרָם בַּר פַּפָּא, אָמַר רַב חִסְדָּא: זוֹ דִּבְרֵי רַבִּי יְהוּדָה וְרַבִּי יוֹסֵי, אֲבָל חכ"א: [ג]כְּבֵיצָה וּמֶחֱצָה שׂוֹחֲקוֹת. *וּמַאן חֲכָמִים — רַבִּי יוֹחָנָן בֶּן בְּרוֹקָה. פְּשִׁיטָא! שׂוֹחֲקוֹת אֲתָא לְאַשְׁמוֹעִינַן. כִּי אֲתָא רַב דִּימִי, אֲמַר: שִׁיגֵּר בּוֹנְיוֹס לְרַבִּי מוֹדְיָא דְּקוּנְדִּים דְּמִן נָאוּסָא, וְשִׁיעֵר רַבִּי מָאתָן וּשְׁבַע עֶשְׂרֵה בֵּיעִין. הָא סְאָה דְּהֵיכָא? אִי דְּמִדְבָּרִית — קמ"ד הָוְיָא, וְאִי דִּירוּשַׁלְמִית — קע"ג הָוְיָא. וְאִי דְּצִיפּוֹרִית — ר"ז הָוְיָין! לְעוֹלָם דְּצִיפּוֹרִית, אַיְיתֵי חַלְּתָא שְׁדֵי עֲלַיְיהוּ. חַלְּתָא כַּמָּה הָוְיָין — תְּמָנֵי, אַכַּתִּי בָּצַר לֵיהּ?! אֶלָּא: אַיְיתֵי וְעוֹדוֹת דְּרַבִּי שְׁדֵי עֲלַיְיהוּ. אִי הָכִי, הָוֵי לֵיהּ טְפֵי! כֵּיוָן דְּלָא הָוֵי כַּבֵּיצָה — לָא חָשֵׁיב לֵיהּ. ת"ר: סְאָה יְרוּשַׁלְמִית יְתֵירָה עַל מִדְבָּרִית שְׁתוּת, וְשֶׁל צִיפּוֹרִית יְתֵירָה עַל יְרוּשַׁלְמִית שְׁתוּת. נִמְצֵאת שֶׁל צִיפּוֹרִית יְתֵירָה עַל מִדְבָּרִית שְׁלִישׁ. שְׁלִישׁ דְּמַאן? אִילֵימָא שְׁלִישׁ דְּמִדְבָּרִית, מִכְּדִי שְׁלִישׁ דְּמִדְבָּרִית כַּמָּה הָוֵי — אַרְבְּעִין וּתְמַנְיָא, וְאִילּוּ עוֹדְפָא — שִׁיתִּין וּתְלָת! וְאֶלָּא שְׁלִישׁ דִּירוּשַׁלְמִית, שְׁלִישׁ דִּידָהּ כַּמָּה הָוֵי — חַמְשִׁין וּתְמַנְיָא, נְכֵי תִּילְתָּא. וְאִילּוּ עוֹדְפָא שִׁתִּין וּתְלָת! וְאֶלָּא דְּצִיפּוֹרִי שְׁלִישׁ דִּידָהּ כַּמָּה הָוֵי — שִׁבְעִין נְכֵי חֲדָא, וְאִילּוּ עוֹדְפָא — ס"ג! אֶלָּא א"ר יִרְמְיָה, ה"ק: נִמְצֵאת סְאָה שֶׁל צִיפּוֹרִי יְתֵירָה עַל מִדְבָּרִית קָרוֹב לִשְׁלִישׁ שֶׁלָּהּ, וּשְׁלִישׁ שֶׁלָּהּ קָרוֹב לְמֶחֱצָה דְּמִדְבָּרִית. מַתְקִיף לָהּ רָבִינָא: מִידֵי "קָרוֹב" "קָרוֹב" קָתָנֵי?! אֶלָּא אָמַר רָבִינָא, ה"ק: נִמְצֵאת שְׁלִישׁ שֶׁל צִיפּוֹרִי בְּוְעוֹדִיּוֹת שֶׁל רַבִּי, יְתֵירָה עַל מֶחֱצָה שֶׁל מִדְבָּרִית שְׁלִישׁ בֵּיצָה. תָּנוּ רַבָּנַן: [ד]"רֵאשִׁית עֲרִיסוֹתֵיכֶם" (במדבר טו) — כְּדֵי

רש"י

וַחֲצִי חֲצִי חֶצְיָהּ לְטַמֵּא טוּמְאַת אוֹכָלִין. לְרַבִּי יוֹחָנָן בֶּן בְּרוֹקָה כִּדְאִית לֵיהּ דְּהַיְינוּ כְּבֵיצָה חָסֵר רְבִיעַ — שֶׁהֲרֵי הוּא שִׁיעֵר בְּכִכָּר שֶׁל רוֹבַע הַקַּב, כִּדְאָמַר מֶחֱצָה שָׂכָר לַחֶנְוָנִי. נִמְצָא כִּכָּר בְּפוּנְדְּיוֹן רוֹבַע קַב, וְהֵן ו' בֵּיצִים חֶצְיָהּ, ג' בֵּיצִים לְבֵית הַמְנוּגָּע, וַחֲצִי חֶצְיָהּ בֵּיצָה וּמֶחֱצָה — לִפְסוֹל אֶת הַגְּוִיָּה וּלְטוּמְאַת אוֹכָלִין ג' רְבִיעֵי בֵּיצָה. וּלְר"ש שֶׁשִּׁיעֵר בְּכִכָּר מִג' לְקַב, כִּכָּר שְׁלֵימָה — ח' בֵּיצִים, חֶצְיָהּ ד' חֲצִי חֶצְיָהּ — ב' חֲצִי חֲצִי חֶצְיָהּ — בֵּיצָה: דְּלָא שָׁווּ שִׁיעוּרַיְיהוּ לַהֲדָדֵי. לָא הָוְיָא שִׁיעוּר טוּמְאַת אוֹכָלִין חֲצִי שִׁיעוּר פְּסוּל גְּוִיָּה מְכוּוָּן, אֶלָּא יֵשׁ שֶׁאוֹמְרִים פָּחוֹת וְיֵשׁ שֶׁאוֹמֵר יוֹתֵר: דְּתַנְיָא כַּמָּה שִׁעוּר חֲצִי פְּרָס. לִפְסוֹל אֶת הַגְּוִיָּה: חָסֵר קִימְעָא. בֵּיצִים קְטַנִּים שִׁיעֲרוּהָ, וְאַלִּיבָּא דְּר"ש דְּאָמַר בְּמַתְנִי' ב' בֵּיצִים: שִׁיעֵר רַבִּי. סְאָה אַחַת שֶׁהוּבְאָה לְפָנָיו, וּמָצָא לְמִנְיַן קַבִּין שֶׁבָּהּ יוֹתֵר מִכ"ד בֵּיצִים לְקַב, דְּהַיְינוּ לְכִכָּר שֶׁל שְׁלִישִׁית הַקַּב יוֹתֵר מֵח' וְחֶצְיָהּ יוֹתֵר עַל ד' וַחֲצִי חֶצְיָהּ ב' בֵּיצִים וְעוֹד אֶחָד מִכ' בְּבֵיצָה לְכָל בֵּיצָה, דְּהַיְינוּ לַחֲצִי פְּרָס אֶחָד מֵעֶשֶׂר בְּבֵיצָה תּוֹסֶפֶת. וְיֵשׁ שֶׁשּׁוֹנִין: אֶחָד מִמ' בְּבֵיצָה, וּמְפָרְשִׁי לְב' הַבֵּיצִים תּוֹסֶפֶת אֶחָד מִמ' וְתוּ לָא. וְהַמְדַקְדֵּק בַּלָּשׁוֹן הַזֶּה א"א לְהַעֲמִידוֹ לְקַמָּן, וַאֲנִי שְׁנֵיהֶן שָׁמַעְתִּי: כָּמוֹהָ וּכְקְלִיפָּתָהּ. אַלְמָא: לָא שָׁוֵי לַחֲצִי שִׁיעוּר דִּפְסוּל גְּוִיָּה, דְּאִי לְרַבִּי יְהוּדָה — חָסֵר קִימְעָא בָּעֵי מִיהֱוֵי, וְאִי לְרַבִּי יוֹסֵי — בֵּיצָה וּקְלִיפָּתָהּ שׂוֹחֲקוֹת בָּעֵי מִיהֱוֵי, וְאִי לְרַבִּי — וְעוֹדוֹת בָּעֵי דְּהַיְינוּ טְפֵי: בְּלֹא קְלִיפָּתָהּ. נַמִּי זוּטַר טְפֵי אֲפִילּוּ מִפַּלְגֵי שִׁיעוּרֵיהּ דַּחֲצִי פְּרָס דְּרַבִּי יְהוּדָה: זוֹ דִּבְרֵי ר' יְהוּדָה. הָךְ בָּרַיְיתָא דַּחֲצִי פְּרָס דִּלְעֵיל: ר' יוֹחָנָן בֶּן בְּרוֹקָה. וְאוֹקִימְנָא אַלִּיבֵּיהּ דְּבְכִכָּר שֶׁל רוֹבַע הַקַּב ו' בֵּיצִים, שִׁיעוּר לְעֵירוּב חֶצְיָהּ — ג', חֲצִי חֶצְיָהּ — בֵּיצָה וּמֶחֱצָה: פְּשִׁיטָא. דְּהָא רַב חִסְדָּא גּוּפֵיהּ הָכִי אוֹקְמָא לְעֵיל גַּבֵּי מֵהֶן מֶחֱצָה לַחֶנְוָנִי: בּוֹנְיוֹס. שֵׁם הָאִישׁ: מוֹדְיָא קוּנְדָּסָא. שֵׁם הַסְּאָה: דְּמִן נָאוּסָא. מֵאוֹתוֹ מָקוֹם: דְּמִדְבָּרִית. שֶׁהֵן ו' קַבִּין, וְקי"ל: קַב ד' לוּגִּין, וְלוֹג ו' בֵּיצִים — הֲרֵי כ"ד בֵּיצִים לְקַב, קמ"ד לִסְאָה: וְאִי דִּירוּשַׁלְמִית. דְּאָמַר לְקַמָּן דְּעוֹדֶפֶת שְׁתוּת עַל סְאָה שֶׁהָיְתָה בִּימֵי מֹשֶׁה, וּשְׁתוּת הֵבִיאוּ מִבַּחוּץ — דְּהַיְינוּ חֲמִישִׁית כַּשִּׁיעוּר הָרִאשׁוֹן, הֲרֵי נִיתּוֹסְפוּ כ' עַל ק' וְנִיתּוֹסְפוּ חֲמִישִׁית עַל מ' דְּהַיְינוּ ח' וּבֵיצָה חָסֵר חוֹמֶשׁ עַל ד' — הֲרֵי תּוֹסֶפֶת כ"ט חָסֵר חוֹמֶשׁ, תְּנֵם עַל קמ"ד — הֲרֵי קע"ג, וּבַהֲהוּא בְּצִיר חוּמְשָׁא לָא דָּק: וְאִי דְּצִיפּוֹרִית. דְּאָמַר לְקַמָּן יְתֵירָה עַל יְרוּשַׁלְמִית שְׁתוּת מִלְּבַר: מָאתַן וְשֶׁבַע הָוְיָין. לְמֵאָה עֶשְׂרִים תּוֹסֶפֶת לְע' י"ד תּוֹסֶפֶת שֶׁהֵן חוֹמֶשׁ שֶׁל ע' שֶׁנִּיתּוֹסֵף עָלֶיהָ חֵלֶק חֲמִישִׁי שֶׁמִּתְּחִילָּה, שֶׁהוּא חֵלֶק שִׁשִּׁי לַמִּדָּה הַגְּדוֹלָה דְּהַיְינוּ שְׁתוּת מִלְּבַר, כְּלוֹמַר: עַל הַחֲמִשָּׁה הֵבִיאוּ שִׁשִּׁי מִן הַחוּץ, הֲרֵי תּוֹסֶפֶת ל"ד. תְּנֵם עַל קע"ג — הֲרֵי ר"ז. וּבְתוֹסֶפֶת שֶׁל ג' הַבֵּיצִים חוּמְשִׁין לָא דָּק, שֶׁהֲרֵי מֵחֶשְׁבּוֹן הָרִאשׁוֹן חָסֵר חוֹמֶשׁ, גַּם מִג' אֵלֶּה חוֹמֶשׁ — לֹא נִשְׁאַר אֲפִילּוּ חֲצִי בֵּיצָה: אַיְיתֵי חַלְּתָא שְׁדֵי עֲלַיְיהוּ. בִּסְאָה זוֹ שֶׁהוּבְאָה לְפָנָיו הָיְתָה סְאָה צִיפּוֹרִית וְחַלָּתָהּ שֶׁכְּשֶׁיִּטְּלוּ חַלָּתָהּ תַּעֲמוֹד עַל סְאָה וְשִׁיעוּר חַלָּה אֶחָד מִכ"ד, כִּדְאָמַר בְּפֶרֶק "חַלּוֹן שֶׁבֵּין ב' חֲצֵירוֹת" (לעיל פא.): כַּמָּה הָוְיָין תְּמָנֵי. שֶׁהֵן אֶחָד מִכ"ד בְּקנ"ב. וְלָא דָּק בְּחַלָּתָן שֶׁל ט"ו בֵּיצִים הַנּוֹתָרִין, וְעוֹלָה לְיוֹתֵר מֵחֲצִי בֵּיצָה: אַיְיתֵי וְעוֹדוֹת דְּר'. שֶׁשִּׁיעֵר וּמָצָא לְכָל ב' בֵּיצִים שֶׁל מִדְבָּרִית אֶחָד מִמ' בְּבֵיצָה, כִּדְאָמַר דְּהָוֵי לְפ' בֵּיצָה, לְק"ם ב' בֵּיצִים, וּלְמ"ז הַנּוֹתָרִין יוֹתֵר מֵחֲצִי בֵּיצָה: אִי הָכִי טְפֵי הָוֵי לְהוּ. מִמָּאתַן וְשִׁיבְסַר. וּמְשַׁנֵּי: כֵּיוָן דְּלָא הָוֵי בֵּיצָה לָא חָשֵׁיב לֵיהּ. כָּךְ שָׁמַעְתִּי בְּלָשׁוֹן אֶחָד. וְקַשְׁיָא לִי בְּגַוַּהּ: דְּאִי דָּיְיקַתְּ בָּהּ שַׁפִּיר — טְפֵי מִבֵּיצָה הָוֵי, שֶׁהֲרֵי בְּוְעוֹדוֹת שֶׁל מ"ז בֵּיצִים שֶׁלֹּא חָשַׁבְתָּ יֵשׁ יוֹתֵר מֵחֲצִי בֵּיצָה, וּבְחַלָּתָן שֶׁל ט"ו בֵּיצִים שֶׁלֹּא חָשַׁבְתָּ יֵשׁ יוֹתֵר מֵחֲצִי בֵּיצָה וְגַם לְמַעְלָה בְּתוֹסֶפֶת צִיפּוֹרִית עַל יְרוּשַׁלְמִית נִשְׁאֲרוּ ב' חוּמְשִׁין שֶׁלֹּא דִּקְדַּקְנוּ בָּהֶן. וּבְלָשׁוֹן אַחֵר שָׁמַעְתִּי: אֶלָּא אַיְיתֵי וְעוֹדוֹת שֶׁל ר' שְׁדֵי עֲלַיְיהוּ, וְדַל חַלָּתָן מֵהָכָא. וְכִי פָּרְכִינַן מָאתַן וְשֵׁב הָווּ, אַיְיתֵי וְעוֹדוֹת דְּר' אַחַת מִכ' לְכָל בֵּיצָה שְׁדֵי עֲלַיְיהוּ, דְּהָווּ לְמָאתַן י' בֵּיעֵי הָווּ מָאתַן וְשִׁיבְסַר. א"ה טְפֵי לְהוּ וְעוֹדוֹת דְּרַבִּי אֶחָד מִכ' לְכָל בֵּיצָה מִז' בֵּיצִים, וְגַם ב' חוּמְשִׁין שֶׁלֹּא דִּקְדַּקְנוּ בָּהֶן! וּמְשַׁנֵּי: כֵּיוָן דְּלָא הָוֵי בֵּיצָה לָא חָשֵׁיב לֵיהּ: שְׁתוּת. מִלְּבַר: וְשֶׁל צִיפּוֹרִית יְתֵירָה עַל יְרוּשַׁלְמִית שְׁתוּת. יְרוּשַׁלְמִית, וּשְׁתוּת מִלְּבַר: תִּילְתָּא. דְּקמ"ד הָוֵי מ"ח: וְאִילּוּ עוֹדֶפֶת. דְּלְצִיפּוֹרִית עַל מִדְבָּרִית ס"ג. דְּהָא סְאָה לְצִיפּוֹרִית ר"ז, כִּדְאָמְרַן לְעֵיל, וּמִדְבָּרִית קמ"ד: וְאֶלָּא שְׁלִישׁ יְרוּשַׁלְמִית. קָאָמַר: שְׁלִישׁ דִּידָהּ כַּמָּה הָוֵי נ"ח נְכֵי תִּילְתָּא. דְּהָא סְאָה יְרוּשַׁלְמִית קע"ג, כִּדְאָמְרִינַן לְעֵיל: קָרוֹב לִשְׁלִישׁ דִּידָהּ. דִּשְׁלִישׁ דִּידָהּ ס"ט, וְעוֹדְפָהּ ס"ג: וּשְׁלִישׁ דִּידָהּ. דְּהוּא ס"ט קָרוֹב הוּא לְמֶחֱצָה מִדְבָּרִית, דְּהוּא ע"ב: בְּוְעוֹדוֹת דְּרַבִּי. כִּי מְשַׁעֲרַתְּ לָהּ בְּוְעוֹדוֹת דְּאַשְׁכַּח בָּהּ רַבִּי, דְּשִׁיעֵר בָּהּ מָאתַן וְשִׁיבְסַר וְהָוֵי שְׁלִישׁ דִּידְהוּ ע"ב וּשְׁלִישׁ בֵּיצָה, וִיתֵירָה עַל מֶחֱצָה דְּמִדְבָּרִית שְׁלִישׁ בֵּיצָה, דְּמֶחֱצָה דְּמִדְבָּרִית ע"ב:

תוספות

וחצי חצי חציה לטמא טומאת אוכלין. אכולהו תנאי קאי כדמפרש בקונטרס. לר"י בן ברוקה כדאית ליה, דהיינו כביצה חסר רביע, ולר"ש כביצה שלימה. והא דאמר בכל דוכתא: כביצה לטמא טומאת אוכלין — היינו כרבי שמעון, ולא כרבי יוחנן בן ברוקה.

קע"ג הויא ר"ז הויא. אין החשבון מכוון, כדפי' בקונט', ולא דק:

חלתא כמה הויין תמני מאתן וחמיסר הויין. ר"ח גרים: חלתן כמה הויין — תשעה מאתן ושיתסר הויין. וכן הוא אמת, כדאמר בפ' "חלון" (לעיל דף פא.) דשיעור חלה א' מכ"ד. ולריך בילה לכ"ג בילים ותשעה פעמים כ"ג הם ר"ז:

שליש דידה כמה הוי שיתין נכי תרתי. לא דק, דמעט חסר. וכיון דלא חסר אלא מיעוט בילה לא חיים. ויש דגרס שיתין נכי תרתי ונכי פורתא:

נמצאת שליש[(א)] ציפורי. בועודות ושליש דקתני בברייתא קאי אשליש ליפורי ואשליש בילה:

יתירה על מחצה של מדברית שליש ביצה. לפי שמונה שליש דלפורי ס"ט וס"ט, ועודות ג' בילים וט' ועודות. ואם כן שליש לפורי עם הועודות ע"ב בילים ומחלה חסר ועוד. כיון דלא הוי חלי בילה קרי לה שליש. אבל אי דייקת בה שפיר הוי יותר מחלי בילה. דהא סאה ליפורי הויא יתירה על ר"ז קרוב לב' חומשים, ונמלא שליש שלה ס"ט בילים וחלי חומש, וכשתלטרף עם הועודות — הוי יותר מע"ב בילה ומחלה. ואמר מהר"י: דהך ברייתא קיימא אקבלת רב דימי, דקאמר: ושיער רבי מאתן ושיבסר, ולא חשיב ועודות של ז' בילים הואיל ואינו עולה לבילה ושליש ממאתן ושיבסר עולין שבעין ותרין ושליש. ומה שמקשין שכולה שמעתין חשיב ועודות של ליפורי, ושל מדברית לא חשיב, דהא ועודות איכא בכולהו דלא הוסיפו אלא שתות שבירושלמית וכן בליפורי! אור"י: דבירושלים ובליפורי לא הוסיפו כי אם למנין בילים של סאה מדברית. והקדמונים שלפני רבי דקדקו בדבר שאין בתוספת שלהן שתות מלומלמת. כי בילים מדבריות היו גסין יותר מאותן של יום התוספת, והוסיפו על מדת ליפורית שהיתה מאתן וז' ביעין ושני חומשין חסר קימעא י' בילים אחד מכ' לכל בילה: על מחצה של מדברית שליש ביצה. מפרש מהר"י: נמלא שליש של ליפורי מלגאו, יתירה על שליש של מדברית מלבר שליש בילה. וקאי שליש דברייתא אתרוייהו, אבילה. ורבינא מפרש דברי רבי ירמיה, ומפרש דה"ק רבי ירמיה: נמלאת סאה ליפורית יתירה על של מדברית קרוב לשליש שלה, פי' לשליש מדברית מלבר. ושליש שלה — פירוש ושליש של ליפורי מלגאו, קרוב למחלה של מדברית. וכעין זה מלינו בפרק "בכל מערבין" (לעיל דף לה:), אמר רבי ירמיה: כשהיה עליה שרך כל בין השמשות, ומפרש' לה רבה ורב יוסף: שבעת

[תענית ו. כ. יבמות מו: קה: כתובות ו: לג: קידושין טו: גיטין כב. מו: טו. ב"ק עא. ב"מ ס: ע"ז ז: סנהדרין סו. שבועות לו: הוריות ג. ה: זבחים מב. מנחות פח: בכורות יד: יז. ל. חולין עט. תמורה ל: לג: נדה ח: נב:]

עין משפט נר מצוה

ט א ב ג מיי' פ"ד מה' טומאת אוכלין הל' א:
י ד מיי' פ"ו מהלכות בכורים הלכה טו סמג עשין קמד טוש"ע י"ד סי' שכב סעיף א:

הגהות הב"ח

(א) תום' ד"ה נמלאת שליש כל ליפורי בועודות וכו' ושליש:

גליון הש"ס

גמ' ותנא דידן מ"ט לא תני. תמוה לי מהיכא פסיקא זה דלריב"ב שיעור ט"א ג' רביעי בילה כיון שהוא חלי חלי דילמא באמת לכ"ע ט"א בכבילה כדדרשי' אוכל הנאכל בבת אחת אלא דהברייתא כר"ש דלדידיה דבילה הוא חלי חליה מש"ה נקט ליה בסדר החשבון דחלי חליה לטמא טומאת אוכלין אבל מתני' חליה לבית המנוגע דקאי ריב"ב ור"ש למר כדאית ליה ולמר כדאית ליה מש"ה לא תני למנקט חלי חליה לטומאת אוכלין דלריב"ב אינו כן וה' יאיר עיני:

רבינו חננאל

אין עירוב אלא בכבר שלם למעוטי פרוסה. ויהיב ר' שמעון דמתני' שיעורא דעירוב דהוא ככר שלם (והוא) שיעור ב' סעודות *) ככר שיש בה שליש קב. חציה לבית המנוגע וחצי חציה לפסול את הגויה. כל חד וחד לפום מאי דאית ליה ככר דיליה. חציה לבית המנוגע כדתניא כתיב והבא אל הבית וכתיב והאוכל והשוכב אלא ליתן שיעור לשוהה שאינו טמא עד שישהא בכדי אכילת פרס פת חטים ולא פת שעורים כו' וחצי חציה לפסול את הגויה. כדתנן כל האוכלין מצטרפין לפסול את הגויה בכחצי פרס פי' אם יאכל אדם אוכלין טמאין שיעור חצי פרס ואע"פ שאינו אוכל מטמא אדם אבל נפסל גופו ואם יאכל תרומה או קדשים חייב שגרם להן טומאה. והאי דקתני בחצי פרס בעינן למהוי ליה רווחא למיכל דאי משלים סעודה דיליה בהא סעודה דתרומה או קדשים קודם שיתאכלו האוכלין הטמאין במעיו חייב. תנא וחצי [חצי] חציה לטמא טומאת אוכלין. ואקשינן ותנא דידן מ"ט לא תני וחצי [חצי] חציה לטמא טומאת אוכלין ופריק משום דלא שוו שיעורייהו להדדי דאילו שיעור חציה בבית המנוגע וחצי חציה לפסול את הגויה שוין ואלו בטומאת אוכלין ר' נתן ור' דוסא אמרו כביצה שאמרו כמוה ובקליפתה וחכ"א כמוה בלא קליפתה והלכתא בפלוגתא לא קמיירי. ותניא כמה שיעור חצי פרס ב' ביצים חסר קמעא דברי ר"י ור' יוסי א' ב' ביצים שוחקות שיער [רבי] ב' ביצים ועוד. וכמה הוא ועוד [אחד] מעשרים בביצה. אמר רב חסדא זו דברי ר' יהודה ור' יוסי אבל חכ"א כביצה ומחצה שוחקות הוא דהוי חצי פרס. ואמרי' מאן חכמים ר' יוחנן בן ברוקה הוא. דיהיב שיעורא דככר חצי קב דהוא בחשבון קמ"ד ביצים לסאה דאי הפת ו' קבין מגיע לכל קב כ"ד ביצים חצי קב י"ב ביצים והוא שיעור הככר קודם שיפרש רב חסדא צא מהן מחצה לחנווני חצי ככר שהן ו' ביצים לבית המנוגע וחצי חציה שהן ג' ביצים לפסול את הגויה וחצי חצי חציה שהיא ביצה ומחצה לטמא טומאת אוכלין. פשיטא דר' יוחנן בן ברוקה היא ושנינן אין מיהו שוחקות אתא רב חסדא לאשמעי' דלא תנן מאי שוחקות עודפות כמעט כי אתא רב דימי אמר שיגר לו בוניים לרבי מודיא קונדיסא דמן ניסא דהוי סאה ושיעורה (ררי"ן) [רי"ז] ביצים ואקשינן הא סאה דשיעורא (ררי"ן) [רי"ז] ביעי דהיכא אי סאה מדברית קמ"ד ביעי היא דהיא ו' קבין כל קב כ"ד ביצה הרי קמ"ד ביעי אי סאה ירושלמית דעודפת על של מדברית חומשא של מדברית דהיא כ"ט ביעי פחות חומש ביצה (כ"ד) [כ"ט]

*) נראה דל"ל דהוא שתי ידות מככר שיש בו שליש קב:

רב נסים גאון

ת"ל האוכל והשוכב אלא ליתן שיעור לאוכל *) וכמה הוא שיעור כדי אכילת פרס פת חיטין ולא פת שעורים מיסב ואוכלה בליפתן ואיתא נמי במשנת נגעים (פרק יג משנה ט) הנכנס לבית המנוגע טמא כולה והיא גרורה בתחלת זו המסכת (דף ד) בפרק מבוי ובתוספתא (נגעים פרק ז) אמרו ר' שמעון אומר כי מזון שתי סעודות שאמרו חכמים בעירובי תחומין רביעו נקרא חצי פרס לפסול את הגויה חציו נקרא פרס לאכול בבית המנוגע מיסב ואוכלה בלפתן. וחצי חציה לפסול את הגויה זו הטומאה גזירה דרבנן היא ופירושה כי כל מי שאכל מאכלים טמאים כשיעור הזה נאסר לאכול בתרומה עד שיטהר ואם נגע בתרומה פסלה וזה אחד מי"ח דבר שגזרו בו ביום דתנן בסוף מסכת זבין ואלו פוסלין את התרומה האוכל אוכל ראשון ואוכל שני כולה והיא קבועה בפרק יציאות השבת (שבת דף יד) ובפרק יום הכפורים (יומא דף פ) אמרו הנה לטומאת גויות דלאו דאורייתא ובמסכת נדה בפרק יוצא דופן אמרי אבל גויה דטומאה דרבנן לא ובמסכת שחיטת חולין בפרק השוחט אחד בעוף (חולין דף לד) אמר עולא האוכל שלישי של חולין שנעשו על טהרת תרומה נפסל גופו מלאכול בתרומה והמשקין הטמאין נמי נידונין כאוכלין כמו ששנינו במסכת זבין (פרק ה משנה יב) והשותה משקין טמאין ושיערו שיעורו ברביעית

*) לפנינו איתא שם ליתן שיעור לשוכב כדי שיאכל וכמה הוא שיעור וכו'.

יא א מיי' פ"ד מהלכות עירובין הלכה טו טוש"ע א"ח סי' שעה סעיף ב:
יב ב מיי' פ"ג מהל' עירובין הלכה טז:

כְּדֵי עִיסּוֹתֵיכֶם. וְכַמָּה עִיסּוֹתֵיכֶם — כְּדֵי עִיסַּת הַמִּדְבָּר. וְכַמָּה עִיסַּת הַמִּדְבָּר — דִּכְתִיב: °"וְהָעוֹמֶר עֲשִׂירִית הָאֵיפָה הוּא". מִכָּאן אָמְרוּ: ז' רְבָעִים קֶמַח וְעוֹד חַיֶּיבֶת בְּחַלָּה, שֶׁהֵן ו' שֶׁל יְרוּשַׁלְמִית, שֶׁהֵן ה' שֶׁל צִיפּוֹרִי. מִכָּאן אָמְרוּ: הָאוֹכֵל כְּמִדָּה זוֹ, ה"ז בָּרִיא וּמְבוֹרָךְ, יָתֵר עַל כֵּן — רַעַבְתָן, פָּחוֹת מִכָּאן — מְקוּלְקָל בְּמֵעָיו.§ **מתני'** *אאַנְשֵׁי חָצֵר וְאַנְשֵׁי מִרְפֶּסֶת שֶׁשָּׁכְחוּ וְלֹא עֵירְבוּ, כֹּל שֶׁגָּבוֹהַּ י' טְפָחִים — לַמִּרְפֶּסֶת, פָּחוֹת מִכָּאן — לֶחָצֵר. חוּלְיַית הַבּוֹר וְהַסֶּלַע גְּבוֹהִים עֲשָׂרָה טְפָחִים — לַמִּרְפֶּסֶת, פָּחוֹת מִכָּאן — לֶחָצֵר. בד"א — בִּסְמוּכָה, אֲבָל בְּמוּפְלֶגֶת — אֲפִילּוּ גָּבוֹהַּ י' טְפָחִים לֶחָצֵר. וְאֵיזוֹ הִיא סְמוּכָה — כֹּל שֶׁאֵינָהּ רְחוֹקָה אַרְבָּעָה טְפָחִים.§ **גמ'** פְּשִׁיטָא; לָזֶה בְּפֶתַח וְלָזֶה בְּפֶתַח — הַיְינוּ *חַלּוֹן שֶׁבֵּין שְׁתֵּי חֲצֵירוֹת. לָזֶה בִּזְרִיקָה וְלָזֶה בִּזְרִיקָה — הַיְינוּ *כּוֹתֶל שֶׁבֵּין ב' חֲצֵירוֹת. לָזֶה בְּשִׁלְשׁוּל וְלָזֶה בְּשִׁלְשׁוּל — הַיְינוּ *חָרִיץ שֶׁבֵּין ב' חֲצֵירוֹת. לָזֶה בְּפֶתַח וְלָזֶה בִּזְרִיקָה — הַיְינוּ *דְּרַבָּה בַּר רַב הוּנָא אָמַר רַב נַחְמָן. לָזֶה בְּפֶתַח וְלָזֶה בְּשִׁלְשׁוּל — הַיְינוּ *דְּרַב שֵׁיזְבִי אָמַר רַב נַחְמָן. לָזֶה בְּשִׁלְשׁוּל וְלָזֶה בִּזְרִיקָה מַאי? אָמַר רַב: בשְׁנֵיהֶן אֲסוּרִין. וּשְׁמוּאֵל אָמַר: נוֹתְנִין אוֹתוֹ לָזֶה שֶׁבְּשִׁלְשׁוּל, שֶׁלָּזֶה תַּשְׁמִישׁוֹ בְּנַחַת וְלָזֶה תַּשְׁמִישׁוֹ בְּקָשֶׁה. *וְכָל דָּבָר שֶׁתַּשְׁמִישׁוֹ לָזֶה בְּנַחַת וְלָזֶה בְּקָשֶׁה — נוֹתְנִים אוֹתוֹ לָזֶה שֶׁתַּשְׁמִישׁוֹ בְּנַחַת. תְּנַן: אַנְשֵׁי חָצֵר וְאַנְשֵׁי מִרְפֶּסֶת שֶׁשָּׁכְחוּ וְלֹא עֵירְבוּ, כֹּל שֶׁגָּבוֹהַּ עֲשָׂרָה טְפָחִים — לַמִּרְפֶּסֶת, פָּחוֹת מִכָּאן — לֶחָצֵר. קָא סָלְקָא דַּעְתָּךְ, מַאי מִרְפֶּסֶת — בְּנֵי

תורה אור: שמות טז

רש"י

כְּדֵי עִיסּוֹתֵיכֶם. שֶׁאַתֶּם לָשִׁים בַּמִּדְבָּר, עוֹמֶר לַגּוּלְגּוֹלֶת: אֵיפָה ג' סְאִין בִּמְנָחוֹת יָלֵיף לָהּ בְּפֶרֶק "הַתּוֹדָה" (דף עז.), דִּכְתִיב (יחזקאל מה): "הָאֵיפָה וְהַבַּת תּוֹכֶן אֶחָד (לָהֶם) [יִהְיֶה]" וּכְתִיב (שם): "מַעְשַׂר הַבַּת מִן הַכּוֹר" וְכוֹר שְׁלֹשִׁים סְאִין, מַעֲשַׂר דִּידֵיהּ כַּמָּה הָוֵי — ג' סְאִין, וְהָעוֹמֶר עֲשִׂירִית שֶׁל ג' סְאִין שֶׁהֵן י"ח קַבִּין, שֶׁהֵן ע"ב לוּגִּין. עֲשִׂירִית דְּע' לוּגִּין ז' לוּגִּין. עֲשִׂירִית שֶׁל ב' לוּגִּין — חוֹמֶשׁ הַלּוֹג, וְהוּא בֵּיצָה וְחוּמְשָׁא. וְהַיְינוּ דְּקָאָמַר ז' רְבָעִים וָעוֹד. רְבָעִים — רִבְעֵי הַקַּב, דְּהַיְינוּ ז' לוּגִּין וְעוֹד בֵּיצָה וְחוּמְשָׁא: שֶׁהֵן ו' יְרוּשַׁלְמִית. שֶׁהֲרֵי ו' מִדְבָּרִיּוֹת נַעֲשׂוּ ה' יְרוּשַׁלְמִיּוֹת, נִשְׁאַר לָנוּ לוֹג מִדְבָּרִי וְחוּמְשׁוֹ. דְּבֵיצָה וְחוּמְשָׁא הָוֵי חוֹמֶשׁ הַלּוֹג, בֵּיצָה חוֹמֶשׁ לְחָמֵשׁ בֵּיצִים וְהַחוֹמֶשׁ בֵּיצָה הוּא תּוֹסֶפֶת לַבֵּיצָה הַשִּׁשִּׁית, הֲרֵי לוֹג וְחוּמְשׁוֹ, וְהֵן נַעֲשִׂין לוֹג יְרוּשַׁלְמִי. שֶׁהֲרֵי ו' חוּמְשִׁין אֵלּוּ נַעֲשׂוּ ה': הֲרֵי זֶה בָּרִיא. שֶׁאוֹכֵל כָּל צָרְכּוֹ: וּמְבוֹרָךְ. שֶׁאֵינוֹ אוֹכֵל יוֹתֵר מִדַּאי וּכְתִיב (משלי יג): "וּבֶטֶן רְשָׁעִים תֶּחְסָר": **מתני'** ה"ג: בְּמַתְנִי' אַנְשֵׁי חָצֵר וְאַנְשֵׁי מִרְפֶּסֶת כו'. וְלֹא עֵירְבוּ אֵלּוּ עִם אֵלּוּ אֲבָל עֵירְבוּ אֵלּוּ לְעַצְמָן וְאֵלּוּ לְעַצְמָן — מִרְפֶּסֶת אֲרוּכָּה הִיא, וְהַרְבֵּה פִּתְחֵי עֲלִיּוֹת פְּתוּחִין לָהּ, וְכוּלָּן יוֹצְאִין בְּסוּלָּם א' לֶחָצֵר, וּמִמֶּנָּה לִרְה"ר. וְאַעפ"כ אֵין אוֹסְרִין, הוֹאִיל וְגָבוֹהַּ מִרְפֶּסֶת י' שֶׁלֹּא הָלְכוּ בְּסוּלָּם אֶלָּא לְהָקֵל, וְאָמְרִינַן תּוֹרַת מְחִיצָּה עָלָיו וְאֵינָן אוֹסְרִין. כִּדְאָמְרִינַן בְּ"כֵיצַד מְעַבְּרִין" (לעיל דף נט:): סוּלָּם תּוֹרַת פֶּתַח עָלָיו וְתוֹרַת מְחִיצָּה עָלָיו, וְהַכֹּל לְהָקֵל. וּמ"מ שְׁנֵי רְשׁוּיוֹת הֵן וְאֵין מוֹצִיאִין מִזּוֹ לָזוֹ: כֹּל שֶׁגָּבוֹהַּ י'. אִם יֵשׁ בֶּחָצֵר תֵּל אוֹ עַמּוּד גָּבוֹהַּ י' סָמוּךְ לַמִּרְפֶּסֶת — רְשׁוּת מִרְפֶּסֶת שׁוֹלֶטֶת בּוֹ, וּמִשְׁתַּמְּשִׁין הֵן בּוֹ, אֲבָל לֹא בְּנֵי חָצֵר: בִּסְמוּכָה. שֶׁהַחוּלְיָא סְמוּכָה לַמִּרְפֶּסֶת: חוּלְיַית הַבּוֹר. קַרְקַע שֶׁנָּטְלוּ בַּחֲפִירַת הַבּוֹר וְהִקִּיפוּ בּוֹ פִּי הַבּוֹר סָבִיב: **גמ'** לָזֶה בְּפֶתַח וְלָזֶה בְּפֶתַח. ב' חֲצֵירוֹת שֶׁלֹּא עֵירְבוּ יֵשׁ רְשׁוּת אַחַת סְמוּכָה לָהֶן וְנוֹחָה לִשְׁתֵּיהֶן לְהִשְׁתַּמֵּשׁ בָּהּ, כְּפֶתַח זֶה שֶׁהוּא נוֹחַ לִיכָּנֵס: הַיְינוּ חַלּוֹן שֶׁבֵּין ב' חֲצֵירוֹת. כְּלוֹמַר: הָא לָא מִיבַּעְיָא לַן מַאי דִּינֵיהּ אִם אָסוּר לִשְׁתֵּיהֶן אוֹ מוּתָּר — דְּהַיְינוּ חַלּוֹן שֶׁבֵּין ב' חֲצֵירוֹת. דִּתְנַן בֵּיהּ: רָצוּ — אֶחָד מְעָרְבִין, רָצוּ — שְׁנַיִם מְעָרְבִין. וְאִם לֹא עֵירְבוּ כְּאַחַד — שְׁנֵיהֶם אֲסוּרִים לְהִשְׁתַּמֵּשׁ בָּהּ, אִם רְשׁוּת שֶׁל אַרְבָּעָה הִיא. דְּאֵין רְשׁוּת פָּחוֹת מִד' וּמְנָלַן דַּאֲסוּרִים בָּהּ, דְּהָא גַּבֵּי כּוֹתֶל שֶׁבֵּין שְׁתֵּי חֲצֵירוֹת תְּנַן (לעיל דף עו:): הָיוּ בְּרֹאשׁוֹ פֵּירוֹת — אֵלּוּ עוֹלִין מִכָּאן וְאוֹכְלִין וְכֵן אֵלּוּ, וּבִלְבַד שֶׁלֹּא יוֹרִידוּ לְמַטָּה. אַלְמָא: כָּל הֵיכָא דְּשָׁוֵי לְתַרְוַיְיהוּ — אָסְרִי אַהֲדָדֵי. וְגַם בִּרְשׁוּת נְמוּכָה מִי' אָמְרִינַן מָקוֹם שֶׁאֵין בּוֹ ד' עַל ד' מוּתָּר לִבְנֵי רה"י וְלִבְנֵי רה"ר לְכַתֵּף עָלָיו, דִּמְקוֹם פְּטוּר הוּא. הָא אִית בֵּיהּ ד' — אָסוּר לְתַרְוַיְיהוּ. כָּל זְרִיקָה — לְמַעְלָה מִי' טְפָחִים, וְכָל שִׁלְשׁוּל — עָמוֹק מִי' טְפָחִים. וְכָל תַּשְׁמִישׁ נוֹחַ דְּקָרֵינַן לֵיהּ פֶּתַח לֹא גָּבוֹהַּ קַרְקָעִיתוֹ י' טְפָחִים וְלֹא נָמוּךְ עֲשָׂרָה טְפָחִים: לָזֶה בִּזְרִיקָה וְלָזֶה בִּזְרִיקָה. כָּל רְשׁוּת שֶׁהִיא בֵּין ב' רְשׁוּיוֹת וְקָשָׁה תַּשְׁמִישָׁהּ לִשְׁתֵּיהֶן, לָזֶה גָּבוֹהַּ י' וְלָזֶה גָּבוֹהַּ עֲשָׂרָה וְאֵינָן יְכוֹלִים לְהִשְׁתַּמֵּשׁ אֶלָּא בִּזְרִיקָה — הָא לָא מִיבַּעְיָא לִי דְּהַיְינוּ כּוֹתֶל שֶׁבֵּין ב' חֲצֵירוֹת וְאִיסּוּרָן מְפוֹרָשׁ בַּמִּשְׁנָה. דְּקָתָנֵי: וּבִלְבַד שֶׁלֹּא יוֹרִידוּ לְמַטָּה, אַלְמָא: אֲסוּרִים עִם שְׁנֵיהֶן: הַיְינוּ חָרִיץ. דְּהָוֵי נַמִּי אָסוּר לְתַרְוַיְיהוּ, דְּהָא הֶפְסֵק רְשׁוּת חָשִׁיב. וְכֵיוָן דְּתַשְׁמִישׁוֹ שָׁוֶה לִשְׁנֵיהֶם — אֲסוּרִין בּוֹ, דְּאָמַר* רַב (לעיל דף עז.): חָרִיץ שֶׁבֵּין ב' חֲצֵירוֹת, עָמוֹק מִזּוֹ י' וְלָזֶה שָׁוֶה לָאָרֶץ — נוֹתְנִין אוֹתוֹ לָזֶה שֶׁשָּׁוֶה לָאָרֶץ, דַּהֲוָה לָזֶה תַּשְׁמִישׁ בְּנַחַת וְלָזֶה בְּקָשֶׁה כו' שָׁמְעִינַן מִינַּהּ דְּאִי לִשְׁנֵיהֶן בְּנַחַת אוֹ לִשְׁנֵיהֶן בְּקָשֶׁה — שְׁנֵיהֶן אֲסוּרִין בּוֹ: לָזֶה בְּפֶתַח וְלָזֶה בִּזְרִיקָה. כְּגוֹן שֶׁחָצֵר זוֹ נְמוּכָה וְחָצֵר זוֹ גְּבוֹהָה — וְתֵל בֵּינֵיהֶם גָּבוֹהַּ מִזּוֹ י' וְלָזוֹ שָׁוֶה לָאָרֶץ: הַיְינוּ דְּרַבָּה בַּר רַב הוּנָא. בְּפֶרֶק "חַלּוֹן" (שם) דְּאָמַר: כּוֹתֶל שֶׁבֵּין ב' חֲצֵירוֹת, גָּבוֹהַּ י' וְלַצְּדוֹ אֶחָד שָׁוֶה לָאָרֶץ — נוֹתְנִין אוֹתוֹ לָזֶה שֶׁשָּׁוֶה לָאָרֶץ: לָזֶה בְּפֶתַח וְלָזֶה בְּשִׁלְשׁוּל. כְּגוֹן חָצֵר גְּבוֹהָה מִן הַתֵּל י' דְּאֵינָהּ מִשְׁתַּמֶּשֶׁת עָלָיו בְּחוֹל אֶלָּא בְּשִׁלְשׁוּל, וַחֲבֶרְתָּהּ שָׁוָה לָהּ: הַיְינוּ דְּרַב שֵׁיזְבִי. בְּפֶרֶק "חַלּוֹן" (שם): לָזֶה בְּשִׁלְשׁוּל וְלָזֶה בִּזְרִיקָה. כְּגוֹן חָצֵר זוֹ גְּבוֹהָה מִזֶּה הַתֵּל י', וְזוֹ נְמוּכָה מִמֶּנּוּ י': מַאי. לִשְׁנֵיהֶם בְּקָשֶׁה הוּא, וַהֲרֵי הֵן שָׁוִין בּוֹ וְאוֹסְרִין זֶה עַל זֶה, דְּהָא כָּל שִׁלְשׁוּל אָמְרִינַן דְּקָשֶׁה הוּא. אוֹ דִּילְמָא לְגַבֵּי זְרִיקָה הֲוָה שִׁלְשׁוּל תַּשְׁמִישׁוֹ בְּנַחַת הוּא, וּמוּתָּר. וְזֶה שֶׁבִּזְרִיקָה — אָסוּר, אִם לֹא עֵירְבוּ אֵלּוּ עִם אֵלּוּ אֶלָּא אֵלּוּ לְעַצְמָן וְאֵלּוּ לְעַצְמָן: בְּנֵי

תוספות

שבעת רבעים קמח ועוד חייבין בחלה. פי': ז' לוגין ועוד, דהיינו ביצה וחומש ביצה, כדפי' בקונטרס, והם שש ירושלמיות וה' ציפוריות. ובסוף "כלל גדול" (שבת דף עו:) היה כתוב בספרים: והתנן, ה' רבעים קמח ועוד חייבים בחלה — ל"ג רש"י(א) "ועוד". התם משמע דבשל ציפורי איירי, והתם ליכא "ועוד", אלא ה' בצמצום. ור"ת מפרש: דאתיא כרבי יוסי, וגרסינן ליה שפיר. דתנן במס' עדיות (פ"א משנה ב), ומייתי לה בפ"ק דשבת (דף טו.), שמאי אומר: מקב לחלה כו'. וחכ"א: חמש רבעים קמח חייבין בחלה. ור' יוסי אומר: חמש — פטורים, חמש ועוד — חייבים. ומפרש ר"ת: דסבר רבי יוסי ד"ראשית עריסותיכם" — היינו דלאחר הפרשת ראשית, דהוא חלה ישאר שיעור עריסותיכם — דהיינו עיסת מדברית. וההוא "ועוד" — היינו כדי חלה. ומהר"י מפרש: דר' יוסי לטעמיה דשמעתין, דקאמר חלי פרס ב' ביצים שוחקות. ושיער רבי ב' ביצים ועוד א' מכ' בביצה, א"כ, מז' רבעים קמח ועוד שהם מ"ג ביצים וחומש ביצה כמנין חלה, יעלה ועודות — ב' ביצים ושלשה ועודות הרי לרבי יוסי מ"ה ביצים וחומש ביצה וג' ועודות. אע"פ שהסאין והקבין ניתוספו, מנין הביצים כדקאי קאי כדמוכח בשמעתין. ולכאורה נראה דאין הלכה כרבי יוסי, כדאמרינן ב"מי שהוליאוהו" (לעיל דף מו: *) דהלכה כר' יוסי מחבירו, ולא מחביריו. ואמרינן נמי, אמר ליה ר' אלעזר לרב אסי: מה אמור רבנן בבי מדרשא? א"ל: הכי אמר ר' יוחנן: הלכה כר' יוסי. וקאמר התלמוד: מכלל דיחידאה פליג עליה. משמע דאי רבים פליגי עליה — אין הלכה כר' יוסי. אבל לפום ריהטא דגרסינן בפ' "כלל גדול" (שבת דף עו:) ובפרק "אלו עוברין" (פסחים דף מח:) דנקט התלמוד חמש רבעים ועוד חייבין בחלה — משמע דהלכה כר' יוסי: **קא** סלקא דעתיך מאי מרפסת בני עלייה. מפרש ר"י: סתם פתח עלייה גבוה עשרה מן מרפסת, והמרפסת גבוה מן החצר י', ודרך סולמות יורדין מעלייה למרפסת וממרפסת לחצר, ודרך חצר יוצאים לרשות הרבים. והמרפסת היא של בני עלייה, ואין בני החצר אוסרים אותה לבני עליות לפי שהמרפסת היא שלהם. והא דקאמר בסמוך בשתי גזוזטראות כשבאין בני תחתונה דרך עליונה למלאות שאוסרת התחתונה על העליונה — היינו כדמפרש בפירקין *משום שעשו מחיצה בשותפות. וכשלא עירבו בני עליות יחד אוסרים המרפסת זה על זה משום לזה בשלשול ולזה בשלשול. אבל מחמת הסולמות שיורדין בהם מן העליות לא היו אוסרין זה על זה, דסולם תורת מחיצה עליו. והשתא פריך לרב שפיר, כיון דפתחי עליות וחלונותיהם גבוהים מן החצר כ' או יותר, אמאי נותנין תל ועמוד שבחצר הגבוהים י', והם כנגד החלונות? דגבוהים לבני עליות בשלשול י' יאסרו לרב בני חצר על בני עליות ע"י זריקה, כיון דתל ועמוד הוי של שניהם ולא דמי למרפסת שהיא לבני עליות לבדה. ואע"פ שתל ועמוד הוא שוה למרפסת, ויכול להשתמש מן המרפסת בתל ועמוד בפתח — מ"מ לא מיקרי לבני עליות בפתח אלא בשלשול. כי במרפסת אין בה דיורין, ואינה יכולה לאסור את התל לחצר אלא ע"י עליות. ואע"פ שיורדין בה מן העליות ומשתמשין בה — אינה אוסרת, כיון דסולם תורת מחיצה עליו. והא דאמרינן בשמעתין דכשבאין בני התחתונה למלאות לא חשיב לבני התחתונה כזריקה — לאו משום דסולם חשיב עליו כפתח לאסור, אלא דע"י סולם חשיב לבני התחתונה תשמישן בנחת כמו בשלשול. אבל כפתח לא חשיב, ולא עדיף טפי משלשול לאסור. ומשני: לאותן הדרים במרפסת. פירוש: שפתחי עליות תוך עשרה למרפסת, דתו ליכא בסולם תורת מחיצה: הכי

הגהות הב"ח

(א) תוס' ד"ה שבעת וכו' לא גרס רש"י התם ועוד דמשמע:

רבינו חננאל

מוספת על קמ"ד הוויין להו קע"ג ביעי אי סאה דציפורי ר"ז ביצים הוויין ואמרין לעולם סאה ששיער (ררי"ן) [רי"ז] ביצים סאה דציפורי היא והאי דאמרת ר"ז (סאה) ביצים בתר דאפיקו חלתן. וכי שיער (ררי"ן) [רי"ז] בהדי חלתן. ואתינן למיחזי חלת סאה של ציפורי כמה ביעי הוויין. ומדתנן במתני' שיעור חלה אחד מכ"ד נמצאו שהורמה חלה מזו הסאה ט' ביצים ודחינן אכתי *) רי"ן ביעי הוויין ור' שיער רי"ז ושבקינן להני חשבני לכלהו ואמרינן אלא אייתי ועוד דר' ושדי עלייהו כלומר של ציפורי הויא ר"ז ביצים שוחקות שהן כל ביצה וביצה ועוד עציבות. וכי שיער (ררי"ן) [רבי רי"ז] ביצים עציבות שיער ופי' אייתי ועוד שהוא חלק אחד מעשרים בביצה שא' ר' ושדי אהני ר"ז ביעי (פי') [דהיינו] ר"ז ועודים. [ופרכינן א"ה הו"ל טפי] ופרקינן כיון דלא הוויין ביצה לא חשיב להו: **ת"ר** סאה ירושלמית עודפת על של מדברית שתות. ושל ציפורי עודפת על של ירושלמית שתות. נמצאת ציפורית עודפת על מדברית שליש שהוא מחצה. האי שליש דהיכא אי דמדברית טפי הוא שליש דמדברית מ"ח הוא כי שדית להו אקמ"ד הוויין קצ"ב **) ואנן קע"ג ביעי הוא דאמרי' (בפיאה) [בסאה] של ירושלמית. ואי דשל ציפורית אכתי בצרן להו א"ר ירמיה ה"ק נמצאת סאה של ציפורי עודפת [על] של מדברית קרוב לשליש שלה כו' ודחי לה רבינא מידי קרוב קתני אלא ה"ק נמצאת [שליש] סאה של ציפורי [ועוד דר'] יתר על מחצה של מדברית שליש ביצה פי' סאה ציפורית בתר דשדית עלה ועוד דר' הוויא רי"ז ביעי שליש [כמה] הוויין ע"ב ביעי ושליש ביצה ומחצה של מדברית דהיא קמ"ד ביעי חציה ע"ב ביעי. אשתכח שליש של ציפורי עודף על מחצה דמדברית שליש ביצה: **ת"ר** סאה ירושלמית עודפת על של מדברית שתות כו'. פי' סאה מדברית הוויא לה קמ"ד ביצים שתותיהן הוויין כ"ט ביעי קמ"ד וכ"ט ביעי קע"ג נמצאת סאה ירושלמית שהיא קע"ג ביצים עודפת על סאה מדברית שתותא מלבר (עד) [ועוד] שתות [של] ק"ע הוא (ל"ד). כשתוסיף ל"ד על קע"ג הוויין רי"ז ביצים נמצאת (עוד) [סאה] של ציפורי עודפת על של ירושלמי שתות מלבר ונשאר שתות שליש ביצים שלא נחשב אלא

כיון שאין בשתותיהן שיעור ביצה לא חשיב להו כדאמרן לעילא. וראינו לרבותינו הגאונים זצ"ל פירוש זולתי זה הפירוש אבל זהו קבלה ומסורה בידינו: ירושלמי מזונו לחול אבל לא לשבת דברי ר"מ סבר לחול דלית (ביה) [ליה] ***) בשש לאכול בו אכיל פיתא ציבחר בשבת דאית ליה מטעמים אכול פיתא סגין. ר' יהודה סבר בחול דלית ליה מה לאכל [אכיל פיתא] סגין בשבת דאית ליה מה לאכול אכיל פיתא ציבחר. איתא חמי ר' יוחנן בן ברוקה אמר הן עביד עגולא תריסר ביעי והדין עביד עיגולא תמני ביעי והוא ר"ש ותני (בן) [כי] קרובין דבריהם להיות שוין רב הונא א' צא מהן שליש ליציאה. **ת"ר** ראשית עריסותיכם כדי עריסותיכם. כמה כדי עיסתכם כדי עיסת מדברי כדכתיב והעומר עשירית האיפה הוא. מיכן אמרו ז' רביעים קמח ועוד חייבין בחלה שהן ו' ירושלמית וה' של ציפורי מיכן אמרו כל האוכל כמדה זו הרי זה בריא (בריך) ומבורך. פחות מיכן הרי זה מקולקל במעיו. פירוש כמו חולה במעיו הוא יתר מיכן הרי זה רעבתן: **מתני'** אנשי חצר ששכחו ולא עירבו כל שגבוה י' טפחים למרפסת מיכן

*) נ"ל אכתי רט"ז הוויין כצ"ל וכ"כ התוס' בשמו בד"ה תלתא: **) אולי צ"ל ואנן ר"ז ביעי הוא דאמרינן בסאה של ציפורית כצ"ל: ***) בשש הוא לפתן וכמ"ש הערוך בערך בשש ופירושו פשוט.

רב נסים גאון

ברביעית ולפיכך לא הצריכוה טומאת ערב מפני שהיא דרבנן כדתניא בתורת כהנים אין האוכל אוכלין טמאין ולא השותה משקין טמאין טמא טומאת ערב ואמרו אין טומאה מן התורה עולה מידי טומאתה בו ביום: **פשיטא** לזה בפתח ולזה בפתח הינו חלון שבין שתי חצרות הינו מתני' דהיא תחילת פרק חלון לזה בזריקה ולזה בזריקה הינו כותל שבין שתי חצרות כלומר מתניתא תנייתא לזה בשלשול ולזה בשלשול היינו חריץ שבין שתי חצרות והינו מתניתא תליתאה לזה בפתח ולזה בזריקה היינו דרבה בר רב הונא אמר רב נחמן קאי אהא דאיתא בתחלת פרק חלון כותל שבין ב' חצרות גבוה עשרה וצדו אחד שוה לארץ כו' לזה בפתח ולזה בשלשול היינו דרב שיזבי אמר רב נחמן ואיתה למימרא דילה בתרה דההיא מימרא דרבה בר רב הונא דכתבנו:

ואזדו

בְּנֵי עֲלִיָּיה(א) וּמַאי קָרוּ לָהּ מִרְפֶּסֶת — דְּקָסָלְקִי בְּמִרְפֶּסֶת. אַלְמָא: כָּל לָזֶה בְּשִׁלְשׁוּל וְלָזֶה בִּזְרִיקָה — נוֹתְנִין אוֹתוֹ לָזֶה שֶׁבְּשִׁלְשׁוּל! כִּדְאָמַר רַב הוּנָא: לְאוֹתָן הַדָּרִים בְּמִרְפֶּסֶת. ה"נ: [א]לְאוֹתָן הַדָּרִין בְּמִרְפֶּסֶת. אִי הָכִי, אֵימָא סֵיפָא: פָּחוֹת מִכָּאן — לֶחָצֵר, אַמַּאי? לָזֶה בְּפֶתַח וְלָזֶה בְּפֶתַח הוּא! מַאי לֶחָצֵר — [ב]אַף לֶחָצֵר, וּשְׁנֵיהֶן אֲסוּרִין. ה"נ מִסְתַּבְּרָא, מִדְּקָתָנֵי סֵיפָא: בד"א — בִּסְמוּכָה, אֲבָל בְּמוּפְלֶגֶת, אֲפִילּוּ גְּבוֹהַּ י' טְפָחִים — לֶחָצֵר. מַאי לֶחָצֵר? אִילֵימָא לֶחָצֵר וְשָׁרֵי; אַמַּאי? רְשׁוּתָא דְּתַרְוַיְיהוּ הוּא! אֶלָּא מַאי לֶחָצֵר — אַף לֶחָצֵר, וּשְׁנֵיהֶן אֲסוּרִין. ה"נ, מַאי לֶחָצֵר — אַף לֶחָצֵר, וּשְׁנֵיהֶן אֲסוּרִין, ש"מ. תְּנַן: חוּלְיַית הַבּוֹר וְהַסֶּלַע שֶׁהֵן גְּבוֹהִין עֲשָׂרָה — לַמִּרְפֶּסֶת, פָּחוֹת מִכָּאן — לֶחָצֵר. אָמַר רַב הוּנָא: לְאוֹתָן הַדָּרִים בַּמִּרְפֶּסֶת. תֵּינַח סֶלַע, בּוֹר מַאי אִיכָּא לְמֵימַר? אָמַר רַב יִצְחָק בְּרֵיהּ דְּרַב יְהוּדָה: הָכָא בְּבוֹר מְלֵאָה מַיִם עָסְקִינַן. וְהָא חָסְרָא! כֵּיוָן דְּכִי מַלְיָא שָׁרְיָא, כִּי חָסְרָא — נַמִּי שָׁרְיָא. אַדְּרַבָּה, [ג]כֵּיוָן דְּכִי חָסְרָא אֲסִירָא, כִּי מַלְיָא נַמִּי אֲסִירָא! אֶלָּא אָמַר אַבַּיֵי: הָכָא בְּבוֹר מְלֵיאָה פֵּירוֹת עָסְקִינַן. וְהָא חָסְרֵי! [ד]בְּטִיבְלָא. דַּיְקָא נַמִּי, דְּקָתָנֵי דּוּמְיָא דְּסֶלַע, ש"מ. וְל"ל לְמִיתְנָא בּוֹר, וְל"ל לְמִיתְנָא סֶלַע? צְרִיכָא, דְּאִי אַשְׁמְעִינַן סֶלַע — דְּלֵיכָּא לְמִיגְזַר, אֲבָל בּוֹר — לִיגְזוֹר, זִמְנִין דְּמַלְיָא פֵּירוֹת מְתוּקָּנִין — צְרִיכָא. תָּא שְׁמַע: [ה]אַנְשֵׁי חָצֵר וְאַנְשֵׁי עֲלִיָּיה שֶׁשָּׁכְחוּ וְלֹא עֵירְבוּ — אַנְשֵׁי חָצֵר מִשְׁתַּמְּשִׁין בַּעֲשָׂרָה הַתַּחְתּוֹנִים, וְאַנְשֵׁי עֲלִיָּיה מִשְׁתַּמְּשִׁין בַּעֲשָׂרָה הָעֶלְיוֹנִים. כֵּיצַד? זִיז יוֹצֵא מִן הַכּוֹתֶל, לְמַטָּה מֵעֲשָׂרָה — לֶחָצֵר, לְמַעְלָה מֵעֲשָׂרָה — לָעֲלִיָּיה. [ו]הָא דְּבֵינֵי בֵּינֵי — אָסוּר! אָמַר רַב נַחְמָן: הָכָא בְּכוֹתֶל תִּשְׁעָה עָשָׂר עָסְקִינַן, וְזִיז יוֹצֵא מִמֶּנּוּ. לְמַטָּה מֵעֲשָׂרָה — לָזֶה בְּפֶתַח וְלָזֶה בְּשִׁלְשׁוּל, לְמַעְלָה מֵעֲשָׂרָה — לָזֶה בְּפֶתַח וְלָזֶה בִּזְרִיקָה.

ת"ש

בני עלייה. דגביהי ממרפסת טובא, אבל דרך מרפסת זו עולין ויורדין. ותל שבחצר שהוא גבוה י' הוי נמוך מן העלייה י' דהוי לזה בשלשול ולזה בזריקה, וקתני דבני עלייה מותרין בו: הדרין במרפסת. כגון שיש בה דיורין, דלדידהו הוי האי תל שבחצר שוה להן בתוך עשרה, או נמוך או גבוה מהם פחות מי': לזה בפתח ולזה בפתח הוא. ותרוייהו בעי איתסורי ביה, דהא סתם מרפסת לא גביהה טובא: אף לחצר. כלומר: שתי הרשויות שולטות בו, ואוסרין זה על זה: ה"נ מסתברא. דמאי לחצר – אף לחצר קאמר, ודיורי מרפסת עסקינן: מדקתני סיפא מופלגת. אפילו גבוה י' הוי לחצר: אי נימא. דשרי ליה לאשתמושי: אמאי. נהי נמי דמאי מרפסת בני עלייה רשותא דתרוייהו היא, דלשניהן תשמישו בקשה; לחצר בזריקת גובה, ולעלייה בזריקה את משך ההפלגה ובשלשול את הנמוכות. ונהי דלשמואל שלשול לגבי זריקת גובה נוח הוא, הכא דאיכא שלשול וזריקת משך – שוין הן לזריקת גובה, ואמאי לחצר: אלא. על כרחך אף לחצר, ואסורין. לרב נמי, דמתרץ לה בדיורי מרפסת, מאי לחצר דקתני – אפחות מכאן אף לחצר קאמר, ואסורין: חוליית הבור. או שיש בחצר סלע: למרפסת. וקס"ד לבני עלייה קאמר, וקשיא לרב: תינח סלע. דהוי לבני מרפסת כפתח, שעל גביו הוי תשמיש דידיה, וגבוה שוה להן הוא: אלא בור. שממלאים הימנו – תשמישתו בשלשול הוא אפילו לבני מרפסת, שהרי מקרקעיתו דולין. וש"מ: דהואיל ולבני חצר תשמישו בזריקה, שאין יכולין למלאות אלא א"כ זורקין דלי למעלה מן החוליא – יהבינן לה לבני מרפסת דבשלשול, כשמואל: מלאה מים. דהוי כפתח לבני מרפסת: בדטיבלא. שהן מוקצין מחמת איסור טבל, ואסורין לטלטל: דומיא דסלע. שאינו חסר: ולמה לי למיתנא. תרוייהו, הואיל ובדטיבלא מוקמת לה. בשלמא אי אמרת בבור מים קאמר – איצטריך בור לאשמעינן, דאע"ג דבשלשול הוא לבני מרפסת – אפ"ה לגבי חצר דתשמישתיה בזריקה – נחת חשיב ליה לשלשול דמרפסת. אלא השתא, דבור וסלע שניהן תשמישתם על גבן – תרוייהו למה לי? ליתני סלע ולא ליתני בור הואיל וסוף כדומיא דסלע בעית לאוקמיה. נהי דבור בלא סלע לא מצי למתני – דאם כן הוה אמינא בבור סתם קאמר – להכי איצטריך סלע, לגלויי עליה דבדטיבלא עסקינן. אלא סלע בלא בור ליתני: ה"ג: צריכא דאי תנא סלע דליכא למיגזר כו'. ולא גרסינן: אי תנא בור אבל סלע לא – דהא בור בלא סלע לא מצי למיתני, כדפרישית: מתוקנין. דשקלי מינייהו וחסרי, ואתו לידי שילשול: ולא עירבו. אלו עם אלו: בעשרה תחתונים. בכותל הבית בחצר, אנשי חצר משתמשין, דלדידהו כפתח, ולבני עלייה בשלשול: בעשרה העליונים. שהן מתחת לעלייה, אנשי עלייה משתמשין – דסמוכין הן לבני עלייה, והוי לדידהו כפתח – ולבני חצר בזריקה: זיז. הבולט חוץ לכותל למעלה מעשרה. קא ס"ד בעלייה גבוה טובא עסקינן, והאי למעלה – לאו מן הקרקע מודד, אלא ה"ק: למעלה – מתחלת טפח עשירי, כשתמדוד מן העלייה ולמטה עשרה – דהיינו כדקתני רישא: בי' עליונים אנשי עלייה משתמשין: הא דביני ביני. שבין י' עליונים לי' תחתונים, דהוי לחצר בזריקה ולעלייה בשלשול: אסור. לתרוייהו, כרב: בכותל תשעה עשר עסקינן. דליכא ביני ביני, דכל למטה מעשרה דידיה – לחצר בפתח ולעלייה בשלשול, וכל למעלה מי' דידיה – לחצר בזריקה ולעלייה בפתח. ובכותל עשרים לא מצי לאוקמיה – דאם כן שמעינן מינה ראש טפח עשירי דלזה בשלשול ולזה בזריקה – אסור, דהא לא שרי תנא קמא אלא למעלה ולמטה. ובזיז רחב ארבעה עסקינן, דבליר מהכי לא הוה רשותא, ומקום פטור הוא, ובטיל להכא ולהכא:

שתי

א] וכן וכו' דיבור אחד עם ד"ה ת"ש וכ"מ מהגהות הגאון מהרי"פ לקמן פז:

הכי נמי מסתברא מדקתני סיפא כו'. אומר ר"י: דהאי ה"נ מסתברא ליתא אלא אליבא דשמואל דוקא, דסבר אדם אוסר על חבירו דרך אויר בשמעתין. אבל לרב, דאמר: אין אדם אוסר על חבירו דרך אויר – הויא הא לחצר דוקא, ומותרין. וא"ת: למה הוצרך לדקדק ה"נ מסתברא מסיפא דסיפא מפחות מכאן לחצר, דקתני גבי חוליית הבור הו"מ לדקדק דאף לשמואל הוי פירושו אף לחצר, דהא חוליית הבור והסלע דקתני שגבוה י' טפחים, ע"כ כשגובה החוליא עשרה טפחים משפת הבור, דהיינו מקרקעית החצר, מדחשיב לה לבני חצר בזריקה. וא"כ, כי קתני עלה פחות מכאן לחצר, שהחוליא פחות משהו מעשרה – א"כ, מראש חוליא עד קרקעית הבור יש יותר מעשרה, ואם כן לא הוי לבני חצר דוקא, דלבני חצר הוי נמי בשלשול כמו לבני עליות, דאין לחלק בין שלשול עשרה לכ'! וי"ל: דמ"מ לא ה"ל למתני לשמואל אף לחצר, גבי חוליית הבור. דנהי דקרקעית הבור הוי אף לחצר, מ"מ תשמיש שעל הסלע וראש החוליא הוי דוקא לחצר לשמואל. אבל לרב – אכולהו הוי, אף לחצר, ה"ל למתני בהדיא אף לחצר. ולהכי מייתי מסיפא דסיפא דלשמואל נמי הוי התם פירוש לחצר אף לחצר, בין אסלע בין אקרקעית הבור, כמו שצ"ל לרב גבי פחות מכאן לחצר: **בור** מאי איכא למימר. וא"ת: בור נמי, הוי לבני מרפסת בשלשול ולבני חצר בזריקה ושילשול, דאמר לקמן (פה.), כיון דלזה בזריקה ושלשול ולזה בשלשול לחודיה – כלזה בזריקה ולזה בפתח דמי! וי"ל: דלקמן בזריקה של הפלגה איירי, דהוי דרך אויר, אבל בזריקת גובה ושלשול – לא עדיף לרב משלשול לחודיה. ואין נראה לר"י חילוק זה, דאם היה אדם אוסר על חבירו דרך אויר לרב – לא היה מפליג בין זריקת גובה לזריקת אויר, מדפריך ליה ר"א לקמן (שם:): והא מר הוא דאמר לזה בזריקה ולזה בשילשול. ונראה לר"י: דהא דאמר לקמן שאני הכא כיון דלזה כו' ולזה בזריקה כלזה בזריקה ולזה בפתח דמי – דיחוי הוא, כלומר: דמצינו למידחי, ולמימר דלרב אדם אוסר על חבירו דרך אויר בעלמא היכא דהוי לתרוייהו בזריקת אויר. אבל לפי המסקנא הוי טעמא דרב משום דאין אדם אוסר על חבירו דרך אויר – לא נאמר דלזה בזריקה ושלשול ולזה בשלשול לחודיה כלזה בזריקה ולזה בפתח דמי, אלא יהיה לזה בזריקה ושלשול ולזה בזריקה כלזה בזריקה ולזה בשלשול, ולא נחלק ביניהן כמו שהיה סבר המקשה לקמן. ועוד י"ל: דלזה בזריקה ושלשול דלקמן – איכא ב' עניני זריקה, זריקת אויר וזריקת גובה אבל היכא דלזה בשלשול לחודיה, ולזה בזריקת גובה ושלשול או בזריקת אויר ושלשול – שניהם אסורין: **כיון** דכי חסרא אסירא כי מליא נמי אסירא. דהוי דבר הניטל בשבת, ואינו ממעט. ומסיק: בפירות של טבל דאין ניטלין בשבת, ולא דמי לעפר ועתיד לפנותו דאמר לעיל (דף עט.) דלא חייץ – דכיון דעתיד לפנותו לא מבטל(ב) ודאי מחילה המפסיק בין ב' חצירות. אבל למעט גובה עשרה, ולשוייה כפתח למרפסת – כיון דאינו ניטל בשבת ממעט, אע"ג דעתיד לפנותו כמו כפה ספל דאמר לעיל (דף עז.) דממעט: **תא** שמע אנשי חצר ואנשי *מרפסת כו'. ל"ג תנן, דאינו משנה בשום מקום, אלא ת"ש גרס. א] וכן ב' גזוזטראות כו'. פי' רש"י: ל"ג וכן. ור"ח גריס לה, דארישא קאי, דקתני בפירקין* "גזוזטרא שהיא למעלה מן כו'":

לא

*[לקמן דף פז:]

יג א ב מיי' פ"ד מה' עירובין הלכה טו טוש"ע סי' שעט ס"ב:

יד ג ד מיי' שם הלכה יח:

טו ה ו מיי' שם הלכה יז וטוש"ע שם ס"ד:

הגהות הב"ח

(א) גמ' בני עלייה ואמאי קרו לה: (ב) תוס' ד"ה כיון וכו' לא מבטל ודאי למחילה המפסיק:

רבינו חננאל

לחצר כו'. פשיטא לזה בפתח ולזה בפתח היינו חלון שבין ב' חצרות שניהן שוין בו וכן לזה בשלשול ולזה בשלשול כלומר אין אחד מהן יכול להשתמש בהריץ שביניהן אלא ע"י (שלשול) [עירוב]. לזה בזריקה ולזה בזריקה היינו כותל שבין ב' חצרות לזה בפתח ולזה בזריקה היינו דרבה אמר רב נחמן דאמר בפ' חלון שבין ב' חצרות. כותל שבין ב' חצרות גבוה י' ורחב ד' וצדו אחד שוה לארץ נותנין אותו לזה ששוה לארץ שתשמישו בנחת כו' לזה בפתח ולזה בשלשול היינו דרב שיזבי אמר רב נחמן דאמר חריץ שבין ב' חצרות עומק י' ורחב ד' וצידו אחד שוה לארץ נותנין לזה ששוה לארץ דהוי ליה תשמישו בנחת לזה בשלשול ולזה בזריקה כגון דהוו להו חד למעלה וחד למטה והכותל ביניהן מאי רב אמר שניהן אסורין עד שיערבו ושמואל אמר נותנין אותו לזה שבשלשול דהוה ליה תשמישו בנחת. ואקשינן לרב מהא דתנן אנשי חצר ששכחו ולא עירבו כל שגבוה י' טפחים למרפסת מאי לאו האי דקתני במרפסת להנהו דדיירי בעלייה דהוה להו בשלשול ולאנשי חצר בזריקה וקתני נותנין אותו למרפסת. ופריק רב לאו להנהו דדיירי בעלייה אלא להני דדיירי במרפסת עצמה דאע"ג דמרפסת ליתה בית דירה מיהו (אי) איכא דדיירי במרפסת אי הכי אימא סיפא פחות מיכן לחצר ואי להני דדיירי במרפסת אמאי לא לזה בפתח ולזה בפתח הוא (אלא) [לא] מאי לחצר אף לחצר ושניהן אסורין בו עד שיערבו הכי נמי מסתברא כו'. ת"ש חוליית הבור והסלע שגבוה י' טפחים למרפסת והא להנהו דדיירי בעלייה בשלשול הוא. ופריק רבינא להני דדיירי במרפסת דהוה תשמישן בנחת. התינח סלע אלא בור לא אפשר אלא בשלשול ופרקינן בבור מלא מים וליכא שלשול. והא כי חסרו מיא הוה ליה בשלשול כו' ופרקינן אלא בבור מלא פירות והא אכיל מינהון וחסרי להו (והיה) [והוה] תשמישתיה בשלשול ואסיקנא בור מלא פירות של טבל דלא (הוה) [חזיא] ליה ולא שקיל מינהון ולא חסרי דיקא נמי דקתני דומיא דסלע דלא חזי ליה כו'. ת"ש אנשי חצר ואנשי עלייה ששכחו ולא עירבו כל שהוא למעלה מעשרה טפחים לבני עלייה למטה מי' לחצר כיצד זיז היוצא מן הכותל למעלה מעשרה טפחים לבני עלייה משתמשין בו למטה מי' בני חצר משתמשין בו הא דביני ביני דהוה לבני עלייה בשלשול ולבני החצר בזריקה שניהן אסורין בו ופריק רב נחמן הכא בכותל [תשעה עשר] עסקינן וזיז היוצא ממנו למטה מי' (הנה) [הוא] לבני חצר בפתח ולבני עלייה בשלשול נותנין אותו לאלו שתשמישן בו ע"י פתח למעלה מעשרה טפחים הוה לבני עלייה בפתח ולבני חצר בזריקה כו' וליכא התם

תא שמע: *שתי גזוזטראות זו למעלה מזו, עשו לעליונה ולא עשו לתחתונה – שתיהן אסורות עד שיערבו! אמר רב אדא בר אהבה: בבאין בני תחתונה דרך עליונה למלאות. אביי אמר: כגון דקיימין בתוך עשרה דהדדי. ולא מיבעיא קאמר; לא מיבעיא עשו לתחתונה ולא עשו לעליונה – דאסירי, דכיון דבגו י' דהדדי קיימין אסרן אהדדי. אלא אפילו עשו לעליונה ולא עשו לתחתונה, סד"א כיון דלזה בנחת ולזה בקשה – ליתביה לזה שתשמישו בנחת, קמ"ל: כיון דבגו עשרה קיימין – אסרן אהדדי. כי הא דאמר רב נחמן, אמר שמואל: גג הסמוך לרה"ר – צריך סולם קבוע להתירו. סולם קבוע – אין, סולם עראי – לא. מ"ט – לאו משום דכיון דבתוך עשרה דהדדי קיימי אסרן אהדדי? מתקיף לה רב פפא: ודילמא כשרבים מכתפין עליו בכומתא וסודרא! אמר רב יהודה, אמר שמואל:

בור

שתי גזוזטראות. מתני' היא: גזוזטרא שהיא למעלה מן *הים. ב' זיזין בולטין מן העלייה שעל שפת הים, וקובעין נסרים מזה לזה, והיא גזוזטרא. ותנן: אין ממלאין ממנה בשבת, לפי שהגזוזטרא רה"י שגבוה ורחבה הרבה, והים כרמלית. אלא א"כ עשו לה מחיצה עשרה, בין מלמעלה בין מלמטה. שחוקקין נקב ארבעה כעין פי בור, ועושין מחיצה סביבותיו למעלה או למטה, ומשלשל דלי וממלא. וחשיב כאילו פיות המחיצה יורדין וסותמין עד תהום, כדאמר בפ"ק (דף יב.): קל הוא שהקילו חכמים במים שמחיצה תלויה מתרת בהן: וכן לא גרסינן: ב' גזוזטראות זו למעלה מזו. ואין מכוונות זו על זו, אלא משוכות זו מכנגד זו בתוך ד' ועשו לעליונה הנקב והמחיצה, ולא עשו לתחתונה. ובשבת זורקין בני תחתונה דלי שלהן על מחיצות העליונה, ויורד לנקב, ומשלשל ומושך ועולה: שתיהן אסורין. למלאות, מפני שרשות שתיהן שולטות בו. וכגון שעשו אותה מחיצה בשותפות, כדמוקמינן לה בפירקין לקמן.* הלכה: לזה בשלשול, לבני עליונה תשמיש מילוי זה בשלשול, שמשלשל לים. ולבני תחתונה בזריקה ושלשול, וקתני: שתיהן אסורות. וכ"ש לזה בשלשול ולזה בזריקה לאודה: בבאין בני תחתונה. ועולין בסולמות דרך עליונה למלאות, דלתרווייהו בשלשול: כגון דקיימי בגו עשרה דהדדי. שאין עליונה גבוהה מתחתונה עשרה, ואע"ג דאמרי לזה בקשה ולזה בנחת הוא, שיש מקלת זריקה עם השלשול, ואמר שמואל לעיל* דכל תשמיש שהוא נחת לזה מזה נותנין אותו לנחת – לא תיקשי, דטעמא דהכא לאו משום תשמיש, אלא משום דכיון דבגו עשרה דהדדי קיימין – אין רשות שלישית לזו בלא זו. ואפילו לזה בפתח ולזה בזריקה, *שאין חלוק רשות ביניהן. וכי אמרינן רשות שלישית הסמוכה לשתים לזה בנחת ולזה בקשה ניתנת לזה בנחת – ה"מ היכא דב' הרשויות חלוקות בגובה י' כגון חצר ועלייה, וכגון ב' חצירות המובדלות י' בגובה קרקעיתן, או מחיצה עשרה ביניהן, או חריץ עשרה: ולא מיבעיא קאמר. כלומר: וכי תימא הואיל ובתוך עשרה קיימין, וטעמא משום דאין לזו רשות בלא זו, ולא לאשמעינן לזה בשלשול ולזה בזריקה(א) נותנין אותו לזה שבשלשול – מה לי עשו לעליונה מה לי עשו לתחתונה: לא מיבעיא קאמר לא מיבעיא עשו לתחתונה ולא עשו לעליונה. דאיכא לאוקומי טעמא דאיסורא משום תשמיש השוה. דהא סמוכות הן במשך הכותל בתוך ד' טפחים, כדמוקמינן לקמן [דף פח.] וגובהה נמי בגו עשרה דהדדי: אלא אפילו כו'. דהוי לזה בשלשול, ולזה במקלת זריקה ושלשול: ליתביה לזה שתשמישו בנחת. כדשמואל, הואיל ומקלת קושי יש לזה מזה: קמ"ל דכיון כו' אסרן אהדדי. בלא שום טעם תשמיש: גג הסמוך לרה"ר. שאינו מוקף חצר לכל צדדיו אלא לצדו אחד רה"ר וסתם גג גבוה עשרה: צריך סולם קבוע. מן העלייה לגג, להתירו לטלטל מן המרפסת לגג. דאי עביד ליה סולם – גלי דעתיה דסלקיה לגג מכח רה"ר, ואיהו ניחא ליה לאשתמושי ביה: סולם עראי. כיון דמסליק ליה כמאן דליתיה הוא: מ"ט. הא גג זה אינו לתשמיש בני רה"ר כלל: לאו משום. דבהכי עסקינן דלא גביהה מרפסת עשרה מרה"ר וממנה עולין לגג, ופחות מעשרה הוא לה. הלכך: אע"ג דמרפסת כפתח. ולבני רה"ר אינו ראוי, כיון דמרפסת ורה"ר בגו עשרה דהדדי קיימי – אסרי אהדדי. דאי לאו הכי – טעמא מאי ניהו? וכגון דמרפסת מגופפת היא למעלה, ופתחה בי' אמות לרה"ר. דאי לאו מגופפת היא סביב, כיון דלא גביהה עשרה – כרמלית היא, וסולם לא מהני לה, דקא מטלטל מכרמלית לרה"י: בכומתא וסודרא. שרגילין לתת עליו בחול כובעין ומעפורת ותשמיש נוחה והגון הוא להם למשאוי קל כזה. ואע"פ שאינו ראוי להם לכיתוף משאוי כבד, כדאמר ב"יציאות השבת" (שבת דף ח.): תשעה חזו לכתוף, אבל י' לא ה"מ – למשאוי כבד. ומיהו, לכומתא וסודרא חזו. כשבני אדם עייפין בימות החמה נוטלין כובעיהן וסודרן מראשיהן עד שיפוח הרוח בהן הלכך, אסרי עלייהו ואפילו לא קיימא מרפסת בגו י' ולא דמו לרשות שבין ב' חצירות לזו בפתח ולזו בזריקה – דחצר לאו תשמישתיה בהני כובעים קלים, אלא בכלים כבדים וכי גבוה כותל י' – לא חזי לתשמישתיה דחצר(ב) ונותנין אותו לזה שבפתח. אבל לבני רה"ר – חזי. ואית דמוקי להא דר"נ בגג פחות מעשרה. וא"א, דא"כ ה"ל כרמלית. דכל רשות שרחבה ד' ואינה גבוהה עשרה אצל רה"ר – כרמלית היא, וכיון דהכי הוא – סולם מאי מהני? ואני שמעתי: בגו עשרה דהדדי – שאינו רחוק מרה"ר עשרה. וא"א לומר כן, שלא שיערו חכמים עשרה לשבת אלא בגובה, ולא שיערו ארבעה אלא במשך:

בור

לא מיבעיא קאמר. דבשלמא לרב נקט עשו לעליונה כו' – לאשמעינן: לזה בזריקה ולזה בשלשול שניהם אסורים. אלא השתא, דקיימי בגו עשרה – מה לי עשו לעליונה, מה לי עשו לתחתונה? כך פירש רש"י. ולרב אדא בר אהבה נמי, דאוקמא בבאין בני תחתונה דרך עליונה למלאות – קמ"ל טובא, אע"ג דאמר בסוף "כיצד מעברין" (לעיל דף נט:) דסולם תורת מחילה עליו, ולא אסר, הכא, לענין ליחשב תשמיש בנחת כלזה בשלשול ולזה בשלשול, אסרי: **גג** הסמוך לרה"ר. פירש בקונטרס שאינו מוקף חצר בכל צדדיו, אלא לידו אחד רה"ר, וסתם גג גבוה עשרה ויש שם מרפסת דלא גבוהה עשרה מרה"ר, וממנה עולין לגג ופחות מעשרה הוא לה. אלמא, אע"ג דלמרפסת כפתח, ולבני רה"ר אינו ראוי כיון דמרפסת ורה"ר בגו עשרה דהדדי קיימי – אסרי אהדדי. דאי לאו הכי טעמא מאי הוי? וכגון דמרפסת מגופפת היא למעלה, ופתוח בעשרה אמות לרה"ר. דאי לא מגופפת היא סביב כיון דלא גבוה עשרה – כרמלית היא, וסולם לא מהני בה, דקא מטלטל מכרמלית לרה"י. וקשה לר"י להעמיד כשיש מרפסת בין רה"ר לגג, דאינו מזכיר הכא מרפסת כלל. ועוד: אי מרפסת מגופפת(ג) – היאך בני רה"ר אוסרין עליה ועל הגג? ואי דליכא גיפופי – הויא לה כרמלית, והגג נפרץ לה בעשרה. ואי בלא מרפסת איירי, וקאי גגה בתוך עשרה, אם כן הוי כרמלית! ואור"י: דמיירי שפיר בלא מרפסת ובני רה"ר משתמשים בו לפי שאינו גבוה עשרה ואינו נפרץ במלואו, וכגון שצידי הגג גבוה עשרה או כל הגג למטה מעשרה ויש לו מעקה ופתוח לרה"ר בעשרה או בפחות. וקאמרינן דצריך סולם קבוע להתירו, אבל בלא סולם – אין בני חצר רגילים בו ומבטלין ממנו בני רה"ר שהרגילו להשתמש(ד) תורת דיורין, ומשוי להו (חד) קרפף ואסור לטלטל ממנו לחצר לרבנן. ולר"ש נמי, כלים ששבתו בבית אסור להוליך מחצר לגג, כיון דנעשה קרפף, ולא דמי לחצר או מבוי שפתוחים לרה"ר בעשרה, דאין בני רה"ר אוסרים עליו דהתם – איכא דיורין גמורין, ואין כח לבני רה"ר לבטלם. וקא אמרינן: דילמא בכומתא וסודרא דרגילין להניח שם בני רה"ר כשהם עייפין, אע"פ שגבוה עשרה – שמשוי קל הוא, כדפירש בקונטרס, ותשמיש נחת(ה). ולא דמי לרשות שבין שתי חצירות לזה בפתח ולזה בזריקה – דחצר אין משתמשין בו בכובעים אלא בכלים כבדים. ור"ת מפרש בענין אחר: גג הסמוך לרה"ר ונמוך בתוך עשרה – צריך סולם קבוע להתירו, דכיון דתוכו רה"י היא, ולא דמי לשאר כרמלית. וסולם קבוע שבחצר ממעט כח כרמלית שבחצר, דלא הוי כרמלית מעליא. ודייק: סולם קבוע – אין, סולם עראי – לא. אף על גב דע"י סולם עראי הוי תשמיש נחת טפי לחצר (ו)מבני רה"ר, דלית להו לבני רה"ר אפילו סולם עראי. ואפ"ה, כיון דבתוך עשרה קיימי – אסרי. ודחי רב פפא: דלבני רה"ר נמי איכא תשמיש נחת – בכומתא וסודרא, דראשו של אדם סמוך לגג והוי תשמישו בנחת בלא סולם כלל, כלבני חצר בסולם. ולהכי צריך סולם קבוע להתיר כרמלית גרוע כזה, דהוי תוכו רשות היחיד:

בור

התם דביני ביני. ת"ש וכן ב' גזוזטראות זו למעלה מזו עשו מחיצה לעליונה ולא עשו לתחתונה שתים אסורות עד שיערבו. ופריק רב אדא בר אהבה בבאין בני תחתונה דרך עליונה למלאות אביי אמר כגון דקיימא תרווייהו סמוכות זו לזו בתוך י' טפחים ולא מיבעיא קאמר כו'. ואסיקנא כל בחדא רשותא לא אמרינן לזה בנחת ולזה בקשה פי' חדא רשותא (או) [אי] קיימין תרווייהו בתוך י' טפחים ומנא תימרא כי הא דאמר רב יהודה אמר שמואל גג הסמוך לרה"ר צריך סולם קבוע להתירו ודייקינן סולם קבוע אין סולם עראי לא אמאי לזה שבסולם עראי תשמישו בנחת היא אמאי לא יהבינן ליה לאו משום דאמרי' כל חדא רשותא לא אמרינן כל שתשמישו בנחת ליה יהבינן (ליה). ודחי רב פפא לאו משום דחדא רשותא אינון אלא משום דמשתמש ביה בכונתא וסודרא. פי' לובש כותנא וסודרא ומעייל להו להאי גג מרה"ר שנמצא משתמש בו ע"י כיתוף. אמר רב יהודה

[במשנה איתא המים]

[לקמן פז:]

[דף פח.]

[דף פג:]

[כיון]

הגהות הב"ח

(א) רש"י ד"ה ולא מבעיי וכו' ולזה בזריקה אי נותנין: (ב) ד"ה בכומתא וכו' לא חזי לתשמישתי דחצר אבל לבני רה"ר חז דאין להם רשו' אחר להשתמש להניח כובעיה ונותנין אותן לזה שבפתח ואית דמוקי להא: (ג) תוס' ד"ה גג וכו' מגופפת היי היאך: (ד) בא"ד להשתמש בו תורת דיורין: (ה) בא"ד ותשמיש נחת הוא ולא: (ו) בא"ד טפי לחצר מלבני רה"ר:

בּוֹר שֶׁבֵּין שְׁתֵּי חֲצֵירוֹת, מוּפְלֶגֶת מִכּוֹתֶל זֶה אַרְבָּעָה וּמִכּוֹתֶל זֶה אַרְבָּעָה — זֶה מוֹצִיא זִיז כָּל שֶׁהוּא וּמְמַלֵּא, וְזֶה מוֹצִיא זִיז כָּל שֶׁהוּא וּמְמַלֵּא. וְרַב יְהוּדָה דִּידֵיהּ אָמַר: אֲפִילּוּ קַנְיָא. אֲמַר לֵיהּ אַבַּיֵּי לְרַב יוֹסֵף: הָא דְּרַב יְהוּדָה — דִּשְׁמוּאֵל הִיא. דְּאִי דְּרַב *הָא אָמַר: אֵין אָדָם אוֹסֵר עַל חֲבֵירוֹ דֶּרֶךְ אֲוִיר. וְדִשְׁמוּאֵל מֵהֵיכָא? אִילֵימָא מֵהָא דְּאָמַר רַב נַחְמָן, אָמַר שְׁמוּאֵל: גַּג הַסָּמוּךְ לִרְשׁוּת הָרַבִּים — צָרִיךְ סוּלָּם קָבוּעַ לְהַתִּירוֹ. דִּילְמָא כִּדְרַב פָּפָּא! אֶלָּא מֵהָא: זֶה מוֹצִיא זִיז כָּל שֶׁהוּא וּמְמַלֵּא, וְזֶה מוֹצִיא זִיז כָּל שֶׁהוּא וּמְמַלֵּא. טַעְמָא — דְּאַפֵּיק, הָא לָא אַפֵּיק — אָמְרִינַן: אָדָם אוֹסֵר עַל חֲבֵירוֹ דֶּרֶךְ אֲוִיר. וּדְרַב מֵהֵיכָא? אִילֵימָא מֵהָא — שְׁתֵּי גְּזוּזְטְרָאוֹת זוֹ לְמַעְלָה מִזּוֹ, עָשׂוּ מְחִיצָה לָעֶלְיוֹנָה וְלֹא עָשׂוּ מְחִיצָה לַתַּחְתּוֹנָה — שְׁתֵּיהֶן אֲסוּרוֹת עַד שֶׁיְּעָרְבוּ. וְאָמַר רַב הוּנָא, אָמַר רַב: לֹא שָׁנוּ אֶלָּא בִּסְמוּכָה, אֲבָל בְּמוּפְלֶגֶת אַרְבָּעָה — עֶלְיוֹנָה מוּתֶּרֶת וְתַחְתּוֹנָה אֲסוּרָה. דִּלְמָא שָׁאנֵי הָכָא, דְּכֵיוָן דְּלָזֶה בִּזְרִיקָה וְשִׁלְשׁוּל, וְלָזֶה בְּשִׁלְשׁוּל לְחוּדֵיהּ — כְּלָזֶה בִּזְרִיקָה וְלָזֶה בְּפֶתַח דָּמֵי. אֶלָּא מֵהָא, דְּאָמַר רַב נַחְמָן, אָמַר רַבָּה בַּר אֲבוּהּ, אָמַר רַב: שְׁנֵי בָתִּים וְשָׁלֹשׁ חוּרָבוֹת בֵּינֵיהֶם — זֶה מִשְׁתַּמֵּשׁ בְּסָמוּךְ שֶׁלּוֹ עַל יְדֵי זְרִיקָה, וְזֶה מִשְׁתַּמֵּשׁ בְּסָמוּךְ שֶׁלּוֹ עַל יְדֵי זְרִיקָה, וְהָאֶמְצָעִי

רש"י

בור שבין שתי חצירות. הפרודות זו מזו, ומפסיק ביניהן כעין מבוי קטן, ואין דיורין פתוחין לו. והבור באותו הפסק. מופלגת מכותל זה ארבעה כו' דאי לאו הכי[א] דמופלג, הוי תשמישו בנחת, והוי כמו שהבור חציה בחצר זו וחציה בחצר זו שרשות שניהן שולטת בה. ותנן במתני':* [לקמן דף פו.] בור שבין שתי חצירות — אין ממלאין הימנה בשבת, שזה אוסר על זה עד שיערבו או עד שיעשו מחיצה תלויה בבור. כך השיב ר"י: זה מוציא זיז כל שהוא. מכתלו עד לבור, וממלא דרך חלונו. וכן זה. דכיון דמופלגת ד' — לא שלטי ביה לאסור זה על זה. ומשום שיהא רשות לשניהן במבוי נמי ליכא — [לקמן פח.] שאין דיוריהן פתוחין לחצר לצאת ולבא ברגל, ואין תשמישתן בכך אלא דרך אויר. ובדין הוא דזיז נמי לא ליבעי, אלא משום היכר בעלמא שלא ישתמשו ברשות אחרת של שניים בלא עירוב — משום הכי מתקני הכא פורתא. ודכוותה אתמר במסכת שבת בפרק "הזורק" (דף ק:), ספינה, רב הונא אמר: מוציא הימנה זיז כל שהוא וממלא, ומוקמינן לה התם דאינו אלא היכר בעלמא דלא לייתי לטלטולי מכרמלית אחרת לרה"י. ויש לגבי מילוי ס"ל דלאו כרמלית היא אלא קרקעיתא, אבל אוירא דמיא — מקום פטור הוא, דמיא כמאן דליתנהו דמו: אפילו קניא. דלא מינכר כולי האי — שרי: והא דרב יהודה. דבעי תיקון כל שהוא: דשמואל היא. משמואל רביה גמר לה דצריך תיקון קצת: דאי דרב. דהוה נמי רביה — מיניה לא גמר לה, דהא אין אדם אוסר על חבירו בתשמיש מופלג כזה שצריך לזרוק דלי באויר ד' טפחים, ואפילו קניא לא צריך: ודשמואל מהיכא. מאיזו מימרא דשמואל סלקא דעתיה דאביי למשמע דרב יהודה משמואל גמר לה. סלקא דעתך השתא דכי שמעה אביי להא דרב יהודה — מילתא באנפי נפשיה שמעה: אמר רב יהודה בור שבין שתי חצירות מופלגת ארבעה מכאן ומכאן — זה מוציא קנה כל שהוא וממלא וכו' ולא שמעה בהדיא הא דשמואל דאי עלה דהא דשמואל דזיז כל שהוא שמעה אביי להא דרבי יהודה — מאי תיבעי לן דשמואל מהיכא — הא הכא אשמעינן שמואל בהדיא דבעי תיקון: צריך סולם קבוע. ואי לא — בני רה"ר אסרי עליה דרך אויר שאין גג זה ראוי לתשמישן אא"כ זורקין עליו שום דבר, דסתם רה"ר איכא חפופי סמוך לכתלים, ומתרחקים על כרחן: דילמא כדרב פפא. שתשמיש גמור הוא להן בכומתא וסודרא: אלא מהא כו'. דאביי שמעה לדרב יהודה אמילתיה דשמואל. והכי קאמר אביי: הא דבעי רבי יהודה קניא — משמואל גמר לה דבעי תיקון. ואתא לאשמעינן דשמואל רביה לאו זיז דוקא אמר, דכיון דלא בעי זיז ד' דהא זיז כל שהוא אמר — יליף רב יהודה מיניה דה"ה לקניא: ודרב מהיכא. שמעינן דאין אדם אוסר על חברו דרך אויר: אלא בסמוכה. שאין עליונה משוכה מכנגד התחתונה במשך הכותל ד' טפחים, ואע"ג דגבוהה ממנה עשרה. רב לטעמיה, דאמר: לזה בשלשול ולזה בזריקה — שניהן אסורין, דתשמיש דשלשול וזריקה חשיב תשמיש. אבל במופלגת מכנגדה ד' כיון דאין לתחתונה כאן אלא תשמיש מופלג במשך — זהו אויר, ולאו תשמיש הוא. לא מצינו לשון הפלגה בתלמוד בגבהה אלא[ב] במשכה, כדתנן במתניתין: בד"א בסמוכה כו': שאני הכא. דכיון דלזה בזריקת אויר וזריקת גובה ושלשול, ולזה בשלשול לחודיה שמשלשל דלי ליים: כלזה בפתח ולזה בזריקה דמי. אבל גבי בור, דשניהן שוין בהפלגה — לעולם אימא לך דאסרי: וג' חורבות ביניהן. מחיצות פרוצות זו לזו ואין בהן דיורין ואין להן בעלים, אלא בני הבתים האלו, ויש חלונות בבתים פתוחין לחורבה: זה משתמש. בחורבה הסמוכה לו דרך חלונות ע"י זריקה, הואיל ואין לו בה תשמיש גמור בחול, שאין לו בה פתח פתוח לה אלא חלון — אין פירצת המחיצה אוסרת, ומותר להשתמש בכולה. והוא אינו יכול להשתמש דרך חלון למרחוק אלא ע"י זריקה. וחבירו אינו אוסר עליו, ואע"פ שמשתמש בה בחול בזריקה, שזורק דרך אויר שלו בפירצה עד תוך חורבה זו — אינו אוסר על חבירו דרך אויר, שאין לו עליו תשמיש אלא ע"י אויר. אבל בסמוכה לחברו — לא ישתמש אפילו בזריקה, הואיל ויש לחברו בה תשמיש נוח בשלשול סמוך לחלונו: והאמצעי

תוספות

בור שבין שתי חצירות מופלגת מכותל זה ד' כו'. פירש בקונטרס: שיש בין שתי חצירות כעין מבוי קטן ואין דיורין פתוחין לו, והבור באותו הפסק. זה מוציא זיז כל שהוא עד לבור וממלא דרך חלונו, וכן זה. דכיון דמופלגת ד' — לא שלטי ביה לאסור זה על זה, ומשום שיהא רשות לשניהם במבוי נמי ליכא, שאין דיורין פתוחין לו לצאת ולבא ברגל, ואין משתמשין בו אלא דרך אויר. ובדין הוא דאפילו זיז נמי לא ניבעי, אלא משום היכר בעלמא שלא ישתמשו ברשות אחרת של שניים בלא עירוב, מש"ה מתקני הכא פורתא. ולרב לא צריך שום תיקון, דאין אדם אוסר על חבירו דרך אויר. ורש"י הקשה בעצמו בסמוך, דגבי שני בתים ושלש חורבות ביניהם דאמצעי אסור, ומוקי להו דקיימי כי שנובא, דכי היכי דאמצעי בכולו אסור לשניהם משום שכל אחד משתמש בד' הסמוכים לו בלא אויר — הכי נמי יאסרו זה על זה מבוי קטן. דכיון דכל אחד יכול להשתמש בארבעה הסמוכים לו. וכיון שהמבוי אסור — היאך יכול לשלשל ולמלאות מן הבור לחצר דרך אויר המבוי האסור? ותירץ: דלא דמי, דאילו חורבה משתמשין בה נמי בסמוך, אבל הכא במבוי — ליכא שום תשמיש אלא מילוי, והוא ע"י הפלגת אויר ד'. ור"י מפרש: כגון שזה הבור מושך כל אורך החצירות, ומפסיק בין ד' הסמוכים לחצר זו לארבעה הסמוכים לחצר אחרת, דחשיב כל חד רשותא לנפשיה. אי נמי אור"י: כגון שאותו הפסק שבין שתי החצירות שהבור עומד שם אינו רה"י אלא רה"ר, או כרמלית, ומחיצות הבור גבוהים עשרה. דכשממלאים מן הבור לחצר מביאין דרך מלמעלה מי', דהוי מקום פטור, כדאמרינן בשמעתין בשני בתים משני לידי רשות הרבים, דמותר לזרוק מזה לזה:

דילמא כדרב פפא. בכומתא וסודרא מעיקרא סלקא דעתיה דאיירי במשאות כבדים, דאותן אין רגילין להתקרב לכתלים, דמשתמשין בגג ע"י זריקה כגון אותם שמפשילין משאות במקלות על כתפיהם, וכשרוצים לכתף מכתפים על הגג, ויש הפסק ד' מן האויר ולגג. ומשני: בכומתא וסודרא, שהוא דבר קל, ורגילין להתקרב לכותל, ולא הוי דרך אויר:

שני בתים ושלש חורבות ביניהם. פירש בקונטרס: שאין לחורבות בעלים אלא בני הבתים האלה. משמע דסבר: דאם יש להם בעלים — דאוסרין אותן הבעלים על בני הבתים, אע"ג דאינם אוסרין את החצר ואת המבוי שפתוחין להם, דקי"ל כרבי יהודה דבית התבן אינו אוסר. ובפירקין* נמי פסקינן כר"ש, דאמר: דירה בלא בעלים — לא שמה דירה. מכל מקום, בתוכה מיהא אסור לטלטל. ובסוף "הדר" (לעיל דף עד.) פירש כן בהדיא, גבי דילמא אתי לאפוקי מאני דבתים לחורבה. פירש: והרי רשות אחרת היא, שיש לה בעלים, ובמבוי לא נשתתפה שאינה אוסרת, כדתניא לעיל* אינה אוסרת אלא מקום דירה בלבד — דהיינו מקום פיתא או מקום לינה. והא דשרינן הכא להשתמש בסמוך לו אע"ג שיש לחבירו כמו כן חלק בה — אינו אוסר על זה, כיון שגם לזה יש חלק בה, דשניהם שותפים בשלשתן ואינם אוסרין זה על זה את הסמוכים, כיון דהוי לזה תשמישו בנחת ולחבירו בקשה. ובשתי גזוזטראות דסוף פרקין עשו לתחתונה — סילקו נפשייהו מעליונה, ואין אוסרין את העליונה אף על פי שעשו אותה בשותפות, ויש להם חלק בה. ואין נראה לר"י לעשות דירה בלא בעלים דירה לחלאין, לאסור לטלטל בתוכו. ואור"י: דהא דאמרינן בסוף "הדר" דילמא אתי לאפוקי מאני דבתים לחורבה — איירי בחורבה הפתוחה לבית, ואיירי שאותו בית פתוח לצד אחר, ואינו רגיל במבוי[ג]. ולכך אין המבוי ניתר בלחי וקורה משום בית אלא משום חורבה, ואיירי שפיר הכא בחורבות שיש להם בעלים, וכיון דלא דיירי בהו — לא אסרי:

לימא

עין משפט נר מצוה

טז א מיי' פ"ג מהל' עירובין הלכה כג טוש"ע א"ח סי' שעו סעיף ב:

יז ב מיי' שם הלכה יז וטוש"ע שם סעיף ג:

רבינו חננאל

אמר שמואל בור שבין ב' חצירות מופלג מכותל זה בארבעה ומכותל זה בארבעה והבור באמצע הסימטא. זה מוציא זיז כל שהוא וממלא וזה מוצא זיז כל שהוא וממלא. ורב יהודה דידיה אמר אפי' קניא דיי לו. אמר אביי הא דרב יהודה דשמואל היא דאי דרב הא אמר רב אין אדם אוסר על חבירו דרך אויר ואפי' קניא לא צריך ודייק מהא דאמר שמואל זה מוציא זיז כל שהוא וממלא טעמא דאפיק זיז הא לא אפיק זיז אסור למלאות מ"ט חבירו שיש לו רשות באויר הא סמטא אוסר עליו ש"מ אדם אוסר על חבירו דרך אויר. ודייקינן לרב מהא דאמר ב' חצרות וג' חורבות ביניהן זה משתמש לו בסמוך לו ע"י זריקה וזה משתמש בסמוך לו ע"י זריקה. ואמצעי שניהן אסורין כו'. ש"מ כיון שכל אחד מהן משתמש בסמוך לו אין אדם אוסר על חבירו דרך אויר. א"ל ר' אלעזר לרב והא מר הוא דאמר כלומר אתה אמרת כל לזה בשלשול ולזה בזריקה שניהן אסורין בו והני חורבות כי לזה בזריקה ולזה בשלשול נינהו. א"ל מי סברת דעבדין כשורה פי' כשורה בסדר אחת [לא] בחצובה דעבדין כמין כף יווני והאמצעית היא בין ב' החצרות ושתים החיצונות נמשכות ויוצאות מחוץ לחצרות ואין משתמשות החצרו' הללו בתוך ב' החורבות הללו אלא ע"י זריקה מיהו זריקה מן החצר על החורבה תבא מלמעלה למטה וזריקה מן החורבה לחצר היא ממטה ולמעלה לפיכך זריקה של חצר היא בנחת וקרובה היא לשלשול לפיכך נותנין לזה [שבנחת] וזריקה של חורבה בקשה היא *).

*) [נראה דצ"ל וקרובה היא לשלשול וזריקה של חורבה בקשה היא לפיכך נותנין לזה שבנחת].

הגהות הב"ח

(א) רש"י ד"ה בור וכו' דמופלג ארבע' הוי: (ב) ד"ה אלא בסמוכה וכו' אלא בהמשכה כדתנן: (ג) תום' ד"ה שני וכו' ואינו רגיל במבוי זה ולכך:

גליון הש"ס

גמ' א"ל אביי לר"י הא דר"י דשמואל היא. לעיל דף ז ע"א יבמות דף יח ע"א כתובות דף יב ע"ב:

עין משפט נר מצוה

יח א ב מיי' פט"ו מהלכות שבת הלכה ח סמג לאוין סה טור ש"ע א"ח סי' שנג סעיף א:

יט ג מיי' פ"א מהלכות עירובין הלכה טז סמג לאוין א טוש"ע א"ח סי' שסו סעיף ג:

כ ד מיי' פ"ד שם הלכה ח סמג שם טוש"ע שם סי' שע סעיף א:

כא ה מיי' פ"א שם הלכה יו יז סמג שם טוש"ע שם סי' שפו סעיף א:

כב ו מיי' שם הלכה יט טוש"ע שם סי' שסו סעיף יא:

וְהָאֶמְצָעִי – אָסוּר. יָתֵיב רַב בְּרוּנָא וְקָאָמַר לְהָא שְׁמַעְתָּא. א"ל רַבִּי *אֱלִיעֶזֶר בַּר בֵּי רַב: אֲמַר רַב הָכִי? א"ל: אִין. *אַחְוֵי לִי אוּשְׁפִּיזֵיהּ. אַחְוֵי לֵיהּ. אֲתָא לְקַמֵּיהּ דְּרַב, א"ל: אֲמַר מָר הָכִי? א"ל: אִין. א"ל: וְהָא מָר הוּא דַּאֲמַר: לָזֶה בְּשִׁלְשׁוּל וְלָזֶה בִּזְרִיקָה – שְׁנֵיהֶן אֲסוּרִין! א"ל: מִי סָבְרַתְּ דְּקָיְימִי כַּשּׁוּרָה? לָא! דְּקָיְימִי כַּחֲצוּבָה.

חלון	בית
חורבה	חורבה
חורבה	חורבה
חלון	בית

א"ל רַב פַּפָּא לְרָבָא: לֵימָא שְׁמוּאֵל לֵית לֵיהּ דְּרַב דִּימִי. *דְּכִי אֲתָא רַב דִּימִי, א"ר יוֹחָנָן: מָקוֹם שֶׁאֵין בּוֹ ד' עַל ד' – מוּתָּר לִבְנֵי רה"ר וְלִבְנֵי רה"י לְכַתֵּף עָלָיו, וּבִלְבַד שֶׁלֹּא יַחֲלִיפוּ. הָתָם רְשׁוּיוֹת דְּאוֹרַיְיתָא, הָכָא רְשׁוּיוֹת דְּרַבָּנַן, *וַחֲכָמִים עָשׂוּ חִיזּוּק לְדִבְרֵיהֶם יוֹתֵר מִשֶּׁל תּוֹרָה. אֲמַר לֵיהּ רָבִינָא לְרָבָא: מִי אָמַר רַב הָכִי? וְהָא אִיתְּמַר, *שְׁנֵי בָתִּים מִשְּׁנֵי צִידֵּי רְשׁוּת הָרַבִּים, רַבָּה בַּר רַב הוּנָא אָמַר רַב: [א]אָסוּר לִזְרוֹק מִזֶּה לָזֶה. וּשְׁמוּאֵל אָמַר: מוּתָּר לִזְרוֹק מִזֶּה לָזֶה! א"ל: לָאו מִי אוֹקִימְנָא – [ב]דְּמִדְּלֵי חַד וּמִתַּתֵּי חַד, זִימְנִין דְּמִגַּנְדַּר וְנָפֵיל וְאָתֵי לְאִיתוּיֵי.§ **מתני'** *[ג]הַנּוֹתֵן אֶת עֵירוּבוֹ בְּבֵית שַׁעַר, אַכְסַדְרָה, וּמִרְפֶּסֶת – אֵינוֹ עֵירוּב. [ד]וְהַדָּר שָׁם – אֵינוֹ אוֹסֵר עָלָיו. בֵּית הַתֶּבֶן, וּבֵית הַבָּקָר, וּבֵית הָעֵצִים, וּבֵית הָאוֹצָרוֹת – הֲרֵי זֶה עֵירוּב, וְהַדָּר שָׁם אוֹסֵר,* רַבִּי יְהוּדָה אוֹמֵר: אִם יֵשׁ שָׁם תְּפִיסַת יָד שֶׁל בַּעַל הַבַּיִת – אֵינוֹ אוֹסֵר*.§ **גמ'** אָמַר רַב יְהוּדָה, בְּרֵיהּ דְּרַב שְׁמוּאֵל בַּר שֵׁילַת: *כָּל מָקוֹם שֶׁאָמְרוּ(א) הַדָּר שָׁם אֵינוֹ אוֹסֵר – הַנּוֹתֵן אֶת עֵירוּבוֹ אֵינוֹ עֵירוּב, חוּץ מִבֵּית שַׁעַר דְּיָחִיד. וְכָל מָקוֹם שֶׁאָמְרוּ חֲכָמִים אֵין מַנִּיחִין בּוֹ עֵירוּב – [ה]מַנִּיחִין בּוֹ שִׁיתּוּף, חוּץ מֵאֲוִיר מָבוֹי. מַאי קמ"ל? תְּנֵינָא: הַנּוֹתֵן אֶת עֵירוּבוֹ בְּבֵית שַׁעַר, אַכְסַדְרָה, וּמִרְפֶּסֶת – אֵינוֹ עֵירוּב. עֵירוּב – הוּא דְּלָא הָוֵי, הָא שִׁיתּוּף – הָוֵי! בֵּית שַׁעַר דְּיָחִיד וַאֲוִיר דְּמָבוֹי אִיצְטְרִיכָא לֵיהּ, דְּלָא תְּנַן. תַּנְיָא נַמִי הָכִי: הַנּוֹתֵן אֶת עֵירוּבוֹ בְּבֵית שַׁעַר אַכְסַדְרָה וּמִרְפֶּסֶת, וּבְחָצֵר וּבְמָבוֹי – ה"ז עֵירוּב. וְהָתְנַן: אֵין זֶה עֵירוּב! אֵימָא: ה"ז שִׁיתּוּף. שִׁיתּוּף בְּמָבוֹי לָא מִינְטַר? אֵימָא בְּחָצֵר שֶׁבַּמָּבוֹי. *אָמַר רַב יְהוּדָה, אָמַר שְׁמוּאֵל: [ו]בְּנֵי חֲבוּרָה שֶׁהָיוּ מְסוּבִּין וְקָדַשׁ עֲלֵיהֶן הַיּוֹם, פַּת שֶׁעַל הַשֻּׁלְחָן סוֹמְכִין עֲלֵיהֶן מִשּׁוּם עֵירוּב. וְאָמְרִי לָהּ: מִשּׁוּם שִׁיתּוּף. אָמַר רַבָּה: וְלָא פְּלִיגִי; כָּאן – בִּמְסוּבִּין בַּבַּיִת, כָּאן – בִּמְסוּבִּין בֶּחָצֵר. אֲמַר לֵיהּ אַבָּיֵי לְרַבָּה, תַּנְיָא דִּמְסַיַּיע לָךְ: *עֵירוּבֵי חֲצֵירוֹת בֶּחָצֵר, וְשִׁיתּוּפֵי מְבוֹאוֹת בַּמָּבוֹי. וְהָוֵינַן בָּהּ: עֵירוּבֵי חֲצֵירוֹת בֶּחָצֵר? וְהָתְנַן: הַנּוֹתֵן אֶת עֵירוּבוֹ בְּבֵית שַׁעַר, אַכְסַדְרָה, וּמִרְפֶּסֶת אֵינוֹ עֵירוּב! אֵימָא: עֵירוּבֵי חֲצֵירוֹת – בַּבַּיִת שֶׁבֶּחָצֵר, שִׁיתּוּפֵי מְבוֹאוֹת – בֶּחָצֵר שֶׁבַּמָּבוֹי.§ "רַבִּי יְהוּדָה אוֹמֵר אִם יֵשׁ שָׁם תְּפִיסַת יָד וכו'.§ הֵיכִי דָּמֵי תְּפִיסַת יָד? כְּגוֹן חֲצֵירוֹ שֶׁל(ג) *בּוֹנְיָים. בֶּן בּוֹנְיָים *)אֲתָא לְקַמֵּיהּ דְּרַבִּי, אֲמַר לְהוּ: פַּנּוּ מָקוֹם לְבֶן מֵאָה מָנֶה. אֲתָא אִינִישׁ אַחֲרִינָא, אֲמַר לְהוּ:

פנו

[בגליון: *) פ"א ת']

רש"י

וְאֶמְצָעִי אָסוּר. לְקַמֵּיהּ מְפָרֵשׁ טַעְמָא: דַּעֲבִידָא כַּחֲצוּבָה, וּשְׁנֵיהֶם הַבָּתִּים סְמוּכִים. וְאַע"ג דְּאִיכָּא לְאַקְשׁוּיֵי דְּבוּר דִּלְעֵיל דָּמֵי לְאֶמְצָעִי, שֶׁהֲרֵי שְׁנֵי הַבָּתִּים סְמוּכִין לַאֲוִיר הַמָּבוֹי. וְאִי מִשּׁוּם שֶׁיֵּשׁ הֶפְסֵק אַרְבָּעָה בֵּינוֹ לְכָל א' – הָכָא נַמִי אִיכָּא הֶפְסֵק כָּל חֲלַל חוּרְבָּה הָאֶמְצָעִית, וְכוּלָּהּ אֲסוּרָה לָזֶה וְלָזֶה אֲפִילּוּ רְחָבָה כַּמָּה אַמּוֹת. וְגַבֵּי חֲלַל הַמָּבוֹי נַמִי לִיסְרוּ אַהֲדָדֵי! לָא תִּיקְשֵׁי, דְּאִלּוּ חוּרְבָּה – מִשְׁתַּמְּשִׁין בָּהּ תַּשְׁמִישׁוֹת הַרְבֵּה, בֵּין בְּסָמוּךְ בֵּין בְּרָחוֹק. אֲבָל הָכָא – לֵיכָּא תַּשְׁמִישׁ אֶלָּא מִילּוּי, וְהַהוּא ע"י הַפְלָגַת אֲוִיר אַרְבָּעָה הוּא: אֲמַר רַב הָכִי. בִּתְמִיָּה. דְּר"א סָבַר: מִדְּאָמַר רַב אֶמְצָעִי אָסוּר וְאַע"פ שֶׁיֵּשׁ הֶפְסֵק אֲוִיר חוּרְבָּה בֵּינוֹ וְלַבָּתִּים – ש"מ: אָדָם אוֹסֵר עַל חֲבֵרוֹ דֶּרֶךְ אֲוִיר סְבִירָא לֵיהּ. וְטַעְמָא דִּסְמוּכִין מוּתָּרִין – מִשּׁוּם דְּתַשְׁמִישָׁן קָשֶׁה לַחִיצוֹנִים: וְהָא מָר הוּא דַּאֲמַר כו'. אַלְמָא: אַף עַל גַּב דְּשִׁלְשׁוּל נוֹחַ מִזְּרִיקָה, הוֹאִיל דְּאֵינוֹ מַמָּשׁ לְאֶחָד מֵהֶן כְּפֶתַח – לָא שָׁרִינַן לֵיהּ לְחַד מִינַּיְיהוּ. וְהָכָא נַמִי, מֵאַחַר דְּאֵינוֹ כְּפֶתַח לֹא לָזֶה וְלֹא לָזֶה, אַע"ג דְּנַחַת לָזֶה מִזֶּה – לִיתַּסְרוּ: מִי סָבְרַתְּ דַּעֲבִידִי כִּי שׁוּרָה. זוֹ אֵצֶל זוֹ, שֶׁתְּהֵא הַחִיצוֹנָה מַפְסֶקֶת בֵּין הַבַּיִת וְלָאֶמְצָעִי, דְּתֵיסַק אַדַּעְתָּךְ אָדָם אוֹסֵר דֶּרֶךְ אֲוִיר סְבִירָא לִי, דְּתִיקְשֵׁי לָךְ: סְמוּכִין נַמִי לִיתַּסְרוּ: לֹא דַּעֲבִידֵי כַּחֲצוּבָ'. וּשְׁלָשְׁתָּן סְמוּכִין לַבָּתִּים. הָאֶמְצָעִי כְּנֶגֶד הַשְּׁתַּיִם כִּשְׁלֹשָׁה רַגְלֵי הַקַּנְקַן, הִלְכָּךְ: הַסְּמוּכִין מוּתָּרִין – דְּאֵין אָדָם אוֹסֵר עַל חֲבֵרוֹ דֶּרֶךְ אֲוִיר, וְהָאֶמְצָעִי אָסוּר – דִּשְׁנֵיהֶן מִשְׁתַּמְּשִׁין בָּהּ בְּשִׁלְשׁוּל, וּרְשׁוּת שְׁנֵיהֶם הִיא. וְאַף עַל גַּב דִּשְׁתַּיִם הַסְּמוּכוֹת פְּרוּצוֹת לָאֶמְצָעִי הָאוֹסֵר – לָא אַחְמוּר רַבָּנַן בְּמָקוֹם שֶׁאֵין לוֹ תַּשְׁמִישׁ גָּמוּר שֶׁיְּהֵא אָסוּר מִשּׁוּם פָּרוּץ: לֵימָא שְׁמוּאֵל. דְּאָמַר אָדָם אוֹסֵר עַל חֲבֵרוֹ דֶּרֶךְ אֲוִיר: לֵית לֵיהּ דְּרַב דִּימִי. דְּהָא מָקוֹם שֶׁאֵין בּוֹ אַרְבָּעָה, כֵּיוָן דְּלֵית בֵּיהּ שִׁיעוּר מָקוֹם – הֲנָחָה דִּידֵיהּ לָאו הֲנָחָה הִיא, וַהֲרֵי הוּא כַּאֲוִיר בְּעָלְמָא. וְקָאָמַר מוּתָּר, בְּלֹא שׁוּם תִּיקּוּן. וּשְׁמוּאֵל הוֹצָאַת זִיז בָּעֵי: רְשׁוּיוֹת דְּרַבָּנַן. שְׁנֵיהֶן רה"י, וְאֵין אוֹסְרִין מִזֶּה לָזֶה אֶלָּא מִדְּרַבָּנַן: מִי אָמַר רַב הָכִי. זֶה מִשְׁתַּמֵּשׁ בְּסָמוּךְ לוֹ עַל יְדֵי זְרִיקָה, וְאֵין חֲבֵירוֹ אוֹסֵר עָלָיו דֶּרֶךְ אֲוִיר: שְׁנֵי בָתִּים. שֶׁל אָדָם אֶחָד אָסוּר לִזְרוֹק וְאַע"ג דְּכִי סָגֵי – בַּאֲוִיר רה"ר לְמַעְלָה מֵעֲשָׂרָה קָא סָגֵי, וְקָאָמַר דְּאוֹסֵר עָלָיו אֲוִירָן שֶׁל בְּנֵי רה"ר, אַע"פ שֶׁאֵין לָהֶם כָּאן תַּשְׁמִישׁ: דְּמִידְלֵי חַד וּמִיתַּתֵּי חַד. א' גָּבוֹהַּ וְא' נָמוּךְ, שֶׁמָּא יִזְרוֹק מִן הַנָּמוּךְ לַגָּבוֹהַּ וְלֹא יַגִּיעַ, וְיִפּוֹל לרה"ר. וְלִשְׁמוּאֵל דְּאָמַר מוּתָּר – לָא קַשְׁיָא דִּידֵיהּ אַדִּידֵיהּ, דְּאָמַר: אָדָם אוֹסֵר עַל חֲבֵירוֹ דֶּרֶךְ אֲוִיר דְּהָא אָמְרִינַן: בִּרְשׁוּיוֹת דְּאוֹרַיְיתָא שְׁמוּאֵל מוֹדֵי: **מתני'** אֶת עֵירוּבוֹ. עֵירוּבֵי חֲצֵירוֹת: וְהַדָּר שָׁם. בְּבֵית שַׁעַר שֶׁבֶּחָצֵר: אֵינוֹ אוֹסֵר. עַל בַּעַל חָצֵר, וְאֵין צָרִיךְ לִיתֵּן אֶת הַפַּת – דְּלָאו דִּירָה הִיא: וְהַדָּר שָׁם. אִם הִשְׁאִיל בַּעַל הַבַּיִת בֵּית הַתֶּבֶן שֶׁלּוֹ לְאַחֵר לָדוּר שָׁם – אוֹסֵר עָלָיו בֶּחָצֵר, הוֹאִיל וּפָתוּחַ לֶחָצֵר: אִם יֵשׁ שָׁם תְּפִיסַת יָד שֶׁל בַּעַל הַבַּיִת. שֶׁיֵּשׁ לְבַעַל הַבַּיִת מָקוֹם בְּדִירָתוֹ שֶׁל זֶה שֶׁנּוֹתֵן שָׁם כֵּלָיו לְהַצְנִיעַ: אֵינוֹ אוֹסֵר עָלָיו. דְּכָל רְשׁוּתָא דְּחָצֵר דִּידֵיהּ הוּא, כְּאִילּוּ דָּר עִמּוֹ בַּבַּיִת: **גמ'** חוּץ מִבֵּית שַׁעַר דְּיָחִיד. דְּחָצֵר שֶׁל יָחִיד, וּמַתְנִי' בְּבֵית שַׁעַר דְּחָצֵר דְּרַבִּים עָסְקִינַן: עֵירוּב מִשּׁוּם דִּירָה. דִּמְעָרֵב לְהוּ לְבָתֵּי דִּירָה כְּאִילּוּ כָּל בְּנֵי הַבָּתִּים דָּרִין כָּאן הִלְכָּךְ, אִי לָא חֲזֵי לְדִירָה – לָא מָצֵי שָׁרֵי. אֲבָל שִׁיתּוּף – לָאו מִשּׁוּם דִּירָה הוּא. דְּהָא לָא בָּתִּים שַׁיְּיכֵי בֵּיהּ אֶלָּא חֲצֵירוֹת, הִלְכָּךְ: לָאו דִּירָה בָּעֵינַן אֶלָּא מָקוֹם הַמִּשְׁתַּמֵּר כְּגוֹן חָצֵר. אֲבָל אֲוִיר דְּמָבוֹי לָאו מִשְׁתַּמֵּר הוּא: תַּנְיָא נַמִי הָכִי. דְּמַנִּיחִין בּוֹ שִׁיתּוּף: מְסוּבִּין בַּבַּיִת. מִשּׁוּם עֵירוּב: מִי מִינְטַר. ל"ג דְּטַעְמָא לָאו מִשּׁוּם נְטִירוּתָא הוּא: בַּבַּיִת שֶׁבֶּחָצֵר. לְאַפּוֹקֵי בַּיִת שֶׁבֶּחָצֵר אַחֶרֶת: בֶּחָצֵר שֶׁבַּמָּבוֹי. לְאַפּוֹקֵי חָצֵר שֶׁאֵינָהּ פְּתוּחָה לוֹ: (בוניים) בֶּן בּוֹנְיָים. עָשִׁיר הָוָה, וּמַשְׁאִיל בָּתִּים שֶׁבֶּחָצֵר לַאֲחֵרִים, וְהָיוּ לוֹ כֵּלִים הַרְבֵּה: פַּנּוּ מָקוֹם לְבֶן מֵאָה מָנֶה. שֶׁמִּתּוֹךְ עָשְׁרוֹ הָיוּ לוֹ כֵּלִים בְּכוּלָּן. כְּלוֹמַר: מָקוֹם חָשׁוּב:

פנו

תוספות

לימא שמואל לית ליה דרב דימי. פירוש רש"י נראה עיקר, דקאי אההיא דבור שבין ב' חצירות, דקסבר שמואל אדם אוסר על חבירו דרך אויר אע"פ שהוא תשמיש גרוע. ומשני: התם רשויות דאורייתא, וליכא למיחש שמא מתוך כך יבא לטלטל מרה"י לרה"ר, דאיסורא דאורייתא מידע ידע. אבל הכא, דאי לאו דאסרי אהדדי – שמא מתוך כך יטלטל מחצר לחצר. ור"ת פירש בע"א ואין נראה פירושו: **ומי** אמר רב הכי. פי': דאין אדם אוסר על חבירו דרך אויר, והא אתמר: שני בתים כו'. וקס"ד: טעמא דאוסר לזרוק – משום דסגי באויר רה"ר למעלה מעשרה, וקאמר דאוסר עליו אוירן של בני רה"ר אף על פי שאין להם כאן תשמיש. וכן פי' בקונטרס. ומדשמואל אדשמואל לא מצי למיפרך, דאין תשמיש דאויר הכא חשיב כההיא דלעיל, אבל לרב פריך מכל שכן. ורש"י פירש דלא פריך שמואל אדשמואל משום דברשויות דאורייתא מודה. **לאו** מי אוקימנא כו'. בשבת פרק "הזורק" (דף צז.) מוקי לה הכי משום פירכא אחריתי. וק"ק דהתם נמי קאמר ולאו מי אוקימנא: **בית** התבן כו' הרי זה עירוב. ואפילו אין שם תבן. דלענין הנחת עירוב – לא בעי אלא דחזי לדירה. אבל הא דקאמר בפ' "הדר" (לעיל ד' עב:) דבית התבן אוסר – היינו דוקא כשיש שם תבן, כמו שלר' יהודה אינו אוסר אלא מקום דירה והיינו דוקא כשדר שם בשבת, דבעינן מקום פיתא או מקום לינה. והא דקתני הכא: הדר שם אוסר עליו – דווקא שאין לבעל הבית שם תבן, דאם יש שם תבן – הוי כאילו דר עמו שם בבית לר' מאיר, דחשיב בית התבן כמקום דירה בפרק "הדר", ולא אסרי אהדדי: **עירוב** הוא דלא הוי הא שיתוף הוי. קשה: דאשכחן דקרי עירוב לשיתוף בפ' "הדר" (לעיל ד' עא.): בעל הבית שהיה שותף לשכניו לזה ביין ולזה ביין – אין צריכין לערב. ולקמן בפרק "כל גגות" (דף צא:) קאמר: מאי לא עירבו – לא נשתתפו:

דעריבי

מסורת הש"ס

[נ"ל אלעזר]

[לעיל עד.]

שבת ח: לעיל ט. עז. ולקמן פז. קא:

[לעיל עז. וש"נ]

שבת לז.

לעיל עו. [סוכה ג:]

בסדר המשנה בירושלמי וברי"ף הגי' עליו

[עי' תוס' לעיל עה: ד"ה ורבי יוחנן]

לעיל עג: [ע"ש]

סוכה ג:

[גירס הערוך ע' סבן בן ננס]

יש גורסין בן בוניים תלמידו של רבי

הגהות הב"ח

(א) גמ' כל מקום שאמרו חכמים הדר: (ג) שם חצירו של בן בוניים:

גליון הש"ס

גמ' שיתופי מבואות בחצר שבמבוי. עיין לעיל דף סח ע"א תד"ה וניקני להו. ועוד לעיל דף עא ע"ב תד"ה בפת:

רבינו חננאל

פי' כחצובה מתלת להדף כשורה עומדת על הסדר אחת עם אחת. ומקשינן ומי אמר רב הכי והא והאתמר ב' בתים בב' צידי רה"ר רבה בר רב הונא אמר רב אסור לזרוק מזה לזה ושמואל אמר מותר. ומפרקינן ולאו אוקימנא דחד מדלי וחד מיתתי וזימנין דמיגנדר ואתי לאתויי א"ל רבינא לרבא נימא שמואל דאמר גג הסמוך לרה"ר צריך סולם קבוע א) להתירו בטלטול מרשות הרבים לית ליה הא דכי אתא רב דימי א"ר יוחנן מקום שאין בו אלא ד' על ד' מותר לבני רה"ר ולבני רה"י לכתף עליו ובלבד שלא יחליפו. אמר ליה ברשויות של תורה הכי נמי דאית ליה כי קאמרי' הכא ברשות דרבנן וחכמים עשו חיזוק לדבריהם יותר משל תורה ותוב אמרינן ומי אמר רב אין אדם אוסר על חבירו דרך אויר והא איהו דאמר בב' גגין בב' צידי רה"ר אסור לזרוק מזה לזה ודחינן ולאו מי אוקימנא כגון חד מידלי וחד מיתתי כו': [מתני'] **הנותן** עירובו בבית שער אכסדרה ומרפסת אינו עירוב. והדר שם אינו אוסר. אמרי משמיה דרב כל מקום שאמרו חכמים הדר שם אינו אוסר על בני חצר [הנותן עירובו שם אינו עירוב] חוץ מבית שער של יחיד ובית שער דקתני במתני' בית שער דרבים: **ירושלמי** הדא את אמרת בבית שער של יחיד אבל בבית שער של רבים הרי זה עירוב והדר שם הרי זה אוסר עליו. ב) דבי ר' ינאי אמרי אפילו יתד לתלות בו מגעלו ואפי' טבלא או עשתות רב [אמר] ובלבד דבר הניטל בשבת כו'. [וכל מקום שאמרו אין מניחין בו עירוב וכו'] בו עירוב כגון אכסדרה ומרפסת וכיוצא בהן עירוב אין מניחין בהן אבל מניחין בהן שיתופי מבוי חוץ מן אויר (למבוי) [המבוי] שאפי' שיתופי מבוי לא. תניא נמי הכי כו'. אמר רב יהודה אמר רב בני חבורה שהיו מסובין וקדש היום עליהם פת שעל השלחן סומכין עליו משום עירוב. והני מילי במסובין בבית שבחצר ושיתופי מבוי בחצר שבמבוי. ר' יהודה אמר אם יש שם תפיסת יד של בעה"ב אינו אוסר עליו פי' אם יש בית בחצר שדר בן אדם אחד ויש שם באותו הבית לבעל החצר כלים או סחורה מונחין באותו הבית ומשתמש בה זכה כיון שיש שם מקצת רשות לבעל החצר הדר שם אינו אוסר עליו. היכי דמי תפיסת יד א"ר חנינא כגון חצרות של

בושם

א) ר"ל שלא יאסרו עליו בני ר"ה. ב) [נראה דדברי הירושלמי אלו בשם ר' ינאי קאי אדברי ר"י במשנה ושייך להלן אחר הדיבור היכי דמי תפיסת יד].

פנו מקום לבן מאתים מנה. אמר לפניו רבי ישמעאל ברבי יוסי: רבי, אביו של זה יש לו אלף ספינות בים וכנגדן אלף עיירות ביבשה! אמר לו: לכשתגיע אצל אביו אמור לו: אל תשגרהו בכלים הללו לפני. רבי מכבד עשירים, ר' עקיבא מכבד עשירים. כדדרש *רבא בר מרי: °"ישב עולם לפני אלהים חסד ואמת מן ינצרהו", אימתי ישב עולם לפני אלהים – בזמן שחסד ואמת מן ינצרהו. רבה בר בר חנה אמר: כגון יתד של מחרישה, אמר רב נחמן, תנא דבי שמואל: [א]דבר הניטל בשבת – אוסר, דבר שאינו ניטל בשבת – אינו אוסר. תניא נמי הכי: יש לו טבל, יש לו עששית, וכל דבר שאינו ניטל בשבת – אינו אוסר.§ **מתני'** *המניח ביתו והלך לשבות בעיר אחרת, אחד נכרי ואחד ישראל – הרי זה אוסר, דברי ר' מאיר. ר' יהודה אומר: אינו אוסר. רבי יוסי אומר: נכרי – אוסר, ישראל [ב] – אינו אוסר, שאין דרך ישראל לבא בשבת. רבי שמעון אומר: אפילו הניח ביתו והלך לשבות אצל בתו באותה העיר – אינו אוסר, שכבר הסיע מלבו.§ **גמ'** *אמר רב: הלכה כר"ש. ודוקא בתו, אבל בנו – לא. דאמרי אינשי: נבח בך כלבא – עול, נבח בך גורייתא – פוק.:

מתני' *בור שבין שתי חצירות אין ממלאין ממנו בשבת, אלא אם כן עשו לו מחיצה גבוה עשרה טפחים, *בין מלמטה, בין מתוך אוגנו. רבן שמעון בן גמליאל אומר, בית שמאי אומרים: מלמטה, ובית הלל אומרים: מלמעלה. א"ר יהודה: לא תהא מחיצה גדולה מן הכותל שביניהם.§ **גמ'** אמר רב הונא: למטה – למטה ממש, למעלה – למעלה ממש. וזה וזה בבור. ורב יהודה אמר: [ג]למטה – למטה מן המים, למעלה – למעלה מן המים. א"ל רבה בר רב חנן לאביי: הא דאמר רב יהודה "למטה – למטה מן המים" מאי שנא למטה ממש דלא – דעריבי מיא, למטה מן המים נמי – הא עריבי מיא! א"ל: לא שמיע לך הא דאמר רב יהודה אמר רב, ומטו בה משום רבי חייא: [ד]צריך שיראו ראשן של קנים למעלה מן המים טפח. ותו, הא דאמר רב יהודה: "למעלה – למעלה מן המים", מאי שנא למעלה ממש דלא – דעריבי מיא, למעלה מן המים נמי – הא עריבי מיא! אמר ליה: לא שמיע לך הא דתני יעקב קרחינאה: [ה]צריך שישקע ראשי קנים במים טפח. ואלא הא *דאמר רב יהודה: קורה ארבע מתרת בחורבה, [ו]ורב נחמן אמר רבה בר אבוה: קורה

תורה אור: תהלים סא

רש"י

פנו מקום לבן מאתים מנה. *כלומר: מקום חשוב יותר, בין גדולים לפי כבוד עשרו: אביו של זה. בוניים: בכלים הללו. בבגדים הללו, שאין נראה עשיר כל כך: אימתי ישב עולם. בזמן שיש בו עשירים, שגומלין(א) ומזמנין מזונות לעניים, והם ינצרוהו: מן. לשון מזונות: כגון יתד של מחרישה. קדיליי"א, הויא תפיסת יד: דבר הניטל בשבת. אינו תפיסת יד, ואוסר. דאי בעי – שקיל ושדי ליה לברא: עששיות. של ברזל חתיכות גדולות: **מתני'** הרי זה אוסר. דדירה בלא בעלים – שמה דירה: אינו אוסר. דלאו שמה דירה: ר' יוסי. נמי סבירא ליה לאו שמה דירה. מיהו, נכרי אוסר שמא יבא היום: הסיע. הסיח דירת ביתו מלבו: **גמ'** ודוקא בתו. דעביד איניש דדייר אצל חתנו. אבל בנו – אין אדם מסיח דעתו מביתו לדור אצל כלתו, שמא תתקוטט ויצא: כלבא. זכר, כגון חתנו: גורייתא. נקבה, כגון כלתו: **מתני'** בור שבין שתי חצירות. חציו בזו וחציו בזו: אין ממלאין הימנו. שזה ממלא מרשות חבירו אא"כ כו': בין מלמטה. בגמרא מפרש: בין מתוך אוגנו. אע"פ שאינה נוגעת במים – קל הוא שהקילו חכמים במים, דאמר ביה גוד אחית למחיצה. ובלבד שתהא בתוך אוגן הבור, שתראה כהפסקה: מן הכותל שביניהם. שמפסקת בין החצירות ומפסקת על פני הבור, ואע"פ שאינה נכנסת לתוך אוגנו: **גמ'** למטה. דקאמרי ב"ש: למטה ממש. סמוך למים, ואין צריכין ראשי קנים ליגע במים: למעלה. דקאמרי ב"ה: למעלה ממש. סמוך (ב)משפתו מלמעלה אם ירצה – דיו בכך: וזה וזה בבור. אפילו לב"ה צריך שתהא כל מחיצת עשרה מאוגן הבור ולפנים: ורב יהודה אמר למטה. דב"ש: למטה מן המים. שתהא המחיצה תחובה בקרקעית הבור: למעלה. דב"ה: למעלה מן המים. ובהא מקילי, שאין קנים צריכין ליגע במים. אבל למעלה ממש – לא. מעלה דרב יהודה הוא מטה דרב הונא: דעריבי מיא. תחת המחיצה: הא עריבי מיא. על המחיצה, פעמים שהמים עמוקים מעשרה: שיראו ראשי קנים. העליונים: ותו. לרב יהודה נמי, אליבא דב"ה דאמרי למעלה מן המים סמוך למים, אבל רחוק מן המים לא: מ"ש למעלה ממש. דהוא רחוק מן המים דלא – שאין מחיצת הפסק ניכרת במים, ועריבי מיא להדיא. למטה נמי, מאי הפסק איכא? הרי אין נוגעין במים: שישקע ראשי הקנים. התחתונים ובהא פליגי, דבית שמאי בעו מחיצה המפסקת עד התהום, וב"ה בעו היכר מחיצה: קורה ד' מתרת בחורבה. קורה התחובה מחומה לחומה בחורבה, כדרך חורבות הנופלות, ונשארים בהן קורות ויש ברחבה ארבעה והיא מוטלת על רחבה – מותר לטלטל תחתיה. דאמר שני חודי' יורדין וסותמין, דסבר לה כרבי ישמעאל בר"י, דאמר [לקמן ע"ב]: מחיצה תלויה מתרת ולית הלכתא כוותיה. ולהכי נקט ארבעה, דכי אמרת חודין יורדין וסותמין – יהא בין חלל המחיצות ארבעה, דמחיצה העשויה לפחות מחלל ארבעה – אינה מחיצה: מתרת

תוספות

דעריבי מיא. פי': ואין היכר הפרשה ביניהם. אבל אם יש היכר, אע"פ שהמים באים מצד זה לצד זה – לא קפיד, דאי הוה קפיד – לא היה מועיל אפילו מחילה של ברזל, כדאמרינן ב"מי שהוציאוהו" (לעיל דף מח.): **צריך** שיראו ראשי קנים למעלה מן המים טפח. ואין נראה כפירוש הקונטרס דב"ש בעו מחילה מפסקת עד התהום, אלא שתהא י' טפחים בתוך המים. ואפילו המים עמוקים הרבה, ועריבי מיא מתחת המחילה – סגי בהכי לב"ש, כיון שיש היכר מחילת עשרה בתוך המים. וב"ה בעו היכר מחילת עשרה למעלה, חוץ מן המים, וטפח בתוך המים כדקאמר: צריך שישקע ראשי קנים במים טפח: **קורה ארבעה** מתרת בחורבה. פי' בקונטרס: להכי נקט רחב ארבעה, דכי אמרת חודין יורדין וסותמין (ג) יהיה בין חלל המחילה ד', דמחילה העשויה לפחות מארבעה חללה – לא שמה מחילה. משמע מתוך פירושו דכי אין בו ד' נמי היה אומר פי תקרה יורד וסותם מרוח אחת, אם הוי שאר הרוחות מוקפות מחילה. והוא עצמו פירש קורה ארבעה מתרת במים בבור שבין שתי חצירות, (ד) ונתן על רחבה באמצע הבור למעלה. ולדבריו התם, למה צריך שם קורה ארבעה? כיון שהחצירות מוקפות מחילה, ואין צריך כי אם להפסיק. ועוד: קי"ל כרב, דאמר פי תקרה יורד וסותם. וקי"ל(ה) נמי כרבא לגבי אביי דקורה משום היכר, ולא משום מחילה – היינו משום דבקורה שאינה רחבה כי אם טפח לא אמר פי תקרה יורד וסותם עד שיהא רחבה ארבעה. והכי נמי מוכח פ"ק דשבת (דף ט.) גבי איסקופה דלפי תקרה בעינן רחבה ארבעה גבי(ו) דקאמר כגון שקירה בשתי קורות, ואין באחד ד' כו'. ולאביי נמי, דקא אמר קורה משום מחילה – נראה לר"י דלא הוי אלא מדרבנן, כמו למאן דאמר משום היכר. אלא דסבר אביי דמשום היכר לא היו מתירין חכמים את המבוי, אלא שעשאוה כמחילה דפי תקרה ולא הוי "קורה משום מחילה" פירושו כמו לחי משום מחילה, דהוי דאורייתא, כדאמרי' בפ"ק (דף יב:): הכשירו בלחי – הזורק לתוכו חייב. והא דקאמר בפ"ק (ג"ז שם:) אמילתיה דרב יהודה, דאמר מבוי שאינו ראוי לשיתוף: הכשירו בלחי – הזורק לתוכו חייב, הכשירו בקורה – הזורק לתוכו פטור. אלמא: לחי משום מחילה, וקורה משום היכר. אינו בא לומר דקורה ע"כ משום היכר ולא משום מחילה, דאפילו הוי משום מחילה – הזורק לתוכו פטור, משום דלא הוי מחילה אלא מדרבנן. אלא, כלומר: לחי – ודאי משום מחילה, אבל קורה – מצינו למימר משום היכר. ומיהו, רב יעקב בר אבא שמקשה שם על רבא מיתר על כן א"ר יהודה, דאפילו קורה משום מחילה דאוריי' – טועה היה, וליתא, דאפילו למ"ד משום מחילה – לא הוי אלא מדרבנן. וכן משמע בסוף "כל גגות" (לקמן נה.) דמוכח אביי לרבה מברייתא דיתר על כן, דשתי מחילות דאורייתא. מדמתיר בקורה מכאן וקורה מכאן אע"ג דסבר אביי דקורה משום מחילה. אלא ודאי לא הוי אלא מדרבנן. מיהו, יש לדחות: דלדבריו דרבה קא מותיב, דסבר דהויא משום היכר: קורה

מסורת הש"ס

יש גורסין כאן סבור היה רבי שזה עשיר יותר מבן בוניים

[גיר' ע"י רבה בר מרי]

לעיל מז. סב:

[לעיל מז. ע"ש]

סוכה טז. [ע"ש כמה שינויים גם בפלוגתא דב"ש וב"ה אותא שם להיפך וע"ע תוס' טז: ד"ה ב"ש] *בסדר המשנה וכו' גרסינן בין מלמטה בין מלמעלה וכו' ועי' תוי"ט ד"ה בין

[לקמן נה.]

עין משפט נר מצוה

כג א מיי' פ"ד מהל' עירובין הלכה יד סמג עשין א טור ש"ע א"ח סי' שע סעיף ב:

כד ב מיי' שם הלכה יג וסמג שם טור ש"ע א"ח סי' שעא ס"א:

כה ג ד ה ו מיי' פ"ג מהלכות עירובין הלכה כא ופט"ו מהלכות שבת הלכה יא סמג עשין א טוש"ע א"ח סי' שנו סעיף א וסי' שעו ס"א:

רבינו חננאל

בושם שהיה עשיר גדול ויש בכל הבתים שבחצירו כלים וסחורות ואין שם בית שלא היה לו חפץ בתוכו שהיו לו נכסים הרבה. ר' עקיבא וגם רבי היו מכבדים עשירים והיו דורשין האי קרא ישב עולם. כלומר מי שנתן לו העוה"ז ישב לפני אלהים בזמן שגומל חסדים כדכתיב חסד ואמת מן ינצרוהו: רבה בר רב הונא אמר אפי' יתד של מחרישה אם יש לו לבעל חצר באותו הבית הרי זה תפיסת יד. דבי שמואל תנא דבר הניטל בשבת אוסר ושאינו ניטל בשבת אינו אוסר. פי' אם יש לבעל החצר בבית ההוא דבר הניטל בשבת יתכן שיזדמן לבעה"ב *) ליטול החצר לבטלו בשבת ויטלנו לבעל החצר שם תפיסת יד. לפיכך הדר שם אוסר עליו עד שיערב אבל [אם] הוא דבר שאינו ניטל בשבת הואיל ואינו ניטל בשבת **) אין רשות לבעל החצר לאותו בית לפיכך הדר שם אינו אוסר עליו: **מתני'** ר' שמעון אומר המניח את ביתו והלך לשבות אצל בתו אפילו באותה העיר אינו אוסר על בני חצר. אמר רב הלכה כר' שמעון ודווקא בתו דאמרינן בתו לא שבקא ליה למיפק לביתיה היום אבל אם הלך לשבות אצל בנו אוסר שיתכן לו שיבא היום בחצרו וכל היכא דחיישינן דלמא אתי בשבת אסור: **מתני'** בור שבין ב' חצרות אין ממלאין ממנה בשבת אא"כ עשו לה מחיצה גבוה י"ט כו'. אמר רב הונא למטה דקתני במתני' למטה בבור קרוב למים למעלה למעלה ממש והוא על שפת הבור מתוכו ורב יהודה אמר למטה מן המים כלומר יהיו הקנים משוקעין במים למטה מן המים [ט'] טפחים ונראין הקנים למעלה מן המים טפח. למעלה מן המים וצ"ל מחיצת הקנים שהיא י' טפחים נשקעת בתוך המים טפח. פי' חייש רב יהודה שלא יהיה זה דולה מחצי הבור שהוא רשות חבירו וכן זה בשל זה לפיכך מצריך ראשי הקנים שיהיו

*) אינו מובן ואולי דצ"ל יתכן שיזדמן לבעל החצר ליטול החפץ בשבת ויבטל לבעל החצר שם תפיסת יד. **) אולי צ"ל הרי יש רשות לבעל החצר וכו'.

הגהות הב"ח (א) רש"י ד"ה אימתי וכו' שגומלין חסד ומזמנין: (ב) ד"ה למעלה ממש סמוך לשפתו: (ג) תוס' ד"ה קורה וכו' יורדין וסותמין יהא בין חלל המחילות ד' וכו' לפחות מארבעה חלל לא: (ד) בא"ד בבור שבין שתי חצירות ונתונה על רחבה וכו' למה צריך קורה כצ"ל ותיבת שם נמחק: (ה) בא"ד וקי"ל נמי כרבא לגבי אביי. נ"ב עי' בתוס' פ"ק דף טו בד"ה אביי לטעמיה: (ו) בא"ד גבי הא דקאמר כגון שקירה:

גליון הש"ס **גמ'** רבי מכבד עשירים. בלקוטי מהרי"ל שמע ממהר"ס סג"ל די"ל מתוך שרבי עצמו היה עשיר מופלג לכך הרגיל עצמו לכבד עשירים כדי להתלמד להעם שיכבדו ג"כ אותו בשביל עשרו ולא בשביל תורתו שלא רצה להשתמש בכתרה של תורה ליטול עטרה להתגדל בה עכ"ל: **תוס'** ד"ה קורה וכו' דאפילו קורה משום מחילה דאורייתא. עיין לעיל דף ח ע"ב תד"ה מניח:

קורה ארבעה מתרת במים, הא קא אזיל דלי לאידך גיסא ומייתי! קים להו לרבנן דאין דלי מהלך יותר מארבעה טפחים. תחת קורה מיהא הא עריבי מיא! אלא: משום דקל הוא שהקילו חכמים במים. *כדבעא מיניה רבי טבלא מרב: מחיצה תלויה, מהו שתתיר בחורבה? א"ל: אין מחיצה תלויה מתרת אלא במים, קל הוא שהקילו חכמים במים.§ "א"ר יהודה: לא תהא מחיצה".§ אמר רבה בר בר חנה, אמר רבי יוחנן: ר' יהודה בשיטת רבי יוסי אמרה, דאמר: מחיצה תלויה מתרת אפילו ביבשה. *דתנן: [א]המשלשל דפנות מלמעלה למטה(א) בזמן שגבוהות מן הארץ ג' טפחים — פסולה, ממטה למעלה, אם גבוהות י' טפחים — כשירה. רבי יוסי אומר: כשם שמלמטה למעלה עשרה(ב) כך מלמעלה למטה עשרה. ולא היא, לא רבי יהודה סבר לה כרבי יוסי, ולא ר' יוסי סבר לה כרבי יהודה. רבי יהודה לא סבר לה כרבי יוסי; עד כאן לא קאמר רבי יהודה — אלא בעירובי חצירות דרבנן, אבל סוכה דאורייתא — לא. ולא ר' יוסי סבר לה כר' יהודה; עד כאן לא קאמר ר' יוסי — אלא בסוכה דאיסור עשה הוא, אבל שבת דאיסור סקילה הוא — לא אמר. ואם תאמר: אותו מעשה שנעשה בציפורי על פי מי נעשה? לא על פי רבי יוסי(ג) אלא על פי רבי ישמעאל בר' יוסי נעשה. *דכי אתא רב דימי, אמר: פעם אחת שכחו ולא הביאו ספר תורה מבעוד יום, למחר פרסו סדין על העמודים, והביאו ספר תורה, וקראו בו. פרסו?! לכתחילה מי שרי? והא *[ב]הכל מודים שאין עושין אהל עראי *בשבת! אלא: מצאו סדינין פרוסין על העמודים, והביאו ספר תורה, וקראו בו. אמר רבה: ר' יהודה ור' חנניא בן עקביא אמרו דבר אחד. ר' יהודה — הא דאמרן. ר' חנניא בן עקביא (*דתנן,) ר' חנניא בן עקביא אומר: גזוזטרא שיש בה ארבע אמות על ארבע אמות — חוקק

רש"י

מתרת במים. בבור שבין ב' חצירות, ונתונה על רחבה באמצע הבור למעלה: לאידך גיסא. תחת כל רוחב הקורה, חוץ לקורה, בחלק חבירו: עריבי מיא. ורב יהודה הפסק מחיצה בעי: אלא קל הוא שהקילו חכמים במים. וליתא לדרב יהודה, אלא כדרב הונא דב"ה למעלה ממש קאמרי. ה"ג: אלא קל הוא כו': מחיצה תלויה מתרת אף ביבשה. הלכך, במים נמי אין צריך שתראה המחיצה עשויה בשביל המים ובתוך אוגני הבור: המשלשל. טריליי"ר בלע"ז: מלמעלה למטה. שהתחיל לארוג מחיצות הסוכה למעלה, ואורג ובא למטה: גבוהות מן הארץ שלשה. דגדיים בוקעים בה, הויא לה תלויה ופסולה: מלמטה למעלה. שנוגעות בקרקע: אם גבוהות עשרה טפחים כשירה. ואע"פ שאינן מגיעות לסכך. והכא לא גרס גבוהות מן הארץ, אלא אם גבוהות עשרה טפחים: כשם שמלמטה למעלה. מכשרת ליה, ואע"ג דלא מטיא לסכך: כך מלמעלה למטה. די לה באריג עשרה, ואע"פ שאינה מגעת לארץ: אבל שבת דאיסור סקילה. אע"ג דברשויות דרבנן ליכא סקילה — כל דתקון רבנן כעין דאורייתא תקון: ואם תאמר. הואיל ור' יוסי לגבי שבת לית ליה מחיצה תלויה: מעשה שנעשה בציפורי. על ידי מחיצה תלויה, כדאמר לקמן: ע"פ מי נעשה. והלא ר' יוסי ראש של ציפורי הוה, ועל פיו היו עושין כולן, כדאמר בסנהדרין (דף לב:): אחר רבי יוסי לציפורי: ה"ג: לא ע"פ ר' יוסי נעשה אלא ע"פ רבי ישמעאל בר ר' יוסי נעשה. שכבר נפטר ר' יוסי. ול"ג לא ע"פ רבי יהודה — דרבי יהודה לאו בציפורי הוה. ועוד: דלר' יהודה שרי, דהא רשויות דרבנן הוו, כדלקמן: ולא הביאו ספר תורה. לבית הכנסת. *ובחצר אחרת הוה, והיו מביאין אותו דרך חצר שאינה מעורבת. ופרסו סדינין על גבי עמודין להיות מחיצה מפסקת אצל מחיצות החצר, מבית שהיה ספר תורה מונח בו ועד בית הכנסת, וכעין מבוי קטן כדי הילוך בין סדינים למחיצות החצר. ולא היו בני החצר אוסרים שם — שלא היה פתח פתוח לו אלא אותו פתח לבדו, והנך סדינים מחיצה תלויה הואי: הכל מודים. ר"א ומחלוקתו שנחלקו בתוספת אהל עראי גבי פקק חלון, דאיכא למ"ד פוקקין בו, ואע"ג דמוסיף על אהל עראי הוא — מודים שאין עושין את כל האהל לכתחלה בשבת, בפ' "כל הכלים" (דף קכה:): אמרו דבר אחד. הקילו הרבה במים: גזוזטרא. שהיא למעלה מן הים: שיש בה ארבעה. מרובעות, שהן כ"ד טפחים על כ"ד טפחים: חוקק

תוספות

*קורה ד' מתרת בחורבה. פי' בקונטרס: דסבר לה כר' ישמעאל ברבי יוסי, דאמר: מחיצה תלויה מתרת, ולית הלכתא כוותיה. ואין נראה לר"י, דרבי ישמעאל לא התיר אלא במבוי, אבל במחיצה תלויה דחורבה הפרוצה לרה"ר — לא. ועוד: דקורה ד' לא מטעם מחיצה תלויה מתרת, דהא ליכא מחיצה כלל אלא מטעם פי תקרה(ד), ופי תקרה לא אשכחנא תנאי דפליגי. ורב נמי, דאית ליה (לקמן דף צ:) פי תקרה יורד וסותם — קאמר הכא בסמוך דאין מחיצה תלויה מתרת אלא במים:

הא קאזיל דלי לאידך גיסא. פירש בקונטרס: דלרב יהודה דוקא פריך, שמצריך לשקע ראשי קנים במים שלא ידלה מרשות חבירו. אבל רב הונא לא בעי רק שיש היכר קצת, שלא יטלטל שם להדיא. (ולא) מצי למימר דרב נחמן כת"ק דשרי מתוך אוגנו — דהא מתוך אוגנו דת"ק היינו מלמעלן דרשב"ג, דכי היכי דבעי רב יהודה שיקוע לרשב"ג — ה"ה לת"ק. וכן הא דפריך: תחת הקורה מיהא עריבי מיא — לרב יהודה פריך. ולא מצי לשנויי דקורה מתרת מחודה ולפנים, ולא תחת הקורה — דכיון דרשות שניהן שולטת בהם תחת הקורה. א"כ בסמוך לקורה נמי ליתסר משום שעריבי מיא שתחת הקורה. ועוד: דמשמע ליה דמתרת לגמרי, אף תחת הקורה:

אלא קל הוא שהקילו חכמים במים. פירש בקונטרס: וליתא לדרב יהודה, אלא כרב הונא דב"ה למעלה ממש קאמרי. ועל זה סומכין העולם שיש להן בתי כסאות על המים, אע"פ שאין המחיצות מגיעות עד המים. והא דאמר בפירקין (דף פח.) אמתניתין דגזוזטרא שהיא למעלה מן המים ועשו לה מחיצה גבוה י' כו' לא שנו אלא למלאות, אבל לשפוך — אסור. דהלכתא כאיכא דאמרי, דאפי' לשפוך נמי שרי, דבטל סופרים הלך אחר המיקל. ומיהו, נראה דאינה מועלת המחיצה העשויה לצניעות בית הכסא ולא לשם מחיצת מים, דאין הלכה כרבי יהודה דאמר לא תהא מחיצה גדולה מן הכותל שביניהן. ודבר תימה הוא שפירש בקונטרס מסקנא דשמעתין דלא כרב יהודה, דהא רב ורבי חייא קיימי כוותיה וברייתא דיעקב(ה) קרחאה. ומלינו לפרש: קל הוא שהקילו חכמים במים — דקורה מתרת בלא שיקוע, אבל מחיצה התלויה מלינו למימר כרב יהודה דבעי שיקוע. ור"ח פירש: דקיימא לן כרב יהודה, ול"ג "אלא". ור"ת נמי לא גרס "אלא", ומפרש: דפריך לרב נחמן אפילו אליבא דרב הונא דלא מצריך שיקוע. וה"פ: קורה ד' מתרת במים — פי': אמת המים, או יש עובר אצל כותלו, דהוי(ו) ככרמלית ויש חלון למטה מן הקורה, והקורה מונחת על גבי הזיזין היוצאין מן הכותל. ופריך: הא קאזיל לאידך גיסא. בשלמא בור שבין שתי חצירות — סגי במחיצות, למר כדאית ליה ולמר כדאית ליה, דליתיה כרמלית אלא רה"י. אבל כרמלית גמורה, דלאו בר איערובי הוא — אית לן למיחש דילמא אתי לאידך גיסא! ומשני: גמירי כו'. ופריך: תחת קורה מיהא עריבי מיא בהדי הנך ומכרמלית הוא דולה! ומשני: קל הוא שהקילו חכמים במים. ולא גרס "אלא", דשינויא דאין דלי מהלך יותר מארבעה — כדקאי קאי. וה"פ: כיון שהדלי לא ילך בכרמלית — לערובי מיא נמי לא חיישינן, משום דהקילו במים ע"י מחילת תקרה, כדאמר לקמן (פז.) באמת המים שעשו לה מחיצה עשרה, דלא חיישינן לאיערובי מיא — הכי נמי גבי תקרה: **עד** כאן לא קאמר ר' יהודה אלא בעירובי חצירות. וא"ת: ולימא משום דבמים הקילו חכמים! ועוד, אמאי קאמר: ר' יהודה בשיטת ר' יוסי אמרה? לימא דכולהו תנאי דמכשרי במחיצה תלויה — בשיטת ר' יוסי אמרו! וי"ל: דאשאר תנאי איכא למימר משום דבמים הקילו, אבל ר' יהודה מסום מים — לא היה מיקל כל כך שמתיר אף במחיצה שלא נעשית לשם מים. ולהכי קאמר: משום דבעירובי חצירות דרבנן: **גזוזטרא** שיש בה(ז) ארבעה על ארבעה כו'. משמע: דכי אין בה ארבעה על ארבעה — אינו ממלא. אבל גזוזטרא עצמה — הויא רה"י. וכן גזוזטרא דמתני'. דקתני אין ממלאין הימנה אא"כ עשה לה מחיצה עשרה. אבל גזוזטרא גופה — הויא רה"י, ומטלטל בכולה. ותימה: כיון דאין לה מחיצות, אמאי הויא רה"י? והא טרסקל לא הוי רה"י אפילו לר' יוסי בר יהודה, אלא משום דהדרא מחיצתא, כדאמרינן בפרק "בכל מערבין" (לעיל דף לג:)! וי"ל: דבקיעת דגים לא הויא בקיעה, ואמרינן גוד אחית. אבל בטרסקל — איכא בקיעת גדיים. א"נ: סתמא פתוח לרה"י, והויא כחור היחיד. ור"י האריך בזה בריש "כל גגות" גבי מחיצות שאינן ניכרות. וא"ת: כי אין בה ד' אמות על ד' אמות, לישתרי למלאות לפ"ה שפירש בסוף "כל גגות" (לקמן דף לד:) דאמר פי תקרה בכל ארבע הרוחות! וי"ל: דהכא איירי דעבידא כי ארזילא באלכסון כעין גגין שלנו, דלא אמרינן פי תקרה יורד, כדאמרינן ב"עושין פסין" (לעיל דף כה:). אי נמי: כגון שהגזוזטרא אינה שוה ומליאה פגימות כל סביבותיה, דאין(ח) פי תקרה. אי נמי: כשאין טפח בעובי הגזוזטרא, דמשמע מפירוש הקונטרס דסוף פרק קמא דסוכה (דף יח:) בשמעתא דאכסדרה שיש לה פצימין — דלא אמר פי תקרה יורד וסותם אלא אם כן יש בעובי התקרה טפח:

אמר

עין משפט נר מצוה

כו א מיי' פ"ד מהלכות סוכה הלכה ד סמג עשין מג טוש"ע א"ח סי' תרל סעיף ט:

כז ב מיי' פכ"ב מהלכות שבת הלכה כז סמג לאוין סה טוש"ע א"ח סי' שטו סעיף א:

מסורת הש"ס

שבת קא. לעיל יב. יז: מח.

שבת קא. סוכה טז.

סוכה טז: ע"ש

[תוס' סוכה פ"א שבת קכה: קכז: לעיל מד. ס"א בתחלה]

ובתלמוד אחת שאינה מעורבת כצ"ל מהרש"א

[צ"ל דתניא]

רבינו חננאל

בולטין מן המים למעלה טפח או חוצבין ראשי הקנים במים טפח למנוע הדלי מלילך ולחצוב המים מרשות חבירו אלא הא דאמר רב יהודה קורה ארבעה מתיר (ברחבה) [בחורבה] ורב נחמן אמר רבה בר אבוה קורה [ארבעה] מתיר במים הא קא אזיל דלי ואייתי מיא מאידך גיסא דבורו ואם תאמר קים להו לרבנן דאין דלי מהלך וחוצב מים חוץ מארבעה תותי קורה מיהא עריבי מיא וקא חציב דלי מיא דביני ביני ופרקינן קל הוא שהקילו חכמים שאין מחיצה תלויה מתרת אלא במים וקל הוא שהקילו חכמים במים קיי"ל כרב יהודה דסוגיא דשמעתין:
פיסקא א"ר יהודה לא תהא מחיצה גדולה מן הכותל שביניהם א"ר יוחנן רבי יהודה בשיטת ר' יוסי אמרה דסבר מחיצה תלויה מתרת דתנן המשלשל דפנות מלמעלה למטה אם גבוה מן הארץ ג' טפחים כו' כבר פירשנו שמועה זו במס' סוכה ואסיקנא לא ר' יהודה סבר כר' יוסי ולא ר' יוסי סבר לה כר' יהודה ואם תאמר מעשה שנעשה בצפורי על פי מי נעשה לא על פי ר' יוסי נעשה (אמרה לא על פי ר' יוסי נעשה) אלא על פי ר' ישמעאל בר' יוסי נעשה שפעם אחת שכחו ולא הביאו ס"ת מע"ש ומצאו סדינין שהיו פרוסין ע"ג העמודים במבוי וסמכו בהן משום מחיצה והביאו ס"ת וקראו בו אמר רבה ר' יהודה ור' חנינא בן עקביא שניהם אמרו מחיצה תלויה מתרת. ר' יהודה הא דאמרן ר' חנינא בן עקביא דתניא ר' חנינא בן עקביא אומר גזוזטרא שהיא תקרה משוכה מן הכותל על הים ועומדת על ארבעה עמודים

הגהות הב"ח

(א) גמ' המשלשל דפנות מלמעלה למטה אם גבוהות: (ב) שם כשם שמלמט' למעל' י' טפחים כך מלמעל' למטה י' טפחים ולא היא וכו' ולא ר' יוסי סבר לה כר' יהודה לא ר' יהודה סבר לה כר' יוסי: (ג) שם לא על פי ר' יוסי נעשה אלא: (ד) תוס' ד"ה קורה וכו' מטעם פי תקרה ובפי תקרה: (ה) ד"ה אלא וכו' דיעקב קרחנאי ומלינו: (ו) בא"ד אצל כותלו דהוי כרמלית כצ"ל ואות כ נמחק: (ז) ד"ה גזוזטרא שיש בה ארבע אמות על ארבע כו' משמע דכי אין בה ארבע אמות על ארבע אמות אינו: (ח) בא"ד סביבותיה דאין כאן פי תקרה:

חוקק בה ד' על ד' וממלא. א"ל אביי: ודילמא לא היא; עד כאן לא קאמר רבי יהודה התם – אלא דאמר: "גוד אחית מחיצתא", אבל כוף וגוד – לא. ועד כאן לא קאמר רבי חנניא בן עקביא התם – אלא בימה של טבריא, הואיל ויש לה אוגנים, ועיירות וקרפיפות מקיפות אותה, אבל בשאר מימות – לא. אמר אביי: ולדברי ר' חנניא בן עקביא, היתה סמוכה לכותל בפחות מג' טפחים – צריך שיהא אורכה ד' אמות ורוחבה אחד עשר ומשהו. היתה זקופה – צריך שיהא גובהה עשרה טפחים, ורוחבה ו' טפחים ושני משהויין. אמר רב הונא בריה דרב יהושע: היתה עומדת בקרן זוית – צריך שיהא גובהה י' טפחים, ורוחבה ב' טפחים ושני משהויין. ואלא הא דתניא, ר' חנניא בן עקביא אומר: גזוזטרא שיש בה ד' אמות על ד' אמות – חוקק בה ד' על ד' וממלא, היכי משכחת לה? דעבידא כי אסיתא.§ **מתני'** [א]אמת המים שהיא עוברת בחצר – אין ממלאין הימנה בשבת, אלא אם כן עשו לה מחיצה גבוה י' טפחים בכניסה וביציאה. ר' יהודה אומר: כותל שעל גבה תידון משום מחיצה. אמר רבי יהודה: מעשה באמה של אבל שהיו ממלאין ממנה על פי זקנים בשבת. אמרו לו: מפני שלא היה בה כשיעור.§ **גמ'** תנו רבנן: עשו לה בכניסה ולא עשו לה ביציאה, עשו לה ביציאה ולא עשו לה בכניסה – אין ממלאין הימנה בשבת, אא"כ עשו לה מחיצה י' טפחים ביציאה ובכניסה. ר' יהודה אומר: כותל שעל גבה תידון משום מחיצה. אמר רבי יהודה: מעשה באמת המים שהיתה באה מאבל לצפורי, והיו ממלאין הימנה בשבת על פי הזקנים. אמרו לו: *משם ראייה?! מפני שלא היתה עמוקה י' טפחים ורוחבה ד'. תניא אידך: [ב]אמת המים העוברת בין החלונות, פחות מג' – משלשל דלי וממלא, ג' – אין משלשל דלי וממלא. רשב"ג אומר: פחות מד' – משלשל דלי וממלא, ד' – אין משלשל דלי וממלא. במאי עסקינן? אילימא באמת המים גופה, *דכי אתא רב דימי, אמר ר' יוחנן: [ג]אין כרמלית פחותה מד' – לימא כתנאי אמרה לשמעתיה? אלא באגפיה, ולהחליף. והא *כי אתא רב דימי, אמר רבי יוחנן: מקום שאין בו ארבעה על ארבעה – מותר לבני רשות היחיד ולבני רשות הרבים לכתף עליו, ובלבד שלא יחליפו! התם רשויות דאורייתא, הכא

רש"י

חוקק בה. נקב באמצעיתה, ואפילו אין לה מחיצות סביב הוויין לה י' טפחים הנשארים סביב הנקב לכל צד, ורואין אותן כאילו היו כפופין למטה כעין מחיצה תלויה על המים. ואמר נמי גוד אחית כאילו יורדות וסותמות עד המים והויין מים שכנגד הנקב רה"י ובליר מהכי לא סגי דאין מחיצה פחות מי' גובה ואין מחיצה פחות מד' טפחים חלל שביניהם: כוף. רוחב הנסר שיהא כפוף למטה כמחיצה ואכתי הויא מחיצה [עמוד ב] תלויה ומבעי לן למימר תו גוד אחית: אלא בימה של טבריא. דהכי אמר לקמן* דלאנשי טבריא התיר: אוגנים. שפה גבוה דהויא כמחיצות סביב לה, דאיכא קצת היכרא דהיתר. דהא כרמלית מדרבנן היא, גזרה משום הוצאה מרה"י לרה"ר. הואיל ויש לה קצת היתר, ואע"ג דאכתי כרמלית היא דהא קרפף יותר מבית סאתים שלא הוקף לדירה הוא, מיהו בתקנתא פורתא כי הא – סגי: היתה סמוכה. שהיתה כותל העליה על שפת המים, ואותו הנסר נתון על שני זיזין היוצאים מן הכותל, ושפת הנסר פחות מג' סמוך לכותל – הויא לה האי כותל חדא מן המחיצות, והאויר פחות משלשה שביניה ולכותל מהני לנקב ומוסיף עליו טפח. ומשהו פגם ברוחב הנסר על פני ד' ארכה להשלים הנקב לד' על ד' וצריך להיות בה רוחב עוד י' טפחים למימר בהו כוף למחיצה שנייה כנגד הכותל – הרי י"א רוחב ומשהו. וארכה ד' אמות, להיות י' טפחים לב' ראשיה עד הנקב, דנימא כוף. וכשאתה כופף את ב' הראשים, אע"פ שהנסר רחב י"א ומשהו – אין מועיל למחיצות חלל הנקב אלא טפח ומשהו מזה וטפח ומשהו מזה, שהרי י' טפחים בולטין מן המחיצה האמצעית ולחוץ לצד המים שהרי המחיצה האמצעית כשכפפנו אותה נמצאת עומדת בשפת הפגם, ואין מחיצות הראשין נמשכין ממנה לצד הכותל אלא טפח ומשהו, והוא מצטרף עם פחות מג' לבוד, והויא מחיצה ד': היתה זקופה. לארכה, צריך שיהא ארכה י' ורחבה ו' ושני משהויין וזקופה רחבה כנגד הכותל מופלג ד' מן הכותל, וכוף שפת רחב טפח ומשהו לכאן לצד הכותל, והרי שפתה עכשיו בפחות מג' סמוך לכותל והוא לבוד – הרי מחיצת ד' לכאן. ועוד כוף טפח ומשהו בשפת רחבה השני לצד הכותל – הרי טפח ומשהו מחיצה, ופחות מג' לבוד – הרי מחיצת ד' מכאן. ומחיצה הג' שכנגד הכותל רחבה ד' שלימין – הרי חלל ד' במחיצותיו. וגובהן י' ופותח חלון בכותלו וממלא: היתה עומדת בקרן זוית. שֶׁשְּׁנֵי כתלים מחיצות למים, ואינה צריכה אלא שתי מחיצות – צריך שיהא גובה ארכה כשהיא זקופה י' טפחים ורחבה ב' טפחים ושני משהויין, ומעמידה זקופה שפת עוביה כנגד כותל האחד מופלג ממנו פחות מג' והוא לבוד, נמצאת כאן מחיצה רחבה ה' ומשהו. וכותל השני מכוון כנגד רחבה מופלג ממנו ד' כוף טפח ומשהו היתירין על מדת רחבה, והטה אותם לצד כותל המופלג ד' – נמצאת שפת הנסר עומדת בפחות מג' והוא לבוד, הרי ב' מחיצות של ד': ואלא הא דבעי ר' חנניא. כ"ד על כ"ד היכי משכחת לה: דעבידא כאסיתא. שאין כותל סמוך לה, וקבועה על יתידות, וצריך להיות כל חללה וכל מחיצותיה ממנה, ונעשה כעין מדוכה. **מתני'** אמת המים. חסיתא מורטי"ר: אפילו ברה"י כרמלית היא: עשו לה מחיצה. בתוך אוגניה על פני רוחבה, שיהא ניכר שבשביל המים נעשית. ומחיצת החצר התלויה ועוברת על גבה אינה מועלת לה. ואע"ג דמחיצה תלויה מתרת במים – ה"מ היכא דנראית מחיצה שנעשית בשביל המים, כגון גזוזטרא דמתני' וכגון מחיצה שבתוך הבור*: של אבל. שם העיר, והיתה עוברת בתוך החצירות וממלאין הימנה בחצירות, דמהניא לה מחיצת כותל בחצר תלויה עליה ור' יהודה לטעמיה, דפליג נמי במתני' חבור: שלא היתה כשיעור. כרמלית, או בעומק י' או ברוחב ד' שאין מים נעשין רשות לעצמן בפחות מעומק י' ברוחב ד' ואם עוברת ברה"ר – הויין רה"ר, כדתנן ב"הזורק" (שבת דף ק:) הזורק ד' אמות בים פטור, דכרמלית היא ואם היה רקק מים ורה"ר מהלכת בו – חייב, דרה"ר הוא. וכמה הוא רקק מים – פחות מי' טפחים. אלמא: מים שאינן עמוקין י' אינם רשות לעצמן, וכי הוו נמי בחצר – הוו להו רה"י: **גמ'** עשו לה בכניסה ולא עשו לה ביציאה. לא מהני מידי, דהא מחוברת למים שחוץ לחצר בילייתה, ונעשית הכל כרמלית. אבל כי עשו בכניסה וביליאה – אינה כרמלית דומה כמי שמתחלת בחצר זו: שלא היתה עמוקה י'. או לא היתה רחבה ד' דלא חשיב פחות מד' למיהוי רשותא לנפשיה: בין החלונות. למבוי או לחצר, ובתים מכאן ומכאן על שפתו, וחלונות פתוחין להן למלאות: פחות מג'. מפרש ואזיל במאי קאמר: במאי עסקינן. האי שיעורא דג' וד': אי נימא ברוחב אמת המים. דקאמר ת"ק ג' רוחב הויא כרמלית, ואין ממלאין ממנה לרה"י: לימא כתנאי אמרה. דהא רבנן בג' רוחב קרו לה כרמלית (ואין ממלאין ממנה ברה"י): אלא באגפיה ולהחליף. דיש באמה שיעור כרמלית, והכא בשיש לה אגפים גבוהים, ומהני למיהוי הנך אגפים מקום פטור כי לית להו רוחב ג' ומשלשלין את הדלי ומניחו על אגפים, ומשם מחליפו לאמה וממלאהו וחוזר ומניחו על אגפים. *ומשמחליפו לרה"י, דהשתא מהני אגפים להחליף המשאוי מכרמלית לרה"י, ומרשות היחיד לכרמלית. וקאמרי רבנן: דאי אית בהו רוחב ג' – תו לא הוי מקום פטור אלא רשותא באנפי נפשיה, ולא בטיל להכא ולהכא: והא כי אתא רב דימי גופיה אמר ובלבד שלא יחליפו. דרך מקום פטור. דהא כיון דאמרינן מותר לאלו ולאלו לכתף עליו – מקום פטור חשיב ליה, וקאמר לא יחליפו: התם רשויות דאורייתא. רשות היחיד ורבים איסורא דאורייתא להוציא מזה לזה, אשתכח דמתעבדא איסורא דאורייתא דרך מקום פטור. אבל מכרמלית לרה"י רשויות דרבנן, ומחליפין דרך מקום פטור. ואע"ג דחשיב רב דימי מקום פטור בפחות מארבעה, והכא קאמרי רבנן דשלשה לא הוי מקום פטור – ליכא למימר דהא שמעתא בתרייתא דרב דימי כתנאי אמרה, דאיכא למימר דגבי רשויות דאורייתא דחשיבי – הוי פחות מד' הסמוך להו בטל אצלן, אבל לגבי כרמלית – לא בטיל מכי הוי רוחב שלשה: והא

תוספות

אמר ר' יהודה מעשה כו'. *אין זה מעשה לסתור, דאמילתיה דלעיל קאי, דלא בעי מחיצה לגס מים: הכא

[עמוד ב] [עי' תוי"ט] [שבת כט: וש"נ] שם ז. שם ח. לעיל ע. עז. ולקמן קא: [לעיל פו.] [ומשם מחליפו]

עין משפט נר מצוה

כח א ב מיי' פט"ו מהלכות שבת הלכה יא סמג עשין א טוש"ע א"ח סי' שנו סעיף א:

כט ג מיי' פי"ד מהל' שבת הלכה ד סמג לאוין סה טוש"ע א"ח סי' שמה סעיף יח:

רבינו חננאל

עמודים שיש בה ד' אמות על ד' אמות חוקק בה ד' טפחים על ד' טפחים וממלא. פי' ד' אמות הן כ"ד טפחים על כ"ד טפחים חוקק באמצע ד' טפחים על ד' טפחים נשארו י' טפחים לכל רוח חזינן להו כאילו עומדות מחיצות גבוהות (ז') [י'] טפחים ותלויות על פי החקק כמו מחיצות של בור ומתירין למלאות מים מתוכו בשבת. ודחי אביי ודלמא לא היא כדאמרת דתרווייהו חדא סברא סבירא להו דלמא עד כאן לא קא שרי ר' יהוד' אלא היכא דקיימא מחיצתא וסבר גוד אחתינהו אבל ר' חנינא בן עקביא דצריך לכוף פי' לאוקומי כדגרסינן בפרק נערה שנתפתתה כפיתו ליה אסיתא בצבור כו' דצריך לאוקומי מחיצות ולאחותינהו לא קא"ר יהודה. אי נמי עד כאן לא קא שרי ר' חנינא בן עקביא כי האי גוונא אלא בימה של טבריא הואיל ויש לו אוגנים שחשובות כמחיצות ועיירות וקרפיפות מקיפות לה. והאי דאצריך הכי חומרא דעלמא הוא דעבד אבל בשאר מימות לא אמרינן דמחיצה תלויה מתרת. אמר אביי לדברי ר' חנינא בן עקביא היתה גזוזטרא זו סמוכה לכותל בפחות מג' טפחים צריך שיהא בה אורך ד' אמות שהן כ"ד טפחים ורחב י"א טפחים *) ומשהו ופחות מג' הסמוכות לכותל שהן כלבוד הרי י"ד טפחים (ד') [י'] טפחים גובהו של כותל הרי כ"ד טפחים על כ"ד טפחים חוקק טפח ומשהו (מכי"א)* ומשהו עם פחות מג' הסמוכות לכותל נמצא חקוק ד' טפחים ועשרה טפחים הנותרים. היתה זו הגזוזטרא זקופה כלומר היא מוטלת בתוך ד' כותלים וכתלי' הללו מקיפות אותה מד' רוחותיה צריך שיהא גובה המחיצות י' וצריך להיות בה בזו הגזוזטרא ו' טפחים וב' משהויין על ו' טפחים וב' משהויין וחוקק בה ד' על ד' נשאר בה טפח ומשהו מכל צד מלא רוחב פרסת הרגל (והוא) [הוא] טפח כדגרסינן בשבת פ' א"ר עקיבא [דף פט] וכמה מלא פרסת הרגל טפח והני מילי בקרקע דלא בעיתה תשמישתיה הוא דסגי ליה להלך בפרסת רגליו רחב טפח אבל בגזוזטרא שהיא תלויה על המים ובעיתה תשמישתה בעיא רחב טפי מטפח משהו לפיכך אמר הני משהויין אמר רב הונא בריה דרב יהושע היתה עומדת בקרן זוית כמו בית טריגון צריך שיהא באלו ב' הכותלים ובכותל גזוזטרא זו יוצאה ממנו גובה עשרה בכל אחד מהן והגזוזטרא עצמה צריך להיות בה תקרה ב' טפחים ושני משהויין טפח ומשהו לכל צד מקום שנמצא בה כותל שיוצאה ממנו. ואמרינן הנה פירשת דין גזוזטרא הסמוכה לכותל ודין הזקופה ודין העומדת בקרן זוית אבל דר' חנינא היכי משכחת לה ופרקינן דגזוזטרא דעבידא כי אסיתא כלומר לא נתן לה ר' חנינא מקום פרסת הרגל אלא אמר אם היא כ"ד על כ"ד חוקק ד' טפחים באמצע נשארו י' טפחים לכל צד כדי שיעור המחיצות בלבד וכאילו פתח אסיתא היא שאין מחיצותיה צריכות רוחב להוליכה מיהו במחשבה הן אלו המחיצות וכיון שהן במחשבה הרי יש לו מקום עמידת הרגל לפיכך לא נתן הוא שיעור לעמידת הרגל (יוצאות הולכות וכלות עד באמצע בראשיהן והן כיטירין רחב רב רחבות מלמטה וקצרות מלמעלה): **ירושלמי** ר' טבלה בשם רב אין חורבה למים היה שם תקרה את רואה כאלו היא יורדת וסותמת. היה שם אמלתרא את רואה כאלו היא יורדת וסותמת. א"ר הונא והוא שתהא מחיצה בולטת לתוך חללו של בור כו' עד פשיטא שמותר לטלטל. בשם רב אמרו והוא שתהא מחיצה משוקעת במים כמלא הדלי ולא נמצא ב' רשויות משתמשות ברשות אחת. אמר רב הונא והוא [שתהא] מחיצה בתוך ג"ט לכצוצטרא: תני ר' חנינא בן עקביא א' בצוצטרא שהיא למעלה מן המים. פוחת המעזיבה ומשלשל וממלא והוא שיש בנקב ד"ט ושיהו המחיצות גבוהות י' טפחים. תמן אמרי אפילו אינן גבוהות י' נעשת כמשמרת [חד] א"ר חייא לא התיר ר' חנינא בן עקביא אלא בים של טבריא שההרים מקיפין אותה: **מתני'** אמת המים שעוברת בחצר אין ממלאין ממנה בשבת. פי' מפני שהיא ככרמלית אא"כ עשו לה מחיצה עשרה טפחים בכניסה וביציאה כו'. ת"ר עשו לה לאמת המים מחיצה גבוה עשרה טפחים בתוך המים כגון מחיצות של בור ששנינו במשנתנו בכניסה ולא עשו לה ביציאה או עשו לה ביציאה ולא עשו לה בכניסה אין ממלאין הימנה עד שיעשו לה מחיצה גבוהה י' טפחים בכניסה וביציאה. א"ר יהודה כותל החצר שעל גבה שהוא כותל החצר נידון משום מחיצה. ומעשה באמת המים שהיתה מביאה מים מאבל לציפורי וממלאין ממנה מים ע"פ זקנים בשבת. אמרו לו משם ראיה שמא אין בעמקה עשרה ולא ברחבה [ד']. תניא אידך אמת המים שעוברת ובתים מצד זה ובתים מצד זה ובהן חלונות. **) אם החלונות פחות מג' משלשל כלי וממלא ג' אין ממלא כלי וממלא. רשבג"א פחות מד' משלשל דלי וכו' ואמרינן במאי עסקינן אי נימא באמת המים גופא כלומר אם יש בה פחות מג' טפחים ת"ק סבר ממלאין ממנה כי מקום פטור הוא ואינו כרמלית אבל ג' אין ממלאין ממנה אלא כרמלית רשבג"א ממלאין עד ד' כאיצטבא [דאינה] כרמלית עד שיהא בה ד' נימא הא דר' יוחנן דא' אין כרמלית פחות מד' כתנאי אמרה לשמעתי' ופרקינן אלא באגפיה כלומר אם אין באגפיה ג' לת"ק ולרשבג"א ד' וכי איצטריך להחליף ליטול מגופה דאמת המים ולהחליף באגפיה לדלות מתוך אמת המים בדלי ולהניח הדלי באגפיה ולחזור ולהכניס דלי בחלון. ואמרינן והא כי אתא רב דימי א"ר יוחנן מקום שאין

*) אולי צ"ל וטפח ומשהו עד פחות מג' וכו'. **) נ"ע דהא מסקינן דפחות מג' אאגפיה קאי ומשמע דבברייתא גרסינן סתמא פחות מג' ואולי דתי' החלונות ט"ס.

ל א מיי' פט"ו מהלכות שבת הלכה טו סמג לאוין סה טוש"ע א"ח סי' שנה סעיף ח:
לא ב מיי' פ"ב מהלכות עירובין הלכה כ טוש"ע שם סעיף ה:
[ג"ל דתנן]
לב ג מיי' פ"ד מהל' טומאת אוכלין הלכה יא:

הָכָא רְשׁוּיוֹת דְּרַבָּנַן. וְהָא ר' יוֹחָנָן בִּרְשׁוּיוֹת דְּרַבָּנַן נַמִי אָמַר, (*דְּתַנְיָא:) *כּוֹתֶל שֶׁבֵּין ב' חֲצֵירוֹת גָּבוֹהַּ י' טְפָחִים וְרוֹחַב אַרְבָּעָה — מְעָרְבִין שְׁנַיִם, וְאֵין מְעָרְבִין אֶחָד. הָיוּ בְּרֹאשׁוֹ פֵּירוֹת — אֵלּוּ עוֹלִין מִכָּאן וְאוֹכְלִין, וְאֵלּוּ עוֹלִין מִכָּאן וְאוֹכְלִין. נִפְרַץ הַכּוֹתֶל, עַד עֶשֶׂר אַמּוֹת — מְעָרְבִין שְׁנַיִם, וְאִם רָצוּ — מְעָרְבִין אֶחָד, מִפְּנֵי שֶׁהוּא כַּפֶּתַח. יוֹתֵר מִכָּאן — מְעָרְבִין אֶחָד וְאֵין מְעָרְבִין שְׁנַיִם. וְהָוֵינַן בָּהּ: אֵין בּוֹ אַרְבָּעָה מַאי? אָמַר רַב: אֲוִיר ב' רְשׁוּיוֹת שׁוֹלֶטֶת בּוֹ, וְלֹא יָזִיז בּוֹ מְלֹא נִימָא. וְרַבִּי יוֹחָנָן אָמַר: אֵלּוּ מַעֲלִין מִכָּאן וְאוֹכְלִין, וְאֵלּוּ מַעֲלִין מִכָּאן וְאוֹכְלִין. וְאַזְדָּא רַבִּי יוֹחָנָן לְטַעְמֵיהּ, דְּכִי אֲתָא רַב דִּימִי, אָמַר רַבִּי יוֹחָנָן: מָקוֹם שֶׁאֵין בּוֹ אַרְבָּעָה עַל אַרְבָּעָה — מוּתָּר לִבְנֵי רה"ר וְלִבְנֵי רה"י לְכַתֵּף עָלָיו, וּבִלְבַד שֶׁלֹּא יַחֲלִיפוּ! הַהִיא זְעֵירִי אֲמָרָהּ. וְלִזְעֵירִי קַשְׁיָא הָא! זְעֵירִי מוֹקִים לָהּ בְּאַמַּת הַמַּיִם גּוּפָהּ. וְרַב דִּימִי תַּנָּאֵי הִיא. וְתֶיהֱוֵי כִּי חוֹרֵי כַּרְמְלִית! אַבַּיֵי בַּר אָבִין וְרַב חֲנִינָא בַּר אָבִין דְּאָמְרִי תַּרְוַיְיהוּ: אֵין חוֹרִין לְכַרְמְלִית. רַב אַשִׁי אָמַר: אֲפִילּוּ תֵּימָא יֵשׁ חוֹרִין לְכַרְמְלִית — ה"מ בִּסְמוּכָה, הָכָא בְּמוּפְלֶגֶת. רָבִינָא אָמַר: כְּגוֹן דַּעֲבַד לָהּ נִיפְקֵי אַפּוּמָּהּ. וְאָזְדוּ *רַבָּנַן לְטַעְמַיְיהוּ, וְר' שִׁמְעוֹן בֶּן גַּמְלִיאֵל לְטַעְמֵיהּ.§

מתני' [א]גְּזוּזְטְרָא שֶׁהִיא לְמַעְלָה מִן הַמַּיִם — אֵין מְמַלְּאִין הֵימֶנָּה בְּשַׁבָּת, אֶלָּא אִם כֵּן עָשׂוּ לָהּ מְחִיצָה גְּבוֹהָה עֲשָׂרָה טְפָחִים, בֵּין מִלְמַעְלָה בֵּין מִלְּמַטָּה. *[ב]וְכֵן שְׁתֵּי גְּזוּזְטְרָאוֹת זוֹ לְמַעְלָה מִזּוֹ, עָשׂוּ לָעֶלְיוֹנָה וְלֹא עָשׂוּ לַתַּחְתּוֹנָה — שְׁתֵּיהֶן אֲסוּרוֹת עַד שֶׁיְּעָרְבוּ.§

גמ' מַתְנִיתִין דְּלָא כַּחֲנַנְיָא בֶּן עֲקַבְיָא. דְּתַנְיָא, חֲנַנְיָא בֶּן עֲקַבְיָא אוֹמֵר: גְּזוּזְטְרָא שֶׁיֵּשׁ בָּהּ ד' עַל ד' אַמּוֹת — חוֹקֵק בָּהּ ד' עַל ד' וּמְמַלֵּא. אָמַר ר' יוֹחָנָן מִשּׁוּם רַבִּי יוֹסֵי בֶּן זִימְרָא: לֹא הִתִּיר רַבִּי חֲנַנְיָא בֶּן עֲקַבְיָא אֶלָּא בְּיַמָּהּ שֶׁל טְבֶרְיָא, הוֹאִיל וְיֵשׁ לָהּ אוֹגְנִים, וַעֲיָירוֹת וְקַרְפֵּיפוֹת מַקִּיפוֹת אוֹתָהּ. אֲבָל בִּשְׁאָר מֵימוֹת לֹא. ת"ר: ג' דְּבָרִים הִתִּיר רַבִּי חֲנַנְיָא בֶּן עֲקַבְיָא לְאַנְשֵׁי טְבֶרְיָא: מְמַלְּאִין מַיִם מִגְּזוּזְטְרָא בְּשַׁבָּת, וְטוֹמְנִין בָּעֵצָה, וּמִסְתַּפְּגִין בַּאֲלוּנְטִית. מְמַלְּאִין מַיִם מִגְּזוּזְטְרָא בְּשַׁבָּת — הָא דַּאֲמַרַן. וְטוֹמְנִין בָּעֵצָה מַאי הִיא? דְּתַנְיָא: *[ג]הִשְׁכִּים לְהָבִיא פְּסוֹלֶת, אִם בִּשְׁבִיל שֶׁיֵּשׁ עָלָיו טַל — הֲרֵי הוּא בְּ"כִי יוּתַּן", וְאִם בִּשְׁבִיל שֶׁלֹּא יִבָּטֵל מִמְּלַאכְתּוֹ — אֵינוֹ בְּ"כִי יוּתַּן". וּסְתָם אַנְשֵׁי

רש"י

וְהָא ר' יוֹחָנָן בִּרְשׁוּיוֹת דְּרַבָּנַן. כְּגוֹן ב' חֲצֵירוֹת: נַמִי אָמַר. דְּלֹא יַחֲלִיפוּ דֶּרֶךְ מְקוֹם פְּטוּר, דְּקָאָמַר: אֵלּוּ מַעֲלִין מִכָּאן לַכּוֹתֶל וְאֵלּוּ מַעֲלִין מִכָּאן, וְהוּא הַדִּין דְּמוֹרִידִין. אֲבָל לְאַחְלוּפֵי לֹא, דְּאָמַר הָתָם: וְאַזְדָּא ר' יוֹחָנָן לְטַעְמֵיהּ וּמַיְיתִי עֲלָהּ לְהָא דְּרַב דִּימִי מָקוֹם שֶׁאֵין בּוֹ ד' עַל ד' בָּטֵל לְאֵלּוּ וּלְאֵלּוּ וּבִלְבַד שֶׁלֹּא יַחֲלִיפוּ: אֲוִיר ב' רְשׁוּיוֹת שׁוֹלֶטֶת בּוֹ. דְּכֵיוָן דְּלָא הָוֵי ד' עַל ד' לָא הָוֵי רְשׁוּתָא לְנַפְשֵׁיהּ וְשׁוֹלְטִין שְׁנֵיהֶם בְּרוֹחְבּוֹ: וְלֹא יָזִיז. בְּרֹאשׁוֹ אֲפִילּוּ כִּמְלֹא נִימָא, וְכ"ש שֶׁלֹּא יוֹרִיד הֵימֶנָּה כְּלוּם, וְלֹא יַעֲלֶה מִן הַחֲצֵירוֹת עָלָיו כְּלוּם: אֵלּוּ מַעֲלִין כו'. דְּבָטֵיל לְגַבַּיְיהוּ לְקוּלָּא: וְאַזְדָּא ר' יוֹחָנָן לְטַעְמֵיהּ. מַסְקָנָא דְּאַתְקַפְתָּא הִיא: הַהוּא. דְּאֵלּוּ מַעֲלִין מִכָּאן וְאֵלּוּ מַעֲלִין מִכָּאן, דְּמַשְׁמַע אֲבָל לְאַחְלוּפֵי לֹא: זְעֵירִי אֲמָרָהּ. מִשְּׁמֵיהּ דְּר' יוֹחָנָן. אֲבָל לְרַב דִּימִי אַלִּיבָּא דְּר' יוֹחָנָן – מוּתָּר לְהַחֲלִיף: וְלִזְעֵירִי קַשְׁיָא הָא. דְּקָתָנֵי לְעֵיל: פָּחוֹת מִג' מְשַׁלְשֵׁל דְּלִי וּמְמַלֵּא וְלֵיכָּא לְאוֹקְמָא אֶלָּא בַּאֲגַפֶּיהָ וּלְהַחֲלִיף אַלְמָא: בִּרְשׁוּיוֹת דְּרַבָּנַן מַחֲלִיפִין דֶּרֶךְ מְקוֹם פְּטוּר: זְעֵירִי מוֹקֵי. פְּלוּגְתַּיְיהוּ דְּרשב"ג וְרַבָּנַן בְּרוֹחַב אַמַּת הַמַּיִם גּוּפָהּ. וְאָמְרִי רַבָּנַן דְּבִשְׁלֹשָׁה מִקְרְיָא כַּרְמְלִית: וּדְרַב דִּימִי. דְּאָמַר אֵין כַּרְמְלִית פְּחוּתָה מִד' תַּנָּאֵי הִיא: וְתֶיהֱוֵי כִּי חוֹרֵי כַּרְמְלִית. הַאי אַמָּה, אֲפִילּוּ לֵית בָּהּ שִׁיעוּר כַּרְמְלִית – לִיתְסַר מִשּׁוּם חוֹרֵי כַּרְמְלִית, כִּי הֵיכִי דְּאָמְרִינַן בְּמַסֶּ' שַׁבָּת (דף ז:): חוֹרֵי רְשׁוּת הָרַבִּים כִּרְשׁוּת הָרַבִּים דָּמֵי. כְּגוֹן כּוֹתֶל הַסָּמוּךְ לִרְשׁוּת הָרַבִּים וְיֵשׁ בּוֹ חוֹר, וְזָרַק אַרְבַּע אַמּוֹת וְנָח שָׁם – חַיָּיב דַּחֲשִׁיבֵי לֵיהּ הֲנָחָה בִּרה"ר – ה"נ, הוֹאִיל וְיֵשׁ בָּהּ שִׁיעוּר כַּרְמְלִית קוֹדֶם שֶׁתִּכָּנֵס לָעִיר – הַשְׁתָּא נַמִי תִּיתְסַר, דְּמִכַּרְמְלִית אָתְיָא: אֵין תּוֹרַת חוֹרִין לְכַרְמְלִית. דְּלָא אַחְמִירוּ בֵּיהּ רַבָּנַן כּוּלֵּי הַאי: בִּסְמוּכָה. כְּגוֹן חוֹר שֶׁבְּכוֹתֶל הַסָּמוּךְ לְקַרְפֵּף יוֹתֵר מִבֵּית סָאתַיִם: בְּמוּפְלֶגֶת. שֶׁאֵין בָּהּ כַּשִּׁיעוּר אֶלָּא לְמֶרְחָק: רָבִינָא אָמַר. הַאי שִׁיעוּרָא דְּג' וְד' דְּרַבָּנַן וְרשב"ג לָא בְּשִׁיעוּרָא דְּאַמָּה גּוּפָהּ וְלָא בַּאֲגַפֶּיהָ, וּלְהַחֲלִיף: אֶלָּא דַּעֲבַד לָהּ נִיפְקֵי. מוֹלָאוֹת: אַפּוּמָּהּ. בִּכְנִיסָה וּבִיצִיאָה, וְהִתְחִיל הַמְּחִיצָה סָמוּךְ לַאֲגַפֶּיהָ בְּתוֹךְ אוֹגְנֶיהָ מִכָּאן וּמִכָּאן, וְלֹא חִיבְּרָהּ בָּאֶמְצַע שֶׁיְּהוּ הַמַּיִם נִכְנָסִין וְיוֹצְאִין דֶּרֶךְ שָׁם. וְאָמְרֵי רַבָּנַן: דְּפָחוֹת מִג' – אָמְרִינַן לָבוּד, אֲבָל ג' – לָא אָמְרִינַן לָבוּד, וְאָסוּר דְּפִירְצָה הִיא: וְרַבָּן שִׁמְעוֹן לְטַעְמֵיהּ. דְּאָמַר בְּפ"ק[א] פָּחוֹת מִד' לָבוּד: **מתני'** אא"כ עָשׂוּ לָהּ. כָּל סְבִיבוֹתֶיהָ, אוֹ סְבִיב הַנֶּקֶב ד' עַל ד' הֶחָקוּק בְּאֶמְצָעִיתָהּ. דְּגוֹד אַחֵית אָמַר לְהַכְשִׁיר, אע"פ שֶׁהִיא תְּלוּיָה. אֲבָל כּוֹף וְגוֹד כַּחֲנַנְיָא בֶּן עֲקַבְיָא – לָא אָמַר: בֵּין מִלְּמַטָּה. מְחוּבֶּרֶת לַגְּזוּזְטְרָא מִתַּחְתֶּיהָ: זוֹ לְמַעְלָה מִזּוֹ. אֲפִילּוּ זוֹ שֶׁלֹּא כְּנֶגֶד זוֹ, וּבִלְבַד שֶׁלֹּא תְּהֵא מוּפְלֶגֶת מִכְּנֶגְדָּהּ בְּמֶשֶׁךְ הַכּוֹתֶל אַרְבָּעָה, כִּדְאָמַר בַּגְּמָרָא: שְׁתֵּיהֶן אֲסוּרוֹת. לְמַלְּאוֹת בַּנֶּקֶב הָעֶלְיוֹנָה עַד שֶׁיְּעָרְבוּ וְהַתַּחְתּוֹנָה בַּנֶּקֶב שֶׁלָּהּ אֵין צ"ל שֶׁהִיא אֲסוּרָה דְּהָא מִכַּרְמְלִית לִרה"י קָא מְמַלֵּא: **גמ'** חוֹקֵק בָּהּ כו'. וְאֵין צָרִיךְ בָּהּ מְחִיצָה אַחֶרֶת, דְּאָמְרִינַן "כּוֹף וְגוֹד" הוֹאִיל וְיֵשׁ עֲשָׂרָה לְכָל רוּחַ לַנֶּקֶב: מְמַלְּאִין מַיִם מִגְּזוּזְטְרָא. שֶׁיֵּשׁ בָּהּ ד' אַמּוֹת עַל ד' אַמּוֹת: וְטוֹמְנִין. פֵּירוֹתֵיהֶן בָּעֵצָה, פְּסוֹלֶת קִטְנִית. וְאַף עַל פִּי שֶׁלִּקְּטוּ מִן הַשָּׂדֶה בְּהַשְׁכָּמָה וְהַטַּל עָלָיו אֵין מַכְשִׁירִין אֶת הַפֵּירוֹת כִּדְמְפָרֵשׁ לְקַמֵּיהּ: אֲלוּנְטִית. בֶּגֶד שֶׁמִּסְתַּפְּגִין בּוֹ כְּשֶׁיּוֹצְאִין מִבֵּית הַמֶּרְחָץ: הִשְׁכִּים. קוֹדֶם הַיּוֹם, לְהָבִיא פְּסוֹלֶת תְּבוּאָה מִן הַשָּׂדֶה לְהַטְמִין בּוֹ פֵּירוֹת. אִם לְכָךְ נִתְכַּוֵּון לְהַשְׁכִּים, שֶׁרוֹצֶה וְנוֹחַ לוֹ בַּטַּל שֶׁעָלָיו, וְהִשְׁכִּים עַד שֶׁלֹּא יִיבַשׁ – הֲרֵי הוּא בְּכִי יוּתַּן: אַנְשֵׁי

תוספות

הכא רשויות דרבנן. בריש "חלון" (לעיל דף עו:) סבר רב איפכא, דברשויות דרבנן כי אין ד' בכותל שבין ב' חצירות לא יזיז אפילו כמלא נימא, דעשו הם חיזוק לדבריהם יותר משל תורה. וא"ת: דלקמן בפ' בתרא (דף קא:) משמע דרב דימי אוסר להחליף אפילו ברשויות דרבנן, גבי הא דתניא וחכ"א אף בזמן שהמנעול למעלה מי' מביא מפתח מע"ש ומניחו באיסקופה, ולמחר פותח ונועל בו ומחזירו לאיסקופה או לחלון שעל גבי הפתח. ואם יש בחלון ד' על ד' – אסור, מפני שהוא כמוציא מרשות לרשות, פי': מאיסקופה כרמלית לחלון שהוא רשות היחיד דרך מנעול שהוא מקום פטור, ואסור להחליף. ומסיק עלה: שמע מינה איתא לדרב דימי. וי"ל: דרב דימי ודאי קסבר דברייתא דלקמן פליגא אהך דשמעתין, והכי פירושא: איתא לדרב דימי, ועדיפא מדידיה, דאפילו ברשויות דרבנן אוסר להחליף, כזעירי דשמעתין: **ולזעירי** קשיא. אע"ג דהברייתא בפ' בתרא אתיא כוותיה, מ"מ בעי לאוקמי גם ברייתא דהכא כוותיה. מיהו, אור"י: דזעירי לא אתי כר' יהודה, דשרי בשבת בסוף "הזורק" (דף קא.) בספינה שגבוהה ועמוקה י' לטלטל מתוכה לים ומן הים לתוכה דרך למעלה מי' שהוא מקום פטור, כדמוכח התם: **גזוזטרא** שהיא למעלה מן[ב] הים פי' לעיל: **אלא** א"כ עשו לה מחיצה כו'. וא"ת: דהכא בעינן מחיצה, ובמסכת שבת בפרק "הזורק" (דף ק:) אמר רב הונא: ספינה מוציא ממנה זיז כל שהוא וממלא! ואור"י: דהתם שהמים עמוקים י', דאמרינן אין ספינה מהלכת בפחות מעשרה, וכרמלית מארעא משחינן והוי מים למעלה מי' מקום פטור. והכא מיירי בשאין המים עמוקים י', דכי אמרינן מארעא משחינן – אכתי מיא כרמלית. אי נמי: אפילו יש כאן עמוק י', גזרו אטו שאר גזוזטרא דאין תחתיה עמוק י', דשם צריך מחיצה למלאות. ולכך לא פליג בשום גזוזטרא. אבל ספינה לעולם מהלכת למעלה מי'. א"נ, אור"י: דהכא אפילו עמוק איכא למיחש שמא יעלה הים שירטון, אבל ספינה דמהלכת כל שעה – ליכא למיחש להכי: [ג]**עושה** מחיצה גבוה י'. והא דאמר רבה בר רב הונא בפ' "הזורק" (שבת ד' ק:): עושה מקום ד' וממלא – ע"י מחיצות י' קאמר, ולהכי בעי מקום ד', כדפי' בקונטרס לעיל* דאין מחיצה לפחות מד', ולא כפירש הקונטרס דהתם: **בין** מלמעלה בין מלמטה. מתוך פירוש הקונטרס משמע דלמעלה – היינו למעלה מן הגזוזטרא, ולמטה – למטה מן הגזוזטרא. ולא רצה לפרש הכל תחת הגזוזטרא כלמעלה ולמטה דלעיל גבי בור, משום[ד] דנקב עשוי ד' על ד' ועושה מחיצה סביב הנקב, אפילו למעלה הוי היכר: **מתני'** דלא כחנניה. אף על גב דחנניה לא אמר אלא בימה של טבריה, מתניתין נמי לא מיפליגא ומיירי בכל מימות:

[פי' ד"ה קורה ד']

רבינו חננאל

שאין בו ד' על ד' מותר לבני רשות הרבים ולבני רשות היחיד לכתף עליו ובלבד שלא יחליפו. הנה ר' יוחנן אוסר להחליף וזה להחליף הוא. ופרקינן התם רה"י ורה"ר שהן של תורה. הכא (ולא מחיצות) ברשויות דרבנן. והא ר' יוחנן בדרבנן נמי אמר שלא יחליפו דתנן כותל שבין ב' חצרות גבוה י' ורחב ד' כו' והוינן בה אין בו ד' מאי ואמר רב אויר ב' רשויות שולטות בו ואין מזיזין בו ואפי' כמלא נימא ור' יוחנן אמר אילו מעלין מיכן ואוכלין ואלו מעלין מיכן ואוכלין. ואזדא ר' יוחנן לטעמיה דכי אתא רב דימי א"ר יוחנן מקום שאין בו ד' על ד' מותר לבני רה"י ולבני רה"ר לכתף עליו ובלבד שלא יחליפו ופרקינן האי דתנינן אין בו ד' על ד' אלו מעלין מיכן ואוכלין ואלו מעלין מיכן ואוכלין דמשמע שאין מחליפין זעירי אמרה ולא ר' יוחנן. תוב אקשין ולזעירי קשיא מתני' דאוקימנא (באונייא) [באגפיה] ולהחליף ופרקינן זעירי מוקים לה באמת המים גופה. והא דכי אתא רב דימי אמר אין כרמלית פחותה מד' מוקי לה כתנאי ואקשינן הני חלונות לגבי אמת המים עצמה כי חורי כרמלית ולישתרי מים מן אמת המים עצמה דהא מכרמלית עצמה (מחורי) [לחורי] כרמלית מפיק ולא תחשביה כמפיק מכרמלית לרה"י דאינו מותר לכתחלה. (ותנינן) [ופרקינן] אין חורין לכרמלית כלומר אין דין חורין לכרמלית. ר' אבינא אמר אפי' תימא [יש חורין] לכרמלית התם כי אמרה חורין בסמוכה אבל הכא במופלגת. כלומר רחוקה היא זו אמת המים מן החלון. רב אשי אמר כגון דעבד לה ד' גפופי אפומה. פי' גפופי כגון אבנים בולטות מצדי החלון שחשובות כמחיצות ועל אלו גפופין א' ת"ק פחות מג' דהוא כלבוד ומוקפת מחיצות דפחות מג' לרבנן ולרשב"ג פחות מד' *) (מקום פטור הוא ומותר להניח עליו מן הכרמלית ולהחליף לרה"י כו'). וכן רשב"ג כו'. פירוש חשובות כמחיצות שלבוד בתוך אמת המים. לכך מותרין. ואזדא רשב"ג לטעמיה. דכל פחות מד' כלבוד דמי. ורבנן לטעמייהו דכל פחות מג' כלבוד ומבואר בפרק ראשון: **מתני'** גזוזטרא שהיא למעלה מן הים אין ממלאין הימנה בשבת אלא אם עשו לה מחיצה גבוהה י' טפחים כו'. פי' כגון שהעמיד עמודים על שפת הים ותקרה עליהן. ואמרינן מתניתין דלא כחנניה בן עקביא דמתיר בלא עשיית מחיצות אלא חוקק בלבד וממלא דתניא ר' חנניה בן עקביא אומר גזוזטרא שיש בה ד' על ד' [אמות] חוקק בה ד' טפחים וממלא בהן א"ר חנניה לא התיר ר' חנניה בן עקביא אלא בים של טבריא הואיל ויש בה אוגנים. פי' אוגנים כגון שפתים מקיפות אותה שלא יפול שם תינוק או בהמה בלילה וכיוצא בהן: **ת"ר** ג' דברים התיר ר' חנניה בן עקביא לאנשי טבריא שיהו ממלאין הגזוזטרא בשבת כדאמרן. וטומנין בעצה. שמענו בה ב' פירושים הטמנת פירות ומשום הכשרה. והטמנה בה בשבת. הטמנת פירות פי' התיר לבני טבריא להטמין פירותיהן בעצה שיש בה לחלוחית והיא תבן של קטנית וברור הוא כדתנן בשבת עצה כמלא ואמר להו אעפ"י שיש בה לחלוחית אין לחלוחית זו מכשרת הפירות לקבל טומאה. לפי שאין כוונת אנשי טבריא בלחלוחית העצה. ומפני מה אין מניחין אותה ליבש לחלוחיתה מפני שהן ממהרין לתולשה ולהביאה משום שכל היום הם טרודין במלאכתן והביא להן ראיה דתנן השכם (להן) [להביא פסולת]. אם בשביל טל שעליו נתכוון והשכים להביאן נתברר שרצונו באותו הטל והרי זה בכי יותן מים על זרע ומכשיר ואם לא השכים אלא כדי שלא יבטל ממלאכתו בשאר היום. אינו בכי יותן. ואמר כי אותם אנשי טבריא לא צריכי ללחלוחית של העצה ומפני שלא יבטלו ממלאכתן ממהרין וטומנים בהם הפירות. ותנן נמי הטומן פירותיו

*) תי' אלו עד תי' לרה"י כו' לכאורה אין לו מקום כאן דהא לפי אוקימתא זו פליגי בלבוד ואזדו לטעמייהו ולא מיירי משעור מקום פטור כלל וצ"ע.

רב נסים גאון

ואזדו רבנן לטעמייהו ורבן שמעון בן גמליאל לטעמיה והיינו דאמרי רבנן פחות מג' כלבוד דמי ורבן שמעון בן גמליאל אמר פחות מארבעה כלבוד דמי והברייתא שנזכר בה חלוקתם בפרק מבוי [דף יד ע"א] וכבר פירשנוה: **וטומנין** בעצה. איתא במס' שבת בפרק כלל גדול (דף עו) מאי עצה אמר רב יהודה תבן של מיני קטניות: **שמעת** מינה כוחו ברשויות [לא] גזרו פירושה ברשויות דרבנן כגון ב' רשויות של יחידין אחת לראובן ואחת לשמעון אי נמי (רשות היחיד וכרמלית) [מרשות היחיד לכרמלית] (דאסורין) [דאסור] מדרבנן לא גזרו חכמים בהם כחו ואיתה פירושה בפרק הזורק במס' שבת (דף ק) כוחו בכרמלית לא גזרו רבנן ומנא תימרה דתניא ספינה שבים כו' ושמע מינה כוחו בכרמלית לא גזרו רבנן שמע מינה:

לעיל עו: לקמן צב.

[לעיל ט.]

לעיל פה: [וכס פירש רש"י דלא גרסי' וכן הגי' תוס' שס סד"ה ת"ש וכו' וכתבו בשם ר"ח לגרס וכן]

[תוספתא מכשירין פ"ב]

הגהות הב"ח

(א) רש"י ד"ה ורבן שמעון לטעמיה דאמר בפ"ק דף ט': (ב) תוס' ד"ה גזוזטרא שהיא למעלה מן המים פי' לעיל: (ג) ד"ה אלא וכו' לכך הס"ד ואח"כ מ"ה עשו לה מחיצה: (ד) ד"ה בין וכו' משום להנקב עשוי:

כל

אַנְשֵׁי טְבֶרְיָא כְּמִי שֶׁלֹּא יִבָּטֵל מִמְּלַאכְתּוֹ דָּמֵי. וּמִסְתַּפְּגִין בַּאֲלוּנְטִית מַאי הִיא? *דְּתַנְיָא: [א]מִסְתַּפֵּג אָדָם בַּאֲלוּנְטִית וּמַנִּיחָהּ בַּחַלּוֹן, וְלֹא יִמְסְרֶנָּה לְאוֹלַיְירִין, מִפְּנֵי שֶׁחֲשׁוּדִין עַל אוֹתוֹ דָּבָר. ר"ש אוֹמֵר: אַף מְבִיאָהּ בְּיָדוֹ לְתוֹךְ בֵּיתוֹ. אָמַר רַבָּה בַּר רַב הוּנָא: לֹא שָׁנוּ אֶלָּא לְמַלְאוֹת, אֲבָל לִשְׁפּוֹךְ – אָסוּר. מַתְקִיף לָהּ רַב שֵׁיזְבִי: וְכִי מַה בֵּין זֶה לְעוּקָה? הָנֵי תָּיְימִי, וְהָנֵי לָא תָּיְימִי. אִיכָּא דְּאָמְרִי, אָמַר רַבָּה בַּר רַב הוּנָא: לָא תֵּימָא לְמַלְאוֹת הוּא דְּשָׁרֵי, לִשְׁפּוֹךְ אָסוּר, [ב]אֶלָּא, לִשְׁפּוֹךְ נַמִי שָׁרֵי. אֲמַר רַב שֵׁיזְבִי: פְּשִׁיטָא! הַיְינוּ עוּקָה! מַהוּ דְּתֵימָא: הָנֵי תָּיְימִי, וְהָנֵי לָא תָּיְימִי, קמ"ל. § "וְכֵן שְׁתֵּי גְזוּזְטְרָאוֹת זוֹ וכו'". § אָמַר רַב הוּנָא, אָמַר רַב: [ג]לֹא שָׁנוּ אֶלָּא בִּסְמוּכָה, אֲבָל בְּמוּפְלֶגֶת – עֶלְיוֹנָה מוּתֶּרֶת. וְרַב לְטַעְמֵיהּ, דְּאָמַר רַב: *אֵין אָדָם אוֹסֵר עַל חֲבֵירוֹ דֶּרֶךְ אֲוִיר. אָמַר רַבָּה, א"ר חִיָּיא וְרַב יוֹסֵף, אָמַר רַבִּי אוֹשַׁעְיָא: יֵשׁ גָּזֵל בַּשַּׁבָּת, וְחוּרְבָּה מַחֲזִיר לַבְּעָלִים. הָא גּוּפָא קַשְׁיָא! אָמְרַתְּ "יֵשׁ גָּזֵל בַּשַּׁבָּת" אַלְמָא(א) קַנְיָא. "וְחוּרְבָּה מַחֲזִיר לַבְּעָלִים" אַלְמָא: לָא קַנְיָא! הָכִי קָאָמַר: יֵשׁ דִּין גָּזֵל בַּשַּׁבָּת. כֵּיצַד – דְּחוּרְבָּה מַחֲזִיר לַבְּעָלִים. אָמַר רַבָּה: *וּמוֹתְבִינַן אַשְׁמַעְתִּין: וְכֵן שְׁתֵּי גְזוּזְטְרָאוֹת זוֹ לְמַעְלָה מִזּוֹ וכו'. וְאִי אָמְרַתְּ יֵשׁ דִּין גָּזֵל בַּשַּׁבָּת, אַמַּאי אֲסוּרוֹת? אָמַר רַב שֵׁשֶׁת: הָכָא בְּמַאי עָסְקִינַן – [ד]כְּגוֹן שֶׁעָשׂוּ מְחִיצָה בְּשׁוּתָּפוּת. אִי הָכִי, כִּי עָשׂוּ לַתַּחְתּוֹנָה נַמִי! כֵּיוָן דְּעָשׂוּ לַתַּחְתּוֹנָה – גַּלּוּיֵי גַּלְּיֵי דַּעְתָּהּ דַּאֲנָא בַּהֲדָךְ לָא נִיחָא לִי. §

מתני' [ה]חָצֵר שֶׁהִיא פְּחוּתָה מֵאַרְבַּע אַמּוֹת, אֵין שׁוֹפְכִין בְּתוֹכָהּ מַיִם בַּשַּׁבָּת אא"כ עָשׂוּ לָהּ עוּקָה מַחֲזֶקֶת סָאתַיִם מִן הַנֶּקֶב וּלְמַטָּה. בֵּין מִבַּחוּץ בֵּין מִבִּפְנִים, אֶלָּא שֶׁמִּבַּחוּץ צָרִיךְ לִקְמוֹר, מִבִּפְנִים אֵין צָרִיךְ לִקְמוֹר. ר"א בֶּן יַעֲקֹב אוֹמֵר: [ו]בִּיב שֶׁהוּא קָמוּר אַרְבַּע אַמּוֹת בִּרה"ר – שׁוֹפְכִים לְתוֹכוֹ מַיִם בַּשַּׁבָּת. וַחכ"א: אֲפִילּוּ גַּג אוֹ חָצֵר מֵאָה אַמָּה לֹא יִשְׁפּוֹךְ עַל פִּי הַבִּיב, אֲבָל שׁוֹפֵךְ הוּא לַגַּג וְהַמַּיִם יוֹרְדִין לַבִּיב. [ז]הֶחָצֵר וְהָאַכְסַדְרָה מִצְטָרְפִין לְאַרְבַּע אַמּוֹת. [ח]וְכֵן שְׁתֵּי דְיוֹטָאוֹת זוֹ כְּנֶגֶד זוֹ, מִקְצָתָן עָשׂוּ עוּקָה, וּמִקְצָתָן לֹא עָשׂוּ עוּקָה, אֶת שֶׁעָשׂוּ עוּקָה – מוּתָּרִין, אֶת שֶׁלֹּא עָשׂוּ עוּקָה – אֲסוּרִין. § **גמ'** מ"ט? אָמַר *רַבָּה: מִפְּנֵי שֶׁאָדָם עָשׂוּי לְהִסְתַּפֵּק סָאתַיִם מַיִם בְּכָל יוֹם, בְּאַרְבַּע אַמּוֹת – אָדָם רוֹצֶה לְזַלְּפָן,

פָּחוֹת

רש"י

אנשי טבריא. בעלי מלאכה היו: מסתפג אדם. ביום טוב. ובשבת אם רחץ בצונן מסתפג באלונטית, ואין חוששין שמא יסחוט: לאוליירין. בלנין: על אותו דבר. סחיטה: אף מביאה בידו. ואין חוששין שמא ישכח ויסחוט: לא שנו. שמחילה תלויה מתרת בגזוזטרא לרבנן, אלא למלאות: אבל לשפוך. שופכין בנקב למים – אסור, מפני שהנהר מוליך השופכין חוץ למחילת הגזוזטרא: מה בין זה לעוקה. דתנן במתני' חצר שפחותה מארבע אמות – אין שופכין לתוכה מים בשבת אא"כ עשו לה עוקה, גומא, מחזקת סאתים. ותני עלה: אע"פ שנתמלאה העוקה מבעוד יום – שופכין לה מים בשבת, ואף על פי שהמים יוצאין הימנה לרה"ר: התם תיימי מיא. המים עשויין לכלות ולהבלע בקרקע, הלכך, כי שפיך – אדעתא דליבלעו בדוכתייהו קא שפיך, ואי נפקי לבר – לאו מחשבתו להכי הוא, ולא נתקיימה מחשבתו ושרי. דאפילו איכוון – איסור ממש ליכא, דהא ברשות היחיד שפיך. אבל הכא – מידע ידיע דודאי נפקי ולא תיימי: אפילו לשפוך נמי שרי. דאיהו לא איכפת ליה דליפקו לבראי. אבל חצר הפחותה מארבע אמות – ניחא ליה דליפוק לבר שלא ילכלך את חצרו, הלכך, בעי עוקה, דבעוקה ניחא ליה דליבלעו: בסמוכה. שאינה רחוקה מתחתונה במשך הכותל ארבעה טפחים. ואני שמעתי: שאינה גבוהה ממנה עשרה. ולא מצינו לשון הפלגה בהתלמוד בגובה אלא במשך, כדתנן במתני' באנשי חצר ומרפסת. ועוד: לרב, מה לי גבוהה או נמוכה? הא איהו דאמר (לעיל ד' פג:): לזה בשלשול ולזה בזריקה – שניהם אסורין! ועוד, מהא מתניתא מותבינן תיובתא לשמואל בפירקין לעיל [פד:] ואי רב גופיה כדקיימן בגו עשרה בהדדי אוקמה, היכי מותיב לה? ואביי דתרלה כגון דקיימן בגו עשרה בהדדי – מאי חדושיה: עליונה מותרת. כדאמרינן דאין תשמיש לתחתונה בעליונה אלא דרך אויר וזריקת משך ארבעה טפחים, ורב לטעמיה, דאמר: אין אדם אוסר על חבירו דרך אויר: יש גזל בשבת וחורבה מחזיר לבעלים. השתא ס"ד דהכי קאמר: מותר לגזול בשבת רשויות, ולהשתמש בה בחורבתו של חבירו הסמוכה לו, כי היכי דרגיל בה בחול. הואיל וסתם חורבה אין הבעלים משתמשין בה כל כך, קני לה האי בגזלתו כשאר גזלנים, ונעשית רשותו. וחורבה מחזיר לבעלים משמע על כרחו איסור שבת מחזירה לבעלים, וצריך להחזירה ואין קונייה לו, אלמא: אסור להשתמש בה: יש דין גזל. דין השבת גזלה נוהג ברשות של שבת דחורבה מחזיר הגזלה לבעלים, ואסור להשתמש בה: אמאי אוסרת. הא רשותא דעליונה היא, ותחתונה זו שלא כדין משתמשת בה בחול. ואפ"ה, כיון דרגילה בה – אסרה עלה: שעשו. אותה מחיצה של עליונה בשותפות: א"ה כי עשו. בני תחתונה לתחתונה, אם יש להם שותפות בעליונה – נמי אסרי עלה: גלויי גליא דעתה. תחתונה לעליונה דסלקה נפשה בשבת מינה, דהא מחיצה זו אינה נעשית אלא להיתר שבת: **מתני'** אין שופכין לתוכה מים כו'. מפרש לה בגמ': עוקא. גומא: סאתים. בגמ' מפרש טעמא דשיעורא: מן הנקב ולמטה שמחזיק סאתים החלל שלה: בין מבפנים. בין שעשאה לעוקה בתוך החצר, בין שעשאה ברה"ר סמוך לחצר: אלא שמבחוץ צריך לקמור. לכסות פיה בנסרים שיפלו המים מידיו לתוך מקום פטור: ביב. חריץ העשוי לקלח שופכין שבחצר לרה"ר: שהוא קמור במשך ארבע אמות ברה"ר. קים לן בארבע אמות יש שיעור ליבלע בהם סאתים מים שאדם עשוי להסתפק בכל יום: שופכין לתוכו. דתיימי מיא. ואי נמי לא תיימי, דיש בו מים מבע"י, כיון דרוב ימות השנה עשוין ליבלע – הכי נמי כי נפקי לבראי לאו להכי איכוון, וכיון דלא נתקיימה מחשבתו – שרי דאפילו מתכוין לאו איסורא דאורייתא איכא הכא, דהא לאו ברה"ר זריק להו איהו גופיה, אלא מאיליהן יוצאין הלכך, כי לא מיכוין שרי לכתחילה: לא ישפוך על פי הביב. כלומר: בתוך החריץ. ואע"פ שיש אורך מכאן עד יציאתו מאה אמה, ויכולין ליבלע, כיון דבגופיה קא שפיך – מקלחי להדיא ובכח לרשות הרבים, והרואה אומר ששופכן סמוך ליציאתו, ובעי דליפקו. כדאמר בגמ': גזרה שמא יאמרו נגורו של פלוני מקלח מים בשבת: דיוטאות. עליות. וחצר פחותה מארבע אמות לפניהם, ששופכין בה מימיהם: מקצתם. בני האחת עשו עוקה בחצר, ובני האחת לא עשו: **גמ'** מ"ט. אחצר פחותה מארבע אמות קאי, דמשמע: הא ארבע אמות – שרי: אדם רוצה לזלפן. שראויה היא לזלף, להרביץ עפרה, שלא יעלה אבקה. דימות החמה מוקמינן לה למתני' לקמן בברייתא, וכיון דרוצה לזלפן – אי נמי שפיך להו ונפקי, לא מתקיימא מחשבתו:

פחות

תוספות

הני תיימי והני לא תיימי. תימה לר"י: דבמס' שבת בפרק "הזורק" (דף ק:) אמרינן דשופכין דספינה שדי להו אדופני דספינה, משום דכחו בכרמלית לא גזרו. ואע"ג דנפלו מיד לכרמלית. ומהאי טעמא נמי ליشתרי הכא! ואפילו ליסנא בתרא לא שריא לשפוך אלא משום שאינו חושש שילאו לכרמלית, כדפי' בקונטרס. ויש לומר: דבגזוזטרא, פעמים כששופכין ממנה המים הולך מיד עד מקום שרשות הרבים מהלכת ברקק מים, והוי כמו ברשות הרבים, ולא פלוג בכל גזוזטראות. אבל ספינה לא שכיחא לגמרי שתהלך סמוך לרקק:

ביב שהוא קמור ד' אמות ברשות הרבים. פירש בקונטרס: בארבע אמות קים ליה שיש שיעור ליבלע סאתים מים שעשוי להסתפק בכל יום. והיינו טעמא דקאמר בגמ' גבי חצר ארבע אמות תיימי. ולפירושו נראה דאיירי בביב שיש לו ארבע על ארבע, דפחות מכאן לא תיימי, כמו גבי חצר, כדפירש רש"י בגמרא, דאיזו שיעור ניתן לרחבו? ולרבינו שמואל נראה טעמא דקמירת ביב – משום חשדא, וכיון דקמור הוא ד' אמות ברה"ר, הרואה מים יוצאין מן הביב – אינו סבור שיוצאין מן החצר, כיון שרחוק מן החצר ד' אמות. ובגמ' משמע כפירוש הקונטרס, דמדמה ארבע אמות דביב לארבע אמות דחצר, דקאמר כולה כר"א בן יעקב כו'. ולפי' רבינו שמואל: סילון שקמור ארבע אמות ברשות הרבים שופכין לו מים בשבת, דקי"ל*: משנת ר"א בן יעקב קב ונקי. אבל לפ"ה, דהטעם משום דמיבלעי – אסור, דבשל עץ לא מיבלעי. ומיהו, אומר ר"י: דאפילו עשוי כעין רצפה של אבנים – מיבלעי, ושרי:

תנא

עין משפט נר מצוה

לג א מיי' פכ"ב מהל' שבת הלכה כ טור ש"ע א"ח סי' שא סעיף מח:

לד ב מיי' פט"ו מהל' שבת הלכה טו סמג לאוין סה טור ש"ע א"ח סי' שנה סעיף א:

לה ג ד מיי' פ"ד מהל' עירובין הלכה כה טוש"ע שם סעיף ה:

לו ה מיי' פט"ו מהל' שבת הלכה טז סמג לאוין סה טוש"ע א"ח סי' שנז סעיף א:

לז ו מיי' שם הלכה יח טוש"ע שם סעיף ב:

לח ז מיי' שם הלכה טז טוש"ע שם סעיף א:

לט ח מיי' פ"ד מהלכות עירובין הלכה כז סמג שם טוש"ע א"ח סי' שעז:

מסורת הש"ס

שבת קמז:

[לעיל פה.]

[קידושין נ: וש"נ]

[גי' רי"ף ורא"ש רבא וכ"י רב]

[לעיל סב:]

הגהות הב"ח

(א) גמ' אלמא קני והדר תני וחורבה מחזיר:

רבינו חננאל

במים מפני הגנבים אינו בכי יותן. מעשה באנשי ירושלים שטמנו דבלותם במים מפני הסיקרים וטיהרו להן חכמים. הנה זה הטעם מי שאומר כי הטמנת פירות משום הכשרן. אבל טעם הטמנת תבשיל בשבת שאין נמנעים מלהטמין בעצה לחה שהיו אומרים תבן הוא. ותנן לא בתבן ולא בזגין ולא במוכין בזמן שהן לחים ואם עשבים הוא גם העשבים הלחים אסור להטמין בהן. ואמר להן ר' חנניא בן עקביא עצה זו אינה לא תבן ולא עשבין שאינה מפורשת מה הן בפי' ועצה זו כיון שאין בני טבריא חפצים בלחלוחית שבהן מותר להטמין בה בשבת ולא גזרינן עצה מפני תבן. גם התיר להן להסתפג באלונטית כדתניא מסתפג אדם באלונטית ומניחה בחלון הפתוח לרה"ר ומביאה לתוך ביתו כו': **אמר** רבה בר רב הונא לא שנו אלא למלאות מן אמת המים או מן הים אבל לשפוך אסור איכא דאמרי לא תימא למלאות שרי הא לשפוך על הים מתוך הגזוזטרא אסור אלא אפילו לשפוך נמי שרי. אמר רב שיזבי הא פשיטא דהיינו עוקה שמותר לשפוך מים לתוכה ואמרינן מה הוא דתימא בעוקה תיימי מיא ונבלעים משום הכי שרי. אבל הכא בים דהמים אין נבלעין הן אלא נמשכים על פני המים ולא תיימי להו אסור קמ"ל דשרי אפילו לשפוך: **מתני'** וכן ב' גזוזטראות. אמר רב הונא אמר רב לא שנו אלא בסמוכה אבל במופלגת עליונה מותרת: מקשינן אהא דאמרינן יש גזל בשבת מחורבה מחזיר לבעלים. הא גופא קשיא אמרת יש גזל בשבת אלמא מאן דגזל רשותא דחבריה ואחזיק בה ובנה קנאה בשינוי ושרי ליה לטלטולי בשבת דהוה לה כולה רשותיה. והדר אמרת דחורבה יחזיר לבעלים כלומר יחזור רשות של חבירו שגזל כמו שהוא בעינה אלמא לא קנה. ופרקינן ה"ק יש דין גזל בשבת. כיצד דין גזל בזמן שהכניסו גזלן לרשותו אבל אם הניחו בחורבה שהיא של נגזל החורבה יחזיר לבעלים. כלומר אם גזל מחבירו חורבתו ולא בנאה לא קנאה שהרי לא עשה בה כלום לקנותה. ולפיכך לא קנאה בחזקה אלא היא עדיין חורבה ויחזיר לבעלים כמות שהיא בעינה דהא לא קנאה (אלא) [אבל] בנה והחזיק בה קנאה. אמר רבה ומותבינן על זו השמועה איני. שהבונה ברשות חבירו. בגזלה והמחזיק בגזלה קנאה. והתנן ב' גזוזטראות זו למעלה מזו עשו לעליונה מחיצה למעלה ולמטה. (עוד עשו לה מחיצה *) ולא עשו לתחתונה שתיהן אסורות. והא עליונה החזיקה מעבר על גבי התחתונה בגזילה. וא"כ הוא שיש דין גזל בשבת וקנה הגזילה אמאי אסורה *). דרגל העליונה דורסתה אלא עליונה אמאי אסורה הרי יש לה מחיצות ורשות התחתונה שעוברת עליה הרי קנאתה בחזקה אלא מדקתני שתיהן אסורות עד שיערבו ש"מ שאין גזל בשבת. וכי כל אחד אוסרת על חברתה. ופריק רב ששת כגון שעשו מחיצ' בשותפות שגלתה דעתה דלאו (מניה) [מחמת] גזילה קאתו ונעשו כאילו ב' בתים בחצר אחת שצריכין עירוב. ומקשינן אי הכי כי עשו לתחתונה נמי מחיצות למעלה ביניהן ועוד עשו למטה תהיינה אסורות עד שיערבו דהא אמרת נעשו כב' בתים בחצר אחת. ופרקינן כיון דחזרו ועשו לתחתונה מחיצה למטה סליקו נפשייהו מן העליונה דגליא דעתא דלא ניחא ליה שותפות בהדיה ומחיצות הוויין חלוקה ביניהן אבל כל אחת זכתה לעצמה לפיכך שתיהן מותרות: **ירושלמי** ר' חנניה בן עקביא התיר ג' דברים. התיר עצה שבים. והבאת אלונטית. והתיר גזוזטרא. ר' אבא ור' יוסי הדא דאת אמרת במשתמשות דרך הנקב אבל משתמשות מחוץ מותר. ותני כן ג' גזוזטראות זו ע"ג זו אסור להשתמש מן העליונה לתחתונה דרך האמצעית. אבל משתמש מן החצר לגג ואינו חושש הדא דקאמר בפנים אבל מבחוץ אסור. ר' זעירא אמר בין מבחוץ בין מבפנים אסור. מתניתא פליגא על ר' זעירא משלשין קדרות בשר מעל גבי זיז שגבוה י"ט ורחב ד' אם היה חלון בינתים של ד"ט אסור. שאין [משתמשין] מרשות לרשות דרך רשות. ר' שמואל בר רב יצחק פתר לה (בשובה) [בשוה]: **מתני'** חצר שפחותה מד' אמות אין שופכין לתוכה מים בשבת אא"כ עשו לה עוקה מחזקת סאתים כו'. פי' עוקה מלשון חקיקה והיא כמו חפירה בארץ להתקבץ בו המים מ"ט אמר רבה

סאתים

*) נראה דחסר כאן וצ"ל אמאי אסורה העליונה בשלמא התחתונה אסורה דרגל העליונה דורסתה וכו'.

מ א ב ג מיי' פכ"ג מהלכות שבת הלכה טז יז סמג שם טוש"ע א"ח סי' שנז סעיף א:

פחות מד' – שופכן. אי דעביד עוקה – שרי, אי לא – אסור. ר' זירא אמר: [א]ד' אמות – תיימי, פחות מד' אמות – לא תיימי. מאי ביניייהו? אמר אביי: אריך וקטין איכא ביניייהו. תנן: חצר ואכסדרה מצטרפין לד' אמות. בשלמא לרבי זירא – ניחא, אלא לרבה קשיא! *תרגמא רבי זירא אליבא דרבה: באכסדרה מהלכת על פני כל החצר כולה. ת"ש: חצר שאין בה ד' אמות על ד' אמות – אין שופכין לתוכה מים בשבת. בשלמא לרבה – ניחא, אלא לר' זירא קשיא! אמר לך ר' זירא: הא מני – רבנן היא, ומתני' ר"א בן יעקב היא. ומאי דוחקיה דר' זירא לאוקמה למתני' כר"א בן יעקב? אמר רבא: מתניתין קשיתיה; מאי איריא דתני "חצר שהיא פחותה" ליתני "חצר שאין בה ד' אמות[א] על ד' אמות"! אלא לאו – ש"מ דר"א בן יעקב היא, ש"מ. והא מדסיפא ר' אליעזר בן יעקב, רישא לאו ר"א בן יעקב! כולה ר"א בן יעקב היא, וחסורי מיחסרא והכי קתני: חצר שהיא פחותה מד' אמות – אין שופכין לתוכה מים בשבת, הא ד' אמות – שופכין, שר"א בן יעקב אומר: ביב הקמור ד' אמות ברה"ר שופכין לתוכו מים בשבת.§ "ר"א בן יעקב אומר: ביב הקמור".§ מתני' דלא כחנניא. דתניא, חנניא אומר: אפילו גג מאה אמה – לא ישפוך, לפי שאין הגג עשוי לבלוע אלא לקלח. תנא: [ב]במה דברים אמורים – בימות החמה, אבל בימות הגשמים – שופך ושונה ואינו נמנע. מ"ט? אמר רבא: אדם רוצה שיבלעו מים במקומן. אמר ליה אביי: והרי שופכין, דאדם רוצה שיבלעו, וקתני "לא ישפוך"!(א) א"ל: התם למאי ניחוש לה? אי משום קלקול חצירו – הא מיקלקלא וקיימא, ואי משום גזירה שמא יאמרו צנורו של פלוני מקלח מים – סתם צנורות מקלחים הם. אמר רב נחמן: בימות הגשמים, עוקה מחזיק סאתים – נותנין לו סאתים, מחזיק סאה – נותנין לו סאה. בימות החמה, מחזיק סאתים – נותנין לו סאתים, סאה – אין נותנין לו כל עיקר. בימות החמה נמי, מחזיק סאה ניתיב ליה סאה! גזרה דלמא אתי ליתן ליה סאתים. א"ה, בימות הגשמים נמי ליגזור! התם מאי ניחוש לה? אי משום קילקול – הא מיקלקלא וקיימא, אי משום גזירה שמא יאמרו צנורו של פלוני מקלח מים – סתם צנורות מקלחין הן. אמר אביי: [ג]הילכך, אפילו כור ואפילו כוריים.§ "וכן שתי דיוטאות זו כנגד זו".§ אמר רבא: אפילו עירבו. אמר (*ליה) אביי: מאי טעמא? אילימא משום נפישא דמיא – והתניא: אחת לי עוקה ואחת לי גיסטרא בריכה ועריבה, אף על פי שנתמלאו מים מערב שבת – שופכין לתוכן מים בשבת! אלא אי איתמר – הכי איתמר: אמר רבא: לא

רש"י

פחות מד'. אינו ראוי לזלף ושופכן. וכי נפקי, מקיימא מחשבתו. וגזור רבנן עליה דילמא אתי למישרי זריקה בהדיא לרה"ר: תיימי. מיא בד' אמות ראוין ליבלע סאתים. הלכך, אי נמי נפקי לבר – לא מקיימא מחשבתו: דאריך וקטין. כגון שישנה ח' אמות על שתים, דאיכא קרקע כשיעור ד' מרובעות, ויש מקום להבלע סאתים, אבל לזלף אינה ראויה. (*לרבה) אסור לשפוך בלא עוקה, לר' זירא לא בעי עוקה. ובין למר ובין למר, ד' אמות דמתני' באורך וברוחב משמע. דאי לא יהיב שיעורא נמי לפותיא – אין כאן שיעור מפורש כלום. ומשמע אפילו רחבה משהו, וליכא לאוקומי בה טעמא: תנן החצר ואכסדרה מצטרפין לד' אמות. לפוטרה מן העוקה. קס"ד באכסדרה העומדת חוץ לחצר כנגד אחד מן המקצועות, ומצטרפת להשלים השיעור. אלמא: טעמא כדי שיהא שם שיעור לבליעת המים הוא, דהא הכא לאו ד' מרובעות נינהו דליתחזו לזלף: באכסדרה מהלכת על פני כל החצר. כגון חצר ארבע על שתים, ואכסדרה מהלכת על פני כולה להשלים ד' על ד': ד' אמות על ד' אמות גרס בברייתא, אלמא: מרובעות בעינן: הא מני רבנן היא. דלא שרו ליה משום שיעור מקום בליעת המים כדתנן במתני' אפילו ביב מאה אמה לא ישפוך לתוכו, אלא על הגג או על החצר. אלמא: טעמא דידהו משום זילוף הוא. וגבי ביב מגלי דעתיה דקא שפיך דלאו בר זילוף הוא. ורישא דמתני' ר"א בן יעקב היא, דאמר: טעמא משום שיעור מקום לבליעה, כדתנן: ביב שהוא קמור ד' אמות: ומאי דוחקיה דרבי זירא. לפרושי מתני' משום דתיימי מיא, ושרי ליה באריך וקטין, ומיבעי ליה לאוקומי כר"א. לוקמה דבעיא ד' אמות מרובעות, ומשום זילוף, וכרבנן: שהיא פחותה. משמע שחסר שיעורה. הא יש בה שיעור ד' אמות על ד' אמות – לא שנא בריבוע, ולא שנא באריך וקטין – שרי: ליתני חצר שאינה ד' על ד' אמות. דמשמע שאינה עשויה בריבוע זה – ואפילו יש בה כשיעור: מתני'. דקתני לרבנן: אבל שופך הוא על הגג והן יורדין לביב, כלומר: לצנור החקוק בו: דלא כחנניא. דלדידיה, בחצר שרי בגג אסור. גגין שלהן לא היו משופעין, אלא חלקין כעין עליות שלנו, וטחין אותו בטיט מעזיבה וחוקקין צנורות לקלח גשמים, ושופכין השופכין שם: במה דברים אמורים. דצריך עוקה: שיבלעו במקומן. ולא איכפת ליה דליפקו, דבלאו הכי חצרו מטונפת ועומדת מפני הגשמים: א"ל אביי והרי שופכין. השופכין לו לביב ארוך מאה אמה, שיש בו שיעור להיבלע בו. וקא אמרי רבנן במתניתין: לא ישפוך. להנך דביב קרי שופכין סתמא, ולהנך דחצר קרי מים, לפי שפעמים הוא מזלפן: התם. בימות הגשמים למאי ניחוש? אי משום דניחא ליה דניפקו משום קלקול חצרו: הא מקלקלא וקיימא. בגשמים: אי משום שלא יאמרו. ואתי למעבד בימות החמה, אי נמי אתי למימר שרי לזרוק בהדיא לרה"ר, דמה לי בצנור ומה לי ברה"ר ממש האי נמי להכי מתכוון – להא ליכא למיחש, דסתם צנורות בימות הגשמים מקלחין הן, ואמרו מי גשמים נינהו. אבל גבי ביב בימות החמה, אע"ג דיש בו שיעור, ואדם רוצה שיבלעו במקומן – איכא למיחש שמא יאמרו: מחזיק סאה. עוקה, נותנין לו רשות להסתפק ולשפוך סאה. והאי דקאמרי לעיל: שופך ושונה ואינו נמנע – ס"ל לר"נ בעוקה קטנה, ושיעור מדתה קאמר תנא דברייתא דשרי: התם למאי ניחוש לה. אי נמי אתי למיתב סאתים – לא איכפת לן, דהא הוא גופיה לא יליף מינה חורבה, למימר כי היכי דשרי ליה לשפוך בעוקה זו כדי לצאת לחוץ, ה"נ שרי למשדינהו לברא – דהא לא מקיימא מחשבתו, ולא ניחא ליה דליפקו מיא, דהא חצרו מקלקלא וקיימא: ואי משום שמא יאמרו. הרואים, הרי צנורו של פלוני כו' וסבורין שהוא מתכוון לכך: סתם צנורות כו'. ומיהו, לכתחלה לא שרינן ליה טפי משיעורא: אמר אביי הלכך. כיון דליכא למיחש למידי: אפילו כור וכוריים. קא שרי תנא דברייתא: ואפילו עירבו. שתי העליות, דליכא למיחש אי שרי להו להני ע"י עוקא דהנך, אתי לאפוקי מאני מן הבתים ולהורידן לחצר בהדיא עד שפת העוקה ברגליהם, וקא מטלטל בחצר דלא מיערב – אפילו הכי אסור: משום נפישא דמיא. דיש כאן ארבע אמות לשני בתים: גיסטרא. כלי חרס שנסדק, ונתנו שם חליו לקבל המים. להכי נקט גיסטרא, דלא חזיא לתשמישא אחרינא: בריכה. חריץ רחב, כעין ביבר שעושין לדגים: עריבה. ספינה קטנה: ה"ג:

תוספות

תנא במה דברים אמורים. פי' הקונט': במה דברים אמורים – דצריך עוקה. ולפירושו צ"ל דלרב נחמן דבסמוך ה"פ: במה דברים אמורים שצריך עוקה – של סאתים, אבל בימות הגשמים אין צריך עוקה של סאתים אבל עוקה של סאה – צריך. ודוקא כדי מלתה שופך ושונה בה. וכן פירש בקונטרס בסמוך. והא דלא מייתי התלמוד הך ברייתא לעיל אמתני' דעוקה – משום דבעי לאקשויי עלה ממתני' דכ"ב. ור"ת מפרש דאמתני' (ב)לא ישפוך על הכ"ב קיימא ברייתא, והא דקאמר והרי שופכין – כלומר: והרי כ"ב. וגרסינן: "אלא למאי ניחוש לה", ולאכ כמו שכתוב בספרים "אלא התם":

מחזיק סאתים נותן לתוכו סאתים. לאו דוקא סאתים, אלא אפילו כוריים. דאי לאו הכי – אין חילוק בין סאתים לסאה: לא

רבינו חננאל

סאתים מים אדם עשוי להסתפק בכל יום בחצר שהיא בד' אמות ולמעל' ניחא ליה לאיניש לזלפן בחצר שהיא פחותה מד' אמות שופכן. אי איכא עוקא להתקבץ בה המים שרי ואי לא נעשה כשופכין מבחוץ לחצר ברה"ר ואסור. רב זירא אמר בד' אמות תיימי מיא פחותה מד' אמות לא תיימי מיא בחצר אלא נפקא ברה"ר ואמר אביי חצר אריכא וקטינא (דאי) איכא בינייהו לרבה אסור דהא לא מזדלפי לרב זירא שרי דהא כיון דאריכא תיימי מיא. תנן חצר ואכסדרא מצטרפין לד' אמות קשיא לרבה. ופריק כגון שהיתה אכסדרה מקפת את החצר שנמצאת החצר והאכסדרה ד' אמות על ד' אמות. ת"ש חצר שפחותה מד' אמות אין שופכין לתוכה מים בשבת. קשיא לר' זירא ומשני הא רבנן היא דבעי ד' אמות על ד' אמות ומתניתין ר' אליעזר בן יעקב היא. דתנן ביב שקמור ד' אמות ברה"ר שופכין לתוכו מים בשבת הנה אע"פ שאין בו ד' אמות על ד' אמות קתני שופכין לתוכה מים בשבת. ומאי דוחקי דרב זירא לאוקומי למתני' כר' אליעזר בן יעקב נוקמה כרבנן. אמר רבא מתני' קשיתיה מאי איריא חצר שפחותה מד' אמות ניתני חצר שאין בה ד' אמות אלא מאי פחותה פחותה מכל צד. הא אריכא וקטינא שופכין. והכי קתני חצר שפחותה מד' אמו' אין שופכין לתוכה מים בשבת. הא יש בה ד' אמות שופכין שר' אליעזר בן יעקב אומר ביב שקמור ד' אמות ברה"ר שופכין לתוכו מים בשבת. פי' ביב קמור (י' קנ"א היא ממיל מיצהד"ג). מתני' דקתני אבל שופך לגג והן יורדין לביב דלא כחנניה דתניא חנניה אומר אפילו גג ק' אמות לא ישפוך לתוכו מים לפי שאין הגג עשוי לבלע אלא לקלח לרה"ר. תנא במד"א בימות החמה אבל בימות הגשמים שופך ושונה ואינו נמנע. מאי איכא למימר שמא יאמרו צינורו של פלוני מקלח מים. סתם צינורות מקלחין הן. אמר רב נחמן בימות הגשמים עוקה מחזקת סאתים נותנין לו סאתים סאה נותנין לו סאה בימות החמה מחזקת סאתים נותנין לו סאתים סאה אין נותנין לו כל עיקר. ואמרינן בימות החמה נמי ניתיב לו סאה גזירה שמא יתן לו בה סאתים אי הכי בימות הגשמים נגזור ופרקינן הכי השתא בימות הגשמים במאי ניחוש לה אי משום חצרו הא קא מיקלקלא וקיימא כו' א' אביי הלכך אפילו כור אפילו כוריים שרי: **פיסקא** וכן ב' דיוטאות ב' חצרות זו כנגד זו מקצ' כו'. אמר רבה אפילו עירבה ב' דיוטאות זו עם זו לשפוך זו שאין לה עוקה (של זו) לשל זו שיש לה עוקה. ומקשה אביי מ"ט גזרינן דלמא אתי לאפושי בעוקה אי הכי אפי' עירבו נגזור דלמא אתי לאפושי יתר מבית סאתים בעוקה. ותוב מי חיישינן לרבויי מיא. והתניא אחת

מסורת הש"ס

[נ"ל לרבה]

[שבת נב: וש"נ]

רש"ל מ"ז

הגהות הב"ח

(א) גמ' וקתני לא ישפוך א"ל נ"ב כן הוא בספרים אחרי' אבל התוס' גרס אלא: (ב) תוס' ד"ה תנא וכו' דאמתניתין דלא ישפוך:

הגהות הגר"א

[א] גמ' תיבות על ד' אמות מוקפות.

לֹא שָׁנוּ אֶלָּא שֶׁלֹּא עֵירְבוּ, אֲבָל עֵירְבוּ — מוּתָּרִין. וְכִי לֹא עֵירְבוּ מַאי טַעְמָא לֹא? אָמַר רַב אַשִׁי: גְּזֵירָה דִּילְמָא אָתֵי לְאַפּוֹקֵי מִמָּאנֵי דְּבָתִּים לְהָתָם.§

הדרן עלך כיצד משתתפין

כָּל גַּגּוֹת הָעִיר רְשׁוּת אַחַת, וּבִלְבַד שֶׁלֹּא יְהֵא גַּג גָּבוֹהַּ י' אוֹ נָמוּךְ י', דִּבְרֵי ר"מ. וחכ"א: כָּל אֶחָד וְאֶחָד רְשׁוּת בִּפְנֵי עַצְמוֹ. *רַבִּי שִׁמְעוֹן אוֹמֵר: אֶחָד גַּגּוֹת וְאֶחָד חֲצֵירוֹת וְאֶחָד קַרְפֵּיפוֹת — רְשׁוּת אַחַת הֵן לְכֵלִים שֶׁשָּׁבְתוּ לְתוֹכָן, וְלֹא לְכֵלִים שֶׁשָּׁבְתוּ בְּתוֹךְ הַבַּיִת.§ **גמ'** יָתֵיב אַבָּיֵי בַּר אָבִין וְרַבִּי חֲנִינָא בַּר אָבִין, וְיָתֵיב אַבָּיֵי גַּבַּיְיהוּ, וְיָתְבִי וְקָאָמְרִי: בִּשְׁלָמָא רַבָּנַן סָבְרִי: כְּשֵׁם שֶׁדִּיוּרִין חֲלוּקִין לְמַטָּה — כָּךְ דִּיוּרִין חֲלוּקִין לְמַעְלָה. אֶלָּא רַבִּי מֵאִיר מַאי קָסָבַר? אִי קָסָבַר כְּשֵׁם שֶׁדִּיוּרִין חֲלוּקִין לְמַטָּה כָּךְ דִּיוּרִין חֲלוּקִין לְמַעְלָה — אַמַּאי רְשׁוּת אַחַת הֵן? וְאִי קָסָבַר אֵין חֲלוּקִין, דְּכָל לְמַעְלָה מִי' רְשׁוּת אַחַת הִיא — אֲפִילּוּ גַּג גָּבוֹהַּ עֲשָׂרָה וְנָמוּךְ י' נָמֵי! אֲמַר לְהוּ אַבָּיֵי: לָא שְׁמִיעַ לְכוּ הָא *דְּאָמַר רַב יִצְחָק בַּר אַבְדִּימִי, אוֹמֵר הָיָה רַבִּי מֵאִיר: כָּל מָקוֹם שֶׁאַתָּה מוֹצֵא שְׁתֵּי רְשׁוּיוֹת וְהֵן רְשׁוּת אַחַת, כְּגוֹן עַמּוּד בִּרה"י גָּבוֹהַּ עֲשָׂרָה וְרָחָב ד' — אָסוּר לְכַתֵּף עָלָיו, גְּזֵירָה מִשּׁוּם תֵּל בִּרה"ר. ה"נ — גְּזֵירָה מִשּׁוּם תֵּל בִּרה"ר. סְבוּר מִינַּהּ: אֲפִילּוּ מַכְתֶּשֶׁת וַאֲפִילּוּ גִּיגִית. אֲמַר לְהוּ אַבָּיֵי, הָכִי אָמַר מָר: לֹא אָמַר ר"מ אֶלָּא עַמּוּד וְאַמַּת הָרֵיחַיִם, הוֹאִיל וְאָדָם קוֹבֵעַ לָהֶן מָקוֹם. וַהֲרֵי כּוֹתֶל שֶׁבֵּין ב' חֲצֵירוֹת דְּקָבוּעַ, *וְאָמַר רַב יְהוּדָה: כְּשֶׁתִּימְצֵי לוֹמַר לְדִבְרֵי ר"מ: גַּגִּין רְשׁוּת לְעַצְמָן, חֲצֵירוֹת רְשׁוּת לְעַצְמָן, קַרְפֵּיפוֹת רְשׁוּת לְעַצְמָן. מַאי לָאו — דִּשְׁרֵי לְטַלְטוֹלֵי דֶּרֶךְ כּוֹתֶל! אָמַר רַב הוּנָא בַּר יְהוּדָה, אָמַר רַב שֵׁשֶׁת: לֹא, לְהַכְנִים וּלְהוֹצִיא דֶּרֶךְ פְּתָחִים.§ "וחכ"א כָּל אֶחָד וְאֶחָד רְשׁוּת בִּפְנֵי עַצְמוֹ".§ אִיתְּמַר, *רַב אָמַר: אֵין מְטַלְטְלִין בּוֹ אֶלָּא בְּד' אַמּוֹת, וּשְׁמוּאֵל אָמַר: מוּתָּר לְטַלְטֵל בְּכוּלּוֹ. בִּמְחִיצוֹת הַנִּיכָּרוֹת — דְּכוּלֵּי עָלְמָא לָא פְּלִיגִי. כִּי פְּלִיגִי — בִּמְחִיצוֹת שֶׁאֵינָן נִיכָּרוֹת. רַב אָמַר: אֵין מְטַלְטְלִין בּוֹ אֶלָּא בְּד' אַמּוֹ', לָא אָמַר גּוּד אַסִּיק מְחִיצָתָא, וּשְׁמוּאֵל אָמַר: מוּתָּר לְטַלְטֵל בְּכוּלּוֹ, דְּאָמַר גּוּד אַסִּיק מְחִיצָתָא. תְּנַן, וַחֲכָמִים אוֹמְרִים: כָּל אֶחָד וְאֶחָד רְשׁוּת

רש"י

הָכִי גָּרְסִינַן: דִּילְמָא אָתֵי לְאַפּוֹקֵי מַיָּא בְּמָאנֵי דְּבָתִּים לְהָכָא. לִשְׂפַת הָעוּקָה לִשְׁפּוֹךְ לְתוֹכָהּ:

הדרן עלך כיצד משתתפין

כָּל גַּגּוֹת הָעִיר רְשׁוּת אַחַת. וְאַף עַל פִּי שֶׁדִּיוּרִין חֲלוּקִין לְמַטָּה לִשְׁנֵי בְּנֵי אָדָם, הַגַּגּוֹת שֶׁאֵין תַּשְׁמִישָׁן תָּדִיר — אֵין בָּהֶם חִילּוּק רְשׁוּת, וְכֵלִים שֶׁשָּׁבְתוּ בְּגַג זֶה מוּתָּרִין לְהוֹצִיאָם לְזֶה: וּבִלְבַד שֶׁלֹּא יְהֵא גַּג גָּבוֹהַּ. מֵחֲבֵירוֹ עֲשָׂרָה. דְּאִם חָלוּק מֵהֶן בְּגוֹבַהּ י' — אָסוּר לְטַלְטֵל מִמֶּנּוּ לַגַּגִּין. וְטַעְמָא מְפָרֵשׁ בַּגְּמָ': וחכ"א כָּל אֶחָד וְאֶחָד רְשׁוּת לְעַצְמוֹ. וְאִם לֹא עֵירְבוּ דִּיוּרִין שֶׁלְּמַטָּה — אָסוּר לְטַלְטֵל מִזֶּה לָזֶה: ר' שִׁמְעוֹן. מֵיקֵל מִכּוּלָּם, וְאָמַר: חֲצֵירוֹת וְגַגּוֹת וְקַרְפֵּיפוֹת שֶׁאֵינָן יוֹתֵר מִבֵּית סָאתַיִם, הוֹאִיל וְכוּלָּם אֵין תַּשְׁמִישָׁן מְיוּחָד וְתָדִיר — רְשׁוּת אַחַת הֵן. וּמְטַלְטְלִין מִזֶּה לָזֶה, אֲפִילּוּ מֵחָצֵר שֶׁל רַבִּים לְחָצֵר רַבִּים בְּלֹא עֵירוּב. וְלֵית לֵיהּ לר"ש עֵירוּבֵי חֲצֵירוֹת אֶלָּא מִשּׁוּם הֶיתֵּר כְּלֵי הַבַּיִת: לְכֵלִים שֶׁשָּׁבְתוּ בְּתוֹכָן. כֵּלִים שֶׁשָּׁבְתוּ בְּאֶחָד מֵהֶן, מוֹלִיכִין אוֹתָן מִזֶּה לָזֶה: אֲבָל לֹא לְכֵלִים שֶׁשָּׁבְתוּ בְּתוֹךְ הַבַּיִת. וְהֶיאָךְ לַחֲצֵירָן ע"י שֶׁעֵירְבוּ בְּנֵי הֶחָצֵר, אָסוּר לְהוֹצִיאָן מֵחֲצֵירוֹ לְחָצֵר אַחֶרֶת, אִם לֹא עֵירְבוּ ב' הַחֲצֵירוֹת יַחַד: **גמ'** כָּל מָקוֹם שֶׁאַתָּה מוֹצֵא שְׁתֵּי רְשׁוּיוֹת. שֶׁעוֹמֶדֶת כָּל אַחַת לְבַדָּהּ: וְהֵן רְשׁוּת אַחַת. שֶׁם אַחַת לָהֶן, שֶׁשְּׁתֵּיהֶן רְשׁוּת הַיָּחִיד: כְּגוֹן עַמּוּד. גָּבוֹהַּ עֲשָׂרָה בֶּחָצֵר: אָסוּר לְכַתֵּף עָלָיו. מִן הֶחָצֵר, וְאע"פ שֶׁרְשׁוּת חָצֵר עוֹלָה עַד לָרָקִיעַ: גְּזֵירָה מִשּׁוּם תֵּל גָּבוֹהַּ י'. בִּרה"ר, דַּהֲוֵה רה"י, דְּלָא לֵיתֵי לְכַתּוֹפֵי עֲלֵיהּ: אַמַּת הָרֵיחַיִם. כָּל בִּנְיָן הַעֲמָדַת הָרֵיחַיִם מְקוֹם מוֹשָׁבָן קָרֵי לֵיהּ אַמַּת הָרֵיחַיִם: הוֹאִיל וְאָדָם קוֹבֵעַ לָהֶן מָקוֹם. דָּמוּ לְתֵל: וְאָמַר רַב יְהוּדָה. לְקַמָּן בְּפִירְקִין: כְּשֶׁתִּימְצֵי לוֹמַר. כְּשֶׁתְּדַקְדֵּק בִּדְבָרֵיהֶם תִּמְצָא כֵּן: חֲצֵירוֹת רְשׁוּת לְעַצְמָן. וּמְטַלְטְלִין מֵחָצֵר שֶׁל רַבִּים לְחָצֵר שֶׁל רַבִּים בְּלֹא עֵירוּב, וְכֵן שֶׁל יָחִיד דְּכִי הֵיכִי דְּאָמַר ר' מֵאִיר גַּגּוֹת רְשׁוּת אַחַת הֵן — שָׁמְעִינַן מִינַּהּ דַּחֲצֵירוֹת נָמֵי רְשׁוּת אַחַת, שֶׁהֲרֵי אֵין תַּשְׁמִישָׁן מְיוּחָד כְּבָתִּים, וְדָמוּ לְגַגִּין. אֲבָל מִגַּג לְחָצֵר — לֹא, כִּדְקָתָנֵי: וּבִלְבַד שֶׁלֹּא יְהֵא גַּג גָּבוֹהַּ מֵחֲבֵירוֹ י' וְכָל שֶׁכֵּן מִגַּג לְחָצֵר: מַאי לָאו. הָא דְּקָאָמְרִינַן חֲצֵירוֹת רְשׁוּת לְעַצְמָן — דְּשָׁרֵי לְטַלְטוּלֵי דֶּרֶךְ כּוֹתֶל, וְלֹא גָּזַר מִשּׁוּם תֵּל, אַלְמָא: גַּג גָּבוֹהַּ וְנָמוּךְ טַעְמָא אַחֲרִינָא הוּא. *וְקַרְפֵּף אִם יֵשׁ יוֹתֵר מִבֵּית סָאתַיִם (הֵן) מְטַלְטְלִין מִזֶּה לָזֶה תּוֹךְ ד' וְאִי שֶׁל בֵּית סָאתַיִם — מְטַלְטְלִין טִלְטוּל גָּמוּר. אֲבָל מֵהֶן לַחֲצֵירוֹת — לֹא, דְּלָא דָּמוּ לַחֲצֵירוֹת, דַּחֲצֵירוֹת רְשׁוּת שׁוּתָּפוּת, וְקַרְפֵּף רה"י: רַב אָמַר אֵין מְטַלְטְלִין. לְרַבָּנַן, בְּגַג הַסָּמוּךְ לַחֲבֵירוֹ: אֶלָּא בְּד' אַמּוֹת. דְּכֵיוָן דִּלְרַבָּנַן כָּל אֶחָד רְשׁוּת לְעַצְמוֹ, וְהֵן פְּרוּצִין זֶה לָזֶה — אוֹסְרִין זֶה עַל זֶה, דְּה"ל רְשׁוּת פְּרוּצָה בִּמְלוֹאָהּ לְמָקוֹם הָאָסוּר לָהּ: מוּתָּר לְטַלְטֵל בְּכוּלּוֹ. שֶׁמְּחִיצּוֹת הַמַּבְדִּילוֹת לְמַטָּה[ב] מִן הַדִּיוּרִין אָמְרִינַן גּוּד אַסְּקִינְהוּ לְמַעְלָה, וְיַפְרִידוּ בֵּינֵיהֶן: בִּמְחִיצוֹת הַנִּיכָּרוֹת. שֶׁאֵין הַבָּתִּים מְחוּבָּרִין, וְיֵשׁ אֲוִיר בֵּינֵיהֶם, וּמְחִיצּוֹת הַבָּתִּים נִרְאִין לָעוֹמְדִין עַל הַגַּג כְּשֶׁמִּסְתַּכְּלִין תַּחַת רַגְלֵיהֶם: כּוּלֵּי עָלְמָא לָא פְּלִיגִי. דְּאָמְרִינַן בְּהוּ גּוּד אַסִּיק, דְּדָמוּ לְעַמּוּד בִּרְשׁוּת הָרַבִּים דַּהֲוֵי רְשׁוּת הַיָּחִיד מִשּׁוּם גּוּד אַסִּיק — מְשׁוֹךְ וְהַעֲלֵה: כִּי פְּלִיגִי בְּשֶׁאֵין הַמְּחִיצוֹת נִיכָּרוֹת. שֶׁהַגַּגִּין מְחוּבָּרִין יַחַד, וּמְכַסִּין הַמְּחִיצּוֹת שֶׁבֵּין הַדִּיוּרִין: לָא אָמְרִינַן גּוּד אַסִּיק. בְּכִי הַאי גַּוְונָא:

תוספות

לא שנו אלא שלא עירבו. וא"ת: אי דלא עירבו – תרוייהו ליתסרו! וי"ל, דאינם שופכין ממש בתוך העוקה שבחצר, אלא שופכין על הדיוטא, והן יורדין על העוקה הסמוכה לה. ואע"ג דהוי חצר שאינה מעורבת – מ"מ לא אסרו חכמים(א) כאן אלא בכרמלית, כעין שפירשנו לעיל. אבל בחצר שאינה מעורבת – לא אסרו כלל. וכן פסק רבינו שמואל, דמותר לשפוך מים אע"פ שהולכין לרשות אחרת שאינה מעורבת. דמרשות לרשות לא בעי קמירה. ואותם שלא עשו עוקה – אסורים, כדאמר: דילמא אתו לאפוקי מיא במנא דבתים להכא, שיורידו מן הדיוטא בכלים מלאים מים לשפת העוקה שרחוקה מהן, דאין רוצין שיפלו המים למטה ויקלקל החצר:

הדרן עלך כיצד משתתפין

כל גגות. גזרה משום תל ברה"ר. אף על גב דקיימא לן כר' מאיר בגזירותיו, אפילו במקום רבים, כדאמרינן בפ' "אע"פ" (כתובות נז.) גבי משהה אדם את אשתו שתים ושלש שנים בלא כתובה – הכא אומר ר"י דאין הלכה כרבי מאיר. דפסקינן לקמן *הלכה כר"ש, דאמר: כולן רשות אחת הן. וכותל שבין שתי חצירות דאסרינן הכא לר' מאיר – שרי ר' יוחנן לעיל בריש "חלון" (דף עז.)(ג), ולקמן בפירקין [דף צב.]:

מאי לאו דשרי לטלטולי דרך כותל. המ"ל: כשאין הכותל רחב ארבעה: **רב** אמר אין מטלטלין בו אלא בד'. אף על גב דרב ושמואל פסקי לקמן כר"ש – הכא אליבא דרבנן פליגי, ולא סברי להו. א"נ: פלוגתייהו נפקא מינה נמי לר"ש לכלים ששבתו בבית. ואף על גב דגבי כלים ששבתו בתוכו הוי נפרץ במילואו למקום המותר לו – מ"מ חשיב שפיר נפרץ במילואו למקום האסור לכלים ששבתו בתוך הבית. כעין שפירש רש"י *בריש "מי שהוציאוהו" (לעיל דף מג.)(ד), דנפרץ במילואו למקום האסור לטלטל מגואי לבראי ומבראי לגואי הוי מקום המותר לו. א"נ: נפקא מינה כשהגגין יחד יתירים מבית סאתים, דאי לא אמר גוד אסיק – אסור כדאמרינן לקמן(ה):

במחיצות שאינן ניכרות. כשהבתים מחוברין, דאין מחילות הבתים ניכרות, כדפירש בקונטרס. ונראה דהוא הדין אם הגג בולט חוץ למחילות הבית, דחשיב נמי מחילות שאינן ניכרות. ואור"י: דגגין שלנו שבולטין ראשיהן לרה"ר ועבידי כי ארזילא, לפירוש רש"י דמפרש*) כי ארזילא בשיפוע כגגין שלנו – הוי כרמלית, דלא מינכרא מחילתא וליכא למימר גוד אסיק, ופי תקרה נמי לא אמרינן, כיון דעבידי כי ארזילא. וגוד אחית נמי לא אמרינן *לרבנן דרבי יוסי בר יהודה גבי טרסקל, משום בקיעת גדיים. דאפילו רבי יוסי בר יהודה לא אמר אלא בטרסקל דהדרן מחילתא, כדאמר בפרק

*) לקמן צ. ד"ה וכו' אמות.

עין משפט נר מצוה

מא א מיי' פ"ד מהל' עירובין הלכה כז סמג שם טוש"ע א"ח סי' שעז:

א ב מיי' פ"ג מהלכות עירובין הלכה יח סמג עשין א טור ש"ע א"ח סי' שעב סעיף א:

מסורת הש"ס

שבת קל: לעיל [כג: לה.] ע"ז. ולקמן נח.

[לקמן צ: שבת ט.]

[לקמן צ:]

[לקמן צב.]

[צ"ל וקרפיפו']

[לקמן צ.]

רבינו חננאל

אחת לי עוקה גזוזטרא בריכה ועריבה אע"פ שנתמלאו מים מע"ש שופכין לתוכו מים בשבת ואסיקנא אמר רבה לא שנו אלא שלא עירבו אבל עירבו הללו ב' דיוטאות שופכין בעוקה אחת. אבל שלא עירבו גזרינן דלא לשפוך מדוכתיה. דלמא אתי למשקל במנא ושדי בעוקה:

הדרן עלך כיצד משתתפין

פ"ט כל גגות העיר רשות אחת ובלבד שלא יהא גבוה י' טפחים או נמוך י' דברי ר' מאיר מ"ט דר' מאיר אי קסבר כשם שדיורין למטה חלוקין כך חלוקין למעלה. אמאי קתני כל גגות העיר רשות אחת (בלבד) ואי אין חלוקין (כ"ע) [דלמעלה מי'] רשות אחת היא [ובלבד שיהא גבוה] י' או נמוך עשרה למה לי ואוקמה רב יצחק אומר היה ר' מאיר כל מקום שאתה מוצא ב' רשויות והן רשות אחת כגון עמוד ברה"י גבוה י' ורחב ד' אסור לכתף עליו [גזירה] משום תל ברשות הרבים סבור מינה [אפילו] מכתשת אפילו גיגית אסור לכתף עליו. אמר אביי הכי קאמר מר והוא רבה בר נחמני לא אסרו אלא בעמוד ואמת הרחיים הואיל ואדם קובע להם מקום דגזרינן בהו אטו תל ברשות הרבים. ואקשינן והא כותל שבין ב' חצרות דקביע ואמר רב יהודה כשתמצא לומר לדברי ר"מ גגין וחצרות רשות לעצמן מאי לאו דשרי לטלטולי דרך כותל ולא קא גזר משום תל ברה"ר ופרקינן לא להכנים ולהוציא מהן דרך פתחים אבל מזה לזה לא. וחכמים אומרים כל גגות רשות בפני עצמו הוא: אתמר

הגהות הב"ח

(א) תום' ד"ה לא שנו וכו' לא אסרו חכמים כאן אלא בכרמלית כעין שפי' לעיל נ"ב בדף פח. ד"ה הני: (ב) רש"י ד"ה מותר לטלטל וכו' למטה בין הדיורין אמרינן בהו גוד אסקינהו: (ג) תום' ד"ה כל גגות וכו' בריש חלון נ"ב עיין בתוס' בד"ה ור' יוחנן ראש דף עז: (ד) ד"ה רב אמר וכו' כעין שפי' רש"י בריש מי שהוציאוהו נ"ב בדף מב וע"ש בתוס' בד"ה לא על ידי משיכה: (ה) בא"ד כדאמרינן לקמן נ"ב דף צ סוף ע"א:

רְשׁוּת לְעַצְמוֹ, בִּשְׁלָמָא לִשְׁמוּאֵל — נִיחָא, אֶלָּא לְרַב — קַשְׁיָא! אָמְרִי בֵּי רַב מִשְּׁמֵיהּ דְּרַב: שֶׁלֹּא יְטַלְטֵל ב׳ אַמּוֹת בְּגַג זֶה וּב׳ אַמּוֹת בְּגַג זֶה. וְהָא א"ר אֶלְעָזָר, כִּי הֲוֵינַן בְּבָבֶל הֲוָה אָמְרִינַן, בֵּי רַב מִשְּׁמֵיהּ דְּרַב אָמְרוּ: אֵין מְטַלְטְלִין בּוֹ אֶלָּא בְּד׳ אַמּוֹת, וְהָנֵי דְּבֵי שְׁמוּאֵל תָּנוּ: אֵין לָהֶן אֶלָּא גַּגָּן. מַאי "אֵין לָהֶן אֶלָּא גַּגָּן" — לָאו דְּשָׁרוּ לְטַלְטוּלֵי בְּכוּלֵּיהּ? וּמִי אַלִּימָא מִמַּתְנִי׳, דְּאוֹקִימְנָא שֶׁלֹּא יְטַלְטֵל שְׁתֵּי אַמּוֹת בְּגַג זֶה וּשְׁתֵּי אַמּוֹת בְּגַג זֶה — ה"נ: ב׳ אַמּוֹת בְּגַג זֶה וּב׳ אַמּוֹת בְּגַג זֶה. *אֲמַר רַב יוֹסֵף: לָא שְׁמִיעַ לִי הָא שְׁמַעְתָּא. א"ל אַבַּיֵי: אַתְּ אֲמַרְתְּ נִיהֲלַן, וְאַהָא אֲמַרְתְּ נִיהֲלַן: גַּג גָּדוֹל הַסָּמוּךְ לְקָטָן — הַגָּדוֹל מוּתָּר וְהַקָּטָן אָסוּר. וְאָמְרַתְּ לָן עֲלָהּ, אָמַר רַב יְהוּדָה, אָמַר שְׁמוּאֵל: לֹא שָׁנוּ אֶלָּא שֶׁיֵּשׁ דִּיּוּרִין עַל זֶה וְדִיּוּרִין עַל זֶה, דְּהָוְיָא לָהּ הָא דְּקָטָן מְחִיצָּה נִדְרֶסֶת. אֲבָל אֵין דִּיּוּרִין עַל זֶה וְעַל זֶה — שְׁנֵיהֶן מוּתָּרִין. א"ל: אֲנָא הָכִי אָמְרִי לְכוּ: ל"ש אֶלָּא שֶׁיֵּשׁ מְחִיצָּה עַל זֶה וּמְחִיצָּה עַל זֶה, דְּגָדוֹל מִישְׁתְּרִי בְּגִיפוּפֵי, וְקָטָן נִפְרָץ בִּמְלוֹאוֹ. אֲבָל אֵין מְחִיצָּה לֹא עַל זֶה וְלֹא עַל זֶה — שְׁנֵיהֶן אֲסוּרִין. וְהָא דִּיּוּרִין אֲמַרְתְּ לָן! אִי אָמְרִי לְכוּ דִּיּוּרִין — הָכִי אָמְרִי לְכוּ: ל"ש אֶלָּא שֶׁיֵּשׁ מְחִיצָּה רְאוּיָה לְדִירָה עַל זֶה וּמְחִיצָּה רְאוּיָה לְדִירָה עַל זֶה, דְּגָדוֹל מִישְׁתְּרִי בְּגִיפוּפֵי וְקָטָן נִפְרָץ בִּמְלוֹאוֹ. אֲבָל יֵשׁ מְחִיצָּה רְאוּיָה לְדִירָה עַל הַגָּדוֹל, וְאֵין רְאוּיָה לְדִירָה עַל הַקָּטָן — אֲפִילּוּ קָטָן שָׁרֵי לִבְנֵי גָּדוֹל. מַאי טַעְמָא — כֵּיוָן דְּלָא עֲבוּד מְחִיצָּה — סַלּוּקֵי סַלִּיקוּ נַפְשַׁיְיהוּ מֵהָכָא. כְּהָא דְּאָמַר רַב נַחְמָן: עָשָׂה סוּלָּם קָבוּעַ לְגַגּוֹ — הוּתַּר בְּכָל הַגַּגִּין כּוּלָּן. אָמַר אַבַּיֵי: בָּנָה עֲלִיָּיה עַל גַּבֵּי בֵּיתוֹ וְעָשָׂה לְפָנֶיהָ דַּקָּה אַרְבַּע — הוּתַּר בְּכָל הַגַּגִּין כּוּלָּן. אָמַר רָבָא: פְּעָמִים שֶׁהַדַּקָּה לְאִיסּוּר. הֵיכִי דָּמֵי — דַּעֲבִידָא לַהֲדֵי תַּרְבִּיצָא דְּבֵיתֵיהּ, דַּאֲמַר לְנְטוּרֵי

רש"י

רְשׁוּת לְעַצְמוֹ. קָא סָלְקָא דַּעְתָּךְ: כָּל אֶחָד יְטַלְטֵל בְּגַגּוֹ מַשְׁמַע: וְהָנֵי דְּבֵי שְׁמוּאֵל תָּנוּ. אִית מַתְנִיתָא בִּידַיְיהוּ דְּמוֹתְבֵי מִינָּהּ תְּיוּבְתָּא לְדְבֵי רַב, דְּקָתָנֵי: אֵין לָהֶן לְכָל אֶחָד אֶלָּא גַּגּוֹ, דְּמַשְׁמַע דְּלָא יְטַלְטְלוּ אֶלָּא בְּגַגּוֹ, הָא בְּגַגּוֹ — יְטַלְטְלוּ: לָא שְׁמִיעַ לִי הָא שְׁמַעְתָּא. דִּשְׁמוּאֵל, דְּנֵימָא גּוּד אַסִּיק בִּמְחִיצּוֹת כִּי הָנֵי, שֶׁאֵין נִיכָּרוֹת: גַּג גָּדוֹל סָמוּךְ לְקָטָן. גָּדוֹל עוֹדֵף עָלָיו לְכָאן וּלְכָאן: הַגָּדוֹל מוּתָּר. לְטַלְטֵל בּוֹ דִּיּוּרִין שֶׁבּוֹ, וַאֲפִילּוּ לְרַב. דְּהָא מְחִיצּוֹת שֶׁל מַטָּה שֶׁיֶּשְׁנָן בְּעוֹדְפוֹ לְכָאן וּלְכָאן — מְחִיצּוֹת הַנִּיכָּרוֹת הֵן, וְגוּד אַסְּקִינְהוּ. וְאִית לְהוּ גִּפּוּפֵי, וְהָךְ פִּירְצָה שֶׁכְּנֶגֶד הַקָּטָן — פִּתְחָא הָוֵי לַגָּדוֹל, וְאֵין קָטָן אוֹסֵר עָלָיו, דְּהָוֵי כִּשְׁתֵּי חֲצֵירוֹת וּפֶתַח בֵּינֵיהֶם: אֲבָל קָטָן אָסוּר. דִּלְדִידֵיהּ הָוֵי מְלוֹאוֹ, וְלָאו פִּתְחָא הוּא, וְאָסְרֵי עֲלֵיהּ בְּנֵי גָּדוֹל: שֶׁיֵּשׁ דִּיּוּרִין עַל זֶה וְעַל זֶה. שֶׁעוֹבְרִין כָּל שָׁעָה מִזֶּה לָזֶה, הִלְכָּךְ, לֵיכָּא לְמֵימַר גּוּד אַסִּיק בַּמְּחִיצָּה הַתַּחְתּוֹנָה שֶׁבֵּינֵיהֶם, מִפְּנֵי שֶׁנִּדְרֶסֶת הִיא: אֲבָל אֵין בָּהֶן דִּיּוּרִים. אָמְרִינַן בָּהּ גּוּד אַסִּיק, וּמוּתָּר אַף הַקָּטָן, אַלְמָא: אַף בִּמְחִיצָּה שֶׁאֵינָהּ נִיכֶּרֶת אִית לֵיהּ לִשְׁמוּאֵל גּוּד אַסִּיק, דְּאִי לָאו דִּמְחוּבָּרִין הֵן — אֵין דְּרִיסָה מִזֶּה לָזֶה: שֶׁיֵּשׁ מְחִיצָּה עַל זֶה וְעַל זֶה. כָּל סְבִיבוֹתֵיהֶן, חוּץ מִכְּנֶגֶד חִבּוּרָן, דְּהַשְׁתָּא מִישְׁתְּרִי גָּדוֹל בְּגִיפוּפֵי: אֲבָל אֵין מְחִיצָּה לֹא לְכָאן וְלֹא לְכָאן שְׁנֵיהֶן אֲסוּרִין. דְּקָטָן נַמִי אָסַר אַגָּדוֹל, דְּהוֹאִיל וְלָא הָווּ גִּיפּוּפֵי מַמָּשׁ אֶלָּא עַל יְדֵי גּוּד אַסִּיק, לָא הָווּ גִּיפּוּפֵי לְשַׁוְּיֵהּ פִּתְחָא לְגַבֵּיהּ, דְּפִתְחָא דְּמִינְכָּר בָּעֵינַן, וּכְה"ג: לָא עָבְדֵי אֱינָשֵׁי: אִי אָמְרִי לְכוּ דִּיּוּרִין. אִם הִזְכַּרְתִּי לָכֶם שׁוּם דִּירָה בַּדָּבָר, כָּךְ אָמַרְתִּי לָכֶם. רַב יוֹסֵף חָלָה וְשָׁכַח תַּלְמוּדוֹ: לֹא שָׁנוּ. דְּקָטָן אָסוּר, בֵּין לְדִיּוּרֵי קָטָן בֵּין לְדִיּוּרֵי גָּדוֹל — אֶלָּא שֶׁיֵּשׁ מְחִיצָּה רְאוּיָה לְדִירָה. כְּלוֹמַר: מְחִיצָּה קָבוּעַ וְקַיָּימָא, דְּתַרְוַיְיהוּ גָּלוּ דַּעְתַּיְיהוּ דְּבָעוּ אִשְׁתַּמּוּשֵׁי כָּל חַד בְּדִידֵיהּ. הִלְכָּךְ, גָּדוֹל מוּתָּר בְּשֶׁלּוֹ — דְּפִתְחָא הוּא, וְלָא אָסַר קָטָן עֲלַיְיהוּ. וְקָטָן אָסוּר לִשְׁנֵיהֶם [א] מִשּׁוּם דְּנִפְרַץ בִּמְלוֹאוֹ לַגָּדוֹל, וְאָסְרֵי עֲלֵיהּ בְּנֵי גָּדוֹל. וּלְדִידְהוּ נַמִי לָא מִישְׁתְּרֵי, דְּכֵיוָן דַּעֲבַד לֵיהּ מָרֵיהּ מְחִיצָּה קְבוּעָה — לָא סַלֵּיק נַפְשֵׁיהּ מִינֵּיהּ, וְלָא אַחְלֵי לְגַבַּיְיהוּ: סַלּוּקֵי סַלִּיקוּ נַפְשַׁיְיהוּ. בְּנֵי קָטָן מִגַּגּוֹ, וְאַחֲלֵיהּ לִבְנֵי גָּדוֹל: הוּתַּר בְּכָל הַגַּגִּין. וַאֲפִילּוּ לְרַבָּנַן, דְּכֵיוָן דְּאִינְהוּ לָא עֲבִיד סוּלָּם — סַלִּיקוּ נַפְשַׁיְיהוּ וְאַחֲלִינְהוּ לְגַבֵּיהּ: בָּנָה עֲלִיָּיה. וְהִקִּיף כָּל גַּגּוֹ מְחִיצּוֹת לַעֲלִיָּיה: דַּקָּה. פֶּתַח קָטָן פָּתוּחַ לְצַד הַגַּגִּין: הוּתַּר בְּכוּלָּן. דְּגַלֵּי דַּעְתֵּיהּ דְּקָא מַחֲזִיק בְּהוּ — וְהֵם לֹא הִקְפִּידוּ לַעֲשׂוֹת כֵּן — אַחֲלִינְהוּ לְגַבֵּיהּ: פְּעָמִים שֶׁהַדַּקָּה לְאִיסּוּר. וַאֲפִילּוּ לְרַבִּי מֵאִיר, דִּמְשַׁוֵּי כָּל הַגַּגּוֹת רְשׁוּת אַחַת אָסוּר בָּהֶן: דַּעֲבָדָהּ לַהֲדֵי תַּרְבִּיצֵיהּ. שֶׁפָּתַח לְצַד גִּינָּתוֹ, וּמְחִיצָּה שֶׁל צַד הַגַּגִּין הִנִּיחַ סְתוּמָה: לְנְטוּרֵי

תוספות

בפ׳ "בכל מערבין" (לעיל דף לג:), והואיל וכן – כל הגג אסור, כי כל הגג נפרץ במילואו לכרמלית – לאותה בליטה הבולטת לרה"ר. ואע"ג דלא שלטי ביה רבים, שהרי גבוה י׳ – נעשה כרמלית, דלא מצינו מקום פטור רוחב ד׳. דהא בית שאין תוכו י׳ וקרויו משלימין ליו"ד הוי תוכו כרמלית, ואין מטלטלין בו אלא בארבע אמות, אע"ג דלא שלטי ביה רבים, שהרי סתום הוא מכל צד. והא דאמר בפ"ק דשבת (דף ז.) דאין כרמלית למעלה מי׳ – היינו שמכח קרקע הכרמלית אין נעשה האויר כרמלית למעלה מי׳, כדאמר התם דאקילו ביה רבנן (ב) קולי רה"ר, שהאויר למעלה מי׳ מקום פטור, וגזוזטרא דלא הויא כרמלית אלא רשות היחיד – היינו משום דגוד אחית, דבקיעת דגים לא הויא בקיעה, כדפיר׳ לעיל. או בפתוח *לרה"ר דהוי כי חורי רשות היחיד. וכן זיז היוצא לרשות הרבים רחב ד׳ דהוי רשות היחיד – היינו סמוך לחלון תוך י׳, דהוי כי חורי רשות היחיד. ומנעול דחשיב ליה ב"המוצא תפילין" (לקמן דף קא:) רה"י – היינו משום דליכא בקיעת גדיים, שהאיסקופה גבוה שלשה. אי נמי: שיש במנעול עצמו גבוה י׳, דהוי רשות היחיד אפילו איכא רה"ר גמורה תחתיו, כמו עגלות דהוו רה"י ותחתיהן רה"ר ב"הזורק" (שבת דף נט.). ורש"י פירש נמי לקמן (ג) אמתניתין דגג גדול הסמוך לקטן, גבי מה אמר דמינכרא מחיצות שלא יהא גג בולט חוצה להן, דאי לא מינכרא – לא אמר גוד אסיק. וגדול נמי אסור, שאין לו שום מחיצה, וכל שאין לו מחיצה אינו רשות היחיד. וכן בשמעתין גבי גגין השוין לר"מ כו׳ דפריך: קשיא דרב אדרב, פי׳ בקונטרס: דלית ליה גוד אסיק ה"נ בגגין השוין לרבי מאיר, נהי דלא אסור כל חד אחבריה, דחדא רשותא משוי להו – מיהו, בני רה"ר העוברים לפניהם ולאחריהם ולצידי החיצונה, אמאי לא אסרי עלייהו? הא ליכא מחיצה לגגין כו׳! מיהו, בירושלמי משמע דלא חשיב כרמלית והכי איתא (ד), אמר ר׳ יוחנן: זיזין וכתלים שהיו גבוהים י׳ ורחבין ד׳ – מותרין כאן וכאן ובלבד שלא יחליף, משמע דחשיב להו מקום פטור, מדשרי לבני רשות הרבים ורשות היחיד, וכתלים דקאמר התם נראה דהיינו אבנים הבולטין מן הכותל, דאילו כותל גבוה י׳ ורחב ד׳ – הוי ודאי רה"י. והא דנקט רחב ד׳ – לרבותא, דאפ"ה הוי מקום פטור, וכל שכן אם אינם רחבים ד׳. ולא קשיא ההיא דבית שאין תוכו י׳ דהוי כרמלית, אע"ג דלא מצי רבים לאשתמושי – דהכא כיון שהוא למעלה מי׳ יש לו ליחשב מקום פטור, אע"ג דרחב ד׳ כיון דלא הוי לא רה"ר ולא רה"י. והא דפריך: קשיא דרב אדרב – לאו משום דרה"ר אוסרת, כדפי׳ בקונטרס – דלעולם אין רה"ר אוסרת למעלה מי׳, אלא משום דידע שפיר דאיירי ביתר מבית סאתים, כדמסיק. ומ"מ פריך לשמואל, משום דאין נראה לו לומר דהני מחיצות למעלה לא עבידן, ולא הוי מוקף לדירה. והא דקאמרינן נמי לקמן: אף גג דמינכרא מחיצה, דאי לא מינכרא גדול נמי אסור – משום דקטן אוסר עליו, אבל כי מינכרא – אין הקטן אוסר עליו, משום גוד אסיק אפילו לשויה פתחא דלא כרב יוסף דבסמוך דאמר אם אין מחיצה לא על זה ולא על זה שניהם אסורין, דלא אמר גוד אסיק לשויה פתחא – משום דפתחא כי האי גוונא לא עבדי אינשי:

וקטן נפרץ במילואו. כגון שהגג קטן נכנס לתוך הגדול, כדאוקימנא פרק קמא (דף ט:) דמתניתין דחצר קטנה שנפרצה לגדולה, בנכנסין כותלי קטנה לגדולה, שלא יהא נראה מבחוץ ושוה מבפנים.

ועשה לפניה דקה ד׳ הותר בכל הגגין. לפי מה שמפרש ב"כיצד מעברין" (לעיל דף נט: ושם סא.) דדקה היא מחיצה, מפרש ר"י הכא דכשבנה עלייה ועשה מחיצה כל סביב גגו, ופתחה לצד הגגין, ועשה לפני הפתח דקה ד׳ – אז הוי תשמיש קבוע. אבל בלא דקה ירא להשתמש שם תשמיש קבוע, מפני בני גגין אחרים. וקשה: דבלא דקה נמי אמר לעיל, דאם יש מחיצה ראויה לדירה על הגדול ולא על הקטן דאפילו קטן נמי שרי לבני גדול. ור"ח גרס: "הותרו כל הגגין", פירוש: אם עירבו אחר הגגין וזה לא עירב עמהם – אינו אוסר עליהם, דכיון דעשה דקה סילק עצמו מהם. וצריך לומר לפירושו דלצד הגגין הוא פרוץ במילואו, או עלייה אינה אלא בחצי הגג. ואם היה כל הגג מוקף מחיצה – בלא דקה נמי לא היה אוסר. ולשון פעמים שהדקה לאיסור צריך ליישב, דהדקה אינה עושה לא איסור ולא היתר:

כרמלית

רבינו חננאל

אתמר רב אמר אין מטלטלין בכל גג אלא בד׳ אמות דלא אמרינן גוד אסיק מחיצתא. ושמואל אמר אמרינן גוד אסיק מחיצתא וכאילו מחיצות כל חצר עולות ומקיפות הגג לפיכך מותר לטלטל בכל הגג כי כמו החצר הוא ואקשינן עליה דרב והתנן וחכ"א כל אחד ואחד רשות לעצמו. ופרקינן רב הכי קתני כל אחד ואחד רשות לעצמו שלא יטלטל ב׳ אמות בגג זה ושתי אמות בגג אחר. אמר רב יוסף בהא דתנן גג גדול סמוך לגג קטן גדול מותר וקטן אסור. אמר רב יהודה אמר שמואל לא שנו אלא שיש מחיצה הראויה לדירה על הגדול ומחיצה הראויה על הקטן דגדול מישתרי בגיפופי. פי׳ גיפופי כמו כתלים קטני׳ שנשארו מכותלי הגדולה ניתרת בהן שהן כמו פסין אבל הקטן שנפרץ במילואו ואין לו מחיצה כלל בזה *) (חצר א׳ חייב) אבל יש מחיצה הראויה על הגדול ואין הראויה לדירה על הקטן קטן נמי משתרי לגבי גדול דכיון [דלא] עבידו מחיצה בנפשייהו סלוקי סליקו נפשייהו מהכא וכי הא דאמר ר"נ אחד שעשה סולם קבוע לגגו מותרין בכל הגגות דהאי סליק נפשיה מהכא אמר אביי בנה עלייה על גבי ביתו ועשה לפניה דקה כמו איצטב׳ רחבה ד׳ טפחים מותרין בני הגגות בגגותיהן דהאי סליק נפשיה מהכא ולא קאסר. אמר רבא ואי עבד׳ להאי דקה בהדיה ביתיה אסיר דלא אמרינן סלוקי סליק

*) [אולי צ"ל בזה אמרינן דגג הקטן אסור].

ל"ל לרה"י

[לעיל י. וש"נ]

הגהות הב"ח

(א) רש"י ד"ה לא שנו וכו׳ למשום דנפרץ: (ב) תוס׳ ד"ה במחיצות וכו׳ דאקילו ביה רבנן מקולי רה"ר: (ג) בא"ד ורש"י פי׳ נמי לקמן. נ"ב דף צב ע"א: (ד) בא"ד וכן איתא התם א"ר יוחנן.

גליון הש"ס

גמ׳ ומי אלימא ממתניתין. שבת דף יג ע"א ודף פג ע"א:

לנטורי תרביצא הוא דעבידא. בעי רמי בר חמא: שתי אמות בגג ושתי אמות בעמוד מהו? אמר רבה: מאי קא מיבעיא ליה? כרמלית ורה"י קא מיבעיא ליה?! ורמי בר חמא *אגב חורפיה לא עיין בה, אלא הכי קמיבעיא ליה: ב' אמות בגג, וב' אמות באכסדרה מהו? מי אמרינן: כיון דלא האי חזי לדירה, ולא האי חזי לדירה – חדא רשותא היא. או דילמא: כיון דמגג לגג אסיר, מגג לאכסדרה נמי אסיר? בעי רב ביבי בר אביי: ב' אמות בגג וב' אמות בחורבה מהו? אמר רב כהנא: לאו היינו דרמי בר חמא? אמר רב ביבי בר אביי: וכי מאחר אתאי ונצאי?! אכסדרה – לא חזיא לדירה, וחורבה – חזיא לדירה. וכי מאחר דחזיא לדירה, מאי קמיבעיא ליה? אם תימצי לומר קאמר; אם תימצי לומר אכסדרה לא חזיא לדירה – חורבה חזיא לדירה, או דילמא השתא מיהא לית בה דיורין? תיקו. גגין השוין לר"מ, וגג יחידי לרבנן, רב אמר: מותר לטלטל בכולו, ושמואל אמר: אין מטלטלין בו אלא בד'. רב אמר: מותר לטלטל בכולו, קשיא דרב אדרב! התם – לא מינכרא מחיצתא, הכא מינכרא מחיצתא. ושמואל אמר: אין מטלטלין בו אלא בד' אמות, קשיא דשמואל אדשמואל! התם – לא הוי יותר מבית סאתים, הכא – הוי יותר מבית סאתים. והני מחיצות למטה עבידן, למעלה לא עבידן, והוה כקרפף יתר מבית סאתים שלא הוקף לדירה, וכל קרפף יותר מבית סאתים שלא הוקף לדירה – אין מטלטלין בו אלא בד'. איתמר; ספינה, רב אמר: מותר לטלטל בכולה, ושמואל אמר: אין מטלטלין בה אלא בד'. רב אמר: מותר לטלטל בכולה, דהא

רש"י

לנטורי תרביצא עבידא. וסילק עצמו מן הגגין: ב' אמות בגג זה. כרב סבירא ליה דאמר: גג שבין הגגין אין מטלטלין בו אלא בד' דאסרי אהדדי: מהו. לטלטל מאחת מהן לעמוד העומד ברה"ר סמוך לו, גבוה י' ורחב ד': כרמלית ורה"י קא מיבעיא ליה. בתמיה. כלומר, פשיטא דאסיר, דהא גג כרמלית הוא כדאמר' אין מטלטלין בו אלא בד' ועמוד רה"י: ורמי בר חמא אגב חורפיה כו'. התלמוד קאמר: ורמי בר חמא נמי ודאי לא איבעי ליה למיבעי הכי, אלא אגב חורפיה מיהר בשאלתו, ולא עיין בה יפה: והכי הוא דמיבעיא ליה ב' אמות בגג. שבין הגגין: וב' אמות באכסדרה. של בעלים אחרים, ע"ג תקרה של אכסדרה יותר מבית סאתים, ואין לה מחיצה ואין לה פי תקרה דנימא יורד וסותם. דעבידא כי אורזילא, בשפוע כגגין שלנו, וכדאמרן ב"עושין פסין" (לעיל כה:) דהשתא הויא לה נמי כרמלית, מהו לטלטל מזה לזה: חדא רשותא הוא. ואף ע"פ שאינן של איש אחד – אין בהם חלוק רשותא, ואפי' לרבנן. דלא דמו לשני גגין. דהתם איכא דיורין למטה בשניהם, וי"ל כשם שיש חלוק רשות למטה בבתים – כך יש חלוק למעלה. דחלוק למטה סליק ואזיל לעיל. אבל באכסדרה – ליכא למימר הכי: או דילמא כיון דמגג לגג אסיר. טעמייהו דרבנן משום דקפדי אשינוי בעלים הוא, ומגג לאכסדרה נמי: בחורבה. של אחרים, ופרוצה לרה"ר דהויא נמי כרמלית כגג בין הגגין: לאו היינו דרמי. מה בין חורבה לאכסדרה: וכי מאחר אתאי ונצאי. מפי אחר באתי ואלקתי? בשאלה ששאלה אחר באתי לקנתר? בתמיה: מאי קא מיבעיא ליה. הא לא דמי לגג, ואסיר: אם תימצי לומר קאמר. כלומר: לא פשיטא לרב ביבי דתיהוי חורבה חזיא לדירה, ולא פשיטא ליה נמי דתיהוי כי אכסדרה, דהא עדיפא מינה פורתא. ובא להוסיף על שאלתו של רמי בר חמא על ידי את"ל. והכי קאמר: אם פשיטא לרמי בר חמא דשרי, הכא מאי? התם הוא דאכסדרה לא חזיא מידי לדירה, אבל חורבה חזיא לדירה בתיקון מועט, או דילמא כו': גגין השוין. שאין בהן גג גבוה מחבירו עשרה, ויש הרבה סמוכין יחד: לר"מ. דמשוי להו כולהו חדא רשותא, ולא אסרי אהדדי: וגג יחידי לרבנן. שאינו סמוך לאחרים, דאפילו לרבנן ליכא דליסר עליה: ושמואל אמר אין מטלטלין בו אלא בד'. והא דקאמר ר' מאיר רשות אחת הן לטלטל ב' אמות בזה וב' אמות בזה, וטעמייהו דרב ושמואל מפרשא ואזלא: קשיא דרב אדרב. דא"ר לעיל (פט.): בגגין השוין לרבנן דאסרי אהדדי, אלמא: לא אמר גוד אסיק מחיצות שביניהם להיות מובדלת. ה"נ בגגין השוין לר"מ, נהי נמי דהאי לא אסר אחבריה, דחדא רשותא משוי להו, מיהו בני רה"ר העוברת לפניהם ולאחריהם ולצידי החיצונות אמאי לא אסרי עלייהו? הא ליכא מחיצות לגגין, ומחיצות תחתונות אמר רב דלא מהני להו. וכן בגג יחידי לרבנן, ליתסרו עליה בני רה"ר וחצירות שסביבותיו: ומשני: התם בין גג לגג לא אמרינן גוד אסיק, דלא מינכרן מחיצתא שהן מכוסות בגגין. הלכך, כיון דאמרו רבנן יש חלוק רשויות למעלה, וגוד אסיק נמי בכי הני לא אמרי – הרי הן פרוזים כל אחד לרשות האסורה לו, לפיכך אסור לטלטל בו: אבל הכא מחיצות מינכרן. וקאמרינן בהו גוד אסיק. הלכך: לר' מאיר דמשוי להו חדא רשותא – ליכא דליסר, דהא מחיצות חיצונות אית להו, והוו כולהו כחד גג מוקף מחיצות, וכן גג יחידי לרבנן: ה"ג: התם לא מינכרא מחיצתא הכא מינכרא מחיצתא: התם ליכא יותר מבית סאתים. כיון דאית ליה לשמואל גוד אסיק אף במחיצות שביניהם, ואע"פ שאינן ניכרים. ופלוגתייהו קמייתא אליבא דרבנן היא, דמשוו לכל חד רשותא באנפי נפשיה – הוי כל גג וגג מוקף בפני עצמו, ובכל חדא ליכא יותר מבית סאתים. אבל הכא(א) דפלגינן אליבא דר' מאיר דמשוי לכולהו כחד, וכולן ניתרין במחיצות חיצונות – יש כאן יותר מבית סאתים, והיקף זה דגוד אסיק אינו היקף לדירה. דהנך מחיצות של מטה אף על פי שנעשו לדירה – למטה עבידן, לדור בחללן למטה, ולא לדירת גג. הלכך: כי מסקינן להו – הוי מוקף יותר מבית סאתים שלא הוקף לדירה וגג יחידי לרבנן נמי, בדאיכא טפי מבית סאתים, דומיא דגגין השוין לרבי מאיר: מותר לטלטל בכולה. ואפילו ישנה יותר מבית סאתים, דהוקף לדירה הוא: להבריח

תוספות

כרמלית ורה"י קמבעיא ליה. וכגון שהעמוד מופלג מן הגג ד'. דאי בסמוך לו – לא הוי עמוד רה"י דנפרך במילואו לגג, וכגג דמי. אבל כשהוא מופלג – אסור, אע"ג דדרך למעלה מעשרה משתמש, דהוי מקום פטור – מ"מ אסור להחליף. ואפילו מאן דשרי לעיל – הכא מודה, כיון דאין נח במקום פטור:

אלא ב' אמות בגג ושתי אמות באכסדרה מהו. פירש בקונטרס: ע"ג תקרה של אכסדרה של בעלים אחרים, יותר מבית סאתים דהשתא הוי ליה כרמלית. אבל תוך אכסדרה לא רצה לפרש, דכיון דמקורה – לא הוי כרמלית במה שהוא יותר מבית סאתים. כדמוכח בפרק "עושין פסין" (לעיל דף כה.), דאמר: קרפף יותר מבית סאתים וקירה בו בית סאה כו'. ומיבעיא ליה באכסדרה, דלא שייך בה כל כך כשם שדיורין חלוקין למטה – דלית בה דיורין כל כך, כדפי' בקונטרס, ובתר הכי בעי בחורבה, דחזי' לדירה טפי. ובעי נמי בגג דחורבה, כמו באכסדרה. ומלשון הקונטרס משמע דבחורבה לא בעי בגג(ב) אלא בקרקע החורבה. ור"ת פי': ב' אמות בגג דהוי רה"י, וב' אמות בעמוד – שהוא כרמלית, שאינו גבוה י' והוא רחב ד'. וחשיבא לגג כרה"י, משום דמהני ביה עירוב לטלטל בכולו ולא הוי כשאר כרמלית:

או דילמא כיון דמגג לגג אסיר. פי' בקונטרס: וטעמא דרבנן – משום דקפדי אשינוי בעלים. קצת קשה: דלקמן (צא:) אמרינן גג וחצר ומרפסת רשות אחת לרבנן, משמע: אע"פ שהן של בעלים הרבה:

ושמואל אמר אין מטלטלין בו אלא בד'. פי' בקונטרס: והא דקאמר ר"מ רשות אחת – היינו לטלטל ב' אמות בזה וב' אמות בזה. אע"ג דלפי המסקנא דמוקי שמואל ביתר מב' סאתים אתי שפיר, דאיכא לאוקומי מתני' דלא הוי יותר מבית סאתים – מ"מ הוצרך לפרש הקונטרס למאי דסלקא דעתיה השתא:

קשיא דרב אדרב. דס"ד דבלא מינכר מחיצה איירי, דאי מינכר מחיצתא לא היה שמואל אומר "אין מטלטלין בו אלא בארבע": **הכא** דהוי יותר מבית סאתים. ולא אמרינן גוד אסיק לר' מאיר בגגין הרבה, אלא במחיצות החיצונות, כיון דכולן רשות אחת הן. אע"ג דלענין כלים ששבתו בבית אינו רשות אחת ואמרינן גוד אסיק לשמואל. ואם תאמר: כיון דשמואל חשיב גג כקרפף לאסור ביתר מבית סאתים, אם כן בבית סאתים או בפחות נמי יחשב כקרפף בית סאתים שלא הוקף לדירה, ויאסר לטלטל מגג לחצר לרבנן כמו מקרפף לחצר. ולקמן (צא.) אמרי': דלרבנן גג וחצר רשות אחת, וקרפיפות רשות אחת! וי"ל: דדירת גג הויא טפי דירה מבקרפף, לענין כשאינו יותר מבית סאתים: **איתמר** ספינה. ביתירה מבית סאתים איירי, כדפי' בקונטרס. ופליגי אי חשיבי מחיצה דספינה כמוקפת לדירה, אי לא. אבל בפחות מבית סאתים – לכולי עלמא הויא מחיצה, ומטלטל בה, דהא נעשה כולה כד"א. דפסקי רב ושמואל כרבן גמליאל בספינה בפ' "מי שהוציאוהו" (לעיל דף מג:). ואי אפילו בפחות מבית סאתים אין מטלטלין בה אלא בד' – לא היתה נחשבת כד"א כמו בשבת(ג) בתל ונקע, דדוקא מד' אמות ועד בית סאתים, אבל יותר מבית סאתים – לא: דהא

רבינו חננאל

נפשיה אלא לנטורי ביתיה הוא דעביד. שתי אמות בגג שהוא רה"י וב' אמות בעמוד שהוא כרמלית כו'. בעי רמי בר חמא ב' אמות בגג וב' אמות באכסדרה כיון דמגג לגג אסור מגג לאכסדרה נמי אסור כו' ועלתה בתיקו בעי רב ביבי בן אביי ב' אמות בגג וב' אמות בחורבה מהו אמר רב כהנא לאו היינו בעי דרמי בר חמא ועלתה בתיקו. איקפד רב ביבי בר אביי רב כהנא מאחר אתי נצי כלומר הנה הוא בא ומריב אכסדרא לא חזיא לדירה כו' ועלתה גם זו בתיקו. גגין השוין לר"מ דתני כל גגות העיר רשות אחת וגג יחידי לרבנן דתנן כל אחד רשות לעצמו. רב אמר מותר לטלטל בכולו דהכא מינכרא מילתא (מיחזקי) [ומתחזי] מחיצתא ואמרינן גוד אסיק מחיצתא ולא דמי לגג בין הגגין דהתם לא מינכרן ולא (מתחזק) [מתחזי] מחיצתא דכל גג וגג לפיכך אמר רב התם אין מטלטלין בו אלא בד' אמות ושמואל אמר הכא בגגין השוין לר' מאיר ולגג יחידי לרבנן אין מטלטלין בהן אלא בד' מאי [טעמא] משום דהני גגין הוויין להו יתר מבית סאתים והני מחיצות למטה עבדין למעלה לא עבדין. והוויין כקרפף שלא הוקף לדירה וכל קרפף יתר מבית סאתים שלא הוקף לדירה אין מיטלטלין בו אלא בד' וכי קאמינא בגג בין הגגין מותר לטלטלו בכולו בגג שיש לו בית סאתים אבל ביתר מבית סאתים לא וכן חלק בספינה רב אמר מותר לטלטל בכל הספינה דהא איכא מחיצות ושמואל אמר הני מחיצתא להבריח מים עשויות ולא לדירה הלכך אין מטלטלין בה אלא בד' אמות.

מסורת הש"ס

[ב"מ נו: ב"ב קטז: נדה לג:]

הגהות הב"ח

(א) רש"י ד"ה התם ליכא וכו' אבל הכא דפליגי אליבא: (ב) תום' ד"ה אלא וכו' לא בעי בגג החורבה אלא בקרקע החורב' ורבינו חננאל פירש וכו' חשיב לגג: (ג) ד"ה איתמר וכו' כמו בשבת כ"ב פ"ק דף טו:

דְּהָא אִיכָּא מְחִיצָתָא. וּשְׁמוּאֵל אָמַר: אֵין מְטַלְטְלִין בָּהּ אֶלָּא בְּאַרְבַּע אַמּוֹת — מְחִיצוֹת לְהַבְרִיחַ מַיִם עֲשׂוּיוֹת. אֲמַר לֵיהּ רַב חִיָּיא בַּר יוֹסֵף לִשְׁמוּאֵל: הִילְכְתָא כְּוָותָךְ, אוֹ הִילְכְתָא כְּרַב? אֲמַר לֵיהּ: [א]הִילְכְתָא כְּרַב. אָמַר רַב גִּידֵּל, אָמַר רַב חִיָּיא בַּר יוֹסֵף: [ב]וּמוֹדֶה רַב שֶׁאִם כְּפָאָהּ עַל פִּיהָ — שֶׁאֵין מְטַלְטְלִין בָּהּ אֶלָּא בְּאַרְבַּע אַמּוֹת. כְּפָאָהּ לְמַאי? אִילֵימָא לָדוּר תַּחְתֶּיהָ — מַאי שְׁנָא מִגַּג יְחִידִי? אֶלָּא שֶׁכְּפָאָהּ לְזוּפְתָהּ. רַב אַשִׁי מַתְנֵי לָהּ אַסְפִינָה, וְרַב אַחָא בְּרֵיהּ דְּרָבָא מַתְנֵי לָהּ אַאַכְסַדְרָא. *דְּאִיתְּמַר: אַכְסַדְרָה בַּבִּקְעָה, רַב אָמַר: [ג]מוּתָּר לְטַלְטֵל בְּכוּלָּהּ, וּשְׁמוּאֵל אָמַר: אֵין מְטַלְטְלִין בָּהּ אֶלָּא בְּאַרְבַּע. רַב אָמַר: מוּתָּר לְטַלְטֵל בְּכוּלָּהּ — אָמְרִינַן: "פִּי תִקְרָה יוֹרֵד וְסוֹתֵם". וּשְׁמוּאֵל אָמַר: אֵין מְטַלְטְלִין בָּהּ אֶלָּא בְּאַרְבַּע — לָא אָמְרִינַן: "פִּי תִקְרָה יוֹרֵד וְסוֹתֵם". וְרַב אַלִּיבָּא דְּר"מ, לִיטַלְטְלִי מִגַּג לְחָצֵר! גְּזֵירָה מִשּׁוּם *דְּרַב יִצְחָק בַּר אַבְדִּימִי. וּשְׁמוּאֵל אַלִּיבָּא דְּרַבָּנַן, נִיטַלְטֵל מִגַּג לְקַרְפֵּף! אָמַר *רָבָא בַּר עוּלָּא: גְּזֵירָה שֶׁמָּא יִפְחַת הַגַּג. א"ה, מִקַּרְפֵּף לְקַרְפֵּף נַמִי לֹא יְטַלְטֵל, דִּילְמָא מִפְּחִית וְאָתֵי לְטַלְטוֹלֵי! הָתָם, אִי מִפְּחִית — מִינְכְּרָא לֵיהּ מִילְּתָא, הָכָא, אִי מִפְּחִית — לָא מִינְכְּרָא מִילְּתָא. *אָמַר רַב יְהוּדָה: כְּשֶׁתִּמְצָא לוֹמַר, לְדִבְרֵי רַבִּי מֵאִיר: גַּגִּין רְשׁוּת לְעַצְמָן, חֲצֵירוֹת רְשׁוּת לְעַצְמָן, קַרְפֵּיפוֹת

רש"י

לְהַבְרִיחַ מַיִם. וְלֹא לְדִירָה: וּמוֹדֶה רַב שֶׁאִם כְּפָאָהּ עַל פִּיהָ. וְגוֹבְהָהּ יוֹתֵר מֵעֲשָׂרָה, אֵין מְטַלְטְלִין בָּהּ אֶלָּא בְּאַרְבַּע: מַאי שְׁנָא מִגַּג יְחִידִי. דְּאָמַר רַב: אֲפִילּוּ לְרַבָּנַן מוּתָּר לְטַלְטֵל בְּכוּלּוֹ, וַאֲפִילּוּ יוֹתֵר מִבֵּית סָאתַיִם. דְּכֵיוָן דִּמְחִיצּוֹת לְדִירָה נַעֲשׂוּ אע"פ שֶׁלֹּא לְדִירַת מַעְלָה עֲשָׂאוּם. כִּי אָמְרִינַן בְּהוּ גּוֹד אַסֵּיק — הָוֵי כְּהֶיקֵּף לְדִירָה. ה"נ, כֵּיוָן דִּכְפָאָהּ לָדוּר — כְּפִיָּיתָהּ זוֹ הִיא עֲשִׂיַּית מְחִיצָּתָהּ לְדִירַת מַטָּן, כִּי אָמְרַתְּ בְּהוּ גּוֹד אַסֵּיק — הָוֵי הֶיקֵּף לְדִירָה: שֶׁכְּפָאָהּ לְזוּפְתָהּ. שֶׁבִּיטֵּל מְחִיצּוֹתֶיהָ מִתּוֹרַת דִּירָה, דְּאֵינָן עוֹמְדוֹת כָּל זְמַן כְּפִיָּיתָהּ לֹא לְדִירַת מַעְלָן וְלֹא לְדִירַת מַטָּן, וְהָווּ כְּעַמּוּד בְּעָלְמָא. וְכִי אָמְרַתְּ בְּהוּ גּוֹד אַסֵּיק — הָוֵי הֶיקֵּף יוֹתֵר מִבֵּית סָאתַיִם שֶׁלֹּא הוּקַּף לְדִירָה, וְכַרְמְלִית הִיא: מַתְנֵי לָהּ. לְהָא דְּרַב חִיָּיא בַּר יוֹסֵף אַאַכְסַדְרָה: אַכְסַדְרָה בַּבִּקְעָה. הַבִּקְעָה כַּרְמְלִית, כִּדְאָמְרִינַן בִּ"יְצִיאוֹת הַשַּׁבָּת" (שבת ו:) וְאַכְסַדְרָה זוֹ פְּרוּצָה מִד' רוּחוֹתֶיהָ, וְעוֹמֵד קֵירוּיָהּ עַל ד' יְתֵידוֹת וְנוֹתְנִין ד' קוֹרוֹת מִיָּתֵד לְיָתֵד, וַעֲלֵיהֶן מְסַדְּרִין הַנְּסָרִין. וְאוֹתָן הַקּוֹרוֹת קָרֵי פִּי תִקְרָה. וְהַאי דְּנָקַט בִּקְעָה — מִשּׁוּם דִּבְעִיר סְתָם אַכְסַדְרָאוֹת סְמוּכוֹת לְהַקִּיף בַּיִת אוֹ חָצֵר, וְאִיכָּא מְחִיצָּה אַחַת אוֹ שְׁתַּיִם. וּמוֹדֶה שְׁמוּאֵל הָתָם דִּמְטַלְטְלִין, כִּדְאָמְרִינַן לְקַמָּן: וְרַב אַלִּיבָּא דר"מ. כֵּיוָן דְּאָמַר בְּגַגִּין הַשָּׁוִין מְטַלְטְלִין בְּכוּלָּן, אַלְמָא: לָאו כַּרְמְלִית נִינְהוּ לִיטַלְטֵל מִגַּג לְחָצֵר. אַלָּמָּה אָמְרִינַן לְקַמָּן לְדִבְרֵי ר"מ גַּגִּין רְשׁוּת לְעַצְמָן, חֲצֵירוֹת רְשׁוּת לְעַצְמָן, דְּאֵין מְטַלְטְלִין מִגַּג לְחָצֵר? וְאַלִּיבָּא דְּרַבָּנַן בְּגַג יְחִידִי — לֵיכָּא לְמִיפְרַךְ לֵיהּ לְרַב לִיטַלְטֵל מִינֵּיהּ לְחָצֵר, דִּלְרַבָּנַן הָכִי נַמִי שָׁרֵי. דְּאָמְרִי' לְקַמָּן (צא.): לְדִבְרֵי חֲכָמִים גַּגִּין וַחֲצֵירוֹת רְשׁוּת אַחַת, וּמְטַלְטְלִין מִגַּג יְחִידִי לְחָצֵר שֶׁל רַבִּים שֶׁיֵּשׁ לוֹ רְשׁוּת בָּהּ וְלִשְׁמוּאֵל לָא מָצֵי לְמִיפְרַךְ אַלִּיבָּא דְּר' מֵאִיר לִיטַלְטֵל מִגַּג לְחָצֵר — דְּהָא שְׁמוּאֵל גַּגִּין הַשָּׁוִין לְר' מֵאִיר כַּרְמְלִית מְשַׁוֵּי לְהוּ, לְפִיכָךְ אֵין מְטַלְטְלִין מֵהֶן לְחָצֵר שֶׁל רַבִּים, דַּהֲוָיָא רְשׁוּת הַיָּחִיד. דַּאֲפִילּוּ לֹא עֵירְבָה קי"ל בְּמַסֶּ' שַׁבָּת בְּפ' "אִם לֹא הֵבִיא כְּלִי" (דף קל:) *דִּמְטַלְטְלִין בְּכוּלָּהּ. וְהָא דְּאָמַר לְקַמָּן לְדִבְרֵי חֲכָמִים גַּגִּין וַחֲצֵירוֹת רְשׁוּת אַחַת — שְׁמוּאֵל מוֹקֵי לָהּ בְּגַג בֵּין הַגַּגִּין, דְּלִשְׁמוּאֵל דְּאִית לֵיהּ גּוֹד אַסֵּיק בִּמְחִיצּוֹת שֶׁבֵּינֵיהֶן — לֵיכָּא לְכָל אֶחָד יוֹתֵר מִבֵּית סָאתַיִם. א"נ: בְּגַג יְחִידִי, דְּלֵיכָּא יוֹתֵר מִבֵּית סָאתַיִם. וְאַשְׁמְעִינַן אע"ג דְּגַג לְרַבָּנַן רְשׁוּת מְיוּחֶדֶת, וְחָצֵר הוּא רְשׁוּת שׁוּתָּפוּת — מְטַלְטְלִין, דְּלָא גְּזוּר רַבָּנַן מרה"י לִרְשׁוּת שׁוּתָּפִין אֶלָּא בְּבָתִּים, כְּגוֹן מִבַּיִת לְחָצֵר: מִשּׁוּם דְּרַב יִצְחָק. בְּרֵישׁ פִּירְקִין, גְּזֵירָה מִשּׁוּם תֵּל בְּרה"ר: וּשְׁמוּאֵל אַלִּיבָּא דְּרַבָּנַן. בְּגַג יְחִידִי יוֹתֵר מִבֵּית סָאתַיִם, כֵּיוָן דְּאָמַר דְּהַאי גּוֹד אַסֵּיק — לָא הָוֵי הֶיקֵּף לְדִירָה, וְכַרְמְלִית הִיא, לִיטַלְטֵל מִינֵּיהּ לְקַרְפֵּף יוֹתֵר מִבֵּית סָאתַיִם שְׁתֵּי אַמּוֹת בָּזֶה וּב' אַמּוֹת בָּזֶה. אַלָּמָּה אָמְרִי' לְקַמָּן: לְדִבְרֵי חֲכָמִים גַּגִּין וַחֲצֵירוֹת רְשׁוּת אַחַת וְקַרְפֵּיפוֹת רְשׁוּת אַחַת, דְּאֵין מְטַלְטְלִין מֵהֶן לְקַרְפֵּף. וְאַלִּיבָּא דר"מ לֵיכָּא לְמִיפְרַךְ לִיטַלְטֵל מִגַּג לְקַרְפֵּף — דְּהָא תַּרְוַויְיהוּ כַּרְמְלִית נִינְהוּ, דְּהָא [א]גַּג יְחִידִי יוֹתֵר מִבֵּית סָאתַיִם אוֹקִימְנָא גְּזֵירָה מִשּׁוּם תֵּל בְּרה"ר. וּלְרַב נַמִי אַלִּיבָּא דְּרַבָּנַן לֵיכָּא לְמִיפְרַךְ, דְּהָא רַב גַּג יְחִידִי יוֹתֵר מִבֵּית סָאתַיִם רה"י מְשַׁוֵּי לֵיהּ, וּבְגַגִּין הַשָּׁוִין לְרַב אַלִּיבָּא דְּרַבִּי מֵאִיר דְּמוּתָּר לְטַלְטֵל בְּכוּלָּן — לֵיכָּא לְמִיפְרַךְ לִיטַלְטֵל מִינַּיְיהוּ לְקַרְפֵּף *פָּחוֹת מִסָּאתַיִם גְּזֵירָה מִשּׁוּם תֵּל. וּלְרַבָּנַן מִגַּג יְחִידִי אַלִּיבָּא דְּרַב דִּמְשַׁוֵּי לֵיהּ רה"י נַמִי לָא פָּרְכִינַן: לִיטַלְטֵל מִינֵּיהּ לְקַרְפֵּף פָּחוֹת מִבֵּית סָאתַיִם. וְכֵן מֵחָצֵר לְקַרְפֵּף בֵּין לְר"מ בֵּין לְרַבָּנַן — מִשּׁוּם דְּקַרְפֵּף חָלוּק מֵחָצֵר, דְּקַרְפֵּף מוּקְצֶה לְתַשְׁמִישׁ שֶׁאֵינוֹ תָּדִיר, אֲבָל חָצֵר וְגַגִּין שָׁוֶה תַּשְׁמִישָׁן. וּלְרַב לָא פָּרְכִינַן בְּגַגִּין הַשָּׁוִין לְרַבָּנַן, דִּמְשַׁוֵּי לְהוּ רַב אַלִּיבַּיְיהוּ כַּרְמְלִית לִיטַלְטֵל מִינַּיְיהוּ לְקַרְפֵּף יוֹתֵר מִבֵּית סָאתַיִם. דְּאע"ג דִּמְשַׁוֵּי לְהוּ רַב כַּרְמְלִית, מִפְּנֵי שֶׁפְּרוּצִין זֶה לָזֶה — הנ"מ לְהַחְמִיר, לֶאֱסוֹר טִלְטוּל שֶׁל כָּל אֶחָד וְאֶחָד בְּיוֹתֵר מִד'. אֲבָל לָא מְשַׁוֵּי לֵיהּ כַּרְמְלִית גְּמוּרָה לְהָקֵל לְטַלְטֵל מִתּוֹכָן לְכַרְמְלִית גְּמוּרָה. דַּאֲמָרַן לְעֵיל לְגַבֵּי גַּג בֵּין הַגַּגִּין לְרַב, דְּאָסוּר לְטַלְטֵל מִמֶּנּוּ לְחוּרְבָּה וּלְאַכְסַדְרָה. וְאע"ג דִּשְׁנֵיהֶן אֲסוּרִין לְטַלְטֵל בְּתוֹכָן אֶלָּא בְּד' אַמּוֹת, מ"מ הוֹאִיל וְאֵין רְשׁוּתַיְיהוּ דּוֹמוֹת *דְּגַג חֲזֵי לְדִירָה טְפֵי[ב] מֵחָצֵר וְאַכְסַדְרָה לְטַלְטֵל מִמֶּנּוּ לְחוּרְבָּה וּלְאַכְסַדְרָה. וכ"ש הָכָא, דְּגַג חֲזֵי לְדִירָה טְפֵי מִקַּרְפֵּף. אֲבָל לִשְׁמוּאֵל דִּמְשַׁוֵּי גַּג יְחִידִי כַּרְמְלִית גָּמוּר דְּיוֹתֵר מִבֵּית סָאתַיִם הוּא פָּרְכִינַן: גְּזֵירָה שֶׁמָּא יִפְחַת הַגַּג. וְיֶחְסַר מִבֵּית סָאתַיִם, וְיַקְּרוּ גַּם אֶת הַבַּיִת לְמִדַּת הַגַּג מִלְּמַטָּה, וְיִתְּנוּ הַמְּחִיצָּה כְּנֶגֶד שְׂפַת הַגַּג דְּהַשְׁתָּא לֵיכָּא יוֹתֵר מִבֵּית סָאתַיִם וַהֲוֵי רה"י, וְאָתֵי לְטַלְטוֹלֵי מִינֵּיהּ לְקַרְפֵּף כְּמֵעִיקָּרָא: א"ה מִקַּרְפֵּף. יוֹתֵר מִבֵּית סָאתַיִם, לְקַרְפֵּף יוֹתֵר מִבֵּית סָאתַיִם — נַמִי לָא לִיטַלְטֵל אֲפִילּוּ בְּתוֹךְ ד' דִּילְמָא מִפְחִית חַד מִינַּיְיהוּ וַהֲוֵי רה"י מַעֲלְיָיתָא, וְאָתֵי לְטַלְטוֹלֵי כְּמֵעִיקָּרָא מִינֵּיהּ לְחוּרְבָּה, וַהֲוֵי כַּרְמְלִית: אִי מִפְּחִית לָא מִינְכְּרָא מִילְּתָא. כֵּיוָן דְּלֵיכָּא מְחִיצּוֹת עַל הַגַּג לָא מִינְכְּרָא מִילְּתָא. וְלָא מִיחֲזֵי כְּפָחוֹת מִבֵּית סָאתַיִם דָּבָר שֶׁאֵין לוֹ מְחִיצּוֹת לָא סָלֵיק לֵיהּ אוּמְדָּנָא שַׁפִּיר, וְסָבְרִי אַכַּתִּי טְפֵי מִבֵּית סָאתַיִם הוּא: כְּשֶׁתִּמְצָא לוֹמַר. כְּשֶׁתַּעֲמוֹד עַל סוֹף דַּעְתָּן, זֶהוּ גְּמַר דִּבְרֵיהֶן: לְדִבְרֵי ר"מ גַּגִּין רְשׁוּת לְעַצְמָן. וּמְטַלְטְלִין מִגַּגּוֹ שֶׁל רְאוּבֵן לְגַגּוֹ שֶׁל שִׁמְעוֹן: וַחֲצֵירוֹת רְשׁוּת לְעַצְמָן. וּמְטַלְטְלִין מֵחֲצֵירוֹ שֶׁל רְאוּבֵן לַחֲצֵירוֹ שֶׁל שִׁמְעוֹן כֵּלִים שֶׁשָּׁבְתוּ בֶּחָצֵר, וְכֵן מֵחָצֵר שֶׁל רַבִּים לְחָצֵר שֶׁל רַבִּים: וְקַרְפֵּיפוֹת

תוספות

דהא איכא מחיצתא. ואפילו לר' זירא דאמר בריש "מי שהוציאוהו" (לעיל דף מג.): מחילות להבריח מים עשויות, היינו דוקא לענין יוצא חוץ לתחום, דלא שרי להלך את כולה: **ורב** אליבא דר"מ ליטלטל מגג לחצר. לשמואל אליבא דר' מאיר לא מצי למיפרך, כדפי' בקונטרס: דלשמואל גגין השוין לר"מ הוי כרמלית, לפיכך אין מטלטלין מהן לחצר. ופחות מבית סאתים נמי, אע"ג דלא הוי כרמלית — מ"מ, כיון דחשיב ליה לשמואל אין מוקף לדירה — ליכא למיפרך דליטלטל מגג לחצר. אע"ג דלרבנן בגג יתר מבית סאתים אסור לטלטל ממנו לחצר לשמואל, בפחות מבית סאתים — שרי, מ"מ יאמר שמואל דלר"מ יש לגג תורת קרפף, בין ביתר מבית סאתים בין בפחות.

ליטלטל מגג לחצר. אע"ג דידע טעמא דר"מ (ג)דגג גבוה ונמוך, דהוי משום דרב יצחק בר אבדימי מגג לחצר ענייהם חלוקים — ס"ד דלא דמו לתל ברה"ר.

לשמואל אליבא דרבנן לטלטל מגג לקרפף. פירש בקונטרס(ד): בגג יתר מבית סאתים, לקרפף יתר מבית סאתים. כיון דחשיב ליה אין מוקף לדירה, והוו תרוייהו כרמלית. וא"ת: ומנא ליה דאסור? דאי משום דאמרי רבנן לקמן דגגין וחצירות רשות אחת, וקרפיפות רשות אחת, התם ע"כ באין יתירים מבית סאתים, כדפירש בסמוך בקונטרס, דביתירים לא יאמר ר"ש דחצר וקרפף רשות אחת, דבהדיא מוכח בפ' "עושין פסין" (לעיל דף כג:) גבי נזרע רובו, דקרפף יתר מבית סאתים לר"ש הוי כרמלית. ונראה לר"י: דבגג דלא הוי יתר מבית סאתים פריך, דליטלטל לקרפף שאינו יתר מבית סאתים לרבנן, אע"ג דדירת גג חשיב טפי משל קרפף, שמותר לטלטל מגג לחצר ומקרפף לחצר אסור — מ"מ הוי לן למישרי מגג לקרפף, דטפי דמי לקרפף מלחצר. דכשהוא יתר מבית סאתים — הוי כרמלית כמו קרפף, וחצר אפילו בית עשרה כורים שריא. ומשני: גזירה שמא יפחת. פי': שמא יפחת הגג באמצעיתו, וישתמשו בני הבית על הגג דרך הפתח, ואז הוי הגג חשוב מוקף לדירה, ואסור לטלטל ממנו לקרפף כמו(ה) מחצר. אע"ג דהוי מוקף ולבסוף פתח, דלא חשיב מוקף לדירה. דדוקא בקרפף שלא הוקף לדירה לא מהני הוקף ולבסוף פתח, אבל בגג דבלאו הכי חשיב קצת מוקף לדירה, דהא מותר לטלטל ממנו לחצר — מהני ליה הפתח לשוייה מוקף לדירה לגמרי, כחצר. ופריך: א"ה, מקרפף בית סאתים לקרפף בית סאתים נמי לא ליטלטל, שמא יפחת, פירוש: יפרוץ האחד יתר מעשר במילואו לרה"ר או לבקעה. ומשום דנקט לשון פחת גבי גג, נקט נמי האי לישנא גבי פירצת קרפף. ומשני: התם אי (ו)פחות — מינכר, אבל הכא גג לא מינכרא מילתא לעומד בקרפף. ולעומד על הגג נמי לא מינכרא, שיהא אסור לטלטל ממנו לקרפף מחמת פחת זה.

לדברי ר"מ גגין רשות אחת הן כו'. גגין הוא בפירוש במתני', וה"ה חצירות או קרפיפות, הואיל ותשמישן שוה כמו גגין. אבל בתים — לא, דתשמישן תדיר. ועוד: דכי היכי דלרבנן הוי קרפיפות או חצירות רשות אחת, דהא אפילו גג וחצר הוי רשות אחת — כ"ש חצר וחצר. ה"נ לר"מ, דר"מ לא פליג ארבנן אלא בגג וחצר, משום דרב יצחק בר אבדימי: אמר

עין משפט נר מצוה

ב א ב מיי' פי"ד מהל' שבת הלכה ב טוש"ע א"ח סי' שסב סעיף ד:
ג ג מיי' פי"ז מהלכות שבת הלכה לה:

רבינו חננאל

ומודה רב היכא דאפכה לספינה על פיה כדי לזופתה שאין מטלטלין בה אלא בד' אמות והני מילי לזופתה אבל לדור תחתיה הרי הוא כבית וכן אכסדרה בבקעה רב אמר מותר לטלטל בכולה ושמואל אמר אין מטלטלין בה אלא בד' אמות והלכתא בכל הני שמעתא כוותה דרב. לרב אליבא דר' מאיר דאמר מותר לטלטל בכולן הגגין השוין כרה"י הן לטלטל מן הגג לחצר דתרווייהו [רשות] היחיד נינהו. ודחינן אמאי אין מטלטלין מגג לחצר משום דרב יצחק בר אבודימי דאמר. אומר היה ר' מאיר כל מקום שאתה מוצא ב' רשויות והן רשות אחת כגון עמוד ברה"י גבוה י' ורחב ד' אסור לכתף עליו משום תל ברה"ר. לשמואל דאמר אין מטלטלין כגון ברשות היחיד גבוה י' ורחב ד' אסור לכתף בגגין השוין ובגג יחידי לרבנן אלא בארבע משום מחיצתא למטה עבידן לחצירות ולא למעלה לגגין דהוויין להו הני גגין בקרפף יתר מבית סאתים נטלטל מגג לקרפף יטלטל *) דלמא מיפחית דהא כי קרפף וקרפף הוא אומר רבה בר עולא גזרה שמא יהיו הגגין דיהו אי הכי מקרפף לקרפף לא יטלטל דלמא מיפחית חד מן הקרפיפות והוי ליה כרה"ר. ופרקי התם גבי קרפיפות אי מיפחית מחיצתא מינכרא מלתא וממנע ולא מטלטל. אמר רב יהודה כשתמצא לומר לדברי ר' מאיר גגין וחצרות רשות לעצמן

*) אולי צ"ל נטלטל מגג לקרפף דהא כי קרפף וקרפף הוא אמר רבה בר עולא גזירה שמא יפחת הגגין אי הכי וכו'.

רב נסים גאון

פ"ט כל גגות העיר ולרב אליבא דר' מאיר ליטלטל מגג לחצר גזירה משום דרב יצחק בר אבדימי והוא שאמר בתחילת הפרק (דף פט) אומר היה ר' מאיר כל מקום שאתה מוצא ב' רשויות והן רשות אחד כו':

ס"א לחד חזי לדירה טפי מחבריה. רש"ל

הגהות הב"ח

(א) רש"י ד"ה ושמואל וכו' תרווייהו כרמלית נינהו דהא בגגים יותר כצ"ל ותיבת יחידי נמחק: (ב) בא"ד דגג חזי לדירה טפי מחורבה ואכסדרה: (ג) תוס' ד"ה לטלטל וכו' דר"מ בגג וכו' דענייהם חלוקים: (ד) ד"ה לשמואל וכו' פי' בקונטרס מגג יתר: (ה) בא"ד ואסור לטלטל ממנו לקרפף כמו מקרפף לחצר ואע"ג דמה: (ו) בא"ד ופריך אי הכי מקרפף וכו' ומשני התם אי מפחית:

מסורת הש"ס

לעיל כה. ולקמן לד: [סוכה יח:]
[שבת ע. לעיל פט.]
בקד"י רבה
[שם]
דמטלטלין בכולהו וכן בגג יחידי לרבנן אליבא דשמואל והא דאמר כו' כצ"ל מהרש"א
וכן לטלטל מינייהו לקרפף פחות מסאתים כצ"ל מהרש"א

קרפיפות רשות לעצמן. לדברי חכמים: גגין וחצירות רשות אחת, קרפיפות רשות אחת הן. לדברי רבי שמעון: כולן רשות אחת הן. תניא כוותיה דרב, תניא כוותיה דרב יהודה. תניא כוותיה דרב: כל גגות העיר רשות אחת הן, ואסור להעלות ולהוריד מן הגגין לחצר ומן החצר לגגין, וכלים ששבתו בחצר — מותר לטלטלן בחצר. בגגין — מותר לטלטלן בגגין, ובלבד שלא יהא גג גבוה י' או נמוך י', דברי ר"מ. וחכ"א: כל אחד ואחד רשות לעצמו, ואין מטלטלין בו אלא בד'. תניא כוותיה דרב יהודה: *אמר רבי: כשהיינו לומדים תורה אצל ר"ש בתקוע, היינו מעלין שמן ואלונטית מגג לגג, ומגג לחצר, ומחצר לחצר, ומחצר לקרפף, ומקרפף לקרפף אחר, עד שהיינו מגיעין אצל המעיין שהיינו רוחצין בו. אמר רבי יהודה: מעשה בשעת הסכנה והיינו מעלין ס"ת מחצר לגג, ומגג לחצר, ומחצר לקרפף, לקרות בו. °אמרו לו: אין שעת הסכנה ראיה. § "ר"ש אומר אחד גגין" וכו'. § *אמר רב: הלכה כר"ש, והוא, שלא עירבו, אבל עירבו — לא, דגזרינן דילמא אתי לאפוקי מאני דבתים לחצר. ושמואל אמר: [א]בין עירבו, בין שלא עירבו. וכן אמר ר' יוחנן: מי לחשך בין עירבו ובין שלא עירבו? מתקיף לה רב חסדא: לשמואל ולרבי יוחנן, יאמרו: שני כלים בחצר אחת, זה מותר וזה אסור! ר"ש לטעמיה דלא גזר. *דתנן, א"ר שמעון: למה הדבר דומה — לשלש חצירות הפתוחות זו לזו ופתוחות לרה"ר, ועירבו שתי החיצונות עם האמצעית, היא מותרת עמהן והן מותרות עמה, וב' החיצונות אסורין זו עם זו. ולא גזר דילמא אתי לאפוקי מאני דהא חצר להא חצר — ה"נ לא גזרינן דילמא אתי לאפוקי מאני דבתים לחצר. מתיב רב ששת, *ר"ש אומר: אחד גגות, אחד חצירות, ואחד קרפיפות — רשות אחת הן לכלים ששבתו בתוכן, ולא לכלים ששבתו בתוך הבית. אי אמרת בשלמא דעירבו — היינו דמשכחת לה מאני דבתים בחצר. אלא אי אמרת בשלא עירבו — היכי משכחת לה מאני דבתים בחצר? הוא מותיב לה והוא מפרק לה: בכומתא וסודרא. ת"ש

רש"י

וקרפיפות רשות לעצמן. ואפילו הן של ב' אנשים, מטלטלין מזה לזה. דהאמר ר"מ כל גגות העיר רשות אחת, שמע מינה דס"ל דאין רשות מתחלקת מחמת שינוי בעלים, אלא בתים לחודייהו, מפני שהם תדירות לדירה. דמה לי גגין ומה לי חצירות ומה לי קרפיפות. אבל מגג לחצר ומגג לקרפף לר"מ לא, ואפילו של איש אחד כדאמרינן: גזירה משום תל ברה"ר. וכ"ש כשהן של שנים. ומחצר לקרפף נמי לא. דשמעינן להו לרבנן לקמן בברייתא דאסור לטלטל מחצר לקרפף. ור"מ לא שמעינן ליה דפליג עלייהו להקל אלא בחלוק רשויות דגגין, הואיל ושמן שוה. אבל ברשויות החלוקות בשמן — לא שמעינן ליה דמיקל. דדוקא קאמר ר"מ גגות דתשמישתן שוה, וכן חצירות וכן קרפיפות. ואפילו הן של שנים, דבשינוי בעלים לא מיתסרי אלא בתים לר"מ, וגגין לרבנן. אבל בחלוק תשמיש ושינוי שם הרשות — קפיד. הלכך: מחצר לקרפף אסור, ואפילו הוא שלו, ואינו יותר מבית סאתים. דעל כרחך הנך קרפיפות בשאין יתירים על בית סאתים קאמר. דאי ביתירים — בהא לימא רבי שמעון מטלטלין? הא כרמלית היא, וליכא מאן דפליג דמחצר המשכן גמרי. ועוד, בהדיא אמרינן בשלהי "עושין פסין"* דפלוגתא דר"ש ורבנן בקרפף בית סאתים היא, ואפילו חצר וקרפף של איש אחד אסרי רבנן, דקאמרי התם: קרפף יותר מבית סאתים שהוקף לדירה, נזרע רובו — הרי הוא כגנה כו' ואמר רב הונא בריה דרב יהושע כו' וכי דייקת ביה שמעינן מינה דלא שרי ר"ש אלא בקרפף בית סאתים, ורבנן אסרי אע"ג דלחד גברא הוא: לדברי חכמים. דלא גזרו משום תל, גגין וחצירות רשות אחת הן, לא שיטלטל מגג לגג אם חלוקין בעליהן. משום דגגין לרבנן כבתים משוי להו על ידי חלוק שלמטה. אבל מחצר של רבים לחצר של רבים — מטלטלין, ומגג לחצר דרבים — מטלטלין. ואע"ג דגג רשותא דידיה, וחצר דשותפות, כדתניא בברייתא לקמן — הואיל וגג תשמיש שאינו תדיר הוא, לא הוי ממש כבית, ומטלטל ממנו לחצר: קרפיפות רשות אחת. ואפילו הן של שנים. דכל רשות ששמו שוה מותר לו, חוץ מן הגגין. אבל מחצר לקרפף, אפילו דחד גברא — אסיר, ולא דמי לגג וחצר. דתשמישתיה דגג שוה לחצר הוא. והכי שמיע ליה לרב יהודה, וממתניתין דייק לה. מדקאמר ר"ש: כולן רשות אחת, מכלל דרבנן לאו חדא רשותא משוי להו לכולהו. וברייתא מסייעא ליה לקמן, דקתני: גג וחצר ואכסדרה ומרפסת כולן רשות אחת הן. וחצר ומרפסת כב' חצירות דמי. ומדוקיא דידיה, דלא תנא ביה קרפף ומבוי — מוקמינן לה כרבנן. דאי ר"ש — אפילו קרפף נמי מישתרי בהדי חצר. ואי ר"מ — גג וחצר לא מישתרו, דהא בהדיא אסר במתני' מנמוך לגבוה: לדברי ר"ש כולן רשות אחת. דלא תימא האי דא"ר שמעון: אחד גגות ואחד חצירות ואחד קרפיפות — כל חדא וחדא רשותא באנפי נפשיה משוי לה, גגין לעצמן וחצירות לעצמן וקרפיפות לעצמן, דהא סברא — לר"מ אית ליה. אבל ר"ש — כולהו חדא רשותא משוי להו. הכי שמיע ליה לרב יהודה, וברייתא מסייעא ליה. דתניא כוותיה לקמן: היינו מעלין שמן ואלונטית מגג לגג, ומגג לחצר, ומחצר לחצר, ומחצר לקרפף: תניא כוותיה דרב. דקאמר לעיל (פט.) בגגין השוין לרבנן דאין מטלטלין בו אלא בד' דקסברי אהדדי, ולא אמרינן "גוד אסיק" במחיצות שאין ניכרות: רשות אחת. ומטלטלין מזה לזה: ואסור להעלות ולהוריד. ר"מ לטעמיה, דגזר משום תל: מותר לטלטלן בחצר. אע"פ שלא עירבה וה"ה לשאר חצירות: רשות לעצמו. ואין מטלטלין מזה לזה: ואין מטלטלין בו. אפילו בגג עצמו: תניא כוותיה דרב יהודה. אליבא דר"ש: שמן. לסוך בו: אלונטית. להסתפג בה: מגג לגג ומגג לחצר, ומחצר לקרפף, ומקרפף לקרפף, כולהו גרסינן: והוא שלא עירבו. בני החצירות כל אחת לעצמה, דהשתא לא שכיחי כלי הבתים בחצר, וליכא למיגזר אי שרית להוציא כלים ששבתו בזו להכניסן לחברתה, אתי לאפוקי נמי לה כלי הבית: אבל עירבו. כל חצר לעצמה ולא עירבו ג' החצירות יחד — אסור לטלטל מזו לזו אפילו כלי החצר, דכיון דשכיחי מאני דבתים בחצר — גזרינן דילמא אתי לאפוקי מאני דבתים שבחצר זו לחצר זו. ור"ש מודה בזו, דקתני: אבל לא לכלים ששבתו בתוך הבית: מי לחשך. לא גרסינן: היינו דמשכחת לה מאני דבתים בחצר. דאיצטריך למיתני: אבל לא לכלים ששבתו בתוך הבית: *בכומתא וסודרא. ששבתו בתוך הבית, והוליכן לחצר דרך מלבוש. אגבי

תוספות

אמר רב הלכה כר"ש והוא שלא עירבו. אין לפרש דר"ש אין מחלק בין עירבו ולא עירבו, ורב בלא עירבו סבר ליה כוותיה. דא"כ בסמוך, דפריך רב חסדא לשמואל ור' יוחנן יאמרו ב' כלים בחצר אחת זה אסור וזה מותר, לרב נמי תיקשי אליבא דר"ש! ורב ששת נמי דפריך לרב: אלא אי אמרת בשלא עירבו, היכי משכחת מאני דבתים בחצר? הא רב נמי מודה דר"ש אפילו בעירבו קאמר! ולכך נראה דרב סבר דר"ש גופיה לא אמר אלא כשלא עירבו, והשתא(א) סברת שמואל איפכא מדרב. דשמואל לא גזר הכא, דאמר בין עירבו בין לא עירבו, וגבי שלש חצירות גזר — דסבר כרבנן דאמרי שלשתן אסורות לשיטת ר"ת ד"מי שהוציאוהו" (לעיל מח: ד"ה רשות). ורב הכא גזר והתם לא גזר, דפסיק התם כר"ש. ועוד: דמשני הכא שמואל דר"ש לטעמיה דלא גזר, משמע דסבר כוותיה בההיא דג' חצירות, ולשיטת ר"ת סבר כרבנן:

ושמואל אומר בין עירבו בין לא עירבו. והא דאמר *שמואל בגיטין ב"הזורק" (דף עט:): לא יעמוד אדם בגג זה ויקלוט מי גשמים בגגו של חבירו, אומר ר"י: דהתם לקלוט(ב) ולהוליך לביתו קאמר, דכמו שאסור לטלטל כלים ששבתו בבית לחצר ולגג שלא עירבו אפילו לר"ש — כן אסור מגג וחצר לבית. ודווקא מגגו של חבירו, אבל מגג של עצמו — יכול לקלוט ולהוליך לביתו, ואין גג של חבירו אוסר עליו. דשמואל לטעמיה, דאמר לעיל גוד אסיק מחיצתא. וא"ת: מאי קמ"ל שמואל. דפשיטא דאסור להוליך לביתו! וי"ל: דאשמעינן דאע"פ שקולט מן האויר, ועדיין לא נגעו מי גשמים בגג:

מי לחשך. רש"י לא גרס ליה. ואור"י: דאיתא בתורת כהנים בכמה מקומות. ור"ת נמי גרס ליה, ומפרש: מי השמיעך הלכה כר"ש בין עירבו ובין לא עירבו, ורבינו שמואל פירש: דקאי ארב. כלומר: מי הגיד לך שאתה מחלק ביניהם? אינו כן, אלא בין עירבו ובין לא עירבו. ואית דגרסי "מלחשך" בתיבה אחת, ומפרשי: שנולד מלחש [כדאיתא ביומא פג.]:

גג

רבינו חננאל

וקרפיפות רשות לעצמן לדברי חכמים גגין רשות לעצמן וחצרות רשות לעצמן וקרפיפות רשו' לעצמן. לדברי ר' שמעון רשות אחת הן. תניא כוותיה דרב כל גגות העיר רשות אחת הן. ואסור להעלות ולהוריד מגג לחצר ומחצר לגג. וכלים ששבתו בחצר מותר לטלטלן בכל החצר וכלים ששבתו בגגין מותר לטלטלן בכל הגגין ובלבד שלא יהי' גג גבוה י' טפחים או נמוך י' טפחים וחכ"א כל אחד ואחד רשות לעצמו. ואין מטלטלין בו אלא בד' אמות. תניא כרב יהודה. א"ר כשהיינו למדין תורה אצל ר' שמעון בתקוע היינו מעלין לו שמן ואלונטית מחצר לגג ומגג לקרפף ודברים פשוטין הן: **פיסקא** ר' שמעון אומר אחד גגות כו' אמר רב יהודה הלכה כר' שמעון והוא שלא עירבו בחצרות אבל עירבו בחצרות חיישינן דלמא אתי לאפוקי מני דשבתו בבתים לחצר ואתי לטלטולי מן החצר לגגין ולקרפיפות. ושמואל ור' יוחנן תרווייהו שוין בין עירבו ובין לא עירבו הלכתא כר' שמעון ואקשינן עלייהו אי בשעירבו ואפיקו מני דבתים לחצר יאמרו ב' כלים בחצר אחד והני מני דקנו שביתה בחצר שרו והני מני דקנו שביתה בבתים אסירי. ופרקינן אין ר' שמעון לטעמי' דלא גזר דתנן א"ר שמעון למה"ד לג' חצרות שפתוחות זו לזו כו' עד הכא נמי לא גזר דלמא אתי לאפוקי מני דבתים לחצר מתיב רב ששת ר' שמעון אומר אחד גגות כו' ואי אמר בשלא עירבו אי לא עירבו מני דבתים לחצר היכי משכחת להו ופריק רב ששת אליבא דרב לעולם בשלא עירבו והני מני דקנו שביתה בבתים ובחצר דמשתכחי בחצר היכי משכחת לה כגון כנתרא וסודרא דאינון כלי מלבוש ולבשם בבית ויצא בחצר ונזדמן לו ופשט אותם מעליו ונשארו בחצר. וכהאי וכיוצא בהן תנן ולא לכלים ששבתו בתוך הבית

עין משפט נר מצוה

ד א מיי' פ"ג מהלכות עירובין הלכה יח סמג עשין א טוש"ע א"ח סי' שעב סעיף א:

[נ"ל רב יהודה אמר שמואל]

מסורת הש"ס

שבת קמו: [מנחות עב.]

דף כג.

לעיל עד.

לעיל מה: עה.

[לעיל פט. וש"נ]

[עי' רש"י לעיל פד:]

הגהות הב"ח

(א) תוס' ד"ה אמר וכו' השתא ניחא סברת שמואל: (ב) ד"ה ושמואל כו' אומר ר"י דהתם לקלוט. נ"ב ע"ל דף לג בד"ה לא יעמוד:

גליון הש"ס

גמ' אמרו לו אין שעת הסכנה ראיה. עי' מג"א סי' שו ס"ק ח:

ת"ש: *אַנְשֵׁי חָצֵר וְאַנְשֵׁי מִרְפֶּסֶת שֶׁשָּׁכְחוּ וְלֹא עֵירְבוּ, כׇּל שֶׁגָּבוֹהַּ י' טְפָחִים — לַמִּרְפֶּסֶת, פָּחוֹת מִכָּאן — לֶחָצֵר. בד"א — שֶׁהָיוּ אֵלּוּ שֶׁל רַבִּים וְאֵלּוּ שֶׁל רַבִּים, וְעֵירְבוּ אֵלּוּ לְעַצְמָן וְאֵלּוּ לְעַצְמָן, אוֹ שֶׁל יְחִידִים שֶׁאֵין צְרִיכִין לְעָרֵב. אֲבָל הָיוּ שֶׁל רַבִּים, וְשָׁכְחוּ וְלֹא עֵירְבוּ — גַּג וְחָצֵר וְאַכְסַדְרָה וּמִרְפֶּסֶת כּוּלָּן רְשׁוּת אַחַת הֵן. טַעְמָא — דְּלֹא עֵירְבוּ, הָא עֵירְבוּ — לָא! הָא מַנִּי — רַבָּנַן הִיא. דַּיְקָא נַמִי, דְּלָא קָתָנֵי קַרְפֵּף וּמָבוֹי, ש"מ. ת"ש: חָמֵשׁ חֲצֵירוֹת הַפְּתוּחוֹת זוֹ לָזוֹ וּפְתוּחוֹת לַמָּבוֹי, וְשָׁכְחוּ כּוּלָּם וְלֹא עֵירְבוּ — אָסוּר לְהַכְנִיס וּלְהוֹצִיא מֵחָצֵר לְמָבוֹי, וּמִן הַמָּבוֹי לֶחָצֵר. וְכֵלִים שֶׁשָּׁבְתוּ בֶּחָצֵר — מוּתָּר לְטַלְטְלָן בֶּחָצֵר, וּבַמָּבוֹי — אָסוּר. וְר"ש מַתִּיר. שֶׁהָיָה ר' שִׁמְעוֹן אוֹמֵר: כׇּל זְמַן שֶׁהֵן שֶׁל רַבִּים וְשָׁכְחוּ וְלֹא עֵירְבוּ, גַּג וְחָצֵר וְאַכְסַדְרָה וּמִרְפֶּסֶת וְקַרְפֵּף וּמָבוֹי — כּוּלָּן רְשׁוּת אַחַת הֵן. טַעְמָא — דְּלֹא עֵירְבוּ, הָא עֵירְבוּ — לָא! מַאי לֹא עֵירְבוּ — לֹא עֵירְבוּ חֲצֵירוֹת בַּהֲדֵי הֲדָדֵי, הָא חָצֵר וּבָתִּים — עֵירְבוּ. וְהָא "לֹא עֵירְבוּ" קָתָנֵי! מַאי לֹא עֵירְבוּ — לֹא נִשְׁתַּתְּפוּ. וְאבע"א: ר"ש לְדִבְרֵיהֶם דְּרַבָּנַן קָאָמַר לְהוּ; לְדִידִי לָא שְׁנָא עֵירְבוּ וְלָא שְׁנָא לֹא עֵירְבוּ, אֶלָּא לְדִידְכוּ — אוֹדוּ לִי מִיהַת דְּהֵיכָא דְּלֹא עֵירְבוּ רְשׁוּת אַחַת הִיא. וְאָמְרוּ לֵיהּ רַבָּנַן: לֹא, שְׁתֵּי רְשׁוּיוֹת הֵן. אָמַר מָר: וּבַמָּבוֹי אָסוּר. לֵימָא מְסַיַּיע לֵיהּ לְרַבִּי זֵירָא אָמַר רַב, *דְּאָמַר רַבִּי זֵירָא, אָמַר רַב: מָבוֹי שֶׁלֹּא נִשְׁתַּתְּפוּ בּוֹ — אֵין מְטַלְטְלִין אֶלָּא בד"א! אֵימָא: וְלַמָּבוֹי אָסוּר. הַיְינוּ רֵישָׁא! מִשְׁנָה יְתֵירָא אִיצְטְרִיכָא לֵיהּ, מַהוּ דְּתֵימָא: כִּי פְּלִיגִי רַבָּנַן עֲלֵיהּ דְּרַבִּי שִׁמְעוֹן — הָנֵי מִילֵּי הֵיכָא דְּעֵירְבוּ, אֲבָל הֵיכָא דְּלֹא עֵירְבוּ — מוֹדוּ לֵיהּ, קמ"ל. אֲמַר לֵיהּ רָבִינָא לְרַב אַשִׁי: מִי

אַנְשֵׁי מִרְפֶּסֶת. דִּיּוּרֵי עֲלִיּוֹת הַרְבֵּה פְּתוּחִין לָהּ: וְלֹא עֵירְבוּ. בְּנֵי חָצֵר עִם בְּנֵי מִרְפֶּסֶת אֲבָל עֵירְבוּ אֵלּוּ לְעַצְמָן וְאֵלּוּ לְעַצְמָן וּבְנֵי מִרְפֶּסֶת אֵין אוֹסְרִים עַל בְּנֵי חָצֵר אע"פ שֶׁיּוֹרְדִין לָהּ בְּסוּלָּם וּדְרִיסַת רַגְלָם עָלֶיהָ לְרה"ר דְּאָמְרִינַן לְעֵיל בְּפ' "כֵּיצַד מְעַבְּרִין" (דף נט:): סוּלָּם תּוֹרַת פֶּתַח עָלָיו, וְתוֹרַת מְחִיצָּה עָלָיו, וְהַכֹּל לְהָקֵל וְהָכָא אָמְרִינַן תּוֹרַת מְחִיצָּה עָלָיו: כָּל שֶׁגָּבוֹהַּ י' טְפָחִים. כְּגוֹן עַמּוּד אוֹ תֵּל: לַמִּרְפֶּסֶת. מוּתָּר לְהִשְׁתַּמֵּשׁ בּוֹ, וְלֶחָצֵר אָסוּר. דְּה"ל לָזֶה בְּפֶתַח וְלָזֶה בִּזְרִיקָה. וּבִסְמוּכָה לַמִּרְפֶּסֶת בְּתוֹךְ ד' עָסְקִינַן, וּכְדְמוֹקְמָא לָהּ בְּפִירְקִין דִּלְעֵיל (דף פד.): פָּחוֹת מִכָּאן לֶחָצֵר. כְּלוֹמַר: אַף לֶחָצֵר, וּשְׁנֵיהֶן אֲסוּרִים בּוֹ. וְהָכִי אוֹקְמִינַן הָתָם: בד"א. דְּמַחְלְקִין רְשׁוּת חָצֵר וּמִרְפֶּסֶת, דְּלָא מִישְׁתָּרוּ בַּהֲדֵי הֲדָדֵי: בִּזְמַן שֶׁהָיוּ אֵלּוּ שֶׁל רַבִּים כו'. שֶׁדִּיּוּרִין הַרְבֵּה בֶּחָצֵר, וְדִיּוּרִין הַרְבֵּה בַּמִּרְפֶּסֶת: וְעֵירְבוּ אֵלּוּ לְעַצְמָן וְאֵלּוּ לְעַצְמָן. דְּהַשְׁתָּא מַפְּקֵי בְּנֵי חָצֵר מָאנֵי דְּבָתִּים לַחֲצֵירָן וּבְנֵי עֲלִיּוֹת מָאנֵי דַּעֲלִיָּיה לַמִּרְפֶּסֶת. וְאִי שָׁרֵית לֵיהּ כֵּלִים שֶׁשָּׁבְתוּ בֶּחָצֵר לְטַלְטֵל בַּמִּרְפֶּסֶת – אָתֵי לְטַלְטֵל בָּהּ נַמִי כְּלֵי הַבַּיִת: אוֹ שֶׁהָיוּ שֶׁל יְחִידִים. שֶׁאֵין בֶּחָצֵר אֶלָּא בַּיִת אֶחָד, וְאֵין בַּמִּרְפֶּסֶת אֶלָּא עֲלִיָּיה אַחַת: שֶׁאֵינָן צְרִיכִין לְעָרֵב. לְעַצְמָן. וְהַשְׁתָּא שְׁכִיחִי מָאנֵי דְּבַיִת בֶּחָצֵר, וּמָאנֵי דַּעֲלִיָּיה בַּמִּרְפֶּסֶת, דְּלֵיכָּא דְּלֵיסַר עֲלַיְיהוּ. הִלְכָּךְ, גָּזְרוּ בְּהוּ רַבָּנַן דְּלָא לִישְׁתְּרוּ בַּהֲדֵי הֲדָדֵי, גְּזֵרָה מִשּׁוּם מָאנֵי דְּבָתִּים: וְשָׁכְחוּ וְלֹא עֵירְבוּ. לְעַצְמָן, דְּלָא שְׁכִיחִי מָאנֵי דְּבָתִּים בֶּחָצֵר וּמָאנֵי דַּעֲלִיָּיה בַּמִּרְפֶּסֶת: כּוּלָּן רְשׁוּת אַחַת הֵן. לַכֵּלִים שֶׁשָּׁבְתוּ בְּתוֹכָם. מָאן שָׁמְעַתְּ לֵיהּ הַאי סְבָרָא – ר"ש, וְקָאָמַר: עֵירְבוּ – לָא: רַבָּנַן הִיא. דְּמוֹדוּ בְּגַגִּין וַחֲצֵירוֹת דִּרְשׁוּת אַחַת הֵן. וְאִינְהוּ וַדַּאי לָא שָׁרוּ הֵיכָא דְּעֵירְבוּ, דְּגָזְרִי כִּדְאָמְרִינַן בְּפֶרֶק "מִי שֶׁהוֹצִיאוּהוּ" (לעיל מט.) גַּבֵּי ג' חֲצֵירוֹת הַפְּתוּחוֹת זוֹ לָזוֹ, דִּפְלִיגִי אַדְּר"ש וְאָמְרוּ: שְׁלָשְׁתָּן אֲסוּרִין, דְּגָזְרִי דִּילְמָא אָתֵי לְאַפּוֹקֵי מָאנֵי דְּבָתִּים דְּחִיצוֹנָה שֶׁבָּאֶמְצָעִית לַחִיצוֹנָה חֲבֶרְתָּהּ. אֲבָל ר"ש לָא גָּזַר: דְּלָא קָתָנֵי. גַּג וְחָצֵר וְאַכְסַדְרָה וּמִרְפֶּסֶת וְקַרְפֵּף וּמָבוֹי, דְּאִי ר"ש – כּוּלְּהוּ חֲדָא רְשׁוּתָא נִינְהוּ: אָסוּר לְהוֹצִיא מִן הֶחָצֵר לַמָּבוֹי. כְּרַבָּנַן, דְּאָסְרִי בְּמָבוֹי כְּקַרְפֵּף: בַּמָּבוֹי אָסוּר. וּלְקַמָּן מְפָרֵשׁ: קס"ד הַשְׁתָּא דַּאֲפִילּוּ כֵּלִים שֶׁשָּׁבְתוּ בְּתוֹכוֹ אָסוּר לְטַלְטוּלֵי בֵּיהּ, דְּכַרְמְלִית מְשַׁוֵּי לֵיהּ כָּל זְמַן שֶׁלֹּא נִשְׁתַּתְּפוּ בּוֹ: וְר"ש מַתִּיר. אַף לְהוֹצִיא כְּלֵי חָצֵר לַמָּבוֹי: כָּל זְמַן שֶׁהֵן שֶׁל רַבִּים. קס"ד דְּה"ק הוֹאִיל וּבְכוּלָּן יֵשׁ דִּיּוּרִין הַרְבֵּה וְשָׁכְחוּ וְלֹא עֵירְבוּ לְעַצְמָן. כֵּיוָן דְּהַשְׁתָּא לָא שְׁכִיחִי כְּלֵי הַבָּתִּים בַּחֲצֵירוֹת – כּוּלָּן מוּתָּרִים זֶה עִם זֶה: לֹא עֵירְבוּ חֲצֵירוֹת בַּהֲדָדֵי. וְכָל חָצֵר עֵירְבָה לְעַצְמָהּ. וְהַאי "כָּל זְמַן שֶׁהֵן שֶׁל רַבִּים" דְּאָמַר – לָאו טַעְמָא לְהֶיתֵּרָא הוּא, אֶלָּא רְבוּתָא הוּא. וְאע"ג דְּלֹא עֵירְבוּ חֲצֵירוֹת בַּהֲדָדֵי, וְכָל חָצֵר עֵירְבָה לְעַצְמָהּ, וְכָל חֲדָא אִית בָּהּ דִּיּוּרִין טוּבָא, וּמַפְּקֵי מָאנֵי דְּבָתִּים לֶחָצֵר וְאִיכָּא לְמִיגְזַר דְּהָיְידֵי דַּחֲשׁוּשֵׁי דִּיּוּרִין לָא מִיזְדַּהֲרֵי שַׁפִּיר, וּמַפְּקֵי מָאנֵי דְּבָתִּים לֶחָצֵר הָאַחֶרֶת – אפ"ה לָא גָּזַר: וְהָא לֹא עֵירְבוּ. לְגַמְרֵי מַשְׁמַע: מַאי לֹא עֵירְבוּ. דְּמַשְׁמַע לְגַמְרֵי – אַשִּׁיתּוּף דְּמָבוֹי קָאֵי, וּבְעֵירוּב דַּחֲצֵירוֹת לָא אַיְירֵי מִידֵּי. דְּלָא אִיכְפַּת לֵיהּ בְּהוּ בֵּין עֵירְבָה כָּל אַחַת לְעַצְמָהּ, בֵּין לֹא עֵירְבוּ קָאָמַר דְּמוּתָּרִים בַּמָּבוֹי בְּלֹא שִׁיתּוּף: וְאָמְרִי לֵיהּ רַבָּנַן לֹא. בְּגַג וְחָצֵר וְאַכְסַדְרָה וּמִרְפֶּסֶת מוֹדִינַן לָךְ, אֲבָל בְּקַרְפֵּף וּבְמָבוֹי – לָא: הָא דְּר' זֵירָא בְּפ' "ר"א דְּמִילָה" (קל:): אֵימָא וְלַמָּבוֹי אָסוּר. לְהוֹצִיא כְּלֵי הֶחָצֵר: הַיְינוּ רֵישָׁא. הָא תְּנָא לֵיהּ אָסוּר לְהַכְנִיס וּלְהוֹצִיא מִן הֶחָצֵר לַמָּבוֹי: מַהוּ דְּתֵימָא. הָא דִּתְנָא רֵישָׁא אָסוּר – בְּעֵירְבוּ לְעַצְמָן קָאָסְרִי רַבָּנַן, וּמִשּׁוּם כְּלֵי בָּתִּים וְהַאי דְּקָתָנֵי לֹא עֵירְבוּ – לָא נִשְׁתַּתְּפוּ הוּא: אֲבָל לֹא עֵירְבוּ לְעַצְמָן אֵימָא מוֹדוּ. אַשְׁמְעִינַן מִשְׁנָה יְתֵירָה, דְּעַל כׇּרְחָךְ חֲדָא לְעֵירְבוּ וַחֲדָא לְלֹא עֵירְבוּ, וַאֲפִילּוּ הָכִי אָסוּר: וּמִי

גג וחצר ואכסדרה ומרפסת כולן רשות אחת הן. לרב דאוקי מתני' ב"כיצד משתתפין" (לעיל דף פד.*) לאותם הדרים במרפסת – אתי הכא שפיר, דכשעירבו בני מרפסת לעצמן, ובני חצר לעצמן דשכיחי מאני דבתים בחצר ומאני דעליות במרפסת, כשהסלע גבוה י' הוי למרפסת שהסלע שוה להן. ולבני חצר אסור להשתמש על הסלע, אפילו כלים ששבתו בחצר, אטו כלים ששבתו בבית, ופחות מכאן אסורין לשניהם. וכשלא עירבו, דלא שכיחי מאני דבתים ודעליות שם – הוי מרפסת וחצר רשות אחת, ואין אוסרין זה על זה. אבל לשמואל, דקרי מרפסת לבני עליות ומיירי כשהסלע כנגד חלונות, ומשתמשין שם בני עליות דרך חלונות כשלא עירבו. ותימה: היאך משתמשין בפחות מי' בני עליות על הסלע כלים ששבתו בעליות דרך חלונותיהן? והלא אין חצר ומרפסת רשות אחת אלא לכלים ששבתו בתוכן, ולא לכלים ששבתו בתוך הבית ועליות! וי"ל: דלשמואל דוקא ארישא קאי, דמיירי בגבוה עשרה, הוא דמפליג בין עירבו בין לא עירבו כדפרשינן לעיל אליבא דשמואל. אבל סיפא, דקתני פחות מיכן לחצר, דהוי דוקא לחצר לשמואל – מיירי ודאי בין עירבו בני עלייה לעצמן ובני חצר לעצמן, בין לא עירבו. ובין הכי ובין הכי, בני חצר מותרין ובני עלייה אסורין לשלשל מחלונותיהם: **וכלים** ששבתו בחצר מותר לטלטל בחצר. פי': בכל חצירות. דאי באותו חצר ותו לא – אפילו שבתו בבית נמי. ומיירי לרב כשלא עירבו חצירות עם הבתים. וקשיא: דא"כ, היכי מייתי סייעתא בסמוך לרב, דאמר מבוי שלא נשתתפו בו אין מטלטלין בו אלא בד'? הא רב גופיה לא אסר אלא כשעירבו בתים עם החצירות, אבל כשלא עירבו – לא אסר, כדמוכח בפרק "אם לא הביא" (שבת דף קל:)! ואדרבה, קשיא מינה לרב דבכה"ג לא אסר רב! ועוד: דרב פסק כר"ש, והכא קאמר דר"ש מתיר! וי"ל: דמייתי דכמו שעירבו לרב אליבא דר"ש אין מטלטלין בו אלא בד', וטעמא כדמפרש שם רש"י: משום דכשעירבו אסור לטלטל מחצר למבוי אפילו כלים ששבתו בתוכה אטו כלים ששבתו בבית. ואין במבוי שום תשמיש, ודמיא לכרמלית כיון דאין בו אלא ג' מחיצות, ולכך אין מטלטלין בו אלא בד'. ה"נ לרבנן, אפילו בלא עירבו – אין מטלטלין בו אלא בד', דאסרי לטלטל מאני דחצר למבוי, דחצר ומבוי לדידהו לאו רשות אחת הן: **מהו** דתימא כי פליגי רבנן עליה דר"ש היכא דעירבו. ואסור לטלטל מחצר למבוי, משום דשכיחי מאני דבתים בחצר. ומיהו, מחצר לחצר לא אסרי, אע"ג דעירבו – דאין תשמיש דחצר זה רגילין בחצר אחרת, אבל רגילות הוא להוציא מחצר למבוי. ואע"ג דרבנן דשלש חצירות (לעיל מה:) – גזרו, וגם בברייתא דגג וחצר אכסדרה ומרפסת אמרינן דוקא לא עירבו, הא עירבו – גזרינן, שמא רבנן דהכא אינם רבנן דהתם. ובלאו הכי צ"ל כן, דבפרק "מי שהוציאוהו" (לעיל דף מו:) אמר דתנא דפליג אדרבי שמעון – היינו ר' יהודה, ובברייתא המסייעה לרב יהודה אית ליה לרבי יהודה דגג וקרפף רשות אחת, ולרבנן דהכא לית להו*. קמשמע לן דבלא עירבו פליגי, וטעמא דאסור מחצר למבוי – דהוי מבוי כמו קרפף, דלא הוי רשות אחת עם החצר: והא

רבינו חננאל

הבית ת"ש אנשי חצר ואנשי מרפסת ששכחו ולא עירבו כל שגבוה י"ט למרפסת פחות מיכן לחצר בד"א בזמן שהיו של רבים ועירבו אלו לעצמן ואלו לעצמן או שהיו של יחידין שאין צריכין לערב אבל אם היו של רבים ששכחו ולא עירבו [גג] וחצר ואכסדרה ומרפסת רשות אחת. טעמא דלא עירבו הוא דהן רשות אחת אבל עירבו לא. קשיא לשמואל ולר' יוחנן ופרקינן הא ברייתא [רבנן] היא כי קאמרי' בין עירבו בין לא עירבו לר' שמעון קאמרינן. ואמרינן דיקא נמי מדלא קתני מבוי (מבוי) [וקרפף] בהדייהו ש"מ לרבנן היא ולא לר"ש דהא שמעינן ליה לר"ש דמבוי וקרפף כגג וכמרפסת חשיב כדבעינן למימר לקמן. ת"ש [חמש] חצרות פתוחות זו לזו ופתוחות למבוי אסור להכנים ולהוציא מחצר למבוי. *) ושנינן משנה יתירא אצטריכא ליה מהו דתימא כי פליג ר' שמעון לרבנן בשלא עירבו אבל בשעירבו מודה להו דאסור קמ"ל משנה יתירא דאפילו בשעירבו פליג עלייהו א"ל רבינא לרב אשי

*) מד' רבינו אילו נראה דגי' אחרת היה לו בסוגיא וגרס משנה יתרה לר"ש אילטריך. ונ"ע:

[ושם איתא רב הונא]

לעיל פג.

שבת קל:

הס"ד ואח"כ מה"ד קמ"ל. כל"ל רש"א

מִי אָמַר ר' יוֹחָנָן הָכִי? *וְהָא אָמַר רַבִּי יוֹחָנָן: הֲלָכָה כִּסְתַם מִשְׁנָה. וּתְנַן: *כּוֹתֶל שֶׁבֵּין שְׁתֵּי חֲצֵירוֹת, גָּבוֹהַּ עֲשָׂרָה וְרוֹחַב אַרְבָּעָה — מְעָרְבִין שְׁנַיִם וְאֵין מְעָרְבִין אֶחָד. הָיוּ בְּרֹאשׁוֹ פֵּירוֹת — אֵלּוּ עוֹלִין מִכָּאן וְאוֹכְלִים, וְאֵלּוּ עוֹלִין מִכָּאן וְאוֹכְלִים, וּבִלְבַד שֶׁלֹּא יוֹרִידוּ לְמַטָּה! מַאי "לְמַטָּה" — לְמַטָּה לַבָּתִּים. וְהָא תָּנֵי רַבִּי חִיָּיא: וּבִלְבַד שֶׁלֹּא יְהֵא זֶה עוֹמֵד בִּמְקוֹמוֹ וְאוֹכֵל, וְזֶה עוֹמֵד בִּמְקוֹמוֹ וְאוֹכֵל! אֲמַר לֵיהּ: *וְכִי רַבִּי לֹא שְׁנָאָהּ, ר' חִיָּיא מִנַּיִן לוֹ?! אִתְּמַר, שְׁתֵּי חֲצֵירוֹת וְחוּרְבָּה אַחַת בֵּינֵיהֶם, אַחַת עֵירְבָה וְאַחַת לֹא עֵירְבָה. אָמַר רַב הוּנָא: נוֹתְנִין אוֹתָהּ לָזוֹ שֶׁלֹּא עֵירְבָה, אֲבָל לְשֶׁעֵירְבָה — לֹא, דִּילְמָא אָתֵי לְאַפּוֹקֵי מָאנֵי דְּבָתִּים לַחוּרְבָּה. וְחִיָּיא בַּר רַב אָמַר: אַף לְשֶׁעֵירְבָה, וּשְׁתֵּיהֶן אֲסוּרוֹת. וְא"ת שְׁתֵּיהֶן מוּתָּרוֹת, מִפְּנֵי מָה אֵין נוֹתְנִין חָצֵר שֶׁלֹּא עֵירְבָה לְחָצֵר שֶׁעֵירְבָה — הָתָם כֵּיוָן דְּמִנְטְרִי מָאנֵי דְּבָתִּים בֶּחָצֵר אָתֵי לְאַפּוֹקֵי, הָכָא בַּחוּרְבָּה כֵּיוָן דְּלָא מִנְטְרִי מָאנֵי דְּחָצֵר בַּחוּרְבָּה — לָא אָתֵי לְאַפּוֹקֵי. אִיכָּא דְּאָמְרִי, חִיָּיא בַּר רַב אָמַר: אַף לְשֶׁעֵירְבָה, וּשְׁתֵּיהֶן מוּתָּרוֹת. וְאִם תֹּאמַר: שְׁתֵּיהֶן אֲסוּרוֹת — לְפִי שֶׁאֵין נוֹתְנִים חָצֵר שֶׁלֹּא עֵירְבָה לְחָצֵר שֶׁעֵירְבָה. הָתָם כֵּיוָן דְּמִנְטְרִי מָאנֵי דְּבָתִּים בֶּחָצֵר לָא שָׁרוּ בְּהוּ רַבָּנַן, דְּאָתֵי לְאַפּוֹקֵי, אֲבָל בְּחוּרְבָּה — לָא מִנְטְרִי.§

מתני' [א]גַּג גָּדוֹל סָמוּךְ לְקָטָן — הַגָּדוֹל מוּתָּר וְהַקָּטָן אָסוּר. *[ב]חָצֵר *גְּדוֹלָה שֶׁנִּפְרְצָה לִקְטַנָּה — גְּדוֹלָה מוּתֶּרֶת וּקְטַנָּה אֲסוּרָה, מִפְּנֵי שֶׁהִיא כְּפִתְחָהּ שֶׁל גְּדוֹלָה.§ **גמ'** לָמָּה לִי' לְמִיתְנֵי תַּרְתֵּי? לְרַב קָתָנֵי גַּג דּוּמְיָא דְּחָצֵר; מַה חָצֵר מִנְכְּרָא מְחִיצָתָא — אַף [ג]גַּג נָמֵי מִנְכְּרָא מְחִיצָתָא. וְלִשְׁמוּאֵל גַּג דּוּמְיָא דְּחָצֵר; מַה חָצֵר דְּקָא דָּרְסִי לָהּ רַבִּים — אַף גַּג נָמֵי דְּקָא דָּרְסִי לֵיהּ רַבִּים. יָתֵיב רַבָּה וְרַבִּי זֵירָא וְרַבָּה בַּר רַב חָנָן, וְיָתֵיב אַבָּיֵי גַּבַּיְיהוּ, וְיָתְבִי וְקָאָמְרִי: שְׁמַע מִינָּהּ מִמַּתְנִיתִין: דִּיוּרֵי גְדוֹלָה בִּקְטַנָּה, וְאֵין דִּיוּרֵי קְטַנָּה בִּגְדוֹלָה. כֵּיצַד? [ד]גְּפָנִים בִּגְדוֹלָה — אָסוּר לִזְרוֹעַ אֶת הַקְּטַנָּה, וְאִם זָרַע — זְרָעִין אֲסוּרִין, גְּפָנִים

[שבת מו. וש"נ]
לעיל עו: פז:
[יבמות מג. נדה סב: ועי' תוס' שם ד"ה ר"ח]
לעיל ת. ע"ש ט: ע"ש וש"נ
שייך לע"ב

ומי אמר ר' יוחנן הכי. הלכה כר' שמעון(א) ואפילו עירבו דחצירות רשות אחת: ובלבד שלא יורידו למטה. אלמא: אסור להוציא מחצר לחבירתה. אי אמרת בשלמא בעירבו אסור אוקימנא להא בעירבו אבל השתא במאי תוקמא: שלא יהא זה עומד במקומו. בקרקעית החצר. ל"א שיהא זה עומד במקומו גרסינן ועל ראש הכותל קאמר: וכי רבי לא שנאה. למשנה זו במשנתינו: רבי חייא. שסידר וסתם את הברייתא ותלמידו היה: מניין לו. זה הפירוש. ולעולם למטה דסתם רבי מתני' — בבתים קאמר, שלא יוריד מראש הכותל ויוליך לביתו: וחורבה אחת ביניהם. לא שנא שלהם ולא שנא של אחרים. דהא אוקמא כר"ש, שאין חילוק רשות אלא בבתים, וכגון שאינה פרוצה לרשות הרבים: אחת עירבה. לעצמה, ושכיחי מאני דבתים בגווה: אמר רב הונא נותנין החורבה לזו שלא עירבה. להוציא לה כלים ששבתו בחצר, דהא לא שכיחי בה מאני דבתים הואיל ולא עירבה אבל לשעירבה — לא, דרב הונא תלמידו דרב הוה. דאמר הלכה כר"ש בשלא עירבו, אבל עירבו — לא: וחייא בר רב אמר אף לשעירבה. אני שמעתי מאבא אף לשעירבה — נותנין אותה, ומדעתי אני מפרש, דהאי דאמר אבא אף לשעירבה — לאסור את שתיהן קאמר, דגזר לא עירבה אטו עירבה. דאי מפקי הני לגווה — הני נמי אתו ומפקי: וא"ת. במה ששמעתי אף לשעירבה להתיר קאמר אבא דשתיהן מותרות, ולא גזר אבא בעירבה משום מאני דבתים — קשיא לי במילתא דאבא, דאמר לעיל הלכה כר"ש והוא שלא עירבו, אבל עירבו — לא. מפני מה אין נותנים חצר שלא עירבה לחצר שעירבה, תכנים כליה לתוך חבירתה ותוציאם, הא לא גזר רב בחורבה! כלומר: נהי נמי דתשני לי דהא דאמר רב לעיל אבל עירבה לא — מודה הוא דאותה שלא עירבה מכנסת ומוציאה כליה לתוך שעירבה, דהא לא שכיחי בה בשלא עירבה מאני דבתים. ואע"ג דבהא שכיחי — לא חיישינן, דסתמא כי משתמש איניש — במאני דידיה משתמש ולא בחבריה. מיהו, קשיא לי אמאי אסר אבא כשעירבה להכניס לשלא עירבה, הא לא גזר לגבי חורבה: התם כיון דמינטר. כלומר: אף לשעירבה דקאמר רב — להיתר קאמר וגבי חצירות אמאי גזר — משום דכיון דמינטרי כלים בחצר, שכיחי לאפוקי מאני טובא, וחיישינן דלמא מחלפי מאני דבתים במאני דחצר, ומפקי לחבירתה, שהרי נשמרים גם בתוכה. אבל חורבה לא עבידי בה איניש לאפוקי מאני טובא: איכא דאמרי חייא בר רב אמר אף לשעירבה ושתיהן מותרות ואם תאמר שתיהן אסורות. וטעמא משום דשמעינן ליה לאבא דקאמר אבל עירבו לא, אלמא: על כרחך, אפילו דחקת למילתיה דאבא לאוקומא להאי דאסר בשעירבה הוא דאסר לטלטל כליה לשלא עירבה, אבל שלא עירבה מותרת לתוך שעירבה — שמעינן מיהא דאין נותנין שלא עירבה לשעירבה. אלמא: גזר בעירבה משום מאני דבתים. ובחורבה נמי, על כרחך שעירבה אסורה בה. וכי אמר אבא דיהבי לה לתרוייהו — לאיסורא קאמר, לא דמי: התם. גבי חצירות, כיון דמינטרי מאני בחצר חבירו כבחצירו — עבידי לאפוקי לה מאני טובא, וחיישינן דלא ליפוק לה מאני דבתים. אבל חורבה לא: **מתני'** הגדול מותר. להכניס לו כלי הבית שלמטה, ואין בני קטן אוסרין עליו. דלגבי גדול הך פרצה פתח הוא דשרי בגיפופי. וכגון דאין הפרצה יותר מעשר. אבל קטן אסור לו להוציא כלי הבית, דבני גדול אסרי עליה דנפרץ לו במלואו ודברי הכל היא דאפילו ר' מאיר לא אמר פגין רשות אחת אלא לכלים ששבתו בתוכן אבל לכלים ששבתו בבתים לא, דומיא דחצר קטנה שנפרצה לגדולה דלכולי עלמא חצירות רשות אחת הן ולענין כלי הבתים אסרה גדולה מותרת. להוציא כלי הבתים שבה אם עירבה לעצמה ולא אסרי עלה בני קטנה: גדולה אקטנה: **גמ'** תרתי. חצר וגג: מה חצר דמינכרא מחיצתא. שהרי יש לה מחיצות: אף גג. נהי נמי דשרינן ליה במחיצות תחתונות משום גוד אסיק, מיהו מחיצות ניכרות בעינן, שלא יהא גג בולט חוצה להם. דאי לא מינכרא — לא אמרינן גוד אסיק. וגדול נמי אסור, דאין לו שום מחיצה וכל שאין לו מחיצות אינו רשות היחיד. כל גגין שלהן חלקין היו ולא משופעין: ולשמואל. דאמר אפילו לא מינכרא אמרינן גוד אסיק, להכי תננהי גבי הדדי. דמה חצר דדרסי לה רבים — אף גג, האי דקתני קטן אסור — משום דדרסי רבים מזה לזה, דהוי לה מחיצה תחתונה שביניהם מחיצה נדרסת ולא מעלית למיגד ואסוקה. אבל אי לא דרסי בהן — אף קטן שרי, דאמרינן גוד אסיק ותפסיק המחיצה ביניהם, ואע"ג דמכסיא ולא מינכרא: דיורי גדולה מושלין בקטנה. ומושכין אותה אצלן: ואין דיורי קטנה. מושלין בגדולה. למושכן אצלן: אסור לזרוע את הקטנה. דכמאן דהויא קטנה כולה בתוך גדולה דמי. ואפילו מרחיק ארבע אמות מן הגפנים, שאפילו בתוך הגדולה מותר להרחיק ולזרוע — הכא אסור, דקתני מתני' מפני שהיא כפתחה של גדולה, אלמא: כולה כחד פתח משוה לה: *גפנים מותרין. דהא אין דיורי קטנה מושלין בגדולה: גפנים

והא אמר רבי יוחנן הלכה כסתם משנה. וקשה: דסתם ואח"כ מחלוקת הוא, ואמר ב"החולץ" (יבמות דף מב:) דאין הלכה כסתם. ואע"ג דלכל הפחות חשיב סתם כרבים כלפי היחיד — הכא אין נפקא מינה, דבלאו הכי פליגי רבנן עליה! ותירץ הרר"א כהן: דעיקר קושיא לר"י אינה אלא דלא גזר, ובזה הדבר הוי מחלוקת ואח"כ סתם, מחלוקת בשלש אלירות ב"מי שהוליאוהו" (לעיל דף מה:) וסתם בפרק "חלון" (לעיל דף עו:), אבל הכא לא פליגי בגזירה:

מפני מה אין נותנין חצר שלא עירבה לחצר שעירבה. משום דאיירי באחת עירבה ואחת לא עירבה, נקט האי לישנא. והוא הדין דהוה מצי למימר: "מפני מה אין נותנין חצר שעירבה לשעירבה". ובקונטרס פירש שפיר:

איכא דאמרי אף לשעירבה ושתיהם מותרות. לפי האיכא דאמרי קשיא הא דאמר בפרק "הדר" (לעיל דף עד.), ר' יוחנן אמר*: אף לחורבה. ורבי יוחנן לטעמיה דלא גזר דילמא אתי לאפוקי מאני דבתים לחצר. והכא נמי לא גזר דילמא אתי לאפוקי מאני דבתים לחורבה. ומאי לטעמיה הוא, דהא אפילו רב דגזר הכא, גבי חורבה לא גזר!

אף גג דקא דרסי לה רבים. היינו כלישנא קמא דרב יוסף דלעיל*(ב): **גפנים** בגדולה אסורה לזרוע את הקטנה. למ"ד (לעיל דף ט:) נראה מבחוץ ושוה מבפנים נידון משום לחי ופתח — איירי בנכנסין כותלי קטנה לגדולה: גפנים

ה א טור ש"ע א"ח סי' שעל סעיף ד:
ו ב מיי' פ"ג מהלכות עירובין הלכה כד סמג לאוין סה ועשין א טור ש"ע א"ח שם סעיף ג:
ז ג שם סעיף ד וסי' שמה סעיף טז:
ח ד מיי' פ"ז מהלכות כלאים הלכה יט וטוש"ע י"ד סי' רצו סעיף מט:

[נ"ל אפילו חורבה]
ועי' בריטב"א
[בהרא"ש איתא חצר קטנה שנפרצה לגדולה וכן הובא משנה דהכא לעיל ת. ט: וכ"מ מלשון רש"י דהכא ד"ה הגדול וכו' דומיא דחצר קטנה שנפרצה לגדולה וכו' אבל ברב אלפס יש כגירס' הספרים וכן הובא בסוגיין בע"ב והא תנן חצר גדולה וכו' וכן עוד לקמן דף צג:]

הגהות הב"ח

(א) רש"י ד"ה ומי אמר ר' יוחנן הכי הלכ' כר' שמעון לחצירות רשות אחת ואפילו עירבו הס"ד: (ב) תוס' ד"ה אף וכו' דלעיל. נ"ב דף פ"ט:

רבינו חננאל

ומי א"ר יוחנן הלכה כר' שמעון דתני בין גג בין חצר רשות אחת הן והא איהו דאמר הלכה כסתם משנה ותנן בכותל שבין ב' חצרות דהיא סתמא היו בראשו פירות אלו עולין מיכן ואוכלין ואלו עולין מיכן ואוכלין ובלבד שלא יורידו למטה. ואי רשות אחת הן אמאי לא יורידו למטה. ופרקינן מאי לא יורידו למטה דקתני למטה דבתים. כלומר שיכנס בבתים אבל בחצר שרי. איני והא תני ר' חייא ובלבד שלא יעמוד זה בחצרו ויאכל וזה בחצרו ויאכל הנה אפילו בחצר אסור ודחי כי רבי לא שנאה ר' חייא מנין לו. כלומר דבר שלא שנאו [רבי] במשנתנו ר' חייא תלמיד ר' (אבין) [הביא] בידו משנה שלא שנאה רבי *) מכלל זו שאינה שנויה במשנתנו לאו דסמכה היא. אתמר ב' חצרות וחורבה אחת ביניהן חצר אחת עירבה עם הבתים והאחרת לא עירבה. אמר רב [הונא] נותנין חורבה לזו לאותה שלא עירבה אבל [אין] נותנין אותה לאותה שעירבה גזרה שמא יוציא מני דקנו שביתה בבתים מן הבתים לחצר ומן החצר לחורבה. חייא בר רב כו' איכא דאמרי חייא בר רב אמר אף נותנין זו החורבה גם לחצר שעירבה ושניהן מותרות הן בחורבה וא"ת מפני מה אין נותנין חצר שלא עירבה לחצר שעירבה נאמר כי כל החצרות רשות אחת הן התם בחצרות כיון דמנטרי מני דבתים לחצר אתו לאפוקינהו בחצר שלא עירבה אבל בחורבה לא מינטרי הלכך לא שייך גזירה דלמא אתי לאפוקי מני דבתים לחורבה: **מתני'** גג גדול סמוך לגג קטן כו'. ל"ל למיתנא גג ל"ל למיתנא חצר לרב קתני גג דומיא דחצר מה חצר דמינכרן מחיצתא אף גג דמינכרן מחיצתא הוא [דמותר] לטלטל אבל גג בין הגגין דלא מינכרא מחיצתא אין מטלטלין בו אלא ד' אמות. לשמואל קתני גג דומיא דחצר מה חצר דקא דרסי לה רבים אף גג אע"פ דדרסי לה רבים שרי. חצר גדולה שנפרצה לקטנה גדולה מותרת והקטנה אסורה. כשתימצי לומר דיורי גדולה בקטנה. כלומר כל הדר בגדולה כאלו בקטנה הוא דר שהקטנה מכללה של גדולה היא ואין דיורין קטנה חשובין מכלל דירה הגדולה עכשיו אם יהו בגדולה שריגי גפנים אסור לזרוע בקטנה שחשובין הגפנים שבגדולה כאילו גם בקטנה הן נטועים. ואם זרע בקטנה נאסרו אותן הזורעים אבל הגפנים שבגדולה מותרין

*) נראה דל"ל כגון זו שאינה שנויה לן כו'.

גְּפָנִים מוּתָּרִין. גְּפָנִים בַּקְּטַנָּה — מוּתָּר לִזְרוֹעַ אֶת הַגְּדוֹלָה. **אִשָּׁה בַּגְּדוֹלָה וְגֵט בַּקְּטַנָּה — מִתְגָּרֶשֶׁת. אִשָּׁה בַּקְּטַנָּה וְגֵט בַּגְּדוֹלָה — אֵינָהּ מִתְגָּרֶשֶׁת. בצִבּוּר בַּגְּדוֹלָה וּשְׁלִיחַ צִבּוּר בַּקְּטַנָּה — יוֹצְאִין יְדֵי חוֹבָתָן. צִיבּוּר בַּקְּטַנָּה וּשְׁלִיחַ צִבּוּר בַּגְּדוֹלָה — אֵין יוֹצְאִין יְדֵי חוֹבָתָן. גתִּשְׁעָה בַּגְּדוֹלָה וְיָחִיד בַּקְּטַנָּה — מִצְטָרְפִין. תִּשְׁעָה בַּקְּטַנָּה וְאֶחָד בַּגְּדוֹלָה — אֵין מִצְטָרְפִין. דצוֹאָה בַּגְּדוֹלָה — אָסוּר לִקְרוֹת קְרִיאַת שְׁמַע בַּקְּטַנָּה. צוֹאָה בַּקְּטַנָּה — מוּתָּר לִקְרוֹת קְרִיאַת שְׁמַע בַּגְּדוֹלָה. אֲמַר לְהוּ אַבַּיֵי: א"כ מָצִינוּ מְחִיצָה לְאִיסּוּר, שֶׁאִילְמָלֵי אֵין מְחִיצָה[א] — מַרְחִיק ד"א וְזוֹרֵעַ. וְאִילּוּ הַשְׁתָּא אֲסוּרָה! א"ל רַבִּי זֵירָא לְאַבַּיֵי: וְלֹא מָצִינוּ מְחִיצָה לְאִיסּוּר?! וְהָא תְּנַן: חָצֵר גְּדוֹלָה שֶׁנִּפְרְצָה לִקְטַנָּה — גְּדוֹלָה מוּתֶּרֶת וּקְטַנָּה אֲסוּרָה, מִפְּנֵי שֶׁהִיא כְּפִתְחָהּ שֶׁל גְּדוֹלָה. וְאִילּוּ הִשְׁוָה אֶת גִּיפּוּפֶיהָ — גְּדוֹלָה נַמִי אֲסוּרָה! א"ל: הָתָם סִילּוּק מְחִיצוֹת הוּא. אֲמַר לֵיהּ רָבָא לְאַבַּיֵי: וְלֹא מָצִינוּ מְחִיצָה לְאִיסּוּר? וְהָא אִתְּמַר:

סִיכֵּךְ

גְּפָנִים בַּקְּטַנָּה מוּתָּר לִזְרוֹעַ אֶת הַגְּדוֹלָה. לְכַתְּחִלָּה. דִּלְגַבֵּי גְּדוֹלָה פִּיתְחָא: וְכָל פֶּתַח כִּמְחִיצָּה הוּא. וַאֲפִילּוּ סָמוּךְ לַגְּפָנִים מוּתָּר לִזְרוֹעַ אֶת הַגְּדוֹלָה לְכַתְּחִלָּה, כִּדְתְנַן (ב"ב דף כו.) הָיָה גָּדֵר בֵּינְתַיִים — זֶה סוֹמֵךְ לַגָּדֵר מִכָּאן, וְזֶה סוֹמֵךְ לַגָּדֵר מִכָּאן. וּכְשֶׁיִּגְדְּלוּ הַזְּרָעִים, אע"ג דְּדִיוּרֵי גְּדוֹלָה בַּקְּטַנָּה — אֵין אוֹסְרִים אֶת הַגְּפָנִים. דְּאָמַר בִּמְנָחוֹת פ"ב (דף טו.): מַעֲשֶׂה בְּאֶחָד שֶׁזָּרַע אֶת כֶּרֶם שֶׁל חֲבֵירוֹ, וּבָא מַעֲשֶׂה לִפְנֵי חֲכָמִים וְאָסְרוּ אֶת הַזְּרָעִים וְהִתִּירוּ אֶת הַגְּפָנִים. וְאָמַר: מַאי טַעְמָא — קַנְבּוֹס וְלוּף אָסְרָה תּוֹרָה, שְׁאָר זְרָעִים מִדְּרַבָּנַן אֲסִירֵי. הַךְ(א) דְּלָא עֲבַד אִיסּוּרָא — לֹא קָנְסוּ רַבָּנַן. הָכִי נַמִי, הוֹאִיל וּכְשֶׁזָּרַע אֶת הַגְּדוֹלָה — בְּהֶיתֵּר זְרָעָהּ, אֲפִילּוּ שְׁתֵּיהֶם שֶׁלּוֹ לֵיכָּא לְמִקְנְסֵיהּ. וְכ"ש אִם קְטַנָּה שֶׁל אֲחֵרִים, וּגְפָנִים שֶׁלָּהּ קָדְמוּ: אִשָּׁה. עוֹמֶדֶת בַּגְּדוֹלָה, וְזָרַק לָהּ בַּעֲלָהּ גֵּט לְתוֹךְ קְטַנָּה וּשְׁתֵּיהֶן שֶׁלָּהּ וְאִיכָּא לְמַאן דְּאָמַר בְּמַסֶּ' גִּיטִּין (דף עז:) דְּהָא דִּתְנַן: הַזּוֹרֵק גֵּט לְאִשְׁתּוֹ וְהִיא בְּתוֹךְ בֵּיתָהּ אוֹ בְּתוֹךְ חֲצֵירָהּ הֲרֵי זוֹ מְגוֹרֶשֶׁת — דַּוְקָא עוֹמֶדֶת לְתוֹכָהּ בְּאוֹתָהּ שָׁעָה, אֲבָל אִם אֵינָהּ עוֹמֶדֶת לְתוֹכָהּ בְּאוֹתָהּ שָׁעָה — לֹא, וְאע"ג דְּשֶׁלָּהּ הִיא: מִתְגָּרֶשֶׁת(ב) הִיא. שֶׁהֲרֵי הִיא כְּעוֹמֶדֶת בַּקְּטַנָּה, דְּכוּלָּהּ קְטַנָּה בָּתַר גְּדוֹלָה שַׁיְיכָא: אֵינָהּ מִתְגָּרֶשֶׁת. דִּגְדוֹלָה לָאו בָּתַר קְטַנָּה אָזְלָא, וְגֵט לָא קָנֵי לָאִשָּׁה דְּנֵימָא נִשְׁדֵּי אִשָּׁה בָּתַר גֵּט, דְּאִשָּׁה לָא בָּעֲיָא לְמִקְנֵי גִּיטָּא: יוֹצְאִין. דִּשְׁלִיחַ צִיבּוּר דְּקָאֵי בַּקְּטַנָּה — הָכָא שַׁיָּיךְ: אֵין יוֹצְאִין. דְּהַשְׁתָּא לֹא שַׁיָּיךְ בַּתְרַיְיהוּ. וְצִבּוּר דְּקָיְימִי בַּקְּטַנָּה לָא מָצִינַן לְמֵימַר דְּשָׁיְיכִי בַּתְרֵיהּ, דְּרוּבָּהּ בָּתַר חַד לָא מִשְׁתְּדוּ: מוּתָּר לִקְרוֹת קְרִיאַת שְׁמַע בַּגְּדוֹלָה. דְּגַבֵּי גְּדוֹלָה כִּמְחִיצָּה הִיא, וְלָא מָצֵי קְטַנָּה מְקַלְקְלָא(ג) בְּשׁוּם מִידֵּי: שֶׁאִילְמָלֵי אֵין מְחִיצָה. אִי לָאו הָנָךְ גִּיפּוּפֵי שֶׁעוֹדְפִין בַּגְּדוֹלָה — הָיוּ הַגְּדוֹלָה וְהַקְּטַנָּה שָׁווֹת, הָווּ לְהוּ כְּחָצֵר אַחַת, וּמוּתָּר לִזְרוֹעַ שָׁם עִם הַגְּפָנִים וּמַרְחִיק ד' אַמּוֹת. הַשְׁתָּא, מִשּׁוּם הָנָךְ גִּיפּוּפֵי — שָׁדֵינַן לְכוּלָּהּ קְטַנָּה בָּתַר גְּדוֹלָה וּמִיתַּסְרָא כּוּלָּהּ. מָצִינוּ מְחִיצָּה שֶׁאוֹסֶרֶת: וְאִילּוּ הִשְׁוָה אֶת גִּיפּוּפֶיהָ. שֶׁבָּנָה מְחִיצּוֹת בְּתוֹךְ הַגְּדוֹלָה מִכָּאן וּמִכָּאן, עַד שֶׁיַּעַקְלְרֶנָּה כְּמִדַּת הַקְּטַנָּה, וְסִילֵּק אֶת הַגִּיפּוּפִין עַל יְדֵי מְחִיצּוֹת הַלָּלוּ — אַף גְּדוֹלָה אֲסוּרָה(ד) וְעַכְשָׁיו שְׁתֵּיהֶן שָׁווֹת, נִמְצְאוּ מְחִיצּוֹת הַלָּלוּ בָּאוֹת לְאִיסּוּר: סִילּוּק מְחִיצוֹת. הָאַחֲרוֹנוֹת סִילְּקוּ אֶת הָרִאשׁוֹנוֹת. אֲבָל גַּבֵּי זְרִיעָה חָסַר עוֹדֵף הַגִּיפּוּפִין עַל הַקְּטַנָּה, מִשּׁוּם יִתּוּר מְחִיצָּה:

סִיכֵּךְ

גיפופי	
מחילות / מחילות	חלר קטנה
גיפופי	

גפנים בקטנה מותר לזרוע את הגדולה. פי' בקונטרס: וכשיגדלו הזרעים, אע"ג דדיורי גדולה בקטנה — אין אוסרין את הגפנים, כדאמרינן במנחות בפ' שני (דף טו.): מעשה בא' שזרע כרמו של חבירו, ובא מעשה לפני חכמים, ואסרו הזרעים והתירו הגפנים. מ"ט — קנבוס ולוף אסרה תורה, שאר זרעים דרבנן. הך דעביד איסורא — קנסו, הך דלא עביד איסורא — לא קנסו. וה"נ, הואיל וכשזרע את הגדולה — בהיתר זרעה, אפילו שתיהן שלו — ליכא למיקנסיה. ולפירושו מיירי הכא בשאר זרעים. ותימה: דהיכי שרי להניח הזרעים כשיגדלו? כיון דדיורי גדולה בקטנה, דאפילו עלו מאיליהן תנן במסכת כלאים (פ"ה משנה ו): היה עובר בכרם וראה ירק בתוך כרמו, ואמר לכשאחזור אלקטנו, אם הוסיף מאתים — אסור, כיון שמתייאש מללוקטו. וע"כ ההיא דמנחות איירי שלא ידע בעל הכרם שהזרעים בכרמו! לכך נראה לר"י לפרש טעמא דשמעתין: משום דשם גדולה על הקטנה, ואין שם קטנה על הגדולה. ולהכי גפנים בגדולה — הוי שם כרם על הקטנה, ואע"ג דאין גפנים בקטנה — אסור לזורעה, דרחמנא קפיד על שם כרם, דכתיב: "לא תזרע כרמך כלאים". אבל גפנים בקטנה — מותר לזרוע בגדולה, אע"ג דלכשיזרענה יהיה שם שדה על הקטנה — אין לחוש, דרחמנא לא קפיד אשם שדה, דהא לא כתיב: "שדך לא תטע כרם" דהוה משמע דקפיד אשם שדה: **אשה** בגדולה וגט בקטנה. פי' בקונטרס: ושתיהן שלה. דאיכא למאן דאמר בגיטין (דף עז:), הא דתנן הזורק גט לאשתו והיא בתוך ביתה, או בתוך חצירה הרי זו מגורשת — דדוקא דעומדת בתוכה באותה שעה. אבל אינה עומדת בתוכה — לא, אע"ג דשלה היא. וצריך לומר: הא דקאמרינן התם בגמרא "והוא שעומדה בצד ביתה" — לאו אצל ביתה קאמר, אלא בתוך ביתה ממש קאמר, כדקתני התם במתני' בתוך ביתה. דהא הכא אמרינן אשה בקטנה וגט בגדולה — אינה מגורשת, אע"פ שעומדת אצל הגדולה. ולר"י נראה דהכא מיירי בששאילו להאשה חצר אחת, וקאמרינן דכשהשאילו לה גדולה — הוי שמה גם על הקטנה. אשה בקטנה, שהשאילו לה הקטנה — לא הוי בהכי שמה על גדולה:

תשעה בגדולה ויחיד בקטנה מצטרפין. דוקא ביחיד בקטנה. אבל חמשה בקטנה וחמשה בגדולה — אין מצטרפין. וסיפא דנקט תשעה בקטנה — ה"ה חמשה בקטנה, אלא אגב רישא נקט האי לישנא. והא דתנן בפרק "כילד צולין" (פסחים דף פה:): מן האגף ולפנים — כלפנים ומן האגף ולחוץ — כלחוץ, וקאמר התם רב בגמרא: וכן לתפלה. וריב"ל אמר: אפילו מחילה של ברזל אינה מפסקת בין ישראל לאביהם שבשמים. לכאורה נראה דלענין צירוף פליגי, דלענין לצאת מודה רב דיוצא אפילו חוץ לבית הכנסת, כדתנן בפרק "ראוהו ב"ד" (ר"ה דף כז:): היה עובר אחורי בית הכנסת ושמע קול שופר וקול מגילה, אם כוון לבו — יצא. וקשיא, דאם כן סוגיא דהכא כרב. ובפ' "אלו נאמרין" (סוטה דף לח:) משמע דקי"ל כריב"ל, גבי עם שאחורי הכהנים, ומייתי סתמא דהתלמוד ממילתא דריב"ל? ונראה לפרש: דלצירוף מודה ריב"ל דאין מצטרפין, כדאמרינן הכא. ופליגי לענין לענות קדושה או "ברכו" דקי"ל במגילה (דף כג:) דאין דבר שבקדושה פחות מעשרה, וקסבר רב מן האגף ולחוץ — אינו יכול לענות, דלא הוי בכלל צבור שבפנים. וריב"ל סבר: דאפילו מחילה של ברזל אינה מפסקת, והוי בכלל צבור לעניית ברכת כהנים ולענות דבר שבקדושה:

שאילמלי אין מחיצה מרחיק ארבע אמות וזורע. מגיפופי גדולה פריך, כדפי' בקונטרס. דאי לא הוה גיפופי לצד הקטנה אלא השוה גיפופיה, והוי ליה שתיהן חצר אחת — מרחיק ד' אמות וזורע, אם יש בין כרם ולכותל י"ב אמות כדין מחול הכרם. ועכשיו שיש גיפופי ונראות בכך ליחלק יותר זו מזו — מגרע גרע, ואסור לזרוע בקטנה ואפילו היא מאה אמה. כדמשמע לישנא: מפני שהיא כפתחה של גדולה, דהוי כאילו היא תוך הפתח. ודוקא מכותל הגדולה פריך, אבל מקטנה אינו רוצה להקשות. שאם אין כלל מחילות של קטנה — אין צריך להרחיק אלא זורע סמוך לגדולה, דהפתח הוי כמחילה ועכשיו נאסר ע"י מחילות הקטנות — דאין זה תימה, דכשאין מחילות הקטנות נראה הגיפוף, וע"י מחילות הקטנות אין ניכרין גיפופי גדולה, והוי סילוק מחילות. ואומר ר"י: דלכאורה היה נראה מתוך הסברא דאין להחמיר בקטנה שנפרלה לגדולה יותר מאילו היא תוך מחילת גדולה, שמרחיק ד' אמות וזורע כדין(ה) מחול הכרם, ושיש בין הכרם ולכותל י"ב אמות. והא דמשוינן לה כפתחה של גדולה — היינו לעשות הקטנה כאילו היא תוך מחילות הגדולה, שלא להביא זרע לשם אא"כ ירחיק ד' אמות. אבל להחמיר יותר ממה שהיתה תוך מחילות הגדולה — אינה סברא לכאורה. והיה נראה דה"פ: מלינו מחילה לאיסור, שאם אין מחילה כלל לגדולה — מרחיק ד' אמות בקטנה וזורע, אפילו אין י"ב אמות מהכרם שבחוץ לצד הכותל שבחוץ של קטנה. ולא דמי למחול הכרם, דהתם גם הכרם מוקף מחילות — להכי צריך י"ב אמות. אבל הכא דסביב הכרם אין מחילה, ולא שייך כותל קטנה לכרם — אין צריך י"ב אמה. ועכשיו שיש מחילות לגדולה — צריך י"ב אמה כדין מחול הכרם. אבל אומר ר"י דא"א לפרש כן, דא"כ למה מקשה בסמוך ממחול הכרם? דהא אמחול הכרם קיימא השתא, שאם אין מחילה — לא יהא שם דין מחול הכרם, ואם יש מחילות — יהא שם דין מחול הכרם. ונראה לי פירוש רש"י עיקר: **אמר** ליה רבא לאביי. ר"ת הגיה: "רבה", שהרי רבה ור' זירא ורבה בר רב חנן הוו יתבי ומדקדקו שלשתן ממתני' ש"מ דיורין כו', ואביי הקשה על דקדוק שלהן. וכל אחד ואחד בא לקיים דבריו דמלינו מחילה לאיסור. אע"ג דקצת נראה דרבא היה לו לגרוס, מדקאמר בתר הכי לדידי כשירה ולדידך הוי סילוק מחילות. ורבא ואביי פליגי בהא בסוכה בפ"ק (דף יח.) שמזכירו אחר אביי, ולקמן נמי מייתי לה — מ"מ נראה טפי כמו שהגיה ר"ת:

סיכך

ט א *מיי' פ"ה מהלכות גירושין סמג עשין נ טוש"ע אה"ע סי' קלט סעיף ט

*[לא נמצא בהרמב"ם ולא בטוש"ע ופלא על העין משפט להעיד על מה דליתא]

י ב מיי' פ"ח מהלכות תפלה הלכה ז סמג עשין יט טוש"ע א"ח סי' נה סעיף יז:

יא ג מיי' שם וטוש"ע שם סעיף טז:

יב ד מיי' פ"ח מהלכות תפלה הלכה ח טוש"ע א"ח סי' עט סעיף ג:

רבינו חננאל

מותרין. וכן אם היו הגפנים בקטנה מותר לזרוע בגדולה שהקטנה בכלל הגדולה ולא הגדולה בכלל הקטנה. אשה בגדולה וזרק לה בעלה גיטה בקטנה כיון שכל מה שבקטנה חשוב כאלו בגדולה הוה נמצא גרושה וכאילו עמה הוא והגיע ברשותה. וכן אם היו הצבור בגדולה כו'. אמר אביי א"כ מצינו מחיצה לאיסור. שאילו אין שם מחיצה מרחיק ד' אמות וזורע והשתא איתסרו להו זרעים שבקטנה א"ל ר' זירא ולא מצינו מחיצה לאיסור והתניא בית שחציו מקורה וחציו אינו מקורה גפנים כאן מותר לזרוע כאן. ואילו השוה את הקירוי אסור לזרוע בכולו. א"ל אביי התם כיון דזרעיה סלוקי סלוקינהו למחיצות. אמר ליה רבא לאביי והא

הגהות הגר"א

[א] גמ' שאילמלי אין מחילה זורע ואילו וכו'. כצ"ל [וזה דלא כתו' ד"ה שאילמלי שכתבו אבל מקטנה אינה רולה כו' ואומר ר"י דלכאורה כו' ולפי גירסת רבינו באמת הקושיא רק מקטנה].

[גטין עט.]

הגהות הב"ח

(א) רש"י ד"ה גפנים וכו' מדרבנן אסירי הך דעבד איסורא קנסו רבנן הך דלא עבד: (ב) ד"ה מתגרשת שהרי כצ"ל ותיבת היא נמחק: (ג) ד"ה מותר וכו' מקלקלא לה בשום (ד) ד"ה ואלו וכו' אסורה דעכשיו: (ה) תוס' ד"ה שאילמלי וכו' כדין מחול הכרם כשיש:

גליון הש"ס

בעין משפט אות ט' מיי' פ"ה לא נמצא שם ל' ברמב"ם ולא בש"ע ועי' בתשובת זכרון יוסף חאה"ע סי' יב:

*סיכך על גבי אכסדרה שיש לה פצימין – כשירה, ואילו השוה פצימיה – פסולה! א"ל אביי: לדידי – כשירה, לדידך – סילוק מחיצות היא. א"ל רבה בר רב חנן לאביי: ולא מצינו מחיצה לאיסור? והתניא: בית שחציו מקורה וחציו אינו מקורה, גפנים כאן – מותר לזרוע כאן. ואילו השוה את קרויו – אסור! א"ל: התם סילוק מחיצות הוא. שלח ליה רבא לאביי ביד רב שמעיה בר זעירא: ולא מצינו מחיצה לאיסור? והתניא: יש במחיצות הכרם להקל ולהחמיר; כיצד? כרם הנטוע עד עיקר מחיצה – זורע מעיקר מחיצה ואילך, שאילו אין שם מחיצה מרחיק ד"א וזורע, וזה הוא מחיצות הכרם להקל. ולהחמיר כיצד? היה משוך מן הכותל י"א אמה – לא יביא זרע לשם, שאילמלי אין מחיצה – מרחיק ד"א וזורע, וזהי מחיצות הכרם להחמיר! א"ל: ולטעמיך, אותבן ממתניתין, *דתנן: קרחת הכרם, ב"ש אומרים: כ"ד אמות, וב"ה אומרים: ט"ז אמה. מחול הכרם, ב"ש אומרים: ט"ז אמה, וב"ה אומרים: י"ב אמה. ואיזו היא קרחת הכרם – כרם שחרב אמצעיתו. אם אין שם ט"ז אמה – לא יביא זרע לשם, היו שם ט"ז אמה – נותן לו כדי עבודתו, וזורע את המותר. אי זו היא מחול הכרם – בין הכרם לגדר. שאם אין שם י"ב אמה – לא יביא זרע לשם, היו שם י"ב אמה – נותן לו כדי עבודתו וזורע את המותר. אלא התם לאו היינו טעמא(א) – דכל ד"א לגבי כרם – עבודת הכרם, לגבי גדר – כיון דלא מזדרען – אפקורי מפקר להו. דביני ביני, אי איכא ד' – חשיבן, ואי לא – לא חשיבן. אמר רב יהודה: ג' קרפיפות זה בצד זה, ושנים החיצונים מגופפים והאמצעי אינו מגופף, ויחיד בזה ויחיד בזה נעשה כשיירא ונותנין להן(ג) כל צורכן ודאי. אמצעי מגופף ושנים החיצונים אינן מגופפין, ויחיד בזה ויחיד בזה [ויחיד בזה] אין נותנין להם אלא בית שש, איבעיא להו: אחד בזה ואחד בזה ושנים באמצעי מהו? אי להכא נפקי תלתא הוו, ואי להכא נפקי תלתא הוו. או דילמא: חד להכא נפיק, וחד להכא נפיק. ואם תימצי לומר: חד להכא נפיק וחד להכא נפיק; שנים בזה ושנים בזה, ואחד באמצעי מהו? הכא ודאי, אי להכא נפיק תלתא הוו, ואי להכא נפיק תלתא הוו, או דילמא: אימר להכא נפיק, ואימר להכא נפיק? והלכתא: בעיין לקולא. אמר רב חסדא:

גידוד

רש"י

סיכך על גבי אכסדרה שיש לה פצימין. שתי דפנות שיש לה כהלכתה לאורכה, ועשויה כמבוי. ודופן שלישית ורביעית קבועין עמודים לקרני הזויות ויש להם טפח: כשירה. דתנן (סוכה ו.)* שתים כהלכתן ושלישית אפילו טפח: ואילו השוה את פצימיה. שבנה ג' מחיצות בתוכה אצל מחיצות הראשונות, ונמלאו פצימיה עומדין בין שתי המחיצות מכאן ובין שתי מחיצות מכאן, ובתוך האכסדרה אינן נראין: פסולה. דאין לה אלא ב' מחיצות: לדידי כשירה. דפליגי עלך בהא מילתא לקמן בפירקין* דאפילו אין לה שום מחיצה אמרינן פי תקרה יורד וסותם. דקסבר אכסדרה תחובין קורות למעלה מעמוד לעמוד שעליהן נותנים את התקרה, והנך קורות יש להם פה – דהיינו חודם, שאינה עגולה אלא מרובעת: לדידך. נמי, דאמרת פסולה – אין כאן מחיצה לאיסור. דהכא היינו טעמא משום שסילק מכאן את הפצימין ואת מחיצות הראשונות ע"י מחיצות הללו, והעמידה על אלו לבדן: חציו מקורה. מכוסה בגג חלק, כעין תקרת עלייה: גפנים כאן. תחת הקירוי: מותר לזרוע כאן. חוץ לקירוי מיד, ואין צריך להרחיק, דפי תקרה יורד וסותם, והוי מחיצה מבדלת ביניהם: השוה את קרויו. שקירה כל הבית – אסור, אלמא הרחיק: סילוק מחיצות. שהשלמה זו סילק פי תקרה, ואין כאן מבדיל: ביד רב שמעיה. ליהוי להשיב לאביי תשובה זו: להקל ולהחמיר. פעמים שהמחיצה מתרת לענין כלאים, ופעמים שהיא אוסרת: עד עיקר המחיצה. כלומר: עד יסוד מחיצה, סמוך ודבוק למחיצה: היה משוך. כרם רחוק מן הגדר אחת עשרה אמה, וכ"ש פחות: לא יביא זרע. בין כרם לגדר, וטעמא מפרש לקמן: אותבן ממתני'. דאלימתא לאקשויי טפי(ג) מברייתא: קרחת הכרם. לקמן מפרשה: עשרים וארבע אמות. צריך שיהא בה להתירה, להרחיק ארבע אמות ולזרוע. ואם פחות – אסור לזרוע בה אפילו טפח: מחול. סביב כעין מחולות: אין שם שש עשרה אמה כו'. לפי שיש כרם מכאן ומכאן, וצריך להרחיק וליתן ארבע אמות לכרם לכל צד לעבודתו, כמלא בקר וכליו שהיו חורשין בשוורים. ואם נשארו ח' אמות לכאן ולכאן – יש ד' אמות לכל חלק – חשיבי ולא בטילי, ולא אתי כרם דהאי גיסא ומבטל פלגא, וכרם מהאי גיסא ומבטל פלגא: כדי עבודתו. ארבע אמות לכל צד: י"ב אמות. לקמן מפרש טעמא: לאו היינו טעמא. דהיהוי מחיצה, משוויא ליה להאי מחול כי כרם: הכי גרסינן: ארבע אמות דלהדדי כרם עבודת הכרם. וכיון דצריך לו – הוי כרם עצמו: כיון דלא מזדרען. משום דמקלקל ליה לכותל אבנים, שהמחרישה מעלה עפר תיחוח והכותל נופל כשאין תחתיו קרקע חזקה. והכי תנן בבבא בתרא (דף יט.): מרחיקין את הזרע כו': אפקורי מפקר להו. לגבי גדר, ולא מצטרפי להדי האי קאיש, לאחשובי דלא ליבטיל לגבי כרם: ג' קרפיפות זה בצד זה. כגון שהיו מהלכין בדרך, והקיפו ג' קרפיפות לדירה במחיצה של שתי או של ערב, כגון של קנים. או של ערב – כגון חבלים, שלא התירו בו ליחיד אלא בית סאתים, כדמפרש בפ"ק (דף טז:) דשיירא מותרת להקיף כל צרכן בקנים ובחבלים לדירה, אבל יחיד יותר מבית סאתים – לא, אא"כ עשה שתי וערב, מחיצה קיימת: ושנים החיצונים מגופפין וכו'. שהחיצונים רחבים מן האמצעי, והוא פרוץ לשניהם במלואו, וגיפופיהן עודפין עליו: ויחיד בזה ויחיד בזה [ויחיד בזה] נעשו שיירא ונותנין להן כל צורכן. דאמרינן: דיורי גדולים בקטן, ונמלאו שלשתן באמצעי – האמצעי מלגרפן, ומותר אמצעי זה כל שהוא(ז) גדול היקף במחיצה של שתי או של ערב, וכגון שעירבו: אמצעי מגופף והחיצונים אין מגופפין. שהוא רחב מהן, והן פתוחין לו במלואו, ולדידיה לא הוי מילואו: אין נותנין להם. אלא בית סאתים לכל קרפף, שהרי אין שלשה דיורין באחד. דדיורי אמצעי לא הוו בחיצונים. וזיל להכי תרי הוא דהוו, ובאמצעי ליכא אלא חד. ואם אחד מהן יותר מבית סאתים – הוא אסור. ואם אמצעי יותר מבית סאתים – כולן אסורין, שהרי הן פרוצין לבית האסורה. שנים הוו כיחיד. עד דהוי שיירא, דהיינו שלשה: איבעיא להו. אמצעי מגופף ולא חיצונים, ושני אנשים באמצעי, ויחיד בזה ויחיד בזה, מאי: אי להכא נפקי כו'. והנך דאמצעי, הואיל ושניהם שולטין לכאן ולכאן – שדי תרווייהו להכא ותרווייהו להכא, ולשתרו שני קרפיפות החיצונים היקף בכל צרכן: או דילמא. כולי האי לא מקילינן, דנישדינהו להכא ולהכא וה"נ לא אמרינן דנירמינהו תרווייהו לחד. ולמישרי מיהא חד מן החיצונים בכל צורכו, דמספקא לן הי מינייהו. ולחשוב לכל חד, דלא ניהוי אלא חד:(ח) ואי באמצעי. והוא שליט על החיצונים: ולכל היכא דנפיק תלתא הוו. ולישתרי חד מן החיצונים(ו) בכל צרכי היקף: או דילמא אימר להכא או להכא. ולא ידעינן להי מנייהו, הילכך: אפילו חד נמי לא יהבינן ליה כל צרכו: והלכתא בעיין לקולא. שאלותינו אלו להקל:

גידוד

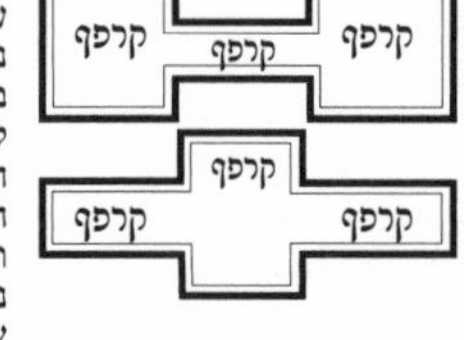

תוספות

סיכך על גבי אכסדרה שיש לה פצימין. אין נראה כמו שפירש בקונטרס שיש שתי דפנות לאורכה, כמבוי מפולש. דבפ"ק דסוכה (דף יח:) מהדר ליה אביי לרבא: בהא מודינא לך, משום דהוי כמבוי מפולש ולא אמרינן פי תקרה יורד וסותם. אלא יש לפרש דהוי כמין גא"ם, ואין להאריך:

חציו מקורה גפנים כאן מותר לזרוע כאן. משום פי תקרה, אע"ג דלענין שבת לא אמרינן פי תקרה לשמואל אלא כשיש ד' מחיצות לגירסת רבינו חננאל ור"ת – [מ"מ] יש לחלק בין כלאים לשבת, כדמשמע בפ"ק (דף יא.). *והא דקא אמרינן לעיל דקטנה הוי כפתחה של גדולה אף לכלאים – מיתורא דקתני במתני' מפני שהיא כפתחה של גדולה משמע ליה: לכל מילי הויא כפתחה:

שנים בזה ושנים בזה. ולא דמי לתשעה בקטנה ויחיד בגדולה, דהכא איכא טעמא כדאמר: דנפיק להכא ולהכא:

גידוד

עין משפט נר מצוה

יג א מיי' פ"ד מהלכות סוכה הלכה ח סמג עשין מג טוש"ע א"ח סי' תרל סעיף ח:

יד ב מיי' פ"ז מהלכות כלאים הלכה יח:

טו ג מיי' שם הלכה יג ופ"ע שם הלכה טו טוש"ע י"ד סי' רצו סעיף כב:

טז ד מיי' פ"ז שם הלכה יא וטוש"ע שם סי' רצו סעיף מב:

[ועי' תוס' סוכה יח: ד"ה אכסדרה וכו' דפירש מותר לכלאים וכו' כדלאיתא בעירובין לעיל יא.]

יז ה מיי' שם הלכה יב טור ש"ע שם סעיף מג:

יח ו ז מיי' פט"ז מהל' שבת הלכה יד טור ש"ע א"ח סי' שסג סעיף ג:

מסורת הש"ס

סוכה יח. לקמן לה.

(דף לה.)

כלאים פ"ד מ"א לעיל ג.

הגהות הב"ח

(א) גמ' לאו היינו טעמא אלא דכל ארבע (ב) שם נותנין להן כל צרכן (ולאו) תז"מ וג"ב ה"א אין זה: (ג) רש"י ד"ה אותבן וכו' טפי מברייתא. נ"ב ר"ל מן הברייתא: (ד) ד"ה ויחיד בזה וכו' כל שהוא גדול היקף גדול במחיצה: (ה) ד"ה והלא ד"ה באמצעי: (ו) באר"ד מן החיצונים בהיקף כל צרכו הס"ד:

רבינו חננאל

סיכך ע"ג אכסדרה שיש לה פצימין כשירה ואלו השוה פצימיה פסולה. א"ל לדידי כשרה היא לדידך סלוקי סלוקינהו למחיצה והתנן חצר גדולה שנפרצה לקטנה גדולה מותרת והקטנה אסורה. ואילו השוה גיפופיה גדולה נמי אסורה ודחינן התם נמי סלוקי סלוקינן למחיצתא והתניא יש במחיצות להקל ולהחמיר להקל כיצד כרם הנטוע עד עיקר מחיצה [זורע מעיקר מחיצה] ואילך שאילו אין שם מחיצה מרחיק ד' אמות וזורע וזו היא מחיצת הכרם להקל. להחמיר כיצד היה משוך מן הכותל י"א אמה לא יביא זרע לשם שאילו אין שם מחיצה מרחיק ד' אמות וזורע וזו מחיצת הכרם להחמיר. הנה מצאנו מחיצה לאיסור. א"ל אדמותבת מברייתא מותיב ממתני' דתנן איזהו מחול הכרם בין הכרם לגדר אם אין שם י"ב אמה [לא] יביא זרע לשם היו שם י"ב אמה נותנין לו כדי עבודתו וזורע את המותר. הנה יש מחיצה לאיסור אלא סברא הוא כל ארבע אמות וכו'. אמר רב יהודה ג' קרפיפות כו' עד ויחיד בכל קרפף נעשו שיירא ובאילו באחד כולן שרויין ונותנין להן כל צרכן אבל אם האמצעית מגופף וב' החיצונות אינן מגופפות ויחיד בכל קרפף אין נותנין להם אלא בית שש בלבד סאתים לכל אחד מהן שאינן שרויין ביחד וכיחידים הן חשובין. איבעיא להו ב' בזה הקרפף ויחיד באמצע מהו. מי אמרינן אי הכין נפיק הא הוו להו ג' ונעשו כשיירא ואי מהכא נפיק הוו להו נמי ג' ונותנין להן כל צרכן. אמר רב

רב נסים גאון

אמר רב יהודה ג' קרפיפות זה בצד זה כו' עשו כשיירא ונותנין להן כל צורכן (ב) שם אם לא תבין איתיה לפירושיה בסוף פרק א' דהא מסכתא (דף טז:) יחיד נותנין לו בית סאתים שנים נותנין להם בית סאתים שלשה עשו שיירא נותנין להן כל צורכן:

אינון שיירא. או דלמא אימ' מהכא לא אמרינן. ב' באמצע ואחד בזה כו' והלכתא דבעיין לקולא. כלומר אמרינן אי מהכא נפיק הוו להו ג' וכן מאידך גיסא ונעשו שיירא ונותנין להן כל צרכן. אמר רב

*גִּידּוּד חֲמִשָּׁה וּמְחִיצָּה חֲמִשָּׁה אֵין מִצְטָרְפִין, עַד שֶׁיְּהֵא אוֹ כּוּלּוֹ בְּגִידּוּד אוֹ כּוּלּוֹ בִּמְחִיצָּה. מֵיתִיבִי: שְׁתֵּי חֲצֵירוֹת זוֹ לְמַעְלָה מִזּוֹ, וְעֶלְיוֹנָה גְּבוֹהָה מִן הַתַּחְתּוֹנָה עֲשָׂרָה טְפָחִים, אוֹ שֶׁיֵּשׁ בָּהּ גִּידּוּד חֲמִשָּׁה וּמְחִיצָּה חֲמִשָּׁה — מְעָרְבִין שְׁנַיִם וְאֵין מְעָרְבִין אֶחָד. פָּחוֹת מִכָּאן — מְעָרְבִין אֶחָד וְאֵין מְעָרְבִין שְׁנַיִם! אָמַר (*רַב:) מוֹדֶה רַב חִסְדָּא בַּתַּחְתּוֹנָה, הוֹאִיל וְרוֹאֶה פְּנֵי עֲשָׂרָה. אִי הָכִי, תַּחְתּוֹנָה תְּעָרֵב שְׁנַיִם וְלֹא תְּעָרֵב אֶחָד, עֶלְיוֹנָה לֹא תְּעָרֵב לֹא אֶחָד וְלֹא שְׁנַיִם! אָמַר רַבָּה בַּר עוּלָּא: כְּגוֹן שֶׁהָיְתָה עֶלְיוֹנָה מְגוּפֶּפֶת עַד עֶשֶׂר אַמּוֹת. אִי הָכִי, אֵימָא סֵיפָא: פָּחוֹת מִכָּאן — מְעָרְבִין אֶחָד וְאֵין מְעָרְבִין שְׁנַיִם. אִי בָּעְיָא — חַד תְּעָרֵב, אִי בָּעְיָא — תְּרֵי תְּעָרֵב! אָמַר רַבָּה בְּרֵיהּ דְּרָבָא: כְּגוֹן שֶׁנִּפְרְצָה הַתַּחְתּוֹנָה בִּמְלוֹאָהּ לָעֶלְיוֹנָה. אִי הָכִי, תַּחְתּוֹנָה — חַד תְּעָרֵב תְּרֵי לֹא תְּעָרֵב. עֶלְיוֹנָה, אִי בָּעְיָא — תְּרֵי תְּעָרֵב, אִי בָּעְיָא — חַד תְּעָרֵב! אִין הָכִי נַמִי. וְכִי קָתָנֵי: "פָּחוֹת מִכָּאן מְעָרְבִין אֶחָד וְאֵין מְעָרְבִין שְׁנַיִם" — אַתַּחְתּוֹנָה. *דָּרֵשׁ מָרֵימָר: גִּידּוּד חֲמִשָּׁה וּמְחִיצָּה חֲמִשָּׁה מִצְטָרְפִין. אַשְׁכְּחֵיהּ רָבִינָא לְרַב אַחָא בְּרֵיהּ דְּרָבָא(א) אֲמַר לֵיהּ: תָּנֵי מָר מִידֵּי בִּמְחִיצָּה? אֲמַר לֵיהּ: לָא. א וְהִלְכְתָא: גִּידּוּד חֲמִשָּׁה וּמְחִיצָּה חֲמִשָּׁה — מִצְטָרְפִין. בָּעֵי רַב הוֹשַׁעְיָא: דִּיּוּרִין הַבָּאִין בְּשַׁבָּת מַהוּ שֶׁיַּאַסְרוּ? אֲמַר רַב(ב) חִסְדָּא: תָּא שְׁמַע, *חָצֵר גְּדוֹלָה שֶׁנִּפְרְצָה לִקְטַנָּה — הַגְּדוֹלָה מוּתֶּרֶת וְהַקְּטַנָּה אֲסוּרָה, מִפְּנֵי שֶׁהִיא כְּפִתְחָהּ שֶׁל גְּדוֹלָה. אָמַר רַבָּה: אֵימַר מִבְּעוֹד יוֹם נִפְרְצָה. אֲמַר לֵיהּ אַבַּיֵּי: לָא תֵּימָא מָר "אֵימַר" אֶלָּא "וַדַּאי מִבְּעוֹד יוֹם נִפְרְצָה". דְּהָא מָר הוּא דַּאֲמַר: *בְּעַי מִינֵּיהּ מֵרַב הוּנָא, וּבְעַי מִינֵּיהּ מֵרַב יְהוּדָה: עֵירֵב דֶּרֶךְ הַפֶּתַח וְנִסְתַּם הַפֶּתַח, עֵירֵב דֶּרֶךְ חַלּוֹן וְנִסְתַּם הַחַלּוֹן, מַהוּ? וְאָמַר לִי: שַׁבָּת, כֵּיוָן שֶׁהוּתְּרָה — הוּתְּרָה. אִתְּמַר, כּוֹתֶל שֶׁבֵּין שְׁתֵּי חֲצֵירוֹת שֶׁנָּפַל, רַב אָמַר: אֵין מְטַלְטְלִין בּוֹ אֶלָּא בְּד"א, וּשְׁמוּאֵל אָמַר: זֶה

רש"י

גִּידּוּד חֲמִשָּׁה. חָצֵר שֶׁקַּרְקָעִיתָהּ גְּבוֹהָ חֲמִשָּׁה טְפָחִים, וְהוֹסִיפוּ עַל אוֹתוֹ גּוֹבַהּ מְחִיצָּה ה': מוֹדֶה רַב חִסְדָּא בַּתַּחְתּוֹנָה. דִּלְגַבָּהּ הָוְיָא מְחִיצָּה. אֲבָל לְגַבֵּי עֶלְיוֹנָה — לָאו מְחִיצָּה הִיא, שֶׁאֵינָהּ רוֹאָה אֶת פְּנֵי עֲשָׂרָה לִמְחִיצָּתָהּ. וְאִי הָוְיָא כּוּלַּהּ בְּגִידּוּד — שַׁפִּיר טְפֵי, מִשּׁוּם דְּמִשְׁתַּמְּשָׁא לְהֶדְיָא עַד סוֹף הַגִּידּוּד, וְרוֹאָה גּוֹבְהָהּ יוֹתֵר עַל חֲבֶרְתָּהּ עֲשָׂרָה, וּמִינְכְּרָא מְחִיצָּתָהּ: תַּחְתּוֹנָה תְּרֵי תְּעָרֵב. כְּלוֹמַר: לְעַצְמָהּ תֵּיעָרֵב דְּיוּרֶיהָ, וְלֹא עִם עֶלְיוֹנָה, שֶׁהֲרֵי מְחִיצָּה בֵּינֵיהֶם. אֲבָל עֶלְיוֹנָה — אֲפִילּוּ לְעַצְמָהּ אֲסוּרָה, שֶׁהַתַּחְתּוֹנָה אוֹסַרְתָּהּ שֶׁאֵין כָּאן מְחִיצָּה. וְלֹא חַד נַמִי תְּעָרֵב עִם תַּחְתּוֹנָה — שֶׁהֲרֵי אֵין כָּאן פֶּתַח, דִּלְגַבֵּי תַּחְתּוֹנָה הַכֹּל סָתוּם: בִּמְגוּפֶּפֶת. מְחִיצָּה עֲשָׂרָה עַל הַגִּידּוּד עַד עֶשֶׂר אַמּוֹת אֶמְצָעִיּוֹת, שֶׁהִנִּיחוּהָ כְּעֵין פֶּתַח וְלֹא הִנִּיחוּ שָׁם הַמְּחִיצָּה עֲשָׂרָה אֶלָּא מְחִיצָּה חֲמִשָּׁה, וְהַגִּידּוּד חֲמִשָּׁה. הִלְכָּךְ: שְׁתֵּיהֶן מְעָרְבוֹת לְעַצְמָן, וְאֵין זוֹ אוֹסֶרֶת עַל זוֹ. דִּלְגַבֵּי תַּחְתּוֹנָה כּוּלָּהּ סְתוּמָה הִיא, וּלְגַבֵּי עֶלְיוֹנָה [מְחִיצָּה] וּפִתְחָא הִיא. וּמִיהוּ, כִּי הֲדָדֵי לָא מָצוּ מְעָרְבֵי מִשּׁוּם דִּלְגַבֵּי תַּחְתּוֹנָה הַכֹּל סָתוּם: אֵימָא סֵיפָא כו'. וְעַל כָּרְחָךְ הַאי פָּחוֹת מִכָּאן — אַמְּחִיצַּת חֲמִשָּׁה שֶׁבְּעֶשֶׂר הָאַמּוֹת קָאֵי, דְּהָא בְּכָל הַהֶיקֵּף מְחִיצָּה עֲשָׂרָה אִיכָּא: אִי בָּעֵי חַד תְּעָרֵב. דְּהָא פֶּתַח גָּמוּר הוּא אֵצֶל שְׁתֵּיהֶן: בִּמְלוֹאָהּ. שֶׁאֵין בְּרָחְבָּהּ אֶלָּא עֶשֶׂר אַמּוֹת, הִלְכָּךְ, אָסְרָה עֶלְיוֹנָה עָלֶיהָ(ג) וְלֹא מְעָרְבָה בַּהֲדָהּ. כְּדִתְנַן: גְּדוֹלָה מוּתֶּרֶת וּקְטַנָּה אֲסוּרָה: אִי הָכִי תַּחְתּוֹנָה חַד תֵּיעָרֵב. עִם הָעֶלְיוֹנָה: תְּרֵי לֹא תְּעָרֵב. בִּפְנֵי עַצְמָהּ דְּעֶלְיוֹנָה אוֹסֶרֶת אא"כ עֵירְבָה עִמָּהּ: דִּיּוּרִין הַבָּאִין בְּשַׁבָּת. כְּגוֹן כּוֹתֶל שֶׁבֵּין שְׁתֵּי חֲצֵירוֹת שֶׁנָּפַל בְּשַׁבָּת דְּהַיְינוּ דִּיּוּרַיְיהוּ הַשְׁתָּא כִּי הֲדָדֵי: מַהוּ שֶׁיַּאַסְרוּ. זֶה עַל זֶה: וּקְטַנָּה אֲסוּרָה. [וְס"ד] שֶׁנִּפְרְצָה בְּשַׁבָּת: אֶלָּא וַדַּאי. עַל כּוֹרְחֵיךְ הָכִי תּוֹקְמָא דְּהָא אַתְּ אָמַרְתְּ דִּיּוּרִין הַבָּאִין בְּשַׁבָּת אֵין אוֹסְרִין: דְּאָמַרְתְּ בְּעַאי מִינֵּיהּ מֵרַב הוּנָא עֵירֵב דֶּרֶךְ הַפֶּתַח. שְׁתֵּי חֲצֵירוֹת שֶׁעֵירְבוּ יַחַד עַל יְדֵי פֶּתַח שֶׁבֵּינֵיהֶם: וְנִסְתַּם. בְּשַׁבָּת, שֶׁנָּפְלָה מַפּוֹלֶת כְּנֶגְדּוֹ: מַהוּ. לְטַלְטֵל מִזּוֹ לָזוֹ דֶּרֶךְ גּוֹבַהּ הַכּוֹתֶל וְחוֹרִין וּסְדָקִין, מִי אָמְרִינַן הוֹאִיל וְהוּתַּר לְמִקְצָת שַׁבָּת — הוּתַּר לְכוּלָּהּ אוֹ לָא: כּוֹתֶל שֶׁבֵּין שְׁתֵּי חֲצֵירוֹת. שֶׁלֹּא הָיָה פֶּתַח בֵּינֵיהֶם, וְלֹא עֵירְבוּ בּוֹ יַחַד, וְנָפַל: רַב אָמַר אֵין מְטַלְטְלִין בּוֹ אֶלָּא בְּאַרְבַּע. רַב לֵית לֵיהּ: הוֹאִיל וְהוּתְּרָה הוּתְּרָה, וּכְחַד חָצֵר לָא מְשַׁוֵּינַן לֵיהּ, דְּקַיְ"ל חָצֵר שֶׁלֹּא עֵירְבָה דִּבְרֵי הַכֹּל מְטַלְטְלִין כֵּלִים שֶׁשָּׁבְתוּ בַּחֲצֵירָהּ — דְּהַהִיא כּוּלָּהּ חֲדָא רְשׁוּתָא הִיא, אֲבָל הָכָא ב' רְשׁוּיוֹת הָאֲסוּרוֹת זוֹ עִם זוֹ הָיוּ, וְנִמְצֵאת כָּל אַחַת פְּרוּצָה בִּמְלוֹאָהּ לְמָקוֹם הָאָסוּר לָהּ. אע"ג דְּקַיְ"ל דַּחֲצֵירוֹת רְשׁוּת אַחַת הֵן — הָכָא בְּשֶׁעֵירְבָה כָּל אַחַת לְעַצְמָהּ עָסְקִינַן. וְרַב לְטַעְמֵיהּ, דְּאָמַר: *הֲלָכָה כְּר"ש, וְהוּא שֶׁלֹּא עֵירְבוּ. אֲבָל עֵירְבוּ — שְׁתֵּי רְשׁוּיוֹת הֵן: זֶה

תוספות

גידוד חמשה ומחיצה חמשה אין מצטרפין. בפרק שני דגיטין (דף טו:) פי' בקונטרס: כגון *בית עמוק חמשה ויש לו מחילות חמשה – אין מצטרפין להיות תוכו רה"י. וקשיא לר"ת: דהא אמר בפרק בתרא (דף לט:) דבור וחוליתה מצטרפין, ובשמעתא נמי אמר דמודה רב חסדא בתחתונה הואיל ורואה פני י'. אלא יש לפרש: גידוד חמשה – גבוה חמשה. ונפקא מינה בשתי חצירות זו למעלה מזו, ולעליונה כדאמר הכא. ונ"ע לענין שבת, אם יש(ד) *(לפרש כשים) תל ברה"ר גבוה חמשה ורחב ארבעה, ועל גביו עשו מחיצה חמשה שהזורק מרה"ר לתוכו חייב, ומתוכו לרה"ר פטור: **וכי** קתני פחות מכאן מערבין אחד ואין מערבין שנים אתחתונה. וא"ת: לעיל כדפריך עליונה לא תערב לא חד ולא תרי, אמאי לא משני: הא דקתני מערבין שנים ואין מערבין אחד, אתחתונה? ויש לומר: משום דמשמע ליה מערבין שנים – אתרוייהו:

לא תימא אימר אלא ודאי מבעוד יום נפרצה. קשה: דהכא אמר אביי דרבה סבר כשמואל, דאמר שבת הואיל והותרה הותרה. וא"כ תיקשי, דאביי גופיה אמר (שבת דף כב.): כל מילי דמר עביד כחומרי דרב, בר מהני תלת דעביד כשמואל: מתירין מבגד לבגד כו'. ואין לומר דמש"ה לא חשיב(ה) הא, דהכא משום דרב הונא ורב יהודה נמי סברי כשמואל – דהא בגרירא איכא דסברי כשמואל, דהא בפרק "המוציא" (שבת פא.) משמע דסבר רבי יוחנן כסתם משנה דנזיר תופף ומפספס. ומיהו, י"ל דהכי פריך ב"המוציא": ומי מצי ר' יוחנן למימר דבר שאין מתכוין אסור, דלא כסתם משנה דנזיר – אפילו איכא סתמא אחרינא כדאשכחן בבילה (דף כג:) – מאי אולמיה האי סתמא מהאי? ואין לרבי יוחנן נמי לפסוק כשום אחת בלא ראייה. אי נמי יש לומר: הא דעביד כחומרי דרב – היינו בעלמא, לבד מעירוב ואבל, דהלכה כדברי המיקל בהם. או שמא: כיון דזימנין הך קולא הויא חומרא, כגון דנאסר במקצת שבת, דמהאי טעמא נאסר לכל השבת – לא חשיב ליה מחומרי דרב, דלרב לית ליה הואיל והותרה הותרה, ולית ליה נמי הואיל ונאסר נאסר: **שבת** כיון שהותרה הותרה. פירשתי בפרק קמא (דף יז. ד"ה עירוב): **אין** מטלטלין בה אלא בארבע. בכלים ששבתו בבית לר"ש.

*) **חייב** דברי ר"א. בגמ' מוקי לה במקום מחילה הפרוצה, וכגון שבשני ראשיה לא נשאר כלל משתי מחילות שבצידה, שמקום מחילה זו שנפרצה אינו תוך מחילות הנשארות. ובלישנא קמא מוקי לה כגון שאבדה להם דרך באותו מקום, ובררו להם מקום מחילות להיות שלהן ללכת דרך שם בשביל דרכם שאבדו שם. ור"א לטעמיה, דאית ליה מה שבררו ברור, ורבנן סברי דאין להם כח לברור, הלכך: אף על פי שעוברים שם – אינו רה"ר, כיון שלא נמסר לרבים, ואינו של רבים. כדאמרינן בפרק שני (דף כב:) גבי שבילי בית גלגול קאמרת. ו"מתוכה" דקאמר ר"א – לאו דוקא מתוכה, אלא משום דנקטו רבנן "מתוכה" – קאמר איהו נמי "מתוכה", כדקאמר בגמרא. והכי קמהדרי ליה רבנן: אי אתה מודה שאם הוציא מתוכה לרה"ר שהוא פטור אבל אסור, שאין לרבים כח שם ולכך אינה נעשית רה"ר אפילו נפלו כל המחילות סביב והוי כרמלית – הכא נמי מקום מחילה תודה שיהיה כרמלית, שאין להם כח בבירתן. והא דשבקי רבנן רה"י כדנקט ר"א, ונקטי רה"ר – משום דר"א דיבר על מקום מחילה שיהא רה"ר, וקאמר שאם הוציא מתוך החצר שהיא רה"י למקום מחילה חייב. אבל רבנן דמיירי במוציא ומכניס לתוכו ממש, ואפילו כשנפלו כל מחילותיה – נקטי רה"ר שאלה הנזכר במשנה, ולא רצו למינקט שאם הוציא מתוכה לחצר שאלה – משום דלא נזכר במשנתנו שהיה חצר אלא. אי נמי: להכי נקטי רה"ר – להוכיח שתוכה חלוק הרבה מרה"ר, שאם לא היה חלוק הרבה – היה מותר להכניס מרה"ר לתוכה. אבל במה שפטור המוציא מרה"י לתוכה – אין להוכיח שחלוק הרבה, דאפילו אין חלוק אלא מעט מרה"ר פטור המוציא מרה"י לתוכה, כיון שאין רה"ר ממש:

ואיבעית

עין משפט נר מצוה

[התם איתא חרין]

יט א מיי' פט"ו מהלכ' שבת הלכה טו טור ש"ע א"ח סי' שסב סעיף ב וסי' שעב סעיף ו:

מסורת הש"ס

גיטין טו:

[נ"ל רבא]

[גיטין טו:]

[לעיל נב.]

לעיל יז.

רש"ל מ"ז

שייך לדף לד ע"ב במתניתין

[לעיל לח.]

רבינו חננאל

רב חסדא גידור ה' טפחים. פי' כמו סלע גבוה ה' טפחים ובנה מחיצה עליה ה' טפחים אין מצטרפין לעשרה דבעינן אי כולו בגידו' אי כולו במחיצה. מיתיבי ב' חצרות זו למעלה מזו כו' הנה גידור ה' ומחיצה ה' מצטרפו. ופריק רבה מודה רב חסדא בתחתונ' הואיל ורואה פני עשרה כלומר הואיל ויש למעל' ממנה עשרה טפחים ואקשינן אי הכי תחתונה תיערב לעצמה דהא סלקו ממנה מחיצות אבל העליונה לא תיערב אפילו לעצמה דהא לית ליה מחיצתא והנה התחתונה אוסרת עליה. וזהו פי' לא תיערב לא אחד ולא שנים כלומר לא תיערב לא לעצמה ולא עם התחתונ' ופריק רבא בר עולא כגון שהיתה העליונה מגופפת פי' סתומה והולכת עד עשר אמות לפיכך העליונה מערבה לעצמה והתחתונה לעצמה. אי הכי שהעליונה מגופפת עד עשר אמות אימא סיפא פחות מיכן מערבין אחד ואין מערבין שנים. אמאי איבעיא העליונה תיערב חד דהא ליכא ביניהן מחיצה עשרה טפחים ואיבעיא תיערב שנים כלומר תערב לעצמה דהא מגופפת עשרה ודחי רבה כגון שנפרצה תחתונה במלואה לעליונה אי הכי תחתונה תיערב עם העליונה דהא אית לה מחיצתא. והנה רואה פני עשרה ונעשית עכשיו העליונה והתחתונה כאחד. אבל עליונה לא חד תערב ולא תרי תיערב דהא נפרצה עליה התחתונה *) חד נמי לא תיערב דהא לה מחיצה ופריק אין הכי נמי כו' ואסיקנא הלכתא גידור ה' ומחיצתא ה' מצטרפין. בעי רב הושעיא דיורין שבאו בשבת מהו שיאסרו. ופשטנא מהא דתנן חצר גדול כו' ואוקימנא בשנפרצה מבעו"י. אבל נפרצה בשבת מותרת אפילו הקטנה. דאיבעיא לן עירב דרך חלון ונסתם החלון מהו לטלטל מזה לזה דרך פתח וכיוצא בו וכן מי שעירב מחצר לחצר דרך הפתח ונסתם הפתח בשבת מה לטלטל מחצר זו לחצר זו דרך חלון אחר שנסתם הפתח ואיפשטא שבת שהותרה למקצתה הותרה כולה ש"מ דיורין הבאין בשבת אין אוסרין ולא מתירין. איתמר כותל שבין שתי חצרות שנפל רב אמר אין מטלטלין באותה חצר אלא בד' אמות כו'.

*) משמע דרבינו גרס דעליונה לא חד תערב ולא תרי תערב ותמוה דא"כ היכי תחתונה יכולה לערב עם העליונה וצ"ע. והא

גליון הש"ס

גמ' גידוד חמשה ומחיצה חמשה אין מצטרפין. עי' לעיל דף עט ע"א תוס' ד"ה כותל:

הגהות הב"ח

(א) גמ' אשכחיה רבינא לרב אחא בריה דרבא אמר ליה וכו' לא) תא"מ ונ"ב ס"א אמר ליה אמר אמימר מידי בגידוד חמשה ובמחילה חמשה אמר ליה לא: (ב) שם מה שיאסרו אמר רב חיננא ת"ש חצר: (ג) רש"י ד"ה במלואה וכו' עליונה עלה אי לא ערבה: (ד) תום' ד"ה גידוד וכו' לענין שבת אם יש הא כל"ל ותיבת לפרש כשים נמחק: (ה) ד"ה לא תימא וכו' לא חשיב להא דהכא וכו' בפרק המוציא יין משמע וכו' פריך בהמוציא ומי:

כ א מיי׳ פ״ג מהלכות עירובין הלכה כה סמג לאוין סה טוש״ע א״ח סי׳ שעב סעיף ב:
כא ב טור ש״ע שם וסי׳ שמה סעיף ב:

זה מטלטל עד עיקר מחיצה, וזה מטלטל עד עיקר מחיצה. והא דרב *לאו בפירוש אתמר, אלא מכללא אתמר. דרב ושמואל הוו יתבי בההוא חצר, נפל גודא דביני ביני. אמר להו שמואל: שקולו גלימא נגידו בה. אהדרינהו רב לאפיה. אמר להו שמואל: אי קפיד *אבא — שקולו *(הימניה) וקטרו בה. *ולשמואל למה לי הא? הא אמר: זה מטלטל עד עיקר מחיצה, וזה מטלטל עד עיקר מחיצה! שמואל עביד לצניעותא בעלמא. ורב, אי סבירא ליה דאסיר — לימא ליה! *אתריה דשמואל הוה. אי הכי, מאי טעמא אהדרינהו לאפיה? דלא נימרו כשמואל סבירא ליה, (*והדר ביה משמעתיה.)§

מתני׳ חצר שנפרצה לרשות הרבים, המכנים מתוכה לרה״י או מרה״י לתוכה — חייב, דברי רבי אליעזר. וחכמים אומרים: מתוכה לרשות הרבים או מרשות הרבים לתוכה — פטור, מפני שהיא ככרמלית.§

גמ׳ ורבי אליעזר, משום דנפרצה לרשות הרבים הויא לה רשות הרבים?! אין, רבי אליעזר לטעמיה. דתניא, *רבי יהודה אומר משום רבי אליעזר: רבים שבררו דרך לעצמן — מה שבררו ברור. איני?! והאמר *רב גידל, אמר רב: והוא שאבדה להן דרך באותו שדה. וכי תימא: הכא נמי כגון שאבדה לה דרך באותה חצר — והאמר רבי חנינא: עד מקום מחיצה מחלוקת! אימא: על מקום מחיצה מחלוקת. ואיבעית אימא: בצידי רשות הרבים קמיפלגי; *דרבי אליעזר סבר: צידי רשות הרבים — כרשות הרבים דמו, ורבנן סברי: צידי רשות הרבים — לאו כרשות הרבים דמו. וליפלוג בצידי רשות הרבים (א) בעלמא! אי איפליגו בצידי רשות הרבים בעלמא — הוה אמרינן: כי פליגי רבנן עליה דרבי אליעזר — הני מילי היכא דאיכא חיפופי, אבל היכא דליכא חיפופי — אימא מודו ליה, קא משמע לן. והא "מתוכה" קאמר! איידי דאמור רבנן "מתוכה", אמר איהו נמי "מתוכה". ורבנן, אמר רבי אליעזר צידי רשות הרבים, ומהדרו ליה אינהו "מתוכה"?! הכי קאמרי ליה רבנן לרבי אליעזר: מי לא קא מודית לן היכא דטילטל מתוכה לרשות הרבים, ומרשות הרבים לתוכה דפטור — מפני שהיא כרמלית, צידי נמי לא שנא. ורבי אליעזר — התם לא קא דרסי לה רבים, הכא — קא דרסי לה רבים.§

מתני׳ *חצר שנפרצה *)לרה״ר משתי רוחותיה, וכן בית שנפרץ משתי רוחותיו, וכן מבוי שנטלו קורותיו או לחייו — מותרים באותו שבת, ואסורים לעתיד לבא, דברי רבי יהודה. רבי יוסי אומר: אם מותרין לאותו שבת — מותרין לעתיד לבא, ואם אסורין לעתיד לבא — אסורין לאותו שבת.§

גמ׳ במאי עסקינן? אילימא בעשר — מאי שנא מרוח אחת — דאמר "פיתחא הוא", משתי רוחות נמי פיתחא הוא! אלא ביתר מעשר — א״ה אפילו מרוח אחת נמי! אמר רב: לעולם בעשר, וכגון

*) ירושל׳ ורי״ף לא גרסו לרה״ר

רש״י

זה מטלטל עד עיקר מחיצה. כדמעיקרא דאמרינן: הואיל והותרה הותרה. ובכלי הבית קאמר שמואל, דאי בששבתו בחצר — אפילו מחצר לחצר נמי דהא שמואל הוא דאמר *הלכה כר״ש. ואפי׳ עירבה כל אחת לעצמה — לא גזר משום מאני דבתים. ואע״ג דהשתא הוו להו חצר אחת כשנפל — לא אסרי להו בתים, דהא שרי לאפוקי מבתים לחצר הואיל והותר למקצת שבת: שקולו גלימא נגידו. קחו טלית ופרסו אותה שם להיות מחיצה: אהדרינהו רב לאפיה. דקסבר: אסור לטלטל הכלים שבתוכה: שקולו המיינה וקטרו בה. קחו אבנטו וקשרו בו את הטלית למחיצה: מתני׳ חצר שנפרצה לרה״ר. במלואה, או יותר מעשר: חייב. דרה״ר הוא. ובגמרא קא בעי לה: פטור. אבל מותר לכתחלה — לא, אפי׳ תוך ארבע אמות דלאו רה״ר היא אלא כרמלית היא, והוא הדין נמי מתוכה לרה״י: גמ׳ שבררו דרך לעצמן. בשדה אחת: מה שבררו ברורו. ואינו רשאי לגודרה אלמא: קנו לה: שאבדה להן דרך באותו שדה. שהיה להן דרך בו, ואינו יודע אי בצפונו אי בדרומו. ובררו להן אחת מן הרוחות: וכי תימא הכא נמי כשאבדה להן הדרך באותה חצר. שאין מקום המחיצה ניכר, ובני רה״ר מרחיבין רה״ר לתוכה במקצת, ואמרו שעד כאן היה רשותן. וכי קאמר ר״א רה״ר היא — באותו מקום מחיצה קאמר, שאלו עוררין עליו: והאמר רבי חנינא עד מקום מחיצות מחלוקת. דמשמע כל החצר כולה עד מקום המחיצה היו חכמים עושין אותה כרמלית, אבל במקום מחיצה מודו. מכלל דר״א משוי ליה לכוליה(ב) רה״ר: ואיבעית אימא. לעולם בשמקומות מחיצות ניכרות, ואפילו הכי משוי ליה ר״א למקום מחיצה רה״ר, דקא סבר: צידי רה״ר כרה״ר דמו: הני מילי היכא דאיכא חיפופי. סתם צידי רה״ר איכא חיפופי, נועצין יתידות אבנים גדולות סמוך לכותל שלא יזיקוהו קרונות, והאויר שבינייהם לכותל קרי צידי רשות הרבים. ובההוא הוה אמינא הוא דפליגי רבנן, ואמרו לאו רשות הרבים הוא, ואסור לטלטל מתוכו לרשות הרבים משום דאיכא הפסק, ולא עיילי בהא רבים להדיא, אבל הכא — אימא מודו ליה: והא מתוכה. לרשות היחיד קאמר ר״א חייב, אלמא: כולה חצר רה״ר משוי ליה: איידי דאמרי רבנן מתוכה כו׳. ואנן פרכינן לרבנן אמאי נקטי מתוכה, הא רבי אליעזר בתוכה מודה דכרמלית היא דמקום מחיצה הוא דקא משוי רה״ר: מתני׳ חצר שנפרצה. בשבת לרשות הרבים: מותרין לאותה שבת. הואיל והותר למקצתה: שניטלה קורתו או (*לחייו) גרסינן: לעתיד לבא. לשבת הבאה: אם מותרין כו׳. בגמרא מפרש דרבי יוסי מחמיר והכי קאמר: כשם שאסורין לעתיד לבא — כך אסורין היום: גמ׳ במאי עסקינן. דאצטריך ליה למנקט משתי רוחותיו: אילימא בעשר. ומשום הכי מרוח אחת לא, דאמרינן פתחא הוא: משתי רוחותיו(ג) נימא נמי פתחא הוא. דקא סלקא דעתיה משתי רוחות זו כנגד זו קאמר, כגון מזרח ומערב:

תוספות

ואיבעית אימא בצידי רה״ר פליגי. ולא מיירי באבדה להם דרך: וליפלגו בצידי רה״ר דעלמא. ואם תאמר: דילמא דוקא הכא פליגי, משום דמקום מחילה שלו! ואור״י: דסתם צידי רשות הרבים הם שלו, שרגיל אדם להיות כונס תוך שלו ובונה: אבל היכא דליכא חיפופי מודו ליה קא משמע לן. משמע דר״א איירי בדאיכא חיפופי. והקשה ריב״א: דבפרק קמא דשבת (דף ו.) אמרינן: מתקיף לה רב אחא בריה דרב איקא, אימר דשמעת ליה לר״א היכא דליכא חיפופי, היכא דאיכא חיפופי מי שמעת ליה? וי״ל: דסוגיא דהכא כרב פפא דהתם: מאי שנא מרוח אחת דאמר פתחא הוא. ואם תאמר: מרוח אחת, אע״ג דפרוץ מרובה אמרינן בפ״ק (דף י:) דניתרת בפס ד׳ או בשני משהויין לכאן ולכאן, אבל בשתי רוחות לא משתרי בהכי, דג׳ מחילות דאוריי׳, [*כמו סתם מבוי דהוי בלחי וקורה]! וי״ל: דהכא פריך לר׳ יהודה, דאית ליה לקמן (נה.) שתי מחילו׳ דאורייתא, ועוד אור״י: דסתם חצר אין לה אלא ג׳ מחילות וברביעית פס ד׳ או ב׳ משהויין, ואיירי(ד) שנפרצו ב׳ רוחות מאותן ג׳ מחילות ואף על גב דהשתא כשנפרצה הוי מפולש, ואמרינן בפ״ק (דף יא.): דבעי לכל הפתוח צורת הפתח — היינו דוקא כשנפרצה לרה״ר או לבקעה. אבל הכא איירי כשנפרצה למבוי או לחצר אחרת, דהא לא קתני שנפרצה לרה״ר: *מאי שנא מרוח אחת דאמרי׳ פי תקרה כו׳. השתא לא קאמר פתחא הוא, דאפילו נפרץ במילואו או ביתר מעשר רוצה להתיר בבית, מטעם פי תקרה: *בשתי רוחות נמי נימא פי תקרה יורד וסותם. רש״י מפרש: דרב ושמואל דפליגי בפי תקרה — היינו דווקא באכסדרה בבקעה שאין לה כלל מחילות. אבל דיש לה אפי׳ מחילה אחת — מודה שמואל דבשלש מחילות אמרינן פי תקרה יורד וסותם. ואתי שפיר הא דנקט אכסדרה בבקעה — לפי שבבקעה דווקא פליגי, שאין שם מחילה. וגרס בתר הכי: כי לית ליה — בד׳, אבל בג׳ — אית ליה. ולפי זה פירוש כל הסוגיא. ואין נראה, דאפילו לרב בשתי מחילות זו כנגד זו לא אמר פי תקרה יורד וסותם, דהוי מפולש, כדאמר בפרק קמא דסוכה (דף יח:). לכך נראה לר״י: דסתם אכסדרה יש לה ג׳ מחילות, כדאמר ב״לא יחפור״ (ב״ב דף כה:): העולם לאכסדרה הוא דומה, דרוח צפונית אינה מסובבת. ולית ליה לשמואל פי תקרה יורד וסותם אלא אם כן יש שם ארבע מחילות. ומיהו, לרב אפי׳ פרוץ משתי רוחות

רבינו חננאל

והא דרב לא אתמר בפירוש אלא מכללא דרב ושמואל הוו יתבי בחצר נפל גודא דביני ביני אמר שמואל אייתו גלימא נגידו ביה משום צניעותא דשרי לטלטולי בכולה עד מקום גודא אהדרינהו רב לאפיה דלא לימרו הדר ביה רב משמעתיה דהוה אסר ולא אמר להו ולא מידי דאתר דשמואל הוה. ואמר שמואל אי קפיד אבא שקילו הימייניה וקטרו ביה האי גלימא: מתני׳ חצר שנפרצה לרה״ר המכנים לתוכה לרה״ר כו׳. ואקשינן וכי [ס״ל] לר׳ אליעזר משום דנפרצה לרה״ר הויא לה רה״ר ופרקינן אין ר׳ אליעזר לטעמיה דכיון שעוברין ושבין רבים בתוכה הויא כרה״ר. דתניא ר׳ יהודה אמר משום ר׳ אליעזר רבים שבירו דרך לעצמן מה שבירו בירו. ואוקמה כשאבדה להן דרך באותה חצר. ועל מקום מחיצה מחלוקת איבעית אימא בצידי רה״ר פליגי ר׳ אליעזר סבר צידי רה״ר כרה״ר דמו. והאי חצר כיון שנפרצה לרה״ר ורבים דרסו לה כצידי רה״ר הוא ורבנן אמרי (לה) [לאו כר״ה דמי] ואמאי לא פליגי בצידי רשות דעלמא. (לא) [דלא] תימא כי פליגי רבנן עליה דר׳ אליעזר דאמרי ליה לאו כרשות [הרבים] דמי אלא היכא דאיכא גיפופי פי׳ גיפופי שנראין כפסין וככתלים קטנים שעושין שלא (יתחברו) [יתחככו] בכתלים. אבל היכא דליכא גיפופי לא קא משמע לן חצר זו שנפרצה דלית ליה גיפופי. ואקשינן והא מתוכה לרה״ר קתני מכלל דאית ליה גיפופי דאי לית ליה גיפופי מאין לה תוך. ופרקינן לעולם לית ליה גיפופי ולית ליה תוך ואיידי דאמור רבנן מתוכה א׳ נמי מתוכה. ואקשינן והיכי מהדרי ליה רבנן מתוכה והוא לא אמר מתוכה. ופרקינן הכי קאמרו ליה רבנן מי לא מודי דהיכא דטילטל מתוכה לרה״ר דפטור מפני שהיא ככרמלית צידי רה״ר לא שנא. ור׳ אליעזר התם בחצר *) דדרסי לה רבים הכא בצידי רה״ר דאית ליה גיפופי לא דרסי לה רבים: מתני׳ חצר שנפרצה מב׳ רוחותיה וכן בית כו׳ ואוקמה רב שנפרצה מב׳ רוחותיה בי׳ אמות בקרן זוית ומפני

*) לשון רבינו תמוה לכאורה וצ״ל דל״ל התם בחצר לא דרסי לה רבים הכא בצידי ר״ה אע״ג דאית ליה גיפופי מ״מ דרסי לה רבים.

לעיל מח. · [ברכות ט. וש״נ] · [נ״ל המיינה] · [חולין נג:] · רש״ל נ״ג · [ב״ב ק.] · [שם] · שבת ו. כתובות לא: · לעיל יז. · [נ״ל לחיו ועי׳ תוס׳ לעיל יז. ד״ה קורותיו]

[עמ״ש לעיל דף עח. על הגליון] · גי׳ רש״ל והיכי עביד שמואל הכי והא

הגהות הב״ח

(א) גמ׳ וליפלוג בצידי רה״ר דעלמא וכו׳ דעלמא הוה אמינא: (ב) רש״י ד״ה והאמר וכו׳ לכוליה חצר רה״ר הס״ד: (ג) ד״ה משתי רוחותיו נמי נימא פתחא: (ד) תוס׳ ד״ה מאי שנא וכו׳ ואיירי נמי שנפרצו:

גליון הש״ס

גמ׳ זה מטלטל עד עיקר מחיצה. עי׳ לעיל דף עט ע״ב: תוס׳ ד״ה בשתי רוחות וכו׳ בבקעה שאין לה כלל. עי׳ לעיל דף עו ע״ב תוס׳ ד״ה גזוזטרא:

א) וכגון שנפרצה בקרן זוית, *דפיתחא בקרן זוית לא עבדי אינשי. § "וכן בית שנפרץ משתי רוחותיו". § מאי שנא מרוח אחת – דאמרינן "פי תקרה יורד וסותם", משתי רוחות נמי, לימא "פי תקרה יורד וסותם"! אמרי דבי רב משמיה דרב: ב) כגון שנפרץ בקרן זוית, וקירויו באלכסון, דליכא למימר "פי תקרה יורד וסותם". ושמואל אמר: אפילו ביתר מעשר. אי הכי, מרוח אחת נמי! משום בית. ובית גופיה תקשי, מאי שנא מרוח אחת – דאמרי' "פי תקרה יורד וסותם", מב' רוחות נמי נימא "פי תקרה יורד וסותם"! ותו: מי אית ליה לשמואל פי תקרה יורד וסותם? והא איתמר, *אכסדרה בבקעה; רב אמר: מותר לטלטל בכולה, ושמואל אמר: אין מטלטלין בה אלא בד' אמות! הא לא קשיא, כי לית ליה – בד', אבל בשלש – אית ליה. מ"מ קשיא! כדאמרי בי רב משמיה דרב: כגון שנפרץ בקרן זוית וקירויו באלכסון, הכא נמי: כגון שנפרץ בקרן זוית וקירויו בארבע. שמואל לא אמר כרב – אלכסון לא קתני. ורב לא אמר כשמואל – אם כן הויא ליה אכסדרה, ורב לטעמיה, דאמר: אכסדרה מותר לטלטל בכולה. *דאיתמר, אכסדרה בבקעה, רב אמר: מותר לטלטל בכולה, ושמואל אמר: אין מטלטלין בה אלא בארבע אמות. רב אמר: מותר לטלטל בכולה, אמרינן "פי תקרה יורד וסותם", ושמואל אמר: אין מטלטלין בה אלא בארבע אמות, לא אמרינן "פי תקרה יורד וסותם". בעשר כולי עלמא לא פליגי, כי פליגי – ביתר מעשר. ואיכא דאמרי: ביתר – כולי עלמא לא פליגי, כי פליגי – בעשר. והא *דאמר רב יהודה:
קורה

רש"י

כגון שנפרצה. בה פרצה אחת, שתופסת בשתי רוחותיה – דהיינו בקרן זוית: דפיתחא בקרן זוית לא עבדי. דלאו אורחיה הוא: משתי רוחות נמי וכו'. אלא סלקא דעתיה: שתי רוחות ממש: אמרי בי רב. הא נמי בקרן זוית, אע"ג דבעשר אוקימנא – לא אמרינן פתחא הוא, דפתחא בקרן זוית לא עבידי. ומשום פי תקרה נמי לא, כגון שקירויו באלכסון בשיפוע, כגון גגין שלנו, דליכא פה, דהיינו כעין ארזילא דאמרינן ב"עושין פסין" (לעיל דף כה:): ושמואל אמר מתניתין אפילו ביתר מעשר. ולא מיתנא ליה אלא בשתי רוחות, כדמפרש ואזיל. ואסבר קא מהדר שמואל: משום בית. דלא אפשר ברוח אחת, משום פי תקרה יורד וסותם: ותו מי אית ליה לשמואל פי תקרה יורד וסותם. דמוקמינן לה מתני' ביותר מעשר, וקאמר דבית לא מיתסר. והאמר שמואל בריש פרקין באכסדרה בבקעה, דאין מטלטלין בה אלא בארבע אמות: כי לית ליה בארבע. במקום שצריך לעשות ארבע מחיצות בסתימת פי תקרה יורד וסותם, כגון אכסדרה: אבל בשלש. דאי היתה בה מחיצה כהלכתה, ופי תקרה לשלש מחיצות מכשיר: מ"מ קשיא. שתי רוחות אמאי לא אמרינן פי תקרה יורד וסותם! ושמואל לא מצי מוקי בקירוי אלכסון – דא"כ ברוח אחת נמי תיתסר, הואיל דיותר מעשר: (א) כדאמרי בי רב. דהאי שתי רוחות קרן זוית קאמר: וקירויו. נמי, אף ע"ג דלא איירי ביה מתניתין מבעי ליה לאוקומי שאינו כשאר תקרות אלא משופע, לדידי נמי האי שתי רוחות חדא קרן זוית הוא. וכגון שנפרץ זה הכותל מן הקירוי על פני כל הפרצה סמוך לה במזרח ובצפון חמש אמות לכאן ברוחב ד' (ג) אמות וחמש אמות ועוד לכאן ברוחב ארבע. נמצאו כאן ארבע פיות שצריך לסתום פי תקרה בחמש אמות למזרח, וחמש ועוד לצפון – הרי שתי סתימות. ועכשיו נמצאו סתימות הללו נמשכות לפנים בחלל הבית מרוחקות ממקום המחיצה ד' לכאן וד' לכאן, וצריך לסתום פי תקרה ארבע בשפת מקלוע פרצת הקירוי המזרחי בדרומה משפת המזרחי ולכותל וכן ארבע בשפת מקלוע פרצת הצפונית. לשון אחר: שנפרץ (ג) בקרן זוית וקירויו נפרץ בארבע ברוחב לפנים למזרח, וכן לצפון, ואורך פרצת הקירוי חמש אמות לכאן וחמש אמות ועוד לכאן, כמדת פרצת הכותל, שיש כאן ארבע פיות תקרה: אחת למזרח חמש אמות ארכה ואחת אורך ארבע סמוך לה בדרום, ועוד אחת לנגד פרצת כותל הצפוני חמש אמות ארכה ואחת סמוך לה ארכה (ארבע) במקלוע *מזרחית, ובארבע לית לשמואל פי תקרה יורד וסותם: ה"ג: שמואל לא אמר כרב אלכסון לא קתני. להכי לא אוקמא שמואל בעשר ובקירוי שלם כרב, דבית קתני סתמא, וכל הבתים קירוין חלקין ולא באלכסון. הלכך, נהי נמי דפתחא לא הוי בקרן זוית נסתמה פי תקרה בשתי רוחות. אבל פרצת הקירוי, איכא למימר דקתני בית שנפרץ בית וקירויו עמו קאמר, ובשתי רוחות כגון קרן זוית אצטריכא ליה. דאי ברוח אחת – אפילו נפחת הקירוי בד' רוחב כנגד כל הפרצה, דהיינו אורך יותר מעשר – אין כאן אלא שלש פי תקרה, אחת ארוך ושנים קצרים, ובשלש אית ליה יורד וסותם: ורב לא אמר כשמואל. דא"כ דנפרץ הקירוי עמהן, ויש כאן ארבע פיות – אפילו הכי איכא למימר בכולהו יורד וסותם, דהכי סבירא ליה באכסדרה בבקעה: בעשר כולי עלמא לא פליגי. דבלאו סתימת פי תקרה נמי פתחים הם: *קורה ארבעה מתיר בחורבה. חורבה הפרוצה ברשות הרבים ונאסרה בטלטול. ויש בה קורה, ראשיה נתונים על שני יתידות – מותר לטלטל תחתיה, דארבע פיותיה יורדין וסותמין ב' בגדה וב' בראשיה:
שיש

תוספות

רוחות אית ליה פי תקרה, ובלבד שלא יהא מפולש. ומשום הכי נקט בבקעה – דבחצר סתם אכסדרה יש לה ג' מחיצות, דסתמא מושכת בכל החצר באורך או ברוחב. אלא שהיא עד אמצע החצר, ופרוצה לפנים במילואו. להכי נקט בבקעה, דאפילו אין לה אלא שתי מחיצות, ופרוצה משני צדדין – אית ליה לרב פי תקרה. ובסמוך גרס: "כי לית ליה – בשלש, אבל בארבע – אית ליה". וכן גרסי רבינו חננאל ורבינו תם. *והכי פי': בשלש – שיש שלש מחיצות, והרביעית פרוצה במלואה. אבל בארבע, שיש ברביעית לחי או פס, דאיכא שם מחיצה, אע"פ שפרוצה מרובה או שפרוצה יתר מעשר – אמרי' פי תקרה. ופריך: מ"מ קשיא, דנימא פי תקרה אפי' בשתי רוחות, כיון דאין פרוצים במילואן, ויש בכל רוח שם מחיצה. דבין לרב ובין לשמואל אין חילוק בין מרוח אחת לשתים ואי נפרץ במילואו אפילו מרוח אחת לא אמרינן פי תקרה יורד וסותם. ומשני: שנפרץ בקרן זוית, וקירויו בארבע. שנפרץ ונפל גם מן הקרוי, עד שמופלג מן הכותל ארבע מכל רוח ורוח. דאף ע"פ דיש כאן ד' מחיצות שלא נפרץ במילואו – לא חשיבי הנך מחיצות לסייע לקירויו, ולימא פי תקרה – כיון דמופלג מהן ארבע. וה"ה דאפילו ברוח אחת בכי האי גוונא לא אמרי' יורד וסותם. ולא נקט קרן זוית אלא משום דאורחא דמילתא, דכשנפרץ שם רגיל להיות נופל מן הקירוי עמו. אי נמי: דוקא בקרן זוית משום דאיכא תרתי לריעותא. דטעמא דפי תקרה – משום דדמי לפתח, כדמפליג בסמוך בין עשר ליתר מעשר. ובקרן זוית לא דמי לפתח, משום דפתחא בקרן זוית לא עבדי אינשי. וא"ת: מאי פריך משתי רוחות נמי נימא פי תקרה, נוקי שתי רוחות דמתניתין שנפרץ זה כנגד זה, דהוי מפולש ולא אמרינן פי תקרה? וי"ל: דניחא ליה לאוקומא בכל ענין. ועוד: דומיא דחצר דלא הוי מפולש, דהא "וכן בית" קתני:

וקירויו באלכסון. פי' בקונטרס: בשיפוע, כעין גגין שלנו דליכא פה, היינו כי ארזילא כדאמרי' ב"עושין פסין" (לעיל כה:). ותימה: דהוה ליה למינקט כי ארזילא, כדנקט התם! ואור"י: דמיירי שנפרץ הקירוי באלכסון עם המחיצות בקרן זוית*, וכי האי גוונא לא אמרינן פי תקרה:

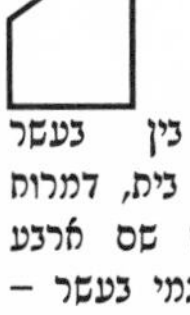

ושמואל אמר אפי' ביתר מעשר. ואיירי בין בעשר בין ביותר מעשר. ונקט שתי רוחות – משום בית, דמרוח אחת מהני פי תקרה אפילו ביתר מעשר, כיון דאיכא שם ארבע מחיצות. ולא מצי למימר דנקט שתי רוחות משום דאיירי נמי בעשר – דלא הוה ליה משום הכי למינקט שתי רוחות כי אם נפרצה סתם, דהוי מרוח אחת, והוי משמע כשהם פרצה שהיא יתר מי' ולא רצה רב להעמיד אף ביתר מעשר ומשום בית, כמו שמואל – דקסבר רב דאי הוה מיירי ביתר מעשר לא לתני שתי רוחות כלל, אלא הוה ליה למיתני דווקא ביתר מעשר מרוח אחת, ולא הוה ליה למנקט שתי רוחות משום בית. אי נמי: סבר רב דביתר מי' לא יתיר רבי יהודה אף לאותה שבת, כמו שמיקל בעשר בקרן זוית, אע"פ שזו וזו נחשב לו כפרצה ולא פתח:

וקירויו בארבע. רש"י פירש שנפרץ הכותל חמש מכאן וחמש לכאן ולא דק, דאם כן לא הויא פרצה יתר מעשר, אלא אלכסון של חמש על חמש, דהיינו שבע אמות, ולא אש לדקדק בזה:

שמואל לא אמר כרב דלא קתני אלכסון. אע"ג דלא קתני נמי שנפרץ הקירוי ברחב ארבע – מ"מ חשיב כמאן דתני ליה בהדיא, כיון דקתני שנפרצה משתי רוחות – שאז רגיל הקירוי ליפול, אבל אין דרכו לפרוץ באלכסון:

רב לא אמר כשמואל דא"כ הוי ליה אכסדרה. כלומר: אפי' נפרצה רביעית ושלישית במילואו, אמר פי תקרה כמו באכסדרה:

בעשר כולי עלמא לא פליגי. פירש בקונטרס: דבלאו סתימת פי תקרה נמי פתחים הם. וקשה לפירושו: דלאיכא דאמרי דמוקי פלוגתייהו בעשר, ולית ליה לשמואל פי תקרה, ולא אמרינן פתחא הוא! אלא נראה דמכח פי תקרה חשבינן ליה פתח ללישנא קמא, כי אע"פ שהוא במילואו, דפי תקרה הוי מטעם פתח, כדפרישית לעיל:
ושמואל

עין משפט נר מצוה

כב א ב מיי' פי"ז מהל' שבת הלכה לה סמג עשין א טוש"ע א"ח סי' שסא סעיף ב:

[וע' תוס' ב"ב יא: ד"ה הכא אפשר]

רבינו חננאל

ומפני מה אין אומרין פתחא הוא ולשתרי משום דפתחא בקרן זוית (שני) [בשני] כתלים זהו מב' רוחותיה ואע"פ שאין שם פילוש אסורה וכן בית שנפרץ מב' רוחותיו ואקשינן מאי שנא מרוח אחת דאמרינן פי תקרה יורד וסותם מב' רוחותיו נמי נימא הכי ואמרינן מתניתין כגון שנפרץ בקרן זוית דכל קרן זוית הוה ליה קירויו באלכסון וכי האי גוונא לא אמרינן פי תקרה יורד וסותם. ושמואל אמר מתניתין בשנפרצה החצר ביתר מעשר ובדין הוא דאפילו מרוח אחת אסורה אלא משום דבעי למיתנא נפרץ בית מב' רוחותיה תנא נמי בפריצות חצר מב' רוחותיה ואקשינן (וכי) [ובית] גופיה למה ליה למיתנא מב' רוחותיו דמרוח א' אפילו יתר מי' אמרינן פי תקרה יורד וסותם. לפיכך מותיב מב' רוחות נמי נימא פי תקרה יורד וסותם. ועוד לשמואל לית ליה פי תקרה יורד וסותם. דאתמר אכסדרה בבקעה רב אמר מותר לטלטל בכולה פי תקרה יורד וסותם. ושמואל אמר אין מטלטלין בה אלא בד' אמות ככרמלית דלא אמרינן פי תקרה יורד וסותם והויא לה רה"י ופרקינן לא קשיא כי לית ליה לשמואל פי תקרה יורד וסותם היכא דאיכא ג' מחיצות והרביעית כולה פתוחה אבל היכא דאיכא ד' מחיצות ונפרץ מקצת מאחת מהן כגון מחיצות בית זה ונשארה מן המחיצה הרביעית אית ליה פי תקרה יורד וסותם. מכל מקום קשיא. כלומר אי אית ליה לשמואל פי תקרה יורד וסותם מרוח אחת הוא הדין מב' רוחות ופרקינן כגון שנפרץ האי בית בקרן זוית וקירויו רחוק ממנו ד' טפחים דהוא מקום פתוח לדברי הכל. ואפילו לרשב"ג דאית ליה פחות מד' כלבוד אבל ד' דברי הכל לא ומשום הכי לא אמרינן פי תקרה יורד וסותם. מרוח אחת אמרינן פתח הוא *) מב' רוחות הוה ליה בקרן זוית כדאמרן ובג' מחיצות לא אמר שמואל פי תקרה יורד וסותם אלא במחיצה רביעית בלבד ואם **) תאמר פתח הוא פתחא בקרן זוית לא עבדי אינשי משום הכי תני ב' רוחות. שמואל לא תני כרב דלא קתני מתני' באלכסון. רב לא אמר כשמואל דאם פרצה זו הויא לה יתר מעשר הויא לה אכסדרה (כב') [ופי] תקרה יורד וסותם ומותר לטלטל בכולה. והוא הדין לבית ***) אמות בפרצה

מסורת הש"ס

[לעיל ו.]

[לעיל כה. וש"נ]

לעיל כה. נ:

לעיל פו

שייך לדף לג.

הגהות הב"ח

(א) רש"י ד"ה כדאמרי הכ"א עם ד"ה וקירויו נמי וכו' קרן זוית שנפרץ זה הכותל ועל פני כל הפרצה נפרץ הקירוי סמוך לה במזרח כל"ל ותיבת וכגון ותיבת מן הקירוי נמחק: (ב) בא"ד ברוחב ארבע וחמש אמות כל"ל ותיבת אמות נמחק: (ג) בא"ד בקרן זוית וקירויו גם הוא נפרץ בארבע וכו' כמדת פרצת הכותל נמצא שיש כאן וכו' לית ליה לשמואל:

רב נסים גאון

אלא כדאמרי בי רב משמיה דרב. איתא בסוף פרק ראשון דסנהדרין (דף יח) אמרי בי רב הונא:

*) כולי עלמא לא פליגי דפתחא הוא ושרי כי פליגי ביתר מי' (היכא דאמרי) [ואיכא דאמרי ביותר מי'] כולי עלמא לא פליגי דאסור כי פליגי בי' ורב לטעמיה ושמואל לטעמיה אלא הא דאמר רב יהודה

*) אולי צ"ל לע"פ הפי תקרה נעשה כפתח וכמ"ש התוס' א"נ דווקא בקרן זווית. **) נראה דר"ל דאם הפרצה אינו אלא י' אמות וכמ"ש התוס' בד"ה ושמואל דאיירי בין בעשר בין ביותר מעשר ודו"ק. ***) נראה שצ"ל וה"ה לבית שנפרץ ביותר מי' אמות.

קוֹרָה ד' מַתִּיר בַּחוּרְבָּה. וְרַב נַחְמָן אָמַר רַבָּה בַּר אֲבוּהּ: קוֹרָה ד' מַתִּיר בַּמַּיִם. מַנִּי? לְהָךְ לִישָּׁנָא דְּאָמְרַתְּ בְּעֶשֶׂר לָא פְּלִיגִי — בְּעֶשֶׂר, וְדִבְרֵי הַכֹּל. לְהָךְ לִישָּׁנָא דְּאָמְרַתְּ בְּעֶשֶׂר פְּלִיגִי — כְּרַב. לֵימָא אַבַּיֵי וְרָבָא בִּפְלוּגְתָּא דְּרַב וּשְׁמוּאֵל קָמִיפַּלְגִי; *דְּאִיתְּמַר: סִיכֵּךְ עַל גַּבֵּי אַכְסַדְרָה שֶׁיֵּשׁ לָהּ פַּצִּימִין — כְּשֵׁירָה. אֵין לָהּ פַּצִּימִין, אַבַּיֵי אָמַר: כְּשֵׁירָה, וְרָבָא אָמַר: פְּסוּלָה. אַבַּיֵי אָמַר: כְּשֵׁירָה — אָמַר: "פִּי תִקְרָה יוֹרֵד וְסוֹתֵם". וְרָבָא אָמַר: פְּסוּלָה — לֹא אָמַר "פִּי תִקְרָה יוֹרֵד וְסוֹתֵם". לֵימָא אַבַּיֵי כְּרַב, וְרָבָא כִּשְׁמוּאֵל! אַלִּיבָּא דִּשְׁמוּאֵל כּוּלֵּי עָלְמָא לָא פְּלִיגִי, כִּי פְּלִיגִי — אַלִּיבָּא דְּרַב. אַבַּיֵי, כְּרַב. וְרָבָא, עַד כָּאן לָא קָאָמַר רַב הָתָם — אֶלָּא דְּהָנֵי מְחִיצוֹת לְאַכְסַדְרָה עֲבִידִי. אֲבָל הָכָא, דְּהָנֵי מְחִיצוֹת לָאו לְסוּכָּה עֲבִידִי — לָא.§ "רַבִּי יוֹסֵי אוֹמֵר אִם מוּתָּרִין".§ אִיבַּעְיָא לְהוּ: רַבִּי יוֹסֵי לֶאֱסוֹר אוֹ לְהַתִּיר? אָמַר רַב שֵׁשֶׁת: [א]לֶאֱסוֹר. וְכֵן אָמַר רַבִּי יוֹחָנָן: לֶאֱסוֹר. תַּנְיָא נַמִּי הָכִי, אָמַר רַבִּי יוֹסֵי: כְּשֵׁם שֶׁאֲסוּרִין לֶעָתִיד לָבֹא, כָּךְ אֲסוּרִין לְאוֹתוֹ שַׁבָּת. אִיתְּמַר, רַב חִיָּיא(א) בַּר יוֹסֵף אָמַר: [ב]הֲלָכָה כְּרַבִּי יוֹסֵי. וּשְׁמוּאֵל אָמַר: הֲלָכָה כְּרַבִּי יְהוּדָה. וּמִי אָמַר שְׁמוּאֵל הָכִי? וְהָתְנַן, *א"ר יְהוּדָה: בד"א — בְּעֵירוּבֵי תְחוּמִין, אֲבָל בְּעֵירוּבֵי חֲצֵירוֹת — מְעָרְבִין בֵּין לָדַעַת בֵּין שֶׁלֹּא לָדַעַת, לְפִי שֶׁזָּכִין לָאָדָם שֶׁלֹּא בְּפָנָיו וְאֵין חָבִין שֶׁלֹּא בְּפָנָיו. *וְאָמַר רַב יְהוּדָה, אָמַר שְׁמוּאֵל: הֲלָכָה כְּרַבִּי יְהוּדָה. וְלֹא עוֹד אֶלָּא, כָּל מָקוֹם שֶׁשָּׁנָה רַבִּי יְהוּדָה בְּעֵירוּבִין — הֲלָכָה כְּמוֹתוֹ. וא"ל רַב חָנָא בַּגְדָּתָאָה לְרַב יְהוּדָה: אָמַר שְׁמוּאֵל אֲפִילּוּ בְּמָבוֹי שֶׁנִּיטַּל קוֹרָתוֹ אוֹ לְחָיָיו? וא"ל: בְּעֵירוּבִין אָמַרְתִּי לָךְ, וְלֹא בִּמְחִיצוֹת. אָמַר רַב עָנָן: לְדִידִי מִיפָּרְשָׁא לִי מִינֵּיהּ דִּשְׁמוּאֵל, כָּאן — שֶׁנִּפְרְצָה לְכַרְמְלִית, כָּאן — שֶׁנִּפְרְצָה לִרְשׁוּת הָרַבִּים.§

מתני' הַבּוֹנֶה עֲלִיָּיה עַל גַּבֵּי שְׁנֵי בָתִּים, וְכֵן גְּשָׁרִים הַמְפוּלָּשִׁים — מְטַלְטְלִין תַּחְתֵּיהֶן בַּשַּׁבָּת, דִּבְרֵי רַבִּי יְהוּדָה. וַחֲכָמִים אוֹסְרִין. וְעוֹד א"ר יְהוּדָה: מְעָרְבִין לְמָבוֹי הַמְפוּלָּשׁ, וַחֲכָמִים [ג]אוֹסְרִין.§

גמ' אָמַר רַבָּה: לָא תֵּימָא הַיְינוּ טַעְמָא דְּרַבִּי יְהוּדָה מִשּׁוּם דְּקָא סָבַר ב' מְחִיצוֹת דְּאוֹרָיְיתָא, אֶלָּא מִשּׁוּם דְּקָסָבַר: "פִּי תִקְרָה יוֹרֵד וְסוֹתֵם". אֵיתִיבֵיהּ אַבַּיֵי: *"יָתֵר עַל כֵּן א"ר יְהוּדָה: מִי שֶׁיֵּשׁ לוֹ שְׁנֵי בָתִּים מִשְּׁנֵי צִידֵּי רה"ר — עוֹשֶׂה לֶחִי מִכָּאן וְלֶחִי מִכָּאן, אוֹ קוֹרָה מִכָּאן וְקוֹרָה מִכָּאן, וְנוֹשֵׂא וְנוֹתֵן בָּאֶמְצַע. אָמְרוּ לוֹ: אֵין מְעָרְבִין רה"ר בְּכָךְ! א"ל: מֵהַהִיא — אִין, מֵהָא — לֵיכָּא לְמִשְׁמַע מִינַּהּ. אָמַר רַב אַשִׁי: מַתְנִיתִין נַמִּי דַּיְקָא, מִדְּקָתָנֵי "וְעוֹד א"ר יְהוּדָה מְעָרְבִין בְּמָבוֹי הַמְפוּלָּשׁ וַחֲכָמִים אוֹסְרִין". אִי אָמְרַתְּ בִּשְׁלָמָא מִשּׁוּם דְּקָא סָבַר "פִּי תִקְרָה יוֹרֵד וְסוֹתֵם" — הַיְינוּ דְּקָתָנֵי "וְעוֹד", אֶלָּא אִי אָמְרַתְּ מִשּׁוּם דְּקָא סָבַר שְׁתֵּי מְחִיצוֹת דְּאוֹרָיְיתָא — מַאי "וְעוֹד"? שְׁמַע מִינַּהּ.§

הדרן עלך כל גגות

הַמּוֹצֵא *תְּפִילִּין — [ד]מַכְנִיסָן זוּג זוּג. ר"ג אוֹמֵר: שְׁנַיִם שְׁנַיִם. בד"א — בִּישָׁנוֹת, אֲבָל בַּחֲדָשׁוֹת — פָּטוּר. *מְצָאָן צְבָתִים אוֹ כְּרִיכוֹת — מַחְשִׁיךְ עֲלֵיהֶן וּמְבִיאָן. וּבַסַּכָּנָה

רש"י

שֶׁיֵּשׁ לָהּ פַּצִּימִין. עַמּוּדִין קְבוּעִין בִּמְחִיצוֹתֶיהָ פָּחוֹת מִג': אַלִּיבָּא דִּשְׁמוּאֵל כ"ע לָא פְּלִיגִי. כְּלוֹמַר: וַדַּאי כִּדְקָאָמְרַתְּ אַבַּיֵי כְּרַב וְלֹא כִּשְׁמוּאֵל, דְּמוֹדֶה אַבַּיֵי דְּלִשְׁמוּאֵל פְּסוּלָה. דְּכֵיוָן דְּבְאַכְסַדְרָה דְּהָנָךְ פֵּיוֹת תִּקְרָה לְאַכְסַדְרָה נַעֲשׂוּ, וַאֲפ"ה אָסַר בְּטִלְטוּל שַׁבָּת — כ"ש דְּלָא מְהַנֵּי לְעִנְיַן סוּכָּה, דְּלָאו לְסוּכָּה עֲבִידִי: כִּי פְּלִיגִי אַלִּיבָּא דְּרַב. כְּלוֹמַר: הָא דְּאָמַר רָבָא כִּשְׁמוּאֵל וְלֹא כְּרַב לָא הִיא, דְּרָבָא נַמִּי כְּרַב אֲמָרָהּ לְמִילְּתֵיהּ, וְאָמַר לָךְ: ע"כ לָא קָא שָׁרֵי רַב לְעִנְיַן שַׁבָּת: אֶלָּא דְּהָנֵי מְחִיצוֹת. פֵּי' אוֹתָן הַקּוֹרוֹת הַנְּתוּנִים עַל אַרְבָּעָה עַמּוּדִים, דְּאִינְהוּ פִּי תִקְרָה — לְאַכְסַדְרָה עֲבִידִי: לָאו לְסוּכָּה. לְשֵׁם סוּכָּה, אע"ג דְּלָא בָּעֵי מְחִיצוֹת לְשָׁם — כּוּלֵּי הַאי מִיהָא לָא מְקִילִינַן: בַּמֶּה דְּבָרִים אֲמוּרִים. דְּצָרִיךְ לְהוֹדִיעַ בְּפֶרֶק "חַלּוֹן" (לעיל פ:): עֵרוּבֵי חֲצֵירוֹת. לְעוֹלָם הוּא זְכוּת לָהֶן. אֲבָל עֵירוּבֵי תְּחוּמִין — פְּעָמִים שֶׁהוּא חוֹב, שֶׁמַּפְסִידִין לָרוּחַ שֶׁכְּנֶגְדָּהּ: נִפְרְצָה לְכַרְמְלִית. שָׁרֵי כְּר' יְהוּדָה. דְּאִי נַמִּי אָתֵי לְאַפּוּקֵי לְבַר — לָאו אִיסּוּרָא דְּאוֹרָיְיתָא אִיכָּא: **מתני'** עַל גַּבֵּי שְׁנֵי בָתִּים. וְהֵם בִּשְׁנֵי צִידֵּי רה"ר — מְטַלְטְלִין תַּחַת הָעֲלִיָּיה, דְּפִי תִקְרָה מִכָּאן וּמִכָּאן יוֹרֵד וְסוֹתֵם: וְכֵן גְּשָׁרִים הַמְפוּלָּשִׁים. שֶׁיֵּשׁ לָהֶם מְחִיצוֹת מִלְּמַטָּה בִּשְׁנֵי הַצְּדָדִים: מְעָרְבִין לְמָבוֹי הַמְפוּלָּשׁ. הוֹאִיל וְאִיכָּא שְׁתֵּי מְחִיצוֹת: **גמ'** דְּאוֹרָיְיתָא. הֲלָכָה לְמֹשֶׁה מִסִּינַי, כִּדְאָמְרִינַן בְּפ"ק (דף ד.): שִׁיעוּרִין חֲצִיצִין וּמְחִיצוֹת הֲלָכָה לְמֹשֶׁה מִסִּינַי. וַהֲרֵי יֵשׁ כָּאן ב' מְחִיצוֹת מִשְּׁנֵי הַבָּתִּים, דְּאִי לָאו מִשּׁוּם פִּי תִקְרָה — לָא הֲוָה שָׁרֵי: יָתֵר עַל כֵּן וכו'. רֵישָׁא דְּבָרַיְיתָא: אֶחָד חַלּוֹן שֶׁבֵּין שְׁנֵי בָּתִּים, וְאֶחָד חַלּוֹן שֶׁבֵּין שְׁתֵּי חֲצֵירוֹת וּגְשָׁרִים וּנְפָשׁוֹת ורה"ר הַמְקוֹרָה — מְטַלְטְלִין תַּחְתֵּיהֶן בַּשַּׁבָּת, דִּבְרֵי ר' יְהוּדָה. יָתֵר עַל כֵּן אָמַר ר' יְהוּדָה: דַּאֲפִילּוּ רה"ר גְּמוּרָה, וְאֵין שָׁם תִּקְרָה לְמֵימַר יוֹרֵד וְסוֹתֵם — שָׁרֵי בִּשְׁתֵּי מְחִיצוֹת שֶׁל שְׁנֵי צִידֵּי רה"ר: מֵהַהִיא אִין. מָצֵית לְמִשְׁמַע דִּשְׁתֵּי מְחִיצוֹת דְּאוֹרָיְיתָא. אֲבָל מִמַּתְנִי' לָא שָׁמְעִינַן לָהּ דְּטַעְמָא מִשּׁוּם סְתִימַת פִּי תִקְרָה הוּא: מַתְנִי' נַמִּי דַּיְיקָא. דְּאִית לֵיהּ לְרַב יְהוּדָה שְׁתֵּי מְחִיצוֹת דְּאוֹרָיְיתָא: אִי אָמְרַתְּ בִּשְׁלָמָא. טַעְמֵיהּ דְּר' יְהוּדָה(ג) דְּקַמַּיְיתָא מִשּׁוּם דִּשְׁתֵּי מְחִיצוֹת דְּאוֹרָיְ' — הַיְינוּ דְּקָתָנֵי "וְעוֹד זוֹ" דְּמַשְׁמַע: וְעוֹד זוֹ, אע"ג דְּלֵיכָּא פִּי תִקְרָה — מַתִּיר ר' יְהוּדָה מִשּׁוּם הַאי טַעְמָא. אֶלָּא אִי אָמְרַתְּ טַעְמֵיהּ בְּקַמַּיְיתָא מִשּׁוּם פִּי תִקְרָה — מַאי וְעוֹד? הָא בְּמָבוֹי לֵיכָּא פִּי תִקְרָה. לָשׁוֹן אַחֵר: מַתְנִי' נַמִּי דַּיְיקָא כְּרַבָּה, דְּטַעְמָא דְּקַמַּיְיתָא מִשּׁוּם פִּי תִקְרָה הוּא. וְה"ג: אא"ב דְּטַעְמָא דְּר"י בְּקַמַּיְיתָא מִשּׁוּם דְּקָסָבַר פִּי תִקְרָה יוֹרֵד וְסוֹתֵם, וּבַתְרַיְיתָא מִשּׁוּם שְׁתֵּי מְחִיצוֹת — הַיְינוּ דְּקָתָנֵי "וְעוֹד זוֹ מַתִּיר רַבִּי יְהוּדָה" וְאע"ג דְּלֵיכָּא פִּי תִקְרָה — מִשּׁוּם שְׁתֵּי מְחִיצוֹת. אֶלָּא אִי אָמְרַתְּ קַמַּיְיתָא נַמִּי מִשּׁוּם שְׁתֵּי מְחִיצוֹת — מַאי וְעוֹד? הִיא הִיא וּפְשִׁיטָא דִּמְעָרְבִין. — רִאשׁוֹן שָׁמַעְתִּי. וְאִית דְּגָרְסִי כְּלִישָּׁנָא בַּתְרָא, וּמִסְתַּבְּרָא כְּוָותַיְיהוּ:

הדרן עלך כל גגות

הַמּוֹצֵא תְּפִילִּין. בַּשָּׂדֶה, בְּמָקוֹם שֶׁנֶּאֱבָדִין: מַכְנִיסָן. לָעִיר וְלַבַּיִת: זוּג זוּג. אֶחָד בָּרֹאשׁ וְאֶחָד בַּזְּרוֹעַ. וְהַיְינוּ זוּג. כְּדֶרֶךְ שֶׁלּוֹבְשָׁן בְּחוֹל, וְחוֹזֵר תָּמִיד וּמַכְנִיסָן זוּג אַחַר זוּג, עַד שֶׁיְּכַלּוּ: שְׁנַיִם שְׁנַיִם. זוּג בָּרֹאשׁ וְזוּג בַּזְּרוֹעַ. וּבַגְּמָרָא בָּעֵי: טַעְמָא מַאי נִינְהוּ: בִּישָׁנוֹת. שֶׁנִּיכָּר הַקֶּשֶׁר הֶעָשׂוּי כְּמִין שַׁדַּי, דְּוַדַּאי תְּפִילִּין הֵן, וְיֵשׁ בָּהֶן קְדוּשָּׁה, וְאָסוּר לְהַנִּיחָן בְּבִזָּיוֹן: אֲבָל בַּחֲדָשׁוֹת פָּטוּר. מִלְּהַכְנִיסָן. דִּילְמָא קָמֵיעַ הֵן בְּעָלְמָא, וְאֵין בָּהֶן קְדוּשָּׁה אֶלָּא בְּנַעֲשִׂים כְּהִלְכָתָן, וְהַיְינוּ לְשְׁמָן, הִלְכָּךְ: לָא מְחַלְּלִינַן שַׁבְּתָא עֲלַיְיהוּ: צְבָתִים. קְשָׁרִים קְשָׁרִים הַרְבֵּה תְּפִילִּין בְּכָל קֶשֶׁר. וּבַגְּמָ' מְפָרֵשׁ מַאי צְבָתִים וּמַאי כְּרִיכוֹת: מַחְשִׁיךְ עֲלֵיהֶן. יַמְתִּין עַד שֶׁתֶּחְשַׁךְ, וְיֵשֵׁב שָׁם וִישַׁמֵּר, וְלִכְשֶׁתֶּחְשַׁךְ יִטְּלֵם יַחַד. וּבַגְּמָ' פָּרֵיךְ: וְלִיעַיְילִינְהוּ זוּג זוּג:

תוספות

וּשְׁמוּאֵל אמר הלכה כרבי יהודה. בסמוך מוקי לה בנפרלה לכרמלית. ונראה דהלכתא כרב באיסורי ואפי' בנפרלה לכרמלית הלכה כרבי יוסי דמחמיר. והיכא דאיתנהו למחילות, אפילו ר' יוסי מודה, דאמר: שבת הואיל והותרה הותרה, כדאמרי'(ג) פ' קמא (דף יז.):

אֵיתִיבֵיהּ יתר על כן. פריך מברייתא, משום דממתניתין דקתני: ועוד א"ר יהודה מערבין במבוי המפולש — לא שמעינן ברשות הרבים גמורה:

הדרן עלך כל גגות

הַמּוֹצֵא תפילין. הך פירקא במסכת שבת ה"ל למיתני גבי הוצאות, אלא משום דקתני סיפא: רבי יהודה אומר נותן אדם לחבירו וחבירו לחבירו, ואפילו חוץ לתחום. ועוד: משום דקתני בסוף פרקין, רבי שמעון אומר: כל מקום שהתירו לך חכמים — משלך נתנו לך, ומפרש בגמ' דקאי אסוף "מי שהוציאוהו".

מַכְנִיסָן זוג זוג. בספ"ק דבילה (דף טו.) מוכח דאיירי דלא מינטרי מחמת כלבי. אבל מינטרי מחמת כלבי, אע"ג דלא מינטרי מחמת גנבי — לא:

אֲבָל בחדשות פטור. איסור נמי איכא, דלקמן (לז.) תניא אוסר בחדשות: לימא

רבינו חננאל

קורה מתיר בחורבה פי' כשמניחה ע"ג פסין ומותר לטלטל בחורבה הסמוכה לו לביתו ורב נחמן אמר קורה ד' אם תלויה או עומדת מתיר במים כלומר באילין חלוקות המים כמחיצה בתוך המים לפיכך מותר לו למלאות מים ולהכניסו לביתו כמאן אמרה לשמעתייהו ופרשינן להההוא לישנא דאמרינן בי' פליגי הני כרב דאמר בעשר אמרינן פי תקרה יורד וסותם קורה חזינן לה כאלו פיה במקום פי תקרה זו אינה מתרת. אבל לשמואל דלית ליה פי תקרה יורד וסותם גם קורה זו אינה מתרת דמחיצה מעליא בעי. ולההוא לישנא דאמר ביותר מי' פליגי אבל בי' לדברי הכל אית להו פי תקרה יורד וסותם. האי תקרה כפי תקרה דמי ולדברי הכל שרי. נימא אביי ורבא בפלוגתא דרב ושמואל פליגי דאתמר סיכך ע"ג אכסדרה שיש לה פצימין כגון אבני בניין היוצאות מן הכותל אחת למעלה מחברתה וביניהן חלל לקבל אחרת כשרה שאלו הפצימין כמו מחיצה הן. אין לה פצימין אביי אמר פי תקרה יורד וסותם כרב רבא אמר פסולה כשמואל. ודחינן אליבא דשמואל כ"ע לא פליגי דלא חד מינייהו אמר כוותיה דהא לית הלכתא כוותיה כי פליגי אליבא דרב אביי כרב. אביי אמר עד כאן לא אמר רב התם אלא משום דהני תלת מחיצתא וקירויה כולהו לאכסדרה עבידן. אבל הכא גבי סוכה דמחיצתא לבתים עבידי ולאו להאי סוכה עבידי אפילו רב מודה דלא אמרינן פי תקרה יורד וסותם: איבעיא להו ר' יוסי לאסור או להתיר קא בעי ואסיקנא רב ששת ור' יוחנן אמרי לאסור תניא נמי הכי ר' יוסי אמר הואיל ואסורין לעתיד אסורין נמי לאותה שבת רב אמר הלכה כר' יוסי ושמואל אמר הלכה כר' יהודה. ומי אמר שמואל הלכה כר' יהודה בהא. והאמר רב יהודה אמר שמואל כל מקום ששנה ר' יהודה בעירובין הלכה כמותו. ואוקימנא להא דתנן א"ר יהודה בד"א בעירובי תחומין אבל בעירובי חצרות מערבין לאדם לדעתו ושלא לדעתו שזוכין לו לאדם שלא בפניו ואין חבין לו [אלא בפניו] וא"ל רב חנא בגדתאה לרב אמר שמואל הלכה כר' יהודה אפילו במבוי שניטלה קורתו או לחייו. ואמר ליה בעירובין אמר ולא במחיצות. ופרקינן בשנפרץ לכרמלית הלכתא כוותיה. אבל בשנפרץ לרה"ר אפילו שמואל לא אמר הלכתא כוותיה. וקיי"ל כרב דאמר הלכתא כר' יוסי: הבונה עלייה ע"ג ב' בתים כו' דייקא מתני' דטעמא דר' יהודה משום דפי תקרה יורד וסותם ולא משום דב' מחיצות דאורייתא הן. ור' יהודה תרתי אית ליה אית ליה שפי תקרה יורד וסותם מיהא ואית ליה ב' מחיצות דאורייתא הן מהא דתניא יתר על כן אמר ר' יהודה מי שיש [לו] ב' בתים בב' כו'. אמר רב אשי מתני' נמי דייקא דקתני ועוד אמר ר' יהודה מערבין במבוי המפולש אמרינן בשלמא רישא פי תקרה יורד וסותם וסיפא ב' מחיצות היינו דקתני ועוד [אלא] אי אמרת אידי ואידי ב' מחיצות ניערבינהו וניתנינהו או ניתי חדא ש"מ: **הדרן עלך כל גגות**

עין משפט נר מצוה

כג א ב מיי' פי"ז מהל' שבת הלכה לד סמג עשין א טור ש"ע א"ח סי' שסא ס"ב וסי' שסה סעיף ז:

כד ג מיי' פי"ז מהל' שבת הלכה יח סמג שם טוש"ע א"ח סי' שסד סעיף א:

א ד מיי' פי"ט מהל' שבת הלכה כג סמג לאוין סה טור ש"ע א"ח סי' שא סעיף מב:

מסורת הש"ס

לעיל נג. סוכה יח:

לעיל מו: פא:

[לעיל פא:]

שבת ו. וקיז. לעיל ו. יב: כב. נט:

שבת סב. ביצה טו.

[עי' תוספות לקמן לז. ד"ה מאן]

הגהות הב"ח

(א) גמ' איתמר רב חייא בר אשי אמר רב הלכה כר' יוסי: (ב) רש"י ד"ה אי אמרת בשלמא וכו' בקמייתא משום וכו' דקתני ועוד דמשמע כנ"ל ותיבת זו נמחק: (ג) תום' ד"ה ושמואל וכו' כדאמרינן סוף פרק קמא:

גליון הש"ס

גמ' איתיביה אביי יתר על כן. עיין לעיל דף פו ע"א תוס' ד"ה קורה הרבעה: שם א"ל מההיא אין. כתובות דף נח ע"ב שבועות דף לא ע"ב:

וּבְסַכָּנָה מְכַסָּן וְהוֹלֵךְ לוֹ. *רַבִּי שִׁמְעוֹן אוֹמֵר: נוֹתְנָן לַחֲבֵירוֹ, וַחֲבֵירוֹ לַחֲבֵירוֹ, עַד שֶׁמַּגִּיעַ לֶחָצֵר הַחִיצוֹנָה. *וְכֵן בְּנוֹ — נוֹתְנוֹ לַחֲבֵירוֹ, וַחֲבֵירוֹ לַחֲבֵירוֹ, אֲפִילּוּ מֵאָה. רַבִּי יְהוּדָה אוֹמֵר: [א]נוֹתֵן אָדָם חָבִית לַחֲבֵירוֹ, וַחֲבֵירוֹ לַחֲבֵירוֹ אֲפִילּוּ חוּץ לַתְּחוּם. אָמְרוּ לוֹ: לֹא תְּהַלֵּךְ זוֹ יוֹתֵר מֵרַגְלֵי בְּעָלֶיהָ.§ **גמ'** זוּג אֶחָד — אִין, טְפֵי — לָא. לֵימָא תְּנַן סְתָמָא דְּלָא כְּרַבִּי מֵאִיר. דְּאִי כְּרַבִּי מֵאִיר — הָאָמַר: לוֹבֵשׁ כָּל מַה שֶּׁיָּכוֹל לִלְבּוֹשׁ, וְעוֹטֵף כָּל מַה שֶּׁיָּכוֹל לַעֲטוֹף. *דִּתְנַן: וּלְשָׁם מוֹצִיא כָּל כְּלֵי תַשְׁמִישׁוֹ, וְלוֹבֵשׁ כָּל מַה שֶּׁיָּכוֹל לִלְבּוֹשׁ, וְעוֹטֵף כָּל מַה שֶּׁיָּכוֹל לַעֲטוֹף! וְהַהִיא סְתָמָא, מִמַּאי דְּרַבִּי מֵאִיר הִיא, דְּקָתָנֵי עֲלָהּ: לוֹבֵשׁ וּמוֹצִיא, וּפוֹשֵׁט וְלוֹבֵשׁ וּמוֹצִיא וּפוֹשֵׁט, אֲפִילּוּ כָּל הַיּוֹם כּוּלּוֹ, דִּבְרֵי ר"מ. אָמַר רָבָא: אֲפִילּוּ תֵּימָא רַבִּי מֵאִיר. הָתָם — דֶּרֶךְ מַלְבּוּשׁוֹ — כַּחוֹל שַׁוְיֵיהּ רַבָּנַן, וְהָכָא דֶּרֶךְ מַלְבּוּשׁוֹ — כַּחוֹל שַׁוְיֵיהּ רַבָּנַן. הָתָם דְּבַחוֹל כַּמָּה דְּבָעֵי לָבֵישׁ — לְעִנְיַן הַצָּלָה נַמִי שָׁרוּ לֵיהּ רַבָּנַן. הָכָא דְּבַחוֹל נַמִי, זוּג אֶחָד — אִין, טְפֵי — לָא, לְעִנְיַן הַצָּלָה נַמִי: זוּג אֶחָד — אִין, טְפֵי לָא.§ "רַבָּן גַּמְלִיאֵל אוֹמֵר שְׁנַיִם שְׁנַיִם".§ מַאי קָסָבַר? אִי קָסָבַר שַׁבָּת זְמַן תְּפִילִּין הוּא — זוּג אֶחָד — אִין, טְפֵי — לָא. וְאִי קָסָבַר שַׁבָּת לָאו זְמַן תְּפִילִּין הוּא, וּמִשּׁוּם הַצָּלָה דֶּרֶךְ מַלְבּוּשׁ שָׁרוּ לֵיהּ רַבָּנַן — אֲפִילּוּ טְפֵי נַמִי! לְעוֹלָם קָסָבַר: שַׁבָּת לָאו זְמַן תְּפִילִּין הוּא, וְכִי שָׁרוּ רַבָּנַן לְעִנְיַן הַצָּלָה — דֶּרֶךְ מַלְבּוּשׁ בִּמְקוֹם תְּפִילִּין. אִי הָכִי, זוּג אֶחָד[(א)] נַמִי — אִין, טְפֵי — לָא! *אָמַר רַב שְׁמוּאֵל בַּר רַב יִצְחָק: מָקוֹם יֵשׁ בָּרֹאשׁ לְהַנִּיחַ בּוֹ שְׁתֵּי תְּפִילִּין. הָנִיחָא דְּרֹאשׁ, דְּיַד מַאי אִיכָּא לְמֵימַר? כִּדְרַב הוּנָא; דְּאָמַר רַב הוּנָא: פְּעָמִים שֶׁאָדָם בָּא מִן הַשָּׂדֶה וַחֲבִילָתוֹ עַל רֹאשׁוֹ, וּמְסַלְּקָן מֵרֹאשׁוֹ וְקוֹשְׁרָן בִּזְרוֹעוֹ. אֵימַר דְּאָמַר רַב הוּנָא שֶׁלֹּא יִנְהַג בָּהֶן דֶּרֶךְ בִּזָּיוֹן, רָאוּי מִי אָמַר? אֶלָּא כִּדְאָמַר רַב שְׁמוּאֵל בַּר רַב יִצְחָק: מָקוֹם יֵשׁ בָּרֹאשׁ שֶׁרָאוּי לְהַנִּיחַ בּוֹ שְׁתֵּי תְּפִילִּין. הָכָא נַמִי: מָקוֹם יֵשׁ בַּיָּד שֶׁרָאוּי לְהַנִּיחַ בּוֹ שְׁתֵּי תְּפִילִּין. *תָּנָא דְּבֵי מְנַשֶּׁה: °"עַל יָדְךָ" — [ב]זוֹ קִיבּוֹרֶת, "בֵּין עֵינֶיךָ" — זוֹ קׇדְקֹד. הֵיכָא? אָמְרִי דְּבֵי רַבִּי יַנַּאי: [ג]מָקוֹם שֶׁמּוֹחוֹ שֶׁל תִּינוֹק רוֹפֵס. לֵימָא בִּדְרַב שְׁמוּאֵל בַּר רַב יִצְחָק קָמִיפַּלְגִי; דְּת"ק לֵית לֵיהּ דְּרַב שְׁמוּאֵל בַּר רַב יִצְחָק, וְרַבָּן גַּמְלִיאֵל אִית לֵיהּ דְּרַב שְׁמוּאֵל בַּר רַב יִצְחָק! לָא, דְּכוּלֵּי עָלְמָא אִית לְהוּ דְּרַב שְׁמוּאֵל בַּר רַב יִצְחָק. וְהָכָא *בְּ"שַׁבָּת זְמַן תְּפִילִּין" קָמִיפַּלְגִי. דְּת"ק סָבַר: שַׁבָּת זְמַן תְּפִילִּין הוּא, וְרַבָּן גַּמְלִיאֵל סָבַר: שַׁבָּת לָאו זְמַן תְּפִילִּין הוּא. וְאִיבָּעֵית אֵימָא: דְּכ"ע — שַׁבָּת זְמַן תְּפִילִּין הוּא. וְהָכָא *בְּ"מִצְוֹת צְרִיכוֹת כַּוָּונָה" קָמִיפַּלְגִי. ת"ק סָבַר: לָצֵאת בָּעֵי כַּוָּונָה, וְרַבָּן גַּמְלִיאֵל סָבַר: לָא בָּעֵי כַּוָּונָה.

וְאִיבָּעֵית

תורה אור: דברים ו

וּבַסַּכָּנָה. שֶׁאֵינוֹ יָכוֹל לְהַמְתִּין שָׁם, וּמִתְיָירֵא מִפְּנֵי הַלִּיסְטִים: נוֹתְנָן לַחֲבֵירוֹ וַחֲבֵירוֹ לַחֲבֵירוֹ. דְּכָל חַד וְחַד לָא מַמְטֵי לְהוּ אַרְבַּע אַמּוֹת: לֶחָצֵר הַחִיצוֹנָה. שֶׁל עִיר שֶׁהוּא מָקוֹם הַמִּשְׁתַּמֵּר רִאשׁוֹן: וְכֵן בְּנוֹ. שֶׁיְּלָדַתּוּ אִמּוֹ שָׁם בַּשָּׂדֶה בַּשַּׁבָּת: לֹא תְּהַלֵּךְ זוֹ יוֹתֵר מֵרַגְלֵי בְּעָלֶיהָ. אֵינָן יְכוֹלִין לְהַרְחִיקָהּ מִתְּחוּם שְׁבִיתַת בְּעָלִים, הַכֹּל לְפִי מַה שֶּׁעֵירְבוּ הַבְּעָלִים: **גמ'** לוֹבֵשׁ כָּל מַה שֶּׁיָּכוֹל לִלְבּוֹשׁ. לְעִנְיַן הַצָּלַת דְּלֵיקָה תְּנַן בְּ"כָל כִּתְבֵי הַקּוֹדֶשׁ" (שבת דף קכ.): וּלְשָׁם הוּא מוֹצִיא. לֶחָצֵר שֶׁסְּמוּכָה לַדְּלֵיקָה: הָתָם. דְּקָאֵי בִּשְׁאָר מַלְבּוּשִׁין, דְּכַמָּה דְּבָעֵי לָבֵישׁ בְּחוֹל: זוּג אֶחָד אִין. דְּקָסָבַר: שַׁבָּת זְמַן תְּפִילִּין הוּא וּמִשּׁוּם הָכִי שָׁרֵי[(ב)] וּבְלָאו הַצָּלָה נַמִי, אִם בָּא לְהַנִּיחַ תְּפִילִּין — מַנִּיחַ, וּמִשּׁוּם הַצָּלָה לָא שָׁרֵינַן לֵיהּ טְפֵי: מַאי קָסָבַר. דְּקָא שָׁרֵי שְׁנַיִם שְׁנַיִם, אֲבָל טְפֵי לָא: אִי קָסָבַר שַׁבָּת זְמַן תְּפִילִּין הוּא. מִשּׁוּם הָכִי שָׁרֵי, אֲבָל לְאַסּוּלֵי טְפֵי מִן הַמִּצְוָה — לָא: לָאו זְמַן תְּפִילִּין הוּא. וְשָׁרוּ לֵיהּ רַבָּנַן דֶּרֶךְ מַלְבּוּשׁ — מִשּׁוּם דְּתַכְשִׁיט הוּא לְגַבֵּיהּ, וְלָא מַשּׂאוֹי. וְאַע"ג דְּלָאו אוֹרְחֵיהּ, הָכָא מִשּׁוּם הַצָּלָה — שָׁרֵי: בִּמְקוֹם תְּפִילִּין. הָרָאוּי לְהַנִּיחַ בּוֹ תְּפִילִּין, שֶׁאֵין כָּל הָרֹאשׁ כָּשֵׁר לְהַנִּיחַ תְּפִילִּין אֶלָּא קׇדְקֹד לְבַד, וְצָרִיךְ יֵשׁ שָׁם שֶׁהַתְּפִילִּין יוֹשְׁבִים בּוֹ וְאֵינָן בּוֹלְטִין כׇּל כָּךְ כִּדִלְקַמָּן. וּבְשַׁבָּת נַמִי, בְּאַתְרָא דְּלָא חֲזוּ לֵיהּ — לָאו תַּכְשִׁיט הוּא, שֶׁבּוֹלְטִין יוֹתֵר מִדַּאי וַהֲוֵי כְּמַשּׂאוֹי: דְּיַד[(ג)]. אֵין כָּל הַזְּרוֹעַ כָּשֵׁר לִתְפִילִּין אֶלָּא קִיבּוֹרֶת, כִּדִלְקַמָּן: מִנְהַג בִּזָּיוֹן. לְהַנִּיחַ חֲבִילָה עֲלֵיהֶן, שָׁרֵי לֵיהּ לְמִנְטְרִינְהוּ הָתָם: רָאוּי מִי אָמַר. דְּגַבֵּי שַׁבָּת לֵימָא דְּתַכְשִׁיט הוּא: קִיבּוֹרֶת. אֵבֶר אֶמְצָעִי שֶׁבַּזְּרוֹעַ, וּבְלַעַ"ז רבדי"ן: רוֹפֵס. רַךְ, וּבְלַעַ"ז פונטינ"א: תַּנָּא קַמָּא סָבַר שַׁבָּת זְמַן תְּפִילִּין הוּא. וּמִשּׁוּם הַצָּלָה לָא מִישְׁרוּ בֵּיהּ טְפֵי מִן הַמִּצְוָה, דְּלָאו תַּכְשִׁיט נִינְהוּ. וְכׇל שֶׁכֵּן דְּכֵיוָן דִּזְמַן תְּפִילִּין הוּא, וְאִיכָּא "בַּל תּוֹסִיף" אָתֵי אִיסּוּר בַּל תּוֹסִיף וּמְשַׁוֵּי לְהוּ עֲלֵיהּ כְּמַשּׂאוֹי: ר"ג סָבַר לָאו זְמַן תְּפִילִּין הוּא. וְהַיְינוּ טַעְמָא דְּשָׁרוּ לֵיהּ רַבָּנַן לְהַצָּלָה — מִשּׁוּם דְּתַכְשִׁיט הוּא. הִלְכָּךְ, כׇּל כַּמָּה דַּהֲוֵה תַּכְשִׁיט — שָׁרֵי, וּמִשּׁוּם "בַּל תּוֹסִיף" לֵיכָּא הָכָא, דְּאֵין כָּאן מִצְוַת תְּפִילִּין כְּלָל, אֶלָּא כִּשְׁאָר מַלְבּוּשׁ בְּעָלְמָא: אִיבָּעֵית אֵימָא דְּכ"ע שַׁבָּת זְמַן תְּפִילִּין הוּא. וּדְכוּלֵּי עָלְמָא אֵינָהּ תַּכְשִׁיט, וּבְמִצְוֹת צְרִיכוֹת כַּוָּונָה קָא מִיפַּלְגִי: ת"ק סָבַר מִצְוֹת צְרִיכוֹת כַּוָּונָה. שֶׁהָעוֹשֶׂה מִצְוָה צָרִיךְ שֶׁיְּכַוֵּין בָּהּ, הִלְכָּךְ, זוּג אֶחָד — אִין, טְפֵי — לָא. דְּאִי מְכַוֵּין לְמִצְוָה — אִיכָּא "בַּל תּוֹסִיף" בְּחַד, וְאִי לָא מְכַוֵּין לְמִצְוָה — תַּרְוַויְיהוּ מַשּׂאוֹי נִינְהוּ, וְאֵין כָּאן מִצְוָה: וְרַבָּן גַּמְלִיאֵל סָבַר מִצְוֹת אֵין צְרִיכוֹת כַּוָּונָה. הִלְכָּךְ: מִצְוָה — אִיכָּא, "בַּל תּוֹסִיף" לֵיכָּא. דְּאֵין עוֹבֵר עַל "בַּל תּוֹסִיף" אֶלָּא אִם כֵּן נִתְכַּוֵּון לְמִצְוָה, וְזֶה לֹא נִתְכַּוֵּון. וּבְכׇל חַד אָמְרֵי הַאי לְמִצְוָה. וְלִבִּי מְגַמְגֵּם לוֹמַר דְּכֵיוָן דְּלָאו תַּכְשִׁיט נִינְהוּ, נְהִי דְּ"בַל תּוֹסִיף" לֵיכָּא, אִיסּוּר שַׁבָּת מִיהָא לָא פָּקַע? וְהָא לֵיכָּא לְמֵימַר דִּלְכוּלֵּי עָלְמָא תַּכְשִׁיט הֵם, דְּאִם כֵּן לְתַנָּא קַמָּא אַמַּאי אָסוּר? לָא לִיכַוֵּין וְלָא לִיתְסַר. וְלֵיכָּא לְמֵימַר נַמִי דִּלְתַנָּא קַמָּא לָא הָווּ תַּכְשִׁיט, וּלְרַבָּן גַּמְלִיאֵל הָווּ תַּכְשִׁיט — דְּאִם כֵּן לוֹקֵי פְּלוּגְתַּיְיהוּ בְּהָכִי. וְעוֹד: הַיְינוּ פְּלוּגְתָּא דִּלְעֵיל דִּזְמַן וְלָאו זְמַן. וְנִרְאֶה לִי דְּהָכִי גָּרְסִינַן: תַּנָּא קַמָּא סָבַר מִצְוֹת אֵין צְרִיכוֹת כַּוָּונָה, וּלְכוּלֵּי עָלְמָא תַּכְשִׁיט הֵן. הִלְכָּךְ, כֵּיוָן דִּלְעִנְיַן מֵיפַק יְדֵי חוֹבָתֵיהּ נָפֵיק בְּלֹא כַּוָּונָה — לְעִנְיַן בַּל תּוֹסִיף נַמִי, אַף עַל גַּב דְּלָא מְכַוֵּין לְהוּ לְמִצְוָה — אִיכָּא בַּל תּוֹסִיף, כֵּיוָן דִּזְמַן תְּפִילִּין הוּא. וְר"ג סָבַר: צְרִיכוֹת כַּוָּונָה, לָצֵאת יְדֵי חוֹבָתוֹ, הִלְכָּךְ, בְּבַל תּוֹסִיף נַמִי לָא עָבַר עַד דִּמְכַוֵּין לְמִצְוָה:

וְאִיבָּעֵית

לימא תנן סתמא דלא כרבי מאיר. אברייתא דלקמן, *דקתני בהדיא: רבי מאיר אומר מכניסן זוג זוג הוי מצי למיפרך דר"מ אדר' מאיר, אלא דניחא ליה טפי לאקשויי אמתניתין. ומכח דקתני עלה בברייתא: ר' מאיר אומר מכניסן זוג זוג — לא היה יכול להוכיח דמתני' רבי מאיר כדמוכח בסמוך אההיא דשבת, ולאקשויי דר"מ אדרבי מאיר. דאדרבה, לקמן מוכח דמתניתין דלא כר"מ, דמתני' קתני "במה דברים אמורים" בישנות וברייתא קתני, רבי מאיר אומר: אחד חדשות ואחד ישנות: **אי** קסבר שבת זמן תפילין. פירש בקונטרס: משום הכי שרי, אבל לאסולי טפי מן המצוה — לא. וקשה: דאם מכח זה בא לדקדק דזוג אין טפי לא — אם כן, בסמוך דקאמר "לעולם לאו זמן תפילין הוא" ה"נ דמצי למימר לעולם זמן תפילין הוא! אלא י"ל: דאי זמן תפילין הוא — איכא "בל תוסיף" אע"ג דלא מיכוון, כדמסיק רבא בפרק "ראוהו בית דין" (ר"ה דף כח.), ולהכי, זוג אחד — אין, טפי — לא: **וכי** שרו רבנן לענין הצלה דרך מלבוש במקום תפילין. פירש בקונטרס: דשלא במקום תפילין הן בולטין יותר מדאי, ונראה משאוי, ולכך אסור. ואין זו סברא. אלא נראה דהטעם משום דלא מיקרי מלבוש אלא במקום שרגיל להניחו בחול: **מקום** יש בראש שראוי להניח בו ב' תפילין. מסופק היה ר"י: איזה שיעור יש ברוחב תפילין, דיש עושין גדולים מחבריהם, ויש שעושין אותם קטנים ביותר, ומדקאמר: מקום יש בראש להניח ב' תפילין — משמע דשיעור רחבו שיתמלא מקום השנים. ואור"י, דמצא במדרש: דשיעורן כב' אצבעות, וסמך לדבר[(ד)]: דליך רוחבו ב' אצבעות, כדאמר בפ' קמא דסוכה (ד' ה.). ואמרי' בפ"ק דערכין (דף ג:): שערו היה נראה בין ליך למנפת, ששם מניח תפילין. ודומה דליך היה במקום הראוי להניח תפילין. אע"ג דגבי ליך כתיב (שמות כח): "מצחו" ומתרגמינן: "בין עינוהי", גבי תפילין נמי כתיב (דברים יא): "בין עיניכם" ודרשינן: בגובה שבראש*: **ידך** זו קיבורת. הוא קבוצת בשר שבזרוע, שבין המרפק שקורין קודא[(ה)] בלע"ז ובין הכתף. ו"קיבורת" כמו קיבורת דאהיני*), ולא כמו שמפרש "קיבורית" הוא קבוצת בשר שבין פיסת היד למרפק סמוך למרפק — דבכל מקום משמע דתפילין הן בזרוע, ובמסכת אהלות (פ"א משנה ח) משמע דזרוע הוא בין המרפק ולכתף, דקאמר: שלשים בפיסת יד[(ו)] כו', שנים בקנה ושנים במרפק, אחד בזרוע וארבע בכתף. וב"הקומץ רבה" (מנחות ד' לז:) נמי אמרי' דבעינן שתהא שימה כנגד הלב:

*) [ב"ב ה. סנהדרין כו:]

ימים

[ועי' תוס' סוכה ה: ד"ה אל יוכיח]

ב א מיי' פי"ב מהל' שבת הלכה יז סמג לאוין סה טור ש"ע א"ח סי' שמט סעיף ג:

ג ב מיי' פ"ד מהלכות תפילין הלכה ב סמג עשין כב טור ש"ע א"ח סי' כז סעיף א:

ד ג מיי' שם הלכה א טוש"ע שם סעיף ט:

רבינו חננאל

פ"י המוצא תפילין מכניסן זוג זוג כו'. זוג אחד אין טפי לא לימא תנן סתם דלא כר' מאיר דאי ר' מאיר האמר כל מאן דבעי מציל דתנן ולשם הוא מוציא כל כלי תשמישו ולובש כו'. אמר רבא אפילו תימא ר' מאיר כדרך מלבושו בחול התירו לו להוציא בשבת התם דבחול כמה דבעי לביש אצולי נמי כמה דבעי מציל הכא דבחול כו'. רבן גמליאל ב' ב' כו'. אוקימנא דר"ג סבר שבת לאו זמן תפילין הוא ומשום בזיון כתבי קודש שרו ליה רבנן וכי שרו ליה רבנן לא שרו ליה אלא דרך מלבוש במקום תפילין וסבר לה כר' שמואל בר רב יצחק דאמר כו' וגם בזרועו נמי יש בו מקום להניח [שני] תפילין. פי' קיבורת הזרוע שכנגד בית השחי והיא בצעת אדרע וי"א טהר או כף. פי' צבתים מעוכין אלו על אלו מלשון וגם שול תשולו לה מן הצבתים ולישנא דרבנן שנים מדובקין זה על זה נקראין צבותין מלשון צבת בצבת עשויה והן אחד כל בתי זו הני צבותין מתקיימה לימא תנן סתמא ור"ג בהא דר' שמואל בר רב יצחק פליגי ודחינן לא דכ"ע אית להו דר' שמואל בר רב יצחק ובשבת זמן תפילין פליגי דת"ק סבר שבת זמן תפילין הוא ולא שרי אלא זוג אחת בלבד. ור"ג סבר שבת לאו זמן תפילין הוא ומשום כתבי הקודש שרו ליה רבנן דרך מלבוש כדרך שראוי לו ללבוש וכיון שיש לו מקום ללבוש בו ב' תפילין התירו לו שנים איכא דאמרי כ"ע שבת זמן תפילין הוא ובלצאת בעי כוונה פליגי ת"ק סבר לצאת לא בעי כוונה ור"ג סבר לצאת נמי בעי כוונה

הגהות הב"ח

(א) גמ' אי הכי זוג אחד אין כל"ל ותיבת נמי נמחק: (ב) רש"י ד"ה זוג אחד וכו' דבלאו הלכה: (ג) ד"ה דיד מאי איכא למימר אין כל: (ד) תוס' ד"ה מקום וכו' וסמך לדבר לאו ליך לרוחבו: (ה) ד"ה ידך זו קיבורת וכו' שקורין קודל"א. נ"ב ע' בתוס' פ' המנוגע דף כ"ב ע"ב ד"ה במרפק: (ו) בא"ד שלשים בפיסת יד אצבע שנים בקנה:

[ע' תוס' לקמן לז: ד"ה ר"ש]

[ע' תוס' שם ד"ה ה"ג]

שבת קכ.

ע"א מד.

מנחות לז. [ערכין יט:]

[שבת סא. וש"נ]

[ברכות יג. פסחים קיד:]

ואיבעית אימא: דכ"ע לצאת לא בעי כוונה. והכא, לעבור משום "בל תוסיף" קמיפלגי. דתנא קמא סבר: לעבור משום "בל תוסיף" — לא בעי כוונה, ורבן גמליאל סבר: לעבור משום "בל תוסיף" — בעי כוונה. ואיבעית אימא: אי דסבירא לן דשבת זמן תפילין — דכ"ע לא לעבור בעי כוונה, ולא לצאת בעי כוונה. והכא ב"לעבור שלא בזמנו" קמיפלגי. תנא קמא סבר: לא בעי כוונה, ורבן גמליאל סבר: "לעבור שלא בזמנו" בעי כוונה. אי הכי, לרבי מאיר זוג אחד נמי לא! ועוד: *הישן בשמיני בסוכה ילקה! אלא מחוורתא כדשנינן מעיקרא. ומאן שמעת ליה שבת זמן תפילין — ר' עקיבא. *דתניא: ○"ושמרת את החקה הזאת למועדה מימים ימימה" — אימים ולא לילות. "מימים" — בולא כל ימים, פרט לשבתות וימים טובים, דברי רבי יוסי הגלילי. ר' עקיבא אומר: לא נאמר חוקה זו אלא לענין פסח בלבד. ואלא הא *דתנן: גהפסח דוהמילה מצות עשה, לימא דלא כרבי עקיבא; דאי ר"ע — כיון דמוקי לה בפסח, לאו נמי איכא, כדרבי אבין א"ר אילעאי; *דאמר רבי אבין, אמר רבי אילעאי: כל מקום שנאמר "השמר" "פן" ו"אל" אינו אלא בלא תעשה. אפילו תימא רבי עקיבא: *"השמר" דלאו — לאו, "השמר" דעשה — עשה. וסבר רבי עקיבא שבת זמן תפילין הוא?! והתניא, *ר"ע אומר: יכול יניח אדם תפילין בשבתות וימים טובים — ת"ל: ○"והיה לך לאות על ידך" — מי שצריכין אות, יצאו אלו שהן גופן אות! אלא, האי תנא הוא: דתניא, הניעור בלילה, רצה — חולץ, רצה — מניח, דברי רבי נתן. יונתן הקיטוני אומר: אין מניחין תפילין בלילה. מדלילה לתנא קמא זמן תפילין — שבת נמי זמן תפילין.(א) דילמא ס"ל: לילה זמן תפילין הוא, שבת — לאו זמן תפילין הוא. דהא שמעינן ליה לרבי עקיבא, דאמר: *לילה זמן תפילין הוא, שבת לאו זמן תפילין הוא! אלא האי תנא הוא, דתניא: מיכל בת כושי היתה מנחת תפילין הולא מיחו בה חכמים. ואשתו של יונה היתה עולה לרגל ולא מיחו בה חכמים. מדלא מיחו בה חכמים — אלמא קסברי מצות עשה שלא הזמן גרמא היא. ודילמא סבר לה כרבי

(שמות יג | סס | יומא פא. מנחות לו:)

ואיבעית אימא. לענין לצאת, כולי עלמא לא פליגי דידי חובתיה נפיק, אע"ג דלא איכוון. ולענין "בל תוסיף" פליגי. לת"ק, כי היכי דלענין מפיק נפיק, לענין "בל תוסיף" נמי עבר. ולרבן גמליאל, אי לא מכווין למצוה — לא עבר: **ואיבעית אימא אי סבירא לן.**(ב) דלכ"ע שבת זמן תפילין, לא לעבור ולא לצאת בעי כוונה ואיכא "בל תוסיף". אלא, שבת לאו זמן תפילין הוא. ובהא פליגי: דת"ק סבר שלא בזמנו נמי, אפי' בלא כוונה — מצוה היא, ותוספת עמה. ולרבן גמליאל שלא בזמנו ואינו מתכוין, אין כאן רמז מצוה, ואין כאן תוספת: **זוג א' נמי לא.** דיש כאן תוספת, שמוסיף שבת על החול למצות תפילין: **ועוד הישן בשמיני בסוכה ילקה.** דמוסיף שמיני על השביעי. ואנן מיתב יתבינן בשמיני בספק שביעי לכתחלה! אלא שלא בזמנו בלא כוונה — לאו תוספת הוא ולהכי שרינן. דאי שמיני הוא — לא מכוונינן למצות סוכה: **מחוורתא כדשנינן מעיקרא.** בשבת זמן ולאו זמן תפילין הוא(ג) קא מיפלגי: **ומאן.** תנא דשמעת ליה דאמר: שבת זמן תפילין, דמוקים מתני' אליביה: **ושמרת את החוקה.** בפרשת "קדש לי" כתיב, והיא אחת מד' פרשיות של תפילין: **אלא לענין פסח.** דאיירי בה לעיל מיניה. והאי "מימים ימימה" — משנה לשנה, דמתרגמינן "מזמן לזמן". אלמא: מדלא דריש ר' עקיבא האי קרא בתפילין — ש"מ דס"ל לילה ושבת זמן תפילין, דלא קא ממעט להו קרא: **והא דתנן.** בפ"ק דכריתות [דף ג.]: הפסח והמילה. אע"פ שיש בהן כרת, הואיל ואין בהן לאו אלא מצות עשה הן — אין מביאין על שגגתן חטאת, שאין חטאת באה אלא על לאו דכרת, כדכתיב (ויקרא ד): "אשר לא תעשינה" וגו': **לאו נמי איכא.** דהא כתיב "ושמרת" וכל שמירה — אזהרת לאו היא, כדר' אבין: **השמר דלאו לאו והשמר דעשה עשה.** פירוש השמר שלא תעשה כן, כגון "השמר לך פן תכרות ברית" וגו' (שמות לד) "השמר לך פן תנקש" וגו' (דברים יב) "השמר בנגע הצרעת" (סס כד) — שלא יקוץ בהרתו. השמר דעשה כי האי, ד"ושמרת את החוקה": **מי שצריכין אות.** ימים שישראל צריכין להעמיד אות על עצמן להכיר שהם מחזיקים בתורתו של הקב"ה, יצאו שבתות וימים טובים שהן עצמן אות בין הקב"ה לישראל דכתיב (שמות לא): "כי אות היא ביני וביניכם": **הניעור בלילה.** שאין לו לחוש שמא יפיח בתפיליו: **רצה מניח.** ואינו כמוסיף על המצוה, דלילה זמן תפילין הוא. ורבנן הוא דגזור שמא יפיח כשהוא ישן: **מדלילה לת"ק זמן תפילין.** אלמא: לא דריש מ"ימים ימימה" למעוטי לילות, דמוקים לקרא בפסח: **שבת נמי זמן תפילין הוא.**(ד) מההוא קרא גופיה ממעט שבת: **ודילמא סבירא ליה לילה זמן תפילין.** דלא דריש "מימים ימימה" לענין תפילין. אבל שבת לאו זמן תפילין הוא, ונפקא ליה מ"והיה לך לאות" כדנפקא ליה לר"ע לעיל, דמוקי מימים ימימה לפסח, דלא ממעט לילה מימים וקא ממעט שבת מ"והיה לך לאות": **בת כושי.** בת שאול כדכתיב (תהלים ז): "על דברי כוש בן ימיני" דהיינו שאול, כדאמרי' ב"אלו מגלחין" (מו"ק דף טז:): **ולא מיחו בה חכמים.** דהוי כתוספת על דברי תורה, שפטורה נשים ממצות עשה שהזמן גרמא: **של יונה.** בן אמיתי: **שלא הזמן גרמא.** אלמא: מצות תפילין כל שעה גם בלילה גם בשבת, דאי מפקת חד — הוי להו זמן קבוע:

דר'

ימים וכו' פרט לשבתות וי"ט. נראה דאדרש' ד"לאות על ידך" דסמוך קא סמיך. ולכאורה אין להניח תפילין בחוה"מ, שא"צ אות, דאסור במלאכה בדבר שאינו אבד. ועוד: דחייב בסוכה בחג, ובפסח אסור באכילת חמץ. וכן פסקו בהלכות גדולות. אבל בירושלמי (פרק "אלו מגלחין" הלכה ד) משמע דצריך להניח, דגרס: ההוא גברא דאבד תפילין. אתא לקמיה דרב חננאל, שדריה לקמיה דרבה בר בר חנה. אמר ליה לספרא: זיל הב ליה תפילך, ואת כתוב לך. דתנא: כותב אדם תפילין לעצמו. אתא לקמיה דרב, א"ל: זיל כתוב ליה להדיא. מתני' פליגי עליה דרב: כותב אדם תפילין לעצמו אבל לאחרים — לא. רב פתר להניח. פירוש: מעמיד המשנה שרצה להניח לאחר המועד, אבל לצורך המועד — יכול לכתוב אף לאחרים. וכן עמא דבר. עוד מביאין ראיה מספ"ק דבילה (דף טו.) גבי משלחין תפילין:

ושמרת את החוקה הזאת. מכאן אור"ת דאפי' בני מערבא *דהוו מברכין כשהיו חולצין תפילין "לשמור חוקיו" — היינו דוקא כשחולצן סמוך לחשיכה, משום דלילה לאו זמן תפילין הוא, דהא כתיב "חוקה". מיהו, לא קי"ל הכי, ואין צריך לברך אפי' חולצן משום לילה. דקי"ל כר' עקיבא דאמר: לא נאמרה חוקה זו אלא לענין פסח בלבד. וב"הקומץ רבה" (מנחות דף לו:) פסקינן דלילה זמן תפילין עד שעת שינה. ורב אשי ורבינא מסקי התם: הלכה, ואין מורין כן, אלא כל הלילה זמן תפילין, כרבי עקיבא דשמעתין:

השמר דעשה עשה. ואפי' ר' יוחנן דאמר ב"הקומץ רבה" (מנחות דף לו:): "השמר" דעשה נמי לאו הוא, ולהכי המניח תפילין אחר שקיעת החמה — עובר בלאו, מודה הוא שאם לא הניח ביום שאינו לוקה. דלענין הנחת היום השמר דעשה עשה הוא, כמו לענין עשיית פסח, דאמר הכא דהוי עשה משום דהוי קום עשה. ודוקא לענין הנחת תפילין בלילה קאמר ר' יוחנן דלאו הוא, דהוי כמו "השמר בנגע הצרעת" דחשיב ליה לאו בפ' "אם לא הביא" (שבת דף קלב:), אע"ג דכתיב "לשמור ולעשות" — משום דפירושו לאו הוא. השמר שלא תקוץ:

מיכל בת כושי היתה מנחת תפילין. בפסיקתא [רבתי פכ"ב*] דר' חזקיה בשם ר' אבהו אמרו: אשתו של יונה — הושבה, מיכל בת כושי — מיחו בה חכמים. מה שפי' בקונטרס: דאי מצות עשה שהזמן גרמא הוא היו מוחין בידה, שנראה כמוסיפה — אין נראה לר"י. דהא ר' יהודה לית ליה נשים סומכות רשות, ושמעינן ליה בפ"ק דסוכה (דף ב:) דאמר: הילני המלכה היתה יושבת בסוכה, וז' בניה. ומיהו, יש ליישב: דמשום בניה היתה יושבת, ולא מיחזי כ"בל תוסיף". אי נמי: משום דשמעינן ליה לרבא בפרק "ראוהו ב"ד" (ר"ה דף כח:) דלעבור שלא בזמנו בעי כוונה, ולגבי אשה דלא מחייבא — הוי כשלא בזמנו(ה), דכיון דלא מיכווני לה לא עברה. אך נראה דוחק. ונראה לפרש: דטעמא למ"ד(ו) דלא הוי רשות — משום דתפילין צריכין גוף נקי, ונשים אין זריזות ליזהר. ועלייה לרגל — משום דמיחזי כמביאה חולין לעזרה, או משום ראיית פנים בעזרה שלא לצורך. ותקיעת שופר וסמיכה נמי, דמעכבין למאן דלית ליה רשות — לאו משום דמיחזי מוסיף, אלא משום דתקיעה מלאכה דרבנן היא, כדאמר בפ' "כיסוי הדם" (חולין דף פד:) דאין וולאה דוחה שבת. וסמיכה — אפי' בהקפת יד מיחזי כעבודה בקדשים.

דילמא סבר לה כר' יוסי דאמר נשים סומכות רשות. מכאן אר"ת: דמותר לנשים לברך על כל מצות עשה שהזמן גרמא, אע"ג דפטורות. כמו מיכל בת שאול, שהיתה מסתמא גם מברכת. אע"ג דר"מ ור' יהודה פליגי עליה, כדאמר בסמוך — קיימא לן כר' יוסי לגבי תרווייהו. ואע"ג דסתם מתני' דאין מעכבין את התינוקות מלתקוע *דלא כרבי יוסי, דמשמע הא נשים מעכבין כדאמר בסמוך — אפ"ה מעשה רב דמיכל בת שאול ואשתו של יונה, ועובדא דפרק "אין דורשין" (חגיגה דף טז:): דהביאנוהו לעזרת נשים כדי לעשות להם נחת רוח. ועוד הביא ראיה מהא דאמר רב יוסף בפרק "החובל" (ב"ק דף פז.): מעיקרא מאן דאמר לי הלכה כרבי יהודה — עבידנא יומא טבא לרבנן, דלא מפקדנא ועבידנא כו'. ואם במקום שפטור ועושה אסור לברך — אם כן אמאי קאמר דהוה עביד

* ועי' ירושלמי ברכות פ"ב ה"ג

עין משפט נר מצוה

ה א מיי' פ"ד מהל' תפילין הלכה י סמג עשין כב טוש"ע א"ח סי' ל סעיף ב:

ו ב מיי' וסמג שם טור ש"ע א"ח סי' לא סעיף א:

ז ג מיי' פ"א מהל' קרבן פסח הלכה א סמג עשין רכג:

ח ד מיי' פ"א מהלכות מילה הלכה א סמג עשין כח טוש"ע י"ד סי' רס:

ט ה טוש"ע א"ח סי' לח סעיף ג בהג"ה:

רבינו חננאל

איכא דאמרי כ"ע [לצאת] לא בעי כוונה ובלעבור משום בל תוסיף פליגי ת"ק סבר לעבור משום בל תוסיף לא בעי כוונה ור"ג סבר אינו עובר עד שיתכוון לעבור ואיבעית אימא אי סבירא לן דשבת לאו זמן תפילין. (ספר אחר זמן תפילין היא) לא לצאת ולא לעבור (ולא) בעי כוונה והכא בלעבור שלא בזמנה פליגי. אי הכי לר' מאיר דאמר שבת לאו זמן תפילין היא לא לצאת ולא לעבור ולא בעי כוונה אלא אע"פ שאינו מתכוין לא לצאת ולא לעבור חייב אפי' זוג אחד אסור. וכן הישן בשמיני בסוכה ילקה שעובר על בסוכות תשבו שבעת ימים והוא ישב ח' הוסיף על ז' ימים שבתורה ואע"פ שלא נתכוון לעבור אלא מחוורתא כדשנינן מעיקרא ומתני' דלא כר' מאיר. מאן תנא הוא דסבר שבת זמן תפילין הוא ר' עקיבא הוא דתניא ושמרת כו' עד אלא לפסח בלבד אבל תפילין אפילו בשבתות וי"ט. ואקשינן אלא הא דתנן בכריתות פ"א הפסח והמילה מצות עשה הן דלא כתיב בהו לאו כיון דאוקמה לפרשה זו בפסח דכתיב בה ושמרת שמירה זו לאו היא כר' אבין א"ר אלעאי הנה גם בפסח יש בו לאו. ופרקינן ר' עקיבא סבר שמירה דלאו היא לאו והאי שמירה דעשה הוא. וסבר ר"ע שבת זמן תפילין והתניא כו' ונתברר כי ר' עקיבא סבר שבת לאו זמן תפילין היא דשבת גופה אות היא. אבל לילה זמן תפילין היא מדקאמר פרשה זו כולה בפסח נאמרה. ואתינן למפשט דר' נתן הוא דסבר שבת זמן תפילין הוא מדקתני היה נעור בלילה רצה חולץ רצה מניח ש"מ דלילה זמן תפילין הוא סבירא ליה. ודחינן להא דוקיא אלא האי תנא הוא דתניא מיכל בת שאול היתה מנחת תפילין בלילה ולא מיחו בה חכמים לאו משום דסברי תפילין מצות עשה שלא הזמן גרמא היא כלומר זמנם בכל יום ואפי' בשבתות וי"ט לפיכך לא מיחו בה חכמים ש"מ דשבת זמן תפילין סבירא להו. ודחינן ודלמא חכמים סבירא להו הנחת תפילין בנשים רשות כדאמרינן נשים

הגהות הב"ח

(א) גמ' ודילמא סבירא ליה לילה: (ב) רש"י ד"ה ואיבעית אימא אי סבירא לן אי שמעינן לכולי עלמא: (ג) ד"ה מחוורתא וכו' דקא מיפלגי: (ד) ד"ה שבת נמי וכו' דהאי קרא: (ה) תוס' ד"ה מיכל וכו' וכיון דלא מיכוונא וכו': (ו) בא"ד דטעמא למ"ד דלית ליה רשות משום:

[ר"ה כח:] | מנחות לו: | זבחים קו: כריתות ב. | מכות יג: שבועות ד. לו. סוטה ה. ע"ז נא: זבחים קו. מנחות לט: | מנחות לו: | [זבחים יט.] | [ברכות מד.] | ר"ה לג.

עין משפט נר מצוה

י א מיי' פ"ב מהל' שופר הלכה ז טור א"ח סי' תקפט:

יא ב מיי' פ"ג מהל' מעשה קרבנות הל' ח סמג עשין קפג:

יב ג ד מיי' פ"ב מהל' ציצית הלכה ז:

גמרא

כְּרַבִּי יוֹסֵי, דְּאָמַר: נָשִׁים סוֹמְכוֹת רְשׁוּת. דְּאִי לָא תֵּימָא הָכִי – אִשְׁתּוֹ שֶׁל יוֹנָה הָיְתָה עוֹלָה לָרֶגֶל וְלֹא מִיחוּ בָּהּ. מִי אִיכָּא לְמ"ד רֶגֶל לָאו מִצְוַת עֲשֵׂה שֶׁהַזְּמַן גְּרָמָא הוּא? אֶלָּא: קָסָבַר רְשׁוּת, הָכָא נַמִי: רְשׁוּת. אֶלָּא הַאי תַּנָּא הִיא, דְּתַנְיָא: *הַמּוֹצֵא תְּפִילִּין – מַכְנִיסָן זוּג זוּג, אֶחָד הָאִישׁ וְאֶחָד הָאִשָּׁה, אֶחָד חֲדָשׁוֹת וְאֶחָד יְשָׁנוֹת, דִּבְרֵי ר"מ. ר' יְהוּדָה אוֹסֵר בַּחֲדָשׁוֹת וּמַתִּיר בִּיְשָׁנוֹת. ע"כ לָא פְּלִיגִי אֶלָּא בַּחֲדָשׁוֹת וִישָׁנוֹת, אֲבָל בְּאִשָּׁה – לָא פְּלִיגִי. שְׁמַע מִינָּהּ: מִצְוַת עֲשֵׂה שֶׁלֹּא הַזְּמַן גְּרָמָא הוּא, וְכׇל מִצְוַת עֲשֵׂה שֶׁאֵין הַזְּמַן גְּרָמָא נָשִׁים חַיָּיבוֹת. וְדִילְמָא סָבַר לָהּ כְּר' יוֹסֵי, דְּאָמַר: נָשִׁים סוֹמְכוֹת רְשׁוּת? לָא ס"ד, דְּלָא רַבִּי מֵאִיר סָבַר לָהּ כְּרַבִּי יוֹסֵי, וְלָא רַבִּי יְהוּדָה סָבַר לָהּ כְּרַבִּי יוֹסֵי. לָא רַבִּי מֵאִיר סָבַר לָהּ כְּרַבִּי יוֹסֵי *דִּתְנַן: אאֵין מְעַכְּבִין אֶת הַתִּינוֹקוֹת מִלִּתְקוֹעַ. הָא נָשִׁים – מְעַכְּבִין. *וּסְתָם מַתְנִי' רַבִּי מֵאִיר. וְלָא ר' יְהוּדָה סָבַר לָהּ כְּר' יוֹסֵי *דְּתַנְיָא: °"דַּבֵּר אֶל בְּנֵי יִשְׂרָאֵל (ויקרא א) וְסָמַךְ" *ב בְּנֵי יִשְׂרָאֵל סוֹמְכִין וְאֵין בְּנוֹת יִשְׂרָאֵל סוֹמְכוֹת. רַבִּי יוֹסֵי וְר"ש אוֹמְרִים: נָשִׁים סוֹמְכוֹת רְשׁוּת. *וּסְתָם סִיפְרָא מַנִּי(א) – ר' יְהוּדָה. א"ר אֶלְעָזָר: גהַמּוֹצֵא תְּכֵלֶת בַּשּׁוּק, לְשׁוֹנוֹת – פְּסוּלוֹת, חוּטִין – כְּשֵׁרִין. מַאי שְׁנָא לְשׁוֹנוֹת – דְּאָמַר: אַדַּעְתָּא דִּגְלִימָא צָבְעִינְהוּ. חוּטִין נַמִי, נֵימָא: אַדַּעְתָּא דִּגְלִימָא טָוְינְהוּ! דבִּשְׁזוּרִים. שְׁזוּרִים נַמִי, נֵימָא: אַדַּעְתָּא דְּשִׁיפְתָּא דִּגְלִימָא עֲיִיפִינְהוּ! בְּמוּפְסָקִין, דְּכוּלֵּי הַאי וַדַּאי לָא טָרְחִי אֱינָשֵׁי. אָמַר רָבָא: וְכִי אָדָם טוֹרֵחַ לַעֲשׂוֹת קָמֵיעַ כְּמִין תְּפִילִּין? דִּתְנַן: בַּמֶּה דְּבָרִים אֲמוּרִים – בִּיְשָׁנוֹת, אֲבָל בַּחֲדָשׁוֹת – פָּטוּר! א"ר זֵירָא לְאַהֲבָה בְּרֵיהּ, פּוּק תְּנֵי לְהוּ: הַמּוֹצֵא תְּכֵלֶת בַּשּׁוּק, לְשׁוֹנוֹת – פְּסוּלִין, חוּטִין מוּפְסָקִין – כְּשֵׁירִין, לְפִי שֶׁאֵין אָדָם טוֹרֵחַ. אָמַר רָבָא: וּמִשּׁוּם דְּתָנֵי לָהּ אַהֲבָה בְּרֵיהּ דְּרַבִּי זֵירָא *כֵּיפֵי תְּלָא לָהּ?! וְהָתְנַן: בַּמֶּה דְּבָרִים אֲמוּרִים – בִּיְשָׁנוֹת, אֲבָל בַּחֲדָשׁוֹת – פָּטוּר! אֶלָּא אָמַר רָבָא: טָרַח וְלָא טָרַח – תַּנָּאֵי הִיא, דְּתַנְיָא: הַמּוֹצֵא תְּפִילִּין – מַכְנִיסָן זוּג זוּג, אֶחָד הָאִישׁ וְאֶחָד הָאִשָּׁה, אֶחָד

רש"י

דר' יוסי. לְקַמָּן: נָשִׁים סוֹמְכוֹת רְשׁוּת. וְאע"ג דִּכְתִיב (ויקרא א): "דַּבֵּר אֶל בְּנֵי יִשְׂרָאֵל וְאָמַרְתָּ אֲלֵיהֶם אָדָם כִּי יַקְרִיב מִכֶּם" וְסָמִיךְ לֵיהּ "וְסָמַךְ יָדוֹ", בְּנֵי יִשְׂרָאֵל סוֹמְכִים וְלֹא בְּנוֹת יִשְׂרָאֵל סוֹמְכוֹת: אוֹסֵר בַּחֲדָשׁוֹת. לְחַלֵּל עֲלֵיהֶן שַׁבָּת, דִּילְמָא קָמֵיעַ בְּעָלְמָא נִינְהוּ: נָשִׁים סוֹמְכוֹת רְשׁוּת. דְּאֵין כָּאן "בַּל תּוֹסִיף", וּמִשּׁוּם אִיסּוּרָא נַמִי לֵיכָּא, דְּקָסָבַר: תַּכְשִׁיט נִינְהוּ: אֵין מְעַכְּבִין. אֵין ב"ד מוּזְהָרִין לְמוֹנְעָן מִלִּתְקוֹעַ בְּיוֹם טוֹב שֶׁל ר"ה, דְּבָעוּ לְחַנּוּכִינְהוּ בְּמִצְוֹת: הָא נָשִׁים מְעַכְּבִין. אע"ג דְּלָא חִלּוּל י"ט הוּא, כִּדְתָנָא דְּבֵי שְׁמוּאֵל (ר"ה דף כט:): יָגָה תְּקִיעַת שׁוֹפָר וּרְדִיַּית הַפַּת, שֶׁהִיא חָכְמָה וְאֵינָהּ מְלָאכָה. מִיהוּ, נִרְאוֹת כְּמוֹסִיפוֹת: סְתָם סִיפְרָא. תּוֹרַת כֹּהֲנִים: לְשׁוֹנוֹת. לֶמֶר סָרוּק וְצָבוּעַ: פְּסוּלוֹת. שֶׁמָּא לֹא נִצְבַּע לְשֵׁם צִיצִית, וַהֲוַאן עֲשָׂיָיה לְשׁוּמָן בָּעֵינַן: דִּגְלִימָא(ב) טָוָואתֵיהּ. לֶאֱרוֹג מֵהֶן טַלִּית וְלֹא לַעֲשׂוֹת מֵהֶן צִיצִית: שְׁזָרְנָהוּ. טְוָואָם: בִּשְׁזוּרִים. שֶׁאֵין דֶּרֶךְ לְאׇרְגָם: דְּשִׁיפְתָּא דִּגְלִימָא. שֶׁכֵּן דֶּרֶךְ לְהָסֵךְ שְׁזוּרִים בִּשְׂפָתוֹ, שֶׁהוּא גְּדִיל וְנִקְרָא בְּלַעַ"ז לִימוּשׂ", וְהַחוּטִים נִקְרָאִים אוּרִי"ל: בְּמוּפְסָקִין דְּכוּלֵּי הַאי לָא טָרַח. לַחֲזוֹר וּלְקׇשְׁרָם וּלְהָסֵךְ אוֹתָן: וְכִי אָדָם טוֹרֵחַ לַעֲשׂוֹת קָמֵיעַ כְּעֵין תְּפִילִּין. וַאפ"ה חָיְישִׁינַן לָהּ בְּמַתְנִי' דְּקָתָנֵי: חֲדָשׁוֹת פָּטוּר, דִּילְמָא קָמֵיעַ נִינְהוּ, וְלֹא מְחַלְּלִין שַׁבְּתָא עֲלַיְיהוּ: פּוּק תְּנֵי לְהוּ. לְהָנָךְ רַבָּנַן דְּבֵי מִדְרְשָׁא, דְּקָשֵׁי לְהוּ כִּדְר' אֶלְעָזָר, לֹא וּשְׁנֵה לָהֶם שֶׁיֵּשׁ בְּיָדִי בָּרַיְיתָא דִּמְסַיְּיעַ לֵיהּ וּמְפָרֶשֶׁת טַעְמָא בְּהֶדְיָא: לְפִי שֶׁאֵין אָדָם טוֹרֵחַ: *כֵּיפֵי. מַרְגָּלִיּוֹת ל"א: נְזָמִים, וְכֵן עִיקָּר:

תוספות

עביד יומא טבא? והלא מפסיד כל הברכות של כל המצות, וק' ברכות בכל יום. ולא חשיב ברכה לבטלה, כיון שמברך על המצוה שעושה, אע"פ שפטור. ומיהו, אין ראיה מסומא לאשה. דסומא מיחייב מדרבנן. ומ"מ היה שמח רב יוסף, משום דמדאורייתא לא מיפקד ועביד, כדמוכח קצת ב"ערבי פסחים" (דף קטז:), דקאמר: סומא פטור מלומר אגדתא. ופריך מרב יוסף ומרב ששת שהיו אומרים הגדה, ומוציאין בני ביתם. ומשני: דקסבר מצה בזמן הזה דרבנן, משמע דמיחייבי מדרבנן, ולכך היו יכולים להוציא אחרים. ומיהו, יש לדחות: דאפי' רשות יכול להוציא בר חיובא דרבנן, כמו קטן דמברך לאביו בפרק "מי שמתו" (ברכות דף כ:) ועולה למנין ז', *ומוציא אחרים מידי מגילה לר' יהודה, כדאמר במסכת מגילה (דף יט:). [מגילה דף כד.] אבל יש לדקדק בפרק "הקורא מעומד" (מגילה דף כד.), ר' יהודה אומר: כל שלא ראה מאורות מימיו – לא יפרוס על "שמע". משמע: הא ראה, אע"ג דהשתא נסתמא – פורס על "שמע", אע"ג דלר' יהודה סומא פטור מכל המצות! אלא ודאי מיחייב מדרבנן, ויכול לומר "קדשנו במצותיו וצונו", כיון דמחייב מדרבנן. כדאמרי' בפ' "במה מדליקין" (שבת דף כג.): היכן צונו – מ"לא תסור". אבל אשה דאינה מיחויבת אפי' מדרבנן במצות עשה שהזמן גרמא, כדמוכח בהדיא בפרק "מי שמתו" (ברכות דף כ:) גבי נשים חייבות בקדוש היום דבר תורה, ובריש סוכה (דף ב:) גבי הילני המלכה, היכי מצי למימר "וצונו"? ואין לתמוה דסומא חייב מדרבנן ואשה פטרו לגמרי – דהחמירו חכמים בסומא משום דהוי ממין בר חיובא. ועוד: שלא יראה כעו"ג אם היה פטור מכל המצות. אבל לאשה, כי פטורה נמי לגמרי ממצות עשה שהזמן גרמא – אכתי מחויבת בכל שאר מצות. וממה שהאשה עולה למנין ז' ומברכת קריאת התורה, אע"ג דפטורה מתלמוד תורה, כדאמר בפ"ק דקדושין (דף כט.) ובריש ב"כל מערבין" (לעיל דף כז.) – אור"ת דאין זו ראיה. דברכת קריאת התורה לאו משום מצות תלמוד תורה, שאפי' בירך ברכת "הערב נא" או נפטר ב"אהבה רבה" – חוזר ומברך. תדע, דבמקום שאין לוי – כהן קורא במקום לוי ומברך, אע"פ שכבר בירך בקריאה ראשונה. ומקטן דמברך ברכת המזון אע"פ שהוא פטור – אין ראיה לאשה, דקטן אתי לכלל חיוב, ואיבעי לחנכו, ואינו מוזהר על "לא תסור"*: **אבל** באשה לא פליגי. וא"ת: דילמא משום דהוי מלבוש לאיש, כדאמר בפרק "במה אשה" (שבת דף סא.) דתפילין דרך מלבוש עבידי! וי"ל: דהיינו דוקא לאיש, משום דרגיל ללובשן בחול, אבל לאשה – לא, כדאמרי' התם: ותלופיהן באיש. דמידי דחזי לאיש לא חזי לאשה, ומידי דחזי לאשה לא חזי לאיש. **לא** ס"ד לא ר"מ ס"ל כר' יוסי כו'. משמע דר"מ ור' יהודה תרוייהו אית להו דנשים חייבות בתפילין, דלאו זמן גרמא הוא. ותימה: דבפרק "מי שמתו" (ברכות דף כ:) תנן: נשים ועבדים וקטנים פטורין מן התפילין. ופריך עלה בגמרא: פשיטא, ומשני דאיצטריך, משום דאיתקש תפילין למזוזה. והשתא הא איצטריך לאפוקי מדר"מ ור' יהודה! וי"ל: דלמאן דחשיב תפילין זמן גרמא – הוי פשיטא דנשים פטורות, ומשום הכי איצטריך לשנויי טעמא דאיתקש. הקשה ה"ר יום טוב מווין: היכי דייק בסמוך דר"מ לא סבר לה כר' יוסי, מכח ההיא סתמא דאין מעכבין את התינוקות מלתקוע, ומתוך כך אנן צריכין לומר דההיא דפרק "מי שמתו" דלא כר"מ, אדרבה, נימא דההוא סתמא כר"מ, דקסבר נשים פטורות, והא דקתני הכא ר"מ אחד האיש ואחד האשה – משום דסבר לה כר' יוסי, דאמר: נשים סומכות רשות, וסתם מתני' דאין מעכבין – דלא כר"מ! ותירץ לו ר"י: דמה נפשך סתמא דברכות דלא כר"מ, דקא סבר ההוא מתני' דנשים סומכות לאו רשות, דקתני התם: נשים ועבדים וקטנים פטורים מק"ש ותפילין, וחייבין בתפלה ובבהמ"ז ובמזוזה. והנהו קטנים – על כרחין בלא הגיעו לחינוך איירי, דבהגיעו לחינוך – בתפילין נמי חייבין, כדאמר בסוף "לולב הגזול" (סוכה דף מב.): קטן היודע לשמור תפילין – אביו חייב ליקח לו תפילין. אלא בלא הגיעו לחינוך איירי. ולא קאי וחייבין אקטנים אלא אנשים ועבדים, ולא נקט קטנים אלא לענין פטור. והא נמי אינו שום חידוש דפטירי בלא הגיע לחינוך, ולא תני להו אלא לאשמועינן דנשים ועבדים כקטנים לענין תפילין, דאי בעי לאנוחי – לא שבקינן להו משום בזיון תפילין, היכא דלא הגיעו לחינוך. ועוד י"ל: דניחא ליה טפי למימר דההיא דברכות דלא כר"מ – משום דלא מיתרצא מילתיה דר"מ, דאמר: זוג – אין, טפי – לא, אא"כ סבר שבת זמן תפילין הוא, כדאסיקנא לעיל, אם לא נאמר דלית ליה דרב שמואל בר רב יצחק, דאמר: מקום יש בראש להניח בו ב' תפילין: **וסתם** סיפרא ר' יהודה. בפ' בתרא דר"ה (דף לג.) אית דגרסי בה: דברי ר' יהודה, והכא מוכח דלא גרסי' ליה: **המוצא** תכלת בשוק וכו' חוטין כשרין. כדמסיק: בשזורין ומופסקין, דכולי האי לא טרח. וא"ת: ואע"ג דלציצית נעשה, אמאי כשירה? הא אמר בפ' "התכלת" (מנחות דף מג:) דאין תכלת ניקחת אלא מן המומחה, שיודע שטעימה פסולה. אבל ממי שאינו מומחה – לא, דאיכא למיחש לטעימה! וי"ל: דכשמצאן שזורין ומופסקין, שאנו יודעים שלצורך ציצית נפסקו – יש לתלות דמן המומחה נפלו. דכשאינו מומחה – אינו רגיל להתעסק בדבר, שיודע שלא יקנו ממנו, ואפי' לעצמו אינו רגיל לעשות, כיון שיודע בעצמו שאינו בקי בהלכות צביעה: **וכי** אדם טורח לעשות קמיע כמין תפילין. השתא לא מסיק אדעתיה טעמא דמקושרות ואין מקושרין דבסמוך, וס"ד דתרוייהו אין מקושרות. אלא שבישנות ניכר רושם הקשר שבהם, ובחדשות אינו ניכר. וחיישינן בחדשות שמא קמיע היא, אבל בישנות אין לחוש לקמיע, דאם היה קמיע – לא היה עושה קשר, דכולי האי ודאי לא הוה עביד ביה כעין תפילין. ואם תאמר: כיון דאין מקושרות, היאך מכניסן? דבשבת אסור לקשור! וי"ל: דס"ד דבלא קשירה נמי הוי דרך מלבוש. אי נמי: עונבן אפי' לר' יהודה, דס"ד דמסתמא דעתו להתיר העניבה ולעשות קשירה גמורה ולא הוי של קיימא: אמר

רבינו חננאל

נשים סומכות רשות דאי לא תימא הכי רגלים מי איכא מ"ד לעלות ברגל מצות עשה שלא הזמן גרמא הוא אלא ודאי מ"ע שהזמן גרמא הוא ולמה לא מיחו בידה משום דסבירא להו עליית נשים ברגל רשות. אלא האי תנא הוא דסבר שבת זמן תפילין הוא דתניא (המוציא) [המוצא] תפלין כו'. עד ר' יהודה אוסר בחדשות ומתיר בישנות לפי שאין אדם טורח. ודייקינן מדלא פליג באשה ש"מ דסברי מ"ע שלא הזמן גרמא היא ואפי' בשבת זמנם הוא ודחינן ודלמא הני נמי סבירא להו נשי [במ"ע שהז"ג] רשות כר' יוסי דאמר נשים סומכות רשות ודחינן לא יכלת למימר דר' מאיר ור' יהודא כר' יוסי סבירא להו דסבר נשים במצות עשה שהזמן גרמא רשות דתנן אין מעכבין כו' ש"מ דר"מ ור' יהודה לא סבירא להו הא דר' יוסי *) (לא אתבריר) לן מאן האי תנא דסבר שבת זמן תפלין היא: א"ר אלעזר המוצא תכלת בשוק [לשונות] (לשתות) פסולה דאמרינן אדעתא דגלימא צבעינהו אבל אם מצא חוטין תכלת שזורין פי' כפולין ומפוסקין בקרנתא כשרין לציצית דכולי האי לא טרח איניש לעשותן למלאכה כגון עשיית שפתא דגלימא וכיוצא בה. ואע"ג דאמר רבא וכי אדם טורח לעשות קמיע כמין תפלין [דתנן] בד"א בישנות אבל בחדשות פטור דחיישינן שמא קמיע נינהו. הא אסקה רבא טריח ולא טריח תנאי היא דתניא המוצא תפלין מכניסן זוג זוג. ר"י סבר בישנות מותר דכולי האי לא טרח אלא בחדשות טרח ר' מאיר סבר אפילו בחדשות לא טרח והשתא דתני אבוה דשמואל בר רב יצחק אלו הן ישנות כל שיש בהן רצועות ומקושרות חדשות שיש בהן רצועות ואינן מקושרות

*) הדבר צ"ע דהא מסקנא בהכא שלקא דר"מ ור"י ס"ל ע"כ דשבת זמן תפילין ואמאי לא איתברר אולי דט"ס וצ"ל ואיתברר לן דהני תנאי סברי דשבת זמן תפילין הוא.

הגהות הב"ח

(א) גמ' וסתם ספרא מני. נ"ב וע"ע מן מסכת נדה דף מו: (ב) רש"י ד"ה דגלימא שזרינהו טוואם לארוג וכו' ציצית הס"ד ואח"כ מ"ה בשזורים:

מסורת הש"ס

[מגילה דף כד.]

[תוספ' פ"ח ע"ש שבת סב.]

ר"ה לג. [ערכין ב:]

[סנהדרין פו. גיטין ז.]

ר"ה לג. חגיגה טז: חולין פה.

שם וקידושין לו.

[שבת קלו: יומא מח. קידושין נג. סנהדרין פו. שבועות יג. בכורות סח. כריתות כב.]

עי' רש"ש ב"ב נג. ד"ה כיפי

[כתובות פח:]

[וע"ע תוספות חגיגה טז: ד"ה לעשות ותוס' ר"ה לג. ד"ה הא ותוס' קידושין לו. ד"ה דלא ותוס' ב"ק פו. ד"ה וכן]

אֶחָד חֲדָשׁוֹת וְאֶחָד יְשָׁנוֹת, דִּבְרֵי רַבִּי מֵאִיר. רַבִּי יְהוּדָה אוֹסֵר בַּחֲדָשׁוֹת וּמַתִּיר בַּיְשָׁנוֹת. אַלְמָא, מָר סָבַר: טָרַח אִינִישׁ, וּמָר סָבַר לָא טָרַח אִינִישׁ.§ (שיצ"י עצב"י סִימָן).§ וְהַשְׁתָּא דְּתָנֵי אֲבוּהּ דִּשְׁמוּאֵל בַּר רַב יִצְחָק: [א]אֵלּוּ הֵן יְשָׁנוֹת — כָּל שֶׁיֵּשׁ בָּהֶן רְצוּעוֹת וּמְקוּשָּׁרוֹת, חֲדָשׁוֹת — יֵשׁ בָּהֶן רְצוּעוֹת וְלֹא מְקוּשָּׁרוֹת. דְּכוּלֵּי עָלְמָא לָא טָרַח אִינִישׁ. וְלִיעַנְבִינְהוּ מִיעַנַּב! אָמַר רַב חִסְדָּא, זֹאת אוֹמֶרֶת: עֲנִיבָה פְּסוּלָה בַּתְּפִלִּין. אַבַּיֵּי אָמַר: *רַבִּי יְהוּדָה לְטַעְמֵיהּ, דְּאָמַר: עֲנִיבָה קְשִׁירָה מַעַלְיָיתָא הִיא. טַעְמָא דַּעֲנִיבָה קְשִׁירָה מַעַלְיָיתָא הִיא, הָא לָאו הָכִי — עָנֵיב לְהוּ? *וְהָאָמַר רַב יְהוּדָה בְּרֵיהּ דְּרַב שְׁמוּאֵל בַּר שֵׁילַת מִשְּׁמֵיהּ דְּרַב: קֶשֶׁר שֶׁל תְּפִלִּין הֲלָכָה לְמֹשֶׁה מִסִּינַי הוּא. וְאָמַר רַב נַחְמָן: וְנוֹיֵיהֶן לְבַר! דְּעָנֵיב לְהוּ כְּעֵין קְשִׁירָה דִּידְהוּ. אָמַר רַב חִסְדָּא, אָמַר רַב: [ב]הַלּוֹקֵחַ תְּפִלִּין מִמִּי שֶׁאֵינוֹ מוּמְחֶה — בּוֹדֵק שְׁתַּיִם שֶׁל יָד וְאַחַת שֶׁל רֹאשׁ, אוֹ שְׁתַּיִם שֶׁל רֹאשׁ וְאַחַת שֶׁל יָד. מַה נַּפְשָׁךְ; אִי מֵחַד גַּבְרָא קָא זָבֵין — לִבְדּוֹק אוֹ שָׁלֹשׁ שֶׁל יָד אוֹ שָׁלֹשׁ שֶׁל רֹאשׁ. אִי מִתְּרֵי תְּלָתָא גַּבְרֵי זָבֵין — כָּל חַד וְחַד לִיבָּעֵי בְּדִיקָה! לְעוֹלָם מֵחַד גַּבְרָא זָבֵין, וּבָעֵינַן דְּמִיתְמַחֵי בְּשֶׁל יָד וּבְשֶׁל רֹאשׁ. אִינִי?! וְהָא תָּנֵי רַבָּה בַּר שְׁמוּאֵל: בַּתְּפִלִּין בּוֹדֵק שָׁלֹשׁ שֶׁל יָד וְשֶׁל רֹאשׁ. מַאי לָאו אוֹ שָׁלֹשׁ שֶׁל יָד, אוֹ שָׁלֹשׁ שֶׁל רֹאשׁ? לֹא, שָׁלֹשׁ, מֵהֶן שֶׁל יָד מֵהֶן שֶׁל רֹאשׁ. וְהָתָנֵי רַב כָּהֲנָא: בַּתְּפִלִּין בּוֹדֵק שְׁתַּיִם שֶׁל יָד וְשֶׁל רֹאשׁ! הָא מַנִּי רַבִּי הִיא, דְּאָמַר: *בִּתְרֵי זִימְנֵי הָוֵי חֲזָקָה. אִי רַבִּי, אֵימָא סֵיפָא: וְכֵן בַּצֶּבֶת הַשֵּׁנִי, וְכֵן בַּצֶּבֶת הַשְּׁלִישִׁי. וְאִי רַבִּי — שְׁלִישִׁי מִי אִית לֵיהּ? מוֹדֶה רַבִּי בִּצְבָתִים, דְּמִתְּרֵי תְּלָתָא גַּבְרֵי זָבֵין. אִי הָכִי, אֲפִילּוּ רְבִיעִי נַמִי, וַאֲפִילּוּ חֲמִישִׁי נַמִי! אִין הָכִי נַמִי, וְהַאי דְּקָתָנֵי שְׁלִישִׁי — לְאַפּוּקֵי מֵחִזְקִיָּה, וּלְעוֹלָם אֲפִילּוּ רְבִיעִי וַחֲמִישִׁי נַמִי.§ "מְצָאָן צְבָתִים אוֹ כְּרִיכוֹת וכו'"§ מַאי צְבָתִים, וּמַאי כְּרִיכוֹת? אָמַר רַב יְהוּדָה, אָמַר רַב: הֵן הֵן צְבָתִים, הֵן הֵן כְּרִיכוֹת. צְבָתִים זוּוֵי זוּוֵי, כְּרִיכוֹת דִּכְרִיכָן טוּבָא.§ "מַחְשִׁיךְ עֲלֵיהֶן וּמְבִיאָן".§ וְאַמַּאי? לְעַיְּילִינְהוּ זוּג זוּג! אָמַר רַב יִצְחָק בְּרֵיהּ דְּרַב יְהוּדָה: לְדִידִי מִיפָּרְשָׁא לֵיהּ מִינֵּיהּ דְּאַבָּא: [ג]כָּל שֶׁאִילּוּ מַכְנִיסָן זוּג זוּג וְכָלוֹת קוֹדֶם שְׁקִיעַת הַחַמָּה — מַכְנִיסָן זוּג זוּג, וְאִי לֹא — מַחְשִׁיךְ עֲלֵיהֶן וּמְבִיאָן.§ "וּבַסַּכָּנָה מְכַסָּן וְהוֹלֵךְ".§ וְהָתַנְיָא: [ד]וּבַסַּכָּנָה מוֹלִיכָן פָּחוֹת פָּחוֹת מֵאַרְבַּע אַמּוֹת! אָמַר רַב: לָא קַשְׁיָא; הָא — בְּסַכָּנַת גּוֹיִם הָא בְּסַכָּנַת לִסְטִים.

א"ל

רש"י

אֶחָד חֲדָשׁוֹת. שֶׁאֵין אָדָם טוֹרֵחַ: וְהַשְׁתָּא דְּתָנֵי אֲבוּהּ דִּשְׁמוּאֵל. דְּהַאי חֲדָשׁוֹת – כְּשֶׁיֵּשׁ בָּהֶן רְצוּעוֹת וְאֵינָן מְקוּשָּׁרוֹת כְּעֵין קֶשֶׁר שֶׁל תְּפִלִּין הֶעָשׂוּי כְּמִין אוֹתִיּוֹת. וְכֵן הוּא קָבוּעַ תָּמִיד – אַלְמָא: טַעְמָא מִשּׁוּם קֶשֶׁר הוּא דִּקְשִׁירָה אַב מְלָאכָה, וְאָסוּר לִקְשׁוֹר בְּשַׁבָּת קֶשֶׁר שֶׁל קַיָּימָא: דְּכ"ע לָא טָרַח. דְּטַעְמָא דַּחֲדָשׁוֹת לָאו מִשּׁוּם סְפֵק קָמֵיעָא הוּא[א]: ר' יְהוּדָה לְטַעְמֵיהּ. בְּפֶרֶק "אֵלּוּ קְשָׁרִים" (שבת דף קיג.): חֶבֶל דְּלִי שֶׁנִּפְסַק – כּוֹרֵךְ עָלָיו פּוּנְדָּא אוֹ פְּסִיקְיָא, וּבִלְבַד שֶׁלֹּא יַעַנְבֶנּוּ. אַלְמָא: טַעְמָא מִשּׁוּם דִּקְשִׁירָה הוּא, וְחַיָּיבִין עָלֶיהָ מִשּׁוּם אַב מְלָאכָה: הָא לָאו הָכִי עָנֵיב. בִּתְמִיָּה: הֲלָכָה לְמֹשֶׁה מִסִּינַי. הֵיאָךְ הוּא עָשׂוּי, שֶׁדּוֹמֶה לְדל"ת, וּבִתְפִירָתָן עָשׂוּי כְּמִין שי"ן, וּרְצוּעָה קְטַנָּה קְבוּעָה בָּהֶן וְרֹאשָׁהּ כָּפוּף וְדוֹמֶה לְיו"ד הֲרֵי שַׁדַּי: וְנוֹיֵיהֶן. אוֹתוֹ הֶיכֵּר הָאוֹתִיּוֹת: לְבַר. לַחוּץ שֶׁאֵינָס כְּלַפֵּי הַתְּפִלִּין בֵּין הַבָּתִּים, אֶלָּא כְּנֶגֶד מַרְאִית הָעַיִן. לְפִי שֶׁנֶּאֱמַר בָּהֶן "וְרָאוּ" וגו', וְתַנְיָא, *ר"א הַגָּדוֹל אוֹמֵר: אֵלּוּ תְּפִלִּין שֶׁל רֹאשׁ: הַלּוֹקֵחַ תְּפִלִּין. הַרְבֵּה יַחַד, וְלַחֲזוֹר לְמוֹכְרָן, וְלוֹקְחָן מִמִּי שֶׁאֵינוֹ מוּמְחֶה: בּוֹדֵק שְׁתַּיִם שֶׁל יָד וְאַחַת שֶׁל רֹאשׁ. וְכֵיוָן דְּהוּחְזַק בִּשָׁלֹשׁ – הָוֵה מוּמְחֶה, וְלוֹקֵחַ הַשְּׁאָר בְּלֹא בְּדִיקָה: מַה נַּפְשָׁךְ. מַאי דַּעְתָּךְ, אִי קִים לָךְ דְּגַבְרָא דִּמְזַבֵּן תְּפִלִּין טוּבָא מֵחַד גַּבְרָא זָבֵין לְהוּ, וְהַאי מוֹכֵר נַמִי מֵחַד גַּבְרָא קְנָנְהוּ: לִבְדּוֹק שָׁלֹשׁ בְּשֶׁל יָד אוֹ שָׁלֹשׁ בְּשֶׁל רֹאשׁ. וְתִסְגֵּי לֵיהּ בְּהָכִי לְהִתְחַזֵּק בְּכוּלְּהוּ: כָּל חַד וְחַד נַמִי. כָּל תְּפִלִּין וּתְפִלִּין דִּשְׁמָּא מִי שֶׁמָּכַר לוֹ אֶת אֵלּוּ לֹא מָכַר אֶת אֵלּוּ: רַבִּי הִיא. בְּמַסֶּכֶת יְבָמוֹת (דף סד:) הוּא דְּאָמַר בִּתְרֵי זִימְנֵי הָוְיָא חֲזָקָה: נִשֵּׂאת לָרִאשׁוֹן וָמֵת, לַשֵּׁנִי וָמֵת – לַשְּׁלִישִׁי לֹא תִּנָּשֵׂא: וְכֵן בַּצֶּבֶת הַשֵּׁנִי. אִם יִהְיוּ לוֹ צְבָתִים הַרְבֵּה, וּבְכָל צֶבֶת תְּפִלִּין הַרְבֵּה, קָא סָלְקָא דַּעְתֵּיהּ דְּהָכִי קָאָמַר: בָּדַק בַּצֶּבֶת הָרִאשׁוֹן שְׁנֵי תְפִלִּין – הוּחְזַק כָּל אוֹתוֹ צֶבֶת, וְכֵן בַּשֵּׁנִי – הוּחְזַק גַּם הוּא, וְכֵן בַּשְּׁלִישִׁי וְכֵיוָן דְּהוּחְזַק בִּשְׁלֹשָׁה צְבָתִים כְּשֵׁרִין – הוּחְזְקוּ כָּל הַצְּבָתִים, וְאֵין צָרִיךְ עוֹד לִבְדּוֹק כְּלוּם: מוֹדֶה רַבִּי בִּצְבָתִים. דְּאֵין אֶחָד מוּחְזָק בְּשֶׁל חֲבֵירוֹ שֶׁדֶּרֶךְ לִיקַּח צֶבֶת אֶחָד מֵאִישׁ זֶה, וְצֶבֶת אֶחָד מֵאִישׁ אַחֵר. לְשׁוֹן צֶבֶת – כְּמוֹ "שֹׁל תָּשֹׁלּוּ לָהּ מִן הַצְּבָתִים" (רות ב): לְאַפּוּקֵי מֵחִזְקִיָּה. לְאַשְׁמוּעִינַן, דְּאַף עַל גַּב דִּבְעָלְמָא תְּרֵי הָווּ חֲזָקָה – בִּצְבָתִים לֵית לֵיהּ לְרַבִּי חֲזָקָה, מִדְּקָתָנֵי שְׁלִישִׁי וְגַלֵּי בֵּיהּ, וְהוּא הַדִּין לְכוּלָּם: זוּוֵי זוּוֵי. שֶׁל רֹאשׁ וְשֶׁל יָד קְשׁוּרִין יַחַד, וְכֵן הַרְבֵּה קְשׁוּרֵי זוּג בְּצֶבֶת אַחַת: דִּכְרִיכָן טוּבָא. כִּי הַדְדֵי. וְאֵין ב' ב' קְשׁוּרִים: וְאִי לָאו. שֶׁאֵינָם כָּלוֹת קוֹדֶם שְׁקִיעַת הַחַמָּה, הוֹאִיל וְהוּא צָרִיךְ לִטְרוֹחַ וְלַחֲזוֹר מִשֶּׁתֶּחְשַׁךְ – מַחְשִׁיךְ עַכְשָׁיו עֲלֵיהֶם, וְיוֹצֵא בָּם יַחַד: מוֹלִיכָן כּוּלָּם פָּחוֹת פָּחוֹת מד' אַמּוֹת. קוֹדֶם שֶׁיַּגִּיעַ לְאַרְבַּע אַמּוֹת יַעֲמוֹד לָפוּשׁ, וְחוֹזֵר וְהוֹלֵךְ פָּחוֹת פָּחוֹת מֵאַרְבַּע אַמּוֹת, וְכֵן תָּמִיד. דְּהַשְׁתָּא כָּל זִמְנָא הָוְיָא עֲקִירָה וְהַנָּחָה, וְאֵין כָּאן הַעֲבָרָה אַרְבַּע אַמּוֹת יַחַד: בְּסַכָּנַת גּוֹיִם. דִּמְבַזּוּ לְהוּ לִתְפִלִּין – מוֹלִיכָן: בְּסַכָּנַת לִיסְטִים. יִשְׂרָאֵל, דְּקָטְלֵי לֵיהּ מִשּׁוּם מָמוֹנוֹ, וְלִתְפִלִּין לָא מְבַזּוּ לְהוּ – מְכַסָּן:

הָכִי

תוספות

אמר רב חסדא זאת אומרת עניבה פסולה בתפילין. תימה: וכי לא ידע רב חסדא דלר"י עניבה קשירה מעלייתא היא, כדקאמר אביי? וי"ל: דניחא ליה לאוקמי מתני' דאוסרת בחדשות כרבנן דר"י, דאמרי לאו קשירה הוא. אי נמי: דקסבר אפילו לר"י שריא עניבה, דסתמא דעתיה להתיר ולעשות קשר גמור בחול, כדפירשתי לעיל:

אביי אמר ר"י לטעמיה כו'. ורבי מאיר דשרי בחדשות קסבר דלאו קשירה היא. ותימה: דבעיא היא בריש "אלו קשרים" *עניבה לר"מ קשירה היא אם לאו, וקאי בתיקו! ואומר ר"י: דהתם בדמיהדק, והכא בלא מיהדק. וקצת נראה דהלכה כר"י דעניבה קשירה היא, מדמסיק אביי: דרבי יהודה לטעמיה, וסתם מתניתין אתיא כרבי יהודה. מיהו, מדפריך סתמא דהתלמוד בפשיטות וליענביה מיענב, משמע דאין הלכה כר' יהודה. ומכאן אר"ת: דאין צריך בכל יום להתיר קשר תפילין ולחזור ולקשור בשעה שמניחן, (א)כגון שהיה אומר רבינו אליהו, דא"כ חדשות אמאי אסר הכא משום קשירה? הא לא הוי קשר של קיימא! ומה שהביא רבינו אליהו ראיה מדאמר בסוף "הקומץ רבה" (מנחות דף לה:): תפילין מאימתי מברך עליהן – משעת הנחה עד שעת קשירה – לאו היינו קשירה ממש, אלא קשירה דהתם היינו הידוק, כמו "שליא קשורה בוולד" (נדה דף כו:) וכן "קשורה בו ככלב" (ע"ג דף ה.):

קשר של תפילין הל"מ. פי' בקונטרס: הל"מ היאך הוא עשוי, שדומה לדל"ת, ובתפירתו עשוי כמין שי"ן, ורצועה קבועה בהם וראשה כפוף ודומה ליו"ד – הרי שדי. ואין נראה לר"י. דאין הל"מ אלא השי"ן בלבד, כדמשמע בפרק "במה מדליקין" (שבת דף כח:), דקאמר: אלא הא דתני רב יוסף לא הוכשרו למלאכת שמים אלא עור בהמה טהורה בלבד (ב) מ"למען תהיה תורת ה' בפיך" – מן המותר בפיך למאי הלכתא? וקאמר לשי"ן. והאמר אביי: שי"ן של תפילין הל"מ. ומשני: אלא לרצועותיהן. ולא פריך מד' ויו"ד, משמע דאין קדושה אלא בשי"ן בלבד והיא דווקא הלכה, ולא מצינו בשום מקום שיהא הקשר קרוי ד'*:

ונוויהן לבר. פי' ר"י: דאקשר קאי, כמו שפי' בערוך. נוי הקשר יפנה לצד חוץ, אותו צד שנראה כעין ד. להכי מייתי לה הכא*:

הלוקח תפילין ממי שאינו מומחה וכו'. תימה דבפרק "התכלת" (מנחות דף מג:) תניא: תפילין יש להן בדיקה, ואין ניקחין אלא מן המומחה. ואין לומר דבלא בדיקה קאמר, דאין ניקחין אלא מן המומחה – דהא קתני סיפא ספרים ומזוזות יש להן בדיקה, וניקחין מכל אדם. ואור"י: דהתם לכתחלה קאמר, דאין ניקחין אלא מן המומחה, שלא יצטרך לקרוע כל התפר ולבודקן ואיכא בזיון תפילין, ואיכא נמי למיחש שמא יתעצל לטרוח לבודקן ויסמוך להניחן בלא בדיקה לצורך שעה, והכא איירי בדיעבד שכבר לקח, או כגון שאינו מוצא מומחה לקנות ממנו. *

מצאן צבתים או כריכות מחשיך עליהן. תימה: בחדשות נמי, דאי אפשר לקשור אמאי לא יצטרך להחשיך עליהן משום בזיון דתפילין? ויש לומר: דישנות דווקא, דחזי להכניס זוג זוג, עשו תקנה אפילו כשהן מרובין ואין כלות קודם שקיעת החמה:

רבי

מסורת הש"ס

[סוכה לג: וש"נ]

מנחות לה:

[ברכות ו.]

[יבמות כו. סד: כתובות מג: ב"מ קו: סנהדרין פא:]

[כרב"א איתא זווי זווי]

[שבת דף קיא:]

[ועי' תוס' ברכות ו. ד"ה אלו וכו']

[ועי' תוס' מנחות לה: ד"ה ונוייהן ועי' בפי' רש"י דהכא ודהתם]

עין משפט נר מצוה

יג א מיי' פי"ט מהלכות שבת הל' כד סמג לאוין סה טוש"ע א"ח סי' שא סעיף מב:

יד ב מיי' פ"ב מהלכות תפילין הלכה י סמג עשין כב טוש"ע א"ח סי' לט סעיף ט:

טו ג ד מיי' פי"ט מהל' שבת הלכה כג כד סמג לאוין סה טוש"ע א"ח סי' שא סעיף מב:

רבינו חננאל

אמר משמיה דרב קשר של תפילין הל"מ אמר רב נחמן ונוייהו לבר (ואי) איכא למימר דעניב להו כעין קשירה דידהו אמר רב חסדא זאת אומרת עניבה פסולה בתפילין אמר רב חסדא הלוקח תפילין כו' ואוקימנא בדזבין מחד גברא ובעינן עד (דמנחי) [דמתמחי] בשל יד ובשל ראש והא דתני רב כהנא בתפילין בודק שתים בשל ראש אוקימנא לר' דאמר בתרי זימני הוי חזקה ומודה ר' בצבתין דמתרי תלתא זבין הלכך צריך לבדוק בכל צבת שתים כדקתני סיפא וכן צבת שני וכן צבת שלישי ואפי' רביעי ואפילו חמישי דינם שוין והא דקתני שלישי לאפוקי מרבי חזקיה ואפילו רביעי ואפילו חמישי הכי דינייהו. מצאן צבתין או כריכות. אמר רב יהודה כו' מחשיך עליהן ומביאן כולן כאחת ובסכנה מכסן והולך לו. אוקימנא בר"א בסכנת גוים כגון שמד אבל בסכנת לסטים מוליכן פחות פחות מארבע אמות

רב נסים גאון

פ"י המוצא תפילין

אביי אמר רבי יהודה לטעמיה דאמר עניבה קשירה מעליותא היא ואיתא הא דר' יהודה במסכת שבת בפרק אלו קשרין (דף קיג) חבל דלי שנפסק לא היה קושרו אלא עונבו ר' יהודה אומר כורך עליו פונדא או פסקיא ובלבד שלא יענבנו ואמרי קסבר ר' יהודה עניבה קשירה היא ואיתא נמי בפרק אור לארבעה עשר (פסחים דף יא): הא מני רבי היא דאמר בתרי זימני הויא חזקה. עיקר דברי רבי (במסכת שבת) [בתוספתא דשבת] בפרק ט"ז נישאת לראשון ומת לשני ומת לשלישי לא תינשא דברי רבי ואיתא בגמ' דיבמות (דף סד) בפרק הבא על יבמתו ובמסכת נדה (דף סד) בפרק האשה שהיא עושה צרכיה:

ומאן

הגהות הב"ח

(א) תוס' ד"ה אביי וכו' בשעה שמניחן כמו שהיה אומר: (ב) ד"ה קשר וכו' אלא עור בהמה טהורה בלבד למאי הלכתא לתפילין (תפילין) בהדיא כתיב בה למען תהיה תורת ה' בפיך מן המותר בפיך וקאמר אלא לעורן ופריך והאמר אביי שי"ן:

הגהות מהר"ב רנשבורג

[א] רש"י ד"ה דכולי עלמא וכו' דטעמא דחדשות לאו משום ספק קמיעא הוא. אלא טעמא דחדשות מפני שאין מקושרות ואסור לקושרן בשבת ואם מניחן בלא קשר אין זה דרך מלבוש בחול והוי ליה משאוי ור"מ דשרי בחדשות משום דס"ל דמותר לקושרן בשבת קשר שאינו של קיימא בקשר מרופה עכ"ל הריטב"א ועי' בדף הקודם בתוס' ד"ה וכי אדם טורח וכו' ודו"ק:

[שייך לעיל לה: במשנה]

מז [א טוש"ע א"ח סי' שנב סעיף א]:

[ג"ז שייך שם]

א"ל אביי: במאי אוקימתא למתניתין — בסכנת גוים, אימא סיפא; ר' שמעון אומר: נותנן לחבירו, וחבירו לחבירו. כל שכן דאוושא מילתא! חסורי מיחסרא, והכי קתני: במה דברים אמורים — בסכנת גוים אבל בסכנת ליסטים — מוליכן פחות פחות מד' אמות.§ "רבי שמעון אומר נותנן לחבירו וכו'.§ במאי קמיפלגי? מר סבר: פחות מארבע אמות עדיף, דאי אמרת נותנן לחבירו וחבירו לחבירו — אוושא מלתא דשבת. ומר סבר: נותנן לחבירו עדיף, דאי אמרת מוליכן פחות מארבע אמות — זימנין דלאו אדעתיה, ואתי לאתויינהו ארבע אמות ברה"ר.§ "וכן בנו".§ בנו מאי בעי התם?! דבי מנשה תנא: בשילדתו אמו בשדה. ומאי אפילו הן מאה — דאע"ג דקשיא ליה ידא, אפילו הכי — הא עדיפא.§ "רבי יהודה אומר נותן אדם חבית".§ ולית ליה לרבי יהודה הא *דתנן: הבהמה והכלים כרגלי הבעלים?! אמר ריש לקיש משום לוי סבא: הכא במאי עסקינן — במערן מחבית לחבית. ורבי יהודה לטעמיה, דאמר: מים אין בהם ממש. *דתנן: רבי יהודה פוטר במים, מפני שאין בהן ממש. ומאי "לא תהלך זו" — לא יהלך מה שבזו יותר מרגלי הבעלים. איתמר דשמעת ליה לר' יהודה היכא דבליען בעיסה, היכא דאיתנהו בעינייהו מי שמעת ליה?! השתא בקדירה אמר רבי יהודה לא בטלי, בעינייהו בטלי?! *דתניא, רבי יהודה אומר: מים ומלח בטלין בעיסה, ואין בטלין בקדירה, מפני רוטבה! אלא אמר רבא: הכא בחבית שקנתה שביתה, ומים שלא קנו שביתה עסקינן, דבטלה חבית לגבי מים. *כדתנן: המוציא החי במטה — פטור אף על המטה, מפני שהמטה טפילה לו. המוציא אוכלין פחות מכשיעור בכלי — פטור אף על הכלי, מפני שהכלי טפל לו. מתיב רב יוסף, ר' יהודה אומר: בשיירא נותן אדם חבית לחבירו, וחבירו לחבירו. בשיירא — אין, שלא בשיירא — לא! אלא אמר רב יוסף: כי תנן נמי במתניתין — בשיירא תנן. אביי אמר: בשיירא — אפילו חבית שקנתה שביתה ומים שקנו שביתה. שלא בשיירא — חבית שקנתה שביתה ומים שלא קנו שביתה. רב אשי אמר: הכא בחבית דהפקר עסקינן, ומים דהפקר עסקינן. ומאן אמרו לו — רבי יוחנן בן נורי היא, *דאמר: חפצי הפקר קונין שביתה. ומאי לא תהלך זו יותר מרגלי הבעלים — לא יהלכו אלו יותר מכלים שיש להם בעלים.§

מתני' *[א]היה קורא בספר על האיסקופה, ונתגלגל הספר מידו, גוללו אצלו. היה קורא בראש הגג ונתגלגל הספר מידו, עד שלא הגיע לעשרה טפחים — גוללו אצלו, משהגיע לעשרה טפחים — הופכו על הכתב. רבי יהודה אומר: אפילו אין מסולק מן הארץ אלא כמלא*(א) מחט — גוללו אצלו. ר' שמעון אומר: אפילו בארץ עצמו — גוללו אצלו, שאין לך דבר משום שבות עומד בפני כתבי הקודש.§ **גמ'** האי איסקופה ה"ד? אילימא איסקופה רשות היחיד, וקמה רשות הרבים, ולא גזרינן דילמא נפיל ואתי לאתויי, מני

*רבי שמעון אומר נותנן לחבירו כו'. נראה דאם אין שם חברים היה מתיר רבי שמעון להוליך פחות מארבע אמות, דלא גרע מכים דפרק "מי שהחשיך" (שבת דף קנג:). והתם נמי, אם היו חברים הרבה, והיו כולן שותפין בו — נראה דלרבי שמעון נותנו לחבירו וחבירו לחבירו, דהכי עדיפא ליה. ***הכי** גרסינן וכן בנו ואפילו הן מאה. ולא כספרים דגרסי ואפי' הן מאה, וכן בנו. דבגמרא מוכח דאפילו הן מאה — אבנו קאי, דמפרש טעמא: אע"ג דקשיא ליה ידא: **את** החי במטה פטור. וא"ת: נהי שהחי נושא את עצמו, להוי כמו זה יכול וזה אינו יכול — דיכול חייב כדמוכח ב"המצניע" (שבת דף צג.)! ואור"י: דמכ"מ מיפטר הכא, משום דגמרינן כל הוצאות ממשכן, ושם לא היו נושאים בעלי חיים. דאילים ותחשים מוליכין ברגליהן, וחלזון מיד כשיוצא מן הים היו מוליאין דמו בעודו בכחו, כי היכי דליזליל ליבעיה כדאמר בסוף פרק "כלל גדול" (שם דף עה.)*:

[ועי' תוס' שבת לה. ד"ה אמאי]

הכא בחבית דהפקר ומים דהפקר עסקינן. דלא קנו שביתה (ו)לזה ולא לזה, ואפילו חוץ לתחום דקאמר — היינו ממקום שביתת המים. אבל חוץ לתחום של הזוכה בהם תחילה — לא יוליכו אותן, למאי דפרישית לעיל בפרק "מי שהוציאוהו" (דף מו.), דכרגלי כל אדם דקתני גבי נהרות המושכין — היינו כרגלי הממלא. והא דקאמר: נותנו לחבירו וחבירו לחבירו — לא משום דלא מצי אזיל התם, אלא משום דאסור להעביר ארבע אמות ברה"ר. ועוד יש לומר: דיכול להוליאם חוץ לתחום(ז) שזכה בהן תחילה, וכגון שלא נתכוון לזכות בהן לא לעצמו ולא לאחרים בהגבהתו, אלא מה ששותים, וכענין זה אפי' בי"ט שייך לשנות נותנן לחבירו וחבירו, לחבירו אע"ג דליכא איסור ד' אמות: ואי

הכי גרסינן: במאי אוקימתא למתני' בסכנת ליסטים אימא סיפא וכו'. כיון דליסטים לא מבזו להו. אמאי קא מזלזל ר"ש באיסורא דשבתא כולי האי! כל שכן דהא דר"ש גריעא(ב) (כולי האי) מתנא קמא, ואיכא זילזול שבת טפי, דאוושא מילתא דהנך גברי דמקילינן כולי האי בשבת וכסוי דת"ק עדיף. לשון אחר ועיקר, ולא לשבש הספרים: מתני' בסכנת עו"ג שגזרו גזירה שלא יניחו תפילין. והאי ובסכנה מכסן והולך לו אכולה מתניתין קאי. והכי קאמר: ובסכנה, שאם ימצאו בידו או ישמע למלכות יהרג בין מעט בין רבים — מכסן בטליתו, שלא יוטלו כ"כ בבזיון ומניחם שם והולך ולא יזיז משם שמא ירגישו בו ויתחייב למלכות. וברייתא — בליסטים גוים, ואסיפא קאי, דקתני: מחשיך עליהן ומביאן, ובסכנת ליסטים שהוא ירא להחשיך שם — מוליכן פחות פחות מד' אמות וכו' ולא יניחם שם — שלא יזלזלו הליסטים בהם וינהגו בהם מנהג בזיון. ובמאי אוקימנא למתניתין בסכנת גוים שלא יתחייב למלכות — אימא סיפא וכו' וכ"ש דאוושא מלתא וישמע למלכות יותר משאם מכניסן זוג זוג או מחשיך עליהם לכולם וזה עיקר, מדלא גרסינן ברישא כל שכן דאוושא מלתא דשבת, כדגרסינן בסיפא מכלל דהאי אוושא דמילתא לאו אזלזולא דשבת קפיד, אלא אסכנת נפשות קפיד: אע"ג דקשיא ליה. שמטלטלין אותו מיד ליד: הא עדיפא. בשבתא, ולא יטלטלנו הוא לבדו פחות פחות מד' אמות: כרגלי הבעלים. שהשואל או לוקח בהמה או כלים מחבירו ביום טוב — אינו יכול להוליכם אלא למקום שהבעלים הראשונים מותרין לילך שם, ואם עירבו לצפון לא יוליכנו זה לדרום: מחבית לחבית. והשניה שלו, וכן עושה תמיד ולקמיה מפרש מאי לא תהלך זו: אין בהם ממש. לקנות שביתה אצל בעליהם הראשונים, וכל אדם מותר להוליכן כרגליו: פוטר במים. פלוגתייהו בפרק בתרא דביצה: האשה ששאלה מחבירתה תבלין לקדירה, ומים ומלח לעיסתה — הרי הן כרגלי שתיהן, אין העיסה הולכת אלא למקום ששתיהן מותרות לילך שם. ואם עירבה זו לצפון וזו לדרום — אין עיסה זזה ממקומה, לפי שאין לזו של צפון אפילו אמה אחת בדרום וה"מ כשנתנו עירובן לסוף אלפים. ר' יהודה פוטר במים, שאין בעלת המים אוסרת על בעלת הקמח כלום: ומאי לא תהלך זו. הא רבי יהודה נמי בחבית לא קאמר דיכולה חבית להלך יותר מרגלי הבעלים, דהא אוקמינן מתני' במערן מחבית לחבית: מפני רוטבה. שניכר ואם השאילה מים לקדירתה, הרי היא כרגלי שתיהן: מים שלא קנו שביתה. שנתמלאו היום ממעין הנובע או מן הנהר, דתניא (לעיל דף מו.): נהרות המושכין ומעיינות הנובעים — הרי הן כרגלי כל אדם: דבטלה חבית לגבייהו. מפני שהיא טפילה להן. ורבנן פליגי למימר דלא תהלך זו, דלא בטלה לגבייהו: פטור אף על המטה. הואיל ופטור על החי, דקיימא לן: חי נושא את עצמו: בשיירא. שחונה בבקעה, שאנוסין הן, שאין להם מים — שרי להו רבנן דתיבטיל: כרבי יוחנן בן נורי. בפרק "מי שהוציאוהו": **מתני'** היה קורא בספר. כל ספרים העשוים בימי הראשונים עשוין (*בגליון) כספר תורה שלנו: גוללו אצלו. הואיל וראשו אחד בידו ובגמרא מפרש לה: לעשרה טפחים. לעשרה התחתונים שברשות הרבים(ג) וכולן מפרש בגמרא: הופכו על הכתב. האותיות כלפי הכותל, שלא יהא מוטל כל כך בבזיון, ומניחו עד שתחשך: משום שבות. כגון זו שלא נפל מידו, שהרי אחז בראשו אחד, ואין כאן אלא משום גזירה דילמא נפיל כוליה מידיה ואתי לאתויי. כל איסור דרבנן הוי שבות: **גמ'** אי נימא איסקופה רשות היחיד. גבוהה עשרה ורחבה ארבעה: וקמה רשות הרבים. ולפניה רשות הרבים וקאמר מתני' אע"ג דמונח ראשו ברשות הרבים — גוללו(ד) ברשות היחיד: ולא גזרינן דלמא(ה) נפל. כוליה מידיה, דאיכא חיוב חטאת, ואתי לאיתויי: מני

[נ"ל בגליון]

רבינו חננאל

ר"ש אמר בשעת סכנת לסטים [אינו] מוליכן פחות פחות מד' אמות זמנין דמשתלי ואתי לאתויינהו ד' אמות ברה"ר [אלא] נותנן לחבירו וחבירו לחבירו עד שמגיע לחצר החיצונה הא עדיפא דהא דאמר פחות פחות מד' אמות זמנין דמשתלי ואתי לאתויינהו ד' אמות ברה"ר ות"ק סבר הא עדיפא דהא כר' שמעון אוושא מלתא ומתיידע לכל. וכן בנו נותנו לחבירו וחבירו לחבירו. מאי בעי התם תנא דבי שמואל בשילדתו אמו בשדה. ואע"ג דקשה ליה לתינוק השלמתו מיד ליד הא עדיפא ליה מלהוליכו פחות פחות מד' אמות. ר' יהודה אמר כו' אתינן לאוקומי לאו חבית ממש אלא מי החבית ובמערה מחבית לחבית [והחבית] קני שביתה ואסור. אבל מיא לית בהו ממש. ור' יהודה לטעמיה דתנן ר' יהודה פוטר במים מפני שאין בהן ממש. ודחינן אימור דשמעת ליה לר' יהודה במיא דלית בהו ממש במיא דבליעי בעיסה במיא בעינייהו מי שמעת ליה והא איהו דאמר מים ומלח אין בטילין בקדירה מפני שהיא רוטבא ואוקמה רבא בחבית שקנתה שביתה ונתמלאת בשבת ממעיין נובע כיוצא בהן דלא קנו שביתה דבטלה לה חבית לגבי מים ומטלטלת אגב מימיה. כדתנן את החי במטה כו'. ואוקמה רב יוסף למתני' בשיירא כדתניא ר' יהודה אומר בשיירא נותן אדם חבית לחבירו וחבירו לחבירו ואתא רב אשי ואוקמה בחבית (דאפקר) [דהפקר] ומים (דאפקר) [דהפקר] ומאן אמרו לו רבי יוחנן בן נורי דאמר חפצי הפקר קונין להן שביתה והכי קאמר ליה לר' יהודה לא תהלך זה יותר מן הכלים שיש להן בעלים וקי"ל כרב יוסף דתניא בהדיה כוותיה. היה קורא בספר כו' אוקמה רב יהודה באיסקופה רה"י וקמה עוברת רה"ר. ולא גזר דלמא נפיל לרה"ר ואתי לאתויי

רב נסים גאון

מאן אמרו לו ר' יוחנן בן נורי הוא דאמר חפצי הפקר קונין שביתה. איתא בפרק מי שהוציאוהו גוים (לעיל דף מז) וכבר כתבנוה בפרק בכל מערבין:

הגהות הב"ח

(א) גמ' במשנה אלא כמלא החוט גוללו [וכן הוא גירסת הירושלמי והרי"ף]: (ב) רש"י ד"ה הכי גרסינן וכו' גריעא מת"ק דאיכא וכו' דמקילי כולי האי: (ג) ד"ה לעשרה וכו' וכולה מפרש בגמ': (ד) ד"ה וקמה וכו' גוללו אצלו ברשות היחיד: (ה) ד"ה ולא גזרינן דילמא נפיק כוליה מידיה ואתי לאתויי דאיכא חיוב חטאת הס"ד: (ו) תום' ד"ה הכא וכו' דלא קני שביתה לא לזה ולא לזה ואפילו: (ז) בא"ד דיכול להוליאן חוץ לתחום של הזוכה בהן תחילה:

[ביצה לז.]

[שם]

[שם לט.]

[שבת צג: קמא.]

[לעיל מה: ביצה לח.]

[שבת ה: לקמן קב.]

[גי' ירושלמי ורי"ף כמלא חוט]

מני ר"ש היא, דאמר: כל דבר שהוא משום שבות אינו עומד בפני כתבי הקודש. אימא סיפא, רבי יהודה אומר: אפילו אין מסולק מן הארץ אלא מלא החוט — גוללו אצלו. רבי שמעון אומר: אפילו בארץ עצמה — גוללו אצלו. רישא וסיפא רבי שמעון, מציעתא רבי יהודה?! אמר רב יהודה: אין, רישא וסיפא ר"ש, מציעתא רבי יהודה. רבה אמר: הכא באיסקופה הנדרסת עסקינן, ומשום בזיון כתבי הקדש שרו רבנן. איתיביה אביי: תוך ד' אמות גוללו אצלו, חוץ לד' — הופכו על הכתב. ואי אמרת באיסקופה(א) נדרסת עסקינן, מה לי תוך ד' אמות מה לי חוץ לארבע אמות? אלא אמר אביי: הכא באיסקופה כרמלית עסקינן, ורשות הרבים עוברת לפניה. תוך ד' אמות, דאי נפיל ומייתי ליה לא אתי לידי חיוב חטאת — שרו ליה רבנן. חוץ לארבע אמות, דאי מייתי ליה אתי לידי חיוב חטאת — לא שרו ליה רבנן. אי הכי, תוך ד' אמות נמי, נגזר דילמא מעייל מרה"ר לרה"י! וכי תימא: כיון דמפסקת כרמלית לית לן בה — *והאמר רבא: המעביר חפץ מתחלת ארבע לסוף ארבע, והעבירו דרך עליו — חייב! הכא במאי עסקינן — באיסקופה ארוכה(ב) אדהכי והכי מידכר. ואיבעית אימא: לעולם באסקופה שאינה ארוכה, וסתם כתבי הקדש עיוני מעיין בהו ומנח להו. וליחוש דילמא מעיין בהו ברה"ר, ועייל להו בהדיא לרה"י! הא מני *בן עזאי היא, דאמר: מהלך כעומד דמי. ודילמא זריק להו מזרק, *דאמר רבי יוחנן: מודה בן עזאי בזורק? אמר רב *אחא בר אהבה: זאת אומרת: *אין מזרקין כתבי הקודש. §"היה קורא בראש הגג" וכו'. § ומי שרי? והתניא: *כותבי ספרים תפילין ומזוזות לא התירו להן להפך יריעה על פניה, אלא פורס עליה את הבגד! התם אפשר, הכא לא אפשר. ואי לא אפיך, איכא בזיון כתבי הקודש טפי. § "הופכו על הכתב". *והא לא נח! [אמר רבא:] בכותל משופע [אמר ליה אביי:] במאי אוקימתא למתניתין — בכותל משופע, אימא סיפא: רבי יהודה אומר: אפילו אינו מסולק מן הארץ אלא מלא החוט — גוללו אצלו. והא נח ליה! חסורי מיחסרא והכי קתני: במה דברים אמורים — בכותל משופע, אבל בכותל

רש"י

מני. מתני' דלא גזר: ר"ש היא דאמר. לא גזרו שבות בכתבי הקדש. דאי ר' יהודה — הא אמר אם מסולק מן הארץ מלא החוט, דלא נח — הוא דגוללו אצלו, דליכא למגזר מידי, דלא דמי לנפילה כלל, אבל הונח כל דהו — אסור, דגזרינן איגודו בידו אטו היכא דנפל כוליה: הנדרסת. לעולם איסקופה רה"י היא אבל נדרסת, דרגל הרבים עוברת דרך לה ובמקום דדריסת רגלי בני אדם עומדין — איכא בזיון כתבי הקדש, ולהכי שריוה לגוללו אצלו. דלא דמיא לקורא בגג, דהתם ליכא בזיון כולי האי. משום הכי, היכא דנח — גזר רבי יהודה, אבל בהא — מודה. דכיון דאוגדו בידו, ושבות בעלמא הוא — לא גזרינן: תוך ארבע אמות. אקורא על האסקופה קאי, ולא ידענא היכא הוא. תוך ארבע אמות שלא נתגלגל הספר עד ארבע אמות בקרקע: מה לי חוץ לארבע. הא כולה שבות היא, דאוגדו בידו. ומה לי מעביר ד' אמות ברשות הרבים, מה לי מכניס מרשות הרבים לאיסקופה רשות היחיד(ג) דהא קשרית לה משום דאוגדו בידו, ויש כאן משום בזיון. וכי היכי דשרית להכניס מרשות הרבים לאיסקופה, הכי נמי אית לן למישרי להעביר ד' אמות ברה"ר: איסקופה כרמלית. רחבה ארבעה ואין גובהה עשרה, וחוצה לה רשות הרבים, ולפנים הימנה רשות היחיד: ומייתי ליה. מרה"ר לאיסקופה אין כאן חיוב חטאת, ואפילו אין אוגדו בידו. דהא מרשות הרבים לכרמלית מעייל, הכא דאוגדו בידו — שרי ליה לכתחלה: חייב חטאת. שמעביר ארבע אמות ברה"ר, הכא דאוגדו בידו לא שרו ליה לכתחלה: נמי נגזר. לרבי יהודה, דגזר שבות אף בכתבי הקדש נגזר דילמא נפל כוליה מידו, ואזיל ושקיל ליה ברשות הרבים ומייתי ליה ברגליו בתוך הבית דרך האיסקופה, וקא מעייל מרשות הרבים לרשות היחיד: וכי תימא וכו' דרך עליו. למעלה מראשו, שעקרו מרשות הרבים והוליכו דרך למעלה מראשו, והניחו לסוף ארבע חייב. ואע"ג דאוירא מקום פטור, דגבוה(ד) ואין בו מקום רוחב ארבע. אלמא: כיון דלא נח במקום פטור — לא מהני — הכא נמי לא מהני — כיון דלא נח באיסקופה, אע"ג דדרים עלה — לאו הנחת גופו הוא, אלא א"כ עמד לפוש: באיסקופה ארוכה. שיש לה משך גדול ברחבה מרשות הרבים עד תוך הבית, דאי נמי נפיל כוליה מידו — לא אתי לידי חיוב חטאת. דאדהכי נזכר ועומד לפוש על האיסקופה, והדר מעייל ליה: סתם כתבי הקודש עיוני מעייני בהו. כי מטי באסקופה, והרי עומד בכרמלית: ודילמא. נפיל כוליה לרה"ר, ושקיל ליה ומעיין ביה התם, ומעייל להו להדיא לבית, ולא קאי אאסקופה מידי: מהלך כעומד דמי. הלכך, ליכא למיגזר מידי. דאי נפיל כוליה ומעייל ליה, כיון דדרים על האסקופה — הרי הוא כעומד בכרמלית, ואין כאן חיוב חטאת: דא"ר יוחנן. בפ"ק דשבת (דף ו.) דזורק לאו כעומד דמי: להפוך. יריעת קלף על פניה להגין עליה שלא יעלה אבק על האותיות: לא אפשר. שאין לו בגד לפרוס: והא לא נח. ואפי' שבות ליכא: בכותל משופע. דכיון דבולט למטה, נח על בליטתו: למטה

תוספות

ואי אמרת באיסקופה הנדרסת מה לי תוך ארבע אמות מה לי חוץ לארבע אמות. משום דקאי עליה דרבה, מקשי לרבה. והוא הדין דהאי פירכא נמי הויא לרב יהודה, דאוקי רישא כר"ש: אלא אמר אביי הכא באיסקופת כרמלית עסקינן. וא"ת: והא לא מפליג אביי בין כרמלית לרה"ר לקמן (צט.), גבי לא יעמוד אדם ברה"י וישתה ברה"ר. ואיבעיא להו: כרמלית מאי? ואמר אביי: היא היא. ואין לומר דדוקא בכתבי הקדש שרי הכא, משום בזיון אבל בשאר מילי אסור — דלקמן (דף קג.) משמע דליכא שבות כלל באיסקופה כרמלית, גבי דחותכין יבלת. דקאמר: ולאו מי אוקימנא באיסקופה כרמלית, ורה"ר לפניה. וכיון דאגודו בידו — אפילו שבות נמי ליכא. משמע: דאי הוי שבות — לא הוה שרינן גבי כתבי הקדש, משום דשבות דמקדש במדינה לא התירו. ואור"י: דגבי שתיה שייך למיגזר טפי שמא יביא אצלו, וכן מחט התחובה לו בבגדו דאסרינן לצאת בה מבעוד יום שמא ישכח ויצא, דמייתי לה אההיא דלקמן בפ"ק דשבת (דף יא:) — בהנהו שייך למגזר טפי גזירה לגזירה מההיא דהכא. וא"ת: כיון *דפרישית דספר דהכא לאו דוקא, מאי איריא דנקט ספר משאר מילי? ולפי ההוא לישנא דמסקינן, דסתם כתבי הקדש עיוני מעיין בהו — ניחא, דספר הוי דווקא. וי"ל: דנקט ספר לאשמועינן דבראש הגג לא יגלול אצלו, לאפוקי מדרבי שמעון דאמר: שאין לך דבר משום שבות עומד בפני כתבי הקדש: **והאמר** רבא המעביר חפץ מתחלת ארבע לסוף ארבע והעבירו דרך עליו חייב. פירש בקונטרס, דרך עליו — למעלה מיו"ד, שהוא מקום פטור. ותימה לר"י: דאדמייתי מדרבא, הוה ליה לאיתויי מת"ק דבן עזאי, דאמר בפ"ק דשבת (דף ה:): המוציא מחנות לפלטיא דרך סטיו — חייב, דהיינו דרך מקום פטור. וע"כ שמיע ליה ההיא ברייתא, דבסמוך מייתי מילתא דבן עזאי. וכן קשה לקמן (צט.) גבי עומד אדם ברה"י ומטלטל ברה"ר, ובלבד שלא יוציא חוץ לד' אמות. וקאמר בגמרא: הא הוציא — חייב חטאת. לימא מסייע לרבא, דאמר: המעביר חפץ כו'. ופירש שם הקונטרס: דמתני' נמי מיירי בעומד על הגג שלמעלה מי', דהוי כעין ההיא דרבא דאיירי במעביר דרך עליו. וקשה לפירושו: דגג מאן דכר שמיה? דרשות היחיד קתני במתני', ולא גג, וע"ק דבפ"ק דשבת (דף ח:) גבי עומד אדם על האיסקופה כו' מסיק: ובלבד שלא יטול מבעל הבית ויתן לעני, ומעני ויתן לבעל הבית. ואם נטל ונתן — שלשתן פטורין. וקאמר: ליהוי תיובתא דרבא, דאמר רבא: המעביר חפץ כו'. ומאי קושיא? ה"ל למימר דרבא סבר כרבנן דבן עזאי! לכך נראה לר"י לפרש "דרך עליו" כפי' ר"ח, שפירש בפ"ק דשבת*: דרך עליו — היינו מימינו לשמאלו. דהוה סלקא דעתך דמעביר מצד ימינו לשמאלו דרך גופו, דהוי חשובה כמונחת — אפ"ה חייב, דחשובה כמהלכת, דהא מהלכת היא. והשתא אתי שפיר, דההיא (ה)עומד אדם על האיסקופה דהכא ודלקמן — איירי שעומד במקום אחד ואינו זז ממקומו, ומעביר מכאן לכאן דרך גופו. ואיירי (*לקמן) כגון שמשליש ארבע על ידי זריקה, ולהכי לא מייתי אלא מדרבא אע"ג דידע לברייתא דבן עזאי: **הכא** לא אפשר. פי' בקונט': משום דאין לו בגד מזומן. ובחנס פי' כן, דאפי' יש לו, מאותו טעם דאסור לגוללו אצלו אסור, לפרוש שום בגד: **והא** לא נח. הוה מצי לאוקמא כר"ע, דאית ליה*) קלוטה כמי שהונחה דמיא. אלא ניחא ליה לאוקמא אפי' כרבנן. ואע"ג דאם הוציא ידו מליאה פירות לחוץ, אמר בריש מסכת שבת (דף ג:) דאסור להחזירה — לא דמי להכא. דהתם גזרינן גופו ברה"י וידו ברה"ר אטו גופו וידו ברה"ר, דאז איכא איסורא דאורייתא אי הדר מעייל לה, דהרי נח. אבל הכא, אפי' הוה כוליה ספר התם — אכתי לא נח:

*) [שבת לז.]

נימא

עין משפט נר מצוה

טז א מיי' פט"ו מהל' שבת הלכה כא סמג לאוין סה טוש"ע א"ח סי' שנב סעיף א:

יז ב מיי' פי"ב מהל' שבת הלכה יד:

יח ג מיי' פ"ו מהלכות ס"ת הלכה ג סמג עשין כה טוש"ע י"ד סי' רפב סעיף ה:

יט ד מיי' פ"י מהל' תפילין הלכה יז טוש"ע י"ד סי' רעו [וכרב אלפס הלכות ס"ת דף סח.]:

דפריך דספר וכו' כצ"ל רש"ל. [וכ"ה ברש"ל מגיה להיפך מן דפריך על דפרישית]

רבינו חננאל

ומתני' ר' שמעון היא דאמר אין דבר משום שבות כגון זה דגולל עומד בפני כתבי הקודש ורישא וסיפא ר' שמעון ומציעתא ר' יהודה ורבה אוקמה באיסקופה נדרסת ומשום דלא נדרסי כתבי [הקודש] שרו רבנן ונדחו דברי רבה ואוקמה (כאביי) [אביי] באיסקופה כרמלית ורה"ר עוברת לפניה. תוך ד' אמות לרה"ר דאי נפיל ומייתו לה לא אתי לידי חיוב חטאת לא גזור רבנן לגוללו אצלו (ככרמלית) [בכרמלית] חוץ לד' אמות ברשות הרבים דאי מייתי ליה נמצא מעביר ד' אמות ברה"ר וחייב חטאת גזור רבנן לגוללו אצלו (ככרמלית) [בכרמלית]. ואקשינן תוך ד' אמות ברה"ר נמי נגזור דלמא מעייל ליה (ולרה"ר) [מרה"ר] לרה"י. וכי תימא כיון דמפסקא ליה כרמלית בין רה"ר לרה"י אי מעייל ליה דרך כרמלית לא מחייב. והא אמר רבא המעביר חפץ מתחלת ד' לסוף ד' והעבירו דרך עליו חייב (והוא) [והא] המעביר דרך עליו כאלו מעביר למעלה מעשרה (כרה"ר) [ברה"ר] הוא שהוא חשוב במקום פטור. ואפ"ה חייב ופריק באיסקופה אריך עסקינן דאדהכי והכי מדכר דשבת הוא ולא אתי לאתויי מרה"ר לרה"י ואע"פ שהוא דרך כרמלית אלא ע"י גלילא איבעית אימא באיסקופה שאינו אריך וסתם כתבי קודש עיוניה מעייני בהו וע"י גלילה הוא העיון לפיכך לא חיישינן דלמא מעייל להו בידים. וניחוש דלמא מעיין בהו ברה"ר והשלים מלעיונה ומעייל להו (בידיה) [בהדיא] לרשות היחיד. ודחינן כיון שלא *) נתכוון לעקור כדי להניח אלא כדי לעיין אע"פ שנמלך והכניסן לא מיחייב אי נמי כבן עזאי דאמר מהלך כעומד דמי **) ואפילו עמד בכרמלית (והניח) [והביא] מרשות הרבים לכרמלית (והכרמלית) [ומכרמלית] עקר והניח ברה"י דכי האי גוונא לא מיחייב. ואקשינן וניחוש דלמא זריק להו מרה"ר לרה"י שאין שם עמידה דהאמר ר' יוחנן

*) לפנינו בגמ' ליתא להאי מילתא אך רבינו הוה גורס כן ועי' בבעהמ"א בכאן ודו"ק. **) תי' אפילו אינו מובן דאדרבה דבעומד בכרמלית והניח בכרמלית בוודאי פטור גם לרבינו ואולי צ"ל דהוי כעומד וכו' וצ"ע.

מסורת הש"ס

[לקמן צט.] שבת ח: וע"ש

[שבת ה: כתובות לא:]

שבת ו.

כד"ו אחא

[מסכ' סופרים פ"ג הל' יב]

[שם הלכה יד וע"ז ע"ש]

הגהות הב"ח

(א) גמ' באיסקופה הנדרסת: (ב) שם דאדהכי והכי: (ג) רש"י ד"ה מה לי וכו' רשות היחיד. הא לא קשרית לה אלא משום דאוגדו: (ד) ד"ה וכי תימא וכו' דגבוה עשרה ואין בו: (ה) תוס' ד"ה והאמר וכו' דההיא דעומד וכו' ומעביר מכאן לכאן דרך גופו והכי נמי לא מייתי אלא מדרבא דלברייתא דבן עזאי ואיירי לקמן כגון שמשליש ארבע על ידי זריקה כס"ד:

רב נסים גאון

הא מני בן עזאי היא דאמר מהלך כעומד דמי עיקר דבריו בפרק יציאות השבת (דף ה:) תנו רבנן המוציא מחנות לפלטיא דרך סטיו חייב ובן עזאי פוטר ואמרי' בשלמא בן עזאי קסבר מהלך כעומד דמי:

עין משפט
נר מצוה

בְּכוֹתֶל שֶׁאֵינוֹ מְשׁוּפָּע, לְמַעְלָה מִשְּׁלֹשָׁה — גּוֹלְלוֹ אֶצְלוֹ, לְמַטָּה מִשְּׁלֹשָׁה — הוֹפְכוֹ עַל הַכְּתָב.§ *"רַבִּי יְהוּדָה אוֹמֵר אֲפִילּוּ אֵינוֹ מְסוּלָּק מִן הָאָרֶץ וכו'.§ דְּבָעֵינַן הֲנָחָה עַל גַּבֵּי מַשֶּׁהוּ. וְאֶלָּא הָא *דְּאָמַר רָבָא: אתּוֹךְ שְׁלֹשָׁה לְרַבָּנָן צָרִיךְ הֲנָחָה, לֵימָא כְּתַנָּאֵי אֲמָרָהּ לִשְׁמַעְתֵּיהּ? אֶלָּא בכּוּלָּהּ רַבִּי יְהוּדָה הִיא, וְחַסּוּרֵי מִיחַסְּרָא, וְהָכִי קָתָנֵי: בַּמֶּה דְּבָרִים אֲמוּרִים — בְּכוֹתֶל מְשׁוּפָּע, אֲבָל בְּכוֹתֶל שֶׁאֵינוֹ מְשׁוּפָּע — אֲפִילּוּ פָּחוֹת מִשְּׁלֹשָׁה טְפָחִים גּוֹלְלוֹ אֶצְלוֹ. שֶׁרַבִּי יְהוּדָה אוֹמֵר: אֲפִילּוּ אֵינוֹ מְסוּלָּק מִן הָאָרֶץ אֶלָּא מְלֹא הַחוּט — גּוֹלְלוֹ אֶצְלוֹ. מַאי טַעְמָא — דְּבָעֵינַן הֲנָחָה עַל גַּבֵּי מַשֶּׁהוּ.§ **מתני'** גזִיז שֶׁלִּפְנֵי חַלּוֹן — נוֹתְנִין עָלָיו וְנוֹטְלִין מִמֶּנּוּ בְּשַׁבָּת.§ **גמ'** הַאי זִיז דְּמַפֵּיק לְהֵיכָא? אִילֵּימָא דְּמַפֵּיק לִרְשׁוּת הָרַבִּים — לֵיחוּשׁ דִּילְמָא נָפֵיל, וְאָתֵי לְאִיתוּיֵי! אֶלָּא דְּמַפֵּיק לִרְשׁוּת הַיָּחִיד — פְּשִׁיטָא! אָמַר אַבָּיֵי: לְעוֹלָם דְּמַפֵּיק לִרְשׁוּת הָרַבִּים, וּמַאי נוֹתְנִין עָלָיו דְּקָתָנֵי — דכֵּלִים הַנִּשְׁבָּרִים.§ תַּנְיָא נַמִי הָכִי: זִיז שֶׁלִּפְנֵי הַחַלּוֹן הַיּוֹצֵא לִרְשׁוּת הָרַבִּים — נוֹתְנִין עָלָיו קְעָרוֹת וְכוֹסוֹת קִיתוֹנִיּוֹת וּצְלוֹחִיּוֹת. וּמִשְׁתַּמֵּשׁ בְּכָל הַכּוֹתֶל עַד עֲשָׂרָה הַתַּחְתּוֹנִים. וְאִם יֵשׁ זִיז אֶחָד לְמַטָּה מִמֶּנּוּ מִשְׁתַּמֵּשׁ בּוֹ, וּבָעֶלְיוֹן אֵין מִשְׁתַּמֵּשׁ בּוֹ אֶלָּא כְּנֶגֶד חַלּוֹנוֹ. הַאי זִיז הֵיכִי דָּמֵי[א] אִי דְּלֵית בֵּיהּ אַרְבָּעָה מְקוֹם פְּטוּר הוּא, וַאֲפִילּוּ כְּנֶגֶד חַלּוֹנוֹ נַמִי לֹא יִשְׁתַּמֵּשׁ. וְאִי אִית בֵּיהּ אַרְבָּעָה — בְּכוּלֵּי הַכּוֹתֶל לִישְׁתַּמֵּשׁ! אָמַר אַבָּיֵי: התַּחְתּוֹן — דְּאִית בֵּיהּ אַרְבָּעָה, וְעֶלְיוֹן — לֵית בֵּיהּ אַרְבָּעָה, וְחַלּוֹן מַשְׁלִימָתוֹ לְד'. כְּנֶגֶד חַלּוֹן — מִשְׁתַּמֵּשׁ, דְּחוֹרֵי חַלּוֹן הוּא, דְּהַאי גִּיסָא וּדְהַאי גִּיסָא — אָסוּר.§ **מתני'** ועוֹמֵד אָדָם בִּרְשׁוּת הַיָּחִיד וּמְטַלְטֵל בִּרְשׁוּת הָרַבִּים, בִּרְשׁוּת הָרַבִּים וּמְטַלְטֵל בִּרה"י, וּבִלְבַד שֶׁלֹּא יוֹצִיא חוּץ מֵאַרְבַּע אַמּוֹת.§ זלֹא יַעֲמוֹד אָדָם בִּרְשׁוּת הַיָּחִיד וְיַשְׁתִּין בִּרה"ר, בִּרה"ר וְיַשְׁתִּין בִּרה"י, וְכֵן לֹא יָרוֹק. רַבִּי יְהוּדָה אוֹמֵר: חאַף מִשֶּׁנִּתְלַשׁ רוּקוֹ בְּפִיו לֹא יְהַלֵּךְ אַרְבַּע אַמּוֹת, עַד שֶׁיָּרוֹק.§ **גמ'** מַתְנֵי לֵיהּ רַב חִינָּנָא בַּר שְׁלָמְיָא לְחִיָּיא בַּר רַב קַמֵּיהּ דְּרַב: לֹא יַעֲמוֹד אָדָם בִּרה"י וּמְטַלְטֵל בִּרה"ר. אָמַר לֵיהּ: שְׁבַקְתְּ רַבָּנַן וַעֲבַדְתְּ כְּר"מ!

הוא

רש"י

לְמַטָּה מִשְּׁלֹשָׁה. הִגִּיעַ רֹאשׁ הַסֵּפֶר לִשְׁלֹשָׁה סָמוּךְ לַקַּרְקַע — אַרְעָא סְמִיכְתָּא הוּא, וַהֲרֵי הוּא כְּמוּנָּח: **אֶלָּא הָא דְּאָמַר רָבָא.** בְּפ' "הַזּוֹרֵק" בְּמַסֶּ' שַׁבָּת (דף ק.): תּוֹךְ שְׁלֹשָׁה לְרַבָּנַן. דִּפְלִיגֵי עֲלֵיהּ דְּר"ע בִּקְלוּטָה כְּמִי שֶׁהוּנְחָה[א] וְאָמְרִי דְּהַזּוֹרֵק מֵרְשׁוּת הַיָּחִיד לִרְשׁוּת הַיָּחִיד דֶּרֶךְ רְשׁוּת הָרַבִּים לְמַטָּה מֵעֲשָׂרָה — לָא אָמְרִינַן הוֹאִיל וְנִקְלְטָה בְּיוּ"ד תַּחְתּוֹנִים, שֶׁהֵן רה"ר הֲרֵי הִיא כְּמִי שֶׁהוּנְחָה לְחַיְּיבוֹ. אֲפִי' זָרַק לְמַטָּה מִשְּׁלֹשָׁה — לָא מִיחַיַּיב, אִם עַד שֶׁלֹּא הִגִּיעַ לָאָרֶץ נִשְׂרַף אוֹ בְּלָעוֹ כֶּלֶב, אֶלָּא אִם כֵּן נָח עַל גַּבֵּי מַשֶּׁהוּ. וַאֲפִילּוּ לָא הָוֵי מְקוֹם אַרְבָּעָה — הָוְיָא הֲנָחָה. וּלְמַעְלָה מִשְּׁלֹשָׁה, אִם נָח — פָּטוּר, וַאֲפִי' לְר"ע. דְּאִי מְקוֹם אַרְבָּעָה הוּא — כַּרְמְלִית הוּא, וְאִי לֵית בֵּיהּ אַרְבָּעָה — מְקוֹם פְּטוּר הוּא: נֵימָא כְּתַנָּאֵי אֲמָרָהּ לִשְׁמַעְתֵּיהּ. דְּהָא תַּנָּא קַמָּא אֲפִילּוּ כִּי לָא נָח נַמִי גָּזַר לְמַטָּה מִג' — מִשּׁוּם דִּילְמָא זִמְנִין דְּאֵין אֲגָדוֹ בְּיָדוֹ. וּלְרָבָא, כִּי אֵין אֲגָדוֹ בְּיָדוֹ נַמִי כִּי הַאי גַּוְונָא דְּלָא נָח לָא מִיחַיַּיב, אִם קְלָטוֹ וְהֶחֱזִירוֹ קוֹדֶם שֶׁנָּח: **מתני'** זִיז שֶׁלִּפְנֵי הַחַלּוֹן. בּוֹלֵט מִן הַכּוֹתֶל, גָּבוֹהַּ י' וְרָחָב ד': נוֹתְנִין עָלָיו. בְּנֵי עֲלִיָּיה, דִּרה"י הוּא: **גמ'** דְּמַפֵּיק לְהֵיכָן. לְהֵיכָן בּוֹלֵט: דְּמַפֵּיק לרה"י. לְחָצֵר: כֵּלִים הַנִּשְׁבָּרִים. כְּלֵי חֶרֶס וּזְכוּכִית, שֶׁאִם נָפְלוּ יִשָּׁבְרוּ. דְּלֵיכָּא *לְמֵימַר דִּילְמָא אָזֵיל וּמַיְיתֵי לְהוּ: קְעָרוֹת וְכוֹסוֹת וְקִיתוֹנִיּוֹת. כּוּלָּם כֵּלִים הַנִּשְׁבָּרִים הֵם, דִּסְתָמַיְיהוּ דְּחֶרֶס: מִשְׁתַּמֵּשׁ בְּכָל הַכּוֹתֶל. אִם הַזִּיז מוּטָל לְאָרְכּוֹ אֵצֶל הַכּוֹתֶל עַל פְּנֵי כּוּלּוֹ, מִשְׁתַּמֵּשׁ בְּכָל הַזִּיז: עַד עֲשָׂרָה הַתַּחְתּוֹנִים. כְּלוֹמַר: כָּל מָקוֹם שֶׁהוּא, בֵּין סָמוּךְ לַחַלּוֹן מִיָּד, בֵּין מוּפְלָג הֵימֶנּוּ הַרְבֵּה, וּבִלְבַד שֶׁלֹּא יְהֵא בְּתוֹךְ עֲשָׂרָה תַּחְתּוֹנִים שֶׁבִּרְשׁוּת הָרַבִּים: לְמַטָּה הֵימֶנּוּ. לְמַעְלָה מֵעֲשָׂרָה: מִשְׁתַּמֵּשׁ בּוֹ. בַּתַּחְתּוֹן, ע"פ כָּל הַכּוֹתֶל, אִם מוּנָּח לְאוֹרְכּוֹ אֵצֶל הַכּוֹתֶל: הַאי זִיז. עֶלְיוֹן, הֵיכִי דָּמֵי: אִי דְּלֵית בֵּיהּ אַרְבָּעָה מְקוֹם פְּטוּר הוּא. וַאֲפִילּוּ כְּנֶגֶד חַלּוֹנוֹ לָא לִשְׁתַּמֵּשׁ. נְהִי דִּמְקוֹם פְּטוּר הוּא וּמוּתָּר לְכַתֵּף עָלָיו, כִּדְקָיי"ל: מָקוֹם שֶׁאֵין בּוֹ אַרְבָּעָה מוּתָּר לִבְנֵי רה"ר וְלִבְנֵי רה"י לְכַתֵּף עָלָיו. מִיהוּ, תַּשְׁמִישׁ תָּדִיר לָא מִשְׁתְּרֵי בֵּיהּ, דְּלָא חֲזִי לְתַשְׁמִישְׁתָּא וּשְׁכִיחֵי כֵּלִים לְמִיפַּל לְרה"ר. וְאע"ג דְּאוֹקְמִינַן בְּכֵלִים הַנִּשְׁבָּרִים — הָנֵי מִילֵּי בִּדְאִית בֵּיהּ ד' דְּלָא שְׁכִיחִי לְמִיפַּל כּוּלֵּי הַאי. אֲבָל הָכָא דְּרוּבָּא נָפְלִי — מֶחֱזֵי כְּמַאן דְּשָׁדֵי לְהֶדְיָא לִרְשׁוּת הָרַבִּים: חוֹרֵי חַלּוֹן הוּא. כְּלוֹמַר: זָוִית הַחַלּוֹן וְהַרְחָבָתוֹ הוּא. וּלְשׁוֹן חוֹרֵי דְּנָקַט — מִשּׁוּם דְּגַבֵּי שַׁבָּת שַׁיָּיךְ לְמֵימַר חוֹרֵי רְשׁוּת הָרַבִּים כִּרְשׁוּת הָרַבִּים, וְכֵן חוֹרֵי רה"י כרה"י דָּמֵי. כְּגוֹן כּוֹתֶל הַסָּמוּכָה לרה"ר וְיֵשׁ בָּהּ חוֹרִין פְּתוּחִין לרה"ר לְמַטָּה מִיּוּ"ד הָוֵי רה"ר: **מתני'** עוֹמֵד אָדָם בִּרה"י. בַּבַּיִת אוֹ עַל הַגַּג, וְשׁוֹחֶה וְנוֹטֵל חֵפֶץ בִּרה"ר כָּאן, וּמַנִּיחוֹ כָּאן: וּבִלְבַד שֶׁלֹּא יוֹצִיאֶנּוּ מֵאַרְבַּע אַמּוֹתָיו. מִמָּקוֹם שֶׁהָיָה מוּנָּח בּוֹ. וְאַשְׁמוּעִי' מַתְנִיתִין דְּלָא גָּזְרִינַן שֶׁמָּא יַכְנִיסֶנּוּ אֶצְלוֹ: וְיַשְׁתִּין בִּרה"ר. דְּמַפֵּיק מֵרה"י לְרה"ר: מִשֶּׁנִּתְלַשׁ רוּקוֹ בְּפִיו. מִשֶּׁנִּתְעַגֵּל וְנֶאֱסַף לָצֵאת: לֹא יְהַלֵּךְ אַרְבַּע אַמּוֹת עַד שֶׁיָּרוֹק. דְּכֵיוָן דִּלְמִשְׁדְּיֵיהּ קָאֵי, מַשּׂאוֹי הוּא: **גמ'** מַתְנֵי לֵיהּ רַב כו'. גְּזֵירָה שֶׁמָּא יַכְנִיסֶנּוּ אֶצְלוֹ: וַעֲבַדְתְּ כְּר"מ. דְּאִיהוּ הוּא דְּגָזַר שֶׁמָּא יָבִיא אֶצְלוֹ כִּדְלְקַמָּן בְּפִירְקִין [דף קא.] לֹא יַעֲמוֹד בִּרְשׁוּת הַיָּחִיד וְיִפְתַּח לִרְשׁוּת הָרַבִּים, שֶׁיִּטּוֹל מַפְתֵּחַ בִּרְשׁוּת הָרַבִּים וְיִפְתַּח בּוֹ פֶּתַח הַסָּמוּךְ לִרְשׁוּת הָרַבִּים שֶׁמָּא יַכְנִיס אֶצְלוֹ בְּמָקוֹם שֶׁהוּא:

מַדְּקִיפָא

תוספות

נימא כתנאי אמרה לשמעתיה. אע"ג דלא ניחא הכא לאוקמי מילתא דרבא בפלוגתא דתנאי דמתני', מ"מ ע"כ אשכחן ברייתא דפליגא עליה במסכת שבת בפ' "הזורק" (דף נז.) גבי הזורק מרה"י לרה"י, ורה"ר באמצע. דקתני בברייתא: תוך ג' – ד"ה חייב, אי נמי, יש לחלק: דהכא שבא החפץ מלמעלה מג' למטה לתוך ג' – הוא דבעי רבא הנחה על גבי משהו, אבל התם – איירי שהיה החפץ תוך ג' משילא מתחת ידו, להכי חשיב כמונח, דהא מודה רבא דהמעביר בתוך שלשה דכמונח בקרקע דמי, כדמוכח בפרק "המוציא יין" (שם דף פ.). והא דלא חשבינן מתגלגל כמונח בסוף "הזורק" (שם דף ק.) – התם איירי כשהיתה תחילת זריקה למעלה מג': **אלא** כולה רבי יהודה היא. תימה דבשבת בפרק "הזורק" (דף נז:) בעי למימר דסבר ר' יהודה קלוטה כמו שהונחה, גבי הזורק מרה"י לרה"ר ועבר ד' אמות ברה"ר. ולמסקנא דהתם ניחא, דמוקי לה כגון דאמר כדנפקא לרה"ר תנוח. דמסתבר טפי למימר התם קלוטה כמו שהונחה, כיון שהיה דעתו ורצונו שתנוח שם. אבל הכא, דאין רצונו שיפול שם הספר – אין לנו לומר שיהא כמונח. אבל למאי דס"ד התם מעיקרא, דמיחייב שתים, ובאומר כל מקום שתרצה שם תנוח – קשה! ויש לחלק: דהתם אינו מקפיד על החפץ אנה שינוח, אבל הכא – מקפיד, ומרצונו היה חפץ שלא היה שם מונח. אבל לרבא קשיא, דאפי' באומר כל מקום שתרצה תנוח בעי רבא הנחה על גבי משהו, דמקפיד, אפילו נח על גבי משהו לא מיחייב, דלא נעשית מחשבתו. וצריך לומר דלמאי דס"ד התם מעיקרא לית ליה דרבא. ועוד יש לומר כדפרישית לעיל, דהתם כשתחילת זריקתו תוך שלשה: **ליחוש** דילמא נפיל ואתי לאיתויי. ואי דמפיק לכרמלית או לחצר שאינה מעורבת, לרבא דלית ליה לקמן (צט.) גזירה לגזירה – פשיטא דשרי, דלא איצטריך למיתני. ולאביי דגזר – אסור כמו במפיק לרה"ר. ועוד נראה: מדמשני אביי לעולם דמפיק לרה"ר, משמע דבמפיק לכרמלית או לחצר שאינה מעורבת – שרי, אפילו כלים שאינן נשברים. ואע"ג דלקמן גזר אביי גזירה לגזירה – יש לחלק, כמו שפירשתי לעיל, ובפרק "כיצד משתתפין" (לעיל דף פד.) גבי אנשי חצר ואנשי עלייה ששכחו ולא עירבו, דקתני: זיז היוצא מן הכותל בעשרה דעלייה – הוי לעלייה, אפילו הניח שם כלים שאינם נשברים: **ומשתמש** בכל הכותל עד עשרה תחתונים. פי' בקונטרס: אם הזיז מוטל לארכו על פני כל הכותל – משתמש בכל הזיז. וקשה לר"י: דהיינו סיפא, דקתני: אם יש זיז למטה הימנו – משתמש בו. ומפרש ר"י: דבחורין שבכותל קאמר דמשתמש, ולשון משתמש בכל הכותל – משמע נמי כן: **אי** דלית(ב) ליה ארבע אפי' כנגד חלונו נמי לא ישתמש. משמע מפירוש הקונט', דברחב ד' משתמש בכלים הנשברים. אבל שאין רחב – לא ישתמש, אפי' כלים הנשברים, דהוי כאילו שדי להו להדיא. וקשה לר"י: דכיון דאפילו ברחב ד' לא ישתמש בכלים שאין נשברין, א"כ אפילו רחב מאה אמה נמי, דלענין שבת חשיב רחב ד' כרחב אלף. ונראה לר"י: דברחב ד' שרי ליתן אפילו כלים שאינן נשברים, ומתני' – ברחב כל שהוא. והא דלא מוקי לה ברחב ד', ובכל כלים – משום דסתם זיז אינו רחב ד'. וכי פריך התלמוד: אי דלית ביה ארבעה אפילו כנגד חלונו לא ישתמש – ה"מ למיפרך אפי' בשלמטה הימנו לא ישתמש. והא דלא משני ליה דבכלים הנשברים איירי – היינו משום דלא מיתוקמא בהכי ע"כ, מדלא שרי בשאר הכותל אלא כנגד חלונו בלבד: **תחתון** דאית ביה ד'. ק"ק דמעליון שמעינן ליה דשרין כנגד חלונו משום דחלון משלימתו לד'! ויש לומר: דאיצטריך לאשמועינן בתחתון, אף על גב דלא ניחא תשמישתא, דהא איכא עליון דמפסיק:

הוא

כ א מיי' פי"ג מהל' שבת הלכה טז:
כא ב מיי' פט"ו מהל' שבת הלכה כא סמג לאוין סה טוש"ע א"ח סי' שנב סעיף ב:
כב ג מיי' שם הל' ז וסמג שם טוש"ע א"ח סי' שנג סעיף ב:
כג ד מיי' שם וטור ש"ע שם סעיף ג:
כד ה מיי' שם הל' ו וטוש"ע שם סעיף ב:
כה ו מיי' פט"ו מהל' שבת הלכה א סמג שם טור ש"ע א"ח סי' שנ סעיף א:
כו ז שם סעיף ב:
כז ח שם סעיף ג:

רבינו חננאל

מודה בן עזאי בזורק שחייב. ופרקינן זאת אומרת אין (מזריקין) [מזרקין] כתבי קודש: היה קורא בראש הגג כו' ואוקימנא מתני' כולה ר' יהודה היא והכי קתני בד"א בכותל משופע דהא נח לפיכך הופכו על הכתב ומניחו. ואע"ג דלא התירו חכמים לכותבי ספרים להפוך יריעה על פניה. אלא אם פירש עליה בגד הכא משום [בזיון] כתבי הקודש התירו להפוך הספר על פניו והני מילי בכותל משופע דנח הספר עליו. אבל בכותל שאינו משופע אפילו למטה מג' טפחים גוללו אצלו דברי ר' יהודה שר' יהודה אמר אפילו אינו מסולק מן הארץ אלא מלא החוט גוללו אצלו דבעינן הנחה ע"ג משהו וכן אמר רבא תוך ג' לרבנן צריך הנחה ע"ג משהו: [מתני'] זיז שלפני החלון כו' אוקימנא בזיז היוצא לרה"ר ונוטלין ממנו. דהא למעלה מי' הוא וכרה"י דמי: **ירושלמי** א"ר יוחנן זיזין וכתלים שגבוהין י' ורחבין ד' מותרין לכאן ולכאן ובלבד שלא יחליף ומאי נותנין עליו דקתני כלים שבורין דאי נפלו לרה"ר לא חיישינן דלמא מעייל להו לרה"י תניא נמי הכי זיז היוצא כו' ועד אין בין זיז לזיז י' אין משתמש בזיז אלא כנגד חלונו ופרשה אביי כגון דאית ביה בזיז ד' טפחים שנעשה (רה"ר) [רה"י] ועליון (דלית) [לית] ביה ד"ט וחלונו משלמתו לד' כנגד החלון שרי ליה לאשתמושי (דחורו) [דחורי] של חלון נינהו. אבל יתרון רחב הזיז דנפיק למעדיף על רוחב החלון (שכנגד החלון בלבד מותר אבל המעדיף) בהאי גיסא ובהאי גיסא אסירי: [מתני'] הא דתנן עומד אדם ברשות הרבים ומטלטל ברשות היחיד עומד אדם ברה"י ומטלטל ברה"ר אוקימנא לרבנן ודלא כר' מאיר דתנן לא יעמוד אדם ברשות הרבים וכו'

מסורת הש"ס

[מתוך הסוגיא נראה שא כאן פסקא]

שבת פ. ק.

[נ"ל למיתח]

הגהות הב"ח

(א) רש"י ד"ה תוך ג' וכו' כמי שהונחה דמיא ואמר וכו' למטה מג' נמי לא: (ב) תוס' ד"ה אי דלית ביה ד' וכו' אפילו בכלים

הגהות הגר"א

[א] אי דלית בי' ארבעה אפילו כנגד חלונו כו' [ותיבות שבנתים מוקפות]

גליון הש"ס

גמ' ליחוש דלמא נפיל. [עיין] ב"ב דף נט ע"ב תוס' ד"ה ואפילו:

הוא סבר: מדסיפא ר"מ — רישא נמי ר"מ, ולא היא: סיפא ר"מ, ורישא רבנן.§ "ובלבד שלא יוציא חוץ".§ הא הוציא — חייב חטאת. לימא מסייע ליה לרבא, *דאמר רבא: המעביר חפץ מתחילת ארבע לסוף ארבע, והעבירו דרך עליו — חייב. מי קתני "אם הוציא חייב חטאת", דילמא, אם הוציא — פטור אבל אסור. איכא דאמרי: הא הוציא — פטור אבל אסור. לימא תיהוי תיובתיה דרבא, דאמר רבא: המעביר מתחילת ד' לסוף ד' והעבירו דרך עליו — חייב! מי קתני, "הוציא פטור אבל אסור"? דילמא: אם הוציא — חייב חטאת.§ "לא יעמוד אדם ברה"י" וכו'§ אמר רב יוסף: [א]השתין ורק — חייב חטאת. והא בעינן עקירה והנחה מעל גבי מקום ד', וליכא! מחשבתו משויא ליה מקום. דאי לא תימא הכי, הא *דאמר *רבא: [ב]זרק ונח בפי הכלב או בפי הכבשן — חייב חטאת. והא בעינן הנחה ע"ג מקום ד' — וליכא! אלא: מחשבתו משויא ליה מקום, ה"נ מחשבה משויא לה מקום. בעי רבא: הוא ברה"י, ופי אמה ברה"ר מהו? בתר עקירה אזלינן, או [ג]בתר יציאה אזלינן? תיקו.§ "וכן לא ירוק. רבי יהודה אומר" וכו'.§ אף על גב דלא הפיך בה? *והתנן: היה אוכל דבילה בידים מסואבות, והכניס ידו לתוך פיו ליטול צרור, רבי מאיר מטמא, ורבי יוסי מטהר. רבי יהודה אומר: [ד]היפך בה — טמא, לא היפך בה — טהור! *אמר רבי יוחנן: מוחלפת השיטה. ריש לקיש אמר: לעולם לא תחליף, והכא במאי עסקינן — בכיחו. והתניא, רבי יהודה אומר: כיחו ונתלש. מאי לאו — רוק ונתלש! לא, כיחו ונתלש. והא תניא(א) ר' יהודה אומר: כיחו שנתלש, וכן רוקו שנתלש, לא יהלך ד' אמות עד שירוק! אלא מחוורתא כדשנינן מעיקרא.§ אמר ר"ל: כיח בפני רבו חייב מיתה, שנאמר: °"כל משנאי אהבו מות", *אל תקרי "למשנאי" אלא "למשניאי". והא מינם אנים! כיח [ה]ורק קאמרינן.§ **מתני'** [ו]*לא יעמוד אדם ברה"י וישתה ברה"ר, ברה"ר וישתה ברה"י, אלא אם כן הכניס ראשו ורובו למקום שהוא שותה. וכן בגת.§ **גמ'** רישא רבנן וסיפא רבי מאיר! אמר רב יוסף: בחפיצין שצריכין לו, ודברי הכל. *איבעיא להו: כרמלית מאי? אמר אביי: היא היא. אמר רבא: *[ז]היא גופא גזירה, ואנן ניקום ונגזור גזירה לגזירה?! אמר אביי: מנא אמינא לה — מדקתני:

וכן

משלי ח

שבת יא. לעיל כ. [ביצה ג.]

רש"י

מדסיפא ר"מ. הא דלא יפתח* דאיירי ר"מ בהו: הא הוציא. הספק מד' אמות – חייב, אע"ג דהוא עומד בגנותו והגביהו למעלה מי' והעבירו – לא אמרי' העברת דרך מקום פטור הוא. אלמא: בתר הנחה ועקירה אזלינן, והרי נטלו מתחילת ארבע והניחו לסוף ארבע: פטור אבל אסור. מדרבנן, דילמא אתי לעבורי דרך למטה מעשרה: מחשבתו. שהוא צריך לכך, משווא לה הולכה חשובה: זרק. מתחילת ד' לסוף ד': בפי הכבשן. שקלטה שלהבת ונשרפה: בתר עקירה. מן הגוף אזלינן. והן נעקרין מן החלל של גוף, וחייב, דמוציא מן הגוף שהוא רה"י לרה"ר: או בתר יציאה. שיוצא מן הגוף ממנו, והרי פי אמה ברה"ר ואין כאן עקירה מרה"י: ואע"ג דלא היפך. בתמיה, דמשום תליש' לחודיה אמר ר' יהודה דאסור, דלמיפק קאי ואפי' דלא היפך בה בתוך פיו: היה אוכל דבילה. של תרומה: בידים מסואבות. סתם ידים שלא נטלו הוו שניות, ופוסלות את התרומה: ר"מ מטמא. שהרי הוכשרה התרומה ברוק שבפיו: ר' יוסי מטהר. דקסבר: כל זמן שהרוק בתוך פיו, לאו משקה הוא, והרי הוא כגופו של אדם ואינו מכשיר: היפך. ברוק, להוציאו לחוץ – טמא דלמשדייה קאי ומכשיר: מוחלפת השיטה. החליף ר' יהודה שיטתו ויצא הימנה: לא תחליף. לא תימא מוחלפת היא. דמתני' דקאמר אע"ג דלא היפך קאי למשדיי' בכיחו עסקינן. ליחה שנתלשה מן הגוף ע"י חולי שקורין טו"ש: כיחו ונתלש. לא יהלך ד' אמות עד שירוק: מאי לאו. תרתי קתני: כיחו, וכן רוקו: כדשנינן מעיקרא. מוחלפת השיטה: חייב מיתה. בידי שמים: כל משנאי אהבו מות. תורה אמרה להאי קרא, בפרשת "ה' קנני": אלא למשניאי. למשניאים דעתו בגנות: והא מינם אנים. שעל כרחו הוא ע"י חולי או הגינה: כיח ורק קאמרינן. שרקק אותו בפני רבו, והיה לו להסתלק משם או להבליעו בכסותו: **מתני'** וישתה ברה"ר. ויושיט צוארו לרה"ר וישתה גזירה שמא יכנים הכלי אצלו: וכן בגת. מפרש בגמ' לענין מעשר: **גמ'** רישא רבנן. לעיל אוקימנא להא דקתני עומד אדם ברה"י ומטלטל ברה"ר כרבנן, דפליגי עליה דר"מ במתני' גבי מפתח, ולא גזרינן שמא יכנים והכא גזר שמא יכנים כר"מ. והא ליכא למימר דשתיית המים חשובי הכנסה כמשתין ורוק – דלא דמי, דהתם קא עקר מרשות זו וקא עבד הנחה ברשות זו. אבל שותה – עביד עקירה והנחה בחדא רשותא, דהא ברשות שהוא שותה בה פיו עומד, ובפיו הן נחין מיד: בחפיצין הצריכין לו. אפי' רבנן מודו דגזר בהו, דמתוך שהוא צריך להם – יכניסם אצלו. הלכך, משקין הללו צריכין לו, וגזרינן: כרמלית מאי. מהו שיעמוד בכרמלית וישתה ברה"י או ברה"ר: היא היא. כי היכי דלא יעמוד ברה"ר וישתה ברה"י, כך לא יעמוד בכרמלית וישתה ברה"י: היא גופה גזירה. אי דעייל לגבייה כלי – ליכא איסורא דאורייתא, אלא גזירה דרבנן, דלא ליתי לאפוקי מרה"י לרה"ר. ואנן ניקום וניגזר שתייה אטו הכנסת כלי:

וכן

תוספות

הוא סבר מדסיפא ר"מ כו'. פי' בקונט': סיפא ההיא דלא יפתח, דאיירי בה ר"מ. וק"ק: דהיא רחוקה יותר מדאי! ונראה לר"י: דסיפא דלא ישתין ולא ירוק, דפליג עליה ר' יהודה, וסתם בר פלוגתא דר' יהודה ר"מ. ומיהו, קשה: דא"כ הוה ליה למיפרך נמי בגמרא ר"מ אדר"מ, למאי דגרסי' ברוב ספרים ר' מאיר מטמא. וכן גרס ר"ת. ולמאי דמסיק מוחלפת השיטה – נמי ניחא דלא תיקשי דר"מ אדר"מ. ושמא מש"ה הניח מלהקשות דר"מ אדר"מ, משום דאיכא דמהפכי דרבי מאיר לדברי רבי יוסי:

זרק ונח ברה"ר בפי כלב כו'. אור"י: דלא גרסי' ונח, דונח משמע דלא נתכוין לכך, כדמוכח בפ"ק דשבת (דף ה.) גבי הא דא"ר יוחנן: זרק חפץ והלך ונח בתוך ידו של חבירו – חייב. הכא איירי במתכוין לכך. ומיהו, ר"ח גריס "ונח", דמלי למימר דונח משמע שפיר מתכוין. דסתם זרק נח החפץ במקום שמתכוין, אבל הלך ונח – משמע שהלך בלא כוונת האדם. ועוד י"ל דבפ"ק דשבת מיתורא דמימרא דייק, דאיירי בלא מתכוין*: **מחשבתו** משוי' ליה מקום. דוקא בכי האי גוונא, דנהנה באותו מקום טפי מבמקום אחר כגון בפי כלב שיאכלנה, ובפי הכבשן שתשרף שם, וכן השתין ורק. אבל זרק על המקלות או על שום דבר, אפי' במתכוין – לא אמרו מחשבתו משויא ליה מקום: **היה** אוכל דבילה בידים מסואבות. פי' בקונט': דבילה של תרומה. ור"י אומר: דאפי' בשל חולין ניחא, דידים הפוסלות תרומה מטמאין את הרוק שהוא משקה להיות תחילה, וחוזר ומטמא את הדבילה, וגם מכשירה, דהוו להו חולין טמאים דפוסלין את הגוייה. דמשקין כל שהוא מטמאין, כדאמרינן בברכות פרק "אלו דברים" (דף נב.): שמא יצאו מים אחורי הכוס ויחזרו ויטמאו את הידים. וסתמא דמאחורי הכוס ליכא רביעית, דבכל נטילתו ליכא אלא רביעית. ובפ"ק דפסחים (דף יד:) נמי משמע שהבשר מטמא מחמת המשקין שעליו, וסתמא ליכא בהו רביעית. והא דקאמר בכמה דוכתי לטמא טומאת משקין ברביעית *גבי יין נסך, ובנזיר [לח.] גבי עשר רביעי' – היינו לפסול את הגוייה, כדתנן במעילה (דף יז:): כל המשקין מצטרפין לפסול את הגוייה ברביעית. אבל ליטמא ולטמא אוכלים – בכל שהוא [משקין] טימאו ומטמו. ורוק חשיב משקה לקבל טומאה, כמו שחשוב משקה להכשיר הדבילה. והשתא ההיא דחגיגה (דף כ:): נימא נפסקה לי וקשרתיה בפה, לפי מה שפירשתי ניחא אפי' ברוק של טהור. וכן פי' הר"ר י"ט: נימא נפסקה לי וקשרתיה בפה, ובשעה שנארג בה כדי לקבל טומאה עדיין היה רוק לח עליה, שניטמא מחמת הידים וטימא את המפה. שהמשקה מטמא בכל שהוא, כדפרישית, ולא כמו שמפרש ר"ת דאיירי ברוק של נדה כמו שפירש שם בקונטרס. לפי שלא היה נראה לו להעמיד ברוק של טהור, משום דלא חשיב רוב משקה לקבל טומאה, דחשיב שפיר משקה כדפרישית:

רבי מאיר מטמא. אית ספרים דגרסי: רבי מאיר מטהר.

וכן בגת. לענין מעשר. פירוש: צריך שיכנים ראשו ורובו על הגת, ועל ידי כן מותר לשתות בכל ענין, והיינו כרבי מאיר:

קולט

עין משפט נר מצוה

כח א מיי' פי"ג מהל' שבת הלכה ג סמג שם:

כט ב מיי' שם הלכה יג סמג שם:

ל ג מיי' שם הלכה ג וסמג שם טוש"ע א"ח סי' שנ סעיף ב:

לא ד מיי' פט"ו מהל' טומאת אוכלין הל' ז:

לב ה טור ש"ע י"ד סי' רמב סעיף כט:

לג ו ז מיי' פט"ו מהל' שבת הלכה ב סמג לאוין סה טוש"ע א"ח סי' שנ סעיף א:

[וע' תוס' שבת ז: ד"ה אלא]

מסורת הש"ס

[לקמן קא.]

שבת ח: ע"ש לעיל לג.

שבת קכ. [וכס"ה רבה]

כלים פ"ח משנה י

[ביצה ג. וש"נ]

[שבת קיז. מגילה כח. ושם איתא אל תקרא משנאי אלא משניאי]

שבת יח.

[שם: ביצה ג. וש"נ]

הגהות הב"ח

(א) גמ' ר' יהודה אומר כיחו וכן רוקו כל"ל ותיבת שנתלש נמחק:

רבינו חננאל

ובלבד שלא יוציא חוץ לד' אמות דייקינן מינה ללישנא בתרא הא הוציא פטור אבל אסור נימא תהוי תיובתא דרבא דאמר המעביר חפץ מתחלת ד' לסוף ד' אם העבירו דרך עליו חייב. ודחי רבא מי קתני בהדיא אם הוציא פטור אבל אסור אבל לעולם אימא לך אם הוציא חייב חטאת: לא יעמוד ברה"י וישתין כו' וכן לא ירוק מרשות לרשות. אמר רב יוסף השתין או רקק בשוגג חייב חטאת ואע"ג דלא עקר מע"ג מקום ד' דהא פיו ופי אמה שלו אין בהן ד' טפחים מחשבתו שחשב כדי לעקור מהן להנאתו משויא להו כמו שיש בו ד' טפחים וכדרבא דאמר רבא זרק ונח בפי הכלב או בפי הכבשן חייב דמחשבתו שויא לפי הכלב ולפי הכבשן [כמקום ד'] הכא נמי פיו ופי אמתו מחשבתו משויא להו כאילו מקום ד' הן. בעי רבא הוא ברשות הרבים ופי אמתו ברשות היחיד או הוא ברה"י ופי אמתו ברה"ר מהו בתר עקירה אזלינן ומרשות לרשות הוא או דלמא בתר יציאה אזלינן ורשות חדא היא ועלתה בתיקו. וקי"ל כל תיקו דאיסורא לחומרא. ר"י [אומר] אע"פ שנתלש רוקו בפיו כו' ואע"ג דלא אפיך ברוק נתלש נקרא *) והתניא האוכל דבילה בידים מסואבות והכנים ידו לתוך פיו ליטול צרור ר' מאיר מטמא שכבר נכשרה ברוקו ונגע בה וידיו מסואבות ור' יוסי מטהר שאין זה הכשר ר' יהודה אמר היפך ברוקו הנה נתלש והכשיר לא היפך טהור פי' לא נתלש עדיין ואינו משקה להכשיר דתנן במכשירין פ"ו ואלו מטמאין ומכשירין זובו של זב ורוקו ושכבת זרעו ומימי רגליו ורביעית מן המת ודם נדה ר' אלעזר אומר ש"ז אינה מכשרת. א"ר יוחנן מוחלפת השיטה. פי' חלוף ואומר במשנה ר' מאיר אומר היפך בו טמא ר' יהודה אומר אע"פ שלא היפך טמא ובא ר"ל ואמר לעולם לא תיפוך והא דתניא בברייתא רוקו ומשנתנו כיחו. פי' כיחו ליחה עבה שהיא כמו חתיכה. ואקשינן עליה והתניא כיחו וכן רוק שנתלש עמו. אם הלך בו ד' אמות חייב אלא מחוורתא כר' יוחנן. אמר ר"ל כיח ורק כו': לא יעמוד אדם ברה"י וישתה ברה"ר כו' ואמרינן רישא דקתני עומד ברה"ר ומטלטל ברה"י כו' רבנן סיפא דקתני לא יעמוד אדם כו' ר' מאיר ופריק רב יוסף בחפצין שצריכין לו לגופו ואפילו רבנן מודו דכי האי גוונא לא שרי ליה אלא מכנים ראשו ורובו למקום שהחפצין נתונים בו. איבעיא להו כרמלית מהו שיעמוד ברה"ר או ברה"י אמר אביי היא היא. כלומר אסור. רבא אמר היא גופא מרשות הרבים לרה"י גזירה היא שמא (יוצא) [יוציא] מרשות לרשות והיא איסורא דאורייתא ניקו

*) משמע מלשון דברייתא הוא וכן לקמן בסמוך אמר והא דתנייא בברייתא וצ"ע דהא משנה הוא בכלים פ"ח.

עין משפט נר מצוה

לד א מיי' פ"ה מהל' מעשר הלכה טז:

לה ב ג ד מיי' פט"ו מהל' שבת הל' ג סמג לאוין סה טוש"ע א"ח סי' שנא:

לו ה ו מיי' שם הל' ט וסמג שם טור ש"ע א"ח סי' שנל סעיף א:

לז ז ח מיי' שם הל' י וטוש"ע שם סעיף ב:

לח ט י מיי' פט"ז מהל' שבת הלכה כד טוש"ע א"ח סי' שסב סעיף א:

תוספות

קולט אדם מן המזחילה למטה מי'. כן גריס בקונטרס. פי': מאויר, אבל לא יצרף פיו או כלי למזחילה, לפי שהמזחילה בפחות מג' סמוך לגג, ואע"פ שהיא למטה מי', מ"מ ה"ל כמוציא מן הגג לרה"ר, כיון דתוך ג' לגג היא: **מן** הצינור מכל מקום שותה. פירוש: אפי' בצירוף כיון שהוא למטה מי', ורחוק שלשה טפחים מן הגג דליכא לבוד. ובגמרא מוקי לה דלית ביה ארבעה, דאי הוי ביה ארבעה – היה אסור לצרף. דמכרמלית לרה"ר קא מפיק. וכפירוש הקונטרס מוכח בתוספתא דמתיר צירוף בצינור למטה מי'. לכך נראה כגרסת הקונט', דגריס גבי מזחילה: למטה מי'. דאי הוי גרסי' למעלה מי' – הוה משמע(ה) צינור אפילו למעלה שרי, ולמטה – אפי' מזחילה שרי. ובתוספתא לא שרי אלא הצינור למטה, אבל צינור למעלה מי' או מזחילה אפילו למטה – אסור. ואית דגרס "ומן הצינור ומ"מ מותר". ובקונטרס הקשה על זאת הגיר' בגמרא. **לא** יעמוד אדם ברה"ר ויגביה ידו למטה מי'. כן גי' ר"ת. אבל בקונטרס גרס: "לא יעמוד אדם ברה"י". והכי פירושא: לא יעמוד על גגו ויצרף מגג חבירו, שגבוה ממנו עשרה טפחים ולא עירבו. ואתיא אפי' *כר"מ, דאמר גגות רשות אחת הן, דבגג גבוה י' מודה. ואפילו לר"ש מצי אתיא. דמצי לפרושי דלצרף אסור, ולהביאם לבית קאמר. וקולט מותר אפילו להביאם – וכגון שלא שבתו בגג חבירו. דאי שבתו – פשיטא דאסור להביאם לבית. ומ"מ, אע"ג דלא שבתו – אסור לצרף ולהביאם לבית, דדמי ממש דמגג לבית קא מייתי. אבל לישנא דברייתא לא משתמע כר"ש, דקאמר: אבל קולט הוא ושותה, משמע במקומו. מכלל דצירוף אפילו במקומו – אסור. והא דאמר בגיטין ב"הזורק" (דף עט:), א"ר יהודה, אמר שמואל: לא יעמוד אדם בגגו ויקלוט מי גשמים מגגו של חבירו – היינו להביאם לבית, כדפרישית לעיל. *צריך לומר דאיירי כששבתו בגג, דבשלא שבתו – שרי, כדאמ' הכא. ומהר"י אומר: דהתם איירי בקולט מאויר גג חבירו, והכא בקולט מאויר גג שלו, בסמוך לגג חבירו: וכן

[ל"ל ד"ה שמואל]

גמרא

וכן בגת. ורבא אמר: לענין מעשר. וכן אמר רב ששת: "וכן בגת" – לענין מעשר. *דתנן: שותין על הגת בין בחמין ובין בצונן ופטור, דברי רבי מאיר. רבי אליעזר בר צדוק מחייב. וחכ"א: [א]על החמין – חייב, ועל הצונן – פטור, מפני שמחזיר את המותר.§ **מתני'** [ב]קולט אדם מן המזחילה למטה מי' טפחים, ומן הצינור מ"מ שותה.§ **גמ'** קולט – אין, אבל מצרף – לא. מ"ט? אמר רב נחמן: הכא במזחילה פחות מג' סמוך לגג עסקינן, דכל פחות מג' סמוך לגג כגג דמי. תניא נמי הכי: [ג]עומד אדם ברה"י ומגביה ידו למעלה מעשרה טפחים לפחות משלשה סמוך לגג, וקולט, ובלבד שלא יצרף. תניא אידך: לא יעמוד אדם ברה"י ויגביה ידו למעלה מעשרה טפחים לפחות מג' סמוך לגג ויצרף, אבל קולט הוא ושותה.§ מן הצינור מ"מ שותה.§ תנא: [ד]אם יש בצינור ד' על ד' – אסור, מפני שהוא כמוציא מרשות לרשות.§ **מתני'** [ה]בור ברה"ר וחולייתו גבוה י' טפחים – חלון שעל גביו ממלאין הימנו בשבת, *אשפה ברה"ר גבוה י' טפחים – חלון שעל גביו שופכין לתוכה מים בשבת.§ **גמ'** במאי עסקינן? אילימא בסמוכה – למה לי חולייא י'? אמר רב הונא: [ו]הכא במאי עסקינן – במופלגת מן הכותל ארבעה. וטעמא – דאיכא חולייא עשרה, הא ליכא חולייא עשרה – קא מטלטל מרה"י לרה"י דרך רה"ר. ורבי יוחנן אמר: אפילו תימא בסמוכה, הא קמ"ל: *דבור וחולייתו מצטרפין לעשרה.§ [ז]"אשפה ברה"ר וכו'.§ ולא חיישינן שמא תנטל אשפה? והא *רבין בר רב אדא אמר רבי יצחק: מעשה במבוי אחד שצידו אחד כלה לים וצידו אחד כלה לאשפה, ובא מעשה לפני רבי ולא אמר בו לא איסור ולא היתר. היתר לא אמר בו – דחיישינן שמא תנטל אשפה ויעלה הים שירטון. איסור לא אמר בו – דהא קיימין מחיצות. לא קשיא; [ח]הא – דיחיד, הא – דרבים.§ **מתני'** *[ט]אילן שהיה מיסך על הארץ, אם אין גופו גבוה מן הארץ שלשה טפחים – מטלטלים תחתיו. שרשיו גבוהים מן הארץ ג' טפחים – לא ישב עליהן.§ **גמ'** *א"ר הונא בריה דרב יהושע: [י]אין מטלטלין בו יתר מבית סאתים. מ"ט? משום

רש"י

וכן בגת. והאי גת מאי היא? אי רה"י, וקאמר דלא יעמוד ברה"ר ויושיט צוארו בגת ויטול כלי וישתה – הא תנא ליה רישא. אלא לאו בגת כרמלית, כגון שאינה גבוהה י': שותין על הגת. עומד על הגת ושותה, דכל זמן שלא הוציאו לחוץ – לאו שתיית קבע היא, ופטור מן המעשר, בין שמזגו בחמין בין שמזגו בצונן: מחייב. במזיגה שמוזגו במים משויא ליה קבע: על החמין חייב. דאין ראוי לחזור המותר שמקלקל היין. הלכך, כי מזג ליה בחמין – אדעתא למשתייה כוליה מזג ליה, ומשויא ליה מזיגת קבע אבל מזיגת צונן – לא משויי' ליה קבע, דילמא שתי פורתא ומהדר. הלכך, כל כמה דשתי הוי עראי. ומתני' דקתני וכן בגת – ר"מ היא. וקתני: לא יעמוד ע"ג קרקע וישתה בגת בלא הפרשת מעשר, אא"כ הכניס ראשו ורובו לגת: **מתני'** קולט אדם מן המזחילה. למטה מי' טפחים. גגין שלהן חלקים היו, וטחים בטיט, ומרזבין קטנים הרבה היו לגג להוציא המים, ונותנין למטה מהם דף כנגד אורך הכותל בשיפוע, וכל המרזבין שופכין עליו והוא מביא כל המים למקום אחד שלא יזיקו את הכותל. ועומד אדם ברה"ר וקולט בכלי למטה מי' טפחים מן המים היורדין מן המזחילה. וקולט דוקא כדמפרש בגמ' אבל לא יצרף פיו או כלי למזחילה, שהוא בפחות משלשה סמוך לגג, ואף על פי שהוא למטה מי', מ"ט – דהואיל ומוטלת לאורך הכותל ובתוך ג' לגג – דמיא לגג, והוי כמוציא מן הגג שהוא רה"י לרה"ר: ומן הצינור מ"מ. כלומר: בין קולט בין מצרף, משום דצינור לעולם ארוך ויוצא לרה"ר, וליכא למימר לבוד. וכיון דלמטה מעשרה הוא(א) – ליכא איסורא. ובגמרא מוקים לה כשאין בפיו ארבעה, ולא גזרינן אטו היכא דאית ביה ארבעה. דאי נמי אית ביה ד' – כרמלית הוא דלא גבוה עשרה. ומש"ה נקט מתני' גבי *מזחילה למטה מי' – משום דבעי' למתני ומן הצינור מ"מ, ואי למעלה מי' לא משתרי צירוף הצינור – גזירה אטו צינור שבפיו ארבע' דקא מפיק מרה"י לרה"ר. אבל קליטה, אפי' למעלה מי' נמי משתרי, דאוירא הוא מקום פטור: **גמ'** מצרף(ב). פיו או חבית למזחילה, והוי כשואב ממנה: תניא נמי הכי. דפחות מג' סמוך לגג כגג דמי והמצרף משם – כמצרף בגג: עומד אדם ברה"י. כגון בגג: וקולט. מן האויר מים שיורדים מגגו של חבירו, אבל לא יצרף. ובמתניתין נמי שמעתי דהכי גרסינן: מן הצינור ומ"מ. ולא גרסינן מכל מקום בלא וי"ו למשרי צירוף, אלא "ומ"מ" כלומר: מ"מ המקלח קולט. ומצאתי בתוספתא דצירוף מותר בצינור למטה מי'. ועוד: הא דקאמר תנא אם יש בצינור ארבעה אסור – אהיכא קאי? אקליטה – מאי מרשות לרשות איכא, ואי אצירוף – מתני' נמי אסר, אפי' כשאין בו ארבעה. ואני שמעתי דאצירופא דמתני' נמי קאי, דאוקימנא בפחות מג' לגג, הא לאו הכי – מצרפין. ואין דרך לשון התלמוד כן לומר תנא אצירוף אמוראים שלא הוזכר במשנה. אלא ה"ג: ומן הצינור מ"מ וכו' מתני' היא, ולמטה מעשרה קאי, ולא סיפא דברייתא היא: תנא אם יש בצינור ארבעה. ברוחב: אסור. לצרף ואע"ג דלמטה מי' הואי ולבוד נמי ליכא אפ"ה כרמלית מיהא הוי ומפיק מכרמלית לרשות הרבים: **גמ'** אי נימא בסמוכה. שהבור סמוכה לכותל בתוך ארבעה טפחים: למה לי חולייא עשרה. בור גופיה רה"י ועמוקה עשרה, והרי אין רשות הרבים מפסקת בינתים: וטעמא דאיכא חולייא עשרה. דלא מטי דלי לרה"ר: הא קמ"ל כו'. ומתניתין לאו כדס"ד דתיהוי חוליא עשרה לבד מבור, אלא ה"ק: בור ברה"ר וחולייתו סביביו, וסך הכל גבוה י' מקרקעית הבור – רה"י, וממלאין ממנה לחלון: שופכין לתוכה. דאשפה רה"י היא: ולא חיישינן שמא תנטל אשפה. ותעמוד על פחות מי' ואתי למשרי ביה נמי כמעיקרא: במבוי. ראשו אחד פתוח לרה"ר, וראשו אחד סתום ושני לצדדיו, אחד ים ונגידודיו גבוהים י' ואחד אשפה ובתים וחצירות פתוחין לו בדופן אמצעי: שירטון. לימו"ן בלע"ז, שמעלה טיט לשפתיו, ומתייבש ונעשה קרקע עולם: דרבים. מתני' באשפה דרבים: דרבים. **מתני'** המיסך. שנופו נוטה למטה מכל צדדיו סביב: מטלטלין תחתיו. דאמרי' לבוד, והרי*) יש כאן מחיצה עשרה(ג): שרשיו גבוהים. שאין הענפים נמוכין אלא בראשן הולכין ומגביהין לצד חיבורן: לא ישב עליהן. דכיון דגבוהין שלשה – כאילן חשיבי, ואין משתמשין באילן: **גמ'** אלא בבית סאתים. אם היה היקיפו יותר על בית סאתים – אין מטלטלין בו אלא בארבע(ד) ואפילו נטעו מתחילה לכך, דהוי מוקף לדירה: מ"ט. הא כל היקף לדירה, אפילו עשרה כורים, מותר:

*) עי' בפירש"י ברי"ף

משום

רבינו חננאל

ניקו ונגזור נמי כרמלית אטו רשות הרבים גזירה לגזירה לא גזרינן ודייק אביי מדתנן וכן בגת ובכרמלית היא. ודחי רבא ואמר וכן בגת לא קתני לענין שבת דלענין שבת מן הגת שרי ואע"ג דלא מעייל רישיה ורובו התם. כי קתני וכן בגת לענין מעשר דפטור כר' מאיר דתנן שותין על הגת בין בחמין ובין בצונן ופטור דברי ר' מאיר ר' אלעזר בר צדוק מחייב. וחכ"א על החמין חייב לעשר שאינו זה עראי אלא קבוע על הצונן פטור כי עראי הוא מפני שמחזיר המותר לו בכום. משא"כ בחמין: קולט מן מזחילה למעלה מי' טפחים ומן הצנור מכל מקום ושותה. פי' קולט מקבל ותופש מן המים היורדין מלמעלה ושותה אבל מצרף לא כלומר לערב המים היורדין מלמעלה עם המים שכבר נחו בקרקע מ"ט אמר רב נחמן הכא במזחילה פחות מג' טפחים סמוך לגג עסקינן דכל פחות מג' סמוך לגג כגג דמי. ואלו המים שקלט מן הגג קלטם שהוא רה"י ולפיכך אינו רשאי לצרפם עם התחתונים שהם ברה"ר תניא נמי הכי כו' ותניא אידך לא יעמוד ברה"ר כו': ירושלמי סילון העומד ברשות הרבים גבוה י' ורחב ד' אין שופכין בתוכו מים שמתגלגלין ויורדין: בור ברה"ר וחולייתו וכו'. אמרינן אי בסמוכה אפי' פחות מי' טפחים כרמלית הוא ושרי ואוקימנא בבור המופלג מן הכותל ד' טפחים אם אין בחולייתו י' טפחים הרי האויר דביני ביני עד הכותל רה"ר נמצא מטלטל המים מן הבור שהוא רה"י לבית שהוא רה"י דרך חלייתו על ד' טפחים שהן רה"ר אבל אם חלייתו גבוהה י' טפחים נמצאו המים כשעולין מפי החוליא למעלה מי' טפחים שהוא רה"י לרה"י ר' יוחנן אמר אפילו תימא בסמוכה לא אמרינן וחולייתו מצטרפין לי'. אשפה ברה"ר כו'. ואקשינן וניחוש שמא תנטל אשפה וישאר המקום רה"ר דהא אמרו משמיה דר' יצחק מעשה במבוי כו' פי' שירטון רפש וטיט וכשייבש נעשה ארץ ובני אדם עוברין ובאין עליו ויעשה המקום רה"ר ונמצא המבוי [פתוח] לרה"ר ופרקינן אשפה דמתניתין אשפה דרבים היא שאין עשויה לפנות ואשפה דמבוי אשפה דיחיד דעבידא לאיפנויי: **אילן** המיסך על הארץ אם אין גופו גבוה מן הארץ שלשה טפחים מטלטלין תחתיו. פירוש כיון שאין גופו גבוה מן הארץ שלשה טפחים חזינן להאי נוף כמאן דמטי על הארץ דכל פחות מג' כלבוד דמי. והא הוי מחיצות לתחת האילן לפיכך נעשה תחת האילן רה"י ומותר לטלטל בכולו. אמר רב הונא בריה דר' יהושע אין מטלטלין בה יתר מבית סאתים כו' שרשיו

הגהות הב"ח

(א) רש"י ד"ה ומן הצינור וכו' דלמטה מעשרה הוא קולט ליכא איסורא: (ב) ד"ה מצרף פיו וכו' נמחק כל הדבור: (ג) ד"ה מטלטלין וכו' מחיצה עשרה שאין הענפים כצ"ל ותיבת שרשיו גבוהין נמחק והד"א: (ד) ד"ה אלא בבית וכו' אלא בארבע אמות ואפילו: (ה) תום' ד"ה ומן הצינור וכו' הוה משמע לצינור אפילו למעלה מעשרה שרי ולמטה מי' אפילו מזחילה שריא ובתוספתא לא שרי אלא בצינור למטה מעשרה אבל וכו' למטה מעשרה אסור:

מסורת הש"ס

שבת יא: [עמ"ש סס מעשרות פ"ד מ"ד]

[לעיל פט.]

[לעיל ח. ע"ש בתוספות ד"ה זורקין]

[לעיל עח. שבת נט.]

לעיל ח.

גי' רש"ל קולט

[לעיל טו. סוכה כד.]

[סוכה כד: ע"ש]

מִשּׁוּם דְּהָוֵי דִּירָה שֶׁתַּשְׁמִישָׁהּ לָאֲוִיר,
וְכָל דִּירָה שֶׁתַּשְׁמִישָׁהּ לָאֲוִיר — אֵין מְטַלְטְלִין
בָּהּ יָתֵר מִבֵּית סָאתַיִם.§ א"שָׁרָשָׁיו גְּבוֹהִין
מִן הָאָרֶץ וכו'.§ אִיתְּמַר, שָׁרְשֵׁי אִילָן
הַבָּאִין מִלְמַעְלָה מִשְּׁלֹשָׁה לְתוֹךְ שְׁלֹשָׁה,
רַבָּה אָמַר: במוּתָּר לְהִשְׁתַּמֵּשׁ בָּהֶן, רַב
שֵׁשֶׁת אָמַר: אָסוּר לְהִשְׁתַּמֵּשׁ בָּהֶן. רַבָּה אָמַר
מוּתָּר לְהִשְׁתַּמֵּשׁ בָּהֶן — דְּכָל פָּחוֹת מִג' דְּאַרְעָא —
אַרְעָא הִיא. רַב שֵׁשֶׁת אָמַר: אָסוּר לְהִשְׁתַּמֵּשׁ
בָּהֶן, דְּכֵיוָן דְּמִכֹּחַ אִיסּוּר קָאָתֵי — אֲסוּרִין. דְּדָמוּ
כְּמִשּׁוּנִיתָא, גדְּסָלְקִין לְעֵילָּא — אֲסוּרִין, דְּנָחְתִּין
לְתַתַּאי — שָׁרוּ. לְצִדְדִין — פְּלוּגְתָּא דְּרַבָּה וְרַב
שֵׁשֶׁת. וְכֵן אַנִּיגְרָא, וְכֵן בְּקֶרֶן זָוִית. הַהוּא דִּיקְלָא
דַּהֲוָה לְאַבַּיֵּי וַהֲוָה סָלֵיק בְּאִיפּוּמָא. אֲתָא לְקַמֵּיהּ
דְּרַב יוֹסֵף וּשְׁרָא לֵיהּ. אָמַר רַב אַחָא בַּר
תַּחְלִיפָא: דִּשְׁרָא לָךְ — כְּרַבָּה שְׁרָא לָךְ. פְּשִׁיטָא! מַהוּ דְּתֵימָא: אֲפִילּוּ לְרַב שֵׁשֶׁת,
בֵּיתָא כְּמַאן דְּמָלֵי דָּמֵי, וְלִישְׁתַּמֵּשׁ בְּפָחוֹת מִג' סָמוּךְ לַגַּג, קמ"ל. תְּנַן: "שָׁרָשָׁיו
גְּבוֹהִין מִן הָאָרֶץ ג' טְפָחִים — לֹא יֵשֵׁב עֲלֵיהֶם". הֵיכִי דָּמֵי? אִי דְּלָא הָדְרִי כָּיְפִי —
פְּשִׁיטָא! אֶלָּא לָאו — אע"ג דְּהָדְרִי כָּיְפִי! לֹא, לְעוֹלָם דְּלָא הָדְרִי כָּיְפִי. וְהָא
קמ"ל: דאע"ג דְּצִידּוֹ אֶחָד שָׁוֶה לָאָרֶץ.§ ת"ר: שָׁרְשֵׁי אִילָן שֶׁגְּבוֹהִין מִן הָאָרֶץ
ג' טְפָחִים. אוֹ שֶׁיֵּשׁ חָלָל תַּחְתֵּיהֶן ג' טְפָחִים, אע"פ שֶׁצִּידּוֹ אֶחָד שָׁוֶה לָאָרֶץ —
ה"ז לֹא יֵשֵׁב עֲלֵיהֶן, לְפִי השֶׁאֵין עוֹלִין בְּאִילָן, וְאֵין נִתְלִין בְּאִילָן, וְאֵין נִשְׁעָנִין
בְּאִילָן, וְלֹא יַעֲלֶה בְּאִילָן מִבְּעוֹד יוֹם וְיֵשֵׁב שָׁם כָּל הַיּוֹם כּוּלּוֹ, אֶחָד אִילָן
וְאֶחָד כָּל הַבְּהֵמָה. אֲבָל בּוֹר שִׁיחַ וּמְעָרָה וְגָדֵר *מְטַפֵּס וְעוֹלֶה מְטַפֵּס
וְיוֹרֵד, וַאֲפִילּוּ הֵן מֵאָה אַמָּה. תָּנֵי חֲדָא: אִם עָלָה — מוּתָּר לֵירֵד, וְתָנֵי חֲדָא:
אָסוּר לֵירֵד. לָא קַשְׁיָא; כָּאן — מִבְּעוֹד יוֹם, כָּאן — מִשֶּׁחֲשֵׁיכָה. וְאִיבָּעֵית אֵימָא:
והָא וְהָא מִשֶּׁחֲשֵׁיכָה, וְל"ק; כָּאן — בְּשׁוֹגֵג, כָּאן — בְּמֵזִיד. וְאִיבָּעֵית אֵימָא: הָא וְהָא
בְּשׁוֹגֵג, וְהָכָא *בִּקְנָסוּ שׁוֹגֵג אַטּוּ מֵזִיד קָמִיפַּלְגִי; מָר סָבַר: קָנְסִינַן, וּמָר סָבַר:
לָא קָנְסִינַן. אָמַר רַב הוּנָא בְּרֵיהּ דְּרַב יְהוֹשֻׁעַ: כְּתַנָּאֵי, *זהַנִּיתָּנִין בְּמַתָּנָה
אַחַת שֶׁנִּתְעָרְבוּ בְּנִיתָּנִין מַתָּנָה אַחַת — יִנָּתְנוּ בְּמַתָּנָה אַחַת. מַתַּן ד' בְּמַתַּן
ד' — יִנָּתְנוּ בְּמַתַּן ד'. מַתַּן אַרְבַּע בְּמַתַּן אַחַת — ר"א אוֹמֵר: יִנָּתְנוּ בְּמַתַּן ד', וְר'
יְהוֹשֻׁעַ אוֹמֵר: יִנָּתְנוּ בְּמַתָּנָה אַחַת. אָמַר לוֹ ר"א: הֲרֵי הוּא עוֹבֵר עַל "בַּל
תִּגְרַע"! אָמַר לוֹ ר' יְהוֹשֻׁעַ: הֲרֵי הוּא עוֹבֵר בְּ"בַל תּוֹסִיף"! *א"ר אֱלִיעֶזֶר: לֹא
אָמְרוּ אֶלָּא כְּשֶׁהוּא בְּעַצְמוֹ. אָמַר לוֹ ר' יְהוֹשֻׁעַ: לֹא נֶאֱמַר "בַּל תִּגְרַע"
אֶלָּא כְּשֶׁהוּא בְּעַצְמוֹ. וְעוֹד א"ר יְהוֹשֻׁעַ: כְּשֶׁנָּתַתָּ — עָבַרְתָּ עַל "בַּל תּוֹסִיף"
וְעָשִׂיתָ מַעֲשֶׂה בְּיָדְךָ, כְּשֶׁלֹּא נָתַתָּ — עָבַרְתָּ עַל "בַּל תִּגְרַע" וְלֹא עָשִׂיתָ
מַעֲשֶׂה בְּיָדְךָ. לְר"א, דְּאָמַר הָתָם: קוּם עֲשֵׂה עָדִיף — ה"נ יֵרֵד. לְר' יְהוֹשֻׁעַ
דְּאָמַר הָתָם שֵׁב וְאַל תַּעֲשֶׂה עָדִיף — ה"נ לֹא יֵרֵד. דִּילְמָא לֹא הִיא, ע"כ לָא קָאָמַר
ר"א הָתָם קוּם עֲשֵׂה עָדִיף *אֶלָּא דְּקָא עָבֵיד מִצְוָה, אֲבָל הָכָא דְּלָא עָבֵיד מִצְוָה —
ה"נ לֹא יֵרֵד. וְאִי נַמִּי, ע"כ לָא קָאָמַר ר' יְהוֹשֻׁעַ הָתָם שֵׁב וְאַל תַּעֲשֶׂה עָדִיף(א) — אֶלָּא
דְּלָא

רש"י

מִשּׁוּם דְּהָוֵי דִּירָה שֶׁתַּשְׁמִישָׁהּ לָאֲוִיר. אֵינָהּ לָדוּר בָּהּ תָּמִיד, אֶלָּא לְהִסְתּוֹפֵף בָּהּ שׁוֹמְרֵי (אֲוִיר) הַשָּׂדֶה: מִלְמַעְלָה מִג' לְתוֹךְ ג'. דִּלְאַחַר שֶׁהִגְבִּיהוּ שְׁלֹשָׁה חָזְרוּ וְכָפְפוּ: דְּדָמוּ כִּי מְשׁוּנִיתָא. כְּשֵׁן סֶלַע, כְּהַר זֶה שֶׁמְּשׁוּפָּע לִצְדָדִין, כָּךְ יוֹצְאִין שָׁרָשָׁיו קְטַנִּים מִתּוֹךְ הַגְּדוֹלִין לִצְדָדִין וְכְפוּפִין לָאָרֶץ מִכָּאן וּמִכָּאן, הַגְּדוֹלִים הוֹלְכִין וּמַגְבִּיהִין בַּאֲלַכְסוֹן יוֹתֵר מִג' כָּזֶה: דְּסָלְקִי לְעֵילַּאי. הַגְּדִילִים מִשֶּׁהִגְבִּיהַּ לְמַעְלָה מִג': אֲסוּרִין. לְדִבְרֵי הַכֹּל: דְּנָחְתִּי לְתַתַּאי. הַגְּדֵילִים לְרֹאשׁוֹ שֶׁל צַד הָאִילָן, כָּל שֶׁלֹּא גָּבוֹהַּ ג' וְכֵן קְטַנִּים הַיּוֹצְאִין מִן הַגְּדֵילִים בְּשִׁיפּוּלוֹ: שָׁרוּ. לְדִבְרֵי הַכֹּל דְּהַכָּא לָאו לִכְלָל אִיסּוּר אָתוּ: לְצִדָּדִין. הַשָּׁרָשִׁים הַקְּטַנִּים הַיּוֹצְאִים מִתּוֹךְ גּוֹבַהּ שֶׁל גְּדוֹלִים, וּמָטִין לָאָרֶץ לְתוֹךְ ג' לְרַב שֵׁשֶׁת אֲסִירִי, דְּמִכֹּחַ אִיסּוּרָא אָתוּ. לְרַבָּה שָׁרוּ: וְכֵן אַנִּיגְרָא. אִילָן הַיּוֹצֵא מִתּוֹךְ חָרִיץ קָצָר הֶעָשׂוּי לְהוֹלִיךְ הַמַּיִם לַשָּׂדוֹת, וּשְׁנֵי לִידֵי הָאִילָן שֶׁל צַד גִּידוּדֵי הֶחָרִיץ נִכְנָסִין בְּגִידוּדָיו. וְאִם בָּא לִמְדּוֹד מִלְּדָדִין שֶׁבְּתוֹךְ הַנֶּגֶר — הֲרֵי הוּא גָּבוֹהַּ ג' וְיוֹתֵר, וְאִם בָּא לִמְדּוֹד מִלְּדָדָיו הַשְּׁנַיִים שֶׁהֵן מִגִּידוּדֵי הֶחָרִיץ וּלְמַעְלָה — אֵין גָּבוֹהַּ ג'. לְרַבָּה(ג) דְּמוֹדֵד הַגִּידוּדִים שָׁרוּ דְּכָל פָּחוֹת מִג' לְאַרְעָא כְּאַרְעָא. לְרַב שֵׁשֶׁת מֵעוּמְקוֹ מוֹדֵד, וַהֲרֵי גָּבוֹהַּ ג' וּמִכֹּחַ אִיסּוּרָא אָתוּ: וְכֵן קֶרֶן זָוִית. אִילָן הָעוֹלֶה בְּמִקְצוֹעַ שְׁנֵי כּוֹתָלִים שֶׁל חָצֵר, וְג' לְדָדָיו נִכְנָסִין בְּתוֹךְ הַמִּקְצוֹעַ שֶׁבַּכּוֹתָלִים, וְאֵין נִרְאֶה אֶלָּא לִדּוֹ שֶׁמִּבַּחוּץ, וְהוֹלֵךְ וְעוֹלֶה עַד לְמַעְלָה לַכּוֹתֶל פָּחוֹת מִג'. לְרַבָּה כָּל פָּחוֹת מִג' לָאו אִילָן הוּא, דְּמֵעוֹלָם לֹא גָּבוֹהַּ שְׁלֹשָׁה, וּלְרַב שֵׁשֶׁת מֵאַרְעָא מָשְׁחִינַן, וּמִכֹּחַ אִיסּוּרָא אָתוּ. וְדַוְקָא קֶרֶן זָוִית, אֲבָל אֵצֶל כּוֹתֶל בְּעָלְמָא — מוֹדֶה רַבָּה, דְּהוֹאִיל וּשְׁלֹשֶׁת לְדָדָיו גְּבוֹהִין וְהָרְבִיעִי שָׁוֶה לָאָרֶץ אוֹ לַכּוֹתֶל — דְּאָסוּר, אֲפִי' לִדּוֹ דְּשָׁוֶה לַכּוֹתֶל: דַּהֲוָה סָלֵיק בְּאִיפּוּמָא. בְּתוֹךְ הַבַּיִת הָיָה עוֹמֵד, וְעוֹלֶה דֶּרֶךְ פִּי אֲרוּבָּה לְמַעְלָה מִן הַגַּג פָּחוֹת מִג': וּשְׁרָא לֵיהּ. דְּאֵינוֹ נִרְאֶה מִן הַגַּג ג' אֲפִי' בְּאֶחָד מִלְּדָדָיו: כְּרַבָּה שְׁרָא לָךְ. דְּאָמַר לָא אָמְרִי' מִכֹּחַ אִיסּוּרָא אָתֵי, דְּהָא הָכָא בְּתוֹךְ הַבַּיִת הוּא דְּאָסוּר שֶׁגּוֹבְהוֹ נִרְאֶה שָׁם: דְּמָלֵי. כְּאַרְעָא סְמִיכְתָּא הִיא. דְּהָא אָמְרַן לְעֵיל: *חַלּוֹן שֶׁבֵּין שְׁנֵי בָּתִּים לְמַעְלָה מִי' כְּמַאן דְּמָלֵי דָּמֵי: דְּהָדְרִי כָּיְפִי. וְאַשְׁמְעִינַן דְּלֹא יֵשֵׁב עַל הַכְּפוּפִין. דְּאִי עַל הַגְּבוֹהִין — פְּשִׁיטָא, אַכַּתִּי לָא אַשְׁמְעִינַן אֵלּוּ הֵן מִשּׁוּם שְׁבוּת: לֹא עוֹלִין בְּאִילָן, בְּמַס' בֵּיצָה (דף לו:): דְּצִידּוֹ אֶחָד שָׁוֶה לָאָרֶץ. שֶׁהַקַּרְקַע גָּבוֹהַּ בְּלִדּוֹ הָאֶחָד, מוֹדֶה רַבָּה הֵיכָא דִּשְׁלֹשֶׁת לְדָדָיו גְּבוֹהִין מִן הָאָרֶץ, דַּאֲסוּרָה צַד הַשָּׁוֶה לָאָרֶץ: וְאֵין נִיתְלִין בְּאִילָן. אסטנדלי"ר: בּוֹר וְשִׁיחַ וּמְעָרָה. בֵּין שֶׁיֵּשׁ בָּהֶן מַיִם, בֵּין שֶׁאֵין בָּהֶם מַיִם: מְטַפֵּס. דנפיי"ר, מְטַפֵּס וְיוֹרֵד. דְּטַעְמָא לָאו מִשּׁוּם דְּטִרְחָא, אֶלָּא שֶׁלֹּא יִתְלוֹשׁ מִן הַמְחוּבָּר בְּמִתְכַּוֵּין: אִם עָלָה. בְּאִילָן, אָסוּר לֵירֵד. דְּכָל דֶּרֶךְ יְרִידָתוֹ הוּא מִשְׁתַּמֵּשׁ בִּמְחוּבָּר: עָלָה מִבְּעוֹד יוֹם. וְקָדַשׁ עָלָיו הַיּוֹם — לָא קָנְסִינַן לֵיהּ, וְיוֹרֵד: הַנִּיתָּנִין בְּמַתָּנָה אַחַת וכו'. כְּגוֹן דַּם הַבְּכוֹר שֶׁנִּתְעָרֵב בְּדַם בְּכוֹר אַחֵר: יִנָּתְנוּ בְּמַתָּנָה אַחַת. וְעוֹלָה אוֹתָהּ מַתָּנָה לָזֶה וְלָזֶה: מַתַּן אַרְבַּע בְּמַתַּן אַרְבַּע. דַּם חַטָּאת זוֹ נִשְׁפַּךְ לְדַם חַטָּאת זוֹ — יִנָּתְנוּ ד' מַתָּנוֹת, וְעוֹלֶה לָזוֹ וְלָזוֹ: יִנָּתְנוּ בְּמַתַּן אַרְבַּע. דְּקָסָבַר: קוּם עֲשֵׂה מִלְּוָה עָדִיף, אע"ג דְּהָאִי מִלְּוָה אִיכָּא צַד עֲבֵירָה דְּעָבַר אַבְּכוֹר אַבַּל תּוֹסִיף, הָאִי עֲשֵׂה דְּחַטָּאת דִּכְתִיב (ויקרא ד): "וְנָתַן עַל קַרְנוֹת" וְדָחֵי לְבַל תּוֹסִיף דִּבְכוֹר: וְר' יְהוֹשֻׁעַ אוֹמֵר נוֹתְנוּ בְּמַתָּנָה אַחַת. כֵּיוָן דְּקַיְימָא לָן: *)כָּל הַנִּיתָּנִין עַל מִזְבֵּחַ הַחִיצוֹן שֶׁנְּתָנָן בְּמַתָּנָה אַחַת כִּיפֵּר, הָכָא דְּלָא אֶפְשָׁר סָמְכִינַן עֲלָהּ אֲפִילּוּ לְכַתְּחִילָּה, וְלָא עָבְרִינַן אַבַּל תּוֹסִיף. וְאִי מִשּׁוּם בַּל תִּגְרַע דְּחַטָּאת, כִּדְקָאָמַר טַעְמָא: מוּטָב שֶׁיֵּעָקֵר "בַּל תִּגְרַע" מֵאֵלָיו, שֶׁהוּא יוֹשֵׁב וְאֵינוֹ עוֹקֵר הַלָּאו בְּיָדַיִם, מֵעֲבוֹר עַל "בַּל תּוֹסִיף" שֶׁהוּא עוֹקְרוֹ בְּיָדַיִם: ה"נ יוֹרֵד. דְּהַךְ יְרִידָה מִלְּוָה הִיא, דְּהָא כָּל זְמַן שֶׁהוּא יוֹשֵׁב מִשְׁתַּמֵּשׁ(ג) וַהֲרֵי זֶה תַּשְׁמִישׁ. הִלְכָּךְ, אע"ג דְּהַשְׁתָּא מִשְׁתַּמֵּשׁ תַּשְׁמִישׁ אַחֵר כְּשֶׁיּוֹרֵד יוֹתֵר וְיוֹתֵר — עָדִיף מִשֶּׁיֵּשֵׁב שָׁם: דְּקָא עָבֵיד מִצְוָה. דִּמְקַיֵּים עֲשֵׂה. פּוֹרֵשׁ מִן הָעֲבֵירָה הוּא ע"י עֲבֵירָה, אֲבָל קִיּוּם מִלְּוָה אֵין כָּאן: דְּלָא

*) [זבחים לו:]

תוספות

וכן בקרן זוית. פי' בקונטרס: שג' לדדיו נכנסין תוך המקצוע, ואין נראה מבחוץ אלא צד רביעי. ואיצטריך למימר תרוייהו קרן זוית, להודיעך כחו דרב ששת, ונגר דמשני לדדיו להודיעך כחו דרבה, דשרי. ומיהו, מודה רבה בסמוך לכותל שאינו שוה לארץ אלא מצד אחד דאסור. והא דנקט ברייתא בסמוך: וצדו אחד שוה לארץ – לא תקשי לרב ששת, דלדידיה לאו דוקא נקט צדו אחד, דהוא הדין משני צדדין: מתן ד' במתן אחת. פי': עולה שהיא מתן שתים שהן ד', בבכור או בפסח. אבל אין לפרש מתן ד' היינו חטאת – דאם נתערבה מתן חטאת בפסח או בבכור אין להם תקנה, לפי שזה למעלה מחוט הסיקרא וזה למטה. וא"ת: וליתי עשה ולידחי לאו ד"בל תוסיף"! וי"ל: דלא דמי כלל לכלאים בציצית, דהכא ע"י פשיעה הוא בא, והיה יכול להתקיים בלא דחיית הלאו: ינתנו במתנה אחת. דקיימא לן: *כל הניתנין (ד)שנתנו במתנה אחת כפר:

לא

רבינו חננאל

שרשיו גבוהין מן הארץ ג' טפחים לא ישב עליהן בשב' שנמצא [משתמש] באילן אבל אם היו שרשיו גבוהין מן הארץ פחות מג' טפחים הרי הן בקרקע ומותר לישב עליהן. אתמר שרשי האילן הבאין למעלה מג' טפחים וחוזרין ונכפפין לתוך ג' רבה אמר מותר לישב עליהן דכל פחות מג' טפחים דארעא כארעא הוא. רב ששת אמר אסור. כיון דמכח איסורא קא אתי אסור. דמו למשוניתא. פי' *) ההוא דיקלא דהוה לבי רב ביבי בר אביי דהוה סליק באיפומא פי' היה עולה אותה תמרה עד הגג ובגג היה לול ויצא מן הלול ועלה באויר הגג והיא עכשיו ענפיה בפחות מג' לגג אתא לקמי (דרבא) [דרב] (רב) יוסף שרא ליה לישב עליו אמר ליה רב אחא בר תחליפא הני דשרו לך כרבה שרו לך דאמר כל פחות מג' לארץ ארץ היא הכא נמי כל פחות מג' לגג גג הוא ואמרינן פשיטא מהו דתימא אפילו לרב ששת ביתא כמאן דמלי דמי [קמשמע לן] היכי דמי אילימא דלא הדרי כיפי צריכא למימר אלא לאו אע"ג דהדרי כיפי שרו. [ומשני לעולם דלא הדרי כיפי] והא קמשמע לן דאף על גב דצידו אחד שוה לארץ אסור דתניא שרשי אילן שגבוהין מן הארץ ג' טפחים או שיש חלל כו'. תני חדא אם עלה באילן ירד והני מילי מבעו"י אבל אם עלה משחשכה אסור. איבעית אימא לעולם בשעלה משחשכה ואם בשוגג ירד במזיד לא ירד. אמר רב הונא בריה דרב יהושע כתנאי דתניא בשחיטת קדשים פ"ח הניתנין מתן ד' כו' לר' אליעזר דאמר התם קום עשה עדיף מותר לירד מן האילן לר' יהושע דאמר שב ואל תעשה עדיף עלה אסור לירד. ודחינן ממאי דלמא עד כאן לא אמר ר' אליעזר התם דכי קא יהיב מצוה קא עביד אבל הכא דכי נחית מן האילן לא עביד [מצוה] הכי נמי לא ירד אבל **) הכא דיתיב באילן עביד איסורא הכי נמי דירד.

תני

*) נראה דחסר בהעתקה פי' ד' רביע על משוניתא ועי' בערוך ערך משנית. **) נראה דחסר כאן וכן צ"ל ואי נמי ע"כ לא אמר ר"י התם שב ואל תעשה עדיף אלא דוקא דלא קעביד איסורא אבל הכא וכו'.

עין משפט נר מצוה

לט א ב ג ד מיי' פכ"א מהל' שבת הל' ח סמג לאוין סה טוש"ע א"ח סי' שלו סעיף כ.
מ ה ו מיי' שם הלכה ט וטוש"ע שם סעיף א:
מא ז מיי' פ"ב מהל' פסולי המוקדשין הלכה יא:

מסורת הש"ס

[ע' לעיל כח. מ"ש על לידו]
[שבת ג: וש"נ]
ר"ה כח: זבחים פ.
[זבחים לו:]
דכי יהיב עביד מצוה כ"ה בס"א
[לעיל עח:]

הגהות הב"ח

(א) גמ' שב ואל תעשה עדיף לאו לא: (ב) רש"י ד"ה וכן אניגרא וכו' לרבה מודד מהגידודים ושרי דכל פחות: (ג) ד"ה ה"נ יורד וכו' שהוא יושב משתמש (והרי זה תשמיש) תא"מ ונ"ב כצ"ל להגיה והדר משתמש: (ד) תוס' ד"ה ינתנו וכו' כל הניתנין על מזבח החיצון שניתנו במתנה:

רב נסים גאון

משום דהואי דירה שתשמישה לאויר וכל דירה שתשמישה לאויר אין מטלטלין בה יותר מבית סאתים ואיתא בתוספתא דעירובין בפרק ב' ואיתא נמי בגמרא דעושין פסין (דף כב) כלל אמר ר' שמעון כל אויר שתשמישו לדירה כו' וכל שתשמישה לאויר כגון בורגנין שבשדה בית סאתים מותר יתר מבית סאתים אסור:

והשתא

גליון הש"ס

תוס' ד"ה מתן ד' וכו' ולדחי לאו דבל תוסיף. במהרי"ק שרש קלט כ' ועוד שהרי תוס' כתבו פרק בתרא דעירובין וז"ל ועי"ל דאין עשה דוחה ל"ת שבמקדש כדאמרינן פרק דם חטאת מיהו יש לדחות דלא דמי דה"ט דל"ת במקדש חמיר ולא מלחי קמי עשה אבל גבי בל תוסיף ל"ש שום חומרא דשייך נמי בעלמא. א"כ מ"מ י"ל כיון דהוי במקדש לא דחי עכ"ל תוס':

מב א מיי' פכ"א מהל' שבת הלכה ו סמג לאוין סה טוש"ע א"ח סי' שלו סעיף א:
מג ב מיי' פ"א שם הל' ה סמג שם טוש"ע שם סעיף ג:
מד ג מיי' פ"ה מהל' דעות הלכה ד ופכ"א מהלכות איסורי ביאה הל' יא סמג לאוין קכו טור ש"ע א"ח סי' רמ סעיף י וטוש"ע אה"ע סי' כה סעיף ב:
מה ד טוש"ע א"ח סי' רמ סעיף א:

דְּלָא קָא עָבֵיד אִיסּוּרָא, אֲבָל הָכָא דְּקָא עָבֵיד אִיסּוּרָא — הָכִי נַמִּי דְּיָרֵד. תָּנֵי חֲדָא: אאֶחָד אִילָן לַח וְאֶחָד אִילָן יָבֵשׁ. וְתַנְיָא אִידָךְ: בד"א — בְּלַח, אֲבָל בְּיָבֵשׁ — מוּתָּר. אָמַר רַב יְהוּדָה: ל"ק; כָּאן — בְּשֶׁגִּזְעוֹ מַחֲלִיף, כָּאן — בְּשֶׁאֵין גִּזְעוֹ מַחֲלִיף. גִּזְעוֹ מַחֲלִיף יָבֵשׁ קָרֵית לֵיהּ? אֶלָּא: לָא קַשְׁיָא; כָּאן — בִּימוֹת הַחַמָּה, כָּאן — בִּימוֹת הַגְּשָׁמִים. בִּימוֹת הַחַמָּה *הָא נָתְרֵי פֵּירֵי! בִּדְלֵיכָּא פֵּירֵי. וְהָא קָא נָתְרֵי קִינְסֵי! *בִּגְרוֹדָא. אִינִי?! וְהָא רַב אִיקְלַע לְאַפְסְטַיָּא, וַאֲסַר בִּגְרוֹדָא! *רַב בִּקְעָה מָצָא, וְגָדַר בָּהּ גָּדֵר.§ אָמַר רָמִי בַּר *אַבָּא, אָמַר רַב אַסִּי: אָסוּר לְאָדָם שֶׁיְּהַלֵּךְ עַל גַּבֵּי עֲשָׂבִים בְּשַׁבָּת, מִשּׁוּם שֶׁנֶּאֱמַר: °"וְאָץ בְּרַגְלַיִם חוֹטֵא". תָּנֵי חֲדָא: מוּתָּר לֵילֵךְ ע"ג עֲשָׂבִים בְּשַׁבָּת, וְתַנְיָא אִידָךְ: אָסוּר. ל"ק; הָא — בְּלַחִים, הָא — בִּיבֵשִׁים. וְאִי בָּעֵית אֵימָא: הָא וְהָא בְּלַחִים, וְלָא קַשְׁיָא; כָּאן — בִּימוֹת הַחַמָּה, כָּאן — בִּימוֹת הַגְּשָׁמִים. וְאִיבָּעֵית אֵימָא: °הָא וְהָא בִּימוֹת הַחַמָּה, וְל"ק; הָא — דְּסַיֵּים מְסָאנֵיהּ, הָא — דְּלָא סַיֵּים מְסָאנֵיהּ. °וְאִיבָּעֵית אֵימָא: הָא וְהָא דְּסַיֵּים מְסָאנֵיהּ, וְל"ק; הָא — דְּאִית לֵיהּ עוּקְצֵי, הָא דְּלֵית לֵיהּ עוּקְצֵי. וְאִיבָּעֵית אֵימָא: הָא וְהָא דְּאִית לֵיהּ עוּקְצֵי, הָא — דְּאִית לֵיהּ *שְׁרָכָא, הָא — דְּלֵית לֵיהּ שְׁרָכָא. *וְהָאִידָּנָא דְּקַיְימָא לַן כְּר"ש — בכּוּלְּהוּ שָׁרֵי.§ וְאָמַר רָמִי בַּר חָמָא, אָמַר רַב אַסִּי: גאָסוּר לְאָדָם שֶׁיָּכוֹף אִשְׁתּוֹ לִדְבַר מִצְוָה, שֶׁנֶּאֱמַר: "וְאָץ בְּרַגְלַיִם חוֹטֵא". וְא"ר יְהוֹשֻׁעַ בֶּן לֵוִי: כָּל הַכּוֹפֶה אִשְׁתּוֹ לִדְבַר מִצְוָה — הָוְיָין לוֹ בָּנִים שֶׁאֵינָן מְהוּגָּנִין. אָמַר רַב אִיקָא בַּר חִינָּנָא: מַאי קְרָאָה °"גַּם בְּלֹא דַעַת נֶפֶשׁ לֹא טוֹב". תַּנְיָא נַמִּי הָכִי: "גַּם בְּלֹא דַעַת נֶפֶשׁ לֹא טוֹב" — זֶה הַכּוֹפֶה אִשְׁתּוֹ לִדְבַר מִצְוָה. "וְאָץ בְּרַגְלַיִם חוֹטֵא" — זֶה הַבּוֹעֵל וְשׁוֹנֶה. אִינִי?! *וְהָאָמַר רָבָא: הָרוֹצֶה לַעֲשׂוֹת כָּל בָּנָיו זְכָרִים — יִבְעוֹל וְיִשְׁנֶה! ל"ק; כָּאן — לָדַעַת, כָּאן — שֶׁלֹּא לָדַעַת.§ *א"ר שְׁמוּאֵל בַּר נַחְמָנִי, א"ר *יוֹחָנָן: כָּל אִשָּׁה שֶׁתּוֹבַעַת בַּעְלָהּ לִדְבַר מִצְוָה — הָוְיָין לָהּ בָּנִים שֶׁאֲפִילּוּ בְּדוֹרוֹ שֶׁל מֹשֶׁה לֹא הָיוּ כְּמוֹתָן. דְּאִילּוּ בְּדוֹרוֹ שֶׁל מֹשֶׁה כְּתִיב: °"הָבוּ לָכֶם אֲנָשִׁים חֲכָמִים וּנְבוֹנִים וִידוּעִים לְשִׁבְטֵיכֶם", וּכְתִיב: "וָאֶקַּח אֶת רָאשֵׁי שִׁבְטֵיכֶם אֲנָשִׁים חֲכָמִים וִידוּעִים", וְאִילּוּ נְבוֹנִים לָא אַשְׁכַּח. וְאִילּוּ גַּבֵּי לֵאָה כְּתִיב: °"וַתֵּצֵא לֵאָה לִקְרָאתוֹ וַתֹּאמֶר אֵלַי תָּבוֹא כִּי שָׂכֹר שְׂכַרְתִּיךָ", וּכְתִיב: °"וּמִבְּנֵי יִשָּׂשכָר יוֹדְעֵי בִינָה לָעִתִּים לָדַעַת מַה יַּעֲשֶׂה יִשְׂרָאֵל רָאשֵׁיהֶם מָאתַיִם וְכָל אֲחֵיהֶם עַל פִּיהֶם". אִינִי?! וְהָאָמַר רַב יִצְחָק בַּר אַבְדִּימִי: *עֶשֶׂר קְלָלוֹת נִתְקַלְּלָה חַוָּה, דִּכְתִיב: °"אֶל הָאִשָּׁה אָמַר הַרְבָּה אַרְבֶּה" — אֵלּוּ שְׁנֵי טִפֵּי דָמִים, אַחַת דַּם נִדָּה, וְאַחַת דַּם בְּתוּלִים. "עִצְּבוֹנֵךְ" — זֶה צַעַר גִּידּוּל בָּנִים. "וְהֵרוֹנֵךְ" — זֶה צַעַר הָעִיבּוּר. "בְּעֶצֶב תֵּלְדִי בָנִים" — כְּמַשְׁמָעוֹ. *"וְאֶל אִישֵׁךְ תְּשׁוּקָתֵךְ" — מְלַמֵּד שֶׁהָאִשָּׁה מִשְׁתּוֹקֶקֶת(א) עַל בַּעְלָהּ בְּשָׁעָה שֶׁיּוֹצֵא לַדֶּרֶךְ. "וְהוּא יִמְשָׁל בָּךְ" — מְלַמֵּד שֶׁהָאִשָּׁה תּוֹבַעַת בַּלֵּב, וְהָאִישׁ תּוֹבֵעַ בַּפֶּה, זוֹ הִיא מִדָּה טוֹבָה בְּנָשִׁים! דכִּי קָאָמְרִינַן — דְּמַרְצְיָא אַרְצוּיֵי קַמֵּיהּ. הָנֵי שֶׁבַע הָוְיָין! כִּי אֲתָא רַב דִּימִי, אֲמַר: עֲטוּפָה כְּאָבֵל, וּמְנוּדָּה מִכָּל אָדָם, וַחֲבוּשָׁה בְּבֵית הָאֲסוּרִין. מַאי מְנוּדָּה מִכָּל אָדָם? אִילֵימָא מִשּׁוּם *דַּאֲסִיר לָהּ יִיחוּד — אִיהוּ נַמִּי אֲסִיר לֵיהּ יִיחוּד! אֶלָּא דַּאֲסִירָא לְבֵי תְרֵי. בְּמַתְנִיתָא תָּנָא: מְגַדֶּלֶת שֵׂעָר כְּלִילִית, וְיוֹשֶׁבֶת וּמַשְׁתֶּנֶת מַיִם כִּבְהֵמָה, וְנַעֲשֵׂית כַּר לְבַעְלָהּ. וְאִידָךְ — הָנֵי, שֶׁבַח הוּא לָהּ. דְּא"ר חִיָּיא: מַאי דִּכְתִיב °"מַלְּפֵנוּ מִבַּהֲמוֹת אָרֶץ וּמֵעוֹף הַשָּׁמַיִם יְחַכְּמֵנוּ", "מַלְּפֵנוּ מִבַּהֲמוֹת" — זוֹ פְּרֵידָה שֶׁכּוֹרַעַת וּמַשְׁתֶּנֶת מַיִם. "וּמֵעוֹף הַשָּׁמַיִם יְחַכְּמֵנוּ" — זֶה תַּרְנְגוֹל שֶׁמְּפַיֵּיס וְאַחַר כָּךְ בּוֹעֵל. א"ר יוֹחָנָן: *אִילְמָלֵא לֹא נִיתְּנָה תּוֹרָה — הָיִינוּ לְמֵידִין צְנִיעוּת מֵחָתוּל, וְגָזֵל *מִנְּמָלָה, וַעֲרָיוֹת מִיּוֹנָה. דֶּרֶךְ אֶרֶץ מִתַּרְנְגוֹל — שֶׁמְּפַיֵּיס וְאַחַר כָּךְ בּוֹעֵל. וּמַאי מְפַיֵּיס לָהּ? אָמַר רַב יְהוּדָה, אָמַר רַב, הָכִי קָאָמַר לָהּ:(ב) זַבֵּינְנָא לִיךְ זִיגָא דְּמָטוּ לִיךְ עַד כַּרְעִיךְ. לְבָתַר הָכִי אָמַר לָהּ: לִישַׁמְּטֵיהּ לְכַרְבַּלְתֵּיהּ דְּהַהוּא תַּרְנְגוֹלָא, אִי אִית לֵיהּ וְלָא זַבֵּינְנָא לִיךְ.§
מתני'

תורה אור: משלי יט | שם | דברים א | בראשית ל | ד"ה א יב | בראשית ג | איוב לה

רש"י — דְּלָא קָא עָבֵיד אִיסּוּרָא. כְּשֶׁהוּא יוֹשֵׁב וְאֵינוֹ נוֹתֵן — הַלָּלוּ דְּבַל תִּגְרַע וְהָעֲשֵׂה דּוֹחֵהוּ עַל קַרְנוֹת נֶעֶקְרִין מֵאֲלֵיהֶן. אֲבָל זֶה — יְשִׁיבָתוֹ תַּשְׁמִישׁ הוּא, שֶׁהוּא מִשְׁתַּמֵּשׁ בָּאִילָן: יָבֵשׁ. שֶׁאֵין בּוֹ לִתְלוֹשׁ, וְלָאו מְחוּבָּר הוּא: בִּימוֹת הַחַמָּה. יָבֵשׁ מוּתָּר, דְּלֵיכָּא אֲפִי' מִשּׁוּם מַרְאִית הָעַיִן, שֶׁהֲרֵי נִיכָּר לַכֹּל שֶׁהוּא יָבֵשׁ שֶׁאֵינוֹ מוֹצִיא עָלִין. וְהָא דְּקָתָנֵי אָסוּר — בִּימוֹת הַגְּשָׁמִים, שֶׁאֵין נִיכָּר בֵּין לַח בֵּין יָבֵשׁ, וְאִיכָּא מִשּׁוּם מַרְאִית הָעַיִן: קָא נָתְרֵי פֵּירֵי. שֶׁנִּשְׁאֲרוּ בּוֹ מִשָּׁנָה שֶׁעָבְרָה, וְאָתֵי לְמִשְׁרֵי(ג) בֵּיהּ תְּלִישָׁה דְּלַח. נְהִי דַּעֲלַיָּה דְּיָבֵשׁ חַטּוּ עֲלָיָה דְּלַח לָא גָּזְרִי' דְּהִיא גּוּפָא גְּזֵירָה. מִיהוּ, תְּלִישָׁה חַטּוּ תְּלִישָׁה נִגְזַר: בִּגְרוֹדָא. יָחוּר שֶׁנִּשְׁרוּ עֲנָפָיו כּוּלָּם: בִּקְעָה מָצָא. כְּלוֹמַר: אֵינָן בְּנֵי תּוֹרָה שֶׁיֵּדְעוּ לְהִזָּהֵר. כְּבִקְעָה זוֹ שֶׁאֵין לָהּ שׁוֹמֵר וְהַכֹּל פָּרוּץ: וְאָץ בְּרַגְלַיִם חוֹטֵא. אַלְמָא: הִלּוּךְ נַמִּי חֵטְא קָרֵי לֵיהּ. וְהָכָא אִיכָּא חֵטְא שֶׁתּוֹלֵשׁ עֲשָׂבִים: לַחִים. אָסוּר, דְּהָוֵי תּוֹלֵשׁ. יְבֵשִׁין כִּתְלוּשִׁין דָּמֵי: סַיֵּים מְסָאנֵי. שָׁרֵי: לָא סַיֵּים מְסָאנֵי. אָסוּר, שֶׁעֲשָׂבִים נִדְבָּקִין בְּקִשְׁרֵי אֶצְבְּעוֹתָיו וְנִתְלָשִׁין: עוּקְצָא. אֶשְׁפִּי"א, (ד)כָּפוּל מִתַּחְתָּיו, וְהָעֲשָׂבִים נִדְבָּקִים שָׁם וְתוֹלְשָׁן: שְׁרָכָא. פְּתִילָה אֲרוּכָּה שֶׁהָעֵשֶׂב אָרוֹךְ אָסוּר:(ה) בִּימוֹת הַחַמָּה. זֶרַע יֵשׁ בַּגִּבְעוֹלִין וּמַשִּׁירָן: כְּר"ש. דְּאָמַר: דָּבָר שֶׁאֵין מִתְכַּוֵּין מוּתָּר: לִדְבַר מִצְוָה. תַּשְׁמִישׁ: בְּרַגְלַיִם. לְשׁוֹן תַּשְׁמִישׁ, דִּכְתִיב (שופטים ה): "בֵּין רַגְלֶיהָ כָּרַע נָפַל שָׁכָב": גַּם בְּלֹא דַעַת. רֵישָׁא דְּהַאי קְרָא אֲתָן בְּרַגְלַיִם הוּא: נֶפֶשׁ לֹא טוֹב. לֹא טוֹבִים הַבָּנִים הַנַּעֲשִׂים בְּלֹא דַעַת הָאִשָּׁה, שֶׁהָיָה בַּעְלָהּ אָץ בְּרַגְלַיִם: הַבּוֹעֵל וְשׁוֹנֶה. שֶׁמַּטְרִיחָהּ: לָדַעַת. הָאִשָּׁה: יִבְעוֹל וְיִשְׁנֶה. שֶׁמְּחַמֶּמֶת בִּיאָה רִאשׁוֹנָה נִתְאַוָּה הָאִשָּׁה וְהוּלְבְּשָׁה תַּאֲוָה, וּכְשֶׁבָּא בִּיאָה שְׁנִיָּה הִיא מַזְרַעַת תְּחִילָּה. וְהֵיכָא דְּהִיא מַזְרַעַת תְּחִילָּה יוֹלֶדֶת זָכָר: לִדְבַר מִצְוָה. תַּשְׁמִישׁ: נְבוֹנִים. מְבִינִים דָּבָר מִתּוֹךְ דָּבָר: יִשָּׂשכָר. לֵאָה תָּבְעָה אֶת יַעֲקֹב לִדְבַר מִצְוָה "וַתֹּאמֶר אֵלַי תָּבוֹא כִּי שָׂכֹר שְׂכַרְתִּיךָ" וגו': צַעַר עִבּוּר. עוּבָּרוֹת חוֹלוֹת הֵן: כְּמַשְׁמָעוֹ. צַעַר הַלֵּידָה: מִשְׁתּוֹקֶקֶת. מִתְאַוָּה לְתַשְׁמִישׁ: וְהוּא יִמְשָׁל בָּךְ. שֶׁהוּא מוֹשֵׁל לוֹמַר בַּפֶּה תַּאֲוַת לִבּוֹ, וְהָאִשָּׁה בַּלֵּב וּבוֹשָׁה לְהוֹצִיא בַּפֶּה: דְּמַרְצְיָא אַרְצוּיֵי קַמֵּיהּ. מַרְאָה לְפָנָיו עִנְיְנֵי חִיבָּה: עֲטוּפָה כְּאָבֵל. בּוֹשָׁה לָצֵאת בְּרֹאשָׁהּ פָּרוּעַ: מְנוּדָּה לְכָל אָדָם. לְקַמֵּיהּ מְפָרֵשׁ שֶׁאֲסוּרָה לְכָל אָדָם חוּץ מִבַּעְלָהּ, וְהָאִישׁ נוֹשֵׂא נָשִׁים הַרְבֵּה: וַחֲבוּשָׁה בְּבֵית הָאֲסוּרִים. כָּל כְּבוּדָּה בַת מֶלֶךְ פְּנִימָה: כְּלִילִית. שֵׁד: כִּבְהֵמָה. שֶׁכּוֹרַעַת כְּשֶׁהִיא מַשְׁתֶּנֶת וְדֶרֶךְ פְּרֵידָה לַעֲשׂוֹת כֵּן: כַּר לְבַעְלָהּ. שֶׁהוּא לְמַעְלָה בִּשְׁעַת תַּשְׁמִישׁ: שֶׁבַח הוּא לָהּ. יוֹשֶׁבֶת וּמַשְׁתֶּנֶת בִּצְנִיעוּת, וְאֵינָהּ חֲסֵרָה כְּלוּם בַּדָּבָר. וְנַעֲשֵׂית כַּר לְבַעְלָהּ — אֵין לָהּ טוֹרַח כָּל כָּךְ, טוֹרְחוֹ מְרוּבֶּה מִשֶּׁלָּהּ: מַלְּפֵנוּ. מְלַמְּדֵנוּ: מִבַּהֲמוֹת אָרֶץ. שֶׁנָּתַן בָּהֶם חָכְמָה לְהוֹרוֹת לָנוּ: שֶׁמְּפַיֵּיס. הוֹלֵךְ וּפוֹשֵׁט כְּנָפָיו, וְהוּא פִּיּוּס כִּדְאָמַר לְקַמָּן, שֶׁאוֹמֵר לָהּ לִקְנוֹת מַלְבּוּשׁ שֶׁמַּגִּיעַ לָאָרֶץ: צְנִיעוּת מֵחָתוּל. שֶׁאֵינוֹ מַטִּיל רְעִי בִּפְנֵי אָדָם, וּמְכַסֶּה צוֹאָתוֹ: וְגָזֵל מִנְּמָלָה. דִּכְתִיב (משלי ו): "(*תָּגֵרָה) בַּקַּיִץ לַחְמָהּ" וְאֵין אַחַת גּוֹזֶלֶת מֵאוֹכֶל חֲבֶרְתָּהּ: וַעֲרָיוֹת מִיּוֹנָה. שֶׁאֵינוֹ נִזְקָק אֶלָּא לְבַת זוּגוֹ: זִיגָא. מַלְבּוּשׁ שֶׁקּוֹרִין קוט"ה: לְבָתַר הָכִי. לְאַחַר בְּעִילָה, שֶׁמְּנַעְנֵעַ וְכוֹפֵף רֹאשׁוֹ לָהּ לָאָרֶץ: אִי אִית לֵיהּ. כַּמָּה לִיקַּח:
* נ"ל תכין

תוספות — לא קשיא הא בלחים הא ביבשים. וא"ת: והא לעיל אסרינן ביבש, דפריך: והא נתרי קינסי כו'! וי"ל: דבאילן שהוא גבוה שייך למגזר טפי, משום דמינכר ביה ניתרי קינסי: והאידנא דקי"ל כר"ש כולהו שרי. פי' ר"ת: דהאי היתר לא קאי אלא אעשבים, דשרי בכל ענין. אבל באילן אין להוכיח שם שום היתר, אפילו יבש. דשייך למיגזר טפי, משום דמנכרא מילתא:

עי' בהגהות רש"ש. ובד"ש ועוד הגי' גם לקמן ואמר רמי בר אבא

רבינו חננאל
תני חדא אחד אילן לח ואחד אילן יבש אסור להשתמש בו ותניא אידך בד"א בלח אבל ביבש דלא משיר עליו מותר ופריק רב יהודה הא דתני *) אסור כשאין גזעו מחליף והא דתני יבש מותר בשגזעו מחליף **). והא דתני אסור בימות הגשמים דאיכא עלין ומשירן. והא דתני יבש מותר בימות החמה ואקשינן בימות החמה הא קא משיר פירי ודחינן באילן דלית ביה פירי. והא איכא קינסי פי' עצים יבשים דקים שנפרכין ברגל או ביד כשעולין או כשיורדין מן האילן ודחינן באילן גרדא פירוש אילן קרח שאין לו עליו לא עלין ולא אמירין אלא הוא יבש כדגרסינן במועד [קטן] ואין משקין שדה גריר במועד. איני והא רב אסר באילן גרדא בשבת ופרקי רב בקעה מצא וגדר בה גדר כלומר מקום שלא היתה בו תורה כמו בקעה ואסר להן אפי' דבר המותר. פ"א קיסני פירוש עלה האילן. תני חדא אסור להלך ע"ג עשבים בשבת שנאמר ואץ ברגלים חוטא ותניא אידך מותר ופרקינן הא דתני אסור ר' יהודה דאמר דבר שאין מתכוין אסור והא דתני מותר ר"ש. ואמרינן אי בעית אימא הא והא ר' יהודה ולא קשיא הא בימות החמה והא בימות הגשמים. [ובדאית להו] שראני עשבים יבשים והן כגון פרוע מתלעתה או דסים מסאני ***) דאית בהו עקוסא בהיזמי והיגי ואסקינ' והשתא דקי"ל כר"ש דאמר דבר שאין מתכוין מותר כולהו שרי בין בימות החמה בין בימות הגשמים בין אית להו שראני בין לית להו שראני בין מסיים מסאני בין לא סיים. בין אית להו עקוסא בין לית להו. בין בהזמי והיגי בין בשאר ציבי בכלהו שרי. אסור לאדם לכוף אשתו לדבר מצוה שנאמר ואץ ברגלים חוטא וכל הכופה הווין לו בנין שאינן מהוגנין דכתיב גם בלא דעת נפש לא טוב נפש היוצאה מביניהם לא טובה. כל אשה שתובעת בעלה כגון לאה שכתוב בה ותצא לאה לקראתו וגו' ונפק מיניה יששכר דכתיב ומבני יששכר יודעי בינה לעתים לדעת מה יעשה ישראל. ובדורו של משה כתיב ואקח את ראשי שבטיכם אנשים חכמים וידועים ואילו נבונים לא אשכח והא דאמרן דתובעת בעלה לאו תובעת ממש תביעה בפה אלא דמרציא ארצויי קמיה בלבישת [בגדים] נאים ותקונם של גוף ודברים בניחותא שמרגילין את האדם לדבר מצוה: י' קללות נתקללה חוה הרבה ארבה כו'. ומנודה מכל אדם דאשה אחת אסורה להינשא לשני אנשים כאחד. א"ר יוחנן אלמלא לא נתנה תורה לישראל למדנו צניעות מחתול שאינו בועל אלא במקום סתר. גזל מנמלה שמכינה בקיץ לחמה. עריות מיונה שאינה מקבלת עליה זכר אלא זכר המיוחד לה. דרך ארץ מתרנגול שמפיים ומראה לתרנגולת בכנפו דוגא דכיפי עבידנא

*) לכאורה נ"ל להיפך הא דתני אסור בשגזעו מחליף והא דתני יבש מותר כשאין גזעו מחליף וצ"ע. **) חסר כאן ונ"ל ופריך גזעו מחליף יבש קרי ליה אלא הא דתני אסור וכו'. ***) רבינו גרס הא דאית ליה עקוסה והיינו דהמנעל יש לו עוקץ חד ושובר את העשבים וכ"ה בערוך ערך עקוס.

הגהות הב"ח
(א) גמ' משתוקקת אל בעלה: (ב) שם הכי קאמר לה זבינא ליך זיגא וכו' שורקא לישמטיה לכרבליתיה וכו' ולא זבינא ליך: (ג) רש"י ד"ה קא נתרי וכו' ואתי למישרי תלישה בלח כצ"ל ותיבת ביה נמחק: (ד) ד"ה עוקצי אשפי"א כפוף מתחתיו: (ה) ד"ה בימות החמה נ"ל קודם ד"ה סיים:

רב נסים גאון
והשתא דקיימא לן כר' שמעון כולהו שרי היינו דאמר ר' שמעון גורר אדם מטה כסא וספסל ובלבד שלא יתכוין לעשות חריץ דקא סבר דבר שאינו מתכוין מותר ואיתא בפרק במה מדליקין (שבת דף כט) וכבר פירשנוהו בפרק כירה ואמרינן נמי דעיקר דברי ר' יהודה דבר שאין מתכוין אסור במשנת יום טוב ובמשנת בכורות איתנהו:
מאי

גליון הש"ס גמ' הא והא בימות החמה. ברי"ף ורא"ש הגי' הא והא בימות הגשמים: **שם** ואי בעית אימא הא והא דסיים מסאניה. הרי"ף כאן השמיט ב' אוקימתות דעוקצי ודשרכא אבל בשבת פרק ואלו קשרים הביאן ובסיפור בתחילת אוקימתא הא דלאית ליה שרכא ואח"כ אוקימתא דסיים מסאניה ואח"כ אוקימתא דעוקצי. וגם איתא ועוקצי והיינו כמו עוקצי. ע' בערוך ערך עקוס:

[ע' תוס' שבת קנ: ד"ה במחובר] [בערוך גריס בגרויא] [לעיל ו. חולין קו.] [בערוך ערך שדך א' גרס שרכי] שבת לה. נדה לא: נדרים כ: [נ"ל יונתן] [אבות דר"נ פרק א ע"ש] יבמות סב: גירסת ע"י דאסירא ליחודי בהדי גברא דלאו דידה איהו נמי אסור ליחודי בהדי איתתא דלאו דידיה ע' תוס' מגילה כח. חולין נז:

מתני' הדלת שבמוקצה, וחדקים שבפרצה, ומחצלות – אין נועלין בהן אלא אם כן גבוהים מן הארץ.§ גמ' ורמינהו: דלת הנגררת, ומחצלת הנגררת, וקנקן הנגרר, בזמן שקשורין ותלויין – נועלין בהן בשבת, ואין צריך לומר ביום טוב! אמר אביי: בשיש להם ציר. רבא אמר: בשהיה להן ציר. מיתיבי: דלת הנגררת, ומחצלת הנגררת, וקנקן הנגרר, בזמן שקשורין ותלויין וגבוהים מן הארץ אפילו מלא נימא – נועלין בהן, ואם לאו – אין נועלין בהן. אביי מתרץ לטעמיה, ורבא מתרץ לטעמיה. אביי מתרץ לטעמיה: או שיש להן ציר, או שגבוהין מן הארץ. רבא מתרץ לטעמיה: כשהיה להן ציר, או שגבוהין מן הארץ.

ת"ר: סוכי קוצים וחבילין שהתקינן לפירצה שבחצר, בזמן שקשורין ותלויין – נועלין בהן בשבת, וא"צ לומר ביו"ט. תני ר' חייא: דלת אלמנה הנגררת – אין נועלין בה. היכי דמי דלת אלמנה – איכא דאמרי: דחד שיפא, ואיכא דאמרי: דלית ליה גשמה. *אמר רב יהודה: האי מדורתא, ממעלה למטה שרי – ממטה למעלה – אסיר. וכן ביעתא, וכן קידרא, וכן פוריא, וכן חביתא. א"ל ההוא צדוקי לרבי יהושע בן חנניה: חדקאה! דכתיב בכו: "טובם כחדק". אמר ליה: שטיא, שפיל לסיפיה דקרא, דכתיב: "ישר ממסוכה". ואלא מאי – "טובם כחדק" – כשם שחדקים הללו מגינין על הפירצה, כך טובים שבנו מגינים עלינו. דבר אחר: "טובם כחדק" – שמהדקין את הרשעים לגיהנם, שנאמר: "קומי ודושי בת ציון כי קרנך אשים ברזל ופרסותיך אשים נחושה והדיקות עמים רבים" וגו'.§ מתני' לא יעמוד אדם ברשות היחיד ויפתח ברשות הרבים, ברשות הרבים ויפתח ברשות היחיד, אא"כ עשה מחיצה גבוה עשרה טפחים, דברי ר' מאיר. אמרו לו: מעשה בשוק של *פטמים שהיה בירושלים שהיו נועלין ומניחין את המפתח בחלון שעל גבי הפתח. רבי יוסי אומר: שוק של צמרים הוה.§ גמ' ורבנן, אמר רבי מאיר רשות הרבים – ומהדרו אינהו כרמלית? *דאמר רבה בר *)בר חנה, אמר רבי יוחנן: ירושלים, אלמלא דלתותיה ננעלות בלילה – חייבין עליה משום רשות הרבים. אמר רב *פפא: כאן – קודם שנפרצו בה פרצות. כאן – לאחר שנפרצו בה פרצות. רבא אמר: סיפא אתאן לשערי גינה. והכי קאמר: וכן לא יעמוד ברשות היחיד ויפתח בכרמלית, בכרמלית ויפתח ברשות היחיד, אלא

*) [גי' הרא"ש רב הונא]

תורה אור: מיכה ז; שם ד

רש"י

מתני' הדלת שבמוקצה. רחבה שאחורי הבתים. ומשום הכי נקט לה, משום שאין משתמשין בה תדיר, ואין בעל הבית חושש לה לעשות לה דלת תלויה כראוי וקבועה, אלא זקופה כנגד הפתח. וכשהוא פותח מטילה לארץ. ויש שתלויות אבל נגררות לארץ: אין נועלין בה. בשבת, משום דעביד בנין. או אפילו כשהיא תלויה ונגררת – אין זה קבועה, וכשהוא מגביהה על המשקוף, כיון דאינה קבועה שם מחזי כבונה: וחדקים שבפרצה. קוצים שעשאם חבילות, והתקינם לסתום בהם פרצה, ופעמים שהוא פותחה: ומחצלת. של קנים, שקורין גליד"א: גמ' קנקן. הוא כלי שאוחזין בו מאחורי המחרישה כשהן חורשין. יש שנועלים ומעמידים אותו במקום דלת כנגד הפתח: בזמן שקשורים ותלויין. אלמא: אתלויין הוא דקפיד, אבל אגבוהים מן הארץ – לא חייש: בשיש להן ציר. דמוכחא מילתא דדלת גמורה היא, והרי היא קשורה ותלויה ולא מחזי כבונה: כשהיה להם ציר. ואע"ג דהשתא ליכא – היכירא הוא דאיכא. ל"א: טעמא דמתני' משום דחופר בארץ. וקשיא לי בגויה, דא"כ מאי תרלתיה דרבא דאמר כשהיה להם ציר? כיון דהשתא ליכא – הא קא עביד חריץ! ועוד: אם כן כר' יהודה בעי לאוקמיה, דאמר דבר שאין מתכוין אסור: וגבוהין. אלמא: תרוייהו בעינן: דלת אלמנה. דלת שהיא אלמנה מתקוניה: דחד שיפא. עשויה מקרש אחד, דהכא ודאי מחזי כבונה ונתן קרש בכותל, שאין בה היכר דלת: גשמה. דילי"ש, בריחים המחברין אותה: מדורתא. היסק גדול: מלמעלה למטה. לאחוז העצים העליונים באויר ולתת תחתונים מלמטה: שרי. ביו"ט, דאין זה בנין אהלים: מלמטה למעלה אסור. לתת התחתונים תחלה לגדדין ברבוע, כדרך שעושין לפני השרים, ולסדר עליונים למעלה. דהיינו כעין בנין אהל וגגו אסור. הכי גרסי': מלמעלה למטה שרי מלמטה למעלה – אסור. וכך מצאתי בתשובת הגאונים, וכן עיקר: וכן ביעתא. לסדר הביצים על הגחלים על כלי ברזל שקורין גרדי"ל, או על גבי שני עצים שמקיפין זה אצל זה, צריך לאחוז ביצים בידו על האור, ואחרו יתן העצים תחתיהן: וכן קדרה. כדתנן במסכת ביצה (דף לב:): אין מקיפין שתי חביות לשפות עליהן את הקדרה. ואמר רב יהודה: אסור להקיף חביות תחלה להקריבן זה אצל זה, ואח"כ יתן הקדרה עליהן, שזה דרך בנין. אבל יאחוז הקדרה באויר, ואחר כך יקיף חביות תחתיה: וכן פוריא. מטה שאוכלין שרים בדרכים, ושל פרקים היא, ויש להם עור ארוך מוקף לולאות, וקושר הלולאות בארוכות המטה. וכשהוא פורקן מתיר הלולאות, והעור נופל. והמתקנו ביו"ט צריך לאחוז העור שטוח מלמעלה, ואח"כ יביאו הרגלים עם הארוכות ויושיבוהו תחתיו. אבל לא יושיבוהו תחלה על רגליו ואח"כ יפשט העור: וכן חביתא. כשמסדר חביות במרתף שורה על שורה חביות של חרס הן כעין כדין גדולים ומדקדק לרב יהודה הכא גבי מתני', ש"מ טעמא דמתני' משום בנין ולא משום חופר: חידקאה. משול כקוץ: טובם כחדק. טובים שבהם כקוצים: שפיל לסיפיה דקרא. השפל עיניך, לשפלו של מקרא, לסופו תראה שלשבח הוא: ישר ממסוכה. הישרים שבנו מגינים עלינו כסוכה: מהדקין כמו: "ושחקת ממנה הדק" (שמות ל). קומי ודושי כו'. סיפיה דקרא: "והדיקות עמים":

מתני' לא יעמוד(א) ברשות היחיד. ויטול מפתח המונח ברשות הרבים, ויפתח בו פתח חנות שברשות הרבים. ואע"פ שאין ממקום מפתח לפתח ארבע אמות – גזירה שמא יכניס המפתח אצלו. וכן לא יעמוד אדם ברשות הרבים ויושיט ידו למעלה גבוה מעשרה ורוחב ארבעה, כגון מפתח חנות המונח על גגו ויטול שם המפתח, ויפתח בה החנות והוא גבוה למעלה מעשרה – גזירה שמא ידיחנה אצלו לתוך עשרה: אא"כ עשו לה מחיצה. ויעמוד בתוכה, ואסיפא קאי: פטמין. קלנים: נועלין. פתח חנותן ועומדין ברשות הרבים והמנעול למעלה מעשרה: צמרים. מוכרי צמר: גמ' ומהדרו ליה אינהו כרמלית. בתמיה דהא ירושלים כולה כרמלית היא, שהיא כולה כחצר של רבים שלא עירבו דהואיל ודלתותיה ננעלות בלילה מערבין את כולה: חייבין עליה. דעיר של רבים היא, שאוכלוסין הרבה באין לה. אבל עכשיו דדלתותיה ננעלות – לאו רשות הרבים, שאינה כדגלי מדבר שהוא דרך פתוח כל שעה. וכיון(ב) דכרמלית לית לן למיגזר שלא יעמוד בה ויפתח ברשות היחיד דילמא מייתי ליה דהא נמי מייתי לגביה שבות בעלמא היא וגזירה לגזירה לא גזרינן: מתניתין לאחר שנפרצה בה פרצות הוא: סיפא אתאן. רבנן אתו לאיפלוגי אשערי גינה לשער גינה שהיא כרמלית, וקאסר ר"מ לעמוד בה ולהושיט ידו על מקום גבוה עשרה ורוחב ארבעה שהוא רשות היחיד, ויטול מפתח(ג) המנעול הגבוה מעשרה: לא יעמוד ברה"י. כגון בחצירו, ויושיט ידו לגנות דרך חור או סדק, ויטול בו מפתח ויפתח בה מנעול מתוך הגינה, שמא ימשך המפתח אליו. ומחמיר רבי מאיר אפילו ברשויות דרבנן. וכן לא יעמוד בגינה ויושיט ידו למקום גבוה עשרה ורוחב ארבעה, שהוא רשות היחיד, ומפתח מונח בו, ויפתח מנעול למעלה מעשרה. גינה כרמלית היא, דהויא יותר מבית סאתים שלא הוקף לדירה: אלא

תוספות

מיתיבי דלת הנגררת. בלאו הכי הוה מצי לאקשויי רישא לסיפא, דקרי לה "נגררת" וקרי לה "גבוהין מן הארץ", והוה מצי למימר "וליטעמיך": דלת אלמנה הנגררת אין נועלין בה. פי' ר"י: דאיירי כשיש להן ציר. דאי אין להן ציר – מאי איריא דלת אלמנה? אפי' דלת אחרינא נמי:

וכן ביעתא. פי' בקונט': שמסדר ביצים על כלי ברזל שקורין גרדי"ל בלע"ז. ואין נראה לר"י(ד) דרך בנין בכך, שהרי כל המחילות עשויות כבר, ולא דמו לחבית ופוריא דמסדר זו אצל זו. ותדע, שהרי היתר פשוט הוא להניח קדירה על גבי טרפידא(ה). ונראה לר"י לפרש: שמסדר עצים או ביצים, ומניח ביצה על גביהן. ומה שאנו מסדרין ככר מכאן וככר מכאן וככר על גביהם, או בספר – ליכא איסורא, אלא כשצריך לאויר שתחתיהם. אי נמי: לא דמי לבנין אלא כשעושה על גבי הקרקע, ולא על השלחן: מביא

עין משפט נר מצוה

מו א ב מיי' פכ"ו מהל' שבת הלכה ח סמג לאוין סה טוש"ע א"ח סי' שיג סעיף ב:

מז ג מיי' שם הל' ט טוש"ע שם סעיף ה:

מח ד ה מיי' פ"ד מהל' יו"ט הל' יד סמג לאוין עה טור ש"ע א"ח סי' תקב סעיף ה:

מט ו מיי' פט"ו מהל' שבת הלכה ה סמג לאוין סה טוש"ע א"ח סי' שנ סעיף א:

מסורת הש"ס

ביצה לב:

[בערוך פירש מוכרי עופות וכ"כ הרב אלפס וע' רש"י ביצה כב: ד"ה פטם]

רבינו חננאל

ליכי גדולים עד דמטו מאוניך עד לארעא. ונשבע לה אם תשיג ידו ולא יעשה לה יהי רצון דנשמטיה שונרא לרישיה דההוא תרנגולא: הדלת שבמוקצה והחדקין שבפרצה כו'. מקום מוקצה שאינו שוה לכרמלית וגבוה ממנה שנעשה מוקצה מן כרמלית והיא כמין דיר וסהר ועשה לאותו מקום דלת. חדקין שבפרצה כדכתיב טובם כחדק והן הקוצין שסותמין בהן הפרצה שלא ליכנס בדיר גנב או חיה רעה והמחצלאות כשמשמען אין נועלין בהן אא"כ גבוהין מן הארץ. ורמינהו דלת הנגררת וקנקן הנגרר בזמן שקשורין ותלויין נועלין בהן בשבת ואין צריך לומר בי"ט. הנה אע"פ שאין גבוהין נועלין בהן. ופריק אביי כשיש להן ציר. כדכתיב הדלת תסוב על צירה והיא עקב אלברוב. רבא אמר כשהיה להם ציר כלומר כיון שהיה להן ציר אין סוגרין להן בדוחק לפיכך אין חוצרין חריץ בעת שסותמין לפיכך מותר. ומותבינן עלייהו דלת הנגררת ומחצלת הנגררת וקנקן הנגרר בזמן שיש להן ציר וגבוהין מן הארץ אפי' כמלא נימא נועלין בהן ואם לאו אין נועלין בהן אביי מתרץ לטעמיה בששיש להן ציר או גבוהין מן הארץ. רבא מתרץ לטעמיה כשהיה להן ציר או כשהיו גבוהין מן הארץ. ת"ר סוכי קוצין וחבילי עצים שהתקינו לפרצה שבחצר [בזמן] שקשורין ותלויין נועלין בהן בשבת: ת"ר דלת אלמנה אמרי לה דחד שיפא. פי' לוח אחד כדכתיב וכפים מעץ יעננו ומתרגמינן שיפא ואמרי לה דלית לה בשימי ויש שגורסין שיבא פי' שיבא שאינה נצמדת משתי צדדיה והוא מלשון צמידים דמתרגמינן שבבין. פי' גשמא בית קבול של ציר שהוא כמלבן אלא יורדת ומשתקעת בארץ. אמר רב יהודה האי מדורתא כו' שמועה זו עיקרה

בי"ט וכבר פירשנוה שם בענין אין מקיפין ב' חביות לשפות עליה את הקדירה ואין סומכין את הקדירה בבקעת. וכן הדלת כל זה שאיסורו משום תולדות בנין וכיון שהזכיר בזה המקום סמיכת הדלת מושבכת גם אלו שהן אסורין משום בנין בשבת. ואמר רב יהודה אם שינה מדרך בנין האי מדורתא ביו"ט ונתן העצים שעליה ממעלה למטה כגון שנתן עץ אחד תלוי בידו למעלה [מן] הכירה ונתן תחתיו עץ אחר עד שהגיע לכירה הרי אלו העצים נתנו בכירה שלא כדרך בנין מותר אבל אם נתן עץ אחד על חבירו ממטה ועלה למעלה הרי זה דרך בנין ואסור וכן קדירה אם אוחזה בידו ומניחה אבנים תחתיה שרי ואם נותן אבנים ושופת הקדרה עליה אסור. וכן ביצים שצריך לצלותן אם אוחז העליונה בידו ונותן אחרות תחתיה שרי ואם זו על זו אסור. וכן חבית כשיבקש להטותה ולסנן יינה מן השמרים אם אוחזה תלויה ומניח אבנים תחתיה נמצאת שלא כדרך בנין ושרי ואם נותן החבית על האבנים אסור וכן פוריא מפורקת לא יחבר העצים התחתונים תחלה אלא אוחז העליונים ומניח התחתונים תחת העליונים ומותר. ואם נותן התחתונים ואח"כ נותן העליונים הרי אלו דרך בנין ואסור: טובם כחדק. פי' טובם שבישראל מחדקין את עובדי כוכבים בגיהנם שנאמר קומי ודושי בת ציון כי קרנך אשים ברזל ופרסותיך אשים נחושה והדיקות עמים רבים וגו': מתני' לא יעמוד ברה"י ויפתח ברה"ר כו' ומקשינן תני ר' מאיר רה"ר ומהדרי ליה רבנן שוק של פטמין שהיה בירושלים שהיא כרמלית דא"ר יוחנן אלמלא דלתותיה ננעלות בלילה חייבין עליה

הגהות הב"ח

(א) רש"י ד"ה לא יעמוד אדם ברשות היחיד וכו' פתח החנות שברשות הרבים ואע"פ שאין ממקום המפתח עד פתח ארבע וכו' למעלה לרשות גבוהים וכו' כגון שהיה מפתח החנות מונח על גגה ויטול שם המפתח ויפתח בה פתח החנות: (ב) ד"ה חייבין וכו' ליכא היא לית לן וכו' דילמא מייתי לה לאו: (ג) ד"ה סיפא וכו' ויטול מפתח ויפתח המנעול: (ד) תוס' ד"ה וכן וכו' ואין נראה לר"י דלדך. נ"ב כלומר שיהא מונח היא כבנין כבר: (ה) בא"ד גבי טרפידא. נ"ב עיין בפ' חולין דף קלח תוס' ד"ה כל הנכו:

אֶלָּא אִם כֵּן עָשָׂה מְחִיצָה גְּבוֹהָה עֲשָׂרָה טְפָחִים, דִּבְרֵי רַבִּי מֵאִיר. אָמְרוּ לוֹ: מַעֲשֶׂה בְּשׁוּק שֶׁל פַּטָּמִים שֶׁהָיָה בִּירוּשָׁלַיִם, שֶׁהָיוּ נוֹעֲלִין וּמַנִּיחִין אֶת הַמַּפְתֵּחַ בַּחַלּוֹן שֶׁעַל גַּבֵּי הַפֶּתַח. רַבִּי יוֹסֵי אוֹמֵר: שׁוּק שֶׁל צַמָּרִים הָיָה.§ תָּנוּ רַבָּנַן: פִּתְחֵי שַׁעֲרֵי גִינָּה, בִּזְמַן שֶׁיֵּשׁ לָהֶן בֵּית שַׁעַר מִבִּפְנִים — פּוֹתֵחַ וְנוֹעֵל מִבִּפְנִים. מִבַּחוּץ — פּוֹתֵחַ וְנוֹעֵל מִבַּחוּץ. מִכָּאן וּמִכָּאן — פּוֹתֵחַ וְנוֹעֵל כָּאן וְכָאן. אֵין לָהֶן לֹא לְכָאן וְלֹא לְכָאן — אֲסוּרִין כָּאן וְכָאן. וְכֵן חֲנוּיוֹת הַפְּתוּחוֹת לִרה"ר, בִּזְמַן שֶׁהַמַּנְעוּל לְמַטָּה מֵעֲשָׂרָה — מֵבִיא מַפְתֵּחַ מֵעֶרֶב שַׁבָּת וּמַנִּיחוֹ בָּאִיסְקוּפָּה, לְמָחָר פּוֹתֵחַ וְנוֹעֵל וּמַחֲזִירוֹ לָאִיסְקוּפָּה. וּבִזְמַן שֶׁהַמַּנְעוּל לְמַעְלָה מֵעֲשָׂרָה — מֵבִיא מַפְתֵּחַ מֵעֶרֶב שַׁבָּת, וּמַנִּיחוֹ בַּמַּנְעוּל, לְמָחָר פּוֹתֵחַ וְנוֹעֵל וּמַחֲזִירוֹ לִמְקוֹמוֹ, דִּבְרֵי רַבִּי מֵאִיר. וַחֲכָמִים אוֹמְרִים: אַף בִּזְמַן שֶׁהַמַּנְעוּל לְמַעְלָה מֵעֲשָׂרָה טְפָחִים — מֵבִיא מַפְתֵּחַ מֵעֶרֶב שַׁבָּת, וּמַנִּיחוֹ בָּאִיסְקוּפָּה, לְמָחָר פּוֹתֵחַ וְנוֹעֵל וּמַחֲזִירוֹ לִמְקוֹמוֹ, אוֹ בַּחַלּוֹן שֶׁעַל גַּבֵּי הַפֶּתַח. אִם יֵשׁ בַּחַלּוֹן אַרְבָּעָה עַל אַרְבָּעָה — אָסוּר, מִפְּנֵי שֶׁהוּא כְּמוֹצִיא מֵרְשׁוּת לִרְשׁוּת. מִדְּקָאָמַר וְכֵן חֲנוּיוֹת — מִכְּלָל דְּבְאִיסְקוּפַּת כַּרְמְלִית עָסְקִינַן. הַאי מַנְעוּל הֵיכִי דָּמֵי? אִי דְּלֵית בֵּיהּ אַרְבָּעָה — מְקוֹם פְּטוּר הוּא, וְאִי אִית בֵּיהּ אַרְבָּעָה — בְּהָא לֵימָא רַבָּנַן: אַף בִּזְמַן שֶׁהַמַּנְעוּל לְמַעְלָה מִי' מֵבִיא מַפְתֵּחַ מֵעֶ"שׁ, וּמַנִּיחוֹ בָּאִיסְקוּפָּה, לְמָחָר פּוֹתֵחַ וְנוֹעֵל בּוֹ וּמַחֲזִירוֹ לָאִיסְקוּפָּה, אוֹ לַחַלּוֹן שֶׁעַל גַּבֵּי הַפֶּתַח? וְהָא קָא מְטַלְטֵל מִכַּרְמְלִית לִרה"י! אָמַר אַבַּיֵי: לְעוֹלָם דְּאֵין בּוֹ אַרְבָּעָה, וְיֵשׁ בּוֹ לָחוֹק וּלְהַשְׁלִימוֹ לְד'. וּבְהָא פְּלִיגִי; *דְּר"מ סָבַר: חוֹקְקִין לְהַשְׁלִים, וְרַבָּנַן סָבְרִי: אֵין חוֹקְקִין לְהַשְׁלִים. אָמַר רַב בֵּיבָי בַּר אַבַּיֵי: ש"מ מֵהָא מַתְנִיתָא תְּלָת; ש"מ: חוֹקְקִין לְהַשְׁלִים, וש"מ: הֲדַר בֵּיהּ ר"מ מִשַּׁעֲרֵי גִינָּה, וְשָׁמְעַתְּ מִינַּהּ: מִדְּרַבָּנַן אִיתָא לִדְרַב דִּימִי. *דְּכִי אֲתָא רַב דִּימִי, א"ר יוֹחָנָן: מָקוֹם שֶׁאֵין בּוֹ אַרְבָּעָה עַל אַרְבָּעָה — מוּתָּר לִבְנֵי רְשׁוּת הָרַבִּים וְלִבְנֵי רְשׁוּת הַיָּחִיד לְכַתֵּף עָלָיו, וּבִלְבַד שֶׁלֹּא יַחֲלִיפוּ.§ **מתני'** נֶגֶר שֶׁיֵּשׁ בְּרֹאשׁוֹ גְּלוּסְטְרָא, רַבִּי אֱלִיעֶזֶר אוֹסֵר, וְרַבִּי יוֹסֵי [א]מַתִּיר. אָמַר רַבִּי אֱלִיעֶזֶר: מַעֲשֶׂה בִּכְנֶסֶת שֶׁבִּטְבֶרְיָא שֶׁהָיוּ נוֹהֲגִין בּוֹ הֶיתֵּר, עַד שֶׁבָּא רַבָּן גַּמְלִיאֵל וְהַזְּקֵנִים וְאָסְרוּ לָהֶן. ר' יוֹסֵי אוֹמֵר: אִיסּוּר נָהֲגוּ בּוֹ, וּבָא רַבָּן גַּמְלִיאֵל וְהַזְּקֵנִים וְהִתִּירוּ לָהֶן.§ **גמ'** בְּנִיטָּל בְּאֶגְדּוֹ — כ"ע לָא פְּלִיגִי, כִּי פְּלִיגִי — בְּשֶׁאֵינוֹ

רש"י

אֶלָּא אִם כֵּן עָשׂוּ וכו'. אַסֵּיפָא קָאֵי, דְּהַשְׁתָּא כִּי קָאֵי בְּגִינָּה קָאֵי בִּרְשׁוּת הַיָּחִיד וְעוֹלָה עַד לָרָקִיעַ: שַׁעֲרֵי גִינָּה. סְתָם מַנְעוּלֵיהֶן גְּבוֹהִין עֲשָׂרָה וּרְחָבִין אַרְבָּעָה, וּרְשׁוּת הַיָּחִיד הֵן: בֵּית שַׁעַר. בַּיִת קָטָן, וּפֶתַח הַגִּינָּה פָּתוּחַ בּוֹ. וּבְשַׁעֲרֵי הַגִּינָּה הַסְּמוּכִין לִרְשׁוּת הָרַבִּים עָסְקִינַן, מִדְּקָתָנֵי סֵיפָא: וְכֵן חֲנוּיוֹת הַפְּתוּחוֹת לִרְשׁוּת הָרַבִּים: פּוֹתֵחַ וְנוֹעֵל[א] בִּפְנִים. דְּבֵית שַׁעַר רְשׁוּת הַיָּחִיד הוּא, וְכֵן כְּשֶׁהוּא מִחוּץ: לֹא לְכָאן וְלֹא לְכָאן אֲסוּרִין מִכָּאן וּמִכָּאן. דְּהַמַּנְעוּל רְשׁוּת הַיָּחִיד הוּא, וְאַע"פ שֶׁהַמַּפְתֵּחַ מוּנָּח עָלָיו — גָּזַר ר' מֵאִיר שֶׁלֹּא יַעֲמוֹד בִּרְשׁוּת הָרַבִּים וְלֹא בְּגִינָּה, וְיִטּוֹל מַפְתֵּחַ שֶׁל רְשׁוּת הַיָּחִיד — שֶׁמָּא יְבִיאֶנּוּ אֶצְלוֹ לִרְשׁוּת הָרַבִּים אוֹ לְכַרְמְלִית: וְכֵן חֲנוּיוֹת. לְקַמָּן מְפָרֵשׁ הַאי "וְכֵן", דְּבְאִיסְקוּפַּת כַּרְמְלִית בְּגִינָּה קָאָמַר. שַׁעֲרֵי חֲנוּיוֹת פְּעָמִים שֶׁמַּנְעוּלֵיהֶם גְּבוֹהִין, וּפְעָמִים שֶׁהֵן נְמוּכִין, לְפִיכָךְ נָתַן בָּהֶן חִילּוּק: (*לְמָחָר פּוֹתֵחַ וּמַנִּיחוֹ עַל הָאִיסְקוּפָּה. לְקַמֵּיהּ מְפָרֵשׁ דְּמֵהָכָא שָׁמְעִינַן דַּהֲדַר בֵּיהּ ר' מֵאִיר מִשַּׁעֲרֵי גִינָּה, וְלֹא גָּזַר בְּעוֹמֵד בִּרְשׁוּת הָרַבִּים שֶׁלֹּא יְטַלְטֵל בְּכַרְמְלִית. דְּהָא אִיסְקוּפָּה כַּרְמְלִית הִיא, דִּרְחָבָה ד' וְאֵינָהּ גְּבוֹהָה י' וּכְשֶׁנּוֹטֵל מַפְתֵּחַ מִשָּׁם וְהוּא עוֹמֵד בִּרְשׁוּת הָרַבִּים, וּמוֹלִיכוֹ דֶּרֶךְ אֲוִיר הָאִיסְקוּפָּה לַמַּנְעוּל שֶׁעַל גַּבָּיו לְמַטָּה מֵעֲשָׂרָה — קָא מְטַלְטֵל מִכַּרְמְלִית לְכַרְמְלִית, וְלֹא גָּזַר רַבִּי מֵאִיר שֶׁמָּא יְבִיאֶנּוּ אֶצְלוֹ חוּץ לְעוֹבִי הָאִיסְקוּפָּה): לְמָחָר פּוֹתֵחַ וְנוֹעֵל וכו'.[ב] וְעַל הָאִיסְקוּפָּה הוּא עוֹמֵד וּמְטַלְטֵל מַפְתֵּחַ מֵאִיסְקוּפָּה לַמַּנְעוּל עַל דֶּרֶךְ אֲוִיר הָאִיסְקוּפָּה, דְּאֵין טִלְטוּל אֶלָּא בְּכַרְמְלִית: וּמַחֲזִירוֹ לִמְקוֹמוֹ. לָאִיסְקוּפָּה: מַנִּיחוֹ בַּמַּנְעוּל. אֲבָל לֹא בָּאִיסְקוּפָּה, דְּכִי מַמְטֵי לֵיהּ מֵאִיסְקוּפָּה לַמַּנְעוּל[ג] הָא מַפֵּיק מִכַּרְמְלִית לִרְשׁוּת הַיָּחִיד: לִמְקוֹמוֹ. לַמַּנְעוּל עַל גַּבָּיו, כְּגוֹן מַנְעוּלִין הַלָּלוּ שֶׁל עֵץ שֶׁעוֹשִׂין עֲנָיִים בְּפִתְחֵיהֶן וְרָאשֵׁיהֶן רְחָבִין, וּבְלַע"ז סרדור"א: וַחֲכָמִים אוֹמְרִים וכו'. לְקַמָּן מְפָרֵשׁ טַעְמָא, דְּלָא מְשַׁוּוּ לֵיהּ לְהַאי מַנְעוּל רְשׁוּת הַיָּחִיד: לִמְקוֹמוֹ. לָאִיסְקוּפָּה, אוֹ לַחַלּוֹן שֶׁאֵין בּוֹ אַרְבָּעָה. דְּאַף עַל גַּב דְּגָבוֹהַּ עֲשָׂרָה — מְקוֹם פְּטוּר בְּעָלְמָא הוּא: שֶׁמּוֹצִיא מֵרְשׁוּת לִרְשׁוּת. מֵאִיסְקוּפָּה שֶׁהוּא כַּרְמְלִית לַחַלּוֹן שֶׁהוּא רְשׁוּת הַיָּחִיד. וְאַף עַל גַּב דְּהִנִּיחוֹ תְּחִילָּה בַּמַּנְעוּל, שֶׁהוּא מְקוֹם פְּטוּר לְרַבָּנַן, וּבָטֵל אֵצֶל כָּל הָרְשׁוּיוֹת — כְּרַב דִּימִי קַיְימָא לָן. דְּאָמַר בְּפ"ק: וּבִלְבַד שֶׁלֹּא יַחֲלִיפוּ: מְקוֹם פְּטוּר הוּא. וְכִי הָוֵי לְמַעְלָה מֵעֲשָׂרָה — הֵיכִי מְשַׁוֵּי לֵיהּ רַבִּי מֵאִיר רְשׁוּת הַיָּחִיד, וְאָסַר: וְיֵשׁ בּוֹ לָחוֹק. בְּתוֹךְ הַדֶּלֶת אֵצֶל רֹאשׁ הַמַּנְעוּל בְּעוֹבְיוֹ שֶׁל דֶּלֶת וּלְהַשְׁלִים רֹאשׁ הַמַּנְעוּל לְאַרְבָּעָה: חוֹקְקִין לְהַשְׁלִים. רוֹאִין אוֹתוֹ כְּאִילּוּ חָקוּק: אֵין חוֹקְקִין. הִלְכָּךְ, מְקוֹם פְּטוּר בְּעָלְמָא הוּא: הֲדַר בֵּיהּ רַבִּי מֵאִיר מִשַּׁעֲרֵי גִינָּה. מִדְּקָא שָׁרֵי לַעֲמוֹד (*בִּרְשׁוּת הָרַבִּים לִיטּוֹל מַפְתֵּחַ מֵאִיסְקוּפַּת כַּרְמְלִית וּלְהוֹלִיכוֹ דֶּרֶךְ אֲוִירָהּ לַמַּנְעוּל שֶׁלְּמַטָּה מֵעֲשָׂרָה וְלֹא גָּזַר שֶׁמָּא יְבִיאֶנּוּ אֶצְלוֹ לִרְשׁוּת הָרַבִּים וש"מ סֵיפָא נַמִי מִדְּקָא שָׁרֵי לַעֲמוֹד) עַל הָאִיסְקוּפָּה כַּרְמְלִית וְלִיטּוֹל מַפְתֵּחַ בַּמַּנְעוּל לְמַעְלָה מֵעֲשָׂרָה בְּאִיסְקוּפַּת כַּרְמְלִית וּלְהוֹלִיכוֹ דֶּרֶךְ אֲוִירָהּ לַמַּנְעוּל וְלֹא גָּזַר שֶׁמָּא יְבִיאֶנּוּ אֶצְלוֹ לָאִיסְקוּפָּה שֶׁהִיא כַּרְמְלִית: וש"מ מִדְּרַבָּנַן.[ד] דְּאָמְרֵי: אִם יֵשׁ אַרְבָּעָה עַל אַרְבָּעָה — אָסוּר לִיטּוֹל מַפְתֵּחַ מֵאִיסְקוּפָּה וְלִנְעוֹל בַּמַּנְעוּל שֶׁהוּא מְקוֹם פְּטוּר וְלִיטְּלוֹ מִשָּׁם וּלְהַנִּיחוֹ בַּחַלּוֹן שֶׁהוּא רְשׁוּת הַיָּחִיד מִשּׁוּם דְּקָא מַחֲלִיף מֵאִיסְקוּפַּת כַּרְמְלִית לַחַלּוֹן שֶׁהוּא רְשׁוּת הַיָּחִיד עַל יְדֵי הֲנָחַת מְקוֹם פְּטוּר: אִיתָא לִדְרַב דִּימִי. דְּאָמַר וּבִלְבַד שֶׁלֹּא יַחֲלִיפוּ: **מתני'** נֶגֶר. קביל"א, שֶׁתּוֹחֲבִין אוֹתוֹ בַּחוֹר שֶׁבָּאִיסְקוּפָּה לִנְעוֹל הַדֶּלֶת: שֶׁיֵּשׁ בְּרֹאשׁוֹ גְּלוּסְטְרָא. שֶׁרֹאשׁוֹ עָבֶה, וְרָאוּי לְבוּכְנָא לִכְתּוֹשׁ וְלִשְׁחוֹק בּוֹ פִּלְפְּלִין. וַאֲפִילּוּ הָכִי, דְּתוֹרַת כְּלִי עָלָיו — ר"א אוֹסֵר, אֶלָּא אִם כֵּן קָשׁוּר וְתָלוּי בַּדֶּלֶת, כִּדְמְפָרֵשׁ בַּגְּמָרָא: וְר' יוֹסֵי מַתִּיר. דְּתוֹרַת כְּלִי עָלָיו, מִשּׁוּם גְּלוּסְטְרָא וְלָא מֵיחֲזֵי כְּבוֹנֶה: **גמ'** בְּנִיטָּל בְּאֶגְדּוֹ. כְּשֶׁהוּא קָשׁוּר וְתָלוּי בְּחֶבֶל שֶׁל קַיָּימָא, וְרָאוּי לְטַלְטְלוֹ עַל יְדֵי אוֹתוֹ חֶבֶל, וְאֵינוֹ נִפְסָק בְּיָדֵיהּ: כּוּלֵּי עָלְמָא לָא פְּלִיגִי. דְּשָׁרֵי, דְּכֵיוָן דְּקָשׁוּר וְתָלוּי יָפֶה — מוֹכְחָא מִלְּתָא דִּלְנְעוֹל קָאֵי, וְלָא מֵיחֲזֵי כְּבוֹנֶה: כְּשֶׁאֵין

תוספות

מביא מפתח ומניח באיסקופה. פירש בקונטרס: דמהא מדקדק דהדר ביה ר' מאיר משערי גינה, ולא גזר לעומד ברשות הרבים שלא יטלטל בכרמלית. דהא איסקופה כרמלית היא, כדאמרינן לקמן. ואין נראה לר"י, דמכאן אין להוכיח דאיכא לאוקמא למחר פותח ונועל, כגון שעומד על האיסקופה. וכן צריך לפרש. דאי ברשות הרבים קאי — מאי "וכן"? דמשמע דומיא דההוא דשערי גינה. ונראה לר"י כמו שהגיה בקונטרס בפירושיו: דמסיפא מוכח דהדר בה רבי מאיר משערי גינה, דקתני: למעלה מי' — מניחו במנעול, ולמחר פותח ונועל. דכי קאי נמי על האיסקופה — הוה ליה מכרמלית לרשות היחיד, דע"כ איסקופה כרמלית היא. דאי מקום פטור — אמאי צריך להניח המפתח במנעול? יניחו באיסקופה!

מדקאמר וכן חניות מכלל דבאיסקופ' כרמלית. דוכן משמע דומיא דשערי גינה. ואי הויא איסקופת רשות היחיד — אם כן היה מטלטל מרשות היחיד לכרמלית. וכן אם היתה רה"ר — היה מטלטל מרשות הרבים לכרמלית, ולא הוי דומיא דשערי גינה דאסרי בכי האי גוונא: **אין** חוקקין. והוי מקום פטור. והא דקאמר ומניחו באיסקופה — הוא הדין ברשות הרבים, אלא דסתמא לא מינטר בקרקע, משום הכי לא נקיט לה: **רבי** יוסי אומר איסור נהגו בו והתירו להם. ואם תאמר: והא אמרינן בנדרים בפרק "ואלו נדרים" (דף פא.) ובפרק "מקום שנהגו" (פסחים דף נא.): דברים המותרים ואחרים נהגו בהם איסור — אי אתה רשאי להתירן בפניהם! ויש לומר: דהיינו כשיודעים שמותר, ומחמירין על עצמן שלא ירגילו בני אדם להקל, ויבאו להתיר איסור. אבל אם מחמירין מחמת טעות — מותר להתיר בפניהם*: **כי** פליגי בשאין ניטל באיגודו. ר"י מפרש דדוקא הכא שרי, משום דבראשו גלוסטרא. אבל באין בראשו גלוסטרא — מודה דאסור, אפי' קשור בדלת. וסבירא ליה כרבנן דרבי יהודה בנגר הנגרר. אי נמי: סבירא[ה] ליה כר' יהודה דשרי בנגרר, והכא איירי בקשור בעיברא דדשא, דמודה רבי יהודה בשאינו ניטל באיגודו, כדמוכח בסמוך. ומשום הכי בעי במתניתין שיהא בראשו גלוסטרא

עין משפט נר מצוה

נ א מיי' פכ"ו מהל' שבת הלכה י סמג לאוין סה טוש"ע א"ח סי' שיג סעיף א:

רבינו חננאל

עליה משום רה"ר ופריק רב פפא לא אהדרו ליה ירושלים אלא לאחר שנפרצו בה פרצות יתר מעשר שהיא רה"ר. וכן שערי גינה לא יעמוד בכרמלית ויפתח ברה"י או ברה"י ויפתח בכרמלית דברי ר' מאיר. אמרו לו מעשה בשוק של פטמין כו': **ת"ר** פתחי גינה בזמן שיש לה שער מבפנים כו' האי מנעול היכי דמי אי דלית ביה ד' מקום פטור הוא. אי דאית ביה ד' בהא נמרו רבנן למעלה מעשרה למחר פותח ונועל בו ומחזירו לאיסקופה הא קא מטלטל מכרמלית לרה"י ופריק אביי לעולם דלית ביה ד' ויש בה לחוק ולהשלימו לד' ר' מאיר סבר חוקקין להשלים ורבנן סברי אין חוקקין להשלים ובמקום פטור הוא אמר רב ביבי בר אביי ש"מ מהא מתני' תלת כו': **מתני'** נגר שיש בראשו גלוסטרא רבי אליעזר אוסר ורבי יוסי מתיר בנגר הניטל באיגודו פי' הניטל באיגודו אם קשור בדלתיה בדבר שיכול להעמידו דברי הכל מותר כי פליגי

[וע"ע תוס' פסחים דף נא. ד"ה אי אתה]

הגהות הב"ח

(א) רש"י ד"ה פותח ונועל מבפנים וכו' כשהוא מבחוץ הס"ד: (ב) ד"ה למחר פותח ונועל וכו' עומד ברשות הרבים ומטלטל כנ"ל ותיבת ועל האיסקופה נמחק: (ג) ד"ה ומניחו במנעול וכו' למנעול קא מפיק: (ד) ד"ה וש"מ מדרבנן דאמרי אם יש בחלון ארבעה: (ה) תוס' ד"ה כי פליגי וכו' אי נמי סבירא להו כר' יהודה:

מסורת הש"ס

כס"א אינו

[לעיל יח: לג: שבת ז: יומא יח:]

[שבת ח: לעיל ע. עז. פ פז.]

רש"ל מ"ז

בְּשֶׁאֵינוֹ נִיטָּל בְּאִיגְדוֹ — דְּמָר סָבַר: כֵּיוָן דְּיֵשׁ בְּרֹאשׁוֹ גְלוּסְטְרָא — תּוֹרַת כְּלִי עָלָיו, וּמָר סָבַר: כֵּיוָן דְּאֵינוֹ נִיטָּל בְּאִיגְדוֹ — לָא.§ **מתני'** *נֶגֶר הַנִּגְרָר — נוֹעֲלִין בּוֹ בַּמִּקְדָּשׁ, אֲבָל לֹא בַּמְּדִינָה. וְהַמּוּנָּח — כָּאן וְכָאן אָסוּר. ר' יְהוּדָה אוֹמֵר: הַמּוּנָּח — מוּתָּר בַּמִּקְדָּשׁ, וְהַנִּגְרָר — בַּמְּדִינָה.§ **גמ'** *תָּנוּ רַבָּנַן: אֵיזֶהוּ נֶגֶר הַנִּגְרָר שֶׁנּוֹעֲלִין בַּמִּקְדָּשׁ אֲבָל לֹא בַּמְּדִינָה — כֹּל שֶׁקָּשׁוּר וְתָלוּי, וְרֹאשׁוֹ אֶחָד מַגִּיעַ לָאָרֶץ. רַבִּי יְהוּדָה אוֹמֵר(א) זֶה — אַף בַּמְּדִינָה מוּתָּר, אֶלָּא אֵיזֶהוּ נֶגֶר שֶׁנּוֹעֲלִין בַּמִּקְדָּשׁ אֲבָל לֹא בַּמְּדִינָה — כֹּל שֶׁאֵינוֹ לֹא קָשׁוּר וְלֹא תָלוּי, וְשׁוֹמְטוֹ וּמַנִּיחוֹ בְּקֶרֶן זָוִית. אָמַר רַב יְהוּדָה, אָמַר שְׁמוּאֵל: [א]הֲלָכָה כְּרַבִּי יְהוּדָה בַּנִּגְרָר. אָמַר רָבָא: [ב]וְהוּא שֶׁקָּשׁוּר בַּדֶּלֶת. אִינִי?! וְהָא רַבִּי טַבְלָא אִיקְּלַע לִמְחוֹזָא, וַחֲזָא לְהַהוּא דַּהֲוָה תָּלֵי בְּעִיבְרָא דְּדַשָּׁא, וְלָא אֲמַר לְהוּ וְלָא מִידֵּי! [ג]הַהוּא נִיטָּל בְּאִיגְדוֹ הֲוָה. רַב אַוְיָא אִיקְּלַע לִנְהַרְדְּעָא, חַזְיֵיהּ לְהַהוּא גַּבְרָא דַּהֲוָה קָא קָטֵיר בְּגֶמִי, אֲמַר: דֵּין לָא נִטְרוֹק. בָּעֵי רַבִּי זֵירָא: נִקְמָז מַהוּ? אֲמַר רַב יוֹסֵף: מַאי תִּיבָּעֵי לֵיהּ? לָא שְׁמִיעַ לֵיהּ הָא דְּתַנְיָא: *נִשְׁמָט — אָסוּר, נִקְמָז — מוּתָּר. וְרַבִּי יְהוּדָה אָמַר: נִקְמָז אַף עַל פִּי שֶׁאֵינוֹ נִשְׁמָט — אָסוּר. וְאָמַר רַב יְהוּדָה, אָמַר שְׁמוּאֵל: הֲלָכָה כְּרַבִּי יְהוּדָה בְּנִקְמָז. וְטַעְמָא מַאי? אָמַר אַבַּיֵי: מִשּׁוּם דְּמִיחֲזֵי כְּבוֹנֶה. בְּעָא מִינֵּיהּ רַב נְחוּמֵי בַּר זְכַרְיָה מֵאַבַּיֵי: עָשָׂה לוֹ בֵּית יָד, מַהוּ? אֲמַר לֵיהּ: בּוּכְנָא קָאָמְרַתְּ. אִיתְּמַר, אָמַר רַב נְחוּמֵי בַּר אַדָּא: עָשָׂה לוֹ בֵּית יָד — מוּתָּר. הַהוּא [ד]שָׁרִיתָא דַּהֲוָה בֵּי רַבִּי פְּדָת, דַּהֲוָה מִדְּלוּ לָהּ בֵּי עֲשָׂרָה וְשָׁדוּ לָהּ אַדַּשָּׁא, וְלָא אֲמַר לְהוּ וְלָא מִידֵּי. אֲמַר: תּוֹרַת כְּלִי עָלֶיהָ. הַהִיא אֲסִיתָא דַּהֲוַת בֵּי מָר שְׁמוּאֵל, דַּהֲוָה מַחֲזֶקֶת *אַדְרִיבָא, שְׁרָא מָר שְׁמוּאֵל לְמִישְׁדְּיֵיהּ אַדַּשָּׁא, אֲמַר: תּוֹרַת כְּלִי עָלֶיהָ.§ שְׁלַח לֵיהּ רָמֵי בַּר יְחֶזְקֵאל לְרַב עַמְרָם: נֵימָא לָן מָר מֵהָלֵין מִילֵּי מַעַלְיָיתָא דַּאֲמַרְתְּ לָן מִשְּׁמֵיהּ דְּרַב אַסִּי בְּכֵיפֵי דְּאַרְבָּא! שְׁלַח לֵיהּ, הָכִי אֲמַר רַב אַסִּי: [ה]הָנֵי כֵּיפֵי דְּאַרְבָּא, בִּזְמַן שֶׁיֵּשׁ בָּהֶן טֶפַח, אִי נַמִי, אֵין בָּהֶן טֶפַח וְאֵין בֵּין זֶה לָזֶה שְׁלֹשָׁה — לְמָחָר מֵבִיא מַחֲצֶלֶת וּפוֹרֵס עֲלֵיהֶן. מַאי טַעְמָא — מוֹסִיף עַל אֹהֶל עֲרַאי הוּא, וְשַׁפִּיר דָּמֵי. הָנְהוּ דִּכְרֵי דַּהֲווּ לֵיהּ לְרַב הוּנָא, דְּבִימָמָא בְּעוּ טוּלָּא וּבְלֵילְיָא בְּעוּ אֲוִירָא. אֲתָא לְקַמֵּיהּ דְּרַב. א"ל: [ו]זִיל כְּרוֹךְ בּוּדְיָיא, וְשַׁיֵּיר בָּהּ טֶפַח. לְמָחָר פַּשְׁטֵהּ, וּמוֹסִיף עַל אֹהֶל עֲרַאי הוּא, וְשַׁפִּיר דָּמֵי. *אָמַר רַב מִשּׁוּם רַבִּי חִיָּיא: [ז]וִילוֹן מוּתָּר לִנְטוֹתוֹ וּמוּתָּר לְפוֹרְקוֹ בַּשַּׁבָּת. *[ח]כִּילַּת חֲתָנִים מוּתָּר לְפוֹרְקָהּ וְלִנְטוֹתָהּ בַּשַּׁבָּת. אָמַר רַב שֵׁשֶׁת בְּרֵיהּ דְּרַב אִידִי: [ט]לָא אֲמַרַן אֶלָּא שֶׁאֵין בְּגַגָּהּ טֶפַח, אֲבָל יֵשׁ בְּגַגָּהּ טֶפַח — אָסוּר. וְכִי אֵין בְּגַגָּהּ טֶפַח(ב) לָא אֲמַרַן אֶלָּא שֶׁאֵין בְּפָחוֹת מִשְּׁלֹשָׁה סָמוּךְ לַגַּג טֶפַח, אֲבָל יֵשׁ בְּפָחוֹת מִשְּׁלֹשָׁה סָמוּךְ לַגַּג טֶפַח — אָסוּר. וְכִי אֵין בְּפָחוֹת מִשְּׁלֹשָׁה סָמוּךְ לַגַּג טֶפַח נַמִי, לָא אֲמַרַן אֶלָּא שֶׁאֵין בְּשִׁיפּוּעָהּ

רש"י

בשאין ניטל באיגדו. שהחבל דק, ואם היה רוצה ליטלו משם לטלטלו ע"י אותו חבל – מיד נפסק. ר"א סבר: כיון דאינו ניטל באיגדו – דהוה כמי שאינו קשור, ותנן לקמן: נגר המונח, שאינו קשור בדלת – אין נועלין בו. והאי נמי מונח הוא. משום גלוסטרא לא שרי ליה. ורבי יוסי סבר: גלוסטרא מהניא ליה, דכיון דכלי הוא – לא הוי כבנין: **מתני'** נגר הנגרר. שקשור בדלת אבל אינו תלוי. שהחבל ארוך, ומתוך שנגרר – אינו נראה כקשור, וכשאין בראשו גלוסטרא קאמר: נועלין בו במקדש. דשבות בעלמא הוא, דאינו בונה ממש, הואיל וקשור לכך. אלא הואיל ונגרר – מיחזי כבונה. ואין שבות דרבנן במקדש, דלא גזרו שם: והמונח. שאינו קשור כלל – הוי בנין ממש. ור' יהודה סבר: לאו בנין ממש הוא, אלא דומה לבנין, ובמקדש לא גזרו שבות: **גמ'** זה אפי' במדינה מותר. הואיל וקשור, אף על פי שאינו תלוי: הלכה כר' יהודה בנגרר. דמותר אפילו במדינה אבל לא במונח, דשרי ליה רבי יהודה במקדש – לית הלכתא כוותיה. דכיון שאינו קשור שם – בנין גמור הוא, כשאר נגרים שנועלים בכותלים. והבונה כל שהוא – חייב. ומלאכה דאורייתא לא הותרה במקדש חוץ מהקרבת תמידין ומוספין וקרבנות צבור, שדוחין את השבת מגזירת הכתוב: והוא שקשור בדלת. עצמה, דמוכח שפיר, ולא שקשור במזוזה: ניטל באיגדו. כלומר: קשור היה בחבל חזק: דין לא נטרוק. זה לא ינעול שאינו קשור, דכמאן דליתיה לגמי דמי: נקמז מהו. שנכנס הנגר בחור האסקופה, ונפחת אותו החור ויוצא הנגר לצד הקרקע, ונועץ בקרקע. ועד השתא איירי כשהאסקופה גבוהה, ואין החור ניקב עד לארץ: נשמט. שנפסק החבל שהוא קשור בו, והרי הוא מונח בקרן זוית כשפותח אותו: עשה לו בית יד. לנגר שאינו קשור כלל, ותחב בית יד באמצעיתו, ודומה למקבת. דהשתא ודאי מוכח מילתא הוא דכלי הוא, מהו לנעול בו: בוכנא קאמרת. הא ודאי שרי. בוכנא מקבת, וכותשין בו חטין ותבלין: שריתא. קורה. כמו: "בצל קורתי" (בראשית יט)(ג) בטלל שרותי: בי עשרה. כלומר: משאוי עשרה בני אדם היה בה, ואפילו הכי לא אסר עלייהו: ושדו ליה אדשא. לסומכה בלילה: תורת כלי. שראויה לישב עליה: אסיתא. מורטיי"ר: אדריבא. לתך חטין, ט"ו סאין, חצי כור: כיפי דארבא. אולמות שעושין בספינה, שעולין כעין מעגלין שקורין גרק"ל, ראשו אחד בדופן זה של ספינה וראשו שני בדופן זה, והוא כפוף כמו אולם, ועומד כמו כיפה. ומרחיק כחצי אמה ונועץ אחר, וכן על פני כולה ופורסין בגדים ומחצלות של גמי להגין מפני החמה והגשמים: שיש בהם טפח. שרוחב של מעגל טפח, דבציר מטפח לא הוי אהל. אבל כשרוחב טפח – מקרי אהל. נמצא יש אהל עליו מבעוד יום, וכשהוא פורס עליו הבגד למחר אינו אלא מוסיף: אי נמי אין ברחבו טפח ואין בין זה לזה שלשה. דאיכא למימר לבוד: דכרי. אילים: דבימממא בעו טולא. מפני השרב: ובליליא בעו אוירא. הנאת הקור, מפני הבל הקיץ. ובימות החול היו פורסין עליהן מחצלות ביום, ונוטלין בלילה: אתא לקמיה דרב. מה נעביד להו בשבתא: כרוך בודיא. כשתסתלק המחצלת מעליהן לפנות ערב שבת, אל תסלקנה כולה משם, אלא הוי גולל אותה וכורך מעל הגג, ושייר בה טפח פרוסה דלהוי עליה שם אהל: ולמחר פשטיה. דהוי תוספת ושרי: וילון. כנגד הפתח, לצניעות: מותר לנטותו. דלאו אהל הוא, דלא קביעא התם, אלא כן דרכו לינתן ולהסתלק כדלת בעלמא: כילת חתנים. לאו אהל הוא, מפני שאין לה גג למעלה רוחב טפח, מפני שהיא נתונה בשיפוע. והיא יריעה שפורסין סביב למטה לישן: שאין בפחות משלשה סמוך לגג טפח. שנתונה באלכסון קצר, שכשחתה מודד רחבה למטה משלשה לגגה – אין בו רוחב טפח, דהוי כולה דופן, ואין כאן אהל כלל. אבל הרחיבה עד טפח בתוך שלשה לגגה – כאילו גגה טפח דמי, ואסור לנטותה: בשיפועה

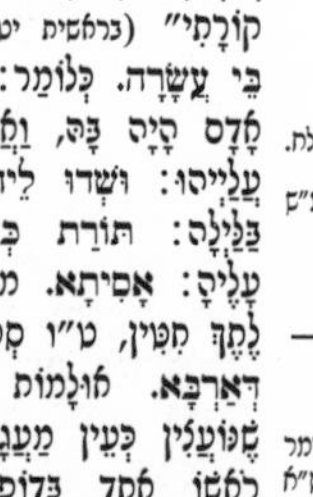

תוספות

גלוסטרא. ומתניתין דלעיל דדלת שבמוקצה והדקין שבפירצה, דבעי שיהו גבוהים מן הארץ, נראה לפרש: אע"ג דיכול לעמוד ע"י אותו חבל, מ"מ אינו ניטל באיגודו, שאם היו רוצים לטלטלו ממקום למקום ע"י אותו חבל היה נפסק, משום הכי צריך שיהיו גבוהים מן הארץ. ואתיא נמי כר' יהודה, דכוותיה פסקינן, דאי הוה ניטל באיגודו – אפילו נגרר ובלא גלוסטרא, ואפילו קטיר בעיברא דדשא, מתיר רבי יהודה כדמוכח הכא:

הלכה כר"י בנגרר. פירש בקונטרס: דנועלין בו במדינה, אבל במאי דשרי מונח במקדש – לית הלכתא כוותיה:

נקמז מהו. פירוש: עד השתא הוה איירי כשהאסקופה גבוהה, ואין החור נוקב עד לארץ. והשתא בעי: אם החור הולך עד שנכנס ונועץ בקרקע, ודמי טפי לבונה:

ההוא שריתא דהוו מדלו לה בי עשרה. ואם תאמר: דאמרינן סוף "במה מדליקין" (שבת דף לה.) גבי חלתא, אמר אביי: בעי מיניה דמר אפילו בת תרי כורי ולא שרי לי! ויש לומר דלא דמי, דחלתא אין רגילות לטלטלה בחול כלל, אבל האי שריתא – דרכה לטלטלה תמיד בחול לנעול הדלת, משום הכי שרי*.

לא אמרן אלא שאין בשיפועה טפח. פירש בקונטרס: שיש כילות קטנות סמוכות זו לזו, ואין בכל אחת טפח. ותימה: דלימא לבוד מכילה זו לכילה זו, ונמצא שיש בשיפועה טפח. ויש לומר: דהא דחשיב ליה אהל לעיל על ידי לבוד – היינו לענין שיוכל להוסיף למחר בשבת, אבל לא מסתבר שיחשב בכי האי גוונא עשיית אהל לאסור עליו לעשות בשבת. דאטו יהיה אסור לנטות בשבת שני חוטין תוך שלשה משום עשיית אהל?!

הא

[וע"ע תוספות שבת לה. ד"ה ואפילו]

עין משפט נר מצוה

נא א ב ג מיי' פכ"ו מהל' שבת הלכה י:

נב ד מיי' פכ"ב מהל' שבת הלכה כ סמג לאוין סה טוש"ע א"ח סימן שח סעיף ב [וברב אלפס שבת פרק י"ז דף נ:]:

נג ה ו מיי' פכ"ב מהל' שבת הלכה כט סמג שם טוש"ע א"ח סי' שטו סעיף ב:

נד ז מיי' שם טוש"ע שם סעי"א בהג"ה:

נה ח ט מיי' שם הלכה ל טוש"ע שם סעיף יא:

מסורת הש"ס

שבת קכו.

שם

[תוספתא פ"ח ע"ש]

[גיר' הערוך ארדבה פי' ארדב חצי לתך]

שבת קלח.

שם: מה: ע"ש

הגהות הב"ח

(א) גמ' רבי יהודה אומר (זה אף) תא"מ ונ"ב ס"א אף זה: (ב) שם וכי אין בגגה טפח נמי לא אמרן: (ג) רש"י ד"ה שריתא וכו' קורתי מתרגמינן בטלל:

רבינו חננאל

בשאינו ניטל באיגודו כגון שהיה קשור בגמי ר' סבר כיון דיש בראשו גלוסטרא. פי' רומנא והיא כמין אחיזת מאנא תורת כלי עליו ומותר לטלטלו. ור' אלעזר סבר כיון דאינו ניטל באיגודו לא מטלטלין ליה. ומפורש בתלמוד א"י אמר רב יוסי מי שמתיר עושה הנגר טפל לגלוסטרא והאוסר עושה לגלוסטרא טפילה לנגר. איזהו נגר א"ר יוחנן קשור אעפ"י שאינו תלוי ודברי הכל כי הגלוסטרא כלי הוא: **נגר** הנגרר נועלין בו במקדש אבל לא במדינ'. והמונח כאן וכאן אסור. ר' יהודה אומר המונח במקדש כו': ת"ר איזהו נגר הנגרר שנועלין בו במקדש כו' אמר רב יהודה אמר שמואל הלכה כרבי יהודה. אמר רב יהודה והוא שקשור ותלוי בדלת. ואם ניטל באיגודו אפי' תלוי אלא בבריח של דלת מותר כר' טבלא. רב הונא איקלע לנהרדעא חזייה לנגר דהוה קטיר בגמי. אמר דין אינו ניטל באיגודו שאינו קשור בדבר שיכול להעמידו. וכיון דאינו ניטל באיגודו לא ניקטור. כלומר אין סוגרין כדגרסינן טרוקו גלי סגרו הפתחים. פי' ניקמן. אמר רב יהודה אמר שמואל הלכה כר' יהודה דאוסר (בניקמן) [בנקמז] משום דמיחזי כבונה (דמפורש) [ומפורש] בירושלמי ר' יעקב בר אחא בשם רבנן מדדו זהו הנקמן בראשי אצבעותיו *) וכיון דמדדהו נראה כי בונה אמר שמואל ואם עשה לו בית יד נעשה (ככוכנא) [כבוכנא] ושרי: ההיא שריתא [כו']. פי' דהוה שקלי לה עשרה ושדו לה אדשא והוה חזי להו ר' פדת ולא אמר להו ולא מידי אמר זו תורת כלי עליה והוא הדין לאסיתא שהיא מכתשת גדולה מחזקת אדרב ואמר מר שמוא' תורת כלי עליה ושרי לטלטולה. פי' הני כיפי דארבא כמין קרשים כפופין ע"ג הספינה. ויש טבעות קבועות וכשתהיה החמה קושרין באותן טבעות מחצלאות ופורסין אותה ע"ג הספינה מפני החמה. (עכשיו) ואי הני כיפי דארבא בהן טפח הנה הן חשיבין כאהלים דקי"ל אוהלי טומאה טפח. ואם אין בכל אחד מהן רחב טפח ואין בין זה הקרש לזה הקרש ג' טפחים כיון דקי"ל כל פחות מג' כלבוד דמי נעשו כל הקרשים כולן כאילו לבודין והנה הם אהל למחר בשבת מביא מחצלת ופורם עליהן דמוסיף על אהל עראי הוא ושרי: הנך דכרי פי' אילים דהוו לרב הונא בימא בעי טולא ובלילה בעו אוירא ואתא לקמיה דרב וא"ל זיל כרוך בודייא ושייר בה טפח (פרום) [פירוש] ושדייה (לדיר) [לבודייא] ע"ג עצים מע"ש וליהוי הבודיא כרוכה על גבי העצים ליליי

*) עיין בירושלמי בפירקין הלכה י' וצ"ע ואולי דרבינו היה לו גי' אחרת בירושלמי.

רב נסים גאון

מאי טעמא מוסיף על אהלי עראי הוא ושפיר דמי עיקר דיליה בפ' כל הכלים ניטלין בשבת (שבת קכה) דתנן פקק החלון ר' אליעזר אומר בזמן שהוא קשור ותלוי פוקקין בו ובגמ' גרסי אמר רבה בר בר חנה אמר ר' יוחנן הכל מודין שאין עושין אהלי עראי בתחלה ביום טוב ואין צריך לומר בשבת לא נחלקו אלא להוסיף שר' אליעזר אומר אין מוסיפין ביו"ט ואין צריך לומר בשבת וחכמים אומרים מוסיפין

בשיפועה טפח, אבל יש בשיפועה טפח – שיפועי אהלים כאהלים דמו. *ואמר רב ששא בריה דרב אידי: [א]סיינא שרי. והתניא: אסור! לא קשיא; הא – דאית ביה טפח, הא – דלית ביה טפח. אלא מעתה שרביב בגלימיה טפח הכי נמי דאסור! אלא לא קשיא; [ב]הא – דמיהדק, הא – דלא מיהדק.§ **מתני'** מחזירין ציר התחתון במקדש, אבל לא במדינה. והעליון – כאן וכאן אסור. רבי יהודה אומר: העליון במקדש, והתחתון במדינה.§ **גמ'** תנו רבנן: [ג]ציר דלת שידה תיבה ומגדל, במקדש – מחזירין, במדינה – דוחקין. והעליון – כאן וכאן לא יחזיר, גזרה שמא יתקע. ואם תקע – חייב חטאת. של בור ושל דות ושל יציע – לא יחזיר, ואם החזיר – חייב חטאת.§ **מתני'** *[ד]מחזירין רטיה במקדש, אבל לא במדינה. אם בתחילה – כאן וכאן אסור.§ **גמ'** תנו רבנן: רטיה שפרשה מעל גבי מכה – מחזירין בשבת. ר' יהודה אומר: הוחלקה למטה – דוחקה למעלה, למעלה – דוחקה למטה. [ה]ומגלה מקצת הרטיה ומקנח פי המכה, וחוזר ומגלה מקצת רטיה, ומקנח פי המכה. ורטיה עצמה לא יקנח, מפני שהוא ממרח. ואם מירח – חייב חטאת. אמר רב יהודה, אמר שמואל: הלכה כר' יהודה. אמר רב חסדא: לא שנו אלא שפירשה על גבי כלי, אבל פירשה על גבי קרקע – דברי הכל אסור! אמר מר בר רב אשי: הוה קאימנא קמיה אבא! נפלה ליה אבי סדיא וקא מהדר ליה. אמינא ליה: לא סבר לה מר להא דאמר רב חסדא: מחלוקת – שפירשה על גבי כלי, אבל פירשה על גבי קרקע – אסור. ואמר שמואל: הלכה כרבי יהודה! אמר לי: *לא שמיע לי. כלומר: לא סבירא לי.§ **מתני'** [ו]קושרין נימא במקדש, אבל לא במדינה. ואם בתחילה – כאן וכאן אסור.§ **גמ'** ורמינהו: נימת כנור שנפסקה – לא היה קושרה, אלא עונבה! לא קשיא; הא – רבנן, והא – ר' אליעזר. לרבי אליעזר דאמר: "מכשירי מצוה דוחין את השבת" – קושרה, לרבנן דאמרי אין דוחין – עונבה. אי רבי אליעזר – אפילו לכתחילה נמי! אלא, לא קשיא; הא *רבי יהודה, והא – רבנן. ורבי יהודה אליבא דמאן? אי

בשיפועה. מכנגד אמצעית גגה עד מקום ששפת יריעה כלה שם. לא הרחיב טפח דהוי כולה כדופן ואין כאן אהל כלל אבל הרחיבה כל דופן ודופן באלכסונה טפח – הוי ההוא אלכסון, אע"פ שהוא משופע קרוי אהל, כרבנן דפליגי אדרבי אליעזר במסכת סוכה (דף יט:) כך שמעתי, וקשיא לי: איזו מטה שאין ברחבה שני טפחים או ג' חסר משהו, שיהיה בגגה פחות מטפח ושני שיפועיה כל אחד פחות מטפח? וי"ל: שהמטה רחבה כמשפטה, ונקליטין הרבה יוצאין הימנה לשני ראשיה, ועולין למעלה סדורין אחד נמוך ואחד גבוה, וקנים נתונים עליהם מנקליטין שבראשה לנקליטין שברגליה, ופורס על המטה שתים ושלש כילות קטנות בגגה, ויריעה גדולה פרוסה סביב המטה לדפנות:

כזה

מטה

סיינא שרי. כובע של לבד, שקורין פלטר"י, מותר לצאת בו בשבת: הא דאית ביה טפח. שיוצא טפח רוחב שפתו להלן מראשו – אסיר, דהוי אהל: שרביב בגלימיה. האריך בטליתו להלן מראשו, והוציאה טפח – הכי נמי דאסור: אלא הא דמיהדק הא דלא מיהדק. וטעמא לאו משום אהל הוא, אלא דילמא נפיל מרישיה ואתי לאתויי. הלכך, כי מיהדק וקשור ברצועה תחת צוארו – שרי, ואי לא – אסור: **מתני'** מחזירין ציר התחתון. של דלת חלון שידה תיבה ומגדל שפתחיהם מצדיהן. דציר התחתון, כל זמן שלא יצא העליון – נוח להחזירו. ואין כאן בנין: אבל לא במדינה. גזירה שמא יתקע בגרזן או במקבות, דהויא מלאכה: והעליון כאן וכאן אסור. דכיון שיצא העליון – כולו נופל, והוי כבונה. וקא סבר: יש בנין בכלי, ומלאכה לא הותרה אפילו במקדש: **גמ'** במקדש מחזירין. כגון שצריכין לו לדבר קרבן, כגון שהיה שם מלח או לבונה או קטורת, ואין שבות במקדש: ובמדינה דוחקין. אם לא יצא כולו מחור האסקופה, אלא התחיל לשמט – דוחקין לחור בלע"ז אנפיינדר"א: והעליון כאן וכאן אסור להחזיר. דהוי בונה ממש: שמא יתקע. שמא יחזיקנו במקבות ובגרזן, והויא מלאכה. ואתחתונה במדינה קאי, דאי אעליון קאי, ובמקדש, הוה ליה שבות, דהך חזרה גזירה משום שמא יתקע, ואמאי מיתסר במקדש דאמר והעליון כאן וכאן אסור, והא שבות במקדש לא גזרו: של בור ושל דות. דהוי בנין המחובר לקרקע, חשיב בנין בכל דהו: בור בחפירה דות בבנין בתוך הקרקע, אישקדיינ"א: **מתני'** מחזירין רטיה. כהן שלקה בידו, ונתן עליה רטיה מבעוד יום, והולך לעבוד עבודה בשבת או ביו"ט ונטל רטיה מעל ידו שלא תהא חוצצת בינו ובין ידו לעבודה. דחציצה פוסלת בה, דבעינן "ולקח הכהן" וכיון דקיים לא הוי לקיחה בכהן – מחזירה במקדש. דאי לא שרית ליה להחזירה – לא שקיל ליה מידיה, וממנע ולא עביד עבודה. וזה אחד משלשה דברים האמורים במסכת ביצה *שהותרו סופן משום תחלתן: אבל לא במדינה. גזירה שמא ימרח הרטיה. ומירוח היינו(א) מוחק האמור באבות מלאכות של שבת: אם בתחלה. שלא היתה קשורה מבעוד יום, וכהן זה לא סלק' לצורך עבודה: כאן וכאן אסור. והכא ליכא למימר אין שבות במקדש, דהא ודאי האי שבות לאו לצורך גבוה הוא, אלא לצורך עצמו: **גמ'** רטיה שפרשה. שנפלה. ובמדינה קא מיירי, ולהכי נקט פרשה, שהרי לא נטלה מדעת: מחזירין. דמילתא דלא שכיחא הוא, ולא גזור בה רבנן: רבי יהודה אומר. אם נפלה – אין מחזירין, אבל אם הוחלקה – דוחקה [*ומחליקה למכה]: שהוא ממרח. מחליק גומות שברטיה. מירוח חייב משום ממחק: לא שנו. דתנא קמא שרי להחזירה: אלא שפרשה ע"ג כלי. על הכר או על הכסת: ע"ג קרקע. כלכתחלה דמי: אבי סדיא. נפלה לו על הכר שבמרגלותיו. כמו שמתרגם "מרגלותיו" – איסדוהי: לא סבר לה מר להא דרב חסדא. דמוקי לפלוגתייהו בשנפלה על הכלי, ואפילו הכי אסר כרבי יהודה ואמר שמואל: הלכה כרבי יהודה: לא שמיע לי. הא דרב חסדא, דאנא סבירא לי דכי פליג ר' יהודה – בנפילה על גבי קרקע, אבל בנפילה על גבי כלי – מודה, דהוה כהוחלקה בעלמא: **מתני'** קושרין נימא. נימת כנור של שיר הלוים לקרבן, אם נפסקה בשבת. ובגמרא מפרש טעמא, דקסבר מכשירי מצוה שלא היה יכול לעשותן מאתמול, דהא היום נפסקה – דוחה את השבת. ואף על גב דקשר אב מלאכה הוא במסכת שבת (דף עג.): ואם בתחילה. שלא היתה שם מעולם, דיכול לעשות מאתמול – אסור: **גמ'** פלוגתא דר"א ורבנן גבי מילה (שבת דף קל.) שר"א מתיר לחטוב עצים ולעשות פחמין בשבת לעשות איזמל למול בו: קרבן לבור הוה מצוה הדוחה את השבת, ושיר הוי מכשירין דידה: אפי' לכתחילה נמי. דאפי' לעשות פחמין שהוא מכשיר – שרי: לר' יהודה. דאמר: עניבה אב מלאכה, במסכת שבת (דף קיג.) אין חילוק בין עניבה לקשירה, וקושר. דקסבר: מכשירי מצוה דוחין. והא דתניא עונבה – רבנן, דאמרי לאו מלאכה היא, וכיון דאפשר בעניבה – לא מחללינן שבת: ורבי יהודה. דמוקמינן מתני' אליביה, וקושר אב מלאכה היא, אליבא דמאן: אי

הא דמיהדק הא דלא מיהדק. פירש בקונטרס: דטעמא לאו משום אהל הוא. ולפי זה מותרין אותן כובעין של לבד, אע"פ שמאהיל טפח, ובלבד שיהיה קשור תחת גרונו, שלא יפול, ואתי לאיתויי ד' אמות ברה"ר. אבל ר"ת מפרש דמיהדק אסור, כשהטפח היוצא מן הכובע חזק שאינו נכפף ונראה אהל. ולפי זה כובעים אסורין: **והעליון** כאן וכאן אסור. פי' בקונטרס: דקסבר יש בנין וסתירה בכלים, דעל שידה תיבה ומגדל קאמר לה בגמרא. ותימה: אטו מתני' כב"ש? דלב"ה אין בנין וסתירה בכלים, בפ"ב דביצה (דף כב.)! ועוד קשה: דבגמרא גבי והעליון כאן וכאן אסור שמא יתקע, דחק לפרש דשמא יתקע קאי על תחתון, דאי אעליון – לא היה אסור במקדש, דאין שבות במקדש. ודוחק גדול הוא. ונראה לר"י: דאפילו ציר העליון הוא דרבנן, דשבות גדולה כזה לא התירו במקדש. וטובא אשכחן דלא התירו במקדש(ג), כגון סידור הקנים ונטילתן דאינו דוחה את השבת*: **מחזירין** רטיה במקדש אבל לא במדינה. פי' בקונט': גזירה שמא ימרח. אבל לשחיקת סממנין ליכא למיחש, כיון דמאתמול הוה עילויה. וקשה: דבפרק "במה אשה" (שבת דף סד:) אמר: אשה יוצאה בפילפל ובגרגיר מלח, ואם נפל – לא תחזיר. ואמאי? כיון דכבר הוי עילויה! ויש לומר: דהתם טעמא לפי שנראית כמו שמתכוון להוציא לחוץ, ואתי למשרי הוצאה. והר"ר יוסף פירש לשם – הטעם משום שחיקת סממנים, וכן יש לפרש בשמעתין. ונקט רטיה לרבותא, אף על גב דאיכא למיחש לשחיקת סממנין ולמירוח – אפי' הכי מחזירין במקדש: **רטיה** שפירשה מחזירין אותה. וא"ת: ומ"ש דאמר גבי פילפל וגרגיר מלח, נפל לא תחזיר? וי"ל: דהך דפילפל איירי שנפל על גבי קרקע, והכא שנפל על גבי כלי, כדקאמר רב חסדא בסמוך. ורב אשי דקאמר בסמוך לא שמיע לי – לא קאי אדרב חסדא כדפירש בקונטרס, אלא קאי אהלכה כר' יהודה. אבל אמילתא דרב חסדא – לא פליג, ומודה דלא שרו רבנן אלא בכלי. ועוד י"ל: ההיא דגרגיר מלח – אתי כרבי יהודה דאסר הכא: **אמר** מר בר רב אשי הוה קאימנא קמיה דרבא. ר"ח גרס: "קמיה דאבא". וכן נראה דל"ג "קמיה דרבא", *דיום שמת רבא נולד רב אשי. **קושרין** נימא כו' ואם לבתחילה כאן וכאן אסור. פירש בקונטרס: שלא היתה שם מאתמול. ור"י מפרש: לכתחילה – אפילו נפסקה היום, ורוצה לשלשלה ולעשותה בלא קשר – זהו לכתחילה: הא

(שבת קלח:) (ביצה יח:) (פסחים מח. מו"ק יב: כתובות פג: לז. ב"ב יג: קסה. סנהדרין כח: חולין נג: סב.) (סוכה לג: וש"נ) (דף יא:) (רש"ל) (שבת קכג: ומנחות לו: ועי' תוס' שם ד"ה לא סודר) (קדושין עב:)

עין משפט נר מצוה

נו א ב מיי' פכ"ב מהלכות שבת הלכה לא וסמג שם טוש"ע א"ח סי' שא סעיף מא:
נז ג מיי' פכ"ב שם הל' כה סמג שם טוש"ע א"ח סי' שיג סעיף ה:
נח ד מיי' פכ"א מהל' שבת הלכה כז סמג שם טוש"ע א"ח סימן שכח סעיף כה:
נט ה מיי' שם וטוש"ע שם סעיף כו:
ס ו מיי' פ"י מהל' שבת הלכה ו:

רבינו חננאל

לילי שבת כדי שיהא האויר נכנס על הצאן ומחר בשעת החמה פרוס גם שאר הבודיא וכסה בה העצים להיות להן צל דכיון דהוה בה מאתמול פריסה מקצת הבודיא טפח נעשה אותו טפח מאתמול אהל עכשיו מוסיף על אהל עראי אתה ושרי לך. וילון פי' פרוכת. אמר שמואל משום ר' חייא כילת חתנים מותר לנטותה כו' אבל יש בגגה טפח או פחות מג' סמוך לגג רחב טפח או נחתא מפוריא טפח או אית בשיפועא טפח. אי אית חד מהנך אסיר ושיפועי אהלים כאהלים דמו. סייאנא. פי' הכובע שעל ראש האדם שיש לו כנפים יוצאות כגון שפתים פשוטות גועות על הפנים מפני השמש אם מהדק אפי' יש בו טפח *) שרי ואי לא אסיר: **מתני'** מחזירין ציר התחתון במקדש. ת"ר ציר דלת של שידה ושל תיבה ושל מגדל כו'. פי' שמא יתקע בה מסמר. **) יהודה אמר פרשה אין מחזירין אותה כלל אלא הוחלקה במכה למטה דוחקה למעלה על גבי מכה וכן אם הוחלקה למעלה דוחקה למטה ומגלה מקצת רטיה ומקנח פי המכה וחוזר ומגלה מקצת רטייה ומקנח פי המכה כו'. אמר רב חסדא לא שנו אלא שפירשה ע"ג כלי דת"ק מתיר להחזירה ור' יהודה אוסר. אבל פירשה ע"ג קרקע דברי הכל אסור להחזירה. אמר מר בר רב אשי הוינא קאים קמיה אבא כו'. וקי"ל כרב אשי דהוה בתרא. ואם בתחילה [להניח] רטיה [אפילו] במקדש אסור כל שכן במדינה

*) עיין בתוס' כאן ד"ה הא ובשבת קל"ח וברא"ש שם דכתבו על שם רבינו להיפך. וגם בדברי רבינו שם בהדיא הגי' בהיפך ע"ש דאם מהודק אסור וכו' וצ"ע: **) נראה לחסר כאן וצ"ל ת"ר רטיה שפירשה מעל גבי מכה מחזירין בשבת ר' יהודה אומר וכו':

רב נסים גאון

בשבת ואין צריך לומר ביו"ט ואיתא נמי (שם קלז) תולין את המשמרת: **מחזירין** רטיה במקדש אבל לא במדינה במס' יו"ט בפרק א' (דף יא) גרסי מאי טעמא התירו חזרת רטייה במקדש ואוקמוה בכהן שעובד עבודה והיינו דאמר עולא ג' דברים התירו סופן משום תחילתן ואלו הן עור לפני הדריסה ותריסי חנויות וחזרת רטיה במקדש קא משמע לן הותרו סופן משום תחילתן כהן דבר עבודה אין דלאו בר עבודה לא: **רבי** אליעזר אומר מכשירי מצוה דוחה את השבת עיקר דבריו במס' שבת בפ' ר' אליעזר אומר אם לא הביא כלי מע"ש (דף קל) דתנן ועוד אמר ר' אליעזר כורתין עצים לעשות פחמים ולעשות ברזל ותניא מילה וכל מכשיריה דוחין

הגהות הב"ח

(א) רש"י ד"ה אבל לא וכו' ומירוח היינו ממחק האמור: (ב) תוס' ד"ה והעליון וכו' דלא התירו במקדש. נ"ב עיין בתוספות פרק המצניע דף צ"ה בד"ה שרא ובפרק כל הכלים דף קכג בסופו:

גליון הש"ס

מתני' קושרין נימא. עיין סוכה דף נ ע"ב ד"ה ורבנן:

אי אליבא דר"א קאמר. כלומר: כמאן ס"ל במכשירין, על כרחך כר"א ס"ל. וכיון דכר"א ס"ל – אמאי הוי לכתחילה אסור: אלא הא ר' שמעון והא רבנן. מתני' רבנן דפליגי עליה דר"ש, ואמרי קושרה – דסבירא להו כר"א בחדא, דמכשירי מצוה דוחין וכו' וכגון בשאי אפשר לעשות מאתמול, כדקתני: שנפסקה לו נימא בכנורו, ופליגי עליה בשאפשר לעשות מבעוד יום. הלכך, בתחילה אסור ומעיקרא כי הוה מוקמינן לה כר' יהודה מ"ט לא שנינן הכי, משום דלא שמעינן בהדיא דאית ליה האי סברא למפלג בין אפשר לאי אפשר וכל כמה דלא אשכח תנא דאמר הכי בהדיא מיבעיא לן סתמא דמתניתין מני: אף היא. אם היה עונבה או קושרה אינה משמעת את הקול, והואיל וקשירה נמי אב מלאכה היא – הא עדיפא שמשמיע את הקול, וטוב לנו לחלל את השבת בשלשולו לקיים השמעת קול שיר של לוים מלחלל שבת בקשירה, שהיא אב מלאכה, ולא נקיים בה שום מצוה. דלא מצי[(ה)] השמע קול: משלשל מלמטה וכורך מלמעלה. שהרי יש יתדות מלמעלה ולמטה, שראשי הנימין כרוכין בהן וכשהוא רוצה – מגלגל היתד והנימא נארכת, כעין שעושין למיני כלי זמר ארפ"א, דמאריך עד שיגיע ליתד שלמעלה וכורכה בו, והרי היא כבתחלה. ומגלגלין היתד עד שמתפשטת כהלכתה ומשמעת קולה. ולרבנן עדיפא למיסרי קשירה, דהא משלשל נמי אב מלאכה הוא, דמתקן כלי כהלכתו וכיון (דדמי) [דשרי] לכתחלה, מחליף ואתי נמי להתיר נימין בכנור חדש לכתחלה, הלכך, קשירה עדיפא: הא והא רבנן. דמכשירין שא"א מבעוד יום דוחין. והא דקתני מתניתין קושרה – כשנפסקה באמצעית, שאילמלי עונבה לא תשמע קולה והא דקתני עונבה – כשנפסקה בראשיה, שאין צריכה שם חיזוק כל כך, וסגי ליה בעניבה: ואי בעית אימא הא והא באמצע. הא ר"ש והא רבנן, וברייתא דקתני לא היה קושרה – מדאורייתא שרי, דס"ל לר"ש מכשירין דמצוה דוחין היכא דלא אפשר להו מאתמול. ומשום גזירה הוא דגזר אמצע אטו מן הצד, אבל בעלמא, דליכא למיגזר מידי דחי: מתני' יבלת. ורוא"ה. והוא מום לתמיד, שדוחה את השבת. כדכתיב (ויקרא כב): "או חרוץ או[(ו)] יבלת" יבלת דקרא קרינן יבלת, שאין שם דבר אלא כמו חיגרת, דומיא דשבור ולא כתיב שבר, ועורת נמי לא כתיב עירון. אבל יבלת דמתני' – הוא שם דבר של המום: חותכין יבלת. ביד קאמר: אם בכלי כאן וכאן אסור. ולא"ג דכי עביד נמי ביד מתקן הוא והוה ליה חותך מבעלי חיים והוי תולדה דגוזז את הצמר אפ"ה כיון דכלאחר יד קא עביד שאין כן דרך לחותכה אלא בסכין אין כאן אלא שבות: ואם בכלי כאן וכאן אסור. דאב מלאכה הוי, הואיל ואינו משנה מכמות שעושין בחול: גמ'[(ז)] הרכיבו. בפסח הבא בשבת קאמר: הרכיבו על כתיפו כרה"ר או להביאו מחוץ לתחום: וחתיכת יבלתו אין דוחין. קשיא סתמא אסתמא: הא. דפסחים בכלי. וה"נ קאמר תנא דמתני' ור"א אפילו בכלי שרי. דס"ל מכשירי מצוה דוחין שבת כגון מלאכה שאפשר לעשותה מבעוד יום כגון בקור המום מכשירי קרבן הוא והקרבן דוחה השבת ובמכשירין פליגי: מתני' ביבישה. ואפ"ה בכלי אסור, משום דמתקן לה, ועיין מלאכה קא עביד. ודפסחים בלחה, ותרווייהו ביד: אמר לך בכלי. למה לי לאשמועינן בפסחים דאסור הא כבר שמעינן לה הכא ולמה ליה לתנא לסתמיה בתרי דוכתי: ואידך. להכי הדר תנייה התם משום פלוגתא דרבי אליעזר, לאשמועינן דאפילו בכלי שרי: ואידך. להכי לא מוקמינן להאי דפסחים בלחה, ובכלי. דאם כן הוה ליה אב מלאכה, והתם הא דשבות הוא דאיירי: דומיא דהרכיבו. דלא מיתסר אלא מדרבנן, דחי נושא עצמו. ותחומין נמי דרבנן, ואפ"ה: הואיל ואפשר מאתמול – לא דחי: ואידך. הרכיבו והבאתו גופה מלאכה גמורה היא, דלא ס"ל להאי תנא בפסחים כר' נתן, דאמר במס' שבת בפ' "המצניע" (דף לד.): חי נושא את עצמו. ובתחומין סבר לה כרבי עקיבא, דאמר במס' סוטה בפ' "כשם שהמים בודקין" (דף כז:) תחומין דאורייתא: א"ר אליעזר ק"ו. התם גבי פלוגתייהו תנינן לה בפ' "אלו דברים" (פסחים סה:): אלו שמשום שבות. אלמא: ת"ק משום שבות קא אסר להו, וש"מ דלאו בכלי מתוקמא: אלא אמר רב יוסף הא והא ביד. ומיהו, מתני' ביבישה לא מוקמינן לה. דאם כן – אפילו בכלי שרי. אלא בלחה וביד היינו טעמא דשרי – דשבות הוא. ובמקדש, שתמידין וקרבנות לצור במקדש הם מבקרין אותן. ובפסחים היינו טעמא דאסור, דאע"ג דשבות הוא, ולורך מקדש הוא – אפ"ה כיון דכל אחד ואחד מבקר פסחו, ומתקנו בביתו ואח"כ מביאו למקדש – לא התירו לעבור על השבות במדינה: להא שמעתא. דרב יוסף: גוללו אצלו. דכיון דאיגדו בידו, אע"ג דאיכא שבות – דילמא נפיל כוליה לרה"ר ואתי לאיתויי. ספר נמי שבות דמקדש קרי ליה, שהרי קדש הוא. אלמא: שבות דלורך מקדש הותר אף במדינה: הא אוקימנא. בריש פירקין באסקופה כרמלית וכו' דאפילו שבות ליכא למגזר. דא"נ נפיל כוליה, כי ממטי ליה לתוך הבית דרך האסקופה – אין כאן חיוב חטאת: משלשלין וכו'. לצלותו, והוא יצלה מעצמו. ובבשר דעלמא אמרינן אין צולין בשר בצל וביצה אלא כדי שיצולו מבעוד יום, גזירה שמא יחתה בגחלים, בפ"ק דשבת (יט:). והא הכא. דכל אחד צולה פסחו בביתו, וקשרי ליה נמי במדינה: בני חבורה. הנמנין על הפסח זריזין הן, דכל העוסקין בקדשים זריזין וחכמים, הלכך, לא מחתי: ואביי. דאישתיק, סבר: כהנים זריזין הן, אמרינן בכמה דוכתי. דכיון שנכנס לעבודה בידוע שלמדוהו הלכות קדש. אבל בני חבורה זריזין הן – לא אמרינן, שאין לך אדם שאינו עושה פסח: רבא אמר. הא והא ביד כדאמר, דבכלי ליכא לאוקמי לפסחים משום מלאכה. והא והא בלחה, דאי ביבישה – לא מיתסר בכלי. אלא מתני' דקתני שבות דאפשר לה מאתמול מידחי מקמי מכשירי מצוה – ר"א היא, דפליג נמי עלה דההוא דפסחים, ואמר דוחין – דאפילו אב מלאכה מידחי מקמייהו, וכ"ש שבות. והא דקתני במתני' דבכלי אסור – מודה ר"א דכמה דאפשר לשנויי משנינן ליה, ולא מחללינן שבתא. והיכא דלא אפשר, כגון גבי איזמל – דחינן אפילו אב מלאכה:

מאי

אי אליבא דר' אליעזר קאמר – אפי' לכתחילה נמי! אלא לא קשיא; הא – ר"ש, הא – רבנן. דתניא: בן לוי שנפסקה לו נימא בכנור – קושרה, ר' שמעון אומר: עונבה. רבי שמעון בן אלעזר אומר: אף היא אינה משמעת את הקול, אלא משלשל מלמטה וכורך מלמעלה, או משלשל מלמעלה וכורך מלמטה. ואיבעית אימא: הא והא רבנן, ולא קשיא; כאן – באמצע, כאן – מן הצד. ואיבע"א: הא והא באמצע, מר סבר: גזרינן, ומר סבר: לא גזרינן.§ **מתני'** [א]חותכין יבלת במקדש, אבל לא במדינה. ואם בכלי – כאן וכאן אסור.§ **גמ'** ורמינהו[(א)] *[ב]הרכיבו והבאתו מחוץ לתחום וחתיכת יבלתו אין דוחין, רבי אליעזר אומר: דוחין! *רבי אלעזר ורבי יוסי *)(בן) חנינא; חד אמר: [ג]הא והא בלחה, ולא קשיא; כאן – ביד, כאן – בכלי, וחד אמר: הא והא ביד, ולא קשיא; הא – בלחה, הא – ביבישה. ולמאן דאמר "הא – ביד, הא – בכלי" מאי טעמא לא אמר הא – בלחה, הא – ביבישה? אמר לך: יבישה אפילו בכלי נמי שרי. מ"ט – איפרוכי איפרכא. ולמ"ד "הא – בלחה, והא – ביבישה" מאי טעמא לא אמר "הא – ביד, הא – בכלי"? אמר לך: בכלי – הא תנן: אם בכלי – כאן וכאן אסור. ואידך: הא דקתני התם – משום דקא בעי איפלוגי ר' אליעזר ורבנן. ואידך: דומיא[(ב)] דהרכיבו והבאתו מחוץ לתחום קתני, דרבנן. ואידך: הרכיבו דלא כרבי נתן, *דאמר: החי נושא את עצמו. הבאתו מחוץ לתחום *כר"ע, דאמר: תחומין דאורייתא. מתיב רב יוסף, אמר רבי אליעזר: ק"ו *ומה שחיטה שהיא משום מלאכה – דוחה את השבת, אלו שמשום שבות – אינו דין שידחו את השבת? אלא אמר רב יוסף: הא והא – ביד, ושבות[(ג)] מקדש במקדש – התירו, שבות דמקדש במדינה – לא התירו. יתיב אביי וקאמר להא שמעתא. איתיביה רב ספרא לאביי: *היה קורא בספר על האסקופה, ונתגלגל הספר מידו – גוללו אצלו. והא הכא, דשבות דמקדש במדינה הוא ולא גזרי' דילמא נפיל ואתי לאיתויי! ולא אוקימנא באסקופה כרמלית, ורה"ר עוברת לפניה! דכיון דאיגדו בידו – אפילו שבות נמי ליכא. איתיביה: *[ד]משלשלין את הפסח לתנור עם חשיכה. והא הכא, דשבות דמקדש במדינה[(ד)] ולא גזרינן שמא יחתה בגחלים! אישתיק. כי אתא לקמיה דרב יוסף, א"ל: הכי אמר לי רב ספרא. אמר ליה: מאי טעמא לא תשני ליה: *בני חבורה זריזין הן? ואביי, *כהנים זריזין הן – אמרינן, בני חבורה זריזין הן – לא אמרינן. רבא אמר: רבי אליעזר היא, דאמר מכשירי מצוה דוחין את השבת. ומודה ר' אליעזר, דכמה דאפשר לשנויי – משנינן.

מאי

*) [נ"ל כר']

הא בלחה הא ביבישה. [מתניתין ביבישה], ואפילו הכי אסרינן בכלי – דשבות גדול הוא.

יבישה אפילו בכלי שרי. ולא מסתבר להחמיר עליו, כיון דאפרוכי מפריך:

ולאו אוקימנא באסקופה כרמלית. תימה, דאמר לעיל (דף לז.) גבי מלאן נבתים או כריכות: מביאן פחות פחות מד' אמות, אלמא: שבות דמקדש במדינה התירו! וי"ל דשבות כי האי גוונא ודאי שמוטלין בבזיון, התירו:

מה

פסחים סה: וסח:

[שם סח: רוב הסוגיא ע"ש]

שבת לג.

[סוטה כז: וש"נ]

[פסחים סה:]

לעיל לז: [שבת ה:]

שבת יט:

[שבת כ. קיד. פסחים נט: סה. פס. ביצה יח. ב"ב ל. חולין קכג: זבחים לה:]

סא א מיי' פ"ט מהל' שבת הלכה ח סמג לאוין סה טוש"ע א"ח סימן שמ סעיף ב:

סב ב ג מיי' פ"א מהל' קרבן פסח הלכה יח סמג עשין רכג:

סג ד מיי' פ"ג מהל' שבת הלכה טו:

רבינו חננאל

קושרין נימא במקדש כו' ורמינהו (נימא) [נימת] כנור שנפסקה לא היה קושרה אלא עונבה ופרקינן לא קשיא מתני' ר' אליעזר ברייתא ר' עקיבא דפליגי במכשירי מילה ובמכשירי פסח ר' אליעזר סבר מכשירי מצוה דוחין את השבת כו' ונדחה ואסיקנ' אלא ל"ק הא ר"ש הא רבנן דתניא בן לוי שנפסקה לו נימא בכנורו קושרה קשר של קיימא כו'. איבעית אימא הא והא ר' שמעון ולא קשיא מתניתין באמצע ברייתא' מן הצד איבעית אימא הא והא באמצע ות"ק סבר לא גזרינן באמצע אטו מן הצד ותנא (כד"א) [דברייתא] סבר גזרינן: **מתני'** חותכין יבלת במקדש אבל לא במדינה ואם בכלי כאן וכאן אסור. והתנן בפסח חתיכת יבלת אינה דוחה את השבת. ופרקינן מתני' ביבישה ומתני' דפסח בלחה. ואיבע"א לעולם בלחה ומתני' ביד. ומתני' דפסח בכלי. מ"ד הא ביד הא בכלי מ"ט לא אמר הא בלחה הא ביבישה. יבישה מיפרך פריכה אין צריך חתיכה. ומ"ד הא בלחה הא ביבשה מ"ט לא אמר הא ביד הא בכלי. אמר לך בכלי א"צ למיתנייה התם [הא] קתני במתני' ואם בכלי כאן אסור בין במקדש בין במדינה אסור ואידך אמר לך הא דקתני התם משום דבעי איפלוג ר' אליעזר ור' יהושע. ואקשינן והא חתיכת יבלתו דומיא (דהכרתו) [דהרכבתו] והבאתו מחוץ לתחום קתני מה הללו משום שבות אף חתיכת יבלת משום שבות ואי בכלי איסור מלאכה הוא. ופרקינן הרכיבו דלא כר' נתן דאמר החי נושא את עצמו והא דר' נתן מפורש בשבת פרק [המצניע דף ל"ד] הבאתו מחוץ לתחום כר"ע דאמר תחומין דאורייתא ומפורש (בסוכה) [בסוטה] פרק [כשם שהמים דף כ"ז] ואילו נמי איסור מלאכה נינהו ומותבינן איני דהני איסור מלאכה נינהו והתנן א"ר אליעזר ומה אם שחיטה שהיא משום מלאכה דוחה שבת אלו שמשום שבות [וכו'] *) מיהו שבות דמקדש במקדש התירו אבל האי דפסח שבות דמקדש. [במדינה לא

*) נ"ל אלא אמר רב יוסף הא והא ביד מיהו שבות דמקדש וכו'.

הגהות הב"ח

(א) גמרא ורמינהו הרכבתו והבאתו וכו' ולא קשיא הא ביד הא בכלי: (ב) שם דומיא דהרכבתו והבאתו וכו' ואידך הרכבתו דלא: (ג) שם ושבות דמקדש במקדש: (ד) שם במדינה הוא ולא גזרינן: (ה) רש"י ד"ה אף הוא וכו' דלא מצי משמעת קול: (ו) ד"ה יבלת וכו' חרוץ או יבלת יבלת דקרא קרינן יבלת שאינה שם דבר אלא כמו חיגרת דומיא דשבור ולא כתיב שבר ועורת נמי לא כתוב עורון אבל יבלת דמתניתין: (ז) ד"ה הרכבתו בפסח הבא בשבת קאמר הרכבתו להרכיבו על כתיפו:

רב נסים גאון

דוחין את השבת דברי ר' אליעזר ורבנן דפליגי עליה סברי כר' עקיבא דאמר מילה עצמה דאי אפשר לעשותה מע"ש דוחה את השבת אבל מכשיריה דאפשר לעשותן מערב שבת אין דוחין את השבת: **פלוגתא** דר' אליעזר ור' יהושע אתא לאשמועינן היינו מתני' דבפ' אלו דברים בפסח דוחין את השבת (פסחים דף סה) ותנן ר' אליעזר אומר דוחין אמר ר' אליעזר ומה אם שחיטה שהיא כו' אמר לו ר' יהושע יום טוב יוכיח כו'. הרכיבו דלא כר' נתן דאמר חי נושא את עצמו הבאתו מחוץ לתחום כר' עקיבא דאמר תחומין דאורייתא ועיקר דברי ר' נתן בפרק המצניע (שבת דף לג) ר' נתן אומר על השחוטין חייב על חיים פטור שהחי נושא את עצמו ועיקר דברי ר' עקיבא במשנת סוטה (דף כז) בפרק כשם שהמים בודקין אותה וכבר פירשנוה: **ולא** קא גזרינן שמא יחתה בגחלים איתא בסוף פרק יציאות השבת (דף יח) לא תמלא אשה קדירה עססיות כו' ואמרינן אפילו תימא בית הלל בהא אסור גזירה שמא יחתה בגחלים. כיון דאמרי רבנן בעלמא משום שבות הכא

מה

מַאי הִיא? דְּתַנְיָא: כֹּהֵן שֶׁעָלְתָה בּוֹ יַבֶּלֶת – חֲבֵירוֹ חוֹתְכָהּ לוֹ בְּשִׁינָּיו. בְּשִׁינָּיו – אִין, בִּכְלִי – לָא. חֲבֵירוֹ – אִין, אִיהוּ – לָא. מַנִּי? אִילֵימָא רַבָּנַן וּבַמִּקְדָּשׁ, כֵּיוָן דְּאָמְרִי רַבָּנַן בְּעָלְמָא מִשּׁוּם שְׁבוּת – הָכָא מַה לִּי הוּא מַה לִּי חֲבֵירוֹ? אֶלָּא לָאו ר"א, דְּאָמַר בְּעָלְמָא חַיָּיב חַטָּאת, וְהָכָא – אע"ג דְּמַכְשִׁירֵי מִצְוָה דּוֹחִין אֶת הַשַּׁבָּת – כַּמָּה דְּאֶפְשָׁר לְשַׁנּוּיֵי מְשַׁנֵּינַן. לֹא, לְעוֹלָם רַבָּנַן, וְאִי עָלְתָה בִּבְרֵיסוֹ – הָכִי נַמִי. הָכָא בְּמַאי עָסְקִינַן – כְּגוֹן שֶׁעָלְתָה לוֹ נְשִׁיכָה בְּגַבּוֹ וּבְאַצִּילֵי יָדָיו, דְּאִיהוּ לָא מָצֵי שָׁקֵיל לָהּ. וְאִי רַבָּנַן, נִשְׁקְלֵיהּ נִיהֲלֵיהּ בַּיָּד, וְתִפְשׁוֹט דְּרַבִּי אֶלְעָזָר. דְּאָמַר רַבִּי אֶלְעָזָר: מַחֲלוֹקֶת בַּיָּד, אֲבָל בִּכְלִי – דִּבְרֵי הַכֹּל – חַיָּיב! וְלִיטַעְמִיךְ, לְרַבִּי אֱלִיעֶזֶר נַמִי: לִישְׁקְלֵיהּ נִיהֲלֵיהּ בַּיָּד! הַאי מַאי? אִי אָמְרַתְּ בִּשְׁלָמָא רַבִּי אֱלִיעֶזֶר – הַיְינוּ דְּגָזַר יָד אַטּוּ כְּלִי. אֶלָּא אִי אָמְרַתְּ רַבָּנַן הִיא – נִשְׁקְלֵיהּ נִיהֲלֵיהּ בַּיָּד, *וְתוּ לָא מִידֵּי.§ **מתני'** *[א]כֹּהֵן שֶׁלָּקָה בְּאֶצְבָּעוֹ – כּוֹרֵךְ עָלֶיהָ גֶּמִי בַּמִּקְדָּשׁ, [ב]אֲבָל לֹא בַּמְּדִינָה. (א)אִם לְהוֹצִיא דָּם – כָּאן וְכָאן אָסוּר.§ **גמ'** *אָמַר *רַב יְהוּדָה בְּרֵיהּ דְּרַבִּי חִיָּיא: לֹא שָׁנוּ אֶלָּא גֶּמִי, אֲבָל צִלְצוֹל קָטָן – הָוֵי יִתּוּר בְּגָדִים. וְרַבִּי יוֹחָנָן אָמַר: לֹא אָמְרוּ יִתּוּר בְּגָדִים אֶלָּא בִּמְקוֹם בְּגָדִים, אֲבָל שֶׁלֹּא בִּמְקוֹם בְּגָדִים – לָא הָוֵי יִתּוּר בְּגָדִים. וְתֵיפּוֹק לֵיהּ מִשּׁוּם חֲצִיצָה! בִּשְׂמֹאל, אִי נַמִי: בְּיָמִין, וְשֶׁלֹּא בִּמְקוֹם עֲבוֹדָה. וּפְלִיגָא דְּרָבָא, דְּאָמַר רָבָא, אָמַר רַב חִסְדָּא: [ג]בִּמְקוֹם בְּגָדִים – אֲפִילּוּ נִימָא אַחַת חוֹצֶצֶת, [ד]שֶׁלֹּא בִּמְקוֹם בְּגָדִים – שָׁלֹשׁ עַל שָׁלֹשׁ חוֹצְצוֹת, פָּחוֹת מִשָּׁלֹשׁ עַל שָׁלֹשׁ – אֵינָן חוֹצְצוֹת. אַדְּרַבִּי יוֹחָנָן וַדַּאי פְּלִיגָא, אַדְּרַב יְהוּדָה בְּרֵיהּ דְּרַבִּי חִיָּיא מִי נֵימָא פְּלִיגָא? [ה]שָׁאנֵי צִלְצוֹל קָטָן דַּחֲשִׁיב. לִישָּׁנָא אַחֲרִינָא, אָמְרִי לָהּ, אָמַר רַב יְהוּדָה בְּרֵיהּ דְּרַבִּי חִיָּיא: לֹא שָׁנוּ אֶלָּא גֶּמִי, אֲבָל צִלְצוֹל קָטָן – חוֹצֵץ. וְרַבִּי יוֹחָנָן אָמַר: לֹא אָמְרוּ חֲצִיצָה בְּפָחוֹת מִשָּׁלֹשׁ עַל שָׁלֹשׁ אֶלָּא בִּמְקוֹם בְּגָדִים, אֲבָל שֶׁלֹּא בִּמְקוֹם בְּגָדִים, שָׁלֹשׁ

רש"י

מַאי הִיא. מְנָא תֵּימְרָא דְּמוֹדֵי ר' אֱלִיעֶזֶר דְּכַמָּה דְּאֶפְשָׁר לְשַׁנּוּיֵי מְשַׁנֵּינַן – דְּתַנְיָא: כֹּהֵן שֶׁעָלְתָה בּוֹ יַבֶּלֶת וכו': בְּשִׁינָּיו אִין. דִּשְׁבוּת הוּא, בִּכְלִי – לָא. וַאֲפִי' בְּשִׁינָּיו, חֲבֵירוֹ – אִין, וְאִיהוּ – לָא, דַּחֲבֵירוֹ לָא מְתַקֵּן לֵיהּ שַׁפִּיר. וְהָכִי אָמַר בְּמַסֶּכֶת שַׁבָּת בְּפֶרֶק "הַמַּצְנִיעַ" *דִּפְלִיגֵי רַבִּי אֱלִיעֶזֶר וְרַבָּנַן בְּנוֹטֵל צִפָּרְנָיו זוֹ בָּזוֹ אוֹ בְּשִׁינָּיו, שֶׁר"א מְחַיֵּיב חַטָּאת וַחֲכָמִים אוֹסְרִין מִשּׁוּם שְׁבוּת. וְאוֹקִימְנָא הָתָם דְּכִי מְחַיֵּיב ר"א – בְּנוֹטֵל לְעַצְמוֹ, אֲבָל לַחֲבֵירוֹ – דִּבְרֵי הַכֹּל פָּטוּר: מַנִּי. הָא דְּקָאָמַר בִּכְלִי לָא וּבְעַצְמוֹ לָא: אִילֵימָא רַבָּנַן. דְּאָמְרִי: מַכְשִׁירֵי מִצְוָה לָא דָּחוּ אַב מְלָאכָה, וְאַשְׁמְעִינַן דִּשְׁבוּת דָּחוּ – כְּגוֹן בְּשִׁינָּיו בַּחֲבֵירוֹ, וּכְגוֹן שֶׁעָלְתָה לוֹ בְּשַׁבָּת, דְּלָא אֶפְשָׁר לֵיהּ לְמִשְׁקְלֵיהּ מֵאֶתְמוֹל: כֵּיוָן דְּאָמְרִי רַבָּנַן. לְגַבֵּי דְּבַר הָרְשׁוּת דְּנוֹטֵל לְעַצְמוֹ זוֹ בָּזוֹ אוֹ בְּשִׁינָּיו – אֵין כָּאן אֶלָּא מִשּׁוּם שְׁבוּת: הָכָא. דְּקָשְׁרוּ בַּחֲבֵירוֹ מִשּׁוּם שְׁבוּת דְּמִקְדָּשׁ – לִישְׁתְּרֵי נַמִי לְעַצְמוֹ, דְּהָא אִיהוּ גּוּפֵיהּ נַמִי שְׁבוּת הוּא: אֶלָּא לָאו ר' אֱלִיעֶזֶר הִיא. דְּאָמַר בְּנוֹטֵל בְּשִׁינָּיו לְעַצְמוֹ, דְּעָלְמָא שֶׁלֹּא לְמִצְוָה – דְּחַיָּיב חַטָּאת. וּמש"ה, ה"נ כֵּיוָן דְּאֶפְשָׁר בַּחֲבֵירוֹ דְּהָוֵי שְׁבוּת – לָא שָׁרֵינַן לֵיהּ לְמִידְחֵי אַב מְלָאכָה וּלְמִשְׁקְלֵיהּ לְנַפְשֵׁיהּ. וְאע"ג דְּאָמַר ר"א מַכְשִׁירֵי מִצְוָה דּוֹחִין אַב מְלָאכָה – כַּמָּה דְּאֶפְשָׁר לְשַׁנּוּיֵי מְשַׁנֵּינַן: לְעוֹלָם רַבָּנַן. דְּאִי לְר' אֱלִיעֶזֶר לָא בָּעֵי שִׁינּוּי, וַאֲפִילּוּ לְעַצְמוֹ וַאֲפִי' בִּכְלִי שָׁרֵי, וּדְקַשְׁיָא לְרַבָּנַן, כֵּיוָן דְּנוֹטֵל לְעַצְמוֹ נַמִי שְׁבוּת הוּא, נִישְׁקְלֵיהּ אִיהוּ לְנַפְשֵׁיהּ: אִי דְּעָלְתָה לוֹ בִּבְרֵיסוֹ. מָקוֹם שֶׁאֶפְשָׁר לוֹ לִיטְּלָהּ בְּיָדוֹ אוֹ בְּשִׁינָּיו – ה"נ: הָכִי גָּרְסִינַן: וְאִי רַבָּנַן לִישְׁקְלֵיהּ נִיהֲלֵיהּ בַּיָּד וְתִפְשׁוֹט דְּר"א וכו'. כְּלוֹמַר: אִי אָמְרַתְּ בִּשְׁלָמָא ר"א הִיא וּמִשּׁוּם שִׁינּוּי – מְתּוֹקְמָא שַׁפִּיר, כְּמוֹ שֶׁמְּתָרֵץ לְקַמֵּיהּ. אֶלָּא אִי אָמְרַתְּ רַבָּנַן, וְטַעְמָא דְּבִכְלִי לָא מִשּׁוּם דְּמַכְשִׁירִין לָא דָּחוּ אַב מְלָאכָה, וְרַבָּנַן אַשְּׁבוּת הוּא דְּמַהַדְרִי. נְהִי דְּאִיהוּ גּוּפֵיהּ מְשַׁנֵּי' לֵיהּ – דְּלָא אֶפְשָׁר לְמִשְׁקְלֵיהּ, דִּבְגַבּוֹ הוּא. חֲבֵירוֹ מִיהָא לַשְׁמַעִינַן דְּנוֹטְלָהּ בַּיָּד, דְּהָא יָדוֹ נַמִי שְׁבוּת הִיא וְהָכִי שַׁפִּיר לְמִתְנֵי. דְּשָׁמְעִינַן מִינֵּיהּ תַּרְתֵּי. חֲדָא: דְּמַכְשִׁירִין שְׁבוּת דָּחוּ, וְלָא אַב מְלָאכָה, כִּדְמַשְׁמַע לָן הַשְׁתָּא. וְעוֹד שָׁמְעִינַן מִינֵּיהּ: מִדְּשָׁרֵי לֵיהּ בַּיָּד וְלָא בִּכְלִי – דְּהָכָא הוּא כְּדר"א. דְּאָמַר הָתָם בְּפֶרֶק "הַמַּצְנִיעַ" (שבת דף צד:): מַחֲלוֹקֶת בַּיָּד, אֲבָל בִּכְלִי – מוֹדוּ רַבָּנַן דְּחַיָּיב חַטָּאת, דְּחַשְׁבִינַן לֵיהּ תּוֹלָדָה דְּגוֹזֵז אֶת הַצֶּמֶר, שֶׁהוּא חוֹתֵךְ מִן הַמְחוּבָּר לְבַעֲלֵי חַיִּים. אֲבָל הַשְׁתָּא לָא מָצֵינוּ לְמִיפְשְׁטֵיהּ מִינָּהּ, וּלְמֵידַק – דְּהָא(ג) בִּכְלִי לָא מִשּׁוּם דְּאַב מְלָאכָה הוּא, דְּהָא בַּיָּד נַמִי שְׁבוּת הוּא, וְלָא קָשָׁרֵי לֵיהּ: וְלִטַעְמִיךְ לר"א נַמִי. נְהִי דְּטַעְמָא מִשּׁוּם שִׁנּוּי הֲוָה, נִשְׁקְלֵיהּ נִיהֲלֵיהּ בַּיָּד – דְּהָא אִיכָּא שִׁנּוּי, דְּמוֹדֶה ר"א בְּנוֹטֵל לַחֲבֵירוֹ שֶׁאֵינוֹ אֶלָּא שְׁבוּת: אִי אָמְרַתְּ בִּשְׁלָמָא ר"א. לְגַבֵּי מַכְשִׁירֵי מִצְוָה שְׁבוּת וְאִיסּוּר דְּאוֹרַיְיתָא הֵיתֵר מְשַׁוֵּי לְהוּ, וְטַעְמָא – מִשּׁוּם דְּאֶפְשָׁר לְשַׁנּוּיֵי מְשַׁנֵּינַן, כִּי הֵיכִי דִּמְשַׁנֵּינַן מֵאַב מְלָאכָה לִשְׁבוּת – מְשַׁנֵּינַן נַמִי מִשְּׁבוּת הַחֲמוּרָה לִשְׁבוּת הַקַּלָּה. הִלְכָּךְ, יָד חֲמוּרָה מִשִּׁינַּיִם, דְּאוֹרְחֵיהּ בְּהָכִי וְדוֹמֶה לִכְלִי, וְאִיכָּא לְמִגְזַר בָּהּ טְפֵי יָד אַטּוּ כְּלִי: אֶלָּא אִי רַבָּנַן. וְטַעְמַיְיהוּ מִשּׁוּם דְּאַב מְלָאכָה לָא מִידְחֵי לָמָּה לְהוּ לְאַהֲדוּרֵי (אֶלָּא) אַשְּׁבוּת כָּל דְּהוּ: וְתוּ לֵיכָּא. לְאַקְשׁוּיֵי מִידֵּי: **מתני'** כּוֹרֵךְ עָלֶיהָ גֶּמִי. וְאע"פ שֶׁהַגֶּמִי מְרַפֵּא אֶת הַמַּכָּה הוֹאִיל וְהַשְׁתָּא מִיהָא לוֹרֶךְ עֲבוֹדָה הִיא, דְּלָאו אוֹרַח אַרְעָא שֶׁתֵּרָאֶה מַכָּתוֹ עִם הָעֲבוֹדָה – מְכַסֶּה אוֹתָהּ בַּגֶּמִי: אֲבָל לֹא בַּמְּדִינָה. שֶׁמְּרַפְּאָה בְּשַׁבָּת, וּרְפוּאָה בְּשַׁבָּת שְׁבוּת הִיא, וְאָסוּר: וְאִם לְהוֹצִיא דָּם. שֶׁמְּהַדְּקָהּ בַּגֶּמִי כְּדֵי לְהוֹצִיא דָּמָהּ: כָּאן וְכָאן אָסוּר. שֶׁאֵין זֶה לוֹרֶךְ עֲבוֹדָה. וְעוֹד: דַּהֲוָה לֵיהּ חוֹבֵל, וְאַב מְלָאכָה לָא מִשְׁתְּרֵי לְגַבַּיְיהוּ: **גמ'** צִלְצוֹל קָטָן. אֵזוֹר קָטָן נָאֶה. כְּמוֹ: "הָיְתָה חֲגוּרָה בְּצִלְצוֹל (*קָטָן)" דְּסוֹטָה (דף ט:) וּבְלַעַ"ז בנדי"ל: הָוֵי יִתּוּר בְּגָדִים. וְתַנְיָא בִּשְׁחִיטַת קָדָשִׁים בְּפֶרֶק שֵׁנִי (זבחים דף יח.) לָבַשׁ שְׁנֵי מִכְנָסַיִם, שְׁנֵי אַבְנֵטִים, חָסֵר אַחַת אוֹ יוֹתֵר אַחַת, אוֹ שֶׁהָיְתָה לוֹ רְטִיָּה עַל(ג) בְּשָׂרוֹ תַּחַת בִּגְדוֹ וְעָבַד עֲבוֹדָה – עֲבוֹדָתוֹ פְּסוּלָה. וְיָלֵיף לָהּ הָתָם מִקְּרָאֵי "בְּנֵי אַהֲרֹן הַכֹּהֲנִים" – בִּכְהוּנָּם. כְּלוֹמַר: בְּבִגְדֵי הֶדְיוֹט הַזְּקוּקִין לָהֶם(ד) כֹּהֵן הֶדְיוֹט שֶׁלָּבַשׁ בִּגְדֵי כֹּהֵן גָּדוֹל וְעָבַד – עֲבוֹדָתוֹ פְּסוּלָה דְּהַיְינוּ יִתּוּר בְּגָדִים: לֹא אָמְרוּ. בְּאוֹתָהּ מִשְׁנָה יִתּוּר בְּגָדִים – אֶלָּא בִּמְקוֹם בְּגָדִים, אֲבָל שֶׁלֹּא בִּמְקוֹם בְּגָדִים כְּגוֹן בָּאֶצְבַּע – לָא הָוֵי יִתּוּר בְּגָדִים: וְתֵיפּוֹק לֵיהּ. בֵּין גֶּמִי בֵּין צִלְצוֹל, מִשּׁוּם דְּהָוֵי חֲצִיצָה בֵּין יָדָיו לָעֲבוֹדָה, וְאָנַן (וְלָקַח בָּעֵינַן) "וְלָקַח הַכֹּהֵן" "וְזָרַק הַכֹּהֵן", בָּעֵינַן דְּמַשְׁמַע בְּעַצְמוֹ עַל יָדוֹ, וְלֹא ע"י אֲחֵרִים: בִּשְׂמֹאל. שֶׁאֵין עֲבוֹדָה כְּשֵׁרָה בָּהּ, כִּדְאָמַר בִּשְׁחִיטַת חוּלִּין: *כָּל מָקוֹם שֶׁנֶּאֱמַר אֶצְבַּע אוֹ (כֹּהֵן) [כֹּהֵן] – אֵינוֹ אֶלָּא יָמִין: אִי נַמִי בְּיָמִין שֶׁלֹּא בִּמְקוֹם עֲבוֹדָה. כְּגוֹן עַל גַּב הָאֶצְבַּע: וּפְלִיגָא. הָא דְּר' יוֹחָנָן, דְּקָאָמַר שֶׁלֹּא בִּמְקוֹם בְּגָדִים לָא הָוֵי יִתּוּר בְּגָדִים, וַאֲפִי' בֶּגֶד ג' עַל ג' מַשְׁמַע דְּלָא פָּסֵיל: אַדְּרַבָּא.(ה) דְּקָאָמַר: בִּמְקוֹם בְּגָדִים, אֲפִי' נִימָא אַחַת חוֹצֶצֶת. וְאע"ג דְּמִשּׁוּם יִתּוּר בְּגָדִים לֵיכָּא לְמֵימַר, דְּהָא לָאו בֶּגֶד הוּא – חֲצִיצָה מִיהָא הָוְיָא, דִּכְתִיב (ויקרא ו): "וּמִכְנְסֵי בַד יִלְבַּשׁ עַל בְּשָׂרוֹ" – שֶׁלֹּא יְהֵא דָּבָר חוֹצֵץ: ג' עַל ג' חוֹצְצוֹת. דְּכֵיוָן דְּבֶגֶד מִקְרֵי הָוֵי יִתּוּר בְּגָדִים. וְהַאי דְּנָקַט בִּלְשׁוֹן חֲצִיצָה – מִשּׁוּם דְּרֵישָׁא אַיְּירֵי בְּנִימָא אַחַת בִּמְקוֹם בְּגָדִים, דְּלָא מָצֵי לְמִתְנְיֵיהּ יִתּוּר בְּגָדִים דְּלָאו בֶּגֶד הוּא: פָּחוֹת מִג' אֵין חוֹצְצוֹת. דְּאַיְּידֵי דְּלָא חָשֵׁיב בֶּגֶד – יִתּוּר בְּגָדִים אֵין כָּאן, דְּלָאו בֶּגֶד הוּא. וַחֲצִיצָה נַמִי אֵין כָּאן – דְּשֶׁלֹּא בִּמְקוֹם בְּגָדִים הוּא, וְשֶׁלֹּא בִּמְקוֹם עֲבוֹדָה: אַדְּר' יוֹחָנָן וַדַּאי פְּלִיגָא. הָא דְּרָבָא, כִּדְאָמְרַן שֶׁלֹּא בִּמְקוֹם בְּגָדִים ר' יוֹחָנָן לָא חָשֵׁיב יִתּוּר כְּלָל אֲפִי' בְּבֶגֶד גָּדוֹל: אַדְּרַב יְהוּדָה בְּרֵיהּ דְּר' חִיָּיא מִי נֵימָא פְּלִיגָא. הָא דְּרָבָא, דְּקָאָמַר שֶׁלֹּא בִּמְקוֹם בְּגָדִים פָּחוֹת מִג' אֵין חוֹצְצוֹת וְאִיהוּ קָאָמַר: דְּצִלְצוֹל קָטָן חָיֵיץ, וְאַף עַל גַּב דְּלָא הָוֵי שָׁלֹשׁ עַל שָׁלֹשׁ: צִלְצוֹל קָטָן חוֹצֵץ. מִשּׁוּם יִתּוּר בְּגָדִים. וְהַיְינוּ נַמִי כְּלִישָּׁנָא קַמָּא, וְאֵין בָּהּ חִילּוּק אֶלָּא בְּמִילְּתֵיהּ דְּר"י. וְהַאי דְּנָקְטֵי לָהּ בְּמִילְּתֵיהּ דְּרַב יְהוּדָה בִּלְשׁוֹן חֲצִיצָה – מִשּׁוּם הַךְ פְּלוּגְתָּא דְּר' יוֹחָנָן דְּלָא מָצֵי לְמִתְנְיֵיהּ מִשּׁוּם יִתּוּר בְּגָדִים, דְּקָאָמַר פָּחוֹת מִשָּׁלֹשׁ עַל שָׁלֹשׁ חוֹצֵץ בִּמְקוֹם בְּגָדִים, וּפָחוֹת מִג' לָא מָצֵי לְמֵימַר יִתּוּר בְּגָדִים אֶלָּא מִשּׁוּם חֲצִיצָה, לְהָכִי נָקַט לָהּ לְכוּלָּהּ בִּלְשׁוֹן חֲצִיצָה:

שָׁלֹשׁ

תוספות

מה לי הוא ומה לי חבירו. וא"ת: וכר' אליעזר מי ניחא? והא לא שרי הכא אלא בשיניו, ובמתני' שרי ביד, מדקתני: אם בכלי – כאן וכאן אסור. משמע הא ביד – שרי! וי"ל דגבי בהמה דאיכא מיאוס לחתוך בשיניו – לא הולרכו לחתוך בשיניו אלא ביד. וא"ת: והיכי מלינו למימר אליבא דר"א דהיכא דאפשר לשנויי משנינן? והא קאמר בפרק אם לא הביא (שבת דף קל.) דמביא סכין למול אפי' דרך רה"ר, אע"ג דאפשר לשנויי ולהביאו דרך גגות וקרפיפות וחלירות! וי"ל: דהתם מקלר דרכו לילך דרך רה"ר, אבל הכא דיכול לחותכו ביד כמו בכלי – מודה ר' אליעזר דמשנינן:

שעלתה לו נשיכה בגבו. תימה: דלשמעינן רבותא טפי כגון שעלתה במקום שיכול הוא בעצמו ליטול, ואפ"ה שרי הוא בעצמו ליטול, אף על גב דלא הוי כלאחר יד! ויש לומר: דאי לא אשמעינן בחבירו – הוי סלקא דעתך דלא שרינן לחבריה ליטול כדי שיעבוד חבירו:

(ו)**הכי** גרסינן: ואי רבנן נשקליה ביד ותפשוט דר' אלעזר. פירוש: דשמעינן מינה תרתי, חדא: דמכשירי מצוה לא דחו אב מלאכה, ועוד: דשמעינן דבכלי מודו דחייב חטאת. אבל השתא לא מלינו למיפשטיה, ולמידק דבכלי לא – משום דאב מלאכה היא, דהא ביד נמי שבות הוא ולא קשרו: **אא"ב** ר' אליעזר. פי': כי היכי דמשנינן מאב מלאכה לשבות – משנינן נמי משבות חמור לשבות הקל. אלא אי אמרת רבנן – למה להו לאהדורי (אלא) אשבות כל דהו? והקשה השר מקולי: דאמאי ניחא ליה למיעבד הרחקה לר"א טפי מלרבנן? והיה נראה להפך, דהא ר"א מיקל טפי! ותירץ דהיא הנותנת, אליבא דרבנן יש להתיר כל שבות, דלא נפיק מינה חורבה, כיון דאית להו דמשום הכשר לא דחינן שבת. אבל ר' אליעזר, דאית ליה דמכשירי' דוחה, ומיהו, באפשר לשנויי – משנינן, יש לנו לחזור אחר שבות הקל שלא יבא להתיר בלא שינוי, באפשר לשנויי:

ליסמעינן

עין משפט נר מצוה

סד א מיי' פ"י מהלכות כלי מקדש הלכה ט סמג עשין קעג:
סה ב מיי' פכ"א מהל' שבת הל' כה סמג לאוין סה טוש"ע א"ח סי' שכח סעיף כד בהג"ה:
סו ג מיי' פ"י מהלכות כלי מקדש הלכה ו סמג עשין סה:
סז ד ה מיי' שם הל' ח:

רבינו חננאל

התירו (* על האיסקופה ונתגלגל הספר מידו גוללו אצלו והא הכא שבות (דכתיבי) [דכתבי] הקדש במדינה הוא ולא גזרינן דילמא נפיל ואתי לאיתויי. אמר ליה ולאו מי אוקימנא לההוא באסקופה כרמלית והה"ר עוברת לפניה דכיון דאיגודו בידו שבות נמי ליכא. איתיביה משלשלין הפסח בתנור עם חשיכה והא הכא דשבות דמקדש במדינה היא ולא גזרינן שמא יחתה בגחלים. ופריק רב יוסף בני חבורה זריזין הן לפיכך לא גזרו ואביי כהנים זריזין הן אמרי' בני חבורה זריזין הם לא אמרינן רבא אמר ר' אליעזר לטעמיה דאמר מכשירי מצוה דוחין את השבת ומודה ר' אליעזר דכמה דאפשר לשנויי משנינן ומנא תימא דתניא כהן שעלתה לו יבלת חבירו חותכה לו (בשיש) [בשיניו] חבירו אין איהו לא. בשיניו אין בכלי לא מני הא אילימא רבנן כיון דאמר משום שבות מה לי הוא ומה לי חבירו. אלא לאו ר' אליעזר היא דאמר בעלמא חייב חטאת כו': **מתני'** כהן שלקה באצבעו כורך עליה גמי במקדש אבל לא במדינה. א"ר יהודה בריה דר' חייא לא שנו אלא גמי אבל צלצול קטן חוצץ. ור' יוחנן אמר לא אמרו חציצה בפחות מג' אצבעות אלא במקום בגדים אבל אצבע וכל כיוצא בה שאינה מקום לבישת בגדים עליה שלש על שלש חוצצות פחות משלש על שלש אינן חוצצות. והיינו דרבא אמר רב חסדא במקום בגדים אפילו נימא אחת חוצצת שלא במקום בגדים

*) נ"ל איתיביה רב ספרא לאביי היה קורא בספר על האסקופה וכו'.

רב נסים גאון

מה לי הוא מה לי חברו אלא לאו רבי אליעזר היא דאמר בעלמא חייב חטאת עיקרה במס' שבת בפ' המצניע (דף לא) דתנן הנוטל ציפורניו כו' ר' אליעזר מחייב חטאת וחכמים אומרים משום שבות: **ודקתני** כורך עליה גמי איתא בטהרות בתוספות מסכת כלים פ' ו' ר' יוסי מטמא בגמי מפני שהרופא נותנו על המכה שמוציץ הלחה. לא שנו אלא גמי אבל צילצול קטן הוי יתור בגדים טעמא דמילתא שהכהן אינו ראשי לשמש במקדש ולעשות עבודה אלא בבגדים האמורים בתורה דילמא מוסיף עליהם ותהיה עבודתו פסולה אם הוסיף עליהן ואיתא בשחיטת קדשים בפרק כל הזבחים שקבל דמן זר אונן (דף יח) לבש ב' מכנסים ב' אבנטים ב' כתנות כו' פסולה עבודתו. ותיפוק לי משום חציצה בשמאל טעמא דמילתא כי הכהן אינו ראשי לקשור על ידו דבר שיהא חוצץ בין ידו ובין כלי שרת וכן לא יהא דבר חוצץ בין ידו ובין הדם כמפורש לשם (זבחים דף כד) מה כלי שרת אין דבר חוצץ בין כלי שרת ובינו כו' וכן היינו פירוקא דפרקינן

מסורת הש"ס

[דף לא:]
[סוכה לו: וש"נ]
זבחים יט:
שם. [ושם אית' רבי יהודה וכ"ג כאן הגאון יעב"ץ ז"ל]
[עד סוף כל הענין]
[ליתא שם]
[דף כד ע"א]

הגהות הב"ח

(א) במשנה ואם להוציא: (ב) רש"י ד"ה הכי גרסינן וכו' דהא דבכלי לא: (ג) ד"ה הוי יתור וכו' רטיה על מכה בבשרו תחת בגדו ועבד עבודתו כנ"ל ותיבת עבודה נמחק: (ד) בא"ד הזקוקין להן הא כהן: (ה) ד"ה ופליגא הא וכו' דלא פסיל אדרבא הס"ד ואח"כ מ"ה דאמר רבא במקום: (ו) תוס' ד"ה הכי וד"ה אא"ב ר' אליעזר הכ"ל:

שָׁלשׁ עַל שָׁלשׁ – חוּצְצוֹת, פָּחוֹת מִשָּׁלשׁ – אֵין חוּצְצוֹת. וְהַיְינוּ דְּרָבָא אָמַר רַב חִסְדָּא. לֵימָא פְּלִיגָא דְּרַב יְהוּדָה בְּרֵיהּ דְּרַבִּי חִיָּיא? שָׁאנֵי צִלְצוֹל קָטָן דַּחֲשִׁיב. וּלְרַבִּי יוֹחָנָן, אַדְּאַשְׁמְעִינַן גֶּמִי, לִישְׁמְעִינַן צִלְצוֹל קָטָן(א) מִילְּתָא אַגַּב אוֹרְחֵיהּ קמ"ל, דִּגְמִי מַסֵּי.§ **מתני'** [א]בּוֹזְקִין מֶלַח עַל גַּבֵּי כֶּבֶשׁ בִּשְׁבִיל שֶׁלֹּא יַחֲלִיקוּ, וּמְמַלְּאִין *מִבּוֹר הַגּוֹלָה וּמִבּוֹר הַגָּדוֹל בְּגַלְגַּל בְּשַׁבָּת, וּמִבְּאֵר הַקַּר בְּיוֹם טוֹב.§ **גמ'** רָמֵי לֵיהּ רַב אִיקָא מִפַּשְׁרוֹנְיָא לְרָבָא, תְּנַן: בּוֹזְקִין מֶלַח עַל גַּבֵּי הַכֶּבֶשׁ בִּשְׁבִיל שֶׁלֹּא יַחֲלִיקוּ. בַּמִּקְדָּשׁ – אִין, בַּמְּדִינָה – לָא. וּרְמִינְהִי: חָצֵר שֶׁנִּתְקַלְקְלָה בְּמֵימֵי גְשָׁמִים – מֵבִיא תֶּבֶן וּמְרַדֶּה בָּהּ! שָׁאנֵי תֶּבֶן דְּלָא מְבַטֵּיל לֵיהּ. א"ל רַב אַחָא בְּרֵיהּ דְּרָבָא לְרַב אַשִׁי: הַאי מֶלַח ה"ד? *אִי דִּמְבַטְּלֵיהּ – קָא מוֹסִיף אַבִּנְיָן, (וּכְתִיב: °"הַכֹּל בִּכְתָב מִיַּד ה' עָלַי הִשְׂכִּיל") וְאִי דְּלָא קָא מְבַטְּלֵיהּ – קָא הָוְיָא חֲצִיצָה! בְּהוֹלָכַת אֵבָרִים לַכֶּבֶשׁ, דְּלָאו עֲבוֹדָה הִיא. וְלָא? וְהָא כְּתִיב: °"וְהִקְרִיב הַכֹּהֵן אֶת הַכֹּל וְהִקְטִיר הַמִּזְבֵּחָה", *וְאָמַר מָר: זוֹ הוֹלָכַת אֵבָרִים לַכֶּבֶשׁ! אֶלָּא אֵימָא: [ב]בְּהוֹלָכַת עֵצִים לַמַּעֲרָכָה, דְּלָאו עֲבוֹדָה הִיא. דָּרֵשׁ רָבָא: [ג]חָצֵר שֶׁנִּתְקַלְקְלָה בְּמֵימֵי גְשָׁמִים – מֵבִיא תֶּבֶן וּמְרַדֶּה בָּהּ. אָמַר לֵיהּ רַב פַּפָּא לְרָבָא, וְהָתַנְיָא: [ד]כְּשֶׁהוּא מְרַדֶּה – אֵינוֹ מְרַדֶּה לֹא בְּסַל וְלֹא בְּקוּפָּה אֶלָּא בְּשׁוּלֵי קוּפָּה! הֲדַר אוֹקִים רָבָא אָמוֹרָא עֲלֵיהּ וְדָרַשׁ: *דְּבָרִים שֶׁאָמַרְתִּי לִפְנֵיכֶם טָעוּת הֵן בְּיָדִי, בְּרַם כָּךְ אָמְרוּ מִשּׁוּם רַבִּי *אֱלִיעֶזֶר: וּכְשֶׁהוּא מְרַדֶּה אֵינוֹ מְרַדֶּה לֹא בְּסַל וְלֹא בְּקוּפָּה אֶלָּא בְּשׁוּלֵי קוּפָּה.§ "מְמַלְּאִין מִבּוֹר הַגּוֹלָה".§ עוּלָּא אִיקְּלַע לְבֵי רַב מְנַשֶּׁה, אֲתָא הַהוּא גַּבְרָא טְרַף אַבָּבָא. אֲמַר: מַאן *הַאי? לִיתְחַל גּוּפֵיהּ, דְּקָא מְחִיל לֵיהּ לְשַׁבְּתָא. א"ל *רַבָּה: [ה]לֹא אָסְרוּ אֶלָּא קוֹל שֶׁל שִׁיר. אֵיתִיבֵיהּ אַבַּיֵּי: *מַעֲלִין בְּדִיּוּפֵי, וּמַטִּיפִין *מֵיאָרֵק לַחוֹלֶה בְּשַׁבָּת. לַחוֹלֶה – אִין, לַבָּרִיא – לָא. ה"ד? לָאו דָּנִים וְקָא בָּעֵי דְּלִיתְעַר? ש"מ: אוֹלוּדֵי קָלָא אָסִיר! לָא, דְּתִיר וְקָא בָּעֵי דְּלֵינַם, דְּמִשְׁתַּמַּע כִּי קָלָא דְּזַמְזוּמֵי. אֵיתִיבֵיהּ: [ו]הַמְשַׁמֵּר פֵּירוֹתָיו מִפְּנֵי הָעוֹפוֹת וּדְלָעָיו מִפְּנֵי הַחַיָּה – מְשַׁמֵּר כְּדַרְכּוֹ בְּשַׁבָּת, וּבִלְבַד שֶׁלֹּא יְסַפֵּק וְלֹא יְטַפֵּחַ וְלֹא יְרַקֵּד כְּדֶרֶךְ *שֶׁהֵן עוֹשִׂין בַּחוֹל. מַאי טַעְמָא – לָאו דְּקָמוֹלִיד קָלָא, וְכָל אוֹלוּדֵי קָלָא אָסִיר! אָמַר רַב אַחָא בַּר יַעֲקֹב: גְּזֵירָה שֶׁמָּא יִטּוֹל צְרוֹר. וְאֶלָּא הָא דְּאָמַר רַב יְהוּדָה אָמַר רַב: [ז]נָשִׁים הַמְשַׂחֲקוֹת בֶּאֱגוֹזִים – אָסוּר. מַאי טַעְמָא – לָאו דְּקָא מוֹלִיד קָלָא, וְכָל אוֹלוּדֵי קָלָא אָסִיר? לָא, דִּלְמָא אָתֵי לְאַשְׁוּוּיֵי גּוּמוֹת. דְּאִי לָא תֵּימָא הָכִי – הָא דְּאָמַר רַב יְהוּדָה: נָשִׁים מְשַׂחֲקוֹת בְּתַפּוּחִים אָסוּר, הָתָם מַאי אוֹלוּדֵי קָלָא אִיכָּא? אֶלָּא: דִּילְמָא אָתֵי לְאַשְׁוּוּיֵי גּוּמוֹת. תְּנַן: מְמַלְּאִין מִבּוֹר הַגּוֹלָה וּמִבּוֹר הַגָּדוֹל בְּגַלְגַּל בְּשַׁבָּת. בַּמִּקְדָּשׁ – אִין, בַּמְּדִינָה – לָא. מַאי טַעְמָא – לָאו מִשּׁוּם דְּאוֹלוּדֵי קָלָא וַאֲסִיר? [ח]לָא, גְּזֵירָה שֶׁמָּא יְמַלֵּא לְגִינָּתוֹ וּלְחוּרְבָּתוֹ. [ט]אַמֵּימָר שְׁרָא לְמִימְלָא בְּגִילְגְּלָא בְּמָחוֹזָא, אֲמַר: מַאי טַעְמָא גָּזְרוּ רַבָּנַן – שֶׁמָּא יְמַלֵּא לְגִינָּתוֹ וּלְחוּרְבָּתוֹ, הָכָא לָא גִּינָּה אִיכָּא וְלָא חוּרְבָּה אִיכָּא. כֵּיוָן דְּקָא חָזֵא דְּקָא

תָּרוּ

(Margin beside Gemara: תורה אור; ד"ה א כח; ויקרא א; גליון אדם ע"ב)

רש"י

שָׁלשׁ עַל שָׁלשׁ חוּצְצוֹת. וּמִשּׁוּם יִתּוּר בְּגָדִים: לֵימָא פְּלִיגָא. הָא דְּרָבָא אַדְּרַב יְהוּדָה בְּרֵיהּ דְּרַבִּי חִיָּיא, דְּחָשֵׁיב גְּלָגוֹל קָטָן יִתּוּר בְּגָדִים: שָׁאנֵי צִלְצוֹל דַּחֲשִׁיב. וְאִיכָּא לְמֵימַר דְּמוֹדֶה בָּהּ רָבָא. אֲבָל רַבִּי יוֹחָנָן פָּלֵיג עֲלֵיהּ, דְּהָא עֲלָהּ קָאֵי וּפָלֵיג: וּלְרַבִּי יוֹחָנָן. דְּאָמַר גְּלָגוֹל נַמִי שָׁרֵי: לִישְׁמְעִינַן. תַּנָּא דְּמַתְנִיתִין גְּלָגוֹל קָטָן דְּלָא חָיֵיץ, וכ"ש גֶּמִי: דִּגְמִי מַסֵּי. מִשּׁוּם שַׁבָּת אִיצְטְרִיךְ לְמִתְנֵי גֶּמִי, דְּאַף עַל גַּב דְּמַסֵּי שָׁרֵי בַּמִּקְדָּשׁ: **מתני'** בּוֹזְקִין מֶלַח. מְפַזְּרִין וּמְכַתְּתִין עַל הַכֶּבֶשׁ, מִפְּנֵי שֶׁחָלָק הוּא. וּכְשֶׁהַגְּשָׁמִים נוֹפְלִין עָלָיו הוּא מַחֲלִיק. בּוֹזְקִין – לְשׁוֹן כִּיתּוּת, כִּדְאָמַר בְּפֶרֶק ב' דְּיוֹמָא (דף כב:): מַמַּאי דְּהַאי "וַיִּפְקְדֵם בְּבָזֶק" מִידֵי דְּמִיבְזַק הוּא, וְעוֹד "כְּמַרְאֵה הַבָּזָק" מְפָרֵשׁ בַּחֲגִיגָה (דף יג:) כְּאוֹר הַיּוֹצֵא בֵּין הַחֲרָסִים שֶׁצּוֹרְפִין בָּהֶן זָהָב, וְהֵם נְקוּבִים וּסְדוּקִים, וְלַהַב הַיּוֹצֵא בַּנֶּקֶב יֵשׁ בּוֹ כְּמַרְאֶה יַרְקְרַק אוֹ אֲדַמְדָּם: וּמְמַלְּאִין מִבּוֹר הַגָּדוֹל כו'. כָּךְ שְׁמָן, וּשְׁנֵיהֶם בְּלִשְׁכַּת הָעֲזָרָה: בְּגַלְגַּל. טור"ן בְּלע"ז. אֲבָל בַּמְּדִינָה לֹא, טַעְמָא מְפָרֵשׁ בַּגְּמָרָא מִשּׁוּם שֶׁמָּא יְמַלֵּא לְגִינָּתוֹ וּלְחוּרְבָּתוֹ: וּמִבְּאֵר הַקַּר בְּי"ט. וְלֹא בְּשַׁבָּת, וּבַגְּמָרָא מְפָרֵשׁ מַאי נִיהוּ: **גמ'** מִפַּשְׁרוֹנְיָא. מָקוֹם: וּמְרַדֶּה בָּהּ. שׁוֹטֵחַ בָּהּ: דְּלָא מְבַטֵּל לֵיהּ. וְלֵיכָּא מִשּׁוּם אַשְׁוּוּיֵי גּוּמוֹת דִּמְלָאכָה הוּא בְּשַׁבָּת, דְּהָוֵי כְּבִנְיָן דְּמִידֵי דַּחֲזֵי לְמַאֲכַל בְּהֵמָה אוֹ לְטִיט הַחוֹמוֹת לָא מְבַטֵּיל לֵיהּ הָתָם. אֲבָל מֶלַח מִשֶּׁנִּדְרָס בָּרֶגֶל לָא חֲזֵי וּמִסְתָּמָא מְבַטֵּיל לֵיהּ וּבַמְּדִינָה אָסוּר: קָא מוֹסִיף אַבִּנְיָן. וַאֲפִילּוּ בְּחוֹל אָסוּר לְהוֹסִיף עַל הַמִּזְבֵּחַ, דִּכְתִיב: "הַכֹּל בִּכְתָב מִיַּד ה' עָלַי הִשְׂכִּיל" שֶׁהַבִּנְיָן נִמְסַר לְדָוִד עַל יְדֵי הַנְּבִיאִים, שֶׁלֹּא לְהוֹסִיף וְשֶׁלֹּא לִגְרוֹעַ. וְאִית דְּנָקְטֵי לֵיהּ מִשּׁוּם שַׁבָּת, וְלָא הִיא. דְּהָא בְּ"כִסּוּי הַדָּם" בִּ"שְׁחִיטַת חוּלִּין" (חולין פג:) דְּאַיְירֵי בְּחוֹל, הָכִי נַמִי פָּרְכִינַן: הָא קָא הָוֵי חֲצִיצָה. בֵּין רַגְלֵיהֶם לַכֶּבֶשׁ, וַחֲלִילָה כִּי הַאי גַּוְונָא פְּסוּלָה, דִּתְנַן בִּ"שְׁחִיטַת קָדָשִׁים" (זבחים טו:): כָּל הַזְּבָחִים שֶׁקִּבֵּל דָּמָן זָר וְאוֹנֵן וְעָרֵל, יוֹשֵׁב וְעוֹמֵד עַל גַּבֵּי כְּלִי, עַל גַּבֵּי רֶגֶל בְּהֵמָה, וְע"ג רֶגֶל חֲבֵירוֹ – פָּסוּל. וְהָתָם יָלֵיף טַעְמָא: בְּהוֹלָכַת אֵבָרִים לַכֶּבֶשׁ דְּלָאו עֲבוֹדָה הִיא. לְעוֹלָם לָא מְבַטֵּל לֵיהּ, אֶלָּא לְאַחַר דְּרִיסָה מוֹלְחִין מִמֶּנּוּ עוֹרוֹת קָדָשִׁים. וּדְקַשְׁיָא לָךְ הָא הָוֵי חֲצִיצָה – לָא תִּקְשֶׁה, דְּהָא דְּקָתָנֵי בּוֹזְקִין מֶלַח – בְּהוֹלָכַת אֵבָרִים לַכֶּבֶשׁ קָאָמַר, דְּלָאו עֲבוֹדָה. דְּקָא ס"ד הַשְׁתָּא דְּכֵיוָן דְּכָל הַכַּפָּרָה תְּלוּיָה בַּדָּם, אע"ג דְּהֶקְטֵר חֲלָבִים הָוֵה עֲבוֹדָה – הוֹלָכָה דִּידְהוּ מִיהָא לָא חָשֵׁיב: וְהִקְרִיב אֶת הַכֹּל. רֵישָׁא דִּקְרָא: "וְהַקֶּרֶב וְהַכְּרָעַיִם יִרְחַץ בַּמָּיִם" אַלְמָא: בְּאֵבָרִים קָמִשְׁתָּעֵי קְרָא, וּמִדְּבָעֵי כְּהוּנָּה – שְׁמַע מִינָּהּ עֲבוֹדָה הִיא: וּמְרַדֶּה בָּהּ. לִדְרוֹס עָלֶיהָ: לֹא בְּסַל וְלֹא בְּקוּפָּה. כְּדֶרֶךְ חוֹל: שׁוּלֵי הַקּוּפָּה. שֶׁנִּשְׁבְּרָה, וְנִשְׁאֲרוּ הַשּׁוּלַיִם: טְרַף אַבָּבָא. הִקִּישׁ עַל הַדֶּלֶת בְּאֶגְרוֹפוֹ, וְהִשְׁמִיעַ קוֹל: דְּקָא מֵחִיל שַׁבָּת. דְּקָסָבַר: כָּל אוֹלוּדֵי קָלָא אָסִיר: בְּקוֹל שֶׁל שִׁיר. הַנִּשְׁמָע כְּעֵין שִׁיר, בִּנְעִימָה וּבְנַחַת: מַעֲלִין בְּדִיּוּפֵי. מַעֲלִין יַיִן מֵחָבִית לְחָבִית ע"י שְׁנֵי קָנִים הַחֲתוּכִים בַּאֲלַכְסוֹן, וּמַנִּיחַ רָאשֵׁין הַמְשׁוּפָּעִים זֶה כְּנֶגֶד זֶה, וְנוֹתֵן אֶחָד מִן הַקָּנִים בֶּחָבִית וּמוֹצֵץ בְּפִיו בְּרֹאשׁ הַקָּנֶה הָאַחֵר מְעַט מִן הַיַּיִן אֵלָיו, וּמְסַלֵּק מִשָּׁם וְהַיַּיִן יוֹצֵא כּוּלּוֹ מֵאֵלָיו. דִּיּוּפֵי – שְׁתֵּי פִּיּוֹת*: וּמַטִּיפִין מֵיאָרֵק לַחוֹלֶה. כְּלִי הוּא, וּפִיו צַר, וְשֶׁל מַתֶּכֶת הוּא וּמְנוּקָּב בְּתַחְתִּיתוֹ נְקָבִים דַּקִּין, וּמְמַלֵּא מַיִם וְסוֹתֵם פִּיו הָעֶלְיוֹן. וְכָל זְמַן שֶׁפִּיו סָתוּם – אֵין הַמַּיִם יוֹצְאִין בַּנְּקָבִים הַתַּחְתּוֹנִים, וּכְשֶׁרוֹצֶה – נוֹטֵל פְּקַק הָעֶלְיוֹן, וְהַמַּיִם יוֹצְאִין בַּנְּקָבִים טִיף אַחַר טִיף. וְנוֹתֵן כְּלִי מַתֶּכֶת וְכוֹפֵהוּ תַּחְתָּיו, וְקוֹלָן נִשְׁמָע לַחוֹלֶה: וְקָא בָּעֵי לְאִתְעוּרֵי. ע"י קוֹל זֶה, וּמִתְיָרְאִין לַהֲקִיצוֹ בְּיָדַיִם שֶׁמָּא יִבָּעֵית. וְכֵיוָן דִּלְהָקִיץ הוּא – לָא בִּנְעִימָה וּבְנַחַת נִשְׁמָע, שֶׁהֲרֵי קוֹל נָעִים מַרְדִּימוֹ וְהוֹלֵךְ. אפ"ה – לַבָּרִיא לָא: זַמְזוּמֵי. לינצ"ש: לֹא יְטַפֵּחַ. יָדָיו עַל לִבּוֹ: יְסַפֵּק. כַּף אֶל כַּף: יְרַקֵּד. בָּרֶגֶל, לְהַשְׁמִיעַ קוֹל לְהַבְעִית הָעוֹפוֹת: שֶׁמָּא יִטּוֹל צְרוֹר. וְיִזְרוֹק לְרה"ר לְהַבְרִיחַ הָעוֹפוֹת: מְשַׂחֲקוֹת בֶּאֱגוֹזִים. לְגַלְגְּלָן דֶּרֶךְ דַּף, וּמַכּוֹת זוֹ אֶת זוֹ, כְּדֶרֶךְ שֶׁמְּשַׂחֲקוֹת הַנָּשִׁים: לְאַשְׁוּוּיֵי גּוּמוֹת. לְהָכִין דֶּרֶךְ לְגַלְגֵּל הָאֱגוֹז: בְּתַפּוּחִים. נַמִּי כה"ג: אוֹלוּדֵי קָלָא. שֶׁהַגַּלְגַּל מַשְׁמִיעַ קוֹל: גְּזֵירָה שֶׁמָּא יְמַלֵּא לְגִינָּתוֹ. מִתּוֹךְ שֶׁמְּמַלְּאִין בּוֹ בְּלֹא טוֹרַח, אָתֵי לְהַשְׁקוֹת בּוֹ בְּגִינָּתוֹ וְחוּרְבָּתוֹ בְּשַׁבָּת:

(Margin beside Rashi: [סוף מסכת מדות]; [חולין פג.]; רש"ל מ"ז; [פסחים סה. חגיגה יח. יומא כז. זבחים יד: כד: מנחות י.]; [שבת סג: וכו' נסמן]; בר"י אלעזר; [תו"ק י. ע"ש פירש"י]; הרי"ף והרא"ש גרסו רבא; [תוספתא שבת פ"ב]; עי' רש"י שבת פ: ד"ה אנדיפי)

תוספות

לישמעינן צלצול קטן. אי גלגול אסור במדינה – פריך שפיר לישמעינן גלגול, דבמקדש מותר ובמדינה אסור. אבל נראה לר"י דגלגול שרי במדינה. וקשיא: דאם כן, מאי פריך? ומפרש ר"י דפריך הכי: דליתני במתניתין כהן שלקה באצבע כורך לו גלגול, בין במקדש בין במדינה, ואם להוציא דם – כאן וכאן אסור:

דרש רבא חצר שנתקלקלה. הלכתא כדמסיק, דלא ירדה לא בסל ולא בקופה אלא בשולי קופה, שנשתברה ונשארו בה השוליים כדפירש בקונטרס. אי נמי: הופך הקופה ונותנה על שוליה, דהיינו על ידי שינוי. אבל ביד – נראה לר"י דאסור:

הכי גרים בקונטרס: אלא הא דאמר רב נשים המשחקות באגוזים כו'. לא משום אשווי גומות, דאי לא תימא הכי כו'. ותימה: תרתי דרב למה ליה? ומיהו, י"ל: דחדא מכלל חברתה איתמר. ור"ח גרס הכי: אלא דאמר רב יהודה נשים המשחקות באגוזים כו' לא, דמשתמע קלא כי זמזומי. פירוש: שזורק אחד ומקבל אחד בהשמעת קול, דאסור. והדר קאמר: ואלא הא דאמר רב יהודה נשים המשחקות בתפוחים כו'. ומשני: לא, משום אשווי גומות. והשתא תרי ענייני איסור אשמעינן. ומיהו, אין למחות בנשים ותינוקות – דמוטב שיהו שוגגין ואל יהו מזידין. פר"ח דהלכתא כעולא, דאפילו קול שאינו של שיר אסור. אף על גב דשני רבה כל הני תיובתא דאקשי ליה – אשנויי לא סמכינן. ורב אלפס והר"ר יהודה בר ברזילי פסקו כרבה, דרב אחא בר יעקב מתרץ אליביה. וקאי אמימר נמי כוותיה, דשרא למימלא בגילגולא במחוזא: **גזרה** שמא ימלא לגינתו ולחורבתו. מפרש רבינו תם: דדוקא בגלגלים גדולים, שממלאין הרבה מים ביחד שייך למיגזר, אבל שלנו קטנים הם, ולא גזרינן:

יצא

עין משפט נר מצוה

סח א ב מיי' פ"ו מהל' תמידין הלכה ג:

סט ג ד מיי' פכ"א מהלכות שבת הל' ד סמג לאוין סה טוש"ע א"ח סי' שיג סעיף י:

ע ה מיי' פכ"ג מהל' שבת הלכה כד סמג שם טור ש"ע א"ח סימן שלח סעי' א:

עא ו שם סעיף ד:

עב ז מיי' פכ"א מהל' שבת הלכה ג סמג שם טור ש"ע שם סעי' ה:

עג ח ט מיי' שם הלכה ה וטוש"ע שם סעיף ו:

רבינו חננאל

שלש על שלש חוצצות פחות מיכן אינן חוצצות נימא הא דרבא אמר רב חסדא פליגא אדר' יהודה בריה דר' חייא דאמר באצבע אפילו צלצול קטן חוצץ ודחינן כגון א) שלקה בשמאל אי נמי שלא במקום צורך עבודה בשלמא לר' יהודה בריה דר' חייא היינו דקתני במתני' גמי מכלל דחתיכת בגד חוצצת אלא לרבי (אחא) [יוחנן] ניתני צלצול קטן וכיוצא בו ופרקינן הא קא משמע לן דגמי מסי: **פיסקא** בוזקין מלח ע"ג כבש בשביל שלא יחליק. ורמינהי חצר שנתקלקלה בימות הגשמים מביא תבן (וממדה) [ומרדה] בה ב) תבן אין מלח לא. ופרקינן אמאי לא בזיק תבן ע"ג הכבש משום דתבן לא מבטיל ליה וכיון דלא מבטיל ליה חוצץ ואשתכח דלא מסגי בכבש ואמרינן האי מלח היכי דמי אי דמבטיל ליה אשתכח דמוסיף על בנין. ואי לא מבטיל ליה הוי חציצה ופרקינן אין בוזקין המלח על הכבש אלא בהולכת אברים לכבש דלאו עבודה היא והא מתניתא והקריב הכהן את הכל המזבחה זו הולכת אברים לכבש. ומדבעיא כהונה ש"מ עבודה היא ואוקימנא בהולכת עצים למערכה דלאו עבודה היא. דרש רבא חצר שנתקלקלה מביא תבן ומרדה. וכשהוא מרדה אינו מרדה לא בסל ולא בקופה (ולא) [אלא] בשולי קופה: **מתני'** ממלאין מים מבור הגולה ומבור הגדל בגלגל בשבת. תנן בסוף מדות לשכת הגולה והגלגל נותן עליו [מים] ומשם מספקין מים לכל העזרה והגלגל הזה כשממלאין בו (מוצא) [מוציא] קול גדול. כדתנן מיריחו היו שומעין קול שעשה בן קטין מוכני לכיור וזה לא התירו אלא במקדש לפיכך כשראה עולא לאותו האיש שהקיש והכה הדלת בשבת והשמיע קול בהקשתו אמר ליתחל גופיה דההוא גברא דקא מחלל שבתא וא"ל רבא לא אסרו השמעת קול עץ כי האי גוונא אלא למקיש ומשמיע קול של שיר בלבד איתיביה אביי מעלין בדייפין ומטיפין מארק לחולה בשבת פי' להודיע שמותר לעלות יין מחבית בדייפי. פי' דייפי כגון מניקות שיש לה שני פיות ומכנים פיו האחד בחבית ושואב בכד ומעלה היין

בכלי ויש פה אחר למעלה מזה פתח הדייף הנתון בפיו כמין דד שהיין בהגעתו לדד מקלח ויוצא ומקבלו בכלי אחר עד שמריק כל היין שבחבית פי' מטיפין מאדק שמענו כי הוא כלי העשוי ולועא כמין [...]ז נקוב בקרקעיתו נקבין דקין דקין ופיו צר ממלאין אותו מים וסותמין פיו כ"ז שפיו סתום אין המים שבתוכו שותתין מן הנקבים שכח הרוח מונע את המים וכשפותחין פיו ויכנס האויר דוחה את המשקה שבתוכו [...]מטיף טפה אחר טפה טפות דקות ונותנין תחתיו כלי נחושת כגון ספל וכיוצא בו. וכשנופלת טפה על הכלי משמעת את הקול טפה אחר טפה או כמין קול משורר. ואמרי' מאי לאו (להני מי ארק) [הני מי יוזק] [...]שהתירו חכמים לחולה לאו בחולה הישן ומבקשים להקיצו ועושין לפניו זה הכלי כדי שיקיץ והנה לחולה בלבד התירו משום סכנה אבל לבריא כי האי גוונא אסור שמוליד קול בשבת. וקשיא לרבה דאמר לא אסרו [...]לא בקול שיר בלבד. ופריק לא לעולם בחולה הניעור ורוצה שישן דמשתמע הללו טיפי דמטיפין מאדק כי זמזומי ג). מיתיבי המשמר זרעים מפני העופות שלא ירדו ויפסידום מקשאן ומדלועין מפני החיות הרי

זה

[...]) גי' אחרת היה לו לרבינו ז"ל בכאן דר"י בר' דר"ח מיירי שלקה בימין במקום עבודה אמנם תמוה דא"כ גמי נמי וצ"ע. ב) [מדברי רבינו אלו נראה דל"ג בגמ' במקדש אין במדינה לא רק גרס תבן אין מלח לא]. ג) עי' בערוך ערך דיופי:

הגהות הב"ח

(א) גמרא לישמעינן גלגול קטן אגב כל"ל ותיבת מילתא נמחק וכו' בפרק ב' דזבחים דף יט דסוגיא מסכתא בחיסור שבת אייריו ועיקר משום שבות נקטו לה הלכך ל"ג מלתא כל"ל [והשאר חסר ולא נודע כוונתו]:

גליון הש"ס

רש"י ד"ה ומטיפין וכו' כלי הוא. עי' מתני' פ"ב מ"ז דכלים:

רב נסים גאון

ופרקינן בשמאל לפי שהעבודה לא הותרה אלא בידו הימנית אבל בשמאלו לא כדתנינן התם (זבחים דף טו) קיבל בשמאל פסול: **בוזקין** מלח. מפזרין על הכבש של מזבח והתם במס' יומא (פ"ב דף כב) אמרו

עד א ב מיי' פ"ג מהל' ביאת מקדש הלכה כ:
עה ג מיי' פ"א מהל' מקוואות הלכה ג:
עו ד מיי' פ"ה מהל' טומאת מת הל' ו:
עז ה מיי' פ"ג מהל' ביאת מקדש הל' טז:

תָּרוּ בָּהּ כִּיתְנָא, אֲסַר לְהוּ.§ "וּמִבְּאֵר הַקֵּר". מַאי בְּאֵר הַקֵּר? אָמַר שְׁמוּאֵל: בּוֹר שֶׁהִקְרוּ עָלֶיהָ דְּבָרִים וְהִתִּירוּהָ. מֵיתִיבִי: לֹא כָּל הַבּוֹרוֹת הַקָּרוֹת הִתִּירוּ, אֶלָּא זוֹ בִּלְבַד. וְאִי אָמְרַתְּ "שֶׁהִקְרוּ דְּבָרִים עָלֶיהָ" מַאי "זוֹ בִּלְבַד"? אֶלָּא אָמַר רַב נַחְמָן בַּר יִצְחָק: בְּאֵר מַיִם חַיִּים, שֶׁנֶּאֱמַר: °"כְּהָקִיר בַּיִר מֵימֶיהָ" וגו'. (ירמיהו ו) גּוּפָא: לֹא כָּל הַבּוֹרוֹת הַקָּרוֹת הִתִּירוּ, אֶלָּא זוֹ בִּלְבַד. וּכְשֶׁעָלוּ בְּנֵי הַגּוֹלָה חָנוּ עָלֶיהָ, וּנְבִיאִים שֶׁבֵּינֵיהֶן הִתִּירוּ לָהֶן. וְלֹא *נְבִיאִים שֶׁבֵּינֵיהֶן, אֶלָּא מִנְהַג אֲבוֹתָם בִּידֵיהֶם.§

מתני' שֶׁרֶץ שֶׁנִּמְצָא בַּמִּקְדָּשׁ — כֹּהֵן מוֹצִיאוֹ בְּהֶמְיָינוֹ, שֶׁלֹּא לְשַׁהוֹת אֶת הַטּוּמְאָה, דִּבְרֵי רַבִּי יוֹחָנָן בֶּן בְּרוֹקָה. רַבִּי יְהוּדָה אוֹמֵר: אבִּצְבָת שֶׁל עֵץ, שֶׁלֹּא לְרַבּוֹת אֶת הַטּוּמְאָה. מֵהֵיכָן מוֹצִיאִין אוֹתוֹ — מִן הַהֵיכָל, וּמִן הָאוּלָם, וּמִבֵּין הָאוּלָם וְלַמִּזְבֵּחַ, דִּבְרֵי ר"ש בֶּן נַנָּס. רַבִּי עֲקִיבָא אוֹמֵר: בכָּל מָקוֹם שֶׁחַיָּיבִין עַל זְדוֹנוֹ כָּרֵת וְעַל שִׁגְגָתוֹ חַטָּאת, מִשָּׁם מוֹצִיאִין אוֹתוֹ. *וּשְׁאָר כָּל הַמְּקוֹמוֹת — כּוֹפִין עָלָיו *פְּסַכְתֵּר. רַבִּי שִׁמְעוֹן אוֹמֵר: מָקוֹם שֶׁהִתִּירוּ לְךָ חֲכָמִים — מִשֶּׁלְּךָ נָתְנוּ לָךְ. שֶׁלֹּא הִתִּירוּ לְךָ אֶלָּא מִשּׁוּם שְׁבוּת.§

גמ' אָמַר רַב טָבִי בַּר קִיסְנָא, אָמַר שְׁמוּאֵל: הַמַּכְנִיס טָמֵא שֶׁרֶץ לַמִּקְדָּשׁ — חַיָּיב. *שֶׁרֶץ עַצְמוֹ — פָּטוּר. מַאי טַעְמָא? אָמַר קְרָא: °"מִזָּכָר וְעַד נְקֵבָה תְּשַׁלֵּחוּ" (במדבר ה) — מִי שֶׁיֵּשׁ לוֹ טׇהֳרָה בַּמִּקְוֶה, יָצָא שֶׁרֶץ שֶׁאֵין לוֹ טׇהֳרָה. לֵימָא מְסַיֵּיעַ לֵיהּ: "מִזָּכָר עַד נְקֵבָה תְּשַׁלֵּחוּ" *פְּרָט לִכְלִי חֶרֶשׂ, דִּבְרֵי רַבִּי יוֹסֵי הַגְּלִילִי. מַאי טַעְמָא — לָאו מִשּׁוּם *)גדְּלֵית לֵיהּ טׇהֳרָה בַּמִּקְוֶה? לֹא, מִי שֶׁנַּעֲשֶׂה אַב הַטּוּמְאָה — יָצָא דכְּלִי חֶרֶס שֶׁאֵינוֹ נַעֲשֶׂה אַב הַטּוּמְאָה. לֵימָא כְּתַנָּאֵי: שֶׁרֶץ שֶׁנִּמְצָא בַּמִּקְדָּשׁ — כֹּהֵן מוֹצִיאוֹ בְּהֶמְיָינוֹ, שֶׁלֹּא לְשַׁהוֹת אֶת הַטּוּמְאָה, דִּבְרֵי רַבִּי יוֹחָנָן בֶּן בְּרוֹקָה. רַבִּי יְהוּדָה אוֹמֵר: בִּצְבָת שֶׁל עֵץ מוֹצִיאוֹ, שֶׁלֹּא לְרַבּוֹת אֶת הַטּוּמְאָה. מַאי לָאו בְּהָא קָא מִיפַּלְגִי: דְּמַאן דְּאָמַר שֶׁלֹּא לְשַׁהוֹת — קָסָבַר: הַמַּכְנִיס שֶׁרֶץ לַמִּקְדָּשׁ — חַיָּיב, ומ"ד שֶׁלֹּא לְרַבּוֹת — קָסָבַר: הַמַּכְנִיס שֶׁרֶץ לַמִּקְדָּשׁ — פָּטוּר! לֹא, הדְּכוּלֵּי עָלְמָא חַיָּיב, וְהָכָא בְּהָא קָא מִיפַּלְגִי; מָר סָבַר: שְׁהוּיֵי טוּמְאָה עָדִיף, וּמָר סָבַר אַפּוּשֵׁי טוּמְאָה עָדִיף. אֶלָּא כְּהָנֵי תַּנָּאֵי, דִּתְנַן: מֵהֵיכָן מוֹצִיאִין אוֹתוֹ כו'? מַאי לָאו בְּהָא קָא מִיפַּלְגִי; דְּמַאן דְּאָמַר מֵעֲזָרָה — לָא, קָסָבַר: הַמַּכְנִיס שֶׁרֶץ לַמִּקְדָּשׁ פָּטוּר, וּמַאן דְּאָמַר מִכּוּלָּהּ עֲזָרָה — קָסָבַר: חַיָּיב. אָמַר

רש"י

תָּרוּ בָּהּ כִּיתְנָא. שׁוֹרִין בּוֹ פִּשְׁתָּן בְּחוֹל. וְאִית דְּגָרְסִי: בּוּנְאָה כּוֹסְמִין: תָּרוּ. שׁוֹרִין: שֶׁהִקְרוּ עָלֶיהָ דְּבָרִים. כְּשֶׁעָלוּ מִן הַגּוֹלָה הוּלְרְכוּ לָהּ, כִּדְלְקַמָּן וְנִימְנוּ וְהִתִּירוּהָ, וּבִטְּלוּ תַּקָּנַת הַשְּׁבוּת מִמֶּנָּה לְמַלְאוֹת הֵימֶנָּה בַּגַּלְגַּל וְלֹא הִתִּירוּ אֶלָּא אוֹתָהּ לְבַדָּהּ. הִקְרוּ — לְשׁוֹן קְרִיאָה (ע"י מִקְרֶה) שֶׁהֵבִיאוּ(א) בָּהּ רְאָיוֹת לְדִבְרֵיהֶם, שֶׁיֵּשׁ בָּהֶן כֹּחַ לַעֲקוֹר שְׁבוּת מִפְּנֵי דּוֹחְקָן: מַאי זוֹ בִּלְבַד. הֵיאָךְ יִקְרְאוּ לִשְׁאָר בּוֹרוֹת בּוֹר הַקֵּר? הֲרֵי לֹא הוּקְרוּ דְּבָרִים אֶלָּא עַל זוֹ. וּמִדְּקָתָנֵי בּוֹר הַקֵּר — פְּשִׁיטָא דְּהַהוּא לְחוּדֵיהּ קָשְׁיֵי: אֶלָּא אָמַר רַב נַחְמָן בַּר יִצְחָק. ע"י שֶׁמַּיִם חַיִּים הָיְתָה קָרֵי לֵיהּ בּוֹר הַקֵּר, לְשׁוֹן מָקוֹר. כְּמוֹ "כְּהָקִיר בַּיִר מֵימֶיהָ" כְּמוֹ שֶׁמַּעְיַן מָקוֹר (מֵימֶיהָ) הַנּוֹבֵעַ מִתְחַדֵּשׁ וְהוֹלֵךְ וּמוֹסִיף תָּמִיד, כָּךְ הִקְרָה רָעָתָהּ: בַּיִר. כְּמוֹ בְּאֵר: נְבִיאִים שֶׁבֵּינֵיהֶם. חַגַּי זְכַרְיָה וּמַלְאָכִי: מִנְהַג אֲבוֹתֵיהֶם. בְּאוֹתוֹ הַבּוֹר: **מתני'** כֹּהֵן מוֹצִיאוֹ בְּהֶמְיָינוֹ. בְּשַׁבָּת וְלָא חָיֵישׁ לְטִלְטוּל דְּאֵין שְׁבוּת בַּמִּקְדָּשׁ. בְּהֶמְיָנוֹ בְּאַבְנֵטוֹ. וְאַף עַל גַּב דְּמִטַּמֵּי לֵיהּ לְאַבְנֵט שֶׁהוּא קָדוֹשׁ — הָכִי עָדִיף, שֶׁלֹּא לְשַׁהוֹת אֶת הַטּוּמְאָה בָּעֲזָרָה, וְלַחֲזוֹר אַחַר צְבָת שֶׁל עֵץ שֶׁהִיא פְּשׁוּטֵי כְּלֵי עֵץ שֶׁאֵינָהּ מְקַבֶּלֶת טוּמְאָה. וְיָדָיו לֹא נָגַע בָּהּ — דְּלָא נִיטַמֵּי כֹּהֵן גּוּפֵיהּ. הִלְכָּךְ, בְּהֶמְיָינוֹ אוֹחֲזוֹ, דְּלָא נָגַע בֵּיהּ. וְשֶׁרֶץ אֵינוֹ מְטַמֵּא בְּמַשָּׂא, וְהָאַבְנֵט שֶׁמִּיטַּמֵּא בַּשֶּׁרֶץ — אֵינוֹ מְטַמֵּא הַכֹּהֵן הָאוֹחֲזוֹ, דַּהֲוָה לֵיהּ אַבְנֵט רִאשׁוֹן לְטוּמְאָה. וַהֲלָכָה רוֹוַחַת הִיא בְּכָל הַתַּלְמוּד שֶׁאֵין אָדָם וְכֵלִים מְקַבְּלִין טוּמְאָה אֶלָּא מֵאַב הַטּוּמְאָה בִּלְבַד. וְגַם בַּמִּקְרָא לֹא מָצִינוּ טוּמְאָה לְכֵלִים וּלְאָדָם אֶלָּא מִן הַשֶּׁרֶץ וְהַנְּבֵלָה וְכַיּוֹצֵא בָּהֶן, שֶׁהוּא אַב הַטּוּמְאָה. אֲבָל רִאשׁוֹן לַטּוּמְאָה מְטַמֵּא אוֹכָלִין וּמַשְׁקִין, כִּדְכְתִיב (ויקרא יא): "וְכָל כְּלִי חֶרֶשׂ אֲשֶׁר יִפּוֹל מֵהֶם" וגו' דַּהֲוָה לֵיהּ כְּלִי חֶרֶס רִאשׁוֹן לַטּוּמְאָה, מִכֵּיוָן שֶׁנִּתְלָה שֶׁרֶץ בַּאֲוִירוֹ. וְאַף עַל פִּי שֶׁלֹּא נָגַע וְהַכְּלִי חוֹזֵר וּמְטַמֵּא מַה שֶּׁבְּתוֹכוֹ, יָכוֹל אִם(ג) כֵּלִים הָיוּ בְּתוֹכוֹ יִטָּמְאוּ מֵחֲמַת כְּלִי רִאשׁוֹן. תַּלְמוּד לוֹמַר: כֹּל אֲשֶׁר בְּתוֹכוֹ יִטְמָא, וְסָמִיךְ לֵיהּ: מִכָּל הָאוֹכֶל אֲשֶׁר יֵאָכֵל, אוֹכָלִין וּמַשְׁקִין מְקַבְּלִין טוּמְאָה מֵחֲמַת הַכְּלִי, וְאֵין כְּלִי אַחֵר מִיטַּמֵּא מֵחֲמָתוֹ בִּשְׁלְהֵי "הַכֹּל שׁוֹחֲטִין": בִּצְבָת שֶׁל עֵץ. שֶׁהִיא פְּשׁוּטֵי כְּלֵי עֵץ: שֶׁלֹּא לְרַבּוֹת אֶת הַטּוּמְאָה. לְטַמֵּא הָאַבְנֵט וְנוֹחַ לוֹ לְהַשְׁהוֹתוֹ שָׁם וְלַחֲזוֹר אַחֲרֵי הַצְּבָת, מִלְּרַבּוֹת הַטּוּמְאָה: מֵהֵיכָן מוֹצִיאִין אוֹתוֹ. בְּשַׁבָּת: מִן הַהֵיכָל וּמִן הָאוּלָם. אֲבָל בָּעֲזָרָה, אִם נִמְצָא שָׁם — מְכַסֵּהוּ בְּסִיר, וּמַנִּיחוֹ עַד שֶׁתֶּחְשַׁךְ: כָּל מָקוֹם שֶׁחַיָּיבִין עַל זְדוֹנוֹ כָּרֵת. אִם יִכָּנֵס לוֹ בְּטוּמְאָה, דְּהַיְינוּ כּוּלָּהּ עֲזָרָה: וּשְׁאָר כָּל מְקוֹמוֹת. לְמָר כִּדְאִית לֵיהּ וּלְמָר כִּדְאִית לֵיהּ. לְבֶן נַנָּס — כּוּלָּהּ עֲזָרָה, לְרַבִּי עֲקִיבָא — לְשָׁכוֹת: כּוֹפִין עָלָיו פְּסַכְתֵּר. סִיר שֶׁל נְחֹשֶׁת, לְכַסּוֹתוֹ עַד שֶׁתֶּחְשַׁךְ לְמוֹצָ"שׁ. "סִירֹתָיו" (שמות כז) — מְתַרְגְּמִינַן פִּסַכְתְּרָוָותֵיהּ: ר"ש אוֹמֵר. מְפָרֵשׁ בַּגְּמָרָא אַהֵיכָא קָאֵי: מִשֶּׁלְּךָ נָתְנוּ לָךְ. כִּדִמְפָרֵשׁ בַּגְּמָרָא: **גמ'** הַמַּכְנִיס טָמֵא שֶׁרֶץ. כְּלִי שֶׁנִּטְמָא בַּשֶּׁרֶץ: חַיָּיב. חַטָּאת בְּשׁוֹגֵג, [א] וְכָרֵת עַל זְדוֹנוֹ, מִשּׁוּם "כִּי אֶת מִקְדַּשׁ ה' טִמֵּא" (במדבר יט): מִזָּכָר וְעַד נְקֵבָה תְּשַׁלֵּחוּ. בַּמִּקְדָּשׁ קָאֵי, כִּדְכְתִיב בְּסֵיפֵיהּ: "וְלֹא יְטַמְּאוּ אֶת מַחֲנֵיהֶם אֲשֶׁר אֲנִי שׁוֹכֵן בְּתוֹכָם" דּוּמְיָא דְּזָכָר וּנְקֵבָה, אָדָם שֶׁיֵּשׁ לוֹ טׇהֳרָה בִּטְבִילָה: פְּרָט לִכְלִי חֶרֶס. טָמֵא, שֶׁאִם הִכְנִיסוֹ לַמִּקְדָּשׁ — פָּטוּר: דְּאֵין לוֹ טׇהֳרָה. *דִּכְתִיב (ויקרא יא): "וְאוֹתוֹ תִשְׁבֹּרוּ" שֶׁאֵין לוֹ טׇהֳרָה אֶלָּא בִּשְׁבִירָתוֹ: לֹא. לְעוֹלָם אֵימָא לָךְ הַמַּכְנִיס שֶׁרֶץ חַיָּיב, וְטַעְמָא דִּכְלִי חֶרֶס — מִשּׁוּם שֶׁאֵינוֹ רָאוּי לְמִדְרָס וְלִהְיוֹת אַב הַטּוּמְאָה, (מִי שֶׁנַּעֲשָׂה אַב הַטּוּמְאָה) דְּבָעֵינַן דּוּמְיָא דְּזָכָר וּנְקֵבָה — פְּעָמִים שֶׁהוּא אַב הַטּוּמְאָה כְּגוֹן זָב וְזָבָה וּטְמֵא מֵת. וְכֵן הַכֵּלִים נַמִּי, הוֹאִיל וּרְאוּיִן לֵיעָשׂוֹת אַב הַטּוּמְאָה כְּגוֹן זָכָר וּנְקֵבָה. כְּגוֹן כְּלִי שֶׁהוּא רָאוּי לְמִדְרָס וּלְמוֹשַׁב הַזָּב — הָוֵי אַב הַטּוּמְאָה ע"י מִדְרָס שֶׁל זָב, וּמְטַמְּאִין אָדָם וְכֵלִים, כִּדְכְתִיב (ויקרא טו): "וְהַיּוֹשֵׁב עַל הַכְּלִי אֲשֶׁר יֵשֵׁב עָלָיו הַזָּב יִטְמָא", הַמַּכְנִיסָן לַמִּקְדָּשׁ, אֲפִילּוּ כְּשֶׁהֵן רִאשׁוֹנִים, כְּגוֹן שֶׁנִּטְמְאוּ בְּמַגַּע הַזָּב אוֹ נָגְעוּ בְּמִדְרַס הַזָּב אוֹ בִּשְׁאָר אֲבוֹת הַטּוּמְאָה — חַיָּיב. יָצָא כְּלִי חֶרֶס שֶׁאֵינוֹ נַעֲשֶׂה אַב הַטּוּמְאָה, שֶׁאֵין לָךְ כְּלִי נַעֲשֶׂה אַב הַטּוּמְאָה לְטַמֵּא אָדָם אוֹ כְּלִי אֶלָּא מִדְרַס הַזָּב, כִּדְפָרֵישִׁית לְעֵיל, אוֹ מַגַּע הַמֵּת. דְּמֵת אֲבִי אֲבוֹת הַטּוּמְאָה, כִּדְכְתִיב בְּ"זֹאת חֻקַּת" "בִּכְלִי אוֹ בְּאָדָם" שֶׁנָּגַע בְּמֵת "וְכֹל אֲשֶׁר יִגַּע בּוֹ הַטָּמֵא יִטְמָא וְהַנֶּפֶשׁ הַנּוֹגַעַת תִּטְמָא עַד הָעָרֶב" פֵּי' נֶפֶשׁ הַנּוֹגַעַת בּוֹ בְּטָמֵא זֶה, שֶׁנִּטְמָא בְּמֵת — תִּטְמָא עַד הָעָרֶב. וְהָא לָא מָצֵית לְמֵימַר דְּהַאי וְהַנֶּפֶשׁ הַנּוֹגַעַת בְּנוֹגֵעַ בְּמֵת עַצְמוֹ קָאָמַר, דְּא"כ — טוּמְאַת שִׁבְעָה אִיכָּא. אַלְמָא: טְמֵא מֵת אַב הַטּוּמְאָה מְשַׁוֵּי לֵיהּ קְרָא לְטַמֵּא אָדָם. הִלְכָּךְ: כְּלִי חֶרֶס אֵינוֹ נַעֲשֶׂה אַב הַטּוּמְאָה כְּלָל, דִּלְמִדְרָס לָא חָזֵי — מִשּׁוּם דְּנִשְׁבָּר, וְתַנְיָא בְּהֶדְיָא בְּפֶרֶק "רַבִּי עֲקִיבָא" בְּמַסֶּכֶת שַׁבָּת (דף פד.): מִדְרַס כְּלִי חֶרֶס טָהוֹר. וְע"י מַגַּע נַמִּי לָא הָוֵי אַב הַטּוּמְאָה, דִּכְתִיב לְעֵיל מֵהַהוּא קְרָא: "וְחִטְּאוֹ בַּיּוֹם הַשְּׁלִישִׁי" וגו' "וְכֹל אֲשֶׁר יִגַּע בּוֹ הַטָּמֵא" וגו' כָּל הֵיכָא דְּקָרֵינַן בֵּיהּ וְחִטְּאוֹ, דְּיֵשׁ לוֹ טׇהֳרָה בִּטְבִילָה — קָרֵינַן בֵּיהּ "וְהַנֶּפֶשׁ הַנּוֹגַעַת תִּטְמָא". וְכָל הֵיכָא דְּלָא קָרֵינַן בֵּיהּ "וְחִטְּאוֹ" — לָא קָרֵינַן בֵּיהּ "וְהַנֶּפֶשׁ הַנּוֹגַעַת": מַאן דְּאָמַר שֶׁלֹּא לְשַׁהוֹת קָסָבַר. שֶׁרֶץ טָעוּן שִׁילּוּחַ מִדְּאוֹרַיְיתָא, הִלְכָּךְ, לָא מִידְחֵי מִקַּמֵּי רִבּוּי הַטּוּמְאָה דְּאַבְנֵט: הַמַּכְנִיס שֶׁרֶץ גָּרְסִינַן: שְׁהוּיֵי(ג) עָדִיף. מֵאַפּוּשֵׁי טוּמְאָה. דְּהָא אַבְנֵט נַמִּי מִידֵּי דְּקֹדֶשׁ הוּא: מַאי לָאו בְּהָא קָא מִיפַּלְגִי דְּמַאן דְּאָמַר מֵעֲזָרָה לָא. מַפְּקִינַן לֵיהּ בְּשַׁבָּת: קָסָבַר הַמַּכְנִיס שֶׁרֶץ לַמִּקְדָּשׁ פָּטוּר. דְּלָא בָּעֵינַן שִׁילּוּחַ מִדְּאוֹרַיְיתָא. הִלְכָּךְ, לָא מִדְחֵיָא שְׁבוּת מִקַּמֵּיהּ. וּמֵהֵיכָל וּמֵאוּלָם הוּא דְּמַפְּקִינַן לֵיהּ, דְּמִשּׁוּם כְּבוֹד שְׁכִינָה לֹא הֶעֱמִידוּ חֲכָמִים דִּבְרֵיהֶם: אָמַר

תוספות

יצא כלי חרס שאין נעשה אב הטומאה. פירש בקונטרס: דלמדרס לא חזי, וגבי טומאת מת כתיב (במדבר יט): "וחטאו ביום השביעי", וכלי חרס לאו בר חיטוי הוא, דכתיב (ויקרא יא): "ואותו תשברו":

לא דכולי עלמא חייב. ושמואל דאמר פטור אית ליה דתנאי היא, וסבירא ליה כמ"ד פטור. ור"ח גרס: "דכולי עלמא פטור". וקשיא לפי': דמאי טעמא דמאן דאמר בהמיינו, הא בהמיינו איכא איסורא דאורייתא להשהותו במקדש, דהא אית ליה טהרה במקוה. ובשרץ ליכא איסורא דאורייתא, דלית ליה טהרה במקוה! לכך נראה גירסת הקונטרס עיקר: אמר

רבינו חננאל

זה משמר כדרכו והולך ובלבד שלא יספק ולא יטפח ולא ירקד כדרך שעושה בחול אמאי קאסר להו משום דאולודי קלא אסיר. ופירק רב אחא בר יעקב אליבא דרבה לא אסרו משום אולודי קלא אלא גזירה שמא יטול צרור ויזרוק עליהן ואלא הא דאמר רב יהודה משמיה דרב נשים משחקות באגוזים אסיר להו דאולודי קלא אסיר ופריק לא *) אלא משום דמשתמע קלא דאגוזים כי זמזומי ואלא הא דאמר רב יהודה אמר שמואל נשים משחקות בתפוחים אסור התם מאי אולודי קלא איכא ופריק התם משום דלמא אתי לאשוויי גומות וכיון שמשחקות ומושכות התפוחים בארץ גזירה שמא כשהן מושכות התפוחים אצלן יש נקב בקרקע ומתמלא. ת"ש ממלאין מים מבור הגולה ומבור הגדול בגלגל בשבת. במקדש אין במדינה לא. מ"ט לאו משום דאולודי קלא בשבת אסיר. ופריק לא גזירה שמא ימלא לגינתו ולחורבתו ואע"ג דשני רבה כל הני תיובתא דמקשי עליה אשינויי לא סמכינן ולא דחינן לשמועה דעולא. אמימר שרא למימלא בגילגלא במחוזא אמר טעמא מאי אסרו במדינה שמא ימלא לגינתו ולחורבתו הכא לא גינה ולא חורבה איכא כיון דחזא דקא תרו כינתי פי' ממלאין מים ושורין טיט לעשות ממנו כנדי [אסר להו]. וממלאין מים מבור הקר ביום טוב מאי בור הקר אמר רב יהודה אמר שמואל בור שחקרו עליה נביאים והתירוה ונדחו דבריו ופירש רב נחמן בור מים חיים כדכתיב כהקיר ביר מימיה כן הקרה רעתם. גופא לא כל בורות הקירות התירו אלא זו בלבד וכשעלו בני הגולה חנו עליה והתירוה ולא נביאים שביניהם התירוה להן אלא מנהג אבותיהם בידיהם: ירושל' לא כל בורות הקירות התירוהו שיהו ממלאין מהן בגלגל אלא אותה הבאר שחנו עליה בלבד: **מתני'** שרץ שנמצא במקדש כהן מוציאו בהמיינו שלא לשהות את הטומאה דברי ר' יוחנן בן ברוקה ר' יהודה אומר בצבת של עץ שלא לרבות הטומאה. אמר רב טוב' בר קיסנא אמר שמואל המכנים טמא שרץ במקדש חייב שרץ עצמו פטור שנאמר מזכר ועד נקבה תשלחו. פרט לכלי חרס דברי ר' יוסי הגלילי. מ"ט פטר לאו משום דלית טהרה לכלי חרס במקוה ודחינן לא טעמא דר' יוסי הגלילי מי שנעשה אב הטומאה יצא כלי חרס שאינו עושה אב הטומאה אבל השרץ הנה הוא אב הטומאה. נימא שמואל אמרה לשמעתיה כתנאי דתנן שרץ שנמצא במקדש כהן מוציאו בהמיינו כו'. מאי לאו בהא קמיפלגי ר' יוחנן בן ברוקה דחייש לשהייה קסבר המכנים שרץ במקדש חייב. ור' יהודה דחייש לטומאת המיינו וא' שלא לרבות את הטומאה קסבר המכנים שרץ במקדש פטור ודחינן לא כ"ע כשמואל דאמר פטור והכא בהא

*) עי' בתוס' לעיל עמוד א' מש"כ בשם רבינו.

הגהות הב"ח

(א) רש"י ד"ה שהקרו וכו' לשון קריאה שהביאו ראיות כנ"ל ותיבת על ידי מקרה ותיבת בה נמחק: (ב) ד"ה כהן וכו' יכול אם היו כלים בתוכו: (ג) ד"ה שהויי טומאה עדיף:

הגהות הגר"א

[א] רש"י ד"ה חייב חטאת בשוגג כו'. נ"ב הוא ט"ס דבהדיא אמרי' בתורת כהנים (פ' א"מ) דלאו אלא [חייב מלקות] בארבעים והביאו רש"י בעצמו (שם יז טז) וכ"כ הרמב"ד (בפ"ג מהלכות ביאת המקדש) וכ"ה בירושל' [נזיר פרק כ"ג]:

גליון הש"ס

רש"י ד"ה חייב חטאת בשוגג. עיין תי"ט רפ"ד דנדה ד"ה ואין חייבין:

רש"ל מ"ז

ס"א הם התירו

תמיד לג:

[גי' הערוך פסקטר ומביא ראיה מן התרגום ע"ש]

*[עי' תוס' סוטה כ: ד"ה לא ותוספות מנחות לה: ד"ה אין ותוס' נדה כח: ד"ה פרט]

*) [שבת פד.]

[עיין פרש"י שבת פד. ד"ה לאפוקי]

רב נסים גאון

ממאי דהאי בזק מידי דמיבדרי הוא: **ר'** עקיבא אומר ממקום שחייבין על זדונו כרת ועל שגגתו חטאת משם מוציאין אותו. בתחילת משנת טהרות (כלים פרק א' מ"ח) שנינו עזרת ישראל מקודשת ממנה שאין מחוסר כיפורים נכנס לשם וחייבין עליה חטאת ובתוספ' (שם) כל הטמאין שנכנסו משערי ניקנור ולפנים אפי' מחוסרי כפרה חייבין על זדונן כרת ועל שגגתן חטאת ואין צריך לומר טבולי יום ושאר כל הטמאים ותניא (שם) משערי ניקנור ולפנים מחנה שכינה והן הן קלעים שבמדבר: **יצא** כלי חרס שאין נעשה אב הטומאה. עיקרה מדכתיב (ויקרא יא) וכל כלי חרש אשר יפול מהם מכל האוכל הרי נתברר מאלו המקראות שכלי חרס אינו מטמא אלא אוכלין ומשקין בלבד מכלל שאינו נעשה אב הטומאה לפי שאב הטומאה מטמא אדם וכלים ולא מצינו כלי חרס שמטמא לא אדם ולא כלים מיכן ראייה שאינו נעשה אב הטומאה כלל והמעלה שלו אינה אלא כמעלת ולד הטומאה שאינו מטמא אלא אוכלין ומשקין בלבד כדאמרינן בתחילת נזיקין (ב"ק דף ב) ותניא בתורת כהנים יכול אף הכלים יהו מטמאין מאויר כלי חרס ת"ל אוכל אוכלין מטמאין באויר כלי חרס ואין הכלים מטמאין באויר כלי חרס ובפרק אור לארבעה עשר (פסחים דף כ) אמרינן תני תנא קמיה דרב ששת שרץ מטמא את המשקין ומשקין מטמאין את הכלי וכלי מטמא את האוכלין ואוכלין את המשקין למדנו ג' טמאות בשרץ א"ל הני ד' הויין אמר [גוז] משקין דרישא נתברר מכל אלו הדברים כי השרץ מטמא הכלי והכלי את האוכלין והאוכלין את המשקין (חדא) [ומיהו] מדרבנן משקין נמי מטמאין כלי חרס כדאיתא בת"כ וכבר פירשנוה בפרק אלו דברים דברכות ואמרינן עלה [בפסחים שם] אמר ליה רב אדא בר אהבה לרבא וליחזי האי תנורא כמאן דמלי טומאה ותיהוי פת ראשונה אמר ליה לא אמרינן כמאן דמלי טומאה דתניא יכול כו' והאי ברייתא שכבר הזכרנוה זהו עיקר דאין כלי חרס נעשה אב הטומאה ואיתא בתורת כהנים נפש אשר תגע בכל דבר טמא ר' עקיבא אומר יכול אפילו באוכלין ומשקין ובכלי חרס יהא חייב ת"ל בבהמה מה בהמה מיוחדת שהיא אב הטומאה יצאו אלו שאינן אב הטומאה לטמא ובגמרא דאור לארבעה עשר דבני מערבא (הלכה ז) גרסי הוא טמא אינו נעשה לטמא ועיקר

תורה אור

אמר רבי יוחנן: ושניהם מקרא אחד דרשו: (דה"ב כט) "ויבאו הכהנים לפנימה בית ה' לטהר ויוציאו את כל הטומאה אשר מצאו בהיכל ה' לחצר בית ה' ויקבלו הלוים להוציא לנחל קדרון חוצה". מר סבר: מדאשתני בעזרה בלוים — טומאה בעזרה ליכא. ומר סבר: עד היכא דלא אפשר בלוים — מפקי כהנים, השתא דאפשר בלוים — תו לא מטמאי כהנים. *תנו רבנן: [א]הכל נכנסין בהיכל לבנות לתקן ולהוציא את הטומאה, ומצוה בכהנים. אם אין שם כהנים — נכנסין לוים, אין שם לוים — נכנסין ישראלים. ואידי ואידי טהורין — אין, טמאין — לא. אמר רב הונא: *רב כהנא מסייע כהני, דתני רב כהנא: מתוך שנאמר: (ויקרא כא) "אך אל הפרוכת לא יבא" יכול לא יהו כהנים בעלי מומין נכנסין בין האולם ולמזבח לעשות ריקועי פחים — תלמוד לומר: *"אך" — חלק. [ב]מצוה בתמימים, אין שם תמימים — נכנסין בעלי מומין. מצוה בטהורין, אין שם טהורין — נכנסין טמאין. אידי ואידי, כהנים — אין, ישראלים — לא. איבעיא להו: טמא ובעל מום איזו מהן נכנס? רב חייא בר אשי אמר רב: טמא נכנס, דהא אישתרי בעבודת ציבור. ר' אלעזר אומר: [ג]בעל מום נכנס, דהא אישתרי באכילת קדשים. § "רבי שמעון אומר וכו'". § רבי שמעון היכא קאי? התם קאי, דתנן: *)מי שהחשיך חוץ לתחום, אפילו אמה אחת לא יכנס. ר' שמעון אומר: אפי' חמש עשרה אמה יכנס, לפי שאין המשוחות *ממצעין את המדות מפני הטועים. דקאמר תנא קמא לא יכנס, ואמר ליה רבי שמעון יכנס. § "שלא התירו לך אלא משום שבות". § היכא קאי? התם קאי, דקאמר תנא קמא: *קושרה, ואמר ליה רבי שמעון: עונבה. עניבה דלא אתי לידי חיוב חטאת — שרו ליה רבנן, קשירה דאתי לידי חיוב חטאת — לא שרו ליה רבנן. §

[לעיל נב:] [לעיל לב:]

הדרן עלך המוצא תפילין וסליקא לה מסכת עירובין

רש"י

אמר רבי יוחנן. לענין עיולי, כולי עלמא המכניס שרץ חייב. ולענין להוציא הטומאה בעזרה בשבת — בהאי קרא פליגי: ויבאו הכהנים (א) פנימי בית ה'. בהיכל ויוציאו הטומאה. ע"ז ותקרובתיה, שהן מטמאין באהל: לחצר בית ה'. עזרה: ויקבלו הלוים להוציא משם לנחל קדרון. אבל כהנים אחרים לא מיטמאין אע"פ שהיו צריכים לאנשים הרבה. אלו מוציאין מן ההיכל לעזרה, ואילו משם ולחוץ — לוים הוא דמיטמאין ולא כהנים. בן ננס סבר: מדאשתני טומאת עזרה מכהנים ללוים, שמע מינה היכא דאיתא בעזרה — לא מפקינן ליה בעבירה, אלא מהדרינן אהתירא. ובשבת נמי לא דחינן שבות: טומאה בעזרה ליתא. כלומר: היכא דאיתא התם — לא חמירא כולי האי: דלא אפשר. בהיכל לא עיילי לוים, דאפי' כהנים אסירי למיעל אלא לעבודה, כדכתיב (ויקרא טז): "ואל יבא בכל עת אל הקדש" — זה היכל, "מבית לפרוכת" — זה לפני ולפנים: תו לא מטמאינן לכהנים. שהרי אפשר בלוים, אבל לשהויי עד אורתא — לא: מסייע כהני. דאמר לקמן: כהנים טמאין עדיפי מטהורי ישראלים: אך אל הפרוכת וגו'. בבעלי מומין כתיב: רקועין. טסין של זהב, שמחפין בהן בית קדשי הקדשים מתוכו: אך חלק. כלומר: אכין ורקין מיעוטין. כל אתין וגמין רבויין. חלק — מיעט. דלמלאכה שרי לעיולי: טמא ובעל מום. אי אפשר אלא באחד מהן, איזה מהן מכניסין: דהא אישתרי בעבודת צבור. דכתיב (במדבר כח): "במועדו" — ואפילו בטומאה, אבל בעל מום לא הותר, דתניא בתורת כהנים: מום בו את לחם אלהיו לא יגש להקריב, אין לי אלא תמידין, שהן קרויין לחם, כענין שנאמר: "את קרבני לחמי לאשי" שאר קרבנות צבור מנין? ת"ל שוב: לחם, קרא אחרינא, וכתיב בתריה: "לחם אלהיו מקדשי הקדשים" וסמיך ליה אקרא קמא, דמשמע הכי: לא יגש להקריב לחם אלהיו: דהא אישתרי באכילת קדשים. מהאי קרא "לחם אלהיו מקדשי הקדשים (ב) ומן הקדשים יאכל": המשוחות. (ג) מודדין התחומין, ומציבין סימן כשהן מודדין מדתן: מפני טועי המדה. שמא יטעו בה, הלכך, מקצרין אותה, נמצא שעדיין התחום לא הגיע, ומי שהחשיך לו חוץ לתחום — כבר נכנס בתוך אלפים ט"ו אמות, כדפרישית ב"מי שהוציאוהו" (לעיל דף נב:) ל"א: מפני הטועין — ששוכחין ויוצאין וחוזרין ונכנסין, לפיכך מקצרין המודדין את התחום הסימן, ומציבין בתוך התחום. שאם יצא — לא עביד איסורא: יכנס. דמשלך נתנו לך, שכבר הוא בתוך תחומו. והכא אתא ר' שמעון למיתב טעמא למילתיה, דלא תימא מיקל אני באיסור שבת — אלא משלו נתתי לו. והכא נקט לה משום פלוגתא דנימת כנור, כדמפרש ואזיל: קושרה. נימת כנור שנפסקה, ופליג רבי שמעון ואמר בברייתא: עונבה. ואמר הכא טעמא למילתא, ופליג אתנא דלעיל, ואמר: לא הותרו במקדש אלא שבות. ובתרתי מיפלגא מילתא דרבי שמעון: רישא במחשיך חוץ לתחום, וסיפא בנימת כנור, והכי קאמר רבי שמעון לתנא קמא: אע"פ שהקלתי במחשיך חוץ לתחום, מחמיר אני בנימת כנור דהתם משלך נתנו לך אבל כאן לא התירו אלא שבות: קשירה דאתיא לידי חיוב חטאת. במדינה (ד) גזרה שמא יקשור קשר של קיימא: הדרן עלך המוצא תפילין וסליקא לה מסכת עירובין

תוספות

אמר רבי יוחנן ושניהם מקרא אחד דרשו. פירש בקונטרס: שבא לתרץ דכולי עלמא מכניס שרץ חייב, ולענין הוצאת טומאה פליגי. ותימה: דלכאורה אין חילוק, דאי מכניס שרץ חייב — הוא הדין דמוזהר להוציא מ"וישלחו מן המחנה", דכל היכא דקרינן "לא יטמאו את מחני" — קרינן "וישלחו", וא"כ, מאי טעמא דמאן דאמר מעזרה לא? ונראה דמילתא באפי נפשה היא, ולא קאי לדחויי הא דקאמר לעיל כתנאי (ה), ופליג בין במכניס בין במוציא, דאין חילוק, כדפירשנו. אלא בא לאסמוכי קרא למאן דאמר חייב, ולמאן דאמר פטור:

אמר ר' שמעון יכנס. והכי קאמר ליה רבי שמעון לתנא קמא: אע"פ שמיקל אני במחשיך חוץ לתחום — מחמיר אני בנימת הכנור, דהתם לאו קולא הוא, אלא משלך נתנו לך. וגם כאן לא נתנו לך אלא משלך, דהיינו עניבה, דהוה דבר המותר. והא דנטר עד הכא — משום דבעי לאסוקי מילי דמקדש אבל לא במדינה:

הדרן עלך המוצא תפילין וסליקא לה מסכת עירובין

עין משפט נר מצוה

עח א ב ג מיי' פ"ז מהל' בית הבחירה הלכה כג:

מסורת הש"ס

תוספתא דכלים פ"א

[חולין מט.]

[פסחים ה. וש"נ]

*)לעיל נב: ושם אית' מי שיצא

הגהות הב"ח

(א) רש"י ד"ה ויבאו הכהנים לפנימה: (ב) ד"ה דהא אישתרי וכו' מקדשי הקדשים וגו' לא יגש כי מום בו וסמיך ליה אקרא: (ג) ד"ה המשוחות וכו' מדתן הס"ד ואחר כך מ"ה מפני הטועין מפני טועי המדה: (ד) ד"ה קשירה וכו' במדינה גזור שמא: (ה) תוס' ד"ה א"ר יוחנן וכו' כתנאי ומפליג בין מכנים למוציא דאין חילוק:

רבינו חננאל

בהא קמיפלגי כו' ואלא לימא דשמואל כי הני תנאי דתנן מהיכן מוציאין אותו מן ההיכל כו' מאי לאו בהא קמיפלגי דר"ש דאמר מכל העזרה מוציאין אותו כו' ועמדה כתנאי. א"ר יוחנן ושניהם מקרא אחד דרשו ויבאו הכהנים פנימה בית ה' לטהר ויוציאו את כל הטומאה אשר מצאו בהיכל ה' לחצר בית ה' ויקבלו הלוים להוציא אל נחל קדרון חוצה *) ר"ע סבר מדאפקו הכהנים מן ההיכל עד לחצר בית ה' מכלל דעזרה לא מקבלה טומאה. ור"ש בן ננס סבר בהיכל דלא אפשר ללוים למיעל מטמינן להו לכהנים אבל בחוצה דאפשר בלוים תו לא מטמינן להו לכהנים. ת"ר הכל נכנסין לתקן ולבנות ולהוציא את הטומאה כהנים לוים וישראלים מצוה בכהנים אם אין שם כהנים נכנסין לוים מצוה בלוים אם אין שם לוים נכנסים ישראלים. אמר רב הונא רב כהנא דכהנא הוא ומסייע כהני. דתני רב כהנא אך אל הפרוכת לא יבא ואל המזבח כו'. יכול [לא] יהו כהנים בעלי מומין נכנסין לבין האולם ולמזבח לעשות ריקועין למזבח ת"ל אך חלק מצוה בתמימים אין שם תמימים נכנסין בעלי מומין מצוה בטהורין אין שם טהורין נכנסין טמאין ואלו ואלו כהנים [אין] אבל ישראלים לא: איבעיא להו טמא ובעל מום איזה מהן נכנס רב חייא בר אשי אמר רב טמא נכנס דהא אישתרי ליה עבודת ציבור. ר' אליעזר אמר בעל מום נכנס דהא אישתרי באכילת קדשים: מתני' ר"ש אומר כל [מה] שהתירו לך חכמים משלך נתנו לך. ר"ש (אומר) התם קאי (בהא) [אהא] דתנן מי שהחשיך חוץ לתחום אפילו אמה אחת לא יכנס. רבי [שמעון] אומר אפי' ט"ו אמה יכנס שאין המשוחות ממצין את המדות מפני הטועין כלומר הניחו מקום שלא הכניסוהו במקום אלפים אמה **) אותם שמדדו התחום יתר מזה וכאילו מכלל תחומך הן ולפיכך התירו לך שלא התירו לך אלא משום שבות גם דבריו הללו במשנה (זו משיב) [משיב על] שאמר ת"ק קושרין. א"ל קשירה דאתיא לידי חיוב חטאת גזרו בה רבנן עניבה דלא קשירה היא ולא אתיא לידי חיוב חטאת אלא משום שבות לא גזרו בה רבנן דכל מקום דהתירו לא התירו שם אלא מקום שהוא מותר והם שגזרו עליו משום שבות הוא אבל במקום איסורא דאורייתא לא: הדרן עלך המוצא וסליקא לה מסכת עירובין

*) [נראה מזה דרבינו גרס במשנה להיפך דר"ע סבר דמוציאין אותו מן ההיכל וכו' ור"ש בן ננס סבר דכל מקום שחייבין וכו' וצ"ע]. **) [אולי צ"ל מפני אותם שמדדו וכו' והוא פי' על מפני הטועין].

רב נסים גאון

ועיקר הדבר הוא מה שהזכרנוהו: **טמא** נכנס דהא אישתרי בעבודת ציבור. בפ' א' דמסכת יומא (דף ו) גרסינן איתמר טומאת המת רב נחמן אמר היתר היא בציבור ואסיקנה כל טומאת המת בציבור רחמנא שרייה ותניא [שם ד' ז] (שמות כח) ונשא אהרן את עון הקדשים וכי איזה עון הוא נושא אם עון פיגול וכו' הא אינו נושא אלא עון טומאה שהותרה מכללה בציבור ובמס' פסחים בפר' אלו דברים בפסח דוחין את השבת (דף סו) גרסי' ופסח גופיה מנא לן כול' יכול לא יהו עושין את השני אלא טמאין וכו' אלא ה"ק אינו נדחה לפסח שני אלא עושין בטומאה וציבור נמי דעביד בטומאה בטמא נפש אבל בשאר טמאות לא ובפ' כיצד צולין (דף עט) שנינו נטמא קהל או רובו או שהיו הכהנים טמאין והקהל טהור (יעשה) [יעשו] בטומאה בעל מום נכנס דהא אישתרי באכילת קדשים וזהו מן התורה דכתיב (ויקרא כא) כל איש אשר בו מום מזרע אהרן הכהן לחם אלהיו מקדשי הקדשים ומן הקדשים יאכל:

סליקא לה מסכת דעירובין בסיעתא דשמיא ברוך נותן ליעף כח

The following paragraph is recited three times:

הַדְרָן עֲלָךְ מַסֶּכֶת עֵירוּבִין וְהַדְרָךְ עֲלָן, דַּעְתָּן עֲלָךְ מַסֶּכֶת עֵירוּבִין וְדַעְתָּךְ עֲלָן, לָא נִתְנְשֵׁי מִנָּךְ מַסֶּכֶת עֵירוּבִין וְלָא תִתְנְשֵׁי מִנָּן, לָא בְּעָלְמָא הָדֵין וְלָא בְּעָלְמָא דְאָתֵי.

יְהִי רָצוֹן מִלְּפָנֶיךָ יהוה אֱלֹהֵינוּ וֵאלֹהֵי אֲבוֹתֵינוּ, שֶׁתְּהֵא תוֹרָתְךָ אֻמָּנוּתֵנוּ בָּעוֹלָם הַזֶּה, וּתְהֵא עִמָּנוּ לָעוֹלָם הַבָּא. חֲנִינָא בַּר פַּפָּא, רָמֵי בַּר פַּפָּא, נַחְמָן בַּר פַּפָּא, אֲחַאי בַּר פַּפָּא, אַבָּא מָרִי בַּר פַּפָּא, רַפְרָם בַּר פַּפָּא, רָכִישׁ בַּר פַּפָּא, סוּרְחַב בַּר פַּפָּא, אַדָּא בַּר פַּפָּא, דָּרוּ בַּר פַּפָּא.

הַעֲרֶב נָא יהוה אֱלֹהֵינוּ אֶת דִּבְרֵי תוֹרָתְךָ בְּפִינוּ וּבְפִי
עַמְּךָ בֵּית יִשְׂרָאֵל, וְנִהְיֶה אֲנַחְנוּ וְצֶאֱצָאֵינוּ (וְצֶאֱצָאֵי
צֶאֱצָאֵינוּ) וְצֶאֱצָאֵי עַמְּךָ בֵּית יִשְׂרָאֵל, כֻּלָּנוּ יוֹדְעֵי
שְׁמֶךָ וְלוֹמְדֵי תוֹרָתְךָ לִשְׁמָהּ. מֵאֹיְבַי תְּחַכְּמֵנִי מִצְוֹתֶךָ תהלים קיט
כִּי לְעוֹלָם הִיא־לִי: יְהִי־לִבִּי תָמִים בְּחֻקֶּיךָ לְמַעַן לֹא
אֵבוֹשׁ: לְעוֹלָם לֹא־אֶשְׁכַּח פִּקּוּדֶיךָ כִּי־בָם חִיִּיתָנִי:
בָּרוּךְ אַתָּה יהוה לַמְּדֵנִי חֻקֶּיךָ: אָמֵן אָמֵן אָמֵן סֶלָה
וָעֶד.

מוֹדִים אֲנַחְנוּ לְפָנֶיךָ יהוה אֱלֹהֵינוּ וֵאלֹהֵי אֲבוֹתֵינוּ
שֶׁשַּׂמְתָּ חֶלְקֵנוּ מִיּוֹשְׁבֵי בֵּית הַמִּדְרָשׁ, וְלֹא שַׂמְתָּ חֶלְקֵנוּ
מִיּוֹשְׁבֵי קְרָנוֹת. שֶׁאָנוּ מַשְׁכִּימִים וְהֵם מַשְׁכִּימִים,
אָנוּ מַשְׁכִּימִים לְדִבְרֵי תוֹרָה, וְהֵם מַשְׁכִּימִים לִדְבָרִים
בְּטֵלִים. אָנוּ עֲמֵלִים וְהֵם עֲמֵלִים, אָנוּ עֲמֵלִים וּמְקַבְּלִים
שָׂכָר, וְהֵם עֲמֵלִים וְאֵינָם מְקַבְּלִים שָׂכָר. אָנוּ רָצִים וְהֵם
רָצִים, אָנוּ רָצִים לְחַיֵּי הָעוֹלָם הַבָּא, וְהֵם רָצִים לִבְאֵר
שַׁחַת, שֶׁנֶּאֱמַר: וְאַתָּה אֱלֹהִים תּוֹרִדֵם לִבְאֵר שַׁחַת תהלים נה
אַנְשֵׁי דָמִים וּמִרְמָה לֹא־יֶחֱצוּ יְמֵיהֶם וַאֲנִי אֶבְטַח־בָּךְ:

יְהִי רָצוֹן מִלְּפָנֶיךָ יהוה אֱלֹהַי, כְּשֵׁם שֶׁעֲזַרְתַּנִי לְסַיֵּם
מַסֶּכֶת עֵירוּבִין כֵּן תְּעַזְרֵנִי לְהַתְחִיל מַסֶּכְתּוֹת וּסְפָרִים
אֲחֵרִים וּלְסַיְּמָם, לִלְמֹד וּלְלַמֵּד לִשְׁמֹר וְלַעֲשׂוֹת וּלְקַיֵּם
אֶת כָּל דִּבְרֵי תַלְמוּד תּוֹרָתְךָ בְּאַהֲבָה, וּזְכוּת כָּל
הַתַּנָּאִים וְאָמוֹרָאִים וְתַלְמִידֵי חֲכָמִים יַעֲמֹד לִי וּלְזַרְעִי
שֶׁלֹּא תָמוּשׁ הַתּוֹרָה מִפִּי וּמִפִּי זַרְעִי וְזֶרַע זַרְעִי עַד
עוֹלָם, וְיִתְקַיֵּם בִּי: בְּהִתְהַלֶּכְךָ תַּנְחֶה אֹתָךְ בְּשָׁכְבְּךָ משלי ו
תִּשְׁמֹר עָלֶיךָ וַהֲקִיצוֹתָ הִיא תְשִׂיחֶךָ: כִּי־בִי יִרְבּוּ יָמֶיךָ משלי ט
וְיוֹסִיפוּ לְךָ שְׁנוֹת חַיִּים: אֹרֶךְ יָמִים בִּימִינָהּ בִּשְׂמֹאולָהּ משלי ג
עֹשֶׁר וְכָבוֹד: יהוה עֹז לְעַמּוֹ יִתֵּן יהוה יְבָרֵךְ אֶת־עַמּוֹ תהלים כט
בַשָּׁלוֹם:

The following paragraph is recited three times:

הַדְרָן We shall return to you, tractate *Eiruvin,* and your glory is upon us. Our thoughts are upon you, tractate *Eiruvin,* and your thoughts are upon us. We will not be forgotten from you, tractate *Eiruvin,* and you will not be forgotten from us; neither in this world nor in the World-to-Come.

יְהִי רָצוֹן May it be Your will, Lord our God and God of our ancestors, that Your Torah will be our avocation in this world and will accompany us to the World-to-Come. Ḥanina bar Pappa, Ramei bar Pappa, Naḥman bar Pappa, Aḥai bar Pappa, Abba Mari bar Pappa, Rafram bar Pappa, Rakhish bar Pappa, Surḥav bar Pappa, Adda bar Pappa, Daru bar Pappa.

הַעֲרֶב נָא Please, Lord our God, make the words of Your
Torah sweet in our mouths and in the mouths of Your
people, the house of Israel, so that we, our descendants
(and their descendants), and the descendants of Your
people, the house of Israel, may all know Your name and
study Your Torah for its own sake. Your commandments *Psalms 119*
make me wiser than my enemies, for they are ever with
me. Let my heart be undivided in Your statutes, in order
that I may not be put to shame. I will never forget Your
precepts, for with them You have quickened me. Blessed
are You, O Lord; teach me Your statutes. Amen, Amen,
Amen, Selah, Forever.

מוֹדִים We give thanks before You, Lord Our God and
God of our ancestors, that You have placed our lot
among those who sit in the study hall and that you have
not given us our portion among those who sit idly on
street corners. We rise early and they rise early. We rise
early to pursue matters of Torah and they rise early to
pursue frivolous matters. We toil and they toil. We toil
and receive a reward and they toil and do not receive a
reward. We run and they run. We run to the life of the
World-to-Come and they run to the pit of destruction,
as it is stated: But You, God, will bring them down into *Psalms 55*
the pit of destruction; men of blood and deceit shall not
live out half their days; but as for me, I will trust in You.

יְהִי רָצוֹן May it be Your will, Lord my God, just as you
have assisted me in completing tractate *Eiruvin* so assist
me to begin other tractates and books and conclude
them to learn and to teach, to observe and to perform,
and to fulfill all the teachings of Your Torah with love.
And may the merit of all the *tanna'im* and *amora'im* and
Torah scholars stand for me and my descendants so that
the Torah will not move from my mouth and from the
mouths of my descendants and the descendants of my
descendants forever. And may the verse: When you *Proverbs 6*
walk, it shall lead you, when you lie down, it shall watch
over you; and when you awaken, it shall talk with you
be fulfilled in me. For in the Torah your days shall be *Proverbs 9*
multiplied, and the years of your life shall be increased.
Length of days is in her right hand; in her left hand are *Proverbs 3*
riches and honor. May the Lord give strength to His *Psalms 29*
people; the Lord will bless His people with peace.

The following קדיש *requires the presence of a* מנין.

יִתְגַּדַּל וְיִתְקַדַּשׁ שְׁמֵהּ רַבָּא
בְּעָלְמָא דְּהוּא עָתִיד לְאִתְחַדָּתָא
וּלְאַחֲיָאָה מֵתַיָּא, וּלְאַסָּקָא יָתְהוֹן לְחַיֵּי עָלְמָא
וּלְמִבְנֵא קַרְתָּא דִירוּשְׁלֵם, וּלְשַׁכְלָלָא הֵיכְלֵהּ בְּגַוַּהּ
וּלְמֶעְקַר פָּלְחָנָא נֻכְרָאָה מֵאַרְעָא
וְלַאֲתָבָא פָּלְחָנָא דִשְׁמַיָּא לְאַתְרֵהּ
וְיַמְלִיךְ קֻדְשָׁא בְּרִיךְ הוּא בְּמַלְכוּתֵהּ וִיקָרֵהּ
(נוסח ספרד: וְיַצְמַח פֻּרְקָנֵהּ וִיקָרֵב מְשִׁיחֵהּ)
בְּחַיֵּיכוֹן וּבְיוֹמֵיכוֹן וּבְחַיֵּי דְכָל בֵּית יִשְׂרָאֵל
בַּעֲגָלָא וּבִזְמַן קָרִיב, וְאִמְרוּ אָמֵן.

יְהֵא שְׁמֵהּ רַבָּא מְבָרַךְ לְעָלַם וּלְעָלְמֵי עָלְמַיָּא.

יִתְבָּרַךְ וְיִשְׁתַּבַּח וְיִתְפָּאַר וְיִתְרוֹמַם וְיִתְנַשֵּׂא
וְיִתְהַדָּר וְיִתְעַלֶּה וְיִתְהַלָּל
שְׁמֵהּ דְּקֻדְשָׁא בְּרִיךְ הוּא
לְעֵלָּא מִן כָּל בִּרְכָתָא
/בעשרת ימי תשובה: לְעֵלָּא לְעֵלָּא מִכָּל בִּרְכָתָא/
וְשִׁירָתָא, תֻּשְׁבְּחָתָא וְנֶחֱמָתָא, דַּאֲמִירָן בְּעָלְמָא
וְאִמְרוּ אָמֵן. (קהל: אָמֵן)

עַל יִשְׂרָאֵל וְעַל רַבָּנָן
וְעַל תַּלְמִידֵיהוֹן וְעַל כָּל תַּלְמִידֵי תַלְמִידֵיהוֹן
וְעַל כָּל מָאן דְּעָסְקִין בְּאוֹרַיְתָא
דִּי בְּאַתְרָא (בארץ ישראל: קַדִּישָׁא) הָדֵין, וְדִי בְּכָל אֲתַר וַאֲתַר
יְהֵא לְהוֹן וּלְכוֹן שְׁלָמָא רַבָּא
חִנָּא וְחִסְדָּא, וְרַחֲמֵי, וְחַיֵּי אֲרִיכֵי, וּמְזוֹנֵי רְוִיחֵי
וּפֻרְקָנָא מִן קֳדָם אֲבוּהוֹן דִּי בִשְׁמַיָּא
וְאִמְרוּ אָמֵן.

יְהֵא שְׁלָמָא רַבָּא מִן שְׁמַיָּא
וְחַיִּים (טוֹבִים) עָלֵינוּ וְעַל כָּל יִשְׂרָאֵל
וְאִמְרוּ אָמֵן.

Bow, take three steps back, as if taking leave of the Divine Presence, then bow, first left, then right, then center, while saying:

עֹשֶׂה שָׁלוֹם/ בעשרת ימי תשובה: הַשָּׁלוֹם/ בִּמְרוֹמָיו
הוּא יַעֲשֶׂה בְרַחֲמָיו שָׁלוֹם, עָלֵינוּ וְעַל כָּל יִשְׂרָאֵל
וְאִמְרוּ אָמֵן.

The following Kaddish requires the presence of a minyan.

Magnified and sanctified may His great name be,
in the world that will in future be renewed,
reviving the dead and raising them up to eternal life.
He will rebuild the city of Jerusalem
and in it re-establish His Temple.
He will remove alien worship from the earth
and restore to its place the worship of Heaven.
Then the Holy One, blessed be He,
will reign in His sovereignty and splendor.
May it be in your lifetime and in your days,
(*Nusaḥ Sepharad:* make His salvation flourish,
and hasten His messiah,)
and in the lifetime of all the House of Israel,
swiftly and soon – and say: Amen.

May His great name be blessed for ever and all time.

Blessed and praised,
glorified and exalted,
raised and honored,
uplifted and lauded
be the name of the Holy One,
blessed be He,
beyond any blessing,
song, praise and consolation uttered in the world –
and say: Amen.

To Israel, to the teachers,
their disciples and their disciples' disciples,
and to all who engage in the study of Torah,
in this (*in Israel add:* holy) place or elsewhere,
may there come to them and you great peace,
grace, kindness and compassion,
long life, ample sustenance and deliverance,
from their Father in Heaven –
and say: Amen.

May there be great peace from heaven,
and (good) life for us and all Israel –
and say: Amen.

Bow, take three steps back, as if taking leave of the Divine Presence, then bow, first left, then right, then center, while saying:

May He who makes peace in His high places,
in His compassion make peace for us and all Israel –
and say: Amen.